AMA DRUG EVALUATIONS

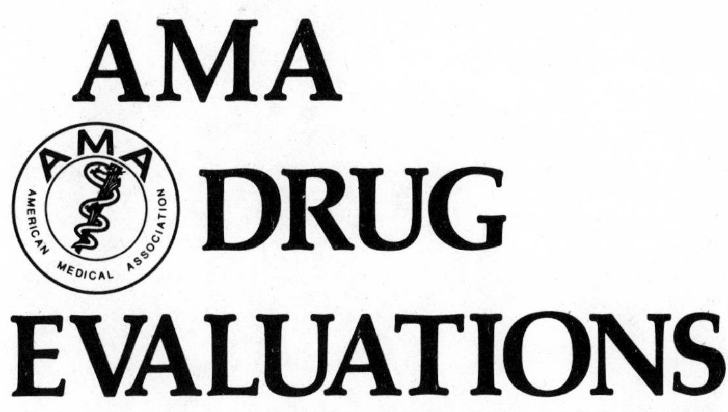

SECOND EDITION

Prepared by the
AMA DEPARTMENT OF DRUGS

PUBLISHING SCIENCES GROUP, INC.
ACTON, MASSACHUSETTS

Printed in the United States of America.

International Standard Book Number: 0-88416-003-3

Library of Congress Catalog Number: 75-147249

PREFACE

The second edition of *AMA Drug Evaluations (AMA-DE)* was compiled by the AMA Department of Drugs under the direction of the former AMA Council on Drugs. It provides reliable and current scientific information for those who prescribe, dispense, and administer drugs.

Readers familiar with the first edition will detect significant new features and changes in format. Among these are (1) a smaller, more convenient size, (2) a hard cover, (3) indexing by trade name as well as generic name, (4) inclusion of structural formulas, (5) use of conventional prose instead of telegraphic style in the individual evaluations, and (6) expanded coverage of information on drug interactions. The New Drugs Section and the Indications Index have been eliminated.

AMA-DE describes uses, routes of administration, or dosages that may not be found in the "package ihsert." FDA-approved labeling limits the use of drugs for purposes of marketing and advertising but does not rigidly constrain a physician's use of the drug for individual patients. Accordingly, *AMA-DE* describes all scientific, recognized uses of drugs irrespective of their status in approved labeling in the "package insert."

In the 2½ years since the first edition, many drug products have been removed from the market by the FDA as the result of the Drug Efficacy Study by the National Academy of Sciences-National Research Council. Every effort has been made to delete these products from the text. Because of the time lag between preparation of final copy and publication, however, some drugs are described that are no longer available.

The American Medical Association hopes that the second edition of *AMA-DE* will be a valuable and useful service to the medical profession and to others working in the field of medical care.

ERNEST B. HOWARD, M.D.
Executive Vice President

CONTENTS

GENERAL INFORMATION

I CARDIOVASCULAR-RENAL AGENTS

II AGENTS AFFECTING BLOOD FORMATION, VOLUME, AND COAGULABILITY

III HOMEOSTATIC AND NUTRIENT AGENTS

IV DRUGS USED IN ANESTHESIA

V ANALGESICS, NARCOTIC ANTAGONISTS, AND AGENTS USED TO TREAT SPECIFIC PAINFUL DISORDERS

VI DRUGS AFFECTING THE CENTRAL NERVOUS SYSTEM

VII HORMONES AND AGENTS AFFECTING HORMONAL MECHANISMS

VIII DRUGS USED IN RESPIRATORY AND ALLERGIC DISORDERS

XIII OTOLOGIC AGENTS

XIV DRUGS USED TO TREAT NEUROMUSCULAR DISORDERS

XV DIAGNOSTIC AGENTS

XVI GASTROINTESTINAL AGENTS

XVII SMOOTH MUSCLE STIMULANTS

XVIII ONCOLYTIC AGENTS

XIX IMMUNOLOGIC AGENTS

XX HEAVY METAL ANTAGONISTS, ENZYMES, AND MISCELLANEOUS AGENTS

ACKNOWLEDGMENTS

Appreciation is expressed for the assistance of the following members of the professional staff of the Department of Drugs:

John D. Archer, M.D.
Morton S. Comer, Ph.D.
Michael H. M. Dykes, M.D.
Howard G. Glass, M.D., Ph.D.
Kathryn S. Huss, M.D.
Joseph B. Jerome, Ph.D.
Mary Ellen Kosman, Ph.D.
Roland E. Lapointe, M.D.
John Reed Lewis, Ph.D.
Karl Mayer, D.V.M.
Russell R. Miller, Ph.D.
Barbara F. Murphy, M.S.
Edward L. Platcow, Ph.D.
Donald O. Schiffman, Ph.D.
Philip G. Seitner, Ph.D.
Leon H. Warren, M.D.

The editorial, technical, and administrative aid furnished by the following Department staff is also acknowledged and appreciated:

Joquain Chang
Susan Connors
Barbara M. Eckel
Helena Suen Fu
Medina Gross
Sandra Kodani
Marilyn Krause
John W. Richardson
Beverly J. Rodgers
Linda A. Schoen
Jill Senrick
Marjorie Spence
Karen Steffensen

The valuable help of the following secretarial staff is recognized:

Lerinee Allen
Barbara Bates
Beverly Blumenshine
Nancy Jo Carpenter
Bonnie Christiansen
Patricia L. Danzinger
Rhonda Dobbs
Barbara J. Fisher
Jeanne M. Kelso
Hei Sung Kim
Melenie Lester
Jean Rawn
Rhonda A. Reese
Offie Robinson
Wanda Ryska
Barbara Schweisheimer
Ellen Skalnik
Carol Strauss
Christine Swiatek
Patricia Washington

The contributions of those pharmaceutical companies that supplied information on products of their manufacture to assist in the preparation of the evaluative statements in this volume are gratefully acknowledged.

JOHN C. BALLIN, PH.D.
Director
Department of Drugs

Consultants for AMA Drug Evaluations

The staff of the Department of Drugs expresses its appreciation to the following consultants for their cooperation and assistance in reviewing the content of this edition of *AMA Drug Evaluations*:

Robert Abel, M.D.
Robert S. Abernathy, M.D.
Charles F. Abildgaard, M.D.
F.S. Abuzzahab, M.D., Ph.D.
*John Adriani, M.D.
Edward H. Ahrens, Jr., M.D.
Thomas P. Almy, M.D.
Joel J. Alpert, M.D.
Thomas T. Amatruda, Jr., M.D.
William W. Anderson, M.D.
Vincent T. Andriole, M.D.
Leonard Apt, M.D.
Jay M. Arena, M.D.
Charles D. Aring, M.D.
Leslie R. Arnett, D.D.S.
Harry L. Arnold, Jr., M.D.
Malcolm Artenstein, M.D.
Joseph F. Artusio, Jr., M.D.
*Daniel L. Azarnoff, M.D.

William Bageant, M.D.
Irving W. Bailit, M.D.
Charles L. Baird, Jr., M.D.
Andre Barbeau, M.D.
Charles F. Barlow, M.D.
*Allan D. Bass, M.D.
Joseph Bateman, M.D.
William T. Beaver, M.D.
J. Weldon Bellville, M.D.
John Benson, Jr., M.D.
Leonard B. Berman, M.D.
Jerrold G. Bernstein, M.D.
Ernest Beutler, M.D.
Edwin Bierman, M.D.
Hugh Biller, M.D.
Harvey Blank, M.D.
Morton D. Bogdonoff, M.D.
Herbert Borison, Ph.D.
Kenneth M. Brinkhous, M.D.
Harold W. Brown, M.D.
Heinrich G. Brugsch, M.D.
Gerald Burke, M.D.
Philip J. Burke, M.D.
Robert P. Burns, M.D.

John R. Calverley, M.D.
John Canary, M.D.
Craig J. Canfield, M.D.
Paul P. Carbone, M.D.
Denis Cavanagh, M.D.
M.H. Charlton, M.D.
Maynard B. Chenoweth, M.D.
Nicholas L. Christy, M.D.
Harold O. Closson, M.D.
David F. Clyde, M.D., Ph.D.
Jay D. Coffman, M.D.
Irvin M. Cohen, M.D.
Jonathan O. Cole, M.D.
Jerome W. Conn, M.D.
Julius M. Coon, M.D., Ph.D.
Herbert L. Cooper, M.D.
George C. Cotzias, M.D.
Henry G. Cramblett, M.D.
William H. Crosby, M.D.
J. Richard Crout, M.D.
*John J. Curry, M.D.

Donald J. Dalessio, M.D.
Willy H. Dam, M.D.
*Norman A. David, M.D.
Paul T. Davidson, M.D.
Edward H. Davis, M.D.
John M. Davis, M.D.
Russell DeJong, M.D.
Thomas J. DeKornfeld, M.D.
Francesco del Greco, M.D.
Herman C.B. Denber, M.D.
Daniel Deykin, M.D.
Seymour Diamond, M.D.
Alberto Di Mascio, Ph.D.
Joseph F. Dingman, M.D.
John W. Ditzler, M.D.
Malin R. Dollinger, M.D.
David A. Dolowitz, M.D.
Edward F. Domino, M.D.
Alan K. Done, M.D.
*Harry F. Dowling, M.D.
Leonard S. Dreifus, M.D.
Harriet Dustan, M.D.

Charles E. Edwards, M.D.
Joel Elkes, M.D.
Philip P. Ellis, M.D.
Rose Ruth Ellison, M.D.
Mark Entman, M.D.
Stephen E. Epstein, M.D.

*Former member of Council on Drugs

William L. Epstein, M.D.
Audrey E. Evans, M.D.

Paul Fasal, M.D.
Samuel Feinberg, M.D.
Harry A. Feldman, M.D.
Gerald Fenichel, M.D.
L.S. Filer, Jr., M.D.
S.K. Fineberg, M.D.
Max Fink, M.D.
Maxwell Finland, M.D.
Frank A. Finnerty, Jr., M.D.
Delbert A. Fisher, M.D.
Thomas B. Fitzpatrick, M.D.
Anthony P. Fletcher, M.D.
Francis F. Foldes, M.D.
Noble O. Fowler, M.D.
Daniel X. Freedman, M.D.
*Edward D. Freis, M.D.
Walter J. Friedlander, M.D.
Arnold P. Friedman, M.D.
Dale G. Friend, M.D.

Donald M. Gallant, M.D.
Ronald B. George, M.D.
Samuel Gershon, M.D.
Ray W. Gifford, Jr., M.D.
Aaron J. Gissen, M.D.
Gilbert H. Glaser, M.D.
Louis Gluck, M.D.
Marian Goble, M.D.
Leon I. Goldberg, M.D., Ph.D.
Douglas Goldman, M.D.
Joseph Goldman, M.D.
Grace A. Goldsmith, M.D.
Franz Goldstein, M.D.
Raymond H. Goodale, M.D.
David J. Goode, M.D.
Edgar S. Gordon, M.D.
W. Morton Grant, M.D.
Jared Grantham, M.D.
*William C. Grater, M.D.
J.S. Gravenstein, M.D.
Norton J. Greenberger, M.D.
*Theodore H. Greiner, M.D.
Raymond F. Grenfell, M.D.
David Grob, M.D.
Morton Grossman, M.D.

Philip D. Hansten, Ph.D.
Paul V. Harper, M.D.
John Harris, M.D.
M. Coleman Harris, M.D.
Donald C. Harrison, M.D.
James B. Hartney, M.D.
William H. Havener, M.D.
Henry O. Heinemann, M.D.
H.F. Henderson, M.D.
Lowell L. Henderson, M.D.
James Henry, M.D.
Victor Herbert, M.D.
Paul Hoeprich, M.D.
Leo E. Hollister, M.D.
*William J. Hossley, M.D.
Frank M. Howard, Jr., M.D.
*John M. Howard, M.D.
Charles Huguley, Jr., M.D.
Daniel A. Hussar, Ph.D.

Sidney H. Ingbar, M.D.
Franz J. Ingelfinger, M.D.

Jay Jacoby, M.D.
Ralph F. Jacox, M.D.
Murray E. Jarvik, M.D., Ph.D.
Ernest Jawetz, M.D., Ph.D.
J.E. Jelinek, M.D.
Hershel Jick, M.D.
Richard J. Johns, M.D.
Joseph E. Johnson, III, M.D.

Sherwin A. Kabins, M.D.
Werner Kalow, M.D.
Naomi M. Kanof, M.D.
Kenneth Kaplan, M.D.
Samuel Kaplan, M.D.
John E. Kasik, M.D., Ph.D.
Irving Kass, M.D.
Donald G. Kassebaum, M.D.
Harry Irving Katz, M.D.
Ronald L. Katz, M.D.
Sol Katz, M.D.
Arthur S. Keats, M.D.
John H. Killough, M.D., Ph.D.
William M. M. Kirby, M.D.
*Joseph B. Kirsner, M.D., Ph.D.
Harold L. Klawans, Jr., M.D.
Stuart A. Kleit, M.D.
Albert M. Kligman, M.D., Ph.D.
George Koelle, M.D., Ph.D.
M. Glenn Koenig, M.D.
David Kritchevsky, Ph.D.
Donald Krogstad, M.D.
Leslie A. Kuhn, M.D.
Calvin M. Kunin, M.D.

Bert N. La Du, M.D., Ph.D.
Richard Landau, M.D.
Elliot C. Lasser, M.D.
Robert S. Lees, M.D.
Carroll M. Leevy, M.D.
Louis Leiter, M.D.

John M. Leonard, M.D.
*Irving H. Leopold, M.D.
Simmons Lessell, M.D.
William Lester, M.D.
Irving M. Levine, M.D.
Samuel A. Levinson, M.D., Ph.D.
Robert I. Levy, M.D.
George B. Lewis, Jr., M.D.
Richard Lewis, M.D.
Theodore W. Lieberman, M.D.
Harry W. Linde, Ph.D.
J.P. Long, Ph.D.
Francis C. Lowell, M.D.
Peere C. Lund, M.D.

Howard I. Maibach, M.D.
Gerald L. Mandell, M.D.
Leslie B. Mann, M.D.
Alexander Marble, M.D.
Frank I. Marcus, M.D.
Lester C. Mark, M.D.
William R. Martin, M.D.
Richard L. Masland, M.D.
Dean T. Mason, M.D.
J. Kenneth McClatch, Ph.D.
Fletcher McDowell, M.D.
James C. Melby, M.D.
Albert I. Mendeloff, M.D.
Sidney Merlis, M.D.
L.H. Miller, M.D.
Russell R. Miller, Ph.D.
William F. Miller, M.D.
J. Gordon Millichap, M.D.
Daniel R. Mishell, Jr., M.D.
Roger S. Mitchell, M.D.
James Monroe, M.D.
Max M. Montgomery, M.D.
Daniel C. Moore, M.D.
Neil C. Moran, M.D.
Karl M. Morgenstein, M.D.
Howard F. Morrelli, M.D.
J.D. Morrison, M.D.
*John G. Morrison, M.D.
*Robert H. Moser, M.D.
James W. Mosley, M.D.
Harry Most, M.D.
John H. Moyer, M.D.
John F. Mueller, M.D.
Sheila M. Muldoon, M.D.

Alexander S. Nadas, M.D.
Franklin A. Neva, M.D.
S.H. Ngai, M.D.
Mark Nickerson, M.D., Ph.D.
Albert Norris, M.D.

Robert A. O'Reilly, M.D.

Ernest W. Page, M.D.
Frank Parker, M.D.
Madhukar A. Pathak, Ph.D.
*C. Alvin Paulsen, M.D.
James Paximos, R.Ph.
Eugene S. Paykel, M.D.
Rufus F. Payne, M.D.
Gustavus A. Peters, M.D.
Donald Pinkel, M.D.
Carl Pochedly, M.D.
Edwin O. Polish, M.D.
Judith G. Pool, Ph.D.
E.L. Posey, Jr., M.D.
Robin D. Powell, M.D.
Phillip Pratt, M.D.
Edward Press, M.D.
Thaddeus Prout, M.D.
Majorie M. Pyle, M.D.

Armand J. Quick, M.D.

Morton I. Rapoport, M.D.
Richard J. Reitemeier, M.D.
Clayton Rich, M.D.
Karl Rickels, M.D.
J. Alfred Rider, M.D., Ph.D.
John F. Roach, M.D.
Laurence L. Robbins, M.D.
Donald S. Robinson, M.D.
*Daniel M. Rogers, M.D.
Edward C. Rosenow, III, M.D.
Thomas G. Rudd, M.D.
Richard Rudders, M.D.
John Ruedy, M.D.

Max S. Sadove, M.D.
Jay Sanford, M.D.
Howerde E. Sauberlich, Ph.D.
Irwin J. Schatz, M.D.
Maurice Schiff, M.D.
Joseph J. Schildkraut, M.D.
Robert F. Schilling, M.D
Frank R. Schmid, M.D.
Paul H. Schreibman, M.D.
Myron G. Schultz, M.D., D.V.M.
George A. Schumacher, M.D.
Robert S. Schwab, M.D.
John H. Seabury, M.D.
Marvin L. Sears, M.D.
William H. Sebrell, Jr., M.D.
Paul M. Seebohm, M.D.
Harry L. Segal, M.D.
Sarah H. Sell, M.D.

Seth K. Sharpless, Ph.D.
Edward B. Shaw, M.D.
C. Norman Shealy, M.D.
Charles C. Shepard, M.D.
Lawrence Sherman, M.D.
William B. Sherman, M.D.
*Sol Sherry, M.D.
Maurice E. Shils, M.D.
*Harry C. Shirkey, M.D.
David Shoch, M.D.
Howard B. Shookhoff, M.D.
Jonas A. Shulman, M.D.
*F.A. Simeone, M.D.
Stanley Slater, M.D.
Robert E. Slayton, M.D.
David E. Smith, M.D.
*Donn L. Smith, M.D., Ph.D.
Edgar B. Smith, M.D.
J. Ned Smith, M.D.
Morton Smith, M.D.
N. Ty Smith, M.D.
Konrad H. Soergel, M.D.
J. Kenneth Sokol, M.D.
Lawrence M. Solomon, M.D.
William N. Spellacy, M.D.
Herta Spencer, M.D.
Bertram Sprofkin, M.D.
Harold C. Standiford, M.D.
John E. Steinhaus, M.D.
Robert K. Stoelting, M.D.
Marion B. Sulzberger, M.D.
Abraham Sunshine, M.D.

Robert W. Talley, M.D.
Peter A. Theodos, M.D.
Richard A. Theye, M.D.
Jared R. Tinklenberg, M.D.
Donald P. Todd, M.D.
Ross M. Tucker, M.D.

John P. Utz, M.D.

Parker Vanamee, M.D.
Leroy D. Vandam, M.D.
Eugene Van Scott, M.D.
Robert W. Virtue, M.D., Ph.D.
Perry P. Volpitto, M.D.

Burton A. Waisbren, M.D.
Alfred J. Wall, M.D.
Shik-Chun Wang, M.D.
Albert J. Wasserman, M.D.
Irwin M. Weiner, M.D.
Ira Weinstein, Ph.D.
Louis Weinstein, M.D., Ph.D.
Sidney C. Werner, M.D.
Stanford Wessler, M.D.
Frederic B. Westervelt, Jr., M.D.
Jean K. Weston, M.D.
June M. Whaun, M.D.
Frances K. Widmann, M.D.
Joseph A. Wilber, M.D.
Park W. Willis, III, M.D.
Charles S. Winans, M.D.
*Maxwell M. Wintrobe, M.D., Ph.D.
Heinz J. Wittig, M.D.
Robert L. Wolf, M.D.
Donald E. Wood, M.D.
Francis Wood, Jr., M.D.
J. Edwin Wood, M.D.
*Lauren A. Woods, M.D., Ph.D.
Theodore E. Woodward, M.D.
Irving S. Wright, M.D.
James B. Wyngaarden, M.D.

Sumner J. Yaffe, M.D.
Melvin D. Yahr, M.D.

Hyman J. Zimmerman, M.D.
Morton Ziskind, M.D.

GENERAL INFORMATION

SCOPE AND ORGANIZATION OF EVALUATIONS

As with the first (1971) edition of *AMA Drug Evaluations*, this second edition has been organized into chapters and sections that are based, insofar as possible, on therapeutic classifications. Each chapter contains an introductory statement that discusses the overall therapeutic category, followed by brief evaluative monographs for individual drugs in the class. Drugs selected for individual evaluations include virtually all therapeutic agents in the official compendia, *United States Pharmacopeia* (U.S.P.) and *National Formulary* (N.F.); the drugs, including mixtures, most commonly prescribed or administered by physicians in the United States; and single-entity preparations introduced during the past ten years. In addition, other drugs have been selected for evaluative statements if they were judged to be of particular importance to complete a discussion of a therapeutic category. Other nationally distributed preparations that are not individually evaluated are listed and indexed to give information about their therapeutic category and availability.

All chapters have been revised and updated from the first edition, and some of them have also been reorganized (and occasionally renamed). Further, several changes in style have been made. For example, more conventional prose has replaced the telegraphic style in the bodies of the evaluations.

To reduce redundancy, the New Drugs Section has been omitted. Necessary information that would have appeared in this section has been incorporated into appropriate chapters.

In the previous edition, some combinations were singled out for discussion on the basis of frequent use, followed by a listing of similar preparations. In this edition, when several mixtures of analogous composition are considered, usually one evaluative discussion applicable to the group precedes the list and specific dosage information may be omitted. In these instances, the prescriber should usually be able to extrapolate a dose from information given elsewhere for the individual ingredients. To facilitate the latter procedure, the quantitative formulas of active ingredients are customarily given for all mixtures in a list.

Finally, structural formulas are provided for most single-entity drugs. In the previous edition, these were given only for drugs in the New Drugs Section.

The evaluative or interpretive information in the book, particularly on controversial matters, may disagree with opinions from other sources. Statements are based on the convergent trend of information available from scientific literature, unpublished data, and the advice of consultants and review committees of the former Council on Drugs. Reportorial information has been condensed and represents that considered most essential to the physician in his choice and use of the drugs. Accordingly, such information as rare, minor, or unconfirmed reactions, precautions that relate to obvious or remote situations, and unusual or speculative uses of a drug are sometimes omitted. For other details, for basic data, and even for varying points of view, the physician is encouraged to consult and compare the many other sources of information on drugs: journal articles, standard textbooks, official compendia, manufacturers' labeling, prominent bulletins and periodicals on drugs and therpeutics, and symposia.

The mere inclusion of a particular drug in *AMA Drug Evaluations* does not imply endorsement by the American Medical Association, nor should it be a criterion for approving the use of that drug in any institution or for any other purpose. The principal purpose of this volume is to provide the medical profession with an evaluation of selected drugs based on the available evidence. Since an evaluation may be favorable, unfavorable, or a combination of both, depending upon the merits of the preparation, the physician should determine in each individual case the relevancy of the limitations, adverse reactions, contraindications, or precautions given in the text.

An effort has been made to list all nationally distributed products that are dispensed exclusively or principally by prescription. Many drugs are listed or described, of course, that *can* be sold without prescription, but ordinarily their brands are not listed if these are principally advertised for over-the-counter sale.

Inclusion of drugs has been based upon the most recent information available, and in a project of this scope, it is inevitable that some preparations have been inadvertently omitted; such omissions are regretted. In part because of the current regulatory activities of the Food and Drug Administration, some preparations probably will no longer be marketed when this book appears in print. Deletion of products and updating of other information has continued as near as possible to the time of publication. In addition, efforts have been made to include drugs newly introduced to the market as near the publication date as practicable.

Published research and reports of clinical experience often are limited to the products of one or only a few manufacturers. Fully adequate clinical comparisons of all brands of the same drug are rarely available. For this reason a valid comparison of brands has rarely been possible and seldom attempted. However, the reader should bear in mind that not all brands and generically labeled forms of the same drug are necessarily therapeutically equivalent. Differences in coatings, binders, particle size, ease of dissolution, purity of ingredients, and other factors can lead to variations in absorption and biological availability of a drug. Also, the degree of consistency from batch to batch will depend upon the manufacturer's quality control procedures. How frequently really significant differences occur in various brands of alleged equivalent products is difficult to estimate. Nevertheless, the fact that they sometimes do occur should be recognized by the prescribing physician in appraising the information in this book and in writing prescriptions that may be filled with the product of any of several manufacturers.

DOSAGE RECOMMENDATIONS

Usual Doses: The dosage information presented falls within the ranges given in official compendia, those suggested by one or more manufacturers, or those considered appropriate by other authorities. For many drugs, however, the correct dose will depend upon the size, age, and condition of the patient; his response to treatment; his sensitivity or tolerance; and the possible synergistic or antagonistic effect of concomitant medication. The epitome of dosage is to weigh expected benefits against risks. If an illness can be tolerated for a while, establishment of the dose should be cautious and exploratory unless a wide margin of safety prevails. However, if immediate disaster threatens from therapeutic failure, treatment should be aggressive. In either situation the physician should remember that improper dosage with the proper drug is probably as common a cause of failure in therapy as the use of an improper drug.

Accordingly, many usual doses are given as ranges. Even the limits of these ranges are seldom inviolable. The upper limits stated for most ranges, however, do suggest that larger amounts either may increase the risks of toxicity beyond what is ordinarily acceptable or may fail to provide additional therapeutic effect in significant degree; similarly, the lower limits often indicate that smaller doses could not be expected to provide full therapeutic effects for most patients.

In the first edition, dosage information was frequently excluded for some drugs when their use was questioned or not recommended; this practice has largely been discontinued. Although a collateral statement may make it clear that no dosage is suggested on the basis of the evaluation of a particular drug, the dose given in the manufacturer's labeling or that usually employed will ordinarily be included as an item of information.

Dosage in Children and Infants: Many problems attend the choice of drugs and determination of doses in pediatric patients. Whether children and infants will respond to a particular drug in the same manner as adults can only be determined through research and experience, and their responses to many drugs are known to be different. Many of the metabolic mechanisms of premature and newborn infants are not fully developed, and a lethal blood concentration of a drug may accumulate if a dosage regimen is based upon the common criteria for conversion from the adult regimen. In fact, the infant's response to drugs during the first weeks of life probably varies more, overall, from that of a one-year-old than the response of a one-year-old varies from that of an adult. This consideration should be borne in mind not only in treating the newborn but also in treating an expectant mother near the time of delivery.

A common practice in the determination of a child's dose has been to give some fraction of an adult dose, using the age of the patient as a rough guide. Because of the great variation in size among children of the same age, this method can be satisfactory only if there is a wide margin of safety. Usually it is better to consider the dose for *all* patients in terms of mg/kg of body weight or to establish the pediatric dose as a fraction proportionate to the weight of the child in comparison with that of an average adult. However, when it is valid to assume that a child will respond to a drug in the same way as an adult will, the best conversion of dosage is one based on body surface area.

Statements of pediatric doses for individual drugs in this book follow the method of conversion which has been developed generally for that particular drug. Thus, some conversions are based upon age, some upon weight, and some upon body surface area. If adequate dosage information based on actual pediatric use is either nonexistent or not readily available, suggested dosage guidelines sometimes are furnished even though it is recognized that more data would be desirable; at times, lack of data has been specifically acknowledged. When dosage information is inadequate, it is suggested that the body surface area be taken as the criterion—*provided no evidence indicates that a child will react to the drug differently from an adult.* In the clinic or office, repeated calculations of these conversions may be too forbidding to be practical. For convenience, a simple table is provided on the inside back cover of this book.

TIMED-RELEASE PREPARATIONS

Drugs that are rapidly metabolized or excreted, but whose effects must be maintained steadily for prolonged periods, can present serious inconveniences because of the need for repeated administration at short intervals; this is especially true with injectable drugs. Accordingly, pharmaceutical formulations have been developed to provide the release of active ingredients for relatively long periods.

In parenteral preparations, sustained release is achieved by using relatively insoluble salts or esters of the active drug or a special vehicle from which the drug is slowly absorbed. It is doubtful that such techniques can ever deliver a dosage that is as precisely controlled as that with intravenous infusion. Nevertheless, when some latitude is permissible in the range of the safe and effective blood level, substitution of sustained-release preparations for repeated injections may provide a somewhat more uniform blood concentration, and this type of preparation is certainly more convenient. Depot preparations of penicillin provide an outstanding example of a useful sustained-release formulation. In some serious infections, of course, continuous intravenous infusion is still needed. Insulin is another excellent example of a drug which, even though dosage requirements are critical, has been prepared in sustained-release forms that have greatly simplified the management of diabetes. Reasonably satisfactory formulations also are available for various corticosteroids, androgens, estrogens, and a few other agents.

The need for sustained-release formulations for oral medications is less apparent. Nevertheless, many have been prepared, and some can provide a certain convenience over more frequent administration—provided they actually deliver the medication in the even, measured manner that is intended. The general term "timed-release" is the one adopted by the *National Formulary* to describe these oral preparations, and the practice is followed in this text. The term includes formulations variously known as "delayed-action," "extended-release," "prolonged-action," "sustained-action," or "repeat-action," but does not include tablets specifically identified as "enteric-coated."

When a physician chooses a timed-release preparation for the convenience of his patient, he should bear in mind that he is introducing one more potential variable into the predictable physiologic availability of the drug. These preparations are listed in this book to provide information on their availability; such listing does not imply endorsement. Actually, only a few have been evaluated for effectiveness, since data on which to base an evaluation of effectiveness are inadequate or are not available for most timed-release forms. In vitro tests designed to demonstrate product uniformity do not assure in vivo effectiveness. No precise product specifications have been established by the official compendia for timed-release preparations.

One type of timed-release preparation clearly to be condemned is that for drugs with a long half-life after absorption. The half-lives of an increasing number of drugs are now being determined, and, when known, this property should be considered in ascertaining the dosage regimen of a drug. For example, results of recent studies have demonstrated that some drugs (eg, diphenylhydantoin) are equally effective whether the total daily amount is given in a single dose or in divided doses. Little logic can be seen for use of a timed-release form of a phenothiazine, phenobarbital, or diphenylhydantoin. And timed-release preparations have actually been formulated for such drugs as digitalis and thyroid. Such practice represents pure nonsense.

"LABEL AS SUCH" AND RELATED MATTERS

In traditional pharmaceutic practice, the name of a prescription drug does not appear on the label of the package that the pharmacist furnishes the patient. However, the physician may instruct the pharmacist to put information on the label by including on the prescription the direction, "Label as such," "L.A.S.," or merely "Label." For several years, the American Medical Association has encouraged physicians to follow this practice and to make an exception only when such disclosure would be detrimental to the welfare of the patient. The reasons for believing prescription drugs should be labeled with their names and strength have been set forth repeatedly: (1) The patient has the right to be informed about his illness and the medications prescribed. (2) In emergency situations, such as accidental poisoning, overdosage, or attempted suicide, immediate identification of a prescription drug from the label may be lifesaving. (3) The information is valuable when the patient changes physicians, moves to another locality, or contacts the prescribing physician at a time when his records are not readily available. (4) The information on the label is of value in group practices in which the patient may not always have the same attending physician. (5) It is advisable that patients with allergies know what is being prescribed. (6) This specific information on the label helps to prevent mix-ups between two or more drugs being taken concurrently, or between medications being taken by different members of the family. (7) If it becomes necessary to issue a warning against the use of a particular drug, the name on the label serves as a danger signal to those who have been given prescriptions for the product.

The reasons that have been advanced opposing the labeling of prescription drugs with the name and strength are far less persuasive than those just given for labeling. There are, of course, some occasions when such labeling is inadvisable for psychological or other reasons, but in these circumstances, the instruction can be omitted from the prescription.

A related matter involves that of refills. Restrictions on refills are controlled by law for certain narcotics and drugs subject to abuse (see the discussion on Department of Justice in the section on Official and Regulatory Agencies). However, it is advisable for the physician to designate the number of refills, if any, he wishes the patient to have and to prescribe only the number of doses usually required in any specific condition, since adjustments in dosage are often necessary to obtain the desired result in individual patients. Prescriptions may not legally be refilled without the physician's authorization. When this authorization is given in advance (on the prescription at the time of writing) the physician would be well advised to place some time limit on the authorization. The very fact that a drug is dispensed by prescription implies the need for professional control. Yet prescriptions with open-end authorization for refills, especially if marked "refill p.r.n." or "ad lib," remain valid indefinitely. It is not unusual for prescriptions to be refilled repeatedly for years after the prescriber has retired, moved away, or even has long been dead. However, in some circumstances a large-quantity prescription *is* appropriate. If a patient is expected to take a drug for a prolonged period, if his correct dosage has been established, and if he can be trusted to follow instructions properly, a prescription for a large quantity will often be more economical than repeated prescriptions or refills for small quantities.

USE OF LABORATORY STUDIES TO MONITOR ADVERSE REACTIONS

Although nearly all drugs have known and reasonably predictable toxicity in excessive dosage, most are given in doses calculated to be in the safe range. In order to achieve therapeutic effects, however, some drugs must be given in amounts that approach the toxic range or that may even reach it for some patients. Accordingly, appropriate observations are needed to detect the approach or onset of toxicity and to reverse it or at least avoid its progression to intolerable proportions.

Numerous vital organs, such as the hematopoietic system, the liver, and the kidneys, can be adversely affected by drugs. When toxic reactions occur gradually, or when their overt manifestations appear slowly, appropriate laboratory testing may reveal their presence earlier than would be detected by the appearance of symptoms. On the other hand, much routine laboratory testing that is done in the absence of symptoms of a reaction is essentially wasteful and may lead to a false sense of security. This condition prevails when efforts are made to anticipate types of reactions that occur precipitously and cause overt signs and symptoms.

The problem is to know what possible reactions to what drugs are likely to be detected by laboratory tests in asymptomatic patients. When test results are abnormal, especially if only to a mild degree, their interpretation can be difficult.

If a drug must be given that is known to cause such effects as leukopenia, anemia, cholestasis, hepatocellular damage, or nephropathy in a substantial number of recipients, it usually is wise to perform some appropriate baseline tests initially for later comparison should the need arise. Tests should be repeated, of course, if signs or symptoms of the disorder occur during treatment. The need to repeat them at intervals during treatment in the absence of symptoms largely depends upon the likelihood that a serious reaction may develop without overt manifestations.

Clearly, an antileukemic drug requires frequent blood cell counts for safe administration; it will cause marrow depression in all patients and this will reach toxic proportions if too much is given. Periodic counts at arbitrarily chosen intervals is less beneficial with agents that occasionally cause a precipitous agranulocytosis as a hypersensitivity reaction. It is true that the prognosis is improved if one is so lucky as to make the diagnosis by laboratory means before any infection begins. However, in view of the prodigious number of routine hemograms that are performed and the rarity of the diagnosis by such means, the chance of benefiting any given patient is remote. There is no intent in this discussion to advise *against* such tests when a drug that can cause allergic agranulocytosis is given. However, performing them is more a matter of discretion than compulsion, and it is proper to consider the patient's convenience and economic status in making the decision. One thing can be said with confidence: careful observation for signs of sudden infection is a far more important precaution. If such infection occurs, immediate laboratory evaluation is then indicated.

Drugs that cause megaloblastic anemia with prolonged use, such as some anticonvulsants, also warrant monitoring with occasional routine blood studies. The reaction progresses gradually, may be detected well in advance of symptoms, and can be controlled by proper management. This precaution is particularly significant during pregnancy, because megaloblastic anemia may damage the fetus if allowed to progress.

Drug-induced liver disease of an allergic or hypersensitivity type also presents problems regarding the best means of early detection. Monitoring treatment with laboratory tests would be valuable with any drug known to produce gradual, subtle, and serious hepatotoxic injury. Fortunately, however, few modern drugs have such potentiality. Nevertheless, many can produce liver damage, without apparent relation to dosage, in hypersensitive patients. Cholestatic reactions are typically less dangerous than the hepatocellular type, but either must be regarded as potentially serious. (A possible exception is the mild and apparently benign cholestasis that seems to be a direct, dose-related effect of various synthetic androgens.)

It would be advantageous if a hepatic reaction could be detected at its earliest development so that administration of the drug could be stopped. Unfortunately, the serious hypersensitivity reactions tend to develop precipitously. Documentation that such reactions can be diagnosed in any substantial number of patients with routine liver function tests before symptoms develop is scanty. Although such diagnoses might occasionally be made, minor abnormalities are often difficult to assess in terms of cause or importance, and striking ones would seldom precede some symptoms by a significant length of time. By far the most important precaution is to observe the patient for such symptoms as malaise, abdominal discomfort, anorexia, dark urine, and jaundice and to perform proper laboratory studies if these reactions occur.

Occasionally, nephrotoxicity from a drug can occur with dramatic suddenness. Usually, however, drugs that can cause kidney damage are more likely to produce it subtly and well in advance of symptoms than are most of those that cause blood, marrow, or liver damage that is detectable in advance. When such a drug is given for prolonged periods, occasional routine laboratory tests, especially urinalyses, may provide a useful means of early detection.

In preparing this book, the usual custom has been to warn of reactions known or thought to be possible, but not to attempt too detailed advice in how to observe for them. Suggestions for routine, periodic laboratory testing are ordinarily reserved for situations when the tests seem to provide clear-cut value. More commonly, the discussions rely upon the physician's discretion and judgment in determining the details of monitoring a patient's treatment with a drug. Even when advice to perform laboratory tests has been indicated, it seldom has been practical to specify frequency. It is unlikely that a precise routine could be outlined that would be ideal for all patients in all situations.

The most important information that a physician can have about adverse reactions to drugs is advice about which ones to expect, either commonly or uncommonly. It is worth repeating, however, that when damage to an important organ is within the spectrum of known reactions to a drug, appropriate baseline observations before treatment may later prove valuable for comparison.

USE OF DRUGS DURING PREGNANCY

In view of the ease with which substances in the mother's bloodstream pass into the fetus, what was once thought of as the placental barrier would more appropriately be called the "placental sieve." In giving a drug to a pregnant woman, the physician must be aware that he may be simultaneously exposing the developing fetus to a potentially toxic substance. Accordingly, special caution and judgment are mandatory during pregnancy. Of course, it is sometimes necessary to administer drugs to pregnant women, since complications of pregnancy must often be treated with drugs, and serious illness can occur coincidentally with pregnancy.

The fact that a drug has been given during pregnancy without recognized untoward effects is not necessarily proof that it will be safe in all cases. Nevertheless, the fact that a drug has a long history of use without reported fetal damage at least *tends* to place it in higher favor for use in pregnant women than a newer similar drug or one that has been associated with reported injury.

Although studies to determine fetal toxicity in animals are now routinely included in the investigation of new drugs, no technique has been developed that can be translated reliably into expected experience in humans.

In preparing this book, an effort has been made to include information on known or reasonably assumed hazards if the drugs are given during pregnancy. With many drugs, however, and particularly with most new ones, little or no information is available on use in humans. Accordingly, it often has been necessary to resort to some form of warning that a drug should be given only if the expected benefits exceed the risks. This warning admittedly is not too helpful when inadequate data exist to know that risks, if any, are present. It merely can serve as a reminder that unless a systemically absorbed drug has been clearly proved safe for use during pregnancy, it should be given only if an overwhelming need exists, and then the possibility of fetal toxicity should be acknowledged.

CAUTION IN USE OF "POTENT" DRUGS

The administration of virtually all effective drugs is attended by at least some degree of risk that must be weighed against the expected benefits. With drugs of certain classes, however, at least three dangers are involved that can be partly minimized if they are given sufficient consideration. These are the dangers of physical dependence, suicidal ingestion, and impairment of mental or physical performance. A fourth danger might be added, but it pertains to practically any potent drug that may be prescribed for administration at home: the possibility of accidental poisoning. Although the physician's control over this hazard is often limited, he can at least caution patients, when appropriate, against improvising in their dosage, against carelessness in reading labels, and against leaving medicines accessible to small children.

Physical Dependence and Related Problems: The potential for physical dependence, including characteristic tolerance and liability to produce withdrawal symptoms, with use of narcotic analgesics is probably the most widely understood. On the other hand, although dependence on sedative-hypnotic agents is by no means a recently discovered phenomenon, its distinctive features are less commonly understood. Usual hypnotic doses do not produce significant physical dependence although some psychic habituation may occur.

However, when daily intake is gradually increased, marked physical dependence and tolerance to the hypnotic effect develop, and the individual is intoxicated by the drug. In contrast to the narcotics, the tolerance is not complete; it develops to the hypnotic effect but not to the lethal toxic effect. Thus, accidental fatal overdosage is common. Abrupt withdrawal of the drug results in a severe withdrawal illness that progresses to psychosis after a few days and often includes dangerous convulsions resembling grand mal. The illness is similar to alcoholic delirium tremens, which also is a withdrawal illness, but convulsions are even more common after barbiturates. This abstinence syndrome is much more dangerous to life than the one from narcotics.

Virtually any agent whose primary pharmacologic action is hypnotic or sedative, including antianxiety agents, is potentially capable of producing physical dependence similar to that with the barbiturates if daily intake is substantially above ordinary therapeutic doses.

Various central nervous system stimulants are also abused because of their euphoriant action (eg, cocaine, amphetamine and related agents, particularly methamphetamine). The amphetamines can cause prolonged wakefulness, bizarre ideation and behavior, and even hallucinations with large doses. Withdrawal from a regimen of abuse does not cause a syndrome resembling that from either narcotics or hypnotics. Without question, however, withdrawal after prolonged high dosage can leave the individual fatigued and depressed.

Discussion of the management of drug-dependent individuals is beyond the scope of this book. For current medical opinion related to treating withdrawal syndromes, care of the drug-dependent patient, types of patients who abuse drugs, and prevention of drug abuse, the reader is referred to *Drug Dependence—A Guide for Physicians*, published by the AMA, as well as the following articles: Narcotics and medical practice: Medical use of morphine and morphine-like drugs and management of persons dependent on them, AMA Council on Mental Health (*JAMA* 218:578-583, 1971); Treatment of morphine-type dependence by withdrawal methods, AMA Council on Mental Health (*JAMA* 219:1611-1615, 1972); and Oral methadone maintenance techniques in the management of morphine-type dependence, AMA Council on Mental Health (*JAMA* 219:1618-1619, 1972).

Suicide With Prescribed Drugs: Efforts at suicide have been made with most common agents. However, because of the patient population involved, psychotropic drugs tend to be especially popular for suicidal attempts, particularly if the term is used broadly to include hypnotics. Suicidal inclination is a common symptom of psychiatric depression and often is greatest when the depression has partly but incompletely subsided. Moreover, antidepressant drugs themselves can be used for suicidal purposes.

Although the physician faces practical and legal limits in his ability to preclude suicide, he can, as circumstances warrant, limit the size of prescriptions, select a relatively nontoxic drug if possible, recommend hospitalization, and advise family members about needed precautions.

Drugs and Accidents: An array of drug effects can diminish the patient's ability to perform his customary tasks, for example, drowsiness, impaired judgment, decreased coordination, blurred vision, as well as more precipitous reactions like hypoglycemia, postural hypotension, and lowered convulsive threshold. In prescribing drugs that may impair such functions as alertness, judgment, or coordination, a physician is wise to caution patients about the manner in which their activities may be affected. Drugs and circumstances vary too greatly to attempt to make any comprehensive statement on which activities should be forbidden, which should be approached with caution, and which perhaps should be temporarily avoided pending a trial with the drug. A physician must evaluate the individual situation and should advise his patients appropriately of possible hazards. Medicolegal considerations may make it prudent to record the advice in his records.

DRUG INTERACTIONS

Many patients require multiple drug therapy, and in recent years there has been an increasing awareness of the importance of drug interactions. Studies in laboratory animals have shown that many drugs may increase or decrease the efficacy or toxicity of other agents, but considerably less is known about drug interactions in man.

Following is a brief review of the mechanisms of some interactions that are probably of clinical significance. Not included in this review are direct in vitro physicochemical interactions or familiar additive, synergistic, or antagonistic effects. Since there are some important interactions for which the mechanism is at present unknown, this discussion cannot be comprehensive.

Interactions Involving Gastrointestinal Absorption of Drugs and Other Agents

Binding: Drug absorption may be decreased by the formation of inactive or insoluble complexes in the intestinal tract. Antacids containing calcium, magnesium, or aluminum interfere with the absorption of tetracyclines due to the chelating action of the antibiotic. Ferrous sulfate also interferes with the absorption of tetracyclines, but the mechanism is not clearly understood. Formation of insoluble complexes may explain the decreased response to iron therapy that has been observed in patients receiving magnesium trisilicate. Cholestyramine resin interferes with the absorption of levothyroxine sodium, liothyronine sodium, and warfarin by intestinal binding. This ion exchange resin also may form complexes with other agents (thiazide diuretics, phenylbutazone) but this has not been clearly established. The absorption of lincomycin is reduced if kaolin-pectin combinations are administered concomitantly or up to two hours after the antibiotic; this interaction may be caused by the adsorbent effect of the antidiarrheal agents.

pH: Most orally administered drugs cross the membranes of the stomach and small intestine by passive diffusion. Since these cell membranes consist of a lipid-protein structure, drugs are more readily absorbed in their nonionized (lipid-soluble) state. Theoretically, changes in the gastric pH could alter the ionization of drugs, thus affecting their absorption. For example, it has been suggested that antacids may interfere with the absorption of acidic agents by increasing the proportion of ionized drug. The clinical significance of this potential interaction has not been established, and, in view of the large surface area involved in drug absorption, it is unlikely that gastric pH is an important factor in the rate of absorption of most drugs. However, results of one study have demonstrated that a low gastric pH is necessary for complete dissolution of tetracycline capsules; sodium bicarbonate decreases dissolution and, therefore, reduces absorption of this antibiotic.

Motility: It has been suggested that anticholinergic drugs and ganglionic blocking agents may delay drug absorption by reducing gastrointestinal motility. Despite the widespread use of drugs with anticholinergic properties, this theoretical interaction has apparently not been studied in man.

Phenobarbital reduces plasma levels (and possibly the therapeutic effect) of griseofulvin by impairing its absorption from the gastrointestinal tract. One proposed explanation for this effect is that phenobarbital stimulates the secretion of bile which, in turn, stimulates peristalsis. The increase in motility would decrease the transit time in the upper portion of the intestinal tract where griseofulvin is absorbed most efficiently.

Inhibition of Gastrointestinal Enzymes: Diphenylhydantoin inhibits the activity of the intestinal conjugase enzyme involved in the conversion of polyglutamates to readily absorbed monoglutamates. This agent can, therefore, reduce the absorption of folic acid and may cause mild megaloblastic anemia in some patients.

Alterations in Intestinal Flora: The prothrombin time after administration of coumarin anticoagulants is increased by chloramphenicol, neomycin, tetracycline, and possibly by other antibiotics. The mechanism of this interaction has not been established but may involve inhibition of vitamin K synthesis by intestinal bacteria. Other suggested mechanisms include inhibition of hepatic microsomal enzymes (chloramphenicol) and impairment of prothrombin utilization (tetracycline).

Interactions involving gastrointestinal absorption are summarized in Table 1.

Interactions Affecting Distribution of Drugs (Protein Binding)

After absorption, most drugs become reversibly bound to plasma proteins, usually albumin. The extent of protein binding varies considerably. Some agents show a high affinity for albumin (eg, phenylbutazone, coumarin anticoagulants, and the highly bound sulfonamides: sulfadimethoxine [Madribon], sulfamethoxypyridazine [Midicel], sulfamoxole, and sulfisoxazole), whereas others are present largely in the free state (eg, antipyrine). The bound portion of the drug is biologically inactive, while the unbound portion is free to diffuse to receptor sites. Since the number of available binding sites is limited, the

Table 1.—Interactions Involving Gastrointestinal Absorption of Drugs and Other Agents

(? = Clinical significance not clearly established)

Drug 1	Drug 2	Effect
Antacids containing calcium, magnesium, or aluminum Ferrous sulfate	Tetracyclines	Decrease in serum level of tetracyclines
Sodium bicarbonate	Tetracycline capsules	Decrease in excretion rate of tetracycline
Magnesium trisilicate	Iron preparations	Reduced response to iron therapy
Cholestyramine resin [Cuemid, Questran]	Levothyroxine sodium [Letter, Synthroid Sodium] Liothyronine sodium [Cytomel] Warfarin [Coumadin, Panwarfin] ?Other oral anticoagulants	Reduced response to hormone
Kaolin-pectin combinations [Kaopectate]	Lincomycin [Lincocin]	Decrease in serum level of lincomycin
Antacids	Various acidic drugs	Reduced absorption of Drug 2?
Anticholinergic drugs Ganglionic blocking agents	Many drugs	Delayed absorption of Drug 2?
Phenobarbital	Griseofulvin [Fulvicin-U/F, Grifulvin V, Grisactin]	Decrease in serum level of griseofulvin
Diphenylhydantoin [Dilantin]	Folic acid	Mild megaloblastic anemia
Chloramphenicol Neomycin Tetracycline ?Other antibiotics	Coumarin anticoagulants	Enhanced hypoprothrombinemia
Aminosalicylic acid	Rifampin [Rifadin, Rimactane]	Decrease in serum level of rifampin

administration of two highly bound drugs may cause an interaction by mutual displacement. When a highly bound drug is displaced, an increase in its therapeutic or toxic effects may be observed. However, duration of action may be shortened because more of the drug will be available for metabolic degradation and glomerular filtration.

Displacement of the highly bound coumarin anticoagulants increases prothrombin time and can lead to severe bleeding. Chloral hydrate, clofibrate, phenylbutazone, and oxyphenbutazone enhance the anticoagulant effect of the coumarin derivatives, and this interaction appears to be due to drug displacement. A number of other agents also may displace coumarin anticoagulants from protein binding sites but this has not been clearly established in man. The enhanced hypoglycemic effect of tolbutamide which occurs after administration of salicylates or some sulfonamides may, in part, be due to occupation of binding sites by the latter agents. Methotrexate is displaced from plasma protein binding sites by salicylates and sulfisoxazole. Increased levels of free methotrexate have been demonstrated after administration of these agents in man, and three cases of methotrexate toxicity have been described in which concomitant aspirin therapy may have played a role. It has been suggested that various highly bound acidic drugs can displace some sulfonamides from protein binding sites, thereby enhancing the antibacterial effect. It has also been reported that quinine may be displaced by pyrimethamine. These interactions may or may not be clinically significant.

Interactions affecting distribution of drugs are listed in Table 2.

Table 2.—Interactions Affecting Distribution of Drugs (Protein Binding)
(? = Clinical significance not clearly established)

Drug 1 (Displaced Drug)	Drug 2	Effect
Coumarin anticoagulants	Chloral hydrate Clofibrate [Atromid-S] Phenylbutazone [Azolid, Butazolidin] Oxyphenbutazone [Oxalid, Tandearil] ?Ethacrynic Acid [Edecrin] ?Mefenamic Acid [Ponstel] ?Salicylates ?Tolbutamide [Orinase] ?Diphenylhydantoin [Dilantin] ?Indomethacin [Indocin] ?Nalidixic Acid [NegGram] ?Highly bound sulfonamides	Increased prothrombin time. Severe bleeding episodes may occur unless Drug 2 is discontinued or the dose of the oral anticoagulant is reduced.
Tolbutamide [Orinase]	Salicylates Sulfaphenazole [Sulfabid] ?Other highly bound sulfonamides	Enhanced hypoglycemic effect. Drug 2 should be used cautiously in patients receiving tolbutamide.
Methotrexate	Salicylates Sulfisoxazole [Gantrisin] ?Other highly bound sulfonamides	Increased plasma levels of free methotrexate. Three cases of enhanced methotrexate toxicity have been reported with salicylates.
Some sulfonamides	?Coumarin anticoagulants ?Indomethacin [Indocin] ?Phenylbutazone ?Probenecid [Benemid] ?Sulfinpyrazone [Anturane]	Enhanced antibacterial effect of sulfonamide
Quinine	?Pyrimethamine [Daraprim]	Increased plasma levels of free quinine

Interactions Affecting Adrenergic Mechanisms

The adrenergic neurotransmitter, norepinephrine, is synthesized and stored in postganglionic sympathetic nerve terminals and is released by nerve impulse or by the action of certain drugs. Two enzymes are of importance in the metabolic disposition of norepinephrine: intracellular monoamine oxidase (MAO) and extracellular catechol-O-methyltransferase (COMT). Most of the norepinephrine stored within the nerve terminal is found in intragranular pools where it is protected from inactivation by MAO. Following release from the neuron and action at the receptor site, norepinephrine is taken up again by the axonal terminal or is methylated by COMT. Re-uptake appears to be the major factor in terminating the action of the neurotransmitter.

Interactions affecting adrenergic mechanisms may result from administration of drugs that interfere with the metabolic disposition of norepinephrine, block the uptake mechanism, release the neurotransmitter, or act at sympathetic receptor sites (see Table 3, as well as the section on Interactions at Receptor Sites).

Interference with Metabolism of Norepinephrine and Other Amines: Monoamine oxidase inhibition causes an accumulation of norepinephrine in the adrenergic neuron. The pressor effect of various noncatecholamines, such as amphetamines, ephedrine, phenylpropanolamine, and metaraminol bitartrate, is in part due to release of norepinephrine; therefore, a severe hypertensive crisis may occur if these agents are administered to patients receiving MAO inhibitors. Tyramine, dopamine, and phenylephrine are metabolized by monoamine oxidase. Hypertensive crises have followed ingestion of tyramine-containing foods by individuals treated with MAO inhibitors, and excessive pressor effects have been reported because of the interaction of these inhibitors

Table 3.—Interactions Affecting Adrenergic Mechanisms
(? = Clinical significance not clearly established)

Drug 1	Drug 2	Effect
Monoamine oxidase inhibitors	Amphetamines	Excessive pressor effects
	Ephedrine	
	Metaraminol bitartrate [Aramine]	
	Phenylpropanolamine [Propadrine]	
	Tyramine (in foods)	
	Levodopa	
	Phenylephrine (orally administered)	
	Tricyclic antidepressants	CNS stimulation, hyperpyrexia, convulsions; fatalities have occurred.
	Meperidine [Demerol]	CNS stimulation, sweating, rigidity, hypertension or hypotension; fatalities have occurred.
	Antidiabetic agents	Enhanced or prolonged hypoglycemic effect
Tricyclic antidepressants	Guanethidine [Ismelin]	Reduced antihypertensive effect of Drug 2
Reserpine	Adrenergic drugs that act mainly by releasing norepinephrine	Reduced sympathomimetic effect
	Levodopa	Reduced therapeutic effect of Drug 2
	Digitalis glycosides	Arrhythmias ?
	Monoamine oxidase inhibitors	Excitation and hypertension if reserpine is given after MAO inhibitor ?

with orally administered levodopa or phenylephrine. The mechanism of other interactions involving MAO inhibitors is not clearly understood: these agents enhance the hypoglycemic effect of antidiabetic drugs and may interact with tricyclic antidepressants or meperidine to cause severe, sometimes fatal, reactions.

Blocking of the Amine-Uptake Mechanism: The tricyclic antidepressants block the uptake of norepinephrine by the sympathetic nerve terminals. Guanethidine also utilizes the amine-uptake mechanism and is ineffective as an antihypertensive agent if it is not transported into the neuron. Tricyclic antidepressants prevent the uptake of guanethidine and thereby antagonize its antihypertensive effect.

Release of Norepinephrine from Storage Sites: Reserpine depletes stores of norepinephrine by slowly releasing the neurotransmitter from intragranular pools where it becomes accessible to inactivation by monoamine oxidase. Reserpine may, therefore, decrease the sympathomimetic effect of adrenergic drugs that act mainly by liberating norepinephrine. Other biogenic amines are also depleted by reserpine. This agent reduces the therapeutic effect of levodopa in parkinsonian patients, possibly by depleting brain dopamine. There have been a few reports in which reserpine was believed to have precipitated arrhythmias in digitalized patients; this interaction has been attributed to release of amines by reserpine. Interactions between monoamine oxidase inhibitors and reserpine have been demonstrated in animals but have not been reported in man.

Interactions at Receptor Sites

A drug may interact with another drug at the same site of action by competing for receptors or by altering receptor sensitivity. Interactions also may occur between two drugs that act at different receptor sites.

Adrenergic Receptor Sites: Cyclopropane and certain halogenated hydrocarbon anesthetics "sensitize" the heart to catecholamines. Epinephrine, levarterenol, and isoproterenol can produce arrhythmias in the presence of these anesthetic agents. Arrhythmias have also occurred during anesthesia after administration of some adrenergic drugs that lack the catechol nucleus; this may be due to release of norepinephrine by these adrenergic agents.

The beta-adrenergic blocking agent, propranolol, prolongs insulin-induced hypoglycemia. The mechanism of this interaction has not been established but may reflect interference with the glycogenolysis produced by catecholamines. (See Table 4.)

Cholinergic Receptor Sites: The belladonna alkaloids and the synthetic and semisynthetic anticholinergic agents are used specifically for their cholinergic blocking effects. There are many other widely used drugs that possess varying degrees of anticholinergic activity. These

Table 4.—Interactions at Adrenergic Receptor Sites
(? = Clinical significance not clearly established)

Drug 1	Drug 2	Effect
Epinephrine Levarterenol [Levophed] Isoproterenol [Isuprel]	Cyclopropane Chloroform Ethyl Chloride Halothane [Fluothane] Trichloroethylene [Trilene]	Arrhythmias due to sensitization of the heart to catecholamines by Drug 2
Noncatecholamines	Cyclopropane Chloroform Ethyl Chloride Halothane Trichloroethylene	Arrhythmias due to release of catecholamines by Drug 1 (?) and sensitization of the heart to catecholamines by Drug 2
Propranolol [Inderal]	Insulin ?Oral hypoglycemic agents	Prolonged hypoglycemic effect due to interference by Drug 1 with catecholamine-induced glycogenolysis

include phenothiazines, tricyclic antidepressants, antihistamines, quinidine, and procainamide. If any of these agents are used concomitantly, additive anticholinergic effects may be expected (eg, excessive dryness of the mouth, constipation), but severe reactions have not been reported. (See Table 5.)

Neuromuscular Junction: Various antibiotics, some general anesthetics, quinidine, and magnesium sulfate have neuromuscular blocking properties. Prolonged apnea has been reported in patients receiving these agents in conjunction with a nondepolarizing neuromuscular blocking drug (tubocurarine, dimethyl tubocurarine, gallamine). Excessive neuromuscular blockade resulting from these interactions does not appear to be consistently reversed by neostigmine. These antibiotics, anesthetics, quinidine, and magnesium sulfate might also be expected to interact with each other to produce blockade at the myoneural junction. This has occurred in man after administration of ether and certain antibiotics.

The depolarizing neuromuscular blocking agent, succinylcholine, is hydrolyzed by plasma pseudocholinesterase; therefore, prolonged postoperative apnea may occur if succinylcholine is given to patients receiving anticholinesterase drugs. The serum cholinesterase level can be depressed even by

Table 5.—Interactions at Cholinergic Sites

All of the following agents have anticholinergic properties and, if given concomitantly, could produce symptoms of excessive cholinergic blockade:

Belladonna alkaloids and synthetic and semisynthetic anticholinergic agents
(antispasmodics, antiparkinsonism agents)
Phenothiazines
Tricyclic antidepressants
Antihistamines
Quinidine
Procainamide [Pronestyl]

Table 6.—Interactions at the Neuromuscular Junction

(? = Clinical significance not clearly established)

The following agents have neuromuscular blocking properties and may intensify the effects of nondepolarizing neuromuscular blocking agents (tubocurarine, dimethyl tubocurarine, gallamine [Flaxedil]) or may interact with each other:

Antibiotics:

Streptomycin
Neomycin
Kanamycin [Kantrex]
Gentamicin [Garamycin]
Colistin Sulfate [Coly-Mycin S]
Colistimethate Sodium [Coly-Mycin M]
Polymyxin B Sulfate [Aerosporin]
Oxytetracycline [Terramycin]
Rolitetracycline [Syntetrin]
Other Tetracyclines ?
Lincomycin [Lincocin] ?

General Anesthetics:

Ether
Cyclopropane ?
Fluoroxene [Fluoromar] ?
Halothane [Fluothane] ?
Methoxyflurane [Penthrane] ?

Other Agents:

Magnesium Sulfate
Quinidine

The following agents may intensify the neuromuscular blockade produced by succinylcholine:

Anticholinesterase Agents
Magnesium sulfate

topical ophthalmic use of long-acting cholinesterase inhibitors. The blocking effect of succinylcholine may also be prolonged by magnesium sulfate.

Interactions at the neuromuscular junction are summarized in Table 6.

Interactions Affecting Drug Metabolism

Enhancement of Drug Metabolism: Most drugs are more soluble in lipid than in water and must be metabolized into water-soluble derivatives before they can be excreted by the kidney. This biotransformation is effected mainly by microsomal enzymes of the liver. Various agents can increase the activity of these nonspecific enzymes, a process known as enzyme induction. Inducing drugs may accelerate their own metabolism and also may increase the rate of metabolism of other unrelated drugs. Since most metabolites are biologically inactive, enzyme induction can decrease the duration and intensity of drug action, reduce drug toxicity, and contribute to the development of tolerance. However, severe toxic effects may occur if the dosage of an interacting drug is adjusted during administration of an inducing agent and the inducing drug is subsequently discontinued.

Agents that increase the activity of drug-metabolizing enzymes in man are listed in Table 7. Most of the interactions included in this table reflect only a reduction in the plasma concentration of the metabolized drug and may or may not indicate a need for dosage alteration. However, of definite clinical significance is the enhanced metabolism of coumarin anticoagulants that occurs in patients receiving phenobarbital, secobarbital, or amobarbital. In

Table 7.—Interactions Due to Enhancement of Drug Metabolism (Enzyme Induction)

(? = Clinical significance not clearly established)

Drug 1 (Inducing Agent)	Drug 2 (Metabolism Enhanced)
Phenobarbital	Coumarin anticoagulants Hydrocortisone Digitoxin Diphenylhydantoin [Dilantin] Dipyrone ?Chlorpromazine ?Testosterone ?Tricyclic antidepressants
Other barbiturates	Coumarin anticoagulants
Rifampin [Rifadin, Rimactane]	?Coumarin anticoagulants
Glutethimide [Doriden]	Warfarin [Coumadin, Panwarfin] Dipyrone
Ethchlorvynol [Placidyl]	Warfarin
Antipyrine	Warfarin Hydrocortisone
Diphenylhydantoin	Hydrocortisone Dexamethasone Digitoxin
Phenylbutazone [Azolid, Butazolidin]	Aminopyrine Hydrocortisone Digitoxin

order to maintain the desired effect on prothrombin time, a larger than usual dose of the anticoagulant may be required. If the barbiturate is subsequently withdrawn, fatal hemorrhage may occur unless the anticoagulant dosage is reduced. The metabolism of oral anticoagulants also is enhanced by glutethimide [Doriden], ethchlorvynol [Placidyl], and antipyrine.

Inhibition of Drug Metabolism: Some drugs interfere with the metabolism of other agents by inhibiting the activity of hepatic microsomal enzymes or by competing for the same enzyme. The half-life of tolbutamide and chlorpropamide is increased by dicumarol. Severe hypoglycemia has occurred after concomitant administration of tolbutamide and this anticoagulant. Phenindione does not alter the metabolism of tolbutamide and may be used safely in patients receiving this antidiabetic agent. The metabolism of tolbutamide also is inhibited by chloramphenicol, phenylbutazone, and sulfaphenazole.

Several agents increase the serum level and half-life of diphenylhydantoin. These include dicumarol, chloramphenicol, disulfiram, isoniazid, and possibly methylphenidate [Ritalin] and sulfaphenazole. If these drugs are given concomitantly with usual doses of the anticonvulsant, signs of diphenylhydantoin toxicity may appear. With isoniazid, diphenylhydantoin intoxication has developed

Table 8.—Interactions Due to Inhibition of Drug Metabolism
(? = Clinical significance not clearly established)

Drug 1 (Metabolism Inhibited)	Drug 2	Effect
Tolbutamide [Orinase]	Dicumarol Chloramphenicol Phenylbutazone [Azolid, Butazolidin] Sulfaphenazole [Sulfabid]	Enhanced hypoglycemic response
Chlorpropamide [Diabinese]	Dicumarol	Enhanced hypoglycemic response
Diphenylhydantoin [Dilantin]	Dicumarol Chloramphenicol Disulfiram [Antabuse] Isoniazid ?Methylphenidate [Ritalin] ?Sulfaphenazole	Increase in serum level of the anticonvulsant. Signs of diphenylhydantoin toxicity may appear.
Coumarin anticoagulants	Chloramphenicol ?Methylphenidate	Prolonged half-life of the anticoagulant
Warfarin [Coumadin, Panwarfin]	Disulfiram	Enhanced anticoagulant effect
Tricyclic antidepressants	Methylphenidate	Increased serum levels of the antidepressant
Mercaptopurine [Purinethol] Azathioprine [Imuran]	Allopurinol [Zyloprim]	Increased toxic effect of Drug 1
Alcohol	Chloral hydrate	Prolonged effect of alcohol
Oxyphenbutazone [Oxalid, Tandearil]	Methandrostenolone [Dianabol]	Increased plasma levels of oxyphenbutazone

only in patients who are slow inactivators of the antituberculous agent.

These and other interactions involving inhibition of drug metabolism are shown in Table 8.

Interactions at the Site of Excretion

Most drugs or their metabolites are removed from the body by renal excretion. Agents that are not protein bound leave the blood and are filtered through the glomerular membrane. Further along the tubule, they may be secreted or reabsorbed by active transport mechanisms or passively reabsorbed by nonionic diffusion. The retention or loss of many agents is altered by interactions affecting these renal mechanisms. For unmetabolized drugs and active metabolites, these interactions are often of clinical significance.

Active Secretion and Reabsorption: There are two major active transport systems in the renal tubules: one for acids and the other for bases. These transport mechanisms remove drugs from the blood and secrete them into the tubules. Even highly protein-bound drugs are secreted by the active transport system. Many acidic drugs and metabolites are actively secreted and may compete with other acidic agents for the same secretory site. If one drug replaces another drug in the secretory transport mechanism, the renal excretion of the latter will be delayed and its action prolonged. A familiar example of this type of interaction is the use of probenecid to prolong the therapeutic effect of penicillin. Drugs also may compete for active tubular reabsorption and this may explain the urate retention that can occur when some uricosuric agents are used concomitantly. Interactions affecting active secretion and reabsorption of acidic drugs are shown in Table 9. Competition for transport mechanisms concerned with active secretion and reabsorption of basic drugs has been studied in animals but not in man.

Passive Reabsorption: The passive diffusion of drugs from the renal tubules back into the plasma is influenced by the same factors that govern gastrointestinal absorption. Most drugs are weak acids or bases and can be passively reabsorbed only in the nonionized (lipid-soluble) state. Changes in the pH of the tubular fluid will affect the extent of ionization, thereby altering the excretion rate. Weak acids (pKa 3.0-7.5) are excreted more rapidly in alkaline urine, and the

Table 9.—Interactions Due to Competition for Active Transport Systems in the Renal Tubules

Drug 1	Drug 2	Effect
Probenecid [Benemid]	Pyrazinamide	Drug 1 inhibits hyperuricemic effect of Drug 2
	Aminosalicylic acid Cephalothin [Keflin] Indomethacin [Indocin] Dapsone [Avlosulfon]	Increased blood levels of Drug 2
Probenecid Phenylbutazone [Azolid, Butazolidin]	Penicillin	Increased half-life of Drug 2
Dicumarol	Chlorpropamide [Diabinese]	Enhanced hypoglycemic effect of Drug 2
Phenylbutazone	Acetohexamide [Dymelor]	Enhanced hypoglycemic effect of Drug 2
Sulfonamides	Tolbutamide [Orinase]	Enhanced hypoglycemic effect of Drug 2
Salicylates	Probenecid Sulfinpyrazone [Anturane]	Uricosuric effect of Drug 2 inhibited

Table 10.—Effect of Urinary pH on Drug Excretion

Weak Acids (pKa 3.0-7.5)

The rate of excretion of these agents may be increased in alkaline urine and decreased in acid urine:

Phenobarbital
Salicylic acid
Some sulfonamides
Nalidixic acid [NegGram] ?
Phenylbutazone [Azolid, Butazolidin] ?
Streptomycin ?

Weak bases (pKa 7.5-10.5)

The rate of excretion of these agents may be increased in acid urine and decreased in alkaline urine:

Amphetamines
Chloroquine [Aralen]
Mecamylamine [Inversine]
Meperidine [Demerol]
Quinine
Quinacrine [Atabrine]
Quinidine

rate of excretion of weak bases (pKa 7.5-10.5) is increased in acid urine. Drugs may be administered to alter the urinary pH and thereby affect the duration of action of other drugs. Phenobarbital is a weak acid and, in the event of overdose, its rate of excretion can be increased by administering sodium bicarbonate to render the urine more alkaline. Amphetamines are weak bases, and individuals who abuse these stimulants have used sodium bicarbonate to prolong their action. Conversely, the rate of excretion of amphetamines may be increased if the urine is acidified by administration of ammonium chloride or ascorbic acid. Some drugs whose duration of action is affected by urinary pH are listed in Table 10.

Interactions Affecting Microorganisms*

Antimicrobial combinations are used with the hope of controlling infection more effectively. However, a single agent often will accomplish as much as a combination of drugs, and at times adverse reactions will follow the use of several antimicrobial agents. Indications advanced for the use of antimicrobial combinations are (1) synergic effect; (2) delayed emergence of resistant organisms; (3) prevention of superinfection; (4) treatment of intracellular bacteria; (5) treatment of mixed infections; (6) initial treatment of overwhelming undiagnosed infections; and (7) decreased untoward effects. Infections favorably affected by antibiotic combinations are listed in Table 11.

Delayed Emergence of Resistant Organisms: A limited number of infections benefit from the delayed emergence of resistant organisms. When bacteria are resistant to one of the antimicrobial agents, resistance will develop to the other agent as rapidly as if it were used alone.

Prevention of Superinfection: Tetracycline is combined with nystatin or amphotericin B in an attempt to prevent fungal overgrowth in the gastrointestinal tract. Unfortunately, not all fungi are eliminated, and even when the fungal population is decreased, diarrhea may persist. In fact, superinfection may be a contraindication to the use of antimicrobial combinations. Organisms resistant to multiple antimicrobial agents will grow more readily in the gastrointestinal, upper respiratory, and genital areas and in the skin.

Intracellular Bacterial Infections: Brucellosis, tuberculosis, and salmonellosis are intracellular bacterial infections that are difficult to eradicate with antibiotics. Intracellular

*Adapted from Kabins, S.A.: Interactions among antibiotics and other drugs. *JAMA* 219:206-212 (1972). Copyright 1972, American Medical Association, updated by S.A. Kabins. References may be found in the original article.

Table 11.—Infections Favorably Affected by Antibiotic Combinations

Infection	Antibiotic Combination	Mechanism of Effect
Enterococcal endocarditis	Penicillin G and streptomycin; ampicillin and streptomycin; penicillin G, streptomycin, erythromycin, and bacitracin; vancomycin and streptomycin; penicillin G or ampicillin and kanamycin; penicillin G or ampicillin and gentamicin	Synergic
Streptococcal viridans endocarditis	Penicillin G and streptomycin; erythromycin and streptomycin; cephalothin and streptomycin; lincomycin and streptomycin	Synergic
Pseudomonas aeruginosa	Carbenicillin and gentamicin*; carbenicillin and polymyxins; ampicillin and methicillin†	Delayed resistance and synergic
Klebsiella pneumoniae	Celphalothin and kanamycin; streptomycin and tetracycline	Synergic and delayed resistance
Tuberculosis‡	Isoniazid, streptomycin, and aminosalicylic acid; isoniazid, streptomycin, and ethambutol; isoniazid and rifampin	Delayed resistance, synergic, and cellular penetration?
Brucellosis	Streptomycin and tetracycline or penicillin G	Synergic, delayed resistance, and cellular penetration(?)
Salmonella typhi, S paratyphi A	Ampicillin and chloramphenicol§	Cellular penetration(?), synergic(?)
Plasmodium falciparum	Trimethoprim and sulfonamides; pyrimethamine and sulfonamides	Synergic
Overwhelming sepsis	Cephaloridine and gentamicin; clindamycin and gentamicin	Synergic(?); Broad spectrum of coverage
	Ampicillin and gentamicin	Synergic
Candida; cryptococci	Amphotericin B and flucytosine	Synergic

*Carbenicillin can inactivate gentamicin in the severely azotemic patient or if the two agents are mixed together in the same intravenou fluid.
†Clinical application limited to urinary tract infection in patients able to concentrate urine.
‡Combinations cited only for initial or first line therapy.
§Single report; needs to be confirmed by further studies.

Brucella organisms are much less susceptible to streptomycin than are organisms in liquid media, probably due to poor penetration of streptomycin into mammalian cells. The combination of streptomycin and tetracycline, in concentrations that are individually subinhibitory for intracellular *Brucella* organisms, is able to kill the intracellular bacteria. Evidence indicates that subinhibitory concentrations of streptomycin are present in cells before the addition of tetracycline, and the enhanced effect is due to intracellular synergism rather than to enhanced penetration as has been suggested. In tuberculosis, isoniazid penetrates cells more readily than streptomycin and enhances its effect. The combination of ampicillin and chloramphenicol may be more effective than either drug alone in eliminating *S. typhi* and *S. paratyphi A* infections.

Mixed Infections: Gastrointestinal and uterine infections are caused by more than one organism. A single broad-spectrum agent such as tetracycline or ampicillin often will eradicate mixed infections. Antibiotic combinations may be necessary when infections are due to multiple bacteria that are each resistant to different antibiotics. Ideally, the combination should be based on sensitivity tests. Although the combination preferably should not have antagonistic effects against the individual organisms, it may be necessary in practice to abrogate this rule.

Overwhelming Undiagnosed Infections: The need for immediate therapy precludes waiting for the results of in vitro studies in overwhelming undiagnosed infections. In such circumstances, the use of antibiotic combinations can readily be justified, but they should be chosen to avoid antagonistic effects and additive toxicity. In a double-blind prospective study, Martin et al demonstrated that cephaloridine, together with gentamicin, almost fulfills these criteria. This combination was compared to cephaloridine plus polymyxin B or colistin, kanamycin plus polymyxin B, or colistin and gentamicin alone. The combination of cephaloridine and gentamicin gave the best results in the treatment of acute gram-negative bacillary infections. The numbers in each group were too small, however, to be of statistical significance.

Gentamicin and gentamicin plus cephaloridine were compared with the other antibiotic combinations in patients with gram-negative bacillary bacteremia and shock. The best survival rate approaching statistical significance was found in the gentamicin-treated patients with and without concomitant cephaloridine treatment. However, some gram-negative bacilli such as *Bacteroides* may be resistant to this combination; therefore, the combination of clindamycin and gentamicin has been used.

Decreased Adverse Reactions: Sulfonamides (ie, sulfadiazine, sulfamerazine, sulfamethazine) may crystallize in the renal tubules. In combination, their antibacterial activity is additive, while their solubility is independent of each other. Consequently, small doses of each when given together may eradicate organisms and decrease renal untoward effects. The combination of chloramphenicol and the polymyxins may be additive against *Pseudomonas* and therefore may be given in smaller doses when used together. Streptomycin has been combined with dihydrostreptomycin in the hope of decreasing toxicity. Instead, insidious and permanent deafness, caused by dihydrostreptomycin, has led to the abandonment of this combination. As a general principle, the more drugs that are used in therapy, the greater is the chance of untoward effects.

Synergic Effect: A synergic effect occurs when two antimicrobial agents kill greater numbers of bacteria or are more effective in curing infections than would be expected from the algebraic summation of the individual drugs. Mechanisms by which antimicrobial agents may act synergistically are listed in Table 12.

The combination of two bactericidal antibiotics acting on different metabolic pathways may increase the rate of early bacterial kill. The best known example of this mechanism occurs with the combination of penicillin G, which inhibits bacterial cell wall synthesis, and streptomycin, an aminoglycoside antibiotic which inhibits protein synthesis at the bacterial ribosome. At nontoxic blood concentrations, each antibiotic is usually unable to kill enterococci, but when combined in similar concentrations they usually kill these bacteria. The method by which this increased rate of bacterial kill is accomplished is not fully understood. Available data indicate that penicillin, in concentrations that inhibit but do not kill enterococci, alters permeability of the cell which, in turn, allows greater intracellular penetration of streptomycin. Jawetz has postulated that synergism may be due to the action of penicillin on the metabolically active portion of a heterogeneous bacterial population, while streptomycin acts on the metabolically inactive or *levo* phase portion of the population.

In practice, one has to test each bacterial isolate to be sure that a synergistic effect can be obtained by nontoxic concentrations of antibiotics. Jawetz and Sonne found that 20% of enterococci were not subject to the synergistic effect of penicillin and streptomycin. The

Table 12.—Mechanisms of Antimicrobial Synergy

Mechanism	Antimicrobials	Organism
Increased rate of cidal activity; cell envelope altered to increase cellular uptake of aminoglycoside or flucytosine	Penicillin G and streptomycin; amphotericin B and flucytosine	Streptococci, especially enterococci; *Candida* and cryptococci
Sequential blockade; two antimicrobial agents acting on different sites in same metabolic pathway	Trimethoprim and sulfonamides	Plasmodia, gram-negative bacilli, gram-positive cocci
Competitive inhibition of enzymes that inactivate antibiotics	Ampicillin and methicillin	Penicillinase-producing gram-negative bacilli
Delayed emergence of minority population of erythromycin-resistant clones in dissociated resistance to erythromycin	Penicillin G and erythromycin	*Staphylococcus aureus*
Render bacterial receptor site accessible to antibiotic	Polymyxins and sulfonamides	*Proteus mirabilis*

ribosomes of these enterococci, in contrast to those susceptible to the antibiotic combination, are highly resistant to the action of streptomycin and thus are unaffected by the increased intracellular penetration of streptomycin. In general, enterococci susceptible to the combination of penicillin and streptomycin can be detected by inhibition of their growth in 2 mg of streptomycin per milliliter. The antibiotic dosage needed to accomplish synergism is variable. After starting therapy, the patient's serum should be tested for adequate bactericidal activity against the organism involved. It is apparent that fixed-combination preparations of penicillin and streptomycin would be difficult if not impossible to use for this purpose.

Sequential blockade is a mechanism of antimicrobial synergism in which two agents act at different sites in the same metabolic pathway. Sulfonamides, by competing with aminobenzoic acid, inhibit the formation of dihydrofolic acid. Trimethoprim or pyrimethamine, inhibitors of dihydrofolic acid reductase, prevent the formation of tetrahydrofolic acid and thereby potentiate the action of sulfonamides. This combination of bacteriostatic agents is bactericidal against many gram-negative bacilli and gram-positive cocci and has proved effective against chloroquine-resistant *Plasmodium falciparum*. Bacteria and plasmodia, in contrast to mammalian cells, are preferentially affected by this combination since they synthesize their own folates and are unable to utilize exogenous folates. Leucovorin or folic acid will protect mammalian cells while causing little or no alteration in the effect of sulfonamides and their potentiators on bacteria or plasmodia. There is no fixed combination of these agents effective against all susceptible organisms.

Competitive inhibition of enzymes that inactivate antimicrobials is another mechanism of synergism. Aminosalicylic acid, by competing for acetyl coenzyme A, decreases the rate of acetylation of isoniazid and results in increased levels and duration of active isoniazid in the blood.

Penicillinase-producing gram-negative bacilli are not susceptible to penicillin or ampicillin, since they hydrolyze these antibiotics. Penicillinase and cephalosporinase (beta-lactamases)-resistant antibiotics (methacillin, oxacillin, cloxacillin, dicloxacillin, cephalothin, cephaloridine, cephalexin), while unable to inhibit these organisms, may have much higher affinities for the active site of their beta-lactamases than do the hydrolyzable substrates (penicillin, ampicillin). In effect, these beta-lactamase-resistant antibiotics tie up the enzyme, thus preventing hydrolysis of penicillin and ampicillin. Unfortunately, the concentration of beta-lactamase inhibitors necessary to achieve this effect is too high to obtain in the serum. Marginally effective levels, however, may be achieved in the urine.

The remaining mechanisms of synergy listed in Table 12 have limited clinical application.

Antibiotic Antagonism: A major concern in the use of antibiotic combinations is that the effect of two agents may be less than the effect of either agent used alone. This is likely to occur when an antibiotic requiring active bacterial growth for its bactericidal action (penicillins, cephalosporins) is inhibited by the concomitant use of a bacteriostatic drug (tetracycline and chloramphenicol). Inhibition may partially be attributed to the prevention of cell lysis by bacteriostatic drugs that probably interfere with the production of mucopeptidases, enzymes which cause autolysis of the inner mucopeptide layers of the bacterial wall. The aminoglycosides also require active bacterial growth for their bactericidal action but are not as readily inhibited by bacteriostatic drugs. The polymyxins do not require active bacterial growth for their bactericidal effect and therefore are not antagonized by bacteriostatic agents. Erythromycin is a bacteriostatic drug when used in low concentrations, but in high concentrations it is bactericidal for streptococci and therefore may act synergistically with penicillin against these organisms. The sulfonamides are bacteriostatic but frequently do not antagonize bactericidal drugs because their slow onset of action allows early bacterial growth.

Conditional resistance occurs when an organism is resistant to one of two agents competing for the same ribosomal binding site. The inactive drug interferes with the active drug by preventing its ribosomal binding. Antagonism of this type occurs with the bacteriostatic agents (erythromycin, lincomycin, and chloramphenicol), which bind to the 50S subunit of the bacterial ribosome.

There are few clear-cut clinical examples of antibiotic antagonism. Lepper and Dowling studied a group of 43 patients, primarily adults, with pneumococcal meningitis. They found mortality to be significantly greater when penicillin was used with chlortetracycline than when penicillin was used alone. This antagonistic effect may be better understood when one considers that the mortality with penicillin alone was almost 30%. A small decrease in the effectiveness of penicillin drastically affected this delicate balance.

A similar antagonistic effect occurs in children treated for bacterial meningitis with various combinations of ampicillin, chloramphenicol, and streptomycin. In 1967, Mathies et al studied 264 children with bacterial meningitis. They found the mortality to be greater with all the combined regimens (10.5%) than with ampicillin alone (4.3%). The difference was not nearly as marked as in adults. Therefore, a much larger group of patients had to be treated before significant changes became apparent.

Antibiotic concentrations achieved in blood and urine with conventional dosage usually are much greater than those needed to eliminate the causative agent(s) in many infections. Despite the antagonistic effects of some combinations, the concentrations of antibiotic in the blood and urine are often sufficient to eliminate many bacteria provided they are not in unfavorable sites such as the meninges, heart valve, or bone. Therefore, in mixed gastrointestinal or uterine infections in which individual organisms might be subject to antagonism between antibiotics, sufficient antibiotic activity remains to control infection. This should particularly be true if the bactericidal agent is given first and in large dosage.

Guidelines derived to help predict which combinations would be synergistic or antagonistic are given in Table 13. Combinations of bactericidal drugs may usually be used without fear of antagonism, but they cannot be relied upon to be synergistic without appropriate in vitro tests. The combination of two bacteriostatic agents frequently considered to be indifferent or additive actually may be either synergistic or antagonistic, and combinations of bactericidal and bacteriostatic agents frequently have additive or indifferent effects. Fear that the latter combinations may be antagonistic may prevent their combined usage. Yet such combinations in appropriate infections may be useful. Therefore, there is no substitute for adequate in vitro studies to determine the precise effect obtained by antibiotic combinations against specific bacterial isolates.

PHARMACOGENETICS

Many of the wide individual differences which patients exhibit in response to drugs are genetically determined. Some of these hereditary alterations in drug response have been carefully investigated in terms of genetics, biochemistry, and pharmacology, and this field of study has been termed "pharmacogenetics." Most genetically determined variations in drug response are related to alterations in the amount

Table 13.—Guidelines to Synergistic and Antagonistic Antimicrobial Combinations

Combination	Interaction	Organisms*	Antimicrobials
Two bactericidal agents†	Synergic	Streptococci	Penicillin and streptomycin
	Additive or indifferent	Most	Most
Two bacteriostatic agents‡	Additive or indifferent	Most	Most
	Synergic	Many	Sulfonamides and trimethoprims
	Antagonistic	Few gram-positive and few gram-negative	Erythromycin and lincomycin; erythromycin and chloramphenicol; lincomycin and chloramphenicol; novobiocin and tetracycline
One bactericidal and one bacteriostatic agent	Antagonistic	Pneumococci	Penicillin and tetracycline
	Additive or indifferent	Most	Most
	Synergic	*Proteus*	Polymyxins and sulfonamides
		Brucella	Streptomycin and tetracycline
		Streptococci	Erythromycin and streptomycin
		Salmonella	Ampicillin and chloramphenicol

*Includes only selected examples.
†Penicillins, cephalosporins, aminoglycosides, polymyxins.
‡Tetracylines, chloramphenicol, erthyromycin, lincomycin, sulfonamides, novobiocin.

or structure of specific proteins. Some disorders are associated with a deficiency or a defect of an enzyme protein (the inborn errors of metabolism) or to an alteration in protein structure (the molecular diseases). Other anomalies are caused by defects in the regulatory mechanisms controlling protein synthesis or by anatomical defects.

Hereditary Diseases Causing Altered Drug Response

Sensitivity to certain drugs occurs in many hereditary disorders. Some genetic defects cause chronic or intermittent symptoms which are worsened or precipitated by administration of drugs. In other conditions, symptoms occur only after drug administration, and drugs may be used as a diagnostic tool and as a method of detecting heterozygotes. Some hereditary diseases are associated with an enhanced or diminished response to certain pharmacologic agents.

DEFECTS OF ERYTHROCYTES

Hereditary abnormalities in the metabolism of the red blood cell or in the hemoglobin structure may cause hemolytic anemia or methemoglobinemia. Many of these genetic variants are characterized by sensitivity to drugs.

Inborn Errors of Metabolism: Drug-induced hemolysis may occur as the result of a genetic defect involving an enzyme deficiency in the erythrocyte. Although the normal red blood cell may rupture after exposure to excessively large doses of hemolytic drugs, the red cells of the genetically predisposed individual are sensitive to concentrations that have no effect on the normal erythrocyte.

A number of drugs can produce hemolytic anemia in individuals with an inherited lack of the enzyme, glucose-6-phosphate dehydrogenase (G6PD). This enzyme, which is present in the erythrocytes, plays a key role in the aerobic metabolism of glucose. Enzyme-deficient cells cannot protect themselves against the effects of oxidant drugs or their metabolites; in the presence of these agents, essential cell components are oxidized and hemolysis occurs. This genetically transmitted error of metabolism is frequently called "primaquine sensitivity," for it was originally described in investigations of the hemolytic effects of antimalarial drugs. However, a large number of drugs can cause hemolysis in individuals with this genetic defect. In addition to having occurred after use of various antimalarial agents (primaquine, pamaquine, pentaquine, quinacrine, quinine), hemolytic anemia has developed in susceptible individuals after administration of sulfonamides, nitrofurans, sulfones, antipyretics, and analgesics (aspirin, acetanilid, aminopyrine, antipyrine, phenacetin), and a number of miscellaneous agents, including chloramphenicol, methylene blue, and vitamin K. It also has occurred after contact with naphthalene and after ingestion of fava beans. Most individuals with G6PD deficiency have no hematologic abnormalities except after contact with these agents.

G6PD deficiency is transmitted by an X-chromosomal gene (sex linkage) of intermediate dominance. The trait gains full expression in the affected hemizygous male $(\overline{X}Y)$ and homozygous female $(\overline{X}\overline{X})$. Because of the high frequency of the gene, homozygous females are not extremely rare. In the heterozygous female $(\overline{X}X)$, symptoms are less severe because of the presence of a normal allele (X).

The geographical distribution of G6PD deficiency closely follows the distribution of *P. falciparum* malaria, which suggests that the trait provides some selective advantage against this disease. This inborn error of metabolism appears most frequently in African and Mediterranean populations. It occurs in about 13% of Negro American males. Oxidant drugs often cause more severe symptoms in Caucasians with G6PD deficiency than in affected Negroes. Also, hemolysis may be induced in Caucasians by agents that have no hemolytic effect on enzyme-deficient Negroes (eg, chloramphenicol, quinidine, aminosalicylic acid, fava beans). G6PD deficiency can be detected by the Brewer test which is based on the inability of the sensitive erythrocyte to reduce methemoglobin. Unreversed methemoglobin appears in enzyme-deficient cells after incubation with glucose, methylene blue, and sodium nitrite. The cells are then hemolyzed in water, and the methemoglobin appears brown in hemizygous males and homozygous females and dark red in heterozygous females.

Oxidant drugs also cause hemolysis in individuals with a deficiency of glutathione or glutathione reductase in the erythrocytes. These inborn errors of metabolism are uncommon. Another rare inherited metabolic disorder is hereditary methemoglobinemia (NADH diaphorase deficiency). Individuals with this autosomal recessive trait have a chronically high level of methemoglobin in the blood and develop severe methemoglobinemia after administration of nitrites and sulfonamides. The methemoglobin can be converted to hemoglobin by administration of methylene blue.

Hemoglobinopathies: There is considerable biochemical variability in the hemoglobin molecule due to genetically determined differences in amino acid sequences in the globin structure. Some variants are not correlated with any known pathology, but others are associated with a variety of hematologic disorders.

The erythrocytes of some individuals undergo a reversible alteration in shape (sickling) under conditions of reduced oxygen tension. This is due to the presence of a hemoglobin variant, sickle cell hemoglobin (Hb S), which is one of the most common hemoglobinopathies. In the homozygous state (sickle cell anemia), the red cells contain approximately 80% Hb S and the remainder is fetal hemoglobin (Hb F); no normal adult hemoglobin (Hb A) is present. Patients with sickle cell anemia have chronic hemolytic anemia with recurrent attacks of fatigue, weakness, anorexia, abdominal pain, and severe hemolytic crises. In the heterozygous state (sickle cell trait), 55% to 80% of the hemoglobin present is in the normal adult form, while the remainder is Hb S; little or no Hb F is present. Individuals with the sickle cell trait generally are asymptomatic unless they become exposed to reduced oxygen tension. Under conditions of hypoxia, sickling and splenic infarction may occur.

Hb S occurs predominantly in racial groups originating in areas where falciparum malaria is endemic. The sickle cell trait is present in about 10% of American Negroes, and the incidence is higher in many African tribes. There is considerable evidence that the possession of this trait provides protection against death from malaria.

Extreme care should be taken during administration of general anesthesia to individuals who are homozygous or heterozygous for Hb S. Hypoxia must be avoided, for even a slight fall in the oxygen tension of the blood may induce hemolytic crisis in patients with sickle cell anemia. Heterozygotes can tolerate a greater degree of hypoxia than homozygotes. Stasis and hypothermia should also be avoided. Since systemic acidosis enhances sickling, infusion of sodium bicarbonate during anesthesia helps to provide protection. There is some evidence that the risk of adverse reactions to blood transfusions is increased in patients with sickle cell disease. Diagnosis of sickle cell disease can be established by adding a drop of blood to the reducing agent, sodium metabisulphite. If sickling is detected on microscopic examination, electrophoretic confirmation is desirable.

A number of hemoglobin variants are easily oxidized to methemoglobin, and in this state they cannot transport oxygen. With some of these variants (Hb H and Hb Zürich), severe methemoglobinemia and hemolysis may develop after administration of certain drugs. Hemoglobin H disease appears in individuals with an inherited defect in hemoglobin synthesis (in thalassemia and certain related disorders). Patients with this disease generally show 10% to 35% abnormal hemoglobin. They have a chronic anemia because the life span of their erythrocytes is shortened to about 40 days. An acute hemolytic anemia may develop after administration of sulfonamides, nitrates, or methylene blue. Hemoglobin Zürich is associated with a chronic compensated hemolytic disease; severe methemoglobinemia and hemolytic crisis may occur in individuals with this variant after administration of sulfonamides, and probably after other methemoglobin-forming drugs.

PORPHYRIAS

The porphyrias are disorders of the regulatory mechanisms controlling the production of porphyrins, the precursor of heme. There are two forms of porphyria for which a hereditary basis has been established: erythropoietic and hepatic. Erythropoietic porphyria is apparently not associated with any abnormal drug reactions. The hepatic porphyrias, acute intermittent porphyria and porphyria variegata, are caused by a disturbance of porphyrin synthesis in the liver cells. Individuals with the hepatic forms are sensitive to barbiturates and some other drugs.

Acute intermittent porphyria (pyrolia, Swedish genetic porphyria) is an autosomal dominant trait characterized by periodic attacks of severe abdominal pain usually accompanied by neural symptoms. Barbiturates increase production of porphyrins and can precipitate a fatal attack of acute intermittent porphyria. Other agents reported to initiate attacks of acute porphyria include sulfonamides, alcohol, chlordiazepoxide, meprobamate, diphenylhydantoin, methsuximide, aminopyrine, hexachlorobenzene, and griseofulvin. Phenothiazines have not been implicated and may be used safely in patients with this genetic disorder.

Porphyria variegata (South African genetic porphyria) occurs in about 1% of the white population of South Africa. It is transmitted as an autosomal dominant trait. The skin of individuals with this genetic defect tends to erode and form bullae after exposure to sunlight or mechanical trauma. Attacks of abdominal pain and paralysis may be precipitated by barbiturates, alcohol, sulfonamides, and estrogens.

HUNTINGTON'S CHOREA

Huntington's chorea is a dominantly inherited degenerative disorder of the nervous system characterized by progressive choreiform movements and dementia. Genetic counseling of patients at risk is difficult because symptoms of the disease generally do not appear before the age of 30 and no test has yet been developed to differentiate presymptomatic patients from their normal siblings. Recently, levodopa was administered to a group of asymptomatic individuals genetically at risk for Huntington's chorea in an attempt to identify those in whom the disease may develop. This procedure evolved from a theory that the biogenic amine, dopamine, is involved in the production of chorea. The choreiform movements that occur in parkinsonian patients during treatment with levodopa have been attributed to hypersensitivity of denervated striatal dopamine receptors. Since extensive loss of striatal neurons occurs in Huntington's chorea, presymptomatic patients might be expected to develop the abnormal movements with challenged with levodopa.

In this study, levodopa was administered to 28 offspring of patients with Huntington's chorea and to 24 control subjects. The drug was given alone for ten weeks in gradually increasing doses up to 2.5 g daily or with a peripheral decarboxylase inhibitor for ten days at a dose of 800 mg daily. Among the individuals genetically at risk for Huntington's chorea, 35.7% developed choreiform movements during administration of levodopa; these movements subsided when the drug was discontinued. None of the control subjects developed chorea. Although the use of levodopa defined two separate populations among individuals at risk for Huntington's chorea, this test cannot be regarded as predictive until the subjects have been followed for many years.

OTHER DISORDERS

Familial nonhemolytic jaundice (Crigler-Najjar syndrome) is a rare recessive hereditary defect manifested by severe postnatal jaundice and kernicterus. Most homozygotes are severely affected and die within the early weeks or months of life. Those who survive may show no obvious abnormality except for jaundice but demonstrate a delayed excretion of drugs that normally undergo glucuronidation. Decreased glucuronidation of salicylates, adrenal corticosteroids, menthol, and trichloroacetic acid has been found in affected individuals. Heterozygotes can be identified by their response to administration of these drugs, for their excretion level is intermediate between the normal level and that of the homozygotes.

Dobin-Johnson syndrome is a familial disorder characterized by chronic, mild conjugated hyperbilirubinemia, intermittent bilirubinuria, and deposition of a dark pigment in the liver cells. The condition is frequently asymptomatic, but various environmental factors can exacerbate the hyperbilirubinemia, resulting in an overt jaundice. Asymptomatic women with this genetic defect have developed clinical jaundice during the last trimester of pregnancy and following use of oral contraceptives.

Von Gierke's disease, the first known disorder of glycogen metabolism, is caused by an inborn error in the conversion of glycogen to glucose. In individuals with this disorder, there is little or no elevation of the blood glucose level after injection of epinephrine. Phenylketonuria is also characterized by an altered response to epinephrine, in this case an enhancement of the hypertensive effect.

Hyperuricemia occurs frequently during prolonged administration of thiazides and related oral diuretics. The high level of serum uric acid may provoke an attack of gout in individuals with a family history is this disease. These agents also may increase the blood glucose level in diabetics and prediabetics.

When applied topically to the eye, corticosteroids cause an abnormal increase in the intraocular pressure of some individuals. This response appears to be genetically determined and occurs most frequently in patients with primary open-angle glaucoma and in their relatives, as well as in myopic individuals with no family history of glaucoma and in diabetics. Topically applied mydriatic drugs (anticholinergics and adrenergics) may precipitate an attack of acute angle-closure glaucoma in eyes with narrow angles and shallow anterior chambers; this angle configuration is an hereditary trait. Systemically administered anticholinergic agents have only rarely induced angle-closure glaucoma in susceptible individuals.

Genetic Factors That Modify The Response to Drugs

Drug studies have revealed a number of biological differences among healthy individuals. Some of these differences are genetically determined and occur in large segments of a population. These genetic variations account for some adverse drug reactions.

Pseudocholinesterase Variants: Succinylcholine is a potent neuromuscular blocking agent that ordinarily has a short duration of action due to its rapid hydrolysis by the plasma enzyme, pseudocholinesterase. In some individuals, however, prolonged apnea occurs after administration of succinylcholine. This prolonged apnea is associated with low activity of serum pseudocholinesterase due to the presence of a genetically determined variant of the enzyme. Serum cholinesterase is controlled by at least four allelic autosomal genes, and several variants have been identified. The "atypical" variant has been most extensively studied. In populations in which this enzyme type is found, the homozygous state (which is associated with succinylcholine sensitivity) occurs in about 1 in 2,500 individuals. Despite the sensitivity of individuals with abnormal pseudocholinesterase, succinylcholine may be administered if the minimal effective dose is given.

Acetylation of Isoniazid and Other Drugs: Acetylation is a major pathway for the metabolic inactivation of drugs, including the tuberculostatic agent, isoniazid. The general population can be divided into two groups on the basis of the speed of inactivation of this drug: slow and fast inactivators. The ability to acetylate isoniazid is genetically controlled. Rapid inactivators are homozygous or heterozygous for a gene that controls an "acetylating" enzyme, while slow inactivators are homozygous for a gene that produces an inactive enzyme. About one-half of American Caucasians and Negroes are slow inactivators, but this trait occurs infrequently among Japanese and Eskimos. Because of the grossly different acetylation capacity among individuals, strict adherence to the recognized therapeutic schedules is advisable to avoid therapeutic failure or toxic reactions. In slow acetylators, the relatively high level of isoniazid may interefere with the metabolism of other drugs (eg, diphenylhydantoin).

Individual differences have been found in the rate of acetylation of sulfamethazine, hydralazine, and phenelzine, and these differences appear to have the same genetic basis as isoniazid inactivation. Genetic factors also play a role in the rate of metabolism of some anticoagulants (warfarin and dicumarol), anticonvulsants (diphenylhydantoin), tricyclic antidepressants (nortriptyline), antirheumatic agents (phenylbutazone), anesthetics (halothane), and alcohol.

Malignant Hyperpyrexia: This rare and often fatal complication of general anesthesia is characterized by a rapid rise is body temperature to above 106 F, severe respiratory and metabolic acidosis, hypovolemia, and hypertonicity of voluntary muscles. In most reported cases, succinylcholine was used for skeletal muscle relaxation and halothane was the principal anesthetic employed. A causative role of either or both agents has not been established, for occasionally the syndrome has occurred with other anesthetics and, in a small number of patients, when no neuromuscular blocking agent was administered.

Most, if not all, cases of malignant hyperpyrexia appear to have a genetic basis. Abnormally high levels of serum creatine phosphokinase (CPK) have been found in patients who survived an episode of malignant hyperpyrexia and in their relatives. It is currently believed that the high levels of CPK reflect a subclinical myopathy of autosomal dominant inheritance.

Venous Thromboembolism and Oral Contraceptives: In recent years, there has been considerable interest in the relationship between A, B, and O blood groups and susceptibility to disease. An association has been established between blood type and the tendency to develop venous thromboembolism; this association is particularly evident in pregnant and puerperal women and in those using oral contraceptives. Women with blood type O are less susceptible to venous thromboembolism than are women with other blood types. However, the difference among groups is not great enough to preclude the use of oral contraceptives in women with blood types A, B, or AB.

OFFICIAL AND REGULATORY AGENCIES

There are several official governmental and quasi-official voluntary bodies concerned with standards, distribution, labeling, and advertising of drug products. In order that the functions of these agencies may be understood and their spheres of influence as they pertain to medicinal agents defined, the following brief descriptions of their organizations and duties are given:

The United States Pharmacopeial Convention, Inc.: Under the General Committee on Revision, The United States Pharmacopeial Convention, Inc. issues the *United States Pharmacopeia* (U.S.P.) at five-year intervals. The United States Pharmacopeial Convention is a private body incorporated in the District of Columbia and is composed of representatives from medical schools, pharmacy schools, state medical associations, state pharmaceutical associations, the American Medical Association, the American Pharmaceutical Association, the American Chemical Society, many other scientific and trade associations, and various interested federal bureaus and departments.

Under authority of the Federal Food, Drug and Cosmetic Act, the *United States Pharmacopeia* is an official standard for the products described therein. Articles are admitted to this compendium by the Committee on Revision on the basis of demonstrated therapeutic value or pharmaceutic necessity.

The American Pharmaceutical Association: The *National Formulary* (N.F.) is compiled by the National Formulary Board of this Association and is published at five-year intervals. The primary purpose of the Association, stated in the 1967 revision of its constitution, is "to aid in improving, promoting, and safeguarding the public health and welfare by maintaining a compendium of standards and specifications calculated to promote the safety, efficacy, and purity of drugs" under criteria and procedures established by the National Formulary Board elected by the APhA Board of Trustees. Only articles considered by the Board to possess demonstrated therapeutic value and usefulness are admitted to the *National Formulary*.

Under authority of the Federal Food, Drug and Cosmetic Act, the *National Formulary* is an official compendium, and drugs described therein must meet the standards set forth in that publication.

The Food and Drug Administration: The FDA regulates the availability and distribution of drugs, including biological products, in interstate commerce. It is concerned with the safety, effectiveness, and reliability of drugs; the standardization of drug names; the labeling of drugs; and the advertising of prescription drugs.

To ensure the safety, identity, strength, quality, and purity of drugs, adequate quality control measures are required in all manufacturing plants. In addition, certification procedures conducted by the FDA itself are applied to antibiotics intended for use in man, as well as to insulin.

The Secretary of Health, Education and Welfare is iven the authority to designate an official name for any drug if he determines that such action is necessary or desirable in the interest of usefulness and simplicity. This name, then, is to be used in any subsequent issue of any official compendium as the only official title for that drug. In practice, the official name will probably be one that has been recommended by the USAN Council (see following discussion). Any such official, "established" name is the only nonproprietary or "generic" name, other than the chemical name or chemical formula, that may appear on the label of a drug. The label for a prescription drug must state the quantities of all active ingredients, and the established drug name for each active ingredient must appear both on the label and in conjunction with the brand name in other labeling. The label for an over-the-counter drug also must disclose the active ingredients but unfortunately is not required to give the quantities or ratios of these ingredients.

The Federal Food, Drug and Cosmetic Act provides that the labeling for any drug must not be false or misleading. Also, the advertising of prescription drugs must conform to the labeling in specified ways. Standards also exist for advertising over-the-counter drugs, but this advertising is regulated by the Federal Trade Commission rather than the FDA.

To market a new drug in interstate commerce, a manufacturer must have approval, through a New Drug Application (NDA), from the FDA. Among other things, the application must provide for the labeling under which the drug will be distributed. For prescription drugs, this labeling includes a document addressed to physicians and containing the recommended uses and dosage as well as disclosure of the possible adverse reactions and recommended precautions in using the drug. If it is deemed possible to write directions for use of a drug by the layman, such directions *must* be written as part of the manufacturer's labeling, and the drug is not entitled to bear the prescription legend. A physician may, of course, prescribe the drug if he chooses, but the manufacturer may not *restrict* it to prescription sale.

Another of the many components of an NDA is the clinical data that have been developed during the investigation of the drug. These data must support the claims made for the drug in the labeling, and they must be adequate to prove safety and efficacy to the satisfaction of the government. The law and regulations set forth many requirements and procedures that must be followed during the investigational stage of the development of a drug prior to submission or approval of the NDA.

After a new drug is marketed under specific approved labeling, the FDA generally requires further proof of safety and efficacy if the labeling is to be changed to add a new therapeutic indication or a variation in dosage. As a general rule, *whether new claims are added to labeling depends upon whether the pharmaceutical company has sufficient commercial interest in the matter to follow the necessary procedures to obtain approval.* However, manufacturers are required to submit to the FDA all reports of adverse effects, other clinical experience, and other relevant data on drugs on the market. The agency can require updating of labeling to keep precautionary information current. It also can take steps to have claims deleted that it considers no longer warranted, or even to suspend (ie, revoke) an NDA and remove the drug from the market if evidence discloses the drug not to be safe and effective, as originally believed. Legal remedies are available by which manufacturers may contest such actions if they disagree.

The FDA's jurisdiction over uses of marketed drugs, doses, and related matters extends only to what the manufacturer may recommend and must disclose in its labeling and advertising. The jurisdiction does not extend to the way a physician uses the drug in the normal course of his practice.

The physician is well advised to be *aware* of what is in a package insert and to give it due weight. However, his decision on how to use a drug must be based on what is good medicine and best for his patient. This statement is both true and legally sound whether his use of a drug conforms to a package insert or departs from it. In a malpractice suit, such drug labeling *may* have evidentiary weight for or against a physician, but the evidence is subject to refutation; drug labeling, *per se*, does not set the standard for what is good medical practice.

The FDA does not have jurisdiction over extemporaneous drugs that the physician may devise for use in the normal course of his practice, provided the physician does not introduce these drugs into interstate commerce. Such drugs would be those he has compounded from separate ingredients, or certain readily available chemicals or other nonpharmaceutical products that can be used therapeutically. The physician and pharmacist, of course, would be responsible for the suitability of the preparations for the use chosen, but the FDA would not be involved.

The Federal Trade Commission: The Federal Trade Commission (FTC) is an independent agency of the federal government directly responsible to the President. The Commission administers several laws, the principal one being the Federal Trade Commission Act, which deals mainly with the regulation of trade practices.

The principal power of the FTC with respect to drugs is contained in Section 15 of the Federal Trade Commission Act: this Act gives the Commission broad power to prevent the dissemination of false or misleading advertising of foods, drugs, and cosmetics to the general public. This power is circumscribed with respect to advertisements directed to the medical profession. Regulation of prescription drug advertising is the responsibility of the FDA. For drugs sold over the counter to the public, the FTC relies upon FDA determinations and has taken action against advertising claims that are inconsistent with these.

Department of Justice: Responsibility for administration of the Federal Comprehensive Drug Abuse Prevention and Control Act of 1970 is assigned to the Bureau of Narcotics and Dangerous Drugs (BNDD). This Act replaces the former Narcotic Acts and the Drug Abuse Control Amendments of 1965. BNDD issues the physician registration and order forms formerly handled by the Internal Revenue Service. An Informational Outline for Physicians on the Controlled Substances Act of 1970 may be obtained from the Bureau of Narcotics and Dangerous Drugs, Washington, D.C. 20537.

The Comprehensive Drug Abuse Prevention and Control Act is designed to improve the administration and regulation of the manufacturing, distribution, and dispensing of controlled substances by providing a "closed" system for legitimate handlers of these drugs. Every person not specifically exempted who manufactures, distributes, prescribes, administers, or dispenses any controlled substances must register annually with the Attorney General. Accurate records of drugs purchased, distributed, and dispensed must be maintained and kept on file for inspection for two years by all persons legitimately involved in the handling of controlled substances who regularly dispense and charge for such drugs in the course of their practice.

The Act establishes five schedules of controlled drugs, with varying degrees of control for each schedule. Each drug or substance subject to control is assigned to one schedule depending upon the drug's potential for abuse, its medical usefulness, and the degree of dependence if abused. These schedules and the drugs included in them are:

Schedule I: Drugs and other substances having a high potential for abuse and no current accepted medical usefulness. Included are certain opium derivatives (eg, heroin), opiates (synthetic narcotics), and hallucinogenic substances (eg, LSD).

Schedule II: Drugs having a high potential for abuse and accepted medical usefulness; abuse leads to severe psychological or physical dependence. In general, drugs in this schedule were previously controlled under the Narcotic Laws, eg, opium and its derivatives, opiates (synthetic narcotics), cocaine, and other stimulants such as amphetamine and related compounds.

Schedule III: Drugs having a lesser degree of abuse potential and accepted medical usefulness; abuse leads to moderate dependence problems. Included in this schedule are certain other stimulants and depressants (eg, barbiturates not included in another schedule), as well as preparations containing limited quantities of certain narcotic drugs.

Schedule IV: Drugs having a low abuse potential, accepted medical usefulness, and limited dependence problems. Included in this schedule are certain depressants not in another schedule (eg, chloral hydrate, phenobarbital).

Schedule V: Drugs having a low abuse potential, accepted medical usefulness, and limited dependence factors. Preparations containing narcotic and non-narcotic drugs as active ingredients are included in this schedule.

The Act also provides that no prescription for drugs in Schedule II can be refilled. Emergency telephone prescriptions for drugs in this Schedule may be filled if the practitioner furnishes a written, signed prescription to the pharmacy within 72 hours provided the drug prescribed is limited to the amount needed to treat the patient during the emergency period. Prescriptions for drugs in Schedules III and IV may be refilled up to five times within six months after the date of issue if authorized by the prescriber. Prescriptions for Schedule V drugs may be refilled only as expressly authorized by the prescribing practitioner on the prescription.

The Post Office: The Fraud Section of the Post Office, under the direction of the Solicitor, enforces the law pertaining to the fradulent use of the mails. The use of the United States mails is a privilege and may be denied to those who use it to defraud the public. Therefore, the solicitation of customers and the shipping via the mails of drugs for which fradulent claims are made may be the basis for the issuance of a "fraud order" and the suspension of all mail service to the guilty party.

The USAN Council: The United States Adopted Names (USAN) Council, an agency formed to adopt appropriate nonproprietary names for all new drugs, was organized in January, 1964 and was preceded by the AMA-USP Nomenclature Committee. It is sponsored by the American Medical Association, the American Pharmaceutical Association, and the United States Pharmacopeial Convention, Inc. The Council is a five member group, with one member appointed by each sponsor, one member-at-large who must be approved by all three sponsors, and one member from the Food and Drug Administration.

The primary functions of the USAN Council are: (1) to negotiate with pharmaceutical manufacturers in the selection of meaningful and distinctive nonproprietary names for new drug entities; (2) to publicize the adopted names, the guiding principles used in devising these names, and the procedures involved in their adoption; and (3) to cooperate with other national and international agencies, particularly the World Health Organization, in standardizing, as much as possible, the nonproprietary nomenclature for drugs.

The Guiding Principles for Coining United States Adopted Names for Drugs appear in *JAMA* 213:608 (July 27) 1970.

Chapter 1

DIGITALIS GLYCOSIDES

The general term digitalis designates a group of drugs that includes galenicals, purified glycosides, and semisynthetic agents derived from *Digitalis purpurea*, *D. lanata*, *Strophanthus gratus*, and other botanical sources. Products in this group are acetyldigitoxin [Acylanid], deslanoside [Cedilanid-D], digitalis leaf or tincture, digitoxin [Crystodigin, Digitaline Nativelle, Myodigin, Purodigin], digoxin [Davoxin, Lanoxin], gitalin [Gitaligin], lanatoside C [Cedilanid], and ouabain. All possess the same qualitative actions on the heart, peripheral vascular system, central nervous system, and gastrointestinal tract, but they vary in potency, rate of absorption, onset of action, and speed of elimination. Digitalis is indicated in virtually all patients with congestive heart failure and in the treatment of certain arrhythmias. (See Chapter 2, Antiarrhythmic Agents.)

Digitalis increases the strength of contraction and alters cardiac automaticity, excitability, conduction velocity, and refractoriness. The increased contractility of the failing heart following digitalis administration results in an increased stroke volume and cardiac output. There is a greater systolic ejection volume, a reduction in cardiac diastolic volume and pulmonary arterial pressure, and, ultimately, a diminution in blood volume and central venous pressure. Heart size may or may not be decreased. Digitalis also increases the contractility of the normal heart, but homeostatic adjustments usually offset any notable increase in cardiac output.

Digitalis often is useful when treating heart failure resulting from acute myocardial infarction, but it must be given cautiously and at approximately one-half the normal digitalizing dose initially because of its propensity to cause arrhythmias. Patients with ischemic myocardial tissue associated with infarction, angina pectoris, or superimposed pulmonary disease may be particularly sensitive to the effects of digitalis. Under these conditions, toxicity usually can be prevented by the frequent administration of small doses of rapidly eliminated glycosides and by the frequent evaluation of the results of treatment.

Digitalis generally is not desirable for the treatment of left ventricular failure resulting from idiopathic hypertrophic subaortic stenosis, since patients with this condition may develop increased obstruction of the left ventricular outflow tract as a result of increased contractility. Digitalis may have variable effectiveness in treating heart failure associated with hyperthyroidism; slowing the ventricular response usually can be achieved but larger than customary doses are generally required. The use of propranolol [Inderal] or a combination of propranolol and digitalis is often more effective. The thyrotoxicosis must be corrected before much improvement in the heart condition can be expected. In some elderly patients with thyrotoxicosis, digitalis may not be useful. Similarly, digitalis is not very effective in acute high output failure associated with beriberi or in some forms of cardiomyopathy.

The choice of digitalis preparation, dosage, and route of administration depends upon the clinical situation, the ease of administration desired, and the speed with which the therapeutic effects must be achieved. When prompt action is desired (eg, in supraventricular tachycardia or acute left side heart failure), a glycoside with a rapid onset of action may be given intravenously; ouabain, deslanoside, and digoxin are administered by this route. Of these three drugs, ouabain appears to have the most rapid onset but its dosage is the most difficult to regulate for continued digitalization. Digoxin may be the preferred agent because the maintenance dose is easily established after its emergency use intravenously.

In the management of less acute or stabilized congestive failure, digoxin and longer-acting preparations such as digitoxin or digitalis leaf are employed. Here again, many physicians prefer digoxin to either digitoxin or digitalis leaf because, if intoxication occurs, it is less persistent since digoxin has a shorter half-life than either of the other agents. Digoxin can be administered orally (80% to 85% of the drug is absorbed by this route) as well as parenterally. Digitoxin is completely absorbed by the oral route.

Digitalis leaf, a crude galenical containing a mixture of glycosides, is the least potent digitalis preparation on a weight basis. The availability of essentially pure and more accurately measurable dosage forms of glycosides such as digoxin and digitoxin militates against the use of digitalis leaf unless it is the preparation with which a physician is most experienced. The glycosides from the leaf are incompletely absorbed from the gastrointestinal tract. In general, digitalis leaf, digitoxin, and digoxin all possess the practical advantage of being effective when given in a single daily dose. Occasionally, for finer adjustment of maintenance dosage, digoxin may have to be given in two divided doses daily. Ouabain, one of the more potent digitalis glycosides, is poorly absorbed from the intestinal tract.

Despite some claims to the contrary, there is no convincing evidence that the digitalis glycosides differ with respect to therapeutic index. With all the drugs, the therapeutic blood level appears to be approximately 50% to 60% of the toxic level. In advanced congestive failure, toxic drug levels may be reached before satisfactory therapeutic effects are obtained. Young persons with hearts of normal size may tolerate larger doses without toxicity than older persons with greatly dilated hearts, presumably because the metabolism is slowed or the rate of excretion is decreased in the elderly.

The onset of action varies among the digitalis glycosides, even when the preparations are given intravenously; this suggests differences in binding by plasma albumin and in drug equilibration within the heart muscle and other body tissues. Rates of elimination also vary widely; metabolic transformation occurs primarily in the liver, and unchanged glycosides and their degradation products are excreted chiefly through the kidneys. Careful monitoring is necessary throughout the first two to three weeks after initiating an altered dosage regimen until a stable level is reached, because these agents have a long biologic half-life and there is a tendency for digitoxin, either in pure form or from digitalis leaf, to accumulate.

It is recommended that the physician familiarize himself with one or two preparations and then restrict his use to those agents.

The optimal dosage is always the smallest amount that continues to compensate heart failure or to produce a normal rhythm or rate. Even when heart failure is fully compensated, some physicians advocate continued doses of digitalis large enough to control the extravagal effect on atrioventricular conduction in patients with atrial fibrillation or flutter and thus permit more patient activity without an excessive increase in ventricular rate. A satisfactory clinical response includes reduction in heart size, a reduction in pulmonary and systemic venous congestion, and a disappearance of edema. Concomitant use of diuretics is frequently necessary when restriction of sodium in the diet has failed.

Effective digitalis therapy for congestive failure frequently is established as a two-step procedure. A patient who has not received digitalis for at least two weeks is given a loading dose large enough to produce a drug concentration in the heart that will cause the desired therapeutic effect. If digitoxin or digitalis leaf was used previously, more than two weeks should have elapsed or a smaller than usual loading dose should be given because these drugs are eliminated more slowly than other digitalis preparations. Usually one-quarter to one-half of the loading dose is given at once; the remainder is given in divided doses at intervals determined by the time of maximal effect from the preceding doses. Depending upon the preparation chosen, these intervals can be minutes or hours. Since the exact amount needed is difficult to predict accurately, the digitalis dosage is adjusted in accordance with the signs of improvement so that only the necessary amount is given. In less severe cases of congestive failure, the largest amount of digoxin, digitoxin, or digitalis leaf that will not cause overt toxic symptoms is given in divided doses over a period of one to three days. There is good evidence to indicate that a loading dose is not necessary in initiating therapy for mild congestive failure. For example, if digoxin is given, the serum concentration from a dosage of 0.25 mg twice daily is the same after six days whether or not a loading dose is given. Even digitoxin, a drug that may take several weeks to reach a plateau, will eventually reach the same serum level as that obtained if an initial loading dose were given.

There is not necessarily a correlation between the weight of an individual and the dose of digitalis needed to effect improvement in congestive failure. For example, an obese patient may require no more digoxin than one who is less obese to obtain similar blood concentrations, since digoxin is poorly concentrated in adipose tissue. However, a muscular individual will generally require more digoxin than one who has a smaller lean body mass. Thus, dosage schedules are somewhat arbitrary averages to be used with caution. Generally, less digitalis is used to treat cardiac failure associated with myocardial infarction.

Following the initial loading dose, the maintenance dose must equal the amount of digitalis destroyed or excreted each day. The maintenance dose is not necessarily a predictable percentage of the loading dose. Indeed, it will not even remain constant in a given individual but will vary in accordance with changes in body mass, liver or renal function, and electrolyte metabolism, as well as with the presence of other disease states and many other factors.

Radioimmunoassay techniques have been developed for measuring serum levels of the pure digitalis glycosides, especially digoxin. These procedures are specific, sensitive (eg, 0.2 ng/ml for digoxin), and precise. Although not yet available at many hospitals, radioimmunoassays are becoming an increasingly important tool to the cardiologist.

Adverse Reactions and Precautions

Digitalis intoxication usually results from the accumulation of larger than necessary maintenance doses, from overzealous rapid loading, from prescribing digitalis in doses beyond reasonable limits when it is not likely to be effective, or from the presence of disease states in which the drug is poorly metabolized or excreted. Intoxication can be prevented in most instances by evaluating therapy frequently and by decreasing the dosage in the presence of factors that tend to cause excessive accumulation (eg, impaired renal function) or when there is an existing alkalosis, hypokalemia, hypercalcemia, hypomagnesemia, or advanced atrioventricular block of any degree. Intoxication cannot be avoided by selecting one particular digitalis glycoside over another, since there is no significant difference in the therapeutic to toxic dose ratio among the glycosides. However, when the risk of intoxication is high, treatment with a short-acting, rapidly eliminated glycoside may reduce the duration of toxic manifestations after the drug has been discontinued.

Usually the early signs of toxicity are not serious, but they serve as a warning that an overdose is being given and that serious toxicity can result. Indeed, the first signs of toxicity may be rather subtle; for example, frequent early signs of toxicity in elderly patients may amount to no more than a mild anorexia and drowsiness. Anorexia, nausea, vomiting, and, to a lesser extent, diarrhea are the predominant and usual early symptoms of digitalis intoxication. In sufficient dosage, all of the drugs produce nausea and vomiting due to their direct action on the central nervous system. (In addition to its central emetic action, digitalis leaf occasionally has a local emetic effect when given in large doses.) Other toxic effects that may develop more slowly include lethargy, drowsiness, and marked confusion, particularly in older patients. Visual disturbances, including a halo effect around dark objects, modified color perception (ie, a tendency for objects to appear yellow or green), amblyopia, diplopia, and scotoma also are caused by digitalis overdosage. Rarely, retrobulbar neuritis that is usually reversible has been reported. A rather distressing side effect, although benign, is the development of gynecomastia.

Despite the frequent and early occurrence of gastrointestinal symptoms following digitalis administration, as many as one-third of patients develop a disturbance of cardiac rhythm as the first evidence of digitalis intoxication. The most frequent early cardiac signs in adults are premature ventricular contractions and first-degree atrioventricular block. Digitalis can cause any degree of atrioventricular block as well as sinus arrest or sinoatrial block. Similarly, digitalis-induced atrial tachycardia often is associated with some degree of atrioventricular block. Atrioventricular nodal tachycardia and paroxysmal atrial tachycardia with atrioventricular block are two of the more common digitalis-induced arrhythmias; bigeminy or ventricular tachycardia also occur. Atrial flutter and fibrillation are uncommon toxic effects of digitalis therapy.

Digitalis intoxication is always suspect when a rate or rhythm disorder occurs in a patient receiving the drug. Discontinuing therapy for a brief period may relieve the toxic symptoms; however, it often is necessary to employ additional measures.

Various agents have been used to correct digitalis-induced arrhythmias or blocks. Potassium will depress ectopic impulse generation in the presence of digitalis intoxication and is the therapy of first choice to counteract various types of arrhythmias. However, it must be used with caution and given slowly since potassium itself is capable of causing all degrees of atrioventricular block. Diphenylhydantoin [Dilantin] is useful in treating a variety of arrhythmias. Propranolol [Inderal] also has met with some success in converting atrial tachycardia with block or, occasionally, a ventricular tachycardia to a normal sinus rhythm. Lidocaine [Xylocaine] has been given to correct ventricular tachycardia. Premature contractions of both supraventricular and ventricular origin can be abolished by quinidine. Procainamide [Pronestyl] has been used with success in overcoming premature ventricular contractions, atrioventricular nodal tachycardia, and atrial tachycardia with block. Both quinidine and procainamide are contraindicated in the presence of third-degree atrioventricular block. Atropine, in a dose of 0.5 to 1 mg subcutaneously, is, in some cases, one of the most useful drugs for correcting various types of digitalis-induced atrioventricular blocks. (See also Chapter 2, Antiarrhythmic Agents.)

Two other forms of therapy that sometimes are effective in the treatment of selected digitalis-induced arrhythmias are the use of calcium chelating agents such as disodium edetate [Endrate] (see Chapter 90, Chelating Agents) and electrical pacing. Electrical pacing can be beneficial in a patient with second- or third-degree atrioventricular block and a superimposed ventricular arrhythmia. Nevertheless, electrical pacing must be used with caution since it can produce tachyarrhythmias.

Since hypokalemia occurs frequently when chronic congestive failure is treated concomitantly with digitalis and diuretics, serum potassium should be measured and hypokalemia corrected, if present, prior to initiating therapy. If serum potassium levels are low, the cardiotoxic action of digitalis is increased and arrhythmias may occur. These arrhythmias can be treated successfully by the oral or intravenous administration of potassium chloride and the temporary discontinuation of digitalis therapy. On the other hand, administration of potassium salts is hazardous when depressed automaticity or conduction predominate, since a rapid increase in serum potassium may lead to third-degree atrioventricular block or asystole. For this reason it is well to monitor the electrocardiogram while potassium is being administered.

The newborn infant, especially the premature infant, with heart disease is particularly susceptible to digitalis intoxication, and frequent electrocardiographic monitoring is essential in these patients. Similarly, special care must be exercised in elderly patients receiving digitalis because their lean body mass tends to be small and renal clearance is likely to be reduced. Short-acting preparations should be used and close observation is very important. In addition, digitalis must be used with great caution in patients with acute viral or toxic myocarditis.

INDIVIDUAL EVALUATIONS

ACETYLDIGITOXIN [Acylanid]

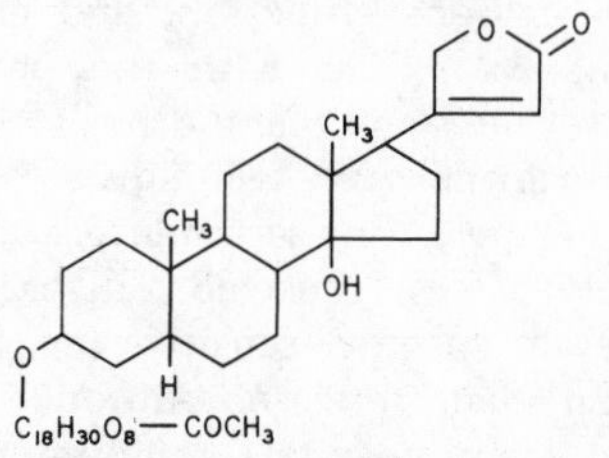

This oral preparation has a more rapid onset of action (one to two hours) and is more quickly eliminated than digitoxin. If signs of intoxication occur, they disappear in one to three days. Acetyldigitoxin is not completely absorbed from the gastrointestinal tract. It is used less commonly than the glycosides available in both oral and injectable forms. The adverse reactions and precautions are the same as those for other digitalis glycosides (see the Introductory Statement).

USUAL DOSAGE.—*Oral: Adults,* for patients with congestive failure who have not received digitalis therapy for at least two weeks, the dose for rapid loading is 1.6 to 2 mg within 24 hours in divided doses. For slower loading, the same amount is given over a two- or three-day period. The maintenance dose is 0.1 to 0.2 mg daily.

For the treatment of a tachycardia, the dose is determined on the basis of clinical response within the limits of adverse reactions (see

Chapter 2, Antiarrhythmic Agents).

PREPARATIONS.—Acylanid (Sandoz). *Oral:* Tablets 0.1 and 0.2 mg.

DESLANOSIDE [Cedilanid-D]

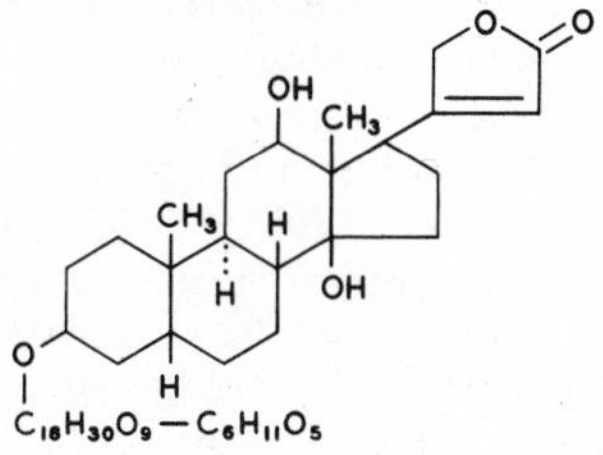

$C_{18}H_{30}O_9-C_6H_{11}O_5$

Deslanoside is a cardioactive glycoside derived from lanatoside C by controlled alkaline hydrolysis. It has essentially the same pharmacologic properties as the natural parent glycoside. It is available as an injectable preparation and although it may be considered the injectable form of lanatoside C, it actually is not lanatoside C but desacetyl lanatoside C; this fact has caused some confusion because of the proclivity of the medical profession to designate deslanoside as lanatoside C in a jargonistic fashion.

Deslanoside frequently is used to attain rapid initial loading. Longer-acting orally administered glycosides then are substituted for maintenance therapy. The onset of action is 10 to 30 minutes and the maximal effect occurs in one to two hours; complete elimination takes three to six days. This glycoside is particularly useful when it is necessary to provide an appreciable digitalis effect within one to two hours (eg, treatment of acute left side heart failure with pulmonary edema or management of supraventricular tachycardia, atrial flutter, or atrial fibrillation).

See the Introductory Statement for a discussion of toxicity.

USUAL DOSAGE.—*Intramuscular, Intravenous: Adults,* for patients with congestive failure who have not received digitalis for at least two weeks, the initial loading dose is 0.8 to 1.6 mg; often one-half of this dose is given immediately, and the remainder is given in divided doses at two-hour intervals. The maintenance dosage is 0.25 to 0.5 mg daily in divided doses at 12-hour intervals until the clinical condition is stable and a longer-acting preparation can be substituted. The smaller dose is recommended for small or elderly patients and for those with metabolic or electrolyte disorders, myocardial hypoxia, or impaired renal function. If a patient who is receiving an inadequate amount of a longer-acting glycoside urgently requires additional digitalis action, 0.2 to 0.4 mg of deslanoside may be given as often as every 30 minutes, depending upon the clinical response.

The initial loading dose for *infants* is 0.02 mg/kg of body weight; for *children 2 to 12 years of age,* 0.025 mg/kg; and for *children 12 years and older,* the adult dose is administered. Maintenance dosage is one-fourth to one-third of the loading dose given in two divided doses at 12-hour intervals.

The dosage used to control tachycardia may be more than that ordinarily employed to treat heart failure and is determined on the basis of the clinical response observed within the limits of adverse reactions (see Chapter 2, Antiarrhythmic Agents).

PREPARATIONS.—Cedilanid-D (Sandoz). *Injection:* Solution 0.2 mg/ml in 2 and 4 ml containers.

DIGITALIS LEAF

This preparation contains a mixture of glycosides as active principles and is the least potent digitalis preparation on a weight basis. Its potency is standardized biologically and it is available as an oral preparation only. Digitalis leaf sometimes is used when loading can be accomplished over several days; it also is satisfactory for maintenance therapy regardless of the drug used for initial loading, but purer and more standardized digitalis preparations are available and are usually preferred. The gastrointestinal absorption of digitalis leaf is fairly uniform. Its onset of action is two to six hours and its maximal effect occurs in 12 to 24 hours. Since digitalis leaf has a long half-life, intoxication can persist for a prolonged period but signs usually abate within several days unless excretion is delayed. (See the Introductory Statement for a discussion of toxicity.)

USUAL DOSAGE.—*Oral: Adults,* for congestive failure in patients who have not received digitalis for at least two weeks, initially 50 to 150 mg three or four times daily for three or four days to a maximum of about 1 g (range, 0.5 to 1.5 g). Maintenance dosage is 100 mg (range, 50 to 200 mg) daily for five to seven days each week. The lower doses should be used for small or elderly patients and for those with myocardial hypoxia, metabolic or electrolyte disorders, or impaired renal function.

For the treatment of supraventricular tachycardia, atrial flutter, or atrial fibrillation, the dosage is determined by therapeutic response and evidence of toxicity. Within the limits of mild adverse reactions, the dosage usually is titrated to a level at which the ventricular rate is slowed to the desired level. (See also Chapter 2, Antiarrhythmic Agents.)

Digitalis leaf is not commonly given to children because the dosage forms are unusually large and difficult for a child to swallow.

PREPARATIONS.—Various oral forms, including capsules and tablets 100 mg, tincture 100 mg/ml.

AVAILABLE TRADEMARKS.—Digitora (Upjohn), Pil-Digis (Davies Rose Hoyt). This drug is marketed by Arnar-Stone, First Texas, Lederle, Lilly, Beecham-Massengill, Upjohn, and other manufacturers under its generic name.

SIMILAR DRUG.—Digifortis (Parke, Davis). Capsules and ampules containing the activity of digitalis leaf.

DIGITOXIN [Crystodigin, Digitaline Nativelle, Myodigin, Purodigin]

$C_{18}H_{31}O_9$

Digitoxin is the chief active glycoside in digitalis leaf. One milligram of digitoxin is therapeutically equivalent to approximately 1 g of digitalis leaf. Although digitoxin is much less commonly used today than a decade ago, it can be given for loading and still remains one of the drugs of choice for maintenance therapy. It is almost completely absorbed from the gastrointestinal tract; therefore, equivalent oral or intravenous doses produce essentially the same therapeutic effect and the drug has a similar onset of action by either route. Thus, intravenous administration is generally unnecessary except when the patient is comatose or is otherwise unable to take medication orally. Onset of action after intravenous injection is one-half to two hours with the maximal effect occurring eight to nine hours later. Following oral administration, onset occurs in two to four hours and the maximal effect is seen within 12 to 24 hours. Two to three weeks may elapse before digitoxin is eliminated.

The chief disadvantages of digitoxin are its slow onset of action and prolonged half-life when compared to a drug such as digoxin. The latter effect can be a particular disadvantage if toxic reactions occur. Nausea and vomiting occasionally are early signs of toxicity, although not infrequently arrhythmias may be observed initially. (See the Introductory Statement for a more detailed discussion of toxicity.)

USUAL DOSAGE.—*Oral*, *Intravenous: Adults,* for patients with congestive failure who have not received digitalis for at least two weeks, initially 1 mg (range, 0.75 to 1.5 mg) is given in divided doses at six- to eight-hour intervals for 12 to 24 hours if there is urgency; this amount is given over a period of two or three days in less acute cases. The maintenance dose is 0.1 mg (range, 0.05 to 0.2 mg) daily for five to seven days each week. The lower loading and maintenance doses should be used in small or elderly patients, in those with metabolic or electrolyte abnormalities, or in those with myocardial hypoxia. Since this drug is metabolized primarily by the liver, often little or no dosage alteration is needed in the presence of renal insufficiency. However, digitoxin should be avoided in patients with severely impaired liver function.

The initial loading dose for *newborn infants* is 0.025 mg/kg of body weight; for *infants under two years of age,* 0.05 mg/kg; for *children 2 to 12 years,* 0.025 mg/kg; and for *children over 12 years,* the adult dose is usually satisfactory. The maintenance dose is approximately 10% of the loading dose, but this amount must be determined individually on the basis of clinical response.

For the treatment of supraventricular tachycardia, atrial flutter, or atrial fibrillation, the dose is determined in the same manner as described for digitalis leaf (see the evaluation on Digitalis Leaf and Chapter 2, Antiarrhythmic Agents).

PREPARATIONS.—

Crystodigin (Lilly).

Oral: Tablets 0.05, 0.1, 0.15, and 0.2 mg.

Injection: Solution 0.2 mg/ml in 1 and 10 ml containers.

Digitaline Nativelle (Fougera).

Oral: Elixir (pediatric) 0.05 mg/ml; solution 0.02 mg/drop; tablets 0.1, and 0.2 mg.

Injection: Solution 0.2 mg/ml in 1 and 2 ml containers.

Myodigin (Davies Rose Hoyt). *Oral:* Tablets 0.1 and 0.2 mg.

Purodigin (Wyeth).

Oral: Tablets 0.05, 0.1, 0.15, and 0.2 mg.

Injection: Solution 0.2 mg/ml in 1 ml containers.

Drug also marketed by other manufacturers under generic name.

DIGOXIN [Davoxin, Lanoxin]

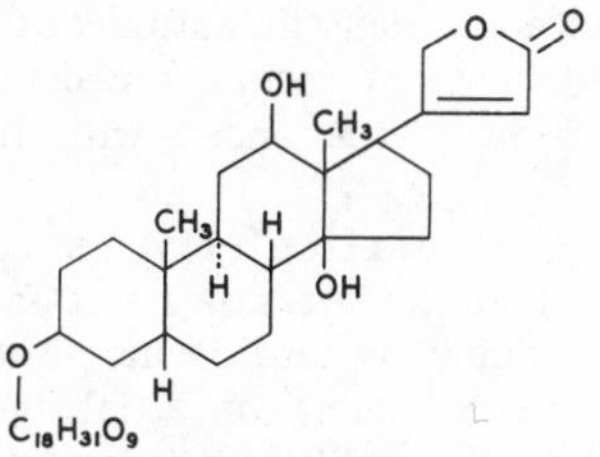

$C_{18}H_{31}O_9$

Digoxin is a prompt-acting glycoside when given orally or parenterally. Onset of action develops within 5 to 30 minutes after an intravenous dose and is somewhat longer following oral administration. The maximal effect occurs within two to five hours, depending upon the route by which the drug is given, and it is eliminated in two to six days (biologic half-life, approximately 18 hours). Digoxin often is used to achieve moderately rapid loading and frequently is used for maintenance. It can be administered as the sole digitalizing agent or, since its onset and duration of action are similar to those of deslanoside, it can be given for maintenance after initial loading with deslanoside. Single daily doses are usually satisfactory for maintenance therapy although it occasionally is necessary to give the drug in two divided doses daily. Many cardiologists feel that this agent is the drug of choice for treating congestive heart failure for the following reasons: (1) It has a rapid onset of action so that effectiveness is not delayed if the drug is needed in an emergency situation. (2) It has a relatively short duration of action, thus minimizing the duration of digitalis intoxication should it occur. (3) It can be administered orally as well as intramuscularly and intravenously. Therefore, digoxin can be given for either rapid or slow digitalization and can be administered parenterally if a patient is unable to take oral medication (eg, a patient undergoing surgery).

See the Introductory Statement for a discussion of toxicity.

USUAL DOSAGE.—

Intravenous: Adults, for patients with congestive failure who have not received digitalis for at least two weeks, the initial loading dose is 0.75 to 1.5 mg. The maintenance dose is 0.125 to 0.75 mg daily (on the average a narrower range of 0.25 to 0.5 mg will usually maintain the majority of patients). The initial loading dose for *newborn infants* is 0.02 to 0.04 mg/kg of body weight; *infants to 2 years of age,* 0.04 to 0.06 mg/kg; *children 2 to 10 years,* 0.02 to 0.06 mg/kg. Maintenance dosage is approximately one-fourth the total loading dosage.

Oral, Intramuscular: Adults, for patients with congestive failure who have not received digitalis for at least two weeks, the initial loading dose is 1 to 3 mg given over a 24-hour period. Maintenance dosage is 0.25 to 0.75 mg daily. The loading dose for *newborn infants* is 0.04 to 0.06 mg/kg of body weight; *infants to 2 years of age,* 0.06 to 0.08 mg/kg; *children 2 to 10 years,* 0.04 to 0.06 mg/kg. Maintenance doses are approximately one-fourth of the total loading dose given daily in single or divided doses.

Occasionally larger oral doses are necessary if digitalization is to be accomplished over a long period of time. For rapid loading, one-half of the dose may be given at once and the remainder given in divided doses at two- to six-hour intervals, depending upon the response. For slower loading, the entire dose may be given in divided amounts over a 24- to 72-hour period, or the loading dose may be omitted entirely, in which case the patient will be digitalized in approximately one week on maintenance dosage alone.

The smaller loading and maintenance dosages given alone should be used in small or elderly patients, and in those with metabolic or electrolyte abnormalities, impaired renal function, or myocardial hypoxia. In patients with impaired renal function, digoxin dosage must be reduced to 30% to 50% of the normal maintenance dosage since the biologic half-life of the drug increases from 18 hours in the normal individual to 72 hours in anuric patients.

The total amount needed to treat tachycardia may be more than that needed to treat heart failure; the dosage is determined on the basis of response within the limits of adverse reactions (see Chapter 2, Antiarrhythmic Agents).

PREPARATIONS.—

Davoxin (Davies Rose Hoyt). *Oral:* Tablets 0.25 mg.

Lanoxin (Burroughs Wellcome).

Oral: Elixir (pediatric) 0.05 mg/ml; tablets 0.125, 0.25 and 0.5 mg.

Injection: Solution 0.1 mg/ml in 1 ml containers and 0.25 mg/ml in 2 ml containers.

Drug also marketed by other manufacturers under generic name.

GITALIN [Gitaligin]

This mixture of amorphous glycosides is available only in oral form and is not commonly used. Any claim of a wider therapeutic index for this preparation than for other digitalis preparations is not substantiated. Gitalin has the same adverse reactions and precautions as other digitalis preparations (see the Introductory Statement).

USUAL DOSAGE.—*Oral: Adults,* for the treatment of patients with congestive heart failure who have not received digitalis therapy for two weeks, the total loading dose is 4 to 6.5 mg over a three- or four-day period; the maintenance dose is 0.25 to 0.75 mg daily.

PREPARATIONS.—Gitaligin (Schering). *Oral:* Tablets 0.5 mg.

LANATOSIDE C [Cedilanid]

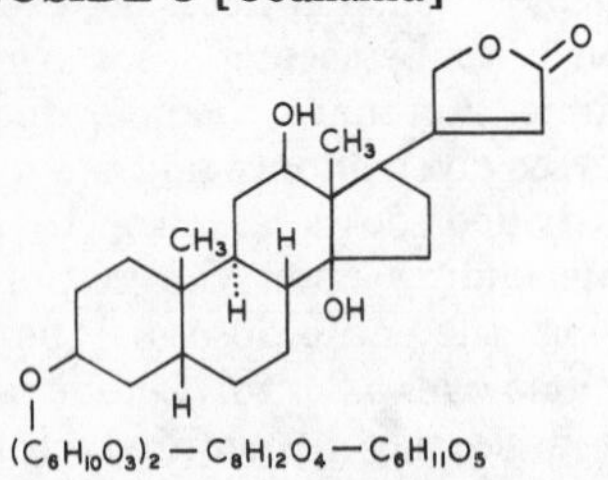

Lanatoside C is marketed only in an oral form. It is rarely used because it is poorly absorbed from the gastrointestinal tract and has a wide range of loading and maintenance dosage. Deslanoside, a derivative of lanatoside C, has the same pharmacologic properties and, therefore, may be considered as the injectable form of this drug. Deslanoside commonly is used for rapid loading.

See the Introductory Statement for a discussion of toxicity.

USUAL DOSAGE.—*Oral: Adults,* for the treatment of congestive heart failure in patients who have not received digitalis for at least two weeks, the initial loading dose is 5 to 10 mg; the maintenance dose is 0.5 to 2 mg.

PREPARATIONS.—Cedilanid (Sandoz). *Oral:* Tablets 0.5 mg.

OUABAIN

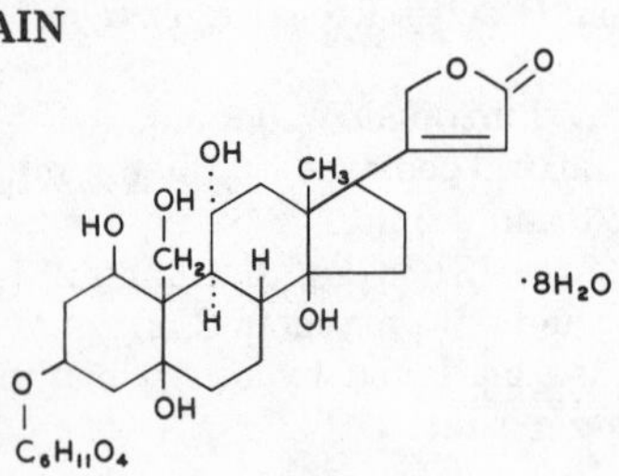

Ouabain is a rapidly acting digitalis glycoside that is administered intravenously. Its onset of action is three to ten minutes and its maximal effect occurs in 30 to 60 minutes; it is eliminated in 24 to 48 hours. Despite its short duration of action, which tends to make toxic manifestations relatively transient, ouabain can easily precipitate digitalis intoxication because of its rapid onset of action, especially when a physician is not experienced with use of the drug.

Ouabain is particularly useful in the treatment of acute left side heart failure with pulmonary edema or cardiogenic shock, and in the rapid management of atrial tachycardia, fibrillation, or flutter. It also is useful in testing the adequacy of digitalis loading, since it can be given in small increments and toxic manifestations are transient if overdosage occurs. Ouabain usually is given only in emergencies; a longer-acting glycoside is given for maintenance after the clinical condition is stabilized.

See the Introductory Statement for a discussion of toxicity.

USUAL DOSAGE.—*Intravenous: Adults,* for patients with congestive heart failure who have not received digitalis therapy for two weeks, the initial loading dose is 0.25 mg, followed by 0.1 to 0.25 mg at 30- to 60-minute intervals until the desired effect is achieved or until 0.8 to 1 mg is given. No patient should receive more than a total loading dose of 1 mg. For the treatment of acute congestive failure, 0.5 mg (range, 0.25 to 0.75 mg) is given as a single dose. The lower dosage should be given to small or elderly patients and to those with certain metabolic and electrolyte disorders, myocardial hypoxia, or impaired renal function. *Children,* the usual daily dose for congestive failure is 0.012 to 0.016 mg/kg of body weight in two equally divided doses; however, this amount may be modified by extenuating clinical factors and unusual response to smaller amounts.

For the treatment of atrial tachycardia, fibrillation, or flutter, it may be necessary to give a larger amount than that ordinarily used to treat heart failure. Also, when treating an arrhythmia, the dosage of ouabain generally is determined by titrating the clinical response against the adverse effects (see Chapter 2, Antiarrhythmic Agents).

PREPARATIONS.—*Injection:* Solution 0.25 mg/ml in 2 ml containers. Drug marketed under generic name.

Chapter 2

ANTIARRHYTHMIC AGENTS

Arrhythmias frequently occur as emergency situations that demand prompt recognition and immediate action. Rational drug therapy depends upon understanding the basic mechanism of the arrhythmia, as well as the underlying physiologic and pharmacologic principles relating to the specific agent to be used. For example, it is important to differentiate between bradycardia caused by a reduced rate of impulse generation and bradycardia due to a reduced number of atrial impulses conducted to the ventricles. Similarly, it must be determined if a rapid ventricular rate is caused by an increased impulse generation in the atria or an increased ventricular autorhythmicity.

The drugs used to treat arrhythmias are derived from many different chemical classes. Individual agents include the digitalis glycosides, quinidine, procainamide [Pronestyl], lidocaine [Xylocaine], diphenylhydantoin [Dilantin], propranolol [Inderal], isoproterenol [Isuprel], ephedrine, and methoxamine [Vasoxyl]. Bretylium, a drug formerly used as an antihypertensive, currently is undergoing clinical trial and shows promise as a new type of antiarrhythmic agent. Time will be needed to assess its usefulness.

Treatment of atrial tachycardia is aimed at converting the arrhythmia to normal sinus rhythm or, if that is not possible, controlling the ventricular rate. The digitalis glycosides (acetyldigitoxin [Acylanid], deslanoside [Cedilanid-D], digitalis, digitoxin, digoxin [Davoxin, Lanoxin], lanatoside C [Cedilanid], and ouabain) are the agents of first choice for this purpose. They are useful in the management of atrial fibrillation and flutter. However, in the presence of organic heart disease, digitalis usually will not convert atrial fibrillation to normal sinus rhythm unless the arrhythmia is of brief duration or has developed secondary to acute left side heart failure. Its effectiveness in treating fibrillation generally lies in its ability to slow conduction through the atrioventricular node, thereby reducing the number of impulses reaching the ventricles. In treating atrial flutter, digitalis protects the ventricles from excessive stimulation and frequently may restore normal sinus rhythm, but this depends largely upon the duration of the arrhythmia. Sinus rhythm is more likely to be restored when the arrhythmia has existed for only a few days. Definitive pharmacologic conversion of fibrillation or flutter to normal sinus rhythm usually requires concomitant therapy with digitalis and quinidine, procainamide, or propranolol. These latter drugs increase the effective refractory period, decrease excitability, and depress conduction in the heart. Digitalis also frequently terminates paroxysmal atrial tachycardia. Since digitalis has a positive inotropic action, it often is helpful in correcting decompensation which may have either caused or been caused by arrhythmia.

The dosage of digitalis used to treat supraventricular tachycardia must be determined individually on the basis of response and signs of toxicity (see Chapter 1, Digitalis Glycosides). The dose usually is increased until the heart rate or rhythm is normal or symptoms of overdosage develop. In the treatment of atrial flutter or fibrillation, the dose is adjusted until the ventricular rate is sufficiently slowed. Since there is more effect on contractility than on electrophysiologic activity per unit of dose, the action of digitalis on automaticity, conduction, and refractoriness, and the interaction of these effects to abolish arrhythmias, may require doses larger than those needed to treat congestive failure.

Quinidine is the prototype antiarrhythmic

drug and is commonly used to abolish atrial or ventricular premature contractions, to prevent paroxysmal supraventricular or ventricular tachycardia, or to convert atrial fibrillation to sinus rhythm. In treating atrial flutter, quinidine should not be administered unless digitalis has been given previously; without the atrioventricular conduction blockade imposed by digitalis, there is danger of converting the flutter to a 1:1 response with a dangerously rapid ventricular rate. The antiarrhythmic actions of procainamide are similar to those of quinidine, and the selection of one drug over the other depends upon the route of administration, onset of effect, desired duration of action, and the occurrence of adverse reactions. When rapid action is necessary, procainamide is generally administered.

Intravenously administered lidocaine and procainamide are the drugs of choice in treating ventricular tachycardia. However, if the condition is life threatening, most cardiologists prefer the use of electrically-induced cardioversion. Lidocaine must be given by continuous intravenous infusion if a sustained effect is desired. Infusion is usually begun following a single intravenous injection of 50 to 100 mg. Either procainamide or quinidine can be used orally for prophylaxis. Occasionally, a digitalis glycoside may be added when the arrhythmia is primarily due to left side failure. Quinidine, procainamide, and lidocaine also have a vagal blocking action on the atrioventricular node. There is no evidence that the combination of quinidine and procainamide is more effective than the use of either agent alone. However, a combination of quinidine and propranolol has been used to treat frequent ventricular premature contractions or tachycardia. This combination may lessen the gastrointestinal reactions that can occur after large doses of either drug alone and may be the treatment of choice.

Quinidine, procainamide, and lidocaine are smooth muscle relaxants and, when given parenterally, their dosage and rate of administration must be carefully adjusted in order to prevent hypotension.

Within the past few years, beta-adrenergic blocking agents have been used to overcome certain cardiac conduction disturbances. The therapeutic rationale for this type of therapy is as follows:

Functionally, a sympathomimetic drug has two types of receptors with which it can react to elicit a response in sympathetic effector cells. While they have not been identified anatomically, the concept of two receptors provides a convenient pharmacologic explanation for the action of both sympathetic agonists and antagonists. These receptors were classified by Alquist in 1948 as alpha or beta depending upon the response observed when certain sympathomimetic amines were administered (eg, phenylephrine acts on alpha receptors and has little or no effect on beta receptors, whereas isoproterenol acts on beta receptors and is essentially devoid of effect on alpha receptors). Most autonomically innervated organs have a preponderance of one or the other receptor. Thus, the heart, the smooth muscle of blood vessels supplying blood to skeletal muscle, and the smooth muscle of the bronchial tree all have a far greater percentage of beta than alpha receptors if, indeed, some of these organs have alpha receptors at all. Stimulation of the beta receptors within these organ systems causes an increase in heart rate and contractile force, a dilation of peripheral blood vessels, and a relaxation of bronchial muscle. Therefore, a beta-adrenergic blocking agent capable of producing a substantial block would inhibit these responses regardless of whether they are produced endogenously by sympathetic stimulation or exogenously by injection of a beta-stimulating catecholamine. (See also Chapter 5, Agents Used in Hypotension and Shock.)

The above paragraph will serve as a brief working foundation for the discussion of propranolol in this chapter. A more detailed discussion of alpha and beta receptor activity is beyond the scope of this book. The interested reader is referred to a suitable textbook of pharmacology such as *The Pharmacological Basis of Therapeutics*, fourth edition, edited by Louis S. Goodman and Alfred Gilman, The Macmillan Company, New York, 1970.

Propranolol has been used for the treatment of essentially every type of tachycardia. This drug may slow the heart rate and decrease the cardiac output at rest. It reduces the inotropic and chronotropic effect of exercise, and decreases the rate of ectopic atrial or ventricular foci and may abolish them. In addition, it consistently slows conduction through the atrioventricular node. Propranolol can sometimes prevent recurrent supraventricular tachycardia. However, it is not commonly used for this purpose and is almost never the drug of first choice. Its use is hazardous when myocardial failure, bradycardia, or atrioventricular block is present.

Bradycardia that occurs as a result of atrioventricular nodal block may have profound negative chronotropic consequences and requires treatment to increase the ventricular rate. In some instances, atropine will reduce or abolish vagal tone, thereby increasing the ventricular rate. Positive chronotropic drugs such as isoproterenol also may be used to increase the autorhythmicity of the nodal or idioventricular pacemaker and the strength of ventricular contraction. Occasionally, ephedrine has been given, but it is considerably less potent than isoproterenol and is not as reliable. Epinephrine, also once widely used to treat bradycardia, has been largely replaced for this purpose by isoproterenol. While epinephrine does have a positive inotropic action, it is less potent than isoproterenol and is more dangerous. It can precipitate or aggravate angina pectoris when myocardial oxygen needs are increased out of proportion to oxygen supply (eg, in ischemic heart disease, as well as various ventricular arrhythmias. Isoproterenol is of value in the treatment of Adams-Stokes syndrome caused by third-degree atrioventricular block; the drug is given intravenously or, rarely, directly into the heart.

Drug therapy for complete heart block is being used less frequently because accumulated experience now indicates that electronic cardiac pacemakers are more reliable in regulating the heart rate.

Recent studies of the mechanism of action of diphenylhydantoin and lidocaine indicate that their antiarrhythmic actions are similar. They decrease automaticity, shorten the effective refractory period, raise the fibrillation threshold, and produce either an increase or no change in conduction velocity. Diphenylhydantoin has been especially useful in the management of arrhythmias produced by digitalis overdosage.

An increasing amount of data indicate that many of the serious arrhythmias are more effectively and safely terminated by use of electric countershock than by drugs. However, countershock should not be used to combat arrhythmias caused by digitalis.

The ability of disodium edetate to bind calcium has led to its use in the treatment of certain arrhythmias such as premature ventricular contractions (see also Chapter 90, Chelating Agents).

Adverse Reactions and Precautions

Adverse reactions caused by antiarrhythmic drugs occur most commonly after overdosage and can be avoided by careful observation of the patient. Successful therapy depends not only upon the electrocardiographic diagnosis of the arrhythmia, but also upon careful assessment of the general condition and the electrolyte balance of the patient. Since the effective dosage of a drug usually is not predictable, the amount and number of individual doses must be determined by evaluating the results during the course of treatment. Blood levels of antiarrhythmic drugs correlate quite well with the therapeutic and toxic levels of the drugs and are very useful in determining correct dosage.

Occasionally, near-toxic doses of digitalis must be given to slow the ventricular rate in atrial flutter or fibrillation. Since gastrointestinal symptoms of digitalis overdosage may not precede signs of cardiac toxicity, it is important to take serial electrocardiograms to determine if additional doses are needed. Evidence of overdosage will generally appear on the electrocardiogram as paroxysmal atrial tachycardia with 2:1 or variable atrioventricular conduction block, or as ventricular premature contractions.

Digitalis frequently must be given at reduced dosage levels to small or elderly individuals or to those with renal insufficiency or certain metabolic and electrolyte abnormalities. For example, metabolic alkalosis and hypokalemia frequently coexist, and either condition may lead to symptoms of digitalis toxicity at normal maintenance doses. See also the individual evaluation and Chapter 1, Digitalis Glycosides.

Common toxic reactions produced by quinidine are known collectively as cinchonism. Quinidine and procainamide produce similar adverse effects on the cardiovascular system. They depress myocardial contractility, especially in large doses, and produce peripheral vasodilatation. In addition, hypotension sometimes occurs, either as a result of the vasodilatation or secondary to the decreased cardiac output caused by the reduced myocardial contractility. It is more likely to occur when procainamide or quinidine is given intravenously. Quinidine and procainamide are contraindicated in complete (third-degree) heart block, unless an electronic pacemaker is used, because of the risk of depressing the automaticity of the ventricular pacemaker. (See also the individual evaluations.) Procainamide is excreted by the kidneys, in large part unmetabolized. Therefore, the dose should be reduced in patients with decreased creatinine clearance.

The obvious aim of antiarrhythmic therapy is to suppress ectopic activity or prevent repetitive re-entry of excitation without altering normal cardiac automaticity and slowing conduction. Overdosage of quinidine or procainamide can depress automaticity and conduction anywhere in the heart. The most common manifestations of overdosage are a delayed repolarization in the ventricles which causes a prolonged Q-T interval, and a prolonged conduction in the atrioventricular node or in the ventricles shown by a long P-R interval or prolonged QRS duration. Larger doses will eventually depress automaticity and conduction in the atria, leading to sinus or atrial arrest or various degrees of atrioventricular block. Electrocardiographic monitoring during treatment may show the early signs of cardiac toxicity, and the more serious complications usually can be averted. Serious toxic effects with quinidine or procainamide must be avoided, because no satisfactory antidote is presently available. Allergic reactions can, of course, be treated symptomatically and hypotensive effects can be counteracted by drugs such as isoproterenol or levarterenol.

Lidocaine and diphenylhydantoin, in effective antiarrhythmic doses, may be less likely to produce hypotension and depression of myocardial contractility than procainamide or quinidine. See the individual evaluations and Chapter 31, Anticonvulsants, and Chapter 18, Local Anesthetics, for a discussion of the toxicity of diphenylhydantoin and lidocaine, respectively.

The negative inotropic effect of propranolol can precipitate or aggravate congestive heart failure. In addition to its effects on the heart, propranolol often produces bronchial constriction in asthmatic patients and may impair the sympathetic response to a decreased blood glucose level in diabetics, thereby depriving these individuals of the subjective warning signs of impending hypoglycemia. Although this drug is useful in treating many types of arrhythmias, including those that are drug-induced, it should not be given without careful consideration of possible consequences to patients with serious myocardial disease, asthma, diabetes, or atrioventricular block. Patients with digitalis-induced paroxysmal atrial tachycardia with block have been treated with propranolol, but this condition is preferably treated by withholding digitalis and infusing potassium or diphenylhydantoin intravenously. The blood pressure as well as heart rate and rhythm should be carefully monitored during intravenous administration. Isoproterenol [Isuprel] or atropine should be infused if hypotension or bradycardia occurs.

The untoward effects of isoproterenol include palpitation, tachycardia, headache, flushing, nausea, tremor, and dizziness. This drug may precipitate angina pectoris when coronary arteriosclerosis exists as a result of the increased myocardial oxygen demands produced by both the chronotropic and inotropic effects. Tachyarrhythmias, including ventricular disturbances, sometimes occur and, in these cases, the drug must be discontinued.

INDIVIDUAL EVALUATIONS

DIGITALIS GLYCOSIDES

The digitalis glycosides are the agents of choice as initial therapy to slow the ventricular rate in atrial fibrillation or flutter. These glycosides are the most useful agents in the treatment of paroxysmal atrial tachycardia if arrhythmia persists after vagal stimulation by carotid sinus massage, valsalva maneuver, or acute hypertension produced by a vasopressor such as methoxamine. They can be used prophylactically to prevent the recurrence of paroxysmal supraventricular tachycardia.

In the treatment of acute tachyarrhythmia, the short-acting digitalis glycosides are more useful than the longer-acting glycosides or digitalis leaf, but the latter drugs are generally used for maintenance. Thus, deslanoside, ouabain, or digoxin usually are used to slow the heart rate when treating tachycardia, and digoxin, digitoxin, or digitalis leaf are used for maintenance after the rate becomes normal and the rhythm stable.

Tachycardia due to digitalis intoxication requires special attention. Atrioventricular and atrial tachycardias obviously cannot be treated with more digitalis and usually do not respond to quinidine or procainamide. Since potassium depletion usually occurs with digitalis intoxication, oral or intravenous administration of potassium chloride may correct the rhythm disturbances. The usual daily oral dose of potassium chloride is 5 to 10 g in milk or other suitable fluid. In an emergency, 80 mEq potassium/liter in 5% dextrose injection can be given by slow intravenous infusion (see also Chapter 16, Replenishers and Regulators of Water, Electrolytes, and Nutrients). Electrocardiographic monitoring is essential, because potassium also may increase

DIGITALIS GLYCOSIDES

Drug	Usual Dosage	Preparations
Acetyldigitoxin Acylanid (Sandoz)	*Oral: Adults*, initially, 1.6 to 2 mg over period of 24 hours; maintenance dose, 0.1 to 0.2 mg daily.	Tablets 0.1 and 0.2 mg
Deslanoside Cedilanid-D (Sandoz)	*Intramuscular, Intravenous: Adults*, initially, 0.8 mg followed by 0.4 mg at 2-hour intervals; maintenance dose, 0.4 to 0.5 mg daily in divided doses. *Children: infants*, 0.05 mg/kg; *2 to 12 years*, 0.025 mg/kg; *12 years and older*, adult dose.	Solution (injection) 0.2 mg/ml in 2 and 4 ml containers
Digitalis Leaf Digitora (Upjohn) Pil-Digis (Davies Rose Hoyt) Also marketed under generic name.	*Oral: Adults*, initially, 1.2 to 1.5 g over period of 24 to 48 hours; maintenance dose, 100 mg daily.	Capsules 100 mg Tablets 100 mg Tincture 100 mg/ml
Digitoxin Crystodigin (Lilly) Digitaline Nativelle (Fougera) Myodigin (Davies Rose Hoyt) Purodigin (Wyeth) Also marketed under generic name.	*Oral: Adults*, initially, 1.2 to 1.5 mg over period of 24 to 48 hours; maintenance dose, 0.1 to 0.2 mg daily. *Children: newborn infants*, 0.075 mg/kg; *under 2 years*, 0.05 mg/kg; *2 to 12 years*, 0.025 mg/kg; *over 12 years*, adult dose. *Intravenous: Adults*, initially, 1 to 1.5 mg daily; maintenance dose, 0.05 to 0.2 mg daily. *Children*, same as oral dose.	Elixir (pediatric) 0.05 mg/ml in 55 ml containers Tablets 0.05, 0.1, 0.15, and 0.2 mg Solution (oral) 1 mg/ml in 10 ml containers Solution (injection) 0.2 mg/ml in 1, 2, and 10 ml containers
Digoxin Davoxin (Davies Rose Hoyt) Lanoxin (Burroughs Wellcome) Also marketed under generic name.	*Oral, Intramuscular: Adults*, initially, 1.5 to 2 mg over period of 24 hours; maintenance dose, 0.25 to 0.50 mg daily. *Children:* initially, *newborn infants*, 0.04 to 0.06 mg/kg; *under 2 years*, 0.06 to 0.08 mg/kg; *2 to 10 years*, 0.04 to 0.06 mg/kg; maintenance dose is approximately one-fourth initial dose. *Intravenous: Adults*, initially, 0.5 to 1 mg; maintenance dose, 0.25 to 0.75 mg daily. *Children:* initially, *newborn infants*, 0.02 to 0.04 mg/kg; *under 2 years*, 0.04 to 0.06 mg/kg; *2 to 10 years*, 0.02 to 0.04 mg/kg.	Elixir (pediatric) 0.25 mg/5 ml Tablets 0.125, 0.25, and 0.5 mg Solution (injection) 0.25 mg/ml in 2 ml containers
Lanatoside C Cedilanid (Sandoz)	*Oral: Adults*, initially 5 to 10 mg; maintenance dose, 1 to 1.5 mg daily.	Tablets 0.5 mg
Ouabain	*Intravenous: Adults*, 0.25 to 0.5 mg. *Children*, 0.012 to 0.016 mg/kg daily.	Solution (injection) 0.25 mg/ml in 2 ml containers

Similar Drugs.—Digifortis (Parke, Davis), Digiglusin (Lilly), Gitalin (Gitaligin [Schering]).

atrioventricular block. When treating ventricular premature contractions or tachycardia caused by digitalis, lidocaine or procainamide is used most often. Propranolol also has been used effectively but it must be given very cautiously, particularly if congestive failure is present. Intravenously administered diphenylhydantoin often is effective in reducing or eliminating ventricular irregularity and, unlike quinidine or procainamide, will not decrease conduction in the ventricle. However, it frequently may cause hypotension, particularly if given rapidly or in large doses. Other serious reactions include atrioventricular block and, rarely, sudden death. Most of the serious complications may be prevented by giving the drug in increments of 100 mg every 10 minutes to a total dosage of 300 mg. See also the Introductory Statement and Chapter 1, Digitalis Glycosides, for a discussion of digitalis toxicity.

USUAL DOSAGE.—It is more difficult to give a meaningful dosage recommendation for the treatment of arrhythmias than for congestive failure because the effects of digitalis on contractility are graded over a narrower range of dosage than on the electrophysiologic action of the heart. Thus, dosage frequently may be higher for treating arrhythmias and must be individualized.

The doses given in the table serve only as a guideline and will have to be adjusted upward until the heart rate and rhythm become normal or downward if symptoms of overdosage develop.

QUINIDINE GLUCONATE [Quinaglute]
QUINIDINE HYDROCHLORIDE
QUINIDINE POLYGALACTURONATE [Cardioquin]
QUINIDINE SULFATE [Quinidex, Quinora]

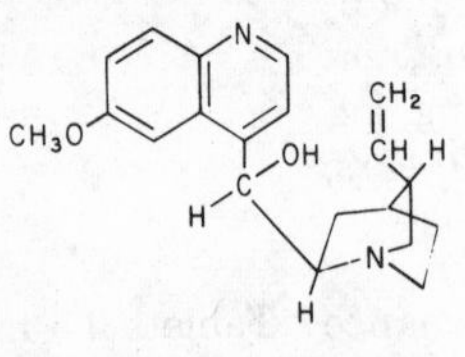

CH₃O … N … OH … C … H … CH₂ … CH … H … N … H

Quinidine generally is given orally as the sulfate. It acts by increasing the effective refractory period and reducing cardiac automaticity. This drug is effective in converting atrial fibrillation and flutter to normal sinus rhythm following administration of digitalis to reduce ventricular rate and produce some degree of atrioventricular block. It prevents ventricular premature contractions and tachycardia and is useful, although less effective, in the prevention and treatment of supraventricular tachyarrhythmias. Usual therapeutic blood levels for quinidine are approximately 5.5 μg/ml.

Untoward effects include manifestations of cinchonism such as headache, vertigo, tinnitus, syncope, a hot flushed skin, nausea, vomiting, diarrhea, and palpitation; diarrhea and a hot flushed face are the most common reactions. Visual disturbances (blurred vision, photophobia, diplopia, disturbed color perception, mydriasis, scotomata, night blindness, and even constricted visual fields) also have been reported. Large doses can produce severe hypotension. Less frequent but extremely serious reactions include hypersensitivity, manifested as a violent allergic response, or, rarely, thrombocytopenic purpura. The reactions largely are dose related, although occasionally they occur after small doses in susceptible people. If the gastrointestinal reactions become a problem, oral administration of procainamide may be substituted for quinidine.

Quinidine may paradoxically increase the ventricular rate in atrial fibrillation or flutter because it may enhance atrioventricular nodal conduction. It is contraindicated in heart block unless an electronic pacemaker is used. Conversion to a normal sinus rhythm with electrical countershock is preferred to large, potentially toxic doses of this drug. Quinidine should not be given with neuromuscular blocking agents and should be used with extreme caution when given with any drug that can depress conduction at the myoneural junction (eg, polymyxin B, neomycin, kanamycin).

USUAL DOSAGE.—

Quinidine Sulfate, Quinidine Gluconate, Quinidine Polygalacturonate:

Oral: Adults, to convert atrial fibrillation or flutter, initially, 200 to 400 mg is given three to five times daily for one to three days. It is important to space doses evenly to prevent lower blood levels during the nighttime hours. Larger doses (400 to 600 mg) may be given up to five times daily for one or two days; generally these amounts are given in the hospital where the patient can be observed for symptoms of cinchonism and signs of toxicity can be detected in the electrocardiogram before each successive dose. To prevent recurrence of atrial irregularity, maintenance doses of 200 to 400 mg are given four times daily. To prevent ventricular premature contractions or tachycardia, 200 to 400 mg can be given every six hours. *Children*, 6 mg/kg of body weight every four to six hours.

Dosage for sustained-release preparations may be larger and may vary more than the amounts listed above. When using these preparations, refer to the manufacturers' literature for specific dosage recommendations.

Quinidine Hydrochloride, Quinidine Gluconate:

Intramuscular, Intravenous: Quinidine is given almost exclusively orally. If this drug is used parenterally, it should be administered only in a hospital. Intramuscularly, 400 mg is given initially and this dose may be repeated every two hours if necessary. The intramuscular route is preferred but, if the situation is acute, 200 mg in dilute solution may be given intravenously, *very slowly* with continuous monitoring of the electrocardiogram and blood pressure. Intravenous administration of quinidine sulfate is dangerous and is not recommended.

PREPARATIONS.—

Quinidine Gluconate:

Quinaglute (Cooper). *Oral:* Tablets (timed-release) 300 mg.

Quinidine Hydrochloride:

Injection: Solution 120 mg/ml in 1.5, 5, and 10 ml containers; solution 800 mg/ml in 10 ml containers.

Quinidine Polygalacturonate:

Cardioquin (Purdue Frederick). *Oral:* Tablets 275 mg (equivalent to 200 mg quinidine sulfate).

Quinidine Sulfate:

Quinidex (Robins). *Oral:* Tablets (timed-release) 300 mg.

Quinora (Davies Rose Hoyt). *Oral:* Tablets 200 and 300 mg.

The various salts also are marketed by other manufacturers under their generic names.

PROCAINAMIDE HYDROCHLORIDE

[Pronestyl]

$$NH_2-C_6H_4-C(=O)-NH-CH_2CH_2N(CH_2CH_3)_2 \cdot HCl$$

The mechanisms of action of this drug are similar to those of quinidine (see the evaluation on Quinidine). However, procainamide may be somewhat less effective than quinidine in converting atrial fibrillation or flutter to normal sinus rhythm and in preventing atrial premature contractions or tachycardia. It prevents ventricular premature contractions and, because it acts immediately when given intravenously, is more effective than quinidine in the treatment of ventricular tachycardia. Effective therapeutic blood levels for procainamide are between 4 and 8 μg/ml.

Adverse effects are similar to those of quinidine. Anorexia, nausea, and vomiting occur frequently. Flushing, bitter taste, asthenia, mental depression, dizziness, and psychosis with hallucinations have been reported. It also may cause hypersensitivity reactions such as fever, urticaria, angioedema, or maculopapular rash. Procainamide is more likely to produce hypotension than quinidine when administered intravenously. Cardiac irregularities occur with large doses. Death has resulted from rapid intravenous injection. Severe toxic effects include leukopenia, agranulocytosis, and a lupus erythematosus-like syndrome. Procainamide is contraindicated in complete heart block, unless an electronic pacemaker is used. Procainamide is excreted by the kidneys, in large part unmetabolized. Therefore, the dose should be reduced in patients with decreased creatinine clearance.

USUAL DOSAGE.—

Oral: Adults and children, 50 mg/kg of body weight daily in divided doses every three hours.

Intramuscular: Adults and children, if it is necessary to obtain high blood levels quickly, a priming dose double the amount of the oral dose can be given by this route. Maintenance dosage can then be given orally at the level indicated above.

Intravenous: Adults, 50 to 100 mg/minute to a maximum of 1 g. Since hypotension may occur with larger doses, an agent that will support blood pressure may have to be given concurrently. For the treatment of ventricular tachycardia, the dosage must be administered in small increments until a sufficient amount has been given to terminate the tachycardia. *Children*, 100 mg is given over a five- to ten-minute period.

Plasma level measurements are the best guide for determining correct dosage in refractory patients, in those with cardiac or renal failure, or in individuals in whom toxicity occurs.

PREPARATIONS.—Pronestyl (Squibb).

Oral: Capsules 250 and 500 mg.

Injection: Solution 100 mg/ml in 10 ml containers.

Drug also marketed by other manufacturers under generic name.

LIDOCAINE HYDROCHLORIDE [Xylocaine Hydrochloride]

$$\text{2,6-}(CH_3)_2C_6H_3\text{-}NH\overset{O}{\overset{\|}{C}}CH_2N(CH_2CH_3)_2 \cdot HCl$$

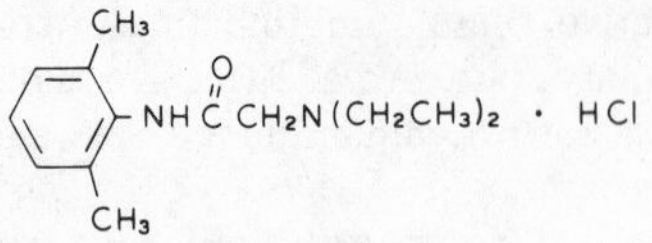

This drug is being used with increasing frequency in the treatment of *ventricular* premature beats and tachycardia because it does not depress conduction in the heart and it has less negative inotropic action than quinidine and procainamide. The incidence of hypotension and depressed myocardial contractility also may be lower than with either of these other agents. (See the Introductory Statement.) Since oral administration is relatively ineffective, a continuous antiarrhythmic effect can be obtained only by intravenous infusion of lidocaine; therefore, this drug is useful only for short-term therapy, and other agents must be used for maintenance. Acceptable therapeutic blood levels for lidocaine range from 2 to 5 μg/ml.

Untoward effects include drowsiness, nervousness, dizziness, blurred vision, nausea, tremor, hypotension, generalized paresthesias, convulsions, and respiratory arrest. Doses larger than 100 mg given as an intravenous bolus injection may depress myocardial contractility. *Lidocaine solutions that contain epinephrine should not be used to treat arrhythmias or administered intravenously.*

USUAL DOSAGE.—*Intravenous:* 1 mg/kg of body weight, usually not to exceed a total dose of 50 to 100 mg, is administered as a single dose. Lidocaine is most commonly given as a continuous intravenous infusion in 5% dextrose in water at a rate of 25 μg/kg/minute in normal adults. This dosage must be reduced in the presence of congestive heart failure or liver disease. A dose of 100 mg is pharmacologically equivalent to 400 to 500 mg of procainamide.

PREPARATIONS.—Xylocaine Hydrochloride (Astra). *Injection:* Solution 2% in 5 and 50 ml containers. Drug also marketed by other manufacturers under generic name.

DIPHENYLHYDANTOIN [Dilantin]
DIPHENYLHYDANTOIN SODIUM [Dilantin Sodium]

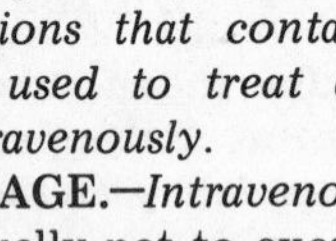

Diphenylhydantoin is less effective as an antiarrhythmic agent than quinidine, procainamide, or lidocaine. It is used orally to treat supraventricular or ventricular premature contractions and intravenously for ventricular premature contractions, ventricular tachycardia, and atrial tachycardia with or without atrioventricular block. This drug reduces automaticity without decreasing conduction in the heart; therefore, it may be particularly useful in the treatment of arrhythmias produced by digitalis overdosage. Although blood levels as low as 2 μg/ml may have antiarrhythmic effects, a mean concentration of 8 to 12 μg/ml is the usual effective therapeutic blood concentration.

Because of the long half-life (approximately 22 hours) of diphenylhydantoin, plateau levels of the drug in plasma can be attained in seven to eight days and these levels can be maintained by this regimen. Moreover, there is no significant difference at any time between plasma levels attained by giving a single daily dose and those attained by giving the same dose in three divided portions several hours apart. However, since wide differences in the plateau levels are observed among individual patients, it is important (if facilities are available) to make periodic plasma level determinations of diphenylhydantoin in patients receiving the drug for long periods.

Common adverse effects include dizziness, nausea, vomiting, pruritus, rash, nystagmus, fatigue, and ataxia, which, if allowed to persist, will become permanent. Gingival hyperplasia can occur after prolonged administration. Diphenylhydantoin rarely causes hepatitis, blood dyscrasias, and pseudolymphoma. (See Chapter 31, Anticonvulsants.) When administered intravenously, it may produce hypotension. Third-degree atrioventricular block and, rarely, sudden death have been reported following administration of this drug. Care must be exercised when giving diphenylhydantoin to patients receiving coumarin derivatives because such patients become more likely to hemorrhage spontaneously.

USUAL DOSAGE.—

Oral: 200 to 400 mg daily.

Intravenous: 100 mg every 10 minutes. Total dose should not exceed 10 mg/kg of body weight.

PREPARATIONS.—

Diphenylhydantoin:

Dilantin (Parke, Davis). *Oral:* Suspension 30 and 125 mg/5 ml; tablets (pediatric) 50 mg.

Diphenylhydantoin Sodium:

Dilantin [sodium] (Parke, Davis).

Oral: Capsules 30 and 100 mg.

Injection: Powder for solution containing approximately 50 mg/ml when diluted with the special solvent provided in the 100 and 250 mg containers.

ADDITIONAL TRADEMARKS.—**Diphenylhydantoin:** Toin (Reid-Provident). **Diphenylhydantoin Sodium:** Kessodanten (McKesson). Drug also marketed by other manufacturers under generic name.

PROPRANOLOL HYDROCHLORIDE
[Inderal]

$$\text{(1-naphthyl)}-OCH_2CH(OH)CH_2NHCH(CH_3)_2 \cdot HCl$$

Propranolol hydrochloride is a beta-adrenergic blocking agent used in the management of certain arrhythmias, hypertrophic subaortic stenosis, pheochromocytoma, angina pectoris, certain hypertensive states, and in overcoming some of the adrenergically mediated symptoms associated with thyrotoxicosis and anxiety neurosis. (See also Chapter 3, Antianginal Agents, and Chapter 6, Antihypertensive Agents.)

When propranolol is administered to a normal individual in a relatively basal state, it may decrease heart rate and cardiac output. It generally does not lower blood pressure when given intravenously for short periods to normal individuals, but it can cause hypotension when administered orally for a prolonged period; this effect may be due to a lowered cardiac output. This drug also attenuates most of the usual cardiac reactions to exercise by modifying the hemodynamic response to sympathetic drive. It competitively blocks both the chronotropic and inotropic effects of catecholamines. In addition to its ability to block beta-adrenergic receptors in the heart, bronchioles, uterus, and vascular bed, propranolol exerts a depressant effect on cardiac muscle similar to that of quinidine. Both the adrenergic antagonism and cardiac depressant effects contribute to its ability to prolong the refractory period and conduction time in the atrioventricular conduction system. Thus, propranolol may precipitate congestive heart failure, particularly when given to a patient with borderline cardiac reserve or to one whose compensation depends upon maintaining a high level of endogenous or exogenous catecholamines. In contrast to other beta-adrenergic blocking agents that have been subjected to clinical trial, propranolol does not have a significant intrinsic beta receptor stimulatory effect. It has limited hypoglycemic action but may potentiate the effects of hypoglycemia due to other factors. It also decreases the rebound of plasma glucose after an insulin tolerance test.

Blockade usually develops within 30 minutes following oral ingestion of propranolol and is maintained for approximately three to eight hours. Almost no blocking action is evident after 12 to 24 hours. When administered by the intravenous route, the onset of action occurs within two minutes and reaches a peak effect in three to five minutes; the total duration of effect is two to four hours.

An oral dose of propranolol is more effective than the same dose given intravenously. This occurs as a result of the "first pass effect." After oral administration, propranolol is present in the liver in relatively high concentration, where it is converted to 4-hydroxypropranolol, a more potent beta blocker than propranolol itself. This conversion does not occur to any appreciable extent when the drug is administered intravenously because the concentration in the liver is lower.

There are no carefully controlled clinical studies comparing propranolol with other antiarrhythmic agents. Nevertheless, the drug does appear to slow the heart rate in patients with supraventricular tachycardias and to be useful in the management of some arrhythmias induced by digitalis or anesthetic agents if prolonged conduction is not present; however, propranolol has not been shown to be superior to lidocaine or diphenylhydantoin (which are preferred drugs for this purpose, often in conjunction with potassium). Propranolol appears to be especially useful in controlling supraventricular arrhythmias in patients with thyrotoxicosis. It also may have prophylactic value in reducing the frequency of paroxysmal atrial tachycardia episodes, especially when this arrhythmia is associated with the Wolff-Parkinson-White syndrome.

Propranolol frequently is effective in treating atrial and ventricular premature contractions and some ventricular tachycardias. Indeed, it may succeed when other antiarrhythmic agents have failed.

When propranolol is used to treat atrial flutter or fibrillation, a decreased ventricular rate usually results from the ability of the drug to decrease atrioventricular conduction time and, occasionally, normal sinus rhythm is restored. The combined use of digitalis and propranolol appears to be an effective regimen for slowing the ventricular response in the presence of atrial flutter and fibrillation.

Propranolol may be useful as the sole therapeutic agent in the long-term treatment and prophylaxis of arrhythmias, particularly when the arrhythmia is caused by sympathetic hyperactivity. Also, it appears to act synergistically with some other antiarrhythmic agents (eg, quinidine), thereby permitting use of a smaller dose of each agent for the management of chronic arrhythmias. This latter application of propranolol may turn out to be its primary therapeutic use in the treatment of arrhythmias.

Adverse Reactions and Precautions.— Propranolol can produce multiple nonspecific untoward effects such as nausea, vomiting, dizziness, mild diarrhea or constipation, fatigue, lethargy, asthenia, insomnia, rash, and, infrequently, mental depression. Most of these reactions are transient and seldom require cessation of therapy.

More serious adverse effects are fever, accompanied by myalgia and sore throat; visual disturbances; marked erythematous rash; paresthesias of the hands; hallucinations; and, rarely, dyspnea or laryngospasm, especially after intravenous administration. In addition, propranolol occasionally may cause hypotension and pronounced bradycardia, dizziness, vertigo, or syncope. Its administration has been associated with an increase in blood urea nitrogen levels. This may be due to decreased renal blood flow secondary to decreased cardiac output rather than to a direct effect of the drug. Serum glutamic oxaloacetic transaminase (SGOT) levels also may be elevated, although no evidence of frank hepatic dysfunction has been observed.

Several deaths have been reported during the use of propranolol. Since the drug is often used in seriously ill patients, its exact role in these deaths is difficult to ascertain.

Unless the need is overwhelming, propranolol must not be used in patients with most types of chronic lung disease or poor respiratory reserve because it will cause a decrease in pulmonary function in most forms of obstructive airway disease. In hypoxic patients, propranolol will increase pulmonary arterial vasoconstriction and cause pulmonary arterial hypertension. Thus, if the drug is used in patients with chronic lung disease, these individuals must be carefully observed for right ventricular failure. Propranolol is contraindicated if right ventricular failure already exists.

Since propranolol may precipitate an acute, severe crisis in asthmatic patients and since these patients may respond poorly to isoproterenol, propranolol usually is contraindicated in the presence of bronchial asthma. It also must be given with extreme caution to patients with borderline cardiac reserve or frank congestive failure, unless the failure is due to an arrhythmia that may be controlled by propranolol. If propranolol therapy must be used in patients with congestive failure, the prior or concomitant administration of digitalis is mandatory to offset to some degree the negative inotropic action of the drug. Propranolol also commonly causes minor electrocardiographic changes such as higher voltage T waves and an increase in the absolute Q-T interval.

Propranolol must be used carefully in diabetics receiving large doses of insulin or other hypoglycemic agents, as well as in patients prone to spontaneous hypoglycemia. In the diabetic patient, the subjective warning signs of acute hypoglycemia are blocked by the drug.

The effects of propranolol on the fetus have not been established. If the drug is used in pregnant patients up to the time of delivery, an unusually short labor frequently occurs.

This beta-adrenergic blocking agent must be used with care in patients receiving catecholamine-depleting drugs (eg, reserpine), as well as in those with impaired renal or hepatic function. It is contraindicated in patients with most types of atrioventricular block and should be used with caution in patients with sinus bradycardia. Propranolol should not be given with anesthetics that depress the myocardium (eg, ether, chloroform) or adrenergic-augmenting psychotropic drugs (including monoamine oxidase inhibitors), or for a period of two weeks following their withdrawal.

USUAL DOSAGE.—

Oral: 10 to 40 mg of propranolol hydrochloride is given three or four times daily before meals and at bedtime or, alternatively, every six hours day and night. Because there is a high degree of variability in the absorption and response to propranolol, it is necessary to individualize the dose. It is always advisable to institute therapy at a low dose, ie, 10 mg every six or eight hours, and gradually increase the amount until the desired effect is obtained or adverse effects appear.

Intravenous: 1 to 3 mg is given initially at a

rate not exceeding 1 mg/minute. Depending upon the response, determined by continuous electrocardiographic monitoring, a second dose may be given after 10 to 15 minutes. Additional doses should be administered only after carefully assessing the clinical status of the patient to insure that there is no evidence of early signs of congestive failure.

If signs of serious myocardial depression (eg, excessive bradycardia) occur following propranolol administration, isoproterenol should be slowly infused intravenously. Since this drug is competitively antagonized by propranolol, the dose required may be quite large; the amount necessary will depend on the dose of propranolol and the elapsed interval since its administration. In addition, the positive inotropic effect of digitalization will partially counteract the negative inotropic action of propranolol. Atropine sulfate (1 mg) given intravenously also may be a useful adjunct, since its ability to block transmission of the vagus nerve will offset the negative chronotropic effect of beta-adrenergic blockade, as well as possibly correct the bradycardia and reverse any existing bronchospasm.

PREPARATIONS.—Inderal (Ayerst).

Oral: Tablets 10 and 40 mg.

Injection: Solution 1 mg/ml in 1 ml containers.

ISOPROTERENOL HYDROCHLORIDE
[Isuprel Hydrochloride]

HO–(C_6H_3)(HO)–$\underset{\text{OH}}{\text{CH}}CH_2NHCH(CH_3)_2 \cdot HCl$

Isoproterenol stimulates beta receptors of the heart, thereby increasing autorhythmicity, excitability, and conduction; it also exerts a positive inotropic effect. In contrast to epinephrine, isoproterenol reduces systemic resistance when given intravenously. This drug is most commonly used in the treatment of third-degree atrioventricular block. It also is used to treat sinus bradycardia, sometimes in conjunction with atropine. Sublingual tablets of isoproterenol are available, but their absorption and duration of action is variable and unreliable. Tachyphylaxis often occurs. For other uses, see Chapter 41, Bronchodilators.

Adverse effects include tachycardia, fear, anxiety, tension, restlessness, tremor, dizziness, headache, flushing, nausea, and palpitation. (Also see the Introductory Statement.)

USUAL DOSAGE.—The dose must always be adjusted within the limits of the adverse effects and according to the actions desired.

Intravenous: In third-degree atrioventricular block, 1 to 2 mg is diluted in 5% dextrose injection in water. The rate of infusion is determined by the chronotropic effect obtained. Rarely, isoproterenol is injected directly into the heart in emergency situations.

PREPARATIONS.—Isuprel Hydrochloride (Winthrop). *Injection:* Solution (aqueous) 1:5,000 (0.2 mg/ml) in 1, 5, and 10 ml containers. Drug also marketed under generic name.

METHOXAMINE HYDROCHLORIDE
[Vasoxyl]

CH_3O–(C_6H_3)(OCH_3)–$\underset{\text{OH}}{\text{CH}}–\underset{NH_2}{\text{CH}}–CH_3 \cdot HCl$

Methoxamine can terminate paroxysmal atrial tachycardia by causing reflex bradycardia. It has no significant stimulatory action on the heart.

Adverse effects include urinary urgency, occasional paresthesia in the extremities, and a feeling of coldness following injection. Large doses may cause sustained, excessive hypertension with severe headache.

For other uses, see Chapter 5, Agents Used in Hypotension and Shock.

USUAL DOSAGE.—

Intravenous: 5 to 10 mg injected slowly.

Intramuscular: 10 to 15 mg.

PREPARATIONS.—Vasoxyl (Burroughs Wellcome). *Injection:* Solution 10 mg/ml in 10 ml containers and 20 mg/ml in 1 ml containers.

Chapter 3

ANTIANGINAL AGENTS

Most antianginal drugs are also called coronary vasodilators on the assumption that they relieve the pain of angina pectoris by dilating the coronary arteries. This assumption is only partially correct. Although these agents do produce coronary vasodilation, neither the cause of the pain nor the mechanism by which drugs prevent or relieve an anginal attack is fully understood. Current evidence indicates that a reduction in the oxygen requirement of the myocardium accounts for the therapeutic action of the drugs.

In considering the value of antianginal agents, it is important to differentiate between drugs used to relieve an acute attack and those used for long-term prophylaxis. The effectiveness of any treatment for preventing attacks of angina pectoris is difficult to determine because the frequency and severity of attacks vary and may be influenced by several unrelated factors (eg, weather, anxiety) and because any antianginal effect is subjective.

The effectiveness of the short-acting agents, nitroglycerin and amyl nitrite, has been established through many years of use. Nitroglycerin is the preferred drug for treatment of acute angina. A sublingual dose at the onset of chest pain usually provides complete relief in one to three minutes. Prompt relief also may be obtained by inhalation of amyl nitrite. Isosorbide dinitrate [Isordil, Sorbitrate] also may relieve the pain of an acute attack when administered sublingually, but its onset of action is slightly slower than that of nitroglycerin.

The actual therapeutic efficacy of these drugs in terminating an established anginal attack may largely be limited to angina occurring at rest. The relief of angina of effort is often probably spontaneous, occurring after cessation of activity and before the effect of the drug has actually become manifest. However, sublingually administered nitrates can prevent an anginal attack when taken shortly before anticipated physical exertion or emotional stress.

The oral administration of the "long-acting" nitrates (eg, pentaerythritol tetranitrate [Peritrate], erythrityl tetranitrate [Cardilate], isosorbide dinitrate, and some timed-release preparations of nitroglycerin) is alleged to reduce the number of episodes and the severity of the pain of angina pectoris. The effectiveness of these agents is even more difficult to determine than that of the short-acting nitrates. The ability of an agent to produce coronary dilatation or to modify favorably the effect of exercise on the electrocardiogram following a single dose has not been definitely shown to be related to the clinical efficacy of the nitrate in preventing angina. In most studies on the treatment of angina pectoris, good to excellent results were achieved in a large percentage of patients, regardless of the drug or nature of the therapeutic procedure being tested. Tolerance to some of the actions of these agents may develop after prolonged oral administration; cross tolerance to the action of nitroglycerin also has been demonstrated, and this may decrease the effectiveness of this drug. Moreover, the results of some studies show that these agents are rapidly destroyed following oral administration. Thus, it cannot be concluded that the prolonged use of long-acting nitrates is of definite therapeutic value.

The non-nitrate compound, dipyridamole [Persantine], is a long-acting coronary dilator; it increases the coronary flow in animals, but is of no value in treating an acute attack of angina pectoris. The evidence that its long-term administration will be beneficial in patients with angina pectoris is not convincing.

The daily use of propranolol [Inderal], a beta-adrenergic blocking drug, has been effective in diminishing the severity of the anginal syndrome in many patients. This drug has provided a significant advance in the treatment of angina pectoris, although its use is not without hazard (see the individual evaluation).

Since papaverine relaxes the coronary vessels in normal animals, use of this drug has been advocated to decrease the incidence of anginal attacks. However, convincing evidence of its effectiveness is not available, and hepatotoxicity has been associated with its administration.

The xanthines, particularly aminophylline, have been used for treatment of angina pectoris because they relax coronary vessels. However, since they also stimulate the myocardium, it is uncertain whether they increase cardiac efficiency. Thus, the efficacy of the xanthines in the management of angina pectoris has not been established.

Since barbiturates, other sedatives, and antianxiety agents reduce the patient's reaction to emotional tension and stress, they may have some value as adjunctive agents. The use of alcohol for its sedative effect also has been suggested; however, recent evidence indicates that even small amounts of alcohol can impair cardiac function in patients with heart disease.

Adverse Reactions and Precautions

Throbbing vascular headaches, flushing of the face, and dizziness often occur during early treatment with the nitrates. Occasionally, generalized systemic vasodilation may cause hypotension, reflex tachycardia (which might induce angina), and syncope. Sudden hypotension has occurred after the ingestion of alcoholic beverages by patients who have been taking nitrates.

Orally administered nitrates occasionally cause gastrointestinal disturbances (eg, nausea, vomiting).

The presence of glaucoma is not a contraindication to the use of the nitrates, since any increase in intraocular pressure is brief and drainage from the eye is not impeded.

SHORT-ACTING ANTIANGINAL AGENTS

NITROGLYCERIN

$$\begin{array}{c} CH_2ONO_2 \\ | \\ CHONO_2 \\ | \\ CH_2ONO_2 \end{array}$$

Nitroglycerin, taken sublingually, is the preferred drug for treatment of acute attacks of angina pectoris. Most patients obtain complete relief in one to three minutes. The drug also may be effective in preventing an attack when taken before physical activity, which, on the basis of the patient's experience, might produce angina. However, the drug should not be taken regularly as a prophylactic measure. Oral administration is unreliable. Despite claims to the contrary, evidence that prolonged use of nitroglycerin orally in timed-release preparations will diminish the severity or frequency of anginal attacks is not convincing. Tolerance may develop, but is rarely a problem with customary intermittent use; tolerance would develop more rapidly with continuous use. Cross tolerance to nitroglycerin may occur when the long-acting nitrates are used for prolonged periods.

Nitroglycerin gradually loses potency through sublimation. Accordingly, the drug must be packaged in glass containers with tightly fitting metal screw caps, and with no more than 100 dosage units in each container. In addition, nitroglycerin must be dispensed in the original unopened container. Patients should be advised to keep the tablets in the original container and close it tightly after each use; it should not be exposed to heat.

The adverse reactions to nitroglycerin are those associated with nitrates in general (see the Introductory Statement). The most common reactions are headache and hypotension. Untoward effects occur less frequently after the patient has become accustomed to using the drug.

USUAL DOSAGE.—

Sublingual: Adults, 0.2 to 0.6 mg. Dosage must be individualized and should be sufficient to be effective without producing untoward effects.

Oral: The efficacy of orally-administered nitrates has not been established. A dose commonly suggested by manufacturers is: *Adults,* 2.5 or 6.5 mg at 12-hour intervals; this may be increased to three times daily at 8-hour intervals.

PREPARATIONS.—

Sublingual: Tablets 0.25, 0.3, 0.4, and 0.6 mg; tablets (hypodermic) 0.15, 0.3, 0.4, and 0.6 mg.

Oral: Capsules (timed-release) 2.5 and 6.5 mg.

AVAILABLE TRADEMARKS.—Nitro-Bid (Marion), Nitrocels (Winston), Nitroglyn (Key), Nitrospan (USV), Vasoglyn (Reid-Provident) [all timed-release oral forms]. Drug also marketed under generic name.

AMYL NITRITE

$$\begin{array}{l} CH_2NO_2 \\ | \\ CH_2 \\ | \\ CH\,CH_3 \\ | \\ CH_3 \end{array}$$

This agent is administered only by inhalation to relieve an acute attack of angina. Because it is volatile and inhaled, the amount of drug absorbed can vary markedly. The marked depressor effect of inhaled amyl nitrite might reduce coronary perfusion more than it decreases myocardial oxygen demands and thereby paradoxically worsen ischemia.

Amyl nitrite is more likely to produce headache and a precipitous drop in blood pressure than nitroglycerin taken sublingually. Reflex tachycardia is more pronounced than with nitroglycerin. See also the Introductory Statement.

USUAL DOSAGE.—*Inhalation: Adults,* 0.18 to 0.3 ml (1 container crushed and inhaled).

PREPARATIONS.—*Inhalation:* Liquid in 0.18 and 0.3 ml containers. Drug marketed under generic name.

BETA-ADRENERGIC BLOCKING AGENT

PROPRANOLOL HYDROCHLORIDE [Inderal]

This beta-adrenergic blocking drug benefits patients with angina pectoris by lessening pain and increasing tolerance to exercise. The mechanism of action is debated, but the principal effect in angina is the reduced cardiac oxygen requirement resulting from decreased sympathetic stimulation of the heart that, in turn, causes a decrease in cardiac work. Propranolol is not useful in abolishing acute attacks, but it may act additively with sublingually administered nitrates given for this purpose. This fact, however, lends no additional credence to the alleged prophylactic value of "long-acting" nitrates administered for prolonged periods by the oral route.

Propranolol is particularly dangerous in patients with asthma or other chronic pulmonary disease, sinus bradycardia, third-degree atrioventricular block, recent myocardial infarction, or congestive heart failure. The drug can induce congestive heart failure in patients with a low cardiac reserve; if this occurs, digitalization and discontinuation of propranolol are necessary. General anesthetics that depress the myocardium are dangerous in patients receiving this agent.

Propranolol may cause serious hypotension in susceptible patients. This may be avoided by starting with small doses, a prudent procedure because of the marked individual variation in susceptibility due to variation in the rate of uptake and metabolism of the drug in the liver. Excessive bradycardia responds to atropine or isoproterenol given intravenously. Nausea, vomiting, diarrhea or constipation, rash, mental depression, visual disturbances, and hallucinations have been reported rarely. Dyspnea has occurred. The drug may both prolong insulin-induced hypoglycemia and obscure the subjective signs of diabetes; thus, its use in diabetics requires special caution. For further details and other uses, see Chapter 2, Antiarrhythmic Agents, and Chapter 6, Antihypertensive Agents.

USUAL DOSAGE.—*Oral: Adults,* 10 to 80 mg every six hours.

PREPARATIONS.—Inderal (Ayerst). *Oral:* Tablets 10 and 40 mg.

LONG-ACTING NITRATES

ERYTHRITYL TETRANITRATE [Cardilate]

$$\begin{array}{l} O_2NOCH\,CH_2ONO_2 \\ \quad\;\;| \\ O_2NOCH\,CH_2ONO_2 \end{array}$$

The effect of *sublingual* administration of erythrityl tetranitrate is apparent in about five minutes and lasts two or three hours. Thus, the drug is not useful for relief of an acute attack of angina pectoris, but it may be effective as a prophylactic measure when taken prior to situations known to precipitate attacks of angina.

As with other long-acting nitrates, there is no convincing evidence that long-term *oral* administration of erythrityl tetranitrate will be of value in managing the anginal syndrome.

Adverse reactions are those associated with the nitrates in general (see the Introductory Statement).

USUAL DOSAGE.—

Sublingual: Adults, for prevention of an acute attack of angina pectoris, 5 to 15 mg.

Oral: The efficacy of orally-administered nitrates has not been established. One recommendation suggested by the manufacturer is: *Adults,* initially, 10 mg three times daily; this may be increased to 30 mg three times daily. (See the manufacturer's literature for other regimens, including some for combined oral and sublingual administration.)

PREPARATIONS.—Cardilate (Burroughs Wellcome).

Sublingual: Tablets 5, 10, and 15 mg.

Oral: Tablets 5, 10, and 15 mg; tablets (chewable) 10 mg.

ISOSORBIDE DINITRATE [Isordil, Sorbitrate]

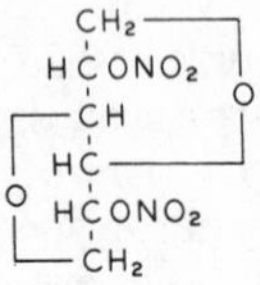

```
       CH2 ──────┐
       HCONO2    │
  ┌─── CH        O
  │    HC ───────┘
  O    HCONO2
  └─── CH2
```

Isosorbide dinitrate, administered *sublingually*, is similar to nitroglycerin in effectiveness and duration of action; relief of angina pectoris may occur in two or three minutes and lasts one to two hours. In addition to its use for relief of acute attacks, this drug may be beneficial for prophylaxis when taken prior to situations known to cause attacks of angina pectoris. The value of routine daily oral administration for the management of the anginal syndrome is unproved.

Adverse reactions are those associated with the nitrates in general (see the Introductory Statement).

USUAL DOSAGE.—

Sublingual: Adults, for relief or prevention of acute attack, 5 mg or more as tolerated.

Oral: The efficacy of orally-administered nitrates has not been established. The manufacturers' suggested dosage is: *Adults*, 5 to 30 mg four times daily. (See the manufacturers' literature for other regimens.)

PREPARATIONS.—

Isordil (Ives).

Sublingual: Tablets 2.5 and 5 mg.

Oral: Capsules (timed-release) 40 mg; tablets 5 and 10 mg; tablets (timed-release) 40 mg.

Sorbitrate (Stuart).

Sublingual: Tablets 2.5 and 5 mg.

Oral: Tablets 5 and 10 mg; tablets (chewable) 5 mg.

MANNITOL HEXANITRATE [Nitranitol]

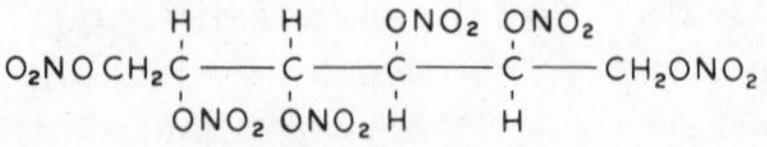

```
            H      H      ONO2   ONO2
O2NOCH2C ── C ──── C ──── C ──── CH2ONO2
            ONO2   ONO2   H      H
```

This long-acting nitrate is administered orally. Like related agents, there is no convincing evidence that long-term daily administration of this drug would be of value in the management of the anginal syndrome.

Adverse reactions are those associated with the nitrates in general (see the Introductory Statement).

USUAL DOSAGE.—The efficacy of orally-administered nitrates has not been established. The manufacturers' suggested dosage is: *Oral: Adults*, 32 to 64 mg every four to six hours.

PREPARATIONS.—Nitranitol (Merrell-National). *Oral:* Tablets 30 mg. Drug marketed by many manufacturers under generic name.

PENTAERYTHRITOL TETRANITRATE [Peritrate]

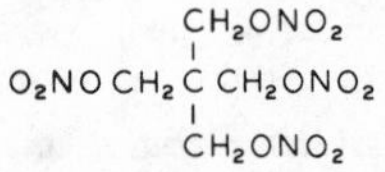

```
          CH2ONO2
          |
O2NOCH2 C CH2ONO2
          |
          CH2ONO2
```

This long-acting nitrate is administered orally; it is not used sublingually because absorption from the oral mucosa is poor. Long-term daily administration is alleged to lessen the frequency and severity of anginal attacks; however, there is no convincing evidence that pentaerythritol tetranitrate is of value in the management of the anginal syndrome.

Adverse reactions are those associated with the nitrates in general (see the Introductory Statement).

USUAL DOSAGE.—The efficacy of orally-administered nitrates has not been established. The manufacturers' suggested dosage is: *Oral: Adults*, 30 to 160 mg daily in divided doses. (See the manufacturers' literature for various regimens.)

PREPARATIONS.—Peritrate (Warner-Chilcott). *Oral:* Tablets 10 and 20 mg; tablets (timed-release) 80 mg.

ADDITIONAL TRADEMARKS.—Duotrate (Marion), El-Petn (Elder), Neo-Corovas (Amfre-Grant), Nitrin (Vale), Pentafin (Tutag), Pentritol (Armour), Perispan (USV), SK-Petn (Smith Kline & French), Steps (Dow), Tetrasule (Arnar-Stone), Tranite (Westerfield), Vasitol (Rowell), Vaso-80 (Reid-Provident). Drug also marketed by many manufacturers under generic name.

TROLNITRATE PHOSPHATE [Metamine]

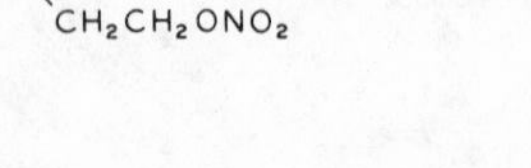

```
  ╱CH2CH2ONO2
N-CH2CH2ONO2  · 2 H3PO4
  ╲CH2CH2ONO2
```

This long-acting nitrate is administered orally. As with related agents, there is no convincing evidence that long-term daily ingestion of trolnitrate is of value in the management of the anginal syndrome.

Adverse reactions are those associated with the nitrates in general (see the Introductory Statement).

USUAL DOSAGE.—The efficacy of orally-administered nitrates has not been established. The manufacturer's suggested dosage is: *Oral: Adults,* 10 mg every six to eight hours (maximum, 40 mg daily); see the manufacturer's literature for details.

PREPARATIONS.—Metamine (Pfizer). *Oral:* Tablets (timed-release) 10 mg.

UNRELATED MISCELLANEOUS AGENTS

AMINOPHYLLINE

This xanthine derivative contains 85% theophylline and 15% ethylenediamine. The use of aminophylline for the treatment of patients with ischemic heart disease and angina pectoris is based on the fact that it is a myocardial stimulant and coronary vasodilator. However, it is uncertain whether the increased need for oxygen caused by myocardial stimulation exceeds the increased supply produced by coronary vasodilatation. Because its effectiveness in the treatment of angina pectoris has not been proved, aminophylline is not recommended for this use.

For adverse reactions and other uses, see Chapter 7, Diuretics, and Chapter 41, Bronchodilators.

USUAL DOSAGE.—The efficacy of this drug by the oral route has not been established for the treatment of angina pectoris. The manufacturers' suggested dosage for this indication is: *Oral: Adults,* 100 to 200 mg three or four times daily.

PREPARATIONS.—*Oral:* Elixir 259 mg/15 ml; tablets 100 and 200 mg.

AVAILABLE TRADEMARK.—Lixaminol (Ferndale). Drug also marketed under generic name.

DIPYRIDAMOLE [Persantine]

This drug is promoted for the long-term treatment of chronic angina pectoris. Carefully controlled double-blind studies have shown that it is not useful in preventing or relieving acute attacks. The alleged beneficial effect in anginal patients after long-term administration is unproved.

Peripheral vasodilatation, headache, vertigo, asthenia, syncope, nausea, and rash have occurred; rarely, the drug has aggravated symptoms of angina pectoris.

USUAL DOSAGE.—The efficacy of this drug has not been established. The manufacturer's suggested dosage is: *Oral: Adults,* 50 mg three times daily taken at least one hour before meals. The manufacturer's literature provides for possible increases in dosage but cautions that side effects increase also.

PREPARATIONS.—Persantine (Geigy). *Oral:* Tablets 25 mg.

PAPAVERINE HYDROCHLORIDE

Although papaverine causes vasodilatation, there is no convincing evidence that it is of value in the treatment of angina pectoris.

This drug has been reported to be hepatotoxic. Other reactions include malaise, intensive flushing of the face, hyperhidrosis, increase in the depth of respiration, tachycardia, a slight rise in blood pressure, drowsiness, and (after oral administration) mild constipation. One manufacturer warns against "uncomfortable and alarming side-effects" if intravenous administration is too rapid.

For other uses of papaverine, see Chapter 4, Peripheral Vasodilators.

USUAL DOSAGE.—The efficacy of this drug has not been established for treatment of angina pectoris. One manufacturer's suggested dosage is:

Oral: Adults, 100 to 300 mg three or four times daily; timed-release form, 150 mg every 12 hours.

Intramuscular, Intravenous (given over a period of one or two minutes): *Adults,* 30 to 120 mg every three hours as indicated.

PREPARATIONS.—

Oral: Capsules (timed-release) 150 mg; tablets 30, 60, 100, 200, and 500 mg.

Injection: Solution 30 mg/ml in 1 and 2 ml containers, 60 mg/ml in 2 ml containers.

AVAILABLE TRADEMARKS.—Cerespan (USV), Pap-Kaps (Sutliff & Case), Pavabid (Marion), Pavacap (Reid-Provident), Pavacen (Central), Pavarine (North American), Pavatest

(Fellows-Testagar), Vasal (Tutag), Vasospan (Ulmer) [all timed-release oral forms]. Drug also marketed under generic name.

MIXTURES

Many products contain two or more antianginal agents or an antianginal agent with a sedative or other drug(s). The sedative agents are acknowledged to be useful as adjuncts in certain patients with angina pectoris. Without exception, however, preparations in the following list contain one or more ingredients of unproved or disproved value when given orally for angina pectoris (the route of administration that the preparations all have in common). Therefore, use of these mixtures is not justified.

Cardilate-P (Burroughs Wellcome): Each tablet contains erythrityl tetranitrate 10 mg and phenobarbital 15 mg.

Cartrax (Roerig): Each tablet contains pentaerythritol tetranitrate 10 or 20 mg and hydroxyzine hydrochloride 10 mg.

Corovas (Amfre-Grant): Each timed-release capsule contains pentaerythritol tetranitrate 30 mg and secobarbital 50 mg.

Diatraegus (Durst): Each tablet contains nitroglycerin 0.22 mg, allobarbital 16.2 mg, crataegus tincture 0.12 ml, and sodium nitrite 65 mg.

Duotrate w/Phenobarbital (Marion): Each timed-release capsule contains pentaerythritol tetranitrate 30 mg and phenobarbital 45 mg.

Equanitrate (Wyeth): Each tablet contains pentaerythritol tetranitrate 10 or 20 mg and meprobamate 200 mg.

Isordil with Phenobarbital (Ives): Each tablet contains isosorbide dinitrate 10 mg and phenobarbital 15 mg.

Maxitate w/Rauwolfia (Pennwalt): Each tablet contains mannitol hexanitrate 30 mg and rauwolfia serpentina 30 mg.

Miltrate (Wallace): Each tablet contains pentaerythritol tetranitrate 10 or 20 mg and meprobamate 200 mg.

Nitranitol w/Phenobarbital (Merrell-National): Each tablet contains mannitol hexanitrate 32 mg and phenobarbital 16 mg.

Nitrovas (Amfre-Grant): Each timed-release tablet contains nitroglycerin 2.6 mg and niacin 35 mg.

Nyomin (Elder): Each tablet contains nitroglycerin 0.25 mg, sodium nitrite 30 mg, potassium nitrate 150 mg, veratrum viride 24 mg, and aconite root 24 mg.

Paveril Phosphate and Amytal (Lilly): Each tablet contains dioxyline phosphate 194 mg and amobarbital 16.2 mg.

Pentoxylon (Riker): Each tablet contains pentaerythritol tetranitrate 10 mg and alseroxylon 0.5 mg.

Pentritol with Butabarbital (Armour): Each timed-release capsule contains pentaerythritol tetranitrate 30 mg and butabarbital 50 mg.

Peritrate with Nitroglycerin (Warner-Chilcott): Each tablet contains pentaerythritol tetranitrate 10 mg and nitroglycerin 0.3 mg.

Peritrate with Phenobarbital (Warner-Chilcott): Each tablet contains pentaerythritol tetranitrate 10 or 20 mg and phenobarbital 15 mg.

Sorbitrate with Phenobarbital (Stuart): Each tablet contains isosorbide dinitrate 10 mg and phenobarbital 15 mg.

Tetrasule-S (Arnar-Stone): Each timed-release capsule contains pentaerythritol tetranitrate 30 mg and amobarbital 30 mg.

Vasitol with Phenobarbital (Rowell): Each tablet contains pentaerythritol tetranitrate 10 or 20 mg and phenobarbital 16 mg.

Vasotrate No. 2 (Reid-Provident): Each tablet contains pentaerythritol tetranitrate 30 mg, nitroglycerin 0.52 mg, and amobarbital 50 mg.

Chapter 4

PERIPHERAL VASODILATORS

Drugs used for their peripheral vasodilating action are of limited clinical value. They may be of some benefit in peripheral vasoconstrictive conditions with no significant organic involvement, but there is little objective evidence that these drugs are useful in patients with obstructive peripheral vascular disease.

Results of studies in normal individuals have clearly demonstrated that there is increased blood flow to various areas with use of vasodilators. However, evidence that such a vasodilator effect occurs in areas of vascular disease is less convincing. Often the effects of ancillary therapeutic measures such as bedrest or cessation of smoking have been ignored in assessing the benefit of a new vasodilator. Regular exercise to the limits of tolerance also may be an aid in therapy.

Because several pharmacodynamic classes of drugs have a vasodilator action, they have been tried in the treatment of peripheral vascular diseases. The first class, the ganglionic blocking agents, have not been useful in treating peripheral vascular disease.

A second group of drugs used to treat peripheral vascular diseases, the alpha-adrenergic blocking agents, dilate vessels in the skin more than those in muscle. Phenoxybenzamine [Dibenzyline] may be worth a trial in the early stages of conditions in which spasm may be a greater factor than organic vascular damage (eg, Raynaud's disease). Phentolamine [Regitine] does not have clinically significant effects on the peripheral vascular system. The alpha-adrenergic blocking drugs have been advocated for the treatment of some types of shock to lessen the severe vasoconstriction produced by reflex sympathetic activity, provided hypovolemia has been corrected, but their effectiveness remains to be established. (See Chapter 5, Agents Used in Hypotension and Shock.)

A third class of drugs, of which papaverine is the prototype, has a direct relaxant effect on vascular smooth muscle. Other drugs in this group include azapetine [Ilidar], cyclandelate [Cyclospasmol], niacin, nicotinyl alcohol [Roniacol], and tolazoline [Priscoline]. Azapetine and tolazoline exert sympatholytic effects in animals after large doses, but it is improbable that the usual clinical doses are sufficient to act in this manner. Both drugs cause cardiac stimulation, azapetine less than tolazoline. They may be of some benefit in conditions in which vasospasm is prominent, but not in those in which organic vascular changes have occurred.

The fourth class of peripheral vasodilators consists of the beta-adrenergic stimulants, isoxsuprine [Vasodilan] and nylidrin [Arlidin]; these drugs cause cardiac stimulation and peripheral vasodilation more in muscle than in skin. Their value in peripheral vascular disorders has not been convincingly demonstrated. That beta-blocking agents do not completely eliminate the effects of isoxsuprine and nylidrin casts doubt on their presumed mode of action or at least suggests a possible second mechanism of action such as a direct smooth muscle relaxant effect.

Although the nitrites are potent vasodilators, they are not used for peripheral vascular disease (see Chapter 3, Antianginal Agents). Results of several studies have indicated that reserpine is effective in treating Raynaud's disease, possibly by diminishing neurogenic vasoconstriction.

Adverse Reactions and Precautions

Since these vasodilating drugs may increase blood flow to normal areas, blood flow to the beds supplied by obstructed arteries may even be decreased. Large doses of any of these agents can cause orthostatic hypotension, which may also reduce blood flow to ischemic areas. Severe hypotension due to toxic doses or unusual sensitivity may be counteracted by vasopressors (eg, levarterenol).

For other adverse reactions and precautions, see the individual evaluations.

INDIVIDUAL EVALUATIONS

AZAPETINE PHOSPHATE [Ilidar]

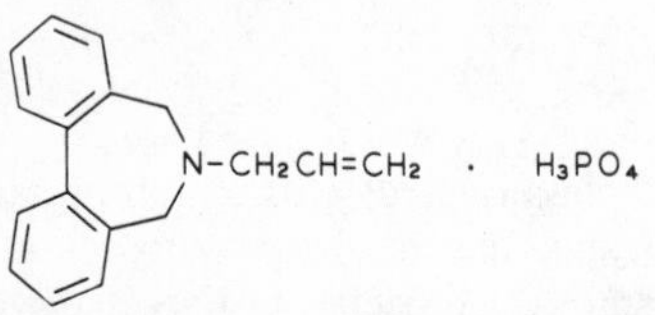

N-$CH_2CH{=}CH_2$ · H_3PO_4

This compound possesses an alpha-adrenergic blocking action, but its vasodilating action is due more to its direct relaxant effect on vascular smooth muscle. It may be useful in conditions in which vasospasm affecting circulation to the skin is predominant (eg, frostbite, Raynaud's disease, acrocyanosis), but it is not useful in diseases in which organic vascular changes are prominent (eg, arteriosclerosis obliterans).

Serious adverse reactions occur only rarely. Untoward effects include nausea, vomiting, dizziness, asthenia, orthostatic hypotension, and syncope; less frequently, azapetine may cause confusion, tachycardia, headache, dryness of the mouth, anorexia, and nasal congestion. This drug is contraindicated in patients with severe coronary disease, and caution is necessary when it is given to those with peptic ulcer, asthma, or cerebrovascular disease.

USUAL DOSAGE.—The efficacy of this drug for treatment of obstructive peripheral arterial diseases has not been established. The manufacturer's suggested dosage for these diseases, as well as the dosage recommended for use in other peripheral vascular diseases, is the same. *Oral: Adults,* initially, 25 mg three times daily. Depending upon the patient's tolerance and response, the dosage may be increased after one week to 50 or 75 mg three times daily.

PREPARATIONS.—Ilidar (Roche). *Oral:* Tablets 25 mg.

CYCLANDELATE [Cyclospasmol]

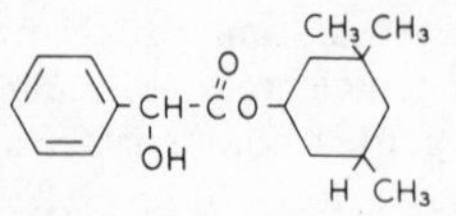

Cyclandelate produces peripheral vasodilation by direct action on peripheral vascular smooth muscle. It is promoted for use to treat intermittent claudication, arteriosclerosis obliterans, thrombophlebitis, nocturnal leg cramps, local frostbite, Raynaud's disease, diabetic and trophic ulcers of the legs, and cerebrovascular insufficiency. The evidence for its efficacy in these disorders is derived from insufficiently controlled studies and is, therefore, unacceptable.

Cyclandelate may cause flushing, headache, asthenia, and tachycardia; gastrointestinal distress (pyrosis, pain, eructation) occurs infrequently. It should not be used in patients in whom a fall in blood pressure is hazardous (eg, those with ischemic heart disease).

USUAL DOSAGE.—Since the efficacy of this drug in peripheral vascular disease has not been established, no meaningful dosage regimen can be given. The manufacturer's suggested dosage is: *Oral: Adults,* initially, 300 to 400 mg four times daily given before meals and at bedtime. When a response occurs, the dosage should be reduced by 200 mg daily until a maintenance dosage is reached (usually 400 to 800 mg daily in two to four doses).

PREPARATIONS.—Cyclospasmol (Ives). *Oral:* Capsules 200 mg; tablets 100 mg.

ISOXSUPRINE HYDROCHLORIDE [Vasodilan]

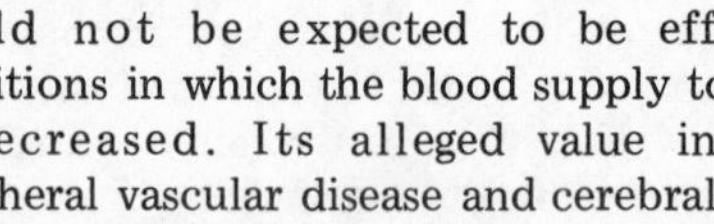

Isoxsuprine, a beta-adrenergic stimulant, is advocated for treatment of peripheral vascular diseases and cerebrovascular disorders. This drug has little effect on cutaneous circulation; thus, it would not be expected to be effective in conditions in which the blood supply to the skin is decreased. Its alleged value in treating peripheral vascular disease and cerebral ischemic episodes has not been convincingly demonstrated. The relaxant effect of isoxsuprine in vitro on uteri of various animals led to its trial in dysmenorrhea, threatened abortion, and premature labor, but proof of the drug's efficacy in these conditions is lacking.

Adverse effects occur infrequently and are usually mild. They include tachycardia, hypotension, nausea, vomiting, dizziness, and asthenia. Large intramuscular doses may produce hypotension and tachycardia.

USUAL DOSAGE.—Since the efficacy of this drug in peripheral vascular disease has not been established, no meaningful dosage regimen can be given. The manufacturer's suggested dosage is:

Oral: 10 to 20 mg three or four times daily.

Intramuscular: 5 to 10 mg two or three times daily.

PREPARATIONS.—Vasodilan (Mead Johnson).

Oral: Tablets 10 mg.

Injection: Solution 5 mg/ml in 2 ml containers.

NIACIN
NICOTINYL ALCOHOL [Roniacol]
NICOTINYL ALCOHOL TARTRATE [Roniacol Tartrate]

The pharmacologic actions of these drugs are similar; niacin is a metabolic product of nicotinyl alcohol. The vasodilator action probably is the result of a direct action on peripheral vascular smooth muscle. These agents act primarily on dermal vessels, especially in the blush area. They are promoted for the treatment of conditions associated with deficient circulation (eg, peripheral vascular disease, arteriospastic disorders), but there is no convincing evidence that their vasodilating action is beneficial in patients with peripheral vascular disease. For other uses of niacin, see Chapter 13, Agents Used to Treat Hyperlipidemia, and Chapter 14, Vitamins and Sources of Vitamins.

The adverse reactions noted include transient flushing of the face and neck, gastrointestinal disturbances (nausea, vomiting, diarrhea), rash, and allergic reactions (urticaria, localized angioedema). Increased anginal episodes in those with pre-existing angina have been reported rarely. These drugs are contraindicated in patients with active peptic ulcer or gastritis.

USUAL DOSAGE.—Since the efficacy of these drugs in peripheral vascular disease has not been established, no meaningful dosage regimen can be given. The manufacturers' suggested dosages are:

Niacin:

Oral: Adults, 50 mg three times daily; alternatively, 125 or 250 mg (in timed-release form) morning and evening.

Nicotinyl Alcohol:

Oral: Adults, 50 or 100 mg three times daily.

Nicotinyl Alcohol Tartrate:

Oral: Adults, 50 or 100 mg three times daily; alternatively, 150 or 300 mg (in timed-release form) morning and evening.

PREPARATIONS.—

Niacin:

Oral: Capsules (timed-release) 125 and 250 mg; tablets 25, 50, 100, and 500 mg.

Nicotinyl Alcohol:

Roniacol (Roche). *Oral:* Elixir 50 mg/5 ml.

Nicotinyl Alcohol Tartrate:

Roniacol Tartrate (Roche). *Oral:* Tablets 50 mg; tablets (timed-release) 150 mg.

AVAILABLE TRADEMARKS.—Niacin: Nico-400 (Marion), Nicobid (Armour). Niacin also marketed under generic name and under the name Nicotinic Acid.

NYLIDRIN HYDROCHLORIDE [Arlidin]

This drug produces vasodilation by stimulating beta-adrenergic receptors. There is no adequate evidence that nylidrin is effective in the treatment of the disorders in which it is being used: peripheral vascular diseases, cerebrovascular insufficiency, and circulatory disturbances of the inner ear.

Infrequent untoward effects include nervousness and palpitation. Because of the risk of tachycardia and hypotension, nylidrin is contraindicated in patients with angina pectoris, acute myocardial infarction, or history of infarction.

USUAL DOSAGE.—Since the efficacy of this drug in peripheral vascular disease has not been established, no meaningful dosage regimen can be given. The manufacturer's suggested dosage is:

Oral: Adults, 3 to 12 mg three or four times daily.

Subcutaneous, Intramuscular: Adults, 2.5 mg one or more times a day as needed. The dose may be increased slowly to 5 mg if necessary.

PREPARATIONS.—Arlidin (USV).

Oral: Tablets 6 and 12 mg.

Injection: Solution 5 mg/ml in 1 and 10 ml containers.

PAPAVERINE HYDROCHLORIDE

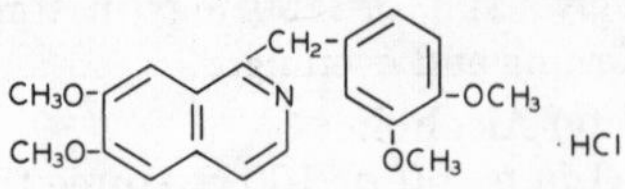

Papaverine is the prototype of the peripheral vasodilators that have a nonspecific relaxant effect on peripheral vascular smooth muscle. This drug is promoted for the treatment of various obstructive and vasospastic peripheral vascular diseases and cerebrovascular insufficiency, but there is no convincing evidence that it has any therapeutic value in these conditions.

For other uses of papaverine, see Chapter 3, Antianginal Agents.

Adverse reactions include nausea, abdominal discomfort, anorexia, constipation, malaise, drowsiness, vertigo, hyperhidrosis, headache, diarrhea, rash, flushing of the face, increase in heart rate and depth of respiration, slight increase in blood pressure, and hepatic reactions due to hypersensitivity (jaundice, eosinophilia, altered results of liver function tests). Intravascular administration should be carried out slowly to avoid arrhythmias.

USUAL DOSAGE.—Since the efficacy of this drug in peripheral vascular disease has not been established, no meaningful dosage regimen can be given. Some dosages suggested by the manufacturers and other sources are:

Oral: Adults, 100 to 300 mg three to five times daily; alternatively, 150 mg (in timed-release form) every 12 hours.

Intravenous, Intra-arterial: Adults, 100 mg given slowly.

PREPARATIONS.—

Oral: Capsules (timed-release) 150 mg; tablets 30, 60, 100, 200, and 500 mg.

Injection: Solution 30 mg/ml in 1 and 10 ml containers and 60 mg/ml in 2 ml containers.

AVAILABLE TRADEMARKS.—Cerespan (USV), Pap-Kaps (Sutliff & Case), Pavabid (Marion), Pavacap (Reid-Provident), Pavacen (Central), Pavarine (North American), Pavatest (Fellows-Testagar), Vasal (Tutag), Vasospan (Ulmer) [all timed-release oral forms]. Drug also marketed under generic name.

RELATED PREPARATIONS.—Dioxyline Phosphate (Paveril Phosphate [Lilly]) and Ethaverine Hydrochloride (Ethaquin [Ascher], Laverin [Lemmon], Neopavrin [Savage]).

PHENOXYBENZAMINE HYDROCHLORIDE [Dibenzyline]

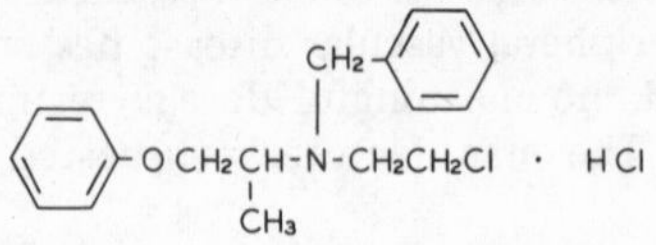

The peripheral vasodilator activity of phenoxybenzamine is attributed to alpha-adrenergic blockade. It sometimes may be effective in the treatment of peripheral vascular disease in which vasospasm is prominent (eg, Raynaud's disease, acrocyanosis, frostbite sequelae). However, there is no adequate evidence that phenoxybenzamine is effective in obstructive peripheral vascular diseases (eg, arteriosclerosis obliterans) and, therefore, its use in these conditions is seriously questioned.

For a discussion of the use of phenoxybenzamine in the management of pheochromocytoma, see Chapter 6, Antihypertensive Agents.

Adverse reactions include orthostatic hypotension, reflex tachycardia, nausea, vomiting, diarrhea, miosis, and nasal congestion. Phenoxybenzamine is contraindicated in patients in whom a fall in blood pressure is hazardous (eg, those with ischemic heart disease).

USUAL DOSAGE.—*Oral: Adults,* for treatment of peripheral vascular diseases other than the obstructive type, initially, 10 mg daily; the dose is increased by 10 mg at four-day intervals until the desired effect is achieved or intolerance occurs (usually 20 to 60 mg daily).

PREPARATIONS.—Dibenzyline (Smith Kline & French). *Oral:* Capsules 10 mg.

TOLAZOLINE HYDROCHLORIDE [Priscoline Hydrochloride]

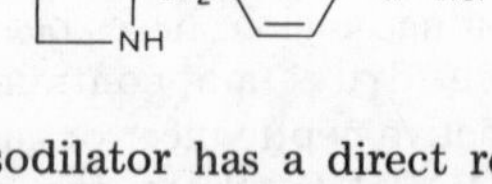

This vasodilator has a direct relaxant effect on smooth muscle. An alpha-adrenergic blocking action is noted after relatively large doses, but this effect is not significant after usual clinical doses. Tolazoline may be useful in diseases in which vasospasm is prominent (eg, frostbite sequelae, Raynaud's disease, acrocyanosis), but there is no adequate evidence that it is useful in conditions in which organic vascular changes are prominent (eg, arteriosclerosis obliterans).

Nausea, epigastric discomfort, tachycardia, flushing, slight increase or decrease in blood pressure, and increased pilomotor activity with pilo-erection, tingling, or chilliness occur after oral, subcutaneous, and intramuscular administration. Vomiting and diarrhea are noted rarely. A feeling of warmth or a burning sensation in the injected extremity usually occurs after intra-arterial administration. Also, intra-arterial injection occasionally produces flushing, pilo-erection, transient vertigo, tachycardia, a sensation of chilliness, formication, transient asthenia, palpitation, apprehension, and a slight increase or decrease in blood pressure. Tolazoline should be used with caution in patients with peptic ulcer or ischemic heart disease.

USUAL DOSAGE.—The efficacy of this drug for treatment of obstructive peripheral vascular diseases has not been established; thus, no dosage is given for this condition. The following are the doses used in the treatment of other peripheral vascular diseases (see above):

Oral: Adults, 25 mg four to six times daily, increased gradually if necessary up to 50 mg six times daily; alternatively, 80 mg (in timed-release form) every 12 hours.

Subcutaneous, Intramuscular, Intravenous: Adults, 10 to 50 mg four times daily. Therapy is begun with the small dose and the amount increased to the limit of the patient's tolerance (appearance of flushing).

Intra-arterial: This route should be used only by those thoroughly familiar with the procedure. *Adults,* initially, 25 mg to test the response of the patient, then 50 to 75 mg once or twice daily. As the patient's condition improves, the dosage is reduced to that amount necessary to sustain the response (usually 50 to 75 mg two or three times weekly).

PREPARATIONS.—Priscoline Hydrochloride (Ciba).

Oral: Tablets 25 mg; tablets (timed-release) 80 mg.

Injection: Solution 25 mg/ml in 10 ml containers.

Drug also marketed under generic name.

Chapter 5

AGENTS USED IN HYPOTENSION AND SHOCK

The goal of therapy in hypotension and shock is to ensure a blood flow that will adequately perfuse vital tissues and sustain their nutrition. In shock characterized by inadequate circulating volume, this is accomplished by administration of blood, fluids, or plasma volume expanders, but in hypotensive states that are essentially normovolemic, therapy usually includes use of a vasoactive drug. Opinions vary on the value of drug therapy, however, and often drugs do not reverse the shock process or reduce mortality.

Adequate tissue perfusion is dependent upon the circulating blood volume, the efficiency of the heart as a pump, and the tone of the resistance and capacitance vessels.[1] The ideal agent for treating shock should increase the perfusion pressure by constricting resistance vessels in tissues that can withstand a reduction in blood flow for relatively prolonged periods (ie, skin, connective tissue, muscle). At the same time, it should improve perfusion in the heart, brain, kidney, and liver. It should also enhance cardiac output (1) by directly stimulating the heart (ideally, at a low oxygen cost) and (2) by constricting the capacitance vessels, thereby preventing venous pooling and increasing venous return. No presently available agent meets all of these requirements. Drugs that increase perfusion pressure generally cause vasoconstriction in both nonvital and some vital areas, while drugs that improve tissue blood flow by vasodilatation either act primarily on resistance vessels in nonvital organs or cause a generalized vasodilatation, thus reducing the effective perfusion pressure.

1. Capacitance is controlled by the venules and veins, which contain the major portion of the blood volume. Resistance is controlled primarily by the small arteries and arterioles (precapillary resistance vessels); to a lesser extent, the venules and veins (postcapillary resistance vessels) also affect resistance. The ratio of precapillary to postcapillary resistance determines the capillary hydrostatic pressure and thus regulates the transfer of fluid between the circulatory system and the tissues.

VASOPRESSORS

The drugs commonly used to treat hypotensive states have traditionally been termed "vasopressors," although these agents vary greatly in their effects on total peripheral resistance and on regional resistance; in addition, they may have pronounced effects on the myocardium. With the exception of the synthetic polypeptide, angiotensin amide [Hypertensin], all so-called vasopressors are adrenergic drugs. These include the catecholamines: levarterenol (norepinephrine) [Levophed] and epinephrine [Adrenalin], as well as the noncatecholamines: ephedrine, hydroxyamphetamine [Paredrine], mephentermine [Wyamine], metaraminol [Aramine], methoxamine [Vasoxyl], and phenylephrine [Neo-Synephrine].

The catecholamines act directly on sympathetic receptor sites. The longer-acting noncatecholamines act directly or indirectly by liberating norepinephrine from tissue stores; the ratio of direct to indirect action varies among the different drugs. Angiotensin amide has a direct effect on vascular smooth muscle that is not due to stimulation of sympathetic receptor sites. Although animal studies have demonstrated that angiotensin also has various indirect actions, it is not certain whether these contribute significantly to its effects in man.

The varied hemodynamic actions of the adrenergic drugs have been attributed to their differential effects on two types of sympathetic receptors: alpha and beta. Although these receptors have not been identified anatomically, this concept has provided a convenient pharmacologic model to explain the action of sympathetic agonists and antagonists. Sympathetic effector cells in different organs generally have a preponderance of one type of receptor. Alpha receptors are most abundant in the resistance vessels of the skin, mucosa, intestine, and kidney, and drugs that act on alpha receptors produce vasoconstriction in these vascular beds. Beta receptors are predominant in the heart, in the arteries and arterioles of skeletal muscle, and in the bronchi, where they subserve cardiac excitation, vasodilatation, and bronchial relaxation. However, drugs that stimulate beta receptors vary in their potency at different sites; some act on all beta receptors, while others act primarily on those in the heart. Both alpha and beta receptors are believed to be present in the veins, but the role of these receptors in activation of the capacitance system needs clarification.

Most adrenergic drugs act on both alpha and beta receptors but differ in their degree of effectiveness in stimulating these two types of receptors. Levarterenol acts mainly on alpha receptors and has little beta-stimulating activity except in the heart. It has a pronounced constrictor action on both resistance and capacitance vessels and positive inotropic and chronotropic effects on the heart. The pressor action of this drug is mainly due to an increase in peripheral resistance. Levarterenol may increase cardiac output because of its positive inotropic effect on the heart, or it may cause reflex bradycardia and reduce cardiac output as a result of its pronounced effect on arterial pressure. The circulatory effects of metaraminol are similar to those of levarterenol; however, metaraminol has a more gradual onset, a longer duration of action, and a less pronounced effect on resistance and capacitance vessels.

Epinephrine acts on beta receptors in the heart and on both alpha and beta receptors in the peripheral blood vessels. It increases the force of cardiac contraction, increases heart rate, constricts capacitance vessels, and constricts resistance vessels in most vascular beds. In small doses, epinephrine dilates the small arteries and arterioles in skeletal muscle; large doses constrict these vessels. The beta receptors in the blood vessels are sensitive to lower concentrations of epinephrine than are the alpha receptors; therefore, in the usual clinical doses, total peripheral resistance is reduced and the pressor effect is due to an increase in cardiac output.

Ephedrine and hydroxyamphetamine stimulate the heart and increase peripheral resistance. Ephedrine constricts capacitance vessels and hydroxyamphetamine may also cause venoconstriction. The pressor effect of these agents is due primarily to an increase in cardiac output. Mephentermine produces similar effects but may increase arterial pressure either by enhancing cardiac output or by constricting resistance vessels.

The alpha-adrenergic stimulant, methoxamine, and the polypeptide, angiotensin amide, are potent constrictors of the resistance vessels but have minimal effects on the capacitance bed and may increase venous pooling and reduce venous return. They increase the work of the left ventricle but have little or no stimulating effect on the heart and may reflexly reduce the heart rate. Although they increase arterial pressure, these agents often reduce cardiac output and effective blood flow, particularly immediately after injection. Phenylephrine also is a potent constrictor of the resistance vessels but has a slight cardiac-stimulating effect.

Clinical Uses of Vasopressors

Hypovolemic Shock: Hypovolemic shock may result from the external or internal loss of blood, plasma, or water following hemorrhage, trauma, burns, or protracted vomiting or diarrhea. In addition to an actual volume deficit (absolute hypovolemia), a relative hypovolemia may occur when there is a significant pooling of blood in the venous circuit, leading to a disproportion between vascular volume and vascular capacitance (eg, in neurogenic shock).

In hypovolemic shock, venous return and cardiac output are reduced and peripheral resistance is generally increased by compensatory mechanisms. Volume replacement is the only effective treatment. Vasopressors have no established value in hypovolemic shock but are sometimes used as adjuncts to volume replacement or as a temporary supportive measure until blood or fluids can be administered. The prolonged use of vasoconstricting drugs can have detrimental effects by reducing blood flow through vital tissues. For the use of blood, plasma, and fluids in the treatment of hypovolemic states, see Chapter 10, Blood, Blood Components, and Blood Substitutes, and Chapter 16, Replenishers and Regulators of Water, Electrolytes, and Nutrients.

Cardiogenic Shock: In shock caused by myocardial infarction, myocardial contractility is impaired because of the myocardial insult and reduced coronary perfusion in the infarcted area. The hemodynamic pattern is not always predictable, but generally cardiac output is reduced and peripheral resistance is either normal or elevated. The goal of therapy is (1) to increase coronary blood flow by raising the systemic blood pressure and (2) to reduce the volume load of the left ventricle by improving the pumping action of the heart.

Although there is no conclusive evidence that vasopressor therapy lowers mortality in shock following myocardial infarction, most clinicians feel that some lives are saved by the use of these agents in conjunction with other measures (eg, administration of oxygen and, if required, digitalis and fluids and regulation of plasma pH). Because of the risks involved in the administration of vasopressors to patients with myocardial infarction, these agents are generally reserved for use only in patients with signs of inadequate perfusion of the brain or heart. Vasopressors with both alpha- and beta-adrenergic effects are usually preferred to those with alpha effects only; levarterenol and metaraminol are most commonly used.

Bacteremic Shock: Shock as a complication of gram-positive bacteremia is uncommon, but invasion of the blood stream by gram-negative organisms can cause rapid circulatory failure and death. No consistent hemodynamic picture has emerged from studies on patients with bacteremic shock, and the response may vary in different stages of the syndrome. Bacteremic shock demands immediate, intensive antibiotic therapy and maintenance of adequate circulating volume. Sodium bicarbonate should be given if metabolic acidosis occurs. The blood gases should be monitored closely, and oxygen should be administered if there is evidence of hypoxemia. Vasopressors are sometimes used as adjuncts in the treatment of bacteremic shock but there is no convincing evidence that they are effective; levarterenol and metaraminol are most commonly given. Corticosteroids are often administered in large doses. (See Chapter 35, Adrenal Corticosteroids.)

Neurogenic Hypotension and Shock: Circulatory depression can result from interference with the neural mechanisms that maintain peripheral resistance, venous return, and cardiac output. Vasopressors are often effective in controlling neurogenic hypotensive states, probably because these are often brief and self-limited.

Hypotension during spinal or epidural anesthesia has been attributed to an increase in vascular capacitance due to the blocking of tonic constrictor impulses to the veins; the subsequent pooling of blood in the venous circuit reduces venous return and cardiac output. Vasopressors are used for both prevention and treatment of the hypotension. However, the routine *prophylactic* use of vasopressors has been criticized because they occasionally cause untoward effects, they are not required by all patients, and they can be administered rapidly if needed. Unless a profound fall in blood pressure demands immediate treatment, vasopressors are generally reserved for patients who have failed to respond to a change in position or to administration of fluids. Ephedrine is often preferred for counteracting the cardiovascular effects of spinal and epidural anesthesia, but hydroxyamphetamine, mephentermine, methoxamine, metaraminol, and phenylephrine also are effective; epinephrine and levarterenol are not commonly used because of their brief duration of action after single doses.

A more serious problem arises when hypotension occurs in the obstetrical patient during labor or delivery, usually after spinal or epidural anesthesia. The hypotension can reduce uterine blood flow sufficiently to cause fetal hypoxia; however, vasopressor therapy can be equally dangerous to the fetus because the uterine blood vessels appear to have only alpha receptors and can only react to pressor drugs by constricting. Before resorting to drug therapy, an attempt should be made to raise the blood pressure by changing the position, displacing the uterus to the left, and administering fluids. If these measures fail, and if the mother develops signs of cerebral or coronary ischemia, a vasopressor should be given. Ephedrine is often preferred.

Some general anesthetics depress the myocardium and the vascular smooth muscle both by a direct action and by interfering with neural mechanisms. Vasopressors are sometimes administered to treat an acute fall in blood pressure during general anesthesia; however, pressor therapy is seldom necessary during well-conducted anesthesia. Agents with minimal cardiac excitatory effects (eg, phenylephrine, methoxamine, angiotensin amide) should be used if pressor therapy is necessary during anesthesia with halothane [Fluothane] or other anesthetics that may sensitize the heart to catecholamines (see Chapter 19, General Anesthetics). Severe, prolonged hypotension during surgery often is the result of blood loss and should be treated by volume replacement.

Venous pooling may occur when ganglionic blocking agents are used to produce controlled hypotension during anesthesia. Vasopressors are effective in controlling severe circulatory depression if other measures fail.

In shock caused by barbiturate intoxication, cardiac output is reduced and peripheral resistance is generally normal or increased. The decrease in cardiac output may be due to venous pooling, to an effect on the myocardium, or to an absolute reduction in plasma volume caused by an increase in vascular permeability and failure of fluid intake. Correction of the circulatory derangement requires administration of blood or fluids to correct the disparity between vascular volume and capacity. Vasopressors are sometimes used as adjuncts to volume replacement, but their value has not been established. Many authorities feel that vasoconstrictors should not be used to treat shock associated with barbiturate intoxication because their prolonged use may intensify the hypovolemia by increasing capillary hydrostatic pressure, thereby promoting the egress of intravascular fluid. In addition, vasopressors may constrict the renal vascular bed and thus prevent excretion of long-acting barbiturates. For a discussion of the treatment of barbiturate intoxication, see Chapter 27, Sedatives and Hypnotics.

Orthostatic hypotension results from a disturbance of the autonomic nervous system: interference with tonic constrictor impulses causes venous pooling in dependent areas and failure of arteriolar constriction when the patient assumes the upright position. Ephedrine, hydroxyamphetamine, and phenylephrine have been used to treat patients with orthostatic hypotension caused by neurologic or neurovascular diseases or that of uncertain etiology; however, vasopressor therapy is often ineffective in these patients. Salt-retaining steroids, which increase vascular volume, may be effective in reversing chronic orthostatic hypotension. Adrenergic drugs should not be used to treat orthostatic hypotension caused by monoamine oxidase inhibitors or tricyclic antidepressants because the combined therapy may precipitate a fatal hypertensive crisis.

Anaphylactic Shock: In anaphylactic shock, cardiac output and systemic blood pressure are reduced because of peripheral vasodilatation and increased capillary permeability. Death can result from acute circulatory failure or bronchospasm. Because of its rapid vasoconstrictor and bronchodilator action, epinephrine is the drug of choice for the emergency treatment of anaphylactic shock. Following initial treatment with epinephrine, and after adequate ventilation is assured, arterial pressure can be maintained by the continuous intravenous infusion of levarterenol or metaraminol. Corticosteroids also should be administered. Antihistamines often are given, but their value has not been established. Prolonged hypotension is usually due to hypovolemia and should be treated by volume replacement.

Shock Due to Removal of Pheochromocytoma: Shock following the surgical removal of a pheochromocytoma is caused by the sudden decline in circulating catecholamine levels and by fluid loss that develops as a result of prolonged constriction of postcapillary vessels. Levarterenol may be used to support the circulation, but it should be given only after the blood volume is restored. This type of shock usually can be avoided by the preoperative administration of an alpha-adrenergic blocking agent (phenoxybenzamine [Dibenzyline] or phentolamine [Regitine]) to allow volume adjustment. Propranolol is sometimes given with the alpha-adrenergic blocking drug. (See also Chapter 6, Antihypertensive Agents.)

DRUGS USED FOR TREATMENT OF REFRACTORY SHOCK

Compensatory hyperactivity of the sympathetic nervous system is a common feature of hypovolemic shock and may also occur in cardiogenic and bacteremic shock. Results of experimental studies on the hemodynamic effects of hemorrhage suggest that this intense sympathetic activity may contribute to the development of irreversible shock. After extensive hemorrhage, blood flow through the tissues, which is already decreased by volume depletion, is further reduced by reflex vasoconstriction. The reduction in blood flow causes local accumulation of metabolites that dilate the precapillary vessels; the postcapillary vessels, which are less sensitive to these metabolites, remain constricted by sympathetic nerve impulses. This leads to a rise in capillary pressure and a loss of fluid from the circulation, thus perpetuating the shock state.

In addition to reducing circulating blood volume, sympathetic hyperactivity produces other deleterious effects which may contribute to the development of irreversible shock. Constriction of resistance vessels greatly compromises blood flow through the kidney, liver, and intestine. Vasoconstriction is more intense in the kidney than in other vascular beds, and the reduction in renal blood flow causes oliguria and, occasionally, acute renal failure. Inadequate oxygenation of the tissues leads to severe metabolic acidosis which cannot be corrected if renal function is curtailed. Myocardial ischemia may result from reduced coronary blood flow. It has also been suggested that tissue ischemia may lead to the production and release of various toxic substances or to the absorption of bacterial endotoxins from the intestine.

These observations explained the frequent failure of vasopressors to reverse the shock process, and led to a search for other agents that might improve effective blood flow. The only drug currently recommended by its manufacturer for this purpose is isoproterenol [Isuprel].

Isoproterenol is an adrenergic drug that acts almost exclusively on beta receptors. It increases the rate and strength of cardiac contraction; dilates the small arteries and arterioles in skeletal and cardiac muscle and in the kidney and intestine; and relaxes bronchial muscle. Effects on the venous capacitance system are unclear; both venoconstriction and venodilatation have been reported. Isoproterenol increases cardiac output, and, at the usual therapeutic doses, the increase may outweigh the vasodilator effect, resulting in a rise in arterial pressure; large doses can cause hypotension.

Isoproterenol has been used to treat patients with bacteremic, cardiogenic, or hypovolemic shock associated with a low cardiac output and a high central venous pressure. Although it has been employed for the initial treatment of cardiogenic and bacteremic shock, its use is generally limited to patients who have not responded satisfactorily to volume replacement or to vasopressors. In hypovolemic states, volume replacement should always precede treatment with this drug.

The rationale for use of isoproterenol in refractory shock is to increase cardiac output and, through peripheral vasodilatation, to reduce the work of the heart and improve tissue perfusion. Although isoproterenol appears to have some potentially beneficial hemodynamic effects, there is as yet no convincing evidence that it reverses the shock process or reduces mortality; metabolic acidosis, oliguria, and other signs of shock may be unaltered.

Several factors may be involved in the failure of isoproterenol to prevent progression of the shock state. A major problem, particularly in cardiogenic shock, is that isoproterenol greatly increases the myocardial oxygen demand because of its positive inotropic and chronotropic effects; however, it may not increase the perfusion pressure sufficiently to maintain an adequate coronary flow, and myocardial ischemia may occur. Isoproterenol also may cause pronounced tachycardia, with a subsequent decrease in diastolic filling time and a reduction in cardiac output. Premature ventricular contractions may occur, particularly in patients with cardiogenic shock. Finally, isoproterenol improves tissue perfusion mainly in a nonvital organ, skeletal muscle, while it acts only as a weak vasodilator in the kidney; in addition, it does not antagonize sympathetic vasoconstriction in vital organs.

Alpha-adrenergic blocking agents, such as phenoxybenzamine [Dibenzyline], also have been used to treat refractory shock. These agents produce vasodilatation by inhibiting sympathetic vasoconstriction. They are believed to act by occupying the alpha-adrenergic receptors, thus preventing activation by the neurotransmitter, norepinephrine. In experimental studies on a variety of forms of shock, these drugs improved the survival rate of laboratory animals; however, their use in man is still in the investigational stage.

The rationale for the use of alpha-adrenergic blocking agents in refractory shock is to reduce the compensatory vasoconstriction (alpha-adrenergic effect) caused by sympathetic hyperactivity without affecting the compensatory cardiac stimulation (beta-adrenergic effect). However, these agents cause a generalized vasodilatation in both vital and nonvital organs that results in severe hypotension and a profound reduction in the effective perfusion pressure. The major value of alpha-adrenergic blocking agents derives from their effect on the capacitance bed, an effect which has led to their use as adjuncts to volume replacement in the treatment of hypovolemic states. By increasing venous capacitance, alpha-adrenergic blockade provides a method of estimating the adequacy of volume replacement and permits administration of a larger volume of fluid without overloading the heart. In the presence of hypovolemia, volume replacement should always precede administration of alpha-adrenergic blocking drugs; fluid should be readily available in case the blocking agent causes an acute fall in blood pressure, indicating that volume replacement was inadequate.

OTHER AGENTS

The catecholamine, dopamine, is currently under investigation for the treatment of shock. Dopamine has certain characteristics that are of potential clinical value. It stimulates the heart by a beta-adrenergic action and constricts resistance vessels by acting on alpha receptors. In addition, it has a *direct* vasodilating action on the renal and splanchnic vascular beds. Because of these unique properties, some investigators feel that dopamine may be of particular value if cessation of renal function is imminent. However, more extensive clinical studies are needed to determine whether dopamine actually improves the rate of survival.

Adverse Reactions and Precautions

Vasopressors: Reliance on pressor agents to treat hypotension and shock may be hazardous because an adequate arterial pressure does not assure that adequate tissue perfusion has been restored. In hypovolemic states, volume replacement is the only effective treatment and vasopressors should be used only as temporary supportive therapy. The rate of infusion of vasopressors must be regulated carefully so that the desired level of blood pressure (ideally, slightly less than the patient's normal pressure) is not exceeded.

Therapeutic doses of vasopressors may cause headache, restlessness, anxiety, weakness, pallor, dizziness, tremor, precordial pain, palpitation, and respiratory distress. Overdosage can cause convulsions, cerebral hemorrhage, and arrhythmias. Patients with hyperthyroidism are particularly sensitive to the untoward effects of these drugs.

Excessive cardiac acceleration can reduce cardiac filling time, myocardial efficiency, coronary blood flow, and cardiac output. Fatal ventricular arrhythmias may be precipitated by vasopressors with cardiac excitatory actions, particularly when used in patients with myocardial infarction or after the administration of anesthetics that sensitize the heart to catecholamines (eg, cyclopropane, halothane [Fluothane]). (Also see Chapter 19, General Anesthetics.) Vasopressors with minimal effects on the heart (eg, phenylephrine [Neo-Synephrine], methoxamine [Vasoxyl], angiotensin amide [Hypertensin]) are preferred if pressor therapy is required during anesthesia with these agents.

Prolonged administration of vasopressors may reduce venous return and cardiac output and increase the work of the heart. The renal blood flow and filtration rate, which are already decreased by compensatory vasoconstriction, may be reduced further by pressor drugs. Severe metabolic acidosis may develop. Plasma volume may be decreased because constriction of the postcapillary vessels increases capillary pressure and facilitates transcapillary fluid loss.

Various pathologic changes have followed the prolonged administration of vasopressors, particularly levarterenol [Levophed]. These include edema, hemorrhage, and necrosis of the intestine, as well as hepatic and renal necrosis, focal myocarditis, subpericardial hemorrhage, and local slough. These changes are seen most commonly in patients in severe shock, and it is not certain whether they are caused by drug therapy or by the shock process alone. However, prolonged administration of levarterenol has produced irreversible shock in experimental animals, and it is probable that overly aggressive vasopressor therapy has caused the death of some patients who might have recovered with only volume replacement.

Recurrent hypotension may follow the sudden withdrawal of vasopressors after they have been used for several days or weeks. This fall in blood pressure may be due to generalized loss of vascular tone, to exudation of fluid from the vascular space, or to depletion of norepinephrine stores. To avoid this complication, an attempt should be made to discontinue therapy as soon as possible. If there is difficulty in withdrawing the drug, dextrose injection should be infused and the blood pressure monitored continually. Use of the pressor drug should not be resumed until the systolic blood pressure falls to 70 to 80 mm Hg. Measurement of the central venous pressure is important to estimate volume loss and to use as a guide for volume replacement. After five or ten minutes, another attempt should be made to discontinue the vasopressor. It may be necessary to repeat this procedure several times. Difficulty in withdrawing vasopressors occurs more commonly with metaraminol [Aramine] than with levarterenol. Patients who have been receiving prolonged metaraminol therapy may have to be given levarterenol to replace tissue stores of norepinephrine before vasopressor therapy can be discontinued.

Isoproterenol Hydrochloride: See the individual evaluation.

INDIVIDUAL EVALUATIONS

LEVARTERENOL BITARTRATE [Levophed Bitartrate]

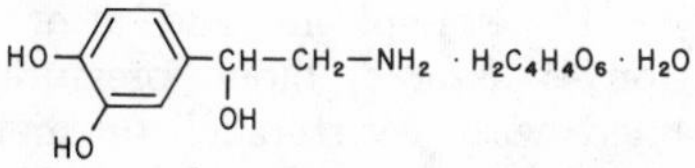

$$HO-C_6H_3(OH)-CH(OH)-CH_2-NH_2 \cdot H_2C_4H_4O_6 \cdot H_2O$$

This adrenergic drug has positive inotropic and chronotropic effects on the heart and a potent constrictor action on resistance and capacitance vessels. Its pressor effect is due largely to an increase in peripheral resistance. Levarterenol is widely used as an adjunct in the treatment of various hypotensive states: It is used in the treatment of shock due to myocardial infarction, bacteremia, or removal of a pheochromocytoma, and in anaphylactic shock after initial treatment with epinephrine. It is also given to control acute hypotension during general anesthesia if cardiac stimulation is not contraindicated. In hypovolemic states levarterenol should be used only as a temporary supportive measure until volume replacement is available.

Levarterenol can cause tissue necrosis at the site of injection. The risk of ischemic injury is reduced if the drug is infused via a catheter in a deeply seated vein. The infusion site should be changed if prolonged administration is necessary. If extravasation occurs, the site should be infiltrated with 10 ml of a solution containing 0.5 to 1 mg of phentolamine per milliliter. To reduce the incidence of venous thrombosis, a sufficient amount of heparin should be added to this infusion solution to supply between 100 and 200 units of heparin per hour.

For a general discussion of adverse reactions and precautions with vasopressors, see the Introductory Statement.

USUAL DOSAGE.—*Intravenous: Adults,* 4 to 8 ml of a 0.2% solution is added to 500 ml of 5% dextrose injection and is given by continuous infusion at a rate adjusted to maintain the systolic arterial pressure at about 90 to 100 mm Hg. Very dilute solutions should not be used because of the danger of overloading the cardiovascular system. *Children,* 1 ml of a 0.2% solution is added to 250 ml of 5% dextrose injection and is given by continuous infusion at a rate of 0.5 ml/minute.

PREPARATIONS.—Levophed Bitartrate (Winthrop). *Injection:* Solution 0.2% (equivalent to 1 mg of base/ml) in 4 ml containers.

ANGIOTENSIN AMIDE [Hypertensin]

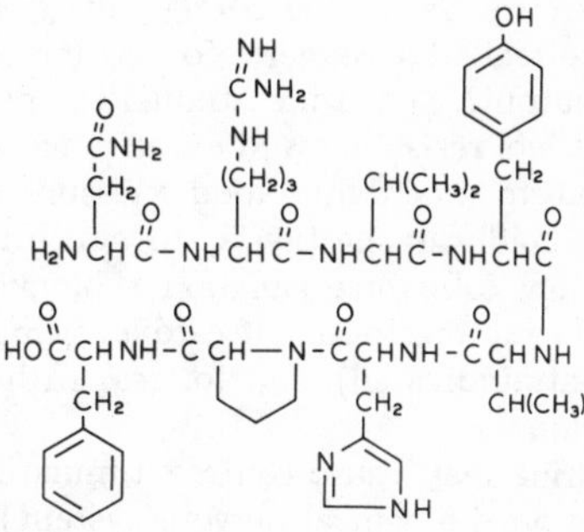

Asn-Arg-Val-Tyr-Val-His-Pro-Phe (structural formula: H_2N-CH(CH_2CONH_2)-CO-NH-CH($(CH_2)_3$NHC(=NH)NH_2)-CO-NH-CH($CH(CH_3)_2$)-CO-NH-CH($CH_2C_6H_4OH$)-CO-NH-CH($CH(CH_3)_2$)-CO-NH-CH(CH_2-imidazolyl)-CO-N(prolyl)-CH-CO-NH-CH($CH_2C_6H_5$)-COOH)

Angiotensin amide, a synthetic polypeptide, acts directly on vascular smooth muscle. The pressor effect of angiotensin is due to an increase in peripheral resistance; it constricts resistance vessels but has little or no stimulating effect on the heart and little effect on the capacitance vessels. Although angiotensin has a greater pressor effect and a more prolonged action than levarterenol, its usefulness is limited because it does not increase, and may reduce, cardiac output. It has been used as an adjunct in various hypotensive states but is mainly of value in controlling acute hypotension during administration of general anesthetics that sensitize the heart to catecholamines (see Chapter 19, General Anesthetics).

Angiotensin may cause dizziness, headache, and mild urticaria. Excessive doses may produce a sharp increase in myocardial oxygen demand and, hence, myocardial hypoxia. Renal vascular constriction and profound reflex bradycardia also may occur. For a general discussion of adverse reactions and precautions with vasopressors, see the Introductory Statement.

USUAL DOSAGE.—*Intravenous: Adults,* 0.5 to 2.5 mg, diluted in 500 ml of sodium chloride injection or 5% dextrose injection, is given by continuous infusion at a rate adjusted to maintain the systolic blood pressure at about 90 to 100 mm Hg.

When whole blood or plasma is indicated, it should be given through a Y-tube or as a separate injection so that the naturally occurring enzymes do not inactivate angiotensin amide.

PREPARATIONS.—Hypertensin (Ciba). *Injection:* Lyophilized powder 2.5 mg (with mannitol 47.4 mg and thimerosal 0.1 mg).

EPHEDRINE SULFATE

$$\left[C_6H_5-\underset{OH}{CH}-\underset{NHCH_3}{CH}CH_3 \right]_2 \cdot H_2SO_4$$

Ephedrine is an adrenergic drug with a pressor effect due largely to an increase in cardiac output. Ephedrine stimulates the heart and constricts resistance and capacitance vessels. It is used to maintain blood pressure during spinal or epidural anesthesia, to control acute hypotension following ganglionic blockade or during general anesthesia (if cardiac stimulation is not contraindicated), and to treat orthostatic hypotension.

Ephedrine may cause central stimulation but its effects on the central nervous system are less pronounced than those of the amphetamines. For a general discussion of adverse reactions and precautions with vasopressors, see the Introductory Statement.

For other uses, see Chapters 41, Bronchodilators; 42, Nasal Decongestants; and 72, Miscellaneous Ophthalmic Preparations.

USUAL DOSAGE.—

Intravenous: Adults, initially, 10 to 25 mg, given slowly. If an adequate response is not obtained, injection may be repeated in five to ten minutes.

Intramuscular, Subcutaneous: Adults, 25 to 50 mg; *children*, 3 mg/kg of body weight daily divided into four to six doses.

Oral: For orthostatic hypotension, *adults*, 25 mg one to four times daily; *children*, 3 mg/kg of body weight daily divided into four to six doses.

PREPARATIONS.—Ephedrine Sulfate, U.S.P. *Injection:* Solution 20 mg/ml in 1 ml containers, 25 mg/ml in 1, 10, and 30 ml containers, and 50 mg/ml in 1 and 10 ml containers.

Oral: Capsules 25 and 50 mg; elixir 5 and 10 mg/5 ml.

Drug marketed by many manufacturers under generic name.

EPINEPHRINE HYDROCHLORIDE [Adrenalin Chloride]

$$(HO)_2C_6H_3-\underset{OH}{CH}-CH_2NH-CH_3 \cdot HCl$$

The adrenergic agent, epinephrine, is the drug of choice for treating anaphylactic shock. It stimulates the heart, constricts the capacitance vessels, and constricts resistance vessels in most vascular beds (but causes vasodilatation in skeletal muscle). It also relaxes bronchial smooth muscle. In the usual clinical doses, the pressor effect of epinephrine is due to an increase in cardiac output.

Following initial treatment of anaphylactic shock with epinephrine and after adequate ventilation is assured, blood pressure may be maintained with levarterenol or metaraminol (see the evaluations on these drugs). In addition, a corticosteroid should be administered. Antihistamines also are given frequently, but their value in anaphylactic shock has not been established. Prolonged hypotension may indicate hypovolemia and should be treated by volume replacement.

For adverse reactions and precautions, see the Introductory Statement.

For other uses, see Chapters 2, Antiarrhythmic Agents; 41, Bronchodilators; 42, Nasal Decongestants; and 69, Agents Used to Treat Glaucoma.

USUAL DOSAGE.—

Intramuscular, Subcutaneous, Intravenous: Adults, initially, 0.5 ml of a 1:1,000 solution injected intramuscularly or subcutaneously, followed by 0.25 to 0.5 ml of a 1:10,000 solution given intravenously every 5 to 15 minutes.

Intramuscular: Children, initially, 0.3 ml of a 1:1,000 solution. This may be repeated at 15-minute intervals for three or four doses if necessary. In an emergency, the drug may be given intravenously.

PREPARATIONS.—Adrenalin Chloride (Parke, Davis). *Injection:* Solution (aqueous) 1:1,000 (1 mg/ml) in 1 and 30 ml containers. Drug also marketed by many manufacturers under generic name.

HYDROXYAMPHETAMINE HYDROBROMIDE [Paredrine]

$$HO-C_6H_4-CH_2\underset{NH_2}{CH}CH_3 \cdot HBr$$

This adrenergic drug does not stimulate the central nervous system, but in other respects its actions are similar to those of ephedrine. Hydroxyamphetamine is occasionally used to treat orthostatic hypotension; however, there is some evidence that, with repeated administration, it may *cause* orthostatic hypotension, due, possibly, to formation of a false neurotransmitter.

For adverse reactions and precautions, see the Introductory Statement.

For other uses, see Chapter 70, Mydriatics and Cycloplegics.

USUAL DOSAGE.—*Oral: Adults,* 60 mg three times daily or 100 to 160 mg once daily 30 to 60 minutes before arising.

PREPARATIONS.—Paredrine (Smith Kline & French). *Oral:* Tablets 20 mg.

ISOPROTERENOL HYDROCHLORIDE
[Isuprel Hydrochloride]

HO, HO — $CHCH_2NHCH(CH_3)_2 \cdot HCl$ (OH)

The adrenergic drug, isoproterenol, acts almost exclusively on beta receptors. It stimulates the heart, dilates resistance vessels (primarily those in skeletal muscle), and relaxes bronchial smooth muscle. The effects of isoproterenol on the capacitance vessels are unclear.

Isoproterenol is used primarily for the treatment of refractory shock associated with myocardial infarction, gram-negative bacteremia, or hypovolemia. However, there is no convincing evidence that this drug reverses the shock process or reduces mortality. In hypovolemic states, volume replacement should always precede administration of isoproterenol. (See also the Introductory Statement.)

Isoproterenol may cause headache, flushing, hyperhidrosis, tremor, dizziness, nausea, palpitation, and tachycardia. Since arrhythmias may occur, continuous monitoring of the cardiac rhythm is advisable during infusion. Fatal ventricular arrhythmias may be precipitated if isoproterenol is given with anesthetics that sensitize the heart to catecholamines (see Chapter 19, General Anesthetics) or with other adrenergic drugs that affect cardiac rhythm. The arterial pressure also should be monitored continuously, for profound hypotension may occur if the inotropic effect of the drug is reduced because of severe depression of the myocardium. Isoproterenol increases the myocardial oxygen demand, but it often fails to raise coronary perfusion pressure proportionately. If the coronary blood flow is not sufficient to meet the increased requirement for oxygen, myocardial hypoxia, manifested by anginal pain and an increase in the production of myocardial lactate, may occur. Isoproterenol should be used cautiously in patients with hyperthyroidism or cardiovascular or renal disease.

For other uses, see Chapter 2, Antiarrhythmic Agents, and Chapter 41, Bronchodilators.

USUAL DOSAGE.—*Intravenous: Adults,* 2.5 mg (12.5 ml of solution) diluted in 500 ml of 5% dextrose injection and infused at a rate of 1 to 10 μg/minute.

PREPARATIONS.—Isuprel Hydrochloride (Winthrop). *Injection:* Solution (aqueous) 1:5,000 (0.2 mg/ml) in 1 and 5 ml containers.

MEPHENTERMINE SULFATE [Wyamine Sulfate]

$C_6H_5-CH_2-C(CH_3)_2-NHCH_3 \cdot \frac{1}{2} H_2SO_4 \cdot H_2O$

The adrenergic drug, mephentermine, stimulates the heart, increases venous tone, and increases peripheral resistance. It is used to maintain blood pressure during spinal or epidural anesthesia or following ganglionic blockade and to control acute hypotension during general anesthesia (if cardiac stimulation is not contraindicated). Occasionally it is given as an adjunct in the treatment of cardiogenic shock. In hypovolemic states, mephentermine should be used only as a temporary supportive measure until volume replacement is available.

Mephentermine stimulates the central nervous system and may cause euphoria. For a general discussion of adverse reactions and precautions with vasopressors, see the Introductory Statement.

For other uses, see Chapter 42, Nasal Decongestants.

USUAL DOSAGE.—

Intravenous: Adults, 600 mg to 1 g diluted in 1 liter of 5% dextrose injection and given by continuous infusion at a rate that will maintain the systolic blood pressure at about 90 to 100 mm Hg. A priming dose of 20 to 60 mg may be injected intravenously prior to infusion. *Children,* 0.4 mg/kg of body weight given slowly.

Intramuscular, Subcutaneous: Adults, 10 to 30 mg. *Children,* 0.4 mg/kg of body weight.

PREPARATIONS.—Wyamine Sulfate (Wyeth). *Injection:* Solution 15 mg/ml in 1, 2, and 10 ml containers and 30 mg/ml in 1 and 10 ml containers.

METARAMINOL BITARTRATE [Aramine]

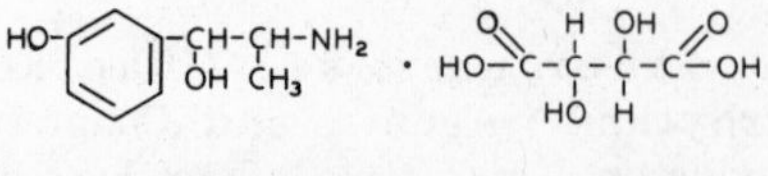

The hemodynamic effects of this adrenergic drug are similar to those of levarterenol; however, metaraminol has a more gradual onset and a longer duration of action, and it appears to have a less pronounced effect on resistance and capacitance vessels. In contrast to levarterenol, it may be given intramuscularly as well as intravenously. Metaraminol is used as an adjunct in the treatment of cardiogenic and bacteremic shock and in anaphylactic shock after initial treatment with epinephrine. It is also given to treat hypotension during spinal or epidural anesthesia and to control acute hypotension during general anesthesia if cardiac stimulation is not contraindicated. In hypovolemic states, metaraminol should be used only as a temporary supportive measure until volume replacement is available.

For adverse reactions and precautions, see the Introductory Statement.

USUAL DOSAGE.—

Intravenous: Adults, 2 to 5 mg as a single injection, or 200 to 500 mg diluted in 1 liter of 5% dextrose injection and administered by continuous infusion at a rate sufficient to maintain the systolic blood pressure at about 90 to 100 mm Hg. Very dilute solutions should not be used because of the danger of overloading the cardiovascular system. *Children,* 0.01 mg/kg of body weight as a single dose or a solution containing 1 mg/25 ml in 5% dextrose injection is administered by continuous infusion at a rate sufficient to maintain the blood pressure at the desired level.

Intramuscular: Adults, 5 to 10 mg; *children,* 0.1 mg/kg of body weight.

Subcutaneous: This drug should not be administered by this route because tissue sloughing may occur.

PREPARATIONS.—Aramine (Merck Sharp & Dohme). *Injection:* Solution 10 mg/ml in 1 and 10 ml containers. Drug marketed under generic name.

METHOXAMINE HYDROCHLORIDE [Vasoxyl]

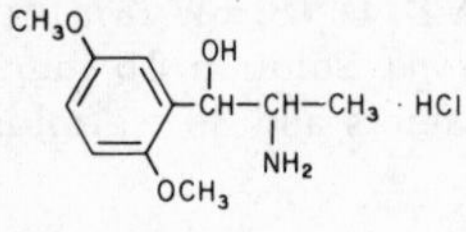

The adrenergic drug, methoxamine, acts almost exclusively on alpha receptors. It constricts resistance vessels, has little effect on venous tone, and does not stimulate the heart. The drug's pressor effect is, therefore, due to an increase in peripheral resistance and is followed by reflex bradycardia. Methoxamine is mainly of value in controlling acute hypotension during general anesthesia when cardiac stimulation is contraindicated. It has also been used to maintain arterial pressure during spinal anesthesia and to control severe hypotension following ganglionic blockade. In addition, methoxamine has slight antiarrhythmic action (usually attributed to its effect on arterial pressure) and is employed to terminate paroxysmal supraventricular tachycardias (see Chapter 2, Antiarrhythmic Agents).

Methoxamine may cause tingling of the extremities, pilomotor stimulation, and a desire to urinate. For a general discussion of adverse reactions and precautions with vasopressors, see the Introductory Statement.

USUAL DOSAGE.—

Intramuscular: Adults, 5 to 20 mg; *children,* 0.25 mg/kg of body weight.

Intravenous: Adults, 5 to 10 mg given slowly in divided doses, or 35 to 40 mg diluted in 250 ml of 5% dextrose injection and infused slowly; *children,* 0.08 mg/kg of body weight given slowly in divided doses.

PREPARATIONS.—Vasoxyl (Burroughs Wellcome). *Injection:* Solution 10 mg/ml in 10 ml containers and 20 mg/ml in 1 ml containers.

PHENYLEPHRINE HYDROCHLORIDE [Neo-Synephrine Hydrochloride]

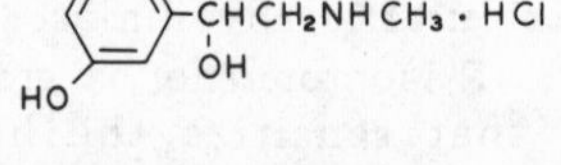

The hemodynamic effects of this adrenergic drug are similar to those of methoxamine; however, phenylephrine may produce slight cardiac stimulation. It appears to have some antiarrhythmic action (usually attributed to its effect on arterial pressure) and is often used to control acute hypotension during anesthesia with agents that sensitize the heart to catecholamines. It is also used to maintain blood pressure during spinal anesthesia and to treat orthostatic hypotension.

For a general discussion of adverse reactions and precautions with vasopressors, see the Introductory Statement.

For other uses, see Chapters 42, Nasal Decongestants; 69, Agents Used to Treat Glaucoma; 70, Mydriatics and Cycloplegics; and 72, Miscellaneous Ophthalmic Preparations.

USUAL DOSAGE.—

Intramuscular, Subcutaneous: Adults, 5 to 10 mg. *Children,* 0.1 mg/kg of body weight.

Intravenous: Adults, 0.25 to 0.5 mg diluted in sodium chloride injection and given slowly, or 10 mg diluted in 500 ml of 5% dextrose injection and infused slowly.

Oral: For orthostatic hypotension, *adults,* 20 mg three times daily; *children,* 1 mg/kg of body weight in 24 hours divided into six doses.

PREPARATIONS.—Neo-Synephrine Hydrochloride (Winthrop).

Injection: Solution 10 mg/ml in 1 and 5 ml containers.

Oral: Elixir 5 mg/5 ml.

Drug also marketed under generic name.

Chapter 6

ANTIHYPERTENSIVE AGENTS

The value of drug therapy in malignant hypertension and other hypertensive emergencies has been accepted for many years. More recently, it has been demonstrated that antihypertensive therapy favorably affects prognosis in less severe forms of hypertension. Results of controlled prospective studies have shown that treatment reduces morbidity and mortality in men with benign essential hypertension who exhibit any evidence of cardiovascular damage or in those with a persistent elevation of diastolic blood pressure of 105 mm Hg or higher. In the patients studied, antihypertensive therapy reduced the incidence of strokes, congestive heart failure, and progressive kidney damage, but had no significant effect on the frequency of myocardial infarction or sudden death. At present, there is no conclusive evidence that antihypertensive therapy improves prognosis in men with early, mild hypertension (diastolic pressure below 105 mm Hg) or in those with labile hypertension. There are no adequate prospective studies on the efficacy of antihypertensive therapy in women; however, actuarial data show a direct relationship between elevated blood pressure and morbidity and mortality.

The major drugs used in the treatment of hypertension are diuretics, agents that depress the activity of the sympathetic nervous system at postganglionic sites, drugs that act directly on vascular smooth muscle, and ganglionic blocking agents. The thiazides (benzothiadiazides) and related compounds are the primary diuretics used for treating hypertension; other diuretic agents include ethacrynate sodium [Sodium Edecrin] and furosemide [Lasix], and the potassium-sparing agents (spironolactone [Aldactone] and triamterene [Dyrenium]). Drugs that depress sympathetic nervous system activity include the commonly used rauwolfia alkaloids (particularly reserpine), methyldopa [Aldomet], and guanethidine [Ismelin]; the beta-adrenergic blocking agent, propranolol [Inderal] which also appears to be an effective antihypertensive drug; and the alpha-adrenergic blocking agents, which have more specialized application. Hydralazine [Apresoline], sodium nitroprusside, and diazoxide [Hyperstat] reduce blood pressure by acting directly on vascular smooth muscle. Agents that block autonomic ganglia include mecamylamine [Inversine], trimethaphan [Arfonad], and pentolinium [Ansolysen]. Monoamine oxidase inhibitors such as pargyline [Eutonyl] have only limited usefulness in the treatment of hypertension. The veratrum alkaloids rarely are prescribed today.

The choice of an appropriate drug depends upon the severity of the disease and the patient's response to a therapeutic trial. The following guidelines are suggested for selection of therapy in patients with hypertension of different degrees of severity. (See also Table 1.)

Chronic Hypertension: Prior to beginning a course of life-long treatment, the patient with moderately elevated blood pressure should be seen on at least three separate visits to determine whether there is a persistent elevation in blood pressure. The extent of organic changes, particularly those affecting the optic fundi, brain, heart, and kidneys, should also be assessed. The goal of therapy is to lower the blood pressure to normal or to the lowest level that the patient will tolerate without untoward effects. Usually, levels of 150/100 mm Hg (lower in the standing position) may be achieved without prohibitive untoward effects. Because of differences in individual responsiveness, the regimen must be individualized. To achieve this, it is often necessary to try various individual drugs or combinations until the optimal effect is

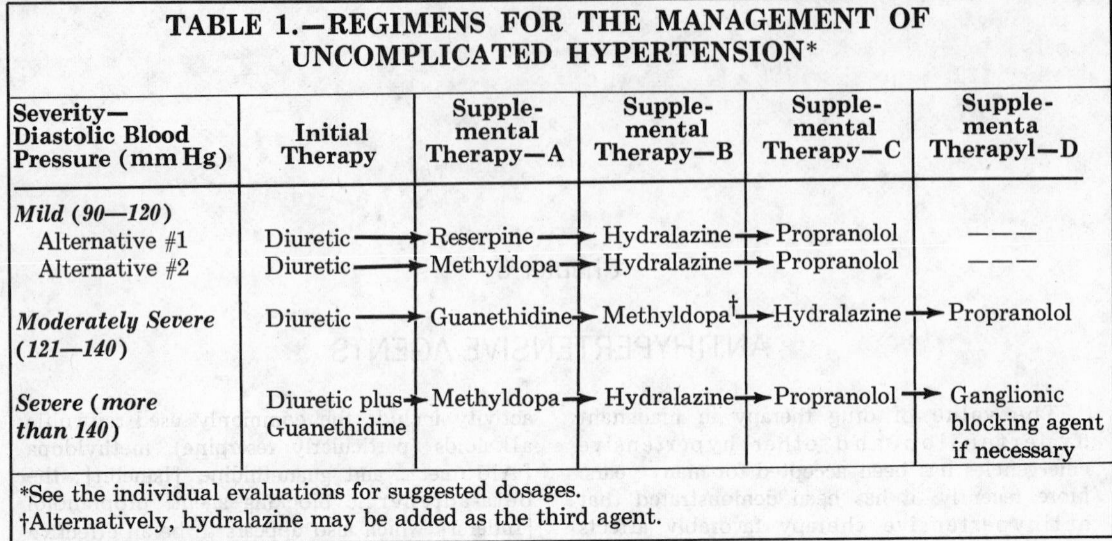

TABLE 1.—REGIMENS FOR THE MANAGEMENT OF UNCOMPLICATED HYPERTENSION*

Severity—Diastolic Blood Pressure (mm Hg)	Initial Therapy	Supple-mental Therapy—A	Supple-mental Therapy—B	Supple-mental Therapy—C	Supple-menta Therapyl—D
Mild (90—120)					
Alternative #1	Diuretic →	Reserpine →	Hydralazine →	Propranolol	---
Alternative #2	Diuretic →	Methyldopa →	Hydralazine →	Propranolol	---
Moderately Severe (121—140)	Diuretic →	Guanethidine →	Methyldopa† →	Hydralazine →	Propranolol
Severe (more than 140)	Diuretic plus Guanethidine →	Methyldopa →	Hydralazine →	Propranolol →	Ganglionic blocking agent if necessary

*See the individual evaluations for suggested dosages.
†Alternatively, hydralazine may be added as the third agent.

obtained. Fixed-dose combinations should be avoided during such a therapeutic trial because they do not permit adequate flexibility in adjusting dosage of the individual agents.

For patients with mild or moderate hypertension (diastolic blood pressure below 120 mm Hg), treatment is usually initiated with an oral diuretic (ie, a thiazide or related compound). The diuretic may control the blood pressure without additional therapy. Even if the diuretic is not effective alone, it is useful to counteract sodium retention and enhance the antihypertensive activity of other agents that are added later (eg, a rauwolfia alkaloid, methyldopa, hydralazine). After the maximal blood pressure reduction from the diuretic has been evaluated, the minimal dose that will maintain the reduction should be continued. This is usually 50 to 100 mg of hydrochlorothiazide daily or its equivalent in the other diuretics (see Table 2). The response to the diuretic should be observed for at least two weeks. Then, if additional reduction in blood pressure is indicated, other agents should be added.

The serum potassium level frequently falls during long-term diuretic therapy; therefore, the patient should maintain an adequate intake of foods that are high in potassium. Thiazide-induced hypokalemia generally needs no correction unless the serum potassium level falls below 3.0 mEq/liter or the patient is receiving digitalis. In these patients, a potassium-sparing diuretic (spironolactone or triamterene) should be given with the thiazide. A fixed-dose combination containing a potassium-sparing and a potassium-losing diuretic [Aldactazide, Dyazide] may be used instead of the single-entity drugs if the dosage ratio meets the needs of the patient. Although potassium supplements are often used to replace the deficit, they are inconvenient, are often poorly tolerated, and may not be as reliable as the combination diuretics.

If the blood pressure is not controlled by diuretic therapy, one of the agents affecting the sympathetic nervous system or the vascular smooth muscle (eg, a rauwolfia alkaloid, methyldopa, hydralazine) should be added. These drugs should be given in conjunction with a diuretic, since the diuretic reduces the dose requirement of other antihypertensive drugs, helps to counteract sodium retention and increased plasma volume that can be produced by long-term administration of some agents, and may discourage the development of tolerance. Possible drug regimens follow and the suggested dosages appear in the individual evaluations.

In patients who can tolerate the depressant effect, the choice of combination therapy would be reserpine and a diuretic. Since reserpine has a delayed onset of action, its full effect often is not observed for as long as six weeks. Therefore, patients started on this combination should be observed for at least six weeks before other drugs are added to the regimen. Alternatively, patients for whom a sedative is undesirable (eg, top level business executives and professional people) can be given methyldopa with a diuretic. Hydralazine can be added to either one of the above regimens if adequate reduction in blood pressure has not been obtained. Hydralazine is better tolerated and probably more effective when used with these agents than when used alone. The action of this drug is relatively brief; therefore, it should be given two or three times daily. This short duration of action makes it valuable for those patients whose blood pressure becomes sharply elevated at regular times during the day.

Each of these agents has advantages and disadvantages which are discussed in more detail in the individual evaluations. Reserpine, if tolerated, is convenient to use because it requires administration only once daily. For patients who respond favorably, a thiazide-reserpine regimen provides a simple and inexpensive means for long-term control of hypertension. However, individuals receiving reserpine must be carefully observed for the appearance of mental depression, and the drug should be discontinued immediately if depression occurs. Methyldopa is preferred by some physicians because of its relative freedom from undesirable effects. The disadvantages of this drug are the wide range of effective dosage (requiring dose titration), the development of tolerance, and the high cost in comparison to reserpine or hydralazine.

The beta-adrenergic blocking agent, propranolol, may be useful in patients with tachycardia and clinical manifestations of intermittent increased cardiac output, in patients with angina, or those who experience significant cardiac stimulation from hydralazine. Individuals who have failed to respond to other regimens also may be helped by the addition of propranolol.

For patients with severe hypertension (diastolic blood pressure over 120 mm Hg but without retinal exudates and hemorrhage), a diuretic plus guanethidine is usually effective. The orthostatic hypotension produced by guanethidine may be troublesome, however, and the dose must be carefully adjusted. In this therapeutic regimen, the diuretic is used initially and, after the response has been evaluated, guanethidine is added. If the diastolic pressure is more than 140 mm Hg, treatment should be initiated with both agents. If orthostatic hypotension or other adverse effects become excessive, the dose of guanethidine may be maintained at the tolerated level and methyldopa or hydralazine added to the regimen. In obstinate cases, hydralazine may be added to the triple regimen of diuretic, guanethidine, and methyldopa; propranolol also may be useful.

Occasionally patients with severe disease cannot be controlled on any of the above regimens. Under these circumstances, the ganglionic blocking agent mecamylamine hydrochloride may be employed. This agent is particularly useful in patients who experience persistent diarrhea with guanethidine which cannot be controlled by an anticholinergic drug. When mecamylamine is added to the regimen, the dose of guanethidine may be reduced without a loss of antihypertensive effect. In addition, the ganglionic blocking drug reduces peristalsis and, therefore, counteracts the diarrhea.

Hypertensive Emergencies: Prompt lowering of the blood pressure is required for patients in the malignant phase of essential hypertension and in other hypertensive emergencies. Malignant hypertension is characterized by a diastolic blood pressure above 130 mm Hg with hypertensive retinopathy. These patients should be hospitalized until the blood pressure is reduced to a reasonable level; this generally requires parenteral administration of antihypertensive drugs. The patient should remain in the hospital until his blood pressure is effectively controlled by oral therapy and optimal doses have been determined.

If the clinical situation permits, a reduction in blood pressure may be obtained within a few hours by parenteral administration of methyldopate hydrochloride or reserpine and a diuretic. However, agents with a more rapid action are required to prevent serious cardiovascular complications when hypertension is complicated by pulmonary edema due to acute left ventricular failure, encephalopathy, cerebral hemorrhage, dissecting aortic aneurysm, or when there is a severe elevation in blood pressure in patients with malignant hypertension, pre-eclampsia, or renal failure.The blood pressure can be reduced within minutes by parenteral administration of trimethaphan or pentolinium. Both agents require careful adjustment in dose and frequent monitoring of blood pressure to prevent excessive hypotension. Hydralazine, given intramuscularly or intravenously, also is useful and often is preferred in the hypertensive patient with acute glomerulonephritis or eclampsia. Some physicians consider sodium nitroprusside to be the most potent and consistently effective agent for treatment of hypertensive crises. This agent, given intravenously, is useful when other drugs have failed to control the blood pressure; however, the infusion must be monitored continuously to prevent excessive hypotension.

Diazoxide is another agent which will produce an immediate fall in blood pressure when given by rapid intravenous injection. The hypotensive effect is due to direct relaxation of vascular smooth muscle. Although diazoxide is a thiazide derivative, it is not a diuretic and actually causes marked sodium and water retention. Diazoxide has been used successfully in many patients with severe or malignant hypertension who have failed to respond to other agents and is considered by many authorities to be the safest and most effective drug for the emergency reduction of blood pressure. It is useful in hypertension associated with impaired renal function, hypertensive encephalopathy, hypertension complicated by left ventricular failure, and in eclampsia.

Fluid overload often makes the hypertensive patient resistant to therapy. In addition, the drugs used to treat hypertensive crisis often cause sodium and water retention. Intravenous administration of furosemide or ethacrynate sodium induces rapid diuresis, enhances the response to antihypertensive agents, and counteracts sodium and water retention. These drugs are particularly useful when hypertensive crisis is associated with acute pulmonary edema or renal failure.

The alpha-adrenergic blocking agents, phentolamine [Regitine] and phenoxybenzamine [Dibenzyline], are used only for hypertensive crises caused by an excess of circulating catecholamines, ie, in phenochromocytoma and in hypertensive crises due to interaction between monoamine oxidase inhibitors and sympathomimetic amines. The beta-adrenergic blocking agent, propranolol, is sometimes used with an alpha-adrenergic blocking drug for the preoperative management of patients with pheochromocytoma.

Adverse Reactions and Precautions

All antihypertensive drugs initially may cause weakness and fatigue and some (rauwolfia alkaloids, methyldopa [Aldomet]) have a pronounced sedative effect. Orthostatic hypotension may occur following administration of the ganglionic blocking drugs, pargyline [Eutonyl], guanethidine [Ismelin], and, to a lesser extent, methyldopa. This is due to interference with the reflex function of the capacitance vessels which results in a reduction in venous return and cardiac output when the patient assumes the upright position. Dosage should be carefully adjusted for each patient, and ambulatory patients should be warned initially, as well as whenever the dosage is increased or another agent is added to the regimen, that episodes of dizziness upon arising and spells of faintness and weakness may occur. These agents should be used only in patients who can be adequately supervised and observed. Some physicians train the patient or a member of his family to record the blood pressure in the home; daily or twice daily recordings, taken in the supine and standing positions and after mild exercise, are used as a guide in regulating dosage.

To maintain adequate perfusion of vital tissues, sudden, marked reductions in blood pressure should be avoided in patients with renal impairment or advanced coronary or cerebral arteriosclerosis. Severe hypotension may occur when antihypertensive drugs are used parenterally to treat hypertensive crises; excessive hypotension should be treated by placing the patient in the head-down, legs-up position. Rarely, intravenous infusion of levarterenol [Levophed] may be needed.

Antihypertensive therapy may lead to electrolyte imbalances, including hypokalemia (thiazides and other potassium-losing diuretics), hyperkalemia (potassium-sparing diuretics), and sodium retention (particularly methyldopa, guanethidine, and diazoxide). These and other adverse effects are discussed in the individual evaluations.

DIURETIC AGENTS

Thiazides and Related Compounds

A thiazide diuretic or related compound (chlorthalidone, quinethazone) commonly serves as the cornerstone of the antihypertensive regimen—as sole therapy in patients with mild hypertension or with other antihypertensive drugs in patients who are not controlled by the diuretic alone. The mechanism by which these agents lower blood pressure is not clearly understood. It may be related to extracellular volume depletion or a negative sodium balance, or to a direct effect on vascular smooth muscle. The advantages of the thiazides and related agents are: (1) they are effective orally; (2) they lower both supine and standing blood pressures; (3) their antihypertensive effect is maintained during long-term administration; (4) their adverse effects are mild; (5) they enhance the

TABLE 2.—THIAZIDES AND RELATED AGENTS

Drug	Usual Initial Oral Dosage*	Preparations
Chlorothiazide Diuril (Merck Sharp & Dohme)	*Adults*, initially, 500 mg twice daily. *Children*, 20 mg/kg daily in 2 divided doses.	Tablets 250 and 500 mg Suspension 250 mg/5 ml
Hydrochlorothiazide Esidrix (Ciba) HydroDiuril (Merck Sharp & Dohme) Oretic (Abbott)	*Adults*, initially, 25 to 50 mg twice daily. *Children*, 2 mg/kg daily in 2 divided doses.	Tablets 25 and 50 mg
Bendroflumethiazide Naturetin (Squibb)	*Adults*, initially, 5 to 20 mg daily; for maintenance, 2.5 to 15 mg daily. *Children*, initially, 0.1 mg/kg daily in 1 or 2 doses; for maintenance, 0.05 to 0.3 mg/kg daily in 1 or 2 doses.	Tablets 2.5 and 5 mg
Benzthiazide Aquatag (Tutag) Diucen (Central) Edemex (Savage) Exna (Robins) Lemazide (Lemmon)	*Adults*, initially, 25 to 50 mg twice daily. *Children*, 1 to 4 mg/kg daily in 3 doses.	Aquatag, Lemazide: Tablets 25 and 50 mg Diucen, Edemex, Exna: Tablets 50 mg
Cyclothiazide Anhydron (Lilly)	*Adults*, initially, 2 mg once daily. *Children*, 0.02 to 0.04 mg/kg once daily.	Tablets 2 mg
Hydroflumethiazide Saluron (Bristol)	*Adults*, initially, 50 to 100 mg daily. *Children*, 1 mg/kg once daily.	Tablets 50 mg
Methyclothiazide Aquatensen (Mallinckrodt) Enduron (Abbott)	*Adults*, initially, 2.5 to 5 mg once daily. *Children*, 0.05 to 0.2 mg/kg once daily.	Aquatensen: Tablets 5 mg Enduron: Tablets 2.5 and 5 mg
Polythiazide Renese (Pfizer)	*Adults*, initially, 1 to 4 mg daily. *Children*, initially, 0.02 to 0.08 mg/kg daily.	Tablets 1, 2, and 4 mg
Trichlormethiazide Metahydrin (Lakeside) Naqua (Schering)	*Adults*, initially, 2 or 4 mg twice daily; for maintenance, 2 or 4 mg once daily. *Children*, 0.07 mg/kg once daily or in divided doses.	Tablets 2 and 4 mg
Chlorthalidone Hygroton (USV)	*Adults*, initially, 50 or 100 mg daily. *Children*, initially, 2 mg/kg 3 times weekly.	Tablets 50 and 100 mg
Quinethazone Hydromox (Lederle)	*Adults*, initially, 50 mg once or twice daily.	Tablets 50 mg

*The initial dosage is subsequently increased or decreased according to the response of the patient.

effect of other antihypertensive drugs, thereby permitting a reduction in dose and reducing the incidence and severity of adverse reactions; and (6) they counteract the sodium retention that may occur after long-term administration of some antihypertensive agents.

The thiazides and related drugs initially may cause weakness, fatigue, and dizziness as a result of excessive diuresis. They increase the urinary excretion of potassium, and during prolonged therapy the serum potassium level falls. The hypokalemia is rarely severe if the diet contains a liberal amount of high potassium foods; however, even a moderate reduction in serum potassium may be dangerous in some patients (eg, those receiving digitalis). In such patients, a potassium-sparing diuretic (spironolactone, triamterene) should be administered with the thiazide. Potassium chloride solution may be given instead of the potassium-sparing agent but is less convenient. Enteric-coated preparations containing a thiazide and potassium chloride may cause small bowel ulceration and are not recommended (see Chapter 7, Diuretics).

Hyperuricemia occurs frequently during prolonged treatment with these oral diuretics.

Rarely, an acute attack of gout may be precipitated in susceptible individuals but this is readily controlled by uricosuric agents or allopurinol. Thiazides may increase the blood glucose level and aggravate pre-existing diabetes; therefore, in diabetic patients, increased doses of hypoglycemic drugs may be needed during diuretic therapy. Reduction in the glomerular filtration rate and an elevation in the blood urea nitrogen level also may occur. For other adverse reactions occasionally associated with thiazides and related drugs, see Chapter 7, Diuretics.

USUAL DOSAGE.—The various thiazides and related drugs differ only in potency on a weight basis and in duration of action. When given in equipotent dosage, no differences in efficacy or toxicity have been demonstrated. (See Table 2 for dosage and preparations.)

Furosemide and Ethacrynate Sodium

These two potent diuretic agents are not chemically related but have similar pharmacologic properties and uses.

FUROSEMIDE [Lasix]

Furosemide is a potent nonthiazide sulfonamide diuretic that is useful as an adjunct in the treatment of hypertensive crises, particularly when the hypertension is associated with acute pulmonary edema or renal failure. When given intravenously, furosemide causes rapid diuresis, enhances the effect of other antihypertensive drugs, and counteracts the sodium retention that may follow use of some of these agents (eg, diazoxide).

Furosemide has also been given orally, alone or with other agents, for treating chronic hypertension. It is useful when hypertension is complicated by congestive heart failure or renal impairment; however, in patients with uncomplicated mild or moderate hypertension, there is nothing to recommend its use in place of a thiazide or related agent. In contrast to the large volume of data attesting to the safety and efficacy of the thiazides, there are few long-term studies on the use of furosemide in mild to moderate hypertension. Also, it should be emphasized that, although furosemide is a potent diuretic, there is no correlation between diuretic potency and antihypertensive effect. Some studies which have compared blood pressures of hypertensive patients treated with furosemide versus those treated with another oral diuretic have found no significant difference between the drugs; in other studies, the thiazide or related agent was found to be more effective.

Electrolyte depletion, hyperuricemia, and elevation of the blood urea nitrogen level are the most common adverse effects of furosemide. Ototoxicity has been reported rarely. For other adverse reactions and precautions, see Chapter 7, Diuretics.

USUAL DOSAGE.—

Intravenous: Adults, for hypertensive crises, 100 to 200 mg administered over a period of one to two minutes. When the glomerular filtration rate is markedly reduced, as in patients with severe renal failure, even larger doses may be required. In acute, oliguric renal failure, some authorities have recommended doses in excess of 1 g, given as a single intravenous injection. An oral diuretic should be substituted for parenteral therapy as soon as practical.

Oral: Adults, for chronic hypertension, 40 mg twice daily.

PREPARATIONS.—Lasix (Hoechst).

Injection: Solution 10 mg/ml in 2 ml containers.

Oral: Tablets 40 mg.

ETHACRYNATE SODIUM [Sodium Edecrin]

Ethacrynate sodium is a potent diuretic chemically unrelated to other diuretic agents. It is useful as an adjunct in the treatment of hypertensive crises, particularly when the hypertension is complicated by acute pulmonary edema or renal failure. When given intravenously, ethacrynate sodium causes rapid diuresis, enhances the effect of other antihypertensive drugs, and counteracts the sodium retention that may follow use of some of these agents (eg, diazoxide).

The most common adverse effects of ethacrynate sodium are electrolyte depletion, hyperuricemia, and elevation of the blood urea nitrogen level. Ototoxicity has been reported rarely. For other adverse reactions and precautions, see Chapter 7, Diuretics.

USUAL DOSAGE.—*Intravenous: Adults,* 50 mg, or 0.5 to 1 mg/kg of body weight, as a single dose. If a second dose is required, it should be injected at another site to avoid possible thrombophlebitis. An oral diuretic should be substituted for parenteral therapy as soon as practical.

PREPARATIONS.—Sodium Edecrin (Merck Sharp & Dohme). *Injection:* Powder 50 mg.

Potassium-sparing Agents

SPIRONOLACTONE [Aldactone]

TRIAMTERENE [Dyrenium]

Spironolactone, an aldosterone antagonist, and triamterene, a drug that acts directly on the renal tubules, produce sodium loss with potassium retention. When used alone, these agents have little or no antihypertensive action, but they may enhance the hypotensive effect of the thiazides. The potassium-sparing diuretics are used to prevent or minimize the hypokalemia induced by the thiazides or other potassium-losing diuretics. This combined therapy is more convenient and reliable than use of a potassium supplement.

The potassium-sparing diuretics can cause hyperkalemia in patients with impaired renal function. For other uses and adverse reactions, see Chapter 7, Diuretics.

USUAL DOSAGE.—

Spironolactone:

Oral: Adults, initially, 50 to 100 mg daily in divided doses. The dosage should then be adjusted according to the response of the patient as determined by serum and urinary electrolyte levels.

Triamterene:

Oral: Adults, initially, 100 mg twice daily after meals. The dosage should be adjusted according to the response of the patient as determined by serum and urinary electrolyte levels. *Children,* initially, 2 to 4 mg/kg of body weight in one or two divided doses daily or every other day. The maximal daily dose for both adults and children is 300 mg.

PREPARATIONS.—

Spironolactone:

Aldactone (Searle). *Oral:* Tablets 25 mg.

Triamterene:

Dyrenium (Smith Kline & French). *Oral:* Capsules 100 mg.

AGENTS THAT DEPRESS THE ACTIVITY OF THE SYMPATHETIC NERVOUS SYSTEM

RAUWOLFIA ALKALOIDS

The actions, uses, and adverse effects of the rauwolfia compounds are similar. Reserpine is regarded as the prototype and is the most commonly used drug in this group. The antihypertensive effect of these agents has been attributed to depletion of catecholamine stores in the sympathetic nerve terminals. With usual oral doses, reflex tonic constrictor impulses to the capacitance vessels are only partially inhibited, and orthostatic hypotension occurs only rarely.

The rauwolfia alkaloids are used orally for treating chronic hypertension. When given alone, these agents are not potent antihypertensive agents except in doses that produce unacceptable adverse effects. They are used most commonly with a thiazide or related agent in patients with mild or moderate hypertension that is not adequately controlled by the thiazide alone. If the desired hypotensive effect is not achieved with the thiazide and reserpine, hydralazine is often added to the regimen.

Reserpine also is used intramuscularly for treating hypertensive crises. The onset of its hypotensive effect is delayed for two or three hours; therefore, it is not useful when *immediate* reduction of blood pressure is required.

Adverse Reactions and Precautions.—Common adverse reactions associated with the rauwolfia alkaloids are mental depression, nasal congestion, bradycardia, lethargy, nightmares, weight gain, and diarrhea. Drowsiness also occurs frequently, and attempts to dissociate the sedative from the hypotensive effect have not been successful. When given parenterally, reserpine may increase gastric acid secretion and should be used cautiously in patients with a history of peptic ulcer. If symptoms suggest recurrence of the ulcer, the drug should be discontinued. Because the rauwolfia alkaloids increase gastrointestinal tone and motility, they should not be given to patients with a history of ulcerative colitis.

The incidence of mental depression after prolonged administration of rauwolfia alkaloids has been reported to be as low as 2% and as high as 18%. Depression can occur with any dose, but is more common when the daily dosage is 1 mg or more. Severe depression, requiring hospitalization or resulting in suicide, has occurred occasionally. If depressive symptoms appear, the drug should be discontinued. The rauwolfia alkaloids should not be given to patients with a history of depression.

Severe hypotension has occurred occasionally when reserpine was administered parenterally to patients in hypertensive crisis. If position change does not relieve the hypotension, an adrenergic drug should be given intravenously. Levarterenol is generally preferred; vasopressors that act in part by liberating norepinephrine may be less effective, since norepinephrine stores are depleted by the rauwolfia alkaloids. Pronounced hypotension also may occur if rauwolfia alkaloids are given with drugs that cause vasodilatation (eg, quinidine).

Sodium and water retention occur occasionally with prolonged administration of a

TABLE 3.—RAUWOLFIA ALKALOIDS

Drug	Chemical Structure
Reserpine Lemiserp (Lemmon) Rau-Sed (Squibb) Resercen (Central) Reserpoid (Upjohn) Rolserp (Robinson) Sandril (Lilly) Serpasil (Ciba) Sertina (Fellows-Testagar) Vio-Serpine (Rowell) Also marketed under generic name.	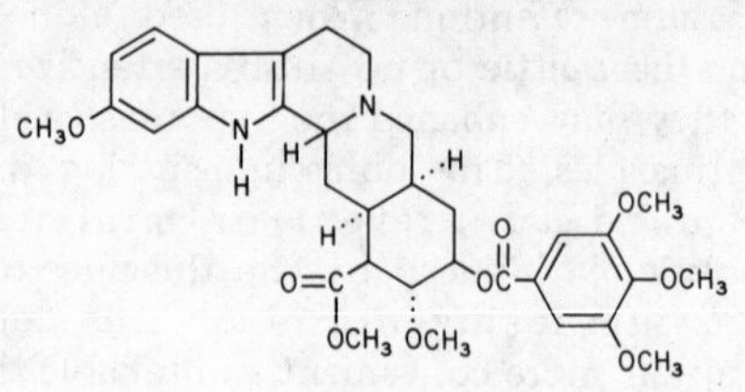
Rauwolfia Serpentina Hyperloid (Person & Covey) Raudixin (Squibb) Rauja (Table Rock) Raulin (Key) Rautina (Fellows-Testagar) Rauval (Vale) Venibar (Ulmer) Wolfina (Westerfield) Also marketed under generic name.	
Alseroxylon Rauwiloid (Riker) Rautensin (Dorsey)	
Deserpidine Harmonyl (Abbott)	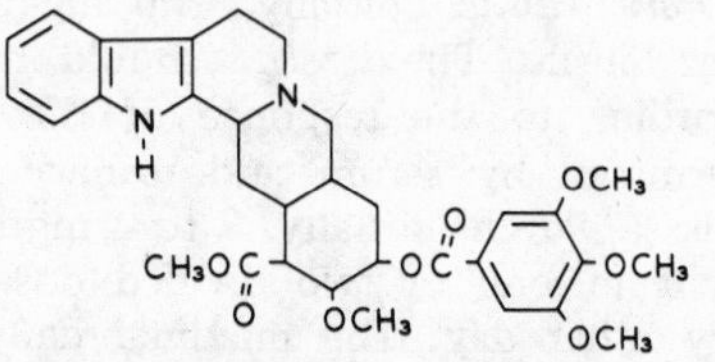
Rescinnamine Cinatabs (Table Rock) Moderil (Pfizer)	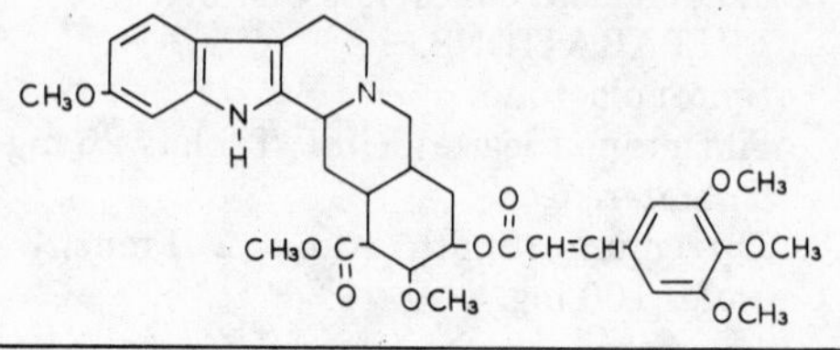
Syrosingopine Singoserp (Ciba)	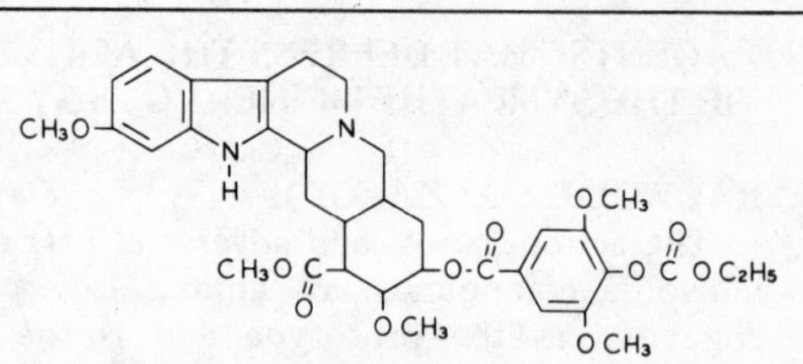

Usual Dosage*	Preparations
Oral: For chronic hypertension, *adults*, initially, 0.25 to 0.5 mg daily; for maintenance, 0.1 to 0.25 mg daily. *Children*, 0.25 to 0.5 mg daily. *Intramuscular:* For hypertensive crisis, *adults*, initially, 0.5 to 1 mg; if there is little or no fall in blood pressure within 3 hours, 2 to 4 mg is given at 3- to 12-hour intervals until the pressure falls to the desired level. *Children weighing less than 36 kg*, initially, 0.02 mg/kg; if there is little or no fall in blood pressure within 4 to 6 hours, 0.04 mg/kg is given at 4- to 6-hour intervals. *Children over 36 kg*, initially, 0.5 to 1 mg with subsequent doses adjusted according to response of the patient.	Elixir 0.25 mg/5 ml Tablets 0.1, 0.25, 0.5, and 1 mg Solution (for injection) 2.5 and 5 mg/ml in 2 and 10 ml containers
Oral: Adults, initially, 200 mg daily in 1 or 2 doses; for maintenance, 50 to 300 mg daily in 1 or 2 doses.	Tablets 50 and 100 mg
Oral: Adults, initially, 2 to 4 mg daily; for maintenance, 2 mg daily.	Tablets 2 mg
Oral: Adults, initially, 0.25 mg 3 or 4 times daily; for maintenance, 0.25 mg daily may suffice in some patients.	Tablets 0.1 and 0.25 mg
Oral: Adults, initially, 0.5 mg twice daily; for maintenance, 0.25 to 2 mg daily.	Tablets 0.25, 0.5, and 1 mg
Oral: Adults, initially, 1 or 2 mg daily in 1 or 2 doses; for maintenance, 0.5 to 3 mg daily.	Tablets 1 mg

*The initial oral dosage is subsequently increased or decreased until the optimal effect is obtained with minimal adverse reactions. The rauwolfia alkaloids have a slow onset and a prolonged duration of action. Adjustments in dosage should, therefore, not be made more frequently than every 7 to 14 days.

rauwolfia alkaloid. This is only rarely a problem during antihypertensive therapy, because these agents are usually administered with a diuretic.

Reserpine has been given parenterally in the treatment of preeclampsia and eclampsia; however, such use may not be advisable, since the drug passes through the placental circulation and may cause drowsiness, nasal congestion, cyanosis, and anorexia in the newborn infant.

The rauwolfia alkaloids lower the convulsive threshold and should be used in reduced dosage in patients with epilepsy. Large doses can cause extrapyramidal reactions; however, this has occurred only rarely with the doses used in antihypertensive therapy.

See Table 3 for dosage and preparations.

METHYLDOPA [Aldomet]
METHYLDOPATE HYDROCHLORIDE
[Aldomet Ester Hydrochloride]

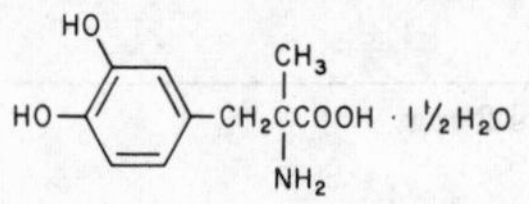

HO–(3,4-dihydroxyphenyl)–$CH_2C(CH_3)(NH_2)COOH \cdot 1\frac{1}{2}H_2O$

Methyldopa is a dopa decarboxylase inhibitor that is useful in the management of mild to severe hypertension. Its antihypertensive effect may or may not be related to displacement of norepinephrine from sympathetic nerve terminals by formation of a false transmitter. A central component also may be involved.

Methyldopa is given orally in mild to moderate hypertension. A thiazide diuretic should be given concomitantly to enhance the antihypertensive effect and prevent sodium and water retention. Tolerance frequently develops after 6 to 12 months of therapy with methyldopa, particularly if a diuretic is not given concurrently in adequate dosage. If the desired hypotensive effect is not achieved with the thiazide and methyldopa, hydralazine may be added as a third agent. In severe hypertension, methyldopa may be added to a thiazide-guanethidine regimen.

When administered intravenously, methyldopa is useful in hypertensive crises. It produces a fall in blood pressure beginning about two hours after injection; therefore, a more rapid-acting agent should be selected if an immediate effect is desired.

Methyldopa often is preferred for use in patients with renal impairment because it sustains (or may increase) renal blood flow; however, since the drug is excreted by the kidney, a reduction in dosage may be necessary.

Methyldopa is generally well tolerated. Drowsiness, which usually subsides with continued therapy, is the most common adverse effect; therefore, increases in dosage should initially be added in the evening. Mental depression is less common with this agent than with reserpine. Dryness of the mouth, nasal congestion, diarrhea, and bradycardia also may occur. Methyldopa produces significantly less orthostatic hypotension than the ganglionic blocking agents, pargyline, or guanethidine, but the patient should be informed of the possible occurrence of dizziness and weakness. Sodium and water retention may occur if methyldopa is administered without a diuretic.

With prolonged treatment, some patients develop a positive Coombs' test, and a few cases of hemolytic anemia have been reported. The hemolytic process generally reverses when the drug is discontinued, but the Coombs' test may remain positive for several months. Reversible agranulocytosis has been reported rarely. Alterations in the results of liver function tests (increased serum glutamic oxaloacetic transaminase and alkaline phosphatase levels) have been noted during the first six weeks of treatment. These abnormalities may be accompanied by fever and malaise and are indicative of hepatitis. The hepatitis is usually mild and is generally reversible following discontinuation of methyldopa.

USUAL DOSAGE.—

Methyldopa:

Oral: For chronic hypertension, *adults,* initially, 250 mg in the morning, which may be increased to 250 mg morning and at bedtime after one week. The twice daily doses may be increased by increments of 250 mg until the blood pressure is controlled or until a total daily dose of 2 g is reached. If patients complain of drowsiness, a larger dose may be given at bedtime than in the morning. *Children,* initially, 10 mg/kg of body weight daily divided into two or three doses. The daily dosage is then increased or decreased according to the response of the patient (maximum, 65 mg/kg daily).

Methyldopate Hydrochloride:

Intravenous: For hypertensive crisis, *adults,* 500 mg to 1 g; this dose may be repeated every six hours if necessary. *Children,* 20 to 40 mg/kg of body weight daily divided into four doses. After the blood pressure has been controlled, oral medication should be substituted.

PREPARATIONS.—

Aldomet (Merck Sharp & Dohme). *Oral:*

Tablets (enteric-coated) 250 mg.

Aldomet Ester Hydrochloride (Merck Sharp & Dohme). *Injection:* Solution 50 mg/ml in 5 ml containers.

GUANETHIDINE SULFATE [Ismelin Sulfate]

$$\text{(azocan-1-yl)}N\text{-}CH_2CH_2NH\overset{NH}{\overset{\|}{C}}NH_2 \cdot H_2SO_4$$

Guanethidine is a potent antihypertensive agent that may act by depleting norepinephrine stores. The maximal hypotensive effect does not occur until two or three days after initial administration and may persist for seven to ten days after withdrawal of the drug. The range of effective dosage is very wide.

Guanethidine is useful in the treatment of moderately severe and severe hypertension. A thiazide diuretic should be given with guanethidine to enhance the antihypertensive effect and prevent sodium and water retention. If the thiazide-guanethidine regimen does not reduce the blood pressure to the desired level, methyldopa or hydralazine may be added.

The most common adverse effects are orthostatic hypotension and hypotension during exercise. The patient should be warned of the possible occurrence of these reactions. During initial therapy and whenever dosage is increased, the blood pressure should be measured in the supine and standing positions and after mild exercise.

Guanethidine causes sodium and water retention and should always be administered with a diuretic. Other common adverse reactions are bradycardia, diarrhea, and retrograde ejaculation.

Guanethidine should not be used in patients with pheochromocytoma, as severe hypertension may occur due to the accelerated release of endogenous amines. The response to exogenous norepinephrine (levarterenol) also may be enhanced. Various noncatecholamines (eg, amphetamines, ephedrine) and the tricyclic antidepressants may antagonize the antihypertensive effect of guanethidine.

USUAL DOSAGE.—*Oral: Adults,* for ambulatory patients, initially, 12.5 mg daily. The dosage may be increased by increments of 12.5 mg every seven days. In hospitalized patients, initially, 25 to 50 mg daily. Because of the drug's long half-life, the maximal effect may not be observed for 7 to 14 days and it may be necessary to reduce the dose slightly after an initial antihypertensive effect has been obtained. *Children,* initially, 0.2 mg/kg of body weight daily, increased by the same amount every seven to ten days if required.

PREPARATIONS.—Ismelin Sulfate (Ciba). *Oral:* Tablets 10 and 25 mg.

Alpha-adrenergic Blocking Agents

PHENOXYBENZAMINE HYDROCHLORIDE [Dibenzyline]

$$C_6H_5\text{-}OCH_2\underset{CH_3}{\underset{|}{C}}H\text{-}\overset{CH_2C_6H_5}{\overset{|}{N}}\text{-}CH_2CH_2Cl \cdot HCl$$

PHENTOLAMINE HYDROCHLORIDE [Regitine Hydrochloride]

PHENTOLAMINE MESYLATE [Regitine Mesylate]

$$\text{(2-imidazolinyl)}\text{-}CH_2\text{-}N(C_6H_4\text{-}CH_3)(C_6H_4\text{-}OH)$$

The alpha-adrenergic blocking agents, phentolamine and phenoxybenzamine, are used only in hypertension caused by an excess of circulating catecholamines; they are not useful in treating essential hypertension. Alpha-adrenergic blocking drugs are administered orally for preoperative management of patients with pheochromocytoma and for long-term treatment of patients who are not suitable candidates for surgery. Phenoxybenzamine is preferred for oral use because it provides more sustained control of the blood pressure. The beta-adrenergic blocking agent, propranolol, may be used concomitantly (see the evaluation on Propranolol Hydrochloride).

Phentolamine is given parenterally immediately prior to surgery for pheochromocytoma and during surgical manipulation of the tumor. It has been administered for diagnosis of pheochromocytoma, but measurement of urinary catecholamines and their metabolites is now the established diagnostic method (see Chapter 77, Miscellaneous Diagnostic Aids). Phentolamine also is used for the treatment of hypertensive crisis caused by interaction between monoamine oxidase inhibitors and sympathomimetic amines.

Orthostatic hypotension and reflex tachycardia are the most common untoward effects of the alpha-adrenergic blocking agents. When these agents are given orally, nasal congestion and gastrointestinal disturbances (nausea, vomiting, diarrhea) may occur.

USUAL DOSAGE.—

Phenoxybenzamine Hydrochloride:

Oral: For preoperative management of pheochromocytoma and for prolonged treatment of patients not suitable candidates for surgery, *adults*, 20 to 60 mg daily in two or three divided doses; *children*, initially 0.2 mg/kg of body weight daily as a single dose. The dosage may be increased gradually at intervals of not less than four days. The maintenance dose is 0.4 to 1.2 mg/kg daily in divided doses.

Phentolamine Hydrochloride:

Oral: For preoperative management of pheochromocytoma or for prolonged treatment of patients not suitable candidates for surgery, *adults*, 50 mg four to six times daily; *children*, 25 mg four to six times daily.

Phentolamine Mesylate:

Intravenous, Intramuscular: To control blood pressure immediately prior to surgery for pheochromocytoma, *adults*, 5 mg; *children*, 1 mg. The dose should be injected one or two hours prior to surgery and repeated if necessary.

Intravenous: During surgery for pheochromocytoma, *adults*, 5 mg; *children*, 1 mg. For diagnosis of pheochromocytoma, *adults*, 5 mg dissolved in 1 ml of sterile water; *children*, 1 mg. A fall in blood pressure of more than 35 mm Hg systolic and 25 mm Hg diastolic suggests pheochromocytoma. For hypertensive crisis due to interaction of a monoamine oxidase inhibitor with sympathomimetic amines, *adults*, 5 mg.

PREPARATIONS.—

Phenoxybenzamine Hydrochloride:

Dibenzyline (Smith Kline & French). *Oral:* Capsules 10 mg.

Phentolamine Hydrochloride:

Regitine [hydrochloride] (Ciba). *Oral:* Tablets 50 mg.

Phentolamine Mesylate:

Regitine [mesylate] (Ciba). *Injection:* Powder (for solution) 5 mg.

Beta-adrenergic Blocking Agent

PROPRANOLOL HYDROCHLORIDE [Inderal]

The role of beta-adrenergic blocking agents in the treatment of chronic hypertension has been a subject of controversy for several years. However, increasing experience with propranolol has demonstrated that, when adequate doses are employed, this agent has a sustained antihypertensive effect in patients with varying degrees of hypertension. The mechanism of action is most commonly attributed to a reduction in cardiac output. Propranolol has been used both alone and with thiazides, hydralazine, methyldopa, and guanethidine. It appears to be particularly useful in hypertensive patients with angina and, when given with hydralazine and a diuretic, in patients with moderate to severe hypertension who cannot tolerate or have failed to respond to other regimens. Propranolol enhances the antihypertensive effect of hydralazine and prevents the reflexly-induced increase in heart rate and cardiac output. This combined therapy is well tolerated by most patients.

Propranolol is sometimes used with an alpha-adrenergic blocking agent for preoperative management of patients with pheochromocytoma and for prolonged treatment of patients who are not suitable candidates for surgery. The rationale is that it may protect the heart from the positive inotropic and chronotropic effects of the high level of circulating catecholamines. There is no general agreement on whether propranolol should be used routinely for this purpose; however, it is of value if there is evidence of excessive cardiac stimulation (eg, premature ventricular contractions).

Propranolol may cause gastrointestinal disturbances, mental depression, fatigue, weakness, and insomnia. Pronounced bradycardia may occur, and the drug should not be used in patients with congestive heart failure unless the failure is due to an arrhythmia that does not respond to other antiarrhythmic agents. It increases airway resistance and should not be used in patients with bronchial asthma. For management of pheochromocytoma, propranolol should be given only with an alpha-adrenergic blocking drug; if used alone, blockade of beta receptors in peripheral vessels may cause a marked hypertensive response.

For other uses and adverse reactions, see Chapter 2, Antiarrhythmic Agents, and Chapter 3, Antianginal Agents.

USUAL DOSAGE.—The metabolism of propranolol varies as much as sevenfold among patients; therefore, the dose must be individualized.

Oral: For chronic hypertension, *adults*, initially, 20 mg administered four times daily. If the desired response is not obtained, the dosage may be increased gradually to 40 mg four times daily. Doses up to 2 g daily have occasionally been administered.

For preoperative management of pheochromocytoma, *adults and children*, 60 mg daily in divided doses for three days prior to surgery (given concomitantly with an alpha-adrenergic blocking agent).

For prolonged treatment of patients with pheochromocytoma not amenable to surgery, *adults and children*, 30 mg daily in divided doses (given concomitantly with an alpha-adrenergic blocking agent).

PREPARATIONS.—Inderal (Ayerst). *Oral:* Tablets 10 and 40 mg.

AGENTS THAT ACT DIRECTLY ON VASCULAR SMOOTH MUSCLE

DIAZOXIDE [Hyperstat I.V.]

Cl, N, CH_3, N-H, SO_2

Diazoxide is a nondiuretic thiazide derivative that is useful in the treatment of hypertensive crises. When given by rapid intravenous injection, diazoxide produces an immediate fall in blood pressure (in one to five minutes), with a return to the pretreatment level within 24 hours. The fall in blood pressure is due to a direct action on the arterioles; capacitance vessels are not affected and cardiac output is increased.

Although diazoxide has not been compared with other antihypertensive agents in controlled studies, it is considered by many investigators to be the drug of choice for emergency reduction of blood pressure. The advantages of diazoxide are: (1) It has a very rapid onset of action. (2) It does not require continuous infusion or careful titration of dosage. (3) It usually does not cause excessive hypotension. (4) The absence of a sedative effect enables the physician to evaluate the patient's mental status. (5) Drug resistance apparently does not occur, provided that an effective diuretic is given concomitantly.

Diazoxide has been used successfully in many patients with severe or malignant hypertension who have failed to respond to other agents. It is useful in hypertensive patients with impaired renal function, hypertensive encephalopathy, hypertension complicated by left ventricular failure, and in eclampsia. Diazoxide is not useful for the treatment of pheochromocytoma.

An oral form of diazoxide, which is available only for investigational purposes, is used in the management of certain juvenile hypoglycemic states.

Sodium and water retention and hyperglycemia are the major adverse effects of diazoxide. Administration of adequate doses of an *effective* diuretic will prevent fluid overload and thereby enhance the antihypertensive effect. A potent, rapid-acting diuretic, such as intravenous furosemide, may be indicated, especially in patients with impaired renal function who may be unresponsive to thiazides. Concomitant use of an effective diuretic is particularly important during repeated injections of diazoxide to avoid congestive heart failure and to discourage the development of drug resistance.

The hyperglycemic effect of diazoxide is usually transitory and can be controlled, if necessary, by oral hypoglycemic agents or insulin. The degree of hyperglycemia is increased by concurrent administration of thiazide diuretics or furosemide. Although severe hyperglycemia has occurred only rarely, blood glucose levels should be measured in patients with diabetes and in those requiring repeated injections of diazoxide. Diabetic patients may require an adjustment in dosage of hypoglycemic drugs during therapy with diazoxide. Two cases of hyperglycemic hyperosmolar nonketoacidotic coma have been reported following repeated oral or intravenous administration of diazoxide; in one patient, the hyperosmolar coma was associated with the appearance of transient lens opacities.

Orthostatic hypotension may occur in patients treated with diazoxide and furosemide. This has been attributed to the decrease in extracellular volume induced by the diuretic. It has been recommended that the patient avoid the erect position for eight to ten hours after combined therapy. Severe hypotension and myocardial or cerebral ischemia have occurred only rarely.

Diazoxide also may cause gastrointestinal disturbances (nausea, vomiting, anorexia), headache, flushing, supraventricular tachycardia, and temporary interruption of labor. Hypersensitivity reactions (rash, leukopenia, fever) are uncommon. Extravasation causes severe local pain but tissue sloughing has not been reported.

Hypertrichosis lanuginosa is a common adverse effect that occurs after the long-term oral use of diazoxide for the management of certain juvenile hypoglycemic states. Alopecia (four cases) and hypertrichosis (one case) have been observed in the offspring of women who were given diazoxide orally during the last 19 to 60 days of pregnancy for treatment of pre-eclampsia. Hypertrichosis and alopecia have not occurred after intravenous use of diazoxide for brief periods.

USUAL DOSAGE.—*Intravenous: Adults,* 300 mg or 5 mg/kg of body weight; *children,* 5 mg/kg. The drug should be injected rapidly (within a period of 30 seconds) to ensure maximal response. A slow rate of administration may be ineffective, possibly because diazoxide is readily bound to plasma protein; the hypotensive effect appears to depend upon an high initial concentration of the drug in the free form. The injection may be repeated, if required, at intervals of one-half to 24 hours. When the blood pressure is stabilized, oral therapy with other antihypertensive agents should be substituted.

PREPARATIONS.—Hyperstat I.V. (Schering). *Injection:* Solution 15 mg/ml in 20 ml containers.

HYDRALAZINE HYDROCHLORIDE

[Apresoline Hydrochloride]

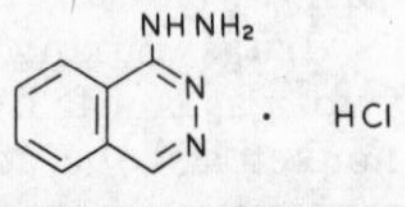

Hydralazine lowers blood pressure by acting directly on arteriolar smooth muscle. It has little effect on capacitance vessels and causes reflex stimulation of the heart; therefore, cardiac output is increased. Hydralazine is given orally for the management of chronic hypertension, preferably in conjunction with other drugs (see the Introductory Statement). When given parenterally, it is useful in hypertensive crises, particularly when an immediate reduction of blood pressure is required. The antihypertensive effect begins within 15 minutes after intravenous administration and lasts three or four hours. Hydralazine is often preferred in patients with renal impairment because it sustains (or may increase) renal blood flow.

The usefulness of hydralazine is limited by its adverse effects. Headache, tachycardia, palpitations, and gastrointestinal disturbances are common. The headache, palpitations, and tachycardia may be minimized by giving hydralazine with reserpine, guanethidine, methyldopa, a thiazide diuretic, or propranolol, and by increasing the dose gradually. The myocardial stimulation caused by hydralazine may produce anginal attacks; therefore, the drug should be used cautiously in patients with angina pectoris. Hydralazine also may cause flushing, dyspnea on exertion, rash, and, rarely, peripheral neuritis and blood dyscrasias.

Prolonged administration of large doses has produced an acute rheumatoid syndrome simulating systemic lupus erythematosus (fever, arthralgia, splenomegaly, edema, and the presence of LE cells in the peripheral blood). This response is dose related and occurs only rarely when the daily dose is below 200 mg. The effects are generally reversible when the drug is withdrawn.

USUAL DOSAGE.—

Oral: For chronic hypertension, *adults,* initially, 10 to 25 mg daily. The daily dose then may be increased by increments of 10 to 25 mg until the blood pressure is reduced to the desired level. The maximal daily dose is 200 mg, usually given in four divided doses. *Children,* initially, 0.75 mg/kg of body weight daily in four divided doses. The dosage may be increased gradually over the next three to four weeks up to 7.5 mg/kg daily.

Intravenous (slow), *Intramuscular:* For hypertensive crises, *adults,* 10 to 20 mg, increased to 40 mg if necessary. The dose should be repeated as needed. *Children,* 1.7 to 3.5 mg/kg of body weight daily divided into four to six doses. If given with reserpine, the dose may be reduced to 0.15 mg/kg every 12 to 24 hours. After the blood pressure is controlled, oral therapy should be substituted.

PREPARATIONS.—Apresoline (Ciba).

Oral: Tablets 10, 25, 50, and 100 mg.

Injection: Solution 20 mg/ml in 1 ml containers.

ADDITIONAL TRADEMARKS.—Dralzine (Lemmon), Lopress (Tutag).

SODIUM NITROPRUSSIDE

This potent vasodilator agent is preferred by some physicians for treatment of hypertensive crises when other agents have been ineffective. It acts rapidly (within two minutes) but continuous infusion is required to maintain the hypotensive effect.

Adverse reactions include transient restlessness, agitation, muscular twitching, retching, and rash. Bone marrow depression has occurred rarely.

USUAL DOSAGE.—*Intravenous: Adults,* the solution is infused at a rate of 10 to 30 drops/minute. The blood pressure should be monitored frequently while the drip rate is initially established and every five minutes thereafter. If used continuously, a fresh solution must be prepared every 12 hours. The solution should be protected from light. After the blood pressure is controlled, oral therapy with other antihypertensive agents should be substituted.

PREPARATIONS.—Sodium Nitroprusside. No single-entity pharmaceutical dosage form available. A solution must be prepared by the hospital pharmacy (60 mg of sodium nitroprusside per liter of 5% dextrose injection).

GANGLIONIC BLOCKING AGENTS

Ganglionic blocking agents are useful in treating hypertensive crises when an immediate reduction in blood pressure is required. They are of limited value in the long-term management of chronic hypertension because of their untoward effects: severe orthostatic hypotension (due to blockade of sympathetic ganglia), adynamic ileus, and urinary retention (due to blockade of parasympathetic ganglia).

MECAMYLAMINE HYDROCHLORIDE
[Inversine Hydrochloride]

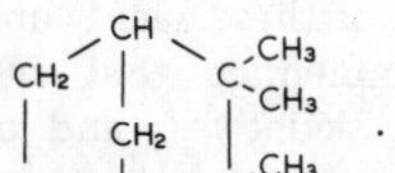

Mecamylamine is used orally to treat moderately severe to severe hypertension. It is not a preferred drug because of the availability of guanethidine, which has an equivalent antihypertensive action but causes fewer untoward effects. However, since mecamylamine reduces peristalsis, it is a useful addition to a thiazide-guanethidine regimen in patients who experience persistent diarrhea with guanethidine.

Adynamic ileus is the most dangerous adverse effect of this long-acting ganglionic blocking drug. It is most likely to occur when excretion of the drug is delayed because of impaired renal function; therefore, mecamylamine should be used cautiously in patients with renal impairment and is contraindicated in those with severe uremia. Other serious adverse effects are orthostatic hypotension and urinary retention. The patient should be warned that weakness and faintness may occur when standing, particularly immediately after arising. Mecamylamine readily crosses the blood-brain barrier and large doses have occasionally caused mental disturbances, convulsions, choreiform movements, and tremor.

USUAL DOSAGE.—*Oral: Adults,* initially, 2.5 mg twice daily. The dose may be increased by increments of 2.5 mg at intervals of not less than two days until the desired response is obtained or until adverse effects become incapacitating. A very small increase in the dose may make the difference between tolerable and intolerable untoward effects.

PREPARATIONS.—Inversine Hydrochloride (Merck Sharp & Dohme). *Oral:* Tablets 2.5 and 10 mg.

TRIMETHAPHAN CAMSYLATE [Arfonad]

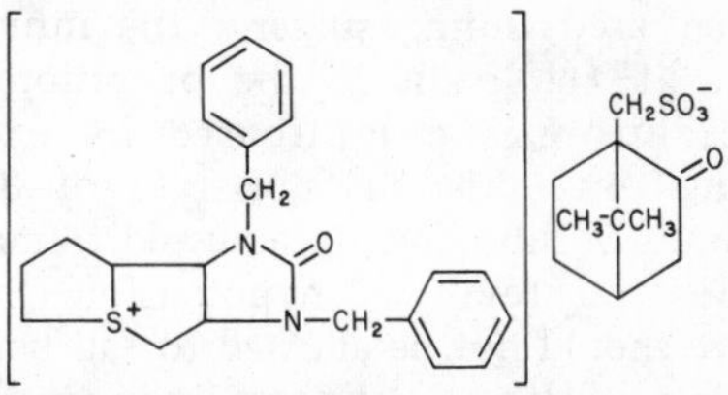

This short-acting ganglionic blocking drug is administered intravenously in hypertensive crises requiring immediate reduction of blood pressure. It has been found particularly useful for the initial control of blood pressure in patients with acute dissecting aneurysms of the aorta. Trimethaphan also is used to produce controlled hypotension for short periods in order to avoid excessive blood loss during neurosurgery and in some cardiovascular operations. In addition to ganglionic blocking properties, trimethaphan has a direct vasodilating action that increases the hypotensive response.

Continuous infusion is necessary to maintain the antihypertensive effect. The blood pressure should be monitored frequently while the rate of administration is initially established and every five minutes thereafter. The hypotensive effect of ganglionic blocking agents is largely dependent upon posture; if the blood pressure fails to drop sufficiently with the patient in the supine position, the head of the bed should be elevated on four- to six-inch blocks. The patient may become refractory to trimethaphan within 48 hours after initiation of therapy.

Trimethaphan may cause urinary retention and orthostatic hypotension, and may precipitate anginal attacks in patients with angina pectoris. Adynamic ileus is not a problem because of the short action of this drug. Other adverse effects include anorexia, nausea, vomiting, dryness of the mouth, mydriasis, and cycloplegia.

USUAL DOSAGE.—*Intravenous: Adults,* trimethaphan is administered by continuous intravenous infusion as a 0.1% solution (1 mg/ml) in 5% dextrose injection. The rate of infusion is determined by the response of the patient.

In hypertensive crises, the infusion may be started at a rate of 0.5 to 1 mg/minute and increased gradually until the blood pressure falls 20 mm Hg or more. After several minutes, the rate can again be increased until the desired level of blood pressure is achieved. Generally, systolic blood pressure should not be allowed to fall below two-thirds of the usual pressure.

When used during surgery, the infusion is begun at the point in the operation when visualization is complicated by excessive bleeding. An initial infusion rate of 3 to 4 mg/minute is subsequently adjusted to maintain the desired level of hypotension. Systolic pressure should not be allowed to fall below 60 mm Hg. When surgery is completed, administration of the drug should be discontinued gradually.

PREPARATIONS.—Arfonad (Roche). *Injection:* Solution 50 mg/ml in 10 ml containers.

MONOAMINE OXIDASE INHIBITORS

Monoamine oxidase inhibitors have a hypotensive effect (predominantly postural) which appears after several weeks of daily administration. There has been no completely satisfactory explanation of their mechanism of action; production of a false transmitter has been the most commonly accepted theory. All monoamine oxidase inhibitors appear to have similar cardiovascular effects, but pargyline is the only one that was introduced specifically as an antihypertensive agent.

PARGYLINE HYDROCHLORIDE [Eutonyl]

$C_6H_5{-}CH_2N(CH_3){-}CH_2C{\equiv}CH \cdot HCl$

This nonhydrazine monoamine oxidase inhibitor is used in the treatment of moderately severe to severe hypertension. Its antihypertensive effect is approximately equal to that of guanethidine and is enhanced by the concomitant administration of a thiazide diuretic. The usefulness of pargyline is greatly limited, however, by its potential adverse reactions. This drug should be reserved for patients who respond poorly to other regimens and who clearly benefit from its use.

The major disadvantage of pargyline derives from possible interactions with other agents. Severe hypertensive crises, occasionally fatal, have occurred as a result of the interaction between monoamine oxidase inhibitors and adrenergic drugs (eg, amphetamines, ephedrine). Hypertensive crises have also occurred when patients receiving monoamine oxidase inhibitors have ingested foods containing pressor amines, particularly tyramine (eg, certain cheeses, wine, beer, chicken livers, pickled herring, broad beans). Reserpine should not be given parenterally to patients receiving pargyline because the sudden release of catecholamines could cause a severe hypertensive reaction. Monoamine oxidase inhibitors also may interact with imipramine or related antidepressants (causing hyperpyrexia and circulatory failure) and with methyldopa or dopamine (resulting in hyperexcitability). Monoamine oxidase inhibitors have prolonged effects; therefore, pargyline should be discontinued at least two weeks before any of these agents are used. It has also been recommended that antihistamines, strong analgesics, sedatives, and other central nervous system depressants should be used cautiously with pargyline.

Pargyline causes orthostatic hypotension, and patients should be warned that weakness and faintness may occur, particularly immediately after arising. Like other monoamine oxidase inhibitors, pargyline has pronounced effects on the central nervous system. Euphoria, insomnia, nightmares, and, occasionally, psychotic reactions may occur. Other adverse effects include sodium and water retention and gastrointestinal disturbances.

USUAL DOSAGE.—*Oral: Adults,* initially, 25 mg once daily. The dosage may be increased once a week by 10 mg increments until the desired response is obtained. In patients over 65 years of age and in those who have undergone sympathectomy, the initial daily dose is 10 to 25 mg. Dosage for *children under 12 years of age* has not been established because experience in this age group is limited.

PREPARATIONS.—Eutonyl (Abbott). *Oral:* Tablets 10, 25, and 50 mg.

VERATRUM ALKALOIDS

These agents cause reflex hypotension and

bradycardia by stimulating pressor receptors in the carotid sinus area and in the heart. The veratrum alkaloids are available in oral form for the management of chronic hypertension and as a parenteral solution for treating hypertensive crises. However, they are rarely used today because of the narrow margin between the therapeutic and the toxic dose and because equally or more effective agents are available.

The most common adverse effects of the veratrum alkaloids are nausea and vomiting. These agents also may cause epigastric distress, hiccup, salivation, hyperhidrosis, blurred vision, paresthesias, excessive hypotension, and bradycardia.

Available preparations are:

Alkavervir:

Veriloid (Riker). *Oral:* Tablets 2 and 3 mg.

Cryptenamine Acetates:

Unitensen Aqueous (Mallinckrodt). *Injection:* Solution 2 mg/ml in 5 ml containers.

Cryptenamine Tannates:

Unitensen (Mallinckrodt). *Oral:* Tablets 2 mg.

Protoveratrines A and B:

Veralba (Dow). *Oral:* Tablets 0.2 mg.

Veratrum Viride:

Vertavis (Mallinckrodt). *Oral:* Tablets 130 C.S.R. units.

MIXTURES

In order to maintain an effective reduction in blood pressure, the concomitant use of two or three antihypertensive agents may be necessary. The place of mixtures in antihypertensive therapy depends upon the requirements of the patient. Although a combination product offers the patient the convenience of taking a single tablet instead of two or three, the fixed ratio of drugs prevents the adjustment of each component to fit the needs of each patient. Thus, increasing the dose of a combination product to supply an increased need of one of the components may result in excessive doses of the other component(s).

Therapy should never be initiated with a fixed-ratio mixture; instead, the dosage of each antihypertensive agent should be determined separately. Some patients may not require more than a single agent. Additional agents should be added to the regimen one at a time, and only if needed. When satisfactory results are obtained from concomitant use of two or more drugs, a mixture may be substituted only if it contains nearly the same proportions of drugs that were found to be optimal.

All of the adverse reactions associated with each individual component of a mixture can occur when the drug is present in a mixture. Therefore, the physician using a mixture must be familiar with the undesirable effects produced by each of the components. For information on adverse reactions, see the Introductory Statement and the individual evaluations.

PREPARATIONS CONTAINING AN ORAL DIURETIC AND A RAUWOLFIA ALKALOID

A number of combination products are available that contain a thiazide or related agent and a rauwolfia derivative. These mixtures are useful if the dosage ratio meets the optimal requirements of the patient.

USUAL DOSAGE.—The dosage depends upon the requirements of the patient as determined previously by use of the individual drugs separately.

PREPARATIONS.—

Diupres-250, Diupres-500 (Merck Sharp & Dohme). *Oral:* Each tablet contains chlorothiazide 250 or 500 mg and reserpine 0.125 mg.

Enduronyl (Abbott). *Oral:* Each tablet contains methyclothiazide 5 mg and deserpidine 0.25 or 0.5 (Forte) mg.

Exna-R (Robins). *Oral:* Each tablet contains benzthiazide 50 mg and reserpine 0.125 mg.

Hydromox R (Lederle). *Oral:* Each tablet contains quinethazone 50 mg and reserpine 0.125 mg.

Hydropres-25, Hydropres-50 (Merck Sharp & Dohme). *Oral:* Each tablet contains hydrochlorothiazide 25 or 50 mg and reserpine 0.125 mg.

Metatensin (Lakeside). *Oral:* Each tablet contains trichlormethiazide 2 or 4 mg and reserpine 0.1 mg.

Naquival (Schering). *Oral:* Each tablet contains trichlormethiazide 4 mg and reserpine 0.1 mg.

Oreticyl (Abbott). *Oral:* Each tablet contains hydrochlorothiazide 25 mg and deserpidine 0.125 mg (Oreticyl 25); hydrochlorothiazide 50 mg and deserpidine 0.125 mg (Oreticyl 50); hydrochlorothiazide 25 mg and deserpidine 0.25 mg (Oreticyl Forte).

Rauzide (Squibb). *Oral:* Each tablet contains bendroflumethiazide 4 mg and rauwolfia serpentina 50 mg.

Regroton (USV). *Oral:* Each tablet contains chlorthalidone 50 mg and reserpine 0.25 mg.

Renese-R (Pfizer). *Oral:* Each tablet contains polythiazide 2 mg and reserpine 0.25 mg.

Serpasil-Esidrix No. 1, No. 2 (Ciba). *Oral:* Each tablet contains hydrochlorothiazide 25 mg (No. 1) or 50 mg (No. 2) and reserpine 0.1 mg.

Singoserp-Esidrix No. 1, No. 2 (Ciba). *Oral:* Each tablet contains hydrochlorothiazide 25 mg and syrosingopine 0.5 (No. 1) or 1 mg (No. 2).

PREPARATIONS CONTAINING A THIAZIDE AND OTHER ANTIHYPERTENSIVE AGENTS

Another type of mixture combines a thiazide diuretic with an antihypertensive agent other than a rauwolfia derivative. The use of mixtures composed of a thiazide plus either methyldopa or guanethidine is not advisable because of the wide variation in the effective doses of both of these latter drugs. Successful regulation of blood pressure with these agents, particularly with guanethidine, requires careful adjustment of dosage. The effective dose of methyldopa may vary between 500 mg and 2 g daily and of guanethidine between 10 and 300 mg daily. In addition, an adjustment of dose is required from time to time during the course of continuous therapy. These considerations make such fixed-dose combinations impractical and undesirable. Thiazides also are available in fixed-dose combination with pargyline. However, pargyline is not a preferred drug for treating hypertension, either alone or in combination with a diuretic.

Mixtures containing a thiazide and potassium-sparing diuretics, hydralazine, or veratrum alkaloids are discussed in the following evaluations.

PREPARATIONS.—

Aldoclor-150, Aldoclor-250 (Merck Sharp & Dohme). *Oral:* Each tablet contains methyldopa 250 mg and chlorothiazide 150 or 250 mg.

Aldoril-15, Aldoril-25 (Merck Sharp & Dohme). *Oral:* Each tablet contains methyldopa 250 mg and hydrochlorothiazide 15 or 25 mg.

Esimil (Ciba). *Oral:* Each tablet contains guanethidine monosulfate 10 mg and hydrochlorothiazide 25 mg.

Eutron (Abbott). *Oral:* Each tablet contains pargyline hydrochloride 25 mg and methyclothiazide 5 mg.

MIXTURES CONTAINING A THIAZIDE AND A POTASSIUM-SPARING DIURETIC

The potassium-sparing diuretics, spironolactone and triamterene, are often given with thiazides to prevent or minimize hypokalemia. These agents are available in fixed-dose combination with a thiazide [Aldactazide, Dyazide]. The combination products are useful if the dosage ratio meets the needs of the patient.

USUAL DOSAGE.—

Aldactazide:

Oral: Adults, initially, two to four tablets daily in divided doses. The dosage should then be adjusted according to the response of the patient.

Dyazide:

Oral: Adults, initially, 50 mg twice daily. The dosage should then be adjusted according to the response of the patient.

PREPARATIONS.—

Aldactazide (Searle). *Oral:* Each tablet contains spironolactone 25 mg and hydrochlorothiazide 25 mg.

Dyazide (Smith Kline & French). *Oral:* Each capsule contains triamterene 50 mg and hydrochlorothiazide 25 mg.

PREPARATIONS CONTAINING HYDRALAZINE AND OTHER ANTIHYPERTENSIVE AGENTS

Mixtures containing hydralazine and either a thiazide or reserpine may be useful if the dosage ratio meets the optimal requirements of the patient as determined by prior use of the drugs individually. A mixture containing all three agents presents greater difficulty in manipulating doses. Although hydralazine, a thiazide, and reserpine are often effective in combination, each should be added one at a time in order to judge the effect of each component and to adjust the dose to achieve the optimal response. After the need for all three agents and their optimal doses have been determined, it is often preferable to substitute a diuretic-reserpine combination tablet with the hydralazine prescribed separately.

PREPARATIONS.—

Apresoline-Esidrix (Ciba). *Oral:* Each tablet contains hydralazine hydrochloride 25 mg and hydrochlorothiazide 15 mg.

Dralserp (Lemmon). *Oral:* Each tablet contains hydralazine hydrochloride 25 mg and reserpine 0.1 mg.

Ser-Ap-Es (Ciba). *Oral:* Each tablet contains hydralazine hydrochloride 25 mg, hydrochlorothiazide 15 mg, and reserpine 0.1 mg.

Serpasil-Apresoline No. 1 and No. 2 (Ciba). *Oral:* Each No. 1 tablet contains hydralazine hydrochloride 25 mg and reserpine 0.1 mg; each No. 2 tablet contains hydralazine hydrochloride 50 mg and reserpine 0.2 mg.

PREPARATIONS CONTAINING A VERATRUM ALKALOID AND OTHER ANTIHYPERTENSIVE AGENTS

The dosage of the veratrum alkaloids must be adjusted carefully because of the narrow margin between therapeutic and toxic doses. For this reason, the use of fixed-dose combinations containing veratrum alkaloids is not advisable.

PREPARATIONS.—

Diutensen (Mallinckrodt). *Oral:* Each tablet contains methyclothiazide 2.5 mg and cryptenamine tannates 2 mg.

Diutensen-R (Mallinckrodt). *Oral:* Each tablet contains methyclothiazide 2.5 mg, cryptenamine tannates 1 mg, and reserpine 0.1 mg.

Protalba-R (Dow). *Oral:* Each tablet contains reserpine 0.08 mg and protoveratrine A 0.2 mg.

Rauvera (Dorsey). *Oral:* Each tablet contains alseroxylon 1 mg and alkavervir 3 mg.

Rauwiloid + Veriloid (Riker). *Oral:* Each tablet contains alseroxylon 1 mg and alkavervir 3 mg.

Salutensin (Bristol). *Oral:* Each tablet contains reserpine 0.125 mg, hydroflumethiazide 50 mg, and protoveratrine A 0.2 mg.

Unitensen-R (Mallinckrodt). *Oral:* Each tablet contains reserpine 0.1 mg and cryptenamine tannates 1 mg.

Veralba-R (Dow). *Oral:* Each tablet contains reserpine 0.08 mg and protoveratrines A and B 0.4 mg.

Vertina (Elder). *Oral:* Each tablet contains rauwolfia serpentina 50 mg and veratrum viride extract 1.1 mg.

PREPARATIONS CONTAINING AN ANTIHYPERTENSIVE AGENT AND A BARBITURATE

Mixtures containing a barbiturate have no place in antihypertensive therapy. Barbiturates are not effective in lowering blood pressure except when given in hypnotic doses. If sedation is necessary for a tense or anxious patient, a barbiturate or antianxiety agent should be given separately in the required dosage.

PREPARATIONS.—

Besertal (Central). *Oral:* Each tablet contains reserpine 0.0625 mg, phenobarbital 15 mg, and thiamine hydrochloride 5 mg.

Butiserpazide (McNeil). *Oral:* Each tablet contains reserpine 0.1 mg, hydrochlorothiazide 25 or 50 mg, and butabarbital 30 mg.

Butiserpine (McNeil). *Oral:* Each tablet contains reserpine 0.1 mg and butabarbital sodium 15 mg; each tablet (timed-release) contains reserpine 0.2 mg and butabarbital sodium 30 mg.

Butizide (McNeil). *Oral:* Each tablet contains hydrochlorothiazide 25 or 50 mg and butabarbital 30 mg.

Harmonyl-N (Abbott). *Oral:* Each tablet contains deserpidine 0.25 mg and pentobarbital calcium 30 mg.

Nembu-Serpin (Abbott). *Oral:* Each tablet contains reserpine 0.25 mg and pentobarbital calcium 30 mg.

Neo-Slowten (Smith, Miller & Patch). *Oral:* Each tablet contains reserpine 0.1 mg, phenobarbital 16.2 mg, and thiamine hydrochloride 5 mg.

Theobarb-R (Mallinckrodt). *Oral:* Each tablet contains reserpine 0.1 mg, phenobarbital 10 mg, and theobromine 324 mg.

Theominal R.S. (Winthrop). *Oral:* Each tablet contains alseroxylon 1.5 mg, phenobarbital 10 mg, and theobromine 320 mg.

Unitensen-Phen (Mallinckrodt). *Oral:* Each tablet contains cryptenamine tannates 1 mg and phenobarbital 15 mg.

Veratrite (Mallinckrodt). *Oral:* Each tablet contains cryptenamine tannates 40 C.S.R. units, phenobarbital 16.2 mg, and sodium nitrite 65 mg.

Vertavis-Phen (Mallinckrodt). *Oral:* Each tablet contains veratrum viride 130 C.S.R. units and phenobarbital 16.2 mg.

PREPARATIONS CONTAINING ANTIHYPERTENSIVE AGENTS AND POTASSIUM CHLORIDE

Mixtures containing a combination of potassium chloride with antihypertensive drugs should not be used because of the occurrence of small bowel ulcerations from enteric-coated preparations containing potassium chloride. If supplemental potassium is necessary, the use of a liquid preparation of potassium chloride is preferable. (See also Chapter 7, Diuretics.)

PREPARATIONS.—

Naturetin $\bar{c}$ K (Squibb). *Oral:* Each tablet contains bendroflumethiazide 2.5 or 5 mg and potassium chloride 500 mg.

Rautrax (Squibb). *Oral:* Each tablet contains rauwolfia serpentina 50 mg, flumethiazide 400 mg, and potassium chloride 400 mg.

Rautrax-N (Squibb). *Oral:* Each tablet

contains rauwolfia serpentina 50 mg, bendroflumethiazide 4 mg, and potassium chloride 400 mg.

Rautrax-N Modified (Squibb). *Oral:* Each tablet contains rauwolfia serpentina 50 mg, bendroflumethiazide 2 mg, and potassium chloride 400 mg.

Miscellaneous Mixtures

These miscellaneous mixtures contain components that, if needed, should be given separately in the required dosage. These combinations contain ingredients that are not appropriate for antihypertensive therapy.

Maxitate w/Rauwolfia Compound (Pennwalt): Each tablet contains rauwolfia serpentina 30 mg and mannitol hexanitrate 30 mg.

Nyomin (Elder): Each tablet contains veratrum viride 24 mg, sodium nitrate 30 mg, potassium nitrate 150 mg, nitroglycerin 0.25 mg, and aconite root 24 mg.

Pentoxylon (Riker): Each tablet contains alseroxylon 0.5 mg and pentaerythritol tetranitrate 10 mg.

Ruhexatal w/Reserpine (Lemmon): Each tablet contains reserpine 0.1 mg, mannitol hexanitrate 30 mg, and ascorbic acid 10 mg.

Sandril c̄ Pyronil (Lilly): Each tablet contains reserpine 0.25 mg and pyrrobutamine 7.5 mg.

Chapter 7

DIURETICS

Diuretics are used to reduce the volume of extracellular fluid and to prevent or eliminate edema. They act by enhancing the urinary excretion of sodium and water, usually by inhibiting reabsorption of sodium in the renal tubules. The resulting diuresis is influenced by the site of action of the drug in the nephron (proximal tubule, loop of Henle, distal tubule) and by hormonal regulatory mechanisms which enhance the reabsorption of sodium.

The diuretics may be classified into the following six groups, listed according to their order of introduction: xanthines, osmotically active agents, mercurial compounds, carbonic anhydrase inhibitors, thiazides and related compounds, and a group of chemically unrelated agents.

XANTHINES

Caffeine, theobromine, and theophylline belong in this class. However, only the soluble salt of theophylline, aminophylline (theophylline ethylenediamine), has current limited usefulness as a diuretic.

AMINOPHYLLINE

Aminophylline is occasionally used as a diuretic, but generally it has been superseded for this purpose by newer, orally effective drugs. The drug produces a significant diuretic effect only when given intravenously. In the past, it was used to supplement mercurial diuretics in patients with refractory congestive heart failure.

For other uses, see Chapter 3, Antianginal Agents, and Chapter 41, Bronchodilators.

Reactions ranging from dizziness, faintness, and palpitation to hypotension, syncope, and sudden death have been reported, especially following rapid intravenous injection.

USUAL DOSAGE.—*Intravenous: Adults,* as diuretic, 250 to 500 mg up to three times daily.

PREPARATIONS.—Aminophylline, U.S.P. Drug marketed by many manufacturers under generic name.

OSMOTIC DIURETICS

Urea [Ureaphil, Urevert] and mannitol [Osmitrol], given intravenously, have an osmotic effect. These agents appear in the glomerular filtrate, remain in the tubular fluid, and limit the reabsorption of sodium.

To produce equivalent diuresis, it is necessary to inject a larger volume of mannitol than urea; this added volume is a disadvantage in patients with congestive heart failure. However, mannitol is less irritating, less likely to cause thrombophlebitis, and does not cause tissue necrosis following accidental extravasation. Thus, in general, mannitol is preferred over urea, particularly when renal failure may be present.

Osmotic agents have been used to prevent and treat oliguria which is sometimes associated with surgery, burns, and other trauma, and to reduce cerebral edema associated with increased intracranial pressure. They also have been used to reduce intraocular pressure in acute glaucoma, although orally administered glycerin is safer and usually adequate for this purpose (see Chapter 69, Agents Used to Treat Glaucoma). Mannitol has been specifically recommended for induction of diuresis in certain drug intoxications and in edema and ascites of nephrotic or cirrhotic origin. Although osmotic diuretics have been suggested for treatment of cardiac edema, the indication is of dubious validity since heart failure is, in effect, a contraindication for this form of therapy.

Urea and mannitol formerly were used to measure the glomerular filtration rate, but more accurate results can be obtained with other drugs. (See Chapter 77, Miscellaneous Diagnostic Aids.)

Adverse reactions occur after rapid intravenous infusion, administration of a large total volume, or both. For a detailed discussion, see the evaluations on Urea and Mannitol.

UREA [Ureaphil, Urevert]

$$\begin{array}{c} NH_2 \\ | \\ C{=}O \\ | \\ NH_2 \end{array}$$

In the past, this drug was administered orally to treat edema accompanying cardiac failure. It is rarely used for this purpose today because large doses are required, its taste is unpleasant, and, compared to newer agents, it is relatively ineffective in removing sodium and water.

Urea is presently given intravenously to temporarily reduce intracranial or cerebrospinal pressure in the control of cerebral edema. It is also used to reduce intraocular pressure, but orally administered glycerin is safer and usually satisfactory for this purpose (see also Chapter 69, Agents Used to Treat Glaucoma). Urea is being used experimentally in the treatment of sickle cell anemia.

Headache, nausea, vomiting, syncope, disorientation, and transient agitated confusion have occurred during infusion of urea. Electrolyte depletion resulting in hyponatremia or hypokalemia also can occur; therefore, early signs of depletion such as muscle weakness or lethargy should be noted. Extravasation of urea can cause local reactions ranging from irritation to necrosis. Phlebitis and thrombosis near the injection site have been observed infrequently. Urea should not be infused into the veins of the lower extremities because superficial and deep thrombosis may occur.

Urea should be used cautiously in patients with cardiac, hepatic, or renal disease. It is contraindicated in patients with severely impaired renal function, liver failure, active intracranial bleeding, or dehydration, and its use is never justified in the presence of elevated blood urea nitrogen or creatinine values.

USUAL DOSAGE.—*Intravenous:* To avoid hemolysis, the rate of infusion should not exceed 4 ml/minute of a 30% solution and the drug should never be mixed with blood in a transfusion set. Urea for injection is prepared by adding an appropriate volume of 5% or 10% dextrose injection or 10% invert sugar in water. Solutions can be stored safely in the refrigerator for no more than 48 hours after preparation.

To prepare 135 ml of a 30% solution of urea for injection, the contents of one 40 g vial are mixed with 105 ml of diluent. Each milliliter of 30% solution provides 300 mg of urea (7.5 g/25 ml).

To reduce intracranial or intraocular pressure, *adults*, 1 to 1.5 g (3.3 to 5 ml of 30% solution)/kg of body weight. *Children*, 0.5 to 1.5 g/kg; *children under 2 years of age*, as little as 100 mg/kg has been used.

PREPARATIONS.—

Ureaphil (Abbott). *Injection:* Powder (for solution) 40 g with citric acid buffer 1 g in 250 ml containers.

Urevert (Travenol). *Injection:* Powder (for solution) 40 and 90 g with 93 and 210 ml of invert sugar solution diluent, respectively.

MANNITOL [Osmitrol]

$$HOCH_2CH(OH){-}CH(OH){-}CH(OH){-}CH(OH)CH_2OH$$

Mannitol is primarily used as an adjunct in the prevention or treatment of oliguria and anuria associated with major surgery. It is also used pre- and postoperatively to reduce intraocular pressure in the surgical management of glaucomatous patients and as an adjunct to eye surgery in nonglaucomatous patients. (See Chapter 69, Agents Used to Treat Glaucoma.) Nondiuretic uses of mannitol include its employment as an irrigating fluid during transurethral prostate resection and as a test for renal function. (See Chapter 77, Miscellaneous Diagnostic Aids.)

Serious adverse reactions are uncommon if recommended doses are not exceeded. During infusion, transient headache, nausea, chills, thirst, slight dizziness, and subjective sensations of constriction or pain in the chest have been observed after doses of 1 to 3 g/kg of body weight. Clinical signs resembling water intoxication with tremors and convulsions have occurred in critically ill patients who received more than 200 g in an eight-hour period. Transient pulmonary congestion, probably caused by an increase in plasma volume, has been reported with large doses (400 to 440 g).

Mannitol must be administered slowly, since rapid administration of large amounts will draw intracellular water into the extracellular space and cause cellular dehydration, hyponatremia, and overexpansion of the intravascular space (pulmonary edema, congestive heart failure).

Care should be taken to avoid extravasation. Fluid and electrolyte balance, urinary volume, and vital signs must be monitored, particularly in severely ill patients or in those receiving more than the recommended dosage of 100 g in 24 hours. Hyponatremia may be prevented by administering 0.45% sodium chloride injection with the mannitol, unless the patient retains sodium or is being treated for fluid retention. When mannitol is used as an adjunct in the treatment of oliguria, hydration must be restored and hypotension corrected. Hypertonic solutions of mannitol should never be mixed with blood, because increased osmotic pressure will cause crenation and agglutination of red blood cells.

Mannitol is contraindicated in patients with severely impaired renal function who fail to respond to a test dose of 200 mg/kg of body weight. This drug also is contraindicated in patients with congestive heart failure when the test dose causes any manifestations of increased congestion or pulmonary edema. The safety of infusion during pregnancy has not been determined.

USUAL DOSAGE.—*Intravenous:* As a diagnostic test or an adjunct in the management of oliguria and anuria, *adults,* initially, a test dose of 200 mg/kg of body weight is given. A satisfactory response is indicated by the excretion of 40 ml of urine/hour over a two- to three-hour period. If there is no response, the injection is stopped and the patient's condition is reevaluated before continuing therapy. Otherwise, hydration with appropriate fluid is then continued and up to 100 g of mannitol as a 10%, 15%, or 20% solution may be given in divided doses every 24 hours to maintain the urine flow at approximately 100 ml/hour.

For reduction of intraocular pressure, *adults,* 1.5 to 2.0 g/kg as a 20% solution (7.5 to 10 ml/kg) given over a 30-minute period. If used preoperatively, the dose should be given one to one and one-half hours before surgery to obtain maximal reduction of intraocular pressure.

PREPARATIONS.—

Osmitrol (Travenol). *Injection:* Solution (aqueous) 5% in 1,000 ml containers, 10% in 500 and 1,000 ml containers, 15% in 150 and 500 ml containers, 20% in 250 and 500 ml containers; 5% (in 0.3% sodium chloride injection) in 1,000 ml containers; 10% (in 0.3% sodium chloride injection) in 1,000 ml containers; 15% and 20% (in 0.45% sodium chloride injection) in 500 ml containers.

Mannitol I.V. (Abbott). *Injection:* Solution 5% and 10% in 1,000 ml containers, 15% and 20% in 500 ml containers.

Mannitol (Cutter). *Injection:* Solution 5% and 10% (in 0.45% sodium chloride injection) in 1,000 ml containers; 15% (in 0.45% sodium chloride injection) in 500 ml containers; 10% in 1,000 ml containers; 15% and 20% in 500 ml containers.

Mannitol (Merck Sharp & Dohme). *Injection:* Solution 25% in 50 ml containers.

Drug also marketed by other manufacturers under generic name.

MERCURIAL COMPOUNDS

The organomercurials act by depressing the renal tubular reabsorption of sodium, chloride, and water. They are administered either orally or parenterally primarily for the treatment of congestive heart failure. The oral mercurial compounds are far less effective than either the parenteral preparations or oral thiazides. Parenteral preparations are usually administered intramuscularly or subcutaneously. They also are effective when given by *slow* intravenous injection; when injected rapidly, they occasionally produce severe systemic reactions, acute tubular necrosis, and sudden death.

Adverse Reactions and Precautions

In sensitive patients, mercurial compounds can cause stomatitis, gastric distress, vertigo, fever, and rash; therefore, small doses should be given to determine sensitivity before full therapeutic doses are administered. When mercurial diuretics are given frequently and produce a pronounced diuresis, hyponatremia with asthenia, leg cramps, and drowsiness may develop. Hypokalemia occurs less frequently than with thiazides. Metabolic alkalosis also may occur and may limit the patient's response to the diuretic. Response may be restored by giving appropriate doses of ammonium chloride, *L*-lysine monohydrochloride, or acetazolamide [Diamox].

Therapy should be discontinued if severe gastric disturbances, vertigo, fever, cutaneous reactions, or electrolyte imbalances develop. These agents are contraindicated in patients with acute nephritis or acute renal failure.

CHLORMERODRIN [Neohydrin]

This oral mercurial diuretic has been replaced by newer, more effective nonmercurial agents.

USUAL DOSAGE.—The manufacturer's

suggested dosage is: *Oral: Adults*, 18.3 to 36.6 mg once daily; this dose may be administered up to three times daily when more intensive therapy is required.

PREPARATIONS.—Neohydrin (Lakeside). *Oral:* Tablets 18.3 mg (equivalent to 10 mg of non-ionic mercury).

MERALLURIDE SODIUM [Mercuhydrin]

$CH_2CHCH_2NHCONHCOCH_2CH_2COONa$, Hg, OCH_3, CH_3, CH_3

This parenteral mercurial diuretic produces prompt diuresis and is used in the treatment of congestive heart failure, nephrotic syndrome, or ascites associated with hepatic disorders. Meralluride should be administered at intervals of several days, since too frequent injections produce metabolic alkalosis and result in reduced response.

For adverse reactions and precautions, see the introduction to this section.

USUAL DOSAGE.—*Intramuscular, Subcutaneous: Adults*, since sensitivity may occur rarely, no more than 0.5 ml should be given initially. Thereafter, 1 to 2 ml may be administered at intervals of several days.

PREPARATIONS.—Mercuhydrin (Lakeside). *Injection:* Solution (aqueous) containing meralluride sodium 88 mg (equivalent to 39 mg of mercury) and theophylline 48 mg per milliliter in 1, 2, and 10 ml containers.

MERCAPTOMERIN SODIUM [Thiomerin]

H_3C, COONa, CH_3, CH_3, OCH_3, $CONHCH_2CHCH_2HgSCH_2COONa$

This mercurial diuretic is used parenterally to treat congestive heart failure, nephrotic syndrome, or ascites associated with hepatic disorders. For adverse reactions and precautions, see the introduction to this section.

USUAL DOSAGE.—*Intramuscular, Subcutaneous: Adults*, 0.2 to 2 ml daily.

PREPARATIONS.—Thiomerin (Wyeth). *Injection:* Powder 1.4 g with 10 ml of sterile water for injection; solution 125 mg (equivalent to 40 mg of mercury)/ml in 1, 2, 10, and 30 ml containers.

Similar Drugs

Mercurophylline

Merethoxylline Procaine (Dicurin Procaine [Lilly]): Each milliliter of solution contains procaine 100 mg and theophylline 50 mg.

Mersalyl and Theophylline (Salyrgan-Theophylline [Winthrop]): Each milliliter of solution contains mersalyl 100 mg and theophylline 50 mg.

CARBONIC ANHYDRASE INHIBITORS

Following the observation in 1949 that large doses of sulfanilamide produced diuresis in edematous patients with congestive heart failure, and the recognition that the diuresis resulted from the inhibition of carbonic anhydrase in the renal tubules, acetazolamide [Diamox], the first orally administered sulfonamide diuretic, was introduced. This drug and its analogues (ethoxzolamide [Cardrase], methazolamide [Neptazane]) are of limited value, however, because tolerance to their diuretic effects develops rapidly when they are administered for longer than 48 hours. The analogues differ from acetazolamide only in dose and duration of action.

For indications, adverse reactions, and precautions, see the following evaluation on Acetazolamide.

ACETAZOLAMIDE [Diamox]
ACETAZOLAMIDE SODIUM [Diamox Parenteral]

$CH_3C(=O)$-NH-C, N—N, C-SO_2-NH_2, S

Acetazolamide was used briefly as an oral diuretic, but because tolerance and renal tubular acidosis develop rapidly with oral administration, its use has been superseded by the thiazides. Since this drug has a tendency to produce metabolic acidosis, acetazolamide has been given with mercurial compounds to potentiate or restore their effect or to reverse the metabolic alkalosis produced by these agents. It also has been used in congestive heart failure associated with cor pulmonale and respiratory acidosis. It is given in the long-term treatment of primary open-angle glaucoma, for the short-term preoperative management of acute angle-closure glaucoma, and as a supplemental agent in epilepsy (see Chapter 31,

Anticonvulsants, and Chapter 69, Agents Used to Treat Glaucoma).

Acetazolamide seldom causes serious adverse reactions; those that do occur are generally transient, since the drug is excreted rapidly. The most common untoward effects are drowsiness and paresthesias of the face and extremities. Fatigue, excitement, and gastrointestinal disturbances have been observed less frequently. Episodes of disorientation may occur in patients with hepatic cirrhosis. Like other sulfonamide derivatives, acetazolamide may produce bone marrow depression, crystalluria, and renal calculi. Fever and allergic-type skin reactions also have been reported.

Acetazolamide is contraindicated in conditions in which sodium ions are depleted (eg, Addison's disease and other types of adrenocortical insufficiency) and in patients with acidosis.

USUAL DOSAGE.—*Oral, Intravenous: Adults,* for diuresis in patients with congestive heart failure, 250 to 375 mg once daily in the morning. Best results are obtained when acetazolamide is given on alternate days or for two days followed by one day without medication. *Children,* 5 mg/kg of body weight daily in the morning.

PREPARATIONS.—

Diamox (Lederle). *Oral:* Capsules (timed-release) 500 mg; tablets 125 and 250 mg.

Diamox Parenteral (Lederle). *Injection:* Powder (for solution) 500 mg.

THIAZIDES AND RELATED COMPOUNDS

The prototype thiazide, chlorothiazide [Diuril], was introduced in 1958. It became widely recognized as a reliable, orally effective diuretic and a number of derivatives were subsequently developed (bendroflumethiazide [Naturetin], benzthiazide [Aquatag, Diucen, Edemex, Exna, Lemazide], cyclothiazide [Anhydron], hydrochlorothiazide [Esidrix, HydroDiuril, Oretic], hydroflumethiazide [Saluron], methyclothiazide [Aquatensen Enduron], polythiazide [Renese], trichlormethiazide [Metahydrin, Naqua]), as well as two similarly acting nonthiazide agents (chlorthalidone [Hygroton], quinethazone [Hydromox]). Although modifications of the chlorothiazide structure have produced longer-acting compounds of greater potency, there is no evidence that they are more effective or safer than the prototype. The demonstrable differences among the various agents in this group involve dosage and duration of action (see the Table); in other respects, they are almost identical, and it is suggested that physicians become familiar with one or two thiazides and use these exclusively.

These related diuretics act by inhibiting the renal tubular reabsorption of sodium, which increases the urinary excretion of both sodium and water. These drugs also increase the urinary excretion of chloride, potassium, and, to a small extent, bicarbonate ions. They are rapidly absorbed from the gastrointestinal tract and diuresis lasts 6 to 72 hours, depending upon the compound used. These agents are suitable for long-term use and cause only mild adverse reactions. More effective diuretics are available for patients who do not respond adequately to the thiazides or for those with impaired renal function.

The thiazides are the drugs of choice for maintenance therapy in ambulatory patients with edema caused by chronic congestive heart failure but with normal renal function. They also have been used in patients with edema associated with nephrosis and certain types of nephritis, liver disease with ascites, pregnancy, and premenstrual tension, as well as edema induced by the administration of corticotropin, adrenal corticosteroids, and some estrogens. The thiazides are generally less effective in these conditions than in congestive heart failure.

These agents also are useful when given alone or with other drugs for the management of hypertension (see Chapter 6, Antihypertensive Agents).

Paradoxically, these diuretics are effective for palliative reduction of the polyuria of nephrogenic and neurohypophyseal diabetes insipidus; in infants and young children, they may be particularly valuable in the prevention of dehydration, fever, and other complications of these diseases. (See also Chapter 40, Antidiuretics.)

Adverse Reactions and Precautions: All thiazides and related agents cause similar adverse reactions. Because of their effects on renal function, these agents may produce electrolyte imbalances. Therefore, patients receiving prolonged thiazide therapy should be examined regularly for evidence of electrolyte imbalance (anorexia, nausea, muscular weakness, and drowsiness), and the serum sodium, potassium, chloride, and bicarbonate levels should be determined periodically. By far the most common electrolyte disturbance is hypokalemia.

THIAZIDES AND RELATED DIURETICS

Thiazides	Chemical Structure	Daily Adult Dosage Range (mg)	Duration of Action (Hours)
Chlorothiazide Diuril (Merck Sharp & Dohme)		500 to 2,000	6 to 12
Hydrochlorothiazide Esidrix (Ciba) HydroDiuril (Merck Sharp & Dohme) Oretic (Abbott)		50 to 200	6 to 12
Benzthiazide Aquatag (Tutag) Diucen (Central) Edemex (Savage) Exna (Robins) Lemazide (Lemmon)		50 to 200	12 to 18
Hydroflumethiazide Saluron (Bristol)		50 to 100	18 to 24
Bendroflumethiazide Naturetin (Squibb)		5 to 20	More than 18
Methyclothiazide Aquatensen (Mallinckrodt) Enduron (Abbott)		2.5 to 10	More than 24
Trichlormethiazide Metahydrin (Lakeside) Naqua (Schering)		2 to 4	Up to 24
Polythiazide Renese (Pfizer)		1 to 4	24 to 48
Cyclothiazide Anhydron (Lilly)		1 to 2	18 to 24
Related Compounds			
Chlorthalidone Hygroton (Geigy)		50 to 200 daily or on alternate days	24 to 72
Quinethazone Hydromox (Lederle)		50 to 200	18 to 24

Patients should be instructed to take food that is high in potassium (eg, raisins, bananas) each day. Even so, many patients may develop hypokalemia (especially those with advanced heart failure, renal disease with edema, or hepatic cirrhosis with ascites, and those receiving digitalis, corticosteroids, or corticotropin). These individuals probably require a potassium-sparing diuretic or potassium chloride solution as a daily supplement. Hypokalemia increases the tendency to develop digitalis-induced arrhythmias. Consequently, careful regulation of digitalis dosage, concomitant use of a potassium-sparing diuretic (eg, spironolactone, triamterene), or administration of potassium supplements, is often necessary in patients receiving digitalis. Patients with ischemic heart disease also may be predisposed to serious arrhythmias if hypokalemia occurs. Data presently available indicate that the sodium:potassium excretion ratio is no more favorable for one thiazide than for another.

Less frequently, thiazide therapy may produce metabolic alkalosis with hypokalemia; patients who lose additional amounts of chloride and potassium due to vomiting, diarrhea, gastrointestinal drainage, sweating, paracentesis, or potassium-depleting disorders of the kidney are especially susceptible. Potassium chloride should be administered to compensate for the deficiencies. If additional chloride is needed, ammonium chloride, sodium chloride, or *L*-lysine monohydrochloride may be used.

Occasionally, dilutional hyponatremia occurs in patients taking oral diuretics. This complication usually exists prior to diuretic therapy and is therefore not attributable to the drug. It usually is encountered in markedly edematous patients with advanced heart failure or hepatic cirrhosis who respond poorly to diuretics. The hyponatremia is a consequence of the combined effects of a disorder of water excretion and excessive intake of sodium-free solutions. Since administration of salt to patients with this condition only increases the edema, its correction depends upon improving the circulatory status, if possible, and rigidly restricting fluid intake. Other untoward effects (eg, gastrointestinal disorders, dizziness, asthenia, fatigue) may be caused by excessive diuresis. These reactions may be prevented by reducing the dose or frequency of administration.

Since these drugs enhance the renal tubular reabsorption of uric acid, they tend to produce asymptomatic hyperuricemia; the development of acute gouty arthritis is rare, except in individuals with a presumed hereditary predisposition to gout or in patients with chronic renal failure. This reaction may be combated by administering uricosuric agents (eg, probenecid [Benemid], sulfinpyrazone [Anturane]) or the xanthine oxidase inhibitor, allopurinol [Zyloprim]. Use of allopurinol is advisable if renal failure is present; probenecid is not effective in the presence of severe renal damage.

Hyperglycemia and aggravation of pre-existing diabetes mellitus have been noted occasionally and are usually reversible upon discontinuation of the drug. The hyperglycemic action should not preclude use of these drugs in diabetics.

Hypotensive episodes during surgery have been observed in some patients receiving thiazides or chlorthalidone [Hygroton].

Blood dyscrasias (leukopenia, aplastic anemia, thrombocytopenic purpura, and agranulocytosis) have been reported infrequently with the older agents but not as yet with the newer derivatives. However, because of the structural similarities of these drugs, such adverse reactions may be anticipated. Hypersensitivity reactions (eg, rash, photosensitivity) are uncommon. Necrotizing vasculitis of the skin and kidney has occurred in elderly patients, but its relationship to the thiazides is still unproved. Rarely, pancreatitis has been observed.

Since small bowel lesions consisting of stenosis with or without ulceration have occurred in patients who received a thiazide combined with potassium chloride in enteric-coated form, this type of mixture should not be used.

The thiazides should be administered cautiously in the presence of severe renal or hepatic disease, and they may be contraindicated when potassium depletion exists. Nitrogen retention following use of the thiazides often is an indication of pre-existing renal impairment. In this situation, the dosage may have to be adjusted or a more effective diuretic (eg, ethacrynic acid, furosemide) used. Patients with liver disease should be observed for signs of impending hepatic coma (eg, asterixis, confusion, drowsinesss) and the thiazides discontinued promptly if any of these signs appear.

When these diuretics are given with other potent hypotensive agents (eg, guanethidine

[Ismelin], methyldopa [Aldomet], hydralazine [Apresoline], pargyline [Eutonyl], or ganglionic blocking agents), the doses of the latter should be determined individually to prevent excessive hypotensive effects, especially orthostatic hypotension.

In elderly patients with advanced arteriosclerosis, the oral diuretics may precipitate myocardial infarction or cerebral thrombosis as a result of severe orthostatic hypotension, especially if the patient is receiving other antihypertensive agents or has undergone a sympathectomy. Since the hypotensive action of the drugs may be enhanced in these patients, the usual doses should be reduced by one-half initially and increased to full doses only if needed.

Although the thiazide diuretics may be indicated in patients with edema and toxemia of pregnancy, they should not be used indiscriminately because of possible adverse effects on the fetus and newborn infant. These hazards include their potential for causing electrolyte disturbances and neonatal thrombocytopenia. Recent reports suggest that thiazides used to treat expectant mothers with preeclampsia or eclampsia may have caused the thrombocytopenia observed in their newborn infants.

The thiazides have been reported to decrease arterial responsiveness to pressor amines (eg, levarterenol [Levophed]) and to augment the neuromuscular blocking action of tubocurarine in surgical patients. Administration of thiazides should be discontinued two to three days prior to elective surgery except in patients with severe hypertension.

USUAL DOSAGE.—Dosages are for diuresis unless otherwise specified. For doses used in hypertension, see Chapter 6, Antihypertensive Agents.

Chlorothiazide [Diuril]:

Oral: Adults, 500 mg to 1 g once or twice daily; *children,* 22 mg/kg of body weight daily in two divided doses; *infants under 6 months of age,* up to 33 mg/kg daily in two divided doses.

Chlorothiazide Sodium [Sodium Diuril]:

Intravenous: Adults, 500 mg twice daily.

Hydrochlorothiazide [Esidrix, HydroDiuril, Oretic]:

Oral: Adults, initially, 50 to 100 mg once or twice daily for several days; for maintenance, 25 to 100 mg daily or intermittently. *Children,* 2 mg/kg of body weight daily in two doses; *infants under 6 months of age,* up to 3 mg/kg daily in two doses.

Bendroflumethiazide [Naturetin]:

Oral: Adults, initially 5 mg daily, preferably in the morning; dose may be increased to 20 mg as a single dose or in two divided doses. For maintenance, 2.5 to 15 mg once daily or intermittently. *Children,* initially, up to 0.4 mg/kg of body weight daily in two divided doses. For maintenance, 0.05 to 0.1 mg/kg daily in a single dose.

Benzthiazide [Aquatag, Diucen, Edemex, Exna, Lemazide]:

Oral: Adults, initially, 50 to 200 mg daily for several days, depending upon the patient's response. For maintenance, dosage is reduced gradually to the minimal effective amount. *Children,* initially, 1 to 4 mg/kg of body weight daily divided into three doses. For maintenance, the dose is reduced as needed. For premenstrual edema, *adults,* 25 to 50 mg once or twice daily for five to seven days prior to the onset of menstruation.

Cyclothiazide [Anhydron]:

Oral: Adults, initially, 1 to 2 mg daily, preferably in the morning; for maintenance, 1 mg on alternate days or two or three times weekly. *Children,* initially, 0.02 to 0.04 mg/kg of body weight daily; for maintenance, the dose is reduced as needed.

Hydroflumethiazide [Saluron]:

Oral: Adults, initially, 50 to 100 mg daily; for maintenance, 25 to 200 mg in divided amounts depending upon the patient's response. *Children,* initially, 1 mg/kg of body weight daily; for maintenance, the dose is adjusted as needed.

Methyclothiazide [Aquatensen, Enduron]:

Oral: Adults, initially, 2.5 to 10 mg once daily; same dose range is used for maintenance. *Children,* 0.05 to 0.2 mg/kg of body weight daily.

Polythiazide [Renese]:

Oral: Adults, initially, 1 to 4 mg daily, depending upon the patient's response and severity of the condition; for maintenance, 0.5 to 8 mg daily adjusted for optimal response. *Children,* initially, 0.02 to 0.08 mg/kg of body weight daily; for maintenance, the dose is adjusted according to response.

Trichlormethiazide [Metahydrin, Naqua]:

Oral: Adults, initially, 2 to 4 mg after breakfast daily or twice daily if needed; for maintenance, 1 to 2 mg once daily. *Children,* 0.07 mg/kg of body weight daily in single or divided doses.

Chlorthalidone [Hygroton]:

Oral: Adults, initially, 50 to 100 mg after

breakfast daily, or 100 mg on alternate days or three times weekly; some patients may require a dose of 200 mg. Maintenance doses should be adjusted individually. *Children,* 2 mg/kg of body weight three times weekly; maintenance dose should be adjusted individually.

Quinethazone [Hydromox]:

Oral: Adults, 50 to 100 mg daily, depending upon the patient's response and severity of the condition. Some patients may require as much as 150 to 200 mg.

PREPARATIONS.—

Chlorothiazide:

Diuril (Merck Sharp & Dohme). *Oral:* Tablets 250 and 500 mg; suspension 250 mg/5 ml.

Chlorothiazide Sodium:

Sodium Diuril (Merck Sharp & Dohme). *Injection:* Powder 500 mg (equivalent to chlorothiazide 500 mg).

Hydrochlorothiazide:

Esidrix (Ciba), HydroDiuril (Merck Sharp & Dohme), Oretic (Abbott). *Oral:* Tablets 25 and 50 mg.

Bendroflumethiazide:

Naturetin (Squibb). *Oral:* Tablets 2.5 and 5 mg.

Benzthiazide:

Aquatag (Tutag), Lemazide (Lemmon). *Oral:* Tablets 25 and 50 mg.

Diucen (Central), Edemex (Savage), Exna (Robins). *Oral:* Tablets 50 mg.

Cyclothiazide:

Anhydron (Lilly). *Oral:* Tablets 2 mg.

Hydroflumethiazide:

Saluron (Bristol). *Oral:* Tablets 50 mg.

Methyclothiazide:

Aquatensen (Mallinckrodt). *Oral:* Tablets 5 mg.

Enduron (Abbott). *Oral:* Tablets 2.5 and 5 mg.

Polythiazide:

Renese (Pfizer). *Oral:* Tablets 1, 2, and 4 mg.

Trichlormethiazide:

Metahydrin (Lakeside), Naqua (Schering). *Oral:* Tablets 2 and 4 mg.

Chlorthalidone:

Hygroton (USV). *Oral:* Tablets 50 and 100 mg.

Quinethazone:

Hydromox (Lederle). *Oral:* Tablets 50 mg.

FUROSEMIDE AND ETHACRYNIC ACID

Furosemide [Lasix] and ethacrynic acid [Edecrin] are similar to the thiazides in their pattern of electrolyte excretion, but have five to ten times the diuretic effect. Hence, dehydration and electrolyte imbalance can occur more frequently than with the thiazide diuretics. They are effective when given orally or intravenously.

Although furosemide and ethacrynic acid are chemically distinct, they are practically identical in their pharmacologic action. Both drugs are effective orally in the control of idiopathic edema and edema associated with congestive heart failure; they are particularly useful in patients who do not respond initially to the less effective but safer diuretics. Such patients include those with chronic renal failure, nephrotic syndrome, or hepatic cirrhosis with ascites. The intravenous route may be used to obtain an immediate diuretic effect in patients with acute pulmonary edema or hypertensive crises. Furosemide also may be given intramuscularly.

The proper use of ethacrynic acid or furosemide requires an understanding and anticipation of the electrolyte and fluid derangements that they may induce. In contrast to other diuretics, both agents continue to exert a diuretic effect in the presence of electrolyte and acid-base disturbances. These drugs are often used intermittently to allow time for the natural correction of these imbalances.

ETHACRYNIC ACID [Edecrin]
ETHACRYNATE SODIUM [Sodium Edecrin]

$$CH_3CH_2C(=CH_2)C(=O)\text{-}C_6H_2Cl_2\text{-}OCH_2COOH$$

Ethacrynic acid is a potent, short-acting diuretic that is chemically unrelated to any other agent in use. Diuresis begins 30 minutes after oral administration, reaches a peak in two hours, and lasts six to eight hours. This diuretic is useful orally for control of idiopathic edema and edema associated with congestive heart failure. It is of value in patients resistant to less potent diuretics, ie, those with chronic renal failure, particularly the nephrotic syndrome, or hepatic cirrhosis with ascites. It also has been used in children with the nephrotic syndrome or congenital heart disease who do not respond to thiazides or spironolactone. Since marked diuresis occurs within minutes following intravenous administration, the parenteral form may be effective in acute pulmonary edema and as an adjunct in the management of hypertensive crises.

Untoward effects are similar to those produced by thiazides, but may be more intense because of the rapid onset of diuresis. Frequent reactions include nausea, vomiting, anorexia, and diarrhea. Hypokalemia is common with prolonged use, and large doses may cause hyponatremia and metabolic alkalosis. Hyperuricemia may occur after prolonged oral administration. Diminished glucose tolerance has been reported occasionally. Gastrointestinal hemorrhage has occurred in patients receiving ethacrynic acid intravenously. Large doses given intravenously or orally have caused vertigo, tinnitus, and reversible as well as permanent deafness, especially in patients with impaired renal function. Rashes, agranulocytosis, and thrombocytopenia have also been documented.

Ethacrynic acid must be used cautiously in elderly patients because it may cause hypovolemia that could lead to circulatory failure, thrombosis, or embolism. Hospitalization should be considered before initiating therapy in patients with hepatic cirrhosis with ascites.

The dose must be individualized. Monitoring of serum electrolyte levels is mandatory during prolonged treatment, since ethacrynic acid continues to exert an effect in the presence of electrolyte imbalances. The patient should be observed for clinical signs of hypovolemia, hyponatremia, and hypokalemia. Its use should be discontinued if increasing azotemia or oliguria is noted. Ethacrynic acid is contraindicated in the presence of anuria, hypotension, dehydration with low sodium levels, metabolic alkalosis with hypokalemia, and in women of childbearing age and nursing mothers.

USUAL DOSAGE.—

Ethacrynic Acid:

Oral: Adults, a single dose of 50 mg is given after a meal on the first day and the effects are evaluated over a 12- to 24-hour period. The dose is adjusted to reduce the weight gradually (about 0.5 to 1 kg/day). For maintenance, the minimal effective dose should be given intermittently with several consecutive drug-free days each week to avoid electrolyte imbalances. In patients with resistant edema (ie, those with cirrhosis or nephrosis) maintenance doses of up to 200 mg twice daily have been given. However, electrolyte and fluid balance must be monitored closely. *Children*, initially, 25 mg. If necessary, the dose is increased by increments of 25 mg daily until a satisfactory response is obtained; total dose should not exceed one-half the maximal daily adult dose.

Ethacrynate Sodium:

Intravenous: Adults, 50 mg or 0.5 to 1 mg/kg of body weight, injected slowly. *Children*, in an emergency, 1 mg/kg is given; this dose may be increased if necessary.

PREPARATIONS.—

Edecrin (Merck Sharp & Dohme). *Oral:* Tablets 25 and 50 mg.

Sodium Edecrin (Merck Sharp & Dohme). *Injection:* Powder 50 mg.

FUROSEMIDE [Lasix]

COOH, NHCH₂, H_2NSO_2, Cl

Furosemide is a short-acting, highly effective nonthiazide diuretic. When administered orally, onset of action occurs within one hour and lasts about six hours; with intravenous or intramuscular administration, the diuretic action is immediate and lasts two hours. It is of particular value in patients with edema associated with congestive heart failure, severe renal failure, nephrotic syndrome, or hepatic insufficiency with ascites who do not respond to or cannot tolerate other diuretics. The drug may be used intravenously or intramuscularly to obtain an immediate diuretic effect in the above conditions and in acute pulmonary edema or hypertensive crisis. Furosemide combined with sodium chloride infusion also has been used to temporarily reduce elevated serum calcium concentrations. Because of its wide dosage range, the dose can be adjusted to produce a graded effect. For use of furosemide in hypertension, see Chapter 6, Antihypertensive Agents.

If excessive doses are administered, rapid loss of water, sodium, potassium, and calcium may cause transient hypotension, asthenia, lethargy, nausea, vomiting, diarrhea, or confusion. During initial therapy, serum electrolyte, carbon dioxide, and blood urea nitrogen levels should be monitored and the drug withdrawn temporarily if abnormalities are noted. Monitoring of serum electrolyte levels is mandatory during prolonged treatment, because furosemide continues to exert an effect in the presence of electrolyte imbalance. Spironolactone or triamterene may be given concomitantly to prevent hypokalemia and associated metabolic alkalosis. Hyperuricemia and impaired glucose metabolism have been observed occasionally. Transient deafness and tinnitus have been observed after rapid injection of large doses, especially in patients with renal failure. Dermatitis, including urticaria with pruritus, and blood dyscrasias (eg, aplastic anemia, leukopenia, thrombocytopenic purpura) may occur.

Furosemide should be discontinued, if possible, one week before surgery because sulfonamide diuretics have been reported to decrease arterial response to pressor amines and enhance neuromuscular blockade caused by tubocurarine. Its use with large doses of salicylates may cause salicylate toxicity because of competitive renal excretion.

Furosemide should be used with caution in elderly patients, since the rapid and profound diuresis may produce dehydration with acute circulatory failure, thrombosis, or embolism. It may be advisable to hospitalize patients with cirrhosis with ascites or those with chronic renal failure prior to initiating therapy. Furosemide should be discontinued if increasing azotemia or oliguria occurs during treatment of severe progressive renal disease. The drug is contraindicated in women of childbearing age.

USUAL DOSAGE.—

Oral: Adults, initially, 40 to 80 mg as a single dose in the morning. Depending upon the patient's response, a second dose can be given six to eight hours later. This dosage schedule can be maintained or reduced. If the initial dose is not effective, successive doses may be increased by increments of 40 mg at intervals of six to eight hours until the desired diuretic effect has been obtained. In patients with severe renal damage and reduced glomerular filtration rates or those with ascites caused by liver disease, the dose may be carefully adjusted up to 600 mg daily. For maintenance, the individually determined dose should be given once or twice daily. It is recommended that the drug be given intermittently (two to four consecutive days per week, followed by a drug-free rest period). *Children*, 2 to 3 mg/kg of body weight daily.

Intravenous, Intramuscular: Adults, initially, 20 to 40 mg given intravenously over a period of one to two minutes or intramuscularly. If the response is not satisfactory, successive doses can be increased by increments of 20 mg no sooner than two hours after the previous dose until the desired diuretic effect is obtained. In emergency situations such as hypertensive crises, initial doses of 100 to 200 mg may be given over a period of one to two minutes, especially in the presence of known or suspected renal disease. When the glomerular filtration rate is markedly reduced, as in patients with severe renal failure, even larger doses may be required. In acute, oliguric renal failure, some authorities have recommended doses in excess of 1 g, given as a single intravenous injection. Such large doses should not be repeated without careful monitoring of fluid and electrolyte balance. It is preferable to administer large initial doses promptly rather than smaller doses which may be ineffective. Oral administration should replace parenteral therapy as soon as practical.

For acute pulmonary edema, *adults*, 40 mg injected intravenously at a slow rate. If indicated, another 40 mg may be given 90 minutes later. In the presence of known chronic renal disease with reduced glomerular filtration rate, doses of 100 to 200 mg may be needed to produce an effective diuresis. *Children*, 1 to 2 mg/kg of body weight as a single dose.

PREPARATIONS.—Lasix (Hoechst).

Oral: Tablets 40 mg.

Injection: Solution 10 mg/ml in 2 ml containers.

DIURETIC AGENTS USED AS ADJUNCTS

AMMONIUM CHLORIDE

Ammonium chloride, an acidifying salt, is of value as a diuretic when used alone and must be used intermittently to avoid tolerance. It is given orally to potentiate the effect of mercurial diuretics or to correct the metabolic alkalosis produced by these compounds, ethacrynic acid, or furosemide.

In adequate doses, ammonium chloride frequently will cause gastric irritation, nausea, and vomiting due to the enteric coating. Absorption may be quite erratic. Occasionally, hepatic coma occurs in patients with severe liver disease because the damaged liver is unable to metabolize ammonia. In patients who cannot tolerate ammonium chloride, *L*-lysine monohydrochloride may be used as an acidifying agent.

USUAL DOSAGE.—*Oral: Adults*, as a diuretic, 1 to 2 g four times daily for three consecutive days per week. As an acidifying agent, 1 to 2 g four times daily.

PREPARATIONS.—Ammonium Chloride, U.S.P. *Oral:* Tablets (enteric-coated) 500 mg. Drug marketed by many manufacturers under generic name.

L-LYSINE MONOHYDROCHLORIDE

$NH_2(CH_2)_4CH(NH_2)COOH \cdot HCl$

This amino acid salt is used to reestablish the patient's response to mercurial diuretics or to correct the metabolic alkalosis induced by other diuretics. It may be given to patients with severely impaired liver function, for it does not cause ammonia intoxication.

Abdominal cramps and transient diarrhea have been noted occasionally. Close clinical observation with monitoring of the blood electrolyte level and carbon dioxide content is necessary to avoid severe metabolic acidosis.

USUAL DOSAGE.—*Oral: Adults,* 10 g four times daily in fruit juice following a meal; this dosage is given for two to four days prior to administering the mercurial diuretic.

PREPARATIONS.—No single-entity pharmaceutical dosage form available; compounding necessary for prescription.

SPIRONOLACTONE [Aldactone]

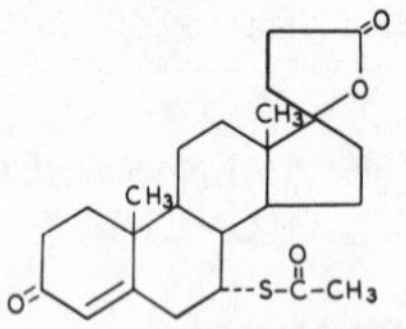

Spironolactone competitively inhibits the action of aldosterone in the renal tubules, thus increasing the excretion of sodium and chloride. At the same time, it retards excretion of potassium and may even cause hyperkalemia.

This drug is used in conditions in which excess aldosterone is produced (ie, in the nephrotic syndrome or hepatic cirrhosis with ascites). The reliability of spironolactone as a diagnostic agent for primary aldosteronism is questionable; there is evidence that it can reduce hypertension in the presence of low aldosterone levels. It also is frequently used as an adjunct to prevent hypokalemia in patients receiving diuretics that deplete potassium. Spironolactone has only a weak diuretic effect in patients with normal levels of aldosterone. Its effect does not appear for three to four days after initiation of therapy and lasts for a similar period after withdrawal. The drug is most effective when administered simultaneously with a thiazide or mercurial diuretic that acts proximally to increase the load of sodium delivered to the distal tubules. Spironolactone also may be used with a thiazide in the treatment of essential hypertension. It should not be used in patients receiving potassium supplements.

Spironolactone is relatively free of adverse effects. Drowsiness, ataxia, rash, and gynecomastia have been observed. The most significant untoward effect is hyperkalemia, which is most likely to occur in patients with renal insufficiency. Therefore, serum electrolyte levels should be monitored during administration, and spironolactone should be used cautiously in patients with impaired renal function or hepatic disease. It is contraindicated in those with acute renal failure, rapidly progressing impairment of renal function, anuria, or hyperkalemia.

USUAL DOSAGE.—*Oral: Adults,* initially, 100 mg daily in four divided doses for five days. *Children,* 3.3 mg/kg of body weight daily in four divided doses.

PREPARATIONS.—Aldactone (Searle). *Oral:* Tablets 25 mg.

TRIAMTERENE [Dyrenium]

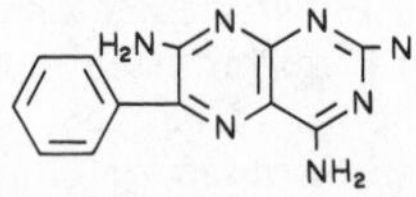

Triamterene does not competitively inhibit the effects of aldosterone but acts directly on tubular transport by inhibiting reabsorption of sodium and chloride. Potassium excretion is not affected. The net effect resembles that produced by spironolactone. Diuresis begins in two hours and a peak effect occurs in four to eight hours.

Triamterene is used to reduce edema associated with congestive heart failure, hepatic cirrhosis, and the nephrotic syndrome; it is also indicated in steroid-induced edema and edema due to secondary aldosteronism. The effect of triamterene is additive to that of other mild diuretics such as thiazides. It also is useful as an adjunct in preventing the hypokalemia induced by the thiazides and other diuretics.

Adverse reactions include nausea, vomiting, mild diarrhea, headache, rash, dryness of the mouth, and azotemia. Since it may produce hyperkalemia, triamterene must be given cautiously to patients with congestive heart failure, hepatic cirrhosis, or renal disease. Regular, frequent determinations of blood urea nitrogen and serum potassium levels should be performed in patients with impaired renal function or azotemia and the drug should be discontinued if the values rise.

Triamterene is contraindicated in patients

with hyperkalemia, edema due to severe and progressive liver disease, or a rising blood urea nitrogen level. Potassium supplements should not be used with triamterene.

USUAL DOSAGE.—*Oral: Adults*, initially, 100 mg twice daily after meals. For maintenance, 100 mg daily or every other day. Daily dosage should not exceed 300 mg. When triamterene is given with a thiazide or other diuretics, each agent should be given in reduced dosage initially, with subsequent adjustment of dosage on an individual basis. *Children*, initially, 2 to 4 mg/kg of body weight divided into one to two doses daily or every other day (maximum, 300 mg daily).

PREPARATIONS.—Dyrenium (Smith Kline & French). *Oral:* Capsules 100 mg.

MIXTURES

ALDACTAZIDE

This combination of spironolactone and hydrochlorothiazide may be useful if the dosage ratio meets the optimal requirements of the patient. The mixture may be effective in patients who do not respond adequately to either drug alone, since excretion of sodium is increased with the concomitant use of spironolactone and a thiazide due to their different sites of action. It is particularly useful when diuresis without hypokalemia is desired (eg, in patients receiving digitalis).

For adverse reactions and precautions, see the discussion on Thiazides and the evaluation on Spironolactone.

USUAL DOSAGE.—*Oral: Adults*, two tablets twice daily at 12-hour intervals. *Children*, dosage is adjusted to provide 1.65 to 3.3 mg/kg of body weight of spironolactone daily.

PREPARATIONS.—Aldactazide (Searle). *Oral:* Each tablet contains spironolactone 25 mg and hydrochlorothiazide 25 mg.

DYAZIDE

This combination of triamterene and hydrochlorothiazide may be useful if the dosage ratio meets the optimal requirements of the patient. Since the diuretic and natriuretic effects of each drug are enhanced when given concomitantly, the reduced doses of this mixture are satisfactory for initial administration. The mixture is useful when diuresis without hypokalemia is desired (eg, in patients receiving digitalis). It is also used as an antihypertensive agent.

For adverse reactions and precautions, see the discussion on Thiazides and the evaluation on Triamterene.

USUAL DOSAGE.—*Oral: Adults*, one capsule twice daily. After edema has been controlled, the patient may be maintained on one capsule daily or every other day. *Children*, dosage has not been established.

PREPARATIONS.—Dyazide (Smith Kline & French). *Oral:* Each capsule contains triamterene 50 mg and hydrochlorthiazide 25 mg.

PREPARATIONS CONTAINING A THIAZIDE AND POTASSIUM CHLORIDE

Since small bowel ulcerations have occurred after use of enteric-coated preparations containing potassium chloride, this type of mixture should not be used. There is no evidence that the thiazide alone contributed to the ulcerations.

A potassium salt should be used only when food sources cannot provide sufficient potassium (eg, in patients receiving prolonged thiazide therapy). A solution of potassium chloride may be used or, alternatively, potassium-retaining diuretics such as spironolactone or triamterene may be combined with the thiazides.

When potassium supplements are indicated, monitoring of the serum potassium level may be helpful to indicate the deficit.

USUAL DOSAGE.—This type of mixture should not be used for the reasons stated above. The dosage is based on the thiazide content.

PREPARATIONS.—Naturetin c K (Squibb): Each tablet contains bendroflumethiazide 5 mg and potassium chloride 500 mg.

Chapter 8

AGENTS USED TO TREAT DEFICIENCY ANEMIAS

Treatment of deficiency anemias is directed toward the replacement of specific chemical substances that are necessary for normal maturation of erythrocytes. However, the therapeutic goal is not only to restore the body nutrient level to normal, but also to determine and, if possible, eliminate the cause of the deficiency. All nutritional deficiencies arise from one or more of five basic causes: inadequate ingestion, absorption, or utilization, or increased requirement or excretion. Knowledge of the food sources and the body metabolism of nutrients is therefore essential to eliminate the causes of such deficiencies. Most deficiency anemias result from inadequate serum and tissue levels of iron, vitamin B_{12}, or folic acid.

Iron Deficiency Anemias: Iron deficiency anemias are caused by inadequate intake, excessive loss, or, rarely, inadequate absorption of iron. In adults, iron deficiency most commonly occurs as a result of blood loss. In women, menstruation is the usual cause of blood loss. In men, blood loss indicates disease (eg, gastrointestinal hemorrhage associated with gastric ulcer). In infants and children, inadequate diet is more likely to be a factor of primary importance.

Since only 10% of food iron is absorbed, the amount of iron ingested must be ten times the daily requirement. The average American diet provides approximately 6 mg of iron per 1,000 kcal. There is a practical limit to how much one can eat and, therefore, iron intake from dietary sources is of borderline adequacy for women and teenage girls and can be inadequate for infants and pregnant women. It has been advocated that iron be given prophylactically to all pregnant women, infants, and small children. Doses equivalent to at least 30 mg of elemental iron per day to pregnant women and 7.5 to 15 mg of elemental iron per day to infants and children 6 months to 6 years of age have been proposed. In the final analysis, this decision must be made by the physician based upon his knowledge of the patient and the patient's dietary habits.

Rational treatment of iron deficiency anemia depends upon accurate diagnosis. Although hypochromic microcytic red blood cells usually indicate iron deficiency, early iron depletion can be confirmed by a decreased or absent marrow hemosiderin. If, in addition to the absent stores, the saturation of transferrin is 15% or less, iron deficiency without anemia is probably present. If the hemoglobin level and packed red blood cell volume also are low, the most likely diagnosis is iron deficiency with anemia. Since the diagnosis of iron deficiency usually can be established quickly and easily, the administration of iron compounds should be delayed until appropriate diagnostic procedures have been completed.

In addition to providing replacement therapy, identification of the source of iron loss is mandatory; the importance of this cannot be overemphasized. Two percent of iron deficiency in adults is caused by neoplastic disease. If no obvious source of blood loss exists, occult bleeding from the gastrointestinal tract should be suspected and, if found, its cause determined and corrected if possible.

Megaloblastic Anemias: Megaloblastic anemias usually result from deficiencies of vitamin B_{12} or folates caused by insufficient intake or inadequate absorption. Existing anemias also may be aggravated by conditions in which these nutrients are required in increased amounts (eg, hemolytic anemias). As with iron deficiency, rational therapy of the megaloblastic anemias depends upon accurate diagnosis. Hematologic findings produced by a deficiency of either vitamin B_{12} or folic acid frequently are identical. However, vitamin B_{12} and folic acid are not interchangeable therapeutic agents; although folic acid may correct most of the hematologic abnormalities due to a vitamin B_{12} deficiency, it will not stop progression of the neurologic damage. The vitamin B_{12} or folate deficiency anemias usually respond so rapidly to specific therapy that transfusion of red blood cells is indicated only when severe anemia is associated with impending pulmonary or circulatory failure. In these patients, the cautious administration of packed red blood cells (up to several units) may produce rapid and dramatic relief.

Testosterone, cobalt, and pyridoxine have been used in the treatment of certain anemias refractory to other types of therapy. However, any response observed after use of these drugs does not represent correction of a deficiency. Testosterone sometimes stimulates erythropoiesis, and large doses of androgenic steroids have been used to treat certain refractory anemias caused by defective production of erythrocytes. Although not all patients benefit from this therapy and the results usually are not dramatic, aplastic and refractory myelophthisic anemias (anemias associated with space-occupying lesions of the marrow, such as myelofibrosis) may respond to the extent that fewer transfusions are needed. In some instances, remission has been induced and sustained. (See also Chapter 36, Androgens and Anabolic Steroids.) Rarely, cobaltous chloride is helpful in the treatment of bone marrow failure, but iron should not be given concomitantly since cobalt blocks certain iron transport enzyme systems. Patients with refractory sideroblastic anemia occasionally respond partially to treatment with large doses of pyridoxine. Refractory megaloblastic anemia, a relatively rare condition, also may be a pyridoxine-responsive anemia. This type of anemia is usually classified as normoblastic on the basis of marrow morphology (about one-fifth of the marrows have been described as megaloblastic or megaloblastoid). Abundant iron is present in the marrow. Thus, it may be worthwhile to institute a trial with pyridoxine in patients with unexplained megaloblastic anemia that does not respond to folic acid or vitamin B_{12}.

IRON COMPOUNDS

The oral route is the method of choice to replace iron in most patients with iron deficiency anemia. Ferrous compounds (ferrous sulfate, ferrous gluconate, and ferrous fumarate [Ircon, Toleron]), are absorbed well and probably to about the same extent; ferric compounds, including chelated compounds such as ferrocholinate [Chel-Iron, Ferrolip], are less readily absorbed. The incidence of untoward effects is approximately the same with both ferric and ferrous compounds and discontinuation of medication is rarely required.

Iron absorption is maximal in the duodenum; sustained-release or enteric-coated preparations, which are at best less well absorbed than the soluble iron salts, are apt to pass beyond the upper gastrointestinal tract and may be ineffective. Most patients respond to ferrous sulfate, the standard against which other oral iron preparations are compared.

Orally administered iron is absorbed best when taken between meals, but is tolerated better when taken with or after a meal. The elemental iron content of different preparations varies greatly and depends upon the type of iron salt in the preparation. Calculation of the dosage for any of these agents always should be in terms of the elemental iron to be administered rather than in terms of the iron salt.

Both the degree of absorption and the adverse effects sometimes observed during iron therapy are directly proportional to the quantity of ionic iron made available from the compound. Therefore, no benefit is gained by changing from one iron compound to another when untoward effects develop. The reactions often may be lessened without reducing the total daily dosage simply by decreasing the size of the individual dose and increasing the number of daily doses.

For iron-deficient adults, a dosage of 50 to 100 mg of elemental iron three times daily usually has been recommended, but current evidence indicates that this regimen may represent overdosage. Oral administration of 30 mg of elemental iron three times daily appears to be sufficient to correct most uncomplicated iron deficiencies rapidly. However, tablets or capsules are not manufactured in units that are convenient for administration of iron at this dosage level. Liquid preparations can be used, but this dosage form has never been too popular with adults. Consequently, the usual dosage recommendations listed in the individual evaluations in this section follow the traditionally recommended regimens; however, smaller doses may be just as satisfactory, particularly if gastrointestinal upset becomes a problem. To lessen gastrointestinal intolerance, small doses can be administered initially, and the medication may be given with meals; after four or five days the doses can be increased gradually as the gastrointestinal tract becomes more tolerant to the iron.

The dosage recommended for premature infants is approximately 2 mg of elemental iron per kilogram of body weight daily, starting five to six weeks after birth. Doses are then decreased gradually to approximately 1 mg/kg daily. Full-term infants and iron-deficient children should receive 25 to 75 mg of elemental iron daily.

The hematologic response to orally administered iron, which begins five to ten days after therapy is started (somewhat earlier in young children), is initiated by a reticulocytosis of 2% to 10%, depending upon the severity of the anemia. The hemoglobin value rises after a period of three to five more days. Thus, a readily perceptible increase is not evident until the end of the second week. Adequate oral dosage increases the hemoglobin production at a rate of 100 to 200 mg/100 ml of blood daily; a normal value is usually attained in two months unless blood loss continues. Parenteral administration produces a similar rise. To replenish depleted body iron stores, an oral preparation should be continued for approximately six months after the hemoglobin content of the blood has returned to normal. If a satisfactory response is not noted after three weeks of therapy, consideration should be given to whether the dosage regimen actually has been followed, whether appreciable blood loss is occurring simultaneously, whether there are other complicating factors (eg, defective iron utilization or absorption, infection), or whether the diagnosis of iron deficiency anemia is correct.

Parenteral iron preparations (iron sorbitex [Jectofer], iron dextran injection [Imferon]) can usually be administered with reasonable safety, but they should not be used until it has been established that oral medication will not correct the deficiency. It is advisable to administer iron parenterally when iron may further irritate an already diseased gastrointestinal tract (eg, in ulcerative colitis), when a patient is unwilling or unable to take iron orally, or when it is suspected that an infant will not get the iron he requires at home. Other drugs (eg, cholestyramine resin [Cuemid, Questran], calcium carbonate) may prevent absorption of iron that is given orally by binding iron or forming insoluble complexes with it; therefore, it may be advisable to administer iron parenterally in patients receiving these drugs.

The so-called malabsorption syndromes (eg, steatorrhea, partial gastrectomy) and apparent intolerance to iron probably do not constitute valid reasons for use of parenteral iron preparations. Malabsorption is exceedingly rare and, at best, is a marginal problem in the pathogenesis of iron deficiency. Intolerance almost always can be corrected by reducing the dose of iron since most symptoms of intolerance are actually symptoms of overdosage. Also, there is generally no reason to correct the iron deficiency rapidly if the bleeding is stopped or known not to be harmful (eg, menorrhagia) and the iron metabolism of the patient is in positive balance.

Parenteral iron preparations should be administered in divided doses, and the response of the patient is probably the best index of adequacy of therapy. Formulas for calculating the amount of iron needed to correct an existing deficiency have value as an overall guide to the total amount of iron needed but generally do not take into account the patient who continues to lose blood; furthermore, they may not compensate for replenishing body stores over and above hemoglobin iron. When a formula is applied, the total dose of iron needed is calculated from the iron content of hemoglobin (0.34%), the approximate blood volume of the patient (about 75 ml/kg of body weight), and the hemoglobin deficit (a normal average value for an adult male is generally about 15.5 g/100 ml, and for an adult female or a child, 14 g/100 ml). One of several formulas that take these various parameters into consideration is as follows:

> Patient's weight (kg) x [Normal hemoglobin value (g/100 mg) — Patient's hemoglobin (g/100 mg)] x 2.5 = Total milligrams of iron needed

The value computed with this formula represents a satisfactory replacement dose in terms of elemental iron for iron dextran injection. (For iron sorbitex, the dose calculated by this formula must be increased by about 30% to compensate for urinary loss of the drug.) However, because the formula determines only the amount of iron needed to restore blood hemoglobin levels to normal, it is necessary to increase the total calculated dose by 10% to 50%

to replenish the depleted iron stores. An adult patient who is not bleeding should not receive more than a total dose of 3 g. Once determined, the total estimated dosage should not be exceeded; if the hemoglobin response is insufficient, other causes of the persisting anemia must be sought.

For a discussion on mixtures containing iron, see the section on Mixtures.

Adverse Reactions and Precautions

Iron compounds are contraindicated in patients with idiopathic pulmonary hemosiderosis or primary hemochromatosis. They should not be used to treat hemolytic anemias unless an iron-deficient state also exists, since storage of iron with possible secondary hemochromatosis can result. Iron overload is particularly likely to occur in patients given excessive amounts of parenteral iron preparations or in those who are taking both oral and parenteral preparations, as well as in patients with hemoglobinopathies or other refractory anemias that might be erroneously diagnosed as iron deficiency anemia. Iron should not be given to patients receiving repeated blood transfusions, since there is a considerable amount of iron in the hemoglobin of transfused red blood cells. Prolonged administration should be avoided except in patients with continued bleeding or repeated pregnancies.

The oral route is preferred whenever possible because toxic reactions, including secondary hemochromatosis with possible tissue damage, are more likely to occur with repeated parenteral administration that bypasses the intestinal regulatory mechanisms. Fever, lymphadenopathy, nausea and vomiting, arthralgias, urticaria, severe peripheral vascular failure, and fatal anaphylactic reactions also have occurred after administration of parenteral iron preparations.

Excessive iron storage is rare following oral administration except in patients with absorption disorders (eg, sideroachrestic anemia, hemochromatosis). Gastrointestinal disturbances, particularly nausea, diarrhea, or constipation, may occur after use of oral preparations. Infants and children appear to tolerate therapeutic doses better than adults. Pregnant women are particularly susceptible to gastrointestinal disturbances; however, there is no absolute intolerance for orally administered iron. These untoward effects tend to subside with continuation of therapy, ingestion of the iron with meals and, if necessary, reduction of the dose; they seldom are severe enough to require discontinuation of the medication. Encouragement by the physician will help the patient though this somewhat difficult time. When iron is administered orally, it may aggravate existing gastrointestinal diseases such as peptic ulcer, chronic ulcerative colitis, or regional enteritis.

Coated tablets and flavored syrups are particularly hazardous because they are attractive to children. *Parents should be warned that iron is toxic when overdoses are ingested by children. Severe reactions and fatalities have occurred.*

INDIVIDUAL EVALUATIONS

FERROUS SULFATE

This iron salt is the most widely used iron preparation. It is probably the agent of choice for treating uncomplicated iron deficiency anemia. Since conditions for iron absorption are favorable only in the upper gastrointestinal tract, sustained-release or enteric-coated preparations that are likely to pass intact beyond the upper gastrointestinal tract may be ineffective.

Adverse effects are generally minimal. Gastrointestinal upset (usually nausea) is the most frequent reaction noted. This drug is absorbed best when taken between meals, but the gastrointestinal reactions may be minimized by reducing the dose and giving it with or shortly after meals. Like other orally administered ferrous compounds, ferrous sulfate may aggravate existing gastrointestinal disease such as peptic ulcer, regional enteritis, and ulcerative colitis.

Severe iron poisoning is uncommon in adults, but can occur in children who ingest iron formulations intended for adults. Toxic symptoms include nausea, vomiting, and shock. The child will appear listless, blanched, and perhaps cyanotic. Death has resulted from acute circulatory failure.

USUAL DOSAGE.—*Oral: Adults*, 300 mg to 1.2 g (equivalent to 60 to 240 mg elemental iron) daily in divided doses. *Children 5 to 12 years of age*, 120 to 600 mg (equivalent to 24 to 120 mg elemental iron) daily in divided doses (elixir or syrup); *children under 5 years and infants*, initially, 1 ml (20 drops) (equivalent to 25 mg elemental iron) of the pediatric preparation; this is gradually increased to as much as 3 ml (equivalent to 75 mg elemental iron) daily in divided doses. See also the Introductory Statement to this section.

PREPARATIONS.—(All strengths expressed in terms of elemental iron.) *Oral:* Capsules 45 and 60 mg; drops (pediatric) 15 mg/0.6 ml; elixir 44 mg/5 ml; syrup 30 mg/5 ml; tablets 65 and 105 mg.

AVAILABLE TRADEMARKS.—Feosol (Smith Kline & French), Fer-In-Sol (Mead Johnson), Fero-Gradumet (Abbott). Drug also marketed by other manufacturers under generic name.

FERROCHOLINATE [Chel-Iron, Ferrolip]

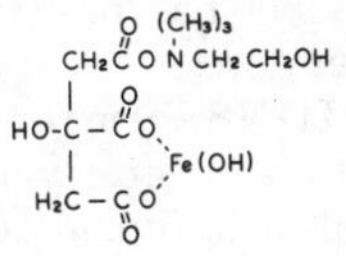

```
          O  (CH3)3
   CH2C  O  N CH2CH2OH
   |    O
HO-C - C O
   |        Fe(OH)
H2C - C O
      O
```

Ferrocholinate is a ferric iron chelate preparation that is useful in treating iron deficiency anemia. It is not as well absorbed as the soluble ferrous salt preparations.

Mild gastrointestinal disturbances are the most common adverse effects. Although ferrocholinate appears to be less toxic on a weight basis than ferrous sulfate or ferrous gluconate, the apparent lesser toxicity is simply a reflection of the smaller quantity of ionic iron that reaches the stomach and intestinal mucosa. It is highly probable that a comparison of equal quantities of ionic iron from ferrocholinate and ferrous sulfate would reveal that the toxicity is equal. The danger of severe iron poisoning still exists, particularly in children. Ferrocholinate may aggravate existing gastrointestinal disease such as peptic ulcer, regional enteritis, and ulcerative colitis. See also the Introductory Statement to this section and the evaluation on Ferrous Sulfate.

USUAL DOSAGE.—*Oral: Adults,* 330 to 660 mg (equivalent to 40 to 80 mg elemental iron) three times daily. *Children,* 1.5 to 2 mg elemental iron/kg of body weight daily. *Infants,* for prophylaxis, 1 to 1.5 mg elemental iron/kg daily. See also the Introductory Statement to this section.

PREPARATIONS.—(All strengths expressed in terms of elemental iron.)

Chel-Iron (Kinney). *Oral:* Drops (pediatric) 25 mg/ml; liquid 50 mg/ml; tablets 40 mg.

Ferrolip (Flint). *Oral:* Syrup 50 mg/5 ml; tablets 40 mg.

FERROUS FUMARATE [Ircon, Toleron]

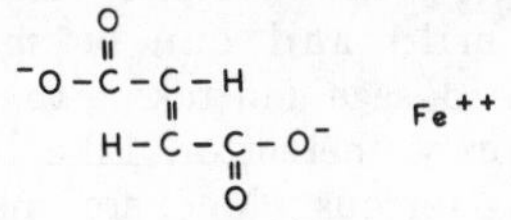

```
       O
       ‖
 ⁻O - C - C - H
           ‖          Fe++
       H - C - C - O⁻
               ‖
               O
```

This agent appears to be as effective as the other orally administered ferrous compounds in treating iron deficiency.

Although ferrous fumarate is alleged to be less irritating than ferrous sulfate or ferrous gluconate, equal amounts of ionic iron from this compound and either of the other two would be equally irritating to the stomach and intestinal mucosa. The gastrointestinal disturbances are usually mild and subside with continuation of therapy. See also the Introductory Statement to this section and the evaluation on Ferrous Sulfate. Severe iron poisoning can result from overdosage, especially in children. Ferrous fumarate may aggravate existing gastrointestinal disease such as peptic ulcer, regional enteritis, and ulcerative colitis.

USUAL DOSAGE.—*Oral: Adults and children over 5 years of age,* 600 to 800 mg (equivalent to approximately 200 to 260 mg elemental iron) daily in three or four divided doses. *Children under 5 years and infants,* 100 to 300 mg (equivalent to 33 to 99 mg elemental iron) daily in three or four divided doses. See also the Introductory Statement to this section.

PREPARATIONS.—

Ircon (Lakeside). *Oral:* Tablets 200 mg (equivalent to 66 mg elemental iron).

Toleron (Mallinckrodt). *Oral:* Suspension 100 mg/5 ml (equivalent to 33 mg elemental iron); tablets 200 mg (equivalent to 66 mg elemental iron).

ADDITIONAL TRADEMARKS.—El-Ped-Ron (Elder), Feostat (Westerfield), Ferranol (Robinson), Fumasorb (Marion), Tolferain (Ascher). Drug also marketed by other manufacturers under generic name.

FERROUS GLUCONATE

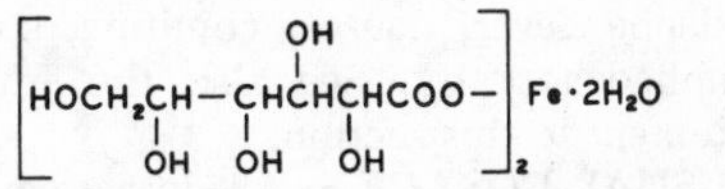

```
[            OH                    ]
[            |                     ]
[ HOCH2CH - CHCHCHCOO-             ]  Fe·2H2O
[       |    |   |                 ]
[      OH   OH  OH                 ]2
```

Ferrous gluconate is probably as effective as the other ferrous compounds used to treat iron deficiency anemia.

Although ferrous gluconate is alleged to be less irritating than ferrous sulfate, equal amounts of ionic iron from both compounds would be equally irritating to the stomach and intestinal mucosa. The gastrointestinal disturbances are generally mild and can be minimized by reducing the dosage and taking the drug with a meal or shortly thereafter. Like other ferrous compounds, ferrous gluconate may aggravate existing gastrointestinal disease such as peptic ulcer, regional enteritis, and ulcerative colitis. Overdosage has caused severe acute iron poisoning, especially in children. See also the Introductory Statement to this section.

USUAL DOSAGE.—*Oral: Adults,* 320 to 640 mg (equivalent to 40 to 80 mg elemental iron) three times daily. *Children,* 100 to 300 mg (equivalent to 12.5 to 37.5 mg elemental iron) three times daily. *Infants,* initially, 120 mg (30 drops of elixir); this amount is increased gradually to 300 mg/5 ml (equivalent to 15 to 37.5 mg elemental iron) daily. See also the Introductory Statement to this section.

PREPARATIONS.—*Oral:* Capsules 435 mg; elixir 300 mg/5 ml; tablets 320 mg.

AVAILABLE TRADEMARK.—Fergon (Breon). Drug also marketed by other manufacturers under generic name.

IRON DEXTRAN INJECTION [Imferon]

Iron dextran injection can be used intramuscularly or intravenously for the treatment of confirmed iron deficiency anemia. The indications for this drug are limited to those situations in which the iron loss is too great to be offset by oral administration of iron (eg, hereditary hemorrhagic telangiectasia) and the cause of loss cannot be corrected, when orally administered iron may further irritate an already diseased gastrointestinal tract (eg, in ulcerative colitis), when a patient is unwilling or unable to take iron orally, or when it is suspected that an infant will not get the iron he requires at home.

Severe anaphylactic reactions, some of them fatal, have occurred after administration of iron dextran injection. It is advisable to give a test dose initially to help detect sensitivity. Staining of the skin and occasional pain occur at the site of injection. This drug also may cause urticaria, headache, fever, nausea, vomiting, and regional lymphadenopathy. See also the Introductory Statement to this section.

USUAL DOSAGE.—(All dosages expressed in terms of elemental iron.) The response of the patient should be closely followed as an index to the effectiveness of therapy. A dosage guide based on the weight of the patient and his degree of anemia is included in the manufacturer's literature.

Intramuscular: Adults over 50 kg of body weight, 50 mg the first day and up to 250 mg every other day or twice weekly thereafter until the total calculated dose is given. *Small adults and children weighing 9 to 50 kg,* no more than 100 mg daily. *Infants 3.5 to 9 kg,* no more than 50 mg daily; *under 3.5 kg,* no more than 25 mg daily.

Intravenous: Adults, 15 to 30 mg initially, increased by increments of 10 mg daily until hemoglobin levels return to normal (maximal daily dose, 50 to 65 mg). The preparation should be given at a rate no faster than 1 ml/2 minutes, and the patient should rest 15 to 30 minutes after each dose. No single dose should ever exceed 100 mg of iron, since the incidence of untoward effects has been reported to be greater after larger doses.

PREPARATIONS.—Imferon (Lakeside). *Injection:* Solution equivalent to 50 mg elemental iron/ml in 2, 5; and 10 ml containers.

IRON SORBITEX [Jectofer]

Iron sorbitex is a chemical complex of iron, sorbitol, and citric acid in stable solution. It is administered only intramuscularly and only in patients in whom the diagnosis of iron deficiency anemia has been established. However, even in proved cases of iron deficiency anemia, iron sorbitex should not be used until a thorough study has been made to determine the cause of the deficiency. This drug is intended for use in patients who are unable to take adequate amounts of iron by mouth because the uptake of orally administered iron cannot keep pace with the iron loss resulting from chronic hemorrhage, or when the patient will not or cannot follow the prescribed regimen (see the evaluation on Iron Dextran Injection).

Minor reactions include transient alteration in taste perception, flushing, malaise, asthenia, myalgia, arthralgia, temporary staining of the skin, and occasional pain at the injection site. Local urticarial reactions, precordial pressure sensations, and palpitations, as well as more pronounced systemic effects such as hyperhidrosis, headache, dizziness, nausea and vomiting, hypotension, and syncope also have occurred. Albuminuria, hematuria, and urinary frequency have been reported in one patient receiving iron sorbitex for a prolonged period. Anaphylaxis, cyanosis, collapse, and death have occurred in at least one patient given this drug.

The more serious reactions to iron sorbitex are more likely to occur in patients who also are taking oral iron preparations. Under these conditions, transferrin becomes rapidly saturated and the iron entering the blood cannot be bound to protein. It is this unbound iron fraction that appears to be responsible for the acute toxic symptoms. *Hence, iron sorbitex should not be used concomitantly with oral iron therapy.*

The use of iron sorbitex is contraindicated in any anemia other than iron deficiency anemia. Other contraindications include renal disease, hepatitis, sensitivity to iron compounds, hemosiderosis, hemochromatosis, and genitourinary tract infections. The prophylactic use of iron sorbitex is unwarranted. *Under no circumstances should iron sorbitex be administered intravenously.*

Patients receiving iron sorbitex should be advised that their urine may darken upon standing. This is due to the formation of iron sulfide and is of no clinical significance.

In one study in which 143 pregnant women received iron sorbitex, no alteration in the course of the pregnancy and delivery and no teratogenic effects in the infant could be detected.

Since adequate clinical observations on the use of iron sorbitex in children have not been conducted, its usefulness in this age group has not been established.

USUAL DOSAGE.—*Intramuscular:* The amount of iron sorbitex given should be sufficient to restore the hemoglobin level to normal and, if indicated, to replenish iron stores. The response of the patient should be closely followed as an index to the effectiveness of therapy.

The usual single daily dose is 1.5 mg of iron/kg of body weight. The average dosage for *adults weighing 60 kg or more* is 100 mg given in the gluteal region. The total dosage should not exceed 200 mg daily, since the incidence of systemic adverse effects is increased significantly with larger doses.

Only one-half of the daily therapeutic dose should be given as the initial injection to help safeguard iron-sensitive individuals who have not received previous iron therapy and may therefore be unaware of their sensitivity.

PREPARATIONS.—Jectofer (Astra). *Injection:* Solution 50 mg elemental iron/ml in 2 ml containers.

VITAMIN B_{12} PREPARATIONS

The most well-known component of the vitamin B_{12} group, cyanocobalamin, has hematopoietic activity apparently identical with that of the antianemia factor in the liver. It is clinically effective in the treatment of vitamin B_{12} deficiency states (eg, pernicious anemia with or without neurologic complications, some cases of tropical sprue or celiac disease, nutritional macrocytic anemia, some cases of megaloblastic anemia in infants). It has no therapeutic value (except as a placebo) in treating any of the nonhematologic conditions for which it has been advocated (eg, acute viral hepatitis, trigeminal neuralgia and various other neuropathies, multiple sclerosis, delayed growth, poor appetite, certain dermatologic and psychiatric disorders, allergies, aging, sterility, thyrotoxicosis, malnutrition). Preparations of liver for injection, although a source of vitamin B_{12} activity, are outmoded and should no longer be used.

The absorption of orally administered cyanocobalamin is facilitated by an intrinsic factor, a glycoprotein secreted by the gastric mucosa. In addition to this specific absorption mechanism, a small fraction (approximately 1%) of an oral dose is absorbed from the gut by simple diffusion. The oral route should be reserved for treating nutritional vitamin B_{12} deficiency (see also Chapter 14, Vitamins and Sources of Vitamins). This route should not be used for treating pernicious anemia because oral preparations of cyanocobalamin are unreliable for obtaining an adequate or sustained therapeutic response. Although patients receiving oral cyanocobalamin-intrinsic factor combinations respond initially, they frequently become refractory within a short period, presumably because they develop antibodies to the transport protein of the intrinsic factor. Since prolonged inadequate oral therapy for pernicious anemia with neurologic complications may lead to permanent damage, parenteral therapy is universally preferred.

The treatment of choice for vitamin B_{12} deficiency is the intramuscular or deep subcutaneous injection of solutions of crystalline cyanocobalamin or hydroxocobalamin. It has been estimated that the total cyanocobalamin deficit in a patient with pernicious anemia is approximately 4,000 to 5,000 μg. Nevertheless, a patient may respond to injections of as little as 1 μg of crystalline cyanocobalamin daily. Demonstrable neurologic damage from pernicious anemia that cannot be reversed in one to one and one-half years of adequate therapy must be considered irreversible. Physical therapy started early is a useful adjunct in the treatment of neuropathy caused by vitamin B_{12} deficiency.

Hydroxocobalamin, an analogue of cyanocobalamin, is equal to cyanocobalamin in hematopoietic activity. Because more of it is bound to blood proteins than cyanocobalamin, less is lost in the urine and thus it is retained in the body a little longer than cyanocobalamin. However, because of the dosages generally used, this is not an important clinical consideration and hydroxocobalamin apparently has no advantage over cyanocobalamin.

Vitamin B_{12}-deficient patients respond dramatically to therapy with cyanocobalamin or hydroxocobalamin. Within a few hours after intramuscular injection, megaloblasts begin developing into mature cells. Often within 24 hours the patient begins to have an increased feeling of well-being. Normoblastic hematopoiesis is restored within 48 to 72 hours. As the condition of the patient continues to improve, the characteristic macrocytic anemia, leukopenia, and thrombocytopenia disappear.

No serious toxic reactions have been reported from the administration of either cyanocobalamin or hydroxocobalamin. Rarely, there may be allergic reactions to the impurities contained in these preparations.

The most important part of any therapeutic regimen is to make the patient with pernicious anemia understand that he must receive injections of vitamin B_{12} at regular intervals for the rest of his life or he will develop irreversible neurologic damage.

INDIVIDUAL EVALUATIONS

CYANOCOBALAMIN

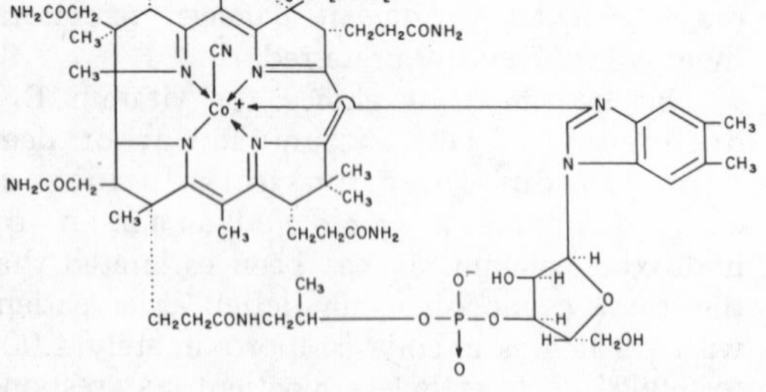

The only established clinical uses for this drug are in the treatment of confirmed vitamin B_{12} deficiency states and in the performance of Schilling's test for pernicious anemia. See the Introductory Statement to this section.

No serious toxic reactions have as yet been reported, but allergic reactions to impurities in the preparation may occur rarely. Injection causes little or no pain, and no adverse local effects have been reported.

USUAL DOSAGE.—

Intramuscular, Intravenous, Subcutaneous: For treatment of uncomplicated pernicious anemia, *adults,* 100 to 1,000 μg daily for one week followed by the same dose weekly until remission is complete; thereafter, 100 to 1,000 μg every four weeks will maintain remission; *children,* a total of 1,000 to 5,000 μg given as single doses of 100 μg over a period of two or more weeks. Thereafter, 30 to 50 μg every four weeks will maintain the remission. For patients with demonstrable neurologic damage, 1,000 μg may be given once weekly for several months, then once or twice monthly for another year; neurologic damage that cannot be reversed within one to one and one-half years must be considered irreversible.

Oral: For treatment of nutritional vitamin B_{12} deficiency, *adults,* 25 μg daily. For uncomplicated pernicious anemia, the manufacturer's suggested dosage is: *Adults,* 1,000 μg daily until remission occurs, followed by 1,000 μg doses as needed to maintain remission. The oral route is markedly inferior to a parenteral regimen and therefore should not be used for treatment of non-nutritional vitamin B_{12} deficiency anemias.

PREPARATIONS.—

Injection: Solution 30 and 50 μg/ml in 10 ml containers; 100 μg/ml in 1, 10, and 30 ml containers; 1,000 μg/ml in 1, 5, and 10 ml containers.

Oral: Capsules 25 μg; tablets 5, 25, 50, 100, and 250 μg (not used to treat pernicious anemia).

AVAILABLE TRADEMARKS.—Belvetin (Durst), Berubigen (Upjohn), Betalin 12 Crystalline (Lilly), Bevite (Key), Cobavite (Lemmon), Cyredin (Merrell-National), Dodex (Organon), Poyamin (Fellows-Testagar), Redisol (Merck Sharp & Dohme), Rubesol (Central), Rubramin PC (Squibb), Ruvite (Savage), Sytobex (Parke, Davis), Vibisone (Invenex), Vi-Twel (Smith, Miller & Patch). Drug also marketed by other manufacturers under the names Cyanocobalamin or Vitamin B_{12}.

SIMILAR PREPARATION.—Vitamin B_{12} with Intrinsic Factor Concentrate (Bifacton [Organon], Biopar Forte [Armour], Intrinase [Upjohn]).

HYDROXOCOBALAMIN

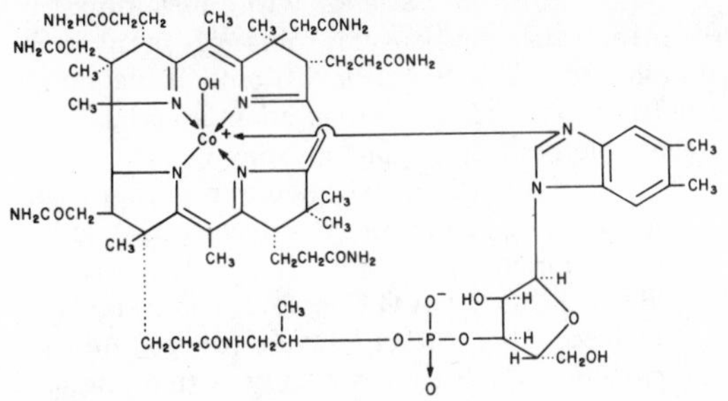

The only established clinical uses of hydroxocobalamin are in the treatment of confirmed vitamin B_{12} deficiency states and in the performance of Schilling's test for pernicious anemia. Its duration of action may be somewhat longer than that of cyanocobalamin. See the Introductory Statement to this section.

Rarely, allergic reactions to impurities in the preparation may occur. Injection causes little or no pain, and no adverse local effects have been observed.

USUAL DOSAGE.—*Intramuscular: Adults,* 1,000 μg two or three times weekly until remission occurs. A dose of 1,000 μg every month will then generally maintain remission. *Children,* see the evaluation on Cyanocobalamin.

PREPARATIONS.—*Injection:* Solution 1,000 μg/ml in 1 and 10 ml containers.

AVAILABLE TRADEMARKS.—AlphaRedisol (Merck Sharp & Dohme), Alpha-Ruvite (Savage), Belvedrox (Durst), Codroxomin (Fellows-Testagar), Droxovite (Kay), Hydroxo B-12 (Philips Roxane), Neo-Betalin 12 (Lilly), Neo-Vitwel (Smith, Miller & Patch), Sytobex-H (Parke, Davis). Drug also marketed by other manufacturers under generic name.

LIVER INJECTION [Pernaemon]

The crude soluble vitamin B_{12} activity of liver is available as a single-entity preparation and in vitamin mixtures for injection. Because crystalline cyanocobalamin for injection is superior to all liver preparations, liver injection should no longer be used.

Adverse reactions include local hypersensitivity, allergy, anaphylactic reactions, and brownish discoloration of the skin at the injection site.

USUAL DOSAGE.—No dosage regimen is given since use of liver injection for treating vitamin B_{12} deficiency states is now obsolete.

PREPARATIONS.—Pernaemon (Organon). Drug also marketed by other manufacturers under generic name.

FOLATES

Folic acid is widely distributed in nature and occurs primarily conjugated with one or more molecules of glutamic acid. These conjugated forms, collectively called folates, are present in nearly all foodstuffs. They are destroyed by prolonged cooking and other types of food processing.

Folates appear to be rapidly absorbed from the small intestine. Folic acid [Folvite] is almost completely absorbed when administered orally, even in the presence of the malabsorption associated with tropical sprue; other folates frequently must be converted by enzymatic hydrolysis in the gut before they can be efficiently absorbed.

Folic acid is specific for the control of folate-deficiency megaloblastic anemias of infancy and pregnancy. It also is effective in the treatment of nutritional macrocytic anemia and most cases of tropical sprue or celiac disease, in which it frequently controls diarrhea.

Many forms of folate may initially correct the anemia of pernicious anemia and other types of vitamin B_{12} deficiency as well, but folates or folic acid should not be used to treat this disease because they do not stop progression of the neurologic symptoms of vitamin B_{12} deficiency. Their indiscriminate prophylactic use may mask symptoms of pernicious anemia and make it difficult to diagnose the vitamin B_{12} deficiency.

The minimal adult requirement for folate is estimated to be 50 μg daily, and the average normal storage of folate in an adult is estimated to be about 7.5 mg. Since the available folate content of the average daily diet in the United States is 200 to 300 μg, dietary sources are generally adequate to maintain a positive folic acid balance in most individuals. However, during pregnancy the fetal requirement for folic acid is large, especially during the last trimester. As a result, plasma levels of folate in the mother gradually fall during pregnancy. At birth, the plasma folate level of the newborn infant averages five times that of the mother. Therefore, a prophylactic dose of 1 mg daily may be given routinely during pregnancy to assure that deficiency will not develop; larger doses may be indicated in women with marked absorption defects.

Although the oral replacement dose of folic acid is 0.25 to 1 mg daily, 100 μg daily produces an adequate hematologic response in patients with uncomplicated folate deficiency. Daily doses greater than 1 mg do not appear to enhance the hematologic effect.

The sodium salt of folic acid (folate sodium) may be given by intramuscular, intravenous, or deep subcutaneous injection. Although parenteral administration has no advantage over oral administration of folic acid, it may be preferred when the folate deficiency is caused by malabsorption rather than by ingestion of inadequate amounts. Doses of 500 to 1,000 μg daily are considered adequate for parenteral therapy.

Folate-deficient patients generally respond rapidly to folic acid. During the first 24 hours there is an improved sense of well-being and within 48 hours the marrow begins to become normoblastic. Reticulocytosis generally begins in two to five days.

When folate deficiency anemia is of dietary origin, correction of the diet is preferred over supplemental medication. Addition of one fresh uncooked fruit or vegetable to the patient's diet each day often constitutes adequate dietary correction.

Individuals taking certain anticonvulsant, antimalarial, or contraceptive drugs may develop folic acid deficiency. The exact mechanisms causing the deficiency are not understood in all cases; however, it is known that some of the drugs act by inhibiting folic acid absorption, whereas others inhibit the enzyme dihydrofolate reductase, thereby blocking the reduction of folic acid to its metabolically active form. Although such folic acid deficiencies can be corrected by withdrawing the drug itself, this is not always possible. Supplementing the diet with folic acid may overcome many of the deficiencies when the mechanism of the deficiency is not enzyme inhibition. If supplemental folic acid fails to correct the deficiency, leucovorin calcium (folinate calcium) should be tried; it is already reduced and is beyond the metabolic step that requires dihydrofolate reductase.

FOLIC ACID [Folvite]
FOLATE SODIUM [Folvite Solution]

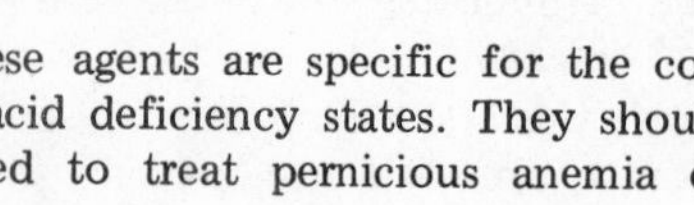

These agents are specific for the control of folic acid deficiency states. They should never be used to treat pernicious anemia or other vitamin B_{12} deficiency states. Indiscriminate use of these drugs in patients with megaloblastic anemias will mask symptoms of pernicious anemia and make diagnosis difficult. If diagnosis and treatment of pernicious anemia is delayed, irreversible neurologic damage may occur.

Except for one questionable report of an allergic reaction, folic acid has been shown to be nontoxic in man.

USUAL DOSAGE.—*Intramuscular, Intravenous, Oral, Subcutaneous* (deep): *Adults and children,* 0.25 to 1 mg daily. When clinical symptoms have subsided and the blood picture has become normal, a maintenance dose of 0.1 to 0.25 mg daily should be given.

PREPARATIONS.—

Folic Acid:

Folvite (Lederle). *Oral:* Tablets 0.25 and 1 mg. Drug also marketed by other manufacturers under generic name.

Folate Sodium:

Folvite Solution (Lederle). *Injection:* Solution equivalent to folic acid 5 mg/ml in 10 ml containers.

SIMILAR PREPARATION.—Calcium Leucovorin Injection (Lederle).

MIXTURES

Deficiency anemias must be properly diagnosed before therapy is initiated. Once diagnosis has been accomplished, the anemic condition generally will respond rapidly to a specific single-entity drug. Many of the antianemic mixtures may delay establishing the correct diagnosis (eg, iron combined with cyanocobalamin or folic acid may obscure the diagnosis of pernicious anemia).

These mixtures contain almost every imaginable combination of two or more of the following compounds or groups of compounds: the iron salts, all the vitamins including folic acid and cyanocobalamin, all the trace minerals, liver extracts, and intrinsic factor. Their use for treating anemias should be discouraged. They are an added expense to the patient when a completely adequate and less expensive regimen is available. For example, while a combination tablet containing an iron salt and a large dose of ascorbic acid may constitute acceptable therapy in the patient having difficulty absorbing iron (ascorbic acid will enhance iron absorption), ingestion of an additional ferrous sulfate tablet instead of the ascorbic acid may be a more economical way to produce the same increase in iron absorption. The supplemental vitamins or minerals present in many iron preparations in no way improve the therapeutic effect of the iron. They are not necessary unless other specific deficiencies also are present. Mixtures of iron with folic acid, cyanocobalamin, and pyridoxine generally should not be used, but a combination of folic acid and iron may be a reasonable prophylactic supplement during pregnancy. There is no sound scientific basis for the inclusion of trace metals such as copper, molybdenum, or cobalt in any preparation.

Combination therapy is indicated only when it can be demonstrated clearly that one type of anemia is superimposed upon another. Even under these circumstances, a combination of *the specific agents lacking in the particular anemias diagnosed are the only agents that should be used to treat the anemias.* Not only is avoidance of mixtures superior therapy, but it also may be absolutely necessary because the preferred route of administration for two therapeutic agents may be different. For example, an anemia caused by deficiencies of iron and vitamin B_{12} would require both iron and cyanocobalamin for treatment. However, the oral route is preferred for administering iron, whereas cyanocobalamin should be given by injection.

Hundreds of mixtures are available. Below is a partial listing of the more widely used preparations. This listing is provided merely as a convenience for the physician who might wish to know the content of a particular mixture. For a discussion of the multiple vitamin and multiple vitamin with mineral preparations used in treating deficiency states not related to anemia therapy, see Chapter 14, Vitamins and Sources of Vitamins.

Cebetinic (Upjohn): Each tablet contains iron 37.5 mg, cyanocobalamin 5 μg, ascorbic acid 25 mg, thiamine mononitrate 2 mg, riboflavin 2 mg, niacinamide 10 mg, and pyridoxine hydrochloride 0.5 mg.

Chromagen Capsules (Savage): Each capsule contains ferrous fumarate 200 mg, cyanocobalamin 10 μg, ascorbic acid 250 mg, and desiccated stomach substance 100 mg.

Chromagen Injectable (Savage): Each 2 ml contains peptonized iron 100 mg, liver injection 5 μg, and cyanocobalamin 25 μg.

C-Ron (Rowell): Each tablet contains ferrous fumarate 100 or 200 mg and ascorbic acid 50 or 100 mg; each Forte tablet contains ferrous fumarate 200 mg and ascorbic acid 600 mg.

C-Ron FA (Rowell): Each tablet contains ferrous fumarate 200 mg, folic acid 0.5 mg, and ascorbic acid 600 mg.

Feosol Plus (Smith Kline & French): Each capsule contains ferrous sulfate 200 mg, desiccated liver 325 mg, cyanocobalamin 1.7 μg, folic acid 0.4 mg, thiamine hydrochloride 2 mg, riboflavin 2 mg, pyridoxine hydrochloride 1 mg, ascorbic acid 50 mg, niacin 10 mg, and pantothenic acid 2 mg.

Feramel (Squibb): Each tablet contains iron 50 mg and ascorbic acid 25 mg.

Ferancee (Stuart): Each chewable tablet contains ferrous fumarate 200 mg and ascorbic acid 150 mg.

Fergon Plus (Breon): Each capsule contains ferrous gluconate 500 mg, vitamin B_{12} with intrinsic factor concentrate 0.5 units, and ascorbic acid 75 mg.

Fero-Folic-500 (Abbott): Each tablet contains iron 105 mg, folic acid 350 μg, and ascorbic acid 500 mg.

Fero-Grad-500 (Abbott): Each tablet contains iron 105 mg and ascorbic acid 500 mg.

Ferritrinsic (Upjohn): Each tablet contains vitamin B_{12} with intrinsic factor concentrate 0.33 units, iron 60 mg, desiccated liver 100 mg, folic acid 0.033 mg, thiamine mononitrate 2 mg, riboflavin 2 mg, and niacinamide 10 mg.

Ferro-Sequels (Lederle): Each timed-release capsule contains ferrous fumarate 150 mg and dioctyl sodium sulfosuccinate 100 mg.

Heptuna Plus (Roerig): Each capsule contains ferrous sulfate 340 mg, iron 100 mg, desiccated liver 50 mg, ascorbic acid 150 mg, cyanocobalamin 5 μg, intrinsic factor concentrate 25 mg, thiamine hydrochloride 3 mg, riboflavin 2 mg, pyridoxine hydrochloride 2 mg, niacinamide 15 mg, pantothenate calcium 1 mg, copper 1 mg, molybdenum 0.2 mg, calcium 37.4 mg, iodine 0.05 mg, manganese 0.033 mg, magnesium 2 mg, phosphorus 29 mg, and potassium 1.7 mg.

Iberet (Abbott): Each tablet or 20 ml of liquid contains iron 105 mg, cyanocobalamin 25 μg, thiamine mononitrate 6 mg, riboflavin 6 mg, niacinamide 30 mg, pyridoxine hydrochloride 6 mg, ascorbic acid 150 mg, and calcium pantothenate 10 mg.

Iberet-500 (Abbott): Each tablet or 20 ml of liquid contains same formulation as Iberet except ascorbic acid 500 mg.

Iberet-Folic-500 (Abbott): Each tablet contains same formulation as Iberet-500 plus folic acid 350 μg.

Iberlate (Abbott): Each 4 g of powder contains iron 15 mg, folic acid 100 μg, cyanocobalamin 3 μg, ascorbic acid 60 mg, niacinamide 4.5 mg, thiamine hydrochloride 1 mg, riboflavin 1.5 mg, and pyridoxine hydrochloride 1 mg.

Iberol (Abbott): Each tablet contains iron 105 mg, cyanocobalamin 12.5 μg, thiamine hydrochloride 3 mg, riboflavin 3 mg, niacinamide 15 mg, pyridoxine hydrochloride 1.5 mg, pantothenate calcium 3 mg, desiccated liver 100 mg, and ascorbic acid 75 mg.

Iberol-F (Abbott): Each tablet contains same formulation as Iberol plus folic acid 1 mg.

Liver Extract with Iron (many manufacturers).

Liver Extract with Vitamin B_{12} (many manufacturers).

Mol-Iron (Schering): Each tablet or 4 ml of liquid contains ferrous sulfate 195 mg and molybdenum sesquioxide 3 mg; each milliliter of drops contains ferrous sulfate 125 mg and molybdenum sesquioxide 2 mg; each timed-release capsule contains ferrous sulfate 390 mg and molybdenum sesquioxide 6 mg.

Mol-Iron Panhemic (Schering): Each capsule contains ferrous sulfate 500 mg, vitamin B_{12} with intrinsic factor concentrate 0.5 units, cyanocobalamin 7.5 μg, folic acid 2.5 mg, molybdenum sesquioxide 7.7 mg, ascorbic acid 75 mg, thiamine hydrochloride 2 mg, riboflavin 2 mg, and niacinamide 10 mg; each timed-release capsule contains ferrous sulfate 390 mg, cyanocobalamin 25 μg, molybdenum sesquioxide 6 mg, thiamine hydrochloride 6 mg, riboflavin 6 mg, pyridoxine hydrochloride 5 mg, niacinamide 30 mg, and ascorbic acid 150 mg.

Norlac (Rowell): Each tablet contains ferrous fumarate 200 mg, folic acid 1 mg, cyanocobalamin 5 μg, calcium carbonate 600 mg, ascorbic acid 100 mg, vitamin A acetate 5,000 units, calciferol 400 units, thiamine mononitrate 2 mg, riboflavin 2 mg, pyridoxine hydrochloride 15 mg, niacinamide 20 mg, pantothenate calcium 10 mg, alpha-tocopheryl acetate 5 units, magnesium 1 mg, copper 1 mg, and iodine 0.15 mg.

Peritinic (Lederle): Each tablet contains iron 100 mg, cyanocobalamin 50 μg, folic acid 0.05 mg, thiamine hydrochloride 7.5 mg, riboflavin 7.5 mg, pyridoxine hydrochloride 7.5 mg, ascorbic acid 200 mg, niacinamide 30 mg, and dioctyl sodium sulfosuccinate 100 mg.

Simron Plus (Merrell-National): Each capsule contains iron 10 mg, folic acid 0.5 mg, vitamin B_{12} activity 3.33 μg, polysorbate 20 400 mg, ascorbic acid 50 mg, and pyridoxine hydrochloride 1 mg.

Stuartinic (Stuart): Each tablet contains ferrous fumarate 305.5 mg, desiccated liver 100 mg, ascorbic acid 50 mg, thiamine hydrochloride 2 mg, riboflavin 2 mg, pyridoxine hydrochloride 0.5 mg, niacinamide 10 mg, and pantothenate calcium 2 mg.

Theragran Hematinic (Squibb): Each tablet contains iron 66.7 mg, cyanocobalamin 50 μg, folic acid 0.5 mg, vitamin A 8,333 units, thiamine hydrochloride 3.3 mg, riboflavin 3.3 mg, pyridoxine hydrochloride 3.3 mg, ascorbic acid 100 mg, vitamin D 133 units, vitamin E 5 IU, niacinamide 3.33 mg, pantothenate calcium 11.7 mg, copper 0.67 mg, and magnesium 41.7 mg.

Trinsicon (Lilly): Each capsule contains liver-stomach concentrate 150 mg, vitamin B_{12} with intrinsic factor concentrate 0.5 units, cyanocobalamin 7.5 μg, iron 110 mg, folic acid 1 mg, and ascorbic acid 75 mg.

Vitron-C (Smith, Miller & Patch): Each tablet contains ferrous fumarate 200 mg and ascorbic acid 125 mg.

Vitron-C-Plus (Smith, Miller & Patch): Each tablet contains cobalamin concentrate activity 10 μg, ferrous fumarate 400 mg, folic acid 1 mg, ascorbic acid 250 mg, thiamine hydrochloride 10 mg, and pyridoxine hydrochloride 3 mg.

Zentron (Lilly): Each chewable tablet or 5 ml of liquid contains iron 20 mg, cyanocobalamin 5 μg, thiamine hydrochloride 1 mg, riboflavin 1 mg, pyridoxine 1 mg, pantothenic acid 1 mg, niacinamide 5 mg, and ascorbic acid 100 mg.

Zymalixir (Upjohn): Each 5 ml of elixir contains ferrous gluconate 130 mg, liver concentrate 65 mg, cyanocobalamin 2 μg, thiamine hydrochloride 1 mg, riboflavin 1 mg, niacinamide 8 mg, and pyridoxine hydrochloride 0.5 mg.

Zymatinic (Upjohn): Each milliliter of drops contains liver concentrate 65 mg, cyanocobalamin 1 μg, ferrous gluconate 65 mg, riboflavin 1 mg, thiamine hydrochloride 1 mg, pyridoxine hydrochloride 0.5 mg, and niacinamide 8 mg.

Chapter 9

ANTICOAGULANTS

Thromboembolic disorders are a leading cause of morbidity and mortality in man. Thrombotic events are frequently encountered in various pathologic conditions such as cardiovascular disorders, sickle cell anemia, peripheral vascular disease, cerebrovascular disease, and trauma, as well as in obstetric, ophthalmologic, otolaryngologic, and orthopedic disorders. It is therefore important that physicians and surgeons be familiar with the major factors responsible for thrombus formation, the mechanisms of coagulation, and the pharmacology of the anticoagulant drugs used in treating these disorders.

The efficacy of anticoagulant therapy has best been documented in orthopedic surgical procedures, traumatic injury to bone or joints, or treatment of pulmonary embolism and thrombophlebitis. The long-term prophylactic use of anticoagulants in survivors of myocardial infarction is one of the more controversial areas in which these drugs are used. In the light of recent knowledge, it appears that therapy should be directed more toward controlling the complications of peripheral venous and mural embolism rather than routine long-term prophylaxis. Some clinical evidence indicates that the routine administration of anticoagulants for up to five years may decrease thrombotic episodes and mortality in patients who have had a myocardial infarction. Treatment of cerebral and peripheral arterial thrombosis is one of the least well-established uses of anticoagulants.

The therapeutic agents used as anticoagulants are heparin, the coumarin derivatives (acenocoumarol [Sintrom], dicumarol, phenprocoumon [Liquamar], warfarin sodium [Coumadin, Panwarfin], and warfarin potassium [Athrombin-K]), and the indandione derivatives (anisindione [Miradon], diphenadione [Dipaxin], and phenindione [Danilone, Hedulin]).

Anticoagulants can be given with relative safety to prevent clotting in certain life-threatening conditions if periodic laboratory testing is conducted. Whole blood clotting time determinations are used to evaluate the effects of heparin therapy; in the usual therapeutic range, the clotting time is at least two and one-half to three times greater than the normal value. However, there is no agreement that clotting time determinations are useful for predicting the appropriate dose of heparin. Some studies show a lack of correlation between clotting times and plasma heparin activity. Thus, some patients may bleed despite close supervision of therapy using this procedure as a guide. Unfortunately, no more reliable laboratory method exists.

During the continuous or intermittent intravenous infusion of heparin, whole blood clotting time should be determined several times daily. If heparin is administered infrequently, clotting time determinations may not be necessary.

The one-stage prothrombin test is commonly used to regulate the dosage of orally administered anticoagulants. This test may be regarded as a means of estimating blood concentrations of factors II (prothrombin), V (proaccelerin), VII (proconvertin), and X (Stuart-Prower factor). Three of these factors (II, VII, X) are depressed when anticoagulants are given orally. However, the depression of each of these multiple factors is not additive. The factor depressed most quickly and profoundly (usually factor VII) acts as the determinant of a routine prothrombin time determination. In the usual dosage range of the orally administered anticoagulants, the one-stage prothrombin test shows a value two to two and one-half times greater than normal when expressed in seconds, or 20% to 30% when the value is expressed as a percentage of normal prothrombin activity interpolated from a standard sodium chloride dilution curve. The prothrombin and proconvertin (P and P) test, the thrombotest, and the partial thromboplastin time (PTT) may be used, but they have no advantage over the one-stage prothrombin test for determining the adequacy of oral anticoagulant dosage. The usual therapeutic range for the P and P test and the thrombotest is 10% to 20% of the control value.

To adjust the dose of oral anticoagulants, prothrombin time should be determined daily until a maintenance dose is established, usually within 7 to 14 days. Thereafter, testing may be performed at daily, twice weekly, weekly, or longer intervals, depending upon the uniformity and predictability of the patient's response. The maintenance dose should be reevaluated periodically in patients with impaired liver function, congestive heart failure, or frequent diarrhea, or when the diet is drastically changed, when the patient receives new drugs (eg, phenobarbital), or when a drug is being withdrawn. (See also the section on Drug Interactions.)

Heparin is a naturally occurring sulfated mucopolysaccharide that produces its primary anticoagulant effect by inactivating thrombin. Heparin is metabolized mainly in the liver and is excreted by the kidneys primarily as a partially desulfated product. Up to 50% may be excreted unchanged, particularly when large doses are administered. The duration of action of heparin depends upon the dose administered. In one study, intravenous doses of 100, 200, and 400 units/kg of body weight were shown to have half-lives of 56, 96, and 152 minutes, respectively.

In the management of pulmonary embolism, one benefit of heparin, in addition to its anticoagulant effect, is that it partially reverses the bronchoconstriction produced by the embolism.

Heparin reduces postprandial lipemia by activating lipoprotein lipase. It also has a slight antihistaminic effect. Because of these actions, claims are made that heparin may be useful as a hypolipidemic or an anti-inflammatory agent. However, there is no evidence that it has any clinical utility for such purposes by any route of administration. Heparin interferes with reactions involving complement and antigen-antibody interaction and depresses aldosterone production; however, these effects have no clinical application. The sublingual administration of heparin, as suggested by some manufacturers, is not advisable because only insignificant amounts of drug are absorbed by this route.

The coumarin and indandione derivatives are administered orally; warfarin sodium also can be given intravenously or intramuscularly. These compounds inhibit hepatic synthesis of factors II (prothrombin), VII (proconvertin), IX (plasma thromboplastin component), and X (Stuart-Prower factor). Although synthesis of these factors may be inhibited by the first dose of the drug, a therapeutic effect is not achieved until the circulating endogenous factors are depleted. The mechanism of action of all members of these two anticoagulant groups is identical. Although the development of individual peak effects is variable, any one drug frequently can maintain the therapeutic responses already established by another. Both abnormal resistance and increased sensitivity to the anticoagulant action of these drugs have been reported. These anticoagulants are metabolized in the liver and their metabolic products are excreted mainly by the kidneys.

The coumarin and indandione derivatives can be classified as short-, intermediate-, or long-acting. Phenindione (plasma half-life, 5 hours) is short-acting. Acenocoumarol (plasma half-life, 24 hours) and warfarin (plasma half-life, 44 hours) are intermediate-acting. Despite the fact that warfarin can be given intravenously, its peak effect is not hastened by using this route. The long-acting anticoagulants are dicumarol (plasma half-life, 1 to 4 days), phenprocoumon (plasma half-life, approximately 6½ days), diphenadione (plasma half-life, 20 days), and anisindione (plasma half-life, 3 to 5 days).

The advantage of using the more rapidly metabolized coumarin and indandione drugs is the rapid return of prothrombin activity when the dosage is reduced or the drug is discontinued. The advantage of using the more slowly metabolized agents is that maintenance therapy is better controlled and alternate-day therapy may be feasible.

Dosage recommendations for the orally administered anticoagulants reflect the long-standing practice of either giving a large loading dose followed by a maintenance dosage regimen or starting with a large initial dose and gradually tapering off to a maintenance dosage over a period of several days. The final maintenance dosage is then adjusted according to prothrombin test responses. However, some authorities feel strongly that the loading dose technique should be discarded; they advocate using a uniform daily dosage slightly larger than the currently recommended maintenance dosage and adjusting the final dosage by using responses to the prothrombin test as a guide. The obvious advantage of the no-load procedure is that it minimizes the danger of hemorrhage, particularly at the inception of treatment in patients with diminished tolerance or unusual sensitivity to an anticoagulant drug. Additional clinical experience will be necessary to fully evaluate this technique.

Whether heparin or a longer-acting orally administered drug is the most appropriate depends upon the purpose of therapy. The direct and immediate physiochemical action of heparin makes it the drug of choice when a rapid anticoagulant effect is desired. The coumarins and indandiones may be preferred when prolonged therapy is indicated and the more convenient oral route is desired. They also are used to continue therapy after the anticoagulant effects of heparin have been established and long-term anticoagulant therapy is indicated.

The action of heparin can be antagonized by the intravenous administration of protamine sulfate (see the evaluation in this chapter). Similarly, the anticoagulant effect of the coumarin and indandione derivatives can be overcome by the administration of phytonadione (vitamin K_1) [AquaMephyton, Konakion, Mephyton, Mono-Kay] (see Chapter 11, Hemostatics); phytonadione usually produces its effect in four to eight hours, depending upon the dose and route of administration. When anticoagulant therapy is resumed after the administration of phytonadione, larger than usual doses may be required initially. The effects of the oral anticoagulants also may be counteracted by the administration of fresh whole blood or plasma, but blood should be used only as a last resort if hemorrhage is severe.

Adverse Reactions

Fever, urticaria, and anaphylaxis occur occasionally after administration of heparin, and alopecia, thrombocytopenia, or a burning sensation of the feet may develop rarely. Myalgia, ostealgia, and osteoporosis sometimes occur with prolonged use. Heparin causes natriuresis and slight hyperkalemia, apparently by inhibiting aldosterone synthesis. Local capillary rupture with subsequent ecchymoses in the area of injection is a complication that must be expected if the subcutaneous route is used; this undesirable effect is more likely to occur following intramuscular injection and this route should be avoided.

Agranulocytosis, leukopenia, leukocytosis, jaundice, hepatitis, nephropathy with acute renal tubular necrosis, severe exfoliative dermatitis, albuminuria, and massive generalized edema have followed the administration of phenindione [Danilone, Hedulin]. These reactions have been fatal in some patients. Although the other indandione derivatives have not been reported to cause these severe adverse effects, all drugs of this group must be considered potentially toxic because of their chemical similarity.

Patients should be advised that the indandione derivatives may produce an orange color in alkaline urine which may be mistaken for hematuria. The color disappears if the urine is acidified. Orange or yellow discoloration of the palms may occur after handling the tablets.

The coumarin compounds are relatively free of untoward effects and have been given for long periods without signs of toxicity. Occasional adverse reactions include gastrointestinal disturbances (especially diarrhea), elevated transaminase levels, urticaria, dermatitis, leukopenia, and alopecia. However, these reactions do not occur uniformly with all coumarin drugs (eg, leukopenia has not been reported with warfarin). Necrotic lesions that are not the result of hemorrhage have developed, usually at sites rich in fat tissue such as the breasts, abdomen, buttocks, thighs, and calves. Rarely, similar cutaneous lesions are seen.

Bleeding is an inherent risk of treatment with any anticoagulant, but its frequency and severity can be minimized by careful management. Gastrointestinal or urinary tract bleeding during anticoagulant therapy may indicate an occult lesion. Adrenal hemorrhage, subdural hematoma, intestinal submucosal hemorrhages with adynamic ileus or colitis, acute hemorrhagic pancreatitis, and cutaneous hemorrhagic necrosis are some of the possible serious complications. It has been reported that the incidence of hemopericardium after myocardial infarction is greater in patients on anticoagulant therapy than in those not receiving anticoagulants.

Precautions

Severe factor IX deficiency has been reported when heparin and the coumarins are used concomitantly. If major hemorrhagic complications occur, the anticoagulant should be discontinued immediately. Bleeding episodes of any kind indicate the need for critical reappraisal of the patient's condition.

Absolute contraindications to the use of anticoagulants are active ulcerative disease of the gastrointestinal tract, hemorrhagic blood dyscrasias, severe liver or kidney disease, open ulcerative wounds, severe hypertension, and recent surgery of the eye, spinal cord, or brain. Anticoagulants should be used with caution in the presence of mild liver or kidney disease, hypertension, alcoholism, subacute bacterial endocarditis, drainage tubes in any orifice, a history of gastrointestinal ulcers, and any occupation that carries a substantial hazard of injury.

Since orally administered anticoagulants cross the placental barrier, discretion must be exercised when administering these drugs to pregnant women. However, if the anticoagulant is discontinued three to four days before delivery, bleeding usually is not a problem. Heparin does not cross the placenta and, therefore, is preferred during pregnancy.

The indandiones should be discontinued promptly if fever or rash develops. Because severe adverse effects do occur in a small precentage of patients, it is recommended that this group of agents be reserved for those who cannot tolerate the coumarins.

A change in the maintenance dose of the orally administered anticoagulants may be required in the presence of conditions that interfere with their actions (eg, the concomitant administration of certain drugs, the existence of a particular pathologic condition, or a change in diet). Thus, careful supervision of a patient on anticoagulant therapy, using the one-stage prothrombin test, is mandatory whenever another drug is added to or withdrawn from the patient's regimen.

Various drugs have been implicated in intensifying or decreasing sensitivity to the coumarins (see the section on Drug Interactions). While not as carefully studied as the coumarins, most indandiones are known to interact with many drugs in a similar manner. One family was shown to have abnormal resistance to the effects of warfarin and dicumarol that appeared to be linked to either a single autosomal dominant or an X-linked dominant gene.

Dicumarol will cause tolbutamide [Orinase] and diphenylhydantoin [Dilantin] to accumulate in the body. Therefore, dosages of these drugs should be reduced when they are given with dicumarol, or an indandione derivative can be substituted.

HEPARIN AND PROTAMINE SULFATE

HEPARIN SODIUM

Heparin is a normal component of the body; it is synthesized in the mast cells and is particularly abundant in the liver and lungs. Its physiologic function is not fully understood, but the sudden release of heparin into the blood following anaphylactic shock indicates that it may play a role in immunologic reactions. The principal therapeutic use of heparin is to reduce the coagulability of blood. Its anticoagulant action apparently plays no significant role in maintaining the normal fluidity of blood.

Heparin requires a protein cofactor, an alpha globulin, for activity. Because of its immediate action, heparin often is given concomitantly with an orally administered anticoagulant until the desired depression of clotting factor activity is reached, at which time heparin is discontinued. Significant quantities of circulating heparin decrease the prothrombin time; therefore, prothrombin time determinations should be made just before the next dose of heparin is administered. Heparin probably should be continued for 24 to 48 hours after a satisfactory depression of prothrombin complex activity is achieved. Heparin can be used in place of sodium citrate as an anticoagulant for donor blood in transfusions for cardiovascular surgery.

This agent may be administered by intermittent subcutaneous and intravenous injections or by continuous intravenous drip. It is inactive orally or sublingually. At full therapeutic dosage, the onset of effect is immediate following intravenous injection, and occurs approximately 20 to 30 minutes after subcutaneous injection.

The normal coagulation system can be activated by nonspecific mechanisms such as the presence of bacterial endotoxins, the formation of antigen- antibody complexes, shock, and leakage of amniotic fluid into the maternal circulation. The release of thromboplastin as a consequence of disease or trauma also may initiate clotting. Fibrin thrombi develop in the small vessels throughout the body, including vital organs such as the brain, kidneys, lungs, and adrenal glands. This clotting condition is generally referred to as disseminated intravascular coagulation (DIC). While it persists, the normal clotting factors (prothrombin, fibrinogen, factors V and VIII) and platelets are being consumed, hence the older term that has been applied to this condition, "consumptive coagulopathy." In patients experiencing DIC, bleeding will occur following needle puncture or other trauma or may be spontaneous. The primary treatment of DIC is to control the underlying pathology. In the meantime, supportive therapy must be given. Transfusion of platelet concentrates may be instituted if thrombocytopenia is severe. However, the administration of clotting factors in an effort to replace those factors being consumed only seems to accelerate DIC. Subjective evidence indicates that the injection of heparin (adults 100 units/kg of body weight, children 50 units/kg, given every four hours intravenously) may reverse the clotting phenomenon and arrest bleeding. Nevertheless, some patients with DIC may not respond to heparin and, rarely, this drug may aggravate bleeding. When this occurs, protamine can be given to counteract the effect of heparin.

Intravenous or subcutaneous injection of heparin seldom causes serious adverse reactions (see the Introductory Statement). However, when administered subcutaneously, it can cause a hematoma, and is even more likely to cause local hematoma or tissue irritation following intramuscular injection; therefore, the latter route should be avoided.

The dosage of heparin should be stated in units rather than in milligrams. The U.S.P. standard for minimal potency is 120 units/mg of dry material derived from lung tissue and 140 units/mg of dry material derived from other sources. The potency of commercial preparations ranges from 140 to 190 units/mg. Physicians who write doses in milligrams do so with the mistaken idea they are being more exact. Precisely the reverse is true because 100 mg of heparin may represent between 12,000 and 19,000 units of effect.

USUAL DOSAGE.—

Intravenous: Adults, 5,000 units initially, followed by individualized doses of 5,000 to 10,000 units every four hours to a total of 25,000 units daily.

Intravenous Infusion: Adults, 100 units/kg of body weight initially followed by 30 units/kg/hour at a rate of 0.5 unit/kg/minute in 5% dextrose injection or isotonic sodium chloride injection. *Children,* 50 units/kg initially, followed by 100 units/kg every four hours. An infusion pump should be used to control the dosage.

Subcutaneous: Adults, 10,000 to 12,000 units every 8 hours or 14,000 to 20,000 units every 12 hours. Different sites should be used for each injection to prevent the development of a massive hematoma.

Intramuscular: This route should not be used.

PREPARATIONS.—Heparin Sodium U.S.P. *Injection:* Solution 1,000, 5,000, 10,000, 20,000, and 40,000 units/ml; gel (for repository injection) 20,000 units/ml.

AVAILABLE TRADEMARKS.—Depo-Heparin Sodium (Upjohn), Hepathrom (Fellows-Testagar), Lipo-Hepin (Riker), Liquaemin Sodium (Organon), Meparin (Elkins), Panheprin (Abbott). Drug also marketed by other manufacturers under generic name.

PROTAMINE SULFATE

Protamine sulfate is a heparin antagonist. Paradoxically, it has anticoagulant action of its own and prolongs clotting time. It is a true antithromboplastin, but is not as active as heparin and therefore is not used clinically as an anticoagulant. When protamine is given in the presence of heparin, the drugs neutralize the action of each other. Each milligram of protamine sulfate neutralizes 80 to 100 U.S.P. units of heparin activity, depending upon the source of heparin. The reaction is almost instantaneous and the effects of protamine persist for approximately two hours.

Protamine usually is well tolerated. Large intravenous doses (up to 200 mg in two hours) have been administered without untoward effects. Toxic manifestations include acute hypotension, dyspnea, and bradycardia; occasionally, a feeling of warmth and flushing of the face also may be observed.

USUAL DOSAGE.—*Intravenous:* Total dosage is determined by the amount of heparin given over the previous three to four hours (each milligram of protamine sulfate, calculated as dry material, neutralizes not less than 80 U.S.P. units of heparin activity derived from lung tissue and not less than 100 U.S.P. units of heparin activity derived from intestinal mucosa). A 1% solution is injected slowly over a period of one to three minutes. The dose should not exceed 50 mg at any one time.

PREPARATIONS.—*Injection:* Powder 50 mg vial with 5 ml of diluent; solution 1% in 5 and 25 ml containers. Drug marketed under generic name.

COUMARIN DERIVATIVES

ACENOCOUMAROL [Sintrom]

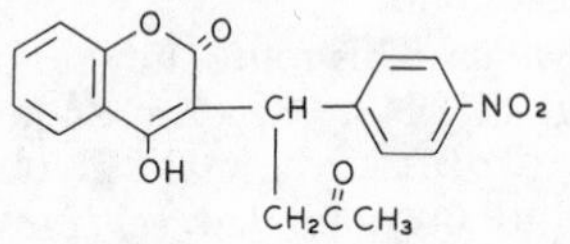

This intermediate-acting, orally administered coumarin derivative inhibits the synthesis of several anticoagulant factors in the liver. It is used in the same manner and with the same precautions as other coumarin derivatives. Following initial administration, the peak effect is reached in 24 to 48 hours, and restoration of normal prothrombin activity occurs two to three days after the last dose is given. The initial dose of acenocoumarol rather than the maintenance dose must be used to maintain the anticoagulant effect of heparin.

Acenocoumarol is relatively free from adverse reactions and, when untoward effects do occur, they are similar to those of the other coumarin derivatives (see the Introductory Statement and the evaluation on Dicumarol). Although this anticoagulant contains a nitrobenzene group, it has not been reported to produce bone marrow depression.

USUAL DOSAGE.—*Oral: Adults,* 20 mg on first day, 12 mg on second day, and 8 mg on third day. A smaller than average initial dose is advisable for patients with impaired hepatic or renal function, or for those in whom an exaggerated response is anticipated. Maintenance dosage should be individualized in accordance with results of prothrombin time determinations; the usual dose is 2 to 10 mg daily.

PREPARATIONS.—Sintrom (Geigy). *Oral:* Tablets 4 mg.

DICUMAROL

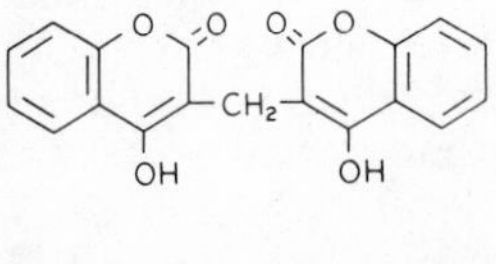

Dicumarol has the same actions and uses as the other oral anticoagulants. This drug is long-acting; it requires three to five days for peak action to develop and, once hypoprothrombinemia is established, the action persists for two to ten days following discontinuation of therapy. Both resistance and sensitivity to its anticoagulant effect have been reported following concomitant use of other drugs. Dicumarol is poorly absorbed from the gastrointestinal tract.

Many factors, including other drugs, affect the prothrombin level and activity in the body and the metabolism of dicumarol; therefore, the dosage of this drug must be individualized and frequently may have to be changed. Dicumarol may cause accumulation of certain drugs and increased destruction or elimination of others. More commonly, other drugs cause an accumulation or increased destruction of the anticoagulant. (See the section on Drug Interactions.) Accordingly, the dose of interacting drugs must be decreased or increased when dicumarol is given concomitantly.

As with all anticoagulants, hemorrhagic complications may occur during therapy. If bleeding occurs, the drug should be discontinued immediately. Phytonadione (vitamin K_1) counteracts the anticoagulant effect, as will fresh whole blood or plasma; blood should be given only if hemorrhage is severe. Phytonadione usually produces its peak effect within four to eight hours following oral administration.

Untoward reactions, which occur infrequently with coumarin derivatives, include dermatitis; necrosis of the breast, buttocks, thighs, abdomen, calves, and skin; alopecia; gastrointestinal irritation; urticaria; leukopenia; and elevated transaminase levels (see the Introductory Statement).

USUAL DOSAGE.—*Oral: Adults,* 300 mg on first day, 200 mg on second day, and 100 mg on third day. Since frequent dosage adjustments may be necessary during the first 7 to 14 days of therapy, the prothrombin time should be determined daily during this period. The maintenance dose is 25 to 150 mg daily, depending upon the results of prothrombin time determinations.

PREPARATIONS.—*Oral:* Capsules 25 and 50 mg; tablets 25, 50, and 100 mg. Drug marketed under generic name and under the name Bishydroxycoumarin.

PHENPROCOUMON [Liquamar]

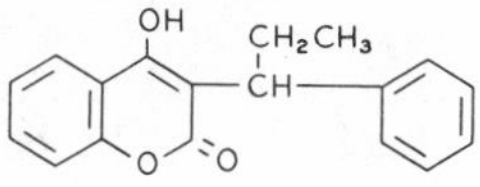

The actions and uses of phenprocoumon, a long-acting coumarin derivative, are qualitatively similar to those of other coumarin and indandione derivatives. The onset of peak action is 48 to 72 hours after administration of the initial dose; recovery may take up to seven days after the last dose is given. This drug frequently maintains the anticoagulant effect established by other anticoagulants.

The precautions, adverse reactions, and general class characteristics described for the other coumarin compounds also apply to phenprocoumon (see the Introductory Statement and the evaluation on Dicumarol).

USUAL DOSAGE.—*Oral: Adults,* 21 mg on first day, 9 mg on second day, 3 mg on third day. Maintenance dosage is individualized and varies between 1 and 4 mg; the exact amount may have to be adjusted to within 0.5 mg. The amount of drug given is determined by results of prothrombin time determinations.

PREPARATIONS.—Liquamar (Organon). *Oral:* Tablets 3 mg.

WARFARIN POTASSIUM [Athrombin-K]
WARFARIN SODIUM [Coumadin, Panwarfin]

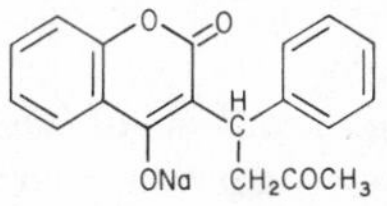

Like dicumarol and other related compounds, warfarin depresses blood prothrombin complex activity. It is readily absorbed from the gastrointestinal tract, and may be used orally, intramuscularly, and intravenously. Warfarin is intermediate-acting with a peak action of 36 to 72 hours and a duration of effect of two to five days. Overdosage can be counteracted by administering phytonadione (vitamin K_1).

The precautions, adverse reactions, and general class characteristics described for the other coumarin compounds also apply to warfarin (see the Introductory Statement and the evaluation on Dicumarol).

USUAL DOSAGE.—*Oral, Intramuscular, Intravenous: Adults,* initially, 15 to 20 mg, followed by a maintenance dose of 2.5 to 10 mg daily. Prothrombin time should be determined before the initial dose is given and every day thereafter until a stable response is attained. After a steady state is achieved, prothrombin time should be determined at regular intervals (see the Introductory Statement).

PREPARATIONS.—

Warfarin Potassium:

Athrombin-K (Purdue Frederick). *Oral:* Tablets 5 and 10 mg.

Warfarin Sodium:

Coumadin (Endo).

Oral: Tablets 2, 2.5, 5, 7.5, 10, and 25 mg.

Injection: Powder 50 mg with 2 ml of diluent and 75 mg with 3 ml of diluent.

Panwarfin (Abbott). *Oral:* Tablets 2, 2.5, 5, 7.5, 10, and 25 mg.

INDANDIONE DERIVATIVES

ANISINDIONE [Miradon]

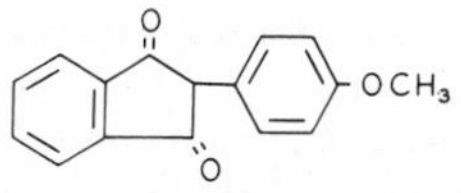

This long-acting, orally effective anticoagulant is chemically related to phenindione and is qualitatively similar in actions and uses to the other coumarin and indandione derivatives presently available. After the initial dose, its peak effect is reached in 48 to 72 hours and coagulation factors gradually return to normal 24 to 72 hours after the drug is discontinued. Phytonadione (vitamin K_1) or fresh whole blood will counteract the effect of this agent.

Hemorrhagic complications may occur (see the Introductory Statement). Dermatitis is the only other untoward reaction reported. However, since other indandione derivatives have produced serious reactions (eg, agranulocytosis, jaundice, nephropathy), anisindione has the potential to cause serious reactions. The drug should be discontinued promptly if fever or rash appears, for these reactions may signal the onset of a more severe complication.

Like other indandione derivatives, anisindione occasionally will impart an orange color to alkaline urine that can be differentiated from hematuria by its disappearance on acidification of the urine. The patient should be advised of this possible occurrence.

USUAL DOSAGE.—*Oral: Adults,* 300 to 500 mg on first day, 200 to 300 mg on second day, and 100 to 200 mg on third day. The average maintenance dose is 25 to 250 mg daily and should be established at the dosage which maintains prothrombin time determinations at two and one-half to three times the normal value.

PREPARATIONS.—Miradon (Schering). *Oral:* Tablets 50 mg.

DIPHENADIONE [Dipaxin]

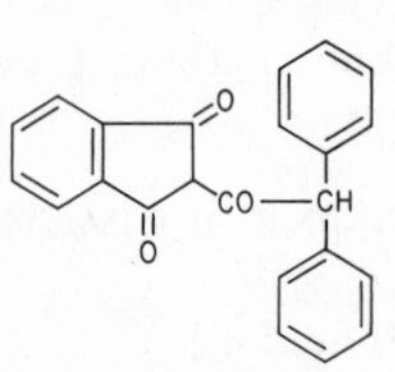

Diphenadione, an orally effective anticoagulant chemically related to phenindione, is one of the most potent and long-acting depressants of prothrombin complex activity. Its peak effect occurs within 48 to 72 hours, and prothrombin depression may persist for 20 days.

This drug has approximately the same ratio between effective and toxic (hemorrhagic) dosage as the other oral anticoagulants; therefore, similar precautions are necessary to avoid overdosage and hemorrhagic complications, particularly in view of its long duration of action. The general class characteristics and precautions described for other indandione compounds also apply to diphenadione (see the Introductory Statement and the evaluation on Phenindione).

No adverse reactions have been reported other than occasional nausea and hemorrhagic complications at toxic dosage levels. However, because of its close chemical similarity to phenindione, which has caused agranulocytosis, diphenadione has the potential to cause similar blood dyscrasias, as well as other severe reactions.

USUAL DOSAGE.—*Oral: Adults,* 20 to 30 mg on first day, 10 to 15 mg on second day. Maintenance dosage is between 7 and 15 mg daily, depending upon the results of prothrombin time determinations.

PREPARATIONS.—Dipaxin (Upjohn). *Oral:* Tablets 5 mg.

PHENINDIONE [Danilone, Hedulin]

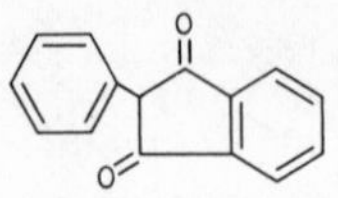

This short-acting anticoagulant is similar in action and uses to the coumarins, but it is chemically unrelated and is effective in smaller doses. Phenindione acts more promptly than dicumarol. Therapeutic levels are usually obtained in 18 to 24 hours, and prothrombin time returns to normal 24 to 48 hours after the drug is discontinued. As with other oral anticoagulants, both resistance and sensitivity to its anticoagulant effect have been reported. Phytonadione (vitamin K_1), fresh whole blood, or plasma will counteract the anticoagulant action of phenindione.

Agranulocytosis, leukopenia, leukocytosis, jaundice, hepatitis, nephropathy with acute renal tubular necrosis, severe exfoliative dermatitis, albuminuria, and massive generalized edema have been reported with use of phenindione. Some of these effects have been fatal. All indandione derivatives are dangerous drugs and should be reserved for use in patients who cannot tolerate the coumarin drugs. Phenindione should be discontinued if evidence of hypersensitivity, leukopenia, or agranulocytosis appears. Patients should be instructed to report prodromal symptoms such as marked fatigue, chills, fever, and sore throat.

Phenindione may produce a harmless orange or reddish discoloration of the urine, and patients should be so advised to avoid creating a false impression of hematuria.

USUAL DOSAGE.—*Oral: Adults,* patients weighing less than 70 kg should be given an initial dose of 200 mg daily; those weighing more than 70 kg should receive 300 mg daily in equally divided doses in the morning and at bedtime. Prothrombin time determinations should be made prior to treatment and then daily until an effective maintenance dose is established. Thereafter, determinations should be made at regular intervals (eg, every 7 or 14 days). The usual maintenance dosage is 50 to 100 mg daily in equally divided doses in the morning and at bedtime.

PREPARATIONS.—

Danilone (Schieffelin). *Oral:* Tablets 50 mg.

Hedulin (Merrell-National). *Oral:* Tablets 20 and 50 mg.

MIXTURES

There is no rationale for using a mixture containing an anticoagulant. Nevertheless, such mixtures are available commercially, and are generally proposed for treating hyperlipidemias or inflammation. These mixtures usually contain heparin, and sometimes are designed to be taken sublingually as well as by injection. At best, use of the injectable preparations can only be classified as experimental, since heparin has no proven hypolipidemic or anti-inflammatory properties. The sublingual preparations are to be universally condemned because heparin is ineffective by this route.

Chapter 10

BLOOD, BLOOD COMPONENTS, AND BLOOD SUBSTITUTES

The use of whole blood and plasma has been the mainstay of transfusion therapy for many years. The introduction of plastic containers with multiple satellite pouches has now made it possible to separate freshly donated blood into red blood cell, white blood cell, or platelet concentrates, fresh frozen plasma, and antihemophilic cryoprecipitates in a closed system. Since these sterile component preparations can now be conveniently prepared, indiscriminate use of whole blood is a practice to be discouraged. Component transfusion therapy is superior because it allows a patient to receive that portion of blood required without needlessly burdening his circulation, and the risk of contracting acute viral (post-transfusion) hepatitis or being exposed to other sensitizing agents or unknown drugs in the blood is minimized or avoided.

In order to use blood and its components properly, the physician must know what preparations are available, what possible effects can be achieved by administering these preparations, and the properties of fresh and stored blood. In addition, he must recognize that every transfusion or administration of an unsterilized blood component carries with it a risk of introducing hepatitis virus and other disease-producing entities (eg, cytomegalic inclusion virus, malaria parasite) and that there is always danger of an incompatibility that may have disastrous results in a particular patient.

As with any drug with known side effects, the physician must weigh the potential danger against the expected benefit before ordering a blood transfusion.

When a blood transfusion is considered essential, there is much the physician can do to reduce the risk of untoward effects. One of the most valuable measures is the use of red blood cell concentrates (packed human blood cells, U.S.P.) rather than whole blood. The use of concentrated blood with a hematocrit value of 60% to 80% reduces the incidence of hypervolemia. Because of the smaller volume of plasma given to the patient, use of red blood cell concentrates also reduces the amount of sodium, potassium, citrate, ammonium, and blood group antibodies infused. Most blood banks now stock red blood cell concentrates as a routine inventory item. The shelf life, requirements for crossmatching, and mode of administration are the same as for whole blood.

Red blood cells should not be used as a plasma volume expander. Other solutions (eg, albumin, Ringer's, dextran, 0.9% sodium chloride, protein fraction) will replace blood loss from acute hemorrhage without the danger of transmitting hepatitis virus. The use of group O, Rh negative, non-crossmatched blood is discouraged because of the possibility of sensitization caused by red blood cell antigen and of infusing incompatible isoagglutinins.

Frozen-thawed red blood cells are now prepared in a number of blood centers. The process produces red blood cells free of irregular antibodies, plasma proteins, and extracellular potassium with few white blood cells. Two techniques are used: low glycerol, fast freezing (liquid nitrogen -196 C) and high glycerol, slow freezing (-85 C). In both techniques, the cryoprotective agent, glycerol, must be washed out of the thawed red blood cells. The washing process can be accomplished in a number of ways but this portion of the procedure still needs refinement. Red blood cells preserved by freezing can be satisfactorily stored for at least five years. This technique will become increasingly important clinically. For example, frozen red blood cells of rare types can provide either autologous or homologous transfusion for patients whose surgery can be scheduled months in advance, or erythroblastosis fetalis requiring rare blood for transfusion therapy can be treated with red blood cells from the mother which have been frozen in advance. This type of preparation also is useful for patients who are scheduled for organ transplantation because the histocompatibility antigens are largely removed with the white blood cells; therefore, the chance of immunization to white blood cells or plasma proteins is minimized and patients already so immunized will not have adverse reactions to these antigens.

Blood platelets provide phospholipid required for formation of the plasma clot and, more important, provide the initial mechanism of hemostasis by aggregating into plugs that seal small openings in blood vessels. The latter function, which occurs only with viable platelets, is an important factor to consider in the storage and transfusion of platelets, since normal platelets have a life span of 9 to 11 days and this aggregating effect of platelet transfusion is usually limited to a time interval considerably less than the life span of the cell. Most patients do not bleed spontaneously unless the platelet count is less than 50,000/mm^3; therefore, platelet transfusions should be given only for severe thrombocytopenia with active or imminent bleeding. Plasmapheresis (collection of blood from a donor, separation of the plasma, and reinfusion of the red blood cells) is one of the processes used to harvest the quantities of platelets needed to control thrombocytopenia. The presence of autologous antibodies (eg, in idiopathic thrombocytopenic purpura) and the post-transfusion induction of homologous antibodies against platelets may impair the usefulness of platelet transfusions.

Platelet-rich (unconcentrated) plasma provides other coagulation factors as well as platelets. However, the relatively large volume needed to arrest bleeding associated with thrombocytopenia limits the number of platelets that can be provided with this material. Although platelet concentrates may contain fewer viable platelets, many more units can be administered safely. The platelets from 1 unit of blood can raise the platelet count of a 70 kg adult approximately 5,000 platelets per microliter. Thus, to raise the platelet count by 50,000 per microliter, 1 unit of platelet concentrate must be transfused for each 7 kg of body weight.

Occasionally, patients with life-threatening agranulocytosis may benefit from the transfusion of white blood cell concentrates prepared from 20 to 30 or more units of fresh blood. These concentrates are not yet routinely available at many centers. Patients with chronic myelocytic leukemia, with white blood cell counts above 100,000/mm^3, have been used as leukocyte donors. The possible hazards of transplantation and subsequent graft versus host or host versus graft reactions must be considered in such transfusions. Leukopheresis, a procedure similar to plasmapheresis but used to prepare leukocytes for transfusion, is still in the experimental stage. Continuous-flow cell-separation devices are being used in a number of blood centers.

Plasma, the cell-free liquid portion of uncoagulated blood, contains the three major groups of blood proteins (albumin, globulin, fibrinogen) and is indicated primarily for treating coagulation deficiencies. The only plasma preparation that currently has official status is antihemophilic human plasma, U.S.P., which is derived from a single donor. However, a deficiency of one or more coagulation factors is preferably treated by administering the appropriate blood component such as antihemophilic factor or fibrinogen (see Chapter 11, Hemostatics). Only when the component products are not readily available or when multiple clotting factor deficiencies exist should the use of single donor antihemophilic plasma, fresh plasma, fresh frozen plasma, or frozen-dried plasma be considered.

Plasma can be given to increase blood volume in counteracting the hypovolemia and hemoconcentration of burn shock and to maintain colloidal osmotic pressure and prevent edema during cardiopulmonary bypass procedures or in patients with hypoproteinemia. However, many physicians now feel that replacement by a balanced electrolyte solution, lactated Ringer's injection, buffered sodium chloride injection (in amounts two to three times the estimated blood loss), a solution of normal human serum albumin, or a partial protein fraction is as effective as plasma for these purposes. These solutions do not carry the inherent risk of transmitting hepatitis virus. Plasma also can be used to restore plasma protein levels to normal, but its ability to supply an adequate amount of protein for metabolic processes is doubtful. Fresh frozen plasma may be useful as an adjunct to control bleeding associated with anticoagulant or massive transfusion therapy, or to counteract hemolytic transfusion reactions. Preferably only single donor plasma should be used so that it can be injected with relative safety when it is crossmatched. If pooled plasma (a mixture of plasma obtained from several donors) is injected, the danger of reactions from agglutinins is less but the probability of contracting acute viral hepatitis is greatly increased. The manufacture of pooled plasma is no longer licensed by the Food and Drug Administration.

The use of plastic bags rather than glass bottles has almost eliminated the hazard of air embolism associated with administration of blood under pressure.

Medications should never be added to blood or plasma.

If temporary maintenance of blood volume is the sole therapeutic objective, blood volume expanders rather than whole blood or plasma can be used. Normal human serum albumin [Albumisol, Albuspan, Buminate, Pro-Bumin, Proserum] and plasma protein fraction [Plasmanate, Plasmaplex, Protenate] are obtained from normal human plasma. They are given primarily in the emergency treatment of shock until whole blood can be obtained, and to correct hypoproteinemia. These preparations are sterile-filtered and pasteurized by heating for ten hours at 60 C to reduce the risk of acute viral hepatitis caused by hepatitis virus B (long-incubation or so-called serum hepatitis); to date, no cases of hepatitis have been reported following their use.

Because of the difficulties involved in maintaining adequate stores of whole blood or plasma, substitutes (eg, dextran solutions) have been developed to improve and support circulation during shock. These plasma substitutes can be given to restore blood volume after hemorrhage when whole blood is not available or until it can be obtained, to correct the oligemia of burn shock, or to temporarily maintain colloidal osmotic pressure. The plasma volume expanders such as dextran 70 [Macrodex] and dextran 75 [Gentran 75] will help maintain the osmotic pressure of plasma in emergencies or during certain types of cardiovascular surgery, but they should not be regarded as substitutes for whole blood or its derivatives in the treatment of anemia or hypoproteinemia. Sodium chloride, balanced electrolyte [Normosol-R, Plasma-Lyte 148, Polyonic R-148], and dextrose injections also can be used for temporary transfusion therapy (see Chapter 16, Replenishers and Regulators of Water, Electrolytes, and Nutrients).

A more detailed discussion of transfusion procedures is beyond the scope of this book. The reader is referred to an AMA publication of the Committee on Transfusion and Transplantation entitled *General Principles of Blood Transfusion* for further information.

Adverse Reactions and Precautions

Despite the greater safety associated with new transfusion techniques, adverse reactions and deaths still occur after the administration of blood, blood components, or blood substitutes. Thus, blood and blood-related products should be used only when there is a clear indication that they are needed. In order to reduce the probability of transfusion reactions, it is essential that all persons associated with the collection, storage, handling, or administration of these agents exercise the greatest possible care at all times.

Viral Hepatitis: One of the most serious adverse reactions is acute viral hepatitis, which may develop after transmission of the virus in such products as packed red blood cells, platelet concentrates or platelet-rich plasma, whole blood, plasma, or fibrinogen; however, the hepatitis may be subclinical and detectable only if liver function tests, including the monitoring of serum enzyme levels, are performed. At present, there is no practical method for sterilizing whole blood nor a fully satisfactory and reliable method for sterilizing plasma. Recently, increased emphasis has been placed on the screening and selection of blood donors in an effort to reduce the incidence of viral hepatitis.

The discovery of hepatitis-associated antigen (HAA, Australia antigen, SH antigen) and the virus-like particles associated with it appears to be a significant advance in developing a diagnostic test for viral hepatitis. Recent work indicates that there are at least two different forms of viral hepatitis caused by immunologically distinct viral agents. The letter designations A (short-incubation or so-called infectious hepatitis, IH virus) and B (long-incubation or so-called serum hepatitis, SH virus) have been applied to these viruses. HAA has not been detected in association with hepatitis virus A, whereas it is present in approximately 75% of the cases caused by hepatitis virus B (one report has indicated an incidence as high as 97%). The Food and Drug Administration now requires all blood banks and plasma collecting and processing facilities to be licensed and they must test all units of blood collected for HAA. However, testing materials currently being used (eg, Ausria-125 [Abbott], Hapindex [Ortho]) are not totally accurate; hepatitis has occurred following a negative result. Part of the problem in detecting HAA is that it is transient in blood and usually reaches its peak concentration several weeks prior to the time that elevated SGPT levels appear and clinical hepatitis is recognized. In spite of our limited understanding of HAA, the difficulties encountered in its determination, and the fact that it has been found only in association with hepatitis virus B, the United States Public Health Service has estimated that routine screening of blood donors and exclusion of those showing a positive HAA test could potentially prevent 20% to 30% of all cases of acute viral (post-transfusion) hepatitis and 1,000 to 2,000 deaths a year. Work also is progressing on the identification and development of testing procedures for another, more labile antigen that has been described in association with hepatitis virus A.

Hypersensitivity Reactions: Donor blood also is directly responsible for allergic responses. Fortunately, most hypersensitivity (allergic) reactions (eg, urticarial rashes, generalized pruritus) are mild and transitory and are not life-threatening. However, severe effects (eg, bronchospasm) occur occasionally and, rarely, cause death. Patients with IgA deficiency may be sensitized by blood transfusion and develop an anaphylactic reaction if the transfusion is repeated. Antihistamines may be helpful in controlling milder reactions, but epinephrine, levarterenol [Levophed], or corticosteroids may be necessary to control serious sensitivity reactions.

Febrile Reactions: These reactions do not occur as often today as in the past, and are not generally dangerous unless they affect other complicating conditions. Pyrogenic reactions are characterized by an increase in body temperature to 39.4 or 40.0 C (103 or 104 F), usually within 15 minutes after the transfusion is begun, and tremors, chills, and headache, which may be severe. Febrile reactions related to leukocyte or platelet agglutinins also occur. When a fever develops, the infusion should be stopped and the cause investigated, since it can be an early manifestation of a more serious reaction, especially hemolytic transfusion reaction.

Hemolysis: This potentially fatal complication of blood transfusion is caused by mislabeling of specimens or, occasionally, by technical errors in blood typing, and results in administration of blood to the wrong recipient. The injection of 100 to 200 ml of incompatible blood may be followed by flushing, tachycardia, restlessness, dyspnea, chills, fever, headache, substernal or flank pain, nausea, and vomiting Hemoglobinuria and hemoglobinemia are present and often are followed by oliguria and acute renal failure. A hemorrhagic diathesis, with thrombocytopenia and spontaneous bleeding, occurs occasionally and may be caused by the intravascular destruction of fibrinogen. Rarely, shock and death may occur within a few minutes after the transfusion has begun. When a hemolytic reaction is suspected, the transfusion must be stopped immediately. The intravenous administration of a suitable osmotic diuretic (eg, mannitol) may help to prevent acute renal failure, and systemically administered corticosteroids may be useful in treating other manifestations.

Jaundice: Stored blood that is approaching its expiration date may produce jaundice if given to patients with inadequate liver function or Gilbert's syndrome. This reaction is caused by a higher percentage of hemolyzed red blood cells than is present in fresh whole blood.

Reactions from Contaminated Products: Transfusion reactions that follow the administration of whole blood, blood components, or plasma contaminated with bacteria are probably the most catastrophic. Fortunately these reactions are rare and can be avoided if proper techniques are carefully followed in the collection and storage of blood. A severe reaction, manifested by chills, fever, profound shock, coma, convulsions, and, frequently, death, may occur after the injection of the first 50 to 100 ml of contaminated product. If the patient survives the initial reaction, he may still develop a bacteremia that will necessitate treatment with a suitable antibiotic. Systemically administered corticosteroids are useful adjuncts to lessen the severity of the reactions.

Hypervolemia: Hypervolemia can be a serious consequence of transfusions with whole blood, plasma, or plasma substitutes, particularly in the elderly, the very young, and patients with pulmonary or cardiac disease. The use of packed red blood cells greatly reduces this hazard. Although hematocrit determinations are commonly used as guides for transfusion therapy, they are not entirely satisfactory. The monitoring of central venous pressure is probably the best means to detect overexpansion of blood volume.

Multiple Transfusion Reactions: The patient who has received multiple transfusions frequently develops leukoagglutinins which, in subsequent transfusions, may cause febrile reactions. Continuous flow centrifugation is more efficient than repeated batch washing to remove the leukocytes and reduce the frequency of these reactions. In the absence of these methods, a nylon filter is effective in removing neutrophils from fresh heparinized blood.

Massive Transfusion Reactions: Hyperkalemia, ionic hypocalcemia, thrombocytopenia, and elevated blood citrate levels may result from massive transfusion. Furthermore, depletion of unstable factors in the blood during storage can cause bleeding during massive transfusion. This condition can be controlled by the intermittent administration of small amounts of fresh blood or plasma. Stored blood also may be adversely affected by anticoagulants; other changes, such as a decrease in pH or increases in ammonia, lactate, and potassium levels, generally are not a problem except in patients with severe renal disease.

The low temperature of stored blood is a hazard of massive transfusion therapy; the administration of 3,000 ml or more of cold blood at a rate of 50 ml per minute causes hypothermia and increases the risk of cardiac arrest. The rapid infusion of massive amounts of blood and the administration of blood to infants and children represent situations in which warmed blood should be used. The safest method of warming is to pass blood through coiled sterile plastic tubing in a heated water bath. Caution must be exercised if a microwave or electromagnetic blood warmer is used. Recent evidence indicates that blood may be overheated with these units even when they are used properly, and the end result of the overheating can be massive hemolysis. Since the microwave heaters are in close proximity to the patient receiving the warmed blood, they are hazardous to patients with pacemakers, and cataracts have developed in some individuals after their use.

INDIVIDUAL EVALUATIONS

NORMAL HUMAN SERUM ALBUMIN

[Albumisol, Albuspan, Buminate, Pro-Bumin, Proserum]

This sterile plasma protein preparation is obtained by fractionating whole human blood. It is sterile-filtered and pasteurized for ten hours at 60 C to remove the hazard of acute viral (so-called serum or post-transfusion) hepatitis. Albumisol is prepared from venous blood that is nonreactive when tested for hepatitis associated antigen (HAA). Normal human serum albumin is used to reduce edema and raise the serum protein level in hypoproteinemia, as a blood volume expander in hypovolemic shock, and in solution as a vehicle for transfusing packed red blood cells. This preparation is useful as an adjunct in exchange transfusions when treating hyperbilirubinemia or erythroblastosis fetalis, and in the prevention and treatment of cerebral edema caused by neurosurgery or anoxia.

Since normal human serum albumin is a constituent of human blood, it is essentially free from toxic effects and does not interfere with normal coagulation mechanisms. However, it should not be administered if the solution is turbid or contains sediment, nor should more than 250 g of albumin be given in 48 hours; if more protein is required, whole blood or plasma should be given instead of additional albumin. This preparation is contraindicated in severe anemia or heart failure, and large amounts should not be given to patients with a low cardiac reserve in order to avoid hypervolemia and possible congestive heart failure.

Normal human serum albumin contains no preservative and should be used promptly once opened. It can be stored at room temperature, but the temperature should not exceed 37 C.

USUAL DOSAGE.—*Intravenous:* Although the following dosage recommendations are useful guides, specific amounts should be determined by the degree of venous and pulmonary congestion and measurement of hemoglobin or hematocrit values. A 5% solution can be given undiluted and a 25% solution can be given undiluted *slowly* or diluted with sterile, nonpyrogenic sodium chloride injection or 5% dextrose injection; dextrose injection is preferred when treating edema. A solution made approximately isotonic with citrated plasma can be prepared by adding 20 ml of 25% albumin solution to 100 ml of sodium chloride injection or 5% dextrose injection. A 25% solution is usually given at a rate of 1 ml/minute and a 5% solution at a rate of 2 to 4 ml/minute.

For hypoproteinemia, *adults*, 25 to 75 g daily. *Children* (in emergency), 25 to 50 g; (nonemergency) one-quarter to one-half adult dose, given more slowly than in an emergency situation.

For shock, *adults and children*, 25 g initially,

repeated in 15 to 30 minutes if necessary. If hemorrhage is a prominent feature, whole blood should be used if available.

For burns, *adults and children*, extent of burn determines amount and duration of administration. The initial dose is 2.2 ml of 25% solution per kilogram of body weight, followed by 5% solution in sufficient quantity to prevent hemoconcentration and maintain near normal electrolyte concentration.

For nephrosis, *adults and children*, 2.2 to 4.4 ml of undiluted 25% solution per kilogram of body weight daily. The preparation should be administered slowly to avoid rapid plasma volume expansion.

For hepatic cirrhosis, *adults*, 25 g daily or 50 g every other day.

PREPARATIONS.—

Albumisol (Merck Sharp & Dohme), Albuspan (Parke, Davis), Buminate (Hyland), Pro-Bumin (Lederle). *Injection:* Solution 5% in 250 and 500 ml containers with intravenous administration sets; solution 25% (salt poor) in 20, 50, and 100 ml containers [Buminate]. The 50 and 100 ml containers are supplied with intravenous administration sets.

Proserum (Dow). *Injection:* Solution 5% in 250 ml containers [Proserum 5] and 25% in 50 ml containers [Proserum 25]. Solutions are supplied with intravenous administration sets.

Drug also marketed under generic name.

WHOLE BLOOD

Whole blood is drawn from a selected donor under rigid aseptic conditions and the ABO blood groups and Rh type are identified. It contains citrate ion or heparin as an anticoagulant. Following crossmatching, it is administered through a filter system when it is necessary to supplement or replace circulating whole blood. Whole blood is stored between 1 and 10 C and the temperature is held constant within a 2 C range, except during shipment when the temperature can be between 1 and 10 C. The expiration date for whole blood is not later than 21 days after the blood is drawn if citrate ion is the anticoagulant, and not later than 48 hours after the blood is drawn if heparin is the anticoagulant.

For adverse reactions and precautions, see the Introductory Statement.

USUAL DOSAGE.—*Intravenous:* 500 ml (1 unit) repeated as necessary. Usually 2 or more units will be given because the danger of transmitting hepatitis is such that the risk is not justifiable unless more than 1 unit is indicated.

PREPARATIONS.—Whole Blood, U.S.P. Available through hospital blood banks.

PACKED HUMAN BLOOD CELLS

Packed human blood cells are prepared by removing the plasma from whole blood. The ABO blood group and Rh type are identified. This preparation is used when it is desirable to increase the number of circulating red cells without appreciably increasing circulating blood volume (eg, in aplastic anemia). It may be prepared from whole blood at any time during the dated period; however, if centrifugation is used for separation, the preparation cannot be made later than six days after the blood has been drawn. Packed human blood cells should be stored at 1 to 6 C, with the temperature held constant within a 2 C range. Its expiration date is not later than that of the whole blood from which it was derived or 24 hours after the hermetic seal is broken.

For adverse reactions and precautions, see the Introductory Statement.

USUAL DOSAGE.—*Intravenous:* The equivalent of 500 ml (1 unit) of whole blood, repeated as necessary. Usually 2 or more units will be given because the danger of transmitting hepatitis is such that the risk is not justifiable unless more than 1 unit is indicated.

PREPARATIONS.—Packed Human Blood Cells, U.S.P. Available through hospital blood banks.

DEXTRAN 40 [Gentran-40, LMD 10%, Rheomacrodex]
DEXTRAN 70 [Macrodex]
DEXTRAN 75 [Gentran 75]

Dextran is a water-soluble glucose polymer biosynthesized by the action of *Leuconostoc mesenteroides* on sucrose. The high molecular weight product thus obtained is further treated by partial acid hydrolysis and differential fractionation to yield finished products of lower and more uniform molecular weight. Both low molecular and high molecular weight products are currently marketed. Dextran 70 and dextran 75 have molecular weights of approximately 70,000 and 75,000, respectively; they are used as plasma expanders in the emergency treatment of shock or impending shock to restore blood volume after hemorrhage when whole blood or blood components are not available. These products also may be used to correct the oligemia of burn shock or to temporarily maintain colloidal osmotic pressure during certain types of cardiovascular surgery. Dextran

40 (low molecular weight dextran) has a molecular weight of approximately 40,000 and is used as a priming fluid (alone or as an additive) for pump-oxygenators during extracorporeal circulation. It also can be used as an adjunct in the treatment of shock or impending shock, but should not replace other established forms of therapy.

Hypersensitivity reactions (rash, pruritus, nasal congestion, dyspnea, chest tightness, and mild hypotension) are the primary untoward effects observed. However, the incidence is low and the reactions generally are mild when adequately hydrolyzed and refined preparations are used. Low molecular weight dextran has considerably less antigenic potential than the higher molecular weight product. Nevertheless, urticaria, angioedema, bronchospasm, and anaphylactic reactions have occurred with both types of preparations. Nausea, vomiting, and, in some cases, acute hypotension also may be seen. Discontinuation of the drug usually relieves the less severe reactions. The immediate subcutaneous administration of epinephrine (0.3 to 0.5 ml) followed by intravenous injection of this drug may be necessary to counteract the more serious adverse effects. This treatment may be supplemented or followed by the administration of an antihistamine and other supportive measures for counteracting shock and hypotension. Equipment for emergency resuscitation should be readily available. Because death from anaphylactic reactions has occurred following intravenous administration of as little as 10 ml of dextran 75 solution, patients receiving any dextran solution should have their blood pressure monitored and should be observed closely for at least the first 30 minutes of infusion.

An increased clotting time occurs in a substantial number of patients receiving dextran, especially when the equivalent of more than 1 unit of plasma is infused. This may or may not be of clinical significance, depending upon the bleeding tendency of the patient under normal conditions. This increase in clotting time may not appear for three to nine hours following the dextran infusion. Dextran will interfere with some laboratory tests (eg, abnormal values in renal and hepatic function studies have been reported following administration of dextran 40). Administration of any dextran preparation also may make crossmatching difficult; therefore, if blood is to be administered, the crossmatch specimen should be drawn prior to dextran infusion. Acute renal failure has been observed in some patients coincident with dextran infusion; however, this effect may be more closely related to the underlying condition being treated than to the dextran infusion itself.

Dextran is contraindicated in patients with known hypersensitivity, severe congestive heart failure, renal failure, hypervolemic conditions, or severe bleeding disorders. It should be used with caution in patients with chronic liver disease, impaired renal function, or in those in whom pulmonary edema or congestive failure is likely to develop.

Dextran may precipitate from solution on storage. It can be redissolved by heating the suspension in a water bath or autoclave for a short period of time at the minimal temperature required to effect solution.

USUAL DOSAGE.—

Dextran 40:

Intravenous: Adults and children, 10 to 20 ml of 10% solution per kilogram of body weight added to the infusion circuit or infused slowly when treating shock. Monitoring central venous pressure is strongly recommended as a guide to determine the amount to be infused. The total daily dose should not exceed 20 ml/kg.

Dextran 70 and Dextran 75:

Intravenous: Adults and children, 500 to 1,000 ml of 6% solution may be infused at a rate of 20 to 40 ml/minute. The total dosage should not exceed 20 ml/kg of body weight during the first 24 hours.

PREPARATIONS.—

Dextran 40:

Dextran 40 (Cutter), Gentran-40 (Travenol), LMD 10% (Abbott), Rheomacrodex (Pharmacia). *Injection:* Solution 10% (in 0.9% sodium chloride solution or 5% dextrose solution) in 500 ml containers.

Dextran 70:

Dextran-70 (Cutter, McGaw), Macrodex (Pharmacia). *Injection:* Solution 6% (in 0.9% sodium chloride solution or 5% dextrose solution) in 500 ml containers.

Dextran 75:

Dextran 6% (Abbott). *Injection:* Solution 6% (in 0.9% sodium chloride solution [Dextran 6%-S] or in 5% dextrose solution [Dextran 6% in D5-W]) in 500 ml containers.

Gentran-75 (Travenol). *Injection:* Solution 6% (in 0.9% sodium chloride solution) in 250 and 500 ml containers.

SIMILAR PREPARATION.—6% Gentran 75 in 10% Travert (Travenol). Contains 6% dextran 75 in a solution of 10% invert sugar (50% fructose and 50% dextrose obtained by hydrolysis of sucrose) in water, in 500 ml containers. This preparation may be used in patients in whom sodium restriction is indicated as may either of the dextran 75 in dextrose preparations listed above.

ANTIHEMOPHILIC HUMAN PLASMA

Antihemophilic human plasma is normal human plasma that has been obtained from a single donor. It is promptly processed to preserve the antihemophilic factor contained in the original blood, and is preserved and stored either in the frozen form or as a dried solid prepared by cryodesiccation. Antihemophilic plasma in the frozen state must be maintained at a temperature not higher than -18 C until just before use; the dried form can be stored at room temperature away from excessive heat. The expiration date of these products is not longer than one year from date of processing if used for antihemophilic purposes and not longer than five years if used for other purposes. Any plasma labeled as human single donor plasma can be used as a source of antihemophilic human plasma if it is used within one year and is frozen within six hours after collection.

For indications, adverse reactions, and precautions, see the Introductory Statement.

USUAL DOSAGE.—*Intravenous:* 250 ml once daily.

PREPARATIONS.—Antihemophilic Human Plasma, U.S.P. Available through hospital blood banks.

PLASMA PROTEIN FRACTION [Plasmanate, Plasmaplex, Protenate]

Plasma protein fraction, a 5% solution of stabilized human plasma proteins in sodium chloride injection, is used for the treatment of hypovolemic shock, as a temporary substitute when whole blood is not available, and as a source of protein in patients with hypoproteinemia. It also is satisfactory for the initial treatment of shock in infants and small children who are dehydrated by diarrhea and in whom the major derangements include hemoconcentration and electrolyte deficiency. Since plasma protein fraction does not provide coagulation factors, it should not be given to correct coagulation defects.

The incidence of adverse reactions following administration of this fraction is low; nausea, vomiting, and hypersalivation have been observed. All patients, especially those with normal or increased circulatory volume, should be carefully observed during infusions of the protein to detect any signs of hypervolemia (eg, pulmonary edema) or cardiac failure. Hypersensitivity reactions or cases of acute viral hepatitis have not been reported. Solutions of plasma protein fraction should not be mixed with or administered through the same sets as other intravenous fluids; this does not preclude concomitant administration of other fluids through another vein.

USUAL DOSAGE.—*Intravenous:* The following amounts will serve as guides; the total amount administered always must be adjusted to meet the needs of each patient. *Adults,* for hypoproteinemia, 1 to 1.5 liters of solution containing 50 to 75 g of protein infused at a rate of 5 to 8 ml/minute. *Infants and young children,* to correct dehydration, 33 ml/kg of body weight infused at a rate of 5 to 10 ml/minute.

PREPARATIONS.—Plasmanate (Cutter), Plasmaplex (Armour), Protenate (Hyland). *Injection:* Solution 5% in 250 and 500 ml containers.

Chapter 11

HEMOSTATICS

A clear understanding of the blood clotting sequence and fibrinolysis is essential for the proper use of hemostatic agents. When bleeding is encountered, it is important that an accurate diagnosis be established quickly if possible. If the bleeding is the result of a specific deficiency (eg, antihemophilic factor), diagnosis may be relatively simple; conversely, when dealing with multiple deficiencies, most of which are acquired, diagnosis and treatment can be difficult.

Some hemostatics are administered systemically to overcome specific coagulation defects, while others are applied locally to control surface bleeding and capillary oozing. The systemic hemostatics include the vitamin K preparations (phytonadione [AquaMephyton, Konakion, Mephyton], menadione, menadione sodium bisulfite [Hykinone], menadiol sodium diphosphate [Kappadione, Synkayvite], and vitamin K_5 [Synkamin]), fibrinogen [Parenogen], aminocaproic acid [Amicar], antihemophilic factor [Antihemophilic Factor (Human), Antihemophilic Globulin, Hemofil, Humafac], cryoprecipitated antihemophilic factor (human), antihemophilic plasma (human), and factor IX complex (human) [Konȳne, Proplex]. Conjugated estrogens [Premarin] are claimed to be useful when given intravenously to control postoperative bleeding, but the evidence is not convincing.

The absorbable, locally applied hemostatics are gelatin sponge [Gelfoam, Gelfilm], oxidized cellulose [Oxycel, Surgicel], thrombin, thromboplastin, and fibrin foam.

VITAMIN K

The vitamin K compounds are fat-soluble naphthoquinones. Phytonadione (vitamin K_1) and vitamin K_2 occur in a variety of natural materials and are produced by bacteria in the gastrointestinal tract; however, phytonadione and two other vitamin K preparations, menadione and vitamin K_5, are now prepared synthetically.

The K vitamins, with the exception of the water-soluble salts of menadione (menadione sodium bisulfite, menadiol sodium diphosphate) and vitamin K_5, are absorbed from the gastrointestinal tract only in the presence of adequate quantities of bile salts and pancreatic lipase. The menadione salts are readily absorbed orally and also can be given intramuscularly or intravenously; phytonadione can be given intravenously as an emulsion. Once absorbed, vitamin K accumulates in the liver, spleen, and lungs, but significant amounts are not stored in the body for long periods. In normal patients, there is no established, measurable daily requirement.

The exact mechanism of action of vitamin K has not been established, but it is known that a deficiency of the vitamin results in a decreased quantity of factor II (prothrombin), factor VII (proconvertin), factor IX (plasma thromboplastin component), and factor X (Stuart-Prower factor) in the liver and blood.

It is improbable that an adult, even one on a deficient diet, will develop vitamin K deficiency. Although only a low concentration of the vitamin is present in meats and milk, leafy green vegetables have a high content. In addition, some vitamin K is produced by colonic bacteria.

True vitamin K deficiency that predisposes the body to hemorrhagic complications is associated with many clinical situations. It is important to differentiate between vitamin K deficiency and defective synthesis of vitamin K-dependent clotting factors if proper therapy is to be instituted. Thus, although true hypoprothrombinemia is caused by a deficiency of vitamin K, in liver disease with severe cellular damage (eg, cirrhosis, hepatitis, hemochromatosis, porphyria cutanea tarda, Wilson's disease), factor II synthesis may be adequate but other vitamin K-dependent clotting factors and factor V may be significantly reduced, even if excess vitamin K is available. Under these conditions, the prothrombin time is prolonged and bleeding may occur, but a true hypoprothrombinemia will not be present.

Individuals receiving long-term intravenous feeding may develop vitamin K deficiency that can be avoided by administering small amounts of the vitamin with the intravenous fluid. Uptake of vitamin K is diminished when a patient receives prolonged oral antibiotic therapy, undergoes prolonged bowel cleansing for colonic surgery, or has a malabsorption syndrome (eg, pancreatic insufficiency, dysentery, intestinal fistula, blind loop syndrome). Moreover, an existing deficiency of vitamin K will be accentuated by alteration of intestinal flora that occurs when drugs are given to treat bacterial diarrhea. When insufficient absorption of vitamin K is caused by biliary disease (obstruction, atresia, fistulas), the prothrombin time will gradually increase; the hypoprothrombinemia and deficiency of other vitamin K-dependent factors will become even more severe if hepatic cell damage also is present. Patients with hereditary hypoprothrombinemia or lack of factors VII and X do not respond to vitamin K therapy.

Competitive inhibition of vitamin K activity in the liver by antagonists such as the coumarin derivatives is one of the most common causes of iatrogenic hemorrhage in man. Other drugs (eg, salicylates, phenylbutazone [Azolid, Butazolidin], quinine, quinidine, sulfonamides) will enhance the hypoprothrombinemic effect of the coumarin derivatives (see also Chapter 9, Anticoagulants, and the section on Drug Interactions).

The prothrombin level in newborn infants is comparatively lower than that of adults, but may not be reflected in prothrombin time determinations. Usually prothrombin time is normal at birth, increases progressively during the next two to seven days, and returns to normal by the fifth to seventh day. Spontaneous hemorrhage caused by deficiency of vitamin K-dependent clotting factors is unlikely by the eighth day. The prothrombin and proconvertin (P and P) test of Owren is more sensitive than the prothrombin test and often yields abnormal results in the newborn. The other vitamin K-dependent clotting factors, factor V, and fibrinogen also are usually lower in the newborn infant. Currently it is thought that the enzyme systems that synthesize these various factors are not fully developed in the newborn. Although the resultant deficiencies can be exacerbated by vitamin K deficiency, administration of the vitamin usually does not correct these deficient levels to comparable adult levels. Other conditions that may contribute to a defect in synthesis of vitamin K-dependent clotting factors by the liver of the newborn are a lack of vitamin K-producing bacteria in the gastrointestinal tract (resulting in less vitamin K absorbed), reduced stores of vitamin K, and maternal drug ingestion (eg, oral anticoagulants, salicylates).

Prophylactic administration of vitamin K to a mother known to be deficient in vitamin K or who has undergone prolonged labor may help prevent hemorrhagic disease in the newborn; however, the more accepted procedure is to administer *small* doses of vitamin K to the newborn infant during the first few days (large doses may cause kernicterus). Phytonadione is the preferred vitamin K preparation because of its greater margin of safety. If hemorrhage is caused by true vitamin K deficiency, this therapy will usually be beneficial. If, however, the deficiency is caused by a lack of vitamin K-dependent clotting factors and fibrinogen, the preferred treatment may be administration of fresh frozen plasma.

Phytonadione (a fat-soluble vitamin) is more effective than the water-soluble vitamin K preparations in the treatment of anticoagulant-induced hypoprothrombinemia. Drug-induced defects in the synthesis of hepatic clotting factor also respond better to this vitamin. The naturally occurring forms of vitamin K and the water-soluble derivatives are equally effective in treating deficiency states or absorptive defects.

Prothrombin levels lower than desired may develop in patients being treated with coumarin derivatives for thromboembolic disorders (thrombophlebitis or phlebothrombosis, pulmonary embolism, and myocardial infarction). A single dose of phytonadione is often all that is necessary to correct the defect. If severe bleeding occurs, the anticoagulant may have to be discontinued and intravenous vitamin K therapy initiated. For immediate therapeutic effect, a transfusion of fresh frozen plasma is indicated. If the need is sufficient to warrant the risk of acute viral hepatitis, factor IX complex (Konÿne, Proplex) may be given.

In vitamin K deficiency caused by poor nutrition or absorption, a single loading dose of vitamin K is frequently sufficient to stop bleeding within a few hours, and additional doses will replenish the vitamin K stores in the body. If an absorptive defect is present and cannot be localized, regular small doses of the vitamin should be given to maintain the patient until the defect is corrected.

A routine laboratory test used to measure vitamin K deficiency is the one-stage prothrombin time. The prothrombin and proconvertin (P and P) test also is being used and is actually more sensitive.

Adverse Reactions

Adverse reactions rarely occur in adults after vitamin K administration, but rapid intravenous injection may cause systemic effects, some of which are serious (flushing of the face, a sense of chest constriction, cyanosis, acute peripheral vascular failure).

When vitamin K is used in treating hemorrhagic diseases in infants, it can produce a significant increase in the plasma levels of unbound bilirubin, as well as kernicterus, hemolytic anemia, and hemoglobinuria. The hemolytic tendency is greatest in infants with relatively low levels of glucose-6-phosphate dehydrogenase (G6PD), but it also is observed in adults with this deficiency. Increased plasma levels of free bilirubin can occur in premature infants if the mother has received large doses of menadione sodium bisulfite [Hykinone], although moderate doses are relatively safe and often needed.

In patients with liver disease, paradoxical hypoprothrombinemia may occasionally be noted after administration of large doses of vitamin K. The etiology of this reduction is unknown.

INDIVIDUAL EVALUATIONS

PHYTONADIONE (Vitamin K_1)
[AquaMephyton, Konakion, Mephyton]

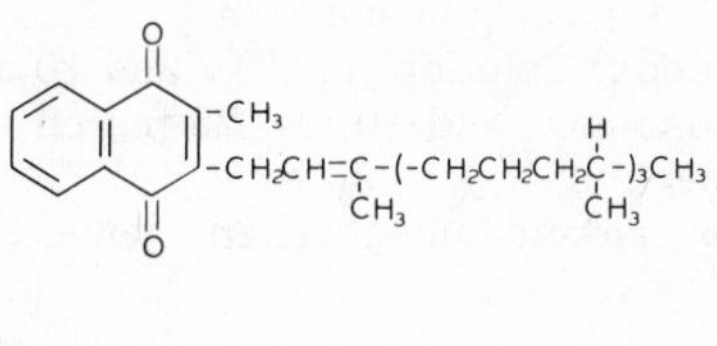

$-CH_3$; $-CH_2CH{=}C(CH_3)-(-CH_2CH_2CH_2CH(CH_3)-)_3CH_3$

Phytonadione is used to reverse anticoagulant-induced hypoprothrombinemia either prophylactically or when bleeding actually has occurred. It will not combat hemorrhage from overdosage of heparin. It also is useful in hypoprothrombinemia caused by inadequate absorption of vitamin K, inadequate gastrointestinal bacterial synthesis of vitamin K, toxic action of certain drugs (eg, salicylates, phenylbutazone [acutely], quinine, quinidine, sulfonamides), neonatal hypoprothrombinemia, and hepatic disease. Phytonadione has a more prompt, potent, and prolonged effect than the vitamin K analogues. In contrast to menadione-type drugs, it will not hemolyze red cells that are deficient in glucose-6-phosphate dehydrogenase (G6PD) and it is safe for use in newborn infants if given in the recommended dosage.

This drug is administered orally, subcutaneously, or intramuscularly for the routine treatment of hypoprothrombinemia. In emergency situations that occur with overdosage of coumarins or indandiones, transfusions of fresh frozen plasma, along with the slow intravenous injection of this drug, may be indicated. Since control of anticoagulant-induced hypoprothrombinemia will reexpose the patient to the same hazards of intravascular clotting that existed prior to anticoagulant therapy, dosage of phytonadione should be kept as low as possible, prothrombin times should be checked at frequent intervals, and heparin should be readily available, because heparin will produce an anticoagulant effect even if large amounts of phytonadione have been given.

Intravenous injection can cause flushing of the face, hyperhidrosis, a sense of chest constriction, cyanosis, and acute peripheral vascular failure. The subcutaneous and intramuscular routes are not as reliable as the intravenous route and may cause delayed nodule formation and pain at the site of injection. Parenteral administration to the newborn has caused a marked increase in the plasma levels of unbound bilirubin, as well as kernicterus, hemolytic anemia, and hemoglobinuria. However, these reactions are less likely to occur with phytonadione than with the water-soluble analogues (menadiol sodium diphosphate, menadione sodium bisulfite, vitamin K_5).

USUAL DOSAGE.—

Oral, Subcutaneous, Intramuscular: Adults and children, 1 to 25 mg.

Intravenous, Intramuscular: For prophylaxis

of hemorrhagic disease of the newborn, 0.5 to 2 mg immediately after birth (umbilical vein may be used); although less desirable, 1 to 5 mg may be given to the mother 12 to 24 hours before delivery. *For treatment of hemorrhagic disease of the newborn,* 1 mg should be given intravenously daily. If no improvement occurs within a few days, the condition of the infant should be reevaluated.

Intravenous: For treatment of hemorrhage due to hypoprothrombinemia caused by overdosage of oral anticoagulants, *adults,* 10 to 50 mg; *children,* 5 to 10 mg. The rate of infusion should not exceed 5 mg/minute by drip, and the preparation should be diluted with 5% dextrose or sodium chloride injection.

PREPARATIONS.—

AquaMephyton (Merck Sharp & Dohme). *Injection:* Solution 2 mg/ml in 0.5 ml containers and 10 mg/ml in 1, 2.5, and 5 ml containers.

Konakion (Roche). *Injection* (intramuscular only): Solution 2 mg/ml in 0.5 ml containers and 10 mg/ml in 1 and 2.5 ml containers.

Mephyton (Merck Sharp & Dohme). *Oral:* Tablets 5 mg.

MENADIOL SODIUM DIPHOSPHATE

[Kappadione, Synkayvite]

This water-soluble dihydro analogue of menadione has the same actions and uses as menadione and phytonadione (see the evaluation on Phytonadione), but phytonadione is generally preferred for prevention and treatment of hemorrhagic disease of the newborn or for treatment of hypoprothrombinemia caused by overdosage of oral anticoagulants. Concomitant administration of bile salts is not necessary for intestinal absorption, but their use is recommended in patients with obstructive jaundice or biliary fistula.

The incidence of adverse reactions, which are similar to those seen with phytonadione, is low when the drug is given at normal therapeutic levels. Like menadione, it will hemolyze red blood cells in individuals deficient in glucose-6-phosphate dehydrogenase (G6PD), as well as in the newborn, especially premature infants. Therefore, menadiol sodium diphosphate probably should not be given to newborn infants or to women during the last few weeks of pregnancy.

USUAL DOSAGE.—

Oral, Subcutaneous, Intramuscular, Intravenous: Adults, for management of hypoprothrombinemic hemorrhagic states, 5 to 10 mg daily; larger doses may be given if the hemorrhage is not controlled. The route chosen will depend upon the urgency of the situation.

Intramuscular: Adults, for management of overdosage of oral anticoagulants, 75 mg repeated as often as necessary. However, phytonadione is more effective and generally preferred (see the evaluation on Phytonadione).

PREPARATIONS.—

Kappadione (Lilly). *Injection:* Solution 5 and 10 mg/ml in 1 ml containers.

Synkayvite (Roche).

Injection: Solution 5 and 10 mg/ml in 1 ml containers and 37.5 mg/ml in 2 ml containers.

Oral: Tablets 5 mg.

MENADIONE

Menadione has the same actions and uses as phytonadione, although it is not as pharmacologically active on a weight basis (see the evaluation on Phytonadione). It is practically insoluble in water and is most frequently used orally; the presence of bile salts is necessary for intestinal absorption.

The incidence of adverse reactions is low when the drug is given at normal therapeutic levels. The reactions are similar to those produced by phytonadione. In addition, menadione can hemolyze red blood cells in individuals deficient in glucose-6-phosphate dehydrogenase (G6PD), as well as in the newborn, especially premature infants. Therefore, it probably should not be given to newborn infants or to women during the last few weeks of pregnancy.

USUAL DOSAGE.—*Oral, Intramuscular:* 2 to 10 mg daily.

PREPARATIONS.—

Oral: Tablets 2, 5, and 10 mg.

Injection: Solution (in oil) 2 and 10 mg/ml in 1 ml containers and 10 and 25 mg/ml in 10 ml containers.

Drug marketed under generic name.

MENADIONE SODIUM BISULFITE
[Hykinone]

Menadione sodium bisulfite is freely soluble in water, and bile salts are not necessary for intestinal absorption. It is used for the same conditions as menadione and phytonadione (see the evaluation on Phytonadione), but phytonadione is preferred for the management of hemorrhagic disease of the newborn.

The incidence of adverse reactions is low when menadione sodium bisulfite is given at normal therapeutic levels. The reactions are similar to those produced by phytonadione; however, like menadione, the sodium bisulfite salt will hemolyze red blood cells in individuals deficient in glucose-6-phosphate dehydrogenase (G6PD), as well as in the newborn, especially premature infants. Therefore, menadione sodium bisulfite probably should not be given to newborn infants or to women during the last few weeks of pregnancy.

USUAL DOSAGE.—

Subcutaneous, Intramuscular: 0.5 to 10 mg daily, depending upon the route and indications for the drug.

Intravenous: For treatment of hypoprothrombinemia caused by overdosage of oral anticoagulants, 50 to 100 mg is given by slow drip if prothrombin activity drops below 15% of normal or signs of bleeding appear (see the evaluation on Phytonadione).

PREPARATIONS.—Hykinone (Abbott). *Injection:* Solution 10 mg/ml in 1 ml containers.

VITAMIN K_5 [Synkamin]

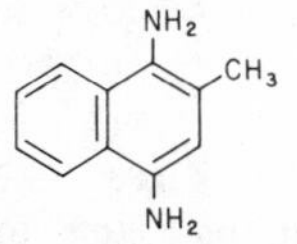

Vitamin K_5 is synthetic and water-soluble. Its actions and uses are similar to those of phytonadione and menadione (see the evaluation on Phytonadione). The presence of bile salts is not needed for intestinal absorption after oral administration; vitamin K_5 also can be administered parenterally.

The incidence of adverse reactions is low at normal therapeutic levels, and the effects are similar to those that occur after overdosage of phytonadione.

USUAL DOSAGE.—

Intramuscular, Intravenous: For hemorrhagic disease of the newborn, 1 mg for prophylaxis or at the first sign of bleeding immediately after birth; however, phytonadione is preferred.

Oral, Intramuscular, Intravenous: For hypoprothrombinemia due to biliary or gastrointestinal dysfunction, *adults*, prophylactically or preoperatively, 1 mg or more daily as needed until the prothrombin level returns to normal; treatment (intravenous), 2 to 5 mg daily.

PREPARATIONS.—Synkamin (Parke, Davis). *Injection:* Solution 1 mg/ml in 1 ml containers.

Oral: Capsules 4 mg.

ANTIHEMOPHILIC FACTORS

Before plasma concentrates became available, bleeding associated with classical hemophilia (hemophilia A) was treated with large and frequent infusions of plasma or, on rare occasions, with whole blood. However, replacement therapy with large volumes of plasma or blood high in protein increased intravascular volume and the possibility of hypervolemia. In addition, transfusion with plasma or blood was inconvenient since these materials had to be used while fresh or factor VIII potency decreased significantly. The introduction of antihemophilic human plasma, which can be stored as a dried product, solved the problem of having to use fresh blood or plasma. Antihemophilic human plasma may be preferred when the etiology of the bleeding is unknown. More recently, the development and use of concentrated antihemophilic factor (AHF, factor VIII) preparations has virtually solved both the problem of hypervolemia resulting from plasma or whole blood transfusions and that of storage so that factor VIII potency is not lost.

Profuse bleeding can occur as a result of mild trauma in patients with severe AHF (antihemophilic factor) deficiency, especially if the individual has taken aspirin. Because of the wide variability in the AHF deficiency defect, a history of bleeding in the patient or his family may be important in establishing the diagnosis of suspected hemophilia; conversely, routine coagulation studies, if performed correctly, can reveal the deficiency in the absence of a history of bleeding. The partial thromboplastin (PTT) test is the screening test used for this purpose; it has replaced both the thromboplastin generation test (TGT) and the prothrombin consumption time (PCT) test. The PTT test is more sensitive and reliable, and gives few false-negative results. (Results are likely to indicate an abnormality with factor VIII levels as high as 30% to 35%, whereas the TGT and the PCT tests will not show abnormality if the concentration of factor VIII is higher than 5% of normal.) However, the PTT test can only indicate that an abnormality exists; it does not identify the specific deficiency. Definitive diagnosis must be established by factor VIII assay unless the deficiency is severe, in which case simple mixture studies with plasma of known deficiency can identify the defect.

AHF is precipitated in the fibrinogen fraction. The first of the precipitates to be prepared and used (fraction I) was obtained by an ethanol precipitation technique. More recently, dried preparations of AHF obtained by purification techniques such as cryoprecipitation, glycine or polyethylene glycol precipitation, and combinations of these techniques have been prepared. Another product, cryoprecipitated antihemophilic factor (human), obtained by a selective rapid-freezing, cold-thawing technique, is widely used because it can be prepared in the hospital blood bank laboratory.

Each type of AHF precipitate has individual advantages and disadvantages. The dried products are stable and are easier to handle, store, and administer than the cryoprecipitates. However, the greater risk of acquiring acute viral hepatitis from preparations made from pooled plasma is a drawback to their wide use. Discovery of hepatitis-associated antigen (HAA, Australia antigen, SH antigen) in the serum of patients with long-incubation (so-called serum) hepatitis and a second, more labile, antigen in the serum of patients with short-incubation (so-called infectious) hepatitis appears to be a significant development in the search for a diagnostic test for viral hepatitis (see also Chapter 10, Blood, Blood Components, and Blood Substitutes). In an effort to decrease the risk of hepatitis, at least one manufacturer of a highly purified AHF preparation (Hyland) screens each unit of plasma for HAA and eliminates those that are positive.

The AHF content of the cryoprecipitates is highly variable; however, the risk of hepatitis is lower than with the commercial products. Also, the modified blood can be reconstituted after removal of the cryoprecipitate and used for other types of transfusions; thus, cryoprecipitated preparations are a more economical approach to the therapy of hemophilia than fresh frozen plasma.

Despite low anti-A and anti-B isoantibody titers, AHF preparations administered in large doses for one week or more will result in the accumulation of anti-A and anti-B antibodies and occasionally will cause a mild hemolytic anemia (see the section on Adverse Reactions). Some AHF preparations also may cause a marked hyperfibrinogenemia (occasionally tenfold more than normal) that interferes with the results of several laboratory tests; although this increased fibrinogen level may not be clinically significant, it has been implicated as a cause of hemolytic anemia, as a stimulus to fibrinolysis, and, more recently, as the cause of an increased bleeding tendency due to a malfunction of platelets. A transient proteinuria with deposits of fibrin and fibrinogen in the kidneys also has been associated with this hyperfibrinogenemia.

Replacement therapy is required when AHF deficiency is associated with active bleeding, as in hemophilia; with spontaneous, traumatic, or surgical bleeding; or with von Willebrand's disease. It is important to note that patients with von Willebrand's disease lack a plasma factor necessary to stimulate their own endogenous factor VIII production and that this stimulating factor is removed from commercial AHF preparations during processing. Hence, only antihemophilic plasma, fresh frozen plasma, or cryoprecipitated AHF is effective in treating von Willebrand's disease. Patients with this disease who are being prepared for surgery should receive cryoprecipitated AHF about 24 hours preoperatively, since factor VIII production does not begin immediately, and every other day after surgery until wound healing is complete.

Bleeding that occurs as a result of a circulating anticoagulant (an immunoglobulin that inactivates circulating factor VIII) also requires replacement therapy. This type of bleeding occurs in about 5% to 10% of hemophilic patients who have received multiple units of AHF concentrates, but it also is observed in healthy individuals, elderly patients, postpartum women, and patients with systemic lupus erythematosus. The presence of an inactivator must be ruled out before performing surgery on a hemophiliac. When the circulating anticoagulant factor is present, AHF concentrates are ineffective in maintaining hemostasis unless antibody titers are low, and they are unlikely to remain low if aggressive therapy is used to prevent surgical bleeding.

Patients with a deficiency of factor VIII, whether severe or mild, should receive plasma factor VIII concentrate before surgery is performed. A base level of factor VIII approximately 30% of normal is necessary for effective hemostasis during surgery, and levels of 20% to 25% should be maintained during the entire postoperative period.

Because of the recognition several years ago that hemophilia B (Christmas disease) is caused by factor IX deficiency, several procedures have been developed to prepare factor IX concentrates, and stable, dried, purified preparations for intravenous use are now available commercially. Because of similar adsorption properties, factors II, VII, and X (the other vitamin K-dependent factors) also are purified in the process when plasma is used as a starting material.

Factor IX complex (human) has been used with success not only in treating factor IX deficiency but also in several other conditions in which one or more of the other factors in the complex are missing (eg, congenital lack of any one of the factors, primary vitamin K deficiency, acquired vitamin K deficiency caused by coumarin therapy).

Adverse Reactions

Acute viral hepatitis is the most common adverse effect encountered with administration of the various precipitated fractions of antihemophilic factor (AHF). The commercial products are usually prepared from pooled plasma and are more likely to cause this complication than the cryoprecipitates. Factor IX complex, like other factors derived from human plasma, also carries the risk of acute viral hepatitis. The use of immune serum globulin (gamma globulin) in an attempt to attenuate the hepatitis virus is neither practical nor reliable since it is unwise to give intramuscular injections to hemophiliacs. If it is absolutely necessary to administer immune serum globulin in conjunction with an AHF product, the immune serum globulin should be given one week and again one month after exposure.

Hemolytic anemia can occur when AHF fractions are given to individuals with group A or B red blood cell antigens because anti-A or anti-B antibodies may be present in the precipitated fraction. The anemia is mild and usually abates after administration of AHF is discontinued. Any commercial AHF preparation that tends to have high titers of anti-A and anti-B antibodies must often be restricted to use in patients with type O blood. On the other hand, blood bank cryoprecipitates are type-specific and can be used in nonmatching patients; hemolysis is rarely encountered because the anti-A or anti-B titer activity in cryoprecipitates is no higher than that of the parent plasma and the volumes administered are usually small.

INDIVIDUAL EVALUATIONS

ANTIHEMOPHILIC FACTOR [Antihemophilic Factor (Human), Antihemophilic Globulin, Hemofil, Humafac]

These products are stable, dried, concentrated preparations of human antihemophilic factor (AHF) or a cryoprecipitated AHF obtained from fresh plasma. They vary widely in degree of purity and concentration. The dried preparations contain relatively small amounts of fibrinogen and other plasma proteins; the cryoprecipitated product contains a higher percentage of non-AHF plasma factors than the dried product. The dried preparations must be stored at 2 to 8 C, and the cryoprecipitated product must be kept frozen. The normal half-life of AHF in the body is biphasic. There is a short phase ($t_{1/2}$ of 4 to 8 hours) consistent with equilibrium within the extravascular space and a longer second phase ($t_{1/2}$ of 12 to 14 hours) consistent with biodegradation of the AHF.

AHF preparations are used in the treatment of classical hemophilia (hemophilia A). They also can be used in patients who are not true hemophiliacs but who have acquired circulating factor VIII inhibitors. However, they should not be given in quantities that totally neutralize *all* circulating inhibitors since residual circulating AHF will tend to stimulate an increase in the inhibitor titer.

Both dried and cryoprecipitated AHF preparations can be administered fairly rapidly without producing significant adverse effects; neither causes hypervolemic reactions. Since the dried forms are prepared from large pools of fresh human plasma, they are capable of causing acute viral hepatitis. Although this danger is lessened with the cryoprecipitated material, both forms should be used only when absolutely essential and when the expected benefit to the patient outweighs the dangers of hepatitis. This is particularly true in infants, especially the newborn, and in patients with liver disease, since morbidity and mortality associated with hepatitis are likely to be higher in these patients. AHF preparations also contain small amounts of groups A and B isohemagglutinins; thus, when large amounts are given to patients with blood groups A, B, or AB, hemolysis can result. Rarely, a chilling sensation or mild fever occurs shortly after administration of AHF.

USUAL DOSAGE.–*Intravenous:* It is generally necessary to have a circulating AHF level 5% to 10% of normal to control hemarthrosis in classical hemophilia. For mild bleeding into muscles or joints not requiring aspiration, the patient should be maintained at 5% to 10% of normal for one to two days. For spontaneous bleeding into a body cavity or joint requiring aspiration, retroperitoneal bleeding, central nervous system bleeding, or hematuria, a level 20% to 30% of normal for three to five days may be indicated. For treatment of severe trauma, a patient may have to be maintained at a level 40% of normal (this level corresponds to a high normal partial thromboplastin time). In surgery, a blood level at least 30% of normal is necessary preoperatively for effective hemostasis; postoperatively, it is desirable to have a circulating level 20% to 25% of normal for seven to ten days.

Although various formulas are available for estimating the amount of the preparation to inject (based on experimental evidence, approximately 4 to 5 units/kg of body weight produce an increase of 10% of normal), appropriate laboratory tests should be performed at frequent intervals to be certain that an adequate level of AHF has been reached and is being maintained. Such determinations may be imperative when using cryoprecipitated AHF because there is no uniformity in the concentration of AHF from one plasma donation to the next. If adequate levels are not reached or if hemorrhage is not controlled at what appears to be adequate dosage, a test for factor VIII inhibitors should be performed.

PREPARATIONS.–

Antihemophilic Factor (Human) (Courtland, Squibb), Antihemophilic Globulin (Michigan State Laboratories), Hemofil (Hyland), Humafac (Parke, Davis). Each bottle is labeled with the number of units it contains. One unit is the antihemophilic factor activity present in 1 ml of average, normal, pooled, human plasma less than one hour old.

Cryoprecipitated Antihemophilic Factor (Human) can be prepared by the hospital blood bank as a by-product of blood banking. There is no way to standardize this product.

FACTOR IX COMPLEX (HUMAN) [Konȳne, Proplex]

These preparations are stable, dried, purified plasma fractions containing coagulation factors II, VII, IX, and X and a relatively small amount of other plasma proteins. Konyne is alleged to be free of thrombin, thromboplastin-like activity, anticomplement activity, depressor activity, and heparin. Similarly, Proplex is stated to be free of these materials except for heparin. Heparin is added to this product to help prevent the possible formation of thrombin under circumstances where the four clotting factors present could inadvertently react after the manufacturing process (eg, increased temperature during storage). Anti-A and anti-B agglutinins are present at clinically insignificant levels; therefore, factor IX complex (human) may be safely used without typing or crossmatching. They cannot cause hypervolemic reactions because of the concentrated nature of these products and the small amount of carrier fluid needed to administer them.

These dried preparations must be stored under refrigeration at 2 to 8 C; freezing should be avoided to prevent breakage of the bottled diluent. Although factor IX complex (human) is stable after reconstitution for at least 12 hours at room temperature, it should be administered promptly. The preparation is only administered intravenously in sterile water for injection and never in a concentration greater than 50 units/ml.

Factor IX complex (human) is used in the treatment of hemophilia B (Christmas disease) or when one or more of the factors contained in this preparation must be increased to correct or prevent hemorrhage. It should be used only under life-threatening circumstances in hemorrhagic disease of the newborn caused by proven deficiency of factors II, VII, IX, or X, or in children or adults who are bleeding or about to undergo surgery and have proven deficiency of factors II, VII, IX, or X. A factor IX level 25% to 30% of normal should be maintained at all times during the healing phase following surgery (this corresponds to a high normal partial thromboplastin time).

Factor IX complex (human) is capable of causing acute viral hepatitis (the incidence with Konȳne is fairly high) and should be used only when the expected benefit to the patient outweighs the dangers of acquiring hepatitis. The risk is particularly great in infants, especially the newborn, and in patients with liver disease, especially that associated with intravascular coagulation or fibrinolysis. Morbidity and mortality associated with hepatitis are likely to be higher in these patients.

Occasionally, transient fever, chills, headache, flushing, or tingling can occur shortly after the administration of factor IX complex, particularly if the injection is given rapidly. Since serious hypersensitivity reactions (eg, anaphylactic shock) have been reported following injection of Konyne, a test dose of this agent should be administered before the full dose is given.

The biological half-life of factor IX is biphasic. It has a short first phase ($t_{1/2}$ of 4.6 + 1.6 hours) consistent with equilibration within the extravascular space and a longer second phase ($t_{1/2}$ of 31.5 + 9.1 hours) consistent with biodegradation.

USUAL DOSAGE.—*Intravenous:* The amount of factor IX complex (human) needed depends upon the patient and nature of the deficiency. Coagulation assays performed prior to therapy and at reasonable intervals during treatment are the best guide to appropriate dosage. Each unit contains the factor IX activity of 1 ml of normal fresh plasma. Overdosage should be avoided because of the long postinfusion half-life of factors II and X; repeated infusion of the complex can cause unnecessarily high levels of these factors to accumulate.

PREPARATIONS.—Konȳne (Cutter), Proplex (Hyland). Each package contains 500 units and a bottle of sterile water for injection, U.S.P.

OTHER SYSTEMIC HEMOSTATICS

FIBRINOGEN [Parenogen]

Fibrinogen, a sterile fraction of normal human plasma, is prepared from fraction I obtained by the Cohn cold ethanol procedure and is one of the normal clotting factors produced in the liver. When added to a solution containing thrombin, it is converted to insoluble fibrin. Maintenance of normal fibrinogen levels requires a high rate of synthesis as well as an active means of disposal. Factors regulating the synthesis of fibrinogen are obscure but probably are activated in response to low fibrinogen levels, increased hormone production, or acute inflammatory conditions.

Although no actual pathogenic relationship has been shown, prolonged shock-like states affect the synthesis of fibrinogen and other clotting factors in the liver. Increased loss of fibrinogen can occur secondary to the deposition of extravascular fibrin or extensive hemorrhage. Loss of one liter of blood will lower the circulatory pool of fibrinogen by approximately 1.8 g and will result in a decrease in plasma concentration of 50 mg/100 ml. This deficiency can be compensated for only by synthesis or mobilization from other sources.

Release of thromboplastic substances into the blood can cause extensive clotting. As a result, there is an excessive consumption of blood coagulation components, including fibrinogen, and a hemorrhagic diathesis ensues. There also will be a physiologic increase in fibrinolysis. Obstetric complications (intrauterine fetal death, abruptio placenta) or incompatible blood transfusions are two clinical situations in which diffuse intravascular clotting (DIC) and overt hemorrhage can occur. Although the evidence is not conclusive, it may be possible to correct intravascular clotting with hemorrhage by administering heparin. This paradoxical treatment serves to neutralize the accelerated rate of thrombin formation, one of the primary causes of the consumption of blood coagulation components (see Chapter 9, Anticoagulants).

Fibrinolysis, a physiologic state that occurs in vivo, is an aseptic enzymatic liquefaction of a fibrin clot. In the nonpathologic state, there are checks and balances in the fibrinolytic system; however, in conditions that predispose an individual to pathologic fibrinolysis (eg, stress, postoperative complications, obstetric complications, neoplastic disease), deficiencies occur in fibrinogen and other clotting factors that also can result in a severe hemorrhagic diathesis. In these acute conditions, administration of fibrinogen not only may not improve hemostasis but may actually increase the fibrinolytic activity by increasing the available substrate. Since most episodes of acquired fibrinolytic bleeding are secondary to intravascular coagulation, an accurate diagnosis must precede a decision to use fibrinogen.

The most common cause of hypofibrinogenemia is severe liver disease. Hepatocellular damage also produces other clotting deficiencies. Indeed, patients with any acquired hypofibrinogenemic condition (fibrinogen levels below 100 mg/100 ml) may have severe bleeding tendencies, probably because there are multiple deficiencies of the various clotting factors. In contrast, only mild bleeding episodes are associated with congenital hypofibrinogenemia.

Administration of fibrinogen may be indicated in extensive surgical procedures (eg, thoracic surgery, pancreatic surgery) when fibrinogen levels are low, as an adjunct in treating hemorrhagic complications secondary to acute afibrinogenemia, and in certain obstetric complications (eg, abruptio placenta, amniotic fluid embolism, intrauterine fetal death), although fresh frozen plasma may be preferred; it also may be used prophylactically to control bleeding in congenital hypofibrinogenemia or acquired fibrinolytic bleeding. Fibrinogen may be indicated in acute hemorrhage, but it should not be used as a substitute for whole blood if hemorrhage is severe; transfusion of fresh or fresh frozen plasma may be more effective.

Adverse Reactions and Precautions.—Fibrinogen is capable of causing acute viral hepatitis (incidence of 15% to 20% reported in some studies). Therefore, the hazard of acquiring serum (SH virus) hepatitis must be weighed carefully against the danger of the hemorrhagic complications. Some manufacturers (eg, Merck Sharp & Dohme) prepare fibrinogen from venous blood that is nonreactive for hepatitis associated antigen (HAA). Also, cryoprecipitated antihemophilic factor (human) can be used as an effective source of fibrinogen, thereby avoiding the hazards of a pooled preparation with its high risk of hepatitis. Adequate blood coagulation studies and determination of plasma fibrinogen levels must be made before fibrinogen is used, except in extreme emergencies when facilities for performing these procedures are not available, or when there is a bleeding state in which fibrinogen levels are known to be low. A plasma fibrinogen level of 50 mg/100 ml is critically low and definitely can be associated with hemorrhage. Levels below 100 mg/100 ml may indicate the need for fibrinogen; however, in chronic, congenital hypofibrinogenemia, low levels may be encountered without significant bleeding.

Fibrinogen can cause thrombosis when it is administered rapidly or in high concentration; cyanosis and tachycardia also are occasionally observed.

This drug must be stored at 2 to 8 C and must be used within one hour following reconstitution.

USUAL DOSAGE.—*Intravenous:* In acute hypofibrinogenemia associated with obstetric complications, 2 to 8 g, depending upon the response of the patient. In other conditions requiring fibrinogen, the dosage must be adjusted according to clinical observations of hemostasis and laboratory studies of blood coagulation, fibrinolysis, and fibrinogen level. The rate of administration in *adults* should be 100 ml every 10 to 20 minutes; the infusion rate must be slower in *infants and children.*

PREPARATIONS.—Parenogen (Cutter). *Injection:* Powder in 1 and 2 g containers (supplied with distilled water for injection). Drug also marketed under generic name.

AMINOCAPROIC ACID [Amicar]

$$H_2N\,CH_2(CH_2)_3CH_2COOH$$

Aminocaproic acid may help control serious hemorrhage associated with excessive fibrinolysis due to increased plasminogen (profibrinolysin) activation. This monoamino carboxylic acid is a potent competitive inhibitor of plasminogen activators; it also inhibits plasmin (fibrinolysin), but to a lesser degree. Therefore, aminocaproic acid prevents the formation of the excessive plasmin responsible for the destruction of fibrinogen, fibrin, and other important clotting components. Since this drug inhibits the dissolution of clots, it may interfere with normal mechanisms for maintaining the patency of blood vessels, particularly in a thrombosis-prone patient.

Aminocaproic acid is well absorbed orally or can be given intravenously, and is excreted rapidly in the urine, largely unchanged. Peak plasma levels are obtained about two hours after a single oral dose. This drug has been used to control hemorrhage that occurs in cardiac bypass, portacaval shunt, and major thoracic surgery; in obstetric complications such as abruptio placenta, amniotic fluid embolism, intrauterine fetal death, and severe menorrhagia; in various neoplastic diseases, particularly fibrinolytic bleeding associated with metastatic prostatic carcinoma or leukemia; in hepatic diseases, especially cirrhosis; and as an adjunct to protect the hemophiliac from bleeding following tooth extraction.

A pathologic fibrinolytic state may be suspected in a patient with a predisposing clinical condition when the results of laboratory tests are also suggestive (increased fibrinolytic activity, prolonged thrombin and prothrombin clotting times, hypofibrinogenemia, and decreased plasminogen levels). However, these conditions and some of the laboratory findings also may be associated with diffuse intravascular coagulation (DIC) due to the release of thromboplastic material.

Aminocaproic acid is concentrated in the urine and inhibits the plasminogen activator, urokinase; therefore, it also has been used in surgical and nonsurgical hematuria arising from the bladder, prostate, or urethra. In patients operated on by the transurethral and suprapubic routes for prostatectomy, a statistically significant reduction of postoperative hematuria has been demonstrated. However, use of aminocaproic acid should be restricted to those patients who are seriously threatened by hemorrhage, and for whom a correctable cause for the bleeding from the prostatic bed has been excluded. If hemorrhage is caused by diffuse intravascular coagulation (DIC), the administration of aminocaproic acid can be dangerous.

Plasminogen activators such as streptokinase and urokinase have been investigated for possible use as thrombolytic agents in the therapy of thromboembolic disorders. Since aminocaproic acid will counteract the thrombolytic effect of these drugs, it may have some usefulness as an antidote.

Aminocaproic acid is of no value in controlling hemorrhage due to thrombocytopenia or most other coagulation defects, although it can be used in the hemophiliac following tooth extraction; when multiple defects exist, other therapeutic measures (eg, administration of fresh frozen plasma, fibrinogen, or vitamin K) may be required.

The drug is not effective in the control of bleeding caused by loss of vascular integrity; therefore, valuable time may be lost if it is used in patients with post-tonsillectomy bleeding, gastrointestinal hemorrhage from ulcers or ruptured esophageal varices, hemoptysis due to bronchiectasis, open surgical wounds, and functional uterine bleeding.

Adverse Reactions and Precautions.—It is important to understand the role of the fibrinolytic system in maintaining the patency and integrity of the vascular system, the laboratory procedures used to determine coagulation defects, and the mechanism of action of aminocaproic acid before use of this drug is attempted.

The untoward effects of aminocaproic acid include pruritus, erythema, rash, hypotension, dyspepsia, nausea, diarrhea, conjunctival erythema, and nasal congestion.

Cardiac and hepatic necroses were found at postmortem examination in one patient who had received therapeutic doses of the drug. Subendocardial hemorrhages and myocardial degeneration have been associated with administration of aminocaproic acid in several animal species. The drug altered protein metabolism in these experiments by inhibiting the utilization of lysine. Although the significance of these findings must await additional studies, prolonged administration is contraindicated in growing children.

Generalized peripheral thrombosis, thrombosis of a portacaval shunt and thrombophlebitis have occurred in several patients after use of aminocaproic acid, and it is theoretically possible that these thrombotic episodes were related to administration of the drug. If the hemorrhagic diathesis is primarily initiated by intravascular coagulation, aminocaproic acid may potentiate a thrombotic disorder which can be fatal. Thus, frequent laboratory tests should be performed to evaluate the hemostatic mechanisms and prevent the development of a hypercoagulable state.

Smaller doses of aminocaproic acid should be used in patients with renal disease or oliguria.

Teratogenic studies in animals have produced variable results, but no significant abnormalities have been noted in humans. Nevertheless, the drug should not be used in pregnant women during the first and second trimester unless absolutely essential. It may be used during the last trimester if specifically indicated and if the potential benefit outweighs the possible hazards to the mother and fetus.

When aminocaproic acid is given during surgery, care must be taken to free the body cavities of blood clots since the acid will remain in high concentration in the clots, thereby inhibiting their physiologic dissolution.

USUAL DOSAGE.—*Intravenous, Oral:* Initially, 5 g orally or by slow intravenous infusion; doses of 1 g then are given at hourly intervals if renal function is normal. This dosage achieves plasma levels of approximately 13 mg/100 ml of plasma, an effective therapeutic level. Administration of more than 30 g in a 24-hour period is not recommended.

When given intravenously, sodium chloride injection, 5% dextrose injection, or Ringer's injection may be used to dilute the aminocaproic acid. Injection of the undiluted drug or rapid injection is not recommended. A reevaluation of the patient's status should be made after eight hours of continuous therapy.

Further evidence is needed to determine the safety of prolonged use of aminocaproic acid in the presently recommended dosages.

PREPARATIONS.—Amicar (Lederle).

Injection: Solution 250 mg/ml in 20 ml containers.

Oral: Syrup 1.25 g/5 ml; tablets 500 mg.

LOCAL ABSORBABLE HEMOSTATICS

The local absorbable hemostatics are absorbable gelatin sponge [Gelfoam], absorbable gelatin film [Gelfilm], oxidized cellulose [Oxycel, Surgicel], and thrombin. They help control surface bleeding and capillary oozing and tend to be fairly innocuous. If infection is present at the site of their application, they can interfere with healing.

ABSORBABLE GELATIN SPONGE [Gelfoam]

This sterile, gelatin-base sponge is insoluble in water and is available in the form of a block, thin film, or powder. Since this preparation is absorbable, it may be left in place after closure of a surgical wound. It is completely absorbed in four to six weeks without causing excessive scar tissue formation or cellular reaction. This product also is useful in controlling capillary bleeding, particularly when saturated or combined with thrombin solution.

USUAL DOSAGE.—*Topical* (in wound or at operative site): Only the minimal amount required to cover the area and control hemorrhage should be applied. Absorbable gelatin sponge should be moistened thoroughly with sterile sodium chloride solution or thrombin solution prior to application.

PREPARATIONS.—Gelfoam (Upjohn). *Topical:* Dental packs 10 x 20 x 7 mm and 20 x 20 x 7 mm; powder (nonsterile) 10 g; powder (sterile) 1 g; prostatectomy cones 13 and 18 cm in diameter; sponge (compressed) 80 x 62.5 x 10 mm, 80 x 125 x 10 mm, 80 x 250 x 10 mm, 20 x 60 x 7 mm, 20 x 60 x 3 mm; sponge pack 80 x 125 x 10 mm.

ABSORBABLE GELATIN FILM [Gelfilm]

This thin absorbable gelatin film is used in neurosurgery, thoracic surgery, or ocular surgery. Depending upon the site and size of implant, eight days to six months are required for absorption.

USUAL DOSAGE.—*Topical:* See the evaluation on Absorbable Gelatin Sponge.

PREPARATIONS.—Gelfilm (Upjohn). *Topical:* Film 25 x 50 mm (ophthalmic) and 100 x 125 mm.

OXIDIZED CELLULOSE [Oxycel, Surgicel]

Oxidized cellulose is a specially treated form of surgical gauze or cotton. It does not enter into the normal physiologic clotting mechanism but, when exposed to blood, swells and is converted into a dark brown or black gelatinous mass that forms an artificial clot. Absorption depends on the size of the implant, the adequacy of the blood supply to the area, and the degree of chemical degradation of the material. It normally occurs between the second and seventh day after implantation of the dry material, but complete absorption of large amounts of blood-soaked material may take six weeks or longer. Under optimal conditions, absorption from a body cavity will occur without cellular reaction or fibrosis.

Oxidized cellulose is useful in surgical procedures to control moderate bleeding when suturing or ligation is technically impractical or ineffective. Such situations include control of capillary, venous, or small arterial hemorrhage encountered in biliary tract surgery; partial hepatectomy; resections or injuries of the pancreas, spleen, or kidneys; bowel resections; amputations; resections of the breast, thyroid, or prostate; and certain types of neurologic and otolaryngologic surgery.

This product should not be used for permanent packing or implantation in fractures because it interferes with bone regeneration and can cause cyst formation. It is less active on surfaces treated by chemical cautery. The Oxycel brand should not be used as a surface dressing except for immediate control of hemorrhage since it inhibits epithelialization, nor should silver nitrate or other corrosive chemicals be applied prior to its use. The hemostatic action of oxidized cellulose is not enhanced by other hemostatic agents; thrombin would be destroyed by the low pH of this material.

USUAL DOSAGE.—*Topical* (in wound or at operative site): The minimal amount required to control hemorrhage should be used to avoid delayed absorption or nonabsorption. It should be placed on the bleeding site or held firmly until hemostasis is obtained.

PREPARATIONS.—

Oxycel (Parke, Davis). *Topical:* Pads (gauze type) 3 x 3 inch 8 ply; pledgets (cotton type) 2 ¼ x 1 x 1 inch; strips (gauze type) 5 x ½ inch 4 ply, 18 x 2 inch 4 ply, 36 x ½ inch 4 ply.

Surgicel (Johnson & Johnson). *Topical:* Knitted fabric strips ½ x 2, 2 x 3, 4 x 8, and 2 x 14 inches.

THROMBIN

This sterile plasma protein substance is prepared from prothrombin of bovine origin and is used topically to control capillary oozing in operative procedures. It is capable of clotting whole blood, plasma, or a solution of fibrinogen without the addition of other substances and also may initiate clot formation when combined with gelatin sponge or fibrin foam. Thrombin alone is ineffective in controlling arterial bleeding.

When applied locally to denuded tissue areas, thrombin is rapidly neutralized by antithrombins, and its activity is reduced as a result of fibrin absorption. There is little danger of thrombin being absorbed into the vascular system.

Thrombin has been instilled into the stomach in an effort to hasten hemostasis in ulcerative disease, but its action is limited because of its rapid transit through the stomach. In addition, sufficient acid must be present in the stomach because thrombin becomes inactive above pH 5.

This compound is stable as a dry powder if stored between 2 and 8 C. In solution, it begins to lose activity within 8 hours at room temperature or within 48 hours if refrigerated. It should never be injected and, particularly, should never be given intravenously, for there is danger of thrombosis and death within a few minutes. Since antigenic reactions have occurred in animals, an allergic phenomenon is a remote possibility in patients being treated with this preparation.

USUAL DOSAGE.—*Topical* (in wound or at operative site): Thrombin is dusted on as a powder, applied as a solution by flooding or spraying the site, or applied with a suitable sponge matrix (eg, absorbable gelatin sponge, fibrin foam).

PREPARATIONS.—

Thrombin (Upjohn). *Topical:* Powder 1,000 units/30 ml container.

Thrombin, Topical (Parke, Davis). *Topical:* Powder 1,000, 5,000, and 10,000 unit containers. The 5,000 unit package also contains a 5 ml container of sterile isotonic sodium chloride diluent with 1:50,000 phemerol chloride as a preservative.

Chapter 12

AGENTS USED TO TREAT HYPERGLYCEMIA

Diabetes mellitus is a hereditary disorder with metabolic and vascular derangements that are probably interrelated. A relative or absolute deficiency of insulin activity is responsible for hyperglycemia associated with alterations in lipid and protein metabolism. The vascular components of the disorder consist of accelerated nonspecific atherosclerosis and a more specific small blood vessel disease primarily affecting the retina and kidney. Diabetic patients may be either ketoacidosis-prone (juvenile, growth-onset) or ketoacidosis-resistant (maturity-onset).

The ketoacidosis-prone patient generally experiences the onset of disease prior to age 20 and is dependent upon exogenous insulin to prevent ketoacidosis. The pancreas contains little or no extractable insulin. Careful dietary regulation is essential in order to maintain blood glucose at levels as nearly normal as possible. It also may be necessary to administer insulin in divided doses individualized so that the peak effect of the insulin matches the maximal elevation of blood glucose.

Ketoacidosis-resistant patients generally experience the onset of diabetes after the age of 40 and tend to be overweight. These patients do not develop ketoacidosis in the absence of insulin therapy, and dietary regulation alone may be adequate to eliminate hyperglycemia and glycosuria. Recommendations of the American Diabetes Association Committee on Food and Nutrition for dietary management of the diabetic patient appear in *Diabetes 20:*633, 1971.

An appropriate diet should be prescribed initially for both symptomatic and asymptomatic patients. If dietary regulation does not establish satisfactory control, the use of insulin should be considered. Insulin currently is preferred over the oral hypoglycemic agents (acetohexamide [Dymelor], chlorpropamide [Diabinese], tolazamide [Tolinase], tolbutamide [Orinase], and phenformin [DBI, Meltrol]) because it is more uniformly effective in controlling hyperglycemia, and because results of recent studies conducted by the University Group Diabetes Program (*Diabetes 19 [suppl 2]:*747-830, 1970 and *JAMA 217:*777-784, 1971), although controversial, suggest that it may be safer with respect to mortality due to cardiovascular complications. Except for their use on an investigational basis, the oral hypoglycemic agents have no place in the treatment of chemical or latent diabetes, subclinical (suspected) diabetes, or prediabetes, and they are contraindicated in patients with diabetic acidosis.

The University Group Diabetes Program (UGDP) study was initiated to determine whether or not the development and progression of vascular complications in patients with maturity-onset, noninsulin-dependent, asymptomatic diabetes mellitus can be influenced by controlling the blood glucose level. The UGDP group concluded the following: (1) The combinations of diet and tolbutamide, diet and phenformin, and diet and insulin therapy for the treatment of mild, noninsulin-dependent diabetes were no more effective than diet alone in prolonging life. (2) Mortality due to cardiovascular complications was increased in those patients who received tolbutamide plus diet or phenformin plus diet as opposed to those who were treated with diet alone or diet plus insulin.

Although there was a statistically significant difference in mortality due to cardiovascular deaths in the groups, the number of deaths in each group was small and the cardiovascular risk factors were not equally distributed in the opinion of some reviewers of this study; thus, interpretation of the data to determine the possible toxicity of the oral hypoglycemic agents is difficult. Only the regimen of diet plus variable insulin produced a significant and sustained decrease in the fasting blood glucose levels. In this study, neither variable nor fixed dosage of insulin was better than diet alone in prolonging life, although insulin in variable dose controlled the blood glucose level most effectively.

It is not possible to state that cardiovascular mortality will be similar for all sulfonylureas. However, it seems prudent to consider these drugs as being similar to tolbutamide until proved otherwise, since the four sulfonylureas that lower blood glucose levels are closely related in structure and mechanism of action.

Results of three other studies of markedly different experimental design (*Postgrad Med J 44 (suppl):*960-965, 1968; *Acta Med Scand,* suppl 507 pp 1-82, 1970; and *Ann Intern Med 76:*586-592, 1972) also do not indicate that there is decrease in cardiovascular morbidity and mortality with the long-term use of tolbutamide and phenformin; however, these studies do not corroborate the UGDP finding of an increased incidence of mortality due to cardiovascular disease.

Although the UGDP study has some flaws, the results clearly indicate that the physician should make every effort to control the hyperglycemia of symptomatic, maturity-onset diabetes with dietary regulation. Should this fail, insulin therapy should be considered prior to the use of the oral hypoglycemic agents. Results of the UGDP study also clearly demonstrate that control of the blood glucose level even with insulin does not alter the progression of cardiovascular disease in the maturity-onset diabetic patient.

INSULINS

The seven forms of insulin available in the United States differ with respect to their rate of onset and duration of action. They may be divided into rapid-, intermediate-, and long-acting groups (see the table on Insulin Preparations). Insulin injection (crystalline zinc insulin, regular insulin) has a rapid onset and a short duration of action. Globin zinc, isophane (NPH), and protamine zinc insulins are conjugated with large protein molecules; as a result, their absorption from subcutaneous sites of injection is delayed and their duration of action is prolonged. Some clinicians prefer insulins in the Lente series because they do not contain a modifying protein, which is theoretically sensitizing. The larger particle size of extended insulin zinc suspension (Ultralente insulin) delays its absorption and prolongs its duration of action. Because of its smaller particle size, prompt insulin zinc suspension (Semilente insulin) is more rapidly absorbed and shorter acting. A combination of 70% Ultralente and 30% Semilente insulin results in insulin zinc suspension (Lente insulin), which has an intermediate duration of action and approximates the general characteristics of isophane insulin.

An intermediate-acting preparation is often chosen for previously untreated ketoacidosis-prone diabetes. In the absence of ketosis or other acute complications, the initial dose may be 10 to 20 units, given one hour before breakfast. Depending on the clinical course, results of urine tests, and postprandial blood glucose levels, this dose may be increased by daily increments of 2 to 10 units or more until satisfactory control is obtained. In another method, 5 to 10 units of a rapid-acting insulin is injected 15 to 30 minutes before each meal and the dose is adjusted gradually by small increments as indicated by the results of urine tests. When reasonably satisfactory control is achieved, an intermediate form of insulin is substituted; this preparation is given before breakfast in a dose approximately equivalent to two-thirds of the previous total daily dose established for the rapid-acting preparation. This latter method generally requires more time to achieve optimal results but control in the unstable ketoacidosis-prone patient is more likely to occur.

Generally, the dose of an intermediate-acting insulin is increased until before-meal urine specimens become aglycosuric or the patient develops hypoglycemic symptoms. A rapid-acting insulin may be given concomitantly with an intermediate preparation if the patient develops hypoglycemic symptoms before supper and the prelunch urine specimen shows significant glycosuria. An increase in the morning dose of the intermediate preparation will generally correct glycosuria that is present before supper or bedtime; on the other hand, prebreakfast glycosuria is often controlled by either reducing the size of the bedtime snack or by giving an additional small dose of an intermediate preparation before supper.

Between-meal and bedtime snacks that represent a shift in mealtime calories but not an

TABLE 1.—INSULIN PREPARATIONS AVAILABLE IN THE UNITED STATES (In Order of Duration of Action)

			Hours After Subcutaneous Administration		
Action	Preparation	Animal Source	Onset of Action	Interval to Maximal Action	Duration Of Action
Rapid	Insulin Injection (regular, crystalline zinc)	Bovine Porcine Mixed Bovine-Porcine	<1	2-3	5-7
	Prompt Insulin Zinc Suspension (Semilente)	Bovine	<1	4-6	12-16
Intermediate	Globin Zinc Insulin Injection (globin)	Bovine	1-2	6-10	12-18
	Isophane Insulin Suspension (NPH)	Bovine Porcine Mixed Bovine-Porcine	2	8-12	18-24
	Insulin Zinc Suspension (Lente)	Bovine Porcine Mixed Bovine-Porcine	2-4	8-12	18-24
Long	Protamine Zinc Insulin Suspension	Bovine Porcine Mixed Bovine-Porcine	4-6	16-18	24-36
	Extended Insulin Zinc Suspension (Ultralente)	Bovine	4-6	16-18	24-36

increase in the total caloric intake help prevent marked postprandial glycosuria and premeal and nocturnal hypoglycemic reactions.

Unstable ketoacidosis-prone diabetes may be difficult to control with intermediate- or long-acting preparations. These patients may require multiple injections of rapid-acting insulin injection. The total daily insulin requirement may be given in divided doses before meals and is based on the results of urine tests. Insulin should not be given at bedtime because of the dangers of nocturnal hypoglycemic reactions, and the prelunch and presupper doses should be small. For example, if the total daily requirement is 40 units, doses of 20 units before breakfast, 6 units before lunch, and 14 units before supper might be given.

Diabetic acidosis requires prompt administration of large doses of regular insulin at intervals dictated by the patient's response and correction of dehydration and electrolyte imbalance. Standard texts may be consulted for details of management.

Hyperosmolar (nonketotic) coma occurs rarely. It is most commonly observed in individuals over 60 years of age who may or may not have a history of diabetes. However, it also may occur in juvenile diabetics. Polydipsia, polyuria, weight loss, rapid onset of coma, severe dehydration, and neurologic disturbances associated with markedly elevated blood glucose levels are observed. Abnormalities in serum electrolytes may be present, but extreme changes in pH or electrolyte or acetone levels are not seen. The insulin requirements vary widely during the first 24 hours. These patients may be more sensitive to the action of insulin than are those with diabetic acidosis. The administration of 10 or more liters of a hypotonic electrolyte solution may be required during the first two days of therapy to correct the imbalance of body fluids.

Specialized texts should be consulted for information on management of the diabetic patient who is undergoing surgery and on adjustment of the increasing insulin requirement during pregnancy and decreasing insulin needs immediately after delivery.

Insulin shock therapy for serious psychiatric disorders is now used infrequently, since it is potentially dangerous and should be administered only by specialists who are thoroughly familiar with all aspects of this procedure.

Adverse Reactions and Precautions

Prompt recognition and appropriate management of the complications of insulin therapy are essential for the safe and effective control of diabetes mellitus.

Hypoglycemia may occur in any patient receiving insulin and is most commonly manifested by hunger, nervousness, warmth and sweating, and palpitations. Patients also may experience headache, confusion, drowsiness, fatigue, anxiety, blurred vision, diplopia, or numbness of the lips, nose, or fingers. Unstable diabetes may occur after repeated hypoglycemic episodes. Hypoglycemic shock (insulin shock) may result from errors in insulin administration (eg, failure to agitate the container before use, improper measurement, faulty injection technique, use of outdated or improperly preserved insulin), omitting a meal, or exercise without concomitant decrease in the insulin dose or increase in carbohydrate intake. In severe cases, syncope and generalized convulsions may develop and may ultimately be fatal.

If the hypoglycemic patient is unable to take soluble carbohydrate or fruit juice orally and if dextrose is not available for intravenous injection, 0.5 to 1 mg of glucagon is given (usually subcutaneously but may be administered intravenously or intramuscularly) every 20 minutes for two or three doses (see the evaluation on Glucagon in Chapter 92, Miscellaneous Drugs).

Local and systemic allergic reactions are seen occasionally in patients receiving insulin for the first time or when therapy is reinstituted. Local inflammatory responses also result from improper cleansing of the skin, contamination of the injection site with alcohol, use of an antiseptic containing impurities, or accidental intracutaneous rather than subcutaneous injection. Local reactions that result from skin-sensitivity phenomena usually subside spontaneously. Allergic urticaria, angioedema, and anaphylactic reactions occur infrequently and usually may be avoided by changing the species source of insulin. Rarely, an intradermal or subcutaneous hyposensitization procedure may be required (see standard texts for details).

Patients susceptible to insulin lipodystrophy, which results in atrophy of the subcutaneous fat tissue at the site of injection, should inject insulin in areas that are not exposed (ie, beneath the skin of the flanks, abdomen, and upper buttocks). Lipodystrophy may possibly be minimized by changing the site frequently.

The presence of insulin antibodies is believed to be of particular significance in the development of insulin resistance. Generally, the term "resistant" has been applied to patients who require more than 200 units daily for several days or more in the absence of acute complications. However, low titers of insulin-binding antibodies can be demonstrated in the serum of nearly all patients who have received insulin injections for several weeks. Occasionally, the hyperglycemia resulting from insulin resistance can be controlled by changing the animal source of the insulin, but the frequent injection of regular insulin is preferred. The possibility of adequately controlling these insulin-resistant patients with diet alone also should be considered, for patients who are insulin resistant are not necessarily insulin dependent. See specialized texts for additional information on this subject.

Visual disturbances in uncontrolled diabetes due to refractive changes are reversed during the early phase of effective management. However, since alterations in osmotic equilibrium between the lens and ocular fluids may not stabilize for a few weeks after initiating therapy, it is wise to postpone prescribing new corrective lenses for three to six weeks.

Hormones that tend to counteract the hypoglycemic effects of insulin include growth hormone, corticotropin, glucocorticoids, thyroid hormone, and glucagon. Epinephrine not only inhibits the secretion of insulin, but also stimulates glycogen breakdown to glucose. Thus, the presence of such diseases as acromegaly, Cushing's syndrome, hyperthyroidism, and pheochromocytoma complicate the control of diabetes.

Every diabetic patient taking insulin should carry an identification card containing pertinent medical information.

INDIVIDUAL EVALUATIONS

INSULIN INJECTION (Regular Insulin, Crystalline Zinc Insulin) [Regular Iletin]

This rapid-acting agent has a short duration of action and is the only insulin preparation that may be given intravenously as well as subcutaneously. (See the Table). Insulin injection may be mixed in the same syringe with isophane (NPH) insulin without altering the characteristics of either form. It also may be mixed with insulin zinc suspension (Lente insulin) if the ratio of regular to Lente insulin does not exceed 1:2, but it should not be mixed with protamine zinc insulin.

Insulin injection is widely used to supplement intermediate- and long-acting preparations. Large doses may be required in diabetic acidosis and other forms of insulin resistance. This is the insulin of choice when glucose tolerance fluctuates rapidly, as in the presence of infection, shock, or surgical trauma.

See the Introductory Statement for further information on this preparation.

USUAL DOSAGE.—

Subcutaneous: No standard dose. Initially, 5 to 10 units 15 to 30 minutes before each meal may be given to patients with newly diagnosed, mild diabetes.

Intravenous: No standard dose can be cited for the treatment of diabetic acidosis.

PREPARATIONS.—

Regular Iletin (Lilly). *Injection:* Solution 40, 80, and 100 units/ml in 10 ml containers; 500 units/ml in 20 ml containers.

Insulin Injection (Squibb). *Injection:* Solution 40, 80, and 100 units/ml in 10 ml containers.

PROMPT INSULIN ZINC SUSPENSION

[Semilente Insulin, Semilente Iletin]

Prompt insulin zinc suspension is rapid-acting. (See the Table.) A preparation combining this form with long-acting, extended insulin zinc suspension (Ultralente insulin) has an intermediate duration of action (see the evaluation on Insulin Zinc Suspension).

This preparation is most commonly used to supplement intermediate- and long-acting forms. See the Introductory Statement for further information on prompt insulin zinc suspension.

USUAL DOSAGE.—*Subcutaneous* (should never be given intravenously): No average dose. Initially, 10 to 20 units one-half hour before breakfast may be used in patients with newly diagnosed, mild diabetes. It usually is necessary to give at least two doses daily.

PREPARATIONS.—Semilente Iletin (Lilly), Semilente Insulin (Squibb). *Injection:* Suspension 40, 80, and 100 units/ml in 10 ml containers.

GLOBIN ZINC INSULIN INJECTION

This is an intermediate-acting insulin preparation. (See the Table.) Globin, a protein prepared from beef blood, delays absorption from the subcutaneous injection site. This preparation is indicated for patients who require more than one daily injection of regular insulin and for those whose condition cannot be controlled by other forms of insulin or who exhibit sensitivity to protamine. It is not recommended for the treatment of diabetic coma.

Hypoglycemic reactions may be less obvious in onset, more prolonged, and occur more frequently than with rapid-acting preparations because of the prolonged effect of the dose. See the Introductory Statement for information on adverse reactions.

USUAL DOSAGE.—*Subcutaneous* (should never be given intravenously): No average dose. Initially, 10 to 20 units daily (about two-thirds to three-fourths of the total daily dose of a rapid-acting insulin preparation) 60 minutes before breakfast. If the patient has been receiving protamine zinc insulin, the dosage on the first day should not exceed one-half of the total dose of all insulin received on the previous day. On the second day, the dose may be increased to two-thirds of the previous total insulin dosage and adjusted slowly thereafter. It often is necessary to give two doses daily. (See the Introductory Statement.)

PREPARATIONS.—

Globin Zinc Insulin Injection (Burroughs Wellcome). *Injection:* Solution 40 and 80 units/ml in 10 ml containers.

Globin Zinc Insulin Injection (Squibb). *Injection:* Solution 40, 80, and 100 units/ml in 10 ml containers.

ISOPHANE INSULIN SUSPENSION

[NPH Iletin, NPH Insulin]

Isophane insulin is an intermediate-acting preparation. Absorption of the insulin in this preparation is delayed because it is conjugated with protamine. It contains less zinc than protamine zinc insulin. (See the Table.) This form of insulin is useful in the control of all forms of diabetes, but it is not suitable for use in the treatment of diabetic acidosis or in emergencies. Either insulin zinc suspension (Lente insulin) or isophane insulin is most often the drug of choice for the previously untreated diabetic patient.

Hypoglycemic reactions may be less obvious in onset, more prolonged, and occur more frequently than with rapid-acting preparations because of the prolonged effect of the dose. See the Introductory Statement for additional information on adverse reactions.

USUAL DOSAGE.—*Subcutaneous* (should never be given intravenously): No average dose. Initially, 7 to 20 units (about two-thirds to the same number of units needed as with a rapid-acting insulin preparation) 30 to 90 minutes before breakfast. A second injection, if needed, may be given 30 minutes before dinner. (See the Introductory Statement.)

PREPARATIONS.—NPH Iletin (Lilly), NPH Insulin (Squibb). *Injection:* Suspension 40, 80, and 100 units/ml in 10 ml containers.

INSULIN ZINC SUSPENSION [Lente Iletin, Lente Insulin]

This intermediate-acting preparation is a mixture of 30% prompt insulin zinc suspension (Semilente insulin) and 70% extended insulin zinc suspension (Ultralente insulin). (See the Table.) It may be used interchangeably with isophane insulin. This preparation or isophane insulin is most frequently the drug of choice for previously untreated diabetics. Insulin zinc suspension is not a suitable substitute for insulin injection (regular insulin) in emergencies.

Hypoglycemic reactions may be less obvious in onset, more prolonged, and occur more frequently than with rapid-acting preparations because of the prolonged effect of the dose. Some physicians prefer insulins in the Lente series because they do not contain a modifying protein. See the Introductory Statement for additional information on adverse reactions.

USUAL DOSAGE.—*Subcutaneous* (should never be given intravenously): No average dose. Initially, 7 to 20 units (about two-thirds to the same number of units needed as with a rapid-acting insulin preparation) 30 to 90 minutes before supper. Patients receiving isophane insulin may be transferred directly to insulin zinc suspension on a unit-for-unit basis. Initially, the total dose should be reduced by 25% in patients who previously had received regular or protamine zinc insulin. (See the Introductory Statement.)

PREPARATIONS.—Lente Iletin (Lilly), Lente Insulin (Squibb). *Injection:* Suspension 40, 80, and 100 units/ml in 10 ml containers.

PROTAMINE ZINC INSULIN SUSPENSION [Protamine, Zinc & Iletin]

This long-acting preparation contains more modifying protein (protamine) and zinc than isophane insulin. (See the Table.) Combining regular insulin with protamine zinc insulin is complicated by the conversion of a portion of the unmodified insulin to an insoluble form. The protamine form of insulin is best suited for mild to moderately severe stable diabetes when sensitivity to insulin timing is not critical. Like extended insulin zinc suspension (Ultralente insulin), it has limited usefulness when given alone. Long-acting preparations are generally less adaptable than intermediate-acting preparations given in divided doses.

Free protamine forms an insoluble complex with prothrombin, and may cause lymphedema around the injection site. The long duration of action of protamine zinc insulin may result in recurrent hypoglycemic reactions if the dosage is not properly adjusted. A soluble carbohydrate (eg, orange juice) may be given to prevent such reactions, but the carbohydrate content of the meal following injection may have to be limited to avoid hyperglycemia. Between-meal snacks are desirable and bedtime snacks are essential. See the Introductory Statement for additional information on adverse reactions.

USUAL DOSAGE.—*Subcutaneous* (should never be given intravenously): No average dose. Initially, 7 to 20 units (about two-thirds to the same number of units needed as with a rapid-acting insulin preparation) given once daily 30 to 60 minutes before breakfast. (See the Introductory Statement.)

PREPARATIONS.—Protamine, Zinc & Iletin (Lilly), Protamine Zinc Insulin (Squibb). *Injection:* Suspension 40, 80, and 100 units/ml in 10 ml containers.

EXTENDED INSULIN ZINC SUSPENSION [Ultralente Iletin, Ultralente Insulin]

The action of this long-acting preparation is similar to that of protamine zinc insulin. (See the Table.) Like prompt insulin zinc suspension (Semilente insulin), it contains no modifying protein to which patients may be sensitive and, like protamine zinc insulin, it has limited usefulness when given alone. This preparation may be combined with insulin zinc suspension (Lente insulin) for patients in whom the blood glucose level in the fasting state is not adequately controlled. It is not suitable for use in emergencies.

The long duration of action of extended

insulin zinc suspension may result in recurrent hypoglycemic reactions if the dose is not properly adjusted. A soluble carbohydrate such as orange juice may be given to help prevent such reactions, but the carbohydrate content of the meal follwoing injection of extended insulin zinc suspension may have to be limited to avoid hyperglycemic. Between-meal snacks are desirable and bedtime snacks are essential. See the Introductory Statement for additional information on adverse reactions.

USUAL DOSAGE.—*Subcutaneous* (should never be given intravenously): No average dose. Initially, 7 to 20 units (about two-thirds to the same number of units needed as with a rapid-acting insulin preparation) given once daily 30 to 90 minutes before breakfast. (See the Introductory Statement.)

PREPARATIONS.—Ultralente Iletin (Lilly), Ultralente Insulin (Squibb). *Injection:* Suspension 40, 80, and 100 units/ml in 10 ml containers.

ORAL HYPOGLYCEMIC AGENTS

Five drugs that can lower the blood glucose level when given orally are available for the treatment of selected patients with diabetes. They include four sulfonylurea compounds (acetohexamide [Dymelor], chlorpropamide [Diabinese], tolazamide [Tolinase], and tolbutamide [Orinase]) and a biguanide compound (phenformin [DBI, Meltrol]), which differs from the sulfonylureas chemically and in its mode of action. None of these agents should be considered either as an oral form of insulin or as a substitute for insulin in the ketoacidosis-prone patient with no functioning source of endogenous insulin.

The absorption of all the hypoglycemic agents is fairly rapid. See the table on Oral Hypoglycemic Agents for the half-lives and duration of action of these agents.

Although the sulfonylureas are classified chemically as sulfonamide derivatives, these agents have no antibacterial action. They appear to act initially by stimulating the release of endogenous insulin from the islet tissue of the pancreas. The insulin thus released appears to act chiefly in the liver to decrease the output of hepatic glucose. The sulfonylureas do not decrease the metabolic destruction of insulin; although the results of some studies suggest that they may potentiate the action of insulin, evidence of this is not clear. The mechanism for the long-term hypoglycemic effect of the sulfonylureas also has not been established.

The mode of action of phenformin is not well understood. This agent appears to increase the rate of anaerobic glycolysis of glucose in vitro, but it has not been shown with certainty that such an effect is responsible for hypoglycemic action in doses used clinically in diabetic patients. The use of phenformin may lead to

TABLE 2.—ORAL HYPOGLYCEMIC AGENTS AVAILABLE IN THE UNITED STATES

Type	Drug	Half-Life (Hours)	Duration (Hours)
Sulfonylurea	Acetohexamide Dymelor (Lilly)	6-8 (includes metabolites)	12-24
	Chlorpropamide Diabinese (Pfizer)	30-36	60
	Tolazamide Tolinase (Upjohn)	7	10-14
	Tolbutamide Orinase (Upjohn)	4-6	6-12
Biguanide	Phenformin Hydrochloride DBI (Geigy) Meltrol (USV)	3	4-6
	Phenformin Hydrochloride (timed-release) DBI-TD (Geigy) Meltrol (USV)	3	8-14

weight loss in the obese, mildly diabetic patient. In addition to inducing anorexia, it appears that it may interfere with the absorption of calorigenic nutriments.

Acetohexamide, chlorpropamide, tolazamide, and tolbutamide lower the blood glucose level in nondiabetic as well as in diabetic individuals. Conversely, phenformin, in usual therapeutic doses, has no hypoglycemic effect in individuals without diabetes; the blood glucose level remains unchanged because an increase in peripheral glucose utilization is exactly compensated by an increase in hepatic glucose output.

In initiating therapy for diabetes, adequate time must be allowed for the patient to learn and practice the necessary dietary habits before other modes of therapy are introduced. Failure to emphasize the principles and the necessity of proper dietary management initially is perhaps the principal shortcoming in the present treatment of diabetes. Mild elevation of blood glucose during this initial period is not life-threatening, and prompt use of oral hypoglycemic agents to lower the blood glucose level before the principles of therapy are understood is detrimental to the long-term care of the patient. If hyperglycemia and symptomatic glycosuria continue after an appropriate trial with diet, it may be necessary to introduce an antidiabetic agent. The use of insulin should be considered prior to the use of the oral hypoglycemic agents for the reasons stated in the Introductory Statement to this chapter.

Oral hypoglycemic agents are useful in symptomatic patients who do not respond to diet alone and who are allergic to insulin or are otherwise unable or unwilling to inject insulin. They are especially useful in the elderly diabetic with poor vision who is living alone and who is in danger of developing hypoglycemia from incorrect insulin dosage.

In changing a patient from insulin to an oral hypoglycemic agent, it is important to have an insulin-free interval to determine whether any therapy other than dietary regulation is in fact needed. Oral hypoglycemic therapy should not be continued or tried again in patients who develop moderate to severe ketonuria or polyuria within 12 to 24 hours after withdrawal of insulin.

An oral hypoglycemic agent should never be used for a patient with unstable diabetes, whatever his age. Similarly, this form of therapy is contraindicated in patients with maturity-onset diabetes complicated by infection, severe trauma, or gangrene or in those recovering from major surgery. Insulin is required when these complications are present. There is no evidence that these drugs, singly or in combination, are more effective than diet alone in preventing cardiovascular complications in the maturity-onset diabetic who has no history of ketosis.

Relapse or secondary failure occurs frequently in patients treated with oral hypoglycemic agents. Only 6% to 12% of patients remain well controlled six to seven years after they started receiving these drugs. For the above reasons, it is advisable to withdraw the drugs from time to time to determine the necessity for their continued use. Such withdrawal will not create a metabolic catastrophe or precipitate ketoacidosis, since oral hypoglycemic agents are not suitable for patients who are ketoacidosis-prone. Oral hypoglycemic agents cannot be expected to prevent insulin dependence. Frequently the test of efficacy will demonstrate that most patients fall into one of two distinct categories: (1) patients who are well controlled on the combination of diet and oral agents and who can continue to be well controlled on diet alone, or (2) patients in whom the dosage of oral hypoglycemic agents had been gradually increased in an attempt to control elevated blood glucose level and in whom the oral hypoglycemic agent, on withdrawal, frequently is found to have made a negligible contribution in controlling the blood glucose value.

Adverse Reactions

Acute toxic effects after the use of oral hypoglycemic agents appear to be relatively rare, but the use of combinations of these drugs increases the risk of untoward reactions. Cholestatic jaundice has occurred rarely after tolbutamide [Orinase], acetohexamide [Dymelor], and chlorpropamide [Diabinese] therapy, and, presumably, it also must be expected to occur with tolazamide [Tolinase]. Jaundice has not been associated with use of phenformin [DBI, Meltrol].

Hypoglycemic reactions, including hypoglycemic shock (eg, hunger, nervousness, warmth and sweating, palpitations, headache, confusion, drowsiness, fatigue, anxiety, blurred vision, diplopia, numbness of the lips, nose, and fingers), have been reported after use of all four sulfonylurea compounds; they are rarely severe but a few fatalities have been reported. Hypoglycemia has occurred in nondiabetic individuals, in diabetic patients, and in those who have received sulfonylureas for other diseases on an investigational basis. It frequently lasts several days so that prolonged or repeated infusions of dextrose are necessary, and the severity often fluctuates during such episodes. Hypoglycemic reactions have occurred after one dose of a sulfonylurea drug, after two or three days of therapy, or after many months of therapy that had previously produced no untoward effects. Hypoglycemia may develop after treatment with a single sulfonylurea, after a change from one oral drug to another, or after a change from insulin to an oral drug. It may occur in patients who receive an inappropriately large dose of a sulfonylurea, in those who do not eat properly, or in those who fail to metabolize or excrete the drug because of hepatic or renal disease. A decreased rate of excretion is most likely to occur after the use of the longer-acting agents, acetohexamide and chlorpropamide.

Allergic skin reactions (pruritus, erythema, urticaria, and morbilliform or maculopapular rash) also have been noted with sulfonylurea compounds. Most of these effects are transient; if they persist, the agent should be discontinued and insulin should be administered. Gastrointestinal disturbances, which occur most frequently with phenformin, can be troublesome. They may be lessened by taking the drug with meals, adjusting the dosage, or substituting the timed-release capsules for the tablets. If symptoms persist, the oral hypoglycemic agent should be discontinued at least temporarily. Hyponatremia has been associated with the administration of chlorpropamide and tolbutamide in a small percentage of patients.

Leukopenia, thrombocytopenia, agranulocytosis, aplastic anemia, hemolytic anemia, and acute intermittent porphyria have been reported rarely after use of the sulfonylurea derivatives but not after use of phenformin.

Clinical data are not adequate to ascertain that the oral hypoglycemic agents have any teratogenic effects. However, the oral hypoglycemic agents are not recommended for use in diabetic women who may become pregnant; insulin is the drug of choice during pregnancy.

Precautions

The transfer of patients from insulin to oral hypoglycemic agents is recommended only under unusual conditions, and extreme care should be used in adjusting the dosage. The patient should be closely observed, preferably in a hospital. If the patient is not hospitalized, he should be seen daily during the first week of therapy and should receive instructions regarding symptoms and signs of hyperglycemia and ketosis. If polyuria or ketonuria occurs during the transitional period, insulin therapy should be reinstituted immediately and no further attempt should be made to substitute oral agents for insulin.

The sulfonylureas are contraindicated in nondiabetic patients with renal glycosuria because their hyperresponsiveness to these agents may result in prolonged or fatal hypoglycemia. Drinks or foods that have a high dextrose content are used to treat relatively mild hypoglycemic reactions in conscious patients. Dextrose should be given intravenously when the patient is unconscious; glucagon also is effective (see the evaluation in Chapter 92, Miscellaneous Drugs).

Drugs that may increase the risk of hypoglycemia in patients taking the sulfonylureas include insulin, phenformin [DBI, Meltrol], the absorbable bacteriostatic sulfonamides, propranolol [Inderal], salicylates, phenylbutazone [Azolid, Butazolidin], oxyphenbutazone [Oxalid, Tandearil], probenecid [Benemid], dicumarol, chloramphenicol [Chloromycetin], monoamine oxidase inhibitors, and alcohol.

Caution is necessary when thiazide diuretics are given with the sulfonylureas, since the thiazides may aggravate the diabetic state, resulting in an increase in the dosage requirement for the oral hypoglycemic agents, temporary loss of control, and even secondary failures.

The sulfonylureas, particularly chlorpropamide [Diabinese], decrease tolerance to alcohol; this is manifested by an unusual flushing of the skin, particularly of the face and neck, similar to that caused by disulfiram [Antabuse].

Chlorpropamide and acetohexamide [Dymelor] should be administered with caution to patients with impaired renal function, and all four sulfonylureas should be administered cautiously to patients with overt hepatic dysfunction.

SULFONYLUREA COMPOUNDS

ACETOHEXAMIDE [Dymelor]

$CH_3CO-\langle\;\rangle-SO_2NHCONH-\langle\;\rangle$

Acetohexamide is similar to other oral hypoglycemic agents in the sulfonylurea class. It has been useful in patients with symptomatic, stable, maturity-onset diabetes who are nonketotic, whose condition cannot be controlled by dietary regulation alone, and who are allergic to insulin or are otherwise unable or unwilling to inject insulin. However, insulin should be considered before an oral hypoglycemic agent is administered because it is more uniformly effective in controlling hyperglycemia. Also, results of studies conducted by the UGDP suggest that it may be safer (see the Introductory Statement). As with other sulfonylureas, secondary failures have occurred after several months of continuous use of acetohexamide.

The incidence of untoward effects is low and reactions are reversible when acetohexamide is discontinued. Nausea, acute gastritis, diarrhea, headache, intolerance to alcohol, nervousness, tingling, and rash occur infrequently. Relatively severe hypoglycemic reactions have been observed occasionally in patients given large doses for a prolonged period without close observation. Rarely, hypoglycemic reactions due to hyperresponsiveness to the drug have occurred in patients given usual therapeutic doses. Although cholestatic jaundice has been reported only rarely, acetohexamide should be administered with extreme caution, if at all, to patients with a history of overt hepatic dysfunction. It also should be given cautiously to patients with impaired renal function.

Thrombocytopenia, agranulocytosis, aplastic anemia, hemolytic anemia, and acute intermittent porphyria also have been reported rarely after use of acetohexamide.

It is essential that patients be carefully selected and educated in the management of diabetes. Initiation or continuation of therapy with acetohexamide is contraindicated in patients with diabetes complicated by ketosis, diabetic coma, infection, severe trauma, major surgery, or gangrene. Insulin should be used when these complications are present, and it remains the drug of choice during pregnancy. Acetohexamide also is contraindicated in nondiabetic patients with renal glycosuria, because prolonged or fatal hypoglycemia may result. See the introduction to this section for further information and discussion on the use of acetohexamide with other drugs.

USUAL DOSAGE.—*Oral:* Dosage should be individualized. The usual range is 250 mg to 1.5 g daily; doses in excess of 1.5 g daily are not recommended. Most patients receiving 1 g or less per day can be given the full amount once daily. The drug should be given twice daily, before the morning and evening meals, if patients require a total of 1.5 g daily. Those who have recently discontinued using a long-acting insulin preparation should be given relatively small initial doses.

PREPARATIONS.—Dymelor (Lilly). *Oral:* Tablets 250 and 500 mg.

CHLORPROPAMIDE [Diabinese]

$Cl-\langle\;\rangle-SO_2NH\overset{O}{\overset{\|}{C}}NH\,CH_2CH_2CH_3$

Chlorpropamide has essentially the same actions, uses, and limitations as the other oral hypoglycemic agents in the sulfonylurea class (see the evaluation on Acetohexamide and the introduction to the section on Oral Hypoglycemic Agents). Both primary and secondary failures have been reported less frequently with chlorpropamide than with tolbutamide.

Untoward reactions have occurred more frequently with chlorpropamide than with the other sulfonylureas and, in a few older patients, hypoglycemic reactions have been severe. Due to its long half-life, maximal accumulation and effect may take one to two weeks. For the same reasons, several weeks may be required for complete elimination of the drug from the body, and chlorpropamide should be given cautiously to patients with impaired renal function. Cholestatic jaundice, usually transient, has been reported only rarely; nevertheless, the drug should be administered with extreme caution, if at all, to patients with a history of overt hepatic dysfunction. Leukopenia, thrombocytopenia, agranulocytosis, aplastic anemia, hemolytic anemia, acute intermittent porphyria, diarrhea, and rash also have occurred rarely.

Hyponatremia has been associated with the administration of chlorpropamide in a small percentage of patients. Serum hypo-osmolality, continued sodium excretion despite hyponatremia, and an impaired ability to dilute urine and to excrete a water load also were reported in these patients. In this phenomenon, chlorpropamide increases the endogenous antidiuretic hormone activity. The abnormalities were corrected by withdrawing the drug but reappeared when chlorpropamide was readministered. (See Chapter 40, Antidiuretics.)

Chlorpropamide is contraindicated in nondiabetic patients with renal glycosuria, because prolonged or fatal hypoglycemia may result.

An intolerance to alcohol may be noted more frequently with this drug than with other sulfonylureas. See the introduction to this section for further information and discussion on the use of chlorpropamide with other drugs.

USUAL DOSAGE.—*Oral:* Dosage should be individualized; the total dose is usually given once daily with breakfast. Initially, for middle-aged patients, 250 mg or less is given daily; for older patients, 100 to 125 mg is given daily. The blood glucose level reaches a plateau five to seven days after initiation of therapy. The dosage may be increased or decreased by 50 to 125 mg at weekly intervals. The maintenance dose varies with the response of the patient and the severity of the disease; the usual range is 100 to 500 mg daily. Patients who do not respond completely to 500 mg daily usually will not respond to larger doses. Maintenance doses greater than 750 mg daily are not recommended.

PREPARATIONS.—Diabinese (Pfizer). *Oral:* Tablets 100 and 250 mg.

TOLAZAMIDE [Tolinase]

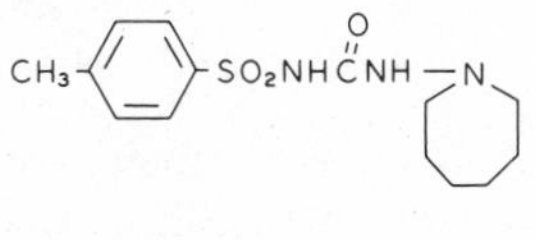

$$CH_3-C_6H_4-SO_2NHC(=O)NH-N(CH_2)_6$$

Tolazamide is chemically and pharmacologically related to other oral hypoglycemic agents of the sulfonylurea type and has the same actions, uses, and limitations (see the evaluation on Acetohexamide and the introduction to the section on Oral Hypoglycemic Agents). Little benefit is likely to be gained by transferring patients to tolazamide if their disease is controlled satisfactorily by another sulfonylurea. As with other sulfonylureas, secondary failures have occurred after several months of continuous use of tolazamide.

Generally, the untoward effects associated with tolazamide are the same as those noted with other sulfonylureas and are reversible when the drug is discontinued. Relatively severe hypoglycemic reactions have been observed occasionally in patients given large doses initially or who received large doses for a prolonged period without close observation. Nausea, anorexia, diarrhea, constipation, vomiting, abdominal cramps, rash, pruritus, asthenia, fatigue, vertigo, nervousness, insomnia, lethargy, and drowsiness have been noted infrequently.

Leukopenia, thrombocytopenia, agranulocytosis, aplastic anemia, hemolytic anemia, and acute intermittent porphyria also have been reported rarely after use of tolazamide.

Tolazamide is contraindicated in nondiabetic patients with renal glycosuria, because prolonged or fatal hypoglycemia may result. See the introduction to the section on Oral Hypoglycemic Agents for further information and discussion on the use of tolazamide with other drugs.

USUAL DOSAGE.—*Oral:* Dosage should be individualized. Initially, 100 to 250 mg daily is given with breakfast; the amount then is adjusted every four to six days as needed. A single daily dose is effective in most patients; if 500 mg or more is required daily, the drug should be given in two doses. Amounts larger than 1 g daily probably will not improve control.

PREPARATIONS.—Tolinase (Upjohn). *Oral:* Tablets 100 and 250 mg.

TOLBUTAMIDE [Orinase]
TOLBUTAMIDE SODIUM [Orinase Diagnostic]

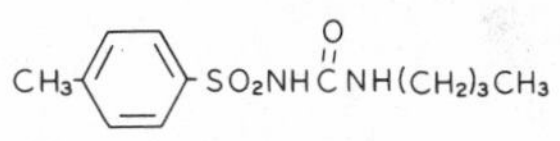

$$CH_3-C_6H_4-SO_2NHC(=O)NH(CH_2)_3CH_3$$

Tolbutamide has the same actions, uses, and limitations as other sulfonylurea compounds (see the evaluation on Acetohexamide and the introduction to the section on Oral Hypoglycemic Agents). Tolbutamide is of greatest value in patients who, because of poor general physical status, should receive a short-acting compound (see the Table).

In patients with pancreatic islet cell tumor, the blood glucose level drops quickly after intravenous injection of tolbutamide sodium and remains low for three hours. Since other hypoglycemic states usually are not affected, tolbutamide sodium may be used in conjunction with estimates of plasma insulin to rule out this condition.

The acute toxicity of tolbutamide appears to be low. Symptomatic hypoglycemia occurs rarely but may be serious, especially in elderly patients who have received a bacteriostatic sulfonamide concomitantly. Other untoward reactions include gastrointestinal disturbances, asthenia, paresthesia, tinnitus, headache, and allergic reactions (pruritus, erythema multiforme, urticaria, and morbilliform or maculopapular rash). Dermatologic reactions are usually transient but, if they persist, phenformin or insulin should be used in place of tolbutamide. Cholestatic jaundice, leukopenia, thrombocytopenia, pancytopenia, and agranulocytosis have been reported rarely. Tolbutamide should be administered with extreme caution, if at all, to patients with a history of overt hepatic dysfunction. The drug is contraindicated in nondiabetic patients with renal glycosuria, since prolonged or fatal hypoglycemia may result.

As with chlorpropamide, hyponatremia has occasionally occurred after the administration of tolbutamide (see the evaluation on Chlorpropamide and Chapter 40, Antidiuretics).

Thrombophlebitis and thrombosis of the vein used for injection of tolbutamide sodium have occurred in a small percentage of patients (0.8% to 2.4%); however, no important sequelae have been reported from this reaction.

The interaction of chloramphenicol and tolbutamide has resulted in the prolonged activity of tolbutamide. See the introduction to this section for further information and discussion on the use of tolbutamide with other drugs.

USUAL DOSAGE.—

Tolbutamide:

Oral: Dosage should be individualized. Initially, 500 mg is given twice daily; the dose then is adjusted gradually until the minimal amount adequate for satisfactory control of blood glucose and glycosuria is established. The maintenance dose, given in divided amounts, is 500 mg to 2 g daily. Amounts greater than 3 g daily produce no better results than smaller doses. Tolbutamide should be given for at least five to seven days to determine its effectiveness.

Tolbutamide Sodium:

Intravenous (diagnostic): 1 g.

PREPARATIONS.—

Orinase (Upjohn). *Oral:* Tablets 500 mg.

Orinase Diagnostic (Upjohn). *Injection* (for diagnostic use only): Powder 1 g (present as 1.081 g tolbutamide sodium).

BIGUANIDE COMPOUND

PHENFORMIN HYDROCHLORIDE [DBI, Meltrol]

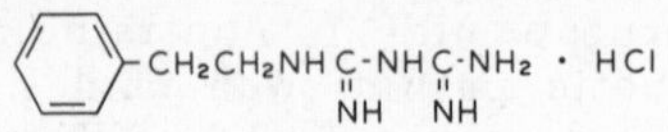

$CH_2CH_2NH\underset{NH}{\overset{\|}{C}}\text{-}NH\underset{NH}{\overset{\|}{C}}\text{-}NH_2 \cdot HCl$

Phenformin is an oral hypoglycemic agent that is not related chemically to the insulins or the sulfonylurea compounds (see the Table). It has been useful in patients with symptomatic, stable, maturity-onset diabetes who are nonketotic, whose condition cannot be controlled by dietary regulation alone, and who are allergic to insulin or are otherwise unable or unwilling to inject insulin. However, insulin should be considered first because it is more uniformly effective in controlling hyperglycemia. Also, results of the studies conducted by the UGDP suggest that it may be safer (see the Introductory Statement).

Concomitant use of a sulfonylurea with phenformin may produce a satisfactory result in patients whose blood glucose cannot be controlled by administering one of these agents alone.

The usefulness of phenformin is limited by the frequency of gastrointestinal reactions such as metallic taste, anorexia, nausea, vomiting, and diarrhea. The incidence and severity of symptoms are proportional to the dose, and may be lessened by taking the drug with meals, by adjusting the dosage, or by using the timed-release preparation. Although there is insufficient evidence to attribute lactic acidosis directly to phenformin, this complication has been described in several diabetic patients who were already seriously ill with conditions accompanied by hypoxia (eg, cardiac, hepatic, or renal failure) or who continued to take phenformin after the ingestion of alcohol or the onset of the severe anorexia or vomiting associated with ketosis.

Occasionally, patients in whom normal blood glucose concentrations are maintained by phenformin may experience loss of weight, asthenia, and ketonuria unless insulin also is administered. In addition to inducing anorexia, it appears that phenformin may interfere with the absorption of calorigenic nutriments.

As with other oral hypoglycemic agents, complete education of the patient concerning his disease and its management is necessary (see the introduction to this section). Phenformin should not be used in the management of diabetes during the early postoperative period, or in the presence of such complications as ketosis, coma, and infection. It is contraindicated in alcoholics, debilitated patients, and those with severe liver or kidney impairment. It also is contraindicated in nondiabetic patients with renal glycosuria because prolonged or fatal hypoglycemia may result. Insulin remains the drug of choice for the treatment of diabetes during pregnancy.

USUAL DOSAGE.—*Oral:* In tablet form, the usual initial dose is 25 to 50 mg daily given with meals. The latter amount is given in divided doses in the morning and evening; if this amount is not effective, the daily dose is increased slowly by increments of 25 mg at intervals of two or three days. Two or three doses daily may produce satisfactory results, but four doses daily will often afford smoother regulation of blood glucose level. The total daily dose is usually limited by gastrointestinal intolerance, which occurs more frequently with doses in excess of 150 mg.

For the timed-release capsule, the usual daily dose is 50 to 100 mg, given with breakfast and the evening meal or before retiring, but a maximal dose of 300 mg daily may be necessary.

When phenformin therapy is initiated in patients receiving insulin, the dose of insulin should be reduced gradually.

PREPARATIONS.—DBI (Geigy), Meltrol (USV). *Oral:* Capsules (timed-release) 50 and 100 mg [DBI-TD, Meltrol-50, -100]; tablets 25 mg [DBI, Meltrol-25].

Chapter 13

AGENTS USED TO TREAT HYPERLIPIDEMIA

The complications of atherosclerosis (eg, ischemic heart disease, myocardial infarction, stroke, renal disease) are the principal underlying causes of death in more than 50% of men in the United States; the incidence in women, until menopause, is somewhat lower. The atherosclerotic process occurs to some degree in all humans and is accelerated by a variety of environmental and genetic factors. Epidemiologic data show that for middle-aged men, the presence of two or more risk factors, even though none may be extreme, markedly increases the probability that atherosclerosis will develop. Among the factors associated with increased risk are hypertension, cigarette smoking, obesity, sedentary habits, strong family history of ischemic heart disease, and elevated serum lipid levels.

Many epidemiologic, clinical, pathologic, and laboratory animal studies have established the fact that elevated cholesterol levels are associated with the development of atherosclerosis and its clinical complications, notably ischemic heart disease. There is no threshold of abnormality but rather a continuous increase in risk from the lowest to the highest serum cholesterol levels. The relationship between serum cholesterol levels and stroke syndrome, the main consequence of cerebrovascular atherosclerosis, is less adequately documented. Risk of ischemic heart disease also may be related to the serum triglyceride concentration, although the correlation is less well substantiated than that for serum cholesterol.

Hyperlipidemia is the general term for abnormally elevated concentrations of lipids in the blood. Cholesterol, triglycerides, phospholipids, and free fatty acids circulate in the blood as part of the protein complexes that impart water solubility to the lipid fraction. Clinically important blood lipid abnormalities also are reflected in changes in the lipoprotein concentrations. The various lipoproteins differ in size, density, electric charge, and protein and lipid content; the higher density lipoproteins have larger ratios of protein to lipid, and the lower density lipoproteins contain a greater proportion of triglycerides. Lipoproteins may be separated into classes by electrophoresis or by ultracentrifugation. Although ultracentrifugation is the more quantitative technique, electrophoresis is more practical and readily available. By either technique, the plasma lipoproteins are separated into four major groups: chylomicrons, very low density (prebeta) lipoproteins, low density (beta) lipoproteins, and high density (alpha) lipoproteins (see Table 1). These groups and their characteristics are:

Chylomicrons are synthesized in the intestinal mucosa and represent mainly exogenous dietary triglycerides; they are the means by which these triglycerides are transported from the intestinal mucosa into the plasma and ultimately to sites of utilization in the tissues. Normally, chylomicrons are rapidly removed from plasma, presumably by a group of enzymes known collectively as lipoprotein lipase or post heparin lipolytic activity (PHLA), since these enzymes are released into plasma following the intravenous administration of heparin. When a deficiency of PHLA exists, chylomicrons accumulate in the plasma.

Very low density lipoproteins (VLDL, prebeta lipoproteins) are rich in all three major serum lipid fractions with a preponderance of triglycerides and are the means by which endogenous triglycerides are transported from the liver to plasma. VLDL accumulate in plasma if they are released from the liver more rapidly than they can be cleared from the plasma.

TABLE 1.—PLASMA LIPOPROTEINS

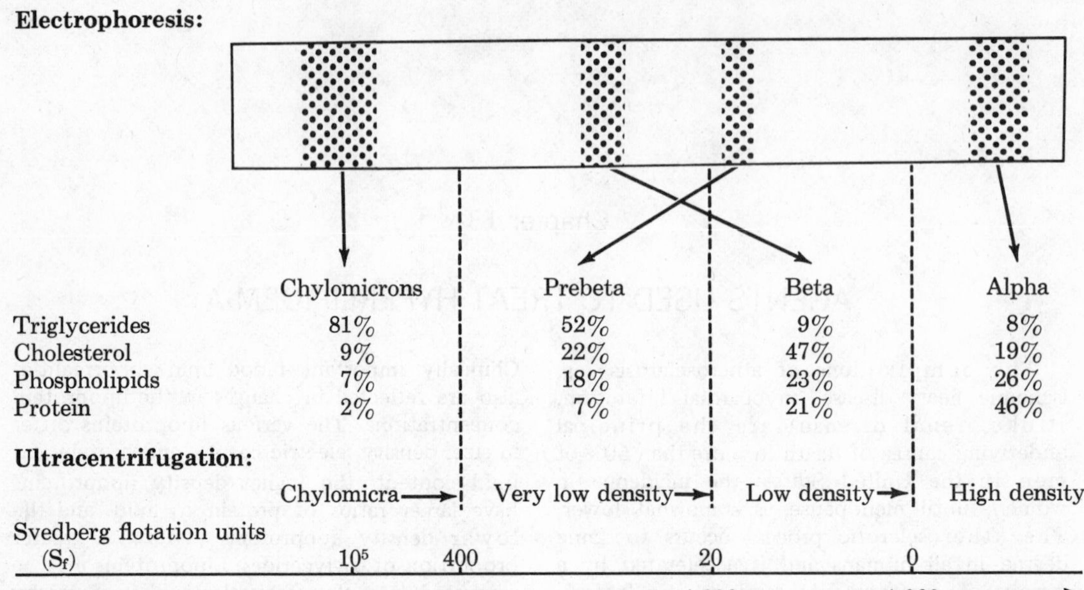

	Chylomicrons	Prebeta	Beta	Alpha
Triglycerides	81%	52%	9%	8%
Cholesterol	9%	22%	47%	19%
Phospholipids	7%	18%	23%	26%
Protein	2%	7%	21%	46%

Release of VLDL into the plasma is usually accelerated by a diet high in carbohydrates. However, in some patients, an abnormal sensitivity to normal amounts of dietary carbohydrate results in a higher and more persistent elevation which is called carbohydrate-induced hypertriglyceridemia.

Low density lipoproteins (LDL, beta lipoproteins) have a high cholesterol and a relatively low triglyceride content, and transport the largest proportion of either exogenous or endogenous plasma cholesterol. Although their exact function is unclear, they appear to be derived from metabolism of VLDL. The plasma concentration of LDL depends on many factors (eg, dietary cholesterol content, intake of saturated fat, VLDL removal rate). It is this group of lipoproteins that has the highest atherogenic potential.

High density lipoproteins (HDL, alpha lipoproteins) at present have no recognized atherogenic significance. However, HDL concentrations are sensitive to estrogens, and hyperestrogenemia usually results in a marked elevation of these lipoproteins; because of the cholesterol component of HDL, total cholesterol occasionally is elevated to abnormal levels.

Of clinical importance are **floating beta lipoproteins** ("broad beta" or beta VLDL). Although these lipoproteins are considered to be normal intermediate forms in the conversion of VLDL to LDL, they may accumulate in abnormal amounts (see discussion of Type III Hyperlipoproteinemia).

Hyperlipoproteinemia may result from (1) increased intake of cholesterol, (2) increased release of endogenous triglycerides and cholesterol from the liver and intestine, (3) failure in peripheral assimilation or clearance from end organs, muscle, and adipose tissue due to defects in enzymes or hormones, or (4) abnormalities in the lipoproteins themselves. All of these factors are modified by the general state of nutrition and the availability of nutritional precursors. Some hormones (insulin, thyroxine, epinephrine, glucagon, growth hormone, estrogens, androgens, glucocorticosteroids) also may affect lipogenesis and lipolysis in different tissues.

In addition to being associated with atherosclerosis, hyperlipoproteinemia may produce lipid deposits (xanthoma) that may be both disfiguring and painful. Also, exogenous hypertriglyceridemia may be associated with episodes of abdominal pain, which may mimic acute surgical emergencies and often lead to unnecessary surgery.

Hyperlipoproteinemia also may be present as

a complication of diabetes mellitus, pancreatitis, nephrotic syndrome, chronic renal failure, obstructive liver disease, hypothyroidism, excessive intake of alcohol, pregnancy, use of oral contraceptives, Von Gierke's disease (glycogenosis type I), dysproteinemias (multiple myeloma, macroglobulinemias), and Cushing's syndrome. In these patients, treatment of the underlying disorder may eliminate or ameliorate the hyperlipidemia. Therefore, *secondary disorders should be considered as possible causes of hyperlipidemia and treated before abnormal lipid pattern is treated by dietary correction or drug therapy.*

Although severe degrees of hyperlipidemia are invariably the result of a genetically determined metabolic abnormality or are secondary to some demonstrable disease, moderate elevations of serum lipid levels frequently occur in individuals who overeat or ingest large amounts of animal fat, cholesterol, or carbohydrate. This type of hyperlipidemia usually responds readily to dietary regulation.

The five lipoprotein patterns do not designate a specific disease mechanism but help to delineate where the deficiency occurs in the complex area of lipid transport: type I represents a defect in metabolizing dietary fat (defect in chylomicron removal); type II is related, at least in part, to the decreased catabolism of LDL; type III, in which abnormal amounts of floating beta lipoproteins are present, represents a defect in conversion of VLDL to LDL; type IV is caused by the overproduction or decreased clearance of VLDL; and in type V there is a defect in utilization of both fat and triglycerides. Each type of hyperlipoproteinemia is heterogeneous; although the present classification into types is oversimplified and incomplete, it is the only current qualitative guideline for treatment.

Hyperlipidemic patients usually have either type II or type IV abnormality. Type II recently has been divided into two subtypes, IIa and IIb; both subtypes are characterized by increased cholesterol levels, but with type IIb there are increased triglycerides as well (see discussion under Type II disorder). Types III and V are somewhat less common, and type I is quite rare. A differential diagnosis is important because dietary and drug management varies significantly.

Therapeutic Goals: The ultimate goal of therapy in hyperlipidemia is to reduce, or even arrest or reverse, the rate of development of atherosclerosis and its complications. On the basis of significant evidence that increased concentrations of certain plasma lipids are associated with increased risk of atherosclerosis, it is assumed, but unproven, that lowering plasma lipids will reduce this risk. However, the studies which suggested that reduction of plasma lipids lessened the morbidity and mortality caused by atherosclerosis included simultaneous changes in other risk factors such as smoking and exercise. Long-term controlled studies on the effect of reducing blood lipids in primary and secondary prevention are in progress.

Although definitive proof is not yet available, early recognition and application of proper therapy before sequelae have developed may offer the best chance of producing beneficial results. Dietary control is the mainstay of therapy. Although drugs are used primarily for their hypolipidemic effect, they also may inhibit platelet aggregation or decrease fibrinogen levels. However, their use must be carefully weighed against their adverse effects and expense. Optimal management also involves detection and elimination of other risk factors, particularly hypertension. The presence of more than one risk factor plus a familial background of atherosclerotic complications make consideration of active intervention more urgent and desirable, especially in younger patients.

Since both types II and IV are relatively common, are frequently genetically determined, and are associated with a high risk of ischemic heart disease, family members, especially children, should be screened for abnormal lipid levels so that treatment can be initiated before irreversible vascular changes have occurred. This appears to be a prudent approach until more definitive studies on therapy become available.

Therapeutic Guidelines: Rational treatment for hyperlipidemia depends upon diagnosis of the definitive type of hyperlipoproteinemia (see discussion under Types of Hyperlipoproteinemia). Proper evaluation also includes complete personal, dietary, and family history; thorough physical examination; and laboratory tests that include evaluation of carbohydrate tolerance, as well as hepatic and renal function. It is essential that an individual be evaluated in a steady state. Emotion, stress, and rapid weight gain or loss all affect lipid concentrations. After an acute myocardial infarction, the concentration of serum triglycerides usually increases and the serum cholesterol level often decreases markedly. Therefore, determination of lipoprotein patterns in these patients is not valid for at least five weeks after the event.

The patient undergoing evaluation should be consuming a conventional American diet and maintaining a steady weight during the week before blood lipids are determined. Cholesterol and triglyceride analyses should be performed on blood samples acquired in the post-absorptive state (after 12 to 14 hours of fasting); patients should be resting and venostasis should be avoided. At least three lipid determinations, obtained at two-week intervals, are essential to confirm the diagnosis and establish a pretreatment baseline. If initial lipid values are elevated, analyses may be repeated and more definitive techniques may be used to establish the type of hyperlipoproteinemia. Plasma for lipoprotein evaluation should be kept cold, but not frozen, until analyzed.

In hyperlipidemic patients, appearance of the plasma after overnight refrigeration is helpful in diagnosis. A definite cream layer indicates the presence of chylomicrons and suggests types I or V (a clear infranatant suggests type I and a cloudy infranatant strongly suggests type V). Diffuse turbidity indicates increased triglycerides (VLDL) and is suggestive of types III or IV or possibly type IIb. The standing plasma in type IIa will be clear; in type IIb it may be slightly turbid. Type III cannot be definitively differentiated from types IIb and IV unless a preparative or analytical centrifugation is done to show the presence of a beta lipoprotein with abnormally low density; this causes it to float at density 1.006. These observations, combined with cholesterol and triglyceride analyses, will suggest the type of abnormality present. After the type of abnormality has been established, cholesterol and triglyceride determinations are adequate for monitoring the effects of diet and drug therapy in most patients with hyperlipidemia.

The diet is the initial consideration in the management of patients with primary hyperlipoproteinemia. Strong patient motivation is a prerequisite if the necessarily long-term therapy is to succeed. Dietary measures, including weight reduction when necessary, are safe and frequently all that is needed.

When prescribing a diet, it is usually necessary to be specific about foods that are contraindicated. It also must be recognized that a single dietary approach is not possible. A handbook for physicians and separate manuals for each of the types of hyperlipoproteinemia which fully describe the recommended diets may be obtained from the Office of Heart Information, National Heart and Lung Institute, Bethesda, Maryland 20014. A summary of dietary restrictions follows:

Type	Diet
I	Low fat (less than 25 g/day) Supplement with medium chain triglycerides High carbohydrate
II	Low cholesterol (less than 300 mg/day) Low saturated fat, supplemented with unsaturated fat (weight reduction has little effect except in type IIb)
III	Weight reduction to ideal body weight Low cholesterol (less than 300 mg/day) Balanced diet (40% fat, 40% carbohydrate) Low alcohol intake
IV	Weight reduction to ideal body weight Low carbohydrate (100-150 g/day) if cholesterol remains elevated Low alcohol intake
V	Weight reduction to ideal body weight High protein Modest fat and carbohydrate reduction Low alcohol intake

Chemotherapy is indicated only if dietary control, including weight reduction when necessary, is unsuccessful. Dietary regulation must continue because the effects of diet and drug therapy are additive. It is essential to determine changes in the lipid pattern as therapy proceeds and to watch for evidence of adverse reactions. The plasma lipids must be evaluated every two weeks initially and then at monthly intervals. In most instances, drug therapy should be modified or changed if no significant reduction of lipoprotein levels occurs after a four- to eight-week trial. Treatment with any of the drugs must be continuous and life-long, for plasma lipid levels usually return to pretreatment concentrations if therapy is discontinued. In addition, treatment must be closely monitored indefinitely. The dose will need adjustment from time to time, as dictated by changes in diet, body weight, concomitant medications, tolerance, and complications.

At present there are two major accepted indications for the use of drugs: prevention of the recrudescence of complications of hypertriglyceridemia (abdominal pain, hepatomegaly, eruptive xanthomas), and reduction of concentrations of certain plasma lipoproteins based on the reasonable presumption that this will decelerate development of atherosclerosis. The second indication is the most common reason for prescribing drugs. It is currently recommended that patients at high risk with primary familial hyperlipidemia be treated on an empirical basis. For the asymptomatic patient with "borderline" concentrations of lipids, dietary regulation after appropriate screening may be sufficient. If diet alone does not lower the lipid levels to normal, the use of a hypolipidemic agent in these patients must be weighed against the risk of long-term toxicity of the drug.

Several drugs have effectively lowered abnormally high concentrations of cholesterol and triglyceride as well as plasma lipoproteins. The plasma concentration of lipids reflects only a fraction of the amount present in the entire body. Results of careful sterol balance studies have shown that the total body pool may be decreased by drug therapy while the plasma concentration remains unchanged. Lipids also may be shifted from one lipoprotein class to another, which may lead to incorrect interpretation of the significance of the lipid value. Although a drug's primary effect may be on one of the lipids (cholesterol, triglyceride, free fatty acid), it is the secondary effect on lipoprotein metabolism that may be most significant. Drugs may directly affect the lipoprotein metabolism by regulating the availability of precursors or altering lipoprotein synthesis and catabolism; the resultant changes in lipoprotein concentrations are reflected in plasma lipid levels. No drug is effective in all types of hyperlipoproteinemia.

At present, the agents primarily advocated for treatment of hyperlipidemias are clofibrate [Atromid-S], cholestyramine [Cuemid, Questran], niacin (nicotinic acid), and neomycin [Mycifradin, Neobiotic]. Estrogens, dextrothyroxine [Choloxin], norethindrone [Norlutate], and sitosterols [Cytellin] are used occasionally. It should be emphasized that current therapy in atherosclerotic disease is essentially experimental in that the effects of long-term use of any of these drugs is essentially unknown.

The use of these agents is discussed under the type of hyperlipoproteinemia in which the drugs are effective. The indications, adverse reactions, and precautions for the individual drugs are unique; therefore, these are discussed in the individual evaluations.

When severe hyperlipidemia causes abdominal pain (this occurs fairly often in types I and V), complete fasting for 24 to 48 hours usually produces dramatic reduction of triglycerides and resolution of pain, and is the only recommended therapy. No drugs are suitable in this acute situation. When the pain is relieved, the diet appropriate to the patient's lipid pattern should be started.

Most therapeutic failures are due to inability of the patient to follow the diet and/or take drugs regularly. However, even with ideal therapy, levels of plasma lipids remain elevated in some patients. Some workers are investigating the concomitant use of two hypolipidemic drugs in these resistant individuals, but such combination therapy has not as yet been adequately evaluated. Also, undesirable drug interactions from such therapy may create undetermined hazards.

Although an increase in alpha lipoprotein rarely is responsible for frank hypercholesterolemia, occasionally women receiving estrogens may have borderline elevated cholesterol level as a result of hyperalphalipoproteinemia. Some drugs also may cause hyperlipidemia. Steroid hormones such as the estrogens in oral contraceptives may induce a hypertriglyceridemia and precipitate an acute bout of abdominal pain. They should be used with caution in patients with type III, IV, or V abnormalities.

A 35% increase in serum cholesterol levels normally occurs during the last trimester of pregnancy. The extent of the increase is much greater in hyperbetalipoproteinemic than in normobetalipoproteinemic females. This increase is independent of the type of diet and cannot be prevented. Furthermore, use of these drugs during pregnancy is not advocated because their safety during this period has not been determined.

Types of Hyperlipoproteinemia

The characteristics of the various types of

TABLE 2.—CHARACTERISTICS OF TYPES OF HYPERLIPOPROTEINEMIA

	Type I	Type II		Type III	Type IV	Type V
	Exogenous hyperlipemia	*a. Hypercholesterolemia*	*b. Combined hyperlipidemia Mixed hyperlipidemia*	*Broad beta pattern Dysbetalipoproteinemia*	*Endogenous hyperlipemia*	*Mixed hyperlipemia*
Incidence	Rare	Common		Relatively uncommon	Common	Relatively uncommon
Lipoprotein Class Elevated	Chylomicrons	LDL (beta lipoproteins)	LDL (beta lipoproteins) VLDL (prebeta lipoproteins)	Floating beta lipoproteins	VLDL (prebeta lipoproteins)	Chylomicrons VLDL (prebeta lipoproteins)
Other Laboratory Abnormalities	Fat tolerance markedly abnormal PHLA low			Carbohydrate sensitivity and glucose tolerance abnormal Uric acid levels often elevated	Carbohydrate sensitivity and glucose tolerance abnormal Uric acid levels often elevated	PHLA sometimes low. Carbohydrate sensitivity and glucose tolerance abnormal. Fat tolerance abnormal. Uric acid levels usually elevated
Age of Detection	Early childhood	Infancy or early childhood (homozygotes) Young adulthood (heterozygotes)		Early adulthood	Adulthood (middle age)	Early adulthood

Clinical Manifestations	Eruptive xanthomas Hepatosplenomegaly Lipemia retinalis Abdominal pain Occasionally: pancreatitis Rarely: iris and retinal xanthomas, lipid keratopathy	Tendon xanthomas Xanthelasma Arcus corneae juvenilis Occasionally: tuberous xanthomas	Planar xanthomas Tuberoeruptive xanthomas Tendon xanthomas Xanthelasma	Rarely: pancreatitis, eruptive xanthomas, xanthelasma retinalis lipemia	Lipemia retinalis Eruptive xanthomas Hepatosplenomegaly Abdominal pain Occasionally: pancreatitis
Ischemic Heart Disease Risk	No association	Greatly accelerated	Primarily peripheral vascular disease accelerated	Accelerated	Data inadequate to determine association
Usual Secondary Causes	Dysgammaglobulinemia	Hypothyrodism Acute intermittent porphyria Multiple myeloma Macroglobulinemia Obstructive liver disease Nephrotic syndrome Excess dietary cholesterol	Hypothyroidism Dysgammaglobulinemia Diabetic acidosis	Hypothyroidism Nephrotic syndrome Diabetes mellitus Pancreatitis Von Gierke's disease (type I glycogenosis) Niemann-Pick disease Gaucher's disease Werner's syndrome Pheochromocytoma	Hypothyroidism Nephrotic syndrome Alcoholism Diabetic acidosis Pancreatitis Von Gierke's disease (type I glycogenosis)

hyperlipoproteinemia are summarized in Table 2 and below:

Type I: Type I is an exogenous, fat-induced hyperlipoproteinemia characterized by massive hyperchylomicronemia due to a severe deficiency in post heparin lipolytic activity (PHLA). Since chylomicrons contain about 85% triglycerides and less than 10% cholesterol, serum triglyceride levels are elevated (to several thousand milligrams per deciliter) far out of proportion to cholesterol; the cholesterol:triglyceride ratio is usually less than 0.2. Patients with this disorder are usually symptomatic before age 10. Adults may experience episodes of pain that may mimic acute abdominal crises and that often are accompanied by fever, leukocytosis, anorexia, and vomiting. Diabetes mellitus may develop after repeated bouts of pancreatitis.

Severely depressed levels of PHLA also have been associated with the hyperchylomicronemia that occasionally accompanies severe hypoinsulinemic diabetes, but PHLA returns to normal when sufficient insulin is provided. Acquired type I hyperlipoproteinemia is seen in some patients with dysgammaglobulinemia associated with multiple myeloma and systemic lupus erythematosus, in which abnormal globulins in the plasma apparently bind heparin and interfere with normal PHLA. This hyperchylomicronemia can be resolved by administration of heparin. PHLA inhibition has been postulated as the cause of the hyperchylomicronemia occasionally observed in alcoholism.

The severity of the disorder may not be proportional to the magnitude of the PHLA depression, because PHLA is only the crude measure of a heterogeneous group of lipolytic enzymes. For example, PHLA is frequently decreased in hypothyroidism, but only rarely is this associated with fasting hyperchylomicronemia. Similarly, administration of estrogens to normal individuals may lower PHLA, although only a small rise in triglyceride and no frank hyperchylomicronemia occur.

Patients with type I hyperlipoproteinemia have abnormal fat tolerance. For those on a normal diet, the plasma in the fasting state appears creamy, and upon standing in the cold, a discrete creamy layer forms over a clear infranatant (diagnostic of type I).

In the familial disorder and those secondary states that do not respond to direct treatment of the underlying disease, a restriction of dietary fat to about 25 g/day will result in marked lowering of triglycerides and resolution of xanthomas and abdominal complaints, although moderate lipemia may remain. This restriction should provide at least 1% of total calories as linoleic acid to meet essential fatty acid requirements and should provide adequate fat-soluble vitamins. The addition of medium-chain triglycerides, which are transported directly to the liver without requiring chylomicron formation, to the diet increases palatability and variation. (See the evaluation on Portagen in Chapter 15, Miscellaneous Nutritional Agents.) To supply adequate calories, carbohydrate should be substituted for fat.

None of the currently available hypolipidemic drugs are effective in type I disorder.

Type II: Type II hyperlipoproteinemia is characterized by an abnormal increase in the plasma concentration of low density (beta) lipoproteins which are normal in composition and electrophoretic and ultracentrifugal properties. This distinction is critical to the separation of type II from type III. Since the LDL contain almost 50% cholesterol, patients have a moderate to marked elevation of serum cholesterol. In both subtypes IIa and IIb, there is increased LDL, however, in IIb an increase in VLDL also occurs, which is manifested by an increase in the concentration of serum triglycerides. The preservation of both patterns under the rubric of type II is important in genetic concepts since either pattern may appear in different hyperlipidemic members of the same family.

The pathophysiology of this syndrome is not established, but studies suggest that the rate of removal of LDL from plasma is reduced. In some persons, an increased cholesterol intake is sufficient to cause an elevated LDL concentration in the plasma.

The standing plasma of the patient with type II is clear, although it may appear slightly turbid in patients with type IIb if the triglycerides are above 400 mg/dl. Definite diagnosis of type II depends upon demonstration of an abnormal increase in LDL, which is most precisely obtained by ultracentrifugation. Type IIa may be suspected from results of cholesterol and triglyceride analyses alone when the cholesterol:triglyceride ratio is greater than 2. The type IIb pattern is difficult to ascertain from analysis of plasma lipids alone.

Familial type II hyperlipoproteinemia is

manifested in early childhood and possibly may be diagnosed at birth. Preliminary results from analysis of cord blood suggests that its incidence is 1 in 200. The main clinical consequences of this disorder are caused by the accumulation of lipids in the arteries, but usually do not appear before age 20 in the heterozygote (see Table). Recurrent severe tendon pain (Achilles tendinitis, tenosynovitis) sometimes accompanied by a migratory polyarthritis has been reported rarely. Polyarthritis may be incorrectly diagnosed as rheumatic fever. Type II hyperlipoproteinemia often is associated with accelerated atherosclerosis and a family history of early death from ischemic heart disease. In the homozygote, ischemic heart disease is almost inevitable before age 20, and for the heterozygote the probability is about 50% by age 50.

If primary type II hyperbetalipoproteinemia is suspected, other family members probably will be affected and should be screened. For definite diagnosis of the familial disorder, the typical lipoprotein pattern must be demonstrated in the patient and in at least one first-degree relative. Xanthomas and ischemic heart disease in childhood strongly suggest the homozygous state.

Many heterozygotes below age 20 can maintain normal lipid levels with strict dietary control. In the adult patient, diet and drug therapy can frequently normalize the plasma lipoproteins. Therefore, because of the striking increase in morbidity and mortality from premature ischemic heart disease in this disorder, the patient and all affected family members should adhere to dietary regulation. The recommended diet for patients with both primary and ''dietary'' type II hyperlipoproteinemia should contain less than 300 mg of cholesterol daily; this can be achieved by removing eggs, high-fat dairy products, shellfish, and fatty meats from the diet. Polyunsaturated fats should be substituted for saturated fats when possible to give a P:S ratio of 2.0 or more, instead of the usual 0.2 or 0.3. Strict adherence to this diet can usually achieve a 20% to 25% reduction of LDL.

When the effect of the diet on the hyperlipidemia is fully established (after one to two months), concomitant drug therapy should be considered. For type IIa, cholestyramine is the agent of choice and will significantly lower serum cholesterol levels. Xanthomas may soften and decrease in size. If a patient cannot tolerate or does not respond to cholestyramine, a cautious trial with other drugs may be undertaken. Dextrothyroxine will effectively lower serum cholesterol in some patients. Its dangers may be minimized by using a small initial dose and increasing it at monthly intervals up to 8 mg daily (see the evaluation on Dextrothyroxine Sodium). Some clinicians advocate the use of small oral doses (2 g daily) of neomycin in young, high-risk patients. At this dosage, neomycin is reported to lower LDL without producing serious adverse effects (eg, nephrotoxicity, ototoxicity). However, until more experience in its long-term use has accumulated, neomycin should not be considered an established mode of therapy.

Type IIb (hyperbetalipoproteinemia with associated hypertriglyceridemia) also may respond to cholestyramine or dextrothyroxine; however, neither drug has an appreciable effect on serum triglycerides. The atherogenic potential of triglycerides is not established, and treatment may not be required unless levels are markedly elevated; in this case, a trial with niacin may be attempted. The adverse effects of niacin possibly outweigh its usefulness in type II, but it does effectively lower both cholesterol and triglyceride levels.

Clofibrate, which has been widely used in the treatment of type II hyperlipoproteinemia, has only a slight effect on serum cholesterol, and has been reported to increase LDL in some patients. It is more likely to be effective in type IIb hyperlipoproteinemia.

No single drug is always completely satisfactory in the treatment of familial type II hyperlipoproteinemia. Therapy usually must be individualized, and combination therapy, though unproven, may possibly control the hyperlipidemia.

Type III: In type III hyperlipoproteinemia, the lipoprotein fraction having beta electrophoretic mobility is abnormally laden with triglycerides and is of lower density. On ultracentrifugation, beta lipoproteins normally will gravitate to the bottom as the LDL fraction; because of its high triglyceride content, in type III patients this lipoprotein fraction will "float" and be found along with the prebeta lipoproteins in the VLDL fraction. Recent work has indicated that VLDL is metabolized through several intermediate stages to form LDL. In type III disease, this conversion is impaired and, as a result, intermediate forms (broad or floating beta lipoproteins) accumulate.

Definitive diagnosis, once requiring ultracentrifugation, now can be achieved by simultaneous electrophoresis on paper, agarose, or cellulose acetate, and on polyacrylamide gel (PGE). The presence of a broadened prebeta band but no beta-migratory lipoproteins (LDL) on PGE, and the concomitant presence of a beta lipoprotein band on other media is considered diagnostic of type III in 95% of patients. When necessary, confirmation of floating beta lipoprotein should be made after ultracentrifugation.

Patients with type III hyperlipoproteinemia usually have similar elevation of both serum cholesterol (400 to 700 mg/dl) and triglyceride (400 to 800 mg/dl) concentrations (cholesterol:triglyceride ratio is usually 1). Depending upon the amount of abnormal lipoprotein present, the plasma may appear clear, cloudy, or milky. Standing plasma is usually turbid, frequently with a faint chylomicron or "cream" layer.

The characteristic planar xanthomas (orange-yellow lipid deposits in the palms of the hands) are presumptively diagnostic although they may also be seen in biliary cirrhosis and, rarely, in type II homozygotes. Corneal arcus senilis may appear at an early age. Premature atherosclerosis affecting the coronary and often the peripheral arteries (manifested by claudication and absent or diminished peripheral pulse) is common and frequently severe. Manifestations occur in men usually in the fourth and fifth decades and in women 10 to 15 years later. Glucose intolerance and hyperuricemia occur in about 40% of patients.

The differential diagnosis of this type of hyperlipoproteinemia is important since the disorder is highly responsive to diet and drug therapy. Obese patients should reduce to ideal body weight by caloric restriction, and then be maintained on a diet low in cholesterol and saturated fat and balanced in fat and carbohydrate. If serum lipid levels are not reduced to normal by diet alone, concomitant administration of clofibrate, the drug of choice in type III, usually reduces serum lipids to within normal range and may resolve cutaneous xanthomas. However, some floating beta lipoproteins may persist in the plasma. There is an apparent improvement in peripheral blood flow, indicating an amelioration of the atherosclerotic process.

Niacin has been reported to be effective and may be used in patients who cannot tolerate clofibrate, but it is not considered a drug of choice because of the frequency and severity of untoward reactions.

Type IV: Type IV hyperlipoproteinemia is characterized by an increase in the concentration of very low density (prebeta) lipoproteins, with resulting hypertriglyceridemia. Type IV is the most common abnormal lipoprotein pattern and reflects an imbalance in the metabolism of endogenous triglycerides. This pattern, undoubtedly genetically heterogeneous, may be due to overproduction of endogenous triglycerides, defects in clearance, or a combination of both. Relatives of patients with types III and V hyperlipoproteinemia often have a type IV pattern. The prevalence of the familial disorder is not known, but the pattern may be secondary to a number of diseases and acute metabolic changes in which the increased mobilization of free fatty acids stimulates the hepatic synthesis of triglycerides. Type IV pattern also may be produced by excessive intake of alcohol, anxiety, and emotional stress. Both the primary and secondary disorders usually are exacerbated by obesity.

This type of hyperlipoproteinemia frequently is associated with premature atherosclerosis. Unlike type II, familial type IV disorder rarely is manifested before 20 years of age, usually exhibits no external symptoms, and often is discovered in the fourth decade or later after the onset of ischemic heart disease. Individuals with a type IV pattern usually do not tolerate carbohydrates; in many, there is an increase in the triglyceride level after ingestion of carbohydrates, and more than 40% have hyperuricemia.

Patients with type IV hyperlipoproteinemia often have normal cholesterol concentrations and the abnormality will not be detected unless triglyceride and/or lipoprotein patterns are determined. Because the level of serum triglycerides fluctuates widely from day to day, it is necessary to demonstrate persistent hypertriglyceridemia on more than one blood specimen to establish diagnosis. Likewise, response to treatment must be ascertained by demonstration of a sustained reduction in the serum triglycerides.

Depending upon the level of triglycerides (200 to several thousand milligrams per deciliter), standing plasma of type IV patients may be clear, turbid, or milky, but without a "cream" layer. In the electrophoretic pattern, there may be trailing of lipoproteins from the prebeta region to the origin, in which case ultracentrifugation is necessary to differentiate type IV from type III abnormality (floating beta lipoprotein).

Patients with this type of hyperlipoproteinemia frequently are overweight. Dietary carbohydrates should be replaced with unsaturated fats if the plasma cholesterol level is elevated. Maintenance of ideal body weight and adherence to this diet will cause complete remission of the hyperlipidemia in a significant number of patients. Alcohol may aggravate hypertriglyceridemia and should be restricted.

If dietary measures are ineffective, drug therapy may be used adjunctively. The drugs that reduce endogenous triglyceride concentrations, clofibrate and niacin, are effective but should be used cautiously. Blood levels should be monitored frequently and therapy reevaluated if LDL rises.

Although clofibrate will significantly reduce triglycerides in most of these patients, some investigators have reported a reciprocal rise in cholesterol and a resultant hyperbetalipoproteinemia in those with severe hypertriglyceridemia.

Niacin (3 to 6 g daily) will reduce triglyceride levels, but activation of peptic ulcer, abnormalities of liver function, exacerbation of diabetes, and hyperuricemia may occur. Since many patients with type IV hyperlipidemia already have hyperuricemia and abnormal glucose tolerance, the untoward effects may outweigh the usefulness of niacin.

Type V: In type V hyperlipoproteinemia there is a defect in the metabolism of both endogenous and exogenous triglycerides. It is characterized by the accumulation of very low density (prebeta) lipoproteins and chylomicrons. Serum cholesterol levels often are normal but may be elevated. The plasma usually is creamy in appearance with a "cream" layer over a turbid infranatant after standing. The serum cholesterol:triglyceride ratio usually is between 0.15 and 0.6.

This disorder is relatively uncommon and may be genetically heterogeneous; relatives of patients with type V often have type IV hyperlipoproteinemia. Patients with the familial type V pattern usually become symptomatic after age 20 rather than in childhood, but otherwise have all the manifestations seen in type I patients. In contrast to those with type I abnormality, patients with type V hyperlipoproteinemia usually have glucose intolerance (this becomes more marked with increasing age) and have hyperuricemia, but they may have normal PHLA. Data on acceleration of atherosclerosis in those with type V abnormality are inadequate.

Since most patients with type V hyperlipoproteinemia are overweight, the first step in management is weight reduction. These patients are sensitive to both fat and carbohydrates; therefore, the diet should have as high a protein content as possible with a balanced proportion of fats (less than 70 g daily) and carbohydrates. Marked reduction in the consumption of alcoholic beverages is necessary to control weight and prevent bouts of abdominal pain. These measures usually control symptoms and lower serum lipids, although not necessarily to the normal range. When the full effects of adherence to the prescribed diet therapy have become established, the concomitant use of drugs may further decrease lipids in some patients. Unless ideal body weight and caloric balance are maintained, however, drug therapy is less than optimal. Clofibrate frequently reduces lipid levels; niacin may be useful if clofibrate is ineffective.

Some investigators recommend use of progestagens in women in whom clofibrate is ineffective; norethindrone acetate in a dose of 5 mg daily has been tried in these patients.

INDIVIDUAL EVALUATIONS

CHOLESTYRAMINE RESIN [Cuemid, Questran]

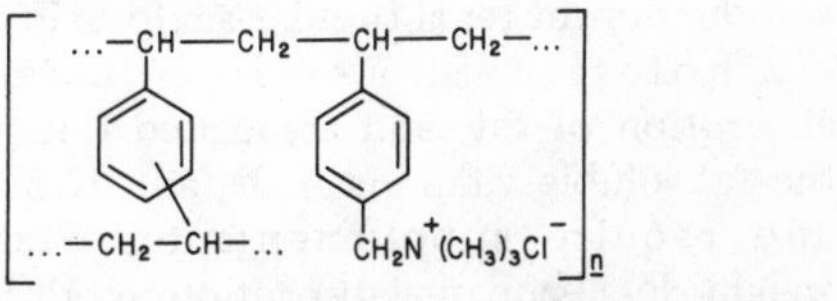

...—CH—CH₂—CH—CH₂—...

...—CH₂—CH—... $CH_2N^+(CH_3)_3Cl^-$ n

Cholestyramine is the insoluble chloride salt of a basic anion exchange resin that binds bile acids in the intestine and prevents their reabsorption. The reduced levels of bile acids increase the rate of conversion of cholesterol to bile acids in the liver which, in turn, increases the de novo synthesis of cholesterol. Recent studies with labeled beta lipoprotein protein demonstrate that the degradation of this moiety is increased whereas synthesis of LDL is not affected. This drug was initially marketed for treatment of pruritus associated with primary biliary cirrhosis and cholestatic jaundice not caused by complete obstruction.

Cholestyramine is the drug of choice for type IIa hyperbetalipoproteinemia. When used as an adjunct to dietary control, a daily dose of 16 to 32 g will reduce beta lipoproteins 25% to 35% with a peak effect in seven to nine days. In type

IIb, cholestyramine will lower the LDL but has no significant effect on VLDL (triglyceride) elevations.

Cholestyramine may decrease prebeta lipoproteins (VLDL) when excessively large doses are used, but this reduction is probably secondary to malabsorption and steatorrhea. In the usual dosage range, cholestyramine is ineffective in hyperprebetalipoproteinemia and is of no benefit in types III, IV, or V hyperlipoproteinemia; it may in fact exacerbate these conditions by producing hypertriglyceridemia.

Cholestyramine probably is one of the safest drugs currently available for treatment of hyperlipoproteinemia; because it is not absorbed from the gastrointestinal tract, there are no systemic toxic effects. Nevertheless, the large doses are unpleasant to take. Since the Cuemid brand has a disagreeable fishy odor, the odorless Questran brand is preferred.

The most frequent untoward effects are mild nausea and constipation, which usually subside with continued therapy. One case of intestinal impaction of cholestyramine has been reported. Other adverse reactions include epigastric distress and, occasionally, diarrhea. Rarely, vomiting, rash, and irritation of the tongue and perianal region have been reported. Because cholestyramine is the chloride form of the resin another potential adverse effect of long-term use is induction of renal tubular acidosis in children.

Cholestyramine may interfere with absorption of fat, and associated deficiency of the fat-soluble vitamins A, D, and K may occur and require supplementation. Steatorrhea, weight loss, and malabsorption syndrome may be noted at doses greater than 30 g daily. For this reason, some investigators consider 24 g daily the maximal dose.

Cholestyramine also may adsorb other drugs given concomitantly; thus, these drugs (particularly chlorothiazide, thyroid, digitalis, iron, phenylbutazone, or warfarin) should be given at least one hour before or four hours after cholestyramine. Mild lengthening of prothrombin time (without bleeding episodes) has been reported. The dosage of anticoagulants given concomitantly should be closely monitored.

USUAL DOSAGE.—*Oral:* Initially, *adults*, 4 g (one packet or one rounded teaspoonful) three times daily before meals. Depending on response, the dose may be increased to 8 g before meals and at bedtime. The drug should never be swallowed dry because of the hazard of esophageal irritation or blockage. It should be mixed with four to six ounces of suitable liquid or pulpy fruit just before taking. Although dosage in *children over 6 years of age* has not been definitively established, 4 g three times daily before meals, with an increase to a maximal total daily dose of 24 g is being given. *Children under 6 years*, dosage has not been established.

PREPARATIONS.—

Cuemid (Merck Sharp & Dohme). *Oral:* Powder in 216 g containers.

Questran (Mead Johnson). *Oral:* Powder in 4 g packets.

CLOFIBRATE [Atromid-S]

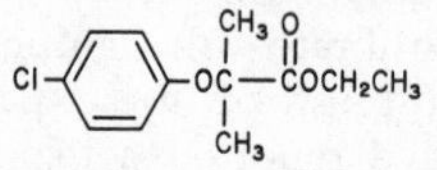

The mechanism of action of clofibrate is unclear, but this agent probably inhibits the hepatic release of lipoproteins, particularly prebeta lipoproteins (VLDL); interferes with the binding of serum free fatty acids to albumin; increases the excretion of fecal neutral sterols; inhibits cholesterol biosynthesis; and affects the metabolism of apoprotein. A few studies indicate that clofibrate may accelerate removal of VLDL. Its major effect in hyperlipoproteinemia is the reduction of VLDL; in most patients the cholesterol-lowering effect is minimal.

Clofibrate, which should be used with appropriate dietary regulation, is uniformly effective and is the drug of choice for type III hyperlipoproteinemia. No untoward lipoprotein shift occurs in these patients. There is reduction of the floating beta lipoproteins, and dramatic improvement in patients with peripheral vascular disease associated with type III hyperlipoproteinemia has been reported.

This drug also may be effective in reducing VLDL levels in patients with types IV and V abnormalities. However, recent reports that clofibrate may increase LDL levels in some type IV patients (iatrogenic conversion of type IV pattern to the more atherogenic type II pattern) require that these patients be carefully observed until further data become available. A similar reciprocal rise in LDL as the VLDL falls also may be noted in type V patients. In both type IV and V hyperlipoproteinemia, the effect of clofibrate should be monitored with serial electrophoretic analyses for changes in intensity of the beta band. If the intensity of this band increases significantly, an undesirable lipoprotein shift has occurred and the drug should be discontinued.

Homozygous type II patients, as well as heterozygous type IIa patients, usually do not respond significantly to clofibrate. However, this drug appears to be effective in reducing VLDL levels in type IIb heterozygotes when VLDL also is increased.

Regression of xanthomas and clearing of diabetic retinopathy has occurred with the reduction of plasma lipid levels in some patients. This agent also has been reported to reduce serum fibrinogen levels and may diminish platelet adhesiveness.

Gastrointestinal effects (nausea, vomiting, diarrhea, dyspepsia, and flatulence) occur in about 10% of patients taking clofibrate, but these are usually transient and disappear with continued therapy. Less frequently, leukopenia, rash, drowsiness, and alopecia areata have been noted. Patients occasionally gain weight.

Clofibrate causes hepatomegaly in animals, but similar changes have not been observed in man. However, elevations in serum transaminase levels, which are reversible when therapy is discontinued, have been noted.

Potentially serious effects on skeletal and cardiac muscle have been reported. Elevation of the level of the muscle enzyme, creatine phosphokinase, occurs, and sometimes is accompanied by frank myositis with asthenia, myalgia, and malaise. Elevated creatine phosphokinase activity may persist when other serum enzymes are normal and the patient is asymptomatic. In a patient with chest pain, increase in transaminase and creatine phosphokinase levels due to clofibrate rather than to myocardial infarction must be considered. A single case of increased ventricular irritability manifested by bigeminy has been reported. In one patient, clofibrate also apparently potentiated the first-degree atrioventricular block induced by propranolol.

This agent is contraindicated in patients with impaired renal or hepatic function, since delayed detoxification and excretion make the duration of action unpredictable. Clofibrate also is contraindicated during pregnancy and should not be given to nursing mothers, for it may be excreted in the milk.

Close supervision of patients on long-term therapy is required. Clofibrate displaces acidic drugs such as coumarin anticoagulants and tolbutamide from binding sites on plasma proteins. The dosage of anticoagulants must be reduced by at least one-third and prothrombin times should be determined frequently, especially during initiation of therapy. SGOT, SGPT, and creatine phosphokinase values should be determined occasionally. A rebound in cholesterol and triglyceride concentrations occasionally is observed after discontinuation of therapy.

Clofibrate should not be used in *children*, since data are insufficient to determine the drug's safety in this age group.

USUAL DOSAGE.—*Oral: Adults*, 500 mg four times daily.

PREPARATIONS.—Atromid-S (Ayerst). *Oral:* Capsules 500 mg.

CONJUGATED ESTROGENS [Premarin]
ETHINYL ESTRADIOL [Estinyl, Feminone, Lynoral, Novestrol]

Estrogens have been used for treatment of hyperlipidemia because of the fact that women have lower serum beta lipoprotein and higher alpha lipoprotein concentrations, as well as decreased susceptibility to atherosclerosis and ischemic heart disease until after the menopause. However, estrogens are unsuitable as antilipidemic agents in men because of their feminizing effects. In women, administration of estrogens may elevate the levels of VLDL and decrease the levels of PHLA. In addition, estrogens are reported to cause abdominal pain and pancreatitis in women with type V hyperlipoproteinemia.

USUAL DOSAGE.—Estrogens are not advisable for treatment of hyperlipoproteinemia because of the reasons cited above.

PREPARATIONS.—See Chapter 37, Estrogens, Progestagens, Oral Contraceptives, and Ovulatory Agents.

DEXTROTHYROXINE SODIUM [Choloxin]

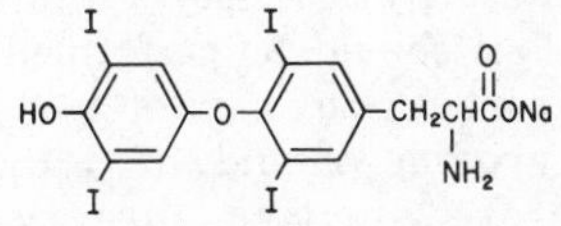

Of all the thyroid analogues, dextrothyroxine has the highest ratio of hypolipidemic to calorigenic activity. The drug effectively reduces beta lipoproteins (LDL) in both euthyroid and hypothyroid patients. Although dextrothyroxine increases the metabolism of cholesterol, the increased rate of synthesis is more than counterbalanced by the increased catabolism; the net effect is a decrease in serum cholesterol concentrations. The magnitude of the decrease may range from 20% to 50% and is greatest in patients with highest baseline concentrations. Maximal effects appear in one to two months. Dextrothyroxine has no consistent effect on elevated prebeta lipoprotein (VLDL) concentrations.

Dextrothyroxine is effective in the treatment of hypothyroidism, but large doses are required. Therefore, its use in hypothyroidism should be reserved for patients in whom hyperbetalipoproteinemia persists despite correction of the hypothyroidism by levothyroxine.

This agent is used in type II hyperbetalipoproteinemia. Since it has no consistent effect on VLDL in the usual dosage range, it is seldom useful in patients with types III, IV, or V patterns.

The untoward effects of dextrothyroxine are usually due to metabolic stimulation and generally mimic symptoms of hyperthyroidism. Loss of weight appears to be the first sign of onset of hypermetabolism. Other reported effects related to the metabolic action of dextrothyroxine include nervousness, insomnia, tremors, hyperhidrosis, and menstrual irregularity. Some patients report altered taste sensations, vertigo, and diarrhea during the first six weeks of therapy, but these reactions subside spontaneously.

Rashes and pruritus may develop in patients who are hypersensitive to iodine. Since this drug raises protein-bound iodine levels, the PBI test cannot be used to measure thyroid function.

In some diabetic patients, long-term administration of dextrothyroxine decreases glucose tolerance and this may necessitate an increase in the dose of hypoglycemic agents. Since dextrothyroxine augments the effect of orally administered anticoagulants, reduction of the dose of the anticoagulant by approximately one-third is usually necessary. Prothrombin time determinations should be performed frequently in patients receiving both drugs. Dextrothyroxine should be withdrawn two weeks before elective surgery if use of anticoagulants is contemplated.

Dextrothyroxine should be used judiciously, if at all, in pregnant patients and nursing mothers, because its effects on the thyroid gland of the fetus or infant are unknown. The drug also must be given cautiously to patients with hypertension or hepatic or renal disease. Dextrothyroxine should not be given to patients with arrhythmias, especially premature ventricular contractions.

USUAL DOSAGE.—*Oral: Adults,* initially, 1 mg daily for one month; the amount may be increased by increments of 1 mg daily at intervals no shorter than one month until a satisfactory lowering of LDL has been achieved or until a maximal daily dose of 8 mg is reached. *Children,* initially, 0.05 mg/kg of body weight daily; this dose may be doubled after one month. The dose is increased by increments of 0.05 mg/kg at monthly intervals until satisfactory reduction of LDL has been observed or until the maximal recommended dose of 4 mg daily has been attained.

PREPARATIONS.—Choloxin (Flint). *Oral:* Tablets 2 and 4 mg.

HEPARIN SODIUM

The use of heparin for hyperlipidemia is of historical interest only. This drug activates lipoprotein lipase and thus catalyzes the lipolysis which enhances removal of chylomicrons from plasma. It is not useful in the treatment of hyperlipoproteinemias because it may induce hemorrhage, and because the required frequent parenteral administration is inconvenient for long-term use.

For other uses of heparin, see Chapter 9, Anticoagulants.

USUAL DOSAGE.—This agent should not be used for hyperlipidemia because of the reasons stated above.

PREPARATIONS.—See Chapter 9, Anticoagulants.

NEOMYCIN SULFATE [Mycifradin Sulfate, Neobiotic]

Neomycin is only slightly absorbed from the gastrointestinal tract. It reduces the absorption of cholesterol from the gastrointestinal tract by precipitating it out of micellar solution. Small doses given for several years have been reported to lower beta lipoprotein (LDL) levels an average of 22% without producing serious adverse effects. Neomycin has variable effects on prebeta lipoproteins (VLDL).

Malabsorption syndrome, development of acute pseudomembranous enterocolitis, nephropathy, and permanent damage to the eighth nerve have occurred after the drug was given parenterally or in large oral doses. It is claimed that these reactions have not occurred at the doses used for treatment of hyperlipidemia. Diarrhea and abdominal cramps, which usually subside spontaneously during continued treatment, have been reported with hypolipidemic doses. Until additional information on safety and efficacy are available, use of this agent should be reserved for patients with refractory type IIa hyperlipoproteinemia with high risk of ischemic heart disease.

Neomycin may potentiate coumarin anticoagulants, and concomitant use of the two types of drugs requires frequent monitoring of prothrombin time.

Neomycin is contraindicated in patients with renal insufficiency, for neomycin may accumulate to toxic levels in these individuals and cause nephrotoxicity and ototoxicity.

For other uses and adverse reactions, see Chapter 57, Aminoglycoside Antibacterial Agents and Miscellaneous Antimicrobial Drugs, and Chapter 72, Miscellaneous Ophthalmic Preparations.

USUAL DOSAGE.—*Oral: Adults,* 0.5 to a maximum of 2 g daily.

PREPARATIONS.—

Mycifradin Sulfate (Upjohn). *Oral:* Solution 125 mg/5 ml; tablets 500 mg.

Neobiotic (Pfizer). *Oral:* Tablets 500 mg.

ALUMINUM NICOTINATE [Nicalex]
NIACIN (Nicotinic Acid)

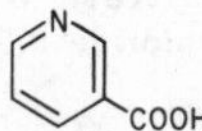

In contrast to other lipid-lowering agents, preliminary studies suggest that niacin reduces the rate of synthesis of beta lipoprotein (LDL). The drug also reduces prebeta lipoproteins (VLDL) and can therefore be effective in all types of hyperlipoproteinemias except type I. It is frequently more effective than other drugs in the severe hypertriglyceridemia of type V disease. However, because niacin produces potentially serious adverse effects, its usefulness is limited; therefore, it cannot be considered an agent of choice for any of the hyperlipoproteinemias, although it may be beneficial in high-risk patients with severe hyperlipidemia who do not respond to other lipid-lowering agents.

Aluminum nicotinate is a complex of aluminum hydroxynicotinate and niacin which is hydrolyzed to aluminum hydroxide and niacin in the gastrointestinal tract. In addition to the reactions caused by the niacin component, aluminum hydroxide may decrease absorption of other drugs, and thus this compound should not be given simultaneously with other agents. Also, if phosphate intake is low, hypophosphatemia and osteomalacia may develop during prolonged administration of large doses. Therefore, niacin is preferred over aluminum nicotinate for treatment of hyperlipidemias.

Flushing occurs initially in practically all patients, and persists in 10% to 15% of them. Other common untoward effects are pruritus, paresthesias, and nausea, vomiting, and other symptoms of gastrointestinal irritation (eg, flatulence, diarrhea). The latter symptoms may subside with continued therapy. Use of small initial doses with gradual increases may reduce the severity of these symptoms in some patients.

More serious reactions are activation of peptic ulcer, impairment of glucose tolerance, hyperuricemia, and liver dysfunction, including cholestatic jaundice. These reactions are usually reversible when the drug is discontinued. It should be noted that many patients with type IV and type V abnormalities already have hyperglycemia and hyperuricemia which would be aggravated by niacin.

This agent can cause histamine release and therefore its use may be dangerous in patients with allergies or asthma. Niacin also potentiates the effects of ganglionic blocking agents and may produce orthostatic hypotension in hypertensive patients when it is used with these agents. Toxic amblyopia also has been reported.

USUAL DOSAGE.—*Oral: Adults,* 1.5 to 6 g niacin or the equivalent 1.87 to 7.5 g aluminum nicotinate divided into three or four doses, given with or after meals.

PREPARATIONS.—

Aluminum Nicotinate:

Nicalex (Merrell-National). *Oral:* Tablets 625 mg.

Niacin:

Drug marketed under generic name and under the name Nicotinic Acid.

NORETHINDRONE ACETATE [Norlutate]

Results of recent studies have shown that this progestational agent, when used in conjunction with appropriate diet, decreases prebeta lipoproteins (VLDL) and chylomicrons in some women with type V hyperlipoproteinemia; its use in men is not advocated because of its estrogenic activity. There is a concurrent increase in PHLA and amelioration of abdominal pain or pancreatitis. Norethindrone also has been tried in women with types III, IV, or V abnormalities in whom estrogens or combination oral contraceptives cause undesirable adverse effects (hypertriglyceridemia and decreased PHLA). However, recent studies have shown that progestagens may elevate serum cholesterol levels. Therefore, until more experience with its use has accumulated, norethindrone should be reserved for use in women with type V hyperlipoproteinemia who are refractory to established therapy.

For other uses and adverse reactions, see Chapter 37, Estrogens, Progestagens, Oral Contraceptives, and Ovulatory Agents.

USUAL DOSAGE.—*Oral:* 5 mg daily. Premenopausal women should receive the drug 21 days per month (to permit regular menses).

PREPARATIONS.—Norlutate (Parke, Davis). *Oral:* Tablets 5 mg.

SITOSTEROLS [Cytellin]

This mixture of plant sterols has been promoted for treatment of hyperbetalipoproteinemia. Sitosterols are poorly absorbed and compete with cholesterol for absorption sites in the intestine. They have no effect on elevated prebeta lipoprotein (VLDL) levels and their effect on beta lipoproteins (LDL) is variable. The long-term effects of sitosterols are unknown. Its use is restricted to patients with mild type IIa hyperlipoproteinemia.

Adverse reactions (eg, anorexia, diarrhea, abdominal cramps) occur rarely.

USUAL DOSAGE.—*Oral: Adults,* 12 to 24 g daily, given in divided doses immediately prior to meals or snacks.

PREPARATIONS.—Cytellin (Lilly). *Oral:* Suspension containing 3 g sitosterols/15 ml (with alcohol 4%).

MIXTURES

The following formulations are marketed for use in hyperlipidemia, but they are not advisable for such use because evidence of the effectiveness of some of these mixtures is lacking and some contain ingredients that are not useful as hypolipidemic agents.

Arcofac (Armour): Each 15 ml of liquid contains linoleic acid 6.8 g, pyridoxine hydrochloride 1 mg, and vitamin E 10 mg.

Lipo-Nicin (Brown): Each tablet contains niacin 100 or 250 mg, niacinamide 150 mg, ascorbic acid 100 mg, thiamine hydrochloride 25 mg, riboflavin 2 mg, and pyridoxine hydrochloride 3 mg.

Vastran Forte (Wampole): Each capsule contains niacin 375 mg, ascorbic acid 50 mg, riboflavin 2.5 mg, thiamine mononitrate 5 mg, cobalamin 1 μg, pyridoxine hydrochloride 0.5 mg, and pantothenate calcium 2.5 mg.

Chapter 14

VITAMINS AND SOURCES OF VITAMINS

The vitamins in purified form are available individually or in various combinations in a wide variety of pharmaceutical preparations: some are for prophylactic use as dietary supplements and others are suitable only for use as therapeutic agents. Both types often are used indiscriminately and inappropriately. Under usual circumstances, healthy persons consuming an adequate balanced diet can expect no benefit from additional vitamins. Moreover, the danger of toxic effects from excessive amounts of vitamins A or D, particularly in infants and children, must be kept in mind.

The AMA Council on Foods and Nutrition states that an adequate diet will supply all the nutrients needed by the normal individual but that both dietary adequacy and nutritional requirements are influenced by many factors. Thus, appropriately formulated vitamin supplements may be indicated to meet temporarily increased demands (eg, in pregnancy and lactation) and to assure proper growth and development during infancy and childhood. Supplementation also may be indicated to compensate for decreased intake or absorption during illnesses or when the diet is inadequate for any reason. It frequently is difficult for the physician to ascertain dietary adequacy, but whenever possible, poor dietary habits due to such factors as ignorance, poverty, food fads, poor dentition, emotional upset, or temporarily changed living pattern should be corrected, thus eliminating further need for supplementation.

Recent surveys reveal that vitamin nutriture is less satisfactory in larger segments of the population than previously believed. For example, levels of some nutrients (eg, vitamin A, ascorbic acid) may be suboptimal or inadequate in the diets of certain low-income families and ethnic groups. These people might benefit from vitamin supplementation at the same time that their diet is being improved. Many disadvantaged preschool children showed evidences of malnutrition, including abnormalities of hair and skin, cheilosis, goiter, mild growth retardation, and decreased stores of vitamin A, iron, folic acid, and thiamine.

Of the fat-soluble vitamins, vitamins A, D, and E are discussed in this chapter. The therapeutic and prophylactic uses of vitamin K in hypoprothrombinemic conditions (eg, hemorrhagic disease of the newborn, overdosage of anticoagulants) are discussed in Chapter 11, Hemostatics.

The water-soluble vitamins to be discussed are ascorbic acid (vitamin C) and the B-complex vitamins, which include niacin (nicotinic acid), pantothenic acid, pyridoxine, riboflavin, and thiamine. Folic acid and cyanocobalamin (vitamin B_{12}), which also are considered members of the B-complex group, will be discussed in this chapter only in relation to their inclusion in supplemental multivitamin preparations. (See also Chapter 8, Agents Used to Treat Deficiency Anemias.)

The Recommended Dietary Allowances (RDA) for individual vitamins established by the Food and Nutrition Board of the National Research Council provide authoritative information to assist the physician in evaluating the formulas of multivitamin preparations. (See also the section on Mixtures.) These allowances, shown in Table 1, represent amounts that will maintain good nutrition in practically all healthy persons, and are usually considerably greater than the Minimum Daily Requirements (MDR) established by the Food and Drug Administration for labeling purposes. The allowances for calories and protein also are shown in Table 1, since the requirements for many of the B vitamins are related to caloric intake. (In nutrition, the calorie used is the

TABLE 1.—RECOMMENDED DAILY DIETARY ALLOWANCES[1]

	Age[3] (years)	*Weight (kg)*	*Height (cm)*	*Kilocalorie (kcal)*	*Protein[4] (g)*	Fat-Soluble Vitamins: *Vitamin A Activity (IU)*	*Vitamin D (IU)*	*Vitamin E Activity (IU)*
Infants	0 to 1/6	4	55	kg x 120	kg x 2.2	1,500	400	5
	1/6 to 1/2	7	63	kg x 110	kg x 2.0	1,500	400	5
	1/2 to 1	9	72	kg x 100	kg x 1.8	1,500	400	5
Children	1 to 2	12	81	1,100	25	2,000	400	10
	2 to 3	14	91	1,250	25	2,000	400	10
	3 to 4	16	100	1,400	30	2,500	400	10
	4 to 6	19	110	1,600	30	2,500	400	10
	6 to 8	23	121	2,000	35	3,500	400	15
	8 to 10	28	131	2,200	40	3,500	400	15
Males	10 to 12	35	140	2,500	45	4,500	400	20
	12 to 14	43	151	2,700	50	5,000	400	20
	14 to 18	59	170	3,000	60	5,000	400	25
	18 to 22	67	175	2,800	60	5,000	400	30
	22 to 35	70	175	2,800	65	5,000	—	30
	35 to 55	70	173	2,600	65	5,000	—	30
	55 to 75+	70	171	2,400	65	5,000	—	30
Females	10 to 12	35	142	2,250	50	4,500	400	20
	12 to 14	44	154	2,300	50	5,000	400	20
	14 to 16	52	157	2,400	55	5,000	400	25
	16 to 18	54	160	2,300	55	5,000	400	25
	18 to 22	58	163	2,000	55	5,000	400	25
	22 to 35	58	163	2,000	55	5,000	—	25
	35 to 55	58	160	1,850	55	5,000	—	25
	55 to 75+	58	157	1,700	55	5,000	—	25
Pregnancy				+200	65	6,000	400	30
Lactation				+1,000	75	8,000	400	30

Adapted from Report of Food and Nutrition Board, National Academy of Sciences-National Research Council, 7th Revised Edition, 1968.

kilocalorie, or the amount of energy required to raise the temperature of 1 kilogram of water 1 C.)

It is often assumed that a dietary intake of less than the Recommended Dietary Allowance by itself indicates substandard nutrition or even a deficiency. There is no justification for such a belief. In the 1968 edition of its publication, *Recommended Dietary Allowances*, the Food and Nutrition Board states:

"Food-consumption survey data cannot be used alone as a measure of nutritional adequacy. In determining nutritional status, the current and past nutrient intake must be taken into consideration, as well as an evaluation of clinical signs and symptoms, growth and development, and biochemical data on tissue and excretory levels of nutrients. Since the RDA are designed to be adequate for practically all of the population of

Water-Soluble Vitamins[2]

Ascorbic Acid (mg)	*Niacin (mg equiv)*[5]	*Riboflavin (mg)*	*Thiamine (mg)*	*Vitamin* B_6 *(mg)*	*Folacin*[6] *(mg)*	*Vitamin* B_{12} *(μg)*
35	5	0.4	0.2	0.2	0.05	1.0
35	7	0.5	0.4	0.3	0.05	1.5
35	8	0.6	0.5	0.4	0.1	2.0
40	8	0.6	0.6	0.5	0.1	2.0
40	8	0.7	0.6	0.6	0.2	2.5
40	9	0.8	0.7	0.7	0.2	3
40	11	0.9	0.8	0.9	0.2	4
40	13	1.1	1.0	1.0	0.2	4
40	15	1.2	1.1	1.2	0.3	5
40	17	1.3	1.3	1.4	0.4	5
45	18	1.4	1.4	1.6	0.4	5
55	20	1.5	1.5	1.8	0.4	5
60	18	1.6	1.4	2.0	0.4	5
60	18	1.7	1.4	2.0	0.4	5
60	17	1.7	1.3	2.0	0.4	5
60	14	1.7	1.2	2.0	0.4	6
40	15	1.3	1.1	1.4	0.4	5
45	15	1.4	1.2	1.6	0.4	5
50	16	1.4	1.2	1.8	0.4	5
50	15	1.5	1.2	2.0	0.4	5
55	13	1.5	1.0	2.0	0.4	5
55	13	1.5	1.0	2.0	0.4	5
55	13	1.5	1.0	2.0	0.4	5
55	13	1.5	1.0	2.0	0.4	6
60	15	1.8	+0.1	2.5	0.8	8
60	20	2.0	+0.5	2.5	0.5	6

[1]The allowance levels are intended to cover individual variations among most normal persons as they live in the United States under usual environmental stresses. The recommended allowances can be attained with a variety of common foods, providing other nutrients for which human requirements have been less well defined.

[2]No allowance has been established for pantothenic acid, but it is estimated that a daily intake of 5 to 10 mg is probably adequate for children and adults.

[3]Entries on lines for age range 22-35 years represent the reference man and woman at age 22. All other entries represent allowances for the midpoint of the specified age range.

[4]Factors for infants assume protein equivalent to human milk. For proteins not 100% utilized factors should be increased proportionately.

[5]Niacin equivalents include dietary sources of the vitamin itself plus 1 mg equivalent for each 60 mg of dietary tryptophan.

[6]The folacin allowances refer to dietary sources as determined by *Lactobacillus casei* assay. Pure forms of folacin may be effective in doses less than ¼ of the RDA.

the United States, they allow a margin of safety for individual variations. Individuals whose diets do not meet the RDA are not necessarily suffering from malnutrition, and diets should not be judged 'poor' on an arbitrary figure based on a comparison with the RDA, which are revised about every five years in order to include new research findings."

Infants most often require supplemental ascorbic acid, vitamin D, and sometimes vitamins A and E. Breast-fed infants should receive a vitamin D supplement. Artificially fed infants should receive ascorbic acid (or orange or tomato juice) and vitamin D, starting within the first week of life, if the formula does not supply 35 mg of ascorbic acid and 400 units of vitamin D. If the formula is high in polyunsaturated fatty acids, they should receive a supplement of vitamin E daily, especially if they are premature.

Infants receiving unfortified skimmed milk formulas should be given 1,500 IU of vitamin A daily. In some situations (eg, infants and children who are not eating and not developing satisfactorily, or who have diarrhea) the physician may deem it advisable to prescribe a B-vitamin supplement.

Healthy growing children consuming an adequate diet require no vitamin supplement unless they do not drink vitamin D-fortified milk and do not have sufficient exposure to sunlight; if a supplement is required, 400 units of vitamin D should be given daily. Similarly, healthy adults require no supplementation except in pregnancy and lactation when vitamin D and possibly certain of the B vitamins may be needed. There is no scientific evidence that elderly persons consuming an adequate diet have higher requirements for vitamins than do other healthy adults.

Because of increased metabolic demands, high potency B-complex and ascorbic acid supplements are indicated in patients with prolonged fever and a large daily fluid intake. These vitamins also are indicated when demand is increased by stress (eg, severe trauma, burns). In order to assure adequate replenishment of these micronutrients when total parenteral nutrition is needed, replacement doses of all the essential water-soluble vitamins should be given daily (see Chapter 16, Replenishers and Regulators of Water, Electrolytes, and Nutrients). The fat-soluble vitamins, A, D, and E, generally are not needed unless the patient's initial nutritional status is poor or his need for total parenteral nutrition is unduly prolonged. However, patients being maintained by total parenteral nutrition (especially infants) may require vitamin K because of reduced synthesis by intestinal bacteria.

Folic acid and ascorbic acid are removed by dialysis, and patients being dialyzed become deficient unless they receive compensatory amounts of these vitamins. The requirement for other vitamins apparently is not increased by dialysis.

Adverse Reactions and Precautions

Therapeutic doses of niacin may cause some transient unpleasant reactions, such as flushing, tingling sensations, and a feeling of warmth; niacinamide does not cause these effects. Hepatotoxic effects have occurred in patients receiving large doses of niacin. Anaphylactic reactions have occurred after the intravenous administration of large doses of thiamine and niacin. Occasionally, B-complex vitamin preparations may cause urticaria, angioedema, pruritus, and contact dermatitis. For precautions in the use of folic acid and cyanocobalamin, see Chapter 8, Agents Used to Treat Deficiency Anemias.

Vitamin E has produced adverse effects only when doses greatly exceeded the Recommended Dietary Allowances, and the effects were reversible when the dosage was lowered.

Excessive doses of vitamins A and D produce hazardous toxic effects. See the individual evaluations on these agents.

VITAMIN A

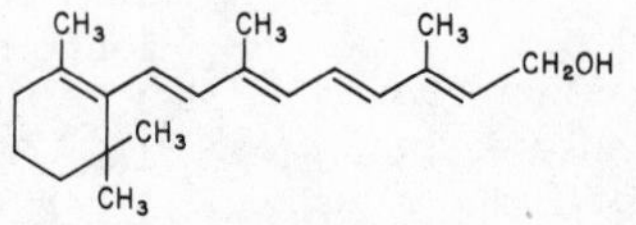

CH_3 CH_3 CH_3 CH_2OH CH_3 CH_3

Vitamin A is essential for normal visual functioning of the retina, normal functioning of various epithelial surfaces, and normal growth and development of bone. Eggs, dairy products, and meat (especially liver) supply preformed vitamin A. Green and yellow vegetables and fruits supply provitamins A, principally beta carotene, which the body converts to active vitamin A. Dietary fat is essential for effective absorption of carotenes, whereas protein is more important in the absorption of preformed vitamin A. Adequate liver reserves of vitamin A can prevent signs of deficiency for prolonged periods of deprivation.

Human milk supplies sufficient vitamin A unless the maternal diet is grossly inadequate. However, infants fed unfortified skimmed milk or milk-free formulas should receive a vitamin A supplement. Premature infants especially may have low liver reserves and may require an additional 500 to 1,000 IU daily to supplement dietary sources. In healthy children and adults consuming an adequate diet, vitamin A supplementation is unnecessary and is potentially hazardous if large doses are given.

Supplementary administration is useful in diseases that interfere with the absorption of vitamin A (eg, tropical sprue, cystic fibrosis, infantile or adult celiac disease, biliary obstruction, total gastrectomy). Severe hypovitaminosis A is rare in the United States, although it is still a serious and sometimes fatal disease in many parts of the world. An early sign is night blindness (nyctalopia). More severe deficiencies, which occur chiefly in children, result in xerophthalmia which, if untreated, progresses to corneal ulceration, perforation, keratomalacia, and blindness.

Epithelial changes in vitamin A deficiency impair local defenses against infection, and deaths from severe deficiency are usually due to bronchopneumonia. These observations led to the designation of vitamin A as the anti-infective vitamin; however, vitamin A in excess of normal requirements is of no value in the prevention or treatment of infections, including common respiratory infections. Neither does evidence warrant the use of vitamin A in the prevention of renal calculi or the treatment of hyperthyroidism, anemia, degenerative conditions of the nervous system, sunburn, or cutaneous ulcerative conditions. Oral administration of vitamin A in large doses has been used as adjunctive therapy in acne, but proof of efficacy is lacking and the treatment is not generally accepted. The topical use of cod liver oil or other preparations containing vitamin A in the treatment of wounds and other local conditions has not been supported by controlled studies.

Vitamin A is toxic in excessive doses, and clinical cases of hypervitaminosis A appear to be increasing. Preparations containing 25,000 IU or more are available without prescription even though such dosages generally should be restricted to patients with severe vitamin A deficiency. Daily doses as low as 18,500 IU in a water-dispersed preparation with vitamin D for one to three months have been reported to produce signs of overdosage in infants 3 to 6 months of age. Manifestations of hypervitaminosis A include anorexia, weight loss, pruritus, cracking and bleeding of lips, fatigue, abdominal discomfort, ostealgia or arthralgia, pseudotumor cerebri, insomnia, alopecia, brittle nails, menstrual irregularities, hyperostoses, and premature closure of the epiphyses. Most of these disorders improve within a week after withdrawal of the drug. Excessive intake of carotene does not cause signs or symptoms of hypervitaminosis A because its conversion to vitamin A is slow and incomplete. A high carotene intake may cause yellowish discoloration of the skin that resembles jaundice, except that it does not involve the sclera; patients with hypothyroidism are especially susceptible to this effect.

USUAL DOSAGE.—

Oral: Infants fed unfortified skimmed milk or other formulas, 1,500 IU. *Adults and children*, for supplementation, dosage should be based on Recommended Dietary Allowance after evaluation of patient's dietary supply. For mild to moderate clinical signs of vitamin A deficiency without corneal involvement, 25,000 to 50,000 IU daily, preferably as an aqueous dispersion, until clinical improvement has occurred; the same dosage should be used after intramuscular therapy in patients with corneal involvement. Daily doses of 50,000 IU or more have been used to treat hypovitaminosis A and other conditions such as hyperkeratotic dermatoses, but such large doses should be restricted to relatively short-term therapy because of the danger of hypervitaminosis A. Correction of the diet or reduction of the dose on the basis of Recommended Dietary Allowances should be substituted for therapeutic administration after response is obtained.

Intramuscular: Adults and children, in severe vitamin A deficiency, 50,000 to 100,000 IU daily for the first several days, preferably in water-dispersible form.

PREPARATIONS.—(Therapeutic; not to be used for prophylaxis.)

Oral: Capsules 25,000, 50,000, 75,000, and 100,000 IU; tablets 50,000 IU.

Injection: Solution 50,000 IU/ml in 5 ml containers.

Amounts of vitamin A suitable for prophylaxis are present in some multivitamin preparations.

AVAILABLE TRADEMARKS.—Vitamin A (water-dispersible): Acon (Endo), Aquasol A (USV), Dispatabs (Person & Covey), Homagenents-Aoral (First Texas), Testavol-S (Fellows-Testagar), Vi-Dom-A (Dome), Vio-A (Rowell). **Vitamin A:** Alphalin (Lilly), Anatola (Parke, Davis), Haliver Oil (Parke, Davis), Super A Vitamin (Upjohn). Drug also marketed by many manufacturers under generic name.

VITAMIN D

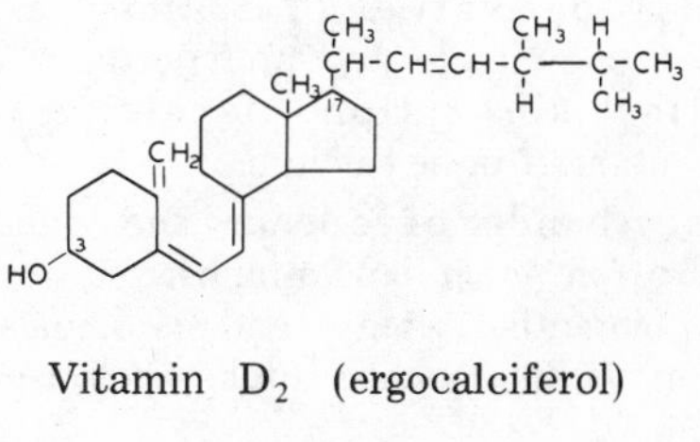

Vitamin D_2 (ergocalciferol)

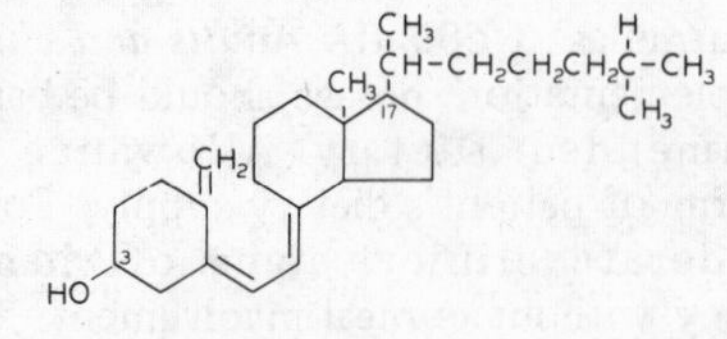

Vitamin D_3 (cholecalciferol)

The term vitamin D refers to either of two sterols, ergocalciferol (vitamin D_2) and cholecalciferol (vitamin D_3), that have equal antirachitic potency in man.

Vitamin D increases the absorption of calcium from the intestine, increases renal tubular reabsorption of phosphate, and aids in the mobilization of bone calcium and maintenance of calcium levels in the serum. Recent evidence concerning the action of this vitamin is of considerable potential clinical importance in the treatment of bone disease associated with chronic uremia (renal osteodystrophy) and certain other diseases that affect bone (eg, familial hypophosphatemias, Fanconi syndrome). Vitamin D itself is an inert storage form in the body and is metabolized to an active form in a series of hydroxylations at specific carbon positions. The principal metabolites identified are 25-hydroxycholecalciferol (25-HCC), which is formed in the liver, and 1,25-dihydroxycholecalciferol (1,25-DHCC), which is formed from 25-HCC in the kidney and has been shown to be the active metabolite in promoting the absorption and mobilization of calcium. The uremic kidney fails to form the active metabolite.

To some extent, both the liver and kidney hydroxylations are regulated by negative feedback mechanisms, and it has been suggested that vitamin D be considered a hormone rather than a vitamin. Nevertheless, the body must obtain vitamin D itself as the precursor of 1,25-DHCC, either from the action of ultraviolet light on sterols in the skin or from exogenous sources. Investigationally, 25-HCC is more rapidly effective in promoting calcium absorption and mobilization than is vitamin D, and 1,25-DHCC is most rapidly effective. Other hydroxy derivatives of 25-HCC have been identified which act preferentially on the intestinal absorption of calcium or the mobilization of bone calcium.

Disturbance of calcium and phosphorus metabolism in hypovitaminosis D results in rickets, infantile tetany, and osteomalacia. In addition to inadequate intake, deficiencies of vitamin D occur as a result of malabsorption (eg, celiac disease, tropical sprue, gastrointestinal resections). Most milk sold in the United States is fortified with at least 400 units of vitamin D per quart, and many other foods such as margarine and breakfast cereals contain added vitamin D. Thus, many individuals in the United States subsisting on the usual foods obtain the recommended daily allowance or more from dietary sources; however, some brands of market milk are not fortified. Irradiation of the skin by sunlight also can meet the requirement for vitamin D.

Breast-fed infants as well as infants receiving an unfortified formula require a daily supplement of vitamin D. Premature infants may have a more critical need for supplementation because they have lower calcium stores (the fetus acquires more than 85% of its calcium stores during the last trimester) and are more susceptible to rickets than are full-term infants. Supplementation is indicated in pregnancy if the diet does not supply 400 units of vitamin D. See also the Introductory Statement.

The margin of safety between prophylactic or therapeutic doses and toxic doses of vitamin D in infants and children appears to be narrower than formerly thought. Manifestations of hypervitaminosis D include hypercalcemia, ectopic calcifications (calcinosis universalis) in soft tissues (eg, heart, blood vessels, kidneys), anorexia, nausea and vomiting, diarrhea, polydipsia, polyuria, and headache. Osteoporosis, hypertension, and decreased renal function also have been observed. Complete recovery follows if the intake of vitamin D is stopped in time.

Hypervitaminosis D may occur in infants and young children receiving supplements in addition to high dietary intake or from overdosage due to parental ignorance or error. It also may be caused by large doses used in the treatment of such diseases as familial hypophosphatemia (vitamin D-resistant rickets) and renal osteodystrophy. There is some evidence of a possible relationship between vitamin D intake and idiopathic infantile hypercalcemia.

There is no satisfactory evidence to indicate that the inclusion of vitamin D in preparations for topical use is beneficial.

For information on the interrelationship of vitamin D and parathyroid hormone and the use of vitamin D and dihydrotachysterol in the treatment of the hypocalcemia of hypoparathyroidism, see Chapter 17, Blood

Calcium Regulators.

USUAL DOSAGE.—

Oral (Supplementation): Premature infants may require a supplement because of their greater susceptibility to rickets. Rarely, an infant is abnormally susceptible to rickets and may require up to 30,000 units daily to prevent deficiency. *Breast-fed infants* or those fed unfortified formulas should receive 400 units daily as a supplement. *Adults*, supplementation ordinarily is needed only during pregnancy and lactation to assure a daily intake of 400 units. *Infants and children* receiving adequate amounts of vitamin D-fortified food require no supplementation; in fact, use of a supplement can result in overdosage.

Oral (Therapeutic): Infants and children, for treatment of rickets, 1,000 to 4,000 units daily until response is obtained; for familial hypophosphatemia (vitamin D-resistant rickets), 50,000 to 200,000 units daily. *Adults*, for osteomalacia in malabsorption syndromes, 10,000 to 50,000 units; for renal osteodystrophy, 50,000 to 500,000 units daily until desired effect is achieved or toxic effects intervene.

PREPARATIONS.—(Therapeutic; not to be used for prophylaxis.)

Ergocalciferol (Vitamin D_2):

Deltalin (Lilly). *Oral:* Capsules 50,000 units.

Drisdol (Winthrop). *Oral:* Capsules 50,000 units; solution 10,000 units/ml.

ADDITIONAL TRADEMARKS.—Geltabs (Upjohn), Viosterol in Oil (Parke, Davis). Also marketed under the names Vitamin D and Calciferol.

VITAMIN E

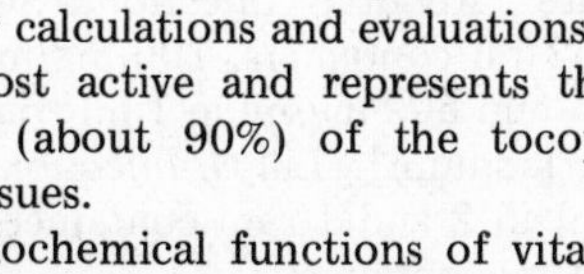

Vitamin E refers to a group of naturally occurring fat-soluble substances, including alpha-, beta-, gamma-, and delta-tocopherol. Generally, only alpha-tocopherol is considered in dietary calculations and evaluations because it is the most active and represents the greatest portion (about 90%) of the tocopherols in animal tissues.

The biochemical functions of vitamin E are not completely understood; it has antioxidant properties and is an essential nutrient apparently having an important role in heme synthesis. Its antioxidant properties protect vitamin A and unsaturated fatty acids both in vitro and in vivo. A number of other substances that occur naturally in foods (eg, certain antioxidants, selenium) can function as partial substitutes for vitamin E.

The requirement for vitamin E increases with the intake of polyunsaturated fatty acids. In the United States, salad oils, shortenings, and margarine commonly supply about 65% of the alpha-tocopherol in the diet. Significant amounts also are supplied by fruits, vegetables, and grain products.

Vitamin E is effective only in the treatment or prevention of vitamin E deficiency, which occurs rarely. Clinical vitamin E-responsive states include macrocytic megaloblastic anemia in some children with severe protein-calorie deficiency (kwashiorkor), hemolytic anemia in premature infants, and autohemolysis of red blood cells in vitro from patients with genetic low-density lipoprotein deficiency. One case of vitamin E-responsive porphyria also has been reported. Specific signs and symptoms of deficiency have not been described with certainty in adults. Vitamin E deficiency due to interference with its absorption may occur in malabsorption syndromes with steatorrhea, and as a result of biliary obstruction, pancreatic disease, and excessive ingestion of mineral oil. Skin lesions, hematologic changes, and edema have been reported in premature infants receiving formulas high in polyunsaturated fatty acids and low in vitamin E; recovery followed administration of 25 to 50 mg (37.5 to 75 IU) of alpha-tocopherol.

Although hypovitaminosis E causes diverse signs (eg, muscular dystrophy, reproductive failure, myocardial necrosis, heart failure) in various animal species, the vitamin has no value in the treatment of similar clinical disorders in man (eg, cardiovascular disease, habitual abortion, sterility, neuromuscular diseases).

No toxic effects have been observed following administration of 800 units of vitamin E per kilogram of body weight for five months. Much larger doses for prolonged periods have caused skeletal muscle weakness, disturbances of reproductive functions, and gastrointestinal upset. Symptoms disappeared within a few weeks when excessive intake was stopped.

USUAL DOSAGE.—*Oral: Adults and children*, in suspected deficiency, four to five times the Recommended Dietary Allowance. *Infants* receiving formulas high in polyunsaturated fatty acids, 5 IU if the formula does not contain at least 0.3 IU/100 kilocalories.

PREPARATIONS.—(Contain forms of alpha-tocopherol unless otherwise indicated.)

Aquasol E (USV). *Oral:* Capsules 30 and 100 IU; drops 50 IU/ml.

E-Ferol (Fellows-Testagar). *Oral:* Capsules 30, 100, 200, 400, and 800 IU.

E-Ferol Succinate (Fellows-Testagar). *Oral:* Capsules 100, 200, and 400 IU; tablets 50 IU.

Eprolin (Lilly) (mixed tocopherols). *Oral:* Capsules 50 mg (50 to 75 IU) and 100 mg (100 to 150 IU).

Epsilan-M (Warren-Teed). *Oral:* Capsules 100 IU.

ADDITIONAL TRADEMARKS.—Ecofrol (Durst), Tocopherex (Squibb), Tokols (Ulmer). Also marketed under the names Vitamin E, Tocopherol, and Tocopheryl Acetate.

ASCORBIC ACID
ASCORBATE SODIUM

```
  ┌──O──┐     H   H
O=C-C=C-C - C - C-OH
    HO OHH  OH  H
```

Ascorbic acid (vitamin C) is essential for many physiologic functions and must be supplied from exogenous sources because man lacks the enzyme necessary to synthesize it. A prolonged deficiency of ascorbic acid causes scurvy. Dietary sources of the vitamin include fresh fruits and juices, vegetables, and liver. If an infant's formula lacks vitamin C, it is especially important that a dietary source or an ascorbic acid supplement be given daily.

Ascorbic acid deficiency leads to degeneration of collagen and intercellular ground substance. Resulting abnormalities include disturbances of bone growth, subperiosteal hemorrhages, loosening of the teeth, swelling and hemorrhages of the gums, and capillary fragility which causes cutaneous hemorrhages. Blood loss in scurvy frequently results in normocytic or macrocytic anemia. Occasionally megaloblastic anemia occurs from a deficiency in both ascorbic acid and folic acid. Deficiency of vitamin C causes delayed wound healing.

If digestive functions are adequate, scurvy can be prevented and cured by including natural food sources of vitamin C in the diet, however, supplemental administration of ascorbic acid may hasten restoration of tissue levels to normal in scorbutic patients. Ascorbic acid may be given intramuscularly as the sodium salt when persistent vomiting, diarrhea, or other conditions preclude its utilization by the oral route.

Ascorbic acid is essential for wound healing, and severely traumatized patients with low blood levels of the vitamin may benefit from its administration. Severe burns cause rapid lowering of blood levels, and clinical evidence suggests that administration of ascorbic acid aids recovery from extensive burns. In controlled studies, normal human subjects showed no discernible benefits from the use of large doses of ascorbic acid for prolonged periods.

Ascorbic acid is of no value in the treatment of pyorrhea and gingival infections. Evidence to support claims that massive doses (as high as 10 g) of ascorbic acid are effective in preventing and aborting colds is unconvincing. Opinions concerning the potential harmful effects of such doses are equally controversial. One case of interference with the anticoagulant action of warfarin has been reported.

After the tissues are saturated, excess ascorbic acid is rapidly excreted by the kidneys. There is no clinical evidence that large doses are harmful.

USUAL DOSAGE.—*Oral, Intramuscular: Infants,* 35 mg daily; if the formula contains two to three times the amount of protein in human milk, 50 mg of ascorbic acid daily for the first few weeks of life is recommended. For the treatment of scurvy, the corrected diet is supplemented with 300 mg of ascorbic acid daily for at least two weeks. In *adults* and *children* with severe burns, 200 to 500 mg daily may be needed to maintain adequate levels in the blood.

PREPARATIONS.—

Ascorbic Acid:

Cecon (Abbott). *Oral:* Solution 500 mg/5 ml.

Cevalin (Lilly). *Oral:* Tablets 50, 100, 250, and 500 mg.

Ce-Vi-Sol (Mead Johnson). *Oral:* Solution 60 mg/ml.

Liqui-Cee (Arnar-Stone). *Oral:* Solution 1 g/5 ml.

Ascorbate Sodium:

Cenolate (Abbott). *Injection:* Solution 50 mg/ml in 2 ml containers, 100 mg/ml in 10 ml containers, and 500 mg/ml in 1 ml containers.

Cevalin [sodium] (Lilly). *Injection:* Solution 100 mg/ml in 2 and 10 ml containers, and 500 mg/ml in 1 ml containers.

ADDITIONAL TRADEMARKS.—Ascorbic Acid: C-Long (Tutag), C-Tabs (Ulmer), Lemascorb (Ascher). Both forms also marketed by many manufacturers under generic name.

NIACIN (Nicotinic Acid)
NIACINAMIDE (Nicotinamide)

The dietary requirement for niacin is expressed in terms of niacin equivalents because the vitamin can be synthesized in the body from dietary tryptophan. Approximately 60 mg of tryptophan is equivalent to 1 mg of niacin. Dietary sources include liver, yeast, meat, and legumes.

Niacin or its amide, niacinamide, is essential for the prevention and cure of pellagra. The two forms are equally effective and are used prophylactically and therapeutically. However, differences in adverse effects make niacinamide the preferred drug, especially for therapeutic use.

Pellagra may be caused by a diet consisting largely of corn (maize), which is deficient in both niacin and tryptophan, and by malabsorption syndromes, alcoholism, and food fads. It also may occur in patients with cirrhosis of the liver, diabetes mellitus, neoplasms, Graves' disease, carcinoid syndrome, and prolonged infections (eg, tuberculosis). Manifestations of pellagra include symmetrically distributed erythematous lesions on exposed surfaces of the body; painful, red swelling of the tongue and oral mucous membranes; gastrointestinal effects such as nausea, vomiting, abdominal distention, and diarrhea; and central nervous system symptoms such as headache, dizziness, insomnia, and confusion. Psychoses (eg, hallucinations) may occur and may be the only manifestation of niacin deficiency; rapid response of such mental disturbances to administration of niacin is useful in differential diagnosis when other symptoms of niacin deficiency are absent. Other manifestations include achlorhydria and anemia due to iron, folic acid, or vitamin B_{12} deficiency. Macrocytic anemia in pellagrous patients is believed most commonly to be due to folic acid deficiency, but neurologic evidence of spinal cord lesions sometimes occurs and, together with the incidence of achlorhydria, suggests vitamin B_{12} deficiency. In addition, pellagra usually is accompanied by deficiencies in other B-complex vitamins.

Since pellagra commonly involves multiple deficiencies, use of a therapeutic vitamin B-complex preparation (eg, one containing niacin, riboflavin, thiamine, pyridoxine, pantothenic acid) in multiples of the Recommended Dietary Allowances is justifiable. If either folic acid or vitamin B_{12} is indicated, these agents should be given separately (see Chapter 8, Agents Used to Treat Deficiency Anemias).

Niacin also has been used in large doses for its vasodilating action, but its beneficial effect for this purpose is unconvincing (see Chapter 4, Peripheral Vasodilators). Niacin is effective in lowering blood lipid levels, but its adverse effects limit its usefulness (see Chapter 13, Agents Used to Treat Hyperlipidemia).

Therapeutic doses of niacin may cause pruritus, flushing, tingling sensations, a feeling of warmth, and mild hypotension; since niacinamide does not cause these effects, it is preferred for therapeutic use. In massive doses, niacin may produce signs of liver damage, which usually are reversible when administration is stopped. Anaphylaxis has been reported following intravenous administration.

USUAL DOSAGE.—

Oral: 50 mg three to ten times daily.

Injection: 25 mg two or more times daily.

PREPARATIONS.—

Niacin, N.F.:

Oral: Tablets 25, 50, 100, and 500 mg.

Injection: Solution (sodium salt) 10 mg/ml in 10 ml containers.

Niacinamide, U.S.P.:

Oral: Tablets 50 and 100 mg.

Injection: Solution 100 mg/ml in 5 and 30 ml containers.

Both forms marketed by many manufacturers under generic names and under names Nicotinic Acid (niacin) or Nicotinamide (niacinamide).

AVAILABLE TRADEMARKS.—Niacin: Nico-400 (Marion), Nicobid (Armour).

PANTOTHENIC ACID

$$HO{-}CH_2C(CH_3)_2{-}CH(OH){-}C(=O){-}NH{-}CH_2CH_2C(=O){-}OH$$

This member of the B-complex group forms a part of coenzyme A and is an essential nutrient for man. However, no proved cases of spontaneously occurring clinical deficiency have been observed.

A Recommended Dietary Allowance has not been established, but a daily intake of 5 to 10 mg is believed to be adequate. Pantothenic acid deficiency seems an unlikely clinical occurrence except possibly in association with other B-vitamin deficiencies (eg, in pellagra, alcoholism). Large doses are ineffective in the prevention or treatment of graying hair or adynamic ileus.

Pantothenic acid is included in multiple vitamin preparations as the calcium or sodium salt or the alcohol, panthenol. It is essentially nontoxic.

USUAL DOSAGE.—For the reasons stated above, this vitamin is not advisable for use alone; 5 to 10 mg is considered suitable for inclusion in multivitamin preparations for dietary supplementation. Topical preparations should not be used.

PREPARATIONS.—

Dexpanthenol:

Injection: Solution 250 mg/ml in 2 and 10 ml containers.

AVAILABLE TRADEMARKS.—Cozyme (Travenol), Ilopan (Warren-Teed), Intrapan (Elkins-Sinn), Pantonyl (Invenex).

Pantothenate Calcium, U.S.P.:

Oral: Tablets 10 and 30 mg.

AVAILABLE TRADEMARK.—Pantholin (Lilly). Drug also marketed under generic name.

Pantothenic Acid:

Oral: Tablets 100 mg. Drug marketed under generic name.

For multivitamin preparations containing pantothenic acid, see listing under section on Mixtures.

PYRIDOXINE HYDROCHLORIDE
(Vitamin B_6)

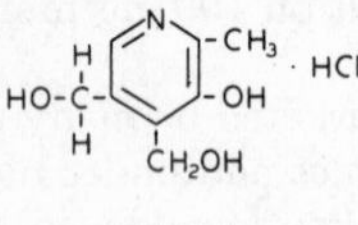

The vitamin B_6 group occurs in a wide variety of foods and consists of three compounds: pyridoxine, which occurs in plant sources, and pyridoxal and pyridoxamine, which are found primarily in foods of animal origin. Because of interconversions in the body, biological differences among these forms are minimal.

The major functions of vitamin B_6 involve protein and amino acid metabolism and, to a lesser degree, carbohydrate and fat metabolism. The requirement for pyridoxine appears to be related to protein intake. Symptoms and signs of deficiency include seborrhea, intertrigo, dermatitis, cheilosis, glossitis, stomatitis, and peripheral neuropathy.

Infants with epileptiform convulsions and hypochromic anemias due to familial type pyridoxine dependency have responded to pyridoxine. The vitamin also has been effective or partially effective in correcting some cases of hypochromic or megaloblastic anemia in patients who had adequate levels of iron but did not respond to other hematopoietic agents. Pyridoxine is indicated for the prevention or treatment of peripheral neuritis caused by administration of certain drugs (eg, isoniazid, hydralazine, penicillamine). The vitamin is of no value in the treatment of nausea and vomiting of pregnancy. However, it reverses the increased levels of certain tryptophan metabolites that occur in pregnant women and in those taking oral contraceptives. Clinical observations suggest that this action may be effective in alleviating some depressive reactions occurring during pregnancy or oral contraceptive administration, but controlled studies to confirm these observations have not been made.

If a vitamin preparation is indicated in a patient receiving levodopa for the treatment of parkinsonism, the intake of pyridoxine should not exceed the Recommended Dietary Allowance in order to avoid possible interference with the beneficial effects of levodopa. See also Chapter 74, Antiparkinsonism Agents.

USUAL DOSAGE.—*Oral, Intramuscular, Intravenous: Infants* with convulsions due to familial type pyridoxine dependency, 10 mg daily. For trial in *adults* and *children* with refractory hypochromic or megaloblastic anemias or peripheral neuritis that may be precipitated in susceptible individuals by isoniazid or other drugs, 20 to 200 mg daily.

PREPARATIONS.—Pyridoxine Hydrochloride, U.S.P.

Oral: Tablets 10, 25, 50, and 100 mg.

Injection: Solution 100 mg/ml in 1, 5, and 10 ml containers.

AVAILABLE TRADEMARKS.—Beesix (Fellows-Testagar), Hexa-Betalin (Lilly), Hexavibex (Parke, Davis), Hydoxin (Mallinckrodt). Also marketed by many manufacturers under generic name.

RIBOFLAVIN (Vitamin B_2)

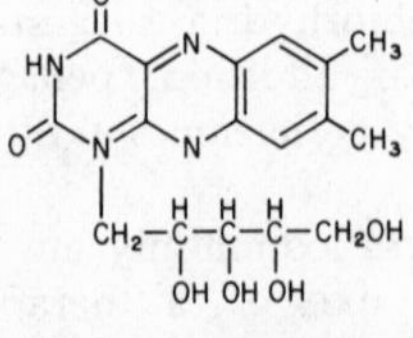

Ariboflavinosis is characterized by cheilosis, glossitis, seborrheic dermatitis of the nose and scrotum, and vascularization of the cornea. Corneal vascularization begins with circumcorneal injection; later, new vessels (digital capillaries) grow into the cornea from the entire circumference of the limbic plexus. Symptoms include pruritus and burning in the eye, photophobia, and visual impairment. Corneal vascularization is an important diagnostic sign, since there are other causes of circumcorneal injection that do not result in vascularization and do not respond to administration of riboflavin. Riboflavin deficiency seldom occurs alone; it often is observed with pellagra and other B-complex deficiency states. Dietary sources of riboflavin include milk, eggs, liver, and meat.

USUAL DOSAGE.—*Oral:* 5 to 10 mg daily.

PREPARATIONS.—Riboflavin, U.S.P. *Oral:* Capsules and tablets 5 and 10 mg.

AVAILABLE TRADEMARK.—Hyrye (Durst). Drug also marketed under generic name.

THIAMINE HYDROCHLORIDE (Vitamin B_1)

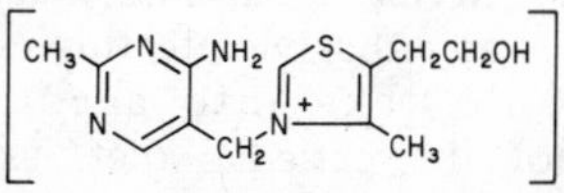

$$\left[\text{CH}_3\text{-pyrimidinyl(NH}_2\text{)-CH}_2\text{-N}^+\text{(thiazolium: 4-CH}_3\text{, 5-CH}_2\text{CH}_2\text{OH)} \right] \text{Cl}^- \cdot \text{HCl}$$

Deficiency of thiamine, an essential coenzyme for carbohydrate metabolism, causes beriberi. This disease has two principal forms: (1) dry beriberi, in which the predominant manifestation is polyneuropathy and (2) acute wet beriberi, in which edema and serous effusions predominate. Other manifestations of beriberi may include muscular weakness, nervousness, fatigue, anorexia, epigastric pain, confusion, ataxia, oliguria, arrhythmias, and increased peripheral blood flow (possibly progressing to high output heart failure). The disease is still endemic in areas where polished, unenriched rice forms a large part of the diet. Severe thiamine deficiency apparently is uncommon in the United States. However, it may occur in alcoholics, pregnant women receiving inadequate diets, and patients with gastrointestinal disorders that interfere with ingestion or absorption.

Since deficiencies of any of the B-complex vitamins tend to involve more than one member of the group, treatment with a multivitamin preparation is rational. However, both dry and acute wet beriberi, as well as some cases of alcoholic neuropathy and neuritis of pregnancy, respond to administration of thiamine alone. In acute wet beriberi, diuresis with rapid disappearance of edema may begin within a few hours after the initial dose. Evidence now available indicates that thiamine deficiency is the cause of Wernicke-Korsakoff syndrome. Thiamine will correct the ophthalmoplegia, ataxia, and nystagmus of Wernicke's encephalopathy, but is of more limited effectiveness in Korsakoff's psychosis since the brain lesions responsible for the amnesia and confabulation are generally irreversible in advanced cases.

Anaphylactoid reactions, a few of which were fatal, have occurred after intravenous administration of large amounts of thiamine in sensitive patients.

USUAL DOSAGE.—*Oral, Intramuscular, Intravenous:* For thiamine-deficiency syndromes, 5 to 10 mg three times daily. Considerably larger parenteral doses have been suggested in severe cases; however, there is no satisfactory evidence that increase in response occurs with doses larger than 30 mg daily. After signs of thiamine deficiency have been corrected, intake of the vitamin should be on the basis of the Recommended Dietary Allowance, supplied by correction of the diet, if possible, or as a daily supplement. Unless evidence indicates that the deficiency is clearly one of thiamine alone, administration of a vitamin B-complex preparation is preferred.

PREPARATIONS.—Thiamine Hydrochloride, U.S.P.

Oral: Elixir 0.25, 1, and 2.25 mg/5 ml; tablets 10, 25, 50, 100, and 250 mg.

Injection: Solution 100 mg/ml in 10, 20, and 30 ml containers.

AVAILABLE TRADEMARKS.—Betalin S (Lilly), Bewon (Wyeth), Thiabev (Key). Drug also marketed by many manufacturers under generic name.

SIMILAR PREPARATION.—Thiamine Mononitrate, U.S.P. Used in some multivitamin preparations and mixtures.

MIXTURES

Properly formulated multivitamin preparations are rational in theory and useful in practice, since clinical vitamin deficiencies are almost always multiple. Such preparations should contain only vitamins shown to be essential ingredients of the diet. However, many formulas contain additional agents such as biotin, choline, and inositol which are so ubiquitous as to be unwarranted. Biotin deficiency can be produced only by the prolonged ingestion of raw egg white, which contains the inactivating protein avidin, because this vitamin normally is synthesized by intestinal bacteria and absorbed. Thus, biotin deficiency is not a clinical problem except under very unusual circumstances. Choline and inositol previously have been considered in the vitamin group of nutrients. Choline has been administered for its lipotropic action in patients with such disturbances as fatty liver, hepatic cirrhosis, and viral hepatitis. However, choline can be synthesized in the human body from methionine, and the dietary measures used in the management of patients with these hepatic diseases supply choline in ample amounts. Inositol also is synthesized in the human body, and there is no evidence substantiating its usefulness in the treatment of any disease.

Multivitamin preparations should contain the individual vitamins in relative amounts approximating a simple multiple of the Recommended Dietary Allowances. Care is necessary in selecting an appropriate preparation because some formulations are qualitatively or quantitatively irrational. Also, many manufacturers use the same general trademark for several preparations having qualitatively and quantitatively different formulas. To evaluate a multiple vitamin preparation, the physician may compare the amount of each vitamin in the formulation with the Recommended Dietary Allowances shown in Table 1. Another convenient reference is the Decavitamin, U.S.P. formula, which is the only official multivitamin preparation and contains supplemental amounts of the essential vitamins as follows: vitamin A 4,000 U.S.P. units, vitamin D 400 U.S.P. units, vitamin E 15 IU, ascorbic acid 70 mg, calcium pantothenate 10 mg, cyanocobalamin 5 μg, folic acid 100 μg, niacinamide 20 mg, pyridoxine hydrochloride 2 mg, riboflavin 2 mg, and thiamine hydrochloride 2 mg. (Certain minor chemical alterations are indicated as acceptable in the U.S.P.)

Table 2 presents an arbitrary simplification of the RDA for different age groups; this may serve as a practical aid in the rapid quantitative evaluation of multivitamin formulas for various supplemental and therapeutic purposes. Until these preparations as a class are brought into greater conformity with current nutritional knowledge, the physician should make an effort to select those having a rational quantitative basis and reject any that violate this criterion. Dosage should take into account the contribution of the patient's diet, especially with reference to vitamins A and D.

Supplemental or Prophylactic Vitamin

TABLE 2.—COMPARATIVE GUIDE FOR SELECTION OF MULTIVITAMIN PREPARATIONS

Recommended Dietary Allowances

Vitamin	*Age (Years)* 1	1-3	3-10	10
A (IU)	1,500	2,000	3,500	5,000*
D (IU)	400	400	400	400†
E (IU)	5	10	15	30
C (mg)	35	40	40	60
Folic Acid (mg)	0.1	0.2	0.3	0.4*
Niacin (mg equiv.)	8	8	15	20
Riboflavin (mg)	0.5	0.5	1.0	2.0
Thiamine (mg)	0.5	0.5	1.0	1.5
Pyridoxine (mg)	0.5	0.5	1.0	2.0
Pantothenic Acid (mg)	5	10	10	10
Vitamin B_{12} (μg)	2	2.5	5	5*

*RDA increased during pregnancy and lactation.

†No RDA after age 22 except during pregnancy and lactation.

Combinations: Prophylactic multivitamin preparations may reasonably contain from one-half to one and one-half times the Recommended Dietary Allowances except for vitamin D, which should not exceed the Recommended Dietary Allowance. Supplemental doses of ascorbic acid and B-complex vitamins larger than those recommended confer no benefits, although they generally are not harmful.

Vitamin supplements should be selected by the physician to fit the needs of a particular situation, and with the understanding that the usefulness of such preparations lies in preventing the possible development of clinical deficiency states or undesirably low tissue levels of the vitamins. Combinations that might be indicated in particular situations would include the water-soluble vitamins, riboflavin, thiamine, and niacin, with or without pyridoxine, pantothenic acid, folic acid, cyanocobalamin, and ascorbic acid; the fat-soluble vitamins, A and D, with or without vitamin E; and preparations containing both water-soluble and fat-soluble vitamins.

These preparations may be useful during special periods of life (such as pregnancy and lactation), during relatively brief illnesses that result in impaired absorption of nutrients, and in patients who for any of numerous reasons are not eating properly. Vitamin administration should be discontinued after the patient has recovered from his illness or adequate dietary habits have been assured. The higher potency preparations (containing one and one-half times the RDA) may be useful for supplementing therapeutic diets (eg, in allergy) or when food intake is drastically reduced (eg, in rapid weight reduction programs, during prolonged illness).

Supplemental amounts of a particular vitamin may sometimes be contraindicated. For example, supplementation with vitamin D should be avoided in normal individuals, especially infants and children, who are receiving adequate amounts in the diet. Pyridoxine may interfere with the effectiveness of levodopa in the treatment of parkinsonsim and concomitant use should be avoided (see Chapter 74, Antiparkinsonsim Agents).

Supplemental multivitamin preparations containing folic acid and cyanocobalamin may be useful in preventing the development of certain deficiency states, such as megaloblastic anemia of pregnancy. The incidence of this anemia, which is usually due to folic acid deficiency, appears to be greater among certain regional or ethnic groups having distinctive cultural and dietary habits. Supplemental multivitamin preparations containing the fat-soluble vitamins A and D, or A, D, and E, in addition to the water-soluble vitamins, also may be useful in persons with increased needs, dietary restrictions, or impaired absorption. However, many such preparations contain vitamin E in amounts representing an insignificant fraction of the Recommended Dietary Allowance.

Therapeutic Multivitamin Preparations: Multivitamin preparations for therapeutic use may contain three to five times the Recommended Dietary Allowances. However, because of the possibility of obscuring the diagnosis of pernicious anemia, therapeutic multivitamin preparations should not contain more than one and one-half times the Recommended Dietary Allowance of folic acid. Larger doses of folic acid should be given separately and on the basis of a definitive diagnosis. The therapeutic uses of folic acid and cyanocobalamin involve critical questions of hematologic diagnosis, dosage, and route of administration, and are discussed in Chapter 8, Agents Used to Treat Deficiency Anemias.

Therapeutic multivitamin preparations should be labeled as such and should be used only for the treatment of deficiency states and for supportive therapy in pathologic states that increase nutritional requirements. *They should not be used as dietary supplements.* They frequently are needed in malabsorption syndromes (eg, patients with gastrointestinal resections, tropical sprue, infantile or adult celiac disease). The type and degree of vitamin therapy needed varies with the clinical condition; for example, in steatorrhea, deficiencies of vitamins A, D, and K may occur if adequate replacement therapy is not given; vitamin K is not available in multivitamin preparations, and must be given on an individual basis (see Chapter 11, Hemostatics). After bowel resection, the need for replacement therapy with water-soluble vitamins depends on the location of the resection, the amount of bowel remaining, and the individual patient. These vitamins should be administered regularly to patients who have diarrhea after bowel resections or bypass operations. Resection of the ileum results in defective absorption of vitamin B_{12}, and thereafter this agent should be administered by injection (see Chapter 8, Agents Used to Treat Deficiency Anemias).

In specific therapeutic situations in which the dose of a vitamin exceeds five times the Recommended Dietary Allowance (eg, vitamin A in acute deficiency), that vitamin should be given separately. The amount of vitamin D in multivitamin preparations should not exceed the Recommended Dietary Allowance.

Vitamin Combinations with Minerals: Although minerals are outside the scope of this chapter, a few general comments are necessary because minerals often are incorporated in vitamin preparations. Iron is one of the most common minerals included in such mixtures, but this element, when indicated for therapy, should be given on an individual basis (see Chapter 8, Agents Used to Treat Deficiency Anemias). Supplemental administration of iron (Recommended Dietary Allowance, 18 mg) may be advisable during childbearing years and especially during pregnancy. Supplemental calcium (Recommended Dietary Allowance, 1.2 g) also may be advisable during pregnancy, and since administration of vitamin D (Recommended Dietary Allowance, 400 units) is recommended if the patient does not consume sufficient vitamin D-fortified milk, preparations containing rational amounts of iron, calcium, and vitamin D are useful for prenatal supplementation. However, vitamin-mineral mixtures are often superfluous or irrational. For example, many such mixtures include trace amounts of essential elements for which either no quantitative human dietary requirement or no proved dietary deficiency has been established (eg, copper, manganese, zinc), or which often are present in amounts representing a small fraction of the recommended allowance (eg, magnesium).

The fluoridation of public water supplies to reduce the incidence of dental caries in children is a public health measure not practiced in all communities. Occasionally, when a need for vitamin supplementation exists and a child's source of drinking water contains less than the optimal amount of fluoride (1 to 1.2 ppm in cooler climates or 0.5 to 0.6 ppm in warmer climates), multivitamin preparations containing 0.5 or 1 mg of fluoride in each daily dose may be an appropriate means for supplying prophylactic fluoride in selected circumstances. However, parents should be warned that the use of the preparation should be discontinued or reviewed if the family moves or there is some other change in the water supply. (For a listing of multivitamin preparations containing fluoride, see Chapter 92, Miscellaneous Drugs.)

Miscellaneous Combinations: Many multivitamin preparations contain unnecessary nutrients (eg, biotin, choline, inositol, betaine, methionine) that have no proven value in the prevention or management of vitamin-deficiency syndromes.

Mixtures of vitamins with other potent drugs such as hormonal agents, antidepressants, and appetite suppressants should not be used (for listings of such combination products, see Chapters 33, Anorexiants; 36, Androgens and Anabolic Steroids; and 39, Thyroid Hormones and Antithyroid Agents).

Following is a partial listing of multivitamin preparations, with and without other substances such as minerals, in common use. The quantitative formulas are included to assist the physician in evaluating preparations and selecting ones suitable for particular applications.

Available Mixtures

Abdec Drops (Parke, Davis): Each 0.6 ml contains vitamin A palmitate 5,000 units, ergocalciferol 400 units, ascorbic acid 50 mg, thiamine hydrochloride 1 mg, riboflavin 1.2 mg, pyridoxine hydrochloride 1 mg, niacinamide 10 mg, and pantothenate sodium 5 mg.

Allbee with C (Robins): Each capsule contains thiamine mononitrate 15 mg, riboflavin 10 mg, pyridoxine hydrochloride 5 mg, niacinamide 50 mg, pantothenate calcium 10 mg, and ascorbic acid 300 mg.

Allbee-T (Robins): Each tablet contains thiamine mononitrate 15 mg, riboflavin 10 mg, pyridoxine hydrochloride 10 mg, pantothenate calcium 25 mg, niacinamide 100 mg, ascorbic acid 500 mg, cyanocobalamin 5 μg, and desiccated liver 150 mg.

Becotin with Vitamin C (Lilly): Each capsule contains thiamine hydrochloride 10 mg, riboflavin 10 mg, pyridoxine hydrochloride 4.1 mg, niacinamide 50 mg, pantothenic acid 25 mg, vitamin B_{12} equivalent 1 μg, and ascorbic acid 150 mg.

Becotin T (Lilly): Each tablet contains thiamine mononitrate 15 mg, riboflavin 10 mg, pyridoxine hydrochloride 5 mg, niacinamide 100 mg, pantothenic acid 20 mg, vitamin B_{12} equivalent 4 μg, and ascorbic acid 300 mg.

Berocca (Roche): Each tablet contains thiamine mononitrate 15 mg, riboflavin 15 mg, pyridoxine hydrochloride 5 mg, niacinamide 100 mg, pantothenate calcium 20 mg, cyanocobalamin 5 μg, ascorbic acid 500 mg, and folic acid 0.5 mg.

Berocca-C Injection (Roche): Each 2 ml contains thiamine hydrochloride 10 mg, riboflavin 10 mg, pyridoxine hydrochloride 20 mg, niacinamide 80 mg, dexpanthenol 20 mg, *d*-biotin 0.2 mg, and ascorbic acid 100 mg.

Betalin Complex Injection (Lilly): Each milliliter contains thiamine hydrochloride 5 mg, riboflavin 2 mg, niacinamide 75 mg, panthenol 2.5 mg, pyridoxine hydrochloride 5 mg, and cyanocobalamin 2.5 μg.

Clusivol Chewable Tablets (Ayerst): Each chewable tablet contains vitamin A acetate 5,000 units, ergocalciferol 400 units, ascorbic acid 75 mg, thiamine mononitrate 1.5 mg, riboflavin 1.5 mg, pyridoxine hydrochloride 1 mg, and niacinamide 15 mg.

Clusivol Tablets (Ayerst): Each tablet contains vitamin A acetate 25,000 units, ergocalciferol 400 units, ascorbic acid 150 mg, thiamine mononitrate 10 mg, riboflavin 5 mg, pyridoxine hydrochloride 0.5 mg, dexpanthenol 1 mg, cyanocobalamin 2.5 μg, niacinamide 50 mg, *dl*-alpha-tocopheryl acetate 0.5 IU, iron 15 mg, calcium 120 mg, manganese 0.5 mg, zinc 0.6 mg, and magnesium 3 mg.

Clusivol Syrup (Ayerst): Each 5 ml contains vitamin A acetate 2,500 units, ergocalciferol 400 units, ascorbic acid 20 mg, thiamine hydrochloride 1 mg, riboflavin 1 mg, pyridoxine hydrochloride 0.6 mg, dexpanthenol 3 mg, cyanocobalamin 2 μg, niacinamide 5 mg, iron 3 mg, manganese 0.5 mg, zinc 0.5 mg, and magnesium 3 mg.

Decavitamin U.S.P.: Each tablet contains vitamin A 4,000 U.S.P. units, vitamin D 400 U.S.P. units, vitamin E 15 IU, ascorbic acid 70 mg, pantothenate calcium 10 mg, cyanocobalamin 5 μg, folic acid 100 μg, niacinamide 20 mg, pyridoxine hydrochloride 2 mg, riboflavin 2 mg, and thiamine hydrochloride 2 mg (certain minor chemical alterations are indicated as acceptable in the U.S.P.).

Dical D Capsules (Abbott): Each capsule contains ergocalciferol 133 units and dicalcium phosphate 500 mg.

Dical D Wafers (Abbott): Each wafer contains ergocalciferol 200 units and dicalcium phosphate 1 g.

En-Cebrin (Lilly): Each capsule contains vitamin A 4,000 units, vitamin D 400 units, thiamine mononitrate 3 mg, riboflavin 2 mg, niacinamide 10 mg, pyridoxine hydrochloride 1.7 mg, vitamin B_{12} equivalent 5 μg, pantothenic acid 5 mg, ascorbic acid 50 mg, calcium carbonate 250 mg, iron 30 mg, iodine 0.15 mg, copper 1 mg, magnesium 5 mg, manganese 1 mg, and zinc 1.5 mg.

Engran (Squibb): Each tablet contains vitamin A acetate 6,000 units, ergocalciferol 400 units, thiamine mononitrate 3 mg, riboflavin 3 mg, pyridoxine hydrochloride 2 mg, cyanocobalamin 2 μg, niacinamide 20 mg, pantothenate calcium 5 mg, ascorbate sodium 75 mg, calcium 100 mg, iodine 0.15 mg, iron 45 mg, copper 1 mg, manganese 1 mg, and zinc 1.5 mg.

Engran-HP (Squibb): Each tablet contains vitamin A acetate 6,000 units, ergocalciferol 400 units, thiamine mononitrate 3 mg, riboflavin 3 mg, pyridoxine hydrochloride 25 mg, cyanocobalamin 2 μg, niacinamide 20 mg, pantothenate calcium 5 mg, ascorbate sodium 100 mg, folic acid 1.5 mg, calcium 100 mg, iodine 0.15 mg, iron 45 mg, copper 2 mg, manganese 1 mg, magnesium 100 mg, and zinc 1.5 mg.

Filibon (Lederle): Each capsule contains vitamin A acetate 4,000 units, vitamin D 400 units, thiamine mononitrate 3 mg, riboflavin 2 mg, pyridoxine hydrochloride 1 mg, ascrobic acid 50 mg, niacinamide 10 mg, vitamin B_{12} equivalent 2 μg, calcium 230 mg, iron 30 mg, magnesium 0.15 mg, potassium 0.835 mg, copper 0.15 mg, iodine 0.01 mg, manganese 0.05 mg, and zinc 0.085 mg.

Filibon FA (Lederle): Each capsule contains same formulation as Filibon plus folic acid 1 mg.

Filibon Forte (Lederle): Each tablet contains vitamin A acetate 6,000 units, vitamin D 400 units, tocopheryl acid succinate 30 IU, ascorbic acid 100 mg, niacinamide 21 mg, pyridoxine hydrochloride 10 mg, pantothenic acid 5 mg, thiamine mononitrate 3 mg, riboflavin 3 mg, folic acid 1 mg, vitamin B_{12} equivalent 5 μg, calcium 350 mg, iron 45 mg, and iodine 0.15 mg.

Filibon OT (Lederle): Each tablet contains same formulation as Filibon plus dioctyl sodium sulfosuccinate 100 mg.

Geriplex FS (Parke, Davis): Each capsule contains vitamin A acetate 5,000 units, ascorbic acid 50 mg, thiamine mononitrate 5 mg, riboflavin 5 mg, cyanocobalamin 2 μg, choline dihydrogen citrate 20 mg, niacinamide 15 mg, *d*-alpha-tocopheryl acid succinate 5 IU, ferrous sulfate 30 mg, manganese sulfate 4 mg, copper sulfate 4 mg, zinc sulfate 2 mg, dibasic calcium phosphate 200 mg, *Aspergillus oryzae* enzymes 162.5 mg, and dioctyl sodium sulfosuccinate 100 mg.

Gevrabon Liquid (Lederle): Each 30 ml contains thiamine hydrochloride 5 mg, riboflavin 2.5 mg, pyridoxine hydrochloride 1 mg, cyanocobalamin 1 μg, niacinamide 50 mg, inositol 100 mg, choline 100 mg, pantothenic acid 10 mg, potassium 10 mg, zinc 2 mg, iodine 0.1 mg, magnesium 2 mg, manganese 2 mg, iron 20 mg, and alcohol 18%.

Larobec (Roche): Each tablet contains thiamine mononitrate 15 mg, riboflavin 15 mg, niacinamide 100 mg, pantothenate calcium 20 mg, folic acid 0.5 mg, cyanocobalamin 5 μg, and ascorbic acid 500 mg.

Mi-Cebrin (Lilly): Each tablet contains thiamine mononitrate 10 mg, riboflavin 5 mg, pyridoxine hydrochloride 1.7 mg, pantothenic acid 10 mg, niacinamide 30 mg, vitamin B_{12} equivalent 3 μg, ascorbic acid 100 mg, vitamin E 5 mg, vitamin A 10,000 units, vitamin D 1,000 units, iron 15 mg, copper 1 mg, iodine 0.15 mg, manganese 1 mg, magnesium 5 mg, and zinc 1.5 mg.

Mi-Cebrin T (Lilly): Each tablet contains thiamine mononitrate 15 mg, riboflavin 10 mg, pyridoxine hydrochloride 2 mg, pantothenic acid 10 mg, niacinamide 100 mg, vitamin B_{12} equivalent 7.5 μg, ascorbic acid 150 mg, vitamin E 5 mg, vitamin A 25,000 units, vitamin D 1,000 units, iron 15 mg, copper 1 mg, iodine 0.15 mg, manganese 1 mg, magnesium 5 mg, and zinc 1.5 mg.

Mission Prenatal (Mission): Each tablet contains iron (as ferrous gluconate) 38.6 mg, ascorbic acid 100 mg, thiamine mononitrate 5 mg, pyridoxine hydrochloride 3 mg, riboflavin 2 mg, niacinamide 10 mg, pantothenate calcium 1 mg, cyanocobalamin 2 μg, vitamin A acetate 4,000 units, ergocalciferol 400 units, and calcium (as gluconate and lactate) 50 mg.

Multicebrin (Lilly): Each tablet contains thiamine mononitrate 3 mg, riboflavin 3 mg, pyridoxine hydrochloride 1.2 mg, pantothenic acid 5 mg, niacinamide 25 mg, vitamin B_{12} equivalent 3 μg, ascorbic acid 75 mg, vitamin E 6 mg, vitamin A 10,000 units, and vitamin D 1,000 units.

Mulvidren (Stuart): Each tablet contains vitamin A palmitate 4,000 units, vitamin D 400 units, ascorbic acid and ascorbate sodium 75 mg, thiamine mononitrate 2 mg, riboflavin 2 mg, pyridoxine hydrochloride 1.2 mg, cyanocobalamin 3 μg, pantothenate calcium 3 mg, and niacinamide 10 mg.

M.V.I. Multivitamin Infusion (USV): Each 10 ml of solution or 5 ml of concentrate contains ascorbic acid 500 mg, vitamin A 10,000 units, ergocalciferol 1,000 units, *d*-alpha tocopheryl acetate 5 IU, thiamine hydrochloride 50 mg, riboflavin 10 mg, pyridoxine hydrochloride 15 mg, niacinamide 100 mg, and dexpanthenol 25 mg.

Myadec (Parke, Davis): Each capsule contains vitamin A palmitate 25,000 units, ergocalciferol 400 units, ascorbic acid 200 mg, thiamine mononitrate 10 mg, riboflavin 10 mg, pyridoxine hydrochloride 5 mg, cyanocobalamin 5 μg, niacinamide 100 mg, *d*-alpha-tocopheryl acetate 15 IU, iodine 0.15 mg, manganese 1 mg, iron 20 mg, copper 2 mg, zinc 1.5 mg, and magnesium 75 mg.

Natabec (Parke, Davis): Each capsule contains vitamin A acetate 4,000 units, ergocalciferol 400 units, ascorbic acid 50 mg, thiamine mononitrate 3 mg, riboflavin 2 mg, pyridoxine hydrochloride 3 mg, cyanocobalamin 5 μg, niacinamide 10 mg, ferrous sulfate 150 mg, and calcium carbonate 600 mg.

Natabec-F.A. (Parke, Davis): Each capsule contains same formulation as Natabec plus folic acid 0.1 mg.

Natabec Rx (Parke, Davis): Each capsule contains same formulation as Natabec plus folic acid 1 mg.

Natalins (Mead Johnson): Each tablet contains iron 40 mg, calcium 250 mg, ascorbic acid 100 mg, vitamin D 400 units, vitamin A 6,000 units, vitamin E 10 IU, thiamine 1.5 mg, riboflavin 2.0 mg, niacinamide 20 mg, pyridoxine hydrochloride 2.5 mg, pantothenate calcium 10 mg, folic acid 0.1 mg, and cyanocobalamin 6 μg.

Obron-6 (Roerig): Each tablet contains vitamin A acetate 5,000 units, ergocalciferol 500 units, thiamine mononitrate 3 mg, riboflavin 2 mg, pyridoxine hydrochloride 10 mg, cobalamin concentrate 2 μg, ascorbic acid 50 mg, niacinamide 20 mg, pantothenate calcium 1 mg, calcium carbonate 243 mg, iron (from ferrous sulfate) 33 mg, manganese 0.3 mg, magnesium 1 mg, potassium 1.7 mg, and zinc 0.4 mg.

One-A-Day (Miles): Each tablet contains vitamin A 5,000 units, vitamin D 400 units, thiamine 1.5 mg, riboflavin 1.7 mg, niacinamide 20 mg, ascorbic acid 60 mg, pyridoxine 2 mg, cyanocobalamin 5 μg, pantothenic acid 10 mg, and folic acid 0.1 mg.

One-A-Day Plus Iron (Miles): Each tablet contains same formulation as One-A-Day plus 18 mg of iron as ferrous fumarate.

Optilets (Abbott): Each tablet contains vitamin A 25,000 units, vitamin D 400 units, thiamine hydrochloride 10 mg, riboflavin 5 mg, niacinamide 100 mg, pyridoxine hydrochloride 5 mg, cyanocobalamin 6 μg, pantothenate calcium 20 mg, and ascorbic acid 200 mg.

Os-Cal (Marion): Each tablet contains ergocalciferol 125 units, calcium 250 mg, and trace minerals from oyster shell.

Poly-Vi-Sol Drops (Mead Johnson): Each milliliter contains vitamin A 2,000 units, vitamin D 400 units, vitamin E 5 units, ascorbic acid 60 mg, thiamine 0.6 mg, riboflavin 0.7 mg, niacin 8 mg, pyridoxine 0.6 mg, and pantothenic acid 4 mg.

Poly-Vi-Sol Tablets (Mead Johnson): Each chewable tablet contains vitamin A 3,500 units, vitamin D 400 units, ascorbic acid 75 mg, thiamine 1.1 mg, riboflavin 1.2 mg, niacinamide 15 mg, vitamin E 4 IU, pyridoxine 1.2 mg, cyanocobalamin 5 μg, pantothenic acid 7 mg, and folic acid 0.1 mg.

Poly-Vi-Sol Liquid (Mead Johnson): Each 5 ml contains vitamin A 4,000 units, vitamin D 400 units, ascorbic acid 75 mg, thiamine 1.2 mg, riboflavin 1.5 mg, and niacinamide 15 mg.

Pramet (Ross): Each tablet contains iron (as ferrous sulfate) 60 mg, vitamin A acetate 4,000 units, ergocalciferol 400 units, ascorbic acid 100 mg, thiamine mononitrate 3 mg, riboflavin 2 mg, pyridoxine hydrochloride 5 mg, cyanocobalamin 3 μg, niacinamide 10 mg, pantothenate calcium 1 mg, iodine 0.1 mg, calcium 250 mg, and copper 0.15 mg.

Pramet FA (Ross): Each tablet contains same formulation as Pramet plus folic acid 1 mg.

Pramilet FA (Ross): Each tablet contains folic acid 1 mg, iron (as ferrous fumarate) 40 mg, vitamin A acetate 4,000 units, ergocalciferol 400 units, ascorbate sodium 60 mg, thiamine mononitrate 3 mg, riboflavin 2 mg, pyridoxine hydrochloride 3 mg, cyanocobalamin 3 μg, niacinamide 10 mg, pantothenate calcium 1 mg, calcium (as calcium carbonate) 250 mg, magnesium (as oxide) 0.15 mg, zinc (as oxide) 0.085 mg, iodine (as calcium iodate) 0.1 mg, and copper (as chloride) 0.15 mg.

Pramilets (Ross): Each tablet contains same formulation as Pramilet FA with the omission of folic acid.

Sigtab (Upjohn): Each tablet contains vitamin A 5,000 units, vitamin D 500 units, thiamine mononitrate 10 mg, riboflavin 10 mg, ascorbic acid 333 mg, niacinamide 100 mg, pyridoxine hydrochloride 2 mg, pantothenate calcium 20 mg, folic acid 0.033 mg, cyanocobalamin 4 μg, and vitamin E 15 IU.

Stresscaps (Lederle): Each capsule contains thiamine mononitrate 10 mg, riboflavin 10 mg, pyridoxine hydrochloride 2 mg, cyanocobalamin 4 μg, ascorbic acid 300 mg, niacinamide 100 mg, and pantothenate calcium 20 mg.

Stuart Prenatal (Stuart): Each tablet contains vitamin A palmitate 6,000 units, ergocalciferol 400 units, ascorbic acid 100 mg, thiamine mononitrate 3 mg, riboflavin 3 mg, pyridoxine hydrochloride 10 mg, cyanocobalamin 5 μg, niacinamide 20 mg, pantothenic acid 5 mg, iron 65 mg, and calcium 350 mg.

Stuart Prenatal with Folic Acid (Stuart): Each tablet contains same formulation as Stuart Prenatal plus folic acid 0.3 mg.

Surbex with C (Abbott): Each tablet contains thiamine 6 mg, riboflavin 6 mg, niacinamide 30 mg, pantothenic acid 10 mg, pyridoxine hydrochloride 2.5 mg, ascorbic acid 250 mg, and cyanocobalamin 2 μg.

Surbex-T (Abbott): Each tablet contains thiamine mononitrate 15 mg, riboflavin 10 mg, niacinamide 100 mg, pyridoxine hydrochloride 5 mg, cyanocobalamin 4 μg, pantothenate calcium 20 mg, and ascorbic acid 500 mg.

Thera-Combex (Parke, Davis): Each capsule contains thiamine mononitrate 25 mg, riboflavin 15 mg, pyridoxine hydrochloride 1 mg, cyanocobalamin 5 μg, niacinamide 100 mg, *dl*-panthenol 20 mg, ascorbic acid 250 mg, and *Aspergillus oryzae* enzymes 162.5 mg.

Thera-Combex H.P. (Parke, Davis): Each capsule contains ascorbic acid 500 mg, thiamine mononitrate 25 mg, riboflavin 15 mg, pyridoxine hydrochloride 10 mg, cyanocobalamin 5 μg, niacinamide 100 mg, and *dl*-panthenol 20 mg.

Theragran Liquid (Squibb): Each 5 ml contains vitamin A palmitate 25,000 units, thiamine hydrochloride 10 mg, riboflavin 10 mg, pyridoxine hydrochloride 5 mg, cyanocobalamin 5 μg, ascorbic acid 200 mg, cholecalciferol 400 units, niacinamide 100 mg, and panthenol 20 mg.

Theragran Tablets (Squibb): Each tablet contains vitamin A acetate 25,000 units, ergocalciferol 400 units, thiamine mononitrate 10 mg, riboflavin 10 mg, pyridoxine hydrochloride 5 mg, cyanocobalamin 5 μg, niacinamide 100 mg, pantothenate calcium 20 mg, ascorbate sodium 200 mg, and *d*-alpha-tocopheryl acid succinate 15 IU.

Theragran M Tablets (Squibb): Each tablet contains same formulation as Theragran Tablets with additional 2 mg copper, 0.15 mg iodine, 12 mg iron, 65 mg magnesium, 1 mg manganese, and 1.5 mg zinc.

Tri-Vi-Sol Drops (Mead Johnson): Each milliliter contains vitamin A 2,000 units, vitamin D 400 units, and ascorbic acid 60 mg.

Tri-Vi-Sol Tablets (Mead Johnson): Each chewable tablet contains vitamin A 3,500 units, vitamin D 400 units, and ascorbic acid 75 mg.

Tri-Vi-Sol with Iron Drops (Mead Johnson): Each milliliter contains same formulation as Tri-Vi-Sol Drops plus 10 mg iron (as ferrous fumarate).

Unicap Capsules (Upjohn): Each capsule contains vitamin A 5,000 units, vitamin D 500 units, thiamine hydrochloride 2.5 mg, riboflavin 2.5 mg, ascorbic acid 50 mg, niacinamide 20 mg, pyridoxine hydrochloride 0.5 mg, pantothenate calcium 5 mg, cyanocobalamin 2 μg, and vitamin E 10 IU.i,

Unicap Tablets (Upjohn): Each chewable tablet contains vitamin A 4,000 units, vitamin D 400 units, thiamine mononitrate 2 mg, riboflavin 2 mg, ascorbic acid 75 mg, niacinamide 18 mg, pyridoxine hydrochloride 1 mg, pantothenate calcium 5 mg, and cyanocobalamin 2 μg.

Unicap Capsules (Upjohn): Each capsule contains vitamin A 5,000 units, vitamin D 500 units, thiamine hydrochloride 2.5 mg, riboflavin 2.5 mg, ascorbic acid 50 mg, niacinamide 20 mg, pyridoxine hydrochloride 0.5 mg, pantothenate calcium 5 mg, cyanocobalamin 2 μg, and vitamin E 10 IU.

Unicap Tablets (Upjohn): Each chewable tablet contains vitamin A 4,000 units, vitamin D 400 units, thiamine mononitrate 2 mg, riboflavin 2 mg, ascorbic acid 75 mg, niacinamide 18 mg, pyridoxine hydrochloride 1 mg, pantothenate calcium 5 mg, and cyanocobalamin 2 μg.

Unicap Therapeutic Tablets (Upjohn): Each tablet contains vitamin A 5,000 units, vitamin D 400 units, thiamine mononitrate 10 mg, riboflavin 10 mg, ascorbic acid 300 mg, niacinamide 100 mg, pyridoxine hydrochloride 2 mg, pantothenate calcium 20 mg, vitamin B_{12} activity 4 μg, vitamin E 30 IU, iron 10 mg, iodine 0.15 mg, copper 1 mg, calcium 50 mg, manganese 1 mg, magnesium 6 mg, and potassium 5 mg.

Vi-Daylin Drops (Ross): Each milliliter contains vitamin A 1,500 units, vitamin D 400 units, ascorbic acid 30 mg, *d*-alpha-tocopheryl acetate 5 IU, thiamine hydrochloride 0.4 mg, riboflavin 0.6 mg, pyridoxine hydrochloride 0.4 mg, and niacinamide 6 mg.

Vi-Daylin Liquid (Ross): Each 5 ml contains vitamin A 3,000 units, vitamin D 400 units, riboflavin 1.2 mg, pyridoxine 1 mg, ascorbic acid 50 mg, thiamine hydrochloride 1.5 mg, cyanocobalamin 3 μg, and niacinamide 10 mg.

Vi-Daylin ADC Drops (Ross): Each milliliter contains vitamin A 1,500 units, vitamin D 400 units, and ascorbic acid 30 mg.

Vi-Daylin Plus Iron ADC Drops (Ross): Each milliliter contains same formulation as Vi-Daylin ADC Drops plus ferrous sulfate 10 mg.

Vi-Daylin Chewable (Ross): Each chewable tablet contains vitamin A 4,000 units, vitamin D 400 units, ascorbic acid 75 mg, thiamine mononitrate 1.5 mg, riboflavin 1.2 mg, pyridoxine hydrochloride 1 mg, cyanocobalamin 3 μg, and niacinamide 10 mg.

Vi-Daylin Plus Iron Chewable (Ross): Each chewable tablet contains same formulation as Vi-Daylin Chewable plus ferrous fumarate 10 mg.

Chapter 15

MISCELLANEOUS NUTRITIONAL AGENTS

This chapter contains descriptions of several products used to provide nutrients orally when normal alimentation is not feasible, ie, when there is interference with digestion, absorption, or metabolism of food; when there is an allergic reaction to food; or when undernourishment occurs in some chronic illnesses. When prescribing these products, the physician should keep in mind all the nutritional requirements of the individual undergoing treatment. These, of course, vary according to the age, weight, and activity of the patient. A description of these requirements is beyond the scope of this book. For detailed information, the reader is referred to a report of the Food and Nutrition Board of the National Research Council: *Recommended Dietary Allowances*, ed. 7, Washington, D.C., National Academy of Sciences, 1968.

Other substances used to provide nutrients when normal alimentation is not feasible are described in Chapter 14, Vitamins and Sources of Vitamins, and in Chapter 16, Replenishers and Regulators of Water, Electrolytes, and Nutrients.

LAMBASE
MBF
MULL-SOY
NEO-MULL-SOY
NUTRAMIGEN
PROSOBEE
SIMILAC ISOMIL

These products are suitable substitutes for cow's milk in individuals with galactosemia, lactase deficiency, allergy to milk, milk-induced steatorrhea, or glycogenosis (glycogen storage disease). They also are useful for newborn infants with a family history of allergy to cow's milk and as diagnostic agents in determining intolerance to milk. The hypoallergenicity of these products is accomplished by substituting either hydrolyzed casein, soy flour, soy protein isolate, or homogenized beef or lamb for the protein in cow's milk. Intolerance to cow's milk sugars (galactose and lactose) is avoided by including either sucrose, maltose, dextrose, dextrins, arrowroot starch, or modified tapioca starch in their formulations. Usually fats, vitamins, and minerals also are present in the formulas. The product usually is used in an aqueous dilution that provides 20 calories per fluid ounce.

USUAL DOSAGE.—*Oral: Adults and children*, used as required by the individual.

PREPARATIONS.—

Lambase (Gerber). Liquid containing lamb, dextrins-maltose-dextrose (from corn), modified tapioca starch, corn oil, sesame oil, vitamin A, thiamine hydrochloride, riboflavin, pyridoxine hydrochloride, ascorbate sodium, vitamin D, tocopheryl acetate, phytonadione, calcium, iron, and phosphorus.

MBF (Gerber). Liquid containing beef hearts, sucrose, sesame oil, modified tapioca starch, vitamin A, thiamine hydrochloride, pyridoxine hydrochloride, ascorbate sodium, vitamin D, tocopheryl acetate, phytonadione, calcium, iron, and phosphorus.

Mull-Soy (Borden). Liquid containing soy protein, soy oil, sucrose, invert sucrose, vitamin A, thiamine, riboflavin, pyridoxine, cyanocobalamin, ascorbic acid, vitamins D and E, niacin, pantothenate calcium, folic acid, inositol, choline, calcium, phosphorus, iron, zinc, magnesium, manganese, copper, and iodine.

Neo-Mull-Soy (Borden). Liquid containing sucrose, soy oil, soy protein isolate, methionine, vitamin A, thiamine, riboflavin, pyridoxine, cyanocobalamin, vitamins D and E, niacin, inositol, choline, pantothenate calcium, folic acid, calcium, phosphorus, iron, iodine, magnesium, zinc, manganese, and copper.

Nutramigen (Mead Johnson). Powder containing hydrolyzed casein, sucrose, arrowroot starch, highly refined corn oil, vitamin A, thiamine, riboflavin, pyridoxine, cyanocobalamin, ascorbic acid, vitamins D and E, niacinamide, folic acid, pantothenate calcium, calcium, phosphorus, iron, iodine, copper, magnesium, potassium, zinc, biotin, and choline.

ProSobee (Mead Johnson). Liquid containing sucrose, soy oil, soy protein isolate, dl-methionine, corn syrup solids, vitamin A, thiamine, riboflavin, pyridoxine, cyanocobalamin, ascorbic acid, vitamins D, E, and K, niacin, folic acid, choline, pantothenic acid, inositol, calcium, phosphorus, magnesium, iron, iodine, copper, zinc, manganese, sodium, potassium, and chloride.

Similac Isomil (Ross). Liquid containing water, sucrose, corn syrup solids, soy protein isolate, corn oil, coconut oil, corn starch, monoglycerides and diglycerides, soy phospholipids, vitamin A, thiamine, riboflavin, pyridoxine, cyanocobalamin, ascorbic acid, vitamin D, alpha-tocopheryl acetate, phytonadione, racemic methionine, choline, niacin, pantothenate calcium, biotin, folic acid, zinc, potassium, iodine, iron, and copper.

LIPOMUL-ORAL

This emulsion containing 67% corn oil with emulsifying, flavoring, and sweetening agents is used as a high calorie dietary supplement. One ounce of emulsion provides about 180 calories, primarily from the corn oil. It is indicated in underweight and malnourished individuals, during prolonged convalescence and chronic illness, and postoperatively to furnish calories and spare dietary protein for body protein deposition.

Nausea or satiety occasionally has occurred after use of this product. Lipomul-Oral should be used cautiously in patients with gallbladder disorders or diabetes.

USUAL DOSAGE.—*Oral: Adults*, 30 to 60 ml two or three times daily. *Children*, 15 to 60 ml one or two times daily.

PREPARATIONS.—Lipomul-Oral (Upjohn). *Oral:* Emulsion containing 10 g of corn oil/15 ml.

PORTAGEN

This product is used when conventional food fats may not be well absorbed, digested, or utilized (eg, in pancreatic insufficiency, bile acid deficiency, lymphatic anomalies, steatorrhea, type I hyperlipoproteinemia). Its fat content consists of more than 95% medium-chain triglycerides (glycerol esters of octanoic and decanoic acids) which are more rapidly absorbed than the triglycerides of the long-chain fatty acids present in conventional food fats. Proteins, carbohydrates (essentially free of lactose), vitamins, and minerals are also included in the product. Portagen is usually used in aqueous dilutions that provide 20 or 30 calories per fluid ounce.

High levels of medium-chain triglycerides in the diet may result in high levels of medium-chain fatty acids in the blood and spinal fluid. These elevated levels may be associated with reversible coma in persons with hepatic cirrhosis and its complications, such as portacaval shunts or the tendency to encephalopathy. This product, therefore, should be used with caution in these individuals.

USUAL DOSAGE.—*Oral: Adults and children*, used as required by the individual.

PREPARATIONS.—Portagen (Mead Johnson). *Oral:* Powder containing sodium caseinate, corn syrup solids, sugar, medium chain triglycerides (fractionated coconut oil), corn oil, lecithin, vitamin A, thiamine, riboflavin, pyridoxine, cyanocobalamin, ascorbic acid, vitamins D and E, and niacinamide.

SIMILAR PREPARATION.—MCT Oil (Mead Johnson). *Oral:* A lipid fraction of coconut oil containing more than 95% medium-chain triglycerides of saturated fatty acids.

LOFENALAC

This product contains a low (average 0.08%) phenylalanine concentration and is used for the management of phenylketonuria. Its administration should be supplemented with other foods to provide all the other essential nutrients and sufficient phenylalanine to support physical and mental development. The use of Lofenalac is contraindicated in all individuals except those with phenylketonuria.

USUAL DOSAGE.—*Oral: Children,* sufficient Lofenalac and other foods to provide 20 to 30 mg of phenylalanine/kg of body weight daily.

PREPARATIONS.—Lofenalac (Mead Johnson). *Oral:* Powder containing corn syrup solids, specially processed casein hydrolysate low in phenylalanine, corn oil, sugar, arrowroot starch, amino acids, vitamin A, thiamine, riboflavin, pyridoxine, cyanocobalamin, ascorbic acid, vitamins D and E, niacinamide, pantothenate calcium, folic acid, iodine, biotin, choline, copper, and zinc.

Chapter 16

REPLENISHERS AND REGULATORS OF WATER ELECTROLYTES, AND NUTRIENTS

Water, electrolytes, and nutrients are used in a wide variety of disorders. In order to prescribe these agents rationally, the physician should understand the physiology and pathophysiology of normal and abnormal fluid and electrolyte balance, and know the fluid, electrolyte, and caloric needs of his patient.

The preparations used in fluid, electrolyte, and nutrient therapy are discussed in broad groups according to their chief indication. The discussion is divided for convenience and, with certain exceptions, the sections do not reflect individual electrolyte abnormalities. The discussion is limited to therapy for larger children and adults; more specialized references should be consulted for information on therapy in infants and smaller children, who are much more vulnerable than adults to fluid and electrolyte imbalances.

Fluid should be given intravenously only when other modes of administration are not feasible, and parenteral therapy should be discontinued as soon as practical. When the patient is dependent on intravenous fluids, it is recommended that the solutions given contain dextrose 5% (or higher percentage, if indicated) to meet minimal caloric needs, prevent ketosis, and decrease protein catabolism.

When drugs are added to parenteral solutions, the physician should be aware of possible physical and chemical incompatibilities. Some incompatibilities are readily noted, but subtle physical, chemical, and pharmacologic incompatibilities also may occur. An example is the inactivation of buffered penicillin G by parenteral solutions containing vitamin B complex with ascorbic acid. A good rule is to add only one drug at a time to an intravenous solution before administration unless it is known that two or more drugs are compatible. Incompatible drugs should be given in separate intravenous solutions.

It is outside the scope of this book to present a comprehensive discussion of the therapy of fluid and electrolyte imbalances. More detailed information on fluid and electrolyte disorders, including methods of calculating the volume of solutions to administer, may be found in *Signs and Symptoms*, 5th edition, edited by C. M. MacBryde and R. S. Blacklow, J. B. Lippincott Company, Philadelphia, 1970, and *Textbook of Medicine*, 13th edition, edited by P. B. Beeson and W. McDermott, W. B. Saunders Company, Philadelphia, 1971.

Abnormal States of Hydration

Because of the dynamic interrelationship between solute and fluid volume control, sodium and water depletion may be considered together. Abnormal states of hydration can be classified as: (1) loss of water in excess of sodium; (2) loss of sodium in excess of water; (3) volume depletion (dehydration); and (4) volume excess (overhydration, hypervolemia).

Loss of Water in Excess of Sodium (eg, from failure of intake, as in coma; diabetes insipidus; hyperhidrosis with no water intake; extensive skin damage from burns): Initially, it is important to provide water without electrolytes. For this purpose dextrose injection 5% or sodium chloride 0.2% to 0.45% with dextrose 5% is recommended. After a normal plasma tonicity has been achieved, more solution may be needed to expand the extracellular fluid volume to normal. Sodium chloride injection 0.9% is recommended for this purpose.

Loss of Sodium in Excess of Water (eg, from chronic renal insufficiency; acute tubular necrosis, especially in the diuretic phase; adrenocortical insufficiency; inappropriate secretion of antidiuretic hormone; vomiting; diarrhea): Sodium depletion occurs when the kidneys are unable to conserve sodium appropriately or when isotonic (or even hypotonic) losses, by any route, are replaced by water without salt. Sodium chloride tablets or sodium chloride injection should be administered to alleviate this condition, depending upon the circumstances. When the serum concentration of sodium is moderately reduced and kidney function is normal, administration of sodium chloride 0.9% is often all that is required. The extracellular fluid volume will be expanded to normal and a normal serum concentration of sodium will be achieved by a water diuresis. In severe degrees of hyponatremia associated with central nervous system symptoms, sodium chloride 3% or 5% may be administered cautiously. Once hyponatremia due to abnormal kidney function has been corrected, dehydration usually will have been corrected only partially; sodium chloride injection 0.9% should then be administered. Hyponatremia due to adrenocortical insufficiency should be treated with sodium chloride injection of appropriate strength, along with hormone replacement therapy. In most cases of inappropriate secretion of antidiuretic hormone, restriction of water intake is enough to correct the condition.

Volume Depletion: Volume depletion is the excessive loss of sodium and water in nearly isotonic proportions (eg, from vomiting, diarrhea, systemic infection, fistula drainage). Sodium chloride injection 0.9% may be used to correct this condition. Actual fluid losses and changes in weight should be measured, and the patient should be carefully observed for signs of water retention.

Solutions that are purported to be similar in composition to lost body fluids in electrolyte concentration (eg, Duodenal Solution) usually offer no advantage over sodium chloride injection 0.9% for short-term use. It is understood that serum electrolytes will be monitored and that potassium and other ions will be added as indicated.

The replacement of normal losses of sodium and water is considered in the section on Carbohydrate, Protein, and Lipid Deficits and Maintenance Therapy. Loss of sodium and water from plasma into the interstitial fluid is discussed in the section on Imbalances Caused by Internal Fluid Shifts.

Volume Excess (eg, from congestive heart failure, nephrotic syndrome, cirrhosis with ascites): Drugs used to treat hypervolemia are discussed in Chapter 1, Digitalis Glycosides, and Chapter 7, Diuretics. Restriction of sodium in the diet, phlebotomy, plasmapheresis, and other measures also are employed in the treatment of this imbalance.

Imbalances Caused by Internal Fluid Shifts

If a shift of extracellular fluid from the plasma to the interstitial fluid is localized (eg, venous thrombosis in a limb, trauma, infiltration of an intravenous solution), usually no treatment is indicated other than to relieve the patient's discomfort by elevating the limb or applying warm compresses. In massive shifts with significant reduction in plasma volume, the use of normal human plasma, dextran, normal human serum albumin [Albumisol, Albuspan, Buminate, Pro-Bumin, Proserum], plasma protein fraction [Plasmanate, Protenate], and/or sodium chloride injection may be indicated. For a discussion on the use of all but the latter, see Chapter 10, Blood, Blood Components, and Blood Substitutes.

Acid-Base Disturbances

Respiratory Acidosis: Hypercapnia and respiratory acidosis are corrected by increasing alveolar ventilation. This, in turn, may be accomplished by treating an underlying infection or toxic reaction, removing a mechanical obstruction, or assisting respiration when trauma, muscle weakness, or poisoning require it.

Respiratory Alkalosis: Since respiratory alkalosis itself usually requires no therapy, treatment is generally directed at the underlying disorder (eg, *Staphylococcus aureus* or gram-negative bacterial sepsis, hepatic failure). Sedatives may be used if indicated.

Metabolic Acidosis: Treatment of metabolic acidosis will vary with the nature of the underlying disorder. In many instances, specific therapy with an alkalizing agent is unnecessary. However, an alkalizing agent, preferably sodium bicarbonate, should be given when the plasma bicarbonate level falls below 16 mEq/liter or the blood pH is below 7.25. Sodium lactate generally is not the preferred therapy because the patient may not be able to convert lactate to bicarbonate and because there is a risk of further complicating a condition of lactic acidosis.

Metabolic Alkalosis: In metabolic alkalosis, attention should be given to the underlying disorder. For example, alkalosis is often caused by a potassium or chloride deficit which, in turn, may be caused by the use of diuretics or hormones, or by a poor diet, vomiting, or gastric suction. Hypokalemia almost invariably accompanies metabolic alkalosis, and is often due to a shift of potassium into cells because of the alkalosis. If total body potassium is decreased, the cause of the deficit must be eliminated and/or potassium administered before or during correction of the alkalosis.

Results of blood chemistry and urine studies should be used as a guide to therapy. Providing chloride ion (potassium chloride and/or sodium chloride) is essential in correcting all types of metabolic alkalosis, because plasma bicarbonate levels will not be reduced and sodium and potassium will not be retained unless chloride is made available. An adequate urinary output must be assured when potassium is given.

Potassium Imbalances

Potassium Deficit: In treating potassium depletion, there is always the risk of producing hyperkalemia; this is particularly true if therapy in patients with organic or functional renal abnormalities is overly aggressive. Therefore, caution is necessary and potassium should be given orally whenever possible. Prolonged therapy is often necessary.

The drug of choice for oral replacement of potassium is potassium chloride solution. Potassium chloride should be used in preference to other salts of potassium since, in most hypokalemic states, hypochloremia is also present and the chloride ion is needed to allow complete potassium replacement. Potassium gluconate [Kaon], potassium bicarbonate and citrate [K-Lyte], and the combination of potassium acetate, potassium bicarbonate, and potassium citrate [Potassium Triplex] are recommended for use in the rare instances in which hypokalemia is associated with hyperchloremia. There is no evidence that any of these preparations is uniformly tolerated better than potassium chloride solution.

If the patient is unable to take potassium orally and if the potassium deficit is severe, potassium chloride must be given intravenously. The electrocardiogram should be checked frequently, because excessive potassium can be detected more rapidly by changes in the electrocardiogram than by measuring serum potassium levels. An adequate urinary output also must be assured. Acidosis, if present, must be treated. Potassium chloride injection is preferably given in concentrations not higher than 40 to 60 mEq/liter; 10 to 15 mEq per hour is a safe rate.

Potassium Excess: The measure or measures to be used in the treatment of hyperkalemia depend upon the degree of hyperkalemia and the severity of its manifestations. In urgent situations (when the electrocardiogram is distinctly abnormal due to hyperkalemia, or the serum potassium level is greater than 6.5 mEq/liter and either the patient's previous history is unknown or this represents a sudden increase), the intravenous infusion of sodium bicarbonate 7.5% is preferred; if electrocardiographic abnormalities persist, 40 to 160 mEq may be injected intravenously over a five-minute period and then repeated after 10 to 15 minutes. Sodium bicarbonate reduces the serum potassium level by causing potassium to shift into cells. If the electrocardiogram reveals absent P waves or a broad QRS complex, it is also advisable to inject 5 to 10 ml of calcium gluconate 10% intravenously over a two-minute period in order to overcome the cardiac toxicity of potassium (but only if the patient is not receiving digitalis). The electrocardiogram should be constantly monitored. If electrocardiographic abnormalities continue, repeated injections of sodium bicarbonate and calcium gluconate (the latter in doses of 1 g [10 ml]) may be given with one- to two-minute intervals between doses. Intravenous infusion of dextrose also causes a shift of potassium into cells, although less rapidly than with sodium bicarbonate. Dextrose solutions should be given with sodium bicarbonate. Usually, 300 to 500 ml of dextrose injection 10% is administered over a 30- to 60-minute period. Insulin injection (crystalline zinc insulin, regular insulin) has been added to the dextrose solution (1 unit/5 g of dextrose) to encourage a further potassium shift; however, insulin given as a separate injection is preferred.

If hyperkalemia cannot be controlled within safe limits by the above procedures, peritoneal or extracorporeal dialysis is indicated. When the infusions are effective but the potassium must be removed from the body because of a continuing excretory problem, an exchange resin (eg, sodium polystyrene sulfonate [Kayexalate]) should be used. Its action will not be evident for at least 24 hours. The exchange resin preferably is given orally, but it may be given rectally in retention enemas or in a dialysis bag.

Magnesium Imbalance

Magnesium Deficit: Magnesium depletion may accompany malabsorption, prolonged intravenous feeding, chronic alcoholism, renal tubular damage, and other diseases when secondary hypocalcemia and hypokalemia develop with or without neurologic abnormalities. Magnesium sulfate may be given parenterally to treat hypomagnesemia. Magnesium (as magnesium acetate) also is included as an essential cation in multiple electrolyte solutions to prevent iatrogenic magnesium deficiency during routine fluid and electrolyte therapy. Magnesium should not be administered if the patient's renal function is impaired.

Magnesium Excess: Hypermagnesemia occurs primarily in patients with chronic renal insufficiency and it results in depression of both the central nervous system and the peripheral neuromuscular junctions. In most situations, patients can tolerate moderately elevated plasma levels of magnesium, but toxic levels may occur with continued administration of magnesium in patients with severe renal impairment. Occasionally, third-degree atrioventricular block and/or respiratory arrest may occur. The administration of calcium salts (see Chapter 17, Blood Calcium Regulators) will counteract the respiratory effects to some extent. Dialysis may be indicated if there is a large excess of magnesium with coexistent renal insufficiency.

Ammonia Imbalance

Certain pathologic conditions (eg, hepatic coma, urea cycle failure) and intravenous hyperalimentation with fibrin or casein hydrolysates may produce an excess of ammonia in the plasma that, in turn, may lead to central nervous system derangements if there is shunting of portal blood. Two ammonia detoxicants (arginine hydrochloride and sodium glutamate) have been used specifically to treat ammonia excess, but their value has not been conclusively demonstrated. Reduction or elimination of protein intake, intravenous administration of dextrose, correction of any electrolyte imbalance, administration of neomycin or other antibiotics to reduce the intestinal flora (to be used with caution because of possible diarrhea), and use of enemas may be more beneficial.

Carbohydrate, Protein, and Lipid Deficits and Maintenance Therapy

Commercially prepared oral nutrients are discussed in Chapter 15, Miscellaneous Nutritional Agents. A well-tolerated, adequate formula given by stomach tube may be more convenient than administering intravenous fluids and can meet nutritional needs more adequately than infusions which supply only carbohydrate calories. Feeding by stomach tube is not without danger, however, for aspiration pneumonia, diarrhea, dehydration, azotemia, and hypernatremia can occur.

However, in patients with serious gastrointestinal disorders or anomalies which require surgery, parenteral alimentation is indicated for nutritional support to sustain life. Furthermore, parenteral nutrition should be provided if the patient is unable to eat, digest, or absorb ingested nutrients normally when tube feeding is not feasible. When patients are unable to eat and drink for approximately one to three days, at least 100 to 150 g of carbohydrate per day should be given intravenously to minimize protein catabolism and the risk of ketosis. For most patients, sodium chloride 0.2% to 0.3% with dextrose injection 5% is useful; this solution supplies water and electrolyte needs as well as calories. Fructose or invert sugar injection (50% dextrose, 50% fructose) offers no advantage over dextrose.

Although insulin (crystalline zinc insulin, regular insulin) sometimes has been added to concentrated dextrose solutions to increase metabolism and decrease hyperglycemia and glycosuria, the current evidence indicates that an appreciable quantity is adsorbed onto the container surface and thus is not available. Therefore, insulin should be given subcutaneously every four to six hours as a separate injection.

When prolonged intravenous maintenance therapy is necessary, the physician should consider giving protein hydrolysate [Aminosol, Amigen, C.P.H., Hyprotigen] or amino acid solution [Fre Amine] concomitantly with large quantities of carbohydrate, vitamins, and minerals to treat or prevent negative nitrogen balance and maintain or increase weight. Simultaneous administration of 100 to 150 carbohydrate calories per gram of nitrogen is necessary for efficient utilization of intravenous amino acids.

Electrolytes are necessary for protein synthesis; commercial preparations of protein hydrolysate injection contain varying amounts of sodium, potassium, magnesium, and other ions, depending on the source of the protein. Supplementation with additional electrolytes, particularly potassium, is usually necessary. Vitamins and salts of calcium, phosphate, magnesium, and iron are added to the intravenous fluids or administered intramuscularly as indicated. For prolonged infusions, certain trace elements (eg, zinc, copper, manganese, cobalt, iodine) also may be supplied.

The technique for providing total parenteral nutrition by the slow and continuous administration of amino acid or protein hydrolysate injection with dextrose solution 20% to 25% is called parenteral or intravenous hyperalimentation. The concentrated, hyperosmotic, and hypertonic nature of the infusate necessitates administering solutions into the vena cava or atrium via an indwelling catheter, and strict aseptic technique must be observed to avoid septicemia. Arteriovenous shunts also have been used.

Since hyperalimentation fluids have limited stability, they are not commercially available as prepared solutions, but kits for the easy preparation of this fluid are commercially available. Prepared solutions are chemically stable for up to 30 days, but because of the possibility of bacterial contamination, it is recommended that these solutions be administered as soon after mixing as possible. Darkened or cloudy solutions should not be used. Because of the risks and potential complications involved, *the physician should be familiar with the techniques before initiating treatment with these preparations.*

Intravenous lipid preparations are of investigational interest since they have a high caloric value. However, at present no commercial lipid preparations are available in the United States for intravenous use.

Vitamin Deficit

Only vitamin preparations used for short-term parenteral therapy are discussed in this chapter; other vitamin preparations are discussed in Chapter 14, Vitamins and Sources of Vitamins.

The B complex vitamins and ascorbic acid may be depleted very rapidly, particularly in stress situations such as severe trauma, major surgery, or severe illness. Therefore, these vitamins are indicated in most patients who require parenteral feeding. Since most commercial parenteral preparations of vitamin B complex with ascorbic acid (eg, Bejectal with C, Berocca C, Solu-B with C, ViCert) contain sufficient vitamins to meet a fivefold increase in demands if administered once daily, it is necessary to add an ampule to only one intravenous solution per day or even less frequently. Large-volume intravenous solutions with vitamins incorporated as part of the finished product can be used, but some commercial products contain doses of B vitamins and ascorbic acid that are far in excess (more than five times) of the recommended daily allowances. Their use, particularly on a continuing basis, is costly and not in the patient's best interest when used needlessly; these solutions are denoted with an asterisk in the Table.

There is no evidence that a significant deficiency of the fat-soluble vitamins A, D, and E develops during an illness of relatively short duration or in patients with severe trauma, but it may be desirable to administer these vitamins once every seven to ten days to patients who are unable to ingest or absorb a normal diet. Vitamin K should be given if the prothrombin time is increased in patients receiving antibiotics that inhibit intestinal synthesis of vitamin K and in patients with an obstructed bile flow or significant fat malabsorption.

AGENTS USED IN ABNORMAL STATES OF HYDRATION

Dextrose injection and sodium chloride injection, in different strengths and combinations, can be used to treat most abnormal hydration states. However, other solutions have been developed for balanced maintenance or replacement of fluid and electrolytes; these provide potassium, magnesium, and bicarbonate precursors such as acetate, in addition to sodium and chloride. Such solutions avoid the excessive amounts of sodium and chloride present in sodium chloride injection which are undesirable for routine maintenance or replacement of these ions. A partial list of commercially available intravenous solutions is given in the Table at the end of this chapter. The evaluation of dextrose injection is included in the section on Agents Used in Carbohydrate and Protein Deficits.

SODIUM CHLORIDE
SODIUM CHLORIDE INJECTION

Isotonic sodium chloride injection is a 0.9% solution containing 154 mEq sodium and 154 mEq chloride/liter. In comparison, plasma contains 137 to 147 mEq sodium and 98 to 106 mEq chloride/liter. Concentrations of 0.11% to 0.45% are hypotonic, and concentrations of 3% and 5% are hypertonic. The concentration and tonicity of sodium chloride solutions determine their usefulness in different disorders.

Sodium chloride should be administered orally whenever possible. A solution containing 3 to 4 g of sodium chloride and 1.5 to 3 g of sodium bicarbonate/liter is satisfactory for oral administration.

Sodium chloride injection 0.9% may be given when fluid and electrolytes have been depleted in isotonic proportions, to maintain stable circulation during and after surgery in patients with normal kidney function, and to reduce the need for blood transfusions by temporarily maintaining plasma volume.

Hypotonic sodium chloride injection or a rotation of containers with dextrose injection 5% and sodium chloride injection 0.9% is indicated primarily when patients are unable to take fluid and nutrients orally for one or more days. Usually dextrose also is indicated as a source of calories.

Hypertonic sodium chloride injection should be reserved for treatment of acute, severe hyponatremia. It should be used with utmost caution in patients with cardiovascular-renal disease.

For other uses of sodium chloride, see Chapter 17, Blood Calcium Regulators, and Chapter 43, Expectorants and Inhalants.

Sodium chloride must be used with caution in patients with congestive heart failure, circulatory insufficiency, kidney failure, or hypoproteinemia. Signs of postoperative intolerance include cellular dehydration, asthenia, disorientation, anorexia, nausea, oliguria, and increased blood urea nitrogen levels. Hypertonic injections should be given slowly and cautiously in small volumes (200 to 400 ml) because of the danger of increased venous pressure. Central venous pressure should be monitored. Overreplacement of extracellular fluid with isotonic sodium chloride injection may lead to both pulmonary and peripheral edema.

USUAL DOSAGE.—

Oral, Intravenous: Adults, as required by the individual. The concentration of ions in plasma and intake-output figures should be used as guides.

Subcutaneous: Generally deemed inadvisable because volume replacement by this route will cause distention of tissues and possibly result in sloughing.

PREPARATIONS.—Sodium Chloride, U.S.P., Sodium Chloride Injection, U.S.P. See Table.

DEXTROSE AND SODIUM CHLORIDE INJECTION

This solution is administered parenterally for the same indications as dextrose injection (see the evaluation on Dextrose) when there is an additional need for electrolyte. Usually it is given intravenously. Subcutaneous administration is not desirable.

USUAL DOSAGE.—

Intravenous: Adults, as required by the individual.

Subcutaneous: Generally deemed inadvisable (see the individual evaluation on Dextrose).

PREPARATIONS.—Dextrose and Sodium Chloride Injection, U.S.P. See Table.

FRUCTOSE AND SODIUM CHLORIDE INJECTION

There is no evidence that fructose and sodium chloride has any advantages over dextrose and sodium chloride injection, and it is considerably more expensive.

USUAL DOSAGE.—No advice on dosage is given.

PREPARATIONS.—Fructose and Sodium Chloride, N.F. See Table.

BALANCED ELECTROLYTE INJECTION

[Isolyte, Normosol, Plasma-Lyte]

The indications for these hypotonic and isotonic electrolyte formulations are similar to those for sodium chloride injection 0.45% and 0.9%. These solutions are claimed to be superior to sodium chloride injection because they more closely approximate normal electrolyte losses. Just as electrolytes must be added to dextrose injection, sodium chloride injection, or dextrose and sodium chloride injection to meet the specific needs of the patient, multiple electrolyte solutions likewise are not intended to correct acidosis, alkalosis, or large deficits of individual electrolytes, nor to replace blood or plasma expanders when these are indicated.

USUAL DOSAGE.—*Intravenous, Subcutaneous* (the intravenous route is preferred): Hypotonic electrolyte preparations, *adults*, 50 ml/kg of body weight daily; *children*, 54 to 84 ml/kg of body weight daily. Isotonic electrolyte preparations, as required to replace acute electrolyte losses.

PREPARATIONS.—See Table.

RINGER'S INJECTION
LACTATED RINGER'S INJECTION

(Hartmann's Solution)

The indications for these solutions are similar to those for isotonic balanced electrolyte injection and isotonic sodium chloride injection; however, the isotonic balanced electrolyte injection more closely resembles the concentration of principal ions of plasma and should be used in preference to Ringer's injection and lactated Ringer's injection. Nevertheless, these solutions are used extensively in the treatment of hypovolemic shock and other conditions in which there is fluid loss.

USUAL DOSAGE.—*Intravenous, Subcutaneous: Adults*, as required by the individual.

PREPARATIONS.—Ringer's Injection, U.S.P., Lactated Ringer's Injection, U.S.P. See Table.

AGENTS USED IN CARBOHYDRATE AND PROTEIN DEFICITS

DEXTROSE
DEXTROSE INJECTION

Dextrose is administered parenterally to provide nutriment and water when oral feeding is not feasible. It usually is administered intravenously as a 5% aqueous infusion; this solution is approximately isotonic with blood and provides about 170 calories/liter. Dextrose 5% or sodium chloride 0.11% to 0.45% with dextrose 5% in water is the preferred solution for intravenous administration of water without electrolytes when there has been a loss of water in excess of sodium. Solutions containing 10% dextrose also are used to provide nutriment, but this concentration is irritating to the veins. Solutions containing 20% and 50% dextrose are used to treat cerebral edema and shock, as sclerosing agents, to cause potassium to shift into cells, and in hyperalimentation.

Subcutaneous administration is not desirable because solutions are irritating, temporarily cause leaching of extracellular water and electrolytes, and may distend tissue and lead to necrosis. Osmotic leaching of extracellular water and electrolytes may result in anuria and oliguria because of circulatory failure, especially in individuals with pre-existing electrolyte and water imbalance. In view of these and other disadvantages, some experts feel that dextrose injection should never be administered subcutaneously.

The rate of utilization of dextrose varies considerably from patient to patient. As an approximate guide, however, the average maximal rate of utilization may be 800 mg/kg of body weight/hour (16 ml/kg/hour of 5% injection). If the individual patient's capacity to utilize dextrose is exceeded, glycosuria and diuresis will occur.

Dextrose injection should not be used as a diluent for blood because it causes clumping of red blood cells and, possibly, hemolysis. This can be avoided by using 5% dextrose in 0.2% or 0.11% sodium chloride injection.

Solutions containing 25% to 50% dextrose are used in parenteral hyperalimentation. These may be administered slowly to provide as much as 3,000 to 4,000 calories daily, and must be given via the superior vena cava or other equally large vein. Solutions containing 50% to 75% dextrose decrease the frequency of dialysis in patients with renal failure.

USUAL DOSAGE.—

Intravenous: Adults, as required by the individual.

Subcutaneous: Generally deemed inadvisable for the reasons discussed above.

PREPARATIONS.—Dextrose, U.S.P., Dextrose Injection, U.S.P. See Table.

FRUCTOSE
FRUCTOSE INJECTION [Levugen]

Fructose offers no advantage over dextrose injection; it may cause increased serum levels of lactate and urate if given rapidly, and it is considerably more expensive.

USUAL DOSAGE.—No advice on dosage is given.

PREPARATIONS.—Fructose, N.F., Fructose Injection, N.F. See Table.

INVERT SUGAR INJECTION

Invert sugar is composed of equal parts of dextrose and fructose. The indications and precautions for its use are the same as for dextrose injection (see the evaluation on Dextrose). Invert sugar offers no advantages over dextrose alone.

USUAL DOSAGE.—

Intravenous: Adults, as required by the individual.

Subcutaneous: Generally deemed inadvisable (see the individual evaluation on Dextrose).

PREPARATIONS.—Invert Sugar Injection. See Table.

HIGH CALORIC SOLUTIONS FOR INJECTION

These solutions contain dextrose injection 20% (see the evaluation on Dextrose) or mixtures of carbohydrates in a multiple electrolyte solution. Two liters per day will provide 1,350 to 2,100 calories. Slow infusion will minimize glycosuria. It has not been determined whether mixtures of carbohydrates are tolerated better than solutions of dextrose injection 20% alone; however, solutions providing maintenance amounts of electrolytes are probably more useful than those without electrolytes.

Alcohol is included in some commercially

prepared high calorie solutions; these preparations probably should not be used because they may be poorly tolerated by some patients and may damage the liver.

High caloric solutions are injected intravenously, but since high concentrations of carbohydrate frequently cause thrombosis and phlebitis, these solutions should be infused slowly with a small needle or catheter into the largest available peripheral vein.

USUAL DOSAGE.—*Intravenous: Adults,* as required by the individual (usually 2 to 3 liters per day).

PREPARATIONS.—Isolyte H 900 Cal (McGaw), Normosol-M 900 Cal (Abbott), Polyonic M-900 (Cutter). See Table.

PROTEIN HYDROLYSATE INJECTION
[Amigen, Aminosol, C.P.H., Hyprotigen]
AMINO ACID SOLUTION [Fre Amine]

These protein hydrolysate solutions of amino acids and short-chain peptides represent the approximate nutritive equivalent of the proteins from which they are derived. Three products are derived from casein [Amigen, C.P.H., Hyprotigen], and one is derived from fibrin [Aminosol]. The preparations may be modified during manufacture by addition of one or more amino acids so that the final solution has a balanced amino acid content for human nutrition. The commercial preparations contain varying quantities of electrolytes. In most, only about 60% of the amino acids are free; the remainder are present as peptides, which presumably are excreted unchanged.

Amino acid solution contains synthetic amino acids but no peptides and is used in hyperalimentation. When mixed with an equal volume of 50% dextrose, it provides 6.25 g of nitrogen and 850 nonprotein calories per liter. The manufacturer claims that patients who cannot tolerate protein hydrolysate have been maintained on amino acid solution and that no toxic effects have occurred.

Protein hydrolysate or amino acid solutions are indicated for intravenous administration when there is interference with ingestion, digestion, or absorption of protein for prolonged periods (usually six days or more) or when parenteral supplementation of oral protein intake is required (eg, in burned or malnourished patients). These solutions must be given with dextrose 20% to 25% or its equivalent to permit protein synthesis, because they serve only as a source of calories when given without or with only low concentrations of dextrose. Infusion by indwelling catheter in the vena cava or atrium is necessary for administering protein hydrolysate or amino acid solution with 20% to 25% dextrose (see the Introductory Statement).

Adverse reactions to protein hydrolysates, noted most commonly with rapid infusion, include nausea, vomiting, headache, fever, flushing, hypotension, abdominal pain, convulsions, phlebitis and thrombosis, and edema at the site of injection. Protein hydrolysate solutions should be given in restricted amounts to patients with acidosis, impaired renal function, and severe liver disease and they should be used cautiously in patients with heart disease.

USUAL DOSAGE.—*Intravenous: Adults,* 250 to 1,500 ml of 5% solution as required by the individual. Caloric intake must be maintained during administration to prevent utilization of protein hydrolysate for energy rather than for protein synthesis. For intravenous hyperalimentation to meet total nutritional requirements, sufficient dextrose must be added to provide 100 to 200 calories per gram of nitrogen. Continuous infusion over each 24-hour period of 2,000 to 4,000 ml of 8.5% amino acid or 5% to 10% protein hydrolysate solution containing 20% to 25% dextrose, plus added vitamins and minerals, is usually adequate to maintain total nutritional balance. *Infants and children,* because of variations in practice, the reader should consult specialized sources. See the manufacturer's literature for dosage of amino acid solution for hyperalimentation.

Protein hydrolysate solutions must be administered immediately after opening. If administration is interrupted, the remainder should be discarded.

PREPARATIONS.—

Protein Hydrolysate Injection, U.S.P.: Amigen (Baxter), Aminosol (Abbott), C.P.H. (Cutter), Hyprotigen (McGaw). See Table.

Amino Acid Solution: Fre Amine (McGaw). See Table.

AGENTS USED IN ACID-BASE DISTURBANCES AND POTASSIUM, MAGNESIUM, AND AMMONIA IMBALANCES

AMMONIUM CHLORIDE

This drug should not be used alone in the treatment of metabolic alkalosis, because it may perpetuate potassium and sodium depletion. However, it may be given with potassium chloride and sodium chloride. Ammonium chloride also is used orally as an expectorant (see Chapter 43, Expectorants and Inhalants) and as a urinary acidifier. It is of little value as a diuretic because of its short duration of action. (See also Chapter 7, Diuretics).

Ammonium chloride tends to cause metabolic acidosis. It must be infused slowly to permit metabolism of ammonium ions by the liver and to avoid ammonia toxicity. Gastric irritation occurs after oral administration, and renal dysfunction has been reported. This agent is contraindicated in patients with impaired hepatic or renal function because of the risk of ammonia toxicity.

USUAL DOSAGE.—

Oral: Adults, 1 to 2 g four times daily.

Intravenous: Adults, 100 to 500 ml of a 2% solution infused over a three-hour period.

PREPARATIONS.—Ammonium Chloride, U.S.P. (powder); Ammonium Chloride Injection, U.S.P.; Ammonium Chloride Tablets, U.S.P. Drug marketed under generic name.

ARGININE HYDROCHLORIDE [R-gene]

Arginine has been used to lower blood ammonia levels, but its value in hyperammonemia has not been demonstrated. See the section on Ammonia Imbalance in the Introductory Statement for other measures used to reduce blood ammonia levels.

This agent may cause metabolic acidosis, and may elevate blood urea nitrogen, creatine, and creatinine levels.

USUAL DOSAGE.—Use of this drug for hyperammonemia is not justifiable because of the reasons stated above. For use as a urinary acidifying agent, see the evaluation on Methenamine in Chapter 57, Aminoglycoside Antibacterial Agents and Miscellaneous Antimicrobial Drugs.

PREPARATIONS.—R-gene (Cutter). *Injection:* Solution 5% in 400 ml containers.

MAGNESIUM SULFATE INJECTION

Magnesium sulfate may be given to treat severe cases of hypomagnesemia, but is primarily used as a central nervous system depressant, especially in eclampsia, although other effective drugs are available for that purpose. When administered orally, it acts as a saline cathartic. The duration of action of an intramuscular dose is several hours; intravenous doses last only 30 minutes.

Overtreatment can cause depression of respiration and heart rate. A calcium salt should be available for intravenous injection to counteract the potential hazard of magnesium intoxication. Magnesium sulfate injection interacts with many other drugs, especially when it is used to depress the central nervous system. It should not be given to patients with impaired renal function or to those who are comatose.

USUAL DOSAGE.—*Intramuscular, Intravenous: Adults and older children*, for severe hypomagnesemia, 2 to 4 g (4 to 8 ml of 50% solution or 17 to 34 mEq) daily in divided doses; administration is repeated daily until serum levels have returned to normal. If the deficiency is not severe, 1 g (2 ml of 50% solution) can be given once or twice daily. Serum magnesium levels should serve as a guide to continued dosage.

For eclampsia, initially, 1 to 2 g in 25% or 50% solution is given intramuscularly. Subsequently, 1 g is given every 30 minutes until relief is obtained. The blood pressure should be monitored after each injection. Magnesium sulfate also may be given intravenously in a 10% solution, but only with great caution; the rate should not exceed 3 ml/minute until relaxation is obtained.

PREPARATIONS.—Magnesium Sulfate Injection, U.S.P. *Injection:* Solution 10%, 25%, and 50%. Marketed under generic name.

ORAL ELECTROLYTE SOLUTION [Lytren, Pedialyte]

Oral electrolyte solution contains dextrose, potassium chloride, and salts of sodium, calcium, and magnesium. It is used to supply water and electrolytes in amounts needed for maintenance as soon as the intake of usual foods and liquids is discontinued and before serious fluid losses or deficits occur. For mild or moderate diarrhea, many physicians use oral electrolyte solution initially in outpatients to prevent or correct mild fluid and electrolyte deficiencies and thereby preclude the need for hospitalization. Oral electrolyte solution should not be given in amounts greater than the total water and electrolyte requirements of the patient. The solution contains only relatively small amounts of carbohydrate; therefore, carbohydrate, protein, and lipids also should be given (see Chapter 15, Miscellaneous Nutritional Agents). Oral electrolyte solution should not be mixed with other fluids (eg, milk, fruit juices).

This preparation should not be used in the presence of severe, continuing diarrhea or other critical fluid losses requiring parenteral fluid therapy, nor should it be used in patients with intractable vomiting, adynamic ileus, intestinal obstruction, or perforated intestine. Oral electrolyte solution should be used with caution in patients with impaired renal function.

USUAL DOSAGE.—*Oral:* Dosage is based on clinical estimation of the patient's requirements and will vary with age, weight, and degree of dehydration. See the manufacturer's literature.

PREPARATIONS.—

Lytren (Mead Johnson). *Oral:* Liquid (for hospitals) in 4 and 32 oz containers. Each liter (80 g) provides 280 calories, 25 mEq sodium, 25 mEq potassium, 4 mEq calcium, 4 mEq magnesium, 32 mEq citrate, 4 mEq sulfate, 30 mEq chloride, 5 mEq phosphate, and 4 mEq lactate.

Pedialyte (Ross). *Oral:* Liquid. Each liter provides approximately 203 calories, 30 mEq sodium, 20 mEq potassium, 4 mEq calcium, 4 mEq magnesium, 30 mEq chloride, 28 mEq lactate, and 50 g dextrose.

POTASSIUM CHLORIDE

Potassium chloride is used in the treatment of hypokalemia, except in the rare instances in which there is an associated hyperchloremia. It may be indicated when hypokalemia results from the use of diuretics, but a potassium-sparing diuretic is preferred in these instances (see Chapter 7, Diuretics). In addition, potassium preparations are used in the treatment of hypokalemic periodic paralysis and Meniere's syndrome, as an antidote to digitalis intoxication (see Chapter 1, Digitalis Glycosides), and as an adjunct to anticholinesterase drugs used in the treatment of myasthenia gravis (see Chapter 75, Agents Used in Myasthenia Gravis).

The liquid form is the preparation of choice for oral therapy. Most commercial preparations contain 10, 20, or 40 mEq of potassium chloride per 15 ml and have been flavored to mask the disagreeable taste. Such preparations *must be diluted* before ingestion (usually with fruit juice or water), and administration after meals is advisable to minimize gastric irritation. Uncoated tablets should not be used because they cause gastric irritation, and enteric-coated tablets should not be used because they may cause small bowel ulceration and their rate of absorption is undependable.

The intravenous route may be indicated if a patient is unable to take potassium orally or if hypokalemia is severe. The serum potassium concentration and electrocardiogram should be checked frequently, and adequate urinary output must be assured. Potassium chloride solutions may cause pain if given in a small vein.

Potassium chloride is preferred to other salts of potassium since, in most hypokalemic states, hypochloremia is also present and chloride ion is needed to allow complete potassium replacement.

Potassium is contraindicated in patients with severe renal impairment with oliguria, anuria, or azotemia; untreated chronic adrenocortical insufficiency (Addison's disease); hyperkalemic periodic paralysis (adynamia episodica hereditaria); heat cramps; and hyperkalemia from any cause. Potassium intensifies the symptoms of myotonia congenita. It should be used with caution in the presence of cardiac failure, and all potassium preparations should be administered as slowly as possible to prevent overtreatment and toxicity. Hyperkalemia must be treated immediately, since lethal potassium blood levels can be reached within a few hours.

USUAL DOSAGE.—

Oral: Adults, 10 to 15 mEq in liquid preparation three or four times daily. Larger or smaller doses may be indicated. Use of tablet forms is deemed inadvisable.

Intravenous: Potassium chloride injection must never be administered undiluted; it should be given at a moderate rate in intravenous solutions at concentrations not greater than 40 to 60 mEq per liter. *Adults,* if serum potassium is greater than 2.5 mEq/liter, neuromuscular and cardiac abnormalities are minimal, and renal function is not impaired, potassium may be given in concentrations usually not higher than 40 mEq/liter at a rate not exceeding 10 to 15 mEq/hour. The total dosage usually should not exceed 100 to 300 mEq/day. Urinary losses of potassium, as well as serum levels, should be checked. In the presence of cardiovascular abnormalities or muscle paralysis (and if the serum potassium level is less than 2 mEq/liter), potassium may be given in a concentration as high as 60 mEq/liter at a rate up to 40 mEq/hour for a total amount of up to 400 mEq/day; however, infusions must be carefully regulated on the basis of results of continuous electrocardiographic monitoring and repeated serum potassium determinations.

PREPARATIONS.—Potassium Chloride, U.S.P., Potassium Chloride Injection, U.S.P., Potassium Chloride Tablets, U.S.P.

AVAILABLE TRADEMARKS.—Kay Ciel Elixir (Cooper), K-Lor (Abbott), K-Lyte-CL (Mead Johnson), Kaochlor Liquid (Warren-Teed). Drug also marketed by many manufacturers under generic name.

POTASSIUM TRIPLEX

This combination of the acetate, bicarbonate, and citrate salts of potassium has the same indications, contraindications, and precautions as potassium chloride (see the evaluation on Potassium Chloride). In addition, Potassium

Triplex is used in the treatment of hypokalemia associated with hyperchloremia (eg, renal tubular acidosis, hypokalemia associated with acidosis). It may be given to patients who cannot tolerate potassium chloride; ammonium chloride, lysine monohydrochloride, or another source of chloride ion should be given concurrently, since the chloride ion is often needed to allow complete potassium replacement.

USUAL DOSAGE.—*Oral: Adults*, 5 ml in fruit juice or water three or four times daily after meals. Larger or smaller doses may be indicated.

PREPARATIONS.—Potassium Triplex (Lilly). *Oral:* Liquid. Each 5 ml contains 10% each of potassium acetate, potassium bicarbonate, and potassium citrate; this supplies approximately 15 mEq of elemental potassium in each 5 ml.

POTASSIUM BICARBONATE AND CITRATE [K-Lyte]

The indications, contraindications, and precautions for potassium bicarbonate and citrate are similar to those for potassium chloride (see the evaluation on Potassium Chloride). In addition, potassium bicarbonate and citrate is used in the treatment of hypokalemia associated with hyperchloremia. This combination may be useful in patients who cannot tolerate potassium chloride; ammonium chloride, lysine monohydrochloride, or some other source of chloride ion should be given concurrently, since chloride ion often is needed to allow complete potassium replacement.

USUAL DOSAGE.—*Oral: Adults*, one tablet (20 mEq elemental potassium) dissolved in 90 to 120 ml of cold water two to four times daily with meals, depending upon the requirements of the patient.

PREPARATIONS.—K-Lyte (Mead Johnson). *Oral:* Tablets (for solution) containing 2.5 g potassium bicarbonate, 2.1 g citric acid, and saccharin.

POTASSIUM GLUCONATE [Kaon]

The indications, contraindications, and precautions for potassium gluconate are similar to those for potassium chloride (see the evaluation on Potassium Chloride). In addition, it is used in the treatment of hypokalemia associated with hyperchloremia. Potassium gluconate may be given to patients who cannot tolerate potassium chloride; ammonium chloride, lysine monohydrochloride, or some other source of chloride ion should also be given concurrently, since chloride ion often is needed to allow complete potassium replacement.

USUAL DOSAGE.—*Oral: Adults*, 15 ml of liquid preparation in 1 oz of water or fruit juice two or four times daily after meals or two tablets four times a day after meals and at bedtime. Larger or smaller doses may be indicated.

PREPARATIONS.—Kaon (Warren-Teed). *Oral:* Elixir 4.68 g (20 mEq elemental potassium)/15 ml; tablets 1.17 g (5 mEq elemental potassium.

SODIUM BICARBONATE

Sodium bicarbonate is the drug of choice in the treatment of metabolic acidosis. In mild to moderate acute acidosis, oral treatment is preferable to intravenous therapy; either tablets, a 2% to 5% solution, or a solution containing sodium bicarbonate 0.15% to 0.3% and sodium chloride 0.3% to 0.4% may be used. In severe acute acidosis, the drug may be given intravenously. Sodium bicarbonate also is used as an antacid (see Chapter 79, Antacids), to alkalize the urine in sulfonamide therapy, and to lessen gastric irritation caused by other drugs. It is used with sodium chloride injection in the treatment of hyponatremia (see the Introductory Statement).

Administration of excessive amounts may lead to metabolic alkalosis. Since potentially large amounts of sodium may be absorbed, the drug should be given cautiously to patients with congestive heart failure or other edematous or sodium-retaining conditions, as well as in those with oliguria or anuria. Sodium bicarbonate is not indicated in patients who are losing chloride as a result of vomiting or continuous gastrointestinal suction, or in those receiving diuretics known to produce a hypochloremic alkalosis.

USUAL DOSAGE.—*Oral, Intravenous: Adults*, as required by the individual.

PREPARATIONS.—Sodium Bicarbonate, U.S.P., Sodium Bicarbonate Tablets, U.S.P., Sodium Bicarbonate Injection. Marketed by many manufacturers under generic name.

SODIUM LACTATE INJECTION

Sodium lactate injection is used in the treatment of metabolic acidosis. Since it must first be metabolized to sodium bicarbonate and since the physician cannot be certain he is not dealing with lactic acidosis, sodium lactate generally is not the preferred drug. Sodium bicarbonate is the drug of choice (see the evaluation on Sodium Bicarbonate).

USUAL DOSAGE.—No advice on dosage is given. A commonly suggested dosage is: *Intravenous: Adults*, 1 liter of one-sixth molar solution given at a rate not greater than 300 ml/hour or approximately 60 drops/minute.

PREPARATIONS.—Sodium Lactate Injection, U.S.P. Marketed by many manufacturers under generic name.

SODIUM POLYSTYRENE SULFONATE
[Kayexalate]

This exchange resin is used in the treatment of hyperkalemia. It is most useful when serum potassium levels are not life-threatening or when other measures have reduced the immediate danger of hyperkalemia, for its action is not evident for at least 24 hours. Sodium polystyrene sulfonate removes potassium from the body by exchanging the sodium ion for potassium in the intestine; the potassium-containing resin is then excreted. This drug should be considered an adjunct to other measures such as a high calorie diet, restriction of electrolyte intake, and control of metabolic acidosis. Other treatment is indicated when electrocardiographic changes signify potassium intoxication (see the section on Potassium Excess in the Introductory Statement). Oral administration is preferred to rectal administration because enemas are not as reliable and often are difficult to recover unless the resin is placed in a dialysis bag. Laxatives must be used if the drug is given orally.

Adverse reactions include anorexia, nausea, vomiting, hypokalemia, hypocalcemia, and constipation. Serum potassium levels should be determined daily during therapy and administration should be discontinued or the dose reduced when the serum potassium level falls to 4 or 5 mEq/liter. Sodium polystyrene sulfonate should be used with caution in patients receiving digitalis preparations, since the action of the digitalis may be intensified in the presence of hypokalemia. Fecal impaction may occur, but this possibility can be decreased by the concomitant administration of a mild laxative.

USUAL DOSAGE.—

Oral: Adults, 15 g (suspended in 150 to 200 ml of water) one to four times daily. The preparation may be given by stomach tube.

Rectal: Adults, 30 to 80 g suspended in 150 to 200 ml of 1% methylcellulose solution or 10% dextrose solution or water is given one to three times a day initially; the frequency of administration may be decreased on succeeding days. The preparations should be retained for six to ten hours if possible and should be followed by use of a cleansing enema. Some authorities believe that the preferred method of rectal administration is to place the drug in a sealed dialysis bag and insert the bag into the rectum.

PREPARATIONS.—Kayexalate (Winthrop). *Oral, Rectal:* Powder 450 g.

TROMETHAMINE FOR INJECTION
(Tromethamine with Sodium and Potassium Chloride)
[Tham-E]

Tromethamine, also known as tris buffer, combines with hydrogen ions, associated acid anions, and carbon dioxide, and the resulting salts are excreted in the urine. Tromethamine with electrolytes is used in the treatment of metabolic acidosis, but it is less effective and more expensive than sodium bicarbonate. Tromethamine with electrolytes also has been used to correct metabolic acidosis associated with cardiac bypass surgery.

This drug may cause metabolic alkalosis, local irritation at the site of injection, venospasm, and thrombosis. Perivascular infiltration may result in inflammation, necrosis, and sloughing of overlying skin. Blood glucose levels may decrease temporarily during administration. When the drug is given rapidly in large doses, respiratory depression may occur, especially in patients with chronic hypoventilation or in those receiving other drugs that depress respiration. The dosage must be carefully adjusted so that the blood pH does not increase above normal; facilities for providing mechanical ventilation should be readily available. Blood pH, carbon dioxide tension, bicarbonate, glucose, and electrolyte levels should be determined before, during, and following administration. Tromethamine may produce hyperkalemia in patients with impaired renal function due to accumulation of the drug. The drug is contraindicated in patients with anuria, uremia, and chronic respiratory acidosis, and during pregnancy. It should not be administered for longer than one day.

USUAL DOSAGE.—See product literature.

PREPARATIONS.—Tham-E (Abbott). *Injection:* Powder (for solution). Each liter contains 36 g of tromethamine, 1.75 g of sodium chloride, and 0.37 g of potassium chloride.

PERITONEAL DIALYSIS SOLUTIONS

Peritoneal dialysis solutions are used to remove excessive body fluid, urea, creatinine, uric acid, serum electrolytes, and toxic ingestions. They are indicated in acute and chronic renal failure, intractable edema, hypercalcemia, hyperkalemia, and poisoning with dialyzable systemic agents. Intermittent peritoneal dialysis should be considered as only part of a total therapeutic program.

Abdominal adhesions may impede peritoneal dialysis by interfering with proper insertion of the catheter and by impairing both instillation and removal of dialyzing fluid. Peritonitis is not an absolute contraindication; antibiotics may be added to the dialysis solution and also administered systemically. Local edema from subcutaneous infiltration of the dialyzing solution may result if the catheter is incompletely inserted or if leakage around the catheter is not controlled. Adynamic ileus may occur, especially with continuous dialysis. If this develops, gastrointestinal decompression should be instituted. Overhydration or too vigorous treatment of edema should be avoided. Hypovolemia may occur and may greatly aggravate renal impairment. Fluid and electrolyte requirements must be maintained during dialysis.

A dialysis solution containing sorbitol is recommended for dialyzing diabetic patients, and solutions containing acetate in place of lactate are recommended for dialyzing patients prone to lactic acidosis. Potassium is added to dialysis solutions as needed.

PREPARATIONS.—Dianeal with 1.5%, 4.25%, or 7% Dextrose (Travenol), Inpersol with 1.5% or 4.25% Dextrose (Abbott). Each liter of solution contains approximately 140 mEq sodium, 4 mEq calcium, 1 mEq magnesium, 101 mEq chloride, 45 mEq lactate, and 15, 42.5, or 70 g of dextrose. McGaw Peritoneal Dialysis Solutions have similar electrolyte and dextrose concentrations except for the substitution of acetate for lactate; they also are available with 1.5% and 4.25% sorbitol. Peridial Chronic 3, Peridial Chronic 1.8, and Peridial Chronic 1.3 (Cutter) have similar electrolyte concentrations except for the substitution of acetate for lactate and the addition of 1.3%, 1.8%, or 3% sorbitol. Peridial also is available with lactate and 1.5% or 7% dextrose for use in emergencies. Inpersol-K with 1.5% Dextrose (Abbott) and Dianeal K with 1.5% Dextrose (Travenol) contain 4 mEq potassium and an additional 4 mEq chloride in addition to the ingredients listed above.

COMMERCIALLY AVAILABLE INTRAVENOUS SOLUTIONS

Generic Name	Manufacturer (Trademark)	Milliequivalents per 1,000 ml							
		$Na+$	$K+$	$Ca+$	$Mg+$	NH_4+	$Cl-$	$HPO_4=$	HCO_3- Precursor
CARBOHYDRATES IN WATER									
Dextrose 2.5%	Abbott, Baxter, Cutter, McGaw, Travenol								
Dextrose 5%	Abbott, Baxter, Cutter, McGaw, Travenol								
Dextrose 10%	Abbott, Baxter, Cutter, McGaw, Travenol								
Dextrose 20%	Abbott, Cutter, McGaw, Travenol								
Dextrose 25%	Cutter								
Dextrose 50%	Abbott, Cutter, McGaw, Travenol								
Fructose 5%	Cutter								
Fructose 10%	Abbott, Baxter (Levugen), Cutter, McGaw								
Invert Sugar 5%	Abbott, Cutter, McGaw								
Invert Sugar 10%	Abbott, Cutter, McGaw								
Dextrose 5%, Alcohol 5%	Abbott, Cutter, McGaw, Travenol								
Dextrose 5%, Alcohol 10%	McGaw								

Generic Name	Manufacturer (Trademark)	Milliequivalents per 1,000 ml. Na+	K+	Ca+	Mg+	NH_4+	Cl−	HPO_4=	HCO_3= Precursor
SINGLE ELECTROLYTE SOLUTIONS									
Sodium Chloride 0.45%	Abbott, Baxter, Cutter, McGaw	77					77		
Sodium Chloride 0.9%	Abbott, Baxter, Cutter, McGaw, Travenol	154					154		
Sodium Chloride 3%	Cutter, McGaw, Travenol	513					513		
Sodium Chloride 5%	Abbott, Cutter, McGaw, Travenol	855					855		
Sodium Lactate (M/6) 1.72%	Abbott, Cutter, McGaw, Travenol	167							Lact 1

Generic Name	Manufacturer (Trademark)	Milliequivalents per 1,000 ml. Na+	K+	Ca+	Mg+	NH_4+	Cl−	HPO_4=	HCO_3− Precursor
SINGLE ELECTROLYTE SOLUTIONS WITH CARBOHYDRATE									
Sodium Chloride 0.11% Dextrose 5%	McGaw	19					19		
Sodium Chloride 0.2% Dextrose 5%	Baxter, Cutter, McGaw, Travenol	34					34		
Sodium Chloride 0.225% Dextrose 5%	Abbott	38.5					38.5		
Sodium Chloride 0.3% Dextrose 3.3%	Cutter	51					51		
Sodium Chloride 0.3% Dextrose 5%	Abbott, Cutter	51					51		
Sodium Chloride 0.33% Dextrose 5%	Baxter, McGaw, Travenol	56					56		
Sodium Chloride 0.45% Dextrose 2.5%	Abbott, Baxter, Cutter, McGaw, Travenol	77					77		
Sodium Chloride 0.45% Dextrose 5%	Abbott, Baxter, Cutter, McGaw, Travenol	77					77		
Sodium Chloride 0.45% Dextrose 10%	McGaw	77					77		
Sodium Chloride 0.9% Dextrose 2.5%	Abbott, Cutter McGaw	154					154		
Sodium Chloride 0.9% Dextrose 5%	Abbott, Baxter, Cutter, McGaw, Travenol	154					154		

Generic Name	Manufacturer (Trademark)	Milliequivalents per 1,000 ml Na+	K+	Ca+	Mg+	NH_4+	Cl−	HPO_4=	HCO_3− Precursor
Sodium Chloride 0.9% Dextrose 10%	Abbott, Baxter, Cutter, McGaw, Travenol	154					154		
Sodium Chloride 0.9% Fructose 10%	Cutter	154					154		
Sodium Chloride 0.9% Invert Sugar 5%	Cutter, McGaw, Travenol (5% Travert in 0.9% Sodium Chloride)	154					154		
Sodium Chloride 0.9% Invert Sugar 10%	Abbott, Cutter, McGaw, Travenol (10% Travert in 0.9% NaCl)	154					154		
Potassium Chloride 0.15% Dextrose 5%	Abbott, Cutter, McGaw (Kadalex L), Travenol		20				20		
Potassium Chloride 0.2% Dextrose 5%	Cutter, McGaw (Kadalex)		27				27		
Potassium Chloride 0.3% Dextrose 5%	McGaw (Kadalex M)		40				40		

Generic Name	Manufacturer (Trademark)	Milliequivalents per 1,000 ml. Na+	K+	Ca+	Mg+	NH_4+	Cl−	HPO_4=	HCO_3= Precursor
MULTIPLE ELECTROLYTE SOLUTIONS									
Balanced Electrolyte Injection Maintenance Formulas	Travenol (Plasma-Lyte 56)	40	13			3	40		Acet 16
	Cutter (Polysal-M), Travenol (Plasma-Lyte M)	40	16	5		3	40		24
Balanced Electrolyte Injection Replacement Formulas	Abbott (Normosol-R and Normosol-R pH 7.4), Cutter (Polyonic R-143), McGaw Isolyte S), Travenol (Plasma-Lyte 148)	140	5			3	98		Acet 27 Gluc 23
	Cutter (Polysal), McGaw (Isolyte), Travenol (Plasma-Lyte)	140	10	5		3	103		55
Duodenal Solution	Abbott (Ionosol D-CM)	138	2	5		3	103		Lact 50
Modified Duodenal Solution	McGaw (Multiple Electrolyte #1), Travenol	80	36	5	3		64		Lact 60

Generic Name	Manufacturer (Trademark)	Milliequivalents per 1,000 ml.							
		Na+	K+	Ca+	Mg+	NH_4+	Cl−	HPO_4=	HCO_3= Precursor
MULTIPLE ELECTROLYTE SOLUTIONS									
Lactated Ringer's (Hartmann's Solution)	Abbott, Baxter, Cutter, McGaw Travenol	130	4	3			109		Lact 28
Acetated Ringer's	Cutter, McGaw	130	4	3			109		Acet 28
Ringer's Hypotonic	McGaw	103	5	5	3		116		
Ringer's	Abbott, Baxter, Cutter, McGaw, Travenol	147	4	4			155		

Generic Name	Manufacturer (Trademark)	Milliequivalents per 1,000 ml.							
		Na+	K+	Ca+	Mg+	NH_4+	Cl−	HPO_4=	HCO_3= Precursor
MULTIPLE ELECTROLYTE SOLUTIONS WITH CARBOHYDRATES									
Balanced Electrolyte, Maintenance Formula, with Dextrose 2.5%	Cutter (Polysal-M)	40	16	5	3		40		24
Balanced Electrolyte, Maintenance Formulas, with Dextrose 5%	Abbott (Normosol-M), Cutter (Polyonic M-56), McGaw (Isolyte H), Travenol (Plasma-Lyte 56)	40	13		3		40		Acet 16
	Cutter (Polysal-M), McGaw (Isolyte R), Travenol (Plasma-Lyte M)	40	16	5	3		40		24
Balanced Electrolyte, Maintenance Formula, with Dextrose 10%	Cutter (Polysal-M)	40	16	5	3		40		24
Balanced Electrolyte, Replacement Formulas, with Dextrose 5%	Abbott (Normosol-R), Cutter (Polyonic R-148), Travenol (Plasma-Lyte 148)	140	5		3		98		Acet 27 Gluc 23
	Cutter (Polysal), McGaw (Isolyte E), Travenol (Plasma-Lyte)	140	10	5	3		103		55
Balanced Electrolyte, Replacement Formula, with Invert Sugar 10%	Travenol (Plasma-Lyte with 10% Travert)	140	10	5	3		103		55
Duodenal Solution with Dextrose 5%	Abbott (Ionosol D-CM)	138	12	5	3		103		Lact 50

Generic Name	Manufacturer (Trademark)	Milliequivalents per 1,000 ml. Na+	K+	Ca+	Mg+	NH_4+	Cl−	HPO_4=	HCO_3= Precursor
Modified Duodenal Solution with Invert Sugar 10%	Abbott (Ionosol D Modified), Cutter, McGaw (Electrolyte No. 1), Travenol (10% Travert with Electrolyte No. 1)	80	23	5	3		64		Lact 60
Lactated Ringer's, Half-Strength, with Dextrose 2.5%	Abbott, Baxter, Cutter, McGaw, Travenol	65	2	1			54		Lact 14
Lactated Ringer's with Dextrose 2.5%	Cutter	130	4	3			109		Lact 28
Lactated Ringer's with Dextrose 5%	Abbott, Baxter, Cutter, McGaw, Travenol	130	4	3			109		Lact 28
Lactated Ringer's with Dextrose 10%	Cutter, McGaw	130	4	3			109		Lact 28
Acetated Ringer's with Dextrose 5%	Cutter, McGaw	130	4	3			109		Acet 28
Ringer's Half-Strength, with Dextrose 2.5%	Abbott, Cutter, McGaw	74	2	2			78		
Ringer's with Dextrose 5%	Abbott, Baxter, Cutter, McGaw, Travenol	147	4	4			155		
Electrolyte No. 2 with Dextrose 5%	Abbott (Ionosol B), Cutter	57	25		5		49	13	Lact 25
Electrolyte No. 2 with Invert Sugar 5%	McGaw, Travenol (Travert)	57	25		5		49	13	Lact 25
Electrolyte No. 2 with Invert Sugar 10%	Abbott (Ionosol B), Cutter, McGaw, Travenol (Travert)	57	25		5		49	13	Lact 25
Electrolyte No. 3 with Dextrose 5%	McGaw (Isolyte G)	63	17			71	151		
Electrolyte No. 3 with Dextrose 10%	Abbott (Ionosol G), McGaw (Isolyte G)	63	17			71	151		
Electrolyte No. 3 with Invert Sugar 10%	Abbott (Ionosol G), Cutter, McGaw (Isolyte G), Travenol (Travert)	63	17			71	151		
Electrolyte No. 4 with Invert Sugar 5%	Travenol (Travert)	30	15		•		22	12.5	Lact 25
Electrolyte No. 48 with Dextrose 5%	Abbott (Ionosol MB), Baxter, Cutter, McGaw (Isolyte P), Travenol	25	20		3		22	3	Lact 23

Generic Name	Manufacturer (Trademark)	Milliequivalents per 1,000 ml. Na+	K+	Ca+	Mg+	NH_4+	Cl−	HPO_4=	HCO_3− Precursor
MULTIPLE ELECTROLYTE SOLUTIONS WITH CARBOHYDRATE									
Electrolyte No. 48 with Fructose 5%	Baxter (Levugen), Cutter, McGaw (Isolyte P)	25	20		3		22	3	Lact 23
Electrolyte No. 48 with Fructose 10%	Baxter (Levugen), Cutter	25	20		3		22	3	Lact 23
Electrolyte No. 75 with Dextrose 5%	Abbott (Ionosol T), Baxter, Cutter, McGaw (Isolyte M), Travenol	40	35				40	15	Lact 20
Electrolyte No. 75 with Fructose 5%	Baxter (Levugen), Cutter, McGaw (Isolyte M)	40	35				40	15	Lact 20
Potassium Chloride 0.15%, Sodium Chloride 0.45%, Dextrose 5%	Cutter	77	20				97		
Potassium Chloride 0.2%, Sodium Chloride 0.15%, Dextrose 3.5% (Ordway's Solution)	Cutter	26	27				53		
Potassium Chloride 0.2%, Sodium Chloride 0.15%, Dextrose 10% (Ordway's Solution)	Cutter	26	27				53		
Potassium Chloride 0.3%, Sodium Chloride 0.45%, Invert Sugar 10%	Cutter, McGaw (Kalavert), Travenol (Travert)	77	40				117		

Generic Name	Manufacturer (Trademark)	Milliequivalents per 1,000 ml. Na+	K+	Ca+	Mg+	NH_4+	Cl−	HPO_4=	HCO_3= Precursor
PROTEIN SOLUTIONS									
Casein Hydrolysate 5%	Baxter (Amigen)	35	19	5	2		22	30	
	Cutter (C.P.H.)	39	18	6	2		14	14	
	McGaw (Hyprotigen)	25	20	5	2		18	25	
Casein Hydrolysate 7%	Cutter (C.P.H.)	39	18	6	2		14	14	

Generic Name	Manufacturer (Trademark)	Milliequivalents per 1,000 ml. Na+	K+	Ca+	Mg+	NH_4+	Cl−	HPO_4=	HCO_3= Precursor
Casein Hydrolysate 10%	McGaw (Hyprotigen) (Also available in a kit with 40% or 50% dextrose for preparing hyperalimentation fluid)	50	36	10	4		36	50	
Fibrin Hydrolysate 5%	Abbott (Aminosol)	10	17						
Amino Acids 8.5%	McGaw (FreAmine) (available in a kit with 50% dextrose for preparing hyperalimentation fluid)	5					22		Acet 12

Generic Name	Manufacturer (Trademark)	Milliequivalents per 1,000 ml. Na+	K+	Ca+	Mg+	NH_4+	Cl−	HPO_4=	HCO_3= Precursor
PROTEIN SOLUTIONS WITH CARBOHYDRATE									
Casein Hydrolysate 5% with Dextrose 5%	Baxter (Amigen)	35	19	5	2		22	30	
	Cutter (C.P.H.)	39	18	6	2		14	14	
	McGaw (Hyprotigen)	25	20	5	2		18	25	
Casein Hydrolysate 5% with Dextrose 5%, Alcohol 5%	Baxter (Amigen)	35	19	5	2		22	30	
	McGaw (Hyprotigen)	25	20	5	2		18	25	
Casein Hydrolysate 5% with Dextrose 5%, Alcohol 6.3%	Cutter (C.P.H.)	39	18	6	2		14	14	
Casein Hydrolysate 5% with Fructose 10%	Baxter (Amigen)	35	19	5	2		22	30	
	McGaw (Hyprotigen)	25	20	5	2		18	25	
Casein Hydrolysate 5% with Fructose 12.5%, Alcohol 2.4%	Baxter (Amigen)	35	19	5	2		22	30	
	McGaw (Hyprotigen)	25	20	5	2		18	25	
Fibrin Hydrolysate with Dextrose 5%	Abbott (Aminosol)	10	17						

Generic Name	Manufacturer (Trademark)	Milliequivalents per 1,000 ml. Na+	K+	Ca+	Mg+	NH_4+	Cl−	HPO_4=	HCO_3= Precursor
HIGH CALORIE SOLUTIONS									
Dextrose 5%, Fructose 15%, Alcohol 4% in Balanced Electrolyte, Maintenance Formula	Abbott, (Normosol-M 900 Cal), Cutter (Polyonic M-900), McGaw (Isolyte H 900 Cal)	40	13		3		40		Acet 16

Generic Name	Trademark (Manufacturer)	Milliequivalents per 1,000 ml. Na+	K+	Ca+	Mg+	NH_4+	Cl−	HPO_4=	HCO_3= Precursor
VITAMIN SOLUTIONS									
	Ascor-B-Sol with Dextrose 5% (Travenol)								
	Beclysyl with Dextrose 5%, Sodium Chloride 0.9% (Abbott)	154					154		
	Beclysyl with Dextrose 5% (Abbott)								
	Dextrose 5% with Vitamins (Travenol)								
	Dextrose 5%, Sodium Chloride 0.9% with Vitamins (Travenol)	154					154		
	*Surbex-T with Dextrose 5% (Abbott)								
	*Surbex-T with Dextrose 5%, Sodium Chloride 0.9% (Abbott)	154					154		
	*Surbex-T with Normosol-M, Dextrose 5% (Abbott)	40	13	3			40		Acet 16
	Travert 10% with Vitamins (Travenol)								
	Trinolyte with Dextrose 5% (McGaw)	132	10	5	3		103		Lact 47
	Vitadex-B with Dextrose 5% (Cutter)								
	Vitadex-B with Dextrose 10% (Cutter)								
	Vitadex-B with Dextrose 5%, Alcohol 5% (Cutter)								
	Vitadex-B with Dextrose 5%, Sodium Chloride 0.9% (Cutter)	154					154		
	Vitadex-B with Dextrose 10%, Sodium Chloride 0.9% (Cutter)	154					154		
	*Vitamin B Complex and 1 g Vitamin C with Dextrose 5%								

*Vitamin content in excess of the recommended daily allowance.

Chapter 17

BLOOD CALCIUM REGULATORS

Regulation of the serum calcium concentration within narrow limits is essential for proper maintenance of important physiological functions, including neuromuscular transmission, blood coagulation, cell membrane permeability, hormone secretion and action, and certain enzyme activities. The Recommended Dietary Allowance of calcium for adults is 800 mg daily. In adults, 15% to 35% is absorbed from the intestine into a rapidly exchangeable extracellular pool. In children, up to 75% is absorbed. Virtually all of the 1,000 to 1,200 g of calcium present in the body of normal adults is in the skeletal tissue. Of the 1% in extracellular fluids, approximately half is bound to serum proteins. Almost all unbound serum calcium is ionized; a small portion is chelated to complex organic anions.

Calcium is excreted primarily in the feces; this loss represents the unabsorbed portion of ingested calcium plus approximately 80 to 180 mg of endogenously secreted calcium. Urinary calcium excretion is usually 100 mg daily, since the renal tubules reabsorb most of the filtered calcium load. Calcium also is excreted in perspiration.

Maintenance of a normal concentration of ionized calcium in serum is achieved by the interactions of three homeostatic agents: parathyroid hormone, vitamin D, and calcitonin. Parathyroid hormone mobilizes calcium from bone by stimulating osteoclastic resorption. Vitamin D is required for this activity. Parathyroid hormone also promotes the renal tubular reabsorption of calcium and causes a slight increase in the intestinal absorption of calcium. Under normal conditions, the serum calcium concentration is maintained within a narrow range, which is determined by age and sex, by means of a negative feedback mechanism involving ionized calcium concentration in serum and parathyroid hormone secretion. Secretion of parathyroid hormone is stimulated by a fall in the level of ionized serum calcium which, in turn, increases mobilization of mineral from bone and urinary excretion of phosphate. A rise in the level of ionized serum calcium, however, inhibits the secretion of parathyroid hormone and stimulates that of calcitonin with a resultant decrease in mobilization of mineral from bone. Calcitonin is synthesized in the parafollicular cells of the thyroid and has also been detected in the parathyroid and thymus glands. In addition to its primary action of inhibiting resorption of bone, calcitonin probably modulates the rate of mineral mobilization and thereby exerts a fine control on the exchange of calcium from bone to extracellular fluids. There is evidence that calcitonin may prevent a sudden increase in serum calcium after ingestion of large amounts of calcium. Vitamin D is not essential for the hypocalcemic action of calcitonin.

Vitamin D is obtained by the ingestion of vitamin D_2 (ergocalciferol) or vitamin D_3 (cholecalciferol) or by ultraviolet irradiation of dehydrocholecalciferol to vitamin D_3 in the skin. Vitamin D is hydroxylated at the 25 position by the liver to produce 25-hydroxycholecalciferol (25-HCC), which is the major metabolite circulating in the plasma; this substance may not act directly in any system, although it is the most effective form when administered in the treatment of rickets. The metabolite, 25-HCC, is further hydroxylated in the kidney to 1,25-dihydroxycholecalciferol, which acts very rapidly to initiate the intestinal transport of calcium and mobilization of minerals from bone. There is evidence that 1,25-DHCC is the biologically active metabolite in the intestine. A deficiency of this metabolite, which is generated primarily in the kidney, may explain the osteodystrophy that accompanies chronic renal disease. Other vitamin D-resistant diseases possibly result from metabolic defects in the formation of active metabolites of the parent vitamin. Less active metabolites have been identified but their roles have not been determined. However, there is evidence that conversion to the more active 1,25-DHCC is enhanced by the presence of parathyroid hormone and conversion to the less active 24,25-DHCC is enhanced by the absence of parathyroid hormone and possibly by the presence of calcitonin.

In certain pathologic states, other hormones (eg, glucocorticoids, growth hormone, thyroid hormone, androgens, estrogens) also affect calcium balance.

HYPERCALCEMIA

The most common cause of hypercalcemia is neoplasm with and without osseous metastases. One cause of hypercalcemia associated with neoplasm without apparent bony metastases is the synthesis and secretion of a parathyroid hormone-like substance by the malignant tumor, most commonly renal cell carcinoma or bronchogenic carcinoma. Other common causes are primary hyperparathyroidism, thiazide therapy, multiple myeloma, sarcoidosis, hypervitaminosis D, and the milk-alkali syndrome. Uncommon causes are leukemias, hyperthyroidism, hypothyroidism, acute adrenocortical insufficiency, "tertiary" hyperparathyroidism, immobilization, infantile idiopathic hypercalcemia, acromegaly, and renal transplants.

The signs and symptoms of hypercalcemia are so variable that diagnosis may be difficult. Primary hyperparathyroidism is characteristically associated with hypercalcemia, hypophosphatemia, and symptoms attributable to recurrent renal calculi, peptic ulceration, and skeletal disease. However, 25% to 30% of patients with primary hyperparathyroidism may have normal levels of calcium and be relatively asymptomatic.

In cases of severe hypercalcemia, an emergency situation (ie, intractable vomiting, profound weakness, and severe dehydration with deterioriation of renal function) can develop rapidly. Coma and death may follow. Sudden death, probably from cardiogenic shock, has occurred.

The clinical manifestations of hypercalcemia involve many organ systems. Gastrointestinal symptoms are anorexia, nausea, vomiting, constipation, and abdominal pain. Hyperchlorhydria may account for the high incidence of peptic ulcer (15% to 25%) in patients with hyperparathyroidism. The use of antacids containing calcium carbonate for the relief of symptoms of ulcer may increase the hypercalcemia and symptoms of ulcer.

Hypercalcemia also affects the central nervous system; symptoms include vague complaints of apathy, depression, amnesia, headaches, and drowsiness. More severe hypercalcemia can produce disorientation, episodes of syncope, hallucinations, coma, and death.

Other symptoms are weakness and hypotonia of both skeletal and smooth muscles, dysphagia, and arrhythmias. Polyuria and polydipsia result from a loss of renal concentrating ability. Calcium may be deposited in various tissues and organs, including the kidneys, conjunctiva, and cornea, where it produces band keratitis. Complications, especially those affecting the kidneys, may be severe. Nephrocalcinosis, usually associated with kidney calculi, can seriously impair renal function and cause uremia, edema, and hypertension, which may be irreversible.

The primary objective in treating hypercalcemic disorders is to control the underlying disease. Surgical excision is the only effective treatment for symptomatic primary hyperparathyroidism. However, when patients with severe hyperparathyroidism develop acute and rapidly progressing hypercalcemia, immediate drug therapy is necessary to reduce serum calcium concentrations and avert a life-threatening situation. Any patient with a serum calcium concentration above 16 mg/100 ml needs intensive care. An abrupt rise in the serum calcium level may cause infarction and necrosis of the renal tubules, with anuria and uremia. Calcium intoxication frequently causes electrocardiographic changes characterized by a short Q-T interval with some degree of heart block; cardiac arrest also may occur. Pancreatitis and multiple venous and arterial thromboses have been reported during a hypercalcemic crisis.

There is great variation in individual tolerance to hypercalcemia and, consequently, in the drug therapy required to treat this complication until specific treatment of the underlying disease has been determined and initiated. Asymptomatic patients with mild hypercalcemia (eg, patients receiving thiazide diuretics) may only require treatment of the underlying cause. After discontinuance of the diuretic, the serum calcium value usually returns to normal in one month or less. Symptomatic patients, however, commonly are dehydrated as the result of vomiting and polyuria. Hydration is the first step in treatment; intravenous fluids, usually isotonic sodium chloride injection, are infused. Loss of other electrolytes (magnesium, potassium) should be corrected. In patients with adequate renal function, the infusion of sodium chloride can be continued in order to increase sodium excretion, which will, in turn, produce a calcium diuresis. Care is necessary to avoid hypervolemia, especially in the elderly, in whom pulmonary edema may develop due to myocardial insufficiency. Natriuretic agents such as furosemide [Lasix] or ethacrynic acid [Edecrin] can be used with the sodium chloride or alone in adequately hydrated patients to increase the renal excretion of calcium. Thiazide diuretics should not be administered, for calciuresis does not accompany natriuresis in patients receiving thiazides and, in addition, serum calcium increases occur in these patients.

Another way to increase the renal excretion of calcium is to administer chelating or binding agents; these drugs form soluble complexes that are not reabsorbed by renal tubules. Sodium sulfate produces a calciuresis, which, in some patients, appears to be greater than could be expected from the natriuresis alone. Sodium citrate is also reported to form a complex with calcium, which increases the renal excretion of calcium.

Disodium edetate is a chelating agent with an affinity for calcium ions. It is very effective in treating severe hypercalcemia, since it increases the urinary excretion of calcium by forming soluble complexes with it, and these are not reabsorbed to any great extent by the renal tubules. Chelation occurs in the blood, which decreases the ionized calcium concentration in serum before calcium is excreted. However, use of this agent is limited to the emergency treatment of calcium intoxication since prolonged use and doses exceeding 3 g have caused acute tubular necrosis of the kidney. (See Chapter 90, Chelating Agents.)

Dialyzing is another technique used to increase the excretion of calcium. Hemodialysis and peritoneal dialysis are able to remove large amounts of calcium by utilization of a calcium-free dialysate; however, these techniques have very short-term effects and are primarily useful preoperatively in patients with severe hypercalcemia and renal insufficiency.

Another approach to the treatment of hypercalcemia is to decrease the absorption of calcium from the gastrointestinal tract. This method is successful only when there is excessive gastrointestinal absorption of calcium (eg, in the milk-alkali syndrome, sarcoidosis, hypervitaminosis D). In milk-alkali syndrome, reduction in dietary calcium is indicated; in sarcoidosis and hypervitaminosis D, glucocorticoids are especially effective, since they reduce absorption by antagonizing the action of vitamin D. A large excess of vitamin D does not modify the effect. The response to oral glucocorticoid therapy is not rapid; a period of one to two weeks may elapse before a decrease in serum calcium occurs.

Although patients with hyperparathyroidism seldom respond to glucocorticoid therapy, patients with myelomas, lymphomas, and leukemias usually do. Patients with solid carcinomas are less responsive, but some decrease in the hypercalcemia can be expected. It is believed that glucocorticoids may have a direct effect on bone to increase accretion or decrease resorption as well as antagonize the action of vitamin D. However, since the prolonged use of glucocorticoids results in osteoporosis, these drugs are limited to short-term use.

The use of inorganic phosphates, either orally or by intravenous infusion in emergencies, is effective in decreasing serum calcium concentration regardless of the cause. Phosphate causes deposition of calcium in bone by increasing accretion, thereby altering the ratio of accretion to resorption. Phosphate has the disadvantage of possibly causing deposition of calcium in soft tissues as well as in bone. Oral phosphate therapy can be given daily for prolonged periods to suppress hypercalcemia.

Calcitonin is secreted in response to increased concentrations of serum ionized calcium and acts by decreasing resorption of bone. Porcine and salmon preparations of this polypeptide hormone are available for investigational use and have been successful in treating osteitis deformans (Paget's disease of the bone) and in a variety of hypercalcemic states. This hormone may prove to be very useful in the treatment of acute hypercalcemia.

Mithramycin, a cytotoxic agent used principally in the treatment of testicular tumors, reduces elevated serum calcium concentrations probably by acting directly on bone. One-fifth to one-tenth of the antineoplastic dose is given; toxic manifestations are minimized at this dosage level. The serum calcium concentration may not be reduced for 24 to 48 hours, but, once the reduction is achieved, mithramycin has a duration of action up to three weeks. The drug is very useful in treating hypercalcemia associated with advanced neoplastic disease.

INDIVIDUAL EVALUATIONS

ADRENAL CORTICOSTEROIDS

Glucocorticoids are effective in the treatment of hypercalcemia due to hypervitaminosis D, sarcoidosis, the milk-alkali syndrome, and adrenocortical insufficiency. They are also useful in some patients with hypercalcemia due to malignant tumors, myelomas, leukemias, and lymphomas. Since patients with primary hyperparathyroidism occasionally may respond to glucocorticoids, its use as a diagnostic test is not recommended.

Glucocorticoids reduce the intestinal absorption of calcium by antagonizing the action of vitamin D. A large excess of the vitamin does not modify this effect. Glucocorticoids also increase the glomerular filtration and calcium clearance rate and probably act directly on bone.

Since their onset of action is slow these drugs are not useful for emergency treatment of hypercalcemia except in patients with renal failure that does not respond to diuretics and fluid. In these patients, parenteral use of glucocorticoids is the only therapy available.

Large doses of steroids may be necessary initially. A diet low in calcium will permit the lowest possible doses to be used to maintain the improvement. The adverse effects of prolonged glucocorticoid therapy (see Chapter 35, Adrenal Corticosteroids) are an important consideration.

USUAL DOSAGE.—

Intravenous, Intramuscular: Adults, in severe hypercalcemia, parenteral preparations are preferred (hydrocortisone sodium succinate 100 to 500 mg daily or prednisolone sodium phosphate 20 to 100 mg daily); these drugs may be given either intramuscularly, intravenously, or, preferably, by intravenous infusion.

Oral: Adults, initially, 40 to 80 mg of prednisone or another glucocorticoid in a therapeutically equivalent dose is given daily until satisfactory control of the serum calcium level is obtained. Dosage then is reduced gradually; final dosage is dependent upon the results of serum calcium determinations.

PREPARATIONS.—

Hydrocortisone Sodium Succinate:

Solu-Cortef (Upjohn). *Injection:* Powder 100, 250, and 500 mg and 1 g.

Prednisolone Sodium Phosphate:

Hydeltrasol (Merck Sharp & Dohme). *Injection:* Solution 20 mg/ml in 2 and 5 ml containers.

Prednisone:

Oral: Tablets 1, 2.5, and 5 mg.

See Chapter 35, Adrenal Corticosteroids, for trademarks of prednisone and for preparations of other glucocorticoids that can be used in equivalent doses.

DISODIUM EDETATE [Endrate, Sodium Versenate]

This chelating agent is used in the treatment of acute hypercalcemia. It forms filterable, soluble complexes with calcium in the blood; these complexes are excreted by the kidneys and not reabsorbed to any extent by the renal tubules.

Although disodium edetate is very effective, the nephrotoxic reactions that may occur limit its use. Renal tubular damage and renal insufficiency have resulted from prolonged use or administration of doses larger than 3 g. Its emergency use is justified in patients with life-threatening hypercalcemia, but treatment should not exceed 48 hours. Disodium edetate should be administered only when the severity of the disease justifies the aggressive treatment.

Other adverse reactions are pain at the site of infusion, hypotension, and hypocalcemia if the drug is not diluted sufficiently or if it is administered too fast. See also Chapter 90, Chelating Agents.

USUAL DOSAGE.—There is wide disagreement about proper dosage; therefore, disodium edetate probably should be regarded as an experimental drug, despite the fact that it has been available for many years, and it should be used with extreme caution. For emergency reduction of severe hypercalcemia, a suggested dosage is 50 mg/kg of body weight infused over a period of four to six hours. Other recommendations for maximal dosage range from 15 to 50 mg/kg of body weight daily. Opinions differ widely on whether dosage may be repeated and, if so, how frequently and how many times.

PREPARATIONS.—

Endrate (Abbott). *Injection:* Solution 150 mg/ml in 20 ml containers.

Sodium Versenate (Riker). *Injection:* Solution 200 mg/ml in 5 ml containers.

FUROSEMIDE [Lasix]

Furosemide lowers serum calcium concentrations by increasing calcium excretion. For patients with very severe hypercalcemia, it is given intravenously in large doses; sodium sulfate or sodium chloride may be infused concomitantly. For mild cases of hypercalcemia, furosemide may be given orally. For adverse reactions, precautions, and contraindications, see Chapter 7, Diuretics.

USUAL DOSAGE.—

Intravenous: 80 to 100 mg every one to two hours until serum calcium levels are normal or sufficiently improved to give oral maintenance therapy.

Oral: 120 mg daily.

PREPARATIONS.—Lasix (Hoechst).

Injection: Solution 10 mg/ml in 2 ml containers.

Oral: Tablets 40 mg.

MITHRAMYCIN [Mithracin]

Mithramycin is a cytostatic antibiotic used primarily in the treatment of testicular neoplasms. It significantly decreases elevated serum calcium levels and also is capable of producing hypocalcemia in patients with normal calcium levels. When used with forced hydration and a reduced calcium intake, mithramycin is useful in treating hypercalcemia associated with carcinoma with or without bony metastases. It has been more effective than glucocorticoids in these patients, and especially in those with tumors producing parathyroid hormone-like polypeptides. A single intravenous injection can effectively reduce elevated plasma calcium levels in some patients without producing serious toxic effects.

In addition to anorexia, nausea, and vomiting, mithramycin can produce hemorrhagic diathesis, thrombocytopenia, and impaired hepatic and renal function. Although lower doses are usually used for treating hypercalcemia than for neoplasms, the same precautions and contraindications apply (see Chapter 88, Antineoplastic Agents).

USUAL DOSAGE.—*Intravenous:* 25 μg/kg of body weight as a single dose by direct injection. If there is no decline in serum calcium levels in 24 to 48 hours, or if the calcium returns to hypercalcemic levels, 25 μg/kg is given daily for two to four days. Additional courses may be given at weekly intervals if the hypercalcemia is not controlled. Alternatively, one to three doses may be given weekly, depending upon the patient's response.

PREPARATIONS.—Mithracin (Pfizer). *Injection:* Powder (for solution) in vials containing mithramycin 2,500 μg, mannitol 100 mg, and sufficient disodium phosphate to adjust the pH to 7.

PHOSPHATE SALTS

Oral administration of inorganic phosphates (monobasic or dibasic sodium or potassium phosphate) may be used in the treatment of mild to moderate hypercalcemia. A reciprocal relationship of ionic calcium and phosphate activity results in a reduction of serum calcium, although not to normal levels in all patients. With the decrease in serum calcium, there is an increase in serum phosphorus, a decrease in urinary excretion of calcium, and a marked increase in urinary excretion of phosphate. The response to oral phosphate salts is delayed for several days. The mechanism of action is not known. Significant ectopic calcification may develop in patients in whom there is a decrease in serum calcium and an improvement in bone lesions, since phosphate therapy does not increase the extracorporeal excretion of calcium. Oral administration may cause vomiting and diarrhea.

The intravenous infusion of phosphate salts is effective and predictable emergency treatment; however, hypotension, acute renal failure, and myocardial infarction have occurred and several deaths have been reported. Tetany has resulted from overdosage. It is important to adhere to the recommended dosage and rate of administration.

USUAL DOSAGE.—*Oral: Adults,* 24 ml of 1 molar dibasic sodium phosphate or a mixed inorganic salt of monobasic and dibasic sodium phosphate four times daily to supply 3 g of phosphorus. Dibasic potassium phosphate may be combined with sodium phosphate to reduce sodium intake when indicated. Following remission, the dose can be reduced to maintain a normal concentration of serum calcium.

Intravenous: Adults, 1 liter of a 0.1 molar solution of phosphate salts (0.081 mole of dibasic sodium phosphate and 0.019 mole of monobasic potassium phosphate) to provide a solution with a pH of 7.4. This is administered at a constant rate over a period of 6 to 12 hours.

PREPARATIONS.—No single-entity pharmaceutical dosage form available; compounding necessary for prescription.

SODIUM CHLORIDE

Infusions of isotonic sodium chloride are used to restore fluid balance and to promote calciuresis in severe hypercalcemia. Rehydration increases the glomerular filtration rate and delivers more calcium to the renal tubules. Natriuresis promotes calciuresis. The hypocalcemic action of sodium chloride is slower in onset and possibly of lesser magnitude than that of sodium sulfate; however, the excretion of sodium is more prolonged. Furosemide or ethacrynic acid given concomitantly increases the calciuresis; thiazides should not be given (see the Introductory Statement).

As with sodium sulfate, intravenous infusions of fluid and sodium may lead to congestive heart failure or hypernatremia, especially in patients with impaired cardiac and renal function. The symptoms of hypernatremia include hyperactivity, confusion, stupor, convulsions, and coma. Hypokalemia and hypomagnesemia also may occur, and an overdosage may cause hypocalcemia. Serum levels of calcium, sodium, potassium, and magnesium should be determined at intervals during infusion of sodium chloride.

See also Chapter 16, Replenishers and Regulators of Water, Electrolytes, and Nutrients.

USUAL DOSAGE.—*Intravenous: Adults*, 1 liter every three to four hours.

PREPARATIONS.—Sodium Chloride, U.S.P.; Sodium Chloride Injection, U.S.P. Marketed under generic name.

SODIUM SULFATE

Intravenous infusions of sodium sulfate increase the renal excretion of calcium in severe hypercalcemia. The treatment can be improved by concomitant administration of furosemide or ethacrynic acid. Thiazide diuretics should not be given (see the Introductory Statement).

In some patients, calcium clearance is greater with diuresis induced by sodium sulfate than with a comparable diuresis induced by sodium chloride, since the non-reabsorbable sulfate anion increases renal excretion of calcium over and above that due to the sodium ion. Electrostatically bound calcium and sulfate ions are not reabsorbed by the renal tubules.

The elevated serum concentration decreases within a few hours but the action is of short duration due to rapid excretion of unmetabolized sulfate (90% to 100% in 24 hours).

The intravenous administration of large amounts of fluids and sodium may lead to congestive heart failure or hypernatremia, especially in patients with impaired cardiac and renal function. The symptoms of hypernatremia include hyperactivity, confusion, stupor, convulsions, and coma. Hypokalemia and hypomagnesemia also may occur and an overdosage may cause hypocalcemia. Serum levels of calcium, sodium, potassium, and magnesium should be determined at intervals during infusion of sodium sulfate.

USUAL DOSAGE.—*Intravenous:* 1 to 4 liters of isotonic solution (38.9 g sodium sulfate decahydrate/liter of water for injection) over a period of 9 to 15 hours. Solution contains 242 mEq/liter of sodium.

PREPARATIONS.—No single-entity pharmaceutical dosage form available; compounding with use of sterile techniques and nonpyrogenic water necessary.

HYPOCALCEMIA

Hypoparathyroidism of any etiology will decrease serum calcium and increase serum phosphorus concentrations. It may occur postoperatively or may be idiopathic. Most commonly, the parathyroid glands or their blood supply are removed or damaged during thyroidectomy or other neck surgery; the hypocalcemia is transient if the glands are only damaged. Idiopathic hypoparathyroidism is rare and occurs most often in girls; some cases appear to be familial. A transitory deficiency of parathyroid hormone may occur in babies of mothers with hyperparathyroidism.

Following parathyroidectomy for hyperparathyroidism associated with osteitis fibrosa cystica with extensive bone resorption, severe hypocalcemia usually will result if all pathologic material is removed in one operation. The low plasma calcium will persist until skeletal homeostasis is re-established.

Hypocalcemia also may result from decreased intestinal absorption of calcium, which is a function of vitamin D activity. Causes are a simple deficiency of vitamin D and conditions associated with intestinal malabsorption (eg, adult celiac disease, tropical sprue, cystic fibrosis, chronic pancreatitis, regional enteritis, gastrectomy, intestinal blind loops and short circuits, multiple jejunal diverticuloses, gastrointestinal fistulas, chronic biliary obstruction). In patients with renal insufficiency, impaired hydroxylation of vitamin D by the kidney causes calcium malabsorption, which results in hypocalcemia and secondary hyperparathyroidism. Excessive secretion of parathyroid hormone increases mobilization of mineral from bone, which probably accounts for the osteodystrophy that occurs with renal disease. The serum calcium concentration may be raised to normal at the expense of bone. Secondary hyperparathyroidism also develops with simple dietary deficiency of vitamin D and with intestinal malabsorption syndromes.

The most prominent symptom attributable to low serum ionized calcium is increased neuromuscular excitability which proceeds to tetany. In overt tetany, the manifestations are numbness and tingling of fingers, toes, and lips; skeletal muscle spasms; twitching of facial muscles; carpopedal spasm; laryngeal stridor; and epileptiform (grand mal or petit mal) convulsions. Chvostek's and Trousseau's signs may be used to detect latent tetany, and a prolonged Q-T interval associated with an inverted T wave is electrocardiographic evidence of hypocalcemia.

Prolonged hypocalcemia may be associated with ectodermal defects involving the nails, skin, and teeth; lenticular cataracts; and a predisposition to candidal infections. Abnormal behavior patterns and personality changes may be observed and, in children, sustained hypocalcemia has resulted in mental retardation. Calcification of the basal ganglia and bilateral cerebellar calcification are found.

Regardless of etiology, the initial treatment of severe hypocalcemia is the immediate intravenous administration of a source of rapidly available calcium ions. A 10% solution of calcium gluconate, given by slow intravenous injection until tetany is controlled, is effective. Calcium chloride or calcium gluceptate also can be used.

For maintenance therapy, a calcium salt (calcium gluconate, calcium lactate, dibasic calcium phosphate, tribasic calcium phosphate, or calcium carbonate, precipitated) is given orally.

Tetany also may occur as a result of the combination of citrate with ionized calcium during exchange transfusions and during massive transfusions with citrated blood, even though total serum calcium may not be reduced appreciably. A calcium salt is given intravenously to prevent this occurrence.

If hypovitaminosis D exists, the vitamin is administered after the acute hypocalcemic symptoms have been controlled.

Adverse Reactions and Precautions

The intravenous administration of calcium salts, injection of parathyroid hormone, or overdosage of vitamin D or dihydrotachysterol may cause hypercalcemia with anorexia, nausea, vomiting, constipation, peptic ulcer pain, polydipsia, and polyuria.

Calcium should be administered with caution in digitalized patients, since it may precipitate arrhythmias.

Calcium salts should always be infused slowly.

Dibasic and tribasic calcium phosphate are contraindicated in the treatment of hypocalcemia with hyperphosphatemia, which may occur in hypoparathyroidism and renal failure. In addition, foods with a high phosphate content such as milk or cheese should be eliminated from the diet and aluminum hydroxide should be given to reduce the intestinal absorption of phosphate.

INDIVIDUAL EVALUATIONS

CALCIUM CARBONATE, PRECIPITATED

This orally administered calcium salt is effective in the treatment of mild and latent hypocalcemic tetany and for maintenance therapy. It is converted in the gastrointestinal tract to soluble calcium salts, which are almost as well absorbed as calcium gluconate; however, patients with achlorhydria may not absorb calcium from this preparation.

USUAL DOSAGE.—*Oral: Adults,* 1 to 2 g three times daily with meals; the preparation is mixed with water or sprinkled on food.

PREPARATIONS.—No single-entity pharmaceutical dosage form available; compounding necessary for prescription.

CALCIUM CHLORIDE

Intravenous administration of calcium chloride is effective in the treatment of severe hypocalcemic tetany. However, it is irritating to the veins and subcutaneous tissue, and care must be taken to avoid extravasation, as necrosis may result. Therefore, other calcium salts are preferable. Calcium chloride should never be administered intramuscularly. Peripheral vasodilatation and a fall in blood pressure may occur.

Calcium chloride can be given orally for milder symptoms of tetany and for maintenance therapy. It is irritating to the gastrointestinal tract and should never be given by gavage.

USUAL DOSAGE.—

Intravenous (slow): *Adults*, 10 to 30 ml of a 5% solution.

Oral: Adults, 4 to 8 g daily in four divided doses, given with demulcent. *Children*, 300 mg/kg of body weight of a 2% solution given daily in four divided doses.

PREPARATIONS.—No single-entity pharmaceutical dosage form available; compounding, using sterile technique and nonpyrogenic water, is necessary for prescription.

CALCIUM GLUCEPTATE

Intravenous administration of calcium gluceptate is effective in the treatment of severe hypocalcemic tetany. A transient tingling sensation and chalk-like taste may be noted after this route of administration. Calcium gluceptate may also be given intramuscularly to infants and other patients in whom intravenous administration is not feasible; it is well tolerated, although mild local reactions may occur.

USUAL DOSAGE.—

Intravenous: Adults and children, 90 to 360 mg or more.

Intramuscular: Adults and children, 36 to 90 mg in gluteal region or lateral aspect of thigh. *Infants*, 36 to 90 mg in several sites in lateral thigh.

PREPARATIONS.—*Injection:* Solution 18 mg/ml in 5 ml containers. Drug marketed under generic name.

CALCIUM GLUCONATE

Calcium gluconate is a source of rapidly available calcium ions and its intravenous administration is the treatment of choice in severe hypocalcemic tetany. The intramuscular route should not be used because of the large quantity of solution that must be injected and the risk of abscess formation. Calcium gluconate is administered orally for mild and latent tetany and for maintenance therapy. It is nonirritating to the veins, subcutaneous tissue, and gastrointestinal tract.

USUAL DOSAGE.—

Intravenous: Adults, initially, 10 to 20 ml of a 10% solution (1 to 2 g) injected slowly; this dose may be repeated until tetany is controlled; a 0.3% solution (30 ml of 10% solution in 1 liter of sodium chloride injection) then is infused by slow drip throughout the day. The maximal daily dose is 15 g (150 ml of a 10% solution). *Children*, 500 mg/kg of body weight daily in divided doses.

Intramuscular: This route of administration should not be used.

Oral: Adults, 3 to 15 g daily in divided doses; *children*, 500 mg/kg of body weight daily in divided doses.

PREPARATIONS.—

Injection: Solution 10% in 10 ml containers.

Oral: Tablets 300, 500, and 600 mg and 1 g.

Drug marketed by many manufacturers under generic name.

CALCIUM LACTATE

This orally administered calcium salt is readily absorbed and is effective in the treatment of mild and latent hypocalcemic tetany and for maintenance therapy.

USUAL DOSAGE.—*Oral: Adults*, 4 g three times daily with meals; *children*, 500 mg/kg of body weight daily in divided doses.

PREPARATIONS.—*Oral:* Tablets 300 and 600 mg. Drug marketed under generic name.

CALCIUM PHOSPHATE, DIBASIC
CALCIUM PHOSPHATE, TRIBASIC

These orally administered calcium salts can be used in the treatment of mild and latent hypocalcemic tetany and for maintenance therapy except in hypoparathyroidism and hypocalcemia associated with advanced renal insufficiency accompanied by hyperphosphatemia. These salts are especially useful when it is desirable to supply both calcium and phosphorus (eg, during pregnancy and lactation).

USUAL DOSAGE.—*Oral: Adults*, 1 to 2 g three times daily with meals.

PREPARATIONS.—No single-entity pharmaceutical dosage form available; compounding necessary for prescription.

PARATHYROID INJECTION

In the past, parathyroid injection was used for the temporary control of tetany in acute hypoparathyroidism. Since it is a preparation of animal origin, the biological activity is uncertain. Parathyroid injection is now considered an obsolete preparation, and is not used for therapy.

USUAL DOSAGE.—Use of this drug is not justified. The manufacturers' suggested dosage is: *Intramuscular, Intravenous, Subcutaneous: Adults*, 40 units every 12 hours; for acute tetany, 50 to 150 units every 12 hours. If parathyroid injection is to be added to other intravenous solutions, 2.5% to 5% dextrose injection should be used. (Sodium chloride solutions often cause a precipitate to form.)

PREPARATIONS.–*Injection:* Solution 100 units/ml in 5 ml containers. Drug marketed under generic name.

VITAMIN D

Vitamin D is used as a therapeutic agent in hypoparathyroidism. As used here, vitamin D is a collective term for ergocalciferol (vitamin D_2) and cholecalciferol (vitamin D_3), the naturally occurring substance found in fish liver oils. A third sterol, dihydrotachysterol, has vitamin D_2 activity and is also administered in the treatment of hypoparathyroidism (see the following evaluation).

For use of vitamin D in vitamin D deficiency, see Chapter 14, Vitamins and Sources of Vitamins.

In parathyroid hormone deficiency, the administration of large doses of vitamin D increases serum calcium levels and decreases serum phosphorus levels. This effect on calcium and phosphorus metabolism is similar to that of parathyroid hormone. Large doses of vitamin D promote phosphaturia, increase mobilization of mineral from bone, and increase calcium and phosphate absorption from the intestine; these effects account for the elevation of serum calcium concentrations.

Ergocalciferol is the most commonly used agent in the long-term treatment of hypoparathyroidism. Its onset of action is slower than that of dihydrotachysterol and the duration of effect is more prolonged.

The dosage of vitamin D should be regulated by frequent estimation of the serum calcium concentration. In the treatment of hypoparathyroidism with vitamin D or dihydrotachysterol, hypercalciuria may occur along with hypocalcemia. Urinary calcium concentrations (Sulkowitch test) do not adequately reflect serum calcium concentrations and cannot be used as a guide to dosage.

Since large doses of vitamin D are required, careful regulation is important to avoid overdosage with resulting hypercalcemia. The complications of hypercalcemia, especially those affecting the kidneys, may be severe and death may result. The possibility of renal damage from excessive doses persists for a considerable period after discontinuing the drug. Adverse effects also occasionally result from a lowered threshold or increased sensitivity in patients not receiving excessively large doses.

Vitamin D is potent and potentially harmful; it is contraindicated in conditions such as arthritis, in which its use has been advocated although no physiologic basis for such use exists.

USUAL DOSAGE.–*Oral: Adults,* initially, 100,000 units twice daily as soon as acute tetany is controlled with intravenous calcium preparations. Adjunctive measures include calcium salts given orally, a diet low in phosphate, and concomitant administration of aluminum hydroxide to inhibit absorption of phosphate. The maintenance dose is usually 50,000 to 100,000 units daily.

PREPARATIONS.–

Ergocalciferol (Vitamin D_2):

Deltalin (Lilly), Geltabs (Upjohn). *Oral:* Capsules 50,000 units.

Drisdol (Winthrop). *Oral:* Capsules 50,000 units; solution 10,000 units/ml.

Viosterol in Oil (Parke, Davis). *Oral:* Solution 10,000 units/g.

Drug also marketed under names Vitamin D and Calciferol.

DIHYDROTACHYSTEROL [Hytakerol]

This form of vitamin D is effective in increasing serum calcium concentrations; it may act somewhat more rapidly in hypocalcemia than vitamins D_2 and D_3. Dihydrotachysterol has been reported to be more effective in raising the serum calcium concentration in patients with renal failure because it can bypass the second hydroxylation step in the kidney.

In comparison to ergocalciferol, the phosphate diuresis produced by dihydrotachysterol is almost as great, the absorption of calcium from the intestine is less, and the serum calcium concentrations rise more rapidly. Because its duration of action is shorter, the potential hazards of accumulation and hypercalcemia are less with dihydrotachysterol than with ergocalciferol.

Dihydrotachysterol has only weak antirachitic activity (about 1/400 that of vitamin D).

USUAL DOSAGE.–*Oral: Adults,* 0.75 to 2.5 mg daily; specific dosage is determined by frequent estimations of serum calcium levels. For maintenance, 0.25 to 1.75 mg weekly has been given.

PREPARATIONS.–

Crystalline Dihydrotachysterol (Philips Roxane). *Oral:* Tablets 0.2 mg.

Hytakerol (crystalline) (Winthrop). *Oral:* Capsules 0.125 mg; solution (in oil) 0.25 mg/ml in 15 ml containers.

MIXTURES

Calcium salts used in the treatment of hypocalcemia are incorporated in mixtures with vitamins C and D and are promoted for oral use as dietary supplements during pregnancy and lactation and in infants and children. There is no evidence that the fixed-ratio mixtures meet the dietary needs of any substantial number of persons; therefore, all of these agents should be prescribed on an individual basis.

There is no evidence that the parenteral proprietary mixtures of calcium salts are more effective than the single-entity agents for the treatment of hypocalcemia.

ORAL PREPARATIONS.–

Calcium Gluconate w/Vitamin D (Lilly): Each capsule contains calcium gluconate 325 mg or 1 g and synthetic vitamin D 330 or 660 units.

Dicalcium Phosphate and Calcium Gluconate with Vitamin D: Capsules and tablets marketed by many manufacturers.

Dicalcium Phosphate Compound with Viosterol (Squibb): Each tablet contains dicalcium phosphate 228 mg, calcium carbonate 45 mg, and vitamin D 330 units.

Dicalcium Phosphate with Vitamin D: Capsules and tablets marketed by many manufacturers.

Dicalcium Phosphate w/Vitamin D and Iron (Lilly): Each capsule contains dicalcium phosphate 500 mg, iron pyrophosphate 87 mg, and vitamin D 330 units.

Dical-D (Abbott): Each capsule contains dicalcium phosphate 500 mg and vitamin D 133 units.

Dical-D w/Iron (Abbott): Each capsule contains dicalcium phosphate 500 mg, vitamin D 133 units, and iron pyrophosphate 87 mg.

Dical-D w/Vitamin C (Abbott): Each capsule contains dicalcium phosphate 500 mg, vitamin D 133 units, and ascorbic acid 15 mg.

Dical-Dee (Barre): Each capsule contains dicalcium phosphate 291 mg, calcium gluconate 194 mg, and vitamin D 350 units.

Dicaldimin (Abbott): Each capsule contains dicalcium phosphate 725 mg, ferrous sulfate 50 mg, thiamine mononitrate 3 mg, riboflavin 3 mg, niacinamide 12 mg, and vitamin D 65 units.

Vio-Cal (Rowell): Each capsule contains dicalcium phosphate 320 mg, calcium gluconate 160 mg, and ergocalciferol 350 units.

PARENTERAL PREPARATIONS.–

Cal-C-Bate (Kay): Each milliliter of solution contains calcium ascorbate 50 mg and calcium gluconate 50 mg with benzyl alcohol 1.5% and sodium bisulfite 0.05% in 5 and 10 ml containers.

Calcium Gluconate-Gluceptate Solution (Abbott): Each milliliter contains calcium gluconate 50 mg and calcium gluceptate 62 mg in 10 ml containers.

Calphosan (Carlton): Each milliliter of solution contains calcium lactate 5 mg and calcium glycerophosphate 5 mg in 10 and 60 ml containers.

Chapter 18

LOCAL ANESTHETICS

Local anesthetics produce loss of sensation and motor activity in a circumscribed area of the body by reversibly blocking conduction in nerve fibers. They interfere with the excitation process in peripheral nerves by several mechanisms, including a decrease in the permeability of the cell membrane to sodium ions, which results in failure of propagation of the action potential.

Local anesthetics may be divided into two main chemical groups: alcohols (eg, benzyl alcohol, phenol) and amines (eg, cocaine, lidocaine [Xylocaine], procaine [Novocain]). The alcohols are used primarily for topical anesthesia but are not important clinically because they destroy tissue. The amines are bases, and they are used both topically and by injection. Chemically, the amines vary widely but most consist of an amine portion, an aliphatic linkage, and an aromatic portion. Certain antihistamines, anticholinergic agents, and adrenergic agents having this configuration also have some local anesthetic action.

Local anesthetic salts are highly ionized, water soluble, and stable. The salt is converted to the nonionized base by the alkalinity of the tissues and thus penetrates the nerve sheath. Depending upon the drug, both the unchanged base and the charged cation (reformed after penetration of the nerve sheath) appear to be responsible for producing nerve block. The base forms are soluble in vehicles used for ointments, while most of the salts are not.

Most amines are either esters (eg, procaine, tetracaine [Pontocaine]) or amides (eg, bupivacaine [Marcaine], lidocaine, mepivacaine [Carbocaine], prilocaine [Citanest]).

The area anesthetized is distal to the point of an injection or, for topical local anesthetics, is the site of application. The duration of the block depends upon the chemical structure of the agent, the concentration and volume of the solution injected, and whether or not a vasoconstrictor was added to the solution. Although local anesthetics act on all parts of a neuron, they are invariably applied to the axons of peripheral nerves, the various fibers of which are blocked in sequence according to their size: first, autonomic fibers (smallest, nonmyelinated); next, those mediating cold, warmth, pain, and touch; and, finally, those mediating somatic motor function and proprioception (largest, myelinated). Function is regained in the reverse order. The degree of penetration depends upon the chemical structure of the agent, the concentration and volume of the solution injected, and the size of the nerve. Greater quantities of more concentrated solutions are required for successful block of larger, centrally located nerve trunks than of smaller peripheral nerves.

Local anesthetics are metabolized primarily in the plasma and liver. The rate and metabolic pathways vary with the type of drug and the age and physical status of the patient. The esters are partly or completely hydrolyzed in the plasma by plasma cholinesterase and metabolites are excreted in the urine. Cocaine is excreted unchanged, predominantly in the urine. The amides are metabolized in the liver, but the mechanism is not entirely clear. Drugs that are eliminated or metabolized slowly tend to be more toxic systemically.

For most local anesthetics, the perineural concentration necessary to produce block is several hundredfold greater than the tolerable plasma level; therefore, the drug should be injected precisely at the appropriate site. *The least amount of the most dilute solution that is effective should be administered.*

Minimal and maximal dosages for a local anesthetic are dependent upon many variables (eg, age of patient, vascularity of tissues at injection site, rate of metabolism, extent of storage in tissues, tolerance, presence of other drugs). Experience in the pediatric use of local anesthetics is limited because many children are emotionally unsuited for regional anesthesia. Their nerve endings and trunks are usually smaller than those in adults, and smaller quantities of more dilute solutions are required for anesthesia. Total maximal dosages used for nerve blocks should be calculated according to body surface area (see table, back cover).

With the exception of solutions for use in spinal anesthesia, local anesthetic solutions should be isotonic to avoid edema, local irritation, and inflammation at the site of injection. Potent drugs such as tetracaine and dibucaine [Nupercaine] may be dissolved directly in physiologic sodium chloride injection, since the amount required is comparatively small and tonicity is not altered by this solvent. Less potent drugs must be used in more concentrated solutions, and adjustment of tonicity is required if they are dissolved in distilled water or another solvent that does not produce an isotonic solution.

Regional (conduction) anesthetic techniques are usually classified according to the site of application of the local anesthetic agent. The classes are: (1) surface (topical), (2) infiltration (local), (3) field block, (4) nerve block, (5) peridural (epidural, extradural, caudal), (6) spinal (intrathecal, subarachnoid), and (7) intravenous regional anesthesia.

Surface Anesthesia: The alcohols or the base form of amines are used to produce surface anesthesia. The salts of the amines do not penetrate intact skin. Wounds, ulcers, and burns are preferably treated with preparations that are relatively insoluble in tissue fluids. Mucous membranes of the nose, mouth, pharynx, larynx, trachea, bronchi, and urethra are readily anesthetized by topical agents. However, since absorption from these areas is rapid, no more than one-fourth to one-third of the dosage used for infiltration should be administered in order to minimize the incidence of systemic toxic reactions. Generally, agents that are most effective topically have the greatest potential to produce systemic toxic reactions.

The drugs used to relieve pruritus, burning, and surface pain on skin and the less sensitive mucous membranes (anus and rectum) include benzocaine, butyl aminobenzoate [Butesin], cyclomethycaine [Surfacaine], dibucaine, dimethisoquin [Quotane], dyclonine [Dyclone], lidocaine, pramoxine [Tronothane], and tetracaine. Piperocaine [Metycaine] is used on the mucous membranes of the anus and rectum but not on the skin.

The following drugs are effective when used topically on various mucous membranes: butacaine [Butyn], cocaine, cyclomethycaine, dibucaine, diperodon [Diothane], dyclonine, hexylcaine [Cyclaine], lidocaine, piperocaine, pramoxine, and tetracaine.

Surface anesthesia is widely used in ophthalmology to anesthetize the cornea and conjunctiva for removal of foreign bodies; for short procedures such as tonometry; for major ocular operations, including cataract extractions and iridectomies; and is combined with retrobulbar injections of a local anesthetic for intraocular or orbital surgery. Drugs most widely used in the eye include dyclonine, lidocaine, proparacaine [Ophthaine], and tetracaine.

Infiltration Anesthesia: In this procedure, the solution is injected in the immediate area of the surgery in order to block nerve endings distributed there. These nerve fibers have no sheath and are readily blocked by very dilute solutions.

Field Block Anesthesia: This is performed by injecting the solution close to the nerves around the area to be anesthetized.

Nerve Block Anesthesia: In this type of anesthesia, a localized perineural injection is made at an access point along the course of a nerve distant from the operative site. More concentrated solutions of drug are required because these nerves have a sheath.

The drugs most commonly used for infiltration, field, and nerve block anesthesia include chloroprocaine [Nesacaine], lidocaine, mepivacaine, prilocaine, and procaine. Tetracaine is seldom used.

Peridural Anesthesia: This technique is accomplished by injecting a local anesthetic into the peridural space. In lumbar epidural anesthesia, the injection is usually made through one of the ligamenta flava between the second lumbar and first sacral vertebrae to avoid injury to the spinal cord, which ends at the second lumbar vertebra in 95% of individuals. In caudal anesthesia, the solution is introduced into the caudal canal (peridural space) through the sacral hiatus. In both techniques, the anesthetic is believed to block the paravertebral and peridural sections of spinal nerves; an insignificant amount of the drug passes into the subarachnoid spaces and the spinal cord itself. In general, the number of spinal segments blocked is determined by the age of the patient (determinant of the rate of escape of drug from the spinal canal) and the volume of solution injected. The physiologic changes are similar but may be less pronounced than those that occur with spinal anesthesia. A test dose of 2 to 5 ml of the solution to be injected should always be administered at least five minutes before the main dose, because an inadvertent spinal (subarachnoid) tap is possible. The relatively large dosage needed and the great vascularity of the peridural space increase the possibility of systemic toxic reactions. Repeated fractional injections through an in situ catheter (continuous peridural anesthesia) may be used to prolong peridural anesthesia.

The drugs most commonly used for this technique are lidocaine and mepivacaine, but procaine, chloroprocaine [Nesacaine], piperocaine (caudal), and prilocaine can also be administered. Only single-dose containers should be used to minimize the chance of injecting a contaminated solution.

Spinal Anesthesia: In this form of anesthesia, a local anesthetic is injected into the spinal subarachnoid space: a needle is inserted through one of the ligamenta flava between the second lumbar and first sacral vertebrae. The drug is believed to anesthetize nerve roots as they emerge from the spinal cord. The number of spinal segments blocked is determined by the volume and concentration of the solution, the rate of injection, motor activity of the patient, the curvature of the spine, and the size of the subarachnoid space. The level of anesthesia is determined by the site of injection; the specific gravity, volume, and concentration of the solution; and the position of the patient. Consciousness is preserved at all times unless profound arterial hypotension develops secondary to the sympathetic block that is always produced. The duration of anesthesia depends upon the chemical nature of the drug and the rate at which the drug leaves the nerve roots. It may be increased 60% to 100% by adding a vasoconstrictor (eg, epinephrine) to the injected solution. Repeated fractional injections through an in situ catheter (continuous spinal anesthesia) may also be used to prolong spinal anesthesia. The drug diffuses within the cerebrospinal fluid and is removed primarily by venous drainage. A small quantity is removed by lymphatic drainage and/or the arachnoid villi. Enzymatic hydrolysis of the drugs in the cerebrospinal fluid is insignificant.

Solutions of local anesthetics for use in spinal anesthesia are prepared in hyperbaric (drug diluted with dextrose) or hypobaric (drug diluted with distilled water) form in order to assure that their specific gravity is higher or lower than that of cerebrospinal fluid, respectively. The hypobaric (light) solutions gravitate caudad and the hyperbaric (heavy) solutions gravitate cephalad when the patient is placed in the head-down position. Tetracaine and lidocaine are widely used for spinal anesthesia, but procaine and dibucaine can also be administered. Hexylcaine is seldom used.

Intravenous Regional Anesthesia: In this technique the entire distal part of an extremity is blocked. The extremity is exsanguinated by elevation and wrapping with elastic bandages, a tourniquet is applied, and the drug is injected intravenously in the distal part of the extremity. The tourniquet must be securely fastened, for inadvertent slipping may cause a severe, possibly fatal, systemic reaction. Chloroprocaine, lidocaine, mepivacaine, procaine, and prilocaine may be used for this technique.

Supplemental Agents: Vasoconstrictors may be added to solutions for infiltration, nerve block, peridural, and spinal anesthesia. These agents produce vasoconstriction, thereby decreasing the rate of absorption. This prolongs the effect of the anesthetic and reduces the risk of systemic toxic reactions. Epinephrine is the vasoconstrictor most commonly used, and the concentration most commonly employed is 1:200,000. Levarterenol [Levophed], nordefrin [Cobefrin], and phenylephrine [Neo-Synephrine] also are used but must be given in higher concentrations.

Some local anesthetics (eg, mepivacaine) allegedly have an inherent vasoconstrictor effect. It has been suggested that use of epinephrine may not be necessary with these drugs and that they may, therefore, be desirable for use in elderly patients; in those with hypertension, severe cardiovascular disease, or thyrotoxicosis; during labor; or in nerve blocks of the ears, fingers, toes, and penis. There is, however, no convincing evidence that any local anesthetic, with the exception of cocaine, has an inherent vasoconstrictor effect.

Hyaluronidase [Alidase, Hyazyme, Wydase] has been added to local anesthetics to facilitate their diffusion into the tissues during infiltration and nerve block anesthesia. However, because a higher incidence of systemic reactions from rapid absorption of the anesthetic and local irritation and sensitization have been reported with use of this enzyme, its value is seriously questioned.

Adverse Reactions

Most systemic reactions from local anesthetics are caused by overdosage (relative overdosage in children) or develop in elderly, debilitated, or acutely ill patients in whom metabolism of the drugs may be impaired. Allergic (hypersensitivity) reactions, including anaphylaxis, are extremely rare. When a substantial quantity of a local anesthetic appears in the blood stream due to overdosage, inadvertent intravenous injection, or rapid absorption from a highly vascular area, the resulting high plasma levels may cause alarming, and sometimes fatal, systemic reactions that are qualitatively similar for all local anesthetics. It is important to note that severe systemic reactions may not occur until approximately 30 minutes after the drug is injected.

The systemic reactions primarily involve the cardiovascular and central nervous systems. The initial manifestations may affect one system or both simultaneously.

The cardiovascular reaction is characterized by hypotension and atrioventricular block that may ultimately progress to cardiac and respiratory arrest; it is the result of myocardial and cardiac conduction depression and systemic vasodilatation. The onset of symptoms is often abrupt, but the manifestations may pass unnoticed in some patients. In severe cases of acute circulatory failure, fluids and vasopressors such as ephedrine, metaraminol [Aramine], and mephentermine [Wyamine] are administered intravenously. If respiratory arrest occurs or asystole is suspected, artificial ventilation and external cardiac massage must be instituted immediately.

The initial phase of the central nervous system reaction is one of excitation, and is characterized by tremors, shivering, and convulsions. If a large amount of drug is absorbed, respiratory depression and, ultimately, arrest may develop as a result of generalized central nervous system depression.

Convulsions may be controlled by the intravenous administration of small increments (50 to 100 mg) of an ultrashort-acting barbiturate such as thiopental [Pentothal], thiamylal [Surital], or methohexital [Brevital]. If none of these are available, a short-acting barbiturate (eg, secobarbital [Seconal], pentobarbital [Nembutal]) may be given in increments of 25 mg every one to two minutes. There may be a latent period of two to three minutes before these drugs become effective. The barbiturate should be given in sufficient quantity to control the seizures, but caution must be exercised because overdosage may occur if sufficient time is not allowed for the anticonvulsant action of the individual doses to become apparent. Artificial ventilation may be required if respiratory depression develops. Hypnotic doses of barbiturates given for prophylaxis are of no value in averting a central nervous system reaction.

Recently, diazepam [Valium] has been recommended to control convulsions. Neuromuscular blocking agents may be used to terminate convulsions, but only if the physician is familiar with their use and with the principles of artificial ventilation.

The predominant local adverse reaction to local anesthetics is eczematoid dermatitis. This is characterized by erythema and pruritus that may progress to vesiculation and oozing, and occurs most commonly among individuals who are frequently exposed to these agents (eg, physicians, dentists). Since the local anesthetic amides were introduced, these reactions have become exceedingly rare.

Systemic signs and symptoms may be produced by the epinephrine added to solutions of local anesthetics for parenteral use. Anxiety, palpitations, dizziness, headache, restlessness, tremors, tachycardia, anginal pain, and hypertension may be observed. These differ from the systemic reactions caused by local anesthetics in that epinephrine does not cause convulsions, but does produce tachycardia. Although these effects of epinephrine tend to be mild and transient, cardiorespiratory failure may develop.

Precautions

Local anesthetics are incompatible with salts of mercury, silver, and other metals, and they are rapidly inactivated by alkalis and antiseptic solutions. Those supplied in multiple-dose containers should not be used for spinal or peridural anesthesia, because of the possibility of adverse reactions to the chemical preservatives or bacterial or chemical contamination from repeated use.

If a patient cannot tolerate a particular local anesthetic, a drug from a different chemical group should be substituted. Skin, conjunctival, and patch tests for hypersensitivity are not necessarily reliable for predicting or excluding the development of an allergic response. If rash, urticaria, edema, or other manifestations of allergy develop during use of a topical local anesthetic, the drug should be discontinued permanently. To minimize the possibility of a serious allergic reaction, topical preparations should not be applied for prolonged periods unless under the continuing supervision of a physician.

Some local anesthetics (eg, lidocaine) have been reported to have neuromuscular blocking effects which may be additive to those of tubocurarine and other muscle relaxants. The clinical significance of this finding remains to be established.

Local anesthetics diffuse readily through the utero-placental barrier, and, particularly if used in excessive quantities, may accumulate in the fetus and cause fetal bradycardia before birth and neonatal depression after birth.

Local anesthetic solutions containing epinephrine should not be used for nerve blocks in areas supplied by end-arteries (eg, digits, ears, nose, penis). Their use in these areas may be followed by ischemia, which may progress to gangrene. These solutions also should not be administered in excessive dosage, intravenously, or with inhalation anesthetics which sensitize the heart to catecholamines, as severe ventricular arrhythmias may result. Local anesthetic solutions for infiltration and nerve blocks in patients in labor should not contain epinephrine in dilutions less than 1:200,000 because of the danger of producing vasoconstriction in uterine blood vessels, which might result in decreased placental circulation, diminished intensity of uterine contractions, and prolonged labor. It also may be undesirable to use anesthetic solutions containing epinephrine in elderly patients or in those with hypertension, severe cardiovascular disease, or thyrotoxicosis.

To prevent accidental intravascular injection, needle placement must always be checked prior to injection of the local anesthetic by aspiration with a syringe. In addition, local anesthetics should not be administered unless an individual capable of conducting resuscitative measures, and the following equipment, are immediately available: syringes and needles, oropharyngeal airways, and anesthesia masks. An apparatus for administering oxygen and artificial ventilation, an apparatus for defibrillating the heart, ultrashort- or short-acting barbiturates, neuromuscular blocking agents, intravenous fluids, vasopressors, and any additional drugs and equipment that may be useful for resuscitation should also be available.

INDIVIDUAL EVALUATIONS

BENOXINATE HYDROCHLORIDE

[Dorsacaine]

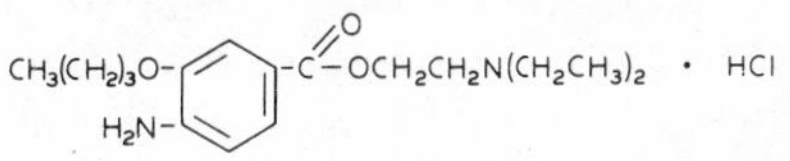

$CH_3(CH_2)_3O-$, H_2N- (benzene ring) $-C(=O)-OCH_2CH_2N(CH_2CH_3)_2 \cdot HCl$

This aminobenzoic acid ester is related to procaine and is used for surface anesthesia in ophthalmology. The average onset of anesthesia is one minute and the duration is 20 to 30 minutes. The corneal reflex is fully restored within one hour. Benoxinate causes minimal ocular irritation but, in contrast to cocaine, little or no mydriasis or cycloplegia; there is less punctate epithelial damage than with tetracaine.

Occasional temporary stinging, burning, and conjunctival erythema have been observed. Rarely, a severe, immediate, apparently allergic corneal reaction (acute, intense, and diffuse epithelial keratitis; a gray, ground-glass appearance; sloughing of large areas of necrotic epithelium; corneal filaments; and, sometimes, iritis with descemetitis) has occurred. For additional information on adverse reactions and precautions, see the Introductory Statement.

USUAL DOSAGE.—*Topical* (ophthalmic): *Adults*, for tonometry, removal of foreign bodies and sutures, and other minor procedures, one or two drops of 0.4% solution in each eye; for more profound anesthesia, two drops of 0.4% solution instilled in each eye at 90-second intervals for three instillations.

PREPARATIONS.—Dorsacaine (Dorsey). *Topical:* Solution (ophthalmic) 0.4% in 15 ml containers.

BENZOCAINE

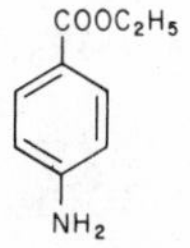

$COOC_2H_5$ (benzene ring) NH_2

Benzocaine, the ethyl ester of aminobenzoic acid, is used for surface anesthesia of the skin and mucous membranes. It is one of the most widely used agents for relief of sunburn, pruritus, and burns. Ointments containing less than 5% benzocaine or acidic preparations are ineffective. Since benzocaine is poorly soluble in water and poorly absorbed, it remains in contact with the skin for a long time, and thus produces a sustained anesthetic effect with a low incidence of systemic toxic reactions.

The possibility of sensitization should always be considered. Preparations containing benzocaine (usually as suppositories) may cause methemoglobinemia in susceptible infants.

For additional information on adverse reactions and precautions, see the Introductory Statement.

USUAL DOSAGE.—*Topical:* Various forms are applied as required.

PREPARATIONS.—*Topical:* Cream 5%; ointment 5%; suppositories 200, 300, and 600 mg. Drug marketed under generic name.

AVAILABLE MIXTURES.—

Americaine Aerosol (Arnar-Stone): Solution containing benzocaine 20% and 8-hydroxyquinoline 0.5%.

Americaine Ointment (Arnar-Stone): Ointment containing benzocaine 20% and benzethonium chloride 0.1%.

Derma Medicone Ointment (Medicone): Each gram of ointment contains benzocaine 20 mg, oxyquinoline sulfate 10.5 mg, menthol 4.8 mg, ichthammol 10 mg, and zinc oxide 137 mg with petrolatum and lanolin.

Derma Medicone-HC Ointment (Medicone): Each gram of ointment contains hydrocortisone acetate 10 mg, benzocaine 20 mg, oxyquinoline sulfate 10.5 mg, ephedrine hydrochloride 1.1 mg, menthol 4.8 mg, ichthammol 10 mg, and zinc oxide 137 mg with petrolatum and lanolin.

Dermoplast Aerosol (Ayerst): Solution containing benzocaine 4.5%, benzethonium chloride 0.1%, menthol 0.5%, 8-hydroxyquinoline benzoate 1.2%, and methylparaben 2% with isopropyl alcohol 1.9%.

Medicone Dressing Cream (Medicone): Each gram of cream contains benzocaine 5 mg and 8-hydroxyquinoline sulfate 0.5 mg with cod liver oil, zinc oxide, and menthol.

Urolocaine (Arner-Stone): Liquid containing benzocaine 10% and benzethonium chloride 0.1%.

BUPIVACAINE HYDROCHLORIDE

[Marcaine Hydrochloride]

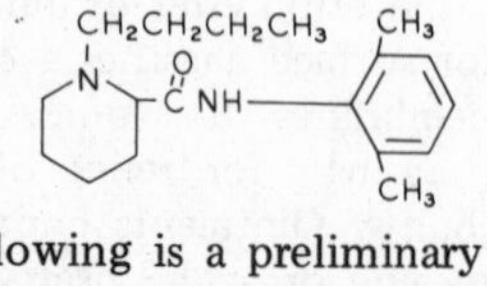

The following is a preliminary evaluation of bupivacaine, an amide that is related chemically to mepivacaine. Its most important property, in comparison to other available local anesthetic agents, is its long duration of action. Bupivacaine is used for infiltration, nerve block, and peridural anesthesia; it is not administered for spinal anesthesia. This agent may prove to be particularly advantageous when administered by continuous peridural techniques to relieve pain during labor, as the need for supplemental doses and, therefore, the probability of rising plasma levels, should be less than with mepivacaine or lidocaine. However, the possibility of accumulation of bupivacaine during continuous peridural anesthesia exists. Bupivacaine should not be used for intravenous regional anesthesia because excessively high blood levels have been observed following release of the tourniquet. Data on use of bupivacaine in children and elderly or debilitated adults are currently incomplete.

The potency of bupivacaine is similar to that of tetracaine and is four times greater than that of mepivacaine, lidocaine, and prilocaine. Although variability exists, the onset of action and period until maximal anesthesia with bupivacaine are comparable to those observed with mepivacaine and lidocaine; the duration of action is two to three times longer than that of mepivacaine and lidocaine and 20% to 30% longer than that of tetracaine. The duration can usually be lengthened by adding epinephrine; some nerve blocks may last more than 12 hours.

Bupivacaine produces systemic toxic reactions that are qualitatively similar to those produced by other local anesthetic drugs. However, it does not cause methemoglobinemia and does not appear to produce fetal depression after its use in obstetrical peridural anesthesia. For additional information on adverse reactions and precautions, see the Introductory Statement.

USUAL DOSAGE.—*Injection:* In *healthy adults*, the maximal single dose should not exceed 200 mg without epinephrine and 250 mg with epinephrine. This dose should not be repeated at intervals of less than three hours and, until further data become available, a total dose of 400 mg in 24 hours generally should not be exceeded.

(Infiltration): Without epinephrine, up to 70 ml of the 0.25% solution; with epinephrine, up to 90 ml of the 0.25% solution. Satisfactory anesthesia can also be produced by infiltration of a 0.1% solution.

(Nerve block): Without epinephrine, up to 70 ml of the 0.25% solution or 35 ml of the 0.5% solution; with epinephrine, up to 90 ml of the 0.25% solution or 45 ml of the 0.5% solution. The 0.5% solution is required to consistently produce a complete motor block of the larger nerves.

(Caudal): With or without epinephrine, for obstetrical analgesia and perineal surgery, up to 30 ml of the 0.25% solution; for surgery of the lower extremities, up to 30 ml of the 0.5% solution. When used for a continuous technique, supplemental doses of the 0.25% or 0.5% solution may produce profound motor block; otherwise these solutions cannot be relied upon to produce such a block. Only single-dose containers should be used.

(Lumbar epidural): With and without epinephrine, for obstetrical analgesia and perineal surgery, up to 20 ml of the 0.25% solution; for surgery of the lower extremities, up to 20 ml of the 0.5% solution. When used for a continuous technique, supplemental doses of the 0.25% or 0.5% solution may produce profound motor block; otherwise these solutions cannot be relied upon to produce such a block. Profound motor block, such as that required for abdominal surgery, can only be obtained consistently by use of up to 20 ml of the 0.75% solution. Repeated doses of the 0.75% solution for continuous peridural anesthesia are not recommended because of the possibility of accumulation and because there appears to be little reason for such use. Only single-dose containers should be used.

PREPARATIONS.—Marcaine [hydrochloride] (Winthrop). *Injection:* Solution 0.25% in 50 ml single- or multiple-dose containers; solution 0.5% in 30 ml single-dose containers and 50 ml multiple-dose containers; solution 0.75% in 30 ml single-dose containers for single-dose use only. All solutions are prepared with or without epinephrine 1:200,000. The solutions that do not contain epinephrine may be reautoclaved.

BUTACAINE SULFATE [Butyn Sulfate]

$NH_2-C_6H_4-COO(CH_2)_3N(C_4H_9)_2$

This aminobenzoic acid ester is used primarily for surface anesthesia of the eye, but also may be applied to the nose, throat, mouth, and urethra. Since butacaine is nine times more toxic than procaine when injected, it should not be administered for infiltration anesthesia. When used in the eye, it does not dehydrate the tissues, cause ischemia, or produce any change in the size of the pupil, accommodation, or intraocular tension. This agent should not be applied to the eye as a powder. Onset of action is within one minute, and the duration is approximately one hour. The potency of butacaine is similar to or slightly greater than that of cocaine, but this anesthetic is two to three times more toxic.

Burning may follow corneal instillation, and repeated use can cause sensitization and local irritation. Prolonged ophthalmic use may cause corneal softening and some loss of the corneal epithelium. For additional information on adverse reactions and precautions, see the Introductory Statement.

USUAL DOSAGE.—*Topical:*

(Eye): For tonometry, removal of foreign bodies and sutures, and other minor procedures, two or three drops of the 2% solution. Application of the 2% ointment three or four times daily will relieve pain for longer periods.

(Nose, throat, mouth): A total dose of 10 ml of the 2% solution should not be exceeded if the drug is applied by swabs, or 5 ml if applied as a spray.

(Urethra): The total dosage should not exceed 4 ml of a 1% solution; the drug should remain in the urethra for three to five minutes. Local anesthesia of the meatus can be obtained by applying a cotton pledget saturated with a 1% solution.

PREPARATIONS.—Butyn Sulfate (Abbott). *Topical:* Ointment (ophthalmic) 2% with nitromersol 1:3,000 in 1/8 oz containers; solution 2% in 30 ml containers. Drug also marketed by other manufacturers under generic and trade names.

BUTYL AMINOBENZOATE PICRATE
[Butesin Picrate]

$NH_2-C_6H_4-COOCH_2CH_2CH_2CH_3 \cdot$ (2,4,6-trinitrophenol: OH, NO_2, NO_2, NO_2)

This derivative of aminobenzoic acid is used on the skin to relieve pruritus and burning. Since this anesthetic is relatively insoluble in water and thus is poorly absorbed, it remains in contact with the skin for a prolonged period and produces a sustained anesthetic effect with a low incidence of systemic toxic reactions.

Butyl aminobenzoate picrate may cause a rash in sensitive individuals; the incidence is increased by the picrate component. For additional information on adverse reactions and precautions, see the Introductory Statement.

USUAL DOSAGE.—*Topical:* The ointment is applied to affected parts as required.

PREPARATIONS.—Butesin Picrate Ointment with Metaphen (Abbott). *Topical:* Ointment 1% with nitromersol 1:5,000 in 1 oz containers.

CHLOROPROCAINE HYDROCHLORIDE

[Nesacaine, Nesacaine-CE]

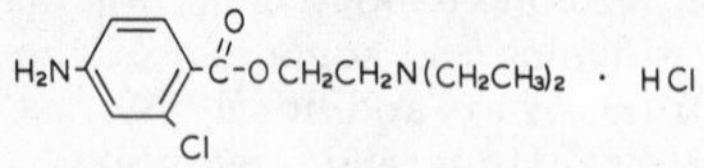

$H_2N-C_6H_3(Cl)-C(=O)-OCH_2CH_2N(CH_2CH_3)_2 \cdot HCl$

Chloroprocaine is a chlorinated analogue of procaine with similar pharmacologic properties. It is used for infiltration, nerve block, peridural, and intravenous regional anesthesia. The drug is not effective topically and has not been studied sufficiently to be used as a spinal anesthetic. Its anesthetic potency is slightly greater than that of procaine, and its duration of action is approximately the same. Nerve blocks performed with chloroprocaine last an average of one hour. The addition of epinephrine 1:200,000 prolongs anesthesia to two hours.

A few cases of thrombophlebitis have been reported following administration of chloroprocaine in intravenous regional anesthesia. This reaction may have been due to the acidity of the solution. For additional information on adverse reactions and precautions, see the Introductory Statement.

USUAL DOSAGE.—*Injection:* The maximal single dose for injection is 800 mg without epinephrine and 1 g with epinephrine 1:200,000. Repeated doses of up to 300 mg without epinephrine and 600 mg with epinephrine 1:200,000 may be given at 50-minute intervals.

(Infiltration): Up to 80 ml of the 1% solution without epinephrine or 100 ml of the 1% solution with epinephrine 1:200,000.

(Nerve block): The dose of the 1% or 2% solution with or without epinephrine 1:200,000 depends upon the type of block and intensity and duration of effect needed.

(Caudal): Initially, 15 to 25 ml (depending upon the size of the patient) of the 2% or 3% Nesacaine-CE solution. Repeated doses may be given at 40- to 60-minute intervals as required; epinephrine 1:200,000 may be used to prolong the action.

(Lumbar epidural): The usual total initial dose is 15 to 25 ml with or without epinephrine 1:200,000 (approximately 2 to 2.5 ml per nerve segment to be blocked) of the 2% or 3% Nesacaine-CE solution. Supplemental doses of 10 to 20 ml may be given at 40- to 50-minute intervals.

(Intravenous regional): 40 ml of a 0.5% solution without epinephrine has been used. The approximate maximal single dose is 800 mg.

PREPARATIONS.—

Nesacaine (Pennwalt). *Injection:* Solution 1% and 2% in 30 ml containers (not for caudal or epidural anesthesia).

Nesacaine-CE (Pennwalt). *Injection:* Solution 2% and 3% in 30 ml containers (for caudal or epidural anesthesia; contains no preservative).

The solutions should not be autoclaved because the potency is impaired.

COCAINE

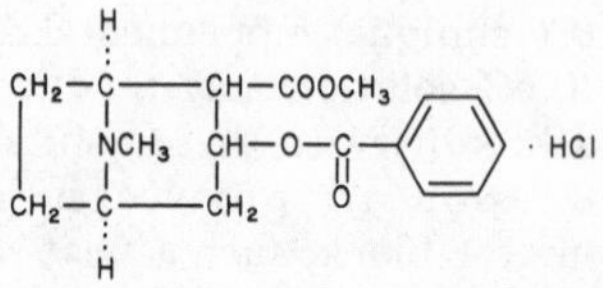

[Structural formula of cocaine hydrochloride: tropane ring with NCH_3 bridge, $CH-COOCH_3$ and $CH-O-C(=O)-C_6H_5$ substituents $\cdot$ HCl]

Cocaine is a naturally occurring alkaloid which produces excellent surface anesthesia with intense vasoconstriction when applied to mucous surfaces. It is not used systemically. Onset of action is rapid (one minute) and the duration is up to two hours, depending upon the dose and concentration applied. Cocaine is used for surface anesthesia in the ear, nose, and throat and in bronchoscopy. The addition of epinephrine not only is unnecessary, but may increase the likelihood of arrhythmias and ventricular fibrillation. The moistening of dry cocaine powder with epinephrine solution to form so-called "cocaine mud" for use on the nasal mucosa is particularly dangerous.

Repeated use of cocaine in the eye in concentrations commonly used for anesthesia may cause the cornea to become cloudy, pitted, and, eventually, ulcerated. This toxic effect is enhanced by inhibition of the normal protective eyelid reflexes, so that drying and contamination with foreign bodies may occur. This effect and mydriasis are the main drawbacks to the ophthalmic use of cocaine to achieve local anesthesia. For uses in the eye not related to anesthesia, see Chapter 70, Mydriatics and Cycloplegics.

Toxic symptoms occur frequently because cocaine is absorbed readily but is eliminated and detoxified slowly. Central nervous system effects include euphoria and cortical stimulation manifested by excitement and restlessness. Stimulation of the lower motor centers causes tremors, while stimulation of the medullary centers causes hypertension, tachycardia, and tachypnea. Acute poisoning produces marked cortical stimulation manifested by excitement, restlessness, confusion, tremor, a rise in blood pressure, tachycardia, tachypnea, nausea, vomiting, abdominal pain, exophthalmos, and mydriasis. Stimulation is followed by depression and, finally, by death from respiratory depression.

Repeated use results in psychic dependence and tolerance; therefore, cocaine is classified as a Schedule II drug under the Controlled Substances Act.

Cocaine exerts an adrenergic effect by potentiating the actions of endogenous and injected epinephrine and norepinephrine; ventricular fibrillation due to absorption of excessive amounts of cocaine may occur, particularly if a general anesthetic which "sensitizes" the myocardium to the catecholamines is also being administered. Solutions of cocaine are unstable and deteriorate on standing. Boiling and autoclaving cause decomposition.

For additional information on adverse reactions and precautions, see the Introductory Statement.

USUAL DOSAGE.—*Topical:*

(Ear, nose, throat, bronchoscopy): Concentrations of 1% to 4% are used. The maximal single dose is 1 mg/kg of body weight. The lowest concentration and smallest volume possible should be applied. Use of concentrations greater than 4% is inadvisable because of the potential for increasing the incidence and severity of systemic toxic reactions.

(Eye): Ophthalmic use of cocaine is deemed hazardous for the reasons stated above.

PREPARATIONS.—Cocaine, N.F., Cocaine Hydrochloride, U.S.P. No single-entity pharmaceutical dosage form available. Compounding necessary for prescription.

CYCLOMETHYCAINE [Surfacaine]

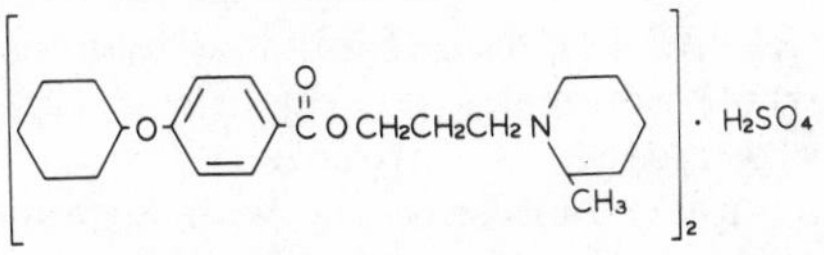

$$\left[C_6H_{11}-O-C_6H_4-\overset{O}{\overset{\|}{C}}-OCH_2CH_2CH_2N(C_5H_9CH_3) \right]_2 \cdot H_2SO_4$$

Cyclomethycaine, a benzoic acid ester, is a topical anesthetic agent used on the skin and on the mucosa of the rectum, vagina, urethra, and urinary bladder in the treatment of thermal or chemical burns; abrasions; dermatologic conditions characterized by pain, pruritus, and irritability; and in various proctologic, gynecologic, and urologic manipulations. This drug is relatively ineffective in anesthetizing the mucous membranes of the mouth, nose, trachea, bronchi, eye, and ear.

Cyclomethycaine may produce transitory stinging or burning in sensitive patients. The ointment form should not be used on vesicular lesions. For additional information on adverse reactions and precautions, see the Introductory Statement.

USUAL DOSAGE.—*Topical:* Preparations are applied as required.

(Skin): 0.5% cream and 1% ointment is used.

(Urethra): 0.75% jelly is used in the untraumatized urethra. The optimal dose is up to 4 ml in women and 10 ml in men.

(Anus): 1% ointment or 0.75% jelly is used for rectal pain.

(Vagina, rectum): The 10 mg suppository gives relief for up to eight hours; the 1% ointment also may be used.

PREPARATIONS.—Surfacaine (Lilly): *Topical:* Cream 0.5% in 1 and 16 oz containers; jelly 0.75% with thimerosal 1:10,000 in 1/8, 1, and 5 oz containers; ointment 1% in 1 and 16 oz containers; suppositories 10 mg.

AVAILABLE MIXTURES.—

Surfadil Cream (Lilly): Cream containing cyclomethycaine 0.5% and methapyrilene hydrochloride 2%.

Surfadil Lotion (Lilly): Each milliliter contains cyclomethycaine 5 mg, methapyrilene hydrochloride 20 mg, and titanium dioxide 50 mg.

DIBUCAINE HYDROCHLORIDE [Nupercainal, Nupercaine Hydrochloride]

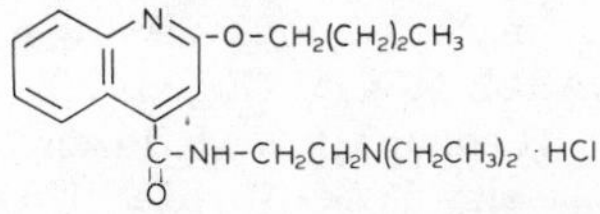

$$\text{(quinoline)}-O-CH_2(CH_2)_2CH_3;\ -\overset{\|}{\underset{O}{C}}-NH-CH_2CH_2N(CH_2CH_3)_2 \cdot HCl$$

Dibucaine, a quinoline derivative, is the most potent and one of the most toxic and long-acting local anesthetics. It is used for spinal and surface anesthesia. Dibucaine is 15 to 20 times more potent than procaine when injected, and 10 to 15 times more potent than cocaine topically. It is five times more toxic than cocaine when applied topically and 15 times more toxic than procaine when injected. The onset of action of this drug is relatively slow (up to 15 minutes). The duration of spinal anesthesia is three to four hours; this can be prolonged to six hours by the addition of epinephrine. The drug is partially metabolized but a portion is eliminated unchanged.

Both hyperbaric (heavy) and hypobaric (light) solutions of the drug are available for spinal anesthesia.

For adverse reactions and additional information on precautions, see the Introductory Statement.

USUAL DOSAGE.—

Topical: Preparations are applied as required.

(Skin): Cream, ointment, or aerosol is used in a concentration of 0.25% to 1%.

(Ear): 0.25% solution is used.

(Pharynx): 0.5% to 2% solution is used.

(Rectum): The ointment or suppository is used morning and night and after each bowel movement.

Injection:

(Infiltration, nerve block, and peridural): Use of dibucaine for these techniques is inadvisable because of the high incidence of local and systemic toxic reactions.

(Spinal): Obstetrical and saddle block, 2.5 to 5 mg (1 to 2 ml hyperbaric solution); lower extremities, 4 mg (6 ml hypobaric solution); lower abdomen, 7.5 to 10 mg (11 to 15 ml hypobaric solution); upper abdomen, 10 to 12 mg (15 to 18 ml hypobaric solution).

PREPARATIONS.—

Nupercainal (Ciba). *Topical:* Ointment 1% in 16 oz containers.

Nupercainal (Madison). *Topical:* Cream 0.5% in 1.5 oz containers; ointment 1% in 1 and 2 oz containers; aerosol spray 0.25% in 6 oz containers; suppositories 2.5 mg.

Nupercaine Hydrochloride (Ciba). *Injection:* Solution 0.25% with dextrose 5% in 2 ml containers (hyperbaric), and 1:1,500 in 20 ml containers (hypobaric).

Drug also marketed under generic name.

AVAILABLE MIXTURES.—

Bucacet (Lemmon): Each lozenge contains dibucaine hydrochloride 0.5 mg and cetalkonium chloride 4 mg.

Dicort Cream (Hickam): Cream containing dibucaine hydrochloride 5% and hydrocortisone 0.5%.

Dicort Suppositories (Hickam): Each suppository contains dibucaine hydrochloride 10 mg and hydrocortisone acetate 10 mg.

DIMETHISOQUIN HYDROCHLORIDE
[Quotane Hydrochloride]

$OCH_2CH_2N(CH_3)_2$ · HCl ; $-CH_2(CH_2)_2CH_3$

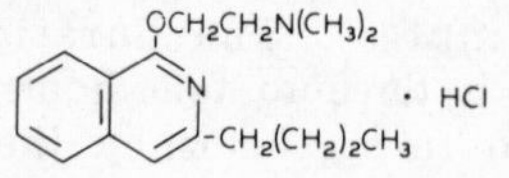

Dimethisoquin is a quinoline derivative which is applied topically on the skin and rectal mucosa for the relief of pruritus, irritation, burning, or pain in a variety of dermatoses, including nonspecific pruritus and mild sunburn. It also may reduce the pain of sutured surgical wounds. It is not used parenterally. Onset of action is rapid (within a few minutes) and the duration is two to four hours.

For adverse reactions and precautions, see the Introductory Statement.

USUAL DOSAGE.—*Topical:* Lotion or ointment is applied not more than four times daily.

PREPARATIONS.—Quotane Hydrochloride (Smith Kline & French). *Topical:* Lotion 0.5% with menthol and zinc oxide in 2 oz containers; ointment 0.5% with thimerosal 1:50,000 in 1 oz containers.

DIPERODON HYDROCHLORIDE [Diothane Hydrochloride]

CH_2-N · HCl ; $CH-O-\overset{O}{C}-NH-$; $CH_2-O-\overset{O}{C}-NH-$

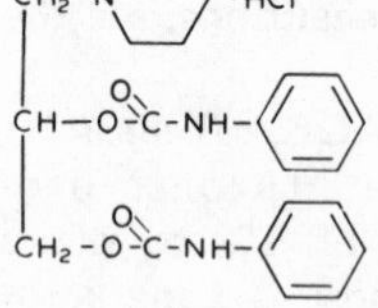

Diperodon is used for surface anesthesia on the skin and mucous membranes. It is as potent as cocaine and has a longer duration of action.

Diperodon may cause burning or stinging on the skin or mucous membranes and allergic reactions (eg, rash). For additional information on adverse reactions and precautions, see the Introductory Statement.

USUAL DOSAGE.—*Topical:* Preparations are applied as required.

(Skin): 1% cream or ointment is applied three or four times daily.

(Rectum): 1% ointment or suppositories are used.

PREPARATIONS.—Diothane Hydrochloride (Merrell-National). *Topical:* Cream 1% with cetylpyridinium chloride 0.1% in 1 oz containers; ointment 1% with oxyquinoline benzoate 0.1% in 1 oz containers; suppositories 1% with urea 10% and oxyquinoline benzoate 0.1%.

AVAILABLE MIXTURE.—Cetyben Troches (Sutliff & Case): Each troche contains diperodon hydrochloride 1 mg and cetylpyridinium chloride 1 mg.

DYCLONINE HYDROCHLORIDE [Dyclone]

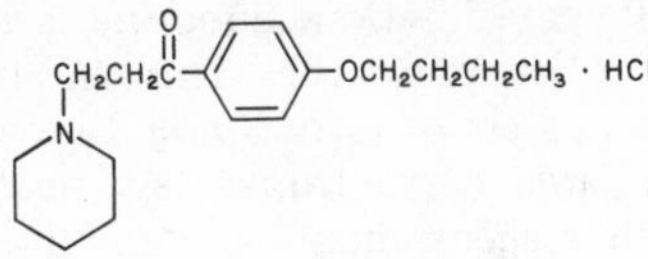

Dyclonine is an effective topical anesthetic. Unlike other local anesthetics, it is a ketone. Therefore, since cross sensitization with other local anesthetic agents does not occur, dyclonine may be useful in patients known to be hypersensitive to local anesthetics of other chemical groups.

Dyclonine is used to anesthetize mucous membranes prior to endoscopy; it also may be applied to relieve the pain of minor burns and gynecologic or proctologic procedures and in the management of pruritus ani or vulvae. When used in the eye, this anesthetic does not produce miosis or mydriasis. The potency of dyclonine is comparable to that of cocaine. Generally, up to ten minutes are required for onset of action and the duration of effect is up to one hour.

The toxicity of dyclonine is low but this drug is contraindicated in cystoscopic procedures following intravenous pyelography because contrast media containing iodine can cause a precipitate to form, and this interferes with visualization. For additional information on adverse reactions and precautions, see the Introductory Statement.

USUAL DOSAGE.—*Topical:* The maximal recommended single dose is 200 mg.

(Skin): 0.5% and 1% solution are applied as required.

(Eye): Because of this drug's irritant property, only the 0.5% solution should be used. For tonometry, removal of foreign bodies and sutures, and minor procedures, one or two drops for one or two instillations. For pterygiums, one drop every three minutes for three instillations. For cataract extraction, one drop every three minutes for five instillations.

(Mouth, esophagus, oral endoscopy): For relief of oral pain, 5 to 10 ml of the 0.5% solution is swabbed, gargled, or sprayed. For esophagoscopy after pharyngeal anesthesia, 10 to 15 ml of the 0.5% solution is swallowed. For relief of esophageal pain, 5 to 15 ml of the 0.5% solution is swallowed.

(Bronchoscopy): The tongue is pulled forward and the larynx and trachea are sprayed with 2 ml of the 1% solution every five minutes until the laryngeal reflex is abolished. This usually requires two or three sprayings. Five minutes should be allowed before instrumentation.

(Urologic endoscopy): 6 to 30 ml of 0.5% to 1% solution (usually 10 to 15 ml) is instilled into the urethra and retained for five to ten minutes before instrumentation.

(Gynecology): 0.5% solution is used as wet compresses or spray.

(Proctology): 0.5% solution is used as wet pledgets for relief of pain and discomfort.

PREPARATIONS.—Dyclone (Dow). *Topical:* Solution 5 mg/ml with chlorobutanol 0.3% and sodium chloride in 30 and 250 ml containers, and 10 mg/ml with chlorobutanol 0.3% and sodium chloride in 120 ml containers.

HEXYLCAINE HYDROCHLORIDE [Cyclaine Hydrochloride]

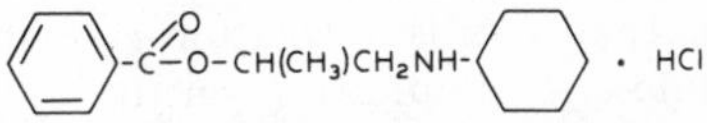

Hexylcaine, a benzoic acid ester, is used for surface anesthesia of the mucous membranes in endoscopy, intubations, and manipulations and for infiltration, nerve block, peridural, and spinal anesthesia. Anesthesia is produced in five minutes and lasts about 30 minutes when the drug is applied topically and approximately two hours when the drug is injected.

Hexylcaine is 25% as toxic as cocaine when applied topically, and is slightly more toxic than procaine when injected. Tissue irritation, burning, swelling, and tissue necrosis with slough have been reported after topical and parenteral administration. For additional information on adverse reactions and precautions, see the Introductory Statement.

USUAL DOSAGE.—*Adults,* the maximal single dose is ordinarily 200 mg for topical use and 500 mg for injection. A 1% or 2% concentration usually gives adequate anesthesia.

Topical:

(Nose): The area is swabbed, packed, or sprayed with a 0.5% to 5% solution. A 1% or greater concentration may be required for antral puncture. The 5% jelly also may be used in the nose and nasopharynx.

(Bronchoscopy and endotracheal intubation): No more than 10 ml (200 mg) of a 2% solution should be used. Before endotracheal intubation, the pharynx and larynx may be anesthetized with 1 to 4 ml of the 5% jelly.

(Gastroscopy): The patient should gargle four times with the 1% or 2% solution; the procedure is repeated twice at five-minute intervals. The excess should not be swallowed. The dose ordinarily should not exceed 200 mg.

(Genitourinary): The dose ordinarily should not exceed 10 ml of the 2% solution; 1 to 4 ml of the 5% jelly may be used to lubricate the cystoscope or sounds before instrumentation.

(Vagina, rectum): The 5% jelly may be used prior to examination and is applied to painful hemorrhoids.

Injection:

(Infiltration): Ordinarily, no more than 500 mg (50 ml of a 1% solution) is used.

(Nerve block): 20 to 100 mg (2 to 10 ml of a 1% solution), depending upon the nerve block. Ordinarily, no more than 100 mg is used.

(Peridural): 200 to 500 mg (10 to 25 ml of a 2% solution).

(Spinal): 15 to 50 mg, depending upon the site, type of surgery, and condition of the patient. The hyperbaric solution is used and the desired dose is withdrawn from the ampule and diluted with an equal volume of cerebrospinal fluid. For low spinal (vaginal delivery), 20 to 25 mg (not diluted with cerebrospinal fluid); for cesarean section, 25 mg (not diluted with cerebrospinal fluid).

PREPARATIONS.—Cyclaine Hydrochloride (Merck Sharp & Dohme).

Injection: Solution 10 mg/ml with propylparaben 0.02% and methylparaben 0.15% in 30 and 100 ml containers (infiltration and nerve block); solution 20 mg/ml in 20 ml containers (peridural); solution 25 mg/ml with 10% dextrose in 2 ml containers (spinal).

Topical: Jelly 5% with thimerosal 0.005% in 30 g containers; solution 50 mg/ml with propylparaben 0.02% and methylparaben 0.15% in 60 ml containers.

LIDOCAINE HYDROCHLORIDE [Xylocaine Hydrochloride]

CH_3 / $NHCOCH_2N(C_2H_5)_2 \cdot HCl$ / CH_3

This effective amide is one of the most widely used topical anesthetics; it also is given for infiltration, nerve block, peridural, spinal, and intravenous regional anesthesia. Lidocaine has been used intravenously for analgesia to suppress the cough reflex, but its use for this purpose may be hazardous. It is superior to procaine or procainamide for the treatment and prophylaxis of arrhythmias (see Chapter 2, Antiarrhythmic Agents).

Compared to procaine, the action of lidocaine is more rapid in onset, more intense, and of longer duration; lidocaine is also more potent than procaine. This anesthetic has excellent powers of diffusion and blocks motor fibers in large nerve trunks (eg, sciatic nerve) where other agents may be ineffective. It has a local vasodilating action but is usually used with epinephrine to delay absorption and prolong the action. Without epinephrine, anesthesia after perineural injection lasts between 60 and 75 minutes; with epinephrine, anesthesia lasts two hours or more.

When administered by extravascular injection, concentrations of 0.5% procaine and lidocaine are approximately equally toxic; however, when higher concentrations of the drugs are so used, lidocaine is one and one-half times as toxic as procaine. When administered intravenously, lidocaine is twice as toxic as procaine. The rapid absorption of large amounts of lidocaine may cause convulsions, but, in some patients, central nervous system depression rather than stimulation occurs. Even in therapeutic doses, lidocaine may cause drowsiness, lassitude, and amnesia. Other systemic reactions are similar to those produced by other local anesthetics. Lidocaine is not irritating and produces relatively little sensitization when used topically. For additional information on adverse reactions and precautions, see the Introductory Statement.

USUAL DOSAGE.—In *healthy adults,* the maximal single dose for topical use is 200 mg; when injected, the maximal single dose should not exceed 300 mg (or 4.5 mg/kg of body weight) without epinephrine and 500 mg (or 7 mg/kg) with epinephrine. This dose should not be repeated at intervals of less than two hours. The site of injection and vascularity of tissue should also be taken into consideration in estimating the total dose. In *normal children,* the dose (preferably of the 0.5% or 1% solution) should be based on body surface area (see table, back cover).

Topical: The 2% solution is generally recommended for topical anesthesia. The 4% solution should be used only when the lower concentration does not provide adequate anesthesia. The maximal dose is 10 ml of the 2% or 5 ml of the 4% concentration.

(Skin): The maximal dose is 35 g of the 2.5% or 5% ointment per day.

(Nose and nasopharynx): 1 to 5 ml of a 1% to 4% solution is sprayed or used on cotton applicators or the 2% jelly is applied, depending upon the procedure. Not more than 30 ml of the 2% jelly should be applied in 12 hours.

(Pharynx and upper digestive tract): The 2% jelly or 2% viscous solution is used. The viscous preparation can be moved around the mouth and pharynx by the cheeks and tongue and then swallowed. The dose of the 2% viscous solution should not exceed 15 ml every three hours or 120 ml in 24 hours. The patient should not eat or drink within one hour because of the danger of aspiration.

(Respiratory tract): 1 to 5 ml of the 4% solution is sprayed or used by applicator or pack to produce anesthesia of the pharynx, larynx, and trachea for laryngoscopy, endotracheal intubation, and bronchoscopy. In addition, 2 to 3 ml of the 4% solution may be injected through the cricothyroid membrane (transtracheal), but a total dose of 5 ml should generally not be exceeded. The 2% jelly or the 2.5% or 5% ointment may be used for lubrication of the endotracheal tube before intubation.

(Urology): A 2% aqueous solution or 2% jelly may be used. *Men*, prior to catheterization, 5 to 10 ml of the 2% jelly is instilled into the urethra and retained for five to ten minutes. The maximal dose is 30 ml in 12 hours. *Women*, application is the same but the dose is 3 to 5 ml.

(Anorectal): The 2% jelly, 5% ointment, or suppositories are used after each bowel movement and before retiring. No more than five suppositories should be used in 24 hours.

Injection:

(Infiltration): Without epinephrine, for extensive procedures, 25 to 60 ml of a 0.5% solution or 10 to 30 ml of a 1% solution; for minor surgery and relief of pain, 2 to 50 ml of a 0.5% solution. With epinephrine 1:200,000, up to 50 ml of a 1% solution.

(Nerve block): Without epinephrine, up to 30 ml of a 1% solution or 15 ml of a 2% solution. With epinephrine 1:200,000, up to 50 ml of a 1% or 25 ml of a 2% solution. Retrobulbar block lasting one to one and one-half hours can be accomplished with 4 ml of the 4% solution. The duration may be extended by adding epinephrine 1:50,000 or 1:100,000.

(Caudal): Without epinephrine, for obstetrical analgesia, up to 30 ml of the 1% solution; for surgical anesthesia, up to 20 ml of the 1.5% solution. With epinephrine 1:200,000, for obstetrical analgesia, up to 30 ml of the 1% solution; for surgical anesthesia, up to 30 ml of the 1.5% solution or up to 25 ml of the 2% solution. Analgesia during labor may be obtained with 20 to 30 ml of a 0.5% solution. Only single-dose containers should be used.

(Lumbar epidural): Without epinephrine, for obstetrical analgesia, 8 to 15 ml of the 1% solution; for surgical anesthesia, 15 to 20 ml of the 1.5% or 10 to 15 ml of the 2% solution. The dose depends on the number of dermatomes to be anesthetized (2 to 3 ml per dermatome is average). With 1:200,000 epinephrine, up to 20 ml of the 1%, 1.5%, or 2% solutions. Analgesia during labor may be obtained with 8 to 10 ml of a 0.5% solution. Only single-dose containers should be used.

(Spinal): The 5% solution with 7.5% dextrose (hyperbaric) is used for spinal anesthesia. For vaginal delivery, 0.8 or 1 ml (40 or 50 mg) will provide perineal anesthesia for about one hour; analgesia lasts an additional 40 minutes. For cesarean section, 1.5 ml (75 mg) may be used. The duration may be prolonged by adding epinephrine.

(Intravenous regional): After occluding the circulation, 30 to 50 ml of a 0.5% solution without epinephrine is injected into a superficial vein of the upper or lower extremity. Satisfactory anesthesia is obtained in four to eight minutes and is maintained as long as the circulation to the extremity is occluded.

PREPARATIONS.—Xylocaine Hydrochloride (Astra).

Injection: Solution 0.5% in 50 ml containers (with or without epinephrine); solution 1% in 2, 5, and 100 ml containers, 20 and 50 ml containers (with or without epinephrine 1:100,000), and 30 ml containers (with or without epinephrine 1:200,000); solution 2% in 2 ml containers (with or without epinephrine 1:100,000), 5 ml containers, 10 ml containers (with or without epinephrine 1:50,000, 1:100,000, or 1:200,000), and 50 ml containers (with or without epinephrine 1:100,000); solution 4% in 5 ml containers; solution 5% with dextrose 7.5% in 2 ml containers.

Topical: Jelly 2% in 30 ml containers; ointment 2.5% in 35 g containers and 5% in 3.5, 15, and 35 g containers; solution (viscous) 2% in 100 and 450 ml containers; solution 4% in 50 ml containers; suppositories 100 mg.

ADDITIONAL TRADEMARKS.—Anestacon (Alcon), Cappicaine (Reid-Provident), Kelocaine (Key), L-Caine (Century), Lida-Mantle (Dome), Nulicaine (Kay), Seracaine (Rachelle), Ultracaine (Ulmer). Drug also marketed under generic name.

AVAILABLE MIXTURES.—

Lida-Mantel-HC Creme (Dome): Cream

containing lidocaine 3% and hydrocortisone acetate 0.5%.

Lidaform-HC Creme, Lotion (Dome): Cream and lotion containing lidocaine 3%, iodochlorhydroxyquin 3%, and hydrocortisone

MEPIVACAINE HYDROCHLORIDE

[Carbocaine Hydrochloride]

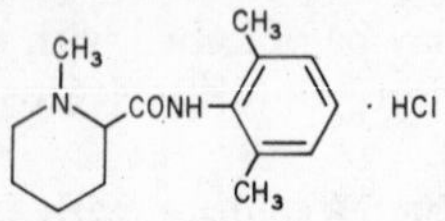

This amide is chemically and pharmacologically related to lidocaine and is used for infiltration, nerve block, peridural, and intravenous regional anesthesia. Mepivacaine is not effective topically except in large doses and therefore should not be used for this purpose. The toxicity and potency of mepivacaine are similar to those of lidocaine; mepivacaine does not diffuse and penetrate as readily, and its action is less rapid in onset and longer in duration. Anesthesia develops in three to five minutes and lasts two to two and one-half hours. Mepivacaine can be used without epinephrine for most purposes; the addition of epinephrine 1:200,000 delays absorption and prolongs the duration of anesthesia.

The systemic reactions observed with mepivacaine are similar to those produced by other local anesthetics, but the drowsiness, lassitude, and amnesia observed with lidocaine do not occur with mepivacaine. For additional information on adverse reactions and precautions, see the Introductory Statement.

USUAL DOSAGE.—*Injection: Adults*, the maximal single dose is 400 mg or 6 mg/kg of body weight. No more than 1 g should be administered during any 24-hour period because the drug accumulates when repeated doses are injected. The dosage should be reduced in *children*.

(Infiltration): Up to 80 ml of a 0.5% or 40 ml of the 1% solution.

(Nerve block): 5 to 20 ml of the 1% or 2% solution. For transvaginal (paracervical plus pudendal) block, up to 40 ml of the 1% solution.

(Peridural): 15 to 30 ml of the 1% solution, 10 to 25 ml of the 1.5% solution, or 10 to 20 ml of the 2% solution. Only single-dose containers should be used.

PREPARATIONS.—Carbocaine Hydrochloride (Winthrop). *Injection:* Solution 1% and 2% with methylparaben 0.1% in 50 ml containers; solution 1% and 1.5% in 30 ml containers; solution 2% in 2 and 20 ml containers.

PHENACAINE HYDROCHLORIDE

[Holocaine Hydrochloride]

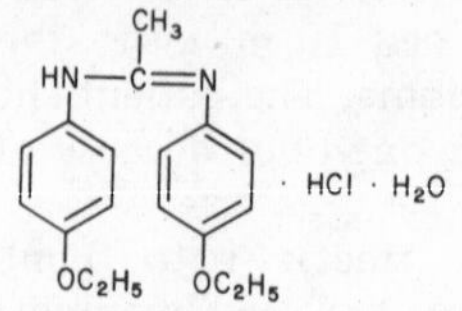

Phenacaine has been supplanted by more effective local anesthetics. It is used solely to produce surface anesthesia in the eye. It does not cause mydriasis. The drug is not given by injection. Compared to cocaine, the onset of action of phenacaine is more rapid (30 seconds) and the duration and potency are similar.

The toxicity of phenacaine is also similar to that of cocaine. This drug is irritating when first instilled into the eye and anesthesia is preceded by temporary smarting. Since phenacaine is precipitated by alkalis, their carbonates, and the usual alkaloid reagents, porcelain rather than glass vessels should be used in preparing solutions. For additional information on adverse reactions and precautions, see the Introductory Statement.

USUAL DOSAGE.—*Topical* (ophthalmic): 0.3 ml of a 1% solution or the 1% or 2% ointment is applied as directed.

PREPARATIONS.—*Topical:* Ointment (ophthalmic) 1% and 2% in 1/8 oz containers; powder for compounding. Drug marketed under generic name and under the trade name Holocaine Hydrochloride.

PIPEROCAINE HYDROCHLORIDE

[Metycaine Hydrochloride]

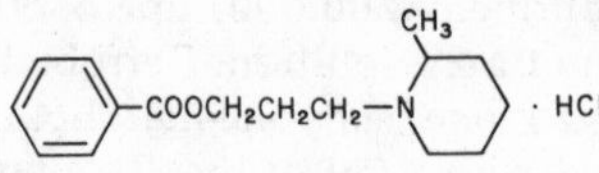

Piperocaine is a benzoic acid ester that is used for surface, infiltration, nerve block, and caudal anesthesia. Its effects are similar to those of procaine, but it is more potent and more toxic. Anesthesia develops more rapidly than with procaine and is of somewhat longer duration.

For adverse reactions and precautions, see the Introductory Statement.

USUAL DOSAGE.—The maximal single dose is 800 mg of a 1% solution or 1 g of a 0.5% solution.

Topical:

(Ophthalmic): One application of the 2% or 4% solution is usually sufficient for minor procedures. Onset of action is in one minute; duration of action is eight to ten minutes. For more profound anesthesia, four instillations at three-minute intervals may be needed. The ointment may be applied one to three times daily.

(Nose, larynx): A 2% spray is used for minor procedures, and a 5% or 10% solution is used for removal of polyps and washing antrums.

(Stomach and other hollow viscus): Not more than 100 ml of a 0.25% solution is instilled.

(Urethra): *Men,* 4 to 8 ml of a 2% to 4% solution is instilled into the urethra and retained for a few minutes, followed by 8 to 16 ml retained for three to ten minutes. *Women,* 15 ml of a 2% to 4% solution is instilled into the bladder; the remaining solution is withdrawn when anesthesia has been established.

(Proctoscopy): A 5% solution is usually used for dilatation and examination, but a 10% or 20% solution may be applied for certain procedures. One to three suppositories may be used per day.

Injection:

(Infiltration): Up to 200 ml of the 0.5% and 80 ml of the 1% solution.

(Nerve block): Up to 200 ml of the 0.5% and 80 ml of the 1% solution. The 2% solution may also be used with caution.

(Caudal): Initially, 8 ml of a 1.5% solution. If signs of intravenous injection or rapid vascular absorption do not occur, another 22 ml is injected for obstetrical analgesia and up to 42 ml is injected for surgical procedures. This dose is given for the average-size sacral canal. Supplementary injections of 20 ml every 30 to 40 minutes will be required.

PREPARATIONS.—Metycaine Hydrochloride (Lilly).

Injection, Topical: Powder for solution 120 mg; solution 2% with chlorobutanol 0.5% in 30 ml containers; tablets 150 mg with lactose.

Injection: Solution 1.5% in Ringer's solution in 200 ml containers (caudal), and solution 2% in 30 ml containers.

AVAILABLE MIXTURES.—

Metycaine Hydrochloride with Merthiolate Ophthalmic Ointment (Lilly): Ointment containing piperocaine hydrochloride 4% and thimerosal 1:5,000 in lanolin, mineral oil, and white petrolatum.

Metycaine Hydrochloride with Zinc Oxide Compound Suppositories (Lilly): Each suppository contains piperocaine hydrochloride 125 mg, belladonna extract 12.5 mg, zinc oxide 250 mg, and bismuth subcarbonate 125 mg.

PRAMOXINE HYDROCHLORIDE

[Tronothane Hydrochloride]

$$CH_3CH_2CH_2CH_2O-C_6H_4-OCH_2CH_2CH_2-N(C_4H_8O) \cdot HCl$$

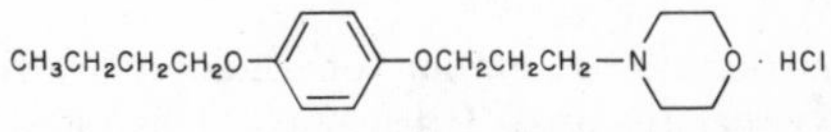

Pramoxine is a local anesthetic agent derived from morpholine. Since it is chemically different from the ester or amide type compounds, it may be useful in patients who are sensitive to these classes of drugs. Pramoxine is applied topically to relieve pain due to burns, wounds, and pruritus. It also may be used to anesthetize laryngopharyngeal surfaces prior to instrumentation and to facilitate sigmoidoscopic examinations. However, it does not abolish the gag reflex. This anesthetic should not be injected or applied to the eye or nasal mucosa, for it may irritate these tissues. Pramoxine acts in three to five minutes, and its potency is comparable to that of benzocaine.

For adverse reactions and precautions, see the Introductory Statement.

USUAL DOSAGE.—*Topical:*

(Skin): The 1% cream or jelly is applied as required, usually every three to four hours. For severe discomfort, the preparations may be applied every two to three hours for one or two days; applications should be decreased thereafter to every four hours.

(Larynx, trachea): The 1% jelly is used on endotracheal and intragastric tubes.

PREPARATIONS.—Tronothane Hydrochloride (Abbott). *Topical:* Cream 1% in 1 oz containers; jelly 1% in 1 oz containers.

AVAILABLE MIXTURES.—

Perifoam (Holland Rantos): Aerosol containing pramoxine hydrochloride 1%, benzalkonium chloride 0.1%, allantoin 0.3%, methylparaben 0.15%, and propylparaben 0.05% with lanolin, witch hazel, and alcohol.

Pramasone Cream (Ferndale): Cream containing pramoxine hydrochloride 1% and hydrocortisone acetate 0.5%.

Pramasone Lotion (Ferndale): Lotion containing pramoxine hydrochloride 1% and hydrocortisone acetate 0.25%.

Quinsone (Sutliff & Case): Ointment containing pramoxine hydrochloride 0.5%, hydrocortisone 1%, and iodochlorhydroxyquin 3%.

PRILOCAINE HYDROCHLORIDE [Citanest Hydrochloride]

$$\text{NHCOCH(CH}_3\text{)NHCH}_2\text{CH}_2\text{CH}_3 \text{ on benzene ring with ortho-CH}_3$$

Prilocaine is similar pharmacologically to mepivacaine and lidocaine. It is used for infiltration, nerve block, peridural, and intravenous regional anesthesia. It is not used topically or for spinal anesthesia. The effectiveness of prilocaine and lidocaine in equivalent dosage is comparable, but the action of prilocaine is slower in onset and of longer duration. This anesthetic is effective without the addition of epinephrine, but epinephrine will prolong its effect. Since prilocaine is more rapidly metabolized and excreted than lidocaine, it is approximately 40% less toxic.

Two of the metabolites of prilocaine, ortho-toluidine and nitroso-toluidine, form methemoglobin. When doses in excess of 600 mg are given, the patient may develop a grayish or slate-blue cyanosis of the lips, mucous membranes, and nail beds, but respiratory and circulatory distress do not appear to occur with the methemoglobinemia. In one clinical study, healthy individuals received 1.2 g of prilocaine and no signs of inadequate oxygen transport developed. The methemoglobinemia is readily reversed by the intravenous administration of methylene blue (1 to 2 mg/kg of body weight of a 1% solution injected over a five-minute period). However, this therapeutic action may cease because of the rapid clearance of methylene blue before the conversion of all the methemoglobin to hemoglobin. Prilocaine should not be administered to patients with idiopathic or congenital methemoglobinemia, anemia, or cardiac or respiratory failure with hypoxia.

For additional information on adverse reactions and precautions, see the Introductory Statement.

USUAL DOSAGE.—*Injection:* In *normal healthy adults*, the maximal single dose is 600 mg or 8 mg/kg of body weight in a two-hour period, or no more than 1.2 g in a four-hour period. A 0.5% to 1% concentration should be used in *children* and the dose adjusted on the basis of body surface area (see table, back cover).

(Infiltration): Up to 30 ml of the 1% or 2% solution.

(Nerve block): Up to 30 ml of the 2% solution or 15 to 20 ml of the 3% solution.

(Caudal): 20 to 30 ml of the 1% solution is adequate for most routine vaginal deliveries. For surgical procedures requiring more profound anesthesia, 20 to 30 ml of the 2% solution or 15 to 20 ml of the 3% solution.

(Lumbar epidural): 20 to 30 ml of the 1% or 2% solution or 15 to 20 ml of the 3% solution.

(Intravenous regional anesthesia): For anesthetizing the arm, 3 mg/kg of body weight of a 0.5% solution.

PREPARATIONS.—Citanest Hydrochloride (Astra). *Injection:* Solution 1% and 2% with methylparaben 0.1% in 30 ml containers, and solution 3% in 20 ml containers.

PROCAINE HYDROCHLORIDE [Novocain]

$$NH_2-C_6H_4-C(=O)-O-CH_2CH_2N(CH_2CH_3)_2 \cdot HCl$$

Procaine, an ester of aminobenzoic acid, was the preferred local anesthetic for injection for many years, but it is now being supplanted by lidocaine and other drugs. This agent is used for infiltration, nerve block, peridural, and spinal anesthesia. It is not applied topically. Procaine has a slower onset of action than lidocaine and prilocaine; its duration of action is about one hour.

Procaine is rapidly metabolized, a factor which accounts for its safety. Much of it is hydrolyzed by plasma cholinesterase; the remainder is metabolized in the liver. The reactions produced by procaine are similar to those of other synthetic local anesthetics. For additional information on adverse reactions and precautions, see the Introductory Statement.

USUAL DOSAGE.—*Injection:* The maximal single dose for *adults* is 1 g; epinephrine 1:200,000 should preferably be used with larger doses.

(Infiltration): Up to 100 ml of a 0.25% or 0.5% solution with or without epinephrine 1:200,000.

(Nerve block): Up to 50 ml of the 1% or 25 ml of the 2% solution with or without epinephrine 1:200,000.

(Caudal): The 1% or 2% solution is administered. For continuous caudal anesthesia, initially, 30 ml of a 1.5% solution, with subsequent doses adjusted as required.

(Epidural): The 1% or 2% solution is used.

(Spinal): The 10% solution diluted with 10% dextrose prepared for spinal anesthesia (hyperbaric) is used. For saddle block (perineum), 0.5 ml of the 10% solution diluted with 0.5 ml of the 10% dextrose solution; for lower extremities, 1 ml of the 10% solution diluted with 1 ml of the 10% dextrose solution; for level to costal margin, 2 ml of the 10% solution diluted with 1 ml of the 10% dextrose solution.

(Intravenous regional): 30 to 50 ml of the 1% solution.

PREPARATIONS.—Novocain (Winthrop). *Injection:* Solution 1% in 2, 6, and 30 ml containers; solution 2% in 30 ml containers; solution 10% in 2 ml containers (for spinal anesthesia). Drug also marketed under generic name.

ADDITIONAL TRADEMARK.—Unicaine (Kay).

AVAILABLE MIXTURE.—Adrocaine Injection (Parke, Davis): Solution containing procaine hydrochloride 1.5% and epinephrine 1:100,000.

PROPARACAINE HYDROCHLORIDE
[Ophthetic, Ophthaine]

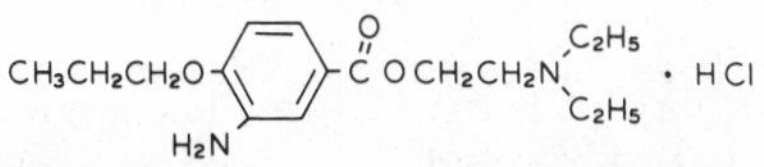

$CH_3CH_2CH_2O$ — (ring, H_2N) — $\overset{O}{\overset{\|}{C}}OCH_2CH_2N(C_2H_5)_2 \cdot HCl$

Proparacaine is an effective surface anesthetic derived from aminobenzoic acid; it is used principally in ophthalmology. Its onset of action is rapid; surface anesthesia of sufficient intensity to permit tonometry can generally be obtained within 20 seconds after instillation of one or two drops of the 0.5% solution. The duration of anesthesia is 15 minutes or more. Because of the high incidence of systemic toxic reactions, proparacaine is not used parenterally.

No untoward effects have occurred after a single application in the eye. With repeated use, proparacaine causes occasional temporary stinging, burning, and conjunctival erythema. A severe, immediate-type, apparently allergic corneal reaction, with acute, intense, and diffuse epithelial keratitis; a gray, ground-glass appearance; sloughing of large areas of necrotic epithelium; corneal filaments; and, sometimes, iritis with descemetitis, has occurred rarely. Allergic contact dermatitis, with drying and fissuring of the fingertips, also has been reported.

USUAL DOSAGE.—*Topical* (ophthalmic): For minor procedures, one or two drops instilled in each eye before surgery. For more profound anesthesia, one drop instilled every five to ten minutes for five to seven doses.

PREPARATIONS.—

Ophthetic (Allergan). *Topical:* Solution (ophthalmic) 0.5% with benzalkonium chloride and glycerin in 15 ml containers.

Ophthaine (Squibb). *Topical:* Solution (ophthalmic) 0.5% with chlorobutanol 0.2% and benzalkonium chloride in 2.5 and 15 ml containers.

PROPOXYCAINE HYDROCHLORIDE
[Blockain Hydrochloride]

$COOCH_2CH_2N(C_2H_5)_2 \cdot HCl$; $OCH_2CH_2CH_3$; NH_2 (ring)

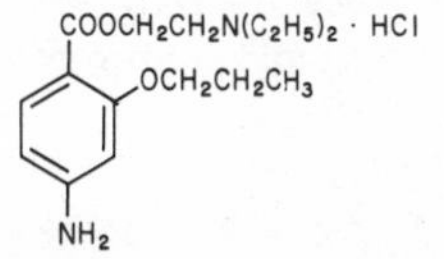

This aminobenzoic acid ester may be used for infiltration and nerve block anesthesia, but more suitable agents are available. It has a more rapid onset and longer duration of action than procaine, and is seven or eight times more potent and toxic.

For adverse reactions and precautions, see the Introductory Statement.

USUAL DOSAGE.—*Injection:* For infiltration and nerve block anesthesia, up to 20 ml of a 0.5% solution with epinephrine 1:200,000. The maximal single dose for *adults* is 100 mg.

PREPARATIONS.—Blockain Hydrochloride (Breon). *Injection:* Solution 0.5% with methylparaben 0.1% and propylparaben 0.04% in 30 ml containers.

TETRACAINE HYDROCHLORIDE [BufOpto Anacel, Pontocaine Hydrochloride]

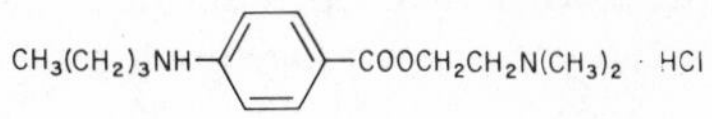

$CH_3(CH_2)_3NH$ — (ring) — $COOCH_2CH_2N(CH_3)_2 \cdot HCl$

This derivative of aminobenzoic acid is used for surface, nerve block, infiltration, caudal, and spinal anesthesia. When used in the eye, tetracaine does not produce mydriasis, cycloplegia, or intraocular hypertension. It is approximately ten times more potent and toxic than procaine when injected, and five to eight times more potent than cocaine when applied topically. When injected, its onset of action is slow (approximately five minutes) but the duration of anesthesia is more than twice as long as that of procaine (two to three hours); topically, the onset of action also develops slowly, and the duration of anesthesia is approximately 15 minutes. Tetracaine is metabolized in the plasma and liver at a slower rate than procaine.

Repeated use in the eye should be avoided because of the possibility that corneal damage may develop. Sulfonamides and mercury and silver salts should not be used concomitantly. For additional information on adverse reactions and precautions, see the Introductory Statement.

USUAL DOSAGE.—The maximal single dose is 50 mg topically and 100 mg with epinephrine 1:200,000 by injection.

Topical:

(Skin, anus): The 0.5% ointment or 1% cream is used. Not more than 1 oz for an adult or ¼ oz for a child should be applied in a 24-hour period.

(Ophthalmic): For minor procedures, one or two drops of the 0.5% solution; the 0.5% ophthalmic ointment may be applied to the lower conjunctival fornix.

(Nose and pharynx): Up to 4 ml of a 1% solution; the 2% solution should not be used because of the higher risk of systemic toxicity. A gauze strip may be saturated with 1 or 2 ml of a solution containing equal parts of 2% tetracaine and epinephrine 1:1,000 and packed into the nose. Alternatively epinephrine solution is applied to the mucous membrane before using the tetracaine solution.

(Esophageal and laryngeal reflexes): 2 ml of a 1% solution or 1 ml of the 2% solution is effective in abolishing the reflexes in preparation for esophagoscopy, bronchoscopy, and bronchography. These doses should not be exceeded because of the risk of systemic toxicity due to rapid absorption of the drug.

Injection:

(Infiltration and nerve block): Tetracaine is seldom used for these procedures now because of the slow onset of action and great systemic toxicity. If used, the recommended concentration is 0.1% to 0.15% with epinephrine 1:200,000.

(Caudal): Up to 30 ml of the 0.15% solution with epinephrine 1:200,000 is used. As anesthesia wears off, subsequent doses of 20 ml may be administered.

(Spinal): The 1% solution, diluted with an equal volume of 10% dextrose prepared for spinal anesthesia (hyperbaric) is used. For saddle block (perineum), 5 mg; for lower extremities and most cesarean sections, 10 mg; for higher levels and to allow intra-abdominal surgery, 12 to 15 mg. Doses exceeding 15 mg are rarely administered. Epinephrine 1:1,000 (0.1 to 0.3 mg) may be added to prolong the duration of anesthesia by 30% to 50% in the average adult. Epinephrine may prolong the duration of anesthesia excessively in elderly patients.

PREPARATIONS.—

Pontocaine Hydrochloride (Winthrop).

Injection: Solution 0.15% in 100 ml containers, and solution 1% in 2 ml containers (spinal).

Topical: Cream 1% in 1 oz containers; ointment 0.5% and 1% in 1 oz containers; ointment (ophthalmic) 0.5% in 1/8 oz containers; solution 2% with chlorobutanol 0.4% in 30 and 118 ml containers; solution (ophthalmic) 0.5% with chlorobutanol 0.4% in 15 and 59 ml containers.

BufOpto Anacel (Professional). *Topical:* Solution (ophthalmic) 0.5% with benzalkonium chloride 1:10,000 and methylcellulose in 5 and 15 ml containers.

Drug also marketed under generic name.

Chapter 19

GENERAL ANESTHETICS

General anesthetics depress the central nervous system and induce varying degrees of analgesia, loss of consciousness, reduced reflex activity, and skeletal muscle relaxation. The ideal general anesthetic should be stable, nonflammable, fast acting, and rapidly eliminated. It should provide adequate analgesia and muscular relaxation but should not produce excitement or have any adverse effects on vital organs and systems, even during prolonged administration. Recovery of consciousness should occur quickly without adverse after effects. No single agent presently available possesses all of these ideal characteristics.

There are two types of general anesthetics: inhalation and intravenous. Inhalation anesthetics are gases or highly volatile liquids that vary greatly in anesthetic potency, safety, and ability to provide adequate muscular relaxation and analgesia. They have an advantage over the intravenous agents in that depth of anesthesia can be regulated by varying the anesthetic concentration. The intravenous anesthetics cause rapid loss of consciousness, are not explosive, provide pleasant induction and recovery, and have a low incidence of unpleasant effects and postanesthetic complications. However, they provide little muscular relaxation or analgesia and frequently do not abolish superficial reflexes. They are sometimes administered rectally for basal anesthesia.

Induction and maintenance of general anesthesia should only be undertaken by individuals who have received adequate training in anesthesia.

Inhalation Anesthetics: The anesthetic *gases* are cyclopropane, nitrous oxide, and ethylene. Cyclopropane produces complete surgical anesthesia with adequate muscular relaxation. The margin of safety between anesthetic and lethal concentrations is very wide, and this agent may be used in all types of surgical procedures. Nitrous oxide has low anesthetic potency, produces little or no muscular relaxation, and generally is used with other drugs (eg, thiopental). It is useful to produce analgesia in dentistry and in the second stage of labor. Ethylene has properties similar to those of nitrous oxide, but is used less frequently because it is explosive and has an unpleasant odor.

The *volatile liquids* are ether, vinyl ether [Vinethene], chloroform, halothane [Fluothane], methoxyflurane [Penthrane], trichloroethylene [Trilene], ethyl chloride, fluroxene [Fluoromar], and enflurane [Ethrane]. In some respects, ether is the ideal anesthetic: it produces complete general anesthesia, has profound analgesic and skeletal muscle relaxant properties, and the margin of safety between the anesthetic and lethal dose is wide. However, induction and recovery are slow, it is explosive, and it is irritating to the respiratory passages. Vinyl ether has properties similar to those of ether, and is less irritating to the respiratory tract. However, it is more potent than ether, and is unsafe for prolonged surgical procedures.

Halothane produces complete general anesthesia, but the degree of analgesia and muscular relaxation is inadequate; therefore, it is generally used with nitrous oxide and a neuromuscular blocking agent. Halothane depresses the myocardium and vascular smooth muscle. Since it dilates the bronchioles and is not irritating to the air passages, it is preferable to other anesthetics for asthmatic patients.

Methoxyflurane is a potent anesthetic with good analgesic and muscle relaxant properties, but induction and recovery are slow because it is highly soluble in tissues. Complete skeletal muscle relaxation can be obtained by use of this agent alone; however, it is generally given with nitrous oxide and a neuromuscular blocking agent because high concentrations can cause circulatory depression and may be associated with renal dysfunction.

Trichloroethylene is used alone as an analgesic for minor diagnostic and surgical procedures and in obstetrics, or it is given with nitrous oxide for general anesthesia. Alone, it is not a satisfactory general anesthetic because the rate of induction and recovery is slow, muscular relaxation is inadequate, and arrhythmias may occur. Ethyl chloride is rapid acting and recovery is fast, but it produces little muscular relaxation. It has been used for minor surgical procedures in children and as an induction anesthetic for ether; however, safer agents are preferred. The anesthetic potency of fluroxene is similar to that of ether. It provides rapid induction and recovery with pronounced analgesia but produces little muscular relaxation. It is used alone for minor surgical procedures or with nitrous oxide for general anesthesia. Enflurane requires further evaluation but appears to combine many of the clinical properties of halothane with those of ether. Chloroform is a potent anesthetic but has been supplanted by other agents because of its toxic effects.

Intravenous Anesthetics: The ultrashort-acting barbiturates, thiopental, [Pentothal], thiamylal [Surital], and methohexital [Brevital], are potent intravenous anesthetics that cause rapid loss of consciousness but their analgesic activity is relatively weak. Except for brief minor procedures, they are seldom used alone for anesthesia. A neuromuscular blocking agent must be given concomitantly to facilitate some procedures.

Ketamine [Ketalar, Ketaject], a derivative of the psychotomimetic agent, phencyclidine [Sernylan], is a short-acting nonbarbiturate intravenous anesthetic. It has been termed a "dissociative" anesthetic because it induces a cataleptic state in which the patient appears to be awake but is disconnected from his surroundings and is unresponsive to pain; the reaction to somatic pain stimuli is blocked more effectively than is the response to visceral pain. After recovery, the patient has no memory of the procedure. Ketamine has been used in various diagnostic procedures and in brief, minor surgical procedures that do not require substantial skeletal muscle relaxation and relief from visceral pain. It also may be used as an induction anesthetic or to supplement agents with low potency such as nitrous oxide.

Adverse Reactions and Precautions

Inhalation Anesthetics: There is generally little danger of respiratory or circulatory failure when anesthetic gases or vapors are administered in proper concentrations by qualified persons. However, some of these agents act on peripheral sites such as the myocardium, vascular smooth muscle, and the mucosa of the respiratory tract to produce undesirable effects. A variety of techniques and drugs can be used to minimize the adverse reactions caused by inhalation anesthetics. For example, the use of basal anesthesia with a short-acting barbiturate reduces the amount of primary anesthetic needed; premedication with atropine or scopolamine combined with morphine or other strong analgesics reduces the incidence of excessive secretions, excitement, and restlessness. (See Chapter 20, Adjuncts to Anesthesia.)

Delirium may occur during induction and recovery with many inhalation anesthetics. Postoperative nausea and vomiting also are noted frequently with some agents.

Inhalation anesthetics have a direct depressant effect on the myocardium and vascular smooth muscle. The degree of depression varies with different agents and is related to the depth of anesthesia. Chloroform, ethyl chloride, and halothane [Fluothane] have pronounced depressant effects on the cardiovascular system, and severe hypotension and circulatory failure may occur with overdosage. Methoxyflurane [Penthrane] produces effects similar to those of halothane, but they are less intense. Although ether and cyclopropane depress the myocardium by a direct action, cardiac output is rarely affected because these drugs also stimulate the sympathetic nervous sytem.

Arrhythmias may develop during the administration of any inhalation anesthetic, especially if anesthesia is prolonged or if hypoxia and hypercapnia are present. Cardiac arrest may occur due to overdosage or hypoxia. Cyclopropane, chloroform, ethyl chloride, halothane, and trichloroethylene [Trilene] sensitize the heart to the actions of the catecholamines; therefore, the administration of epinephrine, levarterenol [Levophed], or isoproterenol [Isuprel] during anesthesia with these agents may be hazardous, since the combined action of the anesthetic and the catecholamine increases the risk of ventricular fibrillation. Arrhythmias occur less frequently with methoxyflurane than with halothane or cyclopropane.

Respiratory depression occurs frequently during general anesthesia with inhalation anesthetics, particularly chloroform, halothane, and methoxyflurane. Although ether has a depressant effect on the respiratory center, respiration is stimulated because of reflex effects.

Reversible mild abnormalities in the results of liver function tests are common, but serious liver damage is rare after the administration of many anesthetics. Some volatile anesthetics have been implicated in the development of severe liver dysfunction. These include vinyl ether and the halogenated compounds, chloroform, ethyl chloride, fluroxene, halothane, methoxyflurane, and trichloroethylene.

Some inhalation anesthetics cause reversible oliguria due to renal vasoconstriction. Chloroform, vinyl ether, and methoxyflurane may cause kidney damage and are contraindicated in patients with impaired renal function. Methoxyflurane should not be used in patients receiving tetracyclines, for renal failure and death have occurred after the concomitant use of these agents.

Nondepolarizing neuromuscular blocking agents (eg, tubocurarine, pancuronium [Pavulon], gallamine [Flaxedil]) should be used in greatly reduced doses with enflurane, ether, halothane, methoxyflurane, or cyclopropane because potentiation of their effects by the anesthetics may enhance neuromuscular blockade.

Cyclopropane, ether, ethyl chloride, ethylene, fluroxene, and vinyl ether are flammable and explosive and must be used with extreme care and only in areas especially designed for their use.

Intravenous Anesthetics: The blood pressure usually is not reduced significantly during anesthesia with barbiturates, although transient hypotension may occur during induction. These agents may cause apnea, coughing, laryngeal spasm, and bronchospasm; pronounced respiratory depression may occur immediately after injection. In the presence of pain, excitement and delirium may occur during recovery.

The barbiturates can cause an exacerbation of acute intermittent porphyria and are contraindicated in patients with this disease. They should be used with care and in small doses in patients with liver disease. Barbiturates stimulate the formation of microsomal liver enzymes that may affect the action of other drugs (eg, anticoagulants).

Care should be taken to avoid extravasation or intra-arterial injection during administration of the barbiturates, as tissue necrosis and gangrene may occur.

The major untoward effects of ketamine are its pressor effect and its tendency to cause hallucinations and other psychic abnormalities during recovery. The psychotomimetic effect, while less pronounced and of shorter duration than that encountered with phencyclidine [Sernylan], limits its clinical usefulness.

INHALATION ANESTHETICS

Gases

CYCLOPROPANE

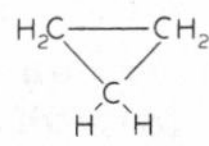

Cyclopropane is a potent, pleasant-smelling, gaseous anesthetic which is explosive at all anesthetic concentrations and should be used in a completely closed system with a carbon dioxide absorber. Induction is rapid (two to three minutes); recovery may be somewhat slower, depending upon the duration of administration. Classical signs described by Guedel for determining depth of anesthesia are not always reliable.

Cyclopropane has a wide margin of safety and is used in all types of surgical procedures. It has good analgesic properties and produces adequate skeletal muscle relaxation except at light planes of anesthesia, when muscle relaxants must be administered concomitantly. It acts synergistically with nondepolarizing neuromuscular blocking agents (tubocurarine, pancuronium, gallamine), but to a lesser extent than ether and halothane. These blocking agents should be used in reduced dosage with cyclopropane.

The cardiovascular system usually is not adversely affected during anesthesia with cyclopropane. Myocardial contractility is maintained, the heart rate is normal or slightly decreased, peripheral resistance is increased, and arterial blood pressure and cardiac output are maintained, or moderately elevated. Cyclopropane is often regarded as the anesthetic of choice for patients in shock.

Cyclopropane increases the irritability of pacemaker tissues. Arrhythmias can occur spontaneously, especially if ventilation is not adequate and hypercapnia develops. Alarming ventricular arrhythmias are likely to occur if epinephrine, levarterenol, or other catecholamines are administered simultaneously; these may progress to ventricular fibrillation. Severe postanesthetic hypotension is observed occasionally This has been attributed to the cessation of sympathetic stimulation produced by cyclopropane.

Both the rate and depth of respiration are progressively depressed, particularly if a narcotic has been used for premedication. Laryngospasm and bronchial constriction may occur occasionally. Undesirable effects due to parasympathetic stimulation may be minimized by using an anticholinergic drug for premedication.

Cyclopropane produces a significant elevation of endogenous catecholamines that may decrease blood flow to the extremities, kidneys, or liver. In the kidneys, this effect may be a contributory factor to a decrease in urinary output; in the liver, glycogen depletion may occur and the blood glucose level may be moderately elevated. Liver function tests may show abnormalities for several days after anesthesia. Other metabolic functions of the body do not appear to be affected significantly.

Although signs of increased capillary bleeding may occur during surgery, no disturbances of the blood clotting mechanism have been demonstrated.

Nausea, vomiting, and headache occur frequently after cyclopropane anesthesia. Postanesthetic delirium is noted more frequently than after other commonly used inhalation agents, particularly if nonanalgesic drugs have been used for premedication.

USUAL DOSAGE.—*Inhalation:* For analgesia, continuous inhalation of 1% to 2% with oxygen. For induction of anesthesia, inhalation of 25% to 50% with oxygen; for maintenance of anesthesia, inhalation of 10% to 20% with oxygen.

PREPARATIONS.—Cyclopropane, U.S.P. Marketed under generic name. Supplied in orange cylinders.

NITROUS OXIDE

Nitrous oxide is a sweet-smelling, nonexplosive gas with low anesthetic potency. At least 20% oxygen should always be administered with nitrous oxide. Induction is not easily achieved with this concentration, but is facilitated by premedication with an analgesic or barbiturate. The practice of inducing anesthesia with hypoxic mixtures is hazardous. Nitrous oxide has good analgesic properties and is useful in dentistry and in the second stage of labor. For surgical anesthesia, it must be supplemented with other agents (eg, volatile liquid anesthetics, strong analgesics, or barbiturates). It does not provide adequate skeletal muscle relaxation; therefore, a neuromuscular blocking agent must be given for procedures requiring muscular relaxation.

This anesthetic has virtually no deleterious effects on the respiratory or cardiovascular systems, or on the kidneys, liver, or metabolic functions, provided that the inhalation mixture contains at least 20% oxygen and ventilation is maintained. Diffusion hypoxia may develop after discontinuing prolonged nitrous oxide anesthesia, and it is advisable to administer oxygen during the initial emergence from anesthesia.

Nitrous oxide is 35 times more soluble in the blood than nitrogen. If an air pocket is present in the body (eg, pneumothorax), the anesthetic will diffuse into this space and increase the pressure. Therefore, this agent should be used cautiously in the presence of conditions such as pneumothorax, pulmonary cysts, or adynamic ileus, and during pneumoencephalography.

Reversible bone marrow depression has occurred, but only after administration of nitrous oxide continuously for more than 24 hours. Nausea and vomiting rarely develop after short exposure unless hypoxia has occurred; the incidence is lower after prolonged administration of nitrous oxide than after cyclopropane or ether. Recovery is relatively brief (two to ten minutes) unless supplementary agents have been used or administration has been prolonged.

USUAL DOSAGE.—*Inhalation:* For analgesia, a 20% concentration of nitrous oxide with 80% oxygen. For induction of anesthesia, 80% nitrous oxide with 20% oxygen for two to three minutes. For maintenance, a mixture of 70% nitrous oxide with 30% oxygen. For the second stage of labor, 80% nitrous oxide with 20% oxygen is given briefly during contractions, and 100% oxygen is administered between contractions.

PREPARATIONS.—Nitrogen Oxide (nitrous oxide), U.S.P. Marketed under generic name. Available in sealed blue metal cylinders.

ETHYLENE

Ethylene is a highly flammable and explosive anesthetic gas with an unpleasant odor. It provides rapid induction and recovery with little excitement and good analgesia but little muscular relaxation. It is easily inhaled without producing bronchospasm or laryngospasm. Although ethylene is more potent than nitrous oxide and is used for the same purposes, nitrous oxide is preferred because it is not explosive.

No appreciable changes in vital functions occur during or after anesthesia with ethylene if hypoxic mixtures are not used. At least 20% oxygen should always be administered during maintenance of anesthesia to avoid hypoxia. If satisfactory anesthesia cannot be attained with ethylene, the gas must be supplemented with a barbiturate, strong analgesic, or other anesthetic vapor (eg, ether, halothane). Diffusion hypoxia may occur at the conclusion of anesthesia; therefore, a high concentration of oxygen should be administered for three to five minutes during the initial emergence from anesthesia.

After prolonged use, there may be a moderate hyperglycemia. Postoperative nausea and vomiting occur more frequently after ethylene than after nitrous oxide but less frequently than after cyclopropane. Unpleasant aftertaste is often experienced for a few hours following ethylene anesthesia.

USUAL DOSAGE.—*Inhalation:* For analgesia, a few inhalations of a 25% to 35% mixture with oxygen. For induction of anesthesia, an 80% to 90% concentration of ethylene with 10% to 20% oxygen is used. However, a 90% concentration of ethylene should be given for no longer than two to three minutes. Patients usually can be maintained on a mixture of 80% ethylene and 20% oxygen.

PREPARATIONS.—Ethylene, N.F. Marketed under generic name as a compressed gas at 750 psi in red (WHO, violet) metal cylinders.

Volatile Liquids

ETHER (Ethyl Ether, Diethyl Ether)

Ether is a potent anesthetic with a pungent, irritating odor. The vapor is flammable and explosive. Induction of anesthesia is relatively slow (10 to 20 minutes) and recovery is prolonged. Induction may be facilitated by the concomitant use of nitrous oxide, ethylene, or other short-acting agents. Ether possesses excellent analgesic properties and produces profound skeletal muscle relaxation. The depth of depression can be followed by observing the signs outlined by Guedel.

This anesthetic generally has benign effects on the cardiovascular system. A direct depressant effect on the heart is counteracted by stimulation of the sympathetic nervous system. At moderate levels of anesthesia, the heart rate is increased, blood pressure is maintained, and cardiac output is sustained or elevated. Ether does not sensitize the heart to catecholamines.

Ether produces excessive salivation, stimulation of bronchial secretions, and irritation of the respiratory passages, which may compromise airway maintenance. The excessive secretions can be minimized by premedication with an anticholinergic drug. Ether stimulates the rate and depth of respiration by reflex mechanisms.

The neuromuscular blocking properties of ether can intensify the neuromuscular blockade produced by nondepolarizing muscle relaxants. When used with this anesthetic, the dose of these blocking agents should be reduced. Ether also may intensify the neuromuscular blockade produced by certain antibiotics (eg, neomycin, polymyxin B).

Ether is not hepatotoxic, but results of liver function tests may show abnormalities for several days after anesthesia. Other transient effects include hyperglycemia, metabolic acidosis, reduction in urinary output, and depression of gastric tone and motility. Postoperative nausea and vomiting occur frequently. Delirium during recovery is not uncommon.

USUAL DOSAGE.—*Inhalation:* Amount required for anesthesia varies with the weight and condition of the patient, the desired depth of anesthesia, and the technique employed. For induction of anesthesia, 10% to 30% of ether vapor in oxygen or a nitrous oxide-oxygen mixture is generally required. For maintenance of stage III anesthesia, 5% to 15% is used.

PREPARATIONS.—Ether, U.S.P. Marketed in airtight, sealed containers of 0.25, 0.5, 1, and 5 lb.

CHLOROFORM

This colorless, sweet-smelling, volatile, nonexplosive liquid is a potent anesthetic with excellent analgesic and muscle relaxant properties. However, it has a pronounced depressant effect on the circulatory system and it can be hepatotoxic and nephrotoxic, particularly when ingested. The depth of anesthesia is difficult to judge because the classical signs described by Guedel do not apply.

Chloroform depresses the myocardium and vascular smooth muscle and reduces cardiac output. Circulatory failure may be the first sign of overdosage. Arrhythmias may develop, and ventricular fibrillation has been reported during difficult mask inductions. Chloroform is not compatible with catecholamines.

Repeated or prolonged administration, excessive dosage, or concomitant hypoxia are believed to predispose the patient to fatal liver necrosis, particularly malnourished, chronically ill patients and those with hepatic disease. The signs of toxicity (nausea, vomiting, prostration, jaundice, and coma) may be delayed for several days; death may occur in four to five days.

USUAL DOSAGE.—Generally, this drug should not be used for anesthesia because of its cardiovascular, hepatic, and renal toxicity.

PREPARATIONS.—Chloroform, N.F. Marketed under generic name.

ETHYL CHLORIDE

Ethyl chloride is a highly volatile, flammable anesthetic which provides rapid induction (one-half to two minutes) and recovery (two to three minutes) and rarely causes excitement and delirium. It does not provide adequate muscular relaxation at safe levels of anesthesia; therefore, neuromuscular blocking agents must be given as adjuncts. Ethyl chloride has been used in children for minor surgical procedures of short duration or as an induction anesthetic; however, safer agents are preferred. It also is used topically for local anesthesia.

Ethyl chloride depresses the myocardium and reduces cardiac output. It is not compatible with catecholamines, and severe arrhythmias may occur if it is given with epinephrine or levarterenol. This highly volatile agent should not be used for prolonged procedures because of the difficulty in maintaining a steady level of anesthesia and the danger of overdosage.

This anesthetic may cause liver damage and is contraindicated in patients with impaired liver function. It should not be administered repeatedly at short intervals.

USUAL DOSAGE.—*Inhalation:* Generally, use of this drug is inadvisable because of the disadvantages noted above. The manufacturers' suggested dosage is: For induction of general anesthesia, 20 to 30 drops on an open-face mask for 30 seconds. For maintenance of anesthesia, inhalation of 4% concentration.

PREPARATIONS.—Ethyl Chloride, N.F. *Inhalation:* Liquid in 5 ml ampules and 30, 40, 80, and 100 g tubes. Drug marketed under generic name.

ENFLURANE [Ethrane]

```
  F   F F
  |   | |
H-C-O-C-C-H
  |   | |
  F   F Cl
```

The following is a preliminary evaluation of enflurane, a clear, colorless, stable, potent, nonflammable, halogenated hydrocarbon anesthetic with a pleasant ethereal odor. The physical, pharmacologic, and clinical properties of enflurane are similar to those of halothane; this drug also possesses some of the clinical advantages of ether. Enflurane may be vaporized in oxygen or nitrous oxide and oxygen, and mild stimulation accompanies induction of anesthesia in some patients. This anesthetic resembles halothane in its induction time (four to six minutes) and time until endotracheal intubation can be accomplished (seven to ten minutes). Airway secretions are not excessive when enflurane is administered. Endotracheal intubation may be facilitated by use of a muscle relaxant if desired. Enflurane appears to provide better analgesia and muscle relaxation than halothane. The latter is provided at a depth of anesthesia associated with almost adequate spontaneous ventilation and often with a normal arterial pressure. Muscle relaxants may be used to facilitate muscle relaxation, but substantial potentiation of nondepolarizing drugs must be anticipated.

Enflurane exerts relatively little effect upon the respiratory system. Some elevation in respiratory rate and decrease in tidal volume results in an approximately normal minute volume. However, spontaneous respiration should be assisted in deeper anesthesia because of decreasing tidal volumes. No difficulty is encountered in assuming manual control of respiration.

The cardiovascular system remains relatively stable. The drug has little effect on the pulse rate and cardiac rhythm, and the arterial pressure, after decreasing moderately following induction, tends to return to normal and then remain stable. Excessive reduction in arterial pressure may be the best indication of overdosage. Studies in animals suggest that enflurane, like halothane, may be incompatible with catecholamines.

Enflurane does not appear to produce significant changes in standard hematologic or urine tests, nor does it appear to affect renal function adversely. However, the clinical implications of the inorganic fluoride known to be produced by biotransformation of the drug require further study. Transient mild abnormalities in results of liver function tests similar to those observed after all anesthetic techniques also have been reported after administration of enflurane. Central nervous system stimulation, manifested by increased electrical activity and seizure-like activity in the EEG, is seen as anesthesia is deepened. Paroxysms of tonic-clonic or twitching movements have developed in a few patients, usually in association with deep anesthesia and hypocarbia. These could be terminated, without sequelae, by lightening the anesthesia and reducing the minute ventilation or by administering another anesthetic agent.

Body temperature falls slightly during surgery in most patients, but shivering is not common during the postoperative period. Recovery from anesthesia is usually rapid and uneventful, and restlessness and delirium are uncommon. Nausea and vomiting are also not common during the postoperative period, and patients tend to request an analgesic soon after recovery.

The safety of enflurane during pregnancy, including its use for labor and delivery, has not been established.

USUAL DOSAGE.—*Inhalation:* For induction, a 2% to 5% concentration vaporized by a flow of oxygen or a nitrous oxide-oxygen mixture. Generally, a 1% to 4% concentration is administered for maintenance. A vaporizor calibrated for enflurane, or from which a known concentration of the drug can be obtained, must be used.

PREPARATIONS.—Ethrane (Ohio Medical Products). *Inhalation:* Liquid in 125 and 250 ml containers.

FLUROXENE [Fluoromar]

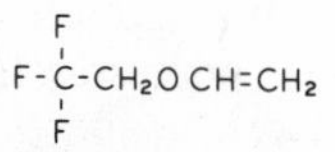

$$\mathrm{F-\overset{\displaystyle F}{\underset{\displaystyle F}{C}}-CH_2O\,CH{=}CH_2}$$

Fluroxene is a fluorinated ether which is potentially flammable and explosive at higher, clinically useful concentrations; however, the energy of the ignition spark is said to be 30 times that required for ethyl ether. It is used alone for minor surgical procedures or with nitrous oxide for general anesthesia.

Unconsciousness is produced quickly but excitement is seen occasionally. Fluroxene has good analgesic properties. Satisfactory muscular relaxation is difficult to obtain even in deeper planes of surgical anesthesia; muscle relaxant drugs must be used as adjuncts, especially for abdominal operations.

Changes in depth of anesthesia may occur rapidly; therefore, the blood pressure and rate and depth of respiration must be observed carefully. The blood pressure is normal or only slightly depressed at usual levels of surgical anesthesia, but severe hypotension may ensue if anesthesia is deepened unduly. Arrhythmias are transient and reversible. Fluroxene apparently does not sensitize the heart to catecholamines and it can be used with epinephrine or levarterenol.

Recovery from anesthesia is rapid, and protective reflexes (cough, gag, swallowing) return early. Postoperative nausea and vomiting are noted infrequently, and excitement or delirium during recovery occurs only rarely.

There have been two anecdotal case reports of hepatotoxic reactions after the use of fluroxene, but no renal toxic reactions have been reported. The bleeding time is prolonged during fluroxene anesthesia, but returns to normal within 24 hours.

USUAL DOSAGE.—*Inhalation:* For analgesia, 1.5% to 2% concentration. For surgical anesthesia, concentrations of 6% to 12% are used for induction, and of 3% to 12% are used for maintenance. If given with 75% nitrous oxide and 25% oxygen, concentrations of 1% to 2% may be adequate. Fluroxene may be introduced into a closed or semiclosed circuit system in combination with oxygen or nitrous oxide-oxygen mixture.

PREPARATIONS.—Fluoromar (Ohio Medical Products). *Inhalation:* Liquid in 125 ml containers.

HALOTHANE [Fluothane]

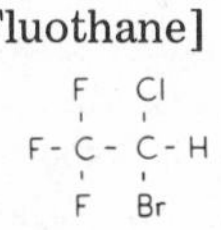

$$\mathrm{F-\overset{\displaystyle F}{\underset{\displaystyle F}{C}}-\overset{\displaystyle Cl}{\underset{\displaystyle Br}{C}}-H}$$

Halothane is a potent, nonflammable, halogenated hydrocarbon anesthetic that provides rapid induction of anesthesia with little or no excitement. It has minimal analgesic properties and, when used in high concentrations, causes circulatory depression; therefore, it is generally given with nitrous oxide. Neuromuscular blocking agents are required because halothane does not produce adequate muscular relaxation. This anesthetic augments the neuromuscular blocking effects of the nondepolarizing muscle relaxants; therefore, these agents should be used in reduced doses with halothane. If succinylcholine has been administered, an anticholinergic drug should be administered to prevent bradycardia or sinus arrest if succinylcholine is to be repeated.

Halothane is not irritating to the respiratory tract. It dilates the bronchioles and is preferable to other anesthetics for patients with bronchial asthma. This anesthetic depresses the respiratory center, and ventilation should be assisted to avoid respiratory acidosis.

The cardiovascular system is profoundly affected by halothane anesthesia: the contractility of the heart and vascular smooth muscle is depressed; sympathetic activity is diminished; vagal tone is augmented; and the blood pressure and pulse rate are reduced, usually in proportion to the depth of anesthesia. Severe hypotension and circulatory failure may occur with overdosage. Arrhythmias may occur during induction or during deep anesthesia, particularly if ventilation is inadequate. Nodal rhythm may develop. Halothane is incompatible with catecholamines and severe arrhythmias may occur if it is used with epinephrine or levarterenol.

Halothane has caused reversible alterations in the results of liver function tests after a single administration; the changes are similar to those observed following administration of other anesthetics. Although fatal liver necrosis has been reported after such use, the incidence is probably no higher than that associated with other general anesthetic techniques. However, it has been suggested that serious liver damage may follow repeated administration of halothane. Although insufficient controlled data have been accumulated to prove this hypothesis, the development of hepatitis in two anesthesiologists, and its recurrence following administration of a subanesthetic concentration of halothane, indicates that the drug is capable of acting as a hepatic sensitizing agent in rare individuals. On this basis, halothane probably should not be given to patients who are known to have developed jaundice and unexplained fever following a prior exposure. This same precaution may apply to those who developed a similar response following exposure to methoxyflurane.

No appreciable metabolic disturbances occur during anesthesia. Aside from reversible oliguria during anesthesia, halothane has no effect on the kidney. It also has no appreciable effect on blood coagulation.

Malignant hyperpyrexia has been reported in patients given halothane and succinylcholine, but a cause-and-effect relationship has not been established.

The incidence of postanesthetic nausea and vomiting is lower after halothane anesthesia than after ether or cyclopropane. Recovery is relatively smooth and rapid after short procedures and is delayed 10 or 15 minutes after long procedures.

USUAL DOSAGE.—*Inhalation:* For induction of anesthesia, a 1% to 4% concentration vaporized by a flow of oxygen or nitrous oxide-oxygen mixture is used. A 0.5% to 2% concentration is used for maintenance. A vaporizer calibrated for halothane, or from which a known concentration of the drug can be obtained, must be used.

PREPARATIONS.—Fluothane (Ayerst). *Inhalation:* Liquid in 125 ml containers.

METHOXYFLURANE [Penthrane]

$$H-\overset{Cl}{\underset{Cl}{C}}-\overset{F}{\underset{F}{C}}-O-CH_3$$

Methoxyflurane is a potent volatile liquid anesthetic with a high blood/gas partition ratio. Because of its solubility in blood, tissues, and certain components of the induction equipment (rubber, soda lime), induction is slow and recovery is prolonged. Methoxyflurane has good analgesic and muscle relaxant properties; however, it is generally used with a nitrous oxide-oxygen mixture and a neuromuscular blocking agent, for high concentrations can cause untoward cardiovascular and renal effects. Methoxyflurane augments the neuromuscular blocking effects of the nondepolarizing muscle relaxants; therefore, these agents should be used in reduced dosage with this anesthetic.

Respiration is not depressed at light levels of anesthesia, but should be assisted or controlled when surgical anesthesia is attained.

Methoxyflurane depresses the cardiovascular system, but to a lesser extent than does halothane. Arrhythmias are uncommon. Methoxyflurane appears not to sensitize the heart to catecholamines.

A number of cases of impaired renal function have been associated with methoxyflurane anesthesia. The symptoms of renal insufficiency include output of a large volume of urine with a low specific gravity, a significant rise in the blood urea nitrogen level, hypernatremia, an elevated concentration of inorganic fluoride in the serum and urine, and an increase in excretion of oxalic acid. High-output renal failure and death have occurred in a few patients. In some cases, autopsy has revealed the presence of renal calcium oxalate crystals. The mechanism of the renal dysfunction is believed to involve an effect of the fluoride ion which renders the distal renal tubules unresponsive to the antidiuretic hormone. At the present time, the major factors contributing to nephrotoxicity are thought to be high concentrations of the anesthetic and prolonged anesthesia. Obesity also is a predisposing factor, probably because large quantities of methoxyflurane or metabolites may be stored in fat for a considerable length of time. It may be unwise to administer methoxyflurane to patients receiving tetracyclines because the concurrent use of these agents has been associated with renal failure. Other anesthetics should be used in patients with renal impairment.

Hepatic necrosis has occurred following anesthesia with methoxyflurane. Thus, this drug probably should not be given to patients who are known to have developed jaundice and unexplained fever after previous administration of methoxyflurane or halothane.

USUAL DOSAGE.—*Inhalation:* For analgesia, 0.5% in air. For induction of anesthesia, 1.5% to 3% concentration vaporized by at least a 1:1 mixture of nitrous oxide and oxygen. For maintenance, a concentration of 0.5% or less is usually adequate. The drug may be administered by either closed or semiclosed circuit systems; in infants and children, the open-drop technique also has been used.

PREPARATIONS.—Penthrane (Abbott). *Inhalation:* Liquid in 15 and 125 ml containers.

TRICHLOROETHYLENE [Trilene]

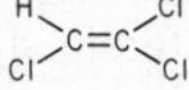

Trichloroethylene is a sweet-smelling, volatile, nonexplosive liquid with potent analgesic properties. It is not satisfactory as a general anesthetic because of its slow induction and recovery rates and inadequate skeletal muscle relaxant properties. It is used primarily as an analgesic in minor diagnostic surgical procedures and in obstetrics and dentistry. It is occasionally used with nitrous oxide for general anesthesia.

Trichloroethylene is relatively safe when given as an analgesic. At anesthetic levels, it causes rapid, shallow breathing that may be followed by respiratory arrest. Arrhythmias may occur spontaneously and may be precipitated by administration of epinephrine or levarterenol.

Occasionally this agent has caused convulsions in children and it should not be used in patients with convulsive disorders. It should never be administered in a closed system with soda lime, because toxic (particularly to the fifth cranial nerve) and explosive by-products may be produced.

USUAL DOSAGE.—*Inhalation:* For analgesia, 0.25% to 0.75% in air. For anesthesia, the concentration of trichloroethylene should not exceed 1% with a 2:1 mixture of nitrous oxide and oxygen as the vaporizing gas.

PREPARATIONS.—Trilene (Ayerst). *Inhalation:* Liquid in 300 ml containers.

VINYL ETHER [Vinethene]

Vinyl ether is a volatile, flammable, liquid anesthetic with a mild ethereal odor. Its effects are similar to those of ethyl ether, but vinyl ether is more potent, provides more rapid induction and recovery, is less irritating to the respiratory tract, and causes less nausea and vomiting. However, it does not provide adequate muscle relaxation at safe levels of anesthesia.

Vinyl ether has been used as the sole anesthetic for brief minor surgical procedures and in obstetrics, and is given as an induction anesthetic when other agents are used for maintenance or to supplement nitrous oxide or ethylene. Because of its possible hepatic and renal toxicity, vinyl ether should not be used for operations lasting more than one hour or for prolonged delivery.

The effects of vinyl ether on the circulatory system are similar to those of ethyl ether. It does not sensitize the heart to catecholamines. It causes a transient hyperglycemia that is less pronounced than that observed with ethyl ether.

Liver damage may occur after prolonged, excessive, or repeated use, or if there is concomitant hypoxia. Renal damage also may occur. Therefore, vinyl ether is contraindicated in patients with hepatic or renal disease. It should not be given repeatedly at short intervals.

Vinyl ether may cause convulsions, particularly in children, and should not be used in patients with a history of convulsive disorders.

This anesthetic decomposes on exposure to light or air; it should not be used if the container has been open for more than 48 hours.

USUAL DOSAGE.—*Inhalation:* Dosage varies depending upon the response of the patient. For induction of anesthesia, 60 to 80 drops per minute on an open face mask usually is sufficient. For maintenance, one-half to two-thirds the induction drop rate; 4% generally maintains anesthesia.

PREPARATIONS.– Vinethene (Merck Sharp & Dohme). *Inhalation:* Liquid in 10, 25, and 50 ml containers.

INTRAVENOUS ANESTHETICS

THIOPENTAL SODIUM [Pentothal Sodium]

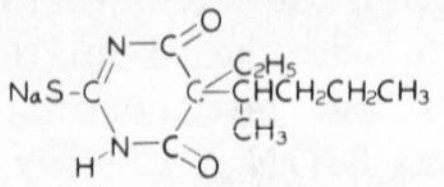

This rapid-acting, potent hypnotic can induce general anesthesia within 30 to 60 seconds after intravenous administration. Once unconsciousness has ensued, basal narcosis can be maintained by additional small increments or by dilute intravenous drip. Thiopental has limited usefulness as the sole anesthetic; for painful surgical procedures or those requiring muscular relaxation, it should be given with analgesics and neuromuscular blocking agents or a potent inhalation anesthetic. It also is given rectally as a basal anesthetic in children.

Thiopental is a potent respiratory depressant, and apnea may occur immediately after intravenous injection. The drug also may cause coughing, laryngeal spasm, and bronchospasm. Adequate ventilation should be assured by orotracheal intubation if necessary. Severe laryngeal spasm (but not bronchospasm) can be relieved promptly by administration of succinylcholine chloride. Thiopental should be used with care in patients with bronchial asthma or respiratory obstruction.

The blood pressure generally is only slightly affected by thiopental. However, a transient hypotensive response may occur immediately after rapid intravenous injection.

Thiopental does not cause hepatic or renal damage, but may cause prolonged somnolence in patients with severe liver disease. It is contraindicated in patients with acute intermittent porphyria.

Care should be taken to avoid extravasation or intra-arterial injection, as necrosis and slough may occur with the former and arteritis, followed by gangrene, with the latter; damage is reduced by use of dilute solutions. If extravasation or intra-arterial injection does occur, local injection (preferably intravenously through the needle used for the thiopental) of 1% procaine (10 ml in an adult) and of heparin will reduce the degree of slough, and sympathetic block or general anesthesia with halothane may relieve pain and arterial spasm and assist in opening collateral circulation.

USUAL DOSAGE.—

Intravenous: The dosage required to produce and maintain anesthesia varies with the body size, physical status of the patient, pre-existing disease, and adequacy of respiratory and circulatory systems.

For induction of anesthesia, *adults,* 2 to 4 ml of a 2.5% solution is injected intermittently every 30 to 60 seconds until the desired effect has been obtained. *Children,* a 2% solution is injected intermittently at 30-second intervals. The total dose recommended for induction is 1.5 ml for *children weighing 15 kg,* 3 ml for *children weighing 30 kg,* 4 ml for *children weighing 40 kg,* or 5 ml for *children weighing 50 kg.* For maintenance, *adults,* 0.5 to 2 ml of a 2.5% solution as required; *children,* a 2% solution is injected intermittently. The recommended dose is 2 ml for *children weighing 30 to 50 kg.*

Rectal: For basal anesthesia in *children,* 30 mg/kg of body weight in a 40% suspension.

PREPARATIONS.—Pentothal Sodium (Abbott).

Injection: Powder (for solution) 0.5, 1, 5, 6.25, 10, and 12.5 g.

Rectal: Suspension 400 mg/g in 2.2 g containers. Drug also marketed under generic name.

THIAMYLAL SODIUM [Surital Sodium]

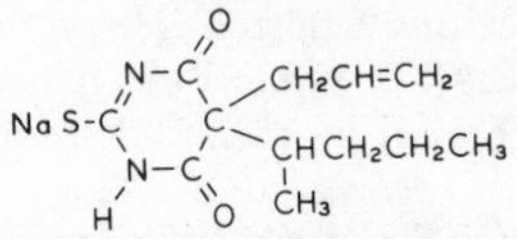

The uses and adverse effects of this rapid-acting barbiturate are similar to those of thiopental.

USUAL DOSAGE.—*Intravenous: Adults,* for induction of anesthesia, 2 to 4 ml of a freshly prepared 2.5% solution is injected intermittently every 30 to 60 seconds until the desired effect has been obtained. For maintenance, 0.5 to 2 ml of a 2.5% solution may be injected as required, or a 0.3% solution may be given by continuous drip.

PREPARATIONS.—Surital Sodium (Parke, Davis). *Injection:* Powder (for solution) 1, 5, and 10 g.

METHOHEXITAL SODIUM [Brevital Sodium]

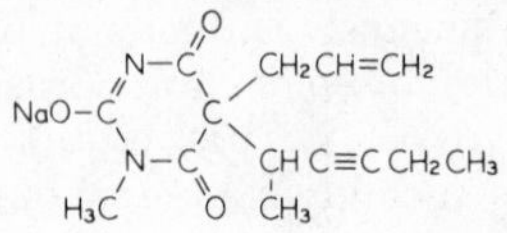

Methohexital is a potent, rapid-acting barbiturate with uses and adverse effects similar to those of thiopental. Hiccups are not uncommon after rapid intravenous injection.

USUAL DOSAGE.—*Intravenous: Adults*, for induction, 5 to 12 ml of a 1% solution at the rate of 1 ml every five seconds. For maintenance, 2 to 4 ml of a 1% solution as required. When given by intravenous drip to supplement other forms of anesthesia, a 0.2% solution is used.

PREPARATIONS.—Brevital Sodium (Lilly). *Injection:* Powder (for solution) 0.5, 2.5, and 5 g.

KETAMINE HYDROCHLORIDE [Ketalar, Ketaject]

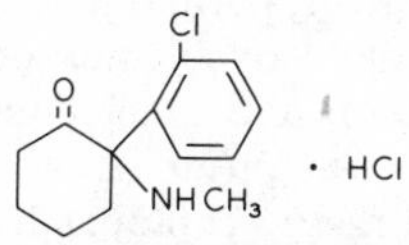

Ketamine is a rapid-acting nonbarbiturate anesthetic that is administered intravenously or intramuscularly. This agent induces a cataleptic state in which the patient appears to be awake but is dissociated from the environment, is unresponsive to pain, and has no subsequent memory of the procedure. The reaction to somatic pain is blocked more effectively than is the response to visceral pain.

Ketamine may be used as the sole anesthetic for diagnostic and minor surgical procedures of short duration. It should not be used as the sole agent for abdominal operations because it does not provide adequate analgesia or skeletal muscle relaxation; for such procedures, ketamine may be used for induction, followed by administration of nitrous oxide or other agents. An anticholinergic drug should be given for premedication to reduce secretions, and a skeletal muscle relaxant should be administered if required.

This anesthetic is particularly useful for diagnostic studies in children and for repeated anesthesia in burned children (burn dressing and skin grafts). It also has been recommended for induction of anesthesia when a barbiturate is not desired or is contraindicated. Some anesthesiologists have found ketamine of value in poor-risk patients of all ages; however, its usefulness in adults is limited because of its adverse effects.

Adverse Reactions and Precautions.—

Psychic: Ketamine is a cyclohexanone that is chemically related to phencyclidine [Sernylan], a drug that was found unsuitable for clinical use because of its psychotomimetic effects during recovery. Psychic disturbances during emergence are common with ketamine, but have been described as of shorter duration than those occurring with phencyclidine. Emergence reactions occur in about 12% of patients and can be highly disturbing to both patient and nursing personnel. Vivid dreams, usually unpleasant, may occur during the recovery period. Psychic changes observed during emergence include irrational behavior, excitement, confusion, euphoria, disturbances of body image, delirium, and hallucinations. Recovery may be prolonged, and the patient may have difficulty in concentrating for several hours after administration of the drug. On subsequent questioning, some patients have expressed unwillingness to have ketamine anesthesia for later operations. The incidence of psychic disturbances during recovery is not closely related to dosage but bears a definite relationship to age of the patient. Emergence reactions occur more frequently in adults than in children. It is not clear to what extent the lower incidence in children may be due to difficulties in detecting these reactions in young children.

Emergence reactions can be minimized if the patient is shielded from auditory and tactile stimulation during the recovery period; however, this precaution may be difficult to achieve if vital signs are to be adequately monitored. Considerably more study is needed on the role of adjunctive drugs in increasing or decreasing the psychotomimetic effects of ketamine. Because of the possibility of emergence reactions, some anesthesiologists feel that ketamine is not suitable for outpatient anesthesia in adults. It is best to avoid this agent in patients with psychosis or severe psychoneurosis.

Cardiovascular: Ketamine usually increases the heart rate and elevates the systolic and diastolic blood pressures. The tachycardia and hypertension occasionally are severe, particularly in elderly patients with arteriosclerosis. The increase in heart rate and blood pressure is more pronounced when the drug is administered intravenously than when it is given intramuscularly. These cardiovascular effects are more prominent in adults than in children, but this may be due to the more frequent use of the intravenous route in adults. It has been reported that excessive elevations in blood pressure are counteracted by administration of halothane.

Bradycardia and hypotension have been observed occasionally, and severe arrhythmias have occurred rarely.

Ketamine should be used with care in patients with mild, uncomplicated hypertension, and is contraindicated in patients with severe hypertension or a history of stroke syndrome.

Respiratory: Ketamine causes minimal depression of respiration, although transient depression may occur immediately after intravenous administration of anesthetic doses. As with other general anesthetics, resuscitative equipment always should be available during administration of ketamine to treat prolonged respiratory depression due to overdosage. Mild respiratory stimulation also has been reported after administration of ketamine.

Muscular and Neurologic: Muscular rigidity, athetoid motions of the mouth and tongue, and random movements of the extremities are not uncommon during anesthesia with ketamine. Laryngeal and pharyngeal protective reflexes usually are active, and mechanical stimulation may cause laryngeal spasm. Ketamine should not be used in surgery involving the pharynx, larynx, or bronchial tree without endotracheal intubation and administration of a muscle relaxant.

Fasciculations, tremors, and clonus have been reported. Generalized convulsions have occurred occasionally; therefore, the drug should be given with care to patients with convulsive disorders.

Ketamine increases cerebrospinal fluid pressure as a result of its hypertensive effect. Some authorities feel that this precludes its use (1) in procedures involving diagnostic cerebrospinal fluid manometry; (2) in cerebral angiography (because the increase in intracranial pressure might cause a holdup of contrast medium); and (3) in patients with evidence of raised intracranial pressure or a space-occupying lesion. Although ketamine has been given in these situations without apparent ill effects, an anesthetic that does not elevate intracranial pressure is preferred.

Gastrointestinal: Many prudent anesthesiologists do not agree with the claim that ketamine can be used safely in patients with full stomachs. Aspiration of vomitus may occur with any general anesthetic, and the same precautions should be taken with ketamine as with other agents. Results of one study showed that postoperative nausea and vomiting occurred more frequently after induction of anesthesia with ketamine than after induction with a barbiturate.

Other Reactions: Ketamine may cause hypersalivation, hyperhidrosis, lacrimation, and shivering. Marked nystagmus occurs frequently during induction and emergence; this precludes the use of ketamine as the sole agent in intraocular surgery. Diplopia has been reported during the recovery period. Transient dermatologic reactions (erythema, rash) may occur.

USUAL DOSAGE.—

Intravenous: For induction, 2 mg/kg of body weight (range, 1 to 4.5 mg/kg), administered over a period of 60 seconds, will generally produce five to ten minutes of surgical anesthesia. For maintenance, one-half to the full induction dose may be repeated as needed.

Intramuscular: For induction, 10 mg/kg of body weight (range, 6.5 to 13 mg/kg) will usually produce 12 to 25 minutes of surgical anesthesia.

PREPARATIONS.—Ketalar (Parke, Davis), Ketaject (Bristol). *Injection:* Solution 10 mg/ml in 20 and 50 ml containers, 50 mg/ml in 10 ml containers, and 100 mg/ml in 5 ml containers [Ketalar].

Chapter 20

ADJUNCTS TO ANESTHESIA

General and regional anesthetics may be supplemented by nonanesthetic drugs, usually for one or more of the following purposes: (1) to reduce preoperative apprehension; (2) to counteract undesirable reflexes; (3) to facilitate induction and provide smooth maintenance and recovery; (4) to fortify anesthetics of low potency; and (5) to reduce the amount of general anesthetic required.

Many of the drugs commonly used as adjuncts to anesthesia are also given therapeutically for other purposes and are presented in more detail in other chapters. General groups and their specific application in surgical and anesthetic procedures are discussed briefly in this chapter. Individual evaluative statements will be limited to those agents not considered in detail elsewhere or to those that appear to possess special merit as adjuncts to anesthesia.

SEDATIVES AND HYPNOTICS

The short-acting barbiturates, particularly secobarbital [Seconal] and pentobarbital [Nembutal], are used as adjuncts to anesthesia to reduce apprehension and produce drowsiness. They are given for preanesthetic medication and for sedation during various diagnostic procedures, during conduction (block) anesthesia, and during labor, as well as for nighttime hypnosis prior to surgery.

The barbiturates have several characteristics that make them good premedicants, provided pain is absent: they reduce preoperative apprehension, which is one of the primary goals of preanesthetic medication; they rarely produce untoward cardiovascular and respiratory reactions; and they do not cause nausea and vomiting. If pain is present, however, emergence excitement is more common after premedication with barbiturates than after use of morphine-like analgesics. Although nonbarbiturate-type hypnotics are qualitatively similar in action to the barbiturates, the barbiturates are preferred by many anesthesiologists.

Adverse Reactions and Precautions: When barbiturates are used for preanesthetic medication, emergence delirium may occur during recovery in the absence of analgesia. Large doses delay recovery from general anesthesia. For other adverse reactions and precautions, see Chapter 27, Sedatives and Hypnotics.

ANTIANXIETY AGENTS

Antianxiety agents are also used to allay preoperative apprehension. This group includes chlordiazepoxide [Librium], diazepam [Valium], hydroxyzine [Atarax, Vistaril], and meprobamate [Miltown, Equanil]. Of these drugs, diazepam has been studied most extensively for this purpose and appears to be highly effective.

For uses and adverse effects of these drugs, see Chapter 28, Antianxiety Agents, and the evaluation on Diazepam in this chapter.

STRONG ANALGESICS

Morphine and the synthetic and semisynthetic narcotics are used to produce analgesia and sedation before and after surgery. They also are given with the anesthetic for additive effects during surgery. When used for preanesthetic medication, most narcotic analgesics produce drowsiness and facilitate induction; they also provide smooth maintenance when anesthetics of low potency are used. By relieving pain, they reduce restlessness during the recovery period.

However, these agents may produce more untoward effects than the barbiturates, and opinion is divided on the advisability of their routine use for preanesthetic medication.

For the use of strong analgesics in the treatment of postoperative pain, see Chapter 21, Strong Analgesics.

Adverse Reactions and Precautions: Respiratory depression is the most serious adverse reaction associated with use of the narcotic analgesics as adjuncts to anesthesia. These agents also cause nausea and vomiting, circulatory instability, urinary retention, and depression of the cough reflex. They occasionally may produce dysphoria when used for preanesthetic medication.

Narcotic analgesics may prolong recovery from general anesthesia. The possibility of hypotension and respiratory depression is increased when they are used with phenothiazines. Monoamine oxidase inhibitors and tricyclic antidepressants also may enhance the depressant effects of some strong analgesics.

PHENOTHIAZINES AND BUTYROPHENONES

Various phenothiazines and the butyrophenone, droperidol [Inapsine], are used in anesthesia to produce drowsiness and to prevent or control nausea and vomiting. These agents produce an outwardly calm and drowsy state from which the patient can be readily aroused. They are potent antagonists of the emetic effects of morphine-like analgesics and other drugs that act on the chemoreceptor trigger zone. In addition, the effects of other central nervous system depressants are increased or potentiated by some of these agents.

The phenothiazines with aliphatic side chains (eg, promethazine [Phenergan]) have the most pronounced sedative effect, but some of these agents may cause significant hypotension during the preoperative and postoperative periods, as well as during induction of anesthesia. Promethazine and propiomazine [Largon] often are preferred because of their low toxicity. The compounds with aliphatic side chains that cause pronounced drowsiness also decrease preoperative apprehension, but there is no convincing evidence that any phenothiazine or droperidol is more effective in reducing anxiety than the barbiturates or the benzodiazepines (eg, diazepam). Agents with a greater tendency to cause extrapyramidal reactions (droperidol and phenothiazines with piperazine side chains) generally do not reduce preoperative apprehension.

The phenothiazines and droperidol are highly effective in preventing and controlling nausea and vomiting during and after surgery. Their routine prophylactic use for this purpose has been questioned, however. These drugs may produce many untoward effects and, since the incidence of severe, protracted postoperative vomiting is low, many authorities feel that emesis should be treated as the need arises. An exception would be procedures in which vomiting could interfere with the results of surgery (eg, intraocular surgery). (See also Chapter 85, Antiemetics.)

The phenothiazines and droperidol are used most commonly in anesthesia in conjunction with morphine-like analgesics. Their concomitant administration results in an additive sedative effect. In addition, the emetic action of the analgesic is counteracted by the phenothiazine or droperidol, while the analgesic reduces akathisia and other extrapyramidal reactions. Combined therapy is given for preanesthetic medication, for obstetrical analgesia, and for neuroleptanalgesia, an anesthetic technique that combines the action of droperidol and the strong analgesic, fentanyl. Neuroleptanalgesia is used for certain diagnostic and surgical procedures requiring a conscious and cooperative patient or as an alternative to general anesthesia when only sedation and analgesia, rather than unconsciousness, are required. When the butyrophenone and the analgesic are supplemented by a general anesthetic and, if needed, a muscle relaxant, the method is termed neuroleptanesthesia and may be used for major surgery.

Although droperidol and fentanyl have traditionally been used for neuroleptanalgesia, droperidol could be replaced by a phenothiazine, and fentanyl appears to offer little advantage over other analgesics except possibly a shorter duration of action. Repeated administration of Innovar, the fixed-dose combination of these agents, may be inadvisable after induction, because this can result in a relative overdose of droperidol. (See the evaluations on Droperidol and Innovar.)

Adverse Reactions and Precautions: Hypotension and extrapyramidal symptoms are the most common untoward effects of the phenothiazines and droperidol. These reactions are most severe when the drugs are given intravenously, but also occur with intramuscular use. Generally the incidence of hypotension is higher with phenothiazines with aliphatic side chains, while the piperazine compounds and droperidol are more likely to cause extrapyramidal reactions.

These agents may prolong recovery time from general anesthesia. The risk of hypotension or respiratory depression may be increased when they are used with other central nervous system depressants such as morphine-like analgesics or barbiturates; therefore, when used concomitantly, the dose of the analgesic or barbiturate should be reduced. For other adverse reactions and precautions, see Chapter 29, Antipsychotic Agents.

ANTICHOLINERGIC AGENTS

Anticholinergic drugs are given before anesthesia to reduce excessive salivary and bronchial secretions caused by some inhalation anesthetics. They are also used to protect against vagally-mediated bradycardia, hypotension, and cardiac arrest induced by succinylcholine or cyclopropane or by certain surgical procedures. Atropine and scopolamine are most commonly used for premedication. Scopolamine is a more potent antisecretory agent than atropine, but it is less effective in blocking the cardiac effects of excessive vagal stimulation. Unlike atropine, scopolamine usually has a pronounced sedative effect and may cause amnesia, particularly when given with a morphine-like analgesic or diazepam. Hyoscyamine [Levsin], the levorotatory isomer of atropine, occasionally is used for premedication. Its actions are similar to those of atropine, but hyoscyamine is more potent.

Adverse Reactions and Precautions: Atropine should be used with caution when tachycardia must be avoided (eg, in patients with mitral stenosis). Scopolamine, administered in small doses, generally does not increase the heart rate. Anticholinergic drugs inhibit heat loss and should be used cautiously in patients with fever, as hyperpyrexia may ensue, particularly in children.

In the dosage used for preanesthetic medication, anticholinergic drugs cause mydriasis and cycloplegia. These agents should be avoided, if possible, in patients predisposed to angle-closure, for atropine has induced acute angle-closure glaucoma when given intramuscularly. If there is a need for anticholinergic premedication in a patient with abnormally shallow anterior chambers and dangerously narrow angles, the hazard of inducing angle-closure glaucoma can be minimized by instilling one drop of 1% pilocarpine in each eye and by giving 500 mg of acetazolamide [Diamox] intravenously or orally. Anticholinergic premedication can be given safely to patients with open-angle glaucoma who are being treated with miotics.

Atropine and scopolamine readily cross the blood-brain barrier. In toxic doses, atropine causes excitation, but in therapeutic doses it rarely produces central nervous system reactions except in elderly patients, in whom it may cause confusion. Scopolamine usually has a pronounced sedative effect, but it may cause excitation and disorientation in elderly patients and in those in pain. (See the evaluations on Atropine Sulfate and Scopolamine Hydrobromide in this chapter and in Chapter 78, Antispasmodics.)

NEUROMUSCULAR BLOCKING AGENTS

Neuromuscular blocking agents are used with general anesthetics to provide sustained skeletal muscle relaxation during surgical procedures, particularly abdominal surgery. The blocking agent provides adequate relaxation without the need for deep general anesthesia and its attendant risks. Neuromuscular blocking drugs also are used to facilitate endotracheal intubation, to relieve laryngeal spasm, to produce apnea so that respiration can be controlled during thoracic surgery, to provide relaxation during brief diagnostic and surgical procedures, to prevent dislocations and fractures during electroconvulsive shock therapy, and to control muscle spasms in tetanus.

These agents are classified as either nondepolarizing (competitive) or depolarizing. The nondepolarizing blocking agents are tubocurarine, dimethyl tubocurarine [Metubine], gallamine [Flaxedil], and pancuronium [Pavulon]. These drugs compete with acetylcholine for the cholinergic receptor sites at the neuromuscular junction of skeletal muscle. By occupying the receptor sites, they block the transmitter action of acetylcholine and produce total paralysis of the muscle fibers that lasts as long as the drug remains bound at the endplate. This competitive block may be reversed by anticholinesterase agents such as neostigmine [Prostigmin] or edrophonium [Tensilon].

The depolarizing agents (succinylcholine [Anectine, Quelicin, Sucostrin, Sux-Cert] and decamethonium [Syncurine]) have a shorter duration of action than the competitive neuromuscular blocking drugs. They are believed to act by producing a sustained depolarization at the motor endplate; paralysis ensues because the endplate receptors are refractory to acetylcholine while in a depolarized state (phase 1 block). Paralysis may be preceded by signs of stimulation (eg, fasciculations). This type of neuromuscular block is intensified by anticholinesterase drugs. In some species, desensitization of the receptors occurs after prolonged administration of the depolarizing relaxants; this gives rise to phase 2 block, which has some similarities to the block produced by the nondepolarizing agents.

The choice of a neuromuscular blocking agent is determined by the expected duration of the procedure, the possibility of interactions between the blocking agent and the general anesthetic or other drugs, and the presence of pathologic conditions which may influence the patient's response to the blocking agent. Generally, a single dose of succinylcholine is used for brief procedures (two or three minutes) such as endotracheal intubation. For longer procedures, doses of the nondepolarizing agents are repeated or succinylcholine is administered by continuous infusion. Occasionally, succinylcholine is given in fractional doses with hexafluorenium [Mylaxen], a pseudocholinesterase inhibitor which increases the intensity and duration of the block.

Nondepolarizing agents are preferred to succinylcholine in conditions in which there are low pseudocholinesterase levels (eg, liver disease, protein depletion, advanced pregnancy, an inborn error of metabolism, after administration of anticholinesterase agents). Gallamine increases the heart rate and elevates blood pressure and may be preferred if bradycardia is present. Gallamine and decamethonium are excreted unchanged by the kidney; since succinylcholine is almost completely hydrolyzed by serum cholinesterase, it may be preferable in patients with severe renal disease. Both the liver and kidneys are involved in the degradation and excretion of tubocurarine; therefore, because it has an alternate route for excretion, tubocurarine may be given in reduced doses to patients with renal disease when a nondepolarizing agent is preferred.

Adverse Reactions and Precautions: Although use of a neuromuscular blocking agent obviates the need for deep general anesthesia, these drugs have no anesthetic or analgesic properties and should never be used in excessive doses to compensate for inadequate anesthesia.

Since the neuromuscular blocking agents affect the respiratory muscles, respiration must be controlled whenever they are used.

The most common untoward effects of the neuromuscular blocking agents are severe hypotension, bradycardia, arrhythmias, bronchospasm, and inadequate postoperative ventilation. These complications are generally due to overdosage, to interactions between the blocking agent and other drugs, or to the presence of pathologic conditions that influence the patient's response to the blocking agent. (See the individual evaluations.)

MISCELLANEOUS ADJUNCTIVE DRUGS

A number of other agents are occasionally given during anesthesia to meet specific problems.

Antiarrhythmic agents are sometimes needed to control arrhythmias caused by the anesthetic, reflex activity, or surgical manipulation of the heart or other organs. Those drugs used include propranolol [Inderal], a beta-adrenergic blocking agent; procainamide [Pronestyl]; lidocaine [Xylocaine] and, more rarely, quinidine sulfate [Quinidex, Quinora]. (See Chapter 2, Antiarrhythmic Agents.)

Ganglionic blocking agents are used to lower blood pressure deliberately and thus avoid excessive hemorrhage during neurosurgery and in some cardiovascular and other operations. (See Chapter 6, Antihypertensive Agents.)

Alpha-adrenergic blocking agents decrease peripheral resistance and relieve vasospasm when excessive norepinephrine is released, such as by a pheochromocytoma. These drugs also are useful when certain accidents occur (eg, the extravasation of levarterenol into the tissue). Drugs in this group include phentolamine [Regitine], tolazoline [Priscoline], and phenoxybenzamine [Dibenzyline] (see Chapter 6, Antihypertensive Agents). The beta-adrenergic blocking agent, propranolol, is sometimes given with an alpha-adrenergic blocking drug for the preoperative management of patients with pheochromocytoma and for the prolonged treatment of cases not amenable to surgery. (See Chapter 2, Antiarrhythmic Agents, and Chapter 6, Antihypertensive Agents.)

Vasopressors are administered systemically to elevate blood pressure in hypotensive states and locally to produce vasoconstriction for control of bleeding and to delay the absorption of drugs such as local anesthetics. (See Chapter 5, Agents Used in Hypotension and Shock, and Chapter 18, Local Anesthetics.)

Analeptics are central stimulants that act on the medullary respiratory centers or the carotid body, or both. They have been given to reverse narcosis, but such use is unjustified. They may cause convulsions in large doses. (See Chapter 34, Analeptics.)

Narcotic antagonists (nalorphine [Nalline], levallorphan [Lorfan], and naloxone [Narcan]) are given specifically to counteract or prevent respiratory depression resulting from the administration of morphine or morphine-like drugs. They are not effective in counteracting the action of methotrimeprazine [Levoprome], and only naloxone is effective against pentazocine [Talwin]. The antagonists are discussed in Chapter 23, Narcotic Antagonists.

ANTIANXIETY AGENTS

DIAZEPAM [Valium]

Diazepam is used for preanesthetic medication and for sedation prior to cardioversion, air encephalography, cardiac catheterization, endoscopy, and dental surgery. It has occasionally been given with nitrous oxide for minor surgical procedures and, in Europe, it has been employed as a component of neuroleptanalgesia.

When given preoperatively, diazepam significantly reduces apprehension and causes pronounced drowsiness. It produces transient antegrade amnesia in almost all patients when given intravenously. There is a lack of agreement on whether or not it produces amnesia when given alone by the intramuscular route. Diazepam greatly potentiates the amnesic effect of scopolamine, particularly when both agents are given intravenously; to a lesser extent, this action is synergistic when diazepam is used with morphine-like analgesics. Comparative data indicate that, because of its pronounced antianxiety effect and low toxicity, diazepam may be more satisfactory for premedication than morphine-like analgesics, phenothiazines, and droperidol. However, its superiority to the barbiturates has not been clearly established.

Diazepam rarely causes untoward effects when given intramuscularly at the recommended dose level. When given intravenously, hypotension, tachycardia, and respiratory depression may occur, particularly when morphine-like analgesics are used concomitantly. Rapid intravenous injection should be avoided, as this may lead to respiratory arrest. Rarely, ventricular arrhythmias have occurred in patients who received diazepam prior to cardioversion; however, a cause-and-effect relationship has not been proved. Although the concomitant administration of diazepam and scopolamine has the advantage of inducing antegrade amnesia, the combination may greatly increase the incidence of excitatory phenomena during induction of anesthesia with a barbiturate. For other adverse reactions and precautions, see Chapter 28, Antianxiety Agents and Chapter 31, Anticonvulsants.

Diazepam should not be mixed with intravenous fluids or solutions of other drugs.

USUAL DOSAGE.—

Intramuscular: Adults, for preanesthetic medication, 10 mg one to two hours before surgery.

Intravenous: Adults, for cardioversion and brief diagnostic procedures, 5 to 15 mg injected slowly five to ten minutes before the procedure.

PREPARATIONS.—Valium (Roche). *Injection:* Solution 5 mg/ml in 2 and 10 ml containers.

PHENOTHIAZINES AND BUTYROPHENONES

PROMETHAZINE HYDROCHLORIDE [Phenergan]

Promethazine is used as an adjunct to anesthesia to produce drowsiness and to prevent or control nausea and vomiting produced by general anesthetics and morphine-like analgesics. It causes pronounced drowsiness and, like other phenothiazines, the sedative effect is increased by the concomitant administration of a morphine-like analgesic. This drug also has antihistaminic properties and is effective in preventing motion sickness.

The adverse effects of promethazine are similar to those of the other phenothiazines with aliphatic side chains. However, in a moderate dose (25 mg intramuscularly), it has little tendency to cause hypotension.

For other uses and adverse reactions and precautions, see Chapter 45, Antihistamines, and Chapter 85, Antiemetics.

USUAL DOSAGE.—

For preanesthetic medication (with reduced dose of a morphine-like analgesic):

Intramuscular: Adults, 25 to 50 mg one to two hours before surgery; *children*, 1.1 mg/kg of body weight one to two hours before surgery.

Rectal: Children over 3 years of age, 50 mg; *under 3 years*, 25 mg.

For obstetrical analgesia (with reduced dose of a morphine-like analgesic):

Intramuscular: Adults, 50 mg; an additional

25 to 50 mg may be given in three or four hours if needed.

For prevention or control of nausea and vomiting, see Chapter 85, Antiemetics.

PREPARATIONS.—Phenergan (Wyeth).

Injection: Solution 25 and 50 mg/ml in 1 and 10 ml containers.

Rectal: Suppositories 25 and 50 mg.

PROPIOMAZINE HYDROCHLORIDE [Largon]

Propiomazine is used as an adjunct to anesthesia to produce drowsiness; it also has antiemetic properties.

Although the adverse effects of propiomazine are similar to those of the other phenothiazines with aliphatic side chains, it rarely causes hypotension when given at the recommended dosage level.

USUAL DOSAGE.—*Intramuscular:* For preanesthetic medication (with reduced dose of a morphine-like analgesic), *adults,* 20 mg one to two hours before surgery; up to 40 mg may be given if needed. *Children 2 to 4 years of age,* 10 mg; *4 to 6 years,* 15 mg; *6 to 12 years,* 25 mg. For obstetrical analgesia (with reduced dose of a morphine-like analgesic), *adults,* 20 to 40 mg; dose may be repeated at three-hour intervals if required.

PREPARATIONS.—Largon (Wyeth). *Injection:* Solution 20 mg/ml in 1 and 2 ml containers.

Other Phenothiazines Used as Adjuncts to Anesthesia

Compounds with aliphatic side chains:
CHLORPROMAZINE [Thorazine (Smith Kline & French)]
TRIFLUPROMAZINE [Vesprin Squibb)]
METHOTRIMEPRAZINE [Levoprome (Lederle)]

Compounds with piperazine side chains:
PROCHLORPERAZINE [Compazine (Smith Kline & French)]
THIETHYLPERAZINE [Torecan (Sandoz)]
PERPHENAZINE [Trilafon (Schering)]

DROPERIDOL [Inapsine]

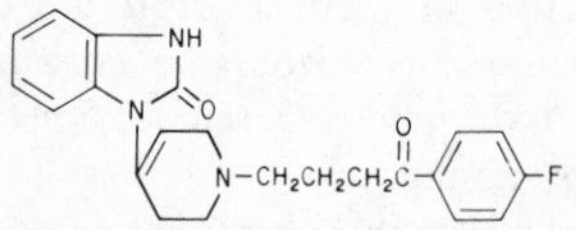

This butyrophenone derivative is used as an adjunct to anesthesia to produce sedation and reduce the incidence of nausea and vomiting. It has been given occasionally as an adjunct to conventional anesthesia, but it is used most commonly with the analgesic, fentanyl, in neuroleptanalgesia (see the evaluation on Innovar). The pharmacologic actions of droperidol are difficult to distinguish from those of the phenothiazines.

When used as the sole agent for preanesthetic medication, droperidol causes considerable drowsiness, but there is no convincing evidence that it reduces preoperative anxiety. In some studies, apprehension, excitement, or restlessness were observed more frequently in patients who received droperidol than in those given a placebo or other preanesthetic medication. The concomitant administration of a morphine-like analgesic reduces the incidence of these reactions; an additive sedative effect also has been observed.

Premedication with droperidol significantly reduces the incidence of postoperative nausea and vomiting in patients who have received strong analgesics. Since the incidence of postanesthetic vomiting is generally low in patients who have not received strong analgesics, studies designed to test the prophylactic value of droperidol in these patients have yielded conflicting results. There is no evidence that, in man, droperidol is any more or less effective than the phenothiazines in preventing or controlling postoperative nausea and vomiting. Like most phenothiazines, droperidol has no effect on motion sickness.

Greater cardiovascular stability is claimed to be one of the advantages of the butyrophenones over the phenothiazines when used as adjuncts to anesthesia. Results of controlled studies have shown that droperidol causes a moderate degree of tachycardia; in moderate doses, it has little effect on blood pressure but large doses may cause hypotension. Comparative clinical data indicate that hypotension occurs more frequently and is more severe in patients who received chlorpromazine than in those given droperidol. However, droperidol appears to offer no advantages over phenothiazines which, in moderate doses, have little effect on the cardiovascular system (eg, promethazine, propiomazine).

Droperidol, administered alone, has no analgesic properties. In animal studies, it potentiated the analgesic effect of fentanyl, but studies designed to measure potentiation in man have yielded conflicting results.

Adverse Reactions and Precautions.—Droperidol may cause extrapyramidal symptoms ranging from a slight localized tremor to a typical parkinsonian crisis. Akathisia is common. Droperidol generally should not be used in patients with parkinsonism. An exception is its use during stereotaxic surgery; cooperation of the patient is needed during this procedure and neuroleptanalgesia has been found useful.

Various psychic disturbances have been reported, including anxiety, excitement, irritability, agitation, and mental depression.

Hypotension and tachycardia may occur immediately after administration of droperidol. Two fatalities have been reported when neuroleptanalgesia was administered to patients receiving vasodilators.

Droperidol may prolong recovery from general anesthesia. The dose of other central nervous system depressants should be reduced when droperidol is used because of its possible additive or potentiating effect.

USUAL DOSAGE.—*Intravenous, Intramuscular:* For premedication (with reduced dose of a morphine-like analgesic), *adults*, 2.5 to 10 mg (1 to 4 ml) 30 to 60 minutes before induction. During induction, 2.5 mg (1 ml)/10 kg of body weight (usually given intravenously). During maintenance of anesthesia, 1.25 to 2.5 mg (0.5 to 1 ml), usually intravenously. *Children 2 to 12 years of age*, 1 to 1.5 mg (0.4 to 0.6 ml)/10 kg.

PREPARATIONS.—Inapsine (McNeil). *Injection:* Solution 2.5 mg/ml in 2 and 5 ml containers.

Mixtures

MEPERGAN

This combination of promethazine and meperidine has been used for preanesthetic medication, for sedation and analgesia during labor, and for control of postoperative pain. For analgesia, the advantage of this combination over an equivalent dose of meperidine alone is questionable (see Chapter 21, Strong Analgesics). The combined use of promethazine and meperidine may have some advantages when used for preanesthetic medication: The two drugs have an additive sedative effect, and promethazine antagonizes the emetic effect of meperidine while meperidine reduces the akathisia and other extrapyramidal symptoms that are sometimes associated with use of promethazine alone. However, this particular fixed-dose combination does not offer any clear advantage over use of the drugs separately. Separate administration would permit the dose of each drug to be adjusted to the requirements of the patient.

The risk of hypotension or respiratory depression is increased when phenothiazines are administered concomitantly with morphine-like analgesics.

For other uses and adverse reactions and precautions of the mixture or individual components, see Chapters 21, Strong Analgesics; 45, Antihistamines; and 85, Antiemetics.

USUAL DOSAGE.—*Intramuscular:* For preanesthetic medication, *adults*, 1 to 2 ml (25 to 50 mg of each component) one to two hours before surgery. *Children*, 0.04 ml (1.1 mg of each component)/kg of body weight one to two hours before surgery. For obstetrical analgesia, *adults*, 2 ml. This dose may be repeated at three- to four-hour intervals.

PREPARATIONS.—Mepergan (Wyeth). *Injection:* Each milliliter of solution contains meperidine hydrochloride 25 mg and promethazine hydrochloride 25 mg in 2 and 10 ml containers.

INNOVAR

Innovar is a combination of the morphine-like analgesic, fentanyl, and the butyrophenone, droperidol. This combination has been used to produce neuroleptanalgesia (see the Introductory Statement). This mixture appears to be most useful for premedication and induction, because fentanyl has a very short duration of action, while the action of droperidol is prolonged. Therefore, repeated administration of the fixed-dose combination can lead to a relative overdose of droperidol. See also the evaluation on Droperidol in this chapter and the evaluation on Fentanyl Citrate in Chapter 21, Strong Analgesics.

USUAL DOSAGE.—

Intramuscular: For premedication, 0.5 to 2 ml administered 45 to 60 minutes preoperatively, according to the physical status, age, and weight of patient. For basal narcosis prior to anesthesia, 0.2 ml/kg of body weight. The dosage should be reduced to 0.1 ml/kg for poor risk or elderly patients.

Intravenous: For induction of anesthesia, 0.1 ml/kg of body weight. For maintenance, 0.5 to 1 ml in response to surgical stress.

PREPARATIONS.—Innovar (McNeil). *Injection:* Each milliliter of solution contains fentanyl citrate 0.05 mg and droperidol 2.5 mg in 2 and 5 ml containers.

ANTICHOLINERGIC AGENTS

ATROPINE SULFATE

Atropine is given before anesthesia to reduce excessive salivary and bronchial secretions caused by some inhalation anesthetics and to prevent vagal cardiac arrest produced by certain drugs (eg, succinylcholine, particularly when used with halothane in children, and cyclopropane) or surgical manipulations (eg, stimulation of the mediastinum, pressure on the eyeball). Atropine is preferred to scopolamine for preventing reflex bradycardia because it has a more sustained effect on the heart. The drug has antiemetic properties and may reduce the incidence of postoperative nausea and vomiting.

In therapeutic doses, atropine causes cycloplegia and mydriasis. Although atropine usually increases the heart rate, initially it may produce bradycardia due to central vagal stimulation. When the cholinergic blockade develops, the pulse rate then is increased. Small intravenous doses frequently cause arrhythmias, which often can be reversed by administration of another dose of atropine. This drug may cause confusion in elderly patients.

See also the Introductory Statement. For other uses of atropine, see Chapters 70, Mydriatics and Cycloplegics; 74, Antiparkinsonism Agents; and 78, Antispasmodics.

USUAL DOSAGE.—*Intramuscular: Adults,* 0.6 mg one-half to one hour before surgery. *Newborn infants,* 0.1 mg; *children,* 0.01 mg/kg of body weight (maximum, 0.4 mg) one-half to one hour before surgery.

PREPARATIONS.—Atropine Sulfate, U.S.P. *Injection:* Solution 0.3, 0.4, 0.5, 0.6, 1, and 1.2 mg/ml in 1, 10, 20, 25, and 30 ml containers; tablets (hypodermic) 0.3, 0.4, and 0.6 mg. Drug marketed by many manufacturers under generic name.

SCOPOLAMINE HYDROBROMIDE

Scopolamine is given before anesthesia to reduce excessive salivary and bronchial secretions caused by some inhalation anesthetics and to produce drowsiness and allay apprehension. This agent is a more potent antisialogogue than atropine. When given in small doses (up to 0.3 mg), it has less effect on the heart than does atropine and is, therefore, preferred for premedication when tachycardia must be avoided. Scopolamine has a pronounced sedative effect and may produce antegrade amnesia, particularly when administered with a morphine-like analgesic or diazepam. It is generally given with a strong analgesic for premedication and for obstetrical analgesia. Scopolamine has antiemetic properties and may reduce the incidence of postoperative nausea and vomiting.

Although scopolamine generally has a sedative effect, it may cause disorientation in elderly patients or in those in pain. For other adverse reactions and precautions, see the Introductory Statement; for other uses of this drug, see Chapter 74, Antiparkinsonism Agents, and Chapter 85, Antiemetics.

USUAL DOSAGE.—

Intramuscular: Adults, 0.4 mg one-half to one hour before surgery or during labor.

Subcutaneous: Children, 0.006 mg/kg of body weight one-half to one hour before surgery.

PREPARATIONS.—Scopolamine Hydrobromide, U.S.P. *Injection:* Solution 0.3 mg/ml in 1 ml containers, 0.4 mg/ml in 0.5 and 1 ml containers, 0.5 mg/ml in 1 and 20 ml containers, 0.6 mg/ml in 1 ml containers. Drug marketed by many manufacturers under generic name.

NEUROMUSCULAR BLOCKING AGENTS

Nondepolarizing (Competitive) Blocking Agents

TUBOCURARINE CHLORIDE

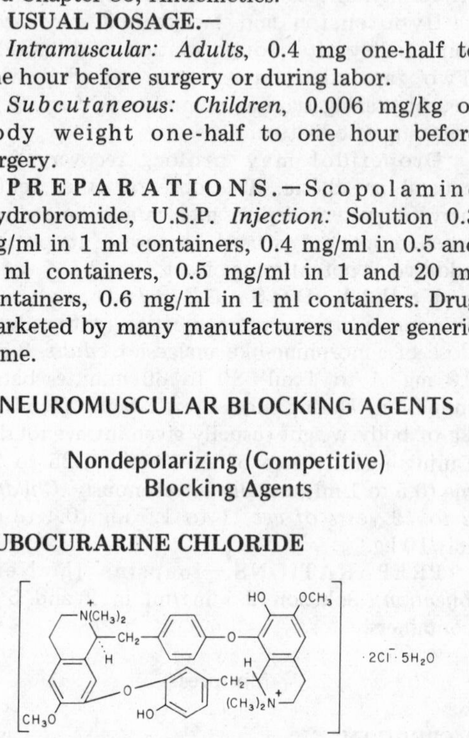

Tubocurarine (curare) is the active alkaloid in the purified extract of *Chondodendron tomentosum* roots. It produces skeletal muscle paralysis by occupying the cholinergic receptor sites at the neuromuscular junction, thereby blocking the action of the neurotransmitter, acetylcholine. Tubocurarine is used to produce muscle relaxation during surgical procedures of moderate or long duration, to reduce the severity of muscle spasms in severe tetanus, and, occasionally, in the diagnosis of myasthenia gravis (see Chapter 75, Agents Used in Myasthenia Gravis). A single intravenous dose of tubocurarine produces paralysis in three to five minutes and the effect persists for 20 to 30 minutes. About one-third of an administered dose is excreted unchanged by the kidneys over a period of several hours. When repeated doses are used in long procedures, the amount of each succeeding fraction should be reduced.

Tubocurarine causes flaccid paralysis of all skeletal muscle. The muscles of the eyes, fingers, and toes are affected first, followed by those of the limbs, neck, and trunk. Then the intercostal muscles and, finally, the diaphragm become paralyzed. The neuromuscular blocking effect of tubocurarine can be antagonized by the intravenous administration of 1 to 3 mg of neostigmine methylsulfate administered with or shortly after 1 to 1.5 mg of atropine. A dose of 10 mg of edrophonium chloride may be given intravenously instead; however, neostigmine is preferred because edrophonium has a very brief duration of action and the patient may become recurarized rapidly as the transient effect wears off. These anticholinesterase agents antagonize only the neuromuscular blocking effects of the nondepolarizing muscle relaxants; they may increase the severity of other adverse reactions such as hypotension and bronchospasm.

Various drugs can potentiate or prolong the action of tubocurarine at the neuromuscular junction. Ether and, to a lesser extent, halothane, cyclopropane, methoxyflurane, and fluroxene act synergistically with the competitive blocking agents. When tubocurarine is given with these anesthetics, the dose of the blocking agent should be reduced by one-third to one-half in some cases. Many antibiotics (eg, streptomycin, neomycin, polymyxin B, colistin, kanamycin, viomycin) can enhance the neuromuscular block produced by tubocurarine and other nondepolarizing agents. If large doses of these agents are used during surgery in patients who have received a nondepolarizing blocking agent, facilities should be available to support respiration postoperatively. Quinidine, magnesium sulfate, and trimethaphan also have been reported to potentiate the neuromuscular blocking action of tubocurarine.

Acidosis enhances and alkalosis diminishes the blocking effect of tubocurarine. Patients with myasthenia gravis are sensitive to the blocking effects of tubocurarine and other nondepolarizing agents; therefore, if administration is required in these patients, the dose of these drugs should be reduced considerably.

Tubocurarine may cause hypotension when given intravenously in large doses. This effect is due to peripheral vasodilatation, which, in turn, is believed to be caused by sympathetic ganglionic block, release of histamine, and diminished venous return as a result of loss of skeletal muscle tone. Tubocurarine also may cause bronchospasm due to the release of histamine.

Tubocurarine does not readily penetrate the blood-brain barrier and is therefore devoid of central nervous system effects when administered in therapeutic doses. It does not cross the placental barrier in significant quantities and may be used safely in obstetrical anesthesia.

USUAL DOSAGE.—

Intravenous: Adults, initially, 0.2 to 0.4 mg/kg of body weight; subsequent doses, 0.06 to 0.08 mg/kg.

Intravenous, Intramuscular: Children, initially, 0.1 to 0.2 mg/kg of body weight; subsequent doses, 0.05 to 0.1 mg/kg.

When used with ether, methoxyflurane, halothane, fluroxene, or cyclopropane, the dose of tubocurarine should be reduced.

PREPARATIONS.—Tubocurarine Chloride. *Injection:* Solution 3 mg/ml in 10 and 20 ml containers; solution (concentrate for dilution only) 15 mg/ml in 1 ml containers (Abbott). Drug marketed by many manufacturers under generic name.

DIMETHYL TUBOCURARINE IODIDE
[Metubine]

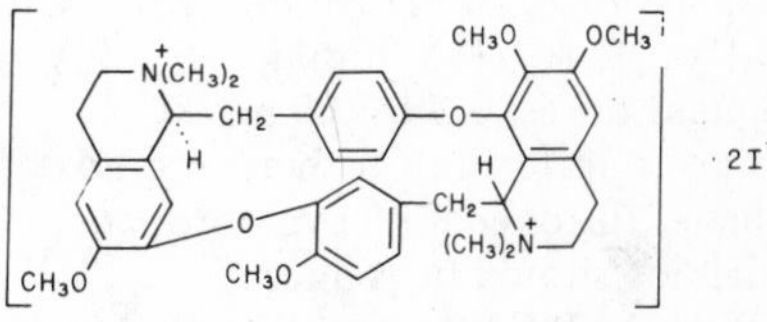

Dimethyl tubocurarine is a semisynthetic derivative of tubocurarine. It is approximately three times as potent as tubocurarine and has a shorter duration of action; in other respects, there is little difference between the two drugs. Dimethyl tubocurarine should not be used in patients sensitive to iodides.

For uses and adverse reactions, see the evaluation on Tubocurarine Chloride.

USUAL DOSAGE.—*Intravenous: Adults,* initially, 0.06 to 0.08 mg/kg of body weight; subsequent doses, 0.02 to 0.03 mg/kg.

When used with ether, methoxyflurane, halothane, fluroxene or cyclopropane, the dose of dimethyl tubocurarine should be reduced.

PREPARATIONS.—Metubine (Lilly). *Injection:* Solution 2 mg/ml in 20 ml containers.

GALLAMINE TRIETHIODIDE [Flaxedil]

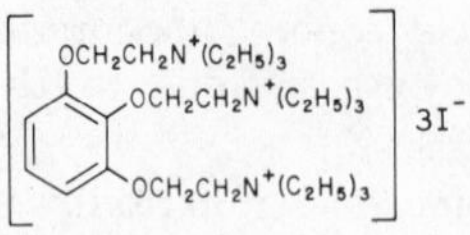

$$\left[C_6H_3(OCH_2CH_2N^+(C_2H_5)_3)_3 \right] 3I^-$$

This synthetic nondepolarizing neuromuscular blocking agent has a shorter duration of action than tubocurarine. Its effects are similar to those of tubocurarine, but gallamine blocks the cardiac vagus and may cause sinus tachycardia and, occasionally, arrhythmias and hypertension. Therefore, it should be used cautiously in patients with pre-existing tachycardia. Gallamine may be the preferred blocking agent for use in patients with bradycardia or various types of heart block. Although studies in experimental animals have shown that gallamine crosses the placental barrier, it has no perceptible effect on newborn infants when used in normal doses for cesarean section. However, tubocurarine or succinylcholine may be preferred for obstetrical use. Since gallamine is excreted unchanged by the kidneys, other blocking agents should be used in patients with renal damage. See also the evaluation on Tubocurarine Chloride.

USUAL DOSAGE.–

Intravenous: Adults, initially, 1 to 2.5 mg/kg of body weight; subsequent doses, 0.3 to 0.4 mg/kg.

Intravenous, Intramuscular: Children, initially, 1 to 1.5 mg/kg of body weight; subsequent doses, 0.3 to 0.5 mg/kg.

When used with ether, methoxyflurane, halothane, fluroxene, or cyclopropane, the dose of gallamine should be reduced.

PREPARATIONS.–Flaxedil (Davis & Geck). *Injection:* Solution 20 mg/ml in 10 ml containers and 100 mg/ml in 1 ml containers.

PANCURONIUM BROMIDE [Pavulon]

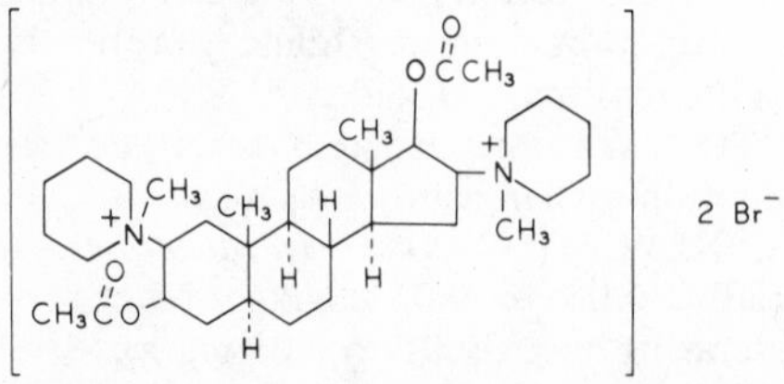

[Structural formula of pancuronium: steroid nucleus with two N-methylpiperidinium groups, two acetoxy ($CH_3\overset{O}{C}O$) groups, CH_3 groups; 2 Br^-]

The following is a preliminary evaluation of pancuronium, a synthetic bisquaternary ammonium steroid that produces a nondepolarizing neuromuscular block but appears to be devoid of endocrine activity. The neuromuscular block is similar to that produced by tubocurarine, and the general spectrum of usefulness of the two drugs appears to be similar (see the Introductory Statement and the evaluation on Tubocurarine Chloride); however, some important differences between the actions of the two drugs exist.

Pancuronium is approximately five times more potent than tubocurarine and has a slightly more rapid onset of action; the duration of action of the two drugs is comparable. Endotracheal intubation can usually be accomplished with ease approximately three minutes after the intravenous injection of 0.1 mg/kg of body weight of pancuronium along with the prior administration of a hypnotic dose of thiopental. Pancuronium has several other apparent advantages over tubocurarine: It does not cause adverse cardiovascular effects (most notably hypotension), presumably because it does not have a ganglionic blocking action, and does not produce bronchospasm, presumably because it does not cause the release of histamine. In addition, there is some evidence that pancuronium may increase the heart rate, cardiac output, and arterial pressure. Like tubocurarine, pancuronium is compatible with all currently used anesthetic agents and techniques and its neuromuscular blocking action can be reversed by neostigmine methylsulfate, given with or after atropine, if more than 30 to 40 minutes have elapsed after the last dose of pancuronium. Limited evidence on the use of pancuronium in children indicates that endotracheal intubation can usually be accomplished with ease in these patients approximately two minutes after the intravenous injection of 0.1 or 0.15 mg/kg of the drug. A rise in pulse rate and arterial pressure normally follows within one minute after administration of the drug and muscular activity reappears suddenly as the effect of the drug wanes. Abundant secretions may tend to develop in children when the drug is used with light planes of anesthesia. There are insufficient data to evaluate the use of pancuronium in pregnant patients, including its use during labor and delivery.

Injection of pancuronium in the alert patient sometimes produces a "burning" sensation that may be due to the added buffer. No toxic effects have been noted in animals when adequate ventilation was maintained. Studies in animals also indicate that 25% to 35% of the drug is excreted in the urine unchanged. There is no evidence that "recurarization" occurs in man following reversal of the neuromuscular blocking action of pancuronium by neostigmine; the effects of this drug in patients with severe electrolyte disturbances or renal or hepatic disease have not been adequately studied.

USUAL DOSAGE.—*Intravenous: Adults*, initially, 0.02 to 0.1 mg/kg of body weight; subsequently, a dose of 0.01 mg/kg, repeated as required, appears to maintain satisfactory muscle relaxation. *Children*, initially, 0.02 to 0.1 mg/kg; one-fifth of the initial dose, repeated as required, appears to maintain satisfactory muscle relaxation.

It must be stressed that these dosages should serve only as guides, that they must be varied according to the basic principles that apply to the use of all nondepolarizing muscle relaxants, and that pancuronium should be used cautiously in children, since only limited data are available on patients in this age group.

PREPARATIONS.—Pavulon (Organon). *Injection:* Solution 2 mg/ml in 2 and 5 ml containers.

Depolarizing Agents

SUCCINYLCHOLINE CHLORIDE [Anectine, Quelicin Chloride, Sucostrin, Sux-Cert]

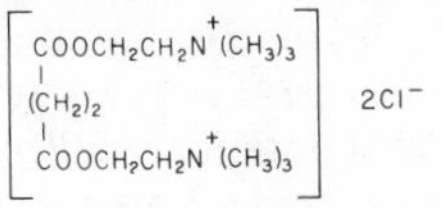

$$\left[\begin{array}{l} COOCH_2CH_2\overset{+}{N}(CH_3)_3 \\ | \\ (CH_2)_2 \\ | \\ COOCH_2CH_2\overset{+}{N}(CH_3)_3 \end{array}\right] 2Cl^-$$

Succinylcholine is a neuromuscular blocking agent which is believed to act by producing a sustained depolarization at the motor endplate. It has a rapid onset (one minute) and a very short duration of action (five minutes); its brief relaxant effect is caused by its rapid hydrolysis by plasma pseudocholinesterase. The drug is used to produce brief relaxation for procedures such as endotracheal intubation, endoscopy, orthopedic manipulation, and electroconvulsive therapy. Prolonged relaxation for major surgery can be produced by infusing it slowly or giving it in fractional doses. It is occasionally used with hexafluorenium bromide. A single dose of succinylcholine causes transient muscle twitching and fasciculations. This brief stimulation is followed by a profound flaccid paralysis of all skeletal muscles, including the intercostals and diaphragm. Tachyphylaxis may occur after repeated administration.

Adverse Reactions and Precautions.—Since succinylcholine is almost completely hydrolyzed by plasma pseudocholinesterase, prolonged postoperative apnea may occur in conditions in which there is low pseudocholinesterase activity, eg, severe parenchymatous liver disease, protein depletion, late pregnancy, the presence of a genetically determined variant of pseudocholinesterase, and administration of anticholinesterase agents. If cholinesterase inhibitors are used in an attempt to antagonize the effect of succinylcholine, they may intensify and prolong the neuromuscular blockade. The serum cholinesterase level can be significantly depressed even by the topical use of long-acting anticholinesterase agents (eg, echothiophate) in open-angle glaucoma or accommodative esotropia. These drugs should be discontinued two to four weeks prior to surgery if succinylcholine is to be given. If this is not possible, the anesthesiologist should be informed that the patient has been receiving anticholinesterase medication and succinylcholine should be given very cautiously.

The response to succinylcholine also may be prolonged in the presence of fluid and electrolyte disturbances. Patients with neuromuscular disorders also may show an abnormal response to the blocking effects of the depolarizing agents. These drugs may produce generalized myotonia in patients with myotonia dystrophica and myotonia congenita. In patients with myasthenia gravis, the uninvolved muscle may be resistant to the depolarizing agents and overdosage may inadvertently occur.

Succinylcholine has been reported to cause both decreases and increases in heart rate and blood pressure. Severe arrhythmias and cardiac arrest have occurred occasionally, particularly in children, when fractional doses have been administered intravenously at short intervals. The complex cardiovascular effects of this blocking agent have been attributed to ganglionic stimulation and blockade, to a direct action on the heart and blood vessels, as well as to other factors. Bradycardia, hypotension, arrhythmias, and cardiac arrest can usually be avoided by the prior administration of atropine.

Succinylcholine can potentiate the effects of digitalis. When given to digitalized patients, it may cause partial or complete atrioventricular block or, rarely, ventricular fibrillation. Severe ventricular arrhythmias and cardiac arrest have followed administration of succinylcholine to patients with severe burns, massive trauma, brain or spinal cord injuries, muscular dystrophy, or multiple sclerosis. These adverse effects on the myocardium have been attributed to a pronounced increase in the plasma potassium level. Although normal individuals show a slight, transient elevation in serum potassium after administration of succinylcholine, patients with severe injuries or neuromuscular disorders (eg, paraplegia, muscular dystrophy) may respond with massive hyperkalemia. Therefore, succinylcholine should be used with extreme caution in these patients. Magnesium sulfate has been reported to potentiate the neuromuscular blockade produced by succinylcholine. Duration of paralysis induced by this blocking agent may be reduced following administration of diazepam.

Succinylcholine causes an initial pronounced increase in the intraocular pressure of unanesthetized or lightly anesthetized patients but does not elevate the intraocular pressure in patients under deep general anesthesia. This ocular hypertensive effect is transient and, because it occurs during the stage of generalized muscle fasciculations and subsides when the extraocular muscles become paralyzed, it may, in part, be due to contraction of the extraocular muscles. Succinylcholine can, therefore, be used safely during intraocular surgery if it is administered at least five minutes before the eye is opened and if adequate levels of the drug are maintained during surgery; it should not be used after the eye has been opened by the surgeon or if the eye is already open at the beginning of surgery (eg, penetrating wounds, iris prolapse). Since succinylcholine has only a brief effect on intraocular pressure, it is not contraindicated in patients with open-angle glaucoma or in patients predisposed to angle-closure. In such patients, one or two drops of pilocarpine may be instilled prior to surgery.

Succinylcholine has no effect on the central nervous system when administered in therapeutic doses. It does not cross the placental barrier in appreciable quantities and may be used safely in obstetrical anesthesia.

A few cases of severe bronchospasm have been reported when succinylcholine was administered with hexafluorenium; therefore, these agents should not be used concomitantly in patients with bronchial asthma.

Administration of succinylcholine has been associated with myoglobinemia and myoglobinuria. The appearance of myoglobin in the serum and urine has been noted most commonly when this blocking agent was given to children by the intravenous route.

Malignant hyperpyrexia is a rare complication of general anesthesia and may have a genetic basis. It is characterized by a rapid rise in body temperature, severe acidosis, hypovolemia, and hypertonicity of the skeletal muscles. In most reported cases, succinylcholine was used to provide muscle relaxation during anesthesia with halothane or other halogenated compounds.

Postoperative pain and stiffness are common after use of succinylcholine. These symptoms generally appear 12 to 24 hours after administration and are believed to be caused by the muscle fasciculations that occur immediately after injection.

USUAL DOSAGE.—

Intravenous: Adults, initially, 0.4 to 0.8 mg/kg of body weight. For continuous or intermittent infusion, a 0.2% solution is administered initially at a rate of 80 to 200 drops per minute; when adequate relaxation is attained, the rate is reduced to 40 to 100 drops per minute. *Children,* initially, 0.4 to 0.8 mg/kg. Continuous infusion of a muscle relaxant in children is considered unsafe.

Intramuscular: Children, 2 mg/kg of body weight.

For use with hexafluorenium, see the evaluation on Hexafluorenium Bromide.

PREPARATIONS.—

Anectine (Burroughs Wellcome). *Injection:* Powder 500 mg and 1 g; solution 20, 50, and 100 mg/ml in 10 ml containers.

Quelicin Chloride (Abbott). *Injection:* Powder 500 mg and 1 g; solution 20 and 50 mg/ml in 10 ml containers, 100 mg/ml in 5 and 10 ml containers, and 25 mg/ml in 20 and 40 ml containers.

Sucostrin (Squibb). *Injection:* Solution 20, 50, and 100 mg/ml in 10 ml containers.

Sux-Cert (Travenol). *Injection:* Powder 500 mg and l g.

Drug also marketed under generic name.

DECAMETHONIUM BROMIDE [Syncurine]

$$(CH_3)_3\overset{+}{N}\text{-}(CH_2)_{10}\text{-}\overset{+}{N}(CH_3)_3 \quad 2\ Br^-$$

This depolarizing neuromuscular blocking agent is not used extensively at the present time. Decamethonium has the same mode of action, indications, and contraindications as succinylcholine; however, it is not hydrolyzed by pseudocholinesterase but is excreted unchanged by the kidneys. It has a longer duration of action than succinylcholine: complete recovery requires about 20 minutes. Succinylcholine, therefore, is preferred for very brief procedures and for patients with renal damage.

For indications and adverse reactions of the depolarizing agents, see the Introductory Statement and the evaluation on Succinylcholine Chloride.

USUAL DOSAGE.—

Intravenous: Adults, 0.04 to 0.06 mg/kg of body weight.

Intravenous, Intramuscular: Children, 0.05 to 0.08 mg/kg of body weight.

PREPARATIONS.—Syncurine (Burroughs Wellcome). *Injection:* Solution 1 mg/ml in 10 ml containers.

MISCELLANEOUS DRUGS

HEXAFLUORENIUM BROMIDE [Mylaxen]

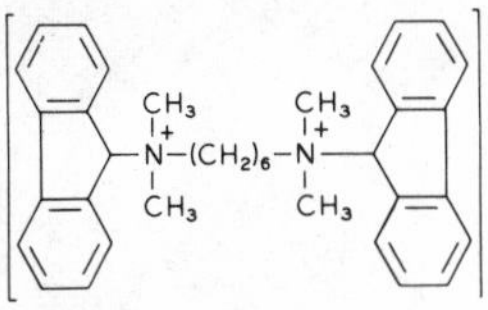

Hexafluorenium is used only to prolong the action of succinylcholine. It is a cholinesterase inhibitor that delays the enzymatic hydrolysis of succinylcholine and thus increases the intensity and duration of its action. The advantages of the combined use of these two agents over the use of fractional doses of succinylcholine alone have not been clearly demonstrated, although hexafluorenium may prevent the muscle fasciculations which are often associated with use of succinylcholine alone.

Since the combined use of succinylcholine and hexafluorenium has occasionally caused bronchospasm, these agents should not be given concomitantly in patients with a history of bronchial asthma.

USUAL DOSAGE.—*Intravenous: Adults,* 0.3 to 0.4 mg/kg of body weight of hexafluorenium, followed in two or three minutes by 0.25 mg/kg of succinylcholine, provides relaxation for 15 to 30 minutes. This relaxation may be sustained with doses of 0.15 mg/kg of succinylcholine repeated every 15 to 30 minutes. When the duration of action of succinylcholine becomes less than 12 to 15 minutes, an additional 0.1 to 0.15 mg/kg of hexafluorenium may be given if the need for relaxation is expected to be more than 30 minutes; if relaxation is required for less than 30 minutes, a larger dose (0.2 to 0.3 mg/kg) of succinylcholine may be given.

PREPARATIONS.—Mylaxen (Mallinckrodt). *Injection:* Solution 20 mg/ml in 10 ml containers.

Chapter 21

STRONG ANALGESICS

Pain is a subjective symptom that varies from patient to patient and in the same patient from time to time, depending upon his emotional and psychological attitude toward the pain, as well as his previous conditioning and mood at the moment. Therapy should attempt to eliminate the cause; when this is not possible, use of an analgesic is indicated. The choice of analgesic will depend largely upon the cause of the pain and its type, location, and severity.

The classification of analgesics is based upon the severity of pain that the drugs are capable of relieving. Those given primarily to relieve moderate to severe pain are designated strong analgesics, while those given to relieve mild to moderate pain are designated mild analgesics (see Chapter 22, Mild Analgesics). The strong analgesics are also classified as potent analgesics by some authors; however, this term may be misleading because the analgesic effectiveness of a drug is not necessarily related to its potency on a miligram basis.

Strong analgesics not only raise the threshold of pain perception, but also alter the psychological response to pain and suppress the patient's anxiety and apprehension. These drugs act on higher nerve centers to relieve pain without causing loss of consciousness, although fully effective doses seldom relieve moderate to severe pain without causing some alteration in consciousness or behavior.

Although most strong analgesics are qualitatively similar in their actions on the central nervous system, their relative usefulness in particular clinical situations is determined by differences in the degree to which some actions and side effects predominate over others at various dose levels, the rapidity of onset of action, and the duration of effectiveness. However, the differences among them are not great and the physician may meet the needs of most patients by becoming familiar with the properties of representative drugs. The availability of several strong analgesics, including the newer agents not subject to narcotic control, permits the physician to exercise greater latitude in selecting those to be used in specific situations.

The strong analgesics are commonly divided into two subgroups: narcotic and non-narcotic. The narcotic analgesics produce morphine-type drug dependence and are included in Schedule II of the Comprehensive Drug Abuse Prevention and Control Act of 1970.

The narcotic analgesics include: (1) opium preparations; (2) purified alkaloids of opium such as morphine; (3) semisynthetic modifications of morphine (hydromorphone [Dilaudid], oxymorphone [Numorphan]); and (4) various synthetic compounds that resemble morphine in many of their actions. The synthetic morphine-like compounds can be classified by chemical structure: (1) phenylpiperidine derivatives (meperidine [Demerol], alphaprodine [Nisentil], anileridine [Leritine], piminodine [Alvodine]); (2) a morphinan (or phenanthrene) derivative (levorphanol [Levo-Dromoran]); (3) a diphenylheptane derivative (methadone); and (4) a propionanilide derivative (fentanyl [Sublimaze]).

Two strong analgesics are classed as non-narcotics because they are not subject to narcotic controls of the Controlled Substances Act: a benzomorphan derivative that is also a weak narcotic antagonist, pentazocine [Talwin], and a phenothiazine derivative, methotrimeprazine [Levoprome].

The narcotic analgesics generally should not be used to treat mild or moderate pain, particularly that caused by benign conditions, or to treat pain that can be relieved satisfactorily by non-narcotic analgesics. On the other hand, narcotics should not be withheld for short-term therapy if their use for relief of moderate to severe pain seems warranted. Moderately severe pain often can be alleviated by an intermediately active agent, but severe pain (eg, that associated with biliary, renal, or ureteral colic or with acute myocardial infarction) can be relieved best by morphine or its potent congeners. The amount required will depend on the intensity of the pain: two to four times the usual dose of morphine may be tolerated for relief of excruciating pain. However, if the pain suddenly subsides or disappears entirely, respiratory depression frequently ensues. An antagonist should be available for use when indicated.

Morphine is the prototype to which other strong analgesics are compared. Small to moderate doses will relieve constant dull pain (eg, of visceral origin) and moderate to large doses will alleviate intermittent, sharp, lancinating pain caused by trauma or of visceral origin. Morphine effectively relieves postoperative pain, as well as that caused by vascular thrombosis (coronary, pulmonary, or peripheral), neoplastic disease, biliary and renal colic, and injuries such as fractures and burns. Special uses of morphine and the other strong analgesics are considered below.

Obstetric Analgesia: Use of a strong analgesic in the obstetric patient requires considerable experience and judgment in order to avoid respiratory depression in the newborn infant and interference with the progress of labor. Meperidine is given most commonly for this purpose because it is less likely to produce these complications than morphine, but depression of fetal respiration is more likely to occur if the time between drug administration and birth is less than 90 minutes. This time interval is even shorter when alphaprodine is used.

Preanesthetic Medication: Strong analgesics are useful for preanesthetic medication because of their sedative, antianxiety, and analgesic effects. These properties afford smoother induction and maintenance of anesthesia and reduce excitement during emergence from anesthesia. However, since a strong analgesic generally should not be used in the absence of pain, a sedative-hypnotic is usually preferred as preanesthetic medication unless pain is present. (See Chapter 20, Adjuncts to Anesthesia.)

Sedation and Hypnosis: There are few exceptions to the statement that a strong analgesic should not be used in the absence of pain. One exception is the patient with dyspnea of "cardiac asthma" (acute left side heart failure with pulmonary edema). The sedative effect of the analgesic relieves anxiety and reduces stimuli from the wet lung. However, these agents generally should not be given to patients with bronchial asthma or with pulmonary edema caused by a chemical respiratory irritant.

Cough: The cough reflex is depressed or abolished by morphine and its congeners, but use of strong analgesics should be restricted to patients with painful cough that cannot be controlled with codeine or non-narcotic agents. (See Chapter 44, Antitussive Agents.) When an active cough reflex is desired along with analgesia, meperidine or oxymorphone may be preferred because of their relative lack of antitussive effect.

Gastrointestinal Tract Disorders: Although morphine and related strong analgesics produce undesirable effects on the gastrointestinal tract (eg, nausea, vomiting, constipation), the spasmogenic effect of the opiates is useful in the symptomatic treatment of diarrhea, and these drugs are used postoperatively in certain patients to "splint the bowel." (See Chapter 80, Antidiarrheals.) However, their prolonged use may lead to severe constipation even after the drug is discontinued. Of the narcotic agents, meperidine is least constipating, although it does have a stimulatory effect on some sphincters of the gastrointestinal tract (eg, sphincter of Oddi).

Adverse Reactions and Precautions

Despite their potent analgesic action, the morphine-like analgesics have disadvantages that limit their usefulness: psychic and physical dependence, respiratory depression, nausea, vomiting, constipation, cardiovascular effects (hypotension, bradycardia), and, in some patients, an increase in intracranial (spinal fluid) pressure. Other adverse reactions include miosis, spasm of the biliary and urinary tracts, and, rarely, hypersensitivity phenomena (urticaria, rash, and anaphylactic reactions).

Although the dependence that occurs with use of narcotic analgesics may be qualitatively and quantitatively different for each member of the group, it is referred to generally as morphine-type dependence to distinguish it from that produced by alcohol, barbiturates, and other types of drugs. The dependence liability is low for pentazocine [Talwin] and appears to be absent for methotrimeprazine [Levoprome].

Respiratory depression is the most potentially dangerous acute action produced by the strong analgesics. It develops most readily in elderly, debilitated patients and in those with disorders characterized by hypoxia (eg, severe pulmonary diseases). Even therapeutic doses may dangerously decrease ventilation in these patients. If severe respiratory depression occurs or appears to be imminent after use of a morphine-like analgesic, the repeated intravenous administration of a narcotic antagonist will counteract this effect. (See Chapter 23, Narcotic Antagonists.) Equipment for administration of oxygen should always be available. Respiratory depression is not as severe with pentazocine as with morphine and its congeners; if severe respiratory depression does occur with pentazocine, it can be counteracted by naloxone [Narcan], but not by other narcotic antagonists.

A strong analgesic should be given in reduced doses or not used at all in patients in shock, since respiratory depression may indirectly further reduce the patient's circulating blood volume, cardiac output, and blood pressure.

Drowsiness and clouding of the sensorium and mental processes are the most prominent central effects of the strong analgesics. Although these effects are desirable in some clinical situations, impaired ability to concentrate and to think clearly limits the usefulness of these agents in ambulatory patients. The strong analgesics should not be administered if pain is necessary for diagnosis.

Depression of ciliary activity also occurs with the narcotic analgesics; thus, these drugs should be used with caution in patients who have excessive respiratory secretions (eg, in chronic obstructive lung disease, chronic bronchitis).

Patients receiving these drugs parenterally should be confined to bed for a period of time to minimize the incidence of hypotension, dizziness, nausea, and vomiting. This is especially important with methotrimeprazine, which causes pronounced orthostatic hypotension and drowsiness.

The narcotic analgesics should be used with caution in patients with inadequately treated hypothyroidism, chronic adrenocortical insufficiency, and hepatic insufficiency, since even small doses may cause stupor or precipitate coma and apnea.

Because morphine and other strong analgesics cause hypoventilation and hypercapnia resulting in cerebrovascular dilatation and increased intracranial pressure, they are contraindicated in patients with head injuries, delirium tremens, and conditions in which intracranial pressure is increased.

The strong analgesics are not necessarily contraindicated in patients with impaired renal function, but these drugs do decrease urinary production by direct action on the kidney and indirectly by stimulating the release of the antidiuretic hormone. Their spasmogenic effect on the sphincter of the urinary bladder results in dysuria and may cause acute urinary retention in patients with prostatic hypertrophy or urethral stricture.

Doses of strong analgesics should be reduced in patients receiving antipsychotic agents, barbiturates, or other drugs that depress respiration. Severe adverse reactions have occurred following the concomitant administration of monoamine oxidase inhibitors and meperidine; these have not been observed with morphine, but can be expected with analgesics related to meperidine.

Dosage should be individualized and based on the severity of the pain. Expert judgment is required by the physician to decide whether to administer repeated doses of a milder analgesic or fewer, fully effective doses of a more potent agent to adequately relieve the patient's pain and anxiety. Ordinarily, morphine or its potent congeners should be given in the smallest effective doses and as infrequently as possible to minimize the development of tolerance and physical dependence. This statement is particularly true when treating chronic diseases or situations that might lead to drug abuse.

The development of tolerance with prolonged use of morphine-like drugs varies from patient to patient; some appear to develop little tolerance to the effects of these drugs, whereas others seem to require an increasing dose. Therefore, an increased need should be evaluated in relation to the individual's problems in order to determine if it is caused by an increase in severity of the pain due to a progression of the pathologic process or increased tolerance to the effects of the drug. The fact that these drugs have actions other than analgesia (eg, relief of anxiety or depression) may lead to abuse by some patients. However, such responses should be recognized and use of the drug controlled to prevent chronic abuse and dependence. The physician should not assume that patients with pathological pain will experience the same effects from morphine-like drugs as the "street addict," or that iatrogenic dependence will consistently develop. Most patients given a morphine-like drug for relief of pain are able to discontinue its use without difficulty even though they have developed mild degrees of dependence; only a small percentage become compulsive abusers.

Strong analgesics must be given parenterally for optimal effectiveness; however, some synthetic analgesics (eg, levorphanol, methadone, anileridine) have a more favorable oral:parenteral ratio than morphine. In some situations, intravenous administration is preferred because onset of action is more rapid and a greater degree of dosage control is possible. Since rapid intravenous injection produces sudden, profound respiratory depression and hypotension, a dilute solution of the drug should be injected slowly over a period of several minutes and an antagonist should be available.

OPIUM ALKALOIDS AND SEMI-SYNTHETIC DERIVATIVES

MORPHINE SULFATE

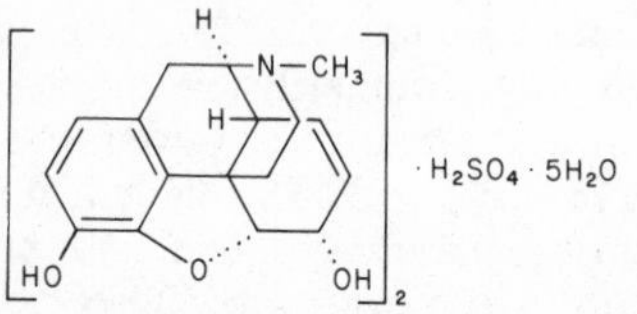

Morphine is the prototype of the narcotic analgesics (see the Introductory Statement for uses, adverse reactions, and contraindications). It must be given parenterally to assure reliable action, for it is considerably less effective after oral administration. Although effects may begin earlier, the maximal analgesic effect occurs about 20 minutes after intravenous injection, 50 to 90 minutes after subcutaneous administration, and 30 to 60 minutes after intramuscular injection. Analgesia persists for approximately four hours, but in some patients it may last up to seven hours.

Some anesthesiologists use morphine to produce anesthesia for open-heart surgery, especially in high-risk patients with cardiac disease. In this technique, large doses (0.5 to 3 mg/kg) of morphine are administered intravenously as the sole anesthetic or with a suitable anesthetic agent (eg, nitrous oxide, halothane). The patients are given oxygen and as long as adequate ventilation is maintained, cardiovascular function is not depressed by morphine. Hypotension may occur, but it can be counteracted with a vasopressor agent and/or a plasma volume expander.

USUAL DOSAGE.—

Intravenous: Adults, 2.5 to 15 mg in 4 to 5 ml of water for injection is injected slowly over a period of four to five minutes. This route of administration is used only rarely.

Subcutaneous, Intramuscular: Adults, the optimal dose is 10 mg/70 kg of body weight (range, 5 to 20 mg), depending upon the use and the individual patient; *children*, 0.1 to 0.2 mg/kg (maximal dose, 15 mg).

Oral: This route should not be used because of reduced effectiveness.

PREPARATIONS.—Morphine Sulfate, U.S.P. *Injection:* Solution 8, 10, 15, and 30 mg/ml in 1 ml containers; 10 and 15 mg/ml in half-filled 2 ml containers; tablets (hypodermic) 8, 10, 15, and 30 mg. Drug marketed under generic name.

OPIUM

Opium and opium preparations, with the exception of Pantopon (see following evaluation), are used infrequently for relief of pain. They have no advantage over pure morphine salts or other strong analgesics. The use of complex mixtures containing opium (eg, Dover's powder, Brown Mixture) has no rational basis and is discouraged.

PANTOPON

This preparation is a mixture of purified opium alkaloids in solution as the hydrochloride salts. It has the same indications as morphine, and is used most commonly in postoperative pain (see the Introductory Statement). Claims that the analgesic and sedative effects of morphine are enhanced, while adverse effects are minimized by other constituents in the mixture, have not been substantiated. The analgesic effect of Pantopon is the same as would be expected from its morphine content; the amount of papaverine present is insufficient to contribute any significant spasmolytic effect. Since Pantopon has no advantage over an equivalent amount of morphine, there is no reason to use it in preference to the latter.

USUAL DOSAGE.—*Intramuscular, Subcutaneous:* The manufacturer's suggested dosage is: *Adults*, 5 to 20 mg.

PREPARATIONS.—Pantopon (Roche). *Injection:* Solution 20 mg/ml in 1 ml containers.

HYDROMORPHONE HYDROCHLORIDE [Dilaudid Hydrochloride]
HYDROMORPHONE SULFATE [Dilaudid Sulfate]

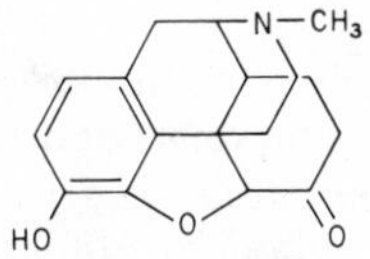

Hydromorphone, a semisynthetic derivative of morphine, has the same actions and uses as morphine (see the Introductory Statement). Results of recent controlled studies have demonstrated that it is approximately eight times more potent on a milligram basis than morphine, which is greater than previous estimates. In addition, hydromorphone is better absorbed orally than is morphine: the former is approximately one-fourth to one-fifth as active orally as intramuscularly.

Adverse reactions are the same as those produced by morphine in equianalgesic doses (see the Introductory Statement).

For other uses, see Chapter 44, Antitussive Agents.

USUAL DOSAGE.—

Hydromorphone Hydrochloride:

Intramuscular, Intravenous (slow), Subcutaneous: Adults, 2 mg as required; dose may be increased to 4 mg for severe pain.

Oral: Adults, 2 mg initially; dose may be increased if necessary.

Rectal: Adults, 3 mg.

Hydromorphone Sulfate:

Intramuscular, Intravenous (slow), Subcutaneous: Adults, same parenteral dosage as for the hydrochloride salt.

PREPARATIONS.—

Dilaudid Hydrochloride (Knoll).

Injection: Solution 1, 2, 3, and 4 mg/ml in 1 ml containers; tablets (soluble) 1, 2, 3, and 4 mg.

Oral: Tablets (soluble) 1, 2, 3, and 4 mg.

Rectal: Suppositories 3 mg.

Drug also marketed by other manufacturers under generic name.

Dilaudid Sulfate (Knoll). *Injection:* Solution 2 mg/ml in 10 and 20 ml containers.

OXYMORPHONE HYDROCHLORIDE [Numorphan Hydrochloride]

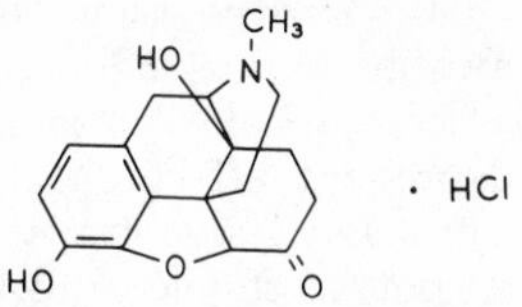

Oxymorphone is a semisynthetic derivative of morphine and is closely related chemically to hydromorphone. Its actions and uses are similar to those of hydromorphone and morphine, except that it possesses no significant antitussive activity (see the Introductory Statement). Although relief of severe pain is achieved with smaller doses than with morphine, the margin of safety and total duration of analgesic action are not greater.

Adverse reactions are similar to those produced by morphine and other narcotic analgesics, but the incidence of nausea and vomiting may be greater with oxymorphone. (See the Introductory Statement.)

USUAL DOSAGE.—

Intramuscular, Subcutaneous: Adults, 1 to 1.5 mg every four to six hours. For obstetric analgesia, 0.5 to 1 mg intramuscularly.

Intravenous: Adults, 0.5 mg initially.

Rectal: Adults, 2 or 5 mg every four to six hours.

PREPARATIONS.—Numorphan Hydrochloride (Endo).

Injection: Solution 1 mg/ml in 1, 1.5, and 15 ml containers, 1.5 mg/ml in 1, 2, and 10 ml containers.

Rectal: Suppositories 2 and 5 mg.

SYNTHETIC COMPOUNDS

Phenylpiperidine Derivatives

MEPERIDINE HYDROCHLORIDE [Demerol Hydrochloride]

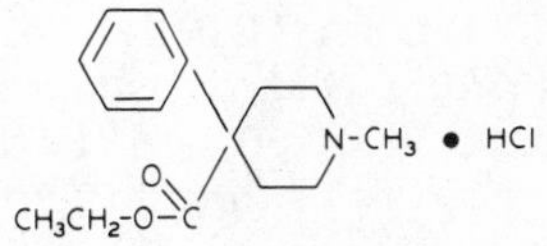

Meperidine is the prototype of the phenylpiperidine derivatives. Although it differs chemically from morphine, it has many similar pharmacologic properties and is used for the same indications. However, it is less effective than morphine in relieving severe pain regardless of dosage. Meperidine is widely used for obstetric analgesia. Although it produces satisfactory pain relief, it has a significant respiratory depressant effect on the newborn. This effect is probably less than with usual doses of morphine, but it should not be regarded lightly. Meperidine may have a spasmogenic or spasmolytic effect on intestinal smooth muscle and, like morphine, it stimulates the biliary tract. It produces little or no depression of the cough reflex. The maximal analgesic effect occurs within 40 to 60 minutes after subcutaneous administration and 30 to 50 minutes after intramuscular injection. The duration of analgesia is two to four hours. Meperidine is considerably less effective orally than parenterally.

Adverse reactions most commonly observed include dizziness, nausea, and vomiting (especially in ambulatory patients), but their incidence with usual doses may be lower than with morphine; meperidine is less constipating. Its sedative effect is comparable to that of morphine. Extreme asthenia, hyperhidrosis, syncope, dysphoria, and unpleasant dreams also have been observed. Convulsions have occurred following very large doses. Equivalent analgesic doses of meperidine and morphine produce a similar degree of respiratory depression; this effect may be reversed by a narcotic antagonist.

Contraindications to the use of meperidine are similar to those for morphine and other narcotic analgesics. They include elevated cerebrospinal pressure and hypersensitivity. Since the drug is inactivated in the liver, the dose should be reduced in patients with severe hepatic insufficiency. (See also the Introductory Statement.) The dose of meperidine also should be reduced in patients receiving antipsychotic agents, sedative-hypnotics, or other drugs that depress the central nervous system. Severe toxic reactions (eg, restlessness, excitement, fever) have occurred following use of meperidine in patients receiving monoamine oxidase inhibitors.

USUAL DOSAGE.—*Intramuscular, Intravenous (slow), Oral, Subcutaneous: Adults,* 100 mg (range, 50 to 150 mg). The dose may be repeated at intervals of three to four hours. For obstetric analgesia, 50 to 100 mg intramuscularly or subcutaneously. The dose may be repeated three or four times at one- to three-hour intervals if necessary; however, the respiration of the newborn may be depressed if the last dose is given less than 90 minutes before birth. *Children,* 1 to 1.5 mg/kg of body weight (maximal dose, 100 mg) administered intramuscularly, orally, or subcutaneously. The dose may be repeated at intervals of three to four hours if necessary.

PREPARATIONS.—Demerol Hydrochloride (Winthrop).

Injection: Solution 50 mg/ml in 0.5, 1, 1.5, 2, 10, and 30 ml containers and half-filled 2 ml containers, 75 mg/ml in 1 ml containers and half-filled 2 ml containers, 100 mg/ml in 1 and 20 ml containers and half-filled 2 ml containers.

Oral: Elixir 50 mg/5 ml; powder 15 g; tablets 50 and 100 mg.

Drug also marketed by other manufacturers under generic name.

ALPHAPRODINE HYDROCHLORIDE
[Nisentil]

CH_3 N-CH_3 · HCl CH_3CH_2C—O

This drug is related chemically and pharmacologically to meperidine. Its uses are the same as those described for meperidine, but it has a more rapid onset and shorter duration of action. Alphaprodine appears to have no significant advantages over meperidine except that its shorter duration of action may make it primarily useful in certain clinical situations (eg, in obstetrics; in urologic examinations and procedures; preoperatively in major surgery; in minor surgical procedures, especially in orthopedics, ophthalmology, rhinology, and laryngology).

Adverse reactions and precautions are similar to those described for meperidine. (See this evaluation and the Introductory Statement.)

USUAL DOSAGE.—

Intravenous: Adults, 0.4 to 0.6 mg/kg of body weight injected slowly over a three- or four-minute interval; total should not exceed 240 mg in 24 hours.

Subcutaneous: Adults, 20 to 60 mg. For obstetric analgesia, initially, 40 to 60 mg; this dose may be repeated at two-hour intervals. Critical period between last dose and birth is shorter than with meperidine. Total amount given should not exceed 240 mg in 24 hours.

PREPARATIONS.—Nisentil (Roche). *Injection:* Solution 40 mg/ml in 1 ml containers and 60 mg/ml in 1 and 10 ml containers.

ANILERIDINE HYDROCHLORIDE [Leritine Hydrochloride]
ANILERIDINE PHOSPHATE [Leritine Phosphate]

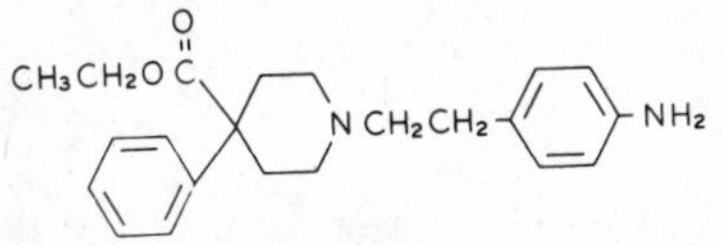

Anileridine is similar chemically and pharmacologically to meperidine and is used for the same indications, but this drug is effective at about one-half the dosage. Its duration of action is slightly shorter and it is relatively more effective when given orally, but otherwise has no advantages over meperidine.

The adverse effects are similar to those produced by meperidine (see this evaluation and the Introductory Statement).

USUAL DOSAGE.–

Anileridine Hydrochloride:

Oral: Adults, 25 to 50 mg; dose may be repeated every four to six hours if necessary.

Anileridine Phosphate:

Intramuscular, Subcutaneous: Adults, for moderate pain, 25 to 50 mg repeated every six hours if necessary; for severe pain, 75 to 100 mg initially. For obstetric analgesia, 50 mg initially; this dose may be repeated in three to four hours if necessary. The total dosage should not exceed 200 mg.

Intravenous (slow): Adults, initially, 5 to 10 mg of well-diluted solution, followed by 0.6 mg/minute until the desired amount is given. For obstetric analgesia, 10 mg of well-diluted solution may be given intravenously at the same time that 40 mg is injected intramuscularly or subcutaneously.

PREPARATIONS.–

Leritine [hydrochloride] (Merck Sharp & Dohme). *Oral:* Tablets 25 mg.

Leritine [phosphate] (Merck Sharp & Dohme). *Injection:* Solution 25 mg/ml in 1, 2, and 30 ml containers.

PIMINODINE ESYLATE [Alvodine Ethanesulfonate]

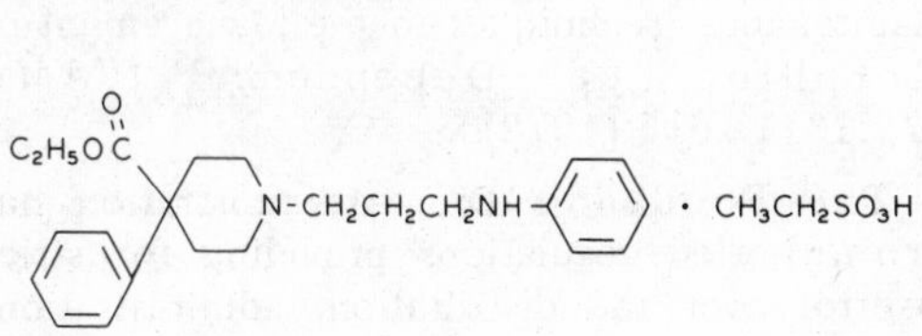

This drug is related chemically and pharmacologically to meperidine. Its analgesic potency on a milligram basis exceeds that of meperidine and is approximately equal to that of morphine. The range of usefulness of piminodine is similar to that of morphine and meperidine. The hypnotic effect of piminodine is less than that of morphine, but the claim that there is almost a complete absence of sedative effect is not supported by available evidence.

Adverse reactions appear to be similar to those produced by meperidine (see this evaluation and the Introductory Statement).

USUAL DOSAGE.–

Intramuscular, Subcutaneous: Adults, 10 to 20 mg every four hours as needed; up to 40 mg has been used for severe pain.

Intravenous (drip): Adults, as adjunct to anesthesia, 2 mg of diluted solution is given slowly and repeated at two-minute intervals; 4 to 6 mg will usually be sufficient.

PREPARATIONS.–Alvodine Ethanesulfonate (Winthrop). *Injection:* Solution 20 mg/ml in 1 ml containers.

Chemically Unrelated Compounds

FENTANYL CITRATE [Sublimaze]

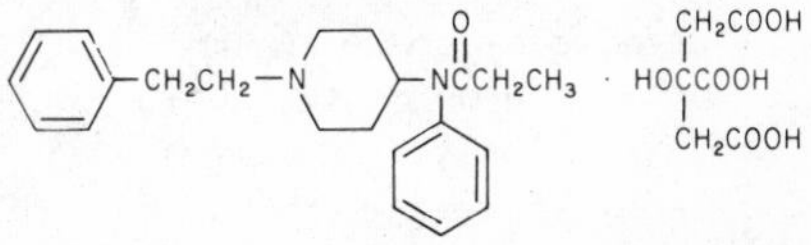

Fentanyl is chemically related to the synthetic phenylpiperidine derivatives. The pharmacologic effects and degree of analgesia produced are similar to those with morphine, but on a weight basis fentanyl is 80 to 100 times more potent. Its duration of action is shorter than that of meperidine or morphine.

The principal use of fentanyl is as an analgesic component in neuroleptanalgesia (see the evaluation on Innovar in Chapter 20, Adjuncts to Anesthesia). Fentanyl has been used as an adjunct for the induction and maintenance of conventional inhalation anesthesia, as a supplement to regional and spinal anesthesia, and for the treatment of postoperative pain; however, it has no significant advantage over morphine or meperidine for these indications.

Adverse reactions are similar to those produced by other morphine-like drugs (see the Introductory Statement). In addition, it can produce muscular rigidity and, hence, respiratory depression after intravenous administration. Doses that produce rigidity often produce apnea as well; this can be controlled promptly by use of small doses of a short-acting muscle relaxant such as succinylcholine chloride. Assisted or controlled respiration is necessary during the period of apnea.

USUAL DOSAGE.—

Intramuscular: Adults, 0.05 to 0.1 mg for preoperative and postoperative pain and pain of short duration.

Intravenous: This route should not be used except in neuroleptanalgesia because it may produce muscular rigidity. The manufacturer's suggested dosage is: *Adults,* 0.05 to 0.1 mg every two to three minutes until the desired effect is achieved. For induction of anesthesia and maintenance, 0.025 to 0.05 mg. *Children,* dosage not established.

PREPARATIONS.—Sublimaze (McNeil). *Injection:* Solution 0.05 mg/ml in 2 and 5 ml containers.

LEVORPHANOL TARTRATE [Levo-Dromoran]

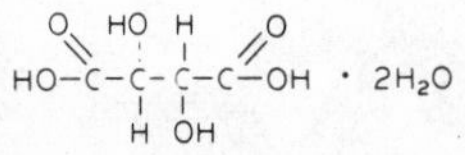

$$HO{-}\overset{O}{\overset{\|}{C}}{-}\overset{HO}{\underset{H}{C}}{-}\overset{H}{\underset{OH}{C}}{-}\overset{O}{\overset{\|}{C}}{-}OH \cdot 2H_2O$$

Levorphanol is a synthetic morphinan-type analgesic related chemically and pharmacologically to morphine, and it is used for the same indications. Levorphanol is four to five times more potent on a milligram basis than morphine and has a somewhat longer duration of action. It is approximately one-half as potent orally as parenterally (intramuscularly), and thus is relatively more effective orally than morphine.

The adverse reactions and precautions of levorphanol are similar to those of morphine. Although some reports suggest that levorphanol is less likely to cause nausea, vomiting, and constipation, any difference in the incidence of adverse reactions is slight. (See the Introductory Statement.)

USUAL DOSAGE.—*Oral, Subcutaneous: Adults,* 2 to 3 mg.

PREPARATIONS.—Levo-Dromoran (Roche). *Injection:* Solution 2 mg/ml in 1 and 10 ml containers.

Oral: Tablets 2 mg.

METHADONE HYDROCHLORIDE

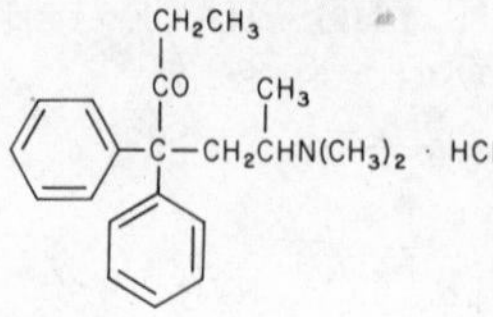

$$(C_6H_5)_2C(COCH_2CH_3){-}CH_2CH(CH_3)N(CH_3)_2 \cdot HCl$$

Methadone is a synthetic analgesic that differs chemically from morphine, but its actions generally are similar. Methadone is slightly more potent than morphine on a milligram basis when administered subcutaneously, and it is relatively more effective orally, a property that makes this drug particularly useful in the treatment of chronic painful conditions (eg, cancer). Although methadone depresses the cough reflex, labeling for use as an antitussive is no longer permitted.

Maximal analgesic doses of methadone depress respiration to a greater extent than do equivalent doses of morphine. They also increase the tone of intestinal smooth muscle, although the latter effect occurs to a lesser degree than with morphine. Nausea, vomiting, constipation, dizziness, dryness of the mouth, and mental depression occur more frequently in ambulatory patients. Contraindications are the same as those for morphine.

Since methadone can prevent or relieve acute withdrawal symptoms of morphine-like drugs, it is useful orally in the detoxification treatment of patients dependent on heroin or other morphine-like agents. The withdrawal of methadone itself produces symptoms that are less intense but more prolonged than those produced by withdrawal of morphine, and the syndrome develops more slowly. Methadone is also useful orally in maintenance treatment programs for individuals dependent on heroin or other morphine-like drugs. A detailed discussion of these uses of methadone is beyond the scope of this book, but may be found in "Narcotics and Medical Practice" *(JAMA 218:*578-583 [1971]), "Treatment of Morphine-Type Dependence by Withdrawal Methods" *(JAMA 219:*1618-1619 [1972]), and "Oral Methadone Maintenance Techniques in the Management of Morphine-Type Dependence" *(JAMA 219:*1611-1615 [1972]).

The Food and Drug Administration has promulgated regulations providing for strict control over the distribution, administration, and dispensing of methadone in order to help reduce the problem of abuse and diversion which resulted from its less restricted availability. Excerpts from these regulations are given below for information; physicians wishing to use methadone should consult the Food and Drug Administration for more complete information.

Under the conditions established by these regulations, methadone may be used for severe pain in hospitalized patients and outpatients, for the detoxification and temporary maintenance treatment of hospitalized narcotic addicts, and for maintenance treatment only under approved methadone programs.

If in a physician's professional judgment methadone would be the drug of choice as an analgesic for treating an outpatient in severe pain, the drug will be available from an approved hospital pharmacy or, in a remote area, from an approved community pharmacy. Prescriptions for analgesia may be filled only if they are written by a physician who has submitted the required statement to the approved hospital or community pharmacy.

USUAL DOSAGE.—

Intramuscular, Subcutaneous: Adults, for relief of pain, 2.5 to 10 mg; dose is repeated only when pain returns. The drug should not be given parenterally in doses larger than 10 mg.

Oral: Adults, for relief of pain, 2.5 to 10 mg every six to eight hours as required.

PREPARATIONS.—Drug available only from approved treatment programs, and hospital and community pharmacies. Information regarding names and locations of programs, hospitals, and selected community pharmacies approved to receive methadone may be obtained from the Food and Drug Administration.

METHOTRIMEPRAZINE [Levoprome]

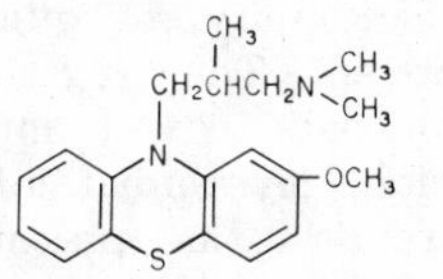

Methotrimeprazine is a strong analgesic related chemically to phenothiazines used as antihistamines and antipsychotics. Its analgesic potency is about one-half that of morphine on a milligram basis; in equianalgesic doses, the onset and duration of action of methotrimeprazine are comparable to morphine. Unlike strong analgesics of the morphine type, methotrimeprazine does not produce psychic or physical dependence and will not suppress the symptoms of morphine withdrawal; thus, it is not subject to narcotic controls.

The most important adverse reactions observed with methotrimeprazine are profound orthostatic hypotension and marked sedation. The prominence of these effects may be disadvantageous or hazardous in surgical and obstetrical patients, and limits use of the drug to nonambulatory patients. Except in terminally ill patients, the degree of sedation produced may be too great to make the drug suitable for use in chronic painful conditions (eg, arthritis). A vasopressor such as methoxamine, phenylephrine, or angiotensin may be indicated to counteract the hypotensive effect.

Many of the other adverse reactions reported (ie, dizziness, disorientation, amnesia, asthenia, slurred speech, blurred vision) can, in part, be attributed to the sedative or hypotensive effect. Nausea and vomiting have occurred in a few patients, and dryness of the mouth, nasal congestion, pain at the site of injection, dysuria, chills, and hypotonic uterine inertia have been reported occasionally.

Like other phenothiazines, methotrimeprazine may produce additive effects when given with some other central nervous system depressants (eg, barbiturates, narcotic analgesics); thus, if these depressants are given concomitantly, the dose must be reduced. Particular attention should be given to the effects on blood pressure when methotrimeprazine is used with atropine or scopolamine.

This drug should be used cautiously in elderly patients or in those with heart disease, and it should not be given with antihypertensive agents or to patients who are in premature labor.

USUAL DOSAGE.—*Intramuscular* (should not be given intravenously or subcutaneously): *Adults,* 10 to 20 mg, repeated every four to six hours if necessary. Smaller doses (5 to 10 mg) should be used initially in elderly patients. On the basis of very limited experience in *children,* a dose of 0.2 to 0.3 mg/kg of body weight is suggested.

PREPARATIONS.—Levoprome (Lederle). *Injection:* Solution 20 mg/ml in 1 and 10 ml containers.

PENTAZOCINE HYDROCHLORIDE [Talwin Hydrochloride]
PENTAZOCINE LACTATE [Talwin Lactate]

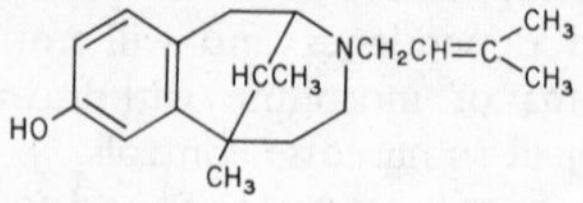

Pentazocine is an analgesic of the benzomorphan series; it also is a weak narcotic antagonist. Thus, it has pharmacologic properties of both agonists of the morphine type and of antagonists of the nalorphine type. Pentazocine is effective in relieving moderate pain; in very severe pain, it may be less effective than morphine. Pentazocine is useful in obstetrics and as a preoperative analgesic and sedative. It may be particularly valuable for relief of chronic pain when used early in the course of disease before the patient has developed appreciable physical dependence on narcotics. The efficacy of pentazocine for relief of the pain of myocardial infarction is controversial. Although it does not cause hypotension as does morphine, pentazocine produces an increase in pulmonary arterial pressure and a rise in central venous pressure, with a tendency to increase cardiac work. Additional studies of the hemodynamic effects of pentazocine are needed before a definitive statement can be made.

The analgesic potency of pentazocine on a milligram basis is approximately one-third that of morphine when administered parenterally and is approximately equal to that of codeine when administered orally. Following intramuscular injection, maximal analgesia usually occurs within 30 to 60 minutes and lasts two to three hours; after oral ingestion, the peak effect occurs in one to three hours and lasts somewhat longer than after intramuscular injection.

Adverse Reactions.—When given in equianalgesic parenteral doses, pentazocine causes drowsiness, hyperhidrosis, and vertigo more frequently than morphine. Pentazocine may produce respiratory depression, but it is less marked than with morphine. The incidence of nausea and vomiting is similar to morphine. Cardiovascular effects seen occasionally include tachycardia, palpitations, and hypertension.

Psychotomimetic effects are relatively rare with usual doses, but occur more frequently following larger doses. These have been described as dysphoria, nightmares, feelings of depersonalization, and, most commonly, visual hallucinations. In addition, epileptiform abnormalities in the electroencephalogram and grand mal convulsions have been observed rarely after large intravenous doses.

Psychic and physical dependence on pentazocine have been reported; most individuals have previously been dependent on other drugs or had abused them. Although proved dependence after the oral use of pentazocine has not occurred, such a possibility should be kept in mind. Following prolonged parenteral use, abrupt withdrawal has caused abdominal cramps, fever, lacrimation, rhinorrhea, anxiety, and restlessness in some patients, but no withdrawal symptoms have been observed in others. When these symptoms have occurred, they have rarely required treatment; however, if symptoms are severe, pentazocine could be readministered and gradually withdrawn. Administration of a benzodiazepine antianxiety agent has been useful to control withdrawal symptoms in some patients. Methadone or other narcotics should not be substituted for pentazocine in the treatment of these symptoms because of their potential for dependence. On the basis of controlled direct addiction studies and clinical experience, the dependence liability of pentazocine appears to be no greater than that of codeine; thus, it is not subject to narcotic controls under the Comprehensive Drug Abuse Prevention and Control Act of 1970. Nevertheless, pentazocine should be prescribed with the same care as are other strong analgesics. Precautions should be taken to avoid increases in dose and frequency of injection if the drug is to be self-administered. Pentazocine should be used with caution, if at all, and carefully monitored in dependence-prone or emotionally unstable individuals.

Precautions.—Pentazocine is relatively contraindicated if increased intracranial pressure, head injury, or other intracranial lesions are present. The drug should be used with caution in patients with impaired renal or hepatic function, myocardial infarction when nausea and vomiting are present, respiratory depression, and in those about to undergo surgery of the biliary tract. Ambulatory patients should be warned not to operate machinery or drive cars while taking the drug.

Pentazocine, like other narcotic antagonists, can precipitate an acute withdrawal syndrome in a patient physically dependent on narcotics. The need for care in its use in these patients should be individually determined, since the incidence and severity of the withdrawal reaction is related to the extent of the patient's prior narcotic experience and the dose of pentazocine given. However, pentazocine should not be given to patients known to be receiving methadone for the treatment of narcotic dependence.

No teratogenic or embryotoxic effects have been reported in animals, but pentazocine should be given with caution to pregnant women. It should not be used in women delivering premature infants.

The narcotic antagonists, levallorphan and nalorphine, are *not effective* in counteracting respiratory depression or overdosage of pentazocine. However, naloxone has been reported to be an effective antagonist in the treatment of overdosage. Oxygen and other supportive measures should be used as needed.

USUAL DOSAGE.—

Pentazocine Hydrochloride:

Oral: Adults, 50 mg every three or four hours as necessary; this may be increased to 100 mg if necessary. The daily dose should not exceed 600 mg. *Children*, dosage not established.

Pentazocine Lactate:

Intramuscular, Intravenous, Subcutaneous: Adults, 30 mg every three to four hours as necessary. [Pentazocine should not be mixed in the same syringe with soluble barbiturates because precipitation will occur.] For obstetric analgesia, a single intramuscular dose of 20 or 30 mg. *Children*, dosage not established; should be reduced according to weight (see table, back cover).

PREPARATIONS.—(Narcotic prescription not required.)

Talwin [hydrochloride] (Winthrop). *Oral:* Tablets 50 mg.

Talwin [lactate] (Winthrop). *Injection:* Solution 30 mg/ml in 1, 1.5, 2, and 10 ml containers.

MIXTURES

MEPERIDINE WITH OTHER ANALGESICS

[APC with Demerol, Demerol-APAP]

Combinations of meperidine with the mild analgesic mixture, APC (aspirin, phenacetin, and caffeine) and with the mild analgesic-antipyretic, acetaminophen [Demerol-APAP], are available for use as oral analgesics. These mixtures may be effective for relief of mild to moderate pain, but they should not be relied on to relieve severe pain because meperidine is less effective orally. There is no conclusive evidence that a synergistic analgesic effect results from the combination of ingredients in these mixtures. Studies comparing them with similar codeine combinations are not available.

Adverse reactions are those of the individual ingredients; the more serious untoward effects are usually produced by meperidine (see the evaluations on Meperidine Hydrochloride in this chapter and on APC and Acetaminophen in Chapter 22, Mild Analgesics).

USUAL DOSAGE.—The advisability of using these mixtures is questionable because of the reasons stated above. The manufacturers' suggested dosages are:

APC with Demerol: *Oral: Adults*, one or two tablets, repeated at intervals of three to four hours if necessary.

Demerol-APAP: *Oral: Adults*, one to two tablets, repeated in four hours if necessary.s,

PREPARATIONS.—

APC with Demerol (Winthrop): Each tablet contains meperidine hydrochloride 30 mg, aspirin 200 mg, phenacetin 150 mg, and caffeine 30 mg.

Demerol-APAP (Breon): Each tablet contains meperidine hydrochloride 50 mg and acetaminophen 300 mg.

MEPERIDINE WITH PROMETHAZINE

[Mepergan]

Promethazine, a phenothiazine, is combined with meperidine in this mixture on the basis of the claim that promethazine potentiates the analgesic and sedative actions of meperidine. The results of some controlled studies indicate that the dose of meperidine required to produce effective analgesia can be reduced by almost one-half when meperidine is combined with promethazine, but other studies do not confirm these findings. Clinical experience with this combination indicates that it is useful for relief of moderate to severe pain; however, whether it has any advantage over an equianalgesic dose of meperidine alone is debatable. The mixture produces more sedation than either drug alone; this sedative effect may be desirable for certain uses (eg, as premedication before surgery [see Chapter 20, Adjuncts to Anesthesia]).

It also is claimed that the incidence of some adverse reactions of meperidine is reduced by promethazine; however, both drugs are potent and produce dissimilar reactions. The tolerance and response to each drug in fixed-ratio combination is unpredictable. Thus, in final analysis, there is insufficient evidence to indicate that Mepergan has any advantage over meperidine alone for analgesia.

USUAL DOSAGE.—This evaluation does not support a suggested dosage of this preparation for analgesia. (See also Chapter 20, Adjuncts to Anesthesia.) The manufacturer's suggested dosage is:

Oral: Adults, one capsule every four to six hours as needed; *children,* dosage not established.

Intravenous: Adults, 1 to 2 ml; *children,* 0.02 ml/kg of body weight. The dose may be repeated every three to four hours.

PREPARATIONS.—Mepergan (Wyeth).

Oral: Each capsule contains meperidine hydrochloride 50 mg and promethazine hydrochloride 12.5 or 25 mg.

Injection: Each milliliter of solution contains 25 mg each of meperidine hydrochloride and promethazine hydrochloride in 2 and 10 ml containers.

Chapter 22

MILD ANALGESICS

The mild analgesics can be divided into two main subgroups: (1) agents chemically related to the strong analgesics (codeine, ethoheptazine [Zactane], and propoxyphene [Darvon]) and (2) analgesic-antipyretics, of which aspirin is the prototype. Although the pharmacologic actions of drugs in the two groups differ, these agents are considered together because of their common therapeutic indication: to relieve mild to moderate pain. They are not useful for relief of severe pain, even in large doses. With the exception of codeine and its congeners, these drugs are not subject to narcotic controls; therefore, they are commonly referred to as "non-narcotic analgesics." However, because some of the newer strong analgesics also are not subject to narcotic controls, the terms "non-narcotic" and "narcotic" are not used as class terms.

When an analgesic is needed, one of the mild agents should be the drug of first choice, except when the pain is severe or when there is some other specific indication for morphine or a comparable strong analgesic (see Chapter 21, Strong Analgesics).

Of the drugs in the first subgroup, codeine is the most efficacious and, although it has a potential for producing physical dependence, the risk from usual oral doses is small. By varying the dosage, the range of pain relieved by codeine is broad. With doses of 32 to 65 mg, its effectiveness is comparable to aspirin in doses of 650 mg; more severe pain may be relieved with larger doses, but the incidence of untoward effects is increased. Although oxycodone, an analogue of codeine, is more potent than codeine on a milligram basis, its dependence potential is higher and it is not available as a single-entity product (see the individual evaluation on Percodan in the section on Mixtures). Propoxyphene is used alone and in mixtures; however, it is less effective on a milligram basis than codeine and is probably no more effective than aspirin in usual doses. The efficacy of ethoheptazine, the other drug of this subgroup, is questionable.

Drugs in the second subgroup have antipyretic as well as analgesic action; some also have an anti-inflammatory effect, which broadens their range of usefulness. These drugs can be divided into four classes, based on chemical structure: salicylates, para-aminophenol derivatives, pyrazolone derivatives, and the newer chemically unrelated agents, mefenamic acid [Ponstel] and indomethacin [Indocin].

In general, the analgesic-antipyretics are most effective in alleviating the pain of headache and of arthritis and other musculoskeletal conditions; they also may relieve mild to moderate postoperative and postpartum pain, dysmenorrhea, and some other types of visceral pain. When drug therapy is indicated to reduce fever, an antipyretic of this group may be useful.

Salicylates: Aspirin is the drug of choice when a mild analgesic or antipyretic is indicated, and is the primary agent used in the management of some rheumatic diseases because it has both analgesic and anti-inflammatory effects. (See Chapter 26, Antirheumatic Agents.) Sodium salicylate and aluminum aspirin have the same actions as aspirin, but are less effective. It has been suggested that the analgesic effect of aspirin is related to blood levels of acetylsalicylate rather than salicylate; however, it has not been possible to correlate these blood levels with the degree of analgesia in man. A compound closely related to the salicylates, salicylamide, has only weak analgesic and antipyretic activity in usual doses; some investigators have found it to be ineffective as an analgesic.

Para-aminophenol Derivatives: Acetaminophen and phenacetin are in this class. Although acetanilid is not an aminophenol, it is metabolized to acetaminophen, and thus may be included in this group. This agent is mentioned primarily to condemn its use as an analgesic because safer and equally effective drugs are available. It is still available as a component of a few analgesic mixtures.

Since phenacetin is less toxic, it has largely replaced acetanilid. Its analgesic effectiveness has been attributed to acetaminophen, which is a metabolic product of acetanilid and phenacetin; however, recent evidence suggests that phenacetin itself has analgesic and antipyretic effects.

The analgesic and antipyretic efficacy of phenacetin and acetaminophen is equal to that of aspirin; however, unlike aspirin, these two analgesics do not have anti-inflammatory or uricosuric effects and thus are not as useful in the treatment of rheumatic diseases. Nevertheless, since they do not antagonize the effects of uricosuric agents as aspirin does, they can be used with these drugs when analgesia is needed in gout (see Chapter 25, Agents Used in Gout). These para-aminophenol derivatives are common ingredients in mixtures.

Pyrazolone Derivatives: There is little difference in actions among the pyrazolone derivatives (antipyrine, aminopyrine, and dipyrone [Dimethone, Key-Pyrone, Narone, Pyral, Pyrilgin]). Like salicylates and para-aminophenol derivatives, they have analgesic and antipyretic properties.

With the recognition that aminopyrine causes agranulocytosis, its use has greatly declined in this country. There is evidence that dipyrone, a derivative of aminopyrine that shares its potential for toxicity, unfortunately is still being misused. This is probably because it is available in injection form and because physicians do not recognize its similarity to aminopyrine since it is marketed under various trademarks. Its only justifiable use is as a last resort to reduce fever when safer measures have failed.

Currently, antipyrine is more widely used topically than systemically for its alleged local analgesic action. (See Chapter 73, Topical Otic Preparations.)

The related compounds, phenylbutazone [Azolid, Butazolidin] and oxyphenbutazone [Oxalid, Tandearil], have some different properties and are discussed in Chapter 25, Agents Used in Gout, and Chapter 26, Antirheumatic Agents.

Miscellaneous Agents: Mefenamic acid [Ponstel], an anthranilic acid derivative, is unrelated chemically to other mild analgesics. Evidence supporting its analgesic efficacy is limited; it has not been shown to be more efficacious than aspirin and other similar mild analgesics and has caused a number of serious adverse reactions.

Indomethacin [Indocin] has analgesic, antipyretic, and anti-inflammatory properties similar to those of aspirin. However, because of its potential to cause serious adverse reactions, it is not used as a simple analgesic; instead, it is indicated only for the treatment of rheumatic disorders (see Chapter 25, Agents Used in Gout, and Chapter 26, Antirheumatic Agents).

In addition to drugs in the two main subgroups of mild analgesics, other agents have been alleged to have an analgesic effect. Notable among these are some of the centrally acting skeletal muscle relaxants, sedative-hypnotics, and central nervous system stimulants (eg, amphetamines, caffeine). There is no conclusive evidence that these agents have an analgesic action when used alone, nor that they enhance analgesia when present as ingredients in analgesic drug combinations.

Adverse Reactions

Most mild analgesics cause relatively few severe adverse reactions when given in doses ordinarily used for relief of mild pain. For discussion of the specific reactions produced, see the individual evaluations.

DERIVATIVES OF STRONG ANALGESICS

CODEINE PHOSPHATE

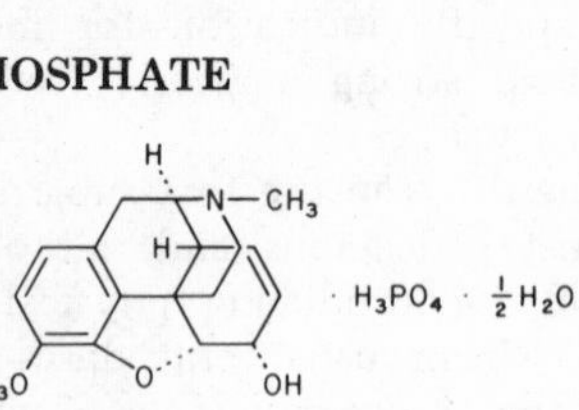

H, N—CH_3, H, CH_3O, O, OH · H_3PO_4 · $\frac{1}{2}H_2O$

CODEINE SULFATE

Codeine is useful in relieving mild to moderate pain from a variety of causes. It also is commonly used to depress the cough reflex (see Chapter 44, Antitussive Agents). This analgesic is most commonly administered orally. Results of controlled studies have shown that 32 to 65 mg of codeine is approximately equivalent to 650 mg of aspirin (oral doses of 15 mg of codeine are usually ineffective). When administered subcutaneously, 120 to 130 mg of codeine is approximately equivalent to 10 mg of morphine sulfate, but the incidence of adverse reactions increases at this dosage level.

Nausea, vomiting, constipation, and drowsiness are minimal after usual oral doses; dizziness may occur in ambulatory patients. However, when the larger doses necessary to relieve more severe pain are used, codeine has most of the disadvantages of morphine, including respiratory depression. Intravenous administration should be avoided, because anaphylactic reactions have been reported with this route. Dependence liability of codeine is less than with morphine or meperidine, and physical dependence occurs only rarely from its use as an oral analgesic; however, the abuse of the drug, particularly in the form of cough syrup, is not uncommon. Codeine is classified as a Schedule II drug under the Controlled Substances Act.

USUAL DOSAGE.—*Oral, Subcutaneous, Intramuscular; Adults,* 30 to 60 mg; *children,* 3 mg/kg of body weight daily divided into six doses.

PREPARATIONS.—

Codeine Phosphate:

Injection: Solution 15, 30, and 60 mg/ml in 1 ml containers; tablets (hypodermic) 15, 30, and 60 mg.

Oral: Tablets (triturates) 15 and 30 mg.

Codeine Sulfate:

Injection: Solution 30 mg/ml; tablets (hypodermic) 15, 30, and 60 mg.

Oral: Tablets (triturates) 15, 30, and 60 mg.

Forms marketed under generic name.

ETHOHEPTAZINE CITRATE [Zactane]

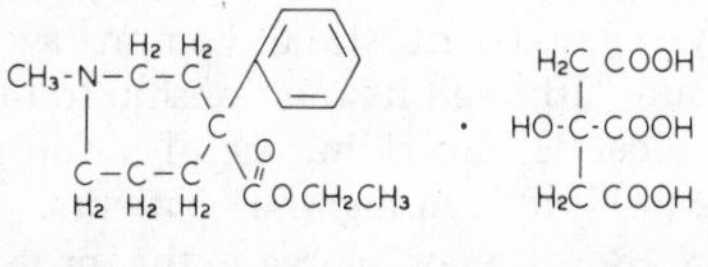

CH_3-N—H_2C—H_2C, C, H_2C—H_2C—H_2C, $COCH_2CH_3$ (O) · H_2C COOH, HO-C-COOH, H_2C COOH

This agent is chemically related to meperidine and has been promoted for relief of mild to moderate pain. It has no anti-inflammatory or antipyretic action. Findings of studies have varied widely and too few well-controlled clinical studies have been done to establish the analgesic efficacy of ethoheptazine. In view of its equivocal effectiveness, more reliable mild analgesics are preferable to this agent. Ethoheptazine is used most frequently in combination with other agents (see the section on Mixtures).

The incidence of adverse reactions after usual doses is relatively low; nausea, vomiting, epigastric distress, dizziness, and pruritus have been observed. Ethoheptazine is not subject to narcotic controls of the Controlled Substances Act.

USUAL DOSAGE.—Since the efficacy of this drug is equivocal, no dosage is given. The manufacturer's suggested dosage is: *Oral: Adults,* 75 to 150 mg three or four times daily.

PREPARATIONS.—Zactane (Wyeth). *Oral:* Tablets 75 mg.

PROPOXYPHENE HYDROCHLORIDE
[Darvon]
PROPOXYPHENE NAPSYLATE
[Darvon-N]

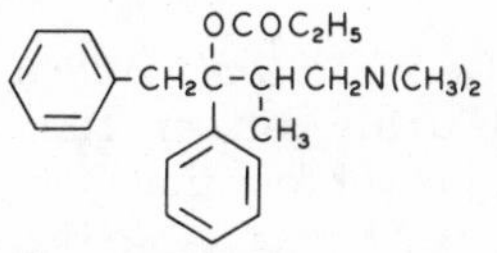

$OCOC_2H_5$; C_6H_5-CH_2C—CH $CH_2N(CH_3)_2$; CH_3 ; C_6H_5

Propoxyphene is related chemically to methadone and is used orally to relieve mild to moderate pain. On the basis of several controlled studies, it is estimated that the milligram potency of propoxyphene hydrochloride is about one-half to two-thirds that of codeine. Results of these studies have demonstrated that 65 mg of propoxyphene hydrochloride was no more effective, and usually was less effective, than 650 mg of aspirin. Comparative studies of the two salts of propoxyphene show that equianalgesic effects are produced by equimolar amounts of the salts (100 mg of napsylate is equivalent to 65 mg of hydrochloride).

Propoxyphene does not possess anti-inflammatory or antipyretic actions, and has little or no antitussive activity, although the levorotatory isomer is used for this purpose (see Chapter 44, Antitussive Agents).

The most frequent adverse reactions are dizziness, drowsiness, nausea, and vomiting. These untoward effects are more prominent in ambulatory patients, and some may be alleviated if the patient is recumbent. Less common adverse reactions include constipation, abdominal pain, rashes, and headache; rarely, asthenia, euphoria, dysphoria, and minor visual disturbances have been reported.

Serious overdosage is manifested by respiratory depression, extreme somnolence progressing to stupor or coma, pupillary constriction, and acute circulatory failure. In addition to these symptoms characteristic of narcotic poisoning, focal and generalized convulsions are prominent in most cases of propoxyphene poisoning, and arrhythmias and pulmonary edema have occasionally been reported. Apnea, cardiac arrest, and death have occurred. The narcotic antagonists (levallorphan, nalorphine, or naloxone) may be useful in overcoming severe depression. Resuscitative and supportive therapy also should be initiated as soon as possible. Analeptics or other central nervous system stimulants should not be used since they may precipitate fatal convulsions.

Abuse of propoxyphene hydrochloride with the development of morphine-type drug dependence has been reported. However, because its potential for abuse is less than that of codeine, propoxyphene is not subject to narcotic controls of the Controlled Substances Act.

USUAL DOSAGE.—*Oral: Adults,* 65 mg of the hydrochloride salt or 100 mg of the napsylate salt three or four times daily.

PREPARATIONS.—

Propoxyphene Hydrochloride:

Darvon (Lilly). *Oral:* Capsules 32 and 65 mg. Drug also marketed under generic name.

Propoxyphene Napsylate:

Darvon-N (Lilly). *Oral:* Suspension 50 mg/5 ml; tablets 100 mg.

ANALGESIC-ANTIPYRETICS

Salicylates

ASPIRIN

COOH

$OCOCH_3$

This agent is the prototype of the analgesic-antipyretic group, and is the drug of choice when a mild analgesic is indicated. It also has an anti-inflammatory effect. Aspirin is more useful in the treatment of headache, neuralgia, myalgia, arthralgia, and other pain arising from integumental structures than it is in acute, severe pain of visceral origin. However, it may be effective in moderate postoperative and postpartum pain or in pain secondary to trauma and cancer. In the latter, aspirin may provide adequate relief and should be tried prior to the use of more potent drugs. This analgesic is the primary agent used in the management of some rheumatic diseases (see Chapter 25, Agents Used in Gout, and Chapter 26, Antirheumatic Agents), although it should not be administered with uricosuric agents in the treatment of gout, since aspirin antagonizes the action of these agents.

When drug therapy is indicated to reduce fever, aspirin is one of the most effective and safest drugs; however, antipyretic therapy is only symptomatic and the cause of the fever must be sought and treated. Doses required in rheumatic fever are larger than usual analgesic doses, but only enough to achieve symptomatic relief should be given; the optimal blood salicylate level is usually 25 to 35 mg/100 ml. Penicillin and other appropriate therapy should be administered concomitantly.

On the basis of available evidence, it appears that salicylate blood levels do not correlate well with analgesic effect. The rate of absorption of aspirin depends upon its dissolution, which may vary among different tablet preparations as a result of variations in formulations. Such differences are eliminated when the drug is given in solution, such as in effervescent preparations (see the discussion on Mixtures of Antacids with Aspirin).

Serious adverse reactions from usual analgesic doses of aspirin occur infrequently; gastrointestinal disturbances (dyspepsia, nausea, vomiting, and occult gastrointestinal bleeding) are most common. With prolonged administration, occult bleeding may lead to iron deficiency anemia. Gastrointestinal effects may be diminished by taking aspirin with milk, food, or large quantities of water. Use of enteric-coated preparations will reduce gastrointestinal reactions, but absorption of aspirin will be delayed and may be quite variable with some of these products. Therefore, when this type of preparation is used, the physician should monitor blood salicylate levels to determine whether absorption is satisfactory. Massive gastrointestinal hemorrhage occurs rarely and, although its relationship to history of peptic ulcer is uncertain, use of a nonsalicylate may be preferable in high-risk patients.

Large doses may increase the prothrombin time, but this is not clinically significant unless patients are also taking anticoagulants. Recent evidence indicates that usual doses of aspirin alter platelet function, and hence the drug may be contraindicated in patients with bleeding disorders.

In individuals who are hypersensitive to aspirin, even usual doses may cause rash or severe urticarial or asthmatic-type anaphylactic reactions. The incidence of these reactions is higher in patients with asthma, hay fever, or nasal polyps.

Signs of salicylism (tinnitus, headache, dizziness, confusion) may occur during prolonged therapy with large doses (eg, in rheumatic disorders); these may be controlled by reducing the dosage (see Chapter 26, Antirheumatic Agents).

Acute intoxication from accidental poisoning is the most common cause of fatal drug poisoning in children. Toxic doses cause a disturbance of acid-base balance, usually manifested as a metabolic acidosis in infants and young children and as a respiratory alkalosis in older children and adults; hyperpyrexia also may occur in infants and young children. The severity of the intoxication is determined by measuring the blood salicylate level. Treatment is aimed at increasing elimination of salicylate from the body and specific therapy for any of the toxic manifestations. Performance of appropriate laboratory tests for diagnosis, use of alkaline diuresis, and, in severe cases, peritoneal dialysis or hemodialysis are necessary.

USUAL DOSAGE.—*Oral, Rectal: Adults,* 600 mg every four hours as necessary; *children,* 65 mg/kg of body weight daily divided into four or six doses.

PREPARATIONS.—Aspirin, U.S.P.

Oral: Capsules 300 mg; tablets 60, 75, 150, 300, and 500 mg; tablets (enteric-coated) 300 and 600 mg.

Rectal: Suppositories 60, 75, 120, 150, 200, 300, and 600 mg and 1 g.

Drug marketed by many manufacturers under generic name.

ALUMINUM ASPIRIN

CH_3OCO — COO—Al—OOC (OH) — $OCOCH_3$

This salt of aspirin contains the equivalent of 80% aspirin. It is practically insoluble in water. Aluminum aspirin is claimed to be more palatable and stable than aspirin, particularly in combination with other drugs. Because of this property, it is used primarily in mixtures. Since aluminum aspirin is slowly and incompletely absorbed from the gastrointestinal tract, effective blood levels may not be reached. In the absence of studies comparing its analgesic efficacy with that of aspirin, aluminum aspirin should not be used alone or with other drugs.

See the evaluation on Aspirin for adverse reactions and precautions.

USUAL DOSAGE.—Since the efficacy of this drug has not been established, a dosage cannot be given. The N.F. suggested dosage is: *Oral: Adults,* 670 mg (equal to about 600 mg of aspirin) every four hours as necessary; *children,* 75 mg every four hours.

PREPARATIONS.—Aspirin Aluminum (Abbott). *Oral:* Tablets (chewable) 75 mg.

SODIUM SALICYLATE

COONa, OH

Although sodium salicylate produces blood salicylate levels as high as or higher than equimolar doses of aspirin, it is less effective than equal doses of aspirin in relieving pain and reducing fever; however, persons who are hypersensitive to aspirin may tolerate sodium salicylate.

In general, sodium salicylate produces the same adverse reactions as aspirin (see that evaluation). This drug does not affect platelet function, but, like aspirin, it does increase prothrombin time. Sodium salicylate should not be used in patients on a low-sodium diet.

USUAL DOSAGE.—*Oral: Adults,* 600 mg every four to six hours as necessary.

PREPARATIONS.—Sodium Salicylate, U.S.P. *Oral:* Tablets (plain, enteric-coated) 300, 500, and 600 mg. Drug marketed by many manufacturers under generic name.

SALICYLAMIDE

OH, CNH_2 (=O)

Salicylamide is the amide of salicylic acid; since it lacks a free carboxyl group, it is not strictly a salicylate, but usually is considered with this group. Results of the few acceptable controlled studies on salicylamide indicate that this agent is much less effective than aspirin as an analgesic or antipyretic when given in the same dose, and therefore is too weak and unreliable to be useful. Salicylamide is conjugated by the intestinal mucosa after oral administration; thus, most of the drug is not absorbed in active form. If doses large enough to saturate the conjugating mechanism are given (1.2 to 1.5 g), blood levels rise rapidly and the potential for toxicity increases significantly.

Although salicylamide has a central depressant action in some animals, there is no evidence that it acts similarly in man except in toxic doses.

The incidence of adverse reactions appears to be lower with salicylamide than with aspirin (see that evaluation), but comparisons at equally effective doses have not been made.

USUAL DOSAGE.—An effective analgesic dosage has not been conclusively established. The manufacturers' suggested dosage is: *Oral: Adults,* 460 to 600 mg three or four times daily; *children,* 65 mg/kg of body weight daily divided into six doses.

PREPARATIONS.—

Amid-Sal (Glenwood). *Oral:* Tablets 230 mg.

Liquiprin (Johnson & Johnson). *Oral:* Solution 60 mg/ml.

Salamide (Philips Roxane), Salicim (Mallinckrodt). *Oral:* Tablets 300 mg.

Salrin (Warren-Teed). *Oral:* Tablets 300 and 600 mg.

Para-aminophenol Derivatives

ACETAMINOPHEN

$CH_3CONH-C_6H_4-OH$

This metabolite of phenacetin and acetanilid is an effective analgesic and antipyretic. It has the same uses as phenacetin (ie, treatment of headache and mild to moderate myalgia and arthralgia) and may be preferable to phenacetin because it is less toxic. Acetaminophen has been substituted for phenacetin in many combination products. This drug lacks the anti-inflammatory effect of the salicylates, but it is probably the analgesic-antipyretic of choice as an alternative to aspirin, particularly in patients allergic to aspirin or with a history of peptic ulcer. Unlike aspirin, acetaminophen does not antagonize the effects of uricosuric agents (see Chapter 25, Agents Used in Gout).

Acetaminophen, unlike phenacetin and acetanilid, produces little or no methemoglobinemia and has not caused hemolytic anemia. It does not cause gastrointestinal bleeding as does aspirin. Although large doses have been reported to potentiate the action of oral anticoagulants, small doses had no effect on prothrombin time. It is not known whether prolonged use of acetaminophen can cause the type of renal injury associated with abuse of analgesic mixtures containing phenacetin. Hepatic necrosis has been observed following overdosage.

USUAL DOSAGE.—*Oral: Adults,* 300 to 600 mg at four-hour intervals if necessary; total daily dose should not exceed 2.4 g. *Children 6 to 12 years of age,* 150 to 300 mg; *1 to 6 years,* 60 to 120 mg; *under 1 year,* 60 mg. These amounts are given as single doses every four to six hours, but the total daily dose should not exceed 1.2 g.

PREPARATIONS.—*Oral:* Drops 60 mg/0.6 ml; elixir or syrup 120 mg/5 ml; tablets 300 or 325 mg; tablets (chewable) 120 mg.

AVAILABLE TRADEMARKS.—Amphenol (Durst), Apamide (Dome), Apap (Ulmer), Conacetol (Consolidated Midland), Elixodyne Elixir (Lemmon), Febrolin (Durst), G-1, G-Lixir (Palmedico), Lestemp (Reid-Provident), Nebs (Eaton), Neopap (Webster), Pyrapap (Savage), SK-APAP (Smith Kline & French), Tempra (Mead Johnson), Tenlap (Dow), Tylenol (McNeil), Valadol (Squibb). Drug also marketed under generic name.

PHENACETIN

$C_2H_5O-C_6H_4-NHCOCH_3$

Phenacetin is closely related to acetanilid and has largely replaced acetanilid because it is less toxic. It is approximately equivalent to aspirin in analgesic and antipyretic effectiveness but has little anti-inflammatory activity. This agent is useful mainly in the treatment of headache and mild to moderate myalgia and arthralgia. Evidence is not convincing that phenacetin decreases anxiety and tension apart from its analgesic effect. Unlike aspirin, it does not antagonize the effects of uricosuric agents (see Chapter 25, Agents Used in Gout).

Absorption is rapid following oral administration; peak plasma levels are reached in one to two hours and the duration of action is about four hours. Phenacetin is rapidly metabolized to acetaminophen, which is excreted in the urine as conjugates. Since acetaminophen is an effective analgesic, the effects of phenacetin have been attributed to acetaminophen; however, studies in rats have shown that phenacetin itself has analgesic-antipyretic activity.

Phenacetin is usually used in mixtures, although there is no reason why it should not be used alone. It is most commonly combined with aspirin and caffeine (see discussion on Mixtures and the evaluation on Aspirin, Phenacetin, and Caffeine [APC]).

Adverse reactions occur infrequently. Although large doses may cause methemoglobinemia, this is seldom clinically significant with usual therapeutic doses. Phenacetin also has produced hemolytic anemia, most commonly after prolonged use of large doses or in individuals with a deficiency of glucose-6-phosphate dehydrogenase. The drug does not have the irritant action of aspirin and therefore does not cause gastrointestinal bleeding. Some patients may develop a rash, but patients sensitive to aspirin may tolerate phenacetin. Prolonged ingestion of large doses has been implicated as a cause of nephrotoxicity. However, in the cases reported, phenacetin was used in an analgesic mixture; thus, evidence for singling out phenacetin as the cause of kidney damage is not convincing. (See evaluation on Aspirin, Phenacetin and Caffeine [APC].)

USUAL DOSAGE.—*Oral: Adults,* 600 mg every three or four hours as needed, but the total daily dose should not exceed 2.4 g. If this dose does not relieve pain, the drug should be discontinued.

PREPARATIONS.—*Oral:* Tablets 300 mg. Drug marketed under generic name.

Pyrazolone Derivatives

DIPYRONE [Dimethone, Key-Pyrone, Narone, Pyral, Pyrilgin]

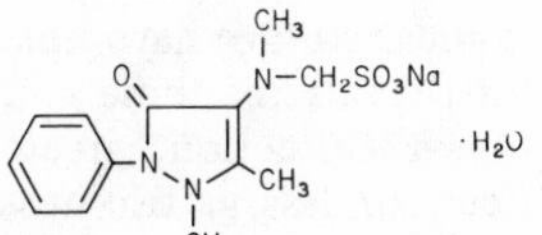

This derivative of aminopyrine has the same actions, including serious adverse effects, as the parent compound. Clinical experience indicates that dipyrone is an effective analgesic and antipyretic, but its relative efficacy compared with that of other analgesics has not been determined. Since dipyrone is more soluble than aminopyrine, it can be administered parenterally in large doses. Although this property may be advantageous when its administration is essential, it probably also contributes to the drug's misuse.

Because dipyrone may produce fatal agranulocytosis and other blood dyscrasias (eg, thrombocytopenic purpura, aplastic anemia), its use as a general analgesic, antiarthritic, or routine antipyretic cannot be condoned. Its only justifiable use is in serious conditions (eg, febrile convulsions in children), in which a parenteral antipyretic preparation may be needed after other measures (eg, sponge baths) and other drugs have failed, or, rarely, in malignant diseases (eg, Hodgkin's disease) when fever cannot be controlled by any other means.

Dipyrone also may produce hemolytic anemia, rash, edema, tremors, nausea and vomiting, gastrointestinal hemorrhage, anuria, allergic reactions (asthma and angioedema), and may accentuate hypoprothrombinemia. Blood studies (white blood cell and differential counts) should be performed frequently. The drug should be discontinued at first evidence of any reduction in blood cell count or sign of agranulocytosis, and the patient should be instructed to discontinue use of dipyrone if sore throat or other sign of infection appears (eg, pain, swelling, tenderness, ulceration).

USUAL DOSAGE.—*Oral, Intramuscular:* No dosage for analgesia is justified. For antipyresis, *adults,* 500 mg to 1 g; total daily dose should not exceed 3 g. *Children,* 250 to 500 mg repeated in three to four hours if necessary; total daily dose should not exceed 1 g for those *under six years of age* or 2 g for those *6 to 12 years.* If the desired effect is not achieved within a few days, the drug should be discontinued.

PREPARATIONS.—

Dimethone (Philips Roxane).

Injection: Solution 500 mg/ml in 10 and 30 ml containers.

Oral: Tablets 300 mg.

Key-Pyrone (Key). *Injection:* Solution 500 mg/ml in 10 and 30 ml containers.

Narone (Ulmer).

Injection: Solution 500 mg/ml in 30 ml containers.

Oral: Tablets 600 mg.

Pyral (Ascher). *Injection:* Solution 500 mg/ml in 30 ml containers.

Pyrilgin (Savage).

Injection: Solution 500 mg/ml in 2, 10, and 30 ml containers.

Oral: Drops (pediatric) 250 mg/ml; liquid 500 mg/5 ml; tablets 500 mg.

Drug also marketed by many manufacturers under generic name.

MISCELLANEOUS AGENTS

MEFENAMIC ACID [Ponstel]

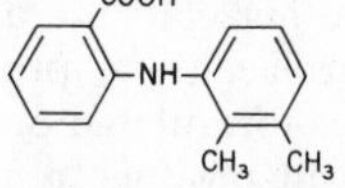

Mefenamic acid is unrelated chemically to other mild analgesics. It is claimed to be useful for relief of pain in conditions ordinarily not requiring the use of strong analgesics. Evidence supporting the analgesic efficacy of mefenamic acid is limited. Few well-designed, double-blind clinical trials have been done using the manufacturer's recommended dosage, and adequate studies comparing this drug with aspirin are lacking. Since mefenamic acid has not been shown to be more effective than aspirin and other mild analgesics and since it has been implicated in a number of serious adverse reactions, other mild analgesics are preferred.

Gastrointestinal symptoms are the most common adverse effects. Diarrhea occurs in a significant number of patients and usually recurs when mefenamic acid is given a second time. Occult gastrointestinal hemorrhage may occur less frequently than with aspirin. Dyspepsia, constipation, nausea, abdominal pain, vomiting, headache, drowsiness, vertigo, and dizziness have been observed. Elevated blood urea nitrogen levels have been noted in one study on human volunteers. Hemolytic anemia, as well as unconfirmed cases of agranulocytosis, thrombocytopenic purpura, and megaloblastic anemia also have been reported.

If diarrhea or rash occurs, the drug should be discontinued and not used thereafter. It is contraindicated in patients with gastrointestinal inflammation or ulceration and in patients with impaired renal function, and should be used with caution in asthmatics because it may exacerbate the condition.

The safety of mefenamic acid for use during pregnancy or in children under 14 years of age has not been established.

USUAL DOSAGE.—Since other mild analgesics are preferred to this drug for the reasons stated above, no dosage is suggested. The manufacturer's suggested dosage is: *Oral: Adults and children over 14 years of age*, 500 mg initially, followed by 250 mg every six hours as needed. Mefenamic acid should not be used longer than one week.

PREPARATIONS.—Ponstel (Parke, Davis). *Oral:* Capsules 250 mg.

MIXTURES

Mixtures of analgesic agents or of an analgesic with drugs of another class are among the most widely used pharmaceutical products. Most of these mixtures are formulated on the theoretical basis that they will produce a greater analgesic effect, provide broader therapeutic uses, or cause fewer or less severe untoward effects than a single ingredient. Despite the widespread use of these products, relatively few well-controlled studies have been performed to determine their effectiveness. Moreover, many of the mixtures are illogical and, with few exceptions, there is no reason for using them in preference to a single analgesic.

The various analgesic mixtures are divided into groups on the basis of similarities in their composition. Examples in each group have been selected for comment because they are popularly prescribed and not because they necessarily have any merit over similar products.

Mixtures of Aspirin with Antacids

Antacids are combined with aspirin in an attempt to reduce the gastric irritation caused by this analgesic; this combination is commonly referred to as buffered aspirin. The relatively small amount of antacid present in most products is insufficient to raise the gastric pH significantly; however, the intimate contact of the antacid with the aspirin particle does increase the dissolution rate of the aspirin, which results in its more rapid absorption. It has been postulated that this increased rate may result in less gastric irritation, and some persons claim that they can tolerate the buffered preparations better; however, results of controlled clinical studies have not conclusively demonstrated that use of these mixtures results in faster onset of action, greater or longer analgesic effect, or less gastric upset than plain aspirin. Thus, the available evidence does not indicate that buffered aspirin tablets are preferable to plain aspirin.

Buffered aspirin is also available in effervescent preparations; when dissolved, the aspirin is present as sodium acetylsalicylate. Results of studies have shown that when aspirin is given in this form, its rate of absorption is faster and the blood salicylate level is higher than with tablet formulations; in addition, the sodium acetylsalicylate in solution with sufficient buffers causes less gastric irritation and gastrointestinal bleeding. Because the effervescent preparations contain more absorbable antacid, repeated use or large doses would alkalize the urine and result in faster excretion and a decrease in the blood level of the salicylate. However, this type of preparation is a useful form of aspirin for occasional use.

The following products are listed as examples only because they are used widely and not to indicate they have any advantage over many similar preparations.

Ascriptin (Rorer): Each tablet contains

aspirin 300 mg and magnesium-aluminum hydroxide 150 mg.

Bufferin (Bristol-Myers): Each tablet contains aspirin 300 mg, aluminum glycinate 45 mg, and magnesium carbonate 90 mg.

Alka-Seltzer (Miles): Each effervescent tablet contains aspirin 324 mg, sodium bicarbonate 1.9 g, citric acid 1.05 g, and calcium phosphate, monobasic 200 mg.

Mixtures of Analgesic-Antipyretic Agents

Many products contain two or more analgesic-antipyretic drugs. Such combinations are alleged to enhance the analgesic action and produce fewer adverse reactions than the individual agents used alone. However, since these drugs apparently have the same mechanism of action, the analgesic effect of a combination would be expected to be no greater than the sum of effects of the individual drugs, and few studies have adequately explored this point. Further, since the common adverse reactions of these agents are not dose related within the therapeutic range, the smaller amount of each agent in the mixture would not necessarily result in fewer or less severe adverse reactions. In fact, results of studies in experimental animals have shown that the acute toxicity of a mixture of aspirin, phenacetin, and caffeine (APC) is a summation of the toxicities of the ingredients. Also, there is a paucity of information about possible interactions between these drugs. Because the rationale for these combinations is open to question, and because adequate studies have not demonstrated their superiority, the use of a single analgesic is preferred.

ASPIRIN, PHENACETIN, AND CAFFEINE (APC)

This is probably the most frequently used mixture of analgesic drugs; however, there is no convincing evidence that the rationale for this combination is sound. Since both aspirin and phenacetin are analgesic-antipyretics, there is no advantage in combining them. Furthermore, since phenacetin has little anti-inflammatory action, the combination would be less effective than an equivalent amount of aspirin alone in treating inflammatory conditions. Although the vascular effect of caffeine may be useful in the treatment of migraine headache, there is no evidence that the small amount contained in the usual APC formulation has an analgesic effect or that it affects the activity of the analgesic components. Despite the assumption of many physicians and patients that APC possesses some advantage over aspirin alone, results of well-controlled clinical studies have not supported this belief. Thus, use of aspirin alone is preferred to use of APC.

Adverse reactions are those of the ingredients. A syndrome termed analgesic nephropathy has been associated with prolonged use of large doses of various analgesic mixtures, usually aspirin, phenacetin, and caffeine. The evidence implicating any single agent as the cause of the renal damage is not convincing. The most common clinical manifestations of the syndrome include sterile pyuria, asymptomatic bacteriuria, and acute pyelonephritis; extrarenal manifestations are dyspepsia, peptic ulcer, anemia, and hypertension. The pathologic changes in the kidney are papillary necrosis and interstitial fibrosis. In addition, malignant tumors of the renal pelvis have been reported in some patients with analgesic nephropathy. There is some evidence that renal function often improves if use of analgesics are discontinued in patients with analgesic nephropathy.

USUAL DOSAGE.—*Oral: Adults*, one or two capsules or tablets every three or four hours. No more than six capsules or tablets should be taken daily. *Children 6 to 12 years of age*, one-half adult dose.

PREPARATIONS.—*Oral:* Tablets containing aspirin 230 mg, phenacetin 150 mg, and caffeine 15 or 30 mg.

AVAILABLE TRADEMARKS.—Anodynos (Otis Clapp), Ansemco No. 1 (Elder), A.S.A. Compound (Lilly), As-Ca-Phen (Ulmer), Aspirin Compound (Parke, Davis), Duradyne (Durst), Empirin Compound (Burroughs Wellcome), P-A-C Compound (Upjohn), Phencasal (Elder), Phensal (Dow). Drug also marketed by many manufacturers under generic name.

Similar Mixtures

Arthralgen (Robins): Each tablet contains salicylamide 250 mg and acetaminophen 250 mg.

Arthra-Zene (Xttrium): Each capsule contains salicylamide 200 mg, acetaminophen 200 mg, and aspirin 200 mg.

Asphac-G (Central): Each tablet contains aspirin 250 mg, phenacetin 120 mg, caffeine 15 mg, and gelsemium tincture 0.2 ml.

Buffadyne (Lemmon): Each tablet contains aspirin 230 mg, phenacetin 150 mg, caffeine 30 mg, dried aluminum hydroxide gel, and magnesium hydroxide.

Causalin (Amfre-Grant): Each tablet contains salicylsalicylic acid 500 mg and aspirin 195 mg.

For-Dyne (First Texas): Each tablet contains salicylamide 300 mg, acetaminophen 120 mg, and caffeine 15 mg.

Phencaset (Improved) (Elder): Each tablet contains aspirin 225 mg, phenacetin 150 mg, caffeine 30 mg, dried aluminum hydroxide gel, and magnesium carbonate 60 mg.

Trigesic (Squibb): Each tablet contains acetaminophen 125 mg, aspirin 230 mg, and caffeine 30 mg.

Mixtures Containing Codeine

Codeine is included in many analgesic preparations to increase their analgesic effectiveness. The combination of codeine or another strong analgesic derivative with an analgesic-antipyretic appears to be rational because the mechanism of action of the drugs in the two groups differs. Results of controlled studies show that the analgesic effects of codeine and aspirin are additive. Thus, this combination may provide a greater degree of pain relief than can be obtained with aspirin alone and the dose of codeine would be smaller than if it were given alone. The combination of codeine with acetaminophen also may provide an additive analgesic effect, but controlled studies demonstrating this are lacking.

Codeine also is included in mixtures containing two or more other mild analgesics (eg, codeine with APC); although codeine may enhance their analgesic effect if present in sufficient amount, such complex combinations are not preferred to the simpler mixture of codeine with aspirin. Several of these mixtures contain sedatives in addition to analgesics (see also the section on Mixtures Containing Analgesics with Sedatives).

CODEINE WITH ASPIRIN

This combination enhances the analgesic effect of both codeine and aspirin, thus providing a greater degree of pain relief than aspirin alone and allowing a reduced dose of codeine. The aspirin component also helps reduce inflammation and fever. See also the introduction to this section. This combination is classified as a Schedule III drug under the Controlled Substances Act.

The adverse reactions are those of the ingredients (see the evaluations on the individual drugs).

USUAL DOSAGE.—*Oral: Adults*, one or two tablets three times daily as required to relieve pain.

PREPARATIONS.—*Oral:* Each tablet contains codeine phosphate 15 or 30 mg and aspirin 325 mg, or codeine phosphate 30 mg and aspirin 600 mg.

AVAILABLE TRADEMARKS.—Ascodeen-30 (Burroughs Wellcome), Codasa (Stayner). Mixture also marketed under generic name.

SIMILAR MIXTURE.—Ascriptin with Codeine (Rorer): Each capsule contains aspirin 300 mg, codeine phosphate 15 mg, and magnesium hydroxide 150 mg.

CODEINE PHOSPHATE, ASPIRIN, PHENACETIN, AND CAFFEINE
(APC with Codeine)

This is an effective analgesic mixture, but there is no evidence that it has any advantage over codeine with aspirin; thus, the latter combination is preferred. See the introduction to this section.

The adverse reactions are those of the ingredients. See the evaluations on the individual drugs.

USUAL DOSAGE.—*Oral: Adults*, one tablet as required to relieve pain.

PREPARATIONS.—

A.S.A. and Codeine Compound (Lilly). *Oral:* Each capsule contains aspirin 230 mg, phenacetin 150 mg, caffeine 30 mg, and codeine phosphate 15, 30, or 60 mg; each tablet contains aspirin 230 mg, phenacetin 150 mg, caffeine 30 mg, and codeine phosphate 15 or 30 mg.

Empirin Compound with Codeine (Burroughs Wellcome). *Oral:* Each tablet contains aspirin 230 mg, phenacetin 150 mg, caffeine 30 mg, and codeine phosphate 8 mg [No. 1], 15 mg [No. 2], 30 mg [No. 3], or 60 mg [No. 4].

P-A-C Compound with Codeine Sulfate (Upjohn). *Oral:* Each capsule or tablet contains aspirin 230 mg, phenacetin 150 mg, caffeine 30 mg, and codeine sulfate 15 or 30 mg.

Mixture also marketed under generic name and under name, APC with Codeine.

FIORINAL WITH CODEINE

This mixture contains APC, codeine, and a barbiturate. If a sedative action is required, the barbiturate should be prescribed separately. See the introduction to this section and the section on Mixtures Containing Analgesics with Sedatives.

Adverse reactions are those of the individual ingredients. See the evaluations on the individual drugs. This combination is classified as a Schedule III drug under the Controlled Substances Act.

USUAL DOSAGE.—Evaluation of this mixture does not support a suggested dosage. The manufacturer's suggested dosage is: *Oral: Adults*, one or two capsules, repeated if necessary (maximum, six per day).

PREPARATIONS.—Fiorinal with Codeine (Sandoz). *Oral:* Each capsule contains codeine phosphate 7.5 mg [No. 1], 15 mg [No. 2], or 30 mg [No. 3]; aspirin 100 mg; phenacetin 130 mg; caffeine 40 mg; and butalbital 50 mg.

PHENAPHEN WITH CODEINE

This mixture contains three analgesics, a sedative, and an anticholinergic agent. This is a needlessly complex preparation and its use is not warranted. See the introduction to this section and section on Mixtures Containing Analgesics with Sedatives.

The adverse reactions are those of the ingredients. See the evaluations on the individual drugs. This combination is classified as a Schedule III drug under the Controlled Substances Act.

USUAL DOSAGE.—No dosage is given for this complex mixture. The manufacturer's suggested dosage is: *Oral: Adults*, No. 2 or No. 3, one or two capsules every three to four hours as needed; No. 4, one capsule every three to four hours as needed.

PREPARATIONS.—Phenaphen with Codeine (Robins). *Oral:* Each capsule contains codeine phosphate 15 mg [No. 2], 30 mg [No. 3], or 60 mg [No. 4]; aspirin 150 mg; phenacetin 200 mg; phenobarbital 15 mg; and hyoscyamine sulfate 0.031 mg.

TYLENOL WITH CODEINE

This combination theoretically would provide the additive analgesic effect of acetaminophen and codeine, which would be comparable to that of aspirin with codeine, but studies on this combination are lacking. The mixture would not provide the anti-inflammatory effect of aspirin alone or of the combination of aspirin with codeine. See also the introduction to this section.

The adverse reactions are those of the ingredients. See the evaluations on Acetaminophen and Codeine. This combination is classified as a Schedule III drug under the Controlled Substances Act.

USUAL DOSAGE.—*Oral: Adults*, one or two tablets every four hours as needed.

PREPARATIONS.—Tylenol with Codeine (McNeil). *Oral:* Each tablet contains acetaminophen 300 mg and codeine phosphate 7.5 mg [No. 1], 15 mg [No. 2], 30 mg [No. 3], or 60 mg [No. 4].

Similar Mixtures

The following mixtures are complex and, on the basis of available evidence, a single analgesic or a combination of codeine with aspirin should be used in preference to these preparations. See the introduction to this section. These mixtures are classified as Schedule III drugs under the Controlled Substances Act.

Asphac-G with Codeine (Central): Each tablet contains codeine sulfate 15 or 30 mg, aspirin 250 mg, phenacetin 120 mg, caffeine 15 mg, and gelsemium tincture 0.2 ml.

Codempiral (Burroughs Wellcome): Each capsule contains codeine phosphate 15 mg [No. 1] or 30 mg [No. 2], aspirin 225 mg, phenacetin 150 mg, and phenobarbital 15 mg.

Donnagesic (Robins): Each timed-release tablet contains codeine phosphate 48.6 mg [No. 1] or 97.2 mg [No. 2], phenobarbital 48.6 mg, hyoscyamine sulfate 0.3111 mg, atropine sulfate 0.0582 mg, and scopolamine hydrobromide 0.0195 mg.

Hasacode (Arnar-Stone): Each tablet contains codeine phosphate 16 mg, phenacetin 162 mg, acetaminophen 162 mg, phenobarbital 16 mg, atropine sulfate 0.00065 mg, scopolamine hydrobromide 0.0011 mg, and hyoscyamine hydrobromide 0.0325 mg.

Percogesic-C (Endo): Each tablet contains codeine phosphate 32.4 mg, acetaminophen 325 mg, and phenyltoloxamine citrate 30 mg.

Soma Compound with Codeine (Wallace): Each tablet contains codeine phosphate 16 mg, phenacetin 160 mg, caffeine 32 mg, and carisoprodol 200 mg.

Mixtures Containing Propoxyphene

DARVON WITH A.S.A.
DARVON-N WITH A.S.A.
DARVON COMPOUND
DARVOCET-N

The rationale for combining propoxyphene with an analgesic-antipyretic is the same as that for similar combinations containing codeine. Propoxyphene hydrochloride is combined with aspirin [Darvon with A.S.A.] and with APC [Darvon Compound, -65]; the napsylate salt is also combined with aspirin [Darvon-N with A.S.A.] and with acetaminophen [Darvocet-N]. Controlled studies with these propoxyphene combinations have been very limited, but the results suggest that the analgesic effects of the individual components are additive in the combinations. However, since it has not been demonstrated that APC has any superiority over a single analgesic-antipyretic, there appears to be no advantage in using the propoxyphene-APC combination in preference to the propoxyphene-aspirin or propoxyphene-acetaminophen combinations. The preparation containing acetaminophen would lack the anti-inflammatory action produced by the preparations containing aspirin, although each combination would have an antipyretic action. Studies comparing the effectiveness of these propoxyphene combinations with similar codeine combinations either have not been performed or the results have been inconclusive.

Adverse reactions of these mixtures are those of the ingredients (see the evaluations on the individual drugs).

USUAL DOSAGE.—

Darvon with A.S.A., Darvon-N with A.S.A.:

Oral: Adults, one capsule or tablet three or four times daily.

Darvon Compound:

Oral: Adults, one or two capsules of Darvon Compound or one capsule of Darvon Compound-65 three or four times daily.

Darvocet-N:

Oral: Adults, two tablets every four hours as needed.

PREPARATIONS.—

Darvon with A.S.A. (Lilly): Each capsule contains propoxyphene hydrochloride 65 mg and aspirin 325 mg.

Darvon-N with A.S.A. (Lilly): Each tablet contains propoxyphene napsylate 100 mg and aspirin 325 mg.

Darvon Compound (Lilly): Each capsule contains propoxyphene hydrochloride 32 mg, aspirin 227 mg, phenacetin 162 mg, and caffeine 32.4 mg.

Darvon Compound-65 (Lilly): Each capsule contains propoxyphene hydrochloride 65 mg, aspirin 227 mg, phenacetin 162 mg, and caffeine 32.4 mg.

Darvocet-N (Lilly): Each tablet contains propoxyphene napsylate 50 mg and acetaminophen 325 mg.

Mixtures Containing Other Strong Analgesic Derivatives

PERCODAN

This mixture contains oxycodone (as the hydrochloride and terephthalate), with aspirin, phenacetin, and caffeine; it is used in the treatment of mild to moderately severe pain.

Oxycodone, a codeine analogue, has pharmacological properties similar to those of codeine; it bears the same chemical relationship to codeine that oxymorphone does to morphine. This drug is effective orally and, on a milligram basis, its analgesic potency, as well as its dependence liability, is greater than that of codeine. In the United States, oxycodone is available only as an ingredient in combination products. Physical dependence on Percodan has been reported; thus, this preparation should be prescribed with the same caution as other narcotics. It is classified as a Schedule III drug under the Controlled Substances Act.

Adverse reactions to Percodan are similar to those of the oral form of codeine (see the evaluation on Codeine). Precautions are the same as for other morphine-like drugs (see Chapter 21, Strong Analgesics).

USUAL DOSAGE.—

Percodan:

Oral: Adults, one tablet every six hours, preferably after meals or with milk.

Percodan-Demi:

Oral: Adults, one tablet every six hours. *Children 12 years of age and over,* one-half tablet every six hours; *6 to 12 years,* one-fourth tablet every six hours.

PREPARATIONS.—

Percodan (Endo): Each tablet contains oxycodone hydrochloride 4.5 mg, oxycodone terephthalate 0.38 mg, aspirin 224 mg, phenacetin 160 mg, and caffeine 32 mg.

Percodan-Demi (Endo): Each tablet contains oxycodone hydrochloride 2.25 mg, oxycodone terephthalate 0.19 mg, aspirin 224 mg, phenacetin 160 mg, and caffeine 32 mg.

ZACTIRIN
ZACTIRIN COMPOUND-100

These mixtures contain ethoheptazine with aspirin or APC. In view of the equivocal analgesic effectiveness of ethoheptazine alone and the lack of evidence demonstrating that these mixtures provide an analgesic effect greater than aspirin alone, the rationale for their use is highly questionable.

The adverse reactions are those of the ingredients. See the evaluations on the individual drugs.

USUAL DOSAGE.—This evaluation does not support a suggested dosage for these mixtures. The manufacturer's suggested dosage is: *Oral:*

Adults, one or two tablets of Zactirin or one tablet of Zactirin Compound-100 three or four times daily.

PREPARATIONS.—

Zactirin (Wyeth): Each tablet contains ethoheptazine citrate 75 mg and aspirin 300 mg.

Zactirin Compound-100 (Wyeth): Each tablet contains ethoheptazine citrate 100 mg, aspirin 227 mg, phenacetin 152 mg, and caffeine 32.4 mg.

Similar Mixtures

The following mixtures are complex and, on the basis of available evidence, use of a single analgesic is preferable to these combinations. See the introduction to this section.

Anexsia-D (Beecham-Massengill): Each tablet contains hydrocodone bitartrate 7 mg, phenacetin 150 mg, aspirin 230 mg, and caffeine 30 mg.

Anodynos-DHC (Otis Clapp): Each tablet contains hydrocodone bitartrate 5 mg, acetaminophen 150 mg, aspirin 227 mg, and caffeine 32.4 mg.

Nucodan (Endo): Each tablet contains oxycodone hydrochloride 4.5 mg, oxycodone terephthalate 0.38 mg, homatropine terephthalate 0.38 mg, and pentylenetetrazol 50 mg.

Percobarb (Endo): Each capsule contains oxycodone hydrochloride 4.5 mg, oxycodone terephthalate 0.38 mg, aspirin 224 mg, phenacetin 160 mg, caffeine 32 mg, hexobarbital 100 mg, and homatropine terephthalate 0.38 mg.

Percobarb-Demi (Endo): Each capsule contains oxycodone hydrochloride 2.25 mg, oxycodone terephthalate 0.19 mg, aspirin 224 mg, phenacetin 160 mg, caffeine 32 mg, hexobarbital 50 mg, and homatropine terephthalate 0.19 mg.

Synalgos-DC (Ives): Each capsule contains drocode (dihydrocodeine) bitartrate 16 mg, aspirin 180 mg, phenacetin 150 mg, promethazine hydrochloride 6.25 mg, and mephentermine sulfate 7.5 mg.

Mixtures Containing Analgesics with Sedatives

Drugs with a sedative action (sedative-hypnotics, antianxiety agents, centrally acting skeletal muscle relaxants) are components of several widely used analgesic mixtures; they allegedly enhance the analgesic effectiveness of the product, provide relief of muscle spasm, or relieve anxiety accompanying pain.

Some of the skeletal muscle relaxants are claimed to possess an inherent analgesic activity, but conclusive clinical evidence supporting this claim is lacking. In addition, it has not been definitely shown that these agents have a selective muscle-relaxing action that is separate from the sedative effect. (See Chapter 30, Centrally Acting Skeletal Muscle Relaxants.) Thus, the effect of these agents in combination with mild analgesics may not differ from that of other analgesic-sedative combinations.

On theoretical grounds, a sedative might be expected to alter a patient's reaction to pain, and a "muscle relaxing" action might be useful in patients with tension headache or certain musculoskeletal problems; however, very few properly controlled studies have been designed to define the patient population that could be expected to benefit from this type of combination or to demonstrate that the combination does, in fact, provide greater symptomatic benefit than the analgesic component administered alone. Also, since the duration of action of the sedative may differ from that of the mild analgesic, the actions of the drugs with repeated use might not coincide. If it is desirable to administer a sedative, it should be given separately as needed rather than in a fixed-dose analgesic combination.

DARVO-TRAN

There is no conclusive evidence that this combination of two analgesics and an antianxiety agent is superior to the mixture containing propoxyphene and aspirin. If a calming action is required, the sedative should be given separately as needed. Thus, the rationale for use of this mixture is questionable. See the introduction to this section and the evaluation on Darvon products in the previous section.

The adverse reactions are those of the ingredients (see the evaluations on the individual drugs).

USUAL DOSAGE.—This evaluation does not support a suggested dosage for this mixture. The manufacturer's suggested dosage is: *Oral: Adults*, one or two capsules three or four times daily.

PREPARATIONS.—Darvo-Tran (Lilly). *Oral:* Each capsule contains aspirin 150 mg, propoxyphene hydrochloride 32 mg, and phenaglycodol 150 mg.

EQUAGESIC

This is a mixture of two analgesics and an antianxiety agent. The analgesic effect of ethoheptazine is questionable, and there is no evidence that meprobamate enhances the analgesic effectiveness of aspirin. If a calming action is required, the sedative should be prescribed separately. Thus, the rationale for use of this mixture is questionable. See the introduction to this section.

The adverse reactions are those of the ingredients (see the evaluations on the individual drugs).

USUAL DOSAGE.—This evaluation does not support a suggested dosage for this mixture. The manufacturer's suggested dosage is: *Oral: Adults,* one or two tablets repeated as necessary three or four times daily.

PREPARATIONS.—Equagesic (Wyeth). *Oral:* Each tablet contains ethoheptazine citrate 75 mg, aspirin 250 mg, and meprobamate 150 mg.

FIORINAL

This mixture contains APC and a barbiturate. If a sedative action is required, the barbiturate should be prescribed separately. Thus, the rationale for use of this mixture is questionable. See the introduction to this section.

The adverse reactions are those of the ingredients (see the evaluations on the individual drugs).

USUAL DOSAGE.—This evaluation does not support a suggested dosage for this mixture. The manufacturer's suggested dosage is: *Oral: Adults,* one or two tablets or capsules, repeated as necessary up to a maximum of six per day.

PREPARATIONS.—Fiorinal (Sandoz). *Oral:* Each tablet or capsule contains aspirin 200 mg, phenacetin 130 mg, caffeine 40 mg, and butalbital 50 mg.

NORGESIC

Norgesic contains APC and a skeletal muscle relaxant. There is no convincing evidence that this mixture is more effective than aspirin alone. If a sedative action is required, this type of drug should be prescribed separately. Thus, the rationale for use of this mixture is questionable. See the introduction to this section.

The adverse reactions are those of the ingredients (see the evaluations on the individual drugs).

USUAL DOSAGE.—This evaluation does not support a suggested dosage for this mixture. The manufacturer's suggested dosage is: *Oral: Adults,* one to two tablets three or four times daily.

PREPARATIONS.—Norgesic (Riker). *Oral:* Each tablet contains aspirin 225 mg, phenacetin 160 mg, caffeine 30 mg, and orphenadrine citrate 25 mg.

PARAFON FORTE

This mixture contains acetaminophen and a skeletal muscle relaxant. Acetaminophen has no anti-inflammatory action, and there is no evidence that the analgesic effectiveness of acetaminophen is increased with the addition of chlorzoxazone. If a sedative action is required, this type of drug should be prescribed separately. Thus, the rationale for use of this preparation is highly questionable. See the introduction to this section.

The adverse reactions are those of the ingredients (see the evaluations on the individual drugs).

USUAL DOSAGE.—This evaluation does not support a suggested dosage for this mixture. The manufacturer's suggested dosage is: *Oral: Adults,* two tablets four times daily.

PREPARATIONS.—Parafon Forte (McNeil). *Oral:* Each tablet contains acetaminophen 300 mg and chlorzoxazone 250 mg.

PHENAPHEN

This mixture contains two mild analgesics, an anticholinergic, and a barbiturate. The basis for combining aspirin and phenacetin is unfounded, and the rationale for including an anticholinergic in this mixture is unproved; moreover, the amount present is insufficient to be effective. If a sedative action is required, this type of drug should be prescribed separately. This mixture is needlessly complex. See the introduction to this section.

The adverse reactions are those of ingredients (see the evaluations on the individual drugs).

USUAL DOSAGE.—This evaluation does not support a suggested dosage for this mixture. The manufacturer's suggested dosage is: *Oral: Adults,* one or two capsules every three or four hours.

PREPARATIONS.—Phenaphen (Robins). *Oral:* Each tablet or capsule contains aspirin 150 mg, phenacetin 180 mg, phenobarbital 15 mg, and hyoscyamine sulfate 0.031 mg.

SOMA COMPOUND

Soma Compound contains phenacetin, caffeine, and a skeletal muscle relaxant. Phenacetin has no anti-inflammatory activity, and there is no evidence that the analgesic effectiveness of phenacetin is increased with the addition of the other ingredients. Moreover, the amount of phenacetin in each tablet would be ineffective at the one-tablet dose level and, at best, marginally effective at the two-tablet dose level. If a sedative action is required, this type of drug should be prescribed separately. Thus, the rationale for use of this preparation is highly questionable. See the introduction to this section.

The adverse reactions are those of ingredients (see the evaluations on the individual drugs).

USUAL DOSAGE.—This evaluation does not support a suggested dosage for this mixture. The manufacturer's suggested dosage is: *Oral: Adults and children over 5 years of age*, one or two tablets four times daily; *children under 5 years*, dosage not established.

PREPARATIONS.—Soma Compound (Wallace). *Oral:* Each tablet contains phenacetin 160 mg, caffeine 32 mg, and carisoprodol 200 mg.

Similar Mixtures

The following mixtures are complex and, on the basis of available evidence, use of a single analgesic is preferred to these combinations. See the introduction to this section.

Acetabar (Philips Roxane): Each tablet contains aspirin 225 mg, phenacetin 150 mg, caffeine 15 mg, and phenobarbital 15 mg.

Algoson (McNeil): Each tablet contains acetaminophen 300 mg and butabarbital sodium 7.5 mg.

Allylgesic (Elder): Each tablet contains acetaminophen 100 mg, aluminum aspirin 100 mg, aspirin 150 mg, and allobarbital 15 mg.

Amsodyne (Elder): Each tablet contains aspirin 300 mg, caffeine 15 mg, phenobarbital 15 mg, and belladonna extract 8 mg.

Amytal and Aspirin (Lilly): Each capsule contains aspirin 325 mg and amobarbital 50 mg.

APAC (North American): Each tablet contains aspirin 226 mg, phenacetin 162 mg, caffeine 16 mg, and phenobarbital 16 mg.

Axotal (Warren-Teed): Each tablet contains aspirin 250 mg, phenacetin 120 mg, and phenobarbital 15 mg.

Bufabar (Philips Roxane): Each tablet contains aspirin 324 mg, caffeine 15 mg, butabarbital 15 mg, aluminum hydroxide, and magnesium carbonate.

Buffadyne A-S (Lemmon): Each tablet contains aspirin 300 mg, phenacetin 150 mg, caffeine 30 mg, amobarbital 15 mg, homatropine methylbromide 2.5 mg, dried aluminum hydroxide gel 75 mg, and magnesium hydroxide 45 mg.

Buffadyne with Barbiturates (Lemmon): Each tablet contains aspirin 300 mg, phenacetin 150 mg, caffeine 30 mg, secobarbital sodium 8 mg, amobarbital 8 mg, dried aluminum hydroxide gel 75 mg, and magnesium hydroxide 45 mg.

Butigetic (McNeil): Each tablet contains acetaminophen 200 mg, phenacetin 150 mg, caffeine 30 mg, and butabarbital sodium 15 mg.

Cephalgesic (Cooper): Each capsule contains aspirin 250 mg, phenacetin 50 mg, anhydrous caffeine 30 mg, and allobarbital 15 mg.

Dialog (Ciba): Each tablet contains acetaminophen 300 mg and allobarbital 15 mg.

Empiral (Burroughs Wellcome): Each tablet contains aspirin 225 mg, phenacetin 150 mg, and phenobarbital 15 mg.

G-2 (Palmedico): Each tablet contains acetaminophen 325 mg and butabarbital 16 mg.

Grillodyne (Fellows-Testagar): Each tablet contains aspirin 225 mg, phenacetin 150 mg, caffeine alkaloid 30 mg, and phenobarbital 15 mg.

Medache (Organon): Each tablet contains acetaminophen 150 mg, salicylamide 150 mg, caffeine 32 mg, and phenyltoloxamine citrate 44 mg.

Nembu-Gesic (Abbott): Each capsule contains aspirin 300 mg and pentobarbital sodium 30 mg.

P-A-C with Cyclopal (Upjohn): Each tablet contains phenacetin 150, aspirin 225 mg, caffeine 30 mg, and cyclopentenyl allylbarbituric acid 50 mg.

Percogesic (Endo): Each tablet contains acetaminophen 325 mg and phenyltoloxamine citrate 30 mg.

Salimeph-C (Kremers-Urban): Each tablet contains salicylamide 250 mg, mephenesin 250 mg, and ascorbic acid 30 mg.

Salimeph Forte (Kremers-Urban): Each tablet contains salicylamide 500 mg, mephenesin 333 mg, and ascorbic acid 50 mg.

Semaldyne (Beecham-Massengill): Each capsule contains aspirin 150 mg, phenacetin 100 mg, phenobarbital 15 mg, and hyoscyamus extract 10 mg.

Tolagesic Tablets (Smith, Miller & Patch): Each tablet contains salicylamide 300 mg and mephenesin 300 mg.

Tranco-gesic (Winthrop): Each tablet contains aspirin 300 mg and chlormezanone 100 mg.

Trancoprin (Winthrop): Each tablet contains aspirin 300 mg and chlormezanone 50 mg.

Miscellaneous Mixtures

Many other nonanalgesic drugs are ingredients of analgesic mixtures, but none of these has been shown to enhance the effectiveness of the analgesic component. Although they may be effective analgesics, these mixtures are illogical because they contain unnecessary ingredients; thus, their use is not preferable to a single analgesic. The following products are listed for information:

Acogesic (Pennwalt): Each capsule contains acetaminophen 330 mg, salicylamide 200 mg, phenyltoloxamine citrate 25 mg, amphetamine phosphate 2 mg, and methylatropine nitrate 0.5 mg.

Cafaryl (Elder): Each capsule contains salicylamide 250 mg, pyrilamine maleate 25 mg, and levamfetamine tartrate 2.5 mg.

Dextrosal (Fellows-Testagar): Each tablet contains aspirin 260 mg, phenacetin 130 mg, and amphetamine sulfate 2.5 mg.

Neocylate (Central): Each tablet contains potassium salicylate 280 mg, aminobenzoic acid 250 mg, ascorbic acid 20 mg, physostigmine salicylate 0.25 mg, and homatropine methylbromide 0.5 mg.

Pentagesic (Kremers-Urban): Each tablet contains aspirin 300 mg, salicylsalicylic acid 100 mg, salicylamide 100 mg, glyceryl guaiacolate 200 mg, and phenyltoloxamine citrate 12.5 mg.

Ponodyne (Fellows-Testagar): Each capsule contains aspirin 250 mg, phenacetin 120 mg, caffeine 30 mg, ascorbic acid 20 mg, and calcium glutamate 75 mg.

Salcedrox (Beecham-Massengill): Each tablet contains sodium salicylate 30 mg, dried aluminum hydroxide gel 120 mg, calcium ascorbate 60 mg, and calcium carbonate 60 mg.

Strascogesic (Pennwalt): Each tablet contains acetaminophen 300 mg and salicylamide 200 mg.

Synalgos (Ives): Each capsule contains aspirin 200 mg, phenacetin 250 mg, promethazine hydrochloride 6.25 mg, and mephentermine sulfate 7.5 mg.

Vio-Sal (Rowell): Each tablet contains potassium salicylate 150 mg, strontium salicylate 150 mg, and calcium salicylate 150 mg.

Chapter 23

NARCOTIC ANTAGONISTS

The available narcotic antagonists, nalorphine [Nalline], levallorphan [Lorfan], and naloxone [Narcan], are the N-allyl analogues of morphine, levorphanol [Levo-Dromoran], and oxymorphone [Numorphan], respectively. The actions of nalorphine and levallorphan are similar; however, naloxone differs from these older narcotic antagonists in that it does not possess agonist or morphine-like properties and, most importantly, has no respiratory depressant action in therapeutic doses.

These antagonists are used primarily to counteract excessive respiratory depression resulting from the administration of morphine or other drugs with a morphine-like effect (hydromorphone [Dilaudid], oxymorphone, methadone, anileridine [Leritine], alphaprodine [Nisentil], levorphanol, meperidine [Demerol], piminodine [Alvodine], fentanyl [Sublimaze]), as well as propoxyphene [Darvon]. Unlike nalorphine and levallorphan, naloxone is effective in antagonizing the action of pentazocine [Talwin]. Because it does not depress respiration, naloxone is the drug of choice in the treatment of respiratory depression of unknown cause but which is suspected of being produced by a narcotic.

When administered to patients with severe depression, the narcotic antagonists promptly increase the respiratory rate and minute volume. However, because the effect of an antagonist may be of shorter duration than that of the analgesic, depression may return as the antagonism wanes and additional doses of these agents may be required.

Administration of nalorphine or levallorphan is effective in the treatment of respiratory depression of the newborn resulting from the administration of large doses of morphine-like drugs to the mother during labor and delivery. These antagonists may be given intravenously shortly before delivery to a mother who had received large doses of morphine-like drugs to reduce or prevent the severity of respiratory depression in the newborn. However, it is preferable to use the antagonist as needed if respiratory depression is present in the infant after delivery. Experience with naloxone is too limited to assess this drug's effectiveness in preventing or treating respiratory depression in newborn infants.

Narcotic antagonists may be used postoperatively to reverse severe respiratory depression resulting from the use of narcotics. However, these antagonists also may decrease the analgesic and sedative effects of narcotics. They have been given concomitantly with various morphine-like analgesics in an attempt to prevent the respiratory depression produced by the morphine-like analgesic while retaining the analgesic effect, but there is little evidence to support this use. The antagonists also counteract most of the gastrointestinal effects of narcotics (eg, biliary spasm produced by morphine); they do not reverse the effects of narcotics on the sensorium.

Narcotic antagonists have been used for the diagnosis of possible narcotic dependence. However, since this test involves considerable risk, it is preferable to use chemical methods to detect narcotic drugs in the urine.

Adverse Reactions and Precautions

Nalorphine and levallorphan, when administered in the absence of narcotics, can themselves produce respiratory depression equal to that caused by usual analgesic doses of the strong narcotic analgesics; however, naloxone does not have this action. Since these agents are specific narcotic antagonists, they are not effective for treating depression caused by other classes of drugs (eg, barbiturates). Naloxone is the drug of choice in patients whose respiratory depression is of unknown cause but is suspected of being produced at least in part by a narcotic; a lack of response is an indication that the depression is not a result of narcotic overdose.

The narcotic antagonists are capable of precipitating a dangerous and possibly fatal withdrawal syndrome in narcotic-dependent individuals; thus, they must be administered cautiously and in small doses to such persons.

INDIVIDUAL EVALUATIONS

NALORPHINE HYDROCHLORIDE [Nalline Hydrochloride]

$N-CH_2CH=CH_2 \cdot HCl$

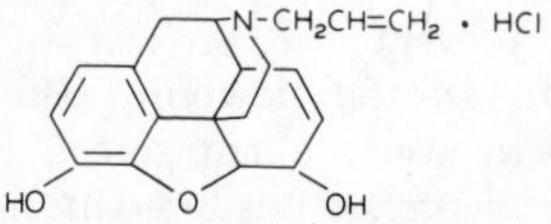

This is the prototype narcotic antagonist. It is effective in the treatment of severe respiratory depression caused by morphine or a morphine-like drug, including that in neonates caused by administration of these drugs to the mother. It also may be used for the diagnosis of possible narcotic dependence. Following subcutaneous administration of nalorphine, a definite increase in pupil size will be noted in persons who are under the influence of narcotic drugs, whereas a miotic effect is usually noted in individuals not under the influence of narcotics. Diagnostic testing should be done only by physicians experienced in performing and interpreting such tests. The development of chemical methods for detection of narcotics in urine provides a more sensitive test that may be preferable to the use of antagonists as a diagnostic procedure.

See the Introductory Statement for details of indications and adverse reactions.

USUAL DOSAGE.—

Intravenous: For treatment of respiratory depression, *adults*, 5 to 10 mg initially; *children*, 0.1 mg/kg of body weight initially. The dose may be repeated at 10- to 15-minute intervals if necessary, but no more than three doses should be given; *neonates*, 0.2 mg is injected directly into the umbilical vein and repeated at close intervals to a maximal dose of 0.5 mg. If depression is severe, up to 0.5 mg may be used initially. Respiration should be supported by mouth-to-mouth resuscitation or mechanical methods until the antagonist becomes effective. If available, oxygen should be administered.

Subcutaneous: For use in the diagnosis of narcotic dependence, consult manufacturer's literature.

PREPARATIONS.--Nalline Hydrochloride (Merck Sharp & Dohme). *Injection:* Solution 5 mg/ml (for use in *adults)* in 1, 2, and 10 ml containers; solution 0.2 mg/ml (for use in *infants)* in 1 ml containers.

LEVALLORPHAN TARTRATE [Lorfan]

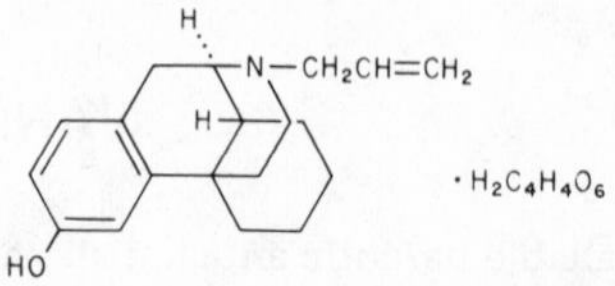

$N-CH_2CH=CH_2 \cdot H_2C_4H_4O_6$

Levallorphan is more potent than nalorphine on a milligram basis, but its actions and uses are similar to those of nalorphine. See the Introductory Statement for details of indications and adverse reactions.

USUAL DOSAGE.—*Intravenous:* For treatment of respiratory depression, *adults*, 1 to 2 mg initially; *children*, 0.02 mg/kg of body weight initially. If the initial response is not adequate, one-third or one-half of initial dose may be repeated at 10-minute intervals one to three times. The total dose generally should not exceed 3 mg; *neonates*, 0.05 to 0.1 mg is injected into the umbilical vein. Respiration should be supported by mouth-to-mouth resuscitation or mechanical methods until the antagonist becomes effective. If available, oxygen should be administered.

PREPARATIONS.—Lorfan (Roche). *Injection:* Solution 1 mg/ml in 1 and 10 ml containers.

NALOXONE [Narcan]

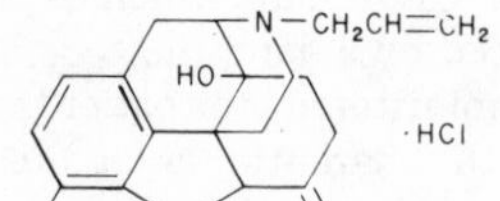

$N-CH_2CH=CH_2 \cdot HCl$

Naloxone differs from the older narcotic antagonists in that it does not possess agonist or morphine-like properties; it has no analgesic, miotic, psychotomimetic, or respiratory depressant actions. It is most useful in the treatment of respiratory depression of unknown cause but which is suspected of being produced by a narcotic. Since naloxone does not depress respiration nor affect the depression produced by barbiturates or other sedative-hypnotics, a lack of response to naloxone is an indication that the depression is not a result of narcotic overdose.

In addition to its use in the treatment of narcotic overdosage, naloxone has been used postoperatively to reverse the depressant effects of narcotics. It also reversed narcotic-induced respiratory depression when administered to a few newborn infants and it did not produce adverse effects. However, there are insufficient data on which to base a recommendation for this use. When given to mothers who had received a narcotic prior to delivery, the infants appeared to have less respiratory depression, but the data are inconclusive.

In addition to antagonizing the effects of narcotics, naloxone is an effective antagonist of depression caused by pentazocine and other antagonists. Also, results of studies in animals showed that naloxone antagonized the convulsive and lethal effects of propoxyphene, and, in man, naloxone reversed the miosis induced by propoxyphene. It might be assumed, therefore, that naloxone would be effective in treating propoxyphene overdosage.

Naloxone is more potent on a milligram basis than either nalorphine or levallorphan. Its onset of action is rapid; an effect usually is noted within two minutes after intravenous injection and only slightly longer after intramuscular or subcutaneous injection. Like other narcotic antagonists, the duration of action of naloxone may be shorter than that of some narcotics. Thus, repeated doses may be necessary to effectively treat the depression from the narcotic, but even larger doses of naloxone would not add to the existing depression. Also, like other narcotic antagonists, naloxone precipitates withdrawal symptoms in individuals dependent on morphine-like drugs; therefore, it must be administered cautiously and in small doses (0.1 mg intravenously) to these persons.

Naloxone has been notably free from adverse reactions. Tolerance or psychic or physical dependence to naloxone does not develop. The drug is not subject to narcotic controls of the Comprehensive Drug Abuse Prevention and Control Act.

USUAL DOSAGE.—*Intravenous, Intramuscular, Subcutaneous: Adults*, 0.4 mg, repeated at two- to three-minute intervals as necessary. *Children*, studies to establish children's dose have not been performed (see table, back cover).

PREPARATIONS.—Narcan (Endo). *Injection:* 0.4 mg/ml in 1 and 10 ml containers.

Chapter 24

AGENTS USED TO TREAT MIGRAINE

Two groups of agents are used to treat the migraine syndrome: those given for the symptomatic relief of pain in the acute attack, and those given prophylactically.

Changes in the intra- and extracranial blood vessels are considered to be of fundamental significance in the migraine syndrome. Ergot alkaloids, which are the most commonly used drugs in the treatment of the acute attack, are vasoconstrictors and are believed to specifically counteract the episodic dilation of certain extracranial arteries and arterioles, primarily branches of the external carotid artery. Other cranial vasoconstrictors (eg, caffeine) may alleviate the pain of migraine headache in some patients. However, the prolonged use of vasoconstrictors can also cause headaches, both during therapy and after withdrawal, possibly as a result of changes in vasomotor activity.

Ergotamine [Ergomar, Gynergen] is the most consistently effective drug for the treatment of acute attacks, and has the most prolonged effect. Relief of the headache after intramuscular administration of 0.5 mg of ergotamine is almost conclusive evidence that the headache is of vascular origin. Dihydroergotamine [D.H.E. 45] may reduce or abolish the headache without inducing nausea or vomiting; however, fewer patients respond to dihydroergotamine than to ergotamine. The other available ergot alkaloids, ergonovine [Ergotrate] and methylergonovine [Methergine], are used principally as oxytocic agents. They are only moderately effective in the treatment of the migraine syndrome and are not used routinely.

Agents that provide nonspecific symptomatic therapy for relief of acute attacks of migraine include the mild analgesics (eg, salicylates, para-aminophenol derivatives, propoxyphene [Darvon], codeine), the strong analgesics (eg, meperidine [Demerol], pentazocine [Talwin]), sedatives, and antianxiety agents. During the acute attack, the sedatives and antianxiety agents may reduce the patient's apprehension and reaction to pain, alleviate nausea and vomiting, and permit sleep. They also may be useful prophylactically to minimize the effects of stressful situations. Drugs that cause dependence and have a liability for abuse (eg, meperidine, pentazocine, codeine, barbiturates) should be avoided or given only infrequently if their use is essential. See Chapters 21, Strong Analgesics; 22, Mild Analgesics; 27, Sedatives and Hypnotics; and 28, Antianxiety Agents for information on these agents.

Methysergide [Sansert], a derivative of methylergonovine, has vasoconstrictor, oxytocic, and antiserotonin actions. It is not effective in the treatment of acute attacks of migraine syndrome, but is useful prophylactically to reduce the frequency and severity of headaches. However, its value is limited because it causes serious toxic reactions (eg, fibrosis of retroperitoneal, pleuropulmonary and cardiac tissues).

Cyproheptadine [Periactin], an antihistamine with mild to moderate antiserotonin activity, may be effective prophylactically in some patients, although recent studies indicate it is only slightly more effective than a placebo. The usual oral dose is 4 mg four times a day, but the amount may be increased to a maximum of 32 mg daily. The patient may experience dryness of the mouth, drowsiness, and stimulation of the appetite with its use. (See Chapter 45, Antihistamines.)

Results of some long-term therapeutic trials in patients with intractable migraine indicate that monoamine oxidase inhibitors may reduce the severity and decrease the frequency of attacks. Initially, 15 mg of phenelzine sulfate

[Nardil] or 10 mg of isocarboxazid [Marplan] is given orally three times daily; after 10 to 14 days the dose is reduced to a maintenance level. The mechanism of action may be related to the relief of depression or the relationship of monoamine oxidase to the release of serotonin. As with all monoamine oxidase inhibitors, paradoxical hypertension and other potentially serious adverse reactions may occur. Also, hypertensive crises in patients taking monoamine oxidase inhibitors may be precipitated by ingestion of foods and beverages with a high tyramine content (eg, cheese, yeast, meat extracts, broad beans, chicken livers, canned figs, herring, chocolate, red wine, beer, game, yogurt) and preparations containing vasopressor agents. (See Chapter 32, Antidepressants.)

The oral contraceptives have been implicated both in the onset and exacerbation of migraine headaches, as well as in the amelioration of the syndrome. (See Chapter 37, Estrogens, Progestagens, Oral Contraceptives, and Ovulatory Agents.)

A variant of the vascular-type migraine headache is now termed cluster headache (also called Horton's syndrome, histamine cephalalgia, facial migraine, and migrainous neuralgia). This headache is characterized by severe, sharp, stabbing pains that occur in clusters in a series of closely spaced attacks, usually at night. The bouts generally last 4 to 12 weeks, with intervals of weeks, months, or years between bouts. The pain of cluster headaches is periorbital or retro-orbital and usually is of short duration; associated signs are infection of the conjunctiva, lacrimation, nasal congestion, flushing of the face, and, occasionally, ptosis and miosis.

The ergot alkaloids help relieve the acute pain of cluster headaches. Adrenal corticosteroids and corticotropin (ACTH) diminish the pain of cluster headaches in some patients, although the mechanism of action is unclear. Total daily doses of 16 mg of triamcinolone [Aristocort, Kenacort] or methylprednisolone [Medrol] may temporarily interrupt the cataclysmic attacks. (See Chapter 35, Adrenal Corticosteroids, and Chapter 38, Anterior Pituitary and Hypothalamic Hormones for adverse reactions.) Ergot preparations may be needed concomitantly. Methysergide, a serotonin antagonist, is the drug of choice for prophylaxis; it is believed that serotonin plays an important role in the genesis of cluster headache.

The use of progestational agents (eg, hydroxyprogesterone [Delalutin] in doses of 500 mg intramuscularly each week for several weeks during the bout of attacks) is under investigation for patients with cluster headache who are unable to take ergot preparations. Results of studies have not been consistent.

Some patients with intractable cluster headaches have been reported to respond favorably to histamine desensitization. A solution of 3 mg of histamine phosphate in 250 ml of isotonic sodium chloride injection is given intravenously at a rate titrated to produce a flush but not a headache. The process requires 18 to 20 days of therapy. Evidence on long-term studies is insufficient to establish the efficacy of histamine desensitization. Some clinicians believe that the effectiveness of other medications may be enhanced after desensitization in those patients whose headaches return.

Adverse Reactions and Precautions

When given in large doses, the ergot alkaloids produce nausea, vomiting, epigastric discomfort, diarrhea, paresthesias of the extremities, cramps and weakness of the legs, myalgia (eg, stiffness of thigh and neck muscles), angina-like precordial pain and distress, transient sinus tachycardia and bradycardia, and, in sensitive patients, localized edema and pruritus. Severe vasoconstriction and endarteritis may occur after long-term, uninterrupted use of these agents. Gangrene of the extremities may result but is rare (1 in 10,000 patients) when the ergot alkaloids are given in recommended doses and in the absence of peripheral vascular disease and other contraindications.

Fibrotic changes in retroperitoneal, pleuropulmonary, and cardiac tissues have been noted in patients receiving long-term methysergide [Sansert] therapy. Prompt withdrawal of the drug is indicated when first signs appear (see the evaluation on Methysergide Maleate).

Ergot preparations are contraindicated in patients with peripheral vascular diseases (eg, Raynaud's disease, thromboangiitis obliterans, thrombophlebitis, marked arteriosclerosis), severe hypertension, ischemic heart disease or a history of anginal pain after exertion, peptic ulcer, renal or hepatic disease, infections, malnutrition, or a history of hypersensitivity to ergot preparations. Ergot preparations have oxytocic properties; therefore, they should not be used during pregnancy and should be used with caution in women who are at risk of becoming pregnant.

For additional adverse reactions and precautions, see the individual evaluations.

INDIVIDUAL EVALUATIONS

ERGOTAMINE TARTRATE [Ergomar, Gynergen]

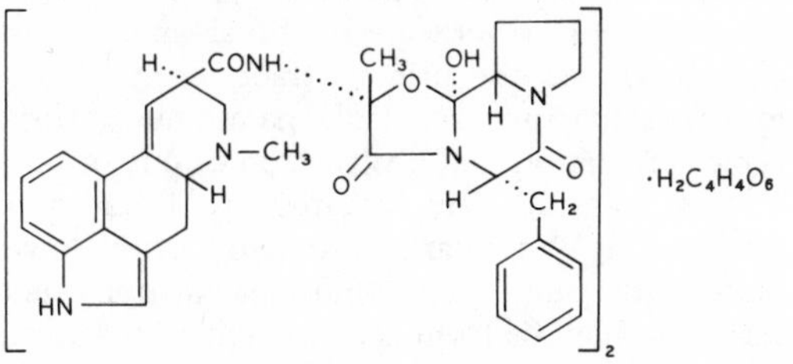

$\cdot H_2C_4H_4O_6$

Ergotamine is the drug of choice in the treatment of acute attacks of migraine headache. It must be administered soon after onset and in adequate dosage to obtain relief. The drug is most effective when given subcutaneously or intramuscularly, but may be given orally, sublingually, or by inhalation.

Daily use of ergotamine for prophylaxis is generally considered inadvisable. However, some specialists treating vascular headaches consider the likelihood of complications a remote possibility in the absence of contraindications; they prescribe ergotamine 0.3 mg four times daily or 0.6 mg twice a day orally for prophylaxis. Patients who have nocturnal attacks of cluster headaches are given 1 to 2 mg orally at bedtime for 10 to 14 days to help terminate the bout. Cyproheptadine or an adrenal corticosteroid may be given concomitantly to reduce the daily dose of ergotamine.

Some authorities believe that ergotamine, because of its vasoconstrictor action, should be given cautiously during the prodromal period in patients who have prolonged, specific neurologic phenomena (visual, sensory, motor). Others have the opposite point of view and believe the drug should not be withheld during the prodromal period because there is no evidence that ergotamine causes intracranial vasoconstriction. For adverse reactions and precautions, see the Introductory Statement.

USUAL DOSAGE.—

Subcutaneous, Intramuscular: Adults, 0.25 to 0.5 mg at start of attack. Dose may be repeated at hourly intervals. If the optimal dose to relieve a headache has been determined for an individual patient, that amount can be given at the onset. The maximal total dose in one week is 1 mg.

Sublingual: Adults, 2 mg at start of attack, followed by 2 mg every 30 minutes if necessary but not more than 6 mg in 24 hours and 12 mg in one week.

Oral: Adults, 1 to 2 mg at start of attack, followed by 1 to 2 mg every 30 minutes up to a total of 6 mg in 24 hours. The maximal dose in one week is 12 mg. *Children over 5 years of age,* 1 mg daily; the maximal daily dose is 2 mg.

Inhalation: Adults, 0.36 mg (single inhalation) at start of attack. Inhalation may be repeated at intervals of no less than five minutes up to a total of six doses in 24 hours. Overdosage should be carefully avoided. The maximal dose in one week is 12 mg.

Intravenous: Adults, 0.25 mg initially; not more than 0.5 mg should be given in 24 hours. Use of this route of administration is rarely indicated.

PREPARATIONS.—

Ergomar (Cooper). *Sublingual:* Tablets 2 mg.

Gynergen (Sandoz).

Injection: Solution 0.5 mg/ml in 0.5 and 1 ml containers.

Oral: Tablets 1 mg.

Medihaler-Ergotamine (Riker). *Inhalation:* Solution 9 mg/ml in 2.5 ml containers. Each dose (a single inhalation) contains approximately 0.36 mg of ergotamine tartrate.

DIHYDROERGOTAMINE MESYLATE [D.H.E. 45 Injection]

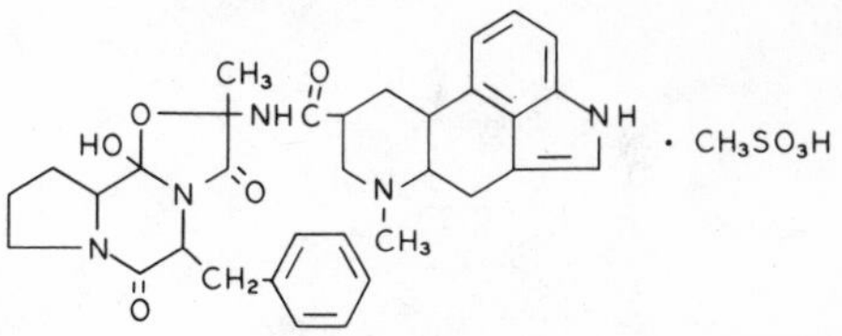

$\cdot CH_3SO_3H$

This preparation is given intramuscularly or intravenously to relieve acute migraine headache. Although the incidence of gastrointestinal reactions appears to be less than with parenteral forms of ergotamine, the effect of dihydroergotamine is less predictable.

For adverse reactions and precautions for the ergot alkaloids, see the Introductory Statement.

USUAL DOSAGE.—

Intramuscular: Adults, 1 mg at start of attack. Dose may be repeated at hourly intervals up to a total of 3 mg.

Intravenous: Adults, 1 mg for rapid effect. Dose may be repeated once after one hour. The total dosage should not exceed 2 mg.

PREPARATIONS.—D.H.E. 45 (Sandoz). *Injection:* Solution 1 mg/ml in 1 ml containers.

ERGONOVINE MALEATE [Ergotrate Maleate]
METHYLERGONOVINE MALEATE [Methergine]

These drugs are used principally as oxytocic agents (see Chapter 87, Oxytocics), and are only about one-half as effective as ergotamine in treating acute attacks of migraine. The incidence of gastrointestinal distress is lower with these drugs than with the oral form of ergotamine. They are not used routinely; however, when they give relief, they may be preferred by patients who experience gastrointestinal reactions with ergotamine.

For adverse reactions and precautions for the ergot alkaloids, see the Introductory Statement.

USUAL DOSAGE.—*Oral: Adults,* 0.2 to 0.4 mg at start of attack. The dose may be repeated every two hours to a total of not more than 1.6 mg in 24 hours. The maximal dose in one week is 12 mg.

PREPARATIONS.—

Ergonovine Maleate:

Ergotrate Maleate (Lilly). *Oral:* Tablets 0.2 mg.

Methylergonovine Maleate:

Methergine (Sandoz). *Oral:* Tablets 0.2 mg.

METHYSERGIDE MALEATE [Sansert]

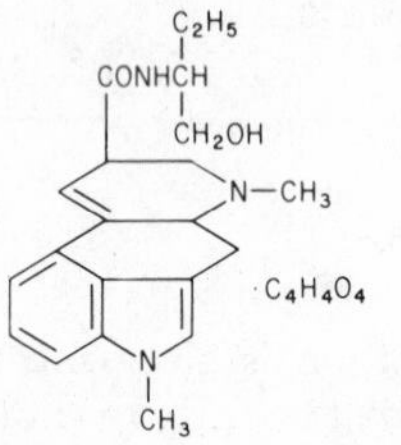

This agent is chemically related to the oxytocic ergot alkaloid derivative, methylergonovine maleate. It is effective as a prophylactic agent in the management of migraine and cluster headaches, and is indicated in patients whose vascular headaches are of sufficient frequency and severity to warrant prophylactic therapy. This drug is of no value in treating acute attacks or in preventing or treating muscle contraction (tension-type) headaches. Methysergide is a serotonin antagonist; however, its mechanism of action in the prevention of migraine syndrome is not known.

Adverse reactions associated with the use of methysergide occur frequently. Many are mild and disappear with continued use of the drug; the serious ones necessitate discontinuance of therapy.

Fibrotic changes have been observed in retroperitoneal, pleuropulmonary, and cardiac tissues. Retroperitoneal fibrosis may cause obstruction of the urinary tract. Early clinical manifestations are flank pain and dysuria; typical deviation and obstruction of one or both ureters may be demonstrated by intravenous pyelography. Vascular insufficiency of the lower limbs with pain, edema, muscular atrophy, and thrombophlebitis from involvement of the aorta, vena cava, and the common iliac vessels may also result from retroperitoneal fibrosis.

Usual signs of pleuropulmonary fibrosis are dyspnea, chest pain, pleural friction rubs, and pleural effusion. Fibrosis of the aortic and mitral valves and of the root of the aorta may also occur and are evidenced by murmurs and dyspnea.

Administration of methysergide should be discontinued if signs of retroperitoneal, pleuropulmonary, or cardiac fibrosis are noted. Partial and even complete regressions of the process may take place after the drug has been discontinued; however, surgical treatment may be necessary. Incompetent valves may have to be replaced.

Methysergide, like other ergot derivatives, has vasoconstrictor properties and may cause vascular insufficiency. Angina-like pain has been precipitated or increased. Symptoms of peripheral vascular insufficiency include cold, numb, painful extremities with or without paresthesias, and diminished or absent pulse. If these symptoms occur, the drug should be discontinued to prevent severe tissue ischemia.

Methysergide is chemically related to lysergic acid diethylamide (LSD) and may act as a central nervous system stimulant. It is not psychotomimetic in the usual dosage range. Central nervous system symptoms that occur include insomnia, nervousness, euphoria, dizziness, ataxia, rapid speech, difficulty in thinking, feeling of depersonalization, nightmares, and hallucinations. Drowsiness, lethargy, loss of initiative, and mental depression also have been reported.

Gastrointestinal reactions (eg, nausea, vomiting, diarrhea, abdominal pain) occur commonly early during the course of therapy.

Administration of methysergide to patients with peptic ulcer has caused pronounced elevations in gastric hydrochloric acid levels. Other adverse reactions include dermatitis, alopecia, peripheral and localized edema, weight gain, arthralgia, and myalgia. Neutropenia and eosinophilia have occurred rarely.

Patients should be seen frequently during therapy with methysergide, and they should be instructed to report symptoms such as chest pain, leg cramps, peripheral edema of ankles or hands, change in skin color, or paresthesias in the extremities. These symptoms can be properly evaluated by careful examination of the blood supply to the extremities, thereby avoiding dangerous sequelae. However, retroperitoneal fibrosis can develop without symptoms or positive results from laboratory studies. Therefore, it is recommended that a urogram be performed initially in all patients who respond favorably to methysergide during a short trial period and who may be candidates for long-term therapy. Urography should then be performed every 6 to 12 months for as long as the patient is taking methysergide to avoid the possible development of a disabling urinary tract disorder.

See the Introductory Statement for contraindications to ergot preparations. In addition, methysergide is contraindicated in patients with pulmonary diseases, valvular heart disease, rheumatoid arthritis and other collagen diseases, and conditions that tend to progress to fibrosis.

Methysergide should not be used continuously for more than six months without imposing a reasonable drug-free period (four to eight weeks). However, the dosage should be gradually reduced during the two to three weeks preceding discontinuation of the drug in order to avoid rebound headache.

USUAL DOSAGE.—*Oral: Adults*, 4 to 6 mg daily in divided doses, taken with food. The maximal recommended daily dose of 6 mg is smaller than the maximal daily dose suggested by the manufacturer.

PREPARATIONS.—Sansert (Sandoz). *Oral:* Tablets 2 mg.

MIXTURES

A number of mixtures containing ergotamine tartrate and one or more other agents (eg, caffeine, belladonna alkaloids, sedatives, analgesics) are available. These fixed-ratio mixtures are of limited usefulness because the dose of each ingredient cannot be individualized to suit the needs of each patient. Caffeine, which acts as a cerebral vasoconstrictor, supposedly enhances the action of ergotamine. The belladonna alkaloids and antihistamines are claimed to assist in allaying gastrointestinal adverse effects. The addition of sedatives and analgesics (phenacetin) limit the use of fixed combinations containing these ingredients, since they are most commonly used by patients with chronically recurring headaches, who are liable to abuse sedatives and analgesics. Their separate prescription is preferred.

CAFERGOT

The ingredients of this extensively prescribed mixture, ergotamine tartrate and caffeine, both act as cranial vasoconstrictors. No comparative clinical trials are available to demonstrate that addition of caffeine to an ergotamine preparation increases the clinical usefulness of the latter; however, sufficient theoretical reasons exist to suggest that the addition of caffeine may be of value in acute attacks of migraine. See the Introductory Statement for adverse reactions and precautions.

USUAL DOSAGE.—The manufacturer's suggested dose is:

Oral: Adults, two tablets at the start of an attack. An additional tablet may be taken every 30 minutes if needed, but the amount generally should be limited to a total of six tablets per attack or not more than 10 tablets per week.

Rectal: Adults, one suppository at the start of an attack. Another suppository may be used in one hour if needed; the total amount should not exceed two suppositories per attack, or not more than four suppositories per week.

PREPARATIONS.—Cafergot (Sandoz).

Oral: Each tablet contains ergotamine tartrate 1 mg and caffeine 100 mg.

Rectal: Each suppository contains ergotamine tartrate 2 mg and caffeine 100 mg.

Mixture also marketed under generic name.

Additional Mixtures

Bellergal (Sandoz): Each tablet contains ergotamine tartrate 0.3 mg, phenobarbital 20 mg, and belladonna alkaloids 0.1 mg; each timed-release tablet contains ergotamine tartrate 0.6 mg, phenobarbital 40 mg, and belladonna alkaloids 0.2 mg.

Cafergot-PB (Sandoz): Each tablet contains ergotamine tartrate 1 mg, caffeine 100 mg, belladonna alkaloids 0.125 mg, and pentobarbital sodium 30 mg; each suppository contains ergotamine tartrate 2 mg, caffeine 100 mg, belladonna alkaloids 0.25 mg, and pentobarbital sodium 60 mg.

Migral (Burroughs Wellcome): Each tablet contains ergotamine tartrate 1 mg, cyclizine hydrochloride 25 mg, and caffeine 50 mg.

Rectalad-Migraine (Wampole): Each 2 ml of solution contains ergotamine tartrate 2 mg, caffeine 25 mg, scopolamine aminoxide hydrobromide 0.4 mg, and chloral hydrate 200 mg.

Wigraine (Organon): Each suppository or tablet contains ergotamine tartrate 1 mg, caffeine 100 mg, belladonna alkaloids 0.1 mg, and phenacetin 130 mg.

Chapter 25

AGENTS USED IN GOUT

Drugs used in gout either terminate attacks of acute gouty arthritis (eg, colchicine) or decrease the uric acid content of the body (ie, uricosuric agents and allopurinol [Zyloprim]). Non-narcotic mild analgesics also may be used adjunctively to relieve the discomfort caused by urate deposits; however, salicylates should not be used with the uricosurics.

Colchicine is specific for treating acute gouty arthritis and is the drug of choice for this purpose. It is not a general purpose analgesic and has no uricosuric action. The proper therapeutic dosage usually will terminate an attack, especially if given early. Colchicine also is used prophylactically: small doses given regularly with a uricosuric agent or allopurinol during the intercritical period may prevent acute attacks and diminish the severity and facilitate treatment of those attacks that do occur.

When colchicine is not effective or is not tolerated, phenylbutazone [Azolid, Butazolidin] or oxyphenbutazone [Oxalid, Tandearil] may relieve acute gouty arthritis. Unlike colchicine, these drugs are not specific for gout. Their value is attributable principally to their nonspecific anti-inflammatory and mild analgesic actions. However, because of their toxicity, these drugs are recommended only for short-term use in acute attacks of gout and should not be used prophylactically or for the treatment of chronic gouty arthritis. Indomethacin [Indocin] also may be effective in relieving acute gouty arthritis, but it is not as effective as colchicine, phenylbutazone, or oxyphenbutazone. Indomethacin probably is somewhat safer than phenylbutazone and oxyphenbutazone.

Corticotropin (ACTH) and the adrenal corticosteroids may be used to treat an acute attack if other drugs are ineffective or are not tolerated.

Uricosuric agents (eg, probenecid [Benemid], sulfinpyrazone [Anturane]) increase the renal excretion of uric acid by decreasing its tubular reabsorption. Thus, they decrease the uric acid content of the blood and tissues and aid in preventing or reducing tophi and the joint changes that occur in chronic gouty arthritis. Uricosurics are of no value in terminating an acute attack, but they eventually reduce the frequency of attacks.

The introduction of allopurinol represents another approach in the management of gout and secondary hyperuricemia. It is a xanthine oxidase inhibitor that decreases the production of uric acid. Although its mechanism of action differs from that of the uricosurics, allopurinol also prevents or reduces the formation of urate deposits and the incidence of attacks of acute gouty arthritis. Also like the uricosurics, allopurinol will not terminate an acute attack once it has begun.

In early, uncomplicated gout, the choice of drugs is optional; probenecid, sulfinpyrazone, or allopurinol may be used. In more severe disease, the choice becomes more critical. Some patients who respond inadequately to probenecid respond satisfactorily to sulfinpyrazone or to concomitant treatment with both. Other patients may respond to allopurinol used alone or with a uricosuric. There is no reason why allopurinol may not be the first drug administered, and it is especially valuable in patients with chronic gouty arthritis complicated by renal insufficiency or uric acid renal calculi.

Uricosurics are sometimes used to treat hyperuricemia in asymptomatic members of families in which gout occurs. If the hyperuricemia is mild, there is no general agreement that treatment is warranted in the absence of other clinical manifestations of gout. There is more agreement for such treatment if the serum uric acid levels are markedly elevated (above 8.5 mg/100 ml).

Adverse Reactions and Precautions

Although the drugs used in gout differ chemically and in their mode of action, some of their adverse reactions and the precautions required with their use are similar. Those drugs used most frequently produce gastrointestinal disturbances that vary in incidence and severity. Nausea and vomiting are relatively common. Phenylbutazone [Azolid, Butazolidin], oxyphenbutazone [Oxalid, Tandearil], indomethacin [Indocin], sulfinpyrazone [Anturane], and corticotropin (ACTH) produce, reactivate, or aggravate peptic ulcers; therefore, these drugs should be avoided in patients with active disease and used cautiously in those with a history of it. Diarrhea, often severe, occurs routinely when maximal therapeutic doses of colchicine are given orally. In fact, the appearance of this reaction often is used as the end point of therapy. Diarrhea is experienced less frequently when colchicine is given intravenously, but more serious toxic reactions occur more frequently.

Rash is most common with phenylbutazone, oxyphenbutazone, allopurinol [Zyloprim], probenecid [Benemid], and sulfinpyrazone; possibly less common with indomethacin; and occurs infrequently with colchicine and corticotropin.

The individual drugs used in gout vary markedly in their potential to produce toxic or hypersensitivity reactions involving the kidneys, liver, bone marrow, cardiovascular system, and central nervous system. See the individual evaluations.

Since the uricosuric agents and allopurinol tend to precipitate attacks of acute gouty arthritis early during their administration, prophylactic doses of colchicine should be given concomitantly, especially in the treatment of primary gout. It may be possible to dispense with colchicine when treating hyperuricemia in patients who have not had attacks of acute gouty arthritis.

Salicylates cannot be used with probenecid or sulfinpyrazone because they block the uricosuric action of these drugs. Other non-narcotic mild analgesics (eg, acetaminophen) are compatible with the uricosurics and, if needed, may be substituted for the salicylates (see Chapter 22, Mild Analgesics).

The uricosuric agents decrease the excretion of some other drugs that may be used concomitantly (eg, penicillins, sulfonamides). See also the individual evaluations that follow.

To help avoid the formation of urate renal calculi, a large flow of alkaline urine should be maintained during therapy. Renal function should be assessed periodically during therapy with uricosuric agents; this also may be advisable during therapy with allopurinol.

Sensitivity to phenylbutazone, oxyphenbutazone, or sulfinpyrazone suggests cross-sensitivity to the other two agents, for they are all chemically related.

Since gout is uncommon in women of childbearing age, data on the effect of antigout regimens on the fetus are limited. Therefore, an assessment of the degree of risk is not possible; however, drugs that are toxic in adults must be suspected of being potentially hazardous to the fetus.

DRUGS FOR ACUTE GOUTY ARTHRITIS

COLCHICINE

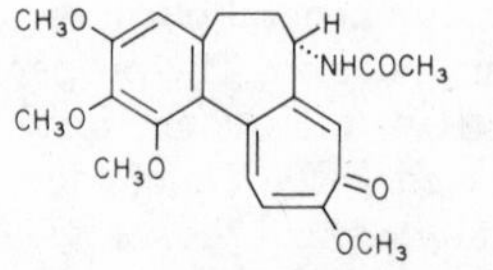

CH_3O, CH_3O, CH_3O, H, $NHCOCH_3$, =O, OCH_3

Colchicine is not a general purpose analgesic and has no uricosuric action, but it is the drug of choice for relief of the inflammation and pain of acute gouty arthritis. Oral administration should begin at the first sign of an attack and continue until symptoms subside or gastrointestinal distress appears. Using these criteria, the dosage may be terminated in 4 to 5 hours or may continue for 14 to 15 hours. It may be difficult to obtain prompt relief with nontoxic doses if there is delay in treatment or inconsistency in the dosage schedule.

Use of colchicine prophylactically during the intercritical period may prevent acute attacks or diminish their severity and facilitate their treatment. Colchicine should be used to prevent attacks of acute gouty arthritis that are precipitated during the early stages of administration of the uricosurics or allopurinol and after surgery in patients with gout. The dosage should be adjusted to provide maximal freedom from acute attacks with no adverse reactions. Patients receiving prophylactic treatment sometimes respond to small therapeutic doses, thus terminating an acute attack without unpleasant complications.

Oral use in the treatment of acute gouty arthritis frequently causes nausea, vomiting, and diarrhea, especially if maximal doses are necessary. The warning provided by this gastric intolerance tends to protect the patient from toxic doses. As soon as these symptoms occur, administration should be discontinued, irrespective of the subsidence of joint symptoms, and drugs to control vomiting and diarrhea should be given. Gastrointestinal distress is less common after intravenous administration, but this route is substantially more dangerous.

Bone marrow depression, purpura, peripheral neuritis, myopathy, anuria, alopecia, liver dysfunction, hypersensitivity reactions, and dermatoses have been reported infrequently. These reactions generally have been associated with overdosage, intravenous administration, delayed excretion caused by kidney damage, and especially with combinations of these factors.

Colchicine should be given with caution to elderly or debilitated patients and to those with renal, cardiovascular, or gastrointestinal disease.

USUAL DOSAGE.—
Oral: Adults, for an acute attack of gout, one or two 0.5 or 0.6 mg tablets are administered, followed by 0.5 or 0.6 mg hourly; alternatively, twice this amount may be given every two hours until articular symptoms subside or gastrointestinal distress occurs. If the intravenous route is used to complement oral administration, the oral form should be discontinued after about 4 mg has been given. For prophylaxis, the dosage depends upon the severity of the condition, including the frequency of acute attacks. If the disease is mild or moderate, 0.5 or 0.6 mg daily is given up to four times weekly; if the disease is severe, 0.5 or 0.6 mg is given one to four times daily.

Intravenous: Adults, for acute attacks, 1 or 2 mg initially, followed by 0.5 mg every three to six hours until a satisfactory response is achieved. The total intravenous dosage for one course of treatment generally should not exceed 4 mg. Subcutaneous extravasation may be painful.

PREPARATIONS.—Colchicine, U.S.P.
Oral: Tablets 0.5 and 0.6 mg.
Injection: Solution 0.5 mg/ml in 2 ml containers.
Drug marketed under generic name.

CORTICOTROPIN (ACTH)
ADRENAL CORTICOSTEROIDS

The antipyretic, euphoric, and anti-inflammatory actions of these agents account for their value in the treatment of attacks of acute gouty arthritis. These drugs should be used only after other drugs have been unsuccessful. They should not be used for the treatment of chronic gouty arthritis.

See Chapter 35, Adrenal Corticosteroids, and Chapter 38, Anterior Pituitary and Hypothalamic Hormones, for other uses, adverse reactions, and precautions.

USUAL DOSAGE.—
Corticotropin:
Intramuscular: Adults, for mild to moderate attacks 60 to 80 units once daily. For severe attacks, 80 to 100 units once daily.

Adrenal Corticosteroids:
The dosages vary greatly depending upon the individual preparation (see Chapter 35).

PREPARATIONS.—
Adrenal Corticosteroids: See Chapter 35.
Corticotropin: See Chapter 38.

INDOMETHACIN [Indocin]

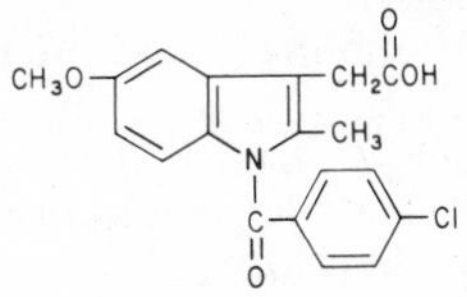

Indomethacin is not specific for gout; however, its anti-inflammatory, antipyretic, and analgesic properties make it useful in the treatment of attacks of acute gouty arthritis. Although it is prompt acting, colchicine, phenylbutazone, and oxyphenbutazone usually are preferred because of their greater effectiveness. Indomethacin should not be used for the treatment of chronic gouty arthritis.

For other uses, adverse reactions, and precautions, see Chapter 26, Antirheumatic Agents.

USUAL DOSAGE.—*Oral: Adults*, for attacks of acute gout, 50 mg three times daily until the symptoms subside. The drug should be taken with food, immediately after meals, or with antacids.

PREPARATIONS.—Indocin (Merck Sharp & Dohme). *Oral:* Capsules 25 and 50 mg.

OXYPHENBUTAZONE [Oxalid, Tandearil]

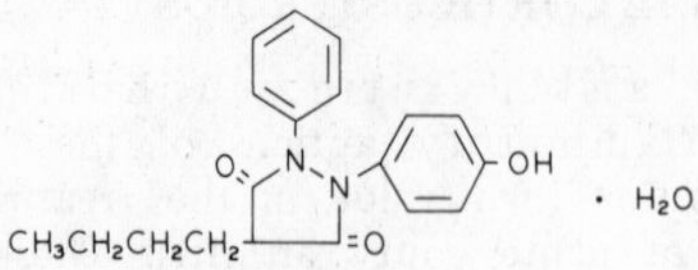

With the exception of its milder gastric irritating properties, this drug has the same mode of action, therapeutic uses, and toxicity as phenylbutazone and should be used with the same precautions (see the evaluation on Phenylbutazone and Chapter 26, Antirheumatic Agents).

USUAL DOSAGE.—*Oral: Adults,* 400 mg initially, followed by 100 mg every four hours until the inflammation subsides. Therapy should not be continued beyond three or four days.

PREPARATIONS.—Oxalid (USV), Tandearil (Geigy). *Oral:* Tablets 100 mg.

PHENYLBUTAZONE [Azolid, Butazolidin]

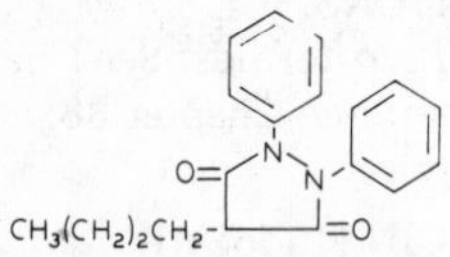

Phenylbutazone is recommended only for short-term use in the treatment of attacks of acute gouty arthritis when colchicine is not effective or is poorly tolerated. It is not specific for gout; its usefulness is attributed principally to its nonspecific anti-inflammatory and mild analgesic actions. Because of its toxicity and the availability of other drugs, phenylbutazone should not be used in the prophylaxis of gout or in the treatment of chronic gouty arthritis.

This agent is poorly tolerated by many patients. The principal adverse reactions reported are nausea, vomiting, epigastric discomfort, peptic ulcer, gastrointestinal bleeding, rash, aphthous stomatitis, aplastic anemia, leukopenia, agranulocytosis, thrombocytopenia, edema, serum sickness-like hypersensitivity reactions, hepatitis, jaundice, anuria, and hematuria. Therapy should be discontinued immediately if any of these reactions occur.

Phenylbutazone should be used with caution in the elderly; in those with renal, hepatic, or cardiovascular disease; and in those with a history or symptoms of peptic ulcer, drug allergy, or blood dyscrasia. It also should be used cautiously in patients receiving coumarin-type anticoagulants, insulin, or oral hypoglycemic agents because of the danger of potentiating the actions of these agents. The drug should not be given to patients with active peptic ulcer.

For other uses, see Chapter 26, Antirheumatic Agents.

USUAL DOSAGE.—*Oral: Adults,* 400 mg initially, followed by 100 mg every four hours until articular inflammation subsides. Therapy should not be continued beyond three or four days.

PREPARATIONS.—Azolid (USV), Butazolidin (Geigy). *Oral:* Tablets 100 mg.

DRUGS FOR CHRONIC GOUTY ARTHRITIS AND OTHER HYPERURICEMIAS

ALLOPURINOL [Zyloprim]

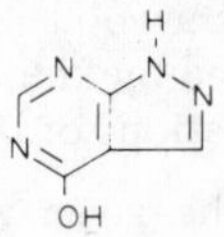

Allopurinol is considered by many to be the drug of choice for the treatment of chronic gouty arthritis and secondary hyperuricemia (eg, that resulting from therapy with antineoplastic agents or thiazide diuretics, or from psoriasis); however, it is not useful in treating attacks of acute gouty arthritis. This agent is especially valuable in patients with chronic gouty arthritis complicated by renal insufficiency or uric acid renal calculi. It acts by inhibiting xanthine oxidase, thus preventing the production of uric acid.

Adverse Reactions and Precautions.—The most common adverse reaction associated with use of allopurinol is a maculopapular rash frequently preceded by pruritus. Exfoliative, urticarial, and purpuric lesions also have been observed. The incidence of rash occurring after the administration of ampicillin is unusually high in patients receiving allopurinol concomitantly. Reactions that occur occasionally include nausea, vomiting, diarrhea, abdominal discomfort, drowsiness, headache, and a metallic taste. Fever and chills with moderate leukopenia or leukocytosis, eosinophilia, arthralgia, and pruritus, which might represent a hypersensitivity reaction, have been reported in a few patients.

Hepatic effects ranging from alterations in liver function tests (increased serum levels of alkaline phosphatase and the transaminases) to hepatitis have been reported; to date, all these effects on the liver have been reversible.

One death associated with bone marrow depression has occurred; however, the question of a causal relationship remains unanswered. Other reactions that have been reported rarely, and in which a causal relationship has not been established, include peripheral neuritis, precipitation of peptic ulcer or increase in ulcer symptoms, tachycardia, pancreatitis, pyelonephritis, increased blood urea nitrogen levels, anemia, retinopathy, and macular degeneration. Several cases of cataracts detected during therapy were thought to be drug-induced, but careful investigation has shown that there is no causal relationship.

Like the uricosurics, allopurinol often increases the frequency of attacks of acute gouty arthritis during the early stages of treatment; therefore, colchicine should be given prophylactically during initial therapy, and patients should receive appropriate treatment for acute attacks that do occur. Attacks usually diminish in number and severity after several months of therapy with allopurinol.

It is advisable to discontinue the drug promptly when a rash occurs, since the rash may become quite serious if treatment is continued after symptoms appear. It may be possible to resume its use at a lower dosage after a period of time.

Although it appears that allopurinol does not increase the storage of iron by the liver, final judgment should be reserved until more information is available. Therefore, it may be advisable to caution patients receiving this drug to refrain from unnecessary ingestion of iron preparations.

Three cases of xanthine renal calculus formation have been reported, but none of them were in individuals who were being treated for gout. Two were in children being treated for hyperuricemia-oligophrenia (Lesch-Nyhan syndrome) and the third was in an individual being treated for lymphosarcoma. As a precaution, a fluid intake sufficient to yield a daily urinary output of at least 2 liters of an alkaline urine is desirable for those using allopurinol.

Studies in animals have shown that allopurinol has no teratogenic effects. However, since there is no information on the effects of xanthine oxidase inhibition on the human fetus, the potential benefits to the patient should be weighed against the possible risk to the fetus before allopurinol is used in pregnant women or women of childbearing age.

Because allopurinol inhibits the oxidation of mercaptopurine, the dose of mercaptopurine must be reduced by 65% to 75% when both drugs are given concomitantly. Since mercaptopurine is a metabolite of azathioprine, similar precautions should be observed when using this drug.

USUAL DOSAGE.—*Oral:* For mild gout, *adults*, 200 to 400 mg daily in two or three doses. For more severe gout with tophi or renal complications, up to 1 g daily in divided doses; however, doses greater than 600 mg/day increase the incidence of toxic reactions and the effect on uric acid production usually is not much greater.

For secondary hyperuricemia, *adults*, 200 to 800 mg daily in divided doses.

For hyperuricemias, *children 6 to 10 years of age*, 100 mg three times daily; *under 6 years*, 50 mg three times daily.

PREPARATIONS.—Zyloprim (Burroughs Wellcome). *Oral:* Tablets 100 mg.

PROBENECID [Benemid]

$$HO-\overset{O}{\overset{\|}{C}}-C_6H_4-SO_2N(CH_2CH_2CH_3)_2$$

Probenecid provides satisfactory uricosuric therapy in most patients with chronic gouty arthritis, particularly in those without complications. It has no significant uricosuric activity in individuals with a glomerular filtration rate of less than 30 ml/minute. This drug is not useful in acute attacks of gouty arthritis, but it prevents or reduces the joint changes and tophi that occur in chronic gouty arthritis.

The drug is well tolerated by most patients. Nausea, headache, rash, and fever are common adverse reactions. Although serious anaphylactoid reactions, hemolytic anemia, aplastic anemia, fatal massive necrosis of the liver, and repeated episodes of a reversible nephrotic syndrome have been reported, these reactions are rare. Massive overdosage may result in convulsions and death from respiratory arrest. Gastrointestinal symptoms are less common than with sulfinpyrazone, but the drug should be used with caution in patients with a history of peptic ulcer.

Acute attacks of gout may occur, especially during the early months of therapy, and colchicine should be given concomitantly for prophylaxis during this period.

A large volume of alkaline urine should be maintained to minimize the renal deposition of urate during therapy; this is particularly important in patients with a history of renal calculi or gouty nephropathy.

Probenecid inhibits the renal transport of penicillin, aminosalicylic acid, the sulfonamides (mostly as inactive conjugates), pantothenic acid, iodopyracet and related iodinated organic acids, aminohippuric acid, phenolsulfonphthalein, sulfinpyrazone, indomethacin, and sulfobromophthalein. The dosage of these agents therefore should be modified when they are administered with probenecid.

Since salicylates diminish the effect of probenecid they should not be used concomitantly.

USUAL DOSAGE.—*Oral: Adults,* 250 mg twice daily for one week, followed by 500 mg twice daily thereafter.

PREPARATIONS.—Benemid (Merck Sharp & Dohme). *Oral:* Tablets 500 mg.

SULFINPYRAZONE [Anturane]

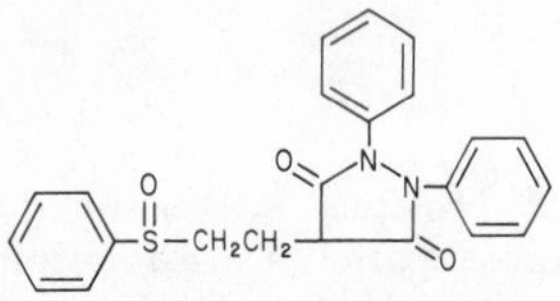

Sulfinpyrazone is the most effective uricosuric agent. However, it is less effective than allopurinol in lowering serum uric acid in complicated cases. This drug is of no value in treating an acute attack of gouty arthritis but it prevents or reduces the joint changes and tophi that occur in chronic gouty arthritis.

The most frequently reported adverse reactions are abdominal pain and nausea. Since reactivation or aggravation of peptic ulcer also has been reported, sulfinpyrazone is contraindicated in the presence of this disease and should be used cautiously in patients with a history of ulcer. Urticaria, often quite mild, is common. Anemia, leukopenia, agranulocytosis, and thrombocytopenia have occurred rarely.

Because acute attacks of gout may increase in frequency or severity during the early months of therapy, colchicine should be given concomitantly.

A large volume of alkaline urine should be maintained to minimize the renal deposition of urate during therapy; this is particularly important in patients with a history of renal calculi or gouty nephropathy. The drug should be used cautiously in patients with renal impairment.

Since sulfinpyrazone reduces the renal tubular excretion of aminohippuric acid, phenolsulfonphthalein, and salicylic acid, diagnostic procedures depending upon the measurement of these substances are invalidated by therapy with this drug. Salicylates diminish the effect of sulfinpyrazone, and therefore should not be used concomitantly.

Like phenylbutazone and oxyphenbutazone, sulfinpyrazone may potentiate the actions of insulin and oral hypoglycemic agents; therefore, it should be used with caution in patients receiving these drugs. Because of its chemical relationship to phenylbutazone and oxyphenbutazone and the similarity of some adverse effects, sulfinpyrazone should be used cautiously, if at all, in patients known to be sensitive to these drugs; however, serious reactions to this agent are less common than with the other two drugs.

USUAL DOSAGE.—*Oral: Adults,* 50 mg four times daily with meals and with milk at bedtime. The dose is gradually increased over a one-week period until a maintenance dosage (ie, the amount required to control blood urate levels) of 400 to 800 mg daily is reached. The dosage then may be reduced to the amount necessary to maintain this control.

PREPARATIONS.—Anturane (Geigy). *Oral:* Capsules 200 mg; tablets 100 mg.

MIXTURES

The following mixtures are used to treat gout; the two discussed in more detail because of their greater current use have limited usefulness because the amount of each ingredient is fixed and cannot be adjusted to meet individual requirements. None of the others are useful because one or more of their ingredients are not fully appropriate in the usual treatment of gout; they are listed only for information.

AZOLID-A
BUTAZOLIDIN ALKA

Use of this combination of phenylbutazone and two antacids is claimed to reduce the gastrointestinal irritation caused by phenylbutazone. The quantities of antacids present are not sufficient to provide adequate therapeutic dosage, assuming that antacids might be helpful in the first place.

For adverse reactions and precautions, see the evaluation on Phenylbutazone and Chapter 79, Antacids.

USUAL DOSAGE.—Dosage is based on the need for phenylbutazone (see the evaluation on Phenylbutazone).

PREPARATIONS.—Azolid-A (USV), Butazolidin Alka (Geigy). *Oral:* Each capsule contains phenylbutazone 100 mg, dried aluminum hydroxide gel 100 mg, and magnesium trisilicate 150 mg.

COLBENEMID

This mixture of probenecid and colchicine is designed to facilitate maintenance therapy in chronic gouty arthritis. The mixture is therapeutically reasonable, but its usefulness is limited because the amount of each ingredient is fixed and cannot be individualized. The usual dosage of probenecid, if given in this mixture, would provide more colchicine than needed by many patients and less than that needed by some.

For adverse reactions and precautions, see the evaluations on Colchicine and Probenecid.

USUAL DOSAGE.—Dosage is based upon the patient's requirement for the individual ingredients, provided that these have been established individually and are consistent with the ratio in this preparation. (See the evaluations on Probenecid and Colchicine.)

PREPARATIONS.—ColBenemid (Merck Sharp & Dohme). *Oral:* Each tablet contains probenecid 500 mg and colchicine 0.5 mg.

Additional Mixtures

Acetycol (Durst): Each tablet contains colchicine (salicylated) 0.25 mg, aspirin 325 mg, aminobenzoic acid 162 mg, ascorbic acid 20 mg, thiamine hydrochloride 5 mg, and niacin 15 mg.

Colsalide (North American): Each enteric-coated tablet contains colchicine 0.43 mg, sodium salicylate 320 mg, and potassium iodide 65 mg.

Pheno-Formasal (First Texas): Each capsule contains colchicine (salicylated) 130 μg, phenobarbital 48.6 mg, and aspirin 455 mg.

Salimeph-C with Colchicine (Kremers-Urban): Each tablet contains colchicine 0.25 mg, salicylamide 250 mg, mephenesin 250 mg, and ascorbic acid 30 mg.

Sodium Salicylate and Iodide with Colchicine (Lilly): Each 20 ml of solution contains colchicine 0.65 mg, sodium salicylate 1 g, and sodium iodide 1 g. [Also marketed under generic name by other manufacturers.]

Sterazolidin (Geigy): Each capsule contains phenylbutazone 50 mg, prednisone 1.25 mg, dried aluminum hydroxide gel 100 mg, and magnesium trisilicate 150 mg.

Chapter 26

ANTIRHEUMATIC AGENTS

The goals in the treatment of rheumatic diseases are to reduce pain and inflammation, maintain joint mobility, and prevent deformity. Whenever possible, the primary therapy should be directed toward correcting the underlying cause of the disorder (eg, infection, abnormal metabolism, allergy, other systemic or localized disease); however, the cause of many arthropathies is not known or is not amenable to specific treatment. Although this discussion is limited to the use of drugs, other measures (orthopedic, physiotherapeutic, psychologic, nutritional, surgical) may be of equal or greater importance in managing some rheumatic diseases, especially the later treatment essential for the restoration of lost motion and correction of deformities. The types of drugs used as antirheumatic agents are nonsteroidal anti-inflammatory drugs (eg, aspirin, phenylbutazone [Azolid, Butazolidin], oxyphenbutazone [Oxalid, Tandearil], indomethacin [Indocin]); other mild analgesics; adrenal corticosteroids; antirheumatic agents of unknown action (eg, gold salts, chloroquine [Aralen], hydroxychloroquine [Plaquenil], immunosuppresive agents); and uricosuric agents.

For additional information on drugs used to treat rheumatic diseases, see Chapters 22, Mild Analgesics; 25, Agents Used in Gout; 35, Adrenal Corticosteroids; 61, Antimalarial Agents; and 88, Antineoplastic Agents.

Drug therapy for active *rheumatoid arthritis* includes use of salicylates (eg, aspirin); these are administered to the point of toxicity, and then the dose is reduced to the maximum that can be tolerated. Aspirin is given primarily for its anti-inflammatory effect and, therefore, should be taken regularly in full therapeutic amounts as long as synovitis is present. Aspirin is also a mild analgesic. Its enzyme-inhibiting effects may enhance its therapeutic value. It relieves pain and stiffness in more than 90% of patients with low-grade disease and little disability. Objective improvement can be documented as well. A small percentage (10%) of patients fail to respond, and some patients are unable to tolerate aspirin. Other measures are needed for these patients and for those with moderately severe disease involving multiple joints that cannot be controlled adequately with aspirin. However, patients who can tolerate aspirin in anti-inflammatory doses should continue to take it even if other drugs also are required. Use of aspirin usually permits smaller doses of more toxic anti-inflammatory agents to be prescribed.

Phenylbutazone and oxyphenbutazone have analgesic and anti-inflammatory properties and are more effective than aspirin in some patients. In addition, other analgesics, sedatives, antianxiety agents, and antidepressants may increase the patient's comfort. The usefulness of the antimalarial agents, chloroquine and hydroxychloroquine, in treating rheumatoid arthritis is controversial and severely limited because of toxicity, particularly their tendency to produce irreversible retinopathy that possibly may lead to permanent blindness. The use of these drugs in children should be avoided. Chloroquine and hydroxychloroquine act slowly; significant improvement is usually noted only after three to six months of therapy, although it may continue for some time after cessation of treatment due to the drugs' slow excretion. A maximum of one year of therapy is specified by many clinicians. Most instances of ocular damage occur with more prolonged therapy, but damage can appear even after the drug is discontinued.

When one or several joints are affected, temporary relief of pain can be obtained by intra-articular injection of corticosteroids. It is possible to control synovitis from two weeks to four months, depending upon the preparation used. Joints should be rested after injections, both to enhance the effect of the corticosteroid and possibly to reduce the chance of cartilage degeneration. Splinting of the joint for two or three weeks is sometimes used to achieve maximal rest.

Other drugs used to treat moderately severe to severe rheumatoid arthritis are gold salts (aurothioglucose [Solganal], gold sodium thiomalate [Myochrysine]), systemically administered adrenal corticosteroids, and various drugs that are under clinical investigation for use in rheumatoid arthritis. These latter drugs include several immunosuppressive agents (eg, cyclophosphamide [Cytoxan], chlorambucil [Leukeran], azathioprine [Imuran]), penicillamine, histidine, dimethyl sulfoxide, radioactive gold, the anthranilates (mefenamic and flufenamic acids), and ibuprofen.

Juvenile rheumatoid arthritis (Still's disease) is more difficult to treat than the adult form because most of the anti-inflammatory drugs have special hazards when they are given to children. Aspirin in large doses is the drug of choice, but infants and young children should be observed carefully for early signs of salicylism. It may take a few days to a month to control the severe systemic manifestations of juvenile rheumatoid arthritis with aspirin. Corticosteroids should be given only to children who do not respond to salicylates. The dangers of inhibiting growth in children who already may have abnormalities of growth and development from the disease, of disturbing endocrine balance, and of decreasing resistance to infection are most significant. Gastric hemorrhage and osteoporosis are other hazards of corticosteroid therapy.

Although gold compounds do not appear to be more toxic in children, serious adverse effects limit their use to patients with rapidly progressive disease that cannot be controlled by other means. Because of reported deaths in children caused by indomethacin and antimalarial agents, and hepatitis and pancytopenia caused by phenylbutazone and oxyphenbutazone, use of these agents should be avoided in children.

In contrast to rheumatoid arthritis, *osteoarthritis* (degenerative joint disease) is not a generalized disease, but instead affects the joints only. Degeneration of articular cartilage and new bone formation are the two basic alterations observed. Drugs help to control symptoms but will not alter the course or outcome of the disease. Aspirin, taken regularly in relatively large doses, is preferred as it is safer than phenylbutazone or oxyphenbutazone. These latter drugs, however, can be very helpful for patients who cannot tolerate aspirin or who fail to respond adequately even with maximal doses. Indomethacin is quite effective in osteoarthritis of the hip, a valid indication for its use.

The value of intra-articular injections of relatively insoluble corticosteroids is controversial. Although they are considered safe and useful for relief of inflammation in a contracted joint in order to permit institution of physical therapy to restore function, there is the danger that the damaged "pain free" joint will be overused and traumatized. The subsequent development of Charcot's joints caused by inhibition of production of chondroitin sulfate by cartilage has been reported.

As in rheumatoid arthritis, aspirin is the preferred anti-inflammatory agent for *ankylosing spondylitis.* Indomethacin, phenylbutazone, or oxyphenbutazone is used when salicylates do not adequately control the disorder or are not tolerated. Systemic corticosteroids are effective as a supplement but are seldom needed.

About 5% of patients with psoriasis develop *psoriatic arthritis*, which has an insidious onset. Any peripheral joint may be affected. Spinal disease with sacroiliitis and spondylitis is not uncommon. Aspirin is the preferred anti-inflammatory agent. Antimalarial drugs are not indicated in psoriatic arthritis, because they may have an adverse effect on the skin disease. Withdrawal of systemically administered corticosteroids also may cause a severe exacerbation of cutaneous psoriasis. Because of its toxicity, use of the immunosuppressive agent, methotrexate, should be reserved for severe, progressive disease, and this agent should be administered only by physicians experienced in its vagaries.

The etiology of *Reiter's syndrome*, which affects the genitourinary, ocular, skeletal, and mucocutaneous systems, is unknown. The joint manifestations are similar to those observed in psoriatic arthritis, although the upper extremities are less frequently affected. The effective drugs are aspirin, phenylbutazone, and oxyphenbutazone. The intra-articular injection of corticosteroids may be helpful in some patients. Systemically administered corticosteroids should be given only when the disease is refractory to other agents.

Adverse reactions to the drugs administered in rheumatic diseases and the precautions necessary for their proper use are diverse. Therefore, they are discussed in the individual evaluations.

NONSTEROIDAL ANTI-INFLAMMATORY AGENTS

ASPIRIN
SODIUM SALICYLATE

Salicylates are the drugs of choice in the treatment of arthropathies. They are used primarily for their anti-inflammatory effect and must be administered to the point of maximal tolerance. All patients with active arthropathies should have an adequate trial with one of these drugs. In addition to a long history of efficacy in relieving pain and stiffness and improving routine task performance, controlled studies using objective measurements have demonstrated the benefits of salicylates. The concurrent use of a salicylate and a more toxic agent (eg, corticosteroids) may permit a reduction in the dosage of the latter agent without an exacerbation of symptoms. For additional information, see Chapter 22, Mild Analgesics.

Gastrointestinal disturbances are the most common reactions. Nausea, vomiting, and gastric distress occur in 10% of patients taking large doses of aspirin; the incidence is higher in patients with peptic ulcer. Occult bleeding occurs in about 70% of patients taking aspirin or sodium salicylate. Up to 10 ml of blood daily (usually 2 to 6 ml) is lost, and iron deficiency anemia may result. Blood loss is not lessened by the use of buffered tablets or the simultaneous ingestion of food or milk. Choline salicylate, enteric-coated sodium salicylate, and, possibly, enteric-coated aspirin may cause fewer gastrointestinal disturbances and less occult blood loss. Acute hemorrhage from gastric erosions may reflect hypersensitivity to salicylates.

Although there is an increased incidence of peptic ulcer in patients with rheumatoid arthritis, salicylates have not been proved to cause the ulcers. Nevertheless, the presence of an active ulcer is considered a relative contraindication to the use of salicylates, since ulcer healing may be impaired.

Tinnitus and hearing loss are the first and most common signs of toxicity (salicylism) in adults and are used to determine the maximal acceptable daily dose. The ototoxic effects are completely reversible even after administration of large doses for many years. However, they are not a reliable indication of toxicity in young and some elderly patients, in whom blood level determinations should be performed if symptoms suggest salicylism. In children, signs of overdosage include hyperventilation with acidosis, an increased metabolic rate, and disturbances in the metabolism of carbohydrates and lipids. The earliest symptoms may be only lethargy and episodic hyperpnea. Children's dosages should be gradually and cautiously increased and frequent measurement of the blood salicylate level is helpful.

Large doses of these drugs prolong prothrombin time, but bleeding occurs only in some patients receiving coumarin anticoagulants concomitantly or in those with severe liver disease. Aspirin may inhibit platelet aggregation, and therefore should be avoided in patients receiving heparin. The synthesis or release of certain prostaglandins may be inhibited by aspirin.

Salicylates interact with other drugs. The effects of probenecid and, possibly, indomethacin are diminished by the salicylates. Since the renal clearance of salicylates is increased by corticosteroids, toxicity may occur when corticosteroids are discontinued in patients receiving large doses of salicylates. For additional information on adverse reactions and interactions, see Chapter 22, Mild Analgesics.

USUAL DOSAGE.—*Oral, Rectal:* The dose for anti-inflammatory effect can be determined in *adults* by giving the amount that produces evidence of ototoxicity, then reducing the dose until there is only brief tinnitus and no discernible hearing loss. Blood levels will range from 15 to 40 mg/100 ml. A safe blood level to maintain in ambulatory adults, determined when the drug is at peak levels (two hours after a fasting dose), is 20 to 30 mg/100 ml. To maintain these levels, most adults require 4.5 to 7.5 g of aspirin daily. In some elderly patients, tinnitus may occur at much lower levels, and it may not be feasible to given sufficient salicylate to obtain an anti-inflammatory effect. Safe blood levels for *children* are 25 to 30 mg/100 ml. The usual daily dosage that will produce these levels is 65 mg/kg of body weight daily. Children with active disease under close supervision may receive 90 to 110 mg/kg daily.

The administration schedule must be adjusted to the patient's living habits. Taking the tablets with meals is preferred by patients who experience gastrointestinal disturbances. Milk or a small meal taken at bedtime delays absorption so that the therapeutic effect is prolonged to allay morning stiffness. Alternatively, a larger dose may be given at bedtime or enteric-coated or timed-release preparations may be used. Enteric-coated tablets, however, have a variable rate of absorption; therefore, the physician must be certain that the patient is receiving the full therapeutic effect if these preparations are used.

PREPARATIONS.—

Aspirin, U.S.P.:

Oral: Capsules 300 mg; tablets 60, 75, 150, 300, and 500 mg; tablets (enteric-coated) 300 and 600 mg; tablets (timed-release) 600 mg.

Rectal: Suppositories 60, 75, 120, 150, 200, 300, and 600 mg and 1 g.

Sodium Salicylate, U.S.P.:

Oral: Tablets (plain, enteric-coated) 300, 500, and 600 mg.

Drugs marketed by many manufacturers under generic names.

SIMILAR DRUG.—Choline Salicylate (Actasal, Arthropan [Purdue Frederick]).

OXYPHENBUTAZONE [Oxalid, Tandearil]

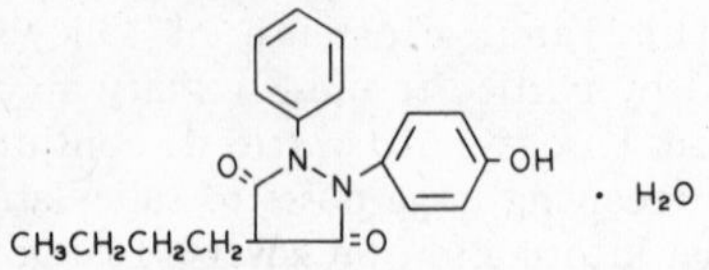

PHENYLBUTAZONE [Azolid, Butazolidin]

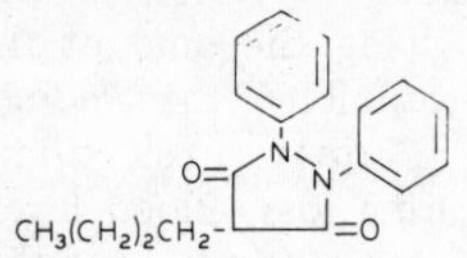

These drugs are often more effective in ankylosing spondylitis and gout than in acute rheumatoid arthritis and other arthropathies. They have anti-inflammatory, antipyretic, and analgesic properties (phenylbutazone has uricosuric properties in addition). However, their usefulness is limited by their potential toxicity. Oxyphenbutazone or phenylbutazone is used with or in place of aspirin when it is ineffective or poorly tolerated. Oxyphenbutazone is purported to produce less gastrointestinal irritation than phenylbutazone.

The most serious adverse reaction is bone marrow depression (eg, leukopenia, pancytopenia, agranulocytosis, aplastic anemia). These effects occur only rarely during a one-week trial, but blood counts, including platelet determinations, should be performed regularly during prolonged treatment. Blood counts, however, cannot always be depended upon to predict blood dyscrasia; therefore, patients who develop a fever, sore throat, or stomatitis should be advised to discontinue the drug and notify their physician immediately.

Gastrointestinal disturbances ranging from mild irritation to ulceration are commonly observed. Other adverse reactions include edema, hepatitis, dermatitis, headache, and vertigo. Susceptibility to toxic effects increases with age; phenylbutazone and oxyphenbutazone should be used only for one-week periods and in reduced dosage in elderly patients.

These drugs are contraindicated in children under 14 years of age and in senile patients; in those with gastrointestinal lesions or a history of recurrent lesions; in those with renal, hepatic, or cardiovascular disease; and in those with a history of blood dyscrasias or drug allergy. They should not be given with other drugs that cause bone marrow depression (eg, gold salts) or antimalarial agents.

Phenylbutazone and oxyphenbutazone may prolong the prothrombin time in patients receiving coumarin anticoagulants concomitantly.

See also Chapter 25, Agents Used in Gout.

USUAL DOSAGE.—*Oral: Adults,* initially, 300 to 400 mg daily in three or four equally divided doses. A one-week trial period is considered adequate to determine response. If symptoms can be controlled with a maintenance dose of 100 to 200 mg daily, the drug may be given for longer periods under careful supervision.

PREPARATIONS.—

Oxyphenbutazone:

Oxalid (USV), Tandearil (Geigy). *Oral:* Tablets 100 mg.

Phenylbutazone:

Azolid (USV), Butazolidin (Geigy). *Oral:* Tablets 100 mg.

INDOMETHACIN [Indocin]

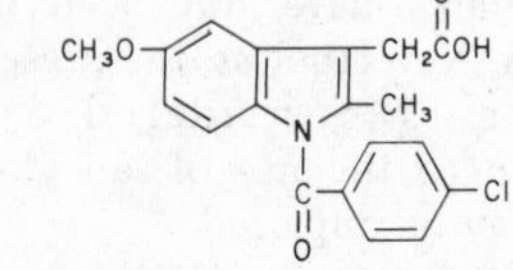

Indomethacin is a nonsteroidal anti-inflammatory compound with antipyretic and analgesic effects. Because of the high incidence of severe adverse effects, it should not be used as an antipyretic or analgesic. Indomethacin is primarily used as an anti-inflammatory agent in ankylosing spondylitis and osteoarthritis (degenerative joint disease) of the hip when salicylates are not effective or tolerated. It is also used for attacks of acute gouty arthritis (see Chapter 25, Agents Used in Gout) and for rheumatoid arthritis. Aspirin can be taken between regularly scheduled doses of indomethacin to permit the use of smaller amounts of the latter drug. If the two drugs are taken together however, aspirin may interfere with the absorption of indomethacin.

Gastrointestinal disturbances (nausea, vomiting, anorexia, indigestion, epigastric burning, stomatitis, diarrhea) have been observed in about 15% of patients. These effects may be reduced by giving the drug with food. Less common, but more significant, effects are single or multiple ulcerations of the esophagus, stomach, duodenum, or small intestine. Perforation and hemorrhage, sometimes fatal, have been reported. Occult bleeding with resultant secondary anemia may occur in the absence of an ulcer. Other gastrointestinal reactions are gastritis and perforation of pre-existing sigmoid lesions. Ulcerative colitis and regional enteritis have occurred rarely.

Central nervous system effects (headaches, usually severe in the morning; vertigo; confusion), which occur during the early weeks of therapy, also are common. If headaches persist, treatment should be discontinued. Drowsiness, confusion, coma, and behavioral disturbances such as depersonalization and depression also have been reported.

Examinations for ocular changes (eg, corneal deposits, retinal disturbances) should be performed regularly. Ototoxic reactions (deafness, tinnitus) occur rarely.

Leukopenia, hemolytic anemia, aplastic anemia, purpura, and thrombocytopenia may develop during therapy with indomethacin. Fatal cases of hepatitis and jaundice have been reported. Dermatologic and hypersensitivity reactions (pruritus, urticaria, rash, angioedema, angiitis, alopecia, acute dyspnea) also may occur.

This drug may mask signs and symptoms of infection.

Indomethacin is contraindicated in pregnant women, nursing mothers, infants, and children under 14 years of age, for safe conditions for use in these patients have not been established. The drug also is contraindicated in patients with active gastrointestinal lesions. It should be used with caution in patients with a history of recurrent gastrointestinal lesions, in the elderly, and in those who have epilepsy, parkinsonism, or emotional or psychiatric problems, since indomethacin may aggravate these conditions.

USUAL DOSAGE.—*Oral:* For ankylosing spondylitis, osteoarthritis of the hip, and rheumatoid arthritis, *adults*, initially, 25 mg two or three times daily. Some patients may respond in four to six days, while others may require up to one month. For exacerbations of chronic arthritis, the daily dose may be increased by increments of 25 mg at weekly intervals until 150 to 200 mg is reached; doses larger than 200 mg daily are not advisable. After the acute phase, the daily dose should be reduced to a maintenance level of 75 mg or less.

PREPARATIONS.—Indocin (Merck Sharp & Dohme). *Oral:* Capsules 25 and 50 mg.

ANTIMALARIAL AGENTS

CHLOROQUINE PHOSPHATE

The anti-inflammatory property of this antimalarial agent, which may derive from its ability to stabilize lysosomal membranes, makes chloroquine useful in the treatment of rheumatoid arthritis and lupus erythematosus but its usefulness is limited by its toxicity. Some patients with rheumatoid arthritis experience moderate relief of symptoms whereas others benefit little, if at all. Clinical improvement is slow: a three- to six-month trial is necessary to obtain maximal benefits. Chloroquine is most commonly used in mild, early rheumatoid arthritis and is usually given with salicylates or small doses of corticosteroids. The arthralgia, arthritis, fever, and acute maculopapular rash of systemic lupus erythematosus have been reported to respond to regimens that include systemic antimalarial agents, but well-controlled studies are lacking. The chronic mucocutaneous manifestations of discoid lupus erythematosus respond to antimalarial agents, but large doses may be required.

For other uses of chloroquine, see Chapter 61, Antimalarial Agents, and Chapter 62, Amebicides.

Ocular toxicity is the most serious complication caused by antimalarial agents. Diplopia and loss of accommodation are dose related and reversible. Blurred vision due to punctate corneal opacities may occur with prolonged treatment, but the drug deposits causing the corneal opacities disappear when chloroquine is discontinued. Serious retinal changes occur infrequently. Retinopathy often results in a progressive impairment of vision even after the drug is discontinued and blindness may result. The retinopathy appears to affect pigmentation; depigmentation starts in the area of the macula. Increased granularity and edema of the retina are the earliest findings. Late changes include narrowing of the retinal vessels, optic nerve atrophy, and diffuse depigmentation. Pigmentary changes in the skin, hair, and eyebrows may indicate the onset of retinal damage. Regular ophthalmic examinations (eg, visual fields, color testing, retinal and corneal visualizations) should be performed at three-month intervals during therapy and possibly during the year following treatment. The drug should be discontinued at the first sign of changes in the ocular fundus.

The retinopathy appears to be dose related; thus, no more than 250 mg daily should be used for the treatment of rheumatoid arthritis, although retinal damage has occurred at lower doses. If control is unsatisfactory with this dose, use of other therapy should be considered.

Other adverse reactions, which are reversible when chloroquine is discontinued, include mild headache, gastrointestinal disturbances (diarrhea, nausea, abdominal cramps), rash, and neuropsychiatric disturbances (eg, emotional changes). Acute intermittent porphyria and neuromyopathy may also occur. The skin lesions of psoriasis may be aggravated and exfoliative dermatitis has been reported; therefore, antimalarial agents are not indicated for use in patients with psoriatic arthritis. Prolonged administration may cause bluish pigmentation of the skin and mucous membranes.

Since chloroquine is known to inhibit some enzymes, patients with glucose-6-phosphate dehydrogenase deficiency should be carefully observed for hematologic abnormalities.

Chloroquine is rapidly absorbed from the gastrointestinal tract and deposited in tissues (eg, lungs, kidney, liver, eyes), where retention is prolonged, as evidenced by its urinary excretion months and even years after therapy is discontinued. Acidification of the urine increases renal excretion, as will treatment with dimercaprol (BAL). Chloroquine is contraindicated in patients with hepatic, renal, or pulmonary disease.

Small amounts of chloroquine can be fatal to children; therefore, patients should be warned to keep the drug out of their reach.

Chloroquine should not be used with gold salts, phenylbutazone, or oxyphenbutazone, as hazards of toxicity are increased.

USUAL DOSAGE.—*Oral: Adults*, a maximum of 250 mg once daily with the evening meal or at bedtime.

PREPARATIONS.—*Oral:* Tablets 250 mg. Drug marketed under generic name.

HYDROXYCHLOROQUINE SULFATE

[Plaquenil Sulfate]

This antimalarial agent has the same actions as chloroquine (see the evaluation on Chloroquine Phosphate). The adverse reactions are also similar, but some patients who develop gastrointestinal symptoms, headache, or rash when taking chloroquine may be able to tolerate hydroxychloroquine.

USUAL DOSAGE.—*Oral: Adults*, 200 mg one or two times daily with meals. If a satisfactory response cannot be maintained with this low dosage, which minimizes the possibility of retinal damage, another form of therapy should be instituted.

PREPARATIONS.—Plaquenil Sulfate (Winthrop). *Oral:* Tablets 200 mg (equivalent to 155 mg of base).

GOLD COMPOUNDS

AUROTHIOGLUCOSE [Solganal]

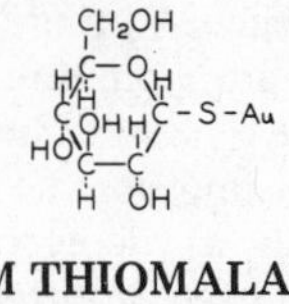

CH_2OH
C—O
H H
C OH H C—S—Au
HO
C—C
H OH

GOLD SODIUM THIOMALATE [Myochrysine]

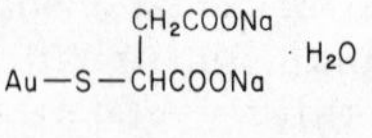

$$\begin{array}{l} \quad\quad\;\; CH_2COONa \\ \quad\quad\quad\; | \\ Au-S-CHCOONa \end{array} \cdot H_2O$$

Active rheumatoid arthritis in adults or children is the only indication for the administration of these agents. Although the exact mechanism of their action is not known, the gold compounds exert an anti-inflammatory effect in rheumatoid arthritis. They are extremely useful and should be considered in early, active rheumatoid arthritis which persists and progresses in spite of faithful adherance to a conservative program of salicylates, rest, and physical therapy over a period of approximately six months. A limited response may occur in moderately advanced disease. Gold compounds are not useful in advanced rheumatoid arthritis with long-standing synovitis and cartilage destruction, osteoarthritis (degenerative joint disease), ankylosing spondylitis, or any other inflammatory arthropathy.

The usefulness of chrysotherapy is limited by the toxicity of gold salts. Dermatitis (ranging from erythema to exfoliative dermatitis), gastrointestinal disturbances, and lesions of the mucous membranes (eg, stomatitis, proctitis, vaginitis) are common and may be serious complications; less frequently, hematologic reactions (eg, eosinophilia, leukopenia, thrombocytopenia, agranulocytosis, aplastic anemia) are observed. Effects on the kidney range from proteinuria to the nephrotic syndrome. Some fatalities have occurred.

Pruritus may signify the early development of a skin reaction. When a skin lesion whose cause is not certain appears, gold therapy must be discontinued *immediately*, for another dose may produce a much more severe skin reaction. The use of gold concomitantly with the antimalarials or the butazones is unwise, since they also tend to produce skin reactions, and thus the etiology of the reaction may be obscured.

Toxic effects may occur after the first injection, throughout the course of therapy, or several months after therapy has been discontinued. Although improvement is not related to toxicity, the incidence and severity of reactions appear to depend somewhat on dosage; severe effects are most common after 300 to 500 mg has been administered. Since the occurrence of these reactions is unpredictable, patients should be questioned about signs of toxicity (eg, rash, pruritus, stomatitis, metallic taste) prior to each injection. A complete blood count, including platelet estimation, and urinalysis should be performed before each injection. If toxicity develops, gold therapy should be discontinued immediately. Treatment with topical or systemic corticosteroids may be necessary, and chelating agents (eg, dimercaprol [BAL], penicillamine) may be used to increase the excretion of gold.

Gold salts are contraindicated in patients with impaired renal or hepatic function, blood disorders, or previous signs of gold toxicity and during pregnancy. They should not be used with antimalarial agents or phenylbutazone or oxyphenbutazone.

USUAL DOSAGE.—*Intramuscular* (gluteal): *Adults*, initially, single weekly injections of 10 mg the first week, 25 mg the second and third weeks, and 50 mg each week thereafter until a total dose of 800 mg to 1 g has been administered. If there is no response by the time 1 g is given, the drug should be discontinued. If the patient has improved and no toxic effects have developed, the dosage can be reduced to 50 mg every two weeks for four doses, every three weeks for four doses, and then monthly. A remission after one year of maintenance therapy is an indication for complete withdrawal of the drug. If a relapse occurs when the interval between doses is increased or when the drug is discontinued, the former schedule should be reinstituted. *Children*, for juvenile rheumatoid arthritis, the dose is adjusted according to weight (1 mg/kg of body weight) and this amount is administered weekly for six months and monthly thereafter as long as therapy is beneficial and there are no signs of toxicity. Single doses for *children under 12 years of age* should not exceed 25 mg.

PREPARATIONS.—

Aurothioglucose:

Solganal (Schering). *Injection:* Suspension 50 and 100 mg/ml in sesame oil with aluminum stearate 2% in 10 ml containers.

Gold Sodium Thiomalate:

Myochrysine (Merck Sharp & Dohme). *Injection:* Solution 10, 25, and 100 mg/ml in 1 ml containers and 50 mg/ml in 1 and 10 ml containers.

ADRENAL CORTICOSTEROIDS

Systemic corticosteroids usually provide distinct improvement in functional capacity with relief of pain and control of inflammation in patients with rheumatoid arthritis, although progression of joint destruction may continue. However, the usefulness of corticosteroids is limited by their numerous adverse effects. Therefore, these drugs should be reserved for patients with moderately severe, rapidly progressing rheumatoid arthritis that does not respond to other antirheumatic agents, for those threatened with severe disability or unemployability, and for those with significant systemic involvement. The minimal dosage that will improve symptoms and signs should be used; complete relief is not sought. In many patients, the corticosteroid can be withdrawn gradually. Other patients require small doses in order to perform their jobs or household duties or simply to take care of themselves.

Prednisone and prednisolone are most commonly used systemically. Other corticosteroids, preferably those with little mineralocorticoid activity, also may be administered in equivalent doses, although their greater potency may make dosage adjustment difficult. For equivalency and adverse reactions, see Chapter 35, Adrenal Corticosteroids.

Intra-articular injection of a long-acting corticosteroid is useful for temporary relief of pain when only a few joints are markedly affected. Effects last two weeks to three or four months, depending upon the preparation used. See Chapter 35, Adrenal Corticosteroids for suitable long-acting preparations and doses.

Because a joint may be traumatized if the injection permits use of the joint or weight to be borne on it without the usual pain or restriction, the patient must be instructed to limit the activity of the injected joint markedly for one to two weeks after injection. Radiologic examinations should be made before intra-articular administration and at intervals after prolonged local use. Usually, one or two injections a year for each involved joint have been suggested as conservative therapy. The two serious adverse effects that sometimes occur with this form of therapy are aseptic necrosis and infection.

USUAL DOSAGE.—

Prednisone, Prednisolone: *Oral: Adults,* initially, 3 to 4 mg daily. Dosage is increased gradually at three- to seven-day intervals to 5 to 7.5 mg daily. Daily doses should not exceed 10 mg except in severely affected patients, such as those with rheumatoid vasculitis. Even at this low dosage, adverse reactions associated with hypercortisonism may occur after prolonged use. *Children,* 1 to 5 mg daily. Alternate-day therapy, in which twice the usual daily dose is given every other morning, can be utilized to minimize growth suppression in children during long-term therapy. This dosage schedule can be followed provided satisfactory control of symptoms continues during the day on which no medication is given.

PREPARATIONS.—

Prednisone, Prednisolone:

Oral: Tablets 1, 2.5, and 5 mg.

AVAILABLE TRADEMARKS.—See Chapter 35, Adrenal Corticosteroids.

IMMUNOSUPPRESSIVE DRUGS

Because of their immunosuppressive properties, use of cytotoxic drugs in disease of undetermined etiology is becoming increasingly popular. These agents are being used experimentally in patients with rheumatoid arthritis who have progressive bone and joint deterioration despite adequate treatment with the drugs already discussed in this chapter, as well as in patients with psoriatic arthritis or systemic lupus erythematosus. The anti-inflammatory properties of these agents may play a large role in their efficacy. Cytotoxic therapy is usually nonspecific; it is not known how these drugs work in the so-called autoimmune diseases.

Most reports on the use of immunosuppressive drugs are from uncontrolled studies. However, in short-term controlled trials, cyclophosphamide [Cytoxan] and azathioprine [Imuran] have been shown to be useful in rheumatoid arthritis and systemic lupus erythematosus, and methotrexate and azathioprine have been beneficial in psoriatic arthritis. Information on the effects of these drugs after long-term use is needed, since short-term benefits may be outweighed by the increased risks which attend prolonged therapy. The use of these drugs is hazardous and they should not be used indiscriminately.

The threat of infection is the major hazard of immunosuppressive therapy; however, at the modest dose levels recommended in rheumatoid arthritis, psoriatic arthritis, and lupus erythematosus, bacterial infections, especially from gram-negative organisms, have not been a major problem. The degree to which a drug produces granulocytopenia may be an important factor. However, infections caused by viral agents and pneumocystis pneumonia, as well as the spread of mycotic and mycobacterial infections are all serious risks.

In youthful patients, the possibility of sterility is an important consideration. Ovarian suppression, premature menopause, and reversible azoospermia have been observed. Because of the mutagenic potential of immunosuppressive agents, conception should be prevented during therapy. These drugs may be teratogenic; therefore, they are contraindicated during the first trimester of pregnancy.

Malignancies have developed in patients treated with immunosuppressive agents after organ transplantation. Whether or not there will be an increase in the prevalence of neoplasia in patients with nonmalignant diseases who receive lower doses has not been determined.

For additional adverse reactions associated with cytotoxic drugs, see Chapter 88, Antineoplastic Agents.

AZATHIOPRINE [Imuran]

This purine antagonist is a derivative of

mercaptopurine. Subjective improvement, a reduction in the number of affected joints, and a corticosteroid-sparing effect have been demonstrated when the drug was given experimentally to patients with rheumatoid arthritis, systemic lupus erythematosus, and psoriatic arthritis. However, further evidence of its efficacy is needed. Azathioprine should not be used indiscriminately for arthropathies because of its toxicity. For other uses of azathioprine, see Chapter 92, Miscellaneous Drugs.

Adverse reactions include gastrointestinal effects (nausea, anorexia, vomiting, diarrhea) and reversible alterations in liver function. The bone marrow depression observed is reversible after discontinuance of the drug. Blood counts, urinalyses, and determinations of alkaline phosphatase and glutamic oxaloacetic transaminase (SGOT) levels should be performed frequently during the initial months of treatment.

USUAL DOSAGE (investigational).—*Oral: Adults*, initially, 50 mg daily. This dose is increased at weekly intervals to a maximum of 150 mg daily.

PREPARATIONS.—Imuran (Burroughs Wellcome). *Oral:* Tablets 50 mg.

CYCLOPHOSPHAMIDE [Cytoxan]

Results of short-term studies have shown that patients with rheumatoid arthritis and systemic lupus erythematosus respond to treatment with cyclophosphamide. A corticosteroid-sparing effect has been demonstrated. However, this drug is very toxic and should not be used indiscriminately for arthropathies. For other uses of cyclophosphamide, see Chapter 88, Antineoplastic Agents.

The incidence of adverse reactions has been as high as 90%. Gastrointestinal symptoms (nausea, cramping, diarrhea), bladder irritation with occasional hemorrhagic cystitis, alopecia, reversible azoospermia, and ovarian suppression have been reported. The bone marrow depression observed is almost always reversible.

USUAL DOSAGE (investigational).—*Oral: Adults*, in one proposed regimen the initial dose is 50 mg daily; this is increased by 50 mg every four weeks until clinical improvement or significant adverse effects occur. The usual maintenance dose is 50 to 100 mg daily. Blood cell counts and urinalyses should be performed weekly during initial therapy, and then monthly.

PREPARATIONS.—Cytoxan (Mead Johnson).

Oral: Tablets 25 and 50 mg.

Injection: Powder 100, 200, and 500 mg.

METHOTREXATE

Methotrexate, a folic acid antagonist, is used to treat progressively disabling psoriatic arthritis that does not respond to other forms of therapy, and it should be administered only by physicians experienced in its vagaries.

The toxicity of methotrexate is great and is usually dose related. Hepatotoxicity, which may result in acute hepatic atrophy, necrosis, fatty changes, periportal fibrosis, or cirrhosis, has occurred in patients receiving long-term therapy for psoriasis. This is particularly significant, since more than one-half of the patients with psoriasis have pre-existing liver disease. Gastrointestinal ulceration and bleeding have also occurred.

Since methotrexate is excreted mainly by the kidneys, impaired renal function may cause accumulation of toxic amounts with further renal damage.

Bone marrow depression, susceptibility to infections, genetic changes, sterility, and possible malignant changes are additional hazards. Salicylates may increase the toxicity of methotrexate, and they should not be given concurrently. See Chapter 68, Dermatologic Agents, and Chapter 88, Antineoplastic Agents for further information on adverse reactions and precautions.

USUAL DOSAGE.—Various dosage regimens are recommended by the manufacturer.

Intravenous, Intramuscular: Adults, initially, 10 to 25 mg once weekly increased until an adequate response is obtained to a maximum of 50 mg weekly.

Oral: Adults, 10 to 25 mg once weekly, increased to a maximum of 50 mg once weekly; or 2.5 mg three or four times in one 36-hour period weekly and increased to a maximum of 30 mg a week; or 2.5 mg daily for five days with at least a two-day rest period, followed by increases in dosage to a maximum of 6.25 mg daily. When optimal clinical improvement has been obtained, the dose should be reduced to the lowest effective amount with the longest possible rest period. Results of available studies suggest that toxicity is lower in patients on intermittent schedules than in those receiving daily doses.

PREPARATIONS.—

Methotrexate (Lederle). *Oral:* Tablets 2.5 mg.

Methotrexate Sodium (Lederle). *Injection:* Solution 2.5 and 25 mg/ml in 2 ml containers.

MIXTURES

Many fixed combinations of drugs are marketed for the treatment of arthritis. None represent good therapy, since individualization of dosage of antirheumatic agents is required and the doses must be altered, when necessary, for maximal effectiveness. In addition, some ingredients in the listed mixtures are not effective in the treatment of arthritis. Antacids are frequently combined with anti-inflammatory agents to reduce gastrointestinal irritation. Often the antacids present either do not provide a substantial dosage or may interfere with the absorption of the active ingredient (eg, corticosteroids).

Arthralgen (Robins): Each tablet contains acetaminophen 250 mg and salicylamide 250 mg.

Azolid-A (USV): Each capsule contains phenylbutazone 100 mg, dried aluminum hydroxide gel 100 mg, and magnesium trisilicate 150 mg.

Butazolidin Alka (Geigy): Each capsule contains phenylbutazone 100 mg, dried aluminum hydroxide gel 100 mg, and magnesium trisilicate 150 mg.

Cordex (Upjohn): Each tablet contains aspirin 300 mg and prednisolone 0.5 or 1.5 mg with or without calcium carbonate 200 mg.

Decagesic (Merck Sharp & Dohme): Each tablet contains dexamethasone 0.25 mg, aspirin 500 mg, and dried aluminum hydroxide gel 75 mg.

Delenar (Schering): Each tablet contains aluminum aspirin 300 mg, dexamethasone 0.15 mg, and orphenadrine hydrochloride 15 mg.

Medaprin (Upjohn): Each tablet contains methylprednisolone 1 mg, aspirin 300 mg, and calcium carbonate 200 mg.

Pabalate (Robins): Each enteric-coated tablet contains sodium salicylate 300 mg and aminobenzoate sodium 300 mg.

Pabalate-SF (Robins): Each enteric-coated tablet contains potassium salicylate 300 mg and aminobenzoate potassium 300 mg.

Parba-K (Elder): Each enteric-coated tablet contains aminobenzoate potassium 100 mg, potassium salicylate 150 mg, and ascorbic acid 100 mg.

Parbocyl (Elder): Each tablet contains aminobenzoic acid 260 mg, sodium ascorbate 21.5 mg, and sodium salicylate 260 mg.

Salcedrox (Beecham-Massengill): Each tablet contains sodium salicylate 325 mg, aluminum hydroxide gel 130 mg, calcium ascorbate 65 mg, and calcium carbonate 65 mg.

Sigmagen (Schering): Each tablet contains prednisone 0.75 mg, aspirin 325 mg, ascorbic acid 20 mg, and dried aluminum hydroxide gel 75 mg.

Sterazolidin (Geigy): Each capsule contains prednisone 1.25 mg, phenylbutazone 50 mg, dried aluminum hydroxide gel 100 mg, and magnesium trisilicate 150 mg.

Stero-Darvon with A.S.A. (Lilly): Each tablet contains paramethasone acetate 0.25 mg, propoxyphene hydrochloride 32 mg, and aspirin 500 mg.

Sylapar (Durst): Each enteric-coated tablet contains salicylamide 250 mg, aminobenzoate potassium 250 mg, and ascorbic acid 20 mg.

Chapter 27

SEDATIVES AND HYPNOTICS

The sedative-hypnotic agents (barbiturates and nonbarbiturates) are used to produce various degrees of central nervous system depression. With increasing dosage, this action ranges from sedation to hypnosis to respiratory depression.

When these drugs are administered during the day in small doses, they often reduce restlessness and emotional tension. The objective of such sedative therapy is to relieve anxiety without lowering sensory perception, reactivity to the environment, and alertness below safe levels. Mild sedation improves mental and psychomotor performance in anxious or inhibited individuals, and facilitates the induction of sleep in irritable or apprehensive patients. Beneficial effects are usually more evident in emotionally upset or neurotic individuals than in psychotic patients. In addition, a sedative often decreases the psychogenic component of gastrointestinal, biliary, cardiovascular, or respiratory disease, and reduces anxiety resulting from these somatic symptoms. The desirable sedative dosage is the amount that is sufficient to alleviate anxiety or tension without causing drowsiness or lethargy.

Although sedatives lack analgesic activity, they help alleviate the anxiety associated with pain or the anticipation of pain. Their central sedative action may be of adjunctive value in relieving painful muscular spasm of local origin, although their skeletal muscle relaxant activity is insignificant in comparison to that produced by neuromuscular blocking agents (eg, tubocurarine). (See Chapter 30, Centrally Acting Skeletal Muscle Relaxants.)

Since the advent of the antianxiety agents, the barbiturates are now used less frequently for daytime sedation and for the management of minor psychiatric disturbances. However, many clinicians prefer barbiturates to the newer agents for controlling the manifestations of mild to moderate anxiety, and it has not been demonstrated conclusively that the antianxiety agents are more effective than the barbiturates (see Chapter 28, Antianxiety Agents).

The most common use of the sedative-hypnotics is to treat insomnia. Many patients have chronic insomnia while other patients have insomnia that is acute but intermittent. Acute insomnia, which can occur during or after plane or train travel or when sleeping in unfamiliar environments, requires only limited treatment. In chronic insomnia, an effort should be made to discover and treat the basic causes of the disorder.

In recent years considerable data have been accumulated in sleep laboratory studies. However, the significance of the presence or absence of a given sleep stage (eg, REM [Rapid Eye Movement] sleep, stage IV sleep [deepest stage of sleep]) with the use of hypnotic doses of these agents is still unclear.

Barbiturates: The classification of barbiturates was originally based on the duration of their hypnotic effects (ie, long-, intermediate-, short-, or ultrashort-acting agents), but the distinction is not always discernible clinically in the usual sedative doses.

The "long-acting" barbiturates (eg, phenobarbital, mephobarbital [Mebaral]) are helpful in maintaining day-long sedation in anxiety-tension states and in treating some convulsive disorders (see Chapter 31, Anticonvulsants).

Barbiturates with an "intermediate" duration of action (eg, amobarbital [Amytal], butabarbital [Bubartal, Butisol], probarbital [Ipral]) or a "short" duration of action (eg, pentobarbital [Nembutal], secobarbital [Seconal]) are effective for the treatment of insomnia and for short-term daytime sedation. They are still widely used for preanesthetic sedation (see Chapter 20, Adjuncts to Anesthesia).

The "ultrashort-acting" barbiturates (eg, thiopental [Pentothal], methohexital [Brevital]) are given intravenously or, occasionally, by retention enema to induce anesthesia (see Chapter 19, General Anesthetics). They also are useful in counteracting convulsions caused by toxins (eg, tetanus) or overdosage of certain drugs (eg, systemic absorption of local anesthetics). Parenteral preparations are of value when a rapid onset of action is necessary or when oral administration is impractical. Sedative-hypnotics are usually ineffective against seizures associated with deficiency states (eg, infantile tetany, hypoparathyroidism, hypoglycemia) which require specific replacement therapy.

Amobarbital, butabarbital, pentobarbital, phenobarbital, and secobarbital are all effective as sedatives and hypnotics. On the basis of clinical experience, they can be recommended as drugs of choice. Available evidence is insufficient to compare the clinical effectiveness of the other barbiturates (aprobarbital [Alurate], mephobarbital, probarbital) with those that can be recommended as drugs of choice.

Nonbarbiturates: The nonbarbiturate sedative-hypnotics include ethchlorvynol [Placidyl], ethinamate [Valmid], flurazepam [Dalmane], glutethimide [Doriden], methaqualone [Optimil, Parest, Quaalude, Somnafac, Sopor], and methyprylon [Noludar]. These drugs generally are somewhat less potent central nervous system depressants than the barbiturates and are used in the treatment of simple insomnia or as daytime sedatives; they are sometimes useful in patients who cannot tolerate the barbiturates or do not respond to them.

The sedative-hypnotics, chloral hydrate and paraldehyde, are safe, rapidly effective, and inexpensive. Their unpleasant taste can be minimized by the use of chilled vehicles; the disagreeable physical properties of chloral hydrate also can be avoided by use of the capsule form, or of the chemical complex, chloral betaine [Beta-Chlor], or of a recently marketed derivative, triclofos [Triclos].

Several bromide salts (eg, ammonium, potassium, sodium) are available in over-the-counter preparations, but their use is deemed inadvisable because of their cumulative toxicity.

Some over-the-counter preparations that are promoted as "safe" agents to ease tension or overcome insomnia contain an antihistamine, usually methapyrilene, as their principal ingredient. However, antihistamines are not reliable remedies for insomnia and, although drowsiness may occur from taking these preparations, this effect is not uniform.

Adverse Reactions and Precautions

Untoward effects commonly observed in sensitive individuals or in those taking excessive doses of the sedative-hypnotics are drowsiness and lethargy. Residual sedation ("hangover") is common after hypnotic doses. Other reactions noted infrequently include skin eruptions (eg, urticaria, angioedema, a generalized morbilliform rash, Stevens-Johnson syndrome, discrete violaceous macules), and gastrointestinal disturbances such as nausea and vomiting. Paradoxical restlessness or excitement or exacerbation of the symptoms of certain organic brain disorders occur in some patients, especially the elderly.

Because the barbiturates and many nonbarbiturates may aggravate symptoms of acute intermittent porphyria, their use is contraindicated in patients with this disease.

Prolonged use of either barbiturates or nonbarbiturates, even in therapeutic doses, may result in psychic or physical dependence. In susceptible individuals, such dependence leads to frequent self-administration until compulsive abuse becomes an established pattern. (See the discussion on Caution in Use of "Potent" Drugs in the General Information section.)

Symptoms of chronic intoxication, which occur most commonly with short-acting barbiturates, are similar to those of acute intoxication with alcohol (eg, disorientation, ataxia, euphoria). Abrupt withdrawal is followed in two or three days by a severe withdrawal syndrome that usually is more serious than the opiate withdrawal syndrome; it may resemble status epilepticus, with grand mal convulsions, delirium, and, sometimes, coma and death. Therefore, substitution of 30 mg of phenobarbital for each 100 mg of the short-acting agent and slow withdrawal (reducing the dose by 10% every 24 hours) is essential when physical dependence is suspected. The use of nonbarbiturates for withdrawal in barbiturate-dependent patients is inadvisable. Phenobarbital also is recommended for withdrawing patients dependent on nonbarbiturate hypnotics.

Tolerance may occur when the drug or another drug given concomitantly causes the sedative to be inactivated by the liver at an accelerated rate, or when a true tolerance of the central nervous system develops. The true tolerance occurs primarily when large doses are being taken; its mechanism is unknown.

When solutions of sodium salts of the barbiturates are administered parenterally, utmost care should be taken to avoid intra-arterial injection or extravasation of these highly alkaline solutions. Accidental injection into an artery provokes intense and prolonged spastic vasoconstriction and ischemia and has caused gangrene of the extremity. When this occurs, acute excruciating pain, edema, erythema, inflammation, and obliteration of the distal pulse are rapidly evident in the affected limb.

Ambulatory patients who are receiving sedative-hypnotics should be specifically warned to avoid activities that require mental alertness, judgment, and physical coordination (eg, driving a vehicle, operating dangerous machinery).

Reducing the dosage of the short- and intermediate-acting barbiturates and the nonbarbiturates (particularly chloral hydrate) should be considered in patients with liver disease (eg, hepatitis, cirrhosis). Bronchopneumonia is a relative contraindication to the use of sedative-hypnotics, since large doses produce respiratory depression.

Routine caution should be exercised when these drugs are used during pregnancy. (See the discussion on Use of Drugs During Pregnancy in the General Information section.)

Drug Poisoning: Overdosage can cause profound shock, hypotension, tachycardia, respiratory depression, areflexia, coma, and death due to depression of the vital medullary centers.

Acute barbiturate or nonbarbiturate poisoning is usually the result of ingestion for suicidal purposes. Some cases of acute poisoning can be attributed to a state of drug-induced confusion (automatism) in which the patient forgets having taken the medication and takes more. In other instances, the additive action of these agents and other central nervous system depressants such as alcohol or opiates often results in death. The usual safeguards are to prescribe small quantities of the drug (10 to 12 hypnotic doses) and to limit the number of times the prescription may be refilled. Under federal regulations, most sedative-hypnotics are classified as Schedule III or Schedule IV agents (see the General Information section for additional information).

Good nursing care is of primary importance in treating poisoning by sedative-hypnotics and may be all that is required if the respiratory rate and depth and the blood pressure are normal, and if there is a positive response to painful stimuli.

Gastric lavage with warm physiologic sodium chloride solution is indicated only after an open airway has been secured; emetics should *not* be used in comatose patients. An adequate airway should be maintained and sufficient oxygen should be given to prevent hypoxemia.

Osmotic diuretics can significantly increase the elimination of those barbiturates that are excreted largely unchanged (eg, phenobarbital). Alkalization of the urine significantly enhances the excretion of phenobarbital. In severe poisoning, hemodialysis may be lifesaving, especially if a vigorous diuresis cannot be maintained.

The prevention of complications includes keeping the patient warm, changing the position hourly to prevent pressure sores and hypostatic pneumonia, and maintaining adequate hydration and nutrition by giving fluids parenterally.

Drug Interactions: Doses of the sedative-hypnotics must be reduced when they are given with other central nervous system depressants (eg, alcohol, antianxiety agents, strong analgesics, antihistamines). Barbiturates must be used with caution in patients receiving monoamine oxidase inhibitors (isocarboxazid [Marplan], pargyline [Eutonyl], phenelzine [Nardil], tranylcypromine [Parnate]), since these drugs may potentiate the depressant effects of the barbiturates.

Recent evidence indicates that administration of some of the sedative-hypnotics for several days increases the rate of hepatic metabolism of many drugs (eg, coumarin anticoagulants) that may be used concomitantly. Thus, adjustment in dosage of these other agents may be necessary. Cross tolerance among the sedative-hypnotic agents is common. (For additional information on drug interactions, see Chapter 9, Anticoagulants, and the section on Drug Interactions.)

BARBITURATES

PHENOBARBITAL
PHENOBARBITAL SODIUM

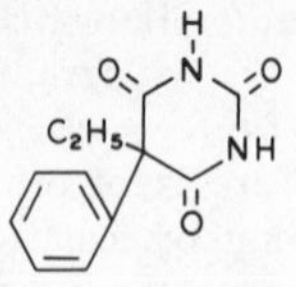

Phenobarbital is long-acting due to its slow excretion in the urine. Although it is commonly considered the prototype of the barbiturate sedative-hypnotics, phenobarbital is not superior to its analogues except for its anticonvulsant properties. It is used primarily as a daytime sedative. It also is given parenterally in status epilepticus and is of value in convulsions caused by drugs that stimulate the central nervous system (eg, conduction-type local anesthetics, atropine, pentylenetetrazol, picrotoxin, and, in children, paradoxically-acting depressants such as diphenhydramine and diphenylhydantoin). (See also Chapter 31, Anticonvulsants.)

Tolerance may occur when the drug or another drug given concomitantly causes the sedative to be inactivated by the liver at an accelerated rate, or when a true tolerance of the central nervous system develops. The true tolerance occurs primarily when large doses are being taken; its mechanism is unknown. Long-term use of larger than usual therapeutic doses may result in physical and psychic dependence. See the Introductory Statement for adverse reactions and information on the use of phenobarbital with other drugs.

USUAL DOSAGE.–

Phenobarbital:

Oral: Adults, as sedative, 30 to 120 mg daily in two or three divided doses; as hypnotic, 100 to 320 mg. *Children*, as sedative, 6 mg/kg of body weight daily in three divided doses. The timed-release preparation does not offer any significant advantage over the ordinary dosage form since phenobarbital has a prolonged half-life.

Phenobarbital Sodium:

Intramuscular, Intravenous: Adults, as hypnotic, 100 to 320 mg. *Children*, as hypnotic, 3 to 6 mg/kg of body weight. Patients should be carefully observed during intravenous injection; the rate must not exceed 100 mg (2 ml of 5% solution) per minute. Relaxation, drowsiness, yawning, and slowing of speech and motor activity usually indicate that only a small additional amount is necessary. Fifteen minutes or longer may be required before a peak concentration in the brain is attained. As sedative, same as oral dose of the base.

PREPARATIONS.–

Phenobarbital:

Oral: Capsules (timed-release) 65 and 100 mg; elixir 20 mg/5 ml; tablets 16, 32, 50, 64, and 100 mg.

Phenobarbital Sodium:

Injection: Powder 120, 130, and 320 mg; solution 130 mg/ml in 1 ml containers, 160 mg/ml in 2 and 10 ml containers.

AVAILABLE TRADEMARKS.– **Phenobarbital:** Barbipil (North American), Barbita (North American), Eskabarb (Smith Kline & French), Lixophen (Elder), Luminal (Winthrop), Solu-Barb (Fellows-Testagar), Stental (Robins). **Phenobarbital Sodium:** Luminal Sodium (Winthrop). Both forms of drug also marketed by other manufacturers under generic name.

AMOBARBITAL [Amytal]
AMOBARBITAL SODIUM [Amytal Sodium]

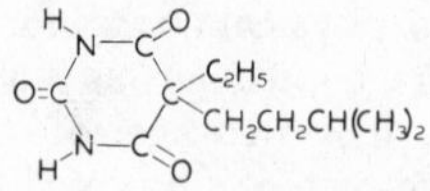

Amobarbital is an effective sedative-hypnotic. Its action is comparable to but of somewhat longer duration than that of secobarbital or pentobarbital. It is most commonly used as a hypnotic.

See the Introductory Statement for adverse reactions and information on the use of amobarbital with other drugs.

USUAL DOSAGE.–

Amobarbital:

Oral: Same as oral dosage for sodium salt.

Amobarbital Sodium:

Intramuscular: Adults, as hypnotic, 65 to 500 mg; *children*, as hypnotic, 3 to 5 mg/kg of body weight. No more than 5 ml of solution should be injected at any one site.

Intravenous (10% aqueous solution): *Adults and children over 6 years of age*, as hypnotic, 65 to 500 mg; the injection rate should not exceed 1 ml/minute. The final dosage is determined largely by the patient's reaction to slow administration.

Oral: Adults and children over 12 years of age, as sedative, 50 to 300 mg daily in divided doses; as hypnotic, 65 to 200 mg at bedtime.

Children under 12 years, as sedative, 6 mg/kg of body weight daily divided into three doses.

PREPARATIONS.—

Amytal (Lilly). *Oral:* Elixir 22 and 44 mg/5 ml; tablets 15, 30, 50, and 100 mg.

Amytal Sodium (Lilly).

Injection: Powder 65, 125, 250, and 500 mg.

Oral: Capsules 65 and 200 mg.

Both forms of drug marketed by other manufacturers under generic name.

BUTABARBITAL SODIUM [Bubartal, Butisol Sodium]

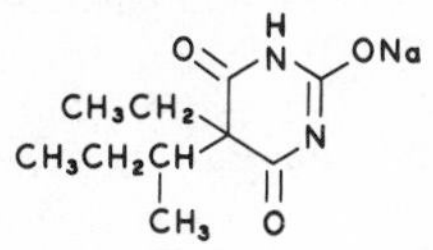

The effectiveness of butabarbital is comparable to that of pentobarbital or secobarbital but it has a longer duration of action. This drug is more commonly used for sedation than as a hypnotic agent.

See the Introductory Statement for adverse reactions and information on the use of butabarbital with other drugs.

USUAL DOSAGE.—

Intramuscular: Adults, as sedative, 90 to 120 mg daily in three or four divided doses; as hypnotic, 100 to 200 mg at bedtime. *Children*, information is inadequate to establish dosage.

Oral: Adults, as sedative, 50 to 120 mg daily in three or four divided doses; as hypnotic, 50 to 100 mg at bedtime. *Children*, as sedative, 6 mg/kg of body weight daily in three divided doses. A timed-release preparation is available, but the bioavailability of the drug in this type of dosage form may frequently be neither uniform nor reliable.

PREPARATIONS.—

Bubartal (Philips Roxane).

Injection: Solution 125 mg/ml in 10 ml containers.

Oral: Tablets (timed-release [Bubartal TT]) 60 mg.

Butisol Sodium (McNeil). *Oral:* Capsules 15, 30, 50, and 100 mg [Buticaps]; elixir 30 mg/5 ml; tablets 15, 30, 50, and 100 mg; tablets (timed-release) 30 and 60 mg.

ADDITIONAL TRADEMARKS.—BBS (Reid-Provident), Butazem (Zemmer), Intasedol (Elder). Drug also marketed by other manufacturers under generic name.

MEPHOBARBITAL [Mebaral]

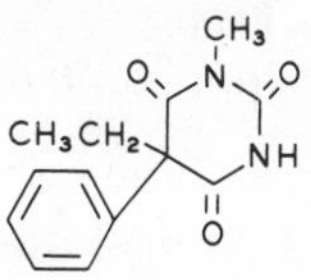

Mephobarbital is metabolized to and has effects and a duration of action similar to phenobarbital, but larger doses are required to produce comparable effects. It is used as an anticonvulsant and daytime sedative (see also Chapter 31, Anticonvulsants).

See the Introductory Statement for adverse reactions and information on the use of mephobarbital with other drugs.

USUAL DOSAGE.—*Oral: Adults*, as sedative, 96 to 400 mg daily in three or four divided doses. *Children*, as sedative, 48 to 128 mg daily in three or four divided doses.

PREPARATIONS.—Mebaral (Winthrop). *Oral:* Tablets 32, 50, 100, and 200 mg. Drug also marketed by other manufacturers under generic name.

PENTOBARBITAL [Nembutal]
PENTOBARBITAL SODIUM [Nembutal Sodium]

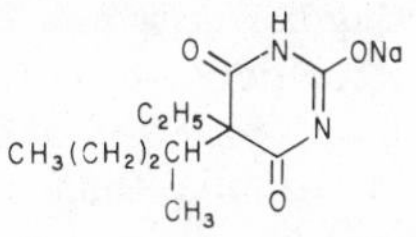

Pentobarbital is an effective, usually short-acting sedative-hypnotic. It is used more frequently for sleep induction than for sedation.

See the Introductory Statement for adverse reactions and information on the use of pentobarbital with other drugs. Pentobarbital apparently is commonly abused by drug-dependent individuals.

USUAL DOSAGE.—

Pentobarbital:

Oral: Same as oral dosage for sodium salt.

Pentobarbital Sodium:

Intramuscular: Adults, as hypnotic, 150 to 200 mg; *children*, as hypnotic, 3 to 5 mg/kg of body weight (maximum, 100 mg). No more than 250 mg or 5 ml of solution should be injected at any one site because of possible tissue irritation.

Intravenous: Adults, as hypnotic, 100 mg initially; after effect is determined (at least one minute), additional doses to a total of 500 mg may be given slowly until desired effect is obtained. *Children*, as hypnotic, 50 mg initially.

Oral, Rectal: Adults, as sedative, 100 to 200 mg daily in three divided doses; as hypnotic, 100 to 200 mg at bedtime. *Children*, as sedative, 6 mg/kg of body weight daily in three divided doses.

PREPARATIONS.—(All strengths expressed in terms of pentobarbital sodium.)

Nembutal (Abbott). *Oral:* Elixir 20 mg/5 ml.

Nembutal Sodium (Abbott).

Injection: Solution 50 mg/ml in 2, 5, 20, and 50 ml containers.

Oral: Capsules 30, 50, and 100 mg; tablets (timed-release) 100 mg.

Rectal: Suppositories 30, 60, 120, and 200 mg.

ADDITIONAL TRADEMARKS.—**Pentobarbital Sodium:** Aquabarb (Webster), Pentosol (Invenex). Drug also marketed by other manufacturers under generic name.

SECOBARBITAL [Seconal]
SECOBARBITAL SODIUM [Seconal Sodium]

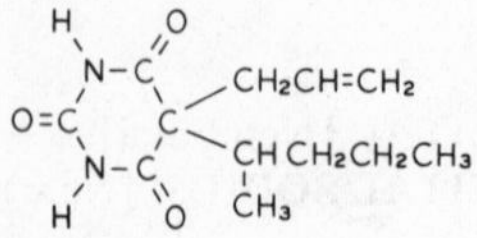

H, O, N–C, $CH_2CH{=}CH_2$, O=C, C, $CH\,CH_2CH_2CH_3$, N–C, CH_3, H, O

This short-acting barbiturate is comparable in effectiveness to pentobarbital sodium. Secobarbital is used more frequently for the treatment of insomnia than as a daytime sedative. For injection, an aqueous solution is preferred to preparations containing a polyethylene glycol vehicle; the latter may be irritating to kidneys, especially in patients with renal insufficiency.

See the Introductory Statement for adverse reactions and information on the use of secobarbital with other drugs. Secobarbital is commonly abused by drug-dependent individuals.

USUAL DOSAGE.—

Secobarbital:

Oral: Same as oral dosage for sodium salt.

Secobarbital Sodium:

Intramuscular: Adults, as hypnotic, 100 to 200 mg. *Children*, as hypnotic, 3 to 5 mg/kg of body weight (maximum, 100 mg).

Intravenous: Adults, as hypnotic, 50 to 500 mg; the injection rate should not exceed 50 mg/15 seconds. Administration should be discontinued as soon as the desired effect is attained.

Oral, Rectal: Adults, as sedative, 100 to 300 mg daily in three divided doses; as hypnotic, 100 to 200 mg at bedtime. *Children*, as sedative, 6 mg/kg of body weight daily in three divided doses.

PREPARATIONS.—

Seconal (Lilly). *Oral:* Elixir 22 mg/5 ml.

Seconal Sodium (Lilly).

Injection: Powder 250 mg; solution 50 mg/ml in 2 and 20 ml containers.

Oral: Capsules 30, 50, and 100 mg; tablets (enteric-coated) 100 mg.

Rectal: Suppositories 30, 60, 120, and 200 mg.

Drug also marketed by other manufacturers under generic name.

Additional Barbiturates

Aprobarbital (Alurate [Roche])
Barbital (Neuronidia [Schieffelin])
Probarbital Calcium (Ipral Calcium [Squibb])
Talbutal (Lotusate [Winthrop])

NONBARBITURATES

CHLORAL BETAINE [Beta-Chlor]

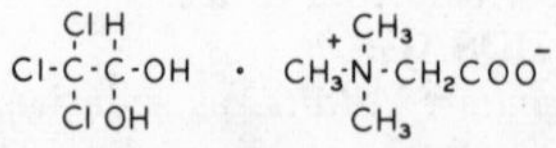

$Cl_3C\text{-}CH(OH)_2 \cdot (CH_3)_3N^+\text{-}CH_2COO^-$

This chemical complex of chloral hydrate and betaine has the same sedative properties and contraindications as chloral hydrate (see this evaluation). However, it does not exhibit the disagreeable physical properties of chloral hydrate. It appears to have no advantage over other sedative-hypnotics, except for patients who cannot tolerate these drugs.

Residual sedation following hypnotic doses occurs infrequently; rarely, sedative doses produce mild euphoria and flatulence. Long-term use of larger than usual therapeutic doses may result in psychic and physical dependence. See the Introductory Statement for information on the use of chloral betaine with other drugs.

USUAL DOSAGE.—*Oral: Adults and children over 12 years of age*, as hypnotic, 870 mg to 1.7 g given 15 to 30 minutes before bedtime; for preoperative sedation, same amounts given 60 to 90 minutes before surgery; as sedative, 870 mg three times daily with additional dose at bedtime if necessary. *Children under 12 years*, information is inadequate to establish dosage.

PREPARATIONS.—Beta-Chlor (Mead Johnson). *Oral:* Tablets 870 mg (equivalent to 500 mg chloral hydrate).

CHLORAL HYDRATE

$CCl_3CH(OH)_2$

Chloral hydrate is a relatively safe, rapidly effective, and reliable sedative-hypnotic. Its unpleasant taste and odor can be minimized by the use of chilled vehicles or of the capsule form. This drug appears to have no advantage over other sedative-hypnotics except for patients who cannot tolerate these drugs.

Gastric irritation occurs in some patients. Paradoxical excitement is rarely observed. Continued use of large doses causes peripheral vasodilation, hypotension, respiratory depression, and some myocardial depression. The dose of chloral hydrate should be reduced in patients with severe hepatic or renal disease. The dose of coumarin anticoagulants should be adjusted during concomitant administration of chloral hydrate, especially when this sedative-hypnotic is given initially or discontinued. Long-term use of larger than usual therapeutic doses may result in psychic and physical dependence. See the Introductory Statement for additional information on the use of chloral hydrate with other drugs. The drug is excreted in the urine in part as trichloroethanol glucuronide which may give false-positive results for glucose.

USUAL DOSAGE.—*Oral, Rectal: Adults,* as sedative, 250 mg three times daily after meals; as hypnotic, 500 mg to 1 g. The daily dosage should not exceed 2 g. *Children,* as sedative, 25 mg/kg of body weight daily divided into three or four doses; as hypnotic, 50 mg/kg. No more than 1 g should be given as a single dose.

PREPARATIONS.—

Oral: Capsules 250 and 500 mg and 1 g; elixir, syrup 500 mg/5 ml.

Rectal: Suppositories 500 and 650 mg and 1.3 g.

AVAILABLE TRADEMARKS.—Amylophene (First Texas), Aquachloral (Webster), En-Chlor (Ulmer), Felsules (Fellows-Testagar), Kessodrate (McKesson), Lycoral (Fellows-Testagar), Noctec (Squibb), Rectules (Fellows-Testagar), Somnos (Merck Sharp & Dohme). Drug also marketed by other manufacturers under generic name.

ETHCHLORVYNOL [Placidyl]

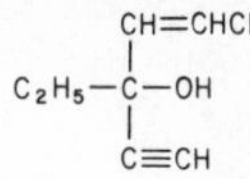

```
        CH=CHCl
        |
C2H5—C—OH
        |
        C≡CH
```

The action of this short-acting agent may be less predictable than that of the barbiturates or chloral hydrate. Ethchlorvynol is primarily used as a hypnotic agent. It appears to have no advantage over other sedative-hypnotics, except for patients who cannot tolerate these drugs.

Hypotension, nausea or vomiting, gastric upset, aftertaste, blurred vision, dizziness, facial numbness, and urticaria occasionally have been reported. Although death has occurred following ingestion of single doses of 7 to 50 g, some individuals have survived such doses. Long-term use of larger than usual therapeutic doses may result in psychic and physical dependence. See the Introductory Statement for information on the use of ethchlorvynol with other drugs.

USUAL DOSAGE.—*Oral: Adults,* as sedative, 100 mg twice daily to 200 mg three times daily; as hypnotic, 500 mg to 1 g at bedtime. *Children,* information is inadequate to establish dosage.

PREPARATIONS.—Placidyl (Abbott). *Oral:* Capsules 100, 200, 500, and 750 mg.

ETHINAMATE [Valmid]

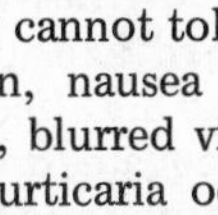

(cyclohexane ring bearing $OCONH_2$ and $C{\equiv}CH$)

Ethinamate is a weak agent with a relatively short onset and duration of action. It is used in the treatment of patients with mild insomnia. Ethinamate appears to have no advantage over other sedative-hypnotics except for patients who cannot tolerate these drugs.

Paradoxical excitement in children, mild gastrointestinal symptoms, and rash occur occasionally. Thrombocytopenic purpura and fever have been reported rarely. Long-term use of larger than usual therapeutic doses may result in psychic and physical dependence. See the Introductory Statement for information on the use of ethinamate with other drugs.

USUAL DOSAGE.—*Oral: Adults,* as hypnotic, 500 mg to 1 g at bedtime; *children,* information is inadequate to establish dosage.

PREPARATIONS.—Valmid (Lilly). *Oral:* Tablets 500 mg.

FLURAZEPAM HYDROCHLORIDE [Dalmane]

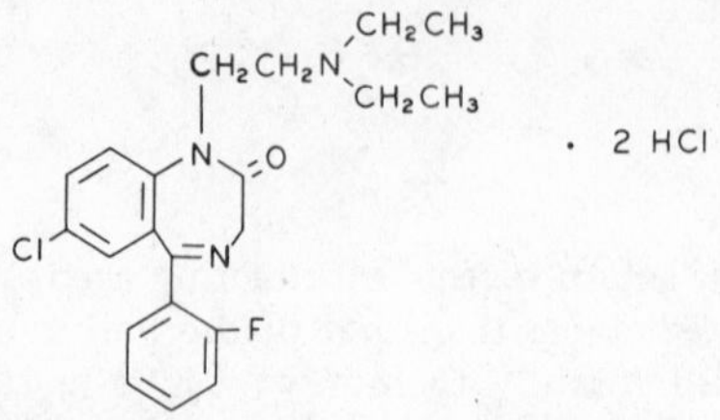

This hypnotic agent is chemically similar to other benzodiazepine derivatives (ie, clorazepate dipotassium, chlordiazepoxide, diazepam, oxazepam), which also are effective as hypnotics when given in adequate dosage. Results of well-controlled studies have shown that flurazepam significantly reduces the sleep-induction time and increases the sleep-duration time. Satisfactory hypnotic effects begin 20 to 45 minutes after oral administration and last seven to eight hours. Flurazepam appears to correct abnormal sleep patterns initially, but its usefulness over prolonged periods has not been established. This drug can be tried in patients who cannot tolerate other hypnotic agents. It is ineffective as a suicidal agent and probably does not interact with the coumarin anticoagulants.

Flurazepam markedly decreases stage IV sleep (deepest stage of sleep) but not dream (REM) time; however, the clinical significance of these results is yet to be determined.

Dizziness and ataxia have occurred, especially in elderly or debilitated patients. Nausea, vomiting, diarrhea, constipation, headache, nervousness, residual sedation, irritability, asthenia, palpitations, arthralgia, and apprehension have been observed less frequently. Paradoxical reactions (eg, excitement, euphoria, hyperactivity), hyperhidrosis, flushes, difficulty in focusing, blurred vision, hypotension, dyspnea, pruritus, rash, eosinophilia, dryness of the mouth, bitter taste, salivation, anorexia, and slurred speech have occurred rarely and were readily reversible when the dosage was reduced or the drug discontinued. Symptoms of overdosage include confusion and coma. Long-term use of larger than usual therapeutic doses may result in psychic and physical dependence. Flurazepam should be used cautiously in patients with impaired liver and kidney function. See the Introductory Statement for information on the use of flurazepam with other drugs.

USUAL DOSAGE.—*Oral: Adults*, as hypnotic, 15 to 30 mg at bedtime; *children*, information is inadequate to establish dosage.

PREPARATIONS.—Dalmane (Roche). *Oral:* Capsules 15 and 30 mg.

GLUTETHIMIDE [Doriden]

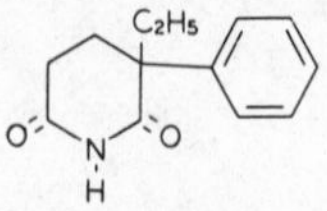

Glutethimide is an effective sedative-hypnotic. It is used more frequently for the treatment of insomnia than as a daytime sedative. Glutethimide appears to have no advantage over other sedative-hypnotics except for patients who cannot tolerate these drugs.

Glutethimide may cause generalized rash, which usually disappears within two or three days after withdrawal of the drug. Nausea, residual sedation, paradoxical excitement, blurred vision, acute hypersensitivity reactions, acute intermittent porphyria, thrombocytopenic purpura, aplastic anemia, urticaria, exfoliative dermatitis, and leukopenia have been reported rarely.

Long-term use of larger than usual therapeutic doses may result in psychic and physical dependence. Overdosage with 20 to 30 times the usual dose has caused prolonged coma, areflexia, and fever. This agent is very insoluble in water and catharsis is helpful in removing residual amounts from the intestines. Most authorities feel that peritoneal dialysis or hemodialysis is ineffective in treating overdosage. Intensive supportive therapy alone frequently yields satisfactory results.

USUAL DOSAGE.—*Oral: Adults and children over 12 years of age*, as sedative, 125 to 250 mg three times daily after meals; as hypnotic, 250 to 500 mg at bedtime; for preoperative sedation, 500 mg given the night before surgery, then 500 mg to 1 g given one hour before surgery. A total daily dosage above 1 g should be avoided. *Children under 12 years*, information is inadequate to establish dosage.

PREPARATIONS.—Doriden (USV). *Oral:* Capsules 500 mg; tablets 125, 250, and 500 mg.

METHAQUALONE [Quaalude, Sopor]
METHAQUALONE HYDROCHLORIDE [Optimil, Parest, Somnafac]

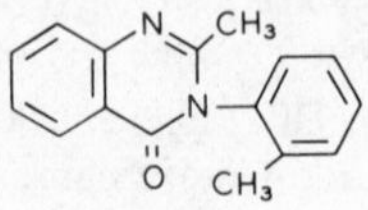

Methaqualone is an effective sedative-hypnotic but appears to have no advantage over other sedative-hypnotics, except for patients who cannot tolerate these drugs.

This agent occasionally produces minor gastric distress, nausea, headache, drowsiness, fatigue, and dryness of the mouth. Acroparesthesia (tingling and numbness in the extremities) has been observed prior to onset of the hypnotic effect, particularly when sleep has not been immediate. Long-term use of larger than usual therapeutic doses may result in psychic and physical dependence. See the Introductory Statement for information on the use of methaqualone with other drugs.

USUAL DOSAGE.--*Oral: Adults*, as sedative, 75 mg four times daily; as hypnotic, 150 to 400 mg at bedtime. *Children*, information is inadequate to establish dosage.

PREPARATIONS.—

Methaqualone:

Quaalude (Rorer). *Oral:* Tablets 150 and 300 mg.

Sopor (Arnar-Stone). *Oral:* Tablets 75, 150, and 300 mg.

Methaqualone Hydrochloride:

Optimil (Wallace), Parest (Parke, Davis), Somnafac (Smith, Miller & Patch). *Oral:* Capsules 200 and 400 mg.

METHYPRYLON [Noludar]

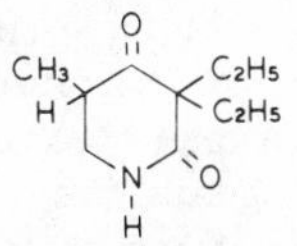

The sedative-hypnotic effect of methyprylon is approximately equivalent to that of glutethimide. Methyprylon is primarily used as a hypnotic. It appears to have no advantage over other sedative-hypnotics, except for patients who cannot tolerate these drugs.

Dizziness, mild to moderate gastrointestinal upset, headache, paradoxical excitement, and rash have been reported occasionally. Long-term use of larger than usual therapeutic doses may result in psychic and physical dependence. See the Introductory Statement for information on the use of methyprylon with other drugs.

USUAL DOSAGE.—*Oral: Adults*, as sedative, 50 to 100 mg three or four times daily; as hypnotic, 200 to 400 mg at bedtime. *Children*, as sedative, 150 to 200 mg daily divided into three or four doses; as hypnotic, a maximum of 200 mg at bedtime. Not deemed advisable for use in *children under 3 months of age.*

PREPARATIONS.—Noludar (Roche). *Oral:* Capsules 300 mg; tablets 50 and 200 mg.

PARALDEHYDE

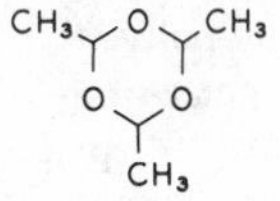

Paraldehyde is a rapidly effective sedative-hypnotic. It is used primarily in the treatment of alcohol withdrawal symptoms; however, some chronic alcoholics and drug abusers develop a liking for its psychic effects. Long-term use of larger than usual therapeutic doses may result in psychic and physical dependence.

Oral administration is the preferred route, but gastric irritation may occur. Intragluteal injection is often irritating but is reasonably safe. Intravenous administration is used only in emergency situations. Only fresh preparations should be administered. Paraldehyde reacts with plastic equipment.

Although the drug is primarily metabolized by the liver, a small portion is excreted through the lungs, which accounts for the characteristic pungent odor of the patient's breath. The sedative effect may be intensified and prolonged in the presence of severe liver damage.

USUAL DOSAGE.—

Intramuscular: Adults, as sedative, 5 ml; as hypnotic, 10 ml. *Children*, as sedative, 0.15 ml/kg of body weight; as hypnotic, 0.3 ml/kg.

Oral, Rectal: Adults, as sedative, 3 to 8 ml; as hypnotic, 10 to 30 ml. *Children*, as sedative, 0.15 ml/kg of body weight; as hypnotic, 0.3 ml/kg. Paraldehyde must be diluted with an equal or double amount of vegetable oil (eg, olive oil) for rectal administration.

PREPARATIONS.—

Injection: Liquid 1 g/ml in 2, 5, 10, 15, and 30 ml containers.

Oral: Capsules 1 g (equivalent to 1 ml); liquid in 15 and 30 ml containers.

Rectal: Liquid in 30 ml containers.

AVAILABLE TRADEMARK.--Paral (Fellows-Testagar). Drug also marketed by other manufacturers under generic name.

TRICLOFOS SODIUM [Triclos]

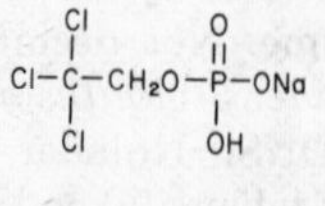

$$Cl_3C{-}CH_2O{-}P(=O)(OH){-}ONa$$

This hypnotic agent has the same properties, adverse reactions, and contraindications as chloral hydrate (see this evaluation). However, it does not exhibit the disagreeable physical properties of chloral hydrate. Triclofos is metabolized prinicipally to trichloroethanol which is also the active metabolite obtained from chloral hydrate. A peak serum level of trichloroethanol is produced in about 1 hour and its half-life is approximately 11 hours. Triclofos appears to have no advantage over other sedative-hypnotics, except for patients who cannot tolerate these drugs.

Residual sedation, flatulence, gastric irritation, nausea, vomiting, ataxia, vertigo, lightheadedness, nightmares, and malaise occur infrequently. Long-term use of larger than usual therapeutic doses may result in psychic and physical dependence. See the Introductory Statement for information on the use of triclofos with other drugs.

USUAL DOSAGE.—*Oral: Adults and children over 12 years of age*, 1.5 g given 15 to 30 minutes before bedtime; *under 12 years*, for sleep induction in electroencephalography, 20 mg/kg of body weight.

PREPARATIONS.—Triclos (Lakeside). *Oral:* Solution 500 mg/5 ml; tablets 750 mg.

BROMIDES

Sodium and potassium are the most commonly used bromide salts in sedative-hypnotic mixtures, but ammonium, calcium, lithium, and magnesium bromides have also been used. The bromides exhibit moderate sedative activity only when used over a period of time; they are useless as hypnotics. Since bromides accumulate in the body and can cause severe drug-induced psychoses, their use is deemed inadvisable.

Skin eruptions (eg, acneiform or generalized morbilliform rash, Stevens-Johnson syndrome) may occur. Treatment of chronic bromide intoxication (bromism) usually consists of supplementing the daily diet with up to 200 mEq of sodium chloride or ammonium chloride. Chloruretics also are useful in treating bromism. The biological half-life of the bromide is thus decreased.

USUAL DOSAGE.—Use of bromide preparations is deemed inadvisable because of the reasons stated above. The manufacturers' suggested dosage is: *Oral: Adults*, for sedation, initially, 1 to 1.5 g three times daily; for maintenance, 250 mg three times daily.

PREPARATIONS.—*Oral:* Elixir, tablets. Bromide salts marketed by many manufacturers.

SIMILAR BROMIDE DRUGS.—

Acetylcarbromal [Sedamyl (Riker)]

Bromisovalum [Bromural (various manufacturers)]

MIXTURES

Many combination products containing one or more barbiturates (most commonly, amobarbital, butabarbital, pentobarbital, phenobarbital, or secobarbital) or other sedative-hypnotics are on the market, but their usefulness is questionable. Fixed-ratio combinations do not permit the careful adjustment of the dosage of each drug, and such adjustment is imperative when administering two or more drugs with different durations of action. Other products contain either such minute amounts of some ingredients that it would be unrealistic to expect any but a placebo effect, or components for which there is no therapeutic rationale. Therefore, use of these mixtures is not advisable.

MIXTURES OF BARBITURATES

This group of mixtures contains two to four barbiturates having different durations of action. Preparations combining "short-acting" and "intermediate-acting" barbiturates have been used extensively for many years. However, when used as hypnotic agents, the administration of supplemental doses of one of the components or of another single-entity barbiturate may be required to produce the desired effect. Thus, use of an appropriate single-entity barbiturate would be preferable, and any alleged advantage of this type of combination is hypothetical. Therefore, mixtures containing two or more barbiturates are not the preferred therapy.

AVAILABLE MIXTURES.—

Ethobral (Wyeth): Each capsule contains butabarbital sodium 15 or 30 mg, phenobarbital 25 or 50 mg, and secobarbital sodium 25 or 50 mg.

Nidar (Armour): Each tablet contains butabarbital sodium 7.5 mg, pentobarbital sodium 25 mg, phenobarbital 7.5 mg, and secobarbital sodium 25 mg.

Pento-Del (Boyle): Each capsule contains pentobarbital 65 mg in an enteric-coated pellet and pentobarbital sodium 97 mg.

Quadra-Sed (Smith, Miller & Patch): Each 5 ml of liquid contains butabarbital sodium 15 mg, pentobarbital sodium 15 mg, phenobarbital sodium 15 mg, and secobarbital sodium 15 mg.

Qui-A-Zone (Walker): Each tablet contains butabarbital 25 mg, pentobarbital 25 mg, phenobarbital 25 mg, and secobarbital 25 mg.

S.B.P. (Lemmon): Each tablet contains butabarbital sodium 30 mg, phenobarbital 15 mg, and secobarbital sodium 50 mg.

Sedobarb (Whittier): Each tablet contains pentobarbital sodium 32 or 65 mg and phenobarbital 16 or 32 mg.

Trinotic (Fellows-Testagar): Each tablet contains amobarbital 40 mg, phenobarbital 25 mg, and secobarbital 65 mg.

Tuinal (Lilly): Each capsule contains 25, 50, or 100 mg each of amobarbital sodium and secobarbital sodium.

MIXTURES OF BARBITURATES AND BROMIDES

Preparations combining barbiturates and bromides or a bromoureide (eg, carbromal) have not been used as extensively as preparations containing only barbiturates. The bromoureides represent a class of weak sedatives that offer no advantage over similarly acting agents; their sedative action is similar to that of the bromides. Bromides have moderate sedative activity but are useless as hypnotics (see the evaluation on Bromides). Therefore, this type of mixture is not considered to be of value.

AVAILABLE MIXTURES.—

Carbrital (Parke, Davis): Each capsule contains pentobarbital sodium 48.6 or 97 mg and carbromal 130 or 259 mg; each 30 ml of elixir contains pentobarbital sodium 130 mg and carbromal 389 mg.

Neo-Sedaphen (Smith, Miller & Patch): Each 5 ml of liquid contains calcium bromide 100 mg, pentobarbital sodium 30 mg, phenobarbital sodium 10 mg, potassium bromide 200 mg, and sodium bromide 300 mg.

Sedaphen (Smith, Miller & Patch): Each 5 ml of liquid contains calcium bromide 100 mg, phenobarbital sodium 20 mg, potassium bromide 200 mg, and sodium bromide 300 mg.

MIXTURES OF BARBITURATES OR CHLORAL HYDRATE AND OTHER SEDATIVE AGENTS

This group of mixtures contains one or more barbiturates or chloral hydrate with other agents that exhibit sedative properties (eg, scopolamine, phenyltoloxamine, mephenesin). This type of mixture is not the preferred therapy because of the reasons stated in the introduction to this section.

AVAILABLE MIXTURES.—

Fello-Sed (Fellows-Testagar): Each 4 ml of liquid contains calcium bromide 500 mg, chloral hydrate 500 mg, and atropine sulfate 0.125 mg.

Hyptran (Wampole): Each tablet contains secobarbital 60 mg and phenyltoloxamine citrate 100 mg.

Loryl (Kremers-Urban): Each capsule contains chloral hydrate 337.5 mg and phenyltoloxamine citrate 37.5 mg.

Neurinase (Fougera): Each tablet contains barbital sodium 200 mg and valerian extract 50 mg; solution contains barbital sodium 3.25 g and valerian extract to make 100 ml.

Plexonal (Sandoz): Each tablet contains barbital sodium 45 mg, butalbital 25 mg, phenobarbital sodium 15 mg, dihydroergotamine mesylate 0.16 mg, and scopolamine hydrobromide 0.08 mg.

Sedadrops (Merrell-National): Each milliliter of liquid contains pentobarbital sodium 8 mg, phenobarbital 16 mg, and homatropine methylbromide 0.27 mg.

Sed-A-Nat (Merrell-National): Each tablet contains phenobarbital 16 mg, hyoscyamus extract 8 mg, passiflora extract 16 mg, and valerian extract 16 mg.

Somorsed (Philips Roxane): Each capsule contains chloral hydrate 250 mg, mephenesin 125 mg, and scopolamine hydrobromide 0.065 mg.

Tranquinal (Barnes-Hind): Each tablet contains acetylcarbromal 130 mg, bromisovalum 250 mg, and scopolamine aminoxide hydrobromide 0.1 mg.

Vellada (Fellows-Testagar): Each tablet contains phenobarbital 16 mg, hyoscyamus extract 8 mg, passiflora extract 16 mg, and valerian extract 16 mg.

Mixtures containing ingredients other than sedatives are discussed in the chapters in which the primary ingredients are evaluated (see Chapters 3, Antianginal Agents; 22, Mild Analgesics; 33, Anorexiants; 41, Bronchodilators; 46, Cold Remedies; 78, Antispasmodics; 83, Miscellaneous Gastrointestinal Agents; and 85, Antiemetics).

Chapter 28

ANTIANXIETY AGENTS

Antianxiety agents are used to control mild to moderate degrees of anxiety and tension in patients with neuroses and depressive states. They also are used in normal individuals who react adversely to unusual environmental stress; however, restraint should be exercised in prescribing antianxiety agents for they are too often misused for the minor stresses of everyday living.

Antianxiety agents include chlormezanone [Trancopal], hydroxyzine [Atarax, Vistaril], meprobamate [Equanil, Miltown], phenaglycodol [Ultran], tybamate [Solacen, Tybatran], and the benzodiazepine derivatives, chlordiazepoxide [Librium], clorazepate [Tranxene], diazepam [Valium], and oxazepam [Serax].

Patients who respond to treatment with antianxiety agents often respond equally well to properly selected doses of barbiturates or other sedatives (see Chapter 27, Sedatives and Hypnotics). However, the antianxiety agents may have a more selective action on subcortical structures than the sedative-hypnotics and therefore may be useful for patients in whom the sedative-hypnotics cause an excessive loss of alertness. In addition, the antianxiety agents may be preferable to the barbiturates for patients with suicidal tendencies, since overdosage is less likely to produce coma or death.

The antianxiety agents share a similar central depressant action: the ability to produce mild sedation in doses that are generally unlikely to cause soporific effects or to adversely affect the clarity of consciousness and the quality of psychomotor performance. Their effects are limited largely to the central nervous system.

When prescribed in a limited number of large oral or parenteral doses, some antianxiety agents (eg, chlordiazepoxide, diazepam, oxazepam) may overcome psychomotor hyperexcitability. These drugs have been used to treat withdrawal symptoms in alcoholism (eg, delirium tremens), to reduce acute psychotic agitation in schizophrenic patients, and to help counteract the confusion, hallucinosis, disorientation, and delusions that often occur in patients with toxic psychoses. Despite their use in treating these symptoms, the antianxiety agents are not effective in the long-term management of chronic schizophrenia or other psychoses.

Because most antianxiety agents have also produced skeletal muscle relaxant effects in animals after large experimental doses, they have been tried in many neuromuscular and musculoskeletal disorders in man. The results of these trials are difficult to evaluate. These agents may be useful as adjuncts in some patients, especially those in whom anxiety and tension tend to intensify the symptoms of spasticity caused by upper motor neuron disorders. However, favorable results may be due to the sedative effect of the drugs rather than to any direct muscle relaxant effect. (See Chapter 30, Centrally Acting Skeletal Muscle Relaxants.) Antianxiety agents have been given preoperatively and postoperatively to allay apprehension (see Chapter 20, Adjuncts to Anesthesia).

The comparative effectiveness of all the antianxiety agents cannot be accurately judged at this time. However, on the basis of clinical experience and the results of controlled studies, chlordiazepoxide and diazepam, followed closely by meprobamate, appear to be more effective than the other antianxiety agents. Controlled studies comparing the efficacies of clorazepate and diazepam are inadequate to make a final judgment. However, available results indicate that the two drugs are apparently equally effective.

Adverse Reactions and Precautions

Overdosage with the antianxiety agents is less likely to result in coma, respiratory depression, and acute circulatory failure than is overdosage with the barbiturates or other sedative-hypnotics. Prolonged administration may produce signs of autonomic imbalance, but, in comparison with the antipsychotic agents, this occurs less frequently and the symptoms are less severe.

Drowsiness is the most common reaction produced by the antianxiety agents; ataxia, dizziness, and headache occur occasionally, especially during the first few days of treatment. The drowsiness and ataxia, which occur more commonly in elderly and debilitated patients, may be avoided by starting with relatively small doses and gradually increasing the dose to amounts that produce the desired calming effect without oversedation. Patients should avoid undertaking activities that require mental alertness, judgment, and physical coordination (eg, driving a car, operating dangerous machinery), especially during the early period of dosage adjustment.

Gastrointestinal discomfort, dryness of the mouth, nausea, and vomiting have been observed. The symptoms of gastrointestinal distress may be reduced by administering the drug with or immediately after meals.

Rash, chills, and fever also have been noted. Blood dyscrasias and a paradoxical aggravation of symptoms of anxiety (increased irritability, insomnia, and hyperactivity) have been reported rarely with the benzodiazepine derivatives and meprobamate [Equanil, Miltown]. An increased frequency of vivid dreams has been associated with use of the benzodiazepine derivatives.

Although serious adverse reactions affecting the skin, blood, and liver are rare, caution is required in prescribing any of these drugs to patients who have a history of allergic dermatoses, marked capillary fragility, blood dyscrasias, impaired renal function, or hepatic disease.

Long-term use of larger than usual therapeutic doses of chlordiazepoxide [Librium], clorazepate [Tranxene], diazepam [Valium], oxazepam [Serax], or meprobamate may cause psychic and physical dependence. Mild to severe withdrawal reactions occur when the drugs are abruptly discontinued. These reactions, including delirium and convulsions, may be as serious as those produced by the barbiturates. However, substantially fewer deaths have been reported from overdoses of the antianxiety agents than from overdoses of the barbiturates. The amount of the benzodiazepine derivatives or meprobamate prescribed for a patient with a history of drug dependence should be limited. Moreover, the physician should maintain close supervision over the amount and duration of use of the antianxiety agents. If patients have been taking large doses for long periods, the benzodiazepine derivatives or meprobamate should not be discontinued abruptly, since this may cause restlessness and other signs of psychomotor excitability, or even severe withdrawal reactions if physical dependence is well established.

Certain psychotropic agents, particularly phenothiazines or monoamine oxidase inhibitors, enhance the action of antianxiety agents. Thus, the antianxiety agents should be given cautiously and in reduced doses with these drugs. An additive effect may occur from the concomitant use of an antianxiety agent and other central nervous system depressants (eg, alcohol).

See the statement on Use of Drugs During Pregnancy in the General Information section.

INDIVIDUAL EVALUATIONS

CHLORDIAZEPOXIDE [Libritabs]
CHLORDIAZEPOXIDE HYDROCHLORIDE [Librium]

NHCH₃ · HCl Cl N O

This benzodiazepine derivative appears to be slightly more effective than meprobamate; however, in comparison to diazepam, another benzodiazepine derivative, chlordiazepoxide is less potent on a milligram basis as an antianxiety agent, has less anticonvulsant activity, and produces less drowsiness. Musculoskeletal disorders in which anxiety and tension intensify the symptoms may respond to its sedative effect (see Chapter 30, Centrally Acting Skeletal Muscle Relaxants). Chlordiazepoxide also may be useful in treating acute withdrawal symptoms in alcoholism (eg, delirium tremens, agitation) but should be used with caution in long-term treatment. It also has been used preoperatively to allay apprehension.

Drowsiness, ataxia, and lethargy have been reported frequently. These effects are more likely to occur in aged or debilitated patients. Hypotension and syncope have occurred with large doses. Rash, nausea, headache, increased or decreased libido, an increase in vivid dreams, agranulocytosis, and jaundice have been observed less frequently. Chlordiazepoxide also may cause excitement, acute rage, depression, and hallucinations.

Certain psychotropic drugs (eg, phenothiazines, monoamine oxidase inhibitors), alcohol, and other central nervous system depressants may enhance the action of chlordiazepoxide or have additive effects when used with this agent. Long-term use of larger than usual therapeutic doses may cause psychic and physical dependence. See the Introductory Statement for additional information on adverse reactions and precautions.

USUAL DOSAGE.—

Oral: Adults, for mild to moderate anxiety and tension, 15 to 40 mg daily divided into three or four doses; for severe anxiety and tension, 60 to 100 mg daily divided into three or four doses. *Elderly or debilitated patients*, 5 mg two to four times daily. Since chlordiazepoxide is excreted slowly, a cumulative increase in effect should be expected for the first several days of administration and dosage adjustments should be made if indicated.

Oral, Intramuscular: Children over 6 years of age, 0.5 mg/kg of body weight daily divided into three or four doses. Information is inadequate to establish dosage for *children under 6 years.*

Intramuscular, Intravenous: Adults, for acute alcoholic withdrawal symptoms, 50 to 100 mg; the dose may be repeated in two to four hours, if necessary, but the total dosage should usually not exceed 300 mg daily. For acute or severe anxiety and tension, 50 to 100 mg initially, then 25 to 50 mg three or four times daily if necessary. For preoperative apprehension, 50 to 100 mg (intramuscularly) one hour before surgery.

PREPARATIONS.—

Chlordiazepoxide:

Libritabs (Roche). *Oral:* Tablets 5, 10, and 25 mg.

Chlordiazepoxide Hydrochloride:

Librium (Roche).

Oral: Capsules 5, 10, and 25 mg.

Injection: Powder 100 mg.

CHLORMEZANONE [Trancopal]

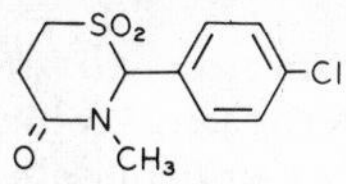

In controlled studies, chlormezanone has been shown to be less effective than diazepam and meprobamate in treating anxiety and tension. Musculoskeletal disorders in which anxiety and tension intensify the symptoms may respond to its sedative effect; however, chlormezanone does not appear to have any specific effect on spasticity or rigidity associated with organic neurologic disorders.

Untoward effects are generally mild and occur relatively infrequently. Drowsiness, lethargy, dizziness, rash, flushing, dryness of the mouth, and nausea have been observed. Jaundice has occurred rarely. Certain psychotropic drugs (eg, phenothiazines, monoamine oxidase inhibitors), alcohol, and other central nervous system depressants may enhance the action of chlormezanone or have additive effects when used with this agent. See the Introductory Statement for additional information on adverse reactions and precautions.

USUAL DOSAGE.—*Oral: Adults*, 300 to 800 mg daily in three or four divided doses. *Children*, 12 mg/kg of body weight daily divided into three or four doses.

PREPARATIONS.—Trancopal (Winthrop). *Oral:* Tablets 100 and 200 mg.

CLORAZEPATE DIPOTASSIUM [Tranxene]

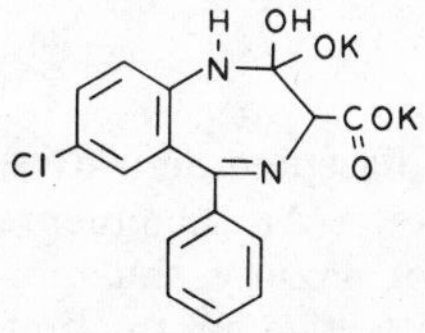

This compound has actions and uses similar to those of other benzodiazepine derivatives (ie, chlordiazepoxide, diazepam, oxazepam). Results of controlled studies show that clorazepate is an effective antianxiety agent. Peak plasma levels of nordiazepam, the principal metabolite of clorazepate, appear within one hour after oral administration, and the half-life of nordiazepam is approximately one day. Controlled studies comparing the efficacies of clorazepate and diazepam are inadequate to make a final judgment; however, available results indicate that the two drugs are apparently equally effective.

The most common adverse effects are drowsiness and ataxia, which occur most frequently in elderly or debilitated patients or in those given large doses. Headache, blurred vision, euphoria, constipation, hiccups, nausea, weakness, dryness of the mouth, dizziness, confusion, rash, insomnia, fatigue, and depression occur occasionally.

Certain psychotropic drugs (eg, phenothiazines, monoamine oxidase inhibitors), alcohol, and other central nervous system depressants may enhance the action of clorazepate or have additive effects when used with this agent. Long-term therapy with larger than usual doses may result in psychic and physical dependence. See also the Introductory Statement.

USUAL DOSAGE.—*Oral: Adults*, for mild to moderate anxiety and tension, 15 to 60 mg daily in divided doses; *elderly or debilitated patients*, initially, 7.5 to 15 mg daily. *Children over 6 years of age*, 7.5 to 60 mg daily in divided doses. Adequate information is not available to establish dosage for *children under 6 years.*

PREPARATIONS.—Tranxene (Abbott). *Oral:* Capsules 3.75, 7.5, and 15 mg.

DIAZEPAM [Valium]

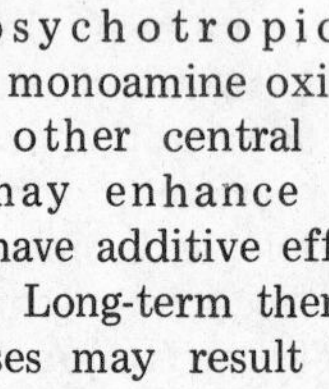

CH_3 N O Cl N

This benzodiazepine derivative appears to be slightly more effective than meprobamate in the management of anxiety and tension. Although diazepam is effective in treating patients with acute agitation due to the withdrawal of alcohol, it should be used with caution in the long-term treatment of alcoholism. Muscular spasms associated with acute musculoskeletal disorders and certain acute and chronic neuromuscular disorders may respond to its sedative effect (see Chapter 30, Centrally Acting Skeletal Muscle Relaxants). Diazepam may be given parenterally as premedication to patients undergoing surgery, cardioversion, or such procedures as gastroscopy and esophagoscopy (see Chapter 20, Adjuncts to Anesthesia). Diazepam also is effective orally and parenterally in counteracting the adverse effects of LSD. Its use in convulsive disorders is discussed in Chapter 31, Anticonvulsants.

The most common adverse effects are drowsiness, fatigue, and ataxia, which occur most frequently in elderly or debilitated patients or when diazepam is given in large doses. Other untoward reactions noted occasionally are nausea, blurred vision, diplopia, dizziness, dysarthria, hypotension, headache, amnesia, an increase in vivid dreams, slurred speech, tremor, rash, urinary incontinence, and constipation; one case of transitory leukopenia has been reported. Like chlordiazepoxide, diazepam can cause excitement, depression, and hallucinations. Apnea and cardiac arrest have occurred, usually following intravenous administration. This has been noted especially in elderly or severely ill patients and in those with limited pulmonary reserve.

Certain psychotropic drugs (eg, phenothiazines, monoamine oxidase inhibitors), alcohol, and other central nervous system depressants may enhance the action of diazepam or have additive effects when used with this agent. Long-term use of larger than therapeutic doses may result in psychic and physical dependence. See also the Introductory Statement.

USUAL DOSAGE.—

Oral: Adults, for mild to moderate anxiety and tension, 4 to 40 mg daily in two to four divided doses; for *elderly or debilitated patients* and when other sedatives are administered concomitantly, 2 to 5 mg daily initially; the dose is increased gradually as needed. *Children*, 0.12 to 0.8 mg/kg of body weight daily divided into three or four doses. Therapy should be initiated with the smallest dose and increased as required.

Intramuscular, Intravenous: Adults, for moderate anxiety and tension, 2 to 5 mg; for severe psychoneurotic reactions, 5 to 10 mg given slowly. The dose may be repeated in three to four hours, but not more than 30 mg should be given within an eight-hour period. For acute alcoholic withdrawal symptoms, 10 mg, then 5 to 10 mg in three to four hours if necessary. *Children*, 0.04 to 0.2 mg/kg of body weight; the dose may be repeated in two to four hours, but the total amount should not exceed 0.6 mg/kg in an eight-hour period. The possibility of inducing kernicterus in newborn infants must be considered, since the parenteral form contains sodium benzoate and benzoic acid as buffers.

The intravenous solution should be injected slowly, taking at least one minute for each 5 mg (1 ml) given. It should not be mixed or diluted with other solutions or drugs, nor added to intravenous fluids.

PREPARATIONS.—Valium (Roche).

Oral: Tablets 2, 5, and 10 mg.

Injection: Solution 5 mg/ml in 2 and 10 ml containers.

HYDROXYZINE HYDROCHLORIDE [Atarax, Vistaril IM]

HYDROXYZINE PAMOATE [Vistaril Pamoate]

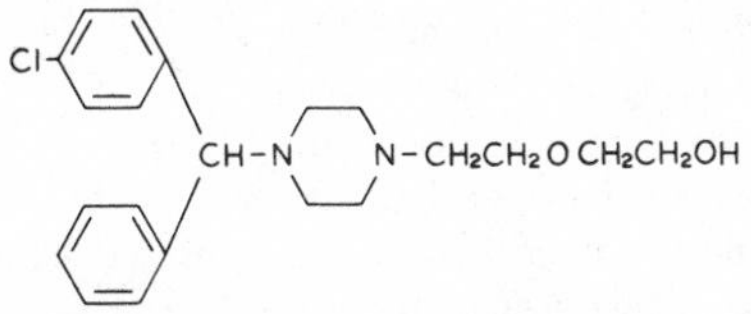

Cl– (chlorophenyl) / (phenyl) CH–N(piperazine)N–$CH_2CH_2OCH_2CH_2OH$

This agent is used to treat anxiety, tension, and agitation. It also may be useful in treating patients with acute agitation due to the withdrawal of alcohol. Hydroxyzine also possesses other potentially useful central and peripheral actions, including antiemetic and antihistaminic effects. Therefore, the drug has been used to manage acute and chronic urticaria as well as other manifestations of allergic dermatoses, postoperative nausea and vomiting, and motion sickness (see Chapter 85, Antiemetics). It also has been used alone and with other central nervous system depressants (eg, opiates, barbiturates) to produce pre- and postoperative sedation.

The incidence of untoward effects appears to be low. Any drowsiness that may develop tends to be transient and does not induce sleep. Hydroxyzine has some teratogenic properties in animals when administered in doses substantially above the human therapeutic range. These findings are difficult to evaluate and inconclusive with respect to human pregnancy (see the statement on Use of Drugs During Pregnancy in the General Information section).

Certain psychotropic drugs (eg, phenothiazines, monoamine oxidase inhibitors), alcohol, and other central nervous system depressants may enhance the action of hydroxyzine or have additive effects when used with this agent. See the Introductory Statement for additional information on adverse reactions and precautions.

USUAL DOSAGE.—

Oral: For anxiety, *adults*, 225 to 400 mg daily divided into three or four doses; *children*, 2 mg/kg of body weight daily divided into four doses.

Intramuscular: Adults, for pre- and postoperative, and pre- and postpartum sedation, 25 to 100 mg; for serious psychiatric conditions and acute alcohol intoxication, 50 to 100 mg immediately and every four to six hours as needed. *Children*, for pre- and postoperative sedation, 1 mg/kg of body weight.

PREPARATIONS.—

Hydroxyzine Hydrochloride:

Atarax (Roerig). *Oral:* Syrup 10 mg/5 ml; tablets 10, 25, 50, and 100 mg.

Vistaril IM (Pfizer). *Injection:* Solution 25 mg/ml in 1 and 10 ml containers, 50 mg/ml in 1, 2, and 10 ml containers, 100 mg/ml in 2 ml containers.

Hydroxyzine Pamoate: (Strengths are expressed in terms of the hydrochloride salt.)

Vistaril [pamoate] (Pfizer). *Oral:* Capsules 25, 50, and 100 mg; suspension 25 mg/5 ml.

MEPROBAMATE [Equanil, Miltown]

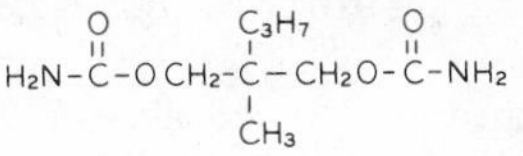

$$H_2N-\overset{O}{\overset{\|}{C}}-OCH_2-\underset{CH_3}{\underset{|}{\overset{C_3H_7}{\overset{|}{C}}}}-CH_2O-\overset{O}{\overset{\|}{C}}-NH_2$$

Meprobamate is useful in the treatment of anxiety and tension, but appears to be somewhat less effective than chlordiazepoxide and diazepam. Psychosomatic and musculoskeletal disorders may respond to its sedative effect. Consistent bioavailability of the timed-release preparation has been demonstrated.

The most common untoward effect is drowsiness. Thrombocytopenia, leukopenia, dermatitis, urticaria, anaphylactic reactions, hypotension and syncope, blurred vision, weakness of the extremities, and paradoxical reactions of euphoria and anger occur rarely. Agranulocytosis and aplastic anemia have been reported, although no causal relationship has been established.

Certain psychotropic drugs (eg, phenothiazines, monoamine oxidase inhibitors), alcohol, and other central nervous system depressants may enhance the action of meprobamate or have additive effects when used with this drug. Meprobamate is a Schedule IV substance and prescriptions for it may not be authorized for refill more than five times in the six-month period after they are written. Long-term use of larger than usual therapeutic doses may result in psychic and physical dependence. Withdrawal symptoms, including convulsions, may occur when the drug is discontinued abruptly after prolonged administration of large doses. See the Introductory Statement for additional information on adverse reactions and precautions.

For other uses, see Chapter 30, Centrally Acting Skeletal Muscle Relaxants, and Chapter 31, Anticonvulsants.

USUAL DOSAGE.—*Oral: Adults,* 1.2 g to 1.6 g daily divided into three or four doses. Doses above 2.4 g daily should not be administered. *Children over 6 years of age,* 25 mg/kg of body weight daily divided into two or three doses. Adequate information is not available to establish dosage for *children under 6 years.*

PREPARATIONS.—

Equanil (Wyeth). *Oral:* Capsules (timed-release) 400 mg; suspension 200 mg/5 ml; tablets 200 and 400 mg; tablets (coated) 400 mg (Wyseals).

Miltown (Wallace).

Injection: Solution 80 mg/ml in 5 ml containers.

Oral: Capsules (timed-release) 200 and 400 mg (Meprospan); tablets 200 and 400 mg; tablets (coated) 400 mg (Meprotabs).

ADDITIONAL TRADEMARKS.—Arcoban (Arcum), Kesso-Bamate (McKesson), Meprocon (Consolidated Midland), SK-Bamate (Smith Kline & French), Tranmep (Reid Provident), Viobamate (Rowell). Drug also marketed by other manufacturers under generic name.

OXAZEPAM [Serax]

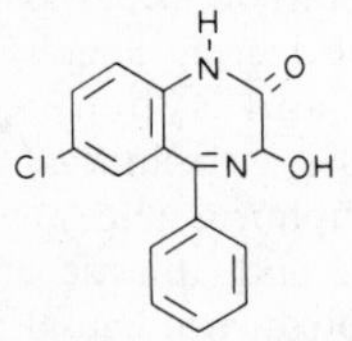

This benzodiazepine derivative, a metabolite of chlordiazepoxide, is less effective than the related agents, chlordiazepoxide and diazepam, in relieving tension, anxiety, and spasm of musculoskeletal disorders. It may be useful as adjunctive therapy for acute agitation due to alcohol withdrawal but should be used with caution in long-term treatment of alcoholism.

The incidence of adverse reactions is low. Drowsiness is the most common untoward effect. Other reactions noted occasionally include rash, nausea, dizziness, syncope, hypotension, tachycardia, edema, nightmares, lethargy, slurred speech, and paradoxical reactions such as excitement and confusion. The incidence of ataxia is less than with the related drugs. Leukopenia, eosinophilia, and hepatic dysfunction have occurred rarely.

Certain psychotropic drugs (eg, phenothiazines, monoamine oxidase inhibitors), alcohol, and other central nervous system depressants may enhance the action of oxazepam or have additive effects when used with this agent. The long-term use of larger than usual therapeutic doses may result in psychic and physical dependence. See the Introductory Statement for additional information on adverse reactions and precautions.

USUAL DOSAGE.—*Oral: Adults,* for mild to moderate anxiety, 30 to 60 mg daily divided into three or four doses; for severe anxiety, 45 to 120 mg daily divided into three or four doses. *Elderly patients,* initially 30 mg daily divided into three doses; if necessary, the dose may be increased cautiously to 45 to 60 mg daily divided into three or four doses. For withdrawal symptoms in alcoholism, 45 to 120 mg daily divided into three or four doses. *Children,* information is inadequate to establish dosage.

PREPARATIONS.—Serax (Wyeth). *Oral:* Capsules 10, 15, and 30 mg; tablets 15 mg.

PHENAGLYCODOL [Ultran]

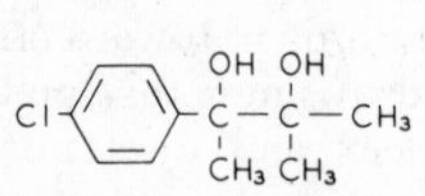

Phenaglycodol is used for the relief of anxiety and tension. Its effectiveness in comparison with similar agents has not been established conclusively.

Drowsiness is the most common untoward effect. Other reactions observed occasionally include dizziness, nausea, gastric distress, dermatitis, and headache. Certain psychotropic drugs (eg, phenothiazines, monoamine oxidase inhibitors), alcohol, and other central nervous system depressants may enhance the action of phenaglycodol or have additive effects when used with this agent. See the Introductory

Statement for additional information on adverse reactions and precautions.

USUAL DOSAGE.—*Oral: Adults*, 800 mg to 1.2 g daily in divided doses; *children*, 13.2 mg/kg of body weight daily divided into three doses.

PREPARATIONS.—Ultran (Lilly). *Oral:* Capsules 300 mg; tablets 200 mg.

TYBAMATE [Solacen, Tybatran]

$$H_2N\overset{\overset{O}{\|}}{C}OCH_2\underset{\underset{CH_2CH_2CH_3}{|}}{\overset{\overset{CH_3}{|}}{C}}CH_2O\overset{\overset{O}{\|}}{C}NHCH_2CH_2CH_2CH_3$$

Tybamate is chemically and pharmacologically related to meprobamate, but it is less effective in the treatment of anxiety and tension.

The incidence of untoward effects is low. Drowsiness, dizziness, and nausea have been reported most frequently. Other reactions noted occasionally include rash, gastrointestinal disturbances, insomnia, euphoria, dryness of the mouth, blurred vision, glossitis, lethargy, pruritus ani, paresthesias, fatigue, ataxia, confusion, depersonalization, and "panic reaction." Grand mal or petit mal seizures have occurred in a few hospitalized psychotic patients who received large doses of tybamate and phenothiazines concomitantly. Other psychotropic drugs (eg, monoamine oxidase inhibitors), alcohol, and other central nervous system depressants also may enhance the action of tybamate or have additive effects when used with this agent. See the Introductory Statement for additional information on adverse reactions and precautions.

USUAL DOSAGE.—*Oral: Adults*, 750 mg to 2 g daily in three or four divided doses. Daily doses larger than 3 g should not be used. *Children 6 to 12 years of age*, 20 to 35 mg/kg of body weight daily in three or four equally divided doses. Adequate information is not available to establish dosage for *children under 6 years.*

PREPARATIONS.—

Solacen (Wallace). *Oral:* Capsules 250 and 350 mg.

Tybatran (Robins). *Oral:* Capsules 125, 250, and 350 mg.

MIXTURES

Several fixed-ratio combinations of two or more antianxiety agents and antianxiety agents with anorexiants, antihypertensive agents, estrogens, mild analgesics, antianginal agents, or antispasmodics are marketed for use in the treatment of anxiety, pain, menopause syndrome, angina pectoris, obesity, hypertension, and musculoskeletal and gastrointestinal disorders. Information and listings of these latter mixtures appear in the appropriate chapters.

Such mixtures have a questionable rationale. When two or more agents with similar indications are combined (eg, Deprol containing meprobamate and benactyzine hydrochloride), the patient is exposed to the possible development of additive effects, often without any compensating advantage. When agents with different actions are combined, an adequate dose of one ingredient may require the administration of supplementary doses of the other components, thus tending to negate the convenience that the combination product would appear to offer.

Chapter 29

ANTIPSYCHOTIC AGENTS

The antipsychotic agents (neuroleptics), formerly called major tranquilizers, modify the symptoms of acute and chronic psychoses. The calming effect produced by these agents is distinguished from that of the barbiturates and other sedative-hypnotics in that large doses do not generally produce unconsciousness or depress vital centers. Therefore, severely disturbed patients can be treated using larger doses with less risk. The value of these agents is well documented in the treatment of acute and chronic schizophrenia, the manic phase of manic-depressive psychosis, and involutional, senile, organic, and toxic psychoses with the exception of delirium tremens, in which their use may be harmful.

These agents are most useful in treating conditions marked by psychotic disorganization of thought and behavior with increased or decreased psychomotor activity. They often rapidly reduce panic, fear, and hostility. Thus, these drugs have helped to decrease combative, destructive, or antisocial and withdrawn behavior in hospitalized patients. More significantly, such patients are better organized and more responsive to their environment, and often may be released from the hospital earlier. In some instances, use of antipsychotic agents obviates the necessity of hospitalization. Maintenance therapy following discharge also may reduce the rate of rehospitalization.

The antipsychotic agents may be of limited value in a few other conditions, although their efficacy in these disorders has not been adequately substantiated by objective studies. They may be useful in ameliorating some of the adverse behavior associated with mental retardation. Most physicians prefer to use antianxiety agents for the treatment of neuroses and psychosomatic conditions because the efficacy of the antipsychotic agents has not been definitively established and fewer adverse reactions are associated with antianxiety agents.

The antipsychotic agents, of which chlorpromazine [Thorazine] is the prototype, fall into three major chemical categories: phenothiazines, thioxanthenes, and butyrophenones. Most of the antipsychotic agents are phenothiazine derivatives. These, in turn, may be chemically divided into three subgroups: (1) aliphatic compounds (chlorpromazine, promazine [Sparine], and triflupromazine [Vesprin]); (2) piperidine compounds (mesoridazine [Serentil], piperacetazine [Quide], and thioridazine [Mellaril]); and (3) piperazine compounds (acetophenazine [Tindal], butaperazine [Repoise], carphenazine [Proketazine], fluphenazine [Permitil, Prolixin], perphenazine [Trilafon], prochlorperazine [Compazine], and trifluoperazine [Stelazine]). The thioxanthene derivatives, chlorprothixene [Taractan] and thiothixene [Navane], are chemically and pharmacologically related to the aliphatic and piperazine phenothiazines, respectively. Haloperidol [Haldol], a butyrophenone derivative, is pharmacologically but not chemically related to the piperazine phenothiazines.

Many investigators have found it difficult if not impossible to distinguish one agent from another on the basis of efficacy. The aliphatic phenothiazines (eg, chlorpromazine) and piperidine phenothiazines (eg, thioridazine) have a significant sedative action, while the piperazine compounds (eg, fluphenazine), the thioxanthenes (chlorprothixene and thiothixene), and the butyrophenone, haloperidol, do not produce marked sedation. It would be logical to assume that the symptoms of agitation and excitement in acute schizophrenia would respond better to the more sedating agents, while withdrawn, apathetic patients with chronic schizophrenia would respond better to the less sedating compounds. However, objective studies have not consistently borne out these assumptions. Therefore, on the basis of clinical experience, all classes of the antipsychotic agents will not only reduce the violent, agitated behavior of the acute schizophrenic patient, but will also make the withdrawn chronic schizophrenic patient more alert, sociable, and communicative.

Because of their secondary pharmacologic actions (eg, antiemesis; potentiation of the effects of hypnotic, analgesic, and anesthetic agents), some antipsychotic agents are used as adjuncts to anesthesia, in the control of nausea and vomiting, and as adjuncts in the control of severe chronic pain. (See Chapter 20, Adjuncts to Anesthesia, and Chapter 85, Antiemetics.)

Some phenothiazines (eg, chlorpromazine, fluphenazine, perphenazine, prochlorperazine) are available as oral timed-release preparations. Since the phenothiazines have prolonged half-lives, these more expensive preparations, which are often erratically absorbed, have no significant advantage over ordinary oral dosage forms.

Lithium carbonate [Eskalith, Lithane, Lithonate] is effective in the treatment of the manic phase of manic-depressive psychosis. A convulsive agent, flurothyl [Indoklon], occasionally is used in treating severe depressive psychoses. (See the individual evaluations.)

Adverse Reactions and Precautions

The antipsychotic agents produce a wide variety of untoward effects; some are idiosyncratic or allergic in nature and others result from their secondary actions on the central and autonomic nervous systems. Although all of the reactions cited may not have been reported with each agent, it is possible that they occur. The pattern of adverse reactions is a factor to be considered in choosing among the compounds.

Extrapyramidal reactions often occur after administration of the antipsychotic agents. The piperazine compounds and haloperidol [Haldol] are more likely to induce a parkinsonian syndrome (tremors, rigidity, akinesia, shuffling gait, postural abnormalities, pill-rolling movements, mask-like facies, hypersalivation) and akathisia (motor restlessness) than the aliphatic compounds. The piperidine compounds are least likely to produce extrapyramidal reactions.

The piperazine compounds and haloperidol are also more likely to induce dyskinetic reactions, especially in younger patients. These reactions, which may be accompanied by hyperhidrosis, pallor, and fever, include perioral spasms (often with protrusion of the tongue), mandibular tics, dysphasia, dysphagia, hyperextension of the neck and trunk, and clonic convulsions. The two most dramatic dyskinetic reactions are torticollis and oculogyric crisis, both of which produce extreme discomfort and may be caused by relatively small doses in either young or elderly patients. Usually the patient remains conscious and fully alert. A rare syndrome, tardive dyskinesia (rhythmic movements of tongue, jaw, and face), occurs in older patients after prolonged administration and may persist after termination of therapy.

It is important to recognize the possible association of these extrapyramidal symptoms with antipsychotic drugs, since acute encephalitis, meningitis, tetanus, and other neurologic disorders have been diagnosed erroneously and patients have been treated accordingly.

Most extrapyramidal symptoms may be relieved promptly by antiparkinsonism drugs (eg, diphenhydramine [Benadryl] in an intramuscular dose of 50 mg) and patients may be able to continue taking the antipsychotic agent at the same or a lower dose level, especially if an orally-administered antiparkinsonism agent is given concomitantly. However, an antiparkinsonism agent should not be given in the absence of extrapyramidal symptoms, since it occasionally can cause delirium or other severe anticholinergic effects, especially in elderly patients. The antiparkinsonism agents often may be discontinued after several weeks without recurrence of extrapyramidal symptoms. (See Chapter 74, Antiparkinsonism Agents.)

Although blood dyscrasias seem least likely to occur with piperazine compounds, such reactions must be presumed to occur with any phenothiazine. Leukopenia, agranulocytosis, purpura, and pancytopenia are the more serious hematologic complications observed. Although their incidence is very low, mortality is high. Therefore, physicians and attendants should be alert to the appearance of such signs as sore throat, cellulitis, fever, and asthenia. If these symptoms appear, the drug should be discontinued and white blood cell and differential counts should be performed; administration may be resumed if the clinical signs are not associated with a blood disorder.

Drug-induced cholestatic jaundice due to hypersensitivity is seen infrequently. It occurs most commonly with aliphatic phenothiazines, usually two to four weeks after treatment is begun. If bilirubinuria and jaundice are detected, the drug should be withdrawn immediately. Although fatalities are rare and clinical recovery from the jaundice seems to occur within a few weeks in most patients, results of liver function tests and serial needle biopsies indicate that the histopathologic changes persist for a much longer time. Thus, if antipsychotic therapy is resumed with another agent, the physician should be alert to the possible recurrence of jaundice. A history of liver disease is not an absolute contraindication to the use of the antipsychotic agents; however, smaller doses are required due to the decreased metabolic rate, and less potent agents (eg, piperidine phenothiazines, thiothixene [Navane], haloperidol) are preferred.

The antipsychotic drugs, especially the aliphatic and piperidine phenothiazines, produce drowsiness, dizziness, and fatigue, particularly when large doses are given; sedation is less pronounced than that caused by the barbiturates and other sedatives and hypnotics. This sedative effect may be therapeutically desirable in some situations. However, significant tolerance to this effect occurs within one to three days after therapy has begun. The phenothiazines may be given at bedtime to patients on maintenance dosages to facilitate sleep and decrease sedation during the day. However, patients should avoid undertaking activities that require mental alertness, judgement, and physical coordination (eg, driving a car, operating dangerous machinery), especially during the early period of dosage adjustment.

The antipsychotic drugs are contraindicated in patients with central nervous system depression, especially in those who are comatose, and they should be given cautiously and in small doses to patients with a history of convulsive disorders.

The antiemetic actions of some of these agents (eg, chlorpromazine [Thorazine], prochlorperazine [Compazine]) may obscure nausea and vomiting associated with various organic disorders.

Orthostatic hypotension occurs more commonly with aliphatic phenothiazines and thioxanthenes than with piperazine or piperidine phenothiazines and haloperidol, especially when they are given parenterally; consequently, patients should be recumbent at the time of parenteral administration and remain so for at least one hour. Large oral doses also may produce orthostatic hypotension and reflex tachycardia. Although tolerance to the hypotensive effect tends to develop with prolonged treatment, caution is always required when these drugs are given to patients in whom a sudden drop in blood pressure is undesirable, such as those with cardiovascular disease.

Since some phenothiazines may induce electrocardiographic alterations, which indicates a disturbance in ventricular repolarization, these agents should be administered cautiously to patients with premature ventricular contractions. These alterations are most likely to occur with mesoridazine [Serentil] and thioridazine [Mellaril], especially when large doses are given.

Many antipsychotic agents have anticholinergic action and should be used cautiously in patients with a history of prostatic hypertrophy. By dilating the pupil, these agents could precipitate an attack of acute glaucoma in patients predisposed to angle closure; this has occurred occasionally after parenteral administration of anticholinergic drugs but has only rarely been reported after oral use. In warm climates, physicians also should be alert for signs of flushing and dryness of the skin in patients receiving large doses of these drugs, since fever and heat exhaustion have been reported. Dryness of the mouth, blurred vision, urinary retention, and constipation also may occur. Such untoward effects are even more likely to be observed when other agents that have anticholinergic effects (eg, tricyclic antidepressants, antiparkinsonism agents) are used concomitantly with the antipsychotic agents. Laxatives or enemas may have to be prescribed to minimize the possibility of fecal impaction.

Delayed ovulation and menstruation, amenorrhea with false-positive pregnancy test, galactorrhea, and weight gain have been reported occasionally; these effects generally are considered to be manifestations of endocrine imbalance caused by depression of hypothalamic function. Retrograde ejaculation of semen into the urinary bladder has occurred rarely.

Skin reactions occur most commonly with aliphatic compounds. With the exception of photosensitivity, most dermatoses are readily controlled by discontinuing the drug, and it often is possible to resume treatment later with another compound, or even with the same one, without recurrence of the allergic skin reaction. An allergic rash also may precede the onset of cholestatic jaundice.

A dark purplish-brown skin pigmentation, induced by light, has occurred in hospitalized psychiatric patients who were given large amounts (1 to 2.5 g daily) of chlorpromazine for a few months, or smaller doses (300 to 400 mg daily) for several years. In approximately 20% of patients on long-term therapy with chlorpromazine, epithelial keratopathy and retinal pigmentary degeneration are observed, and opacities of the cornea and lens due to deposition of fine particulate matter are detectable on slit lamp examination. These ocular changes usually produce no decrease in function and regress after withdrawal of the drug. Patients taking large doses of thioridazine (more than 800 mg daily) have developed retinal pigmentary degeneration with diminished visual acuity; this often does not regress when the drug is discontinued.

When chlorpromazine is abruptly discontinued in patients who have been receiving large doses, symptoms suggesting physical dependence (eg, gastritis, nausea, vomiting, tremors) may occur.

A few patients receiving large doses of phenothiazines for prolonged periods have died suddenly and unexpectedly. Either asphyxia during a convulsive seizure or cardiac arrest seems to be the most likely cause of this rare phenomenon. Results of postmortem examination usually have not revealed any specific cause of death nor established a relationship with administration of the drug. Some of these patients previously had shown characteristic phenothiazine-type electrocardiographic changes.

Routine precautions should be followed when these drugs are used during pregnancy. Extrapyramidal effects may appear in the infant if these agents are given during the last trimester (see the discussion on Use of Drugs During Pregnancy in the General Information section).

Drug Interactions: Because these drugs potentiate the action of other central nervous system depressants, they should be used cautiously in patients who are under the influence of alcohol or barbiturates, and doses of morphine-like analgesics and general anesthetics should be reduced. They also should be used with care in patients who are taking antihypertensive agents or drugs with anticholinergic effects, since they may enhance the action of these drugs. Antipsychotic agents should be temporarily discontinued in patients receiving spinal or epidural anesthesia or adrenergic blocking agents.

PHENOTHIAZINE DERIVATIVES

Aliphatic Compounds

CHLORPROMAZINE [Thorazine]
CHLORPROMAZINE HYDROCHLORIDE
[Thorazine Hydrochloride]

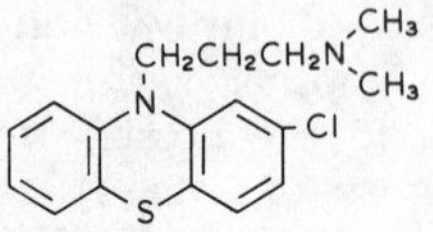

Chlorpromazine is the prototype of the aliphatic phenothiazine compounds. As with other phenothiazines, the value of chlorpromazine is well documented in the treatment of acute and chronic schizophrenia, the manic phase of manic-depressive psychosis, and involutional, senile, organic, and toxic psychoses with the exception of delirium tremens. Most physicians prefer to use antianxiety agents rather than chlorpromazine in treating neurotic patients because its efficacy in this disorder has not been definitively established and fewer adverse reactions are associated with antianxiety agents. The timed-release preparation has no significant advantage over the ordinary dosage forms, since chlorpromazine and other phenothiazines have prolonged half-lives.

All patients, especially children, young adults, and those receiving large doses, should be closely observed for the appearance of extrapyramidal reactions. These reactions can be controlled by reducing the dose or administering an antiparkinsonism agent. Other reactions include drowsiness, dryness of the mouth, blurred vision, weight gain, and photosensitivity.

Orthostatic hypotension may occur when chlorpromazine is given parenterally; consequently, patients should be recumbent when the drug is injected and remain so for at least one hour. Larger oral doses also may produce orthostatic hypotension as well as reflex tachycardia.

Blood dyscrasias (eg, leukopenia, granulocytopenia, agranulocytosis, purpura, pancytopenia) have been observed rarely. Therefore, if such signs as sore throat, cellulitis, fever, and asthenia appear, chlorpromazine should be discontinued and white blood cell and differential counts should be performed. Cholestatic jaundice occurs infrequently, most commonly two to four weeks after treatment has begun. If bilirubinuria and jaundice are detected, the drug should be discontinued and liver function tests should be performed.

See the Introductory Statement for additional information on adverse reactions, precautions, and interactions. For other uses, see Chapter 85, Antiemetics.

USUAL DOSAGE.—

Chlorpromazine:

Rectal: Adults, 100 mg every six to eight hours. *Children*, 1 mg/kg of body weight every six to eight hours.

Chlorpromazine Hydrochloride:

Intramuscular, Oral: Adults, 30 mg to 1 g daily in divided doses. *Elderly patients*, one-fourth to one-half the usual dosage. *Children*, 0.5 mg/kg of body weight every six to eight hours.

PREPARATIONS.—

Thorazine (Smith Kline & French). *Rectal:* Suppositories 25 and 100 mg.

Thorazine [hydrochloride] (Smith Kline & French).

Injection: Solution 25 mg/ml in 1, 2, and 10 ml containers.

Oral: Capsules (timed-release) 30, 75, 150, 200, and 300 mg; liquid (concentrate) 30 and 100 mg/ml; syrup 10 mg/5 ml; tablets 10, 25, 50, 100, and 200 mg.

PROMAZINE HYDROCHLORIDE [Sparine]

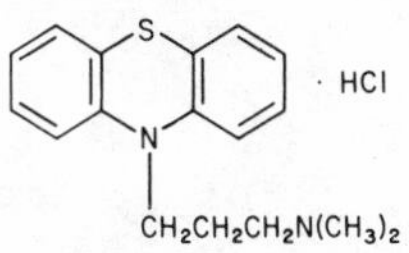

S · HCl
N
$CH_2CH_2CH_2N(CH_3)_2$

Unlike chlorpromazine, this aliphatic compound has not been found to be significantly effective in treating acutely agitated psychotic patients; moreover, the incidence of adverse effects (eg, drowsiness, orthostatic hypotension) is greater with this phenothiazine than with other agents in this group, especially after parenteral administration. For these reasons, other antipsychotic agents are preferred.

See the Introductory Statement and the evaluation on the prototype, Chlorpromazine, for additional information on adverse reactions, precautions, and interactions. For other uses, see Chapter 85, Antiemetics.

USUAL DOSAGE.—There is no reason to use this drug in the treatment of psychosis because more effective and less toxic agents are available. The manufacturer's suggested dosage for psychiatric use is: *Intramuscular, Intravenous, Oral: Adults*, initially, 50 to 150 mg; amount may be increased to a total of 300 mg if the calming effect is not apparent within 30 minutes. For maintenance, 10 to 200 mg at four- to six-hour intervals. Maximal dose is 1 g daily, since convulsions may occur at dosages above this amount. When the drug is used intravenously, the concentration should not exceed 25 mg/ml. *Children over 12 years of age*, 10 to 25 mg every four to six hours; *under 12 years*, information is inadequate to establish dosage.

PREPARATIONS.—Sparine (Wyeth).

Injection: Solution 25 and 50 mg/ml in 1, 2, and 10 ml containers.

Oral: Liquid (concentrate) 30 and 100 mg/ml; syrup 10 mg/ml; tablets 10, 25, 50, 100, and 200 mg.

TRIFLUPROMAZINE HYDROCHLORIDE [Vesprin]

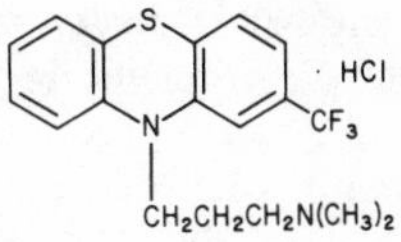

S · HCl
N CF_3
$CH_2CH_2CH_2N(CH_3)_2$

Triflupromazine is useful in treating acute and chronic schizophrenia, the manic phase of manic-depressive psychosis, and involutional, senile, and toxic psychoses, with the exception of delirium tremens. Most physicians prefer to use antianxiety agents in treating neurotic patients rather than triflupromazine because its efficacy in this disorder has not been definitively established and fewer untoward reactions are associated with antianxiety agents.

See the Introductory Statement and the evaluation on the prototype, Chlorpromazine, for additional information on adverse reactions, precautions, and interactions. For use of triflupromazine in controlling nausea and vomiting, see Chapter 85, Antiemetics.

USUAL DOSAGE.—

Intramuscular: Adults, for hospitalized patients, 60 to 150 mg daily; *children*, 0.2 to 0.25 mg/kg of body weight daily.

Oral: Adults, for hospitalized patients, initially, 100 to 150 mg daily; maintenance dose, 30 to 150 mg daily. For those with less serious emotional disorders, 20 to 50 mg daily in divided doses. *Elderly patients*, initially, 20 to 30 mg daily in divided doses. *Children*, 30 to 150 mg daily in divided doses.

PREPARATIONS.—Vesprin (Squibb).

Injection: Solution 10 mg/ml in 10 ml containers, 20 mg/ml in 1 ml containers.

Oral: Suspension 50 mg/5 ml; tablets 10, 25, and 50 mg.

Piperidine Compounds

THIORIDAZINE HYDROCHLORIDE
[Mellaril]

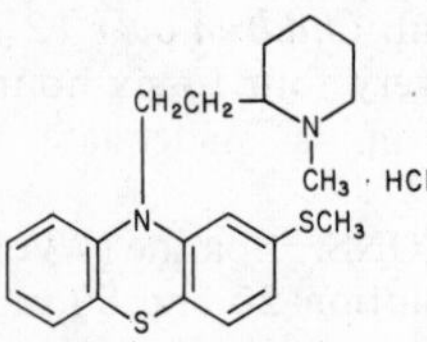

Thioridazine is the prototype of the piperidine compounds. The sedative and behavioral effects produced by thioridazine are similar to those of chlorpromazine. Thioridazine is useful in treating acute and chronic schizophrenia, the manic phase of manic-depressive psychosis, and involutional, senile, organic, and toxic psychoses, with the exception of delirium tremens. Most physicians prefer to use antianxiety agents rather than thioridazine in treating neurotic patients because its efficacy in this disorder has not been definitively established and fewer untoward reactions are associated with antianxiety agents.

Thioridazine produces different adverse effects than do drugs in the other two major phenothiazine subgroups. Extrapyramidal reactions occur rarely compared with the incidence after use of equally effective doses of other phenothiazines. Pronounced sedation and lethargy also are associated less frequently with thioridazine than with aliphatic phenothiazines (eg, chlorpromazine). However, when large doses are given, sedation and lethargy, as well as dryness of the mouth, orthostatic hypotension, and retrograde ejaculation into the urinary bladder, may occur. Other reactions include galactorrhea, gastric irritation, rash, and nasal congestion. Agranulocytosis has been reported; jaundice has not been associated with use of thioridazine.

Patients receiving more than 800 mg daily have developed retinal pigmentary degeneration which has led to blindness in some instances; others receiving smaller daily doses also have experienced visual impairment without detectable retinal changes. Therefore, patients should be closely observed to detect development of pigment deposits and signs of diminished visual acuity, impaired night vision, and brownish discoloration of objects. The use of a piperazine compound or haloperidol is preferred if long-term treatment would require doses in excess of 800 mg daily.

Electrocardiographic alterations, including prolongation of the Q-T interval and lowering and inversion of the T wave, have been associated with large doses. Therefore, the drug should be given cautiously to patients with premature ventricular contractions.

See the Introductory Statement for additional information on adverse reactions, precautions, and interactions.

USUAL DOSAGE.—*Oral: Adults*, for severe psychoses, initially, 150 to 300 mg daily in divided doses. Dose may be increased to as much as 800 mg daily in hospitalized patients. For emotional disturbances, initially, 75 mg daily in divided doses for milder cases and 150 to 200 mg daily in divided doses for severe cases. The maximal daily dose is 200 mg. *Elderly patients*, one-fourth to one-half the usual dosage; *children 2 years of age or more*, 1 mg/kg of body weight daily divided into three or four doses; *under 2 years*, information is inadequate to establish dosage.

PREPARATIONS.—Mellaril (Sandoz). *Oral:* Liquid (concentrate) 30 mg/ml; tablets 10, 15, 25, 50, 100, 150, and 200 mg.

MESORIDAZINE BESYLATE [Serentil]

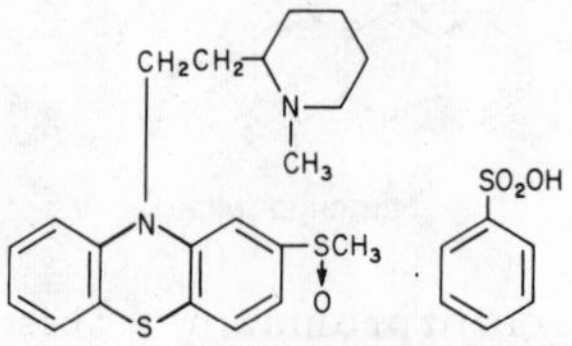

Mesoridazine, a metabolite of thioridazine, is useful in treating acute and chronic schizophrenia, the manic phase of manic-depressive psychosis, and involutional, senile, organic, or toxic psychoses, with the exception of delirium tremens. Most physicians prefer to use antianxiety agents rather than mesoridazine in treating neurotic patients because its efficacy in this disorder has not been definitively established and fewer untoward reactions are associated with antianxiety agents.

See the Introductory Statement and the evaluation on the prototype, Thioridazine Hydrochloride, for additional information on adverse reactions, precautions, and interactions.

USUAL DOSAGE.—

Intramuscular: Adults and children over 12 years of age, 25 to 200 mg daily in divided doses.

Oral: Adults and children over 12 years of age, 100 to 400 mg daily in divided doses. *Elderly patients,* one-fourth to one-half the usual dosage; *children under 12 years,* information is inadequate to establish dosage.

PREPARATIONS.—Serentil (Sandoz).

Injection: Solution 25 mg/ml in 1 ml containers.

Oral: Tablets 10, 25, 50, and 100 mg.

PIPERACETAZINE [Quide]

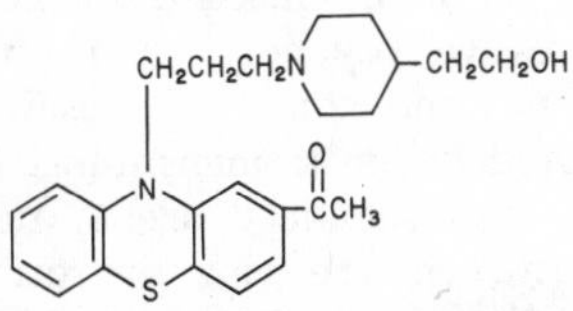

This piperidine phenothiazine is useful in the management of acute and chronic schizophrenia, the manic phase of manic-depressive psychosis, and involutional, senile, organic, and toxic psychoses, with the exception of delirium tremens. Most physicians prefer to use antianxiety agents rather than piperacetazine in treating neurotic patients because its efficacy in this disorder has not been definitively established and fewer untoward reactions are associated with antianxiety agents.

The incidence of extrapyramidal effects is higher with piperacetazine than with other piperidine compounds; piperacetazine more closely resembles the piperazine compounds in this respect. See the Introductory Statement and the evaluation on the prototype, Thioridazine Hydrochloride, for additional information on adverse reactions, precautions, and interactions.

USUAL DOSAGE.—*Oral: Adults and children over 12 years of age,* initially, 20 to 40 mg daily in divided doses. For maintenance, up to 160 mg daily in divided doses has been tolerated by many patients. *Elderly patients,* one-fourth to one-half the usual dosage. *Children under 12 years,* information is inadequate to establish dosage.

PREPARATIONS.—Quide (Dow). *Oral:* Tablets 10 and 25 mg.

Piperazine Compounds

FLUPHENAZINE DECANOATE [Prolixin Decanoate]
FLUPHENAZINE ENANTHATE [Prolixin Enanthate]
FLUPHENAZINE HYDROCHLORIDE [Permitil, Prolixin]

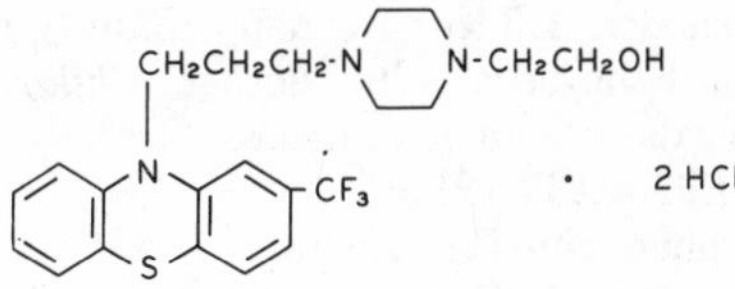

Fluphenazine is the prototype of the piperazine compounds. It is the most potent phenothiazine on a weight basis; it does not, however, have any significant advantage over other phenothiazine compounds when the oral preparations are used in the management of acute and chronic schizophrenia, the manic phase of manic-depressive psychosis, and involutional, senile, organic, and toxic psychoses. Most physicians prefer to use antianxiety agents rather than fluphenazine in treating neurotic patients because its efficacy in this disorder has not been definitively established and fewer adverse reactions are associated with antianxiety agents. Fluphenazine is also used to control nausea and vomiting (see Chapter 85, Antiemetics).

Following intramuscular or subcutaneous administration, the enanthate or the decanoate ester has an average duration of action of two weeks, and they are very useful in patients who refuse to take oral medication. The oral timed-release preparation has no significant advantage over the ordinary oral dosage form, since fluphenazine hydrochloride has a prolonged half-life.

The incidence of extrapyramidal complications is high when large doses are used. Sedative effects and orthostatic hypotension occur less frequently with fluphenazine than with aliphatic or piperidine compounds. Drowsiness, blurred vision, dryness of the mouth, and urinary retention have been reported occasionally. Transient leukopenia and cholestatic jaundice have occurred only rarely. See the Introductory Statement for additional information on adverse reactions, precautions, and interactions.

USUAL DOSAGE.—

Fluphenazine Decanoate:

Intramuscular, Subcutaneous: Adults, 6.25 to

50 mg every two to four weeks.

Fluphenazine Enanthate:

Intramuscular, Subcutaneous: Adults, 6.25 to 100 mg every two to four weeks.

Fluphenazine Hydrochloride:

Intramuscular, Oral: Adults, initially, 2.5 to 10 mg daily in divided doses at six- to eight-hour intervals. Amount may be increased gradually to 20 mg daily in hospitalized patients. For maintenance, 1.5 to 5 mg daily. *Elderly patients*, one-third the usual adult dosage. *Children*, 0.25 to 3 mg daily in divided doses.

PREPARATIONS.—

Fluphenazine Decanoate:

Prolixin Decanoate (Squibb). *Injection:* Suspension (in oil) 25 mg/ml in 1 and 5 ml containers.

Fluphenazine Enanthate:

Prolixin Enanthate (Squibb). *Injection:* Suspension (in oil) 25 mg/ml in 1 and 5 ml containers.

Fluphenazine Hydrochloride:

Permitil (Schering). *Oral:* Liquid (concentrate) 5 mg/ml; tablets 0.25, 2.5, 5, and 10 mg; tablets (timed-release) 1 mg.

Prolixin (Squibb).

Injection: Solution 2.5 mg/ml in 10 ml containers.

Oral: Elixir 2.5 mg/5 ml; tablets 1, 2.5, and 5 mg.

ACETOPHENAZINE MALEATE [Tindal]

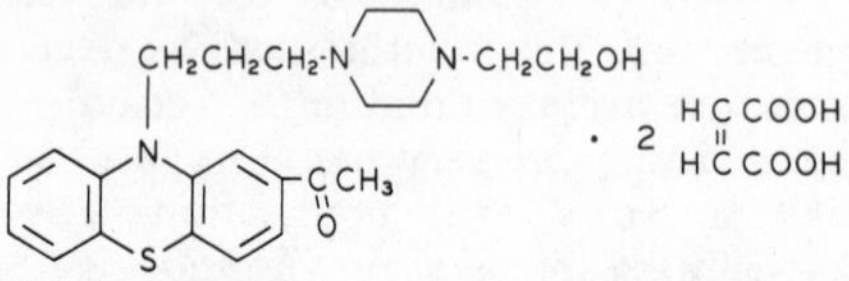

Acetophenazine is used to treat patients with acute and chronic schizophrenia, the manic phase of manic-depressive psychosis, and involutional, senile, organic, and toxic psychoses, with the exception of delirium tremens. Most physicians prefer to use antianxiety agents rather than acetophenazine in treating neurotic patients because its efficacy in this disorder has not been definitively established and fewer adverse reactions are associated with antianxiety agents.

See the Introductory Statement and the evaluation on the prototype, Fluphenazine, for information on adverse reactions, precautions, and interactions.

USUAL DOSAGE.—*Oral: Adults*, for anxiety and tension, 40 to 80 mg daily in divided doses. For hospitalized schizophrenic patients, 80 to 120 mg daily in divided doses; 400 to 600 mg daily has been given in severe cases. *Elderly patients*, one-fourth to one-half the usual dosage. *Children*, 0.8 to 1.6 mg/kg of body weight daily divided into three doses. Maximal dose is 80 mg daily.

PREPARATIONS.—Tindal (Schering). *Oral:* Tablets 20 mg.

BUTAPERAZINE MALEATE [Repoise Maleate]

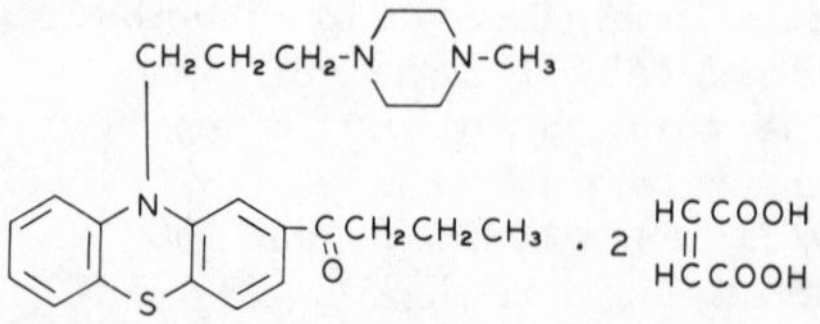

This drug is useful in the treatment of acute and chronic schizophrenia, the manic phase of manic-depressive psychosis, and involutional, senile, organic, and toxic psychoses, with the exception of delirium tremens. Most physicians prefer to use antianxiety agents rather than butaperazine in treating neurotic patients because its efficacy in this disorder has not been definitively established and fewer adverse reactions are associated with antianxiety agents.

See the Introductory Statement and the evaluation on the prototype, Fluphenazine, for information on adverse reactions, precautions, and interactions.

USUAL DOSAGE.—*Oral: Adults*, initially, 15 to 30 mg daily in three divided doses; this may be increased gradually to a maximal daily dose of 100 mg. *Elderly patients*, one-fourth to one-half the usual dosage. *Children under 12 years of age*, information is inadequate to establish dosage.

PREPARATIONS.—Repoise Maleate (Robins). *Oral:* Tablets 5, 10, and 25 mg (expressed in terms of the base).

CARPHENAZINE MALEATE [Proketazine]

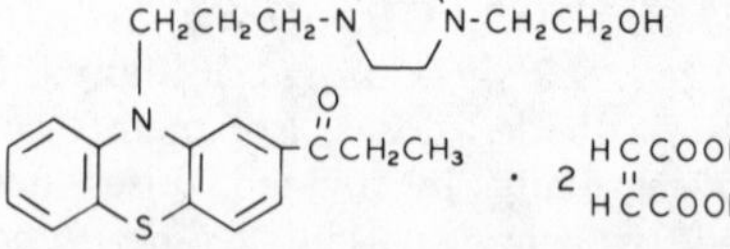

The spectrum of activity of carphenazine is similar to that of other piperazine phenothiazines. The drug is useful in treating patients with chronic or acute schizophrenia, the manic phase of manic-depressive psychosis, and involutional, senile, organic, and toxic psychoses, with the exception of delirium tremens. Most physicians prefer to use antianxiety agents rather than carphenazine in treating neurotic patients because its efficacy in this disorder has not been definitively established and fewer adverse reactions are associated with antianxiety agents.

See the Introductory Statement and the evaluation on the prototype, Fluphenazine, for information on adverse reactions, precautions, and interactions.

USUAL DOSAGE.—*Oral: Adults*, initially, 75 to 150 mg daily in divided doses; the amount may be increased by 25 to 50 mg daily at weekly intervals until optimal therapeutic effects are obtained or adverse reactions supervene. Maximal daily dosage is 400 mg. *Elderly patients*, one-fourth to one-half the usual dosage. *Children*, information is inadequate to establish dosage.

PREPARATIONS.—Proketazine (Wyeth). *Oral:* Liquid (concentrate) 50 mg/ml; tablets 12.5, 25, and 50 mg.

PERPHENAZINE [Trilafon]

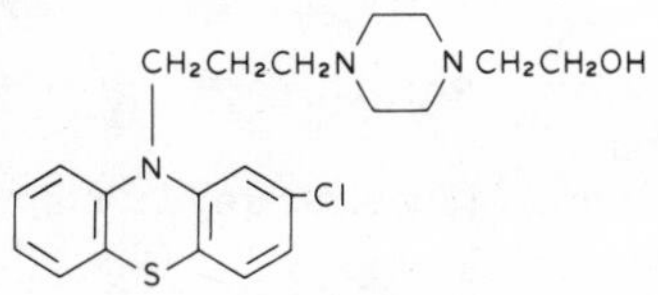

$CH_2CH_2CH_2N$ N CH_2CH_2OH

N

Cl

S

Perphenazine is useful in the treatment of acute and chronic schizophrenia, the manic phase of manic-depressive psychosis, and involutional, senile, organic, and toxic psychoses, with the exception of delirium tremens. Most physicians prefer to use antianxiety agents rather than perphenazine in treating neurotic patients because its efficacy in this disorder has not been definitively established and fewer adverse reactions are associated with antianxiety agents. The timed-release preparation has no significant advantage over the ordinary dosage forms, since perphenazine and other phenothiazines have prolonged half-lives.

See the Introductory Statement and the evaluation on the prototype, Fluphenazine, for information on adverse reactions, precautions, and interactions. For use of perphenazine in controlling nausea and vomiting, see Chapter 85, Antiemetics.

USUAL DOSAGE.—

Intramuscular: Adults, for rapid control of acute psychotic conditions, 5 mg. The dose may be repeated every six hours, but the total daily dosage should not exceed 15 mg in ambulatory patients or 30 mg in hospitalized patients. Oral therapy should be substituted as soon as possible. *Children*, information is inadequate to establish dosage.

Oral: Adults, 16 to 64 mg daily in divided doses; *elderly patients*, one-fourth to one-half the usual dosage. *Children 1 to 6 years of age*, for behavioral disorders, 4 to 6 mg daily in divided doses; *6 to 12 years*, 6 mg daily in divided doses; *over 12 years*, 6 to 12 mg daily in divided doses.

PREPARATIONS.—Trilafon (Schering).

Injection: Solution 5 mg/ml in 1 and 10 ml containers.

Oral: Liquid (concentrate) 16 mg/5 ml; syrup 2 mg/5 ml; tablets 2, 4, 8, and 16 mg; tablets (timed-release) 8 mg.

PROCHLORPERAZINE [Compazine]
PROCHLORPERAZINE EDISYLATE [Compazine Edisylate]
PROCHLORPERAZINE MALEATE [Compazine Maleate]

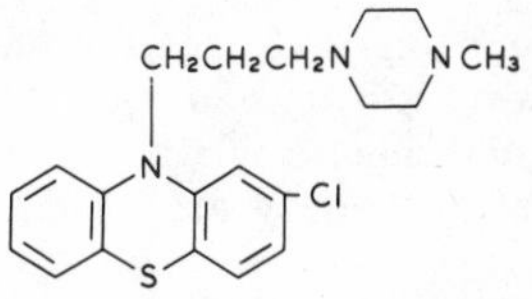

$CH_2CH_2CH_2N$ N CH_3

N

Cl

S

This drug is useful in treating acute and chronic schizophrenia, the manic phase of manic-depressive psychosis, and involutional, senile, organic, and toxic psychoses, with the exception of delirium tremens. Most physicians prefer to use antianxiety agents rather than prochlorperazine in treating neurotic patients because its efficacy in this disorder has not been established and fewer adverse reactions are associated with antianxiety agents. The timed-release preparation has no significant advantage over the ordinary oral dosage form, since prochlorperazine and other phenothiazines have prolonged half-lives.

See the Introductory Statement and the evaluation on the prototype, Fluphenazine, for additional information on adverse reactions, precautions, and interactions. For use of prochlorperazine in controlling nausea and vomiting, see Chapter 85, Antiemetics.

USUAL DOSAGE.—Information is inadequate to establish dosage for *children* weighing less than 10 kg. *Elderly patients* are given one-fourth to one-half the usual adult dosage.

Prochlorperazine:

Rectal: Adults, 50 mg daily in divided doses. *Children,* for behavioral disorders, 0.4 mg/kg of body weight daily divided into three or four doses.

Prochlorperazine Edisylate:

Intramuscular, Intravenous: Adults, to control acutely disturbed patients, 10 to 20 mg at intervals of one to four hours. For maintenance, 10 to 20 mg every four to six hours. *Children* (intramuscular), for behavioral disorders, 0.2 mg/kg of body weight daily divided into three or four doses.

Oral: Adults, for hospitalized patients, initially, 30 to 40 mg daily in divided doses; this dosage may be gradually increased to 50 to 75 mg daily. In more severe disturbances, the optimal dosage is 100 to 150 mg daily. *Children,* for behavioral disturbances, 0.4 mg/kg of body weight daily divided into three or four doses.

Prochlorperazine Maleate:

Oral: Dosage is the same as for the edisylate salt (oral).

PREPARATIONS.—

Prochlorperazine:

Compazine (Smith Kline & French). *Rectal:* Suppositories 2.5, 5, and 25 mg.

Prochlorperazine Edisylate:

Compazine [edisylate] (Smith Kline & French).

Injection: Solution 5 mg/ml in 2 and 10 ml containers.

Oral: Liquid (concentrate) 10 mg/ml; syrup 5 mg/5 ml.

Prochlorperazine Maleate:

Compazine [maleate] (Smith Kline & French). *Oral:* Capsules (timed-release) 10, 15, 30, and 75 mg; tablets 5, 10, and 25 mg.

TRIFLUOPERAZINE HYDROCHLORIDE [Stelazine]

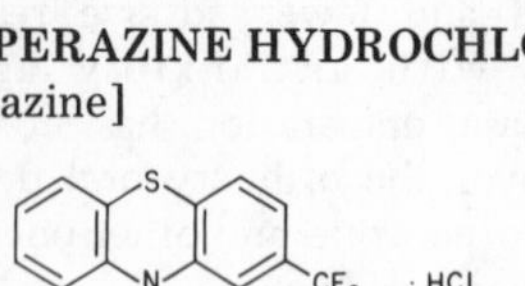

S; N; CF_3 · HCl; $CH_2CH_2CH_2$—N N—CH_3

This phenothiazine is useful in the treatment of acute and chronic schizophrenia, the manic phase of manic-depressive psychosis, and involutional, senile, organic, and toxic psychoses, with the exception of delirium tremens. Most physicians prefer to use antianxiety agents rather than trifluoperazine in treating neurotic patients because its efficacy in this disorder has not been definitively established and fewer adverse reactions are associated with antianxiety agents.

See the Introductory Statement and the evaluation on the prototype, Fluphenazine, for information on adverse reactions, precautions, and interactions.

USUAL DOSAGE.—

Intramuscular: Adults, 1 to 2 mg every four to six hours as needed. The maximal daily dosage is 10 mg. *Children 6 to 12 years of age,* 1 mg once or twice daily.

Oral: Adults, for outpatients, 2 to 4 mg daily in divided doses. For hospitalized patients, initially, 4 to 10 mg daily in divided doses. Optimal dosage for most adults is 15 to 20 mg daily, but some patients may require as much as 40 mg or more daily. *Elderly patients,* one-fourth to one-half the usual dosage. For hospitalized *children 6 to 12 years of age,* 1 mg once or twice daily; the amount may be increased up to 15 mg daily if necessary, but caution should be exercised when such large doses are given.

PREPARATIONS.—Stelazine (Smith Kline & French).

Injection: Solution 2 mg/ml in 10 ml containers.

Oral: Liquid (concentrate) 10 mg/ml; tablets 1, 2, 5, and 10 mg.

THIOXANTHENE DERIVATIVES

CHLORPROTHIXENE [Taractan]

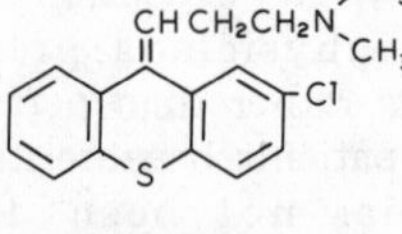

CH_3; CH CH_2CH_2N; CH_3; Cl; S

The chemical structure and pharmacologic actions of chlorprothixene are very similar to those of chlorpromazine and other aliphatic phenothiazine compounds. Its indications are similar to those of the phenothiazines.

Extrapyramidal symptoms occur less frequently than with most of the phenothiazines. Drowsiness, lethargy, dryness of the mouth, orthostatic hypotension, tachycardia, and dizziness occur frequently. Edema, constipation, urinary retention, convulsions, nervousness, syncope, insomnia, nasal congestion, rash, disturbances of accommodation, and an increase in appetite with weight gain also occur. Granulocytopenia and neutropenia are rare. Polyneuropathy and lenticular pigmentation have occurred rarely in patients who received large doses. The antiemetic action of chlorprothixene may obscure nausea and vomiting associated with various organic disorders. All of the known serious untoward effects and precautions associated with phenothiazine therapy should be borne in mind when this agent is used. See the Introductory Statement for additional information on adverse reactions, precautions, and interactions.

USUAL DOSAGE.—

Intramuscular: Adults and children over 12 years of age, 75 to 200 mg daily in divided doses. The oral form should be substituted as soon as possible. *Children under 12 years*, information is inadequate to establish dosage.

Oral: Adults, initially, 75 to 200 mg daily in divided doses, with the amount increased gradually. Dosages exceeding 600 mg daily are rarely required. *Children over 6 years of age*, 30 to 100 mg daily in divided doses; *under 6 years*, information is inadequate to establish dosage.

PREPARATIONS.—Taractan (Roche).

Injection: Solution 12.5 mg/ml in 2 ml containers.

Oral: Liquid (concentrate) 100 mg/5 ml; tablets 10, 25, 50, and 100 mg.

THIOTHIXENE [Navane]

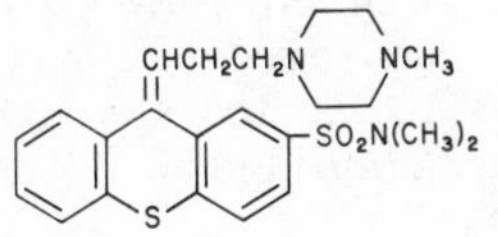

The chemical structure and pharmacologic actions of thiothixene are very similar to those of fluphenazine and other piperazine phenothiazines. Its indications are similar to those of the phenothiazines.

Extrapyramidal symptoms and insomnia occur frequently, especially with large doses. Reactions observed occasionally include drowsiness, asthenia, fatigue, dizziness, dryness of the mouth, polydipsia, blurred vision, hyperhidrosis, tachycardia, orthostatic hypotension, electrocardiographic alterations, impotence, galactorrhea, amenorrhea, rash, convulsions, photosensitivity, and lenticular pigmentation. Transitory leukopenia, a decrease in prothrombin time, and abnormal results of liver function tests have been reported rarely. All of the known serious untoward effects and precautions associated with phenothiazine therapy should be borne in mind when this agent is used. See the Introductory Statement for additional information on adverse reactions, precautions, and interactions.

USUAL DOSAGE.—

Intramuscular: Adults and children over 12 years of age, 8 to 16 mg daily in divided doses; the amount may be increased gradually to a maximal daily dose of 30 mg. The oral form should be substituted as soon as possible. *Children under 12 years*, information is inadequate to establish dosage.

Oral: Adults and children over 12 years of age, initially, 6 to 15 mg daily in divided doses; the amount may be increased gradually to a maximal daily dose of 60 mg. *Children under 12 years*, information is inadequate to establish dosage.

PREPARATIONS.—Navane (Roerig).

Injection: Solution 2 mg/ml in 2 ml containers.

Oral: Capsules 1, 2, 5, and 10 mg; liquid (concentrate) 5 mg/ml.

BUTYROPHENONE DERIVATIVE

HALOPERIDOL [Haldol]

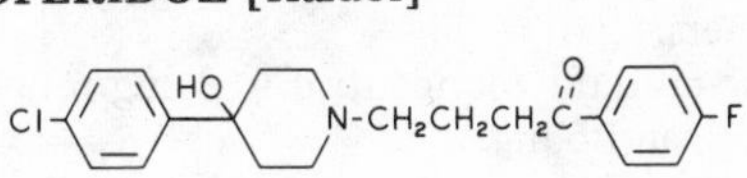

The effectiveness of haloperidol is equivalent to that of some of the phenothiazines, to which it is pharmacologically but not chemically related. It is used in the management of acute and chronic schizophrenia, the manic phase of manic-depressive psychosis, and involutional, senile, organic, and toxic psychoses, with the exception of delirium tremens. Most physicians prefer to use antianxiety agents rather than haloperidol in treating neurotic patients because its efficacy in this disorder has not been definitively established and fewer adverse reactions are associated with antianxiety agents. Haloperidol may control symptoms of Gilles de la Tourette's disease (eg, involuntary tics, utterances). It also has antiemetic properties.

Extrapyramidal symptoms are common, especially after large doses. Of these, akathisia and dystonias occur more frequently with haloperidol than with the phenothiazines. Mental depression, anxiety, apprehension, dizziness, euphoria, lethargy, headache, confusion, dryness of the mouth, anorexia, constipation, hypersalivation, nausea, vomiting, dyspepsia, blurred vision, urinary retention, impotence, edema, and hyperhidrosis occur occasionally. Leukopenia, leukocytosis, and a decrease in the red blood cell count have been reported in several patients. However, agranulocytosis or cholestatic jaundice has not been observed. Haloperidol has little tendency to produce the photosensitivity reactions associated with the phenothiazines. See the Introductory Statement for additional information on adverse reactions, precautions, and interactions.

USUAL DOSAGE.–

Intramuscular: Adults and children over 12 years of age, 6 to 15 mg daily in divided doses. A dosage larger than 15 mg daily is seldom required. The oral form should be substituted as soon as possible. *Children under 12 years*, information is inadequate to establish dosage.

Oral: Adults and children over 12 years of age, initially, 1 to 15 mg daily in two or three divided doses; usual maintenance dosage, 2 to 8 mg daily. The dosage is generally reduced for *elderly and debilitated patients. Children under 12 years*, information is inadequate to establish dosage.

PREPARATIONS.–Haldol (McNeil).

Injection: Solution 5 mg/ml in 1 ml containers.

Oral: Liquid (concentrate) 2 mg/ml; tablets 0.5, 1, 2, and 5 mg.

MISCELLANEOUS PSYCHOTHERAPEUTIC AGENTS

FLUROTHYL [Indoklon]

$$\begin{array}{ccccc} & \mathrm{F} & & \mathrm{F} & \\ & | & & | & \\ \mathrm{F} & \mathrm{C} & \mathrm{CH_2OCH_2} & \mathrm{C} & \mathrm{F} \\ & | & & | & \\ & \mathrm{F} & & \mathrm{F} & \end{array}$$

Flurothyl is a convulsant agent which is given by inhalation. It has the same indications as electroconvulsive therapy, including severe depression in a patient who may be an immediate suicide risk, or depression that has proved refractory to antidepressant drug therapy. The use of a convulsant drug also may be valuable in the treatment of schizoaffective psychoses, especially those with attendant depression, and in acute schizophrenia with excitement or catatonic withdrawal.

In general, untoward effects are similar to those with electroconvulsive therapy, including amnesia and confusion. A few patients may experience prolonged or repeated convulsions; however, since flurothyl is excreted rapidly, these episodes are less common than when pentylenetetrazol is used. Acute circulatory failure, arrhythmias, and myocardial infarction also are possible complications. Concomitant use of psychotherapeutic agents, particularly phenothiazine derivatives and tricyclic antidepressants, may enhance the possibility of acute circulatory failure. Headache, nausea, and vomiting sometimes occur. Fractures and dislocations during convulsive therapy are common unless muscle relaxants are used. Any of the adverse effects of the drugs used as premedication must be anticipated in addition to those of flurothyl itself. Absolute contraindications to convulsive therapy include elevated intracranial pressure, uncontrolled glaucoma, pregnancy, and fever; relative contraindications are cardiovascular disease and bone disease (eg, osteomalacia).

Since flurothyl is excreted by the lungs, a prolonged effect probably can occur in patients with diminished respiratory capacity. Measures for resuscitation should always be available when convulsive therapy is given because of the possibility of prolonged apnea, cardiac arrest, or acute circulatory failure.

USUAL DOSAGE.–*Inhalation: Adults*, the minimal amount of flurothyl necessary to produce a convulsion is given. A total of 0.5 to 1 ml of flurothyl is placed in a vaporizer connected on one side to a 5-liter bag of oxygen and on the other side to a face mask, and forced inhalation is given every five seconds until a convulsion occurs (usually within 40 seconds).

PREPARATIONS.–Indoklon (Ohio Medical Products). *Inhalation:* Liquid in 2 ml containers.

LITHIUM CARBONATE [Eskalith, Lithane, Lithonate]

Lithium carbonate is effective primarily for terminating manic and hypomanic episodes in patients with manic-depressive psychosis. The drug takes effect seven to ten days after initiation of therapy. Smaller doses are used as maintenance therapy during the manic phase of this psychosis. Continued maintenance doses may be given to patients with frequently recurring manic episodes; the ultimate role of this fundamentally prophylactic regimen is currently under study.

Before starting therapy with lithium carbonate, proper diagnosis and categorization of the disease as uncomplicated, clearly-defined manic-depressive illness is mandatory. In addition, the physician must observe the patient frequently, adjust dosages carefully, and monitor lithium blood levels.

There is a difference of opinion regarding whether lithium carbonate is *the* drug of choice or merely *a* drug of choice in treating the mania of manic-depressive illness. In an 18-hospital collaborative controlled study, it was shown that the phenothiazine compound, chlorpromazine, was clearly superior to lithium carbonate in treating the *highly* active patient, whereas lithium carbonate appeared to be the better treatment in the *mildly* active patient. Nevertheless, some physicians prefer lithium carbonate to the phenothiazines for initiating and continuing treatment. Others, however, regard phenothiazines as more rapidly effective and prefer to use a phenothiazine initially, and then maintain the effects with lithium carbonate alone or combined with a phenothiazine. In fact, in severe mania it may be desirable to administer a phenothiazine alone. Further controlled studies should help to determine the relative merits of combination, sequential, or single-drug treatment.

Use of lithium carbonate for psychiatric disorders other than mania has not been adequately investigated; results thus far have been disappointing.

Adverse Reactions.—The severity of toxic symptoms parallels the rise in blood level of lithium carbonate; adverse reactions may occur at doses that are close to therapeutic levels. *Serum lithium levels should not be permitted to exceed 1.4 mEq/liter during the initial treatment phase or 0.8 mEq/liter during maintenance.*

Mild reactions that may be associated with serum levels of less than 2.0 mEq/liter are nausea, diarrhea, malaise, thirst, polyuria, polydipsia, fatigue, and fine hand tremor. The latter five reactions may persist throughout treatment. If these or other symptoms become bothersome, the drug should be withheld for 24 hours and therapy resumed at a lower dosage. Other early symptoms of intoxication at blood levels below 2 mEq/liter are drowsiness, vomiting, muscle weakness, and ataxia.

Other mild to moderately severe reactions that appear to be related to serum levels of 1.5 to 2.5 mEq/liter include anorexia, blurred vision, slurred speech, dryness of the mouth, abdominal pain, weight loss, muscle hyperirritability (eg, fasciculations, clonic movements of whole limbs), drowsiness, lethargy, dizziness, and nystagmus.

Moderate to severe toxic reactions usually associated with serum levels of 2 to 2.5 mEq/liter include, in addition to those listed above, hyperactive deep tendon reflexes, choreoathetoid movements, hyperextension of limbs with grunts and gasps, epileptiform convulsions, toxic confusional state (toxic psychosis), syncope, electroencephalographic changes, acute circulatory failure, stupor, and coma.

Very severe adverse reactions associated with serum levels above 2.5 mEq/liter include generalized convulsions, oliguria, acute circulatory failure, coma, and death.

Other symptoms related to elevated serum levels include albuminuria, allergic vasculitis, drying and thinning of hair, hypoesthesia of the skin, transient scotomata, and dysarthria.

Untoward reactions apparently unrelated to dosage include thyroid effects (goiter formation, decreased protein-bound iodine levels, increased ^{131}I uptake, hypothyroidism), especially when imipramine or other tricylic antidepressants are given concomitantly; transient hyperglycemia; electrocardiographic changes (flattened T waves that may become inverted); headache; cutaneous leg ulcers; pruritus; leukocytosis; peripheral edema; and metallic taste.

No significant unforeseen reactions have been reported when electroconvulsive therapy or antipsychotic agents were used concomitantly with lithium carbonate; however, the possiblity of adverse drug interaction remains.

No specific antidote for lithium poisoning is known. However, in severe cases manifested by frank symptoms of toxicity and serum levels exceeding 2 mEq/liter, lithium carbonate should be discontinued and fluids and electrolytes replaced. Excretion of lithium can be facilitated by the use of urea, sodium bicarbonate, acetazolamide, thiazide diuretics, furosemide, or aminophylline. Hemodialysis may be indicated if renal function is impaired.

Precautions.—Patients should be maintained under close medical supervision at all times. Blood levels should be determined twice weekly during the initial stabilization period and every month or two for the first six to eight months during maintenance therapy. Blood samples should be drawn 8 to 12 hours after the last dose. If the serum level exceeds 1.5 mEq/liter, lithium carbonate should be discontinued and therapy resumed at a lower dosage after 24 hours. The patient, as well as those living in his household, should be cautioned to notify the physician immediately if untoward symptoms or unexplained illnesses occur.

Since lithium is excreted mainly by the kidneys, its normal excretion depends upon unimpaired kidney function and adequate salt and fluid intake. Diminished intake or excessive loss of sodium chloride (through vomiting, perspiration, or use of diuretics) or other electrolytes increases retention of lithium and toxic levels may be reached if the dosage is not reduced. Therefore, the patient must maintain a normal diet, including salt content, and an adequate daily fluid intake (2,500 to 3,000 ml). Lithium carbonate is contraindicated in patients receiving diuretics and in individuals on a low-salt diet. If excessive and prolonged diarrhea, vomiting, or perspiration occur, lithium carbonate should be discontinued and supplemental salt and fluid administered. The drug should not be given to debilitated or dehydrated individuals or to patients with severe infections.

The patient's cardiovascular status, renal function, and general health should be monitored when therapy is continued over long periods. The drug is contraindicated in patients with cardiovascular or renal disease that has led to congestive heart failure or decreased renal blood flow. It also is contraindicated in patients with evidence of brain damage.

Administration of small doses of thyroid hormone to patients who develop a diffuse, nontoxic goiter may stop further enlargement of the thyroid gland or lead to shrinkage, even when administration of lithium carbonate is continued.

If lithium carbonate is considered for use in pregnant or nursing women, the possibility of risk to the fetus or infant should be weighed against the expected therapeutic benefits. In one report, more than 37 mothers who received the drug throughout pregnancy exhibited no evidence of harm to the infant, but two other mothers delivered infants with congenital malformations. No conclusions can be drawn about the etiology at present. One episode of reversible perinatal *toxicity* has occurred: the mother was receiving lithium carbonate and other drugs, including diuretics, and the blood levels of lithium rose markedly in both mother and infant soon after delivery.

USUAL DOSAGE.—*Oral:* Dosage should be individualized according to serum levels and clinical response, and the drug should be discontinued if a satisfactory response is not obtained in 14 days. *Adults,* for acute mania, initially, 1.8 g daily divided into three doses. This regimen normally will produce a serum level of 1.0 to 1.5 mEq/liter. During acute manic episodes, patients show increased tolerance to blood levels that usually would be toxic. The drug should be used cautiously and in reduced doses in *debilitated or elderly patients;* the usual dose in these patients is 600 mg to 1.2 g daily divided into three doses. When an acute attack subsides, the dose should be reduced rapidly to obtain a serum level of 0.5 to 1 mEq/liter. To maintain this level, the usual dosage is 900 mg daily divided into three doses. *Children under 12 years of age,* information is inadequate to establish dosage.

PREPARATIONS.—

Eskalith (Smith Kline & French), Lithonate (Rowell). *Oral:* Capsules 300 mg.

Lithane (Roerig). *Oral:* Tablets (scored) 300 mg.

Drug also marketed under generic name.

MIXTURES

Etrafon (Schering), Triavil (Merck Sharp & Dohme): Each tablet contains perphenazine 2 or 4 mg and amitriptyline hydrochloride 10 or 25 mg. See the evaluation in Chapter 32, Antidepressants.

Chapter 30

CENTRALLY ACTING SKELETAL MUSCLE RELAXANTS

Drugs in this group act on the central nervous system and are claimed to relieve skeletal muscle spasms. Many are similar in chemical structure to drugs used primarily to treat anxiety and tension (see Chapter 28, Antianxiety Agents); therefore, as would be expected, there are few significant differences among drugs in these two groups. In fact, some of these drugs have been promoted first for one purpose and then the other without any substantial evidence for making such changes in therapeutic claims. Barbiturates and other sedatives that have no direct muscle relaxant effect probably may relieve muscular hypertonia in the same manner. Whether relief of pain actually is due to muscular relaxation or to the sedative effects of these drugs has not been conclusively demonstrated.

Skeletal muscle relaxants include carisoprodol [Rela, Soma], chlorphenesin [Maolate], chlorzoxazone [Paraflex], mephenesin, metaxalone [Skelaxin], methocarbamol [Robaxin], and orphenadrine citrate [Norflex], as well as some drugs used primarily as antianxiety agents (eg, chlordiazepoxide [Librium], diazepam [Valium], meprobamate [Equanil, Miltown]). Their central action is entirely different from that of the neuromuscular blocking agents (eg, tubocurarine, succinylcholine), which act at the myoneural junction (see Chapter 20, Adjuncts to Anesthesia).

The centrally acting skeletal muscle relaxants may be most effective in relieving acute muscular spasm of local origin. They are claimed to be helpful when used with physiotherapy in the treatment of sprains and strains, and with salicylates, adrenal corticosteroids, and other agents in the treatment of fibrositis, rheumatoid spondylitis, bursitis, and arthritis. No objective data are available to make reliable comparisons of relative effectiveness and safety among these agents. Some (eg, carisoprodol, chlorzoxazone, diazepam, metaxalone) may be helpful temporarily as adjuncts in relieving muscular spasm accompanying many neurologic disorders (eg, multiple sclerosis, cerebral palsy), but, with the possible exception of diazepam, there is little evidence that they are useful in the long-term management of such conditions. When used intravenously, diazepam, methocarbamol, and orphenadrine citrate may briefly reduce muscular spasms.

In animals, large intravenous doses depress internuncial spinal neurons and presumably reduce multisynaptic spinal reflexes. These drugs also may depress neurons in the brain stem, thalamus, and basal ganglia. These experimental findings cannot be extrapolated to man when the drugs are given orally in much smaller dosage.

Adverse Reactions and Precautions

Drowsiness and dizziness are the most frequently observed adverse reactions. Blurred vision, flushing, asthenia, lethargy, and lassitude are more common after intravenous administration than after usual oral doses. These effects are usually transient. Nausea, vomiting, heartburn, abdominal distress, constipation or diarrhea, ataxia, areflexia, flaccid paralysis, respiratory depression, tachycardia, and hypotension occur occasionally after large oral doses. Acute poisoning rarely is fatal, and is treated in the same manner as barbiturate poisoning (see Chapter 27, Sedatives and Hypnotics).

The drug should be discontinued if a rash, pruritus, or other evidence of hypersensitivity occurs. Serious allergic manifestations (eg, anaphylactic reactions, leukopenia) have occurred rarely. Jaundice has been reported with chlorzoxazone [Paraflex] (see the individual evaluation).

Patients receiving these drugs should not undertake activities that require mental alertness, judgment, and physical coordination (eg, driving a vehicle, operating dangerous machinery) until it is known that the doses used do not cause drowsiness or other incapacitating effects. Caution is necessary if skeletal muscle relaxants and other central nervous system depressants (eg, sedative-hypnotics, antianxiety agents, antipsychotic agents, antidepressants) are used concomitantly, since their effects may be additive.

Psychic or physical dependence may develop after long-term use of large doses of some of these agents (eg, chlordiazepoxide [Librium], diazepam [Valium], meprobamate [Equanil, Miltown]), especially in patients with a known tendency to abuse drugs; abrupt discontinuance after long-term use of large doses may produce severe withdrawal symptoms.

Routine precautions should be followed if these drugs are used during pregnancy (see the discussion in the General Information section on Use of Drugs During Pregnancy).

INDIVIDUAL EVALUATIONS

CARISOPRODOL [Rela, Soma]

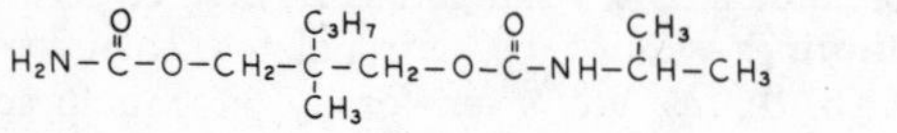

$$H_2N-\overset{O}{\overset{\|}{C}}-O-CH_2-\underset{CH_3}{\underset{|}{\overset{C_3H_7}{\overset{|}{C}}}}-CH_2-O-\overset{O}{\overset{\|}{C}}-NH-\overset{CH_3}{\overset{|}{C}H}-CH_3$$

Carisoprodol, a congener of meprobamate, has approximately the same actions and limited degree of effectiveness as other centrally acting skeletal muscle relaxants. It may be temporarily useful as an adjunct in relieving muscular spasms accompanying many neurologic disorders. Claims that it has analgesic activity have not been substantiated.

Idiosyncratic reactions (eg, extreme asthenia, transient quadriplegia, dizziness, ataxia, diplopia) have occurred rarely after administration of an initial dose of carisoprodol. See the Introductory Statement for additional information on adverse reactions.

USUAL DOSAGE.—*Oral: Adults,* 350 mg four times daily; *children 5 years of age and older,* 25 mg/kg of body weight daily divided into four doses.

PREPARATIONS.—

Rela (Schering). *Oral:* Tablets 350 mg.

Soma (Wallace). *Oral:* Capsules 250 mg; tablets 350 mg.

CHLORDIAZEPOXIDE [Libritabs]
CHLORDIAZEPOXIDE HYDROCHLORIDE [Librium]

This agent is used primarily as an antianxiety agent. It may be effective in treating musculoskeletal hypertonia when anxiety and tension intensify the symptoms; however, the favorable results reported may be attributable to the sedative effect of the drug rather than to any relaxant effect on skeletal muscle.

Ataxia and dysarthria may occur with large doses. See also the Introductory Statement and Chapter 28, Antianxiety Agents, for additional information on adverse reactions and precautions.

USUAL DOSAGE.—

Oral: Adults, 20 to 100 mg daily; *elderly or debilitated patients,* 10 to 20 mg daily. *Children over six years of age,* 0.5 mg/kg of body weight daily divided into three or four doses.

Intramuscular, Intravenous: Adults, 50 to 100 mg initially, then 25 to 50 mg three or four times daily.

Intramuscular: Children over six years of age, 0.5 mg/kg of body weight daily divided into three or four doses.

PREPARATIONS.—

Libritabs (Roche). *Oral:* Tablets 5, 10, and 25 mg.

Librium (Roche).

Oral: Capsules 5, 10, and 25 mg.

Injection: Powder 100 mg.

CHLORPHENESIN CARBAMATE [Maolate]

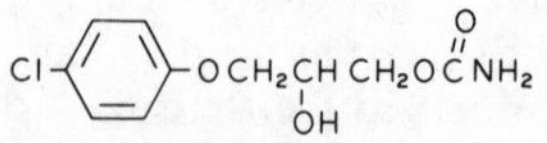

$$Cl-C_6H_4-OCH_2\underset{OH}{\underset{|}{C}H}CH_2O\overset{O}{\overset{\|}{C}}NH_2$$

This analogue of mephenesin has the same limited degree of effectiveness as other agents in this class. It may be useful as an adjunct to physiotherapy and other appropriate measures in the treatment of skeletal muscle spasm of local origin. It is not effective in the management of either congenital or acquired spastic disorders of central nervous system origin.

The most common untoward effects are drowsiness and dizziness. Adverse reactions noted occasionally include gastrointestinal disturbances, paradoxical stimulation, nervousness, insomnia, headache, and asthenia.

Rash and pruritus occur rarely.

USUAL DOSAGE.—*Oral: Adults*, 800 mg initially three times daily until the desired effect is obtained. Maintenance dosage is 400 mg four times daily or less frequently as required. *Children*, dosage has not been determined.

PREPARATIONS.—Maolate (Upjohn). *Oral:* Tablets 400 mg.

CHLORZOXAZONE [Paraflex]

Cl N-H O O

Chlorzoxazone has approximately the same actions and limited degree of effectiveness as other centrally acting skeletal muscle relaxants. It may be temporarily useful as an adjunct in relieving muscular spasms accompanying many neurologic disorders.

This agent should be used cautiously, if at all, in patients with a history of liver disease, since a few cases of jaundice have been reported and since the drug is chemically related to zoxazolamine. Patients should be observed closely for signs of liver damage. See the Introductory Statement for additional information on adverse reactions and precautions.

USUAL DOSAGE.—*Oral: Adults*, 250 to 750 mg three or four times daily; *children*, 20 mg/kg of body weight daily divided into three or four doses.

PREPARATIONS.—Paraflex (McNeil). *Oral:* Tablets 250 mg.

DIAZEPAM [Valium]

This agent is used primarily as an antianxiety agent. It is a useful adjunct in the treatment of muscular spasms in patients with acute musculoskeletal disorders and certain acute and chronic neurologic disorders (eg, cerebral palsy, athetosis, multiple sclerosis, spinal cord injury, stiff-man syndrome). In addition, diazepam is effective orally for minor motor epilepsy and parenterally for status epilepticus.

Ataxia and dysarthria have been associated with large doses.

For additional information, see Chapters 20, Adjuncts to Anesthesia; 28, Antianxiety Agents; and 31, Anticonvulsants.

USUAL DOSAGE.—

Intramuscular, Intravenous: Adults, 5 to 10 mg initially; this amount may be repeated in three or four hours. Larger doses may be necessary for tetanus, but no more than 30 mg should be given within an eight-hour period. *Children*, 0.04 to 0.2 mg/kg of body weight, but the amount should not exceed 0.6 mg/kg in an eight-hour period.

Oral: Adults, 2 to 10 mg three or four times daily; *children*, 0.12 to 0.8 mg/kg of body weight daily divided into three or four doses.

PREPARATIONS.—Valium (Roche).

Injection: Solution 5 mg/ml in 2 and 10 ml containers.

Oral: Tablets 2, 5, and 10 mg.

MEPHENESIN

$-CH_3$
$-OCH_2CH(OH)CH_2OH$

Mephenesin has the same limited degree of effectiveness as other skeletal muscle relaxants. It has been used to relieve acute muscular spasm of local origin.

Untoward effects include vertical nystagmus, diplopia, lassitude, and asthenia or mild ataxia. Gastrointestinal disturbances may be avoided by giving the drug after meals or with milk or fruit juice.

USUAL DOSAGE.—*Oral: Adults*, 2 to 3 g three to five times daily; *children*, 175 mg/kg of body weight daily divided into three to five doses.

PREPARATIONS.—*Oral:* Tablets 500 mg.

AVAILABLE TRADEMARKS.—Romeph (Robinson), Tolax (Sutliff & Case). Drug also marketed by other manufacturers under generic name.

MEPROBAMATE [Equanil, Miltown]

This agent is used primarily as an antianxiety agent. Its reported effectiveness in musculoskeletal disorders is probably attributable to its sedative effect rather than to any direct muscle relaxant effect. Data are insufficient for evaluation of the timed-release preparation.

See Chapter 28, Antianxiety Agents, and Chapter 31, Anticonvulsants, for information on other uses and on adverse reactions and precautions.

USUAL DOSAGE.—

Intramuscular: Adults, 400 mg three or four times daily (maximal daily dose, 2.4 g). For tetanus, *infants*, 600 mg daily divided into four doses; *older children*, 50 to 70 mg/kg divided into six to eight doses (maximal daily dose, 3.2 g).

Oral: Adults, same as intramuscular dose; *older children*, 100 to 200 mg two or three times daily.

PREPARATIONS.—

Equanil (Wyeth). *Oral:* Capsules (timed-release) 400 mg; suspension 200 mg/5 ml; tablets 200 and 400 mg; tablets (coated) 400 mg (Wyseals).

Miltown (Wallace).

Injection: Solution 80 mg/ml in 5 ml containers.

Oral: Capsules (timed-release) 200 and 400 mg (Meprospan); tablets 200 and 400 mg, tablets (coated) 400 mg (Meprotabs).

ADDITIONAL TRADEMARKS.—Arcoban (Arcum), Kesso-Bamate (McKesson), Meprocon (Consolidated Midland), SK-Bamate (Smith Kline & French), Tranmep (Reid-Provident), Viobamate (Rowell). Drug also marketed by other manufacturers under generic name.

METAXALONE [Skelaxin]

Metaxalone may be useful as an adjunct in the treatment of skeletal muscle spasm of local origin. However, clinical benefits reported may be attributable to the drug's sedative effect rather than to any direct relaxant effect on muscular spasm.

Nausea, drowsiness, and dizziness occur frequently. Caution is required when metaxalone is used in patients with a history of liver disease. See the Introductory Statement for additional information on adverse reactions and precautions.

USUAL DOSAGE.—*Oral: Adults*, 800 mg three or four times daily for not more than ten consecutive days; *children*, dosage is reduced (see table, back cover).

PREPARATIONS.—Skelaxin (Robins). *Oral:* Tablets 400 mg.

METHOCARBAMOL [Robaxin]

This analogue of mephenesin carbamate has approximately the same actions and limited degree of effectiveness as other centrally acting skeletal muscle relaxants. When given intravenously, it may briefly reduce muscular spasms.

Dizziness, drowsiness, and mild nausea occur rarely when methocarbamol is used orally. Flushing, metallic taste, nausea, nystagmus, diplopia, mild ataxia, hypotension, and bradycardia have been observed after intravenous administration; these untoward effects may be lessened by giving the injection at a rate not to exceed 3 ml/minute. Parenteral administration is contraindicated in patients with impaired renal function because the polyethylene glycol-300 vehicle may be nephrotoxic.

USUAL DOSAGE.—

Oral: Adults, initially, 1.5 to 2 g four times daily for 48 to 72 hours; maintenance dose, 1 g four times daily. *Children*, 60 mg/kg of body weight daily divided into four doses.

Intramuscular: Adults, 500 mg alternately in each gluteal region every eight hours; *children*, 60 mg/kg of body weight daily divided into four doses.

Intravenous: Adults, 1 to 3 g daily at a rate not exceeding 3 ml/minute; the drug should not be given by this route for more than three days. *Children*, 60 mg/kg of body weight daily divided into four doses.

PREPARATIONS.—Robaxin (Robins).

Injection: Solution (aqueous) 100 mg/ml with 50% polyethylene glycol-300 in 10 ml containers.

Oral: Tablets 500 and 750 mg.

ORPHENADRINE CITRATE [Norflex]

This drug is an analogue of the antihistamine, diphenhydramine. Orphenadrine citrate has approximately the same actions and limited degree of effectiveness as other centrally acting skeletal muscle relaxants. When it is given intravenously, the drug may briefly reduce muscular spasms.

Adverse effects reflect its anticholinergic activity and include blurred vision, dryness of the mouth and skin, and mild excitation. This agent is contraindicated in patients with angle-closure glaucoma or myasthenia gravis. It should be used with caution in patients with tachycardia or signs of urinary retention. (See also Chapter 74, Antiparkinsonism Agents.)

USUAL DOSAGE.—

Oral: Adults, 100 mg twice daily.

Intramuscular, Intravenous: Adults, 60 mg twice daily.

PREPARATIONS.—Norflex (Riker).

Oral: Tablets 100 mg.

Injection: Solution 30 mg/ml in 2 ml containers.

MIXTURES

The centrally acting skeletal muscle relaxants have been combined with analgesics, barbiturates, and adrenal corticosteroids, which suggests that the efficacy of the muscle relaxants leaves much to be desired. Since there is no definitive evidence that any of these fixed combinations are more effective than their components administered separately, there is no justification for prescribing any of these mixtures. See the evaluations on Parafon Forte, Robaxisal and Robaxisal-PH, and Soma Compound in Chapter 22, Mild Analgesics.

Chapter 31

ANTICONVULSANTS

Anticonvulsants are used to terminate convulsive episodes and to prevent or decrease the incidence of seizures in patients with epilepsy. About one in every 200 persons is afflicted with some form of epilepsy, and currently available drugs will usually provide fair to excellent control of the seizures.

The objective of therapy is to control the seizures while maintaining the patient in as normal a physiologic state as possible. Drug therapy must be individualized. The choice of drugs depends upon the type of seizure and the response of the patient; further, many patients with epilepsy have more than one type of seizure, and drugs effective for one type may not help or may even unmask another.

Types of Epilepsy: Although epilepsy may be classified according to various clinical and electroencephalographic criteria, for therapeutic purposes it is convenient to divide the disorders into two broad groups: (1) the grand mal and various focal types; and (2) the petit mal, akinetic, and myoclonic types. The focal seizures include the Jacksonian and the more localized focal motor types; the sensory focal; the psychomotor; and the autonomic, "abdominal," or diencephalic, which are sometimes designated as "nonconvulsive epileptic equivalents." The term petit mal is restricted here to classical absence seizures with three-per-second spikes and waves on the electroencephalogram; akinetic seizures, sometimes considered a form of petit mal, are better regarded separately. Myoclonic seizures can occur as a relatively benign condition, as a manifestation of certain severe, progressive neurologic diseases (eg, infantile massive spasms, myoclonic progressive familial epilepsy), or as a complication of numerous inflammatory, metabolic, or degenerative brain diseases.

Occasional aberrant types may occur, but most epilepsies can be fitted into this classification. Although the term "major epilepsy" is often used synonomously only with grand mal, when discussing prophylactic therapy it is occasionally convenient to regard grand mal and focal motor seizures collectively as major motor seizures. Similarly, the myoclonic and akinetic types may be spoken of as minor motor seizures; however, this does not imply that the underlying disorders are necessarily "minor."

Most idiopathic epilepsy begins during childhood or adolescence. Epilepsy beginning during infancy tends to result from developmental defects, metabolic disease, or birth injury. However, the so-called "benign febrile convulsions" of infancy and early childhood are the most common form of seizures in this age group and the approach to their treatment is controversial. Epilepsy beginning during adulthood usually is caused by trauma, tumors, or other recognizable brain disease.

Drug Treatment: Causes for obscure seizures should be sought, since a specific underlying illness or focal cerebral lesion may be amenable to definitive treatment. With few exceptions, however, the choice of anticonvulsant drugs is based upon the type of seizure rather than on the cause of the seizure.

The appropriate dosage of any drug or combination of drugs depends upon the size, age, and condition of the patient, his response to treatment, and the possible synergistic or antagonistic effect of concomitant medication. The dosage of anticonvulsants for children is usually somewhat larger on a weight basis than that for adults. Except for control of an acute seizure, the patient should be started on a small or moderate dosage of the drug suitable for his type of epilepsy. This dosage should be increased gradually until the seizures are controlled or until the appearance of minor symptoms of toxicity makes further increases inadvisable. If more than minor toxic reactions develop, another drug should be substituted. When the drug used initially is well tolerated but only reduces the frequency of the seizures, an agent of a different chemical class should be added.

With the exception of patients who do not adhere to their prescribed regimen, the largest number of treatment failures results from the administration of insufficient doses of appropriate drugs and failure to use two or more of them concomitantly when indicated. Other common causes of failure include improper classification of type of seizure, use of the wrong drug, failure to recognize progressive neurologic disease, too frequent changes in drug therapy, premature withdrawal of drugs, poor indoctrination of patients, or failure to recognize the social and economic needs of patients. Blood level determinations can be helpful in determining whether a patient is taking the medication as prescribed and whether therapeutic levels have been achieved.

In general, the drugs that are effective in grand mal may be useful in the various focal seizures and vice versa, but they have less or no value in petit mal, akinetic, and myoclonic seizures; the drugs effective in petit mal may be of some help in certain minor motor seizures, but generally are not useful in the grand mal and focal diseases.

Despite the preceding generalizations, phenobarbital is potentially valuable in the management of most epilepsies regardless of the predominant seizure type. Its greatest effectiveness, however, is in grand mal and the various focal epilepsies. Among these, psychomotor seizures are often the most refractory and thus the least likely to respond to this one drug alone.

The other long-acting barbiturates, mephobarbital [Mebaral] and metharbital [Gemonil], are alternate choices; with proper dosage adjustment, their actions closely resemble those of phenobarbital. The shorter-acting barbiturates are not useful prophylactically as anticonvulsants, for their hypnotic action tends to parallel any anticonvulsant effect they might have.

Primidone [Mysoline], which is chemically related to the barbiturates, is frequently useful in refractory grand mal and focal seizures. It is partly metabolized to phenobarbital but also has independent anticonvulsant activity. The drug may have some specific effect against psychomotor seizures, but there is no general agreement on this point.

The hydantoins (diphenylhydantoin [Dilantin], ethotoin [Peganone], and mephenytoin [Mesantoin]) are used primarily in grand mal and focal seizures; they are usually not effective in treating petit mal. Diphenylhydantoin is the drug of choice among the hydantoins; it is more effective than ethotoin and safer than mephenytoin. However, these alternative hydantoins may be considered for trial in special circumstances (see the individual evaluations). The hydantoins have long plasma half-lives; therefore, the dosage schedule must be adjusted gradually over a long period to obtain control without producing toxic reactions.

The *initial* drug used in grand mal and focal epilepsy is usually diphenylhydantoin or phenobarbital. Most neurologists choose diphenylhydantoin, especially for adults. While phenobarbital is somewhat safer, with diphenylhydantoin there is more likelihood of controlling the disease with a single agent. Phenobarbital is more often used initially in children.

Whichever drug is chosen, if an adequate trial fails to control the seizures, the other should be added. If this combination still fails to provide satisfactory control, a third drug from a different chemical class will be needed. If a trial with primidone is elected, this drug should be *substituted* for phenobarbital rather than added to it. Similarly, if a trial with another hydantoin (eg, mephenytoin) is eventually chosen, diphenylhydantoin should be discontinued.

Acetazolamide [Diamox] can sometimes be useful as an adjunct. Also, psychomotor epilepsy may respond to methsuximide [Celontin]. Carbamazepine [Tegretol] is a newer drug that is active against grand mal and focal seizures. Its efficacy in grand mal appears comparable to that of phenobarbital, diphenylhydantoin, or primidone. A precise comparison with other drugs in psychomotor epilepsy is not yet possible, but carbamazepine nevertheless is a valuable addition to the treatment of this disease. Phenacemide [Phenurone] may be effective in controlling psychomotor or other seizures, but since it is extremely toxic, it is only of limited usefulness and should be prescribed only if other medications are ineffective. Inorganic bromides (eg, sodium bromide, potassium bromide) also have anticonvulsant activity, but because of their toxicity and limited efficacy, interest in them has declined. Under special circumstances, however, they still have a place in the treatment of grand mal.

Drugs specifically effective for petit mal include the succinimides (ethosuximide [Zarontin], methsuximide, and phensuximide [Milontin]) and the oxazolidinediones (trimethadione [Tridione] and paramethadione [Paradione]). Ethosuximide is the drug of choice. Nevertheless, phenobarbital retains a prominent role in treating petit mal. Alone, it seldom controls the disorder satisfactorily, but about one-half of the patients with petit mal will also develop grand mal, and the broad anticonvulsant spectrum of phenobarbital makes it very useful. The succinimides and oxazolidinediones are ineffective against grand mal.

If ethosuximide, with or without phenobarbital, fails to control petit mal, another drug from a different chemical class should be added. The selection of a satisfactory second or third drug can sometimes be difficult, as some of those likely to be effective may also be quite toxic. Trimethadione and phenacemide are effective but, because of their hazards, should be prescribed only with reluctance; there is some question whether phenacemide should be used at all. The antimalarial agent, quinacrine [Atabrine] occasionally helps control petit mal when other drugs have failed; however, its potential toxicity also must be considered.

When used alone or as an adjunct, acetazolamide will often help patients with petit mal. Frequently, however, its effectiveness is only temporary. Although a ketogenic diet may enhance its effectiveness, this diet is not pleasant and is difficult to impose upon a child. Nevertheless, acetazolamide should be regarded as a potentially valuable adjunct in refractory petit mal. Preliminary evidence has shown that diazepam [Valium] is frequently effective in petit mal, but its eventual role has not yet been adequately defined. The relative safety of this drug commends it for trial. The use of meprobamate [Equanil, Miltown] has received some support, but its effectiveness is slight. Probably any mild sedative would have some secondary beneficial effect on seizure patterns, and if this is the action sought, phenobarbital would seem preferable.

Minor motor seizures of the akinetic and myoclonic types are often refractory to drug therapy. They may occur alone or in association with petit mal or grand mal. Drugs effective for both seizure types may be used alone or in combination. In general, drugs effective for petit mal may offer some promise in these minor motor types. However, these forms of epilepsy are so heterogeneous and vaguely defined that treatment must essentially be empirical. Among them, only one condition lends itself to a definitive recommendation: For treatment of infantile massive spasms, corticotropin or adrenal corticosteroids offer the greatest promise of effectiveness, despite the fact that these drugs tend to be contraindicated in most epilepsies. Some benzodiazepine derivatives are valuable in minor motor seizures, but the most effective one for this purpose (nitrazepam) is not commercially available in this country. Of those that are available, diazepam appears most suitable for trial.

Sometimes epileptic seizures that initially are satisfactorily controlled by drugs will escape from control. When a barbiturate or hydantoin is involved, the escape may be due to induction of liver enzymes that results in an increased rate of metabolism of the drug. An increase in dosage will ordinarily reestablish control, and once this is accomplished, there is no reason to expect a repetition of the escape unless the disease itself worsens.

Trauma or emotional stress may necessitate an increase in the dosage requirement. This should particularly be borne in mind if a patient requires surgery.

Unless a progressive underlying disease is involved, spontaneous remissions of convulsive disorders are common, especially with the idiopathic forms that usually begin during childhood; the great majority of petit mal, in fact, is limited to childhood. Accordingly, the eventual discontinuation of an anticonvulsant regimen must often be considered. When a decision is made to discontinue medication, the dosage of one drug at a time should be reduced very gradually, since sudden withdrawal of any of these drugs may precipitate a recurrence of seizures and is one of the most common causes of status epilepticus. Only when a serious adverse reaction occurs should a drug be discontinued immediately; another anticonvulsant should be substituted to protect the patient.

Nonepileptic Convulsions: Convulsions are not necessarily epileptic per se. They can occur as a symptom of a vast array of acute conditions (eg, infections, fever, metabolic disturbances, drug overdosage or idiosyncrasy, poisoning, cerebral edema). Treatment in such circumstances is primarily directed at the underlying cause. The prophylactic regimens discussed in this chapter are ordinarily not indicated. Nevertheless, convulsions in some acute conditions (eg, febrile convulsions in children, a convulsion following head trauma) do suggest that chronic epilepsy be considered a possibility.

Convulsions (or impending convulsions) in at least two special circumstances require specific mention. First, generalized (and perhaps myoclonic) seizures are one of the manifestations of congenital and frank pyridoxine deficiency in newborn infants. As expected, pyridoxine is the specific remedy; if the diagnosis is firmly established in these infants, anticonvulsants are not indicated. Pyridoxine, however, should not be regarded as a general-purpose anticonvulsant. (See also Chapter 14, Vitamins and Sources of Vitamins.)

Second, major motor seizures, usually with severe, protracted clonic convulsions, are sometimes associated with the withdrawal syndrome in persons physically dependent on barbiturates, alcohol, or certain other sedatives. In barbiturate dependence, gradual discontinuance of the drug is indicated. In these other dependence syndromes, substitution of phenobarbital and then slow discontinuance will help prevent the convulsions. Diazepam logically deserves further investigation for this use but, at present, its potential role is poorly defined. Although often used, diphenylhydantoin has not been conclusively proved to be of value.

Status Epilepticus: Status epilepticus is a serious emergency that requires prompt and vigorous treatment to prevent permanent harmful effects or death. Diazepam given parenterally is the drug of choice. This condition may also be terminated by the intravenous administration of phenobarbital sodium, which is usually preferred to shorter-acting barbiturates since its effect is almost as rapid and lasts longer. The full calculated anticonvulsant dose should be given initially, as fractional doses may result in the paradoxical situation of barbiturate-induced depression but continued status epilepticus. Diphenylhydantoin sodium may be given intravenously, but its onset of action is delayed for 5 to 15 minutes and it is not very effective in this condition. This drug has the advantage of usually not depressing respiration, but it must be administered slowly to avoid serious hypotension. Paraldehyde given parenterally is regarded quite highly by many neurologists; it can also be given rectally. When anesthetic agents are necessary, they should be given under the supervision of an anesthesiologist, when possible, and resuscitative equipment should be available. A measure of *last resort* for treating status epilepticus is the slow intravenous infusion of the local anesthetic, lidocaine [Xylocaine].

Adverse Reactions and Precautions

Many minor reactions to anticonvulsants may be overcome by reducing the dosage, but this may necessitate the addition of another anticonvulsant to the regimen.

Most anticonvulsants produce gastrointestinal disturbances in some patients, especially during the early stages of treatment. The symptoms may be reduced either by administering the drugs after meals or by decreasing the dosage.

Many anticonvulsants have sedative effects, and drowsiness is sometimes a significant complaint. Again, this effect is most noticeable during the early period of treatment; if it persists, a reduction in dosage may be indicated. Sedative drugs may cause alterations in mood, which occasionally are serious (see Chapter 27, Sedatives and Hypnotics). Other anticonvulsants also can cause mental disturbances. Phenacemide [Phenurone] is particularly prone to cause serious personality changes, including psychoses and suicidal depression.

Ataxia is common with use of the hydantoins and, if persistent, requires a reduction in dosage. There is evidence that these drugs can cause cerebellar damage if a dosage that produces ataxia is administered for a prolonged period. For practical purposes, however, this danger appears remote since the ataxia is so troublesome that it demands correction by dosage adjustment. Very young patients can be exceptions, as drug-induced ataxia may be confused with the natural unsteadiness of the toddler. Ataxia also may occur with the use of barbiturates.

Many anticonvulsants commonly cause skin eruptions; these are usually morbilliform or acne-like and may disappear when the dosage is reduced or the drug is temporarily discontinued and cautiously readministered. However, a skin reaction may herald the development of a severe reaction that may warrant withdrawal of the drug. Systemic lupus erythematosus, Stevens-Johnson syndrome, angioedema, serum sickness, and polyarteritis nodosa have been associated with anticonvulsant medication. Anaphylaxis is extremely rare. Other reactions noted occasionally include alopecia and hypertrichosis.

Because the barbiturates are particularly prone to aggravate acute intermittent porphyria, they should not be used in patients with this disease.

Several anticonvulsants may cause reversible visual disturbances such as diplopia and nystagmus; one of the most notable, hemeralopia (defective vision in a bright light), occurs with the oxazolidinediones, trimethadione [Tridione] and paramethadione [Paradione].

Certain untoward effects characteristic of a particular anticonvulsant may not occur with a chemically related drug; for example, diphenylhydantoin [Dilantin] frequently causes gingival hyperplasia in children, but this reaction seldom occurs with mephenytoin [Mesantoin], and has not been reported with ethotoin [Peganone].

Lymphadenopathies simulating malignant lymphomas have occurred with several anticonvulsants; the hydantoins have been implicated most frequently. Although it is questionable whether diphenylhydantoin [Dilantin] is as prone to cause these pseudolymphomas as is mephenytoin [Mesantoin], it is responsible for a greater number of reactions since it is more widely used. The signs and symptoms may temporarily progress but usually begin to disappear within one to two weeks after discontinuation of therapy. A few cases of true lymphoma and of Hodgkin's disease have been reported in which a causal relationship to hydantoin therapy seems possible.

Megaloblastic anemias, which respond to folic acid, also have been reported with several anticonvulsants, particularly hydantoins, barbiturates, and primidone [Mysoline]. Accordingly, periodic blood studies are indicated when these drugs are taken. Usually the drug may be continued if the anemia responds to treatment with folic acid. However, because folic acid increases the rate of metabolism of diphenylhydantoin and thus may interfere with its anticonvulsant action, folic acid should not be used routinely for prophylaxis in patients without anemia.

Even in the absence of anemia, there is some evidence that folic acid depletion induced by anticonvulsants may be manifested by reversible mental deterioration. Although poor memory, inattentiveness, lethargy, and slow learning may result from other effects of anticonvulsant drugs or may be evidence of brain damage, such symptoms in the presence of low folate blood levels may warrant a trial with folic acid.

Among the most dangerous reactions that develop during therapy with anticonvulsant drugs are those that result from damage to the bone marrow, liver, and kidneys. Severe blood dyscrasias have been associated with phenacemide, mephenytoin, paramethadione, trimethadione, and less frequently with some of the other anticonvulsants. Baseline blood counts should be performed before initiating treatment with these drugs. Although periodic blood studies during treatment will reveal mild leukopenias, they cannot be relied upon to predict the more serious reactions that ordinarily occur precipitously (eg, agranulocytosis, thrombocytopenia, aplastic anemia). An aplastic anemia might be detected before symptoms develop, if one were so fortunate as to have a hemoglobin determination when levels began to decline, but such detection would require an impractical frequency of blood studies in view of the rareness of the reaction. Since early recognition of the dyscrasia and discontinuance of the offending drug are essential, the patient should be advised to report promptly such symptoms as sore throat, fever, easy bruising, petechiae, epistaxis, or other signs of an infection or bleeding tendency. Clinical and laboratory evaluation is necessary if such symptoms occur. Although the risk of dyscrasias is diminished after the first year of treatment, the physician should be constantly alert to their possible occurrence. The mortality from aplastic anemia is particularly high and, if the patient does survive, recovery is slow. Except for mephenytoin and phenacemide, however, this reaction is fortunately very rare.

Severe, sometimes fatal liver disease has occurred with phenacemide and more rarely with some of the other anticonvulsants, including the hydantoins. Before treatment with these drugs is begun, it is advisable to make baseline liver function studies, and patients should be instructed to report promptly any symptoms of hepatitis such as jaundice, dark urine, anorexia, abdominal discomfort, or other gastrointestinal symptoms. Since this drug-induced hepatitis is probably idiosyncratic, the value of performing periodic laboratory studies in asymptomatic patients is doubtful. Phenacemide may be an exception, as there is some evidence that hepatitis can develop insidiously with its use; liver function abnormalities (eg, decreased prothrombin activity) may herald the development of serious disease.

Nephropathies have developed occasionally during treatment with anticonvulsants, especially in patients receiving the oxazolidinediones, trimethadione and paramethadione. Unlike the blood dyscrasias and hepatitis, these reactions may develop insidiously without producing symptoms in the early stages. Therefore, urinalyses should be made before treatment and periodically during treatment. The development of any significant renal abnormality is an indication for discontinuing the drug. See the discussion on Monitoring for Adverse Reactions with Laboratory Studies in the General Information section.

A frequently cited paradoxical effect of anticonvulsants is the tendency of agents effective for one type of seizure to aggravate or precipitate seizures of another type. However, seizure type tends to be mixed in epileptic disorders, and the apparent aggravation of one type may be a manifestation of the natural course of the disease and may reflect the ineffectiveness of the particular drug for that type of seizure. Precipitation of seizures by anticonvulsant drugs probably is rare, and some consultants doubt that it occurs. There is no question, however, that abrupt withdrawal of anticonvulsants can induce seizures. When a drug is to be discontinued, the dosage should be reduced gradually unless rapid withdrawal and substitution of another drug is mandatory because of a serious adverse reaction.

There is strongly suggestive evidence that the incidence of congenital abnormalities is increased with use of trimethadione and paramethadione during pregnancy. Accordingly, these drugs should be avoided in pregnant women if possible. Surveillance for the onset of megaloblastic anemia assumes added importance during pregnancy because of the possible harm to the fetus if the condition is allowed to progress. Infants born to mothers who have received barbiturates, primidone, or hydantoins during pregnancy should be particularly observed for neonatal coagulation defects, which respond to vitamin K (see Chapter 11, Hemostatics).

See the individual evaluations that follow for additional adverse reactions for specific drugs.

Drug Interactions: Possible interactions between anticonvulsants and other drugs, and between each other, must be borne in mind. As an interesting example, phenobarbital has been reported to lower blood levels and decrease the half-life of diphenylhydantoin by increasing its rate of metabolism. This interaction is usually harmless and not clinically apparent, because the net anticonvulsant effect of the two drugs used together is greater than that of either used alone. Nevertheless, the interaction would prevent complete summation of the potential anticonvulsant properties of the drugs.

Drug interactions must be considered if dicumarol is given concomitantly with anticonvulsants. This agent inhibits the metabolism of diphenylhydantoin, possibly leading to drug accumulation and toxicity. On the other hand, the metabolism of coumarin anticoagulants is enhanced by barbiturates, thus necessitating adjustment of anticoagulant dosage when barbiturates are either added or discontinued.

The barbiturates, particularly phenobarbital, stimulate the activity of a number of enzyme systems and affect the metabolism of many drugs. Thus, when a barbiturate is used as an anticonvulsant, possible interactions between it and other drugs the patient may receive should be considered.

Several other drugs (eg, disulfiram [Antabuse], isoniazid, aminosalicylic acid, chloramphenicol) potentiate the action of diphenylhydantoin by interfering with its metabolism. Monoamine oxidase inhibitors potentiate barbiturates. Reserpine antagonizes some anticonvulsants, including diphenylhydantoin. Synergism of toxicity has been reported between mephenytoin and trimethadione or paramethadione.

BARBITURATES

PHENOBARBITAL
PHENOBARBITAL SODIUM

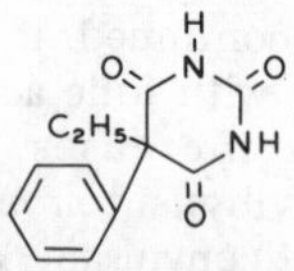

H
O N O
C_2H_5 NH
O

Phenobarbital, a long-acting barbiturate, is the most broadly useful anticonvulsant. Its principal effectiveness is in major motor, psychomotor, and other focal seizures; it can be used as the initial drug, particularly in children, although more commonly it is added if diphenylhydantoin has not completely controlled the seizures. Although its effectiveness in petit mal and minor motor seizures is limited, it nevertheless is often the appropriate initial drug because of its broad spectrum, safety, and the frequency with which grand mal complicates other types of seizures.

Drowsiness, which is usually transient, is the most common adverse effect, although some children become hyperactive. This paradoxical response may indicate underlying "minimal brain dysfunction," causing both the seizures and the response.

If ataxia occurs and persists, a reduction in dosage is required. Gastrointestinal distress occurs occasionally. Skin eruptions are uncommon, with progression to exfoliative dermatitis very rare. Megaloblastic anemia is also uncommon. When the drug is given during pregnancy, the possibility of a coagulation defect in the newborn must be considered. Barbiturates are contraindicated in patients with acute intermittent porphyria. Abrupt termination of therapy in epilepsy may cause withdrawal convulsions, but drug dependence and barbiturate inebriation are unlikely with the usual doses given for epilepsy. (See also the Introductory Statement.)

Phenobarbital sodium is used parenterally in status epilepticus. Although the present trend is to use diazepam instead, phenobarbital remains an important drug for this purpose. The principal danger is respiratory depression. Nevertheless, a full anticonvulsant dose should be given initially, as fractional doses may result in the paradoxical situation of drug-induced depression but continued status epilepticus.

USUAL DOSAGE.—

Phenobarbital:

Oral: Adults, 120 to 200 mg daily, preferably at bedtime; *children,* 1 to 6 mg/kg of body weight daily.

Phenobarbital Sodium:

Intramuscular, Intravenous (slow): For status epilepticus, *adults,* 200 to 320 mg; *children,* 3 to 5 mg/kg of body weight represents a reasonable guide.

PREPARATIONS.—

Phenobarbital:

Oral: Capsules (timed-release) 65 and 100 mg; elixir 20 mg/5 ml; tablets 16, 32, 50, 64, and 100 mg.

Phenobarbital Sodium:

Injection: Powder 120, 130, and 320 mg; solution 130 mg/ml in 1 ml containers, 160 mg/ml in 2 and 10 ml containers.

AVAILABLE TRADEMARKS.—Phenobarbital: Barbipil (North American), Barbita (North American), Eskabarb (Smith Kline & French), Lixophen (Elder), Luminal (Winthrop), Solu-Barb (Fellows-Testagar), Stental (Robins). **Phenobarbital Sodium:** Luminal Sodium (Winthrop). Drug also marketed by other manufacturers under generic name.

MEPHOBARBITAL [Mebaral]

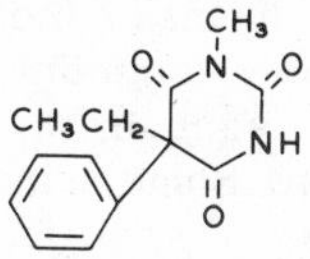

Mephobarbital is metabolized to phenobarbital; thus it has similar properties and uses, but larger doses are given (see the Introductory Statement and the evaluation on Phenobarbital).

USUAL DOSAGE.—*Oral: Adults,* 200 mg at bedtime to 600 mg daily in divided doses, *children under 5 years of age,* 16 to 32 mg three or four times daily; *over 5 years,* 32 to 64 mg three or four times daily.

PREPARATIONS.—Mebaral (Winthrop). *Oral:* Tablets 32, 50, 100, and 200 mg. Drug also marketed under generic name.

METHARBITAL [Gemonil]

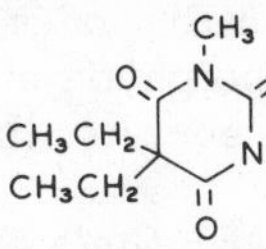

Metharbital has the same structural relation to barbital as mephobarbital has to phenobarbital. Its properties and uses are similar to those of phenobarbital, but this barbiturate is less potent on a weight basis; dosage adjustment is necessary to compensate for this difference. (See the Introductory Statement and the evaluation on Phenobarbital.)

USUAL DOSAGE.—*Oral: Adults,* initially, 100 mg at bedtime to 300 mg daily in divided doses. The dose may be increased to as much as 600 to 800 mg daily if required. *Children,* 5 to 15 mg/kg of body weight daily in divided doses.

PREPARATIONS.—Gemonil (Abbott). *Oral:* Tablets 100 mg.

PRIMIDONE [Mysoline]

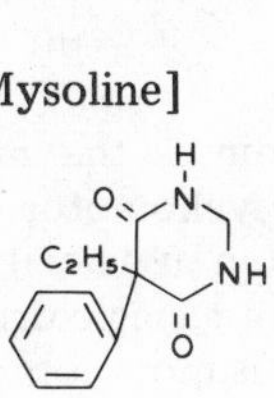

Although not a barbiturate by traditional classification, primidone is considered with this group because of its close chemical relationship. It is partially metabolized to phenobarbital. The principal use of primidone is as a substitute for the barbiturate in patients not responding adequately to a barbiturate-hydantoin regimen. However, larger doses are needed than with phenobarbital. Primidone may be used as the initial "barbiturate" in major motor and focal epilepsy, but it is more commonly reserved for refractory cases because it often causes pronounced sedation. Some clinicians believe that the drug has a specific utility in psychomotor epilepsy. It is not useful in the treatment of petit mal.

Sedation often diminishes with continued administration. If the dosage increase is sufficiently gradual, incapacitating drowsiness may be avoided. Ataxia and some of the more minor reactions resemble those caused by barbiturates. Skin eruptions are noted occasionally. Megaloblastic anemia may occur and responds to folic acid. When the drug is given during pregnancy, the possibility of a coagulation defect in the newborn must be considered. Since primidone is excreted in the milk, drowsiness may occur in nursing infants of mothers receiving the drug. By inference, the contraindication to barbiturates in patients with acute intermittent porphyria also would apply to primidone. (See also the Introductory Statement.)

USUAL DOSAGE.—*Oral: Adults,* 250 mg daily at bedtime to 2 g daily in divided doses; *children under 8 years of age,* one-half adult dosage.

PREPARATIONS.—Mysoline (Ayerst). *Oral:* Suspension 250 mg/5 ml; tablets 50 and 250 mg.

HYDANTOINS

DIPHENYLHYDANTOIN [Dilantin]
DIPHENYLHYDANTOIN SODIUM [Dilantin Sodium]

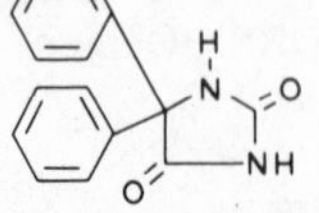

Diphenylhydantoin is the most useful drug for major motor, psychomotor, and other focal epilepsies. It is often used with phenobarbital (or primidone) when a single drug is inadequate. Diphenylhydantoin is most commonly the initial drug chosen, particularly in adults; almost invariably it should be either the first or second agent selected. It is ineffective in petit mal and most minor motor seizures.

Diphenylhydantoin has the advantage of producing little or no sedation in usual doses. Ataxia occurs with larger doses; if persistent, it indicates overdosage, and reduction in the amount is necessary to avoid cerebellar damage. Ocular signs and symptoms such as nystagmus and diplopia also may necessitate reduction of dosage. Peripheral neuropathy may develop after years of use. Skin eruptions occur rather frequently, but are only rarely serious. Gingival hyperplasia is common and often is severe in children; scrupulous oral hygiene helps prevent this troublesome complication, but when it develops, gingivectomy will remedy it. Hirsutism is less common but does occur, especially in the young. Rare but serious idiosyncratic reactions include hepatitis, bone marrow depression, systemic lupus erythematosus, Stevens-Johnson syndrome, and lymphadenopathy resembling malignant lymphomas. Folic acid depletion may occur, and this may progress to megaloblastic anemia. When the drug is given during pregnancy, the possibility of a coagulation defect in the newborn must be considered. (See also the Introductory Statement.)

The sodium salt of diphenylhydantoin is sometimes used parenterally for control of status epilepticus, but it is distinctly inferior to diazepam or phenobarbital sodium. Unlike barbiturates, it seldom depresses respiration. However, the onset of action is relatively slow, and this is a considerable disadvantage. If intravenous administration is too rapid, dangerous hypotension may occur. The high alkalinity of the drug makes intramuscular injection undesirable if the intravenous route is possible, and subcutaneous or perivascular injection must definitely be avoided.

Diphenylhydantoin has been advocated for a large array of disorders besides epilepsy. Evidence of effectiveness is inadequate for all except a few of these disorders. Especially notable is use of the sodium salt intravenously in certain arrhythmias (see Chapter 2, Antiarrhythmic Agents). The oral form may be effective prophylactically for some forms of migraine, but it usually is not the drug of choice (see Chapter 24, Agents Used to Treat Migraine). In addition, trigeminal neuralgia may sometimes be relieved by diphenylhydantoin, but carbamazepine is the drug of choice. Beneficial effects have been reported in a variety of psychoses, neuroses, and other psychiatric disorders, but criteria for selecting patients for trial with the drug are presently too vague for any firm recommendation. The strongest support for such a trial is in psychiatric disorders in which an abnormal electroencephalogram suggests a diagnosis of epilepsy.

USUAL DOSAGE.—

Diphenylhydantoin:

Oral: The dosage must be individualized and adjusted according to the patient's response. *Adults,* initially, 300 mg daily; the most common maintenance dose is 300 to 400 mg daily. *Children,* 3 to 8 mg/kg of body weight daily. Because of the long half-life of diphenylhydantoin, a single daily dose is as effective as divided daily doses. Also, timed-release preparations are unnecessary.

Diphenylhydantoin Sodium:

Intravenous: For status epilepticus, *adults,* 150 to 250 mg injected no faster than 50 mg/minute; *children,* dosage is reduced (see table, back cover). This drug may also be given intramuscularly, but this route is not preferred.

PREPARATIONS.—

Diphenylhydantoin:

Dilantin (Parke, Davis). *Oral:* Suspension 30 and 125 mg/5 ml; tablets (pediatric) 50 mg.

Diphenylhydantoin Sodium:

Dilantin [sodium] (Parke, Davis).

Oral: Capsules 30 and 100 mg.

Injection: Powder for solution containing approximately 50 mg/ml when properly diluted with special solvent provided in 100 and 250 mg containers.

ADDITIONAL TRADEMARKS.— **Diphenylhydantoin:** Toin [timed-release capsules] (Reid-Provident). **Diphenylhydantoin Sodium:** Kessodanten (McKesson), SDPH (Rachelle). Drugs also marketed under generic names.

ETHOTOIN [Peganone]

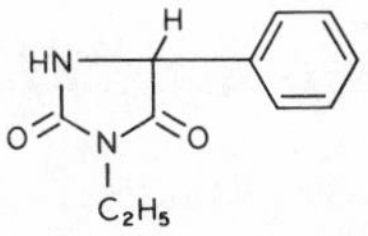

HN, H, O, N, O, C_2H_5

This hydantoin derivative is only moderately effective in grand mal and just slightly so in psychomotor epilepsy. It is usually unsatisfactory if used alone. Its toxicity resembles that of diphenylhydantoin, but the incidence of reactions is generally lower. Thus, this drug is less toxic but also less effective than diphenylhydantoin. (See also the Introductory Statement and the evaluation on Diphenylhydantoin.)

USUAL DOSAGE.—*Oral: Adults,* initially, 1 g daily in divided doses; for maintenance, 2 to 3 g daily in four to six divided doses. *Children,* initially, 750 mg daily; for maintenance, 500 mg to 1 g daily in divided doses.

PREPARATIONS.—Peganone (Abbott). *Oral:* Tablets 250 and 500 mg.

MEPHENYTOIN [Mesantoin]

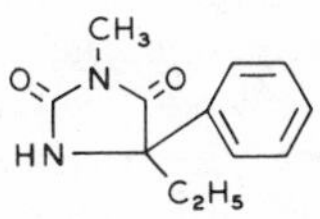

CH_3, O, N, O, HN, C_2H_5

This hydantoin derivative is effective in major motor, psychomotor, and other focal epilepsies, but is more toxic than diphenylhydantoin and should be reserved for patients who do not respond to the drugs of choice.

Mephenytoin has a sedative effect usually absent with diphenylhydantoin; otherwise it lacks or has a lower incidence of some of the more minor adverse effects of diphenylhydantoin (eg, ataxia, gingival hyperplasia, hirsutism, gastric distress). However, life-threatening and other serious reactions are considerably more common: severe skin eruptions, blood dyscrasias (eg, aplastic anemia, leukopenia, agranulocytosis, thrombocytopenia, megaloblastic anemia), hepatitis, systemic lupus erythematosus, and lymphadenopathy simulating malignant lymphomas. Although it has not been reported, mephenytoin would presumably share with diphenylhydantoin the tendency to induce coagulation defects in newborn infants of mothers taking the drug. A toxic synergism occurs between mephenytoin and trimethadione or paramethadione. (See also the Introductory Statement.)

USUAL DOSAGE.—*Oral: Adults,* initially, 50 to 100 mg daily, with weekly increases by the same amount until the maintenance dose is established (usually 200 to 600 mg). Further increases to 800 mg or more occasionally are required. *Children,* initially, same dose as for adults; maintenance dose, usually 100 to 400 mg, depending upon the age of the patient and the severity of the seizures.

PREPARATIONS.—Mesantoin (Sandoz). *Oral:* Tablets 100 mg.

SUCCINIMIDES

ETHOSUXIMIDE [Zarontin]

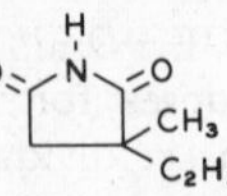

Ethosuximide is the drug of choice for petit mal. It is also effective for minor motor seizures in some patients, but is generally ineffective for psychomotor or grand mal epilepsy, or in patients with considerable organic brain damage.

The most common adverse reactions are gastrointestinal disturbances. Drowsiness, ataxia, headache, dizziness, euphoria, hiccup, rash, and behavioral changes have been reported. Major untoward effects occur considerably less frequently than with the oxazolidinediones (trimethadione and paramethadione). Aplastic anemia, thrombocytopenia, leukopenia, pancytopenia, and eosinophilia are noted rarely. (See also the Introductory Statement.)

USUAL DOSAGE.—*Oral: Adults and children over 6 years of age,* initially, 500 mg daily; the daily dose may be increased if necessary by increments of 250 mg every four to seven days until seizures are controlled or untoward effects develop. Doses exceeding 1 g daily are seldom more effective than smaller doses. *Children under 6 years,* initially, 250 mg daily with increase in dosage same as above.

PREPARATIONS.—Zarontin (Parke, Davis). *Oral:* Capsules 250 mg.

METHSUXIMIDE [Celontin]

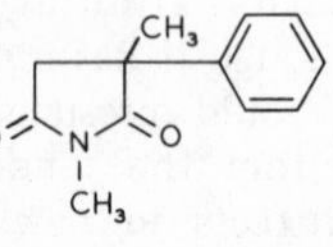

This succinimide may be helpful in petit mal and minor motor seizures, especially when used with other anticonvulsants. It also may be used as an adjunct to other drugs to reduce the incidence of psychomotor attacks. Grand mal, if present, must be controlled with other medication.

Untoward effects occur frequently and may be of minor or major consequence. These include gastrointestinal disturbances and reactions affecting the central nervous system (drowsiness, headache, dizziness, diplopia, and ataxia). Severe mental depression may occur; patients who have psychomotor seizures should be watched closely for behavioral changes, for these may progress to an acute psychosis unless the drug is discontinued. Hypersensitivity reactions, such as skin eruptions, fever, hiccup, and periorbital hyperemia, occur only rarely. Many minor untoward effects may disappear spontaneously or may be controlled by reducing the dose, but a rash may herald the development of a more serious reaction. Renal and hepatic damage may occur. Blood dyscrasias, including aplastic anemia, have been reported rarely. (See also the Introductory Statement.)

USUAL DOSAGE.—*Oral: Adults and children,* initially, 300 mg daily; this may be increased at weekly intervals by increments of 300 mg daily until a daily dose of 1.2 g, given in divided amounts, is attained. The optimal dose is the minimal amount that will control seizures without causing serious untoward effects.

PREPARATIONS.—Celontin (Parke, Davis). *Oral:* Capsules 150 and 300 mg.

PHENSUXIMIDE [Milontin]

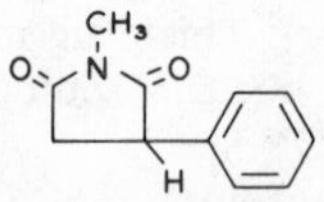

This drug, offered for treatment of petit mal, is the safest of the succinimides. Unfortunately, however, its low potency limits its effectiveness. From the broad view of balancing efficacy and safety, ethosuximide is preferred.

Adverse effects include nausea, asthenia, drowsiness, and rash. The confirmed reaction of greatest concern to date is nephropathy, particularly in children, which apparently is reversible on withdrawal of the drug. Agranulocytosis, if indeed it is caused by phensuximide, has occurred very rarely. (See also the Introductory Statement.)

USUAL DOSAGE.—*Oral: Adults and children,* 500 mg to 1 g two or three times daily.

PREPARATIONS.—Milontin (Parke, Davis). *Oral:* Capsules 250 and 500 mg; suspension 300 mg/5 ml.

OXAZOLIDINEDIONES

TRIMETHADIONE [Tridione]

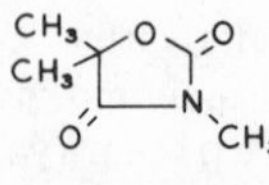

This drug is principally effective in controlling petit mal seizures. Although trimethadione is among the more effective agents for this purpose, it should be reserved for refractory cases because of toxicity.

Serious reactions, some of them fatal, include rash that may progress to exfoliative dermatitis or erythema multiforme, nephropathy, hepatitis, and bone marrow depression with aplastic anemia, neutropenia, or agranulocytosis. Pseudolymphomas, systemic lupus erythematosus, and a myasthenia gravis-like syndrome also have been reported. Drowsiness may occur. Reversible visual disturbances, particularly hemeralopia, are quite common. Hiccup sometimes occurs during early treatment. Hair loss may be noted.

There is suggestive evidence that the use of trimethadione during pregnancy is associated with an increased incidence of congenital abnormalities in the infant. Accordingly, this drug should be avoided in pregnant women if possible. A toxic synergism occurs between trimethadione and mephenytoin. (See also the Introductory Statement.)

USUAL DOSAGE.—*Oral: Adults*, 0.9 to 2.1 g daily in three or four divided doses; *children*, initially, 40 mg/kg of body weight daily in three or four divided doses.

PREPARATIONS.—Tridione (Abbott). *Oral:* Capsules 300 mg; solution 200 mg/5 ml; tablets (chewable) 150 mg.

PARAMETHADIONE [Paradione]

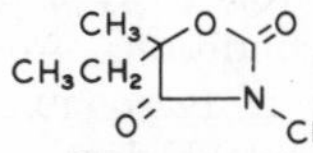

CH_3 O O CH_3CH_2 N O CH_3

This oxazolidinedione is similar to trimethadione and has the same indication, ie, petit mal that is refractory to safer drugs. It is somewhat less toxic than trimethadione, but also is less effective.

Reactions tend to be the same as with trimethadione, but some occur less frequently. A few (eg, pseudolymphoma, systemic lupus erythematosus, myasthenia gravis-like syndrome) have not yet been reported with paramethadione.

As with trimethadione, there is suggestive evidence that the use of paramethadione during pregnancy is associated with an increased incidence of congenital abnormalities in the infant. Accordingly, paramethadione should be avoided in pregnant women if possible. A toxic synergism occurs between paramethadione and mephenytoin. (See also the Introductory Statement.)

USUAL DOSAGE.—*Oral: Adults*, 0.9 to 2.1 g daily in three or four divided doses; *children*, initially, 40 mg/kg of body weight daily in three or four divided doses.

PREPARATIONS.—Paradione (Abbott). *Oral:* Capsules 150 and 300 mg; solution 1.5 g/5 ml.

MISCELLANEOUS ANTICONVULSANTS

Primary

CARBAMAZEPINE [Tegretol]

Carbamazepine is a tricyclic compound chemically related to imipramine. It was introduced in this country for the treatment of trigeminal neuralgia, but it also has important anticonvulsant properties and has been used extensively in Europe for epilepsy. Carbamazepine is useful in major motor and psychomotor epilepsy. Its efficacy in grand mal appears comparable to that of phenobarbital, diphenylhydantoin, or primidone. A precise comparison with other drugs used in psychomotor epilepsy is not yet possible, but carbamazepine nevertheless is a valuable addition to the treatment of this disease, as the older drugs often have proved inadequate. The drug is not effective in petit mal and minor motor epilepsy. However, it has a psychotropic action that may increase alertness and elevate the mood in many patients with epilepsy.

Almost one-fourth of patients receiving carbamazepine experience one or more adverse reactions. For a discussion of these, and for other uses of the drug, see Chapter 92, Miscellaneous Drugs.

USUAL DOSAGE.—*Oral: Children under 6 years of age*, 100 mg daily; *6 to 12 years*, 100 mg twice daily; *adults and adolescents*, 100 mg three times daily. Depending upon response and tolerance, the dosage can be increased by increments of 100 mg each week. The average effective daily dose is 1 g (range, 300 mg to 2 g).

PREPARATIONS.—Tegretol (Geigy). *Oral:* Tablets 200 mg.

DIAZEPAM [Valium]

This benzodiazepine derivative was introduced as an antianxiety agent, but it also has important anticonvulsant properties. Given parenterally, it is potentially lifesaving in status epilepticus and is now regarded as the drug of choice in that condition.

When given orally, diazepam is sometimes helpful in myoclonic seizures, which are often refractory to other drugs; however, it is far less effective than its congener, nitrazepam, which is not commercially available in this country. In infantile massive spasms, this agent has a distinctly secondary role to adrenal corticosteroids (eg, prednisone) or corticotropin, despite the danger of toxicity following their use. Good results have also been reported with diazepam in petit mal, but its exact role has not yet been adequately assessed.

The most common adverse effects with oral use are drowsiness, dizziness, fatigue, and ataxia, all dose-related. Paradoxical excitement or stimulation sometimes occurs. Parenteral administration for status epilepticus requires observation for respiratory depression and hypotension, and the slight possibility of cardiac arrest must be borne in mind. However, the overall safety of the drug appears to compare favorably with other agents used for this emergency. At least one additional consideration is necessary in newborn infants: the injectable form contains sodium benzoate and benzoic acid as buffers, which have been shown in in vitro tests to displace bilirubin from albumin; thus, the possibility of inducing kernicterus must be considered.

For further information on adverse reactions, precautions, and other uses, see Chapters 20, Adjuncts to Anesthesia; 28, Antianxiety Agents; and 30, Centrally Acting Skeletal Muscle Relaxants.

USUAL DOSAGE.—

Oral: Adults, 4 to 40 mg daily in divided doses, beginning with a low dose and increasing it gradually; *elderly or debilitated patients*, initially, 2 mg. *Children*, initially, 2 to 4 mg daily in divided doses; subsequent doses are less than those used for adults.

Intravenous (slow): For status epilepticus, *adults*, 5 to 10 mg; *children*, 2 to 5 mg, depending on size. If the convulsions make slow intravenous injection impossible, intramuscular injection may be substituted. The drug should not be mixed with other agents or diluted with intravenous solutions.

PREPARATIONS.—Valium (Roche).

Injection: Solution 5 mg/ml in 2 and 10 ml containers.

Oral: Tablets 2, 5, and 10 mg.

PARALDEHYDE

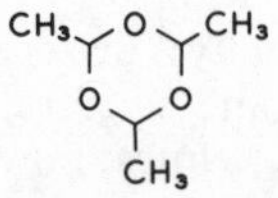

This drug is effective in status epilepticus and still retains considerable popularity. Intravenously, it is sometimes given undiluted, but administration must be slow; otherwise, it induces severe coughing that can add to the difficulty of administration and can even cause pulmonary hemorrhage. Dilution in sodium chloride injection and administration by drip usually is preferred. Intramuscular injection, although often very irritating, is relatively safe if care is taken to avoid peripheral nerves. Rectal administration also is employed, most commonly in children; the dose, however, is more difficult to control by this route. The opinion of consultants has been divided sharply on whether this agent should be used parenterally, and, if so, by which route and technique.

Fatalities have occurred with paraldehyde. Bronchopulmonary disease is a relative contraindication. The sedative effect may be intensified and prolonged in patients with liver damage. Care must be taken to avoid use of decomposed drug.

For other uses of paraldehyde, see Chapter 27, Sedatives and Hypnotics.

USUAL DOSAGE.—

Intramuscular, Intravenous: Adults and children, For status epilepticus, suggested doses have varied, and recommendations of manufacturers are vague. However, dosage for status epilepticus frequently exceeds that given for more benign conditions. About 0.15 ml/kg of body weight is reasonable; sometimes a moderate additional dose will be needed, especially for smaller children. Intravenous injection must be slow, preferably by drip and with the drug diluted with sodium chloride injection. Paraldehyde should be given carefully to avoid extravasation.

Rectal: Children, 0.3 ml/kg of body weight, with the drug dissolved in an equal quantity of olive oil. Alternatively, dilution in milk has been suggested to improve tolerance.

PREPARATIONS.—

Injection: Liquid 1 g/ml in 2, 5, and 10 ml containers.

Rectal: Liquid in 30 ml containers.

AVAILABLE TRADEMARK.—Paral (Fellows-Testagar). Drug also marketed by other manufacturers under generic name.

PHENACEMIDE [Phenurone]

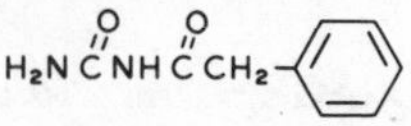

Phenacemide is an effective anticonvulsant that may be useful in refractory psychomotor, grand mal, petit mal, and mixed seizures. However, it is very dangerous and should be used only when adequate control of seizures cannot be achieved with other drugs; there is some question whether it should be used at all.

Potentially fatal reactions include hepatitis, blood dyscrasias (aplastic anemia, agranulocytosis), and toxic psychoses, often accompanied by suicidal depression. Nephropathy occurs occasionally. Rash and gastrointestinal reactions are rather common. (See also the Introductory Statement.)

USUAL DOSAGE.—*Oral: Adults*, initially 250 to 500 mg three times daily. If necessary, an additional 500 mg daily may be added at weekly intervals. The usual maintenance dose is 2 to 3 g daily in divided doses, although some patients have required as much as 5 g daily. *Children 5 to 10 years of age*, approximately one-half adult dosage.

PREPARATIONS.—Phenurone (Abbott). *Oral:* Tablets 500 mg.

Secondary

ACETAZOLAMIDE [Diamox]

This carbonic anhydrase inhibitor, originally introduced as a diuretic, has been used effectively in most forms of epilepsy, most commonly in petit mal. It is most useful as an adjunct to other drugs. A concomitant ketogenic diet enhances the effectiveness if the patient will accept such a regimen. In any event, however, the anticonvulsant action may decline with continued administration. The drug is often most helpful when intermittent administration has some special utility, for example, in a woman whose convulsive tendencies increase with menstruation.

For discussions of adverse reactions and other uses, see Chapter 7, Diuretics, and Chapter 69, Agents Used to Treat Glaucoma.

USUAL DOSAGE.—*Oral: Adults and children*, 8 to 30 mg/kg of body weight daily in divided doses.

PREPARATIONS.—Diamox (Lederle). *Oral:* Capsules (timed-release) 500 mg; tablets 125 and 250 mg.

BROMIDES

Inorganic bromides are of historical interest as the first antiepileptic agents used; they have moderate anticonvulsant activity against all types of seizures. Although bromides are obsolete for routine use, they still have an occasional place, especially in grand mal, when other drugs prove unsuitable. Bromide is usually administered as the sodium or potassium salt.

In its excretory function, the kidney cannot distinguish between the bromide ion and the chloride ion. Therefore, to maintain a consistent anticonvulsant effect, the patient's salt intake should be kept at a fairly constant, low level.

Bromides routinely cause drowsiness, and skin eruptions are frequent. Of greatest importance is cumulative poisoning that causes severe toxic psychoses. Maximal accumulation does not occur for approximately two months.

For other uses, see Chapter 27, Sedatives and Hypnotics.

USUAL DOSAGE.—*Oral: Adults*, 1 g three times daily; the amount may be increased gradually to 2 g three times daily. *Children*, 50 to 100 mg/kg daily in three divided doses.

PREPARATIONS.—*Oral:* Elixir and tablets. Drug marketed under generic name.

LIDOCAINE HYDROCHLORIDE [Xylocaine Hydrochloride]

As an alternative to general anesthesia, this local anesthetic is sometimes infused intravenously in status epilepticus *as a last resort* after the drugs of choice have failed. However, with overdosage, lidocaine itself is a convulsant, and great care is required in its use. For other adverse reactions and uses, see Chapter 2, Antiarrhythmic Agents, and Chapter 18, Local Anesthetics.

USUAL DOSAGE.—*Intravenous:* Lidocaine is administered in a continuous intravenous infusion at the rate of 1 to 3 mg/minute, using a pump, if possible, instead of relying on the uncertainty of a simple drip. Usually, control of seizures will be achieved with the patient maintaining consciousness. The rate is reduced periodically until the drug can be discontinued altogether; this may require several days.

PREPARATIONS.—Xylocaine Hydrochloride (Astra). *Injection:* Solution 0.5%, 1%, 1.5%, and 2% in single and multiple-dose containers of 2 to 100 ml.

ADDITIONAL TRADEMARKS.— Seracaine (Rachelle), Ultracaine (Ulmer). Drug also marketed by other manufacturers under generic name.

QUINACRINE HYDROCHLORIDE [Atabrine Hydrochloride]

This antimalarial agent may be helpful as an adjunct in some cases of refractory petit mal, but it should be used only if other drugs have failed. Its effectiveness as an anticonvulsant is limited.

Yellow discoloration of the skin occurs with use of quinacrine. For a discussion of other adverse reactions and other uses, see Chapters 61, Antimalarial Agents; 65, Anthelmintics; and 88, Antineoplastic Agents.

USUAL DOSAGE.—*Oral: Adults,* 100 mg daily; *children,* 1 to 2 mg/kg of body weight daily.

PREPARATIONS.—Atabrine Hydrochloride (Winthrop). *Oral:* Tablets 100 mg.

MIXTURES

Several fixed-dosage combinations of anticonvulsants are marketed. They are listed below only to acknowledge their availability and not necessarily to encourage their use. Their usefulness is limited since, in the management of epilepsy, the dosage of each drug used concomitantly should be established *individually.* After this has been done, if the doses present in an available mixture correspond to the ratio and quantities required by the patient, the use of such a combination product would seem justified for the convenience of the patient, unless a subsequent adjustment of dosage becomes necessary. However, some available combinations are irrational, since the usual dose of one ingredient carries with it only a trivial dose of the other. Others contain inappropriate ingredients that are not effective for epilepsy. Still others contain more than two ingredients and appear to be entirely too cumbersome for practical use in view of the importance of individualizing the dosage of every drug the patient receives.

Alepsal (Fougera): Each tablet contains phenobarbital 97 mg, belladonna powder 20 mg, and caffeine 26 mg.

Dilantin Sodium with Phenobarbital (Parke, Davis): Each capsule contains diphenylhydantoin sodium 100 mg and phenobarbital 16 or 32.5 mg.

Mebroin (Winthrop): Each tablet contains mephobarbital 90 mg and diphenylhydantoin 60 mg.

Neo-Sedaphen (Smith, Miller & Patch): Each 5 ml of liquid contains pentobarbital sodium 30 mg, phenobarbital sodium 10 mg, sodium bromide 300 mg, potassium bromide 200 mg, and calcium bromide 100 mg.

Phelantin (Parke, Davis): Each capsule contains diphenylhydantoin 100 mg, phenobarbital 30 mg, and methamphetamine hydrochloride 2.5 mg.

Quadra-Sed (Smith, Miller & Patch): Each 5 ml of liquid contains pentobarbital sodium 15 mg, phenobarbital sodium 15 mg, butabarbital sodium 15 mg, and secobarbital sodium 15 mg.

Sedaphen (Smith, Miller & Patch): Each 5 ml of liquid contains phenobarbital sodium 20 mg, sodium bromide 300 mg, potassium bromide 200 mg, and calcium bromide 100 mg.

Sedobarb No. 1 (Whittier): Each tablet contains phenobarbital 16 mg and pentobarbital sodium 32.5 mg.

Chapter 32

ANTIDEPRESSANTS

Depression is one of the most frequently occurring psychiatric disorders. Symptoms of depression also are common in patients with many medical and surgical conditions. Classification of depressive illness as being of endogenous or exogenous (reactive) origin, and as psychotic or neurotic subtype, permits selection of more specifically acting antidepressants. In some patients, use of antidepressants accelerates the rate of improvement, diminishes the intensity of symptoms, reduces the danger of suicide, and promotes social adjustment and occupational rehabilitation.

The tricyclic compounds (imipramine [Presamine, Tofranil], amitriptyline [Elavil], desipramine [Norpramin, Pertofrane], doxepin [Adapin, Sinequan], nortriptyline [Aventyl], and protriptyline [Vivactil]) and the monoamine oxidase inhibitors (isocarboxazid [Marplan], phenelzine [Nardil], and tranylcypromine [Parnate]) have replaced the psychomotor stimulants (amphetamines and methylphenidate [Ritalin]) in the treatment of depression. Other measures, such as supportive psychotherapy, reduction of environmental stress, and improvement of the social milieu, also should be employed in treating patients with exogenous depression. These ancillary measures are of doubtful value in patients with endogenous depression; electroconvulsive therapy, which acts more quickly than the antidepressants, may be indicated in patients with endogenous depression, particularly those who do not respond to the tricyclic compounds or who are suicide risks.

Tricyclic compounds and monoamine oxidase inhibitors also may be useful, alone or with phenothiazines, in the depressive phase of certain types of schizophrenia; however, they will not improve the other symptoms of schizophrenia and may accentuate the basic thought disorder.

Although many studies on the effectiveness of antidepressants have been uncontrolled or poorly controlled, there is good evidence that these drugs produce a satisfactory response (elevation of mood, increased physical activity and mental alertness, improved appetite and sleep patterns, reduction in morbid preoccupation) in approximately 80% of those with endogenous depression. Their efficacy in exogenous depression is not as well documented.

One to four weeks may elapse before improvement is noted with the antidepressants. A gradual increase in dosage may be useful if there are no signs of response. Once optimal improvement is achieved, their use should be continued for three to six months after the patient has passed the depressive phase of his illness. The dosage then may be reduced gradually over a period of several weeks if there are no signs of relapse. Administration should be discontinued if significant improvement is not observed after six to eight weeks at maximal dosage levels.

The tricyclic compounds, which resemble the phenothiazine derivatives chemically, are generally more effective than the monoamine oxidase inhibitors in moderate and severe depression, especially endogenous types. They also may exhibit antianxiety properties. Some of these compounds, chiefly amitriptyline, imipramine, and nortriptyline, may be useful in alleviating enuresis in children and adolescents.

The tricyclic compounds neither inhibit monoamine oxidase activity nor change the concentration of serotonin and catecholamines in the brain. However, by blocking the reuptake of norepinephrine at the adrenergic neurons, they may potentiate the central and peripheral action of adrenergic agents.

Because the monoamine oxidase inhibitors are more toxic than the tricyclic compounds, they should be used only in patients in whom the tricyclic compounds and electroconvulsive therapy were of no value. These agents also may be useful in the migraine syndrome (see Chapter 24, Agents Used to Treat Migraine).

Methylphenidate and the amphetamines have been used for many years in the treatment of depression. However, there is little evidence that they are of value in this condition. These agents are useful as an adjunct to other remedial measures (psychological, educational, or social) in the management of children with the hyperkinetic syndrome. However, they may have a deleterious effect in children with psychopathic personalities. The amphetamines and methylphenidate are effective in controlling the symptoms of narcolepsy, but they are not curative.

The use of amphetamines to alleviate drowsiness and fatigue is unjustifiable except under the most extraordinary circumstances, because elimination of the warning signal of fatigue is dangerous.

Pipradrol [Meratran], which has some of the pharmacologic actions of the amphetamines, has been advocated as a stimulant in some depressive states, but its effectiveness has not been substantiated by controlled studies. Similarly, the effectiveness of deanol acetamidobenzoate [Deaner] as an antidepressant or in the management of children with behavioral and learning problems has not been demonstrated conclusively.

Other classes of drugs such as the antianxiety agents or the sedatives and hypnotics may be useful in alleviating the anxiety, tension, irritability, and agitation often associated with depressive states (see Chapter 28, Antianxiety Agents, and Chapter 27, Sedatives and Hypnotics).

Adverse Reactions

The untoward effects produced by the antidepressants vary widely, and the type and severity of the reaction may depend upon the type of compound used. The most common reactions associated with both tricyclic compounds and monoamine oxidase inhibitors are anticholinergic effects: dryness of the mouth, hyperhidrosis, constipation, blurred vision, and orthostatic hypotension. Adynamic ileus has been reported rarely after the administration of imipramine [Presamine, Tofranil], amitriptyline [Elavil], and nortriptyline [Aventyl]. Elderly patients may be especially susceptible to urinary retention and adynamic ileus. Other untoward effects attributed in part to the anticholinergic activity of these drugs are tachycardia, anorexia, anxiety, and insomnia.

Cholestatic jaundice and agranulocytosis have occurred rarely after use of imipramine, desipramine [Norpramin, Pertofrane], amitriptyline, and nortriptyline. The hydrazine derivatives (isocarboxazid [Marplan] and phenelzine [Nardil]) have occasionally caused hepatitis, presumably a drug-induced hypersensitivity reaction, and leukopenia.

The tricyclic compounds tend to exhibit a quinidine-like effect in that they prolong atrioventricular conduction time; this is manifested in the electrocardiogram by signs of first-degree atrioventricular block.

Paradoxical hypertension has been associated with the concomitant use of monoamine oxidase inhibitors (eg, tranylcypromine [Parnate]) and substances with a high tyramine content. These hypertensive crises are characterized by headache, palpitation, nausea, and vomiting. Occasionally, subarachnoid or intracranial hemorrhage, manifested by stiffness of the neck, decreasing levels of consciousness, and syncope, occurs. Therefore, patients taking monoamine oxidase inhibitors should be warned to avoid foods and beverages with a high tyramine content (eg, cheese [particularly strong, aged varieties], red wines, herring [both kippered (dried, salted) and pickled], chicken livers, canned figs, broad beans [fava beans], chocolate, beer, yeasts, meat extracts, game, yogurt), and compounds containing vasopressor agents (eg, certain cold remedies, nasal decongestants, anorexiants).

For other reactions produced by the tricyclic compounds and monoamine oxidase inhibitors, see the individual evaluations on Imipramine Hydrochloride and Isocarboxazid.

The untoward effects produced by the amphetamines are related to their pharmacologic actions; thus, they may produce nervousness, restlessness, insomnia, cardiovascular disturbances (eg, tachycardia), and gastrointestinal disturbances. Chills and syncope may occur with overdosage. If signs of toxicity appear, these drugs should be discontinued. Susceptible patients may develop psychic dependence and, rarely, physical dependence to the amphetamines; since harmful self-medication also may be fostered in patients' relatives or friends, supervision should remain strict. The amphetamines and methylphenidate are classified as Schedule II drugs under the Controlled Substances Act. (See also Chapter 33, Anorexiants, for further discussion of the amphetamines.)

Precautions

The antidepressants should be used cautiously in hyperactive or agitated patients because they may produce a mild maniacal state (hypomania). In manic-depressive types of psychoses, the risk of suicide is greatest near the end of the depressive cycle; hence particular attention should be given to patients with suicidal tendencies when they begin to respond to therapy.

Antidepressants also should be used with caution in elderly patients and in those with epilepsy, glaucoma, renal failure, or severely impaired liver function. It is advisable to determine the effect of the tricyclic antidepressants on the blood pressure, especially in patients with hypertension or low normal pressure.

The tricyclic compounds are contraindicated in patients with congestive heart failure, angina pectoris, and paroxysmal tachycardia; the monoamine oxidase inhibitors should not be used in patients with a confirmed or suspected cerebrovascular defect, hypertension, cardiovascular disease, or pheochromocytoma.

Routine precautions should be followed for use of these drugs during pregnancy (see the discussion in the General Information section on Use of Drugs During Pregnancy).

Interactions: Special care should be taken when the antidepressants are used with other agents that lower the blood pressure (eg, thiazide diuretics, phenothiazines, alcohol, vasodilators). The tricyclic compounds should not be given to patients receiving guanethidine [Ismelin], since they partially block the action of this antihypertensive agent. The effects of anticholinergic agents, barbiturates, adrenergic agents, and thyroid preparations may be potentiated when these agents are used concomitantly with the tricyclic antidepressants.

The action of barbiturates, insulin, procaine, adrenergic agents, methyldopa [Aldomet], thiazide diuretics, furazolidone [Furoxone], antiparkinsonism agents, phenothiazines, and meperidine [Demerol] may be potentiated when these agents are used with the monoamine oxidase inhibitors; thus, reduced dosage of the potentiated agent is indicated if the drugs are used concomitantly.

The tricyclic compounds usually should not be given with or soon after any of the monoamine oxidase inhibitors, since the latter agents potentiate the anticholinergic actions of the tricyclic antidepressants and may produce a severe atropine-like reaction (tremors, fever, generalized clonic convulsions, delirium, and death). Generally, there should be at least a two-week interval after a monoamine oxidase inhibitor is discontinued before the tricyclic compound is given and at least a four-day interval after a tricyclic compound is discontinued before the monoamine oxidase inhibitor is given. Initial dosage of the second drug should be small and increases should be gradual.

TRICYCLIC COMPOUNDS

IMIPRAMINE HYDROCHLORIDE

[Presamine, Tofranil]

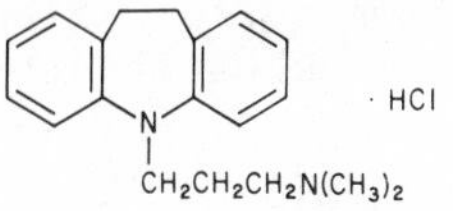

N · HCl

$CH_2CH_2CH_2N(CH_3)_2$

This prototype of the tricyclic compounds is useful in both endogenous and exogenous (reactive) depressions; like other tricyclic compounds, imipramine is more effective in treating the endogenous type. Although it may alleviate the anxiety which sometimes accompanies depression, this symptom often is aggravated. Imipramine may be useful in alleviating enuresis in children and adolescents.

Since the untoward effects associated with the use of imipramine are characteristic for all tricyclic compounds, they are listed only in this evaluation. They may include:

Cardiovascular effects (eg, orthostatic hypotension, palpitations, arrhythmias [tachycardia was the only cardiovascular effect noted in one surveillance study], first-degree atrioventricular block, and stroke syndrome).

Central nervous system and neuromuscular effects (eg, confusion, parkinsonian syndrome [myoclonia, hyperreflexia, fasciculation, tremor], disturbed concentration, disorientation, delusions, hallucinations, excitement, anxiety, restlessness, insomnia, nightmares, paresthesias of the extremities, peripheral neuritis, ataxia, and convulsions).

Allergic reactions (eg, rash, urticaria, photosensitization, and generalized edema or edema of the face and tongue).

Anticholinergic effects (eg, dryness of the mouth, blurred vision, disturbance of accommodation, mydriasis, hyperhidrosis, constipation, adynamic ileus, urinary retention).

Blood dyscrasias (eg, bone marrow depression, including agranulocytosis, eosinophilia, purpura, and thrombocytopenia).

Gastrointestinal effects (eg, nausea, vomiting, anorexia, stomatitis, peculiar taste, diarrhea).

Endocrine effects (eg, testicular swelling, impotence, and gynecomastia in the male; breast enlargement with galactorrhea in the female; increased or decreased libido; and either hyperglycemia or hypoglycemia).

Miscellaneous reactions (eg, dizziness, asthenia, fatigue, headache, weight gain or loss, urinary frequency, drowsiness, cholestatic jaundice, and parotid swelling).

Abrupt cessation of treatment after long-term therapy may produce withdrawal symptoms (eg, headache, malaise, anorexia, fatigue).

See the Introductory Statement for a discussion on precautions and interactions with other drugs.

USUAL DOSAGE.—

Intramuscular: Adults, initially, up to 100 mg daily in divided doses. The oral route should replace parenteral administration as soon as possible.

Oral: Adults (hospitalized), initially, 100 mg daily in divided doses with the amount gradually increased to 200 mg daily; 250 to 300 mg may be given daily if there is no response after two weeks. *Adults* (outpatients), initially, 75 mg daily in divided doses up to a total of 150 mg daily; maintenance, 50 to 150 mg daily. Doses over 200 mg daily should not be used. *Adolescents and elderly patients*, initially, 30 to 40 mg daily; total dose should not exceed 100 mg daily. *Children*, for enuresis, 50 to 100 mg daily divided into two doses.

PREPARATIONS.—Presamine (USV), Tofranil (Geigy).

Injection: Solution 12.5 mg/ml in 2 ml containers.

Oral: Tablets 10, 25, and 50 mg.

AMITRIPTYLINE HYDROCHLORIDE
[Elavil Hydrochloride]

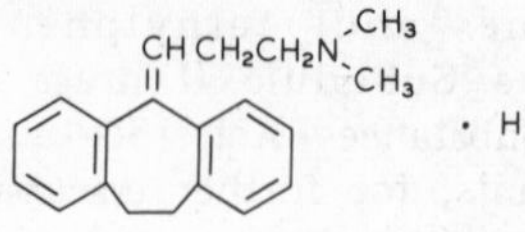

Amitriptyline is as effective as imipramine in the treatment of depression. The indications, adverse reactions, and precautions with its use are similar to those of other tricyclic compounds. However, the incidence of confusional episodes may be greater, especially in elderly patients. See the evaluation on Imipramine Hydrochloride for information on uses and adverse reactions, and the Introductory Statement for a discussion on precautions and interactions with other drugs.

USUAL DOSAGE.—

Intramuscular: Adults, initially, 80 to 120 mg daily in divided doses. The oral route should replace parenteral administration as soon as possible.

Oral: Adults (hospitalized), initially, 100 mg daily in divided doses, with the amount gradually increased to 200 mg daily. A small number of hospitalized patients may require as much as 300 mg daily. *Adults* (outpatients), initially, 75 mg daily in divided doses up to a total of 150 mg daily; for maintenance, 40 to 100 mg daily in divided doses. *Elderly patients and adolescents*, 10 mg three times daily and 20 mg at bedtime. *Children*, for enuresis, dosage is reduced (see table, back cover).

PREPARATIONS.—Elavil Hydrochloride (Merck Sharp & Dohme).

Injection: Solution 10 mg/ml in 10 ml containers.

Oral: Tablets 10, 25, and 50 mg.

DESIPRAMINE HYDROCHLORIDE
[Norpramin, Pertofrane]

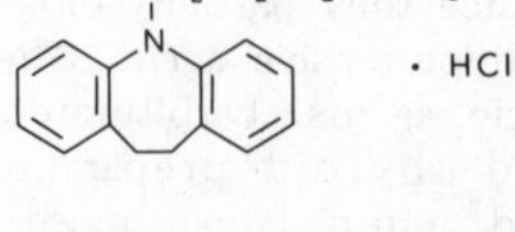

Desipramine, a metabolite of imipramine, has actions and uses similar to other tricyclic compounds. In some patients, the effectiveness of desipramine is reduced after two to six weeks.

Untoward effects occur less frequently than with imipramine, but are similar to those produced by the other tricyclic compounds. See the evaluation on Imipramine Hydrochloride for information on indications and adverse reactions, and the Introductory Statement for a discussion on precautions and interactions with other drugs.

USUAL DOSAGE.—*Oral: Adults*, initially, 75 to 150 mg daily in divided doses for seven to ten days. When necessary, the dosage may then be increased up to a maximum of 200 mg daily in divided doses. For maintenance, 50 to 100 mg daily. *Elderly patients and adolescents*, 25 to 100 mg daily in divided doses. *Children*, for enuresis, 50 to 75 mg daily in divided doses.

PREPARATIONS.—

Norpramin (Lakeside). *Oral:* Tablets 25 to 50 mg.

Pertofrane (USV). *Oral:* Capsules 25 and 50 mg.

DOXEPIN HYDROCHLORIDE [Adapin, Sinequan]

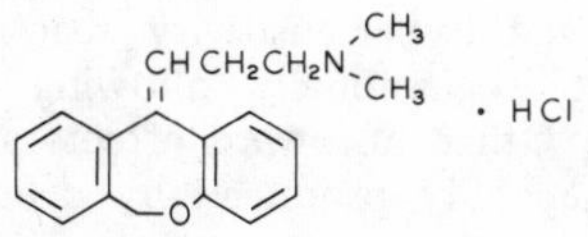

$CHCH_2CH_2N(CH_3)_2 \cdot HCl$

Doxepin possesses the characteristics of other tricyclic compounds and is as effective as imipramine in the treatment of depression.

Untoward effects are similar to those produced by the other drugs of its class. See the evaluation on Imipramine Hydrochloride for additional information on indications and adverse reactions, and the Introductory Statement for a discussion on precautions and interactions with other drugs.

USUAL DOSAGE.—*Oral: Adults*, for depression of mild to moderate severity, initially, 75 mg daily in three divided doses, with an increase or decrease at appropriate intervals according to response of the patient. For more severely depressed patients, initially, 150 mg daily in three divided doses (maximum, 300 mg). *Children*, for enuresis, dosage is reduced (see table, back cover).

PREPARATIONS.—Adapin (Smith Kline & French), Sinequan (Pfizer). *Oral:* Capsules 10, 25, and 50 mg.

NORTRIPTYLINE HYDROCHLORIDE [Aventyl Hydrochloride]

$CHCH_2CH_2NHCH_3 \cdot HCl$

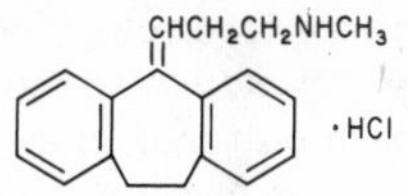

This tricyclic compound has actions similar to other members of this class and appears to be as effective as imipramine in the treatment of depression. See the evaluation on Imipramine Hydrochloride for information on uses and adverse reactions, and the Introductory Statement for a discussion on precautions and interactions with other drugs.

USUAL DOSAGE.—*Oral: Adults* (hospitalized), 75 to 100 mg daily in three or four divided doses. A dosage higher than 100 mg daily should not be used. Lower doses are recommended for *outpatients. Adolescents and elderly patients*, 30 to 50 mg daily in divided doses. *Children*, for enuresis, 1 to 2 mg/kg of body weight daily in divided doses (see also table, back cover).

PREPARATIONS.—Aventyl Hydrochloride (Lilly). *Oral:* Capsules 10 and 25 mg; liquid 10 mg/5 ml.

PROTRIPTYLINE HYDROCHLORIDE [Vivactil Hydrochloride]

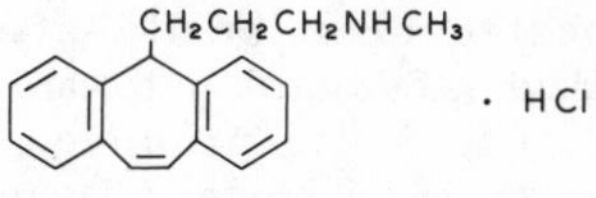

$CH_2CH_2CH_2NHCH_3 \cdot HCl$

Protriptyline, in addition to possessing characteristics of the tricyclic antidepressants as a class, also increases psychomotor activity and, therefore, may be particularly useful in treating depressed patients whose predominant manifestations of illness are psychomotor retardation, apathy, and fatigue. Depressed patients with symptoms of agitation, anxiety, and tension frequently become more disturbed with use of protriptyline.

See the evaluation on Imipramine Hydrochloride for information on indications and adverse reactions, and the Introductory Statement for a discussion on precautions and interactions with other drugs.

USUAL DOSAGE.—*Oral: Adults*, 15 to 60

mg daily in three or four divided doses. Ordinarily, initial doses are small and are adjusted as needed. *Adolescents and elderly patients*, initially, 15 mg daily in three divided doses; the dose is increased gradually if necessary; *in elderly patients*, the cardiovascular system must be monitored closely if the daily dose exceeds 20 mg. *Children*, for enuresis, dosage is reduced (see table, back cover).

PREPARATIONS.—Vivactil Hydrochloride (Merck Sharp & Dohme). *Oral:* Tablets 5 and 10 mg.

MONOAMINE OXIDASE INHIBITORS

ISOCARBOXAZID [Marplan]

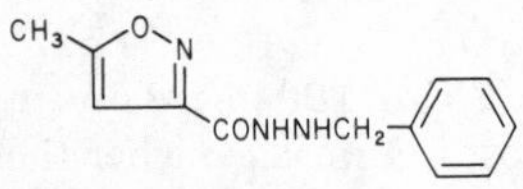

CH_3 O N CONHNHCH$_2$—

Isocarboxazid is a monoamine oxidase inhibitor that may be useful in treating moderate to severe depression but it is more effective in treating the endogenous than the exogenous type. Like other monoamine oxidase inhibitors, however, isocarboxazid is less effective and produces more serious adverse reactions than the tricyclic compounds. It should be used only in patients in whom the tricyclic compounds and electroconvulsive therapy were of no value.

Leukopenia and hepatitis (presumably a drug-induced hypersensitivity reaction) have been reported occasionally after use of isocarboxazid. Additional untoward reactions are similar to those produced by other monoamine oxidase inhibitors. Those observed most frequently include orthostatic hypotension, abnormal cardiac rate and rhythm, dizziness, vertigo, constipation, headache, hyperactivity, hyperreflexia, tremors, fasciculations, hypomanic or manic reactions, nervousness, confusion, amnesia, insomnia, peripheral edema, asthenia, fatigue, dryness of the mouth, blurred vision, hyperhidrosis, anorexia, body weight changes, and rash. Adverse reactions that occur occasionally include restlessness, ataxia, black tongue, coma, dysuria, euphoria, hematologic changes, urinary incontinence, polyneuropathy, changes in libido, spider nevus, photosensitivity, and urinary retention. Hallucinations occur rarely. As with other monoamine oxidase inhibitors, paradoxical hypertension may occur when foods or beverages with a high tyramine content or vasopressors are ingested concurrently.

See the Introductory Statement for additional information on adverse reactions and a discussion on precautions and interactions with other drugs.

USUAL DOSAGE.—*Oral: Adults*, initially, 30 mg daily in single or divided doses; for maintenance, 10 to 20 mg daily or less. The dosage should be reduced as soon as clinical improvement is observed. Daily doses larger than 30 mg should not be given. Information is inadequate to establish dosage for *children under 16 years of age.*

PREPARATIONS.—Marplan (Roche). *Oral:* Tablets 10 mg.

PHENELZINE SULFATE [Nardil]

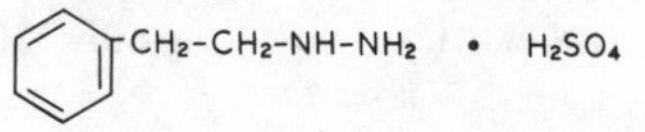

—CH_2-CH_2-NH-NH_2 • H_2SO_4

Phenelzine has essentially the same actions and uses as other monoamine oxidase inhibitors.

Leukopenia and hepatitis (presumably a drug-induced hypersensitivity reaction) have been reported occasionally following the use of phenelzine. Other untoward effects are similar to those generally produced by drugs of this class. See the evaluation on Isocarboxazid for information on indications and adverse reactions, and the Introductory Statement for a discussion on precautions and interactions with other drugs.

USUAL DOSAGE.—*Oral: Adults*, initially, 45 mg daily in three divided doses. After signs of definite improvement have been observed, the dose should be reduced gradually over a period of several weeks to a satisfactory maintenance level, usually 15 mg daily or every other day. The maximal recommended dosage is 75 mg daily in divided doses. Information is inadequate to establish dosage for *children under 16 years of age.*

PREPARATIONS.—Nardil (Warner-Chilcott). *Oral:* Tablets 15 mg.

TRANYLCYPROMINE SULFATE [Parnate]

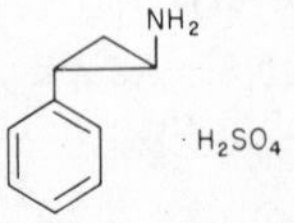

NH_2 · H_2SO_4

This monoamine oxidase inhibitor should be reserved for the symptomatic treatment of patients with severe endogenous depression for whom the tricyclic compounds or electroconvulsive therapy is undesirable or inappropriate. Its efficacy in exogenous depression is not as well documented. The patients should be under close supervision, preferably in the hospital. Tranylcypromine acts more promptly than the monoamine oxidase inhibitors that contain a hydrazine configuration (isocarboxazid, phenelzine).

Untoward effects are similar to those exhibited by the other monoamine oxidase inhibitors. Intracranial hemorrhage (sometimes fatal), associated with paradoxical hypertension and severe occipital headache that may radiate frontally, has occurred in some patients when foods or beverages with a high tyramine content or vasopressors are ingested concurrently. The incidence of this reaction appears to be greater with tranylcypromine than with other monoamine oxidase inhibitors.

See the evaluation on Isocarboxazid for additional information on actions, uses, and adverse reactions, and the Introductory Statement for a discussion on precautions and interactions with other drugs.

USUAL DOSAGE.—*Oral: Adults,* initially 20 mg daily in two divided doses. Subsequent doses should be adjusted according to the patient's response. The lowest effective dose should be used. Amounts above 30 mg daily are not advisable. Information is inadequate to establish dosage for *children under 16 years of age.*

PREPARATIONS.—Parnate (Smith Kline & French). *Oral:* Tablets 10 mg.

AMPHETAMINES AND OTHER PSYCHOMOTOR STIMULANTS

AMPHETAMINE SULFATE [Benzedrine]

Because of the levorotatory component, amphetamine is a less potent central nervous system stimulant than dextroamphetamine on a milligram basis and exhibits more untoward peripheral autonomic effects. Amphetamine has been replaced by the tricyclic compounds and monoamine oxidase inhibitors in the treatment of depression, but it may be useful as an adjunct to other remedial measures (psychological, educational, or social) in the management of children with the hyperkinetic syndrome. However, this form of therapy may have a deleterious effect in children with psychopathic personalities. Amphetamine may be helpful in some patients with narcolepsy. Tolerance to the drug does not appear to develop in these patients when dosage is carefully regulated.

For other uses, see Chapter 33, Anorexiants. For adverse reactions and precautions, see the Introductory Statement. Amphetamine is classified as a Schedule II drug under the Controlled Substances Act.

USUAL DOSAGE.—*Oral:* Use of this drug for depression is not the preferred therapy because more effective agents are available. For narcolepsy, *adults,* 20 to 100 mg; *children 6 to 12 years of age,* initially, 5 mg daily; *12 years and older,* initially, 10 mg daily. Daily dosage may be increased by increments of 5 and 10 mg, respectively, at weekly intervals until an optimal response is obtained. For *children over 5 years* with the hyperkinetic syndrome, initially, 10 mg daily before breakfast and lunch; the amount may be increased gradually to 20 to 30 mg daily in divided doses. A single dose may be given if the timed-release form is used; however, with this type of dosage form, the bioavailability of the drug may be neither uniform or reliable. Amphetamine should not be used for this purpose in *children under 5 years.*

PREPARATIONS.—Benzedrine (Smith Kline & French). *Oral:* Capsules (timed-release) 15 mg; tablets 5 and 10 mg. Drug also marketed under generic name.

DEXTROAMPHETAMINE HYDROCHLORIDE
DEXTROAMPHETAMINE PHOSPHATE
DEXTROAMPHETAMINE SULFATE
[Dexedrine]
DEXTROAMPHETAMINE TANNATE

Like other agents in this class, dextroamphetamine has been used in the treatment of depression, but it has been replaced by the tricyclic compounds and monoamine oxidase inhibitors. On a milligram basis, it is more potent than amphetamine and is preferable to amphetamine in controlling the symptoms of narcolepsy, since it does not contain the levorotatory isomer which produces most untoward peripheral autonomic effects. Tolerance to dextroamphetamine does not appear to develop in patients with narcolepsy when dosage is carefully regulated.

Dextroamphetamine is useful as an adjunct to other remedial measures (psychological, educational, social) in the management of children with the hyperkinetic syndrome. However, this form of therapy may have a deleterious effect in children with psychopathic personalities.

See the Introductory Statement and Chapter 33, Anorexiants, for further information on uses, adverse reactions, and precautions. Dextroamphetamine is classified as a Schedule II drug under the Controlled Substances Act.

USUAL DOSAGE.—*Oral:* This drug should not be used for depression because more effective agents are available. Fro narcolepsy, *adults,* 5 to 60 mg daily; *children,* see the evaluation on Amphetamine Sulfate. For *children over 5 years of age* with the hyperkinetic syndrome, initially, 5 mg daily before breakfast and lunch; the amount may be increased gradually to 10 to 20 mg daily in divided doses. A single dose may be given if the timed-release form is used; however, with this type of dosage form, the bioavailability of the drug may be neither uniform nor reliable. Dextroamphetamine should not be used for this purpose in *children under 5 years.*

PREPARATIONS.—

Dextroamphetamine Hydrochloride:

Oral: Tablets 5 mg; tablets (timed-release) 15 mg.

Dextroamphetamine Phosphate:

Oral: Tablets 5 mg.

Dextroamphetamine Sulfate:

Dexedrine (Smith Kline & French). *Oral:* Capsules (timed-release), 5, 10, and 15 mg; elixir 5 mg/5 ml; tablets 5 mg.

Dextroamphetamine Tannate:

Oral: Tablets (timed-release) 17.5 and 26.25 mg.

ADDITIONAL TRADEMARKS.—**Dextroamphetamine Hydrochloride:** Daro (Fellows-Testagar). **Dextroamphetamine Phosphate:** Dextro-Profetamine (Clark & Clark). **Dextroamphetamine Sulfate:** Amsustaine (Key), Cendex (Central), Dexa-Sequels (Lederle), Dexaspan (USV). **Dextroamphetamine Tannate:** Obotan (Mallinckrodt). Drugs also marketed by many manufacturers under generic name.

METHAMPHETAMINE HYDROCHLORIDE

[Desoxyn, Syndrox]

Like other agents in this class, methamphetamine has been used in the treatment of depression, but it has been replaced by the tricyclic compounds and monoamine oxidase inhibitors. This agent may be helpful in some patients with narcolepsy. Tolerance to this agent does not appear to develop in these patients when dosage is carefully regulated.

Methamphetamine also is useful as an adjunct to other remedial measures (psychological, educational, or social) in the management of children with the hyperkinetic syndrome. However, this form of therapy may have a deleterious effect in children with psychopathic personalities.

Methamphetamine seems to be the favorite of persons who abuse amphetamines. Large doses can produce psychic dependence and a moderate degree of physical dependence. This is classified as a Schedule II drug under the Controlled Substances Act.

See also the Introductory Statement and Chapter 33, Anorexiants, for additional information on uses, adverse reactions, and precautions.

USUAL DOSAGE.—*Oral:* This drug should not be used for depression because more effective agents are available. For narcolepsy, *adults,* 5 to 60 mg daily in divided doses. For *children over 5 years of age* with the hyperkinetic syndrome, initially, 5 mg daily before breakfast and lunch, which may be increased gradually to 10 to 20 mg daily in divided doses. A single dose may be given if the timed-release form is used. However, with this type of dosage form the bioavailability of the drug may be neither uniform nor reliable. Methamphetamine should not be used for this purpose in *children under 5 years.*

PREPARATIONS.—

Desoxyn (Abbott). *Oral:* Tablets 2.5, 5, and 10 mg; tablets (timed-release) 5, 10, and 15 mg.

Syndrox (McNeil). *Oral:* Tablets 5 mg.

ADDITIONAL TRADEMARKS.—Des-Oxa-d (Walker), Oxydess (North American), Semoxydrine Hydrochloride (Beecham-Massengill), Stimdex (Ulmer). Drug also marketed by many manufacturers under generic name and under the name Desoxyephedrine Hydrochloride.

METHYLPHENIDATE HYDROCHLORIDE

[Ritalin Hydrochloride]

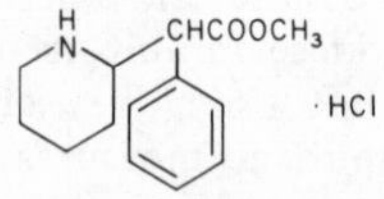

$CHCOOCH_3$ · HCl

Methylphenidate is a mild central nervous system stimulant similar to amphetamine and more potent than caffeine. Although it is widely used in the treatment of mild depression, there is little evidence that it is effective in this condition. Methylphenidate is useful as an adjunct to other remedial measures (psychological, educational, or social) in the management of children with the hyperkinetic syndrome. However, this form of therapy may have a deleterious effect in children with psychopathic personalities. (See also Chapter 34, Analeptics.) It also may be useful in the treatment of narcolepsy.

Nervousness, dyskinesia, insomnia, anorexia, dizziness, palpitation, rash, nausea, abdominal pain, hypertension, hypotension, changes in pulse rate, tachycardia, arrhythmias, and headache occur occasionally. Psychic dependence has occurred after long-term use of large doses; methylphenidate has been used as a substitute for amphetamines by individuals who abuse drugs. It is classified as a Schedule II drug under the Controlled Substances Act.

This agent is contraindicated in patients with marked anxiety, tension, and agitation. It should be used cautiously in patients with epilepsy or hypertension, and in those taking vasopressors or monoamine oxidase inhibitors. The drug should be discontinued in the presence of seizures.

Methylphenidate may potentiate the action of diphenylhydantoin, phenobarbital, primidone, phenylbutazone, tricyclic antidepressants, and coumarin anticoagulants, and may decrease the hypotensive effect of guanethidine. Therefore, the dosage of these agents should be readjusted when they are given with methylphenidate.

USUAL DOSAGE.—*Oral:* This drug should not be used for depression because more effective agents are available. For narcolepsy, *adults,* 10 to 60 mg daily in two or three divided doses. For *children* with the hyperkinetic syndrome, 5 mg before breakfast and lunch. The dosage may be increased gradually by increments of 5 to 10 mg weekly. Daily dosage above 60 mg should not be administered.

PREPARATIONS.—Ritalin Hydrochloride (Ciba). *Oral:* Tablets 5, 10, and 20 mg.

MIXTURES

MIXTURES CONTAINING AN ANTIDEPRESSANT AND ANTIPSYCHOTIC AGENT

Combinations containing amitripytline and perphenazine are available for use in outpatients and hospitalized patients with psychoses or neuroses characterized by anxiety or agitation with symptoms of depression. When these two symptoms coexist, the administration of these agents concomitantly or in a fixed-ratio combination may be more useful than either drug alone. However, the physician may find that the amounts of the drugs supplied in fixed-ratio combinations are not suitable for some of these patients.

See the Introductory Statement and the evaluation on Imipramine Hydrochloride in this chapter and the evaluation on Perphenazine in Chapter 29, Antipsychotic Agents, for information on adverse reactions and precautions.

USUAL DOSAGE.—These mixtures may be substituted for the individual drugs if the dosage sizes available in the fixed-ratio combinations meet the needs of the patient. The manufacturers' suggested dosage is: *Oral: Adults,* in psychoneurotic patients with anxiety and depression, one tablet containing 2 or 4 mg of perphenazine and 25 mg of amitriptyline three or four times daily. In more severely ill patients with schizophrenia, initially, two tablets containing 4 mg of perphenazine and 25 mg of amitriptyline three times daily; a fourth dose may be given at bedtime if necessary. The daily dosage should not exceed nine tablets. *Adolescents and elderly patients,* initially one tablet containing 4 mg of perphenazine and 10 mg of amitriptyline three or four times daily. Usual maintenance dosage for most patients is one tablet containing 2 or 4 mg of perphenazine and 10 or 25 mg of amitriptyline two to four times daily. *Children,* use of these mixtures is inadvisable.

AVAILABLE MIXTURES.—Etrafon (Schering), Triavil (Merck Sharp & Dohme). *Oral:* Tablets containing perphenazine 2 or 4 mg and amitriptyline hydrochloride 10 or 25 mg.

Chapter 33

ANOREXIANTS

Amphetamines and amphetamine-like adrenergic drugs are commonly prescribed as adjuncts in the management of obesity. However, their undesirable effects, including a tendency to produce psychic and, occasionally, physical dependence when used indiscriminately and in large doses, make their use hazardous. In fact, in an attempt to reduce the abuse potential of these agents, many physicians have stopped prescribing amphetamines.

Effective, maintained weight reduction requires an understanding of good nutrition and alteration of underlying psychologic or pathologic factors producing excessive caloric intake. Anorexiants should be given only temporarily, if at all, to suppress the appetite of patients who overeat to gratify inappropriate hunger or who have difficulty in adhering to a prescribed diet because of the discomfort of caloric restriction. They can be used as short-term adjuncts (ie, four to six weeks) in an overall program of weight loss, but their administration is appropriate only as long as weight loss continues without the development of psychic dependence or other undesirable effects or the need for increased dosage. Prolonged use of therapeutic doses or short-term use of large doses of these drugs is usually followed by a short period of fatigue and mental depression.

Although it was originally thought that anorexiants exert their effect in part by stimulation of the central nervous system, results of recent studies have shown that an investigational drug that does not have this action, fenfluramine, is a potent anorexiant. The results of numerous animal studies have suggested, but not proved, that the anorexiants affect the appetite control centers of the hypothalamus. They produce anorexia, a decreased sense of fatigue, and increased alertness, initiative, and motor activity.

The amphetamines (eg, amphetamine [Benzedrine], dextroamphetamine [Dexedrine], methamphetamine [Desoxyn, Syndrox]) were the first drugs prescribed widely to suppress the appetite and are still the standard to which newer drugs are compared. Dextroamphetamine appears to be more useful than amphetamine as an anorexiant, since the dextrorotatory isomer is a more potent appetite suppressant and its effect on the cardiovascular system is less pronounced.

A number of other adrenergic agents with actions similar to those of the amphetamines are used in weight control. These agents (benzphetamine [Didrex], chlorphentermine [Pre-Sate], diethylpropion [Tenuate, Tepanil], phendimetrazine [Plegine], phenmetrazine [Preludin], phentermine hydrochloride [Wilpo], and phentermine resin [Ionamin]) were developed in the hope that they would produce a greater anorexiant effect with fewer untoward reactions than the amphetamines. In spite of minor differences in their actions and untoward effects, none of these agents, with the possible exception of phenmetrazine, has been found to be more effective than dextroamphetamine. Unlike the amphetamines, which have been used as stimulants for other conditions, the amphetamine-like adrenergic agents have been promoted by their manufacturers only for use as anorexiants.

Although timed-release anorexiant preparations are used, the bioavailability of this type of dosage form may be neither uniform nor reliable.

Other drugs not technically classed as anorexiants have been misused in the treatment of overweight patients. These agents include digitalis, diuretics, laxatives, antispasmodics, and thyroid. Digitalis is absolutely contraindicated for treatment of uncomplicated obesity; its use is dangerous since the anorexia it produces is actually a symptom of digitalis intoxication. Diuretics produce impressive temporary decreases in total body weight by increasing the excretion of water, but they do not decrease body fat. Although the judicious administration of diuretics permits the patient to see actual weight loss not masked by fluid retention and encourages him to continue with the difficult regimen of caloric deprivation, dehydration should not be used to delude the patient into thinking he is decreasing adipose tissue. Laxatives used in doses large enough to produce diarrhea can induce both water and nutrient losses, but they should not be prescribed for the treatment of obesity. Antispasmodics exert no effect on body fat or caloric balance.

Thyroid preparations are specific for the treatment of hypothyroidism; their use to promote weight loss in euthyroid patients by increasing the metabolic rate is unsound. The initial dosage of exogenous hormone may increase metabolism, but only until the thyroid gland adjusts with a compensatory decrease in the secretion of endogenous hormone. Increasing the dosage again may cause another brief increase in metabolism until the function of the gland is supressed further or even completely. These temporary increases in metabolic rate may actually stimulate the appetite, making the program of weight reduction more difficult and perhaps preventing even limited success. If the dosage reaches a level significantly greater than the amount that the gland normally would secrete, hyperthyroidism results. Furthermore, when the medication eventually is discontinued, the depressed gland must readjust its secretion toward normal. During this period of readjustment, the patient may experience manifestations of hypothyroidism and may gain weight.

The claim that daily injections of chorionic gonadotropin cause weight loss and redistribution of body fat has not been substantiated.

Phenylpropanolamine, an adrenergic agent with some central stimulant properties, is available without prescription in various proprietary products for weight reduction. This agent is probably ineffective in the dose provided (25 mg).

Miscellaneous Uses of Amphetamines: The amphetamines are of unequivocal usefulness in only a few conditions. These include narcolepsy and, adjunctively to other remedial measures (ie, psychological, educational, social), the management of children with the hyperkinetic syndrome. In addition, in controlled studies on motion sickness the effectiveness of scopolamine was enhanced when it was administered with dextroamphetamine (see Chapter 85, Antiemetics). Although amphetamines have been used in the treatment of depression, there is little evidence that they are effective (see Chapter 32, Antidepressants). The use of amphetamines to allay fatigue is unjustifiable except under the most extraordinary circumstances; they are dangerous for drivers and those engaged in comparable activities, and they have no legitimate role in athletics. Indeed, their use may contribute to increased athletic injuries.

Adverse Reactions and Precautions

The untoward effects produced by the amphetamines are related to their spectrum of pharmacologic actions; thus, these agents may cause nervousness, restlessness, tremors, insomnia, cardiovascular disturbances (eg, tachycardia, hypertension), mydriasis, and gastrointestinal disturbances. Because the amphetamine-like adrenergic agents have a relatively weak peripheral action, usual oral doses of these agents seldom produce these undesirable effects.

Tolerance to the effect of the amphetamines may occur within several weeks. In such instances, the anorexiants should no longer be regarded as acceptable adjuncts in the treatment program and should be discontinued. Weight loss and appetite suppression are not synonymous since the decreased caloric intake may be sufficient to maintain the lower weight. It is emphasized that the dosage should not be unnecessarily increased because this may produce marked restlessness, irritability, and aggressiveness, in addition to the anorexia and insomnia observed with smaller doses.

Acute overdosage results in accentuation of the usual pharmacologic effects: excitement, agitation, hypertension, tachycardia, mydriasis, slurred speech, ataxia, tremor, chills, hyperreflexia, tachypnea, fever, and toxic psychoses characterized by auditory and visual hallucinations and paranoid delusions. If these symptoms occur, the drug should be discontinued, sedatives prescribed, and custodial care and psychotherapy employed when needed. In severe cases, overdosage may cause acute circulatory failure and death.

The physician should be aware that susceptible patients may develop psychic dependence and, rarely, physical dependence from the use of amphetamines and amphetamine-like agents. Further, since harmful self-medication may be fostered in patients' relatives or friends, supervision should remain strict. It is advisable to prescribe small quantities of the drug for short-term therapy. Amphetamine [Benzedrine], dextroamphetamine [Dexedrine], methamphetamine [Desoxyn, Syndrox], phenmetrazine [Preludin], and most of the combination products containing amphetamine compounds are classified as Schedule II drugs under the Controlled Substances Act. They may be dispensed only with a written prescription order, except in an "emergency situation," and the prescription may not be refilled.

Although amphetamine, dextroamphetamine, and methamphetamine are available in sterile solutions for intravenous use, *this dosage form is absolutely contraindicated for any condition.* Individuals who abuse these amphetamines frequently inject the drug four to six times daily with total daily doses as large as several grams. Polyarteritis nodosa (necrotizing angiitis) has been associated with the intravenous administration of large doses of methamphetamine and dextroamphetamine in drug abusers.

Withdrawing amphetamines from abusers may unmask symptoms of chronic fatigue (mental depression, asthenia, tremors, and gastrointestinal disturbances) and, in some individuals, the fatigue may be followed by drowsiness and prolonged sleep.

Generally, the anorexiants should not be prescribed for patients with hypertension, cardiovascular disease, and hyperthyroidism because their sympathomimetic effect may aggravate these conditions. They are contraindicated in those receiving monoamine oxidase inhibitors and guanethidine and should be used with caution in patients who are overly sensitive to adrenergic agents. The drugs should not be given to individuals who are known to be susceptible to drug abuse.

Evidence of teratogenesis has not been observed when these agents are taken during pregnancy although an infant born to a mother who abuses amphetamines may exhibit agitation and have hyperglycemia at birth (see the discussion on Use of Drugs During Pregnancy in the General Information section).

AMPHETAMINES

DEXTROAMPHETAMINE HYDROCHLORIDE
DEXTROAMPHETAMINE PHOSPHATE
DEXTROAMPHETAMINE SULFATE
[Dexedrine]
DEXTROAMPHETAMINE TANNATE

C_6H_5–CH_2–CH(CH_3)–NH_2

Dextroamphetamine appears to be more useful than racemic amphetamine as an anorexiant, since this isomer is a more potent appetite suppressant and its effect on the cardiovascular system is less pronounced. This drug should be prescribed as an adjunct in the treatment of obesity only when combined with a program of caloric restriction, appropriate exercise, and psychologic support. Dextroamphetamine generally should be used no longer than four to six weeks at a time, and new dietary habits should be developed so that decreased caloric intake continues after the drug is discontinued.

Adverse reactions affecting the central nervous system include psychic and, rarely, physical dependence in susceptible individuals, insomnia, restlessness, nervousness, dizziness, tremor, and dystonic movements of the head, neck, and extremities. If insomnia occurs, the last dose should be given in midafternoon. Serious depressive reactions which may sometimes be psychotic in nature have followed the intensive use of dextroamphetamine in a program of strenuous dieting in some individuals. Toxic psychoses have occurred with large dosage. Cardiovascular stimulation may cause increased pulse rate and hypertension, headache, and palpitation. The drug should be discontinued promptly if chest pain or arrhythmias occur. Dryness of the mouth, mydriasis, nausea, diarrhea, and constipation also have been reported. Dextroamphetamine is classified as a Schedule II drug under the Controlled Substances Act. See the Introductory Statement for additional information on adverse reactions and precautions.

For other uses, see Chapter 32, Antidepressants, and the Introductory Statement.

USUAL DOSAGE.—

Oral: Adults, 2.5 to 10 mg three times daily at least 60 minutes before each meal. Alternatively, a timed-release capsule of appropriate size may be taken once daily in the morning, but the bioavailability of this type of dosage form may be neither uniform nor reliable. No information is available on use of dextroamphetamine as an anorexiant in *children under 12 years of age.*

Intravenous: Route should not be used for any purpose.

PREPARATIONS.–

Dextroamphetamine Hydrochloride:

Oral: Tablets 5 mg; tablets (timed-release) 15 mg.

Dextroamphetamine Phosphate:

Oral: Tablets 5 mg.

Dextroamphetamine Sulfate:

Dexedrine (Smith Kline & French). *Oral:* Capsules (timed-release) 5, 10, and 15 mg; elixir 5 mg/5 ml; tablets 5 mg.

Dextroamphetamine Tannate:

Oral: Tablets (timed-release) 17.5 and 26.25 mg.

ADDITIONAL TRADEMARKS.–Dextroamphetamine Hydrochloride: Daro (Fellows-Testagar). **Dextroamphetamine Phosphate:** Dextro-Profetamine (Clark & Clark). **Dextroamphetamine Sulfate:** Amsustain (Key), Cendex (Central), Dexa-Sequels (Lederle), Dexaspan (USV). **Dextroamphetamine Tannate:** Obotan (Mallinckrodt). Drugs also marketed by many manufacturers under generic name.

AMPHETAMINE SULFATE [Benzedrine]

This drug is the racemic form of amphetamine. Amphetamine should not be used as an anorexiant because the dextrorotatory isomer is a more potent appetite suppressant and the levorotatory component has a more pronounced effect on the cardiovascular system.

See the Introductory Statement and the evaluation on Dextroamphetamine for information on adverse reactions and precautions. Amphetamine is classified as a Schedule II drug under the Controlled Substances Act. For other uses, see Chapter 32, Antidepressants.

USUAL DOSAGE.–The use of this agent is not believed to be justifiable (see above). The manufacturer's suggested dosage is: *Oral: Adults,* 5 to 10 mg three times daily at least 60 minutes before each meal. Alternatively, a timed-release capsule of appropriate size may be taken once daily in the morning, but the bioavailability of this type of dosage form may be neither uniform nor reliable. No information is available on the use of amphetamine as an anorexiant in *children under 12 years of age.*

PREPARATIONS.–Benzedrine (Smith Kline & French). *Oral:* Capsules (timed-release) 15 mg; tablets 5 and 10 mg. Drug also marketed by other manufacturers under generic name.

METHAMPHETAMINE HYDROCHLORIDE
[Desoxyn, Syndrox]

$$C_6H_5-CH_2C(CH_3)H-NH-CH_3 \cdot HCl$$

Although methamphetamine is essentially equivalent to dextroamphetamine in its effect on the central nervous and cardiovascular systems as well as in its ability to suppress the appetite, this drug's abuse potential makes it less desirable. Methamphetamine may be prescribed as an adjunct in the treatment of obesity only when used with a program of caloric restriction, appropriate exercise, and psychologic support.

Large doses can produce psychic dependence and, rarely, physical dependence. Methamphetamine seems to be the favorite of individuals who abuse amphetamines. It is classified as a Schedule II drug under the Controlled Substances Act. See the Introductory Statement and the evaluation on Dextroamphetamine for additional information on adverse reactions and precautions.

For other uses, see Chapter 32, Antidepressants.

USUAL DOSAGE.–

Oral: Because of its great abuse potential, the use of this drug is discouraged. The manufacturers' suggested dosage is: *Adults,* 2.5 to 5 mg three times daily 30 to 60 minutes before each meal. Alternatively, a timed-release capsule of appropriate size is taken once daily in the morning, but the bioavailability of this type of dosage form may be neither uniform nor reliable. No information is available on use of methamphetamine as an anorexiant in *children under 12 years of age.*

Intravenous: Route should not be used for any purpose.

PREPARATIONS.–

Desoxyn (Abbott). *Oral:* Tablets 2.5, 5, and 10 mg; tablets (timed-release) 5, 10, and 15 mg.

Syndrox (McNeil). *Oral:* Tablets 5 mg.

ADDITIONAL TRADEMARKS.–Des-Oxa-D (Walker), Oxydess (North American), Semoxydrine Hydrochloride (Beecham-Massengill), Stimdex (Ulmer). Drug also marketed by many manufacturers under generic name and under the name, Desoxyephedrine Hydrochloride.

OTHER ADRENERGIC AGENTS

BENZPHETAMINE HYDROCHLORIDE
[Didrex]

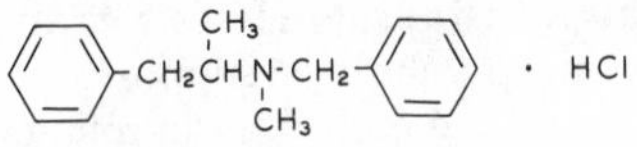

Benzphetamine has the same degree of usefulness in the treatment of obesity as other amphetamine-like adrenergic agents when used in conjunction with caloric restriction, appropriate exercise, and psychologic support.

A minimal number of untoward effects have been associated with use of benzphetamine. Nervousness, euphoria, dizziness, insomnia, tachycardia, palpitations, polyuria, and dryness of the mouth have been reported. Long-term administration, especially of larger than usual therapeutic doses, may result in psychic dependence. See the Introductory Statement for information on precautions.

USUAL DOSAGE.—*Oral: Adults,* 25 to 50 mg one to three times daily. No information is available on use of benzphetamine in *children under 12 years of age.*

PREPARATIONS.—Didrex (Upjohn). *Oral:* Tablets 25 and 50 mg.

CHLORPHENTERMINE HYDROCHLORIDE
[Pre-Sate]

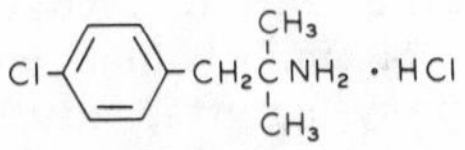

This agent is comparable to dextroamphetamine and other amphetamine-like adrenergic agents in suppressing the appetite when used in conjunction with caloric restriction, appropriate exercise, and psychologic support.

Chlorphentermine produces fewer reactions attributable to central nervous system stimulation (eg, nervousness, palpitation, dizziness, insomnia) than amphetamine and phenmetrazine. Long-term use, especially of larger than usual therapeutic doses, may result in psychic dependence. See the Introductory Statement for information on precautions.

USUAL DOSAGE.—*Oral: Adults,* 65 mg once daily after the morning meal. No information is available on use of chlorphentermine in *children under 12 years of age.*

PREPARATIONS.—Pre-Sate (Warner-Chilcott). *Oral:* Tablets 65 mg.

DIETHYLPROPION HYDROCHLORIDE
[Tenuate, Tepanil]

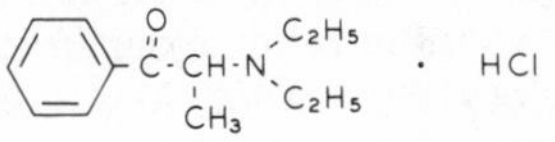

Diethylpropion is less effective as an anorexiant than dextroamphetamine. It should only be used in conjunction with caloric restriction, moderate exercise, and psychologic support.

The incidence of nervousness, excitability, euphoria, and insomnia is lower with diethylpropion than with the amphetamine compounds. Dryness of the mouth, nausea, vertigo, constipation, headache, and drowsiness have been observed occasionally. Long-term use, especially of larger than usual therapeutic doses, may result in psychic dependence. See the Introductory Statement for information on precautions.

USUAL DOSAGE.—*Oral: Adults,* 25 mg three times daily one hour before meals. An additional dose may be taken in the evening for nighttime control of hunger. Alternatively, the timed-release preparation may be taken once daily in the midmorning, but the bioavailability of this type of dosage form may be neither uniform nor reliable. No information is available on use of diethylpropion in *children under 12 years of age.*

PREPARATIONS.—Tenuate (Merrell-National), Tepanil (Riker). *Oral:* Tablets 25 mg; tablets (timed-release) 75 mg.

PHENDIMETRAZINE TARTRATE [Plegine]

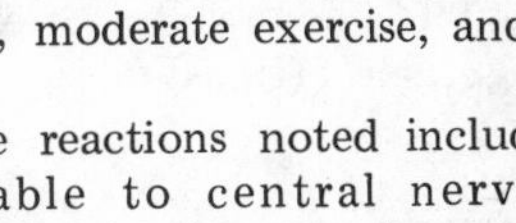

Phendimetrazine is similar to other amphetamine-like adrenergic compounds in its degree of usefulness as an anorexiant. It should only be used in conjunction with caloric restriction, moderate exercise, and psychologic support.

Adverse reactions noted include symptoms attributable to central nervous system stimulation (eg, nervousness, dizziness, insomnia). Other undesirable reactions observed occasionally include glossitis, stomatitis, dryness of the mouth, nausea, abdominal cramps, constipation, headache, and dysuria. Cardiovascular effects such as tachycardia, hypertension, and palpitation have been reported infrequently. Long-term use of this agent, especially of larger than usual therapeutic doses, may result in psychic dependence. See the Introductory Statement for information on precautions.

USUAL DOSAGE.—*Oral: Adults,* 17.5 to 70 mg two or three times daily one hour before meals. No information is available on use of phendimetrazine in *children under 12 years of age.*

PREPARATIONS.—Plegine (Ayerst). *Oral:* Tablets 35 mg.

ADDITIONAL TRADEMARKS.—Melfiat (Reid-Provident), Statobex (Lemmon).

PHENMETRAZINE HYDROCHLORIDE
[Preludin]

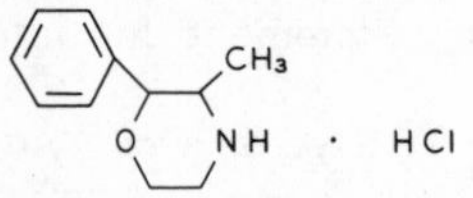

Phenmetrazine is possibly more effective than dextroamphetamine in suppressing appetite in obese individuals. The drug should only be used in conjunction with caloric restriction, moderate exercise, and psychologic support.

Nervousness, excitement, euphoria, insomnia, dizziness, nausea, headache, urticaria, and dryness of the mouth have been observed occasionally. The long-term use of phenmetrazine, especially of larger than usual therapeutic doses, may result in psychic dependence. Phenmetrazine is classified as a Schedule II drug under the Controlled Substances Act. See the Introductory Statement for information on precautions.

USUAL DOSAGE.—*Oral: Adults,* 25 mg two or three times daily one hour before meals. Alternatively, the timed-release preparation may be taken once daily, but the bioavailability of this type of dosage form may be neither uniform nor reliable. No information is available on use of phenmetrazine in *children under 12 years of age.*

PREPARATIONS.—Preludin (Geigy). *Oral:* Tablets 25 mg; tablets (timed-release) 50 and 75 mg.

PHENTERMINE HYDROCHLORIDE [Wilpo]
PHENTERMINE RESIN [Ionamin]

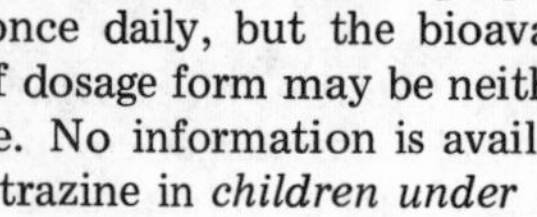

Phentermine is available as the hydrochloride salt and as a complex of the base with an ion-exchange resin. Its usefulness as an anorexiant is comparable to that of dextroamphetamine and other amphetamine-like adrenergic agents, and should only be used in conjunction with caloric restriction, moderate exercise, and psychologic support.

Dryness of the mouth, insomnia, nervousness, and headache have been reported occasionally. Long-term use, especially of larger than usual therapeutic doses, may result in psychic dependence. See the Introductory Statement for information on precautions.

USUAL DOSAGE.—*Oral: Adults,* (hydrochloride) 8 mg three times daily one-half hour before meals; (resin) 15 to 30 mg given before breakfast or 10 to 14 hours before bedtime. Consistent bioavailability of the resin has been demonstrated in unpublished studies. Information is inadequate to establish dosage for *children under 12 years of age.*

PREPARATIONS.—

Phentermine Hydrochloride:

Wilpo (Dorsey). *Oral:* Tablets 8 mg.

Phentermine Resin:

Ionamin (Pennwalt). *Oral:* Capsules 15 and 30 mg.

MIXTURES

A number of mixtures are used in weight control. These include combinations of amphetamine and dextroamphetamine, combinations of amphetamines and barbiturates or antianxiety agents, and preparations containing vitamins, bulk laxatives, or various other ingredients in addition to amphetamines.

A sedative, antianxiety agent, or antipsychotic agent is added to an anorexiant to counteract some of the stimulant effects of the latter. These preparations have the well-recognized disadvantage of a fixed-dosage combination that makes individualization of doses of the constituents in the mixture impossible.

Anorexiant mixtures designed to provide a vitamin supplement to a dieting patient are of minimal value, since well-balanced, low-caloric diets should be adequate to meet the needs of most patients.

Some combination products contain a bulk laxative such as methylcellulose which, when taken with adequate fluid, absorbs water; this increases the bulk in the stomach and induces a sense of satiety. In spite of this, these preparations do not serve a useful purpose in most patients being treated for obesity. Use of harsher laxatives is even less sound.

The use of anorexiant mixtures containing thyroid is condemned (see the Introductory Statement for a discussion on the use of thyroid preparations in the treatment of obesity).

The following list is supplied for information only.

Anorexiants with Sedatives

Ambar (Robins): Each tablet contains methamphetamine hydrochloride 3.33 mg and phenobarbital 21.6 mg; each timed-release tablet contains methamphetamine hydrochloride 10 or 15 mg and phenobarbital 64.8 mg.

Amodex (Fellows-Testagar): Each tablet contains dextroamphetamine hydrochloride 5 mg and amobarbital 20 mg; each timed-release tablet contains dextroamphetamine hydrochloride 7.5 or 15 mg and amobarbital 30 or 60 mg.

Appetrol (Wallace): Each tablet contains dextroamphetamine sulfate 5 mg and meprobamate 400 mg; each timed-release capsule contains dextroamphetamine sulfate 15 mg and meprobamate 300 mg.

Bamadex (Lederle): Each tablet contains dextroamphetamine sulfate 5 mg and meprobamate 400 mg; each timed-release tablet contains dextroamphetamine 15 mg and meprobamate 300 mg.

Biphetamine-T (Pennwalt): Each capsule contains resin complexes equivalent to dextroamphetamine 6.25 or 10 mg, amphetamine 6.25 or 10 mg, and methaqualone 40 mg.

Cendexal (Central): Each timed-release capsule contains dextroamphetamine sulfate 15 mg and amobarbital 60 mg.

Desbutal (Abbott): Each capsule contains methamphetamine hydrochloride 5 mg and pentobarbital sodium 30 mg; each timed-release tablet contains methamphetamine hydrochloride 10 or 15 mg and pentobarbital sodium 60 or 90 mg.

Dexamyl (Smith Kline & French): Each tablet or 5 ml of elixir contains dextroamphetamine sulfate 5 mg and amobarbital 32 mg; each timed-release capsule contains dextroamphetamine sulfate 10 or 15 mg and amobarbital 65 or 97 mg.

Eskatrol (Smith Kline & French): Each timed-release capsule contains dextroamphetamine sulfate 15 mg and prochlorperazine maleate 7.5 mg.

Mepho-d (Walker): Each tablet contains methamphetamine hydrochloride 5 mg, pentobarbital 25 mg, and mephobarbital 24 mg.

Perke Two (Ascher): Each capsule contains dextroamphetamine sulfate 15 mg and amobarbital 60 mg.

Phedoxe 4B (Elder): Each tablet contains methamphetamine hydrochloride 10 mg, amobarbital 10 mg, butabarbital 10 mg, pentobarbital 10 mg, and phenobarbital 10 mg.

15-90 (Elder): Each timed-release capsule contains dextroamphetamine sulfate 15 mg and amobarbital 90 mg.

Anorexiants with Vitamins

Adjudets (Ives): Each troche contains dextroamphetamine phosphate 5 mg, vitamin A 1,500 units, ergocalciferol 150 units, thiamine hydrochloride 0.34 mg, riboflavin 0.67 mg, pyridoxine 0.33 mg, ascorbic acid 20 mg, and niacinamide 2 mg.

Amphedase (Parke, Davis): Each capsule contains dextroamphetamine sulfate 2.5 mg, thiamine mononitrate 5 mg, ascorbic acid 50 mg, niacinamide 25 mg, *Aspergillus oryzae* enzymes 300 mg.

Anorexiants with Sedatives and Vitamins

Obedrin (Beecham-Massengill): Each capsule and tablet contains methamphetamine hydrochloride 5 mg, pentobarbital 20 mg, ascorbic acid 100 mg, thiamine mononitrate 0.5 mg, riboflavin 1 mg, and niacin 5 mg.

Quadamine (Tutag): Each timed-release capsule contains dextroamphetamine sulfate 15 mg, amobarbital 45 mg, vitamin A 6,600 units, vitamin D 400 units, thiamine hydrochloride 1.6 mg, riboflavin 2.5 mg, ascorbic acid 30 mg, niacinamide 15.5 mg, ferrous sulfate 20 mg, copper sulfate 2.8 mg, sodium molybdate 0.45 mg, zinc sulfate 3.9 mg, and potassium iodide 0.13 mg.

Vio-Dex (Rowell): Each capsule contains dextroamphetamine sulfate 5 mg, phenobarbital 16 mg, thiamine mononitrate 1.5 mg, pyridoxine hydrochloride 1.5 mg, ascorbic acid 50 mg, vitamin A acetate 2,500 units, niacinamide 10 mg, pantothenate calcium 5 mg, riboflavin 1.5 mg, and ergocalciferol 200 units; each timed-release capsule contains dextroamphetamine sulfate 10 or 15 mg and twice the amount of the other ingredients in the capsule.

Anorexiants with Bulk-Producing Agents

Cell-O-Dex (Fellows-Testagar): Each tablet contains dextroamphetamine hydrochloride 5 mg, methylcellulose 150 mg, and dicalcium phosphate 90 mg.

Obocell (Mallinckrodt): Each tablet contains dextroamphetamine phosphate 5 mg and methylcellulose 160 mg.

Anorexiants with Bulk-Producing Agents and Vitamins or Sedatives

Obocell Complex (Mallinckrodt): Each capsule contains dextroamphetamine phosphate 5 mg, methylcellulose 100 mg, choline bitartrate 200 mg, inositol 60 mg, thiamine mononitrate 0.8 mg, riboflavin 1.2 mg, and niacinamide 8 mg.

Obocell TF (Mallinckrodt): Each tablet contains dextroamphetamine phosphate 5 mg, methylcellulose 150 mg, and methapyrilene hydrochloride 25 mg.

Opidice (Boyle): Each capsule contains methamphetamine hydrochloride 5 mg, methylcellulose 225 mg, choline bitartrate 150 mg, ascorbic acid 25 mg, vitamin A 1,500 units, vitamin D 150 units, thiamine mononitrate 1 mg, riboflavin 1 mg, niacinamide 10 mg, and ferrous fumarate 2.5 mg.

Anorexiants with Thyroid Preparations and Sedatives

Obestat Ty-Med (Lemmon): Each timed-release capsule or tablet contains methamphetamine hydrochloride 10 mg, amobarbital 60 mg, and thyroid 150 mg.

Perke Three (Ascher): Each capsule contains amphetamine sulfate 15 mg, thyroid 195 mg, atropine sulfate 0.36 mg, aloin 16 mg, and phenobarbital 16 mg.

Miscellaneous Anorexiant Mixtures

Biphetamine (Pennwalt): Each timed-release capsule contains resin complexes equivalent to dextroamphetamine 3.75, 6.25, or 10 mg and amphetamine 3.75, 6.25, or 10 mg.

Ridupois Improved (Elder): Each tablet contains levamphetamine tartrate 10 mg and glyceryl guaiacolate 100 mg.

Chapter 34

ANALEPTICS

Analeptics are central nervous system stimulants. They have had, at best, limited usefulness as adjuncts in the supportive treatment of respiratory depression associated with drug-induced coma. Their use is now considered unwarranted. Unlike the narcotic antagonists, which reverse the respiratory depression produced by morphine-like analgesics, none of these drugs acts as a specific antagonist to any of the barbiturate or nonbarbiturate sedatives and hypnotics.

Analeptics act directly upon the medulla to stimulate respiratory activity, or indirectly to stimulate the carotid chemoreceptors; they do not stimulate the myocardium. Although the action of the analeptics is most apparent in the medulla, the midbrain, cortex, or spinal cord also may be affected as the dose is increased. Convulsions may even occur. The respiratory rate may be increased but this is only a transient effect. Repeated doses of the analeptic may further augment the depressant effects of the central nervous system depressant and arousal from the coma is seldom achieved.

The margin between the analeptic and convulsant dose often is narrow with the older analeptics (picrotoxin, nikethamide [Coramine], pentylenetetrazol [Metrazol]). Accordingly, these agents have generally been supplanted by newer drugs when analeptic therapy is elected. These include ethamivan [Emivan] and doxapram [Dopram].

Analeptics have been used to treat central nervous system depression caused by overdosage of sedatives and hypnotics on the premise that they restore protective reflexes, improve ventilation, and correct hypotension. However, there is no evidence that they produce these beneficial effects. The accepted practice in the treatment of respiratory depression associated with drug-induced coma is to rely entirely upon supportive therapy: establish a patent airway to ensure adequate respiratory exchange, administer oxygen, and assist or control respiration when necessary. Additional supportive therapy to maintain blood pressure and volume often is required. When long-acting barbiturates have caused symptoms of severe poisoning in patients with poor renal function, dialysis has been employed to eliminate the drug rapidly. (See also Chapter 27, Sedatives and Hypnotics.)

Analeptics should not be used to counteract respiratory arrest caused by overdosage of inhalation anesthetics or to shorten the postanesthetic recovery period, since reducing the concentration of the agent in the blood with artificial respiration is more effective. These agents are useless for treating respiratory arrest due to drowning, electrocution, anoxia, carbon dioxide accumulation, carbon monoxide poisoning, neuromuscular blockade (curare), increased intracranial pressure, or shock. Similarly, analeptics are ineffective for treating cardiac arrest, depression caused by an overdosage of central nervous system stimulants, and pulmonary insufficiency caused by chronic lung diseases (eg, emphysema).

Certain central nervous system stimulants have been proposed for use in overcoming the "hangover" effects that may occur during the arousal period in patients recovering from drug-induced coma; these include caffeine, methylphenidate [Ritalin], and the amphetamines (amphetamine [Benzedrine, Leptamine, Monophos, Raphetamine], dextroamphetamine [Dexedrine], methamphetamine). However, their administration for this purpose is neither advisable nor logical. For other uses for the amphetamines, methylphenidate, and also caffeine, see Chapters 32, Antidepressants; 33,

Anorexiants; and 22, Mild Analgesics.

Adverse Reactions and Precautions

Analeptics should not be given in an attempt to restore consciousness. Overdosage may cause hypersalivation, nausea, vomiting, coughing, retching, bradycardia, arrhythmias, hyperreflexia, fasciculations, or convulsions. Delayed psychotic reactions, manifested by euphoria, agitation, manic reactions, confusion, and visual hallucinations have occurred. These effects appear most prominently in patients dependent on barbiturates or barbiturate-type drugs.

INDIVIDUAL EVALUATIONS

CAFFEINE AND BENZOATE SODIUM

This agent should not be used as a respiratory stimulant or to overcome the "hangover" effects that may occur during the arousal period in patients recovering from drug-induced coma. (See the Introductory Statement.)

Large doses cause insomnia, restlessness, excitement, mild delirium, tinnitus, tachycardia, premature heart contractions, and diuresis.

USUAL DOSAGE.—No advice on dosage is given. A commonly employed dosage is: *Intramuscular*, *Intravenous*, *Subcutaneous: Adults*, 500 mg to 1 g. *Children*, 8 mg/kg of body weight (maximum 500 mg). This dose may be repeated every four hours if necessary.

PREPARATIONS.—Caffeine and Benzoate Sodium. *Injection:* Solution 250 mg in 1 ml containers, 500 mg in 2 ml containers. Drug marketed under generic name.

SIMILAR PREPARATIONS.—Caffeine, U.S.P., Caffeine Citrated, N.F.

DOXAPRAM HYDROCHLORIDE [Dopram]

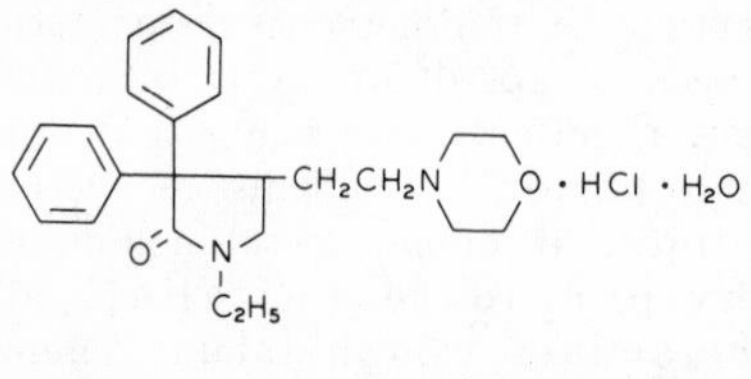

CH_2CH_2N · HCl · H_2O ; C_2H_5

Doxapram has been proposed for use in the management of drug-induced respiratory depression and in hastening arousal during the postoperative recovery period. However, airway management and support of ventilation are more effective in the treatment of respiratory depression; therefore, the use of this analeptic to counteract respiratory depression or shorten postanesthetic recovery time is neither advisable nor logical. (See the Introductory Statement.)

Hyperactivity, fasciculations, hyperreflexia, laryngospasm, tachycardia, hypertension, and convulsions may occur, particularly if large doses are given. Doxapram is contraindicated in patients with convulsive disorders, hypertension, cerebral edema, hyperthyroidism, or pheochromocytoma, and in those taking monoamine oxidase inhibitors or adrenergic agents.

USUAL DOSAGE.—Use of this drug is deemed inadvisable because of the reasons stated above. The manufacturer's suggested dosages are: *Intravenous: Adults*, in the management of respiratory depression following anesthesia, 0.5 to 2 mg/kg of body weight is infused. The calculated total dose is added to dextrose or sodium chloride injection and administered initially at a rate of approximately 5 mg/minute until a satisfactory response is observed; for maintenance, an infusion rate of 1 to 3 mg/minute is suggested. The recommended maximal dosage is 4 mg/kg or 300 mg for adults of average weight. To hasten arousal during the recovery period, 1 to 1.5 mg/kg is injected. The total dose is given as a single dose or in divided doses at five-minute intervals. In the management of drug-induced depression, initially, 0.5 to 2 mg/kg is injected as a single dose. For maintenance, the injection is repeated every one to two hours, or a solution of 1 to 3 mg/kg/hour is infused. The maximal daily dose is 24 mg/kg/day for two days, or a total dose of 3 g for adults of average weight.

Data are not yet available regarding the drug's use in *children.*

PREPARATIONS.—Dopram (Robins). *Injection:* Solution 20 mg/ml in 20 ml containers.

ETHAMIVAN [Emivan]

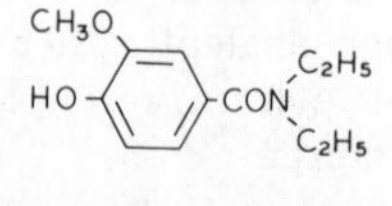

CH_3O ; HO ; CON ; C_2H_5 ; C_2H_5

This analeptic is proposed for treatment of severe respiratory depression caused by overdosage of barbiturates and other sedatives and hypnotics and of pulmonary insufficiency caused by chronic lung disease (eg, emphysema). However, analeptics are of little value in these conditions. Intensive supportive care is more effective in the former. Use of ethamivan may even be harmful in pulmonary insufficiency since an increase in oxygen consumption results; this, in turn may enhance any existing hypoxemia and increase the arterial blood carbon dioxide tension. Temporary stimulation of respiration is of questionable value in the treatment of a chronic disease. The administration of this drug to shorten postanesthetic recovery time is neither advisable nor logical and may be harmful. (See the Introductory Statement.)

Sneezing, coughing, laryngospasm, and fasciculations may occur if the rate of intravenous infusion is too rapid. Excessive doses may cause convulsions. Ethamivan is contraindicated in patients with convulsive disorders and in those taking monoamine oxidase inhibitors or adrenergic agents.

USUAL DOSAGE.—Use of this drug is deemed inadvisable because of the reasons stated above. The manufacturer's suggested dosages are: *Intravenous: Adults*, 2 mg/kg of body weight injected at five-minute intervals until the desired level of consciousness or easy arousal is achieved, or 250 mg may be administered at ten-minute intervals until the eyelid reflex becomes apparent; 100 to 150 mg then is given every hour until the patient is conscious or easily aroused. Alternatively, 1 g is added to 250 ml of dextrose or sodium chloride injection and infused at a rate of approximately 10 mg/minute. *Children*, 0.5 to 5 mg/kg of body weight is injected; dose is repeated at five-minute intervals or followed by infusion of 0.2 mg/kg per minute.

PREPARATIONS.—Emivan (USV). *Injection:* Solution 50 mg/ml in 2 and 10 ml containers.

NIKETHAMIDE [Coramine]

Use of nikethamide in drug-induced coma is of no value and may be dangerous, because the margin between the analeptic and convulsant dose is narrow. Also, its action is often transient and arousal does not occur.

The drug may cause fasciculations and facial pruritus.

USUAL DOSAGE.—Use of this drug is deemed inadvisable because of the reasons stated above. The manufacturer's suggested dosage is: *Intravenous: Adults*, 5 to 10 ml, followed by 5 ml every five minutes for the first hour, then 5 ml every 30 or 60 minutes if necessary.

PREPARATIONS.—Coramine (Ciba). *Injection:* Solution 250 mg/ml in 1.5 and 20 ml containers. Drug also marketed under generic name.

PENTYLENETETRAZOL [Metrazol]

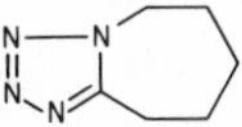

Although pentylenetetrazol was once the mainstay for treating apnea and drug-induced coma, it should no longer be used. Its use as a convulsant in the treatment of psychoses is now obsolete. It is recommended by some manufacturers as a cerebral stimulant for treatment of senility or mental depression; however, there is no adequate evidence to substantiate its effectiveness for these uses.

Pentylenetetrazol may produce convulsions even in heavily narcotized patients; therefore, it should not be used in patients with convulsive disorders or focal cerebral disease.

USUAL DOSAGE.—Use of this drug is deemed inadvisable because of the reasons stated above. The manufacturer's suggested dosages are:

Intravenous: Adults, for treatment of drug-induced coma, 500 mg initially, followed by 1 g every 30 minutes as indicated.

Oral: Adults, for treatment of senility, initially, 200 mg three or four times daily; maintenance, 100 mg three or four times daily.

PREPARATIONS.—Metrazol (Knoll).

Injection: Powder 25 g (for compounding); solution 100 mg/ml in 1 and 30 ml containers.

Oral: Elixir 100 mg/5 ml; tablets 100 mg.

ADDITIONAL TRADEMARK.— Cenalene-M (Central). Drug also marketed under generic name.

PICROTOXIN

Picrotoxin is a potent, long-lasting respiratory stimulant that was formerly widely used in treating overdoses of central nervous system depressants. Its ineffectiveness in hastening arousal and the possible occurrence of severe convulsions have led to its obsolescence.

Doses of 20 mg may produce severe clonic and tonic convulsions.

USUAL DOSAGE.—Use of this drug is deemed inadvisable because of the reasons stated above. Commonly suggested dosages are:

Intravenous: Adults, 3 mg; dose is repeated with caution at three-minute intervals until signs of reflex activity are noted.

Intramuscular, Intravenous: Children, 0.2 mg/kg of body weight; dose is repeated in 15 minutes.

PREPARATIONS.—Picrotoxin, N.F. *Injection:* Solution 3 mg/ml in 20 ml containers. Drug marketed under generic name.

Chapter 35

ADRENAL CORTICOSTEROIDS

Adrenal corticosteroids are used either: (1) in physiologic doses to correct a deficiency (eg, chronic adrenocortical insufficiency, hypopituitarism causing the reduced secretion of adrenocorticotropic hormone [ACTH]) or (2) in pharmacologic doses to treat inflammatory conditions, allergic states, collagen disorders, and certain other diseases.

The major natural adrenal corticosteroids are (1) glucocorticoids (eg, cortisol [hydrocortisone], corticosterone), which primarily have carbohydrate-storing, anti-inflammatory, corticotropin-suppressing, and protein-catabolic activities; and (2) mineralocorticoids (eg, aldosterone, desoxycorticosterone), which primarily have sodium-retaining and potassium-depleting actions. Under basal conditions, the adrenal glands secrete 15 to 30 mg of corticosteroids each day; these corticosteroids are released into the bloodstream in a diurnal pattern, with the greatest amount being secreted between 4 a.m. and 8 a.m. The amounts of the most important corticosteroids secreted daily are: cortisol 10 to 25 mg; corticosterone 0.5 to 2 mg; and aldosterone 30 to 150 μg. This output may increase tenfold during periods of maximal stress. The adrenal glands also secrete androgens (eg, dehydroepiandrosterone, △4-androstendione) and the estrogen, estrone.

The rate of secretion of the glucocorticoids is regulated by fluctuations in the amount of adrenocorticotropic hormone (ACTH) released by the anterior pituitary. The secretion of ACTH, in turn, is modulated primarily by the serum level of cortisol. The other adrenocortical hormones exert only a weak effect in restricting the secretion of ACTH. Evidence exists that corticotropin-releasing hormone (CRH), which is synthesized in the hypothalamus and transported to the anterior pituitary by the hypophyseal-portal blood system, controls the secretion of ACTH. Noxious stimuli (eg, trauma, anxiety, anesthesia, critical illness), acting on the extrahypothalamic central nervous system, increase CRH secretion by the hypothalamus and consequently increase the secretion of ACTH and therefore of cortisol. The stimulus of severe stress overrides the negative feedback effect of cortisol on secretion of ACTH. Secretion of the mineralocorticoid, aldosterone, is controlled chiefly by the renin-angiotensin system of the kidney rather than by ACTH, although adequate blood levels of ACTH are necessary to produce an optimal amount of aldosterone.

Numerous synthetic glucocorticoids have been prepared by varying the chemical structures of the natural hormones. For example, prednisone and prednisolone were produced by introducing a double bond between carbon atoms 1 and 2 (△-1 analogues) of cortisone and hydrocortisone, respectively; this change resulted in an increase in glucocorticoid activity without a corresponding increase in mineralocorticoid action. Other corticosteroids have even less electrolyte activity in proportion to glucocorticoid activity.

The natural and synthetic corticosteroids are used to treat many clinical conditions. Although the precise mechanism of action is not completely understood, a rational approach to the use of these agents is developed from a knowledge of their physiologic and pharmacologic effects. In general, the biological effects of the glucocorticoids are: (1) enhancement of gluconeogenesis, which involves breakdown of endogenous proteins to circulating amino acids, which then are converted to glucose for storage by the liver; (2) modification of the inflammatory response by stabilization of lysosomes; (3) inhibition of fibroblast proliferation and increase in collagen breakdown; (4) reduction in the number of circulating lymphocytes and eosinophils and a decrease in lymphoid tissue; (5) stimulation of erythropoiesis and the production of platelets; (6) maintenance of muscle strength in physiologic amounts and induction of muscle atrophy in excessive amounts; (7) modification of the excitation threshold of the brain; (8) thinning of the gastric mucus; (9) inhibition of bone growth, matrix formation, and calcification; (10) reduction of calcium absorption from the gut and promotion of the renal excretion of calcium; (11) immunosuppression (in large doses only); and (12) suppression of the release of ACTH by the anterior pituitary and therefore suppression of the production of steroids by the adrenal cortex. The biological effects of the mineralocorticoids are enhancement of sodium retention and potassium excretion by the renal tubules.

In considering the therapeutic efficacy of the corticosteroids, it is important to remember that the separation of glucocorticoid and mineralocorticoid activity is incomplete. Some agents that are considered to be primarily glucocorticoids (eg, hydrocortisone, cortisone, prednisone, prednisolone) possess variable mineralocorticoid activity as well, and sodium retention and potassium loss may occur when these drugs are used in pharmacologic amounts. The relative potencies of the corticosteroids used systemically are listed in the table.

Except for sodium retention and potassium loss, there is little difference in the adverse effects produced by the various corticosteroids when therapeutically equivalent doses are given. Hydrocortisone and cortisone are preferred for replacement therapy because of their mineralocorticoid activity, whereas a glucocorticoid with little sodium-retaining effect is usually given in pharmacologic amounts to treat inflammatory, allergic, and other corticosteroid-responsive conditions.

A number of preparations are available for local, oral, and parenteral administration; the latter route is reserved for patients who are either critically ill or unable to take oral medication. Whenever possible, local administration is preferable to systemic therapy (eg, topical application in inflammatory dermatologic conditions, enemas in ulcerative colitis). In addition to circumventing many of the adverse effects of systemic therapy, local administration may achieve a better result. However, since systemic absorption may occur if large doses of a soluble glucocorticoid are used locally, the dose still must be regulated.

Because of the danger of inducing hypercorticism, long-term use of pharmacologic doses of systemic corticosteroids should be reserved for patients with life-threatening conditions or severe symptoms that fail to respond satisfactorily to more benign palliative measures. These agents may be used with comparative safety for brief periods to treat self-limiting diseases or to control acute exacerbations of chronic conditions.

The corticosteroids are dangerous if improperly used; thus, patients must be closely supervised and the dosage individualized in accordance with the severity and prognosis of the disorder, the response of the patient, and the anticipated duration of therapy. It is undesirable to try to suppress all symptoms completely in patients with chronic conditions. Instead, glucocorticoids should be given in the smallest dosage that will control a specific symptom or sign and should be used for the shortest time possible. Measures also must be taken to counteract or prevent undesirable effects. The dosage for children should be regulated according to the severity of the disease rather than by body weight.

A number of chronic diseases for which glucocorticoids are used (eg, asthma, ulcerative colitis, nephrotic syndrome, rheumatoid arthritis) may respond as well to alternate-day therapy with short-acting glucocorticoids as to more frequent administration and the incidence of adverse reactions may be reduced. When glucocorticoids are given daily to children, the rate of growth is decreased since the secretion of growth hormone by the anterior pituitary is suppressed and the peripheral action of growth hormone is antagonized. When short-acting glucocorticoids (prednisone, prednisolone, methylprednisolone) are given on alternate days, children maintain normal growth patterns and other unwanted effects, including pituitary-adrenal suppression, appear to decrease. The observed and theoretical advantages make alternate-day therapy the treatment of choice when feasible. However, many patients become symptomatic or have an exacerbation on the day on which no glucocorticoids are given and, therefore, are not suitable candidates for this regimen.

Indications: The acute symptoms of *collagen diseases* can be controlled with systemically administered glucocorticoids. However, patients with rheumatoid arthritis should be given

RELATIVE POTENCIES OF THE SYSTEMIC CORTICOSTEROIDS

Compound (Or Its Esters)	Glucocorticoid Potency Compared to Hydrocortisone (Mg for Mg Basis)	Mineralocorticoid Potency	Equivalent Dose
Hydrocortisone Cort-Dome (Dome) Cortef (Upjohn) Cortenema (Rowell) Cortril (Pfizer) Hydrocortone (Merck Sharp & Dohme)	1.0	++	20 mg
Cortisone Cortone (Merck Sharp & Dohme)	0.8	++	25 mg
Prednisolone Delta-Cortef (Upjohn) Meticortelone (Schering) Nisolone (Ascher) Sterane (Pfizer) Hydeltrasol (Merck Sharp & Dohme) Hydeltra-T.B.A. (Merck Sharp & Dohme)	4	+	5 mg
Prednisone Delta-Dome (Dome) Deltasone (Upjohn) Deltra (Merck Sharp & Dohme) Meticorten (Schering) Paracort (Parke, Davis) Servisone (Lederle)	4	+	5 mg
Methylprednisolone Medrol, Depo-Medrol, Solu-Medrol (Upjohn)	5	0	4 mg
Triamcinolone Aristocort, Aristospan (Lederle) Kenacort, Kenalog (Squibb)	5	0	4 mg
Paramethasone Haldrone (Lilly) Stemex (Syntex)	10	0	2 mg
Fluprednisolone Alphadrol (Upjohn)	10	0	2 mg
Dexamethasone Decadron (Merck Sharp & Dohme) Deronil (Schering) Dexameth (USV) Gammacorten (Ciba) Hexadrol (Organon)	30	0	0.75 mg
Betamethasone Celestone (Schering)	30	0	0.60 mg
*Fludrocortisone Florinef (Squibb)	15	+++++	

*Used only for mineralocorticoid effect.

corticoids only after conservative treatment with nonsteroidal anti-inflammatory agents, rest, and physical therapy has been tried. Corticosteroids then may be added to the regimen, but they should be used only during the active, reversible phases of the disease. Although most patients experience dramatic relief of symptoms initially, inflammation tends to recur and is sometimes more intense following cessation of treatment. However, by facilitating movement of painful joints that might otherwise become immobilized and ankylosed to the point of complete loss of function, glucocorticoids can prevent invalidism and incapacitation. (See also Chapter 26, Antirheumatic Agents.)

Forms of glucocorticoids that are only slightly soluble (eg, methylprednisolone acetate [Depo-Medrol], prednisolone tebutate [Hydeltra-T.B.A.], triamcinolone acetonide [Aristocort, Kenalog], and triamcinolone diacetate [Aristocort, Kenacort]) are suitable for *local injection* in the treatment of inflamed joints, tendons, bursae, and soft tissues. They have a slower onset but a much longer duration of action (up to two or three weeks) than the soluble esters.

Although the fever, arthritis, and other clinical manifestations of *acute rheumatic fever* respond favorably to glucocorticoid therapy, the underlying disease process is not eliminated. When a significant degree of rheumatic carditis exists, glucocorticoids are the treatment of choice. A duration of treatment exceeding three months is seldom required.

Glucocorticoids also are effective in the symptomatic treatment of *systemic lupus erythematosus*, but their use should be reserved for patients with complications such as hemolytic anemia or thrombocytopenia, those who are critically ill, or those who have renal or neurologic involvement. Massive doses to control the fulminating exacerbations are sometimes lifesaving and the continued use of these agents may prolong life.

Glucocorticoids control the acute arthritic symptoms of *scleroderma* but have no effect on its visceral manifestations. Since renal involvement may be accelerated, they should not be used for long-term therapy. In *polymyositis*, prolonged use is justified when the disease is active. Some acute symptoms of polyarteritis nodosa may be controlled.

Glucocorticoids provide prompt palliation of symptoms in *allergic states*, including bronchial asthma; nonseasonal allergic rhinitis; hay fever (pollinosis, seasonal allergic rhinitis); reactions to drugs, serum, and transfusions; and dermatoses with an allergic component. Their use is preferably reserved for the control of acute episodes; they are not a substitute for conventional measures of management, such as the avoidance of allergens. The glucocorticoids may be lifesaving in patients with anaphylactic reactions or status asthmaticus.

Many patients with allergic, inflammatory, and pruritic *dermatoses* experience remarkable relief of symptoms with topical use of steroids. However, whenever possible, the causal factors should be sought and eliminated. The drugs are of great benefit in severe sunburn, nonvenomous insect bites, and acute, self-limiting cutaneous conditions of the eczematous type. Cutaneous manifestations of some collagen diseases such as systemic lupus erythematosus and dermatomyositis respond to topical therapy.

Glucocorticoids have been injected intralesionally for the treatment of psoriasis, alopecia areata, keloids, and disseminated neurodermatitis. Atrophy of the skin or sloughing may occur at the site of injection.

In *pemphigus vulgaris*, systemic treatment with massive doses of glucocorticoids often produces remission of several months' duration. In most patients, suppression of symptoms requires prolonged treatment with large doses. The manifestations of hypercorticism that result are considered preferable to the symptoms of this otherwise progressive and fatal disease. Nevertheless, these patients should be closely observed for signs of serious and potentially fatal complications (eg, peptic ulcer with hemorrhage and perforation, fulminating infections).

Among the inflammatory *ocular diseases* that respond to treatment with corticosteroids by local application or instillation are nonulcerative (allergic) blepharitis and certain types of anterior uveitis, conjunctivitis, and keratitis. Systemic therapy has been used successfully to suppress inflammatory reactions and prevent irreparable damage to the eye in such conditions as acute posterior uveitis, sympathetic ophthalmia, and optic neuropathy, including retrobulbar neuritis. (See Chapter 71, Anti-infective and Anti-inflammatory Agents Used in Ophthalmology.)

Acute phases of endocrine *exophthalmos* (thyroid ophthalmopathy) with severe proptosis sometimes can be treated successfully with systemic corticosteroid therapy to reduce orbital edema. Patients may respond to 40 to 60 mg of prednisone or its equivalent daily but often doses as large as 120 to 140 mg daily for several weeks are necessary before the amount can be gradually reduced. Corticosteroids have been reported to decrease the need for orbital decompression surgery.

Although data in man does not include double-blind controlled studies, the efficacy of corticosteroids in the management of *cerebral edema* associated with primary and metastatic neoplasms of the brain and postsurgical cerebral edema has strong clinical support and is based on observations of clinical improvement of symptoms and neurological signs. However, the exact mechanisms of action have not been determined. The value of corticosteroids in the management of patients with edema caused by trauma from head injury or cerebral infarction has not been determined. Controlled studies indicate that corticosteroids are not useful in patients with intracerebral hemorrhage or brain stem involvement.

Relatively large doses of glucocorticoids having little mineralocorticoid activity are given initially to treat cerebral edema. Initially, 6 to 10 mg of dexamethasone or its equivalent is given intravenously, followed by 4 to 6 mg intramuscularly every six hours until maximal improvement occurs (generally within two to four days). For maintenance, 3 to 9 mg of dexamethasone daily or its equivalent is given orally, usually for relatively short periods, in accordance with the response of the patient. The anticipated benefits of short-term glucocorticoid therapy for cerebral edema in patients with active gastrointestinal ulcer must be weighed against the risk of gastrointestinal bleeding.

When glucocorticoids are administered to treat *manifestations of an infection*, they may mask symptoms of active progression of the disease; therefore, caution is indicated and appropriate antibacterial therapy is given concomitantly.

Glucocorticoids have been used with antituberculous agents to treat clinical manifestations and complications of *tuberculosis*. Their ability to suppress inflammation and the formation of fibrous tissue is useful in treating pleural and pericardial effusions and pulmonary parenchymal disease. The general condition of patients with pulmonary tuberculosis may improve rapidly with reduction of fever, weight gain, and accelerated clearing of lesions. Patients with tuberculous meningitis show both subjective and objective signs of improvement (reduced cerebrospinal fluid pressure, blood cell count, and protein level). Glucocorticoids also are given to alleviate severe toxicity in preterminal tuberculous patients and to decrease hypersensitivity to the antituberculous drugs (see Chapter 58, Antituberculous Agents). However, certain unwanted effects may occur on withdrawal of steroid therapy (ie, rebound fever, arthralgia, a less favorable roentgenographic picture). Fungal infections occurring with the tuberculous infection or misdiagnosed as tuberculosis may be aggravated.

The role of corticosteroids in the management of patients in *shock* is controversial. Initially, corticosteroids were used in replacement doses for the treatment of shock associated with adrenocortical disease. In the absence of adrenocortical disease or suppression by previously or concurrently administered glucocorticoids, there is no evidence that shock is due to adrenocortical insufficiency. In shock, as in other forms of stress, the cortisol levels are elevated and physiologic doses have no hemodynamic action. There are conflicting opinions concerning the benefits of corticosteroids in the Waterhouse-Friderichsen syndrome.

The therapeutic value of massive doses of glucocorticoids (dexamethasone 5 mg/kg, methylprednisolone 30 mg/kg, or an equivalent, usually infused intravenously over a period of three to five minutes and repeated at four-hour intervals) in shock has not been established. This therapy is advocated by some investigators, especially for bacteremic shock caused by gram-negative organisms, primarily because favorable results have been reported in animals. Hemodynamic changes resulting from decreased resistance of the viscerocutaneous circulation and a slight positive inotropic effect on cardiac muscle are claimed to benefit patients with hypovolemic, cardiogenic, or bacteremic shock. Stabilization of lysosomes is suggested as being particularly important in treating bacteremic shock. (See also Chapter 5, Agents Used in Hypotension and Shock.)

Glucocorticoids are useful in the palliative treatment of certain *neoplastic diseases.* (See also Chapter 88, Antineoplastic Agents.) Favorable effects in acute and chronic leukemias, Hodgkin's disease, multiple myeloma, and other related lymphomas may be attributed to the lymphocytolytic action of these agents. Glucocorticoids, used with antineoplastic agents, have produced remissions in about 60% and clinical improvement in an additional 20% of children with acute lymphoblastic leukemia. Therapeutic responses occur in about 50% of patients with chronic lymphocytic leukemia; the response rate is considerably less in the other diseases. Complications such as autoimmune hemolytic anemia and thrombocytopenia respond to corticoid therapy.

Glucocorticoids are effective in the treatment of *hypercalcemia* associated with hypervitaminosis D, sarcoidosis, myeloma, and adrenocortical insufficiency and in some cases of hypercalcemia associated with malignant disease, with or without bony metastases. (See Chapter 17, Blood Calcium Regulators.)

In addition to being effective in most cases of idiopathic and acquired autoimmune hemolytic *anemia*, the glucocorticoids are effective in some patients with erythroblastopenia and congenital bone marrow failure; they also are useful in the treatment of thrombocytopenic purpuras. There is no convincing evidence that glucocorticoids are beneficial in aplastic anemia (pancytopenia associated with hypocellular bone marrow) or acute agranulocytosis.

Miscellaneous conditions for which glucocorticoids are used include *nephrosis*, *gout*, *ulcerative colitis*, and *multiple sclerosis*. They also are useful as *immunosuppressive agents* when given in large doses. Glucocorticoids possibly suppress immune responses in chronic active *hepatitis* (active juvenile cirrhosis), a disease that occurs in individuals 15 to 30 years of age which usually terminates fatally within a four-year period. It is believed to be caused by disturbed immune mechanisms. Glucocorticoids seem to decrease the number of early deaths (within two years). Although the lives of some patients are prolonged, treatment with glucocorticoids does not cure the disease or prevent cirrhosis. A significant trend toward normal occurs in mean serum bilirubin, total globulin, and albumin levels during the first two to three years.

Replacement therapy with adrenal corticosteroids is required in *adrenocortical insufficiency*, which is caused by atrophy or destruction of the adrenal glands, impaired production of corticotropin, or congenital defects in steroidogenesis.

Primary chronic adrenocortical insufficiency (Addison's disease) is associated with atrophy (autoimmune disease) or destruction of the cortex by metastatic carcinoma, hemorrhage, or infections. Production of both cortisol and aldosterone is deficient. Symptoms include weakness, weight loss, and hyperpigmentation, as well as anorexia, nausea, vomiting, hypoglycemia, hypotension, hyponatremia, and hyperkalemia. The goals of therapy are the reestablishment of strength, weight, normal mental processes, and normal blood pressure.

Hydrocortisone or cortisone is preferred for replacement therapy in chronic adrenocortical insufficiency. If orthostatic hypotension continues in spite of adequate glucocorticoid replacement and a liberal salt intake, a mineralocorticoid should be added to the regimen. The mineralocorticoid most commonly used for this purpose is fludrocortisone [Florinef]; desoxycorticosterone (Doc) [Doca, Percorten], administered intramuscularly, is an alternate drug. During periods of stress, the dose of the glucocorticoid must be increased in proportion to the severity of the stress. During a mild illness, such as a viral upper respiratory tract infection, doubling the maintenance dose usually is sufficient. In the presence of more severe stress, hydrocortisone sodium succinate [Solu-Cortef] or hydrocortisone sodium phosphate [Hydrocortone Phosphate] should be injected intravenously (100 mg every four hours); the doses should then be reduced over four to five days in accordance with the response of the patient. Acute adrenocortical insufficiency (adrenal crisis) may develop unless the dose of the glucocorticoid is increased promptly. Temporary therapy with excessive doses is preferred to inadequate replacement. Dextrose in sodium chloride injection should be given intravenously as needed. Antibiotics are added if an infection is present, and supportive therapy is necessary if shock occurs.

The day before undergoing major surgery, patients with chronic adrenocortical insufficiency should receive twice the maintenance dosage of corticosteroid, with the last dose given at bedtime. Before induction of anesthesia, 100 mg of hydrocortisone sodium succinate or hydrocortisone sodium phosphate should be given intravenously. During prolonged surgery, this dose should be repeated every four hours. After surgery, 50 mg of hydrocortisone sodium succinate or hydrocortisone sodium phosphate should be administered intravenously every four to six hours for two days. Thereafter, providing the postoperative course is uncomplicated, the dosage can be reduced to the usual replacement level over a period of four to five days. Because absorption may be markedly impaired during periods of hypotension, administration of intramuscular preparations is not advisable in patients who are acutely ill.

Corticotropin is ineffective in primary chronic adrenocortical insufficiency, since any adrenal tissue present is secreting at a maximal level.

Secondary adrenocortical insufficiency is caused by deficient secretion of adrenocorticotropic hormone as a result of pituitary disease or the prolonged suppression of pituitary function by large doses of exogenous glucocorticoids. There is less electrolyte disturbance and less pigmentation than in primary chronic adrenocortical insufficiency (Addison's disease). The dosage of hydrocortisone or cortisone used for secondary adrenocortical insufficiency is similar to that given for Addison's disease; the majority of patients do not require the addition of a specific mineralocorticoid. As in primary adrenocortical insufficiency, during periods of stress, the dose of glucocorticoid must be increased in proportion to the severity of the stress. A patient with pituitary suppression from exogenous glucocorticoids will continue to require therapy during periods of stress for as long as one year after discontinuance of glucocorticoid therapy. Complete recovery of pituitary function may take up to nine months.

Clinical manifestations of congenital adrenogenital syndromes vary, depending upon which specific enzyme necessary for the biosynthesis of cortisol by the adrenal cortex is deficient. In each syndrome, synthesis of cortisol is partially or completely interrupted at some point so that an insufficient amount of cortisol is secreted. The low cortisol level causes an excessive amount of adrenocorticotropic hormone to be secreted by the pituitary and adrenal hyperplasia results. In the most common of these syndromes, the simple virilizing form of 21-hydroxylase deficiency, the deficiency is partial and the increased ACTH secretion raises the cortisol level to normal but also increases the secretion of androgens and certain precursors of cortisol. Excessive secretion of androgens during fetal life results in virilization of female infants. About one-half of the patients with 21-hydroxylase deficiency are unable to maintain a normal sodium balance, possibly because a more complete enzyme deficiency also blocks the synthesis of corticosterone, desoxycorticosterone, and aldosterone.

The adrenogenital syndromes are treated in the same manner as other types of adrenocortical insufficiency: the cortisol is replaced and a mineralocorticoid is added for patients with salt-losing forms. Patients with hypertensive adrenocortical hyperplasia secrete an excessive amount of desoxycorticosterone. These patients are best treated by administering a glucocorticoid with minimal mineralocorticoid activity, such as dexamethasone. Doses of the glucocorticoid are determined individually by measuring 17-ketosteroid excretion. In patients with a salt-losing form, careful evaluation of the electrolyte concentration and balance is needed to determine a stable regimen. Mineralocorticoid replacement can usually be discontinued cautiously between the ages of five and seven years. Glucocorticoid therapy must be continued throughout life. The dose should be doubled during periods of moderate stress (eg, upper respiratory infections) and increased further during severe stress (eg, major surgery, severe infection). The usual dose for severe stress is 50 mg of hydrocortisone sodium succinate or hydrocortisone sodium phosphate given intravenously every six hours; the dose may be increased if necessary.

Adverse Reactions and Precautions

The complications of corticosteroid therapy are manifold and, in most instances, are directly related to the pharmacologic effects of these drugs. The likelihood of adverse reactions correlates with the dose, duration of therapy, and underlying disease. The complications should be considered as carefully as the desired effects.

The major adverse reactions with corticosteroid therapy may be divided into the following categories:

Peptic Ulcer: Since glucocorticoids decrease the protective gastric mucous barrier, interfere with tissue repair, and, in some patients, increase gastric acid and pepsin production, gastritis and peptic ulceration are quite common. However, the symptoms of peptic ulcer may be masked by glucocorticoid therapy. Routine prophylactic use of antacids and periodic examination of the stools for occult blood are recommended.

Hypokalemia: Severe hypokalemia may cause asthenia, paralysis, or arrhythmias that may proceed to cardiac arrest. Hypokalemia is related to the mineralocorticoid activity of a specific preparation and can be prevented by supplementary oral administration of potassium (10 to 15 ml of a 10% solution of potassium chloride three or four times daily). Digitalis intoxication may occur as a result of potassium depletion in patients receiving digitalis and desoxycorticosterone or a glucocorticoid with mineralocorticoid properties concurrently. Diuretics may cause a further loss of potassium.

Infections: Tuberculin skin testing is recommended for all patients before the initiation of glucocorticoid therapy, for reactivation of healed or latent tuberculosis in patients receiving glucocorticoids is well documented; isoniazid (300 mg daily) should be given prophylactically to those with positive skin tests.

Impairment of host defenses makes patients receiving large doses of glucocorticoids unusually susceptible to fungal infections, especially candidiasis, pneumocystis pneumonia, cryptococcosis, aspergillosis, and sporotrichosis.

The incidence and severity of bacterial and viral infections also are increased. Since corticoids tend to mask the symptoms, intercurrent infections may become severe before their presence is recognized. Glucocorticoids are especially hazardous when herpes simplex involves the eye. Early recognition and institution of appropriate treatment are the only safeguards against these serious complications. If infections develop during systemic glucocorticoid therapy, the dosage should not be reduced rapidly below the physiologic level because signs of hypocorticism may develop; dosages may have to be increased.

Cutaneous bacterial or yeast infection is the most common complication of topical glucocorticoid therapy. The infection should be treated with appropriate topical or systemic anti-infective agents and the glucocorticoid discontinued if necessary.

Suppression of Growth: Because growth is suppressed in children receiving long-term corticosteroid therapy and because these agents reduce resistance to viral infections, which occur with relative frequency in children, prolonged administration of these drugs in children should be restricted to the most urgent indications.

Central Nervous System Effects: Large doses of corticosteroids cause behavioral and personality changes manifested most frequently by euphoria; other signs include insomnia, nervousness, irritability, and hyperkinesia. Psychotic episodes, including both manic and depressive states, paranoid states, and acute toxic psychoses have been reported occasionally. Although the newer synthetic corticosteroids seem less likely to produce psychoses, the reduced incidence of these disorders may actually be the result of more cautious administration.

Patients with psychoses, severe neuroses, or convulsive disorders are usually poor candidates for corticosteroid therapy. Although a history of emotional disorders does not necessarily preclude use of corticosteroids, these patients should be closely observed for signs of personality changes, including alteration in sleep pattern and other indications of the onset of severe depression or psychosis.

Suppression of Corticotropin Secretion: When glucocorticoids are given for more than one week in amounts greater than physiologic replacement (ie, more than 20 mg of hydrocortisone or its equivalent per day), pituitary function is suppressed to a significant degree. Therefore, the problems that may arise during withdrawal must be considered and the patient should be closely observed. The degree and duration of suppression after therapy is discontinued correlate with the dose of glucocorticoid used and the duration of therapy. The total daily dosage should be reduced slowly to physiologic maintenance levels over a period of one week or more. An exacerbation of the patient's underlying disease may occur during this period. Mild exacerbations may subside within a few days without an increase in the dose of the glucocorticoid, but severe exacerbations require resumption of the prior dosage and a slower withdrawal. Once a physiologic maintenance dose is reached, it should be given as a single daily dose with breakfast for an additional seven to ten days and then discontinued. This schedule allows the pituitary to return to its normal nocturnal corticotropin-secreting activity while the patient is still given a basic maintenance dose of glucocorticoid to cover the relatively deficient period during the day. In the above withdrawal program, administration of corticotropin is not necessary. When the corticosteroid is discontinued, most patients will regain adrenal function in a few days. However, atrophy may persist for months in a small number of patients, particularly in those who had received large doses for a prolonged period. If severe stress occurs within one year following discontinuation of glucocorticoids, the patient should be treated as if he had adrenocortical insufficiency.

When any glucocorticoid is applied to diseased skin under an occlusive dressing, percutaneous absorption can occur. Although clinical signs of hypercorticism resulting from topical therapy have been reported only rarely, suppression of pituitary function is a possible hazard; therefore, when these agents are used topically under occlusive dressings for prolonged periods, use of small doses and intermittent therapy should be considered.

Osteoporosis: This is a common but all too infrequently recognized adverse effect with long-term use of glucocorticoids, for these agents increase all factors causing osteoporosis. Vertebral compression fractures may occur without pain or neurologic symptoms. The incidence of fractures from generalized osteoporosis is high in patients with rheumatoid arthritis regardless of therapy; therefore, prolonged use of glucocorticoids in these patients should be undertaken only after careful consideration of the needs of the patient.

Ocular Effects: Toxic ocular effects associated with topical corticosteroid therapy in the eye include glaucoma, exacerbation of open-angle glaucoma, and increased intraocular pressure in normal eyes. The mechanism responsible for these reactions is still obscure; a hereditary basis with dominant genes has been postulated. (See Chapter 71, Anti-infective and Anti-inflammatory Agents Used in Ophthalmology.)

Pseudotumor cerebri (benign intracranial hypertension) has been reported in some children receiving systemic corticosteroids for prolonged periods; headache, nausea, vomiting, and papilledema tend to subside with reduction of dose.

Posterior subcapsular cataract formation is associated with prolonged systemic therapy. The cataracts are small and cause negligible disturbance of vision. The frequency of occurrence appears to be dose related.

Negative Nitrogen Balance: Negative nitrogen balance results from the excessive breakdown of protein caused by glucocorticoids; this may be modified somewhat by a high protein diet and administration of anabolic agents. However, there is no experimental or clinical evidence to show that anabolic agents protect tissues from atrophy and osteoporosis.

Atrophy of the Skin: The skin may become thin and shiny or may develop striae due to rupture of the subcutaneous collagen fibers if these agents are used topically for prolonged periods in intertriginous areas or under occlusive dressings.

Myopathy: Muscular weakness primarily involves the proximal musculature of the upper extremities and responds to a reduction in dosage. Recovery occurs slowly over a period of months.

Diabetogenic Effect: Glucocorticoids aggravate known diabetes or make latent diabetes chemically apparent. Ketosis is not a problem and the diabetes usually is controlled with diet or antidiabetic agents.

Edema: Since glucocorticoids with little or no mineralocorticoid activity are now available, the problem of electrolyte imbalance is reduced. However, if edema occurs, reduction in sodium intake should be attempted initially and, if it persists, the patient should receive a glucocorticoid that is less likely to retain sodium. However, caution is required if large doses of any corticosteroid are given to patients with cardiovascular or advanced renal disease for prolonged periods; in these patients, even slight fluid retention may be dangerous.

Miscellaneous: Acne, hirsutism, menstrual disorders, facial rounding, development of supraclavicular fat pads, weight gain due to increased appetite, headache, hypertension, hyperhidrosis and flushing, vertigo, asthenia, chronic pancreatitis, intestinal perforation, hepatomegaly, hyperlipidemia, and acceleration of atherosclerosis have been associated with glucocorticoid therapy.

Drug Interactions: The metabolism of hydrocortisone is increased by administration of drugs that induce hepatic enzyme activity (eg, phenobarbital, diphenylhydantoin). If one of these drugs is given concomitantly, an increase in the maintenance dose of hydrocortisone may be necessary.

INDIVIDUAL EVALUATIONS

ADRENAL CORTEX INJECTION

This is an extract of adrenal cortices from beef, sheep, or calf (purified and standardized). Each milliliter contains biological activity equivalent to 0.1 mg of hydrocortisone. Prior to the availability of synthetic corticosteroids, adrenal cortex injection was used to treat adrenocortical insufficiency but it is now obsolete. It is at present widely promoted to the laity to treat hypoglycemia and hypotension purportedly caused by chronic adrenocortical insufficiency. Unfortunately, appropriate diagnostic procedures are rarely performed prior to this use of the drug.

There is no known medical use of this drug.

AVAILABLE TRADEMARKS.—Eschatin (Parke, Davis), Recortex (Fellows-Testagar). Drug also marketed under generic name.

BETAMETHASONE [Celestone]
BETAMETHASONE ACETATE AND BETAMETHASONE SODIUM PHOSPHATE [Celestone Soluspan]
BETAMETHASONE VALERATE [Valisone]

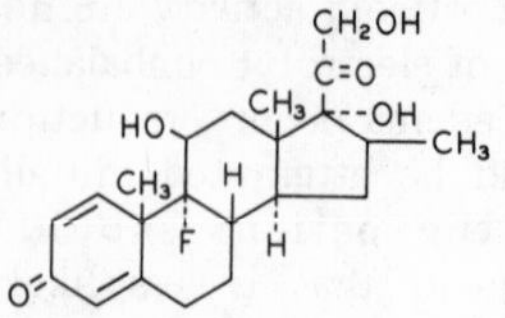

This synthetic analogue of prednisolone closely resembles dexamethasone. It is used in inflammatory and allergic conditions and other glucocorticoid-responsive diseases. In anti-inflammatory effect, 0.6 mg of betamethasone is equivalent to 20 mg of hydrocortisone. This drug lacks the sodium-retaining properties of hydrocortisone; therefore, it is not suitable for replacement therapy in adrenocortical insufficiency.

The base and valerate ester are effective when applied topically to treat inflammation in various skin disorders. The base also is given orally. A suspension containing both the soluble sodium phosphate ester for rapid initiation of action and the slightly soluble acetate ester for sustained action is used intramuscularly, intrasynovially, and injected into the soft tissues.

Undesirable effects are similar to those observed with other glucocorticoids. See the Introductory Statement for specific indications, adverse reactions, and precautions.

USUAL DOSAGE.—

Oral: (Betamethasone) *Adults*, initially 0.6 to 8.4 mg; the dose is reduced for maintenance.

Intramuscular: (Betamethasone Acetate and Betamethasone Sodium Phosphate) 1 to 2 ml containing betamethasone acetate and betamethasone sodium phosphate 3 to 6 mg each.

Intrasynovial, Soft Tissue Injection: (Betamethasone Acetate and Betamethasone Sodium Phosphate) 0.5 to 2 ml (containing betamethasone acetate and betamethasone sodium phosphate 1.5 to 6 mg each), depending upon size of joint or affected area.

Topical: (Betamethasone and Betamethasone Valerate) Appropriate preparation is applied one to three times daily or is used with occlusive dressings.

PREPARATIONS.—

Betamethasone:

Celestone (Schering).

Oral: Syrup 0.6 mg/5 ml; tablets 0.6 mg.

Topical: Cream 2 mg/g in 15 and 45 g containers.

Betamethasone Acetate, Betamethasone Sodium Phosphate (available as combination preparation):

Celestone Soluspan (Schering). *Injection:* Suspension (aqueous). Each milliliter contains betamethasone acetate 3 mg and betamethasone sodium phosphate equivalent to betamethasone 3 mg in 5 ml containers.

Betamethasone Valerate: (Strengths expressed in terms of the base.)

Valisone (Schering). *Topical:* Aerosol 0.15% in 85 g containers; cream, ointment 1.2 mg/g in 5, 15, and 45 g containers.

CORTISONE ACETATE [Cortone Acetate]

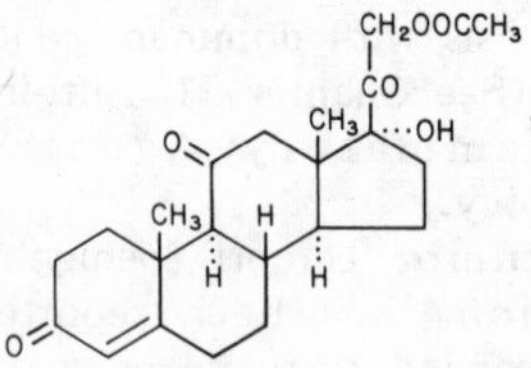

This drug is used primarily for replacement therapy in chronic adrenocortical insufficiency, including congenital adrenogenital syndromes. It also may be given systemically in pharmacologic doses to treat inflammatory or allergic disorders responsive to glucocorticoids. However, cortisone should be given only for short periods as an anti-inflammatory agent because of its strong mineralocorticoid effect. The Δ-1 analogues of cortisone and hydrocortisone have less mineralocorticoid effect and are preferred for maintaining anti-inflammatory action. In anti-inflammatory effect, 25 mg of cortisone is equivalent to 20 mg of hydrocortisone.

Hypertension, sodium and water retention, and hypokalemia can occur; sodium restriction and potassium supplementation may be necessary when cortisone is used as an anti-inflammatory agent.

See the Introductory Statement for specific indications and other adverse reactions and precautions.

USUAL DOSAGE.—

Oral: For chronic adrenocortical insufficiency, 15 to 30 mg daily; for anti-inflammatory effects, 25 to 50 mg daily for milder chronic diseases, and 75 to 150 mg daily for acute and serious chronic diseases.

Intramuscular: For anti-inflammatory effects, 75 to 300 mg daily for serious disease. This route is not suitable for acute situations because of its delayed onset of action and great variation in rate of absorption.

PREPARATIONS.—Cortone Acetate (Merck Sharp & Dohme).

Oral: Tablets 5 and 25 mg.

Injection: Suspension (in sodium chloride) 25 mg/ml in 20 ml containers and 50 mg/ml in 10 ml containers.

Drug also marketed by many manufacturers under generic name.

DESONIDE [Tridesilon]

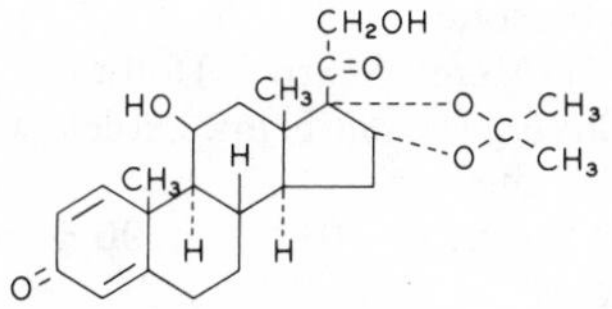

Desonide, a nonfluorinated corticosteroid for topical use, is effective in the treatment of steroid-responsive dermatoses. It is used under occlusive dressings for the management of resistant diseases, such as nummular dermatitis, chronic neurodermatitis, and psoriasis. See the Introductory Statement for specific indications and adverse reactions and precautions.

USUAL DOSAGE.—*Topical:* Preparation is applied two or three times daily or is used under occlusive dressings.

PREPARATIONS.—Tridesilon (Dome). *Topical:* Cream 0.05% in 5, 15, and 60 g containers.

DESOXYCORTICOSTERONE ACETATE
[Doca Acetate, Percorten Acetate]
DESOXYCORTICOSTERONE PIVALATE
[Percorten Pivalate]

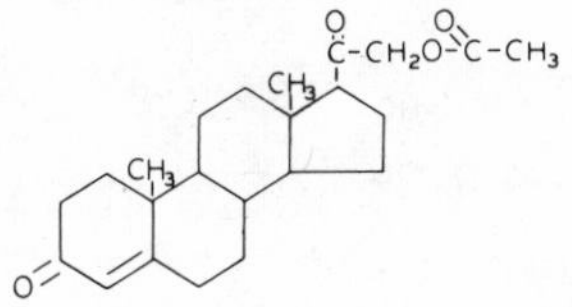

This mineralocorticoid has practically no glucocorticoid effects. It enhances the urinary excretion of potassium and the retention of sodium and water, and is used for mineralocorticoid replacement therapy in the treatment of chronic adrenocortical insufficiency, including salt-losing forms of congenital adrenogenital syndromes. (See the Introductory Statement.) Salt intake must be adjusted individually with use of desoxycorticosterone.

Adverse reactions resulting from excessive retention of sodium and water and elimination of potassium are edema, hypertension, hypokalemia, and cardiac hypertrophy and congestive failure.

USUAL DOSAGE.—

Desoxycorticosterone Acetate:

Intramuscular (solution in oil): Initially, 2 to 6 mg daily; for maintenance, 1 to 5 mg daily.

Buccal: For maintenance, 1 to 5 mg daily.

Subcutaneous Implantation: For maintenance, the number of pellets to be implanted every 8 to 12 months is equal to twice the number of milligrams of desoxycorticosterone acetate solution in oil required daily, plus an extra pellet for each milligram of the daily maintenance dose of the solution in oil in excess of 3 mg. Signs of overdosage or underdosage can be corrected by varying the salt intake or giving the steroid intramuscularly if necessary.

Desoxycorticosterone Pivalate:

Intramuscular: After the daily maintenance dose is determined with desoxycorticosterone acetate in oil, 1 ml (25 mg) of suspension is given for each milligram of the solution in oil required for daily maintenance; the calculated dose is administered every four weeks.

PREPARATIONS.—

Desoxycorticosterone Acetate:

Doca Acetate (Organon). *Injection:* Solution (in oil) 5 mg/ml in 10 ml containers.

Percorten Acetate (Ciba).

Buccal: Tablets 2 and 5 mg.

Implantation: Pellets approximately 125 mg/container.

Injection: Solution (in oil) 5 mg/ml in 10 ml containers.

Drug also marketed under generic name.

Desoxycorticosterone Pivalate:

Percorten Pivalate (Ciba). *Injection:* Suspension 25 mg/ml in 4 ml containers.

DEXAMETHASONE [Decadron, Deronil, Dexameth, Gammacorten, Hexadrol]
DEXAMETHASONE SODIUM PHOSPHATE [Decadron Phosphate, Hexadrol Phosphate]

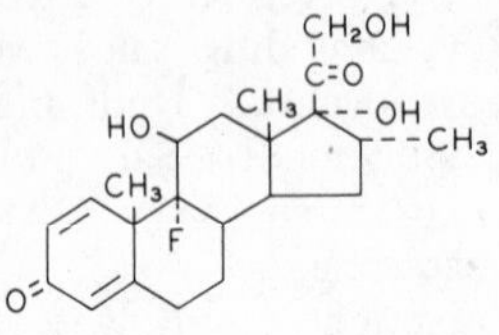

Dexamethasone is a fluorinated derivative of prednisolone and is used primarily in inflammatory and allergic conditions and other glucocorticoid-responsive diseases. In anti-inflammatory effect, 0.75 mg of dexamethasone is equivalent to 20 mg of hydrocortisone. The drug almost completely lacks the sodium-retaining properties of hydrocortisone. Mild diuresis with sodium loss may occur in patients who had been receiving other glucocorticoids. Thus, dexamethasone is not suitable for replacement therapy in acute or chronic adrenocortical insufficiency.

An aqueous solution of dexamethasone sodium phosphate is used intravenously or intramuscularly in acute illnesses and other emergency situations except acute adrenocortical insufficiency. Its intrasynovial use is limited by the short duration of action of this soluble salt. An aerosol preparation of this ester is used for inhalation therapy in bronchial asthma, but dosage by this route is difficult to control and overuse by the patient is a danger. Since systemic absorption occurs with this form of administration, patients should be carefully observed for adverse reactions.

Topical preparations are used for dermatoses and for ophthalmic or nasal therapy (see Chapter 71, Anti-infective and Anti-inflammatory Agents Used in Ophthalmology).

Adverse reactions are similar to those of other glucocorticoids. The drug often causes increased appetite with weight gain.

See the Introductory Statement for specific indications, adverse reactions, and precautions.

USUAL DOSAGE.—

Oral: (Dexamethasone) 0.5 to 10 mg daily; the larger amounts are used for acute, serious conditions.

Intravenous, Intramuscular: (Dexamethasone Sodium Phosphate) 4 to 20 mg, depending on the severity of the infection.

Intrasynovial, Soft Tissue Injection: (Dexamethasone Sodium Phosphate) 0.4 to 6 mg, depending upon size of the joint or area affected.

Inhalation: (Dexamethasone Sodium Phosphate) *Adults,* two inhalations two or three times daily (maximum, twelve inhalations daily); *children,* one or two inhalations two times daily (maximum, eight inhalations daily). Twelve inhalations are approximately equivalent to 0.4 to 0.6 mg.

Topical: (Dexamethasone) Preparation is applied two or three times daily. (Dexamethasone Sodium Phosphate) For nasal use, two sprays in each nostril two or three times daily. For dosage when used in the eye, see Chapter 71.

PREPARATIONS.—(1 mg of sodium phosphate ester is equivalent to 0.84 mg of base)

Dexamethasone:

Decadron (Merck Sharp & Dohme).

Oral: Elixir 0.5 mg/5 ml; tablets 0.25, 0.5, 0.75, and 1.5 mg.

Topical: Aerosol 0.011% in 90 g containers [Decaspray].

Deronil (Schering), Dexameth (USV), Gammacorten (Ciba). *Oral:* Tablets 0.75 mg.

Hexadrol (Organon).

Oral: Elixir 0.5 mg/5 ml; tablets 0.5, 0.75, and 1.5 mg.

Topical: Cream 0.04% in 10 and 30 g containers.

Dexamethasone Sodium Phosphate:

Decadron Phosphate (Merck Sharp & Dohme).

Inhalation: Aerosol (Respihaler) 18 mg/12.6 g container.

Injection: Solution 4 mg/ml in 1 and 5 ml containers.

Topical: Aerosol (intranasal Turbinaire) 0.142% in 12 g containers; cream 0.1% in 15 and 30 g containers.

Hexadrol Phosphate (Organon). *Injection:* Solution 4 mg/ml in 1 and 5 ml containers.

FLUDROCORTISONE ACETATE [Florinef Acetate]

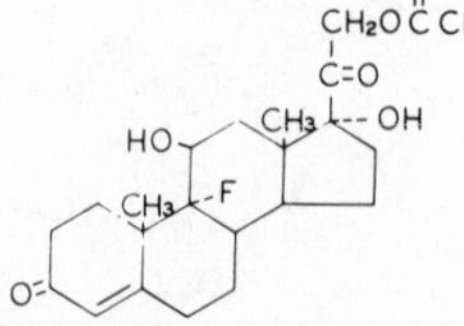

Fludrocortisone is a halogenated derivative of hydrocortisone with potent mineralocorticoid effects and moderate glucocorticoid effects. It is useful for replacement therapy in the treatment of chronic adrenocortical insufficiency, including salt-losing forms of congenital adrenogenital syndromes. Because of its marked effect on electrolyte balance, fludrocortisone should not be used systemically as an anti-inflammatory agent. See the Introductory Statement.

Adverse reactions resulting from the drug's mineralocorticoid effects are edema, hypertension, hypokalemia, and cardiac hypertrophy. In the small doses used, adverse reactions from its glucocorticoid effects are seldom a problem. Salt intake must be adjusted to meet individual requirements.

USUAL DOSAGE.—*Oral:* For chronic adrenocortical insufficiency, 0.05 to 0.1 mg daily; for salt-losing forms of congenital adrenogenital syndromes, 0.05 to 0.2 mg daily.

PREPARATIONS.—Florinef Acetate (Squibb). *Oral:* Tablets 0.1 mg.

FLUMETHASONE PIVALATE [Locorten]

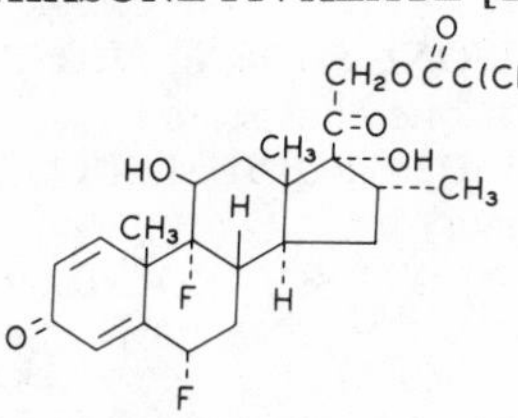

This fluorinated corticosteroid for topical use is effective in the treatment of glucocorticoid-responsive dermatoses. It is used under occlusive dressings for the management of resistant nummular dermatitis, psoriasis, and chronic neurodermatitis. See the Introductory Statement for specific indications, adverse reactions, and precautions.

USUAL DOSAGE.—*Topical:* Preparation is applied to affected area three or four times daily or is used under occlusive dressings.

PREPARATIONS.—Locorten (Ciba). *Topical:* Cream 0.03% in 5, 15, and 60 g containers.

FLUOCINOLONE ACETONIDE [Fluonid, Synalar]

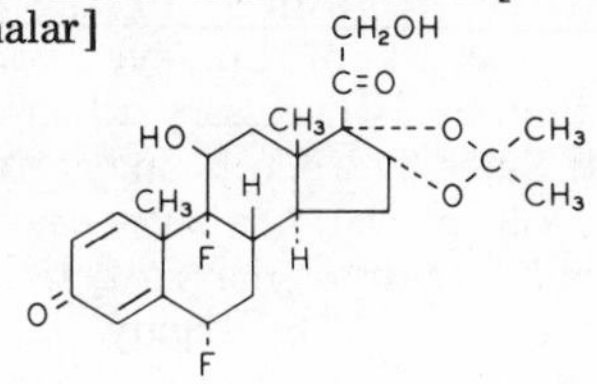

Fluocinolone is a fluorinated corticosteroid for topical use. It is effective in the treatment of glucocorticoid-responsive dermatoses. The drug is used under occlusive dressings for the management of resistant nummular dermatitis, psoriasis, and chronic neurodermatitis.

See the Introductory Statement for specific indications, adverse reactions, and precautions.

USUAL DOSAGE.—*Topical:* Preparation is applied two or three times daily or is used under occlusive dressings.

PREPARATIONS.—

Fluonid (Marion). *Topical:* Cream 0.01% and 0.025% in 15, 60, and 425 g containers; ointment 0.01% in 15 and 60 g containers; solution 0.01% in 20 and 60 ml containers.

Synalar (Syntex). *Topical:* Cream 0.01% in 15, 45, 60, 120, and 425 g containers, 0.025% in 15, 60, 120, and 425 g containers, and 0.2% (Synalar-HP) in 5 and 12 g containers; ointment 0.025% in 15, 60, and 425 g containers; solution 0.01% in 20 and 60 ml containers.

FLUOCINONIDE [Lidex]

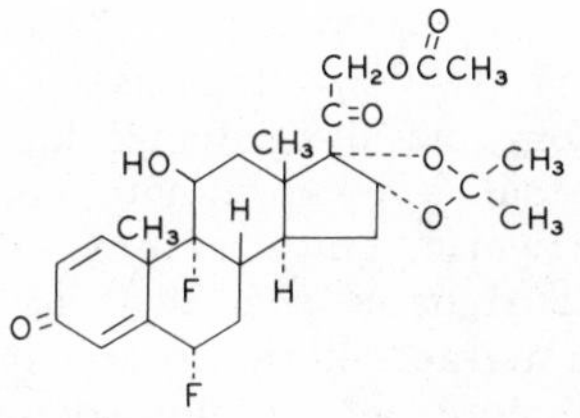

Fluocinonide is a fluorinated corticosteroid for topical use. It is effective in the treatment of glucocorticoid-responsive dermatoses. See the Introductory Statement for specific indications, adverse reactions, and precautions.

USUAL DOSAGE.—*Topical:* Preparation is applied three or four times daily.

PREPARATIONS.—Lidex (Syntex). *Topical:* Cream and ointment 0.05% in 15 and 60 g containers.

FLUOROMETHOLONE [Oxylone]

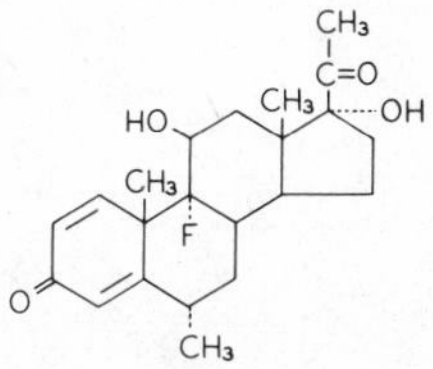

This fluorinated corticosteroid for topical use is effective in the treatment of glucocorticoid-responsive dermatoses. It is used under occlusive dressings to treat resistant nummular dermatitis, psoriasis, and chronic neurodermatitis. See the Introductory Statement for specific indications, adverse reactions, and precautions.

USUAL DOSAGE.—*Topical:* Preparation is applied one to three times daily or is used under occlusive dressings.

PREPARATIONS.—Oxylone (Upjohn). *Topical:* Cream 0.025% in 15, 60, and 120 g containers.

FLUPREDNISOLONE [Alphadrol]

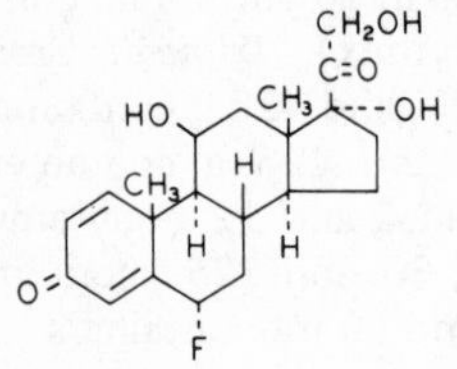

This synthetic glucocorticoid differs from prednisolone by the presence of a fluorine atom at the C-6 position. It is useful in treating inflammatory and allergic conditions and other diseases that respond to glucocorticoids. In anti-inflammatory effect, 1.5 mg of fluprednisolone is equivalent to 20 mg of hydrocortisone. Since its mineralocorticoid effects are poorly defined, fluprednisolone is not suitable for replacement therapy in adrenocortical insufficiency.

Undesirable effects are similar to those observed with other glucocorticoids.

See the Introductory Statement for specific indications, adverse reactions, and precautions.

USUAL DOSAGE.—*Oral:* Initially, 1.5 to 18 mg daily; for maintenance, 1.5 to 12 mg daily.

PREPARATIONS.—Alphadrol (Upjohn). *Oral:* Tablets 0.75 and 1.5 mg.

FLURANDRENOLIDE [Cordran]

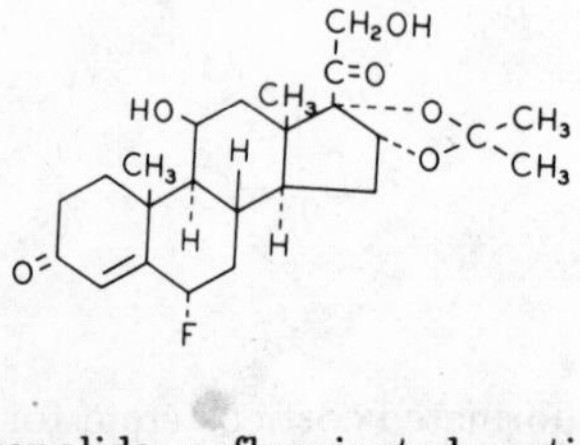

Flurandrenolide, a fluorinated corticosteroid for topical use, is effective in the treatment of glucocorticoid-responsive dermatoses. It is used under occlusive dressings for the management of resistant nummular dermatitis, psoriasis, and chronic neurodermatitis. See the Introductory Statement for specific indications, adverse reactions, and precautions.

USUAL DOSAGE.—*Topical:* Preparation is applied two or three times daily or is used under occlusive dressings. The tape is applied once every 12 hours.

PREPARATIONS.—Cordran (Lilly). *Topical:* Cream and ointment 0.05% in 7.5, 15, 60, and 225 g containers and 0.025% in 30, 60, and 225 g containers; lotion 0.05% in 15 and 60 ml containers; tape 4 $\mu g/cm^2$ in 7.5 cm X 60 cm and 7.5 cm X 200 cm rolls.

HYDROCORTISONE [Cort-Dome, Cortef, Cortril, Heb-Cort, Hydrocortone]
HYDROCORTISONE ACETATE [Cort-Dome Acetate, Cortef Acetate, Cortril Acetate, Hydrocortone Acetate]
HYDROCORTISONE CYPIONATE [Cortef Fluid]
HYDROCORTISONE SODIUM PHOSPHATE [Hydrocortone Phosphate]
HYDROCORTISONE SODIUM SUCCINATE [Solu-Cortef]
HYDROCORTAMATE HYDROCHLORIDE [Ulcort]

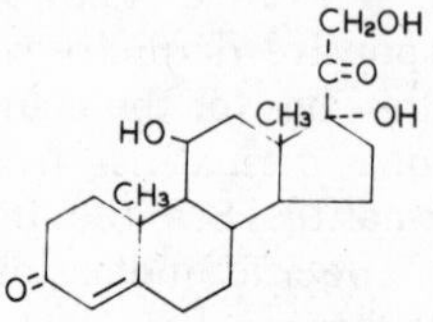

Intravenous and oral preparations of hydrocortisone are given as replacement therapy in acute and chronic adrenocortical insufficiency, including congenital adrenogenital syndromes. Topical forms are used to treat corticosteroid-responsive dermatoses and inflammatory conditions of the vagina or anterior segment of the eye; concomitant antibiotic therapy is necessary when infections are present. Since hydrocortisone acetate is only slightly soluble in water, a suspension injected intrasynovially or into the soft tissues has a long-lasting effect. The highly water-soluble forms (sodium phosphate, sodium succinate) are given parenterally in inflammatory conditions when an immediate response is needed, in acute adrenocortical insufficiency, and in severe stress situations.

The systemic use of hydrocortisone or hydrocortisone acetate for anti-inflammatory action is limited to very short-term administration because of the strong mineralocorticoid effect that causes sodium and water retention, hypertension, and hypokalemia; sodium restriction and potassium supplementation may be necessary. The Δ-1 analogues of cortisone and hydrocortisone have less mineralocorticoid action and are preferred for maintaining anti-inflammatory effects.

See the Introductory Statement for specific indications, adverse reactions, and precautions. For ophthalmic use, see Chapter 71, Anti-infective and Anti-inflammatory Agents Used in Ophthalmology.

USUAL DOSAGE.—(Dosages expressed in terms of the base.)

Oral: (Hydrocortisone, Hydrocortisone Cypionate) For chronic adrenocortical insufficiency, 10 to 25 mg daily; for anti-inflammatory effects, 40 to 80 mg daily.

Intravenous: (Hydrocortisone Sodium Phosphate, Hydrocortisone Sodium Succinate) Initially, 100 to 500 mg; the dose may be repeated if necessary.

Intramuscular: (Hydrocortisone Sodium Phosphate, Hydrocortisone Sodium Succinate) For emergency situations when the intravenous route is not feasible, initially, 100 to 250 mg, followed by doses of 50 mg if necessary.

Intrasynovial, Soft Tissue Injection: (Hydrocortisone, Hydrocortisone Acetate, Hydrocortisone Sodium Phosphate, Hydrocortisone Sodium Succinate) 10 to 50 mg, depending upon the size of the joint.

Topical: (Hydrocortisone, Hydrocortisone Acetate, Hydrocortamate Hydrochloride) Preparation is applied one to three times daily as required.

Rectal: (Hydrocortisone Acetate) One suppository twice daily.

PREPARATIONS.—

Hydrocortisone:

Cort-Dome (Dome). *Topical:* Cream 0.125% and 0.25% in 1, 4, and 16 oz containers and 0.5% and 1% in ½ 1, 4, and 16 oz containers; lotion 0.125% in 6 and 16 oz containers, 0.25% in 4, 6, and 16 oz containers, and 0.5% and 1% in ½, 1, and 4 oz containers.

Cortef (Upjohn).

Injection: Suspension 50 mg/ml in 5 ml containers.

Oral: Suspension 10 mg/5 ml; tablets 5, 10, and 20 mg.

Cortenema (Rowell). *Rectal:* Retention enema 100 mg in 60 ml single-dose units.

Cortril (Pfizer). *Topical:* Ointment 1% in 5 g containers.

Heb-Cort (Barnes-Hind). *Topical:* Cream 0.25% in 1 and 4 oz containers, 0.5% in ½ and 1 oz containers, and 1% in ½, 1, and 16 oz containers; lotion 0.25% in 4 oz containers.

Hydrocortone (Merck Sharp & Dohme). *Oral:* Tablets 10 and 20 mg.

Hydrocortisone Acetate:

Cort-Dome Acetate (Dome). *Rectal:* Suppositories 15 and 25 mg.

Cortef Acetate (Upjohn).

Injection: Suspension 50 mg/ml in 5 ml containers.

Topical: Ointment 1% and 2.5% in 5 and 20 g containers.

Cortril Acetate (Pfizer). *Injection:* Suspension 25 mg/ml in 5 ml containers.

Hydrocortone Acetate (Merck Sharp & Dohme).

Injection: Suspension 25 and 50 mg/ml in 5 ml containers.

Topical: Ointment 1% in 15 and 30 g containers.

Hydrocortisone Cypionate:

Cortef Fluid (Upjohn). *Oral:* Suspension equivalent to hydrocortisone 10 mg/5 ml.

Hydrocortisone Sodium Phosphate:

Hydrocortone Phosphate (Merck Sharp & Dohme). *Injection:* Solution 50 mg/ml in 2 and 10 ml containers.

Hydrocortisone Sodium Succinate:

Solu-Cortef (Upjohn). *Injection:* Powder 100, 250, and 500 mg and 1 g.

Hydrocortamate Hydrochloride:

Ulcort (Ulmer). *Topical:* Ointment 0.5% in 15 g containers.

ADDITIONAL TRADEMARKS.—**Hydrocortisone:** Cetacort (Texas), Dermacort (Rowell), Hautosone (Fellows-Testagar), Hycort (Invenex), Hydrofoam (USV), Lubricort (Texas), Polysorb HC (Fougera), Proctocort (Rowell). **Hydrocortisone Acetate:** Cortifoam (Reed & Carnrick), Fernisone (Ferndale), Mysone (Philips Roxane). Base and acetate also marketed by other manufacturers under generic name.

METHYLPREDNISOLONE [Medrol]
METHYLPREDNISOLONE ACETATE [Depo-Medrol, Medrol Acetate]
METHYLPREDNISOLONE SODIUM SUCCINATE [Solu-Medrol]

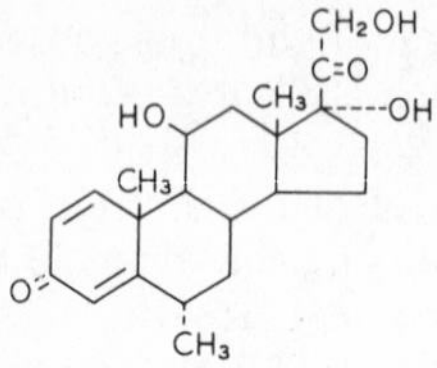

This methyl derivative of prednisolone has the same actions and uses as the parent compound. It is used to treat inflammatory and allergic conditions and other diseases that respond to glucocorticoids. In anti-inflammatory effect, 4 mg of methylprednisolone is equivalent to 20 mg of hydrocortisone. The drug lacks significant sodium-retaining properties; therefore, it is not suitable for replacement therapy in acute or chronic adrenocortical insufficiency.

The base is used orally. Methylprednisolone acetate, when given intramuscularly, has a sustained systemic effect. Since it is relatively insoluble, this form also is suitable for local injection (eg, into joints, soft tissues, cutaneous lesions); it is also used topically in glucocorticoid-responsive dermatoses and rectally as an adjunct in treating ulcerative colitis. Methylprednisolone sodium succinate is highly soluble in water and is used parenterally, preferably intravenously, in emergency situations (except acute adrenocortical insufficiency) when a prompt and intense effect is indicated.

See the Introductory Statement for specific indications, adverse reactions, and precautions.

USUAL DOSAGE.—

Oral: (Methylprednisolone) 4 to 16 mg daily.

Intramuscular: (Methylprednisolone Acetate, Methylprednisolone Sodium Succinate) 40 to 120 mg as needed.

Intravenous: (Methylprednisolone Sodium Succinate) 100 to 250 mg every four to six hours for shock; 10 to 40 mg as needed for other conditions.

Intra-articular, Soft Tissue Injection: (Methylprednisolone Acetate, Methylprednisolone Sodium Succinate) *Adults,* 4 to 80 mg as needed, depending upon size of the joint or affected area.

Topical (skin): (Methylprednisolone Acetate) Preparation is applied one to three times daily.

Rectal: (Methylprednisolone Acetate) 20 to 40 mg as a retention enema three to seven times a week for two or more weeks.

PREPARATIONS.—

Methylprednisolone:

Medrol (Upjohn). *Oral:* Tablets 2, 4, and 16 mg; tablets (timed-release) 2 and 4 mg.

Methylprednisolone Acetate:

Depo-Medrol (Upjohn). *Injection:* Suspension (aqueous) 20 mg/ml in 1 and 5 ml containers, 40 mg/ml in 1, 5, and 10 ml containers, and 80 mg/ml in 1 ml containers.

Medrol Acetate (Upjohn).

Topical: Ointment 0.25% and 1% in 7.5, 30, and 45 g containers.

Rectal: Retention enema 40 mg/unit in 6-unit packs [Medrol Enpak].

Methylprednisolone Sodium Succinate:

Solu-Medrol (Upjohn). *Injection:* Powder 40, 125, and 500 mg and 1 g.

PARAMETHASONE ACETATE [Haldrone, Stemex]

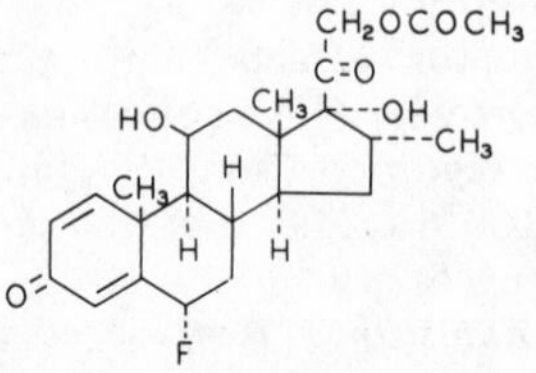

Paramethasone, a synthetic analogue of hydrocortisone, is useful in treating inflammatory and allergic conditions and other diseases that respond to glucocorticoids. In anti-inflammatory effect, 2 mg of paramethasone is approximately equivalent to 20 mg of hydrocortisone. The drug lacks the sodium-retaining properties of hydrocortisone. Sodium may be excreted, although edema and hypertension also are observed infrequently. Thus, paramethasone is not suitable for replacement therapy in adrenocortical insufficiency.

Undesirable effects are similar to those observed with other glucocorticoids. Increased appetite with weight gain occurs in about one-third of patients.

See the Introductory Statement for specific indications and other adverse reactions and precautions.

USUAL DOSAGE.—*Oral:* Initially, 6 to 24 mg daily; for maintenance, 1 to 8 mg daily.

PREPARATIONS.—

Haldrone (Lilly). *Oral:* Tablets 1 and 2 mg.

Stemex (Syntex). *Oral:* Tablets 2 mg.

PREDNISOLONE [Delta-Cortef, Meticortelone, Meti-Derm, Sterane]

PREDNISOLONE ACETATE [Meticortelone Acetate, Nisolone, Sterane Suspension]

PREDNISOLONE SODIUM PHOSPHATE [Hydeltrasol]

PREDNISOLONE SODIUM SUCCINATE [Meticortelone Soluble]

PREDNISOLONE TEBUTATE [Hydeltra-T.B.A.]

This synthetic glucocorticoid is derived from hydrocortisone by the addition of a double bond. In anti-inflammatory effect, 5 mg of prednisolone is equivalent to 20 mg of hydrocortisone. There is less sodium and water retention than with hydrocortisone at equipotent anti-inflammatory doses. Prednisolone is indicated for the treatment of inflammatory and allergic conditions known to respond to glucocorticoids. Because it has no significant mineralocorticoid activity, prednisolone is inadequate as the sole agent in the treatment of adrenocortical insufficiency; a potent mineralocorticoid such as desoxycorticosterone or fludrocortisone also must be given.

The base is used orally or topically. The highly soluble sodium phosphate and sodium succinate esters can be injected intravenously for acute disorders or intramuscularly, intrasynovially, or into soft tissues when rapid onset of effect is desirable. The tebutate form also may be injected intrasynovially or into the soft tissues; the acetate may be given by these routes as well as intramuscularly for a more prolonged effect. The sodium phosphate ester also may be used topically to suppress inflammation in some disorders of the ear or anterior segment of the eye.

See the Introductory Statement for specific indications, adverse reactions, and precautions. For ophthalmic use, see Chapter 71, Anti-infective and Anti-inflammatory Agents Used in Ophthalmology.

USUAL DOSAGE.—(Dosages expressed in terms of the base.)

Oral: (Prednisolone) 5 to 20 mg daily.

Intramuscular: (Prednisolone Acetate, Prednisolone Sodium Phosphate, Prednisolone Sodium Succinate) 10 to 30 mg daily.

Intravenous: (Prednisolone Sodium Phosphate, Prednisolone Sodium Succinate) For emergency situations, 25 to 50 mg; the dose may be repeated if necessary.

Intra-articular, Soft Tissue Injection: (Prednisolone Acetate, Prednisolone Sodium Phosphate, Prednisolone Sodium Succinate, Prednisolone Tebutate) 5 to 50 mg every one to three weeks, depending upon the size of the joint or affected area.

Topical: (Prednisolone) Preparation is applied three or four times daily. (Prednisolone Sodium Phosphate [otic]) Three or four drops applied in the ear two or three times daily. For dosage when used in the eye, see Chapter 71.

PREPARATIONS.—

Prednisolone:

Delta-Cortef (Upjohn), Meticortelone (Schering), Sterane (Pfizer). *Oral:* Tablets 5 mg.

Meti-Derm (Schering). *Topical:* Aerosol 16.6 mg in 50 g containers and 50 mg in 150 g containers; cream 5 mg/g in 10 and 25 g containers.

Prednisolone Acetate:

Meticortelone Acetate (Schering), Nisolone (Ascher), Sterane [acetate] (Pfizer). *Injection:* Suspension 25 mg/ml in 5 ml containers.

Prednisolone Sodium Phosphate:

Hydeltrasol (Merck Sharp & Dohme). *Injection:* Solution 20 mg/ml in 2 and 5 ml containers.

Prednisolone Sodium Succinate:

Meticortelone Soluble (Schering). *Injection:* Powder 50 mg.

Prednisolone Tebutate:

Hydeltra-T.B.A. (Merck Sharp & Dohme). *Injection:* Suspension 20 mg/ml in 1 and 5 ml containers.

ADDITIONAL TRADEMARKS.— Prednisolone: Prednicen (Central), Prednis (USV), Ropredlone (Robinson), Sterolone (Rowell), Ulacort (Fellows-Testagar). **Prednisolone Acetate:** Ropredlone (Robinson), Savacort (Savage), Ulacort (Fellows-Testagar). **Prednisolone Sodium Phosphate:** PSP-IV (Tutag), Sodasone (Fellows-Testagar). Base and acetate also marketed by many manufacturers under generic name.

PREDNISONE [Delta-Dome, Deltasone, Deltra, Meticorten, Paracort, Servisone]

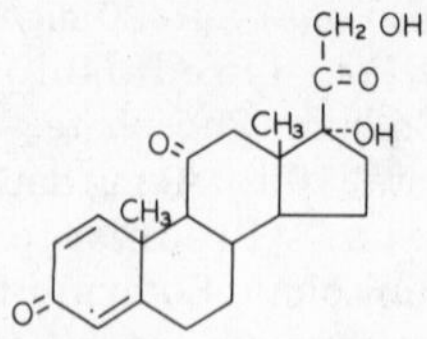

The anti-inflammatory effect of 5 mg of this synthetic glucocorticoid derivative of cortisone is equivalent to 20 mg of hydrocortisone. There is less sodium and water retention than with hydrocortisone at equipotent anti-inflammatory doses. Prednisone is indicated for the treatment of inflammatory and allergic conditions and other diseases that respond to glucocorticoids. Because it has no significant mineralocorticoid activity, prednisone is inadequate as the sole agent in the treatment of adrenocortical insufficiency; a potent mineralocorticoid such as desoxycorticosterone or fludrocortisone also must be given.

See the Introductory Statement for specific indications, adverse reactions, and precautions.

USUAL DOSAGE.—*Oral:* 5 to 20 mg daily.

PREPARATIONS.—

Delta-Dome (Dome), Deltra (Merck Sharp & Dohme), Paracort (Parke, Davis), Servisone (Lederle). *Oral:* Tablets 5 mg.

Deltasone (Upjohn). *Oral:* Tablets 2.5, 5, and 50 mg.

Meticorten (Schering). *Oral:* Tablets 1 and 5 mg.

ADDITIONAL TRADEMARKS.—Lisacort (Fellows-Testagar), Orasone (Rowell), Predsone (Century), Ropred (Robinson). Drug also marketed by other manufacturers under generic name.

TRIAMCINOLONE [Aristocort, Kenacort]
TRIAMCINOLONE ACETONIDE [Aristocort Acetonide, Aristoderm, Kenalog]
TRIAMCINOLONE DIACETATE [Aristocort Diacetate, Kenacort Diacetate]
TRIAMCINOLONE HEXACETONIDE [Aristospan]

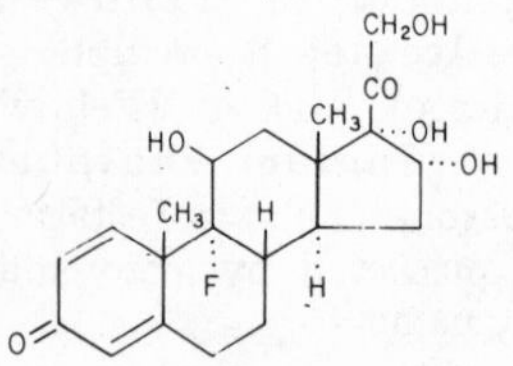

The actions and uses of this fluorinated derivative of prednisolone are similar to those of the parent compound. The drug is used to treat inflammatory and allergic conditions and other diseases that respond to glucocorticoids. It is not suitable as replacement therapy in adrenocortical insufficiency. In anti-inflammatory effect, 4 mg of triamcinolone is equivalent to 20 mg of hydrocortisone. It has less mineralocorticoid effect than prednisolone. Mild diuresis with loss of sodium may occur during the first days of treatment whether or not the patient is frankly edematous. Conversely, edema may occur in patients with a decreased glomerular filtration rate. Triamcinolone does not increase potassium loss except in exceedingly large doses.

The base and diacetate ester are given orally. Aqueous suspensions of the acetonide or diacetate forms are injected intramuscularly to form a depot for sustained systemic action, into joints and soft tissue, and intralesionally for various dermatoses. The acetonide form also is used topically to treat glucocorticoid-responsive dermatoses. Triamcinolone hexacetonide, the least soluble salt, is for intra-articular and intralesional use only.

Adverse reactions are similar to those produced by other glucocorticoids except that triamcinolone does not stimulate the appetite, and produces sedation and depression instead of euphoria.

See the Introductory Statement for specific indications, adverse reactions, and precautions.

USUAL DOSAGE.—

Oral: (Triamcinolone, Triamcinolone Diacetate) Initially, 8 to 16 mg daily. The dosage is reduced for maintenance.

Intramuscular: (Triamcinolone Acetonide, Triamcinolone Diacetate) 40 mg weekly.

Intra-articular: (Triamcinolone Acetonide, Triamcinolone Diacetate, Triamcinolone Hexacetonide) 5 to 40 mg every one to eight weeks, depending upon size of the joint or area affected.

Soft Tissue Injection: (Triamcinolone Acetonide, Triamcinolone Diacetate) Same dosage given as for intra-articular injection.

Topical: (Triamcinolone Acetonide) Preparation is applied three or four times daily.

PREPARATIONS.—

Triamcinolone:

Aristocort (Lederle). *Oral:* Tablets 1, 2, 4, 8, and 16 mg.

Kenacort (Squibb). *Oral:* Tablets 1, 2, 4, and 8 mg.

Triamcinolone Acetonide:

Aristocort [acetonide] (Lederle). *Topical:* Cream 0.025% in 240 mg and 2.4, 15, and 60 g containers, 0.1% in 240 mg and 2.4, 5, 15, and 75 g containers, and 0.5% in 240 mg and 5 and 15 g containers; ointment 0.1% in 240 mg and 5, 15, and 75 g containers and 0.5% in 240 mg and 5 g containers.

Aristoderm (Lederle). *Topical:* Foam 0.1% in 15 g containers.

Kenalog (Squibb).

Injection: Suspension (aqueous) 10 mg/ml in 5 ml containers and 40 mg/ml in 1 and 5 ml containers.

Topical: Cream 0.025% in 2.4, 15, 60, and 80 g containers, 0.1% in 2.4, 5, 15, 60, and 80 g containers; ointment 0.025% in 240 mg and 15 and 60 g containers, 0.1% in 240 mg and 5, 15 and 60 g containers; lotion 0.025% in 60 ml containers, 0.1% in 15 and 60 ml containers; suspension (spray) 0.007% in 50 and 150 g containers.

Triamcinolone Diacetate:

Aristocort [diacetate] (Lederle).

Injection: Suspension 25 mg/ml in 5 ml containers and 40 mg/ml [Aristocort Forte] in 1 and 5 ml containers.

Oral: Syrup 2 mg/5 ml.

Kenacort Diacetate (Squibb). *Oral:* Syrup 4 mg/5 ml.

Triamcinolone Hexacetonide:

Aristospan (Lederle). *Injection:* Suspension 5 mg/ml in 5 ml containers and 20 mg/ml in 1 and 5 ml containers.

MIXTURES FOR SYSTEMIC TREATMENT

Adrenal corticosteroids for systemic use are commonly marketed in fixed combinations with other drugs. Since prolonged systemic use of these potent drugs can produce serious adverse reactions, it is important to individualize the dosage so that the lowest level that will produce satisfactory relief of symptoms is used for the shortest period possible. In addition, the dosage may need to be adjusted during periods of stress. Use of an appropriate amount of glucocorticoid may lead to overdosage or underdosage of the other ingredients in the mixture. For these reasons, use of fixed combinations containing adrenal corticosteroids is discouraged.

The concomitant use of potassium chloride, antibacterial agents, or antifungal agents to prevent or lessen adverse reactions caused by glucocorticoids is frequently indicated. However, it is preferable to prescribe these drugs separately according to individual requirements.

Antacids also are frequently combined with glucocorticoids. Although glucocorticoids may increase gastric secretion, they do not do so consistently. A decrease in resistance of the gastroduodenal mucosa is probably more significant in the development of "steroid ulcers." If antacids are taken with glucocorticoids, it is possible that the adsorbent action of some of them (eg, aluminum hydroxide) may make the glucocorticoid unavailable. (See also Chapter 79, Antacids.)

The addition of ascorbic acid to glucocorticoids is not justified. The only basis for this combination is data showing that a decrease in the concentration of adrenal ascorbic acid occurs in rats after the administration of corticotropin; however, this decrease does not occur consistently in other animals. Although it has been suggested that pantothenic acid improves the ability to withstand stress, any value from the addition of pantothenic acid to glucocorticoid preparations is unproved.

Mixtures of glucocorticoids and antihistamines are marketed for use as adjunctive therapy for patients with respiratory, ocular, or dermatologic allergies. Bronchodilators also are combined with glucocorticoids for the treatment of bronchial asthma. Separate prescription of the necessary, effective ingredients is preferred.

Many mixtures are formulated for use in rheumatoid arthritis and other chronic corticosteroid-responsive arthritides when the condition of the patient warrants the addition of a glucocorticoid to the regimen. These mixtures usually also contain a salicylate or other nonsteroidal anti-inflammatory agent and are designed to be given three or four times daily. Since the regimens used for rheumatoid arthritis and other rheumatic diseases must be highly individualized and the maintenance doses of the glucocorticoid carefully adjusted and subject to change, fixed-dose combinations are not suitable therapy. (See also Chapter 26, Antirheumatic Agents.) The addition of aminobenzoic acid or muscle relaxants to such a mixture offers no therapeutic advantage.

Mixtures Containing Prednisone

Deltasmyl (Roussel): Each tablet contains theophylline 120 mg, ephedrine hydrochloride 15 mg, prednisone

1.5 mg, and phenobarbital 8 mg.

Metreton (Schering): Each tablet contains prednisone 2.5 mg, chlorpheniramine maleate 2 mg, and ascorbic acid 75 mg.

Sigmagen (Schering): Each tablet contains prednisone 0.75 mg, aspirin 325 mg, ascorbic acid 20 mg, and dried aluminum hydroxide gel 75 mg.

Sterazolidin (Geigy): Each capsule contains prednisone 1.25 mg, phenylbutazone 50 mg, dried aluminum hydroxide gel 100 mg, and magnesium trisilicate 150 mg.

Mixtures Containing Prednisolone

Ataraxoid (Pfizer): Each tablet contains prednisolone 2.5 or 5 mg and hydroxyzine hydrochloride 10 mg.

Cordex (Upjohn): Each tablet contains prednisolone 0.5 or 1.5 mg and aspirin 300 mg with or without calcium carbonate 200 mg [Cordex Buffered].

Parafon with Prednisolone (McNeil): Each tablet contains prednisolone 1 mg, chlorzoxazone 125 mg, and acetaminophen 300 mg.

Savacort-S (Savage): Each milliliter of solution contains prednisolone sodium phosphate equivalent to prednisolone phosphate 20 mg, niacinamide 25 mg, disodium edetate 0.05%, sodium bisulfite 0.1%, and phenol 0.5%.

Mixtures Containing Methylprednisolone

Medadent (Upjohn): Each tablet contains methylprednisolone 1.5 mg, aspirin 300 mg, and calcium carbonate 200 mg.

Medaprin (Upjohn): Each tablet contains methylprednisolone 1 mg, aspirin 300 mg, and calcium carbonate 200 mg.

Mixtures Containing Dexamethasone

Decadron Phosphate with Xylocaine Injection (Merck Sharp & Dohme): Each milliliter of solution contains dexamethasone sodium phosphate equivalent to dexamethasone phosphate 1 or 4 mg and lidocaine hydrochloride 5 or 10 mg.

Decagesic (Merck Sharp & Dohme): Each tablet contains dexamethasone 0.25 mg, aspirin 500 mg, and dried aluminum hydroxide gel 75 mg.

Delenar (Schering): Each tablet contains dexamethasone 0.15 mg, orphenadrine hydrochloride 15 mg, and aluminum aspirin 300 mg.

Dronactin (Merck Sharp & Dohme): Each tablet contains dexamethasone 0.25 mg and cyproheptadine hydrochloride 4 mg.

Mixtures Containing Other Glucocorticoids

Aristomin (Lederle): Each capsule contains triamcinolone 1 mg, chlorpheniramine maleate 2 mg, and ascorbic acid 75 mg.

Cortalex (Upjohn): Each tablet contains adrenal cortex extract 0.1 mg and ascorbic acid 15 mg.

Stero-Darvon with A.S.A. (Lilly): Each tablet contains paramethasone acetate 0.25 mg, propoxyphene hydrochloride 32 mg, and aspirin 500 mg.

MIXTURES FOR TOPICAL USE

For an evaluation and listing of various topical mixtures containing glucocorticoids, see Chapters 37, Estrogens, Progestagens, Oral Contraceptives, and Ovulatory Agents; 42, Nasal Decongestants; 56, Nitrofurans; 68, Dermatologic Agents; 71, Anti-infective and Anti-inflammatory Agents Used in Ophthalmology; 73, Topical Otic Preparations; and 82, Anorectal Preparations.

Chapter 36

ANDROGENS AND ANABOLIC STEROIDS

Androgenic hormones are secreted principally by the testis and, to a lesser extent, by the adrenal cortex and ovary. Testosterone, the most potent androgen, is the principal secretion product of the cells of Leydig, which are located in the interstitial spaces of the testis. Leydig cell function is controlled by the anterior pituitary through the gonadotropic hormone which is known both as the luteinizing (LH) and interstitial cell-stimulating (ICSH) hormone. Testosterone, which circulates in a concentration of 280 to 1,400 ng/100 ml in males, is reduced in most tissues to the highly potent 5 α-dihydrotestosterone, which probably is the active intracellular androgen.

Under normal conditions, the adrenal cortex and ovary secrete very little testosterone; instead, they secrete less potent androgens, such as *d*-4-androstenedione and dehydroepiandrosterone, which are metabolized in the liver and kidney to testosterone. The circulating testosterone in normal women (25 to 125 ng/100 ml) is derived primarily from the metabolism of these less potent androgens. When certain pathologic conditions of the adrenal cortex or ovary exist, such as hyperplasia, adenoma, or carcinoma, production of androgens (including testosterone) may be markedly increased. The increased androgenic output causes precocious development in prepuberal boys and virilism in females. If Leydig cell function is lost or markedly impaired, the androgenic products of the adrenal cortex are insufficient to sustain normal male function (eg, libido, sexual potential, muscular strength, endurance).

Testosterone preparations are used primarily to develop or maintain secondary sexual characteristics and other physiologic functions in androgen-deficient males. Decreased testosterone production may be caused by primary testicular failure or it may be secondary to diminished LH (ICSH) secretion associated with anterior pituitary or hypothalamic dysfunction. The primary testicular disorders include Klinefelter's syndrome, testicular atrophy secondary to mumps orchitis or traumatic disruption of testicular vascular supply, surgical castrate syndrome, functional prepuberal castrate syndrome (anorchia), and idiopathic Leydig cell failure (male climacteric). Etiologic factors in secondary testicular failure include pituitary tumors, pituitary insufficiency secondary to trauma and hypothalamic lesions, and selective gonadotropin deficiency that is most likely genetic in origin (hypogonadotropic eunuchoidism).

The diagnosis of androgen deficiency in adult males may be confusing since emotional disturbances can result in diminished sexual desire and impotence. Idiopathic primary Leydig cell failure can occur in later years with all the symptoms usually associated with the menopausal syndrome in women (eg, hot flashes, nervousness, irritability, inability to concentrate, depression). The male differs from the female in that gonadal failure is not related to advanced age per se. Decreased Leydig cell function is caused by testicular disorder or systemic disease not primarily involving the testis. Most men complaining of decreased libido and sexual potential after age 35 are not androgen deficient as can be demonstrated by plasma testosterone determinations. These men are usually psychogenically impotent and do not benefit from testosterone therapy.

In addition to its use as androgen replacement therapy, testosterone may be given therapeutically for its anabolic properties (see the discussion on anabolic agents).

Testosterone may be administered parenterally as intramuscular injections and in pellets that can be implanted subcutaneously; it is much less commonly used than the long-acting esters, testosterone cypionate [Depo-Testosterone] and testosterone enanthate [Delatestryl]. These esters are absorbed slowly from intramuscular sites and produce a steady response that lasts one to two weeks or more. Many clinicians favor this slow steady action for replacement therapy because of convenience and the satisfactory results achieved. In contrast, the more rapid absorption and metabolism of testosterone propionate [Neo-Hombreol, Oreton Propionate] usually necessitates injection of this ester two to four times weekly.

Methyltestosterone [Metandren, Neo-Hombreol (M), Oreton Methyl] and fluoxymesterone [Halotestin, Ora-Testryl, Ultandren], which are alkylated in the C-17α position, are effective orally since they are relatively resistant to inactivation by the liver. However, these preparations must be given daily, and their androgenic potency, milligram for milligram, is less than that of the parenteral forms of testosterone. This difference in potency must be considered when prescribing these preparations.

When testicular failure is secondary to pituitary or hypothalamic disease, treatment with human chorionic gonadotropin (HCG) [Antuitrin-S, A.P.L., Follutein, Pregnyl] is an alternative to testosterone replacement therapy. HCG exerts an LH (ICSH) action in the male that stimulates Leydig cell function and increases the production of endogenous testosterone (see Chapter 38, Anterior Pituitary and Hypothalamic Hormones). Long-term therapy with HCG is often impractical because of its cost; consequently, testosterone preparations are more commonly used.

Androgens have been used in the treatment of certain gynecologic conditions such as uterine hemorrhage, dysmenorrhea, menopause syndrome, premenstrual mastalgia, and postpartum breast enlargement; however, estrogens and oral progestagens are now commonly used in these conditions. (See Chapter 37, Estrogens, Progestagens, Oral Contraceptives, and Ovulatory Agents.) When breakthrough bleeding occurs with estrogen therapy alone, combined estrogen and androgen therapy has been used to treat patients with menopausal and postmenopausal symptoms. Androgens in low doses also have been used to restore libido, especially in menopausal women. However, since administration of even small amounts of androgen for a prolonged period may result in virilism in sensitive women, its use for these purposes should be discouraged.

Advanced or metastatic breast carcinoma in selected cases is the only indication for large-dose, long-term androgen therapy in women. Since the dosage required to induce remissions in breast carcinoma is similar to that used for androgen replacement in the male, patients should be advised that undesirable and distressing effects will occur. These effects include hirsutism, clitoral enlargement, increased libido, oily skin, acne, and deepening of the voice. The short-acting preparations (eg, testosterone propionate, methyltestosterone, fluoxymesterone) are preferred initially, since prompt withdrawal is necessary if symptomatic hypercalcemia develops. Two derivatives of testosterone, dromostanolone propionate [Drolban] and testolactone [Teslac], have been reported to induce remissions with fewer undesirable hormonal effects (see Chapter 88, Antineoplastic Agents).

Experimental evidence suggests that androgens exert an effect on erythropoiesis by stimulating renal and possibly extrarenal production of an erythropoiesis-stimulating factor, erythropoietin. The evidence also suggests that the response is dose related. Accordingly, a variety of androgens, including anabolic steroids, have been used in large doses to treat some refractory anemias caused by the defective production of red blood cells (eg, aplastic, sideroblastic) and refractory anemias such as in myelofibrosis. The results have been variable. Best results have been obtained in idiopathic aplastic anemia in children. Remissions have also occurred in acquired aplastic anemia after prolonged administration of large doses. (See Chapter 8, Agents Used to Treat Deficiency Anemias.)

Weekly administration of relatively large intramuscular doses of testosterone preparations to patients with anemia caused by advanced renal failure indicates that androgenic hormones may significantly decrease requirements for transfusions in patients who are apparently adequately dialyzed, well nourished, and not iron deficient.

Undesirable effects occur with the large doses necessary to treat anemia: virilism in females, precocious puberty in boys, acne, and liver dysfunction. The risk of priapism exists; any increase in erectile frequency is an indication for stopping the androgen. Androgens that do not have an alkyl group substituted in the α position on carbon 17 (ie, testosterone and its esters, nandrolone phenpropionate, nandrolone decanoate) are preferred for prolonged therapy with large doses since liver dysfunction occurs less frequently with their use.

Testosterone and its derivatives have anabolic and somatic growth effects. Attempts to dissociate the anabolic from the androgenic effect by modification of the testosterone molecule have resulted in the development of several synthetic steroids. Results of laboratory tests and bioassays in animals appear to indicate that a separation of anabolic and androgenic effects has been achieved with these compounds, although the dissociation is not as wide in man as the bioassays in animals suggest. All are weak androgens, but nitrogen retention may occur without virilization if dosages are individually determined, if patients are carefully followed up to ascertain particular susceptibility to the androgenic effects, and if therapy is intermittent. There is substantial evidence that nitrogen retention is improved with anabolic agents only when there is sufficient intake of calories and protein. As yet, it is debatable whether the nitrogen-retaining action can be explained as an anticatabolic effect on protein metabolism or whether protein synthesis is favorably influenced. The synthetic anabolic steroids include ethylestrenol [Maxibolin], methandrostenolone [Dianabol], oxandrolone [Anavar], oxymetholone [Adroyd, Anadrol], and stanozolol [Winstrol]; all are oral preparations given daily. Nandrolone phenpropionate [Durabolin] and nandrolone decanoate [Deca-Durabolin] are longer-acting and are given intramuscularly. The metabolism and excretion of the anabolic steroids are largely unknown.

Defective protein metabolism may be a problem in patients with debilitating illness, senile osteoporosis, and in those convalescing from severe acute illnesses, burns, surgery, or trauma. Although testosterone, its derivatives, or the synthetic anabolic steroids may reverse the negative nitrogen and calcium balances, there is no conclusive evidence that the period of recovery from these illnesses has been shortened with use of these drugs. Amelioration of hypercalciuria associated with paralytic poliomyelitis has been reported. Treatment of senile osteoporosis with anabolic steroids may be of some benefit when supplemented with a high protein and high calcium diet.

Androgens may be tried as adjunctive therapy in patients with acute oliguria or chronic renal failure in order to minimize protein catabolism.

Adrenal corticosteroids have catabolic effects and may produce osteoporosis, inhibition of growth, and atrophy of skeletal muscle and skin after long-term therapy; therefore, the concomitant administration of anabolic steroids has been recommended to counteract these effects. Although these steroids exert a positive effect on nitrogen, calcium, and phosphorus retention during corticosteroid therapy, the only clinical benefit shown is that the anabolic steroids may help reverse growth inhibition in children treated with corticosteroids.

Anabolic steroids are proposed for use in various pediatric disorders marked by retarded growth, weakness, or malnutrition. Their use in children or adolescents should be undertaken only after consultation with experts on growth and development. The possibilities of precocious puberty in boys, virilism in females, and accelerated skeletal maturation must always be carefully considered.

Adverse Reactions and Precautions

Virilism: When these steroids are used for indications other than androgen deficiency, the most frequent undesirable effect of therapy is virilism. The first signs in the prepuberal boy are pubic hair development, phallic enlargement, and increased frequency of erections. In females, hirsutism, deepening of the voice, acne, clitoral enlargement, stimulation of libido, and menstrual irregularities may occur; the voice change is irreversible but the clitoral enlargement and hirsutism may be reversible. Combined estrogen and androgen therapy will not delay or prevent the onset of virilism.

Premature epiphyseal closure: Anabolic steroids should not be used to stimulate growth in children who are small but otherwise normal and healthy. When they are used, skeletal maturation may exceed the rate of linear growth and premature closure of the epiphyses may reduce the attainable adult height. The decision to administer anabolic steroids to children for a specific growth indication should be made only after careful evaluation. Bone maturation should be carefully checked by roentgenographic examinations before and at regular intervals during and after treatment. Since stimulation of skeletal growth may continue for six months after therapy is discontinued, anabolic steroids should be discontinued well before bone maturation reaches the norm for the chronologic age. Short courses of therapy at six-month intervals are most satisfactory.

Liver dysfunction: Androgenic and anabolic steroids with an alkyl group substituted in the alpha position on carbon 17 (ie, methyltestosterone [Malogen, Metandren, Neo-Hombreol (M), Oreton Methyl], fluoxymesterone [Halotestrin, Ora-Testryl, Ultandren], ethylestrenol [Maxibolin], methandrostenolone [Dianabol], oxandrolone [Anavar], oxymetholone [Adroyd, Anadrol], and stanozolol [Winstrol]) have produced signs of liver dysfunction. Increases in sulfobromophthalein (BSP) retention and serum glutamic oxaloacetic transaminase (SGOT) levels appear to be dose related. Increased serum bilirubin and alkaline phosphatase values indicate excretory dysfunction. Clinical jaundice is reversible when the drug is discontinued. The histologic findings consist of intrahepatic cholestasis with little or no cellular damage. These drugs, therefore, should be used with caution in patients with pre-existing liver disease. Abnormal results of liver function tests occur less frequently with testosterone and its esters, nandrolone phenpropionate [Durabolin], or nandrolone decanoate [Deca-Durabolin].

Hypercalcemia: Women receiving androgen therapy for disseminated breast carcinoma may develop hypercalcemia. If symptomatic hypercalcemia occurs, the patient should be hydrated and treated with appropriate drugs (see Chapter 17, Blood Calcium Regulators), and the androgen should be discontinued.

Miscellaneous: Retention of sodium and water may cause edema, especially in elderly patients with cardiac or renal disease.

Irregularities of the menstrual cycle have been noted with use of testosterone preparations and several anabolic steroids.

Stomatitis has been reported with the buccal and sublingual forms of testosterone. The use of pellets has caused discomfort and irritation at the site of implantation.

Effects on laboratory tests: Androgens lower the level of circulating thyroxin-binding globulin, thereby decreasing protein-bound iodine levels and increasing triiodothyronine uptake. However, there is no evidence of thyroid dysfunction.

Androgens also alter metyrapone test results, the beta lipoprotein level, 17-ketosteroid secretion, and creatine and creatinine excretion. The anabolic steroids have been reported to enhance blood fibrinolytic activity. The hematocrit value is increased.

Contraindications: Androgens and anabolic steroids are contraindicated in pregnant women because of possible masculinization of the female fetus. Evidence of any beneficial effect of their use in premature and newborn infants is lacking.

They also are contraindicated in men with carcinoma of the prostate or breast. Androgens should not be used in patients with nephrosis or the nephrotic stage of nephritis.

Drug Interactions: Caution is required when C-17-alkylated androgens are administered to patients receiving anticoagulants. Administration of methandrostenolone or ethylestrenol increases the potency of coumarin and indandione anticoagulants given concurrently, and thus increases the risk of hemorrhage (see the Appendix on Drug Interactions). Therefore, when an androgenic steroid is added to or withdrawn from the regimen of a patient receiving an anticoagulant, more frequent prothrombin determinations and the indicated adjustments in dosage of the anticoagulant should be made.

Methandrostenolone also decreases the metabolism of oxyphenbutazone [Oxalid, Tandearil]. A longer, more intense, and unpredictable response to oxyphenbutazone is obtained. Thus, it is advisable to avoid the concomitant use of these two drugs.

INDIVIDUAL EVALUATIONS

FLUOXYMESTERONE [Halotestin, Ora-Testryl, Ultandren]

OH
HO
CH_3
CH_3
CH_3
F
O

Fluoxymesterone is a short-acting preparation which is used orally. It is much less effective as replacement therapy in androgen-deficient males than the long-acting esters of testosterone. Full sexual maturation in patients with prepuberal hypogonadism cannot be achieved with fluoxymesterone, but the drug may be effective when hypogonadism starts in adult life or after secondary sexual characteristics have developed during therapy with a parenteral preparation. Fluoxymesterone also can be used for its anabolic properties and for the palliative treatment of certain cases of metastatic breast carcinoma in women.

See the Introductory Statement for information on adverse reactions.

USUAL DOSAGE.—*Oral:* For androgen

deficiency, 10 to 20 mg daily (this dosage is higher than that recommended by the manufacturers). For metastatic breast carcinoma in women, 10 to 30 mg daily. For anabolic effect, *adults*, 4 to 10 mg daily.

PREPARATIONS.—

Halotestin (Upjohn). *Oral:* Tablets 2, 5, and 10 mg.

Ora-Testryl (Squibb), Ultandren (Ciba). *Oral:* Tablets 5 mg.

METHYLTESTOSTERONE [Metandren, Neo-Hombreol (M), Oreton Methyl]

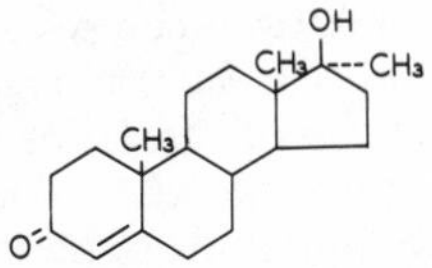

This short-acting preparation, which is used orally and buccally, is much less effective as replacement therapy in androgen-deficient males than the long-acting esters of testosterone. Although methyltestosterone is ineffective in producing full sexual maturation in patients with prepuberal hypogonadism, it may be effective when hypogonadism starts in adult life or after secondary sexual characteristics have developed during therapy with a parenteral preparation. Methyltestosterone also can be used for its anabolic properties and for the palliative treatment of certain cases of metastatic breast carcinoma in women.

See the Introductory Statement for information on adverse reactions.

USUAL DOSAGE.—

Oral: For androgen deficiency, initially 30 to 100 mg daily, and, for maintenance, 20 to 60 mg daily. For metastatic breast carcinoma in women, 50 to 200 mg daily. For anabolic effect, *adults*, 10 to 20 mg daily. Because of marked variation in sensitivity, signs of virilism may occur in women even when less than the virilizing dose cited by the manufacturers (300 mg per month) is given.

Buccal: Adults, one-half of oral dosage (rate of absorption is variable).

PREPARATIONS.—

Metandren (Ciba).

Oral: Tablets 10 and 25 mg.

Buccal: Tablets 5 and 10 mg.

Neo-Hombreol (M) (Organon). *Oral:* Tablets 10 and 25 mg.

Oreton Methyl (Schering).

Oral: Tablets 10 and 25 mg.

Buccal: Tablets 10 mg.

Drug also marketed under generic name.

TESTOSTERONE [Neo-Hombreol (F), Oreton]

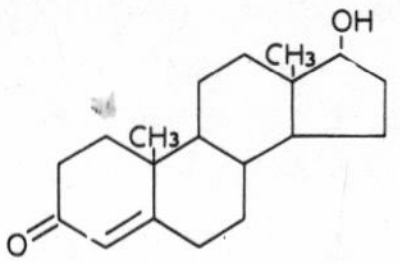

Testosterone is used to develop or maintain secondary sexual characteristics and other physiologic functions in androgen-deficient males. It also may be used for its anabolic properties and for palliative treatment in certain cases of advanced breast carcinoma in women. Testosterone is short-acting when injected intramuscularly and very long-acting when the pellets are implanted subcutaneously. The pellets have been used in place of intramuscular injection of the long-acting esters in oil; however, pellet implantation requires a minor surgical procedure and is expensive. The clinical response to the aqueous suspension of testosterone is somewhat erratic, since the rate of absorption may not be uniform. When androgens are to be used for the palliative treatment of disseminated breast carcinoma, it is desirable to initiate treatment with a short-acting preparation such as the aqueous suspension to determine the patient's tolerance of androgens. The long-acting pellets are not suitable for treating breast carcinoma.

See the Introductory Statement for information on adverse reactions.

USUAL DOSAGE.—

Intramuscular: For androgen deficiency, 50 mg three times weekly. For metastatic breast carcinoma in women, 100 mg three times weekly. For anabolic effect, *adults*, 10 to 25 mg three to seven times weekly. Because of marked variation in sensitivity, signs of virilism may occur in females even when less than the virilizing dose cited by the manufacturers (300 mg per month) is given.

Subcutaneous Implantation: For male hypogonadism, six 75 mg pellets every four to six months. Pellets are implanted subcutaneously into the medial aspect of the thighs (three on each side) by means of a pellet injector.

PREPARATIONS.—

Neo-Hombreol (F) (Organon). *Injection:* Suspension 25 and 50 mg/ml in 10 ml containers.

Oreton (Schering).

Implantation: Pellets 75 mg.

Injection: Suspension 50 mg/ml in 10 ml

containers.

ADDITIONAL TRADEMARKS.—Androlin (Lincoln), Andronaq (Central), Hormale Aqueous (Key), Malogen (Fellows-Testagar), Sterotate (Ulmer). Drug also marketed by many manufacturers under generic name.

TESTOSTERONE CYPIONATE [Depo-Testosterone]
TESTOSTERONE ENANTHATE [Delatestryl]

These long-acting, potent esters of testosterone produce a steady response and are given intramuscularly to develop or maintain secondary sexual characteristics and other physiologic functions in androgen-deficient males. These esters are preferred over other androgens to obtain full sexual development in eunuchoidal males when testicular disease has interfered with normal puberal development, and to treat postpuberal Leydig cell failure. Either ester may be used for the palliative treatment of certain cases of breast carcinoma in women after a favorable response to initial treatment with short-acting preparations. These drugs also may be given as anabolic agents.

See the Introductory Statement for information on adverse reactions.

USUAL DOSAGE.—*Intramuscular:* For androgen deficiency, 200 mg every one to two weeks for two to three years until full sexual development is attained, then 100 to 200 mg every two to five weeks. For metastatic breast carcinoma in women, 200 to 400 mg every two or more weeks. For anabolic effect, *adults*, 200 to 400 mg every four weeks. Because of marked variation in sensitivity, virilism may occur in females even with doses lower than those recommended. Signs of virilism occur frequently in women given more than 150 mg a month.

PREPARATIONS.—

Testosterone Cypionate:

Depo-Testosterone (Upjohn). *Injection:* Solution (in cottonseed oil) 50 mg/ml in 10 ml containers and 100 and 200 mg/ml in 1 and 10 ml containers.

Testosterone Enanthate:

Delatestryl (Squibb). *Injection:* Solution (in sesame oil) 200 mg/ml in 1 and 5 ml containers.

ADDITIONAL TRADEMARKS.—**Testosterone Cypionate:** Durandro (Ascher), Malogen CYP (Fellows-Testagar), T-Ionate-P.A. (Tutag). **Testosterone Enanthate:** Malogen LA (Fellows-Testagar), Repo-Test (Central), Testate (Savage), Testostroval P.A. (Tutag). Drugs also marketed under generic name.

TESTOSTERONE PROPIONATE [Neo-Hombreol, Oreton Propionate]

Testosterone propionate is used to develop or maintain secondary sexual characteristics and other physiologic functions in androgen-deficient males. This short-acting preparation produces a steady response when used parenterally, but this route is not practical for long-term therapy. The drug is useful initially, especially in older men with long-standing androgen deficiency. In these patients, the prostate gland may be sensitive to androgen therapy and bladder neck obstruction may develop; thus, this complication is more easily handled with a short-acting preparation. The buccal route is used for maintenance therapy, but the rate of absorption is less predictable with this route. The short duration of action of testosterone propionate also makes this ester useful for the palliative treatment of certain cases of breast carcinoma in females, because prompt withdrawal of the androgen is necessary if hypercalcemia develops. The propionate ester also may be used parenterally for its anabolic properties.

See the Introductory Statement for adverse reactions.

USUAL DOSAGE.—

Intramuscular: For androgen deficiency, 25 mg two to four times weekly. For metastatic breast carcinoma in women, 50 to 100 mg three times weekly. For anabolic effect, *adults*, 5 to 10 mg daily. Because of marked variation in sensitivity, signs of virilism may occur in females when less than the virilizing dose cited by the manufacturers (300 mg per month) is given.

Buccal: For maintenance therapy in androgen-deficient *males*, 10 to 20 mg daily.

PREPARATIONS.—

Neo-Hombreol (Organon). *Injection:* Solution (in sesame oil) 50 mg/ml in 10 ml containers.

Oreton Propionate (Schering).

Injection: Solution 50 and 100 mg/ml (in sesame oil) in 10 ml containers.

Buccal: Tablets 10 mg.

ADDITIONAL TRADEMARKS.—Hormale Oil (Key), Testonate (Kay). Drug also marketed under generic name.

ANABOLIC STEROIDS

These drugs are weak androgens. When they are given in proper doses for short periods and with appropriate diet in patients with cachexia or debilitating diseases, these agents may produce anabolic effects without clinical signs of virilism. The synthetic androgens have been used in patients recovering from surgery, infections, burns, fractures, emaciating diseases, and severe traumatic injuries, but there is no adequate evidence that their use shortens the period of recovery. They also have been given to patients with increased catabolism due to prolonged corticosteroid therapy. Objective evidence of improvement in patients with senile or corticosteroid-induced osteoporosis has not been demonstrated.

The anabolic agents have been effective in increasing hemoglobin levels in some patients with congenital and idiopathic aplastic anemia (see the Introductory Statement).

Use of androgens for their anabolic properties in prepuberal children with growth failure or inhibition resulting from corticosteroid therapy requires careful consideration because the expected benefits may not justify the risks of precocious puberty in boys, virilism in girls, and premature closure of the epiphyses. If a physician feels that the possible benefits for a specific growth problem outweigh the risks, consultation with experts to determine the dosage regimen is advised.

The table summarizes pertinent dosage information on these synthetic anabolic steroids.

ANABOLIC STEROIDS

Drug	Chemical Structure	Usual Dosage	Preparations
Ethylestrenol Maxibolin (Organon)	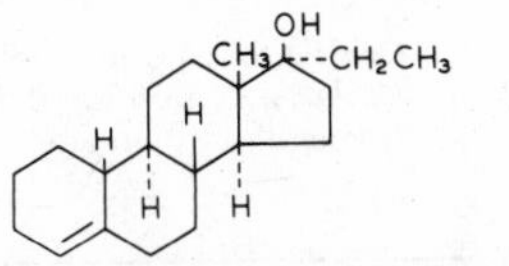 OH, CH_3, CH_2CH_3, H, H, H, H	*Oral: Adults,* 8 to 16 mg daily (this dosage is higher than that recommended by manufacturer). *Children,* 1 to 3 mg daily.	Elixir 2 mg/5 ml Tablets 2 mg
Methandrostenolone Dianabol (Ciba)	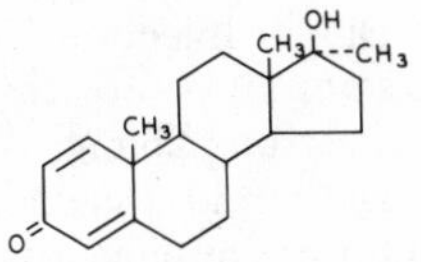 OH, CH_3, CH_3, CH_3, O	*Oral: Adults,* 5 mg daily. *Older children and adults with pituitary dwarfism,* up to 0.05 mg/kg daily.	Tablets 2.5 and 5 mg
Nandrolone Decanoate Deca-Durabolin (Organon)	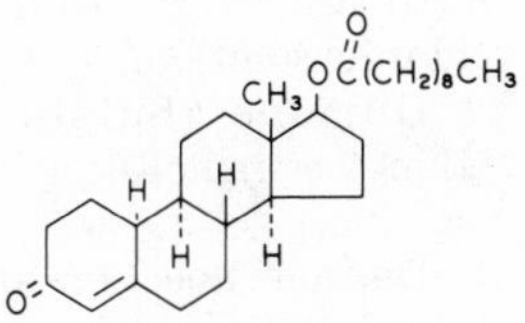 CH_3, $OC(=O)(CH_2)_8CH_3$, H, H, H, H, O	*Intramuscular: Adults,* 50 to 100 mg every 3 to 4 weeks. *Children 2 to 13 years,* 25 to 50 mg every 3 to 4 weeks.	Solution (for injection) 50 mg/ml in 1 and 2 ml containers and 100 mg/ml in 2 ml containers
Nandrolone Phenpropionate Durabolin (Organon)	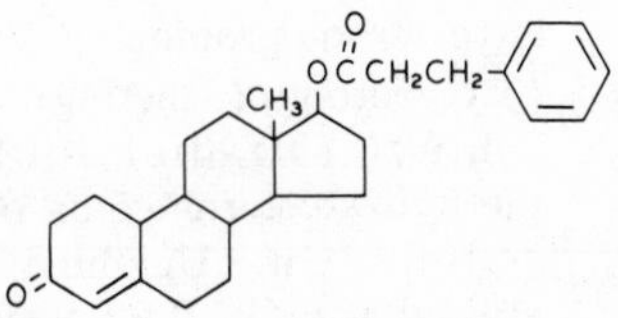 CH_3, $OC(=O)CH_2CH_2-C_6H_5$, O	*Intramuscular: Adults,* 25 to 50 mg weekly. *Children 2 to 13 years,* 25 mg every 2 to 4 weeks.	Solution (for injection) 25 mg/ml in 1 and 5 ml containers and 50 mg/ml in 2 ml containers

ANABOLIC STEROIDS (cont.)

Drug	Chemical Structure	Usual Dosage	Preparations
Oxandrolone Anavar (Searle)	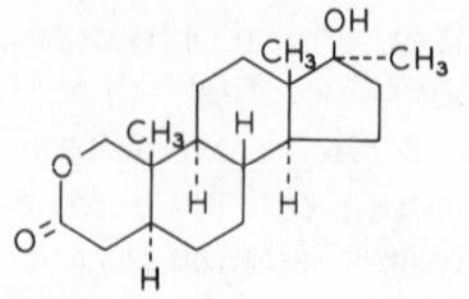	*Oral: Adults,* 5 to 10 mg daily. *Children,* 0.25 mg/kg daily.	Tablets 2.5 mg
Oxymetholone Adroyd (Parke, Davis) Anadrol (Syntex)	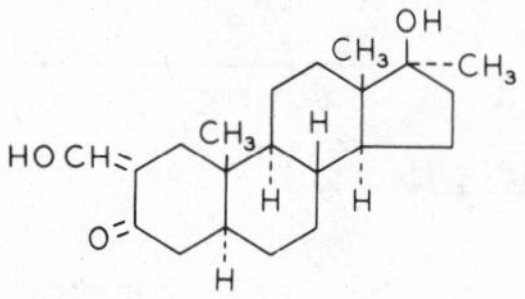	*Oral: Adults,* 5 to 10 mg daily. *Children,* 1.25 to 5 mg daily (depending upon age). For erythropoiesis, *adults and children,* 1 to 2 mg/kg daily.	Adroyd: Tablets 5 and 10 mg Anadrol: Tablets 2.5 and 50 mg
Stanozolol Winstrol (Winthrop)	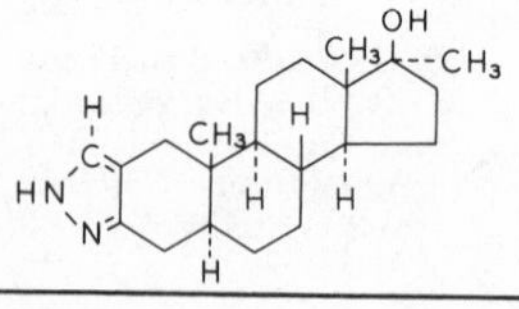	*Oral: Adults,* 6 mg daily. *Children,* 2 to 6 mg daily (depending upon age).	Tablets 2 mg

MIXTURES

ANDROGEN-ESTROGEN PREPARATIONS

Combined estrogen and androgen therapy has been used to avoid breakthrough and withdrawal bleeding from estrogen therapy alone in menopausal and postmenopausal women. However, since administration of androgens to women for any prolonged period may result in virilism, and since the combination of estrogen and androgen therapy will not prevent or delay the onset of virilism, fixed-dosage, combined therapy is discouraged. See the Introductory Statement and the section on Estrogens and Progestagens in Chapter 37.

AVAILABLE MIXTURES.–

Aquadiol with Testosterone Injection (Merrell-National): Each milliliter contains estradiol 0.44 mg and testosterone 12.5 mg.

Deladumone Injection (Squibb): Each milliliter contains estradiol valerate 4 mg and testosterone enanthate 90 mg.

Depo-Testadiol Injection (Upjohn): Each milliliter contains estradiol cypionate 2 mg, testosterone cypionate 50 mg, and chlorobutanol 5 mg in cotton seed oil.

Di-Genik Injection (Savage): Each milliliter contains estrone 2 mg and testosterone 10 mg.

Di-Met Injection (Organon): Each milliliter of suspension contains estrone 2 mg and testosterone 25 mg.

Di-Steroid Injection (Kremers-Urban): Each milliliter contains estrone 2 mg and testosterone 10 mg in isotonic sodium chloride solution or propylene glycol, alcohol, procaine hydrochloride, benzyl alcohol, and sodium chloride solution.

Dumone (Squibb): Each tablet contains ethinyl estradiol 8 μg and methyltestosterone 4 mg.

Duogen Injection (Smith, Miller & Patch): Each milliliter of suspension contains estrone 2 mg and testosterone 25 mg.

Gynetone Injection (Schering): Each milliliter contains estradiol benzoate 1 mg and testosterone propionate 20 mg.

Gynetone (Schering): Each tablet contains ethinyl estradiol 0.02 or 0.04 mg and methyltestosterone 5 or 10 mg.

Halodrin (Upjohn): Each tablet contains ethinyl estradiol 0.02 mg and fluoxymesterone 1 mg.

Mal-O-Fem Injection (Fellows-Testagar): Each milliliter contains estrone 2 mg and testosterone 25 mg.

Mal-O-Fem LA Injection (Fellows-Testagar): Each milliliter contains estradiol valerate 4 or 8 mg and testosterone enanthate 90 or 180 mg.

Premarin with Methyltestosterone (Ayerst): Each tablet contains conjugated estrogens 0.625 or 1.25 mg and methyltestosterone 5 or 10 mg.

TACE with Androgen (Merrell-National): Each capsule contains chlorotrianisene 6 mg and methyltestosterone 2.5 mg.

Theelandrol (Parke, Davis): Each capsule contains esotrogenic substance 5,000 or 10,000 IU and methyltestosterone 5 or 10 mg.

Tylosterone (Lilly): Each tablet or milliliter of injection contains diethylstilbestrol 0.25 mg and methyltestosterone 5 mg.

PREPARATIONS CONTAINING ANDROGENS, ESTROGENS, AND OTHER INGREDIENTS

Numerous mixtures containing androgens and estrogens combined with vitamins, minerals, progesterone, sedatives, stimulants, and other drugs are available. Many are advocated for use in geriatric patients. These "shot-gun" preparations are needlessly complex and may cause virilization of females or feminization of males.

AVAILABLE MIXTURES.—

Biocaps (Amfre-Grant): Each capsule contains ethinyl estradiol 0.01 mg, methyltestosterone 2.5 mg, vitamin A 5,000 units, vitamin D 500 units, thiamine mononitrate 5 mg, riboflavin 4 mg, pyridoxine hydrochloride 0.5 mg, ascorbic acid 75 mg, cyanocobalamin 1 μg, niacinamide 20 mg, vitamin E 10 IU, pantothenate calcium 7.5 mg, *L*-lysine monohydrochloride 50 mg, choline bitartrate 50 mg, inositol 25 mg, ferrous fumarate 30.4 mg, iodine 0.1 mg, calcium 145 mg, phosphorus 110 mg, copper 1 mg, potassium 5 mg, manganese 1 mg, zinc 0.5 mg, and magnesium 1 mg.

Clusivol Geriatric Capsules (Ayerst): Each capsule contains conjugated estrogens 0.125 mg, methyltestosterone 1.25 mg, vitamin A 12,500 units, ergocalciferol 500 units, ascorbic acid 75 mg, thiamine hydrochloride 5 mg, riboflavin 5 mg, pyridoxine hydrochloride 0.5 mg, cyanocobalamin 2.5 μg, vitamin E 0.5 IU, dexpanthenol 0.86 mg, niacinamide 50 mg, biotin 0.05 mg, iron 25 mg, calcium 100 mg, phosphorus 77 mg, copper 0.5 mg, manganese 0.5 mg, iodine 0.75 mg, potassium 2.5 mg, zinc 0.6 mg, magnesium 3 mg, lysine hydrochloride 25 mg, and methionine 12.5 mg.

Combogenic (Smith, Miller & Patch): Each tablet contains estradiol 0.2 mg, methyltestosterone 10 mg, thiamine hydrochloride 10 mg, riboflavin 10 mg, pyridoxine hydrochloride 5 mg, niacinamide 100 mg, panthenol 5 mg, cobalamin concentrate 5 μg, and ascorbic acid 100 mg.

Dumogran (Squibb): Each tablet contains ethinyl estradiol 8 μg, methyltestosterone 4 mg, vitamin A 2,500 units, thiamine hydrochloride 2.5 mg, riboflavin 1.5 mg, pyridoxine hydrochloride 1 mg, cyanocobalamin 1 μg, ascorbic acid 37.5 mg, vitamin D 250 units, vitamin E 2.5 IU, folic acid 0.1 mg, niacinamide 10 mg, pantothenate calcium 2.5 mg, iron 5 mg, iodine 0.05 mg, copper 0.5 mg, manganese 0.5 mg, zinc 0.5 mg, and magnesium 3 mg.

Eldec (Parke, Davis): Each capsule contains estrone 0.167 mg, methyltestosterone 1.67 mg, *Aspergillus oryzae* enzymes 20 mg, pancreatin 133.3 mg, vitamin A 1,667 units, ascorbic acid 33.3 mg, thiamine mononitrate 0.67 mg, riboflavin 0.67 mg, pyridoxine hydrochloride 0.5 mg, folic acid 0.1 mg, choline bitartrate 6.67 mg, niacinamide 16.7 mg, *DL*-panthenol 10 mg, ferrous sulfate 16.7 mg, iodine 0.05 mg, calcium carbonate 66.7 mg, *L*-lysine monohydrochloride 66.7 mg, and methionine 16.7 mg.

Formatrix (Ayerst): Each tablet contains conjugated estrogens 1.25 mg, methyltestosterone 10 mg, and ascorbic acid 400 mg.

Geri-Deimal-H (Boyle): Two tablets provide ethinyl estradiol 0.01 mg, methyltestosterone 5 mg, vitamin A 5,000 units, vitamin D 500 units, vitamin E 2.5 mg, ascorbic acid 75 mg, thiamine hydrochloride 3 mg, riboflavin 3 mg, pyridoxine hydrochloride 1 mg, vitamin B_{12} with intrinsic factor concentrate 0.07 oral unit, niacinamide 50 mg, panthenol 5 mg, choline bitartrate 150 mg, inositol 25 mg, betaine hydrochloride 100 mg, iron 20 mg, iodine 0.15 mg, magnesium 10 mg, pancreatin 97.2 mg, *L*-lysine monohydrochloride 200 mg, amylase 7.5 mg, and proteinase 3 mg.

Gerilets (Abbott): Each tablet contains piperazine estrone sulfate 0.3 mg, methyltestosterone 2.5 mg, inositol 50 mg, betaine hydrochloride 50 mg, niacinamide 20 mg, ascorbic acid 50 mg, iron 15 mg, vitamin E 10 IU, pantothenate calcium 5 mg, riboflavin 5 mg, thiamine mononitrate 5 mg, vitamin A 5,000 units, pyridoxine hydrochloride 1 mg, folic acid 0.25 mg, ergocalciferol 10 μg, and cobalamin 5 μg.

Geritag (Tutag): Each capsule contains ethinyl estradiol 0.01 mg, methyltestosterone 2 mg, vitamin A 5,000 units, ergocalciferol 400 units, vitamin E 10 IU, thiamine mononitrate 2 mg, riboflavin 2 mg, pyridoxine hydrochloride 0.3 mg, cobalamin concentrate 1 μg, ascorbic acid 30 mg, niacinamide 20 mg, pantothenate calcium 3 mg, choline bitartrate 40 mg, inositol 20 mg, methionine 20 mg, iron 10 mg, copper 0.2 mg, molybdenum 0.5 mg, manganese 1 mg, magnesium 5 mg, zinc 1 mg, potassium 2 mg, and iodine 2 mg.

Gevrine (Lederle): Each capsule contains ethinyl estradiol 0.01 mg, methyltestosterone 2.5 mg, vitamin A 5,000 units, ergocalciferol 500 units, cyanocobalamin 1 μg, vitamin E 10 IU, thiamine mononitrate 5 mg, riboflavin 5 mg, niacinamide 15 mg, pyridoxine hydrochloride 0.5 mg, choline bitartrate 50 mg, inositol 50 mg, *L*-lysine monohydrochloride 50 mg, ascorbic acid 50 mg, iron 10 mg, iodine 0.1 mg, calcium 145 mg, phosphorus 110 mg, copper 1 mg, potassium 5 mg, manganese 1 mg, zinc 0.5 mg, and magnesium 1 mg.

Hovizyme (Ayerst): Each tablet contains conjugated estrogens 0.125 mg, methyltestosterone 1.25 mg, amylase 10 mg, protease 5 mg, cellulase 2 mg, methamphetamphetamine hydrochloride 0.5 mg, nicotinyl alcohol tartrate 7.5 mg, dehydrocholic acid 50 mg, ascorbic acid 50 mg, and ferrous fumarate 6 mg.

Mediatric (Ayerst): Each tablet or capsule contains conjugated estrogens 0.25 mg, methyltestosterone 2.5 mg, methamphetamine hydrochloride 1 mg, ascorbic acid 100 mg, cyanocobalamin 2.5 μg, thiamine mononitrate 10 mg, riboflavin 5 mg, niacinamide 50 mg, pyridoxine hydrochloride 3 mg, pantothenate calcium 20 mg, and ferrous sulfate 30 mg.

Mediatric Liquid (Ayerst): Each 15 ml contains conjugated estrogens 0.25 mg, methyltestosterone 2.5 mg, thiamine hydrochloride 5 mg, cyanocobalamin 1.5 μg, and methamphetamine hydrochloride 1 mg.

Os-Cal Mone (Marion): Each tablet contains ethinyl estradiol 5.33 μg, methyltestesterone 2.67 mg, and calcium 400 mg.

Ostone (Rowell): Each tablet contains conjugated estrogens 0.625 mg, methyltestosterone 5 mg, and vitamin D 500 units.

Tylandril (Lilly): Each tablet contains diethylstilbestrol 0.25 mg, methyltestosterone 5 mg, and reserpine 0.1 mg.

Vio-Geric H (Rowell): Each tablet contains conjugated estrogens 0.25 mg, methyltestosterone 2.5 mg, vitamin A 10,000 units, thiamine hydrochloride 10 mg, riboflavin 10 mg, pyridoxine hydrochloride 10 mg, cyanocobalamin 5 μg, ascorbic acid 100 mg, vitamin D 400 units, vitamin E 14 IU, niacinamide 20 mg, pantothenate calcium 15 mg, rutin 20 mg, inositol 25 mg, methionine 50 mg, copper 0.5 mg, iodine 0.1 mg, ferrous fumarate 30 mg, and powdered bone 300 mg.

Chapter 37

ESTROGENS, PROGESTAGENS, ORAL CONTRACEPTIVES, AND OVULATORY AGENTS

Natural and synthetic ovarian hormones are used as replacement therapy in hypogonadism and in menopausal and postmenopausal women; to treat various dysfunctions of the reproductive system; to control fertility; and to treat certain carcinomas in both men and women.

The ovary is the principal site of estrogen production in the nonpregnant premenopausal woman and it secretes chiefly estradiol and estrone. During pregnancy, the placenta produces more estrogens, primarily estriol, than does the ovary. Estrogens are metabolized primarily in the liver by hydroxylation and are conjugated with sulfate and glucuronic acid. The water-soluble, conjugated estrogens are excreted by the kidney. Two peak periods of estrogen production may occur during the menstrual cycle; the major one usually occurs at midcycle, and the second smaller peak usually occurs during the latter part of the cycle when the corpus luteum is secreting maximally.

All known endogenous estrogens are steroids. These natural steroids have an estrogenic action when administered subcutaneously or intramuscularly, but have little effect when given orally. When the natural estrogens are conjugated to form salts (eg, piperazine estrone sulfate, sodium estrone sulfate), they are protected from destruction in the gastrointestinal tract; thus, the conjugated compounds are effective orally. Chemical alterations of estradiol by alkylation at the C 17 position have produced the orally potent estrogenic substances, ethinyl estradiol and mestranol. Certain nonsteroidal chemical substances produce changes similar to those of the steroidal estrogens and are used clinically for their estrogenic effects. Diethylstilbestrol was the first nonsteroidal estrogen discovered and is the most potent when given orally. Closely related stilbene derivatives (hexestrol, benzestrol [Chemestrogen], dienestrol [DV, Synestrol], chlorotrianisene [TACE], promethestrol [Meprane]) and the naphthylene derivative, methallenestril [Vallestril], are additional available nonsteroidal estrogens.

Progesterone is the most abundant known natural progestational substance. The corpus luteum is the main source of this hormone during the menstrual cycle of the nonpregnant woman and during early pregnancy. After the first weeks of pregnancy, the placenta also begins producing progesterone, which is essential for maintenance of a pregnancy. Progesterone is rapidly removed from the blood by excretion of biologically inactive metabolites and by diffusion of active progesterone into the tissues, especially adipose tissue. The urinary pregnanediol level reflects the amount of circulating progesterone. Responsiveness of the genital tissues to progesterone depends upon the priming action of estrogen.

Progestational agents having some of the physiologic activity and pharmacologic effects of progesterone have been synthesized from 19-nortestosterone (testosterone without the 19-methyl group) and from progesterone. These derivatives, called progestagens, have a longer duration of action than progesterone when given parenterally or a greater potency when administered orally, but they may not mimic all of its physiologic activities. Progesterone is antiestrogenic; some progestagens have antiestrogenic activity as well as estrogenic or androgenic properties, depending upon the dose given.

The secretion of pituitary gonadotropins is inhibited by the progestagens (especially the 19-nortestosterone compounds). Progestagens combined with estrogens inhibit secretion more effectively. The endometrial response produced by the various progestagens varies, depending upon the drug's chemical structure, dosage, and potency, but the basic effects are similar. A secretory response of the endometrium may occur during initial administration or with small doses; however, with continued administration or large doses, these agents may suppress glandular growth and secretion and produce stromal edema, pseudodecidual changes, or stromal regression. Not all orally effective progestagens raise basal body temperature.

Indications for Estrogens and Progestational Agents: Hypogonadism with primary amenorrhea may result from decreased gonadotropin secretion; in these cases, the ovary remains infantile. In other instances, ovarian development is inadequate although gonadotropin secretion is increased. Estrogen replacement therapy may be used in both types of abnormality to effect sexual maturation and produce vaginal bleeding as well as to prevent early onset of osteoporosis. In hypogonadism with gonadotropin deficiency, the use of menotropins (human menopausal urinary gonadotropin) [Pergonal] plus human chorionic gonadotropin (HCG) has proved effective replacement therapy in some cases.

A nonpregnant woman with *secondary amenorrhea* that occurs in the absence of either detectable systemic organic disease or disease of the pituitary may be given cyclic therapy. An estrogen may be given alone during the first part of the cycle and a progestagen added during the latter part to ensure withdrawal bleeding. Spontaneous menses may occur if treatment is stopped.

Progestational agents also have diagnostic value in amenorrhea; withdrawal bleeding indicates the production of endogenous estrogen, a responsive endometrium, and a nonpregnant state. The absence of withdrawal bleeding after two to five days of treatment is a fairly reliable *indication of pregnancy*, whereas subsequent bleeding almost always indicates a nonpregnant state. Bleeding fails to occur in 10% to 15% of nonpregnant patients with irregular menstrual cycles. At present, human chorionic gonadotropin assays are more commonly used to indicate pregnancy.

The *menopause* is characteristically accompanied by vasomotor symptoms such as hot flashes and sweating episodes, which are believed to be related to estrogen deficiency, as well as by irritability, headache, anxiety, depression, and fatigability. These emotional symptoms may result from the vasomotor disturbances or may be unrelated. Replacement doses of estrogens usually control vasomotor symptoms and contribute to the patient's comfort. Also, senile (atrophic) vaginitis and pruritus vulvae respond well to either systemic or local estrogen therapy.

There is some evidence that large doses of estrogens administered for a short period during the early part of the menopause will prevent an early loss of bone mass (*osteoporosis*). Large doses of estrogens appear to protect the bone from resorption. However, long-term treatment of postmenopausal women with small doses of estrogens does not appear to affect the osteoporosis which normally occurs with age. Bone formation tends to decrease during prolonged estrogen therapy and the level of bone resorption increases after an initial decrease. Therefore, evidence indicates that the only beneficial effect of estrogens is to slow the loss of bone mass. The ultimate result of long-term treatment may be increased loss of bone mass because of decreased bone formation.

Estrogen therapy during the menopausal and postmenopausal period should be selective and aimed at relief of symptoms associated with vasomotor disturbances or atrophic vaginitis. The prolonged and excessive administration of estrogens to all women "from puberty to the grave," as advocated by some physicians, is not justified. There is no conclusive evidence that the use of estrogens in the postmenopausal period delays progession of atherosclerosis. On the contrary, estrogens may be detrimental to the vascular system, for postmenopausal women who are taking estrogens have increases in plasma triglycerides. The skin changes that accompany aging result from many factors in addition to deficiency of estrogens and progesterone. Although statistics indicate that replacement doses of estrogen do not increase the incidence of breast or uterine carcinomas, the occurrence of cystic endometrial hyperplasia following prolonged administration of estrogens warrants consideration, since adenomatous hyperplasia is known to be associated with endometrial carcinoma. In addition, the induction of cyclic withdrawal bleeding in postmenopausal women may mask the symptoms and delay a diagnosis of uterine carcinoma.

Vaginal cytology may be of value in evaluating the effectiveness of estrogen therapy, although the technique requires training in the interpretation of cytological smears. There is no justification at present for giving oral contraceptives to treat menopausal symptoms.

Dysfunctional uterine bleeding occurs most commonly at the menarche or before the menopause when there is an absence of ovulation. Continued stimulation by estrogen probably results in incomplete sloughing of a hyperplastic proliferative endometrium with prolonged, excessive bleeding. A diagnosis of dysfunctional bleeding should not be made until all indicated diagnostic procedures to rule out pathologic changes have been performed. Hemorrhage can be controlled surgically or by the administration of estrogens and progestagens. Cessation of bleeding usually occurs within 72 hours and a normal withdrawal period follows discontinuance of therapy. A progestational agent may be given at monthly intervals to produce regular withdrawal bleeding and prevent a recurrence.

The value of hormones in the treatment of *premenstrual tension* is not fully established. Changes in hormone levels and electrolyte balance probably are responsible for the premenstrual symptoms of breast engorgement and nipple tenderness and, in part, for the weight gain, tension, and headache. These symptoms may be relieved by decreased sodium intake, a diuretic, or by estrogens and progestagens. The other common symptoms (irritability, hunger, desire for sweets, depression, nausea, vomiting, and lethargy) may be caused by the emotional state.

The effectiveness of hormone treatment for *dysmenorrhea* is also difficult to evaluate, since the relative importance of physiologic and psychologic factors is uncertain. Some favorable results have been reported following the cyclic administration of estrogens and/or progestagens with and without suppression of ovulation.

In *endometriosis*, the continuous administration of progestational agents and estrogens to prevent bleeding from the endometrial implants and to facilitate surgery has met with some success. However, estrogens have a limited duration of effect and produce endometrial hyperplasia. In some patients, long-term administration of large doses of a progestagen with or without an estrogen has caused endometrial fibrosis and prevented reactivation of the implants for prolonged periods. The inconsistent results reported may be attributed to the varied genesis of the implants and the variable degree of hormonal sensitivity.

Although estrogens and progestational agents have been used extensively to treat *habitual and threatened abortions*, evidence of their effectiveness is lacking.

The inadequate production of progesterone by the corpus luteum may result in failure of nidation or deterioration of the cytotrophoblast. Small supplementary amounts of progestational agents have been used during the luteal phase to treat *infertile women* in whom a deficiency can be demonstrated by endometrial biopsy or by determinations of the serum progesterone level.

Estrogens may be helpful in relieving *postpartum breast engorgement* when lactation is to be suppressed and when the baby is being weaned. The precise mechanism by which milk secretion is inhibited is not clear.

Although estrogens and progestagens have been used in an attempt to modify the *size of breasts* considered by normal young females to be over- or underdeveloped, there is no evidence that they are effective for this use except for the breast engorgement that may occur during the period of medication.

Stimulation of the sebaceous glands by androgens may result in *acne*. Increasing the estrogen level in females by the cyclic administration of estrogens with or without progestagens for several months frequently results in an improvement, which may persist after therapy is stopped. The acne may become worse immediately after treatment is started. In adolescent girls, the risk of deranging an immature hypothalamic-pituitary-ovarian relationship with subsequent amenorrhea should be weighed against the potential benefits of estrogen therapy in preventing emotional problems and scarring from severe acne.

Estrogens have been used experimentally in controlling the *height* of girls who are expected to grow extremely tall because of hereditary factors. The role of estrogens in somatic growth and epiphyseal fusion is not clear and the efficacy of this therapy has not been determined. No effect can be expected unless treatment is initiated two years before the menarche. Puberal development will be accelerated. The effect of estrogens on the hypothalamus in girls 9 or 10 years of age is not known.

In metastatic breast *carcinoma*, estrogens are given to women who are more than five years past the natural menopause and they induce remissions of variable length in some patients. Progestational agents also are used to treat breast carcinoma. (See Chapter 88, Antineoplastic Agents.)

Progesterone and progestagens are used to

treat metastatic endometrial carcinoma. Large doses of a progestational agent produce endometrial atrophy, but usually a month of treatment is necessary before objective response is evident. Tumor nodules may decrease in size and pulmonary metastases may disappear from the x-ray film.

Disseminated prostatic carcinoma is usually treated with estrogens and/or bilateral orchiectomy. Endocrine therapy decreases bony metastases and ostealgia and markedly reduces prostatic induration. The main action of estrogens is believed to be feedback suppression of LH, which reduces the secretion of testosterone and consequently produces atrophy of the prostatic glandular epithelium. Although therapy with estrogens appears to reduce the number of deaths from prostatic carcinoma, an increase in the number of deaths from cardiovascular causes has been reported in men receiving diethylstilbestrol orally in a dose of 5 mg daily for long periods. An oral dose of 1 mg daily appears to be as beneficial without being associated with an increase in cardiovascular deaths. Other estrogens have been used for relief of symptoms and regression of the disease in doses ranging up to massive levels, but few studies have been done to determine possible increases in mortality from cardiovascular diseases associated with therapy with estrogens other than diethylstilbestrol.

The use of cyproterone acetate, an antiandrogen with progestational activity, in the treatment of advanced prostatic carcinoma is under investigation. Cyproterone markedly reduces testosterone levels. Ostealgia is relieved and regression of the disease occurs. Mortality from cancer and from other diseases in cyproterone-treated patients as compared to estrogen-treated men is not known.

The ability of estrogens and progesterone to suppress ovulation has resulted in the extensive use of estrogens and progestagens for *controlling fertility* (see the section on Oral Contraceptives).

Estrogens have been used "after the act" as a means of postcoital contraception in volunteers and in rape cases with success. Regimens that have been used effectively include 25 mg of diethylstilbestrol twice daily for five days starting within 72 hours after sexual exposure or 10 mg of conjugated estrogens or 5 mg of diethylstilbestrol daily for 20 to 25 days. Changing the sequence of hormonal influences on the fallopian tube may disturb passage of the ovum and have an antifertility effect. Estrogens may also alter the endometrium and interfere with nidation. The patient should be informed of the association between ingestion of diethylstilbestrol during pregnancy and the occurrence of adenocarcinoma of the vagina in offspring. The possibility of pregnancy from a previous exposure should be considered and ruled out before this regimen is prescribed.

Human chorionic gonadotropin (HCG), one of the first tropic hormones used in the treatment of *anovulation*, seldom induces ovulation when used alone. Its effect is similar to that of LH. When exogenous FSH and LH (menotropins [Pergonal]) are used to induce follicular maturation and are followed by HCG therapy, ovulation occurs in about 90% of women with anovulation. (See Chapter 38, Anterior Pituitary and Hypothalamic Hormones.) Clomiphene [Clomid] is a nonsteroidal compound related chemically to chlorotrianisene [TACE]. When it is administered to women with a potentially functional hypothalamic-pituitary system, evidence of presumptive ovulation occurs in about 70% of patients, but the pregnancy rate is lower (about 30%). The incidence of abortion, approximately 20%, is similar to that in women who conceive after other treatment for infertility or who conceive without treatment. The incidence of multiple births (about 8%) is higher than normal, even when the dosage of clomiphene is carefully individualized to avoid ovarian hyperstimulation. The incidence of fetal abnormalities is not above normal, and infants of clomiphene-treated mothers have developed normally.

Adverse Reactions and Precautions

Adverse reactions include nausea, malaise, irritability, and depression; edema caused by sodium and water retention; weight gain due to nitrogen retention; and fullness and tenderness of the breasts. A rise in thyroxin- and corticosterone-binding protein in the plasma and alterations in the results of liver function tests also are noted.

There is evidence that estrogen therapy is related to an increase in the incidence of thrombophlebitis and thromboembolism. When diethylstilbestrol (5 mg daily) was given to men with prostatic carcinoma, there was an increase in the incidence of death from cardiovascular disturbances, particularly myocardial infarctions and cerebral thrombosis. No such increase was noted when patients were given 1 mg daily.

Women should be examined for breast and genital carcinoma before estrogen therapy is instituted and periodically during administration; the estrogens should be withdrawn if evidence of carcinoma is found or suspected. A family history of carcinoma usually precludes estrogen therapy.

A significant relationship between the maternal ingestion of large doses of diethylstilbestrol during pregnancy and the occurrence of vaginal adenocarcinoma in offspring has been demonstrated. Therefore, diethylstilbestrol and chemically related estrogens are contraindicated during pregnancy.

Masculinization of the female fetus has been associated with use of some progestagens. Therefore, their use during pregnancy is not advisable.

For additional adverse effects of estrogens and progestagens, see the section on Oral Contraceptives.

ORAL CONTRACEPTIVES

The most extensive use of estrogens and progestagens is in the *control of fertility.* Evidence is conclusive that the oral administration of various combinations of an estrogen and progestagen from the 5th through the 24th day of the menstrual cycle or for 21 days followed by a rest period of seven days is almost completely effective in preventing conception. The sequential method, consisting of the administration of an estrogen for 14 or 16 days of the cycle, followed by a progestagen-estrogen combination for five to seven days, also is highly effective. Oral contraceptive preparations containing a progestagen alone (norethindrone), which are given on a continuous daily dosage regimen, are less effective than the combined or sequential contraceptives containing estrogen and progestagen.

When only pregnancies that are not associated with the omission of one or more daily doses (theoretical effectiveness) are included, the pregnancy rate is 0.1 per 100 women per year in those using the combined type of contraceptives and 0.5 per 100 women per year in those using the sequential type. When pregnancies that apparently result from the omission of one or more doses during the cycle are included (use-effectiveness), the pregnancy rate is approximately 0.7 per 100 women per year in those using the combined regimen and 1.4 per 100 women per year in those using the sequential regimen.

In clinical trials with norethindrone alone [Micronor, Nor-Q.D.], the average pregnancy rate was 2.54 per 100 women per year. There was a significant difference in the pregnancy rates between patients who had not taken contraceptives prior to starting norethindrone alone (3.72 per 100 women per year) and those who had been taking estrogen-containing regimens (1.95 per 100 women per year). Tablet omissions by the group not accustomed to taking oral contraceptives may have been a factor in the even greater difference during the first six months.

See the table for the compositions of the oral contraceptives; the chemical structures of the various steroids appear in the figure. The only estrogens and progestagens in these preparations that are available as single-entity drugs are the estrogen, ethinyl estradiol, and the progestagens, norethindrone and norethindrone acetate. (See the individual evaluations.)

The estrogen-progestagen oral contraceptives may suppress ovulation by inhibiting the hypothalamic-releasing hormone (LH-FSH-RH), thereby influencing the release of gonadotropins from the pituitary (see Chapter 38, Anterior Pituitary and Hypothalamic Hormones). In combined products, suppression of FSH and LH by estrogen is enhanced by the progestagen. The sequential products depend on estrogen alone to inhibit FSH and LH release. The later addition of a progestagen ensures prompt endometrial shedding.

The combination estrogen-progestagen preparations also produce changes in the cervical mucus that increase viscosity, inhibit ferning, and presumably render it hostile to penetration by sperm. In addition, alterations of tubal transport, endometrial pattern, and ovarian steroidogenesis may contribute to the contraceptive effect of both types of estrogen-progestagen oral contraceptives. It is possible that other unknown factors may play a role in the mechanism of action.

The progestagen preparation alone probably exerts its contraceptive action by various mechanisms; reduction of the penetrability of the sperm in the cervical mucus and interference with luteal function are possible factors.

Adverse Reactions and Precautions

Ovarian hormones influence all systems of the body directly or through their effects on other endocrine glands and metabolism;

ESTROGENS AND PROGESTAGENS IN ORAL CONTRACEPTIVES

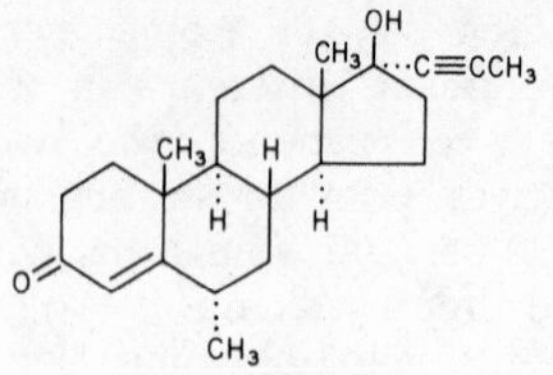

Dimethisterone

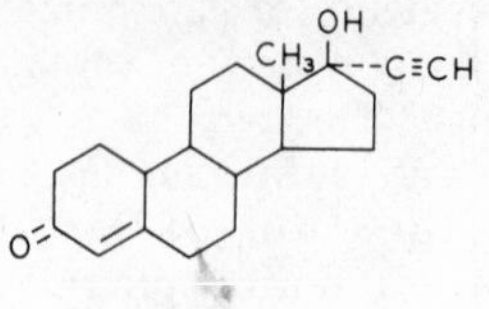

Norethindrone

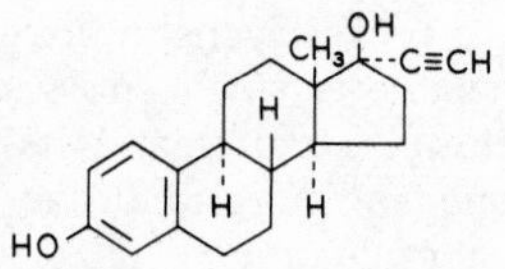

Ethinyl Estradiol

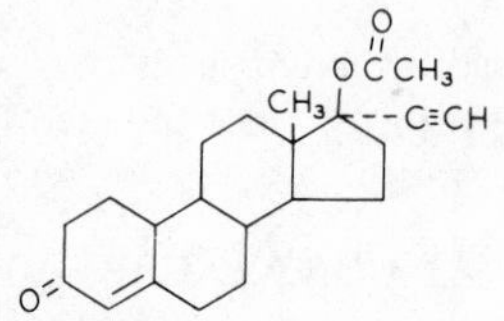

Norethindrone Acetate

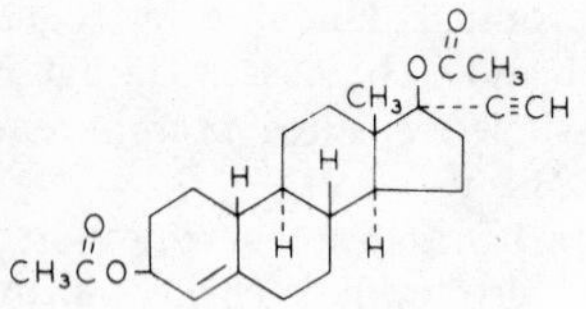

Ethynodiol Diacetate

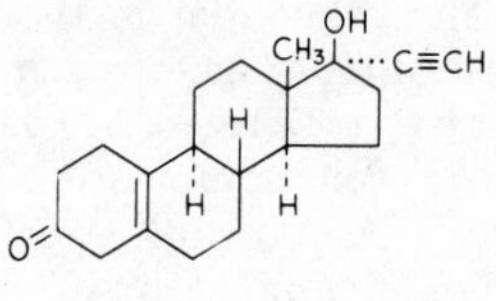

Norethynodrel

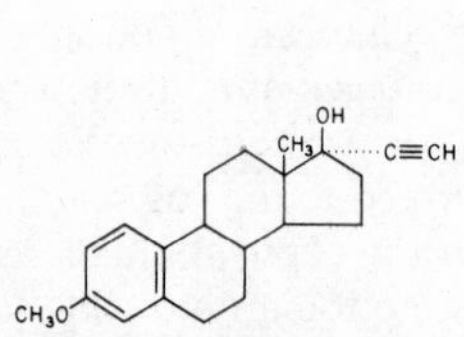

Mestranol

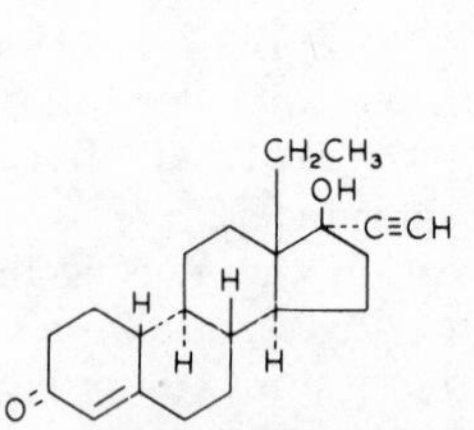

Norgestrel

ORAL CONTRACEPTIVES AVAILABLE IN THE U.S.

Progestagen: Estrogen	*Trade Names Manufacturers*	*Administration*
Combination		
Ethynodiol Diacetate 1 mg: 100μg Mestranol	Ovulen (Searle)	From 5th through 24th or 25th day of cycle
1 mg: 50 μg Ethinyl Estradiol	Demulen (Searle)	or
Norethindrone 10 mg: 60 μg Mestranol	Norinyl 10 mg (Syntex) Ortho-Novum 10 mg (Ortho)	21 days of treatment followed by 7 days during which no pills are taken or inert or iron-containing (75 mg ferrous fumarate) tablets are taken (the numbers 20, 21, or 28 following the trade name indicate number of tablets in package)
2 mg: 100 μg	Norinyl 2 mg (Syntex) Ortho-Novum 2 mg (Ortho)	
1 mg: 80 μg	Norinyl 1 +80 (Syntex) Ortho-Novum 1/80 (Ortho)	
1 mg: 50 μg	Norinyl 1 +50 (Syntex) Ortho-Novum 1/50 (Ortho)	
Norethindrone Acetate 2.5 mg: 50 μg Ethinyl Estradiol	Norlestrin 2.5 mg (Parke, Davis)	
1 mg: 50 μg	Norlestrin 1 mg (Parke, Davis)	
Norethynodrel 5 mg: 75 μg Mestranol	Enovid 5 mg (Searle)	
2.5 mg: 100 μg	Enovid-E (Searle)	
Norgestrel 0.5 mg: 50 μg Ethinyl Estradiol	Ovral (Wyeth)	
Sequential		
Dimethisterone 25 mg: 100 μg Ethinyl Estradiol	Oracon (Mead Johnson)	Ethinyl estradiol for 16 days, then dimethisterone plus ethinyl estradiol for 5 or 6 days
Norethindrone 2 mg: 80 μg Mestranol	Norquen (Syntex) Ortho-Novum SQ (Ortho)	Mestranol for 14 days, then norethindrone plus mestranol for 6 days
Single-Entity		
Norethindrone 0.35 mg	Micronor (Ortho) Nor-Q.D. (Syntex)	One tablet daily

however, an understanding of the extent, mechanisms, and clinical importance of these effects is incomplete. The availability of a variety of oral contraceptive preparations with different pharmacologic components complicates analysis of their effects. Factors such as the chemical alterations that produce the different estrogens and progestagens, the different dosages and regimens, and the prior hormonal milieu of each patient form an infinite number of variables that influence the effect. When information on pharmacologic action is insufficient to establish a causal relationship and a statistical evaluation is attempted, the greatest difficulty is encountered when an observed adverse reaction is rarely caused by the drug whereas it is a common clinical finding in patients with predisposing conditions. Thromboembolic phenomena exemplify reactions of this nature.

The known adverse effects of the oral contraceptives are reviewed below by systems. It is not yet known if all these adverse reactions occur with the norethindrone-alone contraceptive. Some, notably thromboembolic disorders, are believed to be the effect of the estrogen component of the estrogen-progestagen preparations. Since biologically active estrogens form an appreciable portion of the metabolites of norethindrone, it is possible the adverse effects are similar qualitatively. Additional experience with the norethindrone-alone preparation is needed to determine its adverse effects.

Gastrointestinal System: Nausea is a common undesirable effect and occurs most frequently during the first two or three months. Other reported reactions are vomiting, an increase or decrease in appetite, abdominal pain, diarrhea, and constipation.

Oral contraceptives affect the absorption of folate, a water-soluble vitamin. The effect is insufficient to cause a deficiency in most women, but some do develop severe deficiency and anemia.

Alterations in the results of liver function tests have been reported during administration of oral contraceptives. A reversible reduction in hepatic function is evidenced by dose-related sulfobromophthalein (BSP) retention. The defect seems to be in transfer of BSP from liver cells to bile without BSP storage being affected, whereas, in liver disease, both BSP storage and transport are reduced. The reduction in excretory function appears most frequently to be associated with compounds with a 17-alpha-alkyl substitution and a phenolic A-ring structure; these characteristics are present in all oral contraceptives in either the estrogen or progestagen component or in both.

Jaundice occurs rarely in women using oral contraceptives. Results of laboratory tests are similar to those observed in patients with recurrent jaundice of pregnancy and include increases in bilirubin values, alkaline phosphatase, and 5-nucleotidase activity with reduced clearance of BSP. Biopsies reveal cholestasis and, sometimes, minimal amounts of hepatocellular degeneration and necrosis. Predisposing factors may include inherited or acquired defects of hepatic excretory function (eg, familial recurrent jaundice, idiopathic jaundice of pregnancy) and chronic liver disease (eg, hepatitis, cirrhosis).

Cardiovascular System: A possible cause-and-effect relationship between the estrogen-progestagen oral contraceptives and thromboembolic phenomena has been under investigation since 1961. Results of case-matched, retrospective, epidemiologic studies in Great Britain and the United States have led to a general but not universal agreement that the use of oral contraceptives is associated with an increase in morbidity and mortality caused by peripheral venous thrombophlebitis, with or without pulmonary embolism. According to a study in the United States, the increase in morbidity is about fourfold; in studies conducted in the United Kingdom, the increase in morbidity and mortality varied from three- to tenfold. Insufficient data on the incidence of idiopathic thrombophlebitis and thromboembolism in nonusers of oral contraceptives account in part for these variations in results. On the basis of large-scale studies in the United States, it is estimated that the morbidity rate of thrombophlebitis (superficial and deep) and thromboembolism is one per 2,000 women-years of use of oral contraceptives. A similar figure is obtained from a study conducted in the United Kingdom on hospitalized users with idiopathic thromboembolic disease other than superficial thrombophlebitis.

The death rates from British data are, for the age group 20 to 34 years, 15 deaths per 1 million women-years in users and 2 deaths per 1 million women-years in nonusers; for the age group 35 to 44 years, 39 deaths per 1 million women-years in users compared to 5 deaths per 1 million women-years in nonusers.

A retrospective study in the United Kingdom

on the relationship between oral contraceptive usage and postoperative thromboembolic disease indicates the risk is increased three- to fourfold by use of oral contraceptives.

In studies in the United States, a statistical relationship between the use of oral contraceptives and an increase in the incidence of cerebral or coronary thrombosis has not been demonstrated. Cerebral arterial thrombosis has been the most common occlusive disease of the cerebral vasculature reported in women taking oral contraceptives. About one-fourth of these cases involve occlusion of the vertebrobasilar artery, which formerly was considered a rare disorder in young persons. However, the incidence of cerebral thrombosis in users of oral contraceptives has not been shown to be significantly increased over that in the general population in the United States. Cerebral venous thrombosis and cavernous sinus thrombosis associated with the use of oral contraceptives have been reported in the United Kingdom.

Results of retrospective studies performed in the United Kingdom and Scandinavia to determine the risks of thromboembolism associated with different estrogen-progestagen products suggest a positive correlation between the dose of the estrogen component and the incidence of pulmonary embolism and deep venous thrombosis. Differences between regimens of sequential and combined preparations and between the two estrogens, mestranol and ethinyl estradiol, were not evident. These conclusions, although far from definitive, indicate that preparations containing the smallest amount of estrogen which is effective and acceptable for the individual patient should be used. Clinical trials have not revealed decreased efficacy in preventing pregnancies with the low-dose estrogen preparations currently available. However, breakthrough bleeding may result from too low a dose of estrogen.

It is not known at this time if an increased risk of thromboembolic disease is applicable to the norethindrone-alone contraceptive. A few patients developed superficial thrombophlebitis during the clinical trials, but no studies as yet have been done. Since an appreciable amount of norethindrone is metabolized to estrogens, the possibility of an association must be borne in mind.

The effects of estrogen-progestagen oral contraceptives on blood clotting have been investigated. Intravascular clot formation may be influenced by excessive tendency of platelets to aggregate, raised levels of blood clotting factors, and decreased fibrinolysis. Different processes are believed to occur in arteries and in veins. In arteries, platelet adhesion to damaged epithelium appears to be important, and, in veins, hypercoagulability may be primary. Oral contraceptives increase the number of platelets and, possibly, their tendency to clump and increase both blood clotting factors and fibrinolysis. The effects on platelets may partly explain the formation of arterial thrombi; however, in the genesis of venous thrombosis, the effect of an increase in clotting factors occurring with an increase in fibrinolysis is difficult to evaluate. Possibly venous stasis is a factor, as oral contraceptives cause veins to dilate abnormally.

Changes in the walls of arteries and veins have been reported in a small number of estrogen-progestagen oral contraceptive users. Endothelial hyperplasia and intimal thickening have been demonstrated in pulmonary blood vessels and in the vasculature of the endometrium and other sites. The significance of these intrinsic vascular changes has not yet been determined. An interaction between changes in the blood and those in the intima of the vessels, especially the arteries, may provide an explanation for the increased risk of thromboembolism.

Estrogen-progestagen oral contraceptives have been associated both with the initial occurrence of migraine headaches and with their intensification in patients previously affected. The attacks frequently occur during the interval when the steroids are not being taken or during the first two or three days after resumption of medication. In some patients with migraine, symptoms do not worsen and some even appear to improve. However, patients whose migraine attacks begin with use of oral contraceptives or who experience any marked increase in intensity or frequency of headaches should discontinue the medication. Most of the symptoms of migraine are believed to be produced by changes in the cranial vessels; the transient or permanent sensory and motor deficits that occur may result from cerebral ischemia caused by vasoconstriction. However, there are no conclusive data to indicate that the use of oral contraceptives in women with migraine increases the incidence of cerebrovascular disease above that observed in women with migraine who are nonusers.

Increases in systolic and diastolic pressure have developed in some women taking estrogen-progestagen oral contraceptives. Since termination of therapy resulted in a gradual decline in blood pressure to normal in some, an association between oral contraceptives and hypertension was assumed for these women. Estrogen-progestagen combinations consistently increase the amount of renin substrate, which, in turn, increases the production of the potent pressor substance, angiotensin. Normally, the increased amount of angiotensin exerts a negative feedback effect upon the enzyme, renin. The development of hypertension in susceptible individuals may be due to an incomplete feedback effect and, thus, a failure to lower the renin concentration adequately. Headache and an increased tendency to retain fluid may be associated with the hypertension. Blood pressure readings should be taken before starting medication and regularly thereafter.

There are at present no completely adequate criteria for screening patients to determine those with a greater than normal susceptibility to thromboembolic disease. Patients with a history of deep venous thrombosis, pulmonary embolism, cerebral thrombosis, or thrombophlebitis during pregnancy or the puerperium are considered to be in the high-risk category. In addition, patients with hypertension or a history of migraine associated with focal cerebral ischemia require special supervision and those in whom migraine first appears or increases in severity or frequency after starting therapy may be more likely to develop intracranial thrombosis. If signs and symptoms of thromboembolism or neurologic or neuro-ophthalmic disorders occur, oral contraceptives should be discontinued immediately.

A cooperative study performed in the United States, Sweden, and the United Kingdom has provided evidence that the risk of developing venous thromboembolic disease while taking oral contraceptives is lower in women with blood type O than in those with other blood types. The fact that this distinct genetic population differs in tendency to develop venous thromboembolic disease may prove of value as a screening criterion if the underlying mechanisms can be determined.

Endocrine System: Occasionally the first spontaneous menses after discontinuance of estrogen-progestagen contraceptives are delayed for six to ten weeks after termination of therapy; the patient's prior menstrual rhythm then returns. The duration of therapy does not affect return of ovulation, and almost all women ovulate by the third post-treatment cycle. If anovulation persists for six months and intercurrent pathologic causes have been ruled out, therapy with clomiphene [Clomid] or exogenous gonadotropins usually will reverse the inhibition of ovarian function. The cause of the inhibition probably is a disturbance in the highly integrated hypothalamic-pituitary system.

The effect of estrogen-progestagen oral contraceptives on carbohydrate metabolism is complex. Utilization of glucose may be retarded with a compensatory increase in the secretion of insulin. A peripheral anti-insulin effect of HGH may be involved during the first year of use, since these combinations increase the secretion of growth hormone (HGH) by the pituitary. After one year, HGH secretion appears to return to normal in some individuals. If alterations in glucose tolerance continue, other diabetogenic factors may be responsible. Patients who are diabetic during pregnancy but who do not have diabetes in the nonpregnant state are particularly vulnerable to developing an abnormal glucose tolerance. Since oral contraceptives may affect glucose metabolism in these patients, other forms of contraception should be considered. Adverse effects usually are not observed in controlled diabetic patients; however, the status of diabetic patients using oral contraceptives should be reviewed periodically.

The estrogenic component of oral contraceptives increases the level of circulating corticosteroid-binding globulin (CBG, transcortin), which causes a significant increase in protein-bound cortisol in peripheral blood but no increase in free cortisol. Estrogens also slightly decrease the rate of metabolism of corticosteroids. The responsiveness of the pituitary-adrenal system to metyrapone is impaired; however, there is no evidence of resulting adrenocortical insufficiency during stress.

The estrogens in oral contraceptives increase the level of thyroxin-binding globulin. This increased protein binding alters the results of some thyroid function tests: protein-bound iodine (PBI) and butanol-extractable iodine (BEI) levels are elevated and the T^3 (triiodothyronine) uptake is decreased. The basal metabolic rate (BMR), cholesterol levels, ^{131}I uptake, and free thyroxin index (FTI) remain unchanged; these results suggest that thyroid function is not affected. Values of thyroid function tests may return to pretreatment levels within two months after discontinuing therapy.

Reproductive System: The estrogen-progestagen oral contraceptives reduce ovarian size since large follicles and corpora lutea are absent. Although the follicles apparently increase in density, they fail to enlarge beyond a few millimeters in diameter before atresia begins. There is no increase in the storage of ova, and no increase in the reproductive life span has been noted.

The oral contraceptives do not appear to have any adverse effect on the germ cells, and there is little evidence of any increase in the incidence of abortions or congenital anomalies.

The cervix may undergo morphologic changes during therapy, including hypersecretion and hyperplasia of the cervical glands, increased vascularity, and stromal edema. Although these cellular changes may resemble epithelial dysplasia, their prognostic significance has not been determined. A recent study showed that the incidence of carcinoma-in-situ was higher in users than in nonusers. However, a subsequent study showed that more women choosing oral contraceptives have epithelial dysplasia, the precursor of cervical carcinoma, *prior* to using the product than women choosing other contraceptive methods.

Changes in the endometrium depend upon the type of product used. With the combination estrogen-progestagen preparations, there is a rapid progression from a proliferative to a secretory pattern and then glandular atrophy, which accounts for the scant withdrawal bleeding. Regression of the endometrium after a few cycles may be a factor in post-treatment amenorrhea. Sequential estrogen-progestagen products produce less pronounced endometrial changes and heavier withdrawal bleeding.

Menstrual patterns in most patients are altered by the continuous use of a progestagen-alone preparation. Unpredictable bleeding continues throughout the duration of use of these contraceptives. Very short cycles are common. Because of this problem with bleeding patterns, the incidence of discontinuances is higher than with the estrogen-progestagen contraceptives.

Women taking any of the oral contraceptives may experience tenderness and fullness of the breasts.

Estrogens and progestagens have been detected in the milk of mursing mothers. The long-range effect on the nursing infant is not known.

At present, epidemiologic data are lacking to definitely prove or disprove an association between oral contraceptives and carcinoma of the human breast or reproductive organs. The long latent period between the administration of a known carcinogen and the development of cancer makes evaluation of such data difficult. Vaginal adenocarcinoma in offspring after puberty has been associated with the maternal ingestion of synthetic estrogens during pregnancy. Before the advent of oral contraceptives, estrogens were administered chiefly to older, hormone-deficient women, and this replacement-type use does not represent the same situation as the use of potent estrogens and progestagens in healthy women of childbearing age. Therefore, statistics from studies of this older population are not applicable to users of oral contraceptives.

Central Nervous System: Changes in mood have been observed in women using oral contraceptives. Many patients in whom irritability, tension, and depression occur during oral contraceptive use have a history of premenstrual tension before use. On the other hand, some users experience relief of premenstrual tension and a feeling of well-being. Most severe depressions have been noted in women with a history of previous depression. Both decreases and increases in libido have been reported.

Use of oral contraceptives should be discontinued immediately if neuro-ophthalmic disorders (eg, pseudotumor cerebri, optic neuropathy, retinal vascular occlusions, retinal vasculitis [Eales' disease], retinal edema) occur. Results of controlled studies indicate that oral contraceptives apparently have little if any effect on the incidence of minor ophthalmologic abnormalities, which are noted frequently in both users and nonusers. The more serious disturbances are rare and an insufficient number of patients have been studied to permit definitive conclusions at present. Interestingly, users of oral contraceptives experience more difficulties with contact lenses than do nonusers.

Cutaneous System: Chloasma (melasma) is the most frequent skin reaction. Irregular brown macules develop on the face within one month to two years after starting therapy; the macules fade more slowly than chloasma gravidarum and may be permanent. Women who have had chloasma during pregnancy are most susceptible to this reaction. All preparations, including norethindrone-alone, cause the reaction, but the incidence is related to the total amount of estrogen and progestagen (dose and duration).

Acne usually improves during use of oral contraceptives having an estrogenic component, but it may worsen during the initial months and some women previously free of acne may develop it.

An irregular loss of hair can occur during or after use of oral contraceptives. Hirsutism has been reported occasionally in women who, for unknown reasons, are susceptible to the androgenic effects of some of the progestagens.

Other possible cutaneous manifestations include erythema nodosum, erythema multiforme, hemorrhagic eruptions, and pruritus.

Drug Interaction: Since oral contraceptives decrease the hypoprothrombinemic response to coumarin anticoagulants, women taking oral contraceptives may require an increase in dosage of the anticoagulants.

Summary: Of the many adverse effects caused by oral contraceptives, the most important clinically are those affecting blood clotting and the vascular walls, which result in a slight risk of thromboembolic disease; those affecting the angiotensin-renin mechanism that presumably cause hypertension in susceptible individuals; and those affecting the mood. Because the carcinogenic potential of these preparations on the breast and other ovarian hormone-dependent tissues is not yet determined, patients should be carefully examined periodically, and those who have or have had a known or suspected hormone-dependent tumor should not use this method of contraception.

ESTROGENS

ESTRADIOL [Aquadiol, Progynon]
ESTRADIOL BENZOATE [Progynon Benzoate]
ESTRADIOL CYPIONATE [Depo-Estradiol Cypionate]
ESTRADIOL DIPROPIONATE
ESTRADIOL VALERATE [Delestrogen, Duratrad, Estate]

OH
CH_3
HO

Estradiol is the principal and most potent ovarian estrogenic hormone. Most commonly, it is injected intramuscularly; pellets for subcutaneous implantation are seldom used. Oral therapy has been considered to be ineffective because of poor gastrointestinal absorption. Results of preliminary studies with an investigational micronized form of estradiol indicate that this oral form is clinically effective in the treatment of menopausal vasomotor disturbances.

Esters of estradiol are administered intramuscularly in oily solution and have a duration of effect ranging from three or four days to three or four weeks. Long-acting esters given by injection have a gradual and uncertain onset and duration of action and are most suitable for replacement therapy, especially to control symptoms of the menopausal and postmenopausal period and for disseminated breast carcinoma. They are not suitable for treatment of menstrual disorders or for replacement purposes when cyclic therapy is desired.

This drug is not advised for use in men with prostatic carcinoma, since the relationship between the drug given in the manufacturers' suggested dosage and increased mortality from cardiovascular disease has not been determined.

See the Introductory Statement for specific indications and adverse reactions.

USUAL DOSAGE.—

Intramuscular: For replacement therapy, (Estradiol, Estradiol Benzoate) 0.5 to 1.5 mg two or three times weekly; (Estradiol Cypionate) 1 to 5 mg weekly for two or three weeks; (Estradiol Dipropionate) 1 to 5 mg every one to two weeks; (Estradiol Valerate) 5 to 40 mg every two to four weeks. For prevention of postpartum breast engorgement, (Estradiol) 1.5 to 2.2 mg daily.

Subcutaneous Implantation: (Estradiol) One 25 mg pellet every three to four months.

PREPARATIONS.—

Estradiol:

Aquadiol (Merrell-National). *Injection:* Suspension (aqueous) 0.22 mg/ml in 10 ml containers, 0.44 mg/ml in 10 and 25 ml containers, and 1.1 mg/ml in 10 ml containers.

Progynon (Schering).

Injection: Suspension (aqueous) 1 mg/ml in 10 ml containers.

Implantation: Pellets 25 mg.

Estradiol Benzoate:

Injection: Solution (in sesame oil) 0.5 and 1 mg/ml in 10 and 30 ml containers.

Estradiol Cypionate:

Depo-Estradiol Cypionate (Upjohn). *Injection:* Solution (in cottonseed oil) 1 mg/ml in 10 ml containers and 5 mg/ml in 5 ml containers.

Estradiol Dipropionate:

Injection: Solution (in sesame oil) 1 mg/ml in 10 and 30 ml containers.

Estradiol Valerate:

Delestrogen (Squibb). *Injection:* Solution (in sesame oil) 10 mg/ml in 1 and 5 ml containers; solution (in castor oil) 20 mg/ml in 1 and 5 ml containers and 40 mg/ml in 5 ml containers.

Duratrad (Ascher). *Injection:* Solution (in sesame oil) 10 mg/ml in 10 ml containers.

Estate (Savage). *Injection:* Solution (in sesame oil) 10 mg/ml in 10 ml containers.

ADDITIONAL TRADEMARKS.—Estradiol Cypionate: Femogen CYP (Fellows-Testagar). **Estradiol Valerate:** Estraval P.A. (Tutag), Estroval (Reid-Provident), Femogen LA (Fellows-Testagar), RepEstra (Central). Forms marketed by other manufacturers under generic name.

ESTRONE [Estrusol, Glyestrin, Menformon (A), Theelin, Wynestron]
ESTRONE PIPERAZINE SULFATE [Ogen]
ESTRONE POTASSIUM SULFATE [Femspan, Spanestrin P, Theelin R-P]
ESTRONE SODIUM SULFATE [Morestin]

Estrone is an ovarian estrogenic hormone available in aqueous suspension, solution in oil, and vaginal suppositories. The aqueous mixture of the water-insoluble estrone and water-soluble potassium salt of the sulfate ester (estrone potassium sulfate) is claimed to have a more prompt effect than insoluble estrone suspensions. Estrone piperazine sulfate is slightly less potent than estrone sodium sulfate (1.5 mg is equivalent to 1.25 mg of estrone sodium sulfate); both salts are given orally. The potency of most oral mixtures of estrogenic substances is expressed in terms of their estrone sodium sulfate content.

See the Introductory Statement for specific indications and adverse reactions.

USUAL DOSAGE.—

Estrone:

Intramuscular: For replacement therapy in menopausal and postmenopausal women, 0.1 to 1.5 mg weekly in single or divided doses; for dysfunctional uterine bleeding, 2 to 5 mg daily until bleeding is controlled; for prostatic carcinoma, no dosage regimen is recognized, since the relationship between the drug and increased mortality from cardiovascular disease has not been determined; the manufacturers' suggested dosage is 2 to 4 mg two or three times weekly.

Vaginal: One 0.2 mg suppository daily.

Estrone Piperazine Sulfate:

Oral: For replacement therapy in menopausal and postmenopausal women, 1.5 to 3 mg daily; for prevention of postpartum breast engorgement, 4.5 mg every four hours for five doses; for dysfunctional uterine bleeding, 4.5 to 9 mg daily until flow ceases.

Estrone Sodium Sulfate:

Oral: For replacement therapy in menopausal and postmenopausal women, 1.25 to 2.5 mg daily; for prevention of postpartum breast engorgement, 3.75 mg every four hours for five doses; for dysfunctional uterine bleeding, 3.75 to 7.5 mg daily until flow ceases.

PREPARATIONS.—

Estrone:

Estrusol (Smith, Miller & Patch). *Injection:* Suspension (aqueous) 2 and 5 mg/ml in 15 ml containers.

Glyestrin (First Texas). *Vaginal:* Suppositories 0.2 mg.

Menformon (A) (Organon), Wynestron (Wyeth). *Injection:* Suspension (aqueous) 2 mg/ml in 10 ml containers.

Theelin (Parke, Davis).

Injection: Solution (in peanut oil) 1 mg/ml in 1 and 10 ml containers; suspension (aqueous) 1 mg/ml in 1 ml containers, 2 mg/ml in 1 and 10 ml containers, and 5 mg/ml in 1 and 5 ml containers.

Vaginal: Suppositories 0.2 mg.

Drug also marketed by many manufacturers under generic name and under the trade name Theelin.

Estrone Piperazine Sulfate:

Ogen (Abbott). *Oral:* Tablets 0.75, 1.5, 3, and 6 mg (equivalent to estrone sodium sulfate activity 0.625, 1.25, 2.5, and 5 mg, respectively).

Estrone Potassium Sulfate:

Femspan (Fellows-Testagar), Spanestrin P (Savage), Theelin R-P (Parke, Davis). *Injection:* Each milliliter of solution/suspension contains 2 mg of estrone and 1 mg of estrone potassium sulfate in 10 ml containers.

Estrone Sodium Sulfate:

Morestin (Durst). *Oral:* Tablets 1.25 mg.

ETHINYL ESTRADIOL [Estinyl, Feminone, Lynoral, Palonyl]

This steroid is related to estradiol, the principal ovarian estrogen. It is a potent orally effective estrogen. Ethinyl estradiol also is a component of some oral contraceptive estrogen-progestagen mixtures.

See the Introductory Statement for specific indications and adverse reactions.

USUAL DOSAGE.—*Oral:* For replacement therapy in amenorrhea due to hypogonadism, 0.05 mg one to three times daily for the first two weeks of an arbitrary cycle, followed by use of a progestational agent for the last two weeks; for replacement therapy for menopausal symptoms, 0.02 to 0.05 mg daily; for dysfunctional uterine bleeding, 0.5 mg once or twice daily until bleeding is controlled; for postpartum breast engorgement, 0.5 to 1 mg daily for three days, then 0.1 mg for seven days; for breast carcinoma in postmenopausal women, 1 mg three times daily; for prostatic carcinoma, no dosage regimen is recognized, since the relationship between the drug in the suggested dosages and increased mortality from cardiovascular disease has not been determined; the manufacturers' suggested dose is 0.15 to 3 mg daily.

PREPARATIONS.—

Estinyl (Schering). *Oral:* Tablets 0.02, 0.05, and 0.5 mg.

Feminone (Upjohn), Palonyl (Palmedico). *Oral:* Tablets 0.05 mg.

Lynoral (Organon). *Oral:* Tablets 0.01 and 0.05 mg.

Drug also marketed under generic name.

DIETHYLSTILBESTROL
DIETHYLSTILBESTROL DIPHOSPHATE [Stilphostrol]
DIETHYLSTILBESTROL DIPROPIONATE

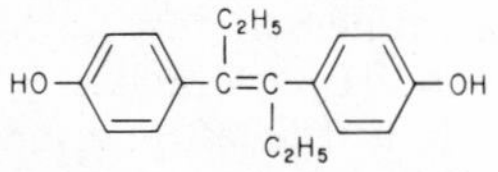

This is the most potent nonsteroidal estrogen and is extensively used. Since diethylstilbestrol is not rapidly inactivated, it can be given in single daily doses even when large doses are required.

Diethylstilbestrol is contraindicated during pregnancy because of an association between the use of this drug during pregnancy and the occurrence of adenocarcinoma of the vagina in offspring.

See the Introductory Statement for specific indications and adverse reactions for this nonsteroidal estrogen.

USUAL DOSAGE.—

Diethylstilbestrol, Diethylstilbestrol Dipropionate:

Oral: For replacement therapy for hypogonadism, 1 mg daily until the desired response is obtained; for replacement therapy for menopausal symptoms, 0.2 to 0.5 mg daily; for dysfunctional uterine bleeding, 5 mg three to five times daily until bleeding is controlled; for postpartum breast engorgement, 5 mg once or twice daily for two to four days; for breast carcinoma in postmenopausal women, initially, 15 mg daily, and the amount is increased according to the tolerance of the patient; for prostatic carcinoma, 1 mg daily.

Diethylstilbestrol Diphosphate:

For prostatic carcinoma, no dosage regimen is recognized, since the relationship between the drug in the suggested dosages and increased mortality from cardiovascular disease has not been determined; the manufacturers' suggested dosage is:

Intravenous: 250 to 500 mg one or two times weekly.

Oral: 50 mg three times daily; the dose may be increased to 200 mg or more three times daily.

PREPARATIONS.—

Diethylstilbestrol:

Oral: Capsules and tablets (plain and enteric-coated) 0.1, 0.25, 0.5, 1, 5, 25, and 100 mg.

Injection: Solution (in sesame oil) 5 and 25 mg in 10 and 30 ml containers.

AVAILABLE TRADEMARKS.—des (Amfre-Grant). Drug also marketed by many manufacturers under generic name.

Diethylstilbestrol Diphosphate:

Stilphostrol (Dome).

Oral: Tablets 50 mg.

Injection: Solution 50 mg/ml in 5 ml containers.

Diethylstilbestrol Dipropionate:

Oral: Tablets 1 and 5 mg. Drug marketed under generic name.

BENZESTROL [Chemestrogen]

This is a nonsteroidal estrogen chemically related to diethylstilbestrol. See the Introductory Statement for indications and adverse reactions.

Benzestrol is contraindicated during pregnancy.

USUAL DOSAGE.—*Oral:* 1 to 5 mg daily.

PREPARATIONS.—Chemestrogen (Watson). *Oral:* Tablets 1, 2, and 5 mg.

CHLOROTRIANISENE [TACE]

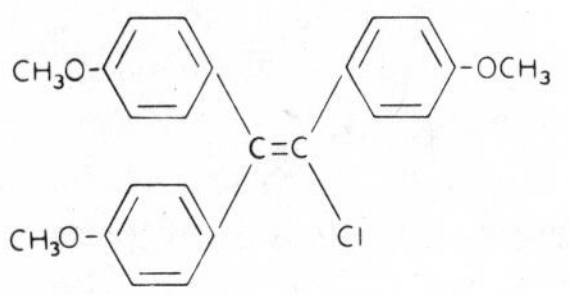

This nonsteroidal estrogen has a long-acting effect that is claimed to be due to a higher degree of storage in adipose tissue. It is sometimes classified as a proestrogen, for it presumably is altered before becoming effective. The drug is used most frequently for the palliative treatment of prostatic carcinoma and postpartum breast engorgement. Results in a small retrospective study of patients with prostatic carcinoma given 12 mg of chlorotrianisene daily (equivalent to approximately 1.5 mg of diethylstilbestrol) were compared with the results obtained in a placebo group in a large Veterans Administration study: the percentage of deaths from cardiovascular disease in patients with Stage III and IV prostatic carcinoma was similar in both studies, but the percentage of deaths from cardiovascular disease in those with Stages I and II disease was almost twice as high in the smaller study. The long duration of action of chlorotrianisene makes this drug less suitable than short-acting oral preparations for the treatment of menstrual disorders and for replacement purposes when cyclic therapy is desired.

See the Introductory Statement for indications and adverse reactions.

USUAL DOSAGE.—*Oral:* For replacement therapy, 12 to 25 mg daily. For prostatic carcinoma, 12 mg daily. For postpartum breast engorgement, 72 mg twice daily for two days; the first dose should be given within eight hours after delivery.

PREPARATIONS.—TACE (Merrell-National). *Oral:* Capsules 12, 25, and 72 mg.

DIENESTROL [DV, Synestrol]

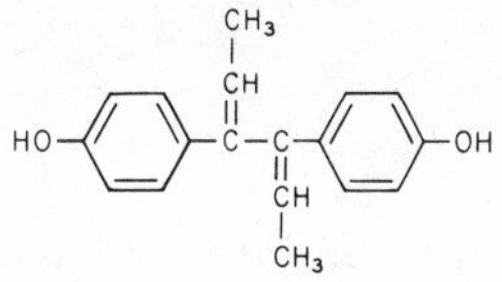

This is a nonsteroidal estrogen chemically related to diethylstilbestrol. See the Introductory Statement for indications and adverse reactions.

Dienestrol is contraindicated during pregnancy.

USUAL DOSAGE.—

Oral: For replacement therapy, 0.1 to 1.5 mg daily; for dysfunctional uterine bleeding, 5 to 20 mg four times daily until bleeding is controlled; for postpartum breast engorgement, 1.5 mg daily for three days, then 0.5 mg daily for seven days; for breast carcinoma in postmenopausal women, 15 mg daily; for prostatic carcinoma, no dosage regimen is recognized, since the relationship between the drug in the suggested doses and increased mortality from cardiovascular disease has not been determined; the manufacturers' suggested dose is 5 to 15 mg daily.

Topical: For atrophic and senile vaginitis, preparation is applied one to two times daily for one to two weeks, then reduced gradually to a maintenance level of one to three times a week.

PREPARATIONS.—

DV (Merrell-National). *Topical* (vaginal): Cream 0.01% in 3 oz containers; suppositories 0.7 mg.

Synestrol (Schering). *Oral:* Tablets 0.5 and 10 mg.

Drug also marketed under generic name.

HEXESTROL

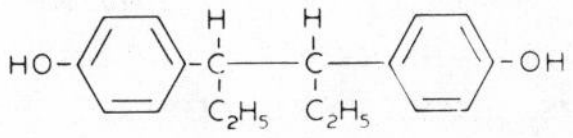

This is a nonsteroidal estrogen chemically related to diethylstilbestrol. See the Introductory Statement for indications and adverse reactions.

Hexestrol is contraindicated during pregnancy.

USUAL DOSAGE.—*Oral:* 2 to 3 mg daily.

PREPARATIONS.—*Oral:* Tablets 1 and 3 mg. Drug marketed under generic name.

METHALLENESTRIL [Vallestril]

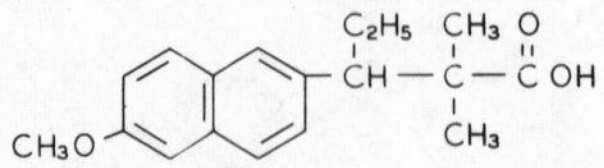

See the Introductory Statement for indications and adverse reactions for this nonsteroidal estrogen.

USUAL DOSAGE.—*Oral:* For replacement therapy in menopausal and postmenopausal patients, 3 to 9 mg daily; for postpartum breast engorgement, 40 mg daily for five days; for prostatic carcinoma, no dosage regimen is recognized, since the relationship between the drug in the suggested dose and increased mortality from cardiovascular disease has not been determined; the manufacturer's suggested dose is 20 mg daily.

PREPARATIONS.—Vallestril (Searle). *Oral:* Tablets 3 and 20 mg.

PROMETHESTROL DIPROPIONATE [Meprane Dipropionate]

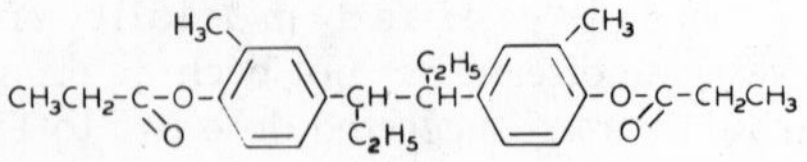

This is a nonsteroidal estrogen chemically related to diethylstilbestrol. See the Introductory Statement for indications and adverse reactions.

Promethestrol is contraindicated during pregnancy.

USUAL DOSAGE.—*Oral:* 1 to 3 mg daily.

PREPARATIONS.—Meprane Dipropionate (Reed & Carnrick). *Oral:* Tablets 1 mg.

CONJUGATED ESTROGENS, U.S.P. [Premarin]

This is a combination of the sodium salts of the sulfate esters of estrogenic substances, principally estrone and equilin; the esters are similar to the type excreted by pregnant mares. The various preparations contain 50% to 65% estrone sodium sulfate and 20% to 35% equilin sodium sulfate. They are effective orally, parenterally, and topically. The parenteral preparation is claimed to control spontaneous capillary bleeding rapidly and to reduce capillary bleeding during surgery; however, evidence of efficacy for this indication is insufficient. The efficacy of topical preparations in the treatment of acne is not proved.

See the Introductory Statement for specific indications and adverse reactions.

USUAL DOSAGE.—

Oral: For replacement therapy in menopausal and postmenopausal women, 0.3 to 1.25 mg daily, cyclically. For replacement therapy for hypogonadism, 2.5 to 7.5 mg daily, cyclically. For dysfunctional uterine bleeding, 3.75 to 7.5 mg daily for three to five days to stop bleeding; this dose is then continued for 20 days. For breast carcinoma in postmenopausal women, 10 mg three times daily for at least three months. For prevention of postpartum breast engorgement, 3.75 mg every four hours for five doses or 5 mg daily for two or more days. For prostatic carcinoma, no dosage regimen is recognized, since the relationship between the suggested dosage of this drug and increased mortality from cardiovascular disease has not been determined; the manufacturers' suggested dosage is 1.25 to 2.5 mg three times daily.

Intramuscular, Intravenous: For emergency treatment of dysfunctional uterine bleeding, 25 mg initially, with the dose repeated in 6 to 12 hours if necessary. No useful dosage is recognized for use of conjugated estrogens for treatment of capillary bleeding because of the reason stated above. The manufacturer's suggested dosage is: *Adults*, 25 mg immediately; this dose may be repeated at hourly intervals up to three doses. *Children*, one-quarter to one-half of adult dose.

Topical: Use of this form for acne lacks evidence of efficacy. The manufacturer's suggested dosage is: 2 to 4 g of cream or 1 ml of lotion applied two times daily.

Topical (vaginal): 2 to 4 g of cream applied daily.

PREPARATIONS.—Premarin (Ayerst).

Oral: Tablets 0.3, 0.625, 1.25, and 2.5 mg.

Injection: Powder 25 mg with 5 ml of diluent.

Topical: Cream containing 0.625 mg/g in 60 g containers; lotion containing 1 mg/ml in 60 ml containers.

Topical (vaginal): Cream containing 0.625 mg/g in 42.5 g containers.

ADDITIONAL TRADEMARKS.—Conestron (Wyeth), Conjutabs (Century), Equgen (Elder), Menotabs (Fleming), Theogen (SIG).

ESTERIFIED ESTROGENS, U.S.P. [Amnestrogen, Evex, Menest, SK-Estrogens]

This is a combination of the sodium salts of the sulfate esters of estrogenic substances, principally estrone; the esters are similar to the type excreted by pregnant mares. Preparations of esterified estrogens contain 75% to 85% estrone sodium sulfate and 6.5% to 15% equilin sodium sulfate.

See the Introductory Statement for indications and adverse reactions.

USUAL DOSAGE.—See dosages for Conjugated Estrogens.

PREPARATIONS.—

Amnestrogen (Squibb), Menest (Beecham-Massengill), SK-Estrogens (Smith Kline & French). *Oral:* Tablets 0.3, 0.625, 1.25, and 2.5 mg.

Evex (Syntex). *Oral:* Tablets 0.625, 1.25, and 2.5 mg.

ADDITIONAL TRADEMARKS.—Estrifol (Premo), Femogen (Fellows-Testagar), Glyestrin (First Texas), Trocosone (Merck), Zeste (Ascher).

MIXTURES OF ESTROGENIC SUBSTANCES

Some mixtures of estrogenic substances do not conform to the U.S.P. definitions of conjugated estrogens or esterified estrogens. Most of these preparations combine estrogens of equine origin, and some also contain synthetic pure conjugates. Their potency is usually expressed in terms of the sodium estrone sulfate content. They have the same indications and adverse effects as conjugated or esterified estrogens (see the Introductory Statement).

AVAILABLE MIXTURES.—Binestro (Ascher), Di-Est (Central), Estronol (Central), Hormonin No. 1, Hormonin No. 2 (Carnrick), Menagen (Parke, Davis), Neo-Amniotin (Squibb), Proliculin (Merrell-National), Semestrin (Beecham-Massengill), Urestrin (Upjohn).

PROGESTERONE AND PROGESTAGENS

PROGESTERONE [Gesterol, Lipo-Lutin, Proluton]

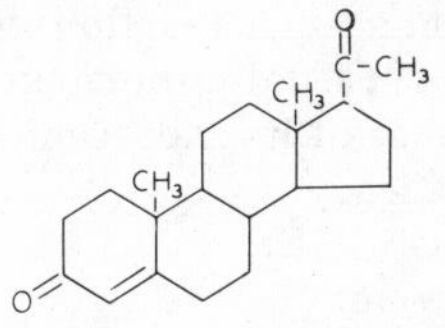

This natural progestational substance acts on target genital tissues and endocrine glands and also has general systemic effects. Parenteral preparations in oil or water are used primarily to treat menstrual disorders. The drug is ineffective when given orally. Responsiveness to progesterone in the target organ depends upon the priming action of estrogen.

See the Introductory Statement for indications and adverse reactions.

USUAL DOSAGE.—*Intramuscular:* For amenorrhea, 25 mg three times weekly during the last two weeks of the menstrual cycle; for dysmenorrhea and premenstrual tension, 10 to 25 mg daily for the week prior to menstruation; for dysfunctional uterine bleeding, 5 to 10 mg daily for five days. The use of this drug for threatened or habitual abortion lacks evidence of efficacy. The manufacturers' suggested dosages are: For threatened abortion, 25 to 50 mg daily; for habitual abortion, 5 to 20 mg three times weekly.

PREPARATIONS.—

Gesterol (Fellows-Testagar). *Injection:* Solution (in oil) 50 mg/ml in 10 ml containers; suspension (aqueous) 50 mg/ml in 10 ml containers.

Lipo-Lutin (Parke, Davis). *Injection:* Solution (in oil) 50 mg/ml in 5 ml containers; suspension (aqueous) 25 mg/ml in 10 ml containers.

Proluton (Schering). *Injection:* Solution (in oil) 50 mg/ml in 10 ml containers.

Drug also marketed by many manufacturers under generic name.

HYDROXYPROGESTERONE CAPROATE [Delalutin]

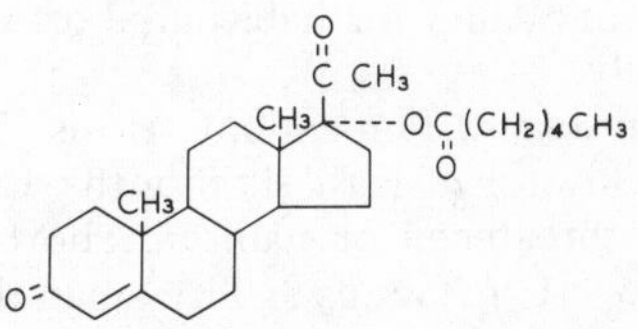

This derivative of progesterone is administered parenterally and is about seven times more potent than progesterone. Its duration of action is about 9 to 17 days. Hydroxyprogesterone has no estrogenic activity. Priming with estrogen is necessary before a response is noted.

See the Introductory Statement for indications and adverse reactions. The drug has not been shown to cause masculinization of the female fetus.

USUAL DOSAGE.—*Intramuscular:* For menstrual disorders, 125 to 250 mg per cycle. Use of this drug for threatened or habitual abortion lacks evidence of efficacy. The manufacturer's suggested dosage is 250 mg or more daily.

PREPARATIONS.—Delalutin (Squibb). *Injection:* Solution (in oil) 125 mg/ml in 2 and 10 ml containers and 250 mg/ml in 1 and 5 ml containers.

MEDROXYPROGESTERONE ACETATE [Depo-Provera, Provera]

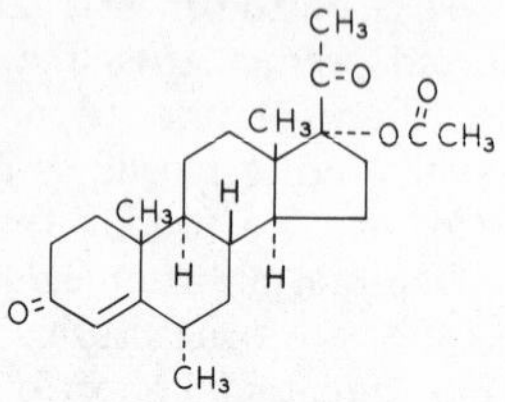

This derivative of progesterone is effective both orally or parenterally. When an aqueous suspension containing 50 mg/ml is administered parenterally, the duration of action is about seven days/50 mg. The drug has no inherent estrogenic activity. Priming with estrogen is necessary before a response is noted.

See the Introductory Statement for indications and adverse reactions.

USUAL DOSAGE.—

Oral: For amenorrhea, dysfunctional uterine bleeding, dysmenorrhea, and premenstrual tension, 2.5 to 10 mg daily for 5 to 20 days, depending upon the indication. Use of this drug for threatened or habitual abortion lacks evidence of efficacy. The manufacturer's suggested dosages are: For threatened abortion, 10 to 30 mg daily; for habitual abortion, 10 to 40 mg daily.

Intramuscular: For endometriosis, 50 mg or more weekly for at least six months. Use of this drug for threatened or habitual abortion lacks evidence of efficacy. The manufacturer's suggested dosages are: For threatened abortion, 50 mg daily when symptoms are present, followed by 50 mg weekly. For habitual abortion, 50 mg weekly.

PREPARATIONS.—

Depo-Provera (Upjohn). *Injection:* Suspension (aqueous) 50 and 100 mg/ml in 1 and 5 ml containers.

Provera (Upjohn). *Oral:* Tablets 2.5 and 10 mg.

MEGESTROL ACETATE [Megace]

This progestagen is used in the palliative treatment of recurrent or metastatic endometrial carcinoma. See Chapter 88, Antineoplastic Agents.

USUAL DOSAGE.—*Oral:* 20 mg twice a day. A trial course of treatment should be continued for two months.

PREPARATION.—Megace (Mead Johnson). *Oral:* Tablets 20 mg.

DYDROGESTERONE [Duphaston, Gynorest]

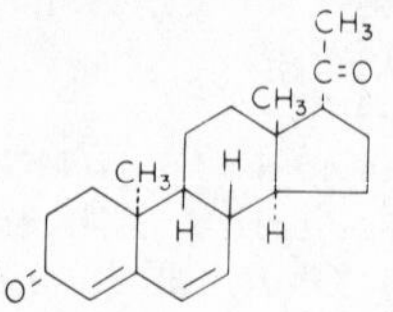

This derivative of retroprogesterone is effective orally. It has no inherent estrogenic activity and no androgenic effects. Priming with estrogen is necessary prior to use. The drug is claimed to be nonthermogenic and does not consistently inhibit ovulation.

See the Introductory Statement for indications and adverse reactions.

USUAL DOSAGE.—*Oral:* For menstrual disorders such as amenorrhea and dysmenorrhea, 10 to 20 mg daily for 5 to 20 days; for endometriosis, 20 mg or more daily. Use of this drug for threatened or habitual abortion lacks evidence of efficacy. The manufacturers' suggested dosages are: For threatened abortion, 10 to 40 mg daily; for habitual abortion, 10 mg daily.

PREPARATIONS.—Duphaston (Philips Roxane), Gynorest (Mead Johnson). *Oral:* Tablets 5 and 10 mg.

NORETHINDRONE [Norlutin]
NORETHINDRONE ACETATE [Norlutate]

This derivative of testosterone is a potent oral progestational agent with inherent estrogenic activity. Its androgenic effects are variable. The acetate salt is approximately twice as potent as the base. Norethindrone is also combined with estrogens for contraceptive use (see the section on Oral Contraceptives).

See the Introductory Statement for indications and adverse reactions. Norethindrone should not be used in threatened or habitual abortion because of its androgenicity and lack of evidence of efficacy.

USUAL DOSAGE.—

Norethindrone:

Oral: For amenorrhea, dysfunctional uterine bleeding, premenstrual tension, and dysmenorrhea, 5 to 20 mg daily; for endometriosis, initially, 10 mg daily for two weeks, then 20 to 30 mg daily for maintenance.

Norethindrone Acetate:

Oral: For amenorrhea, dysfunctional uterine bleeding, premenstrual tension, and dysmenorrhea, 2.5 to 10 mg; for endometriosis, initially, 5 mg daily for two weeks, then 10 to 15 mg daily for maintenance.

PREPARATIONS.—

Norethindrone:

Norlutin (Parke, Davis). *Oral:* Tablets 5 mg.

Norethindrone Acetate:

Norlutate (Parke, Davis). *Oral:* Tablets 5 mg.

ETHISTERONE

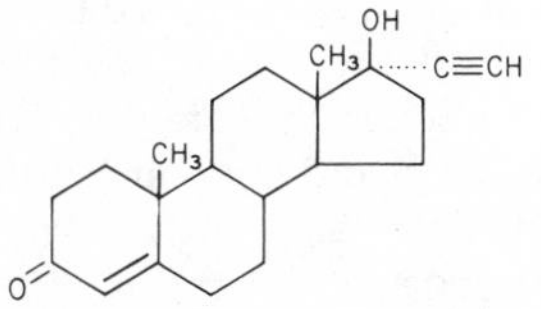

Ethisterone is a derivative of testosterone. Its effectiveness orally is approximately one-fifth that of injectable progesterone preparations. Use in women is undesirable because the drug has androgenic activity.

USUAL DOSAGE.—The manufacturers' suggested dosage is: *Oral:* For dysmenorrhea and premenstrual tension, 25 mg daily for three to eight days before the onset of menstruation.

PREPARATIONS.—*Oral:* Tablets 10, 25, and 50 mg. Drug marketed under generic name.

OVULATORY AGENTS

CLOMIPHENE CITRATE [Clomid]

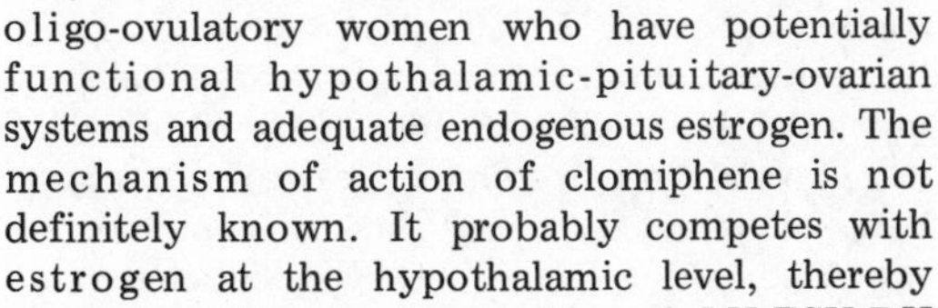

Clomiphene, a nonsteroidal agent related chemically to chlorotrianisene and triparanol, may stimulate ovulation in anovulatory and oligo-ovulatory women who have potentially functional hypothalamic-pituitary-ovarian systems and adequate endogenous estrogen. The mechanism of action of clomiphene is not definitely known. It probably competes with estrogen at the hypothalamic level, thereby causing an increased secretion of LH-FSH-RH and consequently an increase in the pituitary gonadotropins LH and FSH and resultant ovarian stimulation.

In properly selected patients, the incidence of ovulation is 70% to 75% and of pregnancy 25% to 30%. The incidence of multiple pregnancies is eight times the normal.

Human chorionic gonadotropin, in a single injection of 5,000 to 10,000 IU given five to seven days after the last dose of clomiphene, has been used to stimulate the midcycle LH surge. However, there is no evidence that combined therapy gives better results than clomiphene alone.

The major adverse reaction is cystic enlargement of the ovaries. When hyperstimulation occurs, the maximal enlargement takes place several days to two weeks or more after the medication is discontinued. Additional therapy should not be given until the ovaries return to pretreatment size. Conservative treatment of the cystic enlargement is usually adequate.

Although there is no evidence of an increase in the incidence of fetal abnormalities, clomiphene is teratogenic in some subprimate animals. Clomiphene should not be administered to pregnant women.

Visual symptoms of blurred vision and scintillating scotomata are dose related and reversible when the drug is discontinued. Objective signs are rarely found, although measurable loss of visual acuity, definable scotomata, and retinal cell function changes have been reported. The drug should be discontinued if visual abnormalities appear. No changes in the lens as had occurred with use of triparanol have been reported.

Other adverse reactions include nausea, accentuated cyclic ovarian pain (mittelshmerz), breast engorgement, abnormal uterine bleeding, and hot flashes resembling menopausal vasomotor symptoms, which disappeared when therapy was stopped.

USUAL DOSAGE.—*Oral:* Initially, 50 mg daily for five days starting on the fifth day of the menstrual cycle or at any time in the patient who has had no recent menstruation. If ovulation without conception occurs, the same dosage is continued cyclically until conception or for six to eight cycles. If ovulation does not occur, a second course of 100 mg daily should be given for five days in the next cycle, and continued if ovulation without conception occurs. Although the majority of properly selected patients ovulate with doses of 50 to 100 mg, some patients need a larger amount to effect a response. Their minimal ovulatory dose may be 150 or 200 mg.

It should be noted that the manufacturer's recommended regimen does not exceed 100 mg daily for five days per month or more than three months of cyclic therapy. However, with proper monitoring, clomiphene has been used safely in larger doses and/or over a longer period to effect conception in women who fail to ovulate with lower doses or who fail to conceive in three ovulatory months.

PREPARATIONS.—Clomid (Merrell-National). *Oral:* Tablets 50 mg.

MENOTROPINS [Pergonal]

See the evaluation in Chapter 38, Anterior Pituitary and Hypothalamic Hormones.

MIXTURES

Mixtures of progestational agents and estrogens used for contraception are discussed in the section on Oral Contraceptives. These and similar mixtures also are used in various menstrual disorders, including primary and secondary amenorrhea, dysfunctional uterine bleeding, endometriosis, and dysmenorrhea. When given for two to five days, these mixtures also are fairly reliable indicators of pregnancy.

See the Introductory Statement for specific indications and adverse reactions.

OTHER AVAILABLE MIXTURES.—

Cyclogesterin (Upjohn): Each milliliter of solution (in oil) contains conjugated estrogens 1 or 2.5 mg and progesterone 10 or 25 mg; each milliliter of aqueous suspension contains conjugated estrogens 2.5 mg and progesterone 25 mg; each tablet contains conjugated estrogens 1 mg and progesterone 30 mg.

Duosterone (Roussel): Each tablet contains ethinyl estradiol 0.01 mg and ethisterone 10 mg.

MIXTURES OF ANDROGENS AND ESTROGENS

Administration of androgens for a prolonged period of time may cause signs of virilization in women. See Chapter 36, Androgens and Anabolic Steroids, for a listing of androgen-estrogen preparations.

MIXTURES OF ESTROGENS WITH SEDATIVES OR ANTIANXIETY AGENTS

This type of mixture is used for the treatment of menopausal symptoms. Hot flashes and atrophic vaginitis usually respond readily to estrogen therapy alone. However, some patients may have situational anxiety problems that cannot be solved by estrogen therapy alone. In these patients, mild sedatives or antianxiety agents may be helpful. Therefore, if one of the available combinations contains ingredients that are appropriate both quantitatively and qualitatively for an individual patient for a limited period, it may be more convenient and acceptable than use of the drugs separately.

See the Introductory Statement for indications and adverse reactions.

AVAILABLE MIXTURES.—

Menrium (Roche): Each tablet contains esterified estrogens 0.2 or 0.4 mg and chlordiazepoxide 5 mg, or esterified estrogens 0.4 mg and chlordiazepoxide 10 mg.

Meprane with Phenobarbital (Reed & Carnrick): Each tablet contains promethestrol dipropionate 1 mg and phenobarbital 16 mg.

Milprem (Wallace): Each tablet contains conjugated estrogens 0.4 mg and meprobamate 200 or 400 mg.

PMB (Ayerst): Each tablet contains conjugated estrogens 0.45 mg and meprobamate 200 or 400 mg.

Premarin with Phenobarbital (Ayerst): Each tablet contains conjugated estrogens 0.625 mg and phenobarbital 32 mg.

MIXTURES CONTAINING ESTROGENS WITH MISCELLANEOUS SUBSTANCES

Diuretics, oxytocics, thyroid, antihypertensive agents, and vitamins are combined with estrogens for the treatment of menstrual disorders, habitual and threatened abortions, prostatic cancer, and other conditions. Some of these components are of doubtful therapeutic value and the active ones should be prescribed separately.

AVAILABLE MIXTURES.—

Cytran (Upjohn): Each tablet contains medroxyprogesterone acetate 2.5 mg, ethoxzolamide 35 mg, and ectylurea 300 mg.

desPlex (Amfre-Grant): Each tablet contains diethylstilbestrol 5, 10, 25, 50, or 100 mg, hesperidin complex 100 mg, ascorbic acid 50 mg, thiamine hydrochloride 2 mg, riboflavin 2 mg, pyridoxine hydrochloride 1 mg, pantothenate calcium 10 mg, niacinamide 50 mg, folic acid 0.25 mg, and cyanocobalamin 0.5 μg.

Dicorvin (Amfre-Grant): Each tablet contains diethylstilbestrol 100 mg, ascorbic acid 667 mg, and riboflavin 10 mg.

Nugestoral (Organon): Each tablet contains ethisterone 15 mg, hesperidin 162.5 mg, ascorbic acid 175 mg, and vitamin E 3.5 mg.

MIXTURES CONTAINING ESTROGENS AND OTHER DRUGS FOR TOPICAL USE

Hydrocortisone and anti-infectives are combined with estrogens in vaginal and urethral inserts; these are used topically in the treatment of atrophic vaginitis, urethritis, and pruritus vulvae in the postmenopausal patient. Appropriate topical therapy may be used effectively when systemic estrogens are contraindicated. Dienestrol, diethylstilbestrol, and hexestrol are contraindicated during pregnancy.

AVAILABLE MIXTURES.—

AVC with Dienestrol (Merrell-National): Cream containing dienestrol 0.01%, sulfanilamide 15%, aminacrine hydrochloride 0.2%, and allantoin 2%; each suppository contains dienestrol 0.7 mg, sulfanilamide 1.05 g, aminacrine hydrochloride 14 mg, and allantoin 140 mg.

Furacin-E Urethral Inserts (Eaton): Each insert contains diethylstilbestrol 0.1 mg, nitrofurazone 0.2%, and diperodon hydrochloride 2%.

Hist-A-Cort-E (Dome): Cream containing estrone 56,000 IU, hydrocortisone acetate ½% or 1%, vitamin A 100,000 units, and pyrilamine maleate 2%.

Premarin H-C Vaginal Cream (Ayerst): Each gram contains conjugated estrogens 0.625 mg and hydrocortisone acetate 1 mg.

Quinette Vaginal Inserts (Arnar-Stone): Each insert contains diethylstilbestrol 0.1 mg, diiodohydroxyquin 100 mg, and sulfadiazine 500 mg.

Vagi-Plex (Rowell): Each gram of cream contains hexestrol 0.05 mg and sulfamerazine, sulfamethazine, and sulfadiazine 1.25% each.

HORMONE COSMETIC PREPARATIONS

Hormones used topically on the skin are marketed principally as quasi-cosmetic rejuvenating creams. Because of the current FDA restrictions on the concentrations of ovarian hormones that are permitted in such products, there is little likelihood that these products will produce any systemic effects with ordinary use; however, systemic effects occasionally have followed excessive use of hormone creams. There is some experimental evidence that some topically applied steroid hormones (both active and inactive biologically) may cause slight histologic thickening in some areas of the epidermis of aged skin. The dermal changes are questionable and the clinical effects usually negligible.

Topical preparations containing estrogens or natural progesterone in physiologic amounts have no effect on human sebaceous glands and oil secretion. There is no scientific evidence available to indicate that hormone creams are any more effective than simple emollient creams in relieving dryness of the skin nor that hormone creams increase the amount of water that the skin can hold or restore fat to the subcutaneous layer.

Used as directed, topically applied hormones, as presently formulated in cosmetic preparations, appear to be safe.

AVAILABLE PREPARATIONS.—

Ultra Feminine Face Cream with Estrogen and Progesterone (Helena Rubenstein): Each ounce contains estrogens 10,000 IU and progesterone 5 mg.

Hormonex Oil (Mitchum-Thayer): Each ounce of oil contains estrogenic hormone serum 33,000 IU.

Eterna 27 (Revlon): Cream containing pregnenolone acetate 0.5%, niacinamide, and pyridoxine.

Chapter 38

ANTERIOR PITUITARY AND HYPOTHALAMIC HORMONES

The polypeptide hormones secreted by the anterior pituitary are: adrenocorticotropin (ACTH), which regulates the secretion of adrenal corticosteroids (primarily cortisol); thyroid-stimulating hormone (TSH, thyrotropin), which regulates the secretion of thyroid hormones; follicle-stimulating hormone (FSH), which promotes maturation of the graafian follicle and regulates the secretion of estrogen in women; luteinizing hormone (LH), which initiates ovulation and controls progesterone secretion in women and testosterone secretion in men; growth hormone (GH, somatotropin), which promotes growth and modifies the activities of many tissues; prolactin, which initiates lactation; and melanocyte-stimulating hormone (MSH), which causes pigmentary changes.

The synthesis and secretion of the anterior pituitary hormones are regulated by the hypothalamus through the mediation of hypothalamic-releasing and hypothalamic-inhibiting hormones; these are believed to be small polypeptides that are secreted into the pituitary portal circulation. This circulatory system begins as capillaries in the median eminence of the hypothalamus, forms larger vessels that pass down the pituitary stalk, and again breaks up into capillaries in the anterior pituitary. The structure of some hypothalamic hormones has been determined and synthesis accomplished. Secretion by the anterior pituitary of larger polypeptide hormones (ie, ACTH, LH, FSH, TSH, GH, prolactin, and MSH) is stimulated by these small polypeptide-releasing hormones. Control of GH, prolactin, and MSH is accomplished by inhibiting hormones as well as by releasing hormones. ACTH, LH, FSH, and TSH act on specific target organs to stimulate secretion of their respective hormones. For ACTH, LH, FSH, and TSH, there is a closed loop control system by which the hypothalamic-pituitary axis is inhibited by the hormones of the target organs (negative feedback). In addition, for LH and FSH, positive feedback mechanisms exist. Such feedback information is received at the hypothalamic or pituitary levels and also at extra-hypothalamic central nervous system levels.

The specificity of the identified hypothalamic hormones that control the release of pituitary hormones is not absolute. The factor which modulates LH release also modulates FSH release; consequently, this is known as LH-FSH-RH or gonadotropin-releasing hormone (GRH). How it is possible to have either LH or FSH secreted in large amounts when the other gonadotropin is suppressed is not clear, since the same peptide controls both secretions. It is possible that another factor acts on FSH. Lack of absolute specificity is also exhibited by thyroid-releasing hormone (TRH), which appears to possess considerable prolactin-releasing hormone activity.

Thyroid System

Among the factors responsible for the maintenance of normal thyroid secretion are: an adequate supply of iodide; functional integrity of the thyroid gland; adequate secretion of the thyroid-stimulating hormone (TSH, thyrotropin), which is dependent upon the stimulating actions of the hypothalamic hormone, TRH (thyrotropin-releasing hormone); and the inhibiting feedback effect of the level of circulating thyroid hormones, thyroxine and triiodothyronine.

A number of methods are available to evaluate thyroid physiology and hormone availability. For routine clinical use, various measurements of thyroxine concentrations are accurate and widely available. To aid in the diagnosis of subclinical hypothyroidism and to differentiate between thyroidal (primary) and pituitary (secondary) hypothyroidism, TSH (thyrotropin) can be administered to increase iodine uptake and the secretion of thyroid hormone by a gland capable of responding to TSH.

Serum TSH, as determined by radioimmunoassay, is the best single test to determine or confirm thyroidal hypothyroidism and to differentiate thyroidal from pituitary hypothyroidism. The serum TSH rises before any other manifestation of hypothyroidism occurs. In adults, thyroidal hypothyroidism is essentially the only cause of a marked elevation of TSH. TSH assay is also useful to assess the adequacy of thyroid replacement therapy.

Certain patients with hypothyroidism, low serum TSH, and no apparent pituitary disease will respond with a marked rise in FSH following administration of synthetic TRH. It is presumed that these patients have a hypothalamic lesion which impairs secretion of TRH. Hypothyroidism in these patients is termed tertiary or hypothalamic.

INDIVIDUAL EVALUATION

THYROTROPIN (TSH) [Thytropar]

Thyrotropin is isolated from bovine anterior pituitary glands. It acts upon the functioning thyroid to increase iodine uptake and the formation and secretion of thyroid hormones. When radioimmunoassay equipment is not available to determine the level of TSH, and routine tests are inconclusive, thyrotropin can be used diagnostically to determine mild forms of hypothyroidism. It also is possible to differentiate thyroidal (primary) hypothyroidism from pituitary (secondary) hypothyroidism by giving thyrotropin, which will cause a response in thyroid function when the defect is in the pituitary. However, patients with adrenocortical insufficiency are very sensitive to thyroid hormone. Therefore, adrenocortical function should be determined prior to administration of thyrotropin in patients with suspected hypopituitarism.

Thyrotropin can also be used to determine thyroid function in patients receiving thyroid medication. Increased I 131 uptake and serum PBI indicate a potentially normal gland.

Thyrotropin has also been used therapeutically to increase the uptake of radioactive iodine in patients with toxic adenomatous goiters or certain types of thyroid carcinoma.

Thyrotropin is contraindicated in patients with coronary thrombosis and chronic adrenocortical insufficiency (Addison's disease). It should be used with caution in those with angina pectoris or heart failure and in those who are receiving glucocorticoid therapy.

Minor adverse reactions that have been reported include nausea, vomiting, headache, and urticaria. More serious reactions are hypotension, arrhythmias, and thyroid swelling. A few anaphylactic reactions have also been reported.

USUAL DOSAGE.—*Intramuscular, Subcutaneous:* For diagnosis, 10 IU. This dose can be repeated in 24 hours one or two times. For treatment, 10 IU daily for three to eight days prior to a therapeutic dose of radioactive iodine.

PREPARATIONS.—Thytropar (Armour). *Injection:* Powder 10 IU of thyrotropic activity (with diluent).

Adrenal System

Abnormalities in glucocorticoid production may be caused by intrinsic adrenal disease or a response to abnormal levels of adrenocorticotropic hormone (ACTH). Hyperadrenocorticism can result from excessive ACTH being secreted by the pituitary or a non-endocrine tumor, or hypoadrenocorticism can result from hypopituitarism.

In hypopituitarism, ACTH deficiency principally leads to signs of cortisol deficiency. Chronic (primary) adrenocortical insufficiency can be differentiated from that due to hypopituitarism by the presence of hyperpigmentation in Addison's disease since an increase in MSH accompanies elevation of serum ACTH; by different electrolyte abnormalities since the profound aldosterone deficiency of Addison's disease is not present in hypopituitarism; and by signs of deficiencies of other pituitary hormones.

In some patients with hypopituitarism, the hypothalamus may be primarily involved. There is evidence that corticotropin-releasing hormone (CRH), whose structure is unknown at present, controls the secretion of ACTH. Cortisol is the negative feedback modulator. ACTH is secreted in circadian rhythm with maximal ACTH levels in the early morning and minimal levels in the evening. In addition, nervous stimuli affect the secretion of CRH and ACTH.

In primary adrenocortical insufficiency, the level of circulating cortisol is low and that of ACTH is elevated, providing the hypothalamic-pituitary axis is not damaged. When the adrenocortical insufficiency is the result of pituitary or hypothalamic dysfunction, levels of both ACTH and cortisol are low.

In adrenocortical insufficiency, regardless of the cause, there is no early morning peak in serum cortisol and urinary 17-OHCS are below normal. In chronic (primary) adrenocortical insufficiency, exogenous ACTH (corticotropin) will not increase serum cortisol and urinary 17-OHCS, regardless of how much is given or for how long. In patients with limited adrenal reserve, serum cortisol and urinary 17-OHCS may be normal but will not be increased by exogenous ACTH. In hypopituitarism, adrenal responsiveness to ACTH will be retained, although repeated administration may be necessary to eventually increase adrenal steroidogenesis. When the pituitary ACTH reserve is limited, adrenal responsiveness to ACTH is retained although the pituitary will not respond to metyrapone by an increase in ACTH.

Corticotropin (ACTH) [Acthar, Cortrophin] is an open-chain polypeptide consisting of 39 amino acids. Its biological activity is associated with the first 24 amino acids in a sequence common to endogenous ACTH derived from man, cattle, pigs, and sheep. The arrangement of the remaining amino acids (25 to 39) differs from one species to another. The arrangements of amino acids 22 to 39 are clinically important since they may produce antibodies and cause allergic reactions when ACTH of animal origin is injected into humans. In addition, animal preparations, although highly purified, may contain other pituitary proteins or peptides that may be antigenic. These preparations are standardized by bioassay.

Synthetic corticotropin analogues that contain subunits of the 39 amino acid polypeptides have been prepared. Cosyntropin [Cortrosyn] is a 1-24 corticotropin and possesses biological activity. The absence of most of the antigenic part of the molecule reduces the risk of sensitivity reactions, since synthetic polypeptides containing 1-24 amino acids have little immunologic activity. The synthetic compounds can be administered on a weight basis. Cosyntropin is recommended by the manufacturer for use as a diagnostic agent only.

INDIVIDUAL EVALUATIONS

CORTICOTROPIN (ACTH) [Acthar, Cortrophin, Cortrophin Zinc]

Corticotropin is prepared from animal pituitaries, and is bioassayed against a standard preparation of adrenocorticotropic hormones. It stimulates the adrenal cortex to secrete cortisol, desoxycorticosterone, androgens, and other steroids at an accelerated rate.

Corticotropin can be used as a diagnostic agent to determine the competency of the adrenal-pituitary axis, although the synthetic product, cosyntropin, is preferred since the risk of allergic reactions is less. In this test, a maximum of 80 units of corticotropin is administered intravenously or intramuscularly daily for two or more successive days. A rise in plasma cortisol or urinary 17-OHCS indicates a functional adrenal cortex and insufficiency due to pituitary or hypothalamic dysfunction. In primary adrenocortical insufficiency, no increase in the adrenal secretion of steroids occurs.

This hormone is recommended by the manufacturers for the treatment of glucocorticoid-responsive diseases in patients with functional adrenals. (See Chapter 35, Adrenal Corticosteroids, for indications.) However, therapy with corticotropin is less predictable and less convenient and appears to possess no advantages over glucocorticoid therapy in most patients. Some investigators feel that corticotropin is more effective than glucocorticoids in the treatment of ulcerative colitis and multiple sclerosis, but this superiority is not documented by objective evidence. It has been reported that use of corticotropin in children with chronic diseases responsive to long-term glucocorticoid therapy does not inhibit growth to the same extent as do the glucocorticoids. These results need to be confirmed.

Corticotropin has an accepted role in the management of severe myasthenia gravis. This hormone is given in doses of 100 IU daily for a total of 1,000 to 2,000 units. Because marked deterioration of muscle strength occurs two to three days after treatment is started, equipment for assisted respiration should be readily available. Two days to one week after the course of treatment is finished, muscle strength begins to increase and improvement lasts for an average of three months. Some clinicians report better and more prolonged results if a second course is given in two weeks or if the drug is then given once weekly. The use of oral glucocorticoid preparations in place of corticotropin, starting with 60 mg of prednisolone or its equivalent and gradually decreasing the dose to 5 to 15 mg on alternate days, has been tried. The initial deterioration of muscle strength does not occur with the glucocorticoids, but it has not been determined if glucocorticoids are as effective as corticotropin.

Although administration of corticotropin leads to adrenal hyperplasia rather than adrenal atrophy, with prolonged therapy the ability of the pituitary-adrenal axis to respond to stress is impaired. The use of corticotropin during the period of withdrawal of glucocorticoids does not hasten reestablishment of adrenal responsiveness.

In addition to the adverse effects caused by increased secretion of glucocorticoids (see Chapter 35, Adrenal Corticosteroids), corticotropin also can produce undesirable androgenic effects in women (acne, hirsutism, amenorrhea) and electrolyte disturbances. Patients can become sensitized to corticotropin and acute allergic reactions have followed its administration.

The activity of corticotropin is destroyed by proteolytic enzymes in the gastrointestinal tract; therefore, the drug is administered intramuscularly and, occasionally, subcutaneously or intravenously. Since adrenal glands vary in responsiveness to corticotropin, dosage must be individualized to obtain a satisfactory therapeutic effect with minimal dosage and with minimal alteration in metabolism.

USUAL DOSAGE.—

Intramuscular: 40 units of aqueous solution daily in three divided doses or 40 units of gel (repository) or aqueous suspension with zinc hydroxide (repository) every 24 to 72 hours.

Subcutaneous: 40 units of aqueous solution daily in three divided doses or 40 units of gel every 24 to 72 hours.

Intravenous: 10 to 25 units of aqueous solution or 40 to 80 units of gel in 500 ml of 5% dextrose injection given as a continuous infusion for eight hours once daily (no long-acting effect). Sodium chloride injection should not be used as a diluent.

PREPARATIONS.—

ACTH (Merrell-National). *Injection:* Gel (repository) 40 U.S.P. units/ml in 1 and 5 ml containers, and 80 U.S.P. units/ml in 5 ml containers; solution 20 U.S.P. units/ml in 2 and 10 ml containers.

Acthar (Armour). *Injection:* Gel (repository) 40 and 80 U.S.P. units/ml in 1 and 5 ml containers (HP Acthar); powder 25 and 40 U.S.P. units.

Cortrophin (Organon). *Injection (intramuscular and subcutaneous):* Gel (repository) 40 U.S.P. units/ml in 1 and 5 ml containers, and 80 U.S.P. units/ml in 5 ml containers.

Cortrophin-Zinc (Organon). *Injection (intramuscular):* 40 U.S.P. units of corticotropin with 2 mg of zinc/ml in 5 ml containers.

ADDITIONAL TRADEMARKS.—Actest (Fellows-Testagar), Cortigel (Savage). Drug also marketed by other manufacturers under generic name or ACTH.

COSYNTROPIN [Cortrosyn]

Cosyntropin, a synthetic peptide subunit of natural corticotropin, contains the first 24 amino acids in the natural sequence. Cosyntropin is used as a diagnostic agent in patients believed to have adrenal insufficiency. Plasma cortisol determinations are done before and 30 minutes after the injection of 0.25 mg of cosyntropin. In most patients, a normal response is an approximate doubling of the basal cortisol level in 30 to 60 minutes, although some patients with functioning adrenals do not respond to the expected degree in 30 minutes. A cortisol level which exceeds 18 μg/100 ml 30 minutes after the injection of cosyntropin and which shows an increment of at least 7 μg/100 ml above the basal level is considered normal. Lack of a normal response indicates adrenal insufficiency, which could be the result of either adrenal or pituitary dysfunction. To distinguish between the two, cosyntropin (0.25 mg infused over a period of four to eight hours) or corticotropin (80 to 120 units daily for three to four days) is given. This dosage should be adequate to elicit a response in all patients with functional adrenal cortical tissue. The response can be determined by plasma cortisol levels or urinary excretion of steroids. The diagnosis of hypopituitarism in patients who respond can be confirmed by other tests of pituitary function. Little or no response is obtained in patients with Addison's disease.

Hypersensitivity reactions are infrequent and the previous occurrence of one is the only contraindication to use of cosyntropin. Caution should be exercised in giving cosyntropin to patients who are hypersensitive to natural corticotropin.

Patients taking hydrocortisone or estrogen may have abnormally high basal plasma cortisol levels.

USUAL DOSAGE.—*Intramuscular, Intravenous: Adults,* 0.25 mg; *children 2 years of age or less,* 0.125 mg.

PREPARATIONS.—Cortrosyn (Organon). *Injection:* Powder 0.25 mg with mannitol 10 mg.

Gonadal System

The ovary has two functions: to produce ova and to secrete estrogens and progesterone. Feedback control of the hypothalamic-pituitary-ovarian system is modulated by the ovarian hormones. The hypothalamus secretes a decapeptide-releasing hormone (LH-FSH-RH) into the portal blood going to the pituitary. The hypothalamic-releasing hormone stimulates secretion of luteinizing hormone (LH) or follicle-stimulating hormone (FSH) or both, depending upon circumstances, by the anterior pituitary. FSH and LH act upon the ovaries to effect ovulation and the secretion of estrogens and progesterone. Estrogens, particularly estradiol, act both in negative and positive feedback control at the hypothalamic level to regulate secretion of LH-FSH-RH, which, in turn, controls both LH and FSH secretion. The mechanism of this regulation is very complex. Progesterone appears to enhance suppression (negative feedback) of LH and FSH by estrogen and to decrease stimulation (positive feedback) of LH and FSH by estrogen.

The testis has two functions: production of sperm and secretion of testosterone. Each function is served by a different tissue and controlling mechanism. Hypogonadism can cause inadequate secretion of testosterone, aspermatogenesis, or both. The hypothalamic-pituitary-gonad system in the male is similar to that in the female. LH secreted by the pituitary regulates plasma testosterone concentration. However, only negative feedback control of the hypothalamic secretion of LH-FSH-RH exists. Free testosterone and estradiol (formed peripherally from testosterone and also secreted directly) act on the hypothalamus to suppress secretion of LH and FSH. The role of FSH in the regulation of spermatogenesis is not well defined. There is evidence that the germinal epithelium also regulates secretion of FSH.

Drugs available to treat dysfunctions of the hypothalamus-pituitary-gonad system are clomiphene [Clomid], chorionic gonadotropin [Antuitrin-S, APL, Follutein, Pregnyl], and menotropins [Pergonal]. Human pituitary gonadotropins (HPG) from cadaveric pituitaries is available in very limited amounts for investigational use.

Clomiphene is a synthetic nonsteroidal compound used to induce ovulation in women with an intact hypothalamic-pituitary-ovarian axis in whom anovulation is caused by dysfunction. These patients have normal or slightly elevated levels of gonadotropins (LH and FSH) and adequate estrogen secretion; withdrawal bleeding follows administration of progesterone. Clomiphene, both a weak estrogen and a weak estrogen antagonist, acts on the hypothalamus, possibly by competing with estradiol at the binding sites. Increased amounts of FSH and LH are secreted because of its low estrogen activity. (See also Chapter 37, Estrogens, Progestagens, Oral Contraceptives, and Ovulatory Agents.)

Menotropins is a preparation of human gonadotropins isolated from the urine of menopausal women. Ideally, menotropins is indicated for patients with normally developed genital organs in whom anovulation is associated with little or no detectable endogenous FSH or LH. Menotropins, containing FSH in a 1:1 ratio with LH, causes follicular maturation, and ovulation is triggered by the administration of chorionic gonadotropin (HCG) (see the evaluation on Menotropins).

Human chorionic gonadotropin is a placental hormone with many immunologic and biological similarities to human pituitary luteinizing hormone (LH). The major function of endogenous chorionic gonadotropin is to develop and maintain the corpus luteum during pregnancy. Its luteinizing hormone (LH)-like activity makes this preparation useful in the treatment of certain hypogonadal conditions in both men and women (see the evaluation).

INDIVIDUAL EVALUATIONS

CHORIONIC GONADOTROPIN (HCG)

[Antuitrin-S, APL, Follutein, Pregnyl]

This is a placental hormone prepared from the urine of pregnant women. It is cross reactive immunologically with and gives parallel dose response curves to the luteinizing hormone (LH,

ICSH) of the pituitary. However, chorionic gonadotropin differs in part in its carbohydrate composition. Studies indicate that chorionic gonadotropin, which has multiple sites of biological action, is a multivalent hormone.

This hormone is used in the treatment of infertile women in whom anovulation is caused by absent or low gonadotropins; it is given one day after each course of menotropins if urinary estrogen excretion is between 50 and 150 μg every 24 hours. Injection of chorionic gonadotropin simulates the normal ovulatory LH peak.

Ovarian hyperstimulation occurs four to five days after HCG is given in 6% to 7% of patients treated with menotropins and chorionic gonadotropin. It is usually mild and the associated ovarian enlargement and abdominal discomfort require no treatment. Severe hyperstimulation requires hospitalization and careful observation, for ovarian rupture can be life-threatening. Withholding chorionic gonadotropin when the urinary estrogen level is higher than 150 μg every 24 hours minimizes the incidence of ovarian hyperstimulation.

There is no evidence that the addition of chorionic gonadotropin to clomiphene to treat anovulation improves results obtained with clomiphene alone.

In women with presumptive evidence of ovulation, an inadequate luteal phase has been suggested as a cause of infertility and repeated abortions. Although chorionic gonadotropin has been used in these patients, evidence of its efficacy is lacking. This hormone appears to be able to maintain an existing corpus luteum but does not appear to be able to restore a regressing corpus luteum.

Chorionic gonadotropin has been widely used in the male for diagnostic purposes and therapeutically. It specifically stimulates testosterone secretion from Leydig cells. When testicular failure is due to hypothalamic or pituitary dysfunction, chorionic gonadotropin increases endogenous testosterone production. Combined treatment with this hormone and menotropins can result in full spermatogenesis in patients with hypogonadotropic eunuchoidism. However, prolonged treatment with chorionic gonadotropin may have a deleterious effect on the tubules.

Chorionic gonadotropin is used diagnostically to evaluate Leydig cell responsiveness. Short-term administration is not dependable in differentiating primary testicular failure from gonadotropin deficiency. Atrophic testes of long-standing hypopituitarism may require prolonged periods of gonadotropin stimulation to increase testosterone secretion. This preparation is of little use in differentiating between delayed puberty and organic hypogonadotropism in hypogonadal boys.

In cryptorchism, administration of chorionic gonadotropin usually results in descent of the testis if there is no anatomical obstruction. Failure of the testis to descend after an adequate course of therapy is an indication for surgery.

Use of this agent as an aid to weight reduction is unjustified because of lack of evidence of effectiveness and safety.

Evidence of sexual precocity in a prepuberal male is an indication to discontinue therapy until symptoms regress. Edema from the increased secretion of testosterone may occur in some patients.

USUAL DOSAGE.—*Intramuscular:* For cryptorchism, *boys*, 4,000 IU three times weekly for three weeks. For hypogonadism, *men*, 4,000 IU three times weekly. For anovulation, 8,000 to 10,000 IU (see the evaluation on Menotropins).

PREPARATIONS.—

Antuitrin-S (Parke, Davis). *Injection:* Powder 5,000 IU with 10 ml container of diluent.

APL (Ayerst). *Injection:* Powder 5,000 IU, 10,000 IU, and 20,000 IU with 10 ml container of diluent.

Follutein (Squibb), Pregnyl (Organon). *Injection:* Powder 10,000 IU with 10 ml container of diluent.

ADDITIONAL TRADEMARKS.—Libigen (Savage), Riogon (Durst). Drug also marketed by many manufacturers under generic name.

MENOTROPINS [Pergonal]

These pituitary hormones are prepared from the urine of postmenopausal women whose atrophic ovaries are incapable of responding to gonadotropin stimulation. FSH and LH gonadotropin activity is present in a 1:1 ratio. In most patients, use of menotropins alone results only in follicular growth and maturation. To induce ovulation by simulating the preovulatory LH surge, human chorionic gonadotropin (HCG) is given after sufficient follicular maturation has occurred.

Menotropins is used to treat anovulatory women whose ovaries are capable of responding to pituitary gonadotropins but whose gonadotropins are low or absent. The defect responsible for the anovulation is in the hypothalamus or pituitary. Premature ovarian failure must be ruled out.

The individual response to gonadotropin therapy may depend on the patient's endogenous gonadotropin levels. In gonadotropin-deficient women, HP-FSH alone does not produce full follicular maturation as determined by urinary and serum estrogen levels. These patients, however, do have a full follicular response to menotropins. It appears that LH is directly or indirectly essential for the maturation of the ovarian follicle.

Since there is considerable variation in individual response to menotropins and since different dosage regimens have been used, the results of clinical experience are varied. According to a tabulation of pooled data accumulated during the clinical investigation of menotropins, 75% of patients treated with menotropins, with or without the addition of chorionic gonadotropin, showed evidence of ovulation and 25% became pregnant after an average of two courses of treatment. A multiple gestation rate of 19% of completed pregnancies was reported; twins were produced in three-fourths of these pregnancies. The abortion rate was 25%. Fetal abnormalities occurred in 2% of completed pregnancies. The hyperstimulation syndrome occurred in 1.3% of the courses.

Continuing experience has led to the use of larger doses with monitoring of urinary estrogens to determine the state of follicular maturation. Urinary estrogen excretion determinations are also valuable to determine if chorionic gonadotropin should be withheld. In some reports, ovulation rates were as high as 98%, with the incidence of live births up to 45%. Abortions have continued to occur in about 25% of the patients. The incidence of multiple gestation ranged from 17% to 53%. Hyperstimulation occurs more frequently with use of larger doses.

Mild hyperstimulation, evidenced by ovarian enlargement, flatulence, and abdominal discomfort, lasts seven to ten days and requires no treatment. Patients with severe hyperstimulation require hospitalization. The ovarian enlargement is accompanied by weight gain, ascites, pleural effusion, oliguria, hypotension, and hypercoagulability. Treatment is supportive. Ovarian rupture with intraperitoneal hemorrhage may require surgery.

USUAL DOSAGE.—*Intramuscular:* The manufacturer recommends an initial dose of 75 IU of FSH and 75 IU of LH daily for 9 to 12 days, followed by 10,000 IU of chorionic gonadotropin one day after the last dose of menotropins. If there is evidence of ovulation but no pregnancy, this regimen is repeated for two more courses before the dose is increased to 150 IU of FSH and 150 IU of LH daily for 9 to 12 days. The same dose is repeated for two more courses if there is evidence of ovulation but no pregnancy. Doses larger than this are not recommended by the manufacturer.

Clinical experience has demonstrated the marked variability of the individual response. Women with little or no detectable endogenous FSH and LH may require between 1,800 and 3,000 IU of FSH and of LH to develop a follicle ready to ovulate. Vaginal cytology and appearance of the cervical mucus are less reliable as signs of follicular maturation than the urinary excretion of estrogens. Monitoring of urinary estrogens makes it possible to determine the dose and duration of treatment individually during each cycle according to the patient's response. Some clinicians prefer to discontinue the menotropins when estrogen excretion reaches 50 to 100 μg in 24 hours and give chorionic gonadotropin 10,000 IU after a rest period of 24 hours. Pregnancy may be expected in 20% to 45% of these patients within four to six treatment cycles. Other clinicians continue the menotropins until the estrogen level reaches 100 to 150 μg in 24 hours, and administer 10,000 IU of chorionic gonadotropin 24 hours later. A higher pregnancy rate is obtained with the larger doses; however, the degree of hyperstimulation, which is dose related, is also greater. To prevent hyperstimulation, chorionic gonadotropin should be withheld when the urinary estrogen level is higher than 150 μg in 24 hours.

PREPARATIONS.—Pergonal (Cutter). *Injection:* Powder containing 75 IU of FSH and 75 IU of LH plus 10 mg of lactose.

Chapter 39

THYROID HORMONES AND ANTITHYROID AGENTS

THYROID HORMONES

Thyroid hormones are used for the treatment of hypothyroidism, simple nonendemic goiter, chronic fibrous or lymphocytic thyroiditis, and thyrotropin-dependent carcinoma of the thyroid; they also serve to aid in the diagnosis of hyperthyroidism. The prototype of the substances used to treat hypothyroidism is thyroid, U.S.P., which is the powdered thyroid gland of the domesticated animals used for food. This product contains not only the active hormonal substances, triiodothyronine and tetraiodothyronine (thyroxine), but also the iodotyrosines and other organic materials. Other preparations used are thyroglobulin [Proloid], a substance prepared from animal thyroid glands; synthetic salts of the pure thyroid hormones (levothyroxine sodium [Letter, Synthroid], liothyronine sodium [Cytomel]); and a mixture of the synthetic salts of pure thyroid hormones (liotrix [Euthroid, Thyrolar]).

All of these substances produce the same qualitative clinical effects; liothyronine has the most rapid onset and shortest duration of action. The quantitative clinical response to 60 mg of thyroid, U.S.P., is approximately equal to that produced by 60 mg of thyroglobulin, 0.1 mg of levothyroxine, 0.025 mg of liothyronine, or preparations of liotrix containing either 0.06 mg of levothyroxine and 0.015 mg of liothyronine or 0.05 mg of levothyroxine and 0.0125 mg of liothyronine.

Few patients fail to respond satisfactorily to adequate doses of thyroid hormone. Incomplete gastrointestinal absorption is the most common cause of treatment failure and usually results from functional or organic disease of the gastrointestinal tract, use of enteric-coated tablets that do not dissolve, or use of old preparations that have become hardened and thus poorly soluble.

Hypothyroid patients must be informed of their life-long need for replacement therapy. The dosage of the thyroid preparation must be established individually, beginning with a small amount which is increased gradually until an optimal clinical response is produced. The dose required to maintain this response is then given regularly.

Individuals with hypothyroidism respond rapidly to replacement doses of thyroid hormones. Therefore, if the dosage is rapidly increased in an individual with underlying myocardial disease, it is possible to exceed the capacity of the heart to handle the increased metabolic needs of the body. On the other hand, in myxedema coma, the most severe form of hypothyroidism, or in severe myxedema with bowel obstruction, it may be life saving to accept the hazard associated with rapid replacement of the thyroid hormone.

Early diagnosis and prompt, adequate treatment are mandatory for the management of goitrous sporadic cretinism. Most defects associated with this form of hypothyroidism, including inadequate development of the brain, bones, teeth, and muscles, can be avoided if treatment is begun immediately after birth. Maintenance levels of hormone equal to, or slightly above, those required in adults must be established as soon as possible in order to allow the growing child to attain his full potential of physical and mental development. Treatment of the older cretin does not reverse the mental retardation that has already occurred.

Thyroid preparations also may be used to suppress the secretion of thyrotropin, the thyroid-stimulating hormone produced by the anterior pituitary. This action may be beneficial in conditions such as simple nonendemic goiter, in which thyroid therapy may decrease the size of the goiter even though the abnormally functioning thyroid gland is secreting normal amounts of hormones, and in chronic lymphocytic (Hashimoto's) thyroiditis. In the latter disease, exogenous thyroid hormones act not only as replacement therapy for the hypothyroidism that often exists, but they also control the goiter by suppressing the secretion of thyrotropin.

The usefulness of thyroid hormones in granulomatous thyroiditis is not established. Their role in the management of thyroid gland carcinoma also is not clearly defined, but doses just below the toxic level have been recommended for treating carcinoma that may be thyrotropin-dependent. The thyroid hormones are not effective in ameliorating hyperthyroid exophthalmos. When the exophthalmos is severe, large doses of glucocorticoids are usually effective (see Chapter 35, Adrenal Corticosteroids).

Triiodothyronine (T_3), tetraiodothyronine (T_4), and radioactive iodine (^{131}I) are used in the T_3 and T_4 suppression tests to aid in the diagnosis of hyperthyroidism. In these tests, the thyroidal uptake of radioactive iodine is determined before and after the administration of triiodothyronine, which is more commonly used, or tetraiodothyronine. As a result of the inhibition of endogenous thyrotropic hormone (TSH) by these hormones, euthyroid persons usually exhibit a marked decrease in the thyroidal uptake of radioactive iodine, while those with Graves' disease do not. Possible explanations for this difference are (1) thyroid gland function in Graves' disease is increased despite suppression of thyrotropin secretion, perhaps by an abnormal stimulator such as the long-acting thyroid stimulator (LATS) or (2) the pituitary gland is insensitive to such suppressive agents.

The T_3 and T_4 suppression tests also have been used to evaluate the likelihood of remission in individuals with Graves' disease or toxic nodular goiter being treated with antithyroid agents. A test is performed at four- to six-month intervals after initiating therapy; if some degree of suppression of radioactive iodine uptake is noted, the prognosis for current or eventual remission is considered favorable.

Thyroid preparations have been given with some success to reduce the blood cholesterol concentration in euthyroid persons. However, an undesirable increase in calorigenic activity also may occur and cause attacks of angina pectoris or congestive failure in patients with heart disease or hypertension who, theoretically, would benefit from cholesterol-lowering agents. (See Chapter 13, Agents Used to Treat Hyperlipidemia.)

Thyroid hormone has been used inappropriately to effect weight loss in euthyroid obese individuals. Since it is necessary to induce a state of hyperthyroidism to accomplish this, thyroid hormone should not be used for this purpose.

Since hypothyroidism may be associated with abnormalities of reproductive function (amenorrhea, menorrhagia, dysmenorrhea, premenstrual tension, sterility, habitual abortion, and oligospermia), questionable logic has led to the widespread use of thyroid preparations in the treatment of these disorders. There is no evidence, however, that this form of treatment has any benefit unless the patient has hypothyroidism and, therefore, thyroid preparations should not be used.

In the absence of hypothyroidism, thyroid preparations are not effective in accelerating growth or treating skin conditions characterized by excessive dryness, or in mental depression marked by fatigue, lethargy, irritability, or nervousness. Vague symptoms suggestive of hypometabolism should not be treated indiscriminately with thyroid preparations.

Adverse Reactions and Precautions

Except in rare instances of intolerance, possibly due to hypersensitivity to the animal protein in whole thyroid, replacement doses of thyroid hormones do not cause untoward effects. Overdosage will produce signs and symptoms of hyperthyroidism; the amount of hormone that will produce hyperthyroidism varies widely from patient to patient.

Thyroid preparations should be used very cautiously in individuals with cardiovascular disease. The initial dose should be small and should be increased gradually until a state of euthyroidism is achieved or cardiovascular symptoms supervene. If cardiovascular symptoms appear, the dose may have to be reduced and suboptimal therapy accepted.

When hypothyroidism and chronic adrenocortical insufficiency exist concurrently, adequate amounts of cortisone [Cortone] or hydrocortisone [Cortef, Cortril, Hydrocortone] must be given along with thyroid hormone replacement therapy. This is necessary because thyroid hormones increase the metabolic turnover and degradation of adrenocortical hormones and may cause acute adrenocortical insufficiency.

INDIVIDUAL EVALUATIONS

THYROID

This preparation is the cleaned, dried, and powdered thyroid gland of domesticated animals used for food. The U.S.P. standards for all thyroid products from animal sources require that these preparations contain 0.17% to 0.23% iodine by weight in the organic combination peculiar to thyroid tissue. No requirement is made for metabolic potency, which is a function of the proportions of the metabolically active compounds present and which is determined by biological assay. Since the major portion of the iodine in thyroid is present in metabolically inert forms (iodide and iodotyrosines), a given preparation may satisfy the U.S.P. assay requirements and yet not contain sufficient amounts of the metabolically active forms (triiodothyronine and tetraiodothyronine) to produce the desired therapeutic effect. The most useful preparations of thyroid, therefore, are those which have been biologically assayed for metabolic activity. Thyroid is the least expensive marketed product having thyroid hormone activity, although all are relatively inexpensive.

Thyroid is used most commonly as replacement therapy in hypothyroidism. Other uses include the treatment of simple nonendemic goiter, chronic lymphocytic (Hashimoto's) thyroiditis, and thyrotropin-dependent carcinoma of the thyroid (see the Introductory Statement).

Adverse effects result principally from excessive doses. The drug should be used with caution and in reduced doses in patients with cardiovascular disease. (See the Introductory Statement.)

To avoid acute adrenocortical insufficiency in patients with secondary hypothyroidism and chronic adrenocortical insufficiency, a glucocorticoid must be administered concomitantly with thyroid therapy.

USUAL DOSAGE.—*Oral:* For mild hypothyroidism, *young and middle-aged adults*, the initial dose is 30 mg daily; this amount is increased by increments of 30 to 45 mg at two- to three-week intervals to a total of 75 mg daily; thereafter, the dose is increased by increments of 30 to 60 mg at two- to three-week intervals until the desired response is maintained. The maintenance dose ranges from 120 to 180 mg daily. *Older adults*, initially, 7.5 to 15 mg daily for four to six weeks; the dose is doubled at six- to eight-week intervals. *Children*, the initial dose is not more than 30 mg daily; this amount is increased by increments of 15 to 30 mg at intervals of one to three weeks to a total of 60 mg daily. Thereafter, the dose is increased by increments of 30 to 60 mg at intervals of one to three weeks until the desired response is maintained.

For myxedema coma, the use of levothyroxine or liothyronine intravenously is preferred (see individual evaluations). However, if these are not available, thyroid may be used in the following manner: *Adults*, initial dose of 120 to 240 mg is administered by gastric tube; subsequent doses are based on clinical response. The usual maintenance dose is 90 to 180 mg daily in a single morning dose (range, 60 to 240 mg daily).

For cretinism, *children*, initial dose is 15 mg daily, increased by increments of 30 to 60 mg at weekly intervals to a total dose of 60 to 75 mg daily. The dose is then increased by increments of 30 to 60 mg at intervals of one to three weeks until the desired response is maintained. Depending upon the age of the child, 60 to 150 mg daily usually is required.

PREPARATIONS.—*Oral:* Tablets 15, 30, 60, 120, 200, 250, and 300 mg; tablets (enteric-coated) 30, 60, 120, 200, and 300 mg.

AVAILABLE TRADEMARKS.—Thyrar (Armour), Thyrocrine (Lemmon). Drug also marketed by many manufacturers under generic name.

THYROGLOBULIN [Proloid]

Thyroglobulin is obtained from a purified extract of frozen hog thyroid. It meets the U.S.P. standard for iodine in thyroid and also is biologically assayed for metabolic activity. On a weight basis, the potency of this preparation is equal to that of thyroid; however, it is about twice as costly. The indications, adverse effects, and precautions for thyroglobulin are the same as those for thyroid (see the Introductory Statement).

USUAL DOSAGE.—*Oral:* Same doses as those for thyroid are given (see the evaluation on Thyroid).

PREPARATIONS.—Proloid (Warner-Chilcott). *Oral:* Tablets 15, 30, 60, 100, 120, 200, and 300 mg.

LEVOTHYROXINE SODIUM [Letter, Synthroid]

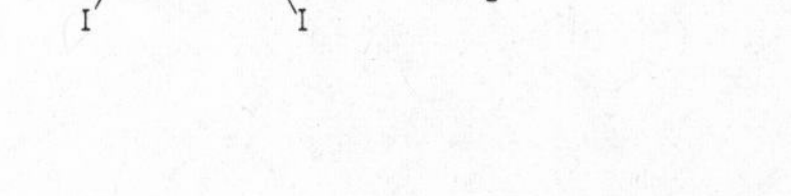

HO–(I,I-phenyl)–O–(I,I-phenyl)–$CH_2CH(NH_2)C(=O)ONa \cdot 5H_2O$

This synthetic sodium salt of the levorotatory isomer of tetraiodothyronine (thyroxine) has the same indications, adverse reactions, and precautions as thyroid (see the Introductory Statement). It is approximately twice as costly as thyroid. Levothyroxine also may be used intravenously in myxedema coma, although some physicians prefer the intravenous administration of liothyronine sodium as initial therapy in such life-threatening situations because of its more rapid onset of action.

USUAL DOSAGE.—

Oral: For hypothyroidism, *young and middle-aged adults,* initially, 0.05 to 0.1 mg daily; this amount is increased by increments of 0.05 to 0.1 mg at two- to three-week intervals until the desired response is maintained. For severe hypothyroidism, the initial daily dose is 0.025 mg; this amount is increased by increments of 0.025 mg at two- to three-week intervals to a total of 0.1 mg daily. Further increases by increments of 0.05 to 0.1 mg may be made at the same intervals until the desired response is maintained. *Older adults,* initially, 0.0125 to 0.025 mg daily for six weeks; this amount is then doubled every six to eight weeks until the desired response is maintained. *Children,* the initial dose should not exceed 0.05 mg; thereafter, the same regimen is followed as for young and middle-aged adults.

For cretinism, *children,* initial dose is 0.025 mg daily; this amount is increased by increments of 0.025 mg at weekly intervals to a total daily dose of 0.1 mg. The dose is then increased by increments of 0.05 to 0.1 mg at intervals of one to three weeks until the desired response is maintained.

Intravenous: For myxedema coma, *adults,* 0.5 mg. The drug is given orally for maintenance.

PREPARATIONS.—

Letter (Armour). *Oral:* Tablets 0.025, 0.05, 0.1, 0.2, 0.3, and 0.5 mg.

Synthroid (Flint).

Oral: Tablets 0.025, 0.05, 0.1, 0.15, 0.2, 0.3, and 0.5 mg.

Injection: Powder (for reconstitution) 0.5 mg.

ADDITIONAL TRADEMARK.—Titroid (Century). Drug also marketed under generic name.

SIMILAR PREPARATION.—Thyroxin Fraction (Squibb).

LIOTHYRONINE SODIUM [Cytomel]

I I NH₂
HO–⟨ring⟩–O–⟨ring⟩–$CH_2CHCOONa$
I

This drug is the synthetic sodium salt of the levorotatory isomer of triiodothyronine. The indications, untoward effects, and precautions of this short-acting drug are the same as those of thyroid, but a longer-acting drug is preferred for most purposes (see the Introductory Statement). It is about four times more costly than thyroid. Some physicians consider liothyronine the drug of choice for intravenous use in myxedema coma because it has a rapid onset and short duration of action, which facilitates the adjustments in dosage often required. Others use levothyroxine sodium as the drug of choice in the therapy of myxedema coma. Although liothyronine sodium is not available commercially in a form suitable for intravenous use, this form will be supplied by the manufacturer upon request.

USUAL DOSAGE.—

Oral: For mild hypothyroidism, *young and middle-aged adults,* initially 25 μg daily; this amount is increased by increments of 12.5 to 25 μg at intervals of one to three weeks until the desired response is maintained. For severe hypothyroidism, initially 5 μg daily. This amount is increased by increments of 5 to 12.5 μg at intervals of one to three weeks until a daily dose of 25 μg is reached; thereafter, this amount is increased by increments of 12.5 to 25 μg at two- to three-week intervals until the desired response is maintained. *Older adults,* initially, 2.5 to 5 μg daily for three to six weeks; the amount is then doubled every six weeks until the desired response is maintained. *Children,* the initial daily dose is 5 μg daily; this amount is increased by increments of no more than 5 μg daily at weekly intervals until the desired response is maintained.

For cretinism, *children,* initial dose is 5 μg daily; the amount is increased by increments of 5 μg at weekly intervals to a total daily dose of 25 μg. Thereafter, the amount is increased by increments of 12.5 to 25 μg at intervals of one to three weeks until the desired response is maintained.

Intravenous: For myxedema coma, *adults,* 10 to 25 μg every eight to twelve hours. The drug is given orally for maintenance.

PREPARATIONS.—Cytomel (Smith Kline & French).

Oral: Tablets 5, 25, and 50 μg.

Injection: Powder (for solution) 114 μg/ml. Not commercially available; manufacturer will supply kit upon request for use in myxedema coma.

LIOTRIX [Euthroid, Thyrolar]

Liotrix is a mixture of synthetic levothyroxine sodium and synthetic liothyronine sodium in a ratio of 4:1, respectively. Indications, adverse reactions, and precautions are the same as those for thyroid (see the Introductory Statement). Unlike some thyroid preparations of biological origin, liotrix closely reproduces the effect of endogenous thyroid hormone secretion without variation in potency. Although it is highly controversial, some authorities believe that, in contrast to the pure synthetic thyroid hormones, liotrix produces laboratory test results (eg, PBI) that are more consistent with the clinical response of the patient. This preparation is about four times more costly than thyroid.

USUAL DOSAGE.—*Oral:* For hypothyroidism, *young and middle-aged adults,* initially, one tablet daily of either a preparation containing in each tablet 30 μg of levothyroxine sodium and 7.5 μg of liothyronine sodium [Euthroid] or 25 μg of levothyroxine sodium and 6.25 μg of liothyronine sodium [Thyrolar]; depending upon the response, the dose is increased by one tablet every two weeks. For maintenance, tablets that conveniently provide between 50 μg and 180 μg of levothyroxine sodium and between 6.25 and 45 μg of liothyronine sodium daily are given. *Older adults,* initially one-fourth to one-half the amount given to young and middle-aged adults; the dose is doubled at six- to eight-week intervals until the desired response is maintained. *Children,* dosage is the same as that for adults, with adjustment in dosage made at intervals of two weeks. The final maintenance dose may be greater in the child than in the adult.

PREPARATIONS.—

Euthroid (Warner-Chilcott). *Oral:* Tablets Euthroid-½, -1, -2, and -3 containing, respectively, 30, 60, 120, and 180 μg of levothyroxine sodium, and 7.5, 15, 30, and 45 μg of liothyronine sodium.

Thyrolar (Armour). *Oral:* Tablets Thyrolar-½, -1, -2, and -3 containing, respectively, 25, 50, 100, and 150 μg of levothyroxine sodium, and 6.25, 12.5, 25, and 37.5 μg of liothyronine sodium.

MIXTURES

The thyroid hormones should be used only when one of the established indications for their use exists (see Introductory Statement). However, they continue to be included in preparations designed for the treatment of various conditions in which they have no proven value. A listing of such preparations appears below only to acknowledge their availability.

Andro-Medicone (Medicone): Each tablet contains thyroid extract 5.5 mg, strychnine sulfate 1 mg, and yohimbine hydrochloride 5.5 mg.

Nobese (Durst): Each capsule contains thyroid 195 mg, phenobarbital 15 mg, amphetamine sulfate 15 mg, atropine sulfate 1.36 mg, and aloin 15 mg; each half-strength tablet contains thyroid 98 mg, phenobarbital 7.5 mg, amphetamine sulfate, 7.5 mg, atropine sulfate 0.18 mg, and aloin 7.5 mg.

Obestat (Lemmon): Each timed-release capsule or tablet contains thyroid 150 mg, methamphetamine hydrochloride 10 mg, and amobarbital 60 mg.

Perke-Three (Ascher): Each capsule contains thyroid 195 mg, amphetamine sulfate 15 mg, atropine sulfate 0.36 mg, aloin 16 mg, and phenobarbital 16 mg.

Thyrobex (McNeil): Each tablet contains thyroid 30 mg, desiccated liver (undefatted) 250 mg, thiamine mononitrate 1 mg, riboflavin 1.2 mg, niacinamide 10 mg, and cyanocobalamin 1 μg.

Vitaroid (Warren-Teed): Each tablet contains thyroid 30 mg, vitamin D 200 units, ascorbic acid 15 mg, riboflavin 1 mg, thiamine hydrochloride 3 mg, and niacinamide 5 mg.

ANTITHYROID AGENTS

The treatment of hyperthyroidism is aimed at decreasing the activity of the thyroid gland with drugs, radiation, or surgery. The criteria for the choice of treatment vary and therapy must be individualized. In general, sodium iodide I^{131} is given most commonly, and surgery is selected as the alternative. Antithyroid drugs usually are reserved to prepare patients for surgery, to treat thyrotoxic crises, to treat hyperthyroidism associated with active ophthalmopathy, or are given before or after radioactive iodine treatment. Roentgen therapy is used infrequently for special situations.

At one time iodine was the only substance available for the management of hyperthyroidism. Its activity is most likely due to its ability to inhibit the release of thyroid hormone from the gland immediately. Unfortunately, its effectiveness usually is only partial and frequently is not sustained (iodine escape). Therefore, use of iodine as an antithyroid drug is now limited to special circumstances: it is administered to treat the potentially fatal thyrotoxic crisis (thyroid storm or thyroid crisis), and to decrease the vascularity of the thyroid gland prior to surgery.

The prototype of the antithyroid drugs in use today is propylthiouracil. It has replaced its parent compound, thiouracil, which is more toxic. Propylthiouracil, a thioamide, inhibits the synthesis of thyroid hormone but, in usual doses, does not inactivate or interfere with the action of thyroid hormone that was previously formed and stored in the gland. Therefore, its effects do not appear until this supply has been utilized, and several days or weeks may elapse before signs of decreased thyroid activity become apparent. Since patients with severe hyperthyroidism dissipate their stores rapidly, they may respond to therapy more quickly than those with mild hyperthyroidism. The drug does not have a permanent effect upon the thyroid gland but it inhibits hormone synthesis and secretion until a spontaneous remission occurs during the course of the disease.

The best results are obtained in women during the childbearing years, particularly those with mild disease and a relatively small goiter. The duration of treatment necessary to secure a prolonged remission may vary from six months to three years, with an average duration of one year. A thyroid suppression test (see the Introductory Statement to the section on Thyroid Hormones) or trial withdrawal of the drug can determine whether a remission actually has occurred. Prolonged remission has been reported in about 50% of patients who received long-term antithyroid therapy (follow-up period of four years or more).

Propylthiouracil frequently increases the vascularity and size of the thyroid gland during treatment. Some clinicians believe that the prognosis for prolonged remission with antithyroid agents will be poor if glandular enlargement does not stabilize or decrease after euthyroidism has been achieved during drug therapy. Exophthalmos also may increase during therapy, and, if severe, may be treated with glucocorticoids.

If signs of hypothyroidism occur during treatment with propylthiouracil, the dose should be reduced or the drug temporarily discontinued. It also may be necessary to administer supplementary doses of thyroid hormones temporarily.

Methimazole [Tapazole] also is commonly used to treat hyperthyroidism; it is related chemically to propylthiouracil and has a similar action and use. On a weight basis, this drug is at least ten times more potent than propylthiouracil although neither drug has an overwhelming advantage over the other. Two other antithyroid drugs with a similar chemistry, activity, and use are carbimazole and methylthiouracil; these agents have had only limited trial in this country.

Potassium perchlorate occasionally may be of value in patients who are unable to tolerate the other drugs.

Guanethidine [Ismelin], reserpine, and propranolol are useful adjuncts in hyperthyroidism and thyrotoxic crisis. They do not affect the hyperactivity of the thyroid gland but do decrease the accompanying increase in adrenergic activity. This relieves the tachycardia, palpitation, and hypertension and may help prevent congestive heart failure (see also Chapter 6, Antihypertensive Agents).

Sodium iodide I^{131} [Oriodide-131, Iodotope I-131, Theriodide-131] has become the drug most commonly used in the treatment of hyperthyroidism. Since radioactive iodine accumulates in thyroid tissue, a single adequate dose cures most patients with Graves' disease by partially destroying the thyroid gland. Repeated doses may be required to cure those with severe disease or large goiters. In toxic nodular goiter, the initial dose may be considerably greater than that used in Graves' disease and additional doses are needed more frequently. It has been recommended that severely hyperthyroid patients be brought to a euthyroid state with propylthiouracil or methimazole before radioactive iodine is given; however, the antithyroid drug must be discontinued two to three days before treatment to avoid interference with uptake of radioactive iodine. Drug therapy may be resumed approximately one week after administration of radioactive iodine to hasten the return to euthyroidism.

Radioactive iodine also is used in the treatment of metastatic thyroid carcinoma. However, only patients whose lesions have an affinity for iodine (primarily follicular carcinoma) benefit from such treatment. Occasionally it has been used as a last resort to decrease thyroid activity in euthyroid patients with intractable angina pectoris.

Radioactive iodine is used in tracer amounts for the evaluation of thyroid function and pathology. All of the procedures are virtually without hazard because the tracer doses are so small (40 microcuries=0.0003 μg of iodine) that they produce no iodine or radiation effects on the thyroid. The procedures used are called radioactive iodine uptake (RAI), TSH stimulation test, triiodothyronine (T_3) suppression test, T_3 test, thyroxine (T_4) displacement test, conversion ratio and 72 hour PBI ^{131} thyroidal clearance, and ^{131}I thyroid scan (also used are ^{123}I, ^{125}I, and ^{99}mTc pertechnetate). A description of the rationale, methodology, and interpretation of these procedures is beyond the scope of this book and the reader is referred to Werner, S.C. and Ingbar, S.H. (eds): *The Thyroid*, 3rd edition, New York: Harper & Row, Publishers, Inc., 1971.

When surgery is chosen to treat hyperthyroidism, the disease first should be controlled by propylthiouracil or methimazole in order to avoid a thyrotoxic crisis. About ten days before surgery, iodine (as Strong Iodine Solution, U.S.P. [Lugol's solution], potassium iodide, or sodium iodide) should be added to the regimen to promote involution of the thyroid and reduce its vascularity, thus reducing the tendency toward excessive bleeding during surgery.

Subtotal thyroidectomy cures a reasonably high percentage of patients with hyperthyroidism. The principal drawbacks to surgery, in addition to operative morbidity and mortality, are the complications that can occur (eg, permanent hypothyroidism, hypoparathyroidism, and damage to the recurrent laryngeal nerve).

Adverse Reactions and Precautions

The adverse effects of iodine administration (iodism) usually include the unpleasant (brassy) taste of iodine, burning in the mouth, sore gums, salivation, acute rhinitis, sialadenitis, conjunctival injection with edema of the eyelids, frontal headache, acneiform rash, and gastric and respiratory tract irritation. Hypersensitivity reactions, which occur only rarely, are manifested by fever, eosinophilia, jaundice, pruritus, angioedema, multiple cutaneous and mucous membrane hemorrhages, serum sickness-like syndrome, bullous ioderma (sometimes fatal), and bronchospasm. Thrombotic thrombocytopenic purpura, nodular nonsuppurative panniculitis (Weber-Christian disease), and collagen-like disorders have been reported, but a causal relationship is unproved.

Hypersensitivity reactions are relatively uncommon with propylthiouracil. Agranulocytosis is the most serious reaction and requires immediate cessation of therapy and institution of supportive measures. Its incidence is approximately 0.2% and appears to be related to duration of therapy; most cases occur in the first two months of treatment, with a gradual decline thereafter. Relying on periodic blood cell counts to detect agranulocytosis is not warranted because of the rapidity with which this complication usually develops. Patients should be instructed to report the occurrence of sore throat or fever immediately, for these symptoms signal the development of agranulocytosis. Milder leukopenias occur more frequently, but are not necessarily an indication for discontinuing therapy or reducing the dose if they are monitored by periodic blood cell counts and do not become severe.

Rash, commonly urticarial or papular, occurs in approximately 3% of patients taking propylthiouracil. It can be severe but usually is quite mild. Patients occasionally experience nausea, abdominal discomfort, arthralgia, headache, dizziness, paresthesia, loss of taste, and drowsiness. Hair loss, depigmentation of the hair, recurrent keratitis, and conjunctival disorders also are seen.

Uncommon reactions include drug fever, sialadenopathy, hepatitis, nephritis, and syndromes resembling connective tissue disorders. These are presumably caused by a polyarteritis. Hypoprothrombinemia and factor VII (proconvertin) deficiency have occurred and can be corrected by parenteral administration of vitamin K.

Propylthiouracil may be given to pregnant women with relative safety, although the dosage should be the smallest amount necessary to be effective (preferably less than 300 mg daily) and particular care must be taken to avoid hypothyroidism. Because the drug can cross the placental barrier, excessive doses, especially during the last trimester of pregnancy, can cause simple nonendemic goiter in the newborn infant. Although evidence is not conclusive, the concomitant administration of thyroid hormones may help to ensure an adequate supply of thyroid hormone to the fetus and thus prevent goiter. Since propylthiouracil is excreted in breast milk, mothers taking the drug should not nurse their babies.

In general, the adverse reactions of methimazole [Tapazole] are similar to those of propylthiouracil. There is some indication that the incidence of agranulocytosis is lower with methimazole, but that the overall incidence of adverse reactions is higher; however, these differences have not been established conclusively. Carbimazole may produce fewer adverse reactions than methimazole, although this has not been substantiated definitely, and methylthiouracil has been reported to cause more adverse reactions than methimazole or propylthiouracil. The incidence of adverse reactions to all antithyroid drugs is dose related: the higher the dose, the greater the incidence of adverse reactions.

Cross sensitivity sometimes exists between the drugs, although it is unusual. Since some mild reactions (eg, slight rash) may disappear spontaneously with continued treatment, opinion is divided on whether to change drugs if a minor adverse reaction occurs. On the other hand, if a severe reaction necessitates withdrawal of one drug, the danger of a recurrence would exist if a related agent is substituted.

For adverse reactions caused by potassium perchlorate, see the individual evaluation.

Radioactive iodine may induce several temporary but potentially serious reactions in the first few days or weeks following therapy. The area over the thyroid gland may become sore as a result of radiation thyroiditis, but the soreness usually disappears when analgesics are given. Occasionally an exacerbation of hyperthyroidism may occur following treatment; this complication is of special significance in patients with severe thyrotoxic heart disease. An unusual but more serious complication, particularly in patients with huge goiters, is an acute swelling of the thyroid gland that has, in very rare instances, produced asphyxiation. (See also the evaluation on Sodium Iodide I^{131}.)

Permanent hypothyroidism apparently is a much more common complication of therapy with radioactive iodine than was previously thought. The incidence appears to be about 10% in the first year, with an increase of approximately 2% to 3% each year following treatment; follow-up studies of ten years or longer do not reveal any evidence of a plateau. Eventually, then, most treated patients develop hypothyroidism and require replacement therapy with thyroid hormones. Therefore, long-term observation is needed to avoid the deleterious effects of unrecognized hypothyroidism.

The concern about possible thyroid carcinoma developing in later years from radioactive iodine given to young adults has now been almost eliminated, although it still exists for patients less than 15 years of age. There also is the theoretical possibility of adverse genetic effects on women of reproductive age who are given radioactive iodine. Pregnant women and nursing mothers should not receive radioactive iodine.

The incidence of acute leukemia following radioactive iodine therapy has been reported to be higher than would be expected in the general population, particularly if the total dose given was relatively large, but this has not been established conclusively.

The potentially fatal thyrotoxic crisis that may occur in hyperthyroid patients who are inadequately prepared for surgery or who experience trauma, infection, or emotional upset has become much less common since the advent of antithyroid drugs. Thyrotoxic crisis is manifested by irritability or apathy, followed by high fever, extreme tachycardia, profound asthenia, possible high output heart failure, and, finally, syncope and coma. Treatment consists of the administration of methimazole or propylthiouracil and iodine as well as use of hypothermic procedures, and administration of fluids and adrenal corticosteroids, guanethidine, reserpine, or propranolol; if heart failure occurs, appropriate treatment should be instituted.

Heart disease is a common complication of hyperthyroidism, especially in the elderly. If congestive heart failure occurs, it must be treated with conventional methods. However, digitalis preparations are less effective than usual in these patients unless the hyperthyroidism is corrected.

INDIVIDUAL EVALUATIONS

POTASSIUM IODIDE
SODIUM IODIDE
STRONG IODINE SOLUTION

Iodine is commonly administered as Strong Iodine Solution, U.S.P., or Potassium Iodide Solution, N.F. Solutions of sodium iodide also are used occasionally. Iodine is used to prepare hyperthyroid patients for thyroidectomy and, with an antithyroid drug, in the treatment of thyrotoxic crisis.

Acute poisoning is relatively rare and is characterized by vomiting, abdominal pain, diarrhea, and gastroenteritis. When poisoning is fatal, the cause is usually aspiration pneumonia, corrosive gastritis, or asphyxiation from edema of the glottis. Symptoms of iodism are more common (see the introduction to this section).

USUAL DOSAGE.—*Oral: Adults and children*, to prepare hyperthyroid patients for thyroidectomy, 6 mg of iodine daily usually provides maximal therapeutic effect in about two to three weeks. However, the unexplained common practice is to administer enough Strong Iodine Solution, U.S.P. or Potassium Iodide Solution, N.F. to achieve a total daily dose of approximately 500 mg of iodine. For treatment of thyrotoxic crisis, an antithyroid drug is administered initially, followed in a few hours by doses of iodine as described above and other appropriate agents and procedures as described in the section on Adverse Reactions and Precautions.

PREPARATIONS.—

Potassium Iodide, U.S.P. *Oral:* Crystals and granules (bulk).

Potassium Iodide Solution, N.F. *Oral:* Solution.

Sodium Iodide, U.S.P. *Oral:* Granules and powder (bulk).

Strong Iodine Solution, U.S.P. *Oral:* Solution containing 5% iodine and 10% potassium iodide.

Forms marketed under generic name; Strong Iodine Solution, U.S.P. marketed under the name Lugol's Solution.

PROPYLTHIOURACIL

$CH_3CH_2CH_2$ H N S NH O

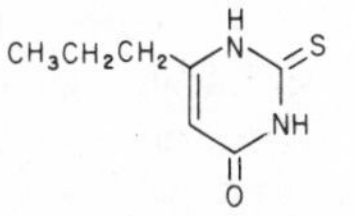

Propylthiouracil, the prototype of the antithyroid drugs, is used for the management of hyperthyroidism associated with active ophthalmopathy; for preoperative preparation of the thyroidectomy patient; and in the treatment of thyrotoxic crisis. It also is given before or after the radioactive iodine treatment of hyperthyroidism. (See also the introduction to this section.) Propylthiouracil inhibits the synthesis of thyroxine, probably by preventing the iodination of tyrosine. Because of its short duration of action, the drug must be given frequently to achieve maximal therapeutic effect. The duration of treatment for hyperthyroidism ranges from six months to three years.

The most frequent adverse reaction is rash, and the most serious is agranulocytosis. There are inconclusive reports that agranulocytosis occurs more frequently with propylthiouracil than with methimazole but that the total incidence of adverse reactions is greater with methimazole. Cross sensitivity to other thioamide derivatives may occur in susceptible patients. During pregnancy, the minimal effective dose should be administered to avoid effects on the fetal thyroid gland and to prevent deleterious effects of maternal hypothyroidism. Postpartum patients should not nurse their babies.

USUAL DOSAGE.—*Oral:* For management of hyperthyroidism, *adults*, initially, 200 to 300 mg daily in divided doses every eight hours; some patients require as much as 900 mg daily for control. These doses are given until the patient is euthyroid; for maintenance, usually 50 to 75 mg (range, 50 to 450 mg) is given daily in two or three doses. *Children 10 years of age and over*, initially, 150 to 300 mg daily in divided doses every eight hours. The usual maintenance dose is 100 mg daily divided into two doses at 12-hour intervals, but some children may require up to 450 mg daily. *Children 6 to 10 years*, initially 50 to 150 mg daily in divided doses every eight hours.

For preoperative preparation of the thyroidectomy patient, the drug is given to *adults and children* in same doses used for hyperthyroidism until the patient is euthyroid; iodine, in a dose of 6 mg daily, is then added to the regimen for 10 days before surgery.

For treatment of thyrotoxic crisis, *adults and children* are given same doses as described above, followed in a few hours by the dose of iodine (see the evaluation on the iodine salts).

PREPARATIONS.— Propylthiouracil, U.S.P. *Oral:* Tablets 50 mg. Drug marketed under generic name.

METHIMAZOLE [Tapazole]

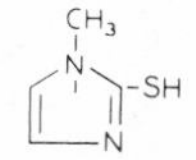

CH_3 N SH N

Methimazole has the same actions, indications, and adverse reactions as propylthiouracil (see the introduction to this section and the evaluation on Propylthiouracil). The drug is approximately ten times more potent than propylthiouracil, but has no distinct advantage over it. The onset of action, degree of response, and incidence of adverse reactions increase with dosage. Cross sensitivity to other thioamide derivatives may occur in susceptible patients.

USUAL DOSAGE.—*Oral: Adults*, the initial daily dose is 15 mg for mild hyperthyroidism, 30 to 40 mg for moderately severe hyperthyroidism, and 60 mg or more for severe hyperthyroidism. These amounts are given in divided doses every eight hours, and are continued until the patient is euthyroid. For maintenance, the amounts are reduced to 5 to 20 mg daily in two or three doses. *Children 6 to 10 years of age*, initially, 5 to 15 mg daily administered in divided doses every eight hours.

For preoperative preparation of the thyroidectomy patient, the drug is given to *adults and children* in same doses used for hyperthyroidism until the patient is euthyroid; iodine, in a dose of 6 mg daily, is then added to regimen for 10 days before surgery.

For treatment of thyrotoxic crisis, same doses as described above are given to *adults and children*, followed in a few hours by the dose of iodine (see the evaluation on the iodine salts).

PREPARATIONS.—Tapazole (Lilly). *Oral:* Tablets 5 and 10 mg.

METHYLTHIOURACIL

This thioamide derivative has had limited use in the United States but is widely used abroad. The actions and indications for its use are similar to propylthiouracil (see the introduction to this section and the evaluation on Propylthiouracil). Adverse reactions are qualitatively similar to those caused by propylthiouracil but their incidence is higher.

USUAL DOSAGE.—*Oral:* For management of hyperthyroidism, *adults*, 50 mg four times daily.

PREPARATIONS.—Methylthiouracil, N.F. *Oral:* No pharmaceutical dosage form available; compounding necessary for prescription. Drug marketed under generic name.

POTASSIUM PERCHLORATE

Potassium perchlorate is the agent of last choice among antithyroid drugs because it can cause fatal aplastic anemia. Its use is limited to the treatment of hyperthyroidism in patients who are unable to tolerate or do not respond to other available forms of therapy. Its thyroid-inhibiting activity depends upon the ability of the perchlorate anion to prevent uptake and cause discharge of iodide by the thyroid gland. The drug acts rapidly and has a short duration of action (only a few hours). Concomitant administration of iodine neutralizes its effect.

Control of hyperthyroidism preferably is accomplished with large doses, but adverse effects are dose-related and include gastric irritation, drug fever, rash, lymphadenopathy, fatal aplastic anemia, nephrotic syndrome, and agranulocytosis. With minimal effective doses, the overall incidence of adverse reactions may be lower than with equally effective doses of propylthiouracil or methimazole.

USUAL DOSAGE.—*Oral:* For hyperthyroidism, *adults*, initially, 1 g daily in four divided doses until the disease is controlled; for maintenance, 200 to 500 mg daily in two or three doses. *Children*, initially, 500 to 750 mg daily in three or four doses until the disease is controlled; for maintenance, 150 to 400 mg daily in two or three doses.

PREPARATIONS.—Potassium Perchlorate. *Oral:* No pharmaceutical dosage form available; compounding necessary for prescription. Drug marketed in bulk form under generic name.

SODIUM IODIDE I^{131} [Iodotope I-131, Oriodide-131, Theriodide-131]

This radioactive isotope of iodine accumulates in the thyroid gland, as does nonradioactive iodine. Most of its biological activity is attributed to ionizing beta radiation that destroys functional and regenerative capacities of thyroid cells within weeks. This isotope also emits gamma radiation which contributes little to its biological activity but is useful in providing an accurate means for determining the amount of isotope uptake.

Radioactive iodine is the most commonly used agent for the treatment of hyperthyroidism. Recurrence of hyperthyroidism after successful sodium iodine I^{131} therapy is very low. It is also used frequently to evaluate thyroid function (see the introduction to this section). Occasionally it has been used in the treatment of intractable angina pectoris and thyroid carcinoma with or without metastases.

Early adverse reactions include mild pain and tenderness in the thyroid area, an acute swelling of the thyroid gland, dysphagia, radiation thyroiditis, exacerbation of thyrotoxicosis (occasionally fatal), and bone marrow depression (with large doses). Adverse reactions reported months or years after treatment include thyroid carcinoma; leukemias, particularly acute forms; chromosomal aberrations; and clinical and subclinical hypoparathyroidism. However, a causal relationship between thyroid carcinoma and leukemia and sodium iodide I ^{131} therapy has not been established. The incidence of hypothyroidism varies between 30% and 70% within 10 to 20 years.

Sodium iodide I ^{131} is contraindicated during pregnancy and lactation; in large toxic nodular goiters, especially those causing mechanical obstruction; and in severe thyrotoxic heart disease.

For additional information on adverse reactions and precautions, see the introduction to this section.

USUAL DOSAGE.—*Oral, Intravenous:* For treatment of suitable patients with Graves' disease and hyperthyroidism, the initial dose for *adults* is calculated on the basis of percentage uptake of radioactive iodine by the thyroid, estimated weight of thyroid tissue, and desired retention of 80 microcuries of radiation per gram of thyroid tissue for the first 50 g of thyroid tissue, and 40 microcuries of radiation per gram of additional thyroid tissue. The total calculated dose may be administered as a single dose or it may be divided into two or more doses given six to eight weeks apart. The usual dose is 4,000 to 10,000 microcuries. If the first treatment is not successful, retreatment with a smaller dose is desirable after a suitable interval (approximately three months). Retreatment doses are based on size and uptake of the gland.

For treatment of suitable patients with toxic nodular goiter and hyperthyroidism, the dose for *adults* is determined as for patients with Graves' disease and hyperthyroidism, but the amount generally is increased by 50%. Two months should elapse before a subsequent dose is considered.

For treatment of thyroid carcinoma and metastases, *adults*, the dose must be individualized.

PREPARATIONS.—

Iodotope I-131 (Squibb).

Oral: Capsules (therapeutic) 6, 7, 8, 9, and 10 millicuries; solution (therapeutic) 1 to 200 millicuries.

Oriodide-131 (Abbott). *Oral:* Solution (therapeutic) 1 to 200 millicuries.

Theriodide-131 (Abbott). *Oral:* Capsules (therapeutic) 1, 3, and 5 millicuries.

Drug also marketed by other manufacturers under generic name.

Chapter 40

ANTIDIURETICS

Antidiuretic agents are used to treat patients with diabetes insipidus. Neurohypophyseal diabetes insipidus occurs uncommonly and is caused by deficient antidiuretic hormone (vasopressin, ADH). Less than one-quarter of the total cases are idiopathic; familial cases are rare. Head trauma, neurosurgery, neoplasms (primary and metastatic), infections, and other factors which damage the hypothalamus or posterior pituitary cause acquired neurohypophyseal diabetes insipidus. Nephrogenic (vasopressin-resistant) diabetes insipidus is a rare hereditary disorder which most frequently affects males. In this disease, the epithelium of the collecting ducts does not respond to antidiuretic hormone, although the hormone is present in normal amounts.

Antidiuretic hormone is synthesized in the hypothalamic nuclei and transported down the neurohypophyseal tract to the posterior pituitary, where it is stored. Osmoreceptors in the hypothalamic nuclei, which are sensitive to changes in extracellular electrolyte concentration, regulate its release into the blood. In the presence of an increased solute concentration of the serum, ADH conserves fluid by making the renal tubular epithelium more permeable to water so that large amounts of water and very little solute are reabsorbed. Physiologic stimuli for the secretion of ADH, other than hypertonicity of extracellular fluid, are a marked reduction in plasma volume, which is monitored by thoracic cardiovascular stretch receptors and baroreceptors; pain and certain emotional states; and various pharmacologic agents (eg, nicotine, morphine, barbiturates). Alcohol inhibits the release of ADH.

Neurohypophyseal diabetes insipidus most commonly is treated with one of several preparations containing natural or synthetic antidiuretic hormone. When the aqueous solution of vasopressin is given intramuscularly or subcutaneously, its effect is brief and frequent administration is required. This brief duration of action makes vasopressin injection useful in initiating therapy following neurosurgery or accidental head injuries and in unconscious patients, for it is possible to control fluid balance precisely. Topical nasal application of powder (posterior pituitary) or spray (vasopressin injection [Pitressin], lypressin [Diapid]) is convenient for short-term administration and the degree of absorption may be adequate to control mild symptoms. For more effective control, the long-acting vasopressin tannate injection [Pitressin Tannate] in oil is given intramuscularly. (See the individual evaluations.)

The oral hypoglycemic sulfonylurea, chlorpropamide [Diabinese], has an antidiuretic effect in patients with neurohypophyseal diabetes insipidus. Relatively short-term studies showed that complete control was attained with chlorpropamide in about one-half of patients with neurohypophyseal disease. Considerable improvement occurred in most of the remaining patients; full control was attained with the addition of a thiazide to the regimen. Experience with chlorpropamide indicates that when used alone for neurohypophyseal diabetes insipidus, it is as effective as the thiazides and does not have the undesirable effect of producing hypokalemia. The antidiuretic action of chlorpropamide has a slow onset and appears to be cumulative.

Results of current studies indicate that chlorpropamide is more effective in patients with less severe disease in whom, presumably, there are small amounts of circulating ADH. This observation supports the suggestion that chlorpropamide reduces free-water clearance by increasing the sensitivity of the renal tubular epithelium to inadequate amounts of ADH, or by providing a central stimulus for increasing the level of circulating ADH from a damaged hypothalamic-neurohypophyseal axis. This drug has not been effective in patients with nephrogenic diabetes insipidus.

Dosage of chlorpropamide, as used experimentally, ranges from 50 mg to 500 mg daily; 250 mg twice daily is commonly administered. Chlorpropamide reduces fasting blood glucose levels in patients with diabetes insipidus and significant, symptomatic hypoglycemia occurs occasionally. In these patients, the dosage should be reduced and a thiazide may be added to the regimen. The effects of long-term chlorpropamide therapy on the β-cells of the normal pancreas in these patients is not known. (See also Chapter 12, Agents Used to Treat Hyperglycemia.)

Thiazide diuretics are effective in the treatment of nephrogenic diabetes insipidus, which is not responsive to antidiuretic hormone or chlorpropamide. Other natriuretic agents, such as ethacrynic acid [Edecrin], also have been tried with reported success. Thiazides also are used in patients with the neurohypophyseal form of the disease who, because of allergic or other reactions, cannot tolerate ADH in any form. The mechanism by which natriuretic diuretic agents produce an antidiuretic effect is not entirely understood, but it is presumed that they indirectly reduce urinary volume by depleting body sodium. Data indicate that they also may potentiate the action of ADH. The thiazides generally reduce the urinary volume in diabetes insipidus by about 30% to 50%; they usually will not decrease the volume to normal except in patients with only slight to moderate polyuria. They may be satisfactory as sole therapy in vasopressin-deficient patients with a daily urine volume of 6 liters or less. The thiazides are given in the same dosage as that used to control edema, and their effectiveness is enhanced by restricting the intake of sodium. The most common untoward effect is hypokalemia. (See Chapter 7, Diuretics, for dosage and adverse reactions.)

Adverse Reactions and Precautions

Water retention and hyponatremia have been observed with all forms of antidiuretic therapy. When the renal excretion of water is impaired, the expanded extracellular volume causes dilution of solutes and also induces sodium diuresis and a negative sodium balance. Signs and symptoms of water intoxication (ie, headache, nausea and vomiting, confusion, lethargy, coma, convulsions) apparently occur as a result of movement of fluid from the extracellular to the intracellular space. This potential danger exists when patients drink an excessive amount of water or require intravenous therapy. Water restriction, administration of sodium chloride, and reduction in dosage of the antidiuretic are indicated in these patients.

Other adverse reactions result from the effects of ADH on vascular smooth muscle. Although the official U.S.P. name for ADH, vasopressin, implies primarily vasoconstrictor activity, only doses much larger than those usually given in the treatment of diabetes insipidus will cause facial pallor and increased blood pressure. Even with large doses, the elevation of blood pressure in normal conscious subjects is slight (10 to 20 mm Hg) and of brief duration.

Vasopressin may cause significant constriction of the coronary arteries, and this effect may be quite serious and even fatal in patients with disease of the coronary arteries. Chest pain, electrocardiographic evidence of myocardial ischemia, and myocardial infarction have been reported after injection of 20 units of vasopressin; a latent period of several hours may precede chest pain. Patients with ischemic heart disease should be given no more than the minimal dose of vasopressin needed to control polyuria. Sometimes even a small dose will cause increased cardiac symptoms in these patients; if this occurs, intake of protein and salt should be restricted, and chlorpropamide [Diabinese] or thiazides should be used instead to control the polyuria.

Large doses of vasopressin (5 to 20 units) stimulate smooth muscle in the gastrointestinal tract and may produce nausea, abdominal cramps, diarrhea, and the urge to defecate. Uterine cramps also may occur after large doses, and menorrhagia has been reported, although the purified pituitary extracts of vasopressin and the synthetic lypressin have very little oxytocic activity. Posterior pituitary injection and posterior pituitary (powder) have significant oxytocic activity and are contraindicated during pregnancy.

Irritation and inflammation of the nasal mucous membranes after the local application of posterior pituitary (powder) is common, and allergic respiratory symptoms such as wheezing, cough, dyspnea, and asthmatic attacks may occur after each dose. Allergic reactions after administration of vasopressin are less common but have included urticaria, disseminated neurodermatitis, fever, flushing, wheezing, and dyspnea. Unexplained shock (which can be treated successfully with epinephrine) has been observed shortly after injection of vasopressin, possibly because of hypersensitivity to foreign protein that was not eliminated during extraction from the gland. Allergic reactions have not been reported after the use of lypressin [Diapid].

INDIVIDUAL EVALUATIONS

LYPRESSIN [Diapid]

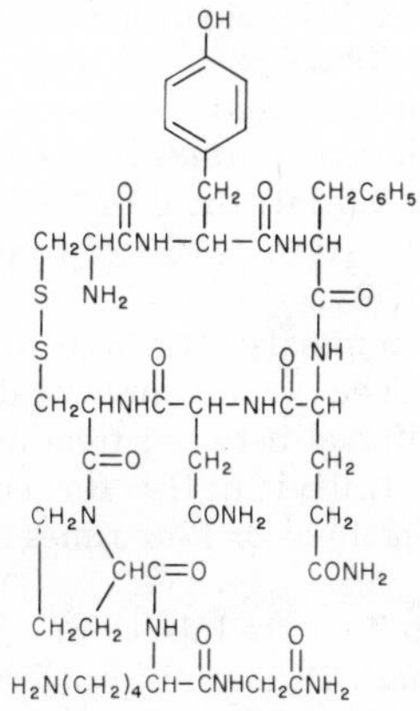

```
                  OH
                  |
              (benzene ring)
                  |
       O         CH2  O   CH2C6H5
       ||         |   ||   |
CH2CHCNH—CH—CNHCH
 |   |                     |
 S  NH2                   C=O
 |                          |
 S          O            O  NH
 |          ||           || |
CH2CHNHC—CH-NHC-CH
     |          |          |
    C=O        CH2        CH2
     |          |          |
CH2N         CONH2      CH2
 |   \                     |
 |    CHC=O              CONH2
 |   /   |
CH2CH2  NH  O         O
         |  ||        ||
H2N(CH2)4CH—CNHCH2CNH2
```

Lypressin solution contains synthetic lysine-8-vasopressin, a polypeptide similar to arginine-8-vasopressin, the antidiuretic hormone found in the posterior pituitary of man. The lysine analogue occurs in swine and is more stable chemically than arginine-8-vasopressin. It has an activity of 50 U.S.P. posterior pituitary (pressor) units per milliliter.

Lypressin is rapidly absorbed from the nasal mucosa. It is effective as sole therapy in mild to moderate neurohypophyseal diabetes insipidus. In more severe cases, the brief duration of effect may cause episodes of abrupt, severe polyuria daily. In these patients, the long-acting vasopressin tannate gives more satisfactory relief. Lypressin can be helpful as adjunctive therapy between injections. This drug is not effective in the nephrogenic form of diabetes insipidus.

There have been no significant local or systemic allergic reactions reported. (See the Introductory Statement for adverse reactions.)

USUAL DOSAGE.—*Topical* (intranasal): One or more sprays applied to one or both nostrils one or more times daily. Each spray delivers approximately 2 U.S.P. posterior pituitary pressor units. The dosage and interval between treatments must be determined individually for each patient. Four sprays in each nostril provides the maximal amount that can be absorbed at one time without excessive wastage. Administration three or four times daily usually is necessary.

PREPARATIONS.—Diapid (Sandoz). *Topical:* Solution (spray) 50 pressor units (0.185 mg)/ml in 5 ml containers.

POSTERIOR PITUITARY
POSTERIOR PITUITARY INJECTION

Both preparations are extracted from posterior pituitary of cattle and swine and contain antidiuretic and oxytocic principles. They are standardized for oxytocic activity, which parallels antidiuretic activity.

Posterior pituitary, a powder made from dessicated posterior pituitary gland, is used for replacement therapy in neurohypophyseal (vasopressin-deficient) diabetes insipidus. It is not effective in the nephrogenic form. The powder is applied topically to the nasal mucous membranes, either by placing in the nose or by inhaling. This form is economical, easy to use, and an alternative to injections. However, it must be applied several times daily, and irritation of the nasal mucous membranes limits its use. Applications may cause sneezing, wheezing, dyspnea, asthmatic attacks, and other signs of hypersensitivity. (See the Introductory Statement for additional adverse reactions.)

Posterior pituitary injection is obsolete since the active principle is available in purer forms (see the evaluations on Vasopressin Injection and Vasopressin Tannate Injection).

USUAL DOSAGE.—

Posterior Pituitary:

Topical (intranasal): *Adults and children,* 5 to 40 mg as required (usually three or four times daily). The dosage and interval between treatment must be determined individually for each patient.

Posterior Pituitary Injection:

No useful dosage is recognized because other purer preparations are available. The manufacturer's suggested dose is: *Intramuscular, Subcutaneous: Adults,* 0.3 to 1 ml (3 to 10 units) three or four times daily.

PREPARATIONS.–

Posterior Pituitary, N.F. *Inhalation:* Powder 3.5 g; capsules 40 mg. Drug marketed under generic name.

Posterior Pituitary Injection, N.F. *Injection:* Solution 10 and 20 units/ml in 1 and 10 ml containers.

AVAILABLE TRADEMARK.–Posterior Pituitary Injection: Pituitrin (Parke, Davis). Drug also marketed by other manufacturers under generic name.

VASOPRESSIN INJECTION [Pitressin]
VASOPRESSIN TANNATE INJECTION [Pitressin Tannate]

Vasopressin injection, a purified extract of the posterior pituitary lobe in aqueous solution, is assayed for pressor activity, which is identical with antidiuretic activity. It contains 20 pressor units and not more than 1 oxytocic unit per milliliter. The brief (two to eight hours) antidiuretic effect produced by intramuscular or subcutaneous injection makes parenteral use of this preparation suitable for precise control of fluid balance when initating therapy following brain surgery or trauma and in acutely ill or unconscious patients with neurohypophyseal diabetes insipidus; the drug is not effective in nephrogenic diabetes insipidus. Vasopressin injection also may be applied topically to the nasal mucous membrane. Topical use provides effective daily maintenance therapy and may cause less nasal irritation than posterior pituitary. This preparation also has been used to treat acute, bleeding esophageal varices, since it reduces the portal venous pressure either by splanchnic vasoconstriction or by decreasing cardiac output. Vasopressin injection also may be given intramuscularly to evaluate the concentrating capacity of the kidneys.

Vasopressin tannate in a peanut oil suspension is the most commonly used injectable preparation for treatment of neurohypophyseal diabetes insipidus; this drug is not effective in the nephrogenic form. Vasopressin tannate provides more complete control of moderate to severe polyuria than do the topical preparations. The antidiuretic effect of a single dose lasts one to three days in most patients. This prolonged action is useful in long-term therapy; however, accumulation of antidiuretic effect with excessive water retention is more likely to occur with this form than with the other preparations. Allergic reactions (fever, rash, wheezing, dyspnea) to the protein derivatives of the posterior pituitary material may occur; the oil vehicle also may occasionally cause an allergic response. (See the Introductory Statement for additional adverse reactions.)

USUAL DOSAGE.–

Vasopressin Injection:

Intramuscular, Subcutaneous: Adults, 5 to 10 units (0.25 to 0.5 ml) three or four times daily; *children*, 2.5 to 10 units (0.125 to 0.5 ml) three or four times daily.

Topical (intranasal): The solution is applied on cotton pledgets, or by spray or dropper. The dosage and interval between treatment must be determined individually for each patient. Administration three or four times daily usually is necessary.

Vasopressin Tannate Injection:

Intramuscular: Adults, 2.5 to 5 units (0.5 to 1 ml) as required, usually every one to three days; *children*, 1.25 to 2.5 units as required, usually every one to three days.

PREPARATIONS.–

Pitressin (Parke, Davis). *Injection:* Solution 20 pressor units/ml in 0.5 and 1 ml containers.

Pitressin Tannate (Parke, Davis). *Injection:* Suspension (in oil) 5 pressor units/ml in 1 ml containers.

Chapter 41

BRONCHODILATORS

Bronchodilators act by relaxing the smooth muscle of the bronchioles. Thus, they are valuable in overcoming acute bronchospasm and as adjuncts in the symptomatic treatment of chronic, obstructive pulmonary diseases (eg, asthma, bronchitis, emphysema). They do not obviate the need for other measures such as elimination of environmental irritants, hyposensitization, bronchial aspiration, and administration of oxygen, expectorants, sedatives, and antibacterial agents.

Bronchodilators comprise two groups: adrenergic (sympathomimetic) agents and the theophylline group of xanthine derivatives. Corticotropin and the adrenal corticosteroids also are useful when bronchodilators alone are ineffective in relieving bronchoconstriction; presumably they act by suppressing inflammation and edema. (See Chapter 35, Adrenal Corticosteroids, and Chapter 38, Anterior Pituitary and Hypothalamic Hormones.)

The most effective bronchodilators are the adrenergic drugs (eg, epinephrine, ephedrine, pseudoephedrine [Sudafed], isoproterenol [Isuprel, Norisodrine], methoxyphenamine [Orthoxine]), which act on the beta receptors of the bronchial smooth muscle to produce relaxation; adrenergic agents with predominantly alpha-receptor and little beta-receptor activity, such as levarterenol (norepinephrine), are not useful as bronchodilators.

Adrenergic bronchodilators may be given orally, sublingually, by aerosol inhalation, by injection, or by rectal instillation; some may be used effectively by several routes. The choice of drug frequently depends upon the route chosen, which, in turn, depends upon the desired speed of onset and duration of action. Rapid relief in an acute attack of asthma may be obtained by subcutaneous injection of epinephrine or by oral inhalation of epinephrine or isoproterenol. A longer duration of action for prophylaxis or treatment of mild attacks of bronchospasm can be obtained by injecting a preparation that is slowly absorbed, such as an aqueous suspension of epinephrine subcutaneously, or by administering other adrenergic agents orally (eg, ephedrine, methoxyphenamine). Isoproterenol may be given sublingually, but its absorption is erratic and unpredictable by this route. No more than one adrenergic compound should be used at a time because these drugs act additively. Tolerance to epinephrine or isoproterenol may develop with too frequent administration.

Theophylline and its derivatives are useful in patients who cannot tolerate the adrenergic drugs or whose bronchospasm is resistant to this group of agents. They apparently act directly on bronchial muscle to relax spasm.

Status asthmaticus and severe asthma refractory to epinephrine are often relieved dramatically by giving aminophylline (theophylline ethylenediamine) intravenously. For oral therapy, dyphylline [Dilor, Lufyllin, Neothylline] and oxtriphylline [Choledyl] may be preferable to theophylline and aminophylline because they produce less gastric irritation and are more uniformly and predictably absorbed. Insufficient evidence is available to substantiate claims that elixirs of theophylline and aminophylline containing 20% alcohol produce less gastric irritation and are absorbed more consistently than other oral forms.

Dyphylline may be given intramuscularly, but other theophylline derivatives should be given by other routes because their injection causes intense local pain. Aminophylline, theophylline olamine [Monotheamin, Fleet Theophylline], and theophylline sodium glycinate [Glynazan, Synophylate, Theoglycinate] can be given rectally as suppositories or by retention enemas. In children, overdosage resulting from erratic absorption following rectal administration may occur less frequently when the drug is given by retention enema.

The concomitant use of an adrenergic drug with theophylline or one of its derivatives often provides bronchodilator action superior to that produced by a drug of either class given alone. This combined action can be especially useful in preventing nocturnal attacks of bronchial asthma in children. Since the dose of each drug should be adjusted individually to the patient's need, fixed-ratio combinations should only be used when an available mixture contains the proper ratio (see the section on Mixtures).

In addition to their bronchodilator effect, the theophylline derivatives increase cardiac output and coronary blood flow and exert a mild diuretic action. When given by slow intravenous injection, aminophylline is frequently of value as an adjunct to therapy for acute pulmonary edema or paroxysmal nocturnal dyspnea due to acute left side heart failure. However, it must never be injected rapidly, for this may result in acute circulatory failure and death. Aminophylline also may afford some relief of Cheyne-Stokes respiration, apparently as a result of its central (medullary) stimulating action.

Corticotropin (ACTH) and the adrenal corticosteroids are often valuable in chronic obstructive lung disease when bronchodilators are ineffective; however, these agents should never be used as the initial treatment. In addition to suppressing allergic responses and reducing inflammation and edema, they also potentiate the bronchodilating effect of adrenergic agents. They should be used cautiously or with appropriate chemotherapy when infection is present.

Adrenal corticosteroid therapy is indicated in severe persistent status asthmaticus or in severe acute or chronic bronchial asthma that is refractory to the adrenergic agents and theophylline derivatives. They also are used occasionally in treating chronic bronchitis and pulmonary emphysema. Usually only a short period of parenteral administration is necessary to treat status asthmaticus, and oral administration can be initiated while the patient is still receiving the corticosteroids by injection. Relief usually can be maintained with oral dosage while the parenteral dosage is gradually decreased. Once status asthmaticus is under control, the patient should be maintained on one or more of the bronchodilators. In contrast, when treating severe chronic bronchial asthma, long-term steroid treatment may be needed despite the hazards of prolonged administration (see Chapter 35, Adrenal Corticosteroids). Consequently, the severity of the asthmatic condition must be carefully evaluated before corticosteroid therapy is instituted. Only the oral route should be considered for long-term administration.

Adverse Reactions and Precautions

Untoward reactions associated with adrenergic bronchodilators primarily involve the cardiovascular or central nervous system.

Epinephrine and isoproterenol [Isuprel, Norisodrine] may cause palpitation, tachycardia, and other disturbances of cardiac rhythm and rate. The adrenergic drugs are contraindicated in most patients with arrhythmias, and their use is dangerous in patients with angina pectoris because they may precipitate episodes of coronary insufficiency and, occasionally, a shock-like state.

Rapid absorption of epinephrine in excessive amounts may cause hypertension, headache, and even cerebral hemorrhage. Since hypertension is less likely to occur with isoproterenol (at concentrations used in the United States), this drug is preferred for use in hypertensive patients.

Central nervous system stimulation, manifested by nervousness, excitability, and insomnia, is common after oral administration of ephedrine, especially in adults, and may require use of a sedative. Rarely, similar reactions follow the subcutaneous injection of epinephrine and the oral or sublingual administration of isoproterenol. Large doses of adrenergic drugs may cause dizziness, asthenia, lightheadedness, nausea, and vomiting.

Long-term use of ephedrine may cause severe urinary retention that necessitates catheterization, particularly in elderly men with an enlarged prostate. Excessive and prolonged administration of epinephrine or isoproterenol by oral inhalation may lead to dryness of the pharyngeal membranes and inflammation of the bronchial mucosa. In sensitive individuals, inhalations of these drugs have precipitated severe, prolonged attacks of asthma. If these preparations are swallowed due to improper administration, they may produce epigastric pain. Refractoriness may develop after repeated use.

Caution should be exercised to avoid hypertension, tachycardia, and increased cardiac oxygen demands when the adrenergic bronchodilators are given to patients with hyperthyroidism or ischemic heart disease. These agents should be used with care in diabetic patients because of their glycogenolytic effect.

The most consistent adverse reactions caused by theophylline and its derivatives are gastrointestinal irritation and central nervous system stimulation. Nausea, vomiting, and epigastric pain, generally preceded by headache, are common following oral administration. These adverse reactions may be obviated by changing the route of administration, although gastrointestinal disturbances may occur even after parenteral administration of many theophylline preparations, including aminophylline. Prolonged use of suppositories may cause irritation of the rectum. The absorption of aminophylline from rectal suppositories is variable; rarely, fatal convulsions and shock have occurred in children after use of suppositories.

Central nervous system stimulation is manifested by irritability, restlessness, and insomnia. These effects may be counteracted by administering sedative doses of barbiturates. Agitation, headache, hyperreflexia, fasciculations, and clonic and tonic convulsions have occurred in young children following overdosage of the theophylline drugs.

Rapid intravenous administration of theophylline and its derivatives has caused severe and even fatal acute circulatory failure. Occasionally, apparent refractoriness to bronchodilators can be corrected by administration of sodium bicarbonate to overcome respiratory acidosis.

Administration of aminophylline by inhalation may cause bronchospasm and should be avoided.

For adverse reactions produced by corticotropin and the adrenal corticosteroids, see Chapter 35, Adrenal Corticosteroids, and Chapter 38, Anterior Pituitary and Hypothalamic Hormones.

ADRENERGIC AGENTS

EPINEPHRINE [Adrenalin in Oil, Asmolin, Sus-Phrine]

EPINEPHRINE BITARTRATE [Asmatane, Medihaler-Epi]

EPINEPHRINE HYDROCHLORIDE
[Adrenalin Chloride]

HO–C_6H_3(OH)–CH(OH)–CH_2NH–CH_3

Epinephrine given parenterally is the treatment of choice for acute asthmatic attacks. Although its principal therapeutic effect in asthma is bronchodilatation produced by beta-receptor activity on bronchial smooth muscle, vasoconstriction and relief of bronchial mucosal edema due to alpha receptor activity may produce additional improvement in vital capacity. Its short duration of action can be prolonged by giving the base in aqueous suspension subcutaneously or a suspension in oil intramuscularly; however, use of the latter route is unwise because bioavailability is not uniform and fatal cases of gas gangrene due to *Clostridium perfringens* have been reported. Care is essential to avoid the inadvertent intravenous injection of intramuscular preparations.

The drug is used in nebulized form by oral inhalation for both prophylaxis and treatment of bronchospasm. Absorption from the respiratory tract may lead to overdosage and produce adverse effects similar to those observed when epinephrine is administered by other routes. Too frequent inhalation also can irritate and dry the bronchial mucosa and increase retention of mucous plugs in the bronchioles. In susceptible patients, inhalation of the drug may cause a severe, prolonged attack of asthma.

Adverse reactions following absorption of epinephrine include excessive sympathetic stimulation (anxiety, palpitation, and headache). Rebound bronchospasm may occur when the effect of epinephrine disappears. Excessive doses cause acute hypertension and arrhythmias. The drug generally is contraindicated in patients with hypertension, diabetes, hyperthyroidism, and ischemic heart disease. Refractoriness may occur after too frequent administration, especially in patients with metabolic acidosis. (See also the Introductory Statement.)

For other uses, see Chapters 2, Antiarrhythmic Agents; 5, Agents Used in Hypotension and Shock; 42, Nasal Decongestants; and 69, Agents Used to Treat Glaucoma.

USUAL DOSAGE.—

Epinephrine, Epinephrine Hydrochloride:

Subcutaneous: Adults, 0.2 to 0.5 mg

(equivalent to 0.2 to 0.5 ml of 1:1,000 solution) every two hours as necessary; *children*, 0.01 mg/kg of body weight every four hours as needed.

Epinephrine:

Intramuscular: For the reasons stated above, use of this route is unwise. The manufacturers' suggested dosage is: *Adults*, 0.4 to 2 mg of the suspension in oil every 8 to 16 hours; *children*, 0.02 to 0.04 mg/kg of body weight every 12 or 24 hours.

Epinephrine Bitartrate, Epinephrine Hydrochloride:

Oral Inhalation: 0.1% to 1% solution or suspension inhaled as a fine mist; repeated when necessary.

PREPARATIONS.—

Epinephrine:

Adrenalin in Oil (Parke, Davis). *Injection:* Suspension 1:500 (2 mg/ml) in peanut oil in 1 ml containers.

Asmolin (Lincoln). *Injection:* Suspension (aqueous) 1:400 (2.5 mg/ml) in 10 ml containers.

Sus-Phrine (Cooper). *Injection:* Suspension (aqueous) 1:200 (5 mg/ml) in 0.5 and 5 ml containers.

Epinephrine Bitartrate:

Asmatane (Riker), Medihaler-Epi (Riker). *Oral Inhalation:* Suspension 7 mg/ml (0.3 mg/measured dose).

Epinephrine Hydrochloride:

Adrenalin Chloride (Parke, Davis).

Oral Inhalation: Solution 1:100 (10 mg/ml).

Injection: Solution 1:1,000 (1 mg/ml) in 1 and 30 ml containers.

Drug also marketed by other manufacturers under generic name.

EPHEDRINE SULFATE

C_6H_5–CH(OH)–CH(CH_3)–NH–CH_3 · ½ H_2SO_4

The actions of ephedrine are similar to those of epinephrine; however, the effects are longer lasting and the drug may be effective for several hours. Ephedrine is not as suitable as epinephrine for severe attacks of bronchial asthma because its bronchodilator action is weaker, but it may be the oral agent of choice for mild attacks of bronchospasm and for patients who require continuous medication. This drug is commonly administered prophylactically at bedtime to prevent nocturnal wheezing.

Adverse reactions are similar to those caused by epinephrine (see the Introductory Statement and the evaluation on Epinephrine). Central nervous system stimulation, manifested by nervousness, excitability, and insomnia, is common. A barbiturate is often given with ephedrine to reduce these effects. Children tend to be more resistant than adults to the stimulation produced by this drug. Rarely, a patient may be allergic to ephedrine. Long-term use may cause urinary retention in men with prostatic hypertrophy.

For other uses, see Chapters 5, Agents Used in Hypotension and Shock; 42, Nasal Decongestants; and 72, Miscellaneous Ophthalmic Preparations.

USUAL DOSAGE.—*Oral: Adults*, 15 to 50 mg every three to four hours; *children*, 3 mg/kg of body weight every 24 hours in four to six divided doses.

PREPARATIONS.—Ephedrine Sulfate, U.S.P. *Oral:* Capsules 25 and 50 mg; tablets 25 mg; syrup 10 and 20 mg/5 ml. Drug marketed under generic name.

ETHYLNOREPINEPHRINE HYDROCHLORIDE [Bronkephrine]

$(HO)_2C_6H_3$–CH(OH)–CH(NH_2)CH_2CH_3 · HCl

This drug is primarily a beta-adrenergic stimulant and is given by injection. Its actions, indications, and adverse reactions are similar to those of isoproterenol, but it is only one-tenth as active in relaxing bronchial smooth muscle. It is not a drug of choice in the management of asthma, but it may be useful in some patients with mild bronchial asthma or in those who do not respond to isoproterenol or epinephrine.

USUAL DOSAGE.—*Intramuscular, Subcutaneous: Adults*, 0.6 to 2 mg; *children*, 0.2 to 1 mg.

PREPARATIONS.—Bronkephrine (Breon). *Injection:* Solution 2 mg/ml in 1 and 10 ml containers.

ISOPROTERENOL HYDROCHLORIDE [Isuprel Hydrochloride, Norisodrine Aerotrol]

ISOPROTERENOL SULFATE [Medihaler-Iso, Norisodrine Sulfate]

$(HO)_2C_6H_3$–CH(OH)$CH_2NHCH(CH_3)_2$ · HCl

Isoproterenol acts primarily on beta-adrenergic receptors and is effective in preventing and relieving bronchoconstriction. It also relaxes smooth muscle of the gastrointestinal tract and blood vessels of the skeletal muscles and increases the rate and force of the heart. Its duration of action is similar to that of epinephrine. Oral inhalation is the preferred route of administration for the treatment of asthmatic attacks. Isoproterenol also may be given intravenously and sublingually; however, the effectiveness of the sublingual route is limited. This drug is preferred over epinephrine in patients with hypertension.

Palpitation, tachycardia and other arrhythmias, and hypotension occur frequently with misuse. Excessive inhalation causes refractory bronchial obstruction. Rarely, sudden death has occurred, presumably from arrhythmia. In susceptible patients, inhalation of the drug may cause a severe, prolonged attack of asthma. Tolerance may develop with too frequent administration. See also the Introductory Statement.

For other uses, see Chapter 2, Antiarrhythmic Agents, and Chapter 5, Agents Used in Hypotension and Shock.

USUAL DOSAGE.—

Isoproterenol Hydrochloride,
Isoproterenol Sulfate:

Oral Inhalation: Adults and children, one or two inhalations from preset nebulizing units, repeated once or twice at five- to ten-minute intervals *if necessary.* If no effect is obtained, the more concentrated solution should be used or, if definite evidence of resistance is present, the patient should be given other medication.

With a hand bulb nebulizer, the dose is 5 to 15 deep inhalations of a mist of the 1:200 solution, repeated in 10 to 30 minutes if necessary. Three to seven deep inhalations will usually suffice if the 1:100 dilution is used. For best results, the breath should be held for a few seconds after each inhalation. When an oxygen aerosol preparation is used, up to 0.5 ml of the 1:200 solution or 0.3 ml of the 1:100 solution may be administered with an oxygen flow of 4 liters/minute for 15 to 20 minutes. Dosage with a powder inhalation device is two to four inhalations of normal force and depth only. *If necessary,* the dose may be repeated after five minutes and once more after ten minutes. If no relief is obtained and there are no adverse reactions with the weaker preparation, the stronger preparation may be tried.

Careful instruction of the patient in the proper use of the device, preferably by demonstration, is essential whenever nebulizers are used. With any nebulized preparation, the least number of inhalations necessary to obtain relief is the most desirable.

Isoproterenol Hydrochloride:

Intravenous: 0.01 or 0.02 mg (0.5 or 1 ml of 1:50,000 solution), repeated when necessary.

Sublingual: Adults, 10 to 15 mg three or four times daily (total daily dose should not exceed 60 mg). *Children,* 5 to 10 mg three or four times daily (total daily dose should not exceed 30 mg).

PREPARATIONS.—

Isoproterenol Hydrochloride:

Isuprel Hydrochloride (Winthrop).

Oral Inhalation: Solution 1:100 (10 mg/ml), 1:200 (5 mg/ml), 1:400 (2.5 mg/ml).

Injection: Solution 1:5,000 (0.2 mg/ml) in 1 and 5 ml containers.

Sublingual: Tablets 10 and 15 mg.

Norisodrine Aerotrol (Abbott). *Oral Inhalation:* Solution 0.25% (2.5 mg/ml).

Isoproterenol Sulfate:

Medihaler-Iso (Riker). *Oral Inhalation:* Suspension 2 mg/ml (0.075 mg/measured dose).

Norisodrine Sulfate (Abbott). *Oral Inhalation:* Powder 10% (10 mg) and 25% (25 mg) aerosol containers.

ADDITIONAL TRADEMARKS.— Isoproterenol Hydrochloride: Iprenol (Vitarine), Proternol (Key), Vapo-N-Iso (USV). Drug also marketed under generic name. **Isoproterenol Sulfate:** Iso-Autohaler (Riker), Vapo-N-Iso Metermatic (USV).

METHOXYPHENAMINE HYDROCHLORIDE

[Orthoxine Hydrochloride]

OCH_3 — $CH_2CH(CH_3)NHCH_3 \cdot HCl$

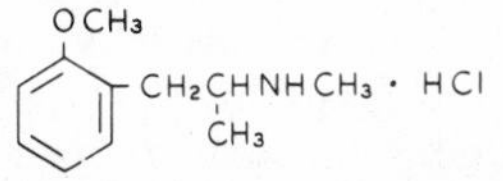

Methoxyphenamine acts primarily on beta-adrenergic receptors of smooth muscle. Its clinical effects are similar to those of ephedrine but methoxyphenamine has fewer cardiovascular effects. It also has weak antihistaminic properties. (See the evaluation on Ephedrine Sulfate.)

USUAL DOSAGE.—*Oral: Adults,* 50 to 100 mg four times daily; *children,* 25 to 50 mg four times daily.

PREPARATIONS.—Orthoxine Hydrochloride (Upjohn). *Oral:* Syrup 50 mg/5 ml; tablets 100 mg.

PSEUDOEPHEDRINE HYDROCHLORIDE
[Sudafed]

$$C_6H_5-CH(OH)CH(NHCH_3)CH_3 \cdot HCl$$

Pseudoephedrine is a physiologically active stereoisomer of ephedrine with similar actions, uses, and adverse reactions (see the evaluation on Ephedrine Sulfate).

USUAL DOSAGE.—*Oral: Adults,* 60 mg three or four times daily; *children,* 4 mg/kg of body weight daily in four divided doses.

PREPARATIONS.—Sudafed (Burroughs Wellcome). *Oral:* Syrup 30 mg/5 ml; tablets 30 and 60 mg.

ADDITIONAL TRADEMARKS.—Besan (Tutag), Ro-Fedrin (Robinson).

THEOPHYLLINE DERIVATIVES

AMINOPHYLLINE (Theophylline Ethylenediamine)

When given by slow intravenous injection, aminophylline often relieves acute bronchospasm or status asthmaticus that is resistant to epinephrine. In addition to its bronchodilator effect, aminophylline increases cardiac output and lowers venous pressure; it is the drug of choice when it is difficult to distinguish bronchospasm from pulmonary edema, and it is frequently of value as an adjunct in the relief of acute pulmonary edema and paroxysmal nocturnal dyspnea due to acute left side heart failure. Aminophylline also may ameliorate Cheyne-Stokes respiration, apparently as a result of its central (medullary) stimulating action. Although preparations for intramuscular use are available, aminophylline should not be given by this route because it tends to produce severe, persistent local pain. The drug also may be administered orally or rectally. The response is variable after oral administration. This formerly was thought to be due to erratic absorption but recently has been shown to be caused by marked differences in the rate of metabolism; since dangerous blood levels can result, the dose must be adjusted for each patient. Absorption after rectal administration also is variable, but less so with retention enemas than with suppositories.

Headache, nausea, vomiting, and epigastric pain occur commonly, especially with oral administration. Severe toxic reactions, manifested by persistent vomiting, agitation, and sometimes convulsions and death, may occur regardless of the route of administration. In children, the triad of hematemesis, central nervous system stimulation, and diuresis may occur. Prolonged use of suppositories often causes irritation of the rectum. Deaths due to convulsions and shock have been reported rarely following insertion of suppositories in asthmatic children. The danger is particularly great if cough preparations containing aminophylline or other theophylline salts are given concomitantly. Rapid intravenous injection causes sudden and profound hypotension. Therefore, intravenous injections must be given slowly and cautiously, especially in patients with myocardial ischemia. See also the Introductory Statement.

For other uses, see Chapter 3, Antianginal Agents.

USUAL DOSAGE.—

Intravenous: Adults, 250 to 500 mg in 10 to 20 ml of diluent, injected over a five- to ten-minute period up to three times daily. If given by continuous intravenous infusion, most patients will require 40 to 50 mg/kg of body weight per hour. The dose should be reduced if signs of gastrointestinal or other toxic effects appear. *Children,* 12 mg/kg daily in three divided doses, injected slowly.

Oral: Adults, 200 or 250 mg every six to eight hours; *children,* this route is not preferred because of limited absorption and gastric irritation.

Rectal: Adults, suppositories, 250 to 500 mg up to three times daily; *children,* 12 mg/kg of body weight daily in three divided doses. *Adults,* retention enema, 500 mg in 10 to 20 ml of water three or four times daily; *children,* 12 mg/kg daily in three divided doses.

Intramuscular: Use of this route is unwise because the injection may cause severe, persistent pain.

PREPARATIONS.—

Injection (Intravenous): Solution 25 mg/ml in 10 and 20 ml containers.

Oral: Tablets (plain and enteric-coated) 100 and 200 mg.

Rectal: Powder for enemas; solution 100 mg/ml in 3 and 4.5 ml containers; suppositories 100, 250, and 500 mg.

AVAILABLE TRADEMARKS.—Aminodur (Cooper), Lixaminol (Ferndale), Rectalad-Aminophylline (Wampole). Drug also marketed by many manufacturers under generic name.

DYPHYLLINE [Dilor, Lufyllin, Neothylline]

Dyphylline is a neutral theophylline derivative having the same actions, uses, and adverse reactions as other theophylline compounds (see the Introductory Statement and the evaluation on Aminophylline). It is freely absorbed from the gastrointestinal tract and is less irritating than theophylline and aminophylline. It can be used intramuscularly without producing local pain because it is a soluble salt and is neutral.

USUAL DOSAGE.—

Oral: Adults, 100 to 300 mg every six to eight hours; *children,* 14 mg/kg of body weight daily in divided doses; *infants,* 4 to 6 mg/kg daily in divided doses.

Intramuscular: Adults, 250 to 500 mg, repeated several times daily if necessary.

PREPARATIONS.—

Dilor (Savage), Neothylline (Lemmon).

Oral: Elixir 50 mg/5 ml; tablets 200 mg.

Injection: Solution 250 mg/ml in 2 ml containers.

Lufyllin (Mallinckrodt).

Oral: Elixir 100 mg/15 ml; tablets 100 and 200 mg.

Injection: Solution 250 mg/ml in 2 ml containers.

ADDITIONAL TRADEMARK.—Brophylline (Tutag).

OXTRIPHYLLINE [Choledyl]

Oxtriphylline is the choline salt of theophylline. Its activity is similar to that of aminophylline (see the Introductory Statement and the evaluation on Aminophylline). It is more consistently absorbed from the gastrointestinal tract and is less irritating than the parent compound.

USUAL DOSAGE.—*Oral: Adults,* 100 to 400 mg four times daily, preferably after meals and at bedtime; *children,* 15 mg/kg of body weight daily in four divided doses.

PREPARATIONS.—Choledyl (Warner-Chilcott). *Oral:* Elixir 100 mg/5 ml; tablets 100 and 200 mg.

THEOPHYLLINE [Aerolate, Aqualin, Elixophyllin, Optiphyllin]

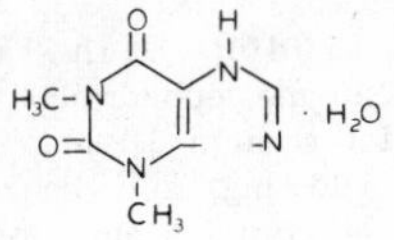

$\cdot H_2O$

Theophylline has the same actions, uses, and adverse reactions as aminophylline (see the Introductory Statement and the evaluation on Aminophylline). It is less soluble and less consistently absorbed from the gastrointestinal tract than some of its salts and derivatives. Evidence that preparations containing 20% alcohol provide more consistent absorption of theophylline and are less irritating is not convincing.

USUAL DOSAGE.—

Oral: Adults, 160 mg every six hours; *children,* 2.5 mg/kg of body weight every six hours.

Rectal (Suppositories): *Adults,* 250 to 500 mg every 8 to 12 hours; *children,* 55 to 110 mg every 8 to 12 hours.

PREPARATIONS.—

Aerolate (Fleming). *Oral:* Capsules 130 and 260 mg.

Aqualin (Webster). *Rectal:* Suppositories 125 and 500 mg.

Elixophyllin (Cooper), Optiphyllin (Fougera). *Oral:* Elixir 25 mg/5 ml.

Drug also marketed by other manufacturers under generic name.

THEOPHYLLINE OLAMINE [Fleet Theophylline, Monotheamin]

Theophylline olamine is administered rectally. It has the same actions, uses, and adverse reactions as aminophylline (see the Introductory Statement and the evaluation on Aminophylline).

USUAL DOSAGE.—*Rectal: Adults,* retention enema, 250 to 500 mg every twelve hours. *Adults,* suppositories, 200 to 400 mg every twelve hours; *children,* dosage not established.

PREPARATIONS.—

Fleet Theophylline (Fleet). *Rectal:* Solution 250 and 500 mg/30 ml in single-dose units.

Monotheamin (Lilly). *Rectal:* Suppositories 500 mg.

THEOPHYLLINE SODIUM GLYCINATE [Glynazan, Synophylate, Theoglycinate]

Theophylline sodium glycinate is administered orally, rectally, or, in emergencies, intravenously. It has the same actions, uses, and adverse reaction as aminophylline (see the Introductory Statement and the evaluation on Aminophylline).

USUAL DOSAGE.—

Oral: Adults, 325 to 750 mg every six to eight hours.

Rectal: Adults, 780 mg every six hours.

Intravenous: For emergency use, *adults*, 400 mg injected slowly; *children*, 4 mg/kg of body weight injected slowly.

PREPARATIONS.–

Glynazan (First Texas). *Oral:* Elixir 325 mg/5 ml; tablets 325 mg.

Synophylate (Central).

Oral: Elixir 110 mg/5 ml; tablets 165 and 325 mg.

Rectal: Suppositories 780 mg.

Injection: Solution 40 mg/ml in 10 ml containers.

Theoglycinate (Brayten). *Oral:* Syrup 130 mg/5 ml; tablets 325 mg.

MIXTURES

One or more of the single-entity drugs discussed will usually control acute attacks of bronchospasm. Concomitant use of drugs in doses which individually are less likely to cause adverse reactions may simplify long-term management. Most available mixtures contain theophylline or a derivative, ephedrine, a sedative to counteract central stimulation, and often an expectorant, which occasionally may slightly enhance the value of a combination. Potassium iodide, a commonly used expectorant, can cause hyperkalemia, iodism, and even goiter or myxedema if given over long periods. Guaiacol is now practically obsolete and has been largely replaced by glyceryl guaiacolate as an expectorant.

Following is a list of available mixtures. The use of fixed-ratio combinations as a substitute for single-entity preparations is generally deemed inadvisable. When additional drugs are indicated, it is advisable to prescribe each agent separately in the dosage that meets the needs of the particular patient. When an available mixture contains the proper ratio, it may be used.

Aerolone Compound (Lilly): Each 100 ml of liquid contains cyclopentamine hydrochloride 500 mg and isoproterenol hydrochloride 250 mg [oral solution].

Amesec (Lilly): Each capsule or enteric-coated tablet contains aminophylline 0.13 g, ephedrine hydrochloride 25 mg, and amobarbital 25 mg.

Aminet (Dome): Each suppository contains aminophylline 500, 250, or 125 mg; pentobarbital sodium 100, 50, or 25 mg; and benzocaine 60, 30, or 15 mg.

Aminodrox (Beecham-Massengill): Each tablet contains aminophylline 100 mg and aluminum hydroxide gel 120 mg with or without phenobarbital 15 mg.

Aminodrox Forte (Beecham-Massengill): Each tablet contains aminophylline 200 mg and aluminum hydroxide gel 250 mg with or without phenobarbital 15 mg.

Amodrine (Searle): Each tablet contains aminophylline 100 mg, racephedrine hydrochloride 25 mg, and phenobarbital 8 mg.

Asbron (Dorsey): Each tablet or 15 ml of liquid contains theophylline sodium glycinate 300 mg, phenylpropanolamine hydrochloride 25 mg, and glyceryl guaiacolate 100 mg.

Ayrcap, AyrLiquid (Ascher): Each timed-release capsule [Ayrcap] contains theophylline 260 mg, pseudoephedrine 50 mg, and butabarbital 15 mg; each 15 ml of liquid contains theophylline 130 mg, pseudoephedrine 25 mg, and butabarbital 8 mg.

Brondecon (Warner-Chilcott): Each tablet or 10 ml of liquid contains oxtriphylline 200 mg and glyceryl guaiacolate 100 mg.

Brondilate (Walker): Each tablet contains isoproterenol hydrochloride 5 mg, ephedrine hydrochloride 15 mg, theophylline calcium salicylate 100 mg, and butabarbital 20 mg.

Bronkolixir (Breon): Each 5 ml of liquid contains theophylline 15 mg, ephedrine sulfate 12 mg, phenobarbital 4 mg, and glyceryl guaiacolate 50 mg.

Bronkometer (Breon): Each measured dose of aerosol delivers isoetharine mesylate 350 μg, phenylephrine hydrochloride 70 μg, and thenyldiamine hydrochloride 30 μg.

Bronkosol (Breon): Each 10 ml of liquid contains isoetharine hydrochloride 1.0%, phenylephrine hydrochloride 0.25%, and thenyldiamine hydrochloride 0.1% [inhalation solution].

Bronkotabs (Breon): Each tablet contains theophylline 50 or 100 mg, ephedrine sulfate 12 or 24 mg, phenobarbital 4 or 8 mg, and glyceryl guaiacolate 50 or 100 mg.

Cardalin (Mallinckrodt): Each tablet contains aminophylline 324 mg, dried aluminum hydroxide gel 162 mg, and benzocaine 32.4 mg with or without phenobarbital 16.2 mg.

Co-Xan (Central): Each 30 ml of elixir contains ephedrine hydrochloride 50 mg, theophylline sodium glycinate 660 mg, codeine phosphate 30 mg, glyceryl guaiacolate 200 mg, and methapyrilene hydrochloride 50 mg.

Dainite (Mallinckrodt): Each tablet contains aminophylline 200 mg, ephedrine hydrochloride 16 mg, pentobarbital sodium 16 mg, dried aluminum hydroxide gel 160 mg, and benzocaine 16 mg; each Night Tablet contains aminophylline 259 mg, pentobarbital sodium 32.4 mg, dried aluminum hydroxide gel 162 mg, benzocaine 16.2 mg, and phenobarbital 24.3 mg.

Dainite-KI (Mallinckrodt): Each tablet contains aminophylline 200 mg, ephedrine hydrochloride 16 mg, phenobarbital 16 mg, potassium iodide 325 mg, dried aluminum hydroxide gel 160 mg, and benzocaine 16 mg.

Deltasmyl (Roussel): Each tablet contains theophylline 120 mg, ephedrine hydrochloride 15 mg, phenobarbital 8 mg, and prednisone 1.5 mg.

Dilor-G (Savage): Each tablet or 10 ml of liquid contains dyphylline 200 mg and glyceryl guaiacolate 200 mg.

Duo-Medihaler (Riker): Each milliliter of liquid contains isoproterenol hydrochloride 4 mg and phenylephrine bitartrate 6 mg [inhalation solution].

Duovent (Riker): Each tablet contains theophylline 130 mg, ephedrine 24 mg, glyceryl guaiacolate 100 mg, and phenobarbital 8 mg.

Dylephrin (Mallinckrodt): Each milliliter of aerosol liquid contains epinephrine hydrochloride 2.5% and atropine sulfate 5 mg.

Elixophyllin-KI (Cooper): Each 15 ml of liquid contains theophylline 80 mg, potassium iodide 130 mg, and alcohol 10% [oral solution].

Ephed-Organidin (Wampole): Each tablet contains ephedrine sulfate 24 mg, iodinated glycerol 60 mg, and methapyrilene fumarate 70 mg; each 5 ml of elixir contains ephedrine sulfate 16 mg, iodinated glycerol 30 mg, and phenobarbital 8 mg.

Ephedrine and Nembutal (Abbott): Each capsule contains ephedrine hydrochloride 25 mg and pentobarbital sodium 25 mg.

Ephedrine and Seconal Sodium (Lilly): Each capsule contains ephedrine sulfate 0.025 g and secobarbital sodium 0.05 g.

Ephoxamine (Unimed): Each tablet or 20 ml of pediatric syrup contains phenyltoloxamine citrate 50 mg and racephedrine hydrochloride 30 mg.

Glynazan/EP (First Texas): Each tablet contains theophylline sodium glycinate 324 mg, ephedrine sulfate 24.3 mg, and phenobarbital 16.2 mg.

Hyadrine (Searle): Each tablet contains aminophylline 150 mg, diphenhydramine 37.5 mg, and racephedrine hydrochloride 25 mg.

Hydryllin with Racephedrine Hydrochloride (Searle): Each tablet contains diphenhydramine 25 mg, aminophylline 100 mg, and racephedrine hydrochloride 25 mg.

Iso-Tabs (Rowell): Each tablet contains theophylline sodium glycinate 300 mg, pseudoephedrine hydrochloride 60 mg, and glyceryl guaiacolate 100 mg.

Isuprel Compound (Winthrop): Each 15 ml of elixir contains isoproterenol hydrochloride 2.5 mg, theophylline 45 mg, ephedrine sulfate 12 mg, phenobarbital 6 mg, and potassium iodide 150 mg.

Kiophyllin (Searle): Each tablet contains aminophylline 150 mg, phenobarbital 15 mg, and potassium iodide 125 mg.

Luasmin (Cooper): Each capsule contains theophylline sodium acetate 200 mg, ephedrine sulfate 30 mg, and phenobarbital sodium 30 mg.

Luftodil (Mallinckrodt): Each tablet contains theophylline 100 mg, ephedrine hydrochloride 24 mg, phenobarbital 16 mg, and glyceryl guaiacolate 200 mg.

Lufyllin-EP (Mallinckrodt): Each tablet contains dyphylline 100 mg, ephedrine hydrochloride 16 mg, and phenobarbital 16 mg.

Lufyllin-GG (Mallinckrodt): Each tablet or 30 ml of elixir contains dyphylline 200 mg and glyceryl guaiacolate 200 mg.

Marax (Roerig): Each tablet or 20 ml of syrup contains theophylline 130 mg, ephedrine sulfate 25 mg, and hydroxyzine hydrochloride 10 mg.

Nebair (Warner-Chilcott): Each 0.05 ml of aerosol contains isoproterenol hydrochloride 63 μg and thonzonium bromide 95 μg.

Neospect (Lemmon): Each tablet contains dyphylline 100 mg, ephedrine sulfate 25 mg, phenobarbital 15 mg, and glyceryl guaiacolate 100 mg.

Neothylline-G (Lemmon): Each tablet or 5 ml of elixir contains dyphylline 100 mg and glyceryl guaiacolate 50 mg.

Norisodrine with Calcium Iodide (Abbott): Each 5 ml of syrup contains isoproterenol sulfate 3 mg and calcium iodide anhydrous 150 mg.

Novalene (Lemmon): Each tablet contains ephedrine sulfate 24 mg, potassium iodide 162 mg, phenobarbital 16 mg, and calcium lactate 162 mg.

Numa (Cooper): Each timed-release tablet contains theophylline 225 mg, ephedrine hydrochloride 50 mg, and butabarbital 25 mg.

Orthoxine and Aminophylline (Upjohn): Each capsule contains aminophylline (hydrous) 100 mg and methoxyphenamine hydrochloride 50 mg.

Phyldrox (Lemmon): Each tablet contains dyphylline 100 mg, ephedrine sulfate 25 mg, and phenobarbital 15 mg.

ProDecadron (Merck Sharp & Dohme): Each 12.6 g of aerosol contains isoproterenol sulfate 18 mg and dexamethasone sodium phosphate equivalent to dexamethasone phosphate 18 mg.

Quadrinal (Knoll): Each tablet or 10 ml of suspension contains theophylline calcium salicylate 130 mg, ephedrine hydrochloride 24 mg, phenobarbital 24 mg, and potassium iodide 320 mg.

Quibron (Mead Johnson): Each liquid filled capsule or 15 ml of elixir contains theophylline 150 mg and glyceryl guaiacolate 90 mg.

Synophedal (Central): Each tablet contains theophylline sodium glycinate 300 mg, racephedrine hydrochloride 25 mg, and phenobarbital 15 mg.

Synophylate with Phenobarbital (Central): Each tablet contains theophylline sodium glycinate 330 mg and phenobarbital 16.2 mg.

Tedral (Warner-Chilcott): Each tablet or 10 ml of pediatric suspension contains theophylline 130 mg, ephedrine hydrochloride 24 mg, and phenobarbital 8 mg; each timed-release tablet contains theophylline (anhydrous) 180 mg, ephedrine hydrochloride 48 mg, and phenobarbital 25 mg.

Tedral-25 (Warner-Chilcott): Each tablet contains theophylline 130 mg, ephedrine hydrochloride 24 mg, and butabarbital 25 mg.

Tedral Anti-H (Warner-Chilcott): Each tablet contains theophylline 130 mg, ephedrine hydrochloride 24 mg, phenobarbital 8 mg, and chlorpheniramine maleate 2 mg.

Tensodin (Knoll): Each tablet contains theophylline calcium salicylate 194 mg, ethaverine hydrochloride 32.4 mg, and phenobarbital 16.2 mg.

Thalfed (Beecham-Massengill): Each tablet contains theophylline (hydrous) 120 mg, ephedrine hydrochloride 25 mg, and phenobarbital 8 mg.

Theokin (Knoll): Each 5 ml of elixir contains theophylline calcium salicylate 149.5 mg and potassium iodide 150 mg.

Theo-Organidin (Wampole): Each 15 ml of elixir contains theophylline 120 mg and iodinated glycerol 30 mg.

Verequad (Knoll): Each tablet or 10 ml of liquid contains theophylline calcium salicylate 130 mg, ephedrine hydrochloride 24 mg, phenobarbital 8 mg, and glyceryl guaiacolate 100 mg.

Chapter 42

NASAL DECONGESTANTS

The vasomotor integrity of the nasal mucosa depends upon a proper balance between sympathetic and parasympathetic efferent impulses. Activation of the parasympathetic division of the autonomic nervous system produces vasodilatation and increased secretion, while activation of the sympathetic division produces vasoconstriction and decreased secretion. Congestion of the nasal mucosa is usually caused by infection, inflammation, allergy, or emotional upset. Treatment may be directed toward eliciting sympathetic responses or blocking parasympathetic responses. (See also Chapter 46, Cold Remedies.)

Adrenergic agents are most commonly used for the symptomatic relief of nasal congestion. They include epinephrine [Adrenalin], ephedrine, phenylephrine [Neo-Synephrine], propylhexedrine [Benzedrex], tuaminoheptane [Tuamine], cyclopentamine [Clopane], methylhexaneamine [Forthane], phenylpropanolamine [Propadrine], and the imidazolines (naphazoline [Privine], oxymetazoline [Afrin], tetrahydrozoline [Tyzine], and xylometazoline [Otrivin]). Cocaine, which potentiates the actions of norepinephrine, also is used for its nasal decongestant effect in special, restricted circumstances.

The adrenergic nasal decongestants act by stimulating the alpha-(excitatory) adrenergic receptors of vascular smooth muscle, thus constricting the dilated network of arterioles within the nasal mucosa and reducing the flow of blood in the engorged, edematous area. Opening of the obstructed nasal passages improves nasal ventilation and aeration and drainage of the sinuses, which may also relieve headache of sinus origin. The ideal drug exerts an effect on surface vessels as well as on the deeper erectile structures.

Antihistamines, which have some antimuscarinic activity, are sometimes combined with an adrenergic agent. Such combinations may be useful in patients with hay fever (pollinosis, seasonal allergic rhinitis), but the antihistamines are of little if any value in nonseasonal (perennial) allergic rhinitis (see Chapter 45, Antihistamines). There is no justification for including other medications such as antibiotics with nasal decongestants (see section on Mixtures). Adrenal corticosteroids (eg, prednisone, prednisolone) or corticotropin (ACTH) may be used systemically for short periods to counteract inflammation of the nasal mucosa that does not respond to other agents (see Chapter 35, Adrenal Corticosteroids).

The nasal decongestants provide temporary symptomatic relief in acute rhinitis associated with the common cold and other respiratory infections, and in hay fever, nonseasonal allergic rhinitis, and other forms of acute and chronic rhinitis and sinusitis. In addition, the topical decongestants are used to facilitate visualization of the nasal and nasopharyngeal membranes during diagnostic procedures and to reduce turgescence of the membranes prior to nasal surgery. Some authorities believe that by opening the obstructed eustachian ostia, the vasoconstrictive action of these drugs may sometimes be useful as an adjunct to antibacterial therapy in middle ear infections or in the relief of serous otitis media.

Most of the nasal decongestants are used topically; a few (eg, ephedrine, phenylephrine) can be used either topically or orally, and phenylpropanolamine is used only orally. The response to topical application of nasal decongestants is prompt and of variable duration, whereas the response to oral therapy is slower and generally of longer duration. However, the topical nasal decongestants may cause swelling of the nasal mucosa, which leads to compulsive overtreatment (see under Adverse Reactions and Precautions).

Topically applied nasal decongestants may not reach all parts of the nasopharyngeal and sinus mucosa. Based on this assumption, systemic therapy with the slower-acting, orally administered drugs and drug combinations has been advocated as being more effective than topical therapy because, after the drug is absorbed, it is carried to ordinarily inaccessible parts of the mucous membranes lining the convoluted nasal passages. It also is claimed that more prolonged relief is produced by the systemically acting adrenergic drugs because topically applied medications tend to be swept away with the respiratory tract fluid by the action of the ciliated cells. There is no convincing clinical evidence to support these contentions. Topically applied dilute aqueous solutions or inhaled vapors of the nasal decongestants have a more rapid onset of action and are more effective than oral doses of the same drugs because of their immediate and direct contact with the nasal mucosa. Also, the duration of action of some topically applied preparations is comparable to that of the orally administered drugs. However, oral preparations are preferable for prolonged use (more than ten days) because the incidence of deleterious effects on the nasal mucosa (eg, dryness, interference with ciliary action, chronic swelling) increases with continued use of the topical agents.

Methods of Topical Application: Nasal decongestants are used topically in the form of vapors or sprays, drops, or solutions applied by means of wet tampons and nasal packs. For short-term, intermittent use, vaporizers containing the volatile bases of certain nasal decongestants (eg, propylhexedrine, tuaminoheptane) are among the most effective means for reaching the desired areas of the nasal mucosa; they are useful when rapid improvement in ventilation of the nose and eustachian orifices is desired (eg, during airplane descent). Drops instilled on the nasal mucosa usually trickle rapidly over the surface and frequently pass to the hypopharynx, where they are swallowed. Swallowing the medication may be avoided by instilling the drops in the lateral, head-low position, but this method is not likely to result in opening of the sinus ostia. Plastic spray packs deliver about three drops of finely divided mist over a much larger area of the nasal mucosa than can be reached by an equal volume in drop form. The mist is sufficiently fine that it does not flow readily, and thus it is less likely to be swallowed than drops. Also, the mist is trapped in the upper respiratory tract so that the possibility of pulmonary absorption is much less than with vapor.

The following regimen for the use of a nasal spray may produce maximal nasal ventilation and opening of the sinus ostia with minimal systemic disturbance: With the patient in the upright position, a spray is delivered into each nostril, and three to five minutes later the nose is thoroughly blown as decongestion begins in the inferior turbinates and part of the middle turbinates. The procedure is then repeated and, if secretions are still being expelled, it may be repeated once more. Congestion of the turbinates high in the nose usually is relieved and the ostia are then more readily accessible for drainage. However, since the total doses provided by this procedure are frequently larger than the usual doses recommended for the same time period, untoward adrenergic effects may be more likely to occur with some of these agents (see the individual evaluations).

Tampons and nasal packs mechanically injure and remove nasal cilia and are no longer used except for diagnostic or surgical procedures in the office or hospital.

Adverse Reactions and Precautions

The topical application of nasal decongestants sometimes causes temporary discomfort such as stinging, burning, or dryness of the mucosa. Inhaled vapors of volatile bases (eg, propylhexedrine [Benzedrex], tuaminoheptane [Tuamine]) particularly may rapidly dry the nasal mucosa and interfere with ciliary action.

Although these agents permit opening of the nasal airways, with drainage and aeration of sinuses, a major disadvantage is the occurrence of rebound congestion after the vasoconstrictive action wears off. Because of this characteristic, topical nasal decongestants, especially naphazoline [Privine], are often abused. Recurrence or exacerbation of the original discomfort may cause the patient to apply or inhale the drug more and more frequently, and overdosage with signs of toxicity may result. Irritation from prolonged and continual use produces chronic swelling of the nasal mucosa. Subsequent topical applications reopen the nasal passages only briefly, and the mucosa becomes pale gray or red, boggy and edematous, and practically identical in appearance to that seen in nonseasonal allergic rhinitis. This condition responds after the medication is discontinued for a week or more. Generally, the topical nasal decongestants should be used only in acute states and for periods not exceeding 10 to 15 days.

The orally administered agents are less apt to induce chronic swelling of the nasal mucosa but are more likely to cause systemic reactions since their action is not selective for the nasal vessels. An oral dosage large enough to bring about nasal decongestion will affect other vascular beds as well, and redistribution of blood flow and cardiac stimulation may occur. Although the vasoconstriction produced usually does not increase blood pressure in most individuals, some patients will experience marked hypertension and arrhythmias.

Topical decongestants also produce systemic reactions, especially in infants and children. Significant absorption may occur from the nasal mucosa or from the gastrointestinal tract when excess solution trickles down the throat and is swallowed. In children and adults, the proper use of nasal sprays (see under Methods of Topical Application) may be the best way to avoid systemic absorption. Use of a nasal spray in the upright position minimizes accumulation since the medication and secretions drip from the nostril and are not swallowed. Use of the drops, when applied in the head-low position, is almost certain to result in systemic absorption.

Systemic effects from overdosage of most adrenergic drugs include transient hypertension, nervousness, nausea, dizziness, palpitation, and, occasionally, central nervous system stimulation. Overdoses of tetrahydrozoline [Tyzine] and naphazoline have caused hypertension, bradycardia, drowsiness, and rebound hypotension; the possibility that such reactions may occur with the other imidazolines (oxymetazoline [Afrin], xylometazoline [Otrivin]) should be kept in mind. These effects are most commonly seen in children. Severe reactions characterized by sweating, drowsiness, deep sleep, coma, and even described as "shock-like," with hypotension and bradycardia, have been reported in children following the absorption of naphazoline and tetrahydrozoline. The imidazolines also may cause arrhythmias, presumably due to coronary vasoconstriction. Because of these effects, the topical nasal decongestants, especially the imidazolines, should be used sparingly and with particular caution in infants, young children, and patients with angina.

Solutions of topical nasal decongestants quickly become contaminated with use and may serve as reservoirs of bacterial and fungal infections. To minimize contamination, the dropper or spray tip should be rinsed in hot water after each use. Patients should be cautioned not to place the dropper in the nostril nor allow more than one person to use the same dropper bottle. The bottle or spray pack should be discarded when the medication is no longer needed. The nasal solutions of many adrenergic agents, especially naphazoline and probably the other imidazolines, should not be used in atomizers made of aluminum or having aluminum parts because of interaction with the metal.

All adrenergic agents should be given sparingly to patients with hyperthyroidism, hypertension, diabetes mellitus, or ischemic heart disease. The nasal decongestants should not be used in patients whose sensitivity to even small doses is manifested by insomnia, dizziness, asthenia, tremor, or arrhythmias, and they should not be given to patients who are receiving monoamine oxidase inhibitors.

INDIVIDUAL EVALUATIONS

COCAINE
COCAINE HYDROCHLORIDE

Cocaine is a local anesthetic and indirect-acting vasoconstrictor. It is effective when marked decongestion and anesthesia of the nasal mucosa is needed, but its use should be limited to office and surgical procedures. It was the first drug to be used as a nasal decongestant. Cocaine potentiates the effects of norepinephrine, apparently by interfering with its reabsorption by the sympathetic nerve endings and thus prolonging its action locally.

Cocaine produces prompt vasoconstriction and temporary paralysis of the cilia. In spite of its local vasoconstrictive action, all mucous membranes may absorb cocaine more rapidly than it can be detoxified and excreted.

Prolonged use of cocaine causes ischemic damage to the nasal mucosa. Systemic absorption resulting from overdosage causes excitement, chills followed by fever, tachycardia, hypertension, and nervousness. See also Chapter 18, Local Anesthetics, and Chapter

70, Mydriatics and Cycloplegics. Epinephrine should not be added to cocaine. Cocaine is classified as a Schedule II drug.

USUAL DOSAGE.—*Topical:* 0.5% to 2% solution is applied as a spray or on a tampon. For a more profound effect, a 10% solution is placed on small cotton pledgets and applied to the nasal mucosa.

PREPARATIONS.—Cocaine, N.F.; Cocaine Hydrochloride, U.S.P. No pharmaceutical dosage form available; compounding by pharmacist necessary.

CYCLOPENTAMINE HYDROCHLORIDE
[Clopane Hydrochloride]

$$C_5H_9-CH_2CH(CH_3)N(H)CH_3 \cdot HCl$$

Cyclopentamine is used topically for temporary relief of nasal congestion. Its effects are similar to those of ephedrine, but it is somewhat more potent as a vasoconstrictor and causes less central nervous system stimulation.

Systemic absorption from overdosage causes transient hypertension, nervousness, nausea, and dizziness. Repeated use of the 1% solution may cause irritation and swelling of the nasal mucosa within a few days. See also the Introductory Statement.

USUAL DOSAGE.—*Topical:* 0.5% solution applied as needed by dropper, spray, or tampon. Drops should be instilled with the head in the lateral, head-low position. If stinging occurs, the solution should be diluted with isotonic sodium chloride solution. A 1% solution may be used for office procedures or prescribed for patients who do not obtain adequate relief with the 0.5% solution.

PREPARATIONS.—Clopane Hydrochloride (Lilly). *Topical:* Solution 0.5% in 500 ml containers, 1% in 30 ml containers; spray 0.5% in 15 ml containers.

EPHEDRINE
EPHEDRINE HYDROCHLORIDE
EPHEDRINE SULFATE

$$\left[C_6H_5-CH(OH)-CH(NHCH_3)CH_3\right]_2 \cdot H_2SO_4$$

Ephedrine has actions similar to those of phenylephrine, but its onset of action is slower. It is effective both topically and orally but is now seldom used because secondary turgescence of the nasal mucosa and tachyphylaxis occur frequently. Other adverse effects include central nervous system stimulation, transient hypertension, and palpitations. See also the Introductory Statement.

Aqueous solutions are preferred; oily solutions are generally contraindicated, especially in children, because of the danger of causing lipid pneumonia. Allergy to ephedrine, which occurs rarely, is a specific contraindication to its use. It also should not be given to patients with heart disease, diabetes, hypertension, or thyroid imbalance. Repeated use of the 3% solution may cause irritation and swelling of the nasal mucosa within a few days. See also the Introductory Statement.

For other uses, see Chapter 5, Agents Used in Hypotension and Shock, and Chapter 41, Bronchodilators.

USUAL DOSAGE.—

Oral: Adults, 25 to 50 mg every three to four hours; *children,* 3 mg/kg of body weight per 24 hours in four to six divided doses.

Topical: 0.5% to 3% solution, generally as drops, applied as needed; drops should be instilled with the head in the lateral, head-low position. The drug may also be applied in pack or tampon. The 1% spray in mineral oil should not be used because of the reason stated above.

PREPARATIONS.—

Oral: Tablets 25 and 50 mg.

Topical: Solution 2% in isotonic sodium chloride solution; spray 1% in light mineral oil. Drug marketed by many manufacturers under generic name.

EPINEPHRINE HYDROCHLORIDE [Adrenalin Chloride]

$$HO(OH)C_6H_3-CH(OH)-CH_2NH-CH_3 \cdot HCl$$

Epinephrine is an effective topical nasal decongestant, but its duration of action is short. It is useful to control epistaxis or to facilitate nasal surgery.

Like other topical nasal decongestants, epinephrine frequently causes rebound nasal congestion. Adverse reactions include anxiety, tremor, apprehension, pallor, restlessness, asthenia, dizziness, throbbing headache, dyspnea, and palpitation. Central nervous system stimulation occurs less frequently than with ephedrine. Adverse effects quickly disappear when the drug is discontinued. Its use with cocaine hydrochloride is contraindicated. See also the Introductory Statement.

For other uses, see Chapters 2, Antiarrhythmic Agents; 5, Agents Used in Hypotension and Shock; 41, Bronchodilators; 69, Agents Used to Treat Glaucoma; and 70, Mydriatics and Cycloplegics.

USUAL DOSAGE.—*Topical:* 1% aqueous solution, instilled as drops or spray, applied as needed. Drops should be instilled with the head in the lateral, head-low position. Some solutions may sting slightly due to presence of 0.1% to 0.2% sodium bisulfite added as antioxidant.

PREPARATIONS.—Adrenalin Chloride (Parke, Davis). *Topical:* Solution (aqueous) 1% in 30 ml containers. Drug also marketed under generic name.

METHYLHEXANEAMINE [Forthane]

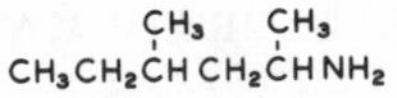

$$CH_3CH_2\overset{CH_3}{\overset{|}{C}}H\,CH_2\overset{CH_3}{\overset{|}{C}}HNH_2$$

Methylhexaneamine is used only by inhalation and is an effective nasal decongestant.

Adverse effects of the adrenergic agents, such as headache, nervousness, central nervous system stimulation, or tremors, are uncommon.

USUAL DOSAGE.—*Topical:* One or two inhalations in each nostril as needed.

PREPARATIONS.—Forthane (Lilly). *Topical:* Inhaler 250 mg.

NAPHAZOLINE HYDROCHLORIDE [Privine Hydrochloride]

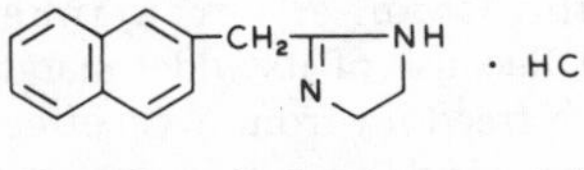

This imidazoline derivative is used topically for relief of local swelling and congestion of the nasal mucous membranes.

Adverse reactions include rebound congestion, "nose-drop dependence," and irritation and swelling of the nasal mucosa from continued use. This swelling is generally alleviated a few days after the medication is discontinued. Naphazoline also may cause paralysis of the nasal cilia and, occasionally, anosmia. Occasional smarting and sneezing also occur. Other adverse reactions include arrhythmias, probably as a result of coronary vasoconstriction, and transient hypertension, bradycardia, sweating, and drowsiness. Systemic absorption from overdosage has caused deep sleep and, in children, coma. Rebound hypotension may follow hypertension and bradycardia. The solution should not be used in atomizers containing any parts made of aluminum. See also the Introductory Statement.

USUAL DOSAGE.—*Topical:* One or two drops or two spray inhalations of 0.05% solution not more often than every three hours. Drops should be instilled with the head in the lateral, head-low position.

PREPARATIONS.—Privine Hydrochloride (Ciba). *Topical:* Solution 0.05% in 30 and 500 ml containers; spray 0.05% in 20 ml containers. Drug also marketed under generic name.

OXYMETAZOLINE HYDROCHLORIDE [Afrin]

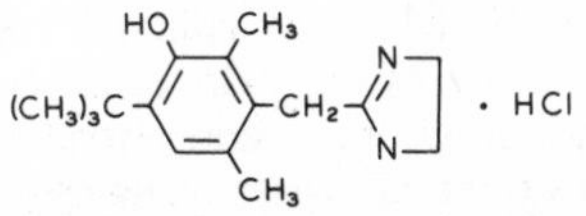

Oxymetazoline is an effective topical nasal decongestant that is somewhat longer acting than the other imidazoline derivatives. Subjective clinical evidence indicates that it is useful in treating nasal congestion associated with nonseasonal allergic rhinitis, hay fever, and other forms of acute and chronic rhinitis or sinusitis.

Mild untoward effects that occur with normal use include local stinging or burning, sneezing, dryness of the nose and throat, headache, dizziness, insomnia, and palpitations. Effects on the central nervous system or blood pressure have not been reported, but presumably overdosage might cause adverse effects similar to those observed with other imidazolines. Prolonged use often causes tolerance and decreased duration of action, necessitating more and more frequent use, and finally rebound congestion and swelling of the mucous membranes. See also the Introductory Statement.

USUAL DOSAGE.—*Topical: Adults and children over 6 years of age*, two to four drops or two or three inhalations of spray in each nostril in morning and at bedtime, or every four to six hours as necessary. With spray inhalations, repetition of treatment in 10 or 15 minutes may be indicated when it is necessary to reach the ostia of the sinuses or eustachian tubes.

PREPARATIONS.—Afrin (Schering). *Topical:* Solution 0.05% in 30 ml containers; spray 0.05% in 3 and 15 ml containers.

PHENYLEPHRINE HYDROCHLORIDE
[Neo-Synephrine Hydrochloride]

$HO-C_6H_4-CH(OH)CH_2NHCH_3 \cdot HCl$

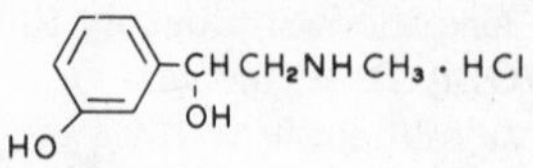

Phenylephrine is the most widely prescribed topical nasal decongestant. It is qualitatively similar in effects to epinephrine but is less potent on a weight basis and has a longer duration of action. Although oral dosage forms are available, this route seldom is effective in producing nasal decongestion at the recommended dosage.

Adverse reactions include all of the untoward effects of ephedrine or epinephrine, except that phenylephrine causes little or no central nervous system stimulation. A concentration of 0.25% is usually effective; the stronger concentrations cause chronic swelling of the nasal mucosa within a few days. See also the Introductory Statement.

USUAL DOSAGE.—

Topical: Adults and older children, several drops of 0.25% to 1% solution instilled in each nostril as needed with the head in the lateral head-low position. Alternatively, the nasal spray may be used or a small amount of the jelly may be placed in each nostril and inhaled. *Infants*, the 0.125% solution is used.

Oral: This route of administration is of limited value because of its uncertain effectiveness. The manufacturer's suggested dosage is: *Adults*, 10 mg three times daily; *children 6 to 12 years of age*, 5 mg three times daily.

PREPARATIONS.—Neo-Synephrine Hydrochloride (Winthrop).

Topical: Solution 0.125% (pediatric) in 15 ml containers, 0.25% and 1% in 30, 120, and 500 ml containers, and 0.5% in 30 ml containers; spray 0.25% and 0.5% in 20 ml containers; jelly (water-soluble) 0.5% in 10 g containers.

Oral: Elixir 5 mg/5 ml.

ADDITIONAL TRADEMARKS.—Alcon-Efrin (Alcon), Biomydrin (Warner-Chilcott), Isohalant Improved (Elder), Isophrin (Broemmel), Synasal (Texas). Drug also marketed by many manufacturers under generic name.

PHENYLPROPANOLAMINE HYDROCHLORIDE [Propadrin]

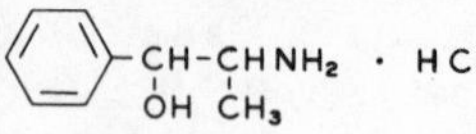

$C_6H_5-CH(OH)-CH(CH_3)NH_2 \cdot HCl$

Phenylpropanolamine is one of the most frequently used oral nasal decongestants. It is similar in actions and adverse effects to epinephrine and ephedrine but has a more prolonged duration of action than epinephrine and produces less central nervous system stimulation than ephedrine. See also the Introductory Statement.

USUAL DOSAGE.—*Oral: Adults*, 25 mg every three or four hours; *children 8 to 12 years of age*, 20 to 25 mg three times daily.

PREPARATIONS.—Propadrine Hydrochloride (Merck Sharp & Dohme). *Oral:* Capsules 25 and 50 mg; elixir 20 mg/5 ml.

ADDITIONAL TRADEMARK.—Protrim (Robinson).

PROPYLHEXEDRINE [Benzedrex]

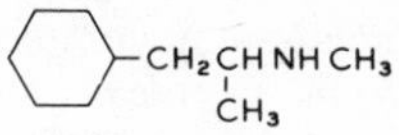

$C_6H_{11}-CH_2CH(CH_3)NHCH_3$

Propylhexedrine is used by inhalation for its decongestant effect on the nasal mucous membranes. It has about one-eighth the pressor effect of amphetamine and produces considerably less central nervous system stimulation than either amphetamine or ephedrine. Because of its wider margin of safety and relative freedom from toxic effects, it is not contraindicated for patients in whom an ephedrine-like pressor or stimulant action would be undesirable. It is considered safe for self-medication by adults, but children should not have unsupervised access to an inhaler. The vapors may dry the nasal mucosa and interfere with ciliary action. See also the Introductory Statement.

USUAL DOSAGE.—*Topical* (inhalation): Two inhalations (0.6 to 0.8 mg) through each nostril as needed. The inhaler usually retains effectiveness for two to three months. If the inhaler is cold, it should be warmed in the hand before use to increase volatility.

PREPARATIONS.—Benzedrex (Smith Kline & French). *Topical:* Inhaler 250 mg.

TETRAHYDROZOLINE HYDROCHLORIDE
[Tyzine]

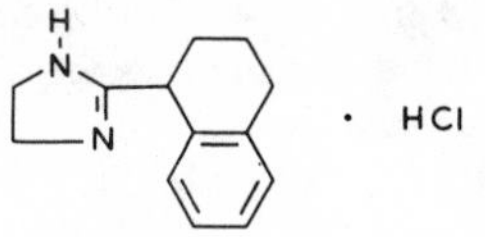

Tetrahydrozoline is an imidazoline derivative that is effective topically for temporary relief of nasal congestion.

Adverse effects include hypertension, bradycardia, severe drowsiness accompanied by sweating, rebound hypotension, and arrhythmias, probably due to coronary vasoconstriction. Chronic swelling of the nasal mucosa may occur with prolonged use. This swelling may not disappear until a week or more after the medication is discontinued. Coma and hypothermia may occur in children, especially infants. Because of these effects, tetrahydrozoline should be used sparingly, if at all, and with particular caution in infants, young children, and patients with angina. See also the Introductory Statement.

USUAL DOSAGE.–*Topical: Adults,* two or three drops of 0.1% solution instilled in each nostril not more often than every three hours. When spray is used, the nozzle may be inserted in each nostril and squeezed sharply one or two times. *Children 6 years of age or older,* one to three drops of 0.05% solution instilled in each nostril, with the head in the lateral head-low position, at intervals of four to six hours. Should be used with extreme caution if at all in *infants and children under 6 years* because of the reasons stated above.

PREPARATIONS.–Tyzine (Pfizer). *Topical:* Solution 0.05% in 15 ml containers; solution 0.1% in 30 and 500 ml containers; spray 0.1% in 15 ml containers.

TUAMINOHEPTANE [Tuamine]
TUAMINOHEPTANE SULFATE [Tuamine Sulfate]

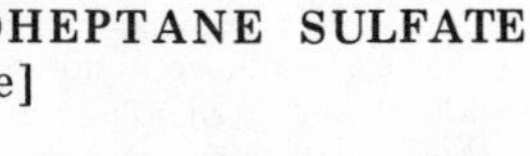

$$[CH_3(CH_2)_4CH(CH_3)NH_2]_2 \cdot H_2SO_4$$

Tuaminoheptane is an effective topical nasal decongestant when the vapor is inhaled or the solution is applied in the form of drops. The vasoconstrictive action of the 1% solution exceeds that of 1% ephedrine solution and the duration of effect is longer.

Adverse reactions are those observed with other adrenergic agents. Tuaminoheptane vapor may dry the nasal mucosa and interfere with ciliary action. The drug is relatively safe for use in infants and young children. It should be used with caution in patients with cardiovascular disease. See also the Introductory Statement.

USUAL DOSAGE.–

Tuaminoheptane:

Topical (inhalation): One or two inhalations in each nostril, repeated at hourly intervals if necessary.

Tuaminoheptane Sulfate:

Topical: Adults and children over 6 years of age, four or five drops; *children 1 to 6 years,* two or three drops instilled in each nostril not more than four or five times daily.

PREPARATIONS.–

Tuamine (Lilly). *Topical:* Inhaler 325 mg.

Tuamine Sulfate (Lilly). *Topical:* Solution 1% in 30 ml containers.

XYLOMETAZOLINE HYDROCHLORIDE
[Otrivin Hydrochloride]

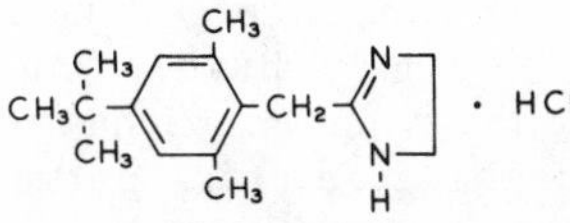

This imidazoline derivative is effective topically for temporary relief of nasal congestion.

Untoward reactions, which are generally mild and occur infrequently, include local stinging or burning, sneezing, dryness of the nose, headache, insomnia, drowsiness, palpitations, and chronic swelling of nasal mucosa. The possibility that overdoses of this drug may cause the more serious reactions reported with other imidazolines should be kept in mind. The solution should not be used in atomizers containing any parts made of aluminum. See also the Introductory Statement.

USUAL DOSAGE.–*Topical: Adults,* two or three drops of 0.1% solution in each nostril or one or two inhalations of 0.1% nasal spray every four to six hours. *Children under 12 years of age,* two or three drops of 0.05% solution or one inhalation of 0.05% nasal spray in each nostril every four to six hours.

PREPARATIONS.–Otrivin Hydrochloride (Ciba). *Topical:* Solution (pediatric) 0.05% in 30 ml containers, 0.1% in 30 and 500 ml containers; spray (pediatric) 0.05% in 15 ml containers, 0.1% in 3 and 15 ml containers.

MIXTURES

Many mixtures combining a nasal decongestant with one or more additional drugs are available; some are designed for topical application and others for oral administration. Frequently the added drug is an antihistamine, antibiotic, glucocorticoid, or a second nasal decongestant. Other compounds occasionally present in the nasal decongestant mixtures include atropine or other anticholinergics, various wetting compounds, and quaternary ammonium salts.

If nasal decongestion is the therapeutic action desired, there is no good evidence that any of the available mixtures are more effective than a single-entity drug preparation. On the other hand, evidence does exist that other agents present in the mixture either do not assist the nasal decongestant and thus simply add cost to the mixture, or are detrimental. For example, antihistamines add no beneficial effect to the topical preparations and, even when administered orally, they produce little or no shrinkage of the engorged nasal mucosa, although they may have some effect in ameliorating the symptoms of hay fever. Also, many added ingredients, particularly the antibiotics, act as sensitizers; in addition, the bacteria present in the nasal discharges are simply the normal flora, and an antibiotic may convert the flora to resistant strains.

Topically applied mixtures are used and abused widely by both the medical profession and the lay public. Careful comparative evaluation of these mixtures with single-entity decongestants has not been made; therefore, their use instead of a single-entity drug should be discouraged. The preparation chosen and the total duration of its use must be determined by the physician on the basis of his experience and the response of the patient. Since individual tolerance and the tendency toward chronic congestion of the mucosa from prolonged use varies among patients, use of these agents should be regulated on an individual basis. A mixture containing a nasal decongestant cannot be expected to perform any better than the same quantity of the decongestant drug alone.

For orally administered decongestant mixtures, see Chapter 46, Cold Remedies.

The following topical mixtures are listed for information and do not constitute approval because of the reasons stated above.

Bihisdin (Philips Roxane): Spray containing phenylephrine hydrochloride 0.25%, pyrilamine maleate 0.1%, and cetylpyridinium chloride 0.05%.

Citra (Boyle): Spray containing phenylephrine hydrochloride 0.5%, gramicidin 0.005%, pyrilamine maleate 0.1%, and cetalkonium chloride 0.05%.

Coricidin Nasal Mist (Schering): Each milliliter of spray contains phenylephrine hydrochloride 5 mg and chlorpheniramine gluconate 3 mg.

Nasocon (Smith, Miller & Patch): Spray containing naphazoline hydrochloride 0.025% and antazoline phosphate 0.5%.

Neo-Vadrin (First Texas): Drops or spray containing phenylpropanolamine hydrochloride 0.4%, phenylephrine hydrochloride 0.15%, chlorobutanol 0.15%, and benzalkonium chloride 0.005%.

NTZ (Winthrop): Solution containing phenylephrine hydrochloride 0.5%, thenyldiamine hydrochloride 0.1%, and benzalkonium chloride 1:5,000.

Pyracort (Lemmon): Suspension containing phenylephrine hydrochloride 0.25%, hydrocortisone acetate 0.02%, and methapyrilene hydrochloride 0.2%.

Pyraphed (Lemmon): Solution containing phenylephrine hydrochloride 0.25% and methapyrilene hydrochloride 0.2%.

Tri-Azo-Mul/AH (First Texas): Each 5 ml of suspension contains trisulfapyrimidines 500 mg and chlorpheniramine maleate 2 mg.

Triaminicin (Dorsey): Spray containing phenylpropanolamine hydrochloride 0.75%, phenylephrine hydrochloride 0.25%, pheniramine maleate 0.125%, and pyrilamine maleate 0.1255%.

Tri-Isohalant (Elder): Liquid containing phenylephrine hydrochloride 0.5%, pyrilamine maleate 0.125%, pheniramine maleate 0.125%, poloxalkol 0.25%, and benzyl alcohol 0.5%.

Chapter 43

EXPECTORANTS AND INHALANTS

Expectorants are used orally to stimulate the flow of respiratory tract secretions. Mucolytic agents are used by inhalation to reduce the viscosity of respiratory tract fluid. Either action allows ciliary motion and coughing to move the loosened material toward the pharynx more easily. This augmentation of bronchial secretions is desirable in the treatment of respiratory disorders in which secretions are purulent, viscid, or excessive. However, the term expectorated sputum is not synonymous with respiratory tract fluid; there may be no correlation between the actions of drugs upon the volume of expectorated sputum and the production of respiratory tract fluid. It is difficult to classify a drug precisely as an expectorant or mucolytic agent, since adequate methods for measuring sputum volume and viscosity or the mucolytic effect of medications have not yet been devised.

The volatile organic oils, of which terpin hydrate is a derivative, are thought to have a direct effect on the bronchial secretory cells. Other agents (ammonium chloride, glyceryl guaiacolate [Robitussin, 2/G], guaiacolsulfonate potassium, syrup of ipecac, iodinated glycerin [Organidin], potassium iodide, hydriodic acid syrup) are believed to act reflexly by irritating the gastric mucosa which in turn stimulates respiratory tract secretion. Although there is experimental evidence to indicate that drugs in each group have an effect on secretion of respiratory tract fluid, such evidence is sparse and unconvincing; thus, the therapeutic efficacy of these agents is doubtful. The use of expectorants is based primarily on tradition and the widespread subjective clinical impression that they are effective.

The inhalation of agents designed to decrease viscosity of respiratory tract secretions and move them up the bronchial tree is an alternative to the oral use of expectorants. The nebulization of water or sodium chloride solution as an adjunct to systemic therapy represents an important advance in the management of acute respiratory diseases. Attempts have been made to increase the efficiency of these humidifying inhalations by adding various compounds to the nebulized fluid. These agents act by several different mechanisms. Hypertonic sodium chloride solutions increase respiratory fluid volume by osmosis. Hygroscopic agents (eg, propylene glycol, glycerin) are added in an attempt to draw more water into bronchial secretions and thus reduce their viscosity. Acetylcysteine [Mucomyst] effectively reduces the viscosity of mucus in vitro, probably by depolymerizing mucopolysaccharides, and several reports indicate that it is also effective clinically. Detergents (eg, tyloxapol [Alevaire]) increase wetting and thereby supposedly increase the liquefaction of mucus; however, special conditions and equipment are required for their administration, and evidence that they are any more effective than plain water or sodium chloride solution is not convincing. Pancreatic dornase [Dornavac] reduces the viscosity of purulent mucus by hydrolysis of deoxyribonucleoprotein; it may be useful as an adjunct in the treatment of paranasal sinus infections although its usefulness is limited because of difficulty in delivering it to an obstructed sinus. In addition to being inhaled as a mist, acetylcysteine and pancreatic dornase can be instilled directly into the trachea or bronchus. This direct administration increases the local concentration and may be more effective than nebulization.

None of the inhalants has been proved to be of greater therapeutic benefit than adequate humidification, and they all present problems in administration. Because inflammatory reactions can result from long-term use of either expectorants or inhalants, these agents generally should be restricted to the short-term management of acute respiratory disease, although occasionally they may be helpful in chronic bronchial conditions.

Adverse Reactions and Precautions

Gastrointestinal disturbances often are associated with the use of expectorants.

Ammonium chloride is readily absorbed and large doses produce metabolic acidosis. Therefore, it should be used with caution in patients with pulmonary, hepatic, or renal insufficiency.

Potassium iodide also is readily absorbed. Prolonged administration of large doses can produce iodism, which is characterized by rash, parotitis, and fever. Anaphylaxis also is an occasional adverse reaction. Sensitivity reactions occasionally occur after administration of any expectorant that contains iodine, including iodinated glycerin and hydriodic acid. Potassium iodide can complicate the interpretation of thyroid function tests and may result in thyroid enlargement or a decrease in thyroid function. It readily crosses the placenta and, when given in large doses, may produce thyroid enlargement in the fetus.

When prescribing ipecac, care must be taken to specify the syrup, because the more potent fluidextract has caused deaths (see also Chapter 84, Emetics).

Inhalant aerosols that contain drugs generally should be used for only a few days because inflammatory reactions occasionally occur during longer periods of administration. Local and systemic sensitivity reactions are most likely to occur with pancreatic dornase [Dornavac], especially after repeated use. Acetylcysteine [Mucomyst] can produce bronchospasm in asthmatic patients.

All inhalant solutions present problems in administration. They must be prepared and diluted under sterile conditions. Although bulb atomizers may be suitable for use under certain conditions, frequently the solutions must be vaporized into a tent, humidified canopy [Croupette], face mask, or mouthpiece. They may be instilled directly into the trachea by bronchoscope or tracheostomy in order to penetrate deeply into the tracheobronchial tree. When a mask or mouthpiece is indicated, intermittent positive pressure breathing (IPPB) techniques are employed using a direct nebulizer-oxygen tank arrangement.

The demonstration of a surface-active agent (surfactant) in the lungs has further complicated the evaluation of inhalation therapy. This surfactant probably assists in preventing osmotic forces from collapsing smaller air passages. The effects of inhalant aerosols on this function have not been fully evaluated, but they may not always be beneficial.

INDIVIDUAL EVALUATIONS

ACETYLCYSTEINE [Mucomyst]

$$\begin{array}{l} HS\,CH_2\underset{|}{C}H\,COOH \\ \quad\quad\quad NH\,CO\,CH_3 \end{array}$$

This drug reduces the viscosity of mucus in vitro. Clinical effectiveness is difficult to assess, but subjective reports and a few controlled studies indicate that acetylcysteine, given by nebulization as an adjunct to other therapy, may be beneficial in reducing the viscosity of abnormal pulmonary secretions in patients with inflammatory lung diseases and in those with cystic fibrosis. The drug also may be instilled directly into the trachea in patients with tracheostomies. This method of administration can be more effective than nebulization.

Adverse reactions are not common but include bronchospasm, especially in asthmatic patients, nausea, and vomiting. Bronchospasm occurs less frequently when the 10% solution is used. Stomatitis, rhinorrhea, and hemoptysis occur occasionally and rare instances of probable sensitization have been reported. Elderly and debilitated patients should be observed closely to avoid aspiration of excessive secretions. Acetylcysteine has an unpleasant odor and reacts irreversibly with metals and rubber.

USUAL DOSAGE.—Open vials should be covered, refrigerated, and used within 96 hours.

Inhalation (nebulization): 2 to 20 ml of a 10% or 1 to 10 ml of a 20% solution nebulized into a face mask or mouthpiece every two to six hours. The solution tends to concentrate and should be diluted with sterile water when three-fourths of the original volume has been used.

Inhalation (instillation): 1 to 2 ml of a 10% to 20% solution instilled into the trachea by tracheostomy or bronchoscope as often as every hour.

PREPARATIONS.—Mucomyst (Mead Johnson). *Inhalation:* Solution (sterile) 10% and 20% in 10 and 30 ml containers.

AMMONIUM CHLORIDE

Ammonium chloride presumably increases the amount of respiratory mucus by reflex stimulation of the gastric mucosa; however, its effectiveness is doubtful. The drug is rarely used alone as an expectorant, but is a common ingredient in mixtures.

Ammonium chloride may produce metabolic acidosis when given in large doses, and should be used cautiously in patients with hepatic, renal, or pulmonary insufficiency.

USUAL DOSAGE.—*Oral: Adults,* 5 ml of syrup containing 300 mg of the drug.

PREPARATIONS.—Ammonium Chloride, U.S.P. Drug marketed under generic name.

TYLOXAPOL [Alevaire]

This detergent is used to lower surface tension and help liquefy mucus. It is reported to be useful for short-term management of many inflammatory and postoperative pulmonary conditions. Results of some reports suggest that detergents exert a beneficial effect when administered intermittently in the long-term management of cystic fibrosis and other chronic pulmonary diseases. However, definitive clinical studies are lacking and it is not known whether solutions containing detergents are more useful than aerosol solutions of sodium chloride or pure water.

Few adverse effects have been reported at recommended concentrations. Prolonged use of tyloxapol irritates the respiratory tract.

USUAL DOSAGE.—*Inhalation:* The solution is given full strength through an aerosol nebulizer attached to a pressurized oxygen or air supply at a rate of 2 to 12 liters of gas/minute, depending upon the nebulizer used. The mist is continuously delivered into a tent for up to a few days, or intermittently for longer periods. The mist may also be delivered through a face mask or through an oral or nasal nebulizer attachment.

PREPARATIONS.—Alevaire (Breon). *Inhalation:* Solution containing tyloxapol 0.125% and glycerin 5% in 60 and 500 ml bottles.

GLYCERYL GUAIACOLATE [Robitussin, 2/G]

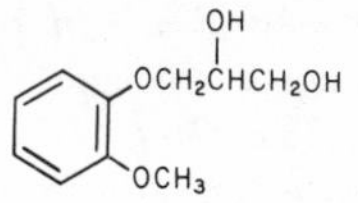

Glyceryl guaiacolate is used alone and as an ingredient of expectorant cough mixtures. It is claimed to act by stimulating receptors in the gastric mucosa thereby initiating a reflex secretion of respiratory tract fluid that increases the volume and decreases the viscosity of bronchial secretions. Few objective studies on its action are available and its effectiveness is doubtful.

Nausea, gastrointestinal upset, and drowsiness occur infrequently. No serious adverse effects have been reported.

USUAL DOSAGE.—*Oral: Adults and children,* 100 to 200 mg two to four times daily.

PREPARATIONS.—Robitussin (Robins), 2/G (Dow). *Oral:* Syrup 100 mg/5 ml. Drug also marketed under generic name.

IODINATED GLYCERIN [Organidin]

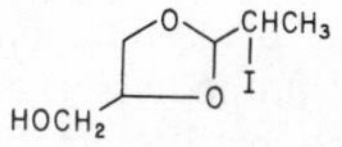

The efficacy of iodinated glycerin is questionable, although it is claimed to have the expectorant actions of iodine and glycerin and does not cause gastric irritation or release inorganic iodine before absorption.

Sensitivity reactions occur occasionally. Therefore, iodinated glycerin is contraindicated in patients who are sensitive to iodine.

USUAL DOSAGE.—*Oral: Adults,* 2 tablets, 20 drops of 5% solution, or 5 ml of elixir four times daily. *Children,* one-half or less of adult dose, depending upon age and weight. All forms should be well diluted with a liquid before ingestion.

PREPARATIONS.—Organidin (Wampole). *Oral:* Elixir 1.2%; solution 5%; tablets 30 mg.

SYRUP OF IPECAC

Syrup of ipecac is believed to increase bronchial secretion by reflex stimulation of gastric mucosa. This time-honored remedy may have some usefulness. It also is an ingredient of many expectorant mixtures. Syrup of ipecac is used as an emetic in higher dosage (see Chapter 84, Emetics). *Caution: This preparation should not be confused with Ipecac Fluidextract which is much more potent and has caused deaths; therefore, it is essential that the physician clearly specify ipecac syrup in prescribing and not use the single word "ipecac."*

USUAL DOSAGE.—*Oral: Adults,* 0.5 to 2 ml every six hours; *children* should not receive this drug as an expectorant.

PREPARATIONS.—*Oral:* Syrup. Drug marketed under generic name.

PANCREATIC DORNASE [Dornavac]

This bovine pancreatic deoxyribonuclease inhalant reduces the viscosity of purulent sputum in vitro by hydrolysis of deoxyribonucleoprotein. Favorable results have been reported in bronchopulmonary infections and in the management of the respiratory complications of cystic fibrosis. It has also been used as an adjunct in the treatment of paranasal sinus infections. Pancreatic dornase is given to facilitate collection of sputum for cytologic examinations.

Local and generalized allergic reactions occur, usually after repeated doses.

USUAL DOSAGE.—*Inhalation:* 50,000 to 100,000 units of powdered pancreatic dornase dissolved in 2 ml of sodium chloride solution and administered immediately either in aerosol form or by direct instillation into the trachea. Ordinary nebulizers may not deliver the drug effectively to the bronchioles; either a direct nebulizer-oxygen tank arrangement or a mechanical respirator should be used. Treatment may be repeated four times daily for seven days.

PREPARATIONS.—Dornavac (Merck Sharp & Dohme). *Inhalation* (aerosol or irrigation): Powder 100,000 units with 2 ml of sterile diluent.

POTASSIUM IODIDE

Potassium iodide is thought to increase bronchial secretion by reflex stimulation of the gastric mucosa. Iodide is secreted in the sputum shortly after oral administration. The effectiveness of potassium iodide as an expectorant is doubtful, and it is preferably used only for short-term management of acute respiratory tract disease. The use of potassium iodide is limited by its unpleasant taste and the frequency of adverse reactions.

Complications include angioedema, laryngeal edema, and occasional anaphylaxis. Prolonged use of large doses can cause iodism (acneiform rash, parotitis, fever, rhinitis). The drug should be discontinued promptly if these reactions occur. Potassium iodide can complicate the interpretation of thyroid function tests and may result in thyroid enlargement or a decrease in thyroid function. It readily crosses the placenta and large doses may produce thyroid enlargement in the fetus.

USUAL DOSAGE.—*Oral: Adults,* 300 mg in a liquid vehicle every four to six hours; *children,* 0.25 to 1 ml of saturated potassium iodide solution in two to four doses daily.

PREPARATIONS.—Potassium Iodide, U.S.P.

AVAILABLE TRADEMARK.—KI-N (Mallinckrodt). Drug also marketed under generic name.

SODIUM CHLORIDE

Inhalation of nebulized isotonic sodium chloride solution assists liquefaction and expectoration of viscid sputum. Inhalation of hypertonic sodium chloride solution has been reported to be effective in cystic fibrosis.

Prolonged inhalation can irritate the bronchial mucosa.

USUAL DOSAGE.—*Inhalation* (solution): Isotonic or 0.5 M sodium chloride is nebulized to form a dense mist in a tent.

PREPARATIONS.—Sodium Chloride, U.S.P. Marketed under generic name.

TERPIN HYDRATE

CH_3, HO (cyclohexane ring) — $C(CH_3)_2$—OH · H_2O

This is one of a large group of miscellaneous volatile oil derivatives claimed to have a direct action on the bronchial secretory cells. This effect is doubtful. The elixir form is used as a vehicle for other cough medications.

USUAL DOSAGE.—*Oral: Adults and children,* 4 to 5 ml every four to six hours.

PREPARATIONS.—Terpin Hydrate Elixir, N.F. Drug marketed under generic name.

MIXTURES

Many mixtures listed in this section appear to have been formulated more for symptomatic relief of minor respiratory disorders than for any other purpose. In addition to one or more ingredients classified as expectorants, most of these combination products contain one or more drugs of the following classes: adrenergics (bronchodilators or nasal decongestants), antitussives (narcotic or non-narcotic), and antihistamines. Occasionally, a local anesthetic or sedative also appears in a formula.

The practitioner occasionally may find some of these preparations useful as relatively harmless supportive therapy for minor respiratory illnesses. However, when expectorant therapy is indicated in serious pulmonary conditions, an appropriate single-entity agent should be used.

Principal disadvantages of the fixed-dosage combination products are that not all ingredients are present in optimal therapeutic amounts and in many instances the ingredients have no therapeutic effect. For example, some preparations supply a suboptimal dose of ammonium chloride (which even at recommended doses is questionably effective as an expectorant) and thus there is little or no assurance of any expectorant action. Many multidrug preparations containing up to six or more different agents can only be condemned as shotgun remedies and should not be used. When mixtures containing antihistamines are used, patients should be warned that drowsiness may occur. See also Chapters 41, Bronchodilators; 42, Nasal Decongestants; 44, Antitussive Agents; 45, Antihistamines, and 46, Cold Remedies.

Actifed-C Expectorant (Burroughs Wellcome): Each 5 ml of liquid contains codeine phosphate 10 mg, glyceryl guaiacolate 100 mg, pseudoephedrine hydrochloride 30 mg, and triprolidine hydrochloride 2 mg.

Acutuss (Philips Roxane): Each 5 ml of liquid contains chlophedianol hydrochloride 15 mg, diphenylpyraline hydrochloride 1 mg, glyceryl guaiacolate 100 mg, and phenylephrine hydrochloride 5 mg; each tablet contains chlophedianol hydrochloride 7.5 mg, diphenylpyraline hydrochloride 0.5 mg, glyceryl guaiacolate 25 mg, phenylephrine hydrochloride 2.5 mg, and acetaminophen 162.5 mg.

Acutuss Expactorant with Codeine (Philips Roxane): Each 5 ml of liquid contains codeine phosphate 10 mg, glyceryl guaiacolate 100 mg, chlorpheniramine maleate 2 mg, phenylpropanolamine hydrochloride 5 mg, phenylephrine hydrochloride 5 mg, and chloroform 13.5 mg.

Ambenyl Expectorant (Parke, Davis): Each 5 ml of liquid contains ammonium chloride 85 mg, codeine sulfate 10 mg, bromodiphenhydramine hydrochloride 4 mg, diphenhydramine hydrochloride 8 mg, and guaiacolsulfonate potassium 85 mg.

Amonidrin (Durst): Each tablet contains ammonium chloride 194 mg, calcium creosotate 16.2 mg, guaiacolsulfonate potassium 194 mg, ephedrine hydrochloride 8.1 mg, and benzocaine 2 mg.

Ayrtab (Ascher): Each tablet contains glyceryl guaiacolate 100 mg and theophylline 100 mg.

Benylin Expectorant (Parke, Davis): Each 5 ml of liquid contains ammonium chloride 130 mg, sodium citrate 54 mg, chloroform 20 mg, and diphenhydramine hydrochloride 13 mg.

Brexin (Savage): Each capsule contains glyceryl guaiacolate 100 mg, pseudoephedrine hydrochloride 60 mg, and methapyrilene hydrochloride 30 mg.

Calcidrine Syrup (Abbott): Each 5 ml contains codeine phosphate 8.4 mg, calcium iodide anhydrous 152 mg, and ephedrine hydrochloride 4.2 mg.

Chlor-Trimeton Expectorant (Schering): Each 5 ml contains ammonium chloride 100 mg, glyceryl guaiacolate 50 mg, chlorpheniramine maleate 2 mg, phenylephrine hydrochloride 10 mg, sodium citrate 50 mg, and chloroform 12.5 mg with or without codeine phosphate 10 mg.

Colrex Expectorant (Rowell): Each 5 ml of syrup contains glyceryl guaiacolate 100 mg and ammonium chloride 100 mg.

Conar Expectorant (Beecham-Massengill): Each 5 ml contains noscapine 10 mg, glyceryl guaiacolate 100 mg, chlorpheniramine maleate 2 mg, phenylephrine hydrochloride 10 mg, chloroform 12 mg, and menthol 0.2 mg.

Dilor-G (Savage): Each tablet or 10 ml of liquid contains glyceryl guaiacolate 200 mg and dyphylline 200 mg.

Dimetane Expectorant (Robins): Each 5 ml contains brompheniramine maleate 2 mg, glyceryl guaiacolate 100 mg, phenylephrine hydrochloride 5 mg, and phenylpropanolamine hydrochloride 5 mg.

Dimetane Expectorant-DC (Robins): Each 5 ml contains brompheniramine maleate 2 mg, glyceryl guaiacolate 100 mg, phenylephrine hydrochloride 5 mg, phenylpropanolamine hydrochloride 5 mg, and codeine phosphate 10 mg.

Ephedrol with Codeine Expectorant (Lilly): Each 30 ml contains guaiacolsulfonate potassium 525 mg, ma huang 3.95 g, squill syrup 1.88 ml, and codeine sulfate 60 mg with tolu balsam and menthol.

GPC-Expectorant (Savage): Each 5 ml contains glyceryl guaiacolate 100 mg, phenylephrine hydrochloride 100 mg, and chlorpheniramine maleate 2 mg.

Hydryllin Compound (Searle): Each 4 ml contains ammonium chloride 30 mg, aminophylline 32 mg, diphenhydramine 8 mg, and chloroform 8 mg.

Ipaterp (Fellows-Testagar): Each tablet contains terpin hydrate 130 mg, ammonium chloride 65 mg, licorice extract 32.5 mg, and ipecac 6.5 mg.

Isoclor Expectorant (Arnar-Stone): Each 5 ml contains codeine phosphate 10 mg, glyceryl guaiacolate 83.3 mg, chlorpheniramine maleate 2 mg, pseudoephedrine hydrochloride 12.5 mg, sodium citrate 162 mg, citric acid 54 mg, and benzoic acid 0.1%.

Novahistine Expectorant (Dow): Each 5 ml contains phenylephrine hydrochloride 10 mg, chlorpheniramine maleate 2 mg, codeine phosphate 10 mg, glyceryl guaiacolate 100 mg, and chloroform 13.5 mg.

Phenergan Expectorant (Wyeth): Each 5 ml contains promethazine hydrochloride 5 mg, ipecac fluid extract 0.01 ml, citric acid anhydrous 60 mg, guaiacolsulfonate potassium 44 mg, chloroform 0.015 ml, and sodium citrate 197 mg with or without codeine phosphate 10 mg.

Phenergan Troches (Wyeth): Each troche contains promethazine hydrochloride 1.5 mg, powdered extract of ipecac 2.3 mg, guaiacolsulfonate potassium 162 mg with or without codeine phosphate 8 mg.

Phenergan Pediatric Expectorant (Wyeth): Each 5 ml contains promethazine hydrochloride 5 mg, fluid extract of ipecac 0.01 ml, guaiacolsulfonate potassium 44 mg, chloroform 0.015 ml, citric acid anhydrous 60 mg, sodium citrate 197 mg, and dextromethorphan hydrobromide 7.5 mg.

Phenergan VC Expectorant (Wyeth): Each 5 ml contains promethazine hydrochloride 5 mg, phenylephrine hydrochloride 5 mg, fluid extract of ipecac 0.01 ml, guaiacolsulfonate potassium 44 mg, chloroform 0.015 ml, citric acid anhydrous 60 mg, and sodium citrate 197 mg with or without codeine phosphate 10 mg.

Polaramine Expectorant (Schering): Each 5 ml contains dexchlorpheniramine maleate 25 mg, pseudoephedrine sulfate 20 mg, and glyceryl guaiacolate 100 mg.

Pyraldine Expectorant (Mallinckrodt): Each 5 ml contains dextromethorphan hydrobromide 15 mg, pyrilamine maleate 12.5 mg, ammonium chloride 65 mg, and alcohol 2%.

Pyribenzamine Expectorant with Ephedrine (Ciba): Each 4 ml contains ammonium chloride 80 mg, ephedrine sulfate 10 mg, and tripelennamine citrate 30 mg.

Pyribenzamine Expectorant with Codeine & Ephedrine (Ciba): Each 4 ml contains tripelennamine citrate 30 mg, codeine phosphate 8 mg, ephedrine sulfate 10 mg, and ammonium chloride 80 mg.

Ryna-Tussadine Expectorant (Mallinckrodt): Each tablet or 5 ml of liquid contains glyceryl guaiacolate 100 mg, phenylephrine hydrochloride 3.75 mg, phenylpropanolamine hydrochloride 6.25 mg, chlorpheniramine maleate 1 mg, and pyrilamine maleate 6.25 mg.

Tedral Expectorant (Warner-Chilcott): Each tablet contains theophylline 130 mg, ephedrine hydrochloride 24 mg, phenobarbital 8 mg, and glyceryl guaiacolate 100 mg.

Triaminic Expectorant (Dorsey): Each 5 ml contains glyceryl guaiacolate 100 mg, phenylpropanolamine hydrochloride 12.5 mg, pheniramine maleate 6.25 mg, and pyrilamine maleate 6.25 mg.

Triaminic Expectorant DH (Dorsey): Each 5 ml contains glyceryl guaiacolate 100 mg, hydrocodone bitartrate 1.67 mg, phenylpropanolamine hydrochloride 12.5 mg, pheniramine maleate 6.25 mg, pyrilamine maleate 6.25 mg, and chloroform 13.5 mg.

TSG-KI (Elder): Each 5 ml of elixir contains theophylline sodium glycinate 300 mg and potassium iodide 100 mg.

Tussi-Organidin Expectorant (Wampole): Each 5 ml contains iodinated glycerol 30 mg, chlorpheniramine maleate 2 mg, and codeine phosphate 10 mg.

Chapter 44

ANTITUSSIVE AGENTS

Cough is a protective reflex that helps clear the respiratory tract of secretions and foreign materials. Frequent or persistent coughing is a symptom associated with a number of diseases of varied etiology. Treatment directed toward suppression of cough is symptomatic and has no direct effect on the underlying disease. However, cough suppressive therapy is frequently indicated to permit rest, facilitate sleep, and reduce the irritation to the respiratory tract that tends to make cough self-perpetuating. The goal is to decrease both the frequency and intensity of the cough while still permitting adequate elimination of tracheobronchial secretions and exudates.

Cough secondary to acute upper respiratory tract infection or irritation generally subsides spontaneously within a few days. Cough arising from irritation of the pharyngeal mucosa sometimes can be managed satisfactorily with demulcents and locally acting sialogogues (eg, hard candy, cough drops). If the cough is nonproductive, an agent that increases the quantity of respiratory tract fluid or decreases its viscosity may be helpful. Severe cough requires treatment with antitussives that specifically suppress the cough reflex.

Antitussives act centrally, peripherally, or both. The centrally acting group includes both narcotic agents (codeine, hydrocodone [Codone, Dicodid], ethylmorphine, morphine, and hydromorphone [Dilaudid]) and non-narcotic agents (dextromethorphan [Romilar], levopropoxyphene [Novrad], noscapine, chlophedianol [Ulo], and benzonatate [Tessalon]). The peripherally acting group encompasses the demulcents (eg, glycerin, honey, acacia, licorice) and the expectorants and mucolytics (ammonium chloride, ammonium carbonate, potassium iodide, ipecac, glyceryl guaiacolate [Cortussin, Dilyn, GG-Cen, Robitussin, 2/G], terebene, terpin hydrate, tolu balsam, creosote, chloroform, and various volatile oils, saponins, and glycosides). Generally, the expectorants and mucolytics are not used alone as antitussives, but commonly are combined with other agents that have antitussive effects (see Chapter 43, Expectorants and Inhalants, for a more detailed discussion of these agents).

Codeine is accepted as the most useful antitussive. On a weight basis, the antitussive effect of ethylmorphine is about the same as that of codeine. Hydrocodone is slightly more potent than codeine but has a greater dependence liability. Morphine and hydromorphone are more potent than either codeine or hydrocodone but are used less frequently for the routine management of cough because of their untoward effects and greater dependence liability; they are reserved for conditions in which cough is associated with pain, anxiety, and restlessness.

The mechanism of action of most of the non-narcotic antitussive agents has not been adequately studied, but their primary action appears to be selective depression of the central cough mechanism. In addition, benzonatate, which has local anesthetic effects, may act by inhibiting stretch receptors in the pharynx and bronchi. Although some of the other non-narcotic drugs also have anesthetic effects, this property does not contribute significantly to their antitussive action. None of them has expectorant action or produces bronchodilation when used in the usual dosage. All of the non-narcotic agents reduce experimentally induced cough, but few have been adequately studied in patients with cough of pathologic origin. Even though patients report subjective improvement, objective measurements often fail to reveal a significant reduction in the frequency of cough.

Demulcents act by coating irritated pharyngeal mucosa and they may have a brief antitussive effect on cough secondary to such irritation. Many syrups and lozenges currently in use have a temporary demulcent effect.

Expectorants and mucolytics supposedly exert their antitussive effect by increasing the quantity and decreasing the viscosity of the respiratory tract fluid, which then is more easily expelled. However, in experimental studies in animals, dosage levels required to accomplish these objectives were higher than doses used therapeutically in man. In clinical studies, these agents generally produced no detectable decrease in sputum viscosity or increase in sputum volume. Controlled clinical studies in patients with chronic or unproductive cough must be made before the efficacy of these drugs can be definitely established. (See Chapter 43, Expectorants and Inhalants, for a more detailed discussion of these drugs.)

Adverse Reactions and Precautions

Adverse reactions to antitussive doses of narcotics occur infrequently because the doses used are less than those usually given for analgesia. Nausea, vomiting, constipation, dizziness, palpitations, drowsiness, pruritus, and, rarely, hyperhidrosis and agitation have been reported. Although narcotics depress respiration, this generally is not a problem with antitussive doses. The depression induced by equianalgesic doses of these agents is roughly comparable in magnitude. Overdosage causes euphoria, convulsions, narcosis, hypotension, and tachycardia. All narcotic antitussives are potentially addicting, but this danger is minimized if they are used only for short periods in the recommended dosage.

The central depressant effects of narcotic antitussives are enhanced by phenothiazines, monoamine oxidase inhibitors, and tricyclic antidepressants, and they are additive to the depression produced by most other centrally-acting depressant drugs. Nalorphine [Nalline], levallorphan [Lorfan], and naloxone [Narcan] will effectively antagonize the respiratory depression produced by the narcotic antitussive agents.

The non-narcotic antitussives produce adverse reactions less frequently than do the narcotic antitussives. Since the non-narcotic agents constitute a group of chemically unrelated compounds, reactions are variable; those that occur are generally mild and subside promptly when the drug is discontinued (see the individual evaluations).

Since definitive investigations to determine the teratogenic effects of the non-narcotic antitussives have not been conducted, their use in pregnant women is deemed inadvisable. Little is known about the toxicity of these drugs in infants and children.

Caution is indicated in the use of antitussives in sedated or debilitated patients. The cough reflex should not be severely obtunded in patients with productive cough. Failure to recognize that cough is suppressed by analgesics used to relieve pain after thoracic, abdominal, or other types of surgery may lead to the retention of secretions postoperatively. Cough and clearing of the respiratory passages are important therapeutic adjuncts to preventing or reversing the development of atelectasis and pneumonitis.

NARCOTIC ANTITUSSIVES

Only rarely is it necessary to give a narcotic antitussive by injection to suppress the cough reflex. Therefore, parenteral dosage forms will not be listed in this section. For available parenteral preparations of these agents, see Chapter 21, Strong Analgesics, and Chapter 22, Mild Analgesics.

CODEINE
CODEINE PHOSPHATE
CODEINE SULFATE

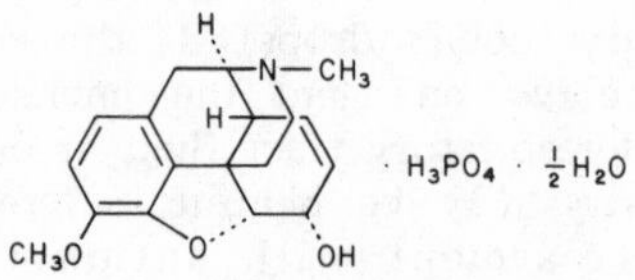

H, N—CH₃, H, · $H_3PO_4 \cdot \frac{1}{2}H_2O$, CH_3O, O, OH

Codeine is considered the most useful narcotic antitussive agent and the drug of choice. Results of clinical studies indicate that there is both subjective and objective relief of cough. Its dependence liability is considerably less than that of morphine or hydromorphone, although cough syrups containing codeine are being misused by drug abusers. Codeine is classified as a Schedule II (C II) substance.

Antitussive doses are generally well tolerated. Adverse reactions reported include nausea, vomiting, dizziness, palpitations, drowsiness, constipation, pruritus, and, rarely, hyperhidrosis, agitation, and allergic reactions.

Dependence and respiratory depression are not common because antitussive use is short term. Overdosage can cause convulsions of spinal origin instead of the anticipated respiratory depression seen with narcotics; this is particularly true in children.

For other uses, see Chapter 22, Mild Analgesics.

USUAL DOSAGE.—*Oral: Adults,* 5 to 10 mg every three to four hours as necessary. *Children,* 1 to 1.5 mg/kg of body weight daily divided into six doses.

PREPARATIONS.—Codeine, N.F., Codeine Phosphate, U.S.P., Codeine Sulfate, N.F. Drug marketed by many manufacturers under generic name. (See the section on Antitussive Mixtures for a listing of combination products containing codeine.)

ETHYLMORPHINE HYDROCHLORIDE

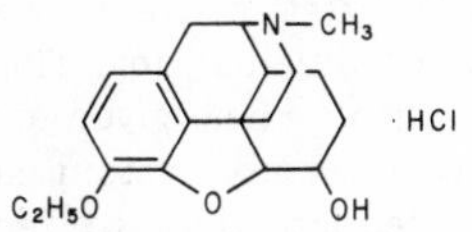

On a weight basis, ethylmorphine is equal to codeine in antitussive potency. It has no advantage over codeine. Controlled clinical studies comparing its efficacy with that of codeine are not available.

Adverse reactions include respiratory depression, dizziness, headache, nausea, vomiting, and constipation. Ethylmorphine is classified as a Schedule II (C II) substance.

USUAL DOSAGE.—*Oral: Adults,* 5 to 15 mg three or four times daily in flavored vehicle. *Children,* 1 mg/kg of body weight daily in four to six divided doses.

PREPARATIONS.—*Oral:* No single-entity pharmaceutical dosage form available; compounding necessary for prescription.

AVAILABLE TRADEMARK.—Dionin (Merck Sharp & Dohme). Drug also marketed under generic name. (See the section on Antitussive Mixtures for a listing of combination products containing ethylmorphine.)

HYDROCODONE BITARTRATE [Codone, Dicodid]

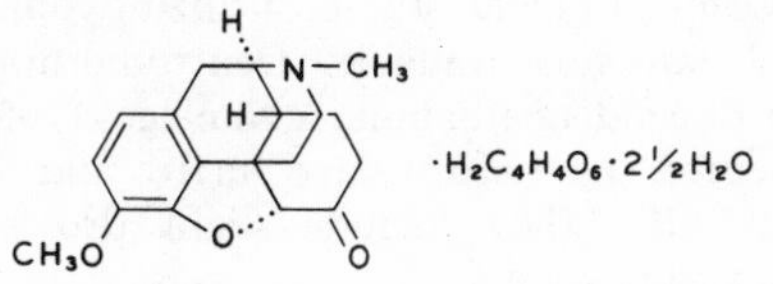

The usefulness of hydrocodone as a narcotic antitussive is similar to that of codeine. Results of subjective studies suggest that the antitussive potency of hydrocodone is slightly greater than that of codeine on a weight basis, but objective confirmation is not available. Its dependence liability is greater than that of codeine. Hydrocodone is classified as a Schedule II (C II) substance.

The most common adverse reactions are nausea, dizziness, and constipation.

USUAL DOSAGE.—*Oral: Adults,* 5 to 10 mg three or four times daily. *Children,* 0.6 mg/kg of body weight daily in three or four divided doses.

PREPARATIONS.—

Codone (Lemmon). *Oral:* Tablets 5 mg.

Dicodid (Knoll). *Oral:* Tablets 5 mg; powder 1 g.

Drug also marketed under generic name. (See the section on Antitussive Mixtures for a listing of combination products containing hydrocodone.)

HYDROMORPHONE HYDROCHLORIDE
[Dilaudid Hydrochloride]

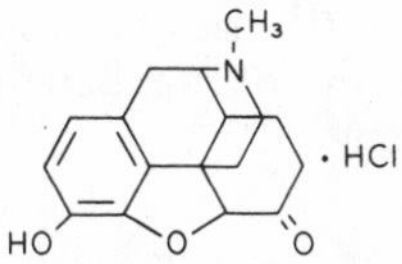

Hydromorphone has greater antitussive potency than codeine on a weight basis. Its dependence liability also is greater than that of codeine. This drug is classified as a Schedule II (C II) substance. Like morphine, its use as an antitussive should be restricted to patients with severely painful cough that cannot be effectively controlled with codeine, hydrocodone, or non-narcotic agents.

Adverse reactions include nausea, vomiting, respiratory depression, dizziness, drowsiness, and constipation.

For other uses, see Chapter 21, Strong Analgesics.

USUAL DOSAGE.—*Oral: Adults,* 1 mg every three or four hours.

PREPARATIONS.—Dilaudid Hydrochloride (Knoll). *Oral:* Tablets 1, 2, 3, and 4 mg.

MORPHINE SULFATE

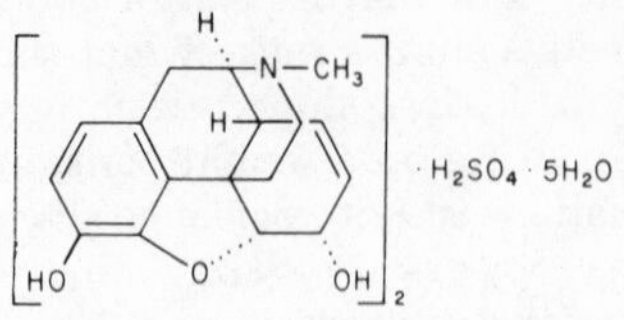

Morphine has greater antitussive potency on a weight basis than either codeine or hydrocodone. Its dependence liability also is much greater, and it is classified as a Schedule II (C II) substance. This drug should only be used as an antitussive when cough is associated with severe pain and cannot be controlled with antitussives having less potential for abuse. It should be administered for a limited period only.

In addition to respiratory depression, adverse reactions include vertigo, headache, nausea, vomiting, and constipation.

For other uses, see Chapter 21, Strong Analgesics.

USUAL DOSAGE.—*Oral: Adults,* 2 to 4 mg three or four times daily. *Children over 1 year of age,* 0.06 mg/kg of body weight three or four times daily.

PREPARATIONS.—Morphine Sulfate, U.S.P. *Oral:* No single-entity pharmaceutical dosage form available; compounding necessary for prescription. (See the section on Antitussive Mixtures for a listing of combination products containing morphine.)

NON-NARCOTIC ANTITUSSIVES

BENZONATATE [Tessalon]

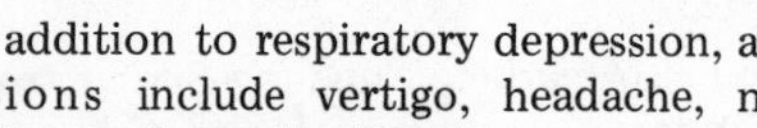

Benzonatate is chemically related to the local anesthetic, tetracaine. Its antitussive effect apparently is due to both a central and peripheral action on the vagal stretch receptors of the lungs. It is less effective than codeine in suppressing cough.

Adverse reactions are mild and include rash, constipation, nasal congestion, slight vertigo, headache, nausea, drowsiness, hypersensitivity reactions, and a vague "chilly" sensation. It has a topical anesthetic action and produces numbness of the oral mucosa if chewed.

USUAL DOSAGE.—*Oral: Adults and children over 10 years of age,* 100 mg three to six times daily; *under 10 years,* 8 mg/kg of body weight daily in three to six divided doses.

PREPARATIONS.—Tessalon (Ciba). *Oral:* Capsules 100 mg.

CHLOPHEDIANOL HYDROCHLORIDE [Ulo]

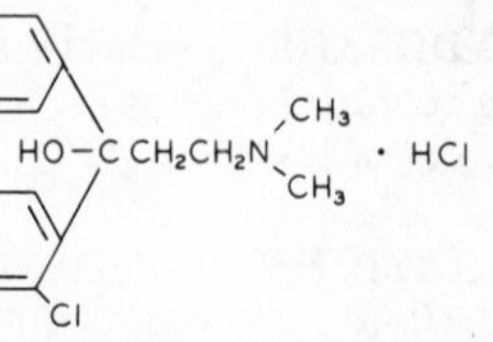

In subjective clinical studies, 25 mg of chlophedianol was as effective as 15 mg of codeine in relieving cough. Objective clinical data are not available.

Adverse reactions include urticaria, dryness of the mouth, nausea, vomiting, vertigo, visual disturbances, drowsiness, excitability, nightmares, and hallucinations. The drug should be used cautiously when given concomitantly with central nervous system stimulants or depressants. Adequate data to recommend its use in infants and pregnant women are not available.

USUAL DOSAGE.—*Oral: Adults,* 25 mg three or four times daily as required; *children over 6 years of age,* 2 mg/kg of body weight in four divided doses.

PREPARATIONS.—Ulo (Riker). *Oral:* Syrup 25 mg/5 ml. (See the section on Antitussive Mixtures for a listing of combination products containing chlophedianol.)

DEXTROMETHORPHAN HYDROBROMIDE [Romilar]

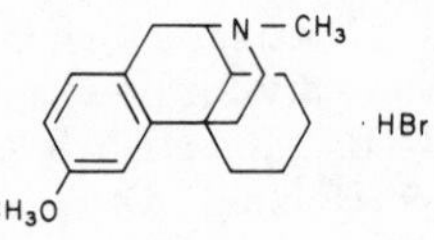

Dextromethorphan is the methyl ether of the dextro isomer of the narcotic analgesic, levorphanol. It has been suggested on the basis of subjective clinical studies that dextromethorphan is an effective cough suppressant. Clinical studies utilizing objective methods are not available. Dextromethorphan has no dependence liability or analgesic effects.

Adverse reactions are mild and occur infrequently; they include slight drowsiness, nausea, and dizziness.

USUAL DOSAGE.—*Oral: Adults*, 15 to 30 mg three or four times daily. *Children*, 1 mg/kg of body weight daily in three or four divided doses.

PREPARATIONS.—Romilar (Sauter). *Oral:* Syrup 7.5 and 15 mg/5 ml. Drug also marketed in bulk form under generic name. (See the section on Antitussive Mixtures for a listing of combination products containing dextromethorphan.)

GLYCERYL GUAIACOLATE [Cortussin, Dilyn, GG-Cen, Robitussin, 2/G]

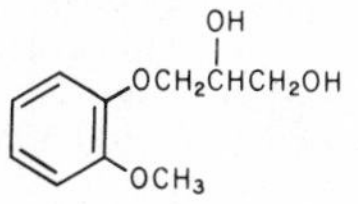

Results of subjective clinical studies suggest that the expectorant action of glyceryl guaiacolate ameliorates a dry, unproductive cough. Clinical studies utilizing objective methods are not available. Experimentally, glyceryl guaiacolate increases respiratory tract secretions in animals when given at a higher dosage level than that used clinically. The drug therefore is of questionable value.

Nausea and drowsiness may occur rarely. Glyceryl guaiacolate may produce a false positive test for 5-hydroxyindoleacetic acid (5-HIAA) in the urine.

USUAL DOSAGE.—*Oral: Adults*, 100 mg every three or four hours as required. *Children 6 to 12 years of age*, 50 mg every three or four hours; *3 to 6 years*, 25 mg every three or four hours.

PREPARATIONS.—

Cortussin (Xttrium), GG-Cen (Central), Robitussin (Robins), 2/G (Dow). *Oral:* Syrup 100 mg/5 ml.

Dilyn (Elder). *Oral:* Tablets 100 mg.

Drug also marketed by other manufacturers under generic name. (See the section on Antitussive Mixtures for a listing of combination products containing glyceryl guaiacolate.)

LEVOPROPOXYPHENE NAPSYLATE [Novrad]

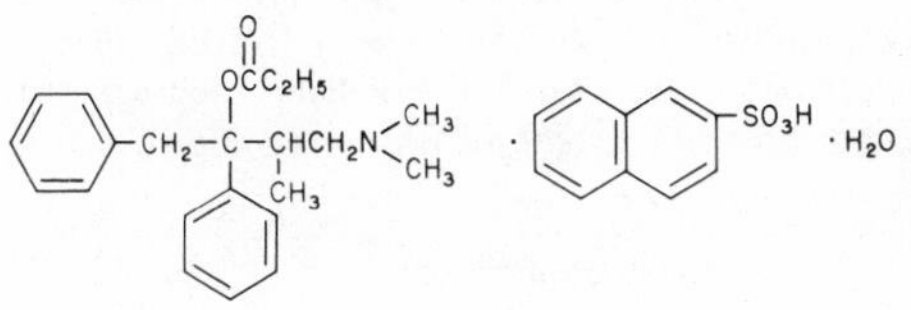

In a few subjective studies, levopropoxyphene has been reported to have an antitussive effect.

Adverse reactions are minor and include headache, dizziness, tremors, nausea, vomiting, abdominal distress, dryness of the mouth, rash, urticaria, and urinary frequency and urgency.

USUAL DOSAGE.—*Oral: Adults*, 50 to 100 mg every four hours as required. *Children*, 6 mg/kg of body weight every 24 hours in six divided doses.

PREPARATIONS.—Novrad (Lilly). *Oral:* Capsules 50 and 100 mg; suspension 50 mg/5 ml.

NOSCAPINE
NOSCAPINE HYDROCHLORIDE

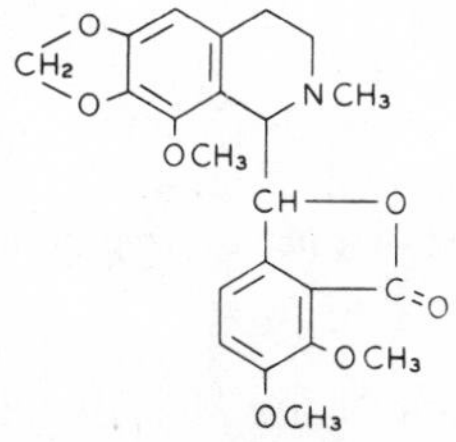

Noscapine is one of the benzylisoquinoline group of opium alkaloids. It has been suggested on the basis of subjective clinical studies that noscapine is an effective cough suppressant. No objective clinical studies in patients with chronic cough are available. Noscapine has no analgesic properties or dependence liability.

Adverse reactions occur infrequently and include drowsiness, headache, nausea, nonseasonal allergic (vasomotor) rhinitis, and conjunctivitis.

USUAL DOSAGE.—*Oral: Adults*, 15 to 30 mg three or four times daily. *Children*, no established dosage available.

PREPARATIONS.—*Oral:* No single-entity pharmaceutical dosage form available; compounding necessary for prescription.

AVAILABLE TRADEMARK.—Nectadon (Merck). Drug also marketed in bulk form under generic name. (See the section on Antitussive Mixtures for a listing of combination products containing noscapine and noscapine hydrochloride.)

MIXTURES

Centrally acting antitussives often are combined with other agents such as bronchodilators, antihistamines, or expectorants. The effectiveness of these mixtures is not known and is difficult to assess because objective clinical studies comparing their efficacy with that of single-entity preparations in patients with chronic cough are lacking. Since most evaluations of single-entity antitussive drugs also are based on subjective rather than objective methods, the effectiveness of mixtures is particularly difficult to assess. The placebo effect undoubtedly is an important factor in subjective studies. Some of the components of these mixtures cause significant toxic effects with overdosage or in sensitive individuals.

The following mixtures are listed for information only and do not constitute approval. It is possible for the physician to exclude many mixtures from consideration because they contain questionably effective ingredients. Mixtures that contain antihistamines promote inspissation of bronchial secretions and thus interfere with a productive cough.

Antitussive Mixtures Containing Chlophedianol

Acutuss (Philips Roxane): Each 5 ml of elixir contains chlophedianol hydrochloride 15 mg, diphenylpyraline hydrochloride 1 mg, glyceryl guaiacolate 100 mg, and phenylephrine hydrochloride 5 mg; each tablet contains chlophedianol hydrochloride 7.5 mg, diphenylpyraline hydrochloride 0.5 mg, phenylephrine hydrochloride 2.5 mg, glyceryl guaiacolate 25 mg, and acetaminophen 162.5 mg.

Ulogesic (Riker): Each tablet contains chlophedianol hydrochloride 7.5 mg, acetaminophen 162.5 mg, diphenylpyraline hydrochloride 0.5 mg, glyceryl guaiacolate 25 mg, and phenylephrine hydrochloride 2.5 mg.

Ulominic (Riker): Each 5 ml of syrup contains chlophedianol hydrochloride 15 mg, diphenylpyraline hydrochloride 1 mg, glyceryl guaiacolate 100 mg, and phenylephrine hydrochloride 5 mg.

Antitussive Mixtures Containing Codeine

Actifed-C Expectorant (Burroughs Wellcome): Each 5 ml contains codeine phosphate 10 mg, glyceryl guaiacolate 100 mg, pseudoephedrine hydrochloride 30 mg, and triprolidine hydrochloride 2 mg.

Acutuss Expectorant W/Codeine (Philips Roxane): Each 5 ml contains codeine phosphate 10 mg, chloroform 13.5 mg, phenylpropanolamine hydrochloride 5 mg, phenylephrine hydrochloride 5 mg, chlorpheniramine maleate 2 mg, and glyceryl guaiacolate 100 mg.

Broncho-Tussin Expectorant (First Texas): Each 30 ml contains codeine phosphate 64.8 mg, terpin hydrate 260 mg, ammonium hypophosphite 520 mg, and guaiacolsulfonate potassium 520 mg.

Calcidrine Syrup (Abbott): Each 5 ml contains codeine 8.4 mg, calcium iodide 152 mg, and ephedrine hydrochloride 4.2 mg.

Cerose Expectorant (Ives): Each 5 ml contains codeine phosphate 10 mg, phenindamine tartrate 10 mg, phenylephrine hydrochloride 5 mg, ipecac fluidextract 0.01 ml, glycerin 2.5 ml, guaiacolsulfonate potassium 86 mg, sodium citrate 195 mg, and citric acid 65 mg.

Cetro-Cirose (Ives): Each 5 ml of syrup contains codeine phosphate 5 mg, ipecac fluidextract 0.01 ml, glycerin 2.5 ml, guaiacolsulfonate potassium 86 mg, sodium citrate 195 mg, and citric acid 65 mg.

Cheracol Syrup (Upjohn): Each 30 ml contains codeine phosphate 65 mg, chloroform 130 mg, guaiacolsulfonate potassium 520 mg, ammonium chloride 520 mg, and antimony and potassium tartrates 5.4 mg.

Chlor-Trimeton Expectorant W/Codeine (Schering): Each 5 ml contains codeine phosphate 10 mg, chlorpheniramine maleate 2 mg, phenylephrine hydrochloride 10 mg, ammonium chloride 100 mg, sodium citrate 50 mg, glyceryl guaiacolate 50 mg, and chloroform 12.5 mg.

Citro-Codea (First Texas): Each 30 ml of liquid contains codeine phosphate 64.8 mg, guaiacolsulfonate potassium 260 mg, sodium citrate 2 g, and citric acid 390 mg.

Colrex Compound (Rowell): Each capsule contains codeine phosphate 16 mg, papaverine hydrochloride 16 mg, aluminum aspirin 300 mg, phenylephrine hydrochloride 5 mg, chlorpheniramine maleate 2 mg, and ascorbic acid 100 mg; each 5 ml of elixir contains codeine phosphate 8 mg, papaverine hydrochloride 8 mg, acetaminophen 120 mg, chlorpheniramine maleate 1 mg, and phenylephrine hydrochloride 5 mg.

Copavin (Lilly): Each capsule or tablet contains codeine sulfate 15 mg and papaverine hydrochloride 15 mg.

Copavin Compound (Lilly): Each 30 ml of elixir contains codeine sulfate 30 mg, papaverine hydrochloride 30 mg, aloin 15 mg, and sodium salicylate 1.3 g.

Cosanyl (Parke, Davis): Each 30 ml of elixir contains codeine phosphate 65 mg, *Euphorbia pilulifera* tincture 7.4 ml, squill compound syrup 1.5 ml, wild lettuce syrup 7.4 ml, cocillana tincture 2.5 ml, cascarin 520 mg, and menthol 5.2 mg.

Cotussis (Merrell-National): Each 30 ml of syrup contains codeine phosphate 60 mg, terpin hydrate 120 mg, chloroform 120 mg, and menthol 15 mg.

Dimetane-DC Expectorant (Robins): Each 5 ml contains codeine phosphate 10 mg, brompheniramine maleate 2 mg, glyceryl guaiacolate 100 mg, phenylephrine hydrochloride 5 mg, and phenylpropanolamine hydrochloride 5 mg.

Emeracol (Upjohn): Each 30 ml of liquid contains codeine phosphate 32.5 mg, chloroform 65 mg, guaiacolsulfonate potassium 520 mg, ammonium chloride 520 mg, and antimony potassium tartrate 2.7 mg.

Emprazil-C (Burroughs Wellcome): Each tablet contains codeine phosphate 15 mg, aspirin 200 mg, caffeine 30 mg, phenacetin 150 mg, and pseudoephedrine hydrochloride 20 mg.

Endotussin-C (Endo): Each 5 ml of syrup contains codeine phosphate 10 mg, homatropine methylbromide 0.5 mg, pyrilamine maleate 12.5 mg, ammonium chloride 60 mg, and sodium citrate 85 mg.

Ephedrol W/Codeine Expectorant (Lilly): Each 30 ml contains codeine sulfate 60 mg, ma huang 3.95 g, squill syrup 1.88 ml, and guaiacolsulfonate potassium 525 mg with tolu balsam and menthol.

Hakriton (Lemmon): Each 15 ml of syrup contains codeine phosphate 5 mg and glyceryl guaiacolate 100 mg.

Histadyl E.C. (Lilly): Each 30 ml of syrup contains codeine phosphate 60 mg, ammonium chloride 660 mg, chloroform 0.06 ml, ephedrine hydrochloride 30 mg, and methapyrilene fumarate 81 mg.

Isoclor Expectorant (Arnar-Stone): Each 5 ml contains codeine phosphate 10 mg, chlorpheniramine maleate 2 mg, pseudoephedrine hydrochloride 12.5 mg, glyceryl guaiacolate 83.3 mg, citric acid 54 mg, and sodium citrate 162 mg.

Mercodol (Merrell-National): Each 30 ml of syrup contains codeine phosphate 60 mg, phenylephrine hydrochloride 30 mg, etafedrine hydrochloride 60 mg, and sodium citrate 1.2 g.

Mercodol W/Decapryn (Merrell-National): Same formulation as Mercodol plus doxylamine succinate 36 mg.

Novahistine Expectorant (Dow): Each 5 ml contains codeine phosphate 10 mg, chloroform 13.5 mg, chlorpheniramine maleate 2 mg, glyceryl guaiacolate 100 mg, and phenylephrine hydrochloride 10 mg.

Novahistine-DH (Dow): Each 5 ml of liquid contains codeine phosphate 10 mg, chlorpheniramine maleate 2 mg, phenylephrine hydrochloride 10 mg, and chloroform 13.5 mg.

Omni-Tuss (Pennwalt): Each 5 ml of suspension contains codeine resin 10 mg, phenyltoloxamine resin 5 mg, chlorpheniramine resin 3 mg, ephedrine resin 25 mg, and guaiacol carbonate 20 mg.

Pediacof (Winthrop): Each 5 ml of syrup contains codeine phosphate 5 mg, chlorpheniramine maleate 0.75 mg, phenylephrine hydrochloride 2.5 mg, and potassium iodide 75 mg.

Phenergan W/Codeine (Wyeth): Each 5 ml of expectorant contains codeine phosphate 10 mg, promethazine hydrochloride 5 mg, ipecac fluidextract 0.01 ml, guaiacolsulfonate potassium 44 mg, chloroform 0.02 ml, citric acid 60 mg, and sodium citrate 197 mg; each troche contains codeine phosphate 8 mg, promethazine hydrochloride 1.5 mg, powdered ipecac extract 2.3 mg, and guaiacolsulfonate potassium 162 mg.

Phenergan-VC W/Codeine (Wyeth): Each 5 ml of expectorant contains codeine phosphate 10 mg, promethazine hydrochloride 5 mg, phenylephrine hydrochloride 5 mg, ipecac fluidextract 0.01 ml, guaiacolsulfonate potassium 44 mg, chloroform 0.02 ml, citric acid 60 mg, and sodium citrate 197 mg.

Prunicodeine (Lilly): Each 30 ml of liquid contains codeine phosphate 60 mg, *Prunus virginiana* 1.58 g, *Pinus strobus* 1.05 g, sanguinaria 262 mg, and terpin hydrate 175 mg.

Pyribenzamine Expectorant W/Codeine and Ephedrine (Ciba): Each 4 ml contains codeine phosphate 8 mg, tripelennamine citrate 30 mg, ephedrine sulfate 10 mg, and ammonium chloride 80 mg.

Pyrroxate W/Codeine (Upjohn): Each capsule contains codeine phosphate 16.2 mg, chlorpheniramine maleate 2 mg, methoxyphenamine hydrochloride 25 mg, phenacetin 162 mg, aspirin 228 mg, and caffeine 37 mg.

Robitussin A-C (Robins): Each 5 ml of liquid contains codeine phosphate 10 mg, glyceryl guaiacolate 100 mg, and pheniramine maleate 7.5 mg.

Sedatole (Merck Sharp & Dohme): Each 5 ml of elixir contains codeine sulfate 5 mg with wild cherry bark, sanguinaria, squill, balm of gilead buds, diluted phosphoric acid, and menthol.

Semcof (Beecham-Massengill): Each 5 ml of syrup contains codeine phosphate 10 mg, sodium citrate 160 mg, ammonium chloride 100 mg, ephedrine hydrochloride 5 mg, and antimony potassium tartrate 0.6 mg.

Synephricol (Winthrop): Each 5 ml of syrup contains codeine phosphate 10.85 mg, phenylephrine hydrochloride 5 mg, thenyldiamine hydrochloride 4 mg, guaiacolsulfonate potassium 87.65 mg, ammonium chloride 69 mg, menthol 1.38 mg, and chloroform 69 mg.

Terhydrol W/Codeine (Mallinckrodt): Each 30 ml of suspension contains codeine sulfate 65 mg, terpin hydrate 1.04 g, chloroform 0.25 ml, and menthol 11.7 mg.

Terpin Hydrate and Codeine Elixir (Various

Manufacturers): codeine, glycerin, sweet orange peel tincture, terpin hydrate.

Tolu-Sed (First Texas): Each 5 ml of expectorant contains codeine phosphate 65 mg, chlorpheniramine maleate 6 mg, glyceryl guaiacolate 600 mg, and chloroform 0.12 ml.

Tussi-Organidin (Wampole): Each 5 ml of expectorant contains codeine phosphate 10 mg, chlorpheniramine maleate 2 mg, and iodinated glycerol 30 mg.

Tussomyl (Elder): Each 5 ml of syrup contains codeine phosphate 3.3 mg, phenylpropanolamine hydrochloride 8 mg, phenindamine tartrate 4 mg, cetylpyridinium chloride 0.05%, and benzyl alcohol 0.3%.

Antitussive Mixtures Containing Dextromethorphan

Cerose-DM (Ives): Each 5 ml of expectorant contains dextromethorphan hydrobromide 10 mg, phenindamine tartrate 5 mg, phenylephrine hydrochloride 5 mg, ipecac fluidextract 0.01 ml, glycerin 2.5 ml, guaiacolsulfonate potassium 86 mg, sodium citrate 194 mg, and citric acid 65 mg.

Cheracol D Cough Syrup (Upjohn): Each 30 ml contains dextromethorphan hydrobromide 60 mg, chloroform 120 mg, glyceryl guaiacolate 84 mg, ammonium chloride 480 mg, and antimony potassium tartrate 5 mg.

Chexit (Dorsey): Each tablet contains dextromethorphan hydrobromide 30 mg, phenylpropanolamine hydrochloride 25 mg, pheniramine maleate 12.5 mg, pyrilamine maleate 12.5 mg, terpin hydrate 180 mg, and acetaminophen 325 mg.

Colrex Syrup (Rowell): Each 5 ml contains dextromethorphan hydrobromide 10 mg, guaiacolsulfonate potassium 80 mg, ammonium chloride 80 mg, phenylephrine hydrochloride 5 mg, and chlorpheniramine maleate 1 mg.

Consotuss Antitussive Syrup (Merrell-National): Each 5 ml contains dextromethorphan hydrobromide 15 mg, chloroform 0.5%, doxylamine succinate 3.75 mg, and glyceryl guaiacolate 100 mg.

Coryban-D Cough Syrup (Roerig): Each 5 ml contains dextromethorphan hydrobromide 7.5 mg, acetaminophen 120 mg, ascorbic acid 12.5 mg, chloroform 0.5%, chlorpheniramine maleate 1 mg, glyceryl guaiacolate 50 mg, and phenylephrine hydrochloride 5 mg.

Cosanyl-DM (Improved Formula) (Parke, Davis): Each 5 ml contains dextromethorphan hydrobromide 15 mg and phenylephrine hydrochloride 5 mg.

Dorcol Pediatric Cough Syrup (Dorsey): Each 5 ml contains dextromethorphan hydrobromide 7.5 mg, glyceryl guaiacolate 37.5 mg, and phenylpropanolamine hydrochloride 8.75 mg.

Duad Koff-Balls (Hoechst): Each liquid-filled sphere contains dextromethorphan hydrobromide 10 mg, sodium citrate 50 mg, and benzocaine 3 mg.

Endotussin-NN (Endo): Each 5 ml of syrup contains dextromethorphan hydrobromide 10 mg, homatropine methylbromide 0.25 mg, pyrilamine maleate 7.5 mg, ammonium chloride 40 mg, and sodium citrate 60 mg; each 5 ml of pediatric syrup contains dextromethorphan hydrobromide 5 mg, homatropine methylbromide 0.15 mg, ammonium chloride 60 mg, and sodium citrate 40 mg.

Ipsatol/DM (Davies Rose Hoyt): Each troche or 5 ml of syrup contains dextromethorphan hydrobromide 10 mg with ipecac, ammonium chloride, and squill.

Orthoxicol (Upjohn): Each 5 ml of syrup contains dextromethorphan hydrobromide 10 mg, methoxyphenamine hydrochloride 17 mg, and sodium citrate 325 mg.

Phenergan Pediatric Expectorant (Wyeth): Each 5 ml contains dextromethorphan hydrobromide 7.5 mg, promethazine hydrochloride 5 mg, ipecac fluidextract 0.01 ml, guaiacolsulfonate potassium 44 mg, chloroform 0.015 ml, citric acid 60 mg, and sodium citrate 197 mg.

Pyraldine (Mallinckrodt): Each 30 ml of syrup contains dextromethorphan hydrobromide 90 mg, pyrilamine maleate 75 mg, ammonium chloride 388 mg, and citric acid 324 mg; each 30 ml of No. 2 syrup contains same formulation as syrup plus phenylephrine hydrochloride 30 mg; each 30 ml of pediatric syrup contains dextromethorphan hydrobromide 45 mg, pyrilamine maleate 75 mg, phenylephrine hydrochloride 30 mg, ammonium chloride 388 mg, and citric acid 324 mg.

Quelidrine (Abbott): Each 5 ml of syrup contains dextromethorphan hydrobromide 10 mg, ammonium chloride 40 mg, chlorpheniramine maleate 2 mg, ephedrine hydrochloride 5 mg, ipecac fluidextract 0.005 ml, and phenylephrine hydrochloride 5 mg.

Robitussin-DM (Robins): Each 5 ml of syrup contains dextromethorphan hydrobromide 15 mg and glyceryl guaiacolate 100 mg; each lozenge contains one-half the dose of each component.

Statuss (Elder): Each capsule or 15 ml of syrup contains dextromethorphan hydrobromide 7.5 mg, chlorpheniramine maleate 1 mg, methoxyphenamine hydrochloride 17.5 mg, and phenylephrine hydrochloride 2.5 mg.

Tacol (Beecham-Massengill): Each tablet contains dextromethorphan hydrobromide 15 mg, chlorpheniramine maleate 2 mg, phenylephrine hydrochloride 10 mg, pyrilamine maleate 12 mg, acetaminophen 325 mg, ascorbic acid 100 mg, and caffeine 20 mg.

3X-Statuss (Elder): Each 5 ml of liquid contains

dextromethorphan hydrobromide 7.5 mg, chlorpheniramine maleate 1 mg, phenylephrine hydrochloride 2.5 mg, and methoxyphenamine hydrochloride 17.5 mg.

Triaminicol (Dorsey): Each 5 ml of syrup contains dextromethorphan hydrobromide 15 mg, ammonium chloride 90 mg, pheniramine maleate 6.25 mg, phenylpropanolamine hydrochloride 12.5 mg, and pyrilamine maleate 6.25 mg.

Tussagesic (Dorsey): Each 5 ml of suspension contains dextromethorphan hydrobromide 30 mg, pheniramine maleate 12.5 mg, phenylpropanolamine hydrochloride 25 mg, pyrilamine maleate 12.5 mg, and terpin hydrate 180 mg; each timed-release tablet contains same formulation as suspension plus acetaminophen 325 mg.

Tussaminic (Dorsey): Each timed-release tablet contains dextromethorphan hydrobromide 30 mg, pheniramine maleate 25 mg, phenylpropanolamine hydrochloride 50 mg, pyrilamine maleate 25 mg, and terpin hydrate 300 mg.

2G/DM (Dow): Each 5 ml of elixir contains dextromethorphan hydrobromide 15 mg and glyceryl guaiacolate 100 mg.

Antitussive Mixture Containing Ethylmorphine

Per-Sed (Philips Roxane): Each 30 ml of liquid contains ethylmorphine hydrochloride 16.2 mg, chloroform 0.12 ml, ammonium chloride 1.04 g, and citric acid 778 mg.

Antitussive Mixtures Containing Glyceryl Guaiacolate

(Many other combination products containing glyceryl guaiacolate are listed with the mixtures.)

Brexin (Savage): Each capsule contains glyceryl guaiacolate 100 mg, pseudoephedrine hydrochloride 60 mg, and methapyrilene hydrochloride 30 mg.

Brondecon (Warner-Chilcott): Each tablet contains glyceryl guaiacolate 100 mg and oxtriphylline 200 mg; each 5 ml of elixir contains glyceryl guaiacolate 50 mg and oxtriphylline 100 mg.

Dilaudid Cough Syrup (Knoll): Each 5 ml contains glyceryl guaiacolate 100 mg and hydromorphone hydrochloride 1 mg.

Dilor-G (Savage): Each tablet or 10 ml of liquid contains glyceryl guaiacolate 200 mg and dyphylline 200 mg.

Dimetane Expectorant (Robins): Each 5 ml contains glyceryl guaiacolate 100 mg, brompheniramine maleate 2 mg, phenylephrine hydrochloride 5 mg, and phenylpropanolamine hydrochloride 5 mg.

Guaiahist (Philips Roxane): Each tablet contains glyceryl guaiacolate 100 mg, phenylephrine hydrochloride 5 mg, and pyrilamine maleate 12.5 mg; each timed-release tablet contains glyceryl guaiacolate 300 mg, phenylephrine hydrochloride 20 mg, and chlorpheniramine maleate 4 mg.

Pavricol (Savage): Each tablet contains glyceryl guaiacolate 100 mg, ethaverine hydrochloride 15 mg, and methapyrilene hydrochloride 30 mg.

Ryna-Tussadine (Mallinckrodt): Each tablet or 5 ml of liquid contains glyceryl guaiacolate 100 mg, phenylephrine hydrochloride 3.75 mg, phenylpropanolamine hydrochloride 6.25 mg, chlorpheniramine maleate 1 mg, and pyrilamine maleate 6.25 mg.

Triaminic Expectorant (Dorsey): Each 5 ml contains glyceryl guaiacolate 100 mg, pheniramine maleate 6.25 mg, phenylpropanolamine hydrochloride 12.5 mg, and pyrilamine maleate 6.25 mg.

Trind (Mead Johnson): Each tablet contains glyceryl guaiacolate 50 mg, phenylephrine hydrochloride 2.5 mg, and acetaminophen 150 mg.

Antitussive Mixtures Containing Hydrocodone

Citra Cough Syrup (Boyle): Each 5 ml of syrup contains hydrocodone bitartrate 1.66 mg, ascorbic acid 30 mg, potassium citrate 150 mg, phenylephrine hydrochloride 2.5 mg, pheniramine maleate 2.5 mg, and pyrilamine maleate 3.33 mg; each 5 ml of Forte syrup contains hydrocodone bitartrate 5 mg, ascorbic acid 30 mg, potassium citrate 150 mg, pheniramine maleate 2.5 mg, and pyrilamine maleate 3.33 mg.

Citra Forte Capsules (Boyle): Each capsule contains hydrocodone bitartrate 5 mg, ascorbic acid 50 mg, methapyrilene hydrochloride 8.33 mg, phenacetin 120 mg, pheniramine maleate 6.25 mg, phenylephrine hydrochloride 10 mg, pyrilamine maleate 8.33 mg, salicylamide 227 mg, and caffeine 30 mg.

Dicoril (Lemmon): Each 30 ml of syrup contains hydrocodone bitartrate 10 mg, pyrilamine maleate 80 mg, and sodium citrate 1 g.

Hycodan (Endo): Each tablet or 5 ml of syrup contains hydrocodone bitartrate 5 mg and homatropine methylbromide 1.5 mg.

Hycomine Pediatric Syrup (Endo): Each 5 ml contains hydrocodone bitartrate 2.5 mg, ammonium chloride 30 mg, homatropine methylbromide 0.75 mg, phenylephrine hydrochloride 5 mg, and pyrilamine maleate 6.25 mg.

Hycomine Compound (Endo): Each tablet contains hydrocodone bitartrate 5 mg, caffeine 30 mg, chlorpheniramine maleate 2 mg, homatropine methylbromide 1.5 mg, acetaminophen 250 mg, and phenylephrine hydrochloride 10 mg.

Triaminic Expectorant DH (Dorsey): Each 5 ml contains hydrocodone bitartrate 1.67 mg, chloroform 13.5

mg, glyceryl guaiacolate 100 mg, pheniramine maleate 6.25 mg, phenylpropanolamine hydrochloride 12.5 mg, and pyrilamine maleate 6.25 mg.

Tussend (Dow): Each tablet or 5 ml of liquid contains hydrocodone bitartrate 5 mg, chlorpheniramine maleate 4 mg, and phenylephrine hydrochloride 20 mg.

Tussionex (Pennwalt): Each capsule, tablet, or 5 ml of suspension contains hydrocodone 5 mg and phenyltoloxamine 10 mg as resin complexes.

Antitussive Mixture Containing Methadone

Methajade (Merck Sharp & Dohme): Each 30 ml of liquid contains methadone hydrochloride 10 mg, phenylpropanolamine hydrochloride 120 mg, potassium citrate 1.2 g, and diluted phosphoric acid 4.5 ml.

Antitussive Mixture Containing Morphine

Terhydrol W/Morphine (Mallinckrodt): Each 30 ml of suspension contains morphine sulfate 16 mg, chloroform 0.25 ml, menthol 11.7 mg, and terpin hydrate 1.04 g.

Antitussive Mixtures Containing Noscapine

Conar (Beecham-Massengill): Each 5 ml of liquid contains noscapine 10 mg, chlorpheniramine maleate 2 mg, phenylephrine hydrochloride 10 mg, chloroform 12 mg, and menthol 0.2 mg; each 5 ml of expectorant contains same formulation as liquid plus glyceryl guaiacolate 100 mg.

Conar-A (Beecham-Massengill): Each tablet or 10 ml of suspension contains noscapine 10 mg, chlorpheniramine maleate 2 mg, phenylephrine hydrochloride 10 mg, acetaminophen 300 mg, and glyceryl guaiacolate 100 mg.

Additional Antitussive Mixtures

Rynatuss (Mallinckrodt): Each tablet contains carbetapentane tannate 60 mg, chlorpheniramine tannate 5 mg, ephedrine tannate 10 mg, and phenylephrine tannate 5 mg; each 5 ml of pediatric suspension contains carbetapentane tannate 30 mg, chlorpheniramine tannate 4 mg, ephedrine tannate 5 mg, and phenylephrine tannate 2.5 mg.

Tuss-Ornade (Smith Kline & French): Each timed-release capsule contains caramiphen edisylate 20 mg, chlorpheniramine maleate 8 mg, isopropamide iodide 2.5 mg, and phenylpropanolamine hydrochloride 50 mg; each 5 ml of liquid contains caramiphen edisylate 5 mg, chlorpheniramine maleate 2 mg, phenylpropanolamine hydrochloride 15 mg, and isopropamide iodide 0.75 mg.

Chapter 45

ANTIHISTAMINES

The antihistamines are useful primarily for the symptomatic relief of certain allergic disorders. They suppress symptoms caused by the release of histamine, one of the chemicals released by the antigen-antibody reaction. Some antihistamines also have other actions: they diminish capillary permeability, act centrally to suppress nausea due to motion sickness, produce sedation, or have a central excitatory effect. In varying degree, most antihistamines exhibit mild local anesthetic and anticholinergic properties; these effects are of little or no therapeutic value for the indications discussed in this chapter.

Only minor variations in properties exist among drugs in the major chemical classes of antihistamines (ethanolamines, ethylenediamines, alkylamines, phenothiazines). See the section on Adverse Reactions and Precautions and the individual evaluations that follow. The evaluations are grouped according to these classes. Other drugs with antihistaminic actions and other uses for some drugs in this chapter are discussed in Chapters 28, Antianxiety Agents; 29, Antipsychotic Agents; 44, Antitussive Agents; 72, Miscellaneous Ophthalmic Preparations; 74, Antiparkinsonism Agents; and 85, Antiemetics.

The antihistamines are most effective in the management of mild hay fever (pollinosis, seasonal allergic rhinitis) and in the treatment of acute allergic urticaria. To a lesser degree, they may be useful when given systemically to treat chronic urticaria, angioedema, and other skin reactions due to various allergens, including drugs, and in the management of nonseasonal (perennial) allergic rhinitis. They are rarely effective in vasomotor rhinitis. Allergic rhinitis usually is managed most effectively by avoiding the allergen and, if this is not practical, by hyposensitization supplemented by antihistamines when needed. Because most antihistamines are weak anticholinergics, they are often claimed to ameliorate symptoms of the common cold by reducing rhinorrhea, but this action is probably insignificant. The allegation that antihistamines prevent or abort the common cold is unfounded. Nevertheless, some (particularly chlorpheniramine maleate) are widely used in cold remedies (see Chapter 46, Cold Remedies).

These agents may relieve pruritus when given systemically. Topical administration, although somewhat effective, is unwarranted because the antihistamine itself can cause an allergic contact dermatitis.

Antihistamines produce some symptomatic relief in serum sickness, but they do not shorten the course of the reaction. They are less effective than epinephrine given subcutaneously to combat acute anaphylactic reactions, but are sometimes useful when given intravenously to patients who do not respond promptly to epinephrine. Diphenhydramine [Benadryl] is the antihistamine of choice for this purpose.

Antihistamines have only limited value in the prevention or treatment of asthmatic attacks of allergic origin, because mediators other than histamine are involved (eg, Slow Reacting Substance of Anaphylaxis [SRS-A]). In acute bronchial asthma, the mild atropine-like drying effect of most antihistamines may cause inspissation of secretions in the bronchi and bronchioles. Infants and young children with allergic bronchitis occasionally respond to some antihistamines, but these agents are contraindicated if bronchospasm develops.

Patients who require penicillin but have a history of sensitivity to it frequently are given an antihistamine. However, there is no convincing evidence that their use affords effective prophylaxis and the false security engendered by this undependable procedure can endanger the life of the patient. There are more effective methods for minimizing the risk of a penicillin reaction. (See Chapter 48, Penicillins.)

Antihistamines may ameliorate mild sensitivity transfusion reactions but do not prevent them. They should not be given routinely to patients receiving a blood transfusion, although some clinicians feel that they may be used prophylactically in patients who have a history of transfusion reactions. Antihistamines should never be added to the blood being transfused.

The central action of some antihistamines is useful in the prophylaxis and treatment of motion sickness and nausea (see Chapter 85, Antiemetics).

Certain over-the-counter preparations promoted as hypnotics contain methapyrilene. However, antihistamines generally are not reliable remedies for insomnia even though they cause drowsiness, since this effect is variable and most persons acquire a tolerance to the central depressant action.

Although timed-release antihistamine preparations are used, the bioavailability of the drug in this type of dosage form may be neither uniform nor reliable.

Adverse Reactions and Precautions

The incidence and severity of untoward effects, and the dose that causes the reactions, vary with each drug. Adverse reactions may be minimized by determining, through trial and error, which antihistamine a particular patient tolerates best.

Manifestations of sedation, the most common untoward effect, include an inability to concentrate, dizziness, ataxia, and deep sleep. Among the most potent and highly sedating antihistamines are two ethanolamines (diphenhydramine [Benadryl], doxylamine [Decapryn]) and a phenothiazine (promethazine [Phenergan]). The incidence of depressant effects with other drugs in these chemical subclasses (carbinoxamine [Clistin], methdilazine [Tacaryl], trimeprazine [Temaril]) is lower. The sedative properties of the ethylenediamines are approximately intermediate, and those of the alkylamines tend to be relatively low.

The sedative effect represents a hazard in ambulatory patients whose activities require mental alertness and motor coordination (eg, driving an automobile). In some cases it may disappear after the antihistamine has been used for two to three days. If sedation persists, the dose should be reduced or another antihistamine should be tried.

Blood dyscrasias (eg, agranulocytosis, thrombocytopenia, pancytopenia, hemolytic anemia) have occurred sporadically; except for the phenothiazines, no generalization is yet possible on whether all drugs in a chemical group would be implicated if one drug in the group causes blood dyscrasias. Although these reactions are rare, the physician should be aware of the possibility of their occurrence when patients are receiving prolonged antihistamine therapy.

Occasionally, the anticholinergic action of an antihistamine may predominate and cause excitation that results in insomnia, tremors, nervousness, irritability, and palpitation. Dryness of the mouth, blurred vision, urinary retention, tachycardia, and constipation also may occur, but these reactions are rare unless large doses are used. Convulsions have been reported in patients with focal lesions of the cerebral cortex and in individuals who had ingested toxic doses. Death may occur in cases of overdosage.

Fever and toxic nephrosis have been observed in children. Disorientation, vertigo, confusion, and delirium have been reported occasionally. Rare reactions include acute labyrinthitis, hysteria, neuropathy, fatigue, hyperhidrosis, early menses, headache, paresthesias, premature heart contractions, urinary frequency, chills, and anaphylactic reactions. Although hypersensitivity reactions may develop when antihistamines are given orally, they more commonly occur after topical application. Therefore, these agents should be given orally rather than topically in the treatment of any dermatitis. Sensitization is manifested by urticarial, eczematous, bullous, or petechial rashes, as well as by fixed drug eruptions. In some cases these eruptions are caused by photosensitization rather than by a primary allergic reaction.

Patients receiving antihistamines should be warned against the concomitant use of alcoholic beverages or other drugs (eg, sedatives, hypnotics) that depress the central nervous system.

ETHANOLAMINES

DIPHENHYDRAMINE HYDROCHLORIDE
[Benadryl]

$(C_6H_5)_2CHOCH_2CH_2N(CH_3)_2 \cdot HCl$

This potent antihistamine is the prototype of the ethanolamine derivatives. Its uses and properties are generally those discussed in the Introductory Statement. Diphenhydramine is the antihistamine of choice for parenteral use in the treatment of anaphylactic and other allergic reactions; this agent may be given with epinephrine, but should not be considered a substitute for it. Diphenhydramine also is an effective antiemetic and antiparkinsonism agent (see Chapter 85, Antiemetics, and Chapter 74, Antiparkinsonism Agents) and has mild antitussive properties, but this effect is of little clinical significance.

The intravenous route is the preferred parenteral route, but deep intramuscular injection also is effective. Subcutaneous, perivascular, and intra-arterial injections should be avoided because they cause pain, irritation, and tissue injury.

The incidence of drowsiness is high. For other reactions, see the Introductory Statement.

Caution is needed when diphenhydramine is given parenterally to patients with hypertension or heart disease, since doses of 100 mg or more may cause hypertension, tachycardia, and changes in the T wave or shortened diastolic interval.

USUAL DOSAGE.—

Intravenous, Intramuscular (deep): *Adults*, 10 to 50 mg every three hours; for severe symptoms, the maximal daily dosage is 400 mg. *Children*, 5 mg/kg of body weight daily in four divided doses (maximal daily dosage, 300 mg).

Oral: Adults, 100 to 250 mg daily in divided doses; *children under 12 years of age*, 5 mg/kg of body weight in four divided doses over a period of 24 hours.

Topical: Use of this route is deemed inadvisable because of the possible sensitizing effect of these preparations (see the Introductory Statement).

PREPARATIONS.—Benadryl (Parke, Davis). *Injection:* Solution 10 mg/ml in 10 and 30 ml containers, 50 mg/ml in 1 and 10 ml containers.

Oral: Capsules 25 and 50 mg; elixir 12.5 mg/5 ml.

Topical: Cream 2% in 1 and 2 oz containers.

ADDITIONAL TRADEMARKS.—Bax (McKesson), Hista-Sed (Century), Niramine (Rachelle), Rohydra (Robinson). Drug also marketed by other manufacturers under generic name.

CARBINOXAMINE MALEATE [Clistin]

$(4\text{-}ClC_6H_4)(C_5H_4N)CHOCH_2CH_2N(CH_3)_2 \cdot HOOCCH{=}CHCOOH$

Carbinoxamine is a potent antihistamine of the ethanolamine type. Its properties, uses, and adverse reactions are generally those discussed in the Introductory Statement. However, the incidence of drowsiness is lower than with other ethanolamines. Its anticholinergic effect is comparatively weak with usual doses, and it does not have a local anesthetic effect.

USUAL DOSAGE.—*Oral: Adults*, 12 to 24 mg daily in divided doses; *children*, 0.4 mg/kg of body weight daily divided into three or four doses. The bioavailability of the drug in timed-release form may be neither uniform nor reliable.

PREPARATIONS.—Clistin (McNeil). *Oral:* Elixir 4 mg/5 ml; tablets 4 mg; tablets (timed-release) 8 and 12 mg.

DOXYLAMINE SUCCINATE [Decapryn]

$(C_6H_5)(C_5H_4N)C(CH_3)OCH_2CH_2N(CH_3)_2 \cdot HOOCCH_2CH_2COOH$

Doxylamine is a potent antihistamine of the ethanolamine type. Its properties, uses, and adverse reactions are generally those discussed in the Introductory Statement. The incidence of drowsiness is high.

USUAL DOSAGE.—*Oral: Adults*, 12.5 to 25 mg every four to six hours; *children*, 2 mg/kg of body weight daily divided into four to six doses.

PREPARATIONS.—Decapryn (Merrell-National). *Oral:* Syrup 6.25 mg/5 ml; tablets 12.5 and 25 mg.

ETHYLENEDIAMINES

TRIPELENNAMINE CITRATE
[Pyribenzamine Citrate]
TRIPELENNAMINE HYDROCHLORIDE
[Pyribenzamine Hydrochloride]

CH_2 N $NCH_2CH_2N(CH_3)_2$

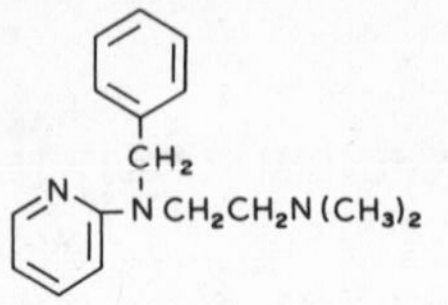

Tripelennamine is a potent antihistamine and is regarded as the prototype of the ethylenediamine group. Its properties and uses are generally those discussed in the Introductory Statement.

Ethylenediamines generally cause less sedation than diphenhydramine. Nevertheless, the major untoward effect is drowsiness, although the drug occasionally causes excitement. Mild to moderate dizziness is common. Mild gastrointestinal irritation (eg, nausea) occurs more commonly with the ethylenediamines than with most antihistamines. Hemolytic anemia, leukopenia, and agranulocytosis have been reported rarely. For other reactions, see the Introductory Statement.

USUAL DOSAGE.—

Tripelennamine Citrate:

Oral: Adults, 200 to 400 mg daily divided into four doses or when indicated (individual doses as large as 150 mg are tolerated by most people); *children,* 100 to 200 mg daily divided into four doses; *infants,* 10 to 20 mg as needed.

Tripelennamine Hydrochloride:

Oral: Adults, 150 to 400 mg daily divided into three or four doses; *children,* 75 to 200 mg daily divided into three or four doses. The bioavailability of the drug in timed-release form may be neither uniform nor reliable.

Topical: Use of this route is deemed inadvisable because of possible sensitizing effects of these preparations (see the Introductory Statement).

PREPARATIONS.—

Pyribenzamine Citrate (Ciba). *Oral:* Elixir 37.5 mg/5 ml.

Pyribenzamine Hydrochloride (Ciba).

Oral: Tablets 25 and 50 mg; tablets (timed-release) 50 and 100 mg.

Topical: Cream 2% in 1 oz containers.

Drug also marketed by other manufacturers under generic name.

METHAPYRILENE HYDROCHLORIDE
[Histadyl]

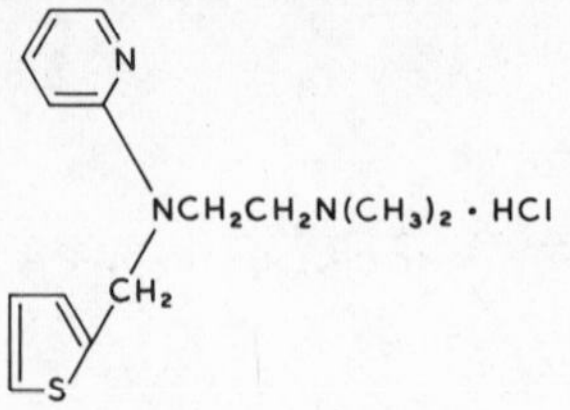

N $NCH_2CH_2N(CH_3)_2 \cdot HCl$ CH_2 S

This antihistamine of the ethylenediamine type has a rapid onset but a short duration of action. Its properties, uses, and adverse reactions are generally those discussed in the Introductory Statement. A parenteral dosage form of methapyrilene is available. However, diphenhydramine is the antihistamine of choice when injection is necessary.

Methapyrilene has a moderate sedative effect, but this action is less pronounced than that of some other antihistamines in therapeutic doses. Nevertheless, it is a common ingredient of many over-the-counter sedative mixtures.

USUAL DOSAGE.—

Oral: Adults, 100 to 250 mg daily divided into four or five doses; *children and infants,* 5 mg/kg of body weight daily divided into five doses (maximal daily dosage, 300 mg).

Intramuscular, Subcutaneous: Adults and children, one-fourth to one-third the oral dose.

PREPARATIONS.—Histadyl (Lilly).

Injection: Solution 20 mg/ml in 10 ml containers.

Oral: Capsules 25 and 50 mg; syrup 20 mg/5 ml.

Drug also marketed by other manufacturers under generic name.

PYRILAMINE MALEATE

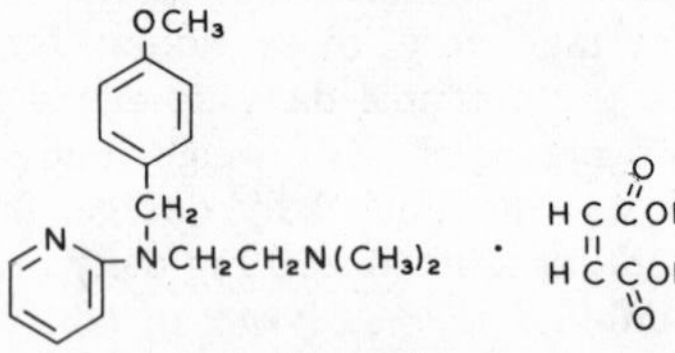

OCH_3 CH_2 N $NCH_2CH_2N(CH_3)_2 \cdot$ HC COOH / HC COOH

Pyrilamine is an effective antihistamine of the ethylenediamine type. Its properties and uses are generally those discussed in the Introductory Statement.

The incidence of drowsiness is low; the incidence of anorexia, nausea, and vomiting is greater than with the ethanolamines.

USUAL DOSAGE.—*Oral: Adults,* 75 to 200

mg daily in divided doses; *children*, information is inadequate to establish dosage.

PREPARATIONS.—*Oral:* Tablets 25 and 50 mg. Drug marketed under generic name.

ALKYLAMINES

CHLORPHENIRAMINE MALEATE [Chlor-Trimeton, Histaspan, Teldrin]

Cl-C6H4-CH(C5H4N)CH2CH2N(CH3)2 · HC(=O)... $ClC_6H_4CH(C_5H_4N)CH_2CH_2N(CH_3)_2 \cdot HCCOOH{=}HCCOOH$

Chlorpheniramine is an effective antihistamine and is regarded as the prototype of the alkylamine group. Its properties and uses are generally those discussed in the Introductory Statement. Chlorpheniramine is a common ingredient in cold remedies. A parenteral dosage form is available. However, diphenhydramine is the antihistamine of choice when injection is necessary.

The incidence of untoward effects is low; drowsiness is the most common reaction but, as with other alkylamines, is less pronounced than with most antihistamines.

USUAL DOSAGE.—

Oral: Adults, 2 to 4 mg every six to eight hours; *children*, 0.35 mg/kg of body weight daily divided into four doses. The bioavailability of the drug in timed-release form may be neither uniform nor reliable.

Intramuscular, Intravenous, Subcutaneous: Adults, 5 to 40 mg (intravenous injection should be made over period of one minute).

Subcutaneous: Children, 0.35 mg/kg of body weight daily divided into four doses.

PREPARATIONS.—

Chlor-Trimeton (Schering).

Oral: Syrup 2.5 mg/5 ml; tablets 4 mg; tablets (timed-release) 8 and 12 mg.

Injection: Solution 10 mg/ml in 1 ml containers, 100 mg/ml in 2 ml containers.

Histaspan (USV), Teldrin (Smith Kline & French). *Oral:* Capsules (timed-release) 8 and 12 mg.

ADDITIONAL TRADEMARKS.—Allerbid (Amfre-Grant), Chlo-Amine (Hollister-Stier), Chloramate (Reid-Provident), Chlormene (Robinson), Drize (Ascher), Histadur (Cooper). Drug also marketed by other manufacturers under generic name.

BROMPHENIRAMINE MALEATE [Dimetane]

$BrC_6H_4CH(C_5H_4N)CH_2CH_2N(CH_3)_2 \cdot HCCOOH{=}HCCOOH$

Brompheniramine is an effective antihistamine of the alkylamine type. Its properties, uses, and adverse reactions are generally those discussed in the Introductory Statement.

The principal untoward effects are drowsiness and rash.

USUAL DOSAGE.—

Oral: Adults, 12 to 32 mg daily divided into three or four doses; *children*, 0.5 mg/kg of body weight daily divided into three or four doses. The bioavailability of the drug in timed-release form may be neither uniform nor reliable.

Intramuscular, Intravenous, Subcutaneous: Adults, 5 to 20 mg every 6 to 12 hours; *children*, 0.5 mg/kg of body weight daily divided into three or four doses.

PREPARATIONS.—Dimetane (Robins).

Oral: Elixir 2 mg/5 ml; tablets 4 mg; tablets (timed-release) 8 and 12 mg.

Injection: Solution 10 mg/ml in 1 ml containers, 100 mg/ml in 2 ml containers.

DEXBROMPHENIRAMINE MALEATE [Disomer]

$BrC_6H_4CH(C_5H_4N)CH_2CH_2N(CH_3)_2 \cdot HC\text{-}COOH{=}HC\text{-}COOH$

This dextrorotatory isomer of brompheniramine maleate is an effective alkylamine-type antihistamine. Its properties, uses, and adverse reactions are generally those discussed in the Introductory Statement.

The most common untoward effect is drowsiness.

USUAL DOSAGE.—*Oral: Adults*, 8 to 12 mg daily divided into two doses; *children*, information is inadequate to establish dosage. The bioavailability of the drug in timed-release form may be neither uniform nor reliable.

PREPARATIONS.—Disomer (Schering). *Oral:* Tablets (timed-release) 4 and 6 mg.

DEXCHLORPHENIRAMINE MALEATE
[Polaramine]

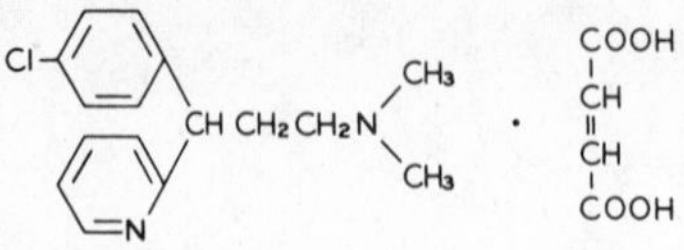

This dextrorotatory isomer of chlorpheniramine is an effective antihistamine of the alkylamine type. Its properties and uses are generally those discussed in the Introductory Statement.

The incidence of untoward effects is low; the most common reaction is drowsiness.

USUAL DOSAGE.—*Oral: Adults,* 3 to 8 mg daily divided into three or four doses; *children,* 0.15 mg/kg of body weight daily divided into four doses. The bioavailability of the drug in timed-release form may be neither uniform nor reliable.

PREPARATIONS.—Polaramine (Schering). *Oral:* Syrup 2 mg/5 ml; tablets 2 mg; tablets (timed-release) 4 and 6 mg.

DIMETHINDENE MALEATE [Forhistal Maleate, Triten]

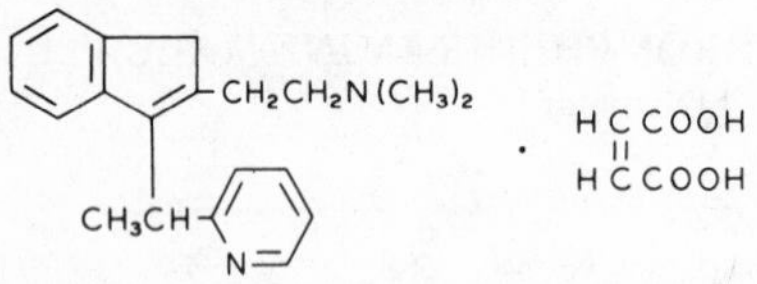

Dimethindene is an effective antihistamine of the alkylamine type. Its properties, uses, and adverse reactions are generally those discussed in the Introductory Statement.

Drowsiness occurs frequently.

USUAL DOSAGE.—*Oral: Adults,* 1 or 2 mg one to three times daily. *Children over 6 years of age,* 0.1 mg/kg of body weight daily in one to three doses; *under 6 years,* dosage has not been established. The bioavailability of the drug in timed-release form may be neither uniform nor reliable.

PREPARATIONS.—

Forhistal Maleate (Ciba). *Oral:* Syrup 1 mg/5 ml; tablets 1 mg; tablets (timed-release) 2.5 mg.

Triten (Marion). *Oral:* Tablets 1 mg; tablets (timed-release) 2.5 mg.

TRIPROLIDINE HYDROCHLORIDE
[Actidil]

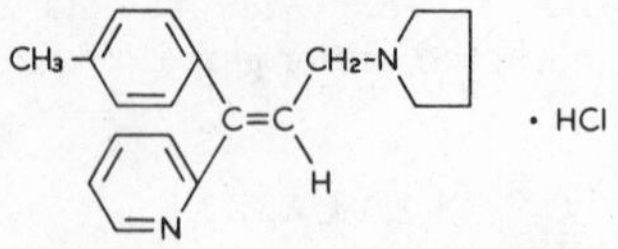

This effective antihistamine of the alkylamine type has a rapid onset of action and a duration up to 12 hours. Its properties and uses are generally those discussed in the Introductory Statement.

The incidence of untoward effects is low; the most common reaction is drowsiness.

USUAL DOSAGE.—*Oral: Adults,* 5 to 7.5 mg daily divided into two or three doses; *children over 2 years of age,* 2.5 mg daily divided into two or three doses; *under 2 years,* 1.25 mg daily divided into two or three doses.

PREPARATIONS.—Actidil (Burroughs Wellcome). *Oral:* Syrup 1.25 mg/5 ml; tablets 2.5 mg.

PHENOTHIAZINES

METHDILAZINE [Tacaryl]
METHDILAZINE HYDROCHLORIDE
[Tacaryl Hydrochloride]

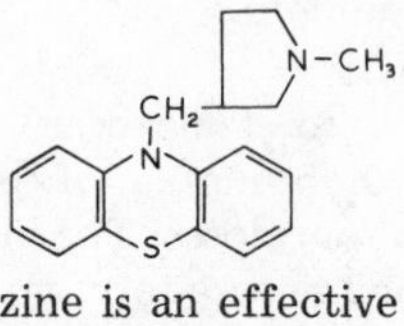

Methdilazine is an effective antihistamine. Its properties and uses are generally those discussed in the Introductory Statement.

The major adverse reactions of other phenothiazines (eg, extrapyramidal effects, blood dyscrasias) have not been observed with methdilazine; cholestatic jaundice has been reported rarely, although a causal relationship has not been established. Drowsiness is the most common untoward effect, but it is less prominent than with other phenothiazines used as antihistamines.

USUAL DOSAGE.—*Oral: Adults,* 16 to 32 mg daily divided into two or four doses; *children,* 0.3 mg/kg of body weight daily divided into two doses.

PREPARATIONS.—

Tacaryl (Mead Johnson). *Oral:* Tablets (chewable) 3.6 mg (equivalent to 4 mg of the hydrochloride salt).

Tacaryl Hydrochloride (Mead Johnson). *Oral:* Syrup 4 mg/5 ml; tablets 8 mg.

PROMETHAZINE HYDROCHLORIDE
[Phenergan]

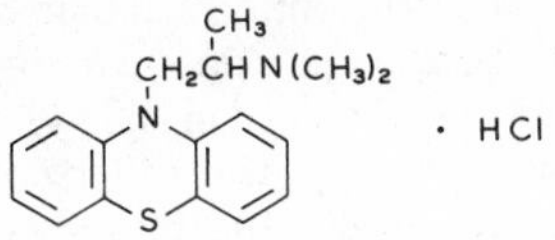

This potent phenothiazine was originally introduced for the treatment of allergic conditions, but its pronounced sedative effect limits its use in many ambulatory patients. For other uses, see Chapter 20, Adjuncts to Anesthesia, and Chapter 85, Antiemetics.

Extrapyramidal reactions (tremors, muscular hypertonia, dystonias), cholestatic jaundice, leukopenia, agranulocytosis, hypotension, and transient myopia have been reported. All precautions applicable to phenothiazines should be observed when using this drug (see Chapter 29, Antipsychotic Agents). Development of photosensitization is a contraindication to further treatment with promethazine.

USUAL DOSAGE.—*Oral, Rectal, Intramuscular, Intravenous: Adults,* 12.5 mg in the morning or when necessary, and 25 mg at bedtime; *children,* 0.13 mg/kg of body weight in the morning or when necessary, and 0.5 mg/kg at bedtime.

PREPARATIONS.—Phenergan (Wyeth).

Oral: Syrup 6.25 and 25 mg/5 ml; tablets 12.5, 25, and 50 mg.

Rectal: Suppositories 25 and 50 mg.

Injection: Solution 25 mg/ml in 1 and 10 ml containers, 50 mg/ml (intramuscular) in 1 and 10 ml containers.

ADDITIONAL TRADEMARKS.—Fellozine (Fellows-Testagar), Ganphen (Tutag).

TRIMEPRAZINE TARTRATE [Temaril]

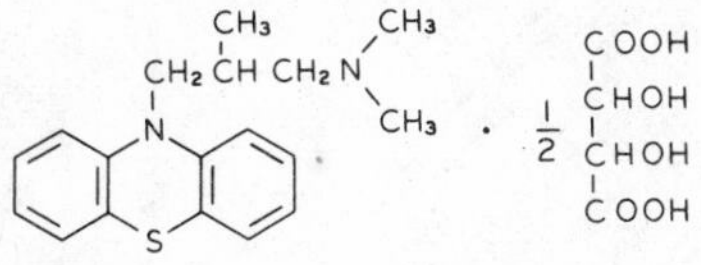

This phenothiazine derivative has properties and uses similar to other antihistamines. (See the Introductory Statement.)

Drowsiness is the most common adverse effect. As with most phenothiazines, cholestatic jaundice, agranulocytosis, leukopenia, and extrapyramidal symptoms (tremors, muscular hypertonia, dystonias) has occurred rarely. All precautions applicable to pheonthiazines should be observed when using trimeprazine (see Chapter 29, Antipsychotic Agents).

USUAL DOSAGE.—*Oral: Adults,* 10 mg daily divided into four doses. Unusually large doses (80 mg daily) have been well tolerated in adults without evidence of untoward effects. *Children under 2 years of age,* 3.75 mg daily divided into three doses; *3 to 12 years,* 7.5 mg daily divided into three doses. The timed-release preparation does not offer any significant advantage over the ordinary dosage form, since trimeprazine and other phenothiazines have prolonged half-lives.

PREPARATIONS.—Temaril (Smith Kline & French). *Oral:* Capsules (timed-release) 5 mg; syrup 2.5 mg/5 ml; tablets 5 mg.

MISCELLANEOUS ANTIHISTAMINES

CYPROHEPTADINE HYDROCHLORIDE
[Periactin Hydrochloride]

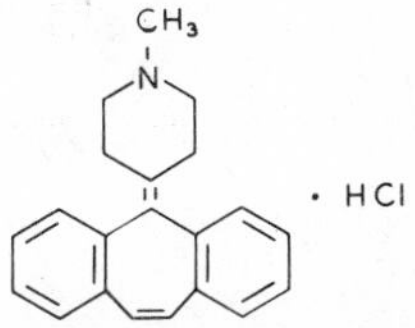

This antihistamine also has mild to moderate antiserotonin activity and is used to relieve pruritus associated with skin disorders such as contact dermatitis, urticaria, and neurodermatitis. When used with a corticosteroid for the control of pruritus, cyproheptadine may permit reduction in the dosage of the steroid. Results of several studies suggest cyproheptadine accelerates weight gain and stimulates linear growth in children, especially in those with asthma. However, most patients lost weight when the drug was discontinued. Some authorities feel that use of an appetite-stimulating agent is unnecessary in healthy children, even if they are below average in weight for age or height.

See Chapter 24, Agents Used to Treat Migraine, for information on use of cyproheptadine in this condition.

Drowsiness is the most common untoward effect. Dryness of the mouth, confusion, ataxia, dizziness, irritability, fatigue, nausea, headache, anorexia, and rash occur occasionally.

USUAL DOSAGE.—*Oral: Adults,* 4 to 20 mg daily in divided doses. Dosage must be individualized and should not exceed 0.5 mg/kg of body weight daily. *Children,* 0.25 mg/kg daily divided into three or four doses.

PREPARATIONS.—Periactin Hydrochloride (Merck Sharp & Dohme). *Oral:* Syrup 2 mg/5 ml; tablets 4 mg.

Other Antihistamines

Bromodiphenhydramine Hydrochloride (Ambodryl [Parke, Davis])
Diphenylpyraline Hydrochloride (Diafen [Riker], Hispril [Smith Kline & French])
Rotoxamine Tartrate (Twiston R-A [McNeil])

MIXTURES

Many fixed-ratio combinations containing two or more antihistamines or antihistamines with analgesics, adrenergic agents, adrenal corticosteroids, or antibacterial agents are marketed for use in allergies and other conditions such as the common cold. Such mixtures have an unsound rationale and should not be used. An adequate dose of one ingredient may require the administration of supplementary doses of the other components, thus tending to negate the minor convenience that the combination product would appear to offer. In addition, when two or more agents with similar action are combined, the patient is exposed to the possible development of sensitivity to any of them, often without any compensating advantage. See Chapters 35, Adrenal Corticosteroids; 44, Antitussive Agents; 46, Cold Remedies; and 55, Sulfonamides for additional information and listings of mixtures containing antihistamines.

Chapter 46

COLD REMEDIES

Acute infections of the upper respiratory tract have diverse etiologies, but symptoms may be similar. Although the common cold is one of the most prevalent acute illnesses, rational therapy for its cure has not been achieved. Consequently, treatment must be directed toward relieving symptoms (postnasal drip, nasal congestion, headache, myalgia, malaise, cough, and, sometimes, fever). Such symptomatic therapy makes an individual feel more comfortable until the natural defense and homeostatic mechanisms of the body can restore him to a healthy state. Administration of an anti-infective agent is indicated only when an infection is presumed to be susceptible to the agent and is serious enough to warrant specific treatment. There is no satisfactory evidence to support allegations that large doses of ascorbic acid (vitamin C) will prevent or cure the common cold (see Chapter 14, Vitamins and Sources of Vitamins).

Some single-entity products afford symptomatic relief of the discomforts of the common cold. They include nasal decongestants (see Chapter 42, Nasal Decongestants), analgesics (see Chapter 22, Mild Analgesics), antitussives (see Chapter 44, Antitussive Agents), and agents used to help dilate the passages of the bronchial tree and keep them clear (see Chapter 41, Bronchodilators, and Chapter 43, Expectorants and Inhalants). In addition, antihistamines (see Chapter 45, Antihistamines) occasionally have a palliative effect on the common cold by helping to counteract postnasal drip, nasal congestion, or bronchial congestion. Similarly, atropine and some of its derivatives are used to dry excessive respiratory tract secretions.

Because no one therapeutic agent can counteract all symptoms associated with the common cold, it has become increasingly popular for manufacturers to market mixtures that are purported to relieve the uncomfortable symptoms of the cold. In most instances these combination products have more sales appeal than actual usefulness. They all have the principal disadvantage of fixed-dosage combination products: when a therapeutic amount of one agent is given, other drugs in the mixture may be administered at higher or lower levels than are optimally therapeutic. This disadvantage is particularly prominent with some of the cold remedies that are sold without prescription, for they may have been formulated to satisfy government safety requirements and contain some ingredients in subtherapeutic quantities.

Despite the shortcomings of cold remedy mixtures, they are widely used and enjoy a certain amount of acclaim and endorsement by both the medical profession and the laity. It is, therefore, probably too simple a generalization to state that these combination products have no usefulness in good medical practice. Nevertheless, a physician who chooses to prescribe a cold remedy must be certain that the mixture is composed of drugs with known effectiveness, that the ingredients are present in adequate therapeutic amounts, and that they are therapeutically rational for the type and severity of symptoms being treated.

PREPARATIONS CONTAINING A MILD ANALGESIC

Hundreds of cold remedies containing a mild analgesic are available for both over-the-counter and prescription dispensing. Unfortunately, this type of mixture does not fulfill the manufacturers' glowing claims. The most widely promoted and probably most widely used cold remedies of this type contain a mild analgesic, an antihistamine, a nasal decongestant, and a mild stimulant (usually caffeine). Some of these preparations may deviate from the prototype by omission of the nasal decongestant or the stimulant, or by also containing an expectorant, a second analgesic or antihistamine, or, occasionally, an antitussive. However, most cold remedies that contain an antitussive are promoted for and more commonly used to relieve cough. (For a listing and discussion of these products, see Chapter 44, Antitussive Agents.)

Adverse reactions vary widely and are characteristic of those produced by the individual drugs in the mixture. When the manufacturer's dosage recommendations are followed, these preparations are relatively devoid of serious undesirable effects. Drowsiness caused by the antihistamine is the most common reaction observed.

Examples of commonly used preparations are listed below; inclusion in this list does not indicate approval for use in the common cold.

Cenagesic (Central): Each tablet contains salicylamide 250 mg, phenacetin 120 mg, phenylephrine hydrochloride 5 mg, pyrilamine maleate 12 mg, ascorbic acid 30 mg, and caffeine 15 mg.

Citra Capsules (Boyle): Each capsule contains salicylamide 227 mg, phenacetin 120 mg, phenylephrine hydrochloride 10 mg, pheniramine maleate 6.25 mg, methapyrilene hydrochloride 8.33 mg, pyrilamine maleate 8.33 mg, caffeine 30 mg, and ascorbic acid 50 mg.

Clistin-D (McNeil): Each tablet contains acetaminophen 300 mg, carbinoxamine maleate 2 mg, and phenylephrine hydrochloride 10 mg.

Colrex Capsules (Rowell): Each capsule contains aluminum aspirin 300 mg, chlorpheniramine maleate 2 mg, phenylephrine hydrochloride 5 mg, ascorbic acid 100 mg, and purified hesperidin 100 mg.

Coricidin (Schering): Each tablet contains aspirin 390 mg, chlorpheniramine maleate 2 mg, and caffeine 30 mg.

Coricidin D (Schering): Each tablet contains aspirin 390 mg, chlorpheniramine maleate 2 mg, caffeine 30 mg, and phenylephrine 10 mg.

Coricidin Demilets (Schering): Each tablet contains aspirin 80 mg, chlorpheniramine maleate 0.5 mg, and phenylephrine hydrochloride 2.5 mg.

Coricidin Medilets (Schering): Each tablet contains aspirin 80 mg and chlorpheniramine maleate 0.5 mg.

Coriforte (Schering): Each capsule contains salicylamide 190 mg, phenacetin 130 mg, chlorpheniramine maleate 4 mg, caffeine 30 mg, and ascorbic acid 50 mg.

Corilin (Schering): Each milliliter of pediatric liquid contains sodium salicylate 80 mg, chlorpheniramine maleate 0.75 mg, and glycine 25 mg.

Co-Tylenol (McNeil): Each tablet contains acetaminophen 325 mg, chlorpheniramine maleate 1 mg, and phenylephrine hydrochloride 5 mg.

Covangesic (Mallinckrodt): Each 5 ml of liquid contains acetaminophen 120 mg, phenylephrine hydrochloride 3.75 mg, phenylpropanolamine hydrochloride 6.25 mg, chlorpheniramine maleate 1 mg, and pyrilamine maleate 6.25 mg; each tablet contains aspirin 324 mg, phenylephrine hydrochloride 7.5 mg, phenylpropanolamine hydrochloride 12.5 mg, chlorpheniramine maleate 2 mg, and pyrilamine maleate 12.5 mg.

Dasikon (Beecham-Massengill): Each capsule contains aspirin 195 mg, phenacetin 130 mg, caffeine 32 mg, chlorpheniramine maleate 2 mg, and atropine sulfate 0.065 mg.

Duadacin (Hoechst): Each capsule contains acetaminophen 120 mg, salicylamide 200 mg, caffeine 30 mg, phenylephrine hydrochloride 5 mg, chlorpheniramine maleate 1 mg, pyrilamine maleate 12.5 mg, and ascorbic acid 50 mg.

Elder Cold-Tabs (Elder): Each tablet contains phenacetin 150 mg, phenylephrine hydrochloride 5 mg, pyrilamine maleate 10 mg, and caffeine 15 mg.

Fiogesic (Sandoz): Each tablet contains calcium carbaspirin equivalent to aspirin 300 mg, phenylpropanolamine hydrochloride 25 mg, pheniramine maleate 12.5 mg, and pyrilamine maleate 12.5 mg.

Histadyl & A.S.A. Compound (Lilly): Each capsule contains aspirin 227 mg, phenacetin 160 mg, caffeine 32.5 mg, and methapyrilene hydrochloride 25 mg.

Kryl (Ayerst): Each tablet contains aspirin 230 mg, phenacetin 160 mg, isothipendyl hydrochloride 4 mg, phenylephrine hydrochloride 5 mg, and ascorbic acid 100 mg.

Neo-Synephrine Compound (Winthrop): Each tablet contains acetaminophen 150 mg, phenylephrine hydrochloride 5 mg, thenyldiamine hydrochloride 7.5 mg, and caffeine 15 mg.

Novahistine Singlet (Dow): Each tablet contains acetaminophen 500 mg, phenylephrine hydrochloride 40 mg, and chlorpheniramine maleate 8 mg.

Opacedrin (Elder): Each capsule contains acetaminophen 50 mg, aspirin 200 mg, chlorpheniramine maleate 1 mg, atropine sulfate 0.12 mg, caffeine 8 mg, and camphor monobromated 8 mg.

Ornex (Smith Kline & French): Each capsule contains acetaminophen 325 mg and phenylpropanolamine hydrochloride 18 mg.

Phenaphen Plus (Robins): Each tablet contains aspirin 162.4 mg, phenacetin 194 mg, hyoscyamine sulfate 0.031 mg, phenobarbital 16.2 mg, pheniramine maleate 12.5 mg, and phenylephrine hydrochloride 10 mg.

Phenergan Compound (Wyeth): Each tablet contains aspirin 600 mg, promethazine hydrochloride 6.25 mg, and pseudoephedrine hydrochloride 60 mg.

Pyrroxate (Upjohn): Each capsule or tablet contains aspirin 228 mg, phenacetin 162 mg, caffeine 37 mg, chlorpheniramine maleate 2 mg, and methoxyphenamine hydrochloride 25 mg.

Rhinex Ty-Med (Lemmon): Each timed-release tablet contains acetaminophen 300 mg, salicylamide 300 mg, phenylpropanolamine hydrochloride 60 mg, and chlorpheniramine maleate 4 mg.

Sinubid (Warner-Chilcott): Each tablet contains acetaminophen 300 mg, phenacetin 300 mg, phenylpropanolamine hydrochloride 100 mg, and phenyltoloxamine citrate 66 mg.

Sinulin (Carnrick): Each tablet contains acetaminophen 325 mg, salicylamide 250 mg, phenylpropanolamine hydrochloride 37.5 mg, chlorpheniramine maleate 2 mg, and homatropine methylbromide 0.75 mg.

Sinutab (Warner-Chilcott): Each tablet contains acetaminophen 150 mg, phenacetin 150 mg, phenylpropanolamine hydrochloride 25 mg, and phenyltoloxamine citrate 22 mg.

Sinutab II (Warner-Chilcott): Each tablet contains phenacetin 150 mg, acetaminophen 150 mg, and phenylpropanolamine hydrochloride 25 mg.

Thephorin-AC (Roche): Each tablet contains aspirin 160 mg, phenacetin 160 mg, caffeine 15 mg, and phenindamine tartrate 10 mg.

Triaminicin (Dorsey): Each tablet contains aspirin 225 mg, acetaminophen 150 mg, caffeine 30 mg, phenylpropanolamine hydrochloride 25 mg, pheniramine maleate 12.5 mg, pyrilamine maleate 12.5 mg, and ascorbic acid 50 mg.

Ursinus (Dorsey): Each tablet contains calcium carbaspirin equivalent to aspirin 300 mg, phenylpropanolamine hydrochloride 25 mg, pheniramine maleate 12.5 mg, and pyrilamine maleate 12.5 mg.

PREPARATIONS CONTAINING A STRONG ANALGESIC

Cold remedies having Dover's powder (powdered opium and ipecac) as a principal active ingredient are still marketed. In addition to that archaic preparation, they contain a mild analgesic. Other substances that may be incorporated into these formulations include caffeine, camphor, ascorbic acid, terpin hydrate, ammonium chloride, and a nasal decongestant or an antihistamine. Since the use of these complex mixtures is not rational therapy, they should not be used in the common cold.

They can produce toxic reactions characteristic of any of the individual drugs in the mixture. Nausea and occasional vomiting are the most common untoward effects seen.

Available mixtures include:

Cenamal (Central): Each capsule contains Dover's powder 24 mg, salicylamide 250 mg, phenacetin 120 mg, racephedrine hydrochloride 5 mg, pyrilamine maleate 12 mg, and ascorbic acid 50 mg.

Dasin (Beecham-Massengill): Each capsule contains opium 3 mg, ipecac 3 mg, phenacetin 100 mg, atropine sulfate 0.12 mg, aspirin 120 mg, camphor 15 mg, and caffeine 8 mg; each ¼ strength tablet contains opium 0.8 mg, ipecac 0.8 mg, phenacetin 30 mg, aspirin 30 mg, camphor monobromated 4 mg, caffeine 2 mg, and atropine sulfate 0.03 mg.

Opasal (Elder): Each capsule contains Dover's powder 15 mg, phenacetin 100 mg, aspirin 200 mg, atropine sulfate 0.12 mg, caffeine 8 mg, and camphor monobromated 8 mg.

Thoryza Improved (Warren-Teed): Each capsule contains Dover's powder 15 mg, methapyrilene hydrochloride 10 mg, acetaminophen 120 mg, phenacetin 100 mg, caffeine 8 mg, and camphor 8 mg.

PREPARATIONS THAT DO NOT CONTAIN AN ANALGESIC

Most of these mixtures contain one or more antihistamines and one or more nasal decongestants. They also may contain an anticholinergic (atropine or an atropine derivative). Although they frequently are promoted as cold remedies, they can only be expected to dry excessive secretions in the respiratory tract. They are far from ideal even for this use, because the oral route is not a particularly good one for obtaining the best results from a nasal decongestant (see Chapter 42, Nasal Decongestants), and the effectiveness of antihistamines in combating congestion of the nose, throat, and bronchial tree is widely variable.

The adverse reactions are characteristic of those produced by the individual drugs in the mixture. Drowsiness caused by the antihistamines is the most frequent untoward effect observed.

Examples of commonly used preparations are listed below; inclusion in this list does not indicate approval for use in the common cold.

Actifed (Burroughs Wellcome): Each tablet contains triprolidine hydrochloride 2.5 mg and pseudoephedrine hydrochloride 60 mg; each 5 ml of syrup contains triprolidine hydrochloride 1.25 mg and pseudoephedrine hydrochloride 30 mg.

Allerstat (Lemmon): Each capsule contains phenylpropanolamine hydrochloride 25 mg, phenylephrine hydrochloride 2.5 mg, pheniramine maleate 12.5 mg, and pyrilamine maleate 12.5 mg.

Coryztime (Elder): Each timed-release capsule contains phenylpropanolamine hydrochloride 50 mg, chlorpheniramine maleate 8 mg, and atropine sulfate 0.37 mg.

Cotrol-D (Beecham-Massengill): Each tablet contains pseudoephedrine hydrochloride 60 mg and chlorpheniramine maleate 4 mg.

Covanamine (Mallinckrodt): Each tablet contains phenylephrine hydrochloride 15 mg, phenylpropanolamine hydrochloride 25 mg, chlorpheniramine maleate 4 mg, and pyrilamine maleate 25 mg; each 5 ml of liquid contains phenylephrine hydrochloride 3.75 mg, phenylpropanolamine hydrochloride 6.25 mg, chlorpheniramine maleate 1 mg, and pyrilamine maleate 6.25 mg.

Deconamine (Smith, Miller & Patch): Each timed-release capsule contains chlorpheniramine maleate 8 mg and pseudoephedrine hydrochloride 120 mg; each tablet contains chlorpheniramine maleate 4 mg and psuedoephedrine hydrochloride 60 mg; each 5 ml of elixir contains chlorpheniramine maleate 2 mg and pseudoephedrine hydrochloride 30 mg.

Demazin (Schering): Each timed-release tablet contains chlorpheniramine maleate 4 mg and phenylephrine hydrochloride 20 mg; each 5 ml of syrup contains chlorpheniramine maleate 1.25 mg and phenylephrine hydrochloride 2.5 mg.

Dimetapp (Robins): Each timed-release tablet contains brompheniramine maleate 12 mg, phenylephrine hydrochloride 15 mg, and phenylpropanolamine hydrochloride 15 mg; each 5 ml of elixir contains brompheniramine maleate 4 mg, phenylephrine hydrochloride 5 mg, phenylpropanolamine hydrochloride 5 mg, and alcohol 2.3%.

Disophrol (Schering): Each tablet contains dexbrompheniramine maleate 2 mg and pseudoephedrine sulfate 60 mg.

Drixoral (Schering): Each timed-release tablet contains dexbrompheniramine maleate 6 mg and pseudoephedrine sulfate 120 mg.

Drize M (Ascher): Each timed-release capsule contains chlorpheniramine maleate 8 mg, phenylephrine hydrochloride 20 mg, and methscopolamine nitrate 2.5 mg.

Extendryl (Fleming): Each timed-release capsule contains chlorpheniramine maleate 8 mg, phenylephrine hydrochloride 20 mg, and methscopolamine nitrate 2.5 mg; each tablet or 5 ml of syrup contains chlorpheniramine maleate 2 mg, phenylephrine hydrochloride 10 mg, and methscopolamine nitrate 1.25 mg.

Fedrazil (Burroughs Wellcome): Each tablet contains pseudoephedrine hydrochloride 30 mg and chlorcyclizine hydrochloride 25 mg.

Histaspan-D (USV): Each timed-release capsule contains phenylephrine hydrochloride 20 mg, chlorpheniramine maleate 8 mg, and methscopolamine nitrate 2.5 mg.

Histaspan-Plus (USV): Each timed-release capsule contains phenylephrine hydrochloride 20 mg and chlorpheniramine maleate 8 mg.

Hista-Vadrin (First Texas): Each tablet contains phenylpropanolamine hydrochloride 40 mg, chlorpheniramine maleate 4 mg, methapyrilene hydrochloride 40 mg, and phenylephrine hydrochloride 5 mg; each 5 ml of syrup contains phenylpropanolamine hydrochloride 20 mg, chlorpheniramine maleate 2 mg, and phenylephrine hydrochloride 2.5 mg.

Hista-Vadrin T.D. (First Texas): Each timed-release capsule contains phenylpropanolamine hydrochloride 50 mg, chlorpheniramine maleate 1 mg, pheniramine maleate 12.5 mg, atropine sulfate 0.024 mg, scopolamine hydrobromide 0.014 mg, and hyoscyamine sulfate 0.122 mg.

Isoclor (Arnar-Stone): Each tablet or 10 ml of liquid contains chlorpheniramine maleate 4 mg and pseudoephedrine hydrochloride 25 mg; each timed-release capsule contains chlorpheniramine maleate 10 mg and pseudoephedrine hydrochloride 65 mg.

Naldecon (Bristol): Each tablet or 10 ml of syrup contains phenylpropanolamine hydrochloride 40 mg, phenylephrine hydrochloride 10 mg, phenyltoloxamine citrate 15 mg, and chlorpheniramine maleate 5 mg; each milliliter of pediatric drops or 5 ml of pediatric syrup contains phenylpropanolamine hydrochloride 5 mg, phenylephrine hydrochloride 1.25 mg, phenyltoloxamine citrate 2 mg, and chlorpheniramine maleate 0.5 mg.

Neotep (Tutag): Each timed-release capsule contains chlorpheniramine maleate 9 mg and phenylephrine hydrochloride 21 mg.

Novahistine (Dow): Each Fortis capsule or Melet chewable tablet contains phenylephrine hydrochloride 10 mg and chlorpheniramine maleate 2 mg; each LP tablet contains phenylephrine hydrochloride 25 mg and chlorpheniramine maleate 4 mg.

Phenergan-D (Wyeth): Each tablet contains pseudoephedrine hydrochloride 60 mg and promethazine hydrochloride 6.25 mg.

Ornade (Smith Kline & French): Each timed-release capsule contains chlorpheniramine maleate 8 mg and phenylpropanolamine hydrochloride 50 mg.

Pyma Timed Capsules (Fellows): Each timed-release capsule contains pyrilamine maleate 50 mg, chlorpheniramine maleate 6 mg, pheniramine maleate 20 mg, and phenylephrine hydrochloride 15 mg.

Rondec (Ross): Each chewable tablet (Rondec C) or tablet (Rondec T) contains carbinoxamine maleate 2.5 mg and pseudoephedrine hydrochloride 60 mg; each milliliter of drops (Rondec D) contains carbinoxamine maleate 1 mg and pseudoephedrine hydrochloride 30 mg; each 5 ml of syrup (Rondec S) contains carbinoxamine maleate 2.5 mg and pseudoephedrine hydrochloride 60 mg.

Rynatan (Mallinckrodt): Each tablet contains phenylephrine tannate 25 mg, chlorpheniramine tannate 8 mg, and pyrilamine tannate 25 mg; each 5 ml of pediatric suspension contains phenylephrine tannate 5 mg, chlorpheniramine tannate 2 mg, and pyrilamine tannate 12.5 mg.

Triaminic (Dorsey): Each timed-release tablet contains phenylpropanolamine hydrochloride 50 mg, pheniramine maleate 25 mg, and pyrilamine maleate 25 mg; each Juvelet timed-release tablet contains phenylpropanolamine hydrochloride 25 mg, pheniramine maleate 12.5 mg, and pyrilamine maleate 12.5 mg; each 5 ml of syrup contains phenylpropanolamine hydrochloride 12.5 mg, pheniramine maleate 6.25 mg, and pyrilamine maleate 6.25 mg; each milliliter of concentrate contains phenylpropanolamine hydrochloride 20 mg, pheniramine maleate 10 mg, and pyrilamine maleate 10 mg.

Triaminic MSC (Dorsey): Each timed-release tablet contains phenylpropanolamine hydrochloride 50 mg, pheniramine maleate 25 mg, pyrilamine maleate 25 mg, and methscopolamine nitrate 4 mg.

Ventilade (Warren-Teed): Each 30 ml of syrup contains phenylpropanolamine hydrochloride 75 mg, methapyrilene fumarate 25 mg, pyrilamine maleate 25 mg, pheniramine maleate 25 mg, and alcohol 5%.

Chapter 47

THERAPEUTIC GASES

Gases used therapeutically include general anesthetics (see Chapter 19); the two gases of the normal metabolic and respiratory processes, oxygen and carbon dioxide; and two pharmacologically inert gases, nitrogen and helium. Of these, oxygen has the greatest therapeutic importance; carbon dioxide has a few uses, and nitrogen and helium are primarily used as diluents for oxygen and other gases or for special therapeutic or diagnostic purposes.

INDIVIDUAL EVALUATIONS

OXYGEN

Oxygen has two primary uses: to form mixtures with inhalation anesthetics and to relieve hypoxemia until the cause of the hypoxia can be corrected by other appropriate measures. It is also used to oxygenate perfusates for tissues being held in readiness for transplantation and to oxygenate blood during pulmonary bypass. Oxygen is sometimes administered by inhalation to facilitate the elimination of nitrogen from the tissues or hollow viscera (eg, after pneumoencephalograms and ventriculograms and in intestinal obstruction).

Selection of the technique of administration depends upon the purpose for which oxygen is to be administered and associated factors such as the cooperative state of the patient, oxygen level demands, anticipated duration of administration, and need for accessibility to the patient. The approximate inhaled oxygen concentrations attainable when currently recommended devices are employed are: short nasal cannula or nasopharyngeal catheter, 30% to 50%; pediatric tents or incubators, 40%; bed tent, 50%; face tent, 70%; loose-fitting mask, 80%; and tight-fitting mask and reservoir bag with unidirectional valves, 100%. Intermittent positive pressure using masks or endotracheal or tracheostomy tubes also permits delivery of 100% oxygen.

Although high concentrations of oxygen may be necessary in life-threatening situations, they should not be used over long periods. When continuous administration is indicated, lower concentrations should be used; for this purpose, delivery of oxygen through a nasal cannula, when practical, offers the greatest patient comfort and accessibility.

Regardless of the concentration provided by the oxygenating system, monitoring of the arterial blood for oxygen saturation is the only means of assuring that therapy is effective.

Oxygen may also be administered in hyperbaric chambers at pressures not exceeding three atmospheres. Hyperbaric oxygen has been used to treat hypoxemia due to carbon monoxide poisoning and various respiratory and circulatory deficiencies. In addition, certain conditions not complicated by hypoxemia (eg, resistant skin lesions, pressure sores, varicose leg ulcers) allegedly respond to this treatment. It also has been used to supplement antibiotics and other therapeutic measures to arrest infections caused by anaerobic bacteria such as *Clostridium* in gas gangrene and tetanus, to avert ischemia and thus to facilitate surgery on the cardiovascular system, and to augment the effects of radiation in treating neoplasms by making them more radiosensitive. Evaluation of the effectiveness and practicality of hyperbaric oxygen for these and other conditions must await the results of further experience.

The basic equipment for administering oxygen consists of a cylinder containing the gas under pressure, a reducing valve (often called a regulator), a flowmeter, and a humidifier. Devices that permit the admixture of air and oxygen in a fixed ratio offer a distinct advantage over those that deliver only pure gas, particularly when the oxygen is to be administered for prolonged periods. When high pressures are required to operate an apparatus, oxygen compressed in steel cylinders at 2,000 psi is delivered to the bedside. In many hospitals, oxygen is piped to individual outlets at the patient's bedside. Only flowmeters are required with piping systems because the oxygen is delivered at low pressures (60 psi).

When oxygen is required for premature infants, the inspired oxygen concentration should not exceed 40% for any substantial period. Concentrations above 40% may cause retrolental fibroplasia and permanent blindness occurs several months later. The brief periods of administration of 100% oxygen necessary for resuscitation of a premature infant impose little risk of retinal injury. Retinal changes are not a problem in full-term infants, although these infants are susceptible to the same pulmonary complications observed in adults.

Adverse Reactions and Precautions.—Prolonged administration of high concentrations of oxygen, even at atmospheric pressure, causes pulmonary irritation that is most commonly manifested by substernal pain. This irritation may be induced by inhalation of 60% oxygen for approximately 12 hours, although most patients have a greater tolerance. Continued administration of high concentrations may cause more severe pulmonary complications (eg, pneumonitis, congestion, and a decrease in vital capacity) which apparently are related to alveolar epithelial and endothelial changes (interstitial edema and fibrosis, alveolar exudation and hemorrhage, and hyaline membrane formation). This potentially irreversible syndrome is often referred to as "oxygen poisoning." Since the toxicity is a response to oxygen tension rather than to the inhaled concentration of the gas, onset of symptoms is more rapid under hyperbaric conditions. In view of this adverse response to oxygen, the concentration should not exceed that required to relieve the hypoxemia.

When administering oxygen through any type of apparatus, the possibility of carbon dioxide retention must be borne in mind. This may derive from rebreathing expired air due to faulty design or malfunction of the apparatus or to failure to provide adequate inflow of fresh gas. Patients with chronic obstructive pulmonary disease are especially susceptible to carbon dioxide retention. In these patients, oxygen may correct the hypoxemia but diminish ventilation by eliminating the hypoxic stimulus mediated via the carotid chemoreceptors, thus leading to further retention of carbon dioxide. Delirium, disorientation, or coma from carbon dioxide narcosis may result. This may be avoided by giving the oxygen mixed with air, together with assisted ventilation, in an intermittent positive pressure ventilator.

Oxygen drawn from cylinders and piping systems is anhydrous and tends to dry the mucous membranes. This causes thickening of the natural or pathologic secretions as well as discomfort. Such dehydrating effects are accentuated when the gas is introduced beyond the normal "air conditioning" area of the nose and pharynx (eg, through tracheostomy tube or nasopharyngeal catheter). Use of humidification apparatus eliminates or reduces these effects.

The risk of fire or explosion in oxygen-enriched atmospheres is directly proportional to the concentration of oxygen in the mixture being supplied. The risk of fire is particularly great with oxygen tents. Electrical appliances must never be used in tents or in the areas close to tents. Smoking should be forbidden in areas where oxygen is being administered.

Contamination of reservoir nebulizers with *Pseudomonas* and other bacteria has been reported; in view of this, all reusable parts should be properly sterilized.

PREPARATIONS.—Oxygen, U.S.P. is prepared by fractional distillation of liquid air. Anhydrous in green-coded cylinders (WHO, white-coded), at about 2,000 psi.

CARBON DIOXIDE

Uses of carbon dioxide, as well as its contraindications, generally reflect the normal physiologic actions of this gas, such as respiratory stimulation, increase in cerebral blood flow, and maintenance of acid-base balance.

Inhalation of carbon dioxide is of therapeutic value in only a few situations. Carbon dioxide is added to oxygen used in pump oxygenators to avoid reduction of the CO_2 tension of the blood. The solid form, carbon dioxide snow, is used by dermatologists to cauterize certain skin lesions. Carbon dioxide (100%) is introduced around the kidney, heart, and other organs to delineate them for x-ray examinations, into the fallopian and other tubes to determine patency, and into the abdominal cavity to produce pneumoperitoneum for peritoneoscopy. While carbon dioxide is the safest of the gases to use for these purposes due to its rapid absorption, large quantities insufflated into the body may cause respiratory acidosis.

Too often carbon dioxide is used inappropriately when it is of little use and possibly may be harmful. Although it often is used in an attempt to relieve *persistent* hiccups, it only occasionally produces transient relief. Use of carbon dioxide has been suggested to improve circulation in cerebrovascular disorders (eg, following cerebral thrombosis), but it is of doubtful value in these conditions and may be harmful because it elevates intracranial pressure. Administration of a mixture of 5% to 7% carbon dioxide with oxygen to treat carbon monoxide poisoning is of limited and questionable usefulness. Carbon dioxide has been used to induce deep breathing and coughing postoperatively in order to avoid atelectasis, but it generally is of no benefit and may aggravate the condition by forcing secretions into the lower air passages or uninvolved portions of the lung.

Carbon dioxide (30% with oxygen) is sometimes used for inhalation for brief periods (one to two minutes) to modify or correct certain mental disorders (Meduna treatment). High concentrations (20% to 30% in oxygen) have been advocated to liquify secretions in respiratory tract diseases. Such concentrations are irritating and augment the acidosis that may exist in such respiratory disorders.

Carbon dioxide, the normal stimulant of the respiratory center, paradoxically depresses the center when inhaled concentrations approach 30%. Acute carbon dioxide retention is characterized by an initial hyperpnea followed by respiratory depression, headache, muscle twitching, severe acid-base imbalances, convulsions, and coma.

Since carbon dioxide is the most potent cerebrovascular dilator known, it should not be used in patients with increased intracranial pressure, intracranial bleeding, expanding lesions, head injury, or in those in coma. Moreover, it is useless and should not be given in an attempt to resuscitate victims of drowning, electric shock, or asphyxiation. Neither should it be used to treat overdosage of central nervous system depressants because the medullary chemoreceptors are depressed and do not respond. Furthermore, a state of acidosis usually exists in these conditions and is aggravated by carbon dioxide.

METHOD OF ADMINISTRATION.—Concentrations of carbon dioxide for inhalation should not exceed 5%, and this gas should be given with a minimum of 20% oxygen. A nonreturn (nonrebreathing) type of inhaler should be used and the patient's condition constantly monitored to detect adverse effects, such as elevations in blood pressure and respiratory depression.

PREPARATIONS.—Carbon dioxide (100%) is supplied in gray-coded cylinders in liquified form, at about 750 psi. The pure gas must be mixed with oxygen and flowmeters and other appropriate apparatus designed to dispense gases should be used.

It is also available premixed with oxygen in gray/green-coded cylinders (WHO, gray/white-coded); the most common concentration is 5% carbon dioxide and 95% oxygen, but it may be as high as 30% carbon dioxide and 70% oxygen. These mixtures are gaseous at room temperature.

HELIUM

Like nitrogen, helium is physiologically inert and it is therefore used as a substitute for nitrogen in inhalation therapy. A mixture of 20% oxygen and 80% helium has one-third the specific gravity of air and therefore reduces the work of breathing as much as 66%. This is especially desirable in patients with obstructive pulmonary disease. It is more beneficial in patients with orifice-type obstructions (eg, acute laryngeal edema, asthma, mucous plug obstructions) than in those with tubular-type obstructions (eg, bronchospasm). Helium increases tidal volume without lengthening the inspiratory phase when used in mechanical ventilators. Many patients with pulmonary insufficiency require oxygen-enriched atmospheres and, since the density of the mixture rises rapidly as the percentage of oxygen is increased, the advantages of using helium are rapidly lost. Therefore, the clinical usefulness of this gas is limited.

Helium also is used to determine pulmonary functional residual capacity. Its very low water and fat solubility makes it an excellent substitute for nitrogen as an oxygen-diluent in high-pressure environments (eg, for divers), thus avoiding the risk of nitrogen narcosis and reducing the time of decompression and the risk of bends.

Helium has been used to inflate the lungs during pulmonary bypass in order to prevent collapse of the aveoli and atelectasis; however, air is equally effective. It also has been given as an inhalant at the conclusion of anesthesia to prevent atelectasis because it is slowly absorbed from occluded lung lobules. Such use merely delays the onset of atelectasis; therefore, this use has no rational basis. The use of helium as a quenching agent in flammable inhalation anesthetic mixtures is not practical.

Helium is nontoxic; however, hypoxia may occur if adequate oxygen is not present in the mixture administered. Helium increases the pitch of sounds from the vocal cords because it is lighter than air. When high concentrations are used, the voice becomes nasal and speech may become unintelligible. This change in voice also is augmented because the gas passes into the paranasal sinuses and resonance is changed.

METHOD OF ADMINISTRATION.—A helium-oxygen mixture usually is administered by a closed system using a face mask and a carbon dioxide absorbent because of the high cost of the gas. The treatment, consisting of inhalation for 10 to 20 minutes, usually is repeated several times daily, alternating with other appropriate inhalation therapy.

PREPARATIONS.—Helium is separated from natural gas. It is supplied in pure, gaseous form in brown-coded cylinders at approximately 1,800 psi and in the form of mixtures that also contain 20% or 40% oxygen in brown/green-coded containers (WHO, brown/white-coded).

NITROGEN

Nitrogen has little therapeutic usefulness. It serves as a diluent for pure oxygen and as a quenching agent in flammable mixtures of gaseous and volatile anesthetics. Nitrogen is sometimes injected into hollow body cavities such as the cerebral ventricles for diagnostic purposes because it is slowly absorbed and permits repeated or serial x-ray examinations. Nitrogen in liquid form is used for cryotherapy in neurologic surgery and for treatment of dermatologic conditions. Nitrogen was at one time given to induce hypoxemia for diagnosis of coronary artery insufficiency and to induce convulsions in the treatment of psychiatric patients, but these uses are obsolete. Inhalation of nitrogen at the conclusion of anesthesia has been recommended to reduce the incidence of atelectasis; however, air is equally effective.

Nitrogen is chemically inert and nontoxic. Hazards in its use are related primarily to the administration of inadequate amounts of oxygen when nitrogen is used as a diluent in gas mixtures. Under hyperbaric conditions, nitrogen dissolves in the blood and lipid tissues in proportion to the increased inhaled partial pressure; embolization (bends) occurs on rapid decompression.

PREPARATIONS.—Compressed nitrogen is supplied in black-coded cylinders containing pure nitrogen in gaseous form at about 2,000 psi.

Chapter 48

PENICILLINS

The generic name, penicillin, encompasses a group of both natural and semisynthetic antibacterial agents. Natural penicillins are extracted from cultures of *Penicillium chrysogenum*, whereas semisynthetic penicillins are prepared by chemical modification of a natural penicillin or by synthesis from the basic penicillin nucleus, 6-aminopenicillanic acid.

The penicillins act by interfering with the synthesis and cross linkage of mucopeptides essential for the formation and integrity of the bacterial cell wall; therefore, they affect growing cells and may not attack bacteria or intracellular microorganisms that are dormant (so-called persisting forms). There is evidence that nondividing organisms continue to undergo restructuring of cell walls and, although in a "resting" phase, may still be somewhat vulnerable to penicillin. Thus, the administration of a bacteriostatic drug (eg, chloramphenicol, an erythromycin, a tetracycline, or a sulfonamide) concomitantly with penicillin does not represent rational therapy since the incomplete suppression of bacterial cell growth by bacteriostatic agents may inhibit the bactericidal action of the penicillin.

Penicillin G (benzyl penicillin) is still the mainstay of antibacterial therapy. In patients not allergic to the penicillins, penicillin G is the drug of choice for treatment and prevention of infections caused by susceptible cocci, including gonococci, alpha-hemolytic streptococci, and group A beta-hemolytic streptococci. Penicllin G also is preferred for infections caused by *Treponema pallidum*, *Clostridium*, *Bacillus anthracis*, *Corynebacterium diphtheriae*, and several species of *Actinomyces*.

Ideally, if the course of the infection permits, bacterial susceptibility to the penicillins should be determined by appropriate in vitro tests before these agents are administered. Since it is possible to be misled by the results of an improperly chosen sensitivity test, the procedure chosen must give reliable results with the penicillins. Sensitivity studies are not usually employed when microscopic examination of a smear indicates that the causative organism is a pneumococcus, meningococcus, gonococcus, treponema, or group A beta-hemolytic streptococcus, but they should be made when the organism is a staphylococcus or enterococcus.

Phenoxymethyl penicillin (penicillin V) [Compocillin-V, Pen-Vee, V-Cillin] and phenethicillin [Darcil, Maxipen, Syncillin] produce somewhat higher blood levels than penicillin G when administered orally at the same dosage level and they are more acid stable, but they have no proven practical therapeutic advantages over larger oral doses of buffered penicillin G.

The more recently introduced semisynthetic derivatives of penicillin are similar in action to the parent compound but, in addition, some are effective against penicillin G resistant penicillinase-producing staphylococci. When a resistant staphylococcal strain is suspected as the causative organism (eg, in hospital-acquired infections), the penicillinase-resistant penicillins are indicated while awaiting the results of laboratory tests. The original concept of restricting penicillinase-resistant penicillins to the treatment of resistant staphylococcal infections is no longer tenable, and any delay in their administration while awaiting the results of laboratory tests contributes to increased mortality in serious infections.

Although it is still too early to determine to what degree the extensive or indiscriminate use of the penicillinase-resistant penicillins may lead to the development of resistant organisms, the rapid emergence of resistant strains of

Staphylococcus aureus feared earlier has not materialized, despite worldwide use of the newer compounds. Nevertheless, these agents should not be used in infections caused by organisms susceptible to penicillin G. The penicillinase-resistant penicillins include cloxacillin sodium monohydrate [Tegopen], dicloxacillin sodium monohydrate [Dynapen, Pathocil, Veracillin], methicillin sodium [Staphcillin], nafcillin sodium [Unipen], and oxacillin sodium [Bactocill, Prostaphlin].

Other semisynthetic derivatives (ampicillin [Alpen, Amcill, Omnipen, Penbritin, Polycillin, Principen], carbenicillin disodium [Geopen, Pyopen], hetacillin [Versapen]) are ineffective against penicillinase-producing staphylococci but are more active than penicillin G against some gram-negative bacteria (eg, *Haemophilus influenzae;* some species of *Salmonella, Shigella,* and *Pseudomonas;* most strains of *Escherichia coli;* and indole-negative *Proteus mirabilis).*

Penicillin preparations for topical use are no longer marketed in the United States, *since there are no indications for this route and hypersensitization is a frequent complication.*

Oral administration is indicated in mild infections, in infections that require prolonged treatment, or for prophylactic purposes. The penicillins should not be used orally for the initial treatment of syphilis, subacute bacterial endocarditis, or actinomycosis. They may be given by this route for prophylaxis of rheumatic fever, but intramuscular injection of benzathine penicillin G is preferred since patients frequently are unreliable about taking drugs orally.

Oral penicillin preparations tend to be absorbed erratically, and most are susceptible to destruction by gastric acid (phenoxymethyl penicillin, oxacillin, and nafcillin are acid resistant). Therefore, to ensure adequate blood and tissue levels, large doses are given frequently, one hour before or two hours after meals.

Transient high blood concentrations can be produced by intramuscular or intravenous injection of an aqueous solution of penicillin G every three to six hours. When massive doses of penicillin G (eg, 50 million units or more daily) are required, the drug must be given by the intravenous route. High tissue levels can be obtained either by continuous or intermittent intravenous infusion. Intrathecal injection of penicillin G potassium has been discarded because of its irritant effect on the central nervous system.

When more sustained effects are needed, less soluble preparations are given intramuscularly. Procaine penicillin G in water or oil may be given every 8 to 12 hours or once daily, depending upon the preparation chosen and the dosage used. An aqueous preparation of benzathine penicillin G is detectable in the body for as long as four weeks after a single intramuscular injection. However, because the blood levels produced are low, these forms of penicillin are effective against only very susceptible bacteria.

Plasma protein binding of penicillins varies. About 20% of ampicillin, between 35% and 50% of penicillin G, 50% of carbenicillin, 50% to 70% of phenoxymethyl penicillin and phenethicillin, and 90% or more of oxacillin, cloxacillin, and dicloxacillin is bound. The protein-penicillin complex easily dissociates: as free drug is withdrawn from the plasma, additional penicillin is unbound from the protein stores. Only the free drug has antibacterial activity.

The claims for clinical superiority of one penicillin over another based on in vitro sensitivity are questionable because such testing does not take into account factors such as stability in gastric acid, rates of absorption and excretion, protein binding, and minimal effective blood and tissue concentrations.

Most penicillins are rapidly excreted in the urine, either unaltered or as metabolites. For this reason, the rate of elimination in very young infants is slow because of their low renal function. Some penicillins, especially ampicillin, nafcillin, cloxacillin, and dicloxacillin, appear in high concentrations in the bile and are reabsorbed from the intestine. Diffusion into cerebrospinal, synovial, and other body fluids is poor unless very large doses are given or inflammation is present (eg, meningitis, pleuritis, arthritis); however, the penicillins do cross the placental barrier, but at a slow rate.

Treatment of Venereal Diseases: The management of venereal diseases is an important public health problem because of the widespread nature of the disease and the fact that *Neisseria gonorrhoeae* is becoming increasingly resistant to drug therapy. The United States Public Health Service has made the following recommendations for the treatment of syphilis and gonorrhea:

I. For primary and secondary syphilis: *Intramuscular: Adults,* benzathine penicillin G 2.4 million units (1.2 million units in each buttock) in a single dose; or procaine penicillin G with aluminum monostearate 2% (PAM) 2.4 million units initially, usually administered as above, followed by two subsequent injections of 1.2 million units at three-day intervals for a total of 4.8 million units; or aqueous procaine penicillin G 600,000 units daily for eight days for a total of 4.8 million units.

II. For latent syphilis: *Intramuscular: Adults*, benzathine penicillin G 2.4 million units administered as for primary syphilis; or procaine penicillin G with aluminum monostearate 2% (PAM) 4.8 million units administered as for primary syphilis; or aqueous procaine penicillin G 4.8 million units administered as for primary syphilis. If no spinal fluid examination is done, treatment must encompass the possibility of asymptomatic neurosyphilis and given according to the schedule below for late syphilis.

III. For congenital syphilis: *Intramuscular: Children under 2 years of age*, benzathine penicillin G 50,000 units/kg of body weight in a single dose; or aqueous procaine penicillin G 100,000 units/kg in divided doses over a ten-day period; *children over 2 years but weighing less than 32 kg*, same dosage as for children under 2 years of age; total dosage should not exceed 3 million units. *Children 12 years and older and/or weighing more than 32 kg*, same as for comparable stages of acquired syphilis.

IV. For late syphilis (includes neurosyphilis, and cardiovascular and late benign syphilis): *Intramuscular: Adults*, initially, benzathine penicillin G 3 million units followed by one or two doses of 3 million units at seven-day intervals for a total of 6 to 9 million units; or procaine penicillin G with aluminum monostearate 2% (PAM) 1.2 million units administered at three-day intervals for a total of 6 to 9 million units; or aqueous procaine penicillin G 600,000 units daily for a total of 6 to 9 million units. Any benefits derived from more than 10 million units have not been demonstrated.

For *Neisseria gonorrhoeae* infection, the preferred drug is penicillin G or ampicillin. The long-acting forms of penicillin have no place in the treatment of gonorrhea. No less than the recommended doses of antibiotics should be given.

I. For uncomplicated gonorrhea (urethral, cervical, pharyngeal, or rectal): *Adults* (men and women), aqueous procaine penicillin G 4.8 million units intramuscularly in two or more divided doses and injected at different sites at one visit, together with probenecid 1 g orally, preferably given at least 30 minutes prior to the injection; or simultaneous oral administration of ampicillin 3.5 g and probenecid 1 g.

II. For treatment of contacts: Patients with known exposure to gonorrhea should receive the same treatment as those known to have gonorrhea.

III. When penicillin or ampicillin is contraindicated (eg, allergy to penicillin, ampicillin, or probenecid, or previous anaphylactic reaction):

Intramuscular: Adults (men), spectinomycin 2 g in a single injection; (women) spectinomycin 4 g in a single injection; or

Oral: Adults (men and women), initially, tetracycline hydrochloride 1.5 g followed by 500 mg four times daily for four days for a total of 9 g. Other tetracyclines are not more effective.

IV. Follow-up urethral specimens should be obtained from men 7 days after completion of treatment; cervical and rectal specimens should be obtained from women 7 to 14 days after completion of treatment.

V. For complications: Although treatment of complications (eg, gonococcal salpingitis, bacteremia, arthritis) must be individualized, repeated large parenteral doses of aqueous crystalline penicillin G have been shown to be effective. The efficacy of alternate antibiotic regimens is unproved. Postgonococcal urethritis can be treated with tetracycline 500 mg orally four times daily for at least seven days.

VI. With syphilis: All patients with gonorrhea should have a serologic test for syphilis at the time of diagnosis. Patients receiving the recommended parenteral penicillin schedule need not have follow-up serologic tests for syphilis. Patients treated with ampicillin, spectinomycin, or tetracycline should have a follow-up serologic test for syphilis each month for four months to detect syphilis that may have been masked by treatment for gonorrhea.

Patients with gonorrhea who also have syphilis should be given additional treatment appropriate to the stage of syphilis.

Adverse Reactions and Precautions

Allergic reactions are common and are among the most serious adverse effects produced by the penicillins. There are two kinds of reactions: an immediate, profound, and often fatal shock characterized by acute circulatory failure and syncope, and possibly facial or laryngeal edema; or a delayed serum sickness-type reaction characterized by rash, urticaria, fever, and, occasionally, diarrhea. Numerous deaths have been caused by anaphylactic reactions following injection of penicillin, but anaphylaxis is less common after oral administration.

The mechanisms of penicillin allergy have not yet been fully explained. It is believed that hypersensitivity reactions are not caused by unaltered penicillin but by degradation products that react with proteins, polypeptides, or amino acids to form antigenic complexes. Penicilloic acid-protein complexes or penicilloyl compounds, chiefly N- (α-benzyl-penicilloyl)-lysine have been implicated as important antigenic determinants.

The incidence of allergic reactions to the penicillins has been estimated to be between 1% and 5%. Hypersensitization occurs most commonly following topical application or exposure to dust or aerosol containing the drug, and considerably less frequently following oral or parenteral administration. The incidence appears to be greater in patients with other allergies and in those with active or latent fungal infections. A positive scratch skin test is not an absolute contraindication to the use of penicillin unless the patient has a history of penicillin sensitivity. Previous medication with penicillin is not a prerequisite to the development of sensitivity.

Since hypersensitivity reactions to penicillin may occur at any time, particularly following parenteral injection, penicillin should not be administered to patients unless certain drugs and resuscitative equipment are immediately available. In acute anaphylactic reactions, the administration of epinephrine (subcutaneously or intramuscularly for mild reactions and intravenously for more serious reactions) can be a life-saving procedure. In addition, prompt administration of oxygen or tracheostomy (if laryngeal edema occurs) may be needed. After primary initial therapy, the administration of a suitable parenteral form of a corticosteroid may prevent a relapse. Although mild hypersensitivity to the penicillins manifested by fever and rashes may eventually be lost, symptoms may recur upon reexposure. For this reason, if penicillin preparations are given at all, they must be used *with extreme caution in any patient with a history of hypersensitivity*.

Penicillinase [Neutrapen] is of little value in the treatment of penicillin-induced hypersensitivity reactions and can produce allergic reactions in its own right. The use of other agents and procedures (as indicated above) is more effective in treating hypersensitivity and frequently is safer.

Attempts have been made to test for hypersensitivity by injecting a small amount of penicillin G intracutaneously. This procedure is dangerous and is contraindicated since even the small amount used can cause serious reactions or death in susceptible patients. Although not available commercially as diagnostic products, a benzylpenicilloyl-polylysine conjugate (BPL) and a minor determinant mixture (MDM) containing benzylpenicillin, sodium benzylpenicilloate, benzylpenicilloate, and sodium-q-benzylpenicilloyl-amine are now sometimes used as test agents. These preparations contain small concentrations of the various agents and are injected intradermally. The BPL and MDM preparations appear to be much safer and more reliable as indicators of potential hypersensitivity than penicillin G. Nevertheless, serious reactions to these agents also have been reported, and they may not detect all types of penicillin sensitivity, although some studies indicate up to a 90% or greater predictability of penicillin sensitivity when both the BPL and MDM are used as a combined testing procedure. Nevertheless, there is no known way to be absolutely sure that a patient will or will not react to penicillin.

The patient must *always* be asked about previous reactions to penicillin before being given the drug. Preparation for possible emergencies following administration of penicillin is advisable; epinephrine should be available for immediate injection. The oral or parenteral administration of an antihistamine prior to the use of penicillin should not be relied upon to provide protection against an allergic reaction. In general, all penicillins are contraindicated in patients who have a history of sensitivity to any penicillin or who have other known or suspected allergies.

Serious superinfections with resistant organisms, especially gram-negative bacteria (eg, *Pseudomonas*, *Proteus*) and *Candida*, may occur following long-term therapy with any of the penicillins.

Nephropathy, manifested as an interstitial nephritis, has been reported following administration of the penicillins. This is a sensitization reaction (except for the reaction caused by methicillin [Staphcillin] which is probably due to direct toxic effects). Kidney damage usually is accompanied by proteinuria, hematuria, and acute renal failure. Fever and eosinophilia also are observed frequently, and pyuria has sometimes been noted. Patients usually recover when the drug is stopped, but fatalities have occurred.

Massive intravenous doses of penicillin G potassium (1.7 mEq of potassium per million units) may cause hyperkalemia and, rarely, convulsions in patients with impaired renal function. Convulsions may accompany rapid intravenous injection of a large single dose (5 million units), especially in epileptics or other susceptible individuals. Although depression of the cell-forming elements of bone marrow has been observed in some patients receiving methicillin, no fatalities have been reported.

The penicillins are relatively nonirritating, but some may cause pain when injected intramuscularly, and phlebitis may occur after repeated intravenous injections, particularly with use of concentrated solutions or when the drug is given by continuous infusion. When injected intrathecally, penicillin preparations are irritating to the central nervous system and may cause convulsions.

INDIVIDUAL EVALUATIONS

PENICILLIN G

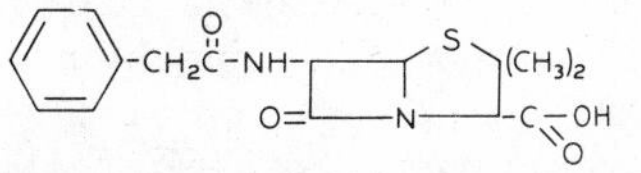

Penicillin G salts are the drugs of choice (in patients not allergic to them) for treating infections caused by group A beta-hemolytic streptococci, pneumococci, gonococci, meningococci, *Treponema pallidum*, *Clostridium*, *Bacillus anthracis*, *Corynebacterium diphtheriae*, and some species of *Actinomyces*.

Since oral preparations are absorbed erratically and penicillin G is destroyed by gastric acid, this route is indicated only for mild infections, stabilized infections, or long-term prophylactic use. Parenteral use of the short-acting penicillin G salts produces transient high blood levels. When massive doses are indicated, the intravenous route is preferred. If sustained, low-level blood concentrations are desirable, they can be achieved by intramuscular injection of procaine penicillin G in water or oil or of benzathine penicillin G in water. When administering procaine penicillin G intramuscularly, inadvertent intravenous injection must be avoided to prevent a reaction to procaine.

Allergic reactions are the most common adverse effects caused by penicillin G (see the Introductory Statement). Intrathecal administration of 10,000 units or more and intravenous doses over 20 million units daily can produce convulsions, although doses larger than this are sometimes used to treat staphylococcal bacterial endocarditis.

USUAL DOSAGE.–

Therapeutic:

Oral: Adults and children, 600,000 to 3 million units daily.

Intramuscular, *Intravenous* (penicillin G sodium or potassium): *Adults*, 300,000 to 1.2 million units daily; doses as high as 60 million units daily may be necessary (by intravenous infusion). *Children*, 300,000 to 1.2 million units daily; doses as high as 10 million units daily may be necessary (by intravenous infusion). *Premature and full-term newborn infants*, 600,000 units daily in two divided doses.

Intramuscular (procaine penicillin G in water or oil, benzathine penicillin G in water): *Adults*, 900,000 to 1.2 million units as a single dose; *children*, 600,000 to 900,000 units. The dose may be repeated at intervals of 48 to 72 hours, depending upon the condition being treated.

Prophylactic:

Oral: In rheumatic fever, *adults and children*, 400,000 units twice daily.

PREPARATIONS.–

Injection: Powder, suspension for injection.

Oral: Capsules, drops, suspension, tablets (buffered, plain).

AVAILABLE TRADEMARKS.–

Benzathine Penicillin G: Bicillin (Wyeth), Permapen (Pfizer).

Penicillin G Potassium: Dramcillin (Schering), G-Recillin (Reid-Provident), Hyasorb (Key), Kesso-Pen (McKesson), Palocillin S-10 (Palmedico), Pedacillin (Durst), Pentids (Squibb), Pfizerpen (Pfizer), Sugracillin (Upjohn).

Procaine Penicillin G: Crysticillin AS (Squibb), Diurnal-Penicillin (Upjohn), Duracillin A.S. (Lilly), Pentids-P (Squibb), Pfizerpen-AS (Pfizer), Wycillin (Wyeth).

Procaine Penicillin G with Aluminum Monostearate (PAM): Procaine Penicillin G sterile, w/Aluminum Stearate Suspension (Squibb).

Forms of penicillin G also marketed by other manufacturers under generic name.

COMBINATIONS OF PENICILLIN G.–

Bicillin All-Purpose Injection (Wyeth): Powder containing benzathine penicillin G 600,000 units, penicillin G potassium 300,000 units, and procaine penicillin G 300,000 units.

Bicillin C-R Injection (Wyeth): Solution containing benzathine penicillin G and procaine penicillin G 150,000 units each in 1 ml containers or 300,000 units each in 1, 2, and 4 ml containers.

Crystifor 400 Injection (Squibb): Powder containing procaine penicillin G 300,000 units and penicillin G sodium 100,000 units.

Duracillin Fortified Injection (Lilly): Powder containing procaine penicillin G 300,000 units and penicillin G sodium 100,000 units.

Duracillin F.A. Injection (Lilly): Powder containing procaine penicillin G 750,000 units and penicillin G sodium 250,000 units.

S-R Injection (Parke, Davis): Powder containing procaine penicillin G 300,000 units and penicillin G sodium 100,000 units.

AMPICILLIN [Alpen, Amcill, Omnipen, Penbritin, Polycillin, Principen]
AMPICILLIN SODIUM [Alpen-N, Amcill-S, Omnipen-N, Penbritin-S, Polycillin-N, Principen/N]

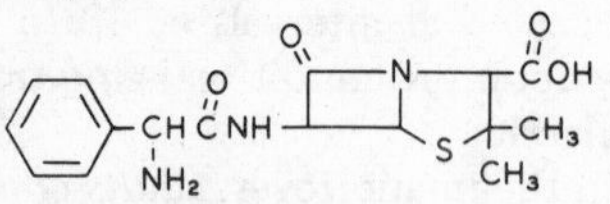

Ampicillin, a semisynthetic penicillin for oral and parenteral use, has the same general spectrum of activity as penicillin G (see the Introductory Statement and the evaluation on Penicillin G), but it is more effective than penicillin G against gram-negative bacteria. Nevertheless, it should not be routinely substituted for penicillin G. In vitro, ampicillin is active against *Haemophilus influenzae*, *Neisseria gonorrhoeae*, *N. meningitidis*, *Salmonella typhi*, nonpenicillinase-producing strains of *Proteus mirabilis*, many strains of *Escherichia coli*, and several strains of shigellae. Present clinical experience indicates that ampicillin also may be effective against *Klebsiella* (most strains of *K. pneumoniae* are resistant). Pseudomonal infections are resistant. Ampicillin also may be useful in treating some infections caused by *Streptococcus faecalis*, but further studies are needed before ampicillin can be routinely recommended in preference to combined penicillin and streptomycin therapy in the treatment of subacute bacterial endocarditis.

Ampicillin is inactivated by penicillinase, and therefore is ineffective against staphylococci resistant to penicillin G. Enteric bacilli, especially *E. coli* and *Proteus*, have become resistant to ampicillin by selective elimination of nonproducers of penicillinase (some strains of *E. coli* also may be resistant to ampicillin by a mechanism other than production of penicillinase), but streptococci, pneumococci, and *H. influenzae* have not become resistant. As with any of the penicillins, indiscriminate use may increase the rate of development of resistant bacterial strains.

Ampicillin is water soluble, acid stable, and readily absorbed from the gastrointestinal tract when given orally. Approximate peak serum levels after a single dose of 500 mg by various routes are: intravenous, 45 μg/ml within five minutes; intramuscular, 8 μg/ml within one hour; and oral, 2.5 to 5 μg/ml within two hours. Low levels of ampicillin are still present six hours after intravenous administration and eight hours after intramuscular or oral administration. Ampicillin is excreted rapidly in the urine; urinary levels of 0.25 to 2.5 mg/ml are attained. About 20% is bound to plasma protein. The usual range of minimal inhibitory concentrations against susceptible bacteria in vitro is 0.02 to 5 μg/ml.

Because ampicillin causes comparatively few adverse reactions, it often is preferable to the tetracyclines or chloramphenicol when a broad spectrum antibacterial agent is desired. For example, if the tetracyclines or chloramphenicol must be avoided because of possible adverse reactions and penicillin G is not indicated because the penicillin-sensitive organism is gram-negative, ampicillin may be used, particularly in infants and pregnant women. Rashes occur more often with ampicillin than with penicillin G and are especially noted in patients with infectious mononucleosis.

The primary clinical indications for ampicillin are urinary, respiratory, and gastrointestinal tract infections, and bacterial otitis and meningitis in children.

Urinary tract infections caused by susceptible bacteria, especially *E. coli*, *P. mirabilis*, nonhemolytic streptococci, and penicillin G-resistant enterococci, appear to respond rapidly to ampicillin, but penicillin G remains the drug of choice for genitourinary infections that are susceptible to it (eg, gonorrheal urethritis).

Penicillin G remains the preferred drug for infections caused by *Diplococcus pneumoniae.* However, respiratory tract infections in which *Haemophilus influenzae* and *Diplococcus pneumoniae* occur together are highly responsive to ampicillin.

The use of ampicillin in biliary tract and intestinal infections caused by sensitive strains of *E. coli*, penicillin G-resistant enterococci, salmonellae, and shigellae appears to be promising because a relatively high concentration of this agent appears in the bile. However, an increasing number of ampicillin-resistant *Salmonella* and *Shigella* species are emerging. The results of treatment of enteritis caused by salmonellae (eg, *S. typhi*, *S. typhimurium)* have been disappointing. Even chloramphenicol has not produced consistently satisfactory results, although it remains the drug of choice except in carrier patients with resistant infections requiring prolonged treatment (see Chapter 54, Chloramphenicol and Derivatives). Results with ampicillin in the treatment of enteritis caused by shigellae appear to be more favorable. Ampicillin also has been used in the treatment of typhoid carriers. For optimal therapy, high doses and long-term therapy should be employed.

In children, bacterial meningitis caused by *N. meningitidis*, pneumococci, or *H. influenzae* appears to respond well to parenteral administration of ampicillin. Large doses appear to be effective, reliable, and relatively nontoxic when compared to results obtained with other therapy. Bacterial meningitis in adults also has been treated successfully.

Ampicillin has been suggested for use in the treatment of subacute bacterial endocarditis and enterococcal infections when the organisms are clinically resistant to penicillin G. Ampicillin also may be preferable in mixed infections (eg, susceptible cocci with gram-negative bacilli) that would otherwise require the use of penicillin G and streptomycin.

For use and dosages of ampicillin in the treatment of gonorrhea, see the Introductory Statement.

Ampicillin is generally well tolerated. Hypersensitivity reactions such as pruritus, rash, urticaria, eosinophilia, fever, and angioedema are the most common reactions observed. These reactions occur more frequently with ampicillin than with penicillin G. Anaphylactic reactions also have been observed, particularly following parenteral use of this drug. Ampicillin generally is contraindicated in patients with a history of sensitivity to any penicillin or with other known or suspected allergies. Local phlebitis has occurred after intravenous infusion, and local pain is common after intramuscular injection. When given orally, ampicillin may cause gastrointestinal disturbances (cramping, diarrhea, nausea, vomiting).

A moderate elevation of the serum glutamic oxaloacetic transaminase (SGOT) levels has been observed in a few infants after use of this drug. It has not been possible to determine whether this reaction is caused by liver disease or the intramuscular injection.

There have been a few reports of nephropathy associated with ampicillin therapy. In two cases this appeared to be an allergic reaction; in other cases, patients with renal disease or prerenal azotemia had deterioration of renal function during therapy. There also have been reports of anemia, thrombocytopenia, leukopenia, and agranulocytosis; these are believed to be hypersensitivity phenomena.

Superinfections, especially of the gastrointestinal tract, have been noted; *Enterobacter*, *Pseudomonas*, and *Candida* are the organisms usually involved. If superinfection occurs, the dosage may have to be reduced or some other antibacterial agent substituted.

Definitive information on the possible toxicity of ampicillin during pregnancy is not available; however, the penicillins in general appear to be nonteratogenic in man.

The parenteral use of ampicillin should be reserved for more severe infections and for patients who are unable to take the drug orally.

USUAL DOSAGE.—

Oral: Adults and children weighing more than 40 kg, 250 to 500 mg four times daily; *less than 40 kg,* 50 to 200 mg/kg of body weight daily in divided doses every six to eight hours. It is not necessary that the stomach be empty when this drug is given orally but peak levels may be higher in fasting patients.

Intravenous: Adults, 1.5 to 2 g every six hours. Patients have been successfully treated for bacterial meningitis with doses of 8 to 14 g daily (150 to 250 mg/kg of body weight daily); therapy can be repeated every three to four hours. *Children,* 25 to 50 mg/kg daily in divided doses every three hours. Daily doses of 200 to 400 mg/kg can be given to treat bacterial meningitis; the drug is administered every three to four hours.

It may be necessary to continue treatment for four weeks or longer (eg, in patients with typhoid fever or chronic bronchitis).

PREPARATIONS.—

Ampicillin (anhydrous):

Omnipen (Wyeth). *Oral:* Capsules 250 and 500 mg; powder for suspension 125 and 250 mg/5 ml.

Penbritin (Ayerst). *Oral:* Capsules 250 and 500 mg; powder for suspension (pediatric) 100 mg/ml; powder for suspension 125 and 250 mg/5 ml.

Ampicillin (trihydrate):

Alpen (Lederle), Principen (Squibb). *Oral:* Capsules 250 and 500 mg; powder for suspension 125 and 250 mg/5 ml.

Amcill (Parke, Davis). *Oral:* Capsules 250 and 500 mg; powder for suspension (pediatric) 100 mg/ml; powder for suspension 125 and 250 mg/5 ml; tablets (chewable) 125 mg.

Polycillin (Bristol).

Oral: Capsules 250 and 500 mg; powder for suspension (pediatric) 100 mg/ml; powder for suspension 125 and 250 mg/5 ml; tablets (chewable) 125 mg.

Injection: Powder for solution 25 mg/ml in 2.5 g containers.

Ampicillin Sodium:

Alpen-N (Lederle). *Injection:* Powder 250 and 500 mg and 1 g.

Amcill-S (Parke, Davis). *Injection:* Powder 125, 250, and 500 mg and 1 g.

Omnipen-N (Wyeth), Polycillin-N (Bristol), Principen/N (Squibb). *Injection:* Powder 125, 250, and 500 mg and 1 and 2 g.

Penbritin-S (Ayerst). *Injection:* Powder 125, 250, and 500 mg and 1, 2, and 4 g.

ADDITIONAL TRADEMARKS.—

Ampicillin: Divercillin (Ascher), Pensyn (Upjohn), Ponecil (Tutag), Ro-Ampen (Rowell), SK-Ampicillin (Smith Kline & French), Totacillin (Beecham-Massengill). Drug also marketed under generic name.

Ampicillin Sodium: SK-Ampicillin-N (Smith Kline & French), Totacillin-N (Beecham-Massengill).

CARBENICILLIN DISODIUM [Geopen, Pyopen]

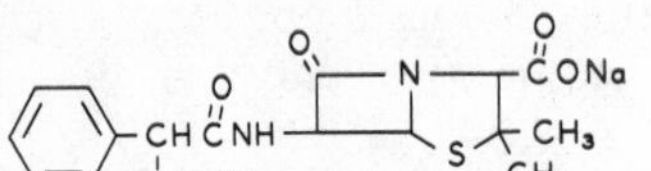

Carbenicillin is a semisynthetic penicillin for parenteral use; it is not absorbed by the oral route. The antibacterial spectrum of carbenicillin is similar to that of ampicillin (see the evaluation on Ampicillin), but this drug is recommended by its manufacturers primarily for the treatment of infections caused by *Pseudomonas aeruginosa*, *Proteus* (particularly the indole-positive strains), and susceptible strains of *Escherichia coli.* Some of the newly emerging pathogenic strains of microorganisms (eg, *Mima, Herella, Citrobacter, Serratia)* also have been shown to be susceptible. Most species of *Klebsiella* are resistant and many strains of *Pseudomonas* develop resistance rapidly. Carbenicillin is susceptible to destruction by penicillinase-producing staphylococci.

The main clinical indications for carbenicillin are infections caused by *Pseudomonas* and indole-positive *Proteus* (eg, *P. vulgaris).* It should not be used as the sole therapeutic agent for deep tissue or systemic infections (including pneumonia) caused by *Pseudomonas* but should be combined with gentamicin. This combination has synergistic effects against *Pseudomonas* in vivo. Since the cost of carbenicillin is very high, its use should be restricted to those situations in which it has a distinct advantage over other antibacterial agents.

Following intramuscular injection, peak blood levels are reached in one to two hours. Serum levels of 10 to 25 μg/ml usually are effective against most susceptible organisms; however, 100 μg/ml or greater are needed for *Pseudomonas.* Carbenicillin is not highly bound to plasma proteins (50%) and is excreted unchanged by the kidney. Urinary levels of 1 to 5 mg/ml can be achieved by giving 2 to 5 g intramuscularly.

Carbenicillin is relatively well tolerated, but hypersensitivity reactions such as pruritus, rash, urticaria, and fever can occur. Serious and occasionally fatal anaphylactic reactions also have occurred.

Patients receiving large doses of carbenicillin have shown blood abnormalities that are common to several other penicillins. These reactions include anemia, thrombocytopenia, leukopenia, neutropenia, and eosinophilia. In addition, several uremic patients on high dosage (24 g daily) developed hemorrhagic conditions associated with abnormal clotting and prothrombin times. The bleeding stopped when the penicillin was discontinued.

As with other penicillins, convulsions can occur if serum levels become excessively high. Local pain at the site of intramuscular or intravenous injection and phlebitis following intravenous administration are common. Nausea has been reported. Elevated serum transaminase (SGOT, SGPT) levels also have been seen.

Carbenicillin usually is contraindicated in patients with a history of allergic reactions to other penicillins, and it should be given cautiously to any person with other known or suspected allergies. If superinfection occurs, the dosage may have to be reduced or some other antibacterial agent substituted.

Definitive information on the possible toxicity of carbenicillin during pregnancy is not available; however, the penicillins in general appear to be nonteratogenic in man.

For use in the eye, see Chapter 71, Anti-infective and Anti-inflammatory Agents Used in Ophthalmology.

USUAL DOSAGE.—

Intramuscular: Adults, 1 to 2 g every six hours; *children*, 50 to 200 mg/kg of body weight daily in divided doses every four to six hours.

Intravenous: Adults, 25 to 30 g daily in divided doses or by continuous or intermittent infusion; *children*, 50 to 200 mg/kg of body weight daily in divided doses every four to six hours.

For urinary tract infections complicated by renal insufficiency, (creatinine clearance less than 5 ml/minute) *adults*, 2 g every 8 to 12 hours; during peritoneal dialysis, 2 g every six hours; during hemodialysis, 2 g every four hours. *Children*, clinical data are insufficient to recommend a dose.

PREPARATIONS.—Geopen (Roerig), Pyopen (Beecham-Massengill). *Injection:* Powder 1, 2, and 5 g.

CLOXACILLIN SODIUM MONOHYDRATE

[Tegopen]

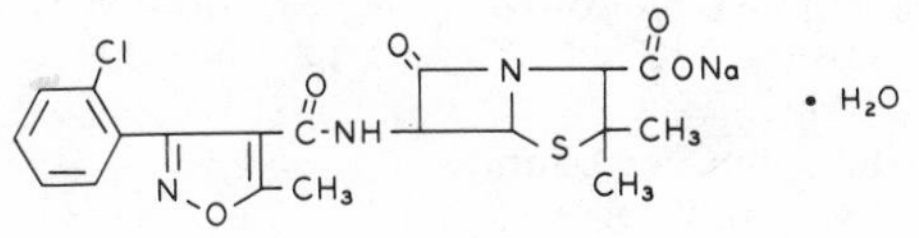

Cloxacillin sodium monohydrate, a semisynthetic penicillin salt used orally, is similar to oxacillin sodium in its in vitro activity against both penicillin G-resistant and penicillin G-sensitive staphylococci, streptococci, and pneumococci. It is used in the treatment of staphylococcal infections of the skin, soft tissues, and respiratory tract; infections of the genitourinary tract or joint spaces; and suppurative osteomyelitis caused by penicillin G-resistant staphylococci. However, penicillin G is preferred for infections caused by penicillin G-sensitive organisms, since in equal doses it is more effective than cloxacillin against these organisms. Cloxacillin also is effective in mixed infections caused by penicillin G-resistant staphylococci and pneumococci or beta-hemolytic streptococci.

Absorption of cloxacillin from the gastrointestinal tract is rapid but variable; some doses may be absorbed inadequately or not at all. Food in the stomach or small intestine reduces absorption and decreases the ultimate plasma level obtainable from a given dose of the drug. Although cloxacillin is more resistant to destruction by gastric acid than many other penicillins, it is degraded to some extent in the stomach.

At equivalent oral doses, somewhat higher plasma levels have been reported with cloxacillin than with either oxacillin or nafcillin. Peak serum levels occur approximately one hour after its administration in capsule form and somewhat sooner after administration of the oral solution. Effective plasma levels can be maintained for four to six hours after a single dose of the drug.

Cloxacillin is distributed throughout the body, but the highest concentrations occur in the kidney and liver. Plasma protein binding is high (90% to 94%). Between 30% and 45% of a single dose is excreted in the urine. Significant amounts also are excreted in the bile.

This penicillin is generally well tolerated. Adverse reactions are essentially the same as those observed with other penicillins (see the Introductory Statement). It may produce allergic reactions (rash, urticaria), epigastric fullness or abdominal discomfort, diarrhea, nausea, and vomiting. A few cases of eosinophilia, mild leukopenia, and elevated serum glutamic oxaloacetic transaminase (SGOT) levels have been reported.

Superinfections with gram-negative organisms have occurred occasionally, especially in patients being treated for pneumococcal pneumonia. If the superinfection is severe, therapy must be discontinued.

Cloxacillin generally is contraindicated in patients with a history of sensitivity to any penicillin or with other known or suspected allergies.

The effect of this drug on the fetus has not been determined, but the penicillins in general appear to be nonteratogenic in man. Cloxacillin has little or no tendency to produce toxic effects on the liver, kidney, or cell-forming elements of bone marrow.

USUAL DOSAGE.—*Oral: Adults and children weighing 20 kg or more*, initially, 500 mg to 1 g every four to six hours given one hour before or two hours after meals; *less than 20 kg*, 50 to 100 mg/kg of body weight daily in four equal doses. The larger initial dosage is reserved for severe infections; if this does not control the infection, it is advisable to substitute a penicillinase-resistant penicillin that can be given parenterally (eg, methicillin).

PREPARATIONS.—Tegopen (Bristol). *Oral:* Capsules 250 mg; granules for solution 125 mg/5 ml.

DICLOXACILLIN SODIUM MONOHYDRATE

[Dynapen, Pathocil, Veracillin]

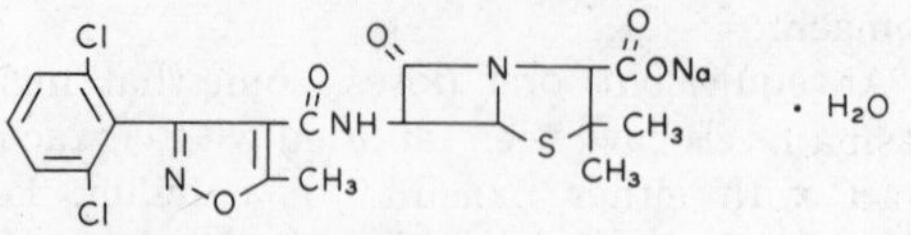

Dicloxacillin sodium monohydrate is a semisynthetic penicillin that is resistant to penicillinase. Higher blood levels are claimed to occur more rapidly than with other penicillins, but evidence that this offers a practical clinical advantage is unconvincing. It appears that this drug is another useful penicillin closely related to cloxacillin in its chemistry, indications, adverse reactions, serum binding, onset and duration of action, and bacterial spectrum (see the Introductory Statement and the evaluation on Cloxacillin Sodium Monohydrate). This drug is not clinically superior to oxacillin, cloxacillin, or any of the other semisynthetic penicillins. Experience with this drug in newborn infants is limited; therefore, dicloxacillin should not be used in neonates until additional information becomes available. The effect of this drug on the fetus has not been determined, but the penicillins in general appear to be nonteratogenic in man.

USUAL DOSAGE.—*Oral: Adults and children weighing 40 kg or more,* 500 mg to 1 g every four to six hours given one to two hours before meals; *less than 40 kg,* 50 to 100 mg/kg of body weight daily in four equal doses every six hours. For control of minor infections due to susceptible organisms, *adults and children weighing 40 kg or more,* 250 to 500 mg every four to six hours; *less than 40 kg,* 25 to 50 mg/kg daily in four equal doses.

PREPARATIONS.—

Dynapen (Bristol), Pathocil (Wyeth). *Oral:* Capsules 125 and 250 mg; powder for suspension 62.5 mg/5 ml.

Veracillin (Ayerst). *Oral:* Capsules 125 and 250 mg.

HETACILLIN [Versapen]
HETACILLIN POTASSIUM [Versapen-K]

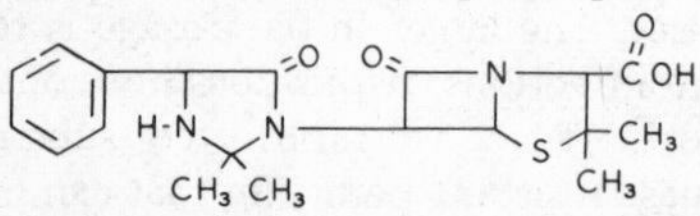

Hetacillin is a semisynthetic penicillin for oral and parenteral use. The drug has no demonstrated antibacterial activity itself, but is converted in the body to ampicillin and acetone. Therefore, this penicillin must be considered as simply another form of ampicillin, and its antibacterial spectrum, indications, susceptibility to penicillinase-producing bacteria, precautions, and adverse reactions are the same as those of ampicillin (see the Introductory Statement and the evaluation on Ampicillin).

Oral preparations of hetacillin are fairly stable in acid and, although food retards it absorption, this drug is fairly consistently absorbed from the gastrointestinal tract. The half-life for conversion of hetacillin to ampicillin at pH 7.1 is approximately 20 minutes.

USUAL DOSAGE.—The manufacturer's dosage recommendations for this penicillin are low. Since the active moiety of hetacillin is ampicillin, the dosages used should be in the same range as ampicillin (see that evaluation) or a little higher, because, upon conversion, 1 g of hetacillin yields less than 1 g of ampicillin. Also, since the intramuscular preparations of hetacillin contain lidocaine, ampicillin is preferred.

PREPARATIONS.—(Strengths expressed in terms of ampicillin.)

Hetacillin:

Versapen (Bristol). *Oral:* Powder for suspension (pediatric) 112.5 mg/ml; powder for suspension 112.5 mg/5 ml; tablets (chewable) 112.5 mg.

Hetacillin Potassium:

Versapen-K (Bristol).

Oral: Capsules 225 and 450 mg.

Injection (intramuscular): Powder (for solution) 225 or 450 mg with 20 and 40 mg of lidocaine hydrochloride, respectively.

Injection (intravenous): Powder (for solution) 225, 450, and 900 mg.

METHICILLIN SODIUM [Staphcillin]

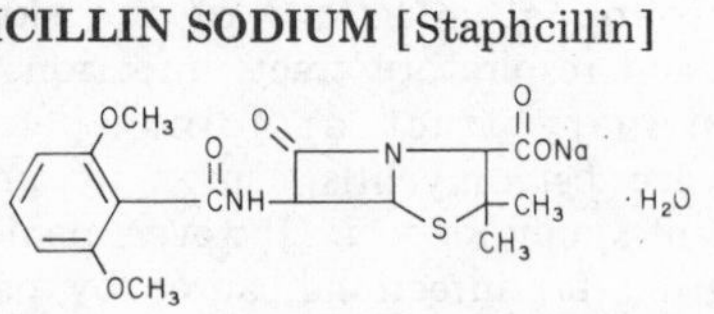

Methicillin sodium is a water-soluble, penicillinase-resistant, semisynthetic salt of penicillin used parenterally to treat infections caused by staphylococci, pneumococci, and beta-hemolytic streptococci. However, penicillin G is still the preferred agent for these organisms. Methicillin is used most frequently for infections of the skin, soft tissues, and respiratory tract caused by penicillin G-resistant staphylococci (eg, bacterial endocarditis, suppurative osteomyelitis, pseudomembranous enterocolitis). Adequate levels can be achieved within the central nervous system for the successful management of staphylococcal meningitis when large doses (12 g daily) are used.

Plasma levels produced by usual intramuscular doses vary between 6 and 10 μg/ml and occasionally are as high as 12 μg/ml; peak plasma levels occur in 30 minutes to one hour and therapeutic concentrations last three to four hours. Approximately 20% of methicillin is bound to plasma proteins and 35% to 50% or more is rapidly excreted unaltered in the urine. The dose should be reduced in the presence of renal disease. Like penicillin G, methicillin is found in the bile and enters other body fluids slowly.

Staphylococci may develop resistance to methicillin by a nonpenicillinase mechanism. This drug also is a powerful inducer of penicillinase.

Methicillin is generally well tolerated; untoward effects are usually mild and consist of the allergic reactions (eg, erythema, rash) typical of all penicillins (see the Introductory Statement). One of the most serious effects reported thus far has been reversible depression of the cell-forming elements of bone marrow, manifested by anemia, neutropenia, or granulocytopenia. Fortunately, this is observed only rarely.

Interstitial nephritis has been associated with the use of methicillin.

Phlebitis has occurred after repeated intravenous injections. This drug has been reported to produce more pain after intragluteal injection than do most other penicillins; however, pain after intramuscular injection is usually about the same as with penicillin G. Sterile abscesses have occurred at the site of injection.

Fatal superinfections with nonsusceptible organisms, especially gram-negative bacteria, have occurred during treatment. Other reactions include diarrhea, edema, vomiting, fever, chills, albuminuria, hematuria, azotemia, eosinophilia, leukocytosis, and one doubtful case of hemolytic anemia.

Since the rate of elimination of methicillin in very young infants is slow because of their inadequate renal function, it should be borne in mind that a sustained high blood concentration of the drug may persist for days following a single dose.

A history of sensitization to other penicillins is usually a contraindication to administration of methicillin. In addition, this drug must be given cautiously to patients with other known or suspected allergies. Because depression of the cell-forming elements of bone marrow may occur, routine blood cell studies are indicated, especially when therapy is prolonged. The effect of this drug on the fetus is not known, but the penicillins in general do not appear to produce teratogenic effects in man.

Although methicillin is stable in dry form, it is very sensitive to heat and storage when dissolved. Therefore, solutions for intramuscular administration must be used within 24 hours if stored at room temperature or within four days if refrigerated. Solutions for intravenous use must be used within eight hours. Moreover, since the drug is extremely unstable in acidic solutions and is destroyed in solutions containing certain basic antibiotics, solutions for parenteral use should have an approximately neutral pH and no other drugs should be added. To help prevent destruction while in solution, methicillin should be administered as intermittent boluses into the infusion tubing rather than being dissolved in the intravenous fluid package. Dextrose solutions with a pH below 5.5 (many commercial solutions may have a pH as low as 3.5) particularly should not be used with methicillin. If the pH of a solution is not known, water for injection or sodium chloride injection should be used as a diluent.

USUAL DOSAGE.—

Intramuscular: Adults, 1 g in 1.5 ml of water for injection or sodium chloride injection every four to six hours (maximum, 1 g every three hours); *children and infants,* 25 mg/kg of body weight every six hours. Since methicillin must be injected frequently, its use for long-term therapy may be inadvisable.

Intravenous: Adults, 1 to 2 g in 50 ml of sodium choride injection every four to six hours. This amount is infused at a rate of 10 ml/minute. For serious infections, up to 12 g daily may be given.

PREPARATIONS.—Staphcillin (Bristol). *Injection:* Powder (buffered) 1, 4, and 6 g (900 mg methicillin base per gram).

NAFCILLIN SODIUM [Unipen]

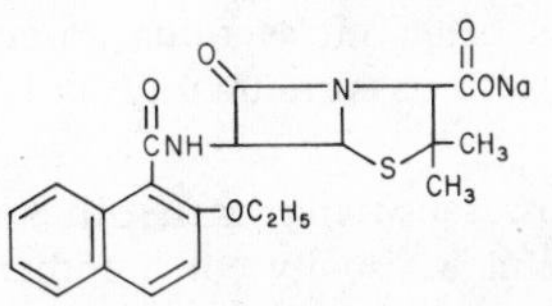

Nafcillin is a semisynthetic penicillin resistant to both penicillinase and acids. It is effective against staphylococci (including penicillin G-resistant strains), beta-hemolytic streptococci, and pneumococci. It also has been used in mixed infections caused by penicillin G-resistant staphylococci with streptococci or pneumococci, and as initial therapy for serious staphylococcal infections in which resistance is suspected but not yet verified by in vitro tests.

This drug is effective in infections of the respiratory tract, soft tissues, and skin caused by susceptible organisms, and in suppurative osteomyelitis. It also has been of some benefit in urinary tract infections.

Nafcillin is used both orally and parenterally. However, it may produce lower blood levels after oral administration than some of the other penicillins because its absorption from the gastrointestinal tract is slower. The minimal concentration necessary for activity against staphylococci in vitro ranges from 0.2 to 2 μg/ml. After oral administration of 500 mg to 1 g, a maximal blood concentration of 1.5 to 5 μg/ml is attained in one hour. The oral route should be used only in mild infections. After intramuscular administration of 500 mg, the average maximal blood level is 5 to 8 μg/ml in one to two hours, and some of the drug persists for four to six hours.

A relatively high concentration of nafcillin is attained in the bile, which represents the major route of excretion for this drug. Some nafcillin is reabsorbed from the gastrointestinal tract. A small amount of the drug is found in synovial fluid after parenteral administration.

Nafcillin is generally well tolerated. Allergic reactions, principally rash, occur most commonly (see the Introductory Statement). Nausea and diarrhea are noted occasionally after administration.

Nafcillin may cause pain and tissue irritation when given intramuscularly. An increase in the level of serum glutamic oxaloacetic transaminase (SGOT) occasionally is observed after intramuscular injection; however, since this reaction subsides rapidly after therapy is discontinued, it may be caused by local tissue injury. Thrombophlebitis has been reported in a few patients after intravenous administration; this effect also is presumably due to tissue injury.

Since cross sensitivity with other penicillins exists, nafcillin is usually contraindicated when there is a history of sensitivity to any penicillin, and it must be administered cautiously to patients with other known or suspected allergies.

USUAL DOSAGE.—

Oral: Adults, 250 mg to 1 g every four to six hours, preferably two hours before meals; *children,* 25 to 50 mg/kg of body weight daily in four divided doses.

Intramuscular: Adults, 500 mg every four to six hours; *children,* 25 mg/kg of body weight twice daily; *newborn infants,* 10 mg/kg twice daily.

Intravenous: Adults, 500 mg to 1 g in 15 to 30 ml of water for injection or sodium chloride injection infused over a 10-minute period every four hours, or dissolved in 150 ml of sodium choride injection and given by slow intravenous drip. Doses up to 8 g daily can be given for serious infections. *Children,* 50 mg/kg of body weight daily in six divided doses.

PREPARATIONS.—Unipen (Wyeth).

Injection: Powder 500 mg and 1 and 2 g.

Oral: Capsules 250 mg; powder for solution 250 mg/5 ml.

OXACILLIN SODIUM [Bactocill, Prostaphlin]

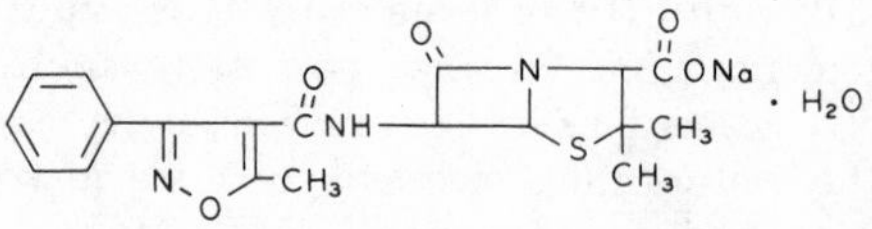

Oxacillin is a semisynthetic penicillin with an action and efficacy close to that of nafcillin and methicillin. Its antibacterial spectrum is similar to that of penicillin G (see the Introductory Statement and the evaluation on Penicillin G); in addition, large doses are effective in the treatment of staphylococcal infections resistant to penicillin G.

Oxacillin is useful in staphylococcal infections of the skin and soft tissues, in respiratory and genitourinary tract infections caused by susceptible organisms, in suppurative osteomyelitis and pseudomembranous enterocolitis caused by penicillin G-resistant staphylococci, and in mixed infections caused by penicillin G-resistant staphylococci with pneumococci or beta-hemolytic streptococci.

This penicillin is more resistant to destruction by gastric acid than penicillin G or methicillin, but is somewhat less resistant than phenoxymethyl penicillin or phenethicillin. Oxacillin also is less susceptible to rapid deterioration in acidic intravenous fluids than methicillin but, like methicillin, is penicillinase-resistant.

The presence of food in the stomach interferes with the absorption of orally administered oxacillin; when the stomach is empty, approximately 60% of the dose is absorbed, and doses of 500 mg to 1 g produce average peak plasma concentrations of 4 to 8 μg/ml in one hour. Intramuscular doses of 500 mg to 1 g produce a blood concentration of 7 to 13 μg/ml, but only a negligible concentration remains after four to six hours.

Oxacillin also appears in bile, in pleural and amniotic fluids, and in milk. Effective antibacterial levels are not achieved in the central nervous system unless inflammation of the meninges is present. Oxacillin has been used effectively in patients with staphylococcal meningitis.

This drug is excreted rapidly by the kidneys, although not as rapidly as penicillin G.

Oxacillin is generally well tolerated. Untoward effects are similar to those produced by the other penicillins (see the Introductory Statement) and include rash, urticaria, and pruritus ani and vulvae. Nausea, vomiting, diarrhea, hairy tongue, fever, and eosinophilia have occurred occasionally. A few serious anaphylactic reactions have been reported, but there have been no deaths. Increased levels of serum glutamic oxaloacetic transaminase (SGOT) have been noted in a few patients. Some infants receiving large doses have developed transient hematuria, albuminuria, and azotemia.

A history of allergic reactions to other penicillins is usually a contraindication to use of oxacillin, although cross reactions do not always occur. In addition, this drug should be administered cautiously to patients with other known or suspected allergies.

The effect of this drug on the fetus has not been determined, but the penicillins in general do not appear to be teratogenic in man.

Hepatic and renal function tests should be performed at regular intervals when therapy is prolonged.

USUAL DOSAGE.—

Oral: This drug should be taken at least one hour before or two hours after meals, and dosage should be continued for at least five days. *Adults and children weighing more than 40 kg,* 500 mg to 1 g every four to six hours; *less than 40 kg,* 50 to 100 mg/kg of body weight daily in four to six doses.

Intramuscular: Adults and children weighing more than 40 kg, 250 mg to 1 g every four to six hours (up to 8 g daily may be given for severe infections); *less than 40 kg,* 50 to 100 mg/kg of body weight daily in four equal doses; *newborn and premature infants,* 25 mg/kg daily.

Intravenous: When administered by direct intravenous infusion, the dose should be well diluted and given over a period of approximately 10 to 15 minutes. Dosages should be comparable to those administered intramuscularly; for severe infections, 1 g or more may be given intravenously every three to four hours depending upon the nature of the infection and the clinical response.

PREPARATIONS.—

Bactocill (Beecham-Massengill).

Oral: Capsules 250 and 500 mg.

Injection: Powder 500 mg and 1 g.

Prostaphlin (Bristol).

Oral: Capsules 250 and 500 mg; solution 250 mg/5 ml.

Injection: Powder 250 and 500 mg and 1 g.

PHENETHICILLIN POTASSIUM [Darcil, Maxipen, Syncillin]

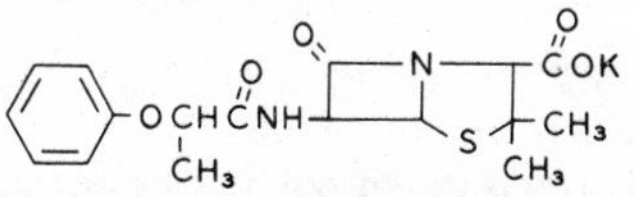

Phenethicillin is a semisynthetic homologue of phenoxymethyl penicillin. It is quite stable in gastric acid. Its absorption from the gastrointestinal tract is rapid but incomplete; absorption is increased if the drug is given when the stomach is empty. Peak blood levels are attained approximately one hour after oral administration.

The indications for use of phenethicillin are the same as for the other orally administered penicillin preparations, ie, the treatment of infections caused by beta-hemolytic streptococci, pneumococci, gonococci, and susceptible staphylococci (see the Introductory Statement). It is not effective against penicillinase-producing staphylococci.

The adverse reactions are similar to those observed with the other penicillins; allergic reactions occur most commonly. (See the Introductory Statement.) Thus, phenethicillin is contraindicated in patients known to be hypersensitive to penicillin, and it may be advisable to use a different antibacterial agent such as erythromycin in patients with a history of other allergic conditions.

If allergic reactions occur, the drug should be stopped immediately and, if necessary, appropriate ameliorative treatment given when indicated (eg, antihistamines for mild rash and pruritus; epinephrine and corticosteroids for anaphylactic reactions). In most instances, discontinuation of phenethicillin is sufficient; another antibacterial agent should be substituted if further treatment of the infection is necessary.

USUAL DOSAGE.—This drug should be given when the stomach is empty. *Oral: Adults,* 125 to 250 mg three times daily for mild to moderate infections and 500 mg three times daily or 250 mg every four hours for severe infections. *Children,* 125 to 250 mg three times daily for mild to moderate infections and 250 mg four times daily for severe infections. *Infants,* 12.5 to 50 mg/kg of body weight in three to six divided doses. For prophylactic treatment of rheumatic fever, *adults and children,* 125 to 250 mg daily.

PREPARATIONS.—

Darcil (Wyeth). *Oral:* Tablets 125 and 250 mg.

Maxipen (Roerig), Syncillin (Bristol). *Oral:* Tablets 250 mg.

PHENOXYMETHYL PENICILLIN [Pen-Vee, V-Cillin]
PHENOXYMETHYL PENICILLIN BENZATHINE [Pen-Vee]
PHENOXYMETHYL PENICILLIN HYDRABAMINE [Compocillin-V]
PHENOXYMETHYL PENICILLIN POTASSIUM [Compocillin-VK, Ledercillin VK, Robicillin VK, Uticillin VK, V-Cillin K, Veetids]

These preparations are phenoxymethyl congeners of penicillin G. They are more resistant to destruction by gastric acid than penicillin G but possess the same antibacterial spectrum. They are available only as oral preparations. When the two drugs are taken in a fasting state, blood levels of phenoxymethyl penicillin are somewhat higher than those produced by an equal quantity of oral penicillin G and, when they are taken with food, blood levels of phenoxymethyl penicillin are considerably higher. However, phenoxymethyl penicillin has no proven advantage over larger oral doses of buffered penicillin G taken on an empty stomach. Even a large oral dose of phenoxymethyl penicillin will not produce blood levels higher than those easily achieved by parenteral preparations of penicillin G.

Allergic reactions are the most common adverse effects. (See the Introductory Statement and the evaluation on Penicillin G.)

USUAL DOSAGE.—*Oral: Adults and children,* 125 to 500 mg four to six times daily; *infants,* 50 mg/kg of body weight daily divided into three doses. For prophylactic treatment of rheumatic fever, *adults and children,* 125 to 250 mg daily.

PREPARATIONS.—

Phenoxymethyl Penicillin:

Pen-Vee (Wyeth). *Oral:* Tablets 125 and 300 mg.

V-Cillin (Lilly). *Oral:* Capsules 125 and 250 mg; powder for drops 125 mg/0.6 ml; powder for suspension (pediatric) 125 and 250 mg/5 ml.

Phenoxymethyl Penicillin Benzathine:

Pen-Vee (Wyeth). *Oral:* Suspension 90 and 180 mg/5 ml.

Phenoxymethyl Penicillin Hydrabamine:

Compocillin-V (Ross). *Oral:* Suspension 180 mg/5 ml; wafers 125 and 250 mg.

Phenoxymethyl Penicillin Potassium:

Ledercillin-VK (Lederle), Robicillin VK (Robins), Uticillin VK (Upjohn), Veetids (Squibb). *Oral:* Powder for solution 125 and 250 mg/5 ml; tablets 250 and 500 mg.

Compocillin-VK (Ross). *Oral:* Granules for solution 125 and 250 mg/5 ml; powder for drops 250 mg/5 ml; tablets 125, 250, and 500 mg.

V-Cillin K (Lilly). *Oral:* Powder for solution 1255 and 250 mg/5 ml; tablets 125, 250, and 500 mg.

ADDITIONAL TRADEMARKS.—Betapen-VK (Bristol), Kesso-Pen-VK (McKesson), Pfizerpen VK (Pfizer), Penapor-VK (Parke, Davis), Pen-Vee K (Wyeth), SK-Penicillin VK (Smith Kline & French).

Chapter 49

CEPHALOSPORINS

The cephalosporins are semisynthetic antibacterial agents that are closely related chemically to the penicillins and, like them, contain a beta lactam ring as part of the nucleus. They are produced by the addition of substituent groups to 7-aminocephalosporanic acid, a chemical nucleus obtained from cephalosporin C, which is elaborated by the fungus *Cephalosporium*. The cephalosporins interfere with the synthesis of the bacterial cell wall by inactivating a transpeptidase, thereby preventing cross-linkage of peptidoglycan chains.

All four currently marketed cephalosporins, cephalothin sodium [Keflin], cephaloridine [Loridine], cephaloglycin dihydrate [Kafocin], and cephalexin monohydrate [Keflex], have similar in vitro spectra that include both gram-positive and gram-negative bacteria. They are effective against most gram-positive cocci and against many gram-negative organisms, most prominently *Escherichia coli*, *Proteus mirabilis*, and *Klebsiella*. *Pseudomonas*, most species of indole-positive *Proteus*, and *Enterobacter* are resistant. Bacterial sensitivity to the cephalosporins preferably should be determined prior to use of these agents; this may be done with the cephalothin test disk. (For a more complete description of the bacterial spectrum of each cephalosporin, see the individual evaluations.)

The cephalosporins are usually penicillinase-resistant, but their susceptibility to destruction by a beta lactamase (designated as cephalosporinase) produced by gram-negative rods, primarily species of *Enterobacter* and *Pseudomonas*, varies. Cross allergenicity between the cephalosporins and penicillins has occurred, but most patients sensitive to a penicillin can be safely treated with a cephalosporin. Bacterial cross resistance between cephalosporins and other antibacterial agents has not been clearly demonstrated, although strains of *Staphylococcus aureus* resistant to methicillin generally are resistant to the cephalosporins.

The cephalosporins are used to treat susceptible infections of the respiratory and urinary tracts, skin and soft tissues, and bone and joints. Some cases of septicemia, peritonitis, septic abortion, bacterial endocarditis, and meningitis caused by sensitive organisms have been successfully treated with the cephalosporins.

Adverse Reactions and Precautions

Minor rashes, urticaria, fever, eosinophilia, and, rarely, neutropenia have been associated with administration of the cephalosporins. The incidence of mild allergic reactions is higher in patients who are hypersensitive to the penicillins. Severe hypersensitivity reactions (eg, anaphylaxis) have been reported, but they are rare.

The most dangerous adverse effect produced by cephaloridine [Loridine] is renal tubular necrosis; renal impairment also has been attributed to cephalothin [Keflin], but the incidence is not as great as with cephaloridine. Some evidence of hepatic dysfunction has been noted following administration of the cephalosporins. Overgrowth of resistant organisms may occur after long-term use.

Diarrhea is the most frequently observed and often the most severe untoward effect seen following administration of cephaloglycin [Kafocin]. It can be severe enough to warrant discontinuing the drug. Diarrhea occurs less frequently with cephalexin [Keflex].

Direct positive Coombs' tests have been observed in patients receiving the cephalosporins. Hemolytic anemia has been reported after the use of cephalothin, but it is not a common or serious adverse reaction.

The intramuscular injection of cephalothin frequently causes pain. Pain occurs less commonly with cephaloridine injections. Intravenous administration of either drug may cause thrombophlebitis. The phlebitis usually can be prevented by alternating veins, slowly injecting a solution diluted with sodium chloride or dextrose injection, and adding a corticosteroid or heparin to the infusion. Intrathecal injection of cephalothin or cephaloridine is not recommended because administration by this route is toxic to the nervous system and causes a variety of effects including nystagmus, hallucinations, and convulsions.

The risk to the fetus when these drugs are given to pregnant patients has not been fully assessed.

INDIVIDUAL EVALUATIONS

CEPHALOTHIN SODIUM [Keflin]

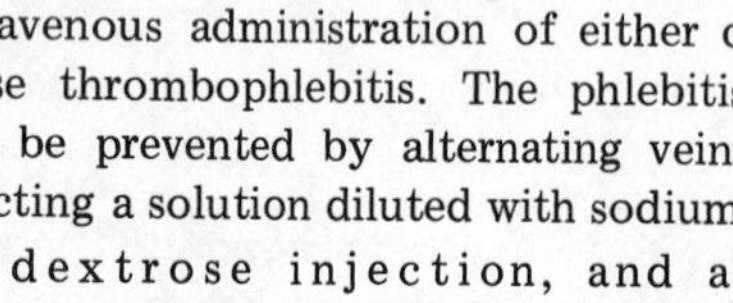

Cephalothin is a broad-spectrum antibiotic that is active in vitro against penicillin-sensitive and penicillinase-producing *Staphylococcus aureus*, beta-hemolytic streptococci, pneumococci, clostridia, *Escherichia coli*, *Klebsiella*, *Proteus mirabilis*, *Neisseria gonorrhoeae*, and some species of *Salmonella* and *Shigella*. Most species of enterococci (eg, *Streptococcus faecalis*) and *Enterobacter* are resistant to concentrations of the drug attainable systemically, but enterococci are susceptible to concentrations that appear in the urine. Cephalothin is ineffective against *Pseudomonas* and many species of indole-positive *Proteus*.

This drug is administered only parenterally, and its use should be restricted to the treatment of serious infections. It has been used successfully in a wide variety of clinical conditions including bacteremias and infections of the respiratory tract, skin, soft tissues, bones, joints, and cardiovascular system. Cephalothin also is suitable for treating urinary tract infections, since a high concentration of active drug is excreted in the urine. It is the drug of choice in staphylococcal infections when parenteral administration is indicated and the patient is known to be hypersensitive to penicillin. Cephalothin may be useful in treating peritonitis, septic abortion, and purulent (staphylococcal or pneumonoccal) meningitis. It is not recommended for meningococcal meningitis. For its use in the eye, see Chapter 71, Anti-infective and Anti-inflammatory Agents Used in Ophthalmology.

Between 60% and 90% of a given dose of cephalothin is excreted by the renal tubules, largely unchanged. This excretion is blocked by probenecid. Of the portion that is metabolized, at least one metabolite has antibacterial activity and is excreted in the urine. Peak urinary concentrations may reach several hundred micrograms per milliliter following usual doses. In normal adults, 60% of the dose is excreted in six hours; therefore, the drug must be administered every four to six hours to maintain effective plasma concentrations unless renal excretion is impaired. Although cephalothin has caused renal tubular necrosis, it is well tolerated and can be used in patients with kidney disease if adjustments are made in dosage.

Intramuscular injection should be made deep into the muscle, since large or repeated doses can cause severe pain, local induration or, rarely, sterile abscesses or necrosis and slough. Local thrombophlebitis may occur after intravenous administration. Intrathecal injection is not recommended.

Other adverse effects are similar to those of the penicillins and include rash, urticaria, fever, and eosinophilia. A direct positive Coombs' test is sometimes observed, particularly in azotemic patients. Rarely, anaphylactic shock, neutropenia, leukopenia, or hemolytic anemia has occurred. Elevated serum glutamic oxaloacetic transaminase (SGOT) levels have been noted. Blood urea nitrogen (BUN) levels may increase but frequently return to normal during therapy. Overgrowth of resistant organisms has been observed. Various organisms, including *Pseudomonas*, can replace pre-existing pathogens in the urinary tract.

Hematologic studies and liver and renal function tests should be performed periodically during prolonged therapy, and blood concentrations should be monitored if possible in patients with impaired renal function to avoid excessive accumulation of the drug.

Cephalothin does not readily accumulate in cerebrospinal and synovial fluids unless these structures are inflamed. However, the drug readily crosses the placenta. Limited trials indicate that cephalothin may be safe for use during pregnancy and in premature and full-term infants.

USUAL DOSAGE.—

Intramuscular: Adults, 500 mg to 1 g four to six times daily depending upon the severity of the infection; *infants and children*, 40 to 80 mg/kg of body weight daily in divided doses.

Intravenous: Adults, 4 to 6 g daily (up to 12 g may be given for serious infections) in sodium chloride or dextrose injection administered in divided doses; this is injected slowly either directly into the vein or into tubing being used for intravenous infusions. *Infants and children*, 40 to 80 mg/kg of body weight daily in divided doses.

PREPARATIONS.—Keflin (Lilly). *Injection:* Powder 1, 2, and 4 g.

CEPHALORIDINE [Loridine]

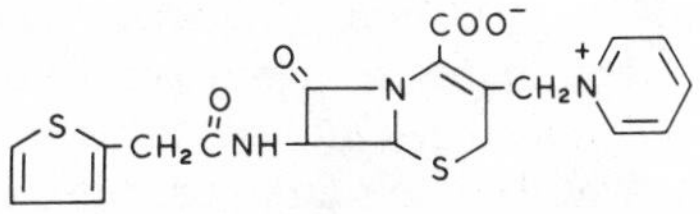

The in vitro spectrum and clinical applications of cephaloridine are almost identical to those of cephalothin; however, because of the potential nephrotoxicity of cephaloridine, the desirability of determining the causative organism and its sensitivity to this agent before initiating therapy cannot be overemphasized. This drug is administered parenterally and should be reserved for use in patients with infections caused by staphylococci or gram-negative bacilli that have been shown to be sensitive to cephaloridine in vitro and who cannot tolerate penicillin or cephalothin. For its use in the eye, see Chapter 71, Anti-infective and Anti-inflammatory Agents Used in Ophthalmology.

Cephaloridine is less resistant to staphylococcal penicillinase than cephalothin, and it is degraded as readily by cephalosporinase produced by some gram-negative species of bacteria (eg, *Enterobacter*, *Pseudomonas*). Injection is less painful than with cephalothin and, when similar doses of the two drugs are administered, cephaloridine produces higher blood levels because its renal clearance rate is one-half that of cephalothin. The rate of excretion is retarded to a limited extent by probenecid. Accumulation in cerebrospinal fluid is poor unless the meninges are inflamed.

Large doses may cause acute renal tubular necrosis, resulting in fatal uremia; therefore, assessment of renal function before and during treatment is essential. Cephaloridine should not be used with other potentially nephrotoxic drugs such as the aminoglycoside antibiotics (eg, kanamycin, gentamicin). Doses for adults should not exceed 4 g daily. This drug must not be confused with cephalothin, which has been used in doses exceeding 12 g daily.

Elevated levels of serum glutamic oxaloacetic transaminase (SGOT) and alkaline phosphatase have been reported. Leukopenia has been associated with cephaloridine therapy, but evidence is insufficient to establish a clear-cut causal relationship. Thus, it is advisable to monitor hepatic and hematopoietic changes, especially when therapy is extended beyond ten days.

Hypersensitivity reactions (urticaria, pruritus, maculopapular or erythematous rashes, and fever) may develop during therapy. Anaphylaxis has been reported. Some patients who are sensitive to penicillin also may be sensitive to cephaloridine. Nausea and vomiting occur rarely.

Colonization by resistant organisms, notably *Pseudomonas*, may occur at multiple sites. Therefore, patients receiving cephaloridine should be observed for signs of superinfection.

Pain at the site of intramuscular injection and thrombophlebitis at the site of intravenous injection have been noted infrequently. Intrathecal administration of this drug is not recommended because it may cause various neurologic reactions (eg, nystagmus, hallucinations, convulsions).

Experience is not adequate to assess the risk to the fetus when this drug is given to pregnant women. For the same reason, it is not recommended for use in premature infants or infants under 1 month of age.

USUAL DOSAGE.—

Intramuscular: Adults, 500 mg to a maximum of 1 g three or four times daily at equally spaced intervals. Since large doses may produce tubular necrosis, an appropriate reduction in dosage should be made in patients with impaired renal function. *Children*, 30 to 50 mg/kg of body weight daily in three divided doses at equally spaced intervals. Up to 100 mg/kg daily has been given in severe infections, but these doses should be used with caution.

Intravenous: Adults and children, 500 mg or 1 g of the drug dissolved in 5 or 10 ml, respectively, of diluent (water for injection, sodium chloride injection, or 5% dextrose injection) and administered as a continuous infusion or by intermittent injections slowly over a period of three to four minutes. Mixing with solutions containing other antibiotics is not recommended.

PREPARATIONS.—Loridine (Lilly). *Injection:* Powder 500 mg and 1 g.

CEPHALOGLYCIN DIHYDRATE [Kafocin]

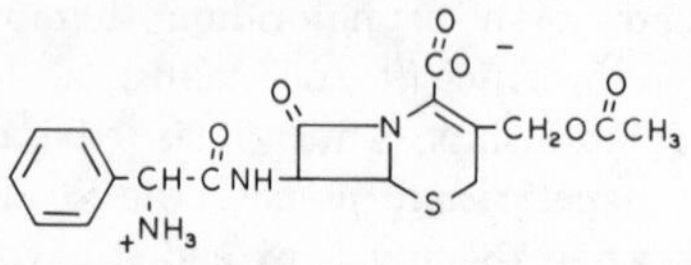

Cephaloglycin is administered only orally. Its in vitro spectrum covers most pathogens that infect the urinary tract, including *Staphylococcus aureus*, *Escherichia coli*, and certain species of *Klebsiella*, *Enterobacter*, *Proteus*, and enterococci. Cephaloglycin is ineffective against *Pseudomonas*. Serum levels of the drug high enough to be useful in treating systemic infections cannot be attained clinically. Since it is excreted almost entirely by the kidney as desacetylcephaloglycin, an active metabolite, cephaloglycin is useful for treating urinary tract infections caused by susceptible organisms. However, it may not be a cephalosporin of first choice for severe urinary tract infections, since cephalothin, cephaloridine, and cephalexin also are excreted by the kidney and each may be capable of achieving higher bactericidal concentrations in the urine than cephaloglycin. The sensitivity of an organism to cephaloglycin should be determined before the drug is administered to make certain that it is the cephalosporin that should be used, since the development of cephalexin has rendered cephaloglycin essentially obsolete.

The presence of food in the stomach does not significantly alter the total amount of cephaloglycin absorbed, but food will delay the appearance of peak serum and urine levels.

Diarrhea is the most common adverse effect. It occasionally has been severe enough to warrant discontinuation of therapy. Nausea and vomiting also may occur. These symptoms usually subside rapidly after discontinuing the drug. Other reactions include rash, urticaria, fever, headache, and vertigo. Eosinophilia occurs infrequently.

Although cephaloglycin can usually be administered safely to patients sensitive to penicillin, laboratory evidence of cross allergenicity has been demonstrated. The safety of this drug in premature infants and those under 1 year of age, and to the fetus during pregnancy, has not been established. Prolonged use may result in overgrowth of nonsusceptible organisms, especially *Pseudomonas*. Cephaloglycin should be administered with caution when marked renal impairment is present.

USUAL DOSAGE.—*Oral: Adults*, 250 to 500 mg four times daily, depending upon the severity of the infection. If larger doses are necessary, one of the injectable cephalosporins should be considered. *Children*, 25 to 50 mg/kg of body weight daily in four divided doses.

PREPARATIONS.—Kafocin (Lilly). *Oral:* Capsules 250 mg.

CEPHALEXIN MONOHYDRATE [Keflex]

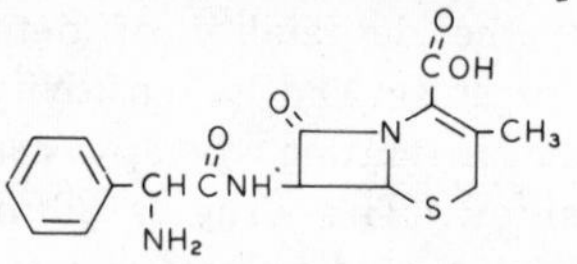

Like cephaloglycin, cephalexin is administered only orally. The in vitro spectrum of cephalexin includes both penicillin-sensitive and penicillinase-producing *Staphylococcus aureus*, beta-hemolytic streptococci, *Diplococcus pneumoniae*, *Escherichia coli*, *Proteus mirabilis*, and some species of *Klebsiella*. It is inactive against *Pseudomonas* and *Herellea*, most *Enterobacter* and indole-positive *Proteus*, and most enterococci (eg, *Streptococcus faecalis*). Some staphylococci that are resistant to methicillin-type penicillins also are resistant to cephalexin.

Unlike cephaloglycin, cephalexin can be used to treat a variety of systemic as well as urinary tract infections. It is useful primarily against sensitive bacteria found in the respiratory and urinary tracts, skin, and soft tissues. Nevertheless, because the susceptibility of even those organisms sensitive to the cephalosporins is variable, sensitivity tests should be performed prior to initiation of therapy with cephalexin. For its use in the eye, see Chapter 71, Anti-infective and Anti-inflammatory Agents Used in Ophthalmology.

Adverse reactions resemble those observed with cephaloglycin. The most frequent untoward effect is diarrhea, which occasionally is severe enough to warrant discontinuing the drug. Pyrosis, nausea, vomiting, and abdominal pain also have been observed. Allergic manifestations are rare. They include rash, genital and anal pruritus, urticaria, angioedema, and anaphylactic reactions. Slight elevations in serum transaminase (SGOT, SGPT) levels have been reported. Eosinophilia and neutropenia, as well as cross sensitivity to the penicillins, have been observed rarely.

Cephalexin is acid stable and the presence of food in the stomach does not interfere with its absorption, although peak serum and urine levels may be somewhat delayed.

Renal function should be determined periodically in patients receiving cephalexin for prolonged periods. Also, the drug should be administered with care and in reduced doses if renal impairment exists.

Long-term use can result in overgrowth of nonsusceptible organisms, frequently *Pseudomonas*. Genital and vaginal candidiasis also is seen. The safety of this drug in pregnant women has not been established. A direct positive Coombs' test and false positive tests for glycosuria have been observed.

USUAL DOSAGE.—*Oral: Adults,* 250 mg every six hours; for severe infections, up to 4 g daily in divided doses. If more than 4 g are needed, a parenteral cephalosporin preparation should be substituted. *Children,* 25 to 50 mg/kg of body weight in four divided doses. For severe infections, this dosage may be doubled.

PREPARATIONS.—Keflex (Lilly). *Oral:* Capsules 250 and 500 mg; drops (pediatric) 100 mg/ml; suspension 125 mg/5 ml.

Chapter 50

ERYTHROMYCIN AND DERIVATIVES

Erythromycin is produced by a strain of *Streptomyces erythreus* and is one of the macrolide group of antimicrobial agents. (The name macrolide is derived from the large lactone ring that is a structural characteristic of these agents.) The exact mode of action of erythromycin has not yet been clearly defined, although it is known to impede protein synthesis in vitro. This drug is considered one of the safest antibiotics in use today.

The antibacterial spectrum of erythromycin is similar but not identical to that of penicillin, and it is a satisfactory and safe alternate drug for infections not requiring high blood levels of penicillin (see Chapter 48, Penicillins). However, if patients can tolerate it, penicillin is preferred for serious infections requiring sustained high blood and tissue levels of this antibiotic.

Erythromycin is active against most gram-positive bacteria, including *Listeria.* Most species of *Neisseria* and some species of *Bordetella*, *Brucella*, *Pasteurella*, and *Haemophilus* are sensitive; most other gram-negative species are not. It also is active against *Mycoplasma pneumoniae* (PPLO, Eaton agent) and certain *Actinomyces* and *Treponema* species.

The principal use of erythromycin is to treat group A beta-hemolytic streptococcal, staphylococcal, and pneumococcal infections. It may be given to patients with nonfulminating staphylococcal infections caused by penicillin-resistant strains, but it is not a drug of first choice for severe infections caused by these organisms because many *Staphylococcus* strains rapidly develop resistance to it. Erythromycin is used in primary atypical pneumonia due to *Mycoplasma pneumoniae*, in acute diphtheria and carriers of *Corynebacterium diphtheriae*, in erythrasma, and in intestinal amebiasis. In addition, it is useful in treating gonorrhea or syphilis when the disease is caused by sensitive organisms and the patient is allergic to penicillin. The use of an ophthalmic ointment and a systemic form of an erythromycin salt or ester is effective in the treatment of blepharitis and trachoma (see also Chapter 71, Anti-infective and Anti-inflammatory Agents Used in Ophthalmology).

Erythromycin is available as the base and as salts and esters of the base. All forms have the same spectrum of activity and essentially the same indications. Erythromycin [E-Mycin, Erythrocin, Ilotycin] is given orally, rectally, and topically (in the eye); erythromycin stearate [Bristamycin, Erythrocin Stearate, Ethril] and erythromycin estolate [Ilosone] are used orally; erythromycin gluceptate [Ilotycin Gluceptate] and erythromycin lactobionate [Erythrocin Lactobionate] are recommended primarily for intravenous use; and erythromycin ethylsuccinate [Erythrocin Ethyl Succinate, Pediamycin] is given both orally and intramuscularly (however, there is no intramuscular form of Pediamycin).

When given orally, erythromycin and its derivatives (with the exception of erythromycin estolate) are inactivated to varying degrees by gastric acid. This can be minimized by administering oral preparations before meals or by administering erythromycin estolate or one of the preparations formulated in acid-resistant tablets. Erythromycin (base) suppositories may be used in children who are unable to take oral preparations. Erythromycin gluceptate and erythromycin lactobionate may be given intravenously when large doses are required but are not tolerated orally. The ethylsuccinate ester can be administered intramuscularly, but these injections usually are painful.

There is evidence that a combination of erythromycin and sulfonamides is effective in children under 3 years of age with otitis media caused by *Haemophilus influenzae.* This combination is useful when the patient is allergic to ampicillin or when erythromycin alone is not effective. Tailoring the dose of the individual components to the need of each patient is essential for best results, since such factors as age, body weight, and severity of disease must be considered.

Adverse Reactions and Precautions

Erythromycin and its derivatives, with the exception of erythromycin estolate [Ilosone], rarely cause serious adverse reactions. When given orally, the erythromycins may produce mild gastrointestinal disturbances (nausea, vomiting, pyrosis, diarrhea), although these reactions occur infrequently and usually only following large doses. Tablets with acid-resistant coating may be given with meals in an effort to reduce these untoward effects, but serum levels will be reduced somewhat. Mild allergic reactions such as urticaria and other rashes have occurred, but serious allergic reactions are rare.

Erythromycin estolate, the lauryl sulfate salt of the propionyl ester of erythromycin, is the only erythromycin ester associated with hepatotoxicity. It can produce jaundice. This reaction is observed most frequently in patients who have previously received the drug but also may occur in those receiving long-term therapy (ten days or more). The jaundice appears to be a hypersensitivity reaction and is reversible when erythromycin estolate is discontinued. There may be accompanying upper right quadrant colic and hepatic enzyme changes suggesting choledocholithiasis. Other erythromycin preparations should be used in preference to the estolate salt in patients with pre-existing liver disease or in those suspected of having impaired liver function.

INDIVIDUAL EVALUATIONS

ERYTHROMYCIN [E-Mycin, Erythrocin, Ilotycin]

ERYTHROMYCIN ESTOLATE [Ilosone]
ERYTHROMYCIN ETHYLSUCCINATE [Erythrocin Ethyl Succinate, Pediamycin]
ERYTHROMYCIN GLUCEPTATE [Ilotycin Gluceptate]
ERYTHROMYCIN LACTOBIONATE [Erythrocin Lactobionate]
ERYTHROMYCIN STEARATE [Bristamycin, Erythrocin Stearate, Ethril]

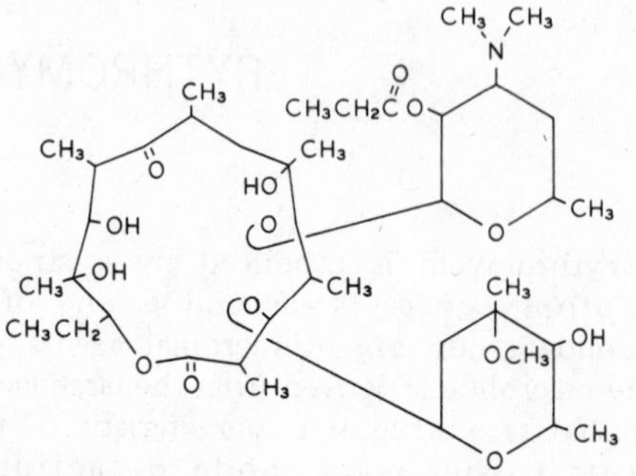

Erythromycin is the free base; the other preparations are salts or esters of the base. All of the erythromycins have the same spectrum of antibacterial activity, the same uses, and the same adverse reactions (with the exception of erythromycin estolate). See the Introductory Statement.

USUAL DOSAGE.—(All doses are expressed in terms of the base.)

Erythromycin:

Oral: Adults, 250 mg every six hours; for severe infections, 250 mg every four hours or 500 mg every six hours. *Children,* 30 mg/kg of body weight daily in divided doses; for severe infections, up to 50 mg/kg daily in divided doses.

Rectal: Children under 9 kg, 125 mg every eight hours; *9 to 18 kg,* 125 mg every six hours. Administration by this route should be replaced by oral therapy as soon as possible.

Erythromycin Estolate:

Oral: Adults and children over 25 kg, 250 mg every six hours. *Children 10 to 25 kg,* 125 mg every six hours; *under 10 kg,* 10 mg/kg of body weight every six hours. For severe infections, all doses may be doubled.

Erythromycin Ethylsuccinate:

Oral: Adults, 400 mg four times daily; for severe infections, 4 g or more daily in divided doses. *Children,* 30 to 50 mg/kg of body weight daily in four divided doses. Doses may be doubled for severe infections.

Intramuscular: (Intramuscular injections are

irritating and painful.) *Adults*, 100 mg. This route should be avoided in children if possible, because they do not have the large muscle mass desirable for deep placement of the injections. If intramuscular injection is essential, the following doses may be given. *Children over 15 kg*, 50 mg; *under 15 kg*, 3 mg/kg of body weight. The interval between injections varies according to the severity of the infection. For severe infections, injections may be given every four to six hours and for mild or moderately severe infections, every six to eight hours, depending upon clinical response.

Erythromycin Gluceptate:

Intravenous: Adults, 250 mg to 1 g every six hours infused over a 20- to 60-minute period or 1 to 2 g given over a 24-hour period as a continuous infusion. In severe infections the dose may be increased to 4 g daily. *Children*, 40 to 50 mg/kg of body weight daily given in divided doses or as a continuous infusion. The amount may be increased to 60 to 70 mg/kg daily for severe infections.

Erythromycin Lactobionate:

Intravenous: Adults, 1 to 4 g daily given in divided doses every six to eight hours or as a continuous infusion. *Children*, 10 to 20 mg/kg of body weight daily given in divided doses or as a continuous infusion.

Erythromycin Stearate:

Oral: Adults, 250 mg every six hours; 4 g or more may be administered daily in severe infections. *Children*, 30 to 50 mg/kg of body weight daily in four divided doses.

PREPARATIONS.—(Preparation strengths are expressed in terms of the base.)

Erythromycin:

E-Mycin (Upjohn). *Oral:* Tablets (enteric-coated) 250 mg.

Erythrocin (Abbott). *Rectal:* Suppositories 125 mg.

Ilotycin (Lilly).

Oral: Tablets (enteric-coated) 250 mg.

Topical: Ointment 1% in 1/2 and 1 oz containers; ointment (ophthalmic) 0.5% in 1/8 oz containers.

Erythromycin Estolate:

Ilosone (Lilly). *Oral:* Capsules 125 and 250 mg; drops 5 mg/drop; granules for suspension 125 mg/5 ml; suspension 125 and 250 mg/5 ml; tablets (chewable) 125 and 250 mg; tablets 500 mg.

Erythromycin Ethylsuccinate:

Erythrocin Ethyl Succinate (Abbott).

Oral: Granules for drops (suspension) 100 mg/2.5 ml; granules for suspension 200 mg/5 ml; tablets (chewable) 200 mg.

Injection: Solution 50 mg/ml in 2 and 10 ml containers.

Pediamycin (Ross). *Oral:* Granules for drops (suspension) 100 mg/2.5 ml; granules for suspension 200 mg/5 ml; tablets (chewable) 200 mg.

Erythromycin Gluceptate:

Ilotycin Gluceptate (Lilly). *Injection:* Powder 250 and 500 mg and 1 g.

Erythromycin Lactobionate:

Erythrocin Lactobionate (Abbott). *Injection:* Powder 500 mg and 1 g.

Erythromycin Stearate:

Bristamycin (Bristol), Ethril (Squibb). *Oral:* Tablets 250 mg.

Erythrocin Stearate (Abbott). *Oral:* Tablets 125 and 250 mg.

Chapter 51

LINCOMYCIN AND CLINDAMYCIN

Lincomycin hydrochloride monohydrate [Lincocin], an antibacterial agent produced by *Streptomyces lincolnensis* var. *lincolnensis*, and its semisynthetic derivatives, clindamycin hydrochloride hydrate [Cleocin Hydrochloride], clindamycin palmitate [Cleocin Palmitate], and clindamycin phosphate [Cleocin Phosphate], have a limited spectrum of activity similar to that of erythromycin. They are active against the common gram-positive pathogens, including *Staphylococcus* (some resistant strains have been reported), *Streptococcus* (except *S. faecalis*), *Diplococcus pneumoniae*, *Clostridium tetani*, *C. welchii*, *Corynebacterium diphtheriae*, several *Actinomyces* species, and some *Nocardia* species. Gram-negative organisms, with the exception of *Bacteroides fragilis* and some strains of *Mycoplasma pneumoniae* (PPLO), are not sensitive to these drugs.

Lincomycin and clindamycin may be used for the treatment of any susceptible infection, but they are particularly indicated in susceptible infections resistant to the penicillins and erythromycin or in patients who cannot tolerate penicillin and erythromycin. Both lincomycin and clindamycin are effective in acute and chronic osteomyelitis caused by susceptible gram-positive organisms.

Clindamycin differs chemically from lincomycin by the substitution of a chlorine atom for a hydroxyl group on the parent compound. With this slight variation, clindamycin has some advantages over lincomycin in that intestinal absorbability is enhanced, potency is increased, and the incidence of adverse effects is lower. Both drugs can be administered orally, intramuscularly, or intravenously.

Staphylococci, especially *Staphylococcus aureus*, develop resistance to lincomycin and clindamycin, but the process occurs slowly. The rate at which clinical resistance develops has not been determined, but natural resistance appears in less than 1% of patients. *Diplococcus pneumoniae* also is rarely resistant to both drugs. Cross resistance occurs between these two agents, as might be expected from their molecular similarities. Cross resistance between lincomycin or clindamycin and most other antibacterial agents has not been encountered clinically, although it has been demonstrated in vitro. However, erythromycin-resistant strains of *S. aureus* may also be resistant to lincomycin or clindamycin. Thus, a member of the lincomycin family should not be selected to treat erythromycin-resistant staphylococcal infections unless in vitro testing indicates that it is effective against the organism. Lincomycin or clindamycin should not be administered with erythromycin because there is competition for the same protein-binding site.

Food may interfere with the oral absorption of lincomycin, but the absorption of clindamycin does not seem to be appreciably retarded by the presence of food in the stomach.

Adverse Reactions and Precautions

Few serious reactions have been observed during treatment with either lincomycin or clindamycin. When given intramuscularly, both drugs can cause pain, irritation, induration, and sterile abscesses. These reactions usually can be minimized or avoided by injecting the drug deep into the muscle. Hypotension also has occurred after intramuscular injection of lincomycin. Intravenous administration of the drugs may cause thrombophlebitis, particularly with prolonged use of indwelling catheters. Rapid intravenous injection of lincomycin has resulted in cardiac arrest.

Minor gastrointestinal disturbances such as nausea, vomiting, and abdominal cramps may occur following administration of either drug. A persistent and occasionally severe diarrhea, sometimes tainted with blood or mucus and pus, has been observed during lincomycin therapy and, less frequently, with clindamycin. The diarrhea is more common after oral administration than after parenteral use, and can result in acute colitis. These agents should be discontinued if severe diarrhea occurs.

Leukopenia (chiefly neutropenia) has been reported rarely following administration of both drugs. In addition, agranulocytosis and thrombocytopenic purpura have been associated with use of lincomycin, and eosinophilia with use of clindamycin. These effects are reversible following withdrawal of the drug.

Both agents rarely cause hypersensitivity reactions. These reactions, which are generally mild, most often consist of pruritus, rash, and urticaria. However, angioedema, exfoliative dermatitis, anaphylactic reactions, and serum sickness have resulted from lincomycin therapy.

Some patients may experience dizziness, headache, generalized myalgia, proctitis, and vaginitis after lincomycin therapy. Superinfections due to nonsusceptible organisms have occurred with both drugs, especially when the duration of therapy exceeded ten days.

The safety of these drugs during pregnancy has not been established, although several hundred women have been given lincomycin with no reported harm to mother or fetus.

Since significant amounts of unchanged lincomycin and clindamycin are excreted in the urine, serum levels in patients with severe renal impairment may be double or triple those seen in patients with normal kidney function who are receiving the same dosage. Accordingly, if these agents are given to patients with impaired renal function, serum levels should be determined at frequent intervals, if possible, and the dosage reduced so that the levels are comparable to those observed in patients with normal kidney function (an average of 1 to 2 μg/ml after oral administration, 4 to 10 μg/ml after intramuscular administration, and 8 to 20 μg/ml after intravenous administration). Transitory changes in many liver function tests have occurred after administration of these drugs, and lincomycin has caused jaundice.

INDIVIDUAL EVALUATIONS

LINCOMYCIN HYDROCHLORIDE MONOHYDRATE [Lincocin]

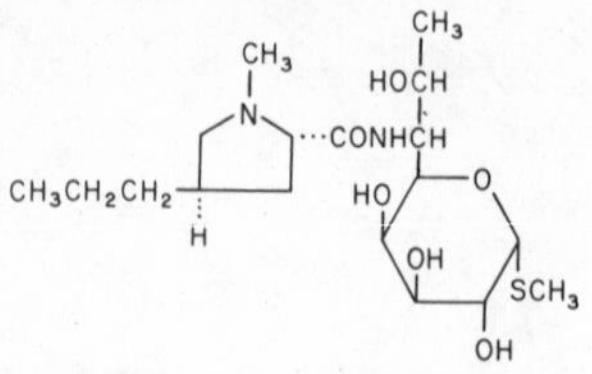

CH_3 HOCH CH_3 N ···CONHCH $CH_3CH_2CH_2$ H HO O OH SCH_3 OH

The spectrum of activity of lincomycin is similar to that of erythromycin. This antibacterial agent is primarily used to treat infections caused by organisms that are resistant to the penicillins and erythromycin but are susceptible to this agent, or in patients who cannot tolerate other antibacterial agents.

For specific uses, adverse reactions, and precautions, see the Introductory Statement.

USUAL DOSAGE.—

Oral: Adults, 500 mg three or four times daily; *children and infants over 1 month of age,* 30 to 60 mg/kg of body weight daily in three or four divided doses.

Intramuscular: Adults, 600 mg every 12 hours; *children and infants over 1 month of age,* 10 mg/kg of body weight every 12 hours. The dose may be administered more frequently in severe infections.

Intravenous: Adults, 600 mg every 8 to 12 hours; *children and infants over 1 month of age,* 10 to 20 mg/kg of body weight daily in two or three divided doses. The solution is added to 0.9% sodium chloride injection or 5% dextrose injection and the preparation is infused slowly.

PREPARATIONS.—(Concentrations expressed in terms of the base.)

Lincocin (Upjohn).

Oral: Capsules 250 and 500 mg; syrup 250 mg/5 ml.

Injection: Solution 300 mg/ml in 2, 3.34 (contains 1 g of the base), 6.67 (contains 2 g of the base), and 10 ml containers.

CLINDAMYCIN PHOSPHATE [Cleocin Phosphate]

CLINDAMYCIN HYDROCHLORIDE HYDRATE [Cleocin Hydrochloride]

CLINDAMYCIN PALMITATE [Cleocin Palmitate]

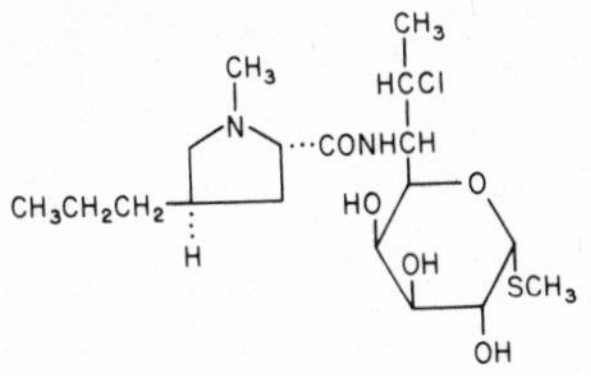

Clindamycin is a semisynthetic derivative of lincomycin and has the same indications as the parent compound. It may be better absorbed and more potent, and may produce fewer adverse effects than lincomycin. For specific uses, adverse reactions, and precautions, see the Introductory Statement.

USUAL DOSAGE.—

Clindamycin Hydrochloride Hydrate, Clindamycin Palmitate:

Oral: Adults, for mild to moderate infections, 150 to 300 mg every six hours; for severe infections, 300 to 450 mg every six hours. *Children and infants over 1 month of age*, for mild to moderate infections, 8 to 16 mg/kg of body weight daily in three or four divided doses; for severe infections, 16 to 20 mg/kg daily in three or four divided doses.

Clindamycin Phosphate:

Intramuscular: Adults, for mild infections, 600 mg daily in two divided doses; for moderate to severe infections, 600 mg to 2.4 g daily in two, three, or four divided doses. Intramuscular injection of more than 600 mg at a single site is not recommended. *Children more than 1 month of age*, for mild infections, 10 to 15 mg/kg of body weight daily in two, three, or four divided doses; for moderate to severe infections, 15 to 30 mg/kg daily in three or four divided doses.

Intravenous: Adults, for moderately severe infections, 900 mg to 1.8 g daily given by continuous infusion or in two or three equal doses infused over a 20-minute period; for severe infections, 1.8 to 2.7 g daily; for life-threatening infections, 2.7 to 4.8 g given by continuous infusion or in three or four divided doses infused over a one-hour period. Administration of more than 1.2 g in a single infusion is not recommended. *Children more than 1 month of age*, for moderately severe infections, 15 to 25 mg/kg of body weight daily given by continuous infusion over a 20-minute period; for severe infections, 25 to 40 mg/kg daily (minimum, 300 mg).

PREPARATIONS.—(Concentrations expressed in terms of the base.)

Clindamycin Hydrochloride Hydrate:

Cleocin Hydrochloride (Upjohn). *Oral:* Capsules 75 and 150 mg.

Clindamycin Palmitate:

Cleocin Palmitate (Upjohn). *Oral:* Granules for suspension 75 mg/5 ml.

Clindamycin Phosphate:

Cleocin Phosphate (Upjohn). *Injection:* Solution 150 mg/ml in 2 and 10 ml containers.

Chapter 52

POLYMYXINS

This group of related polypeptides is produced by strains of *Bacillus polymyxa.* The two antibacterial agents of this group used clinically are polymyxin B and colistin (polymyxin E); the latter compound is produced by *B. polymyxa* var. *colistinus.*

Colistin and polymyxin B have similar in vitro spectra. They are active against a number of gram-negative organisms, the most prominent of which are *Pseudomonas, Escherichia, Klebsiella, Enterobacter, Salmonella, Shigella,* and some *Haemophilus* species. Both drugs exert a bactericidal action in vitro at concentrations attainable in plasma or urine with therapeutic doses. Most species of *Proteus* and *Neisseria* are resistant in vitro at these same levels. *Brucella* is only moderately affected. Colistin and polymyxin B are ineffective against gram-positive bacteria.

The clinical indications for colistin and polymyxin B are similar. They are most commonly used in treating infections caused by strains of *Pseudomonas,* particularly *P. aeruginosa,* and generally should be reserved for use in patients with refractory infections produced by these bacteria, especially individuals with acute bacterial enteritis, urinary tract infections, bacteremia, peritonitis, pneumonia, and meningitis. Colistin and polymyxin B also have been used with success in treating infections caused by strains of *Escherichia, Enterobacter,* and *Klebsiella.* The clinical effectiveness of these agents in infections produced by species of *Salmonella, Shigella, Haemophilus, Brucella,* and some other gram-negative bacilli is not yet proved.

Since bacteria can slowly develop varying degrees of resistance to colistin and polymyxin B, it is advisable to restrict use of these drugs to infections that are known to be refractory to other antibiotics. Cross resistance between colistin and polymyxin B usually is complete.

Colistin is available as the sulfate [Coly-Mycin S] in an oral preparation used only for bacterial enteritis in infants and children, and as the sodium sulfomethyl derivative, colistimethate sodium [Coly-Mycin M], which is administered parenterally. Polymyxin B is available as the sulfate [Aerosporin] in oral, parenteral, and topical preparations. However, if intramuscular administration is required, colistimethate sodium should be used because irritation and severe pain are associated with administration of polymyxin B by this route.

Colistin and polymyxin B are excreted principally by the kidneys. After intramuscular injection of a single dose of colistimethate sodium, peak excretion levels appear in the urine within two hours and 40% to 80% of the dose is recovered within eight hours. Renal excretion of polymyxin B is slower; very little appears in the urine within the first 12 hours after a single dose.

Adverse Reactions and Precautions

The incidence and severity of adverse reactions produced by colistin and polymyxin B are essentially the same except that colistimethate sodium, in contrast to polymyxin B sulfate, is practically nonirritating to tissue.

Dizziness, ataxia, slurred speech, and blurred vision have been observed following administration of these drugs. Muscular weakness, paresis, or complete paralysis due to neuromuscular blockade also have been reported. This effect has resulted in delayed recovery from anesthesia which has progressed to respiratory arrest and death. The blockade produced is not easily reversed and is resistant to neostigmine. The intravenous injection of calcium may be of benefit. Transient circumoral paresthesias and numbness of the extremities are fairly common but disappear as the drug is excreted. These complications should be kept in mind when colistin or polymyxin B is given to patients with neuromuscular disease (eg, myasthenia gravis); those receiving a neuromuscular blocking drug or an anesthetic with a prominent muscle relaxing component (eg, ether), parenterally administered magnesium, quinidine, or quinine; or those receiving potentially neurotoxic drugs (eg, kanamycin [Kantrex]).

Colistin and polymyxin B are nephrotoxic. This is usually manifested as oliguria and an increased blood urea nitrogen (BUN) or serum creatinine level. These drugs, therefore, must be used cautiously and in reduced doses in patients with impaired renal function because they are primarily excreted by the kidneys. The degree of impairment should be estimated with creatinine clearance determinations before the drugs are given, and the dosage reduced accordingly; renal function tests should be performed periodically during treatment.

INDIVIDUAL EVALUATIONS

COLISTIMETHATE SODIUM [Coly-Mycin M]

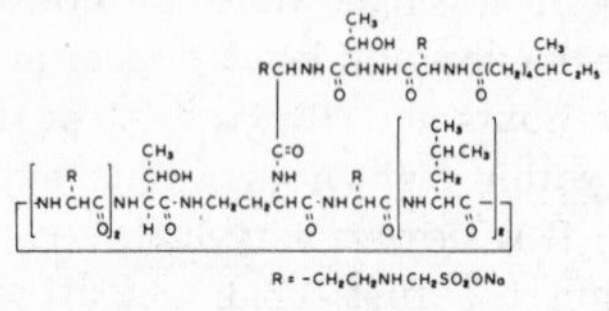

This agent is the sodium salt of the sulfomethyl derivative of colistin. Its antibacterial spectrum includes many gram-negative bacilli (see the Introductory Statement). It is not active against gram-positive bacteria. Colistimethate is useful for treating most infections caused by *Pseudomonas aeruginosa* (eg, bacteremia, meningitis, peritonitis, and, especially, urinary tract infections). However, since the development of gentamicin and carbenicillin, it is no longer the drug of choice for serious *Pseudomonas* infection. Bacterial resistance to this drug and cross resistance to polymyxin B can develop in vitro and perhaps in vivo as well; therefore, colistimethate should be reserved for susceptible infections that do not respond to other antibiotics.

The in vitro antibacterial potency of colistimethate is one-third to one-fifth that of polymyxin B on a weight basis. Therapeutic concentrations do not appear in the cerebrospinal fluid following intramuscular injection. Intestinal infections may not respond to intramuscular administration. Therefore, colistin sulfate, which is given orally, is preferred for these infections.

Colistimethate sodium may adversely affect the kidneys and the central nervous system. Elevated blood urea nitrogen levels, usually reversible, have been reported in a few infants and adults. Symptoms of uremia and acute renal failure as a result of overdosage in patients with impaired renal function also have been observed. (See the Introductory Statement.)

Fever, a few possible cases of neutropenia and granulocytopenia, visual disturbances, dysphonia, vertigo, dizziness, gastrointestinal disturbances, dermatoses, partial deafness, and pain at the site of injection have been reported.

Secondary infections caused by nonsusceptible bacteria may occur during therapy.

Cross sensitivity between colistimethate sodium and polymyxin B has been reported.

In patients with acute renal failure or chronic nephropathies, the dosage of colistimethate must be adjusted according to the degree of impairment of renal function. Because of their possible inadequate renal reserves, the dosage for infants and elderly patients should be carefully regulated. Blood urea nitrogen or serum creatinine levels should be determined periodically. Close attention also should be given to the urinary output, since the onset of oliguria may be a sign of renal damage.

USUAL DOSAGE.—*Intramuscular, Intravenous: Adults and children,* 2.5 to 5 mg/kg of body weight daily in divided doses every eight hours. The total daily dose should not exceed 300 mg.

PREPARATIONS.—Coly-Mycin M Parenteral (Warner-Chilcott). *Injection:* Powder equivalent to 20 or 150 mg colistin base.

COLISTIN SULFATE [Coly-Mycin S]

Colistin sulfate is the water-soluble salt of the

polypeptide antibiotic, colistin. Its in vitro antibacterial potency is approximately equivalent to that of polymyxin B. It is only slightly absorbed from the gastrointestinal tract and, therefore, is used orally in infants and children for the treatment of diarrhea caused by susceptible gram-negative bacilli (see the Introductory Statement for the bacterial spectrum). However, it is suggested that the use of colistin sulfate be restricted to treatment of bacterial enteritis caused by *Escherichia coli* and other susceptible species and only when these species are shown to be refractory to other antimicrobial agents. When there is danger of systemic involvement in severe enteritis, concomitant parenteral therapy should be considered.

Colistin, like polymyxin B sulfate, may be both nephrotoxic and neurotoxic when large doses are given. However, the drug is poorly absorbed from the gastrointestinal tract, and no toxic reactions resulting from usual oral doses have yet been reported. Frequent observations of renal function should be made when this drug is used in infants and children with chronic renal failure.

USUAL DOSAGE.—*Oral: Infants and children*, 3 to 5 mg/kg of body weight daily in three divided doses.

PREPARATIONS.—Coly-Mycin S (Warner-Chilcott). *Oral:* Powder 300 mg, providing the equivalent of 25 mg of colistin base/5 ml when suspended in 37 ml of distilled water.

POLYMYXIN B SULFATE [Aerosporin]

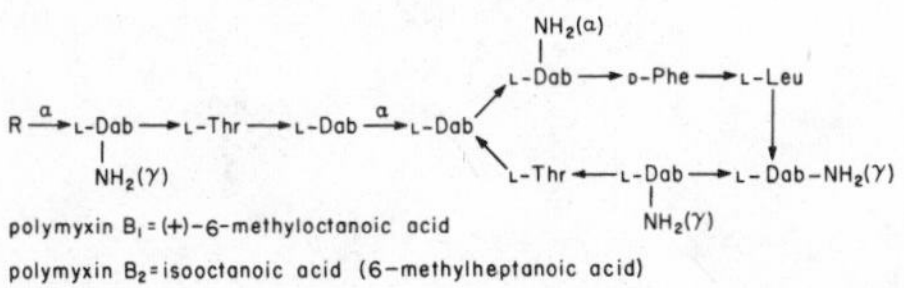

Polymyxin B sulfate is active against many gram-negative bacilli (see the Introductory Statement for the general antibacterial spectrum). It is primarily of value in treating infections caused by *Pseudomonas* species, especially meningitis; however, polymyxin B should be reserved for treatment of susceptible infections that do not respond to other antibiotics. It can be administered by all routes, including intrathecal. Since it is irritating when injected intramuscularly, colistimethate sodium should be given instead when this route is used.

Caution is mandatory when polymyxin is used in patients with impaired renal function, since the drug is nephrotoxic. Parenteral doses that produce blood levels of 1 to 2 μg/ml may cause flushing of the face and dizziness that may progress to ataxia, drowsiness, and paresthesias. Neuromuscular blockade also has been reported following therapeutic doses (see the Introductory Statement).

USUAL DOSAGE.—

Oral: Adults and older children, 75 to 100 mg four times daily. *Children 2 to 5 years of age*, 50 to 75 mg three times daily; *under 2 years*, 25 to 50 mg three times daily (see also table, back cover).

Intramuscular: Adults and children, 1.5 to 2.5 mg/kg of body weight daily divided into three equal doses. The total daily dose should not exceed 200 mg.

Intravenous: Adults and children, 2.5 mg/kg of body weight daily in one or two equally divided doses (total daily dose should not exceed 200 mg); 200 to 500 ml of 5% dextrose injection may be used as a vehicle.

Intrathecal: Adults and older children, 5 mg daily for three to four days, then 5 mg every other day. *Children under 2 years of age*, 2 mg daily for three to four days, then 1 mg daily or 2.5 mg every other day until results of bacterial cultures of cerebrospinal fluid become negative.

Inhalation: Adults and children, 1 to 2 ml of solution containing 1 to 10 mg/ml inhaled four to six times daily; total daily dosage should not exceed an amount equivalent to 2.5 mg/kg of body weight daily.

Topical: Used as required in concentrations of 0.1% to 0.25%.

PREPARATIONS.—

Aerosporin (Burroughs Wellcome). *Injection:* Powder 500,000 units (equivalent to polymyxin standard 50 mg).

Polymyxin B Sulfate (Pfizer).

Oral: Tablets (soluble) 250,000 units (equivalent to polymyxin standard 25 mg).

Injection: Powder 500,000 units (equivalent to polymyxin standard 50 mg).

MIXTURES

A number of mixtures contain polymyxin B in combination with other antibiotics, most frequently neomycin or bacitracin. Some mixtures contain all three antibacterial agents. The proposed rationale for these topical mixtures is that they have a wide antibacterial spectrum that includes both gram-positive and gram-negative organisms. A few mixtures also contain an adrenal corticosteroid. However, there is no evidence that the addition of a corticosteroid enhances the efficacy of these combinations.

Topical antibiotic mixtures are intended to be used on the skin and mucous membranes. Thus, liquid and ointment formulations are available for application to intact and abraded skin, or in the eye or ear.

Fixed-ratio mixtures for topical use that contain polymyxin B have reasonable therapeutic value but also have several disadvantages. Most important, it is possible for sufficient amounts of the drug to be absorbed from abraded skin or mucous membrane sites to cause systemic toxicity. Moreover, these antibiotics are capable of causing hypersensitization following topical application. There is no reasonable rationale for the use of fixed-ratio mixtures by any route other than topical.

Listed below are examples of antibacterial mixtures containing polymyxin B.

Biotres Ointment (Central): Each gram of ointment contains polymyxin B sulfate 4,000 units, zinc bacitracin 200 units, and neomycin sulfate equivalent to neomycin 3 mg.

Cortisporin Ointment (Burroughs Wellcome): Each gram of ointment contains polymyxin B sulfate 5,000 units, zinc bacitracin 400 units, neomycin sulfate equivalent to neomycin 3.5 mg, and hydrocortisone 10 mg.

Neo-Polycin (Dow): Each gram of ointment contains polymyxin B sulfate 8,000 units, zinc bacitracin 400 units, and neomycin sulfate equivalent to neomycin 3 mg.

Neosporin Ointment (Burroughs Wellcome): Each gram of ointment contains polymyxin B sulfate 5,000 units, zinc bacitracin 400 units, and neomycin sulfate equivalent to neomycin 3.5 mg.

Neosporin G.U. Irrigant (Burroughs Wellcome): Each milliliter of solution contains polymyxin B sulfate 200,000 units and neomycin sulfate equivalent to neomycin 40 mg.

Polycidin-HC Otic Drops (Smith, Miller & Patch): Each milliliter of solution contains polymyxin B sulfate 10,000 units, neomycin sulfate equivalent to neomycin 3.5 mg and hydrocortisone 10 mg.

Polysporin Ointment (Burroughs Wellcome): Each gram of ointment contains polymyxin B sulfate 10,000 units and zinc bacitracin 500 units.

Chapter 53

TETRACYCLINES

The tetracyclines are broad spectrum antibacterial agents produced by several species of *Streptomyces;* some of the drugs are semisynthetic chemical modifications of the material elaborated by the microorganism. They are largely bacteriostatic in their action. This group of antibiotics is composed of tetracycline and its hydrochloride salt [Achromycin, Bristacycline, Panmycin, Steclin, Sumycin, Tetracyn], tetracycline phosphate complex [Tetrex], tetracycline buffered with sodium hexametaphosphate [Tetrex-S] or potassium metaphosphate [Panmycin KM, Sumycin], chlortetracycline [Aureomycin], demeclocycline [Declomycin], doxycycline [Vibramycin], methacycline [Rondomycin], minocycline [Minocin], oxytetracycline [Terramycin], and rolitetracycline [Syntetrin].

Although the antibacterial spectra of the tetracyclines are essentially the same, this is not true in all instances. They are drugs of choice in the treatment of infections caused by *Haemophilus ducreyi, Donovania granulomatis, Vibrio comma, V. fetus, Borrelia recurrentis,* and the rickettsiae. They also are primary agents for treating lymphogranuloma venereum, trachoma, inclusion conjunctivitis, and psittacosis. In addition, these drugs may be effective against infections caused by *Mycoplasma pneumoniae* (PPLO), *Streptomyces anaerobius, Bacillus anthracis, Listeria monocytogenes, Clostridium welchii, Francisella tularensis, Pasteurella pestis, Fusobacterium fusiforme, Bacteroides,* and indole-producing strains of *Proteus* (most *Proteus* and *Pseudomonas* are resistant). Respiratory infections and meningitis caused by *Haemophilus influenzae,* as well as intestinal amebiasis, may respond to the tetracyclines. (See also Chapter 62, Amebicides.)

Infections caused by pneumococci can be treated with the tetracyclines when sensitivity tests indicate the presence of a susceptible strain. Similarly, these drugs may be used when penicillin cannot be given to patients with gonococcal, meningococcal, or spirochetal infections. Tetracyclines also are useful in treating mixed bacterial sinusitis. Many infections caused by *Escherichia coli* respond to the tetracyclines, but occasionally resistant strains emerge rapidly. The tetracyclines may be of value in certain malabsorption syndromes such as Whipple's disease. These agents are thought to be useful in acne because they decrease the concentration of free fatty acids in sebum secreted to the skin surface; tetracycline is the most frequently used agent. This treatment is suppressive rather than curative and should be reserved for those patients with inflammatory lesions.

Cross resistance among the tetracyclines usually is complete; organisms resistant to one of these antibiotics frequently will be resistant to all of them with the exception of tetracycline-resistant staphylococci which can be sensitive to minocycline in vitro (this remains to be demonstrated clinically). Thus, in most cases it is necessary to use only one tetracycline in antibiotic susceptibility testing.

Treatment with the tetracyclines, particularly prolonged treatment, may result in replacement of normal oral and intestinal flora by resistant strains of *Staphylococcus aureus* or other species, especially *Pseudomonas, Klebsiella, Enterobacter, Proteus, and Candida.*

The tetracyclines usually are administered orally and are readily but incompletely absorbed when given by this route (doxycycline and minocycline are more completely absorbed than other agents in this group). Since they form insoluble complexes with calcium, magnesium, iron, and aluminum salts, the presence of food, milk and milk products, or cathartics and antacids containing these salts results in decreased and erratic intestinal absorption.

Intravenous and intramuscular preparations are used in patients unable to take medication orally, but intramuscular injection can be extremely painful. Ointments applied topically are of little or no value (except for some ocular infections) and often produce hypersensitivity. Therefore, topical use of these agents is not recommended.

The rates of absorption and development of maximal blood concentrations, as well as duration of action, vary among the tetracyclines. These drugs are bound to plasma proteins but the chemical nature of a tetracycline is more important than the extent of protein binding in determining the duration of its serum half-life. Peak serum levels are generally reached in two to four hours following oral administration. Approximate mean serum half-lives for individual agents are as follows: chlortetracycline, 5.5 hours; tetracycline, 8.5 hours; oxytetracycline, 9.5 hours; methacycline, 15 hours; demeclocycline, 17 hours; minocycline, 17.5 hours; and doxycycline, 19.5 hours.

The tetracyclines are distributed in significant amounts throughout all tissues of the body except adipose tissue and readily cross the placenta. They localize in rapidly growing or metabolizing or calcium-containing structures (eg, liver, bone, teeth, neoplastic tissue).

The tetracyclines are metabolized to varying degrees. All are excreted in the bile where there is considerable reabsorptive cycling from the gastrointestinal tract. Small amounts of these drugs are excreted in the feces, but the major route of excretion for most tetracyclines is through the kidneys. (Minocycline is excreted unchanged in the urine to the extent of only about 10%, whereas 20% to 30% of the unchanged drug is excreted in the feces.)

The tetracyclines fluoresce bright yellow under ultraviolet radiation of 3,600 Angstrom units. This fluorescence may be detected in all tissues except the brain within 24 hours following a loading dose of 3 or 4 g. Thereafter, fluorescence rapidly disappears, except from bone and neoplastic tissue, where it remains visible for several weeks. Tetracycline fluorescence has been used experimentally to measure the rate of formation of urinary calculi and cortical bone, and clinically to help locate and identify neoplastic tumors.

The tetracyclines inhibit the metabolism of microbial cells by blocking the attachment of aminoacyl transfer RNA to ribosomes, which interferes with protein synthesis.

Adverse Reactions and Precautions

All tetracyclines are of relatively low toxicity at recommended dosage levels. Anorexia, pyrosis, nausea, vomiting, flatulence, and diarrhea occur in about 10% of patients receiving 2 g or more daily (this percentage is somewhat higher with prolonged administration). Dizziness is sometimes observed, especially with minocycline [Minocin]; this is usually transient but may last one or two days. Other undesirable reactions include dryness of the mouth; hoarseness; stomatitis, including vesiculopapular oral lesions; glossitis, including black hairy tongue; pharyngitis; dysphagia; enterocolitis; proctitis; and inflammatory lesions (candidal overgrowth) of the vulvovaginal and perianal regions. Most of these effects are related to suppression of normal enteric flora with overgrowth of other organisms. Superinfections, including severe staphylococcal enterocolitis, have occurred during oral and, rarely, during intravenous or intramuscular administration. If diarrhea is observed in a patient receiving a tetracycline, it is important to determine whether it is nonspecific or is caused by overgrowth of *Staphylococcus aureus*. The latter condition can be life-threatening.

Hypersensitivity reactions, which occur uncommonly, include urticaria, angioedema, exfoliative dermatitis, idiopathic nonthrombocytopenic purpura, anaphylactic shock, and exacerbation of systemic lupus erythematosus. Photosensitivity reactions also have been noted, especially with demeclocycline [Declomycin]. As yet, no photosensitivity reactions have been reported for minocycline. Cross sensitization among the tetracyclines has been observed, particularly when they are used topically.

Blood dyscrasias, including neutropenia and hemolytic anemia, have occurred following administration of the tetracyclines, but they are rare. Because these drugs are irritating when given intravenously, they can cause thrombophlebitis.

Pseudotumor cerebri (increased intracranial pressure) has been observed in infants receiving the tetracyclines and, on rare occasions, has been reported in adults as well. This condition disappears within a few hours after therapy is discontinued.

The antianabolic action of these drugs causes a negative nitrogen and riboflavin balance that may result in elevated blood levels of nonprotein nitrogen (doxycycline does not appear to increase blood urea nitrogen levels) and increased excretion of urinary nitrogen. Ordinarily, this poses no problem in patients with adequate renal function and is most likely to occur in individuals receiving diuretics concomitantly. In patients with significant kidney impairment, however, higher serum levels of tetracycline can cause varying degrees of azotemia, hyperphosphatemia, hyperkalemia, and acidosis. (Doxycycline does not accumulate as readily in the serum as the other tetracyclines and, therefore, may not require reduced dosage levels in patients with impaired renal function.) Increasing levels of blood urea nitrogen (BUN) may not accurately reflect changes in renal function; the serum creatinine level provides a more reliable index.

Hepatotoxicity, sometimes associated with pancreatitis, occasionally is observed during tetracycline therapy. This reaction commonly is produced by prolonged oral or parenteral use of large doses, but it may occur when tetracyclines are used for short periods in the presence of renal or hepatic insufficiency or when other potentially hepatotoxic agents are administered concomitantly. This serious reaction is observed most often in pregnant or postpartum patients with pyelonephritis or other renal disease and has caused a number of deaths.

Deposition of the tetracyclines in the teeth and bones of fetuses, infants, and young children has been associated with yellowing of the teeth, enamel defects, and slowing of bone growth. The latter effect is temporary if the drug is not given for too long a period. However, the deposition of tetracycline in teeth during calcification may result in permanent staining. The staining may occur in primary dentition in the fetus as a result of transplacental transfer of tetracycline taken by the mother. This effect appears to be dose-related, but the exact amount of tetracycline that can be given before such staining occurs is not known. Fluorescence of the nails may be demonstrable after prolonged therapy; rarely, discoloration and onycholysis can be seen.

Degradation products of tetracycline may affect renal tubular function and damage the kidneys. The symptoms produced resemble acute Fanconi syndrome (nausea, vomiting, albuminuria, glycosuria, aminoaciduria, hypophosphatemia, hypokalemia, acidosis). The condition is usually reversed slowly after withdrawal of the tetracycline, although fatalities have been reported. This effect has occurred in patients given tetracycline hydrochloride capsules containing citric acid that were stored beyond their expiration date under conditions of increased heat and humidity. As with other dated medication, the expiration dates should be carefully noted and heeded.

When it is essential to administer any of the tetracyclines intravenously in a daily dose of more than 1 g, the dose must be divided and given well-diluted over a period of several hours. Blood levels should not exceed 15 μg/ml.

Since the tetracyclines delay blood coagulation, the effects of coumarin anticoagulants may be potentiated when the two agents are used concomitantly. This anticoagulant effect has been attributed to an alteration in the physiochemical properties of certain lipoproteins. Interference with vitamin K synthesis in the intestinal tract, particularly in elderly patients with marginal hepatic function, also may contribute to this effect.

INDIVIDUAL EVALUATIONS

CHLORTETRACYCLINE HYDROCHLORIDE
[Aureomycin]

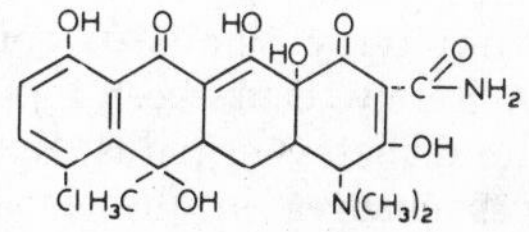

This tetracycline was the first introduced and, therefore, in many respects is regarded as the prototype for this group of drugs. It is comparable in effectiveness to the other tetracyclines and produces similar adverse reactions (see the Introductory Statement). It should not be used topically except for ocular infections.

USUAL DOSAGE.—

Oral: Adults, 1 g daily in four divided doses. In severe illness, 2 g daily may be used. *Children*, 25 to 50 mg/kg of body weight daily in four doses.

Intravenous: Adults, 500 mg every 12 hours; the dose may be given every six hours in severe infections. *Children*, 10 to 15 mg/kg of body weight daily.

Topical: This route generally should not be used because of the danger of hypersensitization. The manufacturer's suggested dosage is: *Adults and children*, a small amount of ointment applied up to several times daily or as needed or as directed by the physician.

Topical (ophthalmic): See Chapter 71, Anti-infective and Anti-inflammatory Agents Used in Ophthalmology.

PREPARATIONS.—

Aureomycin (Lederle).

Oral: Capsules 250 mg.

Injection: Powder 500 mg.

Topical: Ointment 3% in ½ and 1 oz containers; ointment (ophthalmic) 1% in 1/8 oz containers.

DEMECLOCYCLINE [Declomycin]
DEMECLOCYCLINE HYDROCHLORIDE [Declomycin Hydrochloride]

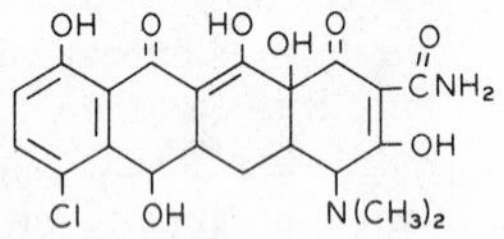

The indications and degree of effectiveness of demeclocycline are comparable to those of the other tetracyclines (see the Introductory Statement).

It may produce the same adverse reactions as the other tetracyclines; however, photosensitivity reactions occur more frequently. Rarely, it has been reported to cause nephrogenic diabetes insipidus; this may be due to chemical changes in the antibiotic during storage.

USUAL DOSAGE.—*Oral: Adults*, 600 mg daily in two or four divided doses. If unusually high blood concentrations are necessary, the intravenous form of one of the other tetracyclines should be used (see the Introductory Statement). *Infants and children*, 6 to 12 mg/kg of body weight daily in two or four divided doses; in severe infections, the dose may be doubled for the first few days of therapy.

PREPARATIONS.—(Strengths expressed in terms of the hydrochloride.)

Declomycin [base] (Lederle). *Oral:* Drops (pediatric) 60 mg/ml; syrup 75 mg/5 ml.

Declomycin [hydrochloride] (Lederle). *Oral:* Capsules 150 mg; tablets 75, 150, and 300 mg.

DOXYCYCLINE HYCLATE [Vibramycin Hyclate]

DOXYCYCLINE MONOHYDRATE [Vibramycin Monohydrate]

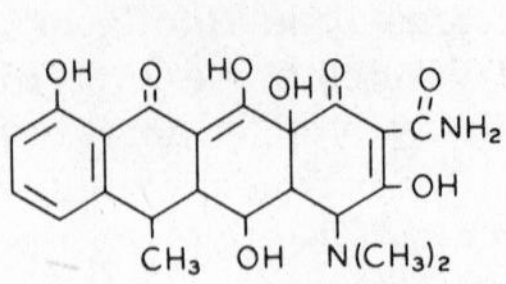

The indications and degree of effectiveness of doxycycline are comparable to those of the other tetracyclines. It is more completely absorbed and, like demeclocycline and minocycline, is more slowly excreted than most other tetracyclines; as a result, smaller and less frequent doses are both an advantage and a necessity. The serum half-life of doxycycline (approximately 19 to 20 hours) is essentially the same for patients with normal or impaired renal function. Therefore, this drug may be safe for use in individuals with decreased renal function.

The adverse reactions are similar to those produced by the other tetracyclines (see the Introductory Statement). Untoward effects reported rarely include allergic reactions, asthenia, and dysuria. It has a somewhat greater tendency to cause untoward gastrointestinal symptoms than other tetracyclines.

USUAL DOSAGE.—*Oral: Adults and children weighing 45 kg or more*, 200 mg on the first day of treatment (100 mg every 12 hours); the maintenance dose is 100 mg daily. For severe infections, the maintenance dose is 100 mg every 12 hours. *Children weighing less than 45 kg*, 4.4 mg/kg of body weight in two divided doses on the first day, followed by 2.2 mg/kg given as a single dose on subsequent days.

PREPARATIONS.—(Strengths expressed in terms of the base.)

Vibramycin Hyclate (Pfizer). *Oral:* Capsules 50 and 100 mg.

Vibramycin Monohydrate (Pfizer). *Oral:* Powder for suspension 25 mg/5 ml.

METHACYCLINE HYDROCHLORIDE [Rondomycin]

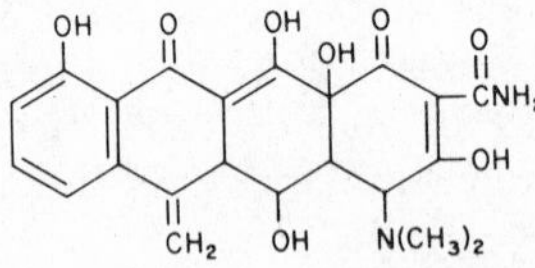

This agent is produced synthetically from oxytetracycline. The indications, antibacterial spectrum, and degree of effectiveness of methacycline are similar to those of the other tetracyclines (see the Introductory Statement).

Methacycline causes the same untoward reactions as the other tetracyclines. Photosensitivity reactions are somewhat less likely to occur than with other drugs in this group.

USUAL DOSAGE.—*Oral: Adults*, 600 mg daily in two or four divided doses; *children*, 6.5 to 13 mg/kg of body weight daily in two or four divided doses.

PREPARATIONS.—Rondomycin (Wallace). *Oral:* Capsules 150 and 300 mg; syrup 75 mg/5 ml.

MINOCYCLINE HYDROCHLORIDE
[Minocin]

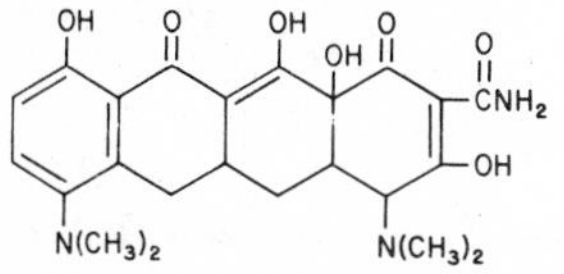

This semisynthetic tetracycline derivative has an antibacterial spectrum and activity comparable to the other agents in this group. Although in vitro activity against certain strains of staphylococci that are resistant to other tetracyclines exists, this effect has not been demonstrated clinically. There is evidence that minocycline may be effective prophylactically against meningococcal infections.

Minocycline appears to be more completely metabolized in the body than other tetracyclines. Therefore, unchanged drug does not accumulate to the same extent as most of the other tetracyclines in patients with renal failure. Nevertheless, if renal impairment exists, even usual oral doses may lead to excessive systemic accumulation of the drug and possible hepatic toxicity. Under such conditions, lower than usual doses are indicated and, if therapy is prolonged, serum level determinations of the drug should be conducted.

The indications, degree of effectiveness, and untoward effects are similar to those of the other tetracyclines (see the Introductory Statement). In addition, this drug may cause transient dizziness more frequently. As yet, photosensitivity reactions have not been reported with minocycline. The use of compounds containing aluminum, magnesium, or calcium will impair absorption.

USUAL DOSAGE.—*Oral: Adults and children over 12 years of age*, 200 mg initially; maintenance dose, 100 mg every 12 hours.

PREPARATIONS.—Minocin (Lederle). *Oral:* Capsules 100 mg.

OXYTETRACYCLINE [Terramycin]
OXYTETRACYCLINE CALCIUM
[Terramycin Calcium]
OXYTETRACYCLINE HYDROCHLORIDE
[Terramycin Hydrochloride]

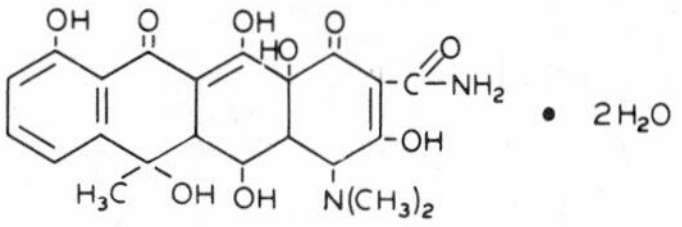

This agent has a spectrum of activity similar to that of the other tetracyclines and may produce similar adverse reactions (see the Introductory Statement).

USUAL DOSAGE.—

Oral (base, calcium, hydrochloride): *Adults*, 1 g daily in divided doses; a total of 2 to 4 g may be given to severely ill patients. *Children*, 25 to 50 mg/kg of body weight daily in four divided doses.

Intramuscular (base): *Adults*, 200 to 400 mg in two or three divided doses depending upon the severity of illness; *children*, 15 to 25 mg/kg of body weight daily in two or three divided doses. Intramuscular injection can be extremely painful.

Intravenous (hydrochloride): *Adults*, 500 mg to 1 g daily in two doses (250 mg dissolved in 10 ml of sterile water for injection and then diluted to a final volume of 100 ml with 5% dextrose or sodium chloride injection); *children*, 10 to 20 mg/kg of body weight daily in two divided doses; drug is diluted as described for adults.

PREPARATIONS.—(Strengths expressed in terms of the base.)

Oxytetracycline:

Terramycin [base] (Pfizer).

Injection: Solution (intramuscular) 50 mg/ml in 2 and 10 ml containers and 125 mg/ml in 2 ml containers.

Oral: Tablets 250 mg.

Oxytetracycline Calcium:

Terramycin [calcium] (Pfizer). *Oral:* Drops (pediatric) 100 mg/ml; syrup 125 mg/5 ml.

Oxytetracycline Hydrochloride:

Terramycin [hydrochloride] (Pfizer).

Oral: Capsules 125 and 250 mg.

Injection: Powder (intravenous) 250 and 500 mg.

ADDITIONAL TRADEMARKS.—**Oxytetracycline Hydrochloride:** Otetrin (Trent),

Oxy-Kesso-Tetra (McKesson), Oxy-Tetrachelle (Rachelle). Drug also marketed under generic name.

ROLITETRACYCLINE [Syntetrin]

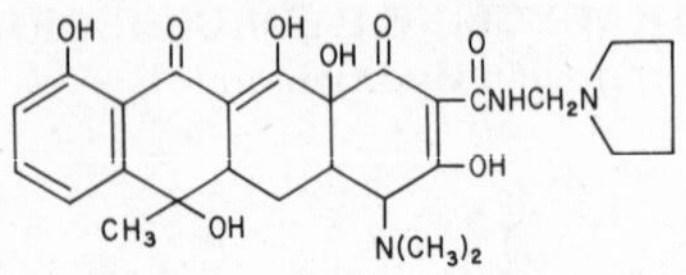

This synthetic derivative of tetracycline is more soluble over a wider range of pH than the parent compound; this facilitates its parenteral use. The indications, degree of effectiveness, and adverse reactions of rolitetracycline are identical to those of the other tetracyclines. (See the Introductory Statement.)

USUAL DOSAGE.—

Intramuscular: Adults, 150 mg every 8 to 12 hours. Doses up to 350 mg every 12 hours may be used in severe infections or to initiate therapy. *Children,* 15 to 20 mg/kg of body weight daily in one or two doses. Intramuscular injection can be extremely painful.

Intravenous: Adults, 350 to 700 mg every 12 hours. The powder may be dissolved in 5 or 10 ml of water for injection and then diluted in sodium chloride injection or dextrose injection to a final volume of 300 to 500 ml for slow infusion. *Children,* 15 to 20 mg/kg of body weight daily in one or two doses.

PREPARATIONS.—Syntetrin (Bristol). *Injection:* Powder (intramuscular) 150 and 350 mg; powder (intravenous) 700 mg.

TETRACYCLINE [Achromycin, Panmycin, Panmycin KM, Sumycin, Tetracyn, Tetrex-S]
TETRACYCLINE HYDROCHLORIDE [Achromycin, Bristacycline, Panmycin, Steclin, Sumycin, Tetracyn]
TETRACYCLINE PHOSPHATE COMPLEX [Tetrex]

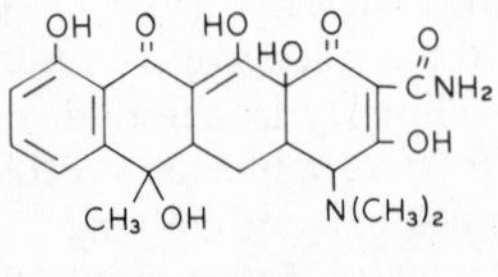

Tetracycline base, its hydrochloride salt, and tetracycline phosphate complex have essentially the same spectrum of antibacterial activity and their effectiveness is similar to that of the other tetracyclines.

Tetracycline phosphate complex is a fairly insoluble complex of sodium metaphosphate and tetracycline. Tetracycline base also is available buffered with sodium hexametaphosphate or potassium metaphosphate.

Relatively low toxicity is associated with these agents (see the Introductory Statement).

USUAL DOSAGE.—

Oral (all forms): *Adults,* 1 g daily in four equally divided doses. In severe illness, the dose may be increased to 2 g. *Children,* 25 to 50 mg/kg of body weight daily in four divided doses.

Intramuscular (hydrochloride, phosphate complex): *Adults,* 200 mg to 1 g daily in two or three divided doses; *children,* 15 to 25 mg/kg of body weight daily in two or three divided doses. *Children weighing more than 40 kg* should be given the adult dose. Intramuscular injection can be extremely painful.

Intravenous (hydrochloride): *Adults,* 500 mg twice daily at 12-hour intervals. Contents of vial should be diluted to at least 1 mg/ml using sodium chloride injection or 5% dextrose injection. *Children,* 10 to 20 mg/kg of body weight daily in two divided doses; the drug is diluted as described for adults.

PREPARATIONS.—

Tetracycline:

Achromycin (Lederle). *Oral:* Drops (pediatric) 100 mg/ml [Achromycin V]; granules for suspension 250 mg/5 ml [Achromycin V]; powder for suspension 250 mg/5 ml [Achromycin]; syrup 125 mg/5 ml [Achromycin, Achromycin V].

Panmycin (Upjohn). *Oral:* Drops (pediatric) 100 mg/ml; syrup 125 mg/5 ml.

Tetracyn (Roerig). *Oral:* Syrup 125 mg/5 ml.

ADDITIONAL TRADEMARKS.—Kesso-Tetra (McKesson), Retet-S (Reid-Provident), Robitet (Robins), T-125 (Elder), Tetrachel-S (Rachelle), TetraMAX S (Century). Drug also marketed by other manufacturers under generic name.

Tetracycline (buffered with potassium metaphosphate):

Panmycin KM (Upjohn), Sumycin (Squibb). *Oral:* Syrup 125 mg/5 ml.

Tetracycline (buffered with sodium hexametaphosphate):

Tetrex-S (Bristol). *Oral:* Drops (pediatric) 100 mg/ml; syrup 125 mg/5 ml.

ADDITIONAL TRADEMARK.—SK-Tetracycline (Smith Kline & French).

Tetracycline Hydrochloride:

Achromycin (Lederle).

Oral: Capsules 100, 250, and 500 mg [Achromycin V].

Injection: Powder (intramuscular) 100 and 250 mg; powder (intravenous) 100, 250, and 500 mg.

Bristacycline (Bristol).

Oral: Capsules 250 and 500 mg.

Injection: Powder (intravenous) 250 and 500 mg.

Panmycin (Upjohn).

Oral: Capsules 250 mg.

Injection: Powder (intramuscular) 100 mg; powder (intravenous) 250 and 500 mg.

Steclin (Squibb).

Oral: Capsules 250 mg.

Injection: Powder (intramuscular) 250 mg; powder (intravenous) 250 and 500 mg.

Sumycin (Squibb). *Oral:* Capsules 250 and 500 mg; tablets (coated) 250 and 500 mg.

Tetracyn (Roerig).

Oral: Capsules 250 and 500 mg.

Injection: Powder (intramuscular) 100 and 250 mg; powder (intravenous) 250 and 500 mg.

ADDITIONAL TRADEMARKS.—Cyclopar (Parke, Davis), Dema (USV), Kesso-Tetra (McKesson), Piracaps (Tutag), Retet (Reid-Provident), Retet-S (Reid-Provident), Robitet (Robins), Ro-Cycline (Rowell), SK-Tetracycline (Smith Kline & French), T-250 (Elder), Tetrachel (Rachelle), TetraMAX (Century). Drug also marketed by other manufacturers under generic name.

Tetracycline Phosphate Complex:

Tetrex (Bristol).

Oral: Capsules 100, 250, and 500 mg.

Injection: Powder (intramuscular) 100 and 250 mg.

MIXTURES

The use of fixed combinations of tetracyclines and other antibacterial agents (eg, novobiocin, troleandomycin) has a questionable rationale. Careful individualized adjustment of dosage often requires the administration of supplementary doses of one of the constituents, thus tending to negate the minor convenience offered by the combination product. In addition, when two agents are combined, the patient is exposed to the possible development of sensitivity to either of them.

Other types of mixtures provide a tetracycline in combination with an antifungal agent (eg, nystatin, amphotericin B) and are designed to prevent the overgrowth of intestinal fungi. Opinion is divided on whether this combined therapy is necessary for transient or mild illness in otherwise healthy patients. The precaution of prescribing an antifungal agent may have a rational basis in diabetic, debilitated, and young or elderly patients; in those receiving antineoplastic agents or adrenal corticosteroids; in those receiving relatively prolonged tetracycline therapy; and in those in whom cultures have already yielded growth of fungi. However, although the numbers of fecal fungi are reduced with oral antifungal therapy, there is no convincing evidence that the incidence of clinical infection is lower. (See also Chapter 60, Antifungal Agents.)

Several mixtures containing a tetracycline, hydrocortisone, and an antibacterial agent (polymyxin B) or a nasal decongestant (phenylephrine) are promoted for superficial skin conditions or rhinitis, respectively. These mixtures also have questionable value and should not be used because of the danger of hypersensitization. (See also Chapter 35, Adrenal Corticosteroids, and Chapter 42, Nasal Decongestants.)

AZOTREX

This product contains a tetracycline, a sulfonamide, and a urinary analgesic and is promoted for the treatment of urinary tract infections; however, its effectiveness has not been established. Since no synergistic action has been demonstrated between tetracycline and sulfamethizole, the use of either agent alone is preferred. Phenazopyridine is contraindicated in patients with renal insufficiency and hepatitis. (See the Introductory Statement and Chapter 55, Sulfonamides.)

USUAL DOSAGE.—Since this mixture appears to be of doubtful value, no dosage regimen is given. The manufacturer's suggested dosage is: *Oral: Adults,* 1 or 2 capsules four times daily. Patients with severe urinary tract infection or those who respond slowly may require larger doses. Therapy should be continued until urine specimens become sterile (usually 7 to 14 days). *Children,* no dosage has been established.

PREPARATIONS.—Azotrex (Bristol): Each capsule contains tetracycline phosphate complex equivalent to tetracycline hydrochloride 125 mg, sulfamethizole 250 mg, and phenazopyridine hydrochloride 50 mg.

MYSTECLIN-F

This mixture provides tetracycline phosphate complex in combination with the antifungal agent amphotericin B, and is designed to prevent the overgrowth of intestinal fungi. The rationale for use of this fixed-ratio combination is weak. Intestinal candidiasis does not occur frequently and there is no clinical evidence that the routine prophylactic administration of an antifungal agent reduces its incidence. If the use of an antifungal drug is indicated to treat intestinal candidiasis in a patient receiving an antibacterial agent, it is preferable to give the antibacterial and antifungal compounds separately. (See also Chapter 60, Antifungal Agents.)

USUAL DOSAGE.—This evaluation does not support a useful dosage recommendation. The manufacturer's suggested dosage, based upon the tetracycline content, is: *Oral: Adults*, 250 to 500 mg four times daily; *children*, 25 to 50 mg/kg of body weight daily in divided doses.

PREPARATIONS.—Mysteclin-F (Squibb): Each capsule contains tetracycline phosphate complex equivalent to tetracycline hydrochloride 125 or 250 mg and amphotericin B 25 or 50 mg; each milliliter of liquid (drops) contains tetracycline phosphate complex equivalent to tetracycline hydrochloride 100 mg and amphotericin B 20 mg; each 5 ml of syrup contains tetracycline phosphate complex equivalent to tetracycline hydrochloride 125 mg and amphotericin B 25 mg.

TERRA-CORTRIL

The various forms of this topical fixed-ratio combination are promoted for treatment of superficial skin conditions or infections of the eye or ear when anti-inflammatory and antibacterial effects are desired. Tetracycline ointments applied topically are of little or no value (except for some ocular infections) and often produce hypersensitivity. The addition of hydrocortisone does not enhance the antibacterial action of the preparation, nor does the inclusion of oxytetracycline provide an advantage for anti-inflammatory use over an ointment containing just the steroid. (See also Chapter 71, Anti-infective and Anti-inflammatory Agents Used in Ophthalmology, and Chapter 73, Topical Otic Preparations.)

USUAL DOSAGE.—Since this preparation is considered to have little merit, no meaningful dosage schedule can be given. The manufacturer's suggested dosage is: *Topical: Adults and children*, a small amount of ointment is applied to the affected area two to four times daily, or the area is sprayed, holding the container 15 cm from the skin for one or two seconds two to four times daily.

PREPARATIONS.—Terra-Cortril (Pfizer): Each gram of ointment contains oxytetracycline hydrochloride equivalent to oxytetracycline 30 mg and hydrocortisone 10 mg; each 85 g aerosol can contains oxytetracycline hydrochloride equivalent to oxytetracycline 300 mg, hydrocortisone 100 mg, and polymyxin B sulfate 100,000 units.

TETRACYCLINES WITH NYSTATIN

These mixtures provide a tetracycline in combination with an antifungal agent; nystatin is present to prevent the overgrowth of intestinal fungi. In most therapeutic regimens using these mixtures, the fixed combinations provide an amount of nystatin that is the minimal or less than the minimal dosage. Accordingly, it is preferable to give nystatin separately on an individual basis when combined therapy with the broad spectrum antibiotic is considered desirable. (See the introduction to the section on Mixtures, the evaluation on Mysteclin-F, and Chapter 60, Antifungal Agents.)

USUAL DOSAGE.—Because there is no convincing evidence that the prophylactic administration of a small amount of an antifungal agent protects the patient against intestinal candidiasis, no meaningful dosage for this fixed-ratio combination can be given. The manufacturers' suggested dosage, based upon the tetracycline content, is: *Oral: Adults*, 250 to 500 mg four times daily; *children*, 25 to 50 mg/kg of body weight daily in four divided doses.

PREPARATIONS.—

Achrostatin V (Lederle): Each capsule contains tetracycline hydrochloride 250 mg and nystatin 250,000 units.

Comycin (Upjohn): Each capsule contains tetracycline phosphate complex equivalent to tetracycline hydrochloride 250 mg and nystatin 250,000 units.

Declostatin (Lederle): Each capsule contains demeclocycline hydrochloride 150 mg and nystatin 250,000 units; each 5 ml of suspension contains demeclocycline equivalent to demeclocycline hydrochloride 75 mg and nystatin 125,000 units; each tablet contains demeclocycline hydrochloride 300 mg and nystatin 500,000 units.

Terrastatin (Pfizer): Each capsule contains

oxytetracycline 250 mg and nystatin 250,000 units; each 5 ml of suspension contains oxytetracycline 125 mg and nystatin 125,000 units.

Tetrastatin (Roerig): Each capsule contains tetracycline hydrochloride 250 mg and nystatin 250,000 units; each 5 ml of suspension contains tetracycline equivalent to tetracycline hydrochloride 125 mg and nystatin 125,000 units.

Tetrex-F (Bristol): Each capsule contains tetracycline phosphate complex equivalent to tetracycline hydrochloride 250 mg and nystatin 250,000 units; each 5 ml of suspension contains tetracycline equivalent to tetracycline hydrochloride 125 mg and nystatin 125,000 units.

UROBIOTIC

This mixture contains a tetracycline, a sulfonamide, and a urinary analgesic and is promoted for the treatment of urinary tract infections. Any advantage of this mixture over an effective dose of the tetracycline or the sulfonamide alone has not been established. Phenazopyridine, a urinary analgesic, is contraindicated in patients with renal insufficiency or hepatitis. (See the introduction to the section on Mixtures and Chapter 55, Sulfonamides.)

USUAL DOSAGE.—This fixed-ratio combination is not considered to be useful and no suggested dosage is given. The manufacturer's dosage is: *Oral: Adults*, 1 to 2 capsules four times daily. *Children weighing 27 to 45 kg*, 1 capsule (Urobiotic-125) four times daily; *under 27 kg*, 1 capsule (Urobiotic-125) three times daily.

PREPARATIONS.—Urobiotic (Pfizer): Each capsule contains oxytetracycline hydrochloride equivalent to oxytetracycline 125 or 250 mg, sulfamethizole 250 mg, and phenazopyridine hydrochloride 50 mg.

Chapter 54

CHLORAMPHENICOL AND DERIVATIVES

Chloramphenicol [Amphicol, Chloromax, Chloromycetin, Mychel] is an antibiotic originally derived from *Streptomyces venezuellae* but now produced synthetically. It should be used in serious infections caused by susceptible organisms when other less potentially dangerous agents are ineffective or contraindicated. This antibiotic should not be used in trivial infections or in infections in which it is not indicated (eg, colds, influenza), nor to prevent bacterial infections of the respiratory tract except as part of the regimen for treating cystic fibrosis. However, in life-threatening, overwhelming infections of doubtful etiology, the generally good tolerance to large doses and the wide spectrum of activity makes chloramphenicol a valuable drug.

This agent is clinically effective against many strains of gram-positive and gram-negative bacteria, *Rickettsia*, and the psittacosis-lymphogranuloma group. It is the most effective antibiotic for treating acute typhoid fever and other serious infections caused by various salmonellae. Typhoid relapses also respond to retreatment with chloramphenicol. This drug is not effective against chronic typhoid, which should be treated with ampicillin or, if cholecystitis or cholelithiasis is present, by cholecystectomy. In one clinical study with a limited number of patients, chloramphenicol was more effective than ampicillin in treating paratyphoid A. In gastroenteritis caused by salmonellae other than *S. typhi*, administration of an antimicrobial agent may not only be ineffective in shortening the period of illness, but may result in a more prolonged period of elimination of the organisms. However, chloramphenicol appears to be the drug of choice in bacteremia and localized infections (eg, arthritis, osteitis, meningitis) caused by salmonellae.

Chloramphenicol is frequently used in life-threatening infections caused by *Bacteroides;* many strains of this genus are sensitive only to this drug. It is effective systemically in eye infections caused by susceptible organisms (occasionally including nonpigment-producing *Pseudomonas* species) because it readily penetrates ocular tissues (see Chapter 71, Anti-infective and Anti-inflammatory Agents Used in Ophthalmology).

Since ampicillin and the tetracyclines are as effective as chloramphenicol against most *Haemophilus influenzae* infections, they are preferred in the majority of these infections. Chloramphenicol may be used for the treatment of meningitis caused by *H. influenzae*, particularly in patients who are sensitive to penicillin.

Chloramphenicol ordinarily is not indicated in *Proteus* or *Escherichia coli* infections, but a few strains are susceptible to this drug only. This antibiotic is as effective as the tetracyclines for treating Rocky Mountain spotted fever and other rickettsial infections, and it may be preferred if the tetracyclines are contraindicated because of renal or hepatic disease. Chloramphenicol may be used for melioidosis (*Pseudomonas pseudomallei* infection) if the sulfonamides or tetracyclines cannot be used.

Adverse Reactions and Precautions

Blood dyscrasias, including aplastic anemia, have occurred following therapy with chloramphenicol. Despite the seriousness of these reactions, including some fatalities, the incidence of blood dyscrasias probably compares favorably with the incidence of severe anaphylactic reactions caused by penicillin or fatal hepatic toxicity and severe staphylococcic diarrhea associated with tetracycline therapy.

The most severe toxic effect observed following use of chloramphenicol is *aplastic anemia with pancytopenia.* Other forms of blood dyscrasias include aplastic anemia without pancytopenia, thrombocytopenia with no change in red or white blood cells, leukopenia, and agranulocytosis. Aplastic anemia has occurred after a single dose of the drug as well as after prolonged therapy. The other forms of blood dyscrasias appear more likely to be associated with large doses, prolonged therapy, or hepatic or renal insufficiency, and also are more likely to be reversible if administration of chloramphenicol is discontinued. Aplastic anemia that later terminated in leukemia has occurred in patients receiving chloramphenicol. These reactions must be distinguished from the transient leukopenia that is reversible and that commonly occurs with chloramphenicol therapy.

Allergic reactions (eg, rashes, angioneurotic edema, urticaria) have been observed following administration of chloramphenicol. Adverse gastrointestinal symptoms include nausea, vomiting, glossitis, stomatitis, diarrhea, and enterocolitis. Mild fever, headache, depression, or confusion also is not uncommon. Neurologic reactions that occur infrequently are delirium, optic neuropathy, or peripheral neuritis. Rarely, anaphylactic reactions and Herxheimer-like reactions have been reported during treatment of typhoid. Sensitization to chloramphenicol may occur after its topical use. An overgrowth of nonsusceptible bacterial or fungal organisms may be seen when this drug is given for prolonged periods. Severe hemorrhage in association with hypoprothrombinemia has been observed in a few patients; some forms of this condition can be prevented or corrected by the administration of phytonadione.

The plasma concentration of chloramphenicol is higher in premature infants and those under two weeks of age than in older infants because of inadequate metabolic inactivation. High blood levels in both premature and full-term infants, frequently have produced a toxic reaction referred to as the gray syndrome or gray baby syndrome; this is characterized by abdominal distention, progressive pallid cyanosis, ashen color, and acute circulatory failure. Since it can be fatal, administration of this antibacterial agent to either premature or full-term infants during the first two weeks of life is not recommended except under unusual circumstances. If chloramphenicol therapy is essential in infants, the dosage recommendations should not be exceeded and plasma levels should be monitored if possible.

When a drug is known to cause blood dyscrasias, it usually is advisable to perform appropriate blood counts to obtain baseline values for later comparisons. Blood studies may reveal early peripheral blood changes (eg, leukopenia or granulocytopenia) caused by the direct marrow depressant effects of chloramphenicol before they become irreversible; however, none of the studies will predict the future occurrence of aplastic anemia or precipitous agranulocytosis. It has been recommended that leukocyte and differential counts be made every 48 hours while a patient is receiving chloramphenicol. In view of the prodigious number of routine hemograms that are performed and the rarity of diagnosing serious blood disorders by such means, the chance of benefiting any given patient by routine examination is remote. Careful observation for sudden sore throat or development of new infection may be a far more important precaution than routine blood studies. If such signs appear, immediate laboratory evaluation is then indicated.

The dosage of chloramphenicol should be reduced in patients with impaired hepatic or renal function.

Interactions: Therapeutic doses of chloramphenicol can interfere with the anamnestic response to tetanus toxoid. Therefore, the concomitant administration of this antibiotic and active immunizing agents should be avoided if possible. Chloramphenicol may lower prothrombin levels by suppressing the vitamin K_1-producing bacterial flora in the gastrointestinal tract. Therapeutic doses of chloramphenicol inhibit the biotransformation of tolbutamide [Orinase], diphenylhydantoin [Dilantin], dicumarol, and other drugs metabolized by the liver microsomal enzymes.

CHLORAMPHENICOL [Amphicol, Chloromax, Chloromycetin, Mychel]
CHLORAMPHENICOL PALMITATE [Chloromycetin Palmitate]
CHLORAMPHENICOL SODIUM SUCCINATE [Chloromycetin Sodium Succinate, Mychel-S]

$$O_2N-C_6H_4-CH(OH)-CH(CH_2OH)NHC(=O)CHCl_2$$

For indications for chloramphenicol and adverse reactions or precautions associated with its use, see the Introductory Statement.

Since high blood titers of chloramphenicol are achieved rapidly following oral administration of the various preparations, this route is preferred except in cases of overwhelming sepsis. Parenteral forms should be given only when oral administration is contraindicated or impractical, and use of oral forms should be substituted as quickly as possible. The sodium succinate ester may produce a bitter taste for a few minutes after injection, and intramuscular administration may cause moderate local pain. As with other antibiotics that are effective systemically, topical use of chloramphenicol generally should be avoided, except by local instillation into the eye (see Chapter 71, Anti-infective and Anti-inflammatory Agents Used in Ophthalmology) and the ear (see Chapter 73, Topical Otic Preparations).

USUAL DOSAGE.—If doses higher than the following recommendations are used because of the severity of an infection, they should be reduced as soon as clinical improvement occurs.

Chloramphenicol:

Oral: Adults, children, and infants over two weeks of age, 50 mg/kg of body weight daily in divided doses every six or eight hours. In typhoid and paratyphoid fever, some authorities recommend that this dosage be continued for at least two weeks and, in severe illness, the dosage may be doubled initially until clinical improvement occurs. In patients in whom the half-life of the drug may be increased (eg, those with impaired hepatic function), the interval between doses may have to be increased. *Premature infants,* 25 mg/kg of body weight daily in divided doses, usually at 12-hour intervals. *Full-term newborn infants under two weeks of age,* 25 mg/kg daily in divided doses every four to six hours. For all infants, it is advisable (but seldom feasible) to monitor chloramphenicol blood levels frequently and, ideally, to maintain the blood level of drug between 10 to 20 μg/100 ml.

Intravenous: Adults may be given the same dosage as that used orally. This drug should not be used parenterally in *children* except to initiate therapy for meningitis or severe sepsis, when 100 mg/kg of body weight daily can be given (the sodium succinate ester is more commonly used in children).

Topical: This route generally should be avoided (see Chapter 71 and 73).

Chloramphenicol Palmitate:

Oral: The palmitate is hydrolyzed to chloramphenicol before absorption from the gastrointestinal tract but it yields lower blood levels than the base. The dosage is the same as that for the parent compound.

Chloramphenicol Sodium Succinate:

Intravenous: A solution is prepared for intravenous use by dissolving the powder in water for injection or other suitable aqueous diluent to make a solution containing 100 mg/ml. The dosage for *adults and children* is the same as that for the base.

Intramuscular: Although the sodium succinate is not labeled for intramuscular use, blood levels produced by intramuscular doses of 1 g every eight hours appear to be within the therapeutic range. As yet, it is uncertain whether intramuscular administration is as effective as intravenous administration. Recommended solutions for this route have ranged from 25% to 40% (250 to 400 mg/ml).

PREPARATIONS.—

Chloramphenicol:

Amphicol (McKesson), Chloromax (Century), Mychel (Rachelle). *Oral:* Capsules 250 mg.

Chloromycetin (Parke, Davis).

Oral: Capsules 50, 100, and 250 mg.

Injection: Solution 250 mg/ml in 2 ml containers.

Topical: See Chapter 71 for topical ophthalmic preparations and Chapter 73 for topical otic preparations.

Chloramphenicol Palmitate:

Chloromycetin Palmitate (Parke, Davis). *Oral:* Suspension equivalent to chloramphenicol 125 mg/4 ml.

Chloramphenicol Sodium Succinate:

Chloromycetin Sodium Succinate (Parke, Davis), Mychel-S (Rachelle). *Injection:* Powder 1 g.

Chapter 55

SULFONAMIDES

The sulfonamides currently used as antibacterial agents are all congeners of sulfanilamide, the prototype of this group. Sulfonamides used for other therapeutic purposes, which include the thiazides (see Chapter 6, Antihypertensive Agents, and Chapter 7, Diuretics), sulfonylureas (see Chapter 12, Agents Used to Treat Hyperglycemia), and carbonic anhydrase inhibitors (see Chapter 69, Agents Used to Treat Glaucoma), also contain the same basic chemical nucleus. Cross sensitization can occur between any of these sulfonamides, regardless of their therapeutic classification.

The sulfonamides that have a free amino group on the benzene ring (eg, sulfadiazine) exert their antibacterial effect by acting as a competitive antimetabolite. Except in special circumstances (eg, the high concentrations achieved in treating urinary infections), all of the sulfonamides are bacteriostatic rather than bactericidal. Therefore, combinations of sulfonamides with penicillin are theoretically of questionable utility, because penicillin is effective only against bacteria which are actively synthesizing cell wall, a process that is inhibited by bacteriostatic agents. However, enhancement of activity, as opposed to inhibition or no effect, has been reported in a few infections following concomitant use of therapeutic doses of both agents (see the section on Mixtures).

Estimates of effective concentrations of the sulfonamides in the blood vary between 6 and 15 mg/100 ml. The drugs are inactivated primarily in the liver by acetylation of the free amino group or by conjugation with glucuronic acid. Either acetylation or conjugation may increase or decrease the solubility of the drug in the urine, the major route of excretion.

The specific uses and the relative importance of the sulfonamides in the treatment of various infections change from time to time, depending upon such factors as increased frequency of bacterial resistance and development of more effective or less toxic antimicrobial compounds.

Certain bacteria can develop a high degree of resistance to these drugs during therapy and, once resistance to a particular agent develops, cross resistance to other sulfonamides is usual. Development of resistance may be minimized by initiating treatment promptly with adequate doses and continuing treatment for a sufficient period to eradicate the infection. Although some strains of *Klebsiella*, *Enterobacter*, or *Proteus* may be readily inhibited by the sulfonamides, particularly in vitro, other strains are totally resistant. Resistance of *Haemophilus influenzae*, *Diplococcus pneumoniae*, and species of *Pseudomonas*, as well as *Streptococcus faecalis* and other enterococci, staphylococci, anaerobic streptococci, spirochetes, and clostridiae frequently has been reported. Resistance to sulfonamides is common in many strains of organisms causing gonorrheal infections, bacillary dysentery, and epidemics of meningococcic meningitis.

Sulfonamides are almost always given orally. When parenteral administration is indicated, sulfisoxazole [Gantrisin] diolamine or a sodium salt (eg, sulfadiazine sodium) may be given subcutaneously or intravenously. When the intravenous route is used, the drug must be well diluted and should be injected slowly with care to avoid extravasation. The alkaline sodium salts of sulfonamides are rarely administered intramuscularly because they are irritating.

Topically applied sulfonamides are generally ineffective in the management of infections in wounds and infections of the skin and mucous membranes, possibly because pus and cellular debris readily inhibit their action. They also have a greater tendency to produce sensitization, which can preclude their later systemic administration. However, in eye infections, ophthalmic solutions or ointments of sulfacetamide sodium or certain other sulfonamides are often useful (see Chapter 71, Anti-infective and Anti-inflammatory Agents Used in Ophthalmology).

Mafenide [Sulfamylon] acetate is used topically to prevent sepsis and reduce mortality in patients with severe burns. The topical use of sulfadiazine silver in the treatment of burns is still investigational. Available data indicate that this compound has a high degree of effectiveness.

Sulfonamides are the agents of choice in the treatment of nocardiosis and chancroid. They are now infrequently used in the treatment of meningococcic meningitis because of the increase in resistant strains; however, the sulfonamides are effective when meningococcic meningitis is caused by sensitive strains. Those preferred include sulfadiazine or, because it can be given by injection and is more soluble in the urine, sulfisoxazole diolamine. Sulfonamides are among the effective agents for trachoma and inclusion conjunctivitis. They also may be used in the long-term suppressive treatment of urinary tract infections caused by sensitive organisms, especially those caused by some strains of *Escherichia coli* and *Proteus mirabilis*. Since resistance commonly develops during the course of suppressive therapy, sulfonamides may be alternated with other agents (eg, nitrofurantoin, nalidixic acid [NegGram]) as sensitivity is lost and reappears. They may be given in the long-term prophylaxis of streptococcic infections, such as rheumatic fever, when penicillin cannot be used; however, these agents should not be used for the treatment of acute infections caused by group A hemolytic streptococci or other pathogenic bacteria that may be sensitive to their action but are more effectively treated with other antibacterials. The usefulness of the sulfonamides in the group prophylaxis and treatment of shigellal enteritis has decreased, since many strains are no longer susceptible and resistance can develop rapidly. Certain sulfonamides also are used preoperatively to suppress intestinal flora.

Administration of a sulfonamide (sulfadiazine or trisulfapyrimidines) and pyrimethamine [Daraprim] is currently the treatment of choice against the protozoan, *Toxoplasma gondii*, in symptomatic toxoplasmosis. The sulfonamides also appear to be useful as adjuncts in the treatment of patients with malaria caused by strains of *Plasmodium falciparum* resistant to chloroquine (see Chapter 61, Antimalarial Agents).

It is difficult to recommend specific drugs within the subdivisions of the sulfonamides since there are few comparative clinical studies and since comparisons based on studies in normal subjects or in the laboratory may not correlate well with therapeutic efficacy or safety. The antibacterial ranges of the various sulfonamides are comparable, and it is not known to what degree, if any, the sensitivities of bacteria to each drug may differ.

The older sulfonamides, sulfanilamide and sulfathiazole, have now been largely discarded either because of their relatively low efficacy or the high incidence of untoward effects that follows their use. Sulfapyridine is outmoded for the same general reasons, but is effective as suppressant therapy in dermatitis herpetiformis (see Chapter 68, Dermatologic Agents).

Short-Acting Sulfonamides: In general, the short-acting sulfonamides should be used for systemic therapy because exposure may be terminated rapidly if a serious adverse reaction develops. Sulfadiazine is one of the best of these agents for general application. It may be used in the treatment of meningococcic meningitis caused by sensitive strains and in the long-term prophylaxis of rheumatic fever and glomerulonephritis. It may also be used in the group prophylaxis of meningococcic infection or bacillary dysentery in outbreaks that have been proved to be due to sulfonamide-sensitive strains of *Neisseria meningitidis* or *Shigella*. Sulfisoxazole has similar applicability and is less likely to cause crystalluria because of its high solubility. Sulfamethoxazole [Gantanol] resembles sulfisoxazole, but it is absorbed from the intestinal tract and excreted in the urine more slowly and must be given less frequently to avoid excessive blood levels. Sulfadiazine, sulfamerazine, and sulfamethazine are used together as trisulfapyrimidines to reduce the risk of crystalluria. Although trisulfapyrimidines is still popular, the mixture is used less often now because of the availability of newer agents that are more soluble in urine than sulfadiazine. Sulfamerazine is seldom used alone and sulfamethazine apparently is not used in this country except in combinations.

For greatest effectiveness in the treatment of urinary tract infections, it is desirable to choose a sulfonamide that is excreted in high antibacterial concentration (largely in the active rather than in the acetylated form), is reasonably soluble at acidic pH values, and maintains adequate antibacterial levels in the blood and tissues during the period of high urinary excretion. The short-acting drugs that most nearly meet these criteria are sulfamethizole [Thiosulfil], sulfisoxazole, and sulfachlorpyridazine [Sonilyn]. Sulfamethoxazole and sulfacetamide also have been used to treat infections of the urinary tract. Prompt response of the bacteriuria is a clinical indication of effectiveness; therapy then should be continued for a minimum of two weeks.

The sulfonamides used topically in ophthalmic preparations include sulfacetamide sodium and sulfisoxazole diolamine. The latter agent also is applied as a vaginal cream for the treatment of susceptible infections. It should be borne in mind that topical use may result in sensitization.

Long-Acting Sulfonamides: The long-acting sulfonamides include sulfadimethoxine [Madribon], sulfamethoxypyridazine [Midicel], sulfamethoxypyridazine acetyl [Midicel Acetyl], and sulfameter [Sulla]. These drugs have a 35- to 40-hour half-life in the blood as compared to 5 to 15 hours for most of those excreted rapidly. Because of this slow rate of excretion, a smaller dose or less frequent administration can maintain an adequate blood level. Although a less frequent dosage schedule may be convenient for the patient, the low urinary concentration of active drug may make the sulfonamide less effective in treating urinary tract infections.

The long-acting sulfonamides offer no clinical advantages over the short-acting agents. In addition, the long-acting sulfonamides may not penetrate into cerebrospinal fluid as well as the shorter-acting agents. Because of their slow rate of excretion, accumulation with excessive concentrations in the blood can occur more easily than with the shorter-acting agents if these drugs are given in frequent or large doses, or to patients with impaired renal function. Because of these hazards, the use of the long-acting agents is justified only under extraordinary circumstances.

Adverse Reactions and Precautions

Hypersensitivity reactions affecting the skin and mucous membranes occur frequently with sulfonamide therapy. They include urticaria, purpura, and other types of rashes that are often accompanied by pruritus and fever; less common sensitivity reactions include photosensitization, erythema nodosum, exfoliative dermatitis, and a serum sickness-like syndrome. The sulfonamides also have been implicated in precipitating polyarteritis nodosa and systemic lupus erythematosus. Nausea, vomiting, and malaise occur frequently. Reactions involving the nervous system include headache, lassitude, dizziness, mental depression, psychoses, and peripheral neuritis. The sulfonamides may cause mild or serious blood dyscrasias, such as leukopenia, granulocytopenia, agranulocytosis, aplastic anemia, thrombocytopenia, and hypoprothrombinemia. Cyanosis also has been reported. Hemolytic anemia may occur both in persons with and those without a deficiency of erythrocytic glucose-6-phosphate dehydrogenase (G6PD). Reactions involving the urinary tract include toxic nephrosis with oliguria and anuria, crystalluria, and gross or microscopic hematuria with or without crystalluria. The hepatotoxic properties of these drugs may result in hepatitis with focal or diffuse necrosis and cholestatic jaundice.

The sulfonamides occasionally may cause Stevens-Johnson syndrome, especially in children. This complication is particularly hazardous, since it is fatal in approximately 25% of susceptible patients; therefore, therapy should be stopped immediately if a rash develops. The short-acting sulfonamides are generally effective in treating conditions for which a long-acting sulfonamide also might be used, and their more rapid elimination is an advantage when toxic reactions occur.

As with all drugs that are excreted primarily in the urine, the absorbable sulfonamides must be used cautiously in patients with impaired renal function. The urinary volume must be adequate (about 1.5 liters per day) before therapy is even begun and, if the urine is highly acidic, sodium bicarbonate or another alkalizing agent should be given concomitantly.

When adequate urinary volume cannot be maintained, sulfonamides may be contraindicated because of their tendency to produce crystalluria. However, if renal function is normal, even patients who have only one kidney may be given the more soluble sulfonamides with relatively little danger of crystalluria. Since sulfamethizole [Thiosulfil] and sulfathiazole may form insoluble precipitates with formaldehyde in the urine, concomitant therapy with methenamine compounds (eg, methenamine mandelate

[Mandelamine]) should be avoided. The reduced conjugation of sulfonamides in patients with severely impaired liver function should be borne in mind.

When given to pregnant women and nursing mothers, sulfonamides can pass into the fetus and into milk and cause kernicterus by displacing protein-bound bilirubin. Sulfonamides also may cause kernicterus in jaundiced or newborn infants; presumably, therefore, these drugs should not be given to premature or full-term infants less than two months of age. The use of long-acting sulfonamides in pregnant women near term is not advisable, since these drugs may persist in the infant after birth.

Blood cell studies made at regular intervals may be of value during prolonged therapy with any sulfonamide, since such studies are useful in detecting the milder leukopenias. However, clinical signs such as a sore throat, fever, pallor, purpura, or jaundice are more useful as early indicators of possible serious blood disorders than are routine blood cell counts.

The possibility of producing hemolytic anemia should be borne in mind if there is a family history or a suspicion of possible congenital erythrocytic glucose-6-phosphate dehydrogenase (G6PD) deficiency; this is most common in Negroes and people of Mediterranean ethnic groups.

Sensitivity to one sulfonamide usually but not always indicates a sensitivity to others; therefore, caution is essential if these agents are administered to patients with a history of sensitivity to any sulfonamide.

Since hypoglycemia has been reported after administration of antibacterial sulfonamides in a few patients receiving tolbutamide [Orinase], these agents should be given cautiously to patients receiving an oral hypoglycemic agent. Sulfonamides also should be used cautiously in those receiving coumarin anticoagulants or methotrexate, since they have been reported to enhance the actions of these agents.

SHORT-ACTING SULFONAMIDES

SULFACETAMIDE
SULFACETAMIDE SODIUM

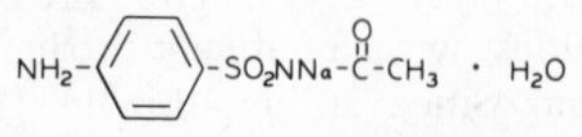

$NH_2-C_6H_4-SO_2NNa-C(=O)-CH_3 \cdot H_2O$

This highly soluble compound has been used for urinary tract infections caused by susceptible organisms but is less effective than other sulfonamides. The sodium salt is useful topically in the treatment of ophthalmic infections (see Chapter 71, Anti-infective and Anti-inflammatory Agents Used in Ophthalmology).

For adverse reactions and precautions, see the Introductory Statement.

USUAL DOSAGE.—

Oral: For urinary tract infections, *adults,* 1 g three times daily; *children over 2 months of age,* 60 mg/kg of body weight daily in three or four divided doses.

Topical: See Chapter 71.

PREPARATIONS.—

Sulfacetamide, N.F. No single-entity pharmaceutical dosage form available; compounding necessary for prescription.

Sulfacetamide Sodium (See Chapter 71.)

SULFACHLORPYRIDAZINE [Sonilyn]

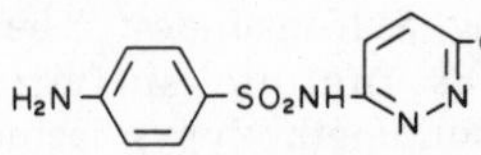

$H_2N-C_6H_4-SO_2NH-$(6-chloropyridazin-3-yl) [structure: pyridazine ring with Cl]

The actions of sulfachlorpyridazine are similar to those of sulfisoxazole. This drug is used primarily in urinary tract infections caused by susceptible organisms. Although its solubility is relatively greater than that of other sulfonamides, crystalluria still may occur because high concentrations are present in the urine. Frequent administration is necessary to maintain constant blood levels (see the Introductory Statement).

USUAL DOSAGE.—*Oral:* The dosage depends on the severity of the infection. *Adults,* 2 to 4 g initially, then 2 to 4 g daily in three to six divided doses. *Children and infants over 2 months of age,* one-half the calculated daily dose initially, then 150 mg/kg of body weight daily (maximum, 6 g) in four to six divided doses.

PREPARATIONS.—Sonilyn (Mallinckrodt). *Oral:* Tablets 500 mg.

SULFADIAZINE
SULFADIAZINE SODIUM

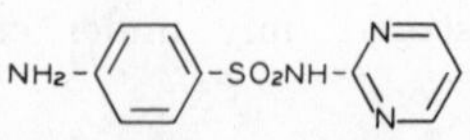

$NH_2-C_6H_4-SO_2NH-$(pyrimidin-2-yl)

This sulfapyrimidine compound is one of the best agents for general use in short- or long-term therapy, in individual prophylaxis (eg, preventing recurrences of rheumatic fever), or in group prophylaxis (eg, acute bacillary dysentery) of infections caused by sensitive organisms. Its low solubility necessitates the maintenance of an adequate urinary volume (at least 1,200 ml daily); concomitant alkalization of the urine reduces the tendency to cause crystalluria but accelerates the urinary excretion of the drug.

The sodium salt is highly alkaline and irritating. It may be given subcutaneously if diluted, but the intravenous route is preferred; it must not be given intrathecally.

For adverse reactions and precautions, see the Introductory Statement.

USUAL DOSAGE.—The blood level should be maintained at 10 to 15 mg/100 ml.

Oral: Adults, 2 to 4 g initially, then 1 g every four to six hours. *Children and infants over 2 months of age,* one-half of calculated daily dose initially, then 150 mg/kg of body weight daily in four to six divided doses. The total daily dose should not exceed 6 g. For prophylaxis of rheumatic fever, 500 mg once daily for *patients under 30 kg* and 1 g daily for *patients over 30 kg.*

Intravenous: Adults, 100 mg/kg of body weight up to a total of 5 g initially, then 30 to 50 mg/kg every six to eight hours. *Children over 2 months of age,* one-half of calculated daily dose initially, then 100 mg/kg daily in four divided doses. Oral therapy should be substituted as soon as possible.

PREPARATIONS.—

Sulfadiazine, U.S.P. *Oral:* Suspension 500 mg/5 ml; tablets 500 mg; tablets (chewable) 300 mg.

Sulfadiazine Sodium, U.S.P. *Injection:* Solution 250 mg/ml in 10 ml containers.

AVAILABLE TRADEMARKS.—**Sulfadiazine:** Coco-Diazine (Lilly), Microsulfon (Consolidated Midland). Drug also marketed by many manufacturers under generic name.

SULFAMERAZINE
SULFAMERAZINE SODIUM

$NH_2-C_6H_4-SO_2NH-C_4H_2N_2-CH_3$

This sulfapyrimidine compound is seldom used as a single-entity drug because newer, more soluble sulfonamides produce less crystalluria. It is now used principally as an ingredient in sulfonamide combinations (eg, trisulfapyrimidines).

Peripheral neuritis has been reported following use of sulfamerazine (see also the Introductory Statement).

USUAL DOSAGE.—*Oral: Adults,* 2 to 3 g initially, then 1 g every eight hours. *Infants and children,* recommended only in trisulfapyrimidines.

PREPARATIONS.—*Oral:* Tablets 500 mg. Drug marketed under generic name.

SULFAMETHAZINE

$NH_2-C_6H_4-SO_2NH-C_4HN_2(CH_3)_2$

This sulfapyrimidine compound apparently is no longer used as a single-entity drug in this country, but is given in combination with sulfadiazine and sulfamerazine (see the evaluation on Trisulfapyrimidines).

SULFAMETHIZOLE [Thiosulfil]

$H_2N-C_6H_4-SO_2-NH-C_2N_2S-CH_3$

This highly soluble, rapidly excreted sulfonamide compound is similar to sulfadiazine, sulfisoxazole, and sulfisomidine in its actions, uses, and adverse effects. Its principal use is in the treatment of urinary tract infections caused by susceptible organisms. About 90% of the drug in the urine is in the active form, which is highly soluble in acid urine. The risk of crystalluria is much less than with sulfadiazine, and alkalization of the urine is not necessary. Mixtures containing sulfamethizole and antibiotics should not be used. See also the Introductory Statement.

USUAL DOSAGE.—*Oral: Adults and children over 34 kg,* 500 mg to 1 g three or four times daily. *Infants over 2 months of age and up to 9 kg,* 50 to 60 mg/kg of body weight daily in four divided doses. *Children 9 to 23 kg,* up to 600 mg daily in four divided doses; *23 to 34 kg,* up to 1.2 g daily in four divided doses.

PREPARATIONS.—Thiosulfil (Ayerst). *Oral:* Suspension 250 mg/5 ml; tablets 250 and 500 mg.

ADDITIONAL TRADEMARK.—Utrasul (Alcon).

AVAILABLE MIXTURE.—Azotrex Syrup (Bristol): Each 5 ml of suspension contains sulfamethizole 250 mg and tetracycline phosphate complex 125 mg.

SULFAMETHOXAZOLE [Gantanol]

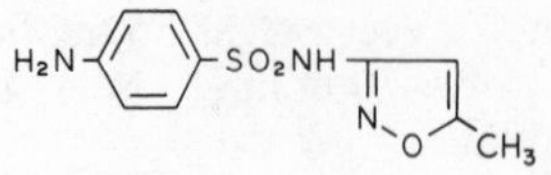

The effectiveness of sulfamethoxazole is similar to that of sulfisoxazole. However, excretion of the unconjugated drug, as well as its absorption from the intestine, is slower; thus, smaller dosage is mandatory to avoid excessive blood levels. It is useful in acute urinary tract infections and infections of soft tissues caused by susceptible organisms. See also the Introductory Statement.

USUAL DOSAGE.—*Oral: Adults*, 2 g initially, then 1 g two or three times daily. *Children over 2 months of age*, 60 mg/kg of body weight (not to exceed 2 g) initially, then one-half of this amount every 12 hours.

PREPARATIONS.—Gantanol (Roche). *Oral:* Suspension 500 mg/5 ml; tablets 500 mg.

SULFISOXAZOLE [Gantrisin]
SULFISOXAZOLE ACETYL [Gantrisin Acetyl]
SULFISOXAZOLE DIOLAMINE [Gantrisin Diolamine]

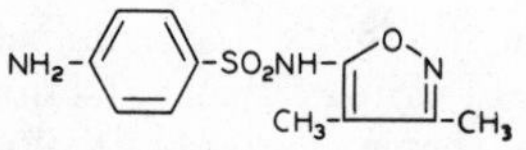

The actions and uses of sulfisoxazole are generally similar to those of sulfadiazine, and it is effective in meningococcic meningitis caused by sensitive strains. This drug is rapidly absorbed and excreted. Since the solubility of both the free and acetylated forms in acidic urine is relatively high compared to that of sulfadiazine, the risk of crystalluria is much less and alkalization of the urine is not necessary. However, adequate fluid intake should be maintained.

A vaginal cream containing sulfisoxazole may be effective in the treatment of vaginitis caused by sensitive strains of streptococci, diphtheroids, or coliform organisms.

Sulfisoxazole acetyl, which is tasteless, is used for liquid oral preparations. This compound is acetylated on the amide of the sulfonamide rather than on the free amino group. Substitution at this position does not inactivate the compound. It is split to sulfisoxazole in the intestine. Sulfisoxazole diolamine, because of its solubility and minimal irritation, is used topically in the eye and for injection.

It should be borne in mind that topical application of sulfonamides may cause sensitization, and that these agents are inactivated by blood and pus. For adverse reactions and precautions, see the Introductory Statement.

USUAL DOSAGE.—

Sulfisoxazole, Sulfisoxazole Acetyl:

Oral: Adults, 4 g initially, then 1 to 2 g every four to six hours. *Children over 2 months of age*, 60 mg/kg of body weight initially, then one-half of this amount every four hours. A concentrated, timed-release preparation [Lipo Gantrisin] is given in approximately the same milligram doses but less frequently (every 12 hours).

Topical (vaginal): (Base) 2.5 to 5 ml (one-half to one applicatorful) applied intravaginally twice daily.

Sulfisoxazole Diolamine:

Intravenous, Subcutaneous: Adults, same as oral dosage. *Children over 2 months of age*, 50 mg/kg of body weight initially, then 100 mg/kg daily in three or four divided doses.

Topical: See Chapter 71, Anti-infective and Anti-inflammatory Agents Used in Ophthalmology.

PREPARATIONS.—(All concentrations expressed in terms of base.)

Sulfisoxazole:

Gantrisin (Roche).

Oral: Tablets 500 mg.

Topical: Cream (vaginal) 10% in 3 oz containers.

Sulfisoxazole Acetyl:

Gantrisin [acetyl] (Roche). *Oral:* Liquid (timed-release) 1 g/5 ml [Lipo Gantrisin]; suspension (pediatric) 500 mg/5 ml; syrup 500 mg/5 ml.

Sulfisoxazole Diolamine:

Gantrisin [diolamine] (Roche).

Injection: Solution 400 mg/ml in 5 and 10 ml containers.

Topical: Ointment (ophthalmic) 4% in 1/8 oz containers; solution (ophthalmic) 4% in 15 ml containers.

ADDITIONAL TRADEMARKS.—**Sulfisoxazole:** SK-Soxazole (Smith Kline & French), Sodizole (First Texas), Sosol (McKesson), Soxomide (Upjohn), Sulfisocon (Consolidated Midland). Drug also marketed under generic name.

Combination Short-Acting Sulfonamides

TRISULFAPYRIMIDINES

This combination of equal parts of sulfadiazine, sulfamerazine, and sulfamethazine appears to produce somewhat higher total blood levels of sulfonamide than do equal doses of sulfadiazine alone, but the effectiveness remains the same.

The incidence of crystalluria (but not of other untoward effects) is reduced with trisulfapyrimidines. See also the Introductory Statement. The rationale for use of trisulfapyrimidines is less cogent with the availability of newer, more soluble sulfonamides.

USUAL DOSAGE.—*Oral: Adults,* 3 to 4 g initially, then 1 g every six hours. *Children and infants over 2 months of age,* one-half the calculated daily dose initially, then 150 mg/kg of body weight daily in four to six divided doses.

PREPARATIONS.—Trisulfapyrimidines, U.S.P. *Oral:* Suspension 500 mg/5 ml; tablets 500 mg.

AVAILABLE TRADEMARKS.—Neotrizine (Lilly), Sulfaloid (Westerfield), Sulfose (Wyeth), Terfonyl (Squibb), Tri-Azo-Tabs (First Texas), Triosulfon DMM (Consolidated Midland), Trisem (Beecham-Massengill), Trisulfazine (Central). Mixture also marketed under generic name.

SULFACETAMIDE, SULFADIAZINE, AND SULFAMERAZINE

This combination of equal amounts of sulfacetamide, sulfadiazine, and sulfamerazine offers no advantage over trisulfapyrimidines.

USUAL DOSAGE.—*Oral:* Same as for trisulfapyrimidines.

PREPARATIONS.—Sulfacetamide, Sulfadiazine, and Sulfamerazine, N.F. *Oral:* Suspension 250 and 500 mg/5 ml; tablets 250 and 500 mg.

AVAILABLE TRADEMARKS.—Buffonamide (Tutag), Cetazine (Bowman), Incorposul (Blue Line), Trizyl (Central).

SULFADIAZINE AND SULFAMERAZINE

This combination of equal amounts of sulfadiazine and sulfamerazine reduces the incidence of crystalluria (as compared to sulfadiazine alone) less than do the preparations containing three sulfonamides and offers no advantages over them.

USUAL DOSAGE.—*Oral:* Same as for trisulfapyrimidines.

PREPARATIONS.—Sulfadiazine and Sulfamerazine, N.F. *Oral:* Suspension 500 mg/5 ml; tablets 500 mg.

AVAILABLE TRADEMARKS.—Aldiazol-M (Beecham-Massengill), Merdisul (Bowman), Sulfonamide Duplex (Lilly).

SULFATHIAZOLE, SULFACETAMIDE, AND NITROBENZOYL SULFANILAMIDE [Sultrin]

A combination containing sulfathiazole, sulfacetamide, and nitrobenzoyl sulfanilamide (each at a different concentration and apparently most active at a different pH) is promoted for the prophylaxis or treatment of cervical and vaginal infections; however, evidence is insufficient to evaluate its efficacy accurately. It should be borne in mind that sensitization may occur from topical application of sulfonamides.

PREPARATIONS.—Sultrin (Ortho). *Topical* (vaginal): Cream containing sulfathiazole 3.42%, sulfacetamide 2.86%, and nitrobenzoyl sulfanilamide 3.7% with urea 0.64% in 78 g containers; each tablet contains sulfathiazole 171 mg, sulfacetamide 143 mg, and nitrobenzoyl sulfanilamide 185 mg with urea 13 mg.

LONG-ACTING SULFONAMIDES

SULFADIMETHOXINE [Madribon]

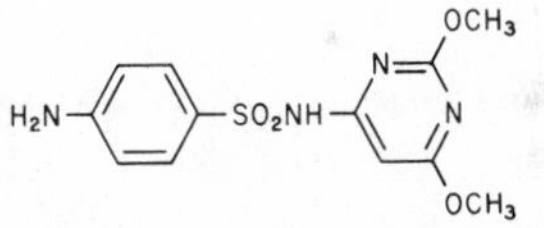

H_2N–C₆H₄–SO_2NH–(pyrimidine, 2,6-OCH_3)

Although 80% of the urinary concentration of this drug is in the form of the inactive glucuronide, sulfadimethoxine is effective in the treatment of urinary tract infections caused by sensitive organisms, as well as in infections of soft tissues and the respiratory tract. Peak blood levels occur within four to eight hours after the initial dose and are maintained thereafter by administration once daily; 85% of the drug in the blood is in the active form. Since its slow elimination from the body increases the hazard to the patient if a serious adverse reaction occurs, the use of sulfadimethoxine instead of a short-acting sulfonamide is justified only under extraordinary circumstances. See also the Introductory Statement.

USUAL DOSAGE.—*Oral: Adults*, 1 g initially, then 500 mg once daily. *Children over 2 months of age*, 25 mg/kg of body weight initially, then 12.5 mg/kg once daily. These doses may be doubled in severe infection, but caution is indicated in the use of this drug (see above).

PREPARATIONS.—Madribon (Roche). *Oral:* Suspension 250 mg/5 ml; tablets 500 mg.

SULFAMETER [Sulla]

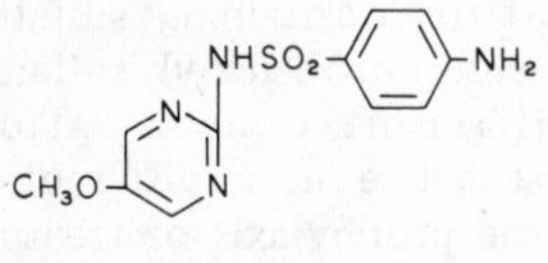

Sulfameter is effective in urinary tract infections caused by susceptible strains of bacteria, especially *Escherichia coli.* About 60% to 70% of the drug in the urine is in the unchanged, active form. Since its slow elimination from the body increases the hazard to the patient if a serious adverse reaction occurs, the use of sulfameter instead of a short-acting sulfonamide is justified only under extraordinary circumstances. See also the Introductory Statement.

USUAL DOSAGE.—*Oral: Adults and children over 12 years of age*, 1.5 g initially, then 500 mg once daily. Caution is indicated in the use of this drug (see above). It should be used with considerable care in *children under 12 years.*

PREPARATIONS.—Sulla (Robins). *Oral:* Tablets 500 mg.

SULFAMETHOXYPYRIDAZINE [Midicel]
SULFAMETHOXYPYRIDAZINE ACETYL [Midicel Acetyl]

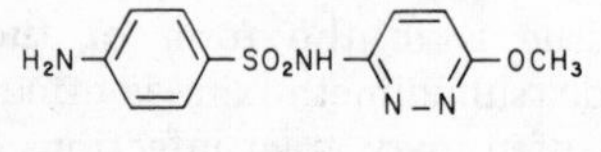

Sulfamethoxypyridazine is effective in systemic and urinary tract infections caused by sensitive organisms. The acetyl derivative, which is tasteless, is used in liquid pediatric preparations. Since its slow elimination from the body increases the hazard to the patient if a serious adverse reaction occurs, use of sulfamethoxypyridazine instead of a short-acting sulfonamide is justified only under extraordinary circumstances. See also the Introductory Statement.

USUAL DOSAGE.—*Oral: Adults and children over 36 kg*, 1 g initially, then 500 mg once daily or 1 g every other day. *Children 9 to 36 kg*, 30 mg/kg of body weight initially, then 15 mg/kg once daily. Caution is indicated in the use of this drug (see above).

PREPARATIONS.—

Sulfamethoxypyridazine:

Midicel (Parke, Davis). *Oral:* Tablets 500 mg.

Sulfamethoxypyridazine Acetyl:

Midicel Acetyl (Parke, Davis). *Oral:* Suspension (pediatric) 250 mg/5 ml.

MISCELLANEOUS SULFONAMIDES

MAFENIDE ACETATE [Sulfamylon Acetate]

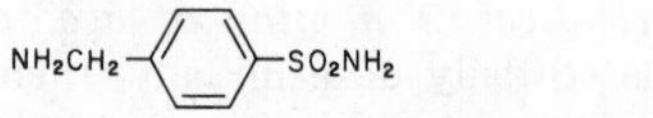

Mafenide acetate is used topically to prevent sepsis and reduce mortality in patients with burns; it is particularly effective against *Pseudomonas aeruginosa.* Unlike other sulfonamides, this drug is not inhibited by pus and body fluids. It diffuses into the burned tissues but produces very low blood levels.

Adverse effects include pain at the site of application, allergic skin reactions, and acid-base disturbances (metabolic acidosis, respiratory alkalosis).

USUAL DOSAGE.—*Topical:* Preparation is applied once or twice daily in 1/16-inch thickness on the burn wounds with a sterile gloved hand.

PREPARATIONS.—Sulfamylon Acetate (Winthrop). *Topical:* Cream equivalent to 85 mg of base/g in 2, 4, and 16 oz containers.

SALICYLAZOSULFAPYRIDINE [Azulfidine]

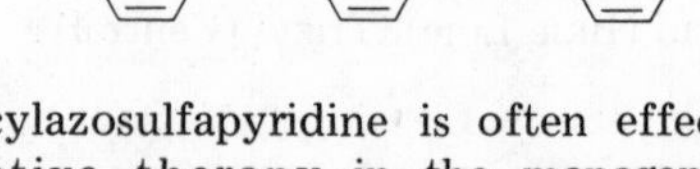

Salicylazosulfapyridine is often effective as adjunctive therapy in the management of ulcerative colitis. It is converted to sulfapyridine in the intestine. Its effect in ulcerative colitis apparently is not due to its antibacterial action since it does not alter the intestinal flora.

Adverse reactions (eg, headache, nausea, vomiting, fever, rash) are common with therapeutic doses and may necessitate discontinuation of salicylazosulfapyridine. Agranulocytosis, with some deaths, has been reported rarely (see also the Introductory Statement).

USUAL DOSAGE.—*Oral: Adults*, initially, 4 to 8 g daily in four to eight divided doses. For maintenance, 2 g daily in four divided doses. *Children and infants over 2 months of age*, initially, 75 to 100 mg/kg of body weight daily in four to eight divided doses. For maintenance, 40 mg/kg daily in four divided doses.

PREPARATIONS.—Azulfidine (Pharmacia). *Oral:* Tablets 500 mg; tablets (enteric-coated) 500 mg.

MIXTURES

Fixed-ratio combinations of various sulfonamides and antibiotics have been popular in practice, but the rationale for their use in general is questionable. Most have been removed from the market. Injection of more than one antibacterial agent may be indicated in severe infections when treatment must be initiated empirically pending determination of the specific etiologic factor; however, when the causative organism has been identified, the drug that best meets the needs of the particular clinical situation should be given.

There is no substantial evidence that there are any significant mixed infections requiring the combined use of the antibacterial agents available in these fixed-ratio combinations. Also, whether a sulfonamide given concomitantly will add to the effect of a bactericidal agent such as penicillin in any particular patient cannot be predicted, and the use of such combinations subjects patients to the potential adverse effects of two potent drugs rather than one (see the Introductory Statement to this chapter, and Chapter 48, Penicillins). However, the effectiveness of penicillin and of erythromycin in the treatment of otitis media caused by *Haemophilus influenzae* has been reported to be increased when a sulfonamide is given concomitantly with either of these antibiotics; the dosage of each antibacterial agent should be the same as when it is used alone. See also Chapter 50, Erythromycin and Derivatives. Other mixtures containing sulfonamides are listed in the section on Estrogens and Progestagens in Chapter 37, and in Chapters 57, Aminoglycoside Antibacterial Agents and Miscellaneous Antimicrobial Drugs; 71, Anti-infective and Anti-inflammatory Agents Used in Ophthalmology; and 80, Antidiarrheals.

Evaluations of types of available mixtures follow.

MIXTURES CONTAINING ANTIBACTERIAL AGENTS AND PHENAZOPYRIDINE

Phenazopyridine, a urinary tract analgesic, is combined with antibacterial agents, primarily sulfonamides, in some fixed-ratio preparations promoted for the treatment of urinary tract infections. Since phenazopyridine may relieve such symptoms as pain, burning, urgency, and frequency, its concomitant use with sulfonamides is effective therapy. However, it preferably is given separately rather than in a fixed combination and should be eliminated from the regimen as soon as the symptoms are controlled. (See also Chapter 92, Miscellaneous Drugs.) Those preparations that contain other antibacterials in addition to sulfonamides needlessly subject patients to the potential hazards of two potent drugs rather than one, since marginal doses can only be additive, and full therapeutic doses generally are no more effective than the individual agents alone.

USUAL DOSAGE.—Preparations containing only a sulfonamide component rather than an antibiotic in addition should be used. Dosage is the same as that for the sulfonamide without phenazopyridine (see the evaluation on the appropriate sulfonamide).

PREPARATIONS.—

Azo Gantanol (Roche). *Oral:* Each tablet contains sulfamethoxazole 500 mg and phenazopyridine hydrochloride 100 mg.

Azo Gantrisin (Roche). *Oral:* Each tablet contains sulfisoxazole 500 mg and phenazopyridine hydrochloride 50 mg.

Azo-Sodizole (First Texas). *Oral:* Each tablet contains sulfisoxazole 500 mg and phenazopyridine hydrochloride 75 mg.

Azo-Sulfisoxazole (Fellows). *Oral:* Each tablet contains sulfisoxazole 500 mg and phenazopyridine hydrochloride 50 mg.

Azotrex Capsules (Bristol). *Oral:* Each capsule contains sulfamethizole 250 mg, tetracycline phosphate complex 125 mg, and phenazopyridine hydrochloride 50 mg.

Ro-Sulfa-A (Rowell). *Oral:* Each tablet contains sulfamethizole 250 mg, trisulfapyrimidines 250 mg, and phenazopyridine hydrochloride 75 mg.

Suladyne (Stuart). *Oral:* Each tablet contains sulfamethizole 125 mg, sulfadiazine 125 mg, and phenazopyridine hydrochloride 75 mg.

Sulfid Forte (Philips Roxane). *Oral:* Each tablet contains sulfacetamide 500 mg, phenazopyridine hydrochloride 100 mg, hyoscyamine sulfate 0.1037 mg, atropine sulfate 0.0194 mg, and hyoscine hydrobromide 0.0065 mg.

Thiosulfil A, Thiosulfil A Forte (Ayerst). *Oral:* Each tablet contains sulfamethizole 250 or 500 mg and phenazopyridine hydrochloride 50 mg.

Urobiotic (Pfizer). *Oral:* Each capsule contains sulfamethizole 250 mg, oxytetracycline hydrochloride 125 or 250 mg, and phenazopyridine hydrochloride 50 mg.

Chapter 56

NITROFURANS

Although the nitrofurans frequently are effective for treating bacterial, protozoal, and fungal infections, they are not agents of choice for infections caused by any of these organisms. Systemically administered nitrofurans are used primarily in treating urinary tract infections. The drugs are active in vitro against a fairly extensive range of gram-positive and gram-negative bacteria at concentrations ranging from 0.1 to 30 μg/ml, but they are not active against all species of *Proteus* and rarely affect *Pseudomonas* species. They have the advantage that bacterial resistance in vivo develops slowly and to a limited degree. Cross resistance of bacteria and cross sensitization in patients occur infrequently.

Adverse Reactions and Precautions

Hypersensitivity reactions occasionally develop within a few days when these agents are used either topically or systemically. Therapy should be discontinued if a rash develops after topical administration, since severe dermatitis may develop with continued administration. Caution should be exercised in treating chronic ulcerative lesions with abnormally sensitive surrounding skin.

Although usual therapeutic doses of nitrofurantoin [Cyantin, Furadantin, Macrodantin, N-Toin, Trantoin] and furazolidone [Furoxone] have had no effect on spermatogenesis in man, larger doses appear to have a highly specific ability to depress spermatogenesis by acting directly on the seminiferous tubules. Large doses of some nitrofurans also can cause hypotension, but the blood pressure is not affected by usual doses.

The systemically administered nitrofurans may cause hemolytic anemia in patients with congenital erythrocytic glucose-6-phosphate dehydrogenase (G6PD) deficiency. This occurs most often in Negroes and certain Mediterranean peoples.

Although no reports of fetal toxicity are available, the possibility of adverse effects on the fetus should be considered. (See the discussion in the General Information section on Use of Drugs During Pregnancy.) Adequate information on the use of nitrofurans in newborn infants is lacking.

INDIVIDUAL EVALUATIONS

FURAZOLIDONE [Furoxone]

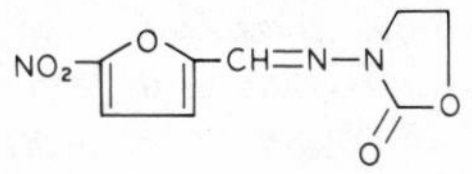

This antibacterial and antiprotozoal agent is moderately effective against a variety of gram-negative and gram-positive enteric organisms, including species of *Salmonella, Shigella, Escherichia, Proteus, Streptococcus,* and *Staphylococcus.* It is used for the treatment of bacterial enteritis and dysentery and for giardiasis, and also may be effective in the treatment of cholera. For other indications, see Chapter 80, Antidiarrheals.

Nausea and vomiting occur frequently, and vesicular or morbilliform pruritic rash has been reported occasionally. The drug is incompletely absorbed but traces appear in the urine. Some of the metabolic degradation products may tint the urine brown.

Furazolidone can produce a disulfiram [Antabuse]-type reaction in some patients after ingestion of alcohol. A metabolite of furazolidone markedly inhibits the activity of monoamine oxidase. Therefore, use of furazolidone with adrenergic agents or with certain foods with significant amounts of tyramine (eg, cheese, yeast extracts, broad beans, chicken livers, pickled herring, chocolate) may cause a hypertensive reaction and is contraindicated. Similarly, its concomitant use with the tricyclic antidepressants is contraindicated. (See Chapter 32, Antidepressants.)

USUAL DOSAGE.—*Oral: Adults*, 100 mg four times daily. *Children*, 6 mg/kg of body weight daily divided into four doses. The drug should not be given to infants under one month of age.

PREPARATIONS.—Furoxone (Eaton). *Oral:* Tablets 100 mg.

AVAILABLE MIXTURE.—Furoxone Liquid (Eaton): Each 15 ml of liquid contains furazolidone 50 mg, kaolin 3 g, pectin 225 mg.

NITROFURANTOIN [Cyantin, Furadantin, Macrodantin, N-Toin, Trantoin]
NITROFURANTOIN SODIUM [Furadantin Sodium]

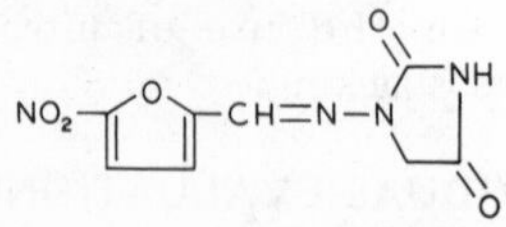

This drug exhibits a wide spectrum of antibacterial activity against both gram-positive and gram-negative organisms, including most strains of *Escherichia coli*, *Staphylococcus pyogenes* var. *albus and aureus*, *Streptococcus pyogenes*, *Aerobacter aerogenes*, and *Paracolobactrum* species. Concentrations of this agent achieved in the urine are bactericidal to sensitive organisms. Nitrofurantoin is effective in the treatment of pyelonephritis and cystitis caused by sensitive organisms. Insufficient evidence is available to ascertain its usefulness in other types of genitourinary tract infections (eg, prostatitis). Administration for longer than 14 days is rarely necessary.

When administered orally, nitrofurantoin is rapidly absorbed from the gastrointestinal tract. Although it is tightly bound to serum protein, it is rapidly excreted by the kidneys; thus, it produces ineffective concentrations of unbound drug in the serum, but high levels in the urine. Effectiveness is reduced when nitrofurantoin is taken orally with antacids.

Nitrofurantoin may produce nausea and vomiting. When administered orally, the possibility of nausea is diminished if the drug is given with meals or if the macrocrystalline form [Macrodantin] is given. Hypersensitivity reactions (diffuse, erythematous, maculopapular rash; urticaria; eczematoid eruption; pruritus), hyperbilirubinemia, cholestatic jaundice, headache, dizziness, and drowsiness have been noted occasionally. Polyneuropathy has occurred, especially in patients with impaired renal function, anemia, diabetes, electrolyte imbalance, or vitamin B deficiency. Serious but nonfatal anaphylactic reactions, as well as allergic pulmonary infiltration with effusion and eosinophilia (Loeffler syndrome), have been observed rarely. This pulmonary reaction is characterized by sudden onset of cough, dyspnea, chills, and fever. See the Introductory Statement for additional information on adverse reactions and precautions.

USUAL DOSAGE.—

Nitrofurantoin:

Oral: The individual doses of nitrofurantoin, administered four times daily, are: *adults*, 50 to 100 mg. *Children up to 7 kg*, 1.5 mg/kg of body weight; *7 to 11 kg*, 12.5 mg; *12 to 21 kg*, 25 mg; *22 to 31 kg*, 37.5 mg; *32 to 40 kg*, 50 mg. The drug should not be given to infants under one month of age. These doses should be reduced by one-half if administration is continued beyond ten days; after another ten days, the amounts should be reduced to one-quarter.

Nitrofurantoin Sodium:

Intramuscular: Adults and adolescents over 55 kg, 180 mg in 3 ml of sterile water for injection twice daily. *Adults and adolescents under 55 kg*, 6.5 mg/kg of body weight daily divided into two doses. Each ml of solution represents 60 mg of nitrofurantoin sodium. Information is inadequate to establish dosage in children under 12 years of age. After five days, the oral or intravenous route should be used.

Intravenous: Adults and adolescents over 55 kg, 180 mg in at least 500 ml of diluent twice daily (crystals are dissolved in 15 ml of 5% dextrose injection or sterile water for injection and then added to 500 ml of sodium chloride injection, 5% dextrose in water, or 5% dextrose in sodium chloride injection). *Adults and adolescents under 55 kg*, 6.5 mg/kg of body weight daily divided into two doses (1 ml of the original 15 ml of solution is added to 33 ml of sodium chloride injection, 5% dextrose in water, or 5% dextrose in sodium chloride injection). The final solution should be infused at the rate of 60 drops per minute. Each ml of solution represents 12 mg of nitrofurantoin sodium. Information is inadequate to establish dosage in children under 12 years of age.

PREPARATIONS.—

Nitrofurantoin:

Cyantin (Lederle). *Oral:* Tablets 50 mg.

Furadantin (Eaton). *Oral:* Suspension 25 mg/5 ml; tablets 50 and 100 mg.

Macrodantin (Eaton). *Oral:* Capsules 25, 50, and 100 mg.

N-Toin (Upjohn), Trantoin (McKesson). *Oral:* Tablets 50 and 100 mg.

Nitrofurantoin Sodium:

Furadantin Sodium (Eaton). *Injection:* Powder 180 mg in 20 ml containers.

ADDITIONAL TRADEMARKS.— Nitrofurantoin: Furachel (Rachelle), Furalan (Lannett). Drug also marketed under generic name.

NITROFURAZONE [Furacin]

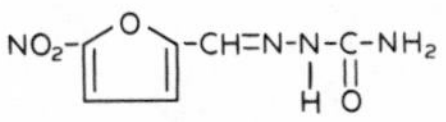

NO_2–(furan ring)–CH=N–N(H)–C(=O)–NH_2

Nitrofurazone is bactericidal for many gram-negative and gram-positive organisms present in surface infections, but strains of *Pseudomonas* and *Proteus* are often resistant. It is useful topically in the treatment of infections of the skin and mucous membranes (eg, infected lacerations, impetigo, otitis externa) caused by sensitive organisms. For other uses, see Chapter 63, Antitrypanosomal Agents, and Chapter 71, Anti-infective and Anti-inflammatory Agents Used in Opthalmology.

Hypersensitization may necessitate discontinuing therapy with this agent. See the Introductory Statement for additional information on adverse reactions and precautions.

USUAL DOSAGE.—*Topical:* The appropriate preparation is applied to the lesion. The frequency of application depends upon the type of preparation used and the patient's response.

PREPARATIONS.—Furacin (Eaton). *Topical:* Cotton, gauze pads, and gauze rolls (impregnated) 0.2%; cream 0.2% in 14 and 28 g containers; cream (vaginal) 0.2% in 85 g containers; powder 0.2% in 14 g containers; soluble dressing 0.2% in 28, 56, 135, and 454 g containers; solution 0.2% in 60 and 473 ml containers; suppositories (vaginal) 6 mg.

ADDITIONAL TRADEMARKS.—Dynazone (Richlyn), Eldezol (Elder). Drug also marketed under generic name.

AVAILABLE MIXTURES.—

Eldezol w/Hydrocortisone (Elder): Ointment containing nitrofurazone 0.2% and hydrocortisone 0.125%.

Furacin Nasal (Eaton): Solution containing nitrofurazone 0.02% and phenylephrine hydrochloride 0.25%.

Furacin Otic (Eaton): Solution containing nitrofurazone 0.2%, nifuroxime 0.375%, and diperodon hydrochloride 2%.

Furacin Urethral Inserts (Eaton): Suppositories containing nitrofurazone 0.2% and diperodon hydrochloride 2%.

Furacin-E Urethral Inserts (Eaton): Suppositories containing nitrofurazone 0.2%, diethylstilbestrol 0.007%, and diperodon hydrochloride 2%.

Furacin-HC Otic (Eaton): Solution containing nitrofurazone 0.2% and hydrocortisone acetate 1%.

Furacin-HC Urethral Inserts (Eaton): Suppositories containing nitrofurazone 0.2%, hydrocortisone acetate 1%, and diperodon hydrochloride 2%.

Furacort (Eaton): Cream containing nitrofurazone 0.2% and hydrocortisone acetate 1%.

Chapter 57

AMINOGLYCOSIDE ANTIBACTERIAL AGENTS AND MISCELLANEOUS ANTIMICROBIAL DRUGS

A varied assortment of antibacterial agents is discussed in this chapter. Several of these compounds (gentamicin [Garamycin], kanamycin [Kantrex], neomycin [Mycifradin, Myciguent, Neobiotic], and streptomycin) may be considered as a class since they all can be grouped chemically as aminoglycosides. Paromomycin also is an aminoglycoside antibiotic, but it is used only for the treatment of intestinal amebiasis (see Chapter 62, Amebicides). In addition, these aminoglycosides share many pharmacologic properties, have similar antibacterial spectra, and exhibit certain common toxic effects.

Since antibacterial activity is the only common bond between the remaining drugs discussed in this chapter, the use of morphologic, chemical, or pharmacologic properties as a basis of classification is not applicable.

AMINOGLYCOSIDE ANTIBACTERIAL AGENTS

GENTAMICIN SULFATE [Garamycin]

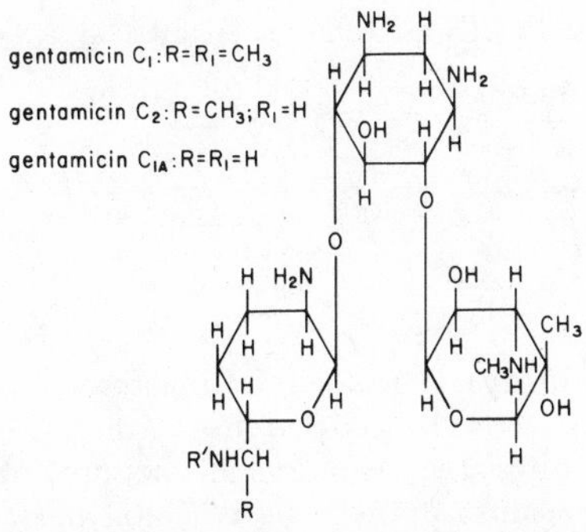

gentamicin C_1: $R = R_1 = CH_3$

gentamicin C_2: $R = CH_3$; $R_1 = H$

gentamicin C_{1A}: $R = R_1 = H$

Gentamicin sulfate, obtained from cultures of *Micromonospora purpurea,* is a mixture of three closely related antibacterial agents. Preparations are available for both parenteral and topical use. It is not given orally since it is poorly absorbed from the gastrointestinal tract. The spectrum and therapeutic activity of gentamicin are similar to those of neomycin, except that this drug is more active against *Pseudomonas* and is somewhat more potent than neomycin on a weight basis. Gentamicin is active against *Enterobacter aerogenes, Escherichia coli,* and *Klebsiella pneumoniae;* indole-positive and indole-negative *Proteus* species; *Pseudomonas aeruginosa;* some species of *Neisseria* and nonpigmented *Serratia;* and most species of *Salmonella* and *Shigella.* It has limited activity against some gram-positive bacteria (eg, *Staphylococcus*). Resistant genera include *Clostridium, Pneumococcus,* and *Streptococcus.* Gentamicin is not effective against *Bacteroides,* fungi, or viruses.

The systemic use of gentamicin should be restricted to the treatment of serious infections caused by susceptible gram-negative bacteria. Most gram-negative septicemias are so severe that if such an infection is suspected, gentamicin may be given empirically while awaiting identification and determination of antibacterial sensitivity of the causative organism. The demonstration of sensitivity is important, since not all strains of susceptible genera are sensitive to gentamicin. When treating urinary tract infections, it is helpful to make the urine alkaline, since the antibiotic is more active in an alkaline than an acid medium.

A wide variety of infected dermatitides respond to topical treatment with gentamicin. Nevertheless, this drug generally should not be used topically because resistant organisms may develop, thereby depriving the patient of a valuable antibacterial agent that can be used systemically. Serious gram-negative infection in burn patients represents one of the few valid topical uses of gentamicin. Topical preparations also are used in the eye (see Chapter 71, Anti-infective and Anti-inflammatory Agents Used in Ophthalmology).

Although bacterial resistance to gentamicin develops infrequently, it does occur, particularly with widespread topical use. Organisms resistant to this drug have shown cross resistance to other aminoglycoside antibiotics.

The average half-life of gentamicin after intramuscular injection is slightly more than two hours. Most of the antibiotic is excreted in the urine unchanged.

Gentamicin can cause renal damage as well as damage to both the cochlear and vestibular portions of the eighth cranial nerve. Auditory impairment is maximal in the high-tone range, although patients ordinarily retain normal conversational hearing function. Vestibular damage is seen more often than auditory damage and complete loss of vestibular function has occurred during gentamicin therapy. Ototoxicity is most likely to occur in patients with impaired renal function. To minimize this possibility, the interval between doses must be lengthened in proportion to the degree of renal failure as estimated by creatinine clearance. (See the manufacturer's literature for a chart suggesting dosage ranges in individuals with impaired renal function.) Serum concentrations of gentamicin also can be a useful guide to dosage: therapeutic blood levels are usually in the range of 5 to 7 μg/ml; serum concentrations in excess of 12 μg/ml are generally considered to be hazardous. Gentamicin should not be given with other ototoxic drugs since the effects might be additive.

Infrequently reported reactions include anemia, purpura, fever, hypotension, nausea, vomiting, arthralgia, and convulsions. Laboratory abnormalities include increased transaminase (SGOT, SGPT) activity and increased unbound serum bilirubin.

Because gentamicin crosses the placental barrier, it can cause renal and otic toxicity in the fetus; therefore, it is contraindicated in pregnant women unless a life-threatening infection exists that does not respond to other antibiotics. Superinfection with fungi or other organisms can occur during therapy.

Gentamicin may produce neuromuscular blockade that enhances the action of other neuromuscular blocking drugs, general anesthetics, parenterally administered magnesium, or other agents with muscle relaxant properties. This drug is incompatible with heparin, with which it reacts to form a precipitate. Gentamicin is inactivated when mixed with carbenicillin and allowed to stand.

USUAL DOSAGE.—

Intramuscular, Intravenous: Adults and children with normal renal function (ie, creatinine clearance equal to or in excess of 70 ml/minute/1.73 M^2 of body surface) may safely be given up to 5 mg/kg of body weight daily. The total daily dosage usually is given in equally divided amounts every eight hours. If renal function is impaired, the interval is lengthened (see the manufacturer's dosage chart). *Premature infants and infants less than 5 days old,* 1 to 3 mg/kg daily in three divided doses.

When administered intravenously, the drug can be given in either 5% dextrose injection or isotonic sodium chloride injection. The concentration should not exceed 1 mg/ml and the dose should be administered over a period of at least 30 minutes. The total duration of therapy by either route should not exceed 10 days.

Topical: The topical use of this drug is not advisable except under unusual circumstances (see above). The manufacturer's suggested dosage is: *Adults and children,* a small quantity of ointment or cream is carefully applied to the lesion three or four times daily. The treated area may be covered with a loose gauze dressing if indicated.

PREPARATIONS.—(Strengths are expressed in terms of the base.)

Garamycin (Schering).

Injection: Solution 10 and 40 mg/ml in 2 ml containers.

Topical: Cream and ointment 0.1% in 15 g containers; ointment (ophthalmic) 3 mg/g in 1/8 oz containers; solution (ophthalmic) 3 mg/ml in 5 ml containers.

KANAMYCIN SULFATE [Kantrex]

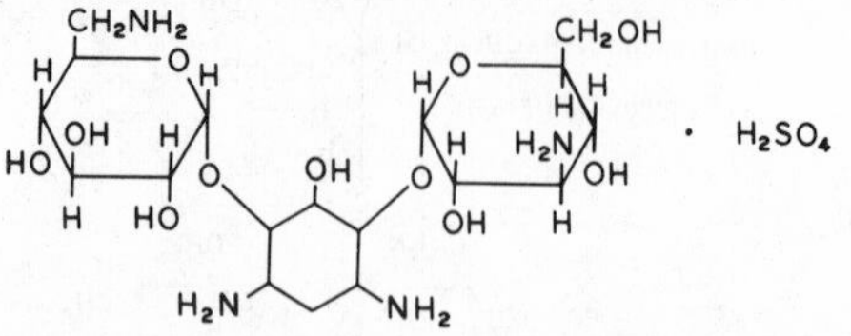

· H_2SO_4

Kanamycin has an antibacterial spectrum similar to that of other aminoglycoside antibiotics (eg, gentamicin, neomycin). It is active against *Escherichia coli* and most strains of *Enterobacter, Klebsiella, Mycobacterium, Neisseria, Proteus, Salmonella, Shigella, Staphylococcus,* and *Vibrio.* Resistant genera include *Bacteroides*, *Clostridium*, *Enterococcus*, *Pneumococcus*, *Streptococcus*, and *Pseudomonas*. Kanamycin has no effect on fungi or viruses. Some organisms (eg, *E. coli*, *Mycobacterium*, *Staphylococcus)* develop resistance rapidly. These same organisms also become resistant to neomycin, gentamicin, paromomycin, and streptomycin.

Kanamycin is used parenterally to treat infections caused by susceptible organisms, and it is used orally to diminish the bacterial content of the gastrointestinal tract prior to surgery or to treat enteritis caused by susceptible organisms. It can reduce bacterial production of ammonia and therefore may be useful in cirrhotic patients with gastrointestinal bleeding in whom hepatic coma is a threat. Although there is little intestinal absorption, caution must be used when giving this drug orally if renal insufficiency exists since some absorption occurs and toxic levels may result.

For other uses of kanamycin, see Chapter 58, Antituberculous Agents, and Chapter 71, Anti-infective and Anti-inflammatory Agents Used in Ophthalmology.

Parenteral use of kanamycin may permanently damage both the cochlear and vestibular portions of the eighth cranial nerve, and the danger is enhanced if renal disease is present. The susceptibility of a patient to auditory or vestibular damage increases with advancing age. Also, kanamycin is more likely to affect the eighth cranial nerve if it is given with other ototoxic drugs or rapid-acting diuretic agents (eg, ethacrynic acid), and it may be contraindicated in patients who have already sustained drug-induced damage to the eighth cranial nerve. Kanamycin should be discontinued if tinnitus, dizziness, or vertigo occurs.

Hypersensitivity reactions such as fever, pruritus, rash, and eosinophilia occur with kanamycin therapy. Other untoward effects include renal damage, headache, and paresthesias. Stomatitis, diarrhea, and proctitis may result from oral administration. Pain and, occasionally, sterile abscesses may occur when kanamycin is injected.

Kanamycin exerts a neuromuscular blocking effect that may enhance the action of other neuromuscular blocking drugs, general anesthetics, parenterally administered magnesium, or other compounds with muscle relaxant properties. Therefore, it must be used with caution in patients receiving these agents.

USUAL DOSAGE.—Daily parenteral doses of 15 mg/kg of body weight probably should not be exceeded in order to minimize toxicity; the maximal daily *adult* dose is 1.5 g. In patients with renal disease, it may be necessary to give the drug at a reduced dosage level every third or fourth day in order to keep the serum level within the therapeutic dosage range of 15 to 20 μg/ml. Toxicity has been observed at levels above 25 μg/ml.

Intramuscular: Adults and children, 15 mg/kg of body weight daily in divided doses every eight hours.

Intravenous: This route is used only when it is essential to obtain high blood levels of the drug rapidly. The drug should be diluted to a concentration of 2.5 mg/ml in sodium chloride injection or 5% dextrose injection and the same amount given intramuscularly is infused slowly.

Intrapleural, *Intraperitoneal:* The administration of kanamycin by these routes is hazardous because a potentially toxic amount of the drug can be absorbed. The manufacturer's suggested regimen is to irrigate the cavity with a solution containing 2.5 mg/ml.

Oral (not for systemic effects): *Adults*, up to 8 g daily in divided doses (eg, for cleansing the bowel, 1 g every four hours for 24 hours followed by 1 g every six hours for 36 to 72 hours). *Infants and children*, 50 mg/kg of body weight daily in four to six divided doses for five to seven days.

PREPARATIONS.—(Strengths are expressed in terms of the base.)

Kantrex (Bristol).

Injection: Solution 37.5 and 250 mg/ml in 2 ml containers and 333 mg/ml in 3 ml containers.

Oral: Capsules 500 mg.

NEOMYCIN SULFATE [Mycifradin Sulfate, Myciguent, Neobiotic]

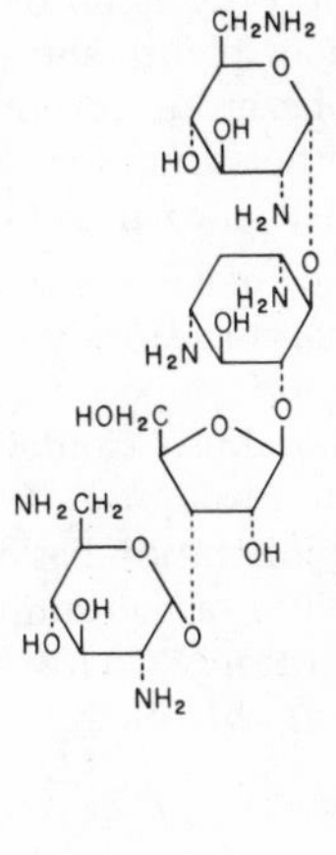

This aminoglycoside antibiotic is probably as effective as kanamycin but is more toxic; both drugs are bactericidal. Neomycin is effective against *Escherichia* and most species of *Enterobacter*, *Klebsiella*, *Salmonella*, *Shigella*, and *Proteus*. Many strains of *Staphylococcus aureus* are sensitive. Genera that have developed moderate to marked resistance include *Clostridium*, *Pneumococcus*, *Enterobacter*, and most strains of *Streptococcus*. This antibiotic is ineffective against *Pseudomonas*, fungi, and viruses.

Neomycin is most commonly used topically but has been administered orally, intramuscularly, and intraperitoneally. However, because of the availability of safer, effective antibiotics, circumstances in which use of the injectable form is justified are virtually nonexistent. Neomycin is used orally in cirrhotic patients with gastrointestinal bleeding in whom hepatic coma is a threat, in order to decrease ammonia-producing organisms in the gastrointestinal tract. It also is given orally to eliminate most pathogenic bacteria from the bowel prior to intestinal surgery, although this use is infrequent.

For other uses, see Chapter 71, Anti-infective and Anti-inflammatory Agents Used in Ophthalmology and Chapter 13, Agents Used to Treat Hyperlipidemia.

When given parenterally, neomycin is ototoxic and nephrotoxic; these effects are dose related. As with gentamicin and kanamycin, the nephrotoxicity caused by neomycin may be reversible, but the ototoxicity involving the cochlear portion of the eighth cranial nerve is usually irreversible and may progress insidiously after the drug is discontinued. Although neomycin is poorly absorbed from the gastrointestinal tract or from topical lesions, enough absorption can occur to produce deafness, particularly in patients with renal impairment. The drug is absorbed readily from the peritoneum or pleura and its use to irrigate these cavities is hazardous. Neomycin should not be given with other drugs that cause ototoxicity or nephrotoxicity since the effects are additive.

Diarrhea and malabsorption are the most common adverse reactions observed following oral administration; superinfections may result from prolonged oral use. Contact dermatitis may occur after topical use. Intraperitoneal or intravenous administration has caused apnea.

Neomycin has a neuromuscular blocking effect and enhances the action of other neuromuscular blocking drugs, general anesthetics, parenterally administered magnesium, and other agents with muscle relaxant properties.

USUAL DOSAGE.—

Topical: An appropriate preparation is applied one or two times daily.

Oral: For hepatic coma, *adults*, 4 to 12 g daily in four doses for five to six days. For infectious diarrhea, *adults*, 100 mg/kg of body weight daily divided into four doses; *newborn and premature infants*, 50 mg/kg daily divided into four doses; *older infants and children*, 100 mg/kg daily divided into four doses.

Intramuscular: This evaluation does not support a useful dosage regimen by this route. The manufacturer's suggested dosage is: *Adults*, 15 mg/kg of body weight daily (maximum, 1 g) divided into four doses. *Newborn and premature infants*, 54 mg/kg daily divided into four doses. *Older infants and children*, 7.5 to 15 mg/kg daily divided into four doses for severe infections (daily maximum, 1 g). The full initial dose can be given to patients with renal impairment, but subsequent doses should be reduced to maintain blood levels below 30 μg/ml, since nephrotoxicity and irreversible ototoxicity may occur. The manufacturer suggests that use of neomycin by this route be limited to the treatment of urinary tract infections in hospitalized patients in whom no other antibacterial agent is effective.

PREPARATIONS.—

Mycifradin Sulfate (Upjohn).

Oral: Solution 125 mg/5 ml; tablets 500 mg.

Injection: Powder (sterile) 500 mg.

Myciguent (Upjohn). *Topical:* Cream 5 mg/g in ½ oz containers; ointment 5 mg/g in ½, 1, and 4 oz containers; ointment (ophthalmic) 5 mg/g in 1/8 oz containers.

Neobiotic (Pfizer). *Oral:* Tablets 500 mg.

Drug also marketed by other manufacturers under generic name.

STREPTOMYCIN SULFATE

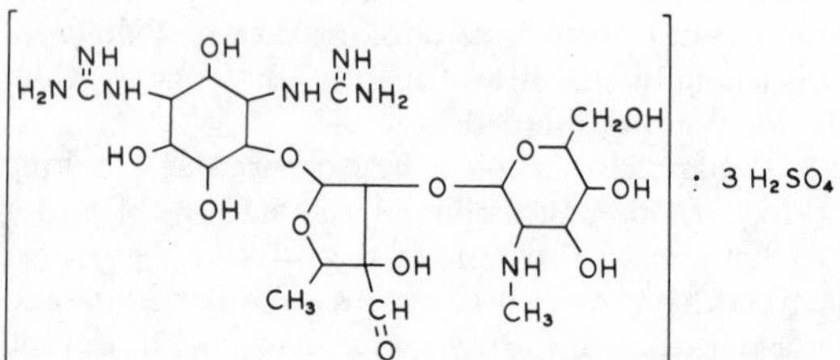

Streptomycin is active against a variety of

gram-positive, gram-negative, and acid-fast organisms. Like other members of the aminoglycoside group, it usually is bactericidal for sensitive organisms. The most sensitive genera are *Brucella, Francisella, Pasteurella, Mycobacterium*, and *Shigella. Bacteroides, Clostridium, Rickettsia*, viruses, and fungi are totally resistant. Since more effective aminoglycoside antibiotics exist (ie, gentamicin, kanamycin), the clinical use of streptomycin is limited to the treatment of very few infections. These include tuberculosis (see Chapter 58, Antituberculous Agents), tularemia, and bubonic plague. However, physicians treating acutely ill patients with plague prefer not to use streptomycin, because it is so rapidly bactericidal that a Herxheimer-like reaction, which can be fatal, is virtually always precipitated. Streptomycin also is used with large doses of penicillin in the treatment of enterococcal endocarditis, but fixed-dose combinations of streptomycin and penicillin are not recommended for this use (see the discussion on Mixtures in Chapter 48, Penicillins). Streptomycin is effective in infections caused by *Haemophilus influenzae* and some strains of *Klebsiella pneumoniae.* Its value in urinary tract infections is limited because of the rapid development of resistant organisms and the hazard of superinfection. This drug exerts its greatest activity in an alkaline medium and in the presence of oxygen. For use of streptomycin in the eye, see Chapter 71, Anti-infective and Anti-inflammatory Agents Used in Ophthalmology.

Many organisms develop resistance to streptomycin rapidly; in fact, some become streptomycin-dependent. Cross resistance between streptomycin and neomycin has been reported, and similar resistance is possible between streptomycin and gentamicin or kanamycin.

The intramuscular route is commonly used, and injection should be deep into the muscle since pain and sterile abscesses have occurred with more superficial injection. The intrapleural and intrathecal routes also have been used, but intrathecal injections should never be made with any preparation containing a preservative. The topical application of streptomycin is contraindicated because of poor absorption and the high risk of sensitization.

Streptomycin causes hypersensitivity reactions ranging from rash to exfoliative dermatitis and anaphylactic shock; hematopoietic damage, including neutropenia, agranulocytosis, aplastic anemia, and, rarely, thrombocytopenic purpura; renal damage; and neurologic changes, including peripheral neuritis, damage to the cochlear and vestibular portions of the eighth cranial nerve (a fairly common occurrence) and, less commonly, damage to the optic nerve. Dizziness is the usual warning sign of labyrinthine dysfunction, and tinnitus the sign of auditory damage. Administration to pregnant women has damaged the eighth cranial nerve of the fetus. Streptomycin should not be given with other ototoxic drugs since effects may be additive. Intrathecal administration has produced radiculitis, transverse myelitis, arachnoiditis, nerve root pain, and even paraplegia. The more serious adverse reactions usually are related to the size of the dose and the duration of administration.

Streptomycin has a weak neuromuscular blocking effect that may enhance the action of other neuromuscular blocking drugs, general anesthetics, parenterally administered magnesium, and other agents with muscle relaxant properties. Therefore, it must be used with caution in patients receiving these agents.

High concentrations of this drug are excreted in the urine, which may account for the renal damage sometimes seen. The possibility of renal damage may be lessened by maintaining an alkaline urine with administration of 500 mg each of sodium citrate and sodium bicarbonate every three hours. Dosage for patients with renal impairment must be based upon the degree of impairment as determined by creatinine clearance.

USUAL DOSAGE.—

Intramuscular: Adults, 15 to 25 mg/kg of body weight daily in two divided doses for seven to ten days and 1 g daily thereafter; *children*, 20 to 30 mg/kg daily in two divided doses.

Intrapleural: Adults, 500 mg to 1 g in sodium chloride injection not more than once every 24 to 48 hours.

Intrathecal: Adults, 75 to 100 mg dissolved in 10 ml of isotonic sodium chloride injection and given over a ten-minute period after withdrawal of 10 ml of cerebrospinal fluid. *Children*, 1 mg/kg of body weight daily.

PREPARATIONS.—*Injection:* Powder (for solution) 1 and 5 g; solution 200 mg/ml in 5 ml containers, 400 mg/ml in 2.5 and 12.5 ml containers, 500 mg/ml in 1, 2, and 10 ml containers. Drug marketed under generic name.

MISCELLANEOUS ANTIBACTERIAL AGENTS

BACITRACIN [Baciguent]
BACITRACIN ZINC

```
                                  S
                                 / \
                                |   C—CH—CHCH₂CH₃
                                |   ‖   |    |
                                 \_N    NH₂  CH₃
                                  |
                                 C=O
                                  |
              D-Asp(NH₂)       L-Leu
                  |              |
 D-Phe—L-His—L-Asp             D-Glu
   |                             |
 L-Ileu—D-Orn—L-Lys————————L-Ileu
```

Bacitracin, a mixture of polypeptide antibiotics produced by a strain of *Bacillus subtilis*, and its zinc salt are bactericidal against gram-positive organisms and *Neisseria;* they are inactive against most other gram-negative organisms. The development of resistant strains is rare, but some strains of *Staphylococcus* are inherently resistant. Since nephrotoxicity, primarily in the form of epithelial degeneration of the convoluted tubules, may occur after injection and since other effective agents with similar antibacterial spectra are available, parenteral use of bacitracin has been abandoned. Oral administration is ineffective because the drug is not absorbed from the gastrointestinal tract. Bacitracin is available in ointment form and as a component of mixtures for topical application; the zinc salt is used only in mixtures (see the section on Topical Mixtures). For use of bacitracin in the eye, see Chapter 71, Anti-infective and Anti-inflammatory Agents Used in Ophthalmology. Bacitracin is stable in petrolatum but not in water-miscible bases.

Hypersensitivity reactions occur rarely when this drug is applied topically.

USUAL DOSAGE.—*Topical: Adults and children,* ointment is applied to lesions once or twice daily.

PREPARATIONS.—Baciguent (Upjohn). *Topical:* Ointment 500 units/g in ½, 1, and 4 oz containers; ointment (ophthalmic) 500 units/g in 1/8 oz containers. Drug also marketed by many manufacturers under generic name.

GRAMICIDIN

Gramicidin is available only as a component of antibacterial mixtures (see the evaluation on Tyrothricin and the section on Topical Mixtures).

METHENAMINE [Uritone]
METHENAMINE MANDELATE [Mandelamine]
METHENAMINE HIPPURATE [Hiprex]

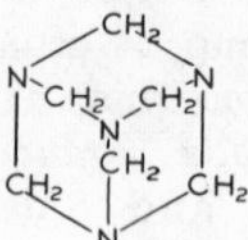

Methenamine is a urinary antiseptic that acts by liberating formaldehyde in an acid medium. It has either a bacteriostatic or bactericidal effect, depending upon the amount of formaldehyde produced by its hydrolysis. This drug is active against a variety of gram-positive and gram-negative organisms including *Escherichia coli,* a common cause of urinary tract infections. Methenamine should not be used as the sole therapeutic agent for the treatment of many acute urinary tract infections, including acute pyelonephritis. Since this agent is active only in acid media, its effectiveness is markedly diminished in patients infected with urea-splitting organisms such as *Proteus* and some *Pseudomonas* species. To assure a urinary pH of 5.5 or below, large doses of ascorbic acid, arginine hydrochloride, or methionine can be used. Alternatively, ammonium chloride may be given three or four times daily; however, large doses of ammonium chloride may induce a metabolic acidosis in patients with diminished renal function. Use of methenamine often is restricted to patients with infections refractory to more effective antibacterial agents because of such problems as structural abnormalities or indwelling catheters. Methenamine is readily absorbed from the gastrointestinal tract and rapidly excreted.

The usually low level of toxicity makes methenamine a relatively safe drug. Release of formaldehyde may account for the mild gastric irritation that sometimes occurs. Formulation of enteric-coated preparations has met only with limited success in preventing this reaction. Large doses of methenamine may cause acute inflammation of the urinary tract. If this occurs, the drug should be discontinued and an alkalizing salt such as sodium bicarbonate given. On rare occasions, hypersensitivity reactions (usually manifested as a rash) have occurred.

Methenamine mandelate combines the antibacterial activity of methenamine with the weak antibacterial effects of mandelic acid. This compound also is effective only in acidic urine, a condition which mandelic acid helps to establish. However, urinary pH frequently will not be made sufficiently acid by methenamine mandelate alone to permit antibacterial action.

Therefore, in many patients, additional measures must be taken to decrease the pH (eg, 4 to 10 g of ascorbic acid daily in divided doses).

The hippurate salt of methenamine frequently acidifies the urine adequately for maximal action of the methenamine. Nevertheless, the recommended daily dose of 2 g occasionally may be less than optimal and additional acidification may be necessary.

Methenamine salts can be given for prolonged periods without the development of resistant organisms. These salts generally are well tolerated but have caused nausea, gastric distress, rash, and dysuria in some patients. They are contraindicated in dehydrated patients and in those with severe renal disease or hepatic insufficiency.

Patients taking methenamine compounds should be taught to measure urinary pH, just as the diabetic tests his urine, and they should know how to adjust the acidity if these agents are to be used effectively.

Since sulfamethizole and sulfathiazole may form insoluble precipitates with formaldehyde in the urine, methenamine compounds should be avoided during therapy with these two agents.

USUAL DOSAGE.—

Methenamine, Methenamine Mandelate:

Oral: Adults, 1 g four times daily; *children under 6 years of age,* 50 mg/kg of body weight daily divided into three doses; *children 6 to 12 years,* 500 mg four times daily.

Methenamine Hippurate:

Oral: Adults and children over 12 years of age, 1 g twice daily; *children 6 to 12 years,* 500 mg to 1 g twice daily.

PREPARATIONS.—

Methenamine:

Uritone (Parke, Davis). *Oral:* Elixir 400 mg/5 ml; tablets 325 mg.

Methenamine Mandelate:

Mandelamine (Warner-Chilcott). *Oral:* Suspension 250 and 500 mg/5 ml; tablets (enteric-coated) 250 and 500 mg and 1 g.

Methenamine Hippurate:

Hiprex (Merrell-National). *Oral:* Tablets 1 g.

ADDITIONAL TRADEMARKS.—Methenamine Mandelate: Mandacon (Alcon), Methendelate (Century), Prov-U-Sep (Reid-Provident), Renelate (Fellows-Testagar). Drugs also marketed by other manufacturers under generic name.

METHENAMINE AND SODIUM BIPHOSPHATE

This product is used for the same purposes and has essentially the same efficacy as the other methenamine preparations (see the preceding evaluation). Sodium biphosphate is added to methenamine to provide an acid urine. If acidification is inadequate, an additional acidifying agent may be needed.

USUAL DOSAGE.—*Oral:* 1 tablet four times daily.

PREPARATIONS.—Methenamine and Sodium Biphosphate, N.F. *Oral:* Each tablet contains 500 mg each of methenamine and sodium biphosphate. Several preparations also are available containing various quantities and ratios of the ingredients.

OTHER URINARY ANTISEPTIC MIXTURES CONTAINING METHENAMINE

The following combinations are listed only to acknowledge their availability. The ratios of drugs in these mixtures prevent proper dosage adjustment of individual ingredients. In addition, some are too complex to provide rational therapy, and some also contain ingredients of dubious merit.

PREPARATIONS.—

Azolate (Amfre-Grant): Each tablet contains methenamine mandelate 250 mg, methionine 50 mg, and phenazopyridine hydrochloride 25 mg.

Azo-Mandelamine (Warner-Chilcott): Each tablet contains methenamine mandelate 500 mg and phenazopyridine hydrochloride 50 mg.

Donnasep (Robins): Each tablet contains methenamine mandelate 500 mg, atropine sulfate 0.0097 mg, scopolamine hydrobromide 0.0033 mg, hyoscyamine sulfate 0.0519 mg, phenazopyridine hydrochloride 50 mg, and phenobarbital 8.1 mg.

Donnasep-MP (Robins): Each tablet contains the same formulation as Donnasep without phenazopyridine hydrochloride.

Hexalol (Central): Each tablet contains methenamine 41 mg, methylene blue 5.4 mg, atropine sulfate 0.03 mg, hyoscyamine 0.03 mg, benzoic acid 4.5 mg, phenyl salicylate 18 mg, and gelsemium 6 mg.

Hexatropine (Elder): Each tablet contains methenamine 130 mg, ammonium chloride 130 mg, atropine sulfate 0.1 mg, and sulfacetamide 130 mg.

Mesulfin (Ayerst): Each tablet contains methenamine mandelate 250 mg and sulfamethizole 250 mg.

Renaltabs (Fellows-Testagar): Each tablet contains methenamine 130 mg, phenyl salicylate 32.4 mg, benzoic acid 8 mg, hyoscyamine sulfate 0.03 mg, atropine sulfate 0.06 mg, and methylene blue 6.5 mg.

Septamide (Lemmon): Each tablet contains methenamine mandelate 250 mg, sulfacetamide 250 mg, and homatropine methylbromide 2.5 mg.

Urised (Alcon): Each tablet contains methenamine 40.8 mg, atropine sulfate 0.03 mg, benzoic acid 4.5 mg, hyoscyamine 0.03 mg, methylene blue 5.4 mg, and phenyl salicylate 18.1 mg.

Urisedamine (Alcon): Each tablet contains methenamine mandelate 500 mg and hyoscyamine 0.15 mg.

NALIDIXIC ACID [NegGram]

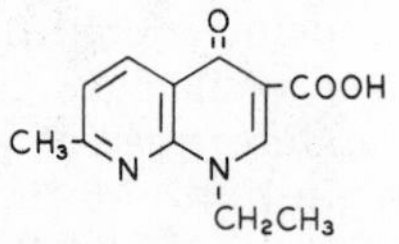

O, COOH, CH_3, N, N, CH_2CH_3

Nalidixic acid is used orally in the treatment of urinary tract infections. It is effective clinically against certain gram-negative bacteria, especially *Escherichia coli* and most species of *Proteus;* treatment of infections caused by *Proteus* organisms is the most important indication for this drug since many strains are resistant to other antibacterial agents. Nalidixic acid is less active against other coliform bacteria such as *Enterobacter* and *Klebsiella. Streptococcus faecalis* and most species of *Pseudomonas* are usually resistant. This drug is relatively ineffective against gram-positive bacteria.

Nalidixic acid has a fairly narrow antibacterial spectrum; therefore, bacterial sensitivity tests are useful in determining when this agent should be used. However, since *S. faecalis* and *Pseudomonas* infections are uncommon, this drug might be used initially in suspected gram-negative infections pending the results of bacterial culture. Nalidixic acid also can be used in acute uncomplicated cystitis in women without prior sensitivity testing, since this condition is almost always caused by sensitive organisms. As with any antibacterial agent used to treat urinary tract infections, follow-up cultures are indicated to determine if the infection has been eliminated. The low concentration of nalidixic acid in the blood and its susceptibility to inhibition by plasma proteins makes this antibiotic unsuitable for use in the treatment of systemic infections.

The degree of resistance and the speed with which some organisms develop resistance to nalidixic acid during therapy is so great that the drug is useless as a therapeutic agent against these bacteria. This is an important drawback to use of nalidixic acid, since therapy often must be continued for two weeks or longer. There appears to be no cross resistance to other antibacterial agents.

The frequency of untoward effects associated with nalidixic acid is usually low. The most common reactions are nausea, vomiting, rash, and urticaria. Diarrhea, fever, eosinophilia, photosensitivity, and bleeding from the gastrointestinal tract occur occasionally. Increased levels of blood urea nitrogen (BUN) and serum glutamic oxaloacetic transaminase (SGOT) have been observed in a few patients. Hemolytic anemia attributed to nalidixic acid also has been reported; patients with a deficiency of glucose-6-phosphate dehydrogenase (G6PD) seem most susceptible. Leukopenia and thrombocytopenia also have occurred.

This drug occasionally causes neurologic reactions (headache, malaise, drowsiness, dizziness, myalgia, muscular weakness, visual abnormalities, excitement, confusion, hallucinations). Overdosage has caused convulsions in both children and adults; thus, care must be exercised in treating children at home, or in treating any patient with a history of convulsive disorders or with central nervous system damage. Also, since nalidixic acid may accumulate in patients with renal and hepatic insufficiency, it should be used cautiously in these patients, especially if neurologic damage is present.

Nalidixic acid can cause increased intracranial pressure and false-positive reactions to nonenzyme tests for glucose in the urine. Caution is indicated if this drug is used during pregnancy, although some pregnant women have taken it during the second and third trimesters without undesirable effects on the mother or fetus. This antibiotic should not be used in infants under 1 month of age. Superinfection with fungal organisms has not been noted.

USUAL DOSAGE.—*Oral: Adults,* 4 g daily in four divided doses for at least one week and preferably for two weeks. Dosage is then reduced to 2 g daily. *Children,* 55 mg/kg of body weight daily in two to four divided doses. For prolonged therapy, the daily dose may be reduced to 33 mg/kg.

PREPARATIONS.—NegGram (Winthrop).

Oral: Tablets 250 and 500 mg.

NOVOBIOCIN CALCIUM [Albamycin Calcium]
NOVOBIOCIN SODIUM [Albamycin Sodium]

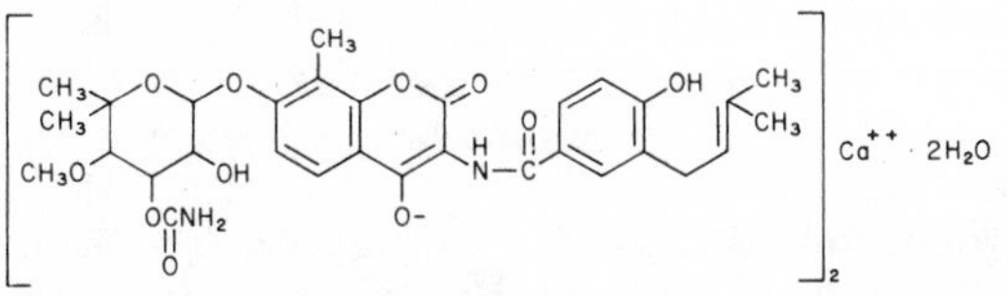

Novobiocin has a narrow antibacterial spectrum; it is effective against most gram-positive pathogens and some species of *Proteus* and *Pseudomonas pseudomallei.* Staphylococci rapidly develop resistance, and the drug is ineffective against the common gram-negative pathogens. Novobiocin is not the drug of first or second choice for any infection.

The high incidence of adverse reactions (up to 20%), including a variety of rashes, various blood dyscrasias, fever, myocarditis, and pneumonitis, strongly indicates that use of novobiocin should be abandoned in favor of less toxic antibiotics. Its irritant action causes pain on injection. Nausea, vomiting, and diarrhea occur after oral administration. A metabolite of this drug can produce yellowish discoloration of skin and sclerae 24 hours after administration. Superinfections are not uncommon. Novobiocin should not be used in newborn and premature infants because it interferes with the metabolism of bilirubin.

USUAL DOSAGE.—Since this preparation is considered to have questionable merit, no useful dosage regimen is recognized. The manufacturer's suggested dosage is:

Oral: Adults, 250 to 500 mg every 6 hours or 500 mg to 1 g every 12 hours; administration is continued for 48 hours after the temperature returns to normal. *Children,* 15 to 45 mg/kg of body weight daily in divided doses every six hours.

Intravenous, Intramuscular: Adults, 500 mg at 12-hour intervals. Oral administration should replace injection as soon as possible; *children,* 15 to 30 mg/kg of body weight daily in divided doses every 12 hours.

PREPARATIONS.—

Novobiocin Calcium:

Albamycin [calcium] (Upjohn). *Oral:* Syrup 125 mg/5 ml.

Novobiocin Sodium:

Albamycin [sodium] (Upjohn).
Oral: Capsules 250 mg.

Injection: Solution 100 mg/ml in 5 ml containers.

SPECTINOMYCIN DIHYDROCHLORIDE PENTAHYDRATE [Trobicin]

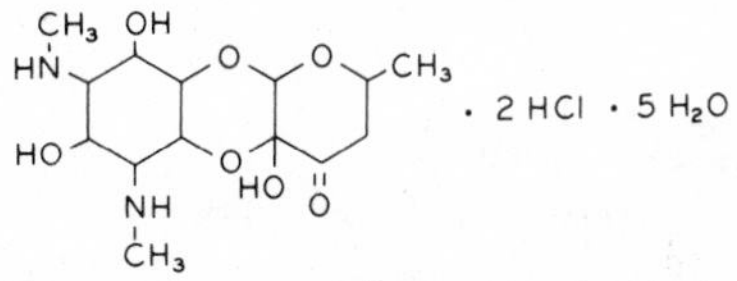

Spectinomycin is an aminocyclitol antibiotic produced by a strain of *Streptomyces spectabilis.* It is active against most strains of *Neisseria gonorrhoeae* in vitro; however, penicillin G is preferred in the treatment of gonorrhea unless patients have known resistant organisms or are allergic to penicillin. The resistance of the gonococcus to penicillin is still relative and can usually be overcome by increasing the dose of penicillin G. Cross resistance between spectinomycin and penicillin in the treatment of gonorrhea has not as yet been demonstrated. Spectinomycin is not bound by plasma protein to any appreciable extent.

Clinically, spectinomycin may be used to treat acute gonorrheal urethritis and proctitis in men and acute cervicitis and proctitis in women when these conditions are caused by susceptible strains of *N. gonorrhoeae.* It is not effective in treating syphilis and, as with several other antibiotics, use of large doses may mask or delay the symptoms of incubating syphilis.

Adverse effects following administration of a single dose occur infrequently and include pain at the site of injection, nausea, chills, fever, insomnia, urticaria, and oliguria. Laboratory abnormalities reported following multiple dosage regimens include a decrease in hemoglobin, hematocrit, and serum creatinine clearance, and an elevation of serum alkaline phosphatase, blood urea nitrogen (BUN), and serum glutamic pyruvic transaminase (SGPT).

Effects on the fetus when the drug is used during pregnancy and the safety of its use in infants and children has not been established.

USUAL DOSAGE.—*Intramuscular: Adults,* in men, 2 to 4 g. The larger doses are indicated for re-treatment after other antibiotic therapy has failed or for patients living in areas where resistance to penicillin is known to be prevalent. In women, 4 g. In both men and women, the dose should be divided between two gluteal injection sites.

PREPARATIONS.—Trobicin (Upjohn). *Injection:* Powder (for solution) 2 and 4 g (supplied with 3.5 and 6.5 ml of diluent, respectively).

TROLEANDOMYCIN [Cyclamycin, TAO]

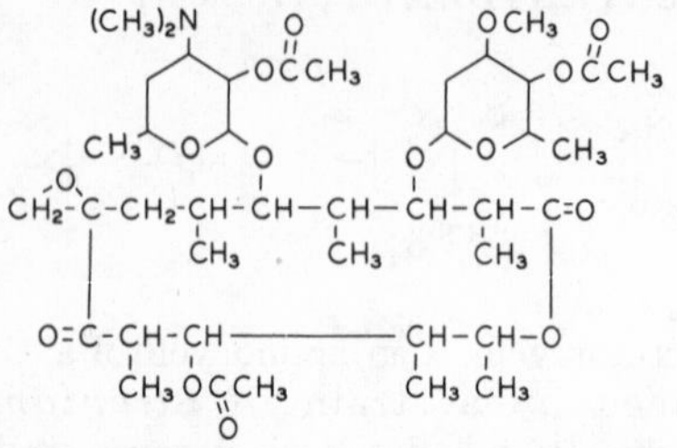

Troleandomycin has an in vitro antibacterial spectrum similar to that of erythromycin, but it has no advantage over erythromycin. This antibacterial agent should be used only when an organism is not sensitive to more effective drugs since it is no longer the drug of first or second choice for any infection. Troleandomycin is given orally and is most active against species of the gram-positive genera, *Clostridium*, *Corynebacterium*, *Pneumococcus*, *Streptococcus*, and some species of *Staphylococcus.* It also is active against some species of the gram-negative genera *Brucella*, *Haemophilus*, and *Neisseria*, but is ineffective against species of *Enterobacter*, *Escherichia*, *Klebsiella*, *Proteus*, and *Pseudomonas*.

This drug may cause hepatic changes if administered for two weeks or longer. These changes are usually reversible if troleandomycin is discontinued promptly. Signs include jaundice, hyperbilirubinemia, and abnormal results of liver function tests. The most common adverse reactions are hypersensitivity, nausea, vomiting, diarrhea, rectal burning, and headache. Anaphylactic reactions have occurred. Because of its potential toxicity, troleandomycin should not be administered for more than ten days. It is contraindicated in chronic conditions such as acne or pyoderma, in patients with hepatic disease or dysfunction, and in patients sensitive to the drug.

USUAL DOSAGE.—*Oral: Adults*, 250 to 500 mg four times daily; *children*, 7 to 12 mg/kg of body weight every six hours.

PREPARATIONS.—Cyclamycin (Wyeth), TAO (Roerig). *Oral:* Capsules 250 mg; suspension 125 mg/5 ml.

TYROTHRICIN

Tyrothricin is a mixture of two polypeptide antibiotics, gramicidin (20%) and tyrocidine (80%). Gramicidin itself is probably a mixture of closely related peptides. Both components are bactericidal for common gram-positive pathogens, and tyrocidine is active against some gram-negative species. Tyrothricin is used topically and is effective in a variety of infections (eg, ulcers, pyodermas). It is not absorbed from the intestine when given orally and is too hemolytic for parenteral use.

Application of tyrothricin to fresh wounds has caused hemolysis and hemorrhage. The drug should not be used for infections of the nasal sinuses, since this use has produced anosmia and chemical meningitis. Resistant organisms have not appeared and hypersensitivity reactions occur rarely.

USUAL DOSAGE.—*Topical:* The available dosage forms of this drug are probably ineffective and should not be used.

PREPARATIONS.—Tyrothricin is available as an ingredient of various mixtures (see the section on Topical Mixtures) and also is marketed as a wet dressing and cream under its generic name.

VANCOMYCIN HYDROCHLORIDE

[Vancocin Hydrochloride]

Vancomycin is a glycopeptide antibiotic of unknown chemical structure. It is bactericidal for gram-positive cocci. Since this antibacterial agent is quite toxic, it should only be used in patients allergic to less toxic antibiotics. There are two indications for use of vancomycin: oral administration to treat staphylococcal enteritis, and intravenous administration to treat infections caused by gram-positive cocci *(Enterococcus, Staphylococcus, Streptococcus)* resistant to less toxic antibiotics. Staphylococci that are resistant to methicillin are frequently susceptible to vancomycin. For use of vancomycin in the eye, see Chapter 71, Anti-infective and Anti-inflammatory Agents Used in Ophthalmology.

Large doses or prolonged therapy has caused permanent deafness and fatal uremia. Other untoward effects include thrombophlebitis, anaphylactic shock, fever, and macular rash. Renal function tests are indicated if treatment is continued for more than one week.

USUAL DOSAGE.—

Intravenous: Adults, 2 g daily in two to four divided doses. Doses of 3 to 4 g daily are used for seriously ill patients with normal renal function. *Children*, 40 mg/kg of body weight daily. The dose should be diluted with 100 to 200 ml of sodium chloride injection or 5% dextrose injection and given slowly to lessen the possibility of thrombophlebitis.

Oral: Adults, the maximal daily dose of 4 g is given as an aqueous solution in doses of 500 mg to 1 g every six hours; *children*, the dosage is reduced (see table, back cover).

Solutions are stable for two weeks at room temperature or longer if refrigerated.

PREPARATIONS.—Vancocin Hydrochloride (Lilly). *Injection, Oral:* Powder 500 mg.

Topical Mixtures

The antibiotics bacitracin, gramicidin, neomycin, and polymyxin B are components of antibacterial mixtures for topical application; frequently the combinations contain two or more of these agents. The rationale for use of these mixtures is that by a judicious choice of at least two antibiotics, one is assured of activity against most pathogens because of an overlapping of the antibacterial spectra. In the special situation of topical infections, the use of mixtures appears justified because of the difficulty of identifying the organisms and because of the relative safety of these agents when given by this route. Also, with topical use of these antibiotics, the development of resistant organisms is rare and hypersensitivity reactions occur infrequently. However, combinations that include a steroid are not considered rational.

Topical preparations are widely and effectively used in treating a variety of dermatitides infected with susceptible bacteria (eg, ulcers, sycosis, paronychia, otitis externa). Ophthalmic preparations also are useful in treating superficial bacterial infections of the eye (see Chapter 71, Anti-infective and Anti-inflammatory Agents Used in Ophthalmology).

Superinfections, especially with fungi, have occurred with use of these topical preparations, and this possibility should be considered if an initial improvement in the lesions is followed by a relapse.

The following preparations are among the better known and more frequently prescribed topical antibacterial mixtures.

USUAL DOSAGE.—*Topical: Adults*, the preparations are applied to the affected area two to five times daily.

PREPARATIONS.—

Mycitracin (Upjohn). *Topical:* Each gram of ointment contains bacitracin 500 units, neomycin sulfate equivalent to neomycin 3.5 mg, and polymyxin B sulfate 5,000 units in ½ and 1 oz containers.

Neo-Polycin (Dow). *Topical:* Each gram of ointment contains neomycin sulfate equivalent to neomycin 3 mg, bacitracin zinc 400 units, and polymyxin B sulfate 8,000 units in ½ oz containers; each gram of otic suspension contains neomycin sulfate equivalent to neomycin 2 mg, polymyxin B sulfate 4,000 units, and dyclonine hydrochloride 10 mg in 7 g containers.

Neosporin (Burroughs Wellcome). *Topical:* Each gram of ointment contains polymyxin B sulfate 5,000 units, neomycin sulfate equivalent to neomycin 3.5 mg, and bacitracin zinc 400 units in 1/32, ½, and 1 oz containers; each milliliter of lotion contains polymyxin B sulfate 10,000 units and neomycin sulfate equivalent to neomycin 3.5 mg in 20 ml containers; each 90 g container of powder (aerosol) contains polymyxin B sulfate 100,000 units, neomycin sulfate equivalent to neomycin 70 mg, and bacitracin zinc 8,000 units; each gram of sterile powder contains polymyxin B sulfate 5,000 units, neomycin sulfate equivalent to neomycin 3.5 mg, and bacitracin zinc 400 units in 10 g containers.

Neosporin-G (Burroughs Wellcome). *Topical:* Each gram of cream contains polymyxin B sulfate 10,000 units, neomycin sulfate equivalent to neomycin 3.5 mg, and gramicidin 0.25 mg in 15 g containers.

Neosporin G.U. Irrigant (Burroughs Wellcome). Solution containing neomycin sulfate equivalent to neomycin 40 mg and polymyxin B sulfate 200,000 units in 1 ml containers. Each milliliter of solution is diluted to 1 liter with sodium chloride for slow drip into the bladder over a period of 24 hours.

Polysporin (Burroughs Wellcome). *Topical:* Each gram of ointment contains polymyxin B sulfate 10,000 units and bacitracin zinc 500 units in ½ and 1 oz containers.

SIMILAR MIXTURES.—

Bacimycin (Merrell-National). *Topical:* Each gram of ointment contains bacitracin 500 units and neomycin sulfate equivalent to neomycin 3.5 mg in ½ oz and 100 g containers.

Biotres (Central). *Topical:* Each gram of ointment contains bacitracin zinc 200 units, neomycin sulfate equivalent to neomycin 3 mg, polymyxin B sulfate 4,000 units, and benzalkonium chloride 5 mg in 1/8 and ½ oz containers.

Spectrocin (Squibb). *Topical:* Each gram of ointment contains gramicidin 0.25 mg and neomycin sulfate equivalent to neomycin 2.5 mg in ½ and 1 oz containers.

Chapter 58

ANTITUBERCULOUS AGENTS

The development of effective chemotherapeutic agents has contributed to the sharp decline in morbidity and mortality due to tuberculosis during the past 25 years. At the present time, the chemotherapy of tuberculosis is undergoing intense reevaluation. Not only are new drugs being introduced, but the choice as well as the dosage schedule for older drugs are being reconsidered.

Isoniazid (INH) [Hyzyd, Niconyl, Nydrazid], streptomycin, ethambutol [Myambutol], and aminosalicylic acid (PAS) [Pamisyl, Parasal, Rezipas] are currently considered "primary" drugs because of their overall safety and effectiveness against the tubercle bacillus, *Mycobacterium tuberculosis.* The "secondary" agents include capreomycin [Capastat], cycloserine [Seromycin], ethionamide [Trecator-SC], kanamycin [Kantrex], pyrazinamide (PZA), and viomycin [Viocin]. They are generally less effective and more toxic than the primary drugs. When retreatment is necessary, rifampin [Rifadin, Rimactane] plus one or two other agents (eg, isoniazid, ethambutol, streptomycin) is the regimen of choice. Rifampin, in combination with other agents, should not be used routinely for the *initial* treatment of pulmonary tuberculosis because less costly regimens are effective.

The drug regimen selected to treat tuberculosis depends on the type of infection, severity of the disease, and previous therapy and, if possible, is guided by organism susceptibility tests. An antituberculous agent should not be administered alone to treat *active* disease because of the almost inevitable development of bacterial resistance. In patients with minimal tuberculosis, a two-drug regimen (isoniazid plus streptomycin or ethambutol) is believed to be as effective as a three-drug regimen. Isoniazid may be given alone when the disease has been relatively well controlled after 24 months of multidrug therapy. The regimen combining streptomycin with aminosalicylic acid is not a regimen of choice for initial treatment. A three-drug regimen (eg, isoniazid, streptomycin, and ethambutol or aminosalicylic acid) is indicated in patients with advanced or moderately advanced tuberculosis when a large bacterial population is observed in multiple samples of sputum. A three-drug regimen is preferred when primary drug resistance has occurred.

Therapy should be continued for a minimum of 24 months in original-treatment cases. In patients with slow reversal of infectiousness (ie, positive sputum cultures after more than three months of therapy) or in whom the disease is very severe, active treatment may be necessary for three years or more.

Appropriate bacterial susceptibility tests (if available) should be performed before and during therapy to detect possible bacterial resistance.

If a serious adverse reaction occurs or a significant degree of bacterial resistance develops to one or more primary drugs, an effective alternative regimen, based on bacterial susceptibility studies and including two secondary drugs, may be substituted.

Drug therapy for extrapulmonary tuberculous infections is the same as that used for pulmonary infections, and generally the use of two primary agents is adequate.

For infections caused by *Mycobacterium kansasii* and Battey (group III) organisms, combinations of at least three antituberculous drugs are chosen on the basis of bacterial susceptibility studies.

Corticosteroids also have been used to treat certain clinical manifestations and complications of tuberculosis (see Chapter 35, Adrenal

Corticosteroids).

Adverse Reactions and Precautions

Close supervision of the patient on antituberculous therapy should be maintained because of the adverse reactions that may occur during the prolonged course of therapy. For some patients, unannounced urine tests may be necessary in order to verify that the drugs are actually being taken.

Hypersensitivity reactions (fever, rash, and lymphadenopathy) may develop with any antituberculous agent, especially the aminosalicylates. All drugs should be discontinued at the first sign of hypersensitivity to avoid exfoliative dermatitis or fatal hepatotoxicity. After the reaction has subsided, each agent should be reintroduced individually in small doses in order to identify the responsible one. The tolerated drugs may be given again in the regular dose and, if possible, another agent should be substituted for the one causing the reaction. Desensitization may permit the reintroduction of a drug found to be the cause of hypersensitivity reactions. However, desensitization with isoniazid is contraindicated if the reaction is hepatotoxic in nature; other drugs should be substituted.

Other adverse reactions and the precautions necessary in the use of antituberculous agents are diverse and are discussed in the individual evaluations.

INDIVIDUAL EVALUATIONS

AMINOSALICYLIC ACID [Pamisyl, Parasal, Rezipas]
AMINOSALICYLATE CALCIUM [Parasal Calcium]
AMINOSALICYLATE POTASSIUM [Parasal Potassium, Paskalium]
AMINOSALICYLATE SODIUM [Natri-PAS, Pamisyl Sodium, Parasal Sodium, Pasara Sodium, Pasna]

O
COH
H_2N OH

Aminosalicylic acid is much less effective than isoniazid, ethambutol, or streptomycin in the treatment of pulmonary tuberculosis, but it supplements these agents. For maximal benefit, relatively large doses are required. Strains of tubercle bacilli resistant to aminosalicylic acid gradually emerge with prolonged therapy.

The sodium salt should not be used when sodium restriction is indicated, and it should be given cautiously to those receiving digitalis or diuretics; the potassium salt should not be used in patients with severely impaired renal function or hyperkalemia, and the calcium salt should be used with caution if massive calcium intake is contraindicated (eg, in hypercalcemia, nephrocalcinosis).

The most common adverse reactions are gastric irritation, abdominal pain, nausea, vomiting, and diarrhea. Reducing the dose temporarily or administering a salt or the congener, benzoylpas calcium, may be helpful. Of all the antituberculous agents, the aminosalicylates are most likely to cause hypersensitivity reactions (eg, fever, rash, headache, sore throat, malaise), which are often followed by signs of liver damage; the drug should be discontinued immediately if these adverse reactions occur. Hypokalemia, metabolic acidosis, hemorrhagic tendencies, blood dyscrasias (ie, leukopenia, agranulocytosis, eosinophilia, thrombocytopenia, acute hemolytic anemia), and goitrogenic effects occur rarely.

The effects of diphenylhydantoin may be potentiated, since aminosalicylic acid interferes with metabolism of this drug. Further potentiation may occur when isoniazid is also used concomitantly.

USUAL DOSAGE.—*Oral: Adults*, 8 to 15 g daily in single or divided doses, preferably after meals. *Children*, 200 to 300 mg/kg of body weight daily in single or divided doses after meals.

PREPARATIONS.—

Aminosalicylic Acid:

Pamisyl (Parke, Davis). *Oral:* Tablets 500 mg.

Parasal (Panray). *Oral:* Tablets 500 mg; tablets (buffered) 500 mg; tablets (effervescent) 2 g; tablets (enteric-coated) 500 mg; tablets (timed-release) 1 g; powder in bulk form.

Rezipas (Squibb). *Oral:* Powder 500 mg of aminosalicylic acid/g in 8 g packets and in bulk form.

Aminosalicylate Calcium:

Parasal Calcium (Panray). *Oral:* Capsules and tablets 500 mg.

Aminosalicylate Potassium:

Parasal Potassium (Panray). *Oral:* Capsules and tablets 500 mg; powder in bulk form.

Paskalium (Glenwood). *Oral:* Powder in 3 and 100 g and in bulk form; tablets 500 mg.

Aminosalicylate Sodium:

Natri-PAS (Glenwood). *Oral:* Powder in bulk form; tablets 500 mg.

Pamisyl Sodium (Parke, Davis). *Oral:* Powder 730 mg of aminosalicylate sodium/g in 250 g containers; tablets 500 and 690 mg.

Parasal Sodium (Panray). *Oral:* Capsules 500 mg; crystals 4.18 g/packet; powder in bulk form; tablets 500 and 690 mg and 1 g; tablets (enteric-coated) 500 mg and 1 g.

Pasara Sodium (Dorsey). *Oral:* Powder in bulk form; tablets 500 and 690 mg and 1 g.

Pasna (Barnes-Hind). *Oral:* Granules 5.5 g of aminosalicylate sodium/6.25 g packet; powder in bulk form; tablets 500 mg and 1 g.

Forms also marketed by other manufacturers under generic name.

SIMILAR PREPARATION.—Benzoylpas Calcium [Benzapas (Dorsey)].

AVAILABLE MIXTURES.—

Neopasalate (Mallinckrodt): Powder or 500 mg or 1 g tablets containing aminosalicylate sodium and aminosalicylic acid.

Neopasalate-K (Mallinckrodt): Tablets containing 500 mg or 1 g aminosalicylate potassium and aminosalicylic acid.

PAS-C (Pascorbic) (Hellwig): Tablets containing 500 mg aminosalicylic acid (recrystallized in the presence of ascorbic acid).

CAPREOMYCIN SULFATE [Capastat Sulfate]

Capreomycin sulfate, a polypeptide antibiotic isolated from *Streptomyces capreolus*, is chemically and pharmacologically related to viomycin. Like viomycin, it is a secondary antituberculous agent and is given with other appropriate drugs to patients having strains of tubercle bacilli resistant to the primary agents (isoniazid, aminosalicylic acid, ethambutol, streptomycin) but sensitive to capreomycin. When capreomycin is used with one or more other antituberculous agents, sputum conversion occurs in a significant percentage of the patients treated. This drug should not be used alone in pulmonary tuberculosis, because tubercle bacilli become resistant in most patients receiving only one antituberculous agent. Capreomycin may be effective in infections caused by atypical mycobacteria when bacterial susceptibility to this agent has been demonstrated.

Cross resistance has occurred frequently between capreomycin and viomycin and, in varying degrees, between capreomycin and kanamycin or neomycin. No cross resistance has been observed between capreomycin and isoniazid, aminosalicylic acid, cycloserine, streptomycin, ethionamide, ethambutol, or rifampin.

Adverse Reactions and Precautions.—The most serious untoward effects are similar to those observed with viomycin and involve the kidneys and the eighth cranial nerve. Therefore, capreomycin should be used cautiously in patients with renal insufficiency or auditory impairment, and the risk of additional eighth nerve impairment or renal injury should be weighed against the possible benefits.

Slight elevation in the blood urea nitrogen or blood nonprotein nitrogen levels, as well as the appearance of casts, albumin, and red and white blood cells in the urine, are observed frequently. The reactions apparently are reversible when capreomycin is discontinued. The dosage should be reduced or the drug discontinued if blood urea nitrogen levels are elevated above 30 mg/100 ml or if other evidence of renal dysfunction is noted.

Since hypokalemia may occur during treatment, serum potassium levels should be determined frequently.

Fatal toxic nephritis was reported in one patient with tuberculosis and portal cirrhosis who was treated with capreomycin and aminosalicylic acid daily for one month.

Vertigo, tinnitus, and deafness have been reported, especially after prolonged therapy in elderly patients or in those with renal dysfunction. Thus, audiometric measurements and tests for vestibular function should probably be performed before initiation of therapy and occasionally thereafter.

Transient abnormalities in the results of liver function tests (ie, hyperbilirubinemia and elevated levels of sulfobromophthalein, alkaline phosphatase, and serum transaminases) and jaundice have been observed rarely in patients receiving capreomycin with other antituberculous agents, many of which also are known to produce hepatotoxicity. Therefore, capreomycin should be used cautiously in patients with liver disease and it is advisable to perform liver function tests when indicated in all individuals taking this agent.

Leukocytosis, leukopenia, eosinophilia, urticaria, and maculopapular rashes associated with febrile reactions have been reported occasionally when capreomycin and other antituberculous drugs were given concomitantly. Pain, induration, excessive bleeding, and sterile abscesses at the site of injection have occurred rarely.

As with some other antibacterial agents (eg, streptomycin, kanamycin, neomycin), capreomycin produces neuromuscular blockade after large intravenous doses. This action is potentiated by ether and is antagonized by neostigmine or calcium gluconate.

Since streptomycin, kanamycin, and viomycin produce similar, sometimes irreversible untoward effects, these agents should not be administered concomitantly with capreomycin. Capreomycin should be used cautiously with other antibacterial agents that may produce ototoxic or nephrotoxic reactions (eg, polymyxin B, colistin sulfate, gentamicin, neomycin).

Teratogenic effects have been noted in rats receiving large doses of capreomycin. The expected benefits should be weighed carefully against the possible hazards if this drug is used in women who are or are likely to become pregnant.

USUAL DOSAGE.—*Intramuscular* (deep): *Adults*, 20 mg/kg of body weight (approximately 1 g) daily for 60 to 120 days followed, if necessary, by 1 g two or three times weekly for 18 to 24 months. Information is inadequate to establish dosage for *children*. The drug should be dissolved in 2 ml of sodium chloride injection or sterile water for injection; two to three minutes should be allowed for complete dissolution.

PREPARATIONS.—Capastat Sulfate (Lilly). *Injection:* Powder 1 g.

CYCLOSERINE [Seromycin]

O NH
H_2N O

Cycloserine inhibits the growth of both gram-negative and gram-positive organisms, but is less active than most other antibiotics. While this agent exerts a definite antituberculous effect, it is considered a secondary agent because it is less effective than streptomycin or isoniazid and produces severe toxic effects. Therefore, use of cycloserine should be restricted to patients who cannot tolerate or do not respond to other antituberculous agents. It is always administered as part of a multidrug regimen.

Toxic effects are dose-related and principally involve the central nervous system. Convulsions may occur, especially with doses of more than 500 mg daily. Other untoward reactions include headache, vertigo, lethargy, tremor, dysarthria, paresthesia, coma, mental depression, confusion, elevated serum transaminase levels, and hallucinations. Concomitant use of pyridoxine may reduce the incidence of neurologic reactions. Cycloserine is contraindicated in patients with a history of epilepsy, and should be avoided in patients with severe anxiety, mental depression, or psychosis since it may precipitate a suicide attempt. It also is contraindicated in patients who are hypersensitive to the drug, in patients with severe renal insufficiency, and in those who consume alcoholic beverages excessively.

USUAL DOSAGE.—*Oral: Adults*, initially, 500 mg daily in single or divided doses for two weeks. For maintenance, 500 mg to a maximum of 1 g daily in single or divided doses, with the exact amount determined by blood levels. Toxic effects may be minimized by maintaining blood levels of the drug below 30 μg/ml. *Children*, initially, 10 mg/kg of body weight daily in single or divided doses for two weeks; for maintenance, the dose should be adjusted to give a blood level of 20 to 30 μg/ml.

PREPARATIONS.—Seromycin (Lilly). *Oral:* Capsules 250 mg.

ETHAMBUTOL HYDROCHLORIDE [Myambutol]

C_2H_5
$CH_2NH\ C\ CH_2OH$
CH_3
$\cdot\ 2\ HCl$
CH_3
$CH_2NH\ C\ CH_2OH$
C_2H_5

Ethambutol is used as a primary agent in the treatment of pulmonary tuberculosis because of its relatively low toxicity. It is commonly used with rifampin in retreatment regimens. This drug should not be used alone because resistant organisms develop in a high percentage of patients if other antituberculous drugs are not given concomitantly.

The incidence and severity of adverse reactions associated with ethambutol are dose-related. Optic neuropathy, which occurs rarely, results in loss in visual acuity, red-green color discrimination, and peripheral visual fields. These changes may be unilateral or bilateral and usually regress when the drug is discontinued; however, irreversible changes have been reported. Close monitoring of vision is essential before and during therapy. The drug must be discontinued if there is a progressive decrease in visual acuity. Other untoward reactions include anaphylactic shock, peripheral neuritis with numbness and tingling of extremities, arthralgia, dermatitis, pruritus, fever, gastrointestinal upset, nausea, dizziness, anorexia, malaise, confusion, and headache. Hyperuricemia and decreased liver function (elevated transaminase levels) have been reported in some patients, but the evidence for a causal relationship is inconclusive. It is desirable to assess the renal, hepatic, and neurologic status of patients periodically. Dosage should be reduced in patients with renal disease.

USUAL DOSAGE.—*Oral: Adults,* for initial treatment, 25 mg/kg of body weight daily as a single dose for 10 to 12 days, followed by 15 mg/kg daily as a single dose. For retreatment, 25 mg/kg daily as a single dose. After 60 days of treatment, the dose of ethambutol may be reduced to 15 mg/kg daily. Therapy should be continued until bacteriologic conversion occurs, or until maximal clinical improvement is noted. Information is inadequate to establish dosage for *children under 13 years of age.*

PREPARATIONS.—Myambutol (Lederle). *Oral:* Tablets 100 and 400 mg.

ETHIONAMIDE [Trecator-SC]

$S{=}C\ NH_2$

$N \quad C_2H_5$

Ethionamide, like isoniazid, is derived from isonicotinic acid, but it is less effective and much more toxic than isoniazid. It should be given only to patients who cannot tolerate or who do not respond to other antituberculous drugs. Ethionamide should be administered with at least two other drugs and, whenever possible, their selection should be based on results of bacterial susceptibility tests.

Some degree of gastrointestinal intolerance (loss of weight, burning sensation in stomach, nausea, vomiting, metallic taste) usually occurs. The drug may be hepatotoxic and occasionally cause jaundice. Elevation of transaminase values (SGOT, SGPT) are the earliest abnormalities observed. Thus, one or both tests should be performed prior to administration and once a month during treatment. Therapy must be discontinued if evidence of significant liver damage becomes apparent. Other reactions are purpura, orthostatic hypotension, thrombocytopenia, gynecomastia, impotence, amenorrhea, mental depression, drowsiness, asthenia, hypersalivation, dysuria, acne, severe allergic rash, and increased difficulty in the management of diabetes mellitus. Neurotoxic reactions (peripheral neuritis, optic neuropathy) have been reported rarely; pyridoxine may be administered with ethionamide in an effort to prevent this neuropathy.

USUAL DOSAGE.—*Oral: Adults,* 500 mg to 1 g daily in single or divided doses, depending on tolerance. *Children,* 12 to 15 mg/kg of body weight daily (maximum, 750 mg) in single or divided doses. The drug should be given with meals.

PREPARATIONS.—Trecator-SC (Ives). *Oral:* Tablets 250 mg.

ISONIAZID [Hyzyd, Niconyl, Nydrazid]

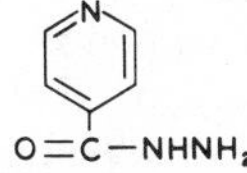

Isoniazid is the best tolerated, most effective, and most economical drug used in the management of active tuberculosis. However, cultures from previously untreated patients sometimes contain a small number of isoniazid-resistant organisms, and treatment with isoniazid alone may lead to overgrowth of these resistant forms and ultimately to therapeutic failure. The use of a second and even a third drug with isoniazid greatly reduces this risk, especially in patients with extensive disease.

For prophylaxis, isoniazid may be used alone in patients who have a recently converted positive tuberculin test, in those who react positively to tuberculin tests but have no other evidence of tuberculosis and are epidemiologically at high risk, and in those with inactive tuberculosis who are at risk of reactivation (eg, those with silicosis or diabetes). When this agent is given prophylactically, administration should be continued for at least one year.

Isoniazid is generally well tolerated. However, the rate of inactivation varies among individuals. The most significant adverse reactions are those affecting the nervous system. Symmetrical peripheral neuritis occurs most commonly and is more likely to develop in those who metabolize the drug slowly. Optic neuropathy has been observed rarely. These neurotoxic effects, which occur because isoniazid acts as an antimetabolite to pyridoxine, may be prevented by administering 50 to 100 mg of pyridoxine daily. Concomitant administration of pyridoxine is recommended in malnourished patients, adolescents, and those predisposed to neuropathy (eg, diabetics). Some degree of amnesia, which is dose-related, also is common. Neurotoxic effects not due to pyridoxine deficiency include toxic psychosis, mental depression, vertigo, hallucinations, and convulsions. Hypersensitivity reactions (eg, fever, lymphadenopathy, or morbilliform, maculopapular, purpuric, or exfoliative rashes), hematologic reactions (eg, agranulocytosis, hemolytic anemia, aplastic anemia, thrombocytopenia, eosinophilia), gastrointestinal reactions (eg, nausea, vomiting, epigastric distress), hyperglycemia, metabolic acidosis, and gynecomastia occur infrequently. Vasculitis of the systemic lupus erythematosus-type with antinuclear antibodies also has been reported. Isoniazid may exacerbate symptoms of rheumatoid arthritis. Minimal elevation of serum glutamic oxaloacetic transaminase levels is common, but the drug should not necessarily be discontinued for this single evidence of hepatotoxicity. Its prophylactic use should be deferred in individuals with liver disease. Hyposensitization with gradually increasing doses of isoniazid is contraindicated if the hypersensitivity reaction is hepatotoxic in nature.

The rate of inactivation of isoniazid is decreased, and thus higher plasma levels of the active form of the drug are present, when aminosalicylic acid is given concomitantly. In some slow inactivators, the effects of diphenylhydantoin may be potentiated, since isoniazid interferes with metabolism of this drug.

USUAL DOSAGE.—*Oral, Intramuscular:* For treatment of active tuberculosis, *adults*, 5 mg/kg of body weight daily in a single dose (maximum, 300 mg daily); *children* inactivate this drug faster than adults and may be given 30 mg/kg daily in a single dose (maximum, 300 mg daily). The larger doses should be used for atypical infection. For prophylactic use, *adults*, 300 mg daily in a single dose; *children*, 10 mg/kg daily in a single dose (maximum, 300 mg daily).

PREPARATIONS.—

Hyzyd (Mallinckrodt). *Oral:* Tablets 100 and 300 mg.

Niconyl (Parke, Davis). *Oral:* Tablets 100 mg.

Nydrazid (Squibb).

Oral: Syrup 50 mg/5 ml; tablets 100 mg.

Injection: Solution 100 mg/ml in 10 ml containers.

ADDITIONAL TRADEMARKS.—Rolazid (Robinson), Teebaconin (Consolidated Midland). Drug also marketed by other manufacturers under generic name.

KANAMYCIN SULFATE [Kantrex]

CH_2NH_2 H O H H OH H HO O OH O H HO H_2N NH_2 CH_2OH H O H H H H_2N OH OH H $\cdot H_2SO_4$

The in vitro antibacterial activity of kanamycin is similar to that of neomycin. It is active against many aerobic gram-positive and gram-negative bacteria. However, since its effectiveness against mycobacteria is limited and it is ototoxic, kanamycin is seldom used in this country for tuberculosis. If used, it should not be given alone or for prolonged periods.

The auditory and vestibular portions of the eighth nerve are affected by kanamycin. Hearing loss is often preceded by tinnitus, dizziness, and disturbance of equilibrium; if these symptoms occur, the drug should be discontinued immediately. Deafness may be partial or complete and in most cases has been irreversible. In patients with impaired renal function, partial and even total deafness has occurred two to seven days after the drug was withdrawn. Rapid development of deafness also has been reported in patients with impaired renal function who had received kanamycin and one of the rapidly-acting intravenous diuretics (eg, ethacrynic acid, furosemide, mannitol) concomitantly. Kanamycin should not be used with other antituberculous agents that produce similar, sometimes irreversible ototoxic effects (eg, capreomycin, streptomycin, viomycin). Less serious adverse reactions include proteinuria and casts in the urine, pain at the site of injection, and hypersensitivity reactions. (See also Chapter 57, Aminoglycoside Antibacterial Agents and Miscellaneous Antimicrobial Drugs.)

USUAL DOSAGE.—*Intramuscular* (deep): *Adults and children*, 15 mg/kg of body weight (maximum, 1 g), usually in a single dose, three to five times weekly.

PREPARATIONS.—(Strengths expressed in terms of the base.) Kantrex (Bristol). *Injection:* Solution 37.5 mg/ml in 2 ml containers (pediatric) and 250 mg/ml in 2 ml containers.

PYRAZINAMIDE

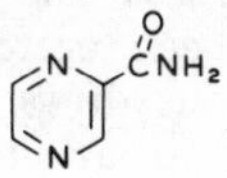

Pyrazinamide is a more effective tuberculostatic agent than aminosalicylic acid, cycloserine, or viomycin but is less effective than streptomycin, rifampin, or isoniazid. Since bacterial resistance develops rapidly, it is considered a secondary agent by most authorities and should only be administered with other effective antituberculous agents in retreatment regimens.

The risk of liver damage with use of pyrazinamide is dose-related; symptoms of hepatotoxicity appear in about 15% of patients when doses of 3 g/day are given. Elevation of transaminase levels (SGOT, SGPT) are the earliest abnormalities observed. Thus, one or both tests should be performed prior to administration and once a month during treatment. Hypoprothrombinemia, hyperfibrinogenemia, and reduced plasma albumin and globulin levels are other manifestations of hepatotoxicity. Therapy must be discontinued if evidence of significant liver damage becomes apparent. Other adverse reactions are arthralgia, anorexia, nausea, vomiting, dysuria, malaise, and fever. Pyrazinamide frequently causes hyperuricemia, occasionally manifested clinically as gout. Control of diabetes mellitus may become difficult during therapy.

USUAL DOSAGE.—*Oral: Adults*, 20 to 35 mg/kg of body weight daily in single or divided doses (maximum, 3 g daily); *children*, information is inadequate to establish dosage.

PREPARATIONS.—*Oral:* Tablets 500 mg (sold to hospitals only). Drug marketed under generic name.

RIFAMPIN [Rifadin, Rimactane]

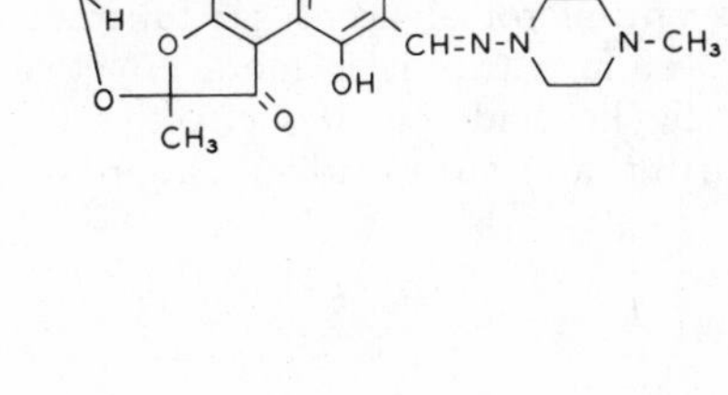

Rifampin, a semisynthetic antibiotic derived from *Streptomyces mediterranei*, is an effective antituberculous agent. It is a drug of choice in patients requiring retreatment, and should be administered with one or preferably two other antituberculous agents; the drugs should be selected on the basis of bacterial susceptibility studies and the knowledge that the patient had not received these agents previously. The routine use of rifampin with other agents in the initial treatment of pulmonary tuberculosis is not ordinarily warranted because less costly regimens are effective. However, rifampin may be given initially if a patient develops serious untoward effects attributable to other agents or if the organisms are resistant to these agents. As with other drugs used in pulmonary tuberculosis, resistant organisms develop in a high percentage of patients if rifampin is given alone.

Rifampin may be used with other appropriate antituberculous agents to treat infections caused by *Mycobacterium kansasii* and other atypical mycobacterial organisms sensitive to this agent. This drug also is indicated for the short-term treatment of asymptomatic carriers of *Neisseria meningitidis;* however, it should be given only when the risk of meningococcal meningitis is high. Rifampin is not recommended for the treatment of symptomatic meningococcal infections. This agent also has been used investigationally in leprosy.

Adverse Reactions and Precautions.—Untoward effects generally occur infrequently. Transient abnormalities in results of liver function tests (ie, hyperbilirubinemia and elevated levels of sulfobromophthalein, alkaline phosphatase, and serum transaminases) have been reported. Several fatalities associated with jaundice have occurred in patients with pre-existing liver disease or in those who had taken other hepatotoxic agents concomitantly. Therefore, rifampin should be used cautiously in patients with liver disease, and it is advisable to perform liver function tests when indicated in all individuals taking this agent.

Transient leukopenia and thrombocytopenia have been noted. Gastrointestinal effects (eg, nausea, vomiting, diarrhea, flatulence) have been severe enough to warrant discontinuing use of rifampin in some patients. Confusion, lethargy, difficulty in concentration, ataxia, dizziness, fever, painful extremities, generalized numbness, pruritus, urticaria, rash, and eosinophilia also have occurred.

Teratogenic effects have been noted in rats and mice receiving large doses. The expected benefits should be weighed carefully against the possible hazards if this drug is used in women who are or are likely to become pregnant.

Patients taking rifampin should be informed that urine, feces, saliva, sputum, tears, and sweat may be orange-red in color.

Drug Interactions.—Since rifampin inhibits the activity of the coumarin anticoagulants, prothrombin times should be determined daily until the effective dosage of the anticoagulant has been established.

The mean plasma half-life of rifampin was decreased in 12 patients who were receiving isoniazid concomitantly and who were slow inactivators of this drug.

The concomitant administration of aminosalicylic acid may delay absorption of rifampin and adequate serum levels may not be attained. Therefore, these two agents should be given separately at intervals of 8 to 12 hours. Adequate serum levels also may not be attained if barbiturates are administered concomitantly.

USUAL DOSAGE.—*Oral:* For pulmonary tuberculosis, *adults*, 600 mg in a single daily dose; *children over 5 years of age*, 10 to 20 mg/kg of body weight (maximum, 600 mg) in a single daily dose; *under 5 years*, no dosage information is available. The drug should be given either one hour before or two hours after eating. Administration should be continued for one to two years after consistent negative cultures have been obtained, as determined by bimonthly cultures, and after maximal improvement has occurred.

For meningococcus carriers, rifampin should be administered in the same dosage as for pulmonary tuberculosis. It should be given for four consecutive days at least two hours after eating.

PREPARATIONS.—Rifadin (Dow), Rimactane (Ciba). *Oral:* Capsules 300 mg.

STREPTOMYCIN SULFATE

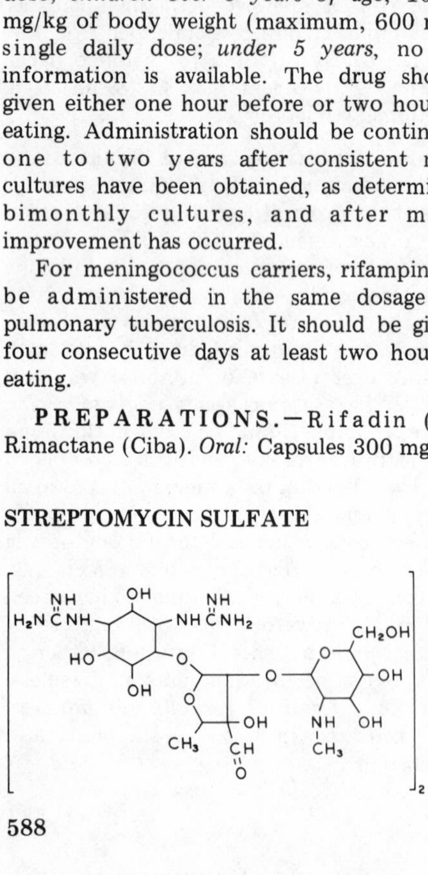

Streptomycin is effective against many gram-negative bacteria and *Mycobacterium tuberculosis*, and has been regarded as one of the primary antituberculous drugs. However, some physicians prefer to administer it at the initiation of therapy only and for relatively short periods. Emergence of streptomycin-resistant organisms will occur if the drug is used alone, especially when response to treatment is delayed. Thus, streptomycin must always be used with other drugs. Other effective drugs which are less toxic are gradually replacing streptomycin in the treatment of tuberculosis.

The most common adverse reaction is damage to the vestibular portion of the eighth cranial nerve. Deafness is less common. Since the drug is excreted by the kidneys, impaired renal function may result in high blood levels and the rapid development of vestibular dysfunction. Eighth nerve damage is often preceded by headache, tinnitus, dizziness, vertigo, nausea, or vomiting. Other ototoxic drugs should not be administered concomitantly. Other central nervous system effects are dysfunction of the optic nerve (scotoma) and, rarely, peripheral neuritis. Exercise immediately following injection may accentuate dizziness, ataxia, paresthesia, and headache. Renal damage occurs with large doses. Hypersensitivity reactions (rash, exfoliative dermatitis, stomatitis, angioedema, pruritus, and fever) and hematopoietic reactions (eosinophilia, neutropenia, agranulocytosis, aplastic anemia, and thrombocytopenia) have been reported. Anaphylaxis has occurred rarely. Adverse effects are more common in elderly patients. Intramuscular administration may be irritating. (See also Chapter 57, Aminoglycoside Antibacterial Agents and Miscellaneous Antimicrobial Drugs.)

USUAL DOSAGE.—*Intramuscular: Adults*, 250 mg to 1 g daily in a single dose. Smaller doses are used in older patients and in those with renal impairment. *Children*, 20 mg/kg of body weight daily in a single dose.

PREPARATIONS.—*Injection:* Powder 1 and 5 g; solution 200 mg/ml in 5 ml containers, 400 mg/ml in 2.5 and 12.5 ml containers, and 500 mg/ml in 2 and 10 ml containers. Drug marketed under generic name.

VIOMYCIN SULFATE [Viocin]

This antimicrobial agent has tuberculostatic properties; in vitro, it is more effective than aminosalicylic acid, but less effective than the remaining antituberculous agents. Since viomycin produces severe toxic effects and strains of *Mycobacterium tuberculosis* become resistant to this agent, it should only be used when patients are unable to tolerate or benefit from other antituberculous drugs. This agent should always be given with other antituberculous agents.

Adverse reactions are similar to those associated with streptomycin but occur more frequently. The most serious toxic effects affect the vestibular portion of the eighth cranial nerve and electrolyte balance. The incidence of vestibular damage is higher than with streptomycin and partial deafness is common. Audiometric determinations should be performed before and during treatment, and viomycin should never be administered with another ototoxic agent.

Viomycin should not be given to patients with renal insufficiency unless there are compelling reasons, for it is nephrotoxic and causes albuminuria, cylindruria, hematuria, nitrogen retention, and serious disturbances in electrolyte balance due to urinary loss of calcium, potassium, and chloride and to increased levels of serum bicarbonate. The electrolyte imbalance may result in fluid retention, edema, dizziness, and electrocardiographic abnormalities. The hypokalemia that can result may produce muscle weakness; tetany is associated with hypocalcemia. Although these renal changes are rapidly reversible when treatment is discontinued, electrolyte disturbance occasionally requires intensive replacement therapy. Rashes, which occur frequently, may be controlled with antihistamines.

USUAL DOSAGE.—*Intramuscular: Adults*, 2 g in two divided doses 12 hours apart; dosage is repeated every third day. In severe cases, the same dosage may be given daily but for no longer than one month. *Children*, 40 mg/kg of body weight in two divided doses 12 hours apart; dosage is repeated every third day.

PREPARATIONS.—Viocin (Pfizer), Viomycin (Parke, Davis). *Injection:* Powder 1 and 5 g.

MIXTURES

The usefulness of fixed-ratio combinations of antituberculous agents is limited since, in the management of tuberculosis, the dosage of each drug used in a multidrug regimen must be established individually.

Pyridoxine is often used with isoniazid to prevent the symmetrical peripheral neuritis and optic neuropathy associated with use of isoniazid, and several preparations containing these two ingredients are available. The dosage of pyridoxine is dependent upon the dosage of isoniazid and the nutritional state of the patient and a fixed combination of these drugs is useful only if it meets the needs of the individual patient.

AVAILABLE MIXTURES.—

Hyzyd Plus B_6 (Mallinckrodt): Each tablet contains isoniazid 100 mg and pyridoxine hydrochloride 10 mg.

Niadox (Barnes-Hind): Each tablet contains isoniazid 100 mg and pyridoxine hydrochloride 10 mg.

Pasna Tri-Pack (Barnes-Hind): Each 5.5 gram packet contains isoniazid 100 or 200 mg, pyridoxine hydrochloride 10 or 20 mg, and aminosalicylate sodium 4.5 mg.

Teebaconin with Vitamin B_6 (Consolidated Midland): Each tablet contains isoniazid 100 mg and pyridoxine hydrochloride 5, 10, or 50 mg.

Chapter 59

ANTILEPROSY AGENTS

Generally, the treatment of leprosy is best managed by specialists who, in the United States, almost always are associated with Public Health Service hospitals or outpatient clinics. Chemotherapy, while not yet completely satisfactory, is the mainstay in the treatment of this disease, and this chapter describes the agents currently being used.

Dapsone [Avlosulfon], a sulfone, is the drug of choice and the agent most commonly used for the treatment of all forms of leprosy. The other available sulfones, sulfoxone [Diasone] and acetosulfone [Promacetin], are seldom used because there is not as much evidence of their efficacy and they are more expensive. Results of studies on the investigational repository sulfone, acedapsone (DADDS), suggest that it will be useful for the treatment and prophylaxis of all forms of leprosy. It has been administered intramuscularly in a dose of 225 mg every 75 days for treatment and prophylaxis in adults and children over 5 years of age, and in a dose of 150 mg every 75 days for prophylaxis in children 6 months to 5 years of age.

The leprosy bacilli *(Mycobacterium leprae)* have become resistant to the sulfones in a few individuals (less than 1%); clofazimine (Lamprene, B663), which is available only for investigational use in the United States, has been used to treat these patients. For adults, it is administered orally in a dose of 100 mg daily.

Rifampin [Rifadin, Rimactane], marketed in the United States for the treatment of tuberculosis (see Chapter 58, Antituberculous Agents), is available for investigational use in the treatment of leprosy. Early reports indicate that this drug, in an oral dose of 600 mg daily for adults, is more rapidly effective than dapsone in the treatment of leprosy. It also appears to be bactericidal for *M. leprae* while all the other drugs currently in use are considered to be bacteriostatic. Its exact role in the treatment of leprosy must await the outcome of studies to determine the efficacy of long-term administration.

Initially favorable results have been reported with the long-acting sulfonamides, sulfadimethoxine [Madribon], sulfalene, sulfamonomethoxine, and sulfadoxine. The therapeutic ratio of these drugs is low, however, and the consequences of drug resistance are great since cross resistance with dapsone develops readily. Initially favorable results also have been reported with thiambutosine, ditophal, amithiozone, vadrine, and isoniazid. However, none of these drugs has been able to sustain its initial effect. Of these drugs, only sulfadimethoxine and isoniazid are marketed in the United States.

The reactions (eg, lepra reactions) which occur during the course of all forms of leprosy are treated with the lowest dose of an agent that will control their worst features. For the milder reactions, aspirin (adults, 600 mg every four hours as necessary; children, 65 mg/kg of body weight daily) or antimonials (stibophen [Fuadin] and antimony potassium tartrate in amounts sufficient to provide adults with 40 to 60 mg of antimony every other day) usually are given. Corticosteroids (eg, prednisolone, 5 to 10 mg daily for adults) usually are used for treatment of the more severe debilitating reactions. Thalidomide, although available only for investigational use in the United States, also is used to treat these reactions and probably is the most effective of all the agents given for this purpose. Adults receive an initial dose of 400 mg daily, and the amount is then decreased over a period of two weeks to 100 mg daily. The dose is repeated if the reactions recur. Thalidomide may cause drowsiness, urticaria, rash, peripheral edema, headache, nausea, constipation, transient leukopenia, and dizziness when used to treat these reactions, and it is contraindicated in women of childbearing age. Other measures used to treat the reactions include discontinuing the sulfone or reducing its dosage, or substituting large doses of clofazimine (adults, 300 to 400 mg daily) for the sulfone.

Adverse Reactions and Precautions

Sulfones: All sulfones except acedapsone (DADDS) cause similar adverse reactions; these are mild and occur infrequently when the drugs are used in the doses recommended (see the individual evaluations). No toxic effects have been reported after the administration of acedapsone.

Transient cyanosis and pallor occur initially and, in some cases of lepromatous leprosy, a bluish discoloration of the skin may continue throughout the course of therapy.

Nausea, vomiting, headache, dizziness, and tachycardia are uncommon if the dosage is increased very gradually.

Methemoglobinemia, leukopenia, agranulocytosis, allergic dermatitis (sometimes exfoliative with concurrent liver damage, fever, and lymphadenitis) have been observed only occasionally after small doses of the sulfones but are common with doses above 100 mg daily.

Hemolysis and hemolytic anemia have been reported infrequently after recommended doses but occur frequently after doses of 200 mg or more daily. Both reactions are noted more frequently in those who have erythrocyte glucose-6-phosphate dehydrogenase (G6PD) deficiency.

Psychoses, which are usually reversible on discontinuing sulfone therapy, have been observed after doses greater than 400 mg weekly. Peripheral neuritis also has occurred rarely after large doses.

Miscellaneous Drugs: Because clofazimine is a red-colored compound that is deposited in the tissues, it discolors the skin and conjunctivae. The skin becomes red at first and changes to mahogany brown later, while the leprosy lesions darken and appear mauve, slate-gray, or black. The conjunctivae become varying shades of red-brown. In addition, a red tint may appear in the urine, sputum, and sweat. All of these effects subside slowly after therapy is discontinued. Nausea, diarrhea, and skin irritation occur rarely.

As yet there have been no reports of adverse effects after the use of rifampin [Rifadin, Rimactane] in treating leprosy. For those that occur as a result of its use in the treatment of tuberculosis, see Chapter 58, Antituberculous Agents.

For information on the adverse effects produced by sulfadimethoxine [Madribon] and isoniazid, see Chapter 55, Sulfonamides, and Chapter 58, Antituberculous Agents, respectively.

INDIVIDUAL EVALUATIONS

ACETOSULFONE SODIUM [Promacetin]

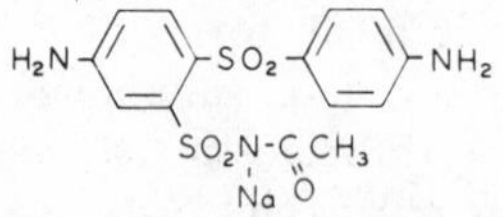

H_2N — SO_2 — NH_2; $SO_2N(Na)$-C(=O)CH_3

This sulfone is indicated for the treatment of all forms of leprosy. It may be as effective as dapsone but, because of the relative lack of clinical evidence, a definite evaluation cannot be made. In addition, it is more costly than dapsone.

The adverse reactions produced by acetosulfone are similar to those of the sulfones as a group (see the Introductory Statement).

USUAL DOSAGE.—*Oral: Adults,* 500 mg daily for the first two weeks; thereafter the dose is increased every two weeks by increments of 500 mg to 1.5 g until a maximal daily dose of 3 to 4 g is reached. *Children,* 7.1 mg/kg of body weight administered in the same schedule as for adults.

PREPARATIONS.—Promacetin (Parke, Davis). *Oral:* Tablets 500 mg.

DAPSONE [Avlosulfon]

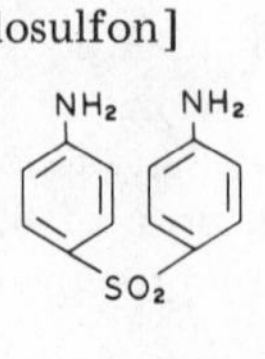

NH_2 NH_2 SO_2

Dapsone is the sulfone of choice for the treatment of all forms of leprosy. Continuous treatment with this drug assures bacterial negativity in almost all cases of the most severe, lepromatous form of the disease. However, five years or more may be required to achieve the bacteria-free state. Some authorities recommend that administration be continued for five to ten years after bacterial negativity has been achieved; others recommend that the drug be continued for life. In tuberculoid leprosy, a milder form of the disease, dapsone probably should be given for one and one-half years after clinical manifestations of the disease have disappeared.

The adverse reactions produced by dapsone are similar to those of the sulfones as a group (see the Introductory Statement).

For other uses, see Chapter 68, Dermatologic Agents.

USUAL DOSAGE.—*Oral: Adults*, for lepromatous leprosy, first and second weeks, 25 mg twice weekly; third and fourth weeks, 50 mg twice weekly; thereafter, 50 mg daily. A maintenance dosage of 100 mg daily also has been used. For tuberculoid and borderline (dimorphous) leprosy, similar regimens are used but maintenance doses of 50 mg or less daily are frequently given. *Children*, 0.35 mg/kg of body weight administered in the same schedule as for adults.

PREPARATIONS.—Avlosulfon (Ayerst). *Oral:* Tablets 25 and 100 mg.

SULFOXONE SODIUM [Diasone Sodium]

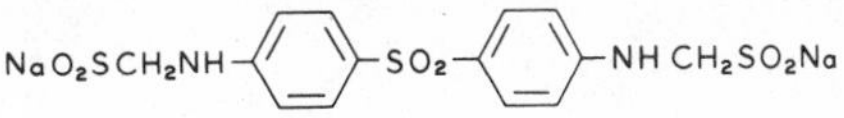

$NaO_2SCH_2NH-C_6H_4-SO_2-C_6H_4-NHCH_2SO_2Na$

This sulfone is indicated for the treatment of all forms of leprosy and dermatitis herpetiformis. It may be as effective as dapsone in the treatment of leprosy but, because of the relative lack of clinical evidence, a definite evaluation cannot be made. It is also more costly than dapsone.

The adverse reactions produced by sulfoxone are similar to those of the sulfones as a group (see the Introductory Statement).

For other uses, see Chapter 68, Dermatologic Agents.

USUAL DOSAGE.—*Oral: Adults*, for leprosy, first and second weeks, 330 mg twice weekly; third and fourth weeks, 330 mg four times weekly; thereafter, 330 mg daily for six days of each week. *Children*, 4.7 mg/kg of body weight administered in the same schedule as for adults.

For dermatitis herpetiformis, *adults*, 330 mg daily for one week; the dose then may be increased to 660 mg daily if necessary. Maintenance dose, 330 mg daily.

PREPARATIONS.—Diasone Sodium (Abbott). *Oral:* Tablets (enteric-coated) 165 mg.

Chapter 60

ANTIFUNGAL AGENTS

Fungal infections can be divided into three therapeutic categories. The first includes the systemic fungal infections, the most important of which are histoplasmosis, coccidioidomycosis, North American blastomycosis, paracoccidioidomycosis (South American blastomycosis), sporotrichosis, and cryptococcosis (torulosis). Uncommon infections in this category are penicilliosis, geotrichosis, aspergillosis, and mucormycosis.

The second category comprises the dermatophytic infections, which are limited to the skin, hair, and nails. About 20 species of *Epidermophyton*, *Trichophyton*, and *Microsporum* cause these infections.

The third category includes only candidiasis (moniliasis). *Candida albicans* is the most common species causing human disease, but *C. krusei*, *C. tropicalis*, *C. pseudotropicalis*, and, more rarely, other species have also been implicated. Candidiasis usually affects moist skin or mucous membranes, including the gastrointestinal tract; occasionally, however, these fungi cause systemic disease.

Systemic Infections: Amphotericin B [Fungizone] is lifesaving in almost all systemic fungal infections, including candidiasis, but instructions for parenteral use must be followed carefully to minimize its many toxic effects. The drug also is effective topically in candidal infections of the skin and nails. Amphotericin B has been combined with broad spectrum antibiotics and such mixtures are used orally to prevent overgrowth of candidal organisms in the gastrointestinal tract, but there is no evidence that this is an effective or desirable adjunct to antibacterial therapy. (See the section on Mixtures of Oral Antifungal Agents with Antibacterial Agents.)

Iodides, the first drugs effective in the treatment of systemic fungal infections, remain the preferred agents for some forms of sporotrichosis. Patients who cannot tolerate or do not respond to iodide should be treated with a parenteral preparation of amphotericin B.

Hydroxystilbamidine is used in North American blastomycosis. It also is effective in leishmaniasis, but the drug of choice in the primary treatment of this disease is stibogluconate sodium [Pentostam], which is not marketed in the United States; however, this agent is available to licensed physicians from the Parasitic Disease Drug Service, Center for Disease Control, Atlanta, Georgia 30333.

It is essential that therapy for systemic fungal infections be continued for a sufficient period to minimize the possibility of relapse. For example, recurrences of North American blastomycosis have been reported several months and even years after arrest of the disease following therapy with either hydroxystilbamidine or amphotericin B; patients who have been treated with hydroxystilbamidine are more apt to have a relapse than those treated with amphotericin B. Remissions, therefore, should not be interpreted as cures until patients have been observed for prolonged periods.

Dermatophytic Infections: The drugs of choice for infections caused by dermatophytic fungi are griseofulvin [Fulvicin U/F, Grifulvin V, Grisactin] orally or tolnaftate [Tinactin] topically. Both drugs may be used simultaneously in extensive or severe infections. Haloprogin [Halotex] also may be used topically as may iodochlorhydroxyquin, especially if bacteria also are present. If the area of infection is inflamed or weeping, initial treatment with wet dressings such as tap water, aluminum acetate solution (Burow's solution), or potassium permanganate solution (1:4,000) may be desirable. The concomitant use of an adrenal corticosteroid may facilitate treatment of an eczematous eruption. Appropriate systemic antibacterial agents may be indicated if bacteria are cultured from lesions or if their presence is suggested by a complicating cellulitis or lymphangitis.

In infections of heavily keratinized areas, especially the soles of the feet, benzoic and salicylic acid ointment (Whitfield's ointment) may be useful to remove heavy layers of keratin and thus permit penetration of more potent antifungal drugs to the base of the infection.

Many proprietary preparations are available for treating dermatophytic infections, especially tinea pedis (athlete's foot). These include dyes such as carbol-fuchsin solution [Carfusin] and gentian violet; salicylanilide; triacetin [Enzactin]; sodium propionate; thymol; and the organic acids: benzoic, salicylic, propionic, caprylic, and undecylenic. Some are available only in combination products (see the section on Mixtures). Evidence for the effectiveness of any of these agents is unimpressive, although undecylenic acid may be useful in milder, uncomplicated dermatophytic infections. The keratolytic agents do give temporary, symptomatic relief. The use of the dyes is no longer justified, for these agents may cause irritation in addition to staining the skin and clothing.

Acrisorcin [Akrinol] is useful only in the treatment of tinea versicolor (pityriasis versicolor). Selenium sulfide detergent suspension [Selsun], tolnaftate, and haloprogin also have been effective in this infection.

Candidiasis: Nystatin [Mycostatin, Nilstat] is effective topically in the treatment of candidal infections of the skin or mucous membranes. It is too toxic for parenteral use. Like amphotericin B, its oral use in combination with broad spectrum antibiotics has been promoted to prevent candidal overgrowth in the gastrointestinal tract of patients being treated with a broad spectrum antibiotic; however, there is no evidence that the use of such mixtures is beneficial. Flucytosine [Ancobon] is useful orally for the treatment of serious candidal or cryptococcal infections.

Mycotic vaginitis usually responds to amphotericin B, nystatin, or candicidin [Candeptin, Vanobid]. Sporostacin, a mixture of chlordantoin and benzalkonium chloride, also is used for mycotic vaginitis and for candidal infections of the skin or mucous membranes, but it is less effective than the three antibiotics previously mentioned.

Other Infections: The organisms causing actinomycosis *(Actinomyces israelii)* and nocardiosis *(Nocardia* species) are now considered to be higher forms of bacteria and do not respond to any antifungal agent. The drug of choice for actinomycosis is penicillin (2 to 20 million units daily for at least six weeks); less effective drugs include lincomycin, the tetracyclines, and erythromycin. For nocardiosis, treatment with an absorbable sulfonamide (eg, sulfadiazine 4 to 6 g daily in four divided doses, adjusted to maintain a plasma level of 10 mg or more per 100 ml) for at least two to three months is often curative. Some patients require concomitant therapy with another antibacterial agent (eg, tetracycline, streptomycin). Drainage of abscesses and debridement is essential.

Adverse Reactions and Precautions

An etiologic diagnosis should be made before treating any infection with an antifungal drug because most of these agents are not active against bacteria; bacterial, fungal, or mixed infections cannot always be differentiated solely on the basis of clinical symptoms. In dermatomycoses, it is necessary to identify the type of organism, since no drug is effective against both the dermatophytes and *Candida.*

Some of the topical preparations used for treating dermatomycoses are irritating or contain potentially sensitizing ingredients. A topical antifungal agent should be discontinued if evidence of sensitization or irritation develops. No confirmed adverse reactions to tolnaftate [Tinactin] have been reported, and only a few local reactions following use of acrisorcin [Akrinol] have occurred. Haloprogin [Halotex] may cause local irritation, burning sensation, and vesicle formation.

Nystatin [Mycostatin, Nilstat] and amphotericin B [Fungizone], administered orally or topically, are essentially devoid of toxicity. The infrequent reactions to either have been mild and transitory and have consisted chiefly of nausea, vomiting, or diarrhea after oral administration. Both drugs are nonirritating to mucous membranes and skin, but a few cases of local allergic reactions have been reported. Resistance has not been a clinical problem, although resistance of *Candida* species has been produced in vitro with both drugs. Flucytosine [Ancobon] is less toxic than amphotericin B, but still may cause reactions related to the gastrointestinal tract, blood, and central nervous system. See the evaluation on flucytosine for additional information.

When given parenterally, amphotericin B causes unpleasant and potentially dangerous reactions in most patients. These effects can be minimized by proper preparation and administration of the solution and use of appropriate adjunctive therapy. See the evaluation on Amphotericin B for additional information.

Serious untoward effects have been observed during or immediately after intravenous administration of hydroxystilbamidine (see the evaluation). These reactions may be minimized by using a dilute solution and infusing it slowly.

Untoward effects following the use of candicidin [Candeptin, Vanobid] have been mild and infrequent; slight irritation of the vulva and surrounding area after vaginal application has occurred most commonly.

Reactions associated with use of griseofulvin [Fulvicin U/F, Grifulvin V, Grisactin] have generally been mild; they include transient urticaria and other skin eruptions, gastrointestinal disturbances, headache, drowsiness, and fatigue.

INDIVIDUAL EVALUATIONS

ACRISORCIN [Akrinol]

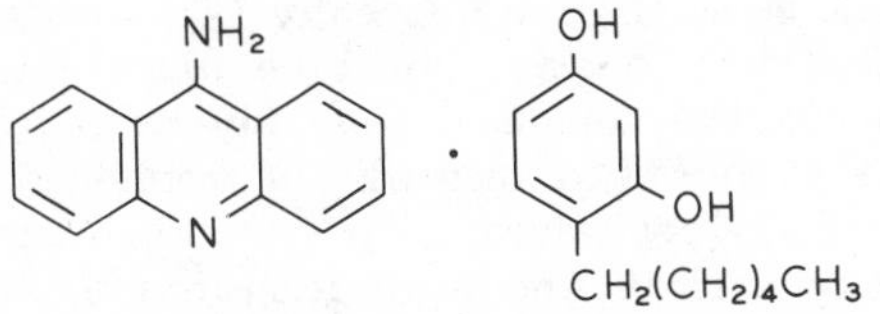

Acrisorcin is useful in the treatment of tinea versicolor (pityriasis versicolor), a chronic fungal infection of the skin caused by *Malassezia furfur.* The drug is not effective in any other infection. Relapses are common in tinea versicolor, and clinical evidence that the drug will produce permanent cure is not conclusive.

A few local reactions (eg, blisters, erythematous vesicular eruptions, urticaria) have been reported. Acrisorcin should not be used near the eyes. Treatment should be discontinued if signs of irritation or sensitization occur.

USUAL DOSAGE.—*Topical:* A small quantity of the cream is applied to lesions morning and night. Before night application, the lesions should be scrubbed with a stiff brush and soap, and the area rinsed thoroughly thereafter to avoid inactivation of the drug by residual soap. Treatment should be continued for at least six weeks.

PREPARATIONS.—Akrinol (Schering). *Topical:* Cream 0.2% in 50 g containers.

AMPHOTERICIN B [Fungizone]

Amphotericin B is an antibiotic produced by *Streptomyces nodosus.* It is used intravenously and intrathecally in the treatment of systemic fungal infections and meningitis and topically in candidiasis of the skin, nails, or mucous membranes including perleche and candidal paronychia. It is fungistatic rather than fungicidal except in higher concentrations than those obtainable systemically.

Amphotericin B is the only available drug for the treatment of the following systemic mycoses: coccidioidomycosis, paracoccidioidomycosis (South American blastomycosis), histoplasmosis, cryptococcosis, candidiasis, aspergillosis, and chromoblastomycosis (usually treated by intralesional injection). It may be effective in occasional cases of maduromycosis (mycetoma) and mucormycosis. For sporotrichosis, amphotericin B should be used only in patients who cannot tolerate or do not respond to iodides; it is preferred in disseminated sporotrichosis. Amphotericin B is the drug of choice for systemic North American blastomycosis; however, hydroxystilbamidine is effective in many patients and probably is less toxic than amphotericin B. Amphotericin B has some effect in mucocutaneous leishmaniasis caused by the protozoan, *Leishmania braziliensis,* but the drug of choice in primary therapy is stibogluconate sodium (see the Introductory Statement).

Investigationally, amphotericin B has been effective in mycotic keratitis by topical application, in fungal endophthalmitis by intraorbital injection (although recovery of vision has generally been poor), and in pulmonary aspergillosis by intrabronchial administration.

The value of amphotericin B in geotrichosis is unproved. It is ineffective in penicilliosis.

Preparations combining amphotericin B with broad spectrum antibiotics have been promoted to prevent candidal overgrowth in the intestine during antibacterial therapy. The rationale for use of this fixed-ratio combination is weak. Intestinal candidiasis does not occur frequently and there is no evidence that routine prophylactic administration of an antifungal agent reduces its incidence. If the use of an antifungal agent with an antibiotic is indicated, it is preferable to give the compounds separately. (See the section on Mixtures of Oral Antifungal Agents with Antibacterial Agents, and Chapter 53, Tetracyclines.)

Amphotericin B may be used intrathecally in meningitis due to a susceptible fungus to increase its effectiveness and reduce the danger of renal toxicity. Local instillations have been effective in fungal cystitis and pyelitis. The drug is excreted slowly by the kidneys, and blood levels are demonstrable for several days after injection of a single dose.

There is no substantial clinical evidence of acquired resistance to amphotericin B, although resistance of *Coccidioides immitis* and some species of *Candida* has been acquired in vitro.

Adverse Reactions and Precautions.—Reactions that have occurred with topical preparations include pruritus, local irritation, and, occasionally, allergic dermatitis. Oral administration may cause nausea, vomiting, and diarrhea.

Adverse reactions following intravenous administration include chills, hyperhidrosis, fever, myalgia, arthralgia, general malaise, anorexia, abdominal cramps, nausea, vomiting, diarrhea, headache, vertigo, phlebitis, and thrombophlebitis. Reactions that occur rarely include hemorrhagic gastroenteritis with melena, thrombocytopenia, leukopenia, agranulocytosis, hypotension, ventricular fibrillation, cardiac arrest (after rapid injection), maculopapular rash, blurred vision or diplopia, polyneuropathy, convulsions, and anaphylactic reactions. Anemia may develop during prolonged therapy. Acute hepatic failure and jaundice also have occurred.

Systemic reactions may be minimized by reducing the rate of infusion, administering the drug on alternate days, and giving ancillary therapy (eg, heparin, antipyretics, antihistamines, antiemetics). If a severe reaction occurs during the course of an infusion, therapy should be interrupted for 15 minutes or discontinued for the day. If the reaction recurs, therapy should be resumed at a lower dosage the next day.

Intrathecal injection may cause pain in the back, legs, or abdomen; headache; paresis (usually transient); paresthesias; impaired vision; nausea and vomiting; and urinary retention.

Evidence of renal damage (increased blood urea nitrogen and nonprotein nitrogen; decreased glomerular filtration, renal plasma flow, and creatinine clearance; appearance of granular and hyaline casts and, sometimes, microhematuria) occurs in many patients. Permanent renal damage has been reported in patients who had received large doses for prolonged periods, especially when the total dosage exceeded 5 g. Renal fibrosis, hyalinization, thickening of the basement membranes, hypercellularity, tubular necrosis, and nephrocalcinosis have been observed. Hypokalemia is common and potassium salts may have to be administered orally to overcome the deficiency.

Renal toxicity may be lessened if the initial dose is small and is gradually increased to the least amount that will produce a plasma level twice the in vitro inhibitory concentration for the fungus cultured from the patient. Also, alkalization of the urine may hasten excretion of the drug and thus prevent or minimize the renal tubular acidosis.

Determinations of blood urea nitrogen (BUN) or serum creatinine should be made on alternate days while the dose is being increased and weekly thereafter during therapy. If levels exceed 40 mg/100 ml or 3 mg/100 ml, respectively, the dose is too large and the drug should be discontinued for a few days or until more nearly normal levels are obtained. Some authorities believe that weekly determinations of serum creatinine clearance rates permit better evaluation of renal function than serum creatinine levels. Serum potassium levels also should be determined frequently.

Systemic therapy should be used only in patients who are under close observation and have a confirmed diagnosis of a progressive, potentially fatal form of a susceptible fungal infection. There is no justification for use of this drug in vague and undiagnosed conditions merely because a skin or serologic test for one of the fungi may have been positive.

Detailed instructions for the storage, preparation, and administration of amphotericin B should be closely followed because of this drug's toxicity and instability under unfavorable conditions (eg, exposure to heat and light, low pH). Since the intravenous preparation is a colloidal suspension, membrane filters in intravenous infusion lines may remove significant amounts of the drug.

Therapy must be continued for a sufficient period, usually two to four months. Antineoplastic agents or large doses of corticosteroids should not be used with amphotericin B unless absolutely necessary to control reactions to amphotericin B or to treat an underlying disease such as chronic adrenocortical insufficiency (Addison's disease).

Systemic fungal infections during pregnancy have been successfully treated with amphotericin B without obvious adverse effects on the fetus.

USUAL DOSAGE.—Amphotericin B is heat labile and sensitive to light. Hence, the dry powder should be stored in the refrigerator and protected against exposure to light. Solutions prepared for parenteral injection should be used promptly and protected from light during intravenous administration.

Intravenous (infusion): Dosage must be adjusted individually according to the severity of the disease and tolerance of the patient. A concentration containing 0.1 mg/ml in 5% dextrose injection having a pH above 4.2 should be used. The solution is prepared by adding 10 ml of water for injection to 50 mg of amphotericin B and shaking the vial until the solution is clear; the contents are then added to the dextrose injection. Bacteriostatic agents must not be present and sodium chloride injection must not be used, because they will cause precipitation of the drug. The infusion must be given slowly. Initially, approximately 0.25 mg/kg of body weight should be administered. The total amount should be increased daily by 5 to 10 mg to a maximal daily dose of 1 mg/kg of body weight. In seriously ill patients who do not respond, the dose on alternate days may be exceeded cautiously to a maximum of 1.5 mg/kg. Therapy should be resumed gradually according to this same schedule whenever administration is interrupted for longer than seven days.

Intrathecal: (50 mg of amphotericin B is diluted with at least 150 ml of 5% dextrose injection [without preservative] to a final concentration of about 0.3 mg/ml; before injection, the dose is mixed in the syringe with 10 to 30 ml of spinal fluid.) The usual dose is 0.5 mg (maximum, 0.75 mg) every 24 to 48 hours. One authority recommends initiating therapy with 0.1 ml of a solution containing 0.25 mg/ml and gradually increasing the dose until the patient can tolerate 0.5 mg without excessive discomfort.

Topical: For candidiasis, preparations are applied by rubbing well into the infected area two to four times daily; the duration of treatment varies from one to two weeks for intertrigo (diaper rash) to many months for tinea unguium (onychomycosis). Persistent or recurrent infection with *Candida* species may be due to continued fecal contamination; under these circumstances, oral administration of an antifungal preparation to eliminate the enteric infection also may be indicated.

For use in the eye, see Chapter 71, Anti-infective and Anti-inflammatory Agents Used in Ophthalmology.

PREPARATIONS.—Fungizone (Squibb).

Injection: Powder 50 mg.

Topical: Cream 3% in 20 g containers; lotion 3% in 30 ml containers; ointment 3% in 20 g containers.

CANDICIDIN [Candeptin, Vanobid]

This fungistatic and fungicidal antibiotic is derived from a soil actinomycete similar to *Streptomyces griseus.* It is effective only for the treatment of mycotic vaginitis (vaginal candidiasis, moniliasis). To avoid reinfection, coitus should be avoided or a condom should be used, and consideration should be given to treating the sexual partner simultaneously.

During pregnancy, manual insertion of the capsule or tablet is preferable to use of the tablet inserter or ointment applicator. Slight irritation of the vulvar and perivulvar area is the most common adverse reaction. Sensitization has been reported only rarely.

USUAL DOSAGE.—*Topical* (vaginal): One applicatorful of ointment or one capsule or tablet is inserted high in the vagina morning and night for 14 days. The course is repeated if symptoms persist or reappear.

PREPARATIONS.—

Candeptin (Julius Schmid). *Topical* (vaginal): Capsules (vaginal); ointment 0.06% in 75 g containers; tablets (vaginal). Activity in each capsule, applicator of ointment (5 ml), or tablet is equivalent to 3 mg of candicidin.

Vanobid (Merrell-National). *Topical* (vaginal): Ointment 0.06% in 75 g containers; tablets (vaginal). Activity in each applicatorful of ointment (5 ml) or tablet is equivalent to 3 mg of candicidin.

CARBOL-FUCHSIN SOLUTION [Carfusin]

This dye has been used to treat tinea. It causes staining, and has been superseded by more effective agents.

USUAL DOSAGE.—(Carbol-Fuchsin Solution, N.F. contains basic fuchsin 0.3%, phenol 4.5%, resorcinol 10%, acetone 5%, ethyl alcohol 10%.) *Topical:* Before application, the area is washed with soap and water and dried. The solution is applied to affected areas once or twice daily for one week.

PREPARATIONS.—Carfusin (Rorer). *Topical:* Solution in 30 and 118 ml containers. Drug also marketed by other manufacturers under the name, Castellani's Paint.

FLUCYTOSINE [Ancobon]

Flucytosine is a synthetic antifungal agent chemically related to fluorouracil and floxuridine. It is administered orally and is indicated only for the treatment of serious systemic infections caused by susceptible strains of *Candida* or *Cryptococcus*, particularly meningitis caused by *Cryptococcus neoformans* or endocarditis due to various strains of *Candida*.

Forty to fifty percent of the pretreatment clinical isolates of *Candida* are resistant to flucytosine and both candidal and cryptococcal organisms may develop resistance during therapy. Therefore, it is advisable to perform culture susceptibility tests initially and at weekly intervals during treatment of cryptococcal infections and it is mandatory that such tests be performed for all infections caused by *Candida* species. Care must be taken to assure that erroneous results are not obtained. The commonly used mediums (including those used for testing amphotericin B sensitivity) interfere with the in vitro activity of flucytosine by competing with the drug for incorporation by the fungi. Reproducible, reliable results can be obtained using synthetic mediums free of cytosine and uridine.

Flucytosine is widely distributed in tissue. Levels achieved in the liver, kidney, spleen, heart, and lung are equal to those in the serum. Levels in the cerebrospinal fluid and central nervous system are one-half those in the serum.

Flucytosine is less toxic than amphotericin B; however, it may cause nausea, vomiting, diarrhea, rash, anemia, leukopenia, thrombocytopenia, and elevation of hepatic enzymes (SGOT, SGPT), blood urea nitrogen (BUN), and creatinine levels. Headache, drowsiness, confusion, vertigo, and hallucinations also have been reported.

Flucytosine must be used with extreme caution in patients with impaired renal function, since the drug is excreted primarily (approximately 90%) by the kidneys. It also must be administered with great care to those with bone marrow depression (eg, patients with certain hematologic diseases or those being treated with radiation or drugs that depress bone marrow). Flucytosine is contraindicated in patients known to be hypersensitive to the drug itself.

The safety of flucytosine during pregnancy has not been established. Therefore, the potential benefits must be weighed against the possible hazards if flucytosine is considered for use in women of childbearing age.

USUAL DOSAGE.—*Oral: Adults and children,* 150 mg/kg daily in divided doses at six-hour intervals.

PREPARATIONS.—Ancobon (Roche). *Oral:* Capsules 250 and 500 mg.

GENTIAN VIOLET

This dye has been used to treat intertriginous candidiasis. It causes staining and has been superseded by more effective agents.

USUAL DOSAGE.—

Genapax Tampon (intravaginal): One tampon (contains 5 mg gentian violet) is inserted and retained for three to four hours once or twice daily for 12 days.

GVS: One applicatorful (contains 1.35% gentian violet) of cream every other day for four to six applications, or one insert (contains 0.4% gentian violet) nightly for 12 consecutive nights.

AVAILABLE TRADEMARKS.—Genapax (Davies Rose Hoyt), GVS (Savage). Drug also marketed by other manufacturers under generic name.

AVAILABLE MIXTURE.—Hyva Gentian Violet (Holland Rantos): Each vaginal tablet contains benzethonium chloride 0.5 mg, methylrosaniline chloride 1 mg, polyethylene glycol tert-dodecylthioether 5 mg, and nonoxynol 9 10 mg.

GRISEOFULVIN [Fulvicin-U/F, Grifulvin V, Grisactin]

Griseofulvin is a fungistatic antibiotic derived from a species of *Penicillium*. It is the only drug effective orally against the species of *Epidermophyton*, *Microsporum*, and *Trichophyton* that cause dermatophytic (tinea, ringworm) infections. The drug is ineffective against other fungi, including *Candida*, and bacteria; hence, identification of the infecting organism is required before griseofulvin is used. If dermatophytic infections are complicated by *Candida* or bacterial infections, concomitant use of a drug active against the second organism is necessary. Griseofulvin is most effective in tinea infections of the scalp and glabrous skin; it is less active against chronic infections of the feet, palms, and nails. Adjunctive therapy with keratolytic agents generally is indicated in areas of hyperkeratosis.

Griseofulvin is contraindicated in patients with acute intermittent porphyria or a history of that condition, hepatocellular failure, and in those who are hypersensitive to the drug itself.

Serious reactions occur infrequently. Relatively minor reactions include headache (which may disappear even if the drug is continued), dryness of the mouth, gastrointestinal disturbances (nausea, vomiting, diarrhea), arthralgia, peripheral neuritis, vertigo, and fever. Other untoward effects include confusion, syncope, blurred vision, leukopenia, photosensitization, rash, candidiasis, insomnia, impaired performance, and proteinuria. The drug rarely may cause serum sickness and angioedema. It also may produce estrogen-like effects in children. Patients sensitive to penicillin are very rarely sensitive to griseofulvin.

USUAL DOSAGE.—(Microcrystalline form; larger crystals are outmoded.) *Oral: Adults*, 500 mg daily in single or divided doses after meals; 1 g or more daily in divided doses has sometimes been given in stubborn infections. *Children*, approximately 10 mg/kg of body weight daily in single or divided doses after meals. Absorption is enhanced after a high-fat meal. In both children and adults, it is necessary to continue therapy until infected keratinous structures have been completely replaced by noninfected tissue; this may vary from about four weeks for tinea capitis to a year or more for tinea unguium. In stubborn cases, concomitant treatment with topical antifungal agents may be helpful.

PREPARATIONS.—(All forms microsize.)

Fulvicin-U/F (Schering). *Oral:* Tablets 125, 250, and 500 mg.

Grifulvin V (McNeil). *Oral:* Suspension 125 mg/5 ml; tablets 125, 250, and 500 mg.

Grisactin (Ayerst). *Oral:* Capsules 125 and 250 mg; tablets 500 mg

Drug also marketed under generic name.

HALOPROGIN [Halotex]

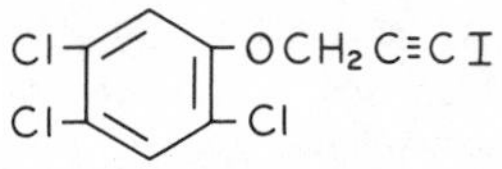

Haloprogin is a synthetic antifungal agent used in the treatment of superficial fungal infections of the skin caused by several *Trichophyton* species, *Microsporum canis*, and *Epidermophyton floccosum*. It also has been used to treat tinea versicolor caused by *Malassezia furfur*.

Adverse reactions include local irritation, burning sensation, and vesicle formation. Haloprogin may increase pruritus and maceration and cause exacerbation of pre-existing lesions. If sensitization is noted, it should be discontinued, and further use is contraindicated. Contact with the eyes must be avoided.

USUAL DOSAGE.—*Topical:* The preparation is applied to the affected area twice daily for two or three weeks. Interdigital lesions may require up to four weeks of therapy. If a patient does not improve after four weeks of treatment, this agent should be discontinued and the diagnosis redetermined.

PREPARATIONS.—Halotex (Mead Johnson). *Topical:* Cream 1% in 30 g containers; solution 1% in 10 and 30 ml containers.

HYDROXYSTILBAMIDINE ISETHIONATE

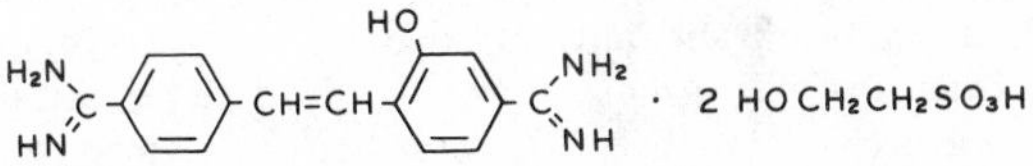

This drug is used to treat North American blastomycosis, but it is less effective than amphotericin B in disseminated disease and relapses occur more frequently. Hydroxystilbamidine appears to be most effective in patients with dermal and noncavitary pulmonary disease and in those whose host defense is adequate. Patients with significant impairment of the host response require amphotericin B. Hydroxystilbamidine also is effective in kala-azar (visceral leishmaniasis) caused by *Leishmania donovani* and mucocutaneous leishmaniasis caused by *L. braziliensis*, but the drug of choice for primary treatment of these diseases is stibogluconate sodium (see the Introductory Statement).

Untoward effects include hypotension, tachycardia, dizziness, headache, flushing, hyperhidrosis, nausea, vomiting, dyspnea, formication, salivation, syncope, fecal and urinary incontinence, and edema of the face and eyelids; these reactions usually disappear within 30 minutes. The neuropathies produced by the parent compound, stilbamidine, have not been observed with hydroxystilbamidine.

USUAL DOSAGE.—*Intravenous* (infusion): A total course of 8 g is given in daily doses of 225 mg in 200 ml of 5% dextrose injection or sodium chloride injection. A freshly prepared solution must be protected from light and heat and is infused immediately over a period of at least 30 minutes or, preferably, 60 minutes. If necessary, the dose may be given intramuscularly in 10 ml of sodium chloride or 5% dextrose injection, but the drug causes pain when given by this route.

PREPARATIONS.—Hydroxystilbamidine Isethionate (Merrell-National). *Injection:* Powder 225 mg.

IODOCHLORHYDROXYQUIN [Vioform]

OH
I
N
Cl

This preparation may be useful in localized dermatophytic infections, especially if bacteria also are present, since the drug has both antibacterial and antifungal activities. (See also Chapters 62, Amebicides; 64, Antitrichomonal Agents; and 68, Dermatologic Agents.) Iodochlorhydroxyquin should not be used near the eyes.

USUAL DOSAGE.—*Topical:* A 3% concentration is applied several times daily; (vaginal) one insert, moistened, is used each evening after a dilute acetic acid douche.

PREPARATIONS.—Vioform (Ciba). *Topical:* Cream 3% in 1 oz containers; inserts (vaginal) 250 mg; ointment 3% in 1 oz containers; powder in ½ oz containers. Drug also marketed under generic name.

NYSTATIN [Mycostatin, Nilstat]

Nystatin is a fungistatic and fungicidal antibiotic derived from *Streptomyces noursei.* It is active against all species of *Candida* that cause human infections. Its usefulness is limited to the treatment of candidal infections of the skin, mucous membranes, gastrointestinal tract, and vagina. The drug is not suitable for treating systemic infections because it is too toxic for parenteral use and is not absorbed from the gastrointestinal tract.

Preparations combining nystatin with broad spectrum antibiotics have been promoted to prevent candidal overgrowth in the intestine during antibacterial therapy. Use of these mixtures is unwarranted since intestinal candidiasis does not occur often and there is no clinical evidence that routine prophylactic administration of an antifungal agent reduces its incidence. (See the section on Mixtures of Oral Antifungal Agents with Antibacterial Agents, and Chapter 53, Tetracyclines.)

Nystatin may cause transient nausea and vomiting after oral administration. Rarely, irritation may occur after topical application, but hypersensitization has not been observed. Resistance to nystatin has not been observed clinically.

USUAL DOSAGE.—

Oral: Adults (tablets), 500,000 to 1,000,000 units three times daily. *Adults and children* (suspension), 400,000 to 600,000 units four times daily (one half of dose in each side of mouth), held in the mouth for a time before swallowing; *infants,* 200,000 units four times daily; *premature and low birth weight infants,* 100,000 units four times daily. Treatment should be continued for at least 48 hours after disappearance of symptoms.

Vaginal: 100,000 to 200,000 units daily for two weeks or longer.

Topical: Ointment or cream is applied to lesions twice daily or as directed. Powder is preferred for moist lesions and is applied two or three times daily. For use in the eye, see Chapter 71, Anti-infective and Anti-inflammatory Agents Used in Ophthalmology.

PREPARATIONS.—

Mycostatin (Squibb).

Oral: Suspension 100,000 units/ml; tablets 500,000 units.

Topical: Cream 100,000 units/g in 15 g containers; ointment 100,000 units/g in 15 and 30 g containers; powder 100,000 units/g in 15 g containers; tablets (vaginal) 100,000 units.

Nilstat (Lederle).

Oral: Drops 100,000 units/ml; tablets 500,000 units.

Topical: Cream 100,000 units/g in 15 g

containers; ointment 100,000 units/g in 15 g containers; tablets (vaginal) 100,000 units.

POTASSIUM IODIDE

Oral administration of potassium iodide is the therapy of choice for cutaneous lymphatic sporotrichosis in patients who can tolerate the drug and do not have a history of iodism. Amphotericin B is preferred in disseminated sporotrichosis.

If symptoms of iodism (rhinitis, salivation, burning of mouth and throat, ocular irritation, sialadenitis, and dermal lesions) occur, administration of potassium iodide may have to be discontinued. Hypothyroidism may develop in patients with goiter (see Chapter 39, Thyroid Hormones and Antithyroid Agents).

USUAL DOSAGE.—*Oral:* 0.6 ml of a saturated solution is given three times daily; the amount is increased each day by 0.06 ml at each dose, depending on tolerance, up to a maximal daily dose of 12 ml. Cure requires six to eight weeks of treatment.

PREPARATIONS.—*Oral:* Solution. Drug marketed under generic name.

SELENIUM SULFIDE DETERGENT SUSPENSION [Selsun]

Selenium sulfide is useful in the treatment of tinea versicolor (pityriasis versicolor), a chronic fungal infection of the skin caused by *Malassezia furfur*. It also is used in the treatment of seborrheic dermatitis of the scalp (see Chapter 68, Dermatologic Agents).

Contact with the eyes and genital area should be avoided because of the irritant properties of the drug. The detergent component of the suspension may cause sensitization.

USUAL DOSAGE.—Affected areas are covered with the suspension and lathered; the preparation is thoroughly rinsed from body areas after five minutes or from facial areas after ten minutes. The preparation is applied once daily for four days.

PREPARATIONS.—Selsun (Abbott). *Topical:* Suspension 2.5% in 125 ml containers.

TOLNAFTATE [Tinactin]

CH_3 — NCSO — (structure: m-tolyl, N-methyl, 2-naphthyl thiocarbamate); CH_3

Tolnaftate is effective topically against all species of *Epidermophyton*, *Microsporum*, and *Trichophyton* that cause dermatophytic (tinea, ringworm) infections in man. It also is active against *Malassezia furfur*, the cause of tinea versicolor (pityriasis versicolor). The drug is not effective against candidal and bacterial species; hence, microscopic or cultural identification of the infecting organisms is necessary before tolnaftate is used. Fungal infections of the scalp, nails, soles, and palms usually do not respond well to tolnaftate, for these lesions are frequently chronic and often refractory to topical medication. However, tolnaftate may be given with griseofulvin for adjunctive local benefit. Patients with *T. rubrum* infections often have a relapse but may respond to a second course of tolnaftate. See also the Introductory Statement.

There have been some subjective claims that tolnaftate is irritating, but no confirmed adverse reactions have been reported.

USUAL DOSAGE.—*Topical:* One or two drops of solution or a small amount of cream or powder is rubbed into lesions twice daily for two to three weeks; treatment for four to six weeks may be required in some cases. The powder or powder aerosol may continue to be used after six weeks to help maintain remission in patients susceptible to tinea.

PREPARATIONS.—Tinactin (Schering). *Topical:* Cream 1% in 15 g containers; powder 1% in 45 g containers; powder (aerosol) 1% in 120 g containers; solution 1% in 10 ml containers.

TRIACETIN [Enzactin]

$$\begin{array}{l} CH_2OOCCH_3 \\ | \\ CHOOCCH_3 \\ | \\ CH_2OOCCH_3 \end{array}$$

Triacetin is used topically in the treatment of superficial fungal infections. It has not been proved by means of controlled clinical trials that this agent provides a therapeutic response greater than that provided by acetic acid, which is released slowly from triacetin by esterases present in fungi, human skin, and serum.

USUAL DOSAGE.—No estimation of a useful dosage regimen can be made since this compound may be no more effective than the acetic acid it releases. The manufacturer's suggested dosage is: *Topical:* After cleansing the lesion with alcohol or soap and water and drying, the aerosol or cream is applied twice daily or the powder is applied each morning.

PREPARATIONS.—Enzactin (Ayerst). *Topical:* Aerosol 15% in 3 oz containers; cream 250 mg/g in 1 oz containers; powder 33.3% in 1 and ½ oz containers.

UNDECYLENIC ACID

$$CH_2{=}CH(CH_2)_8COOH$$

Clinical results suggest that this compound may be the most useful of the proprietary agents used to treat dermatophytic infections. However, controlled clinical trials to prove its effectiveness have not been conducted. It is well tolerated and may be worth a trial in more localized dermatophytic infections.

USUAL DOSAGE.—*Topical:* The concentration should not exceed 10% for application to skin or 1% to mucous membranes. Dosage recommendations vary with different manufacturers. A common practice is to apply a powder or aerosol in the morning and a cream, ointment, or aerosol at night.

PREPARATIONS.—*Topical:* Various forms, including solutions, tinctures, creams, ointments, powders, soaps, and aerosols.

AVAILABLE TRADEMARK.—Desenex Solution (Pharmacraft).

MIXTURES OF ANTIFUNGAL AGENTS

BENZOIC AND SALICYLIC ACID OINTMENT

This mixture contains benzoic acid 6% and salicylic acid 3%. It has no significant antifungal action, but it is an effective keratolytic; prior treatment with this preparation makes infections in deeper layers accessible to more potent antifungal agents. Its use should be discontinued if irritation occurs. See also Chapter 68, Dermatologic Agents.

USUAL DOSAGE.—*Topical:* The ointment is applied once or twice daily to the involved area.

PREPARATIONS.—Mixture marketed under generic name and as Whitfield's Ointment.

COMPOUND UNDECYLENIC ACID [Desenex]

This mixture of undecylenic acid and zinc undecylenate is used topically for the treatment of dermatomycoses. Like the individual agents, it is weakly effective in treating minor lesions. Its use should be discontinued if sensitization or irritation develops.

USUAL DOSAGE.—*Topical:* Ointment or powder is applied once or twice daily to the involved area.

PREPARATIONS.—*Topical:* Powder or ointment containing undecylenic acid 2% (powder) or 5% (ointment) and zinc undecylenate 20%.

AVAILABLE TRADEMARK.—Desenex Powder, Ointment (Pharmacraft).

SPOROSTACIN

Sporostacin, a combination of chlordantoin and benzalkonium chloride, is promoted for topical use in the treatment of candidal infections of the vulvovaginal area. In vitro, chlordantoin inhibits *Candida albicans*, and a combination of chlordantoin and benzalkonium chloride acts synergistically. Cure rates reported following use of the mixture ranged from less than 50% to 70% after a 14-day course of treatment and 90% or better after three courses. Adequate controlled studies to confirm these findings have not been reported. Use of the mixture might be justified in patients who do not tolerate or do not respond to more effective agents such as nystatin or amphotericin B.

Untoward effects caused by this preparation (burning and at least one instance of allergic dermatitis) have been reported in less than 1% of patients.

USUAL DOSAGE.—*Topical:* For candidal infections of the vulvovaginal area, the cream is applied to the affected area once or twice daily as required. For mycotic vaginitis, one applicatorful of cream is applied twice daily for 14 days; the course of therapy may be repeated if necessary.

PREPARATIONS.—Sporostacin (Ortho). *Topical:* Cream containing chlordantoin 1% and benzalkonium chloride 0.05% in 95 g containers.

Additional Mixtures

Hydrophen (Amfre-Grant): Ointment containing zinc undecylenate 6%, benzalkonium chloride 1:1,000, benzocaine 1%, and phenylmercuric nitrate 1:3,000 in 1, 4, and 6 oz containers.

Propion Gel (Wyeth): Gel containing propionate calcium 10% and propionate sodium 10% in 95 g containers.

Quatrasal (Dome): Solution or spray containing salicylanilide 2.5%, benzethonium chloride 0.5%, and isopropyl alcohol 97% (solution) in 1 oz containers or 47% (spray) in 3 oz containers.

Sopronol (Wyeth): Ointment or solution containing caprylate sodium 10%, propionate sodium 12.3%, propionate zinc 5%, and propionic acid 2.7% in 1 and

4 oz containers (ointment) or 2 oz containers (solution); powder containing caprylate sodium 10%, propionate sodium 5%, and propionate zinc 5% in 2 and 5 oz containers.

Verdefam (Texas): Cream containing propionate sodium 1%, caprylate sodium 1%, propionic acid 3%, and copper undecylenate 0.5% in 1 oz containers; solution containing undecylenic acid 5%, copper undecylenate 0.5%, propionic acid 3%, salicylic acid 5%, caprylate sodium 2%, and propionate sodium 2% in 2 oz containers.

MIXTURES OF ANTIFUNGAL DRUGS WITH OTHER TYPES OF AGENTS

Several topical antifungal agents are incorporated into mixtures with antibiotics, corticosteroids, local anti-infectives, coal tar derivatives, or local anesthetics. Some dermatomycoses represent mixed infections of dermatophytes and *Candida* with each other or with bacteria and may not respond unless treated with a specific agent for each organism. Corticosteroids also may be needed to combat inflammation. In such instances, use of a single topical preparation combining rational amounts of the indicated drugs may be appropriate and is more convenient than the use of separate preparations. However, such preparations should be used selectively and not routinely. Their disadvantage is that if irritation or sensitization occurs, the responsible ingredient must be found by a process of trial and error after application of the mixture is stopped. The rationale for the inclusion of local anesthetics and coal tar derivatives in antifungal preparations is highly questionable. These agents lack effective anti-infective action and, like other topically applied drugs, may cause sensitization. Also, pruritus due to infection is rapidly controlled as inflammation, edema, and swelling subside.

Caldecort (Pennwalt): Each gram of ointment contains calcium undecylenate 30 mg, neomycin sulfate equivalent to neomycin 3.5 mg, and hydrocortisone acetate 10 mg in 7 and 28 g containers.

Domeform-HC (Dome): Cream containing iodochlorhydroxyquin 3% and hydrocortisone alcohol 0.5% or 1% in ½ and 1 oz containers.

Heb-Cort V (Barnes-Hind): Cream containing iodochlorhydroxyquin 3% and hydrocortisone alcohol 0.25% or 1% in 1 oz containers; lotion containing iodochlorhydroxyquin 3% and hydrocortisone alcohol 0.25% in 2 oz containers.

Hyquin (Texas): Cream containing iodochlorhydroxyquin 3% and hydrocortisone alcohol 0.5% in ½ and 1 oz containers.

Lidaform-HC (Dome): Cream or lotion containing iodochlorhydroxyquin 3%, hydrocortisone acetate 0.5%, and lidocaine 3% in ½ oz (cream) and 1 oz (lotion) containers.

Mycolog (Squibb): Each gram of cream or ointment contains nystatin 100,000 units, neomycin sulfate equivalent to neomycin 2.5 mg, and triamcinolone acetonide 1 mg in 5, 15, 30, and 120 mg containers.

Myconef (Squibb): Each gram of ointment contains nystatin 100,000 units, neomycin sulfate equivalent to neomycin 2.5 mg, gramicidin 0.25 mg, and fludrocortisone acetate 1 mg in 15 g containers.

Neo-Domeform-HC (Dome): Each gram of cream contains iodochlorhydroxyquin 3%, neomycin sulfate 5 mg, and hydrocortisone alcohol 0.5% in ½ oz containers.

Neo-Nysta-Cort (Dome): Each gram of ointment contains nystatin 100,000 units, neomycin sulfate equivalent to neomycin 0.35%, and hydrocortisone alcohol 1% in ½ oz containers.

Nystaform (Dome): Each gram of ointment contains nystatin 100,000 units and iodochlorhydroxyquin 1% in ½ oz containers.

Nystaform-HC (Dome): Each milliliter of lotion contains nystatin 100,000 units, iodochlorhydroxyquin 3%, and hydrocortisone 0.5% in 1 oz containers; each gram of ointment contains nystatin 100,000 units, iodochlorhydroxyquin 3%, and hydrocortisone 1% in ½ oz containers.

Racet (Lemmon): Cream containing iodochlorhydroxyquin 3% and hydrocortisone 0.5% in 3.5, 30, and 454 g containers; forte cream containing iodochlorhydroxyquin 3% and hydrocortisone 1.5% in 5 g containers.

Racet LCD (Lemmon): Cream containing iodochlorhydroxyquin 3%, hydrocortisone 0.5%, and coal tar solution 5% in 30 g containers.

Topigel (Reed & Carnrick): Gel containing iodochlorhydroxyquin 1%, hydrocortisone 1%, and coal tar extract 5% in ½ and 1 oz containers.

Vioform-Hydrocortisone (Ciba): Cream, lotion, or ointment containing iodochlorhydroxyquin 3% and hydrocortisone 1% in 5 g, 20 g, and 15 ml (lotion) containers.

MIXTURES OF ORAL ANTIFUNGAL AGENTS WITH ANTIBACTERIAL AGENTS

Oral mixtures of a broad spectrum antibiotic (tetracycline or oxytetracycline) and an antifungal drug (amphotericin B or nystatin) have been promoted to prevent the overgrowth of intestinal fungi during antibacterial therapy. The rationale for using such combinations is difficult to justify. Intestinal candidiasis as a complication of broad spectrum antibiotic therapy occurs infrequently, and there is no clinical evidence that the routine administration of an antifungal agent reduces its incidence. The use of an antifungal agent is indicated if symptomatic intestinal candidiasis occurs in a patient receiving an antibacterial drug or if candidal colonization without symptoms occurs in a patient for whom fungal disease represents a special risk. Such patients include diabetics, those receiving antineoplastic agents or corticosteroids, debilitated patients, and infants or elderly patients. However, in these situations, it is preferable to give the antibacterial and antifungal agents separately, since the doses of antifungal agents in fixed combinations may be suboptimal. Thus, the fixed-ratio combinations should not be used. (For a listing of available mixtures, see Chapter 53, Tetracyclines.)

Chapter 61

ANTIMALARIAL AGENTS

Because of its great prevalence, mortality, morbidity, and economic impact, malaria continues to be one of the most grave diseases affecting man. Although its significance in the United States is minimal compared to other parts of the world, the problem is becoming more serious. The annual number of cases of malaria has risen from less than 200 in the period from 1960 to 1965 to about 4,000 in 1970. The increase in number of cases was primarily among military personnel; the number of cases in civilians returning from endemic areas has remained relatively constant. Recognition and treatment of these individuals is necessary if a serious public health problem is to be avoided.

Four species of the parasitic protozoan *Plasmodium* normally are responsible for producing malaria in man. These species and the types of malaria they produce are *Plasmodium vivax* (benign tertian), *P. malariae* (quartan), *P. ovale* (ovale tertian), and *P. falciparum* (malignant tertian).

The main symptoms of disease are fever, severe anemia, hyperhidrosis, malnutrition, and splenomegaly. Falciparum malaria is the most serious because it may be fatal if adequate treatment is not instituted promptly. The other types of malaria are less severe and mortality is usually low, but infection often recurs.

The life cycle of the malaria-causing organisms begins when the infected female anopheline mosquito bites a human and deposits sporozoites, the end-product of the parasite's sexual phase of development in the mosquito. The sporozoites invade the hepatic cells and develop into primary tissue schizonts (primary exoerythrocytic forms); later on in the life cycle, merozoites are produced, and these invade erythrocytes and develop into blood schizonts (asexual erythrocytic forms of malaria parasites).

The schizogenous cycle in the erythrocytes is initiated by the invasion of the merozoites released from the liver or from other infected erythrocytes. The duration of the cycles varies from 42 to 72 hours, depending upon the species of *Plasmodium* involved. When the parasites mature, the infected erythrocytes rupture, releasing merozoites, fragmented erythrocytes, pigment, and other products of the maturation process into the blood-stream. If sufficient numbers of parasites are present, the chills, fever, and sweating of a malarial paroxysm occur.

After a few cycles, gametocytes, the sexual erythrocytic forms, appear. If the infected person then is bitten by a mosquito, gametocytes enter the mosquito with the blood meal. There, the sexual stage of reproduction eventually produces sporozoites, which enter the mosquito's salivary glands to await injection into another human host to complete the cycle.

The antimalarial drugs can be classified on the basis of their action at different stages in the life cycle of the plasmodial organism. Those that destroy primary tissue schizonts are called primary tissue schizontocides or *causal prophylactic agents.* These include primaquine, chloroguanide [Paludrine], and pyrimethamine [Daraprim]. *Causal prophylaxis* implies prevention of red blood cell invasion by malarial parasites but, unfortunately, this objective is not uniformly attainable. The agents that destroy blood schizonts are termed blood schizontocides or *suppressive agents.* These include quinine, quinacrine [Atabrine], chloroquine [Aralen, Roquine], hydroxychloroquine [Plaquenil], amodiaquine [Camoquin], chloroguanide, pyrimethamine, and combinations of sulfones and sulfonamides with pyrimethamine and chloroguanide. When the suppressive agents are used prophylactically, they may prevent malaria by eliminating parasites as they are released from the tissues into the bloodstream, an effect referred to as *clinical prophylaxis.* Used therapeutically, these agents may be of value in terminating acute attacks of malaria and in completely eliminating asexual erythrocytic parasites from the blood. The term *radical cure* implies the complete elimination of parasites from the body so that relapse cannot occur. Primaquine, in conjunction with an effective schizontocide, accomplishes this in all relapsing malarias by virtue of its ability to destroy the secondary tissue schizonts of the responsible plasmodia. In contrast, *clinical cure* denotes the relief of symptoms without necessarily completely eliminating the infection. The blood schizontocides are capable of producing this. Primaquine is the only antimalarial drug in widespread use that destroys gametocytes and is called a gametocytocide. Primaquine, pyrimethamine, and chloroguanide render gametocytes noninfective and thus prevent sporogenous development in the mosquito host. They are called sporontocides. Both of these classes of drugs may be useful in preventing further transmission of malaria.

Although the site of action of the antimalarial drugs primarily determines how they are used against the disease, their ultimate usage is influenced by other factors (eg, plasmodial resistance, relative efficacy, toxicity, availability) and, therefore, drug therapy for treatment and prophylaxis of malaria varies. The most effective regimens are described in the following paragraphs and doses of the drugs are presented in the appropriate evaluation. Regardless of which regimen is used, it frequently is important to provide the patient, particularly if he has falciparum malaria, with ancillary therapy (eg, packed red blood cell transfusions, restoration of fluid and electrolyte balance, steroids).

A course of chloroquine phosphate or amodiaquine hydrochloride is administered orally in acute attacks of malaria produced by *Plasmodium vivax*, *P. ovale*, *P. malariae*, or a susceptible strain of *P. falciparum.* To prevent relapses occurring in those malarias caused by *P. vivax*, *P. ovale*, or *P. malariae*, a course of primaquine phosphate is administered orally, either along with the chloroquine phosphate or amodiaquine hydrochloride or after the patient has recovered from the acute attack. If primaquine phosphate is not tolerated because of severe erythrocytic glucose-6-phosphate dehydrogenase (G6PD) deficiency (hemolysis occurs) and relapses develop, a course of chloroquine phosphate is administered orally each week until the individual is asymptomatic (several months may be required). If chloroquine phosphate is not tolerated or the malarial attack is severe, the hydrochloride salt is administered intramuscularly until it is possible to give chloroquine phosphate orally (see the evaluations on Chloroquine and Amodiaquine Hydrochloride).

When an acute attack of falciparum malaria occurs and the individual has been in an area where *P. falciparum* is resistant to 4-aminoquinoline derivatives (Brazil, Columbia, Venezuela, Thailand, Malaya, Cambodia, and parts of the Philippines and Vietnam), or has transfusion or injection malaria, the malaria is treated with a combination of quinine sulfate and pyrimethamine or quinine sulfate, pyrimethamine, and dapsone given orally. If there is a recrudescence of this malaria, one of several alternative regimens may be given: (1) trimethoprim and sulfalene, two investigational drugs, are administered orally and concomitantly; (2) quinine sulfate and tetracycline are administered orally and sequentially; or (3) pyrimethamine and sulfisoxazole are administered orally and concomitantly together with the continuous intravenous infusion of quinine dihydrochloride (see the evaluations on Quinine and Pyrimethamine). If orally administered quinine sulfate is not tolerated or the malarial attack is severe, quinine dihydrochloride is administered intravenously until it is possible to give quinine sulfate orally.

Chloroquine phosphate or amodiaquine hydrochloride along with primaquine phosphate is given prophylactically to persons entering areas where malaria is endemic. Administration of chloroquine or amodiaquine is begun two weeks before the individual enters the malarious area and is continued for eight weeks after he leaves. Primaquine is administered in a single course immediately after the individual has left the malarious area (see the individual evaluations).

Other Uses of Antimalarial Agents: Quinine has been used in the treatment of nocturnal leg cramps and myotonia congenita; in the diagnosis of myasthenia gravis; as an antipyretic-analgesic; to induce labor; and as a local anesthetic or sclerosing agent. However, with the exception of the use of quinine to treat nocturnal leg cramps, more effective drugs are currently available for these purposes.

Although quinacrine has very little current use in malaria, it is considered the drug of choice for treatment of some tapeworm infections (see Chapter 65, Anthelmintics) and a drug of choice in symptomatic giardiasis. Quinacrine also has been used in petit mal epilepsy and for the palliation of recurrent pleural effusions and ascites associated with certain neoplastic diseases. (See Chapter 31, Anticonvulsants, and Chapter 88, Antineoplastic Agents.) Its use in discoid lupus erythematosus and rheumatoid arthritis has largely been abandoned.

Pyrimethamine is given with sulfonamides in the treatment of toxoplasmosis. Chloroquine, hydroxychloroquine, and amodiaquine are used in the treatment of hepatic amebiasis, and are alternatives to quinacrine or metronidazole [Flagyl] in giardiasis.

Chloroquine and hydroxychloroquine also have been used in the treatment of discoid and systemic lupus erythematosus, rheumatoid arthritis, and polymorphous light eruptions. The restricting factor is the toxicity of these agents when they are given for long periods in the doses necessary to achieve therapeutic effects. The benefits that occur in most patients with discoid lupus erythematosus have led to the rather general acceptance of chloroquine and hydroxychloroquine in the treatment of this condition. In the absence of adequate, well-controlled studies, use of these drugs in systemic lupus erythematosus has been more controversial; their uncertain effectiveness in this form of lupus erythematosus, their hazards, and their possible aggravation of the disease indicate that they have only a very limited place at present in its treatment, except perhaps in the management of the skin lesions. Although chloroquine and hydroxychloroquine are effective in about half of those treated for rheumatoid arthritis, the effects are often only moderate and usually do not occur until after several weeks or months of treatment (see Chapter 26, Antirheumatic Agents).

Adverse Reactions and Precautions

When used as antimalarial agents in properly adjusted doses, these drugs produce few adverse reactions. However, those that are given in large doses for long periods (eg, in discoid lupus erythematosus), produce numerous severe reactions, some of which may be irreversible. The adverse reactions produced by antimalarial agents and the precautions necessary in their use are diverse and are therefore discussed in the individual evaluations.

INDIVIDUAL EVALUATIONS

AMODIAQUINE HYDROCHLORIDE
[Camoquin Hydrochloride]

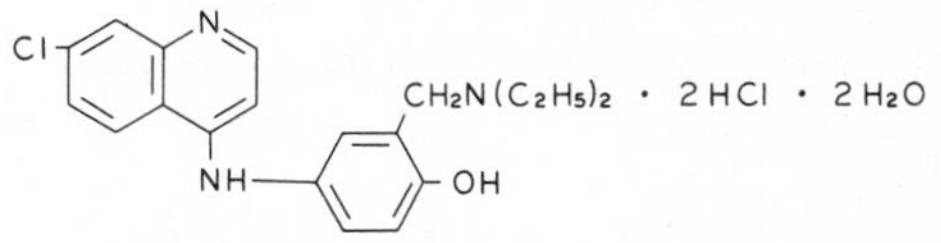

This 4-aminoquinoline derivative is a drug of choice in the prophylaxis and treatment of acute attacks of malaria caused by *Plasmodium vivax*, *P. ovale*, *P. malariae*, and susceptible strains of *P. falciparum* (see the Introductory Statement). Amodiaquine also is used to treat giardiasis and hepatic amebiasis.

Adverse reactions include nausea, vomiting, diarrhea, fatigue, lassitude, vertigo, and pigmentation of the palate, nail beds, and skin. Most of the gastrointestinal reactions can be minimized by administering the drug with meals. The pigmentation reactions occur in 40% of those receiving weekly antimalarial doses over a prolonged period (five weeks to six years). They usually appear after approximately nine months of therapy and disappear four to nine months after the drug is discontinued.

USUAL DOSAGE.—*Oral:* For treatment of acute attacks of malaria (except resistant falciparum) in nonimmune persons, *adults*, 780 mg initially, followed by 520 mg daily for the next two days. *Children less than 2 years of age*, 130 mg twice on the first day, followed by 130 mg once daily for the next four days; *2 to 6 years*, 195 mg twice on the first day, followed by 130 mg once daily for the next four days; *6 to 10 years*, 195 mg three times a day on the first day, followed by 195 mg once daily for the next four days.

For prophylaxis of malaria (except resistant falciparum), *adults*, 520 mg; *children less than 2 years*, 65 to 130 mg; *2 to 10 years*, 130 to 260 mg. This dose is given once weekly on the same day of the week beginning two weeks before the individual enters the malarious area and is continued for eight weeks after he leaves. In addition, a single course of primaquine is administered immediately after the individual has left the malarious area (see the evaluation on Primaquine Phosphate).

For hepatic amebiasis, *adults*, 780 mg daily for ten days; after a rest period of eight to ten days, 780 mg is given daily for eight days.

For giardiasis, *adults*, 260 mg three times daily until the stools are free of *Giardia lamblia*. *Children less than 5 years*, 260 mg daily; *5 to 10 years*, 390 mg daily.

PREPARATIONS.—Camoquin Hydrochloride (Parke, Davis). *Oral:* Tablets 260 mg.

CHLOROGUANIDE HYDROCHLORIDE [Paludrine]

$$Cl-C_6H_4-NH-C(=NH)-NH-C(=NH)-NH-CH(CH_3)_2 \cdot HCl$$

This folic acid antagonist is used for the prophylaxis of malaria in areas where species of *Plasmodium* are not resistant to it. Unfortunately, however, chloroguanide-resistant strains of plasmodia are widespread and this resistance is the major drawback to use of the drug.

The incidence of adverse reactions (vomiting, gastrointestinal discomfort, diarrhea, hematuria, and casts in the urine) is very low. Prolonged use may cause anorexia, malaise, and weight loss. Like pyrimethamine, it should be used with caution during pregnancy, particularly during the first trimester.

USUAL DOSAGE.—*Oral:* For prophylaxis of nonresistant strains of malaria in nonimmune persons, *adults*, 100 mg daily; *children less than 2 years of age*, 25 to 50 mg daily; *2 to 6 years*, 50 to 75 mg daily; *6 to 10 years*, 100 mg daily. This dose is administered when the individual enters the malarious area and is continued for eight weeks after he leaves. In addition, a single course of primaquine is administered immediately after the individual has left the malarious area (see the evaluation on Primaquine Phosphate).

PREPARATIONS.—Paludrine (Ayerst). *Oral:* Tablets 100 mg.

CHLOROQUINE HYDROCHLORIDE [Aralen Hydrochloride]
CHLOROQUINE PHOSPHATE [Aralen Phosphate, Roquine]

7-Cl-quinoline-4-yl: $HN-CH(CH_3)(CH_2)_3N(C_2H_5)_2 \cdot HCl$

Chloroquine phosphate, a 4-aminoquinoline derivative, is given orally and is a drug of choice for the prophylaxis and treatment of acute attacks of malaria caused by *Plasmodium vivax*, *P. ovale*, *P. malariae*, and susceptible strains of *P. falciparum* (see the Introductory Statement). It also is a component of the mixture, Aralen Phosphate with Primaquine Phosphate, which is used for the prophylaxis of malaria in endemic areas.

The hydrochloride salt is used when parenteral administration is required because the phosphate salt is not well tolerated (presence of vomiting, pronounced nausea, or malabsorption), or the infection is severe (associated with coma, confusion, acute circulatory failure, segmenting erythrocytic forms, or falciparum malaria with more than 5% infected erythrocytes), or is present in infants. Oral administration of a 4-aminoquinoline derivative should be substituted as soon as practicable.

For other uses of chloroquine, see the Introductory Statement.

Most adverse effects resulting from antimalarial doses of chloroquine are relatively mild since the amounts used for clinical prophylaxis are small and the larger ones used in treating acute attacks are given for short periods only. The adverse effects are dose related and include gastrointestinal discomfort with nausea, diarrhea, pruritus, headache, central nervous system stimulation, and reversible interference with visual accommodation. For the reactions that may occur with the prolonged use of large doses of chloroquine phosphate in systemic or discoid lupus erythematosus and rheumatoid arthritis, see Chapter 26, Antirheumatic Agents.

Acute overdosage of chloroquine phosphate or hydrochloride can cause acute circulatory failure, convulsions, respiratory and cardiac arrest, and death.

USUAL DOSAGE.—

Chloroquine Hydrochloride:

Intramuscular: For acute attacks of malaria (except resistant falciparum), *adults*, 250 mg initially and repeated, if necessary, at intervals of six hours; dosage should not exceed 1 g in 24 hours. *Children*, 6.25 mg/kg of body weight initially and repeated if necessary in six hours. The total dose for 24 hours should not exceed 12.5 mg/kg.

Chloroquine Phosphate:

Oral: For treatment of acute attacks of malaria (except in resistant falciparum) in nonimmune persons, *adults*, 1 g initially, followed by 500 mg in six hours and 500 mg daily for the next two days. *Children*, 16.66

mg/kg of body weight initially, followed by 8.33 mg/kg in six hours and 8.33 mg/kg daily for the next two days.

For prophylaxis of malaria (except resistant falciparum), *adults*, 500 mg and *children*, 8.33 mg/kg. The dose is given once weekly on the same day of the week. Administration should be started two weeks before the individual enters the endemic area and continued for eight weeks after he returns. A single course of primaquine phosphate also should be administered immediately after the individual has left the malarious area (see the evaluation on Primaquine Phosphate).

For polymorphous light eruptions, *adults*, 250 mg daily.

For giardiasis, *adults*, 500 mg daily for five days.

For dosages in rheumatoid arthritis and lupus erythematosus, see Chapter 26, Antirheumatic Agents.

PREPARATIONS.—

Chloroquine Hydrochloride:

Aralen Hydrochloride (Winthrop). *Injection:* Solution 50 mg/ml in 5 ml containers.

Chloroquine Phosphate:

Aralen Phosphate (Winthrop). *Oral:* Tablets 500 mg.

Roquine (Robinson). *Oral:* Tablets (enteric-coated) 250 mg.

Tablets and enteric-coated tablets also marketed under generic name.

HYDROXYCHLOROQUINE SULFATE

[Plaquenil Sulfate]

CH_3 CH_2CH_2OH NH CH $CH_2CH_2CH_2N$ CH_2CH_3 · H_2SO_4 Cl N

Hydroxychloroquine, a 4-aminoquinoline derivative, is used for the prophylaxis and treatment of malaria caused by *Plasmodium vivax*, *P. malariae*, *P. ovale*, and susceptible strains of *P. falciparum* (see the Introductory Statement).

For other uses of this drug, see the Introductory Statement.

Antimalarial doses may produce headache, dizziness, diarrhea, anorexia, nausea, abdominal cramps and, rarely, vomiting.

USUAL DOSAGE.—*Oral: Adults*, for treatment of acute attacks of malaria (except resistant falciparum) in nonimmune persons, *adults*, 800 mg initially, followed by 400 mg in six or eight hours and 400 mg on each of the next two days; *children 1 year of age or less*, 100 mg initially, followed by three doses of 100 mg at six- or eight-hour intervals; *2 to 5 years*, 400 mg initially, followed by 200 mg eight hours later; *6 to 10 years*, 400 mg initially, followed by two doses of 200 mg at eight-hour intervals; *11 to 15 years*, 600 mg initially, followed by 200 mg eight hours later and 200 mg 24 hours later.

For prophylaxis of malaria (except resistant falciparum), *adults*, 400 mg once weekly on the same day of each week. Administration should be started two weeks before the individual enters an endemic area and continued for eight weeks after he returns. A single course of primaquine phosphate should also be administered after the individual has left the malarious area (see the evaluation on Primaquine Phosphate).

For polymorphous light eruptions, *adults*, initially, 400 mg once or twice daily for weeks or months depending upon the response. For prolonged maintenance therapy, 200 to 400 mg daily.

For giardiasis, *adults*, 200 mg three times daily for five days.

For dosages in rheumatoid arthritis and lupus erythematosus, see Chapter 26, Antirheumatic Agents.

PREPARATIONS.—Plaquenil Sulfate (Winthrop). *Oral:* Tablets 200 mg.

PRIMAQUINE PHOSPHATE

CH_3O N · $2\,H_3PO_4$ NH-CH $CH_2CH_2CH_2NH_2$ CH_3

This drug is the only 8-aminoquinoline derivative now in widespread use for the treatment of malaria. It is administered to prevent relapses (effect a radical cure) of malaria caused by *Plasmodium vivax*, *P. ovale*, or *P. malariae*. It also is used in the prophylaxis of delayed attacks of these malarias that can occur after an individual leaves a malarious area and discontinues prophylactic therapy with amodiaquine hydrochloride, chloroquine phosphate, or another appropriate antimalarial agent. (See the Introductory Statement.)

The most serious adverse effect is acute hemolysis. This occurs in individuals with glucose-6-phosphate dehydrogenase (G6PD) deficiency or other inherited alterations of the pentose phosphate pathway of the red blood cells that predispose to hemolysis. The hemolytic anemia that may result from usual antimalarial doses is generally relatively mild and self-limited, and continued weekly administration of moderate doses of the drug usually mitigates the hemolytic effects. Primaquine also may cause abdominal discomfort, nausea, headache, disturbance of visual accommodation, pruritus, and methemoglobinemia. Leukopenia and agranulocytosis occur most commonly in patients with rheumatoid arthritis; accordingly, the drug should be given with particular caution to patients with collagen diseases.

Primaquine should be discontinued immediately if a marked darkening of the urine or a sudden decrease in the hemoglobin concentration or leukocyte count occurs. It should not be administered to individuals who have received quinacrine recently, since its toxicity is enhanced.

USUAL DOSAGE.—*Oral:* To prevent relapses, *adults*, 26.3 mg and *children*, 13.15 mg/kg of body weight. This dose is given daily for 14 days concomitantly with chloroquine phosphate or amodiaquine hydrochloride during an acute attack or by itself after the patient has recovered from the acute attack. If primaquine is not tolerated because of severe G6PD deficiency and hemolysis, chloroquine phosphate is administered orally each week until the patient is asymptomatic (several months may be required).

For prophylaxis of delayed attacks, *adults*, 26.3 mg and *children*, 13.15 mg/kg daily for 14 days beginning immediately after the individual has left the malarious area. This treatment must be carried out after the administration of chloroquine phosphate, amodiaquine hydrochloride, or another appropriate antimalarial agent (see the evaluations).

PREPARATIONS.—*Oral:* Tablets 26.3 mg. Drug marketed under generic name.

PYRIMETHAMINE [Daraprim]

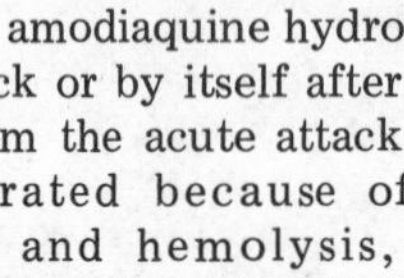

Pyrimethamine is a folic acid antagonist that is used for the prophylaxis of malaria in areas where the species of *Plasmodium* are not resistant to it. Unfortunately, however, pyrimethamine-resistant strains are widespread. This plasmodial resistance is the major drawback to this use of pyrimethamine. The drug also is used in various combinations with dapsone, sulfisoxazole, and quinine to treat acute attacks of malaria caused by resistant strains of *P. falciparum* (see the Introductory Statement and the evaluation on Quinine), and concomitantly with sulfonamides in the treatment of toxoplasmosis (see Chapter 71, Anti-infective and Anti-inflammatory Agents Used in Ophthalmology, and Chapter 55, Sulfonamides).

The hazards from small, suppressive antimalarial doses are minimal. However, the toxicity increases substantially when large daily doses are used with sulfonamides to treat toxoplasmosis. Anorexia, vomiting, megaloblastic anemia, and bone marrow depression with leukopenia and thrombocytopenia may then occur. Although it has been given to many pregnant women in small suppressive antimalarial doses with no apparent complications, large daily doses might be dangerous, particularly during the first trimester.

USUAL DOSAGE.—*Oral:* For prophylaxis of malaria caused by nonresistant strains, *adults and children over 10 years of age*, 25 mg once weekly; *children 4 to 10 years*, 12.5 mg once weekly; *under 4 years*, 6.25 mg once weekly. The drug should be given on the same day each week and administration should begin when the individual enters the malarious area and continued for ten weeks after he leaves. In addition, a single course of primaquine phosphate is administered immediately after the individual has left the malarious area (see the evaluation on Primaquine Phosphate).

For treatment of toxoplasmosis, *adults*, 50 to 75 mg daily with 1 to 4 g of a sulfonamide (eg, sulfadiazine) (see Chapter 55, Sulfonamides). The dose is continued for one to three weeks, depending upon the response and tolerance of the patient. The amount of each drug then may be reduced by about one-half and therapy continued for four or five weeks. *Children*, 1 mg/kg of body weight daily divided into two equal daily doses with the usual pediatric dosage of a sulfonamide. After two to four days, the dose of each drug may be reduced by one-half and therapy continued for approximately one month. The gastrointestinal symptoms produced by these large doses of pyrimethamine disappear promptly upon reduction of dosage and can be minimized by giving the medication with meals.

If hematologic abnormalities appear, administration should be stopped or reduced to no more than 25 mg daily and leucovorin (folinic acid), in doses of 3 to 9 mg, should be administered intramuscularly until the blood cell count returns to safe levels. Alternatively, the concomitant administration of 3 to 9 mg of leucovorin with pyrimethamine will usually prevent the development of the thrombocytopenia and leukopenia without interfering with the action of pyrimethamine (see Chapter 8, Agents Used to Treat Deficiency Anemias, and Chapter 71, Anti-infective and Anti-inflammatory Agents Used in Ophthalmology).

For doses used in the treatment of resistant falciparum or transfusion or injection malaria, see the evaluation on Quinine.

PREPARATIONS.—Daraprim (Burroughs Wellcome). *Oral:* Tablets 25 mg.

QUINACRINE HYDROCHLORIDE
[Atabrine Hydrochloride]

CH_3O – acridine – $NH\,CH(CH_3)CH_2CH_2CH_2N(C_2H_5)_2$, Cl $\cdot\ 2HCl \cdot 2H_2O$

This acridine derivative has been superseded by the 4-aminoquinolines which are more potent and less toxic. It is used for the prophylaxis and treatment of malaria caused by nonresistant strains of *Plasmodium* only when the 4-aminoquinoline derivatives are not available.

For other uses of quinacrine, see the Introductory Statement.

Quinacrine produces a harmless but cosmetically unacceptable yellow pigmentation in all tissues of the body. Headache and gastrointestinal disturbances occur frequently, and corneal edema has been observed. Hypersensitivity reactions in the form of lichenoid and eczematoid dermatitis with secondary exfoliative dermatitis have occurred rarely, and fatal cases of agranulocytosis, aplastic anemia, and hepatitis have been reported. Toxic psychoses also have been attributed to the drug. Quinacrine should not be given with the 8-aminoquinoline antimalarial agent, primaquine, because it increases the toxicity of this drug.

USUAL DOSAGE.—*Oral:* For treatment of acute attacks of malaria (except resistant falciparum) in nonimmune persons, *adults and children over 8 years of age*, 200 mg given with 1 g of sodium bicarbonate every four to six hours for five doses; thereafter, 100 mg three times daily for the next six days. *Children 4 to 8 years*, 200 mg three times the first day, then 100 mg twice daily for six days; *1 to 4 years*, 100 mg three times the first day, then 100 mg once daily for six days. For prophylaxis of malaria, *adults*, 100 mg once daily and *children*, 50 mg once daily for one to three months. Medication should always be taken after meals with a full glass of water, tea, or fruit juice.

For giardiasis, *adults*, 100 mg three times daily for five to seven days; *children*, 8 mg/kg of body weight daily divided in three doses for five days.

PREPARATIONS.—Atabrine Hydrochloride (Winthrop). *Oral:* Tablets 100 mg.

QUININE DIHYDROCHLORIDE
QUININE SULFATE

CH_3O – quinoline – $C(H)(OH)$ – quinuclidine ($CH{=}CH_2$, H, N, H)

Quinine is an alkaloid extracted from the bark of the cinchona tree. The sulfate salt is used orally in various combinations with pyrimethamine, tetracycline, and dapsone in the treatment of an acute attack of malaria in individuals infected with 4-aminoquinoline-resistant *Plasmodium falciparum* (see the Introductory Statement). Unless they are unavailable, safer and more effective agents have superseded quinine sulfate in the treatment of other forms of malaria.

Quinine dihydrochloride is administered intravenously in combination with orally administered pyrimethamine and sulfisoxazole in the treatment of recrudescences of malaria in individuals infected with 4-aminoquinoline-resistant *P. falciparum* (see the Introductory Statement). It is also administered intravenously in the treatment of acute attacks of this disease when quinine sulfate is not tolerated (presence of vomiting, pronounced nausea, or malabsorption), or when the infection is severe (associated with coma, confusion, acute circulatory failure, segmenting erythrocytic forms, proportion of infected erythrocytes more than 5%), or is present in infants.

For other uses of this drug, see the Introductory Statement.

The usual therapeutic antimalarial doses of the sulfate salt frequently cause symptoms of mild to moderate cinchonism (tinnitus, headache, altered auditory acuity, blurred vision, nausea) but these symptoms are seldom severe enough to necessitate cessation of treatment. Serious adverse effects are relatively rare; however, more marked symptoms of cinchonism may develop, particularly when plasma levels exceed 12 mg/liter. These effects include eighth nerve damage resulting in more severe auditory impairment (decreased auditory acuity, vertigo, tinnitus); more severe visual alterations (blurred vision, disturbed color perception, photophobia, diplopia, night blindness, constricted visual fields, scotoma, mydriasis); more pronounced gastrointestinal symptoms (nausea, vomiting, abdominal pain, diarrhea); and other central nervous system symptoms such as excitement, apprehension, delirium, and coma. Irreversible auditory or visual damage has been reported. Asthma may be precipitated in susceptible persons. Urticaria is the most frequent allergic reaction, and pruritus may develop with or without associated urticaria. Other adverse reactions include acute hemolysis, hypoprothrombinemia, symptomatic thrombocytopenic purpura, and agranulocytosis. Malarial hemoglobinuria (blackwater fever) has accompanied the use of quinine sulfate, particularly in patients with falciparum malaria; however, the role played by quinine in precipitating or contributing to the acute hemolysis, hemoglobinuria, and renal failure of this syndrome is uncertain.

Intravenous administration of the dihydrochloride salt may produce hypotension and acute circulatory failure. It should be injected slowly in very dilute solutions, and oral administration of the sulfate salt should be substituted as soon as possible. Any adverse reaction associated with quinine sulfate also must be considered a possibility with the dihydrochloride salt.

Historically, quinine has gained notoriety from its use, often in toxic doses, in attempts to produce abortion. Any reputation it may have as an efficient abortifacient is probably undeserved, but the possibility of adverse effects upon the fetus must be considered if the drug is administered to pregnant women.

USUAL DOSAGE.—

Quinine Dihydrochloride:

Intravenous: For acute attacks of 4-aminoquinoline-resistant falciparum malaria when quinine sulfate is not tolerated, the infection is severe, or recrudescence occurs (for a description of the latter use, see the dosage for quinine sulfate), *adults*, 650 mg in 500 ml of a suitable diluent (eg, sodium chloride injection) infused over an eight-hour period. If the patient is severely ill, this amount may be infused over a one-hour period. This dose may be repeated at eight-hour intervals if necessary, but the total daily amount should not exceed 1.95 g. *Children*, 10 mg/kg of body weight, given by slow (over a one- or two-hour period) intravenous infusion of a very dilute solution; the dose may be repeated in 12 hours, but the total daily amount should not exceed 15 mg/kg of body weight.

Quinine Sulfate:

Oral: For treatment of acute attacks of malaria (except resistant falciparum) in nonimmune persons, *adults*, 650 mg every eight hours for 10 to 12 days. *Children*, 15 mg/kg of body weight three times daily for ten days. For treatment of resistant falciparum, transfusion, or injection malaria, *adults*, 650 mg of quinine sulfate three times a day for 10 to 12 days, together with 25 mg of pyrimethamine twice daily for the first three days; 25 mg of dapsone daily can be added to this regimen beginning on the first day of treatment and continuing for 28 days. Several alternative regimens are available if recrudescence occurs: (1) the simultaneous administration of a single dose each of 1.5 g of trimethoprim and 1 g of sulfalene; (2) 650 mg of quinine sulfate every eight hours for three days, followed by 250 mg of tetracycline every six hours for 10 days; or (3) the intravenous infusion of 1.95 g of quinine dihydrochloride every 24 hours for ten days, along with the oral administration of 500 mg of sulfisoxazole every six hours and 25 mg of pyrimethamine twice daily for the first three days. Information on how to obtain trimethoprim and sulfalene and more information on the chemotherapy of resistant falciparum malaria is available from the Walter Reed Army Institute of Research, Washington, DC 20012 (telephone [202] 576-3268).

For nocturnal leg cramps, *adults*, 200 to 300 mg at bedtime.

PREPARATIONS.—

Quinine Dihydrochloride, N.F. *Injection:* Powder.

Quinine Sulfate, N.F. *Oral:* Capsules and tablets 120, 200, and 300 mg.

Both salts marketed under generic name.

MIXTURES

ARALEN PHOSPHATE WITH PRIMAQUINE PHOSPHATE

This therapeutically rational combination of chloroquine and primaquine is used in the prophylaxis of malaria. It should not be used in the treatment of malaria.

Intestinal cramps, diarrhea, and serious hematologic effects have occurred occasionally in individuals with a personal or family history of glucose-6-phosphate dehydrogenase (G6PD) deficiency. This mixture is contraindicated in patients with granulocytopenia, in those receiving other potentially hemolytic drugs or depressants of myeloid elements of bone marrow, and in those who have received quinacrine recently. It should be used with caution in patients with a history of idiosyncrasy to chloroquine or primaquine and in those with G6PD deficiency, and should be discontinued immediately if marked darkening of the urine, decrease in hemoglobin concentration or leukocyte count, or severe reactions affecting the skin occur.

USUAL DOSAGE.—*Oral: Adults and children over 45 kg,* one tablet weekly on the same day of each week, starting at least one day before entering the malarious area and continuing for eight weeks after leaving the area. *For younger children,* a suspension is made of the tablets so that each 5 ml contains 40 mg of chloroquine base and 6 mg of primaquine base. The following amounts are then given once weekly on the same day of each week. *Children 5 to 7 kg,* 2.5 ml; *7 to 11 kg,* 5 ml; *12 to 16 kg,* 7.5 ml; *16 to 20 kg,* 10 ml; *21 to 25 kg,* 12.5 ml; *25 to 45 kg,* one-half tablet. Recommended doses should not be exceeded.

PREPARATIONS.—Aralen Phosphate with Primaquine Phosphate (Winthrop). *Oral:* Tablets containing chloroquine phosphate 500 mg (equivalent to 300 mg base) and primaquine phosphate 79 mg (equivalent to 45 mg base).

CAMOPRIM

This therapeutically rational combination of amodiaquine and primaquine is active against all stages of malaria.

No adverse reactions have been reported. This mixture is contraindicated in individuals with granulocytopenia and in those receiving other potentially hemolytic drugs or depressants of the myeloid elements of the bone marrow. It should be used with caution in individuals with a history of idiosyncrasy to amodiaquine or primaquine and to those who have G6PD deficiency, and should be discontinued immediately if marked darkening of the urine, decrease in hemoglobin concentration or leukocyte count, or severe skin reaction occurs.

USUAL DOSAGE.—*Oral:* For prophylaxis and eradication of malaria, *adults,* two tablets weekly or on alternate weeks. The following doses for *children* are given weekly or on alternate weeks: *7 to 14 kg,* one-half pediatric tablet; *14 to 20 kg,* one pediatric tablet; *20 to 27 kg,* one and one-half pediatric tablets; *over 27 kg,* two pediatric tablets. For eradication, dose is continued until eradication is achieved.

Suppressive cure (acute clinical case): *Adults,* two tablets on first day, one tablet each on second and third days, followed by two tablets weekly for six weeks. *Children,* dose is the same as for prophylaxis and eradication, and is given daily for three days and weekly thereafter for six weeks.

PREPARATIONS.—Camoprim (Parke, Davis). *Oral:* Tablets containing amodiaquine hydrochloride equivalent to 150 mg amodiaquine base and primaquine phosphate equivalent to 15 mg primaquine base; tablets (pediatric) containing amodiaquine hydrochloride equivalent to 75 mg amodiaquine base and primaquine phosphate equivalent to 15 mg primaquine base.

Chapter 62

AMEBICIDES

Drug therapy for amebiasis is directed at eliminating the causative agent, the protozoan *Entamoeba histolytica*, from the infected individual. This organism commonly infects the intestinal lumen and wall and the liver (the latter is the primary site of extraintestinal infection, although other sites may be involved), and the drugs used in the treatment of amebiasis are effective at one or more of these sites.

Carbarsone, diiodohydroxyquin [Diodoquin, Yodoxin], iodochlorhydroxyquin [Entero-Vioform], and the antibiotic paromomycin [Humatin] act primarily in the intestinal lumen. They are called luminal or contact amebicides and their degree of effectiveness probably is similar.

Tetracycline [Achromycin, Panmycin, Panmycin KM, Sumycin, Tetracyn, Tetrex-S], chlortetracycline [Aureomycin], oxytetracycline [Terramycin], and erythromycin [E-Mycin, Erythrocin, Ilotycin] act indirectly in the intestinal lumen and wall by modifying the intestinal flora necessary for survival of the amebae. Tetracycline, chlortetracycline, and oxytetracycline are much more effective than the other tetracyclines and erythromycin and are regarded as the antibiotics of choice.

Emetine and its analogue, dehydroemetine, and chloroquine [Aralen, Roquine] are called tissue amebicides. Emetine and dehydroemetine, which is as effective as emetine and probably less toxic, act against amebae principally in the intestinal wall and the liver, while chloroquine acts against amebae principally in the liver. Chloroquine is less toxic than emetine and dehydroemetine but is appreciably less effective. Amodiaquine [Camoquin] and hydroxychloroquine [Plaquenil], which are chemically related to chloroquine, also are active against amebae in the liver, but are rarely used in the treatment of amebiasis.

Recently, metronidazole [Flagyl], a trichomonacide (see Chapter 64), has been introduced for the treatment of amebiasis. It is unique in that it acts against amebae at all the sites where they are commonly found. In a short time, it has established itself as a very useful amebicide.

Until the advent of metronidazole, the successful therapy of amebiasis almost always required the combined use of the aforementioned drugs. The doses of the drugs used in the various regimens are given in the individual evaluations.

Asymptomatic intestinal amebiasis is treated with a course of one of the luminal amebicides. Diiodohydroxyquin, iodochlorhydroxyquin, or paromomycin are used most frequently. Alternatively, metronidazole may be given. Although carbarsone is effective, it is rarely used in asymptomatic amebiasis because of its toxicity.

Chronic nondysenteric intestinal amebiasis and amebic dysentery are preferably treated with a course of metronidazole. When this agent cannot be used, a combination of drugs is prescribed: when the dysentery is mild or moderate, a tetracycline, a luminal amebicide, and chloroquine (to protect the liver from amebic invasion) are administered concomitantly; when the dysentery is severe, dehydroemetine or emetine (which protects the liver from amebic invasion in additon to being antidysenteric) is substituted for the chloroquine. Those with severe dysentery also must remain in bed and be given necessary supportive therapy (eg, fluids, electrolytes, gastric suction to relieve abdominal distention, and a bland diet supplemented with vitamins). Relapses should be treated with the drug regimen not used previously.

The usual complications of intestinal amebiasis are treated in various ways. Ameboma (amebic granulomatous tissue) and stricture, peritonitis, and intussusception are treated by the concomitant administration of dehydroemetine or emetine, a luminal amebicide, and a tetracycline. Intussusception also must be surgically reduced at the same time that these drugs are being given. Peritonitis is usually fatal in spite of treatment. Metronidazole is probably as effective as the preceding regimen in treating ameboma. Ulcerative postdysenteric colitis is treated by maintaining an adequate fluid and electrolyte balance, correcting anemia by blood transfusion, and providing a high calorie diet. Prednisolone [Delta-Cortef, Sterane] and salicylazosulfapyridine [Azulfidine] may be administered, but their effectiveness is unpredictable.

Metronidazole appears to be the drug of choice for the treatment of hepatic amebiasis. The second most effective treatment consists of the simultaneous administration of dehydroemetine or emetine, chloroquine, a luminal amebicide, and a tetracycline. The luminal amebicide and the antibiotic are given to treat the intestinal infection that must also be assumed to be present. It is also necessary that liver abscesses be drained by aspiration or, rarely, by surgery, when indicated (ie, when there is a palpable mass, persistent localized tenderness, markedly raised hemidiaphragm, or failure of remission of symptoms with drug therapy). Liver scanning techniques using rose bengal sodium I 131 or gold Au 198 are useful in locating the abscesses so that blind aspiration is unnecessary.

Amebic liver abscesses sometimes rupture into the lungs, pleura, pericardium, or peritoneum. These extraintestinal complications are treated by draining and administering amebicides as for hepatic amebiasis.

Adverse Reactions and Precautions

The untoward effects of the amebicides and the precautions necessary in their use are varied (see the individual evaluations), but all of the drugs have a tendency to cause gastrointestinal effects (eg, anorexia, nausea and vomiting, epigastric burning and pain, increased gastrointestinal motility, diarrhea, or constipation).

INDIVIDUAL EVALUATIONS

CARBARSONE

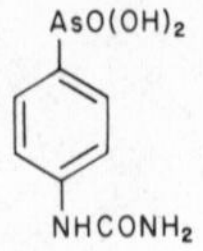

$AsO(OH)_2$

$NHCONH_2$

This organic arsenic compound is active against amebae primarily in the lumen of the intestine. Although carbarsone is effective, it is not used frequently today because less toxic drugs are available. When it is selected, it is given alone in the treatment of asymptomatic intestinal amebiasis and as an adjunct in the treatment of other common forms of the disease (see the Introductory Statement).

The slow excretion of this compound leads to its accumulation and the resulting toxicity. Adverse reactions are nausea, vomiting, abdominal pain, cramps, diarrhea, sore throat, polyuria, weight loss, splenomegaly, hepatitis, jaundice, pruritus, dermatoses, neuritis, visual disturbances, and edema of the ankles, knees, and wrists. Fatalities as a result of exfoliative dermatitis, liver necrosis, or hemorrhagic encephalitis have been reported. Dimercaprol may be effective in the treatment of carbarsone poisoning (see Chapter 90, Chelating Agents). Carbarsone is contraindicated in those with liver and kidney disease, contracted visual or color fields, or hypersensitivity to arsenic.

USUAL DOSAGE.—*Oral: Adults,* 250 mg twice daily for ten days. Additional courses of treatment may be given, if necessary, after an interval of 10 to 14 days to prevent accumulation and toxicity. *Children,* 7.5 mg/kg of body weight in three divided doses daily for ten days.

PREPARATIONS.—*Oral:* Capsules 250 mg; tablets 250 mg. Drug marketed under generic name.

CHLOROQUINE HYDROCHLORIDE [Aralen Hydrochloride]
CHLOROQUINE PHOSPHATE [Aralen Phosphate, Roquine]

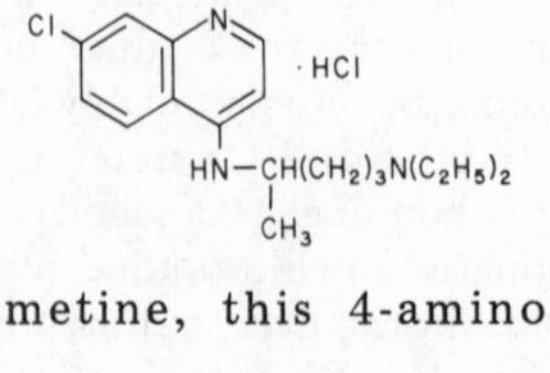

Cl, N, $\cdot HCl$

$HN-CH(CH_2)_3N(C_2H_5)_2$, CH_3

Like emetine, this 4-aminoquinoline

compound is amebicidal in the liver. It is less toxic than emetine, but is much less effective. Chloroquine is used in combination with other drugs for the treatment of chronic nondysenteric intestinal amebiasis, mild or moderate amebic dysentery, and hepatic amebiasis and its complications (see the Introductory Statement). The phosphate salt is administered orally; when it is not tolerated or a rapid effect is desired, the hydrochloride salt is administered intramuscularly.

The adverse reactions and precautions associated with the use of chloroquine in amebiasis are similar to those associated with its use in malaria (see Chapter 61, Antimalarial Agents).

USUAL DOSAGE.—

Chloroquine Phosphate:

Oral: Adults, 1 g daily for two days, followed by 500 mg daily for at least two to three weeks; *children,* 20 mg/kg of body weight daily in two doses for two days, followed by 10 mg/kg daily for at least two to three weeks.

Chloroquine Hydrochloride:

Intramuscular: Adults, 200 to 250 mg daily for 10 to 12 days; *children,* 15 mg/kg of body weight daily for two days, followed by 7.5 mg/kg daily for at least two to three weeks.

PREPARATIONS.—

Chloroquine Phosphate:

Aralen Phosphate (Winthrop). *Oral:* Tablets 500 mg.

Roquine (Robinson). *Oral:* Tablets (enteric-coated) 250 mg.

Drug also marketed by other manufacturers under generic name.

Chloroquine Hydrochloride:

Aralen Hydrochloride (Winthrop). *Injection:* Solution 50 mg/ml in 5 ml containers.

DIIODOHYDROXYQUIN [Diodoquin, Yodoxin]

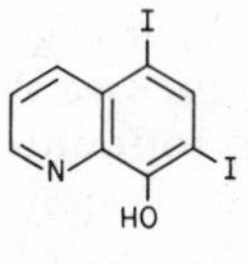

I
N
I
HO

This organic iodine compound is active against amebae primarily in the intestinal lumen. Diiodohydroxyquin is used alone in the treatment of asymptomatic intestinal amebiasis and, in combination with other drugs, in the treatment of other common forms of amebiasis (see the Introductory Statement). This drug also has been used in the prophylaxis of "travelers' diarrhea." Its administration for this purpose is not recommended because there is no satisfactory evidence that it is effective. For other uses, see Chapter 64, Antitrichomonal Agents.

There have been occasional reports of rash, acne, slight enlargement of the thyroid gland, nausea, abdominal cramps, pruritus ani, and optic neuropathy after use of diiodohydroxyquin. This drug interferes with results of thyroid function tests for several months, and it is contraindicated in patients who are hypersensitive to iodine or have liver disease.

USUAL DOSAGE.—*Oral: Adults,* for amebiasis, 650 mg three times daily for 20 days; *children,* 40 mg/kg of body weight daily in two or three doses (maximum, 1.95 g daily) for 20 days. If required, the course may be repeated after a two- or three-week interval.

PREPARATIONS.—

Diodoquin (Searle). *Oral:* Tablets 650 mg.

Yodoxin (Glenwood). *Oral:* Tablets 210 mg; powder 25 g.

Drug also marketed under generic name.

EMETINE HYDROCHLORIDE

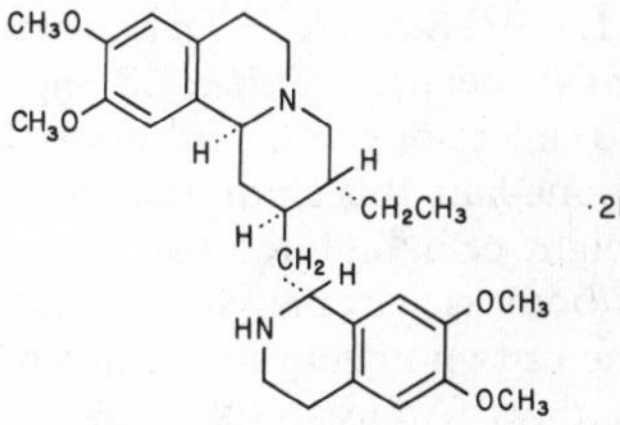

CH_3O
CH_3O
N
H
H
CH_2CH_3
·2HCl
H
CH_2 H
HN
OCH_3
OCH_3

This compound is the salt of an alkaloid of ipecac. Ipecac, although once used in the treatment of amebiasis, has been abandoned because it produces severe gastrointestinal irritation, nausea, and vomiting. Emetine is active against amebae at intestinal (wall) and extraintestinal sites (eg, liver and lungs). It is used in combination with other drugs to treat severe amebic dysentery, complications of intestinal amebiasis, and hepatic amebiasis as well as its complications (see the Introductory Statement). The drug is always administered by deep subcutaneous or intramuscular injection, because oral administration irritates the gastrointestinal tract and intravenous injection is hazardous.

Adverse reactions are observed in approximately 75% of those treated. Emetine accumulates in the body and untoward effects occur with increasing frequency as repeated courses are administered. The most serious reactions occur in the cardiovascular system and include precordial pain, dyspnea, tachycardia, hypotension, electrocardiographic changes, gallop rhythm, cardiac dilatation, congestive failure, and death. The electrocardiographic changes can be of long duration (an average of six weeks) and include prolongation of the Q-T and P-R intervals and flattening or inversion of the T wave. Injury to heart tissue, as well as to other organs, also may occur. Nausea, vomiting, diarrhea, dizziness, headache, debilitating skeletal muscle weakness, stiffness, pain and muscle weakness at the site of injection, as well as eczematous, urticarial, or purpuric lesions also have been observed.

The patient should be hospitalized and remain in bed during treatment with emetine, and electrocardiographic, blood pressure, and heart rate examinations should be performed daily. Unless the amebiasis does not respond to other therapy, emetine is contraindicated during pregnancy, in patients with heart or kidney disease, in children, and in those with recently developed polyneuropathy. It should be used with caution in debilitated or aged patients.

USUAL DOSAGE.—*Intramuscular, Subcutaneous* (deep): *Adults,* 65 mg daily in one or two injections for not more than ten days. Only one-half this amount should be given to underweight or debilitated patients. *Children,* 1 mg/kg of body weight daily (maximum, 65 mg daily) in one or two injections for not more than four to six days. At least six weeks should be allowed between courses of treatment to prevent cumulative toxicity.

PREPARATIONS.—*Injection:* Solution 65 mg/ml in 1 ml containers. Drug marketed under generic name.

SIMILAR DRUG.—Dehydroemetine Dihydrochloride (available from the Parasitic Disease Drug Service, National Communicable Disease Center, Atlanta, Georgia).

ERYTHROMYCIN

Erythromycin is active against amebae in the intestinal lumen and wall. Its amebicidal action is indirect, a result of its ability to modify the intestinal flora necessary for survival of the amebae. It is used with other drugs to treat all the common forms of amebiasis except asymptomatic intestinal amebiasis (see the Introductory Statement). It is used infrequently, however, because the tetracyclines are more efficacious.

For adverse effects and precautions, as well as other uses, see Chapter 50, Erythromycin and Derivatives.

USUAL DOSAGE.—*Oral: Adults,* 1 g daily in divided doses every six hours for 10 to 14 days; *children,* 30 to 50 mg/kg of body weight daily in divided doses every six hours for 10 to 14 days.

PREPARATIONS.—See Chapter 50, Erythromycin and Derivatives.

IODOCHLORHYDROXYQUIN
[Entero-Vioform]

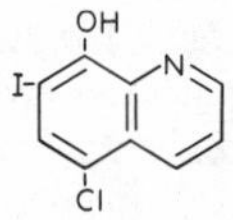

OH
I
N
Cl

This organic iodine compound is active against amebae primarily in the intestinal lumen. It is given alone in the treatment of asymptomatic intestinal amebiasis and as an adjunct to other drugs in the treatment of other common forms of amebiasis (see the Introductory Statement). Although this drug has been widely used in the prophylaxis of "travelers' diarrhea," there is no acceptable evidence that it is effective for this purpose. In addition, use of iodochlorhydroxyquin to prevent diarrhea has been implicated in the production of a severe neurologic disease, subacute myelo-optic neuropathy (SMON). For these reasons, its administration to prevent "travelers' diarrhea" is not recommended. For other uses of iodochlorhydroxyquin, see Chapter 60, Antifungal Agents, and Chapter 64, Antitrichomonal Agents.

The adverse reactions are nausea, vomiting, abdominal cramps, rash, acne, and pruritus ani. Because a severe neurologic disease has been associated with its use (see above), the physician who prescribes iodochlorhydroxyquin for amebiasis should keep in mind the drug's neurotoxic potential. This drug is contraindicated in patients who are hypersensitive to iodine or have liver disease. Furthermore, it interferes with results of thyroid function tests for several months.

USUAL DOSAGE.—*Oral: Adults,* for amebiasis, 500 to 750 mg three times daily for ten days. The course may be repeated after an interval of eight days. No more than two courses should be given.

PREPARATIONS.—Entero-Vioform (Ciba). *Oral:* Tablets 250 mg. Drug also marketed under generic name.

METRONIDAZOLE [Flagyl]

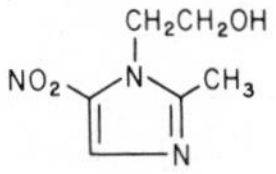

This nitroimidazole compound is amebicidal at both intestinal and extraintestinal sites and it appears to be the drug of choice for all of the commonly encountered amebic infections except asymptomatic intestinal amebiasis. Its status in the latter condition is uncertain at this time, and must await the results of more widespread use. In addition, metronidazole is as good as or better than the most effective treatment for the complications of amebiasis. Unlike the other amebicides, it is used alone. See also the Introductory Statement.

For other uses of metronidazole, see Chapter 64, Antitrichomonal Agents, and Chapter 80, Antidiarrheals.

The usual adverse reactions are nausea, headache, anorexia, vomiting, diarrhea, epigastric distress, abdominal cramping, constipation, and a metallic, sharp, and unpleasant taste. Occasionally, furry tongue, glossitis, stomatitis, and a moderate leukopenia have occurred. Other reactions noted include dizziness, vertigo, incoordination, ataxia, and darkened urine; in addition, it may have a disulfiram-like effect (abdominal distress, nausea, vomiting, or headache, and a modification of the taste of the alcoholic beverage) when taken with alcoholic beverages. Metronidazole is contraindicated in patients with a history of blood dyscrasia (because it is a nitroimidazole), and in those with central nervous system disease. It should not be used during the first trimester of pregnancy, for its effects on fetal development are not definitely known.

USUAL DOSAGE.—*Oral: Adults,* 750 mg three times daily for ten days; *children,* 35 to 50 mg/kg of body weight daily in three divided doses for ten days.

PREPARATIONS.—Flagyl (Searle). *Oral:* Tablets 250 mg.

PAROMOMYCIN SULFATE [Humatin]

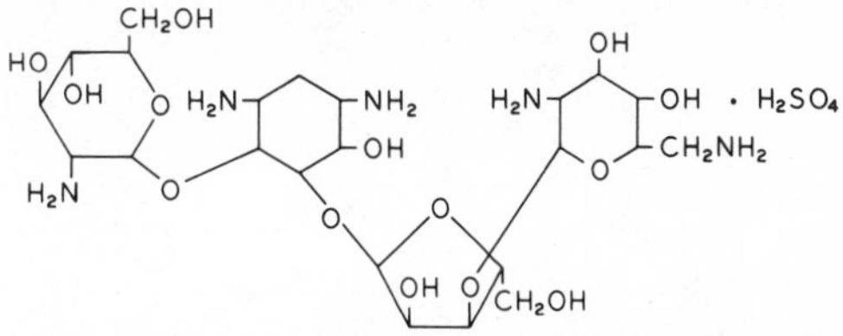

This broad spectrum antibiotic is active against amebae primarily in the intestinal lumen. Unlike other antibiotics used as amebicides, it is directly amebicidal. It is used alone in the treatment of asymptomatic intestinal amebiasis and in combination with other drugs in the treatment of other common forms of amebiasis (see the Introductory Statement).

Frequently reported adverse reactions are nausea, increased gastrointestinal motility, and diarrhea. Rash, headache, vertigo, generalized abdominal pain, and vomiting have been reported occasionally. Patients should be observed for signs of superinfection. Nephrotoxicity may result from absorption of the drug.

USUAL DOSAGE.—*Oral: Adults and children,* 25 mg/kg of body weight daily administered in divided doses with meals for five days. The course may be repeated after a two-week interval.

PREPARATIONS.—Humatin (Parke, Davis). *Oral:* Capsules 250 mg; syrup (pediatric) 125 mg/5 ml.

TETRACYCLINES

This group of broad spectrum antibiotics is active against amebae in the intestinal lumen and wall. The tetracyclines are indirectly amebicidal in that they modify the intestinal flora necessary for amebic viability. Tetracycline, chlortetracycline, and oxytetracycline are the most effective members of this group of drugs and also are more effective than erythromycin and paromomycin. They are used with other drugs in the treatment of all the common forms of amebiasis with the exception of asymptomatic intestinal amebiasis (see the Introductory Statement).

For adverse reactions and precautions, as well as other uses, see Chapter 53, Tetracyclines.

USUAL DOSAGE.—(Oxytetracycline, Chlortetracycline, Tetracycline) *Oral: Adults,* 250 mg every six hours for ten days; *children,* 50 mg/kg of body weight daily in four divided doses for seven days.

PREPARATIONS.—See Chapter 53, Tetracyclines.

Chapter 63

ANTITRYPANOSOMAL AGENTS

Six drugs are used in the modern therapy of African trypanosomiasis (African sleeping sickness): suramin sodium, pentamidine isethionate, melarsoprol, melarsonyl potassium, nitrofurazone, and tryparsamide. The information in this chapter is largely based upon experience in Africa, because African trypanosomiasis is rarely seen in the United States.

Early treatment of patients with African trypanosomiasis is essential; the longer the disease is allowed to progress, the more difficult it is to treat. Death or permanent brain damage is inevitable if significant changes in the central nervous system have occurred before therapy is instituted.

If treatment of African trypanosomiasis is begun in the early (hemolymphatic) stage, before the central nervous system has been invaded, suramin is the drug of choice in both the Rhodesian (East African) and the Gambian (mid-African) forms. Pentamidine isethionate also is used in the hemolymphatic stage of Gambian disease, but it is less effective than suramin. If invasion of the central nervous system is still in the early phase and there is little or no damage, suramin may still be curative; however, more toxic drugs must be used if the leukocyte count and the protein level in cerebrospinal fluid are distinctly abnormal.

Melarsoprol appears to be the most useful drug in the late (meningoencephalitic) stage of both forms of African trypanosomiasis. The cerebrospinal fluid should be examined for trypanosomes, leukocytes, and protein content before and after treatment with melarsoprol in order to assess the results of therapy. If significant neurologic involvement has occurred, it frequently is advisable to administer suramin to stabilize the patient's condition prior to the use of melarsoprol (see the individual evaluations). Melarsonyl potassium also has been used in the late stage of African trypanosomiasis, but there has been only limited experience with this drug.

Nitrofurazone also is used in the meningoencephalitic stage, but it is less effective and much more toxic than melarsoprol. Therefore, it is recommended for use only as a last resort.

A single dose of pentamidine isethionate can be used for group prophylaxis to lower the infection rate of the Gambian form of African trypanosomiasis in the native population, where it is sometimes difficult to examine and treat all inhabitants. However, every effort should be made to exclude persons already infected, since the prophylactic doses of this drug may mask symptoms of the disease and make later diagnosis difficult. Persons going on safari should not be given prophylactic treatment because of the danger of masking an infection, which may develop into serious disease months or years later. These individuals can be examined and treated, if necessary, on return home.

Clinical trials in South America have shown promise for nifurtimox, a nitrofuran derivative, in the treatment of Chagas' disease (American trypanosomiasis). Present data indicate that the drug is clearly effective in the acute form of Chagas' disease; its value in the chronic form is less certain.

The antitrypanosomal agents are not commercially available in this country, as Chagas' disease occurs only rarely and in a mild form in certain southern areas of the United States. However, trypanosomiasis is seen occasionally in persons returning from Africa or South America. When the need for these drugs does arise, suramin sodium, pentamidine isethionate, melarsoprol, and nifurtimox can be obtained from the Parasitic Disease Drug Service, Center for Disease Control, Atlanta, Georgia 30333. The day telephone number is (404) 633-3311, Extensions 3676, 3677, and the night telephone number is (404) 633-2176.

Adverse Reactions and Precautions

All antitrypanosomal agents produce variable toxic effects, and, in general, great caution is necessary in using them. Hospitalization is essential in order to plan and provide the most appropriate dosage regimen and to observe the patient for signs and symptoms of toxicity. Treatment in the field (in Africa) should be restricted to those for whom hospitalization is impossible.

The initial dosage of the antitrypanosomal agents should be based upon the general condition of the patient rather than solely upon body weight.

See the individual evaluations for specific reactions caused by these agents.

INDIVIDUAL EVALUATIONS

MELARSOPROL

This organic arsenical, formerly known as Mel B or melarsen oxide BAL, is the drug of choice in the treatment of the late (meningoencephalitic) stage of both the Rhodesian and Gambian forms of African trypanosomiasis. Although melarsoprol also is very effective in the early (hemolymphatic) stage, because of its toxicity its use can be recommended only in those patients who fail to respond to treatment with suramin or pentamidine. Resistance of trypanosomes to this drug is increasing.

Adverse reactions are common. So-called "reactive encephalopathy," a form of toxic encephalopathy, is the most common of the serious untoward effects and frequently results in death. Clinical manifestations of toxicity usually appear after the first three-day course of therapy. The mechanism is obscure, but it is believed that this toxic encephalopathy is a variety of the Herxheimer reaction and is caused by the rapid liberation of trypanosomal antigen. Consequently, patients with a heavy blood or lymph infection should receive preliminary treatment with suramin sodium (two to four doses of 250 to 500 mg on alternate days). The dose of melarsoprol should be reduced if casts in the urine or evidence of hepatic toxicity are observed. Vomiting and colic may occur, but their incidence may be reduced by injecting the drug slowly. Dimercaprol [BAL] produces little antidotal action but is not contraindicated. Melarsoprol may precipitate erythema nodosum in leprous patients. Severe hemolytic reactions occur in patients with glucose-6-phosphate dehydrogenase (G6PD) deficiency.

USUAL DOSAGE.—*Intravenous* (administered slowly and with care to prevent extravasation): *Hemolymphatic stage without neurologic involvement*, generally not recommended because of toxicity. *Adults in good condition with only slight neurologic involvement*, 3.6 mg/kg of body weight daily for three days, followed by a second course after two weeks. *Adults in good condition with moderate elevation of protein level or leukocyte count in cerebrospinal fluid*, successive daily or alternate-day doses of 1.5, 2.0, and 2.2 mg/kg followed, after a seven-day interval, by 2.5, 3.0, and 3.6 mg/kg on successive days. After an additional seven-day interval, a third course of three daily injections of 3.6 mg/kg is given. The maximal daily dose should not exceed 200 mg. *For children, underweight patients, and those with excessive amounts of protein in cerebrospinal fluid*, a similar pattern of increasing doses should be followed after pre-treatment with suramin.

For treatment of relapse in the hemolymphatic stage after suramin has not been effective, *adults*, three daily doses of 3.6 mg/kg repeated once after an interval of two weeks (maximal daily dose should not exceed 200 mg). For treatment of relapse in the meningoencephalitic stage, *adults*, 3.6 mg/kg per day for three successive days; this dosage is repeated for three courses at two-week intervals.

PREPARATIONS.—Melarsoprol is available in the United States from the Parasitic Disease Drug Service, Center for Disease Control, Atlanta, Georgia 30333; see Introductory Statement for telephone numbers.

AVAILABLE TRADEMARK (FOREIGN).—Arsobal (Rhone-Poulenc, France). *Injection:* Solution 3.6% in 6 ml containers.

MELARSONYL POTASSIUM

This drug, formerly known as Mel W, is a water-soluble derivative of melarsoprol. Like melarsoprol, it also is used in the late stage of African trypanosomiasis; however there has been less experience with its use. It may be less effective in the Rhodesian form than in the Gambian form. Relapses after therapy with melarsonyl potassium do not respond to melarsoprol. This drug is given intramuscularly.

Toxic effects are similar and occur about as frequently as with melarsoprol (see the evaluation on Melarsoprol).

USUAL DOSAGE.—*Intramuscular: Adults and children*, four daily injections starting with a dose of 1 mg/kg of body weight and increasing the amount to 4 mg/kg (maximal single adult dose, 200 mg). Course is repeated at full dosage after an interval of seven to ten days.

AVAILABLE TRADEMARK (FOREIGN).—Trimelarsan (Labs Specia, France). (Not available in the United States.)

NITROFURAZONE

Nitrofurazone is indicated for patients in the late (meningoencephalitic) stage of African trypanosomiasis who do not respond to treatment with melarsoprol. It has a low rate of cure and its primary use is as a last resort when all other forms of therapy have failed.

The toxic effects of the drug are similar to those of other nitrofurans (see Chapter 56, Nitrofurans). It produces hemolytic anemia in patients with congenital deficiency of erythrocytic glucose-6-phosphate dehydrogenase (G6PD), and causes reversible degeneration of the seminiferous tubules and polyneuropathy characterized by severe burning pain in the soles. It also is likely to cause arrhythmias.

USUAL DOSAGE.—*Oral:* A single course should not exceed 500 mg every six hours for one week. Three courses may be given at intervals of one week.

PREPARATIONS.—*Oral:* Tablet form marketed by foreign manufacturers. (Not available in United States for systemic use.)

PENTAMIDINE ISETHIONATE

Pentamidine has been used in the early stage of the Gambian form of African trypanosomiasis, but it is less effective than suramin sodium. Its primary use is in patients with kidney disease. The drug is effective only in the early (hemolymphatic) stage of the disease, because it does not cross the blood-brain barrier. It also is used for group prophylaxis in Gambian trypanosomiasis (see the Introductory Statement).

Intramuscular injection, although painful, is the preferred route of administration because reactions occur more frequently after intravenous administration. These reactions include dyspnea, tachycardia, dizziness, syncope, headache, vomiting, and pruritus. Since pentamidine is a potent histamine liberator, severe pain occurs after subcutaneous injection. Pentamidine should not be used for treating relapses in patients in the early stage of the Gambian form of trypanosomiasis; suramin or melarsoprol should be used instead.

USUAL DOSAGE.—*Intramuscular: Adults and children*, in early Gambian trypanosomiasis, a single injection of 4 mg/kg of body weight is given daily for a total of ten injections; for group prophylaxis, a single injection of 4 mg/kg is given every 6 to 12 months.

PREPARATIONS.—Pentamidine Isethionate is available in the United States from the Parasitic Disease Drug Service, Center for Disease Control, Atlanta, Georgia 30333; see Introductory Statement for telephone numbers.

AVAILABLE TRADEMARK (FOREIGN).—Lomidine (Labs Specia, France).

SURAMIN SODIUM

Suramin sodium is the drug of choice in the early (hemolymphatic) stage of both the Rhodesian and Gambian forms of African trypanosomiasis. Suramin also may be given prior to melarsoprol in the late (meningoencephalitic) stage in order to stabilize the patient's condition. However, because it does not cross the blood-brain barrier, suramin is effective alone only in the early invasive phase of the meningoencephalitic stage of the disease.

Adverse reactions vary in intensity and frequency, depending on the race and nutritional status of the patient and the purity of the drug. Reports of serious toxic reactions appear to be confined to those appearing in older literature, before the necessity of eliminating impure batches of the drug was realized. Nausea, vomiting, shock, and syncope are the most serious immediate reactions; however, their incidence is low. Colic and acute urticaria also can occur immediately. Papular eruptions, paresthesia, photophobia, lacrimation, palpebral edema, and hyperesthesia of the palms and soles occur up to 24 hours after administration. Albuminuria, hematuria, and cylindruria occur even later. Agranulocytosis and hemolytic anemia have been observed very rarely. Suramin causes fetal abnormality in rats, but this effect has not been noted in man.

Moderate albuminuria is usual during the treatment of the acute phase, but persisting, pronounced albuminuria calls for caution and modification of the treatment schedule. This drug should be used cautiously in patients with renal insufficiency.

For other uses, see Chapter 65, Anthelmintics.

USUAL DOSAGE.—*Intravenous: Adults*, initially, 100 mg in a freshly prepared 10% solution is given to test for sensitivity. Then 1 g in a 10% solution is injected slowly on days 1, 3, 7, 14, and 21. *Children*, initially 100 mg is given as a test dose. Then 10 to 15 mg/kg of body weight is injected slowly on days 1, 3, 7, 14, and 21.

PREPARATIONS.—Suramin Sodium is available in the United States from the Parasitic Disease Drug Service, Center for Disease Control, Atlanta, Georgia 30333; see Introductory Statement for telephone numbers.

AVAILABLE TRADEMARKS (FOREIGN).—Antrypol (Imperial Chemical, England), Bayer-205 (Bayer, Germany), Germanin (Bayer, Sweden), Moranyl (Labs Specia, France).

TRYPARSAMIDE

Originally, this drug was used in the late stage of the Gambian form of trypanosomiasis, but it has been superseded by melarsoprol. It is still used in combination with suramin sodium for the treatment of Gambian sleeping sickness in the field. Its primary advantage is that many field dressers in Africa are trained in its use in nonhospitalized patients. Its use is not justified unless melarsoprol is not available.

Evidence of contraction of the visual field has been reported in about one-third of patients; blindness may occur infrequently. Tryparsamide also causes liver damage, various forms of dermatitis, gastrointestinal disturbances, Herxheimer-like reactions, severe nitritoid crises, and allergic responses.

USUAL DOSAGE.—*Intravenous: Adults*, 2 g in 10 ml of water for injection at five- to seven-day intervals for 10 to 12 injections.

PREPARATIONS.—*Injection:* Powder marketed by foreign manufacturers. (Not available in United States.)

NIFURTIMOX (Bayer 2502)

Nifurtimox has been found to be effective in the acute form of Chagas' disease in clinical trials in Argentina, southern Brazil, and Chile; no successful trials have been reported from Venezuela or the northern Andean states. Results reported from Venezuela suggest that this drug may be effective against *Trypanosoma cruzi* in the chronic form of the disease.

Anorexia, weight loss, abdominal pain, nausea, and vomiting are common untoward effects. Convulsions, headache, nervousness, drowsiness, vertigo, insomnia, polyneuropathy, disorientation, amnesia, tremor, myalgia, and a rash that responds to antihistamines also have been observed during nifurtimox therapy. The drug may cause hypoglycemia. Alcohol, antibiotics, and digitalis may reduce the patient's tolerance to nifurtimox. It should not be used during pregnancy or in children less than one year of age.

USUAL DOSAGE.—*Oral: Adults and children over 1 year*, the optimal dosage of this drug has not been fully determined; it varies from 5 to 25 mg/kg of body weight daily.

In acute cases, the effectiveness of treatment may be determined by complement fixation tests supplemented by electrocardiographic examination, direct blood examination, inoculation of culture media, inoculation of laboratory animals, and xenodiagnosis when available.

PREPARATIONS.—Nifurtimox is available in the United States from the Parasitic Disease Drug Service, Center for Disease Control, Atlanta, Georgia 30333; see Introductory Statement for telephone numbers.

AVAILABLE TRADEMARK (FOREIGN).—Lampit (Bayer, Germany).

Chapter 64

ANTITRICHOMONAL AGENTS

Infections of the vagina caused by the parasitic protozoan, *Trichomonas vaginalis*, are common and occur most frequently during the reproductive years when estrogen levels are high. Recurrent infections suggest the possibility that trichomonads persist in extravaginal foci. Occasionally *T. vaginalis* has been found in the urine when it has been absent in the vaginal mucus. *T. vaginalis* also is found in the male urethra and invades the periurethral glands and ducts of both sexes.

Diagnosis of trichomoniasis should be made by microscopic examination of a fresh wet smear of exudate scraped from the vagina, of semen or prostatic fluid obtained by massage, or of urinary sediment. Trichomonal flagella can easily be identified in fresh smears, but special strains are required to identify them in fixed smears. When the patient's symptoms are suggestive of trichomoniasis but the parasites are not present in the smear, cultural procedures should be used to establish diagnosis; cultures are usually necessary to establish a positive diagnosis in the male. When the signs and symptoms disappear and the wet smear is negative, it is reasonable to assume that the initial infection has been controlled, although cultures are mandatory for the evaluation of "cures" in patients of either sex.

Antitrichomonal therapy formerly depended solely on the use of locally-acting agents. Now a systemic trichomonacide, metronidazole [Flagyl], is available and has become the drug of choice.

Local agents may be useful when extravaginal sources of reinfection are not present. Furazolidone, a nitrofuran, and the halogenated hydroxyquinolines such as diiodohydroxyquin [Floraquin] and iodochlorhydroxyquin [Vioform] have been used with some success. Arsonic acid derivatives such as carbarsone and glycobiarsol [Milibis] have trichomonacidal action, although they are used more commonly as amebicides (see Chapter 62, Amebicides). The local anti-infective agents povidone-iodine [Betadine] and aminacrine, which is a constituent of several mixtures, are effective in the treatment of vaginal infections caused by susceptible organisms, but evidence of their value in trichomoniasis is scanty.

Various adjuvants are combined with topical trichomonacides to assist penetration into mucus, pus, and detritus. Such adjuvants include wetting agents such as sodium lauryl sulfate, dioctyl sodium sulfosuccinate, and nonoxynol. Other locally active agents that may be useful as adjuncts and are used with specific trichomonacidal agents include white vinegar, boric acid, and lactic acid; they help restore the vagina to a more normal pH.

The claim is made that the vaginal instillation of lactobacilli is successful in the treatment of vaginitis, regardless of its etiology. However, lactobacilli have no effect in restoring vaginal flora to normal or in eradicating specific pathogens.

Adverse Reactions and Precautions

Hypersensitivity reactions are the principal untoward effects associated with the locally active trichomonacides. They also may cause burning, pruritus, or staining at the site of treatment but these minor effects rarely necessitate discontinuation of therapy. Occasionally a patient may react to the iodine in halogenated hydroxyquinolines or to the arsenic in arsenical compounds. Topical preparations that contain iodine rarely cause iodism, but have been reported to affect the results of thyroid function studies.

The adverse reactions produced by

metronidazole are discussed in the following evaluation.

INDIVIDUAL EVALUATIONS

METRONIDAZOLE [Flagyl]

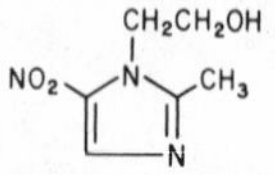

Metronidazole, a systemic trichomonacide, is highly effective when given orally in the treatment of infections caused by *Trichomonas vaginalis* in both the male and female. Topical application by insertion into the vagina is used in combination with oral therapy in the treatment of refractory infections. Topical application alone is much less effective. The drug is biologically active in the semen and urine and, therefore, is active against trichomonads in extravaginal as well as vaginal foci. Metronidazole also is effective in the treatment of trichomonal prostatovesiculitis and urethritis. However, metronidazole should not be used indiscriminately; it should be reserved for those patients in whom the presence of *T. vaginalis* has been demonstrated by wet smear or culture. Sexual partners should receive concomitant treatment, because asymptomatic trichomoniasis in the male partner is a frequent source of reinfection of the female.

This drug appears to be specific for trichomonads. It is inactive against *Candida albicans* and other agents that cause vaginitis. Because activation of latent candidal infections may occur in a substantial percentage of patients with trichomonal infection, either during or following treatment with metronidazole, it usually is advisable to treat both infections simultaneously after laboratory confirmation of the diagnoses. For information on agents used in the treatment of candidal infections, see Chapter 60, Antifungal Agents. Metronidazole does not affect the normal vaginal bacterial flora, including the Doderlein bacillus.

For other uses of metronidazole, see Chapter 62, Amebicides, and Chapter 80, Antidiarrheals.

The incidence of untoward effects with metronidazole is low and no serious reactions have been reported. The most frequent reaction is nausea; diarrhea occurs less commonly. Other adverse effects that have been reported include unpleasant taste, urticaria, vaginal and urethral burning or discomfort, vertigo, headache, and, rarely, an unexplained darkening in the color of the urine.

Metronidazole can produce a disulfiram [Antabuse]-type reaction in some patients after ingestion of alcohol. As with disulfiram, metronidazole may cause an accumulation of acetaldehyde by interfering with the oxidation of alcohol to carbon dioxide and water.

Temporary decreases in total leukocyte and polymorphonuclear leukocyte counts have been reported; therefore, total and differential white cell counts should be made, especially if a second course of therapy is necessary. Metronidazole should be used with caution in patients with blood dyscrasias, especially those involving bone marrow depression.

Metronidazole has been used effectively in the treatment of trichomoniasis during pregnancy; no complications have been recognized and no adverse reactions affecting the fetus have been reported. However, since there is evidence that the drug is transported readily across the placenta, it is recommended that metronidazole be used with discretion in pregnant women, especially during the first trimester, until more data are acquired concerning possible hazards to the fetus at various stages of its growth and development. Metronidazole is excreted in the breast milk of nursing mothers; no adverse effects have been observed in nursing infants.

USUAL DOSAGE.—

Oral: Women, 250 mg three times daily for ten days; *men,* 250 mg two times daily for ten days. If a second course of treatment is needed, there should be a four- to six-week interval between courses.

Topical (vaginal): *Women,* 500 mg daily for ten days; in refractory infections, an oral dosage of 250 mg two times daily should be given concomitantly for ten days.

PREPARATIONS.—Flagyl (Searle).

Oral: Tablets 250 mg.

Topical (vaginal): Tablets 500 mg.

DIIODOHYDROXYQUIN [Floraquin]

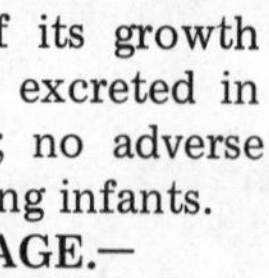

Diiodohydroxyquin is useful in the local treatment of vaginitis caused by *Trichomonas vaginalis,* but it is less effective than systemic treatment with metronidazole. Its acidity helps to reestablish the normal pH of the vagina.

The incidence of reactions is very low because the drug is poorly soluble when used topically. Diiodohydroxyquin can produce a generalized rash in patients with intolerance to iodine and should be discontinued if rash occurs. Enough iodine may be absorbed to affect the results of thyroid function studies.

For other uses of diiodohydroxyquin, see Chapter 62, Amebicides.

USUAL DOSAGE.—*Topical* (vaginal): One to two moistened tablets are inserted each evening after a douche with dilute acetic acid. Treatment is continued for 10 to 15 days.

PREPARATIONS.—Floraquin (Searle). *Topical* (vaginal): Tablets 100 mg.

IODOCHLORHYDROXYQUIN [Vioform]

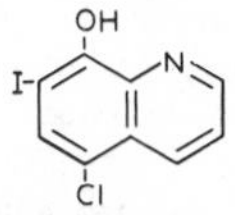

OH, I, N, Cl

Iodochlorhydroxyquin is useful in the local treatment of vaginitis caused by *Trichomonas vaginalis*, but it is less effective than systemic treatment with metronidazole. It also is used in treating vaginitis caused by *Candida albicans*, *Trichophyton* (tinea cruris), or mixed bacteria.

Iodochlorhydroxyquin should be discontinued if a rash appears. Its use may affect results of thyroid function tests based on iodine uptake. The drug may cause staining at the site of treatment, local burning, and pruritus.

For other uses of this drug, see Chapter 60, Antifungal Agents, and Chapter 62, Amebicides.

USUAL DOSAGE.—*Topical* (vaginal): A moistened tablet is inserted each evening after a douche with dilute acetic acid.

PREPARATIONS.—Vioform (Ciba). *Topical* (vaginal): Inserts 250 mg.

POVIDONE-IODINE [Betadine]

This water-soluble complex of polyvinylpyrrolidone and iodine is a mild local anti-infective agent that is used topically on the skin and mucous membranes (see Chapter 67, Antiseptics and Disinfectants). Vaginal preparations are claimed to be useful in trichomoniasis, but systemic treatment with metronidazole is preferred.

Although povidone-iodine does not produce the degree of local irritation associated with the use of tincture of iodine, reactions may occur in patients allergic to iodine. Serum protein-bound iodine levels increase temporarily in some patients.

USUAL DOSAGE.—*Topical* (vaginal): After swabbing the cervix and vagina with a povidone-iodine solution in the office, one applicatorful of the gel is inserted nightly, followed by use of the douche preparation the next morning. Daily applications of gel and douche should be continued throughout the menstrual cycle, including the days of menses, for a minimum of 10 to 15 days.

PREPARATIONS.—Betadine (Purdue Frederick). *Topical* (vaginal): Douche 1% in 8 oz containers; gel 1% in 3 oz containers; solution 1% in ½, 8, 16, and 32 oz containers. (In all preparations, the percentage indicates the amount of available iodine.)

MIXTURES

A number of combination products are available for local application in the treatment of trichomoniasis. Their suitability varies with the ingredients and the goal of treatment in a specific case. It should be noted that some of these preparations are offered not only for trichomoniasis, but also for other vaginal infections characterized as bacterial, candidal, mixed, or "nonspecific." None of these vaginal preparations is as effective as the systemic preparation of metronidazole for treating trichomoniasis.

Preparations containing antibiotics might be helpful against bacteria susceptible to them, although sulfonamides are undesirable for this type of topical application because of their sensitizing properties. The quinoline derivatives may have some degree of effectiveness against a variety of organisms. Evidence for the effectiveness of aminacrine is scanty. The organic mercurial compounds have very limited anti-infective activity clinically.

The estrogens present in some preparations presumably would contribute to the therapeutic effect only if atrophic vaginitis complicates the disease. An occasional preparation contains an adrenal corticosteroid for anti-inflammatory action. Some preparations contain alleged debriding agents such as allantoin as a therapeutic gesture. Detergent and surfactant agents would probably exert some cleansing effect and improve the action of other ingredients. Undoubtedly, the vehicles for some vaginal preparations provide a degree of soothing or cleansing properties.

TRICOFURON

This mixture of furazolidone and nifuroxime is effective in the local treatment of vaginitis caused by *Candida albicans* and *Trichomonas vaginalis*. However, furazolidone applied topically is less effective for the latter condition than systemic treatment with metronidazole. Nifuroxime, which is not available as a single-entity preparation, is useful in treating *Candida* infections.

Localized sensitization occurs occasionally, and one confirmed case of generalized urticaria caused by the suppository preparation has been reported.

USUAL DOSAGE.—*Topical* (vaginal): As an office procedure, entire vaginal vault, cervix, and vulvar mucosa is dusted with powder; the procedure is repeated one or two times weekly except during menstruation.

The suppository is inserted intravaginally after douche each morning and evening for one week. Thereafter, one suppository is inserted in the evening. Treatment should be continued throughout the menstrual cycle.

PREPARATIONS.—Tricofuron (Eaton). *Topical* (vaginal): Each 15 g of powder contains furazolidone 1.5 mg (0.1%) and nifuroxime 7.5 mg (0.5%); each suppository contains furazolidone 5 mg (0.25%) and nifuroxime 7.5 mg (0.375%).

Following is a listing of additional mixtures available for trichomonal and other vaginal infections:

Aquacort (Webster): Each suppository contains aminacrine hydrochloride 3 mg, hydrocortisone acetate 10 mg, tyrothricin 2.5 mg, and phenylmercuric acetate 3 mg.

AVC (Merrell-National): Cream containing aminacrine hydrochloride 0.2%, allantoin 2%, and sulfanilamide 15%; each suppository contains aminacrine hydrochloride 14 mg, allantoin 140 mg, and sulfanilamide 1 g.

AVC-Dienestrol (Merrell-National): Cream containing aminacrine hydrochloride 0.2%, allantoin 2%, dienestrol 0.01%, and sulfanilamide 15%; each suppository contains aminacrine hydrochloride 14 mg, allantoin 140 mg, dienestrol 0.7 mg, and sulfanilamide 1 g.

Baculin (Amfre-Grant): Each vaginal tablet contains diiodohydroxyquin 100 mg, phenylmercuric acetate 3 mg, sodium lauryl sulfate 3 mg, and papain 20 mg.

Lycinate (Hoechst): Each vaginal tablet contains diiodohydroxyquin 100 mg, sodium lauryl sulfate 5 mg, and dioctyl sodium sulfosuccinate 5 mg.

Quinette (Arnar-Stone): Each suppository or 4 g of cream contains diiodohydroxyquin 100 mg, sulfadiazine 500 mg, diethylstilbestrol 0.1 mg, and sodium lauryl sulfate.

Trinalis (Webster): Each suppository contains aminacrine hydrochloride 3 mg, tyrothricin 2.5 mg, and phenylmercuric acetate 3 mg.

Trinalis-HC (Webster): Each suppository contains aminacrine hydrochloride 3 mg, hydrocortisone acetate 10 mg, tyrothricin 2.5 mg, and phenylmercuric acetate 3 mg.

Trisert (Ulmer): Each vaginal tablet contains aminacrine hydrochloride 2 mg, phenylmercuric acetate 3 mg, methylbenzethonium chloride 1.8 mg, and tyrothricin 0.6 mg.

Triva (Boyle): Douche powder contains oxyquinoline sulfate 2% and edetate disodium 0.33%; each 5 g of gel contains aminacrine hydrochloride 10 mg, oxyquinoline benzoate 7.5 mg, and edetate disodium 2.5 mg.

Vagisec (Julius Schmid): Liquid containing nonoxynol 9, edetate sodium, and dioctyl sodium sulfosuccinate.

Vagisec Plus (Julius Schmid): Each suppository contains aminacrine hydrochloride 0.2%, nonoxynol 9 0.175%, edetate sodium 0.022%, and dioctyl sodium sulfosuccinate 0.0024%.

Vagilia (Lemmon): Cream containing sulfisoxazole 10%, aminacrine hydrochloride 0.2%, and allantoin 2%.

Vagitrol (Syntex): Cream containing aminacrine hydrochloride 0.2%, allantoin 2%, and sulfanilamide 15%.

Chapter 65

ANTHELMINTICS

Most common intestinal worms can be eliminated with reasonable certainty by using an appropriate anthelmintic drug; these parasites include *Ascaris lumbricoides* (roundworm), *Necator americanus* and *Ancylostoma duodenale* (hookworms), *Strongyloides stercoralis* (threadworm), *Enterobius vermicularis* (pinworm), and the tapeworms, *Taenia saginata*, *T. solium*, *Diphyllobothrium latum*, and *Hymenolepis nana*. Presently available drugs are less effective against *Trichuris trichiura* (whipworm), and their use does not assure elimination of this parasite.

It often is difficult to evaluate the effectiveness of anthelmintic therapy because the criteria used in various studies to determine the degree of reduction or elimination of parasites differ. In addition, the number of worms present often determines pathogenicity. Thus, by reducing the worm population, clinical improvement may occur, although an anthelmintic agent must eliminate all of the worms to be considered curative. In treating mixed worm infections, the effect that therapy directed against one parasite may have on the other species present should be taken into account.

The relative specificity of anthelmintic drugs requires accurate diagnosis. The clinician must obtain an appropriate specimen (stool, blood, urine, sputum, aspirate, or biopsy) for analysis by a parasitology laboratory. Sometimes the parasites can be identified by gross observation of the stools. In some cases (eg, light *Strongyloides* infections), the parasite may not be immediately detrimental to the patient's health, but treatment is indicated because of the potential danger of severe illness or death due to autoinfection.

Roundworm: A number of drugs are effective in the treatment of roundworm (ascariasis) infections. Piperazine in the form of its various salts [Antepar, Perin] presently is the drug of choice; however, recent studies indicate that pyrantel [Antiminth] may be even more effective than piperazine. Thiabendazole [Mintezol] is a drug of second choice because it is generally less effective than piperazine against ascarides; also, it is less effective in heavy than in light infections, and it may stimulate migration of the parasites. Hexylresorcinol also is an alternate but less effective drug. Thiabendazole is useful for treating mixed infections of roundworms and hookworms because it is clinically effective against both types of parasites. Bephenium hydroxynaphthoate [Alcopara] and hexylresorcinol also are useful in mixed infections.

Hookworm: Tetrachloroethylene and thiabendazole are drugs of choice for hookworm infections (uncinariasis) caused by *N. americanus;* bephenium hydroxynaphthoate is an alternate drug. Bephenium is the drug of choice for hookworm infections caused by *A. duodenale*, and tetrachloroethylene and thiabendazole are alternate drugs. When tetrachloroethylene is chosen to treat hookworm infection complicated by ascariasis, it is advisable to treat the latter parasite first to avoid the possibility that tetrachloroethylene, like its long-discarded predecessor, carbon tetrachloride, might stimulate abnormal migration of the ascarides.

Whipworm: No drug presently available has a reliably high degree of effectiveness in the treatment of whipworm infections (trichuriasis). Repeated oral doses of bephenium hydroxynaphthoate, thiabendazole, or hexylresorcinol have been effective in some patients. Dithiazanine iodide [Delvex] apparently was highly effective in the treatment of trichuriasis, but was removed from the market because of toxicity.

Tapeworm: Quinacrine [Atabrine] is effective and has been the drug of choice for the treatment of infections caused by the large tapeworms *(Taenia solium, T. saginata, Diphyllobothrium latum)* and the dwarf tapeworm *(Hymenolepis nana)*. Dwarf tapeworm infections usually are multiple and generally require intensive treatment to achieve a cure. Niclosamide [Yomesan] also is highly effective in the treatment of infections caused by *T. saginata, D. latum*, or *H. nana*. Aspidium oleoresin, if fresh, is active against tapeworms but is rarely used because of excessive toxicity; it also is somewhat difficult to obtain.

Threadworm: Thiabendazole is the drug of choice for the treatment of threadworm infections (strongyloidiasis). Pyrvinium pamoate [Povan] is an alternate drug that is moderately effective when given once daily for several days.

Pinworm: Piperazine, pyrantel, pyrvinium, and thiabendazole are all highly effective in the treatment of pinworm infections (enterobiasis). Appropriate hygienic measures are essential to prevent reinfection.

Schistosomiasis: Agents used in the treatment of schistosomiasis include trivalent antimony compounds such as antimony potassium tartrate (tartar emetic), which is given intravenously, and stibophen [Fuadin] and stibocaptate (antimony sodium dimercaptosuccinate) [Astiban], which are given intramuscularly. *Schistosoma haematobium* is the most susceptible and *S. japonicum* is the least susceptible to these drugs. Niridazole [Ambilhar] is a new oral agent used in the treatment of *S. haematobium* infections, and it may prove to be the drug of choice. Although antimony potassium tartrate has greater activity, stibophen is the preferred antimonial agent for the treatment of *S. haematobium* and *S. mansoni* infections because it is less toxic; antimony potassium tartrate is the drug of choice for *S. japonicum* infections.

Filariasis: Filariasis caused by *Wuchereria bancrofti, W. malayi, Loa loa*, or *Onchocerca volvulus* is treated with diethylcarbamazine [Hetrazan], a synthetic piperazine derivative. This drug destroys the microfilariae of all these species. It also may either kill or sterilize adult females of *Wuchereria* species and some of the adults of *Loa loa*. The adults of *Onchocerca* are not affected by diethylcarbamazine and either must be removed surgically or killed by treatment with suramin sodium; otherwise the microfilariae reappear a few months after treatment with diethylcarbamazine. Niridazole and thiabendazole have been reported to be effective in the treatment of *Dracunculus medinensis* (guineaworm) infections.

Larva Migrans: Thiabendazole is the drug of choice for treating cutaneous larva migrans (creeping eruption) caused by *Ancylostoma braziliense* or *A. caninum*. Diethylcarbamazine also may be somewhat effective. The use of thiabendazole in visceral larva migrans due to *Toxocara* species is investigational (see also Chapter 71, Anti-infective and Anti-inflammatory Agents Used in Ophthalmology).

Trichinosis: Corticotropin (ACTH) or adrenal corticosteroids are effective in controlling allergic symptoms caused by trichinosis and may be lifesaving in severe infections. Thiabendazole reduces the number of developing trichina larvae in experimentally infected pigs and apparently is clinically useful in man. It is not known if this drug has any activity against the adult *Trichinella spiralis* in the intestine of man.

Liver Fluke: Infections caused by the oriental liver fluke *(Clonorchis sinensis)* are sometimes seen in patients who have been in the Orient. No satisfactory treatment is available, although chloroquine temporarily reduces the egg count. The use of drugs such as emetine and tartar emetic is not justified because of their lack of effectiveness and the questionable pathogenicity of this infection.

Adverse Reactions and Precautions

The anthelmintics are all potentially toxic. Special caution is indicated if they are used in patients with severe hepatic, renal, or cardiac disease; in pregnant women; and in children under one year of age. In some cases (eg, the treatment of schistosomiasis with antimony compounds), anemia and malnutrition should be corrected before anthelmintics are given. In other cases (eg, severe hookworm infection), the parasites can be safely eliminated, and should be, before or at the same time that therapy for anemia (eg, administration of iron) is initiated.

Any of the anthelmintic drugs may cause nausea and vomiting, and the effectiveness of orally administered agents may be reduced if vomiting occurs. Vomiting should be avoided in the treatment of *Taenia solium* (pork tapeworm) because infections with the larval form (cysticercosis) may result from passage of proglottids into the stomach, where they disintegrate and release viable eggs.

The specific reactions produced by the various anthelmintic drugs, and the precautions required in their use are discussed in the individual evaluations that follow.

INDIVIDUAL EVALUATIONS

ANTIMONY POTASSIUM TARTRATE

Antimony potassium tartrate is the most active and most toxic of the trivalent antimony compounds. It is the drug of choice in treating infections caused by *Schistosoma japonicum;* cure rates range from 50% to 90%, depending upon the dosage. Antimony potassium tartrate is not used in the treatment of *S. mansoni* and *S. haematobium* infections because less toxic agents are effective.

Adverse reactions include severe coughing, nausea, vomiting, diarrhea, colic, syncope, bradycardia, severe arthralgia, hypotension, electrocardiographic changes, dyspnea, and, occasionally, jaundice. Anemia and a poor nutritional status should be corrected prior to treatment. Doses should be given two hours after a light meal and the patient should remain recumbent for one hour after treatment. Antiemetics should not be used because they mask nausea and vomiting, which are signs of progressive hepatic necrosis caused by toxic doses.

Treatment should be discontinued if vomiting is severe or persistent or if a blood dyscrasia (eg, thrombocytopenia), albuminuria, purpura, fever, or dermatitis occurs. Contraindications include the presence of a febrile infection, severe cardiac or renal disease, and hepatic damage not caused by schistosomiasis.

USUAL DOSAGE.—*Intravenous: Adults,* the drug should be given extremely slowly in a 0.5% solution freshly prepared in water for injection or 5% dextrose injection; it is administered on alternate days according to the following schedule: for *S. japonicum* infections, 8 ml initially, increased by 4 ml with each subsequent dose until the 11th day, when 28 ml is given; administration of this dose then is continued on alternate days until a total of 500 ml (2.5 g) has been given.

PREPARATIONS.—Antimony Potassium Tartrate, U.S.P. No single-entity pharmaceutical dosage form is available; compounding necessary for prescription.

ASPIDIUM OLEORESIN

This drug is as effective as quinacrine in the treatment of tapeworm infections, but it is rarely used because it is more toxic. Moreover, it often is difficult to obtain.

Adverse effects include nausea, vomiting, and bloody diarrhea. Aspidium may cause abortion in advanced pregnancy because of uterine stimulation. It depresses cardiac and smooth muscle, and sudden cardiac failure may occur. Large doses stimulate the nervous system and may cause tremors and tonic convulsions, followed by ascending depression with respiratory arrest when the medulla is affected. Aspidium affects the optic nerve and may cause blindness.

USUAL DOSAGE.—*Oral* (aspidium oleoresin must be fresh and should be given by stomach tube or, preferably, duodenal tube to avoid vomiting): *Adults,* an emulsion containing 5 to 6 ml of aspidium oleoresin, 8 g of acacia, and water to make 60 ml is given in two divided doses one hour apart. *Children,* 4 ml of the same emulsion/5 kg of body weight is given in two divided doses.

It has been recommended that a fat-free, low-residue diet be taken for several days prior to treatment. On the day before treatment, lunch and supper should consist only of readily absorbed foods (eg, rice, cooked cereal, fruit juice, soup); a saline cathartic such as magnesium sulfate or sodium sulfate (15 g for adults, 7.5 g for children) should be given in the evening.

PREPARATIONS.—Available to pharmacists from Magnus Mabee & Reynard Division, B.F.M. Corp., Paramus, N.J. 07652.

BEPHENIUM HYDROXYNAPHTHOATE
[Alcopara]

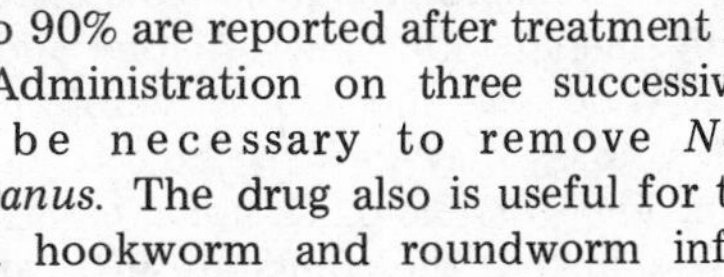

This drug is effective against both species of hookworm. It is the drug of choice in *Ancylostoma duodenale* infections; cure rates of 80% to 90% are reported after treatment for one day. Administration on three successive days may be necessary to remove *Necator americanus.* The drug also is useful for treating mixed hookworm and roundworm infections since usual doses have some effect against *Ascaris lumbricoides.* Bephenium also may be active against *Trichuris trichiura* (whipworm). However, reductions in egg counts of 81% to 100%, which have been reported following the proposed doses, do not necessarily indicate a corresponding reduction in numbers of parasites.

Serious adverse effects have not been reported, but bephenium may cause nausea and vomiting due to its bitter taste. Dehydration, electrolyte imbalance, and diarrhea should be corrected before the drug is used. Information is lacking on the safety of bephenium during pregnancy; therefore, the possible risk to the fetus should be weighed against the expected therapeutic benefits if this agent is considered for use in pregnant women.

USUAL DOSAGE.—*Oral: Adults and children over 22.5 kg,* 5 g twice daily for one day for *A. duodenale;* the same dosage is given for three days for *N. americanus. Children under 22.5 kg,* 2.5 g twice daily for one to three days. For whipworm infection, the proposed dosage is 2.5 g twice daily for three to five days for *children weighing 17 to 33 kg* or 5 g twice daily for several days for *adults.*

PREPARATIONS.—Alcopara (Burroughs Wellcome). *Oral:* Granules 5 g (equivalent to 2.5 g bephenium ion).

DIETHYLCARBAMAZINE CITRATE

[Hetrazan]

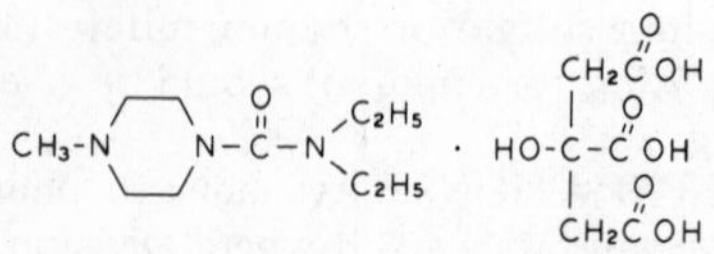

This piperazine derivative is useful in the treatment of filariasis caused by *Wuchereria bancrofti, W. malayi, Onchocerca volvulus,* or *Loa loa.* There also is some evidence that it is effective in cutaneous larva migrans (creeping eruption) caused by larvae of *Ancylostoma braziliense* or *A. caninum.* Diethylcarbamazine has been replaced by more effective drugs (eg, piperazine) for the treatment of roundworm *(Ascaris lumbricoides)* infections.

Diethylcarbamazine quickly kills microfilariae and either kills or sterilizes adult females of *W. bancrofti* and *W. malayi.* A single course of therapy kills microfilariae and some adults of *Loa loa* and stops symptoms, but repeated courses may be necessary to cure the infection. Microfilariae of *O. volvulus* disappear from the skin, but the adults are little affected by diethylcarbamazine and microfilariae and skin lesions reappear in a few months unless the adults are removed surgically or by treatment with suramin.

Adverse reactions include headache, dizziness, nausea, and fever. Destruction of microfilariae in onchocerciasis and loiasis may cause allergic reactions manifested by severe pedal edema, intense pruritus, dermatitis, fever, colic, and lymphadenitis. Rarely, an allergic encephalitic reaction has occurred in patients treated with this drug for loiasis. The concomitant administration of antihistamines or corticosteroids is advisable to minimize allergic reactions. If these reactions are severe, the dosage should be reduced or treatment interrupted. The drug must be administered cautiously in patients with ocular onchocerciasis.

USUAL DOSAGE.—*Oral: Adults and children,* 2 mg/kg of body weight three times daily after meals for 7 to 14 days in wuchereriasis, for 10 days in loiasis, and for 14 to 21 days in onchocerciasis. Patients with onchocerciasis should receive appropriate additional treatment to kill adult parasites. In ocular onchocerciasis, the initial daily dose should be small and increased gradually as follows: 25 mg daily for three days, 100 mg daily for three days, and 150 mg daily for 12 days.

PREPARATIONS.—Hetrazan (Lederle). *Oral:* Tablets 50 mg.

HEXYLRESORCINOL

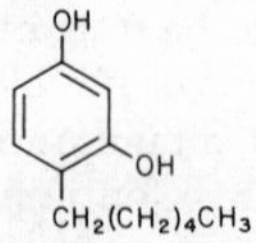

Hexylresorcinol is an alternate drug for the treatment of roundworm *(Ascaris lumbricoides)* and whipworm *(Trichuris trichiura)* infections. Although it is less effective than other drugs against hookworm, pinworm, and dwarf tapeworm, it may be useful in some mixed infections because of its wide anthelmintic spectrum.

The principal untoward effect is burning sensation of the skin and oral and anal mucous membranes; therefore, tablets must be swallowed without chewing and the perianal region should be protected by careful application of petrolatum if the drug ever is administered by retention enema. Hexylresorcinol is contraindicated in patients with ulcerative diseases of the gastrointestinal tract.

USUAL DOSAGE.—*Oral:* The stomach must be empty and no food should be taken for four hours after treatment. *Adults and older children,* 1 g; *children 8 to 12 years of age,* 800 mg; *6 to 8 years,* 600 mg. Treatment may be repeated in three days.

PREPARATIONS.—Jayne's R-W Vermifuge (Glenbrook). *Oral:* Tablets 100 and 200 mg. Drug also marketed in bulk form under generic name.

NICLOSAMIDE [Yomesan]

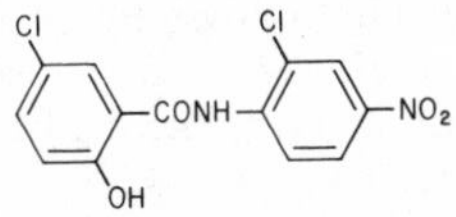

Niclosamide is highly effective against the large tapeworms, *Taenia saginata* and *Diphyllobothrium latum*, and the dwarf tapeworm, *Hymenolepis nana.* The drug causes segments to disintegrate, releasing viable eggs; hence, if it is used in a patient with pork tapeworm *(T. solium)* infection, a purge should be given within one or two hours after treatment to avoid the possibility of cysticercosis. Since tapeworm infections generally are not life-threatening, it is recommended that treatment of pregnant women be postponed until after delivery.

In a limited series, nausea, malaise, and abdominal pain occurred in about 10% of patients.

USUAL DOSAGE.—*Oral: Adults and children over 8 years of age*, two doses of 1 g each one hour apart; *2 to 8 years*, two doses of 500 mg each one hour apart; *under 2 years*, two doses of 250 mg each one hour apart. For *H. nana* infections, the drug should be taken for five successive days. The patient should omit breakfast but may eat two hours after the last dose. The tablets should be chewed and then washed down with water.

PREPARATIONS.—Yomesan. *Oral:* Tablets 500 mg. Not marketed in United States but may be obtained by licensed physicians from the Parasitic Disease Drug Service, Center for Disease Control, Atlanta, Georgia 30333.

NIRIDAZOLE [Ambilhar]

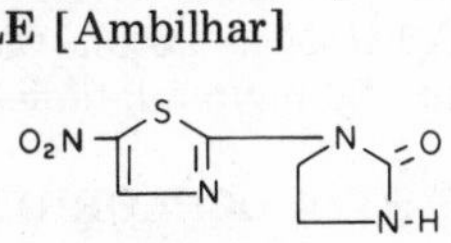

Niridazole is at least as effective as stibophen in the treatment of infections caused by *Schistosoma haematobium* and may be the drug of choice. It is moderately effective against *S. mansoni* and *S. japonicum.* This drug also has been reported to be active against *Dracunculus medinensis* (guineaworm). It is given orally and may be less toxic than stibophen.

Adverse effects include abdominal cramps, headache, anorexia, vomiting, dizziness, electrocardiographic changes, arrhythmias, and neuropsychiatric disturbances. These effects disappear when the drug is discontinued. Additional studies are needed to determine the effects of niridazole on human spermatozoa; transient reduction in spermatogenesis has been reported in some patients. Hemolytic anemia may occur in patients with G6PD deficiency. Niridazole should not be given to patients with a history of liver disease or to those with impaired liver function. It also should not be given to patients with neuropsychiatric or convulsive disorders, and should not be used during pregnancy.

USUAL DOSAGE.—*Oral: Adults and children*, for schistosomiasis, 25 mg/kg of body weight daily in two divided doses for five to seven days; for dracunculiasis, the same dosage is given for seven to ten days.

PREPARATIONS.—Ambilhar (Ciba). *Oral:* Tablets 500 mg. Not marketed in the United States but may be obtained by licensed physicians from the Parasitic Disease Drug Service, Center for Disease Control, Atlanta, Georgia 30333.

PIPERAZINE CALCIUM EDETATE [Perin]
PIPERAZINE CITRATE [Antepar Citrate]
PIPERAZINE PHOSPHATE [Antepar Phosphate]
PIPERAZINE TARTRATE

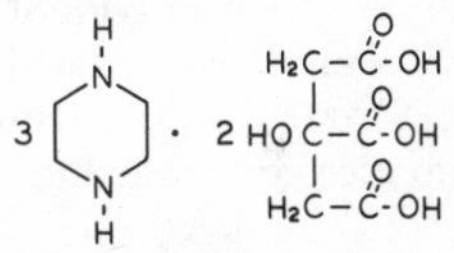

The available piperazine salts form piperazine hexahydrate in solution and all are equally effective. Piperazine is the drug of choice in the treatment of roundworm *(Ascaris lumbricoides)* infections; administration on two successive days cures about 95% of infections. It also is highly effective in the treatment of pinworm *(Enterobius vermicularis)* infections. Roundworms are passed, paralyzed and alive, usually one to three days after treatment. The majority of pinworms are passed alive and active during the first four days of therapy.

Adverse reactions include nausea, vomiting, headache, abdominal cramps, diarrhea, vertigo, tremors, difficulty in visual focusing, asthenia, erythema, and, rarely, urticaria. These effects are transient and disappear when the drug is discontinued. There have been no reports of harmful effects to the fetus after use of piperazine in pregnant women. This drug is contraindicated in patients with grand mal epilepsy.

USUAL DOSAGE.—(Doses of all piperazine salts are expressed in terms of the hexahydrate.) *Oral:* For roundworms, the following doses are given once daily for two consecutive days: *children weighing less than 13.5 kg,* 1 g; *13.5 to 22.5 kg,* 2 g; *22.5 to 45.5 kg,* 3 g; *over 45.5 kg and adults,* 3.5 g. For pinworms, the following doses are given once daily before breakfast for seven consecutive days, and the course may be repeated after three weeks if necessary: *children weighing less than 7 kg,* 250 mg; *7 to 13.5 kg,* 500 mg; *13.5 to 27 kg,* 1 g; *over 27 kg,* 2 g; *adults,* 2.5 g. Fasting before treatment is not necessary.

PREPARATIONS.—(Strengths expressed in terms of the hexahydrate.)

Piperazine Calcium Edetate:

Perin (Endo). *Oral:* Syrup 500 mg/5 ml.

Piperazine Citrate:

Antepar [citrate] (Burroughs Wellcome). *Oral:* Syrup 500 mg/5 ml; tablets 500 mg.

Piperazine Phosphate:

Antepar [phosphate] (Burroughs Wellcome). *Oral:* Wafers 500 mg.

Piperazine Tartrate:

Oral: Tablets 500 mg.

ADDITIONAL TRADEMARKS.— **Piperazine Citrate:** Multifuge (Blue Line), Ta-Verm (Table Rock), Vermidole (Reid-Provident). **Piperazine Phosphate:** Vermizine Tablets (North American). Forms marketed by other manufacturers under generic name.

PYRANTEL PAMOATE [Antiminth]

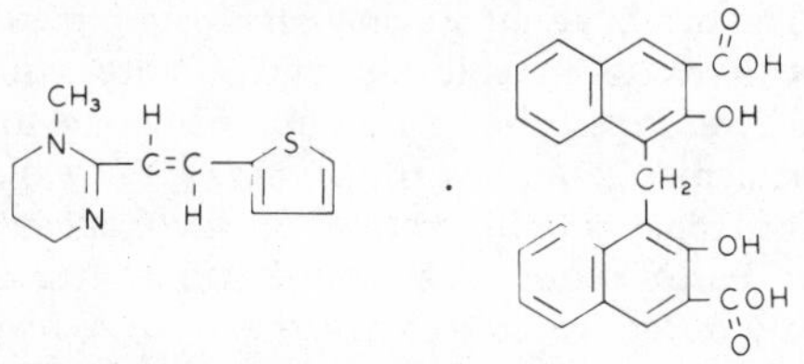

Pyrantel is highly effective in the treatment of roundworm *(Ascaris lumbricoides)* and pinworm *(Enterobius vermicularis)* infections when given in a single oral dose. Three consecutive daily doses are generally more effective in hookworm *(Necator americanus)* infections than a single dose; however, results are conflicting, and clearance rates range from 48% to 93%. The drug is essentially ineffective against whipworm *(Trichuris trichiura).*

Adverse reactions include anorexia, nausea, vomiting, diarrhea, abdominal pain, elevated SGOT levels, headache, dizziness, drowsiness, and rashes.

USUAL DOSAGE.—(Dosage expressed in terms of the base.) *Oral: Adults and children,* for roundworm and pinworm, 11 mg/kg of body weight; for hookworm, this dose is given for three consecutive days. Fasting before treatment is not necessary.

PREPARATIONS.—Antiminth (Roerig). *Oral:* Suspension 250 mg/5 ml.

PYRVINIUM PAMOATE [Povan]

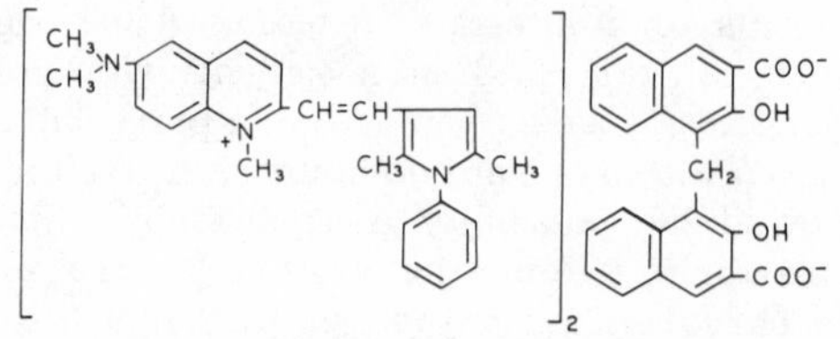

Pyrvinium pamoate is the salt of a cyanine dye. Two doses one or two weeks apart are effective in the treatment of pinworm *(Enterobius vermicularis)* infections; the first dose cures approximately 92% of infections. Daily doses for several days may be useful in threadworm *(Strongyloides stercoralis)* infections.

Pyrvinium pamoate may cause nausea, vomiting, abdominal cramps, and, rarely, photosensitivity. Patients should be told that the drug stains stools bright red and will stain clothing if vomited. Because of this red-staining property, the tablets should be swallowed immediately and not chewed.

USUAL DOSAGE.—(Doses expressed in terms of the base.) *Oral: Adults and children,* 5 mg/kg of body weight. A single dose is repeated in one week for pinworm infections, and the drug is administered daily for five to seven days for threadworm infections.

PREPARATIONS.—Povan (Parke, Davis). *Oral:* Suspension 50 mg/5 ml; tablets 50 mg.

QUINACRINE HYDROCHLORIDE [Atabrine Hydrochloride]

Quinacrine is an effective alternate drug in the treatment of infections caused by the large tapeworms, *Taenia saginata, T. solium,* and *Diphyllobothrium latum* (beef, pork, and fish tapeworms respectively), and the dwarf tapeworm, *Hymenolepis nana.* It may be the drug of choice in *T. solium* infections. The drug is also effective against tapeworms that normally are parasites of animals but occasionally cause human infections (eg, *Dipylidium caninum*, *Hymenolepis diminuta).* Treatment is followed by a saline purge to expel worms, which are stained yellow by the drug. Large tapeworms frequently are eliminated by a single treatment, but, if the scolex is not found, the stools should be examined periodically and shown to be free of worm eggs and segments for the next three to six months to be certain of cure. *H. nana* infections are usually multiple and require more persistent treatment than do the large tapeworm infections.

Nausea and vomiting are the most common adverse effects after anthelmintic dosages of quinacrine. Vomiting reduces the effectiveness of the drug and, in *T. solium* infections, has the potential danger of producing cysticercosis. Other effects include transient dizziness and, less commonly, xanthosis and manifestations of toxic psychosis (eg, hallucinations). The drug should be used cautiously in patients older than 60 years of age and in those with a history of psychosis. Treatment of pregnant women should be postponed until after delivery because quinacrine crosses the placenta and tapeworm infections generally are not life-threatening.

For other uses of quinacrine, see Chapters 31, Anticonvulsants; 61, Antimalarial Agents; and 88, Antineoplastic Agents.

USUAL DOSAGE.—Proper preparation of the patient is important. The diet should be restricted to liquids or semisolid foods on the day before treatment, and no food should be taken after the evening meal. A cleansing enema may be given to reduce the amount of stool that must be searched for scolex on the following day; patients with *H. nana* infection should be given a saline purge (eg, 15 g of magnesium sulfate or sodium sulfate for *adults*, 7.5 g for *children).* The drug is administered the following morning, with breakfast omitted, and a saline purge is given one and one-half to two hours after the last dose. An enema is given if the worms are not expelled by purgation or if the scolex is not recovered. To reduce the possibility of nausea and vomiting, sodium bicarbonate (500 to 600 mg) may be given prior to each dose of quinacrine, an antiemetic such as prochlorperazine may be used, or quinacrine may be given by duodenal tube. Prevention of vomiting is especially important in *T. solium* infections.

Oral: Adults, 800 mg; this amount may be given in two divided doses 30 minutes apart or in four or eight divided doses at 10-minute intervals to help prevent vomiting. *Children weighing 18 to 34 kg*, 400 mg in divided doses; *34 to 45.5 kg*, 600 mg in divided doses. Some sources recommend different dosages and more prolonged treatment for *H. nana* infections.

PREPARATIONS.—Atabrine Hydrochloride (Winthrop). *Oral:* Tablets 100 mg.

STIBOCAPTATE [Astiban]

Stibocaptate (antimony sodium dimercaptosuccinate) is useful in infections caused by *Schistosoma haematobium* and *S. mansoni*, but it should not be used for the treatment of *S. japonicum*. This agent is the least toxic of the trivalent antimony compounds currently in use and is given in fewer injections than the other compounds.

Adverse effects are similar to those produced by the other trivalent antimony compounds. Stibocaptate may cause pain at the site of injection. Gastrointestinal effects include anorexia, diarrhea, constipation, nausea, vomiting, and abdominal pain. Patients may experience asthenia, lassitude, vertigo, headache, fever, arthralgia, and myalgia. The drug also may cause rash, impaired liver function, and electrocardiographic changes (eg, flattening or inversion of the T wave). Coughing or chest pain occurs rarely. Contraindications to the use of stibocaptate include other antimonial therapy within the previous two months, respiratory infections, tuberculosis, fever, jaundice, severe anemia, and cardiac, hepatic, or renal insufficiency. If intestinal helminths are present, they should be treated two weeks before initiating therapy with this agent. Information is lacking on the safety of stibocaptate during pregnancy.

USUAL DOSAGE.—*Intramuscular:* A 10% solution is prepared in water for injection and should be used within 24 hours if unrefrigerated; a refrigerated solution may be used if it remains colorless and clear. The total dose is divided into five equal amounts and is given once or twice a week or, in hospitalized patients, as often as every day, depending upon the patient's tolerance. *Adults*, 40 mg/kg of body weight in five divided doses; *children 6 years of age and older*, 50 mg/kg in five divided doses.

PREPARATIONS.—Astiban (Hoffmann-LaRoche, Switzerland). *Injection:* Powder 500 mg in 5 ml containers and 10 g in 100 ml containers. Not marketed in the United States, but may be obtained by licensed physicians from the Parasitic Disease Drug

Service, Center for Disease Control, Atlanta, Georgia 30333.

STIBOPHEN [Fuadin]

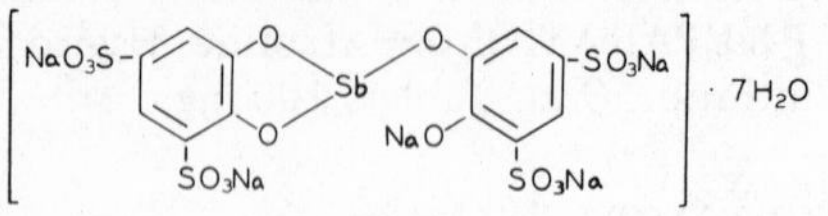

This trivalent antimony compound is useful in the treatment of schistosomiasis caused by *Schistosoma haematobium* or *S. mansoni;* it is preferred over antimony potassium tartrate for these infections because it is less toxic. Stibophen is not effective in *S. japonicum* infections.

The drug is administered intramuscularly; extreme care should be exercised to avoid accidental intravenous administration.

Adverse reactions include nausea, vomiting, diarrhea, severe arthralgia, headache, abdominal pain, coughing, hypotension, and syncope. Thrombocytopenia, hemolytic anemia, ventricular fibrillation, and severe hypersensitivity reactions, sometimes fatal, have been reported. Hepatitis and renal irritation also have been noted. Stibophen may cause transient electrocardiographic changes (eg, increased P wave, decreased or inverted T wave) without cardiovascular symptoms.

Anemia and a poor nutritional status should be corrected prior to giving stibophen. Treatment should be stopped if vomiting is severe or persistent or if a blood dyscrasia (eg, thrombocytopenia), albuminuria, dermatitis, or fever due to infection occurs. Antiemetics should not be used because nausea and vomiting serve as warning signs of progressive hepatic necrosis. The drug is contraindicated in patients with severe renal, cardiac, or hepatic disease not caused by schistosomiasis.

USUAL DOSAGE.—*Intramuscular: Adults,* 1.5 to 2 ml of a 6.3% solution of stibophen on the first day, 3.5 ml on the second day, 5 ml on the third day, then six doses of 5 ml each on alternate days. The drug also may be given in daily doses of 4 to 5 ml five days a week for four weeks for a total of 80 to 100 ml. *Children,* 0.5 ml on the first day, 0.5 ml/10 kg of body weight on the second day, and then 1 ml/10 kg on alternate days until a total of 1 ml/kg has been given. Courses should not be repeated in less than 6 to 12 weeks and not unless viable eggs of *Schistosoma* are found in the stool or demonstrated in rectal biopsy.

PREPARATIONS.—Fuadin (Winthrop). *Injection:* Solution 6.3% in 5 ml containers.

SURAMIN SODIUM

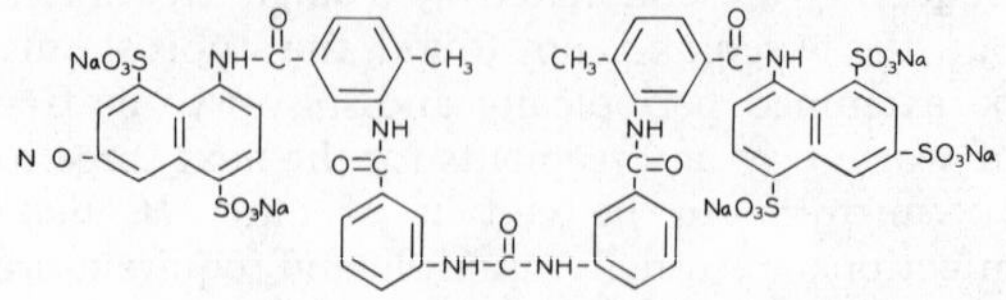

Suramin is a complexed derivative of urea that is used primarily in the treatment and prophylaxis of trypanosomiasis (see Chapter 63, Antitrypanosomal Agents), but it also is used in the treatment of onchocerciasis.

Multiple doses of suramin cause death and degeneration of the adult female *Onchocerca volvulus* within one or two months after treatment; males remain alive for a longer period. Microfilariae gradually die over a period of several months. Diethylcarbamazine is used to kill the microfilariae of *O. volvulus* quickly but is ineffective against the adults.

The need for multiple doses and the potentially dangerous reactions limit the usefulness of suramin; close medical supervision during treatment is essential. Suramin may cause nausea, vomiting, colic, urticaria, and, in very sensitive persons, shock, syncope, and acute circulatory failure. Allergic effects due to proteins released by degenerating microfilariae (eg, pruritus, rash, fever, edema, burning and hyperesthesia of the soles of the feet, photophobia, iritis, lacrimation) occur later, and generally are less intense than with diethylcarbamazine. The drug may cause albuminuria, casts, and hematuria and, rarely, agranulocytosis or hemolytic anemia. It is contraindicated in patients with severe renal or ocular disease.

USUAL DOSAGE.—*Intravenous:* A 10% solution in water for injection is used. For onchocerciasis, *adults,* 200 to 500 mg initially to test tolerance, then 1 g weekly for five weeks; *children,* 100 mg initially to test tolerance, then 10 to 15 mg/kg of body weight weekly for five weeks. The drug may be administered intramuscularly if the intravenous route is impractical.

PREPARATIONS.—Suramin Sodium. Available in United States from the Parasitic Disease Drug Service, Center for Disease Control, Atlanta, Georgia 30333.

TETRACHLOROETHYLENE

$$Cl_2C{=}CCl_2$$

This agent is a drug of choice for hookworm infections caused by *Necator americanus.* A single oral dose cures 80% of infections due to *N. americanus* and about 25% of those due to *Ancylostoma duodenale.* Tetrachloroethylene has been used in severely anemic patients without causing serious untoward effects. The treatment may be repeated one or more times at intervals of four days, or a fecal examination may be made in two weeks and a second dose given if hookworm eggs are present. If *Ascaris lumbricoides* also is present, it is generally recommended that the ascarides be eliminated before tetrachloroethylene is used.

Nausea, vomiting, dizziness, and inebriation occur occasionally. Syncope has been reported rarely.

USUAL DOSAGE.—*Oral: Adults,* 5 ml; *children,* 0.12 ml/kg of body weight to a maximum of 5 ml. Only a low-bulk, low-fat meal should be given the evening before treatment, and the patient should avoid alcohol before and for 24 hours after use of tetrachloroethylene. Breakfast should be omitted and the drug given early in the morning, preferably with the patient remaining recumbent for the next four hours. No purgative should be given since this increases the toxic effects and decreases the effectiveness of the drug.

PREPARATIONS.—*Oral:* Capsules 0.2, 0.5, 1, 2.5, and 5 ml. Available only in veterinary preparations (eg, Nema Worm Capsules [Parke, Davis]), but these are safe and effective for human use.

THIABENDAZOLE [Mintezol]

Thiabendazole is the drug of choice in the treatment of *Strongyloides stercoralis* infection and cutaneous larva migrans (creeping eruption) caused by larvae of *Ancylostoma braziliense* and *A. caninum.* It also is highly effective against pinworm *(Enterobius vermicularis)* infection. Thiabendazole appears to be as active as tetrachloroethylene against hookworm infections caused by *Necator americanus* and of greater effectiveness against *Ancylostoma duodenale.* In heavy roundworm infections, large doses (120 mg/kg) have produced cure rates exceeding 90%. This drug may be active against larvae of *Trichinella spiralis* (trichinosis). Although results in the treatment of whipworm *(Trichuris trichiura)* infections have been variable, it is among the preferred drugs for use in this disease. Thiabendazole (50 to 100 mg/kg of body weight daily for one to three days or 500 mg daily for seven days) has been reported to be effective in the treatment of *Dracunculus medinensis* (guineaworm) infection.

More common untoward effects are dizziness, anorexia, nausea, and vomiting. Diarrhea, fever, abdominal distress, flushing, chills, angioedema, pruritus, lethargy, rash, and headache occur less frequently. Tinnitus, hypotension, and syncope, as well as numbness, hyperglycemia, changes in liver function, and xanthopsia also have been reported. Adverse reactions are transient and appear to be dose related. Thiabendazole should be used cautiously in patients with impaired liver or kidney function. The drug may stimulate aberrant migration of *A. lumbricoides.* Although studies in animals have revealed no teratogenic effects, the expected therapeutic benefits should be weighed against potential harm to the fetus if this drug is used during pregnancy.

USUAL DOSAGE.—*Oral: Adults and children,* 25 mg/kg of body weight twice daily after meals. The maximal daily dose is 3 g. For strongyloidiasis and hookworm and roundworm infection, treatment is given for one or two days; for whipworm infection and trichinosis, for two to four days; for cutaneous larva migrans, for two days; and for pinworm infection, for one day and the dose repeated in seven days.

PREPARATIONS.—Mintezol (Merck Sharp & Dohme). *Oral:* Suspension 500 mg/5 ml; tablets (chewable) 500 mg.

Chapter 66

SCABICIDES AND PEDICULICIDES

The most common infestations caused by parasitic arthropods are scabies and pediculosis. Scabies results from infestation by the itch mite, *Sarcoptes scabiei* var. *hominis.* (In man, less severe infestations with few lesions can be caused by other scabetic parasites that are found on fowl, dogs, cats, and horses.) Pediculosis is caused by *Pediculus capitis* (head louse), which usually attacks the scalp; *P. corporis* (body louse), which becomes embedded in the clothes and attacks the trunk and limbs; and *Phthirus pubis* (crab louse), which causes infestations of the pubis, genitalia, and, occasionally, the axillae, mustache, and eyelashes. The incidence of parasitic infestations has decreased in the United States since World War II, but sharp increases have occurred in other areas of the world.

The chief symptom of these parasitic infestations is pruritus, which results from the injection of the parasite's digestive juices into the skin. Scratching leads to excoriation, and secondary infection may develop and add to the discomfort. The object of treatment is to eliminate the offending organism and to clear or prevent secondary infection. Appropriate antibacterial preparations may be applied topically to treat the infection. The source of infestation and infected contacts should be determined, and clothing should be decontaminated to prevent recurrence.

The treatment of choice for scabies is gamma benzene hexachloride [Kwell]. Other drugs that may be used are benzyl benzoate and crotamiton [Eurax].

Chlorophenothane (DDT) and gamma benzene hexachloride are effective in the treatment of pediculosis corporis, capitis, and pubis; gamma benzene hexachloride is the preferred drug if the lice are resistant to chlorophenothane. Benzyl benzoate also is useful in pediculosis pubis and capitis.

The use of precipitated sulfur and sulfurated lime is outmoded for treating scabetic and louse infestations. However, they may be of some benefit in treating *Demodex folliculorum*, a mite believed to be the cause of rosacea.

Ointments containing mercury or Peruvian balsam and sulfur were widely used in the past to treat scabies and pediculosis, as well as other skin diseases. However, these preparations have no place in the modern therapy of these parasitic infestations. Mercury is absorbed through the intact or damaged skin and may cause renal toxicity.

Adverse Reactions and Precautions

Scabicides and pediculicides may irritate the skin, eyes, and mucous membranes and cause allergic reactions. If signs of intolerance develop, the medication should be discontinued and inflammation of the skin should be allowed to subside before alternative therapy is substituted.

Large-scale use in military and civilian personnel under wartime and disaster conditions has demonstrated that the alleged systemic toxicity of chlorophenothane and gamma benzene hexachloride has not been manifested to any significant degree when these drugs are used as delousing agents.

INDIVIDUAL EVALUATIONS

BENZYL BENZOATE

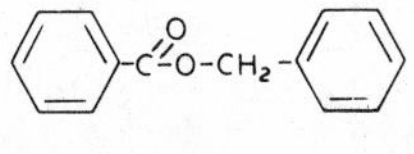

$$C_6H_5-C(=O)-O-CH_2-C_6H_5$$

This agent is useful for pediculosis capitis and pubis. It was once widely used to treat scabies, but has been supplanted by gamma benzene hexachloride, which is the drug of choice.

Benzyl benzoate is relatively nontoxic but may irritate the skin and eyes. Contact with the eyes and urethral meatus should be avoided.

USUAL DOSAGE.—*Topical:* After thorough cleansing with soap and water, a preparation containing approximately 25% of the drug should be applied to the affected areas. When the first application has dried, the preparation may be reapplied and the residue washed off 24 hours later.

PREPARATIONS.—*Topical:* Emulsion 50% in 4, 16, and 64 oz containers; lotion 27% in 16 and 128 oz containers. Drug marketed under generic name.

CHLOROPHENOTHANE

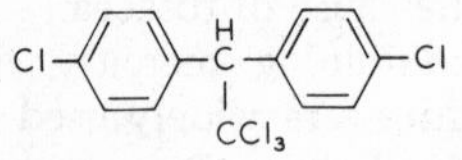

A single application of chlorophenothane (DDT) dusted on the clothing and body is highly effective in treating pediculosis corporis, pubis, and capitis. This drug is not useful in treating scabies. Gamma benzene hexachloride also is effective in eradicating all forms of pediculosis.

Chlorophenothane may cause polyarteritis nodosa and dermatitis. If the drug is absorbed through the skin or inhaled in excessive amounts, systemic toxicity might result. However, since no proved case of poisoning caused by chlorophenothane alone has been reported thus far, respiratory or cutaneous absorption to toxic levels does not appear to be a practical problem when this agent is used as a dusting powder in 10% concentration for delousing. Oily substances on the skin may increase the percutaneous absorption of chlorophenothane and should be avoided.

USUAL DOSAGE.—*Topical:* After throughly cleansing the affected area with soap and water, the clothing, underclothing, and body (for pediculosis corporis and pubis) or the scalp (for pediculosis capitis) are dusted with powder containing chlorophenothane; the treatment is repeated four and eight days later.

PREPARATIONS.—Chlorophenothane, U.S.P. No pharmaceutical dosage form available; compounding necessary for prescription. Usually used as a 5% to 10% powder with talc or other suitable diluent.

CROTAMITON [Eurax]

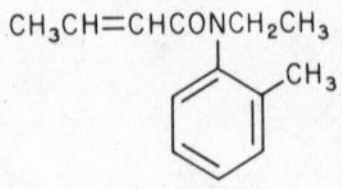

$CH_3CH{=}CHCONCH_2CH_3$

Although crotamiton is an effective scabicide with some antipruritic properties, gamma benzene hexachloride is regarded as the drug of choice in this infestation. Crotamiton should not be used for pruritus without scabies.

This agent rarely may cause contact dermatitis and is irritating to denuded skin. Contact with the eyes and urethral meatus should be avoided.

USUAL DOSAGE.—*Topical:* The preparation should be applied thoroughly to the whole body from the chin down, and especially in the body folds. Two applications, 24 hours apart, are effective for eradication of most scabetic infestations. It often is desirable to repeat the treatment one week later.

PREPARATIONS.—Eurax (Geigy). *Topical:* Cream 10% in 60 g containers; lotion 10% in 6 and 16 oz containers.

GAMMA BENZENE HEXACHLORIDE [Kwell]

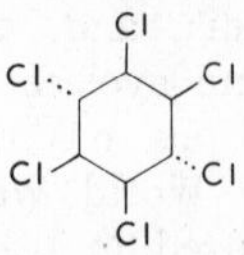

Gamma benzene hexachloride (lindane), in a 1% concentration, is the treatment of choice for scabetic infestations. It is also effective in all forms of pediculosis and is preferred if the lice are resistant to chlorophenothane; this drug kills the nits or eggs as well as the lice. Gamma benzene hexachloride also repels ticks and other arthropods and kills chiggers.

This agent is irritating to the eyes, skin, and mucosa and is toxic if absorbed in excessive amounts. If irritation becomes evident after application, the drug should be washed off and not used again. Application to the eyelashes and urethral meatus should be avoided.

USUAL DOSAGE.—*Topical:* For scabies or pediculosis corporis, 20 to 30 g of the lotion or cream is applied to all parts of the body except the face. The medication is then washed off thoroughly after 24 hours. This treatment is repeated four days later if necessary.

For pediculosis capitis, the scalp is first moistened with water; about an ounce of the shampoo then is applied, worked into a lather, and allowed to remain for five minutes. The scalp is then rinsed thoroughly. This treatment may be repeated in 24 hours, but should not be used more than twice in any one week.

For pediculosis pubis, the shampoo is applied to the pubic, perineal, and axillary areas as above.

PREPARATIONS.—Kwell (Reed & Carnrick). *Topical:* Cream, lotion, and shampoo 1% in 2 and 16 oz containers.

MIXTURES

TOPOCIDE

This mixture of chlorophenothane and benzyl benzoate and a local anesthetic is offered for pediculosis capitis and pubis, as well as for scabies. However, the spectrum of each of these two antiparasitic agents is the same and essentially is confined to pediculosis capitis and pubis (see the evaluations on Benzyl Benzoate and Chlorophenothane); therefore, the rationale for combining these drugs is questionable. Treatment of pediculosis is preferably accomplished by one drug rather than a mixture, and if one is not effective, the other may be tried.

The possible adverse effects are those of the individual ingredients. In addition, use of this combination increases the risk of sensitization to a topical anesthetic. Contact with the eyes and urethral meatus should be avoided.

USUAL DOSAGE.—Use of this mixture is inadvisable because of the reasons stated above. The manufacturer's suggested dosage is: *Topical:* For scabies, after thorough cleansing with soap and water, the lotion is applied to all parts of the body except the face, especially in the body folds. The medication is washed off after 24 hours.

For pediculosis capitis, the hair is first shampooed and dried. The lotion is then applied to the scalp, and the hair combed to spread the preparation thoroughly. The hair is washed after ten days, and the treatment may be repeated in two weeks if necessary.

For pediculosis pubis, the lotion is applied to the affected area and washed off after 48 hours.

PREPARATIONS.—Topocide (Lilly). *Topical:* Each milliliter of lotion contains benzyl benzoate 125 mg, chlorophenothane 10 mg, and benzocaine 20 mg.

Chapter 67

ANTISEPTICS AND DISINFECTANTS

Antiseptics are applied to living tissues either to destroy microorganisms or inhibit their reproduction or metabolic activities. They are used in an attempt to sterilize intact cutaneous and mucous surfaces and contaminated or infected wounds. Since the evidence that these agents may retard the healing of clean wounds is abundant, antiseptics should not be applied to these wounds. Most authorities consider the washing of contaminated wounds with antiseptic solutions an unphysiologic procedure of doubtful value, and possibly harmful. Careful cleansing or irrigation with soap and water or with isotonic sodium chloride solution and removing foreign material by mechanical means to assure free drainage are considered more efficacious and less apt to injure the tissues. Moreover, some antiseptics are inactivated by blood, pus, the protein of necrotic tissue, and other organic matter present in wounds.

The ideal antiseptic should destroy all types of bacteria, fungi, viruses, and other infective agents without harming living tissues. None have this attribute since antiseptics and disinfectants have limited and varying spectra of antimicrobial activity and are general protoplasmic poisons. Some antiseptics have been recommended for the treatment of superficial pyodermas caused by staphylococci, streptococci, and other organisms; however, evidence that they are more effective than meticulous cleansing of the affected areas or administration of antibiotics is not convincing. Other measures must be used in conjunction with antisepsis. For example, washing the hands and arms preoperatively with antiseptics does not obviate the need for prior cleansing with soap and water.

Disinfectants are used on inanimate objects to destroy microorganisms in the nonsporing state. Some disinfectants act as antiseptics in concentrations of sufficient dilution to avoid injury to living tissues; others are not suitable as antiseptics because they require prolonged contact to be effective and thereby cause injury to living tissues. Sterilization is the complete and total destruction of all microbial life, including spores, fungi, growing cells, and viruses. Anything less than this is disinfection or antisepsis. Although most disinfectants are chemical agents, disinfection and sterilization can be accomplished by physical means or agents (eg, heat, ultraviolet light, radiation). Heat sterilization of instruments and utensils is the only dependable method of killing spores, fungi, and viruses. The term "sanitize" is used to denote the reduction of bacterial flora to an acceptable level.

The virucidal effects of some of these agents have not been established with certainty.

The most widely used antiseptics and disinfectants are alcohols, chlorine-containing compounds, elemental and organic iodine preparations, inorganic and organic mercurials, inorganic and organic preparations of silver, quaternary ammonium compounds, phenolic compounds, boric acid and other borates, oxidizing agents, and aldehyde derivatives.

Antiseptics, disinfectants, and sterilizing agents kill cells by coagulation or denaturation of protoplasmic protein, cell lysis (alteration of cell membranes to cause leakage of protoplasm or enzymes), or denaturation or oxidation of enzymes.

Ethylene oxide is used for sterilization of objects that cannot be heated or sterilized by other chemical methods. It has the advantage of being noncorrosive, readily diffusible, and biocidal to all organisms at room temperature. Ethylene oxide is flammable unless mixed with an inert gas, such as carbon dioxide, and is irritating to living tissues. If inhaled, severe irritation to the mucuous membranes of the respiratory tract may result in pulmonary edema. A special sterilizing chamber is required and the objects that are sterilized must remain in contact with the gas for several hours to assure that all the bacteria have been killed.

Since these chemical agents do not act selectively and injure both human and microbial cells, the harm that results may offset any beneficial effects. The effectiveness of antiseptics and disinfectants depends upon many factors, such as concentration, duration of contact with the microbes, pH, temperature, and the presence of inorganic or organic matter that may nullify their activity.

Other agents that may be used topically for specific antimicrobial effects are discussed in Chapters 57, Aminoglycoside Antibacterial Agents and Miscellaneous Antimicrobial Drugs; 60, Antifungal Agents; 64, Antitrichomonal Agents; 71, Anti-infective and Anti-inflammatory Agents Used in Ophthalmology; and 73, Topical Otic Preparations. Other preparations used on the skin are discussed in Chapter 68, Dermatologic Agents.

Adverse Reactions and Precautions

Topically applied antiseptics may irritate the skin and mucous membranes and cause dermatitis or allergic reactions of varying types and severity. If absorbed, systemic toxic reactions may occur. See the individual evaluations for information on specific reactions.

ALCOHOLS

The aliphatic alcohols have varying degrees of antiseptic and disinfecting activity. Those most widely used are ethyl and isopropyl alcohol. Normal propyl alcohol has considerable bactericidal activity, but is seldom used as an antiseptic. Methyl alcohol has no place in antisepsis. Alcohols are applied to the skin to reduce local bacterial flora prior to penetration with needles or other sharp instruments and as a preoperative wash. The disinfecting action of any alcohol can be aided to a considerable degree by gentle rubbing of the skin with sterile gauze while the alcohol is being applied.

The alcohols are flammable and sometimes cause skin irritation.

ETHYL ALCOHOL

Ethyl alcohol is the most widely used agent for disinfection of the skin and is one of the better bactericides because it acts rapidly. It acts by coagulating protein, and also dissolves sebaceous secretions and many foreign chemicals on the skin. The 70% aqueous solution, by weight, is more effective in reducing the surface tension of bacterial cells than undiluted alcohol, which precipitates protoplasm on the periphery of the cell and thus tends to retard penetration of the agent. Ethyl alcohol has tuberculocidal activity. It is not a reliable virucidal agent.

In surgery, the skin is cleansed with a nonflammable defatting agent prior to application of alcohol.

Thorough washing with alcohol shortly after exposure to toxic oils of plants that cause contact dermatitis (eg, poison ivy) may prevent or minimize dermatitis.

Ethyl alcohol is not sporicidal in any concentration; therefore, it is not useful for sterilization of instruments. This antiseptic is undesirable for disinfecting wounds because it causes tissue irritation, painful burning, and stinging. Alcohol also precipitates protein which forms a coagulated mass in which bacteria may grow.

Rubbing alcohol contains about 70% (by volume) of ethyl alcohol. It possesses cleansing and lubricant properties and is used as a rubefacient and skin conditioner for bedridden patients. See also Chapter 68, Dermatologic Agents.

Ethyl alcohol may rarely produce allergic contact dermatitis. High concentrations cause dehydration of the skin. Accidental ingestion results in typical alcoholic intoxication and coma.

METHOD OF APPLICATION.—*Topical.*

PREPARATIONS.—Alcohol, U.S.P., Rubbing Alcohol, N.F. Marketed under generic name.

ISOPROPYL ALCOHOL

Isopropyl alcohol has slightly greater bactericidal activity than ethyl alcohol. This may be due to its greater depression of surface tension. It rapidly kills vegetative forms of most bacteria when used full strength or as a 70% aqueous solution. Isopropyl alcohol has the same uses as ethyl alcohol: it is applied to cleanse and disinfect the skin prior to parenteral injections and surgical incision. As with ethyl alcohol, it is not suitable for sterilizing instruments because it is not sporicidal or virucidal in many cases. It is active against the tubercle bacillus.

Isopropyl rubbing alcohol possesses some solvent and cleansing properties and acts as a lubricant. It is also used as a rubefacient and skin conditioner for bedridden patients. However, since isopropyl alcohol has greater fat-solvent effects than ethyl alcohol, repeated use has a drying effect on the skin.

See also the evaluation on Ethyl Alcohol.

METHOD OF APPLICATION.—*Topical.*

PREPARATIONS.—Isopropyl Alcohol, N.F., Isopropyl Rubbing Alcohol, N.F. Marketed under generic name.

CHLORINE AND CHLORINE-CONTAINING PREPARATIONS

Elemental chlorine is one of the most potent germicidal agents. It is poisonous to all living matter and is used to disinfect inanimate objects, water supplies, and, to a limited extent, tissues. Disinfection and antisepsis with chlorine is accomplished by using gas or chlorine-containing compounds that slowly release hypochlorous acid, which is rapidly bactericidal. The released hypochlorous acid not only acts on organic matter but is also destructive to normal tissues. The germicidal action of chlorine is decreased or nullified by organic matter and an alkaline pH.

As with other antiseptics, none of the chlorine-containing compounds is superior to thorough cleansing of wounds. All cause some injury to tissue protoplasm. They are used in infected wounds only when other methods or agents are not available.

Chlorine is used to disinfect swimming pools. It is not effective against poliomyelitis virus unless the residual chlorine content is maintained at a minimal concentration of 0.5 ppm. Chlorine may be used for disinfecting utensils, but it is not useful for disinfecting medical instruments because it is corrosive.

The commonly used chlorine-containing compounds are solutions of sodium hypochlorite.

SODIUM HYPOCHLORITE SOLUTION

Sodium hypochlorite solution is a potent germicide used to disinfect utensils. The undiluted solution contains approximately 5% sodium hypochlorite; it is irritating to tissues and therefore is not used as an antiseptic. Hypochlorite solution is sometimes used to disinfect swimming pools; it is effective against poliomyelitis virus when used in adequate quantities in the proper manner.

Accidental ingestion of sodium hypochlorite solution (as household bleach) by children is not uncommon. Irritation of the mucous membranes results in a burning sensation, but serious injury is unlikely because the solution is not corrosive; it seldom causes esophageal stenosis or similar complications. Vomiting usually occurs soon after ingestion but if it does not occur spontaneously, emetics or the cautious use of gastric lavage is recommended. The patient should be given water or milk orally to dilute the solution in the stomach. Aluminum hydroxide gel or milk of magnesia may also be given. Acids of any type should not be used in an attempt to neutralize the alkaline solution.

PREPARATIONS.—Sodium Hypochlorite Solution, N.F. Not available as a finished pharmaceutical preparation. Hypochlorite solutions are available as household bleach.

SODIUM HYPOCHLORITE SOLUTION, DILUTED (Modified Dakin's Solution)

This solution contains about 0.5% sodium hypochlorite adjusted to a neutral pH with sodium bicarbonate. It was once widely used to treat suppurating wounds, but its solvent action on sutures may lead to secondary hemorrhage.

METHOD OF APPLICATION.—*Topical:* Applied in concentrations from full strength to 1:4 dilution.

PREPARATIONS.—Diluted Sodium Hypochlorite Solution, N.F.

Additional Chlorine-Containing Compounds

Chloramine-T (Chlorazene [Badger])
Chloroazodine (Azochloramid [Pennwalt])
Oxychlorosene (Clorpactin XCB [Guardian])
Oxychlorosene Sodium (Clorpactin WCS-90 [Guardian])

IODINE COMPOUNDS

Solutions containing elemental iodine and iodine-releasing organic and inorganic compounds are used to disinfect the skin before surgical procedures and as an antiseptic on wounds. The antimicrobial effects of iodine are probably due to its iodinating and oxidizing effects on microbial protoplasm. The activity of iodine is reduced by alkaline substances and in the presence of organic matter.

Iodine is used to disinfect water when other methods are not available. Three drops of tincture of iodine added to one quart of water supposedly kills bacteria, amebae, and other forms of living matter within 15 minutes.

Strong Iodine Solution, U.S.P. (Lugol's solution) is used for the treatment of thyroid disorders, but not as an antiseptic (see Chapter 39, Thyroid Hormones and Antithyroid Agents).

Elemental and organic iodine solutions stain the skin and cause sensitivity in some individuals. Organic iodine compounds are less irritating, less toxic, and less apt to cause skin sensitization than inorganic solutions, but they are also generally less effective.

Solutions of iodine are occasionally taken with suicidal intent. The toxic effects of the elemental iodine in these solutions affect the gastrointestinal mucosa, where the iodine exerts local caustic effects. Abdominal pain, nausea, vomiting, and diarrhea may result. Suspensions of starch or protein or solutions of sodium thiosulfate may be used as an antidote.

These compounds should not be used in patients with known sensitivity to iodine. Systemic absorption may occur and interfere with the results of tests for protein-bound iodine.

IODINE SOLUTION

Iodine Solution, N.F. contains approximately 2% iodine and 2.5% sodium iodide in water. It is applied to superficial lacerations to prevent bacterial infections. The preparation should be kept in tight, light-resistant containers. Iodine Solution should not be confused with Strong Iodine Solution, U.S.P. (Lugol's solution), which is used in the treatment of thyroid disease.

Hypersensitivity reactions may occur after application of this solution.

METHOD OF APPLICATION.—*Topical:* Applied as a 2% solution.

PREPARATIONS.—Iodine Solution, N.F. No single-entity pharmaceutical dosage form available; compounding necessary for prescription.

IODINE TINCTURE

This is a 2% solution of elemental iodine with 2.5% sodium iodide in water and 44% to 50% alcohol. The concentration of alcohol in this tincture is irritating to wounds and does not contribute to the antibacterial action of the iodine. Consequently, the 2% aqueous solution is preferred to the tincture as an antiseptic.

METHOD OF APPLICATION.—*Topical.*

PREPARATIONS.—Iodine Tincture, U.S.P. Marketed under generic name.

IODOFORM

Iodoform, the iodinated analogue of chloroform, has little antibacterial activity itself, but iodine is slowly liberated by body secretions when iodoform is applied to the tissues. This antiseptic is used occasionally as a wound dressing: gauze impregnated with iodoform is packed in abscessed cavities and wounds. However, this preparation is not very effective.

METHOD OF APPLICATION.—*Topical:* Because it has little efficacy, its use is discouraged.

PREPARATIONS.—Iodoform, N.F. Marketed under generic name.

POVIDONE-IODINE [Betadine]

Povidone-iodine is an organic iodine and polyvinylpyrrolidone complex which slowly releases iodine. It is used as an antiseptic on skin and mucous membranes to prevent and control susceptible cutaneous infections, certain infections of the mouth and scalp, and for preoperative preparation of the skin. This preparation is somewhat less effective than aqueous and alcoholic solutions of elemental iodine, but it may be less irritating, less toxic, and nonsensitizing to the skin.

For other uses, see Chapter 64, Antitrichomonal Agents.

Local hypersensitivity reactions occur rarely; these are noted primarily in patients who are sensitive to iodine.

METHOD OF APPLICATION.—*Topical:* The appropriate preparation is applied to cutaneous and mucosal lesions as needed.

PREPARATIONS.—Betadine (Purdue Frederick). *Topical:* Aerosol spray 0.5% in 3 oz containers; gargle 0.1% in 6 and 12 oz containers; ointment 1% in 1 and 16 oz containers; shampoo 0.75% in 4 oz and 1 gal containers; skin cleanser 0.75% in 4 oz containers; solution 1% in ½, 8, 16, and 32 oz and 1 and 2½ gal containers; surgical scrub 0.75% in 16 and 32 oz and 1 and 2½ gal containers; vaginal douche 1% in 8 oz containers; vaginal gel 1% in 3 oz containers. (In all preparations, the percentage indicates the amount of available iodine.)

ADDITIONAL TRADEMARK.—Isodine (Purdue Frederick).

UNDECOYLIUM CHLORIDE-IODINE [Virac]

$$CH_3(CH_2)_nCOOCH_2CH_2NHCOCH_2N^+C_5H_5 \; Cl^- \cdot I_2$$

$n = 6-12$

This is a complex of iodine and a quaternary ammonium compound that gradually releases iodine upon contact with skin and mucous membranes. Undecoylium chloride-iodine is applied topically in the prophylaxis and treatment of surface infections caused by organisms known to be susceptible to the germicidal action of iodine. It is also used for preoperative, postoperative, and therapeutic antisepsis of the skin. Soap interferes with the action of this agent and should not be used concomitantly.

The local irritation associated with use of iodine tincture is rare with this compound. Local hypersensitivity reactions, although uncommon, have occurred. The preparation is contraindicated in persons with known sensitivity to iodine. Since it is irritating to the ocular tissues, contact with the eyes must be avoided.

METHOD OF APPLICATION.—*Topical:* The solution is applied as needed.

PREPARATIONS.—Virac (Chesebrough-Pond's). *Topical:* Solution containing 0.6% and 0.8% available elemental iodine in 2, 4, and 8 oz containers.

MERCURIAL COMPOUNDS

Various mercurial compounds have disinfectant and antiseptic actions, and several inorganic salts of mercury have been used as germicides. Mercuric chloride was one of the original salts used for these purposes. It prevents growth and kills some microorganisms in dilutions of 1:2,000 to 1:4,000. The disinfecting property of mercuric chloride is preserved in fatty vehicles, is enhanced by alcohol, and is reduced by the presence of chloride.

The soluble inorganic salts are not uniformly effective against bacteria. They are ineffective against spore-forming organisms such as *Clostridium tetani.*

Mercurial salts are poor antiseptics for use on abraded skin or open wounds, because the presence of serum and tissue proteins markedly reduces their antibacterial activity. Moreover, they are poisonous because the mercury is absorbed. Soluble salts of mercury are corrosive and therefore are not suitable for sterilizing instruments.

The toxic and caustic properties of inorganic mercury are reduced when the metal is incorporated in an organic compound. Some of the organic salts are more effective than inorganic ones, but alcohol alone has greater bactericidal action than mercurial tinctures.

Acute poisoning with suicidal intent, most often attempted by ingestion of soluble inorganic mercurial compounds, is characterized by injury to the gastrointestinal mucosa and signs of acute gastritis and colitis. Early symptoms include burning pain in the throat and stomach, nausea, retching, vomiting, and diarrhea. Ulceration and hemorrhage occur later. After systemic absorption, mercurials, especially the inorganic compounds, cause severe chemical nephrosis with albuminuria, oliguria, azotemia, and death from irreversible acute renal failure. Renal injury also may occur after prolonged exposure and absorption of small quantities of both inorganic and organic mercurials.

Dimercaprol (BAL) has been effective in treating mercury poisoning if therapy is begun within one or two hours after ingestion, but the extensive renal damage that occurs soon after mercury poisoning cannot be reversed. (See Chapter 90, Chelating Agents.)

NITROMERSOL [Metaphen]

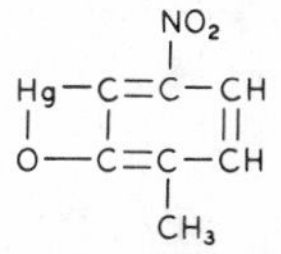

```
          NO2
          |
Hg—C═C—CH
|    |      ||
O—C═C—CH
          |
          CH3
```

This organic mercurial complex derived from mercuricresol is used as an antiseptic for topical application to the conjunctiva and to minor lacerations, abrasions, and wounds; for irrigation of the genitourinary tract; and for preoperative preparation of the skin. It is more effective than the soluble inorganic salts of mercury but less effective than alcohol. Unlike the inorganic salts, nitromersol does not precipitate protein and does not irritate the skin or mucous membranes. It is less likely to cause burns than iodine tincture when applied to scrotal or vulvar skin.

Nitromersol may cause hypersensitivity reactions.

METHOD OF APPLICATION.—*Topical.*

PREPARATIONS.—Metaphen (Abbott). *Topical:* Tincture 1:200 (tinted in acetone, alcohol, and water) in 1 and 16 oz and 1 gal containers.

PHENYLMERCURIC ACETATE [Nylmerate]
PHENYLMERCURIC NITRATE [Phe-Mer-Nite]

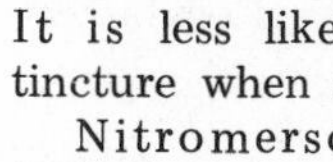

CH_3COOHg—C_6H_5 C_6H_5—HgOH · C_6H_5—$HgNO_3$

Phenylmercuric Acetate 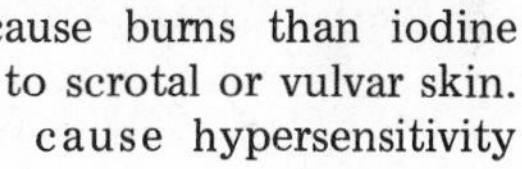   Phenylmercuric Nitrate

Hydrolysis of these salts releases the active phenylmercuric radical. When applied to the skin and mucous membranes, phenylmercuric salts inhibit the growth of gram-positive and gram-negative bacteria, *Trichomonas*, *Candida*, and dermatophytic fungi. However, they are less effective than alcohol. Their activity is unaffected by the presence of serum proteins and soaps. These drugs are claimed to be active against spore-forming organisms such as *Clostridium tetani* and *C. perfringens*, but their sporicidal effects are questionable.

The tincture of phenylmercuric nitrate is used as an antiseptic on the skin. The acetate is used in vaginal jellies and for vaginal irrigation to treat trichomonal, candidal, and nonspecific vaginitis (see Chapter 64, Antitrichomonal Agents). Phenylmercuric acetate is also added to ophthalmic solutions as a preservative.

Although properly diluted solutions are not irritating to tissues, rash due to hypersensitivity has been reported. Treatment should be discontinued if a rash develops or if the infection persists. Solutions should not be applied to extensive denuded areas for prolonged periods of time because enough mercury may be absorbed to cause serious systemic toxicity.

METHOD OF APPLICATION.—*Topical, including vaginal douche.*

PREPARATIONS.—

Phenylmercuric Acetate:

Nylmerate (Holland-Rantos). *Topical* (vaginal): Solution (concentrate) 0.2% in 8 and 16 oz containers; jelly 0.02% in 80 and 136 g containers.

Phenylmercuric Nitrate:

Phe-Mer-Nite (Beecham-Massengill). *Topical:* Tincture (in acetone, alcohol, and water mixture) 1:3,000 in 16 oz and 1 gal containers.

THIMEROSAL [Merthiolate]

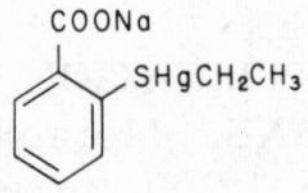

COONa
SHgCH$_2$CH$_3$

This organic mercurial has antibacterial and antifungal activity, but it is less effective than alcohol and is ineffective against spore-forming organisms. Thimerosal is applied as an aqueous solution, cream, or ointment to prevent infection in wounds; in lower concentrations it may be used on the mucous membranes of the nose, throat, and genitourinary tract. Tincture and aerosol preparations (both containing acetone, alcohol, and water) are used for the treatment of wound infections, cutaneous fungal infections (eg, tinea pedis), various pyodermal disorders, preoperative preparation of the skin, and postoperative wound care. Thimerosal (in a 1:10,000 concentration) is used to preserve plasma, serum, immune sera, vaccines, and other biological products.

The mercury ion is tightly bound in the organic complex; therefore, acute systemic toxicity has occurred only rarely. Prolonged use of thimerosal has occasionally resulted in chronic mercury poisoning. Ingestion of the tincture or solution may cause toxic reactions from the alcohol and acetone content of the tincture or the borate content of the solution. This agent is contraindicated in patients with known sensitivity to mercury.

METHOD OF APPLICATION.—*Topical:* Appropriate form is applied as needed. After application, the tincture should be permitted to dry before being covered by bandages or other occlusive dressings. If this is not done, the alcohol and acetone in the solvent may be irritating.

PREPARATIONS.—Merthiolate (Lilly). *Topical:* Aerosol 0.033% in 6 oz containers; cream 0.1% (1:1,000) in 1 oz containers; glycerite 1:1,000 in 1 gal containers; ointment 0.1% (1:1,000) in 1 oz containers; ointment (ophthalmic) 1:5,000 in 1/8 oz containers; solution 1:1,000 in 4 and 16 oz and 1 gal containers; tincture 1:1,000 (in alcohol, acetone, and water) in ¾, 4, and 16 oz and 1 gal containers. Drug also marketed under generic name.

MERBROMIN [Mercurochrome]

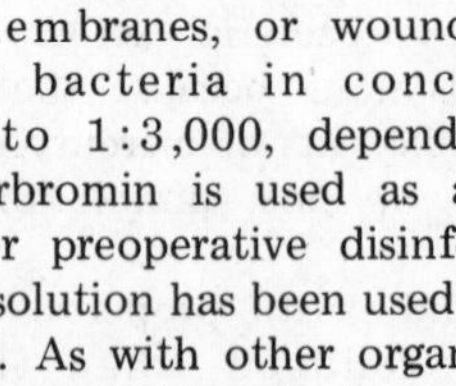

COONa
Br
Br
NaO
O
O
HOHg

This agent is less active than other organic mercurials and is nonirritating to the skin, mucous membranes, or wounds. It inhibits growth of bacteria in concentrations of 1:18,000 to 1:3,000, depending upon the species. Merbromin is used as a 2% aqueous solution for preoperative disinfection of the skin. A 1% solution has been used in the bladder and urethra. As with other organic mercurials, the action of merbromin is reduced by the presence of organic matter and body fluids.

METHOD OF APPLICATION.—*Topical.*

PREPARATIONS.—Mercurochrome (Hynson Westcott & Dunning). *Topical:* Powder; solution (aqueous) 2% in ½ oz containers.

SILVER COMPOUNDS

Soluble silver salts and colloidal silver preparations have been widely used as antiseptics on mucous membranes. However, with the exception of the nitrate, they have been replaced by more effective agents. Silver salts have slight penetrating powers because they are precipitated by the chloride ion present in the cells. The silver ion precipitates protein to produce an antiseptic effect.

Organic compounds containing silver (eg, mild silver protein) are less corrosive but their disinfecting properties do not equal those of the salts because less of the active free silver ion is available.

SILVER NITRATE

Silver nitrate is strongly bactericidal when applied topically in relatively low concentrations; most microorganisms are rapidly destroyed by a 1:1,000 solution, and a 1:10,000 solution is considered to be bacteriostatic. The astringent action of silver nitrate solutions may be useful therapeutically. Aqueous solutions of 1:3,000 to 1:10,000 have been administered for irrigation of the urethra and bladder, and concentrations up to 10% may be applied to treat infected ulcers in the mouth. Strong solutions (5% to 10%) are used to cauterize the mucous membranes.

In many states, instillation of two drops of a 1% or 2% solution into the conjunctival sac of newborn infants is required by law to prevent ophthalmia neonatorum. The solution should be rinsed from the eyes immediately with water (sodium chloride will precipitate silver ions) to prevent chemical conjunctivitis. (See Chapter 71, Anti-infective and Anti-inflammatory Agents Used in Ophthalmology.)

Aqueous solutions containing 0.5% silver nitrate are sometimes applied on dressings for second-degree and debrided third-degree burns to prevent infections caused by *Pseudomonas aeruginosa*, *Proteus*, and other gram-negative organisms. Some authorities consider silver nitrate safe and, if applied early, it will lessen evaporation of water and heat from the burn surface; others warn that loss of large amounts of sodium chloride into the dressing may cause electrolyte imbalance, particularly in infants. (See also Chapter 68, Dermatologic Agents.)

Toughened silver nitrate, a solid prepared in pencil form, is used to remove warts and granulomatous tissue and to cauterize wounds.

METHOD OF APPLICATION.—*Topical.*

PREPARATIONS.--Silver Nitrate, U.S.P. *Topical:* Solution (ophthalmic) 1%; crystals; applicators. Drug marketed under generic name.

Additional Silver Compounds

Silver Protein, Mild (Argyrol [Cooper])
Silver Iodide, Colloidal (Neo-Silvol [Parke, Davis])

SURFACE-ACTING AGENTS

Soaps and detergents play active roles in antisepsis and disinfection by acting as cleansing agents and removing bacteria from the skin. Soaps are anionic surface-acting agents because the effective part of the molecule carries a negative charge. A group of anti-infective detergents whose active portion of the molecule carries a positive charge are referred to as cationic agents.

The quaternary ammonium compounds are cationic surface-acting agents and are effective against both gram-positive and gram-negative bacteria. Gram-negative organisms, including strains of *Pseudomonas aeruginosa*, are more resistant and require longer exposure. Bacterial spores resist even prolonged contact. Aqueous solutions of these compounds are not tuberculocidal.

The keratolytic action of quaternary ammonium compounds aids in the removal of desquamating epithelial cells. These agents also emulsify sebaceous material, which is then removed together with dirt and bacteria. However, the quaternary ammonium compounds tend to be deposited on the skin as an invisible film that is sterile on the outer surface but under which bacteria may remain alive. These compounds are inactivated by soaps, inorganic matter, and, on a mole for mole basis, anionic substances. The mode of action of quaternary ammonium compounds is not yet fully understood but has been ascribed to alteration of cellular membranes, the denaturing of lipoprotein complexes, and possibly other actions.

The quaternary ammonium compounds are inactivated when water deionized by resins is used to prepare the solutions or when cotton fabrics, cellulose sponges, certain plastics (particularly polyvinyl chloride), or other porous materials are immersed in the solution. The surface-acting agents are adsorbed by these materials. For this reason, these agents are of uncertain efficacy in cold sterilization of catheters, flexible endoscopes, or other instruments.

BENZALKONIUM CHLORIDE [Zephiran Chloride]

Benzalkonium, the prototype of the quaternary ammonium compounds, is active against gram-positive and gram-negative bacteria, some fungi (including yeasts), and certain protozoa (eg, *Trichomonas vaginalis*), but aqueous solutions are ineffective against *Mycobacterium tuberculosis*, *Clostridium* species, and other spore-forming bacteria and viruses. It acts rapidly and may be used preoperatively to disinfect intact skin and mucous membranes, and applied to minor lacerations, wounds, and abrasions to prevent infection. Like other cationic detergents, benzalkonium is inactivated by soap and other anionic substances; therefore, soap should be thoroughly rinsed from the skin with water and 70% alcohol before benzalkonium is applied. The sterility of sterilized surgical instruments and other articles may be maintained by keeping them submerged in benzalkonium solution. The addition of an antirust agent containing sodium nitrite is recommended to retard corrosion of metallic instruments stored in solutions of benzalkonium; solutions should be checked periodically for contamination by resistant bacteria and spores.

Accidental contact with concentrated solutions can produce corrosive skin lesions with deep necrosis and scarring. Properly diluted solutions are not ordinarily irritating or sensitizing, although dilute solutions under occlusive dressings or under casts or packs may irritate the skin with prolonged exposure. Caution is suggested when irrigating body cavities with benzalkonium, as systemic absorption may cause muscle weakness.

METHOD OF APPLICATION.—*Topical:* For use on intact skin, minor wounds, and abrasions, 1:750 tincture or aqueous solutions. For use on mucous membranes and broken or diseased skin, 1:20,000 to 1:5,000 aqueous solution. For storage of instruments, 1:750 to 1:5,000 aqueous solution with four antirust tablets per quart (to be changed at least once a week).

PREPARATIONS.—Zephiran Chloride (Winthrop). *Topical:* Solution (aqueous concentrate) 17% in 4 oz and 1 gal containers and 1:750 in 8 oz and 1 gal containers; tincture (spray) 1:750 in 1 and 6 oz containers; tincture 1:750 (tinted) in 8 oz and 1 gal containers.

ADDITIONAL TRADEMARKS.—Benasept (Blue Line), Germicin (Consolidated Midland), Pheneen (Ulmer). Drug also marketed under generic name.

BENZETHONIUM CHLORIDE [Phemerol Chloride]

This cationic antiseptic has a spectrum of action and degree of effectiveness similar to that of benzalkonium chloride. See the evaluation on Benzalkonium Chloride.

METHOD OF APPLICATION.—*Topical.*

PREPARATIONS.—Phemerol Chloride (Parke, Davis). *Topical:* Solution 1:750 in 1 gal containers; solution 3% in 1 gal containers [Phemerol Topical]; tincture 1:500 in 1 gal containers. Drug also marketed under generic name.

METHYLBENZETHONIUM CHLORIDE [Diaparene]

This cationic antiseptic and disinfectant is effective against gram-positive and gram-negative organisms, including those that split urea to form ammonia. Methylbenzethonium is commonly used as a rinse for diapers and for bed linen and underclothes of incontinent adults to prevent ammonia dermatitis; articles should be free of soap to avoid inactivation of the antiseptic. It also is applied topically as a dusting powder around genitalia, rectum, thighs, and intertriginous areas for the prevention and treatment of perianal dermatitis, miliaria rubra, and intertrigo. Methylbenzethonium seldom produces irritation and has a low sensitizing potential.

METHOD OF APPLICATION.—*Topical:* Appropriate form applied as needed.

PREPARATIONS.—Diaparene (Breon). *Topical:* Cream 1:1,000 in 1, 2, 4, and 16 oz containers; dusting powder 1:1,800 in 4, 9, and 12½ oz containers; granules (for solution) 6%; lotion 1:1,500 in 5 oz containers; ointment 1:1,000 in 1, 2, 4, and 16 oz containers; tablets (for solution).

OXIDIZING DISINFECTANTS

The peroxides, permanganates, and cholates release nascent oxygen which is germicidal. Hydrogen peroxide is the most important of the peroxides. Others are sodium peroxide, which is the sodium analogue of hydrogen peroxide, and zinc peroxide. Sodium peroxide is used for dermatologic conditions, such as acne, but its usefulness is limited because its end product, sodium hydroxide, is caustic. Zinc peroxide is used in treating infections caused by microaerophilic and anaerobic organisms.

Potassium permanganate is a vigorous oxidizing agent that is rapidly decomposed in the presence of organic matter. Its use as an antiseptic is obsolete. Potassium chlorate, in a 2% and 4% solution, has been used as a mouthwash and gargle for infections of the mouth and throat. It is potentially toxic and of questionable value, and therefore should not be used.

HYDROGEN PEROXIDE

When hydrogen peroxide comes in contact with catalase, an enzyme found in blood and most tissues, it is rapidly decomposed into oxygen and water. The liberated oxygen has some bactericidal effect. The presence of organic matter in wounds reduces this effect. The duration of action of hydrogen peroxide lasts no longer than the period of decomposition during which oxygen is liberated. Hydrogen peroxide is useful in loosening masses of infected material through the mechanical action of liberating oxygen, and in many instances a wound or cavity may be more thoroughly cleaned than by washing with sodium chloride solution or other disinfectants. When diluted with one or more parts of water, it sometimes is used as a gargle, mouthwash, or vaginal douche. Its use in stomatitis and gingivitis may irritate the tongue and buccal mucosa. Hydrogen peroxide 3% is often instilled in the external ear to aid in removal of cerumen (see Chapter 73, Topical Otic Preparations).

The release of oxygen from hydrogen peroxide on the skin is a very slow process and its use on the intact skin is of doubtful value, but decomposition proceeds at a rapid rate when the agent comes into contact with wounds or mucous membranes. Hydrogen peroxide should never be instilled in a closed body cavity or abscesses from which the gas has no free egress. Hemiplegia has been reported following its use to irrigate the pleural cavity, presumably due to passage of the gas into the vascular system resulting in cerebral embolism.

METHOD OF APPLICATION.—*Topical.*

PREPARATIONS.—*Topical:* Solution 3%. Marketed by many manufacturers under generic name.

BORON COMPOUNDS

Boric acid is a weak acid that has been used as a mild topical antiseptic and eyewash. Borax, the sodium salt of tetraboric acid, is alkaline in aqueous solution and sometimes is used as a disinfectant. Sodium perborate has been used as a cleansing agent, mouthwash, and dentifrice because of its strong oxidizing properties, but its effectiveness is questionable and it is seldom used in present day therapeutics.

BORIC ACID

Boric acid is a weak acid that forms an alkaline sodium salt in solution. A 2.5% solution inhibits growth but does not destroy many forms of bacteria. Boric acid is of little value as a disinfectant but has been used as an antiseptic, particularly as an eyewash. However, since boric acid is of doubtful therapeutic value and fatalities following accidental ingestion or indiscriminate use have been reported, it has no useful place in modern medicine.

This agent produces little or no local irritation. Symptoms of boric acid poisoning include nausea, vomiting, diarrhea, exfoliative dermatitis, headache, restlessness, kidney damage, and acute circulatory failure. Since poisoning may occur from its absorption from burned or denuded areas of skin, boric acid should not be applied to large areas or for prolonged periods. It should not be used to irrigate the bladder or closed body cavities. Solutions should be colored to avoid mistaken identity and accidental ingestion, and containers should be labeled "Poison."

METHOD OF APPLICATION.—This preparation should not be used because of the reasons stated above. A commonly suggested method of application is: *Topical:* A 4% solution or ointment is applied as required.

PREPARATIONS.—Boric Acid. *Topical:* Crystals; ointment 10%; powder; solution 5%. Marketed under generic name.

PHENOLIC COMPOUNDS

Phenols and substituted phenols are all general protoplasmic poisons. In dilute solutions, phenol acts as an antiseptic and disinfectant but its activity varies greatly with the species of microbe. It is used chiefly to disinfect instruments and to cauterize ulcers and infected areas of the skin.

Phenol is bacteriostatic in concentrations of 1:500 to 1:800, and bactericidal and fungicidal in concentrations of 1:50 to 1:100. It is ineffective against spores. Although phenol precipitates and denatures protein, its antibacterial activity continues in the presence of protein. It subsequently becomes freed from the combination and continues to penetrate into sputum, excreta, and other organic materials.

Phenol possesses minor topical local anesthetic activity and is claimed to have an antipruritic effect when added to dermatologic preparations in concentrations of 1:100 to 1:200. Dilute solutions up to 1% are used in mouthwashes but their efficacy is doubtful. Aqueous solutions stronger than 2% are too irritating for topical application. Concentrations of 1:10 to 1:20 in oil and glycerin have been injected into hemorrhoids to obtain a sclerosing effect, and used in neurologic procedures for relief of pain, but these high concentrations may penetrate deeply and cause extensive damage to tissues. Camphorated parachlorophenol is used as an antiseptic on the gums.

The cresols are methyl derivatives of phenol. They are less irritating and less toxic than phenol, and supposedly have a more powerful antiseptic action. The halogenated phenols also are more effective antimicrobial agents than phenol. Phenolic compounds are used principally for disinfecting inanimate objects; they are too caustic and toxic for use on living tissue. Phenol and the cresols should never be used to disinfect rubber, plastic, or fabrics or other objects that may absorb the agent, because burns may result when these come into contact with the skin.

Phenol has been largely replaced by safer and more effective antiseptics and disinfectants and is now mainly of historical interest.

HEXACHLOROPHENE

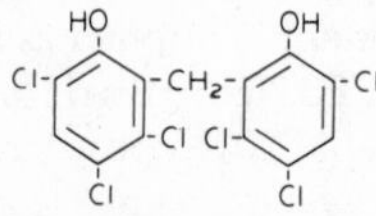

HO OH
Cl- -CH₂- -Cl
-Cl Cl-
Cl Cl

This chlorinated bisphenol compound has strong bacteriostatic activity. It appears to be particularly effective against gram-positive bacteria, including staphylococci. Hexachlorophene is insoluble in water, but has been incorporated in soaps, lotions, ointments, creams, and shampoos.

An emulsion containing hexachlorophene 3% with a detergent (eg, pHisoHex) may be more efficient as a cleansing and antiseptic agent than the same concentration in soap solution. This emulsion is used for handwashing by hospital personnel, preoperatively as a surgical hand scrub, and for preparation of the skin in the operative field. Although single washings of the skin are no more effective than soap in reducing bacterial count, regularly repeated scrubs leave a residual film on the skin that causes a steady decrease in bacterial flora. Alcohol removes the antibacterial residue, but the areas may be painted with antiseptic solutions after washing and rinsing with water.

Hexachlorophene is not irritating to the skin with ordinary use, and hypersensitivity reactions are relatively rare. However, since preparations may cause a burning sensation on the skin and in the eyes, suds containing this agent should be rinsed promptly from the eyes with water.

Significant absorption resulting in neurotoxic effects occurs if hexachlorophene is applied to burned or denuded skin or any mucous membranes. Hexachlorophene is best avoided in premature infants, since it can be absorbed from their unbroken skin. Its use on the skin of full-term infants, children, and adults should be followed by thorough rinsing. Cardiovascular disturbances, convulsions, and respiratory arrest have been reported following accidental ingestion of hexachlorophene detergent emulsion by young children or application of high concentration (6%) to children.

Hexachlorophene should not be used routinely to bathe infants. However, its use may be considered as part of a total program in the control of a hospital nursery infection; the use of a 1% to 3% hexachlorophene preparation for short-term, once daily bathing followed by rinsing may be useful prophylactically in such a program.

METHOD OF APPLICATION.—*Topical.*

PREPARATIONS.—Hexachlorophene, U.S.P. (See Chapter 68, Dermatologic Agents, for listing of available preparations.)

Additional Phenol or Phenol-like Compounds

Chlorothymol
Creosote
Cresol
Cresol Solution, Saponated

ALDEHYDES

FORMALDEHYDE SOLUTION

Formaldehyde is a potent, volatile germicide that has been used both in vapor form and as a 10% solution in water (formalin). The vapor is irritating when inhaled. Formaldehyde is used only in emergencies to disinfect instruments and laboratories contaminated with viruses.

PREPARATIONS.—Formaldehyde Solution, U.S.P. Marketed under generic name.

GLUTARAL [Cidex]

$OCH(CH_2)_3CHO$

Glutaral is a dialdehyde with a wide range of biocidal activity. It is rapidly sporicidal and possesses tuberculocidal action. A 2% aqueous solution buffered with 0.3% sodium carbonate to a pH of 7.5 to 8.5 is useful for the disinfection and sterilization of endosccpic instruments and plastic and rubber apparatus used for inhalation therapy and anesthesia. Cost and lack of stability are prime drawbacks to its use. Glutaral loses activity within two weeks after preparation. It is not used on living tissues.

PREPARATIONS.—Cidex (Arbrook). *Topical:* Solution (aqueous) 2%.

Chapter 68

DERMATOLOGIC AGENTS

A wide variety of compounds are used both systemically and topically in the treatment or prevention of skin disorders. Dermatologic agents described in this chapter include vehicles, single-entity agents, and some widely used dermatologic mixtures. Drugs used for other purposes are discussed elsewhere: see Chapters 18, Local Anesthetics; 35, Adrenal Corticosteroids; 45, Antihistamines; 57, Aminoglycoside Antibacterial Agents and Miscellaneous Antimicrobial Drugs; 59, Antileprosy Agents; 60, Antifungal Agents; 66, Scabicides and Pediculicides; 67, Antiseptics and Disinfectants; 82, Anorectal Preparations; 88, Antineoplastic Agents; and 91, Enzymes Used as Drugs.

VEHICLES AND PHARMACEUTIC AIDS

A vehicle is usually required to incorporate and dilute the active ingredient so that it may be applied to the skin. Although vehicles are generally pharmacologically inert, the choice of a proper carrier is important because its water content or its ability to affect cutaneous water loss influences the overall activity of the finished product; there is great variation in the manner in which a vehicle holds, releases, or assists in the absorption of the active ingredient. In addition, a vehicle must be suitable for use on the portion of the skin for which it is intended (eg, hairy areas, eyelids, groin, mucocutaneous junctions, palms, and soles differ in thickness of epidermis, number and activity of sweat and sebaceous glands, and susceptibility to maceration because of juxtaposition of tissues), and must be suitable for the age of the patient and magnitude of the area to be treated.

Vehicles may be categorized according to their ability to influence the drying or lubrication of affected skin as tinctures, wet dressings, lotions, liniments, powders, pastes, creams, ointments, and oils.

Pharmacists and pharmaceutical manufacturers often must compound mixtures of immiscible liquids such as oil-in-water preparations. Dispersing or emulsifying agents, surfactants, and detergents are used to provide homogeneous, stable preparations. Glyceryl monostearate, polyethylene glycol derivatives (polyoxyl 40 stearate, polysorbate 80), and sodium lauryl sulfate are examples of common constituents of creams, ointments, and soaps containing oily ingredients and water. Spermaceti, a white waxy material consisting mainly of cetyl esters of palmitic acid, is widely used to improve the consistency and appearance of immiscible liquid preparations such as creams. Stearic acid and stearyl alcohol added to creams also act as lubricants, emollients, or antifoaming agents. Methylcellulose and gum tragacanth are inert substances often used as suspending agents in ointments and pastes. The parabens (methylparaben and propylparaben) often are used as preservatives.

Water, ethyl alcohol, and isopropyl alcohol serve not only as vehicles but also as therapeutic agents (see the section on Wet Dressings and Chapter 67, Antiseptics and Disinfectants).

Water is used as a vehicle in lotions, as a moistening agent in creams, or as a bath to restore the normal hydration of the skin. When applied in the form of a hot or cold compress, water increases or decreases skin temperature or macerates the superficial layer of the skin to promote penetration. The alcohols are used to cool the skin and, in varying concentrations, as vehicles for antiseptic, astringent, and rubefacient solutions and lotions.

Glycerin is used as a solvent and emollient in lotions, creams, and pastes, and it is miscible with both water and alcohol.

Preparations containing silicone are limited in their ability to repel water and insulate the skin against contact irritants. Silicone is incorporated into creams, ointments, or sprays, and such preparations can be used on intact skin and, occasionally, on inflamed skin; however, they should not be applied to large areas, to weeping or infected areas, or near the eyes.

Most of these agents are innocuous; however, the parabens have rarely caused sensitivity reactions. Sodium lauryl sulfate increases the permeability of the stratum corneum not only to medicaments but also to noxious agents, and thus may directly or indirectly produce irritation.

WET DRESSINGS

Pruritus in the presence of an acute dermatitis is best alleviated by immersion of the part or the entire body in water for one-half hour or longer. By altering the temperature of the skin, a new sensation is substituted for the itching. Cooling the skin diminishes pruritus safely and effectively in most cases.

Water is the most important ingredient in open wet dressings. In addition to providing evaporative cooling, water also may cleanse and help drain exudates. The vasoconstriction resulting from cooling also combats the first stage of an acute inflammatory response. However, these effects are lost if the wet dressing is occluded by wrapping or covering with plastic or rubber.

Various ingredients such as potassium permanganate, aluminum acetate, or colloidal starch may be added to the water used in baths or wet dressings to contribute a mild antibacterial, astringent, or other action, but the disadvantages of these agents usually outweigh the benefits (see Chapter 67, Antiseptics and Disinfectants). Boric acid, phenol, and cresol should not be used because of their toxicity.

An 0.85% sodium chloride solution is physiologic and is useful for diseased and damaged skin, since no transfer of water into or out of the tissue occurs; more concentrated solutions irritate damaged tissues. Unbroken skin, on the other hand, does not behave as an osmotic membrane; therefore, saturated solutions of sodium chloride or magnesium sulfate do not reduce edema by abstracting water from the skin. As the water evaporates from saline wet dressings, the salt concentration increases and precipitates on the skin, causing irritation.

When baths are used to hydrate the skin for relief of pruritus or dryness, use of an emollient is desirable to keep the skin smooth and moist.

Closed hot wet dressings, changed frequently, soften and macerate the skin surface. They are useful in accelerating the localization and draining of lesions such as furuncles and abscesses, but they should not be used for other types of inflammatory skin disease.

VLEMINCKX SOLUTION [Vlem-Dome]

This sulfurated lime solution is one of the more effective topical preparations used for treatment of severe pustular or cystic acne. It must be freshly prepared.

Vleminckx solution has a disagreeable odor and causes temporary redness and peeling. It may stain some metals (eg, silver, copper) black but does not affect nickel or chrome-plated objects.

METHOD OF APPLICATION.—*Wet Dressings:* Compresses, soaked in a solution prepared by adding 4 ml of liquid concentrate to 500 ml of hot water, are applied for 10 to 20 minutes once daily.

PREPARATIONS.—Vlem-Dome (Dome). *Topical:* Stable liquid concentrate in 4 ml containers. Mixture also marketed under generic name and as individual components for compounding by pharmacists.

ETHYL ALCOHOL
ISOPROPYL ALCOHOL

These alcohols have antipruritic activity due to their cooling effect as well as antiseptic activity (see the introduction to this section and Chapter 67, Antiseptics and Disinfectants). The cooling effect is the result of their volatility. Their descending order of effectiveness is ethyl alcohol, isopropyl alcohol, and water.

Alcohol may irritate inflamed or denuded tissue. Application of an emollient preparation after an alcohol rub helps alleviate the dry feeling of the skin.

METHOD OF APPLICATION.—*Topical.*

PREPARATIONS.—Ethyl Alcohol; Alcohol, U.S.P.; Diluted Alcohol, U.S.P.; Rubbing Alcohol, N.F.; Isopropyl Alcohol, N.F.; Isopropyl Rubbing Alcohol, N.F. Marketed under generic name.

SILVER NITRATE

Silver nitrate solutions are successfully used in the form of wet dressings for antisepsis and to promote protein coagulation in the treatment of second-degree burns and deeper ulcerations.

The most important side effect of silver nitrate therapy is depletion of chloride, due to precipitation of insoluble silver chloride; this is particularly likely to occur if silver nitrate is applied to extensive areas over prolonged periods. Silver nitrate stains the skin black. Small amounts may be absorbed through the skin over prolonged periods resulting in argyria, a permanent bluish-black discoloration of the skin (only one case of argyria has been reported in association with burn therapy). Pain lasting one-half to one hour after application of dressings is common if the concentration of silver nitrate exceeds 0.5% and is occasionally noted with lower concentrations.

METHOD OF APPLICATION.—*Wet Dressings:* All loose skin, debris, oil, and grease must be removed from the surface of the burn. Dressings must remain moist with the solution (0.25% to 0.5%) and changed once or twice daily.

PREPARATIONS.—Silver Nitrate, U.S.P. *Topical:* Crystals for solution. Drug marketed under generic name.

LOTIONS

The term lotion (sometimes called "shake lotion") refers to a suspension of powder in a liquid medium (most frequently water) that requires shaking before application.

Lotions containing anti-inflammatory agents are useful in the management of intertriginous or widespread eruptions; they provide a protective, drying, or cooling effect. A basic white "shake lotion" suitable for anti-inflammatory use contains zinc oxide, talc, glycerin, and water. Calamine may be added to give a flesh tint to the mixture. In addition to the insoluble ingredients, menthol, alcohol, or water-dispersible oils may be added.

A great variety of lotions are commercially available for the treatment of acne. They are designed to cause peeling and drying and vary in effectiveness. Many contain an antibacterial agent, low percentages of salicylic acid, resorcinol, and sulfur, as well as tinted inert powders, a vehicle, and some pleasantly scented material.

BENZOYL PEROXIDE [Benoxyl, Oxy-5, Persadox, Vanoxide]

Benzoyl peroxide is an effective drying agent that causes redness and peeling. It is added to clear or tinted creamy solutions or creams in concentrations of 5% to 10%. Such preparations are sometimes useful in treating acne. They must be fresh because the peroxide is inactivated gradually.

Marked irritation occurs from overuse. Fair-skinned individuals react more violently than those with dark complexions. It should be borne in mind that benzoyl peroxide is a potent contact sensitizer that has other uses (eg, as an ingredient in plastics).

METHOD OF APPLICATION.—*Topical:* Cream or lotion is applied for 15 minutes the first evening, and then is removed with soap and water. The length of exposure is increased by increments of 15 minutes each evening thereafter until the preparation is tolerated for two hours. The preparation then may be left on overnight and washed off in the morning.

PREPARATIONS.—

Benoxyl (Stiefel). *Topical:* Lotion 5% and 10% in 1 and 2 oz containers.

Oxy-5 (USV). *Topical:* Lotion 5% in 1 oz containers.

Persadox (Texas). *Topical:* Cream and lotion 5% in 1 oz containers.

Vanoxide (Dermik). *Topical:* Lotion 5% with 0.25% halquinols in 25 g containers.

TRETINOIN [Aberel, Retin-A]

Tretinoin is the all-trans configuration of retinoic (vitamin A) acid. It is used topically in a polyethylene glycol-ethyl alcohol lotion for the treatment of acne vulgaris, particularly when comedones, papules, and pustules predominate.

This agent is a potent irritant: within 48 hours the skin may become red and begin to peel. One daily application of tretinoin maintains this peeling process which forces epidermal sloughing and prevents blockage of follicles. This process may aggravate acne during the first six weeks of therapy, but good results after three or four months of use are claimed.

The amount and frequency of application should be adjusted to limit the untoward effects associated with irritation while maintaining the peeling action. This agent should not be used on eczematous skin or in patients with a recent history of atopic dermatitis. Contact with the corners of the mouth, nose, eyes, or mucous membranes must be avoided. The patient should avoid exposure to sunlight or sunlamps, concomitant use of other peeling preparations, and the use of after-shave lotions or colognes in the areas in which the preparation is applied. The number of face washings should be limited to three a day.

METHOD OF APPLICATION.—*Topical:* One swab daily before retiring is applied to the skin where acne lesions appear, or the liquid is applied once daily (using fingertips, gauze pad, or cotton swab) before retiring.

PREPARATIONS.—

Aberel (McNeil). *Topical:* Lotion 0.05% in swab form or in 2 oz containers.

Retin-A (Johnson & Johnson). *Topical:* Cream 0.1%; lotion 0.05% in swab form or in 2 oz containers.

WHITE LOTION [Lotioblanc]

White lotion contains zinc sulfate, sulfurated potash, and water and must not be confused with white *shake* lotion. It is sometimes useful for treating mild acne. This preparation has an unpleasant odor and may cause excessive drying and redness of the skin.

METHOD OF APPLICATION.—*Topical:* Applied one or two times daily.

PREPARATIONS.—

Lotioblanc (Arnar-Stone). *Topical:* Stable lotion in 4 oz container.

White Lotion, N.F. (Formerly known as Lotio Alba.) Individual components marketed under generic name for compounding by a pharmacist. Mixture is unstable after three to four weeks of storage.

POWDERS

Zinc oxide, zinc stearate, magnesium stearate, talc, corn starch, bentonite, and titanium dioxide are applied to the skin as dusting powders or in pastes and shake lotions. Their action is primarily mechanical; they increase evaporation, reduce friction, and provide antipruritic and cooling sensations.

Zinc oxide and talc (mainly hydrous magnesium silicate) are protective and absorb some water when applied as a paste in a petrolatum base. Zinc oxide mixed with a small amount of ferric oxide has a pink color; the mixture, calamine, is used in shake lotions. Bentonite (hydrated aluminum silicate) combines with water to form a gel, although it is insoluble in water; it also improves the dispersion of zinc oxide and sulfur in oil-in-water mixtures. Titanium dioxide is opaque and is used in lotions or pastes as a sunscreen.

Precipitated calcium carbonate is a fine white powder that is insoluble in alcohol and water; it gives a dry sensation to the skin and is more absorbent than talc. Starch may be broken down by certain organisms and cause an overgrowth of *Candida albicans*, but this is rare. Talc is capable of causing severe granulomatous reactions when applied to wounds.

OINTMENTS, CREAMS, AND PASTES

These semisolid preparations usually contain pharmacologically active substances. Ointments are greasier than creams or pastes and contain little or no water. They may be of mineral, vegetable, animal, or synthetic origin. Ideally, ointment bases should have a low index of skin sensitization and a pH range of 5.5 to 7, and they should be nontoxic and of uniform consistency. The ingredients should be stable and compatible with each other and with the particular bases to which they are added. Ointment bases may be used alone for their emollient and protective properties.

Creams consist of emulsions of oil and water. The emulsions may contain either droplets of oil in water (water-removable base) or droplets of water in oil (absorption base). The former is more hydrating and less greasy than the latter; however, the absorption base provides more lubrication. Other substances such as spermaceti and sodium borate are frequently added to improve the emulsification, cosmetic appearance, and texture of the preparations.

Simple pastes are made by incorporating a finely divided powder into an ointment base. True pastes contain as much as 50% powder. The resulting mixture protects the skin against external irritants and sunlight. Pastes generally are poor vehicles for delivering active pharmacologic agents to the skin; an exception is a tar-paste mixture in which the paste may reduce any irritant properties of the tar. The ointment base used is usually petrolatum, and the powder is zinc oxide, talc, starch, bentonite, aluminum oxide, or titanium dioxide. Titanium dioxide has particularly good sun screening properties. Coloring matter may be added to make the mixture cosmetically acceptable. A paste containing zinc oxide, talc, and petrolatum in a 1:1:2 ratio is an example of a simple protective paste. Pastes are used in subacute and chronic dermatoses, particularly in infants, but generally should be avoided in weeping lesions and hairy areas.

Generally the more chronic and scaly the lesion, the more an ointment-type preparation is indicated. If the range of an acute weeping lesion to a chronic lichenified state can be considered a spectrum, the order of preferable treatment would be compresses, lotions, creams, and ointments.

ABSORBENT OINTMENT BASES

These bases consist of mixtures of oleaginous materials with emulsifying agents but essentially no water. They are insoluble in water but will take it up. They are difficult to wash off and will not dry out. Examples include hydrophilic petrolatum and anhydrous lanolin.

Hydrophilic petrolatum is composed of white petrolatum, cholesterol, stearyl alcohol, and white wax. It is less greasy than petrolatum but more greasy than hydrophilic ointment, and is often cosmetically more acceptable to patients than petrolatum.

Anhydrous lanolin, an oleaginous substance obtained from the wool of sheep, contains less than 0.25% water but is capable of taking up large amounts of water. It is an ingredient of commercial ointments and some bath oil preparations.

METHOD OF APPLICATION.—*Topical.*

PREPARATIONS.—

Aquaphor (Duke). *Topical:* Ointment base in 2 and 16 oz containers.

Polysorb (Fougera). *Topical:* Ointment base in 1 lb containers.

Qualatum (Schieffelin). *Topical:* Ointment base in 4 and 16 oz containers.

Velvachol (Texas). *Topical:* Ointment base in 1 lb containers.

Hydrophilic Petrolatum and Anhydrous Lanolin are marketed by many manufacturers under their generic names.

EMULSION OINTMENT BASES

Bases of this class are either water-in-oil or oil-in-water emulsions. The oleaginous phase may contain petrolatum, fats, organic alcohols, or other grease-like substances. Both types of bases are insoluble in water but will take it up. The water-in-oil type (eg, lanolin) is difficult to wash off, whereas the oil-in-water type (eg, hydrophilic ointment, so-called vanishing creams) washes off fairly readily.

Hydrophilic ointment contains white petrolatum, stearyl alcohol, and propylene glycol in water along with emulsifying agents and preservatives; it is a good vehicle for water-soluble medicaments. It has good esthetic properties and its texture imparts a pleasant sensation to the skin.

Cold cream is a water-in-mineral oil emulsion (absorption base) that also contains white wax, spermaceti, and sodium borate. It has lubricating qualities, provides some water for hydration of the epidermis, is an excellent vehicle for the incorporation of many medicaments, and has some cooling activity. Cold creams similar to the above formulation are widely used as vehicles.

METHOD OF APPLICATION.—*Topical.*

PREPARATIONS.—

Acid Mantle (Dome). *Topical:* Cream in 1, 4, and 16 oz containers; lotion in 4 and 16 oz containers.

Cetaphil (Texas). *Topical:* Lotion and cream ointment base in 16 oz containers.

Emulsion Base (Schieffelin). *Topical:* Emulsion in 16 oz containers.

Eucerin (Duke). *Topical:* Cream in 16 oz containers.

Lubriderm (Texas). *Topical:* Cream in 1½ and 4 oz containers; lotion in 4 and 8 oz containers.

NeoBase (Burroughs Wellcome). *Topical:* Ointment base in 16 oz containers.

Nivea (Duke). *Topical:* Cream in 1, 2, 2 1/3, 7, and 16 oz containers.

Unibase (Parke, Davis). *Topical:* Ointment base in 16 oz containers.

Cold Cream, U.S.P., Lanolin, Hydrophilic Ointment, and Rose Water Ointment marketed under their generic names.

OLEAGINOUS OINTMENT BASES

These bases consist of hydrophobic hydrocarbons or fats; some are synthetic mixtures with waxes. They are anhydrous, insoluble in water, and will take up little or no water themselves. They are difficult to wash off, will not dry out, and change little with the passing of time (although some may become rancid on aging). Examples of this type of base are petrolatum and lard.

Petrolatum, the most important agent of this group, is a purified mixture of hydrocarbons of high molecular weight obtained from petroleum. It varies in color (yellow to light amber), composition, and consistency depending upon the petroleum source and manner of preparation. White petrolatum, a bleached form of yellow petrolatum, is more esthetically pleasing and, therefore, is the form most commonly used. Petrolatum is protective and emollient when applied to the skin and makes an excellent base or vehicle for topical medicaments.

White ointment is white petrolatum with 5% white wax added. This preparation is firmer at room temperature than petrolatum.

METHOD OF APPLICATION.—*Topical.*

PREPARATIONS.—Petrolatum, White Petrolatum, and White Ointment marketed under their generic names.

WATER-SOLUBLE OINTMENT BASES

Water-soluble bases are greaseless and anhydrous. They not only take up water, but actually are soluble in water. An example is polyethylene glycol ointment.

METHOD OF APPLICATION.—*Topical.*

PREPARATIONS.—Polyethylene Glycol Ointment, U.S.P. Marketed under generic name.

AVAILABLE TRADEMARK.—Carbowax (Union Carbide Corporation, Doak).

SOAPS AND SOAP SUBSTITUTES

Ordinary soaps are sodium or potassium salts of fatty acids. In solution, they are strongly alkaline (pH 9 to 10) and may be irritating to damaged skin. Badly irritated skin should not be exposed to any detergent, soap, or cleanser other than water.

Several soap or soap-like preparations available commercially have a pH of 7.5 or slightly less. Other soaps are superfatted in order to reduce their alkalinity. It has never been established that these products are less irritating than regular sodium or potassium soaps.

Germistatic soaps are used widely because they are promoted as deodorants. Little, if anything, is gained by substituting a germistatic soap or detergent for ordinary soap, and some ingredients in these formulations can be harmful. For example, certain antibacterial agents (eg, halogenated salicylanilides) may cause photosensitization and are best avoided. Similarly, there is little evidence to support the use of other kinds of medicinal agents in soap.

Hexachlorophene has been widely used in germistatic soaps, either alone or combined with additional ingredients such as salicylic acid, sulfur, or tar. (See also Chapter 67, Antiseptics and Disinfectants.) This agent is readily absorbed. It can cause a contact dermatitis in susceptible individuals or with repeated application in high concentrations, and central nervous system toxicity if it is used on mucous membranes or over large dermatitic areas. When hexachlorophene is used in infants or to clean small areas of pyoderma, the residue should be rinsed off thoroughly. Hexachlorophene should not be applied in the form of compresses or for total body bathing.

Modified Soaps or Soap Substitutes:

Neutral Soaps or Soap Substitutes: Dove (Lever Brothers), Lowila (Westwood), Neutragena (Neutragena), pHisoDerm (Winthrop).

Superfatted Soaps: Basis (Duke), Oilatum Soap (Stiefel).

Medicated Soaps and Soap Substitutes:

Acnaveen Bar, Cream (Cooper): Colloidal oatmeal, sulfur, and salicylic acid.

Acne-Dome Medicated Cleanser (Dome): Sulfur and salicylic acid.

Brasivol Scrub Cleansers (Stiefel): Aluminum oxide.

Dial (Armour-Dial): Triclocarban.

Dial Professional (Armour-Dial): Hexachlorophene and triclocarban.

Fostex Cake (Westwood): Sulfur and salicylic acid.

Irish Spring (Colgate-Palmolive): Tribromsalan and triclosan.

Jergens Deodorant Soap (Jergens): Triclocarban.

Lifebuoy (Lever Brothers): Tribromsalan.

Pernox (Westwood): Salicylic acid, sulfur, and polyethylene.

P-300 Soap (Colgate-Palmolive): Tribromsalan and triclosan.

Phase III (Lever Brothers): Tribromsalan and triclocarban.

pHisoHex (Winthrop): Hexachlorophene.

Praise (Lever Brothers): Tribromsalan.

Presulin Cleanser (Schieffelin): Hexachlorophene.

Safeguard (Procter and Gamble): Tribromsalan, triclocarban, and cloflucarban.

Soy-Dome Cleanser (Dome): Hexachlorophene and soya protein complex.

Zest (Procter and Gamble): Tribromsalan and triclocarban.

SHAMPOOS

Shampoos are liquid soaps or detergents used to wash the hair, clean the scalp of scales, and relieve pruritus. Most of the bar soaps described in the previous section also can be used for these purposes. Shampoos also are used as vehicles for applying medication to the scalp for seborrheic dermatitis or psoriasis.

Tar shampoos, zinc pyrithione shampoos or hair-dressings (ZP-11), or selenium sulfide formulations are usually effective temporarily in the treatment of dandruff, but they are not curative. Quaternary ammonium salts are claimed to be effective in the treatment of dandruff. They are present in nonionic shampoos or in products used after the shampoos [Dandricide, Rinse Away]. Hexachlorophene also has been frequently incorporated into medicated shampoos.

The choice of a shampoo depends upon the condition being treated (psoriasis is preferably treated with tar; seborrheic dermatitis often responds well to salicylic acid and sulfur), the color and type of hair being washed (blond hair may become darker with tar shampoos, greasy hair is more effectively treated with sulfur), and the esthetic sensitivity of the individual (if a patient will not use a malodorous sulfur shampoo, he may be just as satisfactorily treated with a salicylic acid-germistatic preparation).

SELENIUM SULFIDE [Selsun]

Preparations containing selenium sulfide in a detergent are temporarily effective for the treatment of dandruff and tinea versicolor (see Chapter 60, Antifungal Agents).

Selenium sulfide has little or no toxicity when applied as directed to normal skin or hair follicles, or even upon accidental ingestion. The drug has an unpleasant odor and taste, and stings conjunctival mucosa on contact. It should not be applied to large areas of skin with marked dermatitic lesions because it can act as a primary irritant under such circumstances.

METHOD OF APPLICATION.—*Topical* (shampoo): One or two teaspoonfuls are applied and allowed to remain on the scalp two to three minutes before rinsing off thoroughly; the application is then repeated. The preparation may be used once or twice weekly. Contact with the eyes should be avoided.

PREPARATIONS.—

Selsun (Abbott). *Topical:* Suspension 2.5% in 4 oz containers.

Selsun Blue (Abbott). *Topical:* Cream 1% in 3.5 oz containers; suspension 1% in 4 and 8 oz containers.

Other Medicated Shampoos:

Breck One Shampoo (Breck): Pyrithione zinc.

Dara Soapless Shampoo (Owen): Protein condensate and coconut fatty acid.

Domerine Medicated Shampoo (Dome): Salicylic acid and allantoin.

Fostex Cream (Westwood): Salicylic acid and sulfur.

Head and Shoulders (Procter and Gamble): Pyrithione zinc.

Ionil (Owen): Salicylic acid and benzalkonium chloride.

Ionil-T (Owen): Same formulation as Ionil plus coal tar solution.

Meted (Texas): Sulfur and salicylic acid.

pHisoDan Shampoo (Winthrop): Sulfur, sodium salicylate, and hexachlorophene.

Presulin Medicated Shampoo (Schieffelin): Hexachlorophene and sulfonated castor oil.

Rezamid Shampoo (Dermik): Colloidal sulfur and salicylic acid.

Sebaveen Shampoo (Cooper): Hexachlorophene, colloidal oatmeal, sulfur, and salicylic acid.

Sebicall Cream Shampoo (Reed & Carnrick): Allantoin and coal tar extract.

Sebulex (Westwood): Sulfur and salicylic acid.

Sebutone (Westwood): Sulfur, salicylic acid, and coal tar.

Tegrin Shampoo (Block): Coal tar and allantoin.

Vanseb (Herbert): Hexachlorophene, sulfur, and salicylic acid.

Zetar Shampoo (Dermik): Chloroxylenal and coal tar.

Zincon (Lederle): Pyrithione zinc.

OILS

Oils are liquid or fluid fats of mineral, vegetable, or animal origin. For topical therapy, vegetable and mineral oils are most widely used. Vegetable oils commonly incorporated in various commercially available creams and lotions are cottonseed oil, corn oil, castor oil, olive oil, and peanut oil. The physical effect of all vegetable oils used on the skin is similar, but their odor and properties of rancidity and emulsification differ. The vegetable oils are generally well tolerated on both normal and chronically diseased skin, but they should not be used alone on weeping dermatoses.

Mineral oil is a mixture of high molecular weight liquid hydrocarbons obtained from petroleum. It is used either alone or as an ingredient in creams, ointments, or lotions. It does not become rancid and, therefore, has advantages over oils of vegetable or animal origin. Nevertheless, many commercial suppliers of mineral oils add stabilizers (eg, tocopherol, butylhydroxytoluene) to the preparation. (The United States Pharmacopeia requires that the stabilizer used be identified on the label.) Topically applied mineral oil is relatively free of untoward effects.

Occasionally it is desirable to add an oil to bath water. Since the oils are not soluble in water, they float and may make the bath an unpleasant experience. To overcome this, emulsifiers are added to disperse the oil; they form a milky mixture of microglobules of oil-in-water. All commercial emulsified oil products contain emulsifiers or surfactants. When these products are used, a fine film of oil remains on the skin after the bath. Use of such products may be desirable to impede the rapid evaporation of water from the epidermis and thereby help overcome dryness of the skin caused by an overheated, underhumidified winter environment. These products also may be helpful in ichthyosis and in pruritic and chronic eczematous dermatoses. Since these surfactant-treated oils impart a pleasant sensation to the skin, they are often used as emollients.

METHOD OF APPLICATION.—*Topical.*

PREPARATIONS.—Mineral Oil and Lanolin: Alpha-Keri (Westwood); **Mineral Oil:** Domol (Dome); **Combined Vegetable Oil Base:** Geri-Bath (Dermik); **Cottonseed Oil:** Lubath (Texas); **Sesame Seed Oil:** Neutragena (Neutragena).

DEODORANTS AND ANTIPERSPIRANTS

Deodorants are applied topically to diminish or mask body odors. Antiperspirants are designed to diminish sweating and may also have deodorant properties. All antiperspirants and some deodorants are classified as drugs under the Food, Drug and Cosmetic Act primarily because their active ingredients are claimed to affect the structure or function of the skin area to which they are applied.

Since body odors are due to bacterial action on perspiration, deodorant preparations exert their effect either by inhibiting bacterial growth directly or by reducing the moisture which is ideal for bacterial proliferation; less ideally, most deodorants attempt to superimpose a more acceptable odor. Both anti-infective agents and antibiotics have been used as bacterial suppressants. Products containing neomycin and similar antibiotics should not be used because they may cause sensitization and a contact dermatitis.

The antiperspirant agents most frequently present in these preparations are aluminum chlorhydroxide and aluminum chloride. Aluminum sulfamate and zinc phenolsulfonate are used less frequently. Two antiperspirants [Secret Cream, Secret Roll-On] contain zirconium hydroxychloride along with aluminum chlorhydroxide, hexachlorophene, and glycine; consumer experience with these two products appears to support the manufacturer's claims of a low level of untoward reactions, including irritation. This is surprising since preparations containing sodium zirconium lactate or zirconium oxide, as well as simple solutions of zirconium hydroxychloride, may produce epithelioid granulomas of the skin.

The most common adverse effects caused by the deodorant or antiperspirant preparations are burning and irritation. Less common reactions include dermatitis, cutaneous granulomas, and, in severe cases, open ulceration. Obviously, these preparations should be discontinued at the first sign of irritation. Usually the irritation will disappear without further complications.

KERATOLYTIC AND DESTRUCTIVE AGENTS

Both mineral and vegetable tars are used to treat chronic lichenified and papulosquamous eruptions. Although they have been largely supplanted by topical corticosteroid preparations in the treatment of psoriasis, seborrheic dermatitis, atopic dermatitis, and lichen simplex chronicus they still are beneficial in these disorders. The tars are soluble in ointments, oils, water-dispersible oils, pastes, and alcohol solutions, but not in water.

The main disadvantage of all tar preparations is their lack of uniformity. Tars are also photosensitizing, have an unpleasant odor, and frequently stain the skin and hair. They may rarely cause allergic sensitization. Their inappropriate use or use in excessive concentrations can aggravate the lesions (particularly in spreading psoriasis) or cause folliculitis.

Coal tar is the most widely used tar. Juniper tar, birch tar, and pine tar cause allergic sensitization more frequently and offer no advantage over coal tar.

Tars incorporated into creams and ointments containing small amounts of a corticosteroid are promoted for use in the treatment of eczema and atopic dermatitis. It has not been determined whether these ingredients in combination are more effective than either agent alone. Several preparations contain a tar and a halogenated quinoline (eg, Ze-Tar-Quin) or a tar, corticosteroid, and halogenated quinoline (eg, Cor-Tar-Quin). The quinoline is added to combat any infection that may be present in chronic eczema and other eruptions for which tars are indicated; however, it has not been established that the quinoline derivative enhances the effectiveness of the tar and/or corticosteroid.

Ichthammol, an irritant and local

antibacterial agent, consists of the ammonium salts of the sulfonic acids of the oils obtained from the destructive distillation of shale. Ichthammol contains not less than 10% of total sulfur in organic and inorganic form. It is less irritating than coal tar and is useful in chronic eczematous dermatoses.

Urea 10% in a suitable cream vehicle or ointment base is used to soften the skin in ichthyotic and other dry, scaly conditions such as psoriasis or atopic dermatitis. There is no evidence that it is toxic or allergenic, but the instability of many urea preparations limits their use.

An ointment in a petrolatum base containing chrysarobin in a 0.1% to 0.2% concentration may be effective in the treatment of psoriasis. Unfortunately the composition of chrysarobin, which is obtained from natural sources, varies widely and standardization has been impossible. Furthermore, it is chemically unstable and irritating to the mucous membranes and conjunctiva; it also stains the skin and can cause primary skin irritation and allergic sensitization. Anthralin, a stable compound, is an available alternative.

When used by experienced physicians, chemical destructive agents are quite versatile and effective. If histologic examination of a lesion is desirable, a biopsy examination should precede use of the chemical. Phenol, which can be absorbed and cause renal toxicity, has been essentially replaced by mono-, bi-, and trichloroacetic acids for the removal of actinic, senile, and seborrheic keratoses. Various dilutions of trichloroacetic acid are used for limited superficial chemosurgical procedures. These acids are markedly corrosive and coagulate skin proteins.

Resorcinol, a keratolytic agent in concentrations of 2% to 10%, is a common ingredient in acne remedies. Its application results in mild irritation that produces some peeling.

A 25% dispersion of podophyllum resin in compound benzoin tincture or as a solution in alcohol is often effective in expert hands in the treatment of condyloma acuminatum.

Cantharidin preparations traditionally have been used to destroy periungual warts, although they also may be used for other types. Application causes a blister to form at the dermal-epidermal junction. The roof of the blister sloughs, taking the wart with it. A stable preparation containing cantharidin 0.7% in collodion [Cantharone] is applied under an occlusive bandage for 48 hours; the bandage should not be removed or the area washed unless severe pain is experienced.

The topical application of fluorouracil in the treatment of multiple premalignant actinic keratoses, particularly of the face and forehead, has become a useful therapeutic procedure (see the individual evaluation).

COAL TAR

This by-product of the destructive distillation of bituminous coal is primarily used for the treatment of psoriasis. Coal tar also is useful in concentrations up to 6% for papulosquamous eruptions and in much higher concentrations for atopic dermatitis and lichen simplex chronicus.

Coal tar has a tendency to produce irritation; this ordinarily is slight in usual concentrations and appears to be negligible in patients with psoriasis. Care should be exercised in using tar preparations in patients with an exacerbation of psoriasis, because tar may precipitate total body exfoliation. Coal tar occasionally is photosensitizing and darkens the color of blond hair when applied to the scalp.

METHOD OF APPLICATION.—*Topical.*

PREPARATIONS.—Coal Tar, U.S.P. *Topical:* Cream, emulsion, lotion, ointment, soap, shampoo, and solution.

AVAILABLE TRADEMARKS.—Balnetar (Westwood), Polytar Bath (Stiefel), Supertah (Purdue Frederick), Tar Distillate (Doak), Tarbonis (Reed & Carnrick), Tarsum (Summers), Zetar (Dermik). Drug also marketed under generic name.

AVAILABLE MIXTURES.—

Alphosyl HC (Reed & Carnrick): Cream or lotion containing coal tar extract 5%, hydrocortisone 0.25% (lotion) or 0.5% (cream), and allantoin 2%.

Bacnelo (Ascher): Lotion containing coal tar solution 2%, zinc oxide, calcium hydroxide solution, precipitated sulfur 3%, and glycerin.

Carbo-Cort (Dome): Cream containing coal tar solution 3% and hydrocortisone 0.25% or 0.5%.

Cor-Tar-Quin (Dome): Cream containing hydrocortisone 0.25%, 0.5%, or 1%, coal tar solution 2%, and diiodohydroxyquin 1%; forte cream containing hydrocortisone 0.5%, coal tar solution 10%, and diiodohydroxyquin 1%.

Pragmatar (Smith Kline & French): Ointment containing coal tar distillate 4%, sulfur 3%, salicylic acid 3%, and cetyl alcohol.

Sebical (Reed & Carnrick): Cream containing coal tar extract 2%, allantoin 2%, and hexachlorophene 1%.

Supertah H-C (Purdue Frederick): Ointment containing coal tar fraction 1.25%, and hydrocortisone 0.5% or 1%.

Tarcortin (Reed & Carnrick): Cream containing coal tar extract 5% and hydrocortisone 0.5%.

Tarpaste (Doak): Coal tar and zinc oxide.

Tegrin Cream (Block): Coal tar and allantoin.

Topigel (Reed & Carnrick): Coal tar extract 5%, iodochlorhydroxyquin 1%, and hydrocortisone 1%.

Ze-Tar-Quin (Dermik): Synthetic crude coal tar, hydrocortisone, and diiodohydroxyquin.

Zetone (Dermik): Crude coal tar and hydrocortisone.

ANTHRALIN [Anthra-Derm, Lasan]

This drug was developed as a stable substitute for chrysarobin in the treatment of psoriasis. Anthralin has been widely accepted in Europe and more recently in the United States for use in this disorder. Usually patients are treated with daily tar baths, exposure to ultraviolet light, and application of anthralin in zinc oxide paste to each psoriatic plaque. Frequency of irritation (due in part to the 24-hour period of exposure to the drug), as well as the need for specialized care in a supervised setting, has limited the use of this treatment.

Anthralin should be applied only to quiescent or chronic patches of psoriasis; it should not be used in the treatment of acute eruptions or excessively inflamed areas. Anthralin should be used with care, if at all, on the face or intertriginous areas. Contact with the eyes may cause conjunctivitis. The drug should be discontinued if sensitivity reactions occur; excessive erythema of adjacent normal skin may require a reduction in the frequency of application. Anthralin may stain fabrics and temporarily stain hair and surrounding skin areas.

Anthralin therapy usually has been withheld from patients with impaired renal function because of the possibility of renal irritation secondary to percutaneous absorption. However, no cases of renal or hepatic toxicity have been reported. Recent toxicologic studies using both paste and ointment forms indicate that topical application in concentrations up to 0.4% does not impair kidney or liver function.

Anthralin preparations in hard paste form are difficult to apply. An effective reformulated anthralin paste in 0.1% or 0.2% concentration is now available. This paste contains at least 0.2% salicylic acid to minimize staining and to act as a preservative. For hairy areas, a fluid preparation, usually in mineral oil and cetyl alcohol vehicles, is preferred. Ointment preparations also are available.

METHOD OF APPLICATION.—*Topical:* Paste is applied without a dressing at bedtime and should remain on the lesions for 8 to 12 hours. The next morning, the paste is removed and the patient is treated with a tar bath and ultraviolet light exposure; a corticosteroid cream is then applied every three hours during the day to control or prevent irritation.

PREPARATIONS.—

Anthra-Derm (Dermik). *Topical:* Oil 0.25% in 2 oz containers; ointment 0.1%, 0.25%, 0.5%, and 1% in 1½ oz containers.

Lasan (Stiefel). *Topical:* Paste 0.1%, 0.2%, and 0.4% in 5 oz containers; pomade 0.4% in 4 oz containers.

Drug also marketed by other manufacturers under generic name.

AVAILABLE MIXTURES.—

Anthra-Tar (Dermik): Anthralin and coal tar.

Anthryl (Reed & Carnrick): Anthralin, allantoin, and coal tar extract.

SALICYLIC ACID

Salicylic acid is a useful keratolytic agent when applied in an ointment base. It is claimed to be keratogenic in concentrations of less than 3%, keratolytic in concentrations between 3% and 6%, and destructive to tissues in concentrations above 6%. Salicylic acid can be used to treat superficial fungal infections, seborrheic dermatitis, acne, psoriasis, and localized neurodermatitis. A 6% concentration in petrolatum is used to thin or remove calluses. As a plaster, it has been used in a 40% concentration with variable success in treating warts and corns.

This drug is absorbed, even from small open lesions. It is slowly excreted in the urine and can cause salicylism. Thus, salicylic acid should not be applied over large areas or for prolonged periods, particularly in the very young. Caution also must be exercised when a 40% plaster is used, particularly on the extremities, in diabetics or in patients with peripheral vascular disease, since acute inflammation and ulceration may occur after overuse. This acid is not effective in a zinc oxide paste (eg, Lassar's paste) because it forms zinc salicylate which is pharmacologically inactive. When applied in the form of an ointment or alcohol lotion, it is odorless and does not stain the skin.

METHOD OF APPLICATION.—*Topical:* To remove calluses, the ointment is applied at bedtime and washed off in the morning. For the treatment of warts and corns, adhesive plaster is applied to the affected area and changed daily; the skin is washed between treatments. A similar regimen is instituted for most other indications, except that the period during which the chemical is in contact with the skin is shortened.

PREPARATIONS.—Salicylic Acid, U.S.P. marketed under generic name. Salicylic Acid Collodion, U.S.P. and Salicylic Acid Plaster, U.S.P. must be compounded by a pharmacist.

BENZOIC AND SALICYLIC ACID OINTMENT

This preparation containing salicylic acid 6% and benzoic acid 3% is used as a keratolytic and fungistatic agent. It has been used with success either alone or with systemically administered griseofulvin for the treatment of chronic superficial fungal infections such as tinea corporis and tinea pedis. See also Chapter 60, Antifungal Agents.

METHOD OF APPLICATION.—*Topical:* The ointment is applied once or twice daily to the involved area.

PREPARATIONS.—Mixture marketed under generic name and under the name Whitfield's Ointment.

FLUOROURACIL [Efudex, Fluoroplex]

Fluorouracil is used topically for the treatment of multiple premalignant actinic keratoses; it is not the treatment of choice for isolated lesions. The drug is most effective in treating keratoses on the face and forehead. Lesions on the hands and arms may require higher concentrations and longer treatment periods. Fluorouracil therapy prevents further development of existing lesions and results in cosmetic improvement. For other uses of this drug, see Chapter 88, Antineoplastic Agents.

Fluorouracil is selectively active against atypical epidermal cells and causes an inflammatory reaction. Even lesions that are not clinically visible respond; for this reason, fluorouracil is applied to the entire affected area. The drug does not react with normal epidermis unless it is applied under occlusive dressings. The healing process may continue for one to two months after therapy is discontinued; restoration of the color and texture of the skin is usually satisfactory.

Commercial preparations provide a choice of concentrations and vehicles. Solutions in propylene glycol are more active than cream preparations containing equivalent concentrations of the drug. Concentrations of 1% to 2% often are adequate for use on the face and forehead.

Before therapy is initiated, the patient should be informed of the inflammatory response, prolonged discoloration of skin, and accompanying burning sensation. The degree of response may be evaluated by limiting the area of initial application. Pruritus and irritation are the most common adverse effects. Allergic reactions have been reported occasionally. Fluorouracil should not be applied to easily irritated areas such as the area around the eyes, the vermilion border of the lips, nasolabial folds, and wrinkles. If normal epidermis exhibits an excessive inflammatory response, the treatment should be discontinued. Exposure to sunlight during treatment should be avoided. The possible hazard of systemic toxicity from topical application can be minimized by applying the weakest effective concentration to small areas. Severe reactions can be averted by careful selection and instruction of patients.

METHOD OF APPLICATION.—*Topical:* Preparation is applied once or twice daily for two to four weeks until a maximal inflammatory response is obtained; frequency of application may have to be adjusted in accordance with the intensity of the response.

PREPARATIONS.—

Efudex (Roche). *Topical:* Cream 5% in 25 g containers; solution 2% and 5% in propylene glycol in 10 ml containers.

Fluoroplex (Herbert). *Topical:* Cream 1% in 3.5 and 30 g containers; solution 1% in 30 ml containers.

Drug also marketed under generic name in injectable form which may be used by pharmacists to prepare topical preparations.

AGENTS AFFECTING PIGMENTATION

Various agents are used in an attempt to increase pigmentation in hypopigmented skin (eg, vitiligo) or to reduce the hyperpigmentation of certain conditions such as severe freckling, chloasma gravidarum, chronic skin inflammation, and photosensitization associated with use of certain perfumes.

HYDROQUINONE [Artra, Derma-Blanch, Eldopaque, Eldoquin]

This agent is claimed to reduce abnormal pigmentation by inhibiting melanogenesis. The results obtained are very variable and often application of hydroquinone is of no value; no adequate explanation is available at this time to account for these variable results. Hypopigmentation or depigmentation caused by hydroquinone may not be permanent, but repigmentation, if it occurs at all, may take a long time.

METHOD OF APPLICATION.—*Topical.*

PREPARATIONS.—

Artra (Pharmaco). *Topical:* Cream 2% in 1, 2, and 4 oz containers.

Derma-Blanch (Brayten). *Topical:* Cream 3% in 1¼ oz containers.

Eldopaque (Elder). *Topical:* 2% and 4% in opaque base in ½ oz containers.

Eldoquin (Elder). *Topical:* Cream 2% in ½ and 1 oz containers; lotion 2% in ½ oz containers.

MONOBENZONE [Benoquin]

This agent causes total, irreversible depigmentation and should only be used to permanently remove the remaining areas of normal pigmentation in patients with generalized vitiligo. Monobenzone is not useful in the treatment of melasma, and postinflammatory and other types of hyperpigmentation. It may cause allergic sensitivity reactions.

METHOD OF APPLICATION.—*Topical.*

PREPARATIONS.—Benoquin (Elder). *Topical:* Lotion 5% in 4 oz containers; ointment 20% in ½, 1¼, and 16 oz containers.

TRIOXSALEN [Trisoralen]

This synthetic psoralen derivative occasionally is used in the treatment of large vitiliginous lesions but its effectiveness is questionable. It is also administered to increase a patient's tolerance to sunlight. Oral administration of trioxsalen must be followed, after approximately two hours, by exposure to sunlight or, in expert hands, to long-wave ultraviolet radiation (320 to 400 nm) from an artificial light source.

During the first few days of therapy, patients are hypersensitive to sunlight and subject to more severe sunburn than under normal circumstances. Dosage of the drug and length of exposure to sun must be closely controlled to prevent injury to the skin; sunglasses and a light-screening lipstick should be used to protect eyes and lips. If overexposure to sunlight inadvertently occurs, vomiting should be induced and the patient should remain in a darkened room for eight hours or until cutaneous reactions subside. In time, trioxsalen increases the tolerance of the skin to ultraviolet light through increased pigmentation and, possibly, by thickening of the stratum corneum.

Trioxsalen is contraindicated in patients with diseases associated with photosensitivity, such as porphyria (porphyria cutanea tarda and erythropoietic protoporphyria), discoid or systemic lupus erythematosus, and xeroderma pigmentosum. It is also contraindicated in vitiligo of infectious origin (eg, leukoderma associated with syphilis, pinta, or leprosy). Other drugs that have photosensitizing properties (eg, phenothiazines) should not be given concomitantly.

Extensive clinical experience indicates that trioxsalen is virtually nontoxic; there are no reported cases of adverse effects.

USUAL DOSAGE.—*Oral: Adults and children over 12 years of age,* for large lesions of vitiligo, 30 mg daily is given two hours before exposure to sunlight at noon. Initial exposure is 30 minutes. As long as erythema develops seven to ten hours after exposure, the patient is maintained on the indicated daily therapy. Once skin tolerance develops and erythema no longer develops, exposure to sunlight is increased by 15-minute increments until a maximal exposure time of 90 minutes is attained. Subsequently, in the absence of erythema, the dose of trioxsalen is increased by increments of 10 mg to a maximum of 50 mg daily. Repigmentation, when it occurs, is usually evident after three to four months of treatment, especially on the face and neck. If no results are obtained after three months of treatment, therapy should be discontinued.

For increasing tolerance to sunlight, the daily dose usually should not exceed 10 mg. Graduated daily exposures to sunlight should follow two hours later. The total period of administration should not exceed 14 days.

PREPARATIONS.—Trisoralen (Elder). *Oral:* Tablets 5 mg.

METHOXSALEN [Oxsoralen]

Topical application of methoxsalen should be restricted to the treatment of small vitiliginous lesions. The drug should be applied to the affected areas and the patient then exposed to sunlight or a long-wave (320 to 400 nm) ultraviolet light source. The procedure preferably should be performed in the physician's office.

Topical use of methoxsalen can cause acute vesicular cutaneous photosensitization in a high percentage of patients; high concentrations of the drug and overexposure of the treated site to long-wave ultraviolet radiation are the major factors contributing to the development of severe erythema and blistering. Dilution of the lotion to concentrations of 1:10,000 or 1:1,000 is helpful to avoid excessive reactions. The chance of overexposure can be minimized by topical application of sunscreens containing benzophenone derivatives or by washing the treated site after exposure to sunlight. If no results are obtained after three months of treatment, topical therapy should be discontinued.

With the availability of trioxsalen and a topical form of methoxsalen, the systemic use of methoxsalen is not justified.

USUAL DOSAGE.—*Topical:* Low concentrations are applied daily to the affected area (50 to 200 $\mu g/in^2$). After two hours, the treated area is exposed to sunlight or long-wave ultraviolet light. Initial light exposures should be limited to 30 to 60 seconds; exposure is increased gradually but increases should not exceed one-half the minimal erythemic dose.

PREPARATIONS.—Oxsoralen (Elder).

Oral: Capsules 10 mg.

Topical: Lotion 1% in 1 oz containers.

SUNSCREENS

Sunscreens are used to help prevent sunburn; some of these products may be helpful in the prevention of actinic damage and skin cancer. These preparations are indicated in (1) individuals who are fair skinned and do not tan well; (2) individuals allergic to sunlight; (3) patients who are using topical or systemic medications with photosensitizing or phototoxic properties; (4) medical personnel and patients who may be exposed to ultraviolet bactericidal lamps; and (5) patients with porphyria (especially erythropoietic protoporphyria).

Individuals with normal skin require only 15 to 20 minutes of exposure to sunlight during summer months to produce a perceptible sunburn reaction. Multiples of this exposure time can lead to an acute, painful sunburn reaction with blisters. Some patients must avoid all exposure to sunlight and are able to venture outdoors only at times when solar irradiation is less intense and with as much protection from opaque clothing and accessories as possible. It is better for such patients to remain indoors between 10 am and 4 pm, especially during summer months.

Physical sunscreens (ointments containing zinc oxide or titanium dioxide) are opaque to all wavelengths of light and may be used on exposed skin surfaces; these products are effective but cosmetically unappealing. The lack of cosmetic appeal also restricts the use of red veterinary petrolatum which filters out a considerable amount of ultraviolet and visible light and thus provides partial protection from sunburn in addition to minimizing skin dryness. Chemical sunscreens which absorb ultraviolet radiation exhibit a wide range of effectiveness depending upon the sunscreen agent itself, its concentration, and the vehicle in the preparation. Increasing the concentration of the sunscreen agent in a preparation increases the amount of protection afforded, but concentration and protection are not directly proportional. Swimming, activities which promote perspiration, or removal of the sunscreen by towelling necessitate reapplication of the preparation to assure continued protection.

The most effective sunscreen appears to be 5% aminobenzoic acid (*p*-aminobenzoic acid or PABA) in 55% to 70% alcohol; padimate (amyl *p*-dimethylaminobenzoate) and glyceryl *p*-aminobenzoate are somewhat less efficient. The benzophenones (dioxybenzone, oxybenzone, and sulisobenzone) are broad spectrum sunscreens and in 10% concentration are especially effective in protecting individuals exposed to ultraviolet bactericidal lamps. They are effective when freshly applied but are readily removed during swimming and give less residual protection.

Preparations containing less effective sunscreens or lower concentrations of effective agents are marketed for individuals who wish to acquire a tan while avoiding sunburn. Such popular commercial preparations are less suitable for protection of patients. Baby oil or mineral oil (with or without iodine), lubricating creams or lotions, cocoa butter, coconut oil, and tanning butters also are used by the laity; these preparations provide no protection against sunburn and their sole virtue is that they minimize skin dryness.

A number of artificial tanning preparations (bronzers, body gels, face colors) are available to give the skin a tanned appearance without exposure to the sun; these preparations provide no protection against sunburn unless a sunscreen is incorporated in the formulation.

METHOD OF APPLICATION.—*Topical.*

PREPARATIONS.—

Block Out (Sea & Ski): Lotion containing padimate 2.5% in 2 and 4 oz containers.

Coppertone (Plough): Cream and lotion preparations containing homosalate (formerly known as homomenthyl salicylate).

Pabafilm (Owen): Greaseless lotion containing padimate 5% in 4 oz containers.

Pabanol (Elder): Aminobenzoic acid 5% in 70% ethanol in 4 oz containers.

PreSun (Westwood): Lotion containing aminobenzoic acid 5% in 4 oz containers.

Sea and Ski (Sea & Ski): Cream, foam, lotion, and oil preparations containing glyceryl aminobenzoate.

Solar Cream (Doak): Cream containing aminobenzoic acid, titanium dioxide, and magnesium stearate in water repellent base in 1 oz containers.

Solbar (Person & Covey): Lotion containing dioxybenzone 3% and oxybenzone 3% in 0.33 and 2.5 oz containers.

Sundare (Texas): Cinoxate lotions in cream base or clear (ethanol) base in 3.7 and 4 oz containers, respectively.

Sungard (Miles): Sulisobenzone 10% in 1 and 2.6 oz containers.

Uval (Dome): Lotion containing sulisobenzone 10% in 75 and 165 g containers.

MISCELLANEOUS TOPICAL PRODUCTS

COLLODION

This mixture of pyroxylin, ether, and alcohol forms a sticky, tenacious film that adheres to the skin. Flexible collodion contains collodion, camphor 0.2%, and castor oil 0.3%. It is used alone as a protectant or as a vehicle for destructive agents such as salicylic acid.

METHOD OF APPLICATION.—*Topical.*

PREPARATIONS.—Collodion, U.S.P. Drug marketed under generic name.

COVERMARK

Covermark is a waterproof, inert, opaque, topical preparation that is a highly effective makeup used to cover deforming pigmentary, vascular, and scarring lesions on exposed areas. It also is a good sunscreen.

METHOD OF APPLICATION.—*Topical.*

PREPARATIONS.—Covermark (O'Leary). *Topical:* Cream.

MENTHOL

Menthol is an alcohol obtained from oils of certain mints or prepared synthetically. A 0.1% to 2% concentration is present in shake lotions and ointments as an antipruritic, but it may be little more effective in relieving pruritus than the vehicle alone. Menthol is incorporated in shaving creams and aftershave lotions to impart a cooling sensation to the skin.

METHOD OF APPLICATION.—*Topical.*

PREPARATIONS.—Menthol, U.S.P. Drug marketed under generic name.

POLYETHYLENE FILM

Polyethylene film is widely used as an occlusive dressing in dermatologic therapy. Occlusion of the skin prevents evaporation of perspiration, increases heat locally, and enhances penetration of certain medications (eg, adrenal corticosteroids) through the epidermal barrier. It is therefore a most useful adjunct in the treatment of psoriasis, atopic dermatitis, and many eczemas.

This form of treatment can cause folliculitis, overgrowth of *Candida*, and other undesirable conditions that result from overmaceration and heating, especially during hot weather.

METHOD OF APPLICATION.—*Topical* (wrapping).

PREPARATIONS.—Glad Wrap (Union Carbide). Also available in tubular form for occlusion of extremities.

SIMILAR PREPARATION.—Saran Wrap (Dow). Vinylidene polymer plastic used in the same manner as polyethylene film for occlusive dressings.

SULFUR OINTMENTS

Sulfur ointments may be simple preparations of sulfur in various ointment bases or a combination of sulfur, salicylic acid, and tar incorporated into a base. The principal indications for sulfur preparations are seborrheic dermatitis, acne, some superficial fungal infections, and certain types of diaper dermatoses. Although sulfur preparations were once widely used for scabies and fungal infections, they have now been replaced by more effective agents (see Chapter 66, Scabicides and Pediculicides, and Chapter 60, Antifungal Agents).

METHOD OF APPLICATION.—*Topical:* Ointments or pastes containing 1% to 40% sulfur, depending upon the indication and type of sulfur used, are applied to the skin. Concentrations of 1% to 3% are used in dandruff shampoos.

PREPARATIONS.—Precipitated Sulfur, U.S.P., Sublimed Sulfur, N.F. Marketed under generic name. Ointments and pastes may be compounded by the pharmacist, although commercially compounded ointments are available under generic name.

TOPICAL HORMONE PREPARATIONS

Hormones used topically (estrogens, progesterone, and related compounds) are marketed principally as quasi-cosmetic rejuvenating creams. Since hormones are present naturally in all body tissues, there is no sound reason to ascribe regional aging changes (such as wrinkles, which are predominantly seen on the face, neck, and hands) to a deficiency of sex hormones.

To be effective in combating changes in aging skin, a sex hormone would have to be active locally. There is evidence that some topically applied steroidal hormones (both active and inactive biologically) cause slight histologic thickening of the epidermis of aged skin. Claims that such products also produce dermal changes are questionable. Commercially available topical estrogen or progesterone preparations have no effect on human sebaceous glands and oil secretion. Large amounts of estrogen or progesterone, however, may produce systemic effects and reduce sebum secretion. There is no scientific evidence to indicate that hormone creams are any more effective than simple emollient creams in relieving dryness of the skin. Hormone creams have not been shown to increase the amount of water that the skin can hold, nor to restore subcutaneous fat. The objective cosmetic effects of hormone creams have never been shown to differ significantly from those obtained by use of the hormone-free cream base.

Topically applied hormones, as presently formulated in cosmetic preparations, have no systemic effects when used as directed and appear to be safe.

MISCELLANEOUS SYSTEMIC AGENTS

METHOTREXATE
METHOTREXATE SODIUM

Methotrexate is a valuable agent for the symptomatic control of severe, recalcitrant, disabling psoriasis which does not adequately respond to other forms of therapy. Diagnosis must be established by biopsy or after dermatologic consultation. Since there have been reports that the drug may cause hepatic cirrhosis and failure, methotrexate must be used cautiously and only by physicians experienced in antimetabolite therapy. The patient should be fully informed of the risks involved and should be under constant supervision by a physician.

Guidelines for the use of methotrexate in the treatment of refractory psoriasis have recently been published by both the Food and Drug Administration and by the Psoriasis Task Force of the National Program for Dermatology.

For information on the use of this drug as an antineoplastic agent and in rheumatoid disorders, see Chapter 88, Antineoplastic Agents, and Chapter 26, Antirheumatic Agents, respectively.

PREPARATIONS.—

Methotrexate (Lederle). *Oral:* Tablets 2.5 mg.

Methotrexate Sodium (Lederle). *Injection:* Solution 2.5 and 25 mg/ml in 2 ml containers.

SULFAPYRIDINE
SULFOXONE SODIUM [Diasone Sodium]
DAPSONE [Avlosulfon]

Clinical experience indicates that these drugs can be particularly useful in treating dermatitis herpetiformis, subcorneal pustular dermatitis, leprosy, and other dermatoses. They also may improve pyoderma gangrenosum. Their mechanism of action in these diseases is unknown, but apparently the antibacterial activity is not solely responsible.

Daily doses of 200 to 300 mg of dapsone will produce, in less than two weeks, hemolysis or methemoglobinemia in many patients; leukopenia has been reported rarely. Therefore, complete blood cell counts should be performed at regular intervals. Sulfapyridine can cause severe gastrointestinal irritation in patients receiving more than 3 g daily.

See also Chapter 59, Antileprosy Agents, for additional information on sulfones.

USUAL DOSAGE.—

Sulfapyridine:

Oral: Adults, 500 mg to 1 g four times daily. Doses up to 6 g daily have been used.

Sulfoxone Sodium:

Oral: Adults, 330 mg daily for one week. Dose may then be increased to 660 mg daily. Maintenance dose, 330 mg daily.

Dapsone:

Oral: Adults, 100 to 200 mg daily.

PREPARATIONS.—

Sulfapyridine:

Oral: Tablets 500 mg. Drug marketed under

generic name.

Sulfoxone Sodium:

Diasone Sodium (Abbott). *Oral:* Tablets (enteric-coated) 165 mg.

Dapsone:

Avlosulfon (Ayerst). *Oral:* Tablets 25 and 100 mg.

TOPICAL DERMATOLOGIC COMBINATIONS

Mixtures Containing Glucocorticoids

Various ointments, creams, and lotions containing a corticosteroid with antibacterial and antifungal agents are marketed for the treatment of a wide range of cutaneous disorders. The addition of antibacterial agents to glucocorticoids may seem logical, but proof of the efficacy of these mixtures is lacking.

In general, glucocorticoids are not preferred for the treatment of cutaneous infections, and antibacterials should not be used as a prophylactic measure in the treatment of noninfectious dermatoses. Also, corticosteroids can suppress signs and symptoms even when they do not cure dermatoses; it is still essential to determine the causal factors of dermatoses and to eliminate them. Thus, while these mixtures may be used with apparent or initial success in the treatment of a wide variety of cutaneous disorders, not all of the components in these mixtures are necessary or desirable.

The use of corticosteroids systemically, intralesionally, and topically in the treatment of dermatoses or the cutaneous manifestations of systemic disease is discussed in Chapter 35, Adrenal Corticosteroids.

Tars have been incorporated into creams and ointments containing small amounts of corticosteroids for the treatment of eczema and atopic dermatitis. It is not clear whether the combination is more effective than either agent alone. However, these mixtures are effective and there appears to be no disadvantage to their use. A quinoline derivative sometimes has been added to act as an anti-infective agent, but it has not been established that this ingredient enhances the effectiveness of the tar or glucocorticoid.

Alphosyl-HC (Reed & Carnrick): Cream or lotion containing coal tar 5%, allantoin 2%, and hydrocortisone 0.5% (cream) or 0.25% (lotion).

Bacimycin-HC Ointment (Merrell-National): Each gram contains bacitracin 500 units, neomycin sulfate 5 mg, and hydrocortisone 5 mg.

Caldecort Ointment (Pennwalt): Each gram contains hydrocortisone acetate 10 mg, undecylenate calcium 30 mg, and neomycin sulfate 5 mg.

Caquin (Durst): Cream containing iodochlorhydroxyquin 3% and hydrocortisone 1%.

Carbo-Cort (Dome): Creme containing coal tar solution 0.5% and hydrocortisone 0.25% or 0.5%.

Cordran-N Cream, Ointment (Lilly): Each gram contains flurandrenolide 0.05% and neomycin sulfate 5 mg.

Cor-Tar-Quin (Dome): Cream containing hydrocortisone 0.25%, 0.5%, or 1%, coal tar solution 2%, and diiodohydroxyquin 1%; forte cream containing hydrocortisone 0.5%, coal tar solution 10%, and diiodohydroxyquin 3%; lotion containing hydrocortisone 0.25% or 0.5%, coal tar solution 2%, and diiodohydroxyquin 1%.

Cortisporin (Burroughs Wellcome): Each gram of cream contains polymyxin B sulfate 10,000 units, neomycin sulfate 5 mg, gramicidin 0.25 mg, and hydrocortisone acetate 5 mg; each gram of ointment contains polymyxin B sulfate 5,000 units, zinc bacitracin 400 units, neomycin sulfate 5 mg, and hydrocortisone 10 mg.

Domeform-HC (Dome): Creme containing hydrocortisone 0.5% and iodochlorhydroxyquin 3%.

Fostril-HC (Westwood): Lotion containing polyoxyethylene lauryl ether 6%, sulfur 2%, and hydrocortisone 0.25%.

Hazel-Balm-HC (Arnar-Stone): Aerosol containing hydrocortisone 0.2% and hamamelis water.

Heb-Cort MC (Barnes-Hind): Lotion containing hydrocortisone 0.25% with menthol and camphor.

Heb-Cort-V (Barnes-Hind): Cream or lotion containing hydrocortisone 0.25% or 1% and iodochlorhydroxyquin 3%.

Hydrelt (Elder): Cream containing iodochlorhydroxyquin 3%, hydrocortisone 0.5%, and aluminum acetate solution 2%.

Hydrelt-C (Elder): Cream containing iodochlorhydroxyquin 3% and hydrocortisone 0.5%.

Kenalog-S Cream, Lotion, Ointment (Squibb): Each gram of cream or ointment or milliliter of lotion contains neomycin sulfate 2.5 mg, gramicidin 0.25 mg, and triamcinolone acetonide 1 mg.

Komed-HC (Barnes-Hind): Lotion containing hydrocortisone acetate 0.5%, sodium thiosulfate 8%, salicylic acid 2%, and isopropyl alcohol 25%.

Lidaform-HC (Dome): Creme or lotion containing iodochlorhydroxyquin 3%, lidocaine 3%, and hydrocortisone acetate 0.5%.

Mantadil (Burroughs Wellcome): Cream containing chlorcyclizine hydrochloride 2% and hydrocortisone acetate 0.5%.

Mycolog Cream, Ointment (Squibb): Each gram contains nystatin 100,000 units, neomycin sulfate 2.5 mg, gramicidin 0.25 mg, and triamcinolone acetonide 1 mg.

Myconef Ointment (Squibb): Each gram contains nystatin 100,000 units, neomycin sulfate 2.5 mg, gramicidin 0.25 mg, and fludrocortisone acetonide 1 mg.

Neo-Cort-Dome (Dome): Creme or lotion containing neomycin sulfate 0.5% and hydrocortisone 0.25%, 0.5%, or 1% (creme) and 0.25% and 0.5% (lotion).

Neo-Cortef Cream (Upjohn): Each gram contains neomycin sulfate 5 mg and hydrocortisone acetate 10 or 25 mg.

NeoDecadron Cream (Merck Sharp & Dohme): Each gram contains dexamethasone sodium phosphate 1 mg and neomycin sulfate 5 mg.

NeoDecaspray Aerosol (Merck Sharp & Dohme): Each 90 g container contains dexamethasone 10 mg and neomycin sulfate 50 mg.

Neo-Delta Cortef Lotion, Ointment (Upjohn): Each gram or milliliter contains prednisolone acetate 5 mg and neomycin sulfate 5 mg.

Neo-Medrol Acetate Topical (Upjohn): methylprednisolone acetate 0.25% or 1% and neomycin sulfate 0.5%.

Neo-Nysta-Cort (Dome): Ointment containing neomycin sulfate 0.5%, nystatin 100,000 units, and hydrocortisone 1%.

Neo-Oxylone Ointment (Upjohn): Each gram contains neomycin sulfate 5 mg and fluorometholone 0.25 mg.

Neo-Polycin HC Ointment (Dow): Each gram contains zinc bacitracin 400 units, neomycin sulfate 4.29 mg, polymyxin B sulfate 8,000 units, and hydrocortisone acetate 10 mg.

Neo-Synalar (Syntex): Cream containing neomycin sulfate 0.5% and fluocinolone acetonide 0.025%.

Nystaform-HC Ointment (Dome): Each gram contains nystatin 100,000 units, iodochlorhydroxyquin 3%, and hydrocortisone 1%.

Tarcortin (Reed & Carnrick): Cream containing hydrocortisone 0.5% and coal tar 5%.

Vioform-Hydrocortisone (Ciba): Cream, lotion, or ointment containing hydrocortisone 0.5% or 1% and iodochlorhydroxyquin 3%.

Mixtures Containing Antibiotics

The less absorbable antibiotics (bacitracin, gramicidin, neomycin, and polymyxin B) are commonly used, usually in combinations of two or more, as components of antibacterial mixtures for topical application on the skin. Combinations of antibiotics for cutaneous therapy have not been proved more effective than single agents unless the infection is caused by more than one organism and the organisms do not respond to a single antibiotic. Cultures may be taken to identify the organisms and in vitro sensitivity tests performed to determine the appropriate antibacterial agent. Certain areas may be prone to mixed infections, particularly the anal-perineal area and the toe webs where gram-positive organisms, gram-negative organisms, and *Candida* can flourish. In these cases, the combination products are possibly helpful.

A number of antibiotics (bacitracin, gentamicin, gramicidin, neomycin, and tyrothricin) that are used alone or in combination are discussed in Chapter 57, Aminoglycoside Antibacterial Agents and Miscellaneous Antimicrobial Drugs. Polymyxin B sulfate is discussed in Chapter 52, Polymyxins.

Topical antibiotic preparations are not likely to provide adequate protection against glomerulonephritis resulting from cutaneous streptococcic infections. Appropriate systemic antibiotics are indicated for all clinically significant pyodermas from which these organisms have been cultured.

The topical application of antibacterial agents commonly used systemically (eg, tetracyclines) should be avoided, since there is risk of sensitization and development of resistant organisms.

Topical antibacterial agents are capable of suppressing local microbial population, but they all have relatively limited spectra of activity, which favors overgrowth of resistant elements of the cutaneous flora. These agents also may be very potent sensitizers of the skin, and can be absorbed to even toxic levels. Furthermore, there is very little evidence that topical antibacterial agents add a great deal therapeutically.

Bacimycin Ointment (Merrell-National): Each gram contains zinc bacitracin 500 units and neomycin sulfate 5 mg.

Biotres Ointment (Central): Each gram contains zinc bacitracin 200 units, neomycin sulfate 3 mg, polymyxin B sulfate 4,000 units, and benzalkonium chloride 5 mg.

Mycitracin Topical Ointment (Upjohn): Each gram contains bacitracin 500 units, neomycin sulfate 5 mg, polymyxin B sulfate 5,000 units.

Neo-Polycin Ointment (Dow): Each gram contains zinc bacitracin 400 units, neomycin sulfate 4.29 mg, and polymyxin B sulfate 8,000 units.

Neosporin (Burroughs Wellcome): Each gram of ointment or powder contains polymyxin B sulfate 5,000 units, zinc bacitracin 400 units, and neomycin sulfate 5 mg; each gram of lotion contains polymyxin B sulfate 10,000 units and neomycin sulfate 5 mg; each 90 g container of aerosol contains polymyxin B sulfate 100,000 units, neomycin sulfate 100 mg, and zinc bacitracin 8,000 units.

Neosporin-G Cream (Burroughs Wellcome): Each gram contains polymyxin B sulfate 10,000 units, neomycin sulfate 5 mg, and gramicidin 0.25 mg.

Polysporin Ointment (Burroughs Wellcome): Each gram contains polymyxin B sulfate 10,000 units and zinc bacitracin 500 units.

Spectrocin Ointment (Squibb): Each gram contains neomycin sulfate 2.5 mg and gramicidin 0.25 mg.

Chapter 69

AGENTS USED TO TREAT GLAUCOMA

The goal in the treatment of glaucoma is to reduce the intraocular pressure sufficiently to prevent damage to the optic nerve, the retinal circulation, and the retinal cells. The drugs used in glaucoma therapy reduce intraocular pressure by increasing the facility of outflow of aqueous humor (miotics, epinephrine), by decreasing the inflow of aqueous humor (carbonic anhydrase inhibitors, epinephrine), or by transiently reducing the volume of the intraocular fluids (osmotic agents.)

MIOTICS

The miotics are cholinergic drugs that stimulate parasympathetic effector cells directly (parasympathomimetics) or indirectly by inhibiting cholinesterase, the enzyme that destroys acetylcholine (anticholinesterase agents). When applied topically to the eye, these drugs cause miosis, spasm of accommodation, and a persistent fall in intraocular pressure that may be preceded by a transitory rise.

In primary angle-closure (acute congestive or narrow-angle) glaucoma, miotics are used to reduce the intraocular pressure prior to iridectomy (which is the treatment of choice) and for the control of residual glaucoma, if present, following surgery. The fall in intraocular pressure is brought about by constriction of the pupil which pulls the iris away from the filtration angle and thus improves the outflow of aqueous humor.

The miotics are the principal drugs used in the treatment of primary open-angle (chronic simple) glaucoma. Drug therapy is the treatment of choice for this condition and miotics must be given indefinitely. The mechanism by which these drugs reduce intraocular pressure in open-angle glaucoma is not well understood. It has been postulated that contraction of the ciliary muscle may cause a spreading of the trabecular interspaces, thereby increasing the facility of outflow of aqueous humor. Vasomotor factors also may be involved.

In general, the treatment of secondary glaucomas should be directed toward control of the underlying disease. Miotics may be useful in some forms, but, in the presence of an active inflammatory process, they are of little therapeutic value and actually may be harmful (see Chapter 70, Mydriatics and Cycloplegics). Miotics are of limited value in the preoperative treatment of congenital glaucoma, which is essentially a surgical problem. They also are applied topically in other ophthalmologic conditions (eg, accommodative esotropia.

Parasympathomimetics: Pilocarpine, which acts directly upon cholinergic receptor sites and thus mimics acetylcholine, has a short duration of action. It is the standard drug used for initial and maintenance therapy in primary open-angle glaucoma; in this condition it should be given in the concentration and at the frequency necessary to maintain a satisfactory reduction in intraocular pressure. It also is used in the emergency treatment of primary angle-closure glaucoma and in congenital glaucoma to reduce intraocular pressure prior to surgery. Pilocarpine generally is tolerated better than the other miotics. It seldom causes local irritation, and systemic effects and hypersensitivity reactions occur infrequently. Carbachol can be substituted if an allergy to pilocarpine does develop. Methacholine chloride [Mecholyl Chloride], a very short-acting miotic, is sometimes used for the emergency treatment of angle-closure glaucoma, usually in conjunction with neostigmine.

Short-Acting Anticholinesterase Agents: Physostigmine (eserine) formerly was widely used in the emergency treatment of primary angle-closure glaucoma, usually in conjunction with pilocarpine. It also has been used in primary open-angle glaucoma but is not as well tolerated as pilocarpine and may cause local irritation and allergic reactions. Neostigmine bromide [Prostigmin Bromide] occasionally has been used in glaucoma therapy, but it is less effective than physostigmine, since it does not penetrate the eye as well.

Long-Acting Anticholinesterase Agents: Demecarium [Humorsol] and the organophosphorus compounds, isoflurophate [Floropryl] and echothiophate [Phospholine], are long-acting, potent cholinesterase inhibitors used in the treatment of primary open-angle glaucoma. Because of their toxicity, these drugs are generally reserved for use in patients in whom the shorter-acting miotics have failed. Resistance to a miotic may develop after prolonged administration; it has been reported that responsiveness can sometimes be restored in patients who have developed resistance to pilocarpine by substituting a long-acting anticholinesterase agent for a period of time. The possibility of serious adverse effects should not preclude the use of the strong miotics in open-angle glaucoma that cannot be controlled by the less toxic drugs; the risk of visual loss due to uncontrolled open-angle glaucoma is considerably greater than the potential hazards of these agents.

The long-acting cholinesterase inhibitors should not be used prior to iridectomy in angle-closure glaucoma because they may precipitate an acute attack; they may, however, be used after iridectomy if continued drug therapy is required.

If two anticholinesterase miotics are given successively, the physician should be aware of their possible antagonistic action. The effects of the organophosphorus compounds, isoflurophate and echothiophate, may be partially blocked by the prior administration of physostigmine or neostigmine. Therefore, administration of the organophosphorus agent should be delayed until the previously administered drug has been excreted.

EPINEPHRINE

Epinephrine has only a slight effect on the intraocular pressure of the normal eye but, when instilled in eyes with primary open-angle glaucoma, it induces a prolonged fall in intraocular pressure, accompanied by a brief mydriasis and vasoconstriction. The mechanism by which epinephrine lowers intraocular pressure is not fully understood; it is believed to involve both a decrease in the production of aqueous humor and an increase in the facility of outflow.

Epinephrine occasionally has been used as the sole therapeutic agent in the initial treatment of primary open-angle glaucoma, but it is most frequently given with pilocarpine or other miotics. The combination of epinephrine and a miotic is more effective in reducing intraocular pressure than either of the two drugs alone; similar effects have been found with the combined use of epinephrine and a carbonic anhydrase inhibitor.

Epinephrine is contraindicated preoperatively for treatment of patients with angle-closure glaucoma, but may be used after iridectomy.

CARBONIC ANHYDRASE INHIBITORS

When adequate control of intraocular pressure cannot be obtained with topically applied agents, the concomitant use of a systemically-administered carbonic anhydrase inhibitor often is of value. These drugs were originally introduced as diuretics, but their effect on intraocular pressure does not depend upon diuresis. They reduce the inflow of aqueous humor and thus lower pressure, possibly by blocking ocular carbonic anhydrase.

Carbonic anhydrase inhibitors are of greatest value in the long-term treatment of primary open-angle glaucoma that cannot be controlled by miotics and epinephrine. They also are used with miotics and osmotic agents in the *short-term* preoperative treatment of acute angle-closure glaucoma, but they should not be given chronically prior to iridectomy. Short-term administration of carbonic anhydrase inhibitors is useful in the self-limited secondary glaucomas (eg, glaucomatocyclitic crisis syndrome, glaucoma secondary to anterior uveitis or trauma), and prolonged therapy may be effective in some cases of chronic secondary glaucoma. These agents are also of value in the preoperative treatment of congenital glaucoma.

Acetazolamide [Diamox], which may be given orally or parenterally, is the most commonly used carbonic anhydrase inhibitor. Newer orally administered analogues include dichlorphenamide [Daranide, Oratrol], ethoxzolamide [Cardrase, Ethamide], and methazolamide [Neptazane]. All of the carbonic anhydrase inhibitors are effective in reducing intraocular pressure and their adverse effects are similar; however, some patients who cannot tolerate one agent may do well on another.

OSMOTIC AGENTS

Hypertonic solutions of glycerin [Glyrol, Osmoglyn], urea [Urevert, Ureaphil], or mannitol [Osmitrol] can be given systemically to reduce intraocular pressure. By increasing blood osmolarity, these agents induce the withdrawal of fluid from the eyeball by an osmotic effect. They cause an immediate, marked fall in intraocular pressure and are often effective in patients who do not respond to miotics and carbonic anhydrase inhibitors.

Osmotic agents are used with miotics and carbonic anhydrase inhibitors in primary angle-closure glaucoma to reduce intraocular pressure prior to iridectomy. In addition, they may be used preoperatively in congenital glaucoma, retinal detachment surgery, routine cataract extraction, and keratoplasty. The osmotic agents also are effective in some secondary glaucomas (eg, glaucoma secondary to anterior uveitis); glycerin and mannitol are preferred in these conditions because urea readily penetrates ocular fluids, particularly in the presence of inflammation. In primary open-angle glaucoma, these agents are generally used only for preoperative treatment of patients in whom surgery has become necessary.

Urea and mannitol usually are given intravenously; they are equally effective in reducing intraocular pressure, but mannitol is less toxic. Glycerin, which is administered orally, is not as rapidly effective as the intravenous agents, but often is preferred because of its safety and convenience.

Adverse Reactions and Precautions

Miotics: Miotics may cause a variety of untoward reactions as a result of their local actions on ocular structures. These occur most frequently with the long-acting anticholinesterase agents and occasionally with the short-acting cholinesterase inhibitors. The parasympathomimetics rarely cause adverse reactions.

Common local effects induced by miotics include twitching of the eyelids, browache, headache, ocular pain, ciliary and conjunctival congestion, accommodative myopia, and poor vision in dim light. Localized allergy occasionally develops, manifested by conjunctivitis and contact dermatitis; this complication occurs frequently with physostigmine solutions.

When the long-acting anticholinesterase drugs are administered for long periods, cysts may develop at the pupillary margin of the iris, particularly in children. These rounded nodules of the pigmentary epithelium sometimes enlarge sufficiently to interfere with vision, but generally disappear when the drug is discontinued. Their incidence can be reduced if one or two drops of a 2.5% solution of phenylephrine [Neo-Synephrine] are instilled simultaneously with the anticholinesterase agent.

Pupillary block and severe local vascular congestion induced by the long-acting anticholinesterase agents may cause a precipitous rise in intraocular pressure in eyes with narrow angles. For this reason, these drugs are contraindicated prior to iridectomy in angle-closure glaucoma. Very rarely, the short-acting miotics have produced pupillary block in predisposed eyes.

Rare complications of topical therapy with the long-acting cholinesterase inhibitors are uveitis, iritis, and the formation of peripheral anterior synechiae and posterior synechiae. These drugs may increase the frequency of hemorrhage during ocular surgery. After filtering operations, they cause an inflammatory response, thus increasing the possibility of the formation of posterior synechiae. The size of the resultant drainage bleb also may be reduced. Pilocarpine should be substituted for the long-acting miotics several weeks prior to filtering surgery or cataract extraction. In secondary glaucomas when there is an active inflammatory process (eg, glaucoma secondary to anterior uveitis) miotics usually are of little therapeutic value and may predispose to development of posterior synechiae.

There is evidence that the incidence of cataracts is increased by prolonged treatment with the long-acting anticholinesterase agents, particularly in patients over 60 years of age. These cataracts are characterized by the early appearance of anterior subcapsular vacuoles. Echothiophate [Phospholine] has been implicated most frequently, possibly because of its wider usage. The incidence of this type of cataract is not increased by long-term treatment with pilocarpine, carbachol, or concomitant use of pilocarpine and physostigmine.

Detachment of the retina has been reported in patients treated with miotics, particularly the long-acting cholinesterase inhibitors. These drugs should be used with caution in patients with a history of retinal detachment.

Topically applied miotics can be absorbed and occasionally cause systemic effects. Systemic reactions are extremely rare following administration of pilocarpine or carbachol, and occur most frequently with the long-acting anticholinesterase drugs, particularly echothiophate. Symptoms include hypersalivation, sweating, nausea, vomiting, abdominal pain, diarrhea, bradycardia, hypotension, and bronchoconstriction. Therefore, these drugs should be used with caution in patients with intestinal or urinary obstruction or in those with a history of bronchial asthma. Toxic doses of the anticholinesterase agents can cause central nervous system effects (ataxia, confusion, convulsions, coma) and muscular paralysis; death can result from respiratory failure. Pressure at the inner canthus after instillation will minimize drainage into the nose and throat, and may reduce the likelihood of systemic reactions.

Prolonged apnea may develop if depolarizing neuromuscular blocking agents (succinylcholine or decamethonium [Syncurine]) are given during anesthesia to patients receiving anticholinesterase drugs (see Chapter 20, Adjuncts to Anesthesia).

Epinephrine: Topically applied epinephrine can cause pupillary dilatation, even when used with potent miotics. It is contraindicated preoperatively for the treatment of angle-closure glaucoma because it may precipitate an acute attack. Epinephrine causes browache, headache, blurred vision, ocular irritation, and lacrimation in some patients. With repeated use, the drug may cause reactive hyperemia and allergic conjunctivitis and contact dermatitis. About 20% of patients cannot tolerate prolonged use of this agent because of these reactions. Corneal edema may occur after prolonged administration.

When instilled without miotics in patients with open-angle glaucoma, epinephrine has rarely caused a temporary elevation of intraocular pressure with initial use. This may be associated with release of many pigment particles into the aqueous humor, presumably from the iris.

With long-term administration of epinephrine, melanin-like pigmentary deposits may appear in the conjunctiva of the lids or in roughened or edematous areas of the cornea. Its prolonged use in aphakic patients may lead to a decrease in visual acuity associated with vascular spasm, edema, and fine hemorrhages about the macula; in most instances, these changes are reversible, but a permanent loss of vision has occurred in some patients. The incidence of maculopathy in aphakic patients has been reported to be as high as 20% to 30%.

Very rare systemic reactions to topically applied epinephrine include tachycardia, premature ventricular contractions, hypertension, headache, sweating, tremors, and blanching. In several instances, systemic effects have occurred when the drug was applied after the corneal epithelium was damaged or its permeability was increased by tonometry or the administration of local anesthetics.

Epinephrine should be used with care in individuals with arrhythmias, hypertension, hyperthyroidism, and arteriosclerotic heart disease. It may cause ventricular premature contractions, tachycardia, and fibrillation in patients undergoing general anesthesia with halothane [Fluothane], cyclopropane, or other agents that sensitize the heart to catecholamines (see Chapter 19, General Anesthetics).

Carbonic Anhydrase Inhibitors: Common systemic adverse effects of the carbonic anhydrase inhibitors include diuresis, paresthesias, gastrointestinal disturbances (anorexia, nausea, vomiting, and diarrhea), drowsiness, and fatigue. Headache, dizziness, depression, and confusion also may occur. These agents occasionally cause ureteral calculus formation with colic, exacerbation of gout, drug fever, rash, transient myopia, and, very rarely, bone marrow depression. Excessive excretion of electrolytes is uncommon; however, the cautious use of a potassium supplement may be desirable to counteract any tendency to develop hypokalemia. Carbonic anhydrase inhibitors are contraindicated in patients with conditions in which sodium and potassium ions are depleted, including chronic adrenocortical insufficiency (Addison's disease) and all types of adrenal failure.

In patients with angle-closure glaucoma, carbonic anhydrase inhibitors should be used only for short-term emergency treatment prior to iridectomy. If surgery is delayed and miotic therapy does not completely open the angle, peripheral anterior synechiae may develop. In such patients, the use of carbonic anhydrase inhibitors will temporarily reduce the intraocular pressure but the progressive destruction of the angle will be obscured.

Eventually the angle may become sufficiently compromised to preclude successful iridectomy.

It has been suggested that the pre- or postoperative use of carbonic anhydrase inhibitors may adversely affect the outcome of filtering operations by reducing the size of the resultant drainage bleb and delaying reformation of the anterior chamber.

Osmotic Agents: The osmotic agents often cause headache, nausea, and vomiting. Serious adverse effects may follow administration of urea or mannitol; these are discussed in the individual evaluations. Glycerin is safer than the intravenously administered agents and often is preferred for this reason.

MIOTICS

Parasympathomimetics

PILOCARPINE HYDROCHLORIDE
PILOCARPINE NITRATE

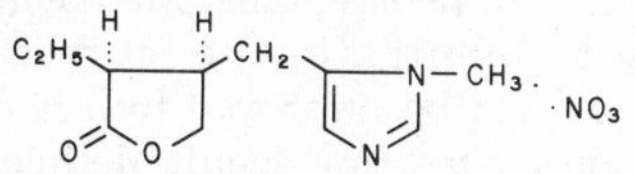

Pilocarpine is the drug of choice for initial and maintenance therapy in primary open-angle glaucoma. It also is used for the emergency treatment of primary angle-closure glaucoma and in congenital glaucoma to reduce the intraocular pressure prior to surgery. In addition, it is used to counteract cycloplegic drugs. Pilocarpine penetrates the eye well; after conjunctival instillation, miosis begins in 15 to 30 minutes and lasts four to eight hours. Reduction of intraocular pressure is maximal in 75 minutes.

Pilocarpine generally is tolerated better than all other miotics. It seldom causes local irritation, and allergic reactions are uncommon. It rarely causes systemic effects, but should be used cautiously in patients with bronchial asthma.

USUAL DOSAGE.—*Topical* (local instillation into conjunctival sac):

In primary open-angle glaucoma, the drug should be given in the concentration and at the frequency necessary to maintain a satisfactory reduction in intraocular pressure. Initially, one or two drops of a 1% or 2% solution are instilled in each eye every six to eight hours. A 0.25% or 0.5% solution may be tried if stronger concentrations are not tolerated. The concentration and frequency of administration may be increased later as needed; in most patients, concentrations above 4% are of little additional benefit, but some patients may be satisfactorily controlled with higher concentrations. If resistance develops during prolonged use, it has been reported that responsiveness may be restored by substituting an anticholinesterase drug for a period of time.

In acute primary angle-closure glaucoma prior to surgery, initially one or two drops of a 2% solution are instilled in the affected eye every minute for five minutes. One or two drops are then instilled every five minutes for 25 minutes, followed by one or two drops three or four times an hour until the angle opens. Three drops of a 1% solution may be instilled in the unaffected eye every eight hours to avoid a bilateral attack.

In congenital glaucoma, some surgeons instill one or two drops of a 2% solution in the affected eye every six hours, then every 10 minutes for 30 minutes immediately prior to surgery.

To counteract mydriasis and restore accommodative power after use of cycloplegics, one or two drops of a 1% or 2% solution are instilled as needed.

PREPARATIONS.—

Pilocarpine Hydrochloride:

Almocarpine (Ayerst). *Topical:* Solution (ophthalmic) 0.5%, 1%, 2%, 3%, and 4% with benzalkonium chloride, boric acid, potassium chloride, and sodium carbonate in 15 ml containers.

BufOpto Pilocel (Professional). *Topical:* Solution (ophthalmic) 0.25%, 0.5%, 1%, 2%, 3%, 4%, and 6% with methylcellulose, benzalkonium chloride, boric acid, sodium citrate, and potassium chloride in 15 and 30 ml containers.

Isopto Carpine (Alcon). *Topical:* Solution (ophthalmic) 0.25%, 0.5%, 1%, 2%, 3%, 4%, 5%, 6%, 8%, and 10% with hydroxypropyl methylcellulose, benzalkonium chloride, phenylmercuric nitrate, boric acid, sodium citrate, citric acid, and sodium chloride (in 1% solution only) in 15 and 30 ml containers.

Mi-Pilo (Barnes-Hind). *Topical:* Solution (ophthalmic) 1%, 2%, and 4% with sodium biphosphate, sodium phosphate, sodium chloride, benzalkonium chloride, and disodium edetate in 15 ml containers.

Pilocar (Smith, Miller & Patch). *Topical:* Solution (ophthalmic) 1%, 2%, and 4% with benzalkonium chloride, disodium edetate, potassium chloride, boric acid, and sodium carbonate in 1 ml containers; solution (ophthalmic) 0.5%, 1%, 2%, 3%, 4%, and 6% with hydroxypropyl methylcellulose, benzalkonium chloride, disodium edetate, potassium chloride, boric acid, and sodium carbonate in 15 ml containers.

Pilomiotin (Cooper). *Topical:* Solution (ophthalmic) 0.5%, 1%, 2%, 3%, and 4% in 15 ml. containers; 1%, 2%, and 4% in 1 ml containers.

Drug also marketed under generic name.

Pilocarpine Nitrate:

P.V. Carpine Liquifilm (Allergan). *Topical:* Solution (ophthalmic) 0.5%, 1%, 2%, 3%, 4%, and 6% with polyvinyl alcohol in 15 ml containers.

CARBACHOL

$$NH_2\overset{O}{\overset{\|}{C}}OCH_2CH_2\overset{+}{N}(CH_3)_3 \cdot Cl^-$$

Carbachol is used in the primary glaucomas as a replacement for pilocarpine when resistance or intolerance to the latter has developed. It is slightly more potent than pilocarpine but does not penetrate the eye as well; however, it is usually prepared with a wetting agent to enhance corneal penetration.

Carbachol may cause more accommodative spasm and headache than pilocarpine and may produce slight conjunctival hyperemia. Other local and systemic adverse reactions occur rarely (see the Introductory Statement).

USUAL DOSAGE.—*Topical* (local instillation into conjunctival sac):

In primary open-angle glaucoma, one or two drops of a 0.75% to 3% solution are instilled in each eye every four to eight hours. The drug should be given in the concentration and at the frequency necessary to maintain a satisfactory reduction in intraocular pressure.

In acute primary angle-closure glaucoma prior to surgery, initially, one or two drops of a 1.5% solution are instilled in the affected eye every minute for five minutes. One or two drops are then instilled every five minutes for 25 minutes, followed by one or two drops three or four times an hour until the angle opens. Three drops may be instilled in the unaffected eye every eight hours to avoid a bilateral attack.

PREPARATIONS.—

BufOpto Carbacel (Professional). *Topical:* Solution (ophthalmic) 0.75%, 1.5%, and 3% with methylcellulose and benzalkonium chloride in 15 ml containers.

Isopto Carbachol (Alcon). *Topical:* Solution (ophthalmic) 0.75%, 1.5%, 2.25%, and 3% with hydroxypropyl methylcellulose, benzalkonium chloride, boric acid, sodium chloride, and sodium borate in 15 and 30 ml containers.

P.V. Carbachol (Allergan). *Topical:* Solution (ophthalmic) 0.75%, 1.5%, and 3% with polyvinyl alcohol, benzalkonium chloride, disodium edetate, sodium chloride, and potassium chloride in 30 ml containers.

METHACHOLINE CHLORIDE

[Mecholyl Chloride]

$$CH_3COOCH(CH_3)CH_2\overset{+}{N}(CH_3)_3 \cdot Cl^-$$

Methacholine is a very short-acting miotic that may be used for the emergency treatment of angle-closure glaucoma; it is generally alternated with neostigmine. Methacholine alone does not penetrate the cornea well, but penetration can be improved by use of a topical anesthetic or a wetting agent. Methacholine also is used for the diagnosis of Adie's pupil, a disorder of pupillary motility which is characterized by supersensitivity to parasympathomimetic drugs; a weak solution of methacholine (without a wetting agent) has no effect on the normal pupil but causes constriction of the sensitized pupil encountered in Adie's syndrome.

Methacholine may cause systemic reactions such as flushing, sweating, and hypotension. It is contraindicated in patients with bronchial asthma.

USUAL DOSAGE.—*Topical* (local instillation into conjunctival sac):

In acute primary angle-closure glaucoma prior to surgery, one or two drops of a freshly-prepared 10% solution are instilled in the affected eye every ten minutes until the angle opens. The drug is generally alternated with a 5% solution of neostigmine. The unaffected eye may be treated every eight hours to avoid a bilateral attack.

For diagnosis of Adie's pupil, one or two drops of a freshly-prepared 2.5% solution are instilled in both eyes. To establish the diagnosis, the pupil of the affected eye should constrict within approximately 30 minutes.

PREPARATIONS.—Mecholyl Chloride (Quinton). *Topical:* Powder (for solution) 25 mg.

Short-Acting Anticholinesterase Agents

PHYSOSTIGMINE
PHYSOSTIGMINE SALICYLATE
PHYSOSTIGMINE SULFATE

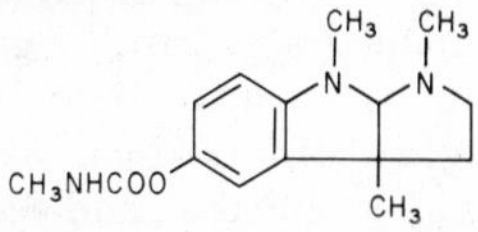

Physostigmine has been used in primary open-angle glaucoma and occasionally is administered in the emergency treatment of angle-closure glaucoma. It also has been used in the treatment of accommodative esotropia, but long-acting cholinesterase inhibitors are more commonly administered for this purpose. Physostigmine produces miosis in about 30 minutes and the effect may last 12 to 36 hours.

Physostigmine is rarely tolerated for prolonged periods because conjunctivitis and allergic reactions occur frequently. Long-term administration can produce follicles in the cul-de-sac. In Negroes, reversible depigmentation of the lid margins occasionally is seen after prolonged treatment with physostigmine ointments. For other adverse reactions and precautions, see the Introductory Statement.

Solutions are sensitive to light and heat and should not be used if discolored. Ointments and preparations of the alkaloid in oil may cause blurred vision and are usually reserved for nighttime use.

USUAL DOSAGE.—*Topical* (local instillation into conjunctival sac):

Physostigmine, Physostigmine Salicylate:

In primary open-angle glaucoma, one or two drops of a 0.25% to 1% solution are instilled in each eye every four to six hours. The ointment may be used at night. The drug should be given in the lowest effective concentration and no more frequently than is necessary to maintain a satisfactory reduction of intraocular pressure.

In acute primary angle-closure glaucoma prior to surgery, one or two drops of a 0.25% solution are instilled in the affected eye every five minutes for 30 minutes, then at 30-minute intervals until the angle opens. The drug may be alternated with pilocarpine if desired. To avoid a bilateral attack, the unaffected eye may be treated every eight hours.

Physostigmine Sulfate:

The sulfate salt is rarely used. For primary open-angle glaucoma, the U.S.P. dose is 0.1 ml of a 0.25% to 1% solution up to four times daily.

PREPARATIONS.—

Physostigmine:

Topical: Ointment (ophthalmic) 0.25%. Drug marketed under generic name.

Physostigmine Salicylate:

Isopto Eserine (Alcon). *Topical:* Solution (ophthalmic) 0.25% and 0.5% with hydroxypropyl methylcellulose, chlorobutanol, sodium bisulfite, sodium chloride, and citric acid in 15 ml containers.

Solution (0.25% to 1%) and ointment 0.25% also marketed by other manufacturers under generic name.

Physostigmine Sulfate:

Topical: Ointment (ophthalmic) 0.25% in 1/8 oz containers; solution (ophthalmic) 0.25% in 15 ml containers. Drug marketed under generic name.

NEOSTIGMINE BROMIDE
[Prostigmin Bromide]

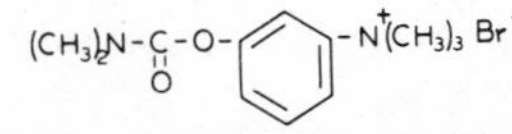

Neostigmine is occasionally used in primary open-angle glaucoma and in the emergency treatment of angle-closure glaucoma to reduce intraocular pressure prior to iridectomy. It also has been administered in accommodative esotropia, but the long-acting anticholinesterase agents are more commonly used for this purpose. Neostigmine is not as effective as physostigmine, since it does not penetrate the eye as well, but it is more stable and less irritating.

For adverse reactions and precautions, see the Introductory Statement.

For other uses of neostigmine, see Chapter 75, Agents Used in Myasthenia Gravis, and Chapter 86, Stimulants of Gastrointestinal and Urinary Tracts.

USUAL DOSAGE.—*Topical* (local instillation into conjunctival sac):

In primary open-angle glaucoma, one or two drops of a 3% to 5% solution are instilled in each eye every four to six hours. The drug should be given in the lowest effective concentration and no more frequently than is necessary to maintain a satisfactory reduction in intraocular pressure.

In acute primary angle-closure glaucoma prior to surgery, one or two drops of a 5% solution are instilled in the affected eye as often as necessary to maintain a reduction in intraocular pressure. Neostigmine may be alternated with pilocarpine or methacholine if desired. To avoid a bilateral attack, the unaffected eye may be treated every eight hours.

PREPARATIONS.—Prostigmin Bromide (Roche). *Topical:* Solution (ophthalmic) 5% with boric acid, methylparaben, and propylparaben in 7.5 ml containers. (Solution may be diluted if desired.)

Long-Acting Anticholinesterase Agents

DEMECARIUM BROMIDE [Humorsol]

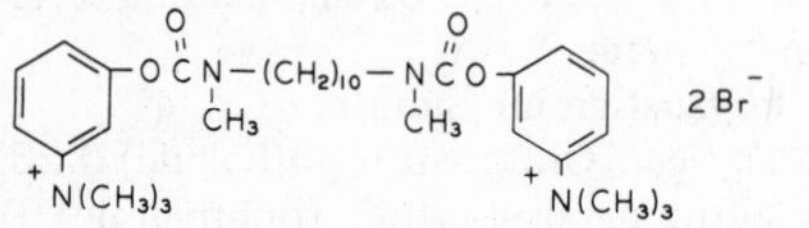

$$\text{C}_6\text{H}_4(\overset{+}{N}(CH_3)_3)\text{-O-}\overset{O}{\overset{\|}{C}}\text{-}\underset{CH_3}{\underset{|}{N}}\text{-}(CH_2)_{10}\text{-}\underset{CH_3}{\underset{|}{N}}\text{-}\overset{O}{\overset{\|}{C}}\text{-O-C}_6\text{H}_4(\overset{+}{N}(CH_3)_3)\quad 2Br^-$$

Demecarium is a potent, long-acting miotic that is used to treat primary open-angle glaucoma, glaucoma (which is not due to pupillary block) in aphakia, and accommodative esotropia. After a single instillation, demecarium causes a reduction in intraocular pressure which is maximal in 24 hours and may persist for nine days or more.

The long-acting anticholinesterase drugs are more toxic than short-acting miotics and should be used in primary open-angle glaucoma only when the short-acting agents have proved inadequate. They should not be used prior to iridectomy in angle-closure glaucoma because they may precipitate an acute attack. With prolonged administration, iris cysts may develop, particularly in children; the incidence of cysts may be reduced by the simultaneous instillation of one or two drops of a 2.5% solution of phenylephrine. For other adverse reactions and precautions, see the Introductory Statement.

USUAL DOSAGE.—*Topical* (local instillation into conjunctival sac):

In primary open-angle glaucoma, one drop of a 0.125% or 0.25% solution is instilled in each eye every 12 to 48 hours. The drug should be used at the lowest effective concentration and no more frequently than is necessary to control intraocular pressure.

In accommodative esotropia, one drop of a 0.125% solution is instilled in each eye daily for two to three weeks, followed by one drop on alternate days for three weeks. Further administration depends upon the clinical response.

PREPARATIONS.—Humorsol (Merck Sharp & Dohme). *Topical:* Solution (ophthalmic) 0.125% and 0.25% with sodium chloride and benzalkonium chloride in 5 ml containers.

ECHOTHIOPHATE IODIDE [Phospholine Iodide]

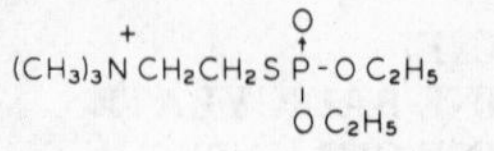

$$(CH_3)_3\overset{+}{N}CH_2CH_2S\overset{O}{\overset{\uparrow}{P}}\text{-}OC_2H_5\quad I^-$$
$$\qquad\qquad\qquad\qquad |\ OC_2H_5$$

Echothiophate is a potent, long-acting miotic that is used to treat primary open-angle glaucoma, glaucoma (which is not due to pupillary block) in aphakia, and accommodative esotropia. After a single instillation, echothiophate causes a reduction in intraocular pressure which is maximal after 24 hours and may persist up to four days.

The long-acting anticholinesterase drugs are more toxic than short-acting miotics and should be used in primary open-angle glaucoma only when the short-acting agents have proved inadequate. They should not be used prior to iridectomy in angle-closure glaucoma because they may precipitate an acute attack. With prolonged administration, iris cysts may develop, particularly in children; the incidence of cysts may be reduced by the simultaneous instillation of one or two drops of a 2.5% phenylephrine solution. For other adverse reactions and precautions, see the Introductory Statement.

USUAL DOSAGE.—*Topical* (local instillation into conjunctival sac):

In primary open-angle glaucoma, initially, one drop of a 0.03% to 0.06% solution is instilled in each eye every 12 to 48 hours. The drug should be given in the lowest effective concentration (maximum, 0.25%) and no more frequently than is necessary to maintain a reduction in intraocular pressure.

In accommodative esotropia, initially, one drop of a 0.125% solution is instilled in each eye once daily for two to three weeks. Subsequent administration depends upon clinical response.

PREPARATIONS.—Phospholine Iodide (Ayerst). *Topical:* Lyophilized powder 1.5, 3, 6.25, and 12.5 mg with 5 ml of diluent to make 0.03%, 0.06%, 0.125%, and 0.25% solutions, respectively.

ISOFLUROPHATE (DFP) [Floropryl]

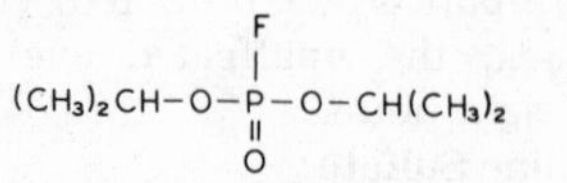

$$(CH_3)_2CH\text{-}O\text{-}\underset{\underset{O}{\|}}{\overset{\overset{F}{|}}{P}}\text{-}O\text{-}CH(CH_3)_2$$

Isoflurophate is a potent, long-acting miotic that is used to treat primary open-angle glaucoma, glaucoma (which is not due to pupillary block) in aphakia, and accommodative esotropia. After a single instillation, isoflurophate causes a reduction in intraocular pressure which is maximal within 24 hours and may persist for a week.

The long-acting anticholinesterase drugs are more toxic than short-acting miotics and should be used in primary open-angle glaucoma only when the short-acting agents have proved inadequate. They should not be used prior to iridectomy in angle-closure glaucoma because they may precipitate an acute attack. With prolonged administration, iris cysts may develop, particularly in children; the incidence of cysts may be reduced by the simultaneous instillation of one or two drops of a 2.5% phenylephrine solution.

Isoflurophate is rapidly hydrolyzed by water; therefore, patients should be instructed not to touch the eyes or lids with the dropper or to transfer tears or water into the container. The solution in oil and the ointment may cause blurred vision. For other adverse reactions and precautions, see the Introductory Statement.

USUAL DOSAGE.—*Topical* (local instillation into conjunctival sac):

In primary open-angle glaucoma, one or two drops of a 0.01% to 0.1% solution are instilled in each eye every 12 to 48 hours. The drug should be given in the lowest effective concentration and no more frequently than is necessary to maintain a satisfactory reduction of intraocular pressure.

In accommodative esotropia, one drop of a 0.025% ointment is instilled every night for two weeks, then one drop every other day to one drop once a week for two months.

PREPARATIONS.—Floropryl (Merck Sharp & Dohme). *Topical:* Ointment (ophthalmic) 0.025% in polyethylene-mineral oil gel in 3.5 g containers; solution (ophthalmic) 0.1% in anhydrous peanut oil in 5 ml containers.

EPINEPHRINE

EPINEPHRINE BITARTRATE
EPINEPHRINE HYDROCHLORIDE
EPINEPHRYL BORATE

Epinephrine is applied topically in the treatment of primary open-angle glaucoma. It is usually given with a miotic but occasionally has been used alone. The intraocular pressure falls rapidly within one hour after instillation and is maintained at a satisfactory level for 12 hours. When epinephrine is given with either a miotic or a carbonic anhydrase inhibitor, the reduction in intraocular pressure is greater than that produced by the individual agents.

Local adverse reactions to epinephrine include browache, headache, blurred vision, ocular irritation, lacrimation, reactive hyperemia, allergic conjunctivitis, and contact dermatitis. Pigmentary deposits may appear in the conjunctiva of the lids or in roughened or edematous areas of the cornea after long-term administration. Macular damage may occur in aphakic patients. Systemic reactions occur infrequently. Epinephrine is contraindicated preoperatively for treatment of angle-closure glaucoma. For other adverse reactions and precautions, see the Introductory Statement.

For other uses of epinephrine see Chapters 2, Antiarrhythmic Agents; 5, Agents Used in Hypotension and Shock; 18, Local Anesthetics; 41, Bronchodilators; 42, Nasal Decongestants; and 70, Mydriatics and Cycloplegics.

USUAL DOSAGE.—*Topical* (local instillation into conjunctival sac): In primary open-angle glaucoma, one drop of a 1% to 2% solution is instilled in each eye once or twice daily. In some patients, the 0.5% concentration may be adequate.

PREPARATIONS.—

Epinephrine Bitartrate:

BufOpto Mytrate (Professional). *Topical:* Solution (ophthalmic) 1% and 2% with methylcellulose, benzalkonium chloride, sodium bisulfite, and disodium edetate in 5 and 15 ml containers.

Epitrate (Ayerst). *Topical:* Solution (ophthalmic) 2% (equivalent to 1.1% base) with chlorobutanol, sodium bisulfite, sodium chloride, poloxalkol, and disodium edetate in 7.5 ml containers.

IOP (Smith, Miller & Patch). *Topical:* Solution (ophthalmic) IOP ¼, IOP ½, IOP 1 (base equivalent to bitartrate salt of 0.5%, 1%, and 2%) with mannitol, benzalkonium chloride, sodium bisulfite, monobasic and dibasic sodium phosphate, and disodium edetate in 10 ml containers.

Lyophrin (Alcon). *Topical:* Powder (ophthalmic) 100 mg with 5 ml of diluent with sodium bisulfite, disodium edetate, benzalkonium chloride, boric acid, and polysorbate 80 to make 2% solution.

Murocoll (Muro). *Topical:* Solution (ophthalmic) 1.82% (equivalent to 1% base) and 3.64% (equivalent to 2% base) with chlorobutanol, sodium bisulfite, and sodium chloride in 7.5 ml containers.

Epinephrine Hydrochloride:

Epifrin (Allergan). *Topical:* Solution (ophthalmic) 0.25%, 0.5%, 1%, and 2% with benzalkonium chloride, sodium metabisulfite, disodium edetate in 5 ml (0.5%, 1%, and 2% solutions) and 15 ml containers (all strengths).

Epinephrine 1:1000 (Cooper). *Topical:* Solution (ophthalmic) as the hydrochloride in 1 ml containers.

Glaucon (Alcon). *Topical:* Solution (ophthalmic) 0.5%, 1%, and 2% in 10 ml containers.

Epinephryl Borate:

Epinal (Alcon). *Topical:* Solution (ophthalmic) 0.5% and 1% with benzalkonium chloride, hydroxypropyl methylcellulose, ascorbic acid, acetylcysteine, boric acid, and sodium carbonate in 7.5 ml containers.

Eppy (Barnes-Hind). *Topical:* Solution (ophthalmic) 0.5% and 1% with sodium bisulfite, oxyquinoline sulfate, and phenylmercuric acetate in 7.5 ml containers.

CARBONIC ANHYDRASE INHIBITORS

ACETAZOLAMIDE [Diamox]
ACETAZOLAMIDE SODIUM [Diamox Sodium]

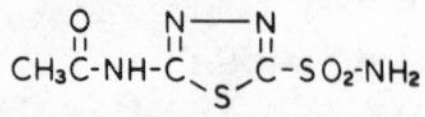

$CH_3C(=O)$-NH-C(=N-N=)C-SO_2-NH_2 (thiadiazole ring, S)

Acetazolamide is given systemically to lower the intraocular pressure. A single oral dose reduces the intraocular pressure for three to five hours. Acetazolamide is useful in the long-term treatment of primary open-angle glaucoma that cannot be managed by miotics and epinephrine. It also is used with miotics and osmotic agents in the *short-term* preoperative treatment of primary angle-closure glaucoma but should not be given chronically prior to iridectomy. Short-term administration also is indicated in the self-limited secondary glaucomas, and prolonged therapy may be effective in some cases of chronic secondary glaucoma.

Gastrointestinal disturbances and paresthesias are the most common adverse effects of acetazolamide. For other adverse reactions and precautions, see the Introductory Statement.

For other uses of acetazolamide, see Chapter 7, Diuretics, and Chapter 31, Anticonvulsants.

USUAL DOSAGE.–

Acetazolamide:

Oral: Adults, 250 mg every six hours (range, 125 mg every 12 hours to 500 mg every 4 hours). The timed-release preparation may be given every 12 hours, but may not be as effective as the regular tablets.

Acetazolamide Sodium:

Intravenous, Intramuscular (used when patients with acute angle-closure glaucoma cannot take oral medication): *Adults,* initially, 500 mg; half is given intravenously and the remainder intramuscularly. The dose may be repeated, if necessary, in two to four hours. *Infants and children,* 5 to 10 mg/kg of body weight every six hours.

PREPARATIONS.–

Diamox (Lederle). *Oral:* Capsules (timed-release) 500 mg; tablets 125 and 250 mg.

Diamox [sodium] (Lederle). *Injection:* Powder 500 mg (reconstituted with at least 5 ml of sterile water for injection).

DICHLORPHENAMIDE [Daranide, Oratrol]

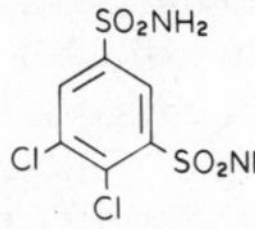

(Structure: benzene ring with two SO_2NH_2 groups and two Cl)

Dichlorphenamide is given systemically to reduce intraocular pressure. Its uses and adverse reactions are similar to those of acetazolamide (see the Introductory Statement).

USUAL DOSAGE.–*Oral: Adults,* 50 to 200 mg every six to eight hours.

PREPARATIONS.–Daranide (Merck Sharp & Dohme), Oratrol (Alcon). *Oral:* Tablets 50 mg.

ETHOXZOLAMIDE [Cardrase, Ethamide]

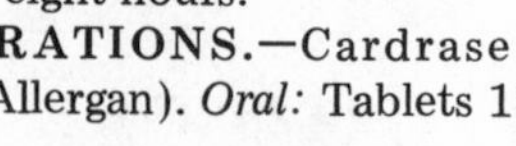

(Structure: C_2H_5O-benzothiazole-SO_2NH_2)

Ethoxzolamide is given systemically to reduce intraocular pressure. Its uses and adverse reactions are similar to those of acetazolamide (see the Introductory Statement).

USUAL DOSAGE.–*Oral: Adults,* 125 mg every six to eight hours.

PREPARATIONS.–Cardrase (Upjohn), Ethamide (Allergan). *Oral:* Tablets 125 mg.

METHAZOLAMIDE [Neptazane]

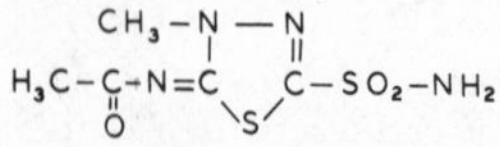

(Structure: H_3C-C(=O)-N=C (thiadiazoline ring with CH_3-N, N, S)-C-SO_2-NH_2)

Methazolamide is given systemically to reduce intraocular pressure. Its uses and adverse reactions are similar to those of acetazolamide; however, patients who are forced to discontinue acetazolamide because of the formation of renal calculi may tolerate methazolamide. This drug appears to cause more drowsiness and fatigue than the other carbonic anhydrase inhibitors. For other adverse reactions and precautions, see the Introductory Statement.

USUAL DOSAGE.—*Oral: Adults,* 50 to 100 mg every eight hours.

PREPARATIONS.—Neptazane (Lederle). *Oral:* Tablets 50 mg.

OSMOTIC AGENTS

GLYCERIN [Glyrol, Osmoglyn]

$$\begin{array}{c} CH_2OH \\ | \\ CHOH \\ | \\ CH_2OH \end{array}$$

Glycerin is given orally to reduce intraocular pressure. A maximal reduction in intraocular pressure occurs about one hour after administration, with a return to the pretreatment level in about five hours. Glycerin is used with miotics and carbonic anhydrase inhibitors in acute primary angle-closure glaucoma to reduce intraocular pressure prior to iridectomy. It also is effective in some secondary glaucomas (eg, glaucoma secondary to anterior uveitis), and may be used preoperatively in congenital glaucoma, retinal detachment surgery, routine cataract extraction, and keratoplasty. Its use in primary open-angle glaucoma is usually confined to preoperative treatment.

Glycerin is safer than the intravenously administered agents, urea and mannitol, but is less rapidly effective. Headache, nausea, and vomiting are the most common untoward effects of this agent. Diarrhea occurs occasionally. Glycerin may cause hyperglycemia and glycosuria and should be used cautiously in diabetics. Any of the systemic effects of dehydration that occur with the intravenous osmotic agents are potential hazards, but are less likely to occur with glycerin.

USUAL DOSAGE.—*Oral: Adults and children,* 1 to 1.5 g/kg of body weight, usually given as a 50% solution. The drug may be administered more than once daily, if necessary. Lemon juice may be added to increase palatability.

PREPARATIONS.—

Glyrol (Smith, Miller & Patch). *Oral:* Solution 75%.

Osmoglyn (Alcon). *Oral:* Solution 50%.

Also marketed under generic name in bulk form (unflavored), but proper dilution is necessary.

MANNITOL [Osmitrol]

$$HOCH_2\underset{OH}{\underset{|}{C}}H-\underset{OH}{\underset{|}{C}}H-\overset{OH}{\overset{|}{C}}H-\overset{OH}{\overset{|}{C}}HCH_2OH$$

Mannitol is given intravenously to reduce intraocular pressure. A maximal reduction in intraocular pressure occurs 30 to 60 minutes after injection and lasts about six hours. Mannitol is used with miotics and carbonic anhydrase inhibitors in acute angle-closure glaucoma to reduce intraocular pressure prior to iridectomy. It also is effective in some secondary glaucomas (eg, glaucoma secondary to anterior uveitis), and may be used preoperatively in congenital glaucoma, retinal detachment surgery, routine cataract extraction, and keratoplasty. Its use in primary open-angle glaucoma is usually confined to preoperative treatment.

If an intravenous osmotic agent is indicated, mannitol is generally preferred because it is less toxic than urea. Renal disease is not a contraindication to its use, and it does not cause tissue necrosis if extravasation of the solution occurs. However, mannitol requires a large volume for injection; therefore, urea or glycerin are preferred when there is danger of overloading the cardiovascular system.

Headache, nausea, vomiting, dehydration, and diuresis are common untoward effects of mannitol. Chills, dizziness, and chest pain also have been reported. The drug has occasionally caused pulmonary edema, agitation, disorientation, and convulsions. Fatalities have occurred after the administration of large doses.

For other uses, adverse reactions, and precautions, see Chapter 7, Diuretics, and Chapter 77, Miscellaneous Diagnostic Aids.

USUAL DOSAGE.—*Intravenous: Adults and children,* 0.5 to 2 g/kg of body weight in a 20% solution is infused slowly over a period of 30 to 60 minutes.

PREPARATIONS.—Osmitrol (Travenol). *Injection:* Solution 20% in 250 and 500 ml containers. Drug also marketed by other manufacturers under generic name in 5%, 10%, 15%, and 25% concentrations.

UREA FOR INJECTION [Urevert, Ureaphil]

$$\begin{array}{c} NH_2 \\ | \\ C{=}O \\ | \\ NH_2 \end{array}$$

Urea is given intravenously to reduce intraocular pressure. A maximal reduction in intraocular pressure appears one hour after injection, with a return to the pretreatment level in five to six hours. Urea is used with miotics and carbonic anhydrase inhibitors in acute primary angle-closure glaucoma to reduce intraocular pressure prior to iridectomy. It also is effective in some secondary glaucomas (eg, glaucoma secondary to anterior uveitis) and may be used preoperatively in congenital glaucoma, retinal detachment surgery, routine cataract extraction, and keratoplasty. Its use in primary open-angle glaucoma is usually confined to preoperative treatment.

Urea is more toxic than mannitol. Headache, nausea, vomiting, dehydration, and massive diuresis are common untoward effects. Dizziness, disorientation, and agitation also have been reported. The drug occasionally has caused pulmonary edema. Convulsions and death from subdural hemorrhage have occurred rarely. Urea is irritating to the tissues; it causes pain at the site of infusion and necrosis may occur if extravasation of the solution occurs. Urea should not be used in patients with severe renal disease.

For other uses, adverse reactions, and precautions, see Chapter 7, Diuretics.

USUAL DOSAGE.—*Intravenous: Adults,* 0.5 to 2 g/kg of body weight of a 30% solution is administered at a rate of 60 drops/minute. *Children,* 0.5 to 1.5 g/kg of a 30% solution is infused over a 30-minute period. The solution should be prepared just prior to use.

PREPARATIONS.—

Urevert (Travenol). *Injection:* Powder 40 and 90 g with diluent to make a 30% solution with 10% invert sugar.

Ureaphil (Abbott). *Injection:* Powder 40 g with diluent to make a 30% solution with 10% invert sugar.

MIXTURES

MIXTURES CONTAINING PILOCARPINE AND PHYSOSTIGMINE

The combination of pilocarpine and the short-acting anticholinesterase, physostigmine, may be used in the treatment of acute angle-closure glaucoma. To avoid the development of resistance to both agents, the use of these combination products is not advisable in primary open-angle glaucoma.

USUAL DOSAGE.—*Topical* (local instillation into conjunctival sac): In acute primary angle-closure glaucoma prior to surgery, one or two drops are instilled in the affected eye as often as necessary to obtain a reduction in intraocular pressure. To avoid a bilateral attack, the unaffected eye may be treated every eight hours.

PREPARATIONS.—

BufOpto Miocel (Professional). *Topical:* Solution (ophthalmic) containing physostigmine salicylate 0.125%, and pilocarpine hydrochloride 2% with methylcellulose, phenylmercuric acid, sodium bisulfite, boric acid and sodium carbonate in 5 and 15 ml containers.

Isopto P-ES (Alcon). *Topical:* Solution (ophthalmic) containing physostigmine salicylate 0.25% and pilocarpine hydrochloride 2% with hydroxypropyl methylcellulose, chlorobutanol, and boric acid in 15 ml containers.

MIXTURES CONTAINING PILOCARPINE AND EPINEPHRINE

Mixtures containing pilocarpine and epinephrine are available for use in the treatment of primary open-angle glaucoma. The usefulness of these fixed combinations is limited because of the difference in duration of action of the two components.

PREPARATIONS.—

E-Carpine (Alcon). *Topical:* Solution (ophthalmic) containing epinephrine bitartrate (equivalent to epinephrine base 0.5%) and pilocarpine hydrochloride 1%, 2%, 3%, 4%, or 6% with sodium bisulfite, benzalkonium chloride, and disodium edetate in 15 ml containers.

Epicar (Barnes-Hind). *Topical:* Solution (ophthalmic) containing epinephrine hydrochloride 0.65% (equivalent to epinephrine base 0.55%) and pilocarpine hydrochloride 1%, 2%, 3%, 4%, or 6% with benzalkonium chloride and disodium edetate in 15 ml containers.

E-Pilo (Smith, Miller & Patch). *Topical:* Solution (ophthalmic) containing epinephrine bitartrate 1% (equivalent to epinephrine base 0.55%) and pilocarpine hydrochloride 1%, 2%, 3%, 4%, or 6% with mannitol, benzalkonium chloride, sodium bisulfite, monobasic and dibasic sodium phosphate, and disodium edetate in 10 ml containers.

P1E1, P2E1, P3E1, and P6E1 (Person & Covey). *Topical:* Solution (ophthalmic) containing epinephrine bitartrate 1% and pilocarpine hydrochloride 1%, 2%, 3%, or 6% with chlorobutanol and benzalkonium in 15 ml containers.

Chapter 70

MYDRIATICS AND CYCLOPLEGICS

Anticholinergic drugs are applied topically to the eye to produce cycloplegia and mydriasis. These agents paralyze accommodation and dilate the pupil by relaxing the ciliary muscle and the sphincter muscle of the iris. They are used primarily as an aid in refraction and for other diagnostic purposes, pre- and postoperatively in intraocular surgery, and in the treatment of anterior uveitis and some secondary glaucomas. The anticholinergic drugs used topically in the eye include atropine, scopolamine, homatropine hydrobromide, cyclopentolate [Cyclogyl], tropicamide [Mydriacyl], and eucatropine.

Adrenergic drugs, such as phenylephrine [Efricel, Neo-Synephrine], are used to produce mydriasis without cycloplegia. These drugs dilate the pupil by causing contraction of the dilator muscle of the iris; they produce only slight relaxation of the ciliary muscle and, therefore, have no significant effect on accommodation. Since adrenergic and anticholinergic drugs act by different mechanisms, wider mydriasis can be obtained with combined therapy than with the individual agents. There is no convincing evidence that combined therapy has any significant effect on the onset, duration, or intensity of cycloplegia.

Phenylephrine is used as an aid in ophthalmoscopy and retinal photography, for pre- and postoperative mydriasis, and as an adjunct in the treatment of anterior uveitis. It is often given to supplement atropine when maximal mydriasis is desired. Other adrenergic drugs occasionally used as mydriatics are epinephrine and hydroxyamphetamine [Paredrine].

DIAGNOSTIC USES

Refraction: Both the cycloplegic and mydriatic actions of the anticholinergic drugs are useful in estimating errors of refraction. Paralysis of accommodation reveals latent refractive errors, and dilatation of the pupil facilitates estimation of the error and permits examination of the interior of the eye. The presence of mydriasis does not necessarily indicate adequate cycloplegia, as mydriasis generally occurs more rapidly than cycloplegia, persists for a longer period, and can be obtained with a lower concentration of the drug than is required for relaxation of accommodation.

Atropine is the most potent cycloplegic drug. It has a slow onset and a long duration of action; residual cycloplegia may persist for six days after instillation. Because of its prolonged action, atropine is not useful for refraction of adults, but it is often preferred for use in children under the age of 6, as accommodation is very active in young children. It is the agent of choice for refraction of all children with accommodative esotropia, for maximal cycloplegia is necessary to determine the total hypermetropic error in these patients. Since an accommodative factor may be present in every type of convergent strabismus, atropine is commonly used for the initial examination of all such cases.

Scopolamine has a cycloplegic effect comparable to that of atropine, but its duration of action is shorter. It is rarely used for refraction except in children who are sensitive to atropine.

The short-acting cycloplegics (homatropine, cyclopentolate, and tropicamide) are used for refraction in older children and adults, and their use in children under the age of 6 is not uncommon. These agents may be less effective in eyes with dark irides than in those with light irides; therefore, more frequent instillation or use of a stronger solution may be required to produce adequate cycloplegia in patients with brown or hazel eyes. Homatropine has the slowest onset and the most prolonged action of the short-acting cycloplegics: residual cycloplegia may persist for 36 to 48 hours after instillation. Cyclopentolate is more potent than homatropine and has a shorter duration of action. It provides adequate cycloplegia between 25 and 75 minutes after instillation, with complete recovery in 6 to 24 hours. Tropicamide has a very brief action and examination must be performed between 20 and 35 minutes after instillation or an additional drop must be applied. This drug generally provides sufficient cycloplegia for most refractive purposes, but residual accommodation may exceed 2.5 diopters in some patients. The major advantage of tropicamide is that complete recovery of accommodation occurs two to six hours after administration.

A 1% to 4% solution of pilocarpine may be used to counteract mydriasis and cycloplegia after use of the short-acting anticholinergics. The 1% solution is usually adequate and is less likely to cause untoward effects (spasm of accommodation and, very rarely, pupillary block). Because its duration of action is shorter than that of atropine and scopolamine, pilocarpine is not useful in counteracting the effects of these drugs.

Ophthalmoscopy and Retinal Photography: Adrenergic and short-acting anticholinergic drugs are used to dilate the pupil to permit ophthalmoscopic examination of the lens and posterior segment of the eye and as an aid in retinal photography. Phenylephrine and hydroxyamphetamine have the advantage of producing mydriasis without cycloplegia, thus sparing the patient the inconvenience of residual blurring of vision. Phenylephrine is considerably more effective than hydroxyamphetamine. For examination of the peripheral retina, more complete mydriasis is required than can generally be obtained with the adrenergic drugs. Cyclopentolate, tropicamide, or eucatropine are commonly used to produce wide pupillary dilation and may be supplemented with an adrenergic drug if required. After the examination, 1% pilocarpine may be instilled to counteract mydriasis.

Eyes with dark irides are often resistant to mydriatic drugs. Combined use of an adrenergic and anticholinergic drug may be necessary to provide adequate pupillary dilation in eyes with brown or hazel irides.

In patients with primary open-angle glaucoma, topically applied adrenergic drugs reduce the intraocular pressure; therefore, phenylephrine may be used safely to produce mydriasis for ophthalmoscopic examination. If wider dilatation is required, tropicamide may be instilled with the phenylephrine. Although anticholinergic drugs may increase the intraocular pressure in eyes with open-angle glaucoma, the pressure rise is reduced or abolished by the adrenergic drug.

Mydriatic drugs can precipitate an attack of acute angle-closure glaucoma in eyes with narrow angles and shallow anterior chambers. If pupillary dilatation is necessary for ophthalmoscopic examination of a patient with potential angle-closure, systemic ocular hypotensive drugs should be administered prior to the examination. Phenylephrine may be used to induce mydriasis or, for examination of only the posterior pole, a wick of cotton moistened with 1:1,000 epinephrine may be placed in the inferior cul-de-sac for three minutes. After the examination, 2% pilocarpine should be instilled as required until miosis is secured. The eye should be observed even after the pupil constricts to make certain that the intraocular pressure is not elevated.

Provocative Test for Angle-Closure Glaucoma: Short-acting anticholinergic drugs may be used to induce mydriasis in the shallow-chambered, narrow-angled eye in order to test the capacity for angle-closure. Eucatropine is preferred for this purpose, but may be difficult to obtain unless it is prepared by a pharmacist. Cyclopentolate and homatropine are occasionally used but the response is more difficult to control if test results are positive. A pressure rise of 8 mm Hg within an hour is considered positive (requiring iridectomy) *if* the angle is gonioscopically closed at the time of the pressure elevation. In the absence of an increase in intraocular pressure, the test is regarded as positive if tonography shows a reduction in outflow facility of 25% to 30% which is accompanied by gonioscopic evidence of increased angle-closure. Gonioscopic examination is essential because open-angle glaucomatous eyes also may show a pressure rise and a reduction in outflow facility after instillation of anticholinergic drugs.

Tonographic tracings detect a larger percentage of eyes capable of closure than do pressure measurements (80% to 85% as contrasted with 50%). If negative results are obtained in provocative testing of an eye with a gonioscopically narrow angle, repeated testing may be required.

Provocative testing may precipitate an attack of acute angle-closure glaucoma; therefore, only one eye should be tested at a time. At the conclusion of the test, 2% pilocarpine should be instilled as needed until miosis is secured. If the pupil does not constrict and the intraocular pressure continues to rise, a carbonic anhydrase inhibitor and an osmotic agent should be given systemically.

USES IN INTRAOCULAR SURGERY

Maximal mydriasis may be desired during intraocular surgery, particularly to facilitate round pupil cataract extraction and to locate the retinal break during retinal detachment operations. Atropine, supplemented with phenylephrine, is commonly used preoperatively for this purpose. If the pupil constricts during cataract surgery, epinephrine may be injected directly into the anterior chamber.

The pupil is usually dilated daily after intraocular surgery to avoid posterior synechiae which may develop as a complication of anterior segment inflammation (see following section). Generally, atropine or scopolamine is instilled one to several times daily until slit-lamp examination shows minimal iritis. Phenylephrine is commonly used in mild postoperative inflammation (eg, after iridectomy). After surgery for congenital cataracts, prolonged administration of both atropine (or scopolamine) and phenylephrine has been recommended; if the drugs are discontinued before all cortex is absorbed, formation of posterior synechiae and acute angle-closure glaucoma are common complications.

USES IN ANTERIOR UVEITIS AND GLAUCOMA SECONDARY TO INFLAMMATION

Anticholinergic drugs are applied locally in the nonspecific treatment of anterior uveitis and in secondary glaucomas associated with ocular inflammation. They are used for inflammations of the anterior segment of either endogenous or exogenous origin. Atropine is generally preferred because of its potent and prolonged action and is often given with phenylephrine to produce maximal mydriasis. Scopolamine also is commonly employed and is particularly useful in patients who become sensitive to atropine. Shorter-acting anticholinergic drugs, especially homatropine, are used in mild inflammatory conditions (eg, glaucomatocyclitic crisis) and are sometimes preferred whenever the intraocular pressure is elevated.

Anticholinergic drugs relieve the pain associated with anterior uveitis by relaxing the inflamed intraocular muscles; they also help prevent severe complications by dilating the pupil and by reducing abnormal vascular permeability.

When the pupil is miotic, the close contact between the inflamed iris and the central portion of the lens encourages the formation of posterior synechiae. These synechiae can completely seal the iris to the lens, preventing the passage of aqueous humor from the posterior to the anterior chamber. The accumulation of aqueous in the posterior chamber causes the iris to bulge forward and close the angle (iris bombe′), with a resultant sharp increase in intraocular pressure. Dilation of the pupil helps prevent the formation of posterior synechiae and may aid in breaking these adhesions once they have formed. Intensive topical therapy with atropine (or scopolamine) and phenylephrine is required if complete posterior synechiae from the iris to the lens have caused pupillary block and acute angle-closure glaucoma. If topical therapy is unsuccessful, subconjunctival injection of a mixture of cocaine, atropine, and epinephrine may break the synechiae.

In acute anterior uveitis, increased permeability of the blood vessels of the iris causes an outpouring of protein and inflammatory cells into the anterior chamber. This inflammatory debris can clog the angle, and permanent obstruction to aqueous outflow may result from the formation of peripheral anterior synechiae from the iris to the trabecular meshwork. Atropine may reduce the abnormal vascular permeability and prevent the development of secondary glaucoma. However, if peripheral anterior synechiae are suspected, it is advisable to avoid prolonged mydriasis and to encourage mobility of the pupil.

In addition to mydriatic-cycloplegic therapy, corticosteroids are used in anterior uveitis to reduce inflammation and anti-infective agents are given if the uveitis is associated with ocular infection. If the intraocular pressure is elevated, systemic ocular hypotensive agents are administered and epinephrine may be applied locally. (See Chapter 69, Agents Used to Treat Glaucoma, and Chapter 71, Anti-infective and Anti-inflammatory Agents Used in Ophthalmology.)

USES IN OTHER SECONDARY GLAUCOMAS

Glaucoma Due to Pupillary Block in Aphakia: Pupillary block may occur after cataract extraction due to formation of posterior synechiae from the iris to the vitreous or to the lens capsule. The intact hyaloid face of the vitreous may herniate through the pupil and press against the posterior cornea, with resultant corneovitreal adhesion and corneal opacification. Predisposing factors include wound leak, a persistent flat anterior chamber, prolonged, severe postoperative inflammation, and ciliary body detachment.

Aphakic pupillary block can often be relieved by intensive topical therapy with atropine (or scopolamine) and phenylephrine in addition to systemic administration of an osmotic agent to reduce vitreous volume. If topical therapy is ineffective, subconjunctival injection of a mixture of cocaine, atropine, and epinephrine may dilate the resistant pupil and break the pupillary block. It has been commonly accepted that the cocaine acts solely by potentiating the mydriatic effect of epinephrine; however, recent data indicate that cocaine may have an additional effect which is unrelated to mydriasis.

Cocaine was instilled topically in the eyes of several patients who developed late shallow or flat anterior chambers with corneovitreal contact after cataract extraction. In these eyes, the intraocular pressure is usually normal or low. In some of these patients, maximal mydriasis with other agents had failed to relieve the vitreous herniation. Cocaine caused rapid regression of the anterior hyaloid membrane from the cornea and a deepening of the anterior chamber. The mechanism by which cocaine caused retraction of the hyaloid face is unknown, but this effect was not associated with enhanced mydriasis. Both cocaine and epinephine appear to be indicated for treatment of vitreous herniation in all patients who have failed to respond to conventional drug therapy. These agents should be tried before attempting air injection or drainage of fluid from the vitreous cavity.

Miotic drugs are used to treat glaucoma in aphakic eyes that is not due to pupillary block (see Chapter 69, Agents Used to Treat Glaucoma).

Malignant Glaucoma: Malignant glaucoma is an uncommon complication of surgery for angle-closure glaucoma in which forward displacement of the lens and iris flattens the anterior chamber, causing angle-closure with pupillary block. Increased vitreous pressure and an abnormal slackness in the zonules of the lens are believed to be causative factors. Therapy with atropine and phenylephrine may break the pupillary block by promoting and maintaining re-formation of the anterior chamber. It has been postulated that mydriatic-cycloplegic therapy increases tension in the zonules and thereby pulls the lens back into position; dilatation of the pupil also may be a factor in breaking the pupillary block. In treating malignant glaucoma, systemic ocular hypotensive drugs are usually administered with the topical agents. After the anterior chamber has re-formed and the intraocular pressure is reduced, the systemic drugs and phenylephrine may be discontinued but atropine must be administered indefinitely; if atropine therapy is stopped, malignant glaucoma may recur and not respond to further therapy. Scopolamine may be substituted if sensitivity to atropine develops.

MISCELLANEOUS USES

Cycloplegic drugs have also been used to discourage accommodation in other ocular disorders. In patients with severe functional spasm of accommodation, atropine is sometimes applied daily for three or four weeks to provide a period of accommodative rest. In suppression amblyopia, cycloplegia has been employed as a form of partial occlusion. When instilled in the fixing eye, atropine reduces visual acuity, thereby forcing fixation with the amblyopic eye. It has been used to maintain equality of vision following total occlusion (patching), or as a substitute for total occlusion in very young or uncooperative patients who refuse to wear a patch. Partial occlusion with atropine is most effective if the fixing eye is severely hypermetropic, because cycloplegia causes greater visual impairment in hypermetropes than in myopes or emmetropes. If atropine does not force fixation with the amblyopic eye, total occlusion should be substituted.

In accommodative esotropia, atropine has occasionally been instilled daily in both eyes to discourage convergence by preventing accommodation. However, since the accommodative power is rarely completely inhibited, the blurring of vision induced by the cycloplegic may increase the accommodative effort, with a resultant exaggeration of convergence and an increase in the amount of esotropia. More commonly, long-acting anticholinesterase agents are used to induce accommodation without the central nervous system effort, thus reducing the amount of convergence associated with a given amount of accommodation (see Chapter 69, Agents Used to Treat Glaucoma).

A few ophthalmologists believe that the daily use of a cycloplegic drug will retard the progression of myopia in children, but the data available at present are not convincing. This treatment is based on a theory that excessive accommodation is a major factor in myopia and that myopic progression is due to continued spasm of the ciliary muscle with resultant nonreversible changes in the shape of the lens. Fundus changes and the increase in axial length of the eyeball have been attributed to "nutritional disturbances" of the retina, choroid, and sclera which are claimed to result from "stretching" of the retinal and choroidal blood vessels by the continued spasm of the ciliary muscle.

Adverse Reactions and Precautions

Mydriatic drugs (anticholinergic or adrenergic) can precipitate an attack of acute angle-closure glaucoma if instilled in eyes with narrow angles and shallow anterior chambers. An abrupt rise in intraocular pressure occurs because pupillary dilatation crowds the iris into the angle and relaxes the peripheral iris, permitting it to be pushed into the trabecular meshwork by pressure in the posterior chamber. Long-acting mydriatics such as atropine or scopolamine should not be used prior to iridectomy in eyes predisposed to angle-closure, and shorter-acting mydriatics should be used cautiously (see the previous discussion on uses).

Topically-applied anticholinergic drugs also increase intraocular pressure in some eyes with primary open-angle glaucoma. It has been estimated that a pressure rise occurs in about one out of three eyes with mild open-angle glaucoma after instillation of anticholinergic agents. This response is not caused by closure of the angle but appears to be due to an increase in resistance to aqueous outflow caused by loss of ciliary muscle tone. Short-acting anticholinergics may be used safely for diagnostic purposes in open-angle glaucomatous eyes when they are given with epinephrine or phenylephrine [Efricel, Neo-Synephrine], because the adrenergic drug will reduce or abolish the pressure rise. Atropine and scopolamine should be used cautiously.

In treating inflammation of the anterior segment, synechiae may form while the pupil is dilated if mydriatic drugs (anticholinergics and adrenergics) are applied for prolonged periods without moving the pupil. If slit-lamp examination shows that synechiae are forming, the mydriatic should be discontinued and a miotic should be substituted for a brief period.

Systemic reactions may occur after ocular instillation of the anticholinergic drugs, particularly in children and elderly patients. Symptoms of systemic toxicity include dryness of the mouth and skin, flushing, fever, rash, thirst, tachycardia, irritability, hyperactivity, ataxia, confusion, somnolence, hallucinations, and delirium. These reactions have been observed most frequently after use of atropine. Rarely, convulsions, coma, and death have occurred after ocular instillation of this drug in young children. Systemic reactions also have been noted after use of scopolamine or homatropine hydrobromide, and central nervous system disturbances have been reported in children following administration of cyclopentolate [Cyclogyl]. Tropicamide [Mydriacyl] has rarely caused systemic reactions. To avoid systemic effects, these drugs should be instilled in the lowest effective concentration and no more frequently than is necessary to obtain the desired response. Pressure at the inner canthus after instillation of solutions will minimize drainage into the nose and throat and may reduce the likelihood of systemic reactions.

Systemic reactions also may occur after ocular instillation of adrenergic drugs, particularly if the drug is applied after the corneal epithelium is damaged or its permeability is increased by tonometry or local anesthesia. The symptoms include tachycardia, premature ventricular contractions, hypertension, hyperhidrosis, tremors, and blanching. Cerebrovascular accident has been reported after adrenergic drugs have been injected subconjunctivally or applied with cotton packs.

Atropine may cause contact dermatitis of the lids and allergic conjunctivitis. Allergic reactions are uncommon after ocular use of the other anticholinergic agents.

The adrenergic drugs may cause browache, headache, blurred vision, hypersensitivity reactions, pain, and lacrimation. Pigment granules, presumably from the iris, may appear in the anterior chamber 30 to 40 minutes after instillation and disappear within 12 to 24 hours. These aqueous floaters occur most commonly in older patients with dark irides. It has been suggested that contraction of the dilator muscle causes rupture of degenerated cells in the pigmentary epithelium resulting in the release of pigment granules into the anterior chamber. Fewer floaters are released if the drug is administered repeatedly at intervals of one to three days, but the number of floaters approaches the original number after a longer interval (one week).

In patients over 50, rebound miosis has been noted 24 hours after instillation of phenylephrine. A diminished mydriatic response was also observed when the drug was instilled again 24 hours later. Limited data suggest that the concomitant administration of an anticholinergic drug (tropicamide) does not prevent these reactions. The effect of other adrenergic drugs has not been studied, but rebound miosis and reduced mydriasis did not occur after instillation of cyclopentolate in a small number of patients.

For adverse reactions associated with prolonged use of epinephrine, see Chapter 69, Agents Used to Treat Glaucoma.

For adverse reactions of cocaine, see the individual evaluation on this drug.

ANTICHOLINERGIC DRUGS

ATROPINE SULFATE

Atropine is a potent, long-acting mydriatic and cycloplegic which is widely used in ophthalmology. Its effect on accommodation may last six days and mydriasis may persist for 12 days. It is often preferred for refraction of children under 6 years of age and is the cycloplegic of choice for use in children with accommodative esotropia. It is also commonly used for the initial refraction in all types of convergent strabismus. Because of its long duration of action, atropine is not useful for refraction in adults. In addition, atropine is used for pre- and postoperative mydriasis, in anterior uveitis, and in some secondary glaucomas.

Atropine can cause acute angle-closure glaucoma if instilled in eyes with narrow angles and shallow anterior chambers. It may also increase the intraocular pressure in open-angle glaucomatous eyes. Systemic reactions may occur, particularly in children and in elderly patients. Contact dermatitis and allergic conjunctivitis are not uncommon. (See the Introductory Statement.)

For other uses of atropine, see Chapters 20, Adjuncts to Anesthesia; 74, Antiparkinsonism Agents; and 78, Antispasmodics.

USUAL DOSAGE.—*Topical* (local instillation into conjunctival sac):

For refraction in *children*, one drop of 0.5% atropine solution (in children under 30 months) or of 1% solution (in children over 30 months) is instilled three times daily for three days prior to refraction and once on the morning of refraction. Administration should be discontinued if systemic effects occur. An ointment (0.5% or 1%) may be used instead of the solution; however, the ointment should not be administered for several hours prior to refraction, as it will impair the transparency of the cornea and alter the regularity of its refraction.

For preoperative mydriasis, one drop of 1% atropine solution supplemented with one drop of 10% phenylephrine solution is instilled prior to surgery. Some surgeons prefer instillation of one drop of a 3% atropine solution several times on the day prior to surgery and once several hours prior to surgery; if adequate mydriasis is not obtained, two drops of 10% phenylephrine solution may be instilled every five minutes for six instillations one hour before surgery.

For postoperative mydriasis after iridectomy, filtering operations, keratectomy, retinal detachment surgery, and senile cataract extraction, one drop of 1% or 2% atropine solution is usually instilled once daily. A stronger concentration or more frequent administration may be required if the inflammation is severe. The frequency of instillation is guided by the pupillary response.

After penetrating keratoplasty, if the anterior chamber is formed and the pupil is miotic, one drop of 1% atropine solution is instilled once daily or as needed to obtain adequate mydriasis. After nonpenetrating keratoplasty, several drops of 2% atropine solution are instilled once daily or as needed to obtain adequate mydriasis.

After cyclodialysis, one drop of 1% atropine solution is instilled once daily, usually beginning on the fourth day after surgery. (For the first three days the pupil should be miotic to hold open the cleft but it should be moved daily with 10% phenylephrine.)

After surgery for congenital cataracts, one drop of 1% atropine solution, supplemented with one drop of 10% phenylephrine solution, is instilled as needed until all cortex is absorbed. The frequency of instillation is guided by the pupillary response.

For anterior uveitis, one or two drops of 1% or 2% atropine solution (or 1% ointment) are instilled one to three times daily. A stronger concentration or more frequent administration may be necessary in very severe inflammations. For maximal mydriasis, atropine may be supplemented with phenylephrine (one drop of a 10% solution instilled three or more times daily). When slit-lamp examination shows minimal flare and cells in the anterior chamber, atropine may be discontinued and a less potent agent (eg, homatropine) may be instilled one or more times daily; as the inflammation subsides, the frequency of administration may be reduced to twice weekly.

For secondary angle-closure glaucoma with pupillary block due to posterior synechiae to the lens or, in aphakia, to the vitreous or lens capsule, one or two drops of a 2% to 4% atropine solution should be instilled every minute for five minutes; one drop of 10% phenylephrine solution may be instilled every minute for three minutes to enhance the mydriatic effect. If the pupil does not dilate within 30 minutes, powdered atropine may be applied directly to the cornea or a cotton pack moistened with atropine solution may be placed in the cul-de-sac for one hour. A 2% topical solution of epinephrine and systemic ocular hypotensive drugs are also administered to reduce the intraocular pressure (see Chapter 69, Agents Used to Treat Glaucoma).

If topical therapy fails to break the synechiae, a mixture of cocaine, atropine, and epinephrine may be injected subconjunctivally at the limbus. A combination of homatropine and phenylephrine may be used in patients sensitive to cocaine. (For dosage, see the evaluations on Cocaine Hydrochloride and Homatropine Hydrobromide.)

If drug therapy is successful in breaking the synechiae, 2% atropine solution and 10% phenylephrine solution may be instilled topically four times daily for continuing therapy.

For malignant glaucoma, initially, one drop of 1% to 4% atropine solution and one drop of 10% phenylephrine solution should be instilled three or four times daily or more frequently if required; an osmotic agent and a carbonic anhydrase inhibitor are generally administered systemically in conjunction with the mydriatic-cycloplegic therapy. This treatment should be continued for at least four days before resorting to surgery. If drug therapy is successful in promoting re-formation of the anterior chamber and reducing the intraocular pressure, the osmotic agent may be discontinued. If the intraocular pressure remains low, the dosage of the carbonic anhydrase inhibitor may be reduced or discontinued. Later, phenylephrine may be discontinued, but atropine must be administered indefinitely. The atropine dosage is gradually reduced; the usual maintenance dosage is one drop of a 1% solution daily or every other day. (For dosage of osmotic agents and carbonic anhydrase inhibitors, see Chapter 69, Agents Used to Treat Glaucoma.)

PREPARATIONS.—

Atropine Sulfate (Allergan). *Topical:* Solution (ophthalmic) 1%, 2%, and 4% in 15 ml containers; ointment (ophthalmic, sterile) 0.5% and 1% with chlorobutanol in 3.5 g containers.

Atropine Sulfate (Lilly). *Topical:* Ointment (ophthalmic) 1% in 1/8 oz containers.

Atropisol (Smith, Miller & Patch). *Topical:* Solution (ophthalmic, sterile) 0.5% in 1 and 5 ml containers, 1% in 1, 5, and 15 ml containers, 2% in 1 and 5 ml containers, and 4% in 5 ml containers; ointment (ophthalmic, sterile) 0.5% and 1% in 1/8 oz containers.

BufOpto Atropine (Professional). *Topical:* Solution (ophthalmic, sterile) 0.5% and 1% with methylcellulose, sodium acid phosphate monobasic and dibasic, sodium chloride, and benzalkonium chloride in 5 and 15 ml containers.

Isopto Atropine (Alcon). *Topical:* Solution (ophthalmic) 0.5%, 1%, and 3% with hydroxypropyl methylcellulose, benzalkonium chloride, boric acid, and hydrochloric acid in 5 ml containers (0.5%, 1%, and 3% solutions) and 15 ml containers (1% solution).

Drug also marketed by other manufacturers under generic name.

CYCLOPENTOLATE HYDROCHLORIDE
[Cyclogyl]

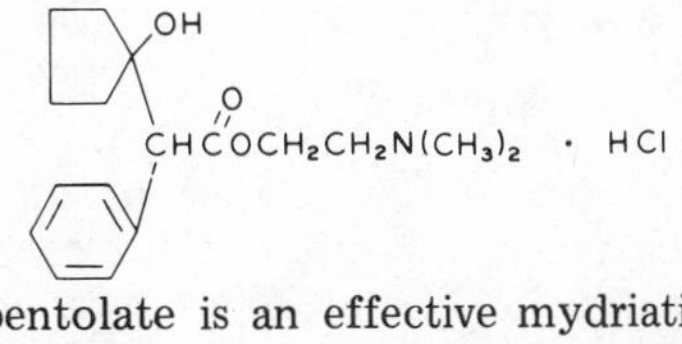

$CHCOCH_2CH_2N(CH_3)_2 \cdot HCl$ (cyclopentyl-OH; phenyl)

Cyclopentolate is an effective mydriatic and cycloplegic with a rapid onset and a relatively short duration of action. It provides adequate cycloplegia between 25 and 75 minutes after instillation, with complete recovery of accommodation in 6 to 24 hours. Cyclopentolate is used as an aid in refraction and for ophthalmoscopy. It is occasionally used for provocative testing in angle-closure glaucoma; however, eucatropine is preferred for this purpose.

Systemic absorption may cause central nervous system disturbances in children. For other adverse reactions and precautions, see the Introductory Statement.

USUAL DOSAGE.—*Topical* (local instillation into conjunctival sac):

For refraction, *adults*, one drop of 1% or 2% solution is instilled once, or one drop of 0.5% solution is instilled and repeated in five minutes; *children*, one drop of 0.5%, 1%, or 2% solution is instilled, followed ten minutes later by one drop of 0.5% or 1% solution. The 2% solution is generally preferred for use in patients with darkly-pigmented irides.

For ophthalmoscopy, one drop of 0.5% solution is instilled prior to the examination. For wider mydriasis, cyclopentolate may be supplemented with one drop of 10% phenylephrine solution.

As a provocative test for angle-closure glaucoma, two drops of 0.5% solution are instilled in only one eye; the other eye should be tested at another time, because the test may precipitate an acute attack of angle-closure glaucoma. In the presence of gonioscopic evidence of occlusion, the test is considered positive if there is an 8 mm Hg rise in intraocular pressure within an hour, or if a 25% to 30% reduction in outflow facility is demonstrated by tonographic tracings. At the conclusion of the test, one or two drops of 2% pilocarpine solution should be instilled every four hours for two or three doses. If the pupil does not constrict and intraocular pressure continues to rise, a carbonic anhydrase inhibitor and an osmotic agent should be given systemically (for dosage, see Chapter 69, Agents Used to Treat Glaucoma).

PREPARATIONS.—Cyclogyl (Alcon). *Topical:* Solution (ophthalmic, sterile) 0.5% and 1% with boric acid, potassium chloride, sodium carbonate monohydrate, and benzalkonium chloride in 2 ml (1% solution) and 15 ml containers (0.5%, 1% solution); solution (ophthalmic, sterile) 2% with boric acid, sodium borate, povidone, and chlorobutanol in 2 and 7.5 ml containers.

EUCATROPINE HYDROCHLORIDE

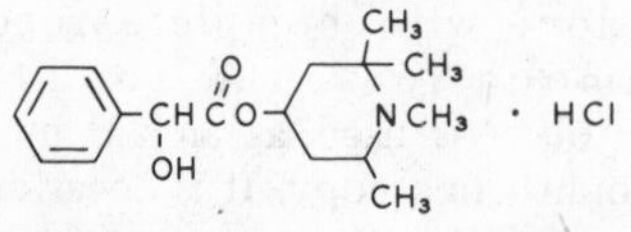

Eucatropine, a weak anticholinergic drug, is an effective mydriatic with a duration of action of two to four hours. It produces little cycloplegia. Eucatropine is used for ophthalmoscopy and is the preferred agent for provocative testing for angle-closure glaucoma. However, this agent generally must be prepared by the pharmacist.

For adverse reactions and precautions, see the Introductory Statement.

USUAL DOSAGE.—*Topical* (local instillation into conjunctival sac):

For ophthalmoscopy, one or two drops of 5% or 10% solution are instilled and repeated in 10 to 15 minutes if necessary.

As a provocative test for angle-closure glaucoma, two drops of a 5% solution are instilled in only one eye; the other eye should be tested at another time, because the test may precipitate an acute attack of angle-closure glaucoma. In the presence of gonioscopic evidence of occlusion, the test is considered positive if there is an 8 mm Hg rise in intraocular pressure within an hour or if a 25% to 30% reduction in outflow facility is demonstrated by tonographic tracings. At the conclusion of the test, one or two drops of 2% pilocarpine solution should be instilled every four hours for two or three doses. If the pupil does not constrict and the intraocular pressure continues to rise, a carbonic anhydrase inhibitor and an osmotic agent should be given systemically (for dosage, see Chapter 69, Agents Used to Treat Glaucoma).

PREPARATIONS.—Eucatropine Hydrochloride, U.S.P. *Topical:* Solution (ophthalmic) 2% and 5%; powder for solution. Drug marketed under generic name.

HOMATROPINE HYDROBROMIDE

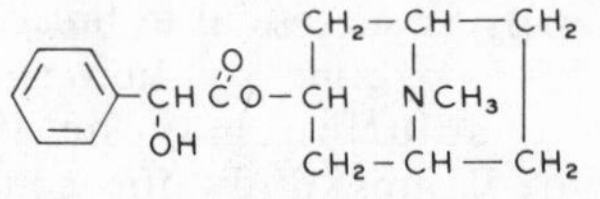

Homatropine is a relatively short-acting mydriatic and cycloplegic. Repeated instillation of the 2% solution at ten-minute intervals produces maximal cycloplegia in 60 minutes. Effects may persist for 36 to 48 hours. Homatropine is applied topically as an aid in refraction. It is occasionally used for provocative testing for angle-closure glaucoma, but eucatropine is preferred for this purpose. Homatropine also is applied topically to treat mild anterior uveitis. A mixture of homatropine and phenylephrine may be injected subconjunctivally to break posterior synechiae, but the combination of cocaine, atropine, and epinephrine is generally preferred.

For adverse reactions and precautions, see the Introductory Statement.

USUAL DOSAGE.—*Topical* (local instillation into conjunctival sac):

For refraction, one or two drops of the 2% solution are instilled every 10 or 15 minutes for five doses, or one or two drops of the 5% solution are instilled once and repeated in 15 minutes.

As a provocative test for angle-closure glaucoma, two drops of the 2% solution are instilled in only one eye; the other eye should be tested at another time because the test may precipitate an attack of angle-closure glaucoma. In the presence of gonioscopic evidence of occlusion, the test is considered positive if there is an 8 mm Hg rise in intraocular pressure within an hour, or if a 25% to 30% reduction in outflow facility is demonstrated by tonographic tracings. At the conclusion of the test, one or two drops of 2% pilocarpine solution should be instilled every four hours for several doses until miosis is secured. If the pupil does not constrict and the intraocular pressure continues to rise, a carbonic anhydrase inhibitor and an osmotic agent should be given systemically (for dosage, see Chapter 69, Agents Used to Treat Glaucoma).

For mild anterior uveitis, one or two drops of 2% or 5% solution are instilled two to four times daily. When homatropine is used for continuing therapy after use of atropine or scopolamine, the drops may be instilled one or more times daily, followed by twice weekly.

For secondary angle-closure glaucoma with pupillary block due to posterior synechiae to the lens or, in aphakia, to the vitreous or lens capsule, if topical therapy with atropine or scopolamine and phenylephrine fails to break the posterior synechiae, 0.2 ml of a solution containing 20 mg of homatropine hydrobromide, 25 mg of phenylephrine hydrochloride, and 5 ml of distilled water may be injected subconjunctivally at one or two areas around the limbus.

PREPARATIONS.—

Homatropine Hydrobromide (Allergan). *Topical:* Solution (ophthalmic) 2% and 5% in 15 ml containers.

Homatropine Hydrobromide (Smith, Miller & Patch). *Topical:* Solution (ophthalmic) 2% and 5% in 1 and 5 ml containers.

BufOpto Homatrocel (Professional). *Topical:* Solution (ophthalmic) 2% and 5% with methylcellulose in 15 ml containers.

Isopto Homatropine (Alcon). *Topical:* Solution (ophthalmic) 2% and 5% with hydroxypropyl methylcellulose, benzalkonium chloride (2% solution) or benzethonium chloride (5% solution), sodium chloride, and hydrochloric acid in 5 and 15 ml containers.

SCOPOLAMINE HYDROBROMIDE

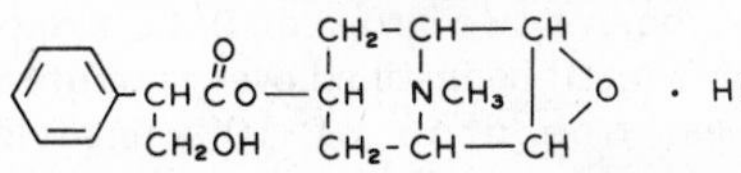

```
                O     CH2-CH——CH
                ‖      |   |    \
 (C6H5)—CH  C—O——CH   NCH3  |   O    · HBr
         |             |   |    /
        CH2OH         CH2-CH——CH
```

Scopolamine is a potent mydriatic and cycloplegic. In the concentrations used clinically, it has a shorter duration of action than atropine; cycloplegia may persist for three days. Scopolamine rarely causes local allergic reactions and is, therefore, useful as a substitute in patients who are sensitive to atropine. It is occasionally used for refraction of children who cannot tolerate atropine, but is used most commonly for postoperative mydriasis, in anterior uveitis, and in some secondary glaucomas.

Scopolamine can cause acute angle-closure glaucoma if it is instilled in eyes with narrow angles and shallow anterior chambers. It may also increase intraocular pressure in open-angle glaucomatous eyes. Systemic reactions may occur, particularly in children and elderly patients (see the Introductory Statement).

For other uses of scopolamine, see Chapters 20, Adjuncts to Anesthesia; 74, Antiparkinsonism Agents; and 85, Antiemetics.

USUAL DOSAGE.—*Topical* (local instillation into conjunctival sac):

For refraction in children, one drop of 0.2% or 0.25% solution or 0.2% ointment is instilled twice daily for two days before the refraction.

For postoperative mydriasis, one drop of 0.2% or 0.25% solution is instilled once daily or more frequently if inflammation is severe. After surgery for congenital cataracts, one drop of 0.2% or 0.25% solution, supplemented with one drop of 10% phenylephrine solution, is instilled as needed until all cortex is absorbed. The frequency of administration is guided by the pupillary response.

For anterior uveitis, one or two drops of 0.2% or 0.25% solution or 0.2% ointment are instilled one to three times daily or more frequently in severe inflammations. For maximal mydriasis, scopolamine may be supplemented with one drop of 10% phenylephrine solution instilled three or more times daily. When slit-lamp examination shows minimal flare and cells in the anterior chamber, scopolamine may be discontinued and a less potent agent (eg, homatropine) may be instilled one or more times daily; as the inflammation subsides, the frequency of administration may be reduced to twice weekly.

For secondary angle-closure glaucoma with pupillary block due to posterior synechiae to the lens or, in aphakia, to the vitreous or lens capsule, one or two drops of 0.2% scopolamine solution should be instilled every minute for five minutes; one drop of 10% phenylephrine solution may be instilled every minute for three minutes to enhance the mydriatic effect. A 2% topical solution of epinephrine and systemic ocular hypotensive drugs are also administered to reduce the intraocular pressure (see Chapter 69, Agents Used to Treat Glaucoma). If topical therapy fails to break the synechiae, a combination of cocaine, atropine, and epinephrine may be injected subconjunctivally. A combination of homatropine and phenylephrine may be used in patients sensitive to cocaine. (For dosage, see the evaluations on Cocaine Hydrochloride and Homatropine Hydrobromide.) If drug therapy is successful in breaking the synechiae, 0.2% scopolamine solution and 10% phenylephrine solution may be instilled topically four times daily for continuing therapy.

For malignant glaucoma, initially, one drop of 0.25% to 0.5% scopolamine solution and one drop of 10% phenylephrine solution should be instilled three or four times daily or more frequently if required. An osmotic agent and a carbonic anhydrase inhibitor are generally administered systemically in conjunction with the mydriatic-cycloplegic therapy. This treatment should be continued for at least four days before resorting to surgery. If drug therapy is successful in promoting re-formation of the anterior chamber and reducing the intraocular pressure, the osmotic agent may be discontinued. If the intraocular pressure remains low, the dosage of the carbonic anhydrase inhibitor may be reduced or discontinued. Later, phenylephrine may be discontinued, but scopolamine must be administered indefinitely. The scopolamine dosage is gradually reduced; the usual maintenance dosage is one drop of a 0.25% solution once daily. For dosage of osmotic agents and carbonic anhydrase inhibitors, see Chapter 69, Agents Used to Treat Glaucoma.

PREPARATIONS.—

Isopto Hyoscine (Alcon). *Topical:* Solution (ophthalmic) 0.25% with hydroxypropyl methylcellulose, benzalkonium chloride, glacial acetic acid, sodium acetate, and sodium chloride in 5 and 15 ml containers.

Scopolamine Hydrobromide (Allergan). *Topical:* Ointment (ophthalmic, sterile) 0.2% with chlorobutanol, white petrolatum, mineral oil, and nonionic lanolin derivatives in 3.5 g containers.

Powder for solution also marketed by other manufacturers under generic name.

TROPICAMIDE [Mydriacyl]

Tropicamide is an effective mydriatic and cycloplegic with a rapid onset and a short duration of action. It is used as an aid in refraction and for ophthalmoscopy and retinal photography. Maximal cycloplegia occurs within 20 to 35 minutes after two drops of the 1% solution are instilled five minutes apart, with complete recovery of accommodation in two to six hours. The 0.5% solution produces maximal pupillary dilatation within 20 to 25 minutes; residual mydriasis persists for about seven hours.

Tropicamide rarely causes severe adverse reactions. For adverse reactions and precautions produced by the anticholinergic drugs, see the Introductory Statement.

USUAL DOSAGE.—*Topical* (local instillation into conjunctival sac):

For refraction, one or two drops of 1% solution are instilled and repeated in five minutes. If the examination cannot be performed within 20 to 35 minutes, an additional drop must be instilled.

For ophthalmoscopy and retinal photography, one or two drops of 0.5% or 1% solution are instilled prior to the procedure. For wider mydriasis, tropicamide may be supplemented with one drop of 10% phenylephrine solution. For examination of patients with primary open-angle glaucoma, one or two drops of a solution containing equal parts of 0.5% tropicamide and 10% phenylephrine may be instilled to produce mydriasis.

PREPARATIONS.—Mydriacyl (Alcon). *Topical:* Solution (ophthalmic) 0.5% and 1% with sodium nitrate, nitric acid, and phenylmercuric nitrate in 15 ml containers.

ADRENERGIC DRUGS

PHENYLEPHRINE HYDROCHLORIDE
[Efricel, Neo-Synephrine Hydrochloride]

Phenylephrine is used to produce mydriasis

for ophthalmoscopy and retinal photography, pre- and postoperatively in intraocular surgery, and as an adjunct in the treatment of anterior uveitis and some secondary glaucomas. It is often used to supplement anticholinergic drugs to achieve maximal mydriasis. After ocular instillation of the 10% solution, maximal mydriasis is obtained in 60 to 90 minutes. Recovery from mydriasis occurs in about six hours.

Adverse reactions to phenylephrine include transient pain, release of aqueous floaters, and occlusion of structurally narrow angles. Systemic effects are uncommon. Rebound miosis and a reduced mydriatic effect with repeated use has been reported. (See the Introductory Statement.)

For the use of phenylephrine in preventing miotic iris cysts, see Chapter 69, Agents Used to Treat Glaucoma, and for its use as an ophthalmic decongestant, see Chapter 72, Miscellaneous Ophthalmic Preparations. For other uses of phenylephrine, see Chapter 5, Agents Used in Hypotension and Shock, and Chapter 42, Nasal Decongestants.

USUAL DOSAGE.—*Topical* (local instillation into conjunctival sac):

For ophthalmoscopy and retinal photography, one or two drops of 10% solution are instilled and may be repeated in 10 or 15 minutes. For wider dilatation, phenylephrine may be used to supplement cyclopentolate or tropicamide. It is also used with tropicamide for examination of eyes with open-angle glaucoma (see the evaluations on Cyclopentolate Hydrochloride and Tropicamide).

For examination of eyes predisposed to angle-closure, one or two drops of 2.5% or 10% solution are instilled two hours after administration of acetazolamide (250 mg orally) and one hour after administration of glycerin (1 to 1.5 g/kg of body weight orally). After the examination, one or two drops of 2% pilocarpine solution should be instilled as required to reestablish miosis.

For preoperative mydriasis, phenylephrine is most commonly used to supplement atropine for maximal mydriasis prior to round pupil cataract extraction or retinal detachment surgery (see the evaluation on Atropine Sulfate); it is occasionally used alone (one or two drops of 10% solution instilled 30 to 60 minutes before surgery).

For postoperative mydriasis after iridectomy, one drop of 10% solution is instilled once or twice daily. Atropine should be substituted if the inflammation is severe. After cyclodialysis, one drop of 10% phenylephrine solution is instilled once daily for three days; after the third day, atropine is substituted. For use of phenylephrine with atropine or scopolamine after congenital cataract extraction and as adjunctive therapy in anterior uveitis and secondary glaucomas, see the evaluations on these drugs.

PREPARATIONS.—

Efricel (Professional). *Topical:* Solution (ophthalmic) 2.5% and 10% with methylcellulose, sodium bisulfite, and benzalkonium chloride in 5 ml containers (10% solution) and 15 ml containers (2.5%, 10% solution).

Neo-Synephrine Hydrochloride (Winthrop). *Topical:* Solution (ophthalmic, sterile) 2.5% with sodium phosphate, sodium biphosphate, benzalkonium chloride, boric acid, and phosphoric acid or sodium hydroxide in 15 ml containers; solution (sterile) 10% with sodium phosphate, sodium biphosphate, benzalkonium chloride, and phosphoric acid or sodium hydroxide in 5 ml containers; solution (viscous, sterile) 10% with sodium phosphate, sodium biphosphate, methylcellulose, and benzalkonium chloride in 5 ml containers.

Phenylephrine Hydrochloride (Smith, Miller & Patch). *Topical:* Solution (ophthalmic) 10% in 1 and 5 ml containers.

Drug also marketed by other manufacturers under generic name.

EPINEPHRINE HYDROCHLORIDE

Epinephrine is occasionally used to produce mydriasis for ophthalmoscopy in eyes predisposed to angle-closure, during round pupil cataract extraction, and (with atropine and cocaine) for breaking posterior synechiae. It is also used for differential diagnosis of a miotic pupil (see the evaluation on Cocaine). Epinephrine is less effective than phenylephrine in the normal eye, but produces adequate pupillary dilatation when the permeability of the eye is increased (eg, during surgery).

For adverse reactions and precautions, see the Introductory Statement.

For use of epinephrine in glaucoma therapy, see Chapter 69, Agents Used to Treat Glaucoma. For other uses, see Chapters 2, Antiarrhythmic Agents; 5, Agents Used in Hypotension and Shock; 41, Bronchodilators; and 42, Nasal Decongestants.

USUAL DOSAGE.—

Topical (local instillation into conjunctival

sac): For ophthalmoscopy in eyes predisposed to angle-closure, when examining only the posterior pole of the retina, a wick of cotton moistened with 1:1,000 solution may be placed in the inferior cul-de-sac for three minutes. Acetazolamide (250 mg orally) should be given two hours prior to the examination and glycerin (1 to 1.5 g/kg of body weight orally) should be administered one hour before the examination. One or two drops of 2% pilocarpine solution should be instilled after ophthalmoscopy as needed to reestablish miosis.

Intracameral (injected into anterior chamber): For mydriasis during round pupil cataract extraction, if pupillary dilatation is not sufficient to deliver the lens through a round pupil, 0.2 ml of a 1:1,000 solution may be injected into the anterior chamber.

Subconjunctival (injected beneath Tenon's capsule): Some surgeons inject 0.1 ml of a 1:1,000 solution subconjunctivally to produce mydriasis prior to congenital cataract surgery.

For use of epinephrine with atropine and cocaine to break posterior synechiae, see the evaluation on Cocaine Hydrochloride.

PREPARATIONS.—Epinephrine Hydrochloride. Solution 1:1,000 marketed by many manufacturers under generic name.

HYDROXYAMPHETAMINE HYDROBROMIDE [Paredrine]

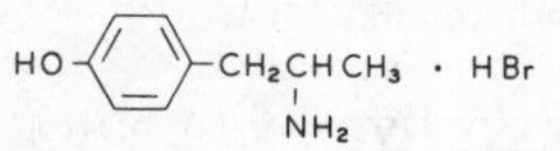

HO—C_6H_4—$CH_2CH(NH_2)CH_3$ · HBr

Hydroxyamphetamine is occasionally used to produce mydriasis for ophthalmoscopy. It produces maximal mydriasis in 45 to 60 minutes, with recovery in about six hours. It is less effective than phenylephrine. Hydroxyamphetamine also has been used with homatropine as an aid in refraction, but there is no convincing evidence that combined therapy has any significant effect on the onset, duration, or intensity of cycloplegia.

For adverse reactions and precautions, see the Introductory Statement.

USUAL DOSAGE.—*Topical* (local instillation into conjunctival sac): For ophthalmoscopy, one or two drops are instilled and may be repeated in ten minutes.

PREPARATIONS.—Paredrine (Smith Kline & French). *Topical:* Solution (ophthalmic) 1% with boric acid and thimerosal in 15 ml containers.

OTHER AGENTS

COCAINE HYDROCHLORIDE

[Structural formula: cocaine · HCl]

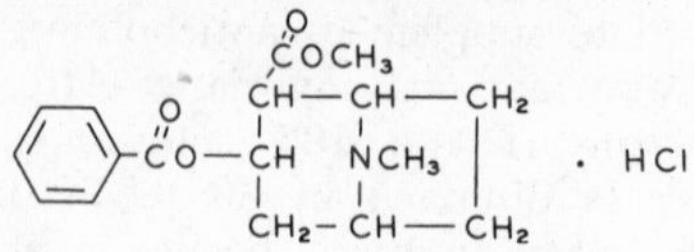

When applied to the eye, cocaine produces mydriasis, vasoconstriction, lid retraction, slight loss of accommodation, exophthalmos, and anesthesia. It usually reduces intraocular pressure but may increase intraocular pressure in eyes predisposed to angle-closure. The sympathomimetic action is due to potentiation of the effects of endogenous or exogenous catecholamines. Cocaine is believed to act by preventing uptake of the neurohumor into the sympathetic nerve terminal. Accumulation of the neurohumor at the sympathetic receptor site then prolongs the response of the effector organ.

In patients who have not responded to intensive topical therapy with mydriatic drugs, subconjunctival injection of a mixture of cocaine, atropine, and epinephrine may dilate resistant pupils and break pupillary block caused by posterior synechiae to the lens or, in aphakia, to the vitreous or lens capsule. When applied topically to aphakic eyes demonstrating flat anterior chambers with corneovitreal contact, cocaine has caused prompt regression of the anterior hyaloid membrane and deepening of the anterior chamber.

The action of cocaine depends upon intact sympathetic innervation; therefore, it may be useful in the differential diagnosis of a miotic pupil. In Horner's syndrome, if the lesion is in the superior cervical ganglion or its postganglionic fibers, mydriasis will not occur after instillation of a 2% solution of cocaine. However, a 1:1,000 solution of epinephrine, which is a poor mydriatic in the normal eye, will produce mydriasis as a result of denervation supersensitivity. A similar response is obtained in patients with Raeder's syndrome, which also involves a postganglionic lesion. If miosis is caused by a preganglionic lesion, the pupil shows a normal response to cocaine or epinephrine.

Topically applied cocaine can cause pitting and sloughing of the corneal epithelium. With repeated use, permanent scars may develop in the corneal stroma. By dilating the pupil, cocaine can precipitate an attack of acute angle-closure glaucoma; the drug should not be instilled in eyes with narrow angles and shallow anterior chambers. Cocaine is rapidly absorbed from the mucous membranes and may cause severe systemic reactions. The symptoms of acute intoxication include tachycardia, hypertension, irregular respiration, chills, fever, euphoria, restlessness, anxiety, delirium, and convulsions. Death may result from acute circulatory failure and respiratory arrest.

USUAL DOSAGE.—

Subconjuctival: To break posterior synechiae to the lens or, in aphakia, to the vitreous or lens capsule, 0.1 ml of a mixture containing equal proportions of 4% cocaine, 1% atropine, and 1:1,000 epinephrine hydrochloride may be injected at the limbus.

Topical (local instillation into conjunctival sac): **To induce retraction of the vitreous face in aphakia,** two drops of a 5% solution of cocaine should cause regression of the vitreous face within approximately 15 minutes. One drop of a 2% solution of epinephrine hydrochloride may be given concomitantly. For continuing therapy, two drops of a 5% solution of cocaine may be instilled one to three times daily until the vitreous assumes a more normal position; 1% atropine and/or 2% epinephrine may be given concomitantly. Continuing therapy is necessary for as long as the vitreous continues to demonstrate contact with the cornea between treatments. If treatment is required for more than one week, more radical measures may be necessary.

For differential diagnosis of a miotic pupil, one drop of a 2% solution of cocaine is instilled in each eye. The pupil of the normal eye will dilate within 20 minutes. The miotic pupil will fail to respond to the drug if miosis is caused by a lesion in the superior cervical ganglion or its postganglionic fibers. Instillation of one drop of a 1:1,000 solution of epinephrine will have no effect on the normal pupil but will dilate the denervated pupil.

PREPARATIONS.—Cocaine Hydrochloride, U.S.P. No pharmaceutical dosage form available; compounding necessary for prescription.

MIXTURE

CYCLOMYDRIL

Cyclomydril is a combination of cyclopentolate and phenylephrine which is designed to produce wide mydriasis. It is used to dilate the pupil for ophthalmoscopic examination of the lens and the posterior segment of the eye and as an aid in retinal photography.

For adverse reactions and precautions, see the evaluations on Cyclopentolate Hydrochloride and Phenylephrine Hydrochloride.

USUAL DOSAGE.—*Topical* (local instillation into conjunctival sac): One drop instilled prior to the examination.

PREPARATIONS.—Cyclomydril (Alcon). *Topical:* Solution (ophthalmic, sterile) containing cyclopentolate hydrochloride 0.2% and phenylephrine hydrochloride 1% with polyvinylpyrrolidone, boric acid, sodium borate, and chlorobutanol in 2 and 7.5 ml containers.

Chapter 71

ANTI-INFECTIVE AND ANTI-INFLAMMATORY AGENTS USED IN OPHTHALMOLOGY

ANTI-INFECTIVE AGENTS

Anti-infective agents are applied locally to treat infections of the lids, conjunctiva, and cornea. They may be applied in the form of drops, ointments, packs, lamellae, corneal baths, iontophoresis, and subconjunctival injection. Intraocular and severe external infections require intensive systemic therapy in addition to local administration. Rarely, anti-infective agents are administered by intracameral injection to achieve a high intraocular concentration.

A number of antibiotics and sulfonamides which are commonly administered systemically are available for topical ophthalmic use to treat external bacterial infections. However, in selecting a drug for topical administration, preference should usually be given to antibacterial agents that are rarely or never administered systemically (ie, bacitracin [Baciguent], polymyxin B [Aerosporin], neomycin sulfate [Mycifradin, Myciguent], sulfacetamide sodium, gramicidin). The choice of these drugs for topical use will avoid possible sensitization to the common systemic anti-infective agents and will discourage the development of resistant strains of organisms. Most external bacterial infections can be controlled by proper selection from among these "topical-only" agents or by use of a combination product. Identification of the causative organism should be attempted, but treatment should not be withheld pending this information.

Since most anti-infective agents do not readily penetrate the eye when given systemically, large doses must be used to treat intraocular infections. Because of its superior penetration, chloramphenicol has been considered by many authorities to be the drug of choice for treating intraocular bacterial infections; however, many other anti-infective agents demonstrate satisfactory penetration when given in the proper dosage. In addition, many agents that do not enter the normal eye will penetrate the inflamed eye, since the blood-aqueous barrier is decreased by injury or inflammation.

Antibacterial agents that are commonly used to treat ocular infections are discussed in the individual evaluations which follow this section. Also included are evaluations of drugs used to treat fungal, viral, protozoal, and helminthic infections of the eye.

Before the advent of antibiotics and sulfonamides, ocular infections were treated with a variety of antiseptics and germicides such as silver nitrate, mild silver protein, copper sulfate, zinc sulfate, thimerosal [Merthiolate], merbromin [Mercurochrome], yellow mercuric oxide, ammoniated mercury, nitromersol [Metaphen], acriflavine [Neutroflavine], benzalkonium chloride, boric acid, and iodine. Most of these agents are no longer used to treat ocular disease because of ineffectiveness or local toxicity, but some still have limited ophthalmic use. Benzalkonium and thimerosal are widely used as preservatives for eyedrops. Benzalkonium also is used to enhance the corneal penetration of drugs and to cleanse the skin and irrigate the eye prior to surgery. Iodine tincture (2%) is applied for chemical cauterization of dendritic ulcers caused by herpes simplex virus. Mild silver protein will color conjunctival secretions, thereby aiding in their identification and removal during preoperative cleansing of the eye.

Local application of silver nitrate is legally required in most states for prophylaxis of gonorrheal ophthalmia neonatorum. Because silver nitrate may cause severe local irritation, some ophthalmologists have suggested that it be replaced by a less irritating topical agent or by a systemically-administered antibiotic. However, most authorities feel that silver nitrate has stood the test of time and should be continued to be used in a 1% solution (preferably packaged in wax ampules) as the prophylactic agent of choice against gonorrheal ophthalmia neonatorum. If an alternate agent is required, bacitracin ointment is considered the drug of choice; bacitracin is bactericidal and is not used systemically. Antibiotics which are commonly used systemically are not recommended for prophylaxis, but may be used for treatment of ophthalmia neonatorum.

Zinc sulfate, usually in combination with phenylephrine, is sometimes used to treat minor ocular irritations but it is a relatively ineffective antiseptic. Boric acid, which also has little merit as an antiseptic, is extensively (and ineffectively) used by the laity as an eyewash. See Chapter 67, Antiseptics and Disinfectants, for additional information on these drugs.

Adverse Reactions and Precautions

Some anti-infective agents readily cause contact dermatitis when applied topically, and individuals sensitized to one drug may show cross reactions when exposed to immunochemically related agents. In such patients, the subsequent *systemic* administration of the sensitizing drug or a related agent may cause eczematous contact-type dermatitis medicamentosa. Penicillin, streptomycin, neomycin, and some sulfonamides are active topical sensitizers. Sensitization rarely occurs following topical use of chloramphenicol, erythromycin, or the tetracyclines. Occasionally, urticarial, anaphylactoid reactions have occurred after systemic administration of an anti-infective agent in an individual who was sensitized by local use of the drug (most commonly, penicillin).

Topically applied anti-infective agents interfere with the normal bacterial flora of the eye and may encourage the growth of nonsusceptible organisms. Widespread use of antibacterial agents which are commonly used systemically can lead to the development of resistant strains of organisms.

Many anti-infective agents cause local irritation when administered topically or by the subconjunctival route. A local anesthetic should be instilled in the eye prior to subconjunctival injection. The interior of the eye will not tolerate high concentrations of most drugs. Uveitis may occur after intracameral administration of anti-infective agents, and corneal edema and lens damage may result from trauma to the corneal epithelium and lens. Intracameral injection should be undertaken only by ophthalmologists and generally should be reserved for infections requiring surgical treatment or for ruptured surgical or traumatic wounds.

When anti-infective agents are administered systemically to treat intraocular infections, large doses must be used. This increases the risk of severe adverse reactions.

ANTIBACTERIAL AGENTS

AMPICILLIN
AMPICILLIN SODIUM

Ampicillin is given systemically and by subconjunctival injection to treat intraocular infections caused by gram-positive and gram-negative organisms. It is active against *Haemophilus influenzae* and some strains of *Escherichia coli*, but is ineffective against penicillinase-producing staphylococci and most strains of *Pseudomonas*. This agent penetrates the eye readily after systemic administration.

For the antibacterial activity and systemic toxic effects of ampicillin, see Chapter 48, Penicillins.

USUAL DOSAGE.—

Oral: Adults, 2 g initially, then 1 g every six hours.

Intravenous, Intramuscular: Adults, 1 g every six hours. *Children*, 200 mg/kg of body weight daily, preferably intravenously, in four divided doses. *Premature and full-term newborn infants*, 100 mg/kg daily in four divided doses.

Subconjunctival (injected beneath Tenon's capsule): 40 to 50 mg in 0.5 ml of isotonic sodium chloride injection or sterile water for injection.

PREPARATIONS.—See Chapter 48, Penicillins.

BACITRACIN [Baciguent]

Bacitracin is applied topically and by subconjunctival injection to treat external ocular infections caused by gram-positive organisms. Its antibacterial spectrum is similar to that of penicillin, but it is preferred to penicillin for topical use because few strains of organisms are resistant, allergic reactions occur less frequently, and future sensitization to penicillin is avoided. Bacitracin is a common ingredient of many ophthalmic mixtures. See also Chapter 57, Aminoglycoside Antibacterial Agents and Miscellaneous Antimicrobial Drugs.

USUAL DOSAGE.—

Topical (local instillation into conjunctival sac): Ointment is instilled in affected eye one to three times daily or more frequently. In severe infections, one or two drops of solution containing 10,000 units/ml are instilled every hour until improvement occurs; the frequency of administration is then reduced.

Subconjunctival (injected beneath Tenon's capsule): 10,000 units in 0.5 ml of isotonic sodium chloride injection once or twice daily.

PREPARATIONS.—Baciguent (Upjohn).

Topical: Ointment (ophthalmic) 500 units/g in 1/8 oz containers. Solution for topical use may be made from powder.

Injection: Powder 10,000 and 50,000 units.

Drug also marketed by many manufacturers under generic name.

CARBENICILLIN DISODIUM [Geopen, Pyopen]

This semisynthetic penicillin is effective against a wide range of gram-positive and gram-negative organisms. Its antibacterial spectrum is similar to that of ampicillin; however, carbenicillin is active against most strains of *Pseudomonas aeruginosa*, indole-positive *Proteus*, and some strains of *Enterobacter* that are not susceptible to ampicillin. This agent is not active against penicillin-resistant staphylococci.

Carbenicillin is given systemically to treat intraocular infections; subconjunctival injection may also be indicated, as the drug penetrates the eye well when given by this route.

Pain, chemosis, and conjunctival hyperemia occur after subconjunctival injection. The chemosis and hyperemia may persist for several days. For the antibacterial activity and systemic adverse effects of carbenicillin, see Chapter 48, Penicillins.

USUAL DOSAGE.—

Intravenous: Adults, 5 to 7 g every four hours.

Intravenous, Intramuscular: Children, 500 mg/kg of body weight daily in four to six divided doses or by continuous drip.

Subconjunctival (injected beneath Tenon's capsule): 250 mg in 0.5 ml of isotonic sodium chloride injection or sterile water for injection.

PREPARATIONS.—Geopen (Roerig), Pyopen (Beecham-Massengill). *Injection, Topical:* Powder (for solution) 1 and 5 g.

CEPHALEXIN MONOHYDRATE [Keflex]

This cephalosporin has a broad spectrum of antimicrobial activity that includes both penicillin-sensitive and penicillin-resistant organisms. Cephalexin penetrates the eye after oral administration and may be useful in treating intraocular infections caused by susceptible gram-positive and gram-negative organisms.

For the antibacterial activity and adverse effects of cephalexin, see Chapter 49, Cephalosporins.

USUAL DOSAGE.—*Oral: Adults,* 2 g initially, then 1 g every eight hours; *children,* 75 mg/kg of body weight daily in four to six divided doses. If daily doses larger than 4 g are required, a parenteral cephalosporin preparation should be substituted.

PREPARATIONS.—Keflex (Lilly). *Oral:* Capsules 250 and 500 mg; suspension 100 mg/ml and 125 mg/5 ml.

CEPHALORIDINE [Loridine]

This cephalosporin is given systemically and by subconjunctival injection to treat intraocular infections caused by sensitive organisms. It has also been administered topically and subconjunctivally to treat corneal ulcers. Cephaloridine has the same antibacterial spectrum as cephalothin, but cephalothin is generally preferred because it is less toxic. Cephaloridine penetrates the eye well after systemic administration.

This drug should not be given in doses larger than 4 g per day because of possible renal damage. See also Chapter 49, Cephalosporins.

USUAL DOSAGE.—

Intravenous, Intramuscular: Adults, 1 g every six hours. *Children,* 100 mg/kg of body weight daily (maximum, 4 g), preferably intramuscularly, in four divided doses. Not recommended for *premature or full-term infants less than 1 month old.*

Subconjunctival (injected beneath Tenon's capsule): 25 to 50 mg in 0.5 ml of isotonic sodium chloride injection or sterile water for injection. Doses as large as 100 mg have been used occasionally.

Topical (local instillation into conjunctival sac): One or two drops of solution containing 50 to 100 mg/ml are instilled every hour until improvement occurs; the frequency of administration is then reduced.

PREPARATIONS.—Loridine (Lilly).

Injection: Powder 500 mg and 1 g.

Topical: No ophthalmic form is available but

solution for topical use may be made from powder.

CEPHALOTHIN SODIUM [Keflin]

Cephalothin is effective against a wide range of organisms, including penicillin-resistant staphylococci, and is useful for initial therapy when the causative agent has not been identified. It is given systemically and by subconjunctival injection to treat intraocular infections. When administered systemically, its intraocular penetration is fair. Cephalothin has also been given topically and subconjunctivally to treat corneal ulcers.

For the antibacterial activity and systemic toxic effects of cephalothin, see Chapter 49, Cephalosporins.

USUAL DOSAGE.—

Intravenous, Intramuscular: Adults, 1 to 2 g every four to six hours.

Intravenous: Children, 200 mg/kg of body weight daily in four divided doses. *Premature and full-term newborn infants,* 100 mg/kg daily in four divided doses.

Subconjunctival (injected beneath Tenon's capsule): 50 mg in 0.5 ml of isotonic sodium chloride injection or sterile water for injection. Doses as large as 100 mg have been administered occasionally.

Topical (local instillation into conjunctival sac): One or two drops of solution containing 50 to 100 mg/ml are instilled every hour until improvement occurs; the frequency of administration is then reduced.

PREPARATIONS.—Keflin (Lilly).

Injection: Powder 1, 2, and 4 g.

Topical: No ophthalmic form is available but solution for topical use may be made from powder.

CHLORAMPHENICOL [Chloromycetin, Chloroptic]

CHLORAMPHENICOL SODIUM SUCCINATE [Chloromycetin Sodium Succinate]

Chloramphenicol is effective against a variety of gram-positive and gram-negative organisms, including some strains of *Pseudomonas.* This agent is useful for topical administration because of its broad spectrum of activity and because it rarely causes sensitization. When given systemically, chloramphenicol readily penetrates the eye and has been regarded as the drug of choice for treating intraocular infections. However, other agents also demonstrate adequate penetration when given in the proper dosage. Chloramphenicol occasionally is given by intracameral injection to treat intraocular infections.

One case of bone marrow hypoplasia has been reported following prolonged (23 months) use of the 0.5% eye drops. Systemic adverse reactions have not occurred after short-term topical ophthalmic use.

For the antibacterial activity and systemic adverse effects of chloramphenicol, see Chapter 54, Chloramphenicol and Derivatives.

USUAL DOSAGE.—

Chloramphenicol:

Oral: Adults, initially, 2 to 3 g, then 1 g every eight hours.

Intravenous: Adults, 1 g every eight hours. *Children,* 100 mg/kg of body weight daily in four divided doses. *Premature infants less than 2 weeks old,* 25 mg/kg daily in four divided doses. *Older premature and full-term infants,* 50 mg/kg daily in four divided doses.

Subconjunctival (injected beneath Tenon's capsule): 1.25 mg in 0.5 ml of isotonic sodium chloride injection once or twice daily.

Topical (local instillation into conjunctival sac): For severe conjunctivitis or corneal ulcers, one drop of a 0.5% aqueous solution every 30 minutes. For mild conjunctivitis, one drop of a 0.5% aqueous solution is applied at one- to two-hour intervals or ointment is instilled three or four times daily.

Intracameral (injected into anterior chamber): 1 to 2 mg in 0.2 to 0.5 ml of isotonic sodium chloride injection.

Chloramphenicol Sodium Succinate:

Subconjunctival (injected beneath Tenon's capsule): 50 to 100 mg in 0.5 ml of isotonic sodium chloride injection once or twice daily.

PREPARATIONS.—

Chloramphenicol:

Chloromycetin (Parke, Davis).

Oral: Capsules 50, 100, and 250 mg.

Injection: Solution 250 mg/ml in 2 ml containers.

Topical (ophthalmic): Ointment 1% with liquid petrolatum and polyethylene in 1/8 oz containers; powder (for suspension) 25 mg in 15 ml containers; solution 0.5% in 5 ml containers.

Chloroptic (Allergan). *Topical* (ophthalmic): Ointment 1% with chlorobutanol, white petrolatum, and mineral oil in 3.5 g containers; solution 0.5% with chlorobutanol, polyethylene glycol 300, poloxyl 40 stearate, and sodium hydroxide or hydrochloric acid in 7.5 ml containers.

Chloramphenicol Sodium Succinate:

Chloromycetin Sodium Succinate (Parke,

Davis). *Injection:* Powder 1 g.

ADDITIONAL TRADEMARKS.— Chloramphenicol: Amphicol (McKesson), Chloromax (Century), Mychel (Rachelle).

COLISTIMETHATE SODIUM (Coly-Mycin M Parenteral)

The spectrum of activity of colistimethate is similar to that of the polymyxins: it is primarily active against gram-negative bacilli, including *Pseudomonas aeruginosa, Escherichia coli, Aerobacter aerogenes,* and *Klebsiella pneumoniae.* It has little effect on *Proteus* organisms and is ineffective against most gram-positive bacteria. Colistimethate may be given topically and by subconjunctival injection to treat external ocular infections; it is also given systemically and occasionally by the intracameral route to treat intraocular infections.

For the antibacterial spectrum and systemic adverse effects of colistimethate, see Chapter 52, Polymyxins.

USUAL DOSAGE.—

Topical (local instillation into conjunctival sac): One or two drops of a solution containing 1.5 to 3 mg/ml are instilled every ten minutes for severe infections and every one to four hours for mild infections.

Subconjunctival (injected beneath Tenon's capsule): 15 to 20 mg in 0.5 ml of isotonic sodium chloride injection or sterile water for injection. Doses as large as 37.5 mg have been used occasionally.

Intramuscular: Adults, 1.5 to 5 mg/kg of body weight daily in two to four divided doses. *Children,* 5 mg/kg daily (maximum, 300 mg) in four divided doses. *Premature and full-term newborn infants,* 2.5 mg/kg daily in four divided doses.

Intracameral (injected into anterior chamber): 0.1 mg in 0.2 to 0.5 ml of isotonic sodium chloride injection.

PREPARATIONS.—Coly-Mycin M Parenteral (Warner-Chilcott).

Topical: No ophthalmic form is available but solution for topical use (1.5 to 3 mg/ml) can be made from powder.

Injection: Powder equivalent to 150 mg colistin base.

ERYTHROMYCIN [E-Mycin, Ilotycin]
ERYTHROMYCIN ETHYLSUCCINATE [Erythrocin Ethyl Succinate]
ERYTHROMYCIN LACTOBIONATE [Erythrocin Lactobionate]

Erythromycin is given systemically, by subconjunctival injection, and, occasionally, by intracameral injection to treat intraocular infections caused by gram-positive organisms. It also may be applied topically to treat external ocular infections, but antibiotics that are rarely used systemically are preferred for this purpose.

Staphylococci often develop resistance to erythromycin. Sensitization occurs rarely following topical use.

For the antibacterial activity and systemic adverse effects of erythromycin, see Chapter 50, Erythromycin and Derivatives.

USUAL DOSAGE.—

Erythromycin:

Oral: Adults, initially, 1 g, then 500 mg every six hours.

Topical (local instillation into conjunctival sac): Ointment preparation is applied one or more times daily.

Erythromycin Ethylsuccinate:

Intramuscular: Adults, 100 mg four times daily. *Children,* 15 mg/kg of body weight daily in four divided doses. *Premature and full-term newborn infants,* 7.5 mg/kg daily in four divided doses.

Erythromycin Lactobionate:

Intravenous: Adults, 1 to 4 g daily in divided doses. *Children,* 50 mg/kg of body weight daily in four divided doses. *Premature and full-term newborn infants,* 10 mg/kg daily in four divided doses.

Subconjunctival (injected beneath Tenon's capsule): Up to 50 mg in 0.5 ml of isotonic sodium chloride injection once or twice daily.

Intracameral (injected into anterior chamber): 1 to 2 mg in 0.2 to 0.5 ml of isotonic sodium chloride injection.

PREPARATIONS.—(Strengths expressed in terms of the base.)

Erythromycin:

E-Mycin (Upjohn). *Oral:* Tablets (enteric-coated) 250 mg.

Ilotycin (Lilly).

Oral: Tablets (enteric-coated) 250 mg.

Topical: Ointment (ophthalmic) 0.5% with mineral oil and white petrolatum in 1/8 oz containers.

Erythromycin Ethylsuccinate:

Erythrocin Ethyl Succinate (Abbott). *Injection:* Solution 50 mg/ml in 2 and 10 ml containers.

Erythromycin Lactobionate:

Erythrocin Lactobionate (Abbott). *Injection:* Powder 500 mg and 1 g.

GENTAMICIN SULFATE [Garamycin]

Gentamicin is a broad-spectrum antibiotic that is applied topically or injected by the subconjunctival route to treat external ocular infections caused by susceptible organisms. It also may be given systemically to treat intraocular infections. The drug is active against a wide variety of gram-negative and gram-positive organisms, and is particularly useful because of its significant activity against *Pseudomonas*, *Proteus*, *Klebsiella*, and *Escherichia coli* and against staphylococci and streptoccocci that have developed resistance to combinations of neomycin, bacitracin, and polymyxin B.

Gentamicin may cause transient local irritation after topical administration. It occasionally causes conjunctival erythema and lacrimation. For the antibacterial activity and systemic adverse effects of gentamicin, see Chapter 57, Aminoglycoside Antibacterial Agents and Miscellaneous Antimicrobial Drugs.

USUAL DOSAGE.—

Topical (local instillation into conjunctival sac): One or two drops of a solution containing 3 to 10 mg/ml are given every one to four hours, or the ointment preparation is applied two or three times daily. (The 10 mg/ml solution is not available in ophthalmic form but may be prepared by diluting the parenteral solution.)

Subconjunctival (injected beneath Tenon's capsule): 1.25 to 20 mg in a 0.5 ml aqueous solution.

Intramuscular: Adults, initially, 0.8 mg/kg of body weight, then 0.4 mg/kg every six hours. *Children over 2 years of age*, initially 2.5 mg/kg, then 5 mg/kg daily in four divided doses. *Children under 2 years*, initially 1.25 mg/kg, then 2.5 mg/kg daily in four divided doses. Information is not sufficient at this time to recommend a dose for use in *newborn infants.*

PREPARATIONS.—(Strengths expressed in terms of the base.)

Garamycin (Schering).

Topical: Ointment (ophthalmic) 3 mg/g with methylparaben, propylparaben, and petrolatum in 1/8 oz containers; solution (ophthalmic) 3 mg/ml with disodium phosphate, monosodium phosphate, sodium chloride, and benzalkonium chloride in 5 ml containers.

Injection: Solution 40 mg/ml in 2 ml containers.

KANAMYCIN SULFATE [Kantrex]

Kanamycin is given intramuscularly and by subconjunctival injection to treat intraocular infections caused by resistant staphylococci and gram-negative organisms. When given systemically, its intraocular penetration is fair. Because of its toxicity, kanamycin often is used only when penicillins or cephalosporins are ineffective or are not tolerated by the patient.

For the antibacterial activity and systemic adverse effects of kanamycin, see Chapter 57, Aminoglycoside Antibacterial Agents and Miscellaneous Antimicrobial Drugs.

USUAL DOSAGE.—

Intramuscular: Adults, 500 mg every eight hours. *Children*, 15 mg/kg of body weight daily in four divided doses. *Premature and newborn full-term infants*, 10 mg/kg daily in four divided doses.

Subconjunctival (injected beneath Tenon's capsule): 10 to 20 mg in 0.5 ml of isotonic sodium chloride injection.

PREPARATIONS.—Kantrex (Bristol). *Injection:* Solution 37.5 and 250 mg/ml in 2 ml containers and 333 mg/ml in 3 ml containers.

LINCOMYCIN HYDROCHLORIDE MONOHYDRATE [Lincocin]

Lincomycin is given systemically to treat intraocular infections; it is effective against most gram-positive organisms, including streptococci, pneumococci, and penicillin-resistant staphylococci. It penetrates the eye adequately after systemic administration. Lincomycin has also been administered topically and subconjunctivally to treat corneal ulcers.

Chemosis and subconjunctival hemorrhages may appear after subconjunctival injection. For the antibacterial activity and systemic adverse effects of lincomycin, see Chapter 51, Lincomycin and Clindamycin.

USUAL DOSAGE.—

Oral: Adults, initially, 2 g, then 1 g every six hours.

Intravenous, Intramuscular: Adults, 600 mg every eight hours. *Children*, 20 mg/kg of body weight daily, preferably intravenously, in four divided doses. Should not be used in *infants under 1 month of age.*

Subconjunctival (injected beneath Tenon's capsule): 0.17 to 0.25 ml of a solution containing 300 mg/ml. Doses as large as 0.5 ml have been used occasionally.

Topical (local instillation into conjunctival sac): One or two drops of solution containing 50 to 150 mg/ml are instilled hourly.

PREPARATIONS.—Lincocin (Upjohn).

Oral: Capsules 250 and 500 mg; syrup 250 mg/5 ml.

Injection: Solution 300 mg/ml in 2 and 10 ml containers.

Topical: No ophthalmic form is available but preparation for topical use may be made by diluting the parenteral solution.

METHICILLIN SODIUM [Staphcillin]

The semisynthetic penicillins are given systemically to treat intraocular infections caused by penicillin G-resistant staphylococci. Methicillin is the drug of choice among these agents. It is often used with chloramphenicol for the initial treatment of intraocular infections caused by unidentified organisms. When given systemically, the intraocular penetration of methicillin is fair. The drug also can be given by the subconjunctival and intracameral routes.

For the antibacterial activity and systemic adverse effects of methicillin, see Chapter 48, Penicillins.

USUAL DOSAGE.—

Intramuscular: Adults, 3 to 4 g every six hours.

Intravenous: Adults, 2 to 3 g every six hours.

Intravenous, Intramuscular: Children, 300 mg/kg of body weight daily in four divided doses (preferably intravenously). *Premature and full-term newborn infants,* 150 mg/kg daily in four divided doses.

Subconjunctival (injected beneath Tenon's capsule): 50 to 150 mg in 0.5 ml of isotonic sodium chloride injection or sterile water for injection.

Intracameral (injected into anterior chamber): 1 mg in 0.2 to 0.5 ml of isotonic sodium chloride injection.

PREPARATIONS.—Staphcillin (Bristol). *Injection:* Powder (buffered) 1, 4, and 6 g (900 mg methicillin base per gram).

NEOMYCIN SULFATE [Mycifradin Sulfate, Myciguent]

Neomycin sulfate is applied topically or by the subconjunctival route to treat external ocular infections caused by susceptible organisms (eg, chronic blepharoconjunctivitis due to *Staphylococcus aureus,* pneumococcic corneal ulcers, infections due to some strains of *Pseudomonas).* It occasionally is given by intracameral injection to treat intraocular infections. Neomycin is a common ingredient of many ophthalmic mixtures. Since it is not generally used systemically, it is often preferred for local use. However, neomycin is an active topical sensitizer. In sensitized individuals, cross reactions may occur which could prevent the subsequent systemic use of kanamycin, paromomycin, gentamicin, and streptomycin.

For antibacterial activity and systemic adverse effects, see Chapter 57, Aminoglycoside Antibacterial Agents and Miscellaneous Antimicrobial Drugs.

USUAL DOSAGE.—

Topical (local instillation into conjunctival sac): Ointment is applied to affected eye one to three times daily.

Subconjunctival (injected beneath Tenon's capsule): 100 to 500 mg in 0.5 ml of isotonic sodium chloride injection or sterile water for injection once or twice daily.

Intracameral (injected into anterior chamber): 2.5 mg in 0.2 to 0.5 ml of isotonic sodium chloride injection.

PREPARATIONS.—

Mycifradin Sulfate (Upjohn). *Injection:* Powder 500 mg.

Myciguent (Upjohn). *Topical:* Ointment (ophthalmic) 5 mg/g with anhydrous lanolin, mineral oil, and white petrolatum in 1/8 oz containers.

Drug also marketed by other manufacturers under generic name.

PENICILLIN G SODIUM

Penicillin G is given intravenously, by subconjunctival injection, and, occasionally, by intracameral injection to treat intraocular infections caused by nonpenicillinase-producing bacteria. It is usually administered with a broad-spectrum antibiotic to treat intraocular infections. When given systemically, its intraocular penetration is fair. Penicillin should not be applied topically because of the high incidence of sensitization that occurs with this route of administration.

For the antibacterial activity and systemic toxic effects of penicillin, see Chapter 48, Penicillins.

USUAL DOSAGE.—

Intravenous: Adults, 8 to 20 million units daily. *Children,* 200,000 to 400,000 units/kg of body weight daily in four divided doses. *Premature and full-term newborn infants,* 40,000 to 80,000 units/kg daily in four divided doses.

Subconjunctival (injected beneath Tenon's capsule): 500,000 to 1 million units in 0.5 ml of isotonic sodium chloride injection or sterile water for injection.

Intracameral (injected into anterior chamber): 1,000 to 4,000 units in 0.2 to 0.5 ml of isotonic sodium chloride injection.

Topical (local instillation into conjunctival sac): Penicillin should not be administered topically because of the high incidence of sensitization.

PREPARATIONS.—

Injection: Powder (for solution) 1 and 5 million units.

Topical: Ointment (ophthalmic) 1,000 units/g in 1/8 oz containers.

Drug marketed under generic name.

POLYMYXIN B SULFATE [Aerosporin]

Polymyxin B is applied topically or injected subconjunctivally to treat external ocular infections caused by gram-negative organisms. It is used frequently in the treatment of corneal ulcers. The drug also may be given intravenously, intramuscularly, or by intracameral injection to treat intraocular infections. Because of its toxicity, polymyxin B is only rarely administered systemically; therefore, it is a preferred drug for topical use and is a common ingredient of many ophthalmic mixtures.

For the antibacterial activity and systemic adverse effects of polymyxin B, see Chapter 52, Polymyxins.

USUAL DOSAGE.—

Topical (local instillation into conjunctival sac): For corneal ulcers due to *Pseudomonas aeruginosa*, one drop of a freshly prepared solution containing 20,000 units/ml is instilled two to ten times hourly; the drug also should be given once or twice daily by subconjunctival injection, and a systemic antibiotic effective against *Pseudomonas* (eg, gentamicin, colistin, carbenicillin) should be given concomitantly. For corneal ulcers due to *Moraxella liquefaciens*, *Escherichia coli*, or *Klebsiella pneumoniae*, one drop of a solution containing 20,000 units/ml is instilled every 30 minutes.

Subconjunctival (injected beneath Tenon's capsule): 5 to 10 mg in 0.5 ml of isotonic sodium chloride injection (with 2% procaine).

Intravenous: Adults, 1.5 to 2.5 mg/kg of body weight daily as a single dose or divided into two doses.

Intravenous, Intramuscular: Children, 2.5 mg/kg of body weight daily (maximum, 200 mg) in four divided doses, preferably intravenously. *Premature and full-term newborn infants*, 1.25 mg/kg daily in four divided doses.

Intracameral (injected into anterior chamber): 0.1 mg in 0.2 to 0.5 ml of isotonic sodium chloride injection.

PREPARATIONS.—Aerosporin (Burroughs Wellcome). *Injection, Topical:* Powder (for solution) 500,000 units (equivalent to 50 mg polymyxin standard). Drug also marketed under generic name.

STREPTOMYCIN SULFATE

Streptomycin is effective against a variety of gram-positive and gram-negative organisms, including some strains of *Pseudomonas*. It penetrates the eye adequately after systemic administration and is used with penicillin to treat intraocular infections caused by susceptible organisms. The drug also may be given by the subconjunctival route and occasionally is administered by intracameral injection. Streptomycin is given with isoniazid or aminosalicylic acid in the treatment of ocular tuberculosis. The diagnosis of ocular tuberculosis is usually difficult to establish; therefore, these drugs are often used together to treat chronic granulomatous uveitis that has not responded to other types of therapy and is presumed to be caused by tuberculous infection.

Streptomycin may cause serious adverse reactions, including damage to the eighth cranial nerve. Because of its toxicity, some authorities feel that streptomycin should be used only in severe infections caused by organisms known to be sensitive to this drug and resistant to less toxic agents (eg, in ocular tuberculosis).

For the antibacterial activity and systemic adverse effects of streptomycin, see Chapter 57, Aminoglycoside Antibacterial Agents and Miscellaneous Antimicrobial Drugs, and Chapter 58, Antituberculous Agents.

USUAL DOSAGE.—

Intramuscular: For ocular tuberculosis, *adults*, 1 g every three days. Isoniazid (100 mg orally three times daily for five days, followed by 50 mg three times daily) or aminosalicylic acid (3 g orally every six hours) should be given concomitantly. *Children*, 40 mg/kg of body weight daily (maximum, 1 g) in one or two divided doses, with isoniazid (20 mg/kg daily, orally or intramuscularly, in two or three doses) or aminosalicylic acid (300 mg/kg daily, orally, in four divided doses). *Premature and full-term newborn infants*, 20 mg/kg daily in four divided doses, with aminosalicylic acid (150 mg/kg daily, orally, in four divided doses). [Note: The dosage for isoniazid in newborn infants has not been well established.] If a favorable response is obtained within 28 days, therapy should be continued for six months.

For other intraocular infections, *adults*, 1 g

initially, then 500 mg every eight hours. *Children*, 20 mg/kg initially, then 40 mg/kg daily in four divided doses. *Premature and full-term newborn infants*, 10 mg/kg initially, then 20 mg/kg daily in four divided doses. This drug should be given with penicillin G or a semisynthetic penicillin.

Subconjunctival (injected beneath Tenon's capsule): 50 mg in 0.5 ml of isotonic sodium chloride injection.

Intracameral (injected into anterior chamber): 0.5 to 5 mg in 0.5 ml of isotonic sodium chloride injection.

PREPARATIONS.—*Injection:* Powder 1 and 5 g; solution 200 mg/ml in 5 ml containers, 400 mg/ml in 2.5 and 12.5 ml containers, and 500 mg/ml in 1, 2, and 10 ml containers. Drug marketed under generic name.

SULFACETAMIDE SODIUM

Because sulfacetamide sodium is available only for topical ophthalmic use, it is preferred for this purpose over sulfonamides that are commonly given systemically. It is effective in treating external ocular infections caused by susceptible organisms (eg, many forms of acute and chronic conjunctivitis, corneal ulcers). The drug occasionally is used in trachoma but orally administered sulfonamides and topically applied tetracyclines are preferred.

Sulfacetamide sodium may cause local irritation. Topically applied sulfonamides often cause sensitization; however, this is not common with sulfacetamide sodium. See also Chapter 55, Sulfonamides.

USUAL DOSAGE.—*Topical* (local instillation into conjunctival sac): For acute catarrhal conjunctivitis caused by *Staphylococcus aureus*, *Diplococcus pneumoniae*, *Haemophilus aegyptius*, *H. influenzae*, or *Neisseria catarrhalis*, one drop of a 10% or 15% solution every 10 to 30 minutes.

For chronic conjunctivitis due to *Proteus* organisms, inclusion conjunctivitis, or acute catarrhal conjunctivitis of the newborn caused by *H. influenzae*, 10% ointment applied three or four times daily.

For chronic blepharoconjunctivitis due to *S. aureus*, one drop of a 30% solution three or four times daily; 10% ointment may be used at bedtime.

For corneal ulcers due to *Moraxella liquefaciens*, *Escherichia coli*, or *Klebsiella pneumoniae*, one drop of a 10% solution every 30 minutes or 10% ointment applied three or four times daily.

PREPARATIONS.—

Blefcon (Madland). *Topical:* Ointment (ophthalmic) 30% in 1/8 oz containers.

Bleph-10 Liquifilm (Allergan). *Topical:* Solution (ophthalmic) 10% with polyvinyl alcohol in 5 and 15 ml containers.

Bleph-30 Liquifilm (Allergan). *Topical:* Solution (ophthalmic) 30% with polyvinyl alcohol in 15 ml containers.

BufOpto Sulfacel-15 (Professional). *Topical:* Solution (ophthalmic) 15% with methylcellulose, sodium thiosulfate, sodium phosphate (dibasic), sodium phosphate (monobasic), propylene glycol, methylparaben, and propylparaben in 5 and 15 ml containers.

Cetamide (Alcon). *Topical:* Sterile ointment (ophthalmic) 10% in white petrolatum, anhydrous liquid lanolin, and mineral oil with methylparaben and propylparaben in 3.5 g containers.

Isopto Cetamide (Alcon). *Topical:* Solution (ophthalmic) 15% with methylcellulose, sodium thiosulfate, methylparaben, propylparaben, dried sodium phosphate, and sodium biphosphate in 5 and 15 ml containers.

Sodium Sulamyd (Schering). *Topical:* Ointment (ophthalmic) 10% with methylparaben, propylparaben, benzalkonium chloride, sorbitan monolaurate, and petrolatum in 1/8 oz containers; solution (ophthalmic) 10% and 30% with methylcellulose (10% solution only), methylparaben, propylparaben, sodium thiosulfate, and sodium dihydrogen phosphate in 5 and 15 ml containers.

Sulf-30 (Smith, Miller & Patch). *Topical:* Solution (ophthalmic) 30% with methylparaben, propylparaben, sodium thiosulfate, and monobasic and dibasic sodium phosphate in 5 ml containers.

Sulfacetamide Sodium (Cooper). *Topical:* Solution (ophthalmic) 10% with hydroxypropyl methylcellulose in 1 and 15 ml containers.

Drug also marketed by other manufacturers under generic name.

SULFADIAZINE
SULFADIAZINE SODIUM

Sulfadiazine may be given systemically to treat intraocular infections or severe external ocular infections. Its ophthalmic use today is confined largely to the treatment of trachoma and, along with pyrimethamine, of ocular toxoplasmosis. Sulfadiazine also is available for topical ophthalmic use, but agents that are rarely used systemically are preferred.

For the antibacterial activity and systemic

adverse effects of sulfadiazine, see Chapter 55, Sulfonamides.

USUAL DOSAGE.—

Oral: For trachoma, *adults,* 3 g daily in divided doses for three to four weeks. *Children,* 100 mg/kg of body weight daily in four divided doses for one week, followed by 60 mg/kg daily in four divided doses for two weeks. It may be necessary to repeat this treatment for several months, alternating three weeks of drug administration with one week without medication. A broad spectrum antibiotic (usually tetracycline) should be applied topically in conjunction with sulfonamide therapy.

For use in ocular toxoplasmosis, see the evaluation on Pyrimethamine.

For intraocular infections, *adults,* 2 g initially, followed by 1 g every six hours.

Intravenous: For intraocular infections, *children,* 120 mg/kg of body weight daily in four divided doses. Should not be used in *newborn infants.*

Topical: (local instillation into conjunctival sac): Ointment is applied three or four times daily.

PREPARATIONS.—

Sulfadiazine, U.S.P:

Oral: Suspension 500 mg/5 ml; tablets 500 mg; tablets (chewable) 300 mg.

Topical: Ointment (ophthalmic) 5% in 1/8 oz containers.

Drug marketed by many manufacturers under generic name.

Sulfadiazine Sodium, U.S.P:

Injection: Solution 250 mg/ml in 10 ml containers.

SIMILAR TOPICAL PREPARATIONS.—

Sulfathiazole:

Topical: Ointment (ophthalmic) 5% in 1/8 oz containers. Drug marketed under generic name.

Sulfisoxazole Diolamine:

Gantrisin Diolamine (Roche). *Topical:* Ointment (ophthalmic) 4% in 1/8 oz containers; solution (ophthalmic) 4% in 15 ml containers.

See Chapter 55, Sulfonamides, for available systemic forms.

TETRACYCLINE HYDROCHLORIDE [Achromycin]

The most common topical ophthalmic uses of tetracycline are in the treatment of infections caused by TRIC agent (trachoma and inclusion conjunctivitis); antibiotics that are rarely used systemically are preferred for other external infections. Tetracycline also is given systemically and by subconjunctival injection to treat intraocular infections and severe external ocular infections. When administered systemically, it does not readily penetrate the eye and large doses must be used; intraocular penetration after subconjunctival administration is also comparatively poor.

Tetracycline rarely causes adverse reactions when administered topically. The antibacterial activity and systemic adverse effects of tetracycline are discussed in Chapter 53, Tetracyclines.

USUAL DOSAGE.—

Topical (local instillation into conjunctival sac): For inclusion conjunctivitis, 1% ointment is applied three or four times daily for 30 days. For trachoma, 1% ointment is applied three or four times daily for six weeks; the drug should be given in conjunction with a systemic sulfonamide preparation. For other external ocular infections, one or two drops of a 0.5% solution are instilled in affected eye every 30 minutes to two hours. Solutions should be freshly prepared every 24 to 48 hours and kept refrigerated.

Subconjunctival (injected beneath Tenon's capsule): 2.5 to 5 mg in 0.5 ml of isotonic sodium chloride injection once or twice daily.

Oral: Adults, 1 g initially, then 500 mg every six to eight hours.

Intravenous: Children, 15 mg/kg of body weight daily in four divided doses. Should not be used in *newborn infants.*

Intramuscular: Children, 25 mg/kg of body weight daily in four divided doses (intravenous route preferred). Should not be used in *newborn infants.*

PREPARATIONS.—Achromycin (Lederle).

Topical: Ointment (ophthalmic) 1% in 1/8 oz containers; suspension in oil (ophthalmic) 1% in 4 ml containers.

Injection: Powder 100, 250, and 500 mg.

For other systemic forms and additional trademarks, see Chapter 53, Tetracyclines.

SIMILAR DRUG.—

Chlortetracycline Hydrochloride:

Aureomycin (Lederle). *Topical:* Ointment (ophthalmic) 1% in 1/8 oz containers.

VANCOMYCIN HYDROCHLORIDE [Vancocin Hydrochloride]

Vancomycin is one of the most effective antibiotics for treating intraocular infections caused by resistant staphylococci. It is given intravenously and by subconjunctival injection. Intraocular penetration is fair when vancomycin is administered systemically.

Vancomycin may cause severe adverse reactions, including deafness and renal damage. For the antibacterial activity and systemic adverse effects of vancomycin, see Chapter 57, Aminoglycoside Antibacterial Agents and Miscellaneous Antimicrobial Drugs.

USUAL DOSAGE.—

Intravenous: Adults, 2 g initially, then 1 g every 12 hours. *Children*, 20 mg/kg of body weight initially, then 40 mg/kg daily in four divided doses. *Premature and full-term newborn infants*, 5 mg/kg initially, then 10 mg/kg in four divided doses.

Subconjunctival (injected beneath Tenon's capsule): 15 to 25 mg in 0.5 ml of sodium chloride injection.

PREPARATIONS.—Vancocin Hydrochloride (Lilly). *Injection:* Powder 500 mg.

Mixtures of Antibacterial Agents

Many antibiotic mixtures are available for topical treatment of external ocular infections. These combination products are useful when therapy must be initiated before the responsible organism has been identified.

AVAILABLE MIXTURES.—

Chloromycetin-Polymyxin Ophthalmic Ointment (Parke, Davis): Each gram contains chloramphenicol 1% and polymyxin B sulfate 5,000 units with liquid petrolatum and polyethylene in 1/8 oz containers.

Mycitracin Ophthalmic Ointment (Upjohn): Each gram contains polymyxin B sulfate 5,000 units, neomycin sulfate 5 mg, and bacitracin 500 units with anhydrous lanolin, mineral oil, and white petrolatum in 1/8 oz containers.

Neo-Polycin (Dow): *Ophthalmic Ointment:* Each gram contains polymyxin B sulfate 10,000 units, neomycin sulfate equivalent to neomycin 3 mg, and bacitracin 500 units with anhydrous lanolin, white petrolatum, and liquid petrolatum in 1/8 oz containers. *Ophthalmic Solution:* Each milliliter contains polymyxin B sulfate 5,000 units, neomycin sulfate equivalent to neomycin 2 mg, and gramicidin 0.02 mg with thimerosal, polyoxyalkylene diol, hydrochloric acid, and sodium chloride in 10 ml containers.

Neosporin (Burroughs Wellcome): *Ophthalmic Ointment:* Each gram contains polymyxin B sulfate 5,000 units, neomycin sulfate 5 mg, and bacitracin 400 units with white petrolatum in 1/8 oz containers. *Ophthalmic Solution:* Each milliliter contains polymyxin B sulfate 5,000 units, neomycin sulfate 2.5 mg, and gramicidin 0.025 mg with alcohol, propylene glycol, polyoxyethylene polyoxypropylene compound, sodium chloride, and thimerosal in 10 ml containers.

Polyspectrin (Allergan): Each gram of sterile ointment contains bacitracin zinc 400 units, polymyxin B sulfate 5,000 units, and neomycin sulfate equivalent to neomycin 3.5 mg with chlorobutanol, white petrolatum, and mineral oil in 3.5 g containers; each milliliter of solution contains polymyxin B sulfate 5,000 units and neomycin sulfate 0.5% with polyvinyl alcohol 1.4% in 10 ml containers.

Polysporin Ophthalmic Ointment (Burroughs Wellcome): Each gram contains polymyxin B sulfate 10,000 units and bacitracin zinc 500 units with petrolatum base in 1/8 oz containers.

Statrol Ophthalmic Drops (Alcon): Each milliliter contains neomycin sulfate equivalent to neomycin 3.5 mg and polymyxin B sulfate 16,250 units with phenylephrine hydrochloride 0.12%, hydroxypropyl methylcellulose, benzalkonium chloride, boric acid, sodium chloride, hydrochloric acid, and sodium hydroxide in 5 ml containers.

ANTIFUNGAL AGENTS

AMPHOTERICIN B [Fungizone]

Amphotericin B is effective against a variety of fungi, particularly *Candida*, *Coccidioides*, *Cryptococcus*, *Histoplasma*, *Blastomyces*, and *Sporotrichum*. It is used topically to treat external fungal infections (eg, mycotic conjunctivitis). It also may be given intravenously or subconjunctivally for severe external infections (eg, fungal corneal ulcers) and for intraocular infections (eg, fungal endophthalmitis).

Severe local irritation may occur with topical use. Intraocular penetration is poor when amphotericin B is administered systemically; therefore large doses must be used, thereby increasing the risk of hepatic and renal toxicity. The patient should be hospitalized if the drug is given systemically. See Chapter 60, Antifungal Agents.

USUAL DOSAGE.—

Topical (local instillation into conjunctival sac): One drop of a suspension containing 0.1 to 1 mg/ml in sterile distilled water every 30 minutes.

Subconjunctival (injected beneath Tenon's capsule): 0.1 to 0.2 mg in a 0.5 ml aqueous suspension.

Intravenous: Adults and children, initially, 0.1 to 0.25 mg/kg of body weight daily infused over a period of three to six hours. The daily dose should be increased gradually up to 1 mg/kg daily. *Premature and full-term newborn infants*, initially, 0.1 mg/kg daily gradually increased to 0.5 mg/kg daily infused over a period of four to six hours.

PREPARATIONS.—Fungizone (Squibb).

Topical: No ophthalmic form available, but aqueous suspension containing 0.1 to 1 mg/ml may be prepared from powder marketed for intravenous use.

Injection: Powder 50 mg.

NYSTATIN [Mycostatin]

Nystatin is used topically or by the subconjunctival route to treat external candidal infections (eg, mycotic conjunctivitis and corneal ulcers). It is of little or no value in the treatment of other fungal infections. See also Chapter 60, Antifungal Agents.

USUAL DOSAGE.—

Topical (local instillation into conjunctival sac): One drop of a suspension containing 25,000 units/ml every 15 minutes, or the powder may be dusted onto the lesion. Alternatively, an ointment preparation containing 100,000 units/g may be applied four times daily.

Subconjunctival (injected beneath Tenon's capsule): 5,000 units in 0.5 ml of isotonic sodium chloride injection once or twice daily.

PREPARATIONS.—Mycostatin (Squibb). No ophthalmic form available, but preparations available for parenteral administration or dermatologic use may be used. Powder should be reconstituted with isotonic sodium chloride injection to make a suspension containing 25,000 units/ml for topical use or 10,000 units/ml for subconjunctival injection. Dermatologic forms include ointment 100,000 units/g in 15 and 30 g containers; powder 500,000 units in 1 ml containers and 100,000 units/g in 15 g containers.

ANTIVIRAL AGENTS

IDOXURIDINE [Dendrid, Herplex, Stoxil]

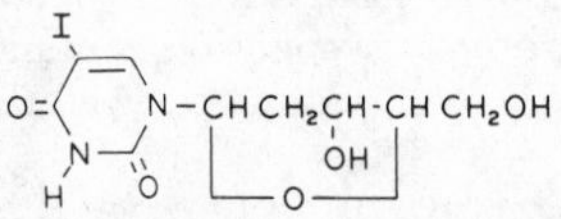

I
O= N–CH CH_2CH–CH CH_2OH
OH
H N O O

Idoxuridine (IDU) is used topically to treat herpes simplex infections of the lids, conjunctiva, and cornea. This agent improves the course of acute dendritic keratitis and also may be of value in controlling recurrences if the infection is confined to the surface. Topically applied idoxuridine does not penetrate the cornea. It has no proved effectiveness in cases of deeper stromal involvement and iritis which may be due to viral invasion or may represent an allergic reaction to a viral toxin or antigen. However, if stromal keratitis is treated with topical corticosteroid preparations, idoxuridine should be given concomitantly to prevent reactivation of the epithelial infection. The drug also has been used experimentally to treat vaccinia infections of the eye.

Idoxuridine may cause slight local irritation, photophobia, and mild edema of the eyelids and cornea. Small punctate defects may appear in the corneal epithelium during the treatment of herpes simplex infections; it is not clear whether these punctate areas are caused by the disease or by the drug. Idoxuridine inhibits corneal stromal healing and probably should not be used for several weeks after corneal transplantation.

USUAL DOSAGE.—*Topical* (local instillation into conjunctival sac): One drop of the solution is instilled every hour during the day and every two hours at night. The ointment is applied four or five times daily or as nighttime medication when the solution is used during the day. Treatment should be continued for at least two weeks.

PREPARATIONS.—

Dendrid (Alcon). *Topical:* Solution (ophthalmic) 0.1% with benzalkonium chloride, phenylmercuric nitrate, and boric acid in 15 ml containers.

Herplex Liquifilm (Allergan). *Topical:* Solution (ophthalmic) 0.1% with polyvinyl alcohol in 15 ml containers.

Stoxil (Smith Kline & French). *Topical:* Ointment (ophthalmic) 0.5% in petrolatum base in 4 g containers; solution (ophthalmic) 0.1% with thimerosal in 15 ml containers.

ANTIPROTOZOAL AGENTS

PYRIMETHAMINE [Daraprim]

The folic acid antagonist, pyrimethamine, is used with sulfonamides (usually sulfadiazine) to treat vision-threatening uveitis when a presumptive diagnosis of ocular toxoplasmosis has been made. Ocular toxoplasmosis is believed to be a common cause of posterior uveitis, but the diagnosis is usually difficult to establish; possibly for this reason, opinion is divided as to the effectiveness of pyrimethamine. Pyrimethamine is synergistic with sulfonamides and combined therapy permits a reduction of the dosage of both drugs. Corticosteroids usually are given concomitantly to reduce inflammation; however, some authorities believe that the proliferative form of toxoplasmosis should not be treated with steroids.

Pyrimethamine may cause bone marrow depression. Red blood cell, white blood cell, and platelet counts should be performed once or twice a week during therapy. If the platelet count falls below 100,000 or the white blood cell count falls below 4,000, leucovorin calcium (folinic acid) should be administered intramuscularly in a dose of 3 to 9 mg/day and pyrimethamine therapy may be continued. If the platelet count falls below 80,000, the pyrimethamine dosage should be reduced or therapy should be discontinued. Alternatively, leucovorin (3 mg daily) may be used prophylactically during therapy.

For other indications and adverse reactions, see Chapter 61, Antimalarial Agents.

USUAL DOSAGE.—*Oral: Adults*, 100 to 150 mg may be given initially. Then 25 mg is administered twice daily for eight weeks, followed by 25 mg once daily for an additional eight weeks. Finally, 25 mg is given every other day until a total of six months of therapy has been completed. Sulfadiazine (4 g daily, orally, in divided doses) should be given concomitantly. *Children*, initially, 4 mg/kg of body weight (maximum, 200 mg) in four divided doses for one day, then 1 mg/kg daily (maximum, 50 mg) in four divided doses for six weeks. Sulfadiazine should be given orally in conjunction with pyrimethamine (sulfadiazine dosage: 100 mg/kg daily [maximum, 4 g] in four divided doses for one to three weeks, then 50 mg/kg daily in four divided doses until a total of six weeks of therapy has been completed).

PREPARATIONS.—Daraprim (Burroughs Wellcome). *Oral:* Tablets 25 mg.

ANTHELMINTICS

DIETHYLCARBAMAZINE CITRATE [Hetrazan]

Diethylcarbamazine is used systemically to treat ocular onchocerciasis. It is effective in destroying the microfilariae but has no effect on the adult worms; therefore, microfilariae generally reappear in two to four months unless the adults are removed surgically or by treatment with suramin.

Destruction of the microfilariae causes pronounced allergic reactions (conjunctivitis, uveitis) which can be controlled by corticosteroid therapy. See also Chapter 65, Anthelmintics.

USUAL DOSAGE.—*Oral: Adults*, the initial dose should not exceed 0.5 mg/kg of body weight, administered once on the first day and twice on the second day. The dosage is then increased to 1 mg/kg three times daily on the third day followed by 3 mg/kg three times daily on the fourth day and continued for a total course of 30 days. *Children*, initially, 1 mg/kg daily. The dosage is gradually increased by increments of 2 mg/kg daily to a maximum of 9 mg/kg in four divided doses for a total course of 30 days.

PREPARATIONS.—Hetrazan (Lederle). *Oral:* Tablets 50 mg.

THIABENDAZOLE [Mintezol]

On the basis of very limited data, thiabendazole has been reported to be of benefit in the treatment of intraocular toxocariasis. However, the treatment of toxocaral endophthalmitis is controversial, and the efficacy of thiabendazole in this condition cannot be regarded as established. Corticosteroids may be of value in reducing the ocular allergic response to the parasite. Thiabendazole also may be effective in treating ocular trichinosis.

See also Chapter 65, Anthelmintics.

USUAL DOSAGE.—*Oral: Adults*, 50 to 60 mg/kg of body weight daily. *Children*, 50 mg/kg daily (maximum, 3 g) in two doses. *Premature and full-term newborn infants*, 25 mg/kg daily in two doses.

PREPARATIONS.—Mintezol (Merck Sharp & Dohme). *Oral:* Suspension 500 mg/5 ml; tablets (chewable) 500 mg.

ANTI-INFLAMMATORY AGENTS

Adrenal corticosteroids are used in the symptomatic treatment of certain nonpyogenic ocular inflammatory disorders. By controlling inflammation, these agents reduce the amount of permanent scarring and can prevent visual loss. They generally are more effective in acute than in chronic conditions.

Adrenal corticosteroids are of value in ocular inflammatory disorders caused by allergy (eg, vernal conjunctivitis, drug or contact sensitivity) and in various inflammatory conditions of uncertain etiology (eg, many types of endogenous uveitis). They also are indicated when significant scarring may be expected after severe ocular injury (eg, severe burns, penetrating wounds) and in the treatment of postoperative iridocyclitis. Corticosteroids generally are contraindicated in ocular infections: Although pyogenic inflammations initially respond to steroid therapy, the course of the disease may be worsened by the weakening of bodily defense mechanisms. However, there are some ocular infectious disorders in which corticosteroid therapy may be helpful. Herpes zoster infections and superficial punctate keratitis (which is believed to be caused by a virus) are improved by corticosteroid therapy. Also, many ophthalmologists use corticosteroids in ocular infections if vision is seriously threatened by an acute, severe uveitis or stromal edema which is believed to be caused by a superimposed allergic reaction (eg, stromal herpes); in this situation, an effective anti-infective agent is generally administered before steroid therapy is begun and continued until after it is terminated.

Corticosteroids are applied topically to treat inflammations of the lids, conjunctiva, cornea, and sclera; they may also be injected subconjunctivally if the disorder does not respond to topical therapy. Anterior uveitis (iritis, iridocyclitis) can occasionally be controlled by local therapy but, in most instances, corticosteroids also must be given systemically. Inflammatory disorders of the posterior segment of the globe (eg, posterior scleritis, chorioretinitis, optic neuritis) require systemic therapy; the drugs also may be given by the subconjunctival route and occasionally are administered by retrobulbar injection. When corticosteroids are given systemically to treat uveitis, large doses may be required to control the inflammation.

Cortisone, dexamethasone [Decadron, Maxidex], fluorometholone [FML], hydrocortisone [Eye-Cort, Hydrocortone, Optef], medrysone [HMS], and prednisolone [Hydeltrasol, Inflamase, Sterofrin] are available as drops or ointments for topical ophthalmic use. Solutions or suspensions of corticosteroids may be injected by the subconjunctival route, or the repository form of methylprednisolone [Depo-Medrol] or triamcinolone [Aristocort, Kenalog] may be preferred for more prolonged action. (See the following individual evaluations.) Systemic doses of corticosteroids are given in Chapter 35, Adrenal Corticosteroids. Corticotropin also may be used to treat intraocular inflammations (see Chapter 38, Anterior Pituitary and Hypothalamic Hormones).

Other anti-inflammatory agents are occasionally used in ophthalmology. Before corticosteroids were available, aspirin was used to treat uveitis and episcleritis; it is still given occasionally in these conditions, either alone or with corticosteroids. Episcleritis and uveitis associated with rheumatoid arthritis have sometimes been treated successfully with indomethacin [Indocin] or phenylbutazone [Azolid, Butazolidin]. Antineoplastic agents have limited usefulness in ophthalmology because of their toxicity, but they have occasionally been administered in inflammatory disorders that did not respond to other agents (eg, cyclitis, uveitis, sympathetic ophthalmia).

Adverse Reactions and Precautions

Topically applied corticosteroids cause discomfort, burning, and lacrimation in some patients. Suspensions given subconjunctivally may cause pain, ulceration, and granulomatous formations. A topical anesthetic should be applied before subconjunctival injection of corticosteroids. Mydriasis, loss of accommodation, and ptosis occasionally follow local use.

In general, the severe adverse reactions associated with systemic use of these agents (eg, electrolyte imbalance, osteoporotic changes, peptic ulcer) do not occur when the corticoids are applied topically, but serious local complications are not infrequent. The corticosteroids are potentially toxic agents and never should be used to treat minor disorders or conditions that can be controlled by safer drugs (eg, allergic reactions of the immediate type that respond to decongestants or to systemic antihistamines). They always should be given in the lowest effective concentration and long-term use should be avoided whenever possible. After prolonged use in some chronic conditions, exacerbation of the disease may occur if the corticosteroid is discontinued abruptly; therefore, the interval between applications should be lengthened gradually.

Corticosteroids lower resistance to infection and, by reducing inflammation, can mask the symptoms of serious ocular disease. Their use should be avoided in most ocular infections and they should not be used to treat ocular inflammatory conditions if the diagnosis is uncertain. Their use also should be avoided in the treatment of minor corneal abrasions. These agents may activate latent ocular herpes simplex infections and worsen the course of active disease. In the initial stages of dendritic keratitis, the nature of the infection may not be recognized without slit-lamp magnification. Frequently, corticosteroids or steroid-antibiotic combinations are prescribed and the eye appears to improve while the infection is spreading. Eventually the deeper corneal structures become involved and the cornea may perforate. Topical corticosteroids, alone or in combination with antibiotics, also increase susceptibility to fungal infections, particularly when the corneal epithelium has been damaged by injury, surgery, or infection. Other ocular diseases that can be activated or worsened by the use of corticosteroids are vaccinia, trachoma, *Pseudomonas* infections, and ocular tuberculosis.

Although corticosteroids are often used prophylactically after ocular surgery to prevent inflammation and scarring, their value has not been clearly established by controlled studies and there is some experimental evidence that they may delay healing. If corticosteroids are employed postoperatively, their use should be postponed until the healing process has begun unless a severe intraocular inflammation demands immediate treatment.

Repeated administration of topical corticosteroids may raise the intraocular pressure by reducing outflow facility. The rise in pressure is minimal in most instances, but in some individuals it is of sufficient magnitude to induce glaucomatous changes with eventual visual loss. The rise in pressure is not accompanied by pain and the condition usually is reversible if it is detected before damage to the optic nerve has occurred. A glaucomatous response to topical corticosteroids is genetically determined and occurs most frequently in patients with primary open-angle glaucoma and in their relatives. This response also is common in myopic individuals with no family history of glaucoma and in diabetics. The magnitude of the steroid-induced ocular hypertension is related to the concentration, frequency of administration, duration of treatment, and anti-inflammatory potency of the drug used. The rise in pressure has been reported most frequently after administration of a 0.1% concentration of dexamethasone [Decadron, Maxidex]. Medrysone [HMS] rarely causes a clinically significant increase in intraocular pressure, but this may be due to low anti-inflammatory potency or to failure to penetrate ocular tissue. Intraocular pressure should be determined every two months in patients receiving prolonged corticosteroid therapy. These agents should be used with extreme caution, and long-term administration avoided, in patients with primary open-angle glaucoma and in their relatives, in myopic individuals, and in diabetics.

Posterior subcapsular cataract formation has been associated with long-term systemic administration of large doses of corticosteroids, and a few cases have been reported after prolonged topical therapy. These lens changes do not regress when corticosteroids are discontinued, but further progression has not been observed.

Topical corticosteroids should be used sparingly in any conditions that cause thinning of the cornea, as perforation may occur.

INDIVIDUAL EVALUATIONS

CORTISONE ACETATE

Cortisone is used topically to treat nonpyogenic inflammations of the lids, conjunctiva, and anterior segment of the globe. A suspension may be given by subconjunctival injection if topical therapy is ineffective. For systemic therapy, corticosteroids with less mineralocorticoid activity are preferred.

For specific uses, adverse reactions, and precautions, see the Introductory Statement to this section.

USUAL DOSAGE.—

Topical (local instillation into conjunctival sac): One or two drops of a 0.5% suspension every one to two hours until a response is obtained; the frequency then is reduced. For severe conditions, a 1.5% or 2.5% suspension may be used. The ointment preparation is applied three or four times daily or as nighttime medication when the suspension is used during the day.

Subconjunctival (injected beneath Tenon's capsule): 0.5 ml of a 2.5% suspension every 7 to 14 days.

PREPARATIONS.—

Topical: Ointment (ophthalmic) 1.5% in 1/8 oz containers.

Injection (subconjunctival), Topical: Suspension 2.5% and 5%.

Ophthalmic preparations marketed under generic name.

DEXAMETHASONE [Maxidex]
DEXAMETHASONE SODIUM PHOSPHATE
[Decadron Phosphate, Hexadrol Phosphate]

Dexamethasone is applied topically to treat

nonpyogenic inflammations of the lids, conjunctiva, and anterior segment of the globe. It also may be given by subconjunctival injection if topical therapy is ineffective. Systemic therapy generally is required for inflammations of the posterior segment of the globe and in severe anterior segment disorders. Dexamethasone is more potent than other available topically applied ophthalmic corticosteroids and, therefore, may be preferred for severe inflammations of the anterior segment; weaker steroids, which are less likely to increase the intraocular tension in susceptible individuals, are preferred for superficial ocular inflammations.

For specific uses, adverse reactions, and precautions, see the Introductory Statement to this section.

USUAL DOSAGE.—

Dexamethasone:

Topical (local instillation into conjunctival sac): One or two drops of a 0.1% suspension every one or two hours until a response is obtained; the frequency then is reduced.

Oral: See Chapter 35, Adrenal Corticosteroids.

Dexamethasone Sodium Phosphate:

Topical (local instillation into conjunctival sac): One or two drops of a 0.1% solution every one or two hours until a response is obtained; the frequency then is reduced. The ointment preparation is applied three or four times daily or as nighttime medication when the solution is used during the day.

Subconjunctival (injected beneath Tenon's capsule): 0.5 ml of a 0.1% solution every 7 to 14 days.

Intravenous, Intramuscular: See Chapter 35, Adrenal Corticosteroids.

PREPARATIONS.—

Dexamethasone:

Maxidex (Alcon).

Topical: Suspension (ophthalmic) 0.1% with benzalkonium chloride, hydroxypropyl methylcellulose, dried sodium phosphate, polysorbate 80, disodium edetate, and citric acid in 5 and 15 ml containers.

Oral: See Chapter 35, Adrenal Corticosteroids.

Dexamethasone Sodium Phosphate:

Decadron Phosphate (Merck Sharp & Dohme).

Topical: Ointment (ophthalmic) 0.05% with white petrolatum and mineral oil in 3.5 g containers.

Injection (subconjunctival), Topical: Solution (sterile ophthalmic) 0.1% with creatinine, sodium citrate, sodium borate, polysorbate 80, sodium hydroxide, sodium bisulfite, phenylethanol, and benzalkonium in 2.5 and 5 ml containers.

Injection (intravenous, intramuscular): Solution 4 mg/ml with creatinine, sodium citrate, sodium hydroxide, sodium bisulfite, methylparaben, and propylparaben in 1 and 5 ml containers.

Hexadrol Phosphate (Organon). *Injection (intramuscular, intravenous):* Solution 4 mg/ml with sodium bisulfite, sodium citrate, sodium chloride, disodium edetate, sodium hydroxide, methylparaben, and propylparaben in 1 and 5 ml containers.

FLUOROMETHOLONE [FML]

Fluorometholone is a new synthetic corticosteroid structurally related to progesterone. It appears to be comparable to medrysone in effects on the intraocular pressure of patients known to experience a rise in pressure with some other corticosteroids. Data are not sufficient to compare the anti-inflammatory potency of fluorometholone with that of other topically applied corticosteroids.

USUAL DOSAGE.—*Topical* (local instillation into conjunctival sac): One or two drops every one or two hours until a response is obtained; the frequency is then reduced.

PREPARATIONS.—FML (Allergan). *Topical:* Suspension (ophthalmic) 0.1% with polyvinyl alcohol; benzalkonium chloride; disodium edetate; sodium chloride; sodium phosphate monobasic, monohydrate; sodium phosphate dibasic, anhydrous; polysorbate 80; and sodium hydroxide in 5 ml containers.

HYDROCORTISONE [Optef]
HYDROCORTISONE ACETATE [Eye-Cort, Hydrocortone Acetate]

Hydrocortisone is applied topically to treat nonpyogenic inflammations of the lids, conjunctiva, and anterior segment of the globe. It is more effective than cortisone against external ocular inflammations. Hydrocortisone also may be given by subconjunctival injection if topical therapy is ineffective. For systemic therapy, corticosteroids with less mineralocorticoid activity are preferred.

For specific uses, adverse reactions, and precautions, see the Introductory Statement to this section.

USUAL DOSAGE.—

Topical (local instillation into conjunctival sac): One or two drops of a 0.5% suspension every one or two hours until a response is obtained; the frequency then is reduced. For severe conditions, a 2.5% suspension may be used. The ointment preparation is applied three or four times daily or as nighttime medication when the suspension is used during the day.

Subconjunctival (injected beneath Tenon's capsule): 0.5 ml of a 2.5% suspension every 7 to 14 days.

PREPARATIONS.—

Hydrocortisone:

Optef (Upjohn). *Topical:* Solution (ophthalmic) 0.2% in 2.5 ml containers.

Hydrocortisone Acetate:

Eye-Cort (Mallard). *Topical:* Suspension (ophthalmic) 0.5%.

Hydrocortone Acetate (Merck Sharp & Dohme).

Topical: Ointment (ophthalmic) 1.5% in 1/8 oz containers.

Injection (subconjunctival), Topical: Suspension (ophthalmic) 2.5% in 5 ml containers.

Drug also marketed under generic name.

MEDRYSONE [HMS]

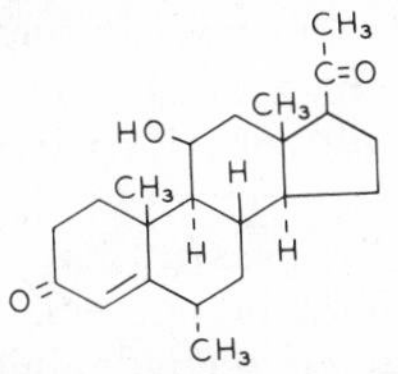

Medrysone is a synthetic corticosteroid structurally related to progesterone. It is effective in the treatment of allergic conjunctivitis and also may be useful in other superficial ocular inflammatory conditions. Available evidence indicates that medrysone seldom increases the intraocular pressure of patients known to experience a rise in pressure with some other corticosteroids. Further studies are needed to determine whether its anti-inflammatory action is actually divorced from an ocular hypertensive effect or whether its lack of effect on intraocular pressure is due to low anti-inflammatory potency or to failure of the drug to penetrate the ocular tissues.

Medrysone may cause stinging and conjunctival irritation. For other adverse reactions and precautions, see the Introductory Statement to this section.

USUAL DOSAGE.—*Topical* (local instillation into conjunctival sac): One or two drops of the 1% suspension every one or two hours until a response is obtained; the frequency then is reduced.

PREPARATIONS.—HMS (Allergan). *Topical:* Suspension (ophthalmic) 1% with polyvinyl alcohol; benzalkonium chloride; disodium edetate; sodium chloride; potassium chloride; sodium phosphate monobasic, monohydrate; sodium phosphate dibasic, anhydrous; methylcellulose; and sodium hydroxide or hydrochloric acid in 2.5, 5, and 10 ml containers.

METHYLPREDNISOLONE ACETATE

[Depo-Medrol]

Methylprednisolone is given by the subconjunctival route to treat nonpyogenic inflammations of the lids, conjunctiva, and anterior segment of the globe that do not respond to topical corticosteroid therapy. When administered by subconjunctival injection, the effect lasts two to four weeks. The drug also may be given systemically to treat intraocular inflammations.

For specific uses, adverse reactions, and precautions, see the Introductory Statement to this section.

USUAL DOSAGE.—

Subconjunctival (injected beneath Tenon's capsule): 0.5 ml of a suspension containing 40 mg/ml is administered every four weeks.

Intramuscular: See Chapter 35, Adrenal Corticosteroids.

PREPARATIONS.—Depo-Medrol (Upjohn). No ophthalmic preparation is available. The aqueous suspension for injection containing 40 mg/ml may be used for subconjunctival injection.

PREDNISOLONE ACETATE [Sterofrin]
PREDNISOLONE SODIUM PHOSPHATE

[Hydeltrasol, Inflamase]

Prednisolone is applied topically to treat nonpyogenic inflammations of the lids, conjunctiva, and anterior segment of the globe. It may also be given by subconjunctival injection if topical therapy is ineffective. Systemic therapy generally is required for inflammations of the posterior segment of the globe and in severe anterior segment disorders.

For specific uses, adverse reactions, and precautions, see the Introductory Statement to this section.

USUAL DOSAGE.—

Prednisolone Acetate:

Topical (local instillation into conjunctival sac): One or two drops of a 0.12% to 1% solution every one or two hours until a response is obtained; the frequency then is reduced.

Prednisolone Sodium Phosphate:

Topical (local instillation into conjunctival sac): One or two drops of a 0.125% to 1% solution every one to two hours until a response is obtained; the frequency then is reduced. The ointment preparation is applied three or four times daily or as nighttime medication when the solution is used during the day.

Subconjunctival (injected beneath Tenon's capsule): 0.5 ml of a 0.5% solution every 7 to 14 days.

Systemic (intramuscular, intravenous): See Chapter 35, Adrenal Corticosteroids.

PREPARATIONS.—

Prednisolone Acetate:

Sterofrin (Alcon). *Topical:* Suspension (ophthalmic) 0.12%, 0.25%, and 1% with hydroxypropyl methylcellulose, benzalkonium chloride, dried sodium phosphate, polysorbate 80, disodium edetate, glycerin, and citric acid in 5 ml containers.

Prednisolone Sodium Phosphate:

Hydeltrasol (Merck Sharp & Dohme).

Topical: Ointment (ophthalmic) 0.25% with white petrolatum and mineral oil in 3.5 g containers.

Injection (subconjunctival), Topical: Solution (sterile ophthalmic) 0.5% with creatinine, sodium citrate, polysorbate 80, disodium edetate, potassium phosphate, hydrochloric acid, phenylethanol, and benzalkonium chloride in 5 ml containers.

Intramuscular: See Chapter 35, Adrenal Corticosteroids.

Inflamase (Smith, Miller & Patch). *Topical:* Solution (ophthalmic) 0.125% and 1% (Inflamase Forte) with benzalkonium chloride, disodium edetate, monobasic and dibasic sodium phosphate, and sodium chloride in 1 and 5 ml containers.

TRIAMCINOLONE ACETONIDE [Kenalog]

Triamcinolone is given by the subconjunctival route to treat nonpyogenic inflammations of the lids, conjunctiva, and anterior segment of the globe that do not respond to topical corticosteroid therapy. The drug also may be given intramuscularly to treat intraocular inflammations.

For specific uses, adverse reactions, and precautions, see the Introductory Statement to this section.

USUAL DOSAGE.—

Subconjunctival (injected beneath Tenon's capsule): 0.5 ml of an aqueous suspension containing 10 mg/ml.

Intramuscular: See Chapter 35, Adrenal Corticosteroids.

PREPARATIONS.—Kenalog-10 (Squibb). *Injection:* Suspension (aqueous) 10 mg/ml in 5 ml containers.

MIXTURES

TOPICAL CORTICOSTEROIDS WITH DECONGESTANTS

Topical corticosteroids also are available in combination products containing the decongestant, phenylephrine. These mixtures have no proved advantage over single-entity corticosteroids.

PREPARATIONS.—

Prednefrin (Allergan): Suspension (ophthalmic) containing prednisolone acetate 0.12% or 2% and phenylephrine hydrochloride 0.12% with methylcellulose, benzalkonium chloride, and antipyrine in 5 and 10 ml containers.

Prednefrin-S (Allergan): Solution (ophthalmic) containing prednisolone 0.2% and phenylephrine hydrochloride 0.12%, with chlorobutanol, antipyrine, and buffers in 5 ml containers.

Predulose (Professional): Suspension (ophthalmic) containing prednisolone acetate 0.25% and phenylephrine hydrochloride 0.125% with propylene glycol, monobasic and dibasic sodium phosphate, sodium thiosulfate, polysorbate 80, and methylcellulose.

Vasopred (Smith, Miller & Patch): Suspension (ophthalmic) containing prednisolone acetate 0.25% and phenylephrine hydrochloride 0.125% with benzalkonium chloride, methylcellulose, and sodium bisulfite in 5 ml containers.

TOPICAL CORTICOSTEROIDS WITH ANTIBACTERIAL AGENTS

Other mixtures contain a corticosteroid in fixed dose combination with an antibacterial agent. These mixtures should not be used for the routine topical treatment of ocular infections. Corticosteroids reduce resistance to infection, and combined therapy may have an adverse effect on the course of the ocular disease if the antibacterial agent is not effective against the invading organism, if it is not present in sufficient concentration, or if nonsusceptible organisms are present. These combination products also have been used to prevent the development of bacterial infections during corticosteroid therapy. This use is not advisable because combined therapy may lead to the development of superinfection by organisms (particularly fungi) that are not susceptible to the antibiotic. In addition, hypersensitivity may develop to the anti-infective agent, and the corticosteroid may mask the allergic response.

There are certain conditions in which both corticosteroids and anti-infective drugs are required (eg, severe corneal burns; ocular infections in which vision is threatened by an acute, severe uveitis or stromal edema; postoperatively in selected patients). In such instances, although a fixed-dose combination offers convenience to the patient, it may not provide the proper dosage schedule. Also, once the inflammation is under control, combined therapy is no longer required and steroid dosage should be reduced gradually and then terminated.

PREPARATIONS.—

Blephamide Liquifilm (Allergan): Ophthalmic suspension containing prednisolone acetate 0.2% and sulfacetamide sodium 10% with phenylephrine hydrochloride and polyvinyl alcohol in 5 and 10 ml containers.

BufOpto Sulfapred (Professional): Ophthalmic suspension containing prednisolone acetate 0.25%, sulfacetamide sodium 10%, and phenylephrine hydrochloride 0.125% with propylene glycol, monobasic and dibasic sodium phosphate, sodium thiosulfate, polysorbate 80, methylcellulose, and methyl- and propylparaben in 5 and 15 ml containers.

Cetapred (Alcon): Each gram of ophthalmic ointment contains sulfacetamide sodium 10% and prednisolone acetate 0.25% with white petrolatum, anhydrous liquid lanolin, mineral oil, and methyl- and propylparaben in 3.5 g containers.

Chloromycetin-Hydrocortisone Ophthalmic Liquid (Parke, Davis): Each 5 ml contains chloramphenicol 12.5 mg and hydrocortisone acetate 25 mg in 5 ml containers.

Chloroptic-P (Allergan): Sterile ophthalmic ointment containing chloramphenicol 1% and prednisolone alcohol 0.5% with chlorobutanol, white petrolatum, mineral oil, polyoxyl 40 stearate, polyethylene glycol 300, and nonionic lanolin derivatives in 3.5 g containers.

Cortisporin Ointment (Burroughs Wellcome): Each gram contains hydrocortisone 10 mg, polymyxin B sulfate 5,000 units, bacitracin zinc 400 units, and neomycin sulfate equivalent to neomycin 3.5 mg with white petrolatum in 1/8 oz containers.

Cortisporin Ophthalmic Suspension (Burroughs Wellcome): Each milliliter contains hydrocortisone 10 mg, polymyxin B sulfate 10,000 units, neomycin sulfate equivalent to neomycin 3.5 mg with thimerosal, cetyl alcohol, glyceryl monostearate, liquid petrolatum, polyoxyl 40 stearate, and propylene glycol in 5 ml containers.

Isopto Cetapred (Alcon): Ophthalmic suspension containing prednisolone acetate 0.25% and sulfacetamide sodium 10% with hydroxymethylcellulose, methyl- and propylparaben, sodium thiosulfate, and sodium biphosphate in 5 and 15 ml containers.

Maxitrol (Alcon): Each gram of ointment contains dexamethasone 0.1%, neomycin sulfate 3.5 mg, and polymyxin B sulfate 6,000 units with white petrolatum, anhydrous liquid lanolin, and methyl- and propylparaben in 3.5 g containers; each milliliter of suspension contains dexamethasone 0.1%, neomycin sulfate 3.5 mg, and polymyxin B sulfate 6,000 units with hydroxypropyl methylcellulose, sodium chloride, polysorbate 80, hydrochloric acid and/or sodium hydroxide and benzalkonium chloride in 5 ml containers.

Metimyd (Schering): Each milliliter of suspension contains prednisolone acetate 5 mg and sulfacetamide sodium 100 mg in 5 ml containers; each gram of ointment contains prednisolone acetate 5 mg and sulfacetamide sodium 100 mg in 1/8 oz containers.

Neo-Cortef Eye-Ear Drops and Ointment (Upjohn): Each milliliter of 0.5% solution contains hydrocortisone acetate 5 mg and neomycin sulfate 5 mg in 5 ml containers; each milliliter of 1.5% solution contains hydrocortisone acetate 15 mg and neomycin sulfate 5 mg in 2.5 and 5 ml containers; each gram of ointment contains hydrocortisone acetate 5 or 15 mg and neomycin sulfate 5 mg in 1/8 oz containers.

Neo-Decadron Ophthalmic (Merck Sharp & Dohme): Each gram of ointment contains dexamethasone sodium phosphate equivalent to dexamethasone phosphate 0.5 mg and neomycin sulfate equivalent to neomycin 3.5 mg in 3.5 g containers; each milliliter of solution contains dexamethasone sodium phosphate equivalent to dexamethasone phosphate 1 mg and neomycin sulfate equivalent to neomycin 3.5 mg in 2.5 and 5 ml containers.

Neo-Delta-Cortef Eye-Ear Ointment and Drops (Upjohn): Each gram of ointment contains neomycin sulfate 5 mg and prednisolone acetate 2.5 or 5 mg in 1/8 oz containers; each milliliter of solution contains neomycin sulfate 5 mg and prednisolone acetate 2.5 mg in 5 ml containers.

Neo-Deltef Eye Drops (Upjohn): Each milliliter contains prednisolone (as free alcohol) 2 mg and neomycin sulfate 5 mg in 2.5 ml containers.

Neo-Hydeltrasol (Merck Sharp & Dohme): Each gram of ointment contains prednisolone sodium phosphate equivalent to prednisolone phosphate 2.5 mg and neomycin sulfate equivalent to neomycin 3.5 mg in 3.5 g containers; each milliliter of solution contains prednisolone sodium phosphate equivalent to prednisolone phosphate 5 mg and neomycin sulfate equivalent to neomycin 3.5 mg in 2.5 and 5 ml containers.

Neo-Medrol Eye-Ear Ointment (Upjohn): Each gram contains methylprednisolone 1 mg and neomycin sulfate 5 mg in 1/8 oz containers.

Neosone Ophthalmic Ointment (Upjohn): Each gram contains cortisone acetate 15 mg and neomycin sulfate 5 mg in 1/8 oz containers.

Neo-Polycin HC Ophthalmic Ointment (Dow): Each gram contains neomycin sulfate 4.29 mg, bacitracin 500 units, polymyxin B sulfate 10,000 units, and hydrocortisone acetate 10 mg in 1/8 oz containers.

Ophthocort (Parke, Davis): Each gram of ointment contains chloramphenicol 1%, hydrocortisone acetate 0.5%, and polymyxin B sulfate 5,000 units in 1/8 oz containers.

Optimyd (Schering): Ophthalmic solution containing prednisolone sodium phosphate 0.5% and sulfacetamide sodium 10% with sodium thiosulfate, disodium edetate, monobasic and dibasic sodium phosphate, sodium hydroxide, benzalkonium chloride, phenylethyl alcohol, and tyloxapol in 5 ml containers.

Terra-Cortril Eye-Ear Suspension (Pfizer): Each milliliter contains hydrocortisone acetate 15 mg and oxytetracycline hydrochloride equivalent to oxytetracycline 5 mg in 5 ml containers.

Tri-Ophtho Ophthalmic Suspension (Maurry): Each milliliter contains sodium sulfacetamide 100 mg and prednisolone acetate 5 mg with phenylephrine hydrochloride, sodium borate, boric acid, carboxymethylcellulose, polysorbate 80, sodium thiosulfate, chlorobutanol, and methyl- and propylparaben.

Vasocidin (Smith, Miller & Patch): Ophthalmic solution containing prednisolone sodium phosphate 0.25%, sulfacetamide sodium 10%, and phenylephrine hydrochloride 0.125% with methyl- and propylparaben, sodium thiosulfate, polysorbate 80, and polyoxyethylene polyoxypropylene compound in 5 ml containers.

Chapter 72

MISCELLANEOUS OPHTHALMIC PREPARATIONS

DIAGNOSTIC AND SURGICAL AIDS

FLUORESCEIN SODIUM

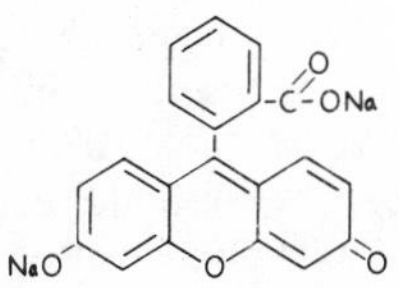

Fluorescein is a water-soluble, nontoxic indicator dye which appears yellow-green in normal tear film and an intense fluorescent green in a more alkaline medium such as the aqueous humor. Fluorescence is activated by ultraviolet light. Because it makes the tear fluid visible, fluorescein is applied topically in the fitting of contact lenses to reveal defects of the corneal epithelium and as an aid in applanation tonometry to delineate the margin of the applanated area. It may also be instilled in the eye to test lacrimal patency; if drainage is normal, the dye will appear in the nasal secretions.

Since the intensity of green fluorescence increases when fluorescein is in contact with the aqueous humor, this dye is useful as an aid in intraocular surgery to indicate when the trephine enters the anterior chamber. In cases of persistent flat anterior chamber after cataract surgery, fluorescein may be used to locate the site of a wound leak. It also is used to detect corneal epithelial defects caused by injury or infection and to locate foreign bodies imbedded in the eye.

In addition to these topical diagnostic uses, fluorescein is given intravenously as an aid in retinal photography. It is useful for detecting occlusion or obliteration of retinal vessels, neovascularization, changes in vascular permeability, and defects in the retinal pigment epithelium. Measurement of the arm-to-retina circulation time is employed for diagnosis of carotid artery occlusion.

A nondiagnostic use of fluorescein is for irrigation of the eye after injury by an indelible pencil. The aniline dye in these pencils causes edema and necrosis of ocular tissue which may result in loss of vision. The dye can be detoxified by irrigation with fluorescein.

Adverse Reactions and Precautions.—The usual preservatives used in ophthalmic preparations are inactivated by fluorescein, and contaminated fluorescein solutions have been a common source of ocular infections, particularly those caused by *Pseudomonas* organisms. These solutions can be sterilized by autoclaving, but are easily contaminated by subsequent use. Sterile, single-dose containers and individually packaged filter-paper strips impregnated with fluorescein are safer than multiple-dose containers.

Nausea and vomiting may occur when fluorescein is given intravenously. Following systemic absorption, this dye causes transient fluorescence of the skin and also appears in the urine. Hypersensitivity reactions have occurred occasionally.

For other uses and adverse reactions, see Chapter 77, Miscellaneous Diagnostic Aids.

USUAL DOSAGE.—

Topical (local instillation into conjunctival sac): For fitting of contact lenses, with the contact lens in place, a fluorescein strip moistened with ophthalmic irrigating solution is lightly touched to the superior sclera. (One drop of a 2% solution may be applied instead.) The patient should be instructed to blink several times to circulate the dye. Under ultraviolet light, areas which lack fluorescein-stained tears appear black, indicating that the contact lens is touching the cornea at those points.

In applanation tonometry, one drop of a 0.25% solution or a fluorescein strip moistened with ophthalmic irrigating solution is applied to the eye immediately before tonometry. A local anesthetic should be instilled prior to application of fluorescein or a combination product containing a local anesthetic and fluorescein may be used. Benoxinate is often preferred for local anesthesia, because it does not reduce fluorescence greatly.

For detection of epithelial defects, a fluorescein strip moistened with ophthalmic irrigating solution or one drop of a 0.5% to 2% solution is placed in the conjunctival sac. To provide contrast between the lesion and surrounding areas, excess dye should be removed by use of an irrigating solution.

To test lacrimal patency, several drops of a 2% solution are instilled in one eye. The patient should be instructed to blink at least four times after the dye is instilled. After six minutes, the patient should blow his nose and clear his throat into paper tissues which are then examined under ultraviolet illumination. If traces of the dye are present in the secretions, the nasolacrimal drainage system is open.

As an aid in ocular surgery, one drop of a 0.5% to 2% solution is instilled in the eye, and a color change indicates when the trephine enters the anterior chamber.

To test for aqueous leak following ocular surgery, several drops of a 2% solution are instilled in the affected eye. Gentle pressure on the globe may be necessary to demonstrate aqueous outflow.

As an antidote to poisoning by aniline dyes, following removal of the pencil point (if still imbedded in the eye) the eye is irrigated with a 2% solution every 10 minutes until a visible precipitate no longer forms. Irrigation is then repeated every 30 minutes for 12 to 24 hours.

Intravenous: Adults, 500 mg (10 ml of a 5% solution or 5 ml of a 10% solution) is injected rapidly into an arm vein. The dye should appear in the central retinal artery in 11 to 13 seconds.

PREPARATIONS.—

Fluor-I-Strip-A.T. (Ayerst). *Topical:* Sterile ophthalmic applicators impregnated with fluorescein in boxes containing 200 individual strips.

Ful-Glo (Barnes-Hind). *Topical:* Sterile ophthalmic applicators impregnated with fluorescein in boxes containing 100 individual strips.

Fluoreseptic (Professional). *Topical:* Solution (ophthalmic) 2% with sodium bicarbonate and phenylmercuric borate in 7.5 and 15 ml containers.

Fluorescein Sodium (Alcon). *Topical:* Solution (ophthalmic) 2% with phenylmercuric nitrate in 15 ml containers.

Fluorescein Sodium (Smith, Miller & Patch). *Topical:* Solution (ophthalmic) 2% in 1 ml container.

Injection: Solution (ophthalmic) 10% in 5 ml containers.

Fluorescite (Alcon). *Injection:* Solution 5% in 10 ml containers and 10% in 5 ml containers.

Drug also marketed by other manufacturers under generic name as powder and 10% solution.

FLURESS

This combination product containing fluorescein and the local anesthetic, benoxinate, is useful for procedures in which simultaneous staining and local anesthesia are required (eg, tonometry, removal of foreign bodies). Fluress is particularly useful as an aid in applanation tonometry because benoxinate causes minimal ocular irritation and does not greatly impair fluorescence. This local anesthetic also may cause less punctate epithelial damage than tetracaine.

For adverse reactions and precautions, see the evaluation on Fluorescein and Chapter 18, Local Anesthetics.

USUAL DOSAGE.—*Topical* (local instillation into conjunctival sac): One drop is instilled before the procedure.

PREPARATIONS.—Fluress (Barnes-Hind). *Topical:* Solution (ophthalmic) containing fluorescein sodium 0.25% and benoxinate hydrochloride 0.4% with boric acid, polyvinylpyrrolidone, and chlorobutanol in 5 ml containers.

ROSE BENGAL

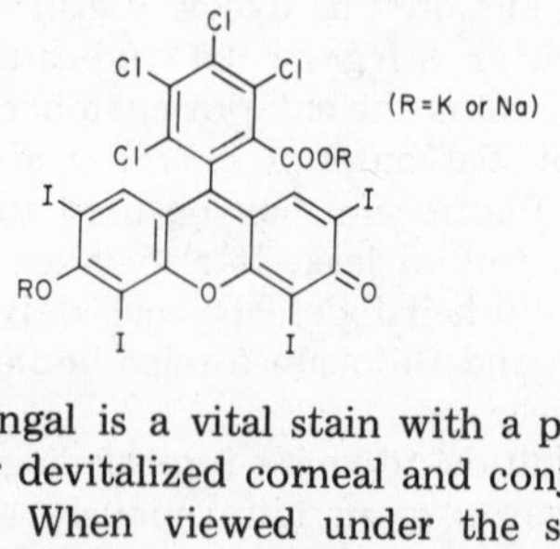

(R=K or Na)

Rose bengal is a vital stain with a particular affinity for devitalized corneal and conjunctival epithelium. When viewed under the slit-lamp, the stain consists of rose-colored dots; if inflammation or hemorrhage interferes with visibility, a green filter will give the stain a purplish-blue cast. Rose bengal is used to determine the extent of epithelial damage in various conjunctival or corneal disorders. It is particularly useful for diagnosis of keratoconjunctivitis sicca and for the fine differentiation of the margin of corneal ulcers.

Rose bengal is more irritating to the eye than fluorescein; however, use of a local anesthetic is generally not necessary.

USUAL DOSAGE.—*Topical* (local instillation into conjunctival sac): One drop of a 1% solution.

PREPARATIONS.—*Topical:* Solution (ophthalmic) 1% in 5 ml containers. Drug marketed under generic name.

ALPHA CHYMOTRYPSIN [Alpha Chymar, Catarase, Quimotrase, Zolyse]

Alpha chymotrypsin is a proteolytic enzyme used for zonulolysis in intracapsular cataract extraction. It is injected behind the iris into the posterior chamber where it dissolves the zonules within one to two minutes, thereby facilitating delivery of the lens. When zonulolysis is complete, the lens may be observed to move forward or to assume a more rounded contour.

Alpha chymotrypsin is used routinely by many surgeons whenever a difficult intracapsular extraction is anticipated. Enzymatic zonulolysis is particularly indicated in young adults, in high myopes, in patients with traumatic cataracts, and after retinal detachment. The zonules of elderly patients are fragile, and alpha chymotrypsin may not be required to facilitate lens extraction. In patients under the age of 20, the lens is firmly attached to the face of the vitreous, and intracapsular extraction can lead to vitreous loss and subsequent retinal detachment. Therefore, zonulolysis is not advisable, and extracapsular extraction is the method of choice in these patients.

Transient glaucoma, usually lasting about one week, is the most common untoward effect of alpha chymotrypsin. The mechanism of this enzyme-induced glaucoma is unclear but may involve accumulation of tissue debris in the trabecular meshwork. Pilocarpine may be effective in reducing the intraocular pressure; corticosteroid therapy is of no value because the glaucoma is not related to an inflammatory process. The use of alpha chymotrypsin has been associated with wound disruption and loss of the anterior chamber. This complication apparently results from the enzyme-induced glaucoma and can be avoided by use of multiple corneoscleral sutures.

The cornea, lens capsule, ciliary body, vitreous face, and lens-vitreous attachments are resistant to the effect of alpha chymotrypsin. However, this enzyme is extremely toxic to the retina and should not be allowed to penetrate into the vitreous, as posterior diffusion could occur.

In patients with fluid vitreous, enzymatic zonulolysis can result in loss of the lens posteriorly and, possibly, to entry of alpha chymotrypsin into the vitreous body.

USUAL DOSAGE.—*Injection:* 0.2 to 0.5 ml of a freshly prepared 1:5,000 solution is slowly injected behind the iris into the posterior chamber. For uniform zonulolysis, the irrigating tip should be manipulated so that the solution is distributed around the anterior lens equator. One to two minutes after injection of the enzyme, the anterior chamber should be irrigated with 2 ml of the diluent, sodium chloride injection, or a balanced salt solution. A second application of the enzyme may be required if the zonules are resistant.

PREPARATIONS.—

Alpha Chymar (Armour), Quimotrase (Smith, Miller & Patch), Zolyse (Alcon). *Injection:* Powder (for solution) 750 units with 10 ml of diluent.

Catarase (Smith, Miller & Patch). *Injection:* Two-compartment vial contains alpha chymotrypsin 300 units in the lower compartment and sodium chloride diluent 2 ml in the upper compartment.

ACETYLCHOLINE CHLORIDE [Miochol]

$$CH_3\overset{O}{\overset{\|}{C}}OCH_2CH_2\overset{+}{N}(CH_3)_3 \cdot Cl^-$$

Acetylcholine is the neurohumoral transmitter at numerous sites in the nervous system, including the neuroeffector junction of the sphincter muscle of the iris. When applied topically to the eye, acetylcholine is of no therapeutic value because of its rapid hydrolysis by acetylcholinesterase and poor corneal penetration. However, it produces prompt, pronounced miosis when introduced into the anterior chamber and is useful during certain surgical procedures on the anterior segment of the eye. Acetylcholine has a shorter duration of action than other miotics; this is an advantage during ocular surgery, because prolonged miosis can cause severe postoperative pain. If miosis is desired during the postoperative period, a longer-acting miotic (ie, carbachol, pilocarpine) must be instilled.

Acetylcholine is commonly used to produce miosis after cataract surgery. By increasing the iris surface, it helps protect the vitreous face and facilitates placement of sutures. It also may prevent formation of peripheral anterior synechiae. During peripheral iridectomy, acetylcholine may be introduced into the anterior chamber to permit excision of only peripheral iris tissue and to aid in repositing of the iris. It is also used during penetrating keratoplasty to facilitate suturing of the graft, to protect the lens, and to prevent incarceration of the iris.

Because of its rapid inactivation, acetylcholine has no adverse local or systemic effects.

USUAL DOSAGE.—*Intracameral:* 0.5 to 2 ml of a freshly prepared 1:100 solution is instilled into the anterior chamber.

PREPARATIONS.—Miochol (Smith, Miller & Patch). *Injection:* Two-compartment vial contains acetylcholine chloride 20 mg and mannitol 100 mg in the lower compartment and sterile water 2 ml in the upper compartment.

CARBACHOL [Intraocular Carbachol]

The parasympathomimetic agent, carbachol, may be preferred to acetylcholine for use during ocular surgery if more prolonged miosis is desired. Carbachol has not been used as extensively as acetylcholine, but the two drugs have been found equally effective in producing prompt, complete miosis after cataract extraction. In contrast to the transient effect of acetylcholine, the miosis induced by carbachol is still evident 15 hours after intracameral injection. An advantage of carbachol is its stability in solution; unlike acetylcholine, it does not have to be freshly prepared prior to instillation.

No toxic effects have been reported from intraocular use of carbachol.

For other uses, see Chapter 69, Agents Used to Treat Glaucoma.

USUAL DOSAGE.—*Intracameral:* 0.4 to 0.5 ml of a 0.01% solution is instilled into the anterior chamber.

PREPARATIONS.—Intraocular Carbachol (Alcon). *Injection:* Sterile solution (ophthalmic, for intraocular use) containing carbachol 0.01% with citric acid, sodium chloride, and dried sodium phosphate in 1.5 ml containers.

OSMOTIC AGENTS

Osmotic agents, such as anhydrous glycerin and hypertonic sodium chloride, are applied topically to reduce corneal edema. By removing fluid, these agents produce a transient clearing of the cornea in the early stages of epithelial edema but are not useful if scarring of the epithelium or stroma has occurred. Glycerin is commonly used prior to ophthalmoscopic and gonioscopic examination when the cornea is too edematous to permit accurate diagnosis. Osmotic agents are also used in the long-term treatment of corneal edema resulting from various ocular diseases (eg, Fuchs' endothelial-epithelial dystrophy). However, they are only of limited therapeutic value because their effects are transient, instillation is painful, and, with progression of the disease, scarring occurs and the osmotic agent no longer will improve visual acuity.

USUAL DOSAGE.—

Anhydrous Glycerin:

Topical (local instillation into conjunctival sac): To facilitate diagnosis, one to three drops are instilled prior to the examination. A local anesthetic should be instilled before the glycerin. For treatment of corneal edema, one or two drops are instilled every three to four hours.

Hypertonic Sodium Chloride:

Topical (local instillation into conjunctival sac): For treatment of corneal edema, one or two drops of solution are instilled three times daily. The ointment may be applied at bedtime.

PREPARATIONS.—

Anhydrous Glycerin:

Ophthalgan (Ayerst). *Topical:* Solution (ophthalmic) with chlorobutanol in 7.5 ml containers.

Hypertonic Sodium Chloride:

Murocoll No. 4 (Muro). *Topical:* Solution (ophthalmic) containing methylcellulose 4,000 cps 0.9% and sodium chloride 5% in 15 and 30 ml containers.

Sodium Chloride Ointment (Muro). *Topical:* Ointment (ophthalmic) 5% in 1/8 oz containers.

IRRIGATING SOLUTIONS

Ophthalmic external irrigating solutions may be used to irrigate the eye following foreign body removal, tonometry, gonioscopy, and use of fluorescein and other dyes. Internal irrigating solutions are balanced salt solutions used during ocular surgery to irrigate the anterior chamber, the extraocular muscles, and the lacrimal system, and to moisten the cornea. The advantage of these irrigating solutions over the use of sterile isotonic sodium chloride solution has not been clearly established.

The boric acid found in most external irrigating solutions may form an insoluble complex with polyvinyl alcohol contained in some contact lens wetting solutions.

PREPARATIONS.—

External Irrigating Solutions:

Blinx (Barnes-Hind). *Topical:* Solution (ophthalmic) containing boric acid, sodium borate, and phenylmercuric acetate in 1 and 4 oz containers.

BufOpto Neo-Flo (Professional). *Topical:* Solution (ophthalmic) containing boric acid, sodium chloride, potassium chloride, sodium carbonate, and benzalkonium chloride in 30 and 110 ml containers.

Collyrium (Wyeth). *Topical:* Solution (ophthalmic) containing boric acid, sodium borate, thimerosal, antipyrine, and sodium salicylate in 6 oz containers.

Eye Stream (Alcon). *Topical:* Solution (ophthalmic) containing sodium chloride, potassium chloride, calcium chloride, magnesium chloride, sodium citrate, and sodium acetate in 1 and 4 oz containers.

Internal Irrigating Solutions:

BSS (Alcon). *Intraocular:* Solution (ophthalmic) containing sodium chloride, potassium chloride, calcium chloride, magnesium chloride hexahydrate, sodium acetate, and sodium citrate dihydrate in 15 ml containers.

Oris (Smith, Miller & Patch). *Intraocular:* Solution (ophthalmic) containing sodium chloride, potassium chloride, calcium chloride dihydrate, magnesium chloride hexahydrate, sodium acetate trihydrate, and sodium citrate dihydrate in 15 ml containers.

LUBRICANTS

Viscous agents are used to replace tears and prevent damage to the cornea in patients with keratoconjunctivitis sicca, exposure keratitis, and neuroparalytic keratitis. They are also used to moisten contact lenses, to lubricate artificial eyes, and to protect the cornea during gonioscopy and other ophthalmic procedures. In addition, these agents are incorporated in many ophthalmic preparations to prolong the contact time of topically applied drugs.

METHYLCELLULOSE
HYDROXYPROPYL METHYLCELLULOSE

Methylcellulose is widely used in ophthalmology to replace tears, to moisten contact lenses, to lubricate artificial eyes, and to protect the cornea during gonioscopy and other procedures. It is also used in ophthalmic preparations to prolong the contact time of drugs.

Methylcellulose is nonirritating to ocular tissue and can be used for prolonged periods without causing damage to the eye. It may cause discomfort if excess solution is allowed to dry on the upper lid.

USUAL DOSAGE.—*Topical:* As artificial tears, one or two drops of a 0.5% solution is applied to the eye as needed. In patients with keratoconjunctivitis sicca, application every 15 minutes may be necessary during warm, dry weather.

To protect the cornea during gonioscopy, one drop of a 1% solution is applied immediately prior to the procedure.

To moisten contact lenses and to lubricate artificial eyes, solution is applied to the contact lens or artificial eye.

PREPARATIONS.—

Methylcellulose:

BufOpto Methulose (Professional). *Topical:* Methylcellulose and benzalkonium in 15 and 30 ml containers.

BufOpto Visculose (Professional). *Topical:* Methylcellulose 0.5% or 1% with benzalkonium chloride in 15 ml containers.

Lacril (Allergan). *Topical:* Methylcellulose 0.5%, polysorbate 80, gelatin, boric acid, and chlorobutanol in ½ oz containers.

Hydroxypropyl Methylcellulose:

Goniosol (Smith, Miller & Patch): *Topical:* Hydroxypropyl methylcellulose 2.5% and benzalkonium in 15 ml containers.

Isopto-Alkaline (Alcon). *Topical:* Hydroxypropyl methylcellulose 1% and benzalkonium in 15 ml containers.

Isopto Plain Ophthalmic Solution (Alcon). *Topical:* Hydroxypropyl methylcellulose 0.5% and alkaline isotonic menstruum with benzalkonium in 15 ml containers.

Isopto Tears (Alcon). *Topical:* Hydroxypropyl methylcellulose 0.5% with benzalkonium chloride in 15 and 30 ml containers.

Lyteers (Barnes-Hind). *Topical:* Hydroxypropyl methylcellulose with benzalkonium chloride and disodium edetate in 15 ml containers.

Tearisol (Smith, Miller & Patch). *Topical:* Hydroxypropyl methylcellulose 0.5% in 15 ml containers.

Ultra Tears (Alcon). *Topical:* Hydroxypropyl methylcellulose 1% with benzalkonium chloride in 15 ml containers.

Wetting Solution (Alcon). *Topical:* Hydroxypropyl methylcellulose, benzalkonium, and phenylmercuric nitrate in 60 ml containers.

POLYVINYL ALCOHOL

Polyvinyl alcohol is a nontoxic viscous compound used as artificial tears and as a contact lens wetting agent. It is useful in prolonging contact time of ophthalmic medications. Polyvinyl alcohol is less viscous than methylcellulose and must be applied more frequently when used as a substitute for tears.

USUAL DOSAGE.—*Topical:* As artificial tears, one or two drops applied to eyes as needed. To moisten contact lenses, solution is applied to lens before insertion.

PREPARATIONS.—

Contique Wetting Solution (Alcon). *Topical:* Polyvinyl alcohol with hydroxypropyl methylcellulose, benzalkonium chloride, and disodium edetate in 1/3, 1, and 2 oz containers.

Lens-Mate (Alcon). *Topical:* Polyvinyl alcohol with hydroxypropyl methylcellulose, benzalkonium chloride, and disodium edetate in 2 oz containers.

Liquifilm Tears (Allergan). *Topical:* Polyvinyl alcohol 1.4% and chlorobutanol in 15 ml containers.

Liquifilm Wetting Solution (Allergan). *Topical:* Polyvinyl alcohol 1.4%, methylcellulose, benzalkonium, and edetic acid in 60 ml containers.

Wetting Solution (Barnes-Hind). *Topical:* Polyvinyl alcohol with disodium edetate and benzalkonium chloride in 35 and 60 ml containers.

Other Available Lubricants

Enuclene (Alcon). *Topical:* Solution containing tyloxapol 0.25% and benzalkonium chloride in 15 ml containers. (Used only for lubrication of artificial eyes.)

DECONGESTANTS

EPHEDRINE
NAPHAZOLINE HYDROCHLORIDE
PHENYLEPHRINE HYDROCHLORIDE
TETRAHYDROZOLINE HYDROCHLORIDE

When applied topically to the eye, adrenergic drugs cause vasoconstriction, mydriasis, and a fall in intraocular pressure. They are useful to control bleeding during ocular surgery, as an aid in ophthalmoscopy and retinal photography, for pre- and postoperative mydriasis, as an adjunct in the treatment of anterior uveitis and some secondary glaucomas, to treat primary open-angle glaucoma, and to prevent formation of miotic iris cysts. (See Chapters 18, Local Anesthetics; 69, Agents Used to Treat Glaucoma; and 70, Mydriatics and Cycloplegics.)

Some adrenergic drugs (phenylephrine, naphazoline, tetrahydrozoline, and, occasionally, ephedrine) are also used as ocular decongestants. These agents improve appearance by whitening the eye. They may temporarily relieve itching and minor irritation caused by chemical or mechanical irritants or by immediate-type allergic reactions (eg, acute atopic conjunctivitis). Decongestants are not effective in treating delayed hypersensitivity reactions (eg, contact dermatoconjunctivitis).

In the concentrations used in decongestant products, adrenergic drugs rarely cause serious untoward effects. However, prolonged or indiscriminate use of these preparations should be avoided, as this could lead to neglect of symptoms of serious eye disease.

When applied locally to the eye, adrenergic drugs may cause browache, headache, blurred vision, irritation, lacrimation, reactive hyperemia, and allergic conjunctivitis and dermatitis. Pigment granules, presumably from the iris, may appear in the anterior chamber after drug instillation, particularly in older patients with dark irides. In patients predisposed to angle-closure glaucoma, these agents can precipitate an acute attack. (For more detailed discussion and for other local adverse effects of adrenergic drugs, see Chapter 69, Agents Used to Treat Glaucoma, and Chapter 70, Mydriatics and Cycloplegics.)

Systemic reactions to topically administered adrenergic drugs may occur, particularly if the drug is applied after the corneal epithelium is damaged or its permeability increased by tonometry or local anesthesia. Symptoms or signs include tachycardia, premature ventricular contractions, hypertension, hyperhidrosis, tremors, and blanching.

Naphazoline and tetrahydrozoline are more stable than phenylephrine. The activity of phenylephrine is greatly reduced by oxidation.

USUAL DOSAGE.—*Topical* (local instillation into conjunctival sac): One or two drops are instilled every two to three hours or as needed until symptoms subside.

PREPARATIONS.—

Phenylephrine Hydrochloride:

BufOpto Efricel (Professional). *Topical:* Solution (ophthalmic) 0.125% with benzalkonium chloride and methylcellulose in 15 ml containers.

Degest (Barnes-Hind). *Topical:* Solution (ophthalmic) 0.2% with benzalkonium chloride, disodium edetate, and sodium chloride in 15 ml containers.

Eye-Gene (Pearson). *Topical:* Solution (ophthalmic) with boric acid, sodium borate, sodium chloride, sodium bisulfite, camphor water, peppermint water, and thimerosal in 1/2 and 1 oz containers.

Isopto Frin (Alcon). *Topical:* Solution (ophthalmic) 0.12% with hydroxypropyl methylcellulose in 15 ml containers.

Prefrin Liquifilm (Allergan). *Topical:* Solution (ophthalmic) 0.12% with polyvinyl alcohol in 2/3 oz containers.

Tear-Efrin (Smith, Miller & Patch). *Topical:* Solution (ophthalmic) 0.12% with hydroxypropyl methylcellulose in 1/2 oz containers.

ADDITIONAL TRADEMARKS.– Op-isophrin (Broemmel), Soothe (Burton, Parsons). Drug also marketed under generic name.

Naphazoline Hydrochloride:

Albalon (Allergan). *Topical:* Solution (ophthalmic) 0.1% with polyvinyl alcohol, benzalkonium chloride, disodium edetate, citric acid, sodium citrate, sodium chloride, and sodium hydroxide in 15 ml containers.

Clear Eyes (Abbott). *Topical:* Solution (ophthalmic) 0.012% with boric acid, sodium borate, methylcellulose, disodium edetate, and benzalkonium chloride in 18 and 45 ml containers.

Naphcon (Alcon). *Topical:* Solution (ophthalmic) 0.012% with benzalkonium chloride in 1/2 oz containers.

Privine Hydrochloride (Ciba). *Topical:* Solution (ophthalmic) 0.1% with boric acid, sodium carbonate, camphor water, and phenylmercuric acetate in 15 ml containers.

Vasocon (Smith, Miller & Patch). *Topical:* Solution (ophthalmic) 0.1% in 15 ml containers.

Tetrahydrozoline Hydrochloride:

Visine (Leeming). *Topical:* Solution (ophthalmic) 0.05% with sodium chloride, boric acid, sodium borate, and benzalkonium chloride in 15 and 30 ml containers.

Ephedrine:

Collyrium with Ephedrine (Wyeth). *Topical:* Solution (ophthalmic) 0.1% with antipyrine, boric acid, borax, and thimerosal in 15 ml containers. Drug also marketed under generic name.

Other Agent Used for Minor Ocular Irritation and Allergy:

Estivin (Alcon). *Topical:* Solution (ophthalmic) containing aqueous infusion of rose petals with sodium ethylmercurithiosalicylate in 1/4 oz containers.

Mixtures

MIXTURES CONTAINING A DECONGESTANT AND ZINC SULFATE

These products are promoted for their decongestant, astringent, and antiseptic properties. They may provide relief of minor ocular irritation because of the action of the adrenergic drug and the mild astringent properties of zinc sulfate. However, zinc sulfate is a relatively ineffective antiseptic, and these combination products are of no established value in treating ocular infections.

PREPARATIONS.–

Allerest Eye Drops (Pharmacraft). *Topical:* Naphazoline hydrochloride 0.012%, zinc sulfate, camphor, potassium chloride, thimerosal, boric acid, and sodium carbonate in 15 ml containers.

Eye-Mo (Winthrop). *Topical:* Phenylephrine hydrochloride, zinc sulfate, berberine sulfate, benzalkonium, and boric acid in 15 ml containers.

M-Z Solution (Smith, Miller & Patch). *Topical:* Phenylephrine hydrochloride 0.12%, zinc sulfate 0.25%, and piperocaine hydrochloride 0.75% in 1/2 oz containers.

Neozin BufOpto (Professional). *Topical:* Phenylephrine hydrochloride 0.125%, zinc sulfate 0.25%, and benzalkonium in 15 ml containers.

Phenylzin (Smith, Miller & Patch). *Topical:* Phenylephrine hydrochloride 0.12%, zinc sulfate 0.25%, and hydroxypropyl methylcellulose in 1/2 oz containers.

Prefrin Z (Allergan). *Topical:* Phenylephrine hydrochloride 0.12%, zinc sulfate 0.25%, benzalkonium, and polyvinyl alcohol in 15 ml containers.

20-20 (S S S). *Topical:* Naphazoline, zinc sulfate, thimerosal, camphor, potassium chloride, and boric acid in 15 ml containers.

Zincfrin (Alcon). *Topical:* Zinc sulfate 0.25%, phenylephrine hydrochloride 0.12%, and benzalkonium in 15 ml containers.

SIMILAR MIXTURE.—Op-isophrin-Z (Broemmel). *Topical:* Phenylephrine hydrochloride, zinc sulfanilate 0.25%, and chlorobutanol in 120 ml containers; same formulation plus methylcellulose in 15 ml containers.

MIXTURES CONTAINING A DECONGESTANT AND ANTIHISTAMINE

These fixed-dose combinations containing a decongestant and an antihistamine are advocated for treatment of ocular allergy. However, topically applied antihistamines are relatively ineffective histamine antagonists and any symptomatic relief obtained from these products is probably due to the local anesthetic properties of the antihistamine and possibly to the vasoconstrictor action of the decongestant.

Antihistamines readily cause eczematous contact dermatitis following topical use. Individuals sensitized to one antihistamine may show cross sensitivity when exposed to other antihistamines or chemically related agents. In sensitized patients, the subsequent *systemic* administration of an antihistamine or chemically related drug may cause eczematous contact-type dermatitis medicamentosa.

These agents dilate the pupil and, in patients predisposed to angle-closure glaucoma, could precipitate an acute attack.

PREPARATIONS.—

BufOpto Vernacel (Professional): Phenylephrine hydrochloride 0.125%, pheniramine maleate 0.5%, methylcellulose, sodium acid phosphate monobasic, sodium phosphate dibasic, sodium chloride, and benzalkonium chloride in 15 and 30 ml containers.

Optihist (Smith, Miller & Patch): Phenylephrine hydrochloride 0.12%, chlorpheniramine maleate 0.2%, and piperocaine hydrochloride 0.75% in 15 ml containers.

Prefrin A (Allergan): Phenylephrine hydrochloride 0.12%, pyrilamine maleate 0.1%, antipyrine, and chlorobutanol in 15 ml containers.

Vasocon-A (Smith, Miller & Patch): Naphazoline hydrochloride 0.05% and antazoline phosphate 0.5% in 15 ml containers.

OTHER AGENTS

PRALIDOXIME CHLORIDE [Protopam Chloride]

The cholinesterase reactivator, pralidoxime, is given intravenously as an adjunct in the treatment of systemic poisoning caused by cholinesterase inhibitors. This oxime does not readily penetrate the blood-aqueous barrier or the cornea; therefore, intravenous or topical administration is generally ineffective in counteracting the ocular effects of anticholinesterase agents (miosis, spasm of accommodation). Pralidoxime does, however, penetrate the eye after subconjunctival injection and could be administered by this route to reverse these ocular effects (eg, if an anticholinesterase agent is accidentally instilled in the eye). Pralidoxime is not equally effective against all cholinesterase inhibitors: it is most active in counteracting the effects of phosphate esters possessing a quaternary nitrogen atom (echothiophate) and is least active against the carbamates (demecarium).

Pralidoxime may also be useful as part of a medical regimen for breaking posterior synechiae. Miotic and mydriatic drugs are sometimes instilled alternately for this purpose. After miosis has been obtained by topical administration of a cholinesterase inhibitor, subconjunctival injection of pralidoxime will counteract the effect within two hours; rapid mydriasis can then be obtained by instillation of atropine and phenylephrine. It has also been reported that wider mydriasis can be obtained with this regimen than with mydriatic drugs alone and this technique has been advocated for dilatation of resistant pupils.

For systemic uses, see Chapters 75, Agents Used in Myasthenia Gravis, and Chapter 92, Miscellaneous Drugs.

Local adverse effects reported after subconjunctival injection of pralidoxime include a burning sensation, conjunctival hyperemia, subconjunctival hemorrhage, and mild iritis. These reactions are more common with use of concentrations exceeding 5%. Allergic reactions or systemic effects have not been observed.

USUAL DOSAGE.—*Subconjunctival* (injected beneath Tenon's capsule): 0.1 to 0.2 ml of a 5% aqueous solution.

PREPARATIONS.—Protopam Chloride (Ayerst). *Injection:* Powder 1 g.

DISODIUM EDETATE [Endrate, Sodium Versenate]

This chelating agent is applied topically to remove corneal calcium deposits that impair vision or, by penetrating the epithelium, cause pain. It dissolves calcium deposits of endogenous origin (eg, band keratopathies and other calcific corneal deposits associated with chronic uveitis, advanced interstitial keratitis, hypercalcemia) and is also useful (after irrigation of the eye) for the early treatment of calcium hydroxide burns of the conjunctiva and cornea.

Disodium edetate will remove calcium from the corneal epithelium and external layers of the stroma, but is ineffective against deposits extending deeper than the level of Bowman's membrane. The removal of superficial calcium deposits should improve vision unless scarring and vascularization have occurred; however, calcium deposits of endogenous origin may recur. Disodium edetate does not penetrate the corneal epithelium. Unless the calcium deposit extends to the surface, the epithelium must be completely removed before application of this chelating agent.

Disodium edetate is well tolerated when applied topically. Transient chemosis may occur. The stronger concentration (1.85%) may cause stromal edema.

For systemic uses, see Chapter 90, Chelating Agents.

USUAL DOSAGE.—*Topical* (local instillation into conjunctival sac): A local anesthetic should be instilled before the procedure; cocaine is preferred because it facilitates epithelial curettage. The corneal epithelium is then completely removed and the denuded area is irrigated with disodium edetate for 15 to 20 minutes. For mild calcium infiltration, a 0.35% solution is employed; for dense infiltration, a 1.85% solution may be used. The solution is applied as a corneal bath or by iontophoresis. After the procedure, the eye should be irrigated with sodium chloride injection or a balanced salt solution.

PREPARATIONS.—No ophthalmic preparation is available. The intravenous solution must be diluted to the desired concentration with isotonic sodium chloride injection.

Endrate (Abbott). *Injection:* Solution 150 mg/ml in 20 ml containers.

Sodium Versenate (Riker). *Injection:* Solution 200 mg/ml in 5 ml containers.

Chapter 73

TOPICAL OTIC PREPARATIONS

The products described in this chapter are applied locally to treat and prevent diseases of the external ear canal and to treat chronic ear infections when the tympanic membrane is perforated. These preparations usually contain two or more drugs combined into a single dosage form. The drugs most commonly used include anti-infective agents, local anesthetics, hydroscopic chemicals, acidifying compounds, adrenal corticosteroids, and nonsteroidal anti-inflammatory agents. Anti-infective agents, adrenal corticosteroids, antihistamines, and analgesics also may be given systemically, when indicated, to supplement topical treatment. Usually, however, systemic therapy is necessary only when there is evidence of cellulitis involving the external meatus or auricle or when pain cannot be controlled by local cleansing, the application of heat, or the use of topical preparations. Drugs instilled into the ear usually are dissolved or suspended in a liquid vehicle, but medicated creams or ointments may be used for dry, crusted lesions. Powders also are used, frequently for their desiccant properties.

The anti-infectives used most commonly in topical otic solutions, suspensions, creams, or ointments are the polymyxins (polymyxin B, colistin) and neomycin. Others include tetracyclines (tetracycline, oxytetracycline, chlortetracycline), sulfonamides, chloramphenicol, gentamicin, nitrofurazone, and nystatin. For the antibacterial or antifungal activity of these agents, see Section IX, Antimicrobial Agents. Antibacterial powders (eg, Aerosporin, chloramphenicol, gentamicin, Furacin) also are used. Additionally, aqueous acetic acid solution 5% is effective against many pathogens (eg, *Pseudomonas*) normally associated with external ear diseases because its acidic pH will prevent growth of the organism. Acetic acid is well tolerated, nonsensitizing, and does not produce resistant organisms when administered as drops, even with routine use.

Infections of the external or middle ear usually are of mixed microbial origin and may occasionally be caused by both bacteria and fungi; only rarely are these infections produced by fungal organisms alone. Broad spectrum antibacterial therapy should be started immediately but may have to be modified following identification of the invading microorganisms. Depending upon the causative organism, there is little reason to expect some drugs to be useful; for example, the tetracyclines are not effective against most *Pseudomonas* and *Proteus*, which are among the most common pathogens found in infections of the ear. Furthermore, despite in vitro testing, some drugs may be inactive or have decreased activity in vivo (eg, the action of sulfonamides can be blocked by metabolites in pus and debris in the affected area).

Various local anesthetics are incorporated into formulations of topical otic preparations in an effort to relieve the pain that usually accompanies acute external otitis or otitis media, and which may be severe. Benzocaine is the agent most commonly used. However, when local anesthetics are applied topically in the ear canal they may cause hypersensitivity reactions and they are rarely effective. The almost complete lack of efficacy of this group of drugs when used in the ear may be due to insufficient absorption. It is often necessary, therefore, to administer systemic analgesics concomitantly to provide adequate relief of pain.

Adrenal corticosteroids relieve pruritus and reduce inflammation in chronic external otitis even when the origin of the disorder is seborrheic, psychogenic, or nonspecific. The drug most commonly included as a component of many topical otic preparations is hydrocortisone. See also Chapter 35, Adrenal Corticosteroids.

Aluminum acetate solution, U.S.P. (Burow's solution) also is used to treat external ear disease. It has anti-inflammatory, antipruritic, and astringent properties, is nonsensitizing, does not produce resistant organisms, and is well tolerated. It is useful as an irrigating solution to remove debris.

External otitis is a general term encompassing all inflammatory processes involving the skin of the external ear canal. Although many different forms of external otitis exist, they may be classified as infectious, eczematoid, or seborrheic, and, in addition, as acute, recurrent, or chronic. Since many of these lesions are not unlike those that occur on other parts of the body, they will respond to similar treatment (see Chapter 68, Dermatologic Agents). *Acute localized external otitis* usually is caused by an infected hair follicle (which may progress to a furuncle) or an infected sebaceous gland. The invading organism almost invariably is a staphylococcus. In *acute diffuse external otitis*, there is a moist, macerating surface; this condition occurs most often when water gets into the ear. *Chronic diffuse external otitis* (otomycosis) is most often observed in southern states. It is caused by a fungus (frequently *Aspergillus niger). Eczematoid external otitis* encompasses all forms of hypersensitivity reactions. *Seborrheic external otitis* is a dry or oily scaling otitis; it is generally associated with seborrheic dermatitis of the scalp and commonly has a secondary bacterial infection superimposed. The organism usually is *Staphylococcus, Pseudomonas*, or *Proteus.*

For topical therapy of the ear to be most effective, it is desirable to maintain a clean and, often, dry ear canal. Failure to do so may permit the existence of a medium conducive to disease. Thus, important principles for managing external otitis are cleansing of the external canal along with the use of a medication suitable for the type and severity of the condition being treated, control of pain (if present), and acidification of the canal to help restore normal flora. Removal of desquamated material, cerumen, purulent secretion, or residual topical preparations without traumatizing the canal is often best accomplished with irrigation followed by suction or the use of small cotton-tipped applicators. For the safety of the patient, this frequently must be done by direct visualization. Suitable irrigation solutions are dilute ethyl alcohol 10% to 20%, hypertonic sodium chloride solution 3% (diluted one to one with water), or aqueous or hydroalcoholic solutions of acetic acid 1%.

When using topical otic preparations, care must be taken to assure that the medication gets into the ear canal or middle ear space (in chronic otitis media with a perforated tympanic membrane) and stays in contact with the affected area long enough for the drug to act. Gentle pressure on the tragus after instilling the drug or use of a saturated cotton wick helps to move the preparation along the canal or into the middle ear space.

When desirable, the ear canal can be dried to prevent "swimmer's ear" and "hot weather ear," two common forms of external otitis most likely to occur in the summer time, by lowering the surface tension of the water so it will drain and evaporate. This usually can be accomplished by instilling a few drops of ethyl or isopropyl alcohol 70% to 95% into the ear. Increased antimicrobial action over that possessed by the alcoholic solution itself can be achieved by adding acetic acid 5% or by using a supersaturated alcoholic solution of boric acid. Both of these preparations help maintain the normal flora of the ear. Various powders, many of which also have antibacterial properties, may be used to dry the ear canal and combat infection (eg, gentamicin powder).

The normal physiologic mechanism for removing cerumen occasionally becomes inefficient and abnormal amounts of this waxy material may accumulate. The most frequent causes for breakdown of this mechanism are persistent use of cotton-tipped applicators by the patient, picking at the ear, lack of moisture or humidity that causes the cerumen to dry and crust, narrow tortuous ear canals, or excessive hair growth in the ear.

Cerumen is made by glands in the outer one-third of the external ear canal. It has hydroscopic and bacteriostatic properties important in keeping the canal in a healthy state. Even when large amounts of cerumen accumulate, it rarely causes enough occlusion to decrease hearing acuity substantially or promote infection. If cerumen must be removed and the tympanic membrane is known to be intact, gentle irrigation with hypertonic sodium chloride solution 3% or warm water and hydrogen peroxide 3% in a one to one ratio are effective, atraumatic procedures. If the tympanic membrane is perforated, or if it is not known whether it is intact, removal of cerumen under direct visualization with ring curettes or suction is preferable. A small Hartman forceps may be useful as well. When instruments are being used in the ear, care must be exercised not to traumatize the canal, for this portion of the ear is extremely sensitive to instrumentation. Also, small children do not tolerate the noise of suctioning well. Hydrogen peroxide 3% always can be instilled carefully into the ear canal (never forced in under pressure) to mechanically break up the cerumen and facilitate its removal.

In patients who have chronic difficulty with hard, impacted cerumen, the occasional instillation of olive oil (sweet oil), sweet almond oil, mineral oil, glycerin, or hydrogen peroxide in the ear canal can soften the cerumen and thereby promote normal removal. Irrigation of the canal with warm water, a mixture of 20% alcohol and water, or Burow's solution by the patient also can prevent the buildup of cerumen.

Products promoted for removal of cerumen (triethanolamine polypeptide oleate-condensate [Cerumenex], carbamide peroxide [Debrox]) are basically no better than the methods outlined above. In addition to being more expensive, Debrox is not significantly different in its activity from hydrogen peroxide and Cerumenex is potentially dangerous.

In the following list of available preparations, several products are described in more detail than others. This is done simply to illustrate the various types of drug combinations available or the more widespread use of a particular product rather than to imply any superiority of one preparation over another of similar formulation.

Adverse Reactions and Precautions

Preparations designed to be instilled and remain in the external ear canal should be used sparingly if other procedures will suffice, since all materials placed in the canal can add to debris already present. Ointments, creams, and powders generally should not be applied to ulcerated surfaces. In addition, they may restrict drainage; this is particularly true of any powder that might form a concretion.

Local adverse reactions have been reported in patients treated with cerumenolytic drugs or agents used to soften cerumen. These effects range from a mild erythema and pruritus of the external canal to a severe eczematoid reaction involving the external ear and periauricular tissue. Reactions generally disappear in two to ten days, but they may last longer and be extremely difficult to cure.

When used topically in the ear, antibacterial agents, particularly neomycin, nitrofurazone, and most sulfonamides, may produce cutaneous sensitivity reactions. The physician must always be alert for this type of reaction since it frequently mimics the disease being treated. Cross sensitization can occur between neomycin and kanamycin, paromomycin, streptomycin, and possibly gentamicin. Such cross sensitization can prevent the use of any or all of these antibacterial agents for the treatment of future infections.

All topical otic preparations containing adrenal corticosteroids should be used with caution and may actually be contraindicated in patients with herpes simplex, vaccinia, or chickenpox, or with tuberculous, fungal, or certain acute purulent infections (eg, furunculosis).

The use of antibacterial preparations for treating eczematoid external otitis is usually contraindicated because these preparations frequently irritate the lesion and may aggravate the allergic response already present.

INDIVIDUAL EVALUATIONS

ALUMINUM ACETATE SOLUTION (Burow's Solution)

This aqueous solution contains approximately 5% aluminum acetate. It has anti-inflammatory, antipruritic, and astringent properties and is indicated primarily for treating external otitis of allergic origin. Aluminum acetate solution is well tolerated, nonsensitizing, and does not produce resistant organisms.

USUAL DOSAGE.—*Topical: Adults and children*, a saturated wick is placed in the ear canal. This preparation can be used either diluted or full strength. If the auricle and postauricular area are involved, diluted aluminum acetate solution can be applied as a wet dressing.

PREPARATIONS.—Aluminum Acetate Solution, U.S.P. *Topical:* Solution containing aluminum subacetate 54.5%, glacial acetic acid 1.5%, and water. No single-entity pharmaceutical dosage form is available; compounding is necessary. For best results, this solution should be prepared fresh before use; the pH is between 3.6 and 4.4.

SIMILAR PREPARATIONS.—Buro-Sol (Doak), Burowets (Panray), Domeboro (Dome).

ANTIPYRINE AND BENZOCAINE SOLUTION [Auralgan]

This solution of antipyrine and benzocaine in

glycerin is intended to be used for the treatment of pain asssociated with acute external otitis and the congestive and secretory stages of acute otitis media. It is rarely effective alone as an analgesic, probably because the local anesthetic in the preparation is poorly absorbed from the squamous epithelium of the external meatus and lateral aspect of the tympanic membrane. This product also is claimed to be useful in facilitating removal of excessive or impacted cerumen. The rationale for inclusion of antipyrine in this formulation is unclear; it may have use as a local irritant and escharotic.

If undue irritation or sensitivity develops, treatment should be discontinued.

USUAL DOSAGE.—*Topical: Adults and children,* in otitis media, the external ear canal is filled and a saturated cotton pledget is inserted into the meatus three or four times a day. For removal of cerumen, the solution is instilled three times daily for two days; the canal is then irrigated with warm water.

PREPARATIONS.—

Antipyrine and Benzocaine Solution, N.F. *Topical:* Solution.

Auralgan (Ayerst). *Topical:* Each milliliter of solution contains antipyrine 54 mg, benzocaine 14 mg, 8-hydroxyquinoline, and glycerin approximately 1 ml in 15 ml containers.

SIMILAR PREPARATION.—E-R-O (First Texas).

CERUMENEX DROPS

Cerumenex is a solution of triethanolamine polypeptide oleate-condensate 10% in propylene glycol. It is promoted as a cerumenolytic because of its ability to emulsify cerumen.

When there is strict adherence to the dosage instructions of the manufacturer, the incidence of adverse reactions appears to be less than 1%. However, clinical studies comparing the efficacy of Cerumenex to other preparations used to soften impacted cerumen are conflicting. Some reports indicate good results, but there is evidence that Cerumenex must be left in the ear canal for longer than 15 to 30 minutes in order to be more effective than other less potentially irritating solutions.

Adverse reactions range from mild pruritus, mild erythema of the external ear canal, and a burning sensation in the ear to a severe eczematoid eruption involving the external ear and periauricular tissue.

USUAL DOSAGE.—Since potential risks may outweigh benefits, no suggested regimen is given. The manufacturer's dosage is: *Topical:* The ear canal is filled with Cerumenex Drops, following which a cotton plug is inserted and the contents allowed to remain in the ear for 15 to 30 minutes. The cotton plug is then removed and the ear canal is flushed with lukewarm water. If a second application is necessary, the procedure may be repeated. The manufacturer warns that large areas of the skin should not be unduly exposed to Cerumenex nor should the drug be left in the ear canal for longer than a 30-minute period.

PREPARATIONS.—Cerumenex Drops (Purdue Frederick). *Topical:* Solution in 8 and 15 ml containers.

COLY-MYCIN S OTIC WITH NEOMYCIN AND HYDROCORTISONE SUSPENSION

This preparation contains colistin, neomycin, hydrocortisone, and a surface-active agent, thonzonium. It is indicated for the treatment of external otitis caused by sensitive organisms and for prophylaxis of "swimmer's ear."

Mild burning or pain in the ear canal occasionally is observed with use of this product. Hypersensitivity reactions also have occurred rarely. This preparation should be used cautiously in patients with a perforated eardrum or long-standing otitis media, and it may be contraindicated in those with herpes simplex, vaccinia, or chickenpox, or with tuberculous, fungal, or acute purulent infections (eg, furunculosis).

USUAL DOSAGE.—*Topical: Adults and children,* for treatment of external otitis, four drops instilled three times daily. For prophylaxis of "swimmer's ear," four drops instilled before and after swimming.

PREPARATIONS.—Coly-Mycin S Otic with Neomycin and Hydrocortisone (Warner-Chilcott). *Topical:* Each milliliter of suspension contains colistin base activity 3 mg (as the sulfate), neomycin base activity 3.3 mg (as the sulfate), hydrocortisone acetate 10 mg, thonzonium bromide 0.5 mg, polysorbate 80, acetic acid, and sodium acetate in a buffered aqueous vehicle with thimerosal 0.002% in 5 and 10 ml containers.

DEBROX DROPS

Debrox is a solution of carbamide peroxide in glycerin. It is similar to hydrogen peroxide in its activity and is indicated in the management of excessive or hardened cerumen. This product also is used empirically in the treatment and prophylaxis of acute external otitis and secretory otitis media.

If undue irritation or sensitivity develops, treatment should be discontinued.

USUAL DOSAGE.—*Topical: Adults and children*, to remove cerumen, five drops instilled twice daily for three or four days. Residual cerumen then may be removed by irrigation with tepid water. For treatment of external otitis and secretory otitis media, ten drops instilled four times daily, followed by use of a saturated wick if necessary. For prophylaxis of external otitis, two drops instilled twice daily.

PREPARATIONS.—Debrox Drops (International). *Topical:* Solution containing carbamide peroxide 6.5% in glycerin in 15 ml containers.

LIDOSPORIN OTIC SOLUTION

This solution containing polymyxin and lidocaine is intended for treatment of external otitis caused by susceptible organisms.

If undue irritation or sensitivity develops, treatment should be discontinued.

USUAL DOSAGE.—*Topical: Adults and children*, three or four drops instilled three or four times daily.

PREPARATIONS.—Lidosporin Otic Solution (Burroughs Wellcome). *Topical:* Each milliliter of solution contains polymyxin B sulfate 10,000 units, lidocaine hydrochloride 50 mg, purified water 0.02 ml, and propylene glycol in 10 ml containers.

OTIC DOMEBORO SOLUTION

This is a solution of acetic acid in a modified Burow's solution that is intended for the treatment of acute external otitis.

USUAL DOSAGE.—*Topical: Adults and children*, four to six drops instilled every two or three hours.

PREPARATIONS.—Otic Domeboro Solution (Dome). *Topical:* Acetic acid 2% in aluminum acetate (modified Burow's) solution in 60 ml containers.

OTOBIOTIC SOLUTION

Otobiotic Solution contains neomycin, sodium propionate, sodium metabisulfite, glycerin, and isopropyl alcohol. It is intended for the treatment of external otitis and chronic otitis media caused by susceptible organisms.

If undue irritation or sensitivity develops, treatment should be discontinued.

USUAL DOSAGE.—*Topical: Adults and children*, for external otitis, three or four drops instilled three or four times daily. A saturated gauze or cotton wick also may be used if desired. For chronic otitis media, the ear canal is partially filled with the solution, which is then allowed to flow out after several minutes. The procedure is repeated three or four times daily.

PREPARATIONS.—Otobiotic (Schering). *Topical:* Each milliliter of solution contains neomycin sulfate 5 mg (equivalent to 3.5 mg neomycin base), sodium propionate 50 mg, sodium metabisulfite 0.1%, glycerin, isopropyl alcohol, and water. The pH of this solution is 6.

VOSOL OTIC SOLUTION
VOSOL HC OTIC SOLUTION

These solutions contain propylene glycol diacetate, acetic acid, and benzethonium chloride in propylene glycol. VoSol HC also contains hydrocortisone. VoSol is indicated in the treatment and prevention of external otitis. VoSol HC is indicated when external otitis is complicated by severe inflammation or is associated with seborrheic or allergic dermatitis, psoriasis, or other noninfectious conditions.

VoSol HC may be contraindicated in individuals with herpes simplex, vaccinia, or chickenpox, or with tuberculous, fungal, or acute purulent infections (eg, furunculosis).

USUAL DOSAGE.—*Topical: Adults and children*, for treatment of external otitis, five drops instilled three or four times daily. For prophylaxis of external otitis (VoSol only), three or four drops instilled as indicated.

PREPARATIONS.—

VoSol Otic Solution (Wampole). *Topical:* Solution containing propylene glycol diacetate 3%, acetic acid 2%, benzethonium chloride 0.02%, and sodium acetate 0.015% in 15 ml containers.

VoSol HC Solution (Wampole). *Topical:* Solution containing the VoSol formulation plus hydrocortisone 1% in 7.5 ml containers.

Additional Preparations

Following is a partial listing of the many preparations that are available for topical use in treating diseases of the external ear canal. All are similar to those described above. Preparations promoted by manufacturers for use either in the eye or the ear are not listed because in order for these preparations to be suitable for use in the eye, they are adjusted to a pH that is not optimal for use in the ear.

Preparations Containing Anti-infective Agents

Aerosporin Otic Solution (Burroughs Wellcome):

Each milliliter contains polymyxin B sulfate 10,000 units, glacial acetic acid 1%, and propylene glycol.

Otos-Mosan Otic Solution (Ayerst): Each milliliter contains urea 125 mg, sodium propionate 60 mg, sulfathiazole 0.6 mg, methylparaben 20 mg, and benzethonium chloride 0.25 mg with aminacrine hydrochloride, lactic acid, isopropyl alcohol, benzyl alcohol, and glycerin.

Preparations Containing Local Anesthetics

Americaine Otic Drops (Arnar-Stone): Solution containing benzethonium chloride 0.1% and benzocaine 20% in glycerin and polyethylene glycol.

Myringacaine Ear Drops (Upjohn): Solution containing benzocaine 4%, ephedrine hydrochloride 0.44%, and ortho-hydroxyphenylmercuric chloride 0.05% in glycerin and propylene glycol.

Otodyne Otic Solution (Schering): Solution containing zolamine hydrochloride 1% and euprocin hydrochloride 0.1% in polyethylene glycol with sodium acetate.

Tympagesic Ear Drops (Warren-Teed): Solution containing benzocaine 5%, phenylephrine hydrochloride 0.25%, antipyrine 5%, and sodium metabisulfite 0.1% in propylene glycol.

Preparations Containing Anti-infective Agents and Local Anesthetics

Chloromycetin Otic Solution (Parke, Davis): Solution containing chloramphenicol 0.5% and benzocaine 1% in propylene glycol.

Furacin Otic Solution (Eaton): Solution containing nitrofurazone 0.2%, nifuroxime 0.375%, and diperodon hydrochloride 2% in polyethylene glycol.

Preparations Containing Anti-infective Agents and Adrenal Corticosteroids

Bro-Parin Ear Drops (Broemmel): Each milliliter of solution contains polymyxin B sulfate 100,000 units, neomycin sulfate equivalent to neomycin 20 mg, heparin sodium 2,000 units, and hydrocortisone 5 mg in polysorbate 80, chlorobutanol, and methylparaben.

Cortisporin Otic Drops (Burroughs Wellcome): Each milliliter of solution contains polymyxin B sulfate 10,000 units, neomycin sulfate equivalent to neomycin 3.5 mg, hydrocortisone 10 mg in polysorbate 80, cetyl alcohol, propylene glycol, and purified water.

Florotic Otic Suspension (Squibb): Each milliliter contains fludrocortisone acetate 1 mg, neomycin sulfate 3.5 mg, polymyxin B sulfate 10,000 units, and nystatin 100,000 units with thimerosal, citric acid, sodium citrate, and glycerin.

Furacin-HC Otic Solution (Eaton): Solution containing nitrofurazone 0.2% and hydrocortisone acetate 1% in polyethylene glycol and glycerin.

Neo-Aristocort Eye-Ear Ointment (Lederle): Ointment containing neomycin sulfate equivalent to neomycin 0.35% and triamcinolone acetonide 0.1%.

Neo-Cortef Eye-Ear Drops (Upjohn): Each milliliter contains neomycin sulfate equivalent to neomycin 3.5 mg and hydrocortisone acetate 5 or 15 mg with myristyl-gamma-picolinium chloride, sodium citrate, polyethylene glycol 4,000, and povidone.

Neo-Cortef Eye-Ear Ointment (Upjohn): Each gram contains neomycin sulfate equivalent to neomycin 3.5 mg and hydrocortisone acetate 5 or 15 mg in anhydrous lanolin, mineral oil, and white petrolatum.

Neo-Delta-Cortef Eye-Ear Drops (Upjohn): Each milliliter of suspension contains neomycin sulfate 5 mg and prednisolone acetate 2.5 mg.

Neo-Delta-Cortef Eye-Ear Ointment (Upjohn): Each gram contains neomycin sulfate 5 mg and prednisolone acetate 2.5 or 5 mg.

Neo-Medrol Eye-Ear Ointment (Upjohn): Each gram contains neomycin sulfate 5 mg and methylprednisolone 1 mg.

Neo-Polycin Otic Suspension (Dow): Each gram contains neomycin sulfate 2.85 mg, polymyxin B sulfate 4,000 units, and dyclonine hydrochloride 10 mg.

Otalgine Drops (Purdue Frederick): Solution containing neomycin undecylenate equivalent to neomycin 0.067%, tyrothricin 0.1%, hydrocortisone alcohol 0.1%, and ethylene oxide-polyoxypropylene glycol condensate 1% in aqueous propylene glycol.

Otic-Neo-Cort-Dome (Dome): Suspension containing neomycin sulfate equivalent to neomycin 0.35%, microdispersed hydrocortisone 1%, and acetic acid 2%.

Otobione Otic Suspension (Schering): Each milliliter contains neomycin sulfate equivalent to neomycin 3.5 mg, prednisolone acetate 5 mg, and sodium propionate 50 mg with polyvinylpyrrolidone and sodium metabisulfite.

Terra-Cortril Eye/Ear Suspension (Pfizer): Each milliliter contains oxytetracycline hydrochloride 5 mg and hydrocortisone acetate 15 mg in mineral oil and aluminum tristearate.

Preparations Containing Anti-infective Agents, Adrenal Corticosteroids, and Local Anesthetics

Auracort Otic Solution (Philips Roxane): Each milliliter contains neomycin sulfate equivalent to neomycin 3.5 mg, polymyxin B sulfate 2,000 units, hydrocortisone 2.5 mg, and pramoxine hydrochloride 10 mg in propylene glycol and glycerin.

Neo-Polycin HC Otic Suspension (Dow): Each gram contains neomycin sulfate 2.85 mg, polymyxin B sulfate 4,000 units, dyclonine hydrochloride 10 mg, and hydrocortisone acetate 10 mg.

Otic Lidaform-HC (Dome): Each milliliter of suspension contains lidocaine 30 mg, iodochlorhydroxyquin 30 mg, hydrocortisone acetate 10 mg, and acetic acid 2%.

Otocort Ear Drops (Lemmon): Each milliliter contains neomycin sulfate 3.5 mg, polymyxin B sulfate 2,000 units, hydrocortisone 0.1%, antipyrine 5%, and dibucaine hydrochloride 0.25%.

Chapter 74

ANTIPARKINSONISM AGENTS

The goal of therapy in parkinsonism is to provide maximal symptomatic relief and to maintain, for the patient's lifetime, some independence of movement and activity. Treatment is palliative and not curative. The major symptoms of the disease-akinesia, rigidity, tremor, and disorders of posture and equilibrium-can be relieved to varying degrees by drug therapy. The best results are obtained in patients who are willing and able to tolerate some degree of toxicity. For successful treatment of parkinsonism, however, drugs should be considered only as part of a total program that also includes physiotherapy, exercise, recreation, and psychological support.

The parkinsonian state is currently believed to reflect an imbalance between cholinergic and dopaminergic mechanisms in the central nervous system. Dopamine, which is normally present in the corpus striatum, is selectively depleted in the brains of patients with idiopathic or postencephalitic parkinsonism. Degeneration of the substantia nigra is a characteristic neuropathologic change, and depletion of striatal dopamine correlates with the degree of cell loss in the substantia nigra. It has been suggested that dopamine acts as an inhibitory neurotransmitter within the nigrostriatal pathways of the extrapyramidal motor system, while acetylcholine has excitatory activity. The symptoms of parkinsonism would thus reflect cholinergic dominance because of the reduced level of dopamine in the brain. Treatment is directed toward inhibition of the cholinergic system by administering drugs with central anticholinergic action, and toward enhancement of the dopaminergic system by replenishing striatal dopamine. Dopamine does not enter the brain in sufficient quantities to be of value in the treatment of parkinsonism, but levodopa, its immediate precursor, readily penetrates the blood-brain barrier.

The discussion in this chapter is divided into three sections: the evaluation on levodopa, an introductory statement on centrally active anticholinergic agents along with individual evaluations, and the evaluation on one miscellaneous agent, amantadine.

INDIVIDUAL EVALUATION

LEVODOPA [Bendopa, Dopar, Larodopa, Levopa]

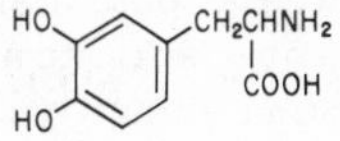

HO, HO (benzene ring) CH_2CHNH_2 / COOH

Levodopa is the most effective agent presently available for treating parkinsonism. When administered in gradually increasing doses for an adequate period of time, it will reduce symptoms and improve functional capacity in the majority of patients. In controlled clinical trials, 50% to 90% of patients have shown moderate to marked improvement; the best results have been obtained when the drug was given for six months or longer. Unlike other antiparkinson drugs, levodopa has not shown reduced effectiveness with continued use.

All of the major symptoms of parkinsonism may be ameliorated by levodopa therapy, although not to the same degree in each patient. Akinesia and rigidity are markedly reduced in most patients. Tremor responds more slowly and may increase in severity during initial therapy. Striking improvements have been observed in balance, posture, gait, speech, and handwriting. Seborrhea and drooling may be completely abolished, and the severity and frequency of oculogyric crises may be reduced. An elevation in mood is common and may precede objective evidence of improvement. Improved intellectual function (ie, a return to the premorbid level) has been reported but there is no convincing evidence that dementia, if present, is favorably affected.

In selecting candidates for levodopa therapy, it is not possible to predict with certainty which patients will benefit, the type or degree of improvement, or the time required to achieve maximal symptomatic relief. The age of the patient and the duration of illness are not closely correlated with therapeutic response. Generally, patients with moderate parkinsonism show the greatest improvement, but some patients with severe impairment have experienced marked relief of symptoms and restoration of functional capacity. Levodopa is effective in both idiopathic and postencephalitic parkinsonism; patients with the postencephalitic form respond to lower doses of the drug but also experience a higher incidence of adverse reactions. Patients with atypical clinical manifestations may show less improvement in functional capacity than those with classical idiopathic or postencephalitic parkinsonism. Prior thalamotomy does not influence the therapeutic response.

All patients with parkinsonism may, therefore, be viewed as potential candidates for levodopa therapy, and some neurologists recommend its use in all newly-diagnosed cases. However, because the treatment schedule is demanding to the patient and the drug has numerous untoward effects, most authorities believe that it should be reserved for those with some degree of functional impairment.

When initiating levodopa therapy in patients who are already receiving anticholinergic drugs, the latter medication should not be discontinued and it is not necessary to reduce the dosage. Abrupt withdrawal of anticholinergic medication often will cause a severe exacerbation of parkinsonian symptoms. In addition, most patients respond better (and possibly experience fewer gastrointestinal side effects) with combined therapy. If treatment is initiated with levodopa, anticholinergic drugs may be added later, if needed, to achieve optimal effects.

Levodopa also has been used successfully to reverse the central nervous system symptoms of chronic manganese poisoning, which have some similarities to the symptoms of parkinsonism. In the rigid akinetic form of Huntington's chorea, levodopa reduces akinesia and rigidity, but it intensifies the choreic movements seen in the classic form of the disease. The drug has been tested in patients with other neurologic diseases associated with extrapyramidal lesions, but there is no convincing evidence that it is of value in these disorders. Unlike the anticholinergic agents, levodopa is not effective in counteracting extrapyramidal reactions induced by the antipsychotic agents (phenothiazines and butyrophenones).

Adverse Reactions and Precautions.—Adverse reactions to levodopa account for a significant proportion of therapeutic failures: some patients cannot tolerate an effective daily dose for an extended period because of severe untoward effects. The most common adverse reactions are gastrointestinal disturbances, cardiovascular symptoms, psychiatric disturbances, and involuntary movements.

Gastrointestinal symptoms: Nausea, vomiting, and anorexia occur in a large percentage of patients, particularly if the initial daily dose is large or if dosage is increased too rapidly. These symptoms can almost always be diminished by temporarily reducing the daily dosage, by administering smaller doses more frequently, or by giving the drug with food. Nausea and vomiting may occur less frequently in patients who are also receiving anticholinergic therapy. Antiemetics also have been found effective, but the phenothiazine compounds may counteract the therapeutic effect of levodopa.

Other gastrointestinal disturbances occasionally reported include abdominal pain, diarrhea, constipation, and peptic ulcer with gastrointestinal bleeding which occasionally has been fatal. Patients with a history of peptic ulcer should be observed carefully for the possible development of gastrointestinal bleeding.

Cardiovascular symptoms: With increasing doses of levodopa, the systolic and diastolic blood pressures often decrease 20 to 30 mm Hg. In most patients the fall in blood pressure is well tolerated, but significant orthostatic hypotension may occur in some individuals. The hypotension tends to diminish with time, and symptoms often can be alleviated by use of elastic bandages or stockings. In some instances, temporary reduction of dosage may be necessary.

Palpitations without arrhythmias may occur but they often disappear despite continued therapy. Some patients may develop minor disturbances of cardiac rate and rhythm (tachycardia and premature ventricular contractions). Severe arrhythmias occur occasionally; these generally can be controlled by antiarrhythmic agents and it is seldom necessary to discontinue levodopa.

Flushing is a common, often transient, side effect of levodopa. Other cardiovascular reactions reported occasionally are hypertension, myocardial infarction, and venous thrombosis. Cardiovascular function should be checked periodically during prolonged therapy, and the drug should be given with care to patients with a history of cardiovascular or cerebrovascular disease.

Psychic symptoms: Levodopa may cause euphoria, restlessness, anxiety, irritability, hyperactivity, insomnia, and vivid dreams. Drowsiness, fatigue, depression, and stupor also have been reported. Occasionally, severe psychic disturbances (agitation, hypomanic and paranoid reactions, delirium, hallucinations, and aggressive or suicidal behavior) have occurred. Severe reactions appear to be most common in patients with pre-existing dementia or a history of mental illness; in some cases, the drug may have unmasked a previously unrecognized dementia. Since most patients with parkinsonism are maintained on both levodopa and anticholinergic agents, it is not clear to what extent the anticholinergic drugs contribute to these adverse psychic reactions. Mental disturbances generally respond to a reduction in levodopa dosage, but occasionally it may be necessary to discontinue the drug. Some authorities regard pre-existing dementia as a relative contraindication to levodopa therapy.

Neurologic symptoms: Abnormal involuntary movements often occur at or just preceding the time of optimal therapeutic response and are the major dose-limiting factor in levodopa therapy. Mild, intermittent dyskinesias involving the mouth, tongue, face, and neck are common after a few months of therapy. Involuntary movements of the limbs, particularly the hands, appear later. Severe, generalized choreo-athetoid movements may occur, particularly after prolonged administration of large doses. These adventitious movements are closely associated with improved control of parkinsonism; therefore, although the dyskinesias disappear when dosage is reduced, the symptoms of parkinsonism will increase. In some patients, involuntary movements recur at progressively lower doses. Small doses of pyridoxine will counteract these movements but also reduce the beneficial effects of levodopa.

A number of other neurologic reactions have occasionally been associated with levodopa therapy (eg, headache, weakness, numbness, dizziness, ataxia, akinetic episodes, convulsions). Exacerbation of oculogyric crises has been reported in a few postencephalitic patients.

Other reactions: Respiratory abnormalities may develop during levodopa therapy, most commonly in patients with postencephalitic parkinsonism. These include coughing, hoarseness, postnasal drip, tachypnea, bradypnea, gasping, panting, sniffing, other bizarre breathing patterns, and feelings of pressure in the chest.

Levodopa occasionally causes mydriasis, blurred vision, diplopia, widening of the palpebral fissures, and activation of Horner's syndrome. Hyperhidrosis, edema, urticaria, alopecia, pallor, malodor, fever, hot flushes, weight gain or loss, urinary frequency or retention, urinary incontinence, nocturia, and muscle twitching, spasm, and pain also have been reported occasionally.

Laboratory Findings.—Results of laboratory studies have not as yet revealed any evidence of serious hematologic, renal, hepatic, or thyroid dysfunction during administration of levodopa. Transitory depression of the white blood cell count has occurred in a few patients. A positive Coombs' test has been noted occasionally, and there have been a few reports of reduced hemoglobin and hematocrit levels that have not been related to a hemolytic process. Mild, transient elevations of the blood urea nitrogen level may occur and usually can be controlled by increasing the intake of fluids. Transient elevation of the serum glutamic oxaloacetic transaminase level has been noted in a few patients, but this returned to normal despite continued drug administration. Increases in blood lactic dehydrogenase, bilirubin, alkaline phosphatase, and protein-bound iodine levels have occurred rarely. Elevations of uric acid have been noted with the colorimetric method of measurement, but have not been reported in tests using the uricase method. Levodopa increases growth hormone levels and may produce carbohydrate intolerance. Dark-colored sweat and changes in the color of the urine (red-tinged when voiding; black when exposed to air) have been reported, but are not indications for discontinuing the drug.

Drug Interactions.—Dopa decarboxylase inhibitors are being used experimentally in an attempt to eliminate the need for large doses of levodopa and thus to decrease the incidence and severity of peripheral side effects. These inhibitors do not readily cross the blood-brain barrier; therefore, when given in small doses, they block the conversion of levodopa to dopamine in the peripheral tissues but do not interfere with this reaction in the central nervous system. The concomitant use of a dopa decarboxylase inhibitor permits a reduction in the daily dosage of levodopa, prolongs the action of a single dose, and reduces the incidence of nausea and vomiting. However, abnormal involuntary movements tend to appear earlier and may be more severe and persistent with combined therapy than with levodopa alone. These inhibitors are hydrazines with the potential untoward effects of this class of drugs. Long-term toxicity studies are still in progress.

Although levodopa is compatible with most drugs, a few adverse interactions have been reported. A hypertensive crisis may occur if levodopa is given with a monoamine oxidase inhibitor. These inhibitors should be discontinued two weeks prior to initiation of levodopa therapy.

The therapeutic effect of levodopa is reduced or abolished by administration of pyridoxine in doses as low as 5 mg daily. Patients receiving levodopa should avoid multiple vitamin preparations containing more than the minimal daily requirement of this vitamin (see Chapter 14, Vitamins and Sources of Vitamins). The effectiveness of levodopa also may be reduced by some antihypertensive drugs (rauwolfia alkaloids). Although phenothiazines have occasionally been used to control nausea, vomiting, and psychotic reactions induced by levodopa, most authorities have found that these agents antagonize the therapeutic effect of levodopa.

If general anesthetics are required during therapy, it has been recommended that levodopa should be discontinued 12 hours before anesthesia and reinstituted (at the same dosage) the morning following surgery. In a number of patients who were given general anesthesia using this procedure, no adverse interactions were observed and the patients' neurologic status did not deteriorate.

USUAL DOSAGE.—*Oral:* Levodopa should be given only under close medical supervision, and the dosage must be carefully adjusted for the individual patient. Patients in good general health with only moderate impairment can be treated as outpatients as long as they are seen at regular intervals and their reliability in taking medicine in proper dosage is not in question. Hospitalization should be reserved for patients with marked disability, those suspected of having systemic disorders which should be monitored on a daily basis, or those for whom drug administration cannot be properly supervised on an outpatient basis.

Levodopa is administered three to seven times daily during the waking hours. It should be given with food to reduce gastrointestinal disturbances. The initial *daily* dosage ranges from 300 mg to 1 g, depending upon the patient's tolerance. The daily dosage should then be increased gradually by increments of 100 to 500 mg as tolerated; generally, increments may be added every two or three days, but in sensitive patients it may be necessary to increase the dosage less frequently. Some authorities have found that adverse reactions can be minimized if the initial daily dose is limited to 300 mg (100 mg three times daily) and if increments are small (100 to 300 mg daily). If adverse reactions are severe, the magnitude and rate of increase should be lowered, the dosage temporarily reduced, or the drug temporarily discontinued. In many patients, parkinsonian symptoms may be better controlled and adverse reactions less severe if the daily dosage is divided into six or seven, rather than three or four, portions.

Dosage should be increased until the desired therapeutic effect is obtained or until adverse reactions preclude a further increase. The daily dosage should be kept as low as possible: the maximal dose should not exceed 8 g daily; doses above this level generally cannot be maintained because of a high incidence of adverse reactions. The optimal therapeutic dosage generally is reached in six to eight weeks and usually ranges from 4 to 6 g daily. After several months to a year of therapy, a satisfactory clinical response may be maintained in some patients with decreasing amounts.

PREPARATIONS.—

Bendopa (Bentex). *Oral:* Capsules 250 and 500 mg.

Dopar (Eaton), Levopa (Smith Kline & French). *Oral:* Capsules 100, 250, and 500 mg.

Larodopa (Roche). *Oral:* Capsules 250 and 500 mg; tablets (scored) 100, 250, and 500 mg.

CENTRALLY ACTING ANTICHOLINERGIC DRUGS

For many years, anticholinergic drugs have been the mainstay in the treatment of parkinsonism. At the present time, these agents are used as adjuncts to levodopa or as sole therapy in patients with mild impairment or in those who cannot tolerate levodopa. The efficacy of these traditional antiparkinson drugs appears to be related to their central cholinergic blocking action: anticholinergic agents that do not readily cross the blood-brain barrier (quaternary ammonium compounds) are ineffective in alleviating parkinsonian symptoms.

The anticholinergic drugs are considerably less effective than levodopa. They can produce slight to moderate improvement of all symptoms of parkinsonism and some improvement in functional capacity. However, their usefulness is limited by side effects which often preclude administration of an adequate dose, and by their tendency to show reduced effectiveness with continued use.

The belladonna alkaloids, atropine and scopolamine, were the first centrally active anticholinergic agents used in parkinsonism. In recent years, they have been largely supplanted by synthetic drugs that are equally effective but that produce fewer peripheral side effects. These include trihexyphenidyl [Artane, Pipanol, Tremin] and its analogues, biperiden [Akineton], cycrimine [Pagitane], and procyclidine [Kemadrin]; the antihistamines, diphenhydramine [Benadryl], chlorphenoxamine [Phenoxene], and orphenadrine [Disipal, Norflex]; the tropanol derivative, benztropine [Cogentin]; and the phenothiazine derivative, ethopropazine [Parsidol].

The optimal daily dosage of any of these agents is that which gives the most symptomatic relief without causing severe untoward effects. Patients with postencephalitic parkinsonism often tolerate larger doses than do those with idiopathic parkinsonism. The patient should be started on a small dose which is gradually increased until maximal benefits are attained or until unacceptable untoward effects require reduction of dosage or substitution of an alternate drug. Such transitions should be accomplished gradually; sudden withdrawal of any agent that has given some degree of relief may cause a marked exacerbation of symptoms. If the initial drug is well tolerated but fails to provide any improvement after adequate trial, an alternate drug should be tried. In most patients who are not receiving levodopa, the maximal tolerated dose of a single anticholinergic drug often does not provide adequate symptomatic relief. In such instances, a second (and, if needed, a third) drug of another class should be added and the dose of each drug individualized.

After long-term administration of anticholinergic agents, some patients who previously had experienced significant symptomatic relief may become refractory to the medication. This frequently is due to progression of the disease, but extraneous factors such as trauma, illness, or emotional stress may cause an exacerbation of the symptoms. An increase in dose can sometimes restore the beneficial effects, or substitution of another drug may be helpful.

Trihexyphenidyl is generally considered the anticholinergic drug of choice for initiating therapy in patients with moderate or severe impairment. Levodopa or an anticholinergic agent of another class may be added later as needed. When therapy is initiated with levodopa, trihexyphenidyl is commonly added to achieve maximal improvement. Patients who are not receiving levodopa are often maintained on a combination of trihexyphenidyl, diphenhydramine, and/or benztropine. Biperiden, cycrimine, and procyclidine are suitable substitutes for trihexyphenidyl.

Benztropine is rarely tolerated in optimal dosage because of its untoward effects. It is most commonly used in small doses to supplement treatment with trihexyphenidyl or levodopa. Because of its long duration of action, this drug is useful for nighttime medication.

The antihistamines have slight antiparkinson activity which has been attributed to their anticholinergic effect. They are used primarily as adjuncts to the more potent antiparkinson drugs; in patients with moderate or severe impairment, diphenhydramine is commonly administered with levodopa, trihexyphenidyl, or benztropine. In addition to their antiparkinson activity, the antihistamines have a sedative effect and may help counteract the insomnia that may follow use of the potent anticholinergics. The antihistamines are also used alone for initial therapy in patients with mild parkinsonism and for maintenance therapy in elderly patients who cannot tolerate the potent anticholinergic drugs.

Ethopropazine also has mild central anticholinergic activity. It is sometimes used as an adjunct to trihexyphenidyl or one of its analogues.

Unlike levodopa, the anticholinergic drugs are useful in controlling most extrapyramidal reactions induced by the antipsychotic agents (phenothiazines and butyrophenones).

Drug-induced rigidity, akinesia, tremor, akathisia, and acute dystonic reactions may be ameliorated by any of the centrally active anticholinergic agents; diphenhydramine is often preferred because of its low toxicity. The tardive dyskinesias, which may occur in 20% of patients after prolonged use of phenothiazines and which occasionally persist after drug withdrawal, do not respond to anticholinergic therapy.

In patients receiving large doses of antipsychotic agents, anticholinergic drugs often are administered prophylactically for the duration of antipsychotic drug therapy. Recent evidence indicates that there is little justification for this practice. Antiparkinson drugs should be prescribed only after extrapyramidal reactions occur and generally they are not required for extended periods. Excluding the tardive dyskinesias, most drug-induced extrapyramidal reactions have a limited course (three months), and symptoms will recur in only a small percentage of patients if anticholinergic drugs are withdrawn after several months of therapy.

Adverse Reactions and Precautions

Most of the untoward effects of the traditional antiparkinson agents are related to their peripheral or central cholinergic blocking activity. These adverse effects are most common with atropine and scopolamine and occur least frequently with the antihistamines and ethopropazine, which have only mild anticholinergic activity. However, some degree of toxicity can be expected to occur with therapeutic doses of any of these centrally active anticholinergic agents.

The most common adverse reactions are dryness of the mouth, mydriasis, cycloplegia, tachycardia, constipation, urinary retention, and psychic disturbances. Because of their mydriatic effect, the anticholinergic drugs could precipitate an attack of acute glaucoma in patients predisposed to angle closure; this has occurred occasionally after parenteral administration of these agents but has only rarely been reported after oral use. Anticholinergic drugs can be given safely to patients with open-angle glaucoma who are receiving miotics. Patients with prostatic hypertrophy should be observed carefully for signs of urinary retention, and those with gastrointestinal disorders should be observed for signs of intestinal obstruction. Patients with a tendency to develop tachycardia should be maintained on the smallest effective dosage.

Impairment of recent memory, mild confusion, insomnia, and restlessness are common psychic effects. More serious mental disturbances include agitation, disorientation, delirium, paranoid reaction, and hallucinations. Psychic disturbances occur most often in elderly patients, particularly in those with pre-existing dementia. The antihistamines are preferred to the more potent agents for use in elderly patients, as they are less likely to cause untoward mental reactions.

Large doses of anticholinergic drugs can cause a marked elevation of body temperature; this potentially life-threatening reaction is more common in children than in adults.

The antihistamines have some adverse effects that are unrelated to their anticholinergic action. Drowsiness and dizziness are common with therapeutic doses of these agents. Anorexia, nausea, and vomiting may occur in some patients. Other reactions which have been reported occasionally include euphoria, hypotension, headache, and weakness, tingling, and heaviness of the hands.

Trihexyphenidyl and Its Analogues

TRIHEXYPHENIDYL HYDROCHLORIDE
[Artane, Pipanol, Tremin]

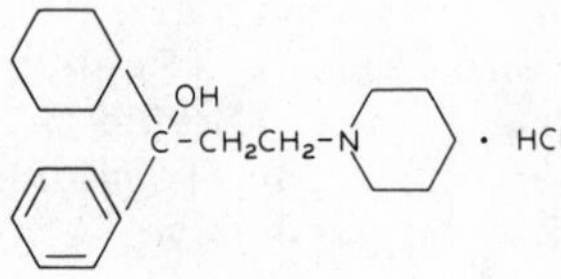

OH
C-CH_2CH_2-N · HCl

Trihexyphenidyl is often preferred for initiating therapy in patients with moderate or severe parkinsonism. It is commonly used as an adjunct to levodopa. Patients who are not receiving levodopa are frequently maintained on a combination of trihexyphenidyl and anticholinergic agents of other classes. This drug also may be used to control drug-induced extrapyramidal reactions.

For more detailed information on usage and for adverse reactions and precautions, see the introduction to this section.

USUAL DOSAGE.—*Oral:* (Tablets or elixir are preferred, as the efficacy of timed-release capsules has not been established.)

For idiopathic and postencephalitic parkinsonism, *adults,* initially, 2 mg two or three times daily. The dosage is gradually increased until the desired therapeutic effect is obtained or until severe adverse reactions preclude a further increase. Doses larger than 15 to 20 mg daily are rarely required or tolerated, but some patients with postencephalitic parkinsonism may tolerate 40 to 50 mg daily.

For drug-induced extrapyramidal reactions, *adults*, initially, 1 mg. If the symptoms are not controlled within a few hours, subsequent doses are increased until symptoms subside. The usual total daily dose is 5 to 15 mg.

PREPARATIONS.—

Artane (Lederle). *Oral:* Capsules (timed-release) 5 mg; elixir 2 mg/5 ml; tablets 2 and 5 mg.

Pipanol (Winthrop), Tremin (Schering). *Oral:* Tablets 2 and 5 mg.

BIPERIDEN HYDROCHLORIDE [Akineton Hydrochloride]

BIPERIDEN LACTATE [Akineton Lactate]

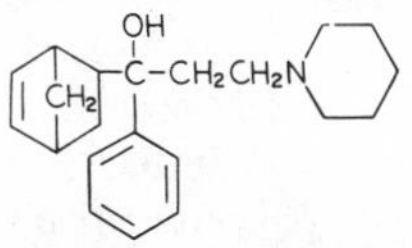

Biperiden is an analogue of trihexyphenidyl with similar actions, uses, and adverse reactions (see the introduction to this section).

USUAL DOSAGE.—

Biperiden Hydrochloride:

Oral: For idiopathic and postencephalitic parkinsonism, *adults*, initially, 2 mg three times daily. The dose may be gradually increased up to 20 mg daily if required and tolerated.

For drug-induced extrapyramidal reactions, *adults*, 2 mg one to three times daily.

Biperiden Lactate:

Intramuscular: For drug-induced extrapyramidal reactions, *adults*, 2 mg; *children*, 0.04 mg/kg of body weight. This dose may be repeated every one-half hour if required, but no more than four consecutive doses should be given within a 24-hour period.

PREPARATIONS.—

Akineton [hydrochloride] (Knoll). *Oral:* Tablets 2 mg.

Akineton [lactate] (Knoll). *Injection:* Solution 5 mg/ml in 1 ml containers.

CYCRIMINE HYDROCHLORIDE [Pagitane Hydrochloride]

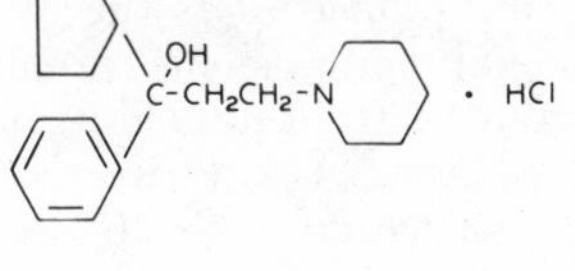

Cycrimine is an analogue of trihexyphenidyl with similar actions, uses, and adverse reactions (see the introduction to this section).

USUAL DOSAGE.—*Oral:* For idiopathic and postencephalitic parkinsonism, *adults*, initially, 1.25 mg three times daily. The dose may be gradually increased to 12.5 to 20 mg daily if required and tolerated.

PREPARATIONS.—Pagitane Hydrochloride (Lilly). *Oral:* Tablets 1.25 and 2.5 mg.

PROCYCLIDINE HYDROCHLORIDE [Kemadrin]

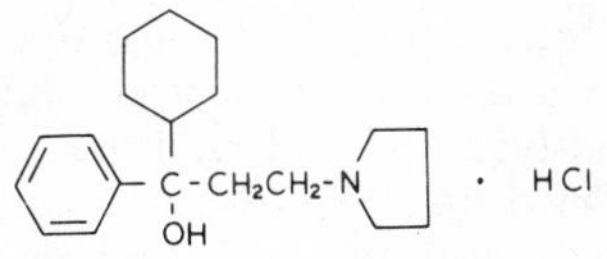

Procyclidine is an analogue of trihexyphenidyl with similar actions, uses, and adverse reactions (see the introduction to this section).

USUAL DOSAGE.—*Oral:* For idiopathic and postencephalitic parkinsonism, *adults*, initially, 5 mg twice daily. The dosage may be gradually increased to 20 to 30 mg daily if required and tolerated.

For drug-induced extrapyramidal reactions, *adults*, initially, 2 to 2.5 mg three times daily. Dosage may be increased by increments of 2 to 2.5 mg daily until symptoms are controlled. Generally, symptomatic relief is obtained with a dose of 10 to 20 mg daily.

PREPARATIONS.—Kemadrin (Burroughs Wellcome). *Oral:* Tablets 2 and 5 mg.

Tropanol Derivatives

BENZTROPINE MESYLATE [Cogentin Mesylate]

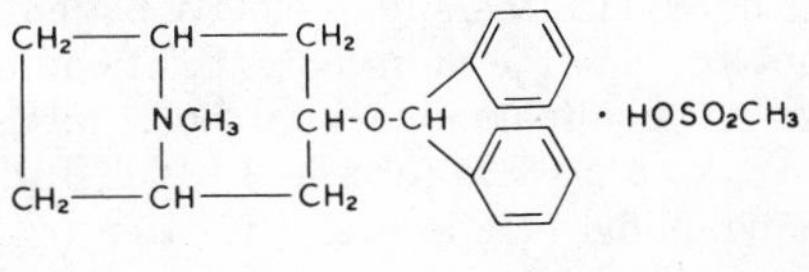

Benztropine is a potent synthetic anticholinergic agent which is chemically related to both atropine and diphenhydramine. It produces intense anticholinergic side effects and can rarely be tolerated in full dosage. Benztropine is useful primarily as an adjunct to other antiparkinsonism drugs; it is commonly used in small doses to supplement levodopa or trihexyphenidyl. Because of its long duration of action, benztropine is useful for nighttime medication. It also is effective in controlling drug-induced extrapyramidal reactions.

For adverse reactions and precautions, see the introduction to this section.

USUAL DOSAGE.—

Oral: For idiopathic and postencephalitic parkinsonism, *adults*, initially, 0.5 to 1 mg at bedtime. Patients with postencephalitic parkinsonism often tolerate an initial dose of 2 mg. The dosage may be gradually increased to 4 to 6 mg daily if required and tolerated.

Oral, Intramuscular, Intravenous: For drug-induced extrapyramidal reactions, *adults*, 1 to 4 mg orally or parenterally once or twice daily. In acute dystonic reactions, initially, 2 mg intravenously; to prevent recurrence, 1 to 2 mg orally twice daily.

PREPARATIONS.—Cogentin Mesylate (Merck Sharp & Dohme).

Oral: Tablets 0.5, 1, and 2 mg.

Injection: Solution 1 mg/ml in 2 ml containers.

Antihistamines

DIPHENHYDRAMINE HYDROCHLORIDE
[Benadryl]

$(C_6H_5)_2CHOCH_2CH_2N(CH_3)_2 \cdot HCl$

Diphenhydramine has mild antiparkinson activity that has been attributed to its central cholinergic blocking action. It is most commonly used as an adjunct to levodopa or to the more potent anticholinergic agents for treating patients with moderate or severe parkinsonism. It is also used alone for initial therapy in patients with mild impairment and for maintenance therapy in elderly patients who cannot tolerate the more potent anticholinergic drugs. Diphenhydramine may be administered parenterally to control drug-induced extrapyramidal reactions and is often preferred because of its low toxicity.

For information on adverse reactions, see the introduction to this section.

USUAL DOSAGE.—

Oral: For idiopathic and postencephalitic parkinsonism, *adults*, initially, 25 mg three times daily. The dosage may be gradually increased to 50 mg four times daily if required.

Intramuscular (deep), *Intravenous:* For drug-induced extrapyramidal reactions, *adults*, 10 to 50 mg. The maximal single dose is 100 mg and the total daily dose should not exceed 400 mg. *Children* (intramuscular), 5 mg/kg of body weight daily. The maximal daily dose should not exceed 300 mg in 24 hours.

PREPARATIONS.—Benadryl (Parke, Davis).

Oral: Capsules 25 and 50 mg; elixir 12.5 mg/5 ml.

Injection: Solution 10 mg/ml in 10 and 30 ml containers, 50 mg/ml in 1 and 10 ml containers.

CHLORPHENOXAMINE HYDROCHLORIDE
[Phenoxene]

$(ClC_6H_4)(C_6H_5)C(CH_3)-OCH_2-CH_2-N(CH_3)_2 \cdot HCl$

Chlorphenoxamine is an analogue of diphenhydramine with similar actions, uses, and adverse effects in patients with parkinsonism. (See the introduction to this section.)

USUAL DOSAGE.—*Oral:* For idiopathic and postencephalitic parkinsonism, *adults*, initially, 50 mg three times daily. The dosage may be gradually increased to 100 mg two to four times daily if needed.

PREPARATIONS.—Phenoxene (Dow). *Oral:* Tablets 50 mg.

ORPHENADRINE HYDROCHLORIDE
[Disipal]

$(C_6H_5)(CH_3C_6H_4)CH\,O\,CH_2CH_2N(CH_3)_2$

Orphenadrine is an analogue of diphenhydramine with similar actions, uses, and adverse reactions in patients with parkinsonism. (See the introduction to this section.)

Orphenadrine citrate [Norflex], is promoted only as a skeletal muscle relaxant for the treatment of painful muscular spasms. Although the manufacturer does not indicate its use for the treatment of parkinsonism, it appears to have the same properties as the hydrochloride salt; however, commercial promotion as a skeletal muscle relaxant has led to an unrealistic distinction between the two uses. Aplastic anemia in association with its use has been reported rarely.

USUAL DOSAGE.—*Oral:* For idiopathic and postencephalitic parkinsonism, *adults*, initially, 50 mg three times daily. The dosage may be gradually increased up to 250 mg daily if required and tolerated.

PREPARATIONS.—Disipal (Riker). *Oral:* Tablets 50 mg.

Phenothiazines

ETHOPROPAZINE HYDROCHLORIDE
[Parsidol]

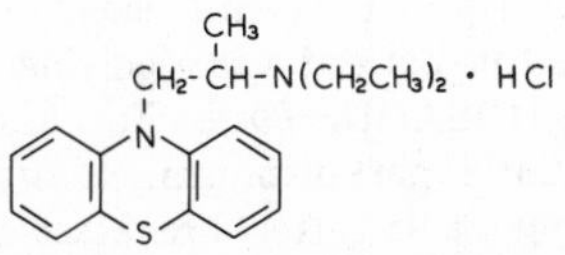

$$CH_2\text{-}CH(CH_3)\text{-}N(CH_2CH_3)_2 \cdot HCl$$

Ethopropazine possesses mild antiparkinson activity which has been attributed to its central cholinergic blocking action. It is used in parkinsonism primarily as an adjunct to trihexyphenidyl or related compounds. Although ethopropazine is a phenothiazine derivative, it is effective in controlling drug-induced extrapyramidal reactions; however, it is not commonly used for this purpose.

Drowsiness, dizziness, inability to concentrate, and confusion are the most common adverse effects of ethopropazine. Mild anticholinergic side effects have also been reported. Muscular cramps, epigastric discomfort, paresthesia, heaviness of the limbs, hypotension, and rash occur occasionally. For additional adverse reactions, see the introduction to this section.

USUAL DOSAGE.—*Oral:* For idiopathic and postencephalitic parkinsonism, *adults*, initially, 50 mg once or twice daily. The dosage may be gradually increased, if required, to a total daily dose of 100 to 400 mg in mild or moderate cases. Patients with severe impairment may require 500 to 600 mg.

PREPARATIONS.—Parsidol (Warner-Chilcott). *Oral:* Tablets 10, 50, and 100 mg.

ADDITIONAL AGENT

AMANTADINE HYDROCHLORIDE
[Symmetrel]

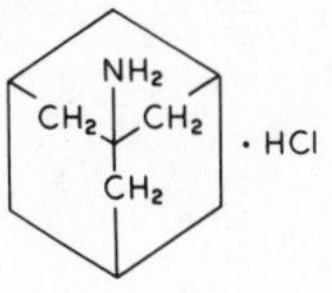

NH_2, CH_2, CH_2, CH_2 $\cdot HCl$

The antiviral agent, amantadine, produces a moderate reduction in the severity of symptoms and an improvement in functional capacity in some patients with parkinsonism. Its mechanism of action is not understood but may be related to the release of dopamine and other catecholamines from neuronal storage sites. Amantadine is considerably less effective than levodopa, but produces more rapid clinical improvement (two to five days) and causes fewer untoward reactions. Its long-term efficacy has not been established; the beneficial effects have been reduced in some patients after four to eight weeks of therapy.

The role of amantadine in the treatment of parkinsonism has not yet been clearly defined. It has been suggested that the drug might be useful for initial therapy in previously untreated patients; however, there is little information on its efficacy when used as the sole agent. In most reported studies, amantadine was given to patients who already were receiving some form of anticholinergic medication; an additive therapeutic effect has been clearly demonstrated with the combined therapy. Amantadine also has been used as an adjunct to levodopa. It is useful in patients who cannot tolerate large doses of levodopa, but is of no additional benefit in those who are already receiving optimal levodopa therapy.

At the present time, there is no convincing evidence that amantadine is of value in treating the tardive dyskinesias induced by antipsychotic agents.

For other uses of amantadine, See Chapter 92, Miscellaneous Drugs.

Adverse Reactions and Precautions.—Livedo reticularis appears to be the most common adverse effect associated with use of amantadine in parkinsonism. Although this cutaneous reaction has not been mentioned by some investigators, others have reported its occurrence in a large percentage of patients receiving the drug for one month or longer in doses of 100 to 600 mg daily. The reported incidence in women has ranged from 55% to 100%, and, in men, from 0% to 80%. In some patients, the livedo has disappeared during continued amantadine therapy, but in others it has persisted throughout the period of administration. It has disappeared gradually over a period of 2 to 12 weeks in all patients from whom the drug has been withdrawn. Laboratory studies in a limited number of patients excluded an association between livedo reticularis and a drug-induced lupus erythematosus. However, more extensive investigation is needed to definitely rule out the possibility of an underlying systemic disorder.

There are apparently no reports of livedo reticularis in patients receiving amantadine for prophylaxis of influenza, although the drug has sometimes been administered in a dose and for a period of time sufficient to reveal this reaction in parkinsonian patients. An interaction with anticholinergic drugs does not appear to explain this discrepancy, as some parkinsonian patients who developed livedo during amantadine therapy were not receiving anticholinergic agents.

Edema of the ankles (usually, but not invariably, associated with livedo) has been noted in a number of patients receiving amantadine. This edema is not associated with sodium retention and appears to be due to an increase in vascular permeability.

Both the peripheral and central adverse effects of the anticholinergic drugs are increased by amantadine. In some patients, combined therapy has induced acute psychotic reactions identical to those caused by atropine poisoning. If signs of central toxicity occur during combined therapy, the dose of the anticholinergic drug should be reduced. Psychotic reactions also have occasionally occurred in patients receiving amantadine in conjunction with levodopa.

Adverse reactions occasionally associated with administration of amantadine alone are dizziness, nervousness, inability to concentrate, ataxia, slurred speech, insomnia, lethargy, blurred vision, dryness of the mouth, gastrointestinal upset, and rash. Convulsions were reported in one elderly parkinsonian patient who was given amantadine in a dose of 800 mg daily; it is not clear what other medications this patient was receiving.

USUAL DOSAGE.—*Oral:* For idiopathic or postencephalitic parkinsonism, *adults*, initially, 100 mg once daily after breakfast for five to seven days. If adverse reactions do not appear during this period, an additional 100 mg is given after lunch. In some patients, the dosage has been gradually increased up to 500 mg daily, but it is generally felt that doses exceeding 200 mg daily provide little additional symptomatic relief.

PREPARATIONS.—Symmetrel (du Pont). *Oral:* Capsules 100 mg; syrup 50 mg/ml.

Chapter 75

AGENTS USED IN MYASTHENIA GRAVIS

The weakness and rapid fatigability of skeletal muscle which characterize myasthenia gravis are caused by an impairment of neuromuscular transmission. The principal agents used in the diagnosis and treatment of this disease are the reversible anticholinesterase compounds. These drugs are believed to alleviate myasthenic symptoms by inhibiting cholinesterase, the enzyme that destroys acetylcholine, thereby increasing the effective concentration of acetylcholine at the motor end-plate.

Treatment of Myasthenia Gravis: Physostigmine (eserine), a tertiary amine, was the first cholinesterase inhibitor used to treat myasthenia gravis. It has now been supplanted by the more effective quaternary ammonium compounds, neostigmine bromide [Prostigmin Bromide], ambenonium chloride [Mytelase], and pyridostigmine bromide [Mestinon]. These compounds are given orally; in severe cases, neostigmine methylsulfate is administered parenterally. The quaternary ammonium compounds may have a direct stimulating effect on skeletal muscle in addition to their anticholinesterase action; however, the therapeutic effect of these agents appears to be due almost exclusively to cholinesterase inhibition. The maximal muscle strength attained following optimal doses of any of the anticholinesterase agents is approximately the same, but the effectiveness of therapy varies among patients. There is marked improvement in many patients, but the response may be far below normal in those with severe myasthenia gravis.

Myasthenic weakness may worsen suddenly without recognizable cause, and such exacerbations are often characterized by decreased responsiveness to drug therapy which cannot be overcome by administration of larger doses. An exacerbation of myasthenia gravis may progress to a myasthenic crisis, characterized by severe muscular weakness with dysphagia and respiratory arrest. The symptoms of a myasthenic crisis may be difficult to distinguish from those of a cholinergic crisis, which is caused by an overdose of an anticholinesterase drug. If differential diagnosis cannot be made on the basis of the signs and symptoms, some authorities prefer to support respiration and to continue to observe the patient until a diagnosis is possible, while others have found that pharmacologic tests may be useful. These tests should be performed only if facilities for endotracheal intubation and artificial respiration are available. A small intravenous dose (1 to 2 mg) of the short-acting cholinesterase inhibitor, edrophonium [Tensilon], usually causes a brief *remission* of a myasthenic crisis or an *exacerbation* of a cholinergic crisis. If an overdose of the anticholinesterase medication is suspected, 500 mg of pralidoxime [Protopam], a cholinesterase reactivator, may be given by slow intravenous injection. This drug should temporarily increase muscle strength if the symptoms are caused by drug intoxication, but usually intensifies a myasthenic crisis. Pralidoxime must be administered cautiously, because too rapid administration or too large a dose may transform a cholinergic crisis into a myasthenic crisis.

Mild exacerbations of myasthenia are treated by increasing the dose of the oral medication as long as symptomatic improvement results. In the presence of severe dysphagia and respiratory distress, neostigmine methylsulfate should be given intramuscularly or intravenously, supplemented by atropine, if needed, to control the side effects of the anticholinesterase compound on the secretory glands, heart, and gastrointestinal smooth muscle. However, a critically ill patient often may become refractory to the medication. When this occurs, responsiveness can sometimes be restored by a temporary reduction in dosage or the complete withdrawal of medication for 72 hours. If there is severe respiratory difficulty, a tracheostomy should be performed and the patient should be placed on artificial respiration before either of these measures is undertaken. If responsiveness is restored by withdrawal of medication, some authorities believe that the symptoms were probably due to drug overdosage.

A number of other drugs have been used to treat myasthenia gravis in addition to the reversible cholinesterase inhibitors. The irreversible anticholinesterase compounds, such as isoflurophate [Floropryl], sarin, and echothiophate [Phospholine], are only of historical interest in the treatment of myasthenia gravis. These agents have a longer duration of action than the reversible cholinesterase inhibitors, but were unsatisfactory in myasthenia therapy because of their toxicity. Oral administration of ephedrine sulfate (25 mg two or three times daily) or potassium chloride solution (2 g four times daily) may help increase muscular strength in some patients who have not shown optimal response to the anticholinesterases. Corticotropin (ACTH) may benefit some patients with severe, refractory myasthenia gravis. Although exacerbation of the disease has been noted during administration of this hormone (intravenous or intramuscular administration of 100 units daily for 10 to 20 days), it is followed by a moderate to marked remission after cessation of therapy. In patients with respiratory difficulty, tracheostomy and assisted respiration are required.

Diagnosis of Myasthenia Gravis: In doubtful cases, diagnosis of myasthenia gravis can usually be established by the parenteral administration of neostigmine methylsulfate or edrophonium. To control side effects, cholinergic blockade with atropine should be instituted before neostigmine and, in patients over 50 years of age, before edrophonium. Improvement in muscle strength usually is observed in patients with myasthenia gravis, whereas those with other disorders develop fasciculations with either no increase in strength or even a slight weakness. If results are equivocal, the test should be repeated at another time.

Rarely, diagnosis cannot be established with the anticholinesterase compounds; in such instances, some authorities recommend the cautious use of tubocurarine (0.1 to 0.5 mg intravenously). Since this drug increases the severity of myasthenic symptoms, facilities for endotracheal intubation and assisted respiration must be available. Neostigmine methylsulfate (0.5 to 1 mg) should be given intravenously to restore muscle function after administration of tubocurarine.

Adverse Reactions and Precautions

Therapeutic doses of the anticholinesterase compounds can cause miosis, hyperhidrosis, hypersalivation, gastrointestinal distress, and bradycardia. These side effects are more severe with neostigmine [Prostigmin] than with ambenonium [Mytelase] or pyridostigmine [Mestinon]. Some myasthenic patients cannot tolerate optimal doses of anticholinesterase drugs unless atropine is given to control these reactions; however, atropine should be given only if indicated because a sudden increase in side effects may be the first sign of an overdose and this may be masked by atropine.

The anticholinesterase compounds are contraindicated in the presence of mechanical obstruction of the intestinal or urinary tract. They should be used with extreme caution in patients with bronchial asthma.

Cholinergic Crisis: Overdosage may occur if a patient in a refractory phase of the disease is given increasing doses of an anticholinesterase drug in an attempt to control symptoms. In these patients, the maximal strength attained after optimal doses of an anticholinesterase agent is below normal, and the administration of excessive amounts of the drug may convert a myasthenic crisis into a cholinergic crisis. Fasciculations and parasympathomimetic side effects, which are common symptoms of overdosage in normal individuals, may be mild or absent in myasthenic patients; instead, generalized weakness may be the principal sign of overdosage. This state may be difficult to distinguish from a myasthenic crisis. The pharmacologic tests previously discussed may be helpful in differentiating between the two conditions.

When signs of serious overdosage appear, the drug should be discontinued temporarily and 1 to 2 mg of atropine should be given intravenously; endotracheal intubation, artificial respiration, and suction also may be necessary. The slow, cautious intravenous administration of pralidoxime [Protopam] may partially reverse respiratory arrest and improve muscle strength; a dose of 50 mg every minute is usually given until symptoms of overdosage subside and muscle strength improves, or until a maximal dose of 1 g has been administered. This drug should be administered with care, because an overdose may convert a cholinergic crisis into a myasthenic crisis.

INDIVIDUAL EVALUATIONS

NEOSTIGMINE BROMIDE
[Prostigmin Bromide]
NEOSTIGMINE METHYLSULFATE
[Prostigmin Methylsulfate]

$(CH_3)_2N-\underset{O}{\underset{\|}{C}}-O-C_6H_4-\overset{+}{N}(CH_3)_3\ Br^-$

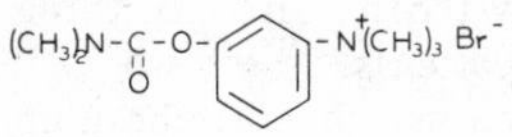

Neostigmine bromide is given orally in the treatment of myasthenia gravis. The therapeutic response is similar to that obtained with ambenonium chloride and pyridostigmine bromide, but neostigmine may have a shorter duration of action. The methylsulfate salt is administered parenterally for the diagnosis of myasthenia gravis, the treatment of exacerbations, and the management of newborn infants with the disease.

Side effects from therapeutic doses occur more frequently with neostigmine than with ambenonium or pyridostigmine. Overdosage can cause a cholinergic crisis (see the Introductory Statement). Neostigmine is contraindicated in the presence of mechanical obstruction of the intestinal or urinary tract. It should be used with extreme caution and in small doses in patients with bronchial asthma. Neostigmine bromide may cause skin reactions in patients sensitive to the bromide ion.

For other uses, see Chapter 69, Agents Used to Treat Glaucoma, and Chapter 86, Stimulants of Gastrointestinal and Urinary Tracts.

USUAL DOSAGE.—The dose and frequency of administration are determined by the severity of the disease and the response of the patient.

Neostigmine Bromide:

Oral: For treatment of myasthenia gravis, *adults,* initially, 15 mg three times daily. This may be increased to 30 mg (or occasionally to 45 mg) administered at two- to four-hour intervals. Atropine (0.6 mg orally or intramuscularly) may be given as needed to control side effects; however, atropine should be used with care because a sudden increase in side effects may be the first sign of overdosage. *Children,* initially, 7.5 to 15 mg three or four times daily; children rarely require more than 45 mg every two hours.

Neostigmine Methylsulfate:

Intramuscular: For diagnosis of myasthenia gravis, *adults,* 0.022 mg/kg of body weight. To control side effects, atropine (0.011 mg/kg intramuscularly) should be given before administration of neostigmine. An improvement in the strength of myasthenic muscle should appear within 10 minutes and last three to four hours. If results are equivocal, the test may be repeated on another day, using a larger dose of neostigmine (0.031 mg/kg) and atropine (0.016 mg/kg). *Children,* 0.025 mg/kg. Atropine (0.011 mg/kg subcutaneously) should be given before neostigmine to control side effects.

Intramuscular, Intravenous: For treatment of exacerbations of myasthenia gravis, *adults,* 0.5 to 2 mg every one to three hours, with atropine (0.2 to 0.6 mg intramuscularly every three to six hours). Dosage should be reduced if the patient is placed in a respirator. (The intramuscular route is preferred.)

Subcutaneous: For treatment of neonatal myasthenia, *infants,* 0.1 to 0.2 mg one to four times daily. Atropine (0.01 mg/kg of body weight subcutaneously) can be given with each dose or with alternate doses to control side effects.

PREPARATIONS.—

Prostigmin Bromide (Roche). *Oral:* Tablets 15 mg.

Prostigmin Methylsulfate (Roche). *Injection:* Solution 1:1,000, 1:2,000, 1:4,000.

Drugs also marketed by other manufacturers under generic names.

AMBENONIUM CHLORIDE
[Mytelase Chloride]

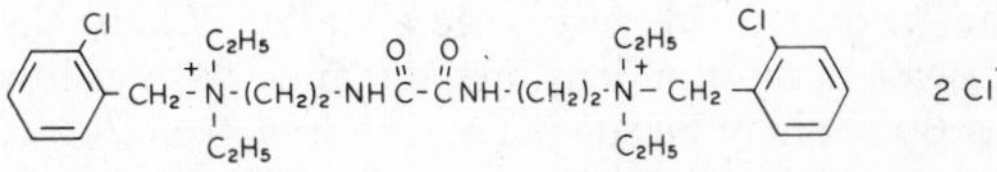

$(2\text{-}ClC_6H_4)-CH_2-\overset{+}{N}(C_2H_5)_2-(CH_2)_2-NH\overset{O}{\overset{\|}{C}}-\overset{O}{\overset{\|}{C}}NH-(CH_2)_2-\overset{+}{N}(C_2H_5)_2-CH_2-(C_6H_4Cl\text{-}2)\quad 2\,Cl^-$

Ambenonium is given orally in the treatment of myasthenia gravis. It produces fewer side effects than neostigmine and may have a longer duration of action. Ambenonium is useful in patients who cannot tolerate neostigmine bromide or pyridostigmine bromide because of sensitivity to the bromide ion.

For adverse reactions and contraindications, see the Introductory Statement.

USUAL DOSAGE.—The dose and frequency of administration are determined by the severity of the disease and the response of the patient.

Oral: Adults, initially, 5 mg. The amount should be increased as required; the usual maintenance dose is 10 to 30 mg at three- to four-hour intervals when the patient is awake. *Children*, initially, 0.3 mg/kg of body weight every 24 hours; the maintenance dose can be increased to 1.5 mg/kg every 24 hours in three or four divided doses.

PREPARATIONS.—Mytelase Chloride (Winthrop). *Oral:* Capsules 10 mg; tablets 25 mg.

PYRIDOSTIGMINE BROMIDE [Mestinon]

$$\text{(1-methylpyridinium-3-yl)}-O-\overset{O}{\overset{\|}{C}}-N-(CH_3)_2 \cdot Br^-$$

Pyridostigmine is used to treat myasthenia gravis. It produces fewer side effects than neostigmine and may have a longer duration of action. The syrup may be given by nasogastric tube and is useful for patients who cannot swallow tablets and for infants and young children. The timed-release preparation is useful for nighttime medication.

Pyridostigmine may cause skin reactions in patients sensitive to bromides. For other adverse reactions and contraindications, see the Introductory Statement.

USUAL DOSAGE.—The dose and frequency of administration are determined by the severity of the disease and the response of the patient.

Oral: Adults, 60 to 300 mg every four hours while the patient is awake; alternatively, one or two timed-release tablets may be given once or twice daily. Larger doses (up to 1.5 g daily) may be required in very severe cases. When the disease is mild, a daily maintenance dose as low as 60 mg may be adequate. *Children*, 7 mg/kg of body weight every 24 hours, divided into five or six doses.

PREPARATIONS.—Mestinon (Roche). *Oral:* Syrup 60 mg/5 ml; tablets 60 mg; tablets (timed-release) 180 mg.

EDROPHONIUM CHLORIDE [Tensilon]

$$\left[CH_3-\overset{C_2H_5}{\overset{|}{\underset{\text{(3-hydroxyphenyl)}}{N^+}}}-CH_3 \right] Cl^-$$

Edrophonium is used in the diagnosis of myasthenia gravis. It has a more rapid onset and shorter duration of action than neostigmine methylsulfate. Administration of atropine is usually not necessary during diagnostic tests with edrophonium in patients under the age of 50, but it should be readily available. After intravenous administration, muscle strength increases within one to three minutes in myasthenic patients.

A smaller dose of edrophonium is also used to differentiate a myasthenic crisis from a cholinergic crisis: an intravenous dose should produce a brief remission of symptoms if they are caused by an exacerbation of the illness, but should further weaken patients suffering from an overdose of medication.

For untoward effects and contraindications, see the Introductory Statement.

USUAL DOSAGE.—

Intravenous: For diagnosis, *adults*, 2 mg injected within 15 to 30 seconds. If no response occurs within 45 seconds, an additional 8 mg should be given. Patients over the age of 50 should be given 0.4 mg of atropine sulfate subcutaneously 10 minutes before administration of edrophonium to prevent bradycardia and hypotension. *Children*, 0.2 mg/kg of body weight; one-fifth of this dose should be given within one minute. If no response occurs, the remainder of the dose should be administered.

Intramuscular, Subcutaneous: For diagnosis, *infants*, 0.05 to 1 mg in a single dose.

Intravenous: For differential diagnosis of myasthenic crisis or cholinergic crisis, *adults*, 1 to 2 mg. This test should be undertaken only if facilities for endotracheal intubation and assisted respiration are immediately available.

PREPARATIONS.—Tensilon (Roche). *Injection:* Solution 10 mg/ml in 1 and 10 ml containers.

Chapter 76

RADIOPAQUE MEDIA

Two general techniques are used in diagnostic roentgenography: the first technique utilizes natural physiologic mechanisms for excretion of the radiopaque agent by a given organ in sufficient concentration to allow opacification of the organ and its excretory ducts (eg, cholescystography, urography); and the second technique depends on the direct instillation of the contrast media into the specific organ or region of the body to be visualized (eg, angiography, bronchography, retrograde pyelography, roentgenography of the alimentary tract).

With the exception of barium sulfate, all radiopaque agents currently used are organic iodine compounds. These can be divided into water-soluble and water-insoluble agents, and their specific use largely depends upon this physical property. A detailed discussion of the methodology employed and the dosages of each agent for each use is beyond the scope of this book. Therefore, only a general discussion of the agents used for the various techniques will be presented.

Barium sulfate is the agent of choice for roentgenographic examination of the alimentary tract. It is administered as a paste for visualization of the esophagus, as a thinner suspension for examination of the stomach and small intestine, and as an enema for examination of the colon. The water-soluble compound diatrizoate, as the meglumine [Gastrografin] or sodium salt [Hypaque Oral] is also used in gastrointestinal radiography. It may be useful when barium is contraindicated (eg, in the presence of obstructions, hemorrhaging). However, this compound may produce more adverse reactions than barium.

The compounds used for roentgenographic visualization of the biliary system include the water-insoluble agents, iopanoic acid [Telepaque], ipodate calcium or sodium [Oragrafin Sodium, Oragrafin Calcium], and tyropanoate sodium [Bilopaque], which are given orally, and the water-soluble compound, iodipamide meglumine [Cholografin Meglumine], which is given intravenously. The orally administered agents are usually absorbed promptly, excreted in the bile, and concentrated in the gallbladder. Satisfactory visualization of the bile ducts may also occur following oral administration of an ipodate salt or tyropanoate sodium. When the ducts or gallbladder cannot be adequately visualized with oral media, iodipamide meglumine may be given intravenously.

Several water-soluble compounds are given intravenously for excretory urography or are instilled directly into the urinary tract through catheters placed in the ureters or urinary bladder for retrograde urography. Those used for excretory urography include salts of diatrizoate, iothalamate [Conray], and methiodal [Skiodan]. In appropriate formulations these compounds, as well as acetrizoate [Cystokon, Pyelokon-R], are used for retrograde urography. After intravenous injection, excretion of these agents is rapid. Since it begins almost immediately when renal function is normal, roentgenographic exposures can be made within five minutes. If renal function is impaired, adequate visualization may be delayed for 30 minutes or longer. For formulations of these agents for specific uses, see the individual evaluations.

In addition to their use in urography, certain specifically formulated water-soluble compounds (eg, meglumine and sodium salts of diatrizoate and iothalamate) are used intra-arterially in various vasographic techniques, including angiocardiography, aortography, and nephrography. These compounds are preferred over other contrast media for this use because they are less toxic in the large quantities that must be administered. The specific uses of each compound are described in the individual evaluations.

Viscous aqueous or oily preparations of radiopaque media are used for the roentgenographic visualization of other organs, body cavities, or fistulous and sinus tracts. Iodized oil [Lipiodol] and ethiodized oil [Ethiodol] are used for sialography, hysterosalpingography, and visualization of sinus and fistulous tracts. Iodized oil and propyliodone oil suspension [Dionosil Oily] are used for bronchography. Other media used for hysterosalpingography are an aqueous mixture of acetrizoate sodium and polyvinylpyrrolidone [Salpix] and an aqueous mixture of diatrizoate meglumine and iodipamide meglumine [Sinografin]. Iophendylate [Pantopaque] is considered the medium of choice for myelography; its toxicity is sufficiently low to permit its introduction into the subarachnoid space.

Adverse Reactions and Precautions

A physician carrying out a diagnostic procedure with radiopaque media should have a thorough understanding of the particular procedure, including the indications for specific contrast media and the associated hazards and possible complications. The final criterion for giving the contrast medium must depend upon the calculated risk and the extent of the need for the diagnostic information.

All contrast media may produce adverse reactions, the nature and severity of which depend upon a number of factors, but especially upon the specific agent and procedure used. The following information is general in nature; for other adverse reactions of specific compounds, see the individual evaluations, and for more complete descriptions, see the manufacturers' literature.

Since iodine-containing contrast agents may alter the results of most thyroid function tests, such tests should be performed prior to the administration of these drugs.

Iodinated contrast media should be used with caution in patients with advanced renal disease, since excretion of the medium may be impaired. Patients with hepatorenal disease present an additional risk.

Contrast media administered orally produce adverse reactions less frequently than when they are given parenterally. Cholecystographic media given orally infrequently may cause nausea, vomiting, and diarrhea. Mild dysuria may be noted occasionally, and false-positive results of tests for urinary protein may occur. Although hypotension and acute renal failure are observed only rarely, they are serious complications. These effects are most commonly observed in patients with hepatic or biliary tract diseases or in those receiving larger than recommended doses. Since satisfactory results in cholecystography depend upon adequate absorption of these agents, the oral cholecystographic media should not be used in patients with gastrointestinal disorders that might interfere with their absorption.

The intravascular injection of contrast media may cause peripheral vasodilation with resultant hypotension and reflex tachycardia shortly after administration. Untoward effects that may occur after administration of most of the intravenous media range from urticaria and angioedema to laryngospasm, bronchospasm, and anaphylactic reactions. Direct toxic effects on tissues may cause vascular damage with increased capillary permeability and disruption of the blood-brain barrier; neural irritation or damage with convulsions and transient or permanent neurologic deficits; and kidney damage with proteinuria, azotemia, or irreversible acute renal failure. Because of the nature and severity of some reactions, it is essential that the patient be observed for at least 15 minutes after the parenteral administration of these agents; appropriate drugs and equipment must be readily available to counteract any reaction.

The use of these agents for excretory urography is contraindicated in patients with anuria. Moreover, this procedure has a definite risk in patients who are known to have multiple myeloma. Although this disease is not a contraindication to excretory urography, partial dehydration in the preparation of these patients is not recommended since this may predispose the patient to precipitation of myeloma protein in the renal tubules. This may progress to anuria with resultant uremia, acute renal failure, and eventually death.

Radiopaque agents should be administered with extreme caution to patients known or suspected of having pheochromocytoma. If they are used, the blood pressure should be assessed throughout the procedure and measures for treatment of a hypertensive crisis should be available.

When contrast media are injected intravascularly, they promote sickling in individuals homozygous for sickle cell disease.

INDIVIDUAL EVALUATIONS

BARIUM SULFATE

This almost insoluble barium salt is the medium of choice for roentgenographic examination of the gastrointestinal tract. It is administered orally or rectally as an aqueous suspension in amounts that vary according to the area of the gastrointestinal tract to be examined and the technique to be employed. Suspensions used orally usually contain sweetening and flavoring agents. Barium Sulfate, U.S.P. is generally substantially less expensive than proprietary preparations; however, the proprietary preparations contain suspending agents which allow easy and rapid preparation (dispersal) of high concentrations. Barium products are also available in special packaging suited to specific procedures (eg, prefilled barium enema bags, esophageal creams).

With the exception of constipation and, occasionally, impaction, adverse effects have not been observed after the oral use of barium sulfate. Rarely, perforation of the bowel wall with peritonitis or formation of a barium granuloma has occurred after the administration of barium sulfate enemas.

USUAL DOSAGE.—

Oral: Adults, 200 to 300 g in a suitable suspension.

Rectal: Adults, 400 to 750 g in a suitable suspension.

In prescribing barium sulfate, the name should be written legibly and in full to avoid the erroneous substitution of the soluble barium salts (eg, barium sulfide, barium sulfite), which are toxic and have caused fatalities.

PREPARATIONS.—Barium Sulfate, U.S.P. *Oral:* Powder in 1 and 5 lb containers and in single-dose units designed for a particular examination. Available with or without flavoring agents.

AVAILABLE TRADEMARKS.—Bari-Shake (Travenol), Barobag (Fleet), Barosperse, Barosperse Esophageal Cream (Mallinckrodt), Barotrast (Barnes-Hind), Colonatrast (Barnes-Hind), Esophotrast (Barnes-Hind), Oratrast (Barnes-Hind), Rugar (McKesson), Travad B.E. (Flint). Drug also marketed under generic name.

ACETRIZOATE SODIUM [Cystokon, Pyelokon-R]

COONa; I; I; NHCOCH$_3$; I

This water-soluble organic iodine compound is used for retrograde pyelography and cystography. The available preparations are not used intravascularly.

For adverse reactions, see the manufacturers' literature.

USUAL DOSAGE.—See the manufacturers' literature.

PREPARATIONS.—

Cystokon (Mallinckrodt). *Injection:* Solution 30% (20% iodine) in 100 and 250 ml containers and 250 and 500 ml dilution units.

Pyelokon-R (Mallinckrodt). *Injection:* Solution 20% (13.3% iodine) in 50 ml containers.

AVAILABLE MIXTURE.—Salpix (Ortho). *Injection:* Solution containing acetrizoate sodium 530 mg/ml and polyvinylpyrrolidone 230 mg/ml in 10 ml containers. For hysterosalpingography.

DIATRIZOATE MEGLUMINE
DIATRIZOATE SODIUM

COONa; I; I; CH$_3$COHN; NHCOCH$_3$; I

Diatrizoate, available as the sodium or meglumine salt and various mixtures thereof, is one of the best tolerated and least toxic of the radiopaque diagnostic media. The uses of the various formulations are given below.

For adverse reactions, see the Introductory Statement and manufacturers' literature.

USUAL DOSAGE.—Since the dosage varies with the procedure, route of administration, and preparation used, the manufacturers' literature should be consulted.

PREPARATIONS.—

Diatrizoate Meglumine:

Cardiografin (Squibb). *Injection:* Solution 85% diatrizoate meglumine (40% iodine) in 50 ml containers. For angiocardiography and thoracic aortography.

Cystografin (Squibb). *Injection:* Solution 30% diatrizoate meglumine (14% iodine) 100 ml in 300 ml containers and 300 ml in 500 ml containers. For retrograde cystourethrography.

Gastrografin (Squibb). *Oral, Rectal:* Solution 76% diatrizoate meglumine (37% iodine) in 120 ml containers. For roentgenography of the gastrointestinal tract.

Hypaque Meglumine 60% (Winthrop). *Injection:* Solution 60% diatrizoate meglumine (28% iodine) in 20, 30, and 50 ml containers. For excretory urography, cerebral angiography, peripheral arteriography, venography, direct cholangiography, splenoportography, arthrography, and diskography.

Meglumine Diatrizoate Injection, U.S.P. 76% (Squibb). *Injection:* Solution 76% diatrizoate meglumine (36% iodine) in 20 and 50 ml containers. For excretion urography, aortography, pediatric angiocardiography, and peripheral arteriography.

Reno-M-30 (Squibb). *Injection:* Solution 30% diatrizoate meglumine (14% iodine) in 50 and 100 ml containers. For retrograde pyelography.

Reno-M-60 (Squibb). *Injection:* Solution 60% diatrizoate meglumine (28% iodine) in 30 and 50 ml containers. For excretion urography, cerebral angiography, peripheral arteriography, venography, operative T-tube or percutaneous transhepatic cholangiography, splenoportography, arthrography, and diskography.

Reno-M-DIP (Squibb). *Intravenous:* Solution 30% diatrizoate meglumine (14% iodine) in 300 ml containers. For drip infusion pyelography.

Diatrizoate Sodium:

Hypaque Sodium Oral (Winthrop). *Oral, Rectal:* Liquid 50 g (24.9% iodine); powder 250 g (60% iodine). For roentgenographic examination of the gastrointestinal tract.

Hypaque Sodium 20% (Winthrop). *Injection:* Solution 20% diatrizoate sodium (12% iodine) in 100 ml containers. For retrograde pyelography.

Hypaque Sodium 25% (Winthrop). *Intravenous:* Solution 25% diatrizoate sodium (15% iodine) in 300 ml containers. For drip infusion pyelography.

Hypaque Sodium 50% (Winthrop). *Injection:* Solution 50% diatrizoate sodium (30% iodine) in 20, 30, and 50 ml containers. For excretory urography, cerebral and peripheral angiography, aortography, intraosseous venography, direct cholangiography, hysterosalpingography, and splenoportography.

Mixtures of Diatrizoate Meglumine and Diatrizoate Sodium:

Hypaque-M, 75% (Winthrop). *Injection:* Solution 25% diatrizoate sodium and 50% diatrizoate meglumine (38.5% iodine) in 20 and 50 ml containers. For angiocardiography, aortography, angiography, and excretory urography.

Hypaque-M, 90% (Winthrop). *Injection:* Solution 30% diatrizoate sodium and 60% diatrizoate meglumine (46.2% iodine) in 20 and 50 ml containers. For angiocardiography, aortography, angiography, excretory urography, and hysterosalpingography.

Renografin-60 (Squibb). *Injection:* Solution 8% diatrizoate sodium and 52% diatrizoate meglumine (29% iodine) in 30 and 50 ml containers. For excretion urography, cerebral angiography, peripheral arteriography, venography, operative T-tube or percutaneous transhepatic cholangiography, splenoportography, arthrography, and diskography.

Renografin-76 (Squibb). *Injection:* Solution 10% diatrizoate sodium and 66% diatrizoate meglumine (37% iodine) in 20 and 50 ml containers. For excretion urography, aortography, pediatric angiocardiography, peripheral arteriography, and selective coronary arteriography.

Renovist II (Squibb). *Injection:* Solution 29.1% diatrizoate sodium and 28.5% diatrizoate meglumine (31% iodine) in 30 and 60 ml containers. For excretion urography, aortography, angiocardiography, peripheral arteriography, peripheral venography, and venocavography.

Mixture of Diatrizoate Meglumine and Iodipamide Meglumine:

Sinografin (Squibb). *Injection:* Solution 40% diatrizoic acid as diatrizoate meglumine and 20% iodipamide as iodipamide meglumine (38% iodine) in 10 ml containers. For hysterosalpingography.

ETHIODIZED OIL [Ethiodol]

This x-ray contrast medium is an iodine addition product of the ethyl ester of the fatty acids of poppyseed oil; it is a low viscosity oil that contains 38% organically bound iodine. Ethiodized oil is used for hysterosalpingography and sialography, and in the visualization of sinus and fistulous tracts. It should not be used for bronchography or myelography because of its toxicity.

For adverse reactions, see the Introductory Statement and manufacturer's literature.

USUAL DOSAGE.—See the manufacturer's literature.

PREPARATIONS.—Ethiodol (Fougera). *Injection:* Liquid (38% iodine) in 2 and 10 ml containers.

IODIPAMIDE MEGLUMINE [Cholografin Meglumine]

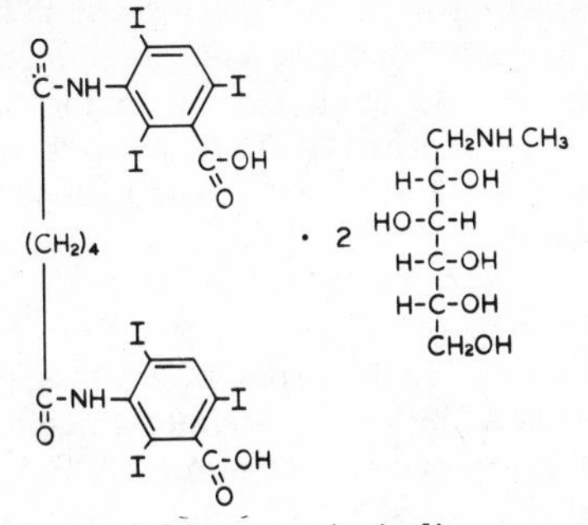

This water-soluble organic iodine compound is administered intravenously. It is the agent of choice in cholangiography. In cholecystography, it is used primarily when orally administered media fail to give adequate visualization of the gallbladder or are not tolerated or when visualization must be accomplished quickly. Cholangiography can be performed 25 minutes after administration of this compound, and cholecystography after about two to two and one-half hours.

For adverse reactions and precautions, see the Introductory Statement and the manufacturer's literature.

USUAL DOSAGE.—See the manufacturer's literature.

PREPARATIONS.—Cholografin Meglumine (Squibb). *Injection:* Solution 52% (about 26% iodine) in 20 ml containers.

IODIZED OIL [Lipiodol]

This iodinated poppyseed oil is used as a radiopaque medium in hysterosalpingography, sialography, bronchography, and in the visualization of sinus and fistulous tracts.

For adverse effects, see the Introductory Statement and manufacturer's literature. Deaths have been reported after use of iodized oil in bronchography (primarily due to anoxia associated with emphysema or bronchospasm) and hysterosalpingography (primarily due to cerebral oil embolism). This agent is contraindicated for use in any area in which bleeding has occurred, in patients taking mercurial salts, in those with disease in which there is inflammation (eg, pulmonary tuberculosis), and in individuals who are sensitive to iodine.

USUAL DOSAGE.—See the manufacturer's literature.

PREPARATIONS.—Lipiodol (Fougera). *Injection:* Solution (10% iodine) in 5 ml containers, and solution (28% and 40% iodine) (Iodized Oil, N.F.) in 5, 10, and 20 ml containers. Solutions that are dark brown in color should not be used.

IOPANOIC ACID [Telepaque]

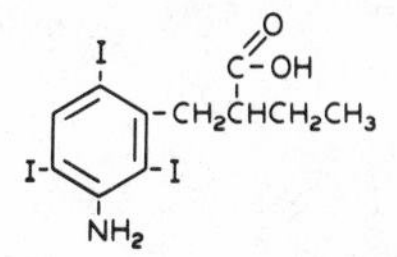

Iopanoic acid is a water-insoluble, organic iodine compound that is administered orally for cholecystography.

Adverse reactions occur infrequently; nausea, vomiting, and diarrhea have been reported. The drug is contraindicated in patients with severe renal or hepatorenal disease or with gastrointestinal disorders that prevent absorption of the drug. For additional information, see the Introductory Statement and manufacturer's literature.

USUAL DOSAGE.—See the manufacturer's literature.

PREPARATIONS.—Telepaque (Winthrop). *Oral:* Tablets 500 mg.

IOPHENDYLATE INJECTION [Pantopaque]

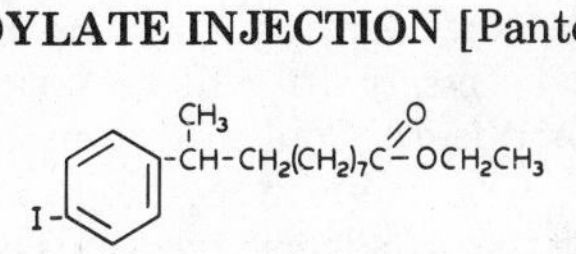

This preparation, a mixture of the isomers of ethyl iodophenylundecanoate, is designed for use in myelography; it is not used intravascularly. The material should be removed as completely as possible after the examination since if it is not removed, complete absorption may take several years.

Severe arachnoiditis that causes headache, fever, meningism, severe back pains, pain in the lower extremities, and elevation of the white cell count and protein content of cerebrospinal fluid occurs infrequently. The incidence of arachnoiditis is greatly increased when active subarachnoid bleeding has been induced by lumbar puncture. In addition, lipid granuloma, obstruction of the ventricular system, and venous intravasation which results in pulmonary embolization are observed rarely. Patients who experience active subarachnoid bleeding during the lumbar puncture or who are hypersensitive to iodine should not be given iophendylate.

USUAL DOSAGE.—For dosage and administration technique, see the manufacturer's literature.

PREPARATIONS.—Pantopaque (Lafayette). *Injection:* Liquid (30.5% iodine) in 1, 3, 6, and 12 ml containers.

IOTHALAMATE MEGLUMINE [Conray, Conray 30, Cysto-Conray]
IOTHALAMATE SODIUM [Angio-Conray, Conray-400]

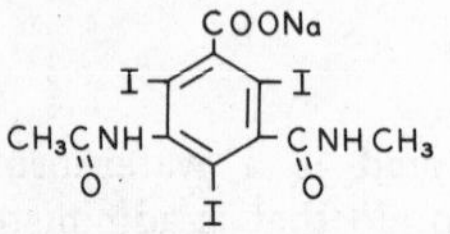

These water-soluble organic iodine compounds are used for roentgenography of the circulatory system and urinary tract. They are among the best media available for intravenous urography, cerebral angiography, peripheral arteriography and venography, intravenous infusion urography, intravascular angiocardiography, aortography, arteriography, excretory urography, and retrograde pyelography, cystography, and cystourethrography.

The specific uses of the various preparations are given below. The 80% solution of iothalamate sodium is used primarily for intravascular angiocardiography and aortography when it is necessary to achieve greater opacity (eg, in the obese). Concentrations higher than 60% are not used in cerebral angiography because the risk of adverse reactions is increased.

For adverse reactions and other precautions, see the Introductory Statement and the manufacturer's literature.

USUAL DOSAGE.—See the manufacturer's literature.

PREPARATIONS.—

Iothalamate Meglumine:

Conray (Mallinckrodt). *Injection:* Solution 60% (28.2% iodine) in 20, 30, and 50 ml containers. For intravenous urography, cerebral angiography, and peripheral arteriography and venography.

Conray 30 (Mallinckrodt). *Injection:* Solution 30% (14.1% iodine) in 300 ml containers. For intravenous infusion urography.

Cysto-Conray (Mallinckrodt). *Injection:* Solution 43% (20% iodine) in 50, 100, and 250 ml containers, and 250 and 500 ml dilution units. For retrograde pyelography, cystography, and cystourethrography.

Iothalamate Sodium:

Conray-400 (Mallinckrodt). *Injection:* Solution 66.8% (40% iodine) in 25 and 50 ml containers. For intravascular angiocardiography, aortography, arteriography, and excretory urography.

Angio-Conray (Mallinckrodt). *Injection:* Solution 80% (48% iodine) in 20 and 50 ml containers. For intravascular angiocardiography and aortography when greater opacity is necessary than that obtained with 66.8% solution.

AVAILABLE MIXTURE.—Vascoray (Mallinckrodt). *Injection:* Solution containing meglumine iothalamate 52% and sodium iothalamate 26% (40% iodine) in 25 and 50 ml containers. Same uses as Conray-400.

IPODATE CALCIUM [Oragrafin Calcium]
IPODATE SODIUM [Oragrafin Sodium]

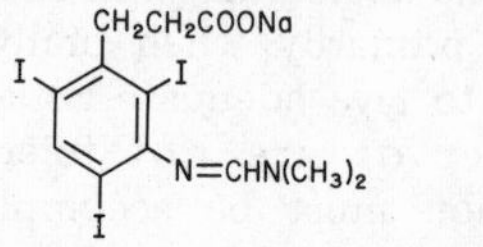

These water-soluble organic iodine compounds are given orally for cholangiography and cholecystography.

Adverse reactions (eg, nausea, vomiting, diarrhea) occur infrequently. The use of these agents is contraindicated in patients with renal or hepatorenal disease, gastrointestinal disease which prevents absorption, and in those who are sensitive to iodine. For additional information, see the Introductory Statement and the manufacturer's literature.

USUAL DOSAGE.—See the manufacturer's literature.

PREPARATIONS.—

Oragrafin Calcium (Squibb). *Oral:* Granules (for suspension) 3 g/8 g packet.

Oragrafin Sodium (Squibb). *Oral:* Capsules 500 mg.

METHIODAL SODIUM [Skiodan Sodium]

This water-soluble radiopaque medium is used for excretory and retrograde urography and for direct injection during surgery into the gallbladder or common duct for cholangiography.

For adverse reactions and precautions, see the Introductory Statement and the manufacturer's literature.

USUAL DOSAGE.—See the manufacturer's literature.

PREPARATIONS.—Skiodan Sodium (Winthrop). *Injection:* Powder (for solution) 500 g (52% iodine); solution (intravenous) 40% (20.8% iodine) in 50 ml containers (for excretory urography); solution 20% (10.4%

iodine) in 50 ml containers and 40% (20.8% iodine) with benzyl alcohol 1% in 50 and 100 ml containers, respectively (for retrograde urography).

PROPYLIODONE [Dionosil Oily]

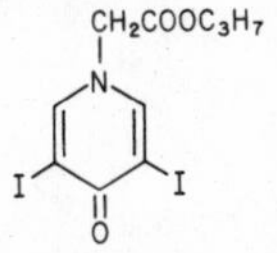

$CH_2COOC_3H_7$

This preparation is a suspension of propyliodone in peanut oil, and it is used for bronchography.

For adverse reactions, see the manufacturer's literature.

USUAL DOSAGE.—For dosage and administration technique, see the manufacturer's literature.

PREPARATIONS.—Dionosil Oily (Picker).

TYROPANOATE SODIUM [Bilopaque Sodium]

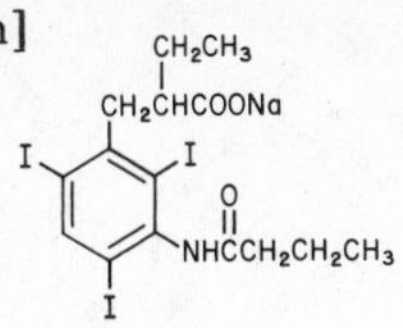

CH_2CH_3
$CH_2CHCOONa$
$NHCCH_2CH_2CH_3$

This organic iodine compound is used orally for cholecystography and cholangiography; it is related chemically to iopanoic acid and ipodate sodium.

Adverse reactions occur infrequently; nausea, vomiting, and diarrhea have been reported. For additional information on adverse reactions and precautions, see the Introductory Statement and the manufacturer's literature.

USUAL DOSAGE.—See the manufacturer's literature.

PREPARATIONS.—Bilopaque Sodium (Winthrop). *Oral:* Capsules 750 mg.

Chapter 77

MISCELLANEOUS DIAGNOSTIC AIDS

The agents discussed in this chapter are used to detect anatomic evidence of disease or pathologic dysfunction. Included are compounds used to test organ function as well as products that aid in the diagnosis of pernicious anemia, tumors, and amyloid disease. Agents used in cutaneous tests to determine immunity to certain diseases, the presence of certain diseases, or the identification of an offending allergen also are described. Both nonradioactive and radioactive compounds are considered, but chemicals used as contrast media in roentgenography are discussed in Chapter 76, Radiopaque Media.

A comprehensive discussion of laboratory diagnostic procedures is beyond the scope of this book; therefore, only selected tests are described in a general fashion in order to supply information on a few of the diagnostic aids that can be classified as drugs in the broadest sense. Several good textbooks contain detailed information on procedures for the various tests discussed in this chapter. Two such texts are *Clinical Laboratory Diagnosis*, 7th edition, by S.A. Levinson and R.P. McFate, Lea & Febiger, Philadelphia, and *Clinical Interpretation of Laboratory Tests*, 6th edition, by R.H. Goodale and F.K. Widmann, F.A. Davis Co., Philadelphia.

AGENTS USED FOR LIVER FUNCTION TESTS

Liver function tests by themselves are not diagnostic, nor is there always good correlation between the functional capacity of the liver and gross pathology. Marked pathologic changes in the liver may exist even when the results of liver function tests are within normal limits. This is due, at least in part, to the great functional reserve of the liver and its considerable regenerative ability.

Despite these limitations, liver function tests are valuable. By use of the appropriate tests, it is possible to determine the presence or absence of certain diseases, to evaluate the severity of disease, and, often, to differentiate between obstructive and nonobstructive jaundice, as well as to evaluate the response to treatment and determine when healing has occurred.

INDOCYANINE GREEN [Cardio-Green]

Indocyanine green is cleared from the circulation very rapidly. Hepatic parenchymal cells transfer almost 100% of this compound directly into the bile in unconjugated form. Excretion is influenced only by the liver and its excretory system, although false high values are sometimes seen in patients with decreased cardiac output or hepatic circulation.

Ear lobe densitometry is reported to be quite accurate for determination of the plasma concentration of indocyanine green; venipuncture can be avoided for collection of samples and the actual rate of disappearance from the plasma can be obtained.

Solutions are unstable and must be prepared immediately before use. The absorption peak is reduced by sodium bisulfite, frequently a component of heparin preparations. The small amount of sodium iodide present in indocyanine green precludes its use in patients allergic to iodides, and a variety of thyroid function tests may be inaccurate for at least a week following administration of this agent.

At normal recommended dosage levels, indocyanine green is usually well tolerated. Allergic reactions, including one case of anaphylactic shock, have been reported when this dye was injected into uremic patients undergoing hemodialysis; therefore, the possibility of allergic reactions in normal individuals receiving the dye must not be discounted.

USUAL DOSAGE.—*Intravenous: Adults*, 0.5 mg/kg of body weight (the manufacturer recommends that the dose not exceed 2 mg/kg).

PREPARATIONS.—Cardio-Green (Hynson, Westcott & Dunning). *Injection:* Powder 10 and 40 mg in disposable units and 25 and 50 mg with diluent.

SULFOBROMOPHTHALEIN SODIUM (BSP)
[Bromsulphalein]

When sulfobromophthalein is injected intravenously, it is bound to plasma proteins and then released to liver cells where about 80% is conjugated with compounds such as glutathione and glycine. These conjugated compounds are excreted in the bile. Clearance of sulfobromophthalein from the blood depends upon the ability of the hepatic parenchymal cells to absorb, conjugate, and excrete this dye.

Great care must be exercised to avoid extravasation or inadvertent intra-arterial injection. If extravasation does occur, the surrounding tissue becomes indurated, painful, and, occasionally, photosensitive. Hypersensitivity reactions also have been reported after extravasation; therefore, caution is necessary if BSP must be injected again.

Anaphylactic reactions, some fatal, have occurred on rare occasions, most commonly in patients with asthma. Milder reactions infrequently encountered include urticaria, pruritus, malaise, generalized flushing, syncope, fever, chills, nausea, vomiting, hypotension, tachycardia, and vertigo. Since newborn and premature infants do not possess enzymes for conjugating BSP, they should not receive this dye.

USUAL DOSAGE.—*Intravenous: Adults*, 5 mg/kg of body weight infused over a period of three minutes. The patient should be closely observed for an additional five minutes.

PREPARATIONS.—Bromsulphalein (Hynson, Westcott & Dunning). *Injection:* Solution 50 mg/mk in 3, 7.5, and 10 ml containers. Drug also marketed by other manufacturers under generic name.

AGENTS USED FOR KIDNEY FUNCTION TESTS

Because the kidneys filter, secrete, and reabsorb substances, a specific test to determine functional loss in pathologic conditions involving the kidney usually will detect a defect in only one of these functions. Thus, the use of several tests is usually necessary to obtain a comprehensive estimate of the functional state of the kidney.

Laboratory determinations of blood urea nitrogen, nonprotein nitrogen, and creatinine concentrations have been used as indexes of renal function, but are inadequate since extrarenal factors (eg, gastrointestinal hemorrhage) can affect blood levels of these compounds in the absence of renal disease. Also, a patient can be near renal failure and still show normal blood values.

The glomerular filtration rate can be estimated by the renal plasma clearance of inulin, mannitol, or creatinine. Of these compounds, inulin clearance is probably the most accurate measure of glomerular filtration; however, this test is complex and not adaptable for routine use. Mannitol has limitations in that approximately 10% is reabsorbed by the tubules. Creatinine has the advantage of being an endogenous compound and, with increased use of automated analysis, is the basis of the method most often used clinically.

Use of iodopyracet and iodohippurate to measure renal plasma flow and tubular functional capacity has largely been discarded in favor of aminohippurate because of greater accuracy and ease of chemical determination. Indigotindisulfonate is used chiefly for ureteral orifice visualization in cystoscopy.

AMINOHIPPURIC ACID
AMINOHIPPURATE SODIUM (PAH)

This compound, which is filtered by the glomeruli and secreted by the renal tubular epithelium, is used to measure the effective renal plasma flow and to determine the functional capacity of the tubular excretory mechanism.

When plasma concentrations of PAH are raised rapidly, patients may experience nausea or vomiting and a sensation of sudden warmth, symptoms that can be avoided by infusing the drug more slowly. PAH diagnostic procedures cannot be used in patients receiving sulfonamide compounds because color reactions develop between sulfonamides and the reagents used to assay PAH. Also, drugs that share a common excretory pathway with PAH (eg, penicillin), those that inhibit renal tubular transport (eg, probenecid), or those that have a uricosuric effect (eg, salicylates) can interfere with PAH clearance.

USUAL DOSAGE.—*Intravenous: Adults*, to determine effective renal plasma flow, enough sterile 20% solution is administered to produce an approximate blood level of 2 mg/100 ml of plasma, based on estimated blood volume of the patient. To determine tubular excretory mass, enough sterile 20% solution is infused to produce an approximate blood level of 40 to 60 mg/100 ml of plasma, based on estimated blood volume of the patient.

PREPARATIONS.—

Reagent Aminohippuric Acid, U.S.P. *Injection:* Powder in 2 g containers for control chemical determination.

Sodium Aminohippurate Injection, U.S.P. *Injection:* Solution 20% in 10 and 50 ml containers.

Drugs marketed under generic name.

INDIGOTINDISULFONATE SODIUM
(Indigo Carmine)

This dye usually appears in the urine within ten minutes after intravenous injection. It is used principally in cystoscopy when each ureteral orifice is under direct observation. Differential appearance of the dye provides an index of relative kidney function.

Occasionally allergic-type, idiosyncratic reactions (eg, pruritus, rash, bronchial constriction) have occurred following injection of this agent; these respond to treatment with antihistamines, epinephrine, or corticosteroids. Patients with a history of allergy should be tested for sensitivity before the drug is given.

USUAL DOSAGE.—*Intravenous: Adults,* 40 to 80 mg.

PREPARATIONS.—*Injection:* Solution 8 mg/ml in 5 ml containers. Drug marketed under generic name and under the name Indigo Carmine.

INULIN

This compound is filtered only by the glomeruli and is neither secreted nor reabsorbed by the tubules. It is used to measure the glomerular filtration rate (ie, milliliters of plasma filtrate that had to cross the glomerular membrane to account for the amount of inulin excreted per unit of time). However, this test is not suitable for routine use.

In the past, inulin frequently caused pyrogenic reactions, but current methods of production seem to have corrected this problem. Massive doses can produce an osmotic diuresis and raise serum osmolality significantly.

USUAL DOSAGE.—*Intravenous: Adults,* 10 g, dissolved in 100 ml of sodium chloride injection, is infused at the rate of 10 ml/minute.

PREPARATIONS.—*Injection:* Powder; solution 100 mg/ml in 50 ml containers. Drug marketed under generic name.

MANNITOL

This drug occasionally is used diagnostically to measure the glomerular filtration rate. It is filtered by the glomeruli but as much as 10% may be reabsorbed by the tubules, thereby introducing an unmeasurable variable. It is not secreted by the tubule cells.

Mannitol also is used as a diuretic (see Chapter 7), in the treatment of glaucoma (see Chapter 69), and, in 2.5% concentrations, as an irrigating fluid in transurethral prostate resection.

The doses used to test renal function rarely cause adverse reactions. When reactions do occur, they are usually mild and include thirst, nausea, vomiting, chills, slight dizziness, headache, hyponatremia, hypochloremia, and subjective sensations of chest constriction or pain. Mannitol should not be administered to patients with edema caused by metabolic abnormalities or cardiac failure or to patients who are not adequately hydrated or whose renal function is known to be severely impaired.

USUAL DOSAGE.—*Intravenous: Adults,* enough sterile solution is given slowly to maintain an adequate measurable plasma concentration. Generally, 80 ml of a 25% solution is diluted with 200 ml of sodium chloride injection and administered at a rate of 20 ml/minute.

PREPARATIONS.—*Injection:* Solution 25% in 50 ml containers. Drug marketed under generic name.

PHENOLSULFONPHTHALEIN (Phenol Red)

Upon injection, all but about 4% of phenolsulfonphthalein is bound to plasma proteins. Since only the free drug can be filtered by the glomeruli, the remaining drug, except for about 20% that is excreted by the liver into the bile, is secreted by the proximal convoluted tubules.

This dye also is used in cystoscopy when the ureters are being observed directly. The time of appearance gives an indication of relative kidney function. Normally, the dye appears at the ureteral orifice within two minutes after intravenous injection.

Another less frequently used procedure is the tubal patency test. If phenolsulfonphthalein is introduced into a patent fallopian tube and enters the peritoneal cavity, it appears quickly in the urine; if the fallopian tube is obstructed, the dye will not appear.

Phenolsulfonphthalein may be given either intramuscularly or intravenously, but the intravenous route is preferred because phenolsulfonphthalein is somewhat erratically absorbed from the intramuscular site.

USUAL DOSAGE.—*Intramuscular, Intravenous: Adults,* 6 mg in 1 ml of physiologic sodium chloride injection. The solution must be made isotonic and alkaline with sodium bicarbonate.

PREPARATIONS.—*Injection:* Solution 6 mg/ml in 1 ml containers. Drug marketed under generic name.

AGENTS USED TO TEST GASTRIC ACID SECRETION

Many chemical agents have the ability to increase gastric secretion. Histamine, betazole [Histalog], and gastrin are potent secretory stimulants. Caffeine and alcohol have been used, but they produce submaximal responses. In appropriate doses, betazole, an analogue of histamine, is capable of stimulating hydrochloric acid output equal to or greater than that produced by histamine and causes fewer untoward effects. Pentagastrin is a safe and potent stimulant, but is not available commercially in this country. The use of either histamine or betazole usually requires the collection of gastric juice by intubation. If it is preferable to determine gastric acidity without collecting a gastric acid sample, azuresin [Diagnex Blue], an ion-exchange resin, may be tried with or without prior stimulation with histamine or betazole, but the results are frequently inaccurate.

AZURESIN [Diagnex Blue]

Azuresin is an ion-exchange resin used to determine gastric acidity without intubation. After oral administration, the blue dye, azure-A, is displaced by hydrogen ions, absorbed by the small intestine, and excreted in the urine. Although this procedure does not furnish quantitative results, visual estimation of the dye content of a urine specimen collected two hours after administration and comparison with a previously prepared control will indicate the presence or absence of hydrochloric acid in the stomach. Unfortunately, false-negative results occur so frequently that this test is of little value. Also, false-positive results have been reported occasionally. When the test indicates the absence of acid, a gastric secretion stimulant such as caffeine, betazole, or even histamine may be used with the resin to further verify achlorhydria. If the presence or absence of gastric juice is critical to diagnosis, intubation should be performed after administration of betazole or histamine.

The drug produces negligible toxicity and tests employing other drugs can be carried out concomitantly. However, the incidence of inaccurate results may be increased in the presence of pyloric obstruction, severe hepatic or renal disease, impaired intestinal absorption, vomiting, marked dehydration, bladder obstruction, or total or subtotal gastrectomy.

The patient may continue to pass blue or green urine for a few days after the test; this phenomenon is of no consequence.

USUAL DOSAGE.—*Oral: Adults,* 2 g.

PREPARATIONS.—Diagnex Blue (Squibb). *Oral:* Granules in 2 g container with a color standard, two 250 mg tablets of caffeine and benzoate sodium, and 300 mg capsules of ascorbic acid (for preparation of a urine control).

BETAZOLE HYDROCHLORIDE [Histalog]

Betazole is an isomer of histamine with similar pharmacologic actions. However, it has a more pronounced effect on glandular secretion than histamine, its onset of action is slower, and its duration of action is more prolonged. Many of the untoward reactions observed with histamine are milder or absent (see the evaluation on Histamine Phosphate); therefore, the concomitant use of antihistamines is unnecessary. It is usually preferable to perform gastric analysis by intubation, but betazole can be combined with azuresin in the so-called tubeless method of acid detection (see the evaluation on Azuresin).

Flushing and hyperhidrosis are observed in about 20% of patients. The incidence of headache is lower than for histamine. Urticaria and syncope have been reported only rarely. Great caution must be exercised when giving betazole to patients with a history of previous hypersensitivity, asthma, heart disease, or recent gastrointestinal bleeding.

USUAL DOSAGE.—*Intramuscular, Subcutaneous: Adults,* 1.5 to 1.7 mg/kg of body weight or, alternatively, 100 mg for the average-sized adult. Up to 2 mg/kg may be administered.

PREPARATIONS.—Histalog (Lilly). *Injection:* Solution 50 mg/ml in 1 ml containers. Drug also marketed under generic name.

HISTAMINE PHOSPHATE

Histamine acts principally on the vascular system, smooth muscle, and exocrine glands. The latter action is the basis for its use in determining gastric acidity. When administered parenterally, histamine stimulates a copious, highly acidic gastric secretion.

Serious adverse effects can occur, especially if histamine is given in excessive dosage or too rapidly; these include asthma, severe headache, acute circulatory failure, shock, and death. Antihistamines given prior to testing generally will diminish or counteract most of the undesirable effects without interfering with stimulation of gastric acid secretion. Epinephrine must always be available to counteract the effects of histamine. The drug must never be used in elderly patients or in those with severe hypertension, hypotension, asthma, heart disease, an unstable vasomotor system, or recent upper gastrointestinal tract hemorrhage. When the drug is injected subcutaneously, care must be taken to avoid its introduction into a vein. Betazole, a histamine analogue, may be as useful as histamine and is less toxic (see the evaluation on Betazole Hydrochloride).

Other diagnostic applications of histamine include its local injection into the skin to produce a wheal in order to determine if blood vessels are normally permeable; this reaction occurs within two minutes. The red flare that surrounds the wheal also is significant in determining the integrity of local peripheral nerves, since this part of the response results from reflex action.

USUAL DOSAGE.—

Subcutaneous: Adults, for gastric analysis, 0.04 mg/kg of body weight. Although this drug can be administered by the intramuscular and intravenous routes, these routes should not be used.

Intradermal: Adults and children, to produce a wheal, 0.1 ml of a solution containing equal parts of 1:1,000 histamine phosphate and 2% procaine.

PREPARATIONS.—Histamine Phosphate, U.S.P. *Injection:* Solution 1:1,000 in 1 ml containers, 0.275 mg/ml in 1 and 20 ml containers, and 2.75 mg/ml in 1 ml containers. Drug marketed under generic name.

AGENTS USED TO DETERMINE BLOOD VOLUME, CIRCULATION TIME, CARDIAC OUTPUT, AND OTHER CARDIOVASCULAR MEASUREMENTS

The measurement of various indexes of vascular system function can be useful in determining the presence or extent of certain pathologic conditions. For example, an assessment of blood volume is a useful guide when treating shock, and the detection of increased cardiac output may help evaluate thyrotoxicosis, severe anemia, or other metabolic and circulatory abnormalities. Although none of the methods currently available is completely adequate, in experienced hands such procedures can yield valuable information when they are part of a thorough diagnostic evaluation.

EVANS BLUE

Evans blue, an azo dye, is used for the colorimetric estimation of blood (plasma) volume. It is tightly bound to plasma albumin and remains within the intravascular compartment. Mixing is usually complete within ten minutes. Plasma volume is estimated from the plasma concentration of dye attained following injection of a known quantity.

No adverse reactions have been reported. Very large doses stain sclerae and skin; this gradually disappears, but may take several weeks.

USUAL DOSAGE.—*Intravenous* (patient in fasting state): *Adults*, 25 mg (5 ml of a 0.5% aqueous solution diluted further with 1 to 2 ml of sodium chloride injection).

PREPARATIONS.—Evans Blue, U.S.P. *Injection:* Powder 25 and 100 g; solution 5 mg/ml in 5 ml containers. Drug marketed under generic name.

FLUORESCEIN SODIUM

Fluorescein is primarily used topically in the diagnosis of certain ophthalmologic abnormalities (see the evaluation in Chapter 72, Miscellaneous Ophthalmic Preparations). However, it also is used to determine circulation time and altered blood vessel permeability or patency, and for visualization of the gallbladder and bile ducts during surgery.

In the presence of brain abscess, hematoma, or neoplasm, the permeability of the blood-brain barrier is altered and the negatively charged dye will diffuse into the abnormal brain tissue. This response is helpful in locating superficial lesions and, if fluorescein tagged with radioactive iodine is used with a scanning technique, deeper lesions may be located.

Fluorescein tints the skin faintly yellow after intravenous injection, but this disappears within 24 hours. Nausea and, occasionally, vomiting occur when the dye is injected intravenously. Solutions for injection must be freshly prepared and sterilized.

USUAL DOSAGE.—

Intravenous: For circulation studies, *adults*, 3 to 4 ml of a 20% solution injected rapidly; *children*, 0.16 ml/kg of body weight of a 5% solution injected rapidly. For gallbladder and bile duct visualization, *adults*, 10 ml of a 5% solution four hours preceding surgery. The solution is preserved with 5% sodium bicarbonate.

Intra-arterial: Adults, 5 ml of a 20% solution.

Oral: Adults, 3 to 6 g in water; *children*, 1.5 to 2 g in water.

PREPARATIONS.—Fluorescein Sodium, U.S.P. *Injection:* Powder; solution 5% in 10 ml containers and 10% in 5 ml containers.

AVAILABLE TRADEMARK.—Fluorescite (Alcon). Drug also marketed under generic name as powder and 10% solution.

INDOCYANINE GREEN [Cardio-Green]

This drug is used for the continuous recording of dye dilution curves to determine cardiac output or circulation time. It frequently is used with oximetry, which does not require withdrawal of blood for determination of dye concentrations. A neglibible amount of drug accumulates in tissues, results are easily calculated, and repetition of measurements is readily possible.

See the evaluation on Indocyanine Green in the section of Agents Used for Liver Function Tests for a discussion of adverse effects and precautions.

USUAL DOSAGE.—*Intravenous: Adults*, 5 mg; *children*, 2.5 mg; *infants*, 1.25 mg. Doses are prepared in 1 ml of water for injection and flushed into the circulation with sodium chloride injection. For continuous infusion, 0.4 to 0.7 mg/minute (total dose not exceeding 2 mg/kg of body weight) can be given during a three-hour period.

PREPARATIONS.—Cardio-Green (Hynson, Westcott & Dunning). *Injection:* Powder 10 and 40 mg in disposable units and 25 and 50 mg with diluent.

AGENTS USED FOR CUTANEOUS IMMUNITY TESTS

Tests for susceptibility to infectious diseases can be of great value in preventive medicine. Mass immunization programs that prevent epidemics often are based on evidence that a population is susceptible to a given infection. Nevertheless, modern medicine relies less on these tests than formerly because routine, elective immunization as a preventive procedure is preferred when specific immunologic agents are available (see Chapter 89, Vaccines, Toxoids, and Serologic Agents). Diphtheria toxin (Schick test), mumps skin test antigen, scarlet fever streptococcus toxin (Dick test), and the tuberculins (Mantoux, von Pirquet, Rosenthal-Tine, and Vollmer tests) are some of the agents used most commonly today to test for susceptibility to infectious diseases.

DIAGNOSTIC DIPHTHERIA TOXIN
(Schick Test)

This sterile solution of the toxic growth products of *Corynebacterium diphtheriae* is used to determine immunity to diphtheria. The preparation must meet the prescribed federal standards for biologicals.

Rarely, a patient will have an allergic reaction to the test material.

USUAL DOSAGE.—*Intradermal: Adults and children*, 0.1 ml (representing 1/50 guinea pig minimal lethal dose of diphtheria toxin).

PREPARATIONS.—Diphtheria Toxin for Schick Test (Diluted) (Wyeth). *Injection:* 10 dose containers. Used without dilution.

There is no commercial source for diphtheria toxin control material. Directions for its preparation are given in the *United States Dispensatory*.

MUMPS SKIN TEST ANTIGEN

Mumps skin test antigen is a sterile suspension of killed mumps virus in sodium chloride injection preserved with 1:10,000 thimerosal. The virus is obtained from monkey tissues and fluids or embryonated chicken eggs which have been inoculated with mumps virus. This test is not as reliable as some of the other cutaneous immunity tests. The antigen is prepared and tested for safety according to federal specifications outlined by the Food and Drug Administration.

The virus obtained from a chicken source is contraindicated in patients with an allergy to chicken, chicken feathers, or eggs, and it must not be used if a sensitivity reaction occurs after use of the chick embryo test antigen.

USUAL DOSAGE.–*Intradermal: Adults and children,* 0.1 ml (20 complement fixing units).

PREPARATIONS.–*Injection:* Suspension 1 ml. Drug marketed under generic name.

PURIFIED PROTEIN DERIVATIVE OF TUBERCULIN(PPD)
OLD TUBERCULIN (OT)

These soluble growth products of *Mycobacterium tuberculosis* are purified and sterilized (old tuberculin) or are prepared in a special medium free of protein (purified protein derivative) for use in skin sensitivity tests. These agents determine sensitivity to tubercle bacillus protein. Of the two preparations, the purified derivative is usually preferred because its potency is more uniform than that of old tuberculin.

All products marketed in the United States must meet the standards of the United States Public Health Act. Doses can be stated in micrograms, milliliters, or international units (IU). There are both United States Standard strengths and International Standards against which either the PPD or OT can be calibrated.

USUAL DOSAGE.–

Intradermal (Mantoux): *Adults and children,* PPD is used. Four dose sizes are available. The first test dose contains 0.02 μg/0.1 ml (1 IU) and is used when close contact with known cases of tuberculosis has occurred, or when great susceptibility to tuberculosis is anticipated. If a negative reaction occurs, the second test dose of 5 μg/0.1 ml (250 IU) can be used. Alternatively, one of the intermediate test doses of 0.1 μg/0.1 ml (5 IU) or 0.2 μg/0.1 ml (10 IU) may be tried first, particularly if a fairly high level of susceptibility is expected and fine calibration is not necessary.

Cutaneous Scarification (von Pirquet): *Adults and children,* OT is used. One drop of the undiluted preparation equal to one drop of undiluted OT reference standard is applied. One drop of a 1:100 or 1:10,000 dilution is then applied to a second scratch site. Sterile sodium chloride solution is the control placed on a third scratch site.

Intradermal (Rosenthal-Tine): *Adults and children,* either PPD or OT can be used. Four punctures are made by a special disposable device that carries on its tines 50 μg of U.S. Standard OT (5 IU) or 0.1 μg of U.S. Standard PPD (5 IU).

Topical (Vollmer): *Adults and children,* OT is used. Each patch unit applied to the skin contains 0.0001 ml (0.1 mg) of U.S. Standard OT.

PREPARATIONS.–Purified Protein Derivative of Tuberculin, U.S.P.; Old Tuberculin, U.S.P. Drugs marketed under generic name.

SCARLET FEVER STREPTOCOCCUS TOXIN
(Dick Test)

This preparation is a refined, highly purified, stabilized, preserved, and diluted toxin derived from virulent hemolytic streptococci. It is made heat-labile by precipitation with alcohol. The toxin is used to detect susceptibility to scarlet fever, but it is not as reliable for this purpose as the Schick test is for detecting susceptibility to diphtheria.

USUAL DOSAGE.–*Intradermal: Adults and children,* 0.1 ml.

PREPARATIONS.–*Injection:* Solution in 0.5 and 5 ml containers. Drug marketed under generic name.

AGENTS USED AS BIOLOGICAL TEST ALLERGENS OR ANTIGENS (OTHER THAN IMMUNOLOGIC AGENTS)

Solutions containing a test allergen or antigen can be helpful in detecting either the nature of a substance causing an allergic reaction or the presence of an infection for which the test material is a specific antigen. Most testing procedures use the intradermal route of administration and the test site is read at some finite time following injection. The occurrence of erythema is always required as evidence of a positive reaction, and frequently an area of induration or even vesiculation is necessary. However, no test by itself is completely diagnostic; a clinical history and possibly other tests will be needed before a conclusion can be drawn. The incidence of systemic toxicity with these test solutions is low.

ALLERGENS

Allergens are substances that evoke various cutaneous, respiratory, or systemic allergic responses (ie, rhinitis, asthma, gastrointestinal distress, urticaria, or, rarely, anaphylactic reaction). These substances may be plant pollens, fungi, animal dander, house dust, (including mites), drugs, chemicals, foods, or a host of other commonly encountered materials.

Several suspected allergens may be screened at the same time using the dermal test technique. A drop of the prepared allergen is applied to the skin which previously has been cleansed with alcohol or ether. The skin under the drop is lightly abraded by one of several common procedures, the simplest of which is to scratch the surface lightly with the tip of a sterile hypodermic needle. Alternatively, 0.05 ml of the allergen preparation can be injected intracutaneously to form a small wheal.

When diagnostic skin tests are used, it is essential to have equipment and drugs available to counteract severe reactions quickly. Fortunately, these reactions are not common. Epinephrine hydrochloride (0.3 to 0.5 ml of a 1:1,000 solution given intramuscularly or 0.5 ml/minute of a 1:10,000 solution given intravenously) is the therapy of choice in an emergency; the use of aminophylline and antihistamines also may be indicated. In addition, many physicians have mechanical devices available for artificial respiration.

Most test allergen suppliers have 500 or more different preparations available, all made according to Food and Drug Administration specifications. These manufacturers supply various test kits containing several of the more common allergens. Less common preparations can be ordered separately, and some manufacturers will even prepare special test materials on request.

BLASTOMYCIN

This preparation is the sterilized, concentrated, soluble growth products of *Blastomyces dermatitidis*. It contains preservatives and an FDA-certified red dye. Blastomycin is used as a dermal indicator for North American blastomycosis, a fungal infection that affects the skin and viscera. Injection of an excessive amount of the extract can cause severe induration and local necrosis.

USUAL DOSAGE.—*Intracutaneous: Adults and children*, 0.1 ml of a 1:100 dilution of the commercially available concentrate.

PREPARATIONS.—*Injection:* Concentrate 0.01 ml supplied with 1 ml of sterile, buffered diluent. Drug marketed under generic name.

COCCIDIOIDIN

Coccidioidin is prepared from broth culture filtrates of *Coccidioides immitis* and is used to help diagnose coccidioidomycosis.

USUAL DOSAGE.—*Intradermal: Adults and children*, 0.1 ml of a 1:1,000 or 1:100 dilution.

PREPARATIONS.—*Injection:* Solution 1:10 and 1:100 in 1 ml containers. Drug marketed under generic name.

HISTOPLASMIN

Histoplasmin contains the concentrated, sterilized, soluble growth products obtained from *Histoplasma capsulatum* in the mycelial phase and an FDA-certified red dye. The preparation is used as a dermal indicator for the diagnosis of histoplasmosis and the differential diagnosis of histoplasmosis from other fungal or bacterial infections and other pulmonary disease.

This material should be injected only intradermally. The amount injected should not be larger than the recommended dose to avoid local necrosis and ulceration.

USUAL DOSAGE.—*Intradermal: Adults and children*, 0.1 ml of a 1:100 dilution prepared by mixing the antigen solution with the diluent provided.

PREPARATIONS.—*Injection:* Solution 0.01 ml in 1 ml containers supplied with 1 ml of diluent. Drug marketed under generic name.

TRICHINELLA EXTRACT

This buffered, phenolic, sodium chloride solution contains a soluble antigen prepared from killed, washed, defatted, and powdered larvae of *Trichinella spiralis*. It is used as a dermal indicator for the diagnosis of trichinosis. There is no official standard of potency, but the solution must meet the prescribed federal standards for biologicals. The solution vehicle is used as a control.

Although no untoward effects from the use of this test have been reported, the possibility of allergic reactions must not be discounted.

USUAL DOSAGE.—*Intradermal: Adults and children*, 0.1 ml of test solution and of control solution is injected into opposite forearms.

PREPARATIONS.—*Injection:* Solution in sodium chloride injection in 1 ml container with appropriate sodium chloride solution control. Drug marketed under generic name.

AGENTS USED FOR PITUITARY FUNCTION TESTS

METYRAPONE [Metopirone]
METYRAPONE TARTRATE [Metopirone Ditartrate]

Metyrapone is used to test pituitary function, particularly to detect partial hypopituitarism. The drug interferes with steroidogenesis in the adrenal cortex, thereby decreasing the production of cortisol, corticosterone, and aldosterone. The depressed production of cortisol causes a greatly increased secretion of corticotropin in normal individuals, but the response is reduced in patients with hypopituitarism or limited pituitary reserve.

In rare instances, intravenous administration of metyrapone has produced thrombophlebitis. Less serious effects that can occur after oral administration include nausea, abdominal discomfort, dizziness, vertigo, headache, and drowsiness. Nausea can be minimized by giving the drug with a small quantity of milk or food. Metyrapone is contraindicated in patients with chronic adrenocortical insufficiency. Since several drugs or pathologic conditions modify the results of the test, whenever possible the test should be performed in patients receiving no other medication.

USUAL DOSAGE.—

Metyrapone:

Oral: Adults, 750 mg every four hours for six doses; *children,* 15 mg/kg of body weight every four hours for six doses. The 24-hour urine collection should begin after the last dose.

Metyrapone Tartrate:

Intravenous: Adults and children, 30 mg/kg of body weight in 1,000 ml of sodium chloride injection infused over a four-hour period beginning between 8 and 10 a.m. The 24-hour urine collection should begin at the start of the test.

PREPARATIONS.—

Metopirone (Ciba). *Oral:* Tablets 250 mg.

Metopirone [ditartrate] (Ciba). *Injection:* Solution 100 mg/ml in 10 ml containers.

AGENTS USED TO DETECT PHEOCHROMOCYTOMA

Actively secreting chromaffin cell tumors elaborate either norepinephrine or a mixture of epinephrine and norepinephrine. These tumors usually cause episodes of either paroxysmal or fluctuating hypertension, although sustained hypertension can occur.

Measuring the urinary excretion of catecholamines and their metabolites is now the established method for diagnosis of pheochromocytoma. Screening methods for determining the urinary excretion of 4-hydroxy-3-methoxymandelic acid or the metanephrines, normetanephrine and metanephrine, are readily available in most laboratories. Pharmacologic tests are used only rarely today because they are less accurate, require more time to perform, and are potentially hazardous. The *pharmacologic test of choice* in the patient with sustained hypertension is the phentolamine test. In normotensive patients with a history of paroxysmal attacks, the histamine test may be helpful in suggesting the diagnosis. However, the diagnosis must be confirmed in patients with positive pharmacologic test results by demonstration of the increased urinary excretion of norepinephrine and epinephrine or their metabolites before exploratory surgery is performed.

Histamine can produce profound hypertension and phentolamine profound hypotension in the presence of pheochromocytoma. Accordingly, these agents must be used with great caution and emergency resuscitative and antidotal measures must be readily available.

AGENT USED TO DETECT AMYLOID DISEASE

CONGO RED

Although this dye has had various medical and diagnostic uses in the past, it is used currently only in the detection of amyloidosis, although this use is of questionable value. As much as 80% (average 60%) of an injected dose can be retained by the abnormal amyloid deposit.

Congo red must be injected slowly to prevent thrombosis. Except for rare idiosyncratic reactions that have sometimes caused death, congo red appears to be free of toxic effects. Water for injection should be used as the carrier for the dye, since congo red may flocculate in sodium chloride injection.

USUAL DOSAGE.—*Intravenous: Adults and children,* 100 to 200 mg (10 to 20 ml of a 1% solution) given slowly.

PREPARATIONS.—Congo Red. *Injection:* Solution 1% in 10 ml containers. Drug marketed under generic name.

RADIOPHARMACEUTICALS

Radioactive isotopes (radionuclides) are used in clinical medicine almost exclusively for diagnostic purposes. A few nuclides (eg, radioactive gold, radioactive iodine) can serve both as diagnostic aids and as therapeutic agents, depending upon the dosages used. The isotopes used most commonly as diagnostic aids include radioactive chromium (sodium chromate Cr 51), cobalt (cyanocobalamin Co 57, cyanocobalamin Co 60), iodine (sodium iodide I 125, sodium iodide I 131, iodohippurate sodium I 131, iodinated I 125 serum albumin, iodinated I 131 serum albumin, rose bengal sodium I 131, thyroxine I 125, thyroxine I 131, liothyronine I 131), iron (ferrous citrate Fe 59), mercury (chlormerodrin Hg 197, chlormerodrin Hg 203), phosphorus (sodium phosphate P 32), and technetium (sodium pertechnetate Tc 99m, technetium Tc 99m sulfur colloid).

All the radiopharmaceuticals used in nuclear medicine are radioactive or contain a radioactive label, essentially do not achieve a pharmacologic effect in the usual sense, and are administered systemically. Because of these characteristics, the production, distribution, and medical uses of radionuclides are more closely supervised than any other group of medicinal agents with the exception, perhaps, of the narcotics. They are packaged in special, distinctive containers, are labeled with internationally recognized symbols of radioactivity, and are available only to specially trained and government-licensed personnel in hospitals, clinics, and laboratories. At the present time, licenses for the use of radioactive substances are obtained directly from the Atomic Energy Commission (AEC). A few states (agreement states) have been granted permission by the AEC to regulate the medical uses of isotopes within their borders, but the same general federal rules and regulations apply.

Exact dosages of radioactive agents used as diagnostic aids cannot be stated unequivocally. Dosages are stated in units of radioactivity, such as millicuries (mCi) or microcuries (μCi), rather than in measures of weight or volume. For diagnostic purposes, the quantity of radiation is the most important consideration when using these drugs; the quantity of drug usually is so small that it is insignificant. For example, the usual dose of ^{131}I for a thyroid-uptake test or scan contains approximately 0.0002 μg of elemental iodine; in contrast, the average person consumes 150 to 200 μg of iodine each day in his diet, and the material for a routine intravenous pyelogram may contain between 5 and 10 g of iodine. Therefore, it is the rate of physical decay of the isotope (physical half-life) and the rate of excretion (biological half-life) that are used to determine acceptable dosage levels. If the isotope decays rapidly (eg, technetium 99m, physical half-life six hours), millicurie amounts may be given to patients with little danger of serious radiation exposure. On the other hand, agents with relatively long physical and biological half-lives (eg, strontium 85, physical half-life 64 days) must be given in microcurie amounts and their use must be limited to serious medical problems in which the radiation risk is less than the possible benefit derived from using the isotope. For practical purposes, a compound is considered to have lost all of its radioactivity after ten half-lives.

Diagnostic uses of radiopharmaceuticals can be divided into either function (tracer) or imaging studies. Sometimes a single dose of isotope will suffice for both types of study (eg, a thyroid-uptake and scan can be done with the same dose of ^{131}I).

Imaging (scintiphoto) techniques represent a rapidly developing area of nuclear medicine in which camera-type imaging devices have contributed significantly. Their potential in the medical application of radioactive material is just beginning to be explored. The older rectilinear scanning techniques are still very much a part of the imaging field, however, and will be for some time to come.

Adverse Reactions and Precautions

Because of the small amounts of isotope generally used for diagnostic testing, allergic reactions are virtually unknown with the exception that, rarely, individuals are allergic to iodine or mercury and anaphylactic reactions have occurred with these compounds. Nevertheless, the small amount of radioactive elemental iodine used for testing usually can be given safely to patients with known iodine sensitivity.

Some drugs, biological tests, hospital procedures, or diseases can interfere with the results of isotope studies. Similarly, special procedures may have to be used with a particular test in order to make its findings valid or to protect a specific organ. For example, when radioactive iodine compounds are being used and the thyroid is not the organ being tested, it sometimes is necessary to protect the thyroid by administering strong iodine (Lugol's) solution orally prior to use of the diagnostic iodine preparation. Sufficient iodine is present in Lugol's solution to cause a reaction in an iodine-sensitive individual. Consequently, possible sensitivity to iodine must be determined before performing the test.

There are no precautions necessary to protect medical personnel from radiation during a properly performed *diagnostic* procedure unless radiation levels are unusually high (eg, 20 millicuries of Tc 99m sometimes used for brain scan work). Similarly, the levels of radiation received by the patient are generally very low, usually less than would be received from a routine x-ray examination. Radioactivity present in stool and urine following diagnostic procedures is negligible and these samples do not require special handling. In contrast, most *therapeutic* uses of radioisotopes do require special precautions.

Sometimes precautions also must be taken to ensure that radiation levels are kept within safe limits when diagnostic tests are performed. Unlike most pharmaceuticals, the concentration stated on the label cannot be accepted since, despite rather careful steps in their production, a number of radiopharmaceuticals contain levels of radioactivity significantly different from the specified amount because of radioactive decay since they were manufactured; therefore, activity of radiopharmaceuticals must be measured immediately prior to administration.

Misreading the units is another obvious source of error which has occurred in a few instances. Mistaking mCi for μCi leads to a thousandfold difference in dosage. For this reason, high-activity radioactive substances that may be used for therapy should *never* be stored in the same location as the same substance of lower radioactivity used for diagnosis.

Other precautions involve the proper performance and interpretation of the diagnostic procedure. Because of gamma ray emissions of similar energies, or because of equipment limitations in the laboratory performing the test, it may be important to administer radiopharmaceuticals in a certain sequence when more than one diagnostic procedure involving isotopes is contemplated. As a general rule, little or no preparation of the patient is required for most radioisotopic procedures.

Chapter 78

ANTISPASMODICS

Antispasmodics are used primarily to reduce the frequency and force of gastrointestinal smooth muscle contractions which, when excessive, often cause intense pain. Although smooth muscle spasm can be relieved by drugs that act at a number of different sites, those most commonly used are anticholinergic agents which act wholly or partly by blocking the action of acetylcholine at postganglionic parasympathetic sites.

Various parasympathetically innervated organs demonstrate different sensitivities to anticholinergic drugs, depending upon the dose. Small doses inhibit the production of saliva, sweat, and bronchial secretions. Slightly larger doses reduce parasympathetic input to the heart and eye; this causes tachycardia, loss of visual accommodation, and mydriasis. Moderate doses block the actions of cholinergic nerves supplying the bladder and gut so that urination is impeded and peristalsis is reduced. Still larger doses diminish gastric secretion. Because of the nonspecificity of these anticholinergic actions, an effective antispasmodic and antisecretory dose of any of these drugs also may be expected to produce side effects (eg, dryness of the mouth, blurred vision, constipation, dysuria).

Anticholinergic antispasmodics, which include the naturally occurring belladonna alkaloids, their derivatives, and numerous synthetic substitutes, are frequently used as adjuncts in the management of peptic ulcer. When adequate doses are administered, these drugs effectively relieve pain by inhibiting motility; their antisecretory effects also may contribute to relief of pain. However, there is no conclusive evidence that they facilitate healing of the ulcer or prevent complications or recurrences. Antispasmodics also are used as adjuncts in the treatment of functional bowel disorders (eg, irritable colon), mild dysentery, diverticulitis, and pancreatitis. They are of little or no value in pylorospasm, diaphragmatic hernia, asymptomatic diverticulosis, biliary dyskinesia, and dysmenorrhea. Opinion is divided on their usefulness in regional enteritis and ulcerative colitis.

Antispasmodics are generally administered orally before meals and at bedtime; long-acting and timed-release preparations are given less frequently. Some antispasmodics may be used parenterally to treat acute symptoms.

Belladonna Drugs: These drugs are available as the naturally occurring alkaloids of belladonna, as the individual active agents, as mixtures of the individual alkaloids, and as quaternary ammonium derivatives of the alkaloids. The naturally occurring anticholinergic alkaloids of belladonna are hyoscyamine and scopolamine (hyoscine). Hyoscyamine, the main active alkaloid, racemizes to atropine on extraction but its antimuscarinic activity is due primarily to the *l*-isomer. There are no qualitative differences in the antimuscarinic effects of atropine and scopolamine. Atropine, the prototype of this group, antagonizes the effect of acetylcholine at peripheral neuroeffector sites. It does not block transmission at the neuromuscular junction of skeletal muscle and has no effect on transmission at autonomic ganglia except when administered in toxic doses. It is readily absorbed from the gastrointestinal tract and readily crosses the blood-brain barrier, where large doses stimulate (presumably by leaving the adrenergic system unopposed) and toxic doses depress the central nervous system.

Atropine reduces both the motility and secretory activity of the gastrointestinal system. It reduces the tone of the ureter and urinary bladder and has a slight relaxant action on the bile ducts and gallbladder. It has little effect on the myometrium. Atropine antagonizes the effects of cholinergic drugs on the gastrointestinal system, but is less effective in counteracting the action of these drugs on the urinary bladder.

Synthetic Anticholinergic Agents: The synthetic anticholinergic agents (see Table 1) are quaternary ammonium compounds, with the exception of oxyphencyclimine [Daricon, Vio-Thene], which is a tertiary amine; thus the latter's actions are similar to those of atropine. The natural alkaloids of belladonna are also tertiary amines, but several quaternary ammonium derivatives are also available. The quaternary ammonium compounds differ from atropine in several important respects: (1) They are less readily absorbed when given orally and there is considerable individual variability in response. (2) They rarely exert an effect on the central nervous system because they do not readily cross the blood-brain barrier. (3) Their duration of action is longer than that of the belladonna alkaloids. (4) In addition to their antimuscarinic effects, these drugs may interfere with transmission in autonomic ganglia, an action that both contributes to the therapeutic effect and may cause such reactions as orthostatic hypotension and impotence. (5) At toxic dose levels they can produce neuromuscular blockade which, in turn, may cause respiratory arrest. Some differences exist in the ratios of ganglionic blocking effect to antimuscarinic effect. However, most of the pharmacologic action of the drugs at usual doses is attributed to the antimuscarinic effect.

There appears to be little clinical evidence that certain quaternary ammonium compounds have selective anticholinergic actions. Clinically effective doses always evoke adverse effects, and such doses may exceed those usually recommended by manufacturers.

Other Synthetic Antispasmodics: A number of synthetic antispasmodics (see Table 2) relax smooth muscle primarily by exerting a nonspecific direct action on muscle fiber. These agents have little or no antimuscarinic activity and exert little effect on gastric secretion; they are most useful in the treatment of gastrointestinal disorders characterized by hypermotility and spasm.

Adverse Reactions and Precautions

Most untoward effects associated with the use of anticholinergic agents are manifestations of their pharmacologic actions: dryness of the mouth, anhidrosis, mydriasis, cycloplegia, tachycardia, constipation, and dysuria may be expected to appear after administration of full therapeutic doses of these drugs. Dermatologic reactions also may occur. Tolerance develops to many of these adverse reactions with prolonged administration, but this may be accompanied by a decrease in therapeutic effectiveness. Toxic doses may produce extreme dryness of the mouth accompanied by a burning sensation, dysphagia, thirst, marked photophobia, flushing of the skin, fever, leukocytosis, rash, nausea, vomiting, and hypertension.

Large doses of the belladonna drugs or other nonquaternary agents may produce signs of central nervous system stimulation (eg, restlessness, tremor, irritability, delirium, hallucinations). Stimulation may be followed by depression and death from medullary paralysis. Children are more susceptible to the toxic effects of these drugs than adults.

Large doses of the quaternary ammonium compounds may cause ganglionic blockade, as evidenced by orthostatic hypotension and impotence, and toxic doses may cause respiratory arrest as a result of neuromuscular blockade. Since quaternary ammonium compounds do not readily cross the blood-brain barrier, central nervous system effects occur only rarely.

Anticholinergic antispasmodics should be used with caution in patients with prostatic hypertrophy, pyloric obstruction, obstruction of the bladder neck, and cardiospasm. Because of their mydriatic effect, the anticholinergic drugs may precipitate an attack of acute glaucoma in patients predisposed to angle-closure. This has occurred occasionally after parenteral administration of these agents but has been reported only rarely after oral use. Anticholinergic drugs can be given safely to patients with open-angle glaucoma who are being treated with miotics. Antacids may interfere with absorption and should not be given simultaneously with anticholinergics.

Reactions observed with the other synthetic antispasmodics in this group are related to their direct action on smooth muscle or, occasionally, to hypersensitivity. Untoward effects reported with some of these drugs include drowsiness, euphoria, dizziness, asthenia, headache, nausea, constipation, diarrhea, hypotension, and rash.

BELLADONNA DRUGS

BELLADONNA EXTRACT

BELLADONNA LEAF
BELLADONNA LEAF FLUIDEXTRACT
BELLADONNA TINCTURE

For actions, indications, and adverse reactions, see the Introductory Statement.

USUAL DOSAGE.—

Belladonna Extract. *Oral: Adults*, 15 mg.

Belladonna Leaf. *Oral: Adults*, 30 to 200 mg.

Belladonna Leaf Fluidextract. *Oral: Adults*, 0.06 ml.

Belladonna Tincture. *Oral: Adults*, 0.6 ml three times daily; *children*, 0.1 ml/kg daily in three or four divided doses.

PREPARATIONS.—

Belladonna Extract, N.F. *Oral:* Tablets 15 mg.

Belladonna Leaf, U.S.P. and Belladonna Leaf Fluidextract, N.F. No single-entity pharmaceutical dosage forms available; compounding necessary for prescription.

Belladonna Tincture, U.S.P. *Oral:* Tincture in 4 oz, pint, and gallon containers.

All forms marketed under generic name.

Mixtures of Belladonna Alkaloids

BELLAFOLINE
DONNA
PRYDON

For actions, indications, and adverse reactions, see the Introductory Statement.

USUAL DOSAGE.—

Bellafoline (total levorotatory alkaloids of belladonna as maleates).

Oral: Adults, 1 or 2 tablets every four to six hours; *children*, 1/2 to 1 tablet every four to six hours.

Subcutaneous: Adults, 0.5 to 1 ml once or twice daily.

Donna. *Oral: Adults*, 1 tablet every 10 to 12 hours.

Prydon. *Oral: Adults*, 1 tablet every 12 hours.

PREPARATIONS.—

Bellafoline (Sandoz).

Oral: Tablets 0.25 mg.

Injection: Solution 0.5 mg/ml in 1 ml containers.

Donna (Robins). *Oral:* Each timed-release tablet contains hyoscyamine sulfate 0.311 mg, atropine sulfate 0.0582 mg, and scopolamine hydrobromide 0.0195 mg.

Prydon (Smith Kline & French). *Oral:* Each timed-release tablet contains belladonna alkaloids 0.4 or 0.8 mg, hyoscyamine sulfate 0.305 mg, atropine sulfate 0.060 mg, and scopolamine hydrobromide 0.35 mg.

MIXTURES

Many widely promoted mixtures contain antispasmodics in combination with other drugs such as barbiturates, antianxiety agents, and phenothiazines, or with antacids. If compatible agents are present in one dosage form in a ratio that satisfies the needs of an individual, use of the preparation may be convenient. However, these fixed-ratio products present certain problems.

Antispasmodics require greater individualization of dosage than most drugs. If the necessary adjustment of dosage of one component of a combination is made, the patient receives an inappropriate dosage of the other component since the dosage adjustments of the ingredients seldom parallel each other.

While sedatives may be appropriate for relieving the anxiety that is a component of many gastrointestinal disorders, a phenothiazine would rarely be the correct choice, because phenothiazines are primarily *antipsychotic* agents. Some antacids (eg, aluminum hydroxide) and charcoal present in other mixtures may interfere with the absorption of the antispasmodics.

For these reasons, the routine use of these mixtures is not advisable; they are listed only to provide information.

Antrenyl-Phenobarbital (Ciba): Each tablet contains oxyphenonium bromide 5 mg and phenobarbital 15 mg.

Banthine W/Phenobarbital (Searle): Each tablet contains methantheline bromide 50 mg and phenobarbital 15 mg.

Barbidonna (Mallinckrodt): Each tablet or 3.7 ml of elixir contains hyoscyamine sulfate 0.1286 mg, atropine sulfate 0.025 mg, scopolamine hydrobromide 0.0074 mg, and phenobarbital 16.2 mg; each No. 2 tablet contains hyoscyamine sulfate 0.1286 mg, atropine sulfate 0.025 mg, scopolamine hydrobromide 0.0074 mg, and phenobarbital 32.4 mg.

Bar-Don (Warren-Teed): Each tablet or 5 ml of elixir contains hyoscyamine hydrobromide 0.1 mg, scopolamine hydrobromide 0.007 mg, atropine sulfate 0.02 mg, and phenobarbital 16.67 mg.

Belap (Lemmon): Each tablet contains belladonna extract 8.1 mg; and phenobarbital 8.1, 16.2, or 32.4 mg; each timed-release tablet contains homatropine methylbromide 7.5 mg and amobarbital 50 mg.

TABLE 1—ANTICHOLINERGIC ANTISPASMODICS

Drug	Chemical Structure
Belladonna Alkaloids:	
Atropine Sulfate, U.S.P.	
Hyoscyamine Cystospaz (Alcon)	
Hyoscyamine Hydrobromide, N.F.	
Hyoscyamine Sulfate, N.F. Levsin (Kremers-Urban)	
Quaternary Ammonium Derivatives of Belladonna Alkaloids:	
Homatropine Methylbromide Homapin (Mission) Malcotran (Pennwalt) Mesopin (Endo) Novatrin (Ayerst) Drug also marketed under generic name.	
Methscopolamine Bromide Pamine Bromide (Upjohn) Drug also marketed under the name Scopolamine Methylbromide.	
Methylatropine Nitrate Metropine (Pennwalt) Drug also marketed under the name Atropine Methylnitrate.	
Synthetic Substitutes:	
Anisotropine Methylbromide Valpin (Endo)	
Diphemanil Methylsulfate Prantal Methylsulfate (Schering)	

Usual Dosage	Preparations
Oral: Adults, 0.3 to 1.2 mg every 4 to 6 hours. *Subcutaneous: Adults,* 0.5 mg every 4 to 6 hours. *Children,* 0.01 mg/kg every 4 to 6 hours.	Tablets 0.3, 0.4, and 0.6 mg Solution (for injection) 0.3, 0.4, 0.5, 0.6 and 1.2 mg/ml in 1, 20, and 30 ml containers Tablets (hypodermic) 0.3, 0.4, and 0.6 mg
Oral: Adults, 0.25 to 0.5 mg 3 times daily. *Children,* 0.125 to 0.25 mg 3 times daily.	Tablets 0.15 mg
Oral, Intramsucular, Subcutaneous, Intravenous: Adults, 0.25 mg every 4 to 6 hours.	No single-entity pharmaceutical dosage form available; compounding necessary for prescription
Oral: Adults, 0.125 to 0.25 mg every 4 to 6 hours. *Children 2 to 10 years,* one-half above dosage range; *children under 2 years,* one-fourth above dosage range. *Intramuscular, Subcutaneous, Intravenous: Adults,* 0.25 to 0.5 mg every 6 hours. When symptoms are controlled, oral medication is substituted. *Children,* dosage not established.	Elixir 0.125 mg/5 ml Tablets 0.125 and 0.25 mg Tablets (timed-release [Levsinex]) 0.375 mg Solution (for injection) 0.25 mg/ml in 1, 10, and 30 ml containers
Oral: Adults, 2.5 to 10 mg 4 times daily. *Children,* 3 to 6 mg 4 times daily (chewable tablets). *Infants,* for colic, 1 mg 4 times daily (elixir).	Homapin: Tablets 5 and 10 mg Malcotran: Tablets 10 mg Mesopin: Elixir 5 mg/5 ml; tablets 5 mg Novatrin: Tablets 5 mg
Oral: Adults, 2.5 to 5 mg 4 times daily. *Children,* 0.2 mg/kg daily in 4 doses. *Intramuscular, Subcutaneous: Adults,* 0.25 to 1 mg every 6 to 8 hours until acute symptoms are controlled and patient can take oral medication. *Children,* dosage not established.	Tablets 2.5 mg Solution (for injection) 1 mg/ml in 1 ml containers
Oral: Adults, 1 to 2 mg every 4 to 6 hours. *Infants and children under 5 years,* 0.25 to 0.5 mg every 3 hours. *Children over 5 years,* 0.5 to 1 mg every 3 hours.	Tablets 1 mg
Oral: Adults, 10 mg 3 or 4 times daily. *Children* dosage not established.	Elixir 10 mg/5 ml Tablets 10 mg
Oral: Adults, initially, 100 mg every 4 to 6 hours; maintenance dose 50 to 100 mg every 4 to 6 hours; timed-release preparation, 100 or 200 mg every 8 hours. *Children,* dosage not established.	Tablets 100 mg Tablets (timed-release) 100 mg

TABLE 1—ANTICHOLINERGIC ANTISPASMODICS (Cont'd.)

Drug	Chemical Structure
Glycopyrrolate Robinul (Robins)	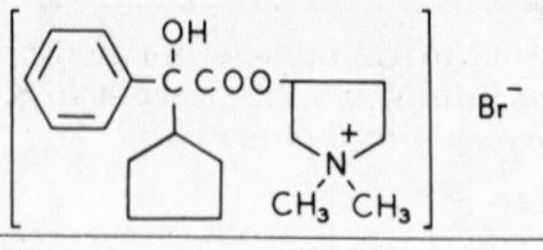
Hexocyclium Methylsulfate Tral (Abbott)	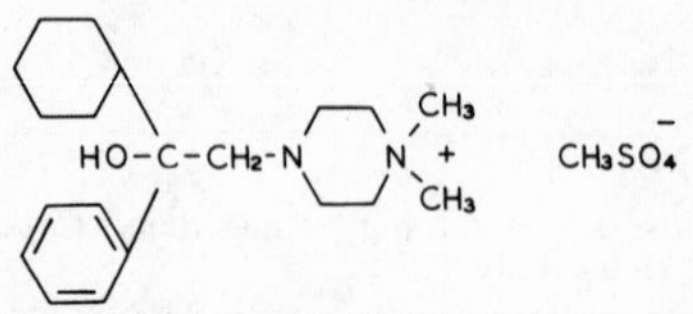
Isopropamide Iodide Darbid (Smith Kline & French)	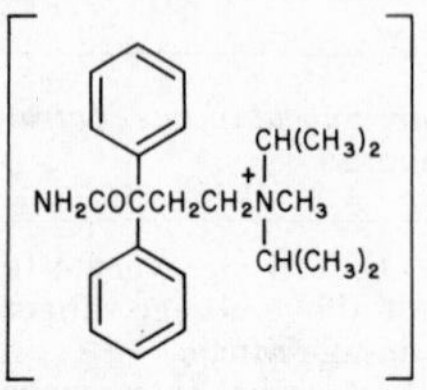
Mepenzolate Bromide Cantil (Lakeside)	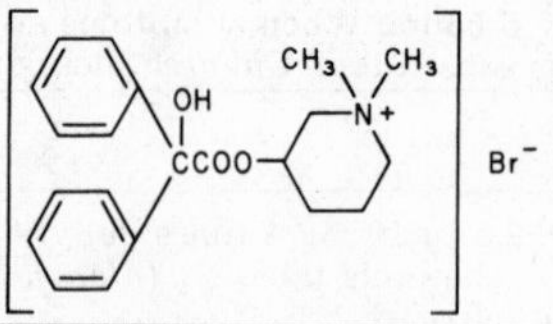
Methantheline Bromide Banthine (Searle)	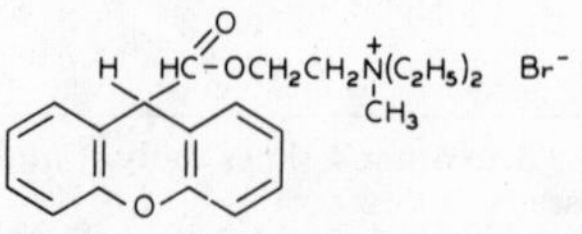
Oxyphencyclimine Hydrochloride* Daricon (Beecham-Massengill) Vio-Thene (Rowell)	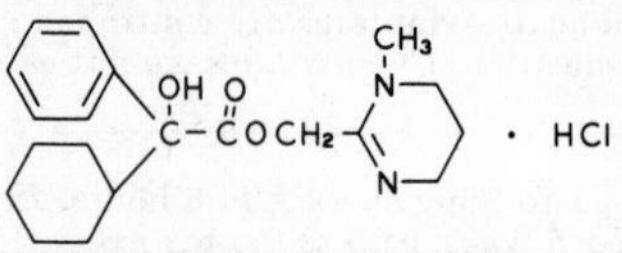
Oxyphenonium Bromide Antrenyl Bromide (Ciba)	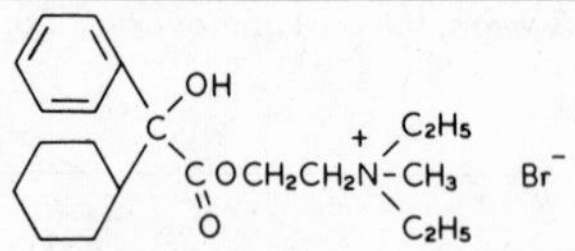
Pentapiperium Methylsulfate Quilene (Warner-Chilcott)	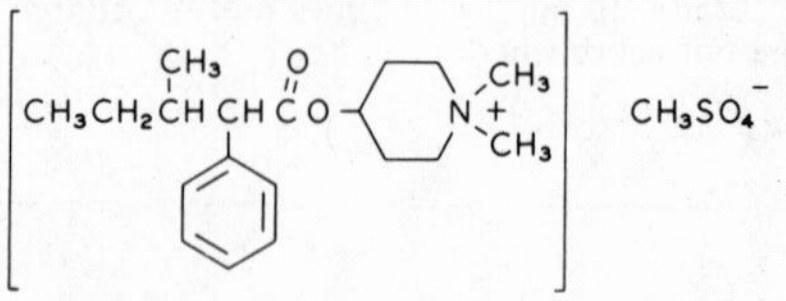
Pipenzolate Bromide Piptal (Lakeside)	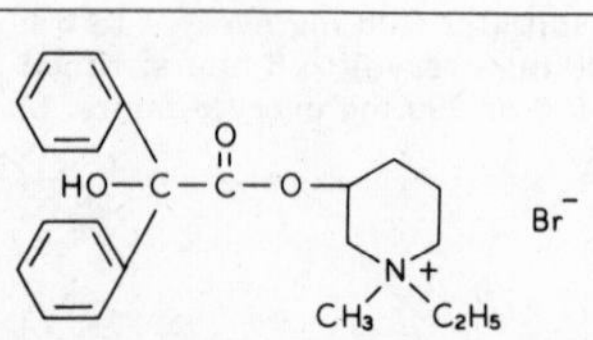

*Tertiary amine. All others are quaternary ammonium compounds.

Usual Dosage	Preparations
Oral: Adults, initially, 1 or 2 mg 3 times daily; maintenance dose, 1 mg 2 times daily. *Children*, dosage not established. *Intramuscular, Intravenous, Subcutaneous: Adults*, 0.1 or 0.2 mg at 4-hour intervals 3 or 4 times daily. *Children*, dosage not established.	Tablets 1 and 2 mg Solution (for injection) 0.2 mg/ml in 1 and 5 ml containers
Oral: Adults, initially, 25 mg 4 times daily. Timed-release tablet, 50 mg 2 times daily; for nocturnal relief, 75 mg at bedtime. Maintenance dosage is adjusted to meet individual needs.	Tablets 25 mg Tablets (timed-release) 50 and 75 mg
Oral: Adults, 5 mg every 12 hours.	Tablets 5 mg
Oral: Adults, 25 mg 4 times daily. Dosage increased gradually to 50 mg if necessary.	Liquid 25 mg/5 ml Tablets 25 mg
Oral: Adults, intially, 50 to 100 mg every 6 hours; dose reduced to 25 mg for patients who cannot tolerate larger doses. Maintenance dose, generally one-half initial dose. *Children*, 6 mg/kg daily in 4 doses. *Intramuscular: Adults*, 50 mg every 6 hours. *Children*, 3 mg/kg in 4 doses.	Tablets 50 mg Powder (for injection) 50 mg
Oral: Adults, 10 mg twice daily; dose gradually increased to 50 mg if untoward effects do not appear.	Daricon: Tablets 10 mg Vio-Thene: Tablets (timed-release) 10 mg
Oral: Adults, 10 mg 4 times daily. *Children*, 0.8 mg/kg divided into 4 doses.	Tablets 5 mg
Oral: Adults, 10 or 20 mg 3 or 4 times daily; additional 10 mg may be required at bedtime. Some patients may require 30 mg 4 times daily.	Tablets 10 mg
Oral: Adults, 5 mg 4 times daily. An additional 5 mg may be required at bedtime. *Children*, dosage not established.	Tablets 5 mg

TABLE 1—ANTICHOLINERGIC ANTISPASMODICS (Cont'd.)

Drug	Chemical Structure
Poldine Methylsulfate Nacton (McNeil)	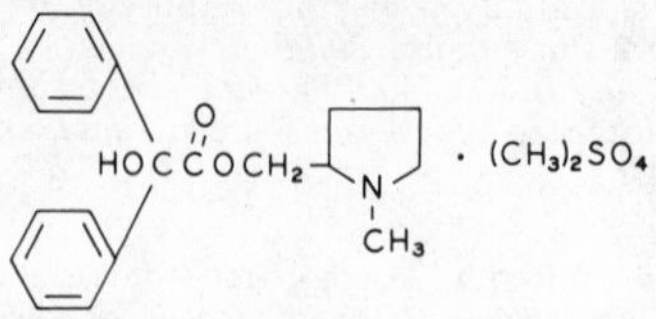 HOC C(=O) OCH₂–(pyrrolidine, N–CH₃) · (CH₃)₂SO₄
Propantheline Bromide Pro-Banthine (Searle)	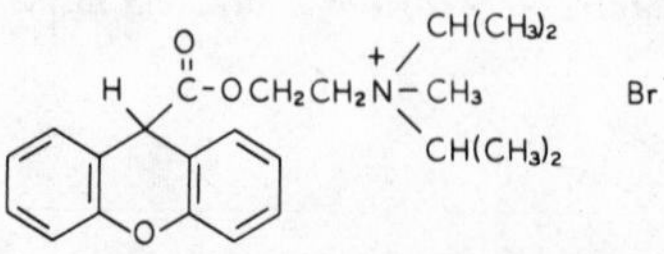 H C(=O)–OCH₂CH₂N⁺(CH(CH₃)₂)₂–CH₃ Br⁻
Tridihexethyl Chloride Pathilon (Lederle)	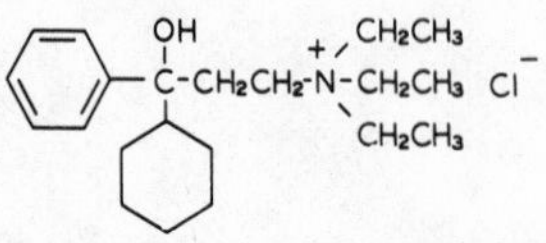 OH, C–CH₂CH₂–N⁺(CH₂CH₃)₃ Cl⁻

TABLE 2—OTHER SYNTHETIC ANTISPASMODICS

Drug	Chemical Structure
Adiphenine Hydrochloride Trasentine Hydrochloride (Ciba) Drug also marketed under generic name.	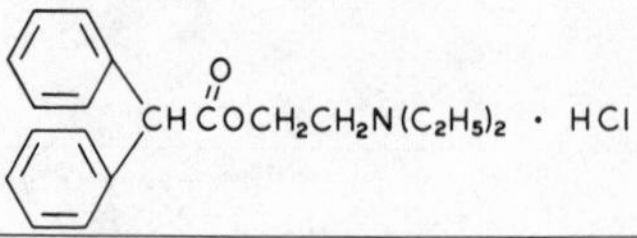 CH C(=O)OCH₂CH₂N(C₂H₅)₂ · HCl
Alverine Citrate Profenil (Smith, Miller & Patch) Spacolin (Philips Roxane)	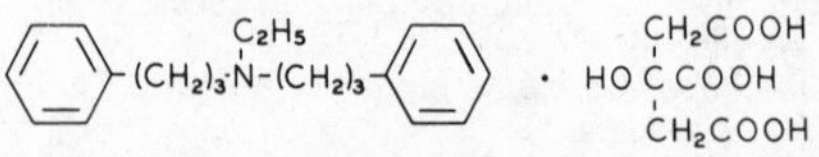 (CH₂)₃N(C₂H₅)–(CH₂)₃ · HO C COOH (CH₂COOH)₂
Dicyclomine Hydrochloride Bentyl (Merrell-National)	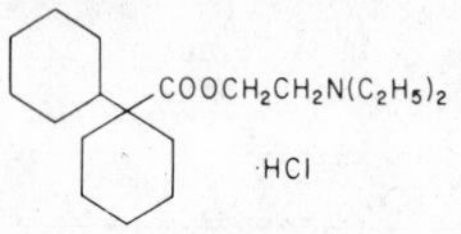 COOCH₂CH₂N(C₂H₅)₂ ·HCl
Isometheptene Hydrochloride Octin Hydrochloride (Knoll) Drug also marketed under generic name.	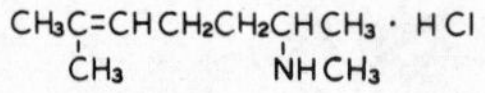 CH₃C(CH₃)=CHCH₂CH₂CH(NHCH₃)CH₃ · HCl
Isometheptene Mucate Octin Mucate (Knoll)	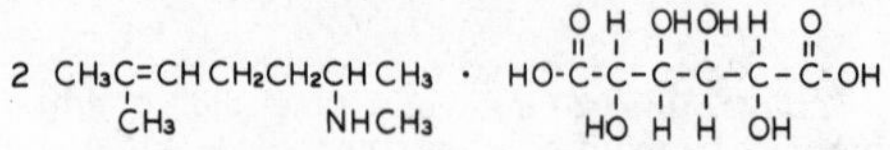 2 CH₃C(CH₃)=CHCH₂CH₂CH(NHCH₃)CH₃ · HO-C(=O)-CH(OH)-CH(OH)-CH(OH)-CH(OH)-C(=O)-OH
Isometheptene Tartrate Isometene (Canfield)	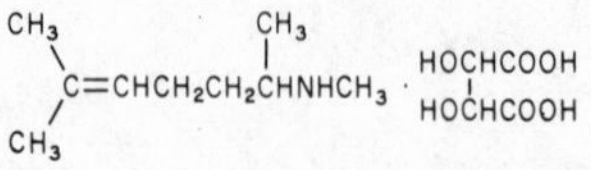 (CH₃)₂C=CHCH₂CH₂CH(CH₃)NHCH₃ · HOCHCOOH–HOCHCOOH
Methixene Hydrochloride Trest (Dorsey)	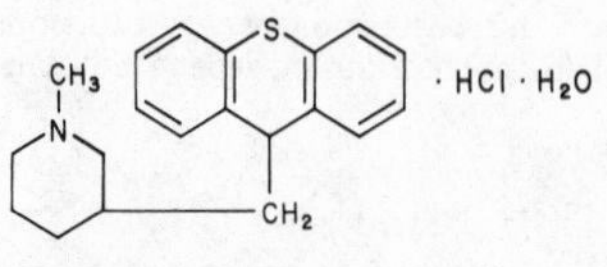 CH₃–N, S, CH₂ · HCl · H₂O

Usual Dosage	Preparations
Oral: Adults, 4 mg 3 or 4 times daily. *Children,* dosage not established.	Tablets 4 mg
Oral: Adults, 15 mg 3 times daily and 30 mg at bedtime, or timed-release preparation given 2 or 3 times daily. *Children,* 1.5 mg/kg daily in 4 doses. *Intramuscular, Intravenous: Adults,* 30 mg every 6 hours. (Powder dissolved in not less than 10 ml of sodium chloride injection for intravenous administration.)	Tablets 7.5 and 15 mg Tablets (timed-release) 30 mg Powder (for injection) 30 mg
Oral: Adults, 25 mg 3 times daily before meals and 50 mg at bedtime. Dosage increased to 50 mg 4 times daily if necessary. Alternatively, timed-release preparation given every 12 hours; if necessary, this dose is given every 6 hours. *Subcutaneous, Intravenous, Intramuscular: Adults,* 10 to 20 mg every 6 hours.	Capsules (timed-release) 75 mg Tablets 25 mg Solution (for injection) 10 mg/ml in 1 ml containers

Usual Dosage	Preparations
Oral: Adults, 75 to 150 mg 3 times daily. *Children,* dosage not established.	Tablets 75 mg
Oral: Adults, 120 mg 1 to 3 times daily.	Tablets 120 mg
Oral, Intramuscular: Adults, 10 to 20 mg 3 or 4 times daily. *Children,* 10 mg 3 or 4 times daily. *Infants,* 5 mg 3 or 4 times daily.	Capsules 10 mg Syrup 10 mg/5 ml Tablets 20 mg Solution (for injection) 10 mg/ml in 2 and 10 ml containers
Intramuscular: Adults, 100 mg repeated once in 4 to 6 hours. *Children,* dosage not established.	Solution (for injection) 100 mg/ml in 1 ml containers
Oral: Adults, 130 mg 3 or 4 times daily. *Children,* dosage not established.	Tablets 130 mg
Intramuscular: Adults, 100 mg repeated once in 4 to 6 hours. *Children,* dosage not established.	Solution (for injection) 100 mg/ml in 10 ml containers
Oral: Adults, 1 mg 3 times daily. Dose increased to 2 mg if necessary. *Children,* dosage not established.	Tablets 1 mg

TABLE 2—OTHER SYNTHETIC ANTISPASMODICS (Cont'd.)

Drug	Chemical Structure
Piperidolate Hydrochloride Dactil (Lakeside)	$(C_6H_5)_2CH{-}C(=O){-}O{-}$(1-$C_2H_5$-3-piperidyl) · HCl
Thiphenamil Hydrochloride Trocinate (Poythress)	$(C_6H_5)_2CHC(=O)SCH_2CH_2N(C_2H_5)_2$ · HCl

Belbarb (Arnar-Stone): Each tablet contains scopolamine hydrobromide 0.0072 mg, atropine sulfate 0.024 mg, hyoscyamine hydrobromide 0.128 mg, and phenobarbital 16 mg; each No. 2 tablet contains scopolamine hydrobromide 0.0072 mg, atropine sulfate 0.024 mg, hyoscyamine hydrobromide 0.128 mg, and phenobarbital 32 mg.

Belladenal (Sandoz): Each tablet or timed-release tablet contains levorotatory alkaloids of belladonna 0.25 mg and phenobarbital 50 mg; each 5 ml of elixir contains levorotatory alkaloids of belladonna 0.078 mg and phenobarbital 15.6 mg.

Bellergal (Sandoz): Each tablet contains levorotatory alkaloids of belladonna 0.1 mg, ergotamine tartrate 0.3 mg, and phenobarbital 20 mg; each timed-release tablet contains levorotatory alkaloids of belladonna 0.2 mg, ergotamine tartrate 0.6 mg, and phenobarbital 40 mg.

Bentyl W/Phenobarbital (Merrell-National): Each capsule, tablet, or 5 ml of syrup contains dicyclomine hydrochloride 10 mg and phenobarbital 15 mg.

Butibel (McNeil): Each tablet or 5 ml of elixir contains belladonna extract 15 mg and butabarbital sodium 15 mg; each timed-release tablet contains belladonna extract 30 mg and butabarbital sodium 30 mg.

Cantil W/Phenobarbital (Lakeside): Each tablet contains mepenzolate bromide 25 mg and phenobarbital 16 mg.

Chardonna (Rorer): Each tablet contains belladonna extract 5 mg, activated charcoal 60 mg, and phenobarbital 20 mg.

Combid (Smith Kline & French): Each timed-release capsule contains isopropamide iodide 5 mg and prochlorperazine maleate 10 mg.

Daricon-PB (Beecham-Massengill): Each tablet contains oxyphencyclimine hydrochloride 5 mg and phenobarbital 15 mg.

Donnalate (Robins): Each tablet contains hyoscyamine sulfate 0.052 mg, atropine sulfate 0.01 mg, scopolamine hydrobromide 0.003 mg, dihydroxyaluminum aminoacetate 500 mg, and phenobarbital 8.1 mg.

Donnatal (Robins): Each capsule, tablet, or 5 ml of elixir contains hyoscyamine sulfate 0.1037 mg, atropine sulfate 0.0194 mg, scopolamine hydrobromide 0.0065 mg, and phenobarbital 16.2 mg; each No. 2 tablet contains same formulation as Donnatal except phenobarbital 32.4 mg; each timed-release tablet contains hyoscyamine sulfate 0.3111 mg, atropine sulfate 0.0582 mg, scopolamine hydrobromide 0.0195 mg, and phenobarbital 48.6 mg.

Donphen (Lemmon): Each tablet contains hyoscyamine sulfate 0.1 mg, atropine sulfate 0.02 mg, scopolamine hydrobromide 6 μg, and phenobarbital 15 mg.

Enarax (Roerig): Each tablet contains oxyphencyclimine hydrochloride 5 or 10 mg and hydroxyzine hydrochloride 25 mg.

Hybephen (Beecham-Massengill): Each tablet or 5 ml of elixir contains hyoscyamine sulfate 0.1277 mg, atropine sulfate 0.0233 mg, scopolamine hydrobromide 0.0094 mg, and phenobarbital 15 mg.

Kinesed (Stuart): Each chewable tablet contains hyoscyamine sulfate 0.1 mg, atropine sulfate 0.02 mg, scopolamine hydrobromide 0.007 mg, simethicone 40 mg, and phenobarbital 16 mg.

Kolantyl (Merrell-National): Each tablet contains dicyclomine hydrochloride 5 mg, dried aluminum hydroxide gel 300 mg, magnesium oxide 185 mg, and methylcellulose 100 mg; each 5 ml of gel contains dicyclomine hydrochloride 2.5 mg, aluminum hydroxide 150 mg, magnesium hydroxide 150 mg, and methylcellulose 50 mg; each wafer contains dicyclomine hydrochloride 2.5 mg, dried aluminum hydroxide gel 180 mg, magnesium hydroxide 170 mg, and methylcellulose 50 mg.

Usual Dosage	Preparations
Oral: Adults, 50 mg 4 times daily. *Children*, dosage not established.	Tablets 50 mg
Oral: Adults, initially, 400 mg every 4 hours. *Children over 6 years*, 200 mg every 4 hours. Dose given less frequently after symptoms are controlled.	Tablets 100 and 400 mg

Levsin W/Phenobarbital (Kremers-Urban): Each tablet or 5 ml of elixir contains hyoscyamine sulfate 0.125 mg and phenobarbital 15 mg; each milliliter of injection contains hyoscyamine sulfate 0.25 mg and phenobarbital 15 mg.

Milpath (Wallace): Each tablet contains tridihexethyl chloride 25 mg and meprobamate 200 or 400 mg.

Pamine PB (Upjohn): Each tablet contains methscopolamine bromide 2.5 mg and phenobarbital 15 mg; each half-strength tablet or 5 ml of elixir contains methscopolamine bromide 1.25 mg and phenobarbital 8 mg; each milliliter of drops contains methscopolamine bromide 0.5 mg and phenobarbital 20 mg.

Pathibamate (Lederle): Each tablet contains tridihexethyl chloride 25 mg and meprobamate 200 or 400 mg.

Pathilon W/Phenobarbital (Lederle): Each tablet contains tridihexethyl chloride 25 mg and phenobarbital 15 mg; each timed-release tablet contains tridihexethyl chloride 75 mg and phenobarbital 45 mg.

Phenobarbital and Belladonna (Upjohn): Each tablet contains belladonna extract 8.1 mg and phenobarbital 16.2 or 32.4 mg.

Pro-Banthine W/Dartal (Searle): Each tablet contains propantheline bromide 15 mg and thiopropazate dihydrochloride 5 mg.

Pro-Banthine W/Phenobarbital (Searle): Each tablet contains propantheline bromide 15 mg and phenobarbital 15 mg.

Prydonnal (Smith Kline & French): Each timed-release capsule contains belladonna alkaloids 0.4 mg and phenobarbital 65 mg.

Robinul-PH (Robins): Each tablet contains glycopyrrolate 1 or 2 mg and phenobarbital 16.2 mg.

Sidonna (Reed & Carnrick): Each tablet contains simethicone 25 mg, hyoscyamine sulfate 0.1037 mg, atropine sulfate 0.0194 mg, scopolamine hydrobromide 0.0065 mg, and butabarbital sodium 16 mg.

Trasentine-Phenobarbital (Ciba): Each tablet contains adiphenine hydrochloride 50 mg and phenobarbital 20 mg.

Valpin-PB (Endo): Each tablet or 5 ml of elixir contains anisotropine methylbromide 10 mg and phenobarbital 8 mg.

Chapter 79

ANTACIDS

Antacids are used to reduce gastric acidity in the symptomatic treatment of peptic ulcer, hyperchlorhydria, gastritis, and other disorders of the stomach and duodenum. There is no conclusive evidence that they hasten the healing of peptic ulcers or reduce the number of relapses, but they are effective in relieving pain when adequate doses are given at sufficiently frequent intervals.

The goal of antacid therapy is to raise the pH of the gastric contents to 5; at this level the damaging effects of acidity are greatly reduced and the proteolytic activity of pepsin is almost completely abolished. In addition to a high neutralizing capacity, the ideal antacid should have a prolonged duration of action and should not cause untoward systemic or local effects. These goals are difficult, if not impossible, to attain. The duration of action is limited by the emptying time of the stomach, and prolonged neutralization requires frequent drug administration. Compounds with low toxicity have little neutralizing capacity, while the potent antacids can cause severe systemic effects. Alterations in normal bowel function usually occur during antacid therapy. Other undesired local effects of some agents are release of carbon dioxide in the stomach and interference with the absorption of other drugs.

Although sodium bicarbonate is highly soluble and has an immediate and pronounced neutralizing effect, its duration of action is very brief, it releases carbon dioxide in the stomach and it produces metabolic alkalosis in some patients. Therefore, sodium bicarbonate has little merit as a gastric antacid.

Calcium carbonate is a highly effective antacid because of its rapid onset of action, high neutralizing capacity, and relatively prolonged action. The pH of the gastric contents can be maintained above 4 by hourly administration of 4 g of calcium carbonate, and the presence of food in the stomach will prolong its action. Calcium carbonate is reconstituted in the intestine or insoluble calcium soaps or calcium phosphate are formed; however, significant amounts of calcium may be absorbed by some patients (see Adverse Reactions and Precautions). Tribasic calcium phosphate also has been used as a gastric antacid, but its neutralizing capacity is less than that of calcium carbonate.

Aluminum hydroxide is a nonabsorbable antacid with demulcent, adsorbent, and astringent properties. It has a slow onset of action and a low neutralizing capacity, but there is no evidence that it is less effective in relieving pain than other more potent antacids. The symptomatic relief obtained may be due to the drug's demulcent action or to other properties unrelated to reduction of acidity. Aluminum hydroxide does not produce systemic effects because insoluble compounds are formed in the intestine (eg, aluminum phosphate). Since the elimination of phosphate in the feces results in a compensatory decrease in the urinary excretion of phosphate, it may be used to treat phosphatic renal calculi; however, basic aluminum carbonate is considered more effective for this purpose. Other aluminum products used as antacids are aluminum phosphate, dihydroxyaluminum aminoacetate [Robalate], and dihydroxyaluminum sodium carbonate. These compounds have properties similar to those of aluminum hydroxide; however, aluminum phosphate does not increase the fecal elimination of phosphate.

Magnesium hydroxide, usually in the form of milk of magnesia, has a rapid and relatively long neutralizing action. Insoluble magnesium compounds are formed in the intestine, but some magnesium ions may be absorbed.

Magnesium carbonate and magnesium oxide also have a high neutralizing capacity, but tribasic magnesium phosphate and magnesium trisilicate are relatively weak antacids. Magaldrate [Riopan] is a chemical union of magnesium and aluminum hydroxides.

Several other drugs have been used to reduce gastric acidity. Resins, such as polyamine-methylene resin [Resinat], have a slight neutralizing effect but are bulky and unpalatable. Insoluble bismuth salts, gastric mucin, methylcellulose, and glycine are common ingredients of mixtures, but their therapeutic value is doubtful.

Adverse Reactions and Precautions

The most common adverse reactions associated with prolonged use of antacids are constipation or diarrhea. Because of the cathartic effects of the magnesium salts, large and frequent doses often cannot be tolerated. Constipation may result from repeated administration of calcium or aluminum preparations; formation of fecal concretions is an occasional complication. Disruption of normal bowel function can be minimized by the use of magnesium salts with calcium or aluminum preparations.

The presence of an antacid in the stomach causes a compensatory increase in the secretion of gastric juice and in the output of hydrochloric acid. There is no convincing evidence that the increased secretion rate outlasts the neutralizing effect of any antacid except possibly calcium carbonate. Rebound gastric hypersecretion has been demonstrated several hours after administration of this antacid. The acid rebound has been variously attributed to a local effect of the calcium ion, to hypercalcemia, or to the superior neutralizing capacity of calcium carbonate. The clinical significance of this phenomenon is unclear. In treating peptic ulcer, the rebound hypersecretion would be buffered by additional doses of the antacid and by frequent feeding. However, it has been suggested that sustained, buffered hypersecretion could lead to hyperplasia of the parietal cells.

The milk-alkali syndrome (Burnett syndrome) is an occasional complication that occurs after the prolonged administration of large doses of sodium bicarbonate or calcium carbonate together with the ingestion of foods containing vitamin D, such as milk. The essential features of this syndrome are hypercalcemia and renal insufficiency with azotemia and metastatic calcinosis. Hematologic findings usually include normal or elevated phosphorus levels, normal alkaline phosphatase levels, and mild metabolic alkalosis. The urinary excretion of calcium is generally not increased. Conjunctival deposition of calcium can occur, manifested by band keratopathy. Nausea is a common symptom. Predisposing factors are preexisting renal disease, hypertension, gastrointestinal hemorrhage, and dehydration and electrolyte imbalance due to excessive vomiting or aspiration of the gastric contents. Magnesium and aluminum salts have not been implicated in this syndrome. Sodium bicarbonate may cause pronounced metabolic alkalosis in patients with impaired renal function.

Antacids containing magnesium can produce severe toxic effects in patients with impaired renal function. The symptoms of magnesium poisoning include lethargy, coma, circulatory failure, and respiratory arrest due to neuromuscular blockade.

Sodium bicarbonate is contraindicated in patients on a low-sodium diet, and some other antacids contain sufficient sodium to preclude their unrestricted use in these patients. Information is not available for all antacids, but chemical analysis has shown that aluminum preparations may contain significant amounts of sodium, although there is considerable variation in products from different manufacturers. Milk of magnesia (magnesium hydroxide) and calcium carbonate, U.S.P., have a relatively low sodium content.

Eructation and flatulence may occur after the administration of carbonates or bicarbonate due to the release of carbon dioxide in the stomach. The gastric distention produced by the carbon dioxide could cause perforation of a gastric ulcer.

Aluminum salts occasionally cause nausea and vomiting. Phosphate deficiency and osteomalacia may develop in patients with a low phosphate intake during prolonged administration of large doses of aluminum preparations, with the exception of aluminum phosphate.

INDIVIDUAL EVALUATIONS

SODIUM BICARBONATE

Sodium bicarbonate is a highly soluble antacid with an immediate and pronounced neutralizing effect; however, it is not a satisfactory antacid because of its brief duration of action and occasional untoward effects.

Adverse reactions include eructation and flatulence, sodium retention, metabolic alkalosis, and the milk-alkali syndrome (see the Introductory Statement).

For other uses, see Chapter 16, Replenishers and Regulators of Water, Electrolytes, and Nutrients.

USUAL DOSAGE.—This agent has little merit as a gastric antacid because of the reasons stated above. The U.S.P. dosage is: *Oral: Adults,* 300 mg to 2 g one to four times daily.

PREPARATIONS.—Sodium Bicarbonate, U.S.P. Drug marketed under generic name.

CALCIUM CARBONATE

Calcium carbonate is regarded by some authorities as the antacid of choice. The powder form has a rapid onset of action, high neutralizing capacity, and relatively prolonged action. The tablets are less effective.

Constipation and lack of palatability are frequent complaints; fecal concretions may occur. The constipating effects of this drug can be minimized by combined therapy with magnesium salts. A mixture of two parts magnesium oxide and one part calcium carbonate will not affect the bowel function of most patients. If constipation or diarrhea does occur, the ratio of the ingredients may be adjusted. Patients receiving prolonged calcium carbonate therapy together with foods containing vitamin D may develop the milk-alkali syndrome; other adverse effects are hypercalcemia and rebound hyperacidity. Liberation of carbon dioxide in the stomach may cause eructation and flatulence.

USUAL DOSAGE.—*Oral:* The dose and frequency of administration depend upon the severity of symptoms and relief obtained. *Adults,* 1 to 4 g with water four or more times daily; to control severe symptoms, 2 to 4 g every hour may be required. The tablets should be chewed before swallowing.

PREPARATIONS.—Calcium Carbonate, U.S.P. *Oral:* Powder (precipitated); tablets 600 mg.

AVAILABLE TRADEMARKS.—Glycate (Durst): Each chewable tablet contains calcium carbonate 300 mg and glycine 150 mg.

Titralac (Riker): Each 5 ml of liquid contains calcium carbonate 1 g and glycine 300 mg; each tablet contains calcium carbonate 420 mg and glycine 180 mg.

Drug also marketed under generic name.

CALCIUM PHOSPHATE, TRIBASIC

This agent is occasionally used as an antacid, but it has only a mild and brief neutralizing action. Tribasic calcium phosphate is also used as a source of calcium and phosphate in deficiency states (see Chapter 17, Blood Calcium Regulators).

For adverse reactions, see the Introductory Statement.

USUAL DOSAGE.—*Oral:* The dose and frequency of administration depend upon the severity of symptoms and relief obtained. *Adults,* 1 to 4 g with water three or more times daily; to control severe symptoms, 2 to 4 g every hour may be required.

PREPARATIONS.—Calcium Phosphate, Tribasic, N.F. *Oral:* Powder. Drug marketed under generic name.

ALUMINUM HYDROXIDE GEL [Amphojel] DRIED ALUMINUM HYDROXIDE GEL [Amphojel Tablets]

Aluminum hydroxide gel is a nonabsorbable antacid with demulcent, adsorbent, and astringent properties. It has a slow onset of action and a low neutralizing capacity. Different preparations of aluminum hydroxide vary in neutralizing potency; tablets are less effective than liquid preparations. The drug increases phosphate excretion in the feces and sometimes is used in the treatment of phosphatic renal calculi.

Aluminum hydroxide is relatively nontoxic; the most common adverse reaction is constipation, which can be controlled by combined therapy with a magnesium compound. Fecal concretions may occur. The astringent action of this agent occasionally causes nausea and vomiting. If phosphate intake is low, patients receiving large doses for long periods may develop hypophosphatemia and osteomalacia. Aluminum hydroxide can interfere with the absorption of other drugs and should not be given simultaneously with such agents as anticholinergics and barbiturates. Aluminum hydroxide preparations contain sodium and should not be administered to patients on a low-sodium diet.

USUAL DOSAGE.—*Oral:* The dose and frequency of administration depend upon the severity of symptoms and relief obtained. *Adults,* 5 to 10 ml of gel or tablets containing 300 or 600 mg given with water four times daily; tablets should be chewed before swallowing. To control severe symptoms, 40 ml of gel every hour may be required; this may be given by intragastric drip after dilution with two to three parts water. In the treatment of phosphatic renal calculi, 40 ml of gel is given after meals and at bedtime; in most patients, this dose will reduce the urinary excretion of phosphate within a few days.

PREPARATIONS.—Amphojel (Wyeth). *Oral:* Suspension (gel); tablets 300 and 600 mg (dried gel). Forms also marketed under generic name.

ADDITIONAL TRADEMARKS.— **Aluminum Hydroxide Gel:** Co-Lu-Gel (Ulmer). **Dried Aluminum Hydroxide Gel:** Algelum (Robinson).

ALUMINUM PHOSPHATE GEL [Phosphaljel]

This nonabsorbable liquid preparation has properties similar to aluminum hydroxide. It is regenerated in the intestine and endogenous phosphate is spared; therefore, it should be used in preference to aluminum hydroxide when a high phosphate diet cannot be maintained.

For adverse reactions, see the Introductory Statement.

USUAL DOSAGE.—*Oral:* Dose and frequency of administration depend upon the severity of symptoms and relief obtained. *Adults,* 15 to 45 ml with water four or more times daily.

PREPARATIONS.—Phosphaljel (Wyeth). *Oral:* Suspension 4%.

DIHYDROXYALUMINUM AMINOACETATE [Robalate]

This agent is a nonabsorbable antacid with properties similar to aluminum hydroxide. In the dried form, dihydroxyaluminum aminoacetate has a greater neutralizing capacity than dried aluminum hydroxide gel, but comparison of liquid preparations has shown that aluminum hydroxide gel is more effective. There is little evidence to support the claim that dihydroxyaluminum aminoacetate is less constipating than aluminum hydroxide.

For adverse reactions, see the Introductory Statement.

USUAL DOSAGE.—*Oral:* The dose and frequency of administration depend upon the severity of symptoms and relief obtained. *Adults,* 500 mg to 2 g with water four or more times daily.

PREPARATIONS.—Robalate (Robins). *Oral:* Suspension 500 mg/5 ml; tablets 500 mg.

ADDITIONAL TRADEMARKS.—Alglyn (Brayten), Alkam (First Texas), Alzinox (Cooper).

Other Aluminum Preparations

Basic Aluminum Carbonate [Basaljel (Wyeth)]

Dihydroxyaluminum Sodium Carbonate [Rolaids (American Chicle)]

MAGNESIUM HYDROXIDE
MAGNESIUM OXIDE
MILK OF MAGNESIA

These antacids have the same properties because magnesium oxide is converted to the hydroxide in water. Milk of magnesia, a suspension of magnesium hydroxide, is used mainly as a laxative. These preparations have a rapid onset of action and a high neutralizing capacity. Their duration of action is longer than that of sodium bicarbonate.

The most common untoward effect is diarrhea; this can be minimized by combined therapy with a calcium or aluminum preparation. Absorbed magnesium may produce toxic effects in patients with impaired renal function (see the Introductory Statement).

For other uses of these preparations, see Chapter 81, Laxatives and Agents Affecting Fecal Consistency.

USUAL DOSAGE.—The dose and frequency of administration depend upon the severity of symptoms and relief obtained.

Magnesium Hydroxide:

Oral: Adults, 300 to 600 mg of powder or one or two tablets with water four or more times daily; *children,* one-half or one tablet. Tablets should be chewed before swallowing.

Magnesium Oxide:

Oral: Adults, 250 mg to 1.5 g with water four or more times daily.

Milk of Magnesia:

Oral: Adults, 5 ml of liquid four or more times daily; *children,* 2.5 to 5 ml of liquid.

PREPARATIONS.—

Magnesium Hydroxide, N.F. *Oral:* Powder; tablets 300 mg.

Magnesium Oxide, U.S.P. *Oral:* Capsules and powder available in both heavy and light form (light form suspends more readily in liquids).

Milk of Magnesia, U.S.P. *Oral:* Suspension.

Drugs marketed under generic name.

MAGNESIUM CARBONATE

This alkaline salt is similar to magnesium hydroxide and magnesium oxide, but differs from these agents in that carbon dioxide is liberated in the stomach during neutralization. Magnesium carbonate has a high neutralizing capacity and is a common ingredient in antacid mixtures.

For adverse reactions and precautions, see the Introductory Statement. For other uses, see Chapter 81, Laxatives and Agents Affecting Fecal Consistency.

USUAL DOSAGE.—*Oral:* The dose and frequency of administration depend upon the severity of symptoms and relief obtained. *Adults,* 500 mg to 2 g with water four times daily; to control severe symptoms, 2 g each hour may be required. Tablets should be chewed before swallowing.

PREPARATIONS.—Magnesium Carbonate, N.F. *Oral:* Powder; tablets 2 g. Drug marketed under generic name.

MAGNESIUM PHOSPHATE, TRIBASIC

The actions of this alkaline powder are similar to those of other magnesium preparations. Its neutralizing capacity is less than that of magnesium carbonate but greater than that of magnesium trisilicate.

For adverse reactions and precautions, see the Introductory Statement.

USUAL DOSAGE.—*Oral:* The dose and frequency of administration depend upon the severity of symptoms and relief obtained. *Adults,* 1 to 2 g with water four times daily; to control severe symptoms, 2 g every hour may be required.

PREPARATIONS.—Tribasic Magnesium Phosphate, N.F. *Oral:* Powder. Drug marketed under generic name.

MAGNESIUM TRISILICATE

Magnesium trisilicate has a slow onset of action and low neutralizing capacity. It is a common ingredient of many antacid mixtures. Magnesium trisilicate reacts with hydrochloric acid to form hydrated silicon dioxide which may provide symptomatic relief by coating the crater of an ulcer. It also has adsorbent properties.

For adverse reactions and precautions, see the Introductory Statement.

USUAL DOSAGE.—*Oral:* The dose and frequency of administration depend upon the severity of symptoms and relief obtained. *Adults,* 1 to 4 g with water four times daily; to control severe symptoms, 2 g or more every hour may be required. Tablets should be chewed before swallowing.

PREPARATIONS.—Magnesium Trisilicate, U.S.P. *Oral:* Powder; tablets 300 and 500 mg.

AVAILABLE TRADEMARK.—Trisomin (Lilly). Drug also marketed under generic name.

MAGALDRATE [Riopan]

Magaldrate is a chemical union of aluminum and magnesium hydroxides. It has a low sodium content.

Prolonged use may cause constipation in some patients. Although some limited absorption might occur, magaldrate is unlikely to cause disturbances of acid-base balance. However, even limited absorption may produce hypermagnesemia in patients with impaired renal function. For other adverse reactions and precautions, see the Introductory Statement.

USUAL DOSAGE.—*Oral:* The dose and frequency of administration depend upon the severity of symptoms and relief obtained. *Adults,* 400 to 800 mg four or more times daily. Hourly administration may be necessary to control severe symptoms.

PREPARATIONS.—Riopan (Ayerst). *Oral:* Suspension 400 mg/5 ml; tablets 400 mg; tablets (chewable) 400 mg.

MIXTURES

Disruption of normal bowel function after prolonged administration of antacids can be minimized by alternating magnesium salts with calcium or aluminum preparations or by using mixtures. Some combination products contain additional ingredients of doubtful therapeutic value, such as gastric mucin, methylcellulose, glycine, simethicone, and oxethazaine. Preparations containing antacids combined with anticholinergics and barbiturates should not be used because the dose of each of these agents should be adjusted individually and because some antacids, such as aluminum hydroxide, may interfere with the absorption of other drugs (for a listing of these mixtures, see Chapter 78, Antispasmodics).

The dose and frequency of administration depend upon the severity of symptoms and relief obtained.

Mixtures Containing Aluminum Hydroxide and Magnesium Salts

Aludrox (Wyeth): Tablets and suspension containing aluminum and magnesium hydroxides.

A-M-T (Wyeth): Tablets and suspension containing dried aluminum hydroxide gel and magnesium trisilicate.

Bidrox (McNeil): Each 5 ml of suspension contains

aluminum hydroxide 400 mg and magnesium hydroxide 100 mg.

Cimadrox (Beecham-Massengill): Each tablet contains dried aluminum hydroxide gel 200 mg, magnesium trisilicate 400 mg, and ascorbic acid 20 mg.

Creamalin (Winthrop): Each tablet or 5 ml of suspension contains aluminum hydroxide gel 320 mg and magnesium hydroxide 75 mg.

Delcid (Merrell-National): Each 5 ml of liquid contains aluminum hydroxide gel 600 mg and magnesium hydroxide 665 mg.

Gaviscon (Marion): Each tablet contains dried aluminum hydroxide gel 80 mg, magnesium trisilicate 20 mg, sodium bicarbonate 70 mg, and alginic acid 200 mg.

Gelusil (Warner-Chilcott): Each tablet or 4 ml of liquid contains aluminum hydroxide 250 mg and magnesium trisilicate 500 mg.

Gelusil-M (Warner-Chilcott): Each tablet or 5 ml of suspension contains aluminum hydroxide 250 mg, magnesium hydroxide 100 mg, and magnesium trisilicate 500 mg.

Maalox (Rorer): Each 5 ml of suspension or No. 1 tablet contains combined hydroxides of aluminum and magnesium 400 mg; each No. 2 tablet contains combined hydroxides of aluminum and magnesium 800 mg.

Malcogel (Upjohn): Each 5 ml of liquid contains aluminum hydroxide 300 mg and magnesium trisilicate 600 mg.

Malcotabs (Upjohn): Each tablet contains dried aluminum hydroxide gel 600 mg and magnesium trisilicate 300 mg.

Mucotin (Warner-Chilcott): Each tablet contains dried aluminum hydroxide gel 250 mg, magnesium hydroxide 65 mg, magnesium trisilicate 450 mg, and gastric mucin 65 mg.

Mylanta (Stuart): Each tablet or 5 ml of liquid contains aluminum hydroxide 200 mg, magnesium hydroxide 200 mg, and simethicone 20 mg.

Neosorb (Lemmon): Each tablet contains aluminum hydroxide gel 250 mg, magnesium trisilicate 460 mg, and methylcellulose 65 mg.

Neosorb Plus (Lemmon): Suspension containing aluminum hydroxide 6%, magnesium hydroxide 3%, and magnesium trisilicate 3%; each tablet contains dried aluminum hydroxide gel 300 mg, magnesium hydroxide 150 mg, and magnesium trisilicate 150 mg.

Neutralox (Lemmon): Each tablet or 5 ml of liquid contains dried aluminum hydroxide gel 300 mg, magnesium hydroxide 150 mg, and magnesium trisilicate 150 mg.

Oxaine-M (Wyeth): Each 5 ml of suspension contains oxethazaine 10 mg in alumina gel with magnesium hydroxide.

Silain-Gel Liquid (Robins): Each 5 ml of liquid contains aluminum hydroxide 282 mg, magnesium hydroxide 85 mg, and simethicone 25 mg.

Silain-Gel Tablets (Robins): Each tablet contains aluminum hydroxide-magnesium carbonate 282 mg, magnesium hydroxide 85 mg, and simethicone 25 mg.

Trigelma (Durst): Each tablet contains aluminum hydroxide gel 250 mg, magnesium hydroxide 60 mg, and magnesium trisilicate 150 mg; each 5 ml of liquid contains aluminum hydroxide gel 2.1 g and magnesium hydroxide paste 300 mg.

Trisogel (Lilly): Each capsule contains aluminum hydroxide gel 100 mg and magnesium trisilicate 280 mg; each 5 ml of liquid contains aluminum hydroxide 140 mg and magnesium trisilicate 540 mg.

WinGel (Winthrop): Each tablet or 5 ml of liquid contains aluminum and magnesium hydroxides 410 mg stabilized with hexitol.

Mixtures Containing Calcium Carbonate and Other Antacids

Alkets (Upjohn): Each tablet contains calcium carbonate 750 mg, magnesium carbonate 120 mg, and magnesium oxide 60 mg.

Buffertabs (Durst): Each tablet contains calcium carbonate 200 mg, magnesium carbonate 120 mg, bismuth subcarbonate 60 mg, aluminum hydroxide 30 mg, and aminoacetic acid 50 mg.

Camalox (Rorer): Each 5 ml of suspension contains calcium carbonate 250 mg, aluminum hydroxide 225 mg, and magnesium hydroxide 200 mg.

Dicarbosil (Arch): Each tablet contains calcium carbonate 489 mg, magnesium carbonate 10 mg, and magnesium trisilicate 6 mg.

Ducon (Smith Kline & French): Each 5 ml of suspension contains calcium carbonate 375 mg, aluminum hydroxide 720 mg, and magnesium hydroxide 350 mg.

Ratio (Warren-Teed): Each tablet contains calcium carbonate 400 mg and magnesium carbonate 50 mg.

Tums (Lewis-Howe): Each tablet contains calcium carbonate 489 mg, magnesium carbonate 10 mg, and magnesium trisilicate 6 mg.

Chapter 80

ANTIDIARRHEALS

Diarrhea is a pathologic acute or chronic increase in the fluidity and frequency of the stools. This symptom may be caused by infection (bacterial, viral, fungal, or parasitic), poisoning (eg, heavy metals, pesticides, bacterial exotoxins), drugs, altered distribution of bile acids, malabsorption, allergy, ischemia, hypermotility, and gastrointestinal lesions, including inflammatory conditions (regional enteritis) and hormone-producing neoplasms (eg, carcinoid).

Many of the drugs discussed in this chapter are nonspecific and useful only for the symptomatic treatment of diarrhea. They include drugs of demonstrated effectiveness (eg, diphenoxylate hydrochloride with atropine [Lomotil], opium tincture), as well as other agents (eg, bismuth subcarbonate, kaolin, pectin) whose supposed effectiveness is supported mainly by tradition. Drugs of the latter group are generally available only as components of mixtures, and until well-controlled clinical studies are available, generally no recommendation is made for these agents.

The specific cause of acute, self-limiting diarrhea often remains unknown. A bacterial toxin is the most common cause in children; viruses also may be responsible. The nonspecific antidiarrheal agents may be useful in mitigating the symptoms of acute diarrhea (eg, opiates in the treatment of *Salmonella* food poisoning). The symptomatic treatment of chronic diarrhea is justified only to give the patient relief while a search is made for the cause or when symptomatic therapy is needed in addition to treatment of the underlying cause.

The drugs used for specific treatment of the various underlying causes of diarrhea include antibacterial agents (eg, neomycin), antiprotozoal agents (eg, metronidazole [Flagyl]), and cholestyramine resin [Cuemid, Questran]. Other drugs useful for the specific treatment of enteric infections resulting in diarrhea (eg, ampicillin, tetracycline, nystatin) are discussed in their respective chapters. These drugs should be used only when there is an established diagnosis or strong presumptive evidence of such a diagnosis and appropriate laboratory service for confirmation is not available. For example, in acute bacterial diarrhea of infants, a bacteriologic diagnostic service is not always available, and antibacterial therapy with an appropriate drug may be initiated on the basis of a careful, informed clinical diagnosis (enteropathogenic serotypes of *Escherichia coli* are the most common etiologic agents).

In any patient with severe diarrhea lasting more than 24 to 48 hours, fluid and electrolyte imbalances should be corrected to avoid dehydration and hypokalemia. In chronic diarrhea, electrolyte and nutrient status should be monitored and appropriate replacement therapy (eg, potassium, magnesium, calcium, albumin, vitamins) given when indicated. A careful investigation should be made to determine the cause of any persisting or continually recurring diarrhea and appropriate specific therapeutic measures (eg, medication, surgery, diet) should be instituted. Many such patients have special problems outside the scope of this book (eg, lactase deficiency, food allergies, carcinoid).

Nonspecific Antidiarrheals: The opiates are the most effective and prompt-acting nonspecific antidiarrheal agents. They act directly on intestinal smooth muscle to produce spasm with decreased peristalsis and increased segmentation. By tradition, the opium preparations, opium tincture and paregoric, are more widely used than the pure alkaloids, but morphine and codeine are equally effective. Paregoric (camphorated opium tincture), which has been characterized as needlessly complex, nevertheless may have an advantage over opium tincture in its more convenient dosage. Since the usual oral doses of these preparations are neither euphoric nor analgesic, they can be used to treat acute, self-limited diarrhea with no risk of producing dependence; there is a real but slight risk of producing physical dependence if opiates are used to treat chronic diarrhea such as that associated with regional enteritis, colitis, or a colostomy. The effectiveness of diphenoxylate with atropine is about the same as that of the opium extracts. The mixture is classified as a Schedule V substance.

Theoretically, anticholinergic-type antispasmodics should be ideal antidiarrheals; however, it usually is not possible to give effective doses of these agents without producing undesirable reactions, since no drug of this class has been shown to exert a selective effect on the gastrointestinal tract. Ordinarily, there is no justification for adding a fraction of the usual clinical dose of an antispasmodic to an effective antidiarrheal agent. Anticholinergics are prescribed by many physicians when diarrhea is a problem in the irritable colon syndrome.

The use of the three bismuth salts (subcarbonate, subgallate, and subnitrate) as antidiarrheals is supported chiefly by tradition. Supposedly they adsorb toxins, bacteria, and viruses and provide a protective coating for the intestinal mucosa, but none of these conjectural actions has been substantiated.

Activated charcoal, once popular as an adsorbent in the treatment of diarrhea, is now used only for the treatment of poisonings, especially those caused by alkaloids, mercuric chloride, aspirin, or iron.

Kaolin and other hydrated aluminum silicate clays (eg, activated attapulgite) and pectin act as adsorbents and protectants. They are customarily available in preparations combining the two. Adequately controlled clinical studies demonstrating the efficacy of these popular but minimally effective antidiarrheal mixtures are lacking, and the usefulness of these agents is supported mainly by tradition. Frequently other ingredients are also present in the mixture.

Polycarbophil is a hydrophilic polyacrylic resin that may be effective in the symptomatic treatment of diarrhea because of its water-binding capacity; it is available only as an ingredient in mixtures.

Viable *Lactobacillus* cultures [Bacid, Lactinex] have been advocated for the treatment of diarrhea due to abnormal intestinal flora, especially for the rather common diarrhea that may occur postoperatively in a patient whose gut has been recolonized (eg, by staphylococci, *Candida*) after "sterilization" by antibacterial agents given in conjunction with gastrointestinal surgery. No well-controlled studies supporting the use of these preparations have been published.

Two amebicides, iodochlorhydroxyquin [Entero-Vioform] and diiodohydroxyquin [Diodoquin, Yodoxin], have been used in the prophylaxis of "traveler's diarrhea"; however, the cause of this diarrhea is not known and the efficacy of these drugs for this use has not been proved. (See Chapter 62, Amebicides.)

Drugs Having Specific Indications: Although furazolidone [Furoxone] is useful in the treatment of symptomatic giardiasis, metronidazole [Flagyl] and quinacrine hydrochloride [Atabrine] are more effective. Metronidazole also is useful in the treatment of intestinal amebiasis (see Chapter 62, Amebicides).

Mild candidal superinfections may respond to cessation of antibacterial therapy. In severe superinfections with penicillinase-producing staphylococci, the broad-spectrum antibiotics should be stopped and treatment should include vancomycin [Vancocin] orally, a penicillinase-resistant penicillin or a cephalosporin parenterally, and measures to combat shock.

Acute gastroenteritis due to *Salmonella* infections other than typhoid fever ordinarily should not be treated with antibacterial agents because there is evidence that antibiotics do not shorten the period of illness and may prolong the excretion of organisms. However, antibiotic therapy is advisable in severe cases, especially in patients who are vulnerable to serious illness and death (eg, infants, the elderly). Many patients with *Salmonella* gastroenteritis benefit from symptomatic therapy with opiates. Restoration of fluid and electrolyte balance is essential if dehydration is present. If specific therapy is needed, chloramphenicol [Chloromycetin] and ampicillin are the agents of choice; the antibiotic should be given for 10 to 14 days.

Orally administered antibiotics are used in the treatment of enteropathogenic *Escherichia coli* infections: neomycin [Mycifradin, Neobiotic] or kanamycin [Kantrex] are drugs of first choice; ampicillin, tetracyclines, furazolidone, polymyxin B [Aerosporin], and paromomycin [Humatin] also are effective.

Ampicillin is the antibiotic of choice in *Shigella* infections. The sulfonamides are effective in bacillary dysentery caused by sensitive strains of *Shigella*, but they are no longer considered as primary therapy because of the prevalence of resistant strains. For sensitive strains, sulfadiazine, sulfisoxazole [Gantrisin], or ampicillin is given for seven to ten days. Alternative drugs for oral use in patients with infections caused by resistant strains of *Shigella* or when clinical failure occurs are kanamycin, tetracyclines, furazolidone, polymyxin B, and paromomycin. Genetic transfer of resistance to one or more antibiotics occurs between *Shigella* and other enteric gram-negative bacteria, so antimicrobial agents must be judiciously selected and used.

Salicylazosulfapyridine [Azulfidine] is used as adjunctive therapy in patients with ulcerative colitis.

Treatment with polymyxin B or gentamicin [Garamycin] plus carbenicillin [Geopen, Pyopen] is useful in acute enteritis due to *Pseudomonas* infection.

Antibiotics effective in the treatment of acute gastroenteritis due to *Proteus* infection include tetracyclines, gentamicin, kanamycin, neomycin, and clindamycin [Cleocin].

See also Chapters 48, Penicillins; 52, Polymyxins; 53, Tetracyclines; 54, Chloramphenicol and Derivatives; 55, Sulfonamides; and 57, Aminoglycoside Antibacterial Agents and Miscellaneous Antimicrobial Drugs.

Cholestyramine resin is useful in the treatment of watery diarrhea caused by changes in the distribution of bile acids; this occurs in patients with distal ileal resections of less than 100 cm and in those with colonization of the upper small intestine by colonic flora.

Adverse Reactions and Precautions

Opiate preparations should not be used for prolonged, unsupervised periods because of their potential for abuse, although this is minimal in doses used for diarrhea. They should not be used in diarrhea caused by poisoning until the toxic material has been eliminated from the gastrointestinal tract. Untoward effects from the usual antidiarrheal doses are uncommon, but larger doses may produce the undesirable effects of the opiates (see Chapter 21, Strong Analgesics). The dependence liability of diphenoxylate hydrochloride with atropine [Lomotil] is slight, and reactions occur infrequently with usual doses (see the evaluation on Diphenoxylate Hydrochloride with Atropine). The opiates must be used with caution in patients acutely ill with ulcerative colitis or ischemic colonic disease, since they can precipitate adynamic ileus of the colon and possibly toxic dilatation. They also should be used cautiously in patients with hepatic dysfunction.

Anticholinergics (eg, propantheline [Pro-Banthine]), when used in therapeutic doses, have caused dryness of the mouth, visual disturbances, dizziness, headache, increased intraocular pressure, dysuria, tachycardia, drowsiness, and rash. Like the opiates, the anticholinergics may facilitate dilatation in acute ulcerative or ischemic disease of the colon. (See Chapter 78, Antispasmodics.)

The adsorbents are usually safe, but their continued use has produced impaction in very young, old, or debilitated patients; they also may interfere with absorption of bile salts and drugs.

The preparations containing poorly absorbed antibiotics are hazardous in patients with extensive intestinal lesions, which might lead to significant absorption. Enough neomycin has been absorbed from the gastrointestinal tract to produce deafness (see the evaluation on Neomycin Sulfate in Chapter 57, Aminoglycoside Antibacterial Agents and Miscellaneous Antimicrobial Drugs). This danger is particularly great in patients with impaired renal function.

Intestinal candidiasis and the dangerous complication of acute pseudomembranous enterocolitis have been observed after therapy with many orally administered antibiotics. The use of vancomycin [Vancocin] should be considered if the latter condition develops.

Fatal secondary staphylococcal intestinal infection has been reported after the prophylactic use of neomycin in adults.

When poorly absorbed antibacterial agents are given for a long period, the physician should be alert for the possible development of hypoprothrombinemia due to reduced vitamin K synthesis by intestinal bacteria.

Many mixtures containing poorly absorbed antibacterial agents with adsorbents and protectants frequently provide suboptimal antibacterial dosages and yet subject the patient to the potential adverse effects of these agents.

Cholestyramine resin [Cuemid, Questran] may cause steatorrhea or constipation.

INDIVIDUAL EVALUATIONS

BISMUTH SUBCARBONATE

Bismuth salts (most commonly bismuth subcarbonate) are used as supposed protectants and adsorbents in the treatment of diarrhea. There is no evidence, other than tradition, that they have any beneficial effect in diarrhea or contribute to the action of any mixtures containing them.

USUAL DOSAGE.—The usual suggested dosage for bismuth subcarbonate is: *Oral: Adults,* 1 to 4 g, suspended in water, every two to four hours.

PREPARATIONS.—*Oral:* Powder; tablets 300 mg. Drug marketed under generic name.

CHOLESTYRAMINE RESIN
[Cuemid, Questran]

Cholestyramine is useful in many patients with diarrhea caused by changes in distribution of the bile acids. These include patients with ileal resections of less than 100 cm, whose diarrhea is caused by an increase in concentration of bile acids in solution in the colon, and those with colonization of the upper small intestine by colonic flora. In patients with extensive ileal resections who are eating a normal diet, cholestyramine generally does not lessen diarrhea and it increases steatorrhea. In these patients, the concomitant use of cholestyramine and a low-fat diet supplemented with medium-chain triglycerides may control diarrhea while permitting caloric balance.

For other uses, see Chapter 13, Agents Used to Treat Hyperlipidemia.

USUAL DOSAGE.—*Oral: Adults,* 4 g four times daily before meals; the preparation is suspended in 180 to 240 ml of water or, when necessary, a fluid. The drug should never be swallowed dry because of the hazard of esophageal irritation or blockage.

PREPARATIONS.—

Cuemid (Merck Sharp & Dohme). *Oral:* Powder in 216 g containers.

Questran (Mead Johnson). *Oral:* Powder in 4 g packets.

DIPHENOXYLATE HYDROCHLORIDE WITH ATROPINE [Lomotil]

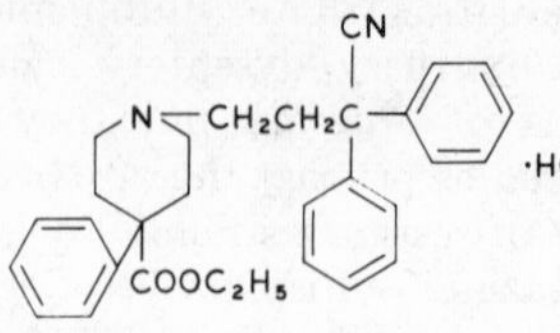

CN
N—CH_2CH_2C
·HCl
$COOC_2H_5$

The effectiveness of diphenoxylate hydrochloride is comparable to that of the opium extracts. It apparently acts by increasing intestinal tone and inhibiting intestinal propulsive motility.

Diphenoxylate hydrochloride with atropine has minimal potential for producing physical dependence when administered in the recommended dosage range, and is classified as a Schedule V substance. The incidence of adverse reactions is relatively low. Untoward effects include rash, drowsiness, dizziness, depression, restlessness, abdominal distention, intestinal obstruction, toxic dilatation of the colon, nausea, headache, and blurred vision. Investigationally, large doses (40 to 60 mg) of diphenoxylate produced a morphine-like euphoria, and toxic doses may cause respiratory depression and coma. Narcotic antagonists are effective antidotes. (See Chapter 23, Narcotic Antagonists.) Diphenoxylate may potentiate the actions of barbiturates, opiates, and other depressants. It should be used cautiously in patients with liver disease, since hepatic coma has been precipitated in a patient with cirrhosis.

USUAL DOSAGE.—*Oral: Adults,* 5 mg three or four times daily. *Children 8 to 12 years of age,* 10 mg daily in divided doses; *5 to 8 years,* 8 mg daily in divided doses.

PREPARATIONS.—Lomotil (Searle). *Oral:* Each tablet or 5 ml of liquid contains diphenoxylate hydrochloride 2.5 mg and atropine sulfate 0.025 mg.

FURAZOLIDONE [Furoxone]

Furazolidone, an antibacterial and antiprotozoal agent, is moderately active against some gram-positive and gram-negative enteric organisms, including species of *Salmonella, Shigella, Escherichia, Proteus, Streptococcus,* and *Staphylococcus.* This drug may be useful in the treatment of severe bacterial enteritis and dysentery caused by susceptible strains of *Salmonella* and *Shigella,* but it will not prevent the carrier state in these infections and more effective drugs are available. Enteropathogenic *E. coli* infections may respond to furazolidone. This agent also is effective in giardiasis. It is poorly absorbed and does not satisfactorily reduce the bacterial population of the intestine when given preoperatively.

The common adverse effects are nausea and vomiting. Arthralgia, fever, and cutaneous hypersensitivity reactions have been reported. The drug may cause hemolysis in patients deficient in erythrocyte glucose-6-phosphate dehydrogenase. Catabolic products color urine brown. Alcohol should not be used during therapy to avoid a disulfiram-type reaction. The monoamine oxidase inhibiting activity of a metabolite of furazolidone enhances the action of sympathomimetic amines. The safety of this drug during pregnancy and in infants less than 1 month of age has not been determined.

See also the Introductory Statement and Chapter 56, Nitrofurans.

USUAL DOSAGE.—*Oral: Adults,* 100 mg four times daily. *Children 5 years of age or older,* 25 to 50 mg four times daily; *1 to 5 years,* 17 to 25 mg four times daily; *infants 1 month to 1 year,* 8 to 17 mg four times daily.

PREPARATIONS.—Furoxone (Eaton). *Oral:* Tablets 100 mg.

LACTOBACILLUS CULTURES

[Bacid, Lactinex]

Bacid is a culture of *Lactobacillus acidophilus,* and Lactinex is a mixed culture of *L. acidophilus* and *L. bulgaricus (L. bulgaricus* does not colonize in the colon). These viable cultures are promoted as an aid in the restoration of normal intestinal flora after administration of antibacterial drugs; many of these drugs suppress intestinal saprophytes such as lactobacilli and *Bacteroides* and potential pathogens such as staphylococci and *Candida* may then emerge. However, no well-controlled studies supporting use of these preparations have been published.

USUAL DOSAGE.—The manufacturers' suggested dosages are:

Bacid: *Oral:* Two capsules two to four times daily.

Lactinex: *Oral:* Four tablets or 1 g packet three or four times daily.

PREPARATIONS.—

Bacid (USV). *Oral:* Capsules containing *Lactobacillus acidophilus* with carboxymethylcellulose sodium 100 mg.

Lactinex (Hynson, Westcott & Dunning). *Oral:* Granules 1 g packet; tablets 250 mg.

METRONIDAZOLE [Flagyl]

Metronidazole, a trichomonacidal and amebicidal agent, appears to be more effective than furazolidone and equally as effective as quinacrine in the treatment of giardiasis.

The incidence of untoward effects is lowest with metronidazole. The drug occasionally causes nausea and, less commonly, diarrhea. Some patients receiving metronidazole experience a disulfiram-type reaction after the ingestion of alcohol.

For other uses and adverse effects of metronidazole, see Chapter 62, Amebicides and Chapter 64, Antitrichomonal Agents.

USUAL DOSAGE.—*Oral:* For treatment of giardiasis, *adults and children over 30 kg,* 250 mg three times daily; *children 19 to 29 kg,* 250 mg twice daily; *14 to 19 kg,* 125 mg three times daily; *under 14 kg,* 125 mg twice daily. Treatment should be continued for seven days.

PREPARATIONS.—Flagyl (Searle). *Oral:* Tablets 250 mg.

OPIUM TINCTURE

Opium tincture is a traditional preparation that is useful for the symptomatic treatment of diarrhea. It is less widely used today than paregoric because the latter is more dilute and teaspoonful doses are more convenient to measure than the smaller amounts of opium tincture prescribed. An effective antidiarrheal dose is not likely to produce euphoria or analgesia because of the relatively small amount needed to produce an effect on the gastrointestinal tract.

Adverse reactions with usual doses are uncommon, but larger doses may produce the undesirable effects of opiates (see Chapter 21, Strong Analgesics). Opium tincture is classified as a Schedule II drug.

USUAL DOSAGE.—*Oral:* 0.6 ml (range, 0.3 to 1 ml) four times daily. The maximal single dose is 1 ml taken at intervals of 2 to 4 hours, and not more than 6 ml should be taken in 24 hours.

PREPARATIONS.—*Oral:* Tincture 10% containing 10 mg of morphine per milliliter. Drug marketed under generic name.

MIXTURES

DONNAGEL
DONNAGEL PG

Donnagel is a mixture containing kaolin, pectin, and three anticholinergic drugs (atropine, scopolamine, and hyoscyamine). It is of doubtful efficacy (see the Introductory Statement and the evaluation on Kaolin Mixture with Pectin). Donnagel PG combines the effects of the basic formula and opium (see the evaluation on Opium Tincture). This mixture is classified as a Schedule V substance.

The adverse effects are those produced by the individual drugs in the mixtures. (See the appropriate evaluations.) Contraindications of the basic mixture include glaucoma and intestinal obstruction. Donnagel should be administered with care to patients with urinary tract obstruction or prostatic hypertrophy.

USUAL DOSAGE.—No useful dosage is recognized. The manufacturer's suggested dosages are:

Donnagel: *Oral: Adults,* 30 ml initially, then 15 to 30 ml after each evacuation. *Children,* 10 ml initially, then 5 to 10 ml after each evacuation.

Donnagel PG: *Oral: Adults,* 30 ml every three hours or as needed. *Children over 1 year of age,* 10 ml every three hours as needed.

PREPARATIONS.—

Donnagel (Robins). *Oral:* Each 30 ml of suspension contains kaolin 6 g, pectin 142.8 mg, hyoscyamine sulfate 0.1037 mg, atropine sulfate 0.0194 mg, and scopolamine hydrobromide 0.0065 mg.

Donnagel PG (Robins). *Oral:* Each 30 ml of suspension contains the same formulation as Donnagel plus powdered opium 24 mg.

FUROXONE LIQUID

Furoxone Liquid is a mixture of the antibacterial and antiprotozoal agent, furazolidone, with pectin and kaolin. The rationale for this mixture is questionable because furazolidone is effective only in giardiasis and specific enteric bacterial infections caused by sensitive strains, and the effectiveness of kaolin and pectin is doubtful (see the Introductory Statement and evaluation on Kaolin Mixture with Pectin). However, if the tablet form of furazolidone is difficult to administer, this preparation may be considered a liquid dosage form of the drug.

USUAL DOSAGE.—This mixture is useful only as a liquid dosage form of furazolidone. (For recommended dosage of the antimicrobial agent, see the evaluation on Furazolidone.)

PREPARATIONS.—Furoxone Liquid (Eaton). *Oral:* Each 15 ml of liquid contains furazolidone 50 mg, kaolin 3 g, and pectin 225 mg.

KAOLIN MIXTURE WITH PECTIN

Kaolin and pectin each have adsorbent and allegedly protective properties and are promoted for use in the symptomatic treatment of diarrhea. They are customarily available only in preparations that contain both agents and often additional antibacterial drugs as well. Adequately controlled clinical studies that demonstrate the efficacy of kaolin-pectin combinations are lacking, and although their use is supported by tradition, they are of doubtful value. It has been suggested, without verification, that kaolin and pectin adsorb viruses and bacterial toxins.

Kaolin and pectin are contraindicated in patients with obstruction of the bowel. These mixtures should not be used for more than two days, or in patients with fever, or in children less than 3 years of age.

USUAL DOSAGE.—Because proof of efficacy is lacking, no useful dosage is recognized. The suggested N.F. dosage is: *Oral: Adults,* 30 ml repeated as necessary.

PREPARATIONS.—Kaolin Mixture with Pectin, N.F. *Oral:* Suspension containing 20% kaolin and 1% pectin in sweetened, peppermint-flavored tragacanth. Marketed under generic name.

KAOPECTATE

The formula of this mixture is a modification of the formula for Kaolin Mixture with Pectin, N.F. Like the latter, it is of doubtful value. It should not be used for more than two days, or in patients with fever, or in children less than 3 years of age. It is contraindicated in patients with obstruction of the bowel.

USUAL DOSAGE.—Because proof of efficacy is lacking, no useful dosage is recognized. The manufacturers' suggested dose (to be taken after each evacuation) is: *Oral: Adults,* 60 to 120 ml. *Children over 12 years of age,* 60 ml; *6 to 12 years,* 30 to 60 ml; *3 to 6 years,* 15 to 30 ml.

PREPARATIONS.—Kaopectate (Upjohn). *Oral:* Each 5 ml of liquid contains kaolin 1 g and pectin 20 mg.

SIMILAR MIXTURES.—Kalpec (Wyeth),

Kao-Con (Upjohn), Paocin (Beecham Massengill), Pargel (Parke, Davis).

PAREGORIC

Paregoric (camphorated opium tincture) is an antidiarrheal mixture that contains 0.04% morphine and provides the convenience of teaspoonful doses. It is as effective as opium tincture in the appropriate dose. Paregoric frequently is combined with other antidiarrheal agents.

Adverse effects are rare, but nausea and other gastrointestinal disturbances occur occasionally; the usual oral doses do not produce euphoria or analgesia, but prolonged use has produced dependence despite the unappealing taste of paregoric. Paregoric is classified as a Schedule III drug. It should not be used in diarrhea caused by poisoning until toxic material is eliminated from the gastrointestinal tract.

USUAL DOSAGE.—*Oral: Adults*, 5 to 10 ml every two hours (but not more than four times daily) or until diarrhea is controlled. *Children*, 0.25 to 0.5 ml/kg of body weight after each loose stool. Customary amount per prescription should be 1 or 2 ounces.

PREPARATIONS.—Paregoric, U.S.P. contains 0.4 mg of morphine per milliliter. Drug marketed under generic name and under the name Camphorated Tincture of Opium.

PAREPECTOLIN

This antidiarrheal mixture contains pectin, kaolin, and opium; its effectiveness is primarily due to the opium content, and thus use of the alkaloid alone is preferred. It is classified as a Schedule V substance.

This mixture has the same adverse effects and contraindications as do opium and kaolin mixture with pectin. (See the Introductory Statement and the evaluations on Opium Tincture and Kaolin Mixture with Pectin.)

USUAL DOSAGE.—No useful dosage is recognized because there is no evidence that pectin and kaolin contribute to the antidiarrheal effect. The manufacturer's suggested dosage is: *Oral: Adults*, 15 to 30 ml after each evacuation for no more than four doses in 12 hours. *Children*, 5 to 10 ml after each evacuation for no more than four doses in 12 hours.

PREPARATIONS.—Parepectolin (Rorer). *Oral:* Each 30 ml of suspension contains opium 15 mg, pectin 162 mg, and kaolin 5.5 g.

SIMILAR MIXTURE.—Pecto-Kalin (Lemmon).

SORBOQUEL

Sorboquel is a mixture of polycarbophil and the anticholinergic-antispasmodic, thihexinol methylbromide. Polycarbophil is a hydrophilic polyacrylic resin that may be useful in both constipation and diarrhea because of its marked capacity for binding water. Evidence in support of an enhanced antidiarrheal effect of polycarbophil by the addition of thihexinol is from uncontrolled clinical studies and is unconvincing.

Overdosage with Sorboquel may cause symptoms of atropine poisoning (see Chapter 78, Antispasmodics). The drug is contraindicated in patients with urinary retention, angle-closure glaucoma, and in those in whom tachycardia would be dangerous.

USUAL DOSAGE.—Use of this mixture is not justified because of the potential adverse effects of thihexinol and inadequate evidence that it contributes to the antidiarrheal effect of polycarbophil. The manufacturer's suggested dosage is: *Oral: Adults and children over 12 years of age*, one tablet four times daily; six to eight tablets daily may be given in severe cases. The dose should be reduced after diarrhea has responded to treatment.

PREPARATIONS.—Sorboquel (Schering). *Oral:* Each tablet contains polycarbophil 500 mg and thihexinol methylbromide 15 mg.

Additional Antidiarrheal Mixtures

The following antidiarrheal mixtures are listed for information only.

Cerebel (Xttrium): Each 5 ml of liquid contains cerium oxalate 300 mg, hyoscyamine sulfate 5.2 μg, scopolamine hydrobromide 3 μg, atropine sulfate 0.01 mg, milk of bismuth 2.5 ml, and phenobarbital elixir 2.02 ml; each capsule contains cerium oxalate 300 mg, bismuth subcarbonate 300 mg, and powdered extract of belladonna alkaloids 8 mg.

Corrective Mixture (Beecham-Massengill): Each 5 ml of elixir contains zinc phenolsulfonate 10 mg, phenyl salicylate 20 mg, bismuth subsalicylate 80 mg, and pepsin 40 mg with or without paregoric 0.6 ml.

Infantol (First Texas): Each 30 ml of suspension contains pectin 260 mg, zinc phenolsulfonate 104 mg, bismuth subsalicylate 518 mg, and chondrus extract with (Pink) or without (White) paregoric 3.6 mg.

Kaomagma (Wyeth): Each 5 ml of suspension contains kaolin 1 g in aluminum hydroxide gel.

Metropectin (Pennwalt): Each tablet contains

methylatropine nitrate 1 mg, kaolin 450 mg, pectin 60 mg, aluminum hydroxide 120 mg, and beta lactose 60 mg.

Mul-Sed (Webster): Each 5 ml of liquid contains paregoric 1.25 ml, pectin 43.2 mg, kaolin 860 mg, and milk of bismuth 0.8 ml.

Parelixir (Purdue Frederick): Each 5 ml of liquid contains tincture of opium 0.03 ml and pectin 24 mg.

Pectocel (Lilly): Each 5 ml of suspension contains pectin 50 mg, kaolin 1 g, and zinc phenolsulfonate 12 mg.

Pektamalt (Warren-Teed): Each 5 ml contains pectin 109 mg and kaolin 1.09 g with potassium gluconate and sodium citrate.

Chapter 81

LAXATIVES AND AGENTS AFFECTING FECAL CONSISTENCY

Laxatives and drugs that affect fecal consistency facilitate the passage of feces through the colon and their elimination from the rectum. The proper uses of these drugs are to ease defecation in those with painful hemorrhoids or other rectal disorders; to avoid excessive straining and concurrent increases in abdominal pressure in those with hernias; to avoid potentially hazardous increases in blood pressure during defecation in patients with hypertensive, cerebral, coronary, or other arterial diseases; to relieve acute constipation; to cleanse the bowels prior to radiologic and proctologic examinations and bowel surgery; to remove parasites and toxic vermifuge after anthelmintic therapy; and to remove the toxic material in some cases of poisoning.

In the past, drugs of this type were classified according to the vigor of their action as laxatives (mildest), cathartics, and drastics (most irritant). The drastics include the resinous drugs, colocynth, gamboge, elaterin, ipomea, jalap, and podophyllum. The violence of their action often produces hemorrhagic enteritis, and thus use of the drastics is not justified. Croton oil, which is similarly violent in action and has been virtually abandoned because of it, also should not be used. Calomel (mercurous chloride), once widely used as a cathartic, should not be used because it is unsafe and unreliable. A more useful classification, based on mechanism of action, is: stimulants, bulk-forming agents, saline cathartics, lubricants, and wetting agents.

Stimulants: The exact mechanism of action of each drug in this group has not been established. In general, however, they produce defecation by stimulating peristalsis either by acting on the intestinal intramural nerve plexus, smooth muscle, electrolyte transport system, or some combination of these.

Castor oil has been classified as a stimulant cathartic because lipolytic action in the small intestine liberates ricinoleic acid, which stimulates the motor activity of the small intestine by an unknown mechanism to produce defecation.

The anthraquinone-containing group of stimulant cathartics (eg, casanthranol, cascara, senna, danthron [Danivac, Dorbane], rhubarb, aloe) is widely used. These drugs act principally on the large intestine which they reach both directly after passage through the small intestine and indirectly by way of the bloodstream, since some is absorbed. Of these, cascara has the mildest action and will produce a soft or formed stool with little or no colic. Danthron, a synthetic anthraquinone, also has a mild effect. Crude senna is somewhat more active. Rhubarb and aloe are the most potent; since they are most likely to cause colic, they should not be used. Casanthranol, a glycoside-containing extract of cascara, is reported to be ten times more potent than cascara.

Phenolphthalein is presumably a stimulant cathartic. It acts primarily on the large intestine and produces a semifluid or soft stool with little or no colic.

Oxyphenisatin is similar pharmacologically to phenolphthalein and is administered rectally to produce defecation. The acetate ester of this compound has been withdrawn from the market because its prolonged oral use caused hepatitis and jaundice.

Bisacodyl [Dulcolax], which also is similar pharmacologically to phenolphthalein, stimulates the sensory nerve endings of the colonic mucosa to initiate reflex peristalsis which, in turn, produces defecation.

Glycerin suppositories promote defecation by stimulating the rectal mucosa; they also may soften inspissated fecal material.

Bulk-Forming Agents: The bulk-producing laxatives (bran, gum tragacanth, chondrus, sterculia [karaya] gum, bassora gum, carboxymethylcellulose, agar, plantago seed, and psyllium hydrophilic colloid) absorb water and expand. This expanded indigestible and unabsorbable material increases the bulk of the intestinal contents, thereby producing a reflex peristalsis and defecation. The absorbed water also softens the stool. Bulk laxatives are most effective if taken with one or more glasses of water. The most commonly used preparations are those containing psyllium hydrophilic colloid which is derived from plantago seeds. Allergic reactions (urticaria, nonseasonal rhinitis, dermatitis, and bronchial asthma) are a serious drawback to the use of the plant gums.

Saline Cathartics: These agents include a group of salts, one or both ions of which are poorly absorbed. A hypertonic solution of such a salt osmotically draws a substantial amount of fluid into the intestine, and the presence of this fluid causes increased peristalsis and defecation. The commonly used salts in this class are magnesium carbonate, oxide, citrate, hydroxide, or sulfate; sodium sulfate or phosphate; and mixed sodium and potassium tartrate. The saline cathartics also are used after the ingestion of anthelmintics or poisons to hasten the evacuation of the worms or toxic materials.

Lubricants: Mineral oil (liquid petrolatum), olive oil, and cottonseed oil usually are considered to be the representatives of this group. However, the digestible oils have now fallen into disuse and only mineral oil is currently used. When administered orally, mineral oil softens the feces and is used when it is important to lessen the strain of evacuation (eg, in patients with hernia or cardiovascular disease). When administered rectally, it eases the passage of impacted fecal material. Its mechanism of action is not known.

Wetting Agents: Dioctyl sodium sulfosuccinate [Colace, Doxinate], dioctyl calcium sulfosuccinate [Surfak], and poloxalkol [Magcyl, Polykol] soften the feces by lowering their surface tension; this permits the fecal mass to be penetrated by intestinal fluids. They are used when it is important to lessen the strain of evacuation.

Adverse Reactions and Precautions

Laxatives should be used only for short-term therapy. Most physicians probably have more patients who should break the habit of taking laxatives than they have patients who need such drugs. The addition to the diet of such natural laxatives as high residue foods, figs, or prunes, and the establishment of a regular time for defecation (eg, after breakfast) may help those in the first group.

A laxative should never be given to a patient with undiagnosed abdominal pain, intestinal obstruction, or fecal impaction. A change in bowel habit that persists must be thoroughly investigated.

The prolonged continuous use of the stimulant drugs may result in spastic colitis, sodium depletion, hypokalemia, dehydration, secondary aldosteronism, steatorrhea, protein-losing gastroenteropathy with hypoalbuminemia, changes in intestinal anatomy, and osteomalacia.

Because it is possible that obstruction or impaction may occur after use of the bulk-forming agents, these drugs should not be used by those with dysphagia or intestinal ulcerations, adhesions, or stenosis.

See also the individual evaluations.

STIMULANTS

BISACODYL [Dulcolax]

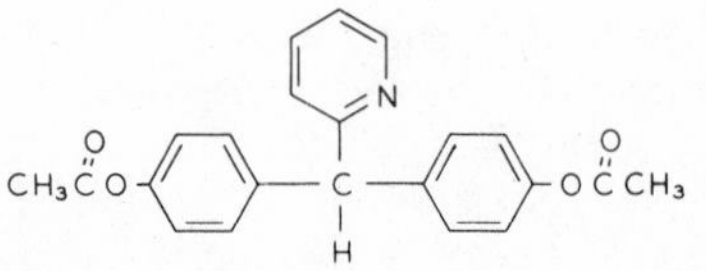

Bisacodyl is a mild stimulant laxative that is active orally and rectally. It produces a copious soft to formed stool within six hours after oral administration and within one hour after rectal administration.

The tablets should be swallowed whole to avoid gastric irritation; they should not be taken within one hour after ingestion of milk or antacids in order to prevent dissolution of the enteric coating, release of the drug, and resultant gastric irritation. Mild colic has been reported. The suppository may produce mild smarting or tenesmus, and continued administration can cause mild rectal irritation. See also the section on adverse reactions and precautions in the Introductory Statement.

USUAL DOSAGE.—

Oral: Adults, 10 to 15 mg; *children,* 5 to 10 mg.

Rectal: Adults and children over 2 years of age, 10 mg; *under 2 years,* 5 mg.

PREPARATIONS.—Dulcolax (Geigy).
Oral: Tablets (enteric-coated) 5 mg.
Rectal: Suppositories 10 mg.

CASANTHRANOL [Peristim Forte]

Casanthranol is a purified mixture of the anthranol glycosides extracted from cascara sagrada. It is a member of the anthraquinone-containing group of stimulant laxatives (see the Introductory Statement), and is reported to be ten times as potent as whole cascara sagrada. In most patients, a semisoft stool is produced by casanthranol in 8 to 12 hours.

Adverse reactions that have been reported are abdominal cramping, diarrhea, and nausea and rectal bleeding in a patient with ulcerative colitis. See also the section on adverse reactions and precautions in the Introductory Statement.

USUAL DOSAGE.—*Oral: Adults,* 90 mg at bedtime; in stubborn cases, 180 mg may be required.

PREPARATIONS.—Peristim Forte (Mead Johnson). *Oral:* Capsules 90 mg.

CASTOR OIL
CASTOR OIL, AROMATIC
CASTOR OIL, EMULSIFIED [Neoloid]

Castor oil is a stimulant laxative which produces one or more copious, watery evacuations approximately two to six hours after ingestion. Normal evacuation may be delayed one or more days after its use. This drug is more active if taken on an empty stomach. Since it thoroughly empties gas and feces from the intestines, castor oil is used in the preparation of patients for proctoscopy, bowel surgery, or radiologic studies of the gastrointestinal tract. Fruit juice or carbonated drinks help disguise the disagreeable taste. Neoloid is a mint-flavored emulsion of castor oil.

No adverse reactions have been reported. For general precautions, see the section on adverse reactions and precautions in the Introductory Statement.

USUAL DOSAGE.—

Castor Oil; Castor Oil, Aromatic:

Oral: Adults, 15 to 30 ml; *children,* 5 to 15 ml.

Castor Oil, Emulsified:

Oral: Adults, 30 to 60 ml; infants, 2.5 to 7.5 ml; *children,* dose adjusted between that used for infants and adults.

PREPARATIONS.—

Castor Oil, U.S.P., Castor Oil, Aromatic, N.F. Marketed under generic name.

Castor Oil, Emulsified: Neoloid (Lederle). *Oral:* Liquid 36.4%.

CASCARA SAGRADA

Cascara is the mildest member of the anthraquinone group of stimulant laxatives. Its effect on the small intestine is slight, but it causes vigorous peristalsis in the large intestine. The drug produces a soft or formed stool in six to eight hours with little or no colic.

The prolonged use of cascara preparations produces benign pigmentation of the colonic mucosa (melanosis coli) that may regress after the drug is discontinued. Since the active principles of cascara are excreted in milk, this laxative should not be given to lactating mothers. The drug imparts a yellowish-brown color to acid urine and a reddish color to alkaline urine. See also the section on adverse reactions and precautions in the Introductory Statement.

USUAL DOSAGE.—*Oral: Adults,* 300 mg of extract, 1 ml of fluidextract, or 5 ml of aromatic fluidextract.

PREPARATIONS.—Cascara Tablets, N.F., Cascara Sagrada, U.S.P., Cascara Sagrada Extract, N.F., Cascara Sagrada Fluidextract, N.F., Aromatic Cascara Fluidextract, U.S.P.

AVAILABLE TRADEMARK.—Cas-Evac (Parke, Davis). Forms also marketed under generic name.

DANTHRON [Danivac, Dorbane]

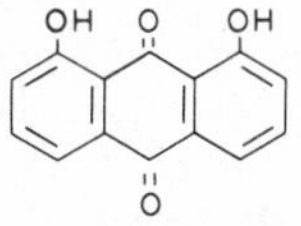

This synthetic anthraquinone derivative has the same mode of action as other stimulant laxatives (see the Introductory Statement). It produces a soft or semifluid stool in six to eight hours. Danthron is much less active than an equivalent dose of the glycosides in the anthraquinone-containing stimulant laxatives.

Brownish discoloration of the rectal mucosa has been reported after prolonged use of danthron. This disappears after the drug is discontinued. Danthron is excreted in milk and should not be given to lacating mothers. It also is excreted in urine and imparts a pink color to alkaline urine. See also the section on adverse reactions and precautions in the Introductory Statement.

USUAL DOSAGE.—*Oral: Adults,* 75 to 150 mg.

PREPARATIONS.—Danivac (Fellows-Testagar), Dorbane (Riker). *Oral:* Tablets 75 mg. Drug also marketed under generic name.

GLYCERIN SUPPOSITORIES

Glycerin suppositories contain by weight approximately 91% glycerin, 9% sodium stearate, and 5% water. They promote fecal evacuation in 15 to 30 minutes by stimulating the rectal mucosa. They also may soften inspissated fecal material.

Glycerin suppositories should not be used in the presence of anal fissures, fistulas, ulcerative hemorrhoids, or proctitis. See also the section on adverse reactions and precautions in the Introductory Statement.

USUAL DOSAGE.—*Rectal: Adults and children,* one suppository.

PREPARATIONS.—Glycerin Suppositories, N.F. Drug marketed under generic name.

OXYPHENISATIN [Lavema Enema Powder]

This drug is a potent stimulant laxative. It is administered rectally, and acts upon the colon to produce defecation within a few minutes. Its efficacy relative to other substances used as enemas (eg, isotonic sodium chloride solution) is, however, as yet unknown.

The acetate ester of this drug was widely used as an orally administered laxative. However, it has been withdrawn from the market because of its toxicity. (See also the Introductory Statement.)

Cramps, diarrhea, nausea, vomiting, sweating, tachycardia, and syncope occur infrequently after the use of this drug.

USUAL DOSAGE.—*Rectal: Adults,* prior to diagnostic or surgical procedures, one-half to one packet dissolved in 1 to 2 liters of water; *elderly or debilitated patients,* one-half packet in 1 liter of water. For severe constipation, one-half to one packet dissolved in 180 ml of water. As a barium enema adjuvant, one-half to one packet mixed with 1 or 2 liters of barium enema suspension; *elderly or debilitated patients,* one-half packet.

PREPARATIONS.—Lavema Enema Powder (Winthrop). *Rectal:* Each packet contains oxyphenisatin 20 mg with disodium edetate, sodium stearate, and lactose in sufficient quantity to make 3 g.

AVAILABLE MIXTURE.—Lavema Compound Solution Disposable Enema Kit (Winthrop): Each 180 ml contains oxyphenisatin 20 mg, tyloxapol 135 mg, and propylene glycol 9 ml.

PHENOLPHTHALEIN

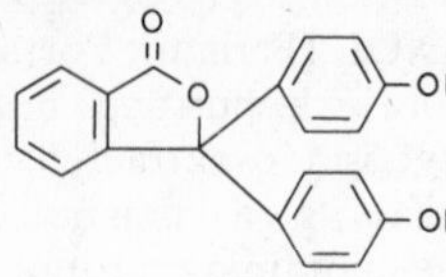

Phenolphthalein is a stimulant laxative which acts primarily on the large intestine to produce a semifluid stool in four to eight hours with little or no colic. Its action may persist for three to four days as a result of the enterohepatic circulation of the small amounts absorbed. Phenolphthalein is the active agent in many proprietary over-the-counter laxative preparations.

Dermatitis, particularly fixed drug eruptions, with pruritus, burning, vesication, and discoloration may occur in hypersensitive patients. Fatal hypersensitivity reactions also have been reported but a causal relationship to phenolphthalein has not been established. Occasional cases of nonthrombocytopenic purpura have occurred. Phenolphthalein imparts a red color to alkaline urine or alkaline feces. See also the section on adverse reactions and precautions in the Introductory Statement.

USUAL DOSAGE.—*Oral: Adults,* 60 mg, but as much as 200 mg has been given.

PREPARATIONS.—Phenolphthalein, N.F.; Phenolphthalein Tablets, N.F.

AVAILABLE TRADEMARK.—Phenolax (Upjohn). Drug also marketed in bulk form under generic name.

SENNA PREPARATIONS

Senna is an anthraquinone-type stimulant laxative with actions similar to those of cascara, but it is more active and produces more colic. Defecation occurs within six hours.

Senna is available as the crude drug, as the crystalline senna glycosides (sennosides A and B), and as a standardized senna concentrate [Senokot] which is purified and standardized. The purified preparations are more commonly used than the crude ones and are claimed to produce colic and loose stools only rarely; however, evidence supporting this claim is limited.

The drug imparts a yellowish-brown color to acid urine and a reddish color to alkaline urine. See also the section on adverse reactions and precautions in the Introductory Statement.

USUAL DOSAGE.—

Senna:

Oral: Senna, N.F.: *Adults,* 2 g; *children,* 4 mg/kg of body weight. Senna Fluidextract, N.F.: *Adults,* 2 ml; *children,* 0.04 ml/kg. Senna Syrup, N.F.: *Adults,* 8 ml; *children,* 0.15 ml/kg.

Senokot:

Oral: (Granules) *Adults,* 1 level teaspoonful to a maximum of 2 level teaspoonsful two times daily; *geriatric, obstetric, or gynecologic patients and children over 27 kg,* dosage reduced by one-half. (Syrup) *Adults,* 2 to 3 teaspoonsful one or two times daily; *geriatric, obstetric, or gynecologic patients,* dosage reduced by one-half; *children 5 to 15 years of age,* 1 to a maximum of 2 teaspoonsful two times daily; *1 to 5 years,* one-half to a maximum of 1 teaspoonful two times daily; *1 month to 1 year,* one-quarter to a maximum of one-half teaspoonful twice daily. (Tablets) *Adults,* two tablets to a maximum of four tablets two times daily; *geriatric, obstetric, or gynecologic patients and children over 27 kg,* dosage reduced by one-half.

Rectal: Adults, one suppository; *children over 27 kg,* one-half suppository.

Glysennid:

Oral: Adults, one or two tablets before retiring; *children over 10 years of age,* one or two tablets; *6 to 10 years,* one tablet.

PREPARATIONS.—

Senna, N.F., Senna Fluidextract, N.F., Senna Syrup, N.F.

Senokot (Purdue Frederick).

Oral: Granules, syrup, tablets.

Rectal: Suppositories.

Glysennid (Sandoz). *Oral:* Tablets.

AVAILABLE TRADEMARKS.—Senna: Aperens (Brayten), Casafru (Davies Rose Hoyt), Roenten (Mallinckrodt). Forms also marketed under generic name.

BULK-FORMING AGENTS

CARBOXYMETHYLCELLULOSE SODIUM

[Bu-Lax, C.M.C.]

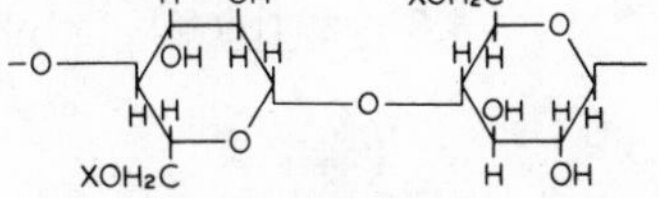

X = H or CH_2CO_2Na

This bulk-forming laxative is a synthetic hydrophilic colloid which is indigestible and nonabsorbable and does not interfere with the intestinal absorption of essential nutrients. It usually produces its laxative effect within 12 to 24 hours but up to three days of medication may be necessary to achieve a full effect. Carboxymethylcellulose is claimed to aid in the treatment of obesity and acute diarrhea, but the evidence supporting these claims is not convincing.

For general precautions, see the section on adverse reactions and precautions in the Introductory Statement.

USUAL DOSAGE.—*Oral: Adults,* 1.5 g two to four times daily; *children,* 500 mg two or three times daily. The drug should be taken with one or two glasses of water and ingested rapidly.

PREPARATIONS.—Bu-lax (Ulmer), C.M.C. (Robinson). *Oral:* Tablets 500 mg. Drug also marketed in bulk form under generic name.

PLANTAGO SEED (Psyllium Seed)

This bulk-forming laxative consists of the whole or powdered seeds of one of three species of *Plantago.* It usually produces its laxative effect within 12 to 24 hours but up to three days of medication may be necessary to achieve a full effect. It is indigestible, nonabsorbable, and does not interfere with absorption of essential nutrients. Plantago seed is alleged to aid in the treatment of obesity and acute diarrhea, but its efficacy for these purposes has not been proved.

For general precautions, see the section on adverse reactions and precautions in the Introductory Statement.

USUAL DOSAGE.—*Oral: Adults,* 4 to 15 g in a glass of water, one to three times daily. The drug should be ingested rapidly.

PREPARATIONS.—Plantago Seed, N.F. Drug marketed under generic name and under the name Psyllium Seed.

PSYLLIUM HYDROPHILIC COLLOID

[Effersyllium, Metamucil, Mucilose, Plantamucin, Testarr]

This bulk-forming laxative is the refined colloid from psyllium seeds. It usually produces its laxative effect within 12 to 24 hours but up to three days of medication may be necessary to achieve a full effect. The preparation is indigestible, nonabsorbable, and will not interfere with the intestinal absorption of essential nutrients. Psyllium hydrophilic colloid is alleged to aid in the treatment of obesity and acute diarrhea, but evidence supporting these claims is not convincing.

For general precautions, see the section on adverse reactions and precautions in the

Introductory Statement.

USUAL DOSAGE.—*Oral: Adults*, 1 rounded teaspoonful (7 g) or one packet (instant mix) is mixed with a glass of water or other suitable fluid; the liquid is ingested rapidly one to three times daily. A second glass of water improves the effect.

PREPARATIONS.—

Effersyllium (Stuart). *Oral:* Granular powder.

Metamucil (Searle). *Oral:* Powder in effervescent (instant mix) and noneffervescent form.

Mucilose (Winthrop). *Oral:* Granules, flakes.

Plantamucin (Elder). *Oral:* Granules.

Testarr (Fellows-Testagar). *Oral:* Powder.

SALINE CATHARTICS

MAGNESIUM AND SODIUM SALTS

Many different salts with essentially the same actions are used as saline cathartics. They produce a watery or semifluid evacuation in two to six hours. Saline cathartics are most effective if taken with substantial amounts (at least 240 ml) of fluid on an empty stomach. They are also useful in eliminating the parasites and toxic vermifuge after anthelmintic therapy and in removing the toxic material in some cases of poisoning.

The magnesium and potassium salts are contraindicated in patients with impaired renal function. The bitter taste of magnesium sulfate may cause nausea. The magnesium salts should not be used with neomycin. The sodium salts are contraindicated in cardiac patients with edema or evidence of congestive heart failure, or in those on a low-sodium diet. For general precautions, see the section on adverse reactions and precautions in the Introductory Statement.

For dosages, see the following table:

PREPARATIONS	USUAL DOSAGE (Adults)*†
Fleet Enema (Fleet) (solution containing 16 g sodium biphosphate and 6 g sodium phosphate/100 ml)	4 oz (rectal only)
Magnesium carbonate, N.F.	8 g
Magnesium citrate solution, N.F. (1.55 to 1.9 g/100 ml magnesium oxide with citric acid and sodium bicarbonate for effervescence)	200 ml
Milk of Magnesia, U.S.P. (7.5% to 8.5% magnesium hydroxide suspension)	15 ml
Magnesium oxide, U.S.P.	4 g
Magnesium sulfate, U.S.P.	15 g
Phospho-Soda (Fleet) (solution containing 48 g sodium biphosphate and 18 g sodium phosphate/100 ml)	10 to 20 ml
Potassium bitartrate	2 g
Potassium phosphate	4 g
Potassium sodium tartrate, N.F.	10 g
Sodium phosphate, N.F.	4 g
Sodium phosphate, effervescent, dried, N.F.	10 g
Sodium sulfate	15 g
Seidlitz powders (blue powder paper, sodium bicarbonate 2.5 g and potassium sodium tartrate 7.5 g; white powder paper, tartaric acid 2.2 g)	Contents of one blue and white powder paper mixed in about 60 ml of water.
Travad Enema (Flint) (solution containing sodium biphosphate 16 g and sodium phosphate 6 g/100 ml)	4.5 oz (rectal only)

*Dosage is reduced for children (see table, back cover).

†Except where indicated, all doses are to be administered orally. Many manufacturers market their own flavored versions of the various saline cathartics, which tend to be more expensive than the official preparations.

LUBRICANTS

MINERAL OIL (Liquid Petrolatum)

Mineral oil is an indigestible hydrocarbon oil of limited absorbability. It is used orally to lessen the strain of evacuation (eg, in patients with hernia or cardiovascular disease) or rectally to ease the passage of impacted fecal material. The emulsified preparations may reduce seepage through the anal sphincter and may be more effective than the nonemulsified preparation.

Prolonged oral use (more than two weeks) reduces the absorption of the fat-soluble vitamins (A, D, E, and K). The user should be alerted to the risk of lipid pneumonia if mineral oil is aspirated and to the possibility of untoward effects from its absorption. Because of this possibility, its use with the wetting agents, which presumably may increase its absorption, is contraindicated. Mineral oil should not be used after anorectal surgery, for it may cause pruritus ani and interfere with healing of tissue. For general precautions, see the section on adverse reactions and precautions in the Introductory Statement.

USUAL DOSAGE.—*Oral, Rectal: Adults,* 15 to 45 ml at bedtime.

PREPARATIONS.—Mineral Oil; Mineral Oil Emulsion, N.F.; Mineral Oil, Light, N.F.

AVAILABLE TRADEMARKS.—Fleet Oil Retention Enema (Fleet), Kondremul (Cooper), Petrogalar, Plain (Wyeth). Forms also marketed under generic name.

WETTING AGENTS

DIOCTYL CALCIUM SULFOSUCCINATE [Surfak]
DIOCTYL SODIUM SULFOSUCCINATE [Colace, Doxinate]

$$\begin{array}{l} \overset{O}{\overset{\|}{C}}OCH_2\overset{C_2H_5}{\overset{|}{C}}H(CH_2)_3CH_3 \\ | \\ CH_2 \\ | \\ CH\,SO_3Na \\ | \\ \underset{O}{\underset{\|}{C}}OCH_2\underset{C_2H_5}{\underset{|}{C}}H(CH_2)_3CH_3 \end{array}$$

These wetting agents soften the feces and are used when it is necessary to lessen the strain of defecation (eg, in persons with hernia or cardiovascular disease). They require one to two days to exert their full effect. These drugs are often combined with other agents, but their use with mineral oil is contraindicated because of the presumption that they may increase the absorption of the oil and thus the possibility of untoward effects.

Diarrhea is the only reported adverse reaction. For general precautions, see the section on adverse reactions and precautions in the Introductory Statement.

USUAL DOSAGE.—*Oral: Adults and children over 12 years of age,* 50 to 240 mg daily; *6 to 12 years,* 40 to 120 mg daily; *3 to 6 years,* 20 to 60 mg daily; *under 3 years,* 10 to 40 mg daily.

PREPARATIONS.—

Dioctyl Calcium Sulfosuccinate:

Surfak (Hoechst). *Oral:* Capsules 50 and 240 mg.

Dioctyl Sodium Sulfosuccinate:

Colace (Mead Johnson). *Oral:* Capsules 50 and 100 mg; solution 10 mg/ml; syrup 20 mg/5 ml.

Doxinate (Hoechst). *Oral:* Capsules 60 and 240 mg; solution 50 mg/ml.

ADDITIONAL TRADEMARKS.—Dioctyl Sodium Sulfosuccinate: D-S-S (Parke, Davis), Definate (Fellows-Testagar), Diomedicone (Medicone), Diosuccin (Consolidated Midland), Doss Capsules (Ferndale), Ilozoft (Warren-Teed), Kosate (Lemmon), Laxinate (Mallard), Parlax (Robinson).

POLOXALKOL [Magcyl, Polykol]

$$HO(C_2H_4O)_a(C_3H_6O)_b(C_2H_4O)_cH$$

The actions and uses of this wetting agent are similar to those of dioctyl calcium sulfosuccinate and dioctyl sodium sulfosuccinate (see the evaluation).

Poloxalkol should not be administered with mineral oil because it is presumed that this drug may increase the absorption of mineral oil and thus the possibility of untoward effects. For general precautions, see the section on adverse reactions and precautions in the Introductory Statement.

USUAL DOSAGE.—*Oral: Adults,* 250 mg two or three times daily; *children 6 to 12 years of age,* 250 to 500 mg daily.

PREPARATIONS.—Magcyl (Elder), Polykol (Upjohn). *Oral:* Capsules 250 mg.

MIXTURES

Sufficient evidence is not available to determine the usefulness of laxative mixtures. The following partial listing of available mixtures is provided only for informational purposes; inclusion does not imply a recommendation for use.

Agoral (Warner-Chilcott): Each 100 ml of emulsion contains phenolphthalein 1.3 mg in mineral oil.

Alophen (Parke, Davis): Each capsule or pill contains aloin 16 mg, belladonna extract 2.7 mg, ipecac 4.3 mg, and phenolphthalein 32.4 mg.

Bassoran, Plain (Merrell-National): Granules containing sterculia gum 87% and magnesium trisilicate 8.7%.

Bassoran with Cascara (Merrell-National): Each 30 mg of granules contains sterculia gum 75%, magnesium trisilicate 7.5%, and cascara extract 4.4 ml.

Bicholax (Elder): Each tablet contains phenolphthalein 32.4 mg with cascara sagrada extract, sodium glycocholate, sodium taurocholate, and aloin.

Billotabs (Fellows-Testagar): Each tablet contains ox bile extract 30 mg, phenolphthalein 30 mg, cascara sagrada extract 30 mg, aloin 8 mg, and podophyllin 3 mg.

Casakol (Upjohn): Each capsule or 5 ml of syrup contains poloxalkol 250 mg and casanthranol 30 mg.

Casyllium (Upjohn): Each 30 ml of granules contains cascara fluidextract aromatic 13.80 ml, psyllium husk powder 19.44 g, and prune powder 5.53 g.

Clysodrast (Barnes-Hind): Each packet contains bisacodyl 1.5 mg and tannic acid 2.5 g.

Dialose (Stuart): Each capsule contains dioctyl sodium sulfosuccinate 100 mg and carboxymethylcellulose sodium 400 mg.

Dialose Plus (Stuart): Each capsule contains casanthranol 30 mg, dioctyl sodium sulfosuccinate 100 mg, and carboxymethylcellulose sodium 400 mg.

Dorbantyl (Riker): Each capsule contains danthron 25 or 50 mg and dioctyl sodium sulfosuccinate 50 or 100 mg.

Doxan (Hoechst): Each tablet contains danthron 50 mg and dioctyl sodium sulfosuccinate 60 mg.

Doxidan (Hoechst): Each capsule contains danthron 50 mg and dioctyl calcium sulfosuccinate 60 mg.

Gentlax (Purdue Frederick): Each tablet or 5 ml of granules contains guar gum 1 g and standardized senna concentrate 326 mg.

Gentlax S (Purdue Frederick): Tablets containing standardized senna concentrate 187 mg and dioctyl sodium sulfosuccinate 50 mg.

Kondremul with Cascara (Cooper): Each 15 ml of emulsion contains mineral oil 55% and cascara extract 660 mg in chondrus extract.

Kondremul with Phenolphthalein (Cooper): Each 5 ml of emulsion contains mineral oil 55% and phenolphthalein 130 mg in chondrus extract.

Milkinol (Kremers-Urban): Liquid containing dioctyl sodium sulfosuccinate and mineral oil.

Modane (Warren-Teed): Each tablet contains pantothenate calcium 25 mg and danthron 75 mg; each tablet (mild) or 5 ml of liquid contains pantothenate calcium 12.5 mg and danthron 37.5 mg.

Neo-Kondremul (Cooper): Each 5 ml of emulsion contains casanthranol 30 mg in mineral oil and chondrus.

Neolax (Central): Each tablet contains dehydrocholic acid 240 mg and dioctyl sodium sulfosuccinate 50 mg.

Oxiphen (Webster): Each tablet contains sodium glycocholate 16.2 mg, sodium taurocholate 16.2 mg, phenolphthalein 32.4 mg, cascara extract 32.4 mg, and aloin 8.1 mg.

Peri-Colace (Mead Johnson): Each capsule contains casanthranol 30 mg and dioctyl sodium sulfosuccinate 100 mg; each 5 ml of syrup contains casanthranol 10 mg and dioctyl sodium sulfosuccinate 20 mg.

Petrogalar, Cascara (Wyeth): An aqueous suspension of mineral oil with cascara 13.2%.

Petrogalar, Phenolphthalein (Wyeth): An aqueous suspension of mineral oil with phenolphthalein 0.3%.

Rectalad Enema (Wampole): Solution containing glycerin, potassium oleate, potassium stearate, and dioctyl potassium sulfosuccinate.

Senokap DSS (Purdue Frederick): Each capsule contains standardized senna concentrate 225 mg and dioctyl sodium sulfosuccinate 50 mg.

Senokot w/Psyllium (Purdue Frederick): Each 5 ml of granules contains senna concentrate 450 mg and psyllium husks 1 g.

Siblin (Parke, Davis): Each tablet contains a water-absorbent ingredient from psyllium 65% and thiamine hydrochloride 0.5 mg with karaya gum, agar, and pectin.

Sof-2 (Savage): Each 15 ml of suspension contains bentonite 2.1 g and magnesium sulfate 2 g.

Syllamalt (Abbott): Powder containing diastatic malt extract powder 15%, malt soup extract powder 35%, and psyllium hydrophilic hemicellulose 50%.

Vacuetts (Dorsey): Suppositories containing sodium biphosphate anhydrous, sodium acid pyrophosphate, sodium bicarbonate, and polyethylene glycols.

Chapter 82

ANORECTAL PREPARATIONS

Hemorrhoids, anal fissures, and related benign conditions are common and often cause pruritus and pain, which may become excruciating, especially during defecation. Of the many proprietary mixtures that are available, a few afford symptomatic relief but none are curative. Most anorectal preparations are suppositories which combine a local anesthetic, emollients, and sometimes a corticosteroid. Some also contain ingredients of questionable rationality such as bismuth salts, menthol, belladonna, opium, vitamins, weak antiseptics, and Peruvian or Nicaraguan balsam. Convincing data that any one mixture is superior to others in relieving symptoms are lacking, although some are probably safer than others.

The local anesthetics commonly incorporated into these preparations include benzocaine, tetracaine, dibucaine, lidocaine, and pramoxine. The bases of local anesthetics penetrate unbroken skin to afford some degree of relief, whereas the salts are effective on mucosa but not on intact perianal skin. In some preparations, the concentration of the base is too low to be active. Benzocaine, one of the most widely used topical anesthetics, exerts no action unless it is present in concentrations of 5% or more. (See also Chapter 18, Local Anesthetics.)

The combinations described in the individual evaluations that follow are those most commonly prescribed; they are not necessarily preferred over similar preparations.

Adverse Reactions and Precautions

Systemic effects may result from absorption of local anesthetics, corticosteroids, and other ingredients from the mucosa of the anus and rectum or excoriated perianal skin. Sensitization may occur after the topical application of some drugs contained in these preparations. Symptoms of overdosage are uncommon because these drugs are used in small quantities.

ANUSOL
ANUSOL-HC

These mixtures are promoted for the relief of pain and pruritus associated with minor anorectal disorders. They supply some symptomatic relief, probably due to the presence of theobroma oil, vegetable oil base, zinc oxide, and hydrocortisone (in Anusol-HC) in the formulation, but they are not curative.

The hydrocortisone in Anusol-HC exerts an anti-inflammatory effect on acutely inflamed lesions, but prolonged treatment may cause undesirable systemic effects (see Chapter 35, Adrenal Corticosteroids).

USUAL DOSAGE.–

Anusol. *Rectal:* One suppository or the liberal application of ointment in the morning, at bedtime, and after each defecation.

Anusol-HC. *Rectal:* One suppository in the morning and at bedtime for three to six days or until the inflammation subsides. Therapy may be continued with the preparation without hydrocortisone.

PREPARATIONS.–

Anusol (Warner-Chilcott). *Rectal:* Ointment and suppositories containing bismuth subgallate 2.25%, bismuth resorcin compound 1.75%, benzyl benzoate 1.2%, Peruvian balsam 1.8%, zinc oxide 11%, and boric acid 5% in theobroma oil or hydrogenated vegetable oil (suppositories) base.

Anusol-HC (Warner-Chilcott). *Rectal:* Suppositories containing same formulation as Anusol suppositories plus hydrocortisone acetate 10 mg.

RECTAL MEDICONE
RECTAL MEDICONE-HC

These preparations are effective for the symptomatic relief of the pain and pruritus associated with minor anorectal disorders, but they are not curative. The mixtures combine a local anesthetic, antiseptic, emollient, protectant, and a corticosteroid (in Rectal Medicone-HC). The steroid, hydrocortisone acetate, exerts an anti-inflammatory effect on acutely inflamed lesions.

Undesirable systemic effects may result from prolonged treatment with Rectal Medicone-HC (see Chapter 35, Adrenal Corticosteroids).

USUAL DOSAGE.–

Rectal Medicone. *Rectal:* One suppository or the liberal application of ointment in the morning, at bedtime, and after each defecation.

Rectal Medicone-HC. *Rectal:* One suppository in the morning and at bedtime for three to six days. Therapy may be continued with the preparation without hydrocortisone.

PREPARATIONS.–

Rectal Medicone (Medicone). *Rectal:* Each gram of ointment contains benzocaine 20 mg, oxyquinoline sulfate 5 mg, menthol 4 mg, zinc oxide 100 mg, Peruvian balsam 12.5 mg, petrolatum 625 mg, and lanolin 210 mg; each suppository contains benzocaine 130 mg, oxyquinoline sulfate 16.2 mg, zinc oxide 194 mg, menthol 9 mg, and Peruvian balsam 65 mg in theobroma oil and vegetable and petroleum oil base.

Rectal Medicone-HC (Medicone). *Rectal:* Each suppository contains the same formulation as Rectal Medicone suppositories plus hydrocortisone acetate 10 mg.

WYANOIDS
WYANOIDS HC

These mixtures are marketed for the relief of pain and pruritus associated with minor anorectal disorders. They supply some symptomatic relief, probably due to the effects of zinc oxide, theobroma oil, and hydrocortisone (in Wyanoids HC) in the formulations. However, they also contain belladonna for no discernible reason. The manufacturer's labeling includes a dire warning about the possible toxic effects from absorption of the belladonna alkaloids if an excessive amount is used.

Undesirable systemic effects may occur after prolonged treatment with Wyanoids HC (see Chapter 35, Adrenal Corticosteroids).

USUAL DOSAGE.–Use of this preparation is inadvisable because of possible toxic effects mentioned above. The manufacturer's suggested dosages are:

Wyanoids. *Rectal:* One suppository at bedtime.

Wyanoids HC. *Rectal:* One suppository twice daily for six days as required.

PREPARATIONS.–

Wyanoids (Wyeth). *Rectal:* Each suppository contains belladonna extract 15 mg, ephedrine sulfate 3 mg, zinc oxide 176 mg, boric acid 543 mg, bismuth oxyiodide 30 mg, bismuth subcarbonate 146 mg, and Peruvian balsam 30 mg in theobroma oil and beeswax.

Wyanoids HC (Wyeth). *Rectal:* Each suppository contains same formulation as Wyanoids plus hydrocortisone acetate 10 mg.

Additional Mixtures

The following mixtures may provide symptomatic relief in some cases. However, inclusion in the list does not imply a recommendation for use; their ingredients should be evaluated in the light of the introduction to this chapter.

'A and D' Hemorrhoidal Suppositories (Schering): Each suppository contains vitamin A 1,500 units and vitamin D 200 units with Peruvian balsam, bismuth subgallate, and zinc oxide in an emollient base of theobroma oil, spermaceti, carnauba wax, and polysorbate 80 (with and without hydrocortisone acetate 10 mg).

Americaine (Arnar-Stone): Ointment containing benzocaine 20% and benzethonium chloride 0.1%.

Anugesic (Warner-Chilcott): Each gram of ointment contains pramoxine hydrochloride 10 mg, bismuth subgallate 22.5 mg, bismuth resorcin compound 17.5 mg, benzyl benzoate 12 mg, Peruvian balsam 18 mg, zinc oxide 107.5 mg, and boric acid 50 mg; each suppository contains pramoxine hydrochloride 25 mg, bismuth subgallate 61 mg, bismuth resorcin compound 47 mg, benzyl benzoate 32.4 mg, Peruvian balsam 48.6 mg, zinc oxide 300 mg, and boric acid 125 mg.

Cort-Dome (Dome): Each suppository contains hydrocortisone acetate 15 or 25 mg in a monoglyceride base.

Diothane (Merrell-National): Ointment containing diperodon 1% and oxyquinoline benzoate 0.1%.

Dorana (Ives): Each suppository or 30 mg of ointment contains phenylmercuric nitrate 1:10,000, shark liver oil 3%, and skin respiratory factor from yeast cells 2,000 units.

Epinephricaine (Upjohn): Ointment containing epinephrine 0.2%, secondary-amyltricresols 1%, zinc oxide 2%, and benzocaine 2.5% in a bland base containing vitamins A and D.

Gentz (Philips Roxane): Jelly and wipes containing pramoxine hydrochloride 1%, alcloxa 0.2%, cetylpyridinium chloride 0.5%, and hamamelis water 50%.

MediConet (Medicone): Wipes impregnated with benzalkonium chloride, ethoxylated lanolin, methylparaben, hamamelis water, and glycerin.

Metycaine & Zinc Oxide Compound (Lilly): Each suppository contains piperocaine hydrochloride 125 mg, belladonna extract 0.125 mg, bismuth subcarbonate 125 mg, and zinc oxide 250 mg.

Nupercainal (Madison): Ointment containing dibucaine 1% in lanolin and petrolatum; suppositories containing dibucaine 2.5% in zinc oxide, bismuth subgallate, and theobroma oil.

P N S Suppositories (Winthrop): Each suppository contains tetracaine hydrochloride 10 mg, phenylephrine hydrochloride 5 mg, tyloxapol 25 mg, and bismuth subcarbonate 100 mg.

Proctodon (Rowell): Each gram of cream contains diperodon hydrochloride 1%, vitamin A palmitate 5,000 units, and vitamin D 1,000 units in a water-miscible base.

Proctofoam-HC (Reed & Carnrick): Foam containing pramoxine hydrochloride 1% and hydrocortisone acetate 1% in a water-soluble mucoadhesive base.

Proctoform (Fellows-Testagar): Each suppository contains bismuth subiodide 8 mg, bismuth subcarbonate 58.5 mg, zinc oxide 162.4 mg, boric acid 259 mg, isobutyl-p-aminobenzoate 65 mg in theobroma oil, spermaceti, and petrolatum.

Rectalgan Liquid (Ayerst): Liquid containing benzocaine 4.5%, benzethonium chloride 0.1%, phenol 0.05%, 8-hydroxyquinoline benzoate 1.2%, menthol 0.5%, and methylparaben 2% with isopropyl alcohol and soya bean and castor oils.

Rectodyne (Beecham-Massengill): Each 30 mg of ointment contains tetracaine hydrochloride 130 mg, powdered opium 130 mg, and stramonium extract 324 mg with phenol, tannic acid, hamamelis water, Peruvian balsam, thymol, and resorcinol; each suppository contains powdered opium 0.38% and belladonna extract 1% with benzocaine, boric acid, ammonium alum, and theobroma oil.

Tanicaine (Upjohn): Each 30 mg of ointment contains phenacaine hydrochloride 324 mg, atropine 16.2 mg, tannic acid 1.6 g, phenol 390 mg, camphor 454 mg, menthol 130 mg, and zinc oxide 5.2 g.

Xylocaine Suppositories (Astra): Each suppository contains lidocaine 100 mg, aluminum subacetate 75 mg, Peruviam balsam 100 mg, bismuth subgallate 115 mg, and zinc oxide 375 mg in neutral glycerides of saturated vegetable fatty acids.

Chapter 83

MISCELLANEOUS GASTROINTESTINAL AGENTS

The gastrointestinal agents described in this chapter are activated charcoal, simethicone, and products intended as replacement therapy in deficiency states (hydrochloric acid, glutamic acid hydrochloride, pepsin, bile acids and salts, and pancreatic enzymes).

The carminatives, which are often aromatic oils of vegetable origin and are given to relieve the feeling of distention after meals, as well as the stomachics (eg, bitters), which are claimed to enhance the functional activity of the stomach, are not discussed in this chapter. These drugs primarily exert a psychic or placebo effect, and the effectiveness of therapy may not be related to their pharmacologic actions. These agents were used much more frequently in the past than at present.

ACTIVATED CHARCOAL

This absorbent was once widely used to treat diarrhea, because it was believed that the presumed toxins adhered to its surfaces. It is now used as an adjunct in the treatment of oral poisonings caused by ingestion of heavy metals, some alkaloids, aniline dyes, and most drugs except cyanide. Contrary to popular belief, burnt toast is not a form of activated charcoal and is useless in the treatment of poisonings.

USUAL DOSAGE.—*Oral: Adults and children*, 1 to 10 g. For emergency treatment, the powder, stirred into water to give a slurry, can be administered and removed soon afterward by gastric tube or by induced vomiting. Alternatively, the charcoal suspension can be used as the gastric lavage fluid.

PREPARATIONS.—Activated Charcoal, U.S.P. *Oral:* Powder, capsules, and tablets. Drug marketed by many manufacturers under generic name.

SIMETHICONE [Mylicon, Silain]

This mixture of dimethylpolysiloxanes and silica gel is promoted for the relief of gaseous distention occurring postoperatively and as a result of aerophagia. However, there are no well-designed, controlled studies to support these claims; thus, the efficacy of simethicone is questionable. The claim is also made that simethicone is useful in the preparation of patients for gastroscopy to eliminate mucus-embedded bubbles that might interfere with the procedure. Since gas bubbles are seldom a problem during gastroscopy, the claim is not a convincing one. Silicon polymers are used in industry as defrothing agents because of their ability to lower surface tension.

No adverse reactions have been reported.

USUAL DOSAGE.—No useful dosage is recognized because evidence of efficacy is lacking. The manufacturers' suggested dosage is: *Oral: Adults*, 40 to 100 mg four times a day (after meals and at bedtime) or as necessary postoperatively.

PREPARATIONS.—

Mylicon (Stuart). *Oral:* Drops 40 mg/0.6 ml; tablets 40 mg.

Silain (Robins). *Oral:* Tablets 50 mg.

HYDROCHLORIC ACID, DILUTED

Hydrochloric acid was once commonly administered to alleviate symptoms such as epigastric distress after meals, abdominal distention, nausea, vomiting, diarrhea, and coated tongue supposedly associated with achlorhydria and hypochlorhydria. However, there is no proof that a decrease in the hydrochloric acid content of the stomach produces any specific symptoms. The usual therapeutic dose is not sufficient to cause free acid to appear in the stomach and there is no evidence that even large doses of hydrochloric acid are beneficial.

Large doses of 10 ml (30 mEq) given during

and after each meal in an attempt to approach the amount of acid normally secreted in response to a meal may produce metabolic acidosis. Alkalizing salts should be taken concurrently. The hydrochloric acid solution must be diluted with water and taken through a glass tube to prevent damage to the dental enamel.

USUAL DOSAGE.—No useful dosage is recognized because proof of efficacy is lacking. The manufacturers' suggested dosage is: *Oral: Adults*, 5 ml (15 mEq) of 10% hydrochloric acid, well diluted in water, taken at mealtime.

PREPARATIONS.—Hydrochloric Acid, Diluted, N.F. Marketed by many manufacturers under generic name.

GLUTAMIC ACID HYDROCHLORIDE
[Acidulin]

$$HOOCCH_2CH_2CH(NH_2)COOH \cdot HCl$$

The proposed uses for this preparation are the same as those for diluted hydrochloric acid but, as with the free acid, there is no sound evidence that this drug has any more than a placebo effect. Capsules or tablets of glutamic acid hydrochloride are prescribed instead of free hydrochloric acid to prevent damage to the dental enamel. This drug does not lower the gastric pH as much as the free acid.

USUAL DOSAGE.—No useful dosage is recognized. The manufacturers' suggested dosage is: *Oral: Adults*, 340 mg to 1 g three times daily before meals.

PREPARATIONS.—Acidulin (Lilly). *Oral:* Capsules 340 mg. Drug also marketed by other manufacturers under generic name.

PEPSIN

This preparation of gastric enzymes is derived from hog stomach. The action of pepsins is not essential to digestion since the proteolytic enzymes of the intestinal tract can convert proteins to peptides and amino acids. Therefore, pepsin is not useful therapeutically.

USUAL DOSAGE.—Suggested dosage from the literature is: *Oral: Adults*, 10 to 30 ml of elixir or 2 g of powder or granules taken with meals three times daily.

PREPARATIONS.—*Oral:* Elixir (plain or lactated), granules, and powder.

AVAILABLE TRADEMARK.—Peptenzyme Elixir (Reed & Carnrick). Drug also marketed by other manufacturers under generic name.

BILE AND BILE ACIDS OR SALTS

The major bile acids are cholic, chenodeoxycholic, and deoxycholic acids. The first two are primary bile acids formed from cholesterol in the liver, and the latter is a secondary acid produced by the action of anaerobic intestinal bacteria on cholic acid. Normally, the bile acids do not occur in bile as free substances but as conjugates with taurine or glycine. Conjugated bile acids are also known as bile salts.

Bile salts pass from the liver into the intestine, where they enhance the absorption of lipids and are necessary for the absorption of fat-soluble vitamins and cholesterol. They are absorbed mainly by the ileum, return to the liver by way of the portal vein, and are reused, thus completing the enterohepatic circulation. Bile salts also regulate the synthesis of bile acid from cholesterol and the secretion of free cholesterol from the liver.

Many conditions (eg, fistula, resection or disease of the ileum, severe liver disease, biliary obstruction, bacterial overgrowth in the small intestine) interrupt the enterohepatic circulation and consequently reduce the concentration of conjugated bile salts in the upper intestine. At present, there is no satisfactory preparation of conjugated bile salts available for replacement therapy. Commercial ox bile preparations do not provide an adequate amount of conjugated bile salts and often cause diarrhea. Their use for replacement therapy or as choleretics in the treatment of various vague symptoms attributed to a deficiency of bile or to intestinal malfunction is not justified, for they are not effective and may be harmful in some instances.

Because bile salts are important for the normal biliary solubilization of cholesterol, disorders of bile acid metabolism may result in the production of abnormal bile and, thereby, cause cholesterol gallstone formation. Recently, reports have suggested that the long-term daily administration of 1 g of chenodeoxycholic acid, one of the primary bile acids, can reduce the size or completely dissolve cholesterol gallstones in selected, asymptomatic patients. There was no decrease in the size of gallstones in patients given cholic acid or placebo therapy.

OX BILE EXTRACT

This is an ineffective preparation proposed for replacement therapy in patients who have an insufficient concentration of bile salts in the intestine. See the introduction to this section.

Diarrhea may occur after use of ox bile extract.

USUAL DOSAGE.—The manufacturers' suggested dosage is: *Oral: Adults*, 300 mg.

PREPARATIONS.—Ox Bile Extract. *Oral:* Capsules, tablets. Drug marketed under generic name.

DEHYDROCHOLIC ACID [Decholin]
DEHYDROCHOLATE SODIUM [Decholin Sodium]

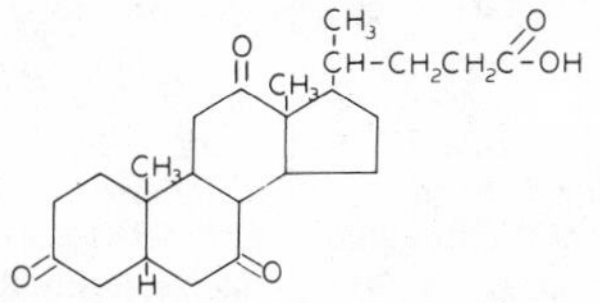

Dehydrocholic acid, a synthetic derivative of cholic acid, is the most active of the hydrocholeretics. Since this drug increases the volume of bile by dilution without increasing the total solids, it is used postoperatively to increase the flow and reduce the viscosity of bile during T-tube drainage. However, there is no evidence to support the claim that hydrocholeretics prevent ascending infection in biliary tract disease or after surgery.

Dehydrocholic acid also is sometimes used to dislodge small calculi from the biliary tract; however, if the calculi are not dislodged and become impacted, an attack of biliary colic may occur. A smooth muscle relaxant, such as a nitrite, may be given with the hydrocholeretic.

Hydrocholeresis may assist in outlining bile ducts to determine obstruction and may improve gallbladder visualization in x-ray diagnosis.

The sodium salt is given intravenously to measure circulation time, since the drug creates a bitter taste when it reaches the tongue.

Anaphylactic reactions occur infrequently.

USUAL DOSAGE.—

Dehydrocholic Acid:

Oral: Adults, 500 mg three times daily.

Dehydrocholate Sodium:

Intravenous: Adults (diagnostic), 3 to 5 ml of a 20% solution.

PREPARATIONS.—

Decholin (Dome). *Oral:* Tablets 250 mg.

Decholin Sodium (Dome). *Injection:* Solution 20% in 5 ml containers.

ADDITIONAL TRADEMARKS.—**Dehydrocholic Acid:** Bili (Reid-Provident), Cholan-DH (Pennwalt), Ketochol (Searle). Both forms also marketed by other manufacturers under generic names.

PANCREATIC ENZYMES

The pancreatic enzymes (amylase, trypsin, and lipase) are obtained from various preparations of hog pancreas. They are effective in patients whose exocrine pancreatic secretion is deficient. Thus, they may be used as replacement therapy in chronic pancreatitis, in ductal obstruction caused by cancer of the pancreas, in cystic fibrosis, and after pancreatectomy. However, these enzymes should be used only after the diagnosis of exocrine pancreatic insufficiency has been established. They are ineffective in gastrointestinal disorders unrelated to pancreatic enzyme insufficiency.

Some preparations are enteric coated to avoid destruction of variable amounts by gastric pepsin.

Although allergic reactions to the animal protein in these preparations occur only rarely, these enzymes should be used cautiously in patients known to be sensitive to pork.

The dosage depends upon the condition of the patient, the amount of fat in the diet, and the qualitative enzyme content of each preparation.

PANCREATIN [Panteric, Viokase]

These preparations of pancreatin are derived from hog pancreas and contain amylase, trypsin, lipase, and other constituents in varying amounts. The N.F. preparation of pancreatin must convert at least 25 times its weight of starch into soluble carbohydrates and of casein into proteoses. The required lipolytic activity is not specified. Preparations containing three or four times N.F. strength also are available.

See the introduction to this section for indications and precautions.

USUAL DOSAGE.—*Oral: Adults*, 4 to 12 g (triple N.F. strength) daily in divided doses at one- or two-hour intervals or before and after meals with an extra dose taken with any food eaten between meals; *children*, initially, 300 to 600 mg with each meal. This dose may be increased if necessary if no nausea, vomiting, or diarrhea occurs.

PREPARATIONS.—

Pancreatin (Lilly). *Oral:* Powder; tablets (enteric-coated) 325 mg (three times N.F. strength); tablets 325 mg (N.F. strength).

Panteric (Parke, Davis). *Oral:* Capsules 325 mg (three times N.F. strength); granules; tablets (enteric-coated) 325 mg (three times N.F. strength).

Viokase (Viobin). *Oral:* Powder; tablets 325 mg (four times N.F. strength).

Drug also marketed by other manufacturers under generic name.

PANCRELIPASE [Cotazym]

The action of pancrelipase is qualitatively similar to that of other pancreatic enzyme preparations; however, it has greater lipase activity as determined by in vitro measurements of the amount of glycerin (free fatty acids) formed by the digestion of fat. This greater lipase activity permits smaller doses to be used to help control steatorrhea. Although pancrelipase may be more acceptable to patients because of the smaller dosage, there are no controlled clinical and metabolic studies to determine the relative efficacy of the various pancreatic enzyme preparations.

See the introduction to this section for indications and precautions.

USUAL DOSAGE.—*Oral: Adults,* 300 to 900 mg with each meal depending upon the amount of fat ingested, and 300 mg with any food eaten between meals. *Children,* 300 to 600 mg with each meal. In severe deficiency, doses of 1 g every waking hour have been given.

PREPARATIONS.—Cotazym (Organon). *Oral:* Capsules 300 mg; powder 600 mg and 1.5 g. Each 300 mg capsule provides: lipase sufficient to digest 17 g dietary fat; trypsin sufficient to digest 34 g dietary protein; and amylase sufficient to digest 40 g dietary starch (based on in vitro assays).

MIXTURES

The following mixtures containing bile constituents and derivatives, enzymes, sedatives, antispasmodics, cellulase, and other ingredients are marketed for the treatment of many ill-defined gastrointestinal syndromes. There are no therapeutic indications for ox bile, pepsin, and hydrocholic acid. Pancreatic enzymes are indicated only when a demonstrated exocrine pancreatic deficiency exists, in which case the pancreatic enzymes should be prescribed alone. Other active ingredients of these mixtures (eg, sedatives, antispasmodics) should be prescribed separately and not in combination with useless drugs or ones whose use is not warranted.

Accelerase (Organon): Each capsule contains pancrelipase approximately 165 mg, mixed conjugated bile salts 65 mg, cellulase 2 mg, and calcium carbonate 20 mg.

Accelerase-PB (Organon): Each capsule contains pancrelipase approximately 165 mg, mixed conjugated bile salts 65 mg, cellulase 2 mg, calcium carbonate 20 mg, belladonna alkaloids as sulfates 0.2 mg, and phenobarbital 16 mg.

Acidol-Pepsin (Winthrop): Each capsule contains betaine hydrochloride 260 mg and pepsin 230 mg.

Bilogen (Organon): Each tablet contains ox bile extract 120 mg, oxidized mixed ox bile acids 75 mg, desoxycholic acid 30 mg, and pancreatin 250 mg.

Bilron (Lilly): Each capsule contains bile salts and iron.

Butibel-Zyme (McNeil): Each tablet contains proteolytic enzyme standardized 10 mg, amylolytic enzyme standardized 20 mg, cellulolytic enzyme standardized 5 mg, lipolytic enzyme standardized 100 mg, iron ox bile 30 mg, butabarbital sodium 15 mg, and belladonna extract 15 mg.

Caripeptic (Upjohn): Each 100 ml of liquid contains standard enzymes of *Carica papaya* with diastase 3.97 g, and alcohol 18%.

Chobile (Mallinckrodt): Each tablet contains ox bile extract 216.4 mg and oxidized ox bile acids 97.4 mg.

Chobile Pan (Mallinckrodt): Each tablet contains ox bile 216.4 mg, oxidized ox bile acids 97.4 mg, and pancreatin 97.4 mg.

Cholan HMB (Pennwalt): Each tablet contains dehydrocholic acid 250 mg, phenobarbital 8 mg, and homatropine methylbromide 2.5 mg.

Cholan V (Pennwalt): Each tablet contains dehydrocholic acid 250 mg and homatropine methylbromide 5 mg.

Choleo-Caps (Smith, Miller & Patch): Each capsule contains ox bile extract 24.3 mg, iron lactate 48.6 mg, calumba 48.6 mg, chamomile 105.5 mg, and rhubarb 105.5 mg.

Convertin (Ascher): Each tablet contains betaine hydrochloride 130 mg and oleoresin ginger 0.1 mg (in outer layer); pancreatin 250 mg and desoxycholic acid 50 mg (in enteric-coated core).

Convertin-H (Ascher): Each tablet contains betaine hydrochloride 130 mg and oleoresin ginger 0.1 mg (in outer layer); pancreatin 250 mg, desoxycholic acid 50 mg, and homatropine methylbromide 2.5 mg (in enteric-coated core).

Converzyme (Ascher): Each 5 ml of liquid contains proteolytic enzyme 10 mg, amylolytic enzyme 80 mg, sorbitol 4.4 g, and homatropine methylbromide 2.5 mg.

Cotazym-B (Organon): Each tablet contains lipase 1,000 units; trypsin, amylase, and other pancreatic enzymes; mixed conjugated bile salts 65 mg; and cellulase 2 mg.

Dactilase (Lakeside): Each tablet contains cellulolytic enzyme 2 mg, amylolytic enzyme 15 mg, proteolytic enzyme 10 mg, pancreatin 100 mg (3 X N.F.), piperidolate hydrochloride 50 mg, and taurocholic acid 15 mg.

Decholin-BB (Dome): Each tablet contains dehydrocholic acid 250 mg, belladonna extract 10 mg, and butabarbital sodium 15 mg.

Decholin with Belladonna (Dome): Each tablet contains dehydrocholic acid 250 mg and belladonna extract 10 mg.

Di-Gel (Plough): Each tablet or 5 ml contains simethicone 25 mg and magnesium carbonate.

Digolase (Boyle): Each capsule contains pancreatin concentrate 80 mg (3 X N.F.), amylase concentrate 15 mg, proteinase concentrate 3 mg, and polysorbate 80, 20 mg.

Donnazyme (Robins): Each tablet contains pepsin 150 mg, pancreatin 300 mg, bile salts 150 mg, hyoscyamine sulfate 0.0518 mg, atropine sulfate 0.0097 mg, hyoscine hydrobromide 0.0033 mg, and phenobarbital 8.1 mg.

Doxegest (Breon): Each tablet contains desoxycholic acid 32.5 mg, papain 15 mg, pancreatin 87.5 mg (3 X N.F.), hemicellulase 25 mg, ketocholanic acid 12.5 mg, and betaine hydrochloride 65 mg.

Doxychol-AS (Cooper): Each tablet contains desoxycholic acid 64.8 mg, dehydrocholic acid 194 mg, hyoscyamine hydrobromide 0.16 mg, phenobarbital 8 mg, and atropine sulfate 0.16 mg.

Desoxychol-K (Cooper): Each tablet contains desoxycholic acid 64 mg and dehydrocholic acid 194 mg.

Entozyme (Robins): Each tablet contains pepsin 250 mg (in outer layer); pancreatin 300 mg and bile salts 150 mg (in enteric-coated core).

Festal (Hoechst): Each enteric-coated tablet contains pancreatic lipase 10 Willstaetter units (WU), pancreatic amylase 10 WU, pancreatic protease 17 WU, hemicellulase 50 mg, and bile constituents 25 mg.

Festalan (Hoechst): Each tablet contains lipase 10 Willstaetter units (WU), amylase 10 WU, protease 17 WU, hemicellulase 50 mg, and bile constituents 25 mg (in enteric-coated core); atropine methylnitrate 1 mg (in outer layer).

Gastroenterase (Wampole): Each tablet contains pepsin 150 mg (in outer layer); pancreatic enzyme concentrate 100 mg, cellulase 25 mg, dehydrocholic acid 50 mg (in enteric-coated core).

Hydro-Bilein (Abbott): Each tablet contains ox bile extract 120 mg and dehydrocholic acid 120 mg.

Hydrochol Plus (Elder): Each tablet contains dehydrocholic acid 200 mg, ox bile 50 mg, methscopolamine nitrate 0.8 mg, and amobarbital 15 mg.

Kanulase (Dorsey): Each tablet contains pepsin N.F. 150 mg, cellulase 9 mg, glutamic acid hydrochloride 200 mg, pancreatin N.F. 500 mg, and ox bile extract 100 mg.

Kanumodic (Dorsey): Each tablet contains pepsin N.F. 150 mg, cellulase 9 mg, glutamic acid hydrochloride 200 mg, pancreatin N.F. 500 mg, ox bile extract 100 mg, pentobarbital 8 mg, and methscopolamine nitrate 2 mg.

Ketosox (Ascher): Each tablet contains desoxycholic acid 65 mg and ketocholanic acids 200 mg.

Kutrase (Kremers-Urban): Each capsule contains phenyltoloxamine citrate 15 mg, hyoscyamine sulfate 0.0625 mg, amylolytic enzyme 30 mg, proteolytic enzyme 6 mg, lipolytic enzyme 75 mg, and cellulolytic enzyme 2 mg.

Ku-Zyme (Kremers-Urban): Each capsule contains amylolytic enzyme 30 mg, proteolytic enzyme 6 mg, lipolytic enzyme 75 mg, and cellulolytic enzyme 2 mg.

Maturon (Ayerst): Each tablet contains amylase 3,000 units, protease 12,000 units, tryptic activity 500 units, dehydrocholic acid 40 mg, vitamin A 2,500 U.S.P. units, ergocalciferol 125 U.S.P. units, ascorbic acid 25 mg, thiamine mononitrate 1.5 mg, riboflavin 1 mg, pyridoxine hydrochloride 0.5 mg, cyanocobalamin 0.5 μg, calcium pantothenate 3.5 mg, nicotinamide 7.5 mg, vitamin E 2.5 IU, calcium 35 mg, phosphorus 27 mg, iron 12.5 mg, manganese 0.15 mg, zinc 0.2 mg, magnesium 2.5 mg, and inositol 10 mg.

Neocholan (Dow): Each tablet contains dehydrocholic acid 250 mg, bile extract 15 mg, phenobarbital 8 mg, and homatropine methylbromide 1.2 mg.

Normacid (Stuart): Each tablet contains pepsin 100 mg and betaine hydrochloride 440 mg.

Nu Leven (Lemmon): Each enteric-coated tablet contains pepsin 150 mg, pancreatic enzyme concentrate 100 mg, and ox bile extract 100 mg.

Oxsorbil (Ives): Each capsule contains dehydrocholic acid 32.4 mg, desoxycholic acid 32.4 mg, ox bile extract 65 mg, oleic acid 178.6 mg, and polysorbate 80, 162.4 mg.

Oxsorbil-PB (Ives): Each capsule contains dehydrocholic acid 32.4 mg, desoxycholic acid 32.4 mg, ox bile extract 65 mg, oleic acid 178.6 mg, phenobarbital 8.1 mg, belladonna powder extract 8.1 mg, and polysorbate 80, 162.4 mg.

Panteric Compound (Parke, Davis): Each tablet contains pancreatin 650 mg (3X equivalent to pancreatin N.F.) and ox bile extract N.F. 97.4 mg.

Paptose (First Texas): Each 30 ml of liquid contains diastase 40 mg, papain 389 mg, rennin 40 mg, and alcohol 15%.

Phazyme (Reed & Carnrick): Each tablet contains pepsin N.F. 100 mg, diastase 25 mg, activated simethicone 20 mg, with and without phenobarbital 15 mg (in outer layer); pancreatin 240 mg and activated simethicone 40 mg (in enteric-coated core).

Pradase (Cooper): Each tablet contains ox bile extract N.F. 150 mg, ketocholanic acid 60 mg, pancreatin N.F. 300 mg, betaine hydrochloride 90 mg, and carminative oils 0.006 ml.

Ro-Bile (Rowell): Each tablet contains pepsin N.F. 260 mg (in outer layer); enzyme concentrate 75 mg (pancreatin 4X N.F. with added standardized lipase), ox bile extract N.F. 100 mg, dehydrocholic acid U.S.P. 30 mg, and belladonna extract N.F. 8 mg (in enteric-coated core).

Sidonna (Reed & Carnrick): Each tablet contains simethicone 25 mg, hyoscyamine sulfate 0.1037 mg, atropine sulfate 0.0194 mg, scopolamine hydrobromide 0.0065 mg, and sodium butabarbital 16 mg.

Silain-Gel (Robins): Each tablet contains simethicone 25 mg, aluminum hydroxide-magnesium carbonate co-dried 282 mg, and magnesium hydroxide 85 mg.

Supligol (Breon): Each enteric-coated tablet contains dessicated whole bile 260 mg and ketocholanic bile acids 65 mg.

Taka-Diastase, Pepsin, and Pancreatin (Parke, Davis): Each tablet contains *Aspergillus oryzae* enzymes 130 mg, pepsin 65 mg, and pancreatin 130 mg.

Therabile (Ascher): Each tablet contains desoxycholic acid 25 mg, ferrated ox bile 200 mg, pancreatin N.F. 250 mg, homatropine methylbromide 2.5 mg, oleoresin ginger 0.1 mg, and dimethionine 100 mg.

Trienzyme (Fellows-Testagar): Each tablet contains amylolytic enzyme 30 mg, proteolytic enzyme 10 mg, and cellulolytic enzyme 3 mg.

Trulase (Cooper): Each tablet contains amylolytic enzyme 30 mg, proteolytic enzymes 6 mg, and lipolytic enzyme 25 mg.

Zymogest (Amfre-Grant): Each tablet contains standardized amylolytic enzyme 25 mg, standardized proteolytic enzyme 10 mg, standardized cellulolytic enzyme 1 mg, dehydrocholic acid 100 mg, hyoscyamine hydrobromide 0.1 mg, hyoscine hydrobromide 0.0065 mg, and atropine sulfate 0.02 mg.

Chapter 84

EMETICS

Emetics (eg, apomorphine hydrochloride, ipecac syrup) are used to induce vomiting after the ingestion of poisons. Small doses of emetics also have been tried with varying degrees of success as a deterrent in chronic alcoholism. Their use as expectorants, usually in about one-fifth the emetic dose, in the treatment of childhood croup, bronchitis, bronchiectasis, asthma, or other conditions associated with unproductive coughing is no longer recommended, for these agents may suppress the appetite and make fluid ingestion and retention difficult. (See Chapter 43, Expectorants and Inhalants.)

Vomiting can be elicited by a direct action of an emetic on the chemoreceptor trigger zone in the medulla, by indirect stimulation of the gastrointestinal tract, or by a combination of these effects. The effectiveness of emetics may be facilitated by having the patient drink 200 to 300 ml of water concomitantly.

Although there is universal agreement that emptying the stomach completely after ingestion of most poisons is desirable, there is disagreement on whether properly performed gastric lavage or drug-induced vomiting is the more effective method. Most of the ingested material still in the stomach is usually recovered with use of an emetic. Although the act of inserting the tube may cause vomiting, especially in children, emptying of the stomach in this way is thought to be less efficient than drug-induced vomiting. Aspiration of vomitus into the bronchial tree also is a potential hazard of both gastric lavage and drug-induced vomiting but the hazard is less with use of emetics.

Antimony potassium tartrate (tartar emetic) and mustard powder have been used as emetics, but the former is too toxic and the latter agent is ineffective. Cupric sulfate is effective, but its potential toxicity is too great to recommend its use.

Adverse Reactions and Precautions

Emetics are contraindicated in patients who are unconscious or semicomatose, inebriated, or in shock. An emetic should not be used if the patient has ingested a caustic substance, since additional injury to the esophagus and possible mediastinitis may result. Gastric lavage would be the treatment of choice if an antiemetic has been ingested recently.

Emetics are generally contraindicated after ingestion of petroleum distillates (eg, kerosene, gasoline) or volatile oils because the patient may aspirate these substances into the bronchial tree while retching and vomiting, and bronchospasm, pulmonary edema, or pneumonia may result. However, definitive data are lacking to indicate that use of an emetic in an alert patient increases the probability of aspiration pneumonia. Some authorities believe that prompt and complete emptying of the stomach achieved by careful aspiration and lavage is effective; when the patient is comatose, a cuffed endotracheal tube is used whenever possible to prevent aspiration. Others prefer that a vegetable oil (eg, corn oil, peanut oil) be given to delay absorption of accidentally ingested petroleum distillates. Neither point of view is established as being superior. The same quantity of petroleum distillates aspirated into the lungs has many times the toxicity it has in the stomach. Thus, in cases of ingestion of known small quantities of petroleum distillates, it is safer to allow the material to remain in the stomach without removal rather than to introduce the risk of aspiration. However, when a petroleum distillate is a solvent for a toxic substance (eg, insecticide) the benefits of employing gastric lavage far outweigh the risks.

INDIVIDUAL EVALUATIONS

APOMORPHINE HYDROCHLORIDE

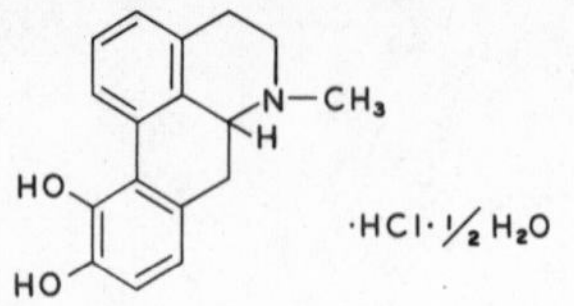

Apomorphine acts directly on the chemoreceptor trigger zone and usually induces vomiting in most adults within five to ten minutes after subcutaneous injection. Generally, the stomach contents are expelled completely and may even contain reflux from the upper intestinal tract. Its action is more efficient when the stomach is full; therefore, 200 to 300 ml of water should be given just before the injection.

Apomorphine usually produces some depression of the central nervous system, but some patients may experience euphoria, restlessness, and tremors. It may produce acute circulatory failure in aged or debilitated patients. Larger or repeated doses *depress* the respiratory center. Overdosage may produce violent vomiting, retching, acute circulatory failure, and death. The depressant actions of apomorphine usually can be reversed by a narcotic antagonist (0.02 mg/kg of body weight of levallorphan, 0.1 mg/kg of nalorphine, or 0.005 mg/kg of naloxone). The narcotic antagonist usually is unnecessary but some physicians administer it routinely to terminate vomiting and alleviate drowsiness. Activated charcoal should be administered orally when an adsorbable substance has been ingested after apomorphine is injected or before if delay in the administration of the emetic is anticipated. (See Chapter 83, Miscellaneous Gastrointestinal Agents.) Apomorphine is a Schedule II controlled drug.

Apomorphine is contraindicated after the ingestion of corrosive substances or alcohol. It also is contraindicated in patients in shock, in comatose or elderly patients, or in those sensitive to morphine derivatives. Apomorphine is not stable and should not be used if the solution is green or brown.

USUAL DOSAGE.—*Subcutaneous: Adults and children,* 0.1 mg/kg of body weight; 200 to 300 ml of water should be taken just before the injection.

PREPARATIONS.—Apomorphine Hydrochloride, N.F. *Injection:* Tablets (hypodermic) 6 mg. Drug marketed under generic name.

IPECAC SYRUP

Ipecac alkaloids act both locally on the gastric mucosa and on the chemoreceptor trigger zone to induce vomiting. An adequate dose causes vomiting in more than 90% of patients within 30 minutes; the average time is usually less than 20 minutes. The stomach is evacuated completely, along with reflux material from the upper intestinal tract. Ipecac syrup is available without prescription in a maximal amount of 30 ml and is labeled in accordance with the requirements of the FDA. This preparation should be available in the home for use in emergencies to avoid delay in treatment if a physician prescribes it by telephone. The emetic action is facilitated if the patient drinks 200 to 300 ml of water concomitantly.

Ipecac syrup should not be confused with ipecac fluidextract. The latter preparation is 14 times more concentrated and has caused several deaths. Fortunately, the fluidextract is no longer official, but it still may be available. Therefore, it is essential that the physician clearly specify ipecac syrup in prescribing and not use the single word "ipecac."

Ipecac syrup is contraindicated in patients who are unconscious, semicomatose, severely inebriated, or in shock. It should not be used if the patient has ingested a corrosive or caustic substance, since regurgitation may further injure the esophagus. It is contraindicated after ingestion of petroleum distillates (eg, kerosene, gasoline) or volatile oils. (See the Introductory Statement.)

Activated charcoal should not be given simultaneously with ipecac syrup, because the charcoal adsorbs the ipecac and nullifies its effect; however, it may be given after vomiting has occurred. (See Chapter 83, Miscellaneous Gastrointestinal Agents.)

USUAL DOSAGE.—*Oral: Adults,* 15 to 30 ml followed by 200 to 300 ml of water; *children over 1 year,* 15 ml followed by about 200 ml of water. Dose may be repeated once after 20 minutes if necessary.

PREPARATIONS.—Ipecac Syrup, U.S.P. Drug marketed under generic name.

Chapter 85

ANTIEMETICS

Vomiting is a complex act that is coordinated by the vomiting center in the medulla. Stimuli are relayed to the center from many peripheral areas (eg, gastric mucosa, peritoneum, joints, tendons), as well as from areas within the central nervous system itself (eg, vestibular apparatus of the ear, chemoreceptor trigger zone, cerebral cortex).

Antiemetic agents prevent or relieve nausea and vomiting by exerting their effects either on the aural vestibular apparatus, the chemoreceptor trigger zone, the cerebral cortex, or the vomiting center itself. Since their mechanism of action is not fully understood in all cases, the choice of drug is often empirical.

Nausea and vomiting may be symptoms of serious organic disturbances or may be produced by infections, drugs, radiation, painful stimuli, emotional disturbances, or motion. Whenever possible, the underlying cause should be determined and corrected. When vomiting accompanies a form of therapy, the use of antiemetics is justified as an adjunct to the treatment.

The selection of an antiemetic should be based upon the cause of the vomiting. Some compounds are effective in preventing or treating vomiting due to motion sickness but are ineffective in controlling vomiting due to other causes. Some agents also relieve vertigo due to labyrinthitis, surgery of the middle and inner ear, or Meniere's disease.

The types of antiemetics include: (1) sedatives and hypnotics (eg, phenobarbital), which act centrally by depressing the cerebral cortex or the vomiting center; (2) scopolamine, an anticholinergic agent, which appears to act primarily by reducing the excitability of the labyrinth receptors and by depressing conduction in the vestibular cerebellar pathways; (3) antihistamines (cyclizine [Marezine], dimenhydrinate [Dramamine], diphenhydramine [Benadryl], meclizine [Antivert, Bonine], hydroxyzine [Atarax, Vistaril]) are assumed to affect neural pathways originating in the labyrinth; (4) the phenothiazines, which act upon the chemoreceptor trigger zone, the vomiting center, or both, and (5) some miscellaneous agents (eg, diphenidol [Vontrol], trimethobenzamide [Tigan]), the former agent acting upon the aural vestibular apparatus and the latter agent acting upon the chemoreceptor trigger zone.

The butyrophenones (eg, droperidol [Inapsine], haloperidol [Haldol]), which are pharmacologically similar to the phenothiazines, also have antiemetic properties. (See also Chapter 20, Adjuncts to Anesthesia, and Chapter 29, Antipsychotic Agents.) Pyridoxine (vitamin B_6) has been used in the management of nausea and vomiting of pregnancy, but it is ineffective. (See Chapter 14, Vitamins and Sources of Vitamins.)

Although the phenothiazines are the most potent and effective antiemetics, they should be prescribed only when vomiting cannot be controlled by less hazardous agents. Those used most commonly for their antiemetic effect include chlorpromazine [Thorazine], fluphenazine [Permitil, Prolixin], perphenazine [Trilafon], prochlorperazine [Compazine], promethazine [Phenergan], thiethylperazine [Torecan], and triflupromazine [Vesprin]. The phenothiazine antiemetics are effective in the management of postoperative nausea and vomiting, radiation sickness, and nausea and vomiting due to toxins. They also are useful in controlling the intractable vomiting of terminal patients with uremia. With the exception of promethazine, the phenothiazines are not useful in preventing or treating motion sickness.

The nonphenothiazine antiemetics are drugs of first choice, particularly for patients receiving long-term antiemetic therapy (eg, those with hyperemesis gravidarum or nausea due to malignancy or administration of antineoplastic agents). They may be less effective and have a shorter duration of action than the phenothiazines, but are safer.

Scopolamine is one of the most effective agents for the prevention of motion sickness. However, its use is limited because of untoward effects and short duration of action. Promethazine, cyclizine, meclizine, and diphenhydramine are less effective, but they have a longer duration of action and produce fewer untoward effects than scopolamine. In controlled studies with individuals who were subjected to severe motion, the combination of scopolamine and ephedrine or dextroamphetamine was shown to be more effective than scopolamine alone.

Routine administration of antiemetics to *prevent* postoperative vomiting may be justified only when vomiting endangers the results of surgery (eg, intraocular or intracranial operations) or when elderly cardiac patients or individuals who might be endangered by dehydration or postoperative electrolyte imbalance must undergo surgery.

These drugs should not be used unless absolutely necessary during pregnancy. If an antiemetic is indicated, one of the well-established antihistamines should be selected (eg, dimenhydrinate). If vomiting persists, consideration may be given to the use of a phenothiazine.

Adverse Reactions and Precautions

Caution is required in the use of antiemetics because they may mask an underlying organic disease or the toxic effects of other drugs.

Drowsiness is the commonest untoward effect and is produced by most antiemetic agents. Individuals whose activities require alertness, such as those operating vehicles or machinery, should use these agents with caution.

Some nonphenothiazine antiemetics (cyclizine [Marezine], hydroxyzine [Atarax, Vistaril], meclizine [Antivert, Bonine]) are teratogenic in animals when given in doses substantially above the therapeutic range in man. Therefore, the possibility that these drugs may be hazardous to the fetus must be borne in mind. (See the discussion on Use of Drugs During Pregnancy in the General Information section.)

Phenothiazines: Phenothiazines in the piperazine group (fluphenazine [Permitil, Prolixin], perphenazine [Trilafon], prochlorperazine [Compazine], and thiethylperazine [Torecan]) are less likely to cause drowsiness, orthostatic hypotension, dryness of the mouth, and nasal congestion than those in the aliphatic group (chlorpromazine [Thorazine], promazine [Sparine], promethazine [Phenergan], and triflupromazine [Vesprin]). Cholestatic jaundice, granulocytopenia, urticaria, dermatitis, thrombocytopenia, leukopenia, agranulocytosis, purpura, pancytopenia, and gastroenteritis also have occurred after use of the phenothiazines. Less common reactions include galactorrhea, photosensitivity, and edema of the extremities.

Extrapyramidal reactions, including dystonia, parkinsonian syndrome, akathisia, and dysphasia, have been associated with the use of all phenothiazines. The incidence of these reactions is higher with drugs in the *piperazine* group than with those in the *aliphatic* group. Drugs in the *piperidine* group (eg, thioridazine [Mellaril]) are least likely to cause extrapyramidal reactions, but they are not effective as antiemetics.

Phenothiazines are contraindicated in patients with a history of dyskinetic reactions or epilepsy or in pregnant women with preeclampsia.

The additive effects (eg, sedation) that occur when phenothiazines are used with other central nervous system depressants should be borne in mind before an antiemetic of this type is given. The additive effect may be desirable in some patients (eg, those with malignancies) but is undesirable in others (eg, those under the influence of alcohol, barbiturates, or strong analgesics). Phenothiazines should not be given to patients who are somnolent or comatose, to those who exhibit other signs of central nervous system depression or hypotension, or to those receiving spinal or epidural anesthesia or adrenergic blocking agents.

Since phenothiazines are detoxified primarily in the liver, these agents should be used with caution in patients with liver dysfunction.

See also Chapter 29, Antipsychotic Agents.

NONPHENOTHIAZINE ANTIEMETICS

SCOPOLAMINE HYDROBROMIDE (Hyoscine Hydrobromide)

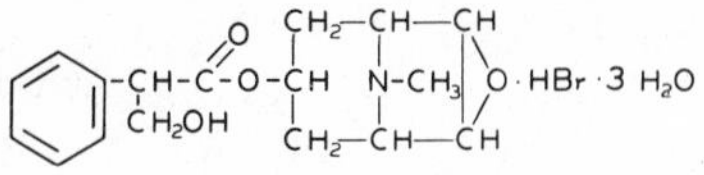

Scopolamine has a rapid onset and short duration of action (one-half to three hours). Although available evidence indicates that this is the most effective agent in the prevention or treatment of motion sickness, it has been largely supplanted by some of the newer antimotion sickness drugs, principally because of its untoward effects. Results of controlled studies with individuals in a selected age group who were subjected to severe motion indicate that there is a synergistic effect when 0.6 mg of scopolamine is given with 50 mg of ephedrine or 10 mg of dextroamphetamine.

Blurred vision, dryness of the mouth, vertigo, increased pulse rate, drowsiness, euphoria, amnesia, and fatigue are associated with use of scopolamine, especially in larger doses. Excitement, restlessness, hallucinations, or delirium also may occur.

For other uses, see Chapter 20, Adjuncts to Anesthesia, and Chapter 74, Antiparkinsonism Agents.

USUAL DOSAGE.—*Oral, Subcutaneous: Adults,* 0.6 to 1 mg; *children,* 0.006 mg/kg of body weight.

PREPARATIONS.—

Oral: Tablets 0.3, 0.4, and 0.6 mg.

Injection: Solution 0.3, 0.4, 0.5, 0.6, 0.8 mg/ml in 1 ml containers.

Drug marketed under generic name.

CYCLIZINE HYDROCHLORIDE [Marezine Hydrochloride]
CYCLIZINE LACTATE [Marezine Lactate]

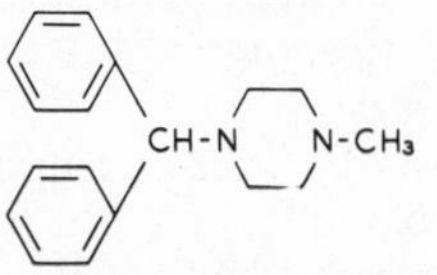

Cyclizine, an antihistamine, is useful in preventing and relieving symptoms of motion sickness and postoperative nausea and vomiting. This drug also relieves vertigo and other symptoms of vestibular disorders of the ear. The duration of action of cyclizine is four to six hours.

Large doses may cause drowsiness and dryness of the mouth. See the Introductory Statement for a discussion on the drug's possible teratogenic effects when used during pregnancy.

USUAL DOSAGE.—

Cyclizine Hydrochloride:

Oral: For motion sickness, *adults,* 50 mg one-half hour before departure, then every four to six hours as necessary (maximal daily dose, 200 mg); *children,* 3 mg/kg of body weight divided into three doses during a 24-hour period.

Rectal: For motion sickness, *adults,* 100 mg three or four times daily as necessary; *children,* 6 mg/kg of body weight divided into three doses during a 24-hour period.

Cyclizine Lactate:

Intramuscular: Adults, for motion sickness, 50 mg three or four times daily as required. To prevent postoperative vomiting, 50 mg preoperatively or 20 to 30 minutes before expected termination of surgery; postoperatively, 50 mg every four to six hours if required. *Children,* for motion sickness, 3 mg/kg of body weight divided into three doses during a 24-hour period.

PREPARATIONS.—

Marezine [hydrochloride] (Burroughs Wellcome).

Oral: Tablets 50 mg.

Rectal: Suppositories 50 and 100 mg.

Marezine [lactate] (Burroughs Wellcome). *Injection:* Solution 50 mg/ml in 1 ml containers.

DIMENHYDRINATE [Dramamine]

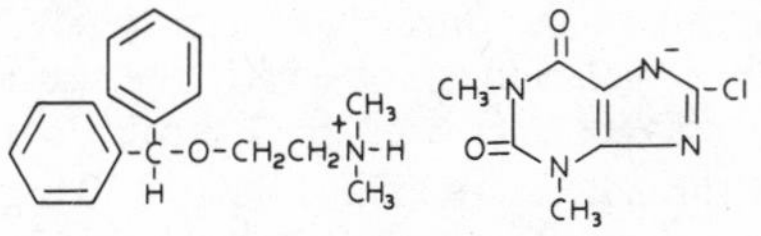

This chlorotheophylline salt of the antihistamine, diphenhydramine, is useful in preventing and treating motion sickness, nausea and vomiting during pregnancy, and postoperative nausea and vomiting. Its duration of action is four to six hours.

Mild drowsiness is associated with use of dimenhydrinate.

USUAL DOSAGE.—

Intramuscular: Adults, 50 mg as needed; *children,* 5 mg/kg of body weight divided into four doses during a 24-hour period (maximal dose, 300 mg/day).

Intravenous: Adults, 50 mg diluted in 10 ml of sodium chloride injection and injected over a period of two minutes; *children*, no dosage has been established.

Oral, Rectal: Adults, 50 to 100 mg every four hours; *children*, 5 mg/kg of body weight divided into four doses during a 24-hour period (maximal dose, 300 mg/day).

PREPARATIONS.—Dramamine (Searle).

Injection: Solution 50 mg/ml in 1 and 5 ml containers.

Oral: Liquid 15 mg/5 ml; tablets 50 mg.

Rectal: Suppositories 100 mg.

ADDITIONAL TRADEMARKS.—Dimen (Robinson), Dimenest (Fellows-Testagar).

DIPHENHYDRAMINE HYDROCHLORIDE [Benadryl]

$CHOCH_2CH_2N(CH_3)_2 \cdot HCl$

This antihistamine is similar to cyclizine in its actions. It is effective in the prevention and treatment of motion sickness, postoperative nausea, and nausea and vomiting of pregnancy. Its duration of action is four to six hours.

The incidence of drowsiness is high; vertigo has occurred occasionally. Individuals whose activities require alertness, such as those operating vehicles or machinery, should use diphenhydramine with caution.

For other uses, see Chapter 45, Antihistamines, and Chapter 74, Antiparkinsonism Agents.

USUAL DOSAGE.—

Intramuscular, Intravenous: Adults, 10 mg initially; if sedation is not severe, the subsequent dosage may be increased to 20 to 50 mg every two or three hours (maximal dose, 400 mg/day). *Children*, 5 mg/kg of body weight divided into four doses during a 24-hour period (maximal dose, 300 mg/day).

Oral: For motion sickness, *adults*, 50 mg one-half hour before departure and 50 mg before each meal; *children*, 5 mg/kg of body weight divided into four doses during a 24-hour period (maximal dose, 300 mg/day).

PREPARATIONS.—Benadryl (Parke, Davis).

Injection: Solution 10 mg/ml in 10 and 30 ml containers, 50 mg/ml in 1 and 10 ml containers.

Oral: Capsules 25 and 50 mg; elixir 12.5 mg/5 ml.

ADDITIONAL TRADEMARKS.—Bax (McKesson), Hista-Sed (Century), Niramine (Rachelle), Rohydra (Robinson). Drug also marketed by other manufacturers under generic name.

DIPHENIDOL [Vontrol]
DIPHENIDOL HYDROCHLORIDE [Vontrol Hydrochloride]

$CH_2CH_2CH_2C\text{-}OH$

N

Diphenidol is useful in the management of nausea and vomiting associated with infectious diseases, malignancies, radiation sickness, general anesthesia, and treatment with antineoplastic agents. In adults, this drug also is effective in the management of vertigo in motion sickness, labyrinthitis following surgery of the middle and inner ear, and Meniere's disease. Its use in the treatment of vertigo in children has not been investigated.

Patients who are receiving diphenidol should be closely supervised, and therapy should be discontinued if auditory and visual hallucinations, disorientation, and confusion occur. Even then, the benefits of using this agent should outweigh the possible risks. The drug occasionally has produced drowsiness, dryness of the mouth, and dizziness. Effects reported rarely include rash, heartburn, headache, nausea, indigestion, blurred vision, malaise, and mild transient hypotension.

USUAL DOSAGE.—

Intramuscular: Adults, 20 to 40 mg four times daily; *children*, 3 mg/kg of body weight daily divided into four doses. No dosage has been established for *infants weighing less than 12 kg.*

Intravenous: Adults, 20 mg initially; dose is repeated in one hour if necessary. No dosage has been established for *children* of any age.

Oral, Rectal: Adults, 25 to 50 mg four times daily; *children*, 5 mg/kg of body weight daily divided into four doses.

PREPARATIONS.—(All strengths expressed in terms of the base.)

Vontrol [base] (Smith Kline & French).

Rectal: Suppositories 25 and 50 mg.

Vontrol [hydrochloride] (Smith Kline & French).

Injection: Solution 20 mg/ml in 2 ml containers.

Oral: Tablets 25 mg.

HYDROXYZINE HYDROCHLORIDE [Atarax, Vistaril IM]
HYDROXYZINE PAMOATE [Vistaril Pamoate]

Hydroxyzine is promoted as an antianxiety agent, but it also possesses antiemetic and antihistaminic properties. It is useful for the prevention and treatment of postoperative nausea and vomiting and motion sickness. The duration of action of hydroxyzine is four to six hours. (Also see Chapter 28, Antianxiety Agents.)

The incidence of drowsiness is low.

USUAL DOSAGE.—

Hydroxyzine Hydrochloride:

Intramuscular: Preoperatively and postoperatively, *adults*, 25 to 100 mg; *children*, 1 mg/kg of body weight.

Hydroxyzine Hydrochloride, Hydroxyzine Pamoate:

Oral: For motion sickness, *adults*, 25 to 100 mg three or four times daily. *Children under 6 years of age*, 50 mg divided into four doses during a 24-hour period; *over 6 years*, 50 to 100 mg divided into four doses during a 24-hour period.

PREPARATIONS.—

Hydroxyzine Hydrochloride:

Atarax (Roerig). *Oral:* Syrup 10 mg/5 ml; tablets 10, 25, 50, and 100 mg.

Vistaril IM [hydrochloride] (Pfizer). *Injection:* Solution 25 mg/ml in 1 and 10 ml containers and 50 mg/ml in 1, 2, and 10 ml containers.

Hydroxyzine Pamoate:

Vistaril [pamoate] (Pfizer). *Oral:* Capsules 25, 50, and 100 mg; suspension 25 mg/5 ml.

MECLIZINE HYDROCHLORIDE [Antivert, Bonine]

Cl–C₆H₄–CH(C₆H₅)–N(piperazine)N–CH₂–C₆H₄(CH₃) · 2 HCl

Meclizine is effective in preventing and treating motion sickness. It has a slower onset and longer duration of action than most of the other antihistamines used for motion sickness; the duration of action of a single oral dose is 12 to 24 hours. Meclizine also is used in the treatment of nausea and vomiting associated with vertigo, labyrinthitis, Meniere's disease, and radiation sickness.

Drowsiness, blurred vision, dryness of the mouth, and fatigue have occurred following administration of meclizine. See the Introductory Statement for a discussion on the drug's possible teratogenic effects when used during pregnancy.

USUAL DOSAGE.—*Oral: Adults*, for motion sickness, 25 to 50 mg once daily. The initial dose should be taken at least one hour prior to departure. For other conditions, 25 to 100 mg daily. *Children*, dosage has not been established.

PREPARATIONS.—

Antivert (Roerig). *Oral:* Tablets 12.5 mg; tablets (chewable) 25 mg.

Bonine (Roerig). *Oral:* Tablets (chewable) 25 mg.

TRIMETHOBENZAMIDE HYDROCHLORIDE [Tigan]

$(CH_3)_2NCH_2CH_2O$–C₆H₄–CH_2NHOC–C₆H₂$(OCH_3)_3$ · HCl

This drug may be useful in alleviating nausea and reducing the frequency of vomiting in the immediate postoperative period after use of a general or spinal anesthetic, as well as in the treatment of nausea and vomiting during pregnancy. Its duration of action is four to six hours. Trimethobenzamide is of little or no value in the prevention and treatment of motion sickness.

The incidence of adverse effects is low; however, drowsiness, vertigo, diarrhea, cutaneous hypersensitivity reactions, extrapyramidal reactions, exaggeration of pre-existing nausea, pain at the site of injection, and local irritation after rectal administration have been noted.

USUAL DOSAGE.—

Intramuscular: Adults, 200 mg three or four times daily. To prevent postoperative vomiting, a single dose of 200 mg may be given before or during surgery; this dose may be repeated three hours after termination of anesthesia if needed.

Oral : Adults, 250 mg three or four times daily; *children*, 15 mg/kg of body weight divided into three or four doses during a 24-hour period.

Rectal : Adults, 200 mg; *children*, 15 mg/kg of body weight divided into three or four doses during a 24-hour period. This route should not be used in *premature or newborn infants.*

PREPARATIONS.–Tigan (Roche).

Injection :Solution 100 mg/ml in 2 and 20 ml containers.

Oral :Capsules 100 and 250 mg.

Rectal : Suppositories 200 mg (with 2% benzocaine).

PHENOTHIAZINE ANTIEMETICS

CHLORPROMAZINE [Thorazine]
CHLORPROMAZINE HYDROCHLORIDE
[Thorazine Hydrochloride]

Chlorpromazine is the prototype of the phenothiazine compounds. In addition to its calming action, it is effective in the management of postoperative nausea and vomiting, radiation sickness, and nausea and vomiting due to toxins. It is not useful in preventing motion sickness. Since chlorpromazine has a prolonged half-life, the timed-release preparation does not offer any significant advantage over the ordinary oral dosage form.

Some patients may become drowsy to an undesirable degree; however, tolerance to excessive sedation usually develops after continued use. Chlorpromazine prolongs postanesthesia sleeping time. Among its more serious untoward reactions, which occur after long-term administration or large doses, are extrapyramidal reactions, orthostatic hypotension, cholestatic jaundice, and leukopenia. Because of the severity of these reactions, the phenothiazines should be used only when vomiting cannot be controlled by less hazardous agents. (See also the Introductory Statement and Chapter 29, Antipsychotic Agents.)

USUAL DOSAGE.–

Intramuscular : *Adults*, 25 to 50 mg every three or four hours until vomiting stops; the drug is then given orally. *Children*, 0.5 mg/kg of body weight every four to six hours.

Oral : *Adults*, 10 to 25 mg every four to six hours; *children*, 0.5 mg/kg of body weight every four to six hours.

Rectal : *Adults*, 100 mg every six to eight hours; *children*, 1 mg/kg of body weight every six to eight hours.

PREPARATIONS.–

Thorazine [base] (Smith Kline & French). *Rectal* :Suppositories 25 and 100 mg.

Thorazine [hydrochloride] (Smith Kline & French).

Injection :Solution 25 mg/ml in 1, 2, and 10 ml containers.

Oral : Capsules (timed-release) 30, 75, 150, 200, and 300 mg; solution (concentrate) 30 and 100 mg/ml; syrup 10 mg/5 ml; tablets 10, 25, 50, 100, and 200 mg.

FLUPHENAZINE HYDROCHLORIDE
[Permitil, Prolixin]

Fluphenazine is effective in the management of postoperative nausea and vomiting, radiation sickness, and nausea and vomiting due to toxins. However, it is not useful in preventing motion sickness. This phenothiazine has virtually no sedative effect and, when given preoperatively, does not appreciably prolong postanesthesia sleeping time. Since fluphenazine hydrochloride has a prolonged half-life, the oral timed-release preparation does not offer any significant advantage over the ordinary oral dosage forms.

The incidence of extrapyramidal reactions is higher with fluphenazine than with most other phenothiazine compounds. This drug has little tendency to produce hypotension; however, blurred vision, dryness of the mouth, and urinary retention have been reported. (See also the Introductory Statement and Chapter 29, Antipsychotic Agents.)

USUAL DOSAGE.–*Intramuscular*, *Oral* : *Adults*, 1 to 2 mg; *children*, dosage is reduced (see table, back cover).

PREPARATIONS.–

Permitil (Schering). *Oral* : Solution (concentrate) 5 mg/ml; tablets 0.25, 2.5, 5, and 10 mg; tablets (timed-release) 1 mg.

Prolixin (Squibb).

Oral : Elixir 2.5 mg/5 ml; tablets 1, 2.5, and 5 mg.

Injection : Solution 2.5 mg/ml in 10 ml containers.

PERPHENAZINE [Trilafon]

This phenothiazine compound is effective in the management of postoperative nausea and vomiting, radiation sickness, and nausea and vomiting due to toxins, but is not useful in preventing motion sickness. Since perphenazine has a prolonged half-life, the timed-release preparation does not offer any significant advantage over the ordinary oral dosage forms.

Untoward effects include extrapyramidal reactions, blurred or double vision, nasal congestion, dryness of the mouth, salivation, headache, and, occasionally, drowsiness. (See also the Introductory Statement and Chapter 29, Antipsychotic Agents.)

USUAL DOSAGE.–

Intramuscular : *Adults*, 5 to 10 mg. *Children 12 years of age and older*, 2 mg; *under 12 years*, dosage has not been determined.

Oral : Adults, 8 to 24 mg daily in divided doses. *Children 1 to 6 years of age,* 4 mg daily divided into three doses; *6 to 12 years,* 6 mg daily divided into three doses; *12 years and older,* 6 to 12 mg daily divided into three doses.

PREPARATIONS.—Trilafon (Schering).

Injection : Solution 5 mg/ml in 1 and 10 ml containers.

Oral : Solution (concentrate) 16 mg/5 ml; syrup 2 mg/5 ml; tablets 2, 4, 8, and 16 mg; tablets (timed-release) 8 mg.

PROCHLORPERAZINE [Compazine]
PROCHLORPERAZINE EDISYLATE [Compazine Edisylate]
PROCHLORPERAZINE MALEATE [Compazine Maleate]

Prochlorperazine is effective in the management of postoperative nausea and vomiting, radiation sickness, and nausea and vomiting due to toxins, especially when minimal sedation is desired. It is not useful in preventing motion sickness. Since prochlorperazine has an intrinsically prolonged action, the timed-release preparation does not appear to offer any significant advantage over the ordinary oral dosage forms.

This piperazine phenothiazine frequently causes extrapyramidal reactions. Although these effects are most likely to occur when large doses are used, signs may appear abruptly in patients taking only moderate doses. Therefore, it is contraindicated in patients with a history of dyskinetic reactions or epilepsy or in pregnant women with pre-eclampsia. (See also the Introductory Statement and Chapter 29, Antipsychotic Agents.)

USUAL DOSAGE.—

Intramuscular (edisylate): *Adults,* 5 to 10 mg every three to four hours; amount should not exceed 40 mg daily. *Children weighing over 10 kg,* 0.2 mg/kg of body weight.

Oral (edisylate, maleate): *Adults,* 5 to 10 mg three or four times daily; *children weighing over 10 kg,* 0.4 mg/kg of body weight divided into three or four doses during a 24-hour period.

Rectal (base): *Adults,* 25 mg twice daily; *children weighing over 10 kg,* 0.4 mg/kg of body weight divided into three or four doses during a 24-hour period.

PREPARATIONS.—

Compazine [base] (Smith Kline & French). *Rectal:* Suppositories 2.5, 5, and 25 mg.

Compazine [edisylate] (Smith Kline & French).

Injection: Solution 5 mg/ml in 2 and 10 ml containers.

Oral: Solution (concentrate) 10 mg/ml; syrup 5 mg/5 ml.

Compazine [maleate] (Smith Kline & French). *Oral:* Capsules (timed-released) 10, 15, 30, and 75 mg; tablets 5, 10, and 25 mg.

PROMAZINE HYDROCHLORIDE [Sparine]

Promazine is effective in the management of postoperative nausea and vomiting, radiation sickness, and nausea and vomiting due to toxins. However, since the incidence of adverse reactions (eg, drowsiness, orthostatic hypotension) is greater with this phenothiazine than with other agents in this group, especially after parenteral administration, other antiemetics are preferred. (See also the Introductory Statement and Chapter 29, Antipsychotic Agents.)

USUAL DOSAGE.—There is no reason to use this drug as an antiemetic because equally effective but safer agents are available. The manufacturer's suggested dosage is: *Intramuscular, Intravenous, Oral: Adults,* 25 to 50 mg; dose may be repeated at four- to six-hour intervals. *Children,* dosage has not been established.

PREPARATIONS.—Sparine (Wyeth).

Injection: Solution 25 and 50 mg/ml in 1, 2 and 10 ml containers.

Oral: Solution (concentrate) 30 and 100 mg/ml; syrup 10 mg/5 ml; tablets 10, 25, 50, 100, and 200 mg.

PROMETHAZINE HYDROCHLORIDE [Phenergan]

Unlike other phenothiazines, promethazine is effective in the prevention and treatment of motion sickness. Its sedative action is of value in the treatment of postoperative nausea and vomiting. Promethazine also exhibits pronounced antihistaminic activity. Results of controlled studies in individuals who were subjected to severe motion indicate that a synergistic effect occurs when 25 mg of promethazine is given with 10 mg of dextroamphetamine or 50 mg of ephedrine.

Promethazine is relatively free of the extrapyramidal stimulation that is associated with some other phenothiazine derivatives. However, the usual precautions recommended for drugs in this class should be observed.

See also the Introductory Statement; Chapter 20, Adjuncts to Anesthesia; and Chapter 45, Antihistamines.

USUAL DOSAGE.—*Intramuscular, Oral, Rectal: Adults,* 12.5 to 25 mg every four to six hours; *children over three months of age,* 0.25 to 0.5 mg/kg of body weight every four to six hours.

PREPARATIONS.—Phenergan (Wyeth).

Injection: Solution 25 and 50 mg/ml in 1 and 10 ml containers.

Oral: Syrup 6.25 and 25 mg/5 ml; tablets 12.5, 25, and 50 mg.

Rectal: Suppositories 25 and 50 mg.

ADDITIONAL TRADEMARKS.—Fellozine (Fellows-Testagar), Ganphen (Tutag).

THIETHYLPERAZINE MALEATE [Torecan Maleate]

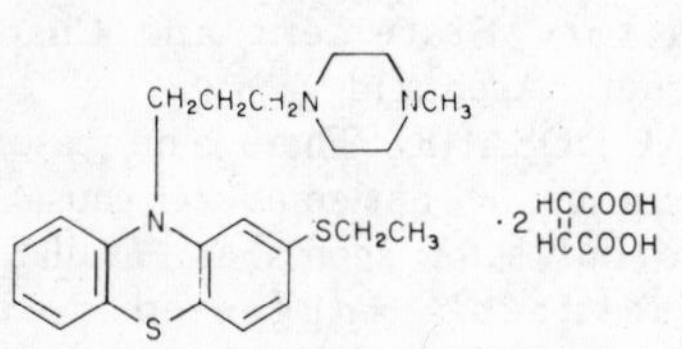

Thiethylperazine is useful in reducing the incidence of nausea and vomiting associated with vertigo and with the administration of general anesthetics, nitrogen mustards, and ionizing radiation. This phenothiazine is not useful in preventing motion sickness and may be ineffective when vomiting is caused by emotional disturbances.

Untoward effects occur infrequently and are mild and transitory with usual doses. Adverse reactions noted occasionally include drowsiness, dizziness, dryness of the mouth and nose, tachycardia, and anorexia. Moderate hypotension also has occurred occasionally within 30 minutes after administration of the drug to patients recovering from general anesthesia. Like other phenothiazine compounds, thiethylperazine may produce extrapyramidal stimulation. Symptoms may appear even after a single dose and abate if therapy is discontinued. (See also the Introductory Statement.)

USUAL DOSAGE.—*Intramuscular, Oral, Rectal :Adults,* 10 to 30 mg daily.

PREPARATIONS.—Torecan Maleate (Sandoz).

Injection : Solution 5 mg/ml in 2 ml containers.

*Oral :*Tablets 10 mg.

*Rectal :*Suppositories 10 mg.

TRIFLUPROMAZINE HYDROCHLORIDE [Vesprin]

This phenothiazine compound is effective in the management of postoperative nausea and vomiting, radiation sickness, and nausea and vomiting due to toxins. It is not useful in preventing motion sickness.

Triflupromazine produces less sedation than some other phenothiazines (eg, promazine), but it prolongs the postanesthesia sleeping time. Extrapyramidal reactions have been observed following even single doses of this compound. (See also the Introductory Statement and Chapter 29, Antipsychotic Agents.)

USUAL DOSAGE.—

Intramuscular : Adults, 5 to 10 mg, repeated in four hours if necessary; *children,* 1 mg for each year of age (maximum, 10 mg daily).

Intravenous : Adults, 1 to 3 mg, repeated in four hours if necessary; *children 7 to 14 years of age,* 2 to 3 mg; *under 7 years,* 1 to 2 mg.

Oral : Adults, 20 to 30 mg daily; *children,* 1 mg for each year of age (maximum, 10 mg daily).

PREPARATIONS.—Vesprin (Squibb).

Injection : Solution 10 mg/ml in 10 ml containers, 20 mg/ml in 1 ml containers.

Oral : Suspension 50 mg/5 ml; tablets 10, 25, and 50 mg.

MIXTURES

Fixed-ratio combinations containing nonphenothiazine antiemetics and other ingredients (eg, pyridoxine, niacin, pentobarbital) are marketed, but there are no controlled studies to support the contention that these combinations, particularly those containing pyridoxine, have any advantage over the nonphenothiazine agent alone; therefore, single-entity preparations are preferred.

Anti-Nausea Supprettes (Webster): Each suppository contains pyrilamine maleate 25 or 50 mg and pentobarbital sodium 30, 45, or 100 mg.

Bendectin (Merrell-National): Each tablet contains dicyclomine hydrochloride 10 mg, doxylamine succinate 10 mg, and pyridoxine hydrochloride 10 mg.

Bucladin (Stuart): Each tablet contains buclizine hydrochloride 50 mg, pyridoxine hydrochloride 10 mg, scopolamine hydrobromide 0.2 mg, hyoscyamine sulfate 0.05 mg, and atropine sulfate 0.05 mg.

Cerebel Liquid (Xttrium): Each 5 ml contains

scopolamine hydrobromide 0.003 mg, phenobarbital 2.02 ml, milk of bismuth 2.5 ml, cerium oxalate 300 mg, hyoscyamine sulfate 0.0052 mg, and atropine sulfate 0.01 mg.

Delkadon (Merck Sharp & Dohme): Each tablet contains scopolamine hydrobromide 0.006 mg, hyoscyamine hydrobromide 0.225 mg, atropine sulfate 0.019 mg, and vinbarbital 30 mg.

Dramamine-D (Searle): Each tablet contains dimenhydrinate 50 mg and dextroamphetamine sulfate 5 mg.

Emesert (Arnar-Stone): Each suppository contains pyrilamine maleate 25 or 50 mg and pentobarbital 30, 45, or 100 mg.

Hytrona (Webster): Each tablet and 5 ml of elixir contains scopolamine hydrobromide 0.005 mg, hyoscyamine hydrobromide 0.180 mg, atropine sulfate 0.015 mg, and phenobarbital 16 mg.

Pyretol (First Texas): Each 5 ml of elixir contains scopolamine hydrobromide 0.0081 mg, chlorpheniramine maleate 2 mg, hyoscyamine sulfate 0.1296 mg, atropine sulfate 0.0242 mg, thiamine mononitrate 12.5 mg, and pyridoxine hydrochloride 25 mg.

Chapter 86

STIMULANTS OF GASTROINTESTINAL AND URINARY TRACTS

Drugs that stimulate the smooth muscle of the gastrointestinal and urinary tracts are used in the treatment of nonobstructive urinary retention and gastrointestinal atony. Those commonly administered are the cholinergic agents, bethanechol [Myocholine, Urecholine] and neostigmine methylsulfate [Prostigmin].

Bethanechol is a choline ester that acts directly on effector cells innervated by the cholinergic system to produce effects similar to those of acetylcholine; however, since bethanechol is relatively resistant to hydrolysis by cholinesterase, its effects are more prolonged than those of acetylcholine. The actions of bethanechol are primarily muscarinic; it produces no significant effects on autonomic ganglia or at the neuromuscular junction. Its actions on the gastrointestinal tract and urinary bladder are more pronounced than those on the cardiovascular system; thus, it is preferred to other cholinergic drugs for stimulation of the gastrointestinal and urinary tracts.

Neostigmine produces its cholinergic effects indirectly by inhibiting acetylcholinesterase, the enzyme that destroys acetylcholine. Inhibition of this enzyme results in an accumulation of acetylcholine at the sites of cholinergic transmission; this, in turn, stimulates the muscarinic receptor sites of effector cells of smooth muscle, exocrine glands, autonomic ganglia, and of the neuromuscular junction of skeletal muscle. The fact that its cholinergic action affects various organ systems is not only the basis for the several therapeutic uses of neostigmine, but is also the cause of its untoward effects.

In addition to its use as a stimulant of the gastrointestinal and urinary tracts, neostigmine is employed in glaucoma therapy (see Chapter 69) and in the diagnosis and treatment of myasthenia gravis (see Chapter 75). Neostigmine antagonizes the action of ganglionic blocking agents at the ganglia, thereby reducing their effects on the cardiovascular and gastrointestinal tracts. It also counteracts the neuromuscular blocking action of the nondepolarizing agents (eg, tubocurarine).

In addition to these two cholinergic agents, dexpanthenol [Cozyme, Ilopan] is promoted for the treatment of adynamic ileus on the theoretical basis that it increases the amount of coenzyme A available for the formation of acetylcholine, which, in turn, increases intestinal tone. However, the theoretical basis for this use of dexpanthenol has not been proved, and since there is no convincing evidence that the drug is effective, dexpanthenol should not be used for intestinal atony.

Adverse Reactions and Precautions

The untoward effects of bethanechol and neostigmine methylsulfate are caused by stimulation of the cholinergic receptors of the autonomic nervous system. See the individual evaluations for specific adverse reactions and precautions.

INDIVIDUAL EVALUATIONS

BETHANECHOL CHLORIDE [Myocholine, Urecholine]

$$CH_3\underset{\underset{\underset{\displaystyle O}{\|}}{OCNH_2}}{\underset{|}{C}}H\,CH_2\overset{+}{N}(CH_3)_3\quad Cl^-$$

Bethanechol is used to restore normal micturition in patients with urinary retention related to surgery, parturition, trauma, or psychic factors. It is also used for the treatment of postoperative gastrointestinal atony, including postvagotomy atony and adynamic ileus secondary to trauma, infection, or neurogenic disorders. It has been administered to counteract the effects of ganglionic blocking agents on the gastrointestinal system and urinary bladder. However, this use is not advised because severe hypotension may occur.

Bethanechol may cause flushing, hyperhidrosis, salivation, and abdominal discomfort. Severe adverse reactions are rare. The drug is contraindicated in patients with mechanical intestinal or urinary obstruction, bronchial asthma, hyperthyroidism, peptic ulcer, severe heart disease, bradycardia, hypotension, vagotonia, or in those receiving anticholinesterase agents.

USUAL DOSAGE.—

Oral: Adults, 10 to 30 mg three or four times daily; *children,* 0.6 mg/kg of body weight daily in three divided doses. This drug should be taken when the stomach is empty.

Subcutaneous: Adults, 2.5 to 5 mg three or four times daily; *children,* 0.15 to 0.2 mg/kg of body weight daily in three divided doses.

Bethanechol should not be given intravenously or intramuscularly because acute severe muscarinic effects may result.

PREPARATIONS.—

Myocholine Chloride (Glenwood). *Oral:* Tablets 10 and 25 mg.

Urecholine Chloride (Merck Sharp & Dohme).

Oral: Tablets 5, 10, and 25 mg.

Injection (subcutaneous): Solution 5 mg/ml in 1 ml containers.

NEOSTIGMINE METHYLSULFATE

[Prostigmin Methylsulfate]

Neostigmine is used for the prevention and treatment of postoperative gastrointestinal atony, but it is not effective in relieving atony that results from bilateral vagotomy. In patients with achalasia of the esophagus, it increases tone and peristalsis. It is also given to prevent or alleviate atony of the urinary bladder. Neostigmine antagonizes the action of ganglionic blocking agents on the cardiovascular and gastrointestinal systems, and is an effective antagonist of nondepolarizing neuromuscular blocking agents (eg, tubocurarine).

For other uses, see Chapter 69, Agents Used to Treat Glaucoma, and Chapter 75, Agents Used in Myasthenia Gravis.

Hyperhidrosis, salivation, gastrointestinal distress, and bradycardia are minor untoward effects of neostigmine. Overdosage can cause a cholinergic crisis. The drug is contraindicated in patients with mechanical obstruction of the intestinal or urinary tract. It should be given with caution and in small doses to patients with bronchial asthma, and should not be given with choline esters or depolarizing neuromuscular blocking agents (eg, decamethonium, succinylcholine).

USUAL DOSAGE.—*Subcutaneous, Intramuscular: Adults,* for *treatment* of atony of the bladder or gastrointestinal system, 0.5 to 1 mg as required. For *prevention* of atony of the bladder or gastrointestinal system, 0.25 mg every four to six hours for two or three days.

PREPARATIONS.—Prostigmin [methylsulfate] (Roche). *Injection:* Solution 0.25 mg/ml in 1 ml containers, 0.5 mg/ml in 1 and 10 ml containers, and 1 mg/ml in 10 ml containers. Drug also marketed by other manufacturers under generic name.

Chapter 87

OXYTOCICS

Oxytocic agents stimulate the motility of the uterus. Only three oxytocics can be recommended for clinical use: the neurohypophyseal hormone, oxytocin [Pitocin, Syntocinon], and, for postpartum use only, the two ergot alkaloids, ergonovine [Ergotrate] and the semisynthetic derivative, methylergonovine [Methergine].

Oxytocin is the only agent that can be relied upon to approximate the pattern of spontaneous uterine contractions. It is the drug of choice to induce labor and to stimulate labor in cases of intrapartum hypotonic inertia. Induction of labor is indicated in selected patients whose pregnancies are associated with various hypertensive disorders with or without proteinuria (preeclampsia, eclampsia, cardiovascular-renal disease), erythroblastosis fetalis, antepartum bleeding, and diabetes mellitus. In these patients, induction of labor after the 36th week and before expected term may reduce maternal and infant morbidity and mortality. Labor also may be induced when premature rupture of the fetal membranes occurs after the 34th week of gestation and spontaneous labor does not begin unless a specific contraindication to oxytocin is present. Other indications for induction are postmaturity (gestation beyond the 41st week of amenorrhea) and intrauterine fetal death if the plasma fibrinogen is diminishing or if there is marked maternal anxiety.

Oxytocin, ergonovine, and methylergonovine may be used postpartum to produce firm uterine contractions and to decrease postpartum uterine bleeding. The ergot alkaloids combine low toxicity, rapid onset, and sustained duration of action and are preferred over oxytocin for these purposes.

Other agents (eg, quinine, quinidine, sparteine sulfate [Spartocin, Tocosamine]) also have oxytocic actions. Quinine and quinidine have been used in the past to initiate labor, but neither drug should be used for this purpose. They are unreliable in safe doses, and there is considerable danger of producing eighth nerve damage in the infant. The uterine response to sparteine is unpredictable.

Two prostaglandin compounds, dinoprostone (PGE_2) and dinoprost ($PGF_{2\alpha}$), are being investigated for use in place of oxytocin. They possess the unique property of producing uterine contractions with essentially equal effectiveness at all stages of pregnancy; hence, they have been utilized for therapeutic abortions as well as for the induction of labor.

Adverse Reactions and Precautions

All oxytocic agents are potentially dangerous. Mothers and infants have been injured and some have died because of their injudicious use. Hyperstimulation of the uterus during labor may lead to uterine tetany with marked impairment of the uteroplacental blood flow, uterine rupture, cervical and perineal lacerations, amniotic fluid embolism, and trauma to the infant (eg, hypoxia, intracranial hemorrhage).

After adequacy of the pelvic outlet is determined, maternal and fetal conditions need to be evaluated to decide whether or not the risk of allowing the pregnancy to continue exceeds that of inducing labor. Factors such as distance from home to hospital and history of rapid labor also may enter into the decision. Induction may prevent an uncontrolled delivery outside the hospital. However, this type of rationalized benefit can be justified only when there is reasonable assurance that no complications will occur. The patient, therefore, must be at or very close to term, with the presenting part fixed and with a favorable cervix. Laboratory examination of the amniotic fluid may be necessary, along with the history and physical examination, to determine maturity. Prematurity represents the major hazard to the fetus and premature induction done without a clear medical indication is inexcusable.

The primary contraindication to the use of oxytocin by any route prior to delivery is the *absence* of a competent observer by the bedside. The only way to prevent complications to mother and fetus during administration is by continuous observation by a knowledgeable professional person using clinical or electronic monitoring to determine uterine contractility, fetal pulse rate, and maternal blood pressure and pulse. If tetany occurs, oxytocin should be discontinued immediately. The intravenous route of administration gives more predictable contraction patterns and more precise control than other routes (ie, intramuscular, nasal, buccal). When these other routes are used prior to delivery, the same careful monitoring by a competent observer is as essential as when oxytocin is administered intravenously.

The oxytocics often will not be effective when given to patients who have been anesthetized with potent uterine relaxants, such as halothane and chloroform, until the anesthetic is completely eliminated.

If vasopressors are administered to correct hypotension during surgical anesthesia, the concurrent administration of an oxytocic may cause severe hypertension and result in cerebral hemorrhage. However, an oxytocic may be administered five to ten minutes after continuous infusion of a short-acting vasopressor has been discontinued. Use of local anesthetic solutions containing 1:200,000 epinephrine is not contraindicated provided that no oxytocic is given within the next 15 minutes.

For further information on adverse reactions and contraindications, see the individual evaluations.

INDIVIDUAL EVALUATIONS

OXYTOCIN [Pitocin, Syntocinon]
OXYTOCIN CITRATE [Pitocin Citrate]

```
Glu(NH2)——Asp(NH2)
|          |
Ileu—Tyr—Cys—Cys—Pro—Leu—Gly(NH2)
```

Only synthetic oxytocin is now available. It is the drug of choice to induce and maintain labor (see the Introductory Statement). It also is used in inevitable or incomplete abortion after the 20th week of gestation; abortions cannot be induced earlier unless large doses are used (eg, 20 to 30 units). Oxytocin may be given postpartum to prevent or control hemorrhage and to correct uterine hypotonicity.

Oxytocin acts to contract the myoepithelium of the mammary glands and to force milk into the large ducts. It occasionally is used successfully to promote milk ejection when ineffective ejection is considered a factor in inadequacy of breast feeding. The intranasal route of administration is most frequently used for convenience. Oxytocin does not have galactopoietic properties.

Hypofibrinogenemia and postpartum bleeding have been observed following use of oxytocin during labor, but these conditions are probably related to the underlying obstetrical problem rather than to the drug. Severe water intoxication with convulsions and coma has been reported, especially when doses larger than 20 milliunits/minute have been infused intravenously for long periods. This is probably due to the small but inherent antidiuretic effect of oxytocin. Maternal deaths due to hypertensive episodes, subarachnoid hemorrhage, or rupture of the uterus have resulted from the injudicious use of oxytocin. Pelvic hematomas and anaphylactoid and other allergic reactions also may occur in the mother. Induced uterine motility may cause sinus bradycardia, premature ventricular contractions, and other arrhythmias in the fetus. Fetal deaths have occurred.

Contraindications to induction of labor are cephalopelvic disproportion; malpresentation; central placenta previa; breech presentation with a small pelvis; uterine scar from previous cesarean section, hysterotomy, or myomectomy; and unengaged head. Induction should be discontinued if fetal distress develops from induced uterine contractions. Extreme caution should be observed in patients with abruptio placenta, partial placenta previa, and overdistention of the uterus resulting from four or more previous pregnancies.

Oxytocin should be used only in the hospital under continuous medical supervision. It should not be used simultaneously by more than one route of administration. Only very dilute solutions of oxytocin should be administered intravenously for induction of labor.

USUAL DOSAGE.—

Intravenous Infusion: A dilute solution, prepared by mixing oxytocin with 500 to 1,000 ml of sodium chloride injection or 5% dextrose injection, is administered with an infusion pump or regulated drip to deliver the desired number of milliunits per minute. The intravenous apparatus is adjusted to begin at the desired infusion rate (0.2 to 4 milliunits/minute) and the rate is carefully increased until an optimal uterine response (three or four contractions of good quality in ten minutes) is obtained. Infusion should be stopped or the rate reduced immediately if changes in fetal heart tones, excessive contractions, or poor relaxation of uterus appear.

Intravenous Injection: In an emergency to help reduce severe postpartum bleeding (to be distinguished from intravenous infusion), 0.6 to 1.8 units (0.06 to 0.18 ml) of oxytocin is diluted with 3 to 5 ml of sodium chloride injection and given slowly.

Intramuscular: To control postpartum bleeding, 3 to 10 units (0.3 to 1 ml).

Buccal: One or more tablets are placed in the parabuccal spaces every 30 minutes until the desired uterine response is obtained or until a total of 15 tablets (3,000 units) has been given. The rate of absorption is unpredictable and buccal administration, although simple, is less precise and less reliable than the intravenous route. The same precaution for continuous careful supervision is essential.

Topical (nasal spray): To promote milk ejection during breast feeding, one spray into one or both nostrils two to three minutes before nursing.

PREPARATIONS.—

Oxytocin:

Pitocin (Parke, Davis). *Injection:* Solution 5 units (5,000 milliunits) in 0.5 ml containers and 10 units (10,000 milliunits) in 1 ml containers.

Syntocinon (Sandoz).

Injection: Solution 5 units (5,000 milliunits) in 0.5 ml containers and 10 units (10,000 milliunits) in 1 ml containers.

Topical: Nasal spray 40 units (40,000 milliunits)/ml in 2 and 5 ml containers.

Injection form also marketed under generic name.

Oxytocin Citrate:

Pitocin Citrate (Parke, Davis). *Buccal:* Tablets 200 units.

ERGONOVINE MALEATE [Ergotrate Maleate]

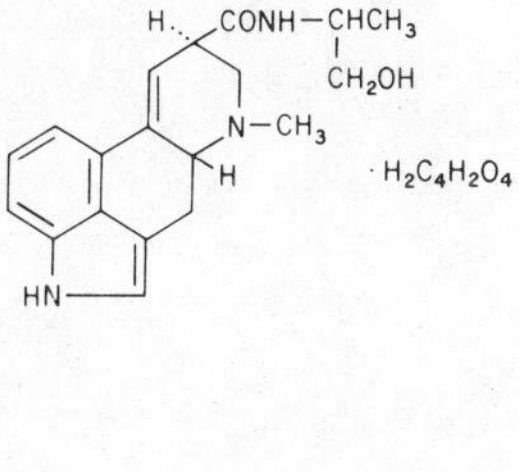

METHYLERGONOVINE MALEATE [Methergine]

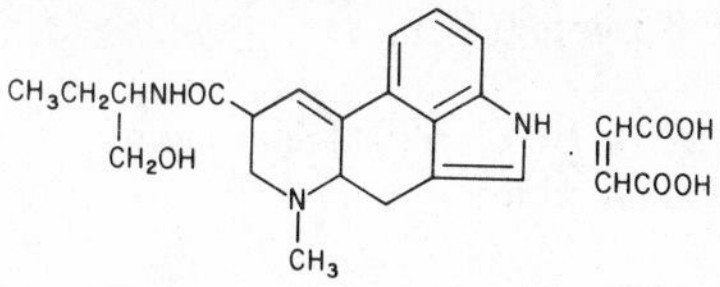

These drugs are used only postpartum, preferably after delivery of the placenta, to produce firm uterine contractions and to decrease uterine bleeding. Ergonovine and methylergonovine are preferred over oxytocin for these purposes. They have a rapid onset and prolonged duration of action.

Nausea and vomiting may occur, especially when ergonovine or methylergonovine is given intravenously. Unusual elevations in blood pressure may occur in some patients for obscure reasons, particularly when spinal or epidural anesthesia is used, or when vasopressors have been administered during anesthesia.

The drugs are contraindicated in pregnant patients and in those who have a history of hypersensitivity to ergot alkaloids. They should be used with caution in those with puerperal infection, obliterative vascular disease, and hepatic, cardiac, or renal disease. Patients with hypocalcemia may be resistant to the oxytocic action of these drugs. Cautious administration of calcium gluconate intravenously may restore uterine sensitivity in these patients, but calcium gluconate should not be given to digitalized patients.

For other uses, see Chapter 24, Agents Used to Treat Migraine.

USUAL DOSAGE.—

Intramuscular: 0.2 mg (1 ml). This dose usually is administered every six hours, but may be repeated in two to four hours if severe bleeding occurs.

Intravenous: 0.2 mg (1 ml) is given in an emergency when excessive uterine bleeding has occurred.

Oral: 0.2 mg two to four times daily in the puerperium, usually for two days (maximum, one week).

PREPARATIONS.—

Ergonovine Maleate:

Ergotrate Maleate (Lilly).

Injection: Solution 0.2 mg/ml in 1 ml containers.

Oral: Tablets 0.2 mg.

Drug also marketed by other manufacturers under generic name.

Methylergonovine Maleate:

Methergine (Sandoz).

Injection: Solution 0.2 mg/ml in 1 ml containers.

Oral: Tablets 0.2 mg.

SPARTEINE SULFATE [Spartocin, Tocosamine]

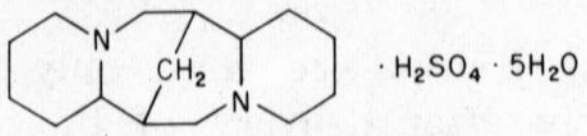

$\cdot H_2SO_4 \cdot 5H_2O$

Hypertonicity and inappropriate frequency of contractions make the oxytocic action of sparteine more like that of the ergot preparations than that of oxytocin. The first dose may result in uterine tetany and fetal sinus bradycardia. Precise control of contractions, which is necessary in the presence of hyperstimulation, is lacking since sparteine is given intramuscularly. Thus, the drug is not suitable for use as an oxytocic agent to induce labor or to treat hypotonic uterine contractions because of its unpredictable action.

USUAL DOSAGE.—No useful dosage is recognized. The manufacturer's suggested dosage is: *Intramuscular:* Initially, 75 mg followed by increments of 75 to 150 mg hourly until a response is obtained. A total dosage of 600 mg should not be exceeded.

PREPARATIONS.—Spartocin (Ayerst), Tocosamine (Trent). *Injection:* Solution 150 mg/ml in 1 ml containers.

Chapter 88

ANTINEOPLASTIC AGENTS

Antineoplastic agents are used clinically to suppress the growth and spread of malignant cells. They should not be administered as primary therapy for malignancies that can be effectively cured with surgery or x-ray therapy alone. However, these agents are given as the primary form of treatment in patients with acute and chronic leukemia, choriocarcinoma, and multiple myeloma, or when a neoplasm cannot be definitely treated by x-ray or surgery (ie, when the malignancy has disseminated and evidence of disease progression is present). When used adjunctively in combination with surgery and irradiation, antineoplastic agents may suppress the growth of microscopic metastases and increase the survival time in patients with severe malignancies.

Drugs, alone or in combination with surgery or irradiation, have produced long-term, complete remissions and even cures in patients with choriocarcinoma, metastatic Wilms' tumor, Burkitt's lymphoma, Hodgkin's disease, and retinoblastoma. Antineoplastic agents can significantly increase the survival time or dramatically improve the condition of patients with acute lymphoblastic leukemia of childhood; to a lesser extent, these agents are effective in acute myeloblastic leukemia in adults, carcinoma of the colon and breast, malignant lymphomas, and multiple myeloma.

Because of their cytotoxic effects on normal hematopoiesis, on the immune system, and on the gastrointestinal tract and skin, considerable experience is required in order to use these agents properly and safely. If the physician has only occasional contact with cancer cases, the patient should be referred to an oncologist or cancer center, particularly for the less responsive tumors for which investigational, multiple-drug therapy is being given (eg, acute leukemia, Hodgkin's disease).

Each antineoplastic agent must be used in the schedule, route, and dosage that is most effective for the particular indication. The dose is based on the patient's height, weight, and body surface area, and must be regulated carefully to avoid prohibitive toxicity. The age, nutritional status, and condition of the patient (particularly renal and hepatic function) also must be considered. Prior chemotherapy, as well as possible interactions between these agents and other drugs being given concomitantly (eg, aspirin, allopurinol, phenobarbital, monoamine oxidase inhibitors) must also be recognized, for these drugs may affect the metabolism or excretion of the antineoplastic agent and possibly enhance its toxicity.

Patients vary in their tolerance to antineoplastic agents and should be evaluated frequently for clinical manifestations of drug toxicity. Hemoglobin, leukocyte, and platelet determinations should be made weekly or more frequently if large doses are being given. Urinalyses should be performed and blood urea nitrogen, uric acid, alkaline phosphatase, and serum glutamic oxaloacetic transaminase levels should be determined before, during, and at the conclusion of a drug trial. In addition, some objective parameter for evaluating results should be chosen and measurements recorded before and during the course of therapy.

The antineoplastic drugs have been classified broadly as alkylating agents, antimetabolites, plant alkaloids, antibiotics, hormones, or miscellaneous agents. The antineoplastic effects of alkylating agents and antimetabolites result from their ability to inhibit malignant cells to varying degrees during various parts of the cell cycle. Alkylating agents kill cells during all phases of the cell cycle and antimetabolic agents kill cells usually during the S phase of the cycle. After mitosis (M), there is a resting period called

G1; the cell is metabolically active during this stage (before the onset of deoxyribonucleic acid [DNA] synthesis). During the S period which follows, DNA is synthesized preparing for cell division. After this period there is a premitotic pause, G2, and then mitosis.

The *alkylating agents* are busulfan [Myleran], chlorambucil [Leukeran], cyclophosphamide [Cytoxan], mechlorethamine (nitrogen mustard) [Mustargen], melphalan [Alkeran], pipobroman [Vercyte], thiotepa, triethylenemelamine, and uracil mustard. Because of their high reactivity with and affinity for DNA in all phases of the cell cycle, the alkylating agents are most effective in malignancies of the reticuloendothelial system (eg, chronic leukemias, lymphomas, myelomas) and in carcinoma of the breast and ovary; they are less effective in carcinoma involving the lung, head, and neck. These agents have little effect on tumors of the gastrointestinal tract.

The *antimetabolites* interfere with the biosynthesis of purine or pyrimidine bases by inhibiting the production of normal precursors and depriving the cell of vital substrates necessary for DNA synthesis or by being incorporated into DNA as fraudulent precursors. These agents usually attack cells that are in the S period of the cell cycle. The purine antagonists are mercaptopurine [Purinethol] and thioguanine. Fluorouracil and its deoxyriboside derivative, floxuridine, are pyrimidine antagonists. Cytarabine [Cytosar], a relatively new agent, acts by inhibiting DNA polymerase.

The antimetabolites have been used to treat the entire spectrum of cancers. Acute leukemias may respond to mercaptopurine, thioguanine, methotrexate, and cytarabine, and chronic myelocytic leukemia may respond to mercaptopurine or thioguanine. Cytarabine appears to be more effective in acute myeloblastic leukemia of adults than in acute lymphoblastic leukemia of children. Fluorouracil is effective in carcinoma of the colon, breast, and ovary, but is less active in carcinoma of the stomach and pancreas. Floxuridine, administered intra-arterially, is used in certain types of malignancies (disseminated breast cancer, carcinoma of the rectum, colon, and liver) that do not respond to surgery or other forms of treatment. Methotrexate or mercaptopurine is curative in most women with choriocarcinoma. Methotrexate is occasionally useful in meningeal leukemia and in carcinoma of the breast, colon, ovary, cervix, testis, and head and neck.

The following *miscellaneous antineoplastic drugs* are synthetic organic agents; they include procarbazine [Matulane], hydroxyurea, mitotane [Lysodren], and the nitrosoureas (BCNU, CCNU, and methyl CCNU), which are under clinical investigation. Procarbazine is primarily indicated for generalized Hodgkin's disease. It is more effective in combination with mechlorethamine, vincristine, and prednisone (MOPP regimen) than as a single agent. Hydroxyurea is useful in chronic myelocytic leukemia, and may be palliative in ovarian carcinoma. Mitotane is indicated only for the treatment of inoperable adrenal cortex carcinoma.

Two plant alkaloids derived from *Vinca rosea*, vinblastine [Velban] and vincristine [Oncovin], act by arresting cells in metaphase. Hodgkin's disease, choriocarcinoma, testicular carcinoma, and, occasionally, breast tumors have responded to vinblastine; acute lymphoblastic leukemias, Wilms' tumor, giant follicular lymphoma, and choriocarcinoma have responded to vincristine.

Several antibiotics are used in antineoplastic therapy: dactinomycin [Cosmegen], an extract of *Streptomyces parvullus;* mithramycin [Mithracin], which is derived from *Streptomyces plicatus;* and daunorubicin, adriamycin, and mitomycin C. The latter three drugs are investigational. Dactinomycin acts by binding directly to DNA; it is highly effective in Wilms' tumor and may be useful in choriocarcinoma and in carcinoma of the testes. Mithramycin inhibits the synthesis of ribonucleic acid (RNA); its primary indication is in the treatment of disseminated testicular carcinoma, especially the embryonal cell type. In addition, mithramycin is useful in the treatment of hypercalcemia and hypercalciuria associated with advanced or metastatic cancer.

The enzyme asparaginase is under investigation and appears to be very effective in the acute leukemias of childhood.

The androgens, dromostanolone [Drolban], fluoxymesterone [Halotestin], testosterone [Neo-Hombreol (F), Oreton], and testolactone [Teslac], a modified testosterone derivative, have been used for palliative therapy in inoperable carcinoma of the breast. Adrenal corticosteroids are used alone or with vincristine to induce remissions in acute leukemias; of these, prednisone [Delta-Dome, Deltasone, Deltra, Meticorten, Paracort] is used most commonly because it is less costly, but prednisolone [Delta-Cortef, Meticortelone,

Sterane, Predne-Dome], cortisone [Cortone], and hydrocortisone [Cortef, Hydrocortone] also are effective. The progestagens, hydroxyprogesterone [Delalutin], medroxyprogesterone [Provera], and megestrol acetate [Megace], are useful as palliative therapy in endometrial carcinoma, and occasionally are effective in renal carcinoma.

The estrogens diethylstilbestrol and ethinyl estradiol are very useful for palliative therapy in carcinoma of the breast.

Special methods of administration of antineoplastic agents include the intracavitary administration of mechlorethamine, thiotepa, fluorouracil, quinacrine, and colloidal radioactive isotopes. Such use appears to be effective in controlling pleural, pericardial, and peritoneal effusions resulting from metastases in 50% of patients receiving mechlorethamine, thiotepa or isotopes, in 85% receiving quinacrine, and in less than 20% receiving fluorouracil.

Regional chemotherapy may be used under certain conditions to produce relatively greater local concentrations of antineoplastic drugs. In one method, low concentrations are infused by continuous intra-arterial injection over prolonged periods (eg, floxuridine); the use of portable infusion pumps to administer the drug by this method is being investigated in ambulatory patients. In extracorporeal perfusion, the area is temporarily isolated from systemic circulation and high local concentrations of the drug are maintained for periods of 30 minutes to one hour. The alkylating agents (eg, thiotepa, melphalan, mechlorethamine) have been used in this manner for the treatment of tumors of the extremities in an attempt to eliminate or reduce serious systemic toxic effects. Although methotrexate and fluorouracil have produced some dramatic results in regional chemotherapy of the head and neck, liver, and pelvis, the benefits generally have been variable.

It is important to realize that the cooperation and skills of the radiotherapist, oncologist, surgeon, and pathologist are necessary in the management of patients with neoplastic diseases. Guidelines for the use of chemotherapeutic agents in specific situations appear in the individual evaluations. The dosages given in these evaluations generally apply only when the drug is administered as a single agent. Combined drug therapy is becoming increasingly important in the management of these patients, and the dosages of the individual agents used in such therapy must be determined individually.

Adverse Reactions and Precautions

All chemotherapeutic agents are capable of producing irreversible toxic effects and death. Therefore, they must be used with caution and, whenever possible, by or under the supervision of a physician trained and experienced in their use.

Suppression of bone marrow activity and gastrointestinal tract and cutaneous reactions have been reported with all types of chemotherapeutic agents except the plant alkaloids, vinblastine and vincristine. Hepatotoxic reactions occur principally with the antimetabolites and occasionally with the alkylating agents. Neurotoxicity is primarily associated with vincristine [Oncovin].

Suppression of hematopoiesis may be manifested by leukopenia, thrombocytopenia, or anemia. Severe leukopenia (white blood cell count less than $2{,}000/mm^3$) or thrombocytopenia (platelet count less than $100{,}000/mm^3$) are indications for immediate cessation of therapy in patients with previously normal hematopoietic systems. In patients with chronic leukemias, the rate of reduction is a much more important indication of the patient's hematopoietic status; the drug should be stopped if the rate of decrease of the leukocyte or platelet count is greater than 50% weekly for two successive weeks. Thrombocytopenia often progresses even though therapy has been stopped; this occurs most commonly with mercaptopurine [Purinethol] and the alkylating agents. If the thrombocytopenia is reversible, evidence of recovery usually is seen within one to two weeks after discontinuing therapy, although it may persist longer in patients in whom bone marrow function was previously depressed. Hemolytic anemia, which occurs in some patients receiving alkylating agents, usually can be corrected by the concomitant administration of prednisone. Megaloblastic marrow changes may be noted with use of any chemotherapeutic drug but do not require discontinuation of therapy or transfusions.

Gastrointestinal disturbances range from mild anorexia or nausea to severe vomiting, hemorrhagic diarrhea, and death. The severe reactions usually are accompanied by aphthous stomatitis. If stomatitis does develop, the drug should be stopped to avoid irreversible damage. These lesions of the oral mucous membranes occur most commonly with methotrexate, fluorouracil, and dactinomycin [Cosmegen].

Cutaneous reactions range from erythema, urticaria, and maculopapular eruptions to exfoliative dermatitis and Stevens-Johnson syndrome; the severe reactions usually require discontinuation of therapy. Alopecia often occurs with administration of cyclophosphamide, vincristine, vinblastine, methotrexate, dactinomycin, and fluorouracil. Regrowth of hair usually takes place when therapy is discontinued. Dactinomycin and, to a lesser extent, cyclophosphamide potentiate the cutaneous reactions produced by radiation therapy, and their concurrent use can produce severe dermatitis.

Any of these agents may indirectly cause hyperuricemic nephropathy and acute renal failure when used to treat patients with leukemia or lymphoma. This is due to breakdown of nucleoproteins and the resultant hyperuricemia that occurs with the excretion of large amounts of uric acid. Symptomatic measures such as hydration, alkalization of urine, and administration of allopurinol [Zyloprim] reduce or prevent hyperuricemia in these patients (see Chapter 25, Agents Used in Gout).

Many antineoplastic drugs have been shown to have some teratogenic properties in experimental animals, but such observations are of relatively little value in predicting the occurrence of adverse effects on the human fetus. Although available information suggests that the administration of these agents during pregnancy may not be as hazardous as had been assumed, their use during the first trimester should be avoided if possible. Methotrexate in particular has been reported to cause abortions. Also, possible indirect effects on the fetus as a result of other toxic actions (eg, hematopoietic, hepatic, renal) should be borne in mind.

Alkylating Agents: The alkylating agents may cause irreversible hematopoietic depression, particularly when given after other antineoplastic drugs or a course of radiation therapy to significant marrow-bearing areas. Blood cell counts should be made weekly during the initial course of therapy. After a maintenance dose is established, blood cell counts should be made at intervals of two or three weeks. Leukopenia and thrombocytopenia are the most common hematopoietic effects that occur after the intra-arterial infusion of thiotepa, melphalan [Alkeran], uracil mustard, and cyclophosphamide. Cyclophosphamide tends to produce less thrombocytopenia than other alkylating agents.

The incidence of gastrointestinal reactions (nausea, vomiting, anorexia, diarrhea) and headache is greater with mechlorethamine than with the other alkylating agents, and extravasation into subcutaneous tissue may cause necrosis and slough at the site of injection. The development of aphthous stomatitis is much less common during therapy with the alkylating agents than with the antimetabolites.

Antimetabolic Agents: In addition to hematopoietic depression and gastrointestinal disturbances (anorexia, vomiting, diarrhea), the antimetabolites may cause aphthous stomatitis; this occurs most frequently in patients treated with methotrexate, fluorouracil, and floxuridine, and occasionally with large doses of mercaptopurine. Stomatitis, diarrhea, thrombocytopenia, leukopenia, or any sudden drop in the white blood cell count is an indication for discontinuing the drug or reducing the dose to avoid the possibility of producing ulceration of the lower gastrointestinal tract, infection, hemorrhage, and death.

Reversible alopecia is noted commonly with fluorouracil and methotrexate, and cutaneous hyperpigmentation may occur with all antimetabolites.

The antimetabolic agents are contraindicated in patients with poor nutritional status, severe leukopenia, or thrombocytopenia. These conditions are likely to be present in patients who recently have had major surgery, radiation therapy, or treatment with other cytotoxic agents. In patients with renal or hepatic impairment, the dose must be adjusted on the basis of the patient's response and the status of renal and hepatic function.

For adverse reactions and precautions for the miscellaneous antineoplastic agents, see the individual evaluations.

ALKYLATING AGENTS

BUSULFAN [Myleran]

$$CH_3SO_2O\text{-}CH_2(CH_2)_2CH_2\text{-}OSO_2CH_3$$

Busulfan is the drug of choice in chronic myelocytic leukemia but is ineffective in the blastic crises. It is also useful in polycythemia vera.

Depression of bone marrow function is the most common adverse effect, and blood cell counts should be performed frequently. Hyperpigmentation may develop during prolonged therapy with busulfan and may be part of an Addisonian-like syndrome. This may consist of asthenia, hypotension, nausea, vomiting, and weight loss, as well as the hyperpigmentation; adrenocortical function is not depressed in all patients. Long-term delayed effects such as cataract formation, bone marrow and interstitial pulmonary fibrosis, aspermia, or ovarian fibrosis can occur. Amenorrhea, testicular atrophy, gynecomastia, anorexia, fatigue, and weight loss also may develop after prolonged use. Serum uric acid levels should be monitored frequently; hyperuricemia, which may result in hyperuricemic nephropathy and acute renal failure, can be treated by hydration, alkalization of the urine, and administration of allopurinol.

See also the Introductory Statement.

USUAL DOSAGE.—*Oral:* 4 to 8 mg (0.06 to 0.1 mg/kg of body weight) daily until leukocyte count decreases by one-half. After determining the nadir of the fall, and rate, maintenance doses of 2 to 4 mg daily are given. If there is a precipitous decrease in leukocyte count, therapy should be discontinued until the leukocyte count begins to increase. Severe leukopenia must be avoided, since this may lead to irreversible bone marrow depression.

PREPARATIONS.—Myleran (Burroughs Wellcome). *Oral:* Tablets 2 mg.

CHLORAMBUCIL [Leukeran]

$(ClCH_2CH_2)_2N-C_6H_4-CH_2CH_2CH_2COOH$

Chlorambucil is useful for the palliative treatment of chronic lymphocytic leukemia, disseminated Hodgkin's disease (Stages III and IV), and lymphosarcoma. Some responses also have been noted in carcinoma of the lung, ovary, and breast; mycosis fungoides; Waldenstrom's macroglobulinemia; and, in combination with methotrexate and dactinomycin, in carcinoma of the testis.

Moderate bone marrow depression can occur after prolonged use and is characterized by leukopenia, thrombocytopenia, and anemia. This myelosuppression is dose dependent and usually reversible. To avoid irreversible damage, hemoglobin determinations, total and differential leukocyte counts, and platelet counts should be made weekly. Chlorambucil is usually withheld for about four weeks after a course of radiation therapy or another drug that depresses bone marrow function. When the white blood cell count falls suddenly or is reduced to 50% of the pretreatment level, the dosage must be reduced or the drug discontinued until leukocyte and platelet counts stabilize or return to a satisfactory level.

Serum uric acid levels should be monitored frequently to avoid possible hyperuricemia and the resultant acute renal failure.

See also the Introductory Statement.

USUAL DOSAGE.—*Oral: Adults,* initially, 0.1 to 0.2 mg/kg of body weight daily for three to six weeks, depending upon the patient's response and the degree of bone marrow depression. Patients with Hodgkin's disease may need 0.2 mg/kg daily, whereas those with other lymphomas or chronic lymphocytic leukemia may require only 0.1 mg/kg daily. When maintenance therapy is necessary, the daily dose should not exceed 0.1 mg/kg, and as little as 0.03 mg/kg may be the largest amount tolerated. The drug should be taken one hour before breakfast or two hours after the evening meal.

PREPARATIONS.—Leukeran (Burroughs Wellcome). *Oral:* Tablets 2 mg.

CYCLOPHOSPHAMIDE [Cytoxan]

$(Cl-CH_2-CH_2)_2N-P(=O)(-NH-CH_2-CH_2-CH_2-O-) \cdot H_2O$

Cyclophosphamide is one of the most versatile and dependable alkylating agents. It is effective in disseminated Hodgkin's disease (Stages III and IV), lymphosarcomas, and reticulum cell sarcomas, particularly when used in combination with a corticosteroid and vincristine. Cyclophosphamide has been used with other drugs in the treatment of acute lymphoblastic leukemia in children. It is one of the primary drugs used for childhood neuroblastoma. When given with dactinomycin and vincristine, it is effective in rhabdomyosarcoma and Ewing's sarcoma. Cyclophosphamide may have a palliative effect in carcinoma of the breast, ovary, and lung and produces remissions in multiple myeloma comparable to those observed with melphalan.

Cyclophosphamide is less destructive to megakaryocytes and platelets than most comparable drugs. It may be given orally or parenterally.

Alopecia, the most frequent untoward reaction, occurs in 50% of patients who receive maximal prolonged therapy. It may begin approximately three weeks after initiation of therapy and hair loss may be total. However, this reaction is reversible on discontinuing therapy. Leukopenia is an expected toxic effect and is used as a guide to therapy. The leukopenia that occurs after large single doses reaches its lowest level in about 10 to 12 days and recovery occurs after 17 to 21 days. Thrombocytopenia usually is less prominent with cyclophosphamide than with other alkylating agents and may occur in the presence of bone marrow depression. A sterile hemorrhagic cystitis has been noted in 20% of children and 10% of adults who receive long-term therapy. The drug also produces anorexia with occasional nausea and vomiting and, rarely, amenorrhea, aphthous stomatitis, cutaneous hyperpigmentation, enterocolitis, jaundice, and hypoprothrombinemia. Cystitis can usually be prevented by liberal fluid intake for four hours following drug administration and frequent emptying of the bladder, especially at bedtime. The urine should be examined for microscopic hematuria.

White blood cell and platelet counts should be made at least weekly until a maintenance dose is determined. The drug must be given cautiously when leukopenia or thrombocytopenia is present. Initial dosage should be reduced by one-third or one-half in patients who have recently received x-ray therapy of large areas, especially of the pelvis. Lower doses also are given to patients with severe hepatic or renal disease. Use of this drug should be avoided, if possible, during the first trimester of pregnancy as it is potentially teratogenic.

See also the Introductory Statement.

USUAL DOSAGE.—Therapy may consist of a short series of injections or prolonged administration.

Oral, Intravenous: Adults, for patients who have not received prior therapy, the maximal initial loading dose should not exceed 35 to 40 mg/kg of body weight given as a single dose over a period of several days; the total loading dose should not exceed 20 to 30 mg/kg in patients who have had prior radiation or chemotherapy.

For *oral* maintenance therapy, 1.5 to 2 mg/kg of body weight daily; dose is adjusted to maintain a balance between toxicity and therapeutic effect. Maintenance dosage may be started as soon as the leukocyte count returns to 3,000 to 5,000/mm^3 and is maintained between 2,500 and 4,000/mm^3. Oral doses preferably are taken on an empty stomach; however, if gastrointestinal upset occurs, the doses may be divided and given with meals. *Children* tolerate larger amounts per kilogram of body weight than adults.

For *intravenous* maintenance therapy, 10 to 15 mg/kg of body weight every seven to ten days. Alternatively, single doses of 30 mg/kg may be given at three- to four-week intervals or when bone marrow recovery is evident.

PREPARATIONS.—Cytoxan (Mead Johnson).

Oral: Tablets 25 and 50 mg.

Injection: Powder 100, 200, and 500 mg.

MECHLORETHAMINE HYDROCHLORIDE

(Nitrogen Mustard) [Mustargen Hydrochloride]

$$CH_3-N(CH_2CH_2Cl)_2 \cdot HCl$$

As a component of the MOPP regimen, mechlorethamine has been effective in advanced stages of Hodgkin's disease (see also the evaluation on Procarbazine Hydrochloride). When given alone, mechlorethamine has produced temporary responses in about 50% of patients with disseminated Hodgkin's disease (Stages III and IV) and lymphomas. Mechlorethamine has produced objective signs of response in up to 50% of patients with mycosis fungoides, and temporary responses in about 10% of patients with pulmonary carcinoma. In the presence of recurring malignant effusions in the pleural, peritoneal, or pericardial spaces, mechlorethamine will decrease the rate of fluid accumulation in about one-half of the patients.

This agent produces nausea and vomiting one-half to three hours after administration; varying degrees of depression of bone marrow function (eg, leukopenia, thrombocytopenia, slight anemia) occur during the first two or three weeks of therapy. When total dosage in a single course of therapy exceeds 0.4 mg/kg of body weight, severe, possibly fatal, leukopenia, anemia, thrombocytopenia, and hemorrhagic diathesis may develop.

Delayed menstruation or amenorrhea may occur after treatment. Hyperuricemia may develop in patients with large tumor masses who are sensitive to the drug; thus, urate precipitation should be minimized by maintaining an adequate fluid intake. Local toxic reactions consist of thrombosis and thrombophlebitis in veins used for infusion. Extravasation into subcutaneous tissues results in painful inflammation and necrosis: prompt infiltration of the area with 1% lidocaine, together with application of an ice compress for 6 to 12 hours, may minimize local reactions. Other untoward effects are alopecia, a metallic taste following injection, asthenia, drowsiness, headache, fever, tinnitus, and deafness. Because mechlorethamine has caused fetal abnormalities in experimental animals, its use should be avoided during the first trimester of pregnancy.

See also the Introductory Statement.

USUAL DOSAGE.—

Intravenous: Adults, 0.4 mg/kg of body weight given as a single dose or on two separate days. Total dosage in patients who have had prior radiation or chemotherapy is 0.2 to 0.3 mg/kg. Solutions, prepared by adding 10 ml of sterile water to 10 mg of drug, are injected into tubing containing sodium chloride injection or 5% dextrose injection. Solutions are highly unstable and should be used immediately; the unused amount should be discarded.

Intracavitary: 0.4 mg/kg of body weight (10 to 20 mg) has been instilled into the intrapleural, intraperitoneal, and intrapericardial space after nearly all accumulated fluid has been removed. The solution is prepared in the same concentration used for the intravenous route. To assure uniform distribution of the drug in the cavity, the patient should be turned every 60 seconds for five minutes to the following positions: prone, supine, right side, left side, and knee chest. Lack of effect is due to failure to move the patient often enough or failure to remove the fluid initially. The remaining fluid may be removed from the pleural or peritoneal cavity by paracentesis 24 to 36 hours later.

PREPARATIONS.—Mustargen Hydrochloride (Merck Sharp & Dohme). *Injection:* Powder 10 mg.

MELPHALAN [Alkeran]

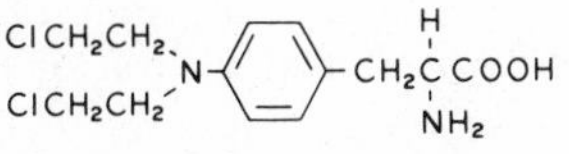

$(ClCH_2CH_2)_2N{-}C_6H_4{-}CH_2CH(NH_2)COOH$

Comparative studies have shown that melphalan is as effective as cyclophosphamide in the treatment of multiple myeloma. One-third to one-half of all patients with multiple myeloma show objective signs of improvement over periods of six months to several years. The objective criteria used as evidence of improvement include decreases in the amount of abnormal proteins in urine or serum, decreases in the number of myeloma cells in bone marrow, increase in hemoglobin level, reduction of hypercalcemia, and, in some patients, reduction of azotemia. Approximately 70% to 80% of patients show subjective signs of remission (relief of pain and increased mobility).

The effectiveness of melphalan in the treatment of other malignant diseases has not been determined; trials have not been comparative and are not yet extensive enough to demonstrate any advantage of this drug over other antineoplastic agents. The results of earlier studies suggest that seminoma, Ewing's sarcoma, chronic lymphocytic leukemia, ovarian carcinoma, and reticulum cell sarcoma are favorably affected by melphalan, whereas mixed tumors of the testes, hemangioendothelioma, and primary carcinoma of the bile duct are less responsive. Melphalan occasionally has produced responses in melanocarcinoma and osteosarcoma in adults and in Burkitt's lymphoma of the jaw in children. Melphalan has been ineffective in acute leukemias; its usefulness in Hodgkin's disease remains to be determined.

Melphalan produces a dose-related depression of bone marrow function resulting in anemia, neutropenia, and thrombocytopenia; mild nausea and vomiting may occur after large doses are administered. Hyperemia and hemorrhage of the gastrointestinal tract have occasionally been associated with aphthous stomatitis. Because it is metabolized slowly, melphalan may accumulate; thus, regular blood cell counts are required to avoid severe bone marrow depression. Melphalan can depress early and late forms of myeloid precursors so that recovery is prolonged. If the leukocyte count falls below $3,000/mm^3$ or the platelet count falls below $100,000/mm^3$, the drug must be discontinued until the counts have improved. The drug should be used with caution in the presence of leukopenia or thrombocytopenia, and the dosage reduced if these reactions appear. If thrombocytopenia is severe, cyclophosphamide may be useful as an alternate drug, since it causes less platelet depression.

Melphalan must be given cautiously to patients receiving radiation or other chemotherapeutic agents that depress bone marrow function, for these treatments may seriously increase a patient's susceptibility to the toxic effects of melphalan. This agent is contraindicated in the presence of severe anemia, leukopenia, or thrombocytopenia, and during the first trimester of pregnancy.

Patients with significant impairment of renal function also may be particularly susceptible to the drug's adverse effects. In these patients, the dosage should be reduced or therapy withheld until renal function has improved.

See also the Introductory Statement.

USUAL DOSAGE.—*Oral:* The following dosages are given to *adults* for treatment of multiple myeloma.

Daily Administration: A loading dose of 0.15 mg/kg is given daily for seven days; this should be followed by a drug-free period of at least two weeks, during which time the leukocyte count will fall. Maintenance therapy can be started after the nadir of the fall has been reached; this may require up to four weeks. The blood cell counts should be monitored during this period, and when the white blood cell and platelet counts begin rising, a maintenance dose of 2 to 4 mg daily may be given.

Intermittent Administration: Advocates of this regimen believe that the use of large doses over short periods produces greater inhibition of tumor cells without permanently damaging normal marrow function; after a dose that causes moderate hematologic toxicity, normal marrow elements recover more rapidly than do tumor cells, which may be more sensitive to the drug. A total of 0.25 mg/kg is given daily for four days every six weeks. The dosage is adjusted to produce mild leukopenia (white blood cell count below 3,500/mm^3) and thrombocytopenia (platelet count less than 100,000/mm^3).

PREPARATIONS.—Alkeran (Burroughs Wellcome). *Oral:* Tablets 2 mg.

PIPOBROMAN [Vercyte]

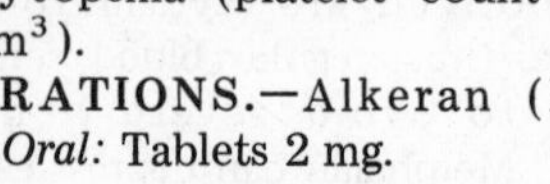

$$BrCH_2CH_2\overset{O}{\overset{\|}{C}}N\langle\;\rangle N\overset{O}{\overset{\|}{C}}CH_2CH_2Br$$

Pipobroman is used in the treatment of polycythemia vera and chronic myelocytic leukemia. Clinical data are limited because of the effectiveness of conventional therapy for polycythemia vera (phlebotomy, sodium phosphate P 32) and chronic myelocytic leukemia (busulfan). Therefore, pipobroman is usually used in patients who do not respond to established therapy.

Adverse gastrointestinal reactions (transient nausea, vomiting, abdominal cramps, and diarrhea) have been reported infrequently. Rash has been observed in a few patients. Anemia sometimes occurs in patients with polycythemia vera and appears to be dose related. Hemoglobin values have been shown to drop 2 g/100 ml with doses as low as 30 mg/kg of body weight.

Patients in whom bone marrow function is still depressed from previous irradiation or other cytotoxic chemotherapy should not receive pipobroman. Clinical experience with this drug is insufficient to recommend its use in children under 15 years of age. Pipobroman also should not be administered during pregnancy, since there is no information on its potential teratogenicity.

See also the Introductory Statement.

USUAL DOSAGE.—*Oral: Adults*, for polycythemia vera, initially, 1 mg/kg of body weight daily. Daily doses of 1.5 to 3 mg/kg may be necessary, but these amounts should not be used until a daily dose of 1 mg/kg has been given for a minimum of 30 days without improvement. Maintenance doses of 0.1 to 0.2 mg/kg daily usually are begun when the hematocrit level has been reduced to 50%.

For chronic myelocytic leukemia, initially, 1.5 to 2.5 mg/kg daily until maximal clinical or hematologic response is obtained. The leukocyte count is used to regulate dosage; if it falls too rapidly, the drug should be discontinued temporarily. Maintenance therapy is started when the leukocyte count approaches 10,000/mm^3; the dose ranges from 25 to 175 mg daily.

PREPARATIONS.—Vercyte (Abbott). *Oral:* Tablets 10 and 25 mg.

THIOTEPA

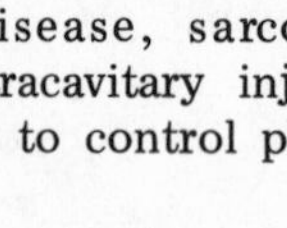

$$(H_2C\text{–}CH_2)N\text{–}\underset{S}{\overset{N(CH_2\text{–}CH_2)}{P}}\text{–}N(CH_2\text{–}CH_2)$$

This is a dangerous drug with unpredictable myelotoxicity. It is effective in the palliative management of carcinoma of the breast and ovary. It has limited usefulness in lymphomas, Hodgkin's disease, sarcomas, and mycosis fungoides. Intracavitary injection of thiotepa may be useful to control pleural or peritoneal effusions.

Thiotepa may produce nausea, anorexia, and headache. It has a toxic effect on the hematopoietic system that is dose related. Initial effects on the bone marrow may not become evident for 5 to 30 days (median, 15 days). As with other alkylating agents, the white blood cell and platelet counts are reliable guides. All of these elements should be checked weekly during maintenance therapy and for at least four weeks after therapy is terminated.

Patients with impaired renal function may not tolerate this drug. Thiotepa is contraindicated during the first trimester of pregnancy. Concomitant radiation therapy should be carried out cautiously, for the depressant effect on the bone marrow will be additive.

See also the Introductory Statement.

USUAL DOSAGE.—Dosage must always be carefully individualized. To avoid too frequent administration, the physician should bear in mind that clinical response to thiotepa is slow and that the drug has a cumulative toxic effect on the bone marrow.

Intrapericardial, Intraperitoneal, Intrapleural: Adults and children over 12 years of age, 0.8 mg/kg of body weight weekly, depending upon the patient's nutritional status. If the leukocyte count is below 3,000/mm^3, therapy should be postponed. For malignant ascites, thiotepa may be given in the abdominal cavity in doses of 10 to 15 mg once a week as long as leukocyte and platelet counts remain adequate.

Intravenous: Adults and children over 12 years of age, 0.8 mg/kg of body weight at two-week intervals.

PREPARATIONS.—Thiotepa (Lederle). *Injection:* Powder 15 mg.

TRIETHYLENEMELAMINE

Triethylenemelamine is used only in the treatment of retinoblastoma. It has also been tried in chronic lymphocytic leukemia, lymphosarcoma, Hodgkin's disease, mycosis fungoides, and polycythemia vera. However, because of its erratic absorption and variable toxicity, triethylenemelamine should not be used in the treatment of these neoplasms.

This agent may produce nausea, vomiting, diarrhea, bone marrow depression, headache, asthenia, and amenorrhea or oligospermia. Hepatic damage has been reported with prolonged use of large doses. The drug should be administered cautiously, and no attempt should be made to achieve a rapid decrease in white blood cell count. Delayed toxic effects (ie, hematuria, albuminuria, azotemia) can occur.

See also the Introductory Statement.

USUAL DOSAGE.—*Oral:* Initially, 2.5 mg. If no adverse effects develop within one week, 2.5 to 5 mg is given twice weekly for four weeks. Complete hemograms must be obtained weekly. Subsequent therapy depends upon the patient's response and tolerance to the drug and results of blood cell counts. A safer schedule is to determine weekly dosage on the basis of body weight (0.05 to 0.1 mg/kg of body weight weekly). Total weekly dosage then is equally divided over the entire week. This schedule may be maintained until therapeutic response or minimal toxic effects occur. Triethylenemelamine should be taken on an empty stomach at least 60 minutes before breakfast with water and at least 2 g of sodium bicarbonate.

PREPARATIONS.—Triethylenemelamine (Lederle). *Oral:* Tablets 5 mg.

URACIL MUSTARD

CH_2CH_2Cl CH_2CH_2Cl

The spectrum of effectiveness of uracil mustard is similar to that of the older alkylating agents: it may be used in the palliative treatment of chronic lymphocytic leukemias and malignant lymphomas including lymphosarcoma, giant follicular lymphoma, and Hodgkin's disease. Uracil mustard also is effective in chronic myelocytic leukemia. Improvement also has been reported in occasional cases of polycythemia vera, mycosis fungoides, and ovarian carcinoma. Some clinicians have noted that uracil mustard is useful in the control of thrombocytosis. Data comparing the effectiveness of uracil mustard and the older agents such as mechlorethamine, cyclophosphamide, and chlorambucil are incomplete, but uracil mustard appears to offer no advantage over these drugs.

Gastrointestinal effects (nausea, vomiting, diarrhea) are the most common untoward reactions. Skin reactions include pruritus, dermatitis, hyperpigmentation, and alopecia, but the incidence of alopecia is less than with cyclophosphamide. Nervousness, irritability, and depression have been reported occasionally. Amenorrhea or oligospermia may occur. Serum uric acid levels should be measured regularly to avoid possible hyperuricemic nephropathy and acute renal failure.

The hematopoietic effects of uracil mustard are cumulative and, as the total dosage approaches 1 mg/kg of body weight, irreversible bone marrow damage may occur. Complete blood cell counts should be made once weekly during the first month of therapy, although maximal bone marrow depression may not occur until two to four weeks after the drug has been discontinued. A critical toxic effect on the bone marrow is indicated by a leukocyte count below $1{,}500/mm^3$ or a platelet count below $50{,}000/mm^3$. Extreme caution is indicated when there is a decrease in the red blood cell count or hemoglobin level of 30% or more below pretreatment level. The drug should be withdrawn immediately if there is a sharp fall in the count of any of the formed elements. Ambulatory patients should not receive more than a one-week supply of the drug at any visit.

Uracil mustard should not be administered for several weeks after completing a course of treatment with another cytotoxic drug or radiation, since it is essential to allow bone marrow function to return to satisfactory levels. Uracil mustard is contraindicated in the presence of pronounced leukopenia, thrombocytopenia, or aplastic anemia. It should not be used during the first trimester of pregnancy to avoid possible abortion and potential damaging effects on the fetus.

USUAL DOSAGE.—*Oral: Adults*, the following are two suggested therapeutic regimens. These recommendations apply to patients who have not recently received suppressive chemotherapeutic agents or extensive irradiation, both of which may markedly reduce tolerance to this drug.

Schedule A: Initially, 1 to 2 mg daily until clinical improvement or bone marrow depression occurs. The drug is then discontinued until the clinical condition deteriorates or the blood cell counts return to satisfactory levels; thereafter, 1 mg may be given daily for three weeks out of each four-week period. Patients may be continued on this regimen for several months or until a relapse occurs.

Schedule B: Initially, 3 to 5 mg daily for seven days; total dosage during this period should not exceed 0.5 mg/kg of body weight. The dose is then decreased to 1 mg daily for three weeks out of each four-week period.

Indications for interrupting or continuing therapy are the same with both schedules, and in each case the dose is adjusted on the basis of the severity of bone marrow depression.

PREPARATIONS.—Uracil Mustard (Upjohn). *Oral:* Capsules 1 mg.

ANTIMETABOLITES

CYTARABINE [Cytosar]

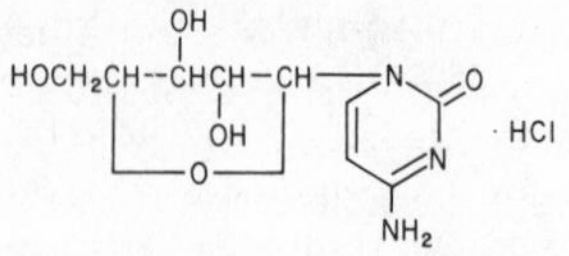

This synthetic nucleoside is effective principally in the treatment of acute myeloblastic leukemia, particularly in adults. In clinical studies using different dosage schedules, complete remission of acute myeloblastic leukemia occurred in 16% to 44% (overall average of 20%) of adults. These results are better than those obtained with other available agents. After induced remission following an initial course of therapy, relapse occurs in approximately three months. With maintenance therapy, remissions last five to eight months in most patients. Limited data indicate that cytarabine can produce remissions in some patients who have become refractory to mercaptopurine, methotrexate, or prednisone; this indicates a lack of cross resistance between cytarabine and these agents.

A combination of cytarabine and thioguanine currently is the treatment of choice for acute myeloblastic leukemia in adults.

Children with acute lymphoblastic leukemias respond better to the older antineoplastic agents. Complete remissions have occurred in 5% and partial remissions in 30% of children given this drug. More clinical testing is necessary to determine the usefulness of cytarabine in children.

Because of its brief plasma half-life (three to four hours), the toxicity of cytarabine depends upon the rate and duration of administration rather than total dose. The drug has been administered in a single large dose, in frequent small doses, and by continuous infusion. Evidence that the varied dosage schedules have any effect on usefulness, however, is not conclusive.

The primary adverse effect is bone marrow depression characterized by leukopenia, thrombocytopenia, and, less frequently, anemia and megaloblastosis. Hematologic depression is more pronounced with continuous infusion than with single large injections. Nausea, vomiting, and diarrhea occur, particularly after rapid intravenous injection. Stomatitis also may develop.

Hepatic dysfunction, manifested by transient

elevated serum transaminase levels, may be noted. Patients should be hospitalized during the initial course of therapy and the drug should be given under the supervision of a physician experienced in the use of antineoplastic agents. Optimal use of the drug is possible only when platelet transfusions are readily available. Because of the variable response, leukocyte and platelet counts should be determined daily during the initial course and at regular intervals during the period of remission. If the platelet count is reduced to less than 50,000/mm^3 or the neutrophils to less than 1,000/mm^3, the dose should be reduced or the drug discontinued. When the bone marrow has recovered, administration is resumed. Liver and kidney function also should be determined regularly during therapy. The use of cytarabine should be avoided during pregnancy because of potential teratogenic effects on the fetus.

USUAL DOSAGE.—Although larger total doses are tolerated by rapid intravenous injection than by slow infusion, the optimal dosage schedule is still to be determined. The preferred regimen depends upon the response of the individual; dosage must be individualized to produce remission with minimal toxicity. The following dosages can be used for both *adults* and *children.*

Intravenous Injection (rapid): 2 mg/kg of body weight is administered daily for ten days. If an antileukemic effect or hematologic depression is not apparent at the end of this period, the dose is increased to 4 mg/kg daily and continued until a remission or hematologic toxicity is noted.

Intravenous Infusion: 0.5 to 1 mg/kg of body weight daily is infused for any desired period (1, 4, 12, or 24 hours); one hour is sufficient for most patients. This dose is administered for ten days. If no toxic or therapeutic response occurs, the dose is increased to 2 mg/kg daily and continued until a remission or hematologic toxicity is noted.

Subcutaneous, Intramuscular: For maintenance of remissions, 1 mg/kg of body weight weekly.

Combined Therapy: To *induce remissions* in acute myeloblastic leukemia, thioguanine is given orally in a dose of 2.5 mg/kg of body weight twice daily and cytarabine is given by intravenous drip in a dose of 2.5 mg/kg (or 100 mg/M^2) twice daily. For maintenance, up to 2.5 mg/kg of thioguanine is given if there is no gastrointestinal or myelosuppressive toxicity, the neutrophil count remains above 1,500/mm^3, and the platelet count is greater than 100,000. In addition, cytarabine is given subcutaneously once weekly in a dose of 0.8 mg/kg (or 30 mg/M^2).

PREPARATIONS.—Cytosar (Upjohn). *Injection:* Powder 100 and 500 mg with 5 and 10 ml sterile water for injection, respectively, and benzyl alcohol 0.9% sufficient to give solutions containing 20 and 50 mg/ml, respectively.

FLUOROURACIL (5 FU)

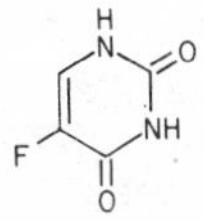

At present, fluorouracil and its deoxyriboside derivative, floxuridine (FUDR), are the only drugs that are effective in the treatment of gastrointestinal cancer. Fluorouracil is less effective in the treatment of carcinomas of the ovary, cervix, urinary bladder, and liver. Objective evidence of a palliative effect has been noted in 40% of patients with carcinomas of the breast (after surgery or hormonal treatment), in 10% to 15% with carcinoma of the rectum, and in 20% with carcinoma of the colon.

The variations in the reported incidence of remissions is primarily due to differences in dosage, selection and condition of patients, and in the criteria used to evaluate objective signs of response. The average duration of remissions induced by repeated courses of therapy at monthly intervals is five to six months, but responses lasting one to four years have been reported.

The use of slow intravenous infusions lasting two to eight hours markedly decreases the toxicity accompanying the administration of fluorouracil. However, results of clinical studies have indicated that rapid injections may be more effective than slow infusions. It has been reported that the weekly administration of fluorouracil without an initial loading dose has produced a comparable response with significantly less toxicity, and this regimen is now being used by most oncologists. There also is some evidence that fluorouracil administered orally once weekly produces antineoplastic effects and is well tolerated.

Leukopenia is the primary adverse effect; it can occur after the first dose but, if so, is usually mild. Recovery occurs when the dose is lowered and only rarely do the injections have to be suspended. Thrombocytopenia is much less prominent. Aphthous stomatitis may develop and is an indication for temporary cessation of therapy. Nausea, vomiting, and diarrhea can occur, as well as a feeling of weakness and lassitude lasting 12 to 36 hours after the injection. Rashes are infrequent with the weekly dose, but may require discontinuation of therapy. Addisonian-like hyperpigmentation is seen in most patients. Alopecia and cerebellar ataxia may develop and are reversible either during therapy or when the drug is discontinued.

USUAL DOSAGE.—*Intravenous: Adults*, the original regimen consisted of a loading dose of 12 mg/kg of body weight once daily for four successive days, and 6 mg/kg every other day until the 12th day. However, all untoward effects are markedly increased and can be very dangerous when this regimen is used. Therefore, oncologists now prefer weekly doses of 15 mg/kg. Treatment is continued as long as there is evidence of clinical improvement. The dosage of each successive course should be regulated on the basis of the patient's previous tolerance to the drug.

PREPARATIONS.—Fluorouracil (Roche). *Injection:* Solution 50 mg/ml in 10 ml containers.

FLOXURIDINE (FUDR)

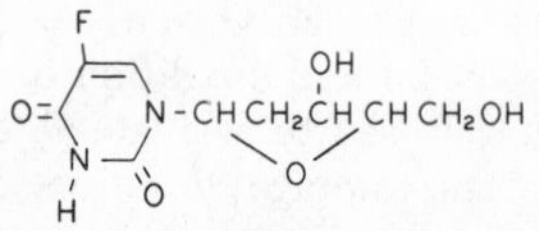

Floxuridine is the deoxyriboside derivative of fluorouracil. Intra-arterial administration of this drug produces a palliative effect in certain malignancies that do not respond to surgery or other forms of treatment. These include disseminated breast cancer, carcinoma of the rectum and colon, and hepatic carcinoma that has metastasized from other primary tumors.

The usefulness of this agent is based on its distinctive metabolism, which depends upon the rate of administration. Following rapid intravenous injection, floxuridine is rapidly broken down to fluorouracil and then to innocuous urea; with this route, its efficacy and adverse effects are the same as those produced by fluorouracil. However, when floxuridine is given by slow, continuous intra-arterial infusion, it is anabolically converted to the active agent, floxuridine monophosphate, which blocks DNA synthesis. This method of administration results in a lower effective dose (30 mg/kg of body weight to 1 mg/kg); it is three times more effective than rapid intravenous injection, and is, therefore, used exclusively.

When administered intra-arterially, local reactions (eg, aphthous stomatitis, erythema) are more prominent than systemic reactions. Systemic reactions are similar to those seen with fluorouracil. The most common of these are nausea, vomiting, diarrhea, and enteritis. Anemia and leukopenia also occur. Other adverse effects include gastrointestinal disorders (anorexia, cramps, duodenal ulcer, gastritis, glossitis, pharyngitis) and dermatologic disorders (alopecia, dermatitis, pruritus, rash, ulceration). Elevated alkaline phosphatase, serum transaminase, serum bilirubin, and lactic dehydrogenase values have been noted.

Because of its toxicity and low therapeutic index, floxuridine should be given under the supervision of a physician who is experienced not only in cancer chemotherapy, but in the technique of intra-arterial infusion. The ambulatory patient must be hospitalized during the first course of treatment and should be informed about toxic manifestations. White blood cell and platelet counts should be performed regularly.

As with fluorouracil, floxuridine should be discontinued immediately when any of the following signs and symptoms appear: stomatitis, esophagopharyngitis, gastrointestinal ulceration and bleeding, diarrhea (five or more loose stools daily), intractable vomiting, leukocyte count of less than $3,500/mm^3$ or a rapidly decreasing count, thrombocytopenia with a platelet count under $100,000/mm^3$, or hemorrhage from any site.

Floxuridine is contraindicated in patients with poor nutritional status or bone marrow depression, and it should be avoided in pregnant women, particularly during the first trimester, because of its potential teratogenicity.

USUAL DOSAGE.—*Intra-arterial: Adults*, the specialized nature of this technique requires the combined skill of a surgeon and oncologist. With the patient under general anesthesia, the artery supplying the tumor is surgically exposed and the catheter is inserted into the lumen and sutured to the vessel wall. A suitable infusion pump is then used to administer 0.1 to 0.6 mg/kg of body weight continuously over a 24-hour period. In hepatic artery infusion, the dosage is 0.4 to 0.6 mg/kg because the drug is metabolized immediately by the liver. Infusion is continued until a local toxic reaction (eg, cutaneous erythema, mucositis) occurs over the region of infusion. The infusion is stopped until the reaction subsides; further courses then are given as long as the response continues. Adequate courses of therapy have varied from one week to several months.

PREPARATIONS.—Floxuridine (Roche). *Injection:* Powder 500 mg in 5 ml containers.

MERCAPTOPURINE [Purinethol]

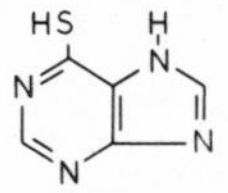

Mercaptopurine produces complete remission in 30% of children with acute lymphoblastic or stem cell leukemia. When administered after a prednisone-induced remission, the incidence of prolonged, complete remissions approaches 80%. Mercaptopurine is less effective in acute myeloblastic leukemia in adults: complete remissions occur in less than 20% of cases and the duration is shorter than in the lymphoblastic type. The drug produces remissions in 80% of adults during the early phase of chronic myelocytic leukemia, but busulfan is still the drug of choice for initial therapy of this condition. In the acute blastic phase, remissions are rare.

Toxic effects include leukopenia, thrombocytopenia, hemorrhage, nausea, vomiting, anorexia (after overdosage), aphthous stomatitis (rare), and jaundice; the latter reaction suggests possible liver damage or biliary stasis. Leukocyte counts should be performed weekly and the drug should be discontinued if an abnormal decrease occurs. The leukocyte count is used to establish a maintenance dose. Smaller doses are recommended in patients with impaired renal or liver function to avoid accumulation. When mercaptopurine is given with allopurinol, the dose of mercaptopurine should be decreased to 33% to 50% of the usual dose. Use of mercaptopurine should be avoided during the first trimester of pregnancy.

USUAL DOSAGE.—*Oral: Adults and children 5 years of age and older,* approximately 2.5 mg/kg of body weight daily in single or divided doses. If clinical improvement and leukocyte depression are not observed in four weeks, the dose may be increased to a maximum of 5 mg/kg daily. The total daily dosage may be given at one time. It is calculated to the closest multiple of 25 mg. Once remission is achieved, administration may be continued for a prolonged period. Therapy should be discontinued if serious toxic effects occur; it may be reinstated at one-half the previous dosage after toxic manifestations disappear.

PREPARATIONS.—Purinethol (Burroughs Wellcome). *Oral:* Tablets 50 mg.

METHOTREXATE
METHOTREXATE SODIUM

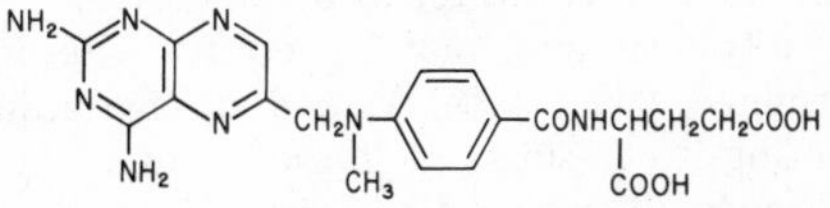

Methotrexate is highly effective in trophoblastic tumors (choriocarcinoma, chorioadenoma destruens, hydatidiform mole): it produces a high rate of response (80%) and long-term survival in one-half the responding patients. Methotrexate, in combination with chlorambucil and dactinomycin, is effective in carcinoma of the testes. It also is effective in Stage III and IV lymphosarcoma, especially in children. It may produce a temporary remission in mycosis fungoides. It is used in combination with several other antineoplastic agents in carcinoma of the breast, lung, and ovary. In acute lymphoblastic leukemia in children, methotrexate alone will produce complete remissions in about 20% of patients, but if administered with prednisone, the incidence of complete remission approaches 80%. Methotrexate, given alone or in combination with other drugs, is being used for intra-arterial infusion of the head and neck, pelvis and limbs. Such treatment is highly specialized and requires the combined skill of an experienced surgeon and oncologist. The use of methotrexate in acute myeloblastic leukemia is obsolete.

For other uses of methotrexate, see Chapter 26, Antirheumatic Agents, and Chapter 68, Dermatologic Agents.

Patients must be carefully observed in order to detect early signs of toxicity (aphthous stomatitis, bone marrow depression, nausea, vomiting, diarrhea). Methotrexate is contraindicated in patients with pre-existing liver, bone marrow, or renal damage, particularly the latter since it is excreted by the kidneys. In patients with renal insufficiency, methotrexate may produce functional and morphologic changes in the kidney. The blood urea nitrogen (BUN) value should be checked every three to four weeks. Intensive, prolonged treatment with methotrexate has produced severe impairment of hepatic function and irreversible fibrosis and cirrhosis. These effects are dose dependent. Therefore, serial liver function tests are recommended. In patients receiving intermittent doses for the treatment of nonmalignant disease (eg, psoriasis), results of liver function tests may be abnormal, but these return to normal after the drug is discontinued.

Methotrexate has been reported to act as an abortifacient and should not be administered during the first trimester of pregnancy.

Leukocyte and platelet counts should be determined twice weekly, and dosage adjusted according to results of these counts and the appearance of signs of toxicity. If severe bone marrow depression occurs, parenteral administration of 3 to 6 mg of leucovorin calcium within one hour following overdosage may prevent serious toxic effects.

The drug should be discontinued if gastrointestinal disturbances occur, and therapy resumed in reduced dosage when symptoms disappear. Dosage then may be gradually increased to the point of tolerance.

USUAL DOSAGE.—

Oral, Intramuscular: For choriocarcinoma, *adults*, 15 mg/M^2 daily for five days. This amount should be given in one dose, for methotrexate is more toxic when given in divided doses. Therapy may be repeated as required when signs of toxicity from the preceding course have disappeared (usually in 7 to 12 days). One to two courses are given after reducing human chorionic gonadotropin titers (less than 50 IU/24 hours).

Oral, Intravenous (combined therapy): For acute leukemia in *children*, 3 mg/M^2 of methotrexate daily and 40 mg/M^2 of prednisone daily in three divided doses are given orally. This usually produces a remission in 80% of patients in four to six weeks. After remission occurs, methotrexate is given intravenously in a dose of 15 mg/M^2 daily for five days for maintenance; this dosage is repeated every 14 days for four courses. After this period, methotrexate (30 mg/M^2 orally twice weekly), prednisone (60 mg/M^2 orally daily for five days once a month), and vincristine (2 mg/M^2 intravenously once a month) are given.

Intrathecal: Initially, methotrexate must be diluted to 1 mg/ml with sodium chloride injection *without* preservative. The solution is filtered through a Millipore filter immediately before administration and given at room temperature. These precautions are essential since severe, sometimes fatal reactions have been reported following intrathecal administration. For meningeal leukemia in *children*, 12 mg/M^2 of methotrexate (diluted to 1 mg/ml as stated above) is given every two or three days until cerebrospinal fluid pressure and cell counts are normal. Leucovorin calcium is given subcutaneously 15 minutes after the methotrexate injection is completed.

PREPARATIONS.—

Methotrexate (Lederle). *Oral:* Tablets 2.5 mg.

Methotrexate Sodium (Lederle). *Injection:* Solution 2.5 and 25 mg/ml in 2 ml containers.

THIOGUANINE

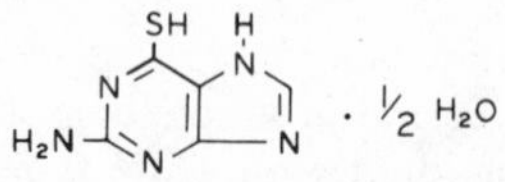

SH H N N N H_2N N · ½ H_2O

Thioguanine is an analogue of mercaptopurine and is effective in the treatment of the same types of leukemia. It is preferred to mercaptopurine because it causes fewer gastrointestinal reactions; in addition, it may be used with allopurinol without adjusting the dose. The percentages and durations of response induced by the two drugs in acute leukemias are similar. As with other antineoplastic agents of the same class, cross resistance exists between thioguanine and mercaptopurine. The combination of thioguanine and cytarabine is the treatment of choice for acute myeloblastic leukemia in adults.

Thioguanine and mercaptopurine also are of comparable effectiveness in early chronic myelocytic leukemia. Busulfan is still the drug of choice for initial therapy in this condition; however, chronic myelocytic leukemia eventually progresses to an acute blastic phase, at which time busulfan should be discontinued and thioguanine, mercaptopurine, or methotrexate substituted. Less often, chronic myelocytic leukemia may become refractory to busulfan and, since increased amounts of busulfan may cause anemia and thrombocytopenia, an alternative drug (usually mercaptopurine) may be tried.

Thioguanine depresses bone marrow function and causes leukopenia, thrombocytopenia, and hemorrhage. Hemoglobin level and white blood cell and platelet counts should be determined at weekly intervals. As with other antineoplastic agents, thioguanine should be discontinued if a sudden decrease in leukocyte or platelet levels occurs. When these cell counts return to normal, therapy may be reinstituted at the same or reduced dosage. Occasionally, nausea, vomiting, anorexia, and aphthous stomatitis may develop if large doses of thioguanine are used.

The use of thioguanine should be avoided

during the first trimester of pregnancy because of potential teratogenic effects.

USUAL DOSAGE.—*Oral: Adults*, initially, approximately 2 mg/kg of body weight daily; the total daily dose is calculated to the closest multiple of 20 mg. If there is no response to this dose after four weeks, the amount may be cautiously increased to 3 mg/kg daily. Absence of clinical or laboratory evidence of improvement with the larger dose is sufficient indication that the patient will not respond, and another class of drugs should be substituted for thioguanine.

For dosage in acute myeloblastic leukemia, see the evaluation on Cytosine Arabinoside.

PREPARATIONS.—Thioguanine (Burroughs Wellcome). *Oral:* Tablets 40 mg.

MISCELLANEOUS AGENTS

HYDROXYUREA [Hydrea]

$$H_2N-\overset{O}{\overset{\|}{C}}-NHOH$$

Hydroxyurea has a limited degree of effectiveness as an antineoplastic agent. It may be useful in patients with chronic myelocytic leukemia who do not respond to busulfan. Hydroxyurea will reduce the leukocyte count within 24 to 48 hours after a single large dose. Because of this predictable leukopenic effect, this agent has been used initially in patients with acute leukemias whose white blood cell counts were high enough to cause thromboembolic complications. Hydroxyurea also has been given concomitantly with radiation therapy in the local control of primary epidermoid (squamous cell) carcinomas of the head and neck, excluding the lip.

As with other antineoplastic agents, hydroxyurea has produced brief objective remissions in melanocarcinomas; however, evaluating the response to treatment is difficult because of the unpredictable behavior of melanomas (erratic growth and occasional spontaneous remissions).

Hydroxyurea may have some palliative effect in advanced ovarian carcinoma. In one study, tumor size was reduced for a mean duration of six months in one-third of a small number of patients treated with this drug.

The most significant adverse effect is bone marrow depression; the granulocytes are primarily affected. The response is rapid and dose dependent; the white blood cell count is reduced to about one-half its initial level in two to four days but recovers rapidly after one week. Because of this, hydroxyurea is tolerated better than other agents that depress the leukocyte count for long periods. Thrombocytopenia and anemia occur rarely. Other rare reactions include gastrointestinal effects (eg, aphthous stomatitis, nausea, vomiting, anorexia, diarrhea), central nervous system disturbances (eg, headache, dizziness, disorientation, hallucinations, convulsions), and minor cutaneous reactions (eg, rash, pruritus). Impairment of renal function with hyperuricemia, uric acid calculi, and elevated blood urea nitrogen levels have been reported.

Blood, bone marrow, renal, and hepatic function should be evaluated prior to and at weekly intervals during therapy. Therapy should be discontinued if the white blood cell count falls below 2,500/mm^3 or the platelet count below 100,000/mm^3. Administration may be resumed when the counts recover. Anemia can be corrected by whole blood transfusions without discontinuing administration of hydroxyurea.

Because it is excreted primarily through the kidneys, hydroxyurea must be used with caution in patients with impaired renal function. The drug is contraindicated in those with bone marrow depression or thrombocytopenia resulting from recent exposure to radiation or chemotherapy. Since hydroxyurea has shown teratogenic effects in experimental animals, it should not be used in women of childbearing age.

USUAL DOSAGE.—*Oral:* For solid tumors, intermittent dosage is 80 mg/kg of body weight as a single dose every third day, and continuous dosage is 20 to 30 mg/kg daily as a single dose.

For resistant chronic myelocytic leukemia, 20 to 30 mg/kg as a single daily dose.

For carcinoma of the head and neck, hydroxyurea is administered with irradiation according to the following schedule: 80 mg/kg of hydroxyurea is given as a single dose every third day at least seven days before initiation of irradiation; this dose is continued during radiotherapy as well as indefinitely afterwards provided that the patient is adequately observed and experiences no unusual or severe reactions. Irradiation should be given at the maximal dose considered appropriate for the particular therapeutic situation; adjustment of irradiation dosage is not usually necessary when hydroxyurea is used concomitantly.

PREPARATIONS.—Hydrea (Squibb). *Oral:* Capsules 500 mg.

MITOTANE [Lysodren]

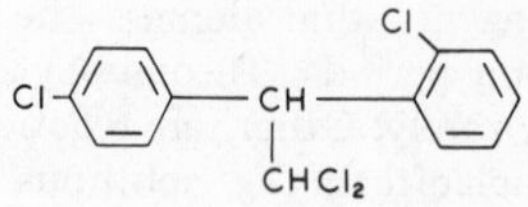

Mitotane is a synthetic organic agent with specific adrenal cytotoxic properties. Its mechanism of action is unknown but there are indications that it modifies the peripheral metabolism of steroids in addition to suppressing adrenal cortical function.

Adrenal cortex carcinoma is rare in man (only an estimated two persons per million are affected). Clinical information on the use of mitotane in this condition is based mainly on individual reports of about 300 cases evaluated by 100 investigators and assembled by the National Cancer Institute.

Primary treatment of adrenal cortex carcinoma is surgery. If the disease recurs or metastasizes and additional surgery is not feasible, treatment with mitotane is indicated. Mitotane reduced measurable tumor masses in about 50% of patients, and excretion of urinary steroids and endocrine symptoms were reduced in about 80% of patients. There was also a reduction in pain, weight loss, fatigue, and anorexia. These responses were palliative with a median duration of about six months.

The incidence of adverse reactions with mitotane is high. The majority of patients experience at least one of the following types of adverse effects: gastrointestinal reactions (anorexia, nausea, vomiting, about 80% of patients), central nervous system reactions (depression, lethargy, vertigo, drowsiness, 40% of patients), and cutaneous reactions (rash, 15% of patients). More infrequent reactions affect the eye (blurred vision, diplopia, lens opacity, retinopathy), genitourinary system (hematuria, cystitis, albuminuria), and cardiovascular system (hypertension, orthostatic hypotension, flushing).

Before initial administration of mitotane, metastatic masses should be resected to prevent possible infarction and hemorrhage due to the rapid onset of effect. Therapy should be supervised by a physician experienced in cancer chemotherapy and patients should be hospitalized until a maintenance dose is established.

Mitotane must be used cautiously in the presence of liver disease not due to metastases of the adrenal cortex neoplasm because of possible interference with metabolism and resultant accumulation.

If shock or severe trauma occurs during treatment, administration of exogenous corticosteroids is mandatory to compensate for the drug-induced depression of adrenocortical function. Supplemental corticosteroids may also be necessary if acute adrenocortical insufficiency develops during treatment.

Because of the prominent central nervous system depressant effects of mitotane (eg, drowsiness, lethargy, vertigo), ambulatory patients must be warned against driving, operating machinery, and performing other tasks involving mental alertness and physical coordination. Prolonged use of the drug may lead to brain damage and impaired function; thus behavioral and neurologic evaluations must be made at regular intervals. The safety of mitotane during pregnancy or lactation is unknown.

USUAL DOSAGE.—*Oral:* Initially, 9 to 10 g daily in three or four divided doses. If adverse effects appear, the dose is reduced until the maximal tolerated dose is determined. This has varied from 2 to 16 g, with an average of 8 to 10 g daily. The treatment is continued as long as clinical benefit occurs. If no improvement is observed after three months at the maximal tolerated dose, the drug should be discontinued.

PREPARATIONS.—Lysodren (Calbio). *Oral:* Tablets 500 mg.

PROCARBAZINE [Matulane]

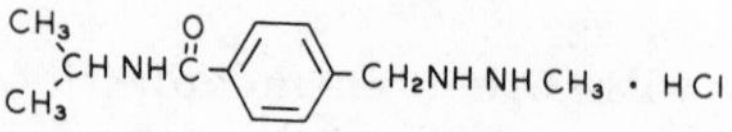

Procarbazine is a synthetic methylhydrazine derivative unrelated to any other antineoplastic agent. Its primary indication is in the treatment of generalized (Stage IIIB or IV) Hodgkin's disease not considered curable by radiation. Because of the availability of alkylating agents and vinblastine, the use of procarbazine as a primary drug has been limited in patients who received no prior chemotherapy. In these patients, it has produced remissions comparable in quality and duration to those achieved with the alkylating agents or vinblastine. Procarbazine has been tested extensively in patients resistant to alkylating agents and vinblastine; in these patients, the incidence of significant responses is lower than when it is used as a primary agent. These results demonstrate a lack of cross resistance between procarbazine and standard radiation, alkylating agents, or vinblastine.

The present preferred treatment of advanced Hodgkin's disease is the MOPP regimen consisting of the simultaneous administration of mechlorethamine, vincristine, procarbazine, and prednisone. Rates and duration of remissions are significantly superior to those produced by single agents. Complete remissions have been reported in as many as 80% of patients on MOPP therapy, with a median duration of remission of several years.

Other lymphomas such as lymphosarcoma and reticulum cell sarcoma have responded to procarbazine alone, but the degree and duration are less than those observed in Hodgkin's disease. Procarbazine has also been tested in a variety of solid tumors without significant effect, except for occasional brief remissions in patients with oat cell sarcoma.

Adverse Reactions and Precautions.—Nausea and vomiting are the most common adverse effects, and usually regress by the end of the first week of administration. Anorexia, stomatitis, dysphagia, diarrhea, and constipation occur less frequently.

Hematopoietic depression, manifested by leukopenia, anemia, and thrombocytopenia, occurs frequently during prolonged administration. Hemorrhage associated with thrombocytopenia has been manifested as petechiae, purpura, epistaxis, hemoptysis, hematemesis, and melena. Severe leukopenia with bacterial infection has been reported.

Central nervous system effects (euphoria, fatigue, depression, lethargy, drowsiness) have occurred less commonly. Paresthesias, headache, dizziness, ataxia, foot drop, and hyporeflexia have also been reported.

Dermatologic effects include dermatitis, pruritus, hyperpigmentation, and alopecia.

Miscellaneous effects (myalgia, arthralgia, chills and fever, hyperhidrosis, asthenia) also may be observed.

A synergistic effect is observed when procarbazine is given with barbiturates, antihistamines, narcotics, antihypertensive agents, or phenothiazines. Alcohol must be avoided because of the possibility of eliciting a disulfiram-like reaction. Since procarbazine exhibits some monoamine oxidase inhibitor activity, hypertensive crises may result if it is used with adrenergic agents, tricyclic antidepressants (eg, amitryptyline, imipramine), or foods and beverages with a high tyramine content (eg, ripe cheese). Procarbazine and other hydrazine derivatives also can cause hemolysis, resulting in anemia.

Peripheral blood and bone marrow function (hemoglobin and hematocrit levels and leukocyte, reticulocyte, and platelet counts) should be determined before the drug is given. During therapy, hematologic data should be checked weekly. Prior treatment with irradiation or other myelosuppressant drugs may limit tolerance to the drug. Renal and hepatic function tests also should be performed before the drug is administered, and it is recommended that urinalysis and levels of transaminases, alkaline phosphatase, and blood urea nitrogen be checked weekly. Toxic effects may be enhanced if renal or hepatic function is impaired.

The drug should be discontinued if central nervous system signs and symptoms, leukopenia (white blood cell count under $4,000/mm^3$), thrombocytopenia (platelet count under $100,000/mm^3$), hypersensitivity reactions, stomatitis, diarrhea, or hemorrhage occur.

Because teratogenic effects occur in animals, the use of procarbazine during the first trimester of pregnancy should be avoided if possible.

USUAL DOSAGE.—*Oral: Adults*, for single-drug therapy, 100 to 200 mg daily in single or divided doses for the first week, followed by 300 mg daily until the white blood cell count falls below $4,000/mm^3$, the platelet count below $100,000/mm^3$, or until maximal response occurs. To minimize nausea and vomiting, 50 mg may be given initially and increased by 50 mg each day until a daily dose of 300 mg is reached. The drug is then discontinued until white cell and platelet counts have returned to satisfactory levels. Maintenance treatment is resumed with doses of 50 to 100 mg daily, depending upon hematologic tolerance.

As part of MOPP combination therapy, *adults and children*, 100 mg/M^2 daily for 14 days of each monthly cycle. Six cycles are administered over a six-month period. The dosage is regulated according to the results of white blood cell and platelet counts.

PREPARATIONS.—Matulane (Roche). *Oral:* Capsules 50 mg.

QUINACRINE HYDROCHLORIDE [Atabrine Hydrochloride]

This antimalarial and anthelmintic agent appears to be as effective as radioactive isotopes and alkylating agents in the management of recurring pleural and peritoneal neoplastic effusions secondary to carcinoma of the lung or breast and in lymphomas or mesotheliomas. Ascites secondary to carcinoma and mesothelioma of the ovary, breast, colon, stomach, and pancreas may respond to intraperitoneal administration. Quinacrine inhibits effusion by producing an inflammatory reaction on serosa which causes fibrous thickening or fibrinous pleurisy.

Toxic effects are fever, regional pain, dyspnea, nausea, vomiting, adynamic ileus, and transient hallucinations. Convulsive seizures have occurred in patients receiving quinacrine and corticosteroids concomitantly.

For other uses of this drug, see Chapters 31, Anticonvulsants; 61, Antimalarial Agents; and 65, Anthelmintics.

USUAL DOSAGE.—*Intracavitary* (intrapleural, intraperitoneal): To determine the tolerance of the patient, a test dose of 50 to 100 mg is given for pleural effusions and 100 to 200 mg for peritoneal effusions. If tolerated, 200 to 400 mg for pleural effusions and 400 to 800 mg for ascites is given daily for three to five days. The course may be repeated after a few weeks, but other treatment should be substituted if there is no permanent effect.

PREPARATIONS.—Atabrine Hydrochloride (Winthrop). *Injection:* Powder 200 mg.

Antibiotics

BLEOMYCIN SULFATE [Blenoxane]

This is a preliminary evaluation of bleomycin, an antibiotic derived from *Streptomyces verticillus*. Bleomycin has a palliative effect in some squamous cell carcinomas in the head and neck region (eg, in the buccal mucosa, tongue, tonsil, and pharynx areas), as well as in the penis, cervix, and vulva. In addition, this agent has shown some degree of effectiveness in lymphomas (eg, Hodgkin's disease, reticulum cell sarcomas, lymphosarcomas) and in testicular carcinomas (eg, embryonal cell type, choriocarcinoma, teratoma).

In contrast to many antineoplastic agents, bleomycin is only slightly myelosuppressive. Because of this, it may be used alone when a low bone marrow reserve is present, or it may be given with agents that have a myelosuppressive action, particularly for the initial induction of remissions. Bleomycin has produced remissions in patients who have become refractory to the older antineoplastic agents.

Adverse reactions most frequently affect the skin and mucous membranes. These are manifested initially by hyperesthesia and swelling of the fingers, which may be followed by vesiculation, hyperkeratosis of the palms, and stomatitis. Hyperthermic reactions (fever with or without chills three to five hours after administration) are common. Headache and nausea and, less frequently, alopecia also may occur.

Pulmonary toxicity has been observed in as many as 10% of patients treated. This potentially serious complication may occur acutely with pulmonary infiltrates or may develop insidiously and progress to pulmonary fibrosis. Since available data indicate that this latter reaction may be dose related, long-term use of bleomycin for maintenance therapy is contraindicated. Regular chest x-rays and auscultation of lungs should be performed every one to two weeks during therapy, and the drug should be discontinued if any signs of pulmonary involvement occur. The incidence of toxic reactions appears to increase markedly when the total dose is over 350 units.

Because of the possible occurrence of anaphylactic reactions, patients with lymphomas should be started with five units or less for the first two doses. If no acute reaction is observed, the regular dosage schedule may be used.

The safety of bleomycin during pregnancy or lactation is unknown.

USUAL DOSAGE.—*Intramuscular, Intravenous:* For squamous cell carcinoma, lymphosarcoma, reticulum cell sarcoma, testicular carcinoma, and Hodgkin's disease, 0.25 to 0.5 units/kg of body weight (10 to 20 units/M^2) once or twice weekly. For Hodgkin's disease, after a 50% response a maintenance dose of 5 units is given once weekly.

For intramuscular or subcutaneous use, the contents of the ampul are dissolved in 1 to 5 ml of sterile water for injection, sodium chloride injection, or 5% dextrose injection. For intravenous or intra-arterial use, the contents of the ampul are dissolved in 5 ml or more of sodium chloride injection or 5% dextrose injection and administered slowly over a period of ten minutes.

PREPARATIONS.—Blenoxane (Bristol). *Injection:* Powder 15 units. Each unit is equivalent to bleomycin A_2 hydrochloride 1.012 mg.

DACTINOMYCIN [Cosmegen]

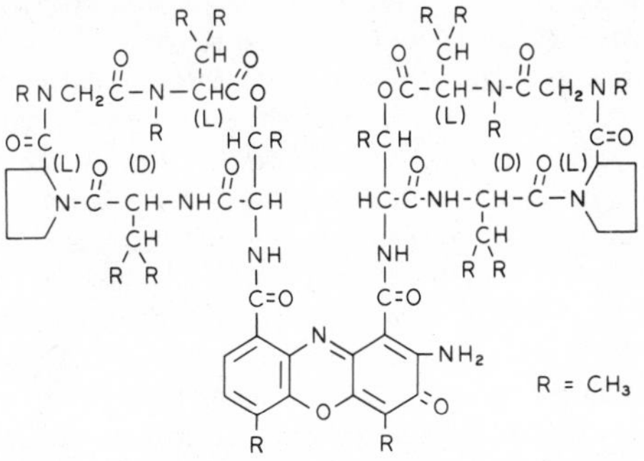

R = CH_3

Dactinomycin is produced by *Streptomyces parvullus.* It is highly effective in Wilms' tumor and has some effect in children with embryonal rhabdomyosarcoma, although remissions may be of short duration. The drug usually has been given in combination with vincristine, cyclophosphamide, and radiation. There is recent data to suggest that the combination of dactinomycin and vincristine suppresses microscopic metastases of embryonal rhabdomyosarcoma and increases the survival rate. In addition, it is useful in choriocarcinoma, carcinoma of the testes, and, possibly, Ewing's sarcoma.

Present therapy of Wilms' tumor depends upon the stage (I [localized] to IV [disseminated]) at the time of diagnosis and includes surgical resection and postoperative irradiation followed by repeated courses of dactinomycin and vincristine. Metastases in the lung, the most frequent site, may be more resistant to treatment and may require additional courses of dactinomycin for control. Vincristine may be equally effective and should be used in patients who have become refractory to dactinomycin.

Use of the combination of dactinomycin, methotrexate, and chlorambucil is of major value in the treatment of metastatic tumors of the testes (seminoma, embryonal carcinoma, teratoma, and choriocarcinoma). This regimen produces signs of objective improvement (as measured by a decrease in the size of pulmonary metastases and by lowered gonadotropin titers) in one-third to one-half of patients. Repeated courses of therapy every one to three months for several years appear to be necessary to maintain the regression. Although methotrexate is the drug of choice for initial use in female patients with choriocarcinoma and related trophoblastic tumors (hydatidiform mole, chorioadenoma destruens), dactinomycin produces complete remission in about one-half of patients who have become resistant to methotrexate. This may be the drug of choice in patients with impaired liver or renal function in whom methotrexate might be contraindicated.

A limited number of patients have received dactinomycin by the perfusion technique. Favorable responses have occurred in patients with Ewing's sarcoma when dactinomycin was given alone or with other antineoplastic agents.

Adverse Reactions and Precautions.—Dactinomycin may cause irritation, phlebitis, or cellulitis at the site of injection. Gastrointestinal tract, cutaneous, or hematologic reactions occur frequently and may be serious, although they usually disappear when the drug is discontinued. The danger of toxic reactions increases when dactinomycin is used with irradiation, with other antineoplastic agents, or with subsequent courses of therapy. Patients also may become more susceptible to infections due to suppression of normal immune mechanisms.

A delayed toxic effect, characterized by erythema and ulceration under the tongue and buccal mucosa (aphthous stomatitis), may develop one to three days after a course of dactinomycin and may last three to five days. Other gastrointestinal reactions include vomiting, nausea, and anorexia, which usually occur four to five hours after an injection. Cheilitis, dysphagia, esophagitis, pharyngitis, abdominal pain, diarrhea, gastrointestinal ulceration, malaise, fatigue, lethargy, fever, myalgia, and proctitis usually do not become apparent until two to four days after a course is completed.

Skin eruptions (eg, acne), erythema, or hyperpigmentation are particularly apt to appear in areas that have been previously irradiated. Reversible alopecia affecting the scalp and sometimes the eyebrows also may occur. Anaphylactic reactions, sometimes fatal, have been reported rarely.

When dactinomycin is given with radiation therapy, the dose of the latter may have to be modified because of the possible potentiation of skin damage.

A decrease in the number of leukocytes (counts as low as $2{,}000/mm^3$ and occasionally as low as $1{,}000/mm^3$) can be expected when dactinomycin is given alone or with radiation therapy. Thrombocytopenia, anemia (possibly to the point of aplastic anemia), agranulocytosis, leukopenia, pancytopenia, and reticulocytopenia also may develop. The combination of low platelet counts and gastrointestinal tract ulcerations may result in gastrointestinal bleeding or infection.

Because of the potential severity of the reactions to dactinomycin, the drug should be used only by physicians experienced in cancer chemotherapy and preferably in hospitalized patients. Because of the local irritating effects of the drug, care should be taken to avoid extravasation into the subcutaneous tissue.

White blood cell counts should be performed daily and platelet counts every three days. Treatment should be discontinued if there is a marked fall in either of these blood elements, since further decreases occur after administration of the drug is stopped.

Determinations of renal and hepatic function should be made periodically in patients receiving dactinomycin.

If dactinomycin is given at or about the time of infection with chickenpox, a severe generalized disease, which is sometimes fatal, may occur.

USUAL DOSAGE.—The dosage varies with the individual patient and depends upon his tolerance, the extent of the neoplasm, and the use of other forms of therapy. Doses are decreased if concomitant therapy (other antineoplastic drugs or radiation) is used or if x-ray therapy has been given previously.

Intravenous: Adults, 0.01 mg/kg of body weight daily for a maximum of five days. Single doses of 2 mg each week for three weeks have been tolerated. *Children,* 15 μg/kg of body weight daily for five days (maximal dose, 0.5 mg). Courses are repeated at six-week to three-month intervals. Alternatively, a total of 2.4 mg/M^2 of body surface may be given in three or four divided doses over a one-week period. Subsequent courses may be given at monthly intervals in adults or children if there are no signs of residual toxic effects.

To avoid extravasation, dactinomycin should be injected into the tubing of a running intravenous infusion; any unused portion must be discarded. The powder is reconstituted by adding 1.1 ml of sterile water for injection to make a 0.5 mg/ml solution.

PREPARATIONS.—Cosmegen (Merck Sharp & Dohme). *Injection:* Powder 0.5 mg with 20 mg of mannitol per vial. Protect from light and excessive heat.

MITHRAMYCIN [Mithracin]

This antibiotic is produced by *Streptomyces plicatus* and acts by forming a complex with DNA and inhibiting cellular and enzymatic RNA synthesis. Its primary indication is in the treatment of disseminated testicular carcinoma, especially the embryonal cell type. Although it is very toxic, its specificity for embryonal carcinoma makes mithramycin useful in selected patients who cannot be treated by surgery or radiation. However, the therapeutic effect has not been consistent. In addition, it has been more effective than corticosteroids in patients with hypercalcemia and hypercalciuria associated with advanced or metastatic cancer, especially in those with tumors producing parathyroid-like hormone. (See also Chapter 17, Blood Calcium Regulators.)

Metastatic lesions in patients with mixed primary tumors of the testes have been only partially reduced or were unaffected by the drug. Usually, these metastases were subsequently identified as teratomas, choriocarcinomas, or seminomas. Use of mithramycin is not recommended for the treatment of metastases due to these cell types.

Because of the low incidence of testicular tumors (estimated 1% of all tumors), the number of cases evaluated is limited.

On the basis of the limited amount of comparative data available, mithramycin alone or in combination with chlorambucil and methotrexate produces the same rate of response (partial and complete) in disseminated embryonal carcinoma of the testes as dactinomycin alone or with chlorambucil and methotrexate. Responses have occurred with mithramycin after the combination of dactinomycin, chlorambucil, and methotrexate has failed and vice versa. Hence, if initial therapy with either regimen fails, all patients with testicular embryonal cell carcinoma probably should receive treatment with the alternate.

Adverse Reactions and Precautions.—Because of the severe toxic reactions produced by mithramycin, this drug should be administered only to hospitalized patients under the supervision of a physician experienced in the use of antineoplastic agents. Patients receiving this drug must be selected on the basis of possible therapeutic benefit after other agents have failed.

Administration of mithramycin produces a characteristic sequence of symptoms and signs. Anorexia, malaise, and nausea with or without vomiting occur shortly after the drug is given; vomiting can be controlled by an antiemetic (eg, chlorpromazine). During the latter phase of a course of injections, central nervous system reactions such as headache, irritability, and lethargy are common. These effects can recur with successive courses, and the patient, anticipating these uncomfortable effects, may resist continuation of therapy.

A striking cutaneous effect has occurred when the drug is given daily until toxic reactions occur. This phenomenon usually has been observed the day before the onset of biochemical changes and is characterized initially by erythema of the face, neck, and upper thorax with periorbital pallor. This is followed by hyperemia with coarsening and thickening of the facial folds and papular lesions. On discontinuing the drug, these features regress but residual pigmentation and desquamation are noted. This phenomenon has not been observed when an alternate-day dosage schedule is used.

Toward the end of a course of daily injections, a characteristic bleeding syndrome occurs in about 50% of patients. It usually begins with epistaxis, and may progress to ecchymoses, hematemesis, or melena. This hemorrhagic diathesis has severely limited the clinical value of mithramycin. Bleeding can occur in the absence of bone marrow depression or liver dysfunction and is unpredictable despite intensive coagulation studies. Other associated hematologic abnormalities are leukopenia, which occurs rarely, and increased prothrombin time, which is noted frequently. Thrombocytopenia is noted to a variable extent in all patients; although it may not be critical, the platelet count is usually less than pretreatment levels and returns to normal after the drug is discontinued. Patients previously treated with radiation are more likely to develop significant thrombocytopenia. The simultaneous elevation of clotting time and bleeding time and abnormal clot retraction also have been observed.

Baseline platelet counts, prothrombin time, and bleeding time should be determined before therapy is begun. These should be monitored during therapy and for several days following the last dose. A significant decrease in the platelet count (25% of pretreatment level) or a significant prolongation of prothrombin or bleeding times are indications for discontinuing the drug. Bleeding is treated with phytonadione (300 mg daily intravenously) and transfusion of platelets and fresh whole blood.

Hepatotoxicity is common during mithramycin therapy. Increased levels of serum enzymes, specifically the transaminases (SGOT, SGPT) and lactic dehydrogenase (LDH), are to be expected. A continuing increase in the LDH level is an indication for stopping the drug. Alkaline phosphatase, ornithine carbamyl transferase, and isocitric dehydrogenase levels are elevated less frequently. Increases in serum bilirubin and sulfobromophthalein (BSP) retention also are noted.

Renal function is affected by mithramycin: increased levels of blood urea nitrogen, serum creatinine, and proteinuria are observed occasionally, and serum calcium, phosphate, and potassium levels are depressed. The extent to which the calcium level is affected appears to be dose dependent, and has been sufficient to produce clinical signs of hypocalcemia. Therefore, it is essential that these levels be monitored during therapy.

All of the toxic manifestations which are described as indications for cessation of therapy can occur as long as 72 hours after discontinuing mithramycin when the drug is administered daily, but delayed toxicity does not occur when the alternate-day dosage schedule is used.

The mortality from causes attributed to mithramycin administration has been as high as 25%; these deaths occurred most frequently when the daily dose schedule was used. Correlation between mortality and individual dose is not apparent; however, hemorrhage, thrombocytopenia, and azotemia were often present. Postmortem examinations of patients who died as a result of mithramycin administration or from terminal malignancies after use of the drug revealed histologic changes in the liver and kidneys.

USUAL DOSAGE.—*Intravenous: Adults*, for the treatment of testicular tumors, doses are based on the patient's ideal weight and must be adjusted to compensate for the presence of abnormal fluid caused by edema or ascites. A course of mithramycin therapy consists of 50 μg/kg of body weight on alternate days for an average of six doses until hematologic or biochemical toxicity requires discontinuation of the drug. Lactic dehydrogenase (LDH), blood urea nitrogen (BUN), prothrombin time, and platelet counts should be determined on the morning of injection. If the LDH level exceeds 2,000 units (except after the first dose), the BUN level exceeds the upper limits of normal by more than 10%, the prothrombin time becomes abnormal, or the number of platelets begins to decline, regardless of how gradually, that course of therapy should be terminated.

An alternative dosage schedule is 25 to 30

μg/kg daily for eight to ten days or until toxic reactions occur.

The calculated dose of mithramycin may be diluted in 1 liter of 5% dextrose injection in water and infused slowly over a period of four to six hours. Extravasation can cause local irritation and cellulitis. If cellulitis occurs, the infusion should be discontinued and resumed later at a different site. Moderate heat at the site of extravasation may aid in dispersing the drug and minimize discomfort and tissue irritation.

For treatment of hypercalcemia or hypercalciuria, when all other forms of therapy have failed, 25 μg/kg is given. If the calcium level is not decreasing at the end of 48 hours, a second dose is given. If hypercalcemia is not controlled by one course, additional courses may be given at weekly intervals. Depending upon the response, one to three doses weekly may be given. The same precautions and contraindications apply to this use as for the treatment of testicular tumors.

PREPARATIONS.—Mithracin (Pfizer). *Injection:* Powder in vials containing mithramycin 2.5 mg, mannitol 100 mg, and sufficient disodium phosphate to adjust the solution to pH 7.

Plant Alkaloids

VINBLASTINE SULFATE [Velban]

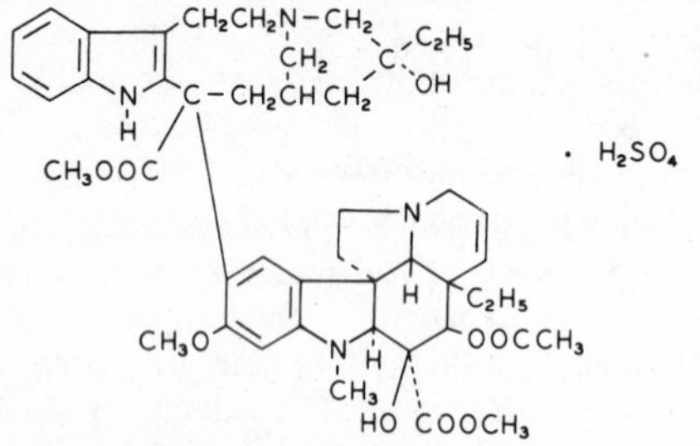

Vinblastine sulfate is a salt of a purified alkaloid extracted from the periwinkle plant, *Vinca rosea.* It is used mainly as a supplemental or alternative drug in Hodgkin's disease and is usually reserved for patients in Stages IIIB and IV (generalized disease) who no longer respond to x-ray therapy or alkylating agents. The duration of remission achieved is comparable to that obtained with use of the alkylating agents; the incidence of nausea and vomiting is less than with the latter agents; and there is no cross resistance between vinblastine and the alkylating agents. Since the leukopenia and bone marrow depression it produces are of short duration, other agents may be administered after vinblastine is discontinued.

In earlier trials, vinblastine had shown some usefulness as a secondary drug in the treatment of choriocarcinoma resistant to methotrexate, but it has been replaced by dactinomycin. Vinblastine may be used as a third drug if necessary.

This agent may have a transient effect on reticulum cell sarcoma and lymphosarcoma. It has occasionally produced a palliative effect in breast carcinomas that did not respond to surgery and hormone therapy.

Leukopenia is the most common untoward reaction caused by vinblastine and may necessitate temporary discontinuation of the drug or adjustment of dosage. Thrombocytopenia and depression of the red blood cell count occur less commonly.

The most common gastrointestinal disturbances are nausea and vomiting, which may be controlled with antiemetics; these effects occur much less frequently than with alkylating agents. Anorexia, diarrhea, stomatitis, constipation, and adynamic ileus, which may be the forerunners of neurotoxic effects, also have been observed. The patient should be informed about the possibility of these reactions, since they occur in 5% to 20% of cases, depending upon the dose. Transient malaise, mental depression, paresthesias, loss of deep tendon reflexes, and headache are the most prominent neurologic effects. The gastrointestinal symptoms, headache, and paresthesias may appear four to six hours after injection, and usually last two to ten hours. Overdosage of vinblastine has caused permanent central nervous system damage and death.

Varying degrees of alopecia occur in 30% to 60% of patients; the alopecia may be reversible when the drug is discontinued or, in some cases, when a smaller maintenance dose is used.

White blood cell and platelet counts should be made once weekly. If these counts are low, the drug should be withheld until the white cell count has recovered to $3,000/mm^3$, and the platelets to $100,000/mm^3$.

Care is essential to avoid extravasation of the drug, since this causes severe irritation and pain and may result in phlebitis or cellulitis at the site of injection. If extravasation occurs, the injection should be stopped immediately and another vein used to complete the dose. Use of cold wet compresses or ice packs may help to disperse the drug and relieve the pain.

Because impaired circulation increases the

possibility of thrombosis, it is inadvisable to inject vinblastine into a vein of an extremity affected by phlebitis, varicosity, or a compressing or invading neoplasm.

Although there is no evidence of adverse effects in infants born of mothers who were treated with vinblastine during the first trimester of pregnancy, it would seem advisable to avoid its use at least during the first three months.

USUAL DOSAGE.—*Intravenous:* Vinblastine sulfate should be administered no more often than once every seven days; dosage is determined on the basis of body weight and the results of weekly white blood cell counts.

Adults (hospitalized or ambulatory patients), initially, 0.1 mg/kg of body weight as a single dose. Successive weekly doses are increased by increments of 0.05 mg/kg until the white blood cell count falls to $3{,}000/mm^3$, a decrease in tumor size occurs, or until a maximal dose of 0.5 mg/kg is reached; thereafter, a maintenance dose one increment smaller than the final dose is given at 7- to 14-day intervals. The requirements of individual patients vary; in most cases the desired response is achieved when a dose of 0.15 to 0.2 mg/kg is reached. Once a remission is induced, some clinicians use a maintenance dose of 10 mg once or twice monthly.

PREPARATIONS.—Velban (Lilly). *Injection:* Lyophilized powder 10 mg.

VINCRISTINE SULFATE [Oncovin]

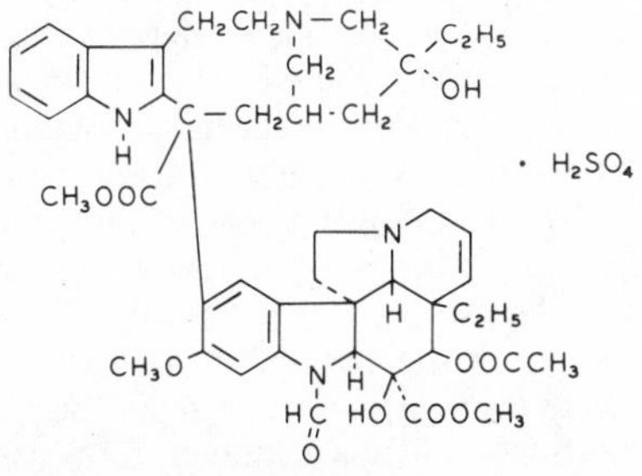

Vincristine sulfate, a salt of a purified alkaloid extracted from the periwinkle plant, *Vinca rosea*, is of value primarily in acute leukemias (acute lymphoblastic leukemia, stem cell leukemia), lymphomas, and solid tumors of childhood. There appears to be no cross resistance between vincristine and other agents used for these conditions (eg, mercaptopurine, methotrexate, dactinomycin, corticosteroids, cyclophosphamide). Vincristine is used frequently with other agents because it only rarely causes hematologic depression.

The use of vincristine as the sole primary drug will induce complete remissions in 50% to 60% of children with acute lymphoblastic leukemia in approximately three to four weeks. When combined with corticosteroids, the remission rate is about 85%; comparable rates of remission are produced with prednisone and mercaptopurine or methotrexate. The combination of vincristine and prednisone is the treatment of choice for induction of remissions. Because of its rapid action and undesirable adverse effects, vincristine is usually reserved for induction of remissions. Methotrexate or mercaptopurine, supplemented by vincristine and prednisone at monthly intervals, are given for maintenance.

Vincristine is quite effective in the childhood neoplasms (eg, neuroblastoma, rhabdomyosarcoma, Hodgkin's disease, Wilms' tumor, Ewing's sarcoma, lymphosarcoma, retinoblastoma). Because remissions tend to be of short duration, it is usually used with other agents to induce remission.

About 50% of adults with Hodgkin's disease respond to vincristine. It is more useful in reticulum cell sarcoma and giant follicular lymphoma than in small cell lymphosarcoma. The usefulness of vincristine is limited by the long-lasting neural damage which may occur during prolonged administration and because the duration of induced remissions may be relatively brief. Vincristine should never be used for maintenance therapy if alkylating agents can be used.

The adverse effects produced by vincristine are reversible, and occur less frequently at dosages below 0.05 mg/kg of body weight weekly. Three groups of reactions occur in children. Reactions in the first group usually disappear in one week or less and, in order of their relative frequency, include constipation, abdominal cramps, and adynamic ileus. Those in the second group are alopecia and peripheral neuritis; these are more troublesome and are reversed more slowly. Toxic manifestations in the third group usually begin with signs of polyneuropathy, and include loss of deep tendon reflexes and, less frequently, neuralgia, paresthesias of fingers and toes, neurotoxicity (eg, foot drop, muscle atrophy), headache, and ataxia. Paresthesias progressing to paresis or paralysis and atrophy of extensor muscles may occur later. Paralysis of certain cranial nerves (II, III, VI, and VII) is observed occasionally. These neurologic complications may persist four months or longer after treatment has been discontinued. Behavioral changes (eg, agitation, depression) also have been observed and may be severe. Convulsions with hypertension have been reported in a few patients.

Similar adverse reactions also occur in adults, and may be more severe; adults, particularly elderly patients, are more likely to develop signs of neuromuscular toxicity. Liver damage, if present, will increase the drug's toxicity.

Since reactions are more likely to persist when vincristine is given in several small doses throughout the week, the use of single weekly doses is recommended. Adverse effects occurring after single weekly doses may decrease or disappear if the dose is reduced.

Neurotoxicity is the main factor limiting the dosage of vincristine. Its effect on bone marrow is less critical than that of most other antineoplastic agents, but mild leukopenia and anemia may occur. Therefore, hemoglobin determinations and white blood cell counts should be made before each dose, and patients should be observed carefully for signs of infection. Since the drug may cause local irritation (phlebitis or cellulitis at the site of injection) care should be taken to avoid extravasation into subcutaneous tissue. A cathartic should be used daily to avoid constipation. Additional prophylactic measures such as stool softeners should be prescribed to maintain bowel movements in hospitalized, bedridden adults.

USUAL DOSAGE.—*Intravenous:* Vincristine sulfate is preferably administered at weekly intervals, since the incidence of complete remission with this schedule has been higher than when smaller doses are given several times a week and toxicity is reduced.

For the treatment of acute leukemias in *children*, the dose may be determined either on the basis of body weight or body surface area. Investigators who recommend the latter method use a weekly dose of 1.5 mg/M^2 of body surface. This corresponds to approximately 0.03 to 0.075 mg/kg of body weight for a 10-year-old child and 0.05 to 0.15 mg/kg for a 1-year-old infant. After remission, the dosage may be reduced to a level as low as 0.025 mg/kg. However, because of potential neural damage, use of vincristine is not advisable for maintenance therapy.

In *patients 12 to 20 years of age*, remissions may be induced with vincristine (weekly dose of 1.5 to 2 mg/M^2 of body surface) and prednisone (40 mg/M^2 once daily). Remission may be maintained with methotrexate (30 mg/M^2 given intramuscularly or orally twice weekly) or mercaptopurine (75 to 90 mg/M^2 daily in one dose).

For *adults*, the suggested dosage (given with prednisone) is 0.025 to 0.075 mg/kg a week, based on 1.4 mg/M^2 of body surface (maximum dose 2 mg/M^2). The dosage of vincristine should be adjusted individually because of the narrow range between therapeutic and toxic levels and individual variations in response. Neurotoxic effects develop in most adults who receive continued weekly doses.

PREPARATIONS.—Oncovin (Lilly). *Injection:* Lyophilized powder 1 and 5 mg with diluent.

Estrogens

CONJUGATED ESTROGENS [Premarin]
DIETHYLSTILBESTROL
ESTERIFIED ESTROGENS [Amnestrogen, Menest, SK-Estrogens]
ETHINYL ESTRADIOL [Estinyl, Feminone, Lynoral, Novestrol]

Estrogens are effective in the treatment of postmenopausal patients with metastatic breast carcinoma and in carcinoma of the prostate.

In *breast carcinoma*, the tumor remission rates from estrogen therapy increase markedly as the number of years since menopause increases. A tumor remission rate of 13% has been reported during the first five years after menopause as compared with 38% after the fifth year. Local soft tissue lesions show a higher remission rate after estrogen therapy than after androgen therapy, whereas the androgens are preferred for skeletal metastases. Evidence of tumor regression is usually not seen for four weeks after therapy is begun, and the trial should be continued for at least two months unless the disease progresses rapidly. Therapy is continued until the patient shows exacerbation of the neoplasm. The tumor may then regress when the hormone is withdrawn. Remission can last from a few months to several years, with an average duration of about 15 months.

Disseminated prostatic carcinoma can be controlled by castration or estrogen therapy. Prostatic acid phosphatase is usually elevated with skeletal involvement and is a useful guide to the efficacy of therapy. Successful treatment becomes evident almost immediately with loss of pain and decreased acid phosphatase levels.

When estrogens are used for breast carcinoma, adverse effects include edema, nausea, anorexia, changes in libido, breast tenderness, abdominal cramps, dizziness, and irritability. Pigmentation of nipples and areola occurs in almost all patients. Since the liver inactivates estrogens, the toxic effects tend to be more severe in the presence of hepatic damage. Urinary incontinence when coughing or straining is a frequent complaint of older women. Patients should be warned that *uterine bleeding* occurs in most postmenopausal women when estrogen therapy is started, interrupted, or discontinued. Bleeding nearly always ceases when the dose is increased.

When estrogens are used for prostatic carcinoma, gynecomastia and impotence are expected adverse effects.

USUAL DOSAGE.—

Conjugated Estrogens:

Oral: For breast carcinoma, 10 mg three times daily; for prostatic carcinoma, 3.75 to 7.5 mg daily.

Diethylstilbestrol:

Oral: For breast carcinoma, 5 mg three times daily (range, 5 to 15 mg daily); for prostatic carcinoma, 1 to 3 mg daily.

Esterified Estrogens:

Oral: For breast carcinoma, 10 mg three times daily; for prostatic carcinoma, 1.25 mg three times daily.

Ethinyl Estradiol:

Oral: For breast carcinoma, 0.5 to 1 mg three times daily; for prostatic carcinoma, 0.15 to 3 mg daily.

PREPARATIONS.—See Chapter 37, Estrogens, Progestagens, Oral Contraceptives, and Ovulatory Agents.

Androgens

DROMOSTANOLONE PROPIONATE [Drolban]
FLUOXYMESTERONE [Halotestin, Ora-Testryl, Ultandren]
TESTOLACTONE [Teslac]
TESTOSTERONE [Neo-Hombreol (F), Oreton]
TESTOSTERONE PROPIONATE [Neo-Hombreol, Oreton Propionate]

Large doses of androgens produce objective signs of regression of disseminated disease in about 20% of women with carcinoma of the breast, the median period of regression being eight months. As with the estrogens, androgens are progressively more beneficial as the period after menopause increases. The tumor remission rate is only 8% in the first year after menopause, about 15% from the second through the fifth postmenopausal year, and 25% thereafter. Local tumors and visceral metastases especially are dependent on postmenopausal age, much more so than bone metastases. Therefore, extensive skeletal lesions usually are preferably treated with androgens.

Adverse effects include virilism with enlargement of the clitoris and hirsutism, edema, and erythrocythemia. These effects appear to be less marked with dromostanolone. Fluoxymesterone is less virilizing than the older androgens. Testolactone is relatively inert hormonally, gives no obvious signs of virilization, and has a similar tumor remission rate as the other androgens. Androgens are contraindicated in patients with cardiorenal disease or hypercalcemia, and during pregnancy or in nursing mothers.

For other uses of these drugs, see Chapter 36, Androgens and Anabolic Steroids.

USUAL DOSAGE.—

Dromostanolone Propionate:

Intramuscular: 100 mg three times weekly for 8 to 12 weeks or as long as there is objective evidence of remission.

Fluoxymesterone:

Oral: 20 to 30 mg daily.

Methyltestosterone:

Oral, Buccal: 200 mg daily.

Testolactone:

Intramuscular: 100 mg three times weekly.

Oral: 50 mg three times weekly.

Testosterone:

Intramuscular: 100 mg three times weekly.

Testosterone Propionate:

Buccal: 200 mg daily.

Intramuscular: 100 mg three times weekly.

PREPARATIONS.—

Dromostanolone Propionate:

Drolban (Lilly). *Injection:* Solution 50 mg/ml in 10 ml containers.

Fluoxymesterone, Methyltestosterone, Testosterone, Testosterone Propionate: See Chapter 36, Androgens and Anabolic Steroids.

Testolactone:

Teslac (Squibb).

Injection: Suspension (aqueous) 100 mg/ml in 5 ml containers.

Oral: Tablets 50 mg.

Adrenal Corticosteroids

PREDNISONE [Delta-Dome, Deltasone, Deltra, Meticorten, Paracort, Servisone]

This adrenal corticosteroid has antineoplastic properties and may control autoimmune complications (hemolytic anemia, thrombocytopenia, leukopenia) associated with reticuloendothelial malignancies. The combination of prednisone and vincristine is the regimen of choice to induce remission in acute leukemia of childhood; mercaptopurine or methotrexate then is given to maintain the remission, supplemented by vincristine and prednisone at monthly intervals. Prednisone also is useful in late stages of chronic lymphocytic leukemia when the clinical picture is one of acute leukemia with a predominantly blastic marrow, when the condition is complicated by hemolytic anemia or thrombocytopenia, or when the patient fails to respond to radiation or chlorambucil. The drug is useful in Hodgkin's disease in special situations or, when more effective drugs have failed, in lymphosarcoma and in carcinoma of the breast.

Prednisone is the most commonly used adrenal corticosteroid because it is less expensive and causes less salt retention, but prednisolone, cortisone, or hydrocortisone also may be given.

For adverse reasons, precautions, and other uses of adrenal corticosteroids, see Chapters 26, Antirheumatic Agents; 35, Adrenal Corticosteroids; 41, Bronchodilators; and 71, Anti-infective and Anti-inflammatory Agents Used in Ophthalmology.

USUAL DOSAGE.—*Oral:* For induction of remission in acute lymphoblastic leukemia, *adults,* initially 60 to 100 mg daily; *children,* 1.5 mg/kg of body weight daily in three divided doses or 45 mg/M^2 daily. Administration is continued for four to six weeks, after which the dose is reduced gradually to maintenance levels or is completely withdrawn over a two-week period in patients with remission. Prednisone in combination with vincristine will produce a higher incidence of remissions than prednisone alone. Caution should be exercised in patients receiving prolonged steroid therapy, since sudden withdrawal or development of stress may result in acute adrenocortical insufficiency.

PREPARATIONS.—

Delta-Dome (Dome), Deltra (Merck Sharp & Dohme), Paracort (Parke, Davis), Servisone (Lederle). *Oral:* Tablets 5 mg.

Deltasone (Upjohn). *Oral:* Tablets 2.5, 5, and 50 mg.

Meticorten (Schering). *Oral:* Tablets 1 and 5 mg.

ADDITIONAL TRADEMARKS.—Lisacort (Fellows-Testagar), Orasone (Rowell), Predsone (Century), Ropred (Robinson). Drug also marketed by other manufacturers under generic name.

Progestagens

HYDROXYPROGESTERONE [Delalutin]
MEDROXYPROGESTERONE [Depo-Provera, Provera]
MEGESTROL ACETATE [Megace]

The primary antineoplastic use of these drugs is in metastatic and recurrent endometrial carcinoma. They produce remissions for prolonged periods in about 25% of patients when the metastases are confined to the pulmonary area. Larger doses are necessary when the disease recurs in osseous, intra-abdominal, or pelvic sites. Progestagens are also used parenterally in renal carcinoma.

These progestational agents are generally well tolerated, but they may cause edema and local reactions at the site of injection.

For other uses, see the section on Estrogens and Progestagens in Chapter 37.

USUAL DOSAGE.—

Hydroxyprogesterone:

Intramuscular: 500 mg to 1.5 g twice weekly for disease involving the pulmonary area, and 2 to 5 g in divided doses weekly for recurring disease in osseous, intra-abdominal, and pelvic sites.

Medroxyprogesterone:

Intramuscular: 400 to 800 mg twice weekly.

Oral: 200 to 300 mg daily.

Megestrol Acetate:

Oral: Adults, 40 mg daily in divided doses.

PREPARATIONS.—

Hydroxyprogesterone:

Delalutin (Squibb). *Injection:* Solution (in oil) 125 mg/ml in 2 and 10 ml containers and 250 mg/ml in 1 and 5 ml containers.

Medroxyprogesterone:

Depo-Provera (Upjohn). *Injection:* Suspension (aqueous) 50 and 100 mg/ml in 1 and 5 ml containers.

Provera (Upjohn). *Oral:* Tablets 10 mg.

Megestrol Acetate:

Megace (Mead Johnson). *Oral:* Tablets 20 mg.

Radioactive Isotopes

GOLD AU 198 [Aurcoloid-198, Aureotope]

Radioactive gold is used principally in the treatment of pleural effusions and ascites secondary to cancer. Its effectiveness in pleural effusions apparently is comparable to that of mechlorethamine. Because radiation sickness may occur in some patients, the dose should be adjusted to insure minimal radiation exposure to the patient and laboratory personnel.

Gold Au 198 is contraindicated in patients with ulcerative tumors, unhealed surgical wounds, exposed cavities, or evidence of loculation. It should not be administered during pregnancy and lactation or to persons less than 18 years of age, nor should it be given more often than once every four weeks unless there is accumulation of fluid. Gold Au 198 is restricted for use by physicians licensed by the Atomic Energy Commission.

USUAL DOSAGE.—*Intrapleural, Intraperitoneal:* For pleural effusions, 35 to 75 millicuries [Aurcoloid-198] or 25 to 100 millicuries [Aureotope]. For ascites, 100 to 125 millicuries [Aurcoloid-198] or 35 to 100 millicuries [Aureotope].

PREPARATIONS.—

Aurcoloid-198 (Abbott). *Injection:* 40 to 90 millicuries per milliliter.

Aureotope (Squibb). *Injection:* 25 to 200 millicuries.

SODIUM PHOSPHATE P 32 [Phosphotope]

Sodium phosphate P 32 is used principally to treat the proliferative phase of polycythemia vera; it reduces the erythrocyte count, packed red blood cell volume, and hypervolemia. It is as effective as the alkylating agents for the palliative treatment of chronic myelocytic leukemia. When used concomitantly with local irradiation, radioactive phosphorus may control enlargement of the spleen in the early stages. It also may be helpful in some patients with chronic lymphocytic leukemia, but this type of leukemia usually responds more readily to other chemotherapeutic agents.

Although usual doses rarely cause radiation sickness, dosage should be adjusted individually to insure minimal radiation exposure to the patient and laboratory personnel. Excessive amounts can cause leukopenia, thrombocytopenia, and anemia. Periodic blood determinations are required. Sodium phosphate P 32 and the alkylating agents cannot be used in sequence to treat chronic myelocytic leukemia, for once resistance has developed to one agent there is no further response to the other. This agent is contraindicated in polycythemia vera when the leukocyte count is less than 5,000/mm^3 or the platelet count less than 150,000/mm^3, and in chronic myelocytic leukemia when the leukocyte count is less than 20,000/mm^3 and the red blood cell count less than 2,500,000/mm^3.

Treatment with sodium phosphate P 32 is restricted for use by physicians licensed by the Atomic Energy Commission.

USUAL DOSAGE.—

Oral: For polycythemia vera, initially, 6 millicuries.

Intravenous: For polycythemia vera, 3 to 5 millicuries (75% of oral dose), depending upon the initial erythrocyte, leukocyte, and platelet counts and the patient's weight. Phlebotomy may be used adjunctively. For chronic myelocytic leukemia, the initial dose is calculated on the basis of results of the leukocyte count (less than 40,000/mm^3, 3 millicuries; 40,000/mm^3 to 100,000/mm^3, 4 millicuries; more than 100,000/mm^3, 5 millicuries); subsequent doses are based upon the response of the patient.

PREPARATIONS.—

Phosphotope (Squibb).

Injection: Available in several potencies up to 50 millicuries.

Oral: Solutions available in several potencies up to 50 millicuries.

Sodium Phosphate P 32 (Abbott).

Injection: 1.5 millicuries/ml in 20, 25, and 30 millicurie containers.

Oral: Solutions in same concentrations as injection.

Chapter 89

VACCINES, TOXOIDS, AND SEROLOGIC AGENTS

Agents that produce either active or passive immunity are used to prevent or modify certain infectious diseases. Their use in routine immunization programs has resulted in a marked decrease in the incidence of some diseases in the United States (eg, diphtheria, pertussis, tetanus, smallpox, measles, poliomyelitis). When such immunization programs have been poorly designed or implemented (particularly among lower socioeconomic groups or in remote rural areas), outbreaks still occur. Recently, epidemics of measles and diphtheria have occurred in some communities, and poliomyelitis epidemics have been feared because of inadequate immunization programs. Thus, the importance of routine immunization procedures for both adults and children is evident. On the other hand, with the eradication of smallpox in this country, routine vaccination and revaccination of children and the general adult population is being abandoned because the hazards of vaccination now exceed the potential hazard of acquiring the disease.

Table 1 presents a suggested sequence for basic immunizations, including the age for initial dosage and a schedule for recall inoculations.

It is generally recommended that a live virus vaccine not be given within one month of any other live virus vaccine. This is to avoid a potential increase in adverse reactions or decrease in antibody response. If the one-month interval is not feasible because of uncertain continuity of the immunization schedule or exposure to more than one disease, the vaccines may be given on the same day, using different injection sites for the parenteral vaccines. Intervals of about two days to two weeks should be avoided because of the increased possibility of interference between the vaccine viruses during that period. However, clinical experience has shown that some live viruses can be given at the same time without interference (eg, smallpox and measles vaccines). Also trivalent and bivalent live virus vaccines combining certain antigens (ie, measles, mumps, rubella; mumps, rubella; measles, rubella) are available for simultaneous routine immunization. Measles vaccine and perhaps other live virus vaccines may interfere with reactivity to the tuberculin test.

Agents discussed in this chapter include those used for routine basic immunizations, those used for immunization procedures related to direct exposure or to enhanced susceptibility to infection (ie, rabies, tuberculosis [BCG], smallpox, influenza vaccines; some gamma globulin preparations), those recommended or required for foreign travel (ie, cholera, typhoid, typhus, yellow fever vaccines), and those for therapeutic use in special situations (eg, snake bite antivenin, various antitoxins, various immunoglobulins, including Rh immune globulin).

For current information on immunization requirements for foreign travel, local or state health departments or an office of the U.S. Public Health Service should be consulted.

Adverse Reactions

Any of the immunizing agents commonly used can produce undesirable, sometimes life-threatening reactions, not only in the individual being immunized, but occasionally in contacts of that individual. However, with few exceptions, the risk of unavoidable reactions is far less than the risk incurred by withholding immunization and, in most instances, does not constitute a valid contraindication to immunization. Adverse reactions may result either from the injected agents or from a foreign protein incorporated with the agent in its manufacture (eg, egg protein from chick embryo

TABLE 1.—RECOMMENDED PROCEDURES FOR IMMUNIZATION

Disease	*Preferred Age for Initial Dose*	*Immunizing Agent*	*Number of Doses*	*Dosage*	*Interval Between Doses*	*Booster*
Diphtheria Tetanus Pertussis[1]	2-3 months	Diphtheria and Tetanus Toxoid and Pertussis Vaccine Combined (DTP)	3	0.5 ml intramuscularly	4-6 weeks	0.5 ml 1 year after primary and 4-5 years later. Td every 10 years thereafter.
Tetanus and Diphtheria (Adult use)[1]	6 years and over	Tetanus and Diphtheria Toxoid, Adult Use (Td)	2	0.5 ml intramuscularly	4-6 weeks	0.5 ml 1 year after primary and every 10 years thereafter.
Poliomyelitis	2-3 months	Live Oral Poliovirus Vaccine Trivalent	4	As directed by manufacturer	6-8 weeks, second and third; 15-18 months, fourth	1 dose at entry into school.
Measles[2]	12 months	Live Measles Vaccine	1	0.5 ml subcutaneously		None now recommended.
Rubella[2]	Between age 1 and puberty	Live Rubella Vaccine	1	0.5 ml subcutaneously		None now recommended.
Mumps[2]	Between age 1 and puberty	Live Mumps Vaccine	1	0.5 ml subcutaneously		None now recommended.
Smallpox	See remarks[3]	Smallpox Vaccine	1			3-year intervals for high-risk groups

[1]When primary immunization or boosters are given over age 6, use Td. Use Td for subsequent boosters at 10-year intervals.

[2]May be given in bivalent or trivalent vaccine.

[3]At present, routine vaccination as part of pediatric immunization schedule is no longer recommended in the United States. Travelers to endemic or infected areas should be vaccinated before leaving, and hospital, medical, public health, and allied professional personnel should be revaccinated at 3-year intervals.

tissue cultures); they often may be avoided with appropriate precautions or minimized with immediate therapy.

Vaccination with live virus currently is contraindicated in patients receiving corticosteroids, antineoplastic agents, immunosuppressive agents, radiation therapy, and in those with agammaglobulinemia. Any vaccination generally should be deferred if the patient has an active infection.

The two major reactions that can follow an injection of hyperimmune serum of animal origin are anaphylaxis and serum sickness. Thus, skin or eye tests to determine sensitivity should be made before any such injection, regardless of whether or not the patient previously has received an injection of animal serum. The skin test dose is 0.02 ml of a 1:100 dilution of the serum injected intradermally; it may be reduced to 0.02 ml of a 1:1,000 dilution in persons with a history of allergy. The test is positive if a wheal appears within 30 minutes. For the eye test, one drop of 1:100 dilution of serum in isotonic sodium chloride solution is instilled in one eye; one drop of sodium chloride solution in the other eye serves as a control. The appearance of lacrimation and conjunctivitis within 30 minutes constitutes a positive reaction; the skin test is preferred because of the risk of a severe ocular reaction with the eye test.

If the sensitivity test is positive and the need for serum is imperative, the tolerance of the patient can be determined by injecting small, graded doses of the serum. For example, at 15-minute intervals, and if no reaction occurs, the following doses are injected: (1) 0.05 ml of 1:20 dilution, subcutaneously; (2) 0.1 ml of 1:10 dilution, subcutaneously; (3) 0.3 ml of 1:10 dilution, subcutaneously; (4) 0.1 ml of undiluted serum, subcutaneously; (5) 0.2 ml of undiluted serum, intramuscularly; (6) 0.5 ml of undiluted serum, intramuscularly; and (7) remaining dose, intramuscularly.

If anaphylactic reactions occur, 0.5 ml of epinephrine 1:1,000 for adults and proportionately less for children is immediately injected intravenously. The dose is repeated in 1 to 15 minutes if necessary. Antihistamines may be given intramuscularly to treat severe urticaria or angioedema.

Serum sickness, manifested by urticaria, lymphadenopathy, arthralgia, and fever, usually appears a few days or weeks after injection of serum. Usually the symptoms can be alleviated by the use of salicylates, antihistamines, and corticosteroids.

ROUTINE IMMUNIZING AGENTS

Diphtheria, Tetanus, and Pertussis

Diphtheria and tetanus toxoids and pertussis vaccine are important in the immunization of infants and are usually given together.

Diphtheria: Diphtheria is primarily a disease of childhood but does occur in all age groups. It is now uncommon in the United States, but localized outbreaks are reported occasionally. Diphtheria toxoid is universally accepted for active immunization against this disease: protective levels of antitoxin have persisted in adequately immunized persons for over ten years. Diphtheria antitoxin is given along with appropriate antibiotics to treat diphtheria.

Pertussis: Immunization against pertussis early in life is strongly recommended because this disease is highly communicable and because three-fourths of the deaths due to this disease occur in infants less than one year old. The widespread use of pertussis vaccine during the past 25 years has resulted in a dramatic decline in the number of cases and deaths. Since morbidity and mortality from pertussis decrease with age, immunization after age 6 (or after entrance into elementary school) usually is not required.

Tetanus: Despite a declining incidence, tetanus remains a public health problem. The solution lies in ensuring 100% active immunization in children and adults through a program of primary immunization and periodic boosters with tetanus toxoid. An immunizing course of tetanus toxoid is highly effective, produces few adverse reactions, and provides protection against tetanus for ten or more years.

A prime consideration in the treatment of contaminated wounds is whether to use tetanus toxoid for active immunization, or tetanus immune globulin or tetanus antitoxin for passive immunization. Tetanus antitoxin of human origin (tetanus immune globulin) is the preferred agent for passive immunization. Tetanus antitoxin of equine or bovine origin may be used if human tetanus immune globulin is not available. However, its use should be preceded by careful testing for sensitivity and *the risk of serious reactions following injection of antitoxin of animal origin should be borne in mind.* Inasmuch as complete primary immunization provides long-lasting protection against tetanus and an anamnestic response to a booster dose develops rapidly in patients who have previously received at least two doses of tetanus toxoid, the use of passive immunization is necessary only when the patient has received less than two doses of tetanus toxoid or treatment of the wound has been delayed for more than 24 hours. Tetanus toxoid should be administered at the same time as tetanus immune globulin but at a different site and with a different syringe. The complete series of primary immunization injections should be given if the patient has had less than two doses of tetanus toxoid previously or if his immunization history is uncertain. The current recommendation of the Public Health Service Advisory Committee on Immunization Practices is that booster doses of tetanus toxoid are necessary no more often than every five years in individuals who have undergone complete primary immunization.

Single Antigens

DIPHTHERIA TOXOID

Diphtheria toxoid, a preparation of detoxified growth products of *Corynebacterium diphtheriae*, is available in fluid form and in precipitated or adsorbed form; the latter is preferred. For primary immunization of infants and young children, it usually is given in combination with tetanus toxoid and pertussis vaccine (DTP). Diphtheria toxoid also is combined with tetanus toxoid without pertussis vaccine in pediatric preparations (DT) and, in reduced amounts, in adult preparations (Td). Diphtheria toxoid is sometimes used alone in infants, young children, and adults who have had severe reactions to DTP.

As with all vaccine preparations, precautions for prevention and arrest of allergic reactions should be observed. Tenderness at the site of injection and, rarely, fever, malaise, myalgia, or sterile abscess may occur.

The Moloney test (0.1 ml of a 1:10 dilution of fluid toxoid intradermally) should be performed before giving diphtheria toxoid to an older child or adult. A positive test (severe pseudoSchick reaction) indicates sensitization to diphtheria toxoid and a need for caution in its administration. See also the evaluations on various combinations of diphtheria toxoid with tetanus toxoid and pertussis vaccine.

USUAL DOSAGE.—*Intramuscular, Subcutaneous (fluid toxoid); Intramuscular (adsorbed toxoid):* For initial active immunization, 0.5 to 1 ml at four- to six-week intervals for a total of two (adsorbed toxoid) or three (fluid toxoid) doses. A booster dose is given 6 to 12 months later.

PREPARATIONS.—Diphtheria Toxoid, U.S.P.; Adsorbed Diphtheria Toxoid, U.S.P. Marketed under generic name.

PERTUSSIS VACCINE

Pertussis vaccine is a suspension of killed pertussis bacilli *(Bordetella pertussis)* and is available in fluid and in precipitated or adsorbed form; the latter is preferred. It usually is given in combination with diphtheria and tetanus toxoids (DTP) but may be used alone for primary immunization of infants when DTP is contraindicated (eg, patients who have experienced an adverse reaction to DTP, especially infants with neurologic disorders). If a central nervous system reaction occurs with this modified schedule, immunization should be deferred until the child is at least one year old and evidence of active cerebral irritation has subsided. Some authorities believe that further injections of pertussis vaccine are contraindicated because of the possible occurrence of severe reactions.

Adverse reactions reported include fever, malaise, and myalgia. Formation of sterile abscesses is rare. Severe central nervous system reactions and some deaths have occurred rarely following administration of pertussis vaccine to individuals of any age. However, the incidence of such adverse reactions is lower than the incidence of similar adverse effects of the disease itself. About 80% of cases of pertussis occur in the first five years of life, and fatal cases rarely occur in older patients. Because of this pattern of morbidity and mortality and an apparent increase in the incidence of adverse reactions with age, use of the vaccine after the sixth year generally is not advisable.

See also the evaluation on Diphtheria and Tetanus Toxoids and Pertussis Vaccine (DTP).

USUAL DOSAGE.—*Subcutaneous: Children 2 months to 6 years of age*, 4 N.I.H. units (0.5 ml) at four-to six-week intervals for three doses; a fourth injection should be given about one year after completion of the initial course, and a recall injection upon entry into school. Recall injections upon intimate exposure to pertussis may be given to *children up to 6 years of age.* If a recall injection is indicated for a *child over 6 years,* one-half of the usual dose of pertussis vaccine should be given. In children with neurologic disorders or those who have had an untoward reaction to DTP, the total dose of 12 protective units for primary immunization should be given in smaller, spaced doses of 0.05 or 0.1 ml.

PREPARATIONS.—Pertussis Vaccine, U.S.P., Adsorbed Pertussis Vaccine, U.S.P. Marketed under generic name.

TETANUS TOXOID

Tetanus toxoid is a sterile preparation of detoxified growth products of *Clostridium tetani*. It is available in fluid and in precipitated or adsorbed form; the latter is preferred. This agent usually is given in combination with diphtheria toxoid and pertussis vaccine (DTP) for primary immunization of infants and young children. Tetanus toxoid alone is indicated for primary immunization of adults and of children in whom DTP is contraindicated, and for prophylaxis of tetanus-prone wounds in previously immunized patients.

Reactions occur infrequently; they include erythema, induration, and tenderness at the site of injection. Fever and malaise may occur more rarely. The incidence of untoward reactions may be higher in individuals over 25 years of age. A small nodule may form at the site of subcutaneous injection of the alum precipitated material, but this usually disappears in a few weeks. See also the evaluations on various combinations of tetanus toxoid with diphtheria toxoid and pertussis vaccine.

USUAL DOSAGE.—*Subcutaneous (fluid); Intramuscular (adsorbed): Adults*, initially, 0.5 ml; this dose is repeated one month later, one year following the second injection, and every ten years thereafter. *Children*, 0.5 ml given at 1½ to 2 months, 2½ to 3 months, 3½ to 4 months, 16 months, 5 years, and every 10 years thereafter.

Opinion is emerging that prophylactic tetanus toxoid booster injections are not necessary unless primary immunization was completed or the last booster injection given more than five years earlier in the case of severe, contaminated wounds or more than 10 years earlier in the case of clean, minor wounds. (See also the Introductory Statement.)

PREPARATIONS.—Tetanus Toxoid, U.S.P.; Adsorbed Tetanus Toxoid, U.S.P. Marketed under generic name.

Combined Antigens

DIPHTHERIA AND TETANUS TOXOIDS (DT)

Diphtheria and tetanus toxoids, pediatric type (DT) may be used for primary immunization and recall injections in children up to 6 years of age when pertussis vaccine should be given separately or omitted. Thus, the indications for its use are limited. This preparation is available in fluid form and in precipitated or adsorbed form; the latter is preferred. Tetanus and diphtheria toxoids, adult type (Td), which contains a reduced amount of diphtheria toxoid, should be used in older children and adults; the triple antigen combination is preferred for routine immunization of infants and preschool age children (see the individual evaluations).

As with other immunization procedures, use of combined diphtheria and tetanus toxoids should be deferred in the presence of active infection or acute respiratory tract disease. (See also the Introductory Statement.)

USUAL DOSAGE.—*Intramuscular, Subcutaneous: Infants and children up to six years of age*, three 0.5 ml doses of fluid DT or two 0.5 ml doses of adsorbed DT at intervals of at least four weeks. A booster injection is given one year later and at the time of entering school.

PREPARATIONS.—Diphtheria and Tetanus Toxoids, U.S.P.; Adsorbed Diphtheria and Tetanus Toxoids, U.S.P. Marketed under generic name.

DIPHTHERIA AND TETANUS TOXOIDS AND PERTUSSIS VACCINE (DTP)

This combination of diphtheria and tetanus toxoids with pertussis vaccine is the recommended preparation for routine primary immunization and recall (booster) injections in children under 6 years of age. It is available both in fluid form and in precipitated or adsorbed form; the latter is preferred because its slower absorption increases its immunogenicity.

The combined triple antigens are not recommended after the sixth year because of the increased possibility of severe local and sometimes generalized reactions. Pertussis antigen is the ingredient most often responsible. Tetanus and diphtheria toxoids, adult type (Td), may be used for primary immunization of patients over six years of age; diphtheria and tetanus toxoids, pediatric type (DT), may be used in younger children. (See the individual evaluations.)

The more common untoward effects include transient fever with localized tenderness, erythema, and induration at the site of injection. If these reactions occur, subsequent doses should be reduced. Reactions involving the central nervous system may occur after any injection in a course and may be manifested by convulsions, infantile massive spasms, hypsarhythmia, pseudotumor cerebri, or acute disseminated encephalomyelitis. The incidence of these reactions has been estimated to be less than 1:1,000,000; however, it is generally recommended that immunizations be withheld or given in fractional doses when the patient has epilepsy or other central nervous system diseases or an allergic disorder. Any central nervous system reaction after one injection is generally regarded as a contraindication to further immunization with pertussis antigen. See also the section on Adverse Reactions in the Introductory Statement.

USUAL DOSAGE.—*Intramuscular, Subcutaneous: Children*, initially, 0.5 or 1 ml at 2 months of age, followed by two more doses at four-week intervals. A fourth dose is given 7 to 12 months after the third and a booster dose is given at five to six years of age. This preparation should not be used in patients over six years of age. (See the manufacturer's recommendations for volume dose of preparation used.)

PREPARATIONS.—Diphtheria and Tetanus Toxoids and Pertussis Vaccine, U.S.P.; Adsorbed Diphtheria and Tetanus Toxoids and Pertussis Vaccine, U.S.P.

AVAILABLE TRADEMARKS.—Infagen (Dow), Tri-Immunol (Lederle), Triogen (Parke, Davis), Triple Antigen (Wyeth), Tri-Solgen (Lilly). Also marketed under generic name.

TETANUS AND DIPHTHERIA TOXOIDS, ADSORBED (Td)

Tetanus and diphtheria toxoids, adsorbed, adult type (Td), is used for primary immunization or recall (booster) injections in adults and children over six years of age. It contains the same amount of tetanus toxoid as other preparations but only 15% to 20% of the amount of diphtheria toxoid.

Reactions to Td are usually mild in patients under 20 years of age. They include erythema, induration, and tenderness at the site of injection; fever and malaise also may occur. Systemic reactions may occur in older patients; these are believed to be due to the diphtheria toxoid component, but because of the reduced amount of diphtheria toxoid present, use of the Moloney test to determine sensitivity and avoid these reactions is not considered necessary. See also the Introductory Statement and evaluations on the individual toxoids.

USUAL DOSAGE.—*Intramuscular: Adults and children over six years of age*, two injections of 0.5 ml with an interval of at least four weeks between injections. A recall (booster) injection is given one year later and every 10 years thereafter.

PREPARATIONS.—Adsorbed Tetanus and Diphtheria Toxoids, U.S.P. Marketed under generic name.

Measles, Mumps, and Rubella

Measles: Widespread use of measles virus vaccines led to a 95% reduction in the overall incidence of measles, but unfortunately immunization efforts have lapsed in some areas with a consequent resurgence of measles cases. At present it is generally believed that a single inoculation with live, attenuated measles virus vaccine will confer lifelong protection. Atypical measles following exposure to natural measles has occasionally appeared in children previously inoculated with killed measles vaccine, and marked local reactions (eg, induration, edema) have occurred when live measles vaccine was administered to patients who had previously received inactivated vaccine. The latter is no longer marketed.

Mumps: Live attenuated mumps virus vaccine provides active immunity in more than 95% of recipients over one year of age. The duration of immunity without revaccination is unknown, but current observations indicate continuing protection after six years. Adverse reactions have been uncommon and mild.

Rubella: Antibodies develop in 96% to 98% of vaccinated individuals receiving live rubella virus vaccines, although titers are lower than those observed following natural infection. Thus far, antibodies have been shown to persist in vaccinees for five years, although at declining levels. Nevertheless, reinfection with wild virus is common in vaccinees and occurs to a lesser extent in naturally immune subjects.

Single Antigens

MEASLES VIRUS VACCINE, LIVE, ATTENUATED

Live attenuated measles virus vaccine is a bacteriologically sterile preparation containing the original Edmonston B strain of modified measles (rubeola) virus or the so-called Schwarz or Moraten further attenuated strains. Edmonston B vaccines are grown in either chick embryo or canine renal cell culture. Further attenuated strains are grown only in chick embryo cell culture.

These vaccines induce active immunity in approximately 99% of recipients after a single dose. They produce a noncommunicable, mild measles infection. With Edmonston B vaccine, about 80% of vaccinated individuals experience a febrile response beginning about the sixth day following inoculation and lasting two to five days; a rectal temperature of 103 F (39.4 C) or higher on at least one reading during this time may be expected in about one-third of patients. A modified measles rash appears in about 40% of patients, usually during defervescence. A few persons develop a mild cough and coryza. Antibody titers produced by the Edmonston B vaccine approximate those occurring after the natural disease. The incidence of fever and rash may be reduced by giving measles immune globulin (0.02 ml/kg of body weight) in another extremity; resulting antibody titers are lower than those following Edmonston B vaccine alone. The Schwarz and Moraten strains are recommended for use without concomitant administration of measles immune globulin; the incidence of hyperpyrexia and rash following administration of Schwarz and Moraten strain vaccines is comparable to that occurring after the administration of Edmonston B vaccine and immune globulin. The level and duration of immunity produced is equally satisfactory. Combinations of measles virus vaccine with live mumps and rubella virus vaccines are available.

Rarely, convulsions associated with fever have occurred after the use of live, attenuated measles virus vaccine. Other reactions that have been observed rarely are thrombocytopenia and purpura and central nervous system reactions (eg, acute disseminated encephalomyelitis). Swelling, erythema, and vesiculation at the site of injection have occurred in children who previously received killed measles virus vaccine. No allergic effects have been reported after administration of live measles vaccine prepared from chick embryo tissue to persons with known allergy to egg protein. However, vaccine prepared from dog renal cell culture is preferred in persons know to have marked hypersensitivity to eggs.

Measles virus vaccine is contraindicated in the presence of leukemias, lymphomas, and other generalized malignancies; untreated active tuberculosis or any febrile illness or upper respiratory tract infection; and during pregnancy. The vaccine also is contraindicated in patients being treated with agents that may interfere with immune mechanisms (eg, corticosteroids, irradiation, antineoplastic agents). Vaccination should be postponed for three months after administration of immune serum globulin, whole blood, or plasma, since the measles virus antibody content may be sufficient to neutralize the vaccine virus.

USUAL DOSAGE.—

Measles virus vaccine, live, attenuated (Edmonston B): The vaccine may be administered alone, although its use with measles immune globulin reduces the incidence of febrile reactions. *Subcutaneous: Children 1 year of age or older*, a single 0.5 ml dose of the reconstituted vaccine is injected in the upper arm. An intramuscular dose of 0.02 ml of measles immune globulin/kg of body weight may be injected concomitantly (with a different syringe) into the deltoid muscle of the opposite arm.

Measles virus vaccine, live, attenuated (Schwarz, Moraten): *Subcutaneous: Children 1 year of age or older*, single dose of the reconstituted vaccine is given in the deltoid muscle.

PREPARATIONS.—Live Attenuated Measles Virus Vaccine, U.S.P. *Injection:* Suspension in single-dose (0.5 ml) containers.

AVAILABLE TRADEMARKS.—

Edmonston B (chick embryo): M-Vac (Lederle). Form also marketed under generic name. **Schwarz:** Lirugen (Dow). **Moraten:** Attenuvax (Merck Sharp & Dohme).

Edmonston B (canine renal cell culture): Measles Virus Vaccine, Live, Attenuated (Philips Roxane).

MUMPS VACCINE

Mumps vaccine is a suspension of killed mumps virus grown in chick embryo. Complement fixation and virus neutralizing antibodies rise within a week or more after a single injection and decline to low levels within six months. A booster injection six months to one year after the first dose induces a secondary response that exceeds the initial one. The duration of immunity is not known; thus, live attenuated mumps virus vaccine is preferred over killed mumps vaccine.

Local and systemic reactions are usually mild, but may be severe in individuals immune to mumps. Adults should receive a skin test for sensitivity to mumps virus; the vaccine should not be administered if the test is positive. The vaccine used for immunization is not suitable for use in skin testing. Mumps skin test antigen is available for this purpose.

USUAL DOSAGE.—*Subcutaneous: Adults and children*, two doses of 1 ml each at an interval of one to four weeks.

PREPARATIONS.—Mumps Vaccine (Lederle, Lilly). *Injection:* Suspension in 2 and 10 ml containers.

MUMPS VIRUS VACCINE, LIVE, ATTENUATED [Mumpsvax]

Live attenuated mumps virus vaccine is a suspension of the Jeryl Lynn strain of mumps virus grown in chick embryo tissue culture. It provides active immunity against mumps in more than 95% of recipients following a single subcutaneous injection. Neutralizing circulating antibodies and continuing protection against mumps are present for at least six years after immunization. Children one year or older may be vaccinated at any time. The vaccine is of particular value in susceptible individuals approaching puberty and in adolescents and adults. Combinations of mumps vaccine with live measles and rubella virus vaccines are available.

Adverse reactions are uncommon and mild. A few instances of fever or tenderness at the site of injection have been reported, but no signs of clinical mumps have been observed. The occasional case of mumps subsequent to vaccination is thought to be due to coincidental occurrence of the natural disease.

The vaccine is contraindicated in patients known to be sensitive to eggs, chicken, chicken feathers, or neomycin, since traces of the latter may remain in the final products. It also is contraindicated during pregnancy, in patients with agammaglobulinemia, in those receiving immunosuppressive therapy (eg, corticosteroids, irradiation, antineoplastic agents), or in those with active infection, unless clinical mumps poses a greater risk. It should not be given within one month of other elective immunization procedures.

USUAL DOSAGE.—*Subcutaneous: Adults and children,* the total volume of reconstituted vaccine is administered. The reconstituted vaccine retains potency for eight hours at 4 C and should be discarded if not used before that time.

PREPARATIONS.—Mumpsvax (Merck Sharp & Dohme). *Injection:* Lyophilized powder in single-dose containers with diluent.

RUBELLA VIRUS VACCINE, LIVE [Cendevax, Meruvax, Rubelogen]

Live rubella virus vaccine is a suspension of attenuated rubella virus derived from either the Parkman and Meyer (HPV-77) or Cendehill strains. The former is grown on either dog kidney or duck embryo cell cultures; the latter is prepared in primary cultures of rabbit kidney cells. Vaccination against rubella is recommended for children between one year of age and puberty; in infants less than one year, the presence of maternal rubella antibody levels may prevent an immune response to rubella virus vaccine. Circulating rubella antibody levels are detectable in 96% to 98% of subjects within the first few weeks following vaccination; these levels have been shown to persist essentially unchanged for as long as five years, suggesting active immunity of long duration. The antibody levels produced by vaccine virus are somewhat lower than those resulting from the natural disease. The vaccine should not be given within one month of any other vaccination, and its use should be deferred six weeks after blood transfusion or immune serum globulin therapy. Since most postpubertal males are immune, the vaccine should not be given to them except during an epidemic. Combinations of rubella virus vaccine with live measles and mumps virus vaccines also are available.

Infrequent adverse reactions include low-grade fever with induration, erythema, and tenderness at the site of injection. Regional adenopathy has occurred. More annoying have been transient arthritis and arthralgia, especially in women, that appear two to six weeks after vaccination. Joint effusions have been noted rarely. The incidence and severity of joint symptoms have been reported to be less with the Cendehill strain.

Depending upon the type of cell culture in which the vaccine virus is grown, care should be exercised in administering these vaccines to persons known to be hypersensitive to dogs, dog dander, ducks, or rabbits. Persons sensitive to neomycin should not be vaccinated. Appropriate precautions should be taken to treat any anaphylactic or acute hypersensitivity reactions that might occur. Vaccination should be avoided in patients with leukemias, lymphomas, or generalized malignancy or in those being treated with corticosteroids, cytotoxic drugs, or irradiation. Vaccination should be postponed in the presence of a febrile illness. Rubella virus vaccine is contraindicated in pregnant women. Women of childbearing age may be considered for vaccination when there is no expectation of pregnancy during the following two months (eg, during the early postpartum period). If vaccination is contemplated, the woman should be tested by the hemagglutination inhibition (HI) test for susceptibility; vaccination is unnecessary if the patient is immune.

The vaccine should be refrigerated and protected from light. It must remain refrigerated after reconstitution and should be discarded if not used within eight hours.

USUAL DOSAGE.—*Subcutaneous: Adults and children*, the total volume of reconstituted vaccine is injected in the outer aspect of the upper arm after suitable cleansing. Vaccine should not be injected intravenously or intramuscularly.

PREPARATIONS.—Cendevax (Smith Kline & French), Meruvax (Merck Sharp & Dohme), Rubelogen (Parke, Davis). *Injection:* Lyophilized powder in single-dose containers with diluent. Vaccine also marketed under generic name.

Combined Antigens

MEASLES, MUMPS, AND RUBELLA VIRUS VACCINE, LIVE [M-M-R]

Live measles, mumps, and rubella virus vaccine is a suspension of the same attenuated viruses present in equivalent monovalent vaccines. The measles and mumps viruses are grown in chick embryo cell cultures, and the rubella virus is grown in duck embryo cell cultures. The vaccine is indicated for simultaneous routine immunization of children one year of age or older. It may be used up to the age of puberty in patients who have not previously been vaccinated against or experienced any of these natural infections. Clinical studies have shown that the vaccine produces antibody levels comparable to those produced by each monovalent vaccine given at properly spaced intervals; the degree of protection against natural disease is also comparable.

Adverse reactions generally are mild and are the same as those associated with the individual monovalent vaccines (eg, fever, rash, local reactions, thrombocytopenia, urticaria, arthritis, arthralgia, polyneuropathy). The vaccine is contraindicated in patients sensitive to neomycin, chicken, duck, or chicken or duck eggs or feathers. It should not be given to patients who should not receive any of the monovalent vaccines (see the individual evaluations).

USUAL DOSAGE.—*Subcutaneous: Children over one year of age up to puberty*, entire single dose.

PREPARATIONS.—M-M-R (Merck Sharp & Dohme). *Injection:* Lyophilized vaccine in single-dose containers.

MEASLES AND RUBELLA VACCINE, LIVE [M-R-Vax]

Live measles and rubella vaccine is a suspension of the same attenuated viruses present in equivalent monovalent vaccines (Moraten strain grown in chick embryo cell cultures and HPV-77 rubella propagated in duck embryo cell cultures). Available evidence indicates that it produces antibodies against measles in 99% of susceptible children and against rubella in 95%.

Adverse reactions and precautions are the same as those associated with the two monovalent vaccines (see the individual evaluations).

USUAL DOSAGE.—*Subcutaneous: Children and adults*, 0.5 ml in outer aspect of upper arm.

PREPARATIONS.—M-R-Vax (Merck Sharp & Dohme). *Injection:* Powder for reconstitution in 1- and 10-dose containers.

RUBELLA AND MUMPS VIRUS VACCINE, LIVE [Biavax]

Live rubella and mumps virus vaccine is a suspension of the same attenuated viruses present in the equivalent monovalent vaccines. The rubella virus is grown in duck embryo cell cultures, and the mumps virus is grown in chick embryo cell cultures. The vaccine is used for simultaneous routine immunization of children one year of age to puberty who have been vaccinated against measles or experienced the natural disease but have no history of immunizing exposure to rubella and mumps viruses. The vaccine produces antibody levels comparable to those produced by each of the monovalent vaccines given separately; the degree of protection against natural disease is also comparable.

Adverse reactions are generally mild and are the same as those associated with the individual monovalent vaccines (eg, fever, rash, local reactions, thrombocytopenia, urticaria, arthritis, arthralgia, polyneuropathy). The vaccine is contraindicated in patients sensitive to neomycin, chicken, duck, or chicken or duck eggs or feathers. It should not be given to patients who should not receive either of the monovalent vaccines. (See the evaluations on Mumps Virus Vaccine, Live, Attenuated and Rubella Virus Vaccine, Live.)

USUAL DOSAGE.—*Subcutaneous: Children one year of age to puberty*, total volume of reconstituted vaccine.

PREPARATIONS.—Biavax (Merck Sharp & Dohme). *Injection:* Lyophilized vaccine in single-dose containers with diluent.

Poliomyelitis

Active immunization against paralytic poliomyelitis may be induced either by oral administration of the attenuated, live oral poliovirus (Sabin) vaccine or by injection of the formaldehyde-inactivated poliomyelitis (Salk) vaccine. The live, oral poliovirus vaccine is available in a trivalent form that combines types I, II, and III, and in individual monovalent forms. Live oral poliovirus vaccine is now the agent of choice because it is easier to administer, does not require booster doses, and produces a longer-lasting immunity resembling that induced by natural poliovirus infection. The separate monovalent types of live oral poliovirus vaccines offer no advantages over the trivalent form for routine immunization but may be useful in a threatened epidemic when the type of the causative virus has been identified.

Routine immunization for adults living in the continental United States is unnecessary because exposure is unlikely. However, any nonimmunized adult who might contact a known case (eg, hospital, medical, and sanitation laboratory employees) or those who live in or travel to epidemic or endemic areas should receive trivalent oral poliovirus vaccine according to the schedule outlined for children and adolescents.

POLIOMYELITIS VACCINE

Poliomyelitis vaccine is a sterile suspension of formaldehyde-inactivated Types I, II, and III strains of poliovirus obtained by propagation in monkey kidney tissue culture. It produces active immunity against paralytic poliomyelitis by stimulating production of serum antibodies specific for Types I, II, and III poliovirus, although it does not decrease the incidence of nonparalytic poliomyelitis. However, repeated booster doses every two years are necessary for maintenance of antibody levels. Poliomyelitis vaccine is now used infrequently.

Local and systemic reactions after inoculation are infrequent and generally mild. Occasionally, headache, stiff neck, sore throat, vomiting, malaise, and a brief, low-grade fever occur. Allergic reactions occur rarely and may be due to small amounts of antibiotics present. It is advisable not to administer the vaccine to patients during an acute illness or under other conditions which could interfere with the immune response mechanism. Allergic individuals should be given an intradermal test dose initially and observed for possible sensitivity to the vaccine.

USUAL DOSAGE.—*Subcutaneous, Intramuscular (dry-needle technique): Adults and children,* a basic course of inoculation requires four 1 ml doses; the first three are given at monthly intervals, and the fourth 6 to 12 months later. For *infants,* the schedule is integrated with other basic immunizations. For maintenance of antibody levels, repeated biennial booster doses are necessary.

PREPARATIONS.—Poliomyelitis Vaccine, U.S.P. *Injection:* Suspension in 10 ml containers. Marketed under generic name.

POLIOVIRUS VACCINE, LIVE, ORAL

Live oral poliovirus vaccine (OPV) contains attenuated poliovirus grown in monkey kidney tissue culture or human cell culture; it is available both in trivalent and monovalent preparations containing Types I, II, and III. It produces an immune response resembling that induced by natural poliovirus infection, ie, it multiplies and stimulates intestinal immunity as well as circulating antibodies, and the immunity is longer lasting than that following administration of killed poliomyelitis vaccine. Poliovirus vaccine is easily administered, and immunity is achieved rapidly. In susceptible individuals, a rise in type-specific serum neutralizing antibody titer begins about one week after ingestion of monovalent vaccine and reaches a peak about three weeks later. A primary series of three adequately spaced doses of trivalent oral poliovirus vaccine will produce an immune response to the three virus types in over 90% of recipients. Both the monovalent and trivalent poliovirus vaccines have been used successfully, but the latter is more commonly used because it is equally effective and record-keeping is simplified.

Live, oral poliovirus vaccine is recommended for all infants and children regardless of the number of doses of inactivated poliomyelitis vaccine that they may have received. Routine immunization of adults living in the United States is unnecessary except for those at increased risk of infection.

Rarely, paralysis has occurred in those receiving oral poliovirus vaccine, or in close contacts, within two months following administration. Tonsillectomy and adenoidectomy are not contraindications to its use, and pregnancy is not a contraindication when immunization is required. The vaccine should not be administered if the patient has diarrhea. Immunization is contraindicated in conditions in which the immune state of the recipient may be altered. These include lymphomas, leukemias, and generalized malignancies, as well as various therapeutic regimens that may lead to lowered resistance (eg, corticosteroids, antineoplastic agents, antimetabolites, irradiation).

USUAL DOSAGE.—

Poliovirus Vaccine, Live, Oral, Trivalent:

Oral: Each dose of trivalent poliovirus vaccine contains approximately 800,000 tissue culture infective doses ($TCID_{50}$) of Type I vaccine, 100,000 of Type II, and 500,000 of Type III in 2 drops or 2 ml, depending upon the concentration used. For primary immunization, three doses are administered. *Infants,* the first dose is given at 2 months of age and the second and third at six- to eight-week intervals thereafter. A fourth dose should be given at approximately 15 to 18 months. *Children and adolescents,* the first two doses should be given six to eight weeks apart, and the third 8 to 12 months after the second dose. All children who have completed the series should be given a single booster dose upon entering school.

Poliovirus Vaccine, Live, Oral, Type I, II, or III:

Oral: Monovalent vaccines (Types I, II, and III) are given separately in three doses. Each dose contains 200,000 to 500,000 tissue culture infective doses ($TCID_{50}$) in 2 or 3 drops, or 2 ml, depending upon the preparation used. For primary immunization, the vaccine is administered in the order of Type I, III, and II. *Infants,* three doses given separately at intervals of six to eight weeks. A fourth dose consisting of trivalent oral poliovirus vaccine should be given at 12 to 15 months of age. *Children and adolescents,* three doses given separately at intervals of six to eight weeks. A fourth dose, consisting of the trivalent vaccine, is given after an interval of 8 to 12 months.

PREPARATIONS.—

Poliovirus Vaccine, Live, Oral, Trivalent (human cell culture):

Diplovax (Pfizer). *Oral:* Suspension 2 drops/dose in 10-dose containers and 0.5 ml/dose in single-dose containers.

Poliovirus Vaccine, Live, Oral, Trivalent (monkey kidney):

Orimune Trivalent (Lederle). *Oral:* Suspension 2 drops/dose in 10-dose containers and 0.5 or 2 ml/dose in single-dose containers.

Poliovirus Vaccine, Live, Oral, Type I, II, or III:

Orimune Monovalent (Lederle). *Oral:* Suspension 2 ml/dose in single-dose containers and 2 drops/dose in 10-dose containers.

MISCELLANEOUS VACCINES

CHOLERA VACCINE

Cholera vaccine is a sterile suspension of killed cholera organisms *(Vibrio cholerae).* It contains eight billion killed vibrio organisms per milliliter. Higher concentrations produce severe local and systemic reactions. Cholera vaccine is indicated only for persons who travel into endemic areas; it should not be given to contacts of imported cases or used for controlling spread of the infection. Many countries require evidence of cholera vaccination (a *validated* International Certificate of Vaccination) for entry, but vaccination is no longer required for persons coming to the United States from cholera-infected areas. The vaccine presently available is of limited usefulness. It provides only about 50% effectiveness for three to six months and does not prevent transmission of the disease.

Serious reactions have been reported rarely. Malaise and fever may occur. Induration and erythema may occur at the site of injection. The vaccine is contraindicated in individuals who have had a serious reaction to previous injections.

USUAL DOSAGE.—*Intramuscular, Subcutaneous:* Primary immunization consists of two doses one week to one month apart; booster doses should be given at six-month intervals. *Adults and children over 10 years of age,* first dose, 0.5 ml; second dose, 1 ml; booster doses, 0.5 ml. *Children under 5 years,* first dose, 0.1 ml; second dose, 0.3 ml; booster doses, 0.3 ml. *Children 5 to 10 years,* first dose, 0.3 ml; second dose, 0.5 ml; booster doses, 0.5 ml. Booster doses are effective no matter how prolonged the interval after the primary series.

PREPARATIONS.—Cholera Vaccine, U.S.P. Marketed under generic name.

INFLUENZA VIRUS VACCINE, BIVALENT

Influenza virus vaccine, bivalent contains formaldehyde-inactivated influenza types A and B grown in embryonated chicken eggs. Because both influenza virus types undergo antigen changes, the influenza vaccine formulation is reviewed regularly and is reformulated when necessary to include the contemporary antigens.

The effectiveness of influenza virus vaccine has been variable and protection is relatively brief. Because of this and the frequency of uncomfortable adverse effects, this preparation is not indicated for use in healthy adults, children, and infants. It use should be considered for persons of all ages for whom influenza infection represents a serious risk (eg, elderly persons; nursing home patients; and those with chronic cardiovascular, bronchopulmonary, or renal diseases, diabetes mellitus, or adrenocortical insufficiency). Annual vaccinations are needed for persons who have chronic debilitating conditions.

Common adverse reactions include fever, malaise, myalgia, and pain at the site of injection. The incidence of adverse reactions may be reduced by use of the new highly purified vaccines. The vaccine is contraindicated in patients sensitive to eggs, chickens, or chicken feathers.

USUAL DOSAGE.—*Subcutaneous:* Primary immunization consists of two doses given six to eight weeks apart, scheduled for completion by mid-November. A single booster dose is sufficient in patients who received a primary series after the 1968-1969 season; others require a primary series to develop immunity against the Hong Kong strain. Doses should be in the volume recommended by the individual manufacturer. For children's dosages, see the manufacturer's labeling.

AVAILABLE TRADEMARKS.—Fluax (Merck Sharp & Dohme), Flu-Imune (Lederle), Fluogen (Parke, Davis), Fluzone (Merrell-National), Zonomune (Lilly). Vaccine also marketed under generic name.

PLAGUE VACCINE

Plague vaccine is prepared from *Yersinia pestis* grown on artificial media, killed with formaldehyde, and preserved with 0.5% phenol. Its use generally is restricted to persons traveling to Vietnam, Cambodia, or Laos; those whose work brings them into frequent contact with wild rodents in plague enzootic areas; and laboratory personnel working with *Yersinia pestis* or infected rodents. Immunization with plague vaccine apparently reduces the incidence and severity of plague, but definitive evaluation has not yet been accomplished.

Possible adverse reactions include myalgia, fever, and pain at the site of injection.

USUAL DOSAGE.—*Intramuscular: Adults and children over 10 years of age,* for primary vaccination, two 0.5 ml doses four or more weeks apart, followed by a third dose of 0.2 ml 4 to 12 weeks after the second injection. Previously vaccinated individuals need only two 0.5 ml doses, 28 days apart. *Children under 10 years of age* receive the same series but at a reduced dosage as follows: *infants under 1 year,* one-fifth adult dose; *1 to 4 years,* two-fifths adult dose; *5 to 10 years,* three-fifths adult dose. Booster doses should be given at 6- to 12-month intervals as long as the risk of infection exists. A satisfactory booster dose is that recommended for the third dose of the primary series.

PREPARATIONS.—Plague Vaccine, U.S.P. Marketed under generic name.

RABIES VACCINE

Rabies vaccine is a sterile suspension of killed, fixed rabies virus obtained from rabbit brain tissues or duck embryo tissues infected with fixed rabies virus. The virus in nervous tissue vaccine from rabbit brain is inactivated with phenol or ultraviolet irradiation, and that in duck embryo vaccine with beta-propiolactone. Although the antigenicity of nervous tissue vaccine is often higher than that of duck embryo vaccine when tested in animals, treatment-failure rates for the two vaccines are not significantly different. Duck embryo vaccine is preferable to nervous tissue vaccine, because severe, neuroparalytic reactions occur more frequently following use of the latter.

Pre-exposure immunoprophylaxis with rabies vaccine (duck embryo) is recommended for persons with an unusually high risk of exposure (eg, veterinarians, animal handlers, persons engaged in experimental canine or feline surgery, laboratory personnel working with rabies virus, spelunkers).

Both laboratory data and clinical experience indicate that postexposure prophylaxis against rabies is usually effective when properly applied, although failures do occur. Postexposure immunoprophylaxis is based on the assumption that every animal biting a person should be considered rabid until proved otherwise; thus, each case must be evaluated individually.

Domestic animals should be isolated and observed by a veterinarian for ten days after the bite. If the animal develops no clinical signs of rabies during this period, it can be considered that no exposure to rabies occurred. However, if the animal suspected of having rabies is killed or dies, the head should be sent to the local health authority for confirmatory diagnosis. According

TABLE 2.—GUIDE FOR POSTEXPOSURE IMMUNOPROPHYLAXIS AGAINST RABIES*

Nature of Exposure	Status of Biting Animal (Whether Vaccinated or Not)		Recommended Treatment (in Addition to Local Treatment)
	At Time of Exposure	During Observation Period of Ten Days	
I. *No Lesion:* *indirect contact*	Rabid	—	None
II. *Licks:*			
(1) Unabraded skin	Rabid	—	None
(2) Abraded skin, scratches, and unabraded or abraded mucosa	(a) Healthy	Clincal signs of rabies or proved rabid (laboratory)	Start vaccine at first signs of rabies in the biting animal
	(b) Signs suggestive of rabies	Healthy	Start vaccine immediately; stop treatment if animal is normal on fifth day after exposure
	(c) Rabid, escaped, killed, or unknown	—	Start vaccine immediately
III. *Bites:*			
(1) Mild exposure	(a) Healthy	Clinical signs of rabies or proved rabid (laboratory)	Start vaccine at first signs of rabies in the biting animal
	(b) Signs suggestive of rabies	Healthy	Start vaccine immediately; stop treatment if animal is normal on fifth day after exposure
	(c) Rabid, escaped, killed, or unknown	—	Start vaccine immediately
	(d) Wild (wolf, jackal, fox, skunk, raccoon, bat, etc.)	—	Serum immediately; start vaccine at same time†
(2) Severe exposure (multiple or face, head, finger, or neck bites)	(a) Healthy	Clinical signs of rabies or proved rabid (laboratory)	Serum immediately; start vaccine at first signs of rabies in the biting animal
	(b) Signs suggestive of rabies	Healthy	Serum immediately; start vaccine at same time† (Vaccine may be stopped if animal is normal on fifth day after exposure)
	(c) Rabid, escaped, killed, or unknown (d) Wild (wolf, jackal, fox, skunk raccoon, bat, etc.)	—	Serum immediately; start vaccine at same time†

*Adapted from the World Health Organization Expert Committee on Rabies, Fifth Report, 1965.
†Course to be followed by supplemental doses given 10 and not less than 20 days after the last dose.

to the U.S. Public Health Service Advisory Committee on Rabies, carnivorous animals (especially skunks, foxes, coyotes, raccoons, dogs, cats) and bats are more likely to be infective than other animals; bites of rabbits, squirrels, chipmunks, rats, and mice seldom, if ever, call for rabies prophylaxis. Properly immunized domestic animals are not likely to develop rabies. In doubtful or unusual cases, the local health authority should be consulted. Even in areas where rabies is enzootic, if adequate data indicate that infection is not present in the particular species, the local authority may recommend that no specific rabies immunoprophylaxis be given.

All bite wounds, scratches, and skin abrasions that are exposed to licks of animals should be immediately and thoroughly cleansed with soap and water and preferably with a cationic detergent such as 1:100 to 1:1,000 benzalkonium chloride [Zephiran] solution. Tincture or aqueous solutions of iodine (dilutions up to 1:10,000) in 50% to 70% alcohol also inactivate rabies virus. If debridement is necessary, the wound area may be infiltrated with a local anesthetic. If possible, bite wounds should not be sutured immediately. If indicated, antibiotics may be given and appropriate tetanus prophylaxis initiated. The management of patients exposed to possibly rabid animals should follow the recommendations set forth by the Expert Committee on Rabies of the World Health Organization (see Table 2, which serves as a general guide to the use of postexposure immunophylaxis).

Mild to severe local erythematous reactions occur in approximately one-third of patients receiving either vaccine. Some patients may develop inflammation and induration at the site of injection, regional lymphadenopathy, and, occasionally, urticaria or serum sickness. Severe abdominal distress with nausea and vomiting occasionally occurs within a few minutes after receiving the vaccine. A systemic reaction characterized by malaise, febrile episodes, and chills has been observed rarely.

Rabies vaccine should be used with caution in patients with known sensitivity to avian or rabbit protein; antihistamines may help prevent or ameliorate reactions in these patients. Although cross sensitization between duck protein and chicken protein has occurred only rarely, caution should be observed in administering duck embryo vaccine to persons known to be highly sensitive to eggs, chicken, or chicken feathers. Epinephrine should be available immediately in case of anaphylactic reaction. Vaccine treatment should be stopped if neurologic reactions develop.

USUAL DOSAGE.—*Subcutaneous: Adults and children*, for pre-exposure immunoprophylaxis (duck embryo vaccine), two 1 ml doses administered in the outer aspect of the upper arm at approximately one-month intervals, followed by a booster dose after six months. A detectable antibody response does not develop in all individuals; therefore, a blood sample should be collected one month after the booster dose is given and submitted to the local health authority for serum antibody determination. If necessary, booster doses may be repeated until an antibody response is detectable. Persons in high-risk occupations should be given a booster dose at least every two years. A person who has had a demonstrated antibody response to pre-exposure rabies prophylaxis needs only a single booster dose of vaccine after a nonbite exposure; if such a person is bitten by a rabid animal, he should receive a course of five daily doses of vaccine, followed by a booster dose 20 days after the last injection.

For postexposure immunoprophylaxis (duck embryo or rabbit brain vaccine), 14 to 21 daily 1 ml doses injected in separate sites. A 23- to 24-gauge needle approximately ½ to ¾ inches long should be used. Two supplemental doses of vaccine should be given 10 to 20 days after completion of the 14- or 21-day course; this is especially important if antirabies serum has been given concomitantly.

PREPARATIONS.—

Rabies Vaccine (Duck Embryo) (Lilly). *Injection:* Powder for resuspension in single-dose (1 ml) containers.

Rabies Vaccine, Human (Rabbit Brain, Phenol Killed) (Merrell-National). *Injection:* Suspension in single-dose (0.5 ml) containers.

ANTIRABIES SERUM

Antirabies serum is a hyperimmune equine serum useful in the prevention of rabies. It should be used in combination with rabies vaccine for prophylaxis of severe exposure. As with all equine sera, tests for sensitivity and precautionary desensitization procedures should be carried out prior to use of antirabies serum (see the Introductory Statement). See also the evaluation on Rabies Vaccine.

USUAL DOSAGE.—*Intramuscular: Adults and children*, for severe exposure (multiple, deep, severe bites, particularly in the region of the head, neck, face, and fingers) and for all bites by animals in which rabies is present or cannot be excluded, 40 IU/kg of body weight; up to one-half of the total dose should be infiltrated around the wound. A full course of 21 doses of rabies vaccine also should be initiated immediately.

PREPARATIONS.—Antirabies Serum, U.S.P. *Injection:* Serum in 1,000 unit containers. Marketed under generic name.

ROCKY MOUNTAIN SPOTTED FEVER VACCINE

Rocky Mountain spotted fever vaccine is prepared from chick embryo tissue. It is not recommended for general use but is intended for active immunization aginst Rocky Mountain spotted fever in laboratory personnel working with *Rickettsia rickettsii* and in those whose occupations result in exposure to ticks in endemic areas. The immunity conferred is of relatively short duration; annual recall injections are necessary for those constantly exposed to ticks. The vaccine is of no therapeutic value.

The vaccine may cause pain at site of injection and, rarely, fever and malaise. It is contraindicated in patients allergic to eggs, chicken, or chicken feathers. It should not be given intravenously.

USUAL DOSAGE.—*Subcutaneous: Adults,* 1 ml every seven to ten days for three doses; *children under 12 years of age,* 0.5 ml every seven to ten days for three doses. For recall injection, *adults,* 1 ml annually; *children under 12 years,* 0.5 ml annually.

PREPARATIONS.—Rocky Mountain Spotted Fever Vaccine, U.S.P. Marketed under generic name.

SMALLPOX VACCINE

Smallpox vaccine is a suspension of infectious vaccinia virus prepared from virus grown on the skin of calves, sheep, or other animals or on chick embryo chorioallantois. Vaccines produced in tissue culture have been used experimentally, but in some trials have proved to be less effective. Vaccines must be refrigerated since they deteriorate rapidly at moderately high temperatures or on exposure to sunlight. Lyophilized vaccines are more stable than liquid vaccines under adverse conditions of transportation and storage, although they are as labile as liquid vaccines upon reconstitution.

In 1971, the U.S. Public Health Service advocated discontinuing routine smallpox vaccination. Shortly thereafter, the Committee on Infectious Diseases of the American Academy of Pediatrics supported this action, which was taken because the hazards of vaccination now exceed the risk of contracting smallpox in this country. Vaccination is still recommended for medical and hospital personnel at risk of exposure to any imported case and for travelers to areas where smallpox has not yet been eradicated. It is believed that spread of the disease from an infected traveler from abroad can be prevented by isolation of the patient and vaccination and surveillance of any contacts.

Successful vaccination produces a limited cutaneous infection with minimal systemic involvement. The vaccinia virus must be deposited in the target cells in the basal layers of the epithelium. The outer aspect of the upper arm is the usual site for primary vaccination and revaccination, although other sites may be used in order to conceal the scar. With good technique, there should be no unsightly scar. The skin should be gently wiped clean; no other special preparation is necessary. Vigorous scrubbing may produce slight abrasions which may result in secondary lesions. Alcohol, acetone, or other chemical agents that might inactivate the virus should not be used, nor should a dressing be applied.

The vaccination site should be inspected after six to eight days. Interpretation of the reactions resulting from vaccination is the same for both the chick embryo and calf lymph vaccines: a successful primary vaccination produces a typical Jennerian vesicle. The absence of a reaction is not an indication of immunity; it is due to inactive vaccine or faulty technique and revaccination is required. Response to revaccination is interpreted as either a major or equivocal reaction. A major reaction is a vesicular or pustular lesion or an area of palpable induration surrounding a central lesion that may be a crust or an ulcer. This indicates a successful revaccination. All other responses are regarded as equivocal reactions. They may represent adequate immunity or an allergic skin response. In this event, the patient should be revaccinated with vaccine from another lot.

Serious and potentially fatal complications of smallpox vaccination include vaccinia gangrenosum, eczema vaccinatum, and acute disseminated (postvaccinal) encephalomyelitis. Therefore, patients with eczema or other forms of chronic dermatitis, or those in household contact with these patients, should not be vaccinated. Smallpox vaccine should not be used for the treatment of herpes infections because it is ineffective and dangerous. Vaccination should be avoided if possible in the presence of any febrile illness, defective or altered immune mechanisms, leukemias, lymphomas, skin infection, and during corticosteroid therapy or pregnancy. If vaccination of such persons is required, vaccinia immune globulin should be used initially. It also is used in the treatment of vaccination eczema and autoinoculation vaccinia of the eye. It is of no value for acute disseminated encephalomyelitis. Vaccinia immune globulin may be obtained from the USPHS Center for Disease Control, Atlanta, Georgia and the quarantine offices in Miami, Seattle, Chicago, Los Angeles, New Orleans, and at Kennedy Airport in New York City.

USUAL DOSAGE.—Multiple pressure method: *Adults and children*, one capillary tube of vaccine expelled on the skin, with scarification as follows: Holding a sterile needle parallel to the skin surface, the side of needle point is moved up and down within the drop of vaccine, applying enough pressure to lightly puncture the skin. For primary vaccinations, 10 pressures should be used; for secondary vaccinations, 30 pressures are desirable. The area covered should not exceed 1/8 inch (3 mm) in diameter. The manufacturer's package insert should be consulted, since specific recommendations for different preparations vary.

PREPARATIONS.—Smallpox Vaccine, U.S.P.

Smallpox Vaccine (Avianized):

Solution in single-dose containers. Vaccine marketed under generic name.

Smallpox Vaccine (Calf Lymph Origin):

Dryvax (Wyeth). Lyophilized powder in 25- and 100-dose containers. Solution in single-dose containers also marketed under generic name.

TUBERCULOSIS VACCINE (BCG)

Tuberculosis vaccine is a suspension of an attenuated strain of the bovine tubercle bacillus *(Mycobacterium bovis)* commonly referred to as BCG (Bacillus Calmette-Guerin) vaccine. Despite a lack of agreement concerning the importance of this vaccine, results of several large controlled studies indicate it confers substantial protection against tuberculosis. It effectively converts individuals with a negative tuberculin skin test to positive reactors; however, evaluation of its effectiveness is complicated by the fact that such a positive skin reaction measures allergic response to tubercular proteins, not degree of immunity to the disease.

The vaccine is recommended for persons restricted to an environment in which they are most likely to develop tuberculosis. Individuals to be vaccinated should be screened by tuberculin test and physical and x-ray examinations. Active tuberculosis must be ruled out before the vaccine is administered.

Adverse reactions are usually rare and mild. After injection, a papule appears which will scale, ulcerate, and dry to leave a smooth, pink or blue scar after about three months. The vaccine is contraindicated in persons who have not been skin tested within the preceding two weeks; in those who are acutely ill or suspected of having respiratory tract, skin, or other infection; in those with agammaglobulinemia; and in patients with a positive tuberculin skin test. Patients who have not reacted to tuberculin after two weeks should be revaccinated. (Tuberculin skin testing is contraindicated in the presence of a skin infection, allergic dermatitis, burns, or a fresh smallpox vaccination.)

USUAL DOSAGE.—*Intradermal or multiple puncture method: Newborn infants,* 0.05 ml; *older infants, children, and adults,* 0.1 ml. Material not immediately used should be discarded.

PREPARATIONS.—BCG Vaccine (Lilly, Research Foundation). *Injection:* Powder for solution in 1 ml containers.

TYPHOID VACCINE

Typhoid vaccine is a sterile suspension of killed typhoid bacilli *(Salmonella typhi)* of a strain selected for high antigenicity. It protects 70% to 90% of recipients, depending upon the degree of subsequent exposure. Routine immunization, while not required in the United States, is recommended for persons exposed to a carrier in the household, living in a community or institution with an outbreak of typhoid fever, or traveling to locations where typhoid is endemic. Flood conditions are not considered an indication for immunization.

Paratyphoid A and paratyphoid B vaccines, which were formerly combined with typhoid vaccine, have been demonstrated to be ineffective. These should not be used because of the increased risk of reactions, which tend to become more severe with each succeeding series of injections.

Adverse reactions to typhoid vaccine include

local erythema, tenderness at the site of injection, malaise, myalgia, headache, and fever. The vaccine is contraindicated in the presence of active illness or in patients with debilitating disease or tuberculosis.

USUAL DOSAGE.—*Subcutaneous: Adults and children over 10 years of age,* two 0.5 ml doses four or more weeks apart or three doses at weekly intervals; *children 6 months to 10 years,* two 0.25 ml doses four or more weeks apart or three doses at weekly intervals. If there is continued or repeated exposure, a booster dose should be given at least every three years. *Adults and children over 10 years,* 0.1 ml is administered intradermally or 0.5 ml subcutaneously; *children 6 months to 10 years,* 0.1 ml intradermally or 0.25 ml subcutaneously.

PREPARATIONS.—Typhoid Vaccine, U.S.P. Marketed under generic name.

TYPHUS VACCINE

Typhus vaccine is a sterile suspension of killed epidemic typhus rickettsiae *(Rickettsia prowazekii)* grown in chick embryo culture. It affords protection against louse-borne typhus only. Vaccination against typhus is necessary only when traveling to certain areas of the world, as recommended by the U.S. Public Health Service, or for special-risk groups.

Vaccination is contraindicated in patients allergic to eggs, chicken, or chicken feathers. Sensitivity testing is required prior to use of the vaccine (see the Introductory Statement). Reported allergic or systemic reactions are minimal, but the possibility of an anaphylactic reaction should be borne in mind. The vaccine is contraindicated in the presence of active illness; in patients with debilitating disease, tuberculosis, or agammaglobulinemia; or in those receiving corticosteroid, antineoplastic, or immunosuppressive drugs.

USUAL DOSAGE.—*Subcutaneous: Adults and children,* two doses at intervals of four weeks: the doses recommended by the manufacturers are given. Yearly booster doses should be administered to individuals in special-risk groups.

PREPARATIONS.—Typhus Vaccine, U.S.P. Marketed under generic name.

YELLOW FEVER VACCINE

Yellow fever vaccine is a suspension of live, attenuated virus prepared from either the 17D or Dakar (French neurotropic) strain of virus, which is grown in chick embryo. The Dakar strain should not be used because of meningoencephalitic reactions associated with its use. The vaccine available in the United States is prepared from the 17D strain, which has caused no significant complications. It is a highly effective vaccine that provides immunity lasting up to ten years. It is recommended for persons six months of age or older traveling to countries in which yellow fever is endemic and for laboratory personnel who might be exposed to the disease.

Yellow fever vaccines that are acceptable for international travel must meet standards of the World Health Organization and must be administered at WHO-approved yellow fever vaccination centers. These centers are located in most cities in the U.S.; specific information may be obtained from city or county public health officers.

Adverse reactions are generally mild and consist of headache, myalgia, or low-grade fever. The vaccine is contraindicated in individuals sensitive to eggs, chickens, or chicken feathers; in patients with febrile illnesses or agammaglobulinemia; or in those receiving corticosteroid, antineoplastic, or immunosuppressive drugs.

USUAL DOSAGE.—*Subcutaneous: Adults and children,* 0.5 ml of reconstituted vaccine. International Sanitary Regulations do not require revaccination more frequently than every 10 years.

PREPARATIONS.—Yellow Fever Vaccine, U.S.P. Marketed under generic name and supplied only to authorized vaccination centers.

ANTIVENINS, ANTITOXINS, AND IMMUNOGLOBULINS

BLACK WIDOW SPIDER ANTIVENIN

[Antivenin *(Latrodectus mactans)* Lyovac]

Black widow spider antivenin is prepared from the serum of horses immunized against the venom of the black widow spider *(Latrodectus mactans).*

Earliest possible use of the antivenin is recommended for greatest effectiveness. If possible, the patient should be hospitalized. Supportive therapy may include warm baths, intravenous injection of morphine or 10 ml of 10% calcium gluconate solution to control myalgia, and barbiturates for extreme restlessness. Central nervous system depressants must be used with caution, because the venom is a neurotoxin that can cause respiratory arrest. Corticosteroids also have been used with varying results. No apparent benefit is gained by local treatment (eg, tourniquets, incision, suction) at the site of the bite.

A test for hypersensitivity to horse serum should be performed prior to use of this agent. Antivenin should not be administered intravenously. (See the Introductory Statement.)

USUAL DOSAGE.—*Intramuscular (deltoid region): Adults and children*, entire contents of one container (2.5 ml restored serum). Although one dose usually is adequate to cause subsidence of symptoms in one to three hours, a second dose may be needed.

PREPARATIONS.—Antivenin *(Latrodectus mactans)* Lyovac (Merck Sharp & Dohme). *Injection:* Powder for suspension 2.5 ml.

CROTALINE ANTIVENIN, POLYVALENT

Polyvalent crotaline antivenin is a suspension of venom-neutralizing antibodies prepared from the serum of horses immunized against the venoms of the pit vipers, *Crotalus adamanteus*, *C. atrox*, *C. durissus terrificus*, and *Bothrops atrox*. It is useful against the venoms of all 17 species of Crotalidae in North and South America. In general, it is effective against North American rattlesnakes, water moccasins, and copperheads, but is of no value against true vipers (eg, puff adder, cobra, mamba), other noncrotalid snakes (eg, cobras, American coral snakes, mambas), or any venomous spiders or scorpions. It should be administered immediately following emergency first aid procedures (eg, immediate application of tourniquet, incision or excision at site of bite, suction, absolute physical rest to minimize lymphatic movement). Tests for sensitivity to horse serum should precede administration. (See the Introductory Statement.)

Lyophilized preparations are active for at least five years; they are readily soluble in water for injection, and should be reconstituted immediately prior to administration.

USUAL DOSAGE.—*Subcutaneous, Intramuscular, Intravenous: Adults*, 1 to 5 containers of reconstituted serum, depending upon the severity of symptoms, time elapsed since the bite, and size of snake. For intravenous use, a 1:10 dilution of antivenin in sterile isotonic sodium chloride injection or 5% dextrose injection is prepared and administered as a constant drip at a rate of 120 drops/minute. *Children* may require twice the adult dosage because they have less resistance and less body fluid with which to dilute the venom.

PREPARATIONS.—Polyvalent Crotaline Antivenin, U.S.P. *Injection:* Powder with 10 ml of bacteriostatic water for injection. Marketed under generic name.

NORTH AMERICAN CORAL SNAKE ANTIVENIN [Antivenin *(Micrurus fulvius)*]

Antivenin *(Micrurus fulvius)* is a concentrated and lyophilized preparation of serum globulins from horses immunized with the venom of eastern coral snakes *(M. fulvius fulvius)*. This antivenin will neutralize the venom of the two subspecies of *M. fulvius;* (1) *M.f. fulvius* found in areas from eastern North Carolina through Florida and in the gulf coastal plain to the Mississippi River; (2) *M.f. tenere* (Texas coral snake) found west of the Mississippi River in Louisiana, Arkansas, and Texas. This antivenin will *not* neutralize the venom of *Micruroides euryxanthus* (Arizona or Sonoran coral snake) found only in southeastern Arizona and southwestern New Mexico.

There are relatively few coral snakebites each year, and it is not possible to predict whether envenomation has occurred even when fang punctures are present. The victim of a coral snakebite should be immobilized immediately and completely, if possible, and carried to the nearest hospital as soon as possible. If complete immobilization is not practical, the bitten extremity should be splinted. If there is any evidence of a break in the skin from the bite, the victim should be hospitalized for observation and treatment.

If symptoms of envenomation occur, the antivenin should be given intravenously as soon as possible. The physician should be familiar with the manufacturer's package brochure, particularly regarding precautions for use of antivenin, as well as for current methods of treatment of venomous snakebites and specifically coral snakebite.

USUAL DOSAGE.—See the manufacturer's recommendation.

PREPARATIONS.—Antivenin *(Micrurus fulvius)* (Equine origin) (Wyeth). *Injection:* Lyophilized preparation with diluent for reconstitution.

BOTULISM ANTITOXIN

Botulism antitoxin is a sterile solution of concentrated antitoxins, chiefly globulins, produced from the blood of horses immunized against the toxins of *Clostridium botulinus*, either type E alone, or types A and B with or without type E. It is the only specific therapy for botulism. Prompt use in exposed individuals sharply decreases mortality, but the value of antitoxin once symptoms have appeared has not been adequately assessed. Patients first should be tested for sensitivity to horse serum. (See the Introductory Statement.) Since type E botulism has been associated almost entirely with eating fish or fish products, type E antitoxin should be given if fish is the suspected source of the toxin. All three types of antisera should be used until the specific type of botulinus toxin has been identified.

Serum sickness may occur 5 to 13 days after administration; the most prominent manifestations are urticaria, fever, and pruritus. Appropriate precautions should be taken for the prevention and arrest of possible allergic and other untoward reactions.

USUAL DOSAGE.—

Intravenous: Adults, 10,000 units of types A, B, and E antitoxin every four hours until the toxic condition has been alleviated. The antitoxin is diluted 1:10 with 10% dextrose injection prior to use. The first 10 ml is injected slowly over a five-minute period; the remainder can be given more rapidly after 15 minutes.

Intestinal instillation: Adults, 10,000 units of types A, B, and E antitoxin instilled every four hours.

PREPARATIONS.—Botulism Antitoxin, U.S.P.

Botulism Antitoxin Bivalent (Types A and B) (Lederle). *Injection:* Solution containing 10,000 units of each type/container.

Type E Botulinus Antitoxin and ABE Trivalent Botulinus Antitoxin are manufactured by the Connaught Laboratories, Toronto, Canada, and may be obtained in the United States from the National Communicable Disease Center, Atlanta, Georgia.

DIPHTHERIA ANTITOXIN

Diphtheria antitoxin is a sterile solution of concentrated antitoxin obtained from the blood of horses hyperimmunized against diphtheria toxin. It is used in the treatment of diphtheria or for prophylaxis in exposed, nonimmunized, susceptible individuals who are not under daily surveillance. Antitoxin should be administered on the basis of a clinical diagnosis of diphtheria without waiting for bacteriologic confirmation. The dose varies according to the site of the diphtheritic membrane, degree of toxicity, and duration of illness. Appropriate antimicrobial therapy (eg, penicillin, tetracyclines, erythromycin) helps clear the infected sites but is of no value against the toxin.

Serum sickness (urticaria, fever, pruritus, malaise, arthralgia) may occur in one week to 12 days. Before injecting diphtheria antitoxin, it is essential to obtain a history of previous injections of serum as well as of pre-existing asthma or allergy. A skin or eye test for sensitivity should be performed in all patients. If a positive reaction occurs, the antitoxin should be administered according to the procedure outlined in the Introductory Statement. Preparation for immediate administration of 1:1,000 epinephrine solution is essential before testing for sensitivity to or administering diphtheria antitoxin. Active immunization with diphtheria toxoid, using a different site, should be initiated at the same time that diphtheria antitoxin is given.

USUAL DOSAGE.—The entire dose required should be given at one time if possible.

Intramuscular: Adults and children, for prophylaxis, 1,000 to 10,000 units.

Intravenous: Adults and children, for treatment, 20,000 to 80,000 units, depending upon duration of illness, degree of toxicity, and site of membrane.

PREPARATIONS.—Diphtheria Antitoxin, U.S.P. Marketed under generic name.

GAS GANGRENE ANTITOXIN

Gas gangrene antitoxin is a sterile solution of specific globulins derived from the serum of horses immunized against the toxins of *Clostridium perfringens*, *C. septicum*, and *C. novyi*. It may be used prophylactically after injuries likely to be followed by gas gangrene or therapeutically for treatment of the infection. The effectiveness of gas gangrene antitoxin has been questioned; however, there is some evidence that, when used concomitantly with appropriate antibacterial agents and debridement of wounds, gas gangrene is, for the most part, prevented.

Antitoxin must be used with caution in sensitive patients; tests for sensitivity to horse serum must precede its use (see the Introductory Statement).

USUAL DOSAGE.—*Intravenous, Intramuscular: Adults and children*, 20,000 to 60,000 units. Total dose injected depends upon the severity of the disease, response to treatment, and manner in which the antitoxin is tolerated. Intramuscular injection of 40,000 units every six hours is advocated in severely ill patients.

PREPARATIONS.—Gas Gangrene Antitoxin. Marketed under generic name.

TETANUS ANTITOXIN

Tetanus antitoxin is a sterile solution of concentrated antibody proteins obtained from the blood of horses hyperimmunized with tetanus toxin or toxoid. It is used prophylactically in nonimmunized patients with tetanus-prone wounds and as a part of therapy in patients with active tetanus. Because of the risks of hypersensitivity reactions, tetanus immune globulin (human) is preferred over tetanus antitoxin; tetanus antitoxin should be used only when the former is not available.

Appropriate eye and skin tests for sensitivity to horse serum should always precede use of tetanus antitoxin (see the Introductory Statement). Epinephrine solution 1:1,000 should be available for prompt treatment of any severe reactions that may occur. When given for prophylaxis, tetanus antitoxin should be administered intramuscularly to lessen the severity of reactions, which can range from pain at the site of injection to serum sickness (arthralgia, urticaria, fever, malaise) and anaphylactic shock. For therapy, the intravenous route is preferred. Active immunization with tetanus toxoid should be initiated at the same time that tetanus antitoxin is given; a different site and a different syringe should be used.

USUAL DOSAGE.—

Intramuscular: Adults and children, for prophylaxis, 5,000 to 10,000 units within 24 hours after injury. If 48 hours have elapsed between time of injury and treatment, a dose of 10,000 to 20,000 units is recommended.

Intravenous: Adults and children, for treatment, 40,000 to 100,000 units or more.

PREPARATIONS.—Tetanus Antitoxin, U.S.P. Marketed under generic name.

IMMUNE SERUM GLOBULIN (HUMAN)

Immune serum globulin is a sterile solution of globulins (chiefly gamma globulin) prepared from pooled normal human plasma. It contains many antibodies normally present in human blood. It is used to prevent infectious hepatitis, rubella, poliomyelitis, and chicken pox. For use in measles, see the evaluation on Measles Immune Globulin.

The value of immune serum globulin in the prevention of mumps or rubella in exposed, susceptible persons or pregnant women is questionable.

Reactions following its use have occurred infrequently and have been mild.

USUAL DOSAGE.—*Intramuscular: Adults and children,* for patients exposed to infectious hepatitis, 0.02 to 0.04 ml/kg of body weight and repeated in three to five months if exposure continues; to poliomyelitis, 0.3 ml/kg of body weight, and repeated five weeks after the first dose if danger of infection still exists; to rubella, 0.25 to 0.44 ml/kg; to chicken pox, 0.55 to 1.3 ml/kg.

PREPARATIONS.—Immune Serum Globulin, U.S.P.

AVAILABLE TRADEMARKS.—Gamastan (Cutter), Gamimune (Hollister-Stier), Gammagee (Merck Sharp & Dohme), Gamulin (Dow), Immu-G (Parke, Davis), Immuglobin (Savage). Also marketed under generic name.

MEASLES IMMUNE GLOBULIN (HUMAN)

Measles may be temporarily prevented or modified by the administration of immune globulin of known measles antibody titer. Effective prevention of measles in susceptible exposed persons depends upon the earliest possible administration within the first six days after exposure. Measles immune globulin should be used to protect exposed nonimmune infants and children with severe or chronic illness and those in hospital wards. Active immunization with live vaccine should be carried out eight or more weeks thereafter.

Occasionally, tenderness at the site of injection and mild fever may develop following use of measles immune globulin. It should never be injected intravenously.

USUAL DOSAGE.—*Intramuscular: Adults and children,* for prevention of measles in nonimmune individuals, 0.22 ml/kg of body weight given within the first six days after exposure. For modification of measles, 0.04 ml/kg given within the first six days after exposure.

PREPARATIONS.—Measles Immune Globulin, U.S.P. Marketed under generic name. Some human immune serum globulin preparations also are standardized for measles.

RH<u>O</u> (D) IMMUNE GLOBULIN (HUMAN)

[Gamulin Rh, HypRho-D, RhoGAM, Rho-Imune]

Rh<u>o</u> (D) immune globulin is a sterile, concentrated solution of gamma globulin prepared from blood plasma of donors having high Rh antibody titers. It is used intramuscularly to prevent formation of active antibodies in Rh negative mothers after delivery of an Rh positive infant or abortion of an Rh positive fetus. To be effective, it must be given within 72 hours after delivery or abortion. When more refined testing reveals that an Rh negative mother is D_u positive (Rh [D] factor variant), Rh immune globulin is not needed since these individuals are not at risk of developing Rh antibodies. Use of Rh immune globulin to prevent active Rh immunization in Rh negative patients inadvertently transfused with Rh positive blood is investigational.

Adverse reactions occur infrequently and are mild and generally confined to the site of injection. Slight elevations of temperature have been reported following injection. Sensitization due to repeated injection of immune serum globulins is unusual, and these agents do not appear to transmit serum hepatitis.

Rh$_{\underline{o}}$ (D) immune globulin is contraindicated in Rh positive patients and in Rh negative patients who have developed Rh antibodies because of a previous delivery, abortion, or transfusion of Rh positive blood. This preparation is to be given only to the postpartum mother. It must not be given to the infant. It should be stored at 2 to 8 C and should not be frozen.

USUAL DOSAGE.—*Intramuscular:* Entire contents of one vial is administered.

PREPARATIONS.—Gamulin Rh (Dow), HypRho-D (Cutter), RhoGAM (Ortho), Rho-Imune (Lederle). *Injection:* Package contains a single dose of the drug and a 1:1,000 dilution for cross matching.

TETANUS IMMUNE GLOBULIN

Tetanus immune globulin is a sterile solution of globulins obtained from the plasma of adults hyperimmunized with tetanus toxoid. It is an effective prophylactic agent in patients with wounds potentially contaminated with *Clostridium tetani.* Tetanus immune globulin is used if the patient has received less than two immunization doses of tetanus toxoid, if the history of immunization is uncertain, or if the wound is more than 24 hours old. Because tetanus immune globulin is of human origin, it is virtually free from risk of hypersensitivity reactions.

Essentially no adverse reactions have been reported; however, as with other gamma globulin preparations, pain and erythema at the site of injection may occur rarely. Tetanus immune globulin should be used intramuscularly only. Active immunization with tetanus toxoid should be initiated either immediately or within one month after administration of tetanus immune globulin; a different site and a different syringe should be used for the injection.

USUAL DOSAGE.—*Intramuscular:* For prophylaxis, *adults,* 250 units; *children,* 4 units/kg of body weight. For treatment, optimal therapeutic dose has not been established; 3,000 to 6,000 units usually are recommended, but doses as large as 10,000 units have been used.

PREPARATIONS.—Tetanus Immune Globulin, U.S.P. *Injection:* Solution in 250 unit containers.

AVAILABLE TRADEMARKS.—Gamatet (Hollister-Stier), Gamulin T (Dow), Homo-Tet (Savage), Hu-Tet (Hyland), Hyper-Tet (Cutter), Immu-Tetanus (Parke, Davis), Pro-Tet (Lederle), T-I-Gammagee (Merck Sharp & Dohme). Also marketed under generic name.

Chapter 90

CHELATING AGENTS

Heavy metal poisoning continues to be an important toxicologic problem, particularly in children. In their elemental state, heavy metals are poorly absorbed from the gastrointestinal tract; however, as neutral salts (eg, mercuric chloride [$HgCl_2$]) they may be absorbed quite rapidly. In addition to absorption following ingestion, these metal ions may enter the body through both intact and abraded skin, by parenteral administration, or by inhalation. Many heavy metal ions produce toxic effects if they are not readily excreted. These effects vary according to the type and amount of metal absorbed, but in general the ions act as irritants to the central nervous system or to various organs such as the kidneys. They also overload and thus inactivate certain intracellular enzyme systems essential to cellular metabolism (eg, those containing sulfhydryl groups).

The only reasonably successful approach in the treatment of heavy metal poisoning is the inactivation of the heavy metal ion by chelation. This is a chemical process whereby certain organic compounds (ligands) exchange less firmly bonded ions for other inorganic ions to form a relatively stable nonionized ring complex. The strength of the binding varies with the chelating agents used. The agents administered primarily for this purpose are calcium disodium edetate [Calcium Disodium Versenate], deferoxamine [Desferal], dimercaprol [BAL], and penicillamine [Cuprimine]. Disodium edetate [Endrate, Sodium Versenate] also is used therapeutically as a chelating agent in the treatment of pathologic states secondary to hypercalcemia, but this drug should not be used for treating heavy metal poisoning because of its high affinity for calcium.

None of the metal-binding compounds presently available has the specificity to form a chelate with only one cation. However, the chelating agents currently used will bind some metals more strongly than others. When a chelate is formed, the cation becomes an integral part of a stable ring structure and ceases to act as a free ion. This soluble complex is readily excreted by the kidneys, if renal excretory function is preserved.

Therapy with a chelating agent is most effective when it is begun immediately after toxic exposure to the heavy metal. If the elapsed time between ingestion of the toxic material and initiation of therapy is sufficient to allow incorporation of the metal into tissue and bone, prolonged administration of the chelating agent will be needed to remove the heavy metal from the body. Furthermore, some irreversible tissue damage will have occurred.

Many factors influence chelation in vivo. Endogenous substances such as hemosiderin, hemoglobin, ferritin, various enzymes, and nucleic acids will interfere with the action of the chelating agents. Changes in the normal pH of blood and urine will alter the degree of ionization of both the chelating drug and the metal ion with which it forms a complex.

Because of the increasing use of radioactive isotopes in medical research and diagnosis, in industry, and in science, accidental poisoning with radioactive metals has become an appreciable hazard, and thus, chelation of radioactive isotopes is an important medical procedure. Nevertheless, when dealing with highly radioactive material that has a long half-life, treatment of toxic symptoms or inactivation of the metal by chelation becomes a secondary consideration to the rapid elimination of the material.

Poisoning with one of the more conventional radioactive metals such as iron or gold can be treated with techniques commonly used to hasten their excretion. However, treatment is more difficult if the toxic reaction is due to one of the more exotic metals such as uranium, radium, strontium, plutonium, or yttrium. Neither radium nor strontium can be removed from the body by chelation with any degree of success because their properties closely resemble those of calcium. The excretion rate of these radioactive elements can be increased by the infusion of calcium salts in conjunction with the oral administration of ammonium chloride. The excretion of uranium, plutonium, yttrium, and some of the other heavier radioactive isotopes can be increased to a limited extent by chelation with calcium disodium edetate. Another chelating agent, trisodium calcium pentetate, currently available only as an investigational drug in this country, hastens the excretion of lanthanum, yttrium, americum, and plutonium. It does not increase the excretion of strontium, polonium, or uranium.

Some chelating drugs have uses other than treating heavy metal poisoning. The capacity of disodium edetate to bind calcium led to its use in the treatment of digitalis-induced arrhythmias. However, its effect is transitory and other definitive treatment must be undertaken quickly. Chelating agents have been tried unsuccessfully in the treatment of porphyria, scleroderma, angina pectoris, nephrocalcinosis, calcified mitral stenosis, otosclerosis, and sarcoidosis.

Adverse Reactions and Precautions

Because of wide variation in the toxic manifestations of the chelating agents, it is not possible to generalize concerning their adverse reactions and precautions. It is sufficient to note that although serious toxic effects can occur with use of compounds such as calcium disodium edetate, dimercaprol, penicillamine, and deferoxamine, the adverse reactions are rarely life-threatening, usually reversible, and generally less severe than the effects of the heavy metal poisoning. (See the individual evaluations.)

INDIVIDUAL EVALUATIONS

CALCIUM DISODIUM EDETATE [Calcium Disodium Versenate]

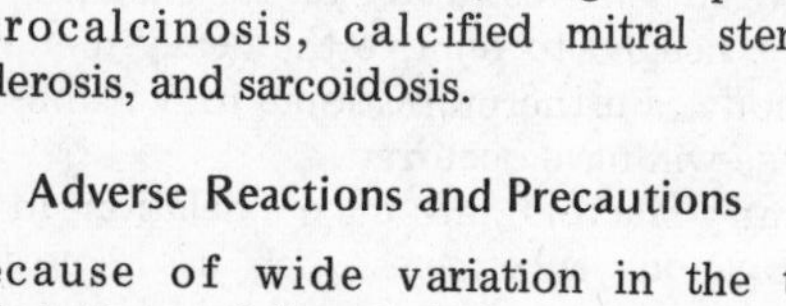

```
         O                        O
         ‖                        ‖
   Na O-C CH2                CH2C-O Na
            \               /
             N-CH2CH2-N                 · x H2O
            /   ↘    ↙    \
         CH2      Ca       CH2
          |      /  \       |
        O=C     /    \     C=O
           \   /      \   /
             O          O
```

This drug is primarily used to treat lead poisoning (plumbism). It is of questionable or unproved value in poisoning caused by copper, cadmium, chromium, manganese, gold, and nickel, and is not effective in mercury or arsenic poisoning. The chelates formed are water soluble, not easily dissociated, and readily excreted by the kidneys. Calcium disodium edetate will not produce negative calcium balance because the drug is fully saturated with calcium. It is capable of binding and inactivating essential trace metals, but this action generally is insignificant. Fortunately, calcium disodium edetate is stable and its optimal pH range for combining with lead includes all physiologic pH values.

When treating lead poisoning, the drug is given intravenously for three to five days to allow continued complex formation and excretion of the heavy metal as it is released from tissues into extracellular fluid. Peak excretion of chelated lead occurs within 24 to 48 hours after intravenous administration.

Calcium disodium edetate should not be given orally as an adjunct to its intravenous administration in the treatment of chronic lead poisoning because it is poorly absorbed from the gastrointestinal tract, its action develops more slowly after oral administration, and it can be given only in small doses. Furthermore, if lead is present in the gut, its absorption may be increased because the lead chelate formed is more soluble than the lead itself. Despite the fact that the chelate has an extremely high stability constant, more chelate will dissociate because more of the chelate is present in the body and, consequently, toxic reactions may occur even though renal excretion of the lead chelate is increased.

The incidence of lead poisoning is reduced when calcium disodium edetate is given orally to workers exposed to high concentrations of lead. Nevertheless, since prophylactic use may enhance absorption of lead, such therapy is of questionable merit. The most effective way to prevent chronic poisoning is to maintain proper industrial hygiene.

Calcium disodium edetate may be given as a diagnostic agent when plumbism is suspected but characteristic symptoms are absent. If the 24-hour urinary excretion of lead is 500 μg or more per liter following administration of calcium disodium edetate, the presence of excessive amounts of lead in the body is indicated. Mortality in patients with untreated lead encephalopathy is high, and permanent brain damage is common in survivors. Thus, early diagnosis and treatment of lead poisoning is important.

Common adverse reactions are gastroenteritis following oral administration and pain at the site of intramuscular injection. Other adverse reactions include transient bone marrow depression, hypotension, cheilosis, chills, fever, and histamine-like reactions (sneezing, nasal congestion, and lacrimation). This drug occasionally causes acute renal tubular necrosis. Fatalities, although rare, have occurred after large doses; therefore, calcium disodium edetate should be used with caution in patients with pre-existing renal disease.

USUAL DOSAGE.—

Intravenous: Adults, 2 to 3 g daily in two divided doses; *children,* 50 to 75 mg/kg of body weight daily in two divided doses. Each dose is administered in 500 ml of sodium chloride injection or 5% dextrose injection by intravenous drip over a period of three to four hours. After five days, therapy should be interrupted for two days to two weeks and a second course then given if necessary. The dosage will depend upon the degree of lead poisoning, the physical size of the patient, and the results obtained, as well as upon any overt signs of adverse reactions to the drug itself. The total dose for the regimen normally should not exceed 550 mg/kg for either adults or children, although at maximal dosage 750 mg/kg will be given. It is not advisable to exceed two courses of therapy in adults. In children, additional courses may be necessary when mobilization of lead from the labile skeletal stores approaches the critical level of 80 μg/100 g of whole blood.

Intravenous (diagnostic): *Adults and children,* up to 75 mg/kg of body weight in three equally divided doses every eight hours.

Intramuscular (diagnostic): This route is used only when intravenous administration is not feasible. A dose of 1 g (as a 20% solution) in 0.5% to 1.5% procaine is injected two or three times daily. The drug is prepared in procaine solution since intramuscular injection is extremely painful.

Oral: Use of this route is not justified because it may enhance lead absorption. The manufacturer's suggested dosage for prophylaxis is 4 g daily in divided doses for *adults* and 60 mg/kg of body weight daily in divided doses for *children.*

PREPARATIONS.—Calcium Disodium Versenate (Riker).

Injection: Solution 200 mg/ml in 5 ml containers.

Oral: Tablets 500 mg.

DISODIUM EDETATE [Endrate, Sodium Versenate]

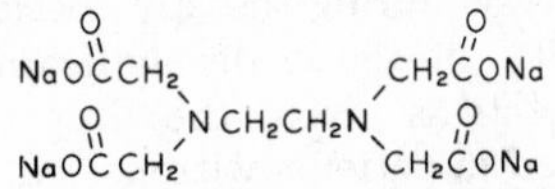

$$\begin{array}{c} NaOOCCH_2 \qquad\qquad CH_2COONa \\ \qquad \diagdown \qquad\qquad \diagup \\ N\,CH_2CH_2N \\ \qquad \diagup \qquad\qquad \diagdown \\ NaOOCCH_2 \qquad\qquad CH_2COONa \end{array}$$

Disodium edetate chelates the same polyvalent cations as calcium disodium edetate; however, disodium edetate has an additional affinity for calcium ions. Therefore, this agent is used in selected patients for the emergency treatment of hypercalcemia (see Chapter 17, Blood Calcium Regulators) and of ventricular arrhythmias associated with digitalis toxicity. It should not be used for heavy metal poisoning because it may produce hypocalcemia.

The effectiveness of disodium edetate in scleroderma, occlusive vascular disease, or other conditions involving calcinosis is controversial. It provides temporary relief in hypercalcemia accompanying metastatic bone disease, but the underlying pathologic condition remains unchanged. It should be used only when the severity of the disease (eg, as indicated by QRS-complex changes or a comatose state) justifies the risk. Disodium edetate is not indicated for treating medial arteriosclerosis or to induce retrograde dissolution of urinary calculi.

Although severe hypocalcemia is unlikely with usual therapeutic dosage, the ECG should be monitored and injectable calcium gluconate should be readily available as precautionary measures during therapy.

Adverse reactions include pain at the site of infusion, thrombophlebitis, chills, fever, back pain, hypotension, muscle cramps (caused by hypocalcemia), vomiting, urinary urgency, erythematous skin eruption, anorexia, nausea, and diarrhea. Although acute renal tubular necrosis has been reported only rarely, periodic urinalysis is recommended during therapy. The drug is contraindicated in patients with renal disease. Chelation of trace metals also may occur, but this has not been found to be of clinical importance.

Rapid injection of concentrated solutions of disodium edetate may produce hypocalcemic tetany and convulsions, as well as respiratory arrest and severe arrhythmias; therefore, the solution should always be well diluted and administered slowly. This agent produces a transient fall in prothrombin time during administration, but coagulability returns to pretreatment levels within 12 hours. Since transient hypotension has occurred during intravenous infusion, blood pressure determinations should be made before and at frequent intervals during therapy. Because there is a possibility of tissue decalcification when disodium edetate is given, the drug usually is contraindicated in patients with healed, calcified tuberculous lesions.

Disodium edetate should be used with caution in patients with clinical or subclinical hypokalemia. In these patients, the serum potassium levels and the ECG should be monitored. The possible occurrence of hypomagnesemia also should be kept in mind. Treatment with disodium edetate may decrease blood glucose and insulin requirements in diabetics.

The disodium edetate preparation contains 1 g of sodium for each 5 g administered; this fact should be borne in mind when treating patients on low-sodium diets or those who are prone to develop congestive heart failure.

USUAL DOSAGE.—*Intravenous* (infusion): *Adults and children*, the daily dosage depends upon the degree of hypercalcemia. Recommendations for maximal dosage range from 15 to 50 mg/kg of body weight daily. The drug is dissolved in 500 ml of sodium chloride injection or 5% dextrose injection and administered over a period of three to four hours. A total of 4 g infused over four hours is usually well tolerated. Kidney function and serum electrolyte levels should be monitored during therapy. Opinions vary widely on whether dosage may be repeated and, if so, how frequently and how many times. One manufacturer suggests daily infusion for five days, followed by two days of rest, and then two more courses until disodium edetate has been given for a total of 15 days. Most authorities feel that a five-day rest period between five- or six-day courses is better and safer than the two-day rest period. In view of the wide disagreement about proper dosage, and the uncertainty about the clinical value of the treatment, disodium edetate probably should be regarded as an investigational drug despite the fact that it has been available commercially for many years.

PREPARATIONS.—

Endrate (Abbott). *Injection:* Solution 150 mg/ml in 20 ml containers.

Sodium Versenate (Riker). *Injection:* Solution 200 mg/ml in 5 ml containers.

DEFEROXAMINE MESYLATE [Desferal]

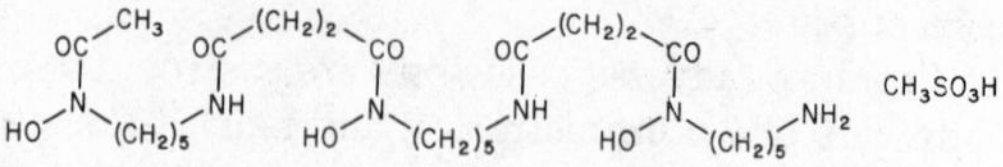

Deferoxamine, a compound obtained from the microorganism *Streptomyces pilosus*, is a potent and highly specific iron chelating agent. It readily complexes with the ferric ion to form ferrioxamine, a colored, stable, water-soluble chelate; it also has some affinity for the ferrous ion. In addition to combining with ionic iron, deferoxamine can remove iron from transferrin, ferritin, and hemosiderin (except from the hemosiderin in bone marrow) without significantly affecting body levels of other metals or trace elements. This drug is useful as an adjunct in the treatment of acute iron intoxication. The ferrioxamine complex formed when deferoxamine combines with iron has a characteristic reddish color. Thus, appearance of a reddish-brown (vin rosé) colored urine after parenteral injection of deferoxamine is presumptive evidence of elevated serum iron levels and an indication for further therapy.

The shorter the interval between iron ingestion and deferoxamine administration, the greater the probability of a successful recovery without complications or sequelae. Indeed, since there is little danger of serious toxicity from this drug when it is used at recommended dosage levels, and since the consequences of iron intoxication are grave, suspected iron poisoning should be treated with deferoxamine even before serum iron levels are known. This is especially true because the serum iron level is not always an accurate indication of the severity of iron intoxication; marked and potentially lethal necrosis of the gastrointestinal tract can occur in the presence of a low serum iron concentration.

Despite the effectiveness of deferoxamine as an iron chelating agent, it should not be used as a substitute for other therapeutic measures such as induced vomiting, lavage, maintenance of a patent airway, peritoneal dialysis, and control of shock and acidosis.

Deferoxamine has been used experimentally in the management of secondary hemochromatosis. It increases iron loss in patients with iron storage associated with sideroachrestic anemia, nocturnal paroxysmal hemoglobinuria (Marchiafava-Micheli syndrome), and other hemolytic anemias (eg, thalassemia major, sickle cell anemia). It also hastens iron excretion in patients who develop hemochromatosis after transfusion. Urinary excretion of iron following administration of this agent usually ranges from 10 to 50 mg daily. Deferoxamine also has been used to treat primary hemochromatosis, but its effect is less marked; phlebotomy can eliminate more iron. However, use of this chelating agent is beneficial when venesection is contraindicated (eg, when the patient is hypoproteinemic or too anemic to tolerate blood loss).

Possible iron deficiency anemia has been postulated as a side effect of prolonged therapy. However, studies using radioactive iron have shown that deferoxamine is incapable of removing iron from hemoglobin, myoglobin, or any of the iron-containing enzymes of the respiratory chain. In fact, experimental observations indicate that a slight increase in the hemoglobin level occurs when deferoxamine is given to patients with hemochromatosis; this is possibly due to a normalizing effect exerted by the drug on porphyrin metabolism.

Deferoxamine generally is well tolerated. Rapid intravenous injection can cause hypotension, tachycardia, erythema, and urticaria. Mild rash or pruritus occurs infrequently. Some patients experience a local histamine-like reaction or local induration following subcutaneous administration; this type of reaction is rare when the drug is given intramuscularly. Deferoxamine also may cause severe, transient pain at the site of injection. Patients receiving long-term deferoxamine therapy have had allergic-type reactions, blurred vision, fever, diarrhea associated with abdominal discomfort, and leg cramps.

There are no absolute contraindications to the use of deferoxamine when treating acute iron intoxication or hemochromatosis. However, since the ferrioxamine complex is largely excreted by the kidneys, large doses should not be given to patients with severe renal insufficiency.

Cataracts occasionally have been reported after prolonged deferoxamine therapy. Apparently this is an uncommon reaction and has not occurred during short-term use of the drug. Nevertheless, prolonged administration of deferoxamine to patients with hemochromatosis is not recommended unless the severity of the disease justifies the risk of possible cataract formation.

USUAL DOSAGE.—

Intramuscular (route of choice): For *adults* and *children* not in shock or severely intoxicated, 1 g initially followed by 0.5 g every four hours for two doses. Subsequently, 0.5 g may be administered every 4 to 12 hours, depending upon the condition of the patient, degree of intoxication (estimated from the amount of iron ingested and the serum iron levels), and response to therapy. The total dosage should not exceed 6 g in a 24-hour period.

Intravenous: Adults and children, for severely ill patients and those beginning to show signs of cardiovascular collapse, 1 g by slow infusion (not exceeding 15 mg/kg/hour) followed by 0.5 g every four hours for two doses. Subsequently, 0.5 g may be administered every 4 to 12 hours, depending upon the condition of the patient. Therapy may have to be continued for two to three days. The intramuscular route should be substituted as soon as it is safe to do so. Both routes should not be used simultaneously. The total dosage should not exceed 6 g in a 24-hour period.

Subcutaneous: This route generally should not be used because induration is likely to occur.

PREPARATIONS.—Desferal (Ciba). *Injection:* Powder (for solution) 500 mg.

DIMERCAPROL [BAL in Oil]

$$\begin{array}{l} CH_2-SH \\ | \\ CH-SH \\ | \\ CH_2-OH \end{array}$$

By forming stable mercaptides, the sulfhydryl groups of dimercaprol remove arsenic, mercury, and gold from cellular enzymes. Dimercaprol is particularly useful in the treatment of acute hemorrhagic encephalitis due to massive arsenotherapy, in arsenic or gold dermatitis, and, reportedly, in postarsenical jaundice. It is not useful in treating hepatic insufficiency or arsine (AsH_3) poisoning, but may be given as an adjunct in arsenical agranulocytosis. The drug is effective in mercury poisoning if therapy is begun within one to two hours following ingestion, but the extensive renal damage that occurs soon after mercury poisoning cannot be reversed. Although dimercaprol removes lead, calcium disodium edetate and penicillamine are preferred for this purpose. Some studies suggest that the combination of dimercaprol with calcium disodium edetate in treating lead encephalopathy hastens excretion of the lead and lowers the incidence of brain damage.

Dimercaprol may be of value in increasing the rate of copper excretion in Wilson's disease (hepatolenticular degeneration), but penicillamine is the drug of choice.

Dimercaprol is of questionable value in poisoning caused by other heavy metals such as antimony and bismuth. It should not be used in iron, cadmium, or selenium poisoning because the resulting dimercaprol-metal complexes are more toxic than the metal alone, especially to the kidneys. If acute renal failure develops during therapy, the drug should be discontinued or used only with extreme caution, since toxic concentrations may occur in the serum.

In usual doses, adverse reactions are generally mild and transitory. They include local pain at the site of injection, paresthesias, lacrimation, blepharal spasm, apprehension, asthenia, salivation, and vomiting. Many of these effects are relieved by the administration of an antihistamine. Dimercaprol has a strong odor and will impart an unpleasant odor to the patient's breath. Large doses cause moderate hypertension and, if the dosage is high enough, coma or convulsions. Dimercaprol also may induce metabolic acidosis associated with elevated serum lactate levels. When the use of large doses is continued, capillary damage resulting in loss of protein and fluid from the circulation occurs. Like all heavy metal chelating agents, dimercaprol is potentially nephrotoxic. Since the chelate rapidly dissociates in an acid medium, releasing the bound metal, the urine should be kept alkaline.

USUAL DOSAGE.—*Intramuscular: Adults and children,* for mild arsenic or gold poisoning, 2.5 mg/kg of body weight four times daily for two days, two times on the third day, then once daily thereafter for ten days; for severe arsenic or gold poisoning, 3 mg/kg every four hours for two days, four times on the third day, then twice daily thereafter for ten days. For mercury poisoning, 5 mg/kg initially, followed by 2.5 mg/kg one or two times daily for ten days.

PREPARATIONS.—BAL in Oil (Hynson, Westcott & Dunning). *Injection:* Solution 100 mg/ml in peanut oil in 3 ml containers.

PENICILLAMINE [Cuprimine]

$$\begin{array}{ccccc} & CH_3 & & H & \\ & | & & | & \\ HS- & C & - & C & -COOH \\ & | & & | & \\ & CH_3 & & NH_2 & \end{array}$$

Penicillamine is an amino acid derived from the degradation of penicillin but it is devoid of antibacterial activity. It is marketed as the dextro isomer which chelates with copper, iron, mercury, lead, and probably other heavy metals to form soluble complexes that are readily excreted by the kidneys. Penicillamine is superior to dimercaprol and calcium disodium edetate as a copper chelating agent. It is effective orally and its primary therapeutic use is to remove excess copper in patients with Wilson's disease (hepatolenticular degeneration). Penicillamine also may be useful in treating cystinuria; in this disorder, the penicillamine combines with cystine to form a soluble, readily excreted disulfide complex. Penicillamine will chelate lead less effectively than calcium disodium edetate, but it has the advantage of being effective orally.

The overall incidence of adverse effects with penicillamine is low, and reactions are most likely to occur shortly after therapy is begun. Most common and serious of the untoward effects are hypersensitivity reactions manifested by a maculopapular or erythematous rash. The rash occasionally is accompanied by fever, leukopenia, thrombocytopenia, eosinophilia, arthralgia, or lymphadenopathy. Purpuric or vesicular ecchymoses are sometimes seen, but the lesions are not progressive and discontinuation of therapy is usually not necessary. The administration of adrenal corticosteroids may be helpful in lessening the hypersensitivity reactions. Nephrotic syndrome, thrombophlebitis, cheilosis, and one case of fatal agranulocytosis also have been reported. Optic neuropathy has occurred in patients given racemic penicillamine, but has not been reported with use of the dextro isomer; the neuropathy disappeared after administration of pyridoxine.

Careful observation of the skin, as well as urinalysis, differential blood cell counts, direct platelet counts, and hemoglobin determinations should be performed every three days during the first two weeks of therapy and at least every ten days for three or four months thereafter.

USUAL DOSAGE.—*Oral:* For Wilson's disease, *adults and older children,* 250 mg four times daily, increased gradually as indicated up to a maximal daily dose of 4 or 5 g. The drug should be given on an empty stomach between meals and at bedtime; the latter dose is given at least three hours after the evening meal. *Young children and infants over 6 months of age,* a single daily dose of 250 mg dissolved in fruit juice. Although these guidelines are helpful, dosage must be individualized, and an adequate amount can be determined only by measuring the urinary excretion of copper. If the patient is on a low-copper diet and is using an oral cation exchange resin, negative copper balance will result if 1 mg or more of copper is excreted in urine each 24 hours.

For lead poisoning, *adults and children*, 250 mg three or four times daily for seven days.

For cystinuria, *adults and older children*, 1 to 4 g daily in four divided doses; *young children and infants*, 30 mg/kg of body weight daily in three or four equally divided doses. If equal doses are not possible or if adverse reactions necessitate a reduction in dosage, the largest amount should be given at bedtime. High fluid intake also is required (about 500 ml of water at bedtime and another 500 ml during the night when the urine is more concentrated and more acidic than during the day). Effective therapy is indicated by the urinary excretion of 100 to 200 mg of free amino acid each 24 hours in patients without a history of renal calculi, and less than 100 mg each 24 hours in patients with a history of calculi or flank pain.

PREPARATIONS.—Cuprimine (Merck Sharp & Dohme). *Oral:* Capsules 250 mg.

Chapter 91

ENZYMES USED AS DRUGS

A wide variety of enzymes and enzyme mixtures have been used as adjunctive therapeutic agents in a number of clinical conditions. They are applied most often in the treatment of traumatically-induced inflammation and edema of soft tissues. These enzymes include the carbohydrase, alpha amylase [Buclamase], and proteolytic or related enzymes such as alpha chymotrypsin [Alpha Chymar, Quimotrase, Zolyse], chymotrypsin [Avazyme], fibrinolysin (bovine) with desoxyribonuclease (bovine) [Elase], sutilains [Travase], trypsin with chymotrypsin [Chymolase Oral, Chymoral, Haugase, Orenzyme], bromelains (plant protease concentrate) [Ananase], proteolytic enzymes from *Carica papaya* [Papase], hyaluronidase [Alidase, Hyazyme, Wydase], and streptokinase-streptodornase [Varidase].

Some enzymes have special applications. Thus, for example, the only clinical use of proteolytic enzymes that has been both established and accepted on the basis of adequate evidence is the ophthalmic (intraocular) use of alpha chymotrypsin to aid in the dissection of the lens zonule in intracapsular cataract extraction (see Chapter 72, Miscellaneous Ophthalmic Preparations). Because of its spreading properties, hyaluronidase has been used to increase diffusion and absorption of fluids given by hypodermoclysis, particularly in children. Less frequently, it is given to enhance diffusion and absorption of other injected drugs (eg, penicillin) or reabsorption of transudates or hematomas. Fibrinolysin with desoxyribonuclease, streptokinase-streptodornase, sutilains, and trypsin have been proposed for use as debriding agents to remove clotted blood or fibrinous or purulent accumulations resulting from trauma, inflammation, empyema, infected wounds or ulcers, chronic suppurations involving draining sinuses, osteomyelitis, or other similar lesions. Fibrinolysin (human) [Thrombolysin], a streptokinase-activated plasminogen, has been used intravenously as an adjunct in the treatment of phlebothrombosis, thrombophlebitis, pulmonary embolism, and arterial thrombosis other than that present in coronary or cerebral arteries. However, its use is limited because dosages are empirical unless special laboratory tests are used to determine the in vivo activity of the preparation. In addition, the streptokinase component is antigenic. Fibrinolysin also has been used in myocardial disease, although some authorities consider its use dangerous.

Other enzymes administered in special situations are penicillinase [Neutrapen], which is promoted for the treatment of hypersensitivity reactions to the penicillins but is of little value and can produce allergic reactions in its own right (see Chapter 48, Penicillins); pancrelipase [Cotazym], a pancreatic enzyme used in replacement therapy for pancreatic exocrine deficiency disorders (see Chapter 83, Miscellaneous Gastrointestinal Agents); and pancreatic dornase [Dornavac], which has replaced crystalline trypsin as a more effective and less irritating agent for loosening pulmonary secretions (see Chapter 43, Expectorants and Inhalants).

The rationale for the oral or parenteral use of proteolytic enzymes in the treatment of traumatically-induced inflammation and edema of soft tissues is based on the claim that the swelling accompanying inflammation is caused by the occlusion of capillary and lymph vessels by fibrin deposits, that the proteolytic enzymes promote the breakdown of fibrin, and that this action thus relieves vascular blockage, reduces edema and inflammation, and enhances healing of tissues. The evidence for this mechanism is based on the unconvincing and incomplete results of studies that were restricted to categorizing the degree of inflammation observed either grossly or microscopically after treatment with enzymes. Controlled studies on the specific alterations induced by enzymes in the various stages of the inflammatory process are not available. Consequently, interpretations of results regarding the efficacy of these agents are entirely subjective. The anti-inflammatory uses of these enzymes are discussed in this chapter only to give information should the physician elect to use them.

Results of experimental studies suggest that the carbohydrase, alpha amylase, may counteract the increased capillary permeability associated with induced inflammation; however, there is no substantiating evidence that it initiates a compensatory physiologic response to inflammation anywhere in the body. The clinical effectiveness of alpha amylase, like that of the proteolytic enzymes, remains unproved.

Adverse Reactions and Precautions

Enzymes intended for the treatment of traumatic injury and edema have caused no serious untoward effects after oral use. When used buccally, alpha amylase [Buclamase], proteolytic enzymes from *Carica papaya* [Papase], and streptokinase-streptodornase [Varidase] have occasionally caused a tingling sensation in the cheek; streptokinase-streptodornase also may produce aphthous stomatitis.

There are no known contraindications to the oral use of chymotrypsin [Avazyme, Chymolase Oral, Chymoral, Haugase, Orenzyme] or to the buccal use of alpha amylase.

The intramuscular administration of chymotrypsin has been abandoned because this agent produces pain and swelling at the site of injection and is antigenic when administered parenterally, especially in patients with allergic tendencies. Also, several cases of anaphylactic reactions (angioedema, erythema, urticaria, acute circulatory failure, and syncope) have been reported.

For adverse reactions caused by the intraocular use of alpha chymotrypsin [Alpha Chymar, Quimotrase, Zolyse], see Chapter 72, Miscellaneous Ophthalmic Preparations.

The topical application of streptokinase-streptodornase [Varidase] as a debriding agent commonly causes fever and local irritation, but these effects can be minimized by regular drainage of closed areas in which the mixture is used. This preparation should not be applied topically in acute cellulitis without suppuration, since the enzymatic action may encourage the spread of nonlocalized infection. When bronchopleural fistulas are present, there is danger of their reopening, especially in patients with active tuberculosis. This preparation may be used with appropriate precautions in the treatment of other fistulas. Pain at the site of injection or febrile reactions have occurred after the intramuscular injection of streptokinase-streptodornase. Allergic reactions (eg, urticaria, rash) have been reported rarely; they disappeared when the medication was discontinued. Streptokinase-streptodornase [Varidase] should never be given intravenously.

The topical mixture, fibrinolysin with desoxyribonuclease [Elase], may produce local hyperemia. It must be used with caution in patients who are sensitive to agents of bovine origin.

Proteolytic enzymes from *Carica papaya* [Papase] or bromelains [Ananase] should not be used in patients receiving anticoagulants, in those with blood clotting disorders, or in those with generalized or systemic infections. They should be used cautiously in patients with hepatic or renal disease.

Fibrinolysin (human) [Thrombolysin] frequently causes febrile reactions (probably due to its streptokinase content). Renal failure also has been reported. This enzyme is contraindicated in the presence of a coagulation defect, severely impaired liver function, or hypofibrinogenemia. Since fibrinolysin may affect coagulation factors, the drug must be administered cautiously after hemorrhage or surgery or with repeated infusions, because bleeding from operative sites or open wounds may occur. Therefore, plasma fibrinogen and prothrombin time determinations should be made periodically in these patients.

Hyaluronidase [Alidase, Hyazyme, Wydase] should not be injected into or near an infected area because of the danger of spreading the infection. Sensitivity to this enzyme is not common, but prior testing is desirable.

Although penicillinase [Neutrapen] is used to counteract anaphylactic reactions to penicillin, it is itself antigenic; however, allergic reactions are rare.

As foreign proteins, all enzymes are potentially antigenic, and may sensitize patients or cause serious anaphylactoid reactions. Any sign of sensitivity (eg, local edema or urticaria, erythema, chills, nausea, vomiting, dizziness, tachycardia, hypotension) is an indication to discontinue therapy and immediately initiate prophylactic measures. Agents such as epinephrine, corticosteroids, and antihistamines should always be available for emergency treatment.

INDIVIDUAL EVALUATIONS

ALPHA AMYLASE [Buclamase]

Alpha amylase is a carbohydrase produced by a strain of nonpathogenic bacteria. It has been proposed for use as an adjunct to conventional therapy in the management of traumatically-induced inflammatory reactions, postoperative tissue reactions, localized skin infections, allergic states, and mesenchymal disorders. However, its therapeutic efficacy has not been established.

Alpha amylase occasionally causes a tingling sensation in the cheek when administered buccally. There are no known contraindications to its use.

USUAL DOSAGE.—This preparation is not considered useful and no dosage is suggested. The manufacturer's dosage is: *Buccal: Adults*, two tablets three or four times daily for a minimum of three days.

PREPARATIONS.—Buclamase (Rystan). *Buccal:* Tablets 10 mg (12,500 Rystan units).

BROMELAINS [Ananase]

This preparation has been proposed as an anti-inflammatory agent. The rationale for use is the same as for other proteolytic enzymes, ie, it is claimed to dissolve fibrin deposits blocking vessels that cause swelling as part of the inflammatory reaction. Results of studies on efficacy and therapeutic usefulness are inconclusive.

There are no known adverse reactions to oral use. The enzyme should be used with caution in patients with hepatic or renal disease. It should not be used in patients with blood coagulation disorders, in those receiving anticoagulants, or in those with generalized or systemic infections.

USUAL DOSAGE.—This evaluation does not support a useful dosage regimen. The manufacturer's suggested dosage is: *Oral: Adults*, initially, 100,000 units four times daily. For maintenance, 100,000 units twice daily or 50,000 units four times daily.

PREPARATIONS.—Ananase (Rorer). *Oral:* Tablets (enteric-coated) 50,000 and 100,000 Rorer units.

CHYMOTRYPSIN [Avazyme]
TRYPSIN WITH CHYMOTRYPSIN [Chymolase Oral, Chymoral, Haugase, Orenzyme]

Chymotrypsin is a proteolytic enzyme of bovine pancreatic origin. It is marketed as a single-entity preparation and as a mixture with trypsin. Results of clinical studies do not show that the combination products are significantly different from or superior to chymotrypsin alone.

This enzyme is proposed for use as an adjunct to the conventional treatment of traumatically-induced inflammation and edema of soft tissues, localized inflammation, and induced trauma, but its clinical effectiveness has not been established.

No contraindications or serious systemic untoward reactions have been observed after oral use.

USUAL DOSAGE.—Since this preparation is considered to be not useful, no meaningful dosage regimen can be given. The manufacturers' suggested dosages are:

Chymotrypsin:

Oral: Adults, for mild conditions, one tablet four times daily. For more severe conditions, two tablets four times daily.

Trypsin with Chymotrypsin:

Oral: Adults, one or two tablets four times daily.

PREPARATIONS.—

Chymotrypsin:

Avazyme (Wampole). *Oral:* Tablets (enteric-coated) 50,000 and 100,000 Wampole units.

Trypsin with Chymotrypsin:

Chymolase (Warren-Teed), Haugase (Wilson). *Oral:* Tablets (enteric-coated) 50,000 Warren-Teed (trypsin:chymotrypsin approximately 3:1) and Haug units, respectively.

Chymoral (Armour). *Oral:* Tablets (enteric-coated) 50,000 and 100,000 Armour units (trypsin:chymotrypsin approximately 6:1).

Orenzyme (Merrell-National). *Oral:* Tablets (enteric-coated) containing trypsin 50,000 or 100,000 N.F. units and chymotrypsin 4,000 or 8,000 N.F. units.

FIBRINOLYSIN (HUMAN) [Thrombolysin]

This preparation is a mixture of profibrinolysin activator (streptokinase) and human fibrinolysin (plasmin) which has the activities of both components.

The manufacturer recommends use of this enzyme in phlebothrombosis, thrombophlebitis, pulmonary embolism, and arterial thrombosis except that involving coronary or cerebral arteries. Fibrinolysin has been used in myocardial disease, although some authorities consider such use dangerous. This preparation should be administered only under carefully controlled conditions by persons who are experienced in its use and who have adequately equipped facilities.

The complex fibrinolytic process in man limits evaluation of a thrombolytic agent. Dosages are empirical unless special assays for continuous evaluation of fibrinolytic activity are conducted during therapy. The initial dosage is based on an assessment of the patient's condition and the urgency of thrombolytic therapy.

Fibrinolysin is contraindicated in the presence of any hemorrhagic disorder, severely impaired liver function, or hypofibrinogenemia. The drug should be used with caution after hemorrhage or extensive surgery or with repeated infusions, and plasma fibrinogen and prothrombin times must be monitored periodically. Since transient febrile responses may occur four to six hours after administration, it also should be given cautiously to patients with pre-existing arrhythmias. Renal failure has been reported. Because of the antigenic nature of streptokinase, suitable antidotes (sedatives, epinephrine, corticosteroids, antipyretics, and antihistamines) should be available in case anaphylactic reactions occur, especially if a second course is given. The incidence of urticarial reactions is less than 1%. Acute viral hepatitis may be a late complication, although the product is now prepared from venous blood that is nonreactive when tested for hepatitis associated antigen (HAA).

USUAL DOSAGE.—Since the dangers of this drug outweigh any supposed benefit, no suggested dosage regimen is given. The manufacturer's dosage is: *Intravenous: Adults*, 50,000 to 100,000 units/hour for one to six hours daily, depending upon the specific situation. If necessary, the dose can be repeated daily for three or four successive days.

PREPARATIONS.—Thrombolysin (Merck Sharp & Dohme). *Injection:* Powder for solution 50,000 MSD units/ml.

HYALURONIDASE [Alidase, Hyazyme, Wydase]

This soluble enzyme product of bovine testicular origin is employed as an adjunct to enhance absorption of drugs in tissue spaces. It is used most advantageously to facilitate administration of fluids by hypodermoclysis, especially in infants and young children; it also is given to aid resolution of transudates, hematomas, and various edemas, and can facilitate diffusion of penicillin as well as diagnostic contrast media when the intravenous route cannot be used. When given with local anesthetic solutions, hyaluronidase increases the diffusion of the local anesthetic; however, its use for this purpose is no substitute for proper technique and neuroanatomic knowledge, and should not be used because the incidence of systemic adverse reactions is increased.

Hyaluronidase should not be injected in or near inflamed or cancerous areas.

Since hypersensitivity reactions may occur, skin or conjunctival testing prior to administration is recommended.

USUAL DOSAGE.—*Injection:* To increase the absorption of drugs (excluding local anesthetics), *adults*, 150 units added to the vehicle containing the drug.

For hypodermoclysis, *adults*, 150 units added to each liter of solution; *children*, 15 units added to each 100 ml of solution. For *premature or very young infants*, not more than 25 ml/kg of body weight daily; *children under 3 years of age*, maximal daily dose is 200 ml. The rate of drip should not exceed 2 ml/minute.

To aid in the resorption of transudates, hematomas, and edemas, *adults*, 150 to 1,500 units infiltrated locally.

PREPARATIONS.—

Alidase (Searle). *Injection:* Powder for solution 150 U.S.P. units/ml.

Hyazyme (Abbott). *Injection:* Lyophilized powder for solution 150 U.S.P. units/ml.

Wydase (Wyeth). *Injection:* Lyophilized powder 150 and 1,500 U.S.P. units; solution 150 U.S.P. units/ml in sterile sodium chloride injection.

Drug also marketed under generic name.

PENICILLINASE [Neutrapen]

Penicillinase hydrolyzes the beta-lactam ring of penicillin and converts it to the inactive penicilloic acid. This enzyme is commercially prepared from fermented culture of a strain of *Bacillus cereus.* It has been given to treat penicillin hypersensitivity reactions but is of little value.

Although repeated administration of penicillinase can cause anaphylactic reactions since the enzyme itself is antigenic, the actual incidence is low. No more than three doses should be given in a single course of treatment.

USUAL DOSAGE.—This drug is considered not useful and the evaluation does not support a dosage recommendation. The manufacturer's suggested dosage is: *Intramuscular: Adults,* 800,000 units are given by deep intragluteal injection. If a second injection is needed, it should be given within three days of the first.

PREPARATIONS.—Neutrapen (Riker). *Injection:* Lyophilized powder 800,000 units with 2 ml of diluent.

PROTEOLYTIC ENZYMES FROM *CARICA PAPAYA* [Papase]

This enzyme has the same proposed uses as other enzymes with proteolytic and alleged anti-inflammatory properties. Studies of efficacy and usefulness are inadequate and results are inconclusive.

Concurrent use of this preparation with anticoagulants is contraindicated, and it should not be used in patients with blood coagulation disorders or generalized or systemic infections. It should be given cautiously to patients with severe renal or hepatic disease. A tingling sensation in the cheek may occur when the preparation is used buccally.

USUAL DOSAGE.—This drug is not considered useful and no suggested dosage regimen is given. The manufacturer's dosage is: *Buccal, Oral: Adults,* for prophylaxis, 20,000 units one or two hours before a trauma-producing procedure; for therapeutic use, 20,000 units four times daily for at least five days.

PREPARATIONS.—Papase (Warner-Chilcott). *Buccal, Oral:* Tablets 10,000 Warner-Chilcott units.

SUTILAINS [Travase]

Sutilains is a sterile preparation of a proteolytic enzyme elaborated by *Bacillus subtilis* in an ointment base. It dissolves and aids in the removal of necrotic tissue and purulent exudate from skin surfaces in second- and third-degree burns, decubitus ulcers, traumatic and pyogenic wounds, and ulcers secondary to peripheral vascular disease.

Untoward effects are mild and consist of transient pain, paresthesia, hemorrhage, and dermatitis. The drug should be discontinued if bleeding or dermatitis occurs. Although no systemic allergic reactions have been reported in humans, immunologic studies have shown that an antibody response may occur.

The concomitant use of detergents or antiseptics (eg, benzalkonium chloride, hexachlorophene, iodine, nitrofurazone) should be avoided because of possible denaturation of sutilains. Sutilains should not be allowed to come in contact with the eyes. If this occurs, the eyes should be rinsed with a copious amount of water (preferably sterile). Use of sutilains is contraindicated for fungating neoplastic lesions or necrotic areas where bone, tendon, fascia, or cartilage is exposed and for wounds involving major body or nerve tissue.

USUAL DOSAGE.—*Topical: Adults and children,* after cleansing and irrigating the wounded area, the ointment is applied in a thin layer and the site covered with a loose wet dressing. Application may be repeated three or four times daily. If there is no demonstrable debriding action within 24 to 48 hours, further application is unlikely to have an effect.

PREPARATIONS.—Travase (Flint). *Topical:* Ointment containing approximately 82,000 casein units/g in 14.2 g containers.

MIXTURES

ELASE

This preparation is a mixture of fibrinolysin (plasmin) and desoxyribonuclease of bovine origin. It is used topically to remove necrotic debris and exudates from skin surfaces in wounds, ulcers, and burns.

Adverse effects are mild. Local hyperemia may occur. Precautions should be taken to prevent allergic reactions in patients with a history of sensitivity to mercury (from the preservative) or bovine products.

USUAL DOSAGE.—*Topical: Adults and children,* the ointment or solution is applied at least twice daily until optimal debridement is obtained.

PREPARATIONS.—Elase (Parke, Davis). *Topical:* Ointment containing fibrinolysin 10 or 30 Loomis units and desoxyribonuclease 6,666 or 20,000 units with thimerosal 0.04 or 0.12 mg in 10 and 30 g containers; powder (for solution) containing fibrinolysin 25 Loomis units and desoxyribonuclease 15,000 units with thimerosal 0.1 mg in 10 ml containers. Desoxyribonuclease units are described as modified Christensen method.

SIMILAR MIXTURE.—Elase-Chloromycetin (Parke, Davis). *Topical:* Each gram of ointment contains fibrinolysin 1 Loomis unit, desoxyribonuclease 666.6 units, and chloramphenicol 10 mg with thimerosal 0.004 mg in 10 and 30 g containers.

STREPTOKINASE-STREPTODORNASE
[Varidase]

This preparation is a mixture of enzymes of bacterial origin. Plasminogen activator (streptokinase) rapidly dissolves blood clots and the fibrinous portion of exudates; streptodornase hydrolyzes desoxyribonucleoprotein to liquefy viscous nucleoprotein of dead cells, but it has no effect on living cells. This mixture is injected into cavities or applied topically as a wet dressing. It is also available for oral, buccal, or intramuscular use to reduce inflammation and edema, but its effectiveness for this purpose has not been substantiated.

Streptokinase-streptodornase has produced the most satisfactory results as a topical debriding agent wherever purulent exudates, clotted blood, or fibrinous deposits are present as the result of trauma and infectious processes. It is used to supplement surgical debridement and drainage in the treatment of hemothorax, empyema, chronic draining sinuses, osteomyelitis, infected wounds, and ulcers.

Pyrogenic reactions and locally irritating effects are the most common adverse reactions. It may produce a tingling sensation in the cheek and aphthous stomatitis when used buccally.

Streptokinase-streptodornase is contraindicated in the presence of active hemorrhage or acute cellulitis without suppuration or when there is a danger of reopening pre-existing bronchopleural fistulas. It should never be given intravenously because of the severe systemic adverse reactions produced by impurities in this preparation.

USUAL DOSAGE.—

Local, Topical: Adults and children, for a hemothorax or thoracic empyema, initially, a solution containing streptokinase 200,000 units and streptodornase 50,000 units is injected in one or several sites. For topical debridement of exudates, a solution containing 5,000 to 10,000 units of streptokinase/ml should remain in direct contact with the affected area. For exudates in small enclosed spaces, a solution containing 5,000 to 10,000 units of streptokinase/ml is used. The dosage and amount of fluid injected generally should depend upon the size of the cavity, and provision should be made for drainage of the liquefied exudate. For surface lesions of the hands, a jelly containing approximately 5,000 units of streptokinase/g may be placed inside a loose rubber glove which is tied at the wrist.

This mixture is not useful by any route for the treatment of inflammation and edema associated with trauma or infection and, therefore, no dosage regimen is given. The manufacturer's suggested dosages are:

Intramuscular (gluteal): *Adults*, 0.5 ml of a solution containing streptokinase 5,000 units twice daily.

Buccal, Oral: Adults, one tablet four times daily for four to six days.

PREPARATIONS.—Varidase (Lederle).

Topical: Powder (for solution or jelly) containing streptokinase 100,000 units and streptodornase at least 25,000 units supplied with or without 15 ml of 4.5% carboxymethylcellulose gel for preparation of jelly.

Intramuscular: Powder (for reconstitution) containing streptokinase 20,000 units and streptodornase at least 5,000 units with 0.2 g thimerosal.

Oral, Buccal: Each tablet contains streptokinase 10,000 units and streptodornase at least 2,500 units with thimerosal 0.2 mg.

Chapter 92

MISCELLANEOUS DRUGS

AMANTADINE HYDROCHLORIDE
[Symmetrel]

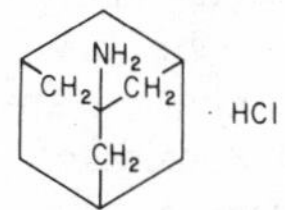

This antiviral agent is useful in preventing illness in persons exposed to respiratory infection during an epidemic confirmed to be due to an A_2 strain of influenza virus and in those above 1 year of age for whom this infection would entail a grave risk. When used prophylactically, it protects 50% to 70% of recipients from infection. Amantadine is not virucidal and apparently produces its effects by impeding penetration of the influenza A_2 virus into the host cell. During a demonstrated influenza A_2 epidemic, amantadine may be used concomitantly with vaccine for prophylaxis.

Although the manufacturer recommends amantadine only for prophylaxis, the drug may have therapeutic value if given promptly after the first symptoms of infection have appeared.

For a discussion of the use of amantadine in parkinsonism, see Chapter 74, Antiparkinsonism Agents.

The most common adverse reactions are irritability, tremor, slurred speech, ataxia, mental depression, insomnia, lethargy, and dizziness. Nausea, anorexia, and vomiting have occurred occasionally. These untoward effects are dose-related; their incidence is low (1% to 2%) when usual doses are used. No renal, hepatic, bone marrow, or other hematologic disturbances have been observed.

Livedo reticularis is a common adverse reaction associated with the use of amantadine in parkinsonism. There are no reports of this reaction in patients receiving the drug for the prophylaxis of influenza.

Patients with a history of epilepsy or those receiving central nervous system stimulants or psychopharmacologic agents should not be given amantadine. If patients have been receiving large amounts of anticholinergic drugs, the dose should be reduced prior to use of amantadine. Those with cerebral arteriosclerosis should be under close medical supervision. Patients who become dizzy after taking amantadine should avoid activities requiring mental alertness (eg, driving) during the course of administration.

USUAL DOSAGE.—*Oral:* For prophylaxis, *adults*, 100 mg twice daily; *children 1 to 9 years of age*, 4 to 9 mg/kg of body weight in two or three equal doses, not to exceed 150 mg daily; *9 to 12 years*, 100 mg twice daily. Administration should be started in anticipation of contact or as soon as possible after contact with individuals who have influenza A_2 respiratory illness. In a planned program of prophylaxis against influenza A_2, amantadine therapy should be continued daily for at least ten days following a known exposure, up to 30 days for possible repeated and unknown exposures, and up to 90 days for possible repeated, uncontrolled, and unknown exposures to influenza A_2 illness.

In the treatment of established A_2 influenza, amantadine should be administered in the same doses used for prophylaxis as soon as possible after the onset of illness; therapy should be continued for ten days.

PREPARATIONS.—Symmetrel (DuPont). *Oral:* Capsules 100 mg; syrup 50 mg/5 ml.

AROMATIC AMMONIA SPIRIT

Aromatic ammonia spirit is a hydroalcoholic solution containing approximately 2% ammonia, 4% ammonium carbonate, and several volatile oils; it is inhaled for treatment of syncope.

Administration brings ammonia in contact with the mucous membranes of the upper respiratory system, where its irritating properties produce sensory stimulation that reflexly stimulates the respiratory and vasomotor centers of the medulla. This produces an increase in respiration and a rise in blood pressure.

Adverse effects have not been reported and are not to be expected from normal use of this preparation.

USUAL DOSAGE.—*Inhalation: Adults and children*, vapor is inhaled as required.

PREPARATIONS.—Aromatic Ammonia Spirit, N.F. Marketed by many manufacturers under generic name.

AZATHIOPRINE [Imuran]

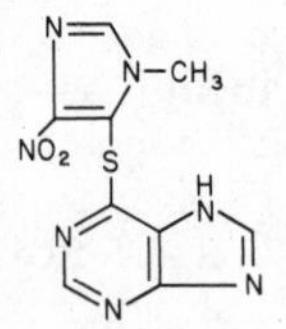

Azathioprine is an imidazolyl derivative of the antineoplastic agent, mercaptopurine, and it has similar actions. It is indicated as an adjunct to prevent rejection in kidney homoplasty. For other investigative uses of azathioprine, see Chapter 26, Antirheumatic Agents. Azathioprine has cytotoxic effects and should be given under the supervision of a physician experienced in the use of antineoplastic agents.

The most common adverse effect is depression of bone marrow function, which is manifested by leukopenia and, less frequently, by thrombocytopenia, anemia, and pancytopenia. Other adverse effects include aphthous stomatitis, rashes, alopecia, and, with larger doses, nausea, vomiting, and diarrhea. Jaundice, accompanied by very high alkaline phosphatase levels suggesting liver damage or biliary stasis, also has been observed.

Complete blood cell counts, including platelets, should be performed every other day during initial administration and at least weekly during maintenance therapy in order to avoid severe and irreversible bone marrow depression. Because azathioprine is excreted in the urine, patients with impaired renal function should be given smaller doses to avoid toxic accumulation.

When cadaveric kidneys are used as transplants, tubular necrosis frequently develops; this affects renal function and clearance of azathioprine and necessitates a reduction in dosage. If patients are also receiving allopurinol for prevention of hyperuricemia, the dose of azathioprine should be reduced by one-third to one-fourth. Azathioprine is inactivated by xanthine oxidase, and in the presence of allopurinol, a xanthine oxidase inhibitor, the metabolism may be delayed; this prolongs the drug's action and can possibly cause severe bone marrow depression.

Since azathioprine lowers immune responses, the development of potentially fatal intercurrent fungal, protozoal, viral, or uncommon bacterial infections requires appropriate therapy and possibly a reduction in dose.

If signs of rejection (decreased urine volume, creatinine clearance rate, and sodium concentration) occur after transplantation, a larger dose may be necessary. If signs of rejection persist, other means of handling the problem should be considered.

Since azathioprine has significant teratogenic potential in animals, its use should be avoided at least during the first trimester of pregnancy.

USUAL DOSAGE.—*Oral:* The dose must be individualized in accordance with the physical condition and tolerance of the patient. The usual initial dose is 3 to 5 mg/kg of body weight given one to five days before surgery. Postoperatively, the dose is adjusted to maintain the homograft without producing toxic effects; as little as 1 to 2 mg/kg daily may be sufficient. Because of a possible delayed action, the dosage may have to be reduced or therapy discontinued if there is an abnormal fall in the leukocyte count and/or prolonged depression of bone marrow function. The adjunctive treatment used to suppress the rejection of renal homografts may enhance the toxicity of azathioprine.

PREPARATIONS.—Imuran (Burroughs Wellcome). *Oral:* Tablets 50 mg.

CARBAMAZEPINE [Tegretol]

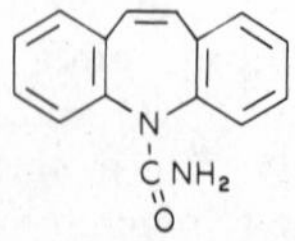

Carbamazepine, a tricyclic compound chemically related to imipramine, has substantially advanced the treatment of trigeminal neuralgia. The drug completely relieves pain in about 80% of the patients treated. Analgesia usually begins within 24 hours and continues as long as carbamazepine is administered. If the drug is withdrawn, the pain usually returns but responds to retreatment. Evidence is accumulating which indicates that the efficacy of carbamazepine declines after prolonged use (ie, about four years). If a relapse occurs during therapy, complete relief may be achieved again in approximately one-half of the patients by increasing the dosage. When this is not effective, the simultaneous administration of diphenylhydantoin and carbamazepine, or of mephenesin, diphenylhydantoin, and carbamazepine, may be helpful. Diphenylhydantoin and mephenesin also are used individually in the treatment of trigeminal neuralgia, but are less effective than carbamazepine. Carbamazepine also is useful in glossopharyngeal neuralgia. These are the only two neuralgias that respond to treatment with this drug.

Carbamazepine is beneficial in treating certain forms of epilepsy (see Chapter 31, Anticonvulsants), and has been used to relieve pain in multiple sclerosis, acute idiopathic polyneuritis (Guillain-Barré disease), peripheral diabetic neuropathy, tabes dorsalis, as well as in individuals with thalamic pain. It also has been administered in the prophylaxis of the migraine syndrome.

Adverse Reactions and Precautions.—About one-fourth of patients receiving carbamazepine experience adverse reactions. Most untoward effects subside spontaneously within a week or after a reduction in dosage, or their occurrence may be minimized by initiating therapy with a small dose and increasing the amount gradually.

Neurologic reactions are reported most commonly (incidence, 15%). They include dizziness, drowsiness, ataxia, confusion, headache, fatigue, blurred vision, transient diplopia and oculomotor disturbances, dysphasia, abnormal involuntary movement, peripheral neuritis and paresthesias, depression with agitation, talkativeness, nystagmus, and tinnitus.

Disorders of the digestive system (nausea, vomiting, gastric distress and abdominal pain, diarrhea, constipation, anorexia, dryness of the mouth, glossitis, and stomatitis) occur in 4% of patients.

Dermatologic reactions (pruritic and erythematous rashes, urticaria, Stevens-Johnson syndrome, photosensitivity, alterations in skin pigmentation, exfoliative dermatitis, alopecia, hyperhidrosis, erythema multiforme, erythema nodosum, and aggravation of systemic lupus erythematosus) occur in 2% of patients.

Hematopoietic reactions include transitory leukopenia, agranulocytosis, eosinophilia, leukocytosis, purpura, aplastic anemia, and thrombocytopenia. The incidence of these reactions is 1%. Four fatalities have been reported from aplastic anemia and thrombocytopenia. Therefore, patients should discontinue the drug and notify their physician if signs of hematologic toxicity appear (eg, fever, sore throat, aphthous stomatitis, easy bruising, petechial or purpuric hemorrhage). Blood and platelet counts also should be performed at regular intervals during therapy.

The overall incidence of cardiovascular, genitourinary, metabolic, hepatic, and miscellaneous reactions is less than 1%. The untoward effects reported include aggravation of hypertension, hypotension, syncope, edema, aggravation of ischemic heart disease, congestive heart failure, recurrence of thrombophlebitis, urinary frequency, acute urinary retention, albuminuria, glycosuria, elevated blood urea nitrogen levels, impotence, cholestatic and hepatocellular jaundice, fever and chills, lymphadenopathy, myalgia and arthralgia, leg cramps, and conjunctivitis.

This drug should be used cautiously in patients with cardiovascular, liver, renal, or urinary tract disease or increased intraocular pressure and in those who are receiving monoamine oxidase inhibitors or tricyclic antidepressants.

Although teratogenicity has not been reported in humans, carbamazepine should not be given to pregnant women unless the benefits outweigh the risks. Also, because toxic effects have been reported in nursing rats, the drug should be administered with caution to nursing mothers.

USUAL DOSAGE.—*Oral:* For trigeminal neuralgia, *adults,* 100 mg twice on the first day; this is increased by increments of 100 mg every 12 hours until freedom from pain is achieved (range, 200 mg to 1.2 g daily). A pain-free condition usually can be maintained with a dose of 400 to 800 mg daily. The drug should always be administered at minimal effective dosage and with meals. Since many individuals have spontaneous prolonged remissions every few months, an attempt should be made to discontinue therapy periodically.

For glossopharyngeal neuralgia, *adults,* 600 mg daily in divided doses (range, 600 mg to 1 g).

For the pain of multiple sclerosis, *adults*, initially 200 mg daily; this amount is increased by increments of 200 mg every other day until relief of pain or toxicity occurs.

For the pain of acute idiopathic polyneuritis (Guillain-Barré syndrome), *adults*, 400 to 600 mg daily in divided doses.

For prophylaxis of the migraine syndrome, *adults*, 200 to 600 mg daily in divided doses, depending upon the tolerance of the individual.

For treatment of the sensory manifestations of peripheral diabetic neuropathy, *adults*, 600 mg daily in divided doses.

For use in epilepsy, see Chapter 31, Anticonvulsants.

PREPARATIONS.—Tegretol (Geigy). *Oral:* Tablets 200 mg.

DISULFIRAM [Antabuse]

$$(C_2H_5)_2N\overset{S}{\overset{\|}{C}}-SS-\overset{S}{\overset{\|}{C}}N(C_2H_5)_2$$

Disulfiram, a thiuram derivative, interferes with alcohol catabolism. Individuals taking this drug who then ingest alcohol show an increase in the blood acetaldehyde concentration, which produces several uncomfortable symptoms. The unpleasantness of this alcohol-disulfiram reaction is the basis for the drug's use. The symptoms consist of flushing, throbbing in the head and neck, dyspnea, nausea, copious vomiting, hyperhidrosis, thirst, chest pain, palpitation, hyperventilation, tachycardia, hypotension, syncope, anxiety, asthenia, vertigo, blurred vision, and confusion. The blood pressure may fall to a shock level. The reaction usually lasts 30 minutes to several hours. Drowsiness and sleep follow. The intensity of the reaction varies but is generally proportional to the amounts of disulfiram and alcohol ingested. In severe reactions, respiratory depression, acute circulatory failure, arrhythmias, myocardial infarction, acute congestive heart failure, syncope, convulsions, and death may occur.

In the absence of alcohol, disulfiram may cause transient mild drowsiness, fatigability, impotence, headache, acneiform eruptions, allergic dermatitis, or a metallic or garlic-like aftertaste during the first two weeks of therapy. These adverse effects usually disappear spontaneously with continued therapy or reduced dosage. Psychotic reactions have been noted; in most cases, these are attributable to large doses, drug interactions (with metronidazole or isoniazid), or the unmasking of underlying psychoses. Polyneuropathy, peripheral neuritis, and, rarely, optic neuropathy also have occurred.

During severe reactions, individuals should be treated as for shock. (See Chapter 5, Agents Used in Hypotension and Shock.) The inhalation of a mixture of 95% oxygen and 5% carbon dioxide and other symptomatic treatment also may be useful. The serum potassium level should be monitored and maintained, particularly in patients receiving digitalis therapy, since hypokalemia has been reported. Because effects persist up to two weeks after termination of therapy, the patient should be warned not to ingest alcohol during this period.

Because disulfiram inhibits the metabolism of several drugs in addition to alcohol, the possible consequences of the accumulation of concomitantly administered drugs should be borne in mind. In particular, toxic levels of diphenylhydantoin or its congeners may accumulate when disulfiram is given concomitantly.

It may be necessary to adjust the dosage of oral anticoagulant preparations upon initiating or discontinuing disulfiram therapy.

Patients should be observed for the appearance of an unsteady gait or marked changes in mental status when isoniazid and disulfiram are given concomitantly; disulfiram should be discontinued if such signs appear.

Disulfiram should be used with great caution in patients with diabetes mellitus, hypothyroidism, epilepsy, cerebral damage, chronic or acute nephritis, hepatic cirrhosis or insufficiency, and during pregnancy. Its use is contraindicated in patients with severe ischemic heart disease, coronary thrombosis, psychosis, in those recently treated with paraldehyde or metronidazole, in those who have recently ingested alcohol or an alcohol-containing product (eg, foods, beverages, elixirs, cough syrups, lotions). Disulfiram should not be used without the patient's full knowledge.

It may be advisable for patients undergoing treatment with disulfiram to carry identification describing the most common symptoms of the disulfiram-alcohol reaction and designating the attending physician. (Identification cards may be obtained from the manufacturer.)

USUAL DOSAGE.—The patient must abstain from using alcohol for at least 12 hours before initiating treatment.

Oral: Adults, initially, 500 mg daily for one

to two weeks. For maintenance, 250 mg daily (range, 125 to a maximum of 500 mg) is given for months to years, depending on the individual.

PREPARATIONS.—Antabuse (Ayerst). *Oral:* Tablets 250 and 500 mg.

FLAVOXATE HYDROCHLORIDE [Urispas]

This drug is used in an effort to reduce symptoms from various disorders of the lower urinary tract. Varying degrees of relief from dysuria, nocturia, suprapubic pain, urinary frequency, urinary urgency, and incontinence associated with cystitis, prostatitis, urethritis, and trigonitis have been reported. Flavoxate appears to compare favorably with propantheline, but conclusive evidence demonstrating its clinical superiority over a placebo is not available. However, the drug tends to increase bladder capacity and decrease pressure in patients with bladder spasm, although these actions have not been demonstrated consistently.

Flavoxate relaxes smooth muscle through a direct musculotropic action. Results of studies in animals indicate that it also has local anesthetic and analgesic properties. The contribution of each of these effects to the relief of symptoms is difficult to appraise clinically. Excretion of the drug in the urine, with the resultant local action upon urinary tissues, may play a role. There is no reason to believe that flavoxate would otherwise be selective in relaxing the musculature of the urinary tract to the exclusion of other smooth muscle.

Flavoxate is not curative; definitive treatment of urologic disease must be provided by other measures.

Adverse reactions are relatively uncommon, although the following have been reported: nausea, vomiting, dryness of the mouth, nervousness, vertigo, headache, drowsiness, blurred vision, increased intraocular pressure, disturbance in visual accommodation, urticaria and other dermatoses, mental confusion (especially in the elderly), dysuria, tachycardia and palpitation, fever, and eosinophilia. One case of leukopenia that was reversible upon discontinuation of the drug has been reported. Some reactions resemble atropine-like effects, although the limited pharmacologic evidence available indicates that flavoxate has little anticholinergic action.

Gastrointestinal obstructions or hemorrhage or lower urinary tract obstructions are contraindications to use of this drug; flavoxate should be used with caution in patients with glaucoma. The safety of the drug in pregnant women has not been established, although no obvious hazards were observed in animal studies.

USUAL DOSAGE.—*Oral: Adults*, 100 or 200 mg three or four times daily; *children under 12 years of age*, dosage has not been established.

PREPARATIONS.—Urispas (Smith Kline & French). *Oral:* Tablets 100 mg.

GLUCAGON

Glucagon, a polypeptide hormone produced by the pancreas, promptly elevates the concentration of glucose in the blood by mobilizing hepatic glycogen. It is given to terminate severe hypoglycemic reactions caused by administration of insulin to diabetic or psychiatric patients when use of dextrose is impractical or difficult. This treatment is useful only when hepatic glycogen is available.

Nausea and vomiting have been the most frequently reported adverse effects. Hypersensitivity reactions are possible because the drug is extracted from animals.

USUAL DOSAGE.—*Intramuscular, Intravenous, Subcutaneous: Adults*, 0.5 to 1 mg, followed by oral ingestion of carbohydrate when the individual responds. Carbohydrate restores liver glycogen and prevents secondary hypoglycemia. There is no contraindication to one or two additional doses or to larger initial doses if desired. If there is no response within 20 minutes, dextrose must be administered intravenously.

PREPARATIONS.—Glucagon (Lilly). *Injection:* Powder 1 and 10 mg.

PHENAZOPYRIDINE HYDROCHLORIDE [Pyridium]

H_2N — N — NH_2 — N=N — phenyl · HCl

This azo dye was introduced as a urinary antiseptic but was found to be of little value for this purpose. Phenazopyridine has some topical anesthetic activity, and currently is used orally as a urinary analgesic to relieve pain in cystitis, prostatitis, and urethritis. Because it provides only symptomatic relief, prompt appropriate treatment of the cause of the pain should be instituted, and phenazopyridine should be discontinued when the symptoms are controlled (usually within four to six days). Many fixed-dose combinations containing antibacterial agents and phenazopyridine are available, but administration of the individual drugs is preferred (see Chapter 55, Sulfonamides, and Chapter 57, Aminoglycoside Antibacterial Agents and Miscellaneous Antimicrobial Drugs).

Gastrointestinal disturbances and headache occur occasionally. Large doses or prolonged use may produce methemoglobinemia; a few cases of hemolytic anemia, skin pigmentation, and acute renal failure also have been reported. The use of phenazopyridine is contraindicated in patients with impaired renal function, uremia, glomerulonephritis, pyelonephritis during pregnancy, or severe hepatitis. The drug will color urine red or orange, and clothing is likely to be stained. (The stain is difficult to remove from fabric.)

USUAL DOSAGE.—*Oral: Adults,* 200 mg three times daily; *children,* 12 mg/kg of body weight daily divided into three doses after meals.

PREPARATIONS.—Pyridium (Warner-Chilcott). *Oral:* Tablets 100 and 200 mg.

PRALIDOXIME CHLORIDE [Protopam Chloride]

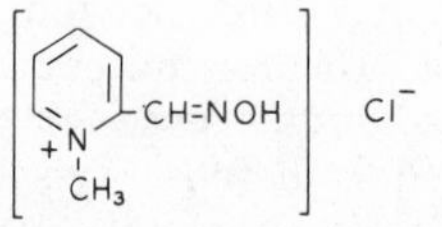

$$\left[\text{(pyridinium ring, } N^{+}\text{–}CH_3\text{)–}CH{=}NOH \right] Cl^{-}$$

Pralidoxime is a cholinesterase reactivator that is used primarily as an adjunct in the treatment of poisoning caused by some cholinesterase inhibitors used as pesticides. It also has been given prophylactically to those who are continually exposed to cholinesterase inhibitors (eg, agricultural workers). Pralidoxime may be used alone in the differential diagnosis of cholinergic crisis or to treat the anticholinesterase-induced symptoms that may occur during treatment of myasthenia gravis (see Chapter 75, Agents used in Myasthenia Gravis). It is used rarely to reverse the ocular effects of topically administered anticholinesterase agents and, in conjunction with other drugs, to produce mydriasis (see Chapter 72, Miscellaneous Ophthalmic Preparations).

Pralidoxime acts by competing with cholinesterase for the carbamate or phosphorous group of the inhibitor, thus displacing the inhibitor and restoring enzyme activity. This reactivation occurs primarily at the neuromuscular junction. Much less takes place at autonomic effector sites and relatively little in the central nervous system. This relative specificity in its site of action determines the role of pralidoxime in the treatment of anticholinesterase poisoning: This oxime is used to reverse muscular paralysis, particularly that of the respiratory muscles. Atropine must be administered to treat symptoms of poisoning that originate at sites where pralidoxime is relatively ineffective. Therefore, atropine is given with pralidoxime to improve central respiratory function and to reduce increased bronchopulmonary secretions, hypersalivation, lacrimation, hyperhidrosis, nausea, vomiting, abdominal cramps, bradycardia, miosis, headache, lethargy, and drowsiness.

Pralidoxime is not equally effective against all cholinesterase inhibitors. Most reports on the successful use of this agent have been in poisonings caused by the organophosphate pesticide, parathion. Pralidoxime also has been used successfully in poisonings caused by the related agents mevinphos, isoflurophate, malathion, Azodrin, dimpylate [Diazinon], disulfoton, EPN, methyl demeton, methyl parathion, phosphamidon, tetraethyl pyrolphosphate (TEPP), and sarin. It is less effective in antagonizing the carbamate-type cholinesterase inhibitors (eg, neostigmine, pyridostigmine, ambenonium) that are used in the treatment of myasthenia gravis. Symptoms of poisoning may become even more severe if pralidoxime is administered after exposure to the carbamate pesticide, carbaryl.

Pralidoxime is most effective if administered immediately after poisoning. Generally, little is accomplished if the drug is given more than 36 hours after termination of the exposure; however, when the poison has been ingested, exposure may continue for some time due to its slow absorption from the lower bowel. Gastric lavage may be employed if ingestion has occurred; however, absorption of the poison may continue and fatal relapses have been reported after initial improvement. Therefore, close supervision of the patient is indicated for at least 48 to 72 hours. If exposure to the poison was through the skin, clothing should be removed and the skin washed thoroughly with sodium bicarbonate or alcohol as soon as possible. Barbiturates may be given cautiously if the patient is having convulsions. Exposure to phosphate ester pesticides should be avoided for several weeks after poisoning.

Pralidoxime may cause dizziness, diplopia, impaired accommodation, headache, drowsiness, nausea, tachycardia, increased systolic and diastolic blood pressure, hyperventilation, and muscle weakness when given parenterally to individuals who have not been exposed to cholinesterase poisoning. No significant toxic effects have been reported after prolonged oral administration.

Although it is not necessary to perform laboratory tests prior to use of pralidoxime, red blood cell and plasma cholinesterase determinations and urinary paranitrophenol measurements (in the case of parathion exposure), if available, may be helpful in confirming the diagnosis and following the course of the illness. The red blood cell cholinesterase determination provides an approximate index of intoxication; a reduction below 50% of normal has been seen only with organophosphate ester poisoning. When pralidoxime is administered soon after onset of poisoning, the red blood cell cholinesterase level may be restored more rapidly than the plasma level. However, both plasma and red blood cell levels may remain depressed for a month or longer after intoxication; they may also be depressed in patients with subclinical chronic exposures.

The dosage of pralidoxime should be reduced in patients with impaired renal function because blood levels are increased in these individuals.

USUAL DOSAGE.—

Intravenous: For severe poisoning (coma, cyanosis, respiratory embarrassment) caused by organophosphate-containing substances, the following treatment program should be instituted: A patent airway is secured and, if necessary, positive pressure artificial respiration is begun. As soon as cyanosis has been relieved, 2 to 4 mg of atropine is given intravenously to adults; this dose may be repeated at five- to ten-minute intervals until signs of toxicity appear. The dosage of atropine in children is 0.5 to 1 mg given intramuscularly or intravenously every 10 to 15 minutes until signs of toxicity appear. Some degree of atropinization should be maintained for at least 48 hours. In *adults*, 1 g of pralidoxime, preferably diluted with 100 ml of sodium chloride injection, is infused over a 30-minute period or injected at a rate not exceeding 200 mg per minute. If response is poor, the dose may be repeated in one hour. *Children* may be given a 5% solution in doses of 20 to 40 mg/kg of body weight. The dose may be increased to 25 to 60 mg/kg if the response is poor.

When the poisoning has been moderately severe, as manifested by hyperhidrosis, lacrimation, hypersalivation, diarrhea, and tightness in the chest, the patient is treated as for severe poisoning but establishment of a patent airway or institution of artificial respiration is not necessary.

For the dosage used in myasthenia gravis, see Chapter 75, Agents Used in Myasthenia Gravis.

Oral: For treatment of mild poisoning (headache, blurred vision, mild muscarinic signs) from organophosphate-containing substances, the exposure to the poison is terminated and 1 to 2 g of pralidoxime is then given. If necessary, this dose is repeated in three hours. The patient should remain under the physician's supervision for at least 24 hours.

For prophylaxis in those who are intermittently exposed to cholinesterase inhibitors for no longer than one working day, *adults*, 3 g for not more than four or five doses. The first dose is taken just before exposure and the second just after exposure; remaining doses are given only if signs and symptoms of poisoning appear. Standard safety procedures in handling pesticides should always be followed.

Subconjunctival Injection: For ophthalmic uses, see Chapter 72, Miscellaneous Ophthalmic Preparations.

PREPARATIONS.—Protopam Chloride (Ayerst).

Injection: Powder 1 g.

Oral: Tablets 500 mg.

SODIUM FLUORIDE

The fluoridation of drinking water is the most widely used method for the mass prevention of dental caries in children. For children living in locations where the community water supply is not adequately fluoridated, however, benefits can be obtained by supplementing the diet with sodium fluoride. Such use must be continued over long periods of time, ie, from infancy until 12 to 14 years of age.

Occasionally, when a need for vitamin supplementation exists and a child's source of drinking water contains less than the optimal amount of fluoride, multivitamin preparations containing 0.5 or 1 mg of fluoride in each daily dose may be an appropriate means for supplying prophylactic fluoride. (See following listing for available preparations.) However, parents should be warned that use of the preparation should be discontinued or reviewed if the family moves or there is some other change in the water supply.

Prevention of caries in children can also be achieved by the topical application of solutions of sodium fluoride or stannous fluoride to the teeth. Certain dentifrices which contain stannous fluoride or sodium monofluorophosphate are also effective.

The use of sodium fluoride, stannous fluoride, and sodium monofluorophosphate to prevent dental caries does not produce toxic reactions. However, accidental poisoning from fluoride-containing compounds (eg, insecticides) does occur, although it is rare. The lethal dose of soluble fluoride compounds for adults is estimated to be between 2 and 5 g. The symptoms of poisoning are nausea, vomiting, hypersalivation, abdominal pain, diarrhea, myalgia, hyperreflexia, tonic and clonic convulsions, paresthesias, and hypotension. Death may result from cardiac failure or respiratory arrest. Treatment should be instituted quickly and should consist of the administration of a soluble calcium salt (eg, calcium chloride solution 5%) by lavage, intravenous administration of fluids and, if signs of tetany appear, calcium gluconate injection.

Chronic toxicity (fluorosis) usually results from the accidental ingestion of fluoride-containing insecticides or continual inhalation of fluoride-containing industrial dusts (eg, in aluminum mining and the phosphate fertilizer industry) or continual use of drinking water containing excessive levels (more than 2 ppm). The toxic effects are manifest in the skeleton (osteomalacia and osteosclerosis) and in the teeth (mottled enamel [dental fluorosis]) if the teeth are developing at the time toxicity occurs. Once the teeth are formed, fluorides have no effect on them. Except for orthopedic and supportive measures, there is no treatment for fluorosis and all efforts should be directed at its prevention.

USUAL DOSAGE.—*Oral: Children 3 to 14 years of age*, sufficient sodium fluoride to provide a daily level of 1 mg of fluoride ion (2.2 mg if there is no fluoride in drinking water; this amount should be adjusted downward in proportion to the amount provided in the drinking water); *2 to 3 years*, half the above amount; *under 2 years*, no specific daily dose has been established.

PREPARATIONS.—Sodium Fluoride, U.S.P. *Oral:* Tablets 2.2 mg.

AVAILABLE TRADEMARKS.—Fluoritab (Fluoritab); Flura-Drops, Flura-Loz, and Flura-Tablets (Kirkman); Karidium (Lorvic); Les-Cav (Cooper); Luride (Davies Rose Hoyt); So-Flo (Professional). Drug also marketed by many manufacturers under generic name.

Mixtures Containing Sodium Fluoride and Vitamins

Abdec Drops W/Fluoride (Parke, Davis): Each 0.6 ml contains vitamin A palmitate 5,000 U, ergocalciferol 400 U, thiamine 1 mg, riboflavin phosphate sodium 1.65 mg, pyridoxine 1 mg, sodium *d*-pantothenate 5.5 mg, nicotinamide 10 mg, ascorbic acid 50 mg, and sodium fluoride 1.1 mg.

Adeflor Chewable Tablets (Upjohn): Each tablet contains sodium fluoride 0.5 or 1 mg, vitamin A 1.2 mg, vitamin D 10 μg, sodium ascorbate 75 mg, thiamine mononitrate 2 mg, riboflavin 2 mg, niacinamide 18 mg, pyridoxine hydrochloride 1 mg, calcium pantothenate 5 mg, and cyanocobalamin 2 μg.

Adeflor B Drops (Upjohn): Each 0.6 ml contains sodium fluoride 0.5 mg, vitamin A 0.6 mg, vitamin D 10 μg, ascorbic acid 50 mg, pyridoxine hydrochloride 1 mg, thiamine hydrochloride 1 mg, riboflavin 1 mg, niacinamide 10 mg, and *d*-pantothenyl alcohol 3 mg.

Funda-Vite (F) (Davies Rose Hoyt): Each 0.6 ml tablet contains ergocalciferol 400 U, ascorbic acid 30 mg, and 1 mg fluoride (from 2.2 mg sodium fluoride).

Novacebrin with Fluoride (Lilly): Each chewable tablet contains sodium fluoride 1 mg, vitamin A 4,000 U, vitamin D 400 U, ascorbic acid 60 mg, thiamine mononitrate 1.5 mg, riboflavin 2 mg, cyanocobalamin 3 μg, niacinamide 12 mg, and panthenol 2.5 mg.

Poly-Vi-Flor (Mead Johnson): Each milliliter contains sodium fluoride 0.5 mg, vitamin A 2,000 U, vitamin D 400 U, vitamin E 5 U, ascorbic acid 60 mg, thiamine 0.6 mg, riboflavin 0.7 mg, niacin 8 mg, pyridoxine 0.6 mg, and pantothenic acid 4 mg.

Poly-Vi-Flor Chewable Tablets (Mead Johnson): Each tablet contains sodium fluoride 1 mg, vitamin A 3,500 U, vitamin D 400 U, vitamin E 4 U, ascorbic acid 75 mg, thiamine 1.1 mg, riboflavin 1.2 mg, niacin 15 mg, pyridoxine 1.2 mg, cyanocobalamin 5 μg, folic acid 0.1 mg, and pantothenic acid 7 mg.

Tri-Vi-Flor Chewable Tablets (Mead Johnson): Each tablet contains sodium fluoride 0.5 mg, vitamin A 4,000 U, vitamin D 400 U, and ascorbic acid 75 mg.

Tri-Vi-Flor (Mead Johnson): Each milliliter contains sodium fluoride 0.5 mg, vitamin A 2,000 U, vitamin D 400 U, and ascorbic acid 60 mg.

Vi-Daylin W/Fluoride (Ross): Each chewable tablet contains sodium fluoride 1 mg, vitamin A 4,000 U, vitamin D_2 400 U, ascorbic acid 75 mg, thiamine mononitrate 1.5 mg, riboflavin 1.2 mg, niacinamide

10 mg, pyridoxine hydrochloride 1 mg, and cobalamin 3 mg.

Vi-Penta Infant Drops (Roche): Each 0.6 ml contains sodium fluoride 0.5 mg, vitamin A 5,000 U, ergocalciferol 10 μg, ascorbic acid 50 mg, and vitamin E 2 U.

SODIUM MORRHUATE

Sodium morrhuate, a sterile solution of the sodium salts of the fatty acids of cod liver oil, is the preferred sclerosing agent in the treatment of simple (without incompetent valves) varicose veins. It is injected into the vein and damages the intimal surface. This induces blood clot formation and, eventually, the formation of fibrous tissue which permanently closes the vein.

Adverse effects include burning, urticaria, or necrosis and slough at the site of injection. Headache, nausea, vomiting, and hypersensitivity reactions also may occur.

USUAL DOSAGE.—*Intravenous: Adults,* 1 ml (range, 0.5 to 5 ml, depending upon the size of the vessel) of a 5% solution.

PREPARATIONS.—Sodium Morrhuate Injection, U.S.P. *Injection:* Solution 5%. Drug marketed by many manufacturers under generic name.

MANUFACTURERS

Abbott Laboratories, 14th and Sheridan Road, North Chicago, Illinois 60064.

Alcon Laboratories, Inc., 6201 South Freeway, P. O. Box 1959, Fort Worth, Texas 76101.

Alcon Specialty Products Division, Alcon Laboratories, Inc., P. O. Box 34630, Dallas, Texas 75234.

Allergan Pharmaceuticals, 2525 DuPont Drive, Irvine, California 92664.

American Chicle Co., Division of Warner-Lambert Pharmaceutical Company, 201 Tabor Road, Morris Plains, New Jersey 07950.

Amfre-Grant, Inc., 520 S. Dean Street, Box 150, Englewood, New Jersey 07631.

Arbrook, Inc., P. O. Box 130, Arlington, Texas 76010.

Arch Laboratories, Division of Lewis-Howe Co., 319 S. 4th Street, St. Louis, Missouri 63102.

Arcum Pharmaceutical Corporation, 225 Mill Street, N.E., Box 38, Vienna, Virginia 22180.

Armour Pharmaceutical Company, Division of Armour & Co., Greyhound Tower, Phoenix, Arizona 85077.

Armour-Dial, Inc., Greyhound Tower, Phoenix, Arizona 85077.

Arnar-Stone Laboratories, Inc., 601 E. Kensington Road, Mount Prospect, Illinois 60056.

B. F. Ascher & Company, Inc., 5100 E. 59th Street, Kansas City, Missouri 64130.

Astra Pharmaceutical Products, Inc., 7 Neponset Street, Worcester, Massachusetts 01606.

Ayerst Laboratories, Division of American Home Products Corporation, 685 Third Avenue, New York, N. Y. 10017.

Badger Pharmacal, Inc., Box 171, Cedarburg, Wisconsin 53012.

Barnes-Hind Pharmaceuticals, Inc., 895 Kifer Road, Sunnyvale, California 94086.

The Barre Drug Co., Inc., 4128 Hayward Avenue, Baltimore, Maryland 21215.

Baxter Laboratories, Inc., 6301 Lincoln Avenue, Morton Grove, Illinois 60053.

Beecham-Massengill Pharmaceuticals, Division of Beecham Inc., 501-551 Fifth Street, Bristol, Tennessee 37620.

Bentex Division, ICN Pharmaceuticals, 12936 Player Road, P. O. Box 35537, Houston, Texas 77045.

Block Drug Co., Inc., 257 Cornelison Avenue, Jersey City, New Jersey 07302.

The Blue Line Chemical Company, 302 S. Broadway, St. Louis, Missouri 63102.

Borden Pharmaceutical Products, Division of Syntex Laboratories, Inc., Stanford Industrial Park, Palo Alto, California 94304.

Bowman Pharmaceuticals, 965 Cleveland Avenue, N.W., Canton, Ohio 44702.

Boyle & Co., 6330 Chalet Drive, Los Angeles, California 90040.

Brayten Pharmaceutical Co., 1715 W. 38th Street, Chattanooga, Tennessee 37409.

John H. Breck, Inc., Berdan Avenue, Wayne, New Jersey 07470.

Breon Laboratories Inc., 90 Park Avenue, New York, N. Y. 10016.

Bristol Laboratories, Division of Bristol-Myers Company, Thompson Road, P. O. Box 657, Syracuse, New York 13201.

Bristol-Myers Products, 345 Park Avenue, New York, N. Y. 10022.

Broemmel Pharmaceuticals, Riker Laboratories, Inc. 19901 Nordhoff Street, Northridge, California 91324.

The Brown Pharmaceutical Co., Inc., 2500 W. Sixth Street, Los Angeles, California 90057.

Burroughs Wellcome Co., 3030 Cornwallis Road, Research Triangle Park, North Carolina 27709.

Burton, Parsons & Co., Inc., 7351 86th Avenue, Washington, D. C. 20027.

Calbio Pharmaceuticals, Division of Calbiochem, P. O. Box 2948, San Diego, California 92112.

C. R. Canfield & Co., 2744 Lyndale Avenue, S., Minneapolis, Minnesota 55408.

The Carlton Corporation, 83 N. Summit Street, Tenafly, New Jersey 07670.

Carnrick Laboratories, Division of G. W. Carnrick Co., 65 Horse Hill Road, Cedar Knolls, New Jersey 07927.

The Central Pharmacal Co., 116-128 E. Third Street, Seymour, Indiana 47274.

Century Laboratories, Inc., 4936 Veterans Memorial Highway, Metairie, Louisiana 70004.

Century Pharmaceuticals, Inc., 4553 Allisonville Road, Indianapolis, Indiana 46205.

Chesebrough-Pond's Inc., 33 Benedict Place, Greenwich, Connecticut 06830.

Ciba Pharmaceutical Company, Division of Ciba-Geigy Corporation, 556 Morris Avenue, Summit, New Jersey 07901.

Otis Clapp & Son, Inc., 143 Albany Street, Cambridge, Massachusetts 02139.

Clark & Clark Corporation, South West Avenue, Wenonah, New Jersey 08090.

Colgate-Palmolive Company, 300 Park Avenue, New York, N. Y. 10022.

Connaught Laboratories, 1755 Steeles Avenue, W., Willowdale, Ontario, Canada.

Consolidated Midland Corporation, 195 E. Main Street, Box 74, Brewster, New York 10509.

Cooper Laboratories, Inc., 546 Bedford Road, Bedford Hills, New York 10507.

Courtland Laboratories, 5555 Valley Boulevard, Los Angeles, California 90032.

Cutter Laboratories, Fourth and Parker Streets, Berkeley, California 94710.

Davies Rose Hoyt, Pharmaceuticals Division of The Kendall Company, 633 Highland Avenue, Needham, Massachusetts 02194.

Davis & Geck, Division of American Cyanamid Company, Middletown Road, Pearl River, New York 10965.

Dermik Laboratories, Inc., 150 Eileen Way, Syosset, Long Island, New York 11791.

Doak Pharmacal Co., Inc., 2000 Shames Drive, Westbury, Long Island, New York 11590.

Dome Laboratories, Division of Miles Laboratories, Inc., 400 Morgan Lane, West Haven, Connecticut 06502.

Dorsey Laboratories, Division of Sandoz-Wander, Inc., N.E. U.S. 6 & Interstate 80, Lincoln, Nebraska 68501.

Dow Pharmaceuticals Division of The Dow Chemical Company, P. O. Box 1656, Indianapolis, Indiana 46206.

Duke Laboratories, Inc., Duke Place, Box 529, South Norwalk, Connecticut 06856.

E. I. du Pont de Nemours & Co., Inc., Pharmaceuticals Division, 1007 Market Street, Wilmington, Delaware 19898.

S. F. Durst & Company, Inc., Division of O'Neal, Jones & Feldman, Inc., 1683 Winchester Road, Philadelphia, Pennsylvania 19020.

Eaton Laboratories, Division of The Norwich Pharmacal Company, 17 Eaton Avenue, Norwich, New York 13815.

Paul B. Elder Company, 705 E. Mulberry Street, P. O. Box 31, Bryan, Ohio 43506.

Elkins-Sinn, Inc., 2 Esterbrook Lane, Cherry Hill, New Jersey 08002.

Endo Laboratories, Inc., 1000 Stewart Avenue, Garden City, New York 11530.

Fellows-Testagar, Division of Fellows Medical Mfg. Co., Inc., 12741 Capital Avenue, Oak Park, Michigan 48237.

Ferndale Laboratories, Inc., 780 W. Eight Mile Road, Ferndale, Michigan 48220.

First Texas Pharmaceuticals, Inc., 1810 N. Lamar Street, P. O. Box 5026, Dallas, Texas 75202.

C. B. Fleet Co., Inc., 4615 Murray Place, P. O. Box 1100, Lynchburg, Virginia 24505.

Fleming and Company, 9730 Reavis Park Drive, St. Louis, Missouri 63123.

Flint Laboratories, Division of Travenol Laboratories, Inc., 6301 Lincoln Avenue, Morton Grove, Illinois 60053.

Fluoritab Corporation, 1927 Copeman Boulevard, Box 361, Flint, Michigan 48501.

E. Fougera & Co., Inc., Cantiague Road, P. O. Box 73, Hicksville, Long Island, New York 11802.

Geigy Pharmaceuticals, Division of Ciba-Geigy Corporation, 556 Morris Avenue, Summit, New Jersey 07901.

Gerber Products Co., 445 State Street, Fremont, Michigan 49412.

Glenbrook Laboratories Inc., Division of Sterling Drug Inc., 90 Park Avenue, New York, N. Y. 10016.

Glenwood Laboratories, Inc., 83 N. Summit Street, Box 518, Tenafly, New Jersey 07670.

Hellwig, Inc., 223 E. Delaware Place, Chicago, Illinois 60611.

G. S. Herbert Laboratories, Division of Allergan Pharmaceuticals, 2525 DuPont Drive, Irvine, California 92664.

Dow B. Hickam, Inc., 5629 Grapevine, P. O. Box 35413, Houston, Texas 77045.

Hoechst Pharmaceuticals, Inc., Route 202-206 North, Somerville, New Jersey 08876.

Holland-Rantos Company, Inc., 865 Centennial Avenue, P. O. Box 5, Piscataway, New Jersey 08854.

Hollister-Stier Laboratories, 3525 N. Regal Street, Box 3145 Terminal Annex, Spokane, Washington 99220.

Hyland Laboratories, Division of Travenol Laboratories, Inc., 3300 Hyland Avenue, P. O. Box 2214, Costa Mesa, California 92626.

Hynson, Westcott & Dunning, Inc., Charles & Chase Streets, Baltimore, Maryland 21201.

International Pharmaceutical Corporation, 400 Valley Road, Warrington, Pennsylvania 18976.

Invenex Pharmaceuticals, 2176 Palou Avenue, San Francisco, California 94124.

Ives Laboratories, Inc., 685 Third Avenue, New York, N. Y. 10017.

The Andrew Jergens Company, 2535 Spring Grove Avenue, Cincinnati, Ohio 45214.

Johnson & Johnson, 500 George Street, New Brunswick, New Jersey 08901.

Kay Pharmacal Co., Inc., 1312 N. Utica Avenue, P. O. Box 50375, Tulsa, Oklahoma 74150.

Key Pharmacal Co., 1252 Heistan Place, Box 4832, Memphis, Tennessee 38104.

Key Pharmaceuticals, Inc., 50 N. W. 176th Street, P. O. Box 3670, Miami, Florida 33169.

Kinney & Company, Inc., 1307 12th Street, P. O. Box 307, Columbus, Indiana 47201.

Kirkman Laboratories, Inc., 934 N. E. 25th Avenue, Portland, Oregon 97208.

Knoll Pharmaceutical Company, 30 N. Jefferson Road, Whippany, New Jersey 07981.

Kremers-Urban Co., 5600 W. County Line Road, P. O. Box 2038, Milwaukee, Wisconsin 53201.

Lafayette Pharmacal, Inc., 522-526 N. Earl Avenue, Lafayette, Indiana 47904.

Lakeside Laboratories, Inc., Division of Colgate-Palmolive Company, 1707 E. North Avenue, Milwaukee, Wisconsin 53201.

The Lannett Co., Inc., 9000 State Road, Philadelphia, Pennsylvania 19136.

Lederle Laboratories, Division of American Cyanamid Company, N. Middletown Road, Pearl River, New York 10965.

Leeming/Pacquin Division, Pfizer, Inc., 235 E. 42nd Street, New York, N. Y. 10017.

Lemmon Pharmacal Company, Temple Avenue, P. O. Box 30, Sellersville, Pennsylvania 18960.

Lever Brothers Company, 390 Park Avenue, New York, N. Y. 10022.

Lewis-Howe Company, 319 S. 4th Street, St. Louis, Missouri 63102.

Eli Lilly and Company, Box 618, Indianapolis, Indiana 46206.

Lincoln Laboratories, Inc., Hickory Point Road, Box 1139, Decatur, Illinois 62525.

The Lorvic Corporation, 8810 Frost Avenue, St. Louis, Missouri 63134.

Madison Laboratories, Division of Ciba-Geigy Corporation, 556 Morris Avenue, Summit, New Jersey 07901.

Madland Laboratories, Inc., 4905 N. 31st Street, Milwaukee, Wisconsin 53209.

Mallard, Inc., 3021 Wabash Avenue, Detroit, Michigan 48216.

Mallinckrodt Pharmaceuticals, Division of Mallinckrodt Chemical Works, Second and Mallinckrodt Streets, St. Louis, Missouri 63160.

Marion Laboratories, Inc., 10236 Bunker Ridge Road, Kansas City, Missouri 64137.

Maurry Biological Co., Inc., 6109 S. Western Avenue, Los Angeles, California 90047.

McGaw Laboratories, 1015 Grandview Avenue, Glendale, California 91201.

McKesson Laboratories, P. O. Box 548, Bridgeport, Connecticut 06602.

McNeil Laboratories, Inc., Camp Hill Road, Fort Washington, Pennsylvania 19034.

Mead Johnson & Co., 2404 W. Pennsylvania Street, Evansville, Indiana 47721.

Medicone Company, 225 Varick Street, New York, N. Y. 10014.

Merck & Co., Inc., 1935 Lincoln Avenue, Rahway, New Jersey 07065.

Merck Sharp & Dohme, Division of Merck & Co., Inc., West Point, Pennsylvania 19486.

Merrell-National Laboratories, Division of Richardson-Merrell Inc., 110 E. Amity Road, Lockland Station, Cincinnati, Ohio 45215.

Miles Laboratories, Inc., 1127 Myrtle Street, Elkhart, Indiana 46514.

Mission Pharmacal Company, 1325 E. Durango Street, Box 1676, San Antonio, Texas 78206.

Mitchum-Thayer, Inc., 2700 W. Wood Street, Paris, Tennessee 38242.

Muro Pharmacal Laboratories, Inc., 121 Liberty Street, Quincy, Massachusetts 02169.

Neutragena Corporation, 5755 W. 96th Street, Los Angeles, California 90045.

North American Pharmacal, Inc., 6851 Chase Road, Dearborn, Michigan 48121.

Ohio Medical Products, Division of Air Reduction Company, Inc., 3030 Airco Drive, Madison, Wisconsin 53701.

Lydia O'Leary, Inc., 41 E. 57th Street, New York, N. Y. 10022.

Organon Inc., 375 Mt. Pleasant Avenue, West Orange, New Jersey 07052.

Ortho Pharmaceutical Corporation, Highway 202, Raritan, New Jersey 08869.

Owen Laboratories, Inc., Division of Alcon Laboratories, Inc., 3737 Belt Line Road, Box 34630, Dallas, Texas 75234.

Palmedico, Inc., 3810 River Drive, P. O. Drawer 3397, Columbia, South Carolina 29203.

Panray Division, Ormont Drug & Chemical Co., Inc., 520 S. Dean Street, Englewood, New Jersey 07631.

Parke, Davis & Company, Joseph Campau Avenue at the River, Detroit, Michigan 48232.

Pearson Products Division, Julius Schmid Inc., 423 W. 55th Street, New York, N. Y. 10019.

Pennwalt Prescription Products Division, Pennwalt Corporation, 755 Jefferson Road,

P. O. Box 1766, Rochester, New York 14623.

Person & Covey, Inc., 616 Allen Avenue, Glendale, California 91201.

Pfizer Laboratories, Division of Pfizer, Inc., 235 E. 42nd Street, New York, N. Y. 10017.

Pharmacia Laboratories Inc., 800 Centennial Avenue, Piscataway, New Jersey 08854.

Pharmaco/Sardo Products, Division of Plough Inc., 3022 Jackson Avenue, Memphis, Tennessee 38101.

Pharmacraft Pharmaceutical Division, Pennwalt Corporation, 755 Jefferson Road, P. O. Box 1212, Rochester, New York 14623.

Philips Roxane Laboratories, Division of Philips Roxane, Inc., 330 Oak Street, Columbus, Ohio 43216.

Picker Corporation, Medical Products Division, 595 Miner Road, Cleveland, Ohio 44143.

Plough, Inc., 3022 Jackson Avenue, P. O. Box 377, Memphis, Tennessee 38101.

Wm. P. Poythress & Co., Inc., 16 N. 22nd Street, P. O. Box 26946, Richmond, Virginia 23261.

Premo Pharmaceutical Laboratories, Inc., 111 Leuning Street, South Hackensack, New Jersey 07606.

The Proctor & Gamble Company, Professional Services Division, P. O. Box 171, Cincinnati, Ohio 45201.

Professional Pharmacal Co., 300 W. Josephine Street, P. O. Box 230, San Antonio, Texas 78212.

The Purdue Frederick Company, 99 Saw Mill River Road, Yonkers, New York 10701.

Quinton Company, Division of Merck & Co., Inc., P. O. Box 1346, Pittsburgh, Pennsylvania 15230.

Rachelle Laboratories, Inc., 700 Henry Ford Avenue, P. O. Box 9095, Long Beach, California 90810.

Reed & Carnrick, 30 Boright Avenue, Kenilworth, New Jersey 07033.

Reid-Provident Laboratories, Inc., 25 Fifth Street, N.W., Atlanta, Georgia 30308.

Research Foundation, 70 W. Hubbard Street, Chicago, Illinois 60610.

Revlon, Inc., 767 Fifth Avenue, New York, N. Y. 10022.

Richlyn Laboratories, 3725 Castor Avenue, Philadelphia, Pennsylvania 19124.

Riker Laboratories, Inc., 19901 Nordhoff Street, Northridge, California 91324.

A. H. Robins Company, 1407 Cummings Drive, Richmond, Virginia 23220.

Robinson Laboratory Inc., 355 Brannan Street, San Francisco, California 94107.

Roche Laboratories, Division of Hoffmann-La Roche Inc., Roche Park, Nutley, New Jersey 07110.

J. B. Roerig & Company, Division of Pfizer, Inc., 235 E. 42nd Street, New York, N. Y. 10017.

William H. Rorer, Inc., 500 Virginia Drive, Fort Washington, Pennsylvania 19034.

Ross Laboratories, Division of Abbott Laboratories, 625 Cleveland Avenue, Columbus, Ohio 43216.

Roussel Corporation, 155 E. 44th Street, New York, N. Y. 10017.

Rowell Laboratories, Inc., Lake of the Woods, Baudette, Minnesota 56623.

Helena Rubinstein, Inc., 767 Fifth Avenue, New York, N. Y. 10022.

Rystan Company Inc., 470 Mamaroneck Avenue, White Plains, New York 10605.

Sandoz Pharmaceuticals, Division of Sandoz-Wander, Inc., Route 10, Hanover, New Jersey 07936.

Sauter Laboratories, Inc., Division of Hoffmann-La Roche, Inc., Nutley, New Jersey 07110.

Savage Laboratories, Inc., P. O. Box 700, Bellaire, Texas 77401.

Schering Corporation, 60 Orange Street, Bloomfield, New Jersey 07003.

Schieffelin & Co., 562 Fifth Avenue, New York, N. Y. 10036.

Julius Schmid, Inc., 423 W. 55th Street, New York, N. Y. 10019.

Sea & Ski Corporation, 1500 Spring Garden Street, Philadelphia, Pennsylvania 19101.

G. D. Searle & Co., P. O. Box 5110, Chicago, Illinois 60680.

SIG Pharmaceuticals, Inc., 13010 Player Street, Houston, Texas 77045.

Smith Kline & French Laboratories, 1500 Spring Garden Street, Philadelphia, Pennsylvania 19101.

Smith, Miller & Patch, Inc., Division of Cooper Laboratories, Inc., 401 Joyce Kilmer Avenue, New Brunswick, New Jersey 08902.

E. R. Squibb & Sons, Inc., Lawrenceville-Princeton Road, P. O. Box 4000, Princeton, New Jersey 08540.

The SSS Company, 71 University Avenue, S. W., P. O. Box 4447, Atlanta, Georgia 30315.

Stayner Corporation, 2531 Ninth Street, Berkeley, California 94710.

Stiefel Laboratories, Inc., Oak Hill, New York 12460.

Stuart Pharmaceuticals, Division of ICA America, Inc., 3411 Silverside Road, Wilmington, Delaware 19899.

Summers Laboratories, Inc., Morris Road and Wissahickon Creek, Fort Washington, Pennsylvania 19034.

Sutliff & Case Company, Inc., 201 Spring Street, P. O. Box 838, Peoria, Illinois 61602.

Syntex Laboratories, Inc., Stanford Industrial Park, Palo Alto, California 94304.

Table Rock Laboratories, Inc., P. O. Box 1968, Greenville, South Carolina 29607.

Texas Pharmacal Company, 307 E. Josephine Street, Dept. R, P. O. Box 1659, San Antonio, Texas 78206.

Travenol Laboratories, Inc., 6301 Lincoln Avenue, Morton Grove, Illinois 60053.

Trent Pharmaceuticals, Inc., 8 Westchester Plaza, Elmsford, New York 10523.

S. J. Tutag & Company, 19180 Mt. Elliott Avenue, Detroit, Michigan 48234.

The Ulmer Pharmacal Company, 1400 Harmon Place, Minneapolis, Minnesota 55403.

Unimed, Inc., Route 202 South, Morristown, New Jersey 07960.

Union Carbide Consumer Products Co., Division of Union Carbide Corp., 270 Park Avenue, New York, N. Y. 10017.

The Upjohn Company, 7000 Portage Road, Kalamazoo, Michigan 49001.

USV Pharmaceutical Corporation, 1 Scarsdale Road, Tuckahoe, New York 10707.

The Vale Chemical Co., Inc., 1201 Liberty Street, Allentown, Pennsylvania 18102.

VioBin Corporation, 226 W. Livingston Street, Monticello, Illinois 61856.

The Vitarine Co., Inc., 227-15 N. Conduit Avenue, Springfield Gardens, New York 11413.

Walker Corp. & Co., Inc., Easthampton Place and N. Collingwood Avenue, Syracuse, New York 13201.

Wallace Pharmaceuticals, Division of Carter-Wallace Inc., Half Acre Road, Cranbury, New Jersey 08512.

Wampole Laboratories, Division of Denver Chemical Mfg. Co., 35 Commerce Road, Stamford, Connecticut 06904.

Warner-Chilcott Laboratories, Division of Warner-Lambert Pharmaceutical Company, 201 Tabor Road, Morris Plains, New Jersey 07950.

Warren-Teed Pharmaceuticals Inc., 582 W. Goodale Street, Columbus, Ohio 43215.

T. E. Watson Co., P. O. Box 133, Briarcliff Manor, New York 10510.

The William A. Webster Company, 3580 Air Park Street, Box 18358, Memphis, Tennessee 38118.

Westerfield Laboratories, Inc., 3941 Brotherton Road, Cincinnati, Ohio 45209.

Westwood Pharmaceuticals, Inc., 468 Dewitt Street, Buffalo, New York 14213.

Whittier Laboratories, 69 Rawls Road, Des Plaines, Illinois 60018.

Wilson Laboratories, Prudential Plaza, Chicago, Illinois 60601.

Winston Pharmaceuticals, Inc., 4706 Kirk Road, Winston-Salem, North Carolina 27103.

Winthrop Laboratories, 90 Park Avenue, New York, N. Y. 10016.

Wyeth Laboratories, Division of American Home Products Corp., Box 8299, Philadelphia, Pennsylvania 19101.

Xttrium Laboratories, Inc., 415 W. Pershing Road, Chicago, Illinois 60609.

The Zemmer Company, Inc., 231 Hulton Road, Oakmont, Pennsylvania 15139.

ADVERSE REACTIONS INDEX

The Adverse Reactions Index is a key to significant adverse drug reactions discussed in the 92 chapters. Adverse reactions appear as main headings; categories of drugs and individual drugs that have been implicated in causing these adverse reactions appear as subheadings. Listing of a drug under an adverse reaction heading does not mean a cause-and-effect relationship has been established; it means only that the drug has been associated with the adverse reaction in some way. Because the list of drugs under some adverse reactions may not be complete, omission of a drug under an adverse reaction heading does not mean the drug has not been implicated in the adverse reaction.

Users of this index should refer to specific reactions. General adverse reaction terms have been included in the index only in reference to those discussions where the authors were unable to give specific information on the nature of the adverse reaction.

Trademarks for most single-entity drugs are given in parentheses following the generic name. For mixtures, only the trademark is given. Mixtures are indicated by (M) following the name.

ADVERSE REACTIONS INDEX

DRUGS INDEX

The Drugs Index is a key to individual drugs and categories of drugs discussed and listed in the 92 chapters. Individual drug names or drug category names appear as main headings; pharmacologic uses, indications, and interactions with other drugs appear as subheadings. Trademarks are capitalized; generic names are not. An (M) follows all names for drug mixtures. Bold face page numbers refer to individual evaluations.

Calculation of Drug Dosage in Children

It must be emphasized that, in both children and adults, any method devised for the calculation of drug dosage provides an estimate only, to be verified or corrected by actual clinical experience. *Moreover, the detoxification and excretion of drugs in premature and newborn infants is markedly different from that which prevails in older children and adults. Thus, dosage schedules based on body surface area may be neither reliable nor safe during this period of immaturity.*

Numerous empirical rules, usually based on age or weight, have been formulated for the determination of dosage in children. However, the dose of many drugs is not always a simple linear function of body weight and to calculate the dose as so much per kilogram of body weight is often inaccurate. Experience has shown that the dose of many drugs is more nearly proportionate to weight to the 0.7 power ($Wt.^{0.7}$). The surface area of the body (in square meters) may also be calculated approximately by $Wt.\ (lb.)^{0.7} \times 0.055$. It is suggested, therefore, that the use of square meters of surface area, rather than weight, provides a more accurate method of adjusting the dosage to the size of the patient. The validity of this method of dosage calculation has been criticized on the grounds that body surface area may not be directly related to physiologic and metabolic function. However, the surface area rule does provide a practical and useful basis for the estimation of drug dosage in children. Thus, dosage may be expressed as grams of milliliters of a given drug per square meter of surface area rather than per unit of body weight. Calculation of a fractional exponential function of weight is too forbidding for practical use, but the task may be simplified by employing the following table.

Determination of Children's Doses from Adult Doses on the Basis of Body Surface Area*

Weight (kg)	Weight (lb)	Approximate surface area in square meters	Approximate percentage of adult dose†
2	4.4	0.15	9
4	8.8	0.25	14
6	13.2	0.33	19
8	17.6	0.40	23
10	22.0	0.46	27
15	33.0	0.63	36
20	44.0	0.83	48
25	55.0	0.95	55
30	66.0	1.08	62
35	77.0	1.20	69
40	88.0	1.30	75
45	99.0	1.40	81
50	110.0	1.51	87
55	121.0	1.58	91

*Adapted from Done, Alan K.: "Drugs for Children," in Modell, W. (editor): *Drugs of Choice 1972-1973*, St. Louis: The C. V. Mosby Co., 1972.

†Based on average adult surface area of 1.73 sq. M.

St. Peter's, Great Falls:
Mr. and Mrs. Broadus A. Lowe
Mr. and Mrs. James E. Neely
Rev. and Mrs. Charles A. Robinson

Christ Church, Greenville:
Mr. and Mrs. J. Mason Alexander
Miss Elizabeth Arnold
Mrs. John W. Arrington, Jr.
John W. Arrington, III
Mr. and Mrs. Nelson B. Arrington
Ralph Bailey, Jr.
H. C. Beattie
Mr. and Mrs. John Edgeworth Beattie, Jr.
Mr. and Mrs. William H. Beattie
Mrs. Ethel Lee W. Bruce
Mr. and Mrs. A. Charles Cannon, Jr.
Mrs. Fedora W. Cole
Miss Laura Smith Ebaugh
Caswell Ellis
Mrs. Carroll A. Gibson
Mr. and Mrs. J. F. Haley
George Harrison
C. E. Hatch, Jr.
Mr. and Mrs. R. Carter Henry
Oscar Hodges, Jr.
Harriet H. Houston
Mrs. Thomas B. Huguenin
Mr. and Mrs. T. S. Inglesby
Dr. and Mrs. J. W. Jervey, Jr.
William Lowndes, Jr.
Seabrook W. Lucas
George E. Lyne
Mrs. Kathryn McKnight Magill
Andrew Burnet Marion
Burnet R. Maybank
Mrs. C. Frederic McCullough
John A. McPherson, Jr.
Mr. and Mrs. Ralph H. McPherson
Mr. and Mrs. Frank P. Morris
Mrs. Margaret Dial Norwood
C. C. Pearce, Jr.
Mr. and Mrs. B. S. Phetteplace
Mrs. Robert Theodore Phillips
Dr. Raymond C. Ramage
Mr. and Mrs. William F. Redmon
Dr. John F. Robinson
Mr. and Mrs. Edward D. Sloan
Mrs. Arthur J. Smith
Annie Donkle Talley
Mrs. C. C. Towers
Mr. and Mrs. Harold R. Turner
Hugh V. Walker
Miss Eva Wrigley

Redeemer, Greenville:
Mr. and Mrs. E. C. Blackwell
Rev. Grant O. Folmsbee
Charles Long
Miss Sue Rogers
Mr. and Mrs. W. L. Walker

St. James', Greenville:
Robert H. Atkinson
Hugh C. Black
Mrs. George Brownlee
Mrs. Elliott P. Cleveland
Mrs. Robert Collier
Mr. and Mrs. John C. Cosby, Jr.
Mr. and Mrs. James T. Flowers
Robert M. Hammond
Mrs. William P. Holifield
Mr. and Mrs. Wales Lowery, Jr.
Mrs. Raven McDavid
Ellida Juell Middleton
Stephen Doar Mitchell
Paul J. Oeland, Sr.
Richard L. Oeland
Ernest Patton
Mr. and Mrs. Hext M. Perry
Rev. John A. Pinckney
Mr. and Mrs. Elmer C. Selmon
L. W. Simkins
Harriet Mitchell Stone
Mrs. T. C. Stone
Edgeworth R. Thomson

Resurrection, Greenwood:
Paul L. Baker
Howard L. Burns
Mr. and Mrs. William S. Davies
Miss Margaret A. Gaillard
James N. Godsey
Dr. and Mrs. Joseph Gwynne Jenkins, Sr.
Mr. and Mrs. Marshall T. Mays
Mrs. J. B. Park
Mr. and Mrs. B. T. Rainsford
W. DuBose Stuckey
Aubrey Bowman White
Samuel H. Zimmerman, Jr.

Good Shepherd, Greer:
Margaret E. Ballenger
Harold V. Cole
Rev. Marshall O. James
Woman's Auxiliary
Mrs. Cora G. Venning
Dr. J. Harvey Venning

Christ Church, Lancaster:
Mrs. Ben C. Hough

Epiphany, Laurens:
Mrs. Evelina H. Barksdale
Dr. and Mrs. Frank L. Culbertson
Mrs. Leroy H. Habenicht
William L. Hubbard

St. Luke's, Newberry:
Dr. and Mrs. E. Gordon Able
Mr. and Mrs. R. T. Albrecht
Thomas E. Davis
Mr. and Mrs. Burlington A. Fretwell
Burlington A. Fretwell, Jr.
Mr. and Mrs. A. C. Garlington
Mrs. Sarah Houseal Goggans
Mrs. Robert McC. Holmes
Foster N. and Abbie LaRoche Martin
Rev. and Mrs. Cannon McCreary

J. Eugene Norris
Mr. and Mrs. R. Houseal Norris
Mr. and Mrs. Thomas H. Pope
Mr. and Mrs. W. F. Rutherford
Mrs. A. Pickens Salley
T. Roy Summer, Jr.
Mrs. C. D. Weeks
Woman's Auxiliary

St. Bartholomew's, North Augusta:

Mrs. R. P. Johnson

St. Paul's, Pendleton:

Fred H. Anthony
Rev. Jack W. Cole
Miss Louise G. Hunter
Miss Henrietta Seabrook

Grace, Ridge Spring:

Mrs. Reuben Asbill
Mrs. Benjamin Boatwright
J. Ernest Boatwright
Mrs. Archie Fripp
Mrs. P. A. Brunson
Mrs. Rod Watson

St. Stephen's, Ridgeway:

Louise Gordon Bradley
Mr. and Mrs. James Spann Edmunds
Mrs. E. Allen Fripp, Jr.
Mrs. Robert H. McKelvey
Mr. and Mrs. Joseph W. Milling, Jr.
Beverly Y. Palmer
Miss Sara McCollough Palmer
Miss Caroline Elizabeth Thomas
Charles Edward Thomas
Mr. and Mrs. Robert Walton Thomas
Mrs. Thomas H. Weir

Our Saviour, Rock Hill:

Deward B. Brittain
Louisa D. Duls
Joseph Hyde Easley
Mr. and Mrs. T. N. Edwards
Dr. Elizabeth F. Johnson
Church of Our Saviour Laymen's Club
Rev. William W. Lumpkin
William J. Neely
Hugh Rock

Mrs. Edna Porter Rodden
Blackburn Wilson Wylie

Advent, Spartanburg:

R. E. Barnwell
Mr. and Mrs. George M. Boyd
Church of the Advent
Ann Wilson Sanders Fraser
Donald Maner Fraser
Mrs. C. B. Fretwell
Francis P. Fretwell
Charles M. Lindsay
Miss Camilla Cordes Lucas
Walter S. Montgomery
Mrs. Moulton A. Phifer
Rev. C. Capers Satterlee, D.D.
Maner Lewton Tonge
Dr. and Mrs. Oscar Britton Wilson

Nativity, Union:

C. F. Baarcke
Rev. William A. Beckham
William E. Broadwell
Mrs. Bessie Young Garner
Mr. and Mrs. J. A. McArthur
Mrs. Henry B. Richardson

St. John's, Winnsboro:

Dr. John C. Buchanan, Jr.
Mrs. U. G. DesPortes
Mrs. Evelyn G. Fergerson
Miss Rebecca A. Hanahan
Edith A. Hilton
Mr. and Mrs. A. E. Jury
Mrs. Daniel Ravenel
Rev. Richard L. Sturgis

Good Shepherd, York:

Mrs. Isabelle L. Cain
James Ravenel Cain
Miss Frank Lindsay Clawson
Herbert Crosland
Mrs. C. L. Harper
Carl H. Hart
Mrs. Joseph E. Hart
Mr. and Mrs. H. Sanford Howie, Jr.
Lettie Harper Knight
Mr. and Mrs. E. B. Lowry
Mr. and Mrs. J. Benjamin White
Church of The Good Shepherd

SOUTH CAROLINA MISCELLANEOUS

Barnwell County Library, Barnwell
Beaufort Township Library, Beaufort
D. R. Bostick, Marion
Calhoun County Library, St. Matthews
Camp Gravatt, Camp and Conference Center
Rev. B. Duvall Chambers, Columbia
Charleston Library Society, Charleston
The Citadel Library, Charleston
Mr. and Mrs. W. M. Clark, Greenville
Mrs. Parker E. Connor, Charleston
The Dalcho Historical Society, Charleston
Department of Christian Education Library, Columbia
Mrs. Eva Hogan Gittman, Columbia
Harry A. Hamiter, Jr., Columbia
Prof. James G. Harrison, Charleston
John James Anthony Henebery, III, Columbia
James Barnwell Heyward, Charleston

Dr. and Mrs. G. F. Hiott, Jr., York
Mr. and Mrs. Jack Hopkins, Greenville
Miss Laura Bellinger Jones, Columbia
F. D. C. Kracke, Charleston
Laurens County Library, Laurens
Andrea Leonardo, Columbia
Lexington County Circulating Library, Batesburg
Marlborough County Public Library, Bennettsville
E. W. McIntosh, Kingstree
Mrs. R. Eugene McLendon, Bishopville
Dr. Chapman James Milling, Columbia
National Society of Colonial Dames of America in South Carolina, Charleston
Mrs. Robert C. Osborne, Orangeburg
William F. Prioleau, Columbia
Mrs. P. Gibbes Richards, Lancaster
Rev. and Mrs. W. J. Roof, Mt. Pleasant
Dr. Donald S. Russell, Columbia
Schindler's Antique Shop, Charleston
Mrs. Margaret W. Smith, Columbia
South Carolina State Library Board, Columbia
Library, University of South Carolina, Columbia
James B. Wessinger, Columbia
Rev. G. Croft Williams, Sc.D., Columbia
Mrs. S. Itly Wilson, Sumter

MISCELLANEOUS OUT-OF-STATE

Mrs. Joseph M. (Rosa Thomas) Armstrong, Baltimore, Md.
Mr. and Mrs. F. P. Bacon, Tryon, N. C.
Edwina McCollough Barr, Orlando, Fla.
Mr. and Mrs. Earl H. Biel, Sr., Philadelphia, Pa.
Misses Ellen and Sarah Blanding, Poughkeepsie, N. Y.
Rev. and Mrs. Alfred P. Chambliss, Jr., Shreveport, La.
Mr. and Mrs. S. E. Boney, Miami, Fla.
Mrs. Catherine Louise Bullock, Jacksonville Beach, Fla.
Julian Calhoun, Tryon, N. C.
Rt. Rev. C. C. J. Carpenter, D.D., Birmingham, Ala.
Arthur Ben Chitty, Sewanee, Tenn.
Rev. Philip G. Clarke, Jr., Raleigh, N. C.
Rev. James McDowell Dick, D.D., Raleigh, N. C.
Mr. and Mrs. Charles A. Dixon, Winston-Salem, N. C.
Rev. Kenneth Donald, Black Mountain, N. C.
Joseph Gantt and Margaret Whaley Ferguson, Mobile, Ala.
Mr. and Mrs. William DeLancey Frierson, II, Coronado, Calif.
Rev. R. Emmet Gribbin, Jr., Tuscaloosa, Ala.
Mrs. Alex Guerry, Chattanooga, Tenn.
Rev. G. Edward Haynsworth, Savannah, Ga.
Mrs. Hugh C. Haynsworth, Washington, District of Columbia
Mrs. Buell David Hendrix, Charlotte, N. C.
Rev. Thomas F. Hudson, Dayton, Ohio
Rev. and Mrs. Roderick H. Jackson, Portsmouth, Va.
Mr. and Mrs. John Earle Jones, Staunton, Va.
Mr. and Mrs. Frank H. (Sarah Thomas) Kendall
Benjamin M. Lee, Knoxville, Tenn.
Miss Monimia Fairfax MacRae, Asheville, North Carolina
Edward McCrady, Ph.D., Sewanee, Tenn.
Raven I. McDavid, Jr., Chicago, Ill.
Rt. Rev. Louis C. Melcher, D.D., Rio de Janeiro, Brazil
Mr. and Mrs. G. E. Middleton, Natchez, Mississippi
Rev. Eugene L. Nixon, Jacksonville, Fla.
Hugh H. Obear, Washington, D. C.
Rev. Fr. Robert E. H. Peeples, Statesboro, Georgia
Miss Katherine H. Porter, Ph.D., Cleveland, Ohio
Rev. Roddey Reid, Jr., Wilmington, Del.
Dr. and Mrs. Shirrell Rogers, Terre Haute. Indiana
Nancy Rogers Saxon, New Canaan, Conn.
Rev. Charles M. Seymour, Jr., St. Augustine, Florida
Rev. Stephen Skardon, New Orleans, La.
Rev. Fred Skinner and Mackie Ramsay Sosnowski, Henderson, Texas
Rt. Rev. Albert R. Stuart, D.D., Savannah, Georgia
Edward Samuel Stuart, Beaumont, Texas
Thomas M. Stubbs, Dillard, Ga.
Rev. L. A. Taylor, O.H.C., Sierre Leone, West Africa
Miss Eleanor Walter Thomas, Ph.D., Cleveland, Ohio
Dr. and Mrs. Henry C. (Mary Russell) Thomas, Chapel Hill, N. C.
Eugene Hester Thompson, Jr., Durham, North Carolina
Mrs. Lucille Hope Newton Thompson, Durham, N. C.
Rev. A. Campbell Tucker, Woodstock, Va.
Library, The University of the South, Sewanee, Tenn.
Miss Ruth Walker, Atlanta, Ga.
Rev. Hallie D. Warren, Jr., Waycross, Ga.
Rev. William Way, D.D., S.T.D., Jacksonville, Fla.
William Whaley, Knoxville, Tenn.
Rev. W. Postell Witsell, D.D., Little Rock, Arkansas

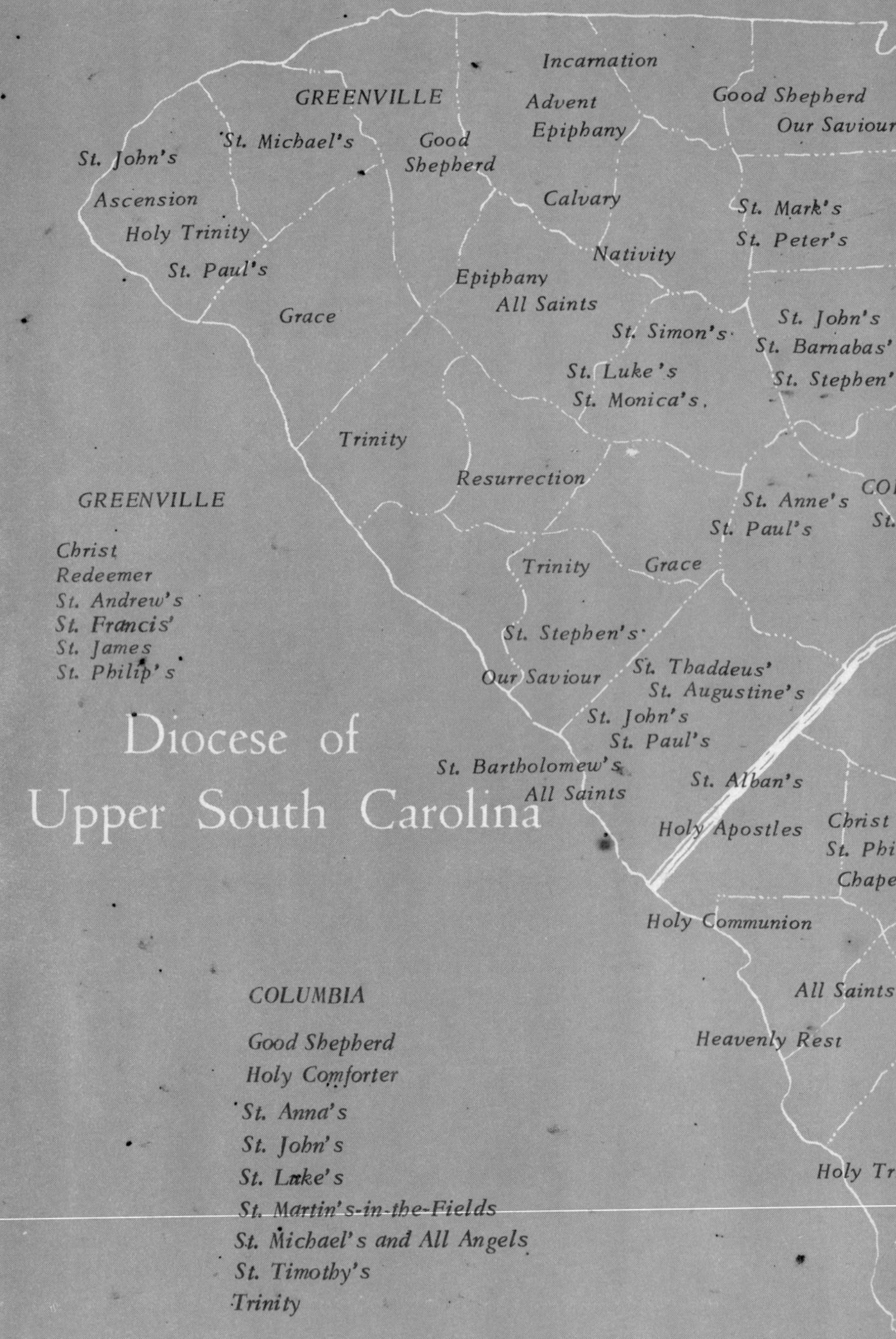
Incarnation
GREENVILLE
Advent
Epiphany
Good Shepherd
Our Saviour
St. John's
St. Michael's
Good
Shepherd
Ascension
Holy Trinity
St. Paul's
Calvary
St. Mark's
St. Peter's
Nativity
Epiphany
All Saints
Grace
St. Simon's
St. John's
St. Barnabas'
St. Luke's
St. Monica's.
Trinity
Resurrection
GREENVILLE
Christ
Redeemer
St. Andrew's
St. Francis'
St. James
St. Philip's
St. Anne's
St. Paul's
Trinity
Grace
St. Stephen's
Our Saviour
St. Thaddeus'
St. Augustine's
St. John's
St. Paul's
Diocese of
Upper South Carolina
St. Bartholomew's
All Saints
St. Alban's
Holy Apostles
Christ
Holy Communion
All Saints
Heavenly Rest
COLUMBIA
Good Shepherd
Holy Comforter
St. Anna's
St. John's
St. Luke's
St. Martin's-in-the-Fields
St. Michael's and All Angels
St. Timothy's
Trinity